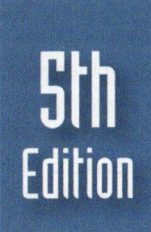

SOCIAL PSYCHOLOGY AND HUMAN NATURE

5th Edition

Roy F. Baumeister
University of Queensland, Australia

Brad J. Bushman
The Ohio State University, USA

Australia • Brazil • Mexico • Singapore • United Kingdom • United States

Social Psychology and Human Nature, Fifth Edition
Roy F. Baumeister and Brad J. Bushman

Senior Vice President, Higher Education & Skills Product: Erin Joyner

Product Director: Laura Ross

Product Manager: Josh Parrott

Senior Content Manager: Tangelique Williams-Grayer

Content Manager: Amanda White

Product Assistant: Kat V. Wallace

Marketing Manager: Tricia Salata

Intellectual Property Analyst: Deanna Ettinger

Intellectual Property Project Manager: Betsy Hathaway

Production Service: Lori Hazzard, MPS Limited

Art Director: Bethany Bourgeois

Text Designer: Terri Wright

Cover Designer: Chris Doughman

Cover Image: Adrian Weinbrecht/The Image Bank/Getty Images

Compositor: MPS Limited

© 2021, 2017 Cengage Learning, Inc.

Unless otherwise noted, all content is © Cengage.

ALL RIGHTS RESERVED. No part of this work covered by the copyright herein may be reproduced or distributed in any form or by any means, except as permitted by U.S. copyright law, without the prior written permission of the copyright owner.

> For product information and technology assistance, contact us at
> **Cengage Customer & Sales Support, 1-800-354-9706**
> or **support.cengage.com**.
>
> For permission to use material from this text or product, submit all requests online at **www.cengage.com/permissions**.

Library of Congress Control Number: 2019911261

Student Edition:
ISBN: 978-0-357-12291-4

Loose-leaf Edition:
ISBN: 978-0-357-12290-7

Cengage
200 Pier 4 Boulevard
Boston, MA 02210
USA

Cengage is a leading provider of customized learning solutions with employees residing in nearly 40 different countries and sales in more than 125 countries around the world. Find your local representative at **www.cengage.com**.

Cengage products are represented in Canada by Nelson Education, Ltd.

To learn more about Cengage platforms and services, register or access your online learning solution, or purchase materials for your course, visit **www.cengage.com**.

Printed at CLDPC, USA, 01-21

ATTITUDES, BELIEFS, AND CONSISTENCY

1

LEARNING OBJECTIVES

1. Define social psychology. Name two key ideas that had a lasting influence on the field.

2. Describe the ABC triad of social psychology.

3. Explain how social psychology relates to other fields of study.

4. Assess the different methods of data collection in social psychology.

5. Describe the benefits and drawbacks of field experiments compared to laboratory experiments, and explain how correlational methods can describe the relationship between variables when traditional laboratory experiments cannot be used.

FOOD FOR THOUGHT
Does Chicken Soup Reduce Cold Symptoms?
17

TRADEOFFS
Research Ethics
20

goja1/Shutterstock.com

YOU are a member of a social world on a planet containing nearly eight billion people. This social world is filled with paradox, mystery, suspense, and outright absurdity. Consider a few examples.

Increasing safety equipment is a no-brainer, right? But studies suggest that requiring bicycle helmets has not diminished the rate of serious injuries among bike riders, because people take more chances.[1] (Meanwhile, fewer people ride bikes, and therefore the health and fitness benefits are missed.) Likewise, requiring seat belts has not reduced the rate of injury and death among automobile occupants, because drivers, feeling safer, take more chances. (And meanwhile, pedestrian deaths have risen, because the seat belts inside the cars do not protect pedestrians from the riskier drivers.) The news magazine *The Economist* proposed, tongue in cheek, that to increase safety, seat belts should be banned, and every car should be fitted with a spike protruding from the steering wheel aimed at the heart of the driver—who would therefore become very careful.[2] The same magazine also proposed banning boxing gloves, which protect their hands so that they can strike more blows—thereby increasing head injuries.

Looking good is important, right? And people spend enormous amounts of time, effort, and money to look good. As a rather weird side effect, the *New York Times* reported in one recent year Americans had spent $62 million dollars on plastic surgery—for their dogs! Tummy tucks and facial beautification and the rest.[3] The latest innovation, and not counted in that $62 million, is that many owners have their male dog spayed so he won't impregnate other dogs—and then splurge to have silicon testicles implanted in him.

Absurdity also seems to know no bounds. For example, two drunk Welsh tourists broke into Sea World in Australia, swam with the dolphins, and stole a penguin named Dirk. When they woke up hungover, they tried to let Dirk go in a canal, but locals saw them and called the police. The magistrate fined each of the tourists 1,000 Australian dollars and told them to drink "a little less vodka."[4]

Can social psychology help us make sense of the baffling diversity of human behavior? The answer to this question is a resounding "Yes!" **Social psychology** is the scientific study of how people affect and are affected by others. Whether you know it or not, social psychology can help you make sense of your own social world. The material discussed in this book is intensely relevant to your life. For example, have you ever asked yourself questions such as these: "How can I get him to go along with my plan?" "Should I ask her right up front to do this big favor, or is there a better way to get her to say yes?" "How can I bring them around to my way of thinking?" Social psychology can also help you understand simpler things, such as taking a coffee break. If your boss told you to make 19,000 decisions before you got your first cup of coffee, you'd probably think you had a cruel boss! The Starbucks chain of coffee shops, however, has advertised that they offered 19,000 beverage options, if you count all the different coffees, teas, cold drinks, and all the things you could add to them. In a sense, therefore, the customer who walks into a Starbucks shop for a morning drink is confronted with more than 19,000 choices. You can even end up with a cup of coffee that costs over $50! It is called the Sexagintuple Vanilla Bean Mocha Frappuccino. It has 60 shots and comes in a 128-ounce (3.79-liter) glass. Isn't having so many choices just a way to frustrate people? How does Starbucks make money? Why don't their customers quit in protest? More to the point (at least for a social psychologist), how do people get by in a world that offers them thousands of options at every turn, even for the simplest decisions? In Chapter 5 we discuss some of the heuristics people use to manage such information overload.

Chances are, something in this book will prove helpful to you in the future. This is not to say that social psychology is a cookbook for how to influence and manipulate others. Social psychology, however, can help you understand basic principles of social influence, as well as many other principles of social behavior. It is also just plain interesting to learn about how and why people act the way they do.

The point is that there are plenty of reasons why you ought to be interested in social psychology. Even if you are only taking the course to satisfy a requirement, you can learn plenty of useful and interesting things. As you learn more, you can profit more and get more enjoyment from what social psychology has to offer. Let's begin by looking at how social psychology became the field it is.

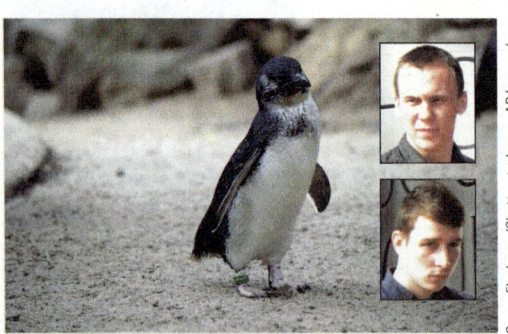

Absurd. Two drunk, Welsh tourists stole Dirk the penguin from Sea World.

2

LEARNING OBJECTIVES

1. Explain how and why the human brain evolved the way it did.

2. Understand how culture and nature work together to affect choices and behavior and make culture a better way of being social.

3. Summarize how the two system of the duplex mind differ and work together.

4. Describe how inner processes serve interpersonal functions.

MONEY MATTERS
Nature, Culture, and Money
45

FOOD FOR THOUGHT
Virtuous Vegetarians
46

THE SOCIAL SIDE OF SEX
Sex and Culture
47

TRADEOFFS
Political Tradeoffs
62

WHAT MAKES US HUMAN?
Putting the Cultural Animal in Perspective
65

iStock.com/Britta Kasholm-Tengve

In 1965 a Canadian woman gave birth to a pair of healthy twin boys. When the boys were eight months old, they were taken to the hospital to be circumcised. Through a series of mishaps, one of the boys had his penis practically burned off by an electric cauterizing machine. Medical technology could not repair the damage. After some long and anxious conversations, the family and medical staff decided that the best thing to do was to remove the rest of the penis and raise the boy as a girl.[1]

The decision was not taken lightly. The family consulted with leading experts on gender and sexuality. In the past, many psychologists and others had believed that men and women were innately different, but the feminist movement had challenged those beliefs as being mere rationalizations for oppressing women. Most expert opinion had come around to agree that boys and girls were not born different but were made different by how they were brought up. Many Canadian and American parents were themselves rethinking how to raise their children so as to undo the constraining stereotypes and perhaps produce more autonomous, stronger daughters and more sensitive, caring sons. If adult personality depended mainly on upbringing, then it should not matter much whether a child was born as a boy or a girl. It should therefore be possible to raise this baby boy as a girl with no untoward consequences. At most, the experts thought that the child would need some injections of female hormones around the time of puberty.

Little Brenda (as the child was named) was not told about the botched circumcision or the gender switch. She grew up wearing long hair and dresses, playing with other girls, and in other ways being introduced to the female sex role. The sex experts kept in touch and reported back to the scientific community that the experiment was working. Brenda was a normal girl.

The reports were not quite right, however. The parents were anxious to avoid displeasing the experts, and perhaps they also wanted to avoid admitting that they might have made a mistake in converting their son into a daughter. But the girl never fit in. She wanted to play rough games like the boys did. She was more interested in sports, race cars, and fighting toys than in dolls, makeup, or tea parties. Her dress was often dirty and disheveled, and her hair was tangled, unlike the other girls'. As the children approached puberty and began to play kissing games or to try dancing at parties, the tensions increased. Brenda did not know what was wrong, but she wanted no part of kissing boys or dancing with them. Her rebellious behavior increased.

Finally it came time for the hormone shots. By now Brenda was in regular therapy. She rebelled and absolutely refused to accept the injections. When her parents broke down and told her the full story of how she had been born as a boy, she finally felt as if she could understand herself. She immediately quit being a girl. She cut her hair, replaced her dresses with boys' clothes, and took a male name. He insisted on having lengthy, agonizing surgeries to remove his breasts and create a sort of penis from the muscles and skin of his legs. Although his body could not biologically father a child, the former Brenda was even able to become a father by virtue of marrying a woman who already had children. But happiness proved elusive, and at age 38 he killed himself.[2,3]

Later, investigative reporters uncovered other such cases. Each time, the person born as a boy and raised as a girl did not turn out to be a typical adult woman. One of them, for example, smoked cigars, refused to wear dresses and skirts, and worked as an auto mechanic.

These stories are important because they suggest limits to the power of socialization. In the 1970s and 1980s, most psychologists accepted the view that the differences between men and women were due to parental care and upbringing. Parents supposedly taught their sons to be aggressive while teaching their daughters to be passive and compliant. For a while, the early part of the "Brenda" story was reported in some textbooks as

Brenda Reimer, after he started to live life as a man. His story is detailed in the book *As Nature Made Him: The Boy Who Was Raised as a Girl*, by John Colapinto.

evidence that sex roles are entirely due to socialization, and Brenda was described as a normal and healthy girl. But the problems that emerged later suggested that the differences between male and female are partly innate. (*Innate* means something you are born with, as opposed to something you learned or acquired during your life. *Innate* is also understood to mean something that cannot be fully or easily changed.) There are limits to how much can be accomplished by teaching, upbringing, and other aspects of socialization.

None of this should be taken to mean that learning and culture are irrelevant. Boys and girls do learn from their culture how to act and how to understand themselves. The power of culture is, however, limited. Apparently, people are predisposed to learn some things more easily than others. If gender identity were entirely a matter of learning, Brenda should have been a normal girl. Parents, teachers, psychologists, and others were all working together to raise her as a girl, and none of her peers or friends was told that she had once been a boy. At times, she seemed to accept herself as a female and to act as girls were expected to act. However, the experiment failed.

Apparently, some parts of who you are come from biology, regardless of what your parents and teachers tell you. And some people do not identify as male or female. Gender is not a binary construct.

Social psychology is aimed at exploring how people think, feel, and act. The ultimate explanations for human behavior lie in nature and culture, and researchers have engaged in many long, bitter debates over which of those is more important. The one clearly correct answer is that both are very important. In this chapter, we will consider the complementary influences of nature and culture. ●

Nature and Social Behavior

Explaining the Psyche

One approach to understanding how people think, feel, and act is to try to understand what the human psyche is designed for. (The **psyche** is a broader term for mind, encompassing emotions, desires, perceptions, and indeed all psychological processes.) To understand something, you have to know what it was designed to do.

Imagine someone who has grown up on a deserted island and has never met another human being or seen any human-made items. Then one day, a box washes ashore containing an electric can opener. How would the person figure out what the can opener does? Having grown up on a deserted island, the person knows nothing about cans or electricity. This hypothetical person might take it apart, analyze it, observe its parts, and see what some of their properties are, but it would be almost impossible for this person to understand it properly.

Understanding the human psyche is somewhat like that. To understand and explain how it works, it is useful to know what the psyche/human mind is designed for. Hence, we turn to nature and culture because those are what made the psyche the way it is. If the psyche was designed to do something in particular, then nature and culture designed it for that purpose. Accordingly, if we can learn what the purpose is, then we can understand people much better.

Why are people the way they are? Why is the human mind set up as it is? Why do people think, want, feel, and act in certain ways? Nature and culture. The nature explanations say that people are born a certain way; their genes, hormones, brain structure, and other processes dictate how they will choose and act. In contrast, the cultural explanations focus on what people learn from their parents, from society, and from their own experiences.

Such debates have raged over many other forms of social interaction and behavior. Are people born with a natural tendency to be aggressive, or is aggression something they pick up from watching violent media, playing with toy

psyche a broader term for mind, encompassing emotions, desires, perceptions, and all other psychological processes

To understand how to work this device, you have to know what it is designed to do.

guns, and copying other people's actions? Are some people born to be homosexuals, or can people choose and change their sexual orientation? Is mental illness the result of how your parents treated you, or is it something in your genes? What about whether someone likes to drink alcohol or gamble? What about heroism, especially when people risk their own lives to protect or save others? How many of the differences between men and women reflect their innate, genetic tendencies, and how many are the product of cultural stereotypes?

Many social scientists have grown tired of nature–nurture debates and wish to put an end to them, though others continue to pursue them vigorously. In recent years, some researchers have stressed that both nature and culture have real influences. The most common resolution tends to favor nature as more important, however, because nature is indispensable. As primatologist Frans de Waal[4] argued, nature versus culture isn't a fair fight because without nature you have nothing. He proposed that the argument should be waged between whether a particular behavior is the direct result of nature or stems from a combination of nature and culture. Your body has to perceive what is happening, your brain has to understand events, and your body has to carry out your decisions (and brain and body are both created by nature). Put more simply, nature comes first, and culture builds on what nature has furnished. That is one view.

This book, however, favors the view that nature and culture have shaped each other. In particular, nature has prepared human beings specifically for culture. That is, the characteristics that set humans apart from other animals (including language, a flexible self that can hold multiple roles, and an advanced ability to understand each other's mental states) are mainly there to enable people to create and sustain culture. This interaction between nature and culture is the key to understanding how people think, act, and feel. But let's start by considering nature and culture separately.

Nature Defined

Nature is the physical world around us, including its laws and processes. It includes the entire world that would be there even if no human beings existed. Nature includes trees and grass, bugs and elephants, gravity, the weather, hunger and thirst, birth and death, atoms and molecules, and all the laws of physics and chemistry. Nature made people too. (People who believe that the original humans were created by a divine power still recognize that the natural processes of reproduction and childbirth create today's people.)

Those who explain human behavior using nature invoke the sorts of processes that natural sciences have shown. For example, neuroscientists look for explanations in terms of what happens inside the brain (chemical reactions, electrical activity). Behavior geneticists seek to understand behavior as the result of genes and show that people are born with tendencies to feel and act in certain ways. Above all, however, the advocates of nature in psychology turn to evolutionary theory to understand behavior patterns. The next section provides an introduction to this theory.

Evolution, and Doing What's Natural

Over the past four decades, many social psychologists have begun looking to the theory of evolution to help explain social behavior. The **theory of evolution**, proposed by the British biologist Charles Darwin in the 1800s, focuses on how change occurs in nature. Over thousands of years, a plant or animal may evolve into a somewhat different kind of creature. Human beings and the great apes evolved from a common ancestor.

Human beings may be different from all other animals, but we are animals nonetheless. As such, we have many of the same wants, needs, and problems that most other animals have. We need food and water on a regular basis, preferably a couple of times every day. We need sleep. We need shelter and warmth. We need air. We suffer illnesses and injuries and must find ways to recover from them. Our interactions with others are sometimes characterized by sexual desire, competition, aggressive impulses, family ties, or friendly companionship. Sometimes we say that certain people are "acting like animals," but this is not surprising, because we are all animals. The implicit criticism in that phrase merely

nature the physical world around us, including its laws and processes

theory of evolution a theory proposed by Charles Darwin to explain how change occurs in nature expresses the point that people are expected to rise above their animal nature, but the animal parts are there inside all of us.

An important feature of most living things, including animals and hence humans, is the drive to prolong life. There are two ways to do this. Obviously, one way is to go on living. (Wouldn't you like to live forever? Death has always been a disturbing threat, and beliefs that death is not the end but merely a transition into a different kind of life, whether as a ghost, a spirit in heaven, or a reincarnated person, have been found all over the earth since prehistoric times.) The other is reproduction: Life makes new life. Indeed, you might say that nature was unable to create an immortal being and therefore settled on reproduction as the only viable strategy to enable any form of life to continue into the future.

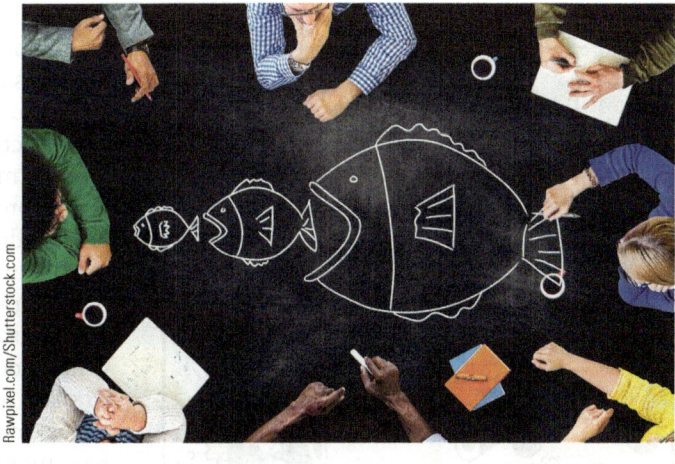

Change is another common trait of living things. Each living thing changes as it grows older, but more important forms of change occur from one generation to the next: Children are different from their parents. Nature cannot plan ahead and design a certain kind of change. Instead, nature produces changes that are essentially random. That is, the complicated processes that mix the genes of two parents to produce a unique set of genes in the baby sometimes produce novel outcomes in the form of new traits. However, powerful forces react to these random changes. As a result, some random changes will disappear, whereas others will endure. The process of **natural selection** decides which traits will disappear and which will continue.

For example, imagine that one baby was born with no ears, another with one leg longer than the other, and the third with eyes that could see farther than the average eye. Having no ears or having legs of unequal length would probably be disadvantages, and natural selection would not preserve these traits for future generations. (That's a polite way of saying that those babies would probably die before being able to pass on their genes by having offspring.) A significant improvement in vision might, however, be selected to remain because the baby who grew up seeing better than other people would be able to find more food and spot danger from a safer distance. The genes for better vision would therefore remain in the gene pool (assuming that this baby would grow up and have babies), and so in future generations more and more people would enjoy this improvement.

Natural selection has two criteria: survival and reproduction. (Remember, these are the two ways of prolonging life.) A trait that improves survival or reproduction will tend to endure for many generations and become more common. A trait that reduces one's chances for survival or reproduction will probably not become common. These are crucial themes because the biological success of any trait is measured in those terms. A novel trait that makes someone happier or gives the person higher self-esteem or fosters a weird sense of humor, will not necessarily be passed on to future generations, unless those changes can translate into better survival or better reproduction.

Survival is not hard to understand. It means living longer. Darwin's contemporary Herbert Spencer coined the phrase "survival of the fittest" to describe natural selection. Animals compete against each other to survive, as in who can get the best food or who can best escape being eaten by larger animals. In a group of zebras, for example, the ones who run the slowest are most likely to be eaten by lions, so the ones born to be fast are more likely to live long enough to pass along their genes.

Survival depends in part on the circumstances in your environment. Consider the coloring of fish. Most fish have a relatively light-colored belly and a relatively dark colored top or back. Why? That coloring is adapted for survival in the water. Most fish live until a bigger fish eats them, making the ability to hide from bigger fish an important trait for survival. Some big fish swim near the surface and look downward for food. The lower (deeper) you go in the water, the darker it gets. When a big fish looks downward, therefore, it can't see dark-colored fish very well, so fish who are dark on the top side are harder to see (and therefore safer). Meanwhile, some big fish lurk in the depths and look upward for their food. Looking upward is looking into the light, so the best way for a fish to blend in is to have a light coloring on its underside. Over millions of years, the fish who were dark on top and light on the bottom survived longest because they were the hardest for the bigger fish to

natural selection the process whereby those members of a species that survive and reproduce most effectively are the ones that pass along their genes to future generations

survival living longer

see, so they were less likely to be eaten and, therefore, more likely to make more baby fish with the same coloring. As a result of this selection process, most fish have this coloring today.

Gradually, biologists have shifted their emphasis from survival to reproduction as the single most important factor in natural selection. Survival is important mainly as a means to achieve reproduction. **Reproduction** means producing babies—though the babies also have to survive long enough to reproduce. Reproductive success consists of creating many offspring who will in turn create many offspring. Put another way, nature judges you by how many grandchildren you produce.

For example, suppose a **mutation** (that is, a new gene or combination of genes) today could double the expected life span of a woman, from about 75 years to about 150. That is, one particular woman was born with the biological makeup to enable her to live 150 years. Would subsequent generations have more and more of this trait, and thus be more and more like this woman (and hence able to live longer)? Possibly not. If the woman was still done having babies around the age of 40, and if her longer life did not improve her quantity or quality of children and grandchildren, then her genetic traits would not spread. Now imagine another woman born with a mutation that doubled the number of children she produced, even though she would die at age 75 just like the others. Subsequent generations might well contain more and more people like her.

Much of the recent work in evolutionary theory has focused on gender differences.[5,6,7] For example, evolution would likely select men to want more sex partners than women want. A woman can only have about one baby a year no matter how many men she has sex with, but a man can father dozens of children each year if he has sex with many women. Moreover, a woman's children would be most likely to survive to adulthood if they were cared for by two parents rather than just their mother. Hence, men today are probably descended from men who desired multiple partners, whereas today's women probably descended from female ancestors who preferred long-lasting monogamous relationships. Current research suggests that this pattern is found all over the world, in many different cultures: Men desire more sex partners than women.[8]

How, exactly, does biological evolution produce changes? The causal processes depend entirely on random changes to physical entities, such as genes. The person (or other creature) is programmed to respond a certain way. Crucially, nothing has to be thought, understood, or spoken in order for these changes to occur. That is, meaning has nothing to do with it. Molecules, chemicals, electrical impulses in the body, and other physical mechanisms produce the results. Behavior changes because the physical makeup of the newborn individual is different. This is quite different from how culture works, as we shall see.

Social Animals

Psychologists study people. Many psychologists have studied other animals, especially rats. But psychologists have never shown much interest in studying trees. Why not?

Trees, like people and all other living creatures, need to get certain things (e.g., water, nutrients) from the world around them. What is inside them is there to enable them to get what they need. The inside parts of trees enable them to draw water from the soil, chemicals from sunlight, and so forth. Trees, however, do not move around in search of food or to escape from predators. They take what comes to them where they are. Facing few decisions and being therefore essentially indifferent to other trees, they do not have much psychology. They don't have much in the way of thoughts, feelings, or behavior because they don't need these things to survive and reproduce. (That's why psychologists don't find them interesting.)

Contrast this with animals that also live as loners. They have to find food, possibly kill it, and eat it. They need more food and produce more waste than trees do. They need to sleep and so must find safe places to do so. Reproduction is more complicated than it is for trees, so they may need to perform a particular set of behaviors in order to reproduce. Like trees, they need to interact with their world, but doing so is more complicated for animals, so what

reproduction producing babies that survive long enough to also reproduce

mutation a new gene or combination of genes

40 | CHAPTER 2 Culture and Nature

is inside them has to be up to the task. Psychologists start to get interested in these processes.

Many animals are not loners. They discovered, or perhaps nature discovered for them, that by living and working together, they could interact with the world more effectively. For example, if an animal hunts for food by itself, it can only catch, kill, and eat animals much smaller and weaker than itself—but if animals band together in a group, they can catch and kill animals bigger and stronger than they are. A pack of wolves can kill a buffalo which can feed the group very well. Thus, more food is available to the same animals in the same forest if they work together than if they work alone. Cooperation has other benefits: The animals can alert each other to danger, can find more food (if they search separately and then follow the ones who succeed in finding food), and can even provide some care to those who are sick and injured. Mating and reproduction are also easier if the animals live in a group than if they live far apart.

"So really, what are you like deep down inside?"

In short, being social provides benefits. Being social is a strategy that enables some animals to survive and reproduce effectively. That is the biological starting point of social psychology: Being social improves survival and reproduction.

The downside of being social is that it is more difficult to achieve than solitary life. As with trees, what is inside social animals is there to enable them to get what they need from the environment. But to be social, one has to have quite a bit going on inside. (Hence, psychologists can find much to study.) Social animals have to have something inside them that makes them recognize each other and want to be together. They must have something that prompts them to work together, such as automatic impulses to copy what the others are doing. (Hunting in groups doesn't happen by mere coincidence.) They must have ways to resolve the conflicts that inevitably arise in social life, as when two animals both want the same piece of food. They need something akin to self-control to enable them to adjust to group life. Social animals need complex, powerful brains.

The Social Brain

Trees don't need brains, and solitary creatures can get by with relatively small ones. Social animals, however, require large brains with additional, flexible capabilities.

The evolutionary anthropologist Robin Dunbar[9,10] compared the brain sizes of many different species to see what behavioral differences went with bigger brains. (Brain size is always adjusted for body weight because bigger animals generally have bigger brains. For example, human men have bigger brains than women, but that's mainly because men are bigger all over. Adult men and women have about the same average intelligence, despite the brain size difference.) Did big-brained species eat better foods, or more complicated foods such as fruit (which ripens and turns rotten rapidly)? Did they roam over larger territories, so that they needed a bigger brain to maintain a more complex mental map? No. Dunbar found that bigger brains were mainly linked to having larger and more complex social groups. Small-brained animals tend to live alone or in small, simple groups, whereas bigger-brained, presumably smarter animals have more relationships with each other and more complicated groups (such as those with dominance hierarchies and competing allies). More recent work has extended this to human beings: People with bigger social networks have been found to be bigger in some key brain parts, notably the orbital prefrontal cortex.[11]

Over time, the size of the human brain has increased to enable us to have rich, complex social lives.

This conclusion is highly important. The human brain did not evolve because it helped us outsmart lions and tigers and bears or build better shelters or invent calculus. It evolved mainly to enable human beings to have rich, complex social lives. The brain is not for understanding the physical world around us so much as it is for understanding each other. It is not so much a calculating brain or a problem-solving brain as it is a social brain.

What aspects of social life are crucial for survival? Current work continues to explore and refine these ideas. One article divided challenges into four types and tried to estimate their effect on the evolution of the big human brain.[12] The traditional emphasis is individual competition (me vs. you). Perhaps surprisingly, they found no evidence that this kind of competition had much effect. In contrast, dealing with challenges in the environment (me vs. nature) was the biggest factor—though they thought much of the brain size came from learning from culture how to deal with nature (e.g., how to make fire, which all human societies but no animal groups master). The next largest challenge was for cooperation (us vs. nature): People work together to get food and shelter. Competition between groups (us vs. them) was a significant but small contributor. (These researchers focused specifically on human females, and so they may have underestimated group vs. group competition, because in prehistory it was mainly males that banded together to fight other groups.) These findings are tentative and provide one intriguing example of what is being learned.

The emphasis on cooperation also fits well with the picture that is emerging from many sources, including evolutionary psychology of morality. Humans cooperate far more effectively and extensively than other animals, who hardly ever engage in true cooperation with non-relatives. Indeed, cooperation is one reason humans live much longer than other apes despite sharing most of their DNA. Adult apes feed themselves, which is fine as long as they are able. But if an ape suffers an injury, such as a broken leg, it cannot get food and may starve to death. In contrast, when humans have such injuries, other group members feed them until they can recover.[13] The same goes for serious illness. These practices help far more people than apes survive to old age.

Again, what is inside enables the creature to satisfy its needs and, ultimately, to survive and reproduce. Social animals (including humans) accomplish those things by means of social interaction. Much of what goes on inside the human mind is designed to help the person relate to others. Social psychologists spend much time studying people's inner processes, including their thoughts and feelings and, recently, how their brains work. They study those things because *inner processes serve interpersonal functions*. Remember that phrase; it will be one of the themes of this book, and it is a good basis for understanding social psychology.

QUIZ YOURSELF
Nature and Social Behavior

1. The finding that kids who watch violent TV programs become more aggressive as adults than do kids who watch nonviolent TV programs can best be explained in terms of _____ influences.
   - (a) biological
   - (b) genetic
   - (c) hormonal
   - (d) societal

2. Suppose that a new baby girl was born with no teeth. Unfortunately, because she had great difficulty eating, she died of starvation before she could have any children. Thus, the trait of having no teeth was not preserved for future generations. This process is called _____.
   - (a) natural selection
   - (b) nurture
   - (c) praxis
   - (d) None of the above

3. What term refers to a new gene or combination of genes?
   - (a) Mutation
   - (b) Natural selection
   - (c) Reproduction
   - (d) Survival

4. Some species have bigger brains (for their body weight) than other species. What do big-brained species primarily use their brains for?
   - (a) Eating better foods
   - (b) Roaming over larger territories
   - (c) Having larger and more complex social structures
   - (d) All of the above

answers: see pg 66

Culture and Human Social Life

Social Animal or Cultural Animal?

Social psychologists like to use the phrase "the social animal" to describe human nature. Many influential thinkers, from the ancient Greek philosopher Aristotle right down to the modern social psychologist Elliot Aronson,[14] have used this phrase. By calling people **social animals**, these thinkers are saying that people seek connections to others and prefer to live, work, and play together with other people.

People are indeed social animals, but using this label may miss the mark of what is special about human beings. Plenty of other animals are social, from ants to elephants (as Aronson and others acknowledge). Human beings are not the only and perhaps not even the most social animals.

Being social animals is not what is most special about human beings. What is special is being cultural animals. Some other animals have bits and scraps of culture, such as when a tribe of monkeys all use stones to open nuts, or learn to rinse their potatoes in the stream to get the dirt off,[15] but none comes anywhere close to having the remarkably rich and powerful cultural systems that humans have. Moreover, human beings have culture everywhere; human life is almost impossible to imagine without it. Culture in animals is typically a bonus or a luxury, something they could live almost as well without. All humans use culture every day and depend on it for their survival.

Not a good idea.

Culture is thus the essence of what makes us human. Yes, we are social beings, but we have plenty of company in that respect. We are also deeply cultural beings, and in that respect we are unique. Let us therefore consider what culture is.

Culture Defined

Culture is harder to define than nature. (In fact, one book listed 164 different definitions of culture that different thinkers have used!)[16] The term originally referred to a system of farming (a usage one can still see in terms like *agriculture*). Then it came to refer to musical and artistic achievements, such as paintings and symphonies. Social scientists eventually began to use the term to refer to what a large group of people have in common. French culture, for example, refers to everything that French people share: language, values, food preferences, a style of government, a place (France), and a shared sense of connection to the artistic and historical achievements of other French people.

For present purposes, the important thing about culture is that it is a kind of social system. Just as a pack of wolves or a school of fish is a social system, so is France. But there are obvious differences. France is much more complex than a pack of wolves. It is rich in symbols, meanings, and information. There are more different kinds of relationships among the French people than among the wolves.

Culture is thus an advanced way of being social. If we think of evolution as proceeding from simple creatures such as plants, to solitary animals, to social animals, then cultural animals are a further step in that same direction.

Following are some important features of culture.

Shared Ideas

Culture is the world of shared ideas. Culture enables you to interact with people you have never met before; by virtue of belonging to the same culture, you have enough in common

social animals animals that seek connections to others and prefer to live, work, and play with other members of their species that you can do things together. If you travel to another city and meet new people, many interactions are possible because of culture: You might talk to them about sports or politics, or you might buy something from them in a store, or you might work together to sail a boat. To say that culture consists of "shared ideas" is to say that no single person has culture.

People may argue about many beliefs and practices, but the arguments occur on the basis of shared underlying beliefs. In the United States, for example, Democrats and Republicans argue about how best to run the country, but they share an underlying faith in certain values such as free elections, help for the sick and needy, a prosperous economy, and good schools. They just disagree about how to provide these things and how to choose between two values when they conflict.

If culture is an important part of what humans evolved to do, then we would expect the human brain to be strongly oriented toward shared ideas. Plenty of evidence confirms this. As one sign, young human children quickly grasp the possibility of shared attention, in the sense that they emphasize looking at the same things that other people (especially their mother or primary caregiver) are looking at. (The expression "look!" is one that very young children understand: they obey it and even say it.)

Recent work in social psychology has provided remarkable evidence of the human brain's attunement to shared ideas. Emotions, for example, seem to be intensified merely by seeing something and knowing that another member of your group is sharing the experience. Participants in these studies saw images, advertisements, or a short video (e.g., the plight of homeless people, or cute puppies cavorting). They were told that other members of the group were viewing the same stimuli at the same time, or one minute earlier, or one minute later, or they were told strangers rather than group members were seeing these things, or in another control condition that they were watching alone. People had the strongest emotional reactions only in the first condition: when another group member was seeing it at exactly the same time.[17] Thus, simultaneous sharing causes the mind to react more strongly to the same information.

Likewise, people learn more quickly and pick up norms for behavior faster when they know another group member is viewing the same information than when they view it alone. If the other person is not a fellow group member, learning is slower, as it is if one's fellow group member is viewing something else.[18]

In fact, people seem especially attuned to knowing that some important information is shared. A clever series of studies required participants to make choices, some of which involved trusting each other, after hearing all the instructions and options. They showed the most trust if the information came by loudspeaker so they were sure the other person heard exactly the same thing they did.[19] Simply being told that the same information was being communicated to the other person had less of an effect. In principle it shouldn't matter whether you are informed that someone else is getting the same information versus you directly experience it together, but it did. The difference is that in one case one has direct, certain knowledge that the other has exactly the same information. In most social settings throughout history, knowing that someone else heard the same story was no guarantee that the other person had exactly the same information, because stories can be told and heard in different ways. This suggests that the brain puts special priority on information that is directly experienced as shared with someone else.

Culture as Social System

Culture exists as a network linking many different people. The idea of a network is useful because it captures the essential point that culture connects many people together and exists in what they share. The problem with the idea of a network is that it doesn't sufficiently capture the dynamic (changing) aspect of culture. Culture never sits still.

Instead of a network, therefore, it is useful to think of culture as a system consisting of many moving parts that work together. Think, for example, of how people get food nowadays: Farmers grow it, factories process it, truckers transport it, stores display it, people buy it and cook it. When a family sits down to dinner, it is likely that 50 or 100 other people have directly helped get that food there (not to mention the thousands of others who were indirectly involved, including the management of the supermarket chain, the banks that financed the farms and the trucking company, the corporations that paid the parents the salaries they used to buy the food, the factories that built the refrigerator and stove, the suppliers of electricity, and so on).

The food system is an initial illustration of one theme of social psychology that we will call *putting people first*. (We will talk more about this later in the chapter, and throughout the book.) Most animals get their food directly from nature, at least after a brief period of infancy. In the modern world, most people get their food from other people. Human survival and success depend more on how we deal with each other than on how we deal with the natural world around us.

Culture as Praxis

Anthropologists now argue among themselves as to whether a culture should be understood more on the basis of shared beliefs and values or shared ways of doing things. (Many use the term **praxis** to refer to practical ways of doing things.) Almost certainly, the answer is both. The culture that people in Philadelphia, Pennsylvania share involves some shared values, such as the value of money, democracy, preferences for some kinds of food, aversion to crime, support for their local sports teams, and so forth. They also share ways of doing things: They drive on the same roads, use the same hospitals when they are sick, buy their food at local supermarkets, borrow money from the same banks, read the same newspapers, and so on. You will not live very well in Philadelphia if you refuse to shop at Philadelphia stores, or insist on driving your car on the left side of the road, or only go to a hospital to play billiards rather than to get treatment for illness.

Often the praxis depends on shared ideas. Money provides a good example: Certain round bits of metal and strips of colored paper are inherently worthless but, by virtue of shared ideas about them, acquire value and can be exchanged for all sorts of things. You can analyze the physics and chemistry of a dollar bill (e.g., its molecular structure) without gaining any clue to its value, because the value depends on shared social understandings. To learn more about the cultural significance of money, see the *Money Matters* box.

praxis practical ways of doing things

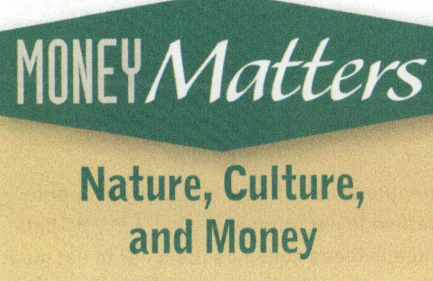

MONEY Matters

Nature, Culture, and Money

Money is such a familiar feature of human life that we take its existence and power for granted. All countries in the world today use money, so culturally it is universal by now. Looked at from the perspective of nature, however, money is quite unusual. No species of plant or animal (other than humans) uses money. Money is thus a product of human culture, but it is estimated to be only about 3,000 years old,[20] which means that early civilizations did not have it. It is much too recent to have shaped human nature biologically. There is no "money instinct."

Clearly people want money, and many people work long and hard to get it. One reason is that money operates as a kind of a tool.[21] Just as animals use tools to get what they want, people use money to get what they want. Biology has programmed humans (like other animals) to want things, so people also come to want money because it enables them to get these things. As a tool, money is desired not for itself but for what can be done with it.

But the money-as-tool analogy failed to explain the widespread human concern with money. For example, some people hoard money, obviously wanting to get it and keep it but not spend it. What good is a tool you never use?

So, theorists have produced a second analogy: Money is not just like a tool; it is also like a drug. People come to want it for its own sake, even though it does not confer any benefit that biology recognizes.[22]

Drugs take advantage of the body's natural capacities for pleasure. People feel happy when they do something that will ultimately lead to survival or reproduction, such as when they have sex or fall in love or find something great to eat. Drugs in a sense trick the body. When you take a drug, you might feel as good as if you had fallen in love, but whereas being in love might help you achieve survival and reproduction, being high on drugs will not normally accomplish either of these. In the same way, money comes to be desired for its own sake, rather than for the sake of the good things one gets for it. That's why people might hoard money, for example. It is as if they are addicted to money.

Although animals never develop money on their own, some of them seem capable of learning aspects of money, if humans teach them. Studies done with monkeys show this.[23] After several months of training, the monkeys learned to trade little coins for treats such as grapes. When the researchers changed the price, the monkeys adjusted their purchases accordingly. Researchers saw few signs of monkeys' using money with each other, except for one enterprising male who managed to trade a coin for sex with a female (who then spent the coin on getting a grape, her favorite treat). Still, their grasp of money remained rudimentary, and the researchers reported that they sometimes tried to use cucumber slices as if they were coins, at least when trading with humans (who did not fall for the counterfeit).

Culture, Information, and Meaning

Another crucial aspect of culture is that it is based on meaningful information. All cultures use language to encode and share information. People act as they do because they process this information. People change their behavior based on information they get from the culture, such as laws and rules, religious teachings and moral principles, historical events, symbols, what they read in books or see on television, and what they learned in school. Nonhuman animals respond to very little information of those kinds.

Human beings can think about and plan for the future, unlike squirrels. If you dig up all a squirrel's nuts and cart them off, the squirrel just goes on burying more nuts at the same pace, not even trying to compensate for the loss. But if humans lose their stores—perhaps because of a power failure that causes all the food in the refrigerator to spoil—then people quickly compensate by replacing the lost supply.

As cultural animals, humans find meaning through connecting with others. For example, researchers on consumer psychology have found that people seem to get more pleasure and value from spending money on experiences (e.g., going out to dinner or theater) than on objects (e.g., buying a new coat or power tool).[24] The reason for this difference has been much disputed. Two social psychologists found the answer: Experiences are generally shared with others, whereas objects are often used by oneself alone. They found, for example, that solitary experiences were no more valued or meaningful than material possessions.[25]

Summary

What, then, is culture? The different components mentioned in this section can be summarized in this way: **Culture** is an information-based system, involving both shared understandings and praxis, that enables groups of people to live together in an organized fashion and to get what they need. Culture can have a significant influence even on basic human needs, such as food and sex. To learn more, read the *Food for Thought* and *Social Side of Sex* boxes.

culture an information-based system that includes shared ideas and common ways of doing things

FOOD FOR *Thought*

Virtuous Vegetarians

Throughout this book, we will feature research relevant to eating. We have selected eating for this treatment because human eating is relevant to both nature and culture.

On the nature side, eating is natural; all animals eat. Eating is a vital means of getting what one needs for survival, which, as we saw, was a crucial goal of biological life. Social animals are social precisely because their social interactions help them get food and thereby survive. Like other animals, humans feel bad when they do not have enough to eat, and these bad feelings motivate people to seek food. Also like other animals, humans quickly learn to dislike and avoid foods that make them sick.

Humans resemble other animals in their need to eat regularly. But eating has been transformed by culture. Unlike all other animals, humans go on diets, have elaborate systems of etiquette and table manners, cook their food, experiment endlessly with recipes, and sometimes serve meals to total strangers.

Another uniquely human trait is the tendency to reject certain categories of food based on ideas. Many religions, for example, prescribe or forbid particular foods, especially on certain days. Based on different religious views, some people will eat beef but not pork, whereas others eat pork but not beef.

Vegetarianism is a revealing example. Some animals eat only plants, but that is the way nature made them. Humans are capable of eating meat and naturally do eat meat, yet cultural reasons convince many people to refuse to eat meat. For example, some people believe that it is morally proper to refuse to eat other animals.[26,27,28,29,30] That means ideas convince them not to eat meat. These ideas include a belief that animals should have rights similar to humans, or a belief that it is better for the planet to have people eat only plant food (because land used for growing livestock is less productive than land used for growing plants).

Nothing like this has been seen in any other species. We have no evidence of any animal that naturally eats meat but sometimes decides, for moral or religious reasons, to eat only plant food. Many human beings do precisely that, however. Such behavior is not found in nature but is well documented among human beings, and it reflects the power of meaning (ideas) to change and determine how people act.

Nature and Culture Interacting

See what sort of explanation you can think of for this: Statisticians began noticing that a large number of professional hockey players in the National Hockey League had birthdays in January and February.[31] Maybe being born in winter makes someone love winter sports more? Getting ice skates for your birthday? But November and December should also be good for that, and those months were marked by relatively few birthdays of NHL players. Also, the same pattern began to emerge in other sports as well, especially soccer, where the effect has been found all over the world.[32] (So obviously it wasn't specifically about cold weather sports in the northern hemisphere.) The pattern is statistically undeniable. What might cause professional athletes to have birthdays in January? Astrology? No.

The unequal birthday pattern emerges from a curious mix of nature and culture. In hockey, as in many sports, pro athletes generally got their start while they were children. Children's

The Social Side of *Sex*

Sex and Culture

Like eating, sexual behavior will be featured through this book as an important category of behavior that is shaped by both nature and culture. Whereas food is needed for survival, sex is needed for reproduction.

Sex has been a bitter battleground between those who explain it on the basis of nature and evolution and those who emphasize cultural construction. Is sex a matter of genes and hormones causing people to feel desires the way nature has prescribed them? Or is culture the principal cause of who wants to do what to whom in bed?

Some features of sexuality are found everywhere and may well be rooted in nature. In all cultures, for example, men seem to desire a greater number of sexual partners than women.[33] Sex is everywhere the main way to make babies. The same basic sex practices are known to most cultures. One sex historian observed that the sex manuals written thousands of years ago in ancient China covered almost all the same techniques one would find in a sex manual today, with only one major exception (sadomasochism).[34]

Some other universal aspects of sex reflect the influence of culture. All known cultures have rules about sex.[35] Cultures know that sex leads to making babies, and efforts to prevent pregnancy have been found all over the world, though the ancient means of preventing conception (except for abstaining from sex) are generally less effective than modern technologies such as the birth control pill and the intrauterine device (IUD). Some form of prostitution, in which people pay money for sex, is found in most large cultures, although many aspects of it (such as whether it is legally tolerated and what it costs) differ substantially.

Cultural differences in sex are also evident. In Turkey, women are expected to be virgins until they marry, and until quite recently it was standard practice for many brides-to-be to have a medical examination to certify their virginity. Lebanese men who have sex with male animals are likewise subject to the death penalty, but it is perfectly legal for them to have sex with female animals. In New Guinea, some tribes regard male–male sex as normal while people are growing up, and boys are expected to perform oral sex on young men as a way of acquiring fluids that produce masculine strength, but after marriage men are supposed to stop their homosexual activities and restrict themselves to their wives.[36] Liberty Corner, New Jersey, has a law prohibiting people from beeping the horn of a parked car during sexual intercourse; one can scarcely imagine what life must have been like in that town before that law restored peace and quiet! Another curious law comes from Liverpool, England: Topless salesgirls are forbidden to work in tropical fish stores, though not in other stores.

Last, there are plenty of differences within a culture too. In the United States today, some people reach their 30th birthdays while still virgins, whereas others have had sex with more than a dozen people by the age of 15. Millions of people go through their entire lives having sex with only one person (their spouse) and only in the missionary position (man on top, woman on bottom), whereas some people have more than a thousand sex partners without ever using the missionary position. Genghis Khan, perhaps the world's most successful lovemaker has more than 16 million direct male descendants alive today! Many people yearn for practices that others regard as dangerous perversions. Some people love to read about sex or watch films of people having sex, whereas others find those materials disgusting and want them to be outlawed.

Nature or culture? Human sexuality provides ample evidence of both.

leagues are grouped by age, but rather than automatically moving from league to league on their birthday (which might disrupt teams), kids are grouped for each season based on a cutoff date—typically January 1. Thus, when the season starts in November, if you're already 9 or will turn 9 by the end of December, you play with the 9-year-olds, but if your birthday isn't until after January 1, you play with the 8-year-olds. Why does that matter? Nine-year-olds are usually bigger and stronger than 8-year-olds. Kids born late in the year grow up always being matched against others who are older, stronger, and faster, so they tend to drop out of the sport. Meanwhile, the lucky kids with birthdays in January will grow up being the oldest (and therefore often the biggest and strongest) children in their league, which puts them at a physical advantage. This advantage helps them be successful and makes the sport fun for them.

You might think the effect would wear off as children grow up. But many of the younger children have already dropped out. Moreover, coaching increases the problem. Coaches want to win, so they bestow their attention and more playing time on their best players—which often means their oldest (hence biggest, strongest, and most coordinated) ones. Children born after January 1 end up getting more training and more opportunities to compete, whereas those born late in the year spend more time on the bench.

The so-called relative age effect[37] is not limited to sports. It has been shown in school performance also.[38,39] Children who end up getting classified as gifted often benefited from starting school later than others, which made them older than their classmates.[40] Before you start planning to have your babies in January, however, note that school cutoff dates are different from sports ones. In many schools, it is the children born in the summer (just before school starts in September) who are destined to be always the youngest in their class and therefore suffer disadvantages in school.[41]

Sport in general is a combination of nature (innate physical abilities) and culture (practice, training, and arbitrary rules). Star pro athletes are thus neither made nor born: They need both the gifts of nature and the benefits of culture. And, it appears, the luck to be born on the right side of the cutoff date also helps!

This chapter began with the story of little Brenda. The failure to raise the boy as a girl suggests that being male has some elements of nature that are not easily overcome by culture. Yet manhood also has strong aspects of culture. Research on "precarious manhood"[42] has shown some cultural differences in beliefs about being a man versus being a woman. Many cultures require boys to prove themselves before they can claim to be men, whereas all girls grow up to be women. Even among modern American college students, manhood is regarded as more tentative and requiring of proof than womanhood. In one of their studies, students read about people who said they felt they were no longer a man, or no longer a woman. Loss of womanhood seemed difficult to fathom, and students thought it must mean that the woman had undergone a sex change operation. Loss of manhood was more readily seen as a result of social factors, such as not being able to provide for one's family.

Thus, in a sense, society regards womanhood as a biological achievement, whereas manhood requires a cultural achievement. (Note that both are cultural opinions, however!) The need for men to prove themselves is relevant to many gender differences. In laboratory studies on precarious manhood, threats to a man's masculinity caused him to feel aggressive and anxious, whereas parallel threats to a woman's femininity produced no such response.[43]

Nature and Culture Shaping Each Other

When people argue whether a behavior is a product of nature or culture, they often seem to assume the two are separate causes. Yet the separation is far from complete. Nature shapes culture, and vice versa.

The influence of nature on culture starts with very basic and simple insights. As we have said, one function of culture is to help people satisfy their biological needs. People need food, water, and shelter, and they often need a good environment for raising their children. Cultures that fail to provide these do not last long.[44,45]

Recent work has shown some surprising ways that cultures are shaped by nature. One big factor is whether the local area has plenty of viruses, bacteria, germs, and similar things, called pathogens, because they make you sick. It turns out that fairly standard differences in cultural practices arise based on whether the local environment is relatively healthy (not very many pathogens) or more risky (abundant pathogens).

In places where there are many pathogens, like southeast Asia and parts of Africa, the cultures that develop put more pressure on people to conform and obey the rules. Nonconformists are more likely to be tolerated where there are few pathogens because the nonconformists will not spread disease so easily there. In fact, in places where abundant pathogens create a high risk of disease, society members are more similar to each other, even in their personalities.[46] Many researchers classify cultures along a continuum from individualism (everyone takes care of themselves and is free to choose how to act) to collectivism (maintaining relationships and getting along with others is more important than doing what you want). Collectivistic cultures tend to be found in places with many pathogens. Individualistic cultures are more common in low-disease environments with few pathogens.[47]

More diseases cause people to be more prejudiced, especially toward people who look different, as if the body automatically suspects strange-looking people of carrying illness.[48] Sexual restraint (such as having fewer sex partners) is a more common and important value when there are many diseases because the close physical contact of sex can spread disease.[49] But even beyond sex, people in such cultures tend to be less oriented toward meeting lots of people, less open to new ideas, and less interested in trying out new experiences.[50]

What about the other way around? Might culture influence nature? In general, nature comes first, but some reversals are increasingly difficult to argue. The human capacity for speech (nature), for example, probably evolved in step with along the emergence of spoken language among humans (culture). (It is hard to imagine why evolution would have favored humans who could talk well, unless they gained some benefit by talking.) Thus, some theorists have begun to speak of "co-evolution," meaning that nature and culture changed together and shaped each other.[51,52] Once the social environment began to include more and more culture, the humans with greater competence for functioning in culture would survive and reproduce better than others. That, after all, is the basic idea of seeing humans as cultural animals![53]

What Makes Cultural Animals?

The human being is a product of both nature and culture. A traditional way of thinking has been that nature provides the foundation, and then culture builds on top of that. That style of thought puts nature first, culture second. However, recent theories have looked for ways to blend the two, such that nature and culture shape each other.[54,55]

Many animals have a little bit of culture. Hence, it is likely that culture existed on earth before humans evolved. If culture was already in the environment, then it could have guided natural selection to endow humans with traits that promoted culture.

Why is culture so rare or rudimentary in nonhuman animals? The answer lies almost certainly in the advanced psychological requirements for culture. We saw earlier that animals need more inner processes to be social than to be solitary. In the same way, they need more inner processes to be cultural than to be merely social. Most animals don't have enough brainpower to sustain culture.

What are some of the main differences between being social and being cultural (or, more precisely, between being merely social and being both social and cultural)? Social animals may act together, as when a swarm of bees or a pack of wolves or a herd of zebras all move together. This mass action is social because the animals know what the others are doing and coordinate their own behavior with it. In contrast, cultural animals often have elaborate division of labor, in which each individual performs a unique function. Compare the collective work of a corporation or a football team with that of a swarm of bees, for example. Although different bees might have different roles (e.g., the queen bee is the mother of all the bees in her hive, worker bees lack reproductive capacity but carry pollen back to the hive to feed the young), the roles are far simpler, less flexible, and fewer than roles in human society.

Social animals may figure out good ways of doing things and may possibly copy something they see another doing. Cultural animals (human beings) deliberately share their knowledge throughout the group, so that it can be preserved and passed on to the next generation. Humans are the only animals to have schools, universities, and libraries, for example. The preservation of knowledge allows for progress, too. One man (Alexander Graham Bell) invented the telephone, and even though he has been dead for decades, many people have and use telephones without having to invent them all over again. Among animals

Still no progress on cooked food, democracy, female liberation, social security, patent law, football, e-mail, or cosmetic surgery.

without culture, each problem has to be solved anew by each generation, and in some cases by each individual.

Social creatures can often communicate, such as with grunts and barks. Their communication refers mainly to events or entities that are present at that moment. Cultural animals use language, which enables them to communicate about many things that are far removed from the here and now. Human children often study history, for example, in which they learn about events that occurred centuries before they were born. Such communication is impossible for merely social animals. No animal knows anything about what happened before it was born, including the history of its social group.

Social animals may help each other, but in general helping is limited to relatives. It is quite rare for any nonhuman animal to make some sacrifice (such as willingly giving away food) in order to benefit another, even if the two animals are related (and especially if they aren't). In contrast, cultural animals have a broader sense of community and sometimes help total strangers. Some people donate large sums of money to alleviate hunger or sickness among people they have never met, who may be of a different race and may live on a faraway continent. Others help people even when it involves great danger to themselves.

When animals live and work together, some degree of conflict is probably inevitable. Social animals have few ways of resolving these disputes other than aggression. If two animals (not related to each other) want the same piece of food, the bigger and stronger one is likely to get it, by force if necessary. In contrast, culture offers many alternative means of resolving disputes. These include moral principles, compromise, and going before a judge in a court of law. Indeed, most modern cultures strongly discourage people from settling their disputes by resorting to violence. Most social animals do not have that luxury.

Thus, the best approach to social psychology is to assume that people are products of both nature and culture. Nature has given humans certain traits and abilities because over time those enabled some people to survive and reproduce better than others. And humans really do survive and reproduce by means of their culture. Hence, we think that natural selection has shaped the human mind to "do" culture. In that sense, it is natural for humans to share information, seek to be together, form groups with multiple roles, communicate with each other about their inner thought processes, and more.

To sum up: Culture is a better way of being social. Being social, and thus being cultural, is a biological strategy. Biology measures success in terms of survival and reproduction. By those measures, human culture has been remarkably successful, even despite its problems such as war, pollution, social inequality, and oppression. Survival has improved remarkably. Indeed, by virtue of research (an important cultural activity), humans have nearly tripled their average life span since the Enlightenment—something no other species has been able to do. Meanwhile, the human population has risen from one woman about 200,000 years ago to nearly 8 billion people now. Our animal relatives such as the great apes all live near the equator, but humans have been able to live in mountains, in forests, in plains, in cold and snowy places, in deserts, in rain-soaked places, and in others, thanks to cultural innovations such as clothing, heated homes, and cooked food.

Are People the Same Everywhere?

At first blush, people are very different. If you have ever visited a foreign country, you probably encountered striking differences. People speak different languages, eat very different foods, etc. These differences reflect the influence of culture.

What could be more natural than sleep? Yet there are important cultural differences in how people sleep. In the United States, most people sleep only at night and wake up with an alarm clock. Many consume coffee or some other substance containing a drug that wakes them up. In Mexico, it is customary for adults to take a nap (a siesta) in the middle of the day, and as a result they may not sleep as much at night. Some cultures and religions disapprove of consuming coffee and similar drugs.

Sleeping arrangements are also quite different, even though most people regard their own sleeping patterns as natural. For example, should small children sleep alone or with their parents? In the United States, the prevailing practice is to keep children out of their parents' bed and even in a separate bedroom. One study of white, middle-class, two-parent families in Cleveland, Ohio, found that only 3% of the babies slept in their parents' bedroom during their first year of life, and only 1% after that.[56]

In other cultures, however, sleeping arrangements are quite different. In a survey of many different non-Western, nonindustrial societies, anthropologists found that the norm everywhere was for infants to sleep with their mothers.[57] Researchers in Japan confirmed that a typical Japanese person hardly ever sleeps alone at any point in life, nor does he or she want to. Roughly half of Japanese children ages 11 to 15 sleep in the same bed with their mother or father; others sleep with siblings. The only Japanese who normally sleep alone are unmarried young adults who are living away from home and old people whose spouse has died and whose children (and grandchildren) are living elsewhere.

People who are accustomed to the middle-class American system might regard it as dangerous, immoral, or even pathological (sick) to let children sleep with their parents. However, when Japanese or people from other cultures learn about the American practice, they have a similar reaction. They think that Americans must not love their children if they put them through the terrifying ordeal of making them sleep by themselves. Some point out that in the animal kingdom, too, babies want to be with their mothers, especially at night, and so it seems "natural" to them to do the same. The American practice thus seems dangerous, immoral, or wrong to them.

In these and countless other ways, people are different, both within and between cultures. Then again, in most respects people are much more similar. Nearly everywhere, people love their children, try to get enough to eat, talk about the weather, wait their turn, make distinctions between right and wrong, compete for status, help each other (and help family and relatives more readily than strangers), worry about money, and drive their cars on the same side of the road. Usually they drive on the right, though in some countries (such as England and Australia) they drive on the left, but the important thing is that they share a rule that tells everyone to drive on the same side.

The question of whether people are the same everywhere, or differ in different cultures, is a vexing one for social psychology. By far the greatest amount of research is done in the United States, most of it at American universities with university students as participants. Some social psychologists despair that the cultural differences are so big that it is impossible to formulate any general conclusions, and some suggest that we should never generalize beyond American college students (or at least not without years of careful checking to verify what patterns are found everywhere).

Others are more optimistic. Although cultural differences are real and important, they are often merely matters of degree rather than opposites. For example, people respond more aggressively to insults and criticism than to praise, people are attracted to others similar to themselves more than to those who are different, and people get jealous when their romantic partners have sex with someone else. There are cultural differences in how these reactions are expressed and perhaps even in how strongly they are felt, but there is no known culture in which the opposite patterns (e.g., disliking similar others, or aggressing more in response to praise than insult) are found. Likewise, basic beliefs about people and the world have broadly similar consequences; for example, social cynicism (expecting that social life will often produce negative outcomes) goes with low conformity, low drive to achieve, and various negative attitudes toward leaders.[58]

In this book, we will present some interesting findings of cultural differences. But our greater quest is for underlying similarities. For example, languages are very different from each other, but underneath they have great similarities, and all known human cultures have and use language. Hence, we think the use of language is part of human nature. Moreover, evolution helped install the necessary equipment (vocal cords, ears that

In some cultures, it is not only acceptable, but desirable, for children to sleep with their parents.

Culture and Human Social Life | 51

can tell thousands of words apart, and brains that can use grammar) for people to use language. Much of social psychology can be understood by assuming that the human psyche was designed by nature (via natural selection) for culture. This means that culture is in our genes, even though cultural differences may not be.

We started with the question of what the human psyche was designed for. Culture is a large, important part of the answer. That is, the human mind, including its emotions, was designed in part to enable it to take part in the advanced kinds of social life that humans have.

QUIZ YOURSELF

Culture and Human Social Life

1. Humans are best described as _____.
   - (a) cultural animals
   - (b) social animals
   - (c) both cultural and social animals
   - (d) neither cultural animals nor social animals

2. In social psychology, the "nature versus nurture" debate _____.
   - (a) is alive and well
   - (b) has largely died out; most social psychologists maintain that human behavior is shaped mostly by social forces
   - (c) has largely died out; most social psychologists maintain that human behavior is shaped mostly by genetic forces
   - (d) has been reframed; the debate now concerns how nature and nurture interact with one another and influence one another

3. All known cultures have rules about _____.
   - (a) agriculture
   - (b) sex
   - (c) sleeping
   - (d) All of the above

4. Most social psychological research has been conducted in _____.
   - (a) Asia
   - (b) Canada
   - (c) Europe
   - (d) the United States

answers: see pg 66

Important Features of Human Social Life

In this section, we will cover several features of human social life that set humans apart from other animals and that are crucial for understanding social interaction among humans. They reflect important ways that human life was shaped by nature to cope with human social life, including culture. These themes will come up repeatedly in the chapters that follow.

The Duplex Mind

The human mind has two main systems. In a sense, this is what Freud said when he distinguished between the conscious ego and the unconscious. Most experts no longer accept Freud's account of how the mind is laid out, but there is a new and exciting version of the theory that the mind has two parts. We call this the **duplex mind**, as in a duplex house with two separate apartments.

Unfortunately, the experts don't agree about what to call these two systems or exactly what goes where. Here, our summary combines many views of the duplex mind, but you should be aware that many different variations exist and that many details are disputed.

duplex mind the idea that the mind has two different processing systems (deliberate and automatic)

Two Systems

We can call the two systems the automatic and the deliberate. The **automatic system** operates mainly outside of consciousness, though it is not a Freudian kind of unconscious full of repressed urges and thoughts you are afraid to think. Instead, it is like a team of little robots doing lots of simple jobs to make your life easier. You are not aware of the robots and the work they are doing. Whereas Freud thought that the unconscious often trips you up by making you say or do the wrong thing, the automatic system is usually very helpful. It handles the endless mundane tasks, such as interpreting, organizing, and categorizing all the information that comes in through your eyes and ears. For example, it might sort through the stream of babbling sounds that your ears hear in order to pick out the score of the game involving your favorite team, and it links that score with relevant information in your memory, such as how your team is doing generally and whether today's outcome will help it qualify for the playoffs.

The **deliberate system** is the other "half" of the duplex mind. (We put "half" in quotation marks because a precise comparison of sizes is not possible given the present state of knowledge. Most likely the automatic system is much bigger than the deliberate system.) The deliberate system mostly operates in consciousness, so it can also be called the conscious system. Though people sometimes think they are conscious of everything in their minds, in reality they are conscious of only one part—but that is a very important part.

The deliberate system is what seems to turn on when you wake up and turn off when you go to sleep. The automatic system continues to operate during sleep, sorting information and making simple judgments.[59] (That is presumably why you wake up if someone softly says your name.) It also moves the body around in bed, as when you bump into your sleeping partner and roll away without waking up. It processes information, too: You will wake up to the sound of your own name spoken more softly than almost any other word, which means that your mind can tell the difference in the meanings of words even when asleep.[60] Telling the difference is the job of the automatic system.

An influential article has called the two systems "impulsive" and "reflective," and these terms capture the gist of how they operate.[61] The automatic system operates by impulse; you feel something and then do it, for example. The deliberate system typically involves reflective thought about what would be the best thing to do.

What Is Consciousness For?

Most people think their conscious minds are in charge of everything they do. They believe the conscious mind constantly directs their actions and their train of thought. These beliefs are false. The automatic system generally runs almost everything. Consider walking, for example, which is something that most people do over and over all day long. Do you consciously control the movements of your legs and feet? Does your conscious mind have to say, "Now pick up the left foot, swing it forward, hold it high enough so it doesn't bump the ground, set down the heel, roll forward, shift weight off the back foot," and so forth? Of course not. Someday watch a small child who is just learning to walk, and you may see what happens when the conscious mind tries to figure out how to make the legs walk. But after walking has been learned, the person almost never thinks about it again. Walking is done automatically, not deliberatively or reflectively.

Over the past couple of decades, there has been a huge shift in psychological theory about the role of consciousness. This change has been driven by the rise in research findings that show how much the automatic system does. Much of behavior is driven and directed by these automatic responses that occur outside of awareness. Many of these findings will be covered in subsequent chapters. The combination of them has led many experts to begin questioning what consciousness is good for—if anything! The automatic system can learn, think, choose, and respond. It has ideas and emotions, or at least simple versions of them. It knows your "self" and other people. Even when people believe they are deciding something, often it can be shown that the automatic system has already decided. Their decisions are swayed by subliminal cues or other bits of information of which the person is unaware that have been processed automatically.

Many experts today believe that consciousness doesn't really do much of anything. One psychobiologist concluded from working with people whose brains had been surgically

automatic system the part of the mind outside of consciousness that performs simple operations

deliberate system the part of the mind that performs complex operations split in half (usually to control epilepsy) that consciousness is just a side effect of other processes and of thinking about the future, and that it doesn't serve any important function.[62,63] Some psychologists think consciousness is simply a kind of emotional signal to call attention to our own actions so we don't confuse them with what other people have done.[64] Others have observed that the automatic system does more than we thought and the deliberate system less, and maybe the field will soon conclude that the conscious part of the mind doesn't do anything at all.[65,66,67,68] With all due respect to these experts, we disagree. We think that the deliberate system was difficult and expensive (in terms of biological requirements) for nature to give us, so most likely some very profound advantages make consciousness worth the trouble. Yes, the automatic system does most of the work of the psyche, but the deliberate system probably does something very important too. Most likely these special jobs involve complex kinds of thought that combine information and follow explicit rules, as in logical reasoning.[69]

Differences Between the Systems

For now, it is important to know that the two systems exist and to appreciate their established differences. These are summarized in **TABLE 2.1**.[70,71]

First, there is a difference in how much each system can do at the same time. The automatic system is like many different little machines doing many unrelated or loosely related things at once. The deliberate system does one thing at a time. As you read, your automatic system converts the visual images of letters into words, converts the words into meanings, and links the information with all sorts of things that are already stored in memory. Meanwhile, you consciously have only one thought at a time. Some recent studies showed that people are less aware of the taste of food if they are distracted.[72] Thus, if they ate foods while mentally rehearsing a phone number, they rated the food as having less taste—and they ate more of it!

The automatic system is quick and efficient. It performs tasks quite effectively and with relatively little effort. In contrast, the deliberate system is slow and cumbersome. Return to the example of walking: Try the experiment of consciously controlling every muscle movement while you are walking. You can do it, but it is very slow and awkward. That is why the mind naturally tries to make everything automatic.

TABLE 2.1 The Duplex Mind: Deliberate and Automatic Systems

Deliberate	Automatic
Slow	Fast
Controllable	Outside of conscious control
Guided by intention	Unintentional
Flexible	Inflexible
Good at combining information	Poor at combining information
Precise, rule-based calculations	Estimates
Can perform complex operations	Can perform simple operations
Does one thing at a time	Can do many things at once
Reasoning	Intuition
Effortful	Effortless
Features full-blown emotions	Features quick feelings of like and dislike, good and bad
Depends on automatic system	Can be independent of conscious processing
"Figure it out"	"Go with your gut feeling"

The deliberate system often requires effort, whereas the automatic system doesn't. In fact, you have to deliberately start to think consciously about something, but the automatic system starts by itself and often cannot be stopped. If we show you a word with a missing letter, you probably cannot stop yourself from filling in the blank. Try to read these letters without thinking of a word: K*SS. Probably you can't. The automatic system is too quick and efficient. It gives you the answer before your conscious mind can even think to formulate the question. The word is KISS.

All the differences mentioned so far favor the automatic system. If it were better at everything, however, we would have to conclude that the deliberate system is just a poorer, dumber, less effective system all around, which would raise the question of why we have it at all. (And that's why some experts, like the ones quoted earlier, have begun to doubt openly that it has any value.) But the deliberate system does have some advantages. First, the deliberate system is much more flexible than the automatic system. The automatic system is like a well-programmed robot or computer. It performs standard, familiar tasks according to the program, and it does them very reliably, quickly, and efficiently. But when the automatic system confronts something novel and unfamiliar, it doesn't know how to deal with it. The conscious mind, slow and cumbersome as it is, is much better at confronting novel, unfamiliar circumstances and deciding how to react.

The advantage of the deliberate system in dealing with novel circumstances is probably one crucial reason that human beings, as cultural animals, developed consciousness. Life in a cultural society is vastly more complicated, in terms of encountering new, unexpected, and unfamiliar dilemmas, than the lives of most other creatures. Imagine a robot that has been programmed to sort red beans from green beans. It will probably do this effectively and quickly, even performing much better than a human being. But then along comes a banana! The robot won't know what to do with a banana, unless it has been programmed for that eventuality too. Unlike a robot, a conscious human mind can deal with the banana even when it was expecting only red and green beans.

Another crucial advantage of the deliberate system is that it is able to combine information in complex, rule-driven ways. An automatic system that has been well trained can estimate that, say, 6 times 53 is a few hundred, but only the deliberate system can calculate that it is precisely 318. The deliberate system alone can perform complex logical reasoning.[73]

The influential social psychologist Daniel Kahneman[74,75] prefers to describe the thinking styles of the two systems as reasoning versus intuition. The automatic system is intuitive, in the sense that it is guided by gut reactions and quick feelings rather than a process of carefully thinking through all the implications of a problem. When you face a decision and someone advises you to "go with your gut feeling," that person is essentially telling you to rely on your automatic system (and its intuitions) rather than trying to reason through the problem logically, as the deliberate system will do. Often that is good advice because the automatic system does produce quick and usually good answers. But the highest achievements and advances of culture depend on the application of careful reasoning, which is the province of the deliberate system and conscious thought.

How They Work Together

The two parts of the duplex mind are not entirely independent of each other. In fact, they often work together.[76,77] The automatic system serves the deliberate system, in the sense that it operates behind the scenes to make conscious thought possible. You may think consciously that something you heard on the radio is illogical. But before that can happen, the automatic system has to have done a great deal of work: It processed the stream of sounds into comprehensible language, understood the gist of the message, and activated various other ideas in your memory that were associated with the core idea. The automatic system also works like an alarm system that signals to the deliberate system that something is wrong and that careful, conscious thinking is needed.

For example, suppose you heard on the news that someone was seriously injured at a campus party last night, and the dean was recommending that all

Go with your gut feeling, or figure out what is best?

further parties be canceled. Your automatic system understands the reasoning: Party caused injury, injury is bad, so parties are bad, so the dean cancels all parties. But the automatic system also connects this news to your feelings, and you realize: Wait! I love parties! I don't want all parties to be canceled! This is about as far as the automatic system can process, but it sends out an alarm to the deliberate system. Now you can reason through the situation consciously: One party caused an injury, but that doesn't reflect badly on all parties; there should be a way to reduce or avoid further injuries without canceling all parties. In that way, the two mental systems work together.

Conscious Override

Sometimes the two systems work against each other, however. One particularly important case is when the deliberate system overrides the automatic impulse. You feel like doing something, but you restrain yourself. For example, if you are looking forward to having a doughnut, and you see someone else take the last doughnut just before you get to the serving tray, you may have a natural impulse to protest. Hey! Give me that doughnut! You might even feel like grabbing it out of the other person's hand. After all, most other animals would act that way if someone took their food. But human beings can restrain that impulse. Rarely do human beings come to blows over the last doughnut. Indeed, the point that people restrain themselves is an important key to the psychology of aggression. We shall see in Chapter 10 that a great many factors cause aggression: violent media, hot temperatures, frustration, and insults. Given that nearly everyone occasionally experiences frustration, wounded pride, media violence, and heat, you might think that human beings would be constantly violent. But in reality, people are not usually aggressive or violent. Why not? People may have many angry impulses, but they restrain them. The conscious mind is often vital for overriding the impulses that the automatic system produces. As we shall see, this pattern is found in many spheres of social behavior, from dieting to prejudice.

Conscious overriding is vital to life in culture. Culture is full of rules about how to behave—norms, guidelines, laws, morals, and expectations. You can't just do whatever you feel like at any moment. Moreover, many situations are complicated and have hidden implications, so it is best to stop and think before acting. Imagine you are driving on a highway when another driver speeds up, passes you, and then slows down to take the next exit. Your natural impulse might be to smash into the back of the other driver's car with your own car, to hold your horn down, or to make angry gestures at the other driver—but that might get you in trouble. It would be better for your conscious mind to override these impulses and exercise self-control over your anger.

The Long Road to Social Acceptance

Living in a culture offers many advantages as compared with living in a merely social group. But it also makes much greater demands.

Consider what it takes to live in a North American city. If you're a bird, maybe you can just fly into town, find an empty tree, build a nest, and then hang around with some other birds until they let you stay. As a human, you need an apartment, which may take you a week of checking advertisements and going around to different addresses. (And to do that, you need to know how to read, how to use a map, and how to get and use a newspaper or the Internet.) You'll probably need to sign a lease promising to live there for a year. You need money to pay the rent, and probably that means you will need a job. A job typically requires credentials, such as education and training, and these may take years to obtain. A better job means more money, but it probably requires more training, and you have to perform well to keep the job. Finding a romantic partner is a much more complicated process in human beings than in other animals. You need to know where to meet people, how to act on a date, how to play the games and roles that are in fashion in this particular group.

This is one of the basic jobs of the human self: to garner acceptance. You need to figure out what other people prefer and expect, and then you need to change yourself to meet those expectations. The requirements for social acceptance are different in different cultures and eras. In the Victorian era (late 1800s), people who picked their noses or said four-letter words aloud were considered socially unacceptable, so most middle- and upper-class people learned to avoid doing those things. Nowadays saying four-letter words is more acceptable in many circles, whereas picking your nose is still not cool.

Outside the lab, people have to do many things to obtain social acceptance. It is not just a matter of etiquette. As previously noted, people need to acquire skills and credentials, gain the discipline to hold down a job, attract and hold relationship partners, and so on.

Built to Relate

The long road that humans travel to social acceptance means that people have to do a great deal of work to get along with others. To do that, they must develop many skills and capabilities. One thing that sets humans apart from other animals is how many inner, psychological traits they have that help them get along. These include the understanding that other humans have inner states like theirs, the capacity for language, and the ability to imagine how others perceive them.

This brings up one very important and broadly helpful theme that we have already mentioned: What is inside people is there because of what happens between people. That is, *inner processes serve interpersonal functions*. The psychological traits people have are designed to enable humans to connect with each other.

When you first consider the matter, it seems the other way around: What is inside people determines what happens between them. Because we are capable of language, we talk to other people. Because we have emotional responses of love and affection, we become attached to others. There is some truth to this view, but only from a relatively narrow perspective. To understand human nature, it is important to recognize that evolution created humans with the capacity for language and the emotional capabilities for love and affection *because* these traits improved people's ability to connect with others.

Earlier in this chapter we discussed the social brain theory, which asserted that evolution made intelligent brains not for understanding the physical environment but rather to increase the capability for having social relations. The intelligent brain is one of the defining traits of human beings. This was a first example of the pattern of inner processes serving interpersonal functions: The inner processes and structures (in this case, the intelligent brain) evolved for the sake of improving interpersonal relations.

Increasing evidence confirms that emotions also serve social functions. When people talk, even about seemingly trivial things, they end up sharing their feelings.[78] The discovery that they have similar emotional reactions creates a bond between them that contributes to a feeling of bonding and even to a willingness to trust each other with money.

People's motivation to do well and achieve is also deeply social. People work harder when a social bond is present, even if the bond is irrelevant to the task. For example, math students worked harder on math problems after reading a brief article about math written by someone whose birthday matched their own than by someone with a different birthday.[79] These findings fit the view of humans as cultural animals, because much of culture is about working together—and the research findings show that feeling connected to others increases one's motivation to work.

Automatic processes (see the earlier section on the duplex mind) also serve interpersonal functions. When cues make people automatically think about a group of others, they respond in ways that suggest preparing to interact with that group. For example, when people think about a group they dislike, they automatically start feeling more aggressive, even if the other group is not aggressive. When they think about the elderly, they change their behavior to prepare for interacting with older people: If they have positive feelings toward the elderly, they become more similar and accommodating (e.g., they walk more slowly, enabling them to walk with old people); if their feelings toward this group are negative, they change in ways that make them less friendly to the elderly (they walk faster, as if making it harder for old folks to keep up!).[80]

Even music may be fundamentally about connecting with others. Music is an important human and cultural phenomenon, and one that has posed a challenge to psychologists to explain. Recent findings have shown that people who like music and are sensitive to it are also more oriented toward working together with group members than musically indifferent people. They favor their group more, give other group members preferential treatment, and desire to belong more. In fact, the threat of being socially rejected from one's group makes people attend more carefully to music.[81] All these findings indicate that music can be partly explained as something that helps bring groups together and strengthen interpersonal ties. It seems that music is indeed the "universal language."

As with other themes, we should be careful not to overstate the case. Not all inner processes are there to serve interpersonal processes. Hunger and thirst, for example, are clearly there to prompt the animal or person to get enough food and water to sustain life. Hunger and thirst are thus inner processes that do not serve interpersonal functions. Still, many of the more advanced, complex, and interesting psychological phenomena do promote social interaction.

Thus, a social psychology approach to human nature will emphasize that many (though not all) inner processes exist for the sake of interpersonal interaction. In the next few chapters, we will see that the self, thinking, and emotion (among others) seem well designed to help people form and maintain relationships with others. Recall our discussion about trees earlier. Trees are neither social nor cultural. They do not need selves, nor the capacity to understand language, nor the knowledge that the inner states of other trees resemble their own. Trees were designed by nature to survive alone and get what they need from their physical surroundings. In contrast, humans were designed by nature to develop relationships and share information with each other. The human psyche is designed for social purposes, and especially for cultural ones, insofar as culture is a better way of being social.

Nature Says Go, Culture Says Stop

What aspects of human behavior come from nature as opposed to culture? There are many different answers, but one broad pattern is a theme that we summarize as "nature says go, culture says stop." That is, people seem naturally to have impulses, wishes, and other automatic reactions that predispose them to act in certain ways. Culture serves not so much to create new wishes and desires as to teach or preach self-control and restraint.

People may naturally feel sexual desires and aggressive urges at many points; they do not seem to need to be taught by culture to have those feelings. In that sense, sex and aggression are natural. But culture does have considerable influence on both sex and aggression. This influence mainly takes the form of restraining behaviors. Culture is full of rules that restrict sex, as by designating certain sexual acts or pairings as unacceptable. Sexual morality is mostly a matter of saying which sexual acts are wrong; likewise, laws about sex mainly prohibit sex acts. (Imagine laws that required people to have sexual intercourse on particular occasions!) Likewise, aggression is subject to a broad variety of cultural restraints, including moral prohibitions and laws that forbid many aggressive acts.

Often, culture works by ideas. Many of those ideas tell people what not to do. Most laws and moral principles say what not to do rather than what one should do. The Ten Commandments of Judeo-Christian religion, for example, mostly begin "Thou shalt not" and then mention some specific behavior. The only two that don't say "not" still imply it to some degree: Keeping the Sabbath holy is mostly a matter of not doing certain things (such as work or shopping) on the Sabbath, and honoring your parents is mostly a matter of refraining from disrespectful treatment. Thus, the most famous list of moral rules in Western culture is basically a list of ideas (rules) about what not to do, probably because people naturally sometimes feel urges to do precisely those things, but the culture (including its religion) disapproves.

To be sure, it would be a gross oversimplification to say that the role of nature is *always* to create positive desires and impulses or that culture *only* says what not to do. There are some important exceptions. Disgust reactions, for example, are quite natural and say "no" in a big way. Likewise, people may start eating because official policy and the clock (representing culture) say it is lunchtime, and they may stop eating because their inner sensations (representing nature) signal them that their bellies are full. In this case, culture says go and nature says stop. People may start engaging in aggression because their government (culture) has declared war, and they may stop aggressing because bodily states (nature) of exhaustion or injury dictate that they cannot continue.

Still, "nature says go and culture says stop" is probably right more often than it is wrong, and it provides a helpful way to understand much of the interplay between nature and culture. Throughout this book, we will see many examples in which impulses arise naturally and are restrained, with difficulty, by individuals who exert themselves to comply with cultural rules. Nature made us full of desires and impulses, and culture teaches us to restrain them for the sake of being able to live together in peace and harmony.

Self-control is one important psychological process that enables people to live in culture and follow cultural rules.[82] And most acts of self-control involve stopping oneself from thinking, feeling, or doing something.[83] With regard to spending money, eating and dieting, engaging in sexual behavior, drinking alcohol or taking drugs, and many similar behaviors, having good self-control means holding oneself back instead of acting on every impulse. Dieters need self-control to keep themselves from eating too much or eating the wrong kinds of food, for example. The desire to eat is natural; the restraints are cultural. Self-control is discussed in Chapter 4.

Selfish Impulse Versus Social Conscience

Selfishness is a particularly important instance of the principle that nature says go and culture says stop. To put the matter in overly simple terms, nature has made us selfish, but culture needs us to resist and overcome selfish impulses.

Selfishness is natural. This is not to say that selfish behavior is good or appropriate, but only that nature programmed us to be selfish. This is probably rooted in the biological processes of evolution. Natural selection favors traits that promote the survival and reproduction of the individual. Some biologists have occasionally proposed "group selection," suggesting that natural selection will promote traits that sacrifice the individual for the sake of the group, but most biologists have rejected those arguments.[84,85] (Some experts think group selection may occur when the individual and group interests are aligned.) Each animal looks out for its own welfare and perhaps that of its children. The natural tendency, reinforced by countless centuries of evolution, is to want what is best for oneself.

In contrast, culture often demands that what is best for society take precedence over the individual's wants and needs. In order to get along with others, people must take turns, respect each other's property, and stifle their anger or at least express it constructively. They may have to share their food and possessions, whether informally through acts of kindness or more systematically through taxes. Many will have to follow commands issued by authority figures.

Compared to humans, animals that live in social groups make only minimal sacrifices for the sake of the group. Culture often imposes far greater requirements in terms of restraining selfishness. All cultures have systems of morality, and one of the main thrusts of morality is to do what is best for the community rather than what is best for the self. To return to the example of the Ten Commandments, note that those rules are divided between commands to uphold the religion (such as by not having other gods) and rules against behaviors that would undermine society (murder, theft, adultery, lying, coveting other people's things, and disrespecting one's parents).

Morality is often effective in small groups. In larger groups, law begins to take the place of morality, but it has the same overarching goal of restraining selfish actions in favor of what is best for the community. The difference seems to be that morality relies on a network of social relationships and therefore works best on people who know each other. The more that social life involves contacts between strangers, the more that laws are needed instead of just morals. Even in modern societies, small groups such as families usually rely on morals and informal rules because these are sufficient in the context of the relationship. Far more people are willing to cheat, betray, or exploit a stranger than a member of their own immediate family. Guilt—an important emotion that pushes people to behave morally instead of selfishly—is far more commonly felt in connection with friends and relatives than strangers.[86,87]

Thus, self-interest is a major battleground between nature and culture. The self is filled with selfish impulses and with the means to restrain them, and many inner conflicts come down to that basic antagonism. That conflict, between selfish impulses and self-control, is probably the most basic conflict in the human psyche.

One place to understand this conflict is in how people react to someone who has a stigma—that is, a trait that others perceive as highly undesirable and that makes them want to avoid the person. Many people have an automatic reaction of wanting to avoid someone who has AIDS or cancer, or who is blind or paralyzed, even if the person is not personally responsible for his or her problem. Researchers have found that the impulse to avoid such people may be rooted in a natural fear of being contaminated by them.[88] The automatic system does not necessarily adjust for whether the person's stigma is contagious or not, so people may irrationally and unfairly avoid people whose presence poses no danger. However, many people recognize consciously that these people do not deserve to be avoided, so the social conscience may motivate them to overcome their initial tendency to avoid the stigmatized person. The automatic reaction does not disappear, but given a moment, people can act on more socially desirable feelings, such as the wish to treat the stigmatized person as a normal human being.[89]

The capacity for consciously overriding impulses, described in the earlier section on the duplex mind, is often used in connection with the battle over self-interest. The natural and selfish impulses arise automatically. Morality, conscience, legal obedience, and other pathways to proper behavior often depend on conscious efforts to know and do the right thing.

Tradeoffs: When You Can't Have It All

When no option is clearly the best in every respect, choices have tradeoffs. A **tradeoff** is a choice in which taking or maximizing one benefit requires either accepting a cost or giving up another benefit. Every option you consider has both advantages and disadvantages. With cars, for example, buying the smaller car improves your gas mileage and is better for the environment but sacrifices safety or comfort. A human being is often faced with such complicated choices, and it is necessary to find some way to add up all the pluses and minuses in order to pick one option.

Tradeoffs are an important feature of human social life. Many decisions and dilemmas involve tradeoffs, so that no one right answer will suit everyone. (In this way, tradeoffs also preserve diversity because there is more than one way to be, with none being the best.) Solving one problem will sometimes create another.

Modern culture confronts individuals with a seemingly endless array of choices, and most of these present tradeoffs. Do you want to eat something delicious or something less fattening? Do you want shoes that will be fashionable or comfortable? Should you take an extra course and thereby learn more or have a lower workload next semester? Should you follow your plan or follow your heart?

One very important set of tradeoffs concerns time. Most commonly, the tradeoff requires choosing between something that has benefits right now versus something that has benefits in the future. Our shorthand term for this sort of tradeoff is "now versus tomorrow." Studies of delay of gratification[90,91] often make the tradeoff between present and future explicit. In a typical study two marshmallows, a child is offered a choice between having one right now—or if the child can wait for 20 minutes.

The ongoing controversy about drug use in sports involves a tradeoff, including a time dimension. Many athletes are tempted to try performance-enhancing drugs. Purists condemn these usages, likening drug use to cheating. But are sports different from everyday life? If you drink a cup of coffee to make yourself more alert for your psychology exam, are you cheating? Are people who use Prozac to make themselves cope better with life, or Viagra to make them perform better in bed, cheaters? And before long, gene splicing may be used to make people stronger, larger, faster, and better in other athletic realms—would those people (who benefited from events before they were born) be cheaters too?

One objection to letting athletes use performance-enhancing drugs is that these may be harmful. Some of them are. The tradeoff of now versus tomorrow is especially apparent in these cases because the so-called sports dopers trade future health problems for current athletic success. Even there, different people will decide the tradeoff differently. The man who founded the National Academy of Sports Medicine once polled 200 Olympic-caliber American athletes about this question. He asked, if you could legally take a performance-enhancing drug that would guarantee that you would win every

tradeoff a choice in which taking or maximizing one benefit requires either accepting a cost or sacrificing another benefit sports competition you entered for the next five years—but that would eventually kill you—would you take it? The overwhelming majority (though not all) said yes.[92]

Natural selection has not favored caring about the distant future. Our sensory organs tell us what is here right now. Our feelings and desires focus on the immediate present. The idea of sacrificing present joy for the sake of greater joy in the future would be foreign, difficult, even incomprehensible to most animals.

A dramatic demonstration of the difference emerged from a study with chimpanzees.[93] They were fed only once a day, always at the same time, and they were allowed to have all the food they wanted. Like humans and many other animals, chimps prefer to eat multiple times during the day, so they were always very hungry in the last couple hours before their next scheduled feeding. A sensible response would have been to keep some of the available food for later, especially for the hungry hours the next morning, but the animals never learned to do this. They would rejoice over the food when it came. They would eat their fill, and then they would ignore the rest, sometimes even engaging in food fights in which they would throw the leftover food at each other. Yet, despite repeated trials, they never learned to store food for later. Even the short span of 24 hours was apparently beyond their cognitive capacity for adjusting their behavior. In contrast, humans routinely acquire and store food for days, or even weeks, months, and years.

Human beings are thus quite different from other animals. In particular, the conscious human mind can form ideas about the distant future, and current behavior can be changed on the basis of those ideas. Going to college is partly an exercise in delay of gratification for many students. A young person can earn money right away by getting a job right out of high school rather than going to college (which costs money rather than earning any). College students often have to live in crowded dormitories with rickety furniture and unappetizing food, whereas if they dropped out and got a job they might be able to rent a nicer apartment and eat better. In the long run, however, college pays off. The U.S. Census Bureau reported that people with college degrees earn, on average, four times as much as those with less than a high school diploma. If you compound that amount by a lifetime of work, the average person with an college degree will likely earn nearly $2 million more than a high school dropout during a 30-year career. Going to college thus sacrifices some immediate pleasures for the sake of a better future life.

The future is more important to cultural beings than to other animals, so the capacity to orient oneself toward the future rather than the present is probably a crucial skill for any cultural being to have. A person who always lived just for today, enjoying the current moment with no regard for the future, would not prosper in human society. Such a person would never pay bills, wash the laundry or dishes, or brush or floss teeth. Such a person would probably eat candy and pastries rather than vegetables. Such a person would probably not go to college or hold down a job. Such a person would make no commitments that required sacrifices, such as to sustain a close relationship. Such a person would never save any money. Such a person would probably disregard any laws that were inconvenient.

That style of life is simply not suited for human cultural life. To live for any length of time in modern society, it is necessary to pay bills, take care of things, eat reasonably healthy food, obey the laws, exercise, and the like. Many of these acts entail some sacrifice in the short run. In the long run, however, the benefits that come from living in such a society make those sacrifices well worthwhile.

Facing up to tradeoffs is not easy. In fact, some research shows that people dislike tradeoffs.[94,95,96] When a decision has to be made, people prefer to think that there is one best or right answer. They like to think that what they choose will bring the best all-around outcomes, and they dislike thinking that they have really lost out on some things in order to get other things. You may find that you don't like the tradeoffs we present throughout this book because it is more comforting to think that there is always a single best answer. It is apparently normal to dislike the idea of tradeoffs, but don't let that prevent you from seeing how widespread and important they really are. The *Tradeoffs* box provides some examples of how political decisions often involve tradeoffs.

Political Tradeoffs

Tradeoffs are abundant in politics. Have you ever wondered why governments keep passing new laws, even though they hardly ever repeal any old ones? You would think that with the addition of more and more laws every year for hundreds of years, we would finally have enough. One explanation is that most laws are designed to remedy an existing problem, but sometimes they create new problems. Tradeoffs are responsible for some of the problems that arise.

As one famous example, in the 1990s the Ohio state legislature heard some sad stories about babies being born in prison (because their mothers were serving time). Taking pity on the babies, the government passed a new law to release pregnant women from prison. This solved one problem but created another, because all the women in Ohio prisons realized that they could get out of prison if they got pregnant, and many women would rather have a baby than be in prison. Female convicts began eagerly trying to have sex with male guards and lawyers. Some inmates would get a weekend pass to attend a relative's funeral—but would skip the funeral and spend the weekend having as much unprotected sex as possible. Thus, there was a tradeoff between preventing babies from being born in prison and encouraging more prisoners to get pregnant. In this case, the law was repealed.

One important political tradeoff links energy issues to environmental ones. Should American oil companies drill for oil in our national forests, where an accident might cause an oil spill that could destroy part of a beautiful forest and kill its wildlife? Many people want to protect the environment, yet they don't want to pay more for gasoline and electricity—and these goals are in conflict. Hence, there is a tradeoff: The more you protect the environment, the more expensive power becomes. It is hard to strike exactly the right balance.

Another tradeoff connects taxes to government services. Everything the government does—maintain an army and police force, collect the garbage, operate public schools, deliver the mail, provide food for the poor—costs money, and the main method for governments to get money is to collect taxes. In general, higher taxes enable the government to provide more services. Here again is a tradeoff because people do not want to pay high taxes, but they do want their government to provide good services.

To what extent do politicians recognize these tradeoffs? Social psychologist Phillip Tetlock[97,98] analyzed the speeches of many politicians, with an eye toward whether they recognized that many problems have two sides. He noted, however, that politicians face another tradeoff in their own careers, because they have to get elected. If one politician says "Everything is expensive, and I can't give you better government services unless we raise taxes," whereas another says "I will give you better services *and* lower taxes," the second one may be more likely to win the election.

Tetlock found that politicians seem to shuffle back and forth as to whether they acknowledge tradeoffs. When running for election, they make simple promises and ignore the political realities of tradeoffs. A successful candidate might well promise cheaper energy *and* better protection for the environment, in order to win the most votes. Once elected, however, politicians suddenly begin to recognize the complexity of tradeoffs, and their speeches often refer frankly to the difficulty of the choices, such as noting with regret that efforts to get cheaper oil may well require some sacrifices in environmental protection.

Is this change a matter of learning? After all, when one is just running for office and does not have any actual responsibilities of governing it may be possible to make all sorts of promises without fully realizing the tradeoffs involved. (Most politicians, like most people, really do want both cheaper energy and a cleaner environment.) Maybe they don't realize the tradeoffs until they actually hold office and have to face up to the difficult choices. But this is not what Tetlock concluded. He found that politicians acknowledge tradeoffs when they are in office—but only until their campaigns for reelection start. At that point, they go back to simple statements that promise all things, disregarding tradeoffs. Tetlock concluded that politicians are dealing with the tradeoff built into the election process: to win an election you must oversimplify the issues and ignore the implicit contradictions.

Putting People First

Can dogs hear better than people? If you have lived with a dog, you know they hear many things that people do not, such as very high or low tones, as well as very soft tones. One of your textbook authors is frequently teased by his wife that his dog is prone to barking at ghosts because the dog will burst into barking for no reason that any person can discern. In that sense, dogs hear better than humans. On the other hand, dogs cannot distinguish between similar sounds. If your dog's name is Fido, he will probably also respond to "buy low," "hi ho," "my dough," and "Shiloh." In that sense, dogs don't hear as well as people.

The explanation is probably rooted in a basic tradeoff in perceptual systems, but it contains an important clue about human nature. Most sense organs (even artificial ones such as cameras) have a tradeoff between detection (how much they can detect) and resolution (how clearly they detect it). For most animals, detection is emphasized over resolution—they perceive something and respond long before they can tell precisely what it is. Humans have more emphasis on resolution, which means perceiving things precisely. Hence, our ears cannot hear as wide a range of sounds as dogs, but we hear them much more distinctly.

More broadly, the sensory organs of most animals are aimed at detecting other species. This is crucial for survival. Animals must spot the predators who want to eat them (in order to run away in time) and the animals they eat (so they can pursue and catch them). The human sensory system is quite unusual in that it is not aimed mainly at other species. Human sense organs, especially eyes and ears, seem designed to help us perceive each other. We can pick our beloved's (or our enemy's) face out of a crowd or a choir up on stage, and we can hear tiny differences in spoken sounds.

Most likely, this unusual feature of human sense organs reflects a change in biological strategy. Nature selected humans to pursue survival and reproduction in a novel fashion. Instead of getting information from the environment, our sense organs are designed to help us get it from each other. And that's what culture is all about—humans getting information from each other in order to survive and reproduce. This is another theme of this book; we call it *putting people first*. And it doesn't stop with information. People get most of what they need from each other, instead of directly from the physical world around them.

Consider food. Many animals spend most of their waking hours looking for food and eating it. They search their environment for things to eat. Some animals search alone, and others search together, but in general they get their food directly from nature. Human food comes from nature too, but most people now get their food from other people. Over the past year, how much of what you ate did you get directly from nature, by picking it from plants or hunting and killing animals? Probably not much: most, if not all, of what you ate came either from supermarkets, where the food prepared by others is sold, or in dining establishments such as restaurants and cafeterias, where food grown by some people is cooked and served by others. If all those institutions abruptly went out of business and people had to get their food directly from nature, most of us would not know how to go about it. Many people would go hungry.

To be sure, humans evolved under conditions different from modern life, and early humans did often get their food directly from the natural environment. But the modern world probably reflects the special aspects of the human psyche better than did the circumstances of prehistoric life. Humans are heavily interdependent and are quite good at developing cultural systems that allow them to benefit from each other's work. As people have learned to make culture work effectively, it is no longer necessary for everyone to hunt, fish, or grow food. Instead, you can become good at one very narrowly specialized task, such as repairing cars or selling shoes or treating broken legs, and your work at this task gives you money with which you can buy the many different things you need and want.

What this tells us about the human psyche is that people have a natural tendency to look to each other first. When people have a problem or a need, they most often look to other people for help, relief, or satisfaction. Even when people just need information, they tend to get it from other people rather than directly from the world around them. Animals learn from their own experience. They deal with the physical world, and they are rewarded or punished depending on how things turn out. Humans, in contrast, rely much less on what they learn from their own direct experience with the physical world. People learn from each other and from the culture.

Some evidence of the importance of putting people first comes from studies pitting money against social acceptance. In one study, some participants gained money but were rejected and ostracized by others; other participants were accepted and included but lost money. The first group felt worse than the second.[99] Money is an important means of getting what you need, but apparently people are more attuned to gaining social acceptance (even from complete strangers) than money.

The culture operates as a kind of "general store" of information. When people don't know what to do, they typically ask someone else who knows the culture's information. How do you get telephone service or a new credit card? Is there sales tax on food? How early (before the scheduled start time) should one arrive for an airline flight, a bus trip, a dinner party, a baseball game, a physician's appointment? Can I get my money back for something, and if so, how? These answers are not the specific wisdom learned by specific individuals, but general rules for getting along in the culture, and any knowledgeable person can tell you the answers—after which you would be able to pass that information along to anyone else.

Putting people first builds on the earlier theme that people are "built to relate." Nature has constructed human beings to turn to each other for food, shelter, support, information, and other needs. The fact that so many inner processes serve interpersonal functions enables people to rely on each other and treat each other as vital resources.

The reliance on other people for information was shown in one of modern social psychology's first experimental investigations, the research on conformity by Solomon Asch.[100,101,102] Asch presented research participants with a line-judging task, in which they simply had to say which of three lines was the best match to a specific line that was presented. The task was easy enough that everyone could get all the answers correct simply by looking at the lines. But Asch introduced a novel twist to this task. He ran the study in groups, and sometimes almost everyone in the group was secretly working with him. Only one person in the group was a real participant. When Asch gave a prearranged signal, all the accomplices (the group members who were working with him and only pretending to be real participants) would give the wrong answer. Thus, the participant suddenly had to decide whether to give the answer that his or her eyes said was correct, or instead to go along with the group and give the answer that everyone else had given. If the human brain were designed mainly to learn from one's own direct experience, participants would still have given the right answer all the time. But they didn't. In a significant number of cases, participants went along with the group, giving the answer that they could see was wrong but that conformed to what everyone else was saying. Thus, sometimes people rely on other people more than on their own direct experience. In Asch's experiment, participants felt it was more important to be accepted by the group than to be correct on the line-judging task.

Recent work has confirmed the importance of getting information from others, with the twist that the effects depend on whether the other is similar to you. Participants heard another person express liking for some music. The participant's own evaluation of that same music was influenced by the other's views. If the other person had come across as similar to the participant in other musical opinions and personal background, then the participant liked the music more. If the other person was dissimilar, however, then his liking for the music made the participant dislike it.[103] The implication is that we put people first—but especially people to whom we have some closeness or connection.

If your brain is like a computer, then culture is like the Internet. Hooking into the system greatly increases the power of what a single computer, and by analogy a single brain, can do. By belonging to culture, you can learn an immense amount of information, whereas if you had to learn from your own direct experiences, you would only have a tiny fraction of that knowledge. Our tendency to put people first enables us to take advantage of the knowledge and wisdom that accumulates in the cultural general store.

QUIZ YOURSELF
Important Features of Human Social Life

1. **The duplex mind contains what two systems?**
   - (a) Automatic; deliberate
   - (b) Cognitive; emotional
   - (c) New; old
   - (d) Short-term; long-term

2. **In humans, the road to social acceptance is _____.**
   - (a) downhill
   - (b) long
   - (c) short
   - (d) smooth

3. **In a classic experiment with lines of different lengths, Solomon Asch found that _____.**
   - (a) perceptual judgments can be influenced by others
   - (b) perceptual judgments cannot be influenced by others
   - (c) large groups of people tend to overestimate the lengths of lines
   - (d) large groups of people tend to underestimate the lengths of lines

4. **In a common analogy used by psychologists, the brain is compared to a computer. In that analogy, culture is like the _____.**
   - (a) hardware
   - (b) Internet
   - (c) keyboard
   - (d) software

answers: see pg 66

What Makes Us Human

Putting the Cultural Animal in Perspective

This chapter has emphasized that human social behavior results from a mixture of nature and culture. Human beings are animals and, as such, have many of the same wants, needs, and behavior patterns that other animals have. According to the theory of evolution, human beings evolved from other animals. The special traits that make us human are thus mostly a result of gradual refinements of traits that animals had. Some notable biological traits differentiate humans from other animals: We have exceptionally large and capable brains, especially in proportion to body size. We walk upright. We can talk.

What makes us human is most apparent, however, in culture. The beginnings of culture can be found in other species, but these little bits of nonhuman culture exist mostly in small, isolated patterns of behavior that make only a relatively minor difference in the animals' life. In contrast, human life is deeply enmeshed in culture; indeed, it is hard to imagine what human life would be like without culture. Culture provides us with food and housing, with languages and things to talk about, with electricity and all the appliances that use it, with all our means of travel other than walking, with our forms of work and play, with science and religion, with medicine, with art and entertainment, and with all the ideas that give our lives meaning.

Cultures are diverse, but they also have many common themes. Phenomena such as language, cooking, clothing, and money are found all over the world, but not in other species. Human life would be vastly different without language, cooking, clothing, and money, but it is only because of culture that we can have them.

Culture also creates problems that are special to humans. Crime cannot exist without laws, nor bankruptcy without money, nor nuclear waste without nuclear technology. Only humans go to war, deliberately commit suicide, or take part in genocide.

Culture is not all good. Still, its benefits far outweigh its costs. Culture has enabled human beings to thrive and multiply. Indeed, nearly all of the animals most closely related to humans (apes and other primates) live near the equator in tropical climates, but human beings have spread all over the globe and live comfortably in mountains and valleys, in sunny and wintry places, in deserts and other seemingly difficult places. Culture has learned to make products (e.g., clothes, plumbing, indoor heating) that make this dispersion possible.

Perhaps most remarkably of all, culture has enabled human beings to increase their life span substantially. Advances in public health and medical care now enable many people to live 80 years or more, about triple what our ancestors could expect. No other animals have been able to develop knowledge that extends their life span.

Many social psychologists have used the phrase "the social animal" to describe human beings, but many other animals are also social. What makes us human is the extent to which we are cultural animals. Culture is a better way of being social. For one thing, it allows humans to accumulate knowledge over time and across generations—something almost no other animals have been able to accomplish. Most social animals start over with each new generation, which must then solve the same problems of how to live comfortably. Each new generation of human beings, however, can learn from previous generations. (Otherwise, instead of reading this textbook, you'd be trying to master how to make fire and forage for food.)

The very fact that we can think about what makes us human is itself an important part of what makes us human. Human beings can think with language and meaning in a way that no other animal can. This makes our social lives much more complicated than they would otherwise be, but it also creates the richness of human life and experience. That is, it makes our social psychology more complicated to study and learn, but it also makes it vastly more interesting!

CHAPTER 2 SUMMARY

Nature and Social Behavior

- The power of socialization to change people is real, but limited.
- Nature is the physical world around us.
- Darwin's theory of evolution focuses on how change occurs in nature.
- Natural selection is a process whereby genetically based traits become more or less common in a population.

- "Survival of the fittest" means that animals compete with each other to survive.
- Reproductive success means creating offspring who will in turn create other offspring.
- A trait that increases an organism's survival rate or leads to better reproductive success is likely to become more common in a population.
- Being social helps humans and other animals survive and reproduce.

- Larger brains evolved to enable animals to function well in complex social structures.
- The human brain evolved to capitalize on culture.

Culture and Human Social Life
- Culture is an information-based system in which many people work together to help satisfy their biological and social needs.
- A culture is what a group of people have in common, including shared beliefs, meanings, and values, as well as shared ways of doing things.
- Both nature and culture are important in shaping behavior.
- Humans, unlike most other creatures, base their actions on meaning and ideas.
- Nature has prepared humans to use ideas.
- Humans and some other animals are social. Humans are far more cultural than any other animal.
- Differences between social and cultural animals include the following:
  - Social animals work together; cultural animals also use extensive division of labor.
  - Social animals may learn things from one another; cultural animals deliberately share knowledge with the group.
  - Social animals may help kin; cultural animals have a broader sense of community and often help strangers.
  - Social animals mainly use aggression to resolve conflict; cultural animals have many alternatives, including moral principles, compromise, and the rule of law.
- Although cultures differ, differences are often merely matters of degree rather than opposites.

Important Features of Human Social Life
- The human mind is a duplex mind, meaning that it has both an automatic and a deliberate system.
- The automatic system is especially useful for the simple tasks we perform, whereas the deliberate system is useful for the more complex tasks.
- The automatic system is fast and relatively effortless, whereas the deliberate system is slow and effortful.
- The automatic and deliberate systems are not independent of one another. Sometimes they work together, and sometimes they work against each other.
- Living in a culture has many advantages, but it makes many demands.
- Inner processes often serve interpersonal functions. That is, the psychological traits people have enable them to connect better with others.
- In general (though not always), nature says go and culture says stop.
- Nature makes us selfish; culture requires us to resist selfish impulses.
- Most choices in life involve tradeoffs, both benefits and costs.
- An important aspect of many tradeoffs is short-term versus long-term gain.
- Humans get most of what they need from other people.
- Culture operates as a "general store" of information.
- Asch's study demonstrated that sometimes people rely more on information from other people than on their own senses.
- If the brain is like a personal computer, then culture is like the Internet. A computer can do a lot more when it is connected to the Internet than when it is a stand-alone machine.

What Makes Us Human? Putting the Cultural Animal in Perspective
- Although human beings evolved from other animals, humans have much larger brains than other animals, especially in proportion to body size.
- Big brains may have evolved to enable more complex social relationships.
- Another main difference between humans and other animals is culture. Culture allows humans to accumulate knowledge over time and across generations.
- Although culture is not all good, its advantages outweigh its disadvantages. For example, culture has enabled modern humans to more than double the life spans of our ancestors.

key terms

automatic system 53
culture 46
deliberate system 53
duplex mind 52
mutation 40
natural selection 39
nature 38
praxis 45
psyche 37
reproduction 40
social animals 43
survival 39
theory of evolution 38
tradeoff 60

quiz yourself ANSWERS

1. Nature and Social Behavior p. 42
   answers: 1.d 2.a 3.a 4.c
2. Culture and Human Social Life p. 52
   answers: 1.c 2.d 3.b 4.d
3. Important Features of Human Social Life p. 64
   answers: 1.a 2.b 3.a 4.b

THE SELF

3

LEARNING OBJECTIVES

1. Explain the importance of a complex self in a cultural animal.

2. Summarize the different sources and motives of self-knowledge.

3. Describe how the sources of self-knowledge lead to self-concept.

4. Analyze the benefits and drawbacks of high self-esteem and positive illusions.

5. Evaluate the different functions of self-presentation.

FOOD FOR THOUGHT
Eating Binges and Escaping the Self
79

MONEY MATTERS
Doing It for Money, Not Love
84

TRADEOFFS
Self-Handicapping
88

THE SOCIAL SIDE OF SEX
Self-Esteem and Saying No to Sex
99

WHAT MAKES US HUMAN?
Putting the Cultural Animal in Perspective
110

iStock.com/RichVintage

In the late 1500s, near the height of the Ottoman Turkish empire, Sultan Suleiman the Magnificent set out with a giant army to conquer as much of Europe as he could. On the way to Vienna, he took offense at some purported remark by a Hungarian nobleman, Count Miklós Zrínyi, and diverted his entire force to conquer the small castle where Zrínyi lived on his lands.[1]

The prospects for the defenders were never very good. They had only a couple of thousand men, as compared to almost 100,000 with the sultan. The castle was not impressive (Suleiman himself called it a "molehill" when he first laid eyes on it). Its best feature was that it was surrounded by a swamp and an artificial lake, which were hard for an attacking army to cross, but the summer had been dry, and this natural advantage was weaker than usual. When the Turks destroyed the dam, the artificial lake drained, leaving the castle exposed. The Turks bombarded the walls with their huge cannon and drilled tunnels, which they exploded to make the walls collapse.

After days of fighting, the defenders knew their cause was hopeless. Only 300 were left alive, their castle walls had huge holes in them, and most of their ammunition was gone. Instead of waiting for the Turks to storm in upon them, Zrínyi decided to die in a blaze of glory. As he prepared for the last moments of his life, he made some curious decisions. He discarded his armor and instead put on his wedding suit of silk and velvet. He hung a heavy gold chain around his neck and stuffed his pockets with gold coins. When asked why he was doing this, he replied that he wanted whoever killed him to know that he was an important person. Thus attired, he flung open the castle doors and led his remaining troops on a suicide charge right into the heart of the Turkish army. All were killed.

The striking thing about this story is the count's concern with self-presentation, which we shall see is the task of making good impressions on other people. It is easily understandable and rational that people want to make good impressions on their bosses, or their dating partners, or their teammates. Zrínyi, however, was trying to make a good impression on someone he did not yet know and who presumably would have already killed him by the time he found the gold coins. There is no practical value to being well regarded after you are dead, especially by the person who took your life. He's not going to be your buddy nor do you any favors. But it mattered to the count anyway.

Concern with making a good impression after you are dead may seem foolish, irrational, or even bizarre, but Count Zrínyi was far from alone in this respect. In fact, news reports in the United States today indicate that more and more people are stipulating plastic surgery to prepare their bodies for their funerals. They want to look their best at their last showing, even though they will be dead and there must be better ways to spend money than for cosmetic operations on a corpse that is about to be buried or cremated!

As cultural beings, people have selves that are much more elaborate and complex than has been found anywhere else in the animal kingdom. The self is an important tool with which the human organism makes its way through human society and thereby manages to satisfy its needs. To be effective at this, the human self has taken shape in a way that it is marked by some deep, powerful drives. Among these drives is a strong concern with how one is perceived by others. This drive mostly serves the goals of survival and reproduction. However, many people care strongly about how others perceive them, even if those other people don't help them survive or reproduce. In some cases, people care about others who will kill them. We may care most about those we depend on, but the fact is that people have a deeply rooted tendency to care, broadly, about how others in general regard them. It's very hard not to care what other people think of you. ●

The monumental work, *Zrinyi's Sortie*, dated 1825, by Peter Krafft (1780–1856). The scene is the sortie of Count Miklós Zrínyi and his men, the heroic defenders of the castle of Szigetvár, against the besieging Turks in 1566, in which Zrínyi lost his life.

What Is the Self?

The self is peculiarly difficult to define. Everyone seems to know what it is and to use the term frequently (especially if you include words like *myself*), but hardly anyone can say exactly what it is. Some brain researchers now say that the self is an illusion, mainly because they cannot find any specific spot in the brain that seems to correspond to the self, but in their everyday lives these researchers act as if they know exactly what the self is, and it is not an illusion. For example, they know the difference between what is their own and what is someone else's (wallet, apartment, feet, ideas, romantic partner). After all, if the self were merely an illusion, there would be no genuine difference between you and me, so how could we talk about whether that $20 bill is yours or mine?

Thus, nearly everyone has a basic understanding of what the self is, even if it is hard to put into words. To develop a more scientific understanding, let us begin by considering what its functions are, what its different main parts or aspects are, and where it comes from.

The Self's Main Jobs

It may sound funny to ask: "Why do we have selves?" Not having a self is not really an option! Everyone has a separate body, and selves begin with bodies, so there is no way for a human being to be completely without a self. Perhaps a more relevant question would concern the structure of the self: "Why are human selves put together the way they are?" One could also ask about their function: "What are selves for?" The structure and function questions are often related, because things are made with a given structure precisely in order to serve that function. (Handles are designed for holding things, for example.) Moreover, as we saw in Chapter 2, many inner traits of human beings serve interpersonal functions. Much of the self is designed to enable you to relate to others, including claiming and sustaining a place in a cultural system that connects you to many other people.

Another theme of this book is the conflict between selfish impulses and social conscience. The self is right in the middle of this battle. On the one hand, selves sometimes naturally feel selfish (hence the very term *selfish*!), and in many situations they have strong impulses to do what is best for themselves. They are designed to know and do what is best for them. On the other hand, selfishness must be kept under control if society is to operate effectively, and selves often incorporate the morals and other values of the culture. Those morals mostly tell you to do what is best for the group instead of what is best for you personally or what you feel like doing. Hence, the self must be able to understand these social morals and other values—plus be able to act on them, even when that requires overriding one's natural, selfish impulses.

The self has three main parts (**FIGURE 3.1**), which correspond to several main things that the self does. The first part consists of **self-knowledge** (sometimes called **self-concept**). Human beings have self-awareness, and this awareness enables them to develop elaborate sets of beliefs about themselves. If someone says, "Tell me something about yourself," you can probably furnish 15 or 20 specific answers without having to think very hard. Consider these experiences, all of which involve self-knowledge and self-awareness: You stop to think about what you would like to be doing in five years. You receive a grade on an exam and consider whether you are good at this particular subject. You check your hair in a mirror or your weight on a scale. You read the results of some medical tests. On a first date, your partner asks you about yourself, and you try to give honest answers that show the kind of person you are. You feel ashamed about something you did last week or last year, or you feel proud about something else you

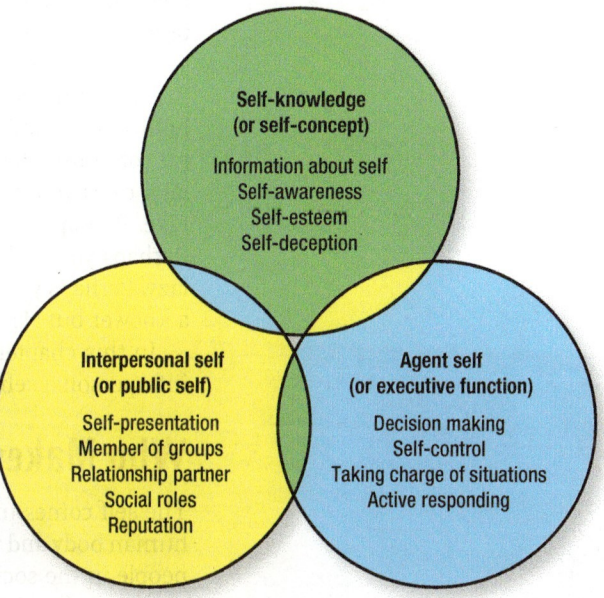

FIGURE 3.1

Three parts of the self: (1) Self-knowledge (or self-concept), (2) Interpersonal self (or public self), and (3) Agent self (or executive function).

self-knowledge (self-concept) a set of beliefs about oneself did. Such moments show the self reflecting on itself and on its store of information about itself.

The **interpersonal self** or **public self** is a second part of the self that helps the person connect socially to other people. Most people have a certain image that they try to convey to others. This public self resembles the self-concept, but the two are not the same. Often, people work hard to present a particular image to others even if it is not exactly the full, precise truth as they know it. Consider some of the things people do to impress others. You dress up for a social event. You show your friends that you are easygoing and fun-loving—but meanwhile you convince your boss that you are serious, reliable, and work-oriented. You spend all day cleaning your home to get it ready for guests. You hold back from arguing for your religious or political views because you think the other people present might not approve of them. You worry about what someone thinks of you. When describing yourself on that first date, you leave out certain unflattering details, such as that nasty foot odor problem, or how you like to burp the words to "Auld Lang Syne." Furthermore, many emotions indicate concern over how one appears to others: You feel embarrassed because someone saw you do something stupid, or even just because your underwear was showing. You feel guilty if you forgot your romantic partner's birthday. You are delighted when your boss compliments you on your good work. These episodes reveal that the self is often working in complex ways to gain social acceptance and maintain good interpersonal relationships.

The third important part of the self, the **agent self** or **executive function** is the part that gets things done. It enables the self to make choices and exert control, including both self-control and control over other people (and things). Sometimes you decide not to eat something because it is unhealthy or fattening. Sometimes you make a promise and later exert yourself to keep it. Sometimes you decide what courses to take or what job to take. Perhaps you cast a vote in an election. Perhaps you sign a lease for an apartment. Perhaps you make yourself go out jogging even though the weather is bad and you feel lazy. Perhaps you place a bet on a sports event. All these actions reveal the self as not just a knower but also as a doer.

In this chapter, we focus on the first two aspects of the self: self-knowledge and the interpersonal self. The next chapter will focus on the self in action.

Who Makes the Self: The Individual or Society?

The self comes into being at the interface between the inner biological processes of the human body and the sociocultural network to which the person belongs (that is, the other people in the society, plus its "general store" of common beliefs and practices.[2] The importance of society is hard to deny; in fact, if you grew up on a deserted island and never met other human beings, you might hardly have a "self" at all in the usual sense. Having a name would be pointless, for example, if you never interacted with other people, nor would you have a reputation, an ethnic identity, or even a set of personal values. (At most you would have preferences, but they would not seem like your personal values if you never met anyone else who might be different.)

Then again, even without meeting other human beings, a person might still have a conception of self as a body separate from its environment. The difference between dropping a stone on your foot and dropping it on a tree root next to your foot is an important sign of self: Your foot is part of your self; the tree is not.

A True or Real Self?

Many people like to think they have an inner "true" self. Most social scientists are skeptical of such notions. If the inner self is different from the way the person acts all the time, why is the inner one the "true" one? By what criterion could we say that someone's "true" self is shy if the person doesn't act shy most of the time? The idea of an inner "true" self different from behavior may have its origins in class prejudices.[3,4,5,6] Back when social mobility began to increase, so that some aristocrats became poor while merchants became rich, the upper classes wanted to continue believing that they were inherently better than other people, even if the others had more money. The upper class could not point to obvious differences in behavior because in point of fact many aristocrats were drunken,

interpersonal self (public self) the image of the self that is conveyed to others

agent self (executive function) the part of the self involved in control, including both control over other people and self-control conceited, stupid, lazy, sexually immoral, and in other respects unworthy. Hence, the upper class settled on the view that the superiority of the blue bloods lay in their inner traits that could not be directly seen.

Even if the inner "true" self is something of a fiction, people still believe in it, and these beliefs affect how they act. A classic article by sociologist Ralph Turner[7] noted that different cultures (and different groups or historical eras within a culture) may differ in their ideas about the true self by placing emphasis on either of two main approaches. One approach emphasizes the inner feelings as the true self. The other focuses on the way the person acts in public, especially in official roles. Many people recognize that they sometimes put on a public performance that differs from how they feel inside.[8] Turner's point was that cultures disagree as to whether the public actions or the inner feelings count as the more real or true side of the self. Suppose, for example, that a soldier is terrified in battle and wants to run and hide, but he steels himself and performs an act of heroism that helps win the battle. Which was the "real" soldier: the terrified coward or the brave hero?

Attitudes toward marriage may reflect different attitudes about the real self. In cultures that emphasize inner feelings as the true self, the actual wedding ceremony and its legal or religious significance are secondary. Marriage is seen as a psychological union of two persons, and what matters is how they feel about each other. If they lose their love for each other, or become attracted to someone else, they may feel justified in abandoning their spouse because to do so is to be true to themselves. A marriage is thus only as good as the current emotional state of the partners. In contrast, a culture that emphasizes public behavior and commitments downplays the inner feelings and instead places great significance on role performance. A couple may have a good marriage even if they cease to love each other, so long as they remain true to their vows and act the way spouses are supposed to act. The actual wedding ceremony counts as much more in such societies than it does among the impulse-oriented societies because it is at the wedding that the real self changes to become married in the eyes of society.

Culture and Interdependence

Selves are somewhat different across different cultures. The most studied set of such cultural differences involves independence versus interdependence. This dimension of difference entails different attitudes toward the self and different motivations as to what the self mainly tries to accomplish, and it results in different emphases about what the self is.

It is at the wedding that a couple becomes married in the eyes of society. Different cultures have different wedding traditions.

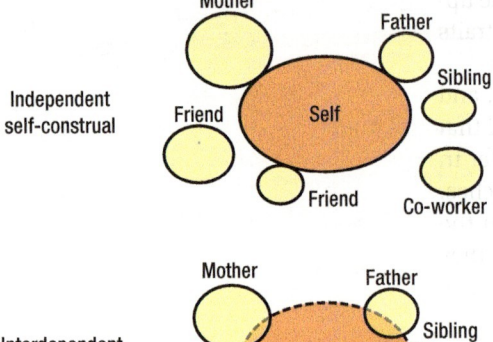

FIGURE 3.2
Depictions of independent and interdependent self-construals.
SOURCE: Markus and Kitayama (1991).

The idea that cultural styles of selfhood differ along the dimension of independence was introduced by an international team of researchers.[9] They proposed that Asians differ from North Americans and Europeans in how they think of themselves and how they seek to construct the self in relation to others. To avoid the overused term *self-concept,* they introduced the term *self-construal,* which means a way of thinking about the self. An **independent self-construal** emphasizes what makes the self different and sets it apart from others. In contrast, an **interdependent self-construal** emphasizes what connects the self to other people and groups. These two types of self-construal are depicted in **FIGURE 3.2**.

To appreciate the difference, it is useful to try a simple exercise such as asking yourself "Who or what am I?" and listing a dozen or more different answers off the top of your head. When you have done this, go through the list again and see how many of your answers express something unique or special about you (such as having an unusual skill or hobby) and how many express connection to others (such as belonging to a particular family, attending a particular university, or coming from a particular place). The relative amounts of those two types of answers indicate where you stand on independence (your unique traits) and interdependence.

It is not inherently better to be either independent or interdependent. Nor is everyone in one culture independent or interdependent. Still, the general finding has been that Easterners (e.g., people from Japan, China, Korea) tend to be more interdependent, whereas Westerners (e.g., people from the United States, Canada, Western Europe) tend to be more independent. Nor are these differences merely superficial ways of talking about the self. Instead, they represent deep-seated differences in what the person strives to become. The American ideal may be the self-made person, who works alone to create or achieve something, possibly overcoming obstacles or other people's resistance in the process, and who eventually becomes a true individual in the sense of a unique person with highly special traits. In contrast, the Asian ideal of selfhood may be more the consummate team player who makes valuable contributions to the group, who does not let personal egotism stand in the way of doing what is best for the group, and who remains loyal to the group and helps it overcome external threats. Asians see the self as deeply enmeshed in a web of personal, family, social, and cultural relationships, outside of which there is meaninglessness and loneliness. Americans see the self as following its own path to autonomy, self-sufficiency, and unique individuality.

A stunning story from the 1976 Olympics concerned a tight battle between the Japanese and the Soviet Russians for the men's team gymnastics medals.[10] It came down to a performance on the rings by Shun Fujimoto in the last event. His performance was nearly perfect except for a slight stutter-step by one leg when he landed at the end. His score was high enough that Japan won the gold medal by a very slight margin over the Russians.

What was remarkable about that story was that Shun had actually broken his leg at the knee in the previous event. He knew that the most intense pain he could imagine was waiting for him at the end of his performance when he landed, and he still managed to concentrate on what he was doing and perform nearly perfectly.

When Americans hear Shun's story, they probably understand it in terms of the independent self. They can imagine Shun wanting the glory of the gold medal, wanting to fulfill his dreams, and wanting to complete what he had worked for years to achieve. They think he would want to be admired for his heroic effort under intensely adverse circumstances.

But Asians probably see the story differently, with a more interdependent construal. It was not personal glory but obligation to the team that pushed him to take on that suffering. If he didn't compete, his team would lose the medal, and he didn't want to let them down. In fact, Shun concealed his injury from his teammates, in case worrying about him or expecting that the team might lose would affect their performances.

Social Roles

Let us return now to the question "What are selves for?" One answer, certainly, is that the self has to gain social acceptance. People are not designed to live by themselves. They

independent self-construal a self-concept that emphasizes what makes the self different and sets it apart from others

interdependent self-construal a self-concept that emphasizes what connects the self to other people and groups need other people to accept them in order to have a job, to have friends and lovers, to have a family. The self is one tool people use to accomplish these goals. By learning how to act properly and how to conform to social rules and norms, people can improve their chances of social acceptance. In Chapter 2 we saw that human beings follow an especially long road to social acceptance. The self is constructed to help them on that road, which includes changing and adapting themselves so as to appeal to others.

Another important purpose of the self is to play **social roles**. A long tradition in psychology and sociology considers social behavior as resembling a play or a movie, in which different people play different roles.[11,12] Indeed some theorists[13] have taken this view to an extreme and analyzed most human behavior and selfhood in terms of actors playing roles. A culture is a large system with many different roles, and everyone has to find a place in it (or several places). You cannot be a senator, or a nurse, or a parent, or a girlfriend, or a police officer unless you can reliably act in appropriate ways. Many roles, such as spouse or engineer, can only be adopted after you have taken a series of steps (such as having a wedding, or getting a college degree with a certain major); the self has to execute these steps just to get into the role. Then, after you have the role, you must perform the duties that define it. To succeed in traveling the long road to social acceptance, the person must have a self capable of all those jobs.

To be sure, humans are not the only creatures to have roles. For example, in ant colonies, ants have different roles, such as one or more fertile "queens," some fertile "drones," and many sterile "workers," "soldiers," or other specialized groups. What is special about the human self is that it is flexible enough to take on new roles and to change roles. A single human being, for example, might work at mowing lawns, writing for the school newspaper, managing the swim team, lifeguarding at several different pools, busing tables in the college dining hall, working with computers, managing others who work with computers, and so forth over the course of a lifetime. Also, a person may perform similar jobs with several different organizations, such as a professor who moves from one university to another but teaches similar courses each time. In contrast, a worker ant almost always does the same job for its entire life and within the same colony of ants; it does not need a self that can adopt and shed different roles.

Where do these roles come from? Often they are part of the social system. If you live in a small peasant farming village, as most people in the history of the world have done, then many roles are not available to you. The limited opportunities in that village's social system mean that you could not be a basketball coach, for example, or a software consultant, or a movie star because the only other people you ever meet are peasant farmers. Most roles are ways of relating to other people within a cultural system. If you lived alone in the forest, it would be silly to describe yourself as a police officer, a bartender, a schoolteacher, or vice president of telemarketing. A person's social identity thus shows the interplay of the individual and the larger cultural system: Society creates and defines the roles, and individual people seek them out, adopt them, and sometimes impose their own style on them. Without society, the self would not exist in full.

But let's start at the beginning. The self has its roots in the human capacity to turn attention back toward its source. Without self-awareness, selfhood and self-knowledge would be impossible. The next section will cover what social psychologists have learned about self-awareness.

The Japanese gymnast Shun Fujimoto completed the last three rotations of the 1976 men's Olympics team competition with a broken kneecap, collapsing in agony after the pain shot through his leg following his dismount from the rings.

social roles the different roles a person plays, as in a play or a movie

self-awareness attention directed at the self

The woman in this picture has at least two roles: (a) she is a soldier, and (b) she is a mother.

Self-Awareness

Self-awareness consists of attention directed at the self. Early in the 1970s, two social psychologists began studying the difference between being and not being self-aware.[14] They developed several clever procedures to

I see room for improvement.

increase self-awareness, such as having people work while seated in front of a mirror, or telling people that they were being videotaped.

Researchers quickly found it necessary to distinguish at least two main kinds of self-awareness: public and private.[15,16] **Private self-awareness** refers to attending to your inner states, including emotions, thoughts, desires, and traits. It is a matter of looking inward. In contrast, **public self-awareness** means attending to how you are perceived by others, including what others might think of you. Public self-awareness looks outward to understand the self. Without public self-awareness, Count Zrínyi would not have dressed as he did on the last day of his life: He wore his wedding suit and gold because he was imagining how he would look to the enemy soldiers outside. Thus, instead of attending to his inner states directly, he thought about himself as seen through other people's eyes.

Researchers have found that self-awareness usually involves evaluating the self, rather than just merely being aware of it. A person looks in the mirror and compares themself against various standards. It is not just "Oh, there I am in the mirror. Is that what I look like? It doesn't matter." Rather, it's "Oh, my hair is a mess. This shirt looks good on me. I should lose a little weight." The essence of self-awareness is comparing oneself against these standards (good-looking hair, nice clothing, fashionable slimness, respectively) and thereby coming up with good or bad evaluations about the self.

Standards

Standards are ideas (concepts) of how things might possibly be. Standards include ideals, norms, expectations, moral principles, laws, the way things were in the past, and what other people have done. Standards are an important example of one theme of this book—namely, the power of ideas to cause and shape behavior. The self is not good or bad in a vacuum, but only when compared to certain standards. Nearly all children start talking about standards (good, bad, nice) when they are around 2 years old, which is also the age at which their self-awareness blossoms,[17] and children begin to develop a concept of themselves as separate from their parents.

Self-awareness is often unpleasant because people compare themselves to high standards such as moral ideals for good behavior or a fashion model's good looks. Researchers have found, for example, that when girls and young women watch television shows featuring especially beautiful actresses and models, they feel less positive about themselves and become more likely to develop eating disorders.[18,19,20,21,22,23,24] But people feel good when they compare themselves to the "average person" or to specific people who are not doing as well because they can usually surpass low standards (at least in their own minds!).

When people are aware that they fall short of standards, the bad feeling leads to either of two reactions: change or escape (**FIGURE 3.3**). One reaction is to try to remedy the problem, such as by improving oneself. This may be as simple as combing one's hair, or as complex as deciding to change basic aspects of one's life. Sometimes changing the standard is easier than changing the self. The other response is to try to avoid or reduce self-awareness, so as to escape from feeling bad.

Recent work suggests that a person's reactions to standards depends on how promising versus hopeless the prospect of meeting the standard seems.[25] When people think they can reach their goals or other standards in a reasonable time, self-awareness makes

private self-awareness looking inward on the private aspects of the self, including emotions, thoughts, desires, and traits

public self-awareness looking outward on the public aspects of the self that others can see and evaluate

standards ideas (concepts) of how things might possibly be

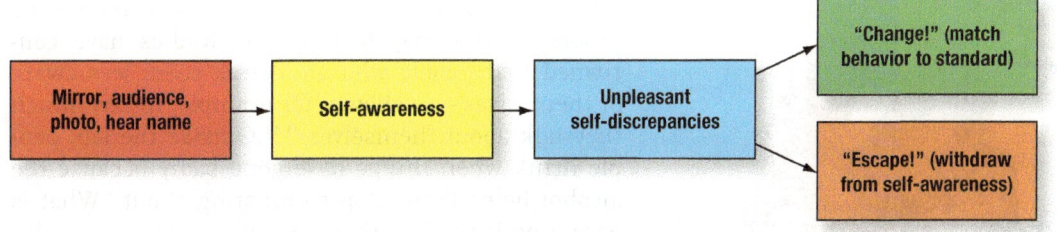

FIGURE 3.3
Self-awareness theory suggests that some situations, such as looking in a mirror, lead to self-awareness. Self-aware people feel bad because they notice any discrepancies between who they are and standards. They can either "change" by matching the behavior to the standard, or "escape" by trying to avoid the self-aware state.
SOURCE: Duval and Wicklund (1972).

them try harder to do so. But if the goal looks unattainable or the person does not feel he or she is making satisfactory progress, then avoiding self-awareness looms as the more appealing solution.

Self-Awareness and Behavior

Self-awareness can make people behave better. Being self-aware makes you compare yourself to moral standards or other ideals. For example, in one study students took a test and had an opportunity to cheat on it. Students who took the test while sitting in front of a mirror were less likely to cheat than students who took the test without a mirror.[26] Another study showed that people are less likely to eat fatty food when they are sitting in front of a mirror than when there is no mirror.[27] Thus, again, self-awareness made people more attuned to societal standards and hence made them act in a more socially desirable manner. Other studies have shown that increasing self-awareness can make people behave less aggressively, conform more to their sexual morals, and stay on their diets.[28,29,30] Increased self-awareness makes people act more consistently with their attitudes about many different issues.[31] Insofar as consistency is a good thing, those findings provide more evidence that self-awareness improves behavior.

The fact that self-awareness enables people to behave better, according to cultural standards, reflects the theme that inner processes serve interpersonal functions. Humans could not get along with each other if they did not have self-awareness. Self-awareness enables people to reflect on themselves and change themselves so as to become more socially desirable—precisely what is needed to improve their ability to get along.

Does self-awareness *always* make people behave better? It does not, of course. For example, terrorists might become more fanatical and more destructive as a result of being self-aware because their standard is to terrorize their enemy. But these exceptions are just that—exceptions. The general effect of high self-awareness is to make people more aware of positive, desirable standards and make them try harder to behave in a positive manner.

One class of largely destructive behaviors, however, does stem from high self-awareness. These behaviors arise when people are aware of themselves in some bad, upsetting aspect, and they cannot solve the problem. In those cases, they may attempt to escape from self-awareness by resorting to destructive or socially undesirable methods. We'll look at this in the next section.

Escaping Self-Awareness

People seek to escape from self-awareness when it feels bad. Research participants who acted contrary to their values and attitudes were told to take a seat in a waiting room afterward. Half the seats faced mirrors (which make a person self-aware), whereas others faced away from the mirrors. The people who had acted against their values generally chose to face away from the mirror.[32] They wanted to avoid self-awareness in order not to be reminded that they had done something wrong. Other participants, who had not done anything wrong, were happy to sit facing the mirror.

Drinking alcohol is one of the most common methods of reducing self-awareness. Alcohol narrows attention, and this usually means directing it away from the self

Alcohol reduces self-awareness, thereby undermining inhibitions.

(although if you get drunk and just think about your problems, you may feel worse). Studies have confirmed that people who are drunk seem less aware of themselves—as shown, for example, in how much they talk about themselves.[33,34] Outside the lab, people drink when things have gone badly because the alcohol helps them stop ruminating about "What is wrong with me?" Perhaps paradoxically, people also turn to alcohol when they feel good and want to celebrate. That's because people want to let down their inhibitions in order to have a good time, and self-awareness is central to most inhibitions. (Remember, self-awareness makes you compare yourself against morals and other standards of proper behavior: that supports inhibitions.)

People use other methods to escape self-awareness. Perhaps the most extreme and destructive of these is suicide. Attempts at suicide, even when unsuccessful, are often intended as ways to escape from a sense of self as being someone who is responsible for some terrible event.[35] Research indicates that even normal, healthy people can experience a rise in suicidal thoughts when they fail to live up to their goals, values, or other standards.[36]

Not all escapes from self-awareness are destructive, but several of them are, possibly because people who are desperate to stop thinking bad thoughts about themselves don't worry about the harm their methods might cause. *Food for Thought* discusses how escaping self-awareness can contribute to binge eating.

Why Do We Have Self-Awareness?

One explanation for human self-awareness is that it is vital for **self-regulation**—the process by which the self controls and changes itself.[37] People deliberately try to alter their responses, such as trying to get out of a bad mood, or to keep their attention and thinking focused on some problem rather than letting their mind wander, or to resist temptation. It is no accident that self-awareness usually involves comparing oneself to meaningful standards because that may be precisely what self-awareness is for. People can reflect on themselves, decide that they are not acting properly, and try to change. Understood in this way, self-awareness is part of the mechanism by which people can bring themselves into line with what other people, including their culture, want and expect. At a simple level, recognizing that your hair is a mess or your socks don't match may be an essential first step toward fixing the problem. (Chapter 4 will have more to say about self-regulation.)

Another explanation for human self-awareness is that it helps us adopt the perspective of other people and imagine how they see us. This reflects the "people first" theme that we introduced in Chapter 2: People are oriented toward other people. To get along, we look to others, and in particular we want to be accepted in social groups. Knowing how we appear to others is a great help toward making ourselves more appealing and acceptable to others. Self-awareness is helpful on the long road to social acceptance. It also indicates, again, that inner processes (in this case, self-awareness) serve interpersonal functions (to help people get along better with others).

At a more complex level, self-awareness can be an exercise in "What am I doing with my life?" Are you making progress toward your goals, such as receiving an education, getting a good job, or finding a suitable partner? People can feel good even though they have not reached their goals, as long as they are making progress toward them.[38] Self-awareness thus can help people manage their behavior over long periods of time so they can reach their goals.

self-regulation the process people use to control and change their thoughts, feelings, and behaviors

public self-consciousness the tendency to think about how others perceive you

private self-consciousness the tendency to think about one's inner thoughts and feelings

FOOD FOR *Thought*

Eating Binges and Escaping the Self

Binge eating is a widespread problem, especially among adolescent and young adult females. Ironically, most of these young women are on a diet and trying to lose weight at the time, and the occasional eating binge thwarts their efforts to restrain their food consumption. Why would a woman who is on a carefully planned, calorie-counting diet suddenly one day eat most of the food in her refrigerator and cupboards?

One answer points to the importance of self-awareness. In this view, the woman may be beset with troubled thoughts and feelings that she is inadequate, unattractive, or otherwise unworthy. The process of eating enables her to escape from those thoughts and feelings.[39] She forgets herself as she becomes absorbed in the activities of tasting, chewing, and swallowing food.

Many chronic dieters are preoccupied with how others perceive them. They may think that other people are whispering about how fat they are, even if they are within the normal weight range. They also tend to be people with high standards and high expectations for themselves (including being ambitious students at good universities). If something goes wrong for them—whether an academic setback, such as a bad test grade, or a personal problem, such as a romantic rejection—this tendency to focus on the self can make them miserable. They find themselves thinking about all their own possible faults and shortcomings that could have caused the problem.

At such times, eating appeals because it provides a distraction from thoughts about the self. The troubling thoughts occur at a highly meaningful level: What's wrong with me? Will I ever be a success in my career? Can I get someone to love me? In contrast, eating focuses the mind at a low level of meaning: take a bite, notice the taste, chew, swallow. Low levels of meaning involve little or no emotion, just sensation. The worries and anxieties about whether you are good enough are replaced by a kind of emotional calm. Eating can thus help turn off bad emotions.

Although dieters are high in **public self-consciousness,** defined as thinking about how others perceive them, they are often low in **private self-consciousness** of their inner states.[40,41] This may be because dieting involves learning to ignore one's inner feelings of hunger. Ignoring hunger may be helpful to dieting, but a common side effect is that the person also loses awareness of inner signals of satiety (that is, of being "full" and having eaten enough). This can contribute to an eating binge because the person keeps on eating even when the stomach is already full. The body sends out its usual "stop eating!" signal, but the mind has learned to ignore it along with other inner signals.

Normally, many dieters count every bite and calorie. This pattern of so-called monitoring helps keep track of food intake, so the dieter can carefully control how much she (or he) eats. This requires a watchful attitude toward the self. During an eating binge, however, self-awareness is often lost, and the person may lose track of how much they are eating. When you stop keeping track, it is hard to regulate. Even people who do not have eating disorders or dieting ambitions find that they eat more when they stop keeping track, such as when their attention is absorbed in a television show or party.

iStock.com/diomoyega

---

1. **Self-knowledge is also known as _____.**
   - ⓐ self-awareness
   - ⓑ self-concept
   - ⓒ self-regulation
   - ⓓ self-presentation

2. **According to self-awareness theory, a self-aware state is _____.**
   - ⓐ pleasant
   - ⓑ unpleasant
   - ⓒ pleasant initially, then unpleasant later
   - ⓓ neutral

3. **Alcohol has been shown to _____ self-awareness.**
   - ⓐ decrease
   - ⓑ increase
   - ⓒ not affect
   - ⓓ reverse

4. **The presence of a mirror has been shown to _____ self-awareness.**
   - ⓐ decrease
   - ⓑ increase
   - ⓒ not affect
   - ⓓ reverse

QUIZ YOURSELF
What Is the Self?

answers: see pg 113

Where Self-Knowledge Comes From

"Tell me something about yourself." Such openings are common, and people will generally oblige by disclosing some information. But where do they get it? How do people amass so much knowledge about themselves? Do people know themselves accurately, or are they mistaken (or do they simply lie a lot)? Humans clearly have a self-concept, or at least a stock of self-knowledge, some of which is true and some of which is distorted. Social psychologists have labored for decades to develop and test theories about how people store this information about themselves.

The next sections examine various theories about the sources of self-knowledge. When reading them, please keep a couple of things in mind: People are not passive receptacles; they actively process information that comes in. Your friend, or your mother, or society may tell you that you are not artistically talented, but you may reject that message. Then again, if all of them tell you that all the time, you may be more inclined to believe it (and they may be right!). Another thing to keep in mind is that people do not get all their self-knowledge from the same source or process. Several of these theories may be simultaneously correct, or at least partly correct.

Looking Outside: The Looking-Glass Self

One influential theory is that people learn about themselves from others. Every day people interact with others, and through these interactions they learn how others perceive them. "Wow, you are really good at sports!" "You're very attractive!" "You're a great cook!" These and many similar comments help give people information about themselves. It may seem surprising that the theme of putting people first extends even to finding out about yourself, but in fact people do learn a great deal about themselves from social interactions, from what other people tell them, and from comparing themselves to other people. These interactions also help cultivate public self-consciousness, which (as noted above) is the tendency to imagine how others perceive us.

The term **looking-glass self** was coined by Charles Horton Cooley[42] to refer to the idea that people learn about themselves from other people. Cooley proposed three components to the looking-glass self: (a) you imagine how you appear to others; (b) you imagine how others will judge you; (c) you develop an emotional response (such as pride or shame) as a result of imagining how others will judge you. It is as if other people hold up a mirror (a looking glass) in which you can see yourself. If you lived on a deserted island and never met anyone else, you would not know yourself nearly as well as you do growing up amid people.

The great American social philosopher George Herbert Mead[43] elaborated on this notion to suggest that most self-knowledge comes from feedback received from other people, whether particular individuals or what he called the **generalized other** (a combination of other people's views). Essentially, other people tell us who and what we are.

The notion of the looking-glass self has been tested extensively. It is partly correct and partly incorrect. Certainly there is ample evidence that people do respond to the feedback they get from others. Then again, if the looking-glass self really were the main source of self-knowledge, there ought to be a pretty good match between how everybody thinks about someone and how the person thinks about themself. But there isn't. Most research suggests that a person's self-concept is often quite different from what friends, family, and coworkers think of them.[44]

Why doesn't the looking-glass self work better? If we were to ask you to describe yourself, and then asked all your friends and acquaintances to describe you, why would there be so many differences? Social psychologists have found that there usually is a good match between your self-concept and how you think others regard you. The gap is between what your friends really think of you and what you think they think. For example,

Failure of the sore thumbs sticking out hypothesis...

Paula Wright 2012

looking-glass self the idea that people learn about themselves by imagining how they appear to others

generalized other a combination of other people's views that tells you who and what you are someone may think of herself as easy to get along with. If so, she probably thinks that everybody sees her as easy to get along with, but in reality other people may think she is a difficult, high-maintenance sort of person.

A person may be mistaken about how other people regard them for two reasons. The first is that people do not always tell the truth. If you ask someone, "Am I a pretty nice person, basically easy to get along with?" that person might just say "Sure!" without really meaning it. People are reluctant to communicate bad news,[45] to criticize someone, to complain, and in other ways to tell people what is wrong with them. (This generalization is subject to cultural differences. In Israel, for example, people supposedly are much more willing to communicate objections and criticisms.) It is very hard to find out if you have bad breath, for example, because almost no one will want to tell you.

The second reason is that people are not always receptive to feedback from others. People may try to tell you that you are hard to get along with, but you may not accept what they say. (You might get angry, or argue that the person is wrong, or change the subject.) As the section on self-deception will show, people are very selective in how they process incoming information about themselves. This is perhaps the biggest fallacy in the notion of the looking-glass self: It seems to depict the person as a passive recipient of information, as if people simply believed whatever other people told them about themselves. In reality, people pick and choose, and sometimes they completely reject what others tell them.

It is no wonder that many people's self-concepts do not match what others think of them. With regard to your unappealing traits, there is a sort of conspiracy of silence: Others don't want to tell you, and you don't want to hear it.

Looking Inside: Introspection

One refreshingly simple explanation of the roots of self-knowledge is that people simply have direct knowledge of what they are like. They don't need to rely on what other people tell them; they just look inward, and they know the answer. **Introspection** refers to the process by which a person examines the contents of his or her mind and mental states. People seemingly can always tell what they are thinking and feeling, probably better than anyone else. The concept of "privileged access" refers to the power of introspection; that is, I have "privileged access" to my own feelings, which I can know directly but you (or anyone else) can only infer. You only know what I am feeling if I tell you, or if you are lucky enough or sharp enough to infer my feelings from observing me.

This certainly rings true. People do know their own thoughts and feelings in ways that others cannot match. Introspection is one source of self-knowledge. It has limits, though. One is developmental. Many children think that their knowledge of their own inner states is no match for parental knowledge. Researchers asked children, "Who knows best what kind of person you really are, deep down inside?" Privileged access would mean that everyone should say, "I know myself best." But up until about the age of 11, children were more likely to say that their parents knew best.[46] The children thought that if they and their parents disagreed about some trait in the child, the parent would more likely be correct. This is remarkable: Children believe that their parents know them better than the children know themselves.

A more systematic and profound attack on introspection began with an influential article by Richard Nisbett and Timothy Wilson in 1977.[47] They proposed that people do not really have much in the way of privileged access, and hence when they look inside, they simply make mistakes, guess, or give what they assume are plausible or socially desirable answers. In a series of studies, Nisbett and Wilson and their colleagues showed that people often do not realize how their minds work. For example, in one study people had to choose which stockings to buy, and by scrambling the sequence the researchers were able to show that most shoppers just chose whichever one they saw last. But the shoppers

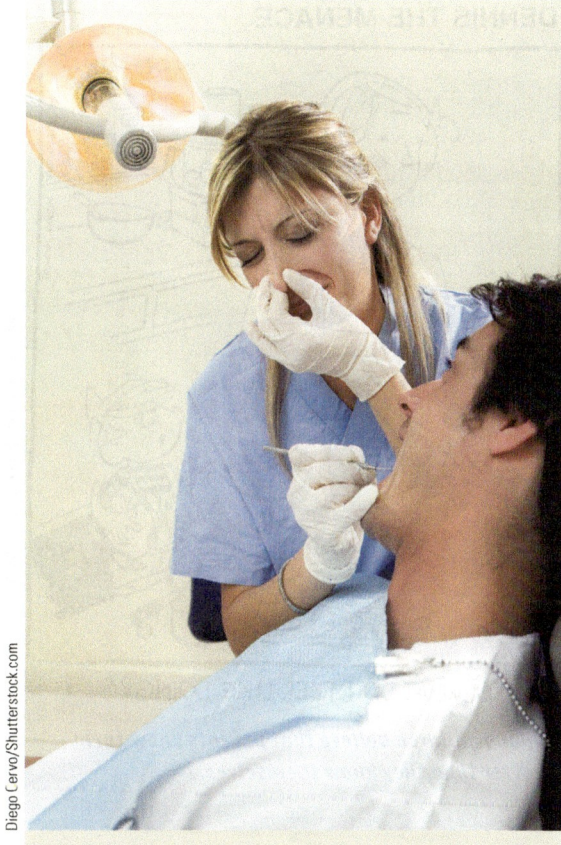

Your dental hygienist will definitely notice whether you have bad breath, but probably won't tell you. Fortunately, you will probably get some mouthwash after your teeth are cleaned. Other people who notice your bad breath, however, may feel awkward offering you mouthwash or a breath mint.

introspection the process by which a person examines the contents of his or her mind and mental states

DENNIS THE MENACE

"MOM, WHAT DO I FEEL LIKE DOING?"

Young children believe that parents know them better than they know themselves.

didn't realize what they were doing. They said they chose based on color or softness instead of saying, "I just chose the last one."[48]

Another failure of introspection was shown in a study of how young men are affected by sexy car ads.[49] The different ads emphasized each car's best features: One got good gas mileage, another had a good safety record, and so forth. One of the ads also featured a pretty young woman wearing only a dark sweater and black lace panties and holding a large spear. In different sessions, the attractive model was paired with different cars. The results showed that the men tended to choose whichever car was paired with the attractive woman. But when asked to explain their choice of car, the men never invoked the scantily clad, spear-carrying young woman; instead, they explained their choice on the basis of whatever was good about that car (e.g., "A good safety record is really important to me"). Note that the experimental design allowed the researchers to establish that the woman in the ad was the true cause of preferences, but the participants were unaware that they had been thus affected. (See Chapter 1 for a discussion of how experimental designs allow researchers to make causal inferences.)

Nisbett and Wilson's[50] claim that people do not know their own minds met fierce resistance in some quarters. We noted in Chapter 1 that science tends to be self-correcting, so that the march of progress can gradually get closer and closer to the truth as new theories are tested and improved. In crucial respects, Nisbett and Wilson were right: People often do not know what goes on inside their minds. In other respects, however, they may have overstated the case. Sometimes people do know what they are thinking and feeling.

The difference lies partly in the duplex mind. As you may recall from Chapter 2, the duplex mind has two parts: one engages in automatic, nonconscious processing of information, whereas the other involves deliberate processes of which we are consciously aware. Introspection is a conscious process. The automatic system does a great deal of work that the deliberate system does not know about or understand.

Is introspection valid? People can correctly know what they think and feel. On the other hand, they may not know *why* they are thinking or feeling something. Terry may be correct when he tells you that he did not like a novel that he read. You can believe his answer (assuming he is not deliberately lying) when he tells you whether he liked it or not. But his explanation of why he liked it or disliked it is less reliable. He may have liked it for many reasons of which he is not aware.

More generally, the self has many traits, some of which are best known to the self, others more easily seen by others. A painstaking study concluded that people are the best judges of their own traits that are hard to observe, such as neuroticism (a tendency to feel unhappy and be bothered by many things). In contrast, for traits that have a strong good-bad dimension, like intelligence and creativity, people may be biased and prone to self-deception, and close acquaintances are better judges than the self.[51]

Looking at Others: Social Comparison

Sometimes self-knowledge requires looking at other people. It may seem surprising that you learn about yourself by looking to others, but other people are vital to self-knowledge. In social comparison, you learn not the facts about yourself, but what those facts mean and how they count—in the context of what other people are like. Suppose, for example, that you score 126 on a test, or you discover that you can swim a mile (1.6 km) in half an hour. Is that good or bad? By itself, it is neither. It is only good or bad in comparison to what others do.

The theory of **social comparison**[52] laid out the power and the processes in which people learn about themselves by comparing themselves to others. Many facts about the self (such as swimming a mile in half an hour) don't carry much weight by themselves and only become meaningful in comparison to others. Social comparison is another instance (like the looking-glass self described earlier) of "putting people first"—we get the information we need, even about ourselves, by focusing on other people.

But to whom do you compare yourself? The most useful comparisons involve people in your same general category, whatever that might be. Comparing your swimming times

social comparison examining the difference between oneself and another person

Olympic gold medalist Michael Phelps is an upward comparison target for swimmers. If you compare yourself as a swimmer to him, you will probably feel badly.

to those of Michael Phelps, the legendary Olympic swimmer, isn't going to be very enlightening, especially if you are a female, middle-aged, overweight swimmer who never learned how to do flip turns.

Sometimes people deliberately compare themselves to others who are better or worse. **Upward social comparisons** involving people better than you, can inspire you to want to do better in order to reach their level. (However, they can also be discouraging.) **Downward social comparisons** against people worse off than yourself, can make you feel good.

Sometimes people compare themselves to others who are close by, such as their friends and family members. Such comparisons can be hard on the relationship, especially for the one who doesn't come out looking good. It's fine for your sister or your husband to be a swimming champ if you aren't a competitive swimmer yourself; in fact, the other's success may reflect favorably on you. But if you are a serious swimmer and your partner consistently does better than you, you may be upset by this comparison, and that can put some distance between the two of you.[53]

People care about these comparisons. A recent study of all bankruptcies in Canada over several years found that when someone wins a big cash prize in the provincial (state) lottery, their neighbors are more likely to go bankrupt.[54] What's more, they went bankrupt buying expensive and visible goods, such fancy cars, not by investing more in invisible goods, such as a stock portfolio. Even things like home furnishings did not change. The neighbors wanted to appear to the world to be as rich and comfortable as their neighbor.

Self-Perception

Yet another theory about where self-knowledge comes from is that people learn about themselves in the same way they learn about others—by observing behavior and drawing conclusions. In a sense, this is the opposite of introspection theory because it dismisses the whole "privileged access" issue. There is no special route to self-knowledge. You see what you do, and you draw conclusions about what you are like. This seemed like a radical theory to many social psychologists when it was proposed in 1965. However, **self-perception theory**[55] does not really claim that people have no privileged access to knowing their inner feelings and states. In fact, the theory proposes that when people did have such information, they might not rely on self-perception processes. But sometimes looking inside is not adequate, and in those cases people are swayed by self-perception. For example, Lucy might say that she believes in God and thinks people ought to go to church, but somehow she never manages to get herself there. At some point she may notice this fact about herself and conclude that her religious convictions are perhaps

upward social comparison comparing yourself to people better than you

downward social comparison comparing yourself to people worse off than you

self-perception theory the theory that people observe their own behavior to infer what they are thinking and how they are feeling, the same way they learn about others somewhat weaker than she had always thought. If religion really mattered to her, she probably would manage to get to church once in a while. At a more mundane level, you may have had the experience of not having eaten for several hours and not feeling hungry but then noticing how eagerly you start to eat when food is available, prompting you to think, "I guess I really was hungry."

One important application of self-perception theory is the overjustification effect, described in the *Money Matters* box.

The Fluctuating Image(s) of Self

So far we have spoken about self-knowledge as the mass of information the person has and carries with themselves all the time. But social psychologists have discovered a smaller, in some ways more important, self-concept that changes much more easily and readily. Called the **phenomenal self**,[56] or the **working self-concept**,[57] it is the image of self that is currently active in the person's thoughts. Put another way, when you are self-aware, you are usually only aware of a small part of all the information you have about yourself. Each

phenomenal self (working self-concept) the image of self that is currently active in the person's thoughts

intrinsic motivation wanting to perform an activity for its own sake

extrinsic motivation performing an activity because of something that results from it

overjustification effect the tendency for intrinsic motivation to diminish for activities that have become associated with rewards

---

MONEY *Matters*

Doing It for Money, Not Love

One of the most important and dramatic instances of self-perception involves motivation. Early on, social psychologists learned to distinguish between intrinsic and extrinsic motivation.[58] **Intrinsic motivation** refers to wanting to perform an activity for its own sake. The activity is an end in itself. Someone might be intrinsically motivated to paint, for example, because he enjoys the process of dabbing colors onto a canvas and takes satisfaction in creating a beautiful or striking picture.

Extrinsic motivation, in contrast, refers to performing an activity because of something that results from it. The activity is a means to some other end—it is pursued for what it accomplishes or leads to, rather than for the activity itself. A person who is extrinsically motivated to paint might paint in order to make money. This painter might be very motivated and might work very hard, even if she did not really like painting much at all. One test would be whether the person would choose to spend free time doing the activity, in the absence of external rewards or incentives. An intrinsically motivated painter might well spend a free Sunday afternoon painting, but an extrinsically motivated painter would not (unless there was money or some other incentive).

Self-perception theory led to the prediction that extrinsic motivations would gradually win out over intrinsic motivations when both were relevant. This is called the **overjustification effect**—the tendency for intrinsic motivation to diminish for activities that have become associated with rewards. Essentially, overjustification means that rewards transform play into work. Mark Twain understood this concept long before psychologists did. In *The Adventures of Tom Sawyer*, Twain wrote:

> There are wealthy gentlemen in England who drive four-horse passenger coaches twenty or thirty miles on a daily line, in the summer, because the privilege costs them considerable money; but if they were offered wages for the service that would turn it into work then they would resign.

Take the intrinsically motivated painter, and suppose that someone then began to pay him to paint. The painter would gradually see himself painting away and getting paid for it. And the logical inference would be that he is painting for the money—which implies that he doesn't really love to paint for its own sake. Accordingly, over time, being paid to paint would make the painter less and less intrinsically motivated to paint.

Extrinsic rewards can create confusion in people who are engaging in an activity they love to do. People begin to wonder why they are doing the activity, for enjoyment or for pay. Reggie Jackson, a baseball player whose salary at the time was then-astronomical $975,000 per year, was once asked why he played baseball. He said, "A lot of it is the money, but I'd be playing if I was making [only] $150,000." Bill Russell, the former basketball star, said, "I remember that the game lost some of its magical qualities for me once I thought seriously about playing for a living."

The overjustification effect has been confirmed in many studies,[59] though there are plenty of exceptions.[60] If people get extrinsic rewards for doing something they intrinsically like to do, eventually the intrinsic motivation grows weaker and the person orients the activity more and more to its extrinsic rewards. In the first demonstrations of this pattern, students performed puzzles and were either paid or not paid for solving them. The researchers then left each student alone for a brief period and secretly observed whether the student continued to work on the puzzles (a sign of intrinsic motivation because it indicated that the person enjoyed the puzzles enough to work on them when there was no reward). Students who had been paid showed a sharp drop in their interest in doing the puzzles once the pay stopped situation summons up only a few relevant aspects of the self, and these constitute the phenomenal self. The difference is comparable to that between all the information you have in your computer and what is currently displayed on the screen. The phenomenal self is what you see on the screen right now: It is only a small part of the total, but it is the part that you can use actively.

Different situations can call up different parts of self-knowledge into the phenomenal self. For one thing, whatever aspects of you stand out as unusual often become prominent in the phenomenal self. Thus, if you are the only woman in a roomful of men, you are probably quite aware of being a woman, whereas if you are among other women, your femaleness does not stand out so much and you may be less aware of it. Note that you are still a woman in either case, and of course you know it. The difference is merely what stands out in your mind.[69,70]

This sense of yourself as standing out is especially important when you are the only member of some category, such as a racial or ethnic group. If you are, say, the only African American on a committee, you may be acutely aware that other people think of you as African American, and you may identify more strongly than you would otherwise

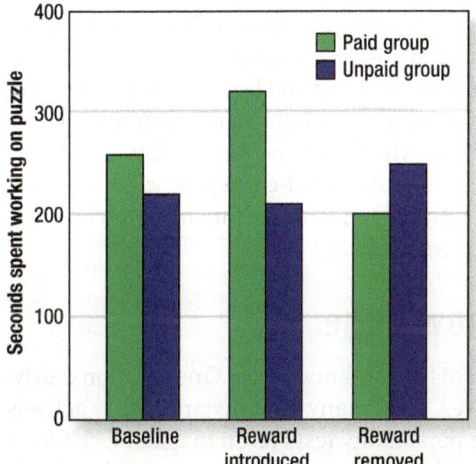

FIGURE 3.4

Average number of seconds participants in paid and unpaid groups spent working on a puzzle at baseline (before a reward was introduced to the paid group), when the reward was introduced, and after the reward was removed.[57]

(see **FIGURE 3.4**). In contrast, students who had done the same number of puzzles but had never been paid continued to find them interesting.[61] Thus, being paid made people think, "I only do these for money," and they no longer liked to do them for their own sake. Extrinsic motivation (money) had replaced intrinsic motivation (fun). Play had become work.

A crucial and revealing factor is whether the rewards are expected during the activity, as opposed to coming as a surprise afterward. You would only infer that somebody is painting for the sake of the money if the person knew in advance that painting would bring money. If the person painted and then received some money afterward, unexpectedly, you would not conclude that money was the driving force. The same logic applies to the self. When people perform an activity and anticipate they will be paid for it, their intrinsic interest in the task diminishes. In contrast, an unexpected reward does not alter their intrinsic motivation.[62,63]

Another factor is initial liking. What if the person does not enjoy the activity? In that case, getting rewards seems to make the activity more attractive, especially if it is possible to discover some pleasure in it.[64] Some things, like swimming, require doing them for a while in order to learn to enjoy them.

You might think that people would know directly whether they desire and enjoy some activity, and that extrinsic rewards would make little difference. (Recall the earlier discussion of introspection and "privileged access.") Certainly people do know to some extent what they want and what they like. But self-perception processes still have some influence. Some experts caution against paying children money to reward them for good grades. The money may cause confusion about why they are trying to get good grades: Is it because learning is fun, or is it because they receive money for good grades? Actually, there is some evidence that when rewards convey a clear message that "you're great!" they do not undermine intrinsic motivation,[65,66] possibly because people like to be good at things. Moreover, sometimes people may say they like something but still not do it as frequently.[67]

A recent study tracked over 10,000 West Point cadets for 10 years to examine how these motives operate outside the lab.[68] Their reasons for attending West Point were sorted into intrinsic and extrinsic. Intrinsic motivation, such as the desire to become an Army officer, led to better outcomes: The higher the intrinsic motivation, the more likely the person was to become one, to get promoted, and to extend military service past the initial term. Extrinsic motivation (e.g., wanting prestige, status, officer's salary) generally reduced those good outcomes, and they greatly weakened the effects of intrinsic motivation—just like the overjustification theory predicts. But among cadets with low intrinsic motivation, having a stronger extrinsic motivation did improve their performance. Thus, again, extrinsic motivation can be good if intrinsic motivation is low, but if intrinsic is high, extrinsic undermines it.

Which ones are most aware of their own race?

with being an African American. (Note that this is ironic, in a way. Some people might guess that you would identify yourself more as an African American if you were in a group that was composed entirely of African Americans.) Being the lone member of some category heightens self-awareness and can impair performance.[71] It can even make you feel that you are responsible for your group's reputation, which greatly increases the pressure. Worrying about how your performance may reflect on your group is called "stereotype threat" and is covered in Chapter 13.

An important aspect of the self is being the same across time. Yet people think of themselves somewhat differently when focused on the present as opposed to the future.[72] When you think about yourself as you are today, the thought tends to be full of specific and concrete facts, such as being a student in this social psychology course and reading this textbook. In contrast, when you think about yourself in the future, such as a year or two from now, your ideas will tend to be more general and abstract, such as whether you will be engaged in studying and learning in general. Future versions of self have broader categories (a man, as opposed to a tall thin man with a beard; a sports fan, as opposed to a pro football fan who favors the Kansas City Chiefs), as compared to present concept of self. In general, the future self-concept is vague, simple, broad, and general, whereas the present self-concept tends to be much more clear-cut, complex, and specific.

Deliberately Seeking Self-Knowledge

In the last section we considered some of the roots of self-knowledge. One additional driving factor is that people want to know themselves, so in many circumstances they actively seek out information about the self. They take personality tests (even magazine self-tests that have little or no scientific validity), consult horoscopes, spend years and thousands of dollars on psychoanalysis or other therapies that promise to improve self-knowledge, learn to meditate, and above all pay close attention to what others say about them. One former mayor of New York, Ed Koch, made a standard joke out of the interest in self-knowledge by acknowledging that most people had an opinion about his performance as mayor. Whenever he met someone, instead of asking, "How are you doing?" as is customary, he would ask, "How am I doing?"

Beginnings of Self-Knowledge

Human beings have a deep thirst for self-knowledge. Some people are more eager than others to learn about themselves, but hardly anyone is indifferent to self-knowledge. The evolutionary origins of the desire for self-knowledge are hard to establish, though one can easily propose many potential benefits that might come from knowing yourself. For example, creatures might have a better idea of which potential mates to pursue if they have a more accurate understanding of their own attractiveness.[73] If you vastly overestimate your sex appeal, you might waste a great deal of time trying to hook up with people who are out of your league. Likewise, if someone challenges you, knowing your own strength and capabilities might dictate whether you choose to fight or back down, and mistakes could be costly.

The long road to social acceptance is one theme of this book, and self-knowledge can be helpful on that road. You need self-knowledge in order to fit in better with others. Will people like me? Am I similar to them? Such questions require self-knowledge. Moreover, as we have seen, cultural groups consist of different roles and different tasks, so it is valuable to know what your strengths and weaknesses are in order to know how best to fit in with the group. You don't want to demand to be the group's cook if you are terrible at cooking, for example, because your bad food might make others dislike and reject you.

Three Reasons for Wanting Self-Knowledge

People want to learn about themselves, but they'd rather learn some things than others. Three main motives shape the quest for self-knowledge. These three motives sometimes compete against each other, and different motives predominate in different people or different circumstances.

The first motive is the simple desire to learn the truth about oneself, whatever it is. This can be called the **appraisal motive**. It consists of a broad, open-minded curiosity, and its main preference is for information that is both important and reliable.[74,75] For example, the appraisal motive may motivate people to start out with tasks of medium difficulty because these offer the most information. If you start out with something that is very easy, then success does not give you much information about whether you have high or low ability because anyone might succeed at an easy task. By the same token, if you start out with something that is very difficult, then failure does not give you much information about whether you have high or low ability because anyone might fail at a difficult task.

The second motive, called the **self-enhancement motive** is the desire to learn favorable or flattering things about the self. Unlike the appraisal motive, the self-enhancement motive can exert considerable bias, driving people to dismiss or ignore criticism while exaggerating or inflating any signs of their good qualities.[76]

The third motive, the **consistency motive** is a desire to get feedback that confirms what the person already believes about themself. Once people have formed ideas about themselves, they are generally reluctant to revise those opinions. In this respect, self-knowledge is no different from knowledge about many aspects of the world: Once people have formed opinions or beliefs about almost anything, they are resistant to change. The consistency motive is also sometimes called the self-verification motive, which implies that people actively seek to "verify" their self-concepts by obtaining confirmation that what they think about themselves is correct.[77,78]

To illustrate these three motives, suppose that you believe that you are not very good at sports. The appraisal motive would make you want to get more information about your sports abilities, regardless of what that information might say. The self-enhancement motive might make you want to learn that you do have some talent at sports after all. (If you can't get such feedback, then the self-enhancement motive might drive you to avoid any more information about yourself at sports, and it might also push you to compensate for your athletic deficiencies by finding out that you are good at other things, such as music or cooking.) And the consistency motive would make you prefer to gain further evidence that you are bad at sports, because that confirms what you already think.

When Motives Compete

When such conflicts arise between motives, which one wins? Logic would suggest that the answer is based on what is most useful. Accurate information is almost always more useful than false information because accurate information furnishes the best basis for making good choices. Hence, the appraisal motive should be the strongest.

It isn't, though. When the three motives were pitted against each other in a series of careful experiments, the appraisal motive emerged as the weakest of the three.[79] Self-enhancement was the strongest. People most want to hear good things about themselves. Their second preference is for confirmation of what they already think (consistency). They do also want accurate information, but the desire for the truth runs a distant third to the desires for favorable and consistent feedback. Although people may prefer positive, flattering feedback, it may not be best for them. Compared to accurate self-evaluation, inflated views of self cause multiple problems, including poor performance, defensiveness, and failing to study and prepare for upcoming challenges.[80] Students who have inflated views of themselves end up getting relatively poor grades in college and end up less satisfied with their lives.[81] People who are prone to use self-enhancing styles of thought tend to lack resilience in the face of personal difficulties, to get poor grades, to lack social skills, and to become narcissistic.[82]

appraisal motive the simple desire to learn the truth about oneself, whatever it is

self-enhancement motive the desire to learn favorable or flattering things about the self

consistency motive a desire to get feedback that confirms what the person already believes about themself

Also, people sometimes have more than one reaction to feedback, especially if feeling and thinking pull in different ways. The self-enhancement motive has an especially strong emotional appeal, whereas the consistency motive has more of a cognitive appeal. People may be more willing to believe and accept consistent feedback in terms of their cognitive reactions, but emotionally they will yearn for and prefer flattering, positive feedback. If someone tells you that you are extremely talented, for example—more talented than you had believed—you may find that your logical mind is skeptical of this news, but emotionally you are happy to hear it.[83,84,85,86]

One way of understanding this ranking of self-knowledge motives is to return to the "people first" theme. It is true that accurate knowledge would be the most useful for making decisions. But probably people want to be accepted by others more than they want a valid basis for making decisions. The human emotional system is set up to promote and reward any signs that the person is likely to be accepted by others. Hence, positive, flattering information is the most appealing because others will like you most if you have good traits.

The fact that the self-enhancement motive is stronger than the appraisal motive means that people want to think well of themselves more than they want to know the truth. One implication is that sometimes people prefer to discredit feedback, even in advance, if they think it might make them look bad. One of social psychology's best documented

self-handicapping putting obstacles in the way of one's own performance so that anticipated or possible failure can be blamed on the obstacle instead of on lack of ability

Trade Offs

Self-Handicapping

Why would someone get drunk before an important job interview? Why do some students stay out partying all night before an important test? Are underachievers all merely too lazy to get their work done?

An intriguing theory has suggested that some people's problems stem from a strategy called **self-handicapping**.[87,88,89,90] Self-handicapping has been defined as putting obstacles in the way of one's own performance, so that anticipated or possible failure can be blamed on the obstacle instead of on lack of ability. The student who parties all night instead of studying before an exam may not get the best grade, but because that low grade can be blamed on not having studied, it does not signify that the student lacks intelligence.

Self-handicapping was first proposed as a possible explanation of alcohol abuse. Alcohol is widely (and correctly) seen as harmful to performance: Drunk people do not perform as well as sober people. Hence, someone who fears that they will perform badly might find alcohol a convenient excuse.

The excuse appeals especially to someone who has already achieved a reputation for being smart or capable. (The importance of what other people think indicates that self-handicapping is primarily a self-presentational strategy, designed to control how one is perceived by others.[91]) Many people who have a big success early in their careers worry that this was just a lucky break, and they fear that they will not be able to do as well again. For example, a rock band might have a big hit with their first recording, which launches them into fame and stardom, but they are afraid that their second recording will not be as good. Fans and critics may hail them as geniuses after the first success, but the band worries that the second album may make everyone reconsider and decide that the band is only a mediocre talent after all. Instead of letting that happen, some band members may develop a drug or alcohol problem. That way, if the second album is not as good, fans and critics can say, "They are really talented, and it's too bad that the drug problem is keeping them from producing more great music." Their reputation as geniuses remains intact. Wouldn't you rather be known as a troubled genius than an diligent mediocrity?

Moreover, if the second performance is good, then people will assign extra credit, so the self-handicapper's reputation is even improved: "Look at what a great report she gave, even though she had been on a drinking binge all week. She must really be amazingly

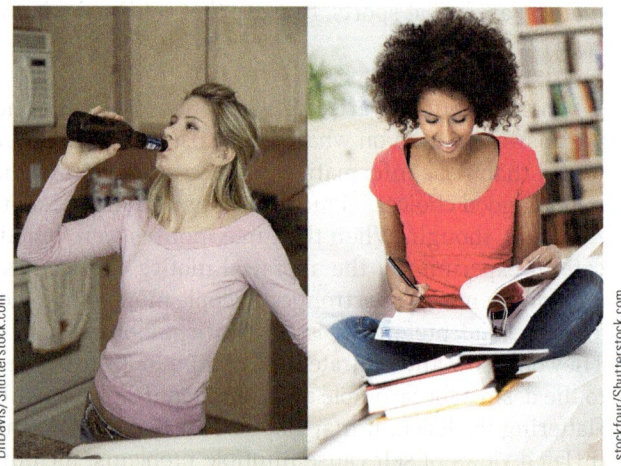

Do some people turn to alcohol in order to provide themselves with a handy excuse for possible failure?

patterns of avoiding feedback that could make them look bad is self-handicapping, which is described in *Tradeoffs*.

Self-Knowledge and the Duplex Mind

The duplex mind is also relevant to the interplay between these conflicting motives. The automatic system tends to favor the self-enhancement motive. When people respond automatically to questions about themselves, they lean toward "everything good is me, and everything bad is not me." Under times of stress, or when people are preoccupied or distracted, this pattern of **automatic egotism** emerges.[92]

Often a conscious override is required in order to furnish a more balanced and consistent view of self. Modesty in particular often seems to require conscious, deliberate control, because people may have a first impulse to say they are wonderful, and they must overcome this impulse in order to offer a humbler account of themselves.[93,94] It is a quick, automatic reaction to feel good about praise or to feel bad when criticized, but it takes a little more thought and effort to question the praise or to admit that the criticism may be valid. Thus, the different parts of the duplex mind may cultivate self-knowledge in different ways. The automatic system favors automatic egotism ("I'm good in general"), whereas the deliberate system can make corrections and strive toward a more balanced, accurate appraisal of the facts.

automatic egotism response by the automatic system that "everything good is me, and everything bad is not me"

smart to do great work despite her drinking problem." Some people, such as those with high self-esteem, are drawn to this advantage because it enriches one's credit for success.[95]

In one series of experiments, participants were told that the purpose was to investigate whether some new drugs had temporary side effects on intelligent performance. The experimenter explained that one drug temporarily made people smarter and the other made people temporarily less smart (like alcohol). Participants then took a first IQ test. On this test, some people were given unsolvable multiple-choice questions, so they had to guess, but to their surprise the experimenter kept telling them their answers were correct. These participants experienced what is called noncontingent success: They were told they did well, but at some level they had to know that they had not really earned their good rating. In another condition, people were given easier problems and accurately told which ones they got correct (thus, contingent success). All participants were then told that their score was the highest that had been seen in the study so far.

Next, the experimenter asked the participant to choose one of the drugs, in preparation for a second IQ test (which would supposedly verify whether performance improved or got worse). One of the drugs (called Actavil) was supposed to increase intellectual performance, whereas the other drug (called Pandocrin) was supposed to decrease intellectual performance. Participants who had experienced the noncontingent success overwhelmingly chose the alcohol-like drug Pandocrin that would supposedly make them perform worse (see **FIGURE 3.5**). Why? They knew the experimenter thought they were brilliant, but they privately doubted they could do as well on the second test, so they wanted the drug that would give them an excuse for poor performance.[96]

In the early 1800s, a European chess champion named Deschappelles won nearly all his matches. As he got old, however, he felt his mental powers waning, and he worried that smart young chess masters would defeat him. He used a self-handicapping strategy to preserve his reputation: He insisted that he would only play games in which his opponent got the first move (a major advantage in chess) and in which he gave up one of his pieces at the start of the game (another disadvantage for him). That way, if he lost, he would not lose respect because the loss would be attributed to his disadvantages; when he won, people

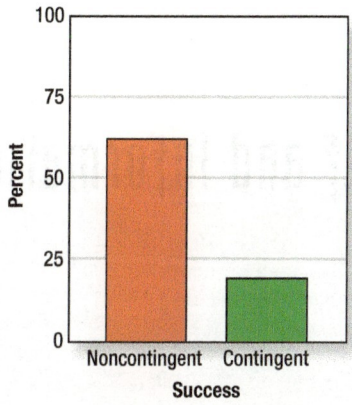

FIGURE 3.5
Percent of participants in the noncontingent and contingent success groups choosing the alcohol-like drug Pandocrin that supposedly decreased intellectual performance.

would marvel at his ability to overcome those handicaps.[97]

Self-handicapping is thus an effective strategy for good self-presentation. It discounts failure and enhances success. The downside of the tradeoff is that it makes failure more likely. Taking a test without having slept, or when hung over, may furnish a handy excuse for failure, but it also increases the odds of failure.

QUIZ YOURSELF

Where Self-Knowledge Comes From

1. The night before an important test, Boozer drinks all night instead of studying. This is an example of _____.
   - (a) self-awareness
   - (b) self-consciousness
   - (c) self-fulfilling prophecy
   - (d) self-handicapping

2. "Do I like parades? Well, each year there have been several parades in town, and I haven't gone to one yet. I must not like parades." Which theory explains this internal dialogue?
   - (a) Cognitive dissonance theory
   - (b) Psychological reactance theory
   - (c) Psychoanalytic theory
   - (d) Self-perception theory

3. A teacher promises one of his preschool students a candy bar for finger painting, a task the student loves to do. The reward is likely to produce _____.
   - (a) cognitive dissonance
   - (b) downward social comparison
   - (c) intrinsic motivation
   - (d) the overjustification effect

4. The simple desire to learn the truth about oneself is called the _____ motive.
   - (a) appraisal
   - (b) consistency
   - (c) extrinsic
   - (d) self-enhancement

answers: see pg 113

Self and Information Processing

Anything That Touches the Self...

Every day people process a great deal of information about their social worlds, and the self often exerts influence over how this information gets processed. For one thing, the self serves as a sign of importance: Anything that bears on the self is more likely to be important than things that do not touch the self. As a result, any link to the self makes the mind pay more attention and think more thoroughly.

One of the earliest and most basic effects of the self on information processing is the **self-reference effect**. Information bearing on the self is processed more thoroughly and more deeply, and hence remembered better, than other information. In the initial studies of this effect,[98] participants simply saw a series of words and were asked a question about each word. Sometimes these questions had nothing to do with the self, such as "Is this a long word?" and "Is it a meaningful word?" Other times, however, the question was "Does this word describe you?" Later on, the researchers gave a surprise test to the participants, asking them to remember as many words on the list as they could. The rate of correct memory depended heavily on which question had been asked, and the questions about the self elicited the best memory (see **FIGURE 3.6**). For example, participants were more likely to remember the word *friendly* if they had been asked whether they were friendly than whether *friendly* was a meaningful word or whether it was a long word.[99,100,101,102,103]

The implication was that simply thinking about a word in connection with the self led to better memory. In fact, even if participants answered "No" to the question about whether the word described them, they still remembered the word better than other words. The self apparently operates like a powerful hook, and whatever gets hung on it (even just for a moment) is more likely to be preserved.

A similar pattern has been called the **endowment effect**. Items gain in value to the person who owns them.[104] If someone asks you how much you would pay for a souvenir

self-reference effect the finding that information bearing on the self is processed more thoroughly and more deeply, and hence remembered better, than other information

endowment effect the finding that items gain in value to the person who owns them mug, you might offer three dollars. If someone gives you the mug and then someone else wants to buy it from you, however, you might find yourself asking for four or five dollars. Somehow the mug became worth more to you during the time you owned it, even if that time was only a few minutes, and you did not have any special experiences with it that might confer sentimental value. Simply being connected to the self gave it more value. Nor does this work only with cash value: People start to like things more when they own them.[105]

Likewise, things gain in value to the self who chooses them. In one famous demonstration, people either were given a lottery ticket or chose one for themselves. Both tickets had identical chances of winning, and therefore objectively they had the same value. But when the researchers asked participants how much they would sell the ticket for, the price of the self-chosen tickets was consistently higher than the price of the randomly given tickets.[106] Somehow the process of choosing the ticket oneself made it seem more valuable to the person who chose it.

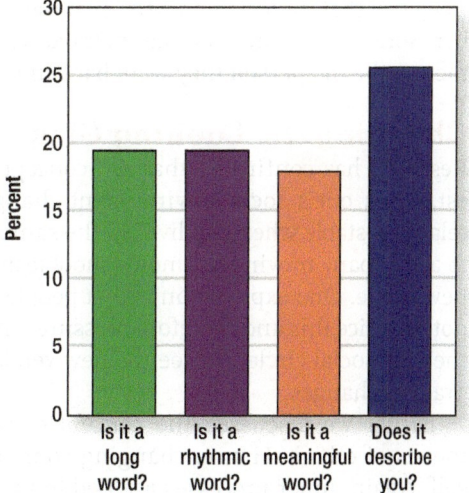

FIGURE 3.6
The self-reference effect refers to the finding that information related to the self (e.g., Does it describe you?) is more memorable than information related to something besides the self (e.g., Is it a long word?).

Can the Self-Concept Change?

People usually believe that they have remained the same person over much of their lives. Your identity certainly changes, but it does so slowly. You have the same social security number, linked to the same tax status. Your name remains the same (even if you decide to change your last name when you marry, your first name is unaffected). You belong to the same family, though you may gradually add new members to this family (such as by marrying or having a baby). Once you start your career, you tend to stay in the same occupation for most of your life, and until recently it was common to spend one's entire career working for the same organization. Your gender remains the same in most cases, and you inhabit the same body for your entire life.

People do change, however. Children add new knowledge and skills as they grow up. Adults may take up new hobbies or break bad habits. Your body is continuous, but it changes too, first growing taller and stronger, then often growing fatter and less flexible, and finally developing wrinkles, shrinking, and acquiring other signs of old age.

Revising Self-Knowledge

When do people change so much that they also revise their self-concept? There are several plausible theories. One is that you can simply decide to change how you think about yourself, and your actions will come around to reflect the new you.[107,108] Another is the reverse: You can decide to change your behavior, and a change in self-concept will follow (see the material on cognitive dissonance in Chapter 7). Both are plausible, but neither gets at the full story.

The evidence suggests that one's social world is a powerful source of stability in the self. Other people expect you to remain pretty much the same. In part, this arises because people see other people in terms of stable traits, even though they do not see themselves that way.[109] Seeing other people in terms of their personality traits reflects the assumption that people mostly remain the same over long periods of time, and indeed there is some evidence that in many respects personality traits do remain fairly stable over long stretches, even from childhood into adulthood.[110,111,112,113]

The expectation that people stay the same can become a kind of pressure to remain constant. Many students notice this when they return home after a year or two at a university, especially if they have not stayed in regular contact with everyone back home.

They feel that their parents still treat them and regard them the way they were years earlier. Sometimes they find that their old friends from high school likewise seem to expect them to be the person they were back in high school.

Changing the Looking Glass

Research has confirmed that self-concept change is most common, and possibly easiest, when one's social environment changes.[114] For example, self-esteem tends to stay relatively stable when one lives in the same social circle, and changes in self-esteem tend to accompany moving to a new school (especially going from high school to college) or a new home. One explanation is that people change gradually, but their social circle tends not to notice this and therefore pressures them to stay the same. When the person moves, the new social circle can see the new version of the person that has emerged from these gradual changes.

Earlier we discussed the concept of the looking-glass self. You know yourself by means of others. Hence, changing your social circle is a promising way to change the self. Again, inner processes are tied to interpersonal relations, so when the social circle changes, the inner self may change too.

A similar conclusion emerged from studies on brainwashing. The techniques of brainwashing first attracted research attention during the Korean War, when Chinese communists sought to change the views of captured American soldiers. The Chinese had no grand theory about how to brainwash Americans, so they just experimented with different methods. At first they tried exposing the prisoners to all-day sessions of propaganda and indoctrination, telling them how great communism was and how bad American capitalism was. This did not work very well. Then the Chinese realized that the problem was not in what happened during the day. Rather, the problem was that every night the prisoners were sent back to the barracks with the other American prisoners, where each man's American identity reasserted itself. The Chinese found that brainwashing became much more successful and effective if they kept the prisoners separate from each other. That way, the American identity and American values were not bolstered by social contacts with other Americans, and the prisoners became much more malleable.[115]

These findings about self-concept change support the view that what goes on inside the person is mainly there to serve interpersonal processes. Many people assume that the inner self is fixed, strong, and stable, and that what they do with other people is simply an expression of an inner "true" self. But that view appears to be mistaken. The important and powerful forces originate in the interactions and relationships between people, and what goes on inside the individual adapts to those interpersonal processes. This is yet another instance of our theme that inner processes serve interpersonal functions.

Promoting Change

When people want to change, therefore, it is helpful to use the social environment rather than fight against it. When people seek to change some aspect of themselves, such as trying to quit smoking or become more physically fit, they do best if they enlist the support of other people in their lives. It is hard to quit smoking if your spouse smokes and wants you to smoke with him or her. In contrast, if your spouse wants you to quit smoking, he or she will probably support your efforts to change, and your chances of success are improved.[116]

Indeed, one effective strategy for change is to persuade everyone else that you have changed. Once they expect you to act in a new and different way, you are more likely to stick to that new line of behavior. Thinking of yourself in the different way is not enough; it is more important and more powerful to get others to think of you in that way. (This also confirms our theme of putting people first: You use other people to help you to change.) In one experiment, people were induced to think of themselves in a new way, either introverted or extraverted. This was accomplished by asking people loaded questions (e.g., "What do you dislike about loud parties?"[117]). Some participants in the experiment answered these questions when sitting alone in a room, talking to a tape recorder, with a guarantee that their responses would be confidential and anonymous. These participants showed no sign of self-concept change. In contrast, other participants answered the same questions by speaking face to face with another person. These participants did change, not only in how they later saw themselves but even in how introverted or extraverted they acted with a new, different person.[118,119] The interpersonal context was necessary for changing the inner self.

Thus, one route to self-concept change involves internalizing your recent behavior. First you act in a certain way, and then gradually you come to think of yourself as being the kind of person who acts that way. Other people play a crucial role as well; acting that way by yourself, in secret, does not seem to produce much effect on the self-concept. In contrast, getting others to see you as that kind of person is helpful toward making you believe that you are that kind of person. Again, self and identity require social validation, a theme to which we will return later in the chapter in the section on self-presentation.

Donald Trump experienced a self-concept change, from businessman to U.S. president.

New Self, New Story

Once the self-concept has changed, people tend to revise their stories about their lives to fit the new version. For example, Donald Trump changed his concept from businessman to U.S. president.

Such revisions of memory have been studied by social psychologists.[120] They have concluded that most of the time people want to believe they remain the same, but sometimes they also want to believe that they have changed, and they shuffle and edit the facts in their memory to fit whichever belief is more relevant. Thus, if people change their attitudes, they may forget what they used to believe, so that they think the new attitude does not reflect a change—rather, they say, "I thought so all along." In contrast, if they want to believe they have changed when they haven't, they may retroactively distort how they used to be. In one memorable demonstration, researchers looked at study skills enhancement programs at universities, which are designed to teach students how to study better. Most universities have such programs, but objective evidence suggests that they do not really accomplish much in the way of making people into better students or enabling them to get better grades. Students who take these programs, however, want to believe that they have improved. They persuade themselves that the program has worked by revising their memory of how bad they were before.[121] For example, if a student's study skills rated a 5 out of 10 before the program, and the program accomplished nothing, the student would rate a 5 after it as well—but she might tell herself afterward that she really had been "more like a 3" before the program, so she can believe that she really did improve.

A vivid demonstration of how memory distorts the facts to fit the self-concept involved a study of women's menstrual periods.[122] An initial survey revealed that some women thought their periods were generally quite unpleasant, whereas others thought theirs were mild and innocuous. The researchers asked the women to record their feelings and sensations on a daily basis through a couple of periods. After a month or more, the women were asked to rate how bad those periods had been. By comparing the daily ratings with the retrospective (a month later) ratings, the researchers could see how memory was distorted. Each woman's beliefs about her general reactions biased her recall. That is, the women who thought their periods were generally bad tended to recall the periods as having been worse than they had said at the time. Conversely, the women who thought their periods were generally not so bad recalled their periods as milder than they had rated them when they were occurring. We constantly revise our memories based on beliefs we hold about ourselves.

Self and Information Processing | 93

QUIZ YOURSELF

Self and Information Processing

1. The finding that we recall information better when it is relevant to the self is called the _____.
   - (a) distinctiveness effect
   - (b) hindsight bias
   - (c) self-importance bias
   - (d) self-reference effect

2. When she visited San Francisco, Letitia bought several handcrafted necklaces for $10 each. When she got home, her sister offered to buy one for $10, but Letitia refused. She wanted $15 for it instead. This example illustrates the _____ effect.
   - (a) distinctiveness
   - (b) endowment
   - (c) intrinsic
   - (d) overjustification

3. During the Korean War, the Chinese found it easier to brainwash American prisoners when _____.
   - (a) the prisoners were kept together
   - (b) the prisoners were kept separate
   - (c) they used one long brainwashing session
   - (d) they used several short brainwashing sessions

4. When a bad event happens to a person, if it is extremely unpleasant, people remember it as being _____, and if it was mildly unpleasant, people remember it as being _____.
   - (a) better than it was; better than it was
   - (b) better than it was; worse than it was
   - (c) worse than it was; better than it was
   - (d) worse than it was; worse than it was

answers: see pg 113

Self-Esteem, Self-Deception, and Positive Illusions

Self-Esteem

Self-esteem refers to how favorably someone evaluates himself or herself. People with high self-esteem hold very favorable views, which usually means they consider themselves to be competent, likable, attractive, and morally good people. In principle, low self-esteem would be the opposite; that is, you might think that people with low self-esteem would regard themselves as incompetent, ugly, unlikable, and morally wicked. In practice, however, few people regard themselves in such strongly negative terms. A more common form of low self-esteem is simply the absence of strong positive views about the self. Thus, the person with high self-esteem says, "I am good," but the person with low self-esteem says, "I am so-so" rather than "I am terrible."

People with high self-esteem are not hard to understand. They think they have good traits, and they want others to share that view; they are willing to take chances and try new things because they think they will succeed. People with low self-esteem are the greater puzzle. What do they want, and what is it like to be one of them? There have been many different theories and assumptions about low self-esteem, but research is converging to show which of them are correct. Here are some of the main conclusions about people with low self-esteem:

- They do not want to fail. (This is contrary to some early theories, including those based on consistency, which assumed that people with low self-esteem would seek to confirm their bad impressions of themselves.) Indeed, people with low self-esteem have the same goals and strivings that people with high self-esteem have, such as to be successful and to get others to like them. The difference is mainly that people with low self-esteem are less confident that they can achieve these positive goals.[123]

- Their ideas about themselves are conflicted and uncertain, a pattern called "self-concept confusion." When asked questions about themselves, people with low self-esteem are more likely than other people to say they do not know or are not sure;

self-esteem how favorably someone evaluates himself or herself

94 | CHAPTER 3 The Self

more likely to give contradictory answers, such as being both "calm" and "nervous"; and more likely to describe themselves differently on different days.[124]

- They focus on self-protection instead of self-enhancement. (**Self-protection** means trying to avoid loss of esteem.) People with low self-esteem go through life looking to avoid failure, embarrassment, rejection, and other misfortunes, even if this means not taking chances or pursuing opportunities.[125]
- They are more prone to emotional highs and lows. Events affect them more strongly than other people, and so they are more vulnerable to mood swings and other emotional overreactions.[126]

In recent decades, many psychologists have turned their attention to self-esteem, both as a research area and as a practical enterprise. The practitioners' focus is on how to increase self-esteem. They believe that low self-esteem lies at the root of many social and psychological problems and that American society as a whole can benefit from widespread efforts to boost nearly everyone's self-esteem.[127]

College students today greatly value self-esteem and love to receive self-esteem boosts such as compliments. Research suggests that college students would rather receive a boost to their self-esteem than eat their favorite food, drink their favorite alcoholic beverage, see their best friend, get their paycheck, or engage in their favorite sexual activity.[128] In addition, college students value self-esteem boosts more than older American adults do.[129]

Is the United States really suffering from an epidemic of low self-esteem? Evidence since the 1970s suggests otherwise; in fact, average self-esteem scores have been rising.[130,131] If anything, self-esteem in the United States is unrealistically high.

One of the first illustrations came in a simple little survey that asked people to rate their driving ability as above average, average, or below average. Almost all (90%) of the people said they were above average.[132] Statistically, one would expect only about half the people to be above average (and about half below it, of course). This finding of 90% above average was at first regarded as a strange and isolated curiosity, but soon similar results began to accumulate from other studies. In a large survey of a million high school students, only 2% said they were below average in leadership ability (70% said they were above average). Even more strikingly, not one student in a million claimed to be below average in the ability to get along with others, whereas 25% claimed to be in the top 1%![133,134]

What about particular groups, such as women and African Americans, who are sometimes thought to suffer from low self-esteem? In fact, their self-esteem is often pretty healthy too, despite various alarmist claims that it is low. Women's self-esteem is only slightly below that of men's.[135] The difference is largest during adolescence, and it seems to be large not because the self-esteem of adolescent girls is especially low but because many teenage boys are very egotistical. Women and girls tend to be critical of their bodies, whereas boys and men think their bodies are just fine, and this discrepancy probably accounts for most if not all of the gender difference in self-esteem. (There is no sign that women regard themselves as less intelligent than men, for example, or less able to get along with others.) Meanwhile, African Americans actually have somewhat higher self-esteem than other Americans, though again the difference is not very large.[136,137,138] Their high self-esteem makes African Americans somewhat unusual because other minority groups average lower than European Americans in self-esteem.[139] Still, no group really scores very low in self-esteem; the differences are just a matter of whether the group regards itself as significantly above average, or closer to average.

Perhaps the most remarkable evidence of such bias was produced in an international study of prison inmates. People who have been convicted of a crime and sent to jail should know they are below average, at least in terms of being morally good people, right? But even these inmates rated themselves above average on a host of moral and prosocial traits.[140] They considered themselves as relatively high on kindness, honesty, trustworthiness, compassion, and self-control—both relative to other prisoners and even relative to other members of the community. The inmates rated themselves as more law-abiding than other prisoners—and although they stopped short of claiming to be more

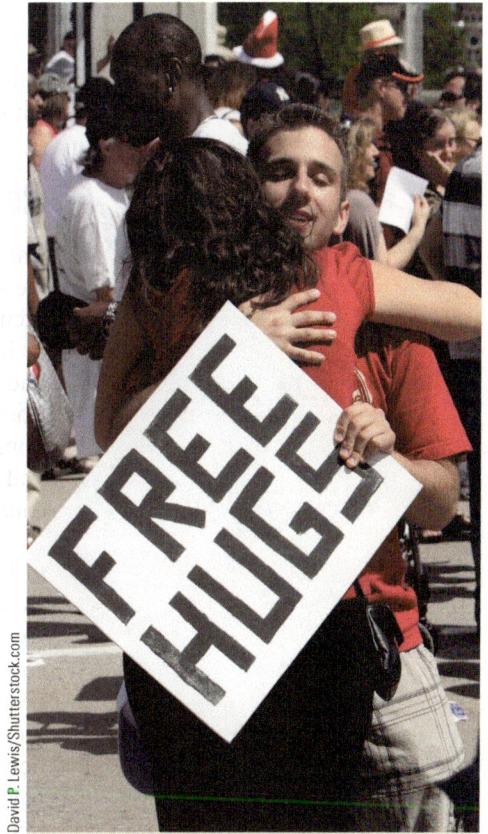

Compliments don't cost any money but are highly valued because they boost one's self-esteem. Recent research shows that college students would rather receive a boost to their self-esteem than eat their favorite food, drink their favorite alcoholic beverage, see their best friend, get their paycheck, or engage in their favorite sexual activity. In addition, college students value self-esteem boosts more than do older American adults.

self-protection trying to avoid loss of esteem

Self-Esteem, Self-Deception, and Positive Illusions | **95** law-abiding than the average person in the community outside the prison, they rated themselves as being about the same. The researchers thought that might be the most remarkable finding: Prisoners consider themselves to be just as law-abiding as people who aren't in prison!

Reality and Illusion

The preceding section focused on self-esteem, which entails how well a person thinks or feels about self. Whether those feelings are accurate is another matter. Are self-concepts accurate, or filled with illusion?

In the 1960s, clinical psychologists noticed that depression is linked to low self-esteem and began to theorize that depressed people have a distorted perception of the world. They began studying the cognitive strategies of depressed people to see how those distortions arose.[141,142,143,144,145,146] For example, do depressed people ignore their own successes and good traits, while exaggerating their faults and failures? Some researchers began to conduct careful studies on how depressed people perceived and interpreted events.

These studies eventually produced a very surprising result. Depressed people don't seem to distort things very much; rather, normal (nondepressed) people are the ones who distort.[147] Depressed people seem to be pretty equal in taking the blame for failure and the credit for success, whereas normal people reject blame for failure while claiming plenty of credit for success. Depressed people are pretty accurate about estimating how much control they have over events, whereas normal people overestimate control.[148] Depressed people are pretty accurate at guessing who likes them and who doesn't, whereas normal people overestimate how much other people like them.[149] Instead of trying to understand how depressed people have learned to distort their thinking in a bad way, it seemed imperative to learn how normal people distort their thinking in a positive way. Somehow depressed people—unlike happy, healthy people—simply fail to put a positive spin on the events in their lives.

In 1988, social psychologists Shelley Taylor and Jonathon Brown provided an influential summary of the ways in which well-adjusted, mentally healthy people distort their perception of events. They listed three "positive illusions" that characterize the thought processes of these normal people.[150]

- People overestimate their good qualities (and underestimate their faults). Normal people think they are smarter, more attractive, more likable, more virtuous, easier to get along with, and in other ways better than they actually are. This explains the "above average effect" already noted, by which most people claim to be better than the average person.

- People overestimate their perceived control over events. Normal people tend to think they are largely in control of events in their lives and that what happens to them is generally the result of their own actions. They believe they have the power to make their lives better and to prevent many misfortunes and problems from occurring.

- People are unrealistically optimistic. They think their own personal chances of getting a good job, having a gifted child, acquiring a great deal of money, and experiencing other positive events are better than the chances of the average person like themselves. Conversely, they think their chances of being unemployed, getting a divorce, having a child with a disability, losing a lot of money, being severely injured in an accident, and experiencing other misfortunes are lower than the average person's chances. Each person tends to see his or her own future as somewhat brighter than other people's.

Don't people get into trouble because of these illusions? You might think that these illusions would create a broad overconfidence that could cause people to make poor decisions, such as overcommitting themselves, taking foolish chances, or investing money unwisely. They may sometimes have that effect, but apparently people have a remarkable capacity to set their illusions aside and be realistic when they have to make a decision. People have a special mind-set that goes with making choices.[151,152] Once the decision is made, people then go right back to their optimistic and confident outlook.

Positive illusions flourish partly because of wishful thinking, also called self-deception. The next section will consider some ways people manage this.

How People Fool Themselves

How do people sustain these positive illusions? Don't everyday experiences burst their bubble and force them to face reality? Someone who believes falsely that they are a genius at math might sign up for an advanced math class, for example, and getting a D would seemingly dispel any such illusions of mathematical brilliance. The fact that people seem able to keep these positive illusions intact for long periods of time has prompted social psychologists to examine **self-deception strategies**—the mental tricks people use to help them believe things that are false. Normally, of course, these are false beliefs that the person wants to be true.

If nobody else can do this, I must be pretty special.

If people's self-concepts were more affected by their failures than by their successes, then most people would probably consider themselves below average! But we have seen that the opposite is true. Self-deception is a pattern of cognitive tricks and strategies that people use to dismiss or diminish the impact of failures and other kinds of bad feedback. The power of bad feedback can be offset by these mental tricks as long as people use them in a biased fashion, so that successes and good feedback are accepted while failures and criticism are questioned, discredited, and forgotten.

One self-deception strategy is called the **self-serving bias**.[153,154,155] This is a common method of interpreting events (and hence an important part of attribution theory—a broad attempt to explain how people interpret all sorts of social events and outcomes—to be discussed in Chapter 5). Essentially, the person claims credit for success but denies blame for failure. Getting a good grade on a test, for example, is taken as a sign that "I'm really smart and good at this." Getting a bad grade is more likely to be chalked up to external factors, such as not having enough sleep, not having studied the right things, a difficult exam, or bad luck. (Also recall the *Tradeoffs* section on self-handicapping, which is a strategy to ensure that the self gets credit for success but no blame for failure.)

A related strategy is to be more skeptical and critical of bad feedback than good feedback. In several studies, researchers had students take a test and then told them at random that they had done either very well or very poorly on the test. Even though they had taken exactly the same test, the people who were told they had done well rated the test as fair and effective, but the people who were told they had done badly thought the test was unfair and poorly designed.[156,157,158] Such tactics enable people to avoid having to revise their self-concepts in light of failure, enabling them to keep their positive illusions intact.

The basic mental processes of attention and memory can also help by being selective. Many people end up remembering good things better than bad things, partly because they spend more time thinking about them and mentally replaying them.[159,160,161,162] Although occasionally failures or criticism stick in one's mind, people usually try not to dwell on them, whereas they enjoy reliving their triumphs and great moments. Selectively focusing on good things can help counteract the power of bad things.

Another strategy makes use of the fact that good and bad are usually relative, as our earlier discussion of social comparison showed. Being able to run a mile (1.6 km) in 7 minutes, for example, is neither good nor bad in itself; the evaluation depends on whom you are comparing yourself against. Compared to the speed of expert runners, a 7-minute mile is pathetically slow, but compared to flatfooted couch-potatoes it is probably terrific. People can turn this to their advantage by choosing their comparison group carefully. People give the most attention to those who are just slightly worse than themselves, because those comparisons make them feel good.[163,164,165] The Japanese have an expression: "Others' misfortunes taste like honey."

In a similar vein, people skew their impressions of other people so as to convince themselves that their good traits are unusual whereas their faults are commonly found

self-deception strategies mental tricks people use to help them believe things that are false

self-serving bias a pattern in which people claim credit for success but deny blame for failure in many other people.[166,167,168] For example, if you are musically talented but have trouble meeting deadlines, you may find yourself thinking that musical talent is rare but procrastination (putting things off, being late, missing deadlines) is common. That makes your fault seem minimal, whereas your good quality makes you special. People are especially inclined to engage in such distortions regarding traits that are central to their self-concepts, and people with high self-esteem are more prone to these distortions than people with low self-esteem. (Probably their high self-esteem is partly sustained by these tricks.)

Yet another strategy relies on the fact that many definitions of good traits are slippery, so people can choose a definition that makes them look good.[169,170,171,172] Most people want to be a good romantic partner, for example, but what exactly defines a good romantic partner? One person can think she is a good romantic partner because they are thoughtful, another can think the same because they are a good listener, and others might think they qualify because they are funny, or easy to get along with, or good in bed, or trustworthy, or able to control their temper. Such shifting criteria may help explain how everyone can regard themselves as above average.

Benefits of Self-Esteem

In recent decades, American society has devoted plenty of effort to boosting self-esteem, especially among schoolchildren and other groups considered to need a boost. This was based on the hope that many benefits would flow from high self-esteem. Would high self-esteem cause people to do better in school? Do you have to love yourself before you can love someone else? Will high self-esteem prevent prejudice, violence, drug addiction, and other ills?

Many results have been disappointing. People with high self-esteem do report that they are smarter, are more successful, have more friends, enjoy better relationships, and are better-looking than other people, but objective measures say they aren't. Often high self-esteem amounts to nothing more than a false belief that one is a terrific, superior person. For example, several studies have shown that people with high self-esteem claim to be especially intelligent, but on an actual IQ test they are no smarter than people with low self-esteem.[173] Likewise, they say they are better-looking than other people, but when researchers get people to judge how good-looking people are from photos, the people with high self-esteem get no higher ratings than anyone else.[174,175,176,177] They think they are better-looking, but no one else can tell the difference.

Students with high self-esteem do have slightly higher grades than people with low self-esteem, but high self-esteem does not lead to good grades.[178,179,180,181,182,183,184,185,186,187] If anything, it is the other way around: Getting good grades and doing well in school lead to high self-esteem. As we saw in Chapter 1, the fact that there is a correlation makes it hard to tell what causes what. Self-esteem and good grades are correlated (though weakly), but studies that track people across time have indicated that self-esteem is the result rather than the cause of the good grades. Also, other factors, such as coming from a good family, contribute to both the high self-esteem and the good grades.

In terms of getting along with others, people with high self-esteem believe that they make a great impression on others and are well liked, but in fact there is no difference in how other people evaluate them.[188,189,190,191,192,193,194,195,196] If anything, sometimes people with high self-esteem are obnoxious and turn people off by thinking they are superior.[197,198]

Sexual activity is another important interpersonal process. To learn how it is related to self-esteem, read *The Social Side of Sex*.

High self-esteem has two main benefits.[199] The first is initiative. High self-esteem fosters confidence that you can do the right thing and should act on your best judgment. People with high self-esteem are more willing than other people to speak up in groups or committees. They are more willing to approach people and strike up new friendships. They are more willing to go against other people's advice and do what they think is best. They resist influence better. They are also more adventurous when it comes to experimenting with sex, drugs, and other activities. This is sadly contrary to the goals of researchers and therapists who hoped that high self-esteem would enable young persons to resist such temptations.

The Social Side of Sex

Self-Esteem and Saying No to Sex

Is there a link between self-esteem and sexual activity? Researchers have multiple reasons for suggesting that there might be. For one thing, people with low self-esteem have been found to be more vulnerable to social influence than people with high self-esteem, a pattern that social psychologists began to uncover in the 1950s.[200,201,202] This led many experts to hope that increasing self-esteem among young people would enable them to resist peer pressures to participate in sex at a young age. In particular, they thought that girls with low self-esteem might be talked into sex before they were ready.

However, the evidence does not show that high self-esteem helps youngsters resist having sex. In one large and well-designed study, self-esteem was measured among more than 1,000 children at age 11; 10 years later, they were asked whether they had engaged in sexual intercourse by the age of 15. Among the boys, there was no relationship between self-esteem and early sex. Among the girls, there was a relationship—but in the opposite direction from what had been predicted. Girls with higher self-esteem at age 11 were more likely (rather than less likely) than others to have had sex by the age of 15.[203] Other studies have failed to find any relationship at all, however.[204,205]

Most people in our society consider children age 15 or younger to be too young to be having sex, and research suggests that most people begin having sex in their late teen years. People who remain virgins until around the age of 20 are therefore of interest. Is there any link between self-esteem and virginity? The answer is yes, but the link differs by gender.

For many women, apparently, virginity is a positive status, and they may take pride in it. Among men, however, virginity has less of a positive aspect, and many male virgins feel ashamed of their virginity. They may feel that they have failed to appeal to women. This is especially true if the men reach an age where they believe most of their peers are having sex and have regular girlfriends. Hence, there is some link between virginity and low self-esteem in men but not in women.[206,207]

For both genders, but especially for women, decisions about whether to have sex are complicated by the potential for pregnancy. Fear of getting pregnant has historically been an important factor holding women back from sexual activity. In this regard, however, high self-esteem seems to be a risk factor because women with high self-esteem tend to downplay or ignore risks. High self-esteem is often marked by a sense of being special or better than others, and it contributes to a feeling that "bad things will not happen to me." In one study, women wrote down a list of their sexual activities, including whether they took precautions against pregnancy. Then they rated their chances of having an unwanted pregnancy. Women with high self-esteem had essentially the same sex lives and took the same chances as women with low self-esteem, but those with high self-esteem regarded themselves as safer.[208] The researchers concluded that high self-esteem causes women to underestimate the dangers of sex.

High self-esteem is thought to solve many social ills, but it frequently does not. For example, boosting self-esteem does not prevent unplanned pregnancy.

The second advantage of high self-esteem is that it feels good. High self-esteem operates like a stock of good feelings that the person can draw on. When life dumps misfortune on your head, such as when you experience failure or trauma, you can bounce back better if you have high self-esteem, because this is a resource that helps you overcome the bad feelings. People with low self-esteem lack this resource, and therefore misfortune hits them harder. If they don't succeed on the first attempt, people with high self-esteem are willing to try again harder, whereas people with low self-esteem are more likely to give up. Most broadly, people with high self-esteem are happier than people with low self-esteem.[209]

FIGURE 3.7

A gas gauge doesn't make the car go, but it tells you how much fuel you have. When gas gauges indicate that fuel is low, people fill up their gas tanks. According to sociometer theory, self-esteem is like a gauge that tells you how much social approval you have. When self-esteem is low, people try to "fill up" using self-esteem boosts.

One study that tracked nearly 2,000 people over a decade confirmed this view of the limited advantages of high self-esteem.[210] Self-esteem produced emotional benefits: People with higher self-esteem at the start of the study later had more positive emotions, were less likely to become depressed, and were more satisfied with their jobs and relationships than other people. But it had no effect at all on objective outcomes, especially career success.

Initiative and good feelings are certainly positive benefits, though they are far less than many self-esteem researchers had hoped. Self-esteem is not the solution to a broad range of psychological and social problems, but it does at least help in those regards.

Why Do We Care?

People are often quite motivated to protect and increase their self-esteem. Indeed, we shall see that many patterns of thinking and acting that social psychologists have demonstrated are based on the desire to maintain one's self-esteem. But why? The preceding section indicated that high self-esteem does not really confer a great many advantages in an objective sense. Why do people care so much about self-esteem if all it does is boost initiative and feel good?

One influential answer is relevant to this book's theme that inner processes serve interpersonal relations. Maybe thinking well of yourself doesn't really matter very much (especially by the basic biological outcome criteria of improving survival or reproduction), but gaining social acceptance does. In this view, self-esteem is essentially a measure of how much you appeal to others. It is noteworthy that self-esteem is mainly based on the reasons that groups use to accept or reject possible members: attractiveness, competence, likability, and morality. Many groups and people avoid and reject people who are unattractive, incompetent, disliked, dishonest, or otherwise immoral. Research has shown social acceptance can raise your self-esteem, whereas rejection can threaten or lower your self-esteem.[211,212]

This view of self-esteem as linked to social acceptance has been called sociometer theory. A **sociometer** (made from the words *social* and *meter*) is a measure of how desirable one would be to other people as a relationship partner, team member, employee, colleague, or in some other way. In this sense, self-esteem is a sociometer because it measures the traits you have according to how much they qualify you for social acceptance. Sociometer theory can explain why people are so concerned with self-esteem: It helps people navigate the long road to social acceptance. Mark Leary, the author of sociometer theory, compares self-esteem to the gas gauge on a car. A gas gauge may seem trivial because it doesn't make the car go forward. But the gas gauge tells you about something that is important—namely, whether there is enough fuel in the car. Just as drivers act out of concern to keep their gas gauge above zero (see **FIGURE 3.7**), so people seem constantly to act so as to preserve their self-esteem.

Sociometer theory is not the only possible explanation for why people might care about self-esteem. Another, simpler theory is that self-esteem feels good (as noted in the previous section), and because people want to feel good, they want to maintain their self-esteem. A more complex variation on that theory invokes the theory of terror management, which holds that fear of death is at the root of all human striving. Terror management theorists assert that having high self-esteem helps shield people from fear of death, so people seek out self-esteem as a way of avoiding a recognition that they are going to die.[213] Another common view is that self-esteem is based mainly on feeling competent rather than on social acceptance. However, evidence suggests that feeling accepted has a bigger impact on self-esteem than does feeling competent (though both matter).[214]

sociometer a measure of how desirable one would be to other people

Is High Self-Esteem Always Good?

Focusing mainly on the benefits of high self-esteem might create the impression that high self-esteem is always a good thing. Alas, the benefits of high self-esteem may be balanced by drawbacks, as is the case with many tradeoffs.

The negative aspects of high self-esteem may be especially apparent in the form of narcissism, a trait that is linked to high self-esteem but that captures its worst aspects. The trait of narcissism is based on the Greek myth of Narcissus, a young man who fell in love with his own reflection in the water and did nothing but stare at it until he died. In psychology, **narcissism** refers to excessive self-love and a selfish orientation. Narcissists think very well of themselves and, as a result, are willing to take advantage of others. Among American college students, levels of narcissism have been increasing over time,[215] though some experts dispute the numbers.[216] This self-centered generation has been dubbed "Generation Me."[217]

A clever test of the idea that self-concepts are changing used lyrics from popular songs. The team of researchers[218] took the most popular American songs from the Billboard Hot 100 year-end list for every year from 1980 to 2007. They ran the lyrics for all these songs (totaling almost 90,000 words!) through a computer program that sorted and counted. As the years went by, the songs contained more and more first-person singular pronouns (e.g., *I, me, my*) and fewer and fewer first-person plural words (*we, our*). Words relating to social interactions (like *talking* and *share*) decreased, as did words expressing positive emotions. In contrast, angry and antisocial words, including swear words, increased over these decades. Altogether, these results suggest that what made songs popular in recent decades has been an increase in focus on the self and on angry, antisocial attitudes, while positive emotion and interpersonal connection have lost their appeal in popular music. These results fit well with the evidence that narcissism has increased.

Narcissism is not the same as high self-esteem, but the two are related. Probably the simplest way to understand the link is to think of narcissism as a subset of high self-esteem. That is, nearly all narcissists have high self-esteem, but many people have high self-esteem without being narcissists. To be sure, there has been some controversy about the self-esteem of narcissists. They often act superior to other people and seem to think they deserve to be treated better than others, but clinical psychologists used to think (and some still think) that this egotistical behavior is a disguise that conceals secret feelings of insecurity and low self-esteem. However, research has not been very successful at finding that narcissists really have low self-esteem; indeed, narcissists seem to be confident if not downright conceited through and through. The only area in which they do not seem to rate themselves especially high concerns getting other people to like them, which narcissists are relatively indifferent about. Admiration is more important to them than liking, and they want and expect others to admire them.[219]

The trait of narcissism is based on the Greek myth of Narcissus, a young man who fell in love with his own reflection in the water. As illustrated in the painting, narcissists are in love with themselves.

narcissism excessive self-love and a selfish orientation

Self-Esteem, Self-Deception, and Positive Illusions

Recent work has begun to highlight more differences between narcissism and self-esteem,[220] though they certainly overlap. High self-esteem often consists of thinking one is as good as other people, and it comes from being brought up by parents who were warm and affectionate. Narcissism, in contrast, consists in thinking oneself superior to other people (and in wanting others to agree), and it comes from being brought up by parents who treated the child as special, superior, and deserving of privileges. Praising your children for everything they do and making a frequent fuss over how wonderful they are leads to narcissism.

Narcissists tend to be more aggressive and violent than other people, especially when they suffer a blow to their egos.[221,222,223] The self-esteem movement had hoped that raising self-esteem would reduce aggression, but there is no sign that that works.

High self-esteem (and not just narcissism) is also associated with higher prejudice.[224,225] People who think well of themselves also tend to think their group is better than other groups, and they discriminate more heavily than other people in favor of their own group.

Narcissists make poor relationship partners in many respects.[226,227,228,229,230] Narcissists typically approach relationships with the attitude "What's in it for me?" and hence do not really try to build a lasting intimacy with another person. They try to associate with glamorous people because they think these others will make them seem glamorous too. They adopt a "game-playing" approach to relationships that helps them maintain power and autonomy without giving much of themselves to the other person. They are also prone to changing relationship partners. If a seemingly more desirable partner comes along, the narcissist will not have many qualms about dumping their current partner and hooking up with the new one. More broadly, narcissists are not as loyal to their partners as other people. They are prone to take advantage of their partners when they get the chance. Narcissists often think they deserve someone better, so even if they have a good relationship, they may still keep an eye out in case a more attractive or desirable partner comes along. Loving someone who loves themselves is no picnic because they will readily dump you in favor of someone else.[231]

As we can see, most of the drawbacks of high self-esteem pertain to the person's relations with others. In tradeoff terms, high self-esteem has both costs and benefits, but they are not distributed fairly. The benefits of someone's high self-esteem mostly go to the person themself, whereas the costs of someone's high self-esteem mostly fall on other people.

The previous section noted that people with high self-esteem have more initiative than those with low self-esteem. In general, initiative may be a good thing, but it certainly can contribute to antisocial actions as well. Research on bullies, for example, began with the old idea that bullies secretly suffer from low self-esteem, but this proved false. The most careful studies have found that bullies have high self-esteem, as do the people who help bullies by joining in to torment their victims. People who stand up to bullies and resist them, including coming to the aid of victims, also have high self-esteem.[232,233] This pattern captures both sides of initiative. People who think well of themselves have more initiative and use it either for bad purposes (bullying others) or for good ones (resisting bullies and protecting victims). Low self-esteem was found mainly among the victims; in fact, the victim role is often a passive one, defined by the absence of initiative.

Persistence in the face of failure also takes initiative (and possibly some resource of good feelings to help overcome discouragement—remember that good feelings were the other benefit of high self-esteem). Many studies have found that people with high self- esteem are more likely than those with low self-esteem to keep trying despite an initial failure.[234,235] In general, we assume that this is a good thing because the chances of eventual success are greater if you keep trying than if you give up. Then again, some endeavors are truly hopeless, lost causes, and continuing to try simply means greater failure. Think of a football coach who keeps calling for a play that never works because the other team knows how to defend against it, or an investor who keeps putting money into a stock that keeps losing, or a scientist who keeps trying to prove a theory that is truly wrong. People with high self-esteem are prone to make that kind of error too. Their persistence in the face of failure can be either a good or a bad thing.[236,237,238,239] In general, though, people with high self-esteem do seem to manage these situations better and make better use of information about when to persist as opposed to when to move on and try something else.[240,241]

Pursuing Self-Esteem

Many people actively pursue self-esteem. Typically they choose some sphere or dimension (such as schoolwork, popularity, or sports) as important to them, invest themselves in it, and try to succeed at it.

Although most people in our culture pursue self-esteem, they go about it in different ways. People who already have high self-esteem pursue it by seeking to dominate others and to increase their competence at valued abilities. People with low self-esteem pursue it by seeking acceptance and validation from others, and especially by trying to avoid failures.[242]

There is increasing evidence that pursuing self-esteem as an end in itself can have harmful consequences.[243] Pursuing self-esteem can compromise the pursuit of competence, as when people choose easy tasks so they can be sure of succeeding. It impairs autonomy because seekers of self-esteem often do whatever others will approve rather than what they themselves might want to do. The pursuit of self-esteem creates feelings of pressure to live up to others' expectations, and therefore it weakens people's intrinsic motivation (their interest in doing something for its own sake). It impairs learning because when self-esteem is on the line people react to setbacks or criticism as threatening events rather than as helpful feedback. It can damage relationships because self-esteem seekers compete against their relationship partners and thereby sometimes undermine intimacy and mutuality. They may also withdraw from partners who are too successful because they feel that they are losing in comparison.[244] Last, the pursuit of self-esteem can be harmful to health, both because it increases stress and because it can lead to unhealthy coping behaviors, such as drinking and smoking, to deal with bad feelings associated with having one's self-esteem on the line.

When people stake their self-esteem on succeeding in some domain, then failure in that domain produces strong negative reactions, including increased anxiety and other negative emotions, as well as drops in self-esteem. If anything, the drops that go with such failures are bigger than the increases that come from success.[245]

QUIZ YOURSELF

Self-Esteem, Self-Deception, and Positive Illusions

1. **A person's overall self-evaluation or sense of self-worth constitutes his or her _____.**
   - (a) possible self
   - (b) self-awareness
   - (c) self-efficacy
   - (d) self-esteem

2. **Depressed people _____ how favorably other people regard them, whereas normal people _____ how favorably other people regard them.**
   - (a) estimate accurately; overestimate
   - (b) estimate accurately; underestimate
   - (c) underestimate; estimate accurately
   - (d) underestimate; overestimate

3. **Which of the following is a positive illusion that people hold?**
   - (a) People overestimate their strengths and underestimate their faults.
   - (b) People overestimate their perceived control over events.
   - (c) People are unrealistically optimistic.
   - (d) All of the above.

4. **When Frank does well on a test, he claims responsibility for the success, but when he does poorly on a test, he denies responsibility and blames his professor for writing a difficult test with ambiguous items. This is an example of _____.**
   - (a) a positive illusion
   - (b) the overjustification effect
   - (c) the self-reference effect
   - (d) the self-serving bias

answers: see pg 113

Self-Presentation

Self-esteem, or egotism, is a common explanation for behavior. Supposedly people do many things—work hard, get in a fight, compete, show off, enjoy compliments, and more—to bolster or protect their self-esteem. Yet why would people care so much about self-esteem? Why would the human psyche be designed to try to prove itself better than other people? Cultural animals do need to care, and care very much, about what *other* people think of them. Could it be that much of what is commonly regarded as egotism, as trying to think well of oneself, is at heart a concern with how others think of you?

Undeniably, people do want to think well of themselves. The self-deception strategies we listed earlier generally work so as to enable people to hold favorable views of themselves. (Actually, though, the line between fooling others and fooling yourself turns out to be much fuzzier than one might think. One theory proposed that self-deception mainly evolved to enable people to deceive others—because you can be more convincing in arguing your case if you believe it than if you do not.)[246] Although people do want to preserve their self-esteem, on closer inspection it often turns out that they are most concerned with having *other people* view them favorably.[247,248,249] It's fine to like yourself, but what matters more is whether other people like you. In fact, if nobody else likes you, it is difficult to like yourself!

Many research studies do not make much of a distinction between private self-esteem and public esteem, but those who do distinguish them often find that the concern with public esteem is greater. As the comedian Billy Crystal used to say, "It is more important to look good than to feel good!"

This chapter opened with the story of Count Zrínyi, who wanted very much to make a good impression on whoever was going to kill him. Clearly feeling good wasn't his goal because he would be dead. Looking good still mattered. Nor is he alone. Studies with American adults and college students found that many of them were quite concerned with their reputations, including how they would be remembered after their death.[250] They were asked questions such as, *Would you rather spend a year in prison now but then be remembered favorably—or escape prison but be remembered after your death as having been a racist or child molester?* Many people chose prison, having their good hand cut off, or even death instead of reputation damage. Of course, these were merely hypothetical questions: the researchers did not cut off any hands or kill anyone. But in lab studies, many people endured putting their hand into a can filled with disgusting giant worms, or putting their hand into painfully cold water, rather than being publicly depicted as a racist.

Probably the concern with looking good to others arises from the basic facts of human nature. Human beings achieve their biological goals of survival and reproduction by means of belonging to social and cultural groups. Getting other people to like you or respect you is very helpful for getting into these groups and staying there. We have said that one theme of human life is the long road to social acceptance. A big part of this road is making good impressions on other people and keeping a good reputation. That is what self-presentation is all about.

Self-presentation is defined as any behavior that seeks to convey some image of self or some information about the self to other people. Any behavior that is intended (even unconsciously) to make an impression on others is included. Self-presentation thus encompasses a wide range of actions, from explicit statements about the self (e.g., "I forgive but I don't forget"), to how you dress or what car you drive, to making excuses or threats, to trying to hide your fear or anger so that other people will think you are cool.

Social networking sites are one medium for self-presentation. People create a site for themselves that presents them as they wish to be seen. One networking site found that most college students participate, but some do not. The nonusers are often disdainful of the time and energy that others invest, and some objected to what they considered phony self-presentations. One woman scornfully told the researchers that someone she knew had listed favorite bands and movies that were chosen simply to make him look cool, as opposed to genuine liking. (She said she had known him for 10 years and he had

The comedian Billy Crystal said, "It is more important to look good than to feel good!" This statement captures the essence of self-presentation.

self-presentation any behavior that seeks to convey some image of self or some information about the self to other people never mentioned these ostensible favorites!) Users and nonusers were similar in many respects, including how much they used the internet for practical purposes (e.g., buying things, getting information) but differed in how much they used it for expressing themselves (e.g., blogging, creating web pages). The urge to express oneself is thus one reason people use social networking sites.[251]

The urge to express oneself is genuine. For example, advice to people on how to act on romantic dates often emphasizes getting the other person to talk about themself. Studies have confirmed this wisdom: People like to talk about themselves and feel good when they do.[252] Brain regions associated with pleasure and reward become more active when someone talks about themself, as opposed to talking about other people. Indeed, participants chose to answer questions about themselves even when they could have earned slightly higher amounts of money answering different (i.e., non-self) questions.

Who's Looking?

A great many behavior patterns studied by social psychologists turn out to depend on self-presentation. Researchers have demonstrated this by comparing how people behave in public conditions, when others are present and one's behavior is identified, with private behavior, when one's actions will remain secret and confidential. If you mainly care about self-esteem, your behavior will be the same regardless of whether someone else is watching. But if you are concerned about what others think (i.e., you are concerned with or motivated by self-presentation), then you will act differently when you are alone than when others are there.

For example, in Chapter 7 you will see that people often change their attitudes to be consistent with their behavior, especially if they have done something out of the ordinary or contrary to their usual beliefs. This pattern occurs mainly when other people are watching; it is much weaker if the behavior is done privately.[253,254] Likewise, when people receive evaluations of their personality or their work, these evaluations have much more impact if they are public (i.e., if other people know about them) than if they are private. Criticism received privately can easily be ignored or forgotten, whereas criticism that is heard by multiple other people must be dealt with. Even if you think the criticism is completely wrong, you cannot just dismiss it or ignore it if other people know about it. That criticism might cause other people to change their impression of you or treat you differently.[255,256,257]

Self-presentation creeps into many behaviors that might not at first seem to have an interpersonal aspect. For example, washing one's hands after using the restroom may seem like a simple matter of personal hygiene. But researchers who have secretly observed how people behave in public restrooms found that washing one's hands is affected by whether other people are watching. Women who used the toilet would usually wash their hands afterward if someone else was in the restroom, but if they believed themselves to be alone, they were more likely to skip washing.[258]

Dieting is also guided by self-presentation. Despite all the talk of how healthy it is to be slim and fit, the strongest motive to lose weight is to make oneself attractive to others. As one expert researcher commented, "No one would diet on a deserted island!"[259]

Even people with severe mental illnesses such as schizophrenia are well attuned to the importance of self-presentation. In a famous study,[260] inmates at a mental hospital were told to report to the head psychiatrist for an interview. On the way, by random assignment, they were told one of two purposes for the interview. Some were told that the purpose of the interview was to evaluate them for possible release from the hospital. You might think that mental patients would be anxious to be released into the outside world, but in fact many have anxieties and fears about that and prefer their safe, structured life in the mental hospital. When the

In his song "Online," Brad Paisley sings about how much cooler he is online. For example, in the real world he works at a pizza joint, drives an old Hyundai, lives with his parents, and is short. Online, however, he is rich, drives a new Maserati, has a black belt in karate, and is tall, thin, and good-looking.

interview began, these patients presented themselves as having serious problems and difficulties, presumably so that the psychiatrist would abandon any plan to release them into the world.

Other patients were told that the purpose of the interview was to decide whether to move them to a locked ward, where more dangerous patients were kept, and where consequently there were fewer comforts and freedoms. These patients presented themselves in the interview as being relatively sane and normal, so as to discourage any thoughts of moving them to the locked ward. Thus, the level of psychopathology (craziness, to put it crudely) displayed by mental patients is at least partly self-presentation. It goes up and down in order to make the desired impression.

When social psychologists first began to recognize the importance of self-presentation, they regarded it as a form of hypocrisy—acting or pretending to be something other than what one is, possibly for bad reasons such as to manipulate others or to feed one's egotism. However, the field gradually recognized that making a good impression and keeping a good reputation constitute a basic and important aspect of human social life. It is not limited to a few phony or hypocritical individuals who seek to convey false impressions. Rather, nearly everyone strives for a good self-presentation as a way of obtaining social acceptance.[261,262] Through self-presentation, people can increase their chances of being accepted by others and can claim a valued identity within the social system, thereby enabling them to maintain their place in the group.

Making an Impression

What makes for a good self-presentation? In many ways, the answers are obvious: One has to show oneself to have good traits and not bad ones. Presenting oneself as competent, friendly, honest, kind, loyal, strong, warm, helpful, and so on, makes for a good self-presentation.[263] The main problem with defining what makes a good self-presentation arises when the values of the self-presenter and the audience diverge. Then the self-presenter faces a tradeoff between being true to their own values and making a good impression on the interaction partner (also called the audience). What the person does depends on a variety of factors, including the importance of one's relationship to the audience and the importance of the issue to the self.

It is perhaps not surprising that people often present themselves along the lines favored by their audience. After all, people want to be liked, and conforming to others' values and expectations is a common strategy for achieving that. What is more surprising is that sometimes people deliberately present themselves in ways that they know their audience will not approve. This isn't the same as being more concerned with private reality than public appearance. For example, if Jason really didn't care what others thought, he wouldn't bother telling them he disagreed with them. But sometimes people deliberately make others see them in ways that the others don't approve.

During the Columbine High School massacre in Colorado, Cassie Bernall was asked by one of the shooters whether she believed in God. She said "yes," and he shot her. She presented herself in a way that the killers didn't like, and she paid with her life.

What kinds of impression are these people trying to make, using their clothing?

If people are playing to the audience but not giving the audience what it wants, they must have some other motive for how they present themselves. This clues us in to a second important function of self-presentation: claiming identity.

A dramatic single instance of refusing to present oneself in a way the audience would approve occurred in the library at Columbine High School on the terrible day that two students brought guns and began shooting their fellow students. Cassie Bernall was in the library during the shootings, on her knees praying out loud. One of the gunmen asked if anyone there believed in God. Witnesses said that Cassie Bernall told him, "Yes, I believe in God." He shot her to death.[264] Although some details of the story are disputed, it does seem that there was pressure on her to deny her religious faith, which she resisted at the cost of her life. Throughout history, many individuals have been pressured to renounce or reject their faith, and many have died for refusing to give the answers that others wanted to hear. Notice, again, that if she really didn't care about how other people saw her, she could easily have lied and denied her faith. She insisted on making a public statement of what she believed in, and that got her killed.

Claiming Identity

People aspire to many identities. A person may wish to be recognized as an artist, a talented athlete, an honest businessperson, a defender of certain values. In general, it is not enough simply to persuade yourself that you hold such an identity. Rather, the claims require social validation: Other people must come to perceive you as holding that identity. In an important sense, you cannot be a great artist, or a sports star, or a brilliant student if you are the only one who believes that you are. It becomes necessary to persuade others to see you in that light. Obtaining social validation for your identity claims is the grander task of self-presentation.

People do use self-presentation to advance their claims to identity. In some studies, participants were made to feel either secure or insecure about their claims. For example, among participants who aspired to become expert guitarists, some were told that their personality profiles differed markedly from those of expert guitarists, which conveyed the message that the participant was not on their way to becoming one of those experts.[265] Others were told that they fit the profile precisely, which made them feel as if they were doing well on their project of becoming an expert guitarist. They were then asked whether they would like to give guitar lessons to beginners, and if so, how many. The people who had been made to feel insecure about their claims to becoming expert guitarists wanted to teach many more lessons than the people who were told they were already looking like expert guitarists. The insecure ones wanted to bolster their claims to being a guitarist by teaching guitar to others because these others would view them as good guitarists.[266]

People will change their behavior to claim identity. One study surveyed citizens shortly before an election. Some were asked about the importance of voting. Others were asked about the importance of "being a voter." This subtle difference in phrasing produced a big difference. The ones who thought about the idea in identity terms ("being a voter") went on to vote at higher rates than those who just thought about voting.[267]

Sometimes, the goal of claiming an identity can motivate a person to engage in self-presentation in a way the audience will not like. This is why people sometimes end up arguing about politics, rather than simply agreeing with what the other person says. They identify with their own political views strongly enough that they would rather stand up for what they believe in than make a good, congenial impression on someone who holds different values. The story about Cassie Bernall and religious faith is another example of this.

Of course, what counts as a good impression changes with the times. In recent years, being environmentally conscious has come to be valued by many people. Studies show that people favor "green" products, which may be more expensive and lower quality than other goods, when they want to make a good impression.[268] They buy such things when they are thinking about their status in other people's eyes, and especially when they are shopping in public—but not when they are shopping privately (e.g., on the internet).

Tradeoff: Favorability Versus Plausibility

By and large, people seek to make good impressions, and so they present themselves favorably. A favorable or self-enhancing way of describing oneself prevails in most social psychology studies.[269] Naturally, people do not go to extremes of claiming to be superstars or geniuses, but they tend to present themselves in the best possible light, within the range of what is plausible. One authority on self-presentation has described this as a tradeoff between favorability and plausibility. In plain terms, people present themselves as favorably as they think they can get away with! They may claim to be smart and attractive, but if they think other people will find out that their claims are exaggerated, then they tone down those claims.[270,271] This tendency toward favorable self-presentations dovetails well with the "automatic egotism" described earlier in this chapter: People automatically tend to furnish a very positive image of themselves, unless circumstances dictate otherwise.[272]

What About Modesty?

The tendency toward favorable self-presentation seems well designed to help people make a good first impression on other people. Not surprisingly, it is less needed and hence less common within established relationships. When people are among friends, they often stop boasting or presenting themselves in the best possible light. If anything, modesty seems more natural and common among friends, and it may even be the default or automatic response.[273] One reason for this is that your friends are probably familiar with your faults and failures. If you claim to be better than you are, they may be quick to point out that you are twisting the facts.

Possibly a deeper reason for the prevalence of modesty within long-term relationships and friendships is that it helps people get along better. Most religions have embraced humility as a virtue and regarded pride as either a sin or an obstacle to salvation. One purported secular goal of religion is to promote group harmony, and people probably can get along with humble, modest individuals better than they get along with puffed-up, conceited narcissists. Groups often must divide up resources that vary in quality, such as who gets the best piece of meat or who gets the better place to sleep. Humility and modesty make such divisions easier: "No, you choose." People who think highly of themselves are more likely to think that they deserve the best, and if a group has several such people, the argument can turn nasty. Indeed, some studies have found that people dislike those who brag and are prone to attack them aggressively.[274] They think that someone who brags probably looks down on them.

Some researchers have found that self-enhancement is especially strong in individualistic cultures that place a high emphasis on individual achievement and merit. In contrast, collectivistic cultures that emphasize group harmony above individual rights are less oriented toward self-enhancement.[275] One team of experts has argued, for example, that the Japanese do not go around trying to prove their individual superiority over others; rather, they seek to improve themselves so as to become better members of their social group. If self-enhancement is found in such cultures, it often takes the form of trying to present oneself as a worthy member of the group or as belonging to a highly valued group.[276] Thus, though Japanese may not strive to prove themselves superior to other Japanese individually, many of them do believe that Japanese culture and people together are good and in many ways superior to others.

Self-Presentation and Risky Behavior

Self-presentation is so important to people that they will sometimes risk illness, injury, or even death in order to make a good impression.[277] Many people try to get a suntan because they believe it makes them look attractive and sexy, but sunbathing exposes the skin to dangerous radiation that can (and often does) cause skin cancer. Many young people smoke cigarettes in an effort to look cool, adult, and sophisticated in front of others. Likewise, adolescent drinking is often driven by the belief that drinkers are perceived as tougher, more adult-like, and more rebellious than nondrinkers. Some people fear that others will think badly of them if they purchase condoms or if they suggest using condoms, so they engage in unprotected sex, thereby risking sexually transmitted infections (including AIDS and unexpected pregnancy). Some people drive fast or refuse to wear seat belts in order to project an image of bravery. Others resist wearing helmets when riding bicycles or playing sports. One of your authors (Bushman) bought a bicycle in Amsterdam. The first thing the

Looking cool, but at what cost?

bike shop salesperson did was remove the safety reflectors from the spokes of the tires, and then threw them in the trash. When Bushman asked why, the bike salesperson said, "You don't want to be seen with these on your bike. That's not cool." (Bushman secretly retrieved the reflectors from the trash, and then put them back on the bike after he left the store.)

The fact that people will take such risks with their health in order to make a good impression on others indicates that, at some level, gaining social acceptance is felt as an even stronger and more urgent motive than the motivation to stay alive and healthy. Self-presentation can be stronger than self-preservation (as suggested by Billy Crystal's remark, quoted earlier, about looking good versus feeling good!). This is yet another sign that the human psyche is designed to gain and keep a place in a social group.

QUIZ YOURSELF
Self-Presentation

1. The comedian Billy Crystal used to say, "It is more important to look good than to feel good!" This concern with looking good to others is called _____.
   - (a) self-awareness
   - (b) self-concept
   - (c) self-handicapping
   - (d) self-presentation

2. John is a young gang member who wants to look tough to his fellow gang members. This concern about looking tough is called _____.
   - (a) self-awareness
   - (b) self-consciousness
   - (c) self-esteem
   - (d) self-presentation

3. Self-presentation concerns often influence people to engage in _____ actions than they would otherwise engage in.
   - (a) less conservative
   - (b) less risky
   - (c) more conservative
   - (d) riskier

4. People tend to furnish a very positive image of themselves, unless circumstances dictate otherwise. This tendency is called _____.
   - (a) automatic egotism
   - (b) private self-awareness
   - (c) public self-presentation
   - (d) self-handicapping

answers: see pg 113

What Makes Us Human

Putting the Cultural Animal in Perspective

No other animal has a self that can begin to approach the human self in complexity and sophistication. Many of the features that make human beings special can be found in the self.

What is special about the human self begins with self-awareness and self-concept. Self-awareness is quite limited or absent in most other species; indeed, very few animals can even recognize themselves in a mirror. In contrast, people have a remarkable ability to be aware of themselves, to think about themselves, to imagine how others regard them, and to change themselves. Self-awareness has at least two crucial dimensions, public and private, and these are useful for different things. Private self-awareness is useful for evaluating oneself, especially toward goals of self-improvement and self-regulation. Public self-awareness is vital for the task of gaining social acceptance because it enables people to anticipate how others will perceive them.

In humans, self-awareness is more than the name implies (i.e., it is more than just paying attention to self). Self-awareness enables people to compare themselves to standards in a way that other animals cannot. They can evaluate whether they are conforming to cultural standards (such as morals and laws), personal standards (such as goals and ambitions), and many others. This ability makes it possible for people to strive to improve and to behave morally. It also produces some distinctively human problems, such as eating disorders and suicide. Regardless, standards are important. They reveal one theme of this book: that human behavior is deeply shaped and guided by ideas. Many people deliberately try to become better people according to moral or cultural ideas. Nothing like it has been identified in any other species.

Self-awareness makes self-knowledge possible. Using language, people can express and remember many things about themselves. This process enables self-knowledge to become efficient, useful, and far-reaching. People develop elaborate theories about themselves. Turn on the television and watch any talk show: Even the most boring and shallow people seem to find endless things to say about themselves.

Know thyself! The quest for self-knowledge is another unique part of being human. Most people are eager to learn about themselves. The various motives for self-knowledge (self-enhancement, consistency, and appraisal) are centrally important among human beings but essentially unknown in other animals. Along with these motives go the concern with self-esteem and the cultivation of positive illusions. Self-deception may also be uniquely human. Some animals occasionally deceive each other, but as far as we can tell, only humans lie to themselves.

Another remarkable and distinctive feature of the human self is its ability to take and leave roles. Almost like a professional actor, the human self can take up a role, perform it well, and then stop and move into a different role that requires acting differently. The self can switch roles during the day as it moves from one situation to another (e.g., from office to home or to a bar with friends). The self can also make more lasting changes, such as when a person gets a promotion or a new job. This ability of the human self to change with changing roles, along the way changing how it thinks and behaves, is vital for cultural beings. Successful cultures are large social systems with many different roles. The human self probably evolved to be able to play different roles.

Intrinsic motivation is found in most animal species, but extrinsic motivation is more specific to humans. One common form of extrinsic motivation involves doing something for money, and of course only humans have money. Extrinsic motivation is important for culture because people will do things for the sake of cultural rewards (including money, prestige, status, and fame). These rewards are often vital for inducing people to do things that enable the culture to function properly. Few people have an intrinsic desire to collect garbage, pay taxes, or go to court, but many people do these things because of extrinsic motivation, and the culture operates more effectively when they do. Extrinsic rewards are the start of economic (money) relations because they motivate people to produce more than they need themselves so they can trade some to others and thus get other things they want.

Humans know the difference between inner states and outward appearances (though not all cultures may be as sensitive to this difference as modern, Western ones). People engage in self-presentation, sometimes to make the optimal impression on the audience and sometimes to cement their claims to a particular social identity, gaining validation from having other people accept them in that role. Sometimes people engage in deceptive self-presentation, trying to present themselves as better than they really are. In general, the desire to communicate information about oneself to others is an important aspect of human life.

In short, the self is something that humans know about and care about in ways that would be impossible for most other animals. Humans strive to learn about themselves, to change themselves to fit cultural and other standards, and to get others to regard them favorably. The self is a vital tool for gaining social acceptance and for participating in culture, in ways that only human beings do.

CHAPTER 3 SUMMARY

What Is the Self?

- The three main parts of the self are:
  - Self-knowledge or self-concept.
  - The interpersonal self or public self.
  - The agent or executive function.
- The main purposes of the self include gaining social acceptance and playing social roles.
- People from collectivistic cultures understand the self as interdependent (connected to others in a web of social relations), whereas people from individualistic cultures lean toward an independent self-construal (seeing the self as a separate, special or unique, self-contained unit).
- Self-awareness is attention directed at the self, and usually involves evaluating the self.
- Private self-awareness refers to attending to one's inner states; public self-awareness means attending to how one is perceived by others.
- Self-awareness is often unpleasant because people often compare themselves to high standards.
- Being self-aware can make people behave better.
- Human self-awareness is far more extensive and complex than what is found in any other species.
- Self-awareness is vital for self-regulation and adopting others' perspectives.

Where Self-Knowledge Comes From

- The looking-glass self refers to the idea that we learn about ourselves from how others judge us.
- People often do not realize how their minds work.
- The overjustification effect is the tendency for intrinsic motivation to diminish for activities that have become associated with external rewards.
- The phenomenal self or the working self-concept is the part of self-knowledge that is currently active in the person's thoughts.
- Three motivations for wanting self-knowledge are the appraisal motive, the self-enhancement motive, and the consistency motive.

- Self-handicapping involves putting obstacles in the way of one's own performance, so that if one fails, the failure can be blamed on the obstacle, and if one succeeds, one looks especially competent.

Self and Information Processing

- The self-reference effect refers to the finding that information bearing on the self is processed more thoroughly and more deeply, and hence remembered better, than other information.
- Self-concept is likely to change to be consistent with the public self, and with what people want to believe about themselves.

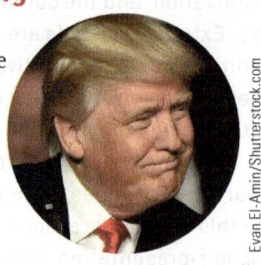

Self-Esteem, Self-Deception, and Positive Illusions

- In many important respects, nondepressed people see the world in a distorted, biased fashion, whereas depressed people can see reality more accurately.
- The self-serving bias leads people to claim credit for success but deny blame for failure.
- People with high self-esteem think they are great, but most people with low self-esteem think they are only mediocre (rather than awful).
- People with low self-esteem do not want to fail, are uncertain about their self-knowledge, focus on self-protection rather than self-enhancement, and are prone to emotional highs and lows.
- Basking in reflected glory refers to people's tendency to want to associate with winners.

- High self-esteem feels good and fosters initiative but does not confer many advantages in an objective sense.
- The sociometer theory suggests that self-esteem is a measure of how socially acceptable you think you are.
- High self-esteem and narcissism are associated with some negative qualities that pertain to relations with others, such as prejudice and aggression.
- Pursuing self-esteem as an end in itself can have harmful consequences.

Self-Presentation

- Most people are more concerned with looking good to others than with private self-esteem.
- Self-presentation is any behavior that seeks to convey some image of self or some information about the self to other people, or that seeks to make an impression on others.
- Nearly everyone strives for a good self-presentation as a way of obtaining social acceptance.
- Self-presentation is so important to people that they sometimes engage in risky or dangerous behavior in order to make a good impression.

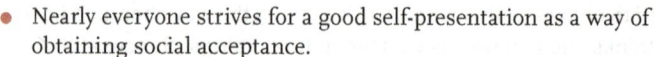

What Makes Us Human? Putting the Cultural Animal in Perspective

- What is special about the human self begins with self-awareness and self-concept.
- The self is a vital and distinctively human tool for gaining social acceptance and for participating in culture.

key terms

agent self (executive function) 72
appraisal motive 87
automatic egotism 89
consistency motive 87
downward social comparison 83
endowment effect 90
extrinsic motivation 84
generalized other 80
independent self-construal 74
interdependent self-construal 74
interpersonal self (public self) 72
intrinsic motivation 84
introspection 81
looking-glass self 80
narcissism 101
overjustification effect 84
phenomenal self (working self-concept) 84
private self-awareness 76
public self-awareness 76
private self-consciousness 78
public self-consciousness 78
self-awareness 75
self-deception strategies 97
self-enhancement motive 87
self-esteem 94
self-handicapping 88
self-knowledge (self-concept) 71
self-perception theory 83
self-presentation 104
self-protection 95
self-reference effect 90
self-regulation 78
self-serving bias 97
social comparison 82
social roles 75
sociometer 100
standards 76
upward social comparison 83

quiz yourself ANSWERS

1. What Is the Self? p. 79
   answers: 1.b 2.b 3.a 4.b
2. Where Self-Knowledge Comes From p. 90
   answers: 1.d 2.d 3.d 4.a
3. Self and Information Processing p. 94
   answers: 1.d 2.b 3.b 4.c
4. Self-Esteem, Self-Deception, and Positive Illusions p. 103
   answers: 1.d 2.a 3.d 4.d
5. Self-Presentation p. 110
   answers: 1.d 2.d 3.d 4.a

CHOICES AND ACTIONS
The Self in Control

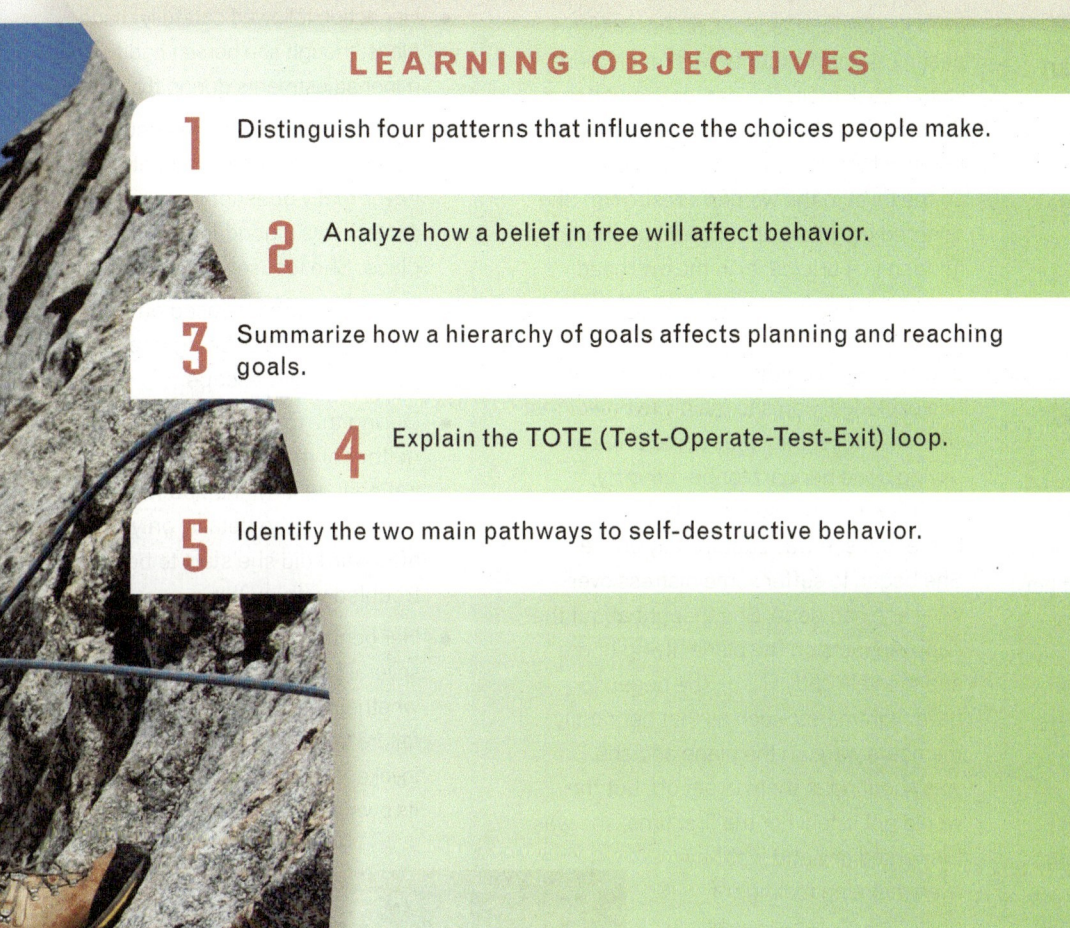

LEARNING OBJECTIVES

1. Distinguish four patterns that influence the choices people make.

2. Analyze how a belief in free will affect behavior.

3. Summarize how a hierarchy of goals affects planning and reaching goals.

4. Explain the TOTE (Test-Operate-Test-Exit) loop.

5. Identify the two main pathways to self-destructive behavior.

Jakub Cejpek/Shutterstock.com

4

MONEY MATTERS
How Money Can Trick You Into Making Bad Decisions
119

THE SOCIAL SIDE OF SEX
Gender, Sex, and Decisions
121

FOOD FOR THOUGHT
Dieting as Self-Regulation
137

TRADEOFFS
Now Versus Tomorrow: Delay of Gratification
142

WHAT MAKES US HUMAN?
Putting the Cultural Animal in Perspective
145

Terrorists have long chosen airplanes as targets for their violent acts. One of the most dramatic was the destruction of Korean Airlines Flight 858 in 1987. Unlike many such events, this act of terror has been recounted in detail by the perpetrator, a young woman named Kim Hyun Hee, in her book *The Tears of My Soul*.[1]

Kim Hyun Hee grew up in North Korea, a totalitarian communist state where all information is tightly controlled by the government. She learned in school that her country (though in fact a starving nation and an international outcast) was the greatest country in the world and blessed with a godlike leader, Kim Il-Sung (the grandfather of Kim Jong-un, North Korea's current Supreme Leader). By virtue of her hard work and her father's connections, she was able to attend the country's only major university, and her good record there earned her an invitation to become a special agent for the Korean foreign intelligence service.

One great day she was summoned to meet the director, who told her that she had been assigned to carry out a mission ordered by the Supreme Leader himself, the most important mission ever attempted by their organization and one that would decide North Korea's national destiny. He explained that she and a comrade would blow up a South Korean commercial airplane. This allegedly would cause the upcoming 1988 Olympics (scheduled for Seoul, South Korea) to be canceled, which in turn would lead to the unification of Korea under the communist government. She said she never understood how destroying a plane and killing some tourists would bring about the country's unification, but she did not question this, and she accepted it on faith. Being assigned such a historic mission was a great honor to her. The director explained that if she succeeded, she would become a national hero, and she and her family would benefit greatly.

At the time, she never thought about the moral issue of killing so many people. "The act of sabotage was a purely technical operation," she recalled later; her attention was focused on the concrete details, rather than guilt or compassion for her victims or even idealistic reflections on her nation's destiny. Airport security was much more casual back then. Her contacts met her at the airport and gave her the parts to the bomb, which she assembled while sitting on the toilet in the women's restroom. She boarded the plane and stowed the bomb (hidden in a briefcase) in the overhead compartment. At a layover she got off the plane, leaving the bomb there. Later that day, she heard on the news that the plane had exploded, and she mainly felt relief that she had succeeded, plus some pride at having done her part for her country.

She was supposed to make her way home, but she was captured by police. She began to suffer some distress over what she had done. She thought about the happy tourists on the plane, flying home and then abruptly killed. She began to have nightmares, such as that her family members were on the plane and she was shouting at them to get off, but they would not listen. For the first time, she was tormented day and night by overwhelming feelings of guilt. She confessed, was sentenced to death, and then was pardoned by the South Korean authorities.

This extraordinary story reveals several important themes about human action:

- Hee's behavior was guided by the values and systems of her culture: Blowing up an airplane was not her idea, but she accepted it and carried it out on faith that it would benefit her nation.
- She trusted that her leaders were good people and knew what they were doing, and she obeyed them without question. She did not notice the moral dilemma in advance and thought only of doing her duty.
- The plans were overly optimistic.
- By herself, she could have achieved very little, but she worked as part of a team.
- Her action followed carefully made plans, though she herself had to make minor adjustments during the mission.
- During the mission, she focused herself on the steps and details, never really questioning whether the project was a good idea in the first place. She focused on how, not why.
- Her nightmares focused on the panicky feeling of being unable to help her family escape.
- During the mission, she thought neither of moral issues nor of national destiny, instead focusing narrowly on the details; only afterward did she start to be troubled with guilt.
- Her behavior was directed toward several goals at different levels; whether you label it a success or a failure depends on which goal you invoke. The mission was a success on its own terms, insofar as the airplane

Kim Hyun Hee, former terrorist and author of *The Tears of My Soul*.

was destroyed and the passengers killed; Hee's capture was the only part that didn't go according to plan. Yet in the broader context, it was a total failure. The 1988 Olympics were held in South Korea as scheduled, and of course the grand goal of uniting the two Koreas under communist rule was not achieved. From the perspective of fulfilling the national destiny, she killed all those people for nothing.

The episode was largely self-defeating insofar as she ended up in prison and (temporarily) sentenced to death. But she did not intend to bring herself to that negative outcome. Instead, she was pursuing highly favorable goals both for herself and her country. Her quest for good backfired.

This chapter focuses on making choices and acting on them. The human self—who and what you are—is defined by the choices you make, but the self is also there precisely to help make choices. Indeed, probably the brain itself evolved to help animals make the choices they faced, and the human brain is so large partly to enable humans to cope with all the complex and difficult choices people have. In this chapter we look at how people make choices and why they sometimes make stupid or destructive ones. ●

What You Do, and What It Means

It is possible to talk about animal behavior without asking what the acts or circumstances "mean" to the animal. Skinnerian behaviorism (an approach that emphasized learning from reward and punishment as the main cause of behavior and that dominated psychology in the 1950s and 1960s) did precisely that, with considerable success. Skinnerian behaviorism, however, failed to provide a satisfactory account of human behavior, precisely because of its failure to deal with meaning. As we saw in Chapter 2, human behavior is often guided by ideas, which is to say that it depends on meanings. A bear may go up the hill or not, but the bear's decision is not based on concepts or ideas such as laws, plans, religious duties, flexible schedules, or promises. In contrast, much of human behavior makes no sense if we fail to appreciate what it *means*.

Culture is a network of meaning, and human beings who live in culture act based on meaning; this is what makes them different from other animals. That doesn't imply the psychologists who studied animals were wasting their time. Many of the principles that apply to animal behavior also apply to human behavior. Humans are animals too. But to explain human behavior, one needs more, and one especially needs meaning.

The importance of ideas—what you do depends partly on what it means—reflects the broad theme that inner processes serve interpersonal functions. Meaning depends on language and is therefore learned only through culture. For example, some religions condemn eating beef, others condemn eating pork, others condemn eating all meat; these rules are all learned from the culture, and only humans (with our inner capacity for understanding meaning) can alter their eating habits based on such rules. To go hungry instead of eating forbidden food reflects another theme, of letting social conscience override selfish impulses.

Thinking enables people to make use of meaning. Many psychologists study thinking for its own sake. Thinking probably evolved to help creatures make better choices for guiding their behavior (though this cannot be proven at present). William James, the father of American psychology, once wrote that "thinking is for doing,"[2] and modern social psychologists have shared that view.[3] The only serious alternative is that conscious thinking is for communicating (e.g., talking)[4]—but much communicating ultimately contributes to doing also. One of the most basic uses of thought is to perform actions mentally before doing them physically. You can imagine yourself running a race, or asking someone for a date, or giving a talk in front of an audience, and these imaginary exercises seem to pave the way for really doing them.

How well does it work? As people imagine something, it becomes more plausible and likely to them.[5,6,7,8,9,10] Salespeople make use of this process: Imagine yourself owning this car, they say, and the more you imagine it, the more likely you are to buy it.

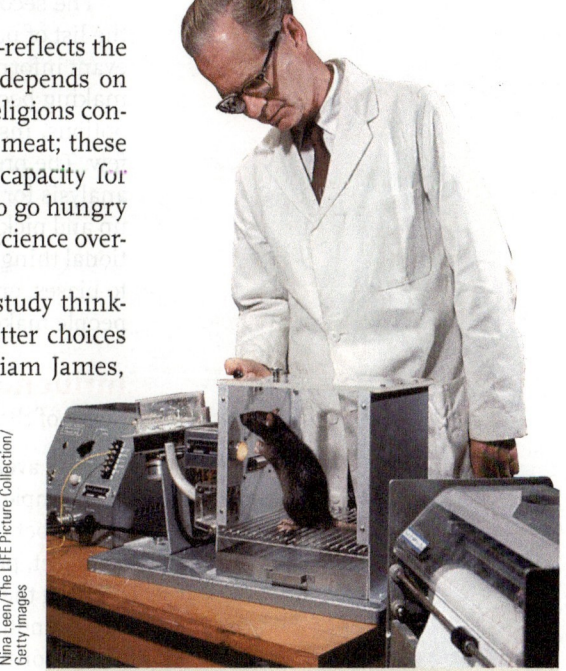

B. F. Skinner and his box. But what does it mean to you?

In one carefully controlled study, some students were told to imagine themselves studying hard for an upcoming exam and doing well on it. These people got significantly higher grades than any other group—an average of 10 points better than the control group. (The control group just kept track of how much they studied without imagining any part of the future.) The ones who imagined themselves studying hard in fact did study longer and harder, which no doubt helped them achieve those high grades. In a different condition, students imagined having done well on the exam, including a vivid scene of looking at the posted grades, following the line across from their number to see a high score, and walking away with a big smile. These people did only slightly (2 points) better than the control group.[11] Apparently just imagining a good outcome isn't as effective as imagining yourself doing all the hard work to produce the success. But all in all, imagination has the power to help make things come true.

Making Choices

Human life is filled with choices. A trip to the grocery store would be a mind-numbing experience if you really confronted all the possible choices, and every year there seem to be more choices to make. One researcher noted that the average American supermarket in 1976 carried 9,000 different products, whereas just 15 years later that figure had risen to 30,000![12] Similar patterns can be found everywhere: more television channels, more hairstyles, more churches and religious denominations, more ways to invest your money, more kinds of blue jeans. The progress of culture seems to offer people more and more choices, which must be desirable because people seem to want more choices. But how do they make them?

Two Steps of Choosing

Social psychologists have uncovered several key features of the process of choosing. It helps to recognize that most people handle choosing in two steps.[13] The first step involves whittling the full range of choices down to a limited few. Out of the many dozens of possible cars you might buy (or of the millions of people you might marry!), you discard most of them and zero in on a few options. This step can be done rather quickly. It entails some risk that a potentially good choice will be rejected without careful consideration, but it is the only way that the human mind can deal with a large set of possible choices.

The second step involves more careful comparison of the highlighted options. Once the list of possible cars is down to four or five, you can test-drive them all and look at relevant information about each one. Most research focuses on this second step of decision making because, typically, researchers study how someone chooses among a few major options, instead of focusing on how someone reduces a large set of choices down to a few. The prevailing assumption is that people perform some sort of mental cost–benefit analysis for each option, looking at the potential good and bad sides, and then add these up and pick the option that comes out best. Although this would seem to be the most rational thing to do, people are often less than fully rational, and their decisions are subject to biases, errors, and other influences. See *Money Matters* to learn about one reason that people make bad decisions.

Influences on Choice

Some of the major patterns that guide people's choices follow:

1. **Risk aversion.** People are more affected by possible losses than by possible gains. In a simple demonstration, participants were asked whether they would take a perfectly fair bet on a coin flip, such that they would win or lose $10. Most people didn't want to bet, presumably because the prospect of losing $10 outweighs the prospect of winning the same amount, even though the odds are exactly equal.[14, 15]

   Another study looked at rational versus irrational (foolish) bets. Rational bets conform to what expert statistical risk appraisal would dictate. (For example, a 50% chance to win $20 is better than a 1% chance of winning $100. You evaluate the bet by multiplying the probability times the outcome: $1/2 \times \$20 = \$10$, whereas $1/100 \times \$100 = \$1$.) Researchers found that people were often rational, but when

risk aversion in decision making, the greater weight given to possible losses than possible gains

MONEY Matters

How Money Can Trick You Into Making Bad Decisions

Suppose you have two job offers. One pays $50,000 per year and seems like it would be reasonably relaxed. The other will be stressful but pays better, at $63,000. Which do you choose?

Or suppose that after you get your job you are choosing between two apartments. They are about the same size and quality. One costs more but would enable you to walk to work. The cheaper one would require you to drive about half an hour each way. Which do you choose?

Many people would make these choices based on money—but this would make them less happy in the long run.[16] This is not because money is irrelevant to happiness. Having more money is better! But there is a particular illusion that is created by the numerical value of money.

Look again at the differences between the options in these examples. The money difference is quantitative: a matter of degree. The other difference is qualitative: Some feature (e.g., walking to work) is present or absent. People tend to overestimate the impact of quantitative differences on happiness, relative to qualitative differences.

The reason for this is rooted in the difference between how one thinks while deciding versus how one experiences life. When you are deciding, you compare the two options (such as the two apartments). You think about them both at the same time. But once you live in one of them, you cease to think about the other one, by and large. The fact that you saved a certain amount of money by renting the cheaper apartment will vanish from your daily awareness. But whether you can walk to work or must drive half an hour in rush-hour traffic will affect you nearly every day. Even though you stop comparing it to what your life would have been like in the other option, that feature remains to intrude on your daily experience.

The difference between comparing multiple options and experiencing a single one was shown in a different way in another study. Participants considered two different ways of resolving a dispute with a neighbor. In one solution, the participant received $600 and the neighbor received $800. In the other solution, the participant and the neighbor each got $500. When participants had both options to compare, they preferred the first one, because it gave them more money ($600 vs. $500). When participants predicted their reaction to only one of the options (i.e., some participants considered only the first solution, and others considered only the second solution), the first solution received fewer favorable ratings than the second because they got less than the neighbor ($600 vs. $800).[17]

In another study, participants imagined shopping for a music dictionary in a used bookstore and were supposed to say how much they would be willing to pay, from $10 to $50. Some saw descriptions of two dictionaries, whereas others only saw a description of one dictionary. One dictionary had 10,000 entries and was in perfect condition. The other had 20,000 entries and was in perfect condition except for a torn cover. When comparing the two, people were willing to pay more for the one with the torn cover (because it had so much more information). Among participants who saw only one option, however, the torn cover reduced what people were willing to pay because they were not able to appreciate the difference in amount of information between 10,000 versus 20,000 entries.[18]

Thus, when choosing between options, people tend to focus on quantitative differences. But after you have made your choice, you have to live with what you chose, and the option you did not choose is probably gone from your life. Remember to focus on what you will live with, not just what scores higher on paper when you compare.

Branden Bushman 2012

This lottery winner chose the lump sum cash option, which means he'll walk away with a whopping $223.3 million prize rather than $344.6 over an extended period of time.

they were not, their irrational behavior was geared toward avoiding losses more often than pursuing gains.[19] That is, people seemed more worried about losing than they were attracted by the possibility of winning.

2. **Temporal discounting.** A second influence is that what happens right now weighs more heavily than what might happen in the future. Would you rather have $1,000 today, or $1,200 two weeks from today? The logical choice would be the delayed one because there is very little chance that you could invest the money wisely enough to turn $1,000 into $1,200 in two weeks, so if you take the delayed reward, you will end up with more money. Most people, however, choose the immediate reward. For example, people who buy lottery tickets often choose the single check (immediate) payment option, which means they get all the money at once if they win (sometimes called a "lump sum")—even though they might get more total money if they accept the winnings in more and smaller check amounts.

   The discounting of the future can be seen in many contexts beyond money. For one such example that mixes sex and money, see *The Social Side of Sex*.

3. **The certainty effect.** Some features of a decision involve possibilities and odds, whereas others are certain. In buying a car, the likelihood that it will need repairs at a certain cost or frequency or that it will safeguard you in a collision are examples of things that might or might not happen, whereas you can be sure of the color and style you are getting. People tend to place undue weight on things that are certain. This is not to say that they completely ignore safety or repair records and just buy cars based on color, but they do end up relying on color a little more than they mean to do. This tendency to place too much emphasis on definite outcomes is called the **certainty effect**.[20]

   For example, suppose you are playing Russian roulette. (A gun has some bullets in it while some of the chambers are empty, and when you play the game you point it at your head and pull the trigger once.) How much would you pay to remove one bullet, assuming either that (a) there are four bullets in the six chambers and two empties, or (b) there is only one bullet and five empties? Reducing the number of bullets from four to three is exactly the same improvement in your chances of surviving the game as is reducing it from one to zero, but most people say they would pay substantially more to eliminate the only bullet. This shows the certainty effect: They want to know they are completely safe. Such processes complicate many decisions about environmental and safety regulations because complete and perfect safety is quite difficult to achieve, yet people might prefer to focus laws and expenditures on trying to reduce risks from 1% to 0% rather than other interventions that might reduce risk from, say, 8% to 4%. Reducing risk from 8% to 4% will save many more people (four times as many) than reducing risk from 1% to 0%.

4. **Keeping options open.** Some people prefer to postpone hard decisions and keep their options open as long as possible. In one study of online shoppers, some were offered a selection of bargains that were only available right away, whereas others had the additional option of coming back later to choose among the same options and bargains. Those who had to buy right away often did so. Those who could put off the decision generally decided to wait, indicating a preference for keeping one's options available until later. Unfortunately for the sellers, the customers who decided to postpone the

temporal discounting in decision making, the greater weight given to the present over the future

certainty effect in decision making, the greater weight given to definite outcomes than to probabilities

The Social Side of Sex

Gender, Sex, and Decisions

Someone of your preferred gender smiles at you and seems to be flirting a bit. There might be a chance to have sex later today. Then again, perhaps the person is just being friendly, and by making romantic or sexual advances you might end up embarrassing yourself and damaging the relationship. Do you make the advances?

The data suggest that the answer may depend on your gender. Men seem much more likely than women to chase after every potential (or even sometimes illusory) chance for sex. The reason for this difference may lie in the fact that evolution has prepared men and women to use different guidelines for making sexual decisions.

One general explanation, called **error management theory**,[21] is that both men and women make decisions so as to minimize the costliest type of error, but men's worst error is not the same as women's. The difference is rooted in a long evolutionary history, during which most males failed to reproduce at all, whereas most females did reproduce. Hence for females the goal is to get the best possible mate, and having sex too readily can defeat that goal. For a woman, to be on the safe side is to say no to sex a little longer, if only to make sure that her partner provides further proof that he is a good man and is devoted to her (and perhaps to make sure no one better is available). In contrast, many male animals will have few or no opportunities to reproduce at all, and so in order to pass along their genes they should take advantage of every chance. It would be folly to pass up a chance for sex today if that opportunity might not be available tomorrow.

These differences are increased by the differences in what the body does to make a baby. If a woman gets pregnant by one man today, and a better partner comes along next week, her body is already committed to the (less attractive) pregnancy, so again it behooves her to wait until she is certain she has the best mate. In contrast, if a man makes one woman pregnant today and then a better partner comes along tomorrow, he is physically capable of impregnating her as well.

A recent study of temporal discounting showed how these sexual impulses can influence even decisions that do not, on the surface, have anything to do with sex. Heterosexual participants in this study had to make choices between sooner smaller rewards (e.g., $5 tomorrow) and larger later ones (e.g., $10 a month from now). After they had made one round of choices, they were exposed to one of four types of stimuli. Some saw 12 pictures of attractive members of the opposite sex. Others saw 12 photos of relatively unattractive members of the opposite sex. Others saw 12 beautiful cars, and a final group saw 12 relatively ugly cars. Then they chose again between sooner smaller and larger later rewards. Only one group showed a substantial shift toward the sooner smaller rewards: men who had looked at the beautiful women. The men in the other three conditions, and the women in all conditions, were relatively unaffected.[22]

Why? Again, evolution has selected men to leap at every mating chance. Apparently, the sight of a pretty woman puts men into a mind-set that emphasizes the present and discounts or ignores the future. A pretty woman can induce a man to spend much of his money right away, even at considerable cost to his future financial circumstances. She doesn't even have to try very hard. This study suggests that simply seeing her is enough to cause the man to forget about long-term financial prudence and focus on the here and now.

decision hardly ever returned to make a purchase. It is hardly surprising that many salespeople make offers that expire immediately.

For some students, keeping a double major is a way of postponing a decision about their future. A double major requires students to divide their time and efforts, so they cannot be as successful at either subject as a single-major student would be, but some people pay this price in order to preserve their options.[23]

Why People Don't Choose

Postponing decisions may be part of a broader pattern called decision avoidance. A review article titled "The Psychology of Doing Nothing"[24] considered different forms this avoidance can take. One, called the **status quo bias** is a simple preference to keep things

error management theory the idea that both men and women seek to minimize the costliest type of error, but that men's and women's goals, and hence worst errors, differ

status quo bias the preference to keep things the way they are rather than change

What type of yogurt should I get? There are too many to choose from. I guess I won't get any.

the way they are instead of changing. Would you want to exchange your home, your romantic partner, your course schedule, for another? The new one is unknown and might have unforeseen problems. People often stick with what they have, even when the alternatives might be better.

Another pattern that leads to doing nothing, called the **omission bias** is taking whatever course of action does not require you to do anything (also called the default option). For example, when you complete a free registration to gain access to a website, often you must mark a particular box if you do not want to receive junk mail and advertisements. Why don't they leave it blank and let you just check it if you want to receive those mailings and ads? Because they want as many people as possible on their mailing list, and they know that many people will not do anything. In principle, it is just as easy for them to make "don't send mail" the default option as to make it "send mail." The omission bias means that many people will do nothing—they will do whatever is the default option—so retailers will get more people on their mailing list by making the default option "send mail" rather than "don't send."

One general theme behind decision avoidance is anticipated regret.[25] People avoid making choices and taking actions that they fear they will regret later on. Apparently, people anticipate less regret over doing nothing than over doing something. They also know the status quo better than the alternatives, so there is a greater risk of regret if you decide to change than if you stand pat.

Another theme is that some decisions become too difficult. An influential study showed that people who visited a table with a display of jams were less likely to buy any of them if the table had 24 different varieties than if it had just 6.[26] Some theorists have proposed that modern life offers too many choices.[27]

Subsequent work has not found that people always recoil from too many choices. People like to have many options. Across many different circumstances, there is no general pattern that having more options leads to more avoidance of decisions.[28] Sometimes having too few choices makes people reluctant to choose; for example, many people refuse to buy when they only see one option, even if it seems okay.[29] Hence, it is necessary to dig a bit deeper to see when this does or does not happen.

Basically, we fail to make a selection from a group of options, whether it is a matter of picking a spouse or a toothbrush or a car, for one of two reasons.[30] One is that none of the options seems good enough. The other is that it is hard to tell which one is the best. These two reasons have opposite relationships to the assortment of options. As the number of options increases, it is less and less plausible that none is good enough—but it gets harder and harder to be sure you've chosen the best one. You might test-drive two cars and decide that neither is good enough, but after you've tried two dozen cars, you should have found at least some satisfactory ones. But of course it's harder to pick the best of 24 than the better of 2.

Reactance

The interest in preserving options is the core of an important psychological theory that has held up well over several decades. Called **reactance theory,** it was first proposed by social psychologist Jack Brehm[31,32,33,34,35] and has much in common with the folk notion of "reverse psychology." The central point of reactance theory is that people desire to have freedom of choice and therefore have a negative, aversive reaction to having some of their choices or options taken away by other people or by external forces. The term *reactance* refers specifically to the negative feelings people have when their freedom is reduced. For example, if someone tells you that you cannot see a concert that you have been looking forward to, you will experience reactance, which is an angry, disappointed feeling.

omission bias the tendency to take whatever course of action does not require you to do anything (also called the default option)

reactance theory the idea that people are distressed by loss of freedom or options and seek to reclaim or reassert them

Reactance produces three main consequences.[36] First, it makes you want the forbidden option more and/or makes it seem more attractive. (If you weren't sure you wanted to see the concert, being told that you can't see it may increase your desire to see it and make you think it is likely to be a really good one.) Second, reactance may make you take steps to try to reclaim the lost option, often described as "reasserting your freedom." (You may try to sneak into the concert after all.) Third, you may feel or act aggressively toward the person who has restricted your freedom.

Many studies have supported reactance theory.[37] Two-year-olds who are told not to play with a particular toy suddenly find that toy more appealing and are more likely to sneak over to it when they think no one is watching. Students who are told they can have their choice of five posters, but then are told that one of them (chosen at random, or even the one that was initially their third choice) is not available, suddenly like that one more and want it more. Labels designed to warn consumers about potentially objectionable material in TV programs, films, video games, and music often have the opposite effect of making people more interested in the "forbidden" media.[38] Most ominously, men who have formed unrealistic expectations of having sex with a particular woman may become angry and even coercive if the woman rejects their advances,[39] especially narcissistic men.[40]

The findings on reactance bring up the broader issues of free will and freedom of action. Regardless of whether someone believes in free will as a genuine phenomenon, one cannot dispute the fact that people are sensitive to how much freedom of choice they have. Reactance theory emphasizes that people are motivated to gain and preserve choices. Having some of their choices taken away by someone else or some external event produces a very negative reaction in most people.

Freedom to Change

Making choices is a major part of life. Animals make simple choices in simple ways, but human beings have a far more complex inner capacity for making choices—which is good because humans face very complex choices. Human choice is also much more momentous than what most animals do. Think of all the choices you make: What courses to take, whom to date, whom to vote for, how to handle your money, what to do on a Sunday afternoon. Understanding choice and decision making is a vital part of any effort to understand human life.

The essence of the idea of freedom is that you can do more than one thing (hence the need to choose among them). This is relevant even to very basic questions such as whether you can choose to change yourself. Some people think their traits are constant and stable, so see little point in trying to change. Others think they can change. For example, some observers have noted that professional (baseball) athletes tend to have different attitudes in the United States and Japan.[41] In general, the American athletes think in terms of innate talent, and hence simply performing up to their ability, whereas the Japanese athletes think of sport in terms of continual improvement through hard work.

That difference in thinking is not confined to athletes. Researcher Carol Dweck[42] has shown that ordinary people and even children can be found exhibiting either style. She uses the term **entity theorists** to refer to people who regard traits as fixed, stable things (entities), as opposed to **incremental theorists** who believe that traits are subject to change and improvement. Entity theorists prefer to do things they are good at, in order that success can gain them credit and admiration. They dislike criticism or bad feedback intensely (partly because they tend to think that bad traits are permanent). In contrast, incremental theorists are more likely to enjoy learning and challenges; they don't mind criticism or initial failure as much because they expect to improve. Entity theorists often choose the easiest task because they want guaranteed success, whereas incremental theorists prefer harder, more challenging tasks where they can learn.[43]

When students move to a new, more challenging environment, such as from elementary school to middle school, or from high school to college, the entity theorists are often

Hideo Nomo played for the Kintetsu Buffaloes, a Japanese professional baseball team, from 1990 to 1994. He signed with the Los Angeles Dodgers in 1995 as the first Japanese player in Major League baseball and won the Rookie of the Year award the same year.

entity theorists those who believe that traits are fixed, stable things (entities) that are not subject to change

incremental theorists those who believe that traits are subject to change and improvement

learned helplessness belief that one's actions will not bring about desired outcomes, leading one to give up and quit trying

discouraged and overwhelmed, and their performance goes down, whereas the incremental theorists keep striving to improve and often show gains in performance.[44] Likewise, in lab studies, failure tends to be devastating to entity theorists and even to produce a kind of **learned helplessness** (they quit trying and give up) because they think the failure is proof that they are incompetent losers. In contrast, when incremental theorists fail, they simply try harder to improve.[45]

Ultimately, the difference is between thinking that people are the way they are, period, versus thinking that people are constantly subject to change. People apply these different outlooks both to themselves and to others. Thus, entity theorists tend to interpret other people's behavior as reflecting their traits, whereas incremental theorists interpret them as caused by temporary states and external factors.[46] (See Chapter 5 for a detailed discussion of the difference between internal and external attributions.)

QUIZ YOURSELF
What You Do, and What It Means

1. Suppose you show up for a paid experiment and receive $10. The researcher says you can double your earnings if the outcome of a coin toss is a head or lose your earnings if the outcome of a coin toss is a tail. What does research show that most people would do?
   - (a) They would flip the coin and try to get $20.
   - (b) They would not flip the coin and keep their $10.
   - (c) There is a 50/50 chance that people will flip the coin because the potential gain equals the potential loss.
   - (d) The research evidence is mixed.

2. Mohammed is 4 years old. His mother, a social psychologist, asks whether he would rather have one cookie today or three cookies tomorrow. Mohammed chooses the one cookie today. This illustrates _____.
   - (a) certainty effect
   - (b) planning fallacy
   - (c) risk aversion
   - (d) temporal discounting

3. Joni wants to see an R-rated (17+) movie with some friends. However, Joni is only 14, and her parents forbid her to go. Which of the following responses could be predicted from Brehm's psychological reactance theory?
   - (a) Joni would behave aggressively toward her parents.
   - (b) Joni would want to see the movie more.
   - (c) Joni would sneak into the movie anyway.
   - (d) All of the above.

4. Entity theorists are to incremental theorists as _____ are to _____.
   - (a) global traits; specific traits
   - (b) specific traits; global traits
   - (c) stable traits; unstable traits
   - (d) unstable traits; stable traits

answers: see pg 147

Freedom of Action

The question of whether people have free will has been debated for centuries, and its importance has been recognized in such fields as theology (religious doctrines), morality, and philosophy.[47] Psychologists are divided on the issue. Many believe that psychology must explain all behavior in terms of causes, and if a behavior is caused, then it is not truly or fully free. Others emphasize the fact that people make choices and could have chosen differently under other circumstances, and in that sense, they believe people do have freedom.

Whether to believe in free will is more than just a philosophical debate. In fact, research suggests that belief in free will is valuable for society. When experimental manipulations induced people to reject their belief in free will, they became more willing to cheat on a test and steal money.[48] Similar manipulations showed that disbelieving in free will causes people to become more aggressive and less helpful toward others.[49] These findings say nothing about whether free will really exists—but the belief in it helps cultural animals act in more prosocial ways, thereby helping the social system function better.

More or Less Free

Whatever the ultimate decision is about free will, one cannot dispute that people perceive that they make some choices and that some of these are freer than others. In particular, people have the subjective experience that sometimes they are constrained by external factors, whereas other times they can freely choose what they think is best. In other words, although absolute freedom is debatable, relative freedom is an important feature of social behavior. Among humans, greater freedom is marked by greater behavioral flexibility, controlled processes (as opposed to automatic ones), and self-regulation (deliberately changing one's own states or responses).

In order to live within a culture and human society, humans need a fairly complex and flexible decision-making apparatus. Most animals face choices to some degree, but these are limited in scope and meaning. An animal may have to choose which direction to walk in seeking food, or where to sleep, or whether to fight over some territory or resource. These are important decisions, but they are not nearly as complicated as the choices faced by human beings in our society, such as what college major or occupation to pursue, whether to lie about past sexual experiences, how much effort and time to spend trying to fix one's car before giving up and getting a new one, how much money to offer for a painting or a house, and whether to yield to family pressures about religious matters. Remember, inner processes serve interpersonal events—so the complex demands of living in human society call for an elaborate inner system for making decisions. This elaborate inner system for making decisions is the basis for the common notion of free will.[50] Whether it truly qualifies as free will depends in large part on which of the competing definitions of free will one uses.

As cultural animals, humans rely on meaning to make their choices, and meaning generally offers multiple ways of understanding and deciding. Unlike most other animals, human beings can decide based on abstract rules, moral and ethical principles, laws, plans, contracts, agreements, and the like. This capacity for thinking about a decision or situation in multiple ways requires a flexible capacity for making those decisions.

Free Action Comes from Inside

Self-determination theory is an important perspective on freedom of action. It builds on the research on intrinsic versus extrinsic motivation discussed in Chapter 3. Not all motivations are equal. As the authors of this theory, Ed Deci and Richard Ryan,[51,52,53] point out, people may be motivated to perform well out of a deep passion for excellence or because of a bribe; they may be motivated to behave honestly out of an inner moral sense or because they fear others are watching them; they may be motivated to work hard because they love what they are doing or because they feel pressure to meet a looming deadline. As those three pairs of motivations indicate, people may be motivated by something originating inside them or by some external pressure or force. Doing things to satisfy external pressures is felt to be less free than acting from one's inner promptings. A central point of self-determination theory is that people have an innate need for autonomy, which means that at least some of their activities must be motivated by their inner drives and choices, rather than by external factors.

Believing you are acting autonomously and from intrinsic motivation has many benefits. People who act on that belief derive more satisfaction, are more interested in and excited about what they are doing, have greater confidence, and often perform better, persist longer, and show greater creativity. Their autonomous actions also contribute to vitality,

self-determination theory the theory that people need to feel at least some degree of autonomy and internal motivation self-esteem, and general well-being (akin to happiness).[54,55,56,57,58,59] They are less prone to fall victim to passivity, alienation, and mental illness. For example, some teachers encourage their students to develop their own interests, make decisions, and in other respects exercise autonomy, whereas other teachers try to control their students. The students of the autonomy-supporting teachers end up more interested in their work, more curious to learn, and more eager for challenges, and they end up learning more.[60,61,62,63,64,65,66,67]

All these studies suggest that different levels of freedom of action have important implications for how people fare. Perhaps most important, when people reach the goals associated with their own autonomous or intrinsic desires, they feel happier and healthier, whereas reaching goals linked to extrinsic motivations is much less able to produce such benefits.[68,69]

Having an Out Versus No Escape

One of the most profound illustrations that perceived freedom produces benefits is the **panic button effect**: Believing that one has an escape option can reduce stress, even if one never makes use of this option. In an early demonstration of this effect, participants were exposed to highly aversive noise stress—blasts of loud noise, delivered at random, unpredictable intervals for irregular lengths of time—while they were trying to solve puzzles. This noise stress made it hard for people to perform their tasks; even afterward, when they sat in a quiet room, people who had been through the noise stress performed worse at a variety of tasks, indicating less concentration, less persistence, and lower frustration tolerance. In this experiment,[70] all participants were exposed to the same noise stress, and all of them had a button on the table in front of them. In reality, the button was not connected to anything, and pressing it would have had no effect.

To some participants, however, the experimenter said that the button would turn off the noise. He said the participant could eliminate the noise if it became too stressful or hard to bear, though he said it would spoil the experiment if the participant pressed it, and he asked the participant not to use the button if possible. No one ever pressed the button. Yet the participants who had this "panic button" available to them did not show all the problems and impairments that the stress had caused. Even though they did not make use of the button to escape the stress, they derived considerable comfort just from knowing it was there.

Thus, even the false belief that one can exert control over events makes them more bearable. Does your neighbor's loud music keep you awake late at night? It may bother you less if you think that you could ask the neighbor to turn it down than if you think you have no choice but to listen to it. Do you suffer when you spend a Friday night alone once in a while? You may feel less lonely if you think you could find some friends or companions than if you think you have no such options.

panic button effect a reduction in stress or suffering due to a belief that one has the option of escaping or controlling the situation, even if one doesn't exercise it

QUIZ YOURSELF
Freedom of Action

1. People who believe in free will are more _____ than people who do not believe in free will.
   - (a) antisocial
   - (b) prosocial
   - (c) extraverted
   - (d) introverted

2. According to self-determination theory, people need to feel that activities are motivated by _____.
   - (a) external factors
   - (b) global factors
   - (c) internal factors
   - (d) specific factors

3. What type of motivation leads to the best goal outcomes?
   - (a) Achievement
   - (b) Attitude
   - (c) Extrinsic
   - (d) Intrinsic

4. Believing that one can exert control over stressful events makes them more tolerable, even if one has no control. This is called the _____.
   - (a) certainty effect
   - (b) panic button effect
   - (c) planning fallacy
   - (d) status quo bias

answers: see pg 147

Goals, Plans, Intentions

Ideas and meanings are centrally important to human action, as discussed earlier in the chapter. Meaning connects things; thus, an action has meaning when it is connected to other things or events. One important type of meaning links an action to a goal. Your current action, such as looking at this page, derives meaning from various future events that are presumably your goals, including learning something about social psychology, doing well in the course, getting an education, earning a degree, and preparing for a career. Without those or similar goals, you might still look at this page, but to do so would be relatively pointless and meaningless.

A **goal** is an idea of some desired future state.[72] Goals, in turn, are the (meaningful) link between values and action.[73,74] That is, most people hold certain values, such as family, friends, religion, honesty, success, and health, but these broad and general preferences must be translated into something much more specific in order to serve as guides for behavior. A goal tells you how to pursue and uphold your values.

Goals can also be called personal projects[75] or personal strivings.[76] Most people have more than one goal or project in their life toward which they work and strive at any given time. In fact, when young adults are asked to list their goals and similar personal projects, the average list contains 15 items.[77] Thus, the typical human life nowadays is characterized by a variety of different goals, some of which may be completely unrelated to others, and some of which may even be in conflict (e.g., if they make competing demands on a limited stock of time or money).

Experts disagree as to how goal-oriented other animals are; hence, they disagree about how unique the goal pursuit of human beings is. The experts who believe that animals do pursue goals, in the sense of having mental ideas about future states and trying to make them come true, generally still concede that human beings do this far better and more extensively than other animals. Animal goals mostly involve the immediate situation and an outcome that is already almost visible, such as climbing a tree or chasing a smaller animal.[78,79] In contrast, human beings pursue goals that may be weeks, years, even decades away, such as in studying and working to become a successful lawyer.

Pursuing distant goals is not as easy as pursuing immediate ones. People may have to interrupt and resume their activities. (While studying to become a lawyer, for example, one must do many things that aren't part of that goal, such as eating, sleeping, and doing laundry!) Self-control is needed to maintain focus and organize one's efforts. Motivation is also likely to fluctuate. During a short-term goal, such as when one is being chased by a bear and wants to get away, motivation stays high throughout, but one's desire to become a lawyer is likely to be stronger on some days than others, and indeed many people change their minds and drop out. Classical motivation theory held that motivation increases as one gets closer to the goal. A modern refinement suggests that the low point for motivation tends to be in the middle of the project. People may start off with high motivation, and it is usually high again as they approach the goal, but during the long slog in the middle, it is likely to wane. Even during tasks done in the same hour, motivation is lower in the middle. For example, when student participants worked on a series of word-making puzzles, they exerted less effort on the middle ones than the early or late ones.[80]

Setting and Pursuing Goals

Where do goals come from? Almost certainly a person's goals reflect the influence of both inner processes and cultural factors. Perhaps the best way to think of this is that the culture sets out a variety of possible goals, and people choose among them depending on their personal wants and needs and also on their immediate circumstances. For example, throughout much of history the goals available to men and women were often quite different; women were barred from many professions, and men were not permitted to be homemakers. Modern Western society has in theory opened up a much wider range of

> "A goal without a plan is just a wish."
> — Antoine de Saint-Exupery (1900–1944), French writer and aviator, author of *The Little Prince*[71]

goal an idea of some desired future state

options to both men and women, though both social and personal factors still steer men and women into some different goals and jobs. For example, pressure to earn enough to support a family causes many more men than women to take jobs that may be stressful, unpleasant, or physically dangerous as long as they offer high pay. In such cases, the man's goal of making enough money to attract a mate and support a family causes him to select some goals over other possible goals, such as having a pleasant job and reducing his risk of dying on the job.[81] Women, in contrast, tend to be less guided by materialistic and financial motives in choosing their careers. They give more emphasis to goals of fulfillment, safety, and flexibility.[82] Again, these differences almost certainly reflect the influence of both individual preferences and cultural realities.

Pursuing goals involves at least two major steps, which involve different mental states. The first step includes setting goals (which may involve choosing among competing goals—you can't do everything at once), evaluating how difficult or feasible a goal is, and deciding how much you want to pursue it. The second step is pursuing the goal, which may include planning what to do and carrying out those behaviors.[83,84,85] Let us consider these two mental states in turn (see **TABLE 4.1**).

Setting goals is a time for being realistic. You may be choosing among different possible goals to pursue, or you may simply be deciding whether to commit yourself to a particular goal or not. People in this state are thoughtful and generally seek all sorts of information (both good and bad) about the goals they are contemplating. In this state, the "positive illusions" that characterize a great deal of normal thinking (see Chapter 3) are typically set aside, and people instead tend to be quite accurate about their own capabilities and their chances of successfully achieving the goal.[86,87]

A very different mind-set accompanies pursuing goals. The time for realism is past; instead, optimism and positive illusions help build confidence and foster better performance. The person zeroes in on the one goal and loses interest in information about other goals. Questions of whether and why to pursue the goal are set aside, in favor of questions of how. The goal dominates information processing, such as by drawing attention to opportunities and obstacles, driving the person to develop workable and detailed plans, and stimulating the person to persist and keep trying even in the face of setbacks or interruptions.

Another benefit of goals is that they can bring the person back to resume an activity after an interruption.[88] To get a good grade in a course, for example, you have to perform many activities that are spaced out in time, such as attending class, studying, and reviewing notes, over a period of several months. The goal (the mental idea of doing well in the class) can be important in helping you turn your efforts to pursuing the relevant activities. Even when you are enjoying a television show or practicing your athletic skills, you may stop those activities to attend class or study. Hardly any other animal is capable of making such decisions to stop one activity in order to resume pursuit of a previously pursued goal. Moreover, people who are most successful in life are those who are good at resuming activities after interruptions because most major successes in life require the person to work on them on many different days, interspersed with other activities such as eating and sleeping.

TABLE 4.1 Mind-Sets and Goals

	Mind-Set	
	Goal Setting	**Goal Pursuit/Striving**
Function	Deciding what to do	Deciding how to do it, and doing it
Attitude	Open-minded	Closed-minded
Mental focus	Feasibility and desirability	Means and obstacles
Core question	Why should I do it?	How do I do it?
Style of thought	Realistic thinking	Optimistic thinking

Both the deliberate and automatic systems help in the pursuit of goals. The deliberate system does much of the goal setting, especially if the decision about whether to pursue a goal is complicated. The automatic system may also help provide the initiative to resume goals that have been interrupted. Also, crucially, if one step toward a goal is blocked, the deliberate system may be helpful in devising an alternate strategy or route to reach the ultimate goal. The automatic system also contributes in an interesting way. Most people experience the so-called **Zeigarnik effect**, which is a tendency to experience automatic, intrusive thoughts about a goal that one has pursued but whose pursuit has been interrupted. (This is the duplex mind at work: The automatic system signals the conscious mind and deliberate system, which may have moved on to other pursuits, that a previous goal was left uncompleted.) That is, if you start working toward a goal and fail to get there, thoughts about the goal will keep popping into your mind while you are doing other things, as if to remind you to get back on track to finish reaching that goal. Because most human activities naturally form themselves into units so that completing them is a goal, any sort of interruption can produce a Zeigarnik effect. One commonplace experience is turning the radio off in the middle of a song—and then having that song running through your mind for the rest of the day.

Recent work has even suggested that the Zeigarnik effect can show how conscious and unconscious mind (or automatic and deliberate systems) work together. Unfinished goals normally keep popping into your mind, but if you make a plan for how to reach the goal, these intrusive thoughts stop.[89] In a sense, then, the Zeigarnik effect is a matter of the unconscious mind nagging the conscious mind to make a plan, like a child tugging at the sleeve of an adult to know when and where they will have lunch. The automatic system is great at executing plans but not so good at making them. The deliberate system is inefficient for carrying out plans but excels at making them.

People perform better if they have goals, but some goals are more helpful than others. In general, it is most helpful to have specific goals and goals that are difficult but reachable—goals you have to stretch to reach.[90,91] A broad goal such as "getting an education" does not necessarily improve performance very much; specific goals such as "getting a good grade on my next test" are more helpful. People who shoot for high goals generally do better than those who set easy goals for themselves, unless the goals are so high as to be unrealistic—and therefore discouraging.

Hierarchy of Goals

Goals are not necessarily independent; in fact, most people have interlinked sets of goals. People usually have a hierarchy of goals, with short-term or proximal goals that operate as stepping-stones toward long-term or distal goals. For example, a high school student might decide she wants to be the Chief Executive Officer (CEO) of a major corporation, which would be a distal goal, but if she had only that goal, she would be unlikely to get very far. To become a CEO, you need to take many steps, such as getting an education, getting an entry-level job at a corporation, gaining experience, and working your way up through the ranks by way of a series of promotions **(FIGURE 4.1)**. It would be silly to drop out of high school and just look through the want ads in the newspaper for job openings as CEO of a major corporation, but if you only had the big, distal goal of becoming a CEO, without the proximal goals that lead up to it, you might not know any better.[92] The person who has a hierarchy of goals, with many steps leading up to the ultimate distal goal, is far more likely to be successful.

The duplex mind is relevant to goal hierarchies. The automatic system can keep track of the goals and initiate behavior to pursue each step along the way. The deliberate system may be useful, however, when an intermediate goal is blocked. Consciousness (associated with the deliberate system) is flexible at processing information, and it can find a substitute goal when the overarching or ultimate goal is blocked. In the previous example, if you had a plan for becoming CEO but discovered that your corporation never hired a CEO from among its own vice presidents, then you might use your deliberate information-processing system to figure out that once you became vice president you would need to look elsewhere (i.e., other corporations) for openings. The automatic system is much less

Zeigarnik effect a tendency to experience automatic, intrusive thoughts about a goal whose pursuit has been interrupted

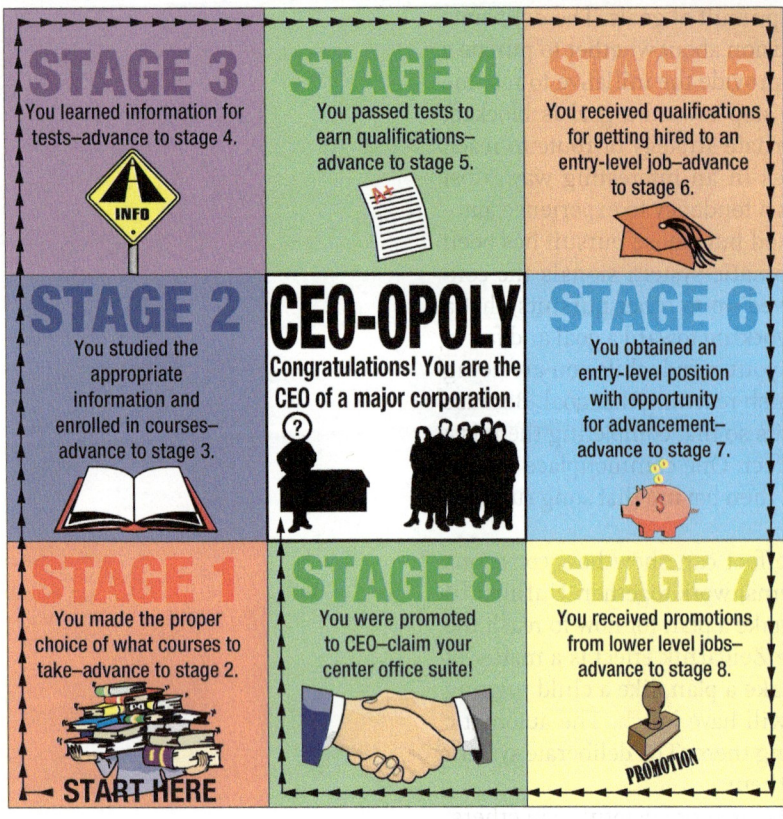

FIGURE 4.1 A hierarchy of goals.

effective at such flexible thinking; if its plan were blocked, it might be at a loss to find an alternative pathway to the ultimate goal.

We have noted the problems that might arise if you have only distal, ultimate goals without forming a hierarchy of proximal goals. Conversely, people who have only proximal (short-term) goals without the distal (long-term) ones also encounter problems.[93] These people essentially go through life dealing with one issue or problem at a time but without a sense of where they should be going in the long run. They may be good at paying the bills, doing their assigned tasks, and responding to immediate needs or problems in their relationships, but where they end up in life is likely to be the result of a series of accidents and may not necessarily be to their liking. Having only proximal goals is not much better than having only distal goals. To live your life effectively within human society and culture, it is important to have both distal and proximal goals (preferably interlinked). In other words, the most effective approach is to have an idea of where you would like to be in five or ten years (even if you change this goal, it is still important to have one) as well as some ideas of what you need to do this week, this month, and this year in order to get there.

Multiple Goals and Goal Shielding

Nearly everyone has many different goals. That presents a problem, however: How do you decide which to work on? Indeed, how do you prevent worries about unmet goals to distract you when you are working toward another goal? For example, just because you are working on a term paper or problem set, your other goals of finding a romantic partner, getting physically fit, and saving money do not magically disappear—but if you think about them all the time, you won't get your paper finished.

In a sense, the different goals compete inside your mind. Each tries to get you to think about it and work toward it. Not only does the mind have to have a way to set priorities and pursue the top goals, it also needs to keep the others from interfering and distracting you from what you are doing. This process of **goal shielding** sometimes has to keep more important goals at bay. For example, you may regard finding a romantic partner as more important than doing your math homework, but if you spend all your time and energy on your love life, you won't get your homework done.

Goal shielding seems to occur naturally, even automatically.[94] When a person starts working toward one goal, the mind automatically shuts other goals away from consciousness. The more committed a person is to the current goal, the more effectively the mind shields this goal by blocking thoughts of other goals.

Different goals are also associated with different people in one's life. Hence being around certain people, or even thinking of them, can shift priorities among goals. As studies have shown, answering questions about a friend made people more helpful than answering questions about a coworker, presumably because the goal of helping is associated with friends more than with coworkers.[95] Thinking of one's mother primed goals of wanting to do well in school; as a result, thoughts of mother motivated people to try harder and perform better, even on laboratory tasks. And the closer people felt emotionally to their mother, the more strongly the thought of her made them want to do well.[96]

Researchers have identified variations on the basic pattern that thinking of a person activates goals that you associate with that person.[97] The more different goals associated with that person, the less any one of them is activated. And if the other person does not

goal shielding occurs when the activation of a focal goal the person is working on inhibits the accessibility of alternative goals care about the goal, then thinking of him or her does not really get you working toward it. If your mother doesn't happen to care about your schoolwork, then thinking of her won't make you study harder.

One of your textbook authors (Bushman) has a photo of Cael Sanderson in his office. As a college student, Sanderson wrestled at Iowa State University, where he never lost a match (his record was 159–0). He went on to win a gold medal in wrestling at the 2004 Olympics in Athens and is currently the head wrestling coach at Penn State University. Bushman remembers Sanderson as a student in his social psychology class. Now his photo inspires Bushman to work harder and strive for excellence in his own life.

Successful people actually seem to manage their social lives partly on the basis of these mental connections.[98] When they have a goal, they automatically think more about people who will help them reach that goal or who at least support them in pursuing it. They draw closer to those helpful people and spend more time with them. It may seem unromantic to choose among your friends based on who is most helpful for reaching your goals, but probably that strategy contributes to success.

Reaching Goals: What's the Plan?

Once you have a goal, you can start to plan. Planning is beneficial because it focuses attention on how to reach the goal and typically offers specific guidelines for what to do. People who make specific plans are more likely to take steps toward their goals than people who fail to make plans; in fact, laboratory studies have indicated that making plans motivates people to get started working toward their goals.[99] In one study, students agreed to furnish reports within 48 hours on how they spent their Christmas holidays. Some were asked to make specific plans as to when and where they would write the report; for others, it was left up to them to decide later on. The first group were more than twice as likely as the latter to complete the reports on time.[100] Thus, those who made specific plans were more likely to reach their goals than those who did not.

Plans have two main drawbacks. One is that if they are too detailed and rigid, they can be discouraging. Students taking part in a study of planning were encouraged to make either detailed daily plans for their studying, monthly plans, or no plans. The researchers expected the students with the daily plans to succeed the best, but they did not; those who planned by the month did best.[101,102] (Actually, among the very best students, daily plans were very effective and sometimes surpassed the monthly plans. For everyone else, though, monthly plans worked best.)

Why? Trying to plan every day had several disadvantages. For one thing, making such detailed plans is tiresome and time-consuming, so many participants in the study soon stopped making plans altogether. Another, more important reason was that daily plans are too rigid, which can create feelings of stress and frustration as soon as anything deviates from the plan. Detailed daily plans leave no scope for making changes and choices day by day, even if one figures out better ways to do things or encounters unexpected delays. People enjoy making some choices along the way, as opposed to having everything laid out precisely in advance. When things go wrong, a monthly plan can still be followed with some revisions, but the day-by-day plans are defeated, and the daily planners felt discouraged and frustrated as soon as they were behind schedule. Thus, plans and even specific plans are good, but too much detail and a lack of flexibility can undermine them.[103]

The second drawback of plans is that they tend to be overly optimistic. When was the last time you heard a story on the news saying, "Construction of the new building has been completed eight months ahead of schedule, and the total cost was $12 million less than had been projected"? Instead, most projects come in late and over budget. As one famous example, the opera house in Sydney, Australia, now recognized as one of the world's most

Few people achieve perfection in sports or any other domain. Cael Sanderson did it in college wrestling, winning all 159 of his matches. He also won a gold medal in wrestling at the 2004 Olympic Games in Greece. Sanderson was head coach of the wrestling team at Iowa State University, where he wrestled as a student. He is currently the head coach of the wrestling team at Penn State, where he has won several national championships.

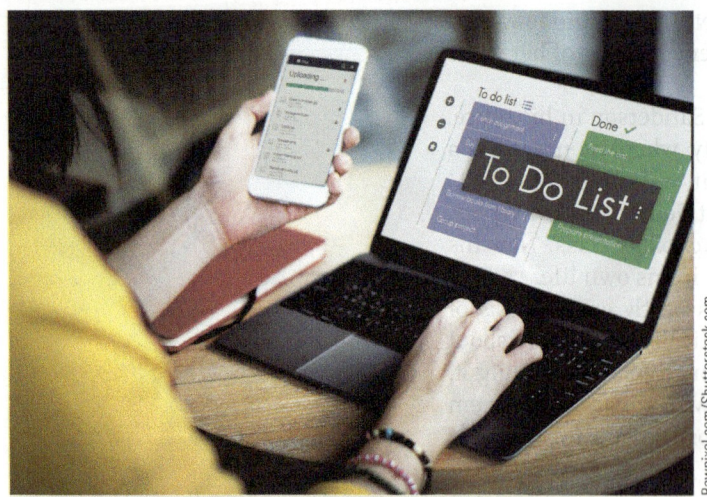

Making daily plans usually is a bad idea.

beautiful and impressive buildings, was started in 1957. The plans said it would cost $7 million and be completed early in 1963. By 1963 it was nowhere near finished and already over budget. The plans were cut back to save time and money, but even so it was not finished until 1973 (10 years late), and the cost had run to more than $100 million![104]

Common Mistakes in Planning

The tendency for plans to underestimate the time and cost probably reflects the optimistic mind-set that people adopt once they have chosen a goal. It is not limited to giant buildings, either. In a very revealing study, students were asked to estimate how long it would take them to finish their thesis, and to furnish both an optimistic estimate and a pessimistic one ("assuming everything went as poorly as it possibly could"). Fewer than a third finished by their best estimate, and fewer than half finished even by their most pessimistic estimate.[105] That is, even when they tried to foresee every possible problem and worst-case scenario, they were still too optimistic. This optimistic bias is related to the **planning fallacy**,[106] defined as the "belief that one's own project will proceed as planned, even while knowing that the vast majority of similar projects have run late."[107]

Another sign that this tendency to make overly optimistic plans comes from people's positive illusions about themselves is that people are pretty accurate at predicting how other people will do. When research participants had to predict how long their roommates or friends would take to complete their projects, the predictions were remarkably accurate. Problems lie not with predicting in general but with the distortions that arise when we think about ourselves. If you want a reliable estimate about how long it will take you to finish some project, don't trust your own judgment—ask someone else who knows you well!

Optimism seems to run wild when the perspective includes a long future; in the short run, people are fairly realistic. People make their short-run decisions based on what seems feasible, whereas long-range decisions are made with less concern for

The Sydney Opera House: Spectacular architectural achievement or catastrophe of planning ... or both?

planning fallacy the tendency for plans to be overly optimistic because the planner fails to allow for unexpected problems practical issues and more attention to how desirable something is. For example, would you rather do a difficult but interesting assignment or an easier but more boring one? If the assignment is due this week, students tend to choose the easy/boring one, whereas if the assignment is not due for a month or two, they pick the difficult/interesting one. In another study, the decision about whether to buy tickets for a show depended mainly on the quality of the show if the show was in the distant future, but if the show was soon, people's decisions depended more on the price of the ticket[108,109] (see **FIGURE 4.2**). As crunch time gets closer, people shift their decision criteria from broad, abstract values toward practical concerns. Thus, one of the biggest differences between long-term planning and dealing with present concerns is the greater pressure of practical constraints on the latter.

In general, people naturally feel more strongly about the present than about the distant future, so the here and now takes precedence over future considerations. But to be successful in life, it is usually necessary to consider the future. Overriding one's immediate wishes and feelings may thus be vital for long-term success. Such overriding requires a powerful ability, called self-regulation, which is far more developed in humans than in other species. Self-regulation, which is important for success in pursuing many goals, is examined in the next section.

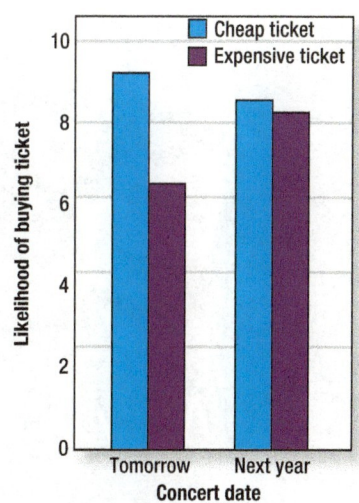

FIGURE **4.2**
The high cost of tickets discouraged people from buying them for an imminent concert, but cost seemed irrelevant if the concert was a year away.[109]

QUIZ YOURSELF
Goals, Plans, Intentions

answers: see pg 147

Self-Regulation and Habits

Control and Willpower

Self-regulation refers to the self's capacity to alter its own responses. It is quite similar to the everyday term "self-control." People regulate their thoughts, their emotions, their impulses and desires, and their task performance. Human beings have a much

self-regulation the self's capacity to alter its own responses; self-control greater capacity for self-regulation than most other creatures, and this is probably a crucial contributor to the human capacity to live in the complex social and cultural worlds we construct. Self-regulation enables people to be flexible, to adapt themselves to many different circumstances, rules, and demands. Self-regulation enables one's social conscience to prevail over selfish impulses, so that people can do what is right and good rather than just indulging their selfish inclinations. In this way, self-regulation enables people to live together and get along much better. This fits the general theme that inner processes serve interpersonal functions. Self-regulation enables people to keep their promises, obey rules, respect others, control their temper, and do other things that make for better interpersonal relations.

Self-regulation predicts success or failure in many different spheres. Most of the problems that afflict people in our society today have some component of inadequate self-regulation: drug and alcohol abuse, addiction, eating disorders, obesity, anxiety and anger control problems, unwanted pregnancy, unsafe sex and sexually transmitted diseases, gambling, overuse of credit cards, debt and bankruptcy, underachievement in school, poor physical fitness, violence and crime, and many more. People who are poor at self-control often end up rejected by their relationship partners, fired by their employers, or even imprisoned for breaking society's laws. People who are good at self-control or self-regulation are more likely to be successful in work, school, relationships, and other important spheres of behavior.[110,111,112,113]

Many people make New Year's resolutions to self-regulate their thoughts and actions. But when you break a resolution, does that mean your self-regulation is poor?

In recent years, various experts have advocated that people make their decisions based on gut feelings, rather than thinking things through. To self-regulation researchers, this sounds like very bad advice, because gut feelings are often swept along by impulsive desires and other momentary feelings. Indeed, the very purpose of self-control is often to restrain gut feelings such as rage, greed, and lust.

Standards: Ideas That Guide Self-Regulation

Effective self-regulation has three main components: standards, monitoring, and strength. The term *standards* was introduced in Chapter 3; it refers to concepts (ideas) of how things might or should be. In Chapter 3 we focused on how people compare themselves to standards, but it is more complicated than that. When people find they do not measure up to their ideals or goals, they often try to change themselves. Having clear standards that do not conflict is important for successful self-regulation. If you don't know what you want to be, it is very difficult to change yourself toward that goal.

Standards can be supplied by the culture. Thus, they represent an important way in which culture can influence behavior. Culture can tell people the right or good way to act. Part of the long road to social acceptance involves learning what the standards are—what is fashionable, acceptable, cool, or morally proper. Many youngsters find the early teen years to be especially difficult and unhappy, because their social life is changing, and it is hard to learn the new standards amid a changing peer group.

Many standards, especially the ones learned from culture, involve what not to do: Don't lie, cheat, steal, spit on the floor, say forbidden words, cut in line, betray a friend, talk back to your teacher, drive when drunk, and so forth. Eight of the Ten Commandments in Judeo-Christian religion specifically say what not to do, and even the other two (honoring parents and keeping the Sabbath day holy) implicitly refer to things that should not be done. As we have repeatedly seen, nature says go and culture says stop. The culture's "stop" rules are standards, and self-regulation is required to implement them.

Monitoring: Watching What You're Doing

The second component of self-control is **monitoring**—keeping track of the behaviors or responses you want to regulate. Indeed, some experts believe that the central purpose of self-awareness (focusing attention on the self) is to promote self-regulation, because as you watch yourself you can monitor how well you are changing to reach your goals or other standards.[114,115] Without self-awareness, self-regulation would be difficult, if not impossible.

The way people monitor themselves is typically summarized as a feedback loop (see **FIGURE 4.3**). An easy-to-remember acronym is **TOTE**, which stands for Test, Operate, Test, and Exit.[116,117] The first test is a comparison of self against the standard. For example, if you have resolved to be nicer to your romantic partner, you may occasionally stop to consider how nice you have been toward that person today. If the test reveals a discrepancy—that is, you are not being as nice as you would like—then you

Culture often tells us those things we cannot do, as displayed in this German sign.

move along to the "operate" phase, in which you exert conscious control to change yourself to become nicer. You might remind yourself to say nice things, or perhaps purchase a small gift to express your appreciation to your partner. At some point in the "operate" phase, you may test the self again. Am I being nice enough now? If the answer is no, then more operations (more changes to the self) are required. Eventually, perhaps, the answer is "yes," indicating that you have met the standard, and at this point you can complete the loop by exiting it.

The concept of feedback loops is borrowed from cybernetic theory, developed during and after World War II to help guide missiles toward their targets despite winds and other difficulties.[118] Its most familiar illustration is the thermostat that helps regulate the temperature in a room: The test involves evaluating whether the current temperature is close to the level at which the thermostat has been set, and the "operate" phase involves turning on the heater or air conditioning unit; when another test reveals that the temperature has reached the desired level, the heater or air conditioner is shut off and the loop is exited.

Monitoring is a key ingredient in self-regulation and often presents the best opportunity for immediate improvement in self-regulation. If you want to keep to an exercise program, write on the calendar each day whether you had a workout. If you want to save money, make a list of what you spend your money on each day, and keep closer track of how much you earn and how much you save.

Dieting furnishes a good example of the importance of monitoring. If you are not dieting, you likely pay little or no attention to how much you eat—you may simply eat your fill. Dieters, in contrast, soon begin to keep a close watch on how much they eat and how fattening these foods are (hence the familiar expression "counting calories"). When dieters eat in settings that undermine monitoring, they eat more. In particular, eating while watching television has long been known to increase calorie intake, mainly because people focus their attention on the television program and not on monitoring how much they consume.[119] Likewise, people overeat at parties, where their attention is focused on the other people and activities rather than on how much they eat.[120]

An important study linked eating binges to failures in monitoring.[121] For this purpose, some dieters were induced to break their diet for the day of the experiment, whereas other dieters kept on their diets. Then both groups, plus a sample of nondieters, ate a snack of as many tiny sandwiches as they wanted. Afterward, the researchers asked everyone to

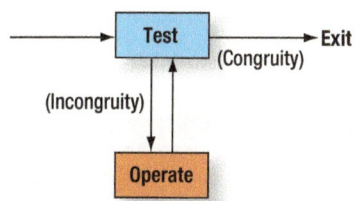

FIGURE 4.3

TOTE (Test, Operate, Test, Exit) model. The first test is a comparison of self against the standard. In the "operate" phase, match behavior to the standard. Then test again to see if the match is close enough. If it is not close enough, keep trying. If it is close enough, stop changing behavior (exit).[115,116]

monitoring keeping track of behaviors or responses to be regulated

TOTE an acronym for the self-regulation feedback loop of Test, Operate, Test, Exit estimate how much she or he had eaten. The nondieters were pretty accurate, as were the dieters whose diets had remained intact. But the dieters who had broken their diets made wildly inaccurate estimates of how many tiny sandwiches they had consumed. Apparently once their diet was broken, they stopped keeping track, which then enabled them to eat a great deal without realizing it.

Many factors interfere with monitoring and thereby undermine self-regulation, including emotional distress and being distracted, but probably the most widely recognized and important factor is alcohol intoxication. One effect of alcohol, even in mild doses, is to reduce attention to self,[122] and as we have seen, without monitoring (attending to) yourself, it is very difficult to self-regulate effectively. Hence, people who have consumed alcohol tend to be worse at self-regulating in almost every sphere of behavior that has been studied. Intoxicated people eat more than sober people, perform more violent and aggressive acts, spend more money, smoke more cigarettes, and engage in more inappropriate sexual behavior—and, yes, drinking alcohol even leads to drinking more alcohol when drinkers stop keeping track of how much they drink.[123,124,125,126,127]

Willpower for Change

The third ingredient of self-regulation is the **capacity for change**. This refers to what goes on in the "operate" phase, during which people actually carry out the changes to their states or responses so as to bring them into line with the standards. This capacity corresponds to the popular notion of "willpower," and in fact it does seem to operate like a strength or energy.

Willpower can become depleted when people use it. In an influential early demonstration of this principle,[128] participants arrived having skipped a meal, so most were hungry. The researchers baked fresh chocolate chip cookies in the laboratory, which filled the room with a delicious and tempting aroma. Each participant was seated at a table in front of a stack of these cookies and delectable chocolates, as well as a bowl of radishes. In the important condition, the experimenter told each participant, "You have been assigned to the radish condition," which meant they were supposed to eat only radishes. The experimenter then left the participant alone for five minutes to eat. This task required considerable willpower to resist the tempting chocolates and cookies and eat only the radishes as instructed. In other conditions, participants were permitted to eat cookies and chocolate instead of radishes, or no food was present at all. After this, the participants were set to work on some difficult (actually unsolvable) problems, and the researchers measured how long people kept trying before they gave up, because willpower is also needed to keep trying when you feel discouraged and want to quit. Consistent with the theory that willpower gets used up, the participants in the radish condition quit sooner than participants in the other two conditions. Thus, resisting temptation (in the form of chocolates and cookies) used up some willpower, so those participants had less left over to help them keep working on the frustrating puzzles. The results are depicted in **FIGURE 4.4**.

capacity for change the active phase of self-regulation; willpower

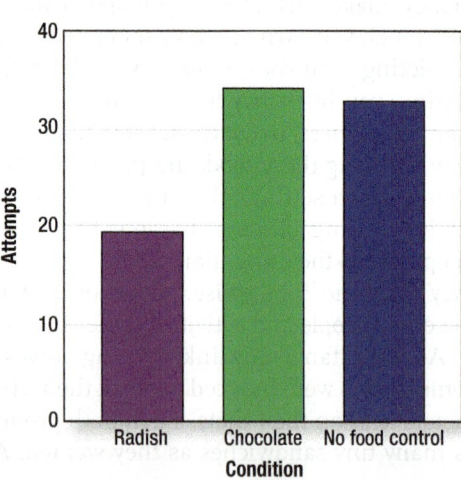

FIGURE 4.4
People who exercised self-control by eating radishes instead of chocolate gave up more easily on difficult tasks.[129]

A more appealing interpretation of these results would be that eating chocolate made people stronger and more effective. Unfortunately for that view, the participants who ate chocolate were no different from the control participants who ate nothing at all. It was resisting temptation, rather than indulging in chocolate, that was responsible for the experimental results.[129] Thus, willpower can be important for regulating one's eating; in fact, dieting is one of the most common behaviors that depends on self-regulation. To learn more about self-regulation in dieting, see *Food for Thought*.

Researchers in many fields have documented different ways that self-control breaks down when people deplete their willpower. Health professionals sometimes stop bothering to wash their hands late in the day, and medical doctors prescribe too many antibiotics. A recent study identified an intriguing source of demands on willpower: jobs that require the worker to put on a happy, cheerful face, such as an airline flight attendant, food server, salesperson, or receptionist.[130] People in such jobs have to regulate their emotional expressions all day. After work, such individuals are especially likely to drink alcohol, including heavy drinking.

FOOD FOR *Thought*

Dieting as Self-Regulation

Many people seek to control and restrain their eating and will therefore refrain from eating some tempting food even when it is readily available to them. (Hardly any nonhuman animals do this!) Partly this reflects the progress of culture at providing food. Like most other animals, humans evolved under conditions of periodic scarcities of food, so nature designed human bodies to keep and store food as much as possible. Now that much of the world lives amid ample available food, the body's natural tendency to store fat has turned from a life-saving asset to a life-endangering liability. Beginning in 2003, experts calculated that more humans worldwide suffer from obesity than are in danger of starving. The problem is too much food, not too little.

Dieting—restricting one's food intake—is the standard response, but it requires self-regulation in order to override the natural desire to eat. What can self-regulation theory tell you about how to succeed? Consider the three main ingredients of self-regulation.

The first is a commitment to standards. A standard would be your goal in terms of weight (or perhaps body measurements such as waist size, or even percentage of body fat). It is helpful to have a realistic idea of what you should weigh. This is a high-level goal that may preside over the whole dieting process (which may take months). It is helpful to set lower-level goals, such as losing a pound or two each week. Many dieters also find it helpful to set standards for food intake, such as not eating more than 1,500 calories per day.

The second ingredient is monitoring. This means keeping track of what you eat, how many calories you consume, and perhaps how much you weigh. External monitoring helps: Rather than relying on memory, keep a journal or diary that records what you eat each day. Also avoid eating in front of the television and other distractions, so you can be aware of how much you eat. If you don't keep track, you are not likely to succeed. Research shows that when dieters break their diets, they often stop keeping track and hence lose any sense of how much they are eating. This can produce an eating binge: You know you are eating too much, but you don't really know how much. The importance of monitoring means that it is important to eat under circumstances in which keeping track of food is possible.

Monitoring weight is another key aspect of dieting. Here the conventional wisdom suggested an exception to the rule to monitor closely. Folk wisdom said that weighing yourself every day can be discouraging because weight fluctuates,

Sometimes, low level thoughts take precedence...

...no matter how high minded we try to be.

Paula Wright 2012

so weighing yourself once a week was supposed to be best. Several well-controlled studies have now shown that self-regulation theory is correct after all: People who weigh themselves every day are most successful at losing weight and at keeping it off.[137]

The third ingredient is willpower, or the capacity for change. The self's strength is used for many different activities, and it can be depleted if there are many other demands. An ideal time for dieting is a period of low stress or pressure, stable relationships, and few demands for major decisions. When your willpower is depleted from coping with stress or deadlines, making hard decisions, resisting temptation, or making other efforts to change the self, you will have less strength available for effective dieting. Experiments have shown that dieters eat more when their willpower is depleted.[138]

How does one acquire or increase willpower? Some evidence indicates that willpower resembles a muscle.[131,132] Regular exercise makes you stronger, even though the muscle is temporarily "tired" after a workout. When people perform regular self-control exercises, they show gradual improvements in their capacity for self-control, even on novel tasks. Such exercises may include trying to improve your posture, keep track of what you eat, speak in complete sentences, and use your nondominant hand (your left hand if you're right-handed) to brush your teeth or open doors. Over the long run, these exercises will strengthen your capacity for self-regulation. Just don't perform them right before you are going to need your willpower because that would be like lifting weights shortly before you have to carry furniture.

Willpower and Decision Fatigue

Many people have an intuitive sense that their willpower fluctuates and so their self-control may get stronger or weaker at different points in the day. But did you know that making decisions also takes willpower? Exerting self-control and making hard choices thus depend on the same supply of energy, and either can affect the other.

One sign that making decisions depletes willpower is that people have poorer self-control after making choices. A series of studies showed that people who made a series of choices later performed worse at self-control.[133] For example, choosing what consumer products they might want caused people to give up faster on a test that required holding one's hand in ice water—a classic lab test of self-control. In a similar vein, students who made choices about what courses to take in the future, or choices about their current course (such as what topics to cover and what educational films to show) did worse thereafter on various lab tests of self-control, such as persevering in solving anagrams.

Such information may have practical consequences. People who have to make many decisions during the day may deplete their willpower, leaving them prone to do things they will regret in the evening, such as eating or drinking too much, or even engaging in sexual or aggressive misbehavior.

Depleted willpower can impair decision making too.[134] When energy is low, decision making changes in various ways, mostly designed to avoid effort. People may prefer to postpone decisions, in effect "deciding not to decide." Their choices are more subject to bias, because they don't think carefully enough to rule out irrelevant factors that could distort the decision. Depleted decision makers also show less tendency to compromise, instead adopting simpler, rigid criteria.

When you have many decisions to make, it is useful to conserve your willpower so as to be able to make the later ones effectively. For example, when you buy a new car, you often must make a long series of decisions. Research has shown that people become increasingly likely to take the standard or default option as they go along, regardless of what the order of decisions is.[135] That is, on the early choices they think hard and choose just what they want, but on the later decisions they tend to take whatever the manufacturer recommends—which can end up increasing the cost of the car significantly. They seemed to suffer from a kind of **decision fatigue**: Having used up their energy on early choices, they took the easy way out on the later ones.

Indeed, a recent study of just this sort of decision fatigue among parole judges raised some disturbing questions about fairness in the legal system. A long-running joke among lawyers asks, "What is justice?" and answers, "Whatever the judge had for breakfast!" Researchers went through the records of parole judges in Israel. These are decisions about whether a particular convict should be released into the community (presumably because he had reformed) or sent back to prison. The easy and safe decision is simply to send him back to prison, because the judge's reputation is at risk if he approves parole and the released convict commits another crime. Nonetheless, some prisoners have earned the right to be paroled, and the judge must decide.

The researchers found a remarkable pattern.[136] As the day wore on, the judge's decisions became increasingly simple and harsh. The prisoners who came before the judge early in the day, when the judge's willpower was high thanks to a good night's sleep and breakfast, had pretty good odds of being granted parole. Those who came before him (all judges and prisoners were men in this study) late in the day were generally sent back to

decision fatigue a state of depleted willpower caused by making decisions, which can affect subsequent decisions by causing people to fail to think and choose carefully prison. The only exceptions came right after the judge was able to replenish his energy: after a mid-morning snack break and especially after lunch.

Habits

The previous section focused on self-control, which consists of using deliberate effort to control your actions. **Habits** are in some ways the opposite. Habits occur with relatively little control by the deliberate system. The human mind appears to be set up to use the deliberate system to acquire new behaviors, but as these become performed over and over, they are gradually transferred to the automatic system. To say someone acted out of habit is to say that the person did not necessarily consider the action or alternatives, did not try to perform or resist that action, and may even have been scarcely aware of what they were doing.

Using a bad habit to satisfy a goal is a bad idea. For example, some students pull an "all-nighter" to prepare for an exam.

How common are habits? Some studies have sought to find out by having people wear beepers and stop and record what they are doing whenever the beeper goes off (at random intervals throughout the day). By assembling these reports, researchers can develop a broad picture of what people do, and how often. One conclusion from these studies is that almost half the actions people do are things they do pretty much every day in the same place.[139] This suggests that most people have plenty of habits and use them often.

Habits may seem like trouble, such as when people apologize that they did something inappropriate because of "force of habit." Someone may set out to drive to a store and instead follow the habitual route to work or home. Yet habits are not generally opposed to one's goals. According to an influential theory,[140] habits are vestiges of past efforts at pursuing goals. In the driving example, the mistake of driving to work instead of the store may occur because usually your goal is to drive to work.

If anything, current goals are often simply missing from the habitual behavior and irrelevant to it. As one performs the same actions in the same situation over and over, that action becomes associated with that situation or with other relevant cues. Being in that situation sets off automatic processes to enact the behavior just like on other occasions. The deliberate system, one's current goals, and other factors may be completely out of the process. Habits become detached from your current goals and operate on their own. Many people report "habit slips," that is, doing something out of habit that is not helpful toward their current goal. Such things happen to the average person about six times each week.[141]

Eating popcorn while watching a movie is a habit for some people and not others. Researchers gave people free popcorn at the start of one movie. Half the people got delicious, fresh popcorn, but the rest got stale popcorn that had been made a week ago. When people were asked to rate the popcorn, not surprisingly, the fresh popcorn was rated as more tasty than the stale popcorn regardless of habit. When it came to how much people ate, however, habits made a big difference. The people who had the habit of eating popcorn at the movies ate just as much popcorn, regardless of whether it was fresh or stale. Meanwhile, people who did not have a popcorn habit ate plenty when it was tasty but ate considerably less of the stale stuff.[142]

But goals are not completely irrelevant to habits. For one thing, they promote the learning of habits. People get the habit of driving a particular way because it took them to their usual goal (e.g., home). Actions that repeatedly help you reach your goals are more likely than others to become habits and indeed strong habits.[143]

Even more important, habits can help sustain pursuit of goals when willpower is low. Success in college, for example, depends on lots of studying. Most students want to succeed, but at various times their motivation (their desire to succeed) may feel weaker than others, and their self-control may also be at a low point. Good study habits can help sustain the effort even when one doesn't feel like it. Recent evidence has shown that during stressful periods, such as exam weeks (when energy is low because of external demands), students act more habitually.[144] For example, those who had a habit of eating a healthy

habit an acquired behavior that, if followed regularly, will become almost automatic breakfast were more likely to do so. Meanwhile those who had a habit of eating unhealthy breakfasts ate more unhealthy foods. In fact, those who had a habit of reading the newspaper became all the more likely to read it during exams week—even though during exams they should in theory be studying for exams, not reading the paper!

Thus, goals can also conflict with habits. What exactly is bad about bad habits? Eating candy at the movies can be a bad habit, because it conflicts with goals to be healthy, fit, and slim. True, the candy probably served another goal, of enjoying oneself and tasting something good. But this merely shows that people sometimes have conflicting goals. One helpful approach is to remove oneself from the situations that trigger the habit. For example, when people want to quit smoking, they may find that it is easier to do on vacation or after moving to a new home because they are not constantly confronted with the cues and situations that usually triggered the impulse to smoke.

Clearly self-control is often needed to break habits. When self-control resources are depleted, people tend to fall back into bad habits. In a field experiment, participants first identified bad habits they were seeking to break, such as drinking alcohol on weeknights, or good habits they wanted to acquire, such as being punctual to class meetings. On some days, they were randomly assigned tasks to deplete their self-control, such as using their left hand for things they normally did with the right hand. Those days were marked by low success at regulating habits: They were more likely to drink alcohol despite its being a weeknight, or more likely to be late to class.[145]

Without habits, life would be exhausting because every action would require deliberate control. As made clear in Chapter 2, the deliberate system takes effort and energy, whereas the automatic system works much more easily and efficiently. The human mind naturally acquires habits to conserve its energy. Sometimes these habits create problems and require considerable mental exertion to break. But that is the price of getting the benefits of being able to do plenty of daily activities without a struggle. Life would be considerably more difficult without habits.

QUIZ YOURSELF
Self-Regulation and Habits

1. **Self-regulation is most similar to which of the following concepts?**
   - (a) Self-awareness
   - (b) Self-consciousness
   - (c) Self-control
   - (d) Self-esteem

2. **Which of the following refers to a concept or idea of how things could be?**
   - (a) Capacity for change
   - (b) Self-consciousness
   - (c) Self-monitoring
   - (d) Standards

3. **Which common household device best illustrates a feedback loop?**
   - (a) Dishwasher
   - (b) Thermostat
   - (c) Toilet
   - (d) Vacuum

4. **What body part does willpower most resemble?**
   - (a) Bone
   - (b) Eye
   - (c) Muscle
   - (d) Stomach

answers: see pg 147

Irrationality and Self-Destruction

Self-regulation, discussed in the previous section, can help people do what is rational, in the sense of what will produce the best results for them in the long run. We turn now from rational behavior and enlightened self-interest to their opposite: irrational and self-destructive behavior.

Self-Defeating Acts: Being Your Own Worst Enemy

"She has self-destructive tendencies." "The other team didn't beat us, we beat ourselves." "I think he has some kind of death wish." How often have you heard such expressions? They refer to the common belief that people sometimes do things to bring failure, suffering, or misfortune upon themselves. The psychological term for such actions is **self-defeating behavior**. In everyday language, when people say what someone did was "stupid," they usually mean that it was self-defeating. The "stupid" actions are those that bring about some result contrary to what the person sought, especially if the person might or should have known better.

Self-defeating behavior is paradoxical. Why would self-destructive behavior ever occur? If rational behavior means doing what serves one's enlightened self-interest, how could rational beings do things that are harmful or detrimental to the self? Self-defeating behavior seems to be irrational in the extreme.

Yet without a doubt people do plenty of self-defeating things. Many smoke cigarettes, thereby exposing themselves to lung cancer and other diseases. They eat unhealthy foods, thereby shortening their lives. They engage in risky sex, thereby increasing their chances of getting diseases or creating an unwanted pregnancy. They waste their money or gamble it away. They fail to take their medicine or follow physicians' orders, thereby preventing themselves from regaining health. The list goes on and on.

Most theories assume that psychological processes are designed to increase safety, security, and happiness, and ultimately to increase survival and reproduction. Self-defeating behavior is the opposite. It challenges psychological theory to explain how self-defeating behavior can be reconciled with the general assumption that people behave in adaptive, rational, self-benefiting ways. Many theories have been proposed, including Sigmund Freud's famous conclusion that people have an innate "death drive" that impels them to pursue their own downfall and death.[146] A more recent version of this theory holds that many people, especially women, suffer from a "fear of success." The fear-of-success theory was proposed by Matina Horner,[147] herself the president of one of the most prestigious women's colleges (Radcliffe), who said that many young women believed that if they became too successful in their work, they would end up lonely, rejected, and unable to find romantic partners. Because of this fear of success, she theorized, many women sabotage, or at least curtail, their careers.

After many decades of research, social psychologists have begun to establish the main facts about self-defeating behavior. A first conclusion is that people almost never directly seek failure, suffering, or misfortune. Freud's theory of a death drive is apparently wrong. People may perform self-destructive acts, but they do not generally do them out of self-destructive intentions. Likewise, carefully controlled studies have discredited the "fear of success" theory.[148] We have no proof that people ever intentionally sabotage their careers or their work because they consciously (or unconsciously) fear what success will mean for them.

Instead, there appear to be two main reasons for self-defeating behavior. One of these involves tradeoffs: Sometimes good and bad outcomes are linked, and in order to get the desired, good outcome, people accept the bad one too. The example of cigarette smoking illustrates this pattern. Yes, smoking causes cancer and other diseases, but hardly anyone decides to smoke in order to get cancer. People smoke for the pleasures and rewards of smoking, including the immediate and pleasant sensations caused by nicotine, and possibly the benefits of impressing others that one is sexy, cool, or mature. They accept some increased risk of lung cancer in order to reap the benefits.

A vivid self-defeating tradeoff was covered in Chapter 3 in *Tradeoffs: Self-Handicapping*. In self-handicapping, you will recall, people create obstacles to their own performance so as to furnish themselves with an excuse for possible failure. The self-handicapper thus sacrifices real chances at success in exchange for protection from the implications of failure.[149] If you are drunk when taking a test, you will likely perform worse than if you were sober—but you are safe from being proven incompetent because even if you perform badly on the test, people will attribute the failure to the alcohol rather than to low ability. (They may question your judgment for getting drunk

self-defeating behavior any action by which people bring failure, suffering, or misfortune on themselves

Many self-defeating behaviors trade off long-term costs for short-term pleasures or benefits.

Irrationality and Self-Destruction | **141**

before the test, but if you are like many people, you'd rather be seen as undisciplined and fun-loving than as stupid and incompetent.)

Self-defeating tradeoffs are especially likely when the reward is immediate and the cost delayed. We noted in Chapter 2 that this was one common kind of tradeoff (now versus the future). Cigarettes offer immediate pleasure, whereas the cancer and death they may bring lie in the distant future. Many self-defeating acts have this characteristic

capacity to delay gratification the ability to make immediate sacrifices for later rewards

Now Versus Tomorrow: Delay of Gratification

Some people spend their money on fun today rather than save for a rainy day. Some people skimp on medical or dental care in favor of things they would rather do. Some people pursue sexual pleasure without worrying about future consequences. In these and other ways, people come to grief. What these self-defeating behaviors have in common is emphasizing the present over the future. However, human beings thrive and prosper best when they can sacrifice some short-term rewards for the sake of a better future. The ability to make those immediate sacrifices for later rewards is called the **capacity to delay gratification**.

During the 1960s, Walter Mischel and his colleagues developed a clever laboratory method for testing children's capacity to delay gratification.[150,151] Each child would be shown some treat, such as a cookie or a marshmallow. The experimenter would explain to each child that the experimenter was going to leave the room, but the child could summon them back by ringing a bell on the table. As soon as the child did this, the child would receive the treat. However, if the child could refrain from ringing the bell and just wait until the adult returned, the child would get a bigger reward (e.g., two cookies instead of one). Some children were able to wait and get the larger reward; others succumbed to temptation and rang the bell.

Mischel's task is a classic tradeoff dilemma: whether to take the sooner smaller reward or wait for the larger later one. As we have seen elsewhere in this book, many tradeoffs involve time, especially pitting something right now versus something in the future. Research using this "delay of gratification" measure has provided the foundations for what we now know about self-regulation, as well as shedding valuable light on self-defeating behavior.

Seeing either the large or the small reward undermined the capacity to hold out. Apparently, seeing what you want stimulates a greater desire for it. Temptation is best resisted by avoiding the sight or thought of it. Many of the children sitting in the room with the bell and the marshmallows came up with this strategy themselves: They would cover their eyes so as not to see the rewards (and be tempted by them), sing, turn around, make up little games, or even take a nap during the waiting period.

Even going to college is an exercise in delay of gratification. Most college students could earn more money, live in a nicer apartment, eat better food, and afford a better car and more expensive clothes if they dropped out and got a job. College often requires living near the poverty line for several years, but its long-term payoffs are immense: As we saw in Chapter 2, a person with a college degree is likely to earn nearly $2 million more than one who does not over the course of a 30-year career.

The benefits of being able to delay gratification also emerged in Mischel's subsequent research. He followed up with many of the children years after they had participated in his experiments. Very few psychological traits seem to remain stable from early childhood into adulthood, and fewer yet have been shown to predict success or failure in life. The children who were good at delaying gratification when they were just 4 years old, however, grew into adults who were more popular with friends and family and more successful in universities and jobs than those who had not been able to resist taking the quick marshmallow in his lab.[152,153] Thus, as they moved through life, being able to resist the impulse to take the immediate payoff really did seem to bring them greater rewards in the long run!

Scholars wonder about whether poor self-control contributes to poverty and inequality. One theory is that people end up poor because they lack self-control and pursue immediate rewards. (Indeed, criminals often have poor self-control, which is a central factor in their criminality.[154]) If poor children lack self-control, perhaps they learned or inherited those traits from their poor parents. A different theory holds that it is rational not to pursue delayed gratification in an unstable, unreliable environment—and poor children are more likely than rich ones to grow up in such an environment. If your parent promises you a treat next week, can you count on it being delivered? If not, then perhaps the sensible thing to do is take what you can get right away. Lab studies have shown that when children get the impression that the adults in the environment are not reliable and trustworthy, they take the immediate reward rather than waiting for delay.[155] Which theory is correct? Further work will tell whether either, neither, or both links poor self-control to low social status.

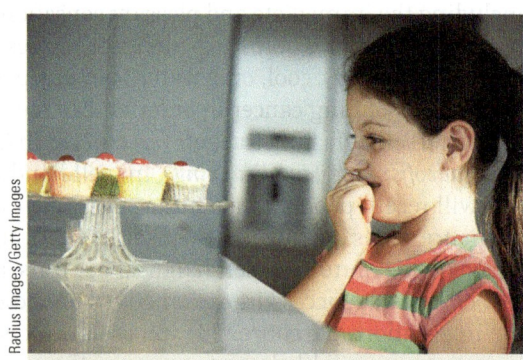

The ability to delay gratification as a child is a good predictor of later success in life.

of sacrificing the future for the sake of the present. Regarding the capacity to give up immediate pleasures for the sake of long-term or delayed benefits, see *Tradeoffs*.

The second pathway to self-defeating behavior involves faulty knowledge and a reliance on strategies that don't work. As with tradeoffs, the person is usually pursuing something positive and good, but the self-defeater chooses a strategy that backfires. Often people do not adequately understand what is effective in the world, either because they do not understand the world, or they do not understand themselves correctly. For example, some people procrastinate because they believe that "I do my best work under pressure"[156]—that work left till the last minute will actually end up being better. This is generally false: Leaving things until the last minute typically makes it harder to do an adequate job. Thus, they think that putting things off will help them do better work, but actually it makes them do poorer work. Students who procrastinate get lower grades than other students.[157] When people are tested under identical laboratory conditions, chronic procrastinators perform worse than others, not better.[158] In short, the claim that "I do my best work under pressure" is a false rationalization for almost everyone, and it is particularly false for procrastinators.

Suicide

Suicide has fascinated psychologists and other social scientists for more than a century. At first blush, suicide is the extreme of irrational, self-destructive behavior because it brings a permanent end to the person's chances for happiness or success. People who believe that humans are created by a divine power generally regard suicide as a major sin because it thwarts their god's wishes. People who believe in evolution cannot understand how natural selection would produce an impulse to end one's own life because it goes against the most basic urges toward survival and reproduction. (At most, they might think that sacrificing oneself for one's children might make biological sense, but that would only explain a tiny minority of suicides.) Suicide is rare among nonhuman animals. Basically, humans are the only creatures who deliberately kill themselves, and many millions have done so.[159] How can this be explained?

Suicide often involves a tradeoff, which as we have seen is one major pathway to self-destructive behavior. Indeed, it often fits the now-versus-future pattern that we have seen as a common tradeoff in human decision making. Suicidal people are often in life circumstances that are acutely unpleasant to them, and their overriding wish is to escape from their emotional distress and feelings of personal worthlessness. They feel miserable and want those feelings to stop. To them, death may seem appealing, not as punishment or violence or suffering (as some theories have proposed) but simply as oblivion. They believe that death will bring peace and an end to their distress and suffering, which looks like an improvement to them. They are willing to trade away their future and all its potential joys in order to gain this immediate relief.

Suicide starts with some discrepancy between expectations (or other standards) and reality. Ironically, suicide rates are often highest in favorable circumstances, such as in rich countries, in places with good climates, or during the fine months of late spring and summer. To be miserable when all around your life seems great for everyone else can be deeply disturbing. Often the suicidal process is set in motion by a significant change for the worse, so that the present seems to fall short of what one has come to expect. For example, rich and poor people commit suicide at about the same rates, but changing from rich to poor produces a big increase in suicide rates. (Going from poor to rich is no problem!) Put another way, suicide does not result from being poor all your life but rather from becoming poor when you are accustomed to being rich. Suicidal college students actually have higher grade point averages than other students—except in their most recent semester, when their grades dipped below average, which probably made them feel that they were falling below what they had come to expect of themselves. Suicidal college students often have parents who expect them to perform well, and the students sometimes feel they cannot meet their parents' expectations.[160,161,162,163,164,165]

Self-awareness is high among suicidal people; indeed, the human capacity for self-awareness may help explain why nonhuman animals hardly ever kill themselves. In the section on self-awareness in Chapter 3, we saw that people sometimes seek to escape from self-awareness when self-awareness is unpleasant. Suicidal people have often reached this point where self-awareness is acutely painful, and the attempt at suicide may be a desperate, extreme effort to stop ruminating about themselves.[166] In the weeks leading up to a suicide attempt, the person is typically full of thoughts of being a failure, a worthless individual, or an immoral person. Some feel cut off from others, and this too is profoundly upsetting.

You might think that suicidal people would be full of emotional distress, such as anxiety, regret, and guilt, but most studies have found the opposite: Suicidal people tend to be emotionally numb. Apparently, their problems are so upsetting that they respond by shutting down emotionally. They try to avoid thinking about the future or the past and avoid all sorts of abstract, meaningful, or emotional material, focusing instead on the concrete here and now. In the movies, suicide notes are often philosophical: "I've had a good run, but I don't find my life worth living any further; please teach my son to be a good man." In reality, suicide notes tend to be mundane and concrete, such as "I paid the electric bill; tell Fred he can have my video games."[167,168,169,170]

The human mind cannot easily stop thinking meaningfully, and these unfortunate people find that they cannot really keep their thoughts and feelings at bay. Suicide starts to look appealing because it is a way to put an end to the distressing thoughts about how bad the self is. Although suicide trades away one's future for the sake of relief in the here and now, the suicidal person often does not reflect on that because he or she is narrowly focused on the present and not thinking about the future. It is not so much a rejection of one's entire life as an attempt to escape from this week's numbing misery. If you are ever confronted with a friend or relative who is suicidal, besides getting professional help, one emphasis should be to help that person refocus on long-term goals and the pleasures and fulfillments that can still be found in the distant future, regardless of how miserable the present or near future may seem.

Another factor that pushes people toward suicide is burdensomeness.[170] Many suicidal individuals are acutely aware of being a burden to others, and they hate that feeling. For example, imagine a man who has long supported his family and after losing his job finds that he has to rely on others to support him. He may start to believe that the people he loves would be better off without him. Therefore, he commits suicide as an act of kindness toward them, relieving them of the burden. Such feelings of guilt may be linked to human nature as cultural animals. People depend on each other and feel bad when they cannot provide for others or reciprocate what others do for them.

No single theory can account for all suicides. The desire to escape from misery may be the most common, but there are other pathways to suicide. This chapter opened with the story of a female terrorist who was prepared to give her own life, and nearly had to do so, in order to destroy a plane full of South Korean tourists. She believed, falsely as it turned out, that killing those people would prevent South Korea from holding the Olympics and would lead to the reunification of her country.

Suicide bombers have been in the news in recent years. The most dramatic were the Arabs who hijacked several airline flights and crashed them into the World Trade Center and the Pentagon on September 11, 2001. Since then, numerous suicide bombers have given their lives to kill other people in various countries in the Middle East and occasionally elsewhere. These people sacrifice themselves to advance a cause such as religion or country, not to escape from a personal hell. (Indeed, some believe they would go directly to heaven for successfully performing their "mission.") Such self-sacrifice represents a commitment to cultural meanings that can override the basic biological drives toward survival and reproduction. Even if one regards them as misguided, futile, or evil, they show how cultural meanings can override biological impulses and cause people to put cultural goals above their own self-interest. Only cultural animals become suicide bombers.

QUIZ YOURSELF
Irrationality and Self-Destruction

1. In everyday terms, self-defeating behavior is defined as _____ behavior.
   - (a) experimental
   - (b) intelligent
   - (c) stupid
   - (d) taboo

2. The two main reasons for self-defeating behavior are _____ .
   - (a) death drive; fear of failure
   - (b) faulty knowledge; tradeoffs
   - (c) fear of failure; tradeoffs
   - (d) faulty knowledge; fear of failure

3. What creatures intentionally kill themselves (i.e., commit suicide)?
   - (a) Chimps
   - (b) Gorillas
   - (c) Humans
   - (d) All of the above

4. Suicidal people are _____ .
   - (a) low in self-awareness
   - (b) high in self-awareness
   - (c) high in self-handicapping
   - (d) focused on future consequences

answers: see pg 147

What Makes Us Human

Putting the Cultural Animal in Perspective

Behavior occurs among all animals, all the time. What sets humans apart (among other things that will be discussed in other chapters) is an elaborate inner system for controlling behavior. The use of meaning enables human beings to make choices in novel ways and to link their here-and-now actions to far distant realities. Other animals, in contrast, just follow their instincts and respond to the here and now.

Only humans vote in elections, pay taxes, hold wedding ceremonies, make blueprints for the buildings they construct, resort to judges and lawsuits to resolve disputes, create and attend schools and colleges, pray, plan their battles, or celebrate events that occurred before they were born. Animals have sex, but only humans distinguish between meaningless and meaningful sexual relationships. Animals play, but only humans keep score, have referees, and distinguish between meaningful and meaningless games (as in whether the game has playoff implications).

Animals may have a limited understanding of what is happening now, but only humans seem to enrich their understanding of the present by thoughtful links to events in the distant past and future. Indeed, human goals often link what one does now to possible outcomes that lie years away. Thus, human action is not just a here-and-now response but is often designed to help bring about something far off, such as graduation or marriage or retirement. it can also be linked to things that have happened elsewhere or long ago, such as when people celebrate Independence Day or a religious holiday. Moreover, people often follow abstract rules made in distant places by people they will never meet. Most Americans pay income tax, for example, though few have any direct contact with the people who make the tax laws.

Consciousness enables people to use complex reasoning processes to make their decisions via the deliberate system. They can think about multiple options and do cost–benefit analyses to decide the best course of action.

Self-regulation is not uniquely human, but it seems far better developed among humans than among other species. Our capacity for self-control makes many aspects of human culture possible because it enables us to change ourselves. We can adjust to new norms and opportunities, to changing fads and fashions, to religious doctrines, to new roles and rules. Self-regulation is the key to morality and virtuous behavior, for without the ability to alter one's actions based on general rules, there would be no point in having moral rules. Humans also use self-regulation in ways that other animals don't, ranging from how American football players abruptly stop trying to knock their opponents down when the ball goes out of bounds, to instances of people passing up delicious and available food just because they are on a diet.

The capacity for self-directed action has its dark side—namely, irrationality. Just as people are capable of altering their behavior on the basis of rational, enlightened plans, they are also capable of altering it to follow foolish and even self-destructive plans. The brilliance of human innovation is one of the wonders of the world, but humans have also done stupid and costly things on a scale that no other creatures can match. Humans are also alone in the animal kingdom in the occasional willingness of individuals to commit suicide.

Despite these occasional problems and misfortunes, however, human behavior is remarkably special. Perhaps the single greatest advance is freedom: By using meaningful thought, reasoning, and self-regulation, people have been able to free their actions from simply responding to their immediate surroundings. People have choices and make choices, and although choosing is sometimes stressful, people generally benefit from this freedom. When people rise up in revolutions or demonstrations, it is almost always to demand greater freedom, not less freedom. The spread of democracy and liberty thus continues in culture what nature and evolution began—namely, progress toward giving individuals greater freedom.

CHAPTER 4 SUMMARY

What You Do, and What It Means

- Human behavior depends on meaning.
- Inner processes such as thoughts, feelings, and motivations serve interpersonal functions.
- Imagining something makes it more likely to happen.
- Making a choice is typically a two-step process, involving whittling many choices down to a few and then doing a careful comparison of those few.
- Risk aversion refers to the finding that people are more affected by possible losses than by possible gains.
- Temporal discounting refers to the finding that the present is more important than the future in decision making. The further in the future something lies, the less influence it has on the decision.
- In an evolutionary perspective, the costliest type of sexual error for a woman was to reproduce with a nonoptimal male, while the most costly sexual error for a man was to miss an opportunity to have sex and thus possibly to reproduce.
- The certainty effect refers to the tendency to place more emphasis on definite outcomes than on odds and probabilities.
- People may prefer to postpone hard decisions and keep their options open as long as possible.
- The status quo bias is a preference to keep things the way they are rather than change.
- The omission bias (sometimes called the default option) denotes taking whatever course of action that does not require you to do anything.
- People often avoid making decisions because they fear they will later regret their choice.
- Reactance occurs when a freedom or a choice is removed, making the person want the lost option more and perhaps take steps to reclaim it.
- People can think of their traits as fixed and stable (entity theorists) or as subject to change and improvement (incremental theorists).
- Learned helplessness occurs when people think they will fail so they quit trying to succeed.

Freedom of Action

- Belief in free will leads people to act in more prosocial ways.
- Although other animals may have free will, among humans free will has greater behavioral flexibility and can be regulated more easily.
- Humans rely on meaning to make their choices.
- Self-determination theory emphasizes that people need to feel that some of their behavior is caused by their own free will.
- The panic button effect refers to the finding that believing there is an escape option can reduce stress, even if the option is never used.

Goals, Plans, Intentions

- Goals are ideas of some desired future state; they are the meaningful link between values and action.
- Goals tell you what to do in order to pursue and uphold your values, and setting and pursuing goals is a vital job of the self.
- Setting goals includes choosing among possible goals and evaluating their feasibility and desirability.
- Pursuing goals includes planning and carrying out the behaviors to reach goals.
- Both conscious and automatic systems help in the pursuit of goals.
- The Zeigarnik effect states that people remember uncompleted or interrupted tasks better than completed ones.
- People have goal hierarchies; some goals are long term, and some are short term.
- Goal shielding is the process of keeping others from interfering with your goals.
- People's plans tend to be overly optimistic, especially over a long time span.

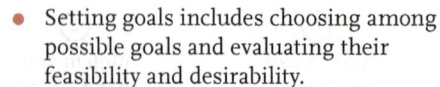

Self-Regulation and Habits

- Self-regulation, or self-control, refers to the self's capacity to alter its own responses; it is essential for cultural animals to adapt to many different demands.
- The three components of self-regulation are standards (concepts of how things should be), monitoring (keeping track of behaviors), and willpower/capacity for change (bringing behavior into line with standards).
- The TOTE model refers to the self-regulation feedback loop of Test, Operate, Test, Exit.
- Willpower is like a muscle, getting depleted after it is used, but getting stronger with exercise.
- A habit is an acquired behavior that, if followed regularly, will become almost automatic.

Irrationality and Self-Destruction

- Self-defeating behavior is defined as any action by which people bring failure, suffering, or misfortune on themselves.
- People engage in self-defeating behavior because they are making tradeoffs or because they are using ineffective strategies, but not usually because they are directly seeking failure.

- The capacity to delay gratification is the ability to make short-term sacrifices in order to get long-term rewards.
- Suicidal people focus on the immediate present at a time when present circumstances may be changing for the worse.

What Makes Us Human? Putting the Cultural Animal in Perspective
- Cultural animals differ from other animals in their elaborate inner systems for controlling behavior.

key terms

capacity for change 136
capacity to delay gratification 142
certainty effect 120
decision fatigue 138
entity theorists 123
error management theory 121
goal 127
goal shielding 130
habit 139
incremental theorists 123
learned helplessness 124
monitoring 135
omission bias 122
panic button effect 126
planning fallacy 132
reactance theory 122
risk aversion 118
self-defeating behavior 141
self-determination theory 125
self-regulation 133
status quo bias 121
temporal discounting 120
TOTE 135
Zeigarnik effect 129

quiz yourself ANSWERS

1. What You Do, and What It Means   p. 124
   answers: 1.b   2.d   3.d   4.c
2. Freedom of Action   p. 126
   answers: 1.b   2.c   3.d   4.b
3. Goals, Plans, Intentions   p. 133
   answers: 1.c   2.a   3.d   4.c
4. Self-Regulation and Habits   p. 140
   answers: 1.c   2.d   3.b   4.c
5. Irrationality and Self-Destruction   p. 145
   answers: 1.c   2.b   3.c   4.b

SOCIAL COGNITION

5

LEARNING OBJECTIVES

1. Identify what most of human thinking is for and relate this to the themes of the duplex mind, people first, and inner processes serving interpersonal functions.

2. Describe the five elements that distinguish automatic from deliberate processes and analyze how schemas, scripts, priming, framing, and thought suppression affect the way we think about other people.

3. Explain how attributions affect our thinking and our behavior, identifying ways that attributions can lead to biases.

4. Describe how the four main heuristics affect the way we think, and debate the value of these shortcuts to human thinking.

5. Identify the biases and fallacies that cause errors in thinking, and describe how and why these could have evolved in a cultural animal.

6. Explain why the shortcuts and styles of thinking described in this chapter have been termed biases and errors, and summarize why they can be beneficial. Describe ways we can reduce the errors in our thinking.

Lucky Business/Shutterstock.com

MONEY MATTERS
Money in the Abstract
158

TRADEOFFS
Conscious and Unconscious Thought
160

FOOD FOR THOUGHT
It's the Thought That Counts (or Doesn't Count!) the Calories
161

THE SOCIAL SIDE OF SEX
Counting Sex Partners
172

WHAT MAKES US HUMAN?
Putting the Cultural Animal in Perspective
181

Diseases that were once largely eradicated in the United States a generation ago (e.g., whooping cough, measles, mumps) are returning, primarily because parents are deciding not to vaccinate their children for these diseases. For example, consider measles vaccinations. Before routine measles vaccinations were given, there were about 500,000 cases of measles in the United States and a high rate of complications from those cases, including 500 deaths.[1] By 2000, it was declared that the endemic spread of measles in the United States had ended. However, in recent years measles outbreaks have increased. For example, there have been recent outbreaks in Texas,[2] Minnesota, Kansas, and Missouri. Measles outbreaks have also occurred in many other developed countries (e.g., Australia, Belgium, Canada, the Czech Republic, Germany, Italy, Japan, The Netherlands, New Zealand, Romania, Singapore, the United Kingdom).[3] Recent years have also seen horrific flu seasons where hundreds of children who did not get a flu vaccine have died from flu.[4] Indeed, opting out of vaccination is now considered a global health threat by the World Health Organization.[5] What has happened?

Typically children received a two-dose vaccine for measles, mumps, and rubella (called the MMR vaccine), with the first dose at age 12–15 months, and the second dose at age 4–6 years.[6] In 1998, a group of 13 researchers led by Andrew Wakefield published an article in the prestigious British medical journal *The Lancet* that reported an examination of 12 children with chronic intestinal disorders who had a history of normal development, followed by severe mental problems.[7] The researchers speculated that the MMR vaccine caused an intestinal infection that damaged the children's brains. Wakefield later coined the term "autistic enterocolitis" for this intestinal disorder. Parents of 8 of the 12 children in the study blamed the MMR vaccine for autistic symptoms in their children. After that, thousands of other parents also claimed that the MMR caused autism in their children. For example, American model Jenny McCarthy blamed vaccinations for her son Evan's autism (even though doctors think Evan has Landau–Kleffner syndrome rather than autism[8]). Despite the evidence, the idea continues to resurface. In December 2018, a newly elected congressman made headlines by saying, without any proof, that vaccines cause autism.[9]

The 1998 article by Wakefield and his colleagues set off a wave of large epidemiological studies, but none of these could replicate the link between vaccination and autism (see Chapter 1 for a discussion of the importance of replication in science). Reviews of the evidence by numerous organizations (e.g., Centers for Disease Control and Prevention, American Academy of Pediatrics, Institute of Medicine, U.S. National Academy of Sciences, U.K. National Health Service, Cochrane Library) all concluded that there is no link between the MMR vaccine and autism. For example, the 2012 Cochrane Library review examined data from nearly 15 million children.[10] It too found no link between the vaccine and autism. A study of 657,461 children from Denmark, published in 2019, came to the same conclusion.[11] The authors stated, "The study strongly supports that MMR vaccination does not increase the risk for autism." A meta-analysis of 10 studies involving more than 1.2 million children found no link between vaccines and autism.[12] (And remember, the original study had only 12 children!)

Undaunted by the contrary evidence, some critics proposed theories to explain why the MMR vaccine might cause autism. One theory was that the mercury-based preservative thiomersal damaged children's brains. In 1999 the Centers for Disease Control and Prevention and the American Academy of Pediatrics asked vaccine makers to remove thiomersal from vaccines, as a precautionary measure. However, removing thiomersal did not affect autism rates. This theory has since been debunked by all scientific and medical organizations.[13]

After the 1998 article by Wakefield and his colleagues was published, vaccination rates plummeted, and the number of measles and mumps cases skyrocketed. Thousands of people have been hospitalized, even though these diseases had been previously controlled.

Since the 1998 study by Wakefield and his colleagues was published, 10 of the 13 authors have retracted the findings.[14] On January 28, 2010, the General Medical Council concluded that the research conducted by Wakefield and his colleagues was unethical, and that the authors had multiple undeclared conflicts of interest (e.g., Wakefield received £55,000—about $69,000—from a group seeking evidence to use against vaccine manufacturers).[15] In 2010, *The Lancet* "fully retract[ed] this paper from the published record," calling it "an elaborate fraud."[16] In 2011, a series of articles reported that Wakefield and his colleagues had also fabricated some of the data. The presumed disorder "autistic enterocolitis" does not exist — it is bogus. Yet, Wakefield said he could make more than $43 million per year by selling diagnostic kits for the bogus disorder.[17]

The vaccine-autism connection has been described as "the most damaging medical hoax of the last 100 years."[18] The well-known pediatrician Rahul Parikh stated that "Refusing to vaccinate a child is dangerous not just for that child but for entire communities," and that "parents who refuse to vaccinate their kids should pay substantially higher health insurance premiums."[19]

It is therefore shocking that some parents still refuse to vaccinate their children. Of the babies born in 2015, 1.3% had received none of the recommended vaccinations by age 2, which is up from 0.3% in 2001.[20] Instead of believing scientific reviews based on millions of children, they believe case reports from single individuals who claim that vaccines cause autism. Peter Hotez, the father of a daughter name Rachel with autism, has tried to counter these unsubstantiated case reports in his book, *Vaccines Didn't Cause Rachel's Autism*. Hotez is also a vaccine scientist heading the Texas Children's Hospital Center for Vaccine Development, a nonprofit that doesn't take vaccine industry funding. As an autism dad, but also an expert in both vaccines and autism, Hotez is a credible source on this topic. In an interview, he argues that children "have a fundamental human right to be protected against deadly infections."[21] He hopes his book will help counter the misinformation parents might read from anti-vaccine websites and social media (see Chapter 7 for a discussion about misinformation).

This chapter sheds light on why things like this occurs. One reason is that misinformation is "sticky"—people can't seem to let go of it.[22] Rejecting information requires cognitive effort. Simply accepting a message as true and the source as credible is much easier than weighing the plausibility of the message and its source. Misinformation is especially "sticky" if the topic isn't very important to you or if you have other things on your mind.

Finally, Nadine had found a doctor who understands her.

What Is Social Cognition?

The rise of social cognition in the 1970s marked a fundamental and sweeping change in how social psychologists studied people. Before the 1970s, social psychology was dominated by behaviorism, which held that in order to be scientific, psychologists should only study visible behavior and not make inferences about what was happening inside the person, such as thoughts and feelings. Social psychologists began to realize, however, that it is impossible to understand people without examining how they think and feel. In the 1970s, social psychologists began to focus their studies on people's thoughts and feelings.

Researchers developed methods and techniques to directly and indirectly observe mental processes so that these processes could be studied scientifically. Among the first mental processes that social psychologists studied were attitudes and the motivation to be consistent in one's attitudes (see Chapter 7). The development of attribution theory in the 1960s and 1970s was one of the most important steps in the scientific study of thinking in social psychology. Attribution theory focuses on how people interpret the causes of events, such as external pressures or internal traits. The term **social cognition** became widely used in the 1980s; it encompassed a broad movement to study any sort of thinking by people about people and about social relationships.[23]

Thinking About People: A Special Case?

Social psychologists study how people think about people. Why this topic in particular? Why not study how people think about frogs, or household appliances, or money, or the weather? Cognitive psychologists might study these other topics, but social psychologists focus on people. Is thinking about people special in some way? In short, yes. People think

social cognition a movement in social psychology that began in the 1970s that focused on thoughts about people and about social relationships

> "It's just a matter of opinions
> You know you keep both in sight
> Why should you bother with the other side
> When you know yours is right."
> — David Gilmour, former guitarist for Pink Floyd, "You Know I'm Right."

about other people more than any other topic, and probably more than about all other topics combined.[24] As a brief test, try turning on the television and scanning the channels. True, some shows are devoted to the physical world, such as those on *Animal Planet* or *The Discovery Channel*. But most shows are about people and their relationships with other people. The news may occasionally cover a hurricane, an earthquake, or a tornado, but even footage of these natural disasters tends to emphasize how they affect people. Most news is about people's activities.

The fact that people think a lot about other people is relevant to several of the themes in this textbook, such as "people first" (see Chapter 2). Remember, one standard theory is that the human brain evolved to solve problems in the physical environment, such as making tools, finding shelter, and obtaining food. In fact, people spend relatively little time thinking about these things. Rather, people use their brains to think about each other, implying that humans evolved to rely on each other for information and help. The human mind is designed to participate in society, and this means its primary job is dealing with other people. Birds get their food from their environment, and so birds' brains are focused on trees and worms and predators. Most humans get their food by interacting with other people, and so people's brains are designed to think about other people.

Research suggests that much thinking is for arguing, in the sense of trying to convince others.[25] In this view, the purpose of the human brain is not even so much for quietly analyzing other people—rather, it is for communicating with others and influencing them. After all, most people spend relatively little time having their own private thoughts but much more time talking and communicating with other people.[26]

The idea that thinking evolved for arguing may seem implausible, especially if you are the sort of person who hates to argue (though if we say "convince" instead of "argue," it will be hard to say you never do this). But as this chapter examines the ways people reason and the sorts of distortions and slip-ups that afflict human logic, we shall see that these suggest a pattern of arguing for a particular side rather than trying to reason out whatever the truth may be. An added advantage of this view is that it starts from a basic fact of social life, which is that people will often have different opinions as to what would be best to do, and so they need to get others to go along with them. Being able to explain why one's own ideas, wishes, plans, or preferences should prevail is a broadly useful skill, and brains may well have evolved to help that along. It is likely that people who were more persuasive (by arguing) would have survived and reproduced better than people who were less persuasive.

The emphasis on thinking about people—and perhaps arguing with them—shows that inner processes serve interpersonal functions (yet another theme from Chapter 2). Nature (evolution) gave us a powerful brain that can think elaborate thoughts, and this brain is used mainly for helping us relate to others—and not only for garnering social acceptance. You need to understand your enemies and rivals almost as well as your friends and lovers. And from time to time you need to convince any and all of them that you are right.

Why People Think, and Why They Don't

Humans can do more and better thinking than any other animal on earth.[27,28,29] Human beings have a brain about the size of a large grapefruit. It weighs about 3 pounds. Although some other animals have larger brains for their body size (e.g., small birds), much of their brain mass is devoted to motor functions (e.g., flying) (see **FIGURE 5.1**). If one compares the size of the cortex (the part of the brain involved in higher-order functions such as thinking) to the rest of the body, humans are at the top of the list.

You might expect that because humans are well equipped to think, they would love to think and would spend all their free time doing it. This is certainly not the case. Researchers have found that often people seem lazy or careless about their

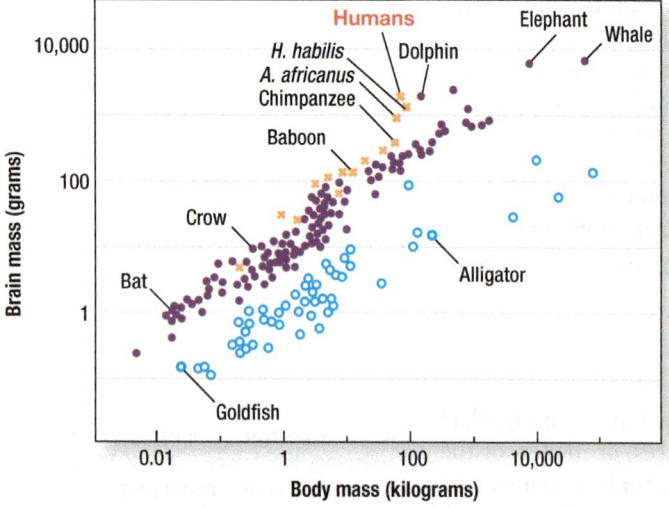

FIGURE 5.1

A plot of brain mass versus body mass for a variety of animals. The open blue circles represent reptiles (including some fish and dinosaurs), the filled purple circles represent mammals (including many birds), and the orange x's represent primates (including humans and their immediate ancestors).

From "Cosmic Evolution - Epoch 7 - Cultural Evolution," Fig. 7.13. Retrieved August 11, 2019 from https://www.cfa.harvard.edu/~ejchaisson /cosmic_evolution/docs/text/text_cult_3.html. Copyright © 2005 by Eric J. Chaisson, Wright Center for Science Education. Reprinted by permission.

thinking. In fact, when experimenters tell people to sit quietly and think, people are unhappy about this, and some would rather receive a mildly painful electric shock[30]. Social psychologists use the term **cognitive miser** to describe people's reluctance to do much extra thinking.[31] Just as a miser tries to avoid spending money, the cognitive miser tries to avoid thinking too hard or too much. Of course, this isn't entirely a matter of laziness. Thinking takes effort. Although people's capacity to think is greater than other animals, it is limited, so people must conserve their thinking. We have ample evidence that when people's capacity for thinking is already preoccupied, they take even more shortcuts to reduce further the need for thought.[32] These mental shortcuts (called heuristics) are discussed later in this chapter. However, people will think hard when arguing with someone else.

Some people seem to be such numskulls that you wonder whether they had a brain at all. For example, one young man went into a liquor store, pointed a gun at the clerk, and demanded all the cash in the register. When the bag was full, he demanded a bottle of whisky too. The clerk refused to give up the whisky, saying that he thought the robber was underage. After a brief argument, the robber showed the clerk his driver's license, thereby finally persuading the clerk to hand over the whisky. Of course, the robber was arrested only two hours later, after the clerk called the police and gave them the robber's name and address!

Then again, people do think at great length about things that are interesting to them. The legendary genius Albert Einstein published an astonishing 258 articles during his lifetime, dealing with the most complicated issues in physics, and his thinking changed the way that scientists understand the world. Some people spend a great deal of effort thinking about their relationship partners (or how to get one). Some people think about particular events, such as the death of a loved one, for many years afterward. Some people think about football or soccer all the time and have a seemingly bottomless appetite for the latest game news, anecdotes, and statistics.

Not all thinking is equally difficult. As the theory of the duplex mind indicates, deliberate thinking requires a lot more effort than automatic thinking. People generally prefer to conserve effort by relying on automatic modes of thought when they can. Unfortunately, the automatic system is not very good at some kinds of thinking, such as logical reasoning and computing probabilities. Therefore, the automatic mind develops various shortcuts, which give rough estimates or pretty good answers. Sometimes, though, people do find it necessary to employ the full power of deliberate thought and analysis.

Automatic and Deliberate Thinking

Humans have a duplex mind, as this book has emphasized (see Chapter 2). Some thinking proceeds by automatic means, whereas other thinking relies on conscious control. To illustrate this point, try the **Stroop test**. In **FIGURE 5.2**, you see several rectangles

FIGURE 5.2
Stroop Test 1: Name the color of each rectangle out loud as quickly as you can.

cognitive miser a term used to describe people's reluctance to do much extra thinking

Stroop test a standard measure of effortful control over responses, requiring participants to identify the color of a word (which may name a different color)

FIGURE 5.3
Stroop Test 2: Name the color of each word as quickly as you can, ignoring what the word says.

BLUE	GREEN	BLACK	RED
RED	BLACK	GREEN	BLUE
RED	BLUE	BLACK	GREEN
BLUE	RED	GREEN	BLACK
BLACK	BLUE	GREEN	RED

FIGURE 5.4
Stroop Test 3: As in Test 2, name the color of each word as quickly as you can, ignoring what the word says.

RED	BLUE	GREEN	BLACK
BLACK	BLUE	RED	GREEN
BLUE	BLACK	GREEN	RED
GREEN	BLUE	BLACK	RED
BLUE	BLACK	RED	GREEN

containing different colors. Say the name of the color in each rectangle out loud as quickly as you can. Go one row at a time, from left to right. If you have a timer on your watch or cell phone, time how long it takes you to do the test. In **FIGURE 5.3**, you see several words written in different ink colors. Say the name of the ink color for each word as quickly as you can, ignoring what the word says. Go one row at a time, from left to right. In **FIGURE 5.4**, do the same thing—say the ink color, ignoring what the word says. For example, if the word **RED** is printed in blue ink, you should say "Blue."

James Ridley Stroop first described the **Stroop effect** in 1935.[33] If you are like most people, it took you longer if the word and ink color didn't match (incongruent) than if they did match (congruent). In the incongruent test (when the word and ink color don't match), the automatic response is to say the word rather than the ink color. It takes conscious effort to override the automatic response and say the ink color instead. One of your textbook authors (Bushman) tried the Stroop test on his son, who was 3-years-old at the time. The boy did very well and said, "This is easy!" (Because he couldn't read, he did not have to contend with the automatic response of the meaning of the printed word and therefore could just say the color of the ink.)

How do we know whether some thought is automatic or deliberate? No one single test can provide the answer because automatic thought has several dimensions. Unfortunately, this makes the definitions of automatic versus deliberate processes somewhat complicated because some thought or response may fit one criterion but not the others. Most phenomena are complex and exist on continuums rather than in one category or another. One study reported the most conclusive evidence yet for two separate systems.[34] It showed that the automatic system and the deliberate system learn in different ways and can't necessarily substitute for each other.

At least five elements distinguish automatic from deliberate processes: *awareness, intention, control, effort,* and *efficiency*. Let's go through these elements. When people

Stroop effect in the Stroop test, the finding that people have difficulty overriding the automatic tendency to read the word rather than name the ink color are engaging in automatic thinking, they may not even be aware that they are thinking. A good example is driving. People who have extensive driving experience don't have to think about how to do it; they just drive. If road conditions become bad, however, deliberate thinking overrides automatic thinking. If it starts to rain or snow, people turn on their windshield wipers, think about whether the roads are slippery, pay more attention to other drivers, and so on. New drivers, in contrast, have to think carefully about what they are doing at all times. Second, automatic thinking is not guided by intention. It may just happen whether you intend it or not. (Indeed, as the Stroop effect shows, automatic thoughts can intrude on your thinking even when you intend to think something else.) Third, automatic thoughts are not subject to deliberate control, so it can be difficult or even impossible to avoid having certain thoughts that have been cued. Fourth, automatic thoughts do not involve effort, whereas deliberate thoughts often involve mental exertion and can feel taxing and tiring. Last, automatic thoughts are highly efficient, unlike deliberate thoughts (which are often slow and cumbersome). To illustrate the difference, suppose we ask you to multiply 3 times 6. The answer comes automatically because you probably memorized it long ago. In contrast, suppose we ask you to multiply 46 times 37, which requires deliberate thought. The differences in intention, control, effort, and efficiency between those two calculations show the relevant differences.

Automatic thinking involves little effort because it relies on knowledge structures. **Knowledge structures** are organized packets of information that are stored in memory. These knowledge structures form when a set of related concepts is frequently brought to mind, or activated. When people think about a concept, it becomes active in memory. Related concepts also become activated (that is, they pop into mind). Over time, as related concepts are frequently activated together, the set of related concepts becomes so strongly linked that activation of one part of the set automatically activates the whole set. For example, the thought of having a cheeseburger might also activate the thought of French fries. Once activated, these knowledge structures simply run their course, like an airplane set on autopilot. The result is automatic thinking.

Different people rely differently on one or the other type of thought. As we have said, both types have advantages. Research shows, however, that the deliberative thinkers are better at knowing what they know[35]. For example, a quick intuitive solution might be close but not quite correct, whereas laboriously thinking through the problem furnishes a different answer. The people who use the deliberate style of thinking thus know there are different possible answers, both the intuitive one and the one reached by thinking things through. In contrast, the intuitive people only know the answer that intuition gives, so they are less likely to know whether they got it right. In other words, intuition is often correct and certainly easier—but intuitive people tend to be overconfident rather than knowing what they know.

Schemas

Schemas are knowledge structures that represent substantial information about a concept, its attributes, and its relationships to other concepts. The concept, for example, could be the self, another person, a social category (e.g., politicians), or an object. A schema for dancing, for example, would include movement, rhythm, repetition, and coordination, as well as connections to music, shoes, romance, fashion, art, and perhaps embarrassment. A schema for bears might include fur, claws, danger, climbing trees, hibernating, and growling, as well as relationships to honey, zoos, countries (e.g., Germany, Russia), U.S. states (e.g., California, Missouri), various sports teams (e.g., Chicago Bears), children's story book characters (e.g., Winnie the Pooh, Paddington Bear), stuffed toys ("Teddy" bears), and drops in stock prices (a "bear market").

Schemas make the complex world much easier to understand. They help organize information by connecting beliefs that are related to each other. They help the mind form expectancies. Hence, if someone asks you to go dancing, you know that person is

knowledge structures organized packets of information that are stored in memory

schemas knowledge structures that represent substantial information about a concept, its attributes, and its relationships to other concepts probably not just telling you to go outside and move around, but perhaps initiating a romantic date, and you should wear nice shoes and be prepared for music.

One type of event that sparks deliberate thinking is a violation of expectancies. In general, people seem to go through their daily lives with a solid idea of what is supposed to happen. When life conforms to what they expect, they don't generally find it necessary to think much about it. But when events depart sharply from what people have learned to expect, they may stop and analyze what happened. This is a very useful pattern. People develop an understanding of their social world, and their expectancies and schemas are part of this understanding. You develop schemas through your experiences, and they guide the way you process information. Getting through daily life is much easier if you have schemas and know what to expect. Events that violate your expectancies show that something might be wrong with how you understand the world, so it is worth pausing to analyze the situation. In a club, you ask someone to dance, and the person sometimes nods and accompanies you to the dance floor, or sometimes politely rejects you; all is as expected, with no need to analyze. But if your invitation to dance is met with a big laugh or a hurried departure, you might stop to wonder what went wrong: Are you not allowed to ask people to dance? Is something wrong with the way you look? Do you smell bad?

Scripts

Scripts are knowledge structures that contain information about how people (or other objects) behave under varying circumstances. In a sense, scripts are schemas about certain kinds of events. In films and plays, scripts tell actors what to say and do. In memory, scripts define situations and guide behavior: The person first selects a script to represent the situation, assumes a role in the script, and behaves accordingly. For example, a restaurant script helps one know what to expect when going to a restaurant (i.e., enter restaurant, wait for a host, host seats you at a table and gives you a menu, waiter/waitress takes your order, cook prepares your order, waiter/waitress brings your food to the table, eat food, ask waiter/waitress for a check, pay for food, leave a tip (in some countries), exit restaurant). Scripts can be learned by direct experience or by observing others (e.g., parents, siblings, peers, mass media characters).

People learn schemas and scripts that influence how they perceive, interpret, judge, and respond to events in their lives. These various knowledge structures develop over time, beginning in early childhood. The pervasiveness, interconnectedness, and accessibility of any learned knowledge structure are largely determined by the frequency with which it is encountered, imagined, and used. With great frequency, even complex knowledge structures can become automatized—so overlearned that we apply them automatically with little effort or awareness.

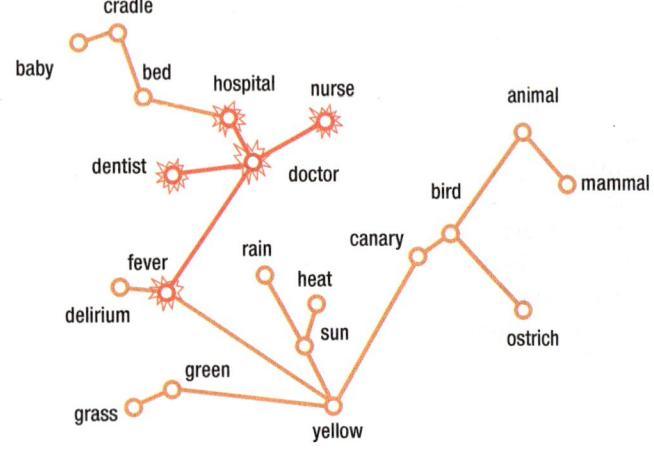

FIGURE 5.5

Human memory can be represented as a network. The nodes represent the concepts. Related concepts are linked in memory.

scripts knowledge structures that define situations and guide behavior

priming activating an idea in someone's mind so that related ideas are more accessible

Priming

You are probably already familiar with the concept of priming. When someone primes an engine (e.g., on a lawn mower, weed eater, snow blower), the person pumps gas into the cylinder so that the spark plug will fire more easily, which makes the engine start more easily. The term "prime the pump" refers to government action taken to stimulate the economy (e.g., cutting taxes, reducing interest rates). Memory is filled with concepts. Related concepts are linked together in memory (e.g., the concepts *doctor* and *dentist*), as depicted in **FIGURE 5.5**. When one concept becomes primed in memory by thinking about it, related concepts in memory become more accessible. Thus, **priming** is the process by which a given stimulus activates mental pathways, thereby enhancing their accessibility. William James, philosopher and psychologist, described priming as the "wakening of associations." Once a concept has been primed, it can influence the way we interpret associated concepts. For example, numerous studies have shown that people are faster at classifying a target word (e.g., *nurse*) when it is preceded by a related word (e.g., *doctor*) than when it is preceded by an unrelated word (e.g., *butter*).[36,37] The prime doesn't have to be conscious either. Some primes are subliminal, or below the level of conscious awareness. For example, a casino in Windsor, Ontario, Canada, was fined because their electronic slot machines flashed the subliminal message "win" to customers. The idea was that priming the concept "win" would make customers more optimistic so that they would shovel more coins into slot machines. Indeed, subsequent research found that subliminally priming participants with the winning image of a jackpot symbol prompted participants to bet more.[38]

"I don't know why. I just suddenly felt like calling."

The power of priming to activate concepts, which then hang around in the mind and can influence subsequent thinking, was demonstrated in an early study.[39] Participants were asked to identify colors while reading words. The words did not seem at all important to the study, but they were actually very important because they were primes. By random assignment, some participants read the words *reckless, conceited, aloof,* and *stubborn*, whereas others read the words *adventurous, self-confident, independent,* and *persistent*. Then all participants were told that the experiment was finished, but they were asked to do a brief task for another, separate experiment. In that supposedly different experiment, they read a paragraph about a man named Donald who was a skydiver, a powerboat racer, and a demolition derby driver, and they were asked to describe the impression they had of Donald. It turned out that the words participants had read earlier influenced their opinions of him. Those who had read the words *reckless, conceited, aloof,* and *stubborn* were more likely to view Donald as having those traits than were participants who had read the other words. That is, the first task had "primed" participants with the ideas of recklessness, stubbornness, and so forth, and once these ideas were activated, they influenced subsequent thinking about Donald.

Research has often used priming as a technique to trigger automatic processes. For example, participants in one study first unscrambled sentences by choosing four out of five words to make a grammatically correct sentence.[40] They were told to do this as quickly as possible. In the rude priming version, one of the five words was rude (e.g., *they/her/bother/see/usually*). In the polite priming version, one of the five words was polite (e.g., *they/her/respect/see/usually*). In the neutral priming version, the polite or rude word was replaced by a neutral word (e.g., *they/her/send/see/usually*). Participants were told that after they completed the task, they should come out into the hallway and find the experimenter. The experimenter waited for the participant, while pretending to explain the sentence task to an accomplice. The accomplice pretended to have a difficult time understanding the task. The experimenter refused to acknowledge the participant, who was waiting patiently for instructions on what to do next. The dependent variable in the study was whether participants interrupted the experimenter within a 10-minute period. Of course, it is rude to interrupt somebody who is speaking to another person. As can be seen in **FIGURE 5.6**, participants primed with rude words were much more likely to interrupt the experimenter than were participants primed with polite words. Thus, priming activated the idea of being rude (or polite), which then lingered in the mind and influenced behavior in a seemingly unrelated context.

Priming people with money changes the way they think about many things. See *Money Matters* to find out how.

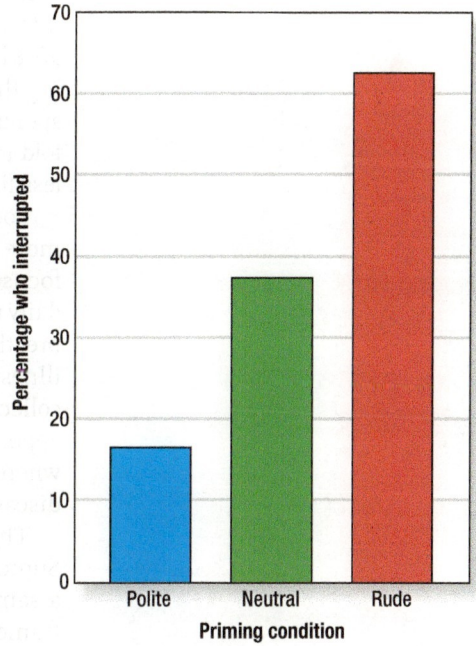

FIGURE 5.6

In one study, participants primed with rude words were much more likely to interrupt the experimenter than were participants in the polite condition.
SOURCE: Bargh et al. (1996).

What Is Social Cognition? | 157

MONEY Matters

Money in the Abstract

Right now, would you describe what you are doing as "moving my eyes along lines of print," "reading," "doing today's assignment," "gaining knowledge about social psychology," or even "advancing my education?" Those descriptions may all be accurate, but their levels of abstraction differ. Moving one's eyes and reading are fairly concrete, whereas pursuing educational goals is more abstract.

Money seems to shift people toward more abstract styles of thinking, as studies showed[41]. Participants had to choose among various groups of descriptions of the same action (like the group in the first sentence of this box). Some previously had the idea of money briefly planted in their minds. These people favored the more abstract descriptions, as compared to others who had not been led to think of money. In another study, people who thought of money sorted objects into fewer, broader categories, as opposites to narrow, specific ones (e.g., birds, vs. seagulls, robins, eagles, hawks, and so forth). Those who had not thought of money sorted into the narrower, more specific categories. Using the larger, more all-encompassing categories indicates more abstract thinking.

Not all primes of money led to abstract thinking. Large amounts of money did, but when people had been led to think of small amounts of money, they did not shift to high levels of abstraction. Also, thinking about prices (a specific application of money) made people think in fairly concrete terms. Thinking about a price is often linked to concrete, specific actions (such as whether to buy something).

Money is itself a rather abstract concept. Money is a symbolic store of value. A dollar may be useful for buying a banana at some point, but the dollar bill itself is not edible, nor good for much else. Perhaps it is no accident that humans engage in far more abstract thought than any other animals—and also are the only ones to invent and use money!

Framing

Politicians call it "spin," but social psychologists call it "framing." **Framing** refers to how information is presented to others. Would you rather eat a hamburger that is 10% fat or 90% lean? Both numbers convey the same fact about the same hamburger, but emphasizing the 90% lean aspect sounds much more appetizing. Research has shown that people spend a lot more money when they are told the money is a "bonus" than when they are told it is a "rebate."[42,43] A rebate is the return of a loss of one's own money, so people are less likely to spend it.

Social psychologists have become very interested in whether health messages are more effective if they are framed in terms of gains or losses. A **gain-framed appeal** focuses on how doing something will make you healthier (e.g., "Flossing your teeth daily removes particles of food in the mouth, avoiding bacteria, thereby promoting fresh breath."); a **loss-framed appeal** focuses on the downside, such as the potential for greater illness (e.g., "If you do not floss your teeth daily, particles of food remain in the mouth, collecting bacteria, thereby causing bad breath."). Research has shown that gain-framed appeals are more effective when targeting behaviors that prevent the onset of disease, whereas loss-framed appeals are more effective when targeting behaviors that detect diseases that people may already have but not be aware of.[44]

The media can also frame stories in different ways. For example, in 2018 the U.S. Supreme Court examined a case in which a Colorado baker refused to bake a cake for a same-sex couple, stating that it was against his religious beliefs. Some news outlets framed the case in terms of anti-LGBTQ+ rights, whereas other news outlets framed in terms of religious freedom.

Framing things sometimes makes unpleasant tasks more palatable. Researchers have even found that framing physical activity as fun rather than exercise reduces overeating later[45]. For example, people who were led to label a hike as an "exercise walk" later ate more dessert at mealtime and consumed more snacks, as compared to people who were led to label the hike as a "scenic walk." Physical activity consumes calories either way, but framing that as exercise apparently makes people feel they should have some delicious treats as reward. Engaging in fun does not produce that same reaction.

framing how information is presented to others

gain-framed appeal focuses on how doing something will add to your health

loss-framed appeal focuses on how not doing something will subtract from your health

Thought Suppression and Ironic Processes

Most people have had thoughts they would like to erase from their minds. When people want to suppress a thought, their mind sets up two processes. One process keeps a lookout for anything that might remind the person of the unwanted thought. It is an automatic process that checks all incoming information for danger. The other is a deliberate process that redirects attention away from the unpleasant thought. For example, if you are upset that you did not do well on a chemistry test and want to avoid worrying about it, your mind may automatically watch for anything that might remind you of tests or chemistry, and when some cue arises (e.g., seeing the person who sits in front of you in chemistry class), your conscious mind quickly turns attention elsewhere (e.g., you don't say hello to that person). The problem with the deliberate system is that whenever conscious control is relaxed, the automatic system is still watching for cues and may therefore flood the mind with them.[46] This chapter's *Tradeoffs* box describes the pros and cons of unconscious and conscious thought.

As a child, the Russian writer Leo Tolstoy (1828–1910) was once challenged by his older brother Nikolenka to remain standing in a corner until he could stop thinking of a white bear.[47] Poor Leo could think of nothing else but a white bear. He quickly learned how difficult it is to control thoughts. Researchers have replicated the informal experiment conducted by young Leo Tolstoy in more formal laboratory settings.[48,49,50] Regardless of the setting, the results are the same: People who are told not to think of a white bear cannot rid their minds of the white, furry creatures. People who are trying to overcome vices are better off not suppressing unwanted thoughts of the things they crave. For example, trying not to think about cigarettes only makes it more difficult for smokers to quit smoking,[51] problem gamblers to quit gambling,[52] and chronic pain patients to quit taking prescription opioids[53]. The paradoxical effects of thought suppression have been linked to a variety of psychological disorders, especially anxiety disorders (e.g., phobias, obsessive-compulsive disorders, panic disorder, post-traumatic stress disorder).[54] Even in dreams, suppressed thoughts are more likely to come to mind.[55,56] One study found that people who tended to suppress their thoughts, dreamt more of negative (but not positive) emotional experiences from waking life, had poorer sleep quality, and had higher levels of depression, anxiety, and stress.[57] One meta-analysis of all previous studies on the topic concluded that suppressing unwanted thoughts often backfires.[58]

If suppressing thoughts does not work, what does work? Research has shown that distraction and even rumination (or contemplation) are more effective than suppression.[59] Mental control is a form of self-regulation, discussed in detail in Chapter 4. *Food for Thought* describes how difficult it is for dieters to control their thoughts and consequently their eating habits.

QUIZ YOURSELF
What Is Social Cognition?

1. Organized beliefs we have about stimuli in our social world are known as _____.
   - (a) automatic processes
   - (b) deliberate processes
   - (c) schemas
   - (d) self-concepts

2. What topic do people spend the greatest amount of time thinking about?
   - (a) Food
   - (b) Money
   - (c) People
   - (d) Weather

3. Which of the following is *not* one of the elements that distinguishes automatic from deliberate processes?
   - (a) awareness
   - (b) efficiency
   - (c) effort
   - (d) relevance

4. During their first year of medical school, many medical students begin to think that they and other people they know are suffering from serious illness. This phenomenon, known as the medical student syndrome, is probably due to _____.
   - (a) counterfactual thinking
   - (b) false consensus
   - (c) false uniqueness
   - (d) priming

answers: see pg 185

Conscious and Unconscious Thought

Suppose you had a tough choice to make, such as choosing the best apartment to rent. What is the best procedure? Conventional wisdom says to make a list of the pros and cons and then use logic to figure out the best option for you. A different approach—to absorb all the information first and then put it out of your mind for a while—is considered a better option by some. Eventually the right answer pops into your mind.

The second approach has gained scientific respectability in the last few years. Two Dutch psychologists have published influential research making the case for what they call "unconscious thought."[60] As they put it, the brain is a giant organ with many neurons and much activity, and only a tiny portion of it goes on in consciousness. The unconscious can therefore be smarter than consciousness. So letting your unconscious mind help make a decision may be a great way to proceed.

To back up their claim, they reported a series of studies with remarkable findings, often showing that unconscious thought outperforms conscious thought. For example, they used a variation on the apartment choice problem that opened this box. Participants were confronted with a huge amount of information: a dozen different features on each of four apartments. The researchers had rigged the information so that one apartment had mostly positive features and another apartment had mostly negative features. They wanted to see whether participants managed to choose what the researchers regarded as the best option.

Some participants had to make their selection immediately after reading all the information. Others had 3 minutes to think consciously about the apartments. A third group, in the unconscious thought condition, had to perform a different mental task that preoccupied their conscious mind for 3 minutes and then choose one of the apartments. These participants in the unconscious thought condition were more likely to make the optimal choice.[61] Unconscious thinking produced seemingly better results than conscious thinking.

These and similar findings led many experts to start recommending that people rely on unconscious thinking for important decisions. Advice to "go with your gut feeling" and "don't overthink it" became common. The Dutch researchers won a huge prize for their main article on unconscious thought. But before long there was a backlash from other researchers, who questioned whether unconscious thought was really superior to conscious thought.

One source of objections was based on follow-up experiments. The superiority of unconscious thought over conscious thought has not been replicated consistently.[62] It may depend on fairly artificial constraints, such as requiring the conscious thought to start and end at precise intervals (e.g., three minutes).

Other work has shown that conscious thought is genuinely superior to unconscious thought at some things (e.g., planning, goal pursuit, self-control, culture). In particular, the unconscious is not very good at logical reasoning.[63] If consciousness is needed for logic, how could the unconscious even keep up with it (let alone surpass it) in the apartment-choosing problem? Problems like that do not require reasoning or indeed combining information in any complex manner. The "right" answer was simply the apartment that had the most positive and fewest negative features. The unconscious is pretty good at tallying up that one option has more good things than another.

Unconscious mind: "you like green and bread—eat it!"

At present, the relative powers and influence of unconscious versus conscious thought comprise an exciting and controversial area, so conclusions are tentative. As time goes on, researchers are discovering that the unconscious mind can process more than we previously thought. For example, it was once thought that the unconscious mind could not perform multistep, effortful arithmetic computations (e.g., 9 – 3 – 4), but some research now suggests that it can.[64] The unconscious mind can also process multiple-word expressions, though nothing like this sentence, let alone stories.[65] Some scholars believe the unconscious mind can perform every fundamental, basic-level function that the conscious mind can perform.[66]

The best bet seems to be that both conscious and unconscious thought processes have important and valuable—but different—functions. Unconscious thought can really help people sort through information and come to good decisions. But conscious thought is also vital, especially when logical reasoning is helpful. So when you face a tough decision, a period of unconscious thought might well be useful. But perhaps that should augment and help rather than replace thinking the matter over consciously.

FOOD FOR *Thought*

It's the Thought That Counts (or Doesn't Count!) the Calories

How much will someone eat? It depends partly on how hungry the person is. Someone who has not eaten anything for hours will eat more than someone who has just eaten a big meal. At least, that would make sense.

Not everyone follows that pattern, and some people even do the opposite. In one research paradigm, participants come to the lab after not having had anything to eat for several hours.[67] By random assignment, participants are initially given nothing to eat, or a moderate milkshake, or a giant double milkshake. Afterward, participants are given three large containers of ice cream (chocolate, strawberry, and vanilla) to taste and rate. In reality, the researchers simply want to find out how much ice cream people will eat, as a function of whether they are already full (milkshake conditions) or hungry (no-milkshake condition).

Dieters react differently from non-dieters in this situation. Non-dieters do what you probably expect. Those who just consumed the milkshake eat less ice cream, just enough to enable them to answer the questions on the rating sheet, whereas those who did not get any milkshake tend to chow down on the ice cream.

Dieters, however, show the opposite pattern (**FIGURE 5.7**). That is, dieters who had not been given any milkshake were very restrained in tasting the ice cream. But dieters who had been assigned to drink a milkshake actually ate significantly more ice cream than the others. Researchers dubbed this tendency **counter-regulation**—or, more informally, the "what the heck" effect—because the dieters seem to be thinking, "My diet is already blown for the day by drinking that milkshake, so what the heck, I might as well enjoy some ice cream too!"[68]

The fact that the "what the heck" effect is driven by peculiar cognitions, rather than any bodily need for food, was demonstrated in a remarkable series of studies.[69] Apparently whether the dieters think their diet is blown for the day depends more on how they think about certain foods than on the actual number of calories consumed. In one study, some dieters were given a snack of cottage cheese with fruit cocktail, which sounds like diet food but actually contained 580 calories. Others ate a small portion of ice cream that contained only 290 calories. Contrary to the actual caloric content, the ones who ate ice cream acted as if their diets were blown and ate more. Those who ate the cottage cheese and fruit cocktail acted as if their diets were still intact, even though their snack had contained twice as many calories as the ice cream.

In another study, dieters had either a high-calorie or a low-calorie salad, or a high-calorie or low-calorie ice cream treat. Regardless of calories, those who ate the ice cream showed the "what the heck" effect, whereas those who had eaten the salads did not. The researchers tried another study in which they told participants precisely how many calories were in the assigned food, and even told them that they would eat this later on. Even under these conditions, dieters who expected to eat ice cream reacted as if their diets were already blown, whereas those who expected to eat salad acted as if their diet were intact, regardless of the caloric content.

None of this makes rational sense. Even if you violate your diet for the day, you should avoid eating more high-calorie foods. Not only do dieters act as if one lapse ruins their diet for the day, so it doesn't matter how much they eat thereafter, they also seem to make those decisions based on rigid ways of thinking about foods, regardless of how many calories the foods contain. Even when the salad contains twice as many calories as the ice cream treat, they act as if salad is good for diets.

If thinking misleads dieters, does it help to avoid thinking? Not really. Trying to suppress thoughts of desired food does not help people restrain their eating.[70,71] Thought suppression only makes people think more about the food they are trying not to think about, called a "rebound effect."

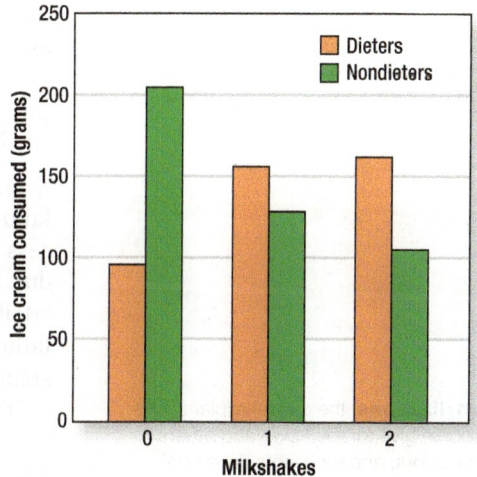

FIGURE 5.7

Nondieters who had had a milkshake ate less ice cream; dieters who had had milkshakes ate more ice cream!

SOURCE: Herman & Mack (1975).

Attributions and Explanations: Why Did That Happen?

Why did he do that? Why did she say that? Is she angry? Is he a fool? Is this job too hard for me? Does this good news mean that I am smarter than other people, or just lucky? People ask and answer these questions in their own minds all the time. Making the

counter-regulation the "what the heck" effect that occurs when people indulge in a behavior they are trying to regulate after an initial regulation failure correct inferences is important, but not easy. There is no perfect way to go from what we actually see (e.g., someone's actions) to drawing firm conclusions about what that person is like inside (e.g., stable personality traits). This applies to ourselves as well as to other people.

Attributions are the inferences people make about events in their lives. Indeed, the study of attributions was a revolutionary step in the history of social psychology because it led social psychologists to abandon once and for all the behaviorist tradition that said psychology should only study observable, objective behavior and not talk about thoughts or other inner processes. Attributions opened the way for the study of thoughts and other cognitive processes.

Attributions are a crucial form of information processing that helps determine behavior. Two people may get identical bad grades on a test, but one of them works harder and does better the next time around, whereas the other gives up and drops out of the course. The attributions they make may help explain the difference. One student looked at the bad grade and thought, "I didn't study hard enough," so that person studied harder and improved. The other student looked at the same grade but thought, "I'm no good at this," or "This is too hard for me," or "This class sucks!" or "This teacher fails everyone." Such conclusions do not spur people to try harder because they imply that all such effort is doomed to failure. Instead, they give up.

Differentiating between seeing behavior caused by internal factors and seeing behavior caused by external factors, first proposed by attribution theorist Fritz Heider[72], has shaped a generation of social psychologists. Research shows, for example, that when students perform poorly in the classroom, teachers tend to make internal attributions (e.g., the student failed because they didn't study hard enough), whereas students tend to make external attributions (e.g., the test was too difficult).[73]

It's Not My Fault: Explaining Success and Failure

One early thrust of attribution theory was to map out how people interpret success and failure. The distinction between internal and external causes is certainly important. Success may be due to internal factors of the person (e.g., effort, intelligence), or could be due to external factors (e.g., luck, task difficulty). Bernard Weiner, another important attribution theorist, proposed a two-dimensional theory of attributions for success and failure.[74] The first dimension was internal versus external; the second dimension was stable versus unstable.

This two-dimensional map of attributions is illustrated in **FIGURE 5.8**. The four possible combinations of internal–external and stable–unstable yield the four main types of attributions that people make when they see themselves or someone else perform a task. Let us briefly consider each.

Internal, stable attributions involve ability. People may think their success reflects intelligence or talent. Conversely, they may decide that they failed at something because they lack the relevant ability. Ability attributions are very important because they invoke relatively permanent aspects of the self. People generally like to think that they have high ability, so their attributions may be biased.[75,76]

Internal, unstable attributions involve effort. Effort is unstable because it can change. If you think someone succeeded because they worked very hard, you have little guarantee that they will do well again (because they might not work as hard the next time). Then again, attributing failure to low effort can be very motivating because people may think that they might succeed if they try harder. There are cultural differences on this dimension. People from collectivist cultures emphasize effort, whereas people from individualistic cultures emphasize ability.[77,78]

External, stable attributions point to the difficulty of the task. Success simply indicates the task was easy, whereas failure indicates the task was hard. Most other people are likely to get the same result because the crucial cause lies in the task, not in the person doing it.

Last, external and unstable attributions involve luck. If you attribute someone's success or failure to luck, there is very little credit or blame due to the person, nor is there any reason to expect the same result the next time. Attributions are not made in a vacuum.

attributions the causal explanations people give for their own and others' behaviors, and for events in general

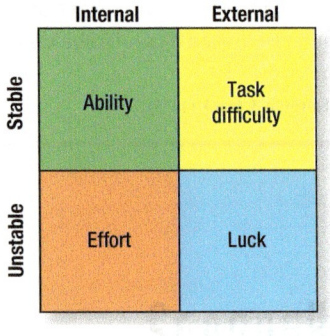

FIGURE 5.8
Two-dimensional attribution theory illustrating the four possible combinations of internal–external and stable–unstable types.

Among other factors, people want to take credit for success but deny blame for failure. This tendency is called the **self-serving bias**. Many studies of attribution have confirmed the widespread operation of the self-serving bias.[79] That is, across many different contexts and settings, people prefer to attribute their successes to ability and effort but tend to attribute their failures to bad luck or task difficulty.[80]

The self-serving bias occurs for several reasons. One reason is simply that interpreting events in that way helps people believe they have high ability and makes them feel good. They can maintain their high opinion of themselves by discounting the misery of their failures and maximizing the glory of their successes. However, evidence suggests that the self-serving bias is especially strong when people are explaining their successes and failures to others.[81,82] This would imply that they care more about what others think of them than about what they think of themselves. In other words, the self-serving bias is an important feature of self-presentation, described as people's efforts to control the impressions they make on others (see Chapter 3). (In a sense, self-presentation is about trying to influence the attributions that other people make about you. Thus, this point fits the theme that much thinking is really about how to convince other people.)

The self-presentational nature of the self-serving bias reflects another theme of this book, which is that inner processes serve interpersonal ends. People learn to think in ways that will help them get along better with others. If others see you as an incompetent loser, your chances of being accepted by them (e.g., hired for a good job) are low. Hence, people want to maximize their credit for success and minimize their blame for failure.

Related to the self-serving bias is the tendency for individuals to overestimate how much they contributed to a group project. If you ask individuals in a group what percentage they contributed to the project, and add up the percentages, the sum is almost always greater than 100 percent—often much greater![83] Part of the explanation for this effect is that individuals tend to view the other group members as a collective rather than as individuals. When individuals "unpack" the collaborations of the other group members, this bias is reduced.[84,85] Still, mostly people will fail to make that sort of correction, and so they will tend to overestimate how much they contributed. This can complicate the process of sharing credit. After all, it's hard to divide up the pay or credit in a fair manner if both people think they did more than half the work!

You Know I'm Right: The Actor/Observer Bias

Suppose you go to a store and see a man shouting at the salesclerk. You might be tempted to conclude that the shouting man is an obnoxious jerk. After all, obnoxious people certainly are more likely to shout at people in stores than are agreeable, easygoing, nice people.

Then again, the shouting man might see things very differently. If you asked him, "Why are you shouting?" he would be unlikely to give the answer "Because I am an obnoxious jerk!" More likely, he would say that the store clerk has treated him badly, and perhaps he has experienced a series of frustrations all day long.

In this example, we saw how you can reach very different conclusions (attributions) about the same behavior. The difference has been called the **actor/observer bias**.[86] It is relevant to any situation in which one person (the observer) is watching someone else's (the actor's) behavior. The actor/observer bias can be defined this way: Actors tend to attribute their own behavior to the situation (external),

self-serving bias the tendency to take credit for success but deny blame for failure; or internal attributions for success, external attributions for failure.

actor/observer bias the tendency for actors to make external attributions and observers to make internal attributions

In many fights and brawls, each side claims that the other side started it.

whereas observers tend to attribute actors' behavior to the person (internal). Put more simply, actors tend to make external attributions, whereas observers tend to make internal attributions.

The actor/observer bias can produce many misunderstandings and disagreements. Indeed, in an argument, it may be common for both sides to see themselves as responding to what the other does. "He started it!" is a common complaint, often heard on both sides, because each side attributes its own behavior to the situation but the others' behavior to their traits and other dispositions. It seems natural to infer that *they* are fighting because they are mean, whereas *we* are fighting because they attacked us. Or, in the simpler words of pro hockey player Barry Beck on a brawl that broke out in one game, "We have only one person to blame, and that's each other!"

Some psychologists have focused on the observer side of the actor/observer bias, labeling it the **fundamental attribution error**. People have a bias to attribute another person's behavior to internal or dispositional causes (e.g., personality traits, attitudes) to a much greater extent than they should. People fail to take full notice and consideration of the external factors (e.g., context, situation, constraints of the social environment) that are operating on the person. The fundamental attribution error is also called the **correspondence bias** because people tend to automatically assume that someone's actions correspond with their personality.

For example, is the person who commits an act of aggression a bully? Is the person who donates money to charity an altruist? To answer this kind of question, people make inferences on the basis of factors such as choice and intention. Intentional behavior that is freely chosen is more informative about a person than is behavior that is coerced. Participants in a classic study[87] read a speech, ostensibly written by a college student, that either favored or opposed Fidel Castro, who was then the communist leader of Cuba and an outspoken enemy of America. The participants were instructed to try to figure out the true attitude of the essay writer. Half of the participants were told that the student who wrote the essay had freely chosen to take this position. The other participants were told that the student was assigned the position by a professor. The study results are depicted in **FIGURE 5.9**. When asked to estimate the student's true attitude, participants were more likely to assume that there was a correspondence between his or her essay (behavior) and attitude (disposition) when the student had a choice than when the student had no choice.

However, crucially, the participants in that study were willing to make internal attributions even when they were told the essay writer had had no choice. Logically, you cannot infer anything about someone's true opinion if the person's behavior was forced by the situation. This is the fundamental attribution error in action: People discounted the situational pressures to write a pro-Castro essay and concluded that the writer must have pro-Castro opinions.

There are several explanations for the fundamental attribution error. First, behavior is more noticeable than situational factors, which are often hidden. Second, people assign insufficient weight to situational causes even when they are made aware of them. Third, people are cognitive misers; they often take quick and easy answers rather than thinking long and hard about things. It takes considerably less cognitive effort to make internal attributions than to make external attributions by thinking about all the external factors that might be operating on the person.

We should note, however, that the fundamental attribution error might not be so fundamental after all. Most research shows that the fundamental attribution error is more common in individualist cultures than in collectivist cultures.[88,89,90] Collectivist cultures tend to place more emphasis on situational explanations of behavior than individualist cultures do.[91] Western civilization pioneered the idea that each person is an individual who can think and act alone. Hence people who live in Western countries (e.g., U.S., U.K., Germany) may be especially prone to attribute actions to causes inside the person. Experiments in China and the USA suggest that the Western style of thinking is designed to improve control over the world, whereas collectivistic thought styles are more about acceptance and harmony. When Asians desire control, they shift and think more like Westerners.[92]

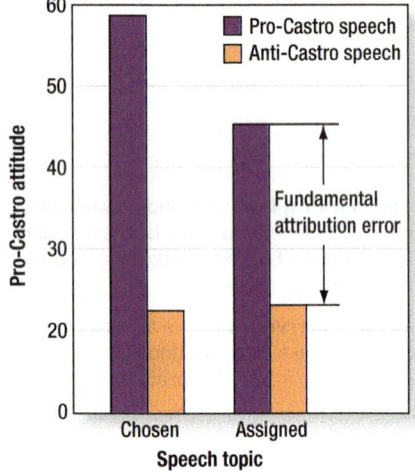

FIGURE 5.9
Participants in a classic study thought that students who wrote a pro-Castro speech had pro-Castro attitudes, even if the speech topic was assigned to them. This is an example of the fundamental attribution error (also called correspondence bias).
SOURCE: Jones and Harris (1967).

fundamental attribution error (correspondence bias) the tendency for observers to attribute other people's behavior to internal or dispositional causes and to downplay situational causes

The fundamental attribution error can also be reduced by perspective taking.[93] When people try to put themselves in the shoes of others, they become more aware of the role of situational factors—that is, observers can begin to understand how actors feel.

Challenging Attribution Theory

Researchers have begun to question the very existence of the actor/observer bias, however, especially when one sorts it out from the self-serving bias. Combining results from many different studies, Bertram Malle has concluded that there was no consistent tendency for observers to make more dispositional attributions than actors.[94] Indeed, he has concluded that the influential theory of the actor-observer bias is wrong. Still, genuine differences exist between how actors and observers explain actions.[95] Actors are more likely than observers to state reasons for how they acted ("I bought a motorcycle to save gas" vs. "He bought a motorcycle because he can't afford high gas prices"). Actors are also more likely to explain their acts by citing their beliefs ("I come here for lunch *because they make* the best hamburgers"), whereas observers point to the actors' desires ("He comes here for lunch *because he likes* the hamburgers").

Thus, the difference between drawing conclusions about self and drawing conclusions about others remains important. People judge others by their actions but judge themselves by their (generally good) intentions.[96] They can discount their own bad actions by saying, "I didn't mean to do that," thus giving themselves a break that they do not give to others.

Taking this a step further, research has shown that people regard others as conformists but do not regard themselves as conformists to the same degree, again because they rely on introspection.[97] That is, if they see another person purchasing the same kind of car or shirt or grill that neighbors already own, they assume that the other person is conforming. When they themselves purchase the same item under the same circumstances, they do not perceive themselves as conforming. Rather, they look inside and perceive that they thought it was a good buy or something that seemed useful to them for personal reasons. For example, in one study,[98] students read about campus issues and were given (false and random) information about what a panel of students had decided. The students generally went along with the panel's recommendations, but they denied doing so out of conformity. However, they thought that other students would go along because of conformity. People do not see in themselves any desire to conform to others, so they do not chalk up their own behavior to conformity. The catch is that conformity pressures and processes may be mostly outside of consciousness, so people do not realize that they are conforming. They can see conformity in others but not in themselves. As the authors put it, the result is that the individual thinks they are "alone in a crowd of sheep".[99] Though we are all doing the same thing, everyone else is conforming, but I am not.

Explaining Actions: A Different Approach

The work by Malle and his colleagues has forced a different look at how people actually explain events.[100] Malle examined people's explanations—rather than relying on rating scales—and concluded that people distinguish between intentional and unintentional action. (Fritz Heider emphasized this in his original book, but even the social psychologists who were most inspired by Heider's work neglected that idea in favor of the internal-external dimension.)

Intentional behavior is typically interpreted and explained on the basis of reasons. If you meant to do it, people assume you have a reason, and that is the explanation. In contrast, unintentional behavior is explained more by causes, which are often outside the person. If the causes are inside the person, they may be something the person is not aware of (e.g., such as if the behavior was a side effect of some medication).

QUIZ YOURSELF
Attributions and Explanations: Why Did That Happen?

1. You and I work on a joint project, and it succeeds. In describing our relative contributions to the project, you assume that your contribution is greater than mine, but I assume that my contribution is greater than yours. This illustrates the _____.
   - (a) actor/observer bias
   - (b) false consensus effect
   - (c) fundamental attribution error
   - (d) self-serving bias

2. Jose reads Sarina's essay that strongly supports capital punishment. Jose knows that Sarina had been assigned the task of writing the essay favoring capital punishment by her debate teacher. Jose is likely to _____.
   - (a) believe that Sarina opposes capital punishment
   - (b) believe that Sarina does, at least to some extent, favor capital punishment
   - (c) believe that Sarina's position on capital punishment is neutral
   - (d) reach no conclusion about Sarina's real position on capital punishment

3. Which of the following is *not* an explanation given for the fundamental attribution error?
   - (a) Behavior is more noticeable than situational factors.
   - (b) People assign insufficient weight to situational causes even when they are made aware of them.
   - (c) People are cognitive misers.
   - (d) People are high in need for cognition.

4. According to Bertram Malle, what is the most important dimension people use when making attributions about the behavior of others?
   - (a) Global/specific
   - (b) Intentional/accidental
   - (c) Internal/external
   - (d) Stable/unstable

answers: see pg 185

Heuristics: Mental Shortcuts

> "Everything should be made as simple as possible, but not simpler."
> —Albert Einstein

People have to make judgments and inferences about uncertain outcomes all the time, and they do it using limited information. What is the likelihood I will get a speeding ticket if I drive at 50 when the speed limit is 40? What is the likelihood of my professor giving an unannounced quiz today in class? What is the likelihood that I will get a high-paying job if I major in psychology? What is the likelihood that this person will say "yes" if I ask them out on a date? What is the likelihood of divorce if I marry this person? What is the likelihood of getting pregnant or catching a sexually transmitted disease if I have unprotected sex with my partner?

As we have seen, deliberate conscious thinking is difficult and requires effort, so most people prefer to rely on automatic processing when they can. Usually the automatic system works very well. The automatic system, however, is not smart enough to perform all the complex operations of reasoning; instead, it relies on shortcuts. These mental shortcuts, called **heuristics**, provide quick estimates (though sometimes inaccurate ones) for decisions about uncertain events. Heuristics greatly simplify our lives. Although people use several heuristics, we will feature four common ones: (a) representativeness, (b) availability, (c) simulation, and (d) anchoring and adjustment.[101] Other shortcuts will be discussed later. For example, stereotypes, sometimes considered to be heuristics, will be covered in Chapter 13 on prejudice and intergroup relations.

Representativeness Heuristic

The **representativeness heuristic** is the tendency to judge the frequency or likelihood of an event by the extent to which it resembles the typical case. For example, in a series of

heuristics mental shortcuts that provide quick estimates about the likelihood of uncertain events

representativeness heuristic the tendency to judge the frequency or likelihood of an event by the extent to which it resembles the typical case

166 | CHAPTER 5 Social Cognition

10 coin tosses, where H is heads and T is tails, most people judge the series HHTTHTHTTH to be more likely than the series HHHHHHHHHH even though both series are equally likely. The reason is that the first series looks more random than the second series. It "represents" our idea of what a random series should look like.

Heavy reliance on the representativeness heuristic leads people to ignore other factors that help shape events, such as rules of chance, independence, and base rate information. Consider the following example:

Thomas is a 41-year-old who reads nonfiction books, reads BBC News on the internet, and solves crossword puzzles in his spare time. Which is more likely?

a. Thomas is an Ivy League professor.
b. Thomas is a truck driver.

Most people answer (a) because Tom seems like a typical Ivy League professor. People fail to consider, however, that there are a lot more truck drivers than there are Ivy League professors. Thus, in making that judgment, people rely on one kind of information (representativeness, which means how well Tom resembles the category of professors) instead of another (how many people are in the category). The representativeness heuristic is related to the base rate fallacy described later in this chapter.

Availability Heuristic

The **availability heuristic** is the tendency to judge the frequency or likelihood of an event by the ease with which relevant instances come to mind. The ease with which relevant instances come to mind is influenced not only by the actual frequency but also by factors such as how salient or noticeable the event is, how recent the event is, and whether attention was paid to the event. Even 4-year-old children use the availability heuristic.[102]

For example, people overestimate the frequency of dramatic deaths and underestimate the frequency of less dramatic deaths.[103] Airplane crash deaths are much more dramatic than deaths caused by tobacco use, and they get a lot more attention from the mass media, which makes them stand out in memory (high availability). As a result, people think they are common. In fact, three jumbo jets full of passengers crashing every day for a year would not equal the number of deaths per year caused by tobacco use. Worldwide, tobacco kills more than 7 million people a year.[104] More than 6 million of these deaths are the results of direct tobacco use, and 890,000 are the result of non-smokers being exposed to second-hand smoke. It also takes tobacco a long time to kill a person, so deaths due to tobacco aren't as salient as deaths due to airplane crashes.

The availability heuristic might also help explain extrasensory perception (ESP) beliefs. Have you had a dream and later found that the dream came true? This has happened to most people. It might be because this event is more salient than the other possible events, as is shown in **FIGURE 5.10**.

It takes a skilled observer to notice when an expected event does *not* occur. For example, consider an incident in the story "Silver Blaze" from Sir Arthur Conan Doyle's *The Memoirs of Sherlock Holmes*.[105] Colonel Ross owned a horse named Silver Blaze, the favorite for the Wessex Cup. Silver Blaze had mysteriously disappeared, and the horse's trainer, John Staker, had been murdered. Inspector Gregory asked Sherlock Holmes to help investigate the case. During the investigation, Colonel Ross asked Sherlock Holmes, "Is there anything else to which you wish to draw my attention?" Holmes replied, "Yes, to the curious incident of the dog in the nighttime." Ross answered, "But the dog did nothing in the nighttime!" Holmes responded, "That is the curious incident." The dog was kept in the same stable as Silver Blaze. Three boys were also in the stable; two slept in the loft while the third kept watch. The stable boy who kept watch had been drugged with opium. Holmes explained, "Though someone had been in and had fetched out a horse, he had not barked enough to arouse the two lads in the loft. Obviously, the midnight visitor was someone whom the dog knew well." From this, the famous detective was able to figure out that it was the trainer who had taken the horse that night.

FIGURE 5.10
The availability heuristic provides one explanation of ESP beliefs. People remember salient events, but forget nonsalient events.

availability heuristic the tendency to judge the frequency or likelihood of an event by the ease with which relevant instances come to mind

Simulation Heuristic

The **simulation heuristic** is the tendency to judge the frequency or likelihood of an event by the ease with which you can imagine (or mentally simulate) it. More easily imagined events are judged to be more likely than other events. When people imagine what might have been, emotional reactions to events are intensified.

Consider the following hypothetical example:[106]

> Mr. Crane and Mr. Tees were scheduled to leave the airport on different flights, at the same time. They traveled from town in the same limousine, were caught in a traffic jam, and arrived at the airport thirty minutes after the scheduled departure time of their flights. Mr. Crane is told that his flight left on time. Mr. Tees is told that his flight was delayed and just left five minutes ago. Who is more upset, Mr. Crane or Mr. Tees?

Most people think Mr. Tees would be more upset than Mr. Crane. The reason is that it is easier for people to imagine how Mr. Tees could have made his flight (e.g., if only the plane had waited a little longer, if only the traffic jam had cleared a few minutes earlier). In contrast, Mr. Crane had no chance of making his flight even if one of those things had been different.

In another study,[107] researchers videotaped television coverage of the Olympic Games. They showed participants the immediate reactions of bronze and silver medalists at the end of the competition, and on the podium when they received their awards. Participants rated the bronze medalists to be happier than the silver medalists! In the movie *I, Tonya*, for example, Tonya Harding's character said the following about Nancy Kerrigan after she won a silver medal in figure skating at the 1994 Winter Olympics: "She goes out and gives a beautiful skate. I never said different. She wins a friggin' silver medal, and when they put that medal round her neck she looked like she stepped in poo." Why does this occur? Although the silver medalists received a higher award than the bronze medalists, it was easier for them to imagine winning the gold medal. For the bronze medal winners, it was a close call to be on the podium with a medal at all. If a few small things had been different, they might have finished in fourth place and received no medal. Satisfaction depends on thoughts about what might have been.

Anchoring and Adjustment Heuristic

In estimating how frequent or likely an event is, people use a starting point (called an anchor) and then make adjustments up and down from this starting point. This mental shortcut or heuristic is called **anchoring and adjustment.** For example, if one party in a negotiation starts by suggesting a price or condition, then the other party is likely to base its counteroffer on this anchor. People use anchors even if they know they are just random numbers. Crucially, most research finds that people remain close, typically too close, to the anchor.[108] The anchor has far more impact than it deserves.

Some research participants were asked to estimate what percentage of the United Nations was comprised of African countries.[109] Before they made their estimate, they were given an anchor that was ostensibly random and had no meaningful link to the correct answer. The researcher spun a *Wheel of Fortune* type wheel that contained the numbers 0–100. The wheel was rigged so that it stopped on 10 for half the participants and on 65 for the other half. These numbers were the anchors. At the time the study was published, there were 39 African countries, which is about half-way between 10 and 65. Participants were asked if the percentage of African countries was higher or lower than the number on the wheel. The estimating task was the same

---

simulation heuristic the tendency to judge the frequency or likelihood of an event by the ease with which you can imagine (or mentally simulate) it

anchoring and adjustment the tendency to judge the frequency or likelihood of an event by using a starting point (called an anchor) and then making adjustments up or down.

Silver medalist Aliaksandra Herasimenia of Belarus (left) does not look very happy compared to gold medalist Ranomi Kromowidjojo (center) of the Netherlands and bronze medalist Marleen Veldhuis of the Netherlands (right) during the medal ceremony Women's 50m Freestyle in the London 2012 Olympic Games.

for both groups, so in theory they should have made similar estimates, but both groups stuck close to their anchor. The average estimate of participants who had been given the random number 10 was 25%, whereas the average estimate of those given the random number 65 was 45%. This study illustrates that people are influenced by an initial anchor value even though it may be unreliable (indeed, it was seemingly chosen at random).

TABLE 5.1 summarizes the definitions and examples of the four heuristics we have discussed. The next section discusses the most common cognitive errors people make.

TABLE 5.1 The Most Common Mental Shortcuts (or Heuristics) That People Use

Heuristic	Definition	Example
Representativeness	The tendency to judge the frequency or likelihood of an event by the extent to which it "resembles" the typical case	In a series of 10 coin tosses, most people judge the series HHTTHTHTTH to be more likely than the series HHHHHHHHHH (where H is heads and T is tails), even though both are equally likely.
Availability	The tendency to judge the frequency or likelihood of an event by the ease with which relevant instances come to mind	People overestimate the frequency of dramatic deaths (e.g., dying in an airplane crash) and underestimate the frequency of less dramatic deaths (e.g., dying from lung cancer).
Simulation	The tendency to judge the frequency or likelihood of an event by the ease with which you can imagine (or mentally simulate) an event	In the Olympics, bronze medalists appear to be happier than silver medalists because it is easier for a silver medalist to imagine being a gold medalist.
Anchoring and adjustment	The tendency to judge the frequency or likelihood of an event by using a starting point (called an anchor) and then making adjustments up and down from this starting point	If one party in a negotiation starts by suggesting a price or condition, then the other party is likely to base its counteroffer on this anchor.

QUIZ YOURSELF

Heuristics: Mental Shortcuts

1. The strategy of judging the likelihood of things by how well they match particular prototypes constitutes the _____ heuristic.
   - ⓐ availability
   - ⓑ matching
   - ⓒ representativeness
   - ⓓ vividness

2. People's greater fear of flying than of driving can probably best be explained by the _____ heuristic.
   - ⓐ anchoring and adjustment
   - ⓑ availability
   - ⓒ representativeness
   - ⓓ simulation

3. "If only I hadn't driven home from work using a different route," thinks Minh, "then my car would not have been hit in the rear by that other driver!" Minh's statement most clearly reflects _____.
   - ⓐ the availability heuristic
   - ⓑ a self-serving bias
   - ⓒ counterfactual thinking
   - ⓓ the self-fulfilling prophecy

4. Masako asked two friends to estimate the number of people living in Tokyo. The correct answer, as of 2019, is about 14 million. She asked the first friend whether it was more or less than 8 million. She asked the second friend whether it was more or less than 20 million. The first friend guessed 10 million people, whereas the second friend guessed 18 million people. The difference in estimates can best be explained using the _____ heuristic.
   - ⓐ anchoring and adjustment
   - ⓑ availability
   - ⓒ representativeness
   - ⓓ simulation

answers: see pg 185

Flawed or Clever Thinking?

Social psychologists have long taken a particular approach to understand human thinking—but objections have led to the consideration of a newer, different approach. We have already seen this with attribution theory. The long-standing assumption was that people first decide whether person versus situation factors cause behavior, but now a different view says people start by distinguishing intended versus unintended actions (though both views are based on Heider's 1958 book).

A similar dispute questions whether people's thinking is full of errors and biases or is instead very effective and well tailored for its purposes. The standard view that people's thinking is full of errors and biases among other flaws has dominated the field for decades (including previous editions of this textbook!). The gist is that the world is full of information that is extensive and complicated, and the human mind is lazy, so people acquire all sorts of mental shortcuts. People favor these shortcuts because they often get the right answer, or at least a good enough answer, while saving plenty of time and effort, but they do open the door for errors and biases. The best approach would be to do the careful, hard thinking of analyzing all the information, using logic, mathematical calculations, and statistical reasoning, but because those are hard, people take the easy way out. The heuristics we covered in the last section are easy to understand in that way, as is the roster of errors and biases we cover in the next section.

Thus, the standard view is that people think in order to find the truth, but their thinking suffers from mistakes and shortcomings stemming largely from laziness and from various motivated biases (e.g., wishful thinking). The alternative view gives people more credit than that. This alternative has two prongs. One was mentioned at the start of the chapter. It says that people evolved to think in order to argue with others and convince them of their side, rather than to figure out the truth alone. (We'll see examples in the next section.) The other prong suggests that the shortcuts and heuristics actually work quite well. It says that it is wrong and foolish to claim that the proper way to think is to perform extensive calculations, using logic and math. Math is good when one has complete and perfect information to work with, but that is rarely true. It says that often people do better with simple rules and guides. People tend to use "psycho-logic" rather than logic.

As a vivid illustration,[110] consider the news story in which an airplane flew into a flock of birds upon takeoff. Several of the birds went into the jet engines and shut them down, leaving the plane coasting through the air with no power. The pilot had to make a quick decision as to whether he could glide back to the airport and land there safely. Such a calculation can be made quite precisely, provided that one knows the plane's current speed and weight, its altitude, the relevant distances, and a few other things (e.g., effects of wind). But of course, the pilot did not have all that information handy, and even if he did, computing them in his head would be risky because a single mistake could mean death for everyone on the plane.

Instead, the pilot relied on one simple heuristic. When you look out the front window of a gliding plane at a point in the horizon, if that point starts to rise in your windshield, you won't make it that far. The pilot looked at the airport in the distance, and when that seemed to rise, that meant the plane was dropping too fast to get there. He abandoned the plan to fly to the airport and instead steered the plane to land in the river, where it stayed afloat long enough for everyone to be rescued. Thus, in this case, he did better by following the simple heuristic than by trying to do the full calculation.

With that in mind, let's take a look at some of social psychology's classic findings about how people think.

QUIZ YOURSELF
Flawed or Clever Thinking?

1. The current view of attributions assumes that people try to explain the behavior of others they start by focusing on _____ actions.
   - (a) external versus internal
   - (b) global versus specific
   - (c) intended versus unintended
   - (d) stable versus unstable

2. Which of the following standard views of heuristic thinking may be incorrect based on the current evidence?
   - (a) automatic
   - (b) effortless
   - (c) flawed
   - (d) quick

3. According to the standard view, people think in order to find _____.
   - (a) the truth
   - (b) a good approximate answer
   - (c) an answer that agrees with what they already believe
   - (d) an answer that will be persuasive to others

4. According to the current view, people think in order to find _____.
   - (a) the truth
   - (b) a good approximate answer
   - (c) an answer that agrees with what they already believe
   - (d) an answer that will be persuasive to others

answers: see pg 185

(So-Called) Errors and Biases

One theme of this book is the duplex mind. The human mind has two main systems: the automatic system and the deliberate system. The automatic system helps people deal with information overload. The job of the automatic system is to make quick, fairly accurate judgments and decisions, whereas the deliberate system works more slowly and thoroughly to make more precise judgments and decisions. Because most people are cognitive misers and do not like to expend mental effort, they rely heavily on the automatic system. The automatic system takes shortcuts, such as by using heuristics. Even though the automatic system is very good at helping people make fast decisions (it can do it in milliseconds!), it is not very good at making precise calculations, such as probabilities. Thus, the automatic system is prone to make several kinds of cognitive errors. Even on such important personal questions as to how many sex partners one has had, people's thinking is subject to biases. For example, many studies have found dramatic but logically implausible differences in how men and women answer the straight-forward question of how many sex partners they have had. Read *The Social Side of Sex* to find out more.

People generally have access to two types of information: (a) statistical information from a large number of people, and (b) case history information from a small number of people (even a single case, such as a friend). Although people would make much better decisions if they paid the most attention to statistical information, they generally pay the most attention to case history information.[111] For example, when buying a new car, people are more influenced by what a few friends tell them about a car (case history information) than they are by what hundreds of people say about the car in *Consumer Reports* (statistical information). Even if the car has an outstanding repair record and is rated very highly by consumers, they won't buy it if their friend owned a similar car once and said it was a "lemon."

Or at least, that is how social psychologists have thought about such patterns for decades: as irrational mistakes. But the newer approach suggests a more positive view.

The Social Side of Sex

Counting Sex Partners

At some point in the development of most intimate relationships, the two individuals ask each other how many people they have previously had sex with. A simple question with a simple answer, right? Hardly! In fact, even when people give supposedly honest answers to physicians or researchers, the answers are subject to distortion from a variety of sources.[112,113] One sign of distortion is that in all surveys, males report many more sex partners than females. For example, the Centers for Disease Control and Prevention surveys find that males report about 6 opposite-sex partners, whereas females report about 4 opposite-sex partners.[114] About 20% of males report at least 15 opposite-sex partners, whereas only about 10% of females report at least 15 opposite-sex partners. These numbers are fairly stable over the past 13 years. Similarly, unequal results have been reported in all other studies.[115,116] These inequalities are logically impossible. If we count only heterosexual behavior, and if there are roughly the same number of males as females, then the average numbers of sex partners must be equal. Every time a male has sex with a new female, the female also has sex with a new male. How can the numbers be so different?

Most experts suspect that tallies of sex partners are affected by motivation. Males want to claim to have had many sex partners because that indicates that they are handsome, charming, and virile. Females, however, want to claim relatively few partners because females value being choosy and look down on others who have had many partners.[117,118,119] As evidence that men and women have different motivations, studies of sexual regret found that women tend to regret sexual things they did, whereas men's regrets focused on things they did not do.[120] Put another way, women regret having had sex with this or that person, whereas men regret missing out on sex with this or that person.

Still, how do these motivations translate into different tallies of sex partners?

One possible answer is that people lie. Males might invent more partners than they have had, and females might deny or conveniently forget some of their past partners. This is not a full explanation either. The gender difference in sex partners is found even on anonymous surveys, in which people would have little to gain by lying and would supposedly not be embarrassed by the truth. Still, there are some signs of it. When researchers hooked people up to lie detectors, they changed their answers to the question about how many sex partners they had. Females, in particular, reported more partners when they were connected to lie detectors than when they could just write a number on a questionnaire.[121]

Another possible answer is that differences are due to sex with prostitutes or homosexual activity. Few surveys include prostitutes, so these women (some of whom have had sex with thousands of men) could skew the data. These sex acts would be counted by the men but not by the women in the research sample (because prostitutes were not included in the female sample). These do contribute something to the finding that men have more sex partners than women. However, some researchers have calculated that there is not nearly enough prostitution to account for the large gender difference in tallies of partners.[122,123] The same goes for homosexual activity. True, gay males typically have more partners than gay females, but gay males are a relatively small segment of the population. Even when data are restricted to heterosexual and non-prostitute sex, males report more partners than females.[124]

Research on social cognition has identified two processes that help explain the difference. One is a difference in how people count. People who have had more than six partners do not always keep an exact count. When asked how many partners they have had, they can either try to make a mental list, or they can estimate. Apparently, females usually answer by making a mental list, but this procedure is prone to underestimating (because it is easy to forget something that may have happened once or twice some years ago). In contrast, males tend to estimate, and estimating tends to produce inflated numbers (because men round up: a true figure of 22 might produce an estimated answer of "about 25"). Accordingly, when males and females try to give honest answers, they may still furnish systematically distorted numbers.[125,126,127]

The other process involves shifting criteria. What exactly counts as sex? Research has shown that males are more likely than females to include borderline cases such as oral sex.[128] There is no truly correct answer, so, as social cognition researchers have found in many spheres, people use criteria that suit them and make them feel good.[129] Females want to report relatively few sex partners, so if they only had oral sex with someone they feel justified in saying they did not have sex. Males want to have higher tallies, so they think it is reasonable to include oral sex. No doubt some people do lie about their sexual histories. But even when they try to tell the truth, they may furnish heavily biased answers. Moreover, these answers are distorted in the directions that give people the answers they prefer.

Maybe people do pretty well by trusting a friend's direct experience than relying on statistics in some magazine. And maybe the issue is for arguing. Suppose your friend complained about a certain car being a lemon, and then you went out and bought the same kind of car, and it too turned out to be a lemon—you'd have a hard time justifying your behavior to your friend. "I told you so!" the friend would say, and your lame response, "But the magazine said its statistics were good" wouldn't help much.

Let's be clear and not overstate. Most experts agree that doing the full calculations is the best way when thorough and clear information is available. But usually it's not. The question is whether to do hard calculations with the available but inadequate data, or to rely on heuristics and rules of thumb. It's also about whether thinking is an often-fallible procedure for reaching the truth or a pretty effective way of arguing one side. Both sides of that debate host lively arguments. (Notice, however, that even scientists often reach the truth by arguing both sides and seeing which one can produce the most convincing evidence!)

Sometimes the consequences are much more important than what car to buy. To return to the story that opened this chapter, parents must decide whether to vaccinate their children. If they ignore the overwhelming statistical evidence and rely instead on personal anecdotes, they might decide not to vaccinate their children, which could prove fatal.

Confirmation Bias

Jonathan Cainer was born in the United Kingdom in 1958.[130] He dropped out of school when he was 15 years old, pumped gas at a service station, and played in a band called *Strange Cloud*. In the early 1980s he moved to the United States and became a manager at a nightclub in Los Angeles. There he met a psychic poet named Charles John Quatro, who told him he would someday write an astrology column read by millions. Cainer returned to the United Kingdom and enrolled at the Faculty of Astrological Studies in London. Today he does indeed write an astrology newspaper column that is read by millions of people all over the world.

Are you impressed by the accuracy of Quatro's prediction regarding Cainer's future as an astrology columnist? We can predict your answer to this question, even though we have never met you (and we are not psychics!). If you believe in astrology, we predict that you will be impressed. If you don't believe in astrology, we predict that you will not be impressed. Were we correct? Told you so!

This example illustrates the **confirmation bias**, defined as the tendency to notice information that confirms one's beliefs, and to ignore information that disconfirms one's beliefs.[131] Philosopher Francis Bacon said, "It is the peculiar and perpetual error of the human understanding to be more moved and excited by affirmatives than by negatives." Beliefs in paranormal phenomena such as telepathy can be explained by the confirmation bias.[132] The confirmation bias isn't limited to paranormal beliefs, however. This bias extends to a wide variety of beliefs.[133]

To learn the truth, it would be best to give equal consideration to confirming and disconfirming evidence. The tendency to pay more attention to confirming than disconfirming evidence has long been regarded as typical of how human thought is sabotaged by bias leading to error. But look at it again from the perspective that human reasoning is designed for arguing, not for figuring out the truth. If you are trying to argue your case, you want evidence that helps you, not evidence that hurts you. It turns out that people are pretty good at finding disconfirming evidence when they have to argue against something.[134] To return to the example of Quatro's prediction about Cainer, people who disbelieve in astrology can probably generate several reasons not to be impressed by that story. Thus, the confirmation bias may not be a flaw in human thinking—it's just a standard pattern that helps people do what thinking is primarily for, namely arguing and convincing.

Illusory Correlations

An **illusory correlation** occurs when people overestimate the link between variables that are related only slightly or not at all.[135] For example, people overestimate the frequency of undesirable behavior by minority group members. One explanation for this tendency is that minority group status and undesirable behaviors are both relatively rare. Because people are sensitive to rare events, the occurrence of two rare events together is especially noticeable.

Consider some experiments on illusory correlation.[136] Participants read a series of sentences describing a desirable or an undesirable behavior from a person belonging to

confirmation bias the tendency to notice and search for information that confirms one's beliefs and to ignore information that disconfirms one's beliefs

illusory correlation the tendency to overestimate the link between variables that are related only slightly or not at all

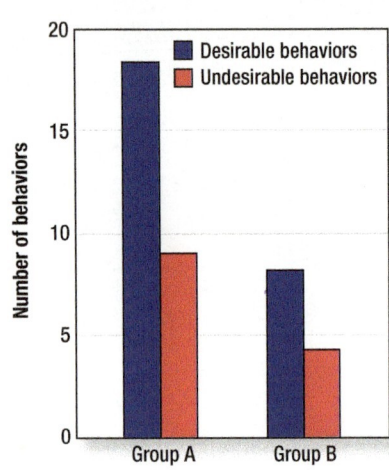

FIGURE 5.11 Actual correlation study. Two-thirds of the behaviors were performed by Group A members (the majority), and two-thirds of the behaviors were desirable for both.
SOURCE: Hamilton and Gifford (1976).

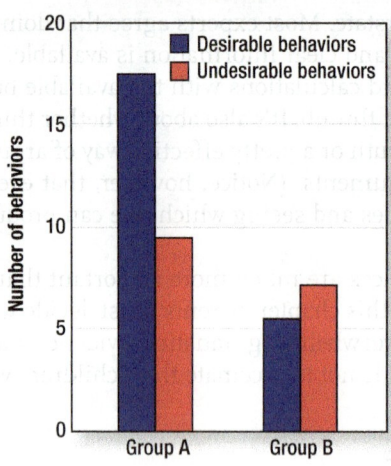

FIGURE 5.12 Illusory correlation study. Even though two-thirds of the behaviors committed by Group B members were desirable, participants "recalled" Group B members committing more undesirable behaviors than desirable behaviors.
SOURCE: Hamilton and Gifford (1976).

group A or B (e.g., "John, a member of Group A, visited a sick friend in the hospital." "Allen, a member of Group B, dented the fender of a parked car and didn't leave his name."). Overall, two-thirds of the behaviors were desirable for both groups, and two-thirds involved a member of Group —the majority (see **FIGURE 5.11**). Participants then estimated the number of desirable and undesirable behaviors performed by members of each group. The ratio of desirable to undesirable behaviors was the same for the two groups, so the estimates should have been the same for the two groups, but they were not. Participants overestimated the number of undesirable behaviors performed by Group B (minority) members; in fact, they estimated more undesirable behaviors than desirable behaviors from Group B members (see **FIGURE 5.12**). Illusory correlations can even occur after exposure to only one unusual behavior performed by only one member of an unfamiliar group (e.g., Ben, a Jehovah's Witness, owns a pet sloth), called **one-shot illusory correlations**.[137]

The mass media contribute to these illusory correlations. For example, if a mentally ill person shoots a famous person (e.g., Mark Chapman shoots Beatles guitarist John Lennon; John Hinckley Jr. shoots former U.S. President Ronald Reagan), the media draw attention to the mental status of the assassin. Assassinations and mental hospitalizations are both relatively rare, making the combination especially noticeable. Such media reporting adds to the illusion of a correlation between mental illness and violent behavior. The rate of violence among those with severe mental illness is not particularly high and is not higher than those without mental illness.[138]

Again, the idea that thinking is for arguing offers a fresh perspective. Illusory correlations are errors if the purpose of thinking is to find the truth. But saying two things go together can be a very convincing argument, and if your opponent is reduced to saying something feeble like, "Well, they don't *always* go together," you have the upper hand in the dispute.

Base Rate Fallacy

The **base rate fallacy** is the tendency to ignore or underuse base rate information (information about most people) and instead to be influenced by the distinctive features of the case being judged. Many cognitive errors are the result of people not paying attention to base rates.

Consider the following example:[139]

A town has two hospitals. In the larger hospital, about 45 babies are born every day; in the smaller hospital, about 15 babies are born every day. In one year, each hospital recorded the number of days on which more than 60% of the babies born were boys. Which hospital recorded more such days?

a. The large hospital
b. The small hospital
c. About the same number of days (within 5% of each other)

one-shot illusory correlation an illusory correlation that occurs after exposure to only one unusual behavior performed by only one member of an unfamiliar group

base rate fallacy the tendency to ignore or underuse base rate information and instead to be influenced by the distinctive features of the case being judged

Most people answer (c). People don't consider the fact that variability decreases as sample size increases. Think about flipping a coin 10 times and getting 6 heads versus flipping a coin 1,000 times and getting 600 heads. You are much more likely to get at least 6 heads in 10 flips (1 in 2.65) than to get at least 600 heads in 1,000 flips (1 in 7.33 billion). Tournaments that eliminate teams after a single loss (e.g., World Cup soccer, National Football League playoffs, college basketball tournaments) allow underdogs a better chance to win, as compared to tournaments in which each round is a series of games (e.g., National Basketball Association playoffs, World Series in baseball). In a single game, the weaker team might get lucky and win. Across many games, the better team will tend to win more often.

Soccer is especially vulnerable to the effects of small samples, because soccer games tend to have low scores such as 1–0. Sometimes only one goal is scored in the entire championship game, and that goal decides the winner. Thus, one moment of luck can crown the underdog as champion. In contrast, a seven-game World Series of baseball may easily contain 40 to 50 points scored, and a seven-game basketball series will typically have over more than 1,000 points, which makes it quite difficult for a relatively inferior team to beat the odds and win just by luck.

The base rate fallacy may simply reflect a broader pattern by which people are not naturally skilled at statistical reasoning. On this point, the newer view of heuristics as adaptive or as designed for arguing is not that helpful, and the base rate fallacy may really be an error. After all, even if you can do the base rate calculations yourself, the person you are arguing against may not understand the argument, and so it won't help you convince that person.

Gambler's Fallacy and the Hot Hand

Suppose you flip a coin 10 times. You flip 9 heads in a row. What is your next flip more likely to be?

a. Heads
b. Tails
c. Heads and tails are equally likely.

Hot hand players answer (a) because they think they have a "hot" hand and their luck will continue. **Gambler's fallacy** players answer (b) because they think their luck will change and that a tails is "due." These biases may both stem from the same source—the representativeness heuristic. The correct answer is (c). If people think about it, they would agree that heads and tails are equally likely on any given flip. They might also agree that the outcome of any flip does not depend on the outcome of the previous flip.

These are both errors if one accepts the assumption that each flip is truly random and independent of the others. But perhaps that is rare in the real world. When dealing with strangers, trust is a big issue. If you saw someone flip "heads" nine times in a row, would you really want to bet on tails the next time, at even money, as the statisticians say you should? More likely, the person has a trick coin. Certainly, if your friends said not to bet on tails, and you did so anyway and lost, they would say "we told you not to bet on tails!" and you'd have a difficult time arguing that what you did was sensible.

To test these biases in the real world, researchers conducted a study in a casino in Nevada.[140] Participants were videotaped while playing roulette. Because a roulette wheel consists of 38 numbers, 1/38, or 2.6%, of the bets should fall on each number. The researchers could look at how each person bet over time. Most players exhibited both biases. Gambler's fallacy players were also more likely to be hot hand players. Statisticians like to say that only people who are really bad at math will choose to gamble. Again, though, the point may simply be that the mind is not designed to deal with truly random events and the statistics that go with them. Predicting future behavior from past behavior is often a sensible strategy and an effective argument.

hot hand the tendency for gamblers who get lucky to think they have a "hot" hand and their luck will continue

gambler's fallacy the tendency to believe that a particular chance event is affected by previous events and that chance events will "even out" in the short run

False Consensus Effect

People tend to overestimate the number of people who share their opinions, attitudes, values, and beliefs. This tendency is called the **false consensus effect**.[141,142] An early demonstration[143] asked students whether they would walk around campus carrying a sign that said, "Eat at Joe's." Later they were asked how many other people they thought would be willing to carry such a sign. Those who agreed to carry the sign said that 62% of other people would also agree to carry the sign, whereas those who refused to carry the sign said that only 33% of other people would carry the sign. Obviously, both can't be right, and one or both groups tended to overestimate the proportion of people who would respond the same way they themselves had.

The availability heuristic provides one possible explanation of the false consensus effect. When asked to predict what other people are like, people use the information that is most readily available—information about themselves and their friends. Because people tend to associate with similar others, this available information might lead people to overestimate the percentage of the population that is similar to themselves. Another explanation is that people want to believe their views and actions are the correct ones, so they assume others would concur. Yet another explanation is that people use their own reaction as an "anchor" (remember the anchoring and adjustment heuristic?) and adjust it when having to furnish a broad prediction about people in general; as usual, they tend to remain too close to the anchor.

A study of over a thousand people on Facebook found that friends routinely overestimated how much they had similar opinions.[144] They failed to realize how much they disagreed, even when they claimed to discuss the issues. People seem to surmise their friends' opinions by projecting their own views and by relying on stereotypes about their friends.

The mood people are in can influence the false consensus effect. In one study,[145] college students chose which of two all-expenses paid vacations to New York they would prefer to take (3-day vacation in a luxury hotel vs. 5-day vacation in a budget hotel). Next, they were induced to feel happy or sad. There was also a neutral mood control group that was not induced to feel an emotion. Afterward, they estimated the percentage of people who would opt for either the same vacation as they chose or the alternate choice. The researchers found a false consensus effect (i.e., the percentage was higher for the vacation participants chose than for the alternative vacation), especially among participants in the happy mood group. We will look at effects of mood more closely in the chapter on Emotions (Chapter 6), but for now it may help to know there is a pattern of taking more mental shortcuts and not thinking as carefully when people are in good moods. Bad moods and negative emotions make people think more carefully, whereas good moods seem to indicate "Everything's fine!" and so errors like the false consensus effect increase.

False Uniqueness Effect

People tend to underestimate the number of people who share their most prized characteristics and abilities. This tendency is called the **false uniqueness effect**.[146] For example, people think their first name is more unique than it actually is, regardless of how rare their name actually is.[147] Similarly, people who engage in desirable health-protective behaviors (e.g., exercising regularly, getting regular checkups, eating healthy foods), underestimate the number of other people who engage in similar behaviors.[148] It appears that people overestimate consensus when it comes to their undesirable characteristics (false consensus) but underestimate consensus when it comes to their desirable characteristics (false uniqueness). As noted in the previous section, they also overestimate consensus for their opinions and preferences.

This mixture of false consensus and false uniqueness effects can be remembered easily by noting that all distortions are in the direction most helpful for self-esteem. That is, you can feel good about yourself if your opinions are correct, and one sign of correctness is that most people agree with you (so you overestimate consensus for opinions). You can feel good about yourself if your faults are ones that many people have (so overestimate consensus regarding faults). And you can feel especially good about yourself if your

false consensus effect the tendency to overestimate the number of other people who share one's opinions, attitudes, values, and beliefs

false uniqueness effect the tendency to underestimate the number of other people who share one's most prized characteristics and abilities talents and virtues are rare and exceptional ones that few people can match (so underestimate consensus regarding good characteristics). Probably this pattern is no accident. As we saw in Chapter 3, people like to think well of themselves, and many patterns of bias and distortion help them achieve and maintain their favorable self-views.

Perseverance of Theories

Generating explanations of social facts is one common mental activity. When research participants read a newspaper article claiming that risk-takers made the best firefighters, they were able to come up with multiple explanations why that would be so. The experimenters, however, had created the newspaper article. Other participants read a different (bogus) newspaper article making the opposite claim, that risk-avoiders made the best firefighters. Those participants were just as good at coming up with explanations. As we said in Chapter 1, common sense can explain most things in hindsight!

But then the experiment took a curious turn. The experimenter told the participants that the news story on which they had based their thinking was a pure fiction created by the researchers for this study. Surprisingly, however, when participants rated their opinions on what sorts of people made the best firefighters, they stuck with what they had been thinking—even though the evidence for it had been completely demolished.[149] These findings were the first demonstration of what came to be known as **theory perseverance** effects. Once the mind draws a conclusion, it tends to stick with that conclusion unless there is overwhelming evidence to change it. Merely losing the evidence on which the conclusion is based does not seem to shake people's belief.

One interpretation of the theory perseverance effect is that the mind is quite impressed with its own activity. Once people had thought about why risk-seekers made the best firefighters, their minds clung to that conclusion. Thus, people may get stuck with false beliefs. Then again, if thinking is designed for arguing, theory perseverance is not surprising. Losing some of the evidence for the side you are arguing does not make you want to switch sides. Indeed, when people argue, if some of the evidence they cite is discredited, they quickly move along to use other arguments.

The cognitive miser may also be relevant. Rejecting information takes more cognitive effort than accepting it.[150]

Statistical Regression

In the 19th century, Sir Francis Galton introduced the concept of **statistical regression** (also called **regression to the mean**), which refers to the statistical tendency for extreme scores or extreme behavior to return toward the average. In his study of men's heights, Galton found that the tallest men usually had sons shorter than themselves, whereas the shortest men usually had sons taller than themselves. In both cases, the height of the children was less extreme than the height of the fathers.

To make it onto the cover of a major sports magazine, such as *Sports Illustrated*, an athlete or team must perform exceptionally well in addition to being lucky. However, appearing on the cover of *Sports Illustrated* got the reputation of being a jinx because athletes consistently performed worse after appearing on the cover. The belief in the *Sports Illustrated* jinx is so strong that some athletes have even refused to appear on the cover.[151]

Many people attribute the subsequent poor performance to internal factors rather than to chance (e.g., after appearing on the cover of *Sports Illustrated*, athletes feel so much pressure that they choke). But the "*Sports Illustrated* jinx" can also be explained by the concept of regression to the mean.[152] The magazine puts a team or athlete on the cover after an exceptionally good performance, and regression to the mean dictates that in most cases the next performance won't be as great, just as really short men don't usually have sons who are even shorter. If the magazine instead used cover photos featuring teams that had performed unbelievably badly that week, the magazine would get a reputation as a miracle worker for improving a team's luck and performance! But that too would be just a misunderstanding of regression to the mean.

In summary, the key to regression to the mean is that when one selects an instance (or a group) for extreme performance, it is almost always true that one will have selected a

theory perseverance proposes that once the mind draws a conclusion, it tends to stick with that conclusion unless there is overwhelming evidence to change it

statistical regression (regression to the mean) the statistical tendency for extreme scores or extreme behavior to be followed by others that are less extreme and closer to average more extreme instance than is warranted. When events deviate from the average, people are more likely to think about the bad exceptions than about the good exceptions.

Illusion of Control

The belief that people can control totally chance situations is called the **illusion of control**.[153,154] For example, gamblers in casinos who are playing craps often roll the dice harder for high numbers and softer for low numbers. People like to be in control of their own fate. The illusion of control has been shown to influence people to take more risks. Research on traders working in investment banks found that traders who had an illusion of control took more risks and lost more money than other traders.[155] Likewise, an illusion of control can influence gamblers to continue gambling in the face of continued losses.[156]

Counterfactual Thinking

Counterfactual means "contrary to the facts." **Counterfactual thinking** involves imagining alternatives to past or present factual events or circumstances.[157] Counter-factual thinking is familiar to everyone, even if they have not heard the term before. We have all thought about "what might have been," if people had only behaved differently. What if you had studied harder in high school? What if your parents had never met? What if the other candidate had won the election? Douglas Hofstadter,[158] cognitive science professor at Indiana University and author of the Pulitzer Prize–winning *Gödel, Escher, Bach: An Eternal Golden Braid*, wrote, "Think how immeasurably poorer our mental lives would be if we didn't have this creative capacity for slipping out of the midst of reality into soft 'what ifs'! Research has confirmed this richness: Counterfactual thinking makes life more meaningful. When people reflect on important life events, like winning scholarship or meeting a romantic partner, these feel all the more meaningful when people consider how they might never have happened.[159]

Counterfactual thinking influences how students take tests.[160] When taking multiple-choice tests, many students choose what they initially think is the correct answer. After thinking about it more, however, they begin to doubt their so-called first instinct and think that another answer is even better. Are students better off staying with their first choice, or should they switch their answer? About 75% of students think it is better to stick with their initial answer. Most college professors also believe that students should stick with their initial answer. Some test preparation guides also give the same advice: "Exercise great caution if you decide to change your answer. Experience indicates that many students who change answers change to the wrong answer."[161] However, virtually all studies show that students are better off switching answers.[162] This tendency has been dubbed the **first instinct fallacy**. It is defined as the false belief that it is better not to change one's first answer even if one starts to think that a different answer is correct.

So why do many students, professors, and test guide writers succumb to this fallacy? Research on counterfactual thinking can shed light on this issue. Assume that you got the answer wrong in the end and therefore engaged in counterfactual thinking about what you might have done to get it right. You'd probably feel the most regret if you had first written down the correct answer and then changed it to a wrong one. You'd feel less regret if you had first written the wrong answer and then refused to change it, because in that scenario you had never put down the right answer. Having first written the correct answer and then erased it makes you feel that you were so close to getting it correct that changing was a terrible mistake. And so you might mistakenly conclude, "I shouldn't ever change away from my initial answer!"

Counterfactual thinking can envision outcomes that were either better or worse than what actually happened. **Upward counterfactuals** involve alternatives that are better than actuality, whereas **downward counterfactuals** are alternatives that are worse than actuality.[163,164] For example, when Nilou looks back on her honeymoon, she can think it could have gone better (e.g., "We should have gone to a more exotic place!") or that it could have been worse (e.g., "Good thing we didn't get robbed!"). People make far more upward than downward counterfactuals, which is probably a good thing because it causes people to consider how to make things better in the future.[165] For example, if Eddie looks back on his exam and regrets not studying harder so he could have earned a higher grade, he will

---

illusion of control the false belief that one can influence certain events, especially random or chance ones

counterfactual thinking imagining alternatives to past or present events or circumstances

first instinct fallacy the false belief that it is better not to change one's first answer on a test even if one starts to think that a different answer is correct

upward counterfactuals imagining alternatives that are better than actuality

downward counterfactuals imagining alternatives that are worse than actuality probably study harder next time. In contrast, if Eddie looks back on his exam with relief that he did not fail it, he probably will not study harder next time.

Downward counterfactuals have their uses, of course. In particular, they help people feel better in the aftermath of misfortune.[166] When something bad happens, people say, "It could have been worse," and contemplating those even more terrible counterfactuals is comforting.

Ultimately, counterfactual thinking is probably one of the crucial traits that help people create and sustain the marvels of human society and culture. Most animals can barely perceive and understand their immediate surroundings, but people can dream of how it can be different. Democracy, women's liberation, and wireless technology did not exist in nature, but human beings were able to look at life as it was and imagine how it could be different, and these imaginings helped them change the world for the better.

The concepts of counterfactual thinking and regret are sometimes used interchangeably. Although the two concepts are related, they are not the same thing.[167] One important difference is that regrets are feelings, whereas counterfactuals are thoughts. **Regret** involves feeling sorry for misfortunes, limitations, losses, transgressions, shortcomings, or mistakes.[168] Counterfactuals involve thinking about how things could have been better or worse.

The various cognitive biases and (so-called) errors discussed in this section are summarized in **TABLE 5.2**.

regret involves feeling sorry for one's misfortunes, limitations, losses, transgressions, shortcomings, or mistakes

TABLE 5.2 Common Cognitive Errors

Error or Bias	Definition	Example
Confirmation bias	The tendency to notice information that confirms one's beliefs and to ignore information that disconfirms one's beliefs	Looking for evidence that your horoscope is true if you believe in astrology, and ignoring evidence that is inconsistent with your horoscope
Illusory correlation	The tendency to overestimate the link between variables that are related only slightly or not at all	Believing that mentally ill individuals are violent and dangerous
Base rate fallacy	The tendency to ignore or underuse base rate information and instead to be influenced by the distinctive features of the case being judged	Thinking that it is equally likely to have 60% of births be male in a small or a large hospital
Gambler's fallacy	The tendency to believe that a particular chance event is affected by previous events, and that chance events will "even out" in the short run	Believing that one is more likely to get a *heads* on a coin toss after the sequence TTTTTTTT than after the sequence THHTTHTHT
Hot hand	The tendency for gamblers who get lucky to think they have a "hot" hand and their luck will continue	Believing that one is more likely to get a *tails* on a coin toss after the sequence TTTTTTTT than after the sequence THHTTHTHT
False consensus effect	The tendency for people to overestimate the number of other people who share their opinions, attitudes, values, and beliefs	Believing that most people have the same religious beliefs as you do
False uniqueness effect	The tendency for people to underestimate the number of other people who share their most prized characteristics and abilities	If a person exercises regularly, underestimating the number of other people who also exercise regularly
Theory perseverance	The tendency to stick with a conclusion unless there is overwhelming evidence to change it	Continuing to dislike someone because you heard she was mean to your friend, even though you later find out she was not mean to your friend
Statistical regression	The statistical tendency for extreme scores or extreme behavior to return toward the average	The *"Sports Illustrated* jinx," in which athletic performance usually declines after appearing on the cover of *Sports Illustrated*
Illusion of control	The belief that one can control totally chance situations	For gamblers, throwing dice softly for low numbers and hard for high numbers
Counterfactual thinking	Imagining alternatives to past or present factual events or circumstances	After getting in a car wreck, thinking "what if" I had gone home using a different route

QUIZ YOURSELF
(So-Called) Errors and Biases

1. Gamblers who throw dice softly to get low numbers and who throw harder to get high numbers are demonstrating _____.
   - a) the base rate fallacy
   - b) the gambler's fallacy
   - c) the illusion of control
   - d) regression to the mean

2. Which sequence of six coin flips is least likely to occur?
   - a) TTTTTT
   - b) TTTTTH
   - c) THHTTH
   - d) All of the above are equally likely to occur.

3. If you scored 99 out of 100 on your first social psychology exam, you are likely to score lower on the second exam, even if you are equally knowledgeable about the material on both exams. This is an example of _____.
   - a) base rate fallacy
   - b) confirmation bias
   - c) false uniqueness effect
   - d) regression to the mean

4. Gustov gets in an accident in which his new car is totaled, but he received only minor injuries. Gustov thinks to himself, "At least I'm still alive. I could have died." This type of thinking illustrates which of the following concepts?
   - a) Downward counterfactual
   - b) Regression to the mean
   - c) Regret
   - d) Upward counterfactual

answers: see pg 185

Are Most People Really Stupid?

> "Some scientists claim that hydrogen, because it is so plentiful, is the basic building block of the universe. I dispute that. I say there is more stupidity than hydrogen, and *that* is the basic building block of the universe."
>
> — Frank Zappa, musician and songwriter

Sometimes social cognition researchers are accused of perpetuating the idea that people are basically stupid, as Frank Zappa suggests in this quotation. This is because these researchers show that people make so many cognitive errors. Would nature have selected stupid people to reproduce and pass on their genes to subsequent generations? We doubt it. The kinds of errors people make are not random—they are quite predictable. Many may not even be errors at all, as we have said: They might just reflect a style of thinking geared toward arguing one's case and convincing others, rather than trying to reason out the truth, whatever it may be.

More often than not, heuristics provide the correct answers, or at least answers that are good enough. The automatic system is also incredibly fast, capable of making decisions in milliseconds. People can even process information outside of conscious awareness. It is possible that some errors may only occur in the social psychological laboratory—not in the real world. Other errors are corrected socially, such as when people give us feedback on what we did wrong. Still other errors can cancel each other out, if they occur in random combinations.

Evolutionary psychologists have argued that when it comes to the really important decisions, those involving survival and reproduction, people make relatively few stupid decisions.[169,170,171] Perhaps this is because they use the deliberate system rather than the automatic system when it comes to making important decisions. The quick and approximate answers provided by the automatic system are not good enough, and people expend the mental energy required to make these important decisions.

Reducing Cognitive Errors

Even if the errors aren't all that serious, who wants to make errors? Several factors can reduce cognitive errors. People can be taught to use relevant statistical probabilities rather

180 | **CHAPTER 5** Social Cognition

than ignore them.[172] Even "crash courses" on statistical reasoning are helpful in reducing cognitive errors[173,174] Making the information easier to process can also improve decision-making ability and reduce cognitive errors.

One of the most effective ways of **debiasing** people from the tendency to make cognitive errors is to get them to use deliberate processing (such as conscious reasoning) rather than automatic processing. Some examples include encouraging people to consider multiple alternatives,[175,176,177] to rely less on memory,[178,179] to use explicit decision rules[180,181] to search for disconfirmatory information,[182] and to use meta-cognition.[183] **Meta-cognition** literally means "thinking about thinking." It is a reflective approach to problem solving that involves stepping back from the immediate problem to examine and reflect on the thinking process. Examples include quizzing oneself to evaluate one's understanding of what one has read in a textbook, planning how to approach a math exam, and evaluating progress toward achieving a learning goal (e.g., memorizing the periodic table of the elements for your chemistry class).

Most attempts to reduce cognitive errors have relied on cognitive approaches such as those described above. However, people often make cognitive errors because they "feel" it is the right choice. Thus, emotions are critical in understanding cognitive errors. Unfortunately, attempts to suppress emotions often backfire (see Chapter 6). A more promising approach is distracting oneself from experiencing emotions. Indeed, a manipulation as simple as "avoid thinking about your feelings" has been shown to reduce cognitive errors.[184]

debiasing reducing errors and biases by getting people to use deliberate processing rather than automatic processing

meta-cognition reflecting on one's own thought processes

QUIZ YOURSELF
Are People Really Stupid?

1. What system is mainly responsible for the cognitive errors that people make?
   - a) Automatic system
   - b) Deliberate system
   - c) Primary system
   - d) Secondary system

2. People make fewer cognitive errors when they are making decisions about _____.
   - a) trivial matters (e.g., what brand of toothpaste to buy)
   - b) important matters (e.g., what major to select in college)
   - c) very serious matters (e.g., survival and reproduction)
   - d) None of the above; cognitive errors are the same for the three types of matters.

3. Which type of graduate training that teaches statistical reasoning is most effective in reducing cognitive errors?
   - a) Business
   - b) Chemistry
   - c) Law
   - d) Psychology

4. The analysis of cognitions is called _____.
   - a) counterfactual thinking
   - b) explicit decision rules
   - c) meta-cognition
   - d) statistical reasoning

answers: see pg 185

What Makes Us Human

Putting the Cultural Animal in Perspective

The special or unique features of human psychology are readily visible in this chapter. Experts debate the question "Do animals think?" (i.e., nonhuman animals), but the debate usually focuses on whether the very simple cognitive activities of animals, such as forming an expectancy and perceiving that it is violated, qualify as thinking. Only a few overly sentimental pet owners believe that animals can formulate complex thoughts or understand long sentences—let alone begin to match the higher flights of human thought, such as in philosophical or religious contemplation, theories of physics and chemistry, poetry, epic narratives, or even arguments about why a sporting event or blind date turned out as it did. Only humans think in those ways.

The remarkable power of human thought is seen not just in the use of symbolism, but in the combining of symbols. People use language to do most of their thinking, and human thought typically combines many small concepts into complex ideas, stories, or theories. A dog can learn several dozen one-word commands, but only humans can string together a long set of words to make sentences, paragraphs, long stories, speeches, or even a book.

The capacity to use language opens up new worlds of thought, as it lets people explore the linkages of meaning. People can do mathematical and financial calculations, conduct cost–benefit analyses, and reason logically. Without language, other animals can engage in only the very simplest, most trivial versions of those forms of thought, or none at all.

The duplex mind is another distinctive feature of human thinking. Automatic processing is probably something both humans and animals have, but the powers of the conscious mind are more uniquely human. Only humans can perform the rule-based, systematic, precise thinking that the deliberate system does, such as complex mathematical calculations, logical reasoning, and detailed cost–benefit comparisons of multiple options when facing a decision.

The simple fact is that most complex patterns of thought are uniquely human. Humans can analyze a complex situation and make attributions about why something happened (and they can also debate with each other about those attributions, to reach a consensual explanation). False consensus and false uniqueness biases are also limited to humans.

Only humans engage in counterfactual thinking, which can be extremely helpful in enabling people to change their behavior in the future. Only humans suffer agonies of rumination and regret about what might have been, but that same power of counterfactual thinking has been a crucial aid to human progress. Over the centuries, people have looked around them at the state of the world and imagined how it could be better. Nature did not give us schools, written language, dental care, recorded music, airplane travel, or the justice system, but counterfactual thinking has enabled people to dream of such improvements—and then to help them become reality.

We saw in Chapter 3 that humans have a much more complex conception of self than other animals. This complex knowledge structure influences thought in many ways. Only humans will show self-serving biases or actor/observer differences, and only humans can learn to correct for these biases.

The remarkable power of human thought creates both unique errors and unique capabilities to understand the truth. In other words, the special properties of the human mind lead to both right and wrong answers that other animals wouldn't get. Only humans can succumb to the base rate fallacy because only humans can use base rates at all, so only humans can learn to use them correctly. Only humans fall prey to the regression fallacy, but only humans can develop an accurate understanding of regression to the mean and can therefore learn to avoid the mistake.

In short, most of the material in this chapter would be absent in a book on the psychology of other animals because human cognition is generally unlike what is found in other species. This sweeping difference is quite unlike what we will see in the next chapter on emotion. That is because advanced cognitive processes are relatively new in evolution and specific to human beings, whereas emotion goes far back in evolutionary time. Thus, many animals have emotional reactions and expressions that resemble human ones in crucial respects. Even so, the fact that we can think about our emotions (and their causes) is likely to change them, as we shall see. For humans and human social life, thinking changes almost everything.

CHAPTER 5 SUMMARY

What Is Social Cognition?

- Social cognition is the study of any sort of thinking by people about people and about social relationships.
- People think about other people more than any other topic, and probably more than about all other topics combined.
- The human mind is designed to participate in society, and this means its primary job is dealing with other people.
- People think about other people in order to be accepted by them, or to compete with or avoid them.
- The term *cognitive miser* refers to people's reluctance to do much extra thinking.
- People generally prefer to conserve effort by relying on automatic modes of thought when they can.
- Knowledge structures are organized packets of information that are stored in memory.
- Schemas are knowledge structures that represent substantial information about a concept, its attributes, and its relationships to other concepts.
- A violation of expectancies sparks deliberate thinking.
- Scripts are knowledge structures that contain information about how people (or other objects) behave under varying circumstances; scripts define situations and guide behavior.
- At least three main types of goals guide how people think:
  - Find the right answer to some problem or question.
  - Reach a particular, preferred conclusion.
  - Reach a pretty good answer or decision quickly.
- In the Stroop effect, the automatic response is to say the word rather than the ink color.

- The four elements that distinguish automatic from deliberate processes are intention, effort, control, and efficiency.
- Priming is the tendency for frequently or recently activated concepts to become more accessible in memory.
- Framing is how something is presented.
- Trying to suppress a thought can have the paradoxical effect of increasing the thought.
- In the counterregulation or "what the heck" effect, dieters eat more if they believe they have broken their diets than if they are hungry.

Attributions and Explanations: Why Did That Happen?

- Attributions are the inferences people make about events in their lives.
- Internal, stable attributions involve ability; internal, unstable attributions involve effort; external, stable attributions point to the difficulty of the task; and external, unstable attributions involve luck.
- The self-serving bias suggests that people want to take credit for success but deny blame for failure.
- The actor/observer bias states that actors tend to make external attributions, whereas observers make internal attributions.
- The fundamental attribution error (also sometimes called correspondence bias) refers to the finding that people have a bias to attribute another person's behavior to internal or dispositional causes.
- A major attribution dimension is whether one believes another person's behavior was intentional versus accidental.

Heuristics: Mental Shortcuts

- Heuristics are mental shortcuts or rules of thumb.
- The representativeness heuristic is the tendency to judge the frequency or likelihood of an event by the extent to which it resembles the typical case.
- The availability heuristic is the tendency to judge the frequency or likelihood of an event by the ease with which relevant instances come to mind.
- The simulation heuristic is the tendency to judge the frequency or likelihood of an event by the ease with which you can imagine (or mentally simulate) an event.
- The anchoring and adjustment heuristic suggests that when people estimate how frequent or likely an event is, they use a starting point (called an anchor) and then make adjustments up and down from this starting point.

Flawed or Clever Thinking

- According to the standard view, the purpose of thinking was to discover the truth. Heuristic and automatic thinking was viewed as flawed and biased.
- According to the current view, thinking is for arguing and persuading others. Heuristic is not viewed as flawed and biased; indeed, it often provides an excellent answer.

(So-Called) Errors and Biases

- People may make cognitive errors because they are more concerned about arguing their point of view than about finding the truth.
- Information overload is the state of having too much information to make a decision or remain informed about a topic.
- Estimation and shifting criteria can result in biased counts of sexual partners.
- People generally have access to two types of information:
  - Statistical information from a large number of people.
  - Case history information from a small number of people.
- People generally pay the most attention to case history information.
- Confirmation bias is the tendency to notice information that confirms one's beliefs and to ignore information that disconfirms one's beliefs.
- An illusory correlation occurs when people overestimate the link between variables that are related only slightly or not at all. It can occur even after one exposure, called one-shot illusory correlations.
- The mass media contribute to illusory correlations by focusing on rare events.
- The base rate fallacy is the tendency to ignore or underuse base rate information and instead to be influenced by the distinctive features of the case being judged.
- The hot hand is the tendency for gamblers who get lucky to think they have a "hot" hand and their luck will continue.
- The gambler's fallacy is the tendency to believe that a particular chance event is affected by previous events and that chance events will "even out" in the short run.
- The false consensus effect is the tendency to overestimate the number of people who share one's opinions, attitudes, values, or beliefs.
- The false uniqueness effect describes the finding that people tend to underestimate the number of people who share their most prized characteristics and abilities.
- The theory perseverance proposes that once the mind draws a conclusion, it tends to stick with that conclusion unless there is overwhelming evidence to change it.
- Statistical regression (also called regression to the mean) refers to the statistical tendency for extreme scores or extreme behavior to return toward the average.
- One major evolutionary purpose of thinking is to decide how to respond when one's goals are blocked.
- The belief that people can control totally chance situations is called the illusion of control.
- Counterfactual thinking involves imagining alternatives to past or present factual events or circumstances.
- Upward counterfactuals posit alternatives that are better than actuality, whereas downward counterfactuals posit alternatives that are worse than actuality.
- Regret involves feeling sorry for misfortunes, limitations, losses, transgressions, shortcomings, or mistakes.
- Regrets are feelings, whereas counterfactuals are thoughts.

Are People Really Stupid?

- More often than not, heuristics provide the correct answers, or at least answers that are good enough.
- Relying less on memory, considering multiple alternatives, using meta-cognition, searching for disconfirmatory information, and using explicit decision rules are all techniques that can reduce cognitive errors.

What Makes Us Human? Putting the Cultural Animal in Perspective

- The remarkable power of human thought creates both unique errors and unique capabilities to find the truth.

key terms

actor/observer bias 163
anchoring and adjustment 168
attributions 162
availability heuristic 167
base rate fallacy 174
cognitive miser 153
confirmation bias 173
counterfactual thinking 178
counter-regulation 161
debiasing 181
downward counterfactuals 178
false consensus effect 176
false uniqueness effect 176
first instinct fallacy 178
framing 158
fundamental attribution error (correspondence bias) 164
gain-framed appeal 158
gambler's fallacy 175
heuristics 166
hot hand 175
illusion of control 178
illusory correlation 173
knowledge structures 155
loss-framed appeal 158
meta-cognition 181
one-shot illusory correlation 174
priming 156
regret 179
representativeness heuristic 166
schemas 155
scripts 156
self-serving bias 163
simulation heuristic 168
social cognition 151
statistical regression (regression to the mean) 177
Stroop effect 154
Stroop test 153
theory perseverance 177
upward counterfactuals 178

quiz yourself ANSWERS

1. What Is Social Cognition? p. 159
   answers: 1.c 2.c 3.d 4.d

2. Attributions and Explanations: Why Did That Happen? p. 166
   answers: 1.d 2.b 3.d 4.b

3. Heuristics: Mental Shortcuts p. 169
   answers: 1.c 2.b 3.c 4.a

4. Flawed or Clever Thinking? p. 171
   answers: 1.c 2.c 3.a 4.d

5. (So-Called) Errors and Biases p. 180
   answers: 1.c 2.d 3.d 4.a

6. Are People Really Stupid? p. 181
   answers: 1.a 2.c 3.d 4.c

EMOTION AND AFFECT

6

LEARNING OBJECTIVES

1. Explain how the two parts of the duplex mind contribute to our emotional experience, and apply your understanding of the duplex mind to contrast conscious emotion and automatic affect.

2. Explain how specific emotions are inner processes that serve interpersonal functions. Describe the role of emotion in feelings of belongingness. Describe how the experience of guilt can help a person maintain good relationships with others, and how feelings of shame, disgust, happiness, and anger can lead to good relationships that enhance survival and reproduction.

3. Identify how human emotions differ from similar responses in animals, relating your knowledge of humans as cultural animals to your explanations. Debate the role of cultural values in specific emotions such as guilt, happiness, anger, and disgust.

4. Describe some of the physiological effects that are related to our experience of emotions. Summarize bodily changes that are associated with happiness, anger, fear, or other emotions, and explain how these physical changes can contribute to our conscious experience of emotions.

5. Summarize why we have emotions, relating the benefits and costs to both interpersonal and evolutionary systems. Explain the relationship between emotions and behavior, and describe the cognitive implications of emotions.

6. Describe the research studying whether emotions differ across gender and across culture, emphasizing the findings on the regulation of emotional expression.

7. Define emotional intelligence and explain how it relates to emotional regulation. Describe how and why people attempt to alter their emotional states.

Jiri Miklo/Shutterstock.com

THE SOCIAL SIDE OF SEX
Can People Be Wrong About Whether They Are Sexually Aroused?
193

TRADEOFFS
Affect Intensity: Emotional Roller Coaster or Even Keel?
200

FOOD FOR THOUGHT
Mood and Food
211

MONEY MATTERS
Emotions and Prices
215

WHAT MAKES US HUMAN?
Putting the Cultural Animal in Perspective
225

187

Some people get very angry when driving a vehicle on the road, and others can be hurt or even killed as a result of their angry outbursts.

In Washington DC, for example, one woman became so angry that she took a car jack out of her car's trunk and started hitting the driver's side window and mirror of a Greyhound bus with it. The driver got out of the bus and stood in front of the woman's car so she could not drive away while he called the police. However, the woman threw the car jack back in her trunk, got in her car, and started driving off anyway, hitting the bus driver with her car and sped off, throwing him to the ground. A passenger on the bus recorded the entire event on his mobile phone.1 Such acts are called "Road Rage." Unfortunately, this woman is not alone. Angry and aggressive driving accounts for more than half of all traffic fatalities in the United States (U.S.), more than texting or alcohol.[2]

Emotions make life rich and colorful, and they influence how people act, though not always in a good way (e.g., crimes of passion!). They still pose something of a mystery. Why do people have emotions? Why is the emotion system set up the way it is? We will try to answer these and other important questions in this chapter.

One clue is that emotions are mostly outside our conscious control, even though we may feel them consciously. Emotions provide a feedback system. They bring us information about the world and about our activities in it. They reward and punish us, so we learn to set up our lives in ways that avoid bad emotions and maximize good emotions. Consider guilt as an example. Guilt helps us know we did something wrong. To avoid guilt, people may change their behavior in advance: They may try to keep their promises, obey the rules, treat other people kindly, and so on. If people could escape guilt just by deciding not to feel guilty, there would be less need to behave well in order to avoid guilt. If you could control your emotions, then anytime you started to feel guilty, you could just turn those feelings off and everything would be fine (at least as far as how you feel is concerned). Guilt can give us feedback and guide our behavior, but only if it and similar emotions are outside of our conscious control. ●

What Is Emotion?

It turns out to be fiendishly difficult to provide a definition of emotion, or even to provide several definitions of distinct concepts related to emotion. Some psychologists use the terms *emotion, affect,* and *mood* interchangeably, whereas others treat the terms as distinct concepts. We treat them as distinct concepts. The most common definitions emphasize **emotion** as a full-blown, conscious state that is clearly linked to some event. Emotion is thus a reaction to something, and the person who has the emotion knows it. You may feel angry because someone insulted you, or happy because you got an "A" on your social psychology test, or sad because your grandmother died. In contrast, **mood** is sometimes defined as a feeling state that is not clearly linked to some event. You may not know why you are in a good or bad mood, but you do know that you feel happy or sad. The third concept, **affect** (pronounced 'AF-ekt; note that this word is a noun, not the verb, which is pronounced ə-'fekt) is sometimes defined as a result of mapping all emotions onto a single good–bad dimension. Positive affect encompasses all good emotions (e.g., joy, bliss, happiness, love, contentment, enthusiasm), whereas negative affect encompasses all bad emotions

emotion a conscious evaluative reaction that is clearly linked to some event

mood a feeling state that is not clearly linked to some event

affect the automatic response that something is good (positive affect) or bad (negative affect)

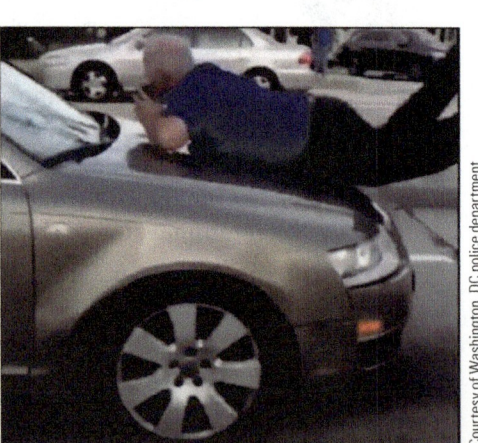

(e.g., anger, anxiety, fear, jealousy, disgust, grief). Most researchers argue that positive and negative affect are separate dimensions, not opposite ends of the same dimension.[4,5,6,7] Other researchers use affect to refer to emotion-type reactions that can occur regardless of consciousness. It makes no sense to say that someone is happy but doesn't know it; in that sense, the conscious feeling is the essence of the emotion. Still, some affective reactions can occur without consciousness. You can have a quick positive or negative feeling about something as simple as a word without being fully conscious of it.

Emotions are very important to humans, and the ability to recognize emotions starts very young. Babies as young as three months old can "hear" emotions. Researchers scanned the brains of 21 babies and found that their brains responded to tapes playing "emotional sounds," such as laughing and crying.[8] The limbic region of the brain, which regulates emotions, responded strongly to negative or sad sounds, but it did not differentiate between neutral and happy sounds. These findings are consistent with the general principle that bad is stronger than good.[9]

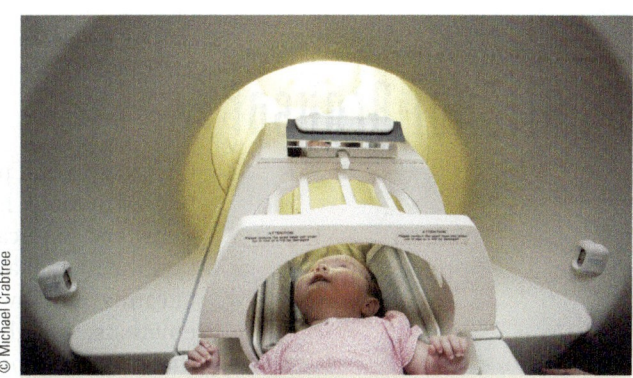

Using brain scan technology, researchers found that babies, three months old, could "hear" different emotions. The limbic brain region of their brains, which regulate emotions, responded strongly to negative or sad sounds, but did not differentiate between neutral and happy sounds.

Conscious Emotion Versus Automatic Affect

Regardless of how people use the terms *emotion*, *mood*, and *affect*, two quite different phenomena need to be distinguished. These correspond roughly to the two dimensions of the duplex mind. One is **conscious emotion**, which is felt as a powerful, single (unified) feeling state. The other is **automatic affect**, which is felt as liking or disliking, or as good or bad feelings toward something, and may occur outside of consciousness.

We will use the term *emotion* to refer to the conscious reaction, often including a bodily response, to something. In contrast, we use the term *affect* to refer to the automatic response that something is good or bad (liking versus disliking). Affective reactions to things that are "good" and "bad" are automatic and very fast, occurring in the first microseconds of thought. As soon as you know what something is, you start to know whether you like or dislike it.[10] This initial evaluation even occurs for things people have never encountered before, such as nonsense words like "juvalamu."[11] In contrast, full-blown emotion takes more time.

There is no point in trying to decide whether automatic affect or conscious emotion is more important. Both are important, and it would be a mistake to assume that everything we learn about one of them applies to the other as well.

Emotions have both mental and physical aspects. In the next section we explore the physical aspects of emotional arousal.

conscious emotion a powerful and clearly unified feeling state, such as anger or joy

automatic affect a quick response of liking or disliking toward something

1. Conscious is to unconscious as _____ is to _____.
   - (a) affect; emotion
   - (b) emotion; affect
   - (c) affect; mood
   - (d) mood; affect

2. Affect is generally mapped onto ___ dimensions.
   - (a) good and bad
   - (b) masculine and feminine
   - (c) specific and universal
   - (d) strong and weak

3. Affective reactions to things that are "good" and "bad" generally occur in the first _____ of thought.
   - (a) microseconds
   - (b) seconds
   - (c) minutes
   - (d) Hours

4. Fatima feels deep sadness because her dog died. What term most accurately describes what Fatima is feeling?
   - (a) Affect
   - (b) Emotion
   - (c) Mood
   - (d) All of the above

What Is Emotion?

answers: see pg 228

Emotional Arousal

One reason that people are fascinated by emotions is that they bridge the mind and the body. Emotions have both mental aspects (such as subjective feelings and interpretations) and physical aspects (such as a racing heartbeat or tears). The challenge is to say how the mental and physical aspects of emotion are linked together. One important area of connection involves the bodily response of arousal, which is linked to most conscious emotions, though not necessarily to automatic affect. **Arousal** is a physiological response that occurs within the body, including a faster heartbeat and faster or heavier breathing. It should not be confused with sexual arousal that we discuss in the *Social Side of Sex Box*, as it is a general bodily state, akin to the everyday term of being "excited."

James–Lange Theory of Emotion

In 1884, American psychologist William James and Danish psychologist Carl Lange both independently proposed a theory linking the mental and physical aspects of emotion, which is now called the **James-Lange theory of emotion**.[12] James[13] described the theory as follows:

> My theory ... is that *the bodily changes follow directly the perception of the exciting fact, and that our feeling of the same changes as they occur is the emotion*. Common sense says: we lose our fortune, are sorry and weep; we meet a bear, are frightened and run; we are insulted by a rival, are angry and strike. The hypothesis here to be defended says that this order of sequence is incorrect, ... we feel sorry because we cry, angry because we strike, afraid because we tremble, and not that we cry, strike, or tremble, because we are sorry, angry, or fearful, as the case may be. [italics in original]

James and Lange proposed that the bodily processes of emotion come first, and then the mind's perception of these bodily reactions creates the subjective feeling of emotion (see **FIGURE 6.1**). When something happens, your body and brain supposedly perceive it and respond to it, and these physiological events form the basis for the emotion you feel.

arousal a physiological reaction, including faster heartbeat and faster or heavier breathing, linked to most conscious emotions

James–Lange theory of emotion the proposition that the bodily processes of emotion come first, and then the mind's perception of these bodily reactions and creates the subjective feeling of emotion

facial feedback hypothesis the idea that feedback from the face muscles evokes or magnifies emotions

Researchers tried for many years to prove the James–Lange theory, but they were largely unsuccessful. One important aspect of the theory is that different emotions must arise from different bodily responses. Data from many studies suggested, however, that the body's response seemed to be very similar for different emotions. Whatever emotion the person felt, the body just showed a standard arousal pattern. Even tears, for example, are not limited to sadness, because people sometimes cry when they are happy or angry or afraid, and many others do not cry when they are sad. Tears, therefore, are not just a sign of sadness, but more likely a sign of intense feeling.

The James–Lange theory did, however, lead to an important contemporary hypothesis—the **facial feedback hypothesis**.[14,15,16] According to the facial feedback hypothesis, facial expressions can evoke or magnify emotions because the brain reacts to what the facial muscles are doing. Several studies have found support for this hypothesis. One of the cleverest manipulations of facial feedback consisted of having participants hold a pen or pencil in either their lips or their teeth (smiling induction) while rating cartoons.[17] The effect was recently replicated in data collected from over 400 undergraduate students collected over nine semesters.[18] This sounds like a trivial difference, but try it: When you hold the pen between your teeth, your face resembles a

In research studies, people who held a pen with their teeth smiled and felt happier, whereas people who held the pen with their lips frowned and felt sad.

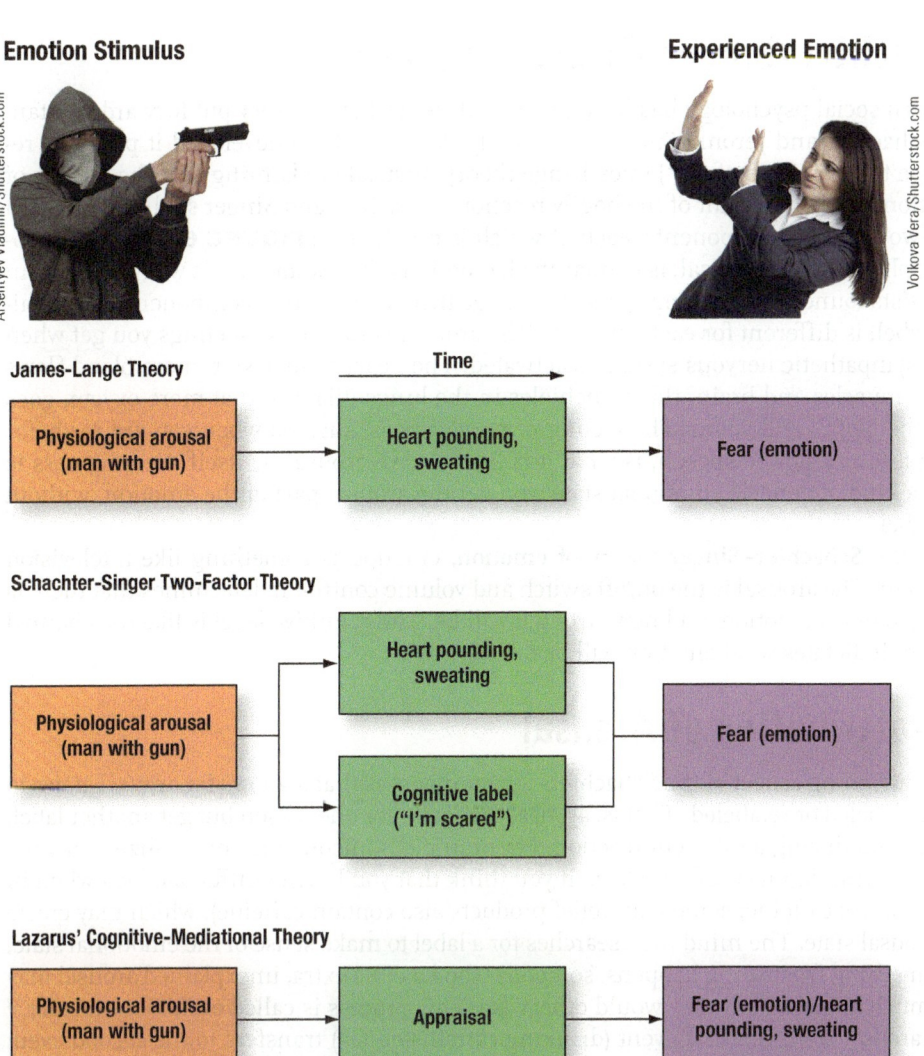

FIGURE 6.1

Three prominent emotion theories.

smile, whereas when you hold it between your lips, your face resembles a frown. The facial feedback hypothesis holds that if you are smiling, you will enjoy things more than if you are frowning, and this is what the researchers found. Participants who held the pen in their teeth thought the cartoons were funnier than did participants who held the pen in their lips. Thus, if you put on a happy face, you will be happier and enjoy external events more.

Facial feedback may also help us recognize emotional expressions in others. A study[19] found that Botox cosmetic injections, which are used to reduce wrinkles and other signs of aging, can have an unintended negative side effect—they reduce muscular feedback from the face, so the brain doesn't get all the usual input that helps it use emotional information. Female patients in cosmetic clinics who received Botox injections were less accurate in recognizing emotional expressions in others than were participants who received dermal filler injections that do not reduce facial feedback. Seeing people smile normally makes you start to smile a little, and that helps your brain understand their emotions. If you've had Botox, your face doesn't react to the other person's smile (or frown or whatever emotional expression they display), and this impairs your ability to understand other people's emotions.

Although Botox cosmetic injections may make people look younger, they can impair the ability to recognize emotional expressions in others.

Emotional Arousal | 191

> "Everyone knows what an emotion is, until asked to give a definition."
> — Beverly Fehr and James Russell[3]

Schachter–Singer Theory of Emotion

Modern social psychology has been greatly influenced by a theory put forward by Stanley Schachter and Jerome Singer in the early 1960s.[20,21] They developed it partly in response to the failure of the James-Lange theory. Instead of claiming that the feeling of emotion is a direct result of the bodily reaction, Schachter and Singer said that emotion has two separate components, each of which is crucial (see **FIGURE 6.1**). One component, physiological arousal, is similar in all emotions. (Remember, this was the problem scientists found when testing the James-Lange theory.) The other component, the cognitive label, is different for each emotion. The arousal is the mix of feelings you get when your sympathetic nervous system is activated: The heart beats faster, more blood flows to the muscles and brain, the bronchioles in the lungs dilate so that more oxygen goes into the blood, and so on. The feeling of nervousness, such as when you are ready for a big test or a public speech, is what it is like to have arousal by itself. Nervousness is thus a kind of generic emotional state: you get the arousal part of the emotion, without the label.

In the **Schachter–Singer theory of emotion**, emotion is something like a television program. The arousal is the on/off switch and volume control: It determines that there is going to be an emotion, and how strong it will be. The cognitive label is like the channel switch: It dictates what emotion will be felt.

Misattribution of Arousal

One intriguing aspect of the Schachter–Singer theory is that it allows for arousal states to be mislabeled or relabeled. That is, arousal may arise for one reason but get another label, thereby producing a different reaction. For example, someone may not realize that what they are drinking has caffeine (e.g., if you think that you have decaffeinated tea when in reality it has caffeine; some pain relief products also contain caffeine), which may create an arousal state. The mind then searches for a label to make sense of the emotional state. If something frustrating happens, someone who has this extra, unexplained arousal may get much angrier than they would otherwise. This process is called **excitation transfer**.[22] The arousal from the first event (drinking caffeinated tea) transfers to the second event (frustration).

There have been several important experimental demonstrations of mislabeling or relabeling arousal. In Schachter and Singer's original studies,[23] participants were told that the researchers were studying the "effects of vitamin injections on visual skills." By the flip of a coin, participants received an injection of either adrenaline (epinephrine) or a placebo (saline solution, which has no effects; it was included just to control for any effects of having someone stick a needle into your arm). Adrenaline is a stimulant that increases your heart rate, blood pressure, and breathing rate. Participants who received the adrenaline shot were either informed or not informed about the "side effects" of the drug (e.g., it causes heart pounding, trembling hands, etc.). Everyone was told that the injection contained the vitamins, but there were no actual vitamins.

Next, participants were exposed to an accomplice who acted either happy and joyous (by playing with paper, rubber bands, pencils, folders, and hula hoops) or angry and resentful (provoked by a questionnaire that asked many nosy, offensive questions, such as "Which member of your immediate family does not bathe or wash regularly?"). The researchers secretly observed to see whether the participant would join in and show similar emotion. The strongest emotional reactions were found among the people who had both received the stimulant (rather than the placebo) and been told that the injection would not have any side effects. The ones who received the stimulant and were told that it was a stimulant attributed their arousal state to the injection rather than to the situation, so they did not label it as an emotional state.

As discussed above, sometimes the mind might not realize that the body is aroused, or why. *The Social Side of Sex* discusses this problem in connection with a particularly interesting form of arousal—sexual arousal. Read the box to find out more about how sexual arousal is related to emotions!

Schachter–Singer theory of emotion the idea that emotion has two components: a bodily state of general arousal and a cognitive label that specifies the emotion

excitation transfer the idea that arousal from one event can transfer to a later event

The Social Side of *Sex*

Can People Be Wrong About Whether They Are Sexually Aroused?

Sexual arousal is one form of arousal. You might think it is simpler and clearer than emotional arousal because emotional arousal can be associated with such a wide spectrum of emotions, whereas sexual arousal is specific and focused. Yet sexual arousal has its ambiguities, too.

One source of ambiguity is that the brain and the genitals are not always "on the same page." Sexual stimulation may affect the brain, or the genitals, or neither, or both. Research suggests that the disconnect between the brain and the genitals is greater among women than men. That is, the link between self-reported arousal (i.e., whether people consciously believe they are sexually aroused) and physiological measures of sexual arousal in the genitals are correlated about 0.60 in men but only about 0.25 in women.[24] Remember, correlations range in size from −1 (a perfect negative correlation) to +1 (a perfect positive correlation). By conventional values, a "small" correlation is .1, a "moderate" correlation is .3, and a "large" correlation is .5.[25] Thus, the correlation is quite large for men, but less than moderate for women.

There is plenty of room for divergence in both genders, especially if the person's attitudes prescribe certain reactions that differ from what the body finds exciting. In one classic study,[26] men's feelings about homosexuality were surveyed, and researchers chose men who were the most tolerant of gay sex and others who were the most strongly opposed to it. Then all the participants watched some films of gay men having sex with each other. The researchers measured both the feelings the men had while watching these films and their physiological response. The latter test used a device (called the penile plethysmograph) that wraps a rubber band around the penis to measure how erect it becomes.

The two measures yielded opposite findings. The men who had said they were most strongly opposed to homosexuality reported that they did not like the gay films at all and that they were not turned on. The physiological sexual data, however, showed that those men were the ones most aroused by the films. This finding lends support to the view that homophobia or anti-gay prejudice is strongest among men who may themselves have homosexual tendencies but find these unacceptable. They react against their own homosexual feelings by claiming to hate gay sex and to find it disgusting.

A comparable finding emerged from research on sex guilt in women.[27] In this work, women watched sexually explicit film clips. Women with high levels of sex guilt reported on questionnaires that they did not enjoy the films, and they rated their sexual arousal to the films as lower than any other women in the study. However, physiological measures of sexual arousal—which assess the degree of lubrication in the vagina (measured using a device called a vaginal photoplethysmograph)—indicated that these women were actually more aroused than the other women in the study. Thus, some women who claim to be turned off by erotic films are actually turned on by them.

Perhaps you can use excitation transfer theory to improve your love life! Take your lover on an exciting date, such as to an amusement park or an action-packed movie, and then hold their hand or kiss them. According to excitation transfer theory, the arousal from the amusement ride or exciting movie will transfer to raise your date's attraction to you. A cup of coffee might also help improve your love life if you drink it with your partner!

Is the bodily arousal state really the same in all emotions? Subsequent research suggested that there is not just one single state underlying all emotions. More plausibly, there are at least two basic arousal states that feel quite different, one pleasant and the other unpleasant. Many research studies have been done with neutral states, such as someone receiving caffeine or another stimulant (e.g., exercising, watching a sexually explicit movie), and it does seem that these states can be converted into almost any emotion, good or bad. However, emotional arousal that comes from events that occur outside the psychological laboratory, is usually already either good or bad. "Good" arousal cannot be converted into "bad" arousal, nor can "bad" arousal be converted into "good" arousal.[28,29] Some studies have explicitly shown that when people experience pleasant arousal, they will not misattribute that state as an unpleasant emotion, or vice versa.[30]

If there are two types of naturally occurring arousal states—one good and one bad—the explanation of why real,

Going on a date? Pick an exciting activity to increase your date's attraction to you. The excitation transfer theory says the arousal activities like an amusement ride or movie will transfer and raise your date's attraction to you.

Emotional Arousal | 193

everyday emotions can't be converted may lie with automatic affect. Remember, conscious emotion takes time to build, but automatic affect arises quickly. If an arousal starts to build to form the basis for a conscious emotional reaction, it will be shaped by the automatic reaction, so it too will feel good or bad. Hence, it will be hard to re-label a bad emotion as a good one, or vice versa. Converting one positive emotion into a different positive one, such as turning joy into pride, will be much easier. A warning to the wise: Always watch out for emotional overreactions fueled by caffeine!

Appraisal Theory of Emotion

In the **appraisal theory of emotion** (see Figure 6.1), cognitions play a central role in emotions, whereas other theories of emotion suggest only a loose connection between thinking and emotions.[31,32] Appraisals are evaluations, interpretations, and explanations of events in the environment, such as whether the event affects your personal well-being. According to appraisal theories, emotions are adaptive responses that reflect appraisals of events in the environment that are significant for the person's well-being. These appraisals lead to different emotional reactions in different people. According to appraisal theory, there are not four, or six, or ten basic emotions, but an infinite number. Similarities and differences among emotions depend on common appraisals. Differences in appraisal account for individual differences in emotion. Although appraisal theories were first proposed decades ago, they are alive and well today.[33]

Appraisal theory of emotion is the idea that emotion is determined by how an event in the environment is appraised (e.g., evaluated, interpreted, explained).

QUIZ YOURSELF
Emotional Arousal

1. **Which theory of emotion predicts that we are angry because we hit someone?**
   - ⓐ Appraisal
   - ⓑ James–Lange
   - ⓒ Schachter–Singer
   - ⓓ None of the above

2. **Which theory of emotion predicts that arousal from an event can be mislabeled?**
   - ⓐ Appraisal
   - ⓑ James–Lange
   - ⓒ Schachter–Singer
   - ⓓ None of the above

3. **Tyrone had a stressful day at the office, so he stopped at the gym on the way home to work out. Even after he gets home, Tyrone still feels wound up. When his wife remarks in passing that he forgot to take out the trash, Tyrone responds by yelling and cursing at his wife. Tyrone's overreaction to his wife's comment illustrates _____.**
   - ⓐ catharsis
   - ⓑ disinhibition
   - ⓒ desensitization
   - ⓓ excitation transfer

4. **What theory predicts that emotion is primarily determined by how an event in the environment is interpreted or evaluated?**
   - ⓐ Appraisal
   - ⓑ James–Lange
   - ⓒ Schachter–Singer
   - ⓓ None of the above

answers: see pg 228

Some Important Emotions

In this section, we describe five important emotions: happiness, anger, guilt, shame, and disgust. Although we could describe many other emotions, these ones are especially important because of their social nature. In reading about each of these emotions, it is helpful to think back to one of this textbook's most important themes—namely, that inner processes serve interpersonal functions. To be sure, some emotions may serve more basic biological needs, especially survival and reproduction. But even there, people mainly achieve survival and reproduction by forming and maintaining good relationships with other people. Hence, for example, we may miss the point if we merely ask, "How could feeling guilty ever benefit the person who feels that way?" Instead, it will be more enlightening to ask, "How does feeling guilty help a person maintain good relationships with others?"

Happiness

One of the most compelling works of fiction to emerge from the Cold War is *One Day in the Life of Ivan Denisovich* by Alexander Solzhenitsyn. The main character has been sent to a prison labor camp in Siberia, Russia for 10 years, and he knows there is no guarantee that he will actually be released when his time is up. The situation is bleak. No family or loved ones ever visit him, and he is only allowed two letters per year. He has to work hard outdoors in freezing temperatures, with worn-out clothes that leave his fingers and toes constantly numb. He has no entertainment, not even something to read, and sleeps on a rock-hard bed in a room full of other prisoners. He has little chance of escape, and anyone who did manage to escape would probably just freeze to death in the vast empty land. Yet on the last page of the book, the hero looks back on his day (remember, the whole book covers just one ordinary day in the middle of his 10-year prison sentence) and reflects that he was pretty lucky—it was "almost a happy day." He falls into a contented sleep.

How could someone have an "almost happy day" in a Siberian prison camp? The writer's goal was to draw attention to the millions of Russians who suffered terribly in the prison camp system. This is what made the story brilliant: Instead of describing a day that was totally awful, the author presented a relatively "good day" in such a miserable setting. The story shows the power of comparisons and expectations. If you expect the worst—and as a Siberian prisoner you would soon come to expect that—then anything slightly better than the very worst can seem quite good by contrast. The good events that surpassed his expectations seem pathetic to most of us. His dinner was two bowls of bad oatmeal, instead of one; he had avoided the worst work assignments; he had managed to get a little tobacco (the camp's only luxury); and he had found a small piece of metal, not useful for anything he could readily imagine, but maybe someday it might come in handy for something.

Defining Happiness

In 1922, a bellboy made a delivery to Albert Einstein, who was staying at Tokyo's Imperial Hotel. Einstein had no change for a tip, but wanted to give the bellboy something, so he wrote his theory of happiness on a piece of hotel stationery: "A calm and modest life brings more happiness than the pursuit of success combined with constant restlessness." He told the bellboy to save the note because it might be valuable in the future, and it was. In a 2017 auction, the note sold for $1.56 million![34]

What is happiness, and how can it be reached? The term *happiness* is used in different ways to refer to slightly different phenomena. Human beings and many animals share one form of happiness, and it refers simply to feeling good right now. When you get something to eat or you warm up in the sun after being cold, you feel good, and you react with happy feelings.

Other forms of happiness are unique to human beings, in part because they involve a broader time span and the meaningful integration of multiple experiences. Thus, someone might be a happy person because they enjoy many positive emotional experiences, or

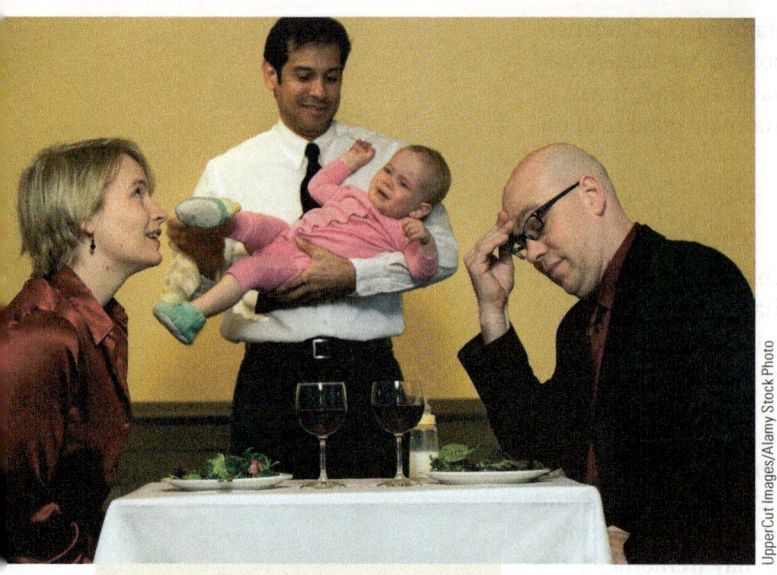

Honey, are you happy we had kids?

because they hardly ever feel bad emotions. Indeed, one measure of happiness is **affect balance:** the frequency of positive emotions minus the frequency of negative emotions.

The most complex form of happiness is sometimes called **life satisfaction.** It involves not only evaluating how your life is generally, but also how it compares to some standard. Probably most animals can feel good or bad, but only humans have life satisfaction because only humans can think meaningfully about their life as a whole and decide whether it measures up to their hopes and goals. Life satisfaction has a much broader time span than current emotion and affect balance.

Objective Roots of Happiness

What would make you happy? Most people answer this question by referring to objective circumstances. They think they would be happy if they had something along these lines: plenty of money, a good job, a happy marriage or at least a good romantic relationship, perhaps children, some friends, good health, and a nice place to live. With one exception, they are correct because people who do have those things are happier than people who do not have them. Note that most of those objective predictors involve succeeding by biological and cultural standards. Thus, if people strive to feel good, they will do things that the culture values (such as marrying and succeeding at a good job), and if everyone were to do those things, the culture would thrive and flourish.

The one odd exception is having children. Couples who have children are less happy than couples who have no children.[35] The drop in happiness due to having children has been shown repeatedly, with many different research samples and methods. It goes against intuitive beliefs, and in fact most parents expect that having children will increase their happiness. What's more, they continue to believe that having children has made them happier, even though the research clearly shows otherwise. Possibly this is because parenthood is riddled with self-deception and illusion. Parents do not want to believe that they made a big mistake by having children, and they also want to rationalize the efforts and sacrifices they have made. Having children is, however, a powerful source of meaning in life, so that even if becoming a parent reduces happiness, it does make life richer and more meaningful.[36]

Culture plays a big role in all this. Nearly all cultures encourage people to have children (by birth or adoption) and therefore help promote the idea (even when false) that having children will make you happy. If enough people expect to become happy by having children, the culture will increase in population, which cultures have generally found to be advantageous. Cultures that do not produce new generations will not survive, so nearly all successful cultures encourage reproduction. Moreover, cultures compete against others, and at some very basic level, those that have more people will triumph over those with fewer. It is not surprising that most cultures glorify parenthood and bestow social approval on those who reproduce most. For a while, the Soviet Union even gave medals to women who had the most children. This may seem odd, but it is merely a more explicit form of the approval that is found all over the world. Most likely it was motivated by urgent pragmatic forces: The Soviet Union suffered more deaths than any other country during World War II, so replenishing the population was more urgently needed there than in other countries.

The fact that having children reduces happiness may actually be a fairly recent, modern phenomenon.[37] Throughout most of history, most people were farmers, and they lived in societies that offered no social security systems, pensions, or other means of support. When you grew too old to work the farm, you would starve, unless you had children to take over the farm and support you. Childlessness was a disaster for a married couple, in terms of their practical and economic prospects. Only when the family changed from an economic partnership into being mainly a group of close relationships did the emotional impact of parenthood shift to become more negative.

affect balance the frequency of positive emotions minus the frequency of negative emotions

life satisfaction an evaluation of how one's life is generally and how it compares to some standard

Some readers become worried when they learn that having children is likely to reduce their happiness. Don't be! Most college students want children.[38] People who decide to have children often end up glad they did, even though along the way they are less happy than they would otherwise have been. The human mind is very good at forgetting bad things and emphasizing good things. Also, if you want to reduce the negative effect on happiness, you can take several steps. The first is to have a stable relationship so as not to suffer the added stresses of being a single parent. The second is to prolong the "newlywed" phase of life between marriage and birth of first child, rather than rushing into parenthood. That phase may allow the relationship to become stronger, enabling it to withstand the stresses of parenthood better. (Also, many studies have confirmed that the interval between the wedding day and the birth of the first child is one of life's happiest times, especially for women.)[39] Third, save up some money, which can be used to cover new expenses and thereby reduce some of the financial stresses that parenthood puts on the couple. After all, children can be expensive! The average cost of raising a child until age 18 is over $250,000.[40] Having a savings cushion can help avoid much unhappiness.

The surprising thing about the objective predictors of happiness, however, is that the effects are weak. Yes, people with plenty of money are happier than people who don't have much money, but the difference is quite small. Apparently, money can buy happiness, but not very much of it. There is only one objective circumstance that has been shown to make a big difference in happiness, and that involves social connections. People who are alone in the world are much less happy than people who have strong, rich social networks. (This strong link shows once again that inner processes, in this case happiness, are linked to interpersonal relationships, in this case forming and maintaining good connections to other people. The human emotional system is set up so that it is very hard for a person to be happy while alone in life.)

For all other circumstances, even including health, injury, money, and career, the differences are small. If you think that reaching your goals will make you happy, you are likely to be disappointed, even though technically you are right. In general, that is, people who meet their goals are briefly happy, but then they go back to where they were before. People who reach their career goal may experience some temporary happiness, but they do not live happily ever after. Most things wear off pretty soon.

After World War II in the former Soviet Union, women who had lots of children were given medals.

The Hedonic Treadmill

The tendency for objective changes to wear off led some social psychologists to speak of the **hedonic treadmill**.[41,42,43,44,45,46] Like a person on a treadmill, you may take big steps forward but end up in the same place. A big success at work or in school will bring joy for a while, but then the person goes back to being as happy or unhappy as before. That doesn't mean that everyone goes back to the same level. Happy people go back to being happy, and unhappy people go back to being unhappy.[47]

In one of the most dramatic illustrations of the hedonic treadmill, researchers studied people who had won the state lottery (thereby gaining hundreds of thousands of dollars) and other people who had been severely paralyzed in an accident.[48] Such events are among the most extremely good or bad things that can happen to someone. At first, of course, the lottery winners were very happy, whereas the accident victims were very unhappy. A year afterward, however, the effects had largely worn off. Winning the lottery was wonderful, but the winners seemed to have lost their ability to appreciate everyday pleasures such as a friendly conversation or a sunset. Additionally, sudden wealth brought a number of problems, such as needy relatives wanting money and tax problems. In general, a year after the big event the differences in happiness were not very noticeable.

It appeared that people got over big good events faster than they got over big bad events. People did not recover emotionally from being paralyzed as fast or as thoroughly as they got over the joy of winning the state lottery. Two large studies that tracked people across many years found that the hedonic treadmill does not work very well when life gets

hedonic treadmill a theory proposing that people stay at about the same level of happiness regardless of what happens to them

Some Important Emotions | 197

worse.[49] That is, people who suffered a disabling injury became less happy than they had been and, though they adjusted somewhat, they tended not to get back to being as happy as they had been before the accident.

Subjective Roots of Happiness

If objective circumstances do not cause happiness, then what does? Happiness appears to lie more in our outlook and personality than in our circumstances. In a sense, some people are "born happy," whereas others remain grumpy and miserable no matter what happens. Longitudinal research has looked at a long list of objective predictors of happiness and, as usual, found very weak relationships to happiness.[50, 51,52] This pattern held true for people who were tracked for a decade. Much can change in 10 years, including most of one's objective circumstances. Ten years from now you will probably have a different job, a different home, different friends, different hobbies, a different amount of money, possibly some different family members. Yet, the strongest predictor of each person's happiness turned out to be how happy the person had been 10 years before.[53] It is not perfect, of course. Some people do change for the better or worse over long periods of time, but they are the exception. In general, people who are happy now will be happy in the future, whereas those who are unhappy now will continue to be so. Major events bring joy or sorrow, but these feelings wear off, and people go back to their own baseline. If you want to be married to a happy person in 10 years, find someone who is happy today (and preferably someone who was happy before meeting you!). Statistically, that person is your best bet for someone who will be happy in the future.

One reason happiness often remains the same across time is that happiness is rooted in one's outlook and approach to life. The importance of one's outlook is evident in the difference between subjective and objective predictors of happiness. In general, subjective predictors are much stronger. *Subjective* refers to how you feel about something, whereas *objective* refers to the something. Thus, how much money you make (objectively) has only a weak relationship to happiness, but how you feel about your income (subjectively) is a strong predictor of happiness. How healthy you are (objectively), measured by how often you got sick this year, has only a weak relationship to your happiness, but how satisfied you are with your health (subjectively) is stronger. Being married has only a weak impact on happiness, but being happily married is a strong factor.

Increasing Happiness

The "positive psychology" movement has begun to look for actions or exercises that can increase happiness. Some findings are promising. Several psychological patterns have been shown to increase happiness, such as investing in relationships, forgiving others, expressing gratitude, "counting your blessings," practicing religious beliefs, meditating, being optimistic, and engaging in physical activity or exercise.[54,55,56,57,58,59,60] These seem to have in common the idea of focusing one's attention on positive things. For example, one exercise you might try if you want to raise your happiness is to sit down once or twice a week and make a list of the good things that have happened to you. Research studies have confirmed that people who do this end up happier than control participants who do not.[61]

Regardless of what causes happiness, happy people are healthy people. For example, consider the results from a fascinating study of Catholic nuns.[62] On September 22, 1930, the Mother Superior of the North American sisters sent a letter requesting that each Catholic nun "write a short sketch of [her] life. This account should not contain more than two to three hundred words and should be written on a single sheet of paper . . . include place of birth, parentage, interesting and edifying events of childhood, schools attended, influences that led to the convent, religious life, and outstanding events." More than 60 years later, these 180 sketches were scored for positive emotions. The researchers found that nuns who expressed high positive emotions lived about 10 years longer than the nuns who expressed low positive emotion! Positive emotions are apparently good for your health, though the results are correlational, so we cannot be sure whether the positive emotion is a cause of good health or merely a sign of it.

In another fascinating study,[63] researchers examined the 1952 Baseball Register photos of 230 Major League Baseball players. Researchers coded whether each player had "no smile" (i.e., stared blankly at the camera), a "partial smile" (i.e., the muscles around his mouth were only slightly raised), or a "full smile" (i.e., a wide grin, with both cheeks raised—also known as a Duchenne smile). Of the 230 players, 46 were still alive. Players who had not smiled in the photos died at age 72.9 years (on average), players with partial smiles died at age 75.0, and players with full smiles died at age 79.9 years. The results remained significant even after controlling for other variables related to mortality (e.g., marital status, BMI). Again, we do not know whether frequent smiling was a cause or just a sign of a long life. But smiling a bit more certainly can't hurt your chances! Remember the facial feedback hypothesis.

It may well be that positive emotions have direct effects on the body that improve health, such as boosting the immune system. It may also be that happiness is linked to good social relations, as we have seen, and perhaps good social relations promote health, whereas being alone in the world weakens bodily health. The link between health and belongingness could also go in either direction or both. Maybe people are drawn to associate with someone who is happy while avoiding sad or grumpy types (thus happiness affects belongingness). Or maybe having good social relations makes people happy whereas being alone reduces happiness (thus belongingness affects happiness). Maybe both are correct. There is even another possibility, which is that some underlying trait predisposes people to get along with others and to be happy.

Where you live also makes a difference. A 5-year study[64] measured the happiness of employees who relocated from the city to greener areas, compared with happiness of employees who relocated in the reverse direction. Results found that relocating to greener areas was associated with more happiness. Other research shows that even imagining yourself outdoors in nature increases happiness.[65]

In sum, happiness is linked to a variety of good outcomes, including health and success in life, but it is not yet clear what causes what. Further research will untangle these possible explanations. For now, it seems plausible that all the possible causal relationships are correct to some extent.

Happy All the Time?

Scholars have even begun to debate whether happiness is always good.[66] There is certainly a case to be made that happiness is simply all good. For one thing, it feels pleasant, and preferring pleasure over pain and good feelings over bad ones is natural. For another, there are many benefits of happiness.[67] Happy people make more money and have superior jobs, are better leaders and negotiators, are more likely to marry and to have fulfilling marriages, and less likely to divorce, have more friends and social support, have stronger immune systems, are physically healthier, live longer, are more helpful and philanthropic, and show more resilience to stress and trauma.

On the other hand, various findings suggest that some people who seem extremely happy are actually less healthy, more rigid, and prone to overlook genuine dangers and threats. Feeling very happy may also be counterproductive in some situations, such as funerals. Happy feelings can blunt negative emotions, leaving people without important signals and other benefits of negative emotion. (As one example, expressing anger is often helpful in a negotiation, and so an overly happy negotiator might not get a good result.)

Indeed, negative emotions presumably serve useful functions, and so sometimes it is appropriate and helpful to feel bad.[68] Interpersonally, bad moods enable people to detect when others are lying and to resist social influence. Bad moods also reduces bias due to stereotypes and prejudice. One possible way of understanding this is that pleasant emotions signal that the external world is fine and so the person can turn inward and take it easy, whereas unpleasant emotions cause people to focus away from the self, attending more to the environment and analyzing things carefully.

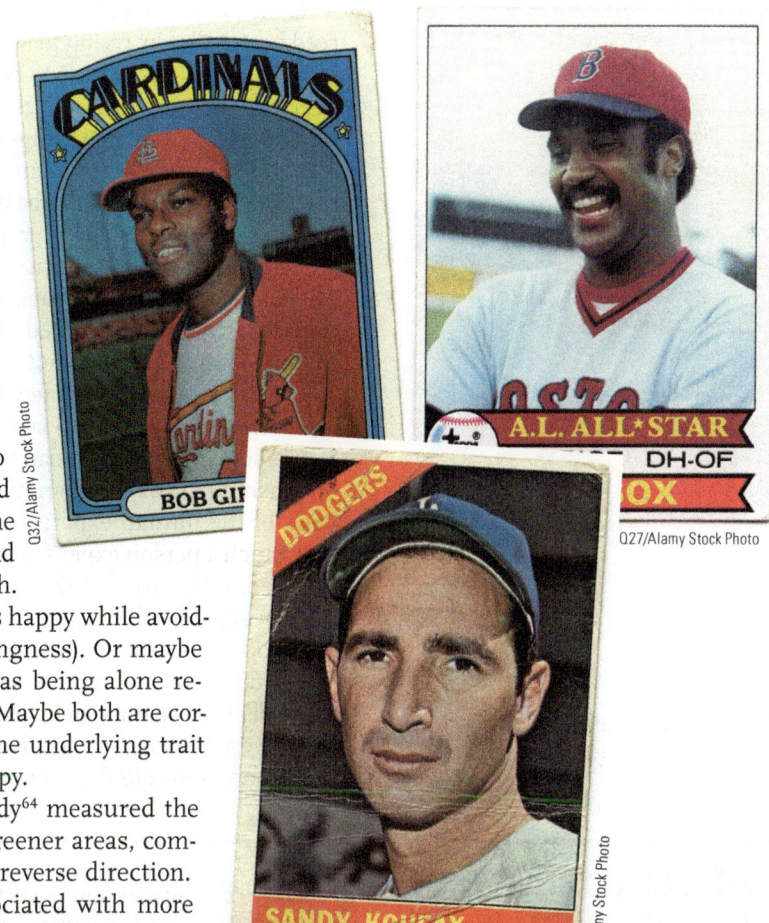

Research shows that baseball players with big smiles (top right) in their official photo lived 5 years longer than those with slight smiles (top left) and 7 years longer than those with no smiles (bottom). Smile—you just might live longer!

Is the pursuit of happiness a good thing? People want to be happy, but perhaps they succeed best at that by trying to do good work and earn the trust and affection of other people, rather than trying directly to be happy. Indeed, some lab studies have found that trying to be happy sometimes backfires, leaving people less happy than those in a control condition who simply experienced things without pushing themselves to feel good.[69] It is perhaps better to let happiness be a reward for good deeds than to make it an end in itself.

Nobody thinks that the best thing would be to be constantly miserable. But perhaps someone can be too happy, or happy at the wrong times. A study[70] of over 2,300 university students from eight countries (U.S., Brazil, China, Germany, Ghana, Israel, Poland, and Singapore) found that although students overall wanted to experience more positive emotions, they especially wanted to experience the emotions that matched what they desired to feel—even negative emotions such as anger. The lead researcher concluded, "If you feel emotions you want to feel, even if they're unpleasant, then you're better off."[71]

Taking the argument a step further, some work has suggested that the healthiest pattern is to experience a broad variety of emotions. People who are happy all the time are only using part of their emotional repertoire and may be missing out on some valuable parts of the human experience. The term **emodiversity** has been introduced to refer to how much a person experiences the variety and abundance of different human emotions. High emodiversity is linked to better mental and physical health,[72] though it is hard to say what causes what.

Emodiversity does not necessarily mean extremity of emotion. A person can have plenty of emodiversity even though all emotions are relatively mild. The extremity of emotional reactions is a separate topic that has interested researchers. Some people often experience intense emotions, both positive and negative, whereas others rarely feel intense emotions of any sort. *Tradeoffs* describes the tradeoff of feeling versus not feeling intense emotions.

Emodiversity refers to how much a person experiences a variety of different emotions

Affect Intensity: Emotional Roller Coaster or Even Keel?

Nearly everyone wants to be happy, and the emotional formula for happiness seems simple: You want to have plenty of good feelings and as few bad ones as possible. Unfortunately, life doesn't always cooperate. Over the last couple of decades, researchers have begun to recognize that some people have many intense experiences, both good and bad, whereas others have relatively few.

One of the most systematic treatments of this difference is based on the Affect Intensity Measure (AIM).[73] Some sample items from the scale are: "When I'm happy, I feel like I'm bursting with joy" and "When I am nervous, I get shaky all over." People who score low on the scale have relatively few emotional reactions, and these tend to be rather subdued. In contrast, people who score high have strong emotions to all sorts of events. Consistent with traditional stereotypes, one study found that advanced art college students had higher scores on the AIM than did advanced science college students.[74] That is, future artists generally live with plenty of extreme emotions, whereas future scientists generally have more subdued emotional lives.

Which is better? Affect intensity appears to be a genuine tradeoff. People who score low on the AIM can go through life on a fairly even keel. They don't become too bothered about problems and stresses, but then again, they don't feel swept away with passionate joy very often either. In contrast, life is an emotional rollercoaster for people with high affect intensity. Thus, you get both the good and the bad, or neither.

The quality of your life circumstances may dictate which is preferable. If your life is in a positive groove, well under control, so that most experiences are good, then you may well get more meaningful enjoyment if you have high affective intensity. In contrast, if your life is filled with unpredictable, uncontrollable events, some of which are very bad, you may well prefer to have low affect intensity. You don't want to take the good with the bad if there is too much bad.

This tradeoff can affect the most intense and personal of relationships. People who have been hurt in love may become reluctant to let themselves fall in love again. Historians have even suggested that in past centuries people were reluctant to love their children because the high rate of child mortality would lead to heartbreak.[75,76] If a woman from a good family had a baby, she would often send it out to the country to be nursed, even though objectively its chances of survival were slightly lower there (because the country was poorer) than if the child stayed with her. Preventing the woman from nursing her own baby kept maternal feelings of love to a minimum, so the mother was less hurt if the baby died. Older children were often sent out to live in other people's households starting when they were 6 or 7, so parents might not develop the lasting emotional bond to their children that comes from living together year after year. Once public health improved, however, and most children could be expected to survive into adulthood, parents could afford the risk of loving their children more, and they began to keep their children with them until they were nearly grown up.

Anger

Anger is an emotional response to a real or imagined threat or provocation. Anger can range in intensity from mild irritation to extreme rage. Anger is different from aggression. Anger is an internal emotion, whereas aggression is an external behavior. (Aggression will be covered in Chapter 10.) Many events make people angry. These events can be interpersonal such as a provocation or a blow to the ego, or they can be stressors such as frustration, physical pain, exposure to violent media, or discomfort caused by heat, crowding, noise, or foul odors.[77] Recent research indicates that lack of sleep can amplify angry feelings.[78] Chemicals inside the body, such as the hormone testosterone, also contribute to getting angry.[79]

Anger is an unusual emotion. One key feature is that it makes people approach things and take action. In their search for ultimate, basic principles that can be used to explain psychological reactions, many researchers have come to focusing on the basic difference between approach and avoidance. These are rooted in simple processes of animal learning (e.g., does the animal move forward to check out the new stimulus, or does it run away?). Much of life can be understood as deriving from approach and avoidance tendencies. In that system, emotions are often helpful signals. Generally, positive emotions signal to approach something, typically because it is good. Conversely, negative emotions are mostly avoidance signals, because they tell you something is bad. Fear, sadness, jealousy, anxiety, depressed feelings, and others tend to motivate people to avoid and withdraw.

Anger is a rare example of an emotion that feels bad but nonetheless signals approach.[80] Being angry often makes people want to confront the problem, such as by fixing it or at least arguing with the person whoever made them angry. Anger is often linked to aggression (as will be explored in Chapter 10), which is one form of approach behavior. The association between anger and approach motivation may thus be due to the increase in aggressive motivation that typically accompanies anger. Anger can be a powerful force in helping people stand up for what they believe is right. The American Revolution, the civil rights movement, the #BlackLivesMatter movement, the feminist movement, the #MeToo movement, and other causes probably were able to use anger to motivate people to take action against things they saw as unfair.

Anger is widely recognized as a problem. It is one of the most heavily regulated emotions, in the sense that cultures have many different norms about anger. Some of these norms conflict with each other. For example, norms say that sometimes it is justifiable to be angry, other times anger is wholly inappropriate, and yet other times there is an obligation to be angry.[81] In another sense, however, anger is one of the least regulated emotions. When people are surveyed about how they control their emotions, they typically report that they have fewer and less effective techniques for controlling anger than for controlling other emotions.[82]

Is Anger Maladaptive?

Anger seems maladaptive today—useless, counterproductive, harmful, divisive, and problematic. When people become angry, they do things they will regret later. They are impulsive, aggressive, and worse. Why would anger exist if it is harmful and maladaptive? It is reasonable to assume that it is (or was) adaptive, or else natural selection would likely have favored people who did not feel anger, and anger would gradually have disappeared from the human repertoire of emotions. In other words, despite all its faults and drawbacks, anger must have some positive value that helps the organism survive—or at least it must have had some positive value in the evolutionary past. Whether anger is suited to today's cultures and social circumstances is another question, however.

One line of explanation is that anger is adaptive because it motivates the person to act aggressively and assertively. The broader context holds that emotions exist in order to motivate actions, and that each emotion points toward a certain kind of act. Anger helps get people ready to defend themselves, assert their rights, pursue their goals that might be blocked, and perform other useful acts.

anger an emotional response to a real or imagined threat or provocation

A second line of explanation begins by objecting to the first: Why not go directly to the aggression? Why become angry first? Anger tips off your foes that you might attack them, allowing them to prepare themselves or even attack you preemptively. The second explanation is that anger helps reduce aggression. This may seem paradoxical because studies show that people are more aggressive when they are angry than when they are not.[83] But that evidence could be misleading, because both anger and aggression occur in situations in which there is conflict, frustration, or provocation. If human beings had evolved to skip feeling anger and go directly to aggression, there would still be plenty of aggression. Hence, in this second view, anger helps warn friends and family that something is wrong and aggression may be coming. This gives people time to resolve the conflict before it reaches the point of violence. Anger may therefore actually reduce aggression, compared to what the world would be like if people went directly into aggressive action as soon as they experienced conflict or frustration. For example, some powerful people manage to get their way with just a brief frown of displeasure or a slight raising of the voice: A hint of anger is enough to make other people scurry to do their bidding, and the powerful person hardly ever has to express a full-blown angry outburst, let alone engage in aggressive action.

Thus, anger may be prosocial in an important sense, and in fact it may help enable people to live together. If anger is a warning sign of impending aggression, anger may help defuse conflict and prevent aggression. Yet as a sign of conflict and problem, anger may be antisocial. Moreover, the action-motivating function of anger may conflict with the social conflict-defusing aspect. Angry people may say or do things that make the problem worse. If one person wants to go out and the other wants to stay in, conflict is already there—but angry, insulting remarks will aggravate it and make it harder to reach a compromise. Research on negotiation has shown some social benefits of anger. When two people are negotiating and one shows anger, the other takes this as a sign to give in. It is a sign that the angry person will not compromise or make concessions, so one had best go along.[84,85,86] Anger is thus useful for a negotiator. To be sure, people dislike angry negotiators, so anger can backfire, especially if the non-angry negotiator has other options. But if they have to settle a negotiation, they concede more to the angry than to the non-angry person.

People seem aware that anger can be useful. Some people actually try to increase their angry feelings when they anticipate a social interaction in which anger might be useful, such as a difficult confrontation with a rival or enemy. Moreover, they are right: Sometimes anger does improve performance in such difficult situations.[87]

A final perspective on the causes of anger is the potential mismatch between people's natural reactions and the complexity of modern social life. Many emotional reactions developed during a time of simpler life circumstances. Anger might help you have the arousal to fight off a predatory animal, but it may be useless and even counterproductive to have the same feelings toward your computer when the hard drive crashes.

Dealing with Anger

Because it is unpleasant, many people want to get rid of their anger when they experience it. There are three possible ways of dealing with anger. One standard approach that has been endorsed by many societies is never to show anger. (Nature supplies the impulse to be angry, but culture tells people to try to stop it.) It can end up prompting people to stuff their anger deep inside and repress it. There is some evidence that this is a costly strategy. Long-term concealed anger can be quite destructive to the person, increasing the risk of such illnesses as heart disease.[88] On the other hand, as we have seen, inner states follow outward expressions (as in the facial feedback hypothesis, discussed earlier), so if people generally act as if to show they are not angry, some anger may be diminished.

A second approach is to vent one's anger. This view treats anger as a kind of inner pressure or corrosive substance that builds up over time and does harm unless it is released. This belief has led to the popularity of "Anger Rooms" (also called "Rage Rooms") around the world, where angry people can wear protective gear and break objects with their hands or baseball bats (e.g., computers, television sets, china plates) as a form of therapy to "let off steam."

The **catharsis theory** falls in this category because it holds that expressing anger (including verbal expression or even aggressive, violent action) produces a healthy release of emotion and is therefore good for the psyche. Catharsis theory, which can be traced back through Sigmund Freud to Aristotle, is elegant and appealing. Unfortunately, the facts and findings do not show that venting one's anger has positive value. On the contrary, it tends to make people more aggressive afterward and to exacerbate interpersonal conflicts.[89] Venting anger is also linked to higher risk of heart disease.[90,91,92] Even among people who believe in the value of venting and catharsis, and even when people enjoy their venting and feel some satisfaction from it, venting anger increases subsequent aggression, even against innocent bystanders.[93]

One variation of venting is intense physical exercise. When angry, some people go running or try some other form of physical workout. Although exercise is good for your heart, it is not good for reducing anger.[94] The reason exercise doesn't work is that it increases rather than decreases arousal levels (recall the earlier section on arousal in emotion). When people become angry, their physiological arousal increases. The goal is to decrease arousal rather than increase it. Also, if someone provokes you after exercising, excitation transfer might occur.[95] That is, the arousal from the exercise might transfer to the response to the provocation, producing an exaggerated and possibly more violent response.

In a nutshell, venting anger may be like using gasoline to put out a fire: It just feeds the flame. Venting keeps arousal levels high and keeps aggressive thoughts and angry feelings alive.

The third approach is to try to get rid of one's anger. This solution is important because the problems of both the other approaches (i.e., stuffing and venting) arise because the person stays angry. The important thing is to stop feeling angry. All emotions, including anger, consist of bodily states (such as arousal) and mental meanings. To get rid of anger, you can change either of those. Anger can be reduced by getting rid of the arousal state, such as by relaxing or by counting to 10 before responding. Thomas Jefferson said, "When angry, count ten. before you speak; if very angry, an hundred." Anger can also be addressed by mental tactics, such as by reframing the problem or conflict, or by distracting oneself and turning one's attention to other, more pleasant topics. Stepping back and taking a more distant third-person perspective—like "a fly on a wall"—is also a helpful way to reduce anger.[96] Certain behaviors can also help get rid of anger. For example, doing something incompatible with anger and aggression can also help, such as petting a puppy, watching a comedy, making love, or performing a good deed.[97] These incompatible behaviors work because it is difficult or impossible to experience anger and another positive emotion at the same time. Perhaps the simplest thing to do is lean back, in your chair for example. As was mentioned above, anger motivates people to approach things. Angry people often lean forward and are "in your face." Recent research has shown that doing the opposite (e.g., leaning backward in your chair) can reduce feelings of anger, especially for people who are prone to anger.[98,99]

Some people also become "hangry" (hungry + angry) when they don't get enough to eat. Thus, don't forget to give your brain the fuel it needs to regulate anger. Although the brain is only about 2% of our body weight, it uses 20%–30% of the calories we consume. It is a very demanding organ. The part of our brain just behind our forehead, called the prefrontal cortex, is in charge of executive functions. One of those functions is controlling our emotions, including anger. We are better able to control our anger when we give our brain the fuel it needs by eating healthy foods (e.g., veggies, whole grains).[100] One "take home" message from this research is that you should not have a discussion about a sensitive topic with your loved one on an empty stomach.[101,]

Anger or Rage Rooms are supposedly therapeutic because they allow customers to "let off steam" by breaking objects, but the scientific research indicates that this approach to reducing anger backfires and actually makes people more angry and aggressive.

catharsis theory the proposition that expressing negative emotions produces a healthy release of those emotions and is therefore good for the psyche

> "[Guilt is] this mechanism we use to control people. It's an illusion. It's a kind of social control mechanism and it's very unhealthy. It does terrible things to our bodies. And there are much better ways to control our behavior than that rather extraordinary use of guilt."[102]

Guilt and Shame

What do you think of the view of guilt expressed in this quotation? Many people agree with it. Guilt does have a bad reputation in our culture. If you visit the "pop psychology" section in a bookstore, you are likely to find several books telling you how to get rid of guilt. The underlying idea is that guilt is a useless (or even harmful) form of self-inflicted suffering. Most people seek to avoid guilt like the plague.

Then again, perhaps guilt deserves more credit than it gets. This quotation was actually from Ted Bundy, a notorious mass murderer who killed at least 30 women in seven different states. Bundy described himself as "the most cold-hearted son of a bitch you'll ever meet."[103] Bundy was executed in an electric chair in Florida in 1989 for his crimes. Perhaps if he had felt a little more guilt himself, Bundy might have refrained from his criminal acts and some of those women (and Bundy himself) would be alive today.

Research by social psychologists has gradually painted a picture of guilt that differs starkly from the negative view held by our culture (and by Ted Bundy). Guilt is actually quite good for society and for close relationships. You would not want to have a boss, a lover, a roommate, or a business partner who had no sense of guilt. Such people exist (they are called psychopaths), but they are often a disaster to those around them.[104] They exploit and harm others, help themselves at the expense of others, and feel no remorse about those they hurt.

Guilt Versus Shame

What is guilt? **Guilt** is negative emotional feeling, and it is usually associated with some implicit reproach that one has acted badly or wrongly. By and large, everyone occasionally does something wrong; the difference between people lies in whether they feel bad about it or not. Research suggests that guilt triggers specific behaviors intended to right the wrong, rather than simply doing anything that might help guilty people feel good about themselves.[105] Guilt is especially associated with acts that could damage a relationship about which one cares.

Guilt must be distinguished from **shame**.[106] The difference lies in how widely the bad feeling is generalized. Guilt focuses narrowly on the action, whereas shame spreads to the whole person. Guilt says, "I did a bad thing." Shame says, "I am a bad person." Research shows that the feelings of shame are very similar across many different cultures.[107]

Research based on that distinction has repeatedly shown that shame is usually destructive, whereas guilt is usually constructive. This may be worth keeping in mind when you deal with your assistants and workers, or your family members, or even your romantic partners. How do you criticize them when they do something wrong? Calling their attention to what they did wrong may seem necessary, but phrasing your criticism in terms of being a bad person (e.g., "you liar") is not nearly as constructive as allowing them to be a person did a bad thing (e.g., "you shouldn't have lied"). Thus, one should avoid making internal negative stable attributions about others (see Chapter 5). There is, after all, no remedy for being a bad person, so shame makes people want to withdraw and hide, or to lash out in anger. In contrast, guilt signifies a person did a bad thing, and there are plenty of ways that a person can remedy an isolated bad act (e.g., apologize, make amends, reaffirm one's commitment to the relationship, promise not to repeat the misdeed, etc.).

Effects of Guilt

Guilt motivates people to do good acts, such as apologizing. Apologies can help repair damage to relationships because they (a) convey the implicit agreement that the act was wrong, (b) suggest that the person will try not to do it again, and (c) counteract any implication that the bad action meant that the person does not care about the relationship. For example, if your partner cooks you a lovely dinner but you arrive an hour late and the food is spoiled, your partner may not care very much about the food itself, but the implication that you do not care about the relationship can be very upsetting. A sincere apology cannot revive the spoiled food, but it may prevent your partner from feeling that you do not care about the relationship.[108,109,110]

Guilt also motivates people to make amends. When people feel guilty about something they have done, they try harder to perform positive or good actions. They are more likely

Ted Bundy in court. Bundy was a serial killer who murdered dozens of women. He was electrocuted in a Florida prison on January 24, 1989.

guilt an unpleasant moral emotion associated with a specific instance in which one has acted badly or wrongly

shame a moral emotion that, like guilt, involves feeling bad but, unlike guilt, spreads to the whole person to learn a lesson and try to behave better in the future. This too can help salvage a relationship from the damage done by some misbehavior.

For example, half the participants in one study[111] were induced to tell a lie. A previous participant (actually an accomplice) told them all about the study and what the correct answers to a test were before the experimenter arrived. Soon thereafter, the experimenter came and asked participants if they had heard anything at all about the study. All participants said no. Thus, half of the participants lied (because in fact they had all heard about the study). After the study was over, the experimenter said that participants were free to go, but added that if they had extra time they could help him fill in bubble sheets for another study (an incredibly boring task). Participants who had not been induced to lie volunteered to help fill in bubble sheets for 2 minutes on average, whereas participants who had been induced to lie volunteered to help fill in bubble sheets for 63 minutes! The lying participants were apparently attempting to wash away their guilt by being more helpful. Guilt made them more willing to do something nice.

Many social psychology studies have found that guilt makes people behave more prosocially.[112,113,114] These research findings suggest that guilt is good for relationships, even though feeling guilty will be unpleasant. Sometimes, in order to make a relationship more successful, people must sacrifice their own selfish interests and do what is best for the other person. (Indeed, one theme of this book has been the need to rely on conscience and self-regulation to overcome selfish impulses in order for civilized society and strong human relationships to survive.) Guilt is one force that pushes people toward making those relationship-enhancing sacrifices.

Thus, guilt can help make you a better person. Does it make your own life better? Guilt benefits relationships, and people are happier when they have good relationships. Even beyond this, there may be benefits of guilt. In a provocative series of studies, researchers showed that guilt can increase pleasure, mainly because people have learned to associate guilt with pleasures such as eating, drinking, and having fun when they should be working. Participants who were primed with the notion of guilt reported higher subsequent enjoyment of various activities, including looking at profiles on a dating website, buying or eating a candy bar, and watching an entertaining film.[115] Thus, ironically, a bit of guilt can increase one's happiness!

Guilt and Relationships

Some forms of guilt do not revolve around doing anything wrong. Sometimes people feel guilty simply because others have suffered more than they have. The term **survivor guilt** emerged after World War II based on observations of victims who had not suffered as much as others. Some people who survived the mass murder campaigns in concentration camps felt guilty for having survived when so many others died. One survivor of the Orlando, Florida mass shooting in which 49 people were killed wrote a poem describing "the guilt of feeling lucky to be alive."[116] Sydney Aiello, a 19-year-old survivor of the Douglas High School mass shooting in Parkland, Florida that left 17 of her classmates dead, struggled with survivor's guilt and was diagnosed with post-traumatic stress disorder. She also feared being in her college classrooms. She committed suicide on March 17, 2019.[117] Likewise, people who survive other natural or human-caused disasters feel guilty for having lived when so many others died. These people had not done anything wrong, but the phenomenon of survivor guilt shows that people are deeply sensitive to a sense of fairness and have some unease when life is "unfair" in their favor. (It is easy to be upset about unfairness when you are the one who got less than others; even some animals react to such unfairness, but animals do not seem to mind getting more than their share.) A more modern version of survivor guilt has been observed during economic recessions, when large firms must lay off many workers. Those who remain often have some feelings of guilt for keeping their jobs when other deserving individuals have lost their jobs.[118]

All of this depicts guilt as a very interpersonal emotion, and it is. The stereotype of guilt depicts it as a solitary emotion, but even if someone feels guilty while alone, most likely the guilt is about something interpersonal. People mainly feel guilty about things they have done to others—hurting them, ignoring them, letting them down, or failing to meet their expectations. Moreover, they mainly feel guilty toward people they care about. Guilt is more linked to close relationships than other emotions. For example, people may often be afraid

survivor guilt an unpleasant emotion associated with living through an experience during which other people died.

Research shows that washing one's hands can actually reduce feelings of guilt, as when Pilate washed his hands after sanctioning the crucifixion of Jesus Christ.

of total strangers, or annoyed by casual acquaintances, or frustrated by someone in a store or restaurant, but guilt is mainly felt toward family, good friends, and other loved ones.[119]

Extending this further, experiments have shown that guilt over hurting someone else depends partly on how useful that other person is.[120] For example, participants felt somewhat guilty when their choices resulted in assigning another person to do an unpleasant task instead of a fun one. They felt much guiltier when they learned that the other person would later decide how to divide the money reward among the group than when the other person had no such power. The transgression and the other person's suffering were the same, so in moral principle the guilt should have been the same. But guilt focuses on relationships that are beneficial to us. That is presumably why people feel more guilt toward their mother or romantic partner than toward strangers.

Many people count on guilt to push their loved ones to behave properly. Others try to help things along a bit. Guilt is one emotion that people actively try to make others feel. Some people become quite skilled at knowing what to say to make someone else feel guilty. As always, though, the guilt depends on the relationship, and a stranger may have a hard time making you feel guilty. The essence of most guilt-inducing strategies is "See how you are hurting me." If you do not care about that person, you may not feel guilty for hurting them. In contrast, if the person is someone you love and care about, you will usually change your behavior to avoid hurting the person.

Guilt is thus an emotion well suited to cultural animals such as human beings. It depends on one's connections to others, and it makes people maintain better relationships with others. It also benefits a large system of interrelationships, which is what a culture is. And it encourages people to live up to cultural standards and rules.[121]

Washing Away the Guilt

The classic literature offers examples of people who try to wash away their guilt by washing their hands. A story in the Bible relates that Pontius Pilate, the Roman governor of Jerusalem, washed his hands and declared himself blameless after decreeing that Jesus would be crucified.[122] Likewise, in Shakespeare's play, *Macbeth,* Lady Macbeth attempted to wash away her guilt of plotting King Duncan's murder by compulsively washing her hands. Research by modern social psychologists has confirmed that the average person actually does feel less guilty after washing his or her hands.[123] Because guilt often makes people do good deeds such as helping, washing one's hands can make people less helpful.[124] Purity is a central notion of morality[125] and cleansing makes one feel pure and clean.[126] In baptisms and other religious rituals, water is often used to wash away sin and make the person clean and virtuous.

Disgust

Disgust may not seem like an emotion, but it is considered to be one—and one that psychologists have begun to recognize as important. **Disgust** can be defined as a strong negative feeling of repugnance and revulsion. It is captured by statements such as "grossed out" or "yuck!" It is different from anger, in that anger motivates people to approach things, whereas disgust motivates people to avoid things.[127] Disgust is "the voice in our heads … the voice of our ancestors telling us to avoid infectious disease and social parasites."[128] The prototype of disgust is the feeling of wanting to vomit after eating something that is intolerable and that the body naturally wishes to expel as fast as possible. It is not confined to humans and may be widespread in the animal kingdom because it helps

disgust a strong negative feeling of repugnance and revulsion motivate animals not to eat things that could make them sick or even kill them. Disgust thus helps keep people healthy.[129]

Disgust may be especially important among humans because our constitution is delicate compared to most other animals, and there are many things we should not eat; yet human children naturally try to learn about things by putting them in their mouths. Paul Rozin led research into disgust by having adult and child research participants watch him put a sterilized dead cockroach into a glass of apple juice and then removing it and offering them a drink from the glass. Most adults said no, and indeed many refused even a fresh drink of apple juice in a different cup, but some of the children had no objection to drinking from the glass that had contained the cockroach.

Women seem to have stronger disgust reactions than men.[130] Men high in masculinity are less willing to show disgust. There are various theories to explain this, including males being socialized to do dirty jobs, but the gender difference may reflect the importance of health for reproduction. Pregnant women typically are highly sensitive to disgust, which nature may have arranged because an infection would endanger the fetus.

Although disgust is unpleasant, it does have its benefits. It can motivate a broad range of healthy behaviors, beyond avoidance of things that will make you sick. Most health workers now appreciate that many people do not wash their hands often enough, including after going to the toilet. Cultivating a sense of disgust helps motivate people to wash more often. Another use of disgust to motivate healthy behavior is in the policies by which some governments (such as Australia's) require cigarette companies to put disgusting pictures on cigarette packs to motivate people to quit smoking.

Disgust can be considered part of a "behavioral immune system" that supports health.[131] The body's inner immune system for fighting off infections requires considerable energy and is not always successful, so it is safer to avoid things that could bring infection. This system does more than stop people from eating spoiled food. It may discourage people from being friendly toward strangers when there are concerns about disease. It may motivate people to avoid having sex or even being friends with people whose faces have ugly marks on them because in the past some diseases left marks on the face. Indeed, sex brings two people into such close contact that many germs can be exchanged, so it carries a disease risk, especially with someone who has slept with many partners. Sexual disgust may therefore motivate people to avoid risky partners, and finding prostitutes or other highly promiscuous people "disgusting" may protect one's health.

Indeed, in our ancestral past, people living together were likely to have had and survived the same diseases, so interacting more with them was relatively safe (because by this point you are probably immune to those illnesses). Strangers, on the other hand, could have diseases you have not yet had, so they posed a greater risk of bringing you new infections. Some thinkers have concluded that prejudice against outgroups may be partly derived from the greater risk of infection that came from socializing with them.[132] The more people feel disgust toward particular groups of other people, the more prejudice they show against those groups,[133] such as obese people,[134] members of the LGBTQ+ community,[135,136] and even some religious groups, such as Muslims[137] and atheists.[138] Groups regarded as disgusting are even viewed as not quite human.[139]

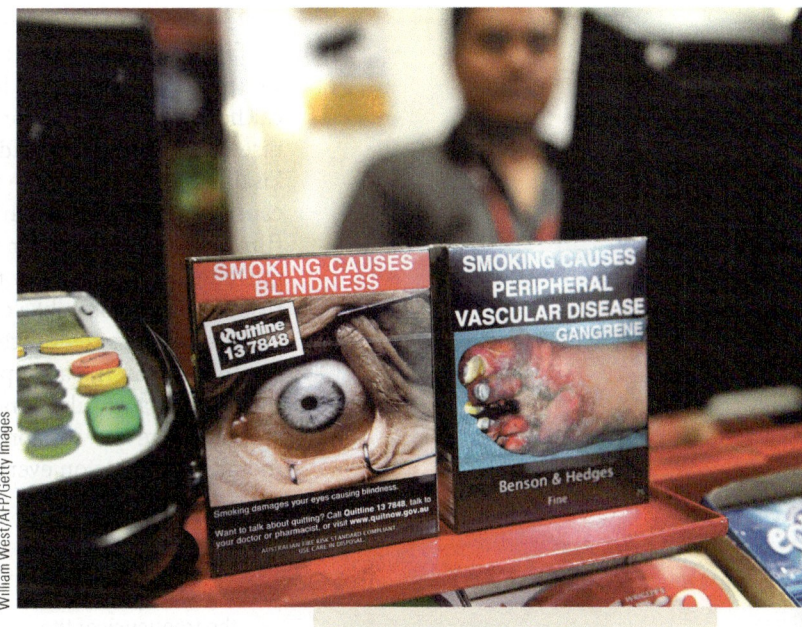

Some governments (such as Australia's) require cigarette companies to put disgusting pictures on cigarette packs to motivate people to quit smoking.

How immoral is sex before dinner?

People also regard some forms of immoral behavior as disgusting, and they elicit similar facial responses and attitudes as do unpalatable foods, filthy restrooms, and bloody wounds.[140] In particular, behaviors associated with purity, such as cleanliness and physical health (also sexual propriety) are particularly linked to disgust. The more strongly research participants find an activity disgusting (like reading about a brother and sister kissing passionately), the more strongly they condemn it. Even being disgusted by a film caused people to make harsher moral judgments about some activity unrelated to the film, when the behavior violated the moral virtue of purity. For example, feeling disgusted caused people to make especially strong moral condemnation of a person they read about who bought a chicken at a supermarket, had sex with it, then cooked and ate it. Disgust had less relevance to moral judgments about unfairness or interpersonal harm.[141] In other research, participants made harsher judgments of immoral behavior if they were in a room that stank (something the researchers achieved by dousing the room with "fart spray" before the session) than in a non-stinky room.[142] The disgusting smell affected moral judgments on everything from sex between first cousins to laziness.

QUIZ YOURSELF
Some Important Emotions

1. One measure of happiness, affect balance, is equal to _____.
   - (a) the frequency of the positive emotions
   - (b) the frequency of positive emotions divided by the frequency of negative emotions
   - (c) the frequency of positive emotions minus the frequency of negative emotions
   - (d) the frequency of positive emotions plus the frequency of negative emotions

2. Mimi just won the lottery in the state where she lives. What is her emotional response likely to be over time?
   - (a) Mimi will be very happy at first and will remain very happy.
   - (b) Mimi will be very happy at first, but she will later return to her level of happiness before she won the lottery.
   - (c) Mimi will be very happy at first, but she will later become very depressed after the good feeling wears off.
   - (d) Mimi's initial and subsequent level of happiness will not change from what it was before she won the lottery.

3. Bill thinks that if he's irritated with his children, he'll feel better and be less inclined to hit them if he just yells and screams. Bill believes in the notion of _____.
   - (a) catharsis
   - (b) displacement
   - (c) excitation transfer
   - (d) negative reinforcement

4. Which statement best describes the research about guilt and shame?
   - (a) Guilt and shame are both good for the individual and society.
   - (b) Guilt and shame are both bad for the individual and society.
   - (c) Guilt is bad and shame is good for the individual and society.
   - (d) Guilt is good and shame is bad for the individual and society.

answers: see pg 228

Why Do We Have Emotions?

If emotions were confusing and destructive reactions that generally made people do stupid things, then probably natural selection would have phased them out long ago because people who had fewer and weaker emotions would fare better than people with plenty of strong emotions. Although some science fiction characters (like the alien Mr. Spock on *Star Trek*) may do fine without emotions, humans who lack emotions seem to have great difficulties in life.[143] It is true that sometimes emotions are confusing and cause people to do stupid, irrational, and even self-destructive things. But all that tells us is that the benefits of emotion must be that much greater, because the benefits have to offset those costs.

One thing seems clear: Emotions comprise an important and powerful feedback system. Emotions tell us whether something is good or bad. You don't have much emotion over things you don't care about! Caring (motivation) is therefore one ingredient necessary for making emotion. As we go through life and things happen to us, emotions follow along afterward and help stamp in the strong sense that each event was good or bad. This is true for both automatic affect and conscious emotion. Whatever else emotions may do, they help formulate our reactions to whatever has just happened.

Emotions Promote Belongingness

Emotions help people get along better. This may seem surprising at first because we are quick to notice when someone else's emotions make that person hard to get along with. Mostly, however, people's emotions promote their ties to others. (Imagine trying to be friends with someone who never showed or felt any emotion.)

The best way to appreciate this is to look at the emotions people have when they either form or break a social bond with someone else. Forming social bonds is linked to positive emotions.[144,145,146,147,148,149,150,151,152,153,154,155] People are happy at weddings (even if they cry!). They are usually delighted when they join a fraternity or sorority (even if they have to go through a hazing process first!). They are excited or at least relieved when they get a job. Having children is revealing: People are usually all full of joyful smiles when they have children, even though in the long run being a parent leads to lower happiness in life, probably because of the stresses and demands of parenting.

Conversely, a host of bad emotions is linked to events that end, damage, or threaten relationships. Having enemies leads to fear or hate. Divorce and other forms of social rejection foster sadness, depression, and anger. Being treated badly or rejected unfairly causes anger. Doing something that hurts a loved one causes guilt. The threat that your partner might leave you for someone else causes jealousy. The prospect of being abandoned and alone causes anxiety. Losing a loved one causes grief.

Positive feelings often reflect healthy relationships,[156] whereas negative feelings often reflect damaged relationships.[157] If you want to feel good and avoid emotional distress, form and maintain good social relationships with other people! Social contact, especially with loved ones, can help people deal with stressful emotions. Female research participants who were anticipating painful electric shocks showed big reductions in stress if they were permitted to hold their husband's hand during the waiting period.[158] The biggest stress-reduction gains were found among the women whose marriages were happiest (indicating they may have felt the strongest positive social connections). There was some benefit, though less, from holding a stranger's hand or holding hands with a husband in a not-so-happy marriage. Thus, a moment of physical contact with another person can reduce bad emotions caused by stress, and the greatest emotional boost comes from holding hands with someone you love. The results from this study are depicted in **FIGURE 6.2**. Research suggests that human touch can also help people with low self-esteem cope with the terror of dying.[159]

The fact that emotions promote belongingness is yet another important instance of our general theme that what happens inside people serves what happens between people. Emotions (inner processes) help promote good interpersonal relations. People want to feel good and avoid bad emotions, and this desire impels them to try to form and maintain good relationships.

Emotions Communicate Social Information

Emotions fit the general pattern that nature says go, culture says stop. Children do not need to be taught to have emotions. Rather, what they learn is to conceal their emotions when appropriate. Apparently, the natural state of an emotion includes visible display, so that others can tell what you are feeling.

FIGURE 6.2

Holding someone's hand reduces how unpleasant stressful events are judged to be and even reduces bodily arousal, especially if the person is your spouse.

SOURCE: Coan et al. (2006).

Emotions are thus not purely for the inside. No one can tell your thoughts unless you choose to speak them, but people can read your emotions. Evolution must have benefited people whose emotions were read by others. Possibly this starts with babies, who cannot take care of themselves and therefore have to let their caregivers know when they feel bad (such as by crying). We have also suggested that anger could help prevent harm by signaling that one is unhappy, so that there is time to discuss the problem rather than having a fistfight.

In Chapter 9, we will see that much prosocial behavior (e.g., helping others) is motivated by empathy, which involves being able to feel what someone else is feeling. Here again, one benefits if one's emotions can be easily read by others. They are more likely to help you if they feel your pain or share your distress.

Indeed, there is a variety of evidence that emotions can be contagious,[160] presumably because there is value (probably for strengthening social bonds) to having people be in a similar emotional state. Some researchers have used social media to examine how emotions spread. One experiment used the News Feed feature of Facebook. It manipulated the emotional content of news about friends, either suppressing more positive or more negative emotional content.[161] People's own posts tended to conform to the emotional content of what they had seen on their News Feed. For example, if positive information was omitted from their News Feed, users tended to post more emotionally negative and less emotionally positive information themselves. The researchers even found a general effect for emotionality: People whose news feed contained less emotional information (good or bad) were less likely to post anything emotional themselves the next day.

Another study looked at the impact of rainy days on millions of Facebook users.[162] To examine how emotions spread, they looked at how Facebook updates changed when it rained. They found that negative updates increased by 1.16% and positive updates decreased by 1.19% when it rained. Then they looked at the friends of the people who posted the updates to see if moods are contagious. They found that every negative update generated an additional 1.29 negative updates, whereas every positive update generated an additional 1.75 positive updates.

Emotions Cause Behavior—Sort Of

Traditionally it has been assumed that emotions guide behavior. This view is consistent with what we know about physiological arousal. Arousal gets the body ready for action.[163,164] Some theorists have proposed that emotion does not exist without a readiness for action.[165] Other theorists have proposed that implicit muscle movements are part of emotion.[166] That is, an emotion naturally and normally starts your body moving.

Then again, maybe emotions do not guide behavior. People have plenty of emotions without doing anything. Additionally, we do not associate most emotions with any single action. Maybe fear prompts you to run away, but it is slow; if you depended on having full-blown fear, you would not escape fast enough. Maybe anger inspires you to fight, but most angry people don't fight. What is the single behavior that is supposed to follow from guilt? From love? From joy?

The objection that emotion is too slow to guide behavior applies mainly to conscious emotion, of course. Automatic affect—the feeling of liking or disliking something—arises in a fraction of a second and therefore can be very helpful. When walking through a crowded room, you may meet someone unexpectedly, and you might have to decide whether to smile at that person or go the other way. The fast, automatic reaction that tells you whether you like or dislike that person can be a big help. If you had to wait around for arousal to build and a full-fledged conscious emotion to occur, it would be too late to help you make that decision.

Food for Thought talks about whether moods guide eating behavior.

When emotion causes behavior, it is often because the person wants to change or escape the emotional state. For example, researchers have long known that sad, depressed moods make people more helpful.[167,168,169,170] This could be true for multiple reasons—for example, that sadness makes people have more empathy for another person's suffering and need, or that sadness makes people less concerned about their own welfare. Then again, perhaps sadness makes people more concerned about themselves, in that they

FOOD FOR *Thought*

Mood and Food

Positive moods lead to preferences for healthy food, whereas negative moods lead to preferences for unhealthy food.[171] People who feel bad often eat badly. For example, people who are depressed or lonely will eat foods that are typically high in sugar, fat, and carbohydrates. Such foods are called "comfort foods" because they are often associated with childhood and home cooking (and thus the comfort of having a parent take care of you). They also provide a sense of well-being—at least until you start feeling guilty after eating them!

Many studies have linked food and mood, as shown in a study of 60 obese women with binge-eating disorders.[172] Binge eaters consume a large amount of food at one time. Sometimes they also feel out of control when eating. By the flip of a coin, half these women were assigned to fast for 14 hours, so they would be very hungry, whereas the rest did not fast. All the women were then induced to have either a negative or a neutral mood, and then they were served a buffet meal (so they could eat as much as they wanted). How much the women ate depended on their mood but not on whether they had fasted. In other words, being in a bad mood had a bigger effect on how much these women ate than how food deprived they were! The bad mood led to more eating, and eating seemed to help cheer the women up.

Other studies have reported similar results: Being in a bad mood leads to binge eating and a feeling of being out of control when eating.[173,174] A comparison of binge-eating-disordered adults, nonclinical binge eaters, and adults who did not binge eat found that all three groups overate in response to negative emotions.[175] The effect of mood on food intake is not limited to people with eating disorders—it applies to all adults. In contrast, inducing a positive mood was shown to reduce the number of cookies people ate.[176]

This doesn't mean that bad moods automatically or directly cause people to eat. Rather, eating seems to be a strategy for making yourself feel better. In one study,[177] half the participants were told that eating would not change their mood. Then all were put into a sad, depressed mood by having them imagine they were the driver in a car accident that killed a child. Those who had been told that eating wouldn't make them feel good did not eat any more than those in a neutral-mood control condition. Only those who thought eating might make them feel better indulged in heavy eating in response to the bad mood. Thus, it is wrong to say simply that emotion "causes" behavior. Emotional distress drives people to want to feel better, and they choose actions that they think will cheer them up. These findings are consistent with mood maintenance theory, which argues that people who are in a good mood try to maintain that good mood as long as they can.[178]

---

want to feel better. One team of researchers hit on an ingenious way to test this theory.[179] They put people in either a happy, sad, or neutral mood. They also gave everyone a pill. Some were told the pill had no side effects, but others were told that the pill would freeze or fix their emotional state for about an hour, which meant that whatever mood or emotion they currently had would continue for another hour. The point of this mood-freezing manipulation was that it made people think it was useless to try to feel better. The group of sad participants whose pills supposedly had no side effects were more helpful than others, consistent with previous findings that sadness increases helping. The mood-freeze participants, however, did not increase in helpfulness. The researchers concluded that sad moods only lead to greater helping if people believe that helping will make them feel better. The emotion (sadness) does not directly cause behavior; rather, it makes people look for ways to escape the bad feeling.

There is another reason to suspect that the purpose of emotion is not directly causing behavior. When emotion does cause behavior, as in the so-called heat of passion, it often produces behaviors that are not wise or beneficial to the individual. For example, angry people often say and do things that they later regret, such as calling their boss an idiot.[180] Evolution favors traits that bring benefits and advantages. If emotions mainly caused foolish actions, then natural selection would have gradually phased emotion out of the human psyche. The irrationality of emotional actions is therefore a reason to suspect that the natural purpose of emotion lies elsewhere.

One seeming exception to the view that emotions do not cause behavior is communication. It seems that emotions are meant to be communicated and, in this sense, emotions do cause behavior. It may be natural to show one's feelings and artificial to hide them. Young children, for example, typically express their emotions freely and without reserve. As they grow up, they slowly learn to hide them sometimes, which is another sign that the influence of socialization is to restrain and conceal feelings rather than to instill them. Once again, nature says go and culture says stop!

Emotions Guide Thinking and Learning

As the previous section showed, emotion may or may not guide behavior directly. The link between emotion and behavior is far from clear, but emotion does influence thinking and learning. As we said earlier, emotions make up a feedback system that helps people process information about the world and their own actions in it. Emotions change the way people think and sometimes help them learn better.

A long-standing stereotype held that emotions undermine rational thinking and make people do foolish, crazy things. However, psychological studies have shown that people who lack emotions (often because of brain injuries or other problems) are not really better off. They have great difficulty adjusting to life and making decisions. For example, a researcher described asking one such patient which of two dates would be better for his next appointment. The man spent most of an hour thinking of all the potential reasons to choose one or the other date, thus showing that he could analyze and think very logically, but he could not manage to choose between them. Finally the researcher just picked one date, and the man immediately said, "Fine!"[181]

Research with such patients has also shown that emotions help people learn from their mistakes. Without emotions, people don't learn. Participants in one study had to draw from various decks of cards.[182] In some decks, the cards generally signaled that the participant would win a small amount of money. In other decks, the amounts of money were larger, but one could lose as well as win. Normal people with normal emotional responses would play the game by sampling each deck, and when they drew a card that cost them a large sum they would then avoid that deck for a while. The negative emotional reaction helped them learn to regard those decks as bad. The patients without emotion (due to damage to a particular brain area) failed to learn. Even after they lost a big sum they would go right back to the same deck, often losing much more money in the process.

Thus, emotions help people learn. The mere fact of having an emotion alters memory: It makes people remember important things better while impairing memory for low-priority information. In lab studies, for example, when people saw an emotionally arousing picture, they remembered the preceding (irrelevant) picture even better than normal—provided it was important to them.[183] If not important, they remembered that previous picture worse than otherwise (i.e., without the later emotional surge). Thus, both positive and negative arousal seem to operate like a filter that puts priorities on what gets into memory and what gets ignored and forgotten.

Emotional also help learning from experience. Bad emotions may help people think about their mistakes and learn how to avoid repeating them. Sometimes this process is aided by counterfactual thinking, which is the process of thinking about what might have been (see Chapter 5). Emotions make people engage in more counterfactual thinking, as in "I wish I hadn't said that" or "If I hadn't wasted time arguing on the phone, I would have gotten there on time" or "I should have asked that attractive person for their phone number."[184]

Emotion can constitute valuable information that people learn about the world. According to the **affect-as-information hypothesis**,[185] people judge something as good or bad by asking themselves, "How do I feel about it?" If they feel good, they conclude that the thing is good. If they feel bad, they conclude that the thing is bad. Research has shown that mood effects are eliminated when people misattribute their mood to an irrelevant source, such as the weather. Researchers in one study sampled phone numbers from the student directory, assigned them to sunny versus rainy conditions by the flip of a coin, and waited for suitable days.[186] The sunny days were the first two sunny spring days after a long period of gray overcast. For the first time in months, students went outside to play Frisbee. The rainy days were several days into a period of low-hanging clouds and rain. The interviewer pretended to call from out of town and asked a few questions about life satisfaction. The crucial manipulation was whether the interviewer first asked as an aside, "By the way, how's the weather down there?" This question was asked to draw students' attention to a plausible source of their present mood. Because the researchers weren't sure that this would work, they also included a condition in which the interviewer told students that the study was about "how the weather affects people's mood." The results showed that students were more satisfied with their lives on sunny days than on

affect-as-information hypothesis the idea that people judge something as good or bad by asking themselves if they feel good or bad about it.

rainy days, but only when their attention was not drawn to the weather. Asking "How's the weather down there?" eliminated the effect of weather on people's life satisfaction.

When people are in an emotional state, they seem to see the world in a more emotional way, and this changes the way they process information. People put things in categories based more on their emotional tone than on their meaning. For example, does the word *joke* go more with *speech* or with *sunbeam*? People who are not having an emotion at the moment tend to group *joke* with *speech* because both involve talking (a logical grouping). In contrast, people who are happy or sad tend to group *joke* with *sunbeam* because both words have positive emotional meanings. Emotion thus attunes you to emotional connections out in the world.[187]

(Anticipated) Emotion Guides Decisions and Choices

We said earlier that emotions are a feedback system in the sense that they give us dramatic and powerful evaluations of whatever has just happened. In a sense, therefore, emotions focus on the recent past. Is that any help toward the future? One way they could help would be with learning, as noted previously. Another, however, is that people can learn to anticipate how they will feel if something happens. As a result, they can begin to guide their behavior based on how they expect to feel. If emotion rewards and punishes behavior, then perhaps people decide how to act based on how they expect to feel afterward. They avoid acts that they expect will make them feel bad, and they favor acts that they expect will make them feel good.

Thus, *anticipated* emotion is important. Indeed, a review found that anticipated emotion has a much stronger effect on human thought and behavior than does actual emotion.[188] Guilt is a good example: Guilt can really organize someone's life even if one hardly ever feels guilty. If guilt does its job, the person will anticipate and avoid acts that might lead to feelings of guilt. The person will end up behaving in a morally and socially desirable manner, and hence will almost never actually have to feel guilty.

Humans are the only animals that can travel mentally through time, preview a variety of different futures, and choose the one they think will bring them the greatest pleasure (or the least pain). **Affective forecasting** is the ability to predict one's emotional reactions to future events.[189] How do you think you would feel, and how long would this emotional state last, if (a) you won first prize in some athletic tournament, (b) you found out your romantic partner was having an affair with another person, (c) you got a great job offer with a high starting salary, or (d) you were wrongly accused of cheating and had to withdraw from the university? Most people are fairly accurate at predicting which emotions they would feel, but they substantially overestimate how long they would feel that way. People also overestimate the intensity of their emotional reactions.[190] The odds are that if any of these things did happen to you, you would get over it and return to your normal emotional state faster than you think. People are rarely happy or unhappy for as long as they expect to be. This error may occur because people focus too much attention on the event in question and not enough attention on other future events.[191]

Is it a problem that our predictive powers are seriously flawed? It may be a blessing rather than a curse, according to social psychologist Dan Gilbert:

> Imagine a world in which some people realize that external events have much less impact than others believe they do. Those who make that realization might not be particularly motivated to change the external events. But one of the reasons we protect our children, for example, is that we believe we would be devastated if they were harmed or killed. So these predictions may be very effective in motivating us to do the things we as a society need to do, even though they might be inaccurate on an individual level. Anyone who wanted to cure affective forecasters of their inferential ills would be wise to measure both the costs and benefits of forecasting errors.[192]

As Gilbert suggests, the benefits of affective forecasting errors generally outweigh the costs. Still, predicting wrongly could carry some costs. Revenge, for example, is something people often pursue on the basis of affective forecasting errors.[193] People believe that punishing someone who did something bad will bring them satisfaction and

affective forecasting the ability to predict one's emotional reactions to future events a feeling of closure. In reality, when people get revenge by punishing someone else, they continue to ruminate about the event and end up feeling worse than people who did not have the opportunity to take revenge. (The latter tend to move on and gradually forget about the issue.) Even when it comes to something as simple as deciding whether to go for a walk indoors (on a treadmill) or outdoors, people lose out because they fail to predict these emotions.[194] The outdoors walk produces a better mood than the indoors walk, but people fail to predict this, and so they miss a chance to feel good. (And note that both these examples involve predicting too little emotion rather than too much—consistent with Gilbert's comment, quoted above, saying that predicting too much emotion may be more helpful than predicting too little!)

Anticipated emotion can be a powerful guide to behavior, though psychologists have just begun to study the ways in which this happens. Thus far, one of the most studied effects of anticipated emotion is anticipated regret. Some researchers have argued that people make decisions more on the basis of how they expect to feel than on the basis of a fully logical, rational analysis of what will yield the greatest reward.[195] Decision making shows a "status quo bias," which means that people tend to stick with what they have and be overly reluctant to make changes, even if changing would logically put them in a better position. These researchers explain the status quo bias on the basis of anticipated regret: If you made the wrong decision, you would probably regret it more if you had made a change (thus relinquished the good situation you had in favor of a worse one) than if you had stuck with what you had.

Imagine this in the context of a romantic relationship: You have a reasonably good relationship, but someone else comes along who seems potentially an even better partner for you, though it is hard to be certain. According to the anticipated emotion theory, your decision will be based on considering how much you will regret either decision if it is wrong. If you stay with your pretty good partner even though the other partner could have been better, you may feel some regret. But you would feel even more regret if you dumped your pretty good partner and went off with the other one, and that turned out to have been a mistake. Anticipating the greater possible regret of making the second kind of mistake (dumping your current partner in favor of the new one) will bias the decision-making process toward staying with the status quo.

Emotions Help and Hurt Decision Making

We have already seen that without emotions, people have trouble making up their minds. They can think through the good and bad features of different choices, but they have trouble settling on which one is best. Decisions are also guided by anticipated emotion, usually for the better. On the other hand, the traditional awareness that people make bad decisions under the influence of emotion suggests that emotion can harm decisions as well as help them. Only recently has decision research started to take seriously the role of emotions in the choices and decisions people make.[196]

Evolution seems to have prepared humans and other primates to experience fear and anxiety in response to certain objects (e.g., snakes, spiders). Anxiety has been called "the shadow of intelligence" because it motivates people to plan ahead and avoid taking unnecessary risks.[197] According to the **risk-as-feelings hypothesis**,[198] people react to risky situations based on how severe the worst outcome is and how likely it is to occur. They do this at a gut level. If their gut tells them the situation is too risky, they avoid it. (In terms of the duplex mind, gut reactions usually refer to the automatic system—in this case, automatic affective reactions.)

Strong conscious emotions can also influence people to engage in risky behavior and ignore future consequences. Sexual arousal often interferes with decision-making ability. For example, male research participants who saw sexually appealing photographs thought they were less likely to contract a sexually transmitted disease from a high-risk partner than did men who saw nonsexual photographs.[199]

Thus, their feeling of sexual arousal prevented them from appraising the danger accurately. Negative emotional responses to sex such as anxiety, guilt, and fear interfere with sexual behavior and also interfere with learning and retaining sexually relevant material,

risk-as-feelings hypothesis the idea that people rely on emotional processes to evaluate risk, with the result that their judgments may be biased by emotional factors

MONEY Matters

Emotions and Prices

Money experts generally advise you to avoid making financial decisions on the basis of emotion. But emotion is an important and common feature of everyday life, and it is unrealistic to expect people to be able to wait until all their emotions have subsided whenever they want to buy or sell anything. Hence, it is useful to know how emotion can affect financial decisions—even emotion that is left over from other events.

The effects of two leftover emotions (disgust and sadness) on buying and selling decisions was investigated in an important study.[200] Participants first watched a film clip designed to induce an emotional state. Some saw a sad scene from a film in which a boy witnesses his father's death. Others saw a disgusting scene in which a man plunges into an unflushed, filthy public toilet in the hope of finding a dose of heroin. Participants in the neutral control condition saw a brief nature scene.

Some participants had received a highlighter pen set as a gift, and they were later asked how much they would sell it for. For the other participants, the price they would pay for the pen set was assessed. (To avoid the problem that some participants might not have much money with them, the researchers asked them to choose between the highlighter set and various amounts of money they could receive instead.) Note that the buying and selling had nothing to do with the emotional states from the film clips, and in fact participants thought they were doing two separate experiments.

Disgust is naturally caused by eating something bad, so it predisposes the body to want to get rid of what is inside it and avoid taking in anything new.[201, 202] In naming prices, people acted as if the highlighter set were the cause of their disgust. They lowered their selling price, which is a good way to get rid of something. They also lowered the price they were willing to pay for it, which reduces the chances of acquiring it.

Sadness reflects a general judgment about something as bad, so the message of sadness is "Let's change something!" As with disgust, sadness induced people to lower their selling price, which increases the odds of selling the item and hence making a change. Unlike disgust, however, sadness caused people to increase what they were willing to pay for the highlighter set, which increased the odds of another kind of change, namely acquiring something.

---

such as contraceptive information.[203] Other negative emotions, such as depression, are also associated with maladaptive decision making.[204] To see how negative emotions affect how much money we spend, see the *Money Matters* box.

In summary, emotions call attention to good and bad outcomes but seem to make people disregard probabilities and odds. Anticipated emotions generally seem to help and inform decision making, but current emotional states can bias the process and lead to risky or foolish choices.

Positive Emotions Counteract Negative Emotions

Positive emotions are studied far less than negative emotions.[205] Compared to negative emotions, there are fewer positive emotions, and they are relatively undifferentiated. For example, it is difficult to distinguish joy, amusement, happiness, and contentment. In contrast, it is easier to distinguish anger, fear, sadness, and disgust.

What adaptive function do positive emotions serve? How did they help our ancestors survive? One possible answer is that positive emotions appear to solve problems of personal growth and development. According to the **broaden-and-build theory** of positive emotions, positive emotions prepare an individual for later hard times.[206, 207, 208] Positive emotions broaden and expand an individual's attention and mind-set. For example, joy broadens by creating urges to play, push the limits, and become creative.[209, 210] These broadened mind-sets, in turn, build an individual's physical, intellectual, and social resources (see **FIGURE 6.3**).

Some research has shown that positive events are strongly related to positive emotions but not negative emotions, whereas negative events are strongly related to negative emotions but not positive emotions.[211] However, in some studies, bad events affected both good and bad emotions, whereas good events mainly affected good emotions.[212, 213] In any case, this line of thought suggests that the value of positive emotions is found mainly in connection with positive events. Against that view, however, research suggests that much of the value of positive emotions may lie in their power to overcome or prevent bad emotions.

broaden-and-build theory the proposition that positive emotions expand an individual's attention and mind-set and promote increasing one's resources

FIGURE 6.3

Positive emotions broaden and expand an individual's attention and mind-set. These broadened mindsets, in turn, build an individual's physical, intellectual, and social resources.

Source: From B.L. Fredrickson, "The value of positive emotions," *American Scientist*, 91, 330–335. Reprinted by permission.

Other Benefits of Positive Emotions

Being in a good mood helps flexibility, creativity, and problem-solving ability. For example, researchers put some physicians in a good mood by giving them some candy.[214] Physicians in the control group received no candy. Both groups of physicians were given a case of a patient with liver disease, and researchers timed how long it took them to diagnose the case. Physicians who received the candy were 19% faster and showed fewer distortions and more flexible thinking in comparison to physicians who received no candy. (The results could not be due to a "sugar high" because the physicians were told to eat the candy after the study was over, and all of them waited.)

Being in a bad mood does not help flexibility and creativity. For example, research participants who thought about the French documentary *Night and Fog,* which is about the World War II concentration camps, did not perform better than individuals in a neutral mood.[215] Thus, the effects are probably not due to mere arousal because both positive and negative moods can increase arousal.

Work can benefit from positive emotions. People in a positive mood also perform better, are more persistent, try harder, and are more motivated than people in a neutral or negative mood.[216, 217] People are more motivated to perform tasks they enjoy doing, and being in a good mood makes tasks more enjoyable.

Being in a good mood can also serve a protective function. People in a good mood tend to avoid risks, such as in gambling.[218] People in a good mood want to remain in a good mood, and they would feel bad if they gambled away their earnings.

Having a positive mood does, however, have a darker side. People in a positive mood are less logical,[219] have poorer short-term memory,[220] and are more easily distracted by irrelevant information.[221] These effects might be due to the fact that positive moods promote heuristic thinking that relies on mental short cuts.

QUIZ YOURSELF

Why Do We Have Emotions?

1. _____ emotions are generally associated with forming social bonds, whereas _____ emotions are generally associated with breaking social bonds.

   a) Unpleasant; pleasant
   b) Pleasant; unpleasant
   c) High arousal; low arousal
   d) Low arousal; high arousal

2. According to the affect-as-information hypothesis, people judge something as good or bad by asking themselves which of the following questions?

   a) "How do I feel about it?"
   b) "What do I think about it?"
   c) "When does it affect me most?"
   d) All of the above

3. People generally _____ how long they will feel a particular emotion.

   a) underestimate
   b) accurately estimate
   c) overestimate
   d) All of the above, depending on whether the emotion is pleasant or unpleasant

4. Which of the following emotions motivates people to plan ahead and avoid taking unnecessary risks?

   a) Anger
   b) Anxiety
   c) Happiness
   d) Sadness

answers: see pg 228

Group Differences in Emotion

Are Emotions Different Across Cultures?

Do people in different cultures have different emotional lives? For many years experts assumed that the answer was "yes." They thought that cultural differences would lead to huge differences in inner lives so that you could not begin to understand how someone from another culture might feel. This view has lost ground, however, and some experts now agree that most emotions may be quite similar across cultural boundaries.

Paul Ekman and his colleagues have identified six basic emotions that can be reliably inferred from facial expressions (see photographs): anger, surprise, disgust, happiness (or joy), fear, and sadness.[222] Their research group showed these photos to people all over the world, and regardless of cultural differences, people interpreted the same facial expression as indicating the same inner emotion. A meta-analysis showed that people living in 37 countries on five continents inferred the same basic emotions from photos of facial expressions.[223] These findings suggest that, based on facial cues, people have similar emotions everywhere and can recognize and understand one another despite their very different cultural backgrounds.

New research produced bodily maps of the six basic emotions, six more complex emotions (anxiety, love, depression, contempt, pride, shame, and envy), and a neutral control.[224] In five separate experiments, 701 participants from Western and Eastern countries were shown two silhouettes of human bodies along with emotional words, stories, movies, or facial expressions. They were asked to color the bodily regions whose activity they felt increasing (in one silhouette) or decreasing (in the other silhouette) while viewing each stimulus. As can be seen in **FIGURE 6.4**, different emotions were consistently associated with different body sensations, regardless of participant gender and the country they lived in. Thus, the bodily sensations experienced for different emotions seem similar for most people. Emotions are not just in your mind or face. Rather, they affect much of the body.

Although it might not be a "basic" emotion, the facial expression for "that's not a good idea" or "I don't like that—called the "not face"—might be universal.[225] Before we learned to say the word "not," we simply make the face. The "not face" is a combination of the facial expressions we use to show disgust, anger and contempt.[226]

Are Women More Emotional Than Men?

"Big Boys Don't Cry," so the saying (and song) goes. A long-standing stereotype depicts men as non-emotional and women as emotional. Women are supposed to be more readily overcome with feelings and to be more guided by them, in contrast to men, who make decisions based on cool, rational deliberation. Is this stereotype accurate?

A large-scale study had adult married men and women carry beepers around.[227] Whenever they heard a beep, they were supposed to stop what they were doing and fill out a quick rating of their current mood and emotional state. The researchers obtained thousands of emotion reports of what men and women felt as they went about their daily activities. Many statistical analyses comparing men and women yielded a general result: no gender differences. Men and women were remarkably alike in the degree to which they reported feelings at any point on the emotional continuum—strong bad emotions, strong good ones, mild bad, mild good, neutral.

Other research with similar methods has obtained similar findings: Daily emotional experience is essentially the same

FIGURE 6.4

Bodily topography of basic (Upper) and nonbasic (Lower) emotions associated with words. The body maps show regions whose activation increased (warm colors) or decreased (cool colors) when feeling each emotion.

SOURCE: Bodily maps of emotions Lauri Nummenmaa, Enrico Glerean, Riitta Hari, and Jari K. Hietanen PNAS January 14, 2014 111 (2) 646–651; https://doi.org/10.1073/pnas.1321664111 Contributed by Riitta Hari, November 27, 2013 (sent for review June 11, 2013).

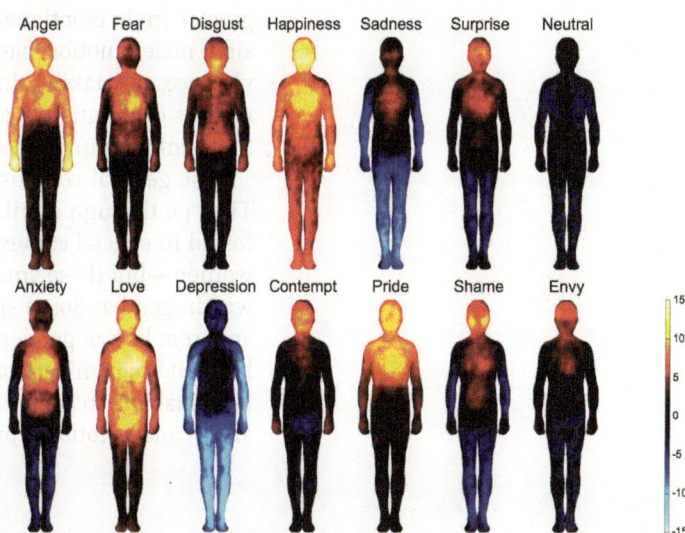

regardless of gender.[228] Adolescent boys do report extreme positive feelings a little less often than girls, although both girls and boys experienced extreme negative emotions such as anger.[229] In laboratory studies, women sometimes report stronger emotional reactions,[230] although this outcome could be affected by social norms that put pressure on men to underreport emotional reactions. Lab studies that use physiological measures do not find women to show stronger reactions. If anything, those measures suggest that men sometimes have stronger emotional reactions than women.[231]

One way to get around social norms (such as exhorting men to restrain emotion) is to look at small children. These studies fail to find greater female emotionality—if anything, the opposite. As far back as 1931, research showed that little boys have more frequent angry outbursts and temper tantrums than girls.[232] Studies of infants either find no difference in emotionality or find that baby boys are more emotionally intense than baby girls.[233,234,235] Observations of boys' play indicate that they seek out exciting, arousing themes but try to learn to manage fear and other emotions.[236] In games, boys put an emphasis on keeping their emotions under control so that feelings do not disrupt the game. Disputes are settled by appealing to abstract rules or, if necessary, replaying the disputed event, whereas girls' games are likely to end when emotion erupts. Partly for this reason, boys' games last longer than girls' games. Boys may find it more difficult than girls to calm themselves down when upset, so they work harder to avoid emotion in the first place. This pattern continues into adulthood and marriage: When married couples argue, husbands show stronger and longer-lasting physiological arousal than wives. As a result, husbands tend to avoid marital conflicts, whereas wives are more willing to argue and confront their spouse with problems.[237]

All these findings begin to suggest a very different conclusion: Men may be slightly *more* emotional than women, whereas women feel more willing to report their emotions and claim to have stronger feelings. Social norms may put pressure on men to stifle their emotions and not admit to having strong feelings, but the greater emotionality of women may be an illusion. Similar patterns are found in empathy research: On self-report measures, women claim to have more empathy than men, but when research uses objective measures of understanding the emotional states of others, no gender difference is found.[238]

What about love? Here too there is scant support for the female emotionality. Men confess "I love you" before women do, and men feel happier than women when someone expresses love to them.[239] Men fall in love faster than women, and women fall out of love faster than men.[240,241,242] Men have more experiences of loving someone who does not love them back, whereas women have more experiences of receiving love but not reciprocating it.[243] When a love relationship breaks up in a heterosexual relationship, men suffer more intense emotional distress than women.[244]

In short, the traditional stereotype of female emotionality is wrong, at least in Western society where most of the research has been conducted. Based on the research findings, one could even speculate that men are more emotional than women. The findings of greater male emotionality in love and work, plus during infancy, fit this pattern. Possibly male emotion has presented problems for society, as when male emotion leads to violence, risk taking, intoxication, and other potential problems. Holding up an ideal of men as cool, rational, and unemotional may be a way for society to keep the dangers of male emotion under control.

The general conclusion is that men and women have fairly similar emotional lives. They go through similar ranges of feeling in their daily lives. Slight differences can be found in special contexts—men get angry at work more often or fall in love faster than women—but these small average differences are overshadowed by the larger differences within gender. Some signs indicate that men's emotions last longer than women's. The apparent lack of gender differences in observed emotion may conceal a pattern such that boys and men are actually by nature more emotional but, as a result of this emotionality (and inability to get over the emotion), develop ways of avoiding emotionally intense situations and emotional provocations.

1. How many "basic" facial emotions have been observed across dozens of different cultures?
   - (a) Two
   - (b) Four
   - (c) Six
   - (d) Eight

2. Which of the following lists contains only "basic" facial emotions (i.e., biologically determined, culturally universal in expression)?
   - (a) Anger, disappointment, disgust
   - (b) Fear, hope, surprise
   - (c) Happiness, indifference, sadness
   - (d) Happiness, sadness, surprise

3. Which group of Americans places the greatest emphasis on emotional moderation?
   - (a) African Americans
   - (b) European Americans
   - (c) Asian Americans
   - (d) Hispanic Americans

4. Which of the following is the conclusion of research evidence regarding emotional expression in males and females?
   - (a) Females are more emotional than males.
   - (b) Males are more emotional than females.
   - (c) Males and females don't differ much in how emotional they are.
   - (d) None of the above

QUIZ YOURSELF

Group Differences in Emotion

answers: see pg 228

Arousal, Attention, and Performance

We noted earlier that emotion contains arousal, in the sense of being physically excited. Many people believe that emotional arousal is harmful—that it is better to calm down, especially when one is trying to make a logical decision or perform effectively in a crisis. Yet the arousal that goes with emotion seems designed by nature to make a person perform better, not worse. For example, when the person is aroused, more oxygen is sent to the brain and muscles than otherwise. So, is emotional arousal good or bad?

One answer is that the relationship between arousal and performance is an upside-down (or inverted) U-shaped curve. That is, increasing arousal first makes for better performance, then for worse. Put another way, some arousal is better than none, but too much arousal can hurt performance. In 1908 Robert Yerkes and John Dodson proposed this view based on their studies with rats.[245] **FIGURE 6.5** illustrates this **Yerkes–Dodson law.** (Psychologists are reluctant to call something a "law," but this finding is so reliable and has been replicated so many times that it is considered a law.) The curve is lower for complex tasks than for simple tasks because performance is generally lower for complex tasks. In both cases, though, the link between arousal and performance resembles an inverted (upside-down) U, going up and then back down.

Arousal also seems good for narrowing and focusing attention. This is probably why people drink coffee, tea, or energy drink when they work: They want to be alert and focused, and consuming a drink that arouses them will produce that state. A famous theory by psychologist J. A. Easterbrook proposed that one major effect of arousal is to narrow attention, and this can explain both slopes of the inverted U-shaped curve that Yerkes and Dodson proposed.[246] Easterbrook's main idea was that arousal makes the mind eliminate information and focus more narrowly. When people have very low arousal, they do

Yerkes-Dodson law the proposition that some arousal is better than none, but too much can hurt performance

FIGURE 6.5
According to the Yerkes-Dodson Law, some arousal is better than none, but too much can hurt performance.

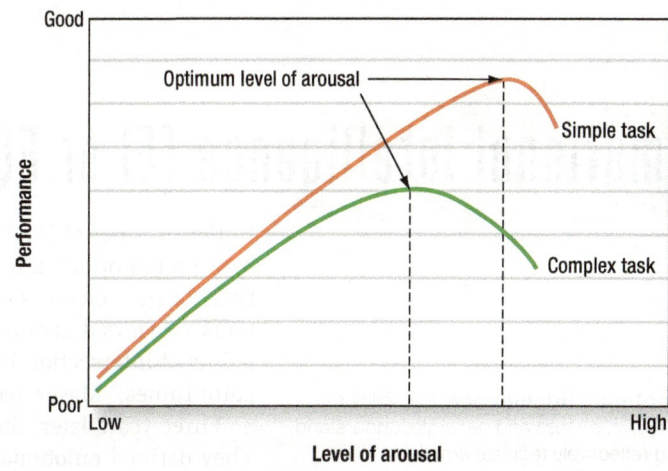

not perform very well because the mind is deluged with all sorts of information (including much that is unhelpful or irrelevant, such as noise outside when you are studying), so it has a difficult time focusing on the task at hand. As arousal increases, the mind begins to screen out irrelevant information, which helps it focus better on the task at hand, and performance improves. At some point, corresponding to the peak on the curve and the best possible performance, the mind is processing all the information relevant to the task and nothing else. That's when you do your best work.

However, as arousal increases beyond that point, the mind continues to focus ever more narrowly—and this further narrowing requires that it throw out helpful, task-relevant information (because all the irrelevant information has already been screened out, so only the good stuff is left). Hence, highly aroused people will be intensely, narrowly focused on what they are doing, but they may miss crucial information that is relevant or helpful. As a result, they end up performing worse than people with a moderate level of arousal.

The effects of stress on thinking appear to go along with Easterbrook's theory.[247] Under stress, people focus more narrowly on the task at hand, so up to a point, stress makes people perform better—but beyond that point, stress makes people ignore relevant information. Research using multiple-choice tests has shown how this can happen. Under stress, people just scan the multiple answers until they find one that seems correct, and they pick that one, sometimes without considering all the options. Thus, if answer B sounds good, they might choose it without even considering answer D. This gets them done faster, but they may make more mistakes, especially if D was really a better answer than B.[248,249]

QUIZ YOURSELF
Arousal, Attention, and Performance

1. According to the Yerkes–Dodson law, there is a(n) _____ curve between arousal and performance.
   - (a) Bell-shaped
   - (b) upside down U-shaped
   - (c) J-shaped
   - (d) U-shaped

2. The curve between arousal and performance is _____ for complex tasks than for simple tasks.
   - (a) broader
   - (b) higher
   - (c) lower
   - (d) narrower

3. According to Easterbrook, arousal influences performance by _____ attention.
   - (a) broadening
   - (b) decreasing
   - (c) increasing
   - (d) narrowing

4. Under high levels of arousal, what answer on a four-item multiple-choice test are students least likely to consider?
   - (a) Answer A
   - (b) Answer B
   - (c) Answer C
   - (d) Answer D

answers: see pg 228

Emotional Intelligence (EI or EQ)

In the summer of 1987, Peter Salovey asked his friend John Mayer to help him paint the living room of his new house.[250] Neither of them was a professional painter. Both were psychology professors who had done research on emotions. Generally, intellect and emotions are viewed as opposites. While painting, Salovey and Mayer wondered if there were points of intersection between the fields of emotion and intelligence. "Maybe it was the paint fumes," Mayer joked.

Three years later, they published an article on the topic of emotional intelligence.[251] They defined **emotional intelligence** as "the ability to perceive emotions, to access and

emotional intelligence the ability to perceive, access and generate, understand, and reflectively regulate emotions generate emotions so as to assist thought, to understand emotions and emotional knowledge, and to reflectively regulate emotions so as to promote emotional and intellectual growth."[252] Emotional intelligence is denoted by EI or EQ rather than IQ.

Emotional intelligence has four parts. The first is Perceiving Emotions, defined as the ability to recognize how you and those around you are feeling. It also involves perceiving emotions in objects, art, stories, music, and other stimuli. The second is Facilitating Thought, defined as the ability to generate an emotion and then reason with this emotion. The third is Understanding Emotions, defined as the ability to understand complex emotions and how emotions can transition from one stage to another. The fourth is Managing Emotions, defined as the ability to be open to feelings, and to modulate them in oneself and others so as to promote personal understanding and growth.

People high on emotional intelligence are better than others at affective forecasting (predicting future emotional states) and less susceptible to common errors. That is, they predict their future emotions more accurately than other people. Scoring high on Managing Emotions was particularly conducive to being able to predict future emotions correctly.[253,254]

Emotional intelligence seems especially important in the business world. For example, employees of a Fortune 400 insurance company who had previously scored high on emotional intelligence scores received greater merit increases, held higher company rank, and received higher ratings from peers and supervisors than did employees with low scores.[255] Emotional intelligence is positive related to job performance in both Western[256] and Eastern[257] cultures, to leadership skills,[258] and to mental and physical health.[259] People with high emotional intelligence have fewer alcohol-related problems than other people,[260] possibly because they know how to manage their emotions without getting drunk. Meta-analyses report that emotional intelligence is also positively related to romantic relationship satisfaction,[261] academic success,[262] and constructive conflict management in leaders.[263]

Recent research suggests that there is a dark side to emotional intelligence. There is a **"dark tetrad" of personality** consisting of narcissism, psychopathy, Machiavellianism, and sadism.[264] Recall from Chapter 3 that narcissists are selfish individuals with inflated egos. Psychopaths show a pervasive disregard for, and violation of, the rights of others. They are callous and unemotional individuals. "Machiavellianism" comes from the Italian philosopher and writer Niccolò Machiavelli. Machiavelli advocated using any means necessary to gain raw political power, including aggression and violence. Sadism is the enjoyment of hurting others. People with these dark personality traits tend to be high in emotional intelligence, but they use their emotional intelligence to manipulate others.[265,266,267] This dark tetrad of personality is also related to aggression (see Chapter 10).

> "Many people with IQs of 160 work for people with IQs of 100, if the former have poor interpersonal intelligence and the latter have a high one."
> — Howard Gardner

dark tetrad of personality four dark personality traits—narcissism, psychopathy, Machiavellianism, and sadism—that are related to emotional intelligence

QUIZ YOURSELF
Emotional Intelligence (EI or EQ)

1. **Which branch of emotional intelligence involves the most basic psychological processes?**
   a. Facilitating thought
   b. Perceiving emotions
   c. Managing emotions
   d. Understanding emotions

2. **Which branch of emotional intelligence involves the most psychologically integrated processes?**
   a. Facilitating thought
   b. Perceiving emotions
   c. Managing emotions
   d. Understanding emotions

3. **Emotional intelligence is negatively related to _____.**
   a. alcohol-related problems
   b. leadership skills
   c. work performance
   d. mental and physical health

4. **What dimension of the "dark triad of personality" is related to emotional intelligence?**
   a. Machiavellianism
   b. Narcissism
   c. Psychopathy
   d. All of the above

answers: see pg 228

Affect Regulation

One reason that emotional intelligence is beneficial is that it can help people control and regulate their feelings. When emotions run out of control, they can wreak havoc on inner and interpersonal processes. Indeed, mental illness is often marked by severe emotional problems, and some experts have concluded that people who are poor at controlling their own emotional reactions are more likely to fall victim to mental illnesses.[268,269,270]

Chapter 4 presented research on self-regulation, and we saw that the ability to self-regulate is important and valuable in many spheres of life. People do regularly seek to control their thoughts, desires, and actions. They often try to control emotions too but encounter an added difficulty: For the most part, emotions cannot be directly controlled. That is, if you are feeling bad, you cannot just decide to be happy and succeed by a simple act of will, in the same sense that you can drag yourself out of bed when you don't feel like getting up. Emotion control is a special case of self-regulation, and generally people have to rely on indirect strategies.

How to Cheer Up

One research group undertook an ambitious attempt to map out people's affect regulation strategies.[271] They used a series of questionnaire studies to find out what strategies people use to cope with a bad mood and make themselves feel better. Their list of strategies points to the different ways that emotion and mood can be altered.

One strategy is simply to do things that produce good feelings. People may cheer themselves up by eating something tasty, having sex, listening to music, or shopping (especially buying oneself a gift).[272,273] A strategy that overlaps with this one involves simply doing something to take one's mind off the problem, such as watching television, changing one's location, avoiding the source of the problem, or taking a shower. Note that neither of these strategies addresses the original problem or source of bad feelings; instead, people seek to create a positive, pleasant state to replace the unpleasant one.

Earlier in this chapter we saw that physical arousal is an important part of emotion. Hence for many people, raising or lowering their arousal is a promising strategy for affect regulation.[274] Arousal control strategies include exercising, drinking coffee or other caffeine products to increase arousal, or drinking alcohol, taking a nap, and using relaxation techniques to decrease arousal. Intense exercise may be an especially interesting strategy because it first increases arousal but later, as one gets tired, decreases it.

Seeking social support is another common strategy for controlling emotion. People may call their friends when they feel bad. Others go out and actively seek others' company. This fits our theme of putting people first: Even to deal with their own problem emotions, people turn to other people. When you are upset about almost anything, you can go spend time with people who like you, and the odds are good that you will end up feeling better. Note that this does not solve the original problem that made you feel bad, but it does help you stop feeling bad.

A very different set of affect regulation strategies is based on trying to deal directly with the problem (the one that gave rise to the bad feelings) in some way. Many people report trying to reframe the problem, such as by putting it into perspective or trying to see a conflict from the other person's side. Some try to use humor to make light of the problem and cheer themselves up. Others seek to vent their feelings, as by pounding a pillow, screaming, or crying (venting might feel good, but it usually just makes things worse). Religious activities such as praying help some people cope with their troubles; indeed, some studies have found religious activities were rated as among the most effective strategies for regulating affect.[275] For example, prayer is an effective way to reduce angry feelings and aggressive behaviors.[276] Imagining the situation from a more distant, third-person perspective, like a fly on a wall, can also reduce angry feelings and aggressive behaviors.[277]

To be sure, many of the strategies may work by more than one means. Exercise might bring both distraction and arousal control. Making jokes may be a way of spending time with others and reframing the problem as less serious than it seemed at first. Having sex may generate good feelings, distract one from the problem, and create a state of tiredness. If you're upset about having lost $100 because of a stupid purchasing decision, then making jokes or having sex or playing tennis does not change the original problem in the least, but it could make you feel better.

Not all strategies are equally effective. The data are very complex, but if people had to choose one strategy as most effective, it might be exercise.[278] If you're feeling sad or depressed, exercise can energize you and lift your mood. However, exercising to get rid of anger might backfire because it keeps arousal levels high rather than reducing them.[279] Listening to music was also rated very highly as effective for changing a bad mood, as was seeking out social support. At the other extreme, watching television and trying to be alone were rated among the least successful ways of coping with a bad mood.

Affect Regulation Goals

In principle, affect regulation can have at least six different goals: One can seek to get into, get out of, or prolong a good mood, and the same three options apply to a bad mood.[280] At first you might wonder why anyone would ever want to get out of a good mood or into a bad one, but in some situations it is inappropriate or even counterproductive to seem (or feel) overly happy. A physician may be in a terrifically happy mood one day, for example, but if she has to tell a patient that his illness is incurable and that he will die soon, a beaming smile may seem out of place. Likewise, an activist who has to present a case of injustice may find that an angry mood will be more effective than a cheerful, happy-go-lucky one.

In particular, people often seek to cultivate neutral moods prior to social interactions. In a series of laboratory studies, researchers first induced good or bad moods by exposing participants to music and then allowed them to select either cheerful or depressing reading material.[281] Some participants expected to meet and talk with someone new; these participants chose reading material *opposite* to their current mood—happy people chose sad readings, and sad people chose happy readings—presumably as a way to bring them out of their current feeling and bring them into a cool, neutral mood. (In contrast, people who did not anticipate an interaction chose mood-congruent readings—happy people chose happy readings, and sad people chose sad ones.) The implication is that people get ready for social interaction with a new partner by trying to get out of either a good or bad mood and into a neutral state.

Further work has shown that how people regulate their emotional states prior to social interaction is often very specific to the context.[282] People who expect to interact with a depressed person often seek out positive stimuli that will make them even happier—possibly because they expect (rightly) that it will be depressing to talk to a depressed person and they want to fortify themselves with an extra good mood to help them resist being brought down. People who are going to interact with a close relationship partner do not seem to change their moods, possibly because they intend to share their good or bad feelings with the partner. In any case, it is clearly wrong to assume that all affect regulation is aimed at trying to feel better right away.

Sometimes people even seek to cultivate anger. People in one study preferred to listen to angry music rather than other types of music when they expected a social interaction that would require confrontation and assertion (see **FIGURE 6.6A**).[283]

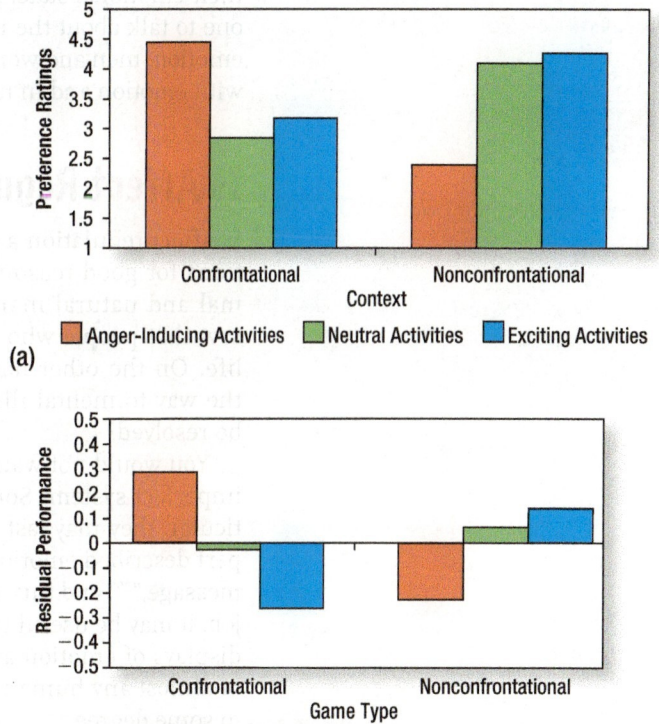

FIGURE 6.6
(a) Preferences for anger-inducing, neutral, and exciting activities (i.e., listening to music and recalling events) when anticipating performing confrontational and nonconfrontational tasks.

(b) Residual performance in the confrontational and nonconfrontational computer games, as a function of music condition.

SOURCE: Tamir et al. (2008).

(In contrast, participants anticipating a cooperative or constructive social interaction chose other types of music.) Thus, people seemed to anticipate that anger might be a useful emotion in the upcoming interaction, so they chose stimuli to help them get and stay mad. What's more, it worked! The angrier participants performed better in the confrontational situation. The results are depicted in **FIGURE 6.6B**.

Thus, people seem to seek out emotions partly on the basis of what will be useful and helpful in their social interactions. This desire to be effective competes with the desire to feel good, of course. Many strategies of emotion regulation are simply aimed at the goal of getting out of a bad mood or into a good one.[284,285]

Gender Differences in Emotion Control Strategies

Men and women may cope with bad moods in some different ways, although in general research shows that men and women are more similar than different.[286] One general theory is that when feeling depressed, women frequently respond with rumination, as in thinking about the problem, whereas men more commonly try to distract themselves with other thoughts or activities.[287] This may contribute to the higher rate of depression among women because ruminating about why you are depressed is more likely to prolong the bad feelings than shifting your attention onto something more cheerful, such as a sports event or hobby. Men often seek to keep themselves busy doing some task or chore, which not only may take their mind off their troubles but may also furnish some good feelings of success and efficacy if they can achieve something useful.

Another difference can be found in what people consume. Women are more likely than men to turn to food when they feel bad.[288,289] In contrast, men turn to alcohol and drugs to cope with the same feelings.[290,291,292,293] In a nutshell, women eat and men drink to regulate their moods. (Both strategies have obvious drawbacks!)

Other gender differences exist in mood regulation strategies.[294] When seeking to feel better, men are more likely than women to use humor to make light of the problem. (A tendency that some women may find annoying if they do not think the problem is funny!) Men are also more prone to report that sexual activity is a good way to improve their emotional state. In contrast, women are more likely to go shopping or to call someone to talk about the issue. Still, overall, as we saw in the earlier section on gender and emotion, men and women are far more similar than different in their overall experiences with emotion and in most other areas as well.

Is Affect Regulation Safe?

Is affect regulation a good idea? This chapter has emphasized that people have emotions for good reasons; if you prevent your emotions from functioning in their normal and natural manner, you may deprive yourself of their valuable guidance. We saw that people who lack emotions often have difficulty finding their way through life. On the other hand, we have seen that poor emotion regulation can also point the way to mental illness and other problems. How can this seeming contradiction be resolved?

You would not want to live without emotions entirely. Then again, emotions are an imperfect system. Sometimes, undoubtedly, emotions overreact to a situation; in particular, they may last past the point at which they have served their function. One expert described emotion regulation as "the ability to hang up the phone after getting the message,"[295] and this seems a very apt characterization. Once emotions have done their job, it may be useful to be able to control them. In any case, culture teaches people that displays of emotion are inappropriate on many occasions. To be a successful member of almost any human society requires the ability to regulate one's emotional reactions to some degree.

QUIZ YOURSELF
Affect Regulation

1. There is a(n) _____ relationship between emotional control and mental health.
   - (a) upside-down U
   - (b) negative
   - (c) null
   - (d) positive

2. What is the most effective strategy for improving a bad mood?
   - (a) Exercise
   - (b) Trying to be alone
   - (c) Watching television
   - (d) All of the above are equally effective for improving a bad mood.

3. Before interacting with someone who is depressed, what type of stimuli do people seek out?
   - (a) Angry
   - (b) Frightening
   - (c) Happy
   - (d) Sad

4. To regulate their moods, women tend to _____, whereas men tend to _____.
   - (a) eat; drink
   - (b) ruminate; distract themselves
   - (c) not use humor; use humor
   - (d) all of the above

answers: see pg 228

What Makes Us Human

Putting the Cultural Animal in Perspective

Humans are hardly the only species to have feelings. Fear, rage, joy, and even something close to love can be found in other animals. But human emotion is special in certain ways. Probably the most important is that human emotion is tied to meaning. People can respond emotionally to ideas, concepts, and the like. They cry at weddings, not because the spectacle of marriage is inherently sad, but because the idea of pledging to love the same person for the rest of one's life is deeply meaningful. Likewise, some ideas, such as freedom, justice, religion, and nationality, have so much emotional power that they can make people willing to sacrifice their lives for them.

The importance of meaning, and thus of ideas, in human emotion is also reflected in Schachter and Singer's theory[296] and appraisal theory,[297] which emphasizes that a bodily reaction needs a cognitive label (an idea) in order to become a full-fledged emotion. Ideas are also central to human happiness. An animal is happy or unhappy depending mainly on what has happened in the last few minutes, but people can reflect on their lives as a whole and be satisfied or discontented. The power of ideas also enables people to suffer (or benefit) from misattribution of arousal because the use of cognitive labels for inner states creates the possibility of switching labels or attaching a mistaken label. One emotion can be converted into another. Ideas can transform emotions, even after the bodily response is already in full gear.

Ideas also give human beings a larger range of subtle emotional differences than is found in most other species. As we said, many animals show fear, rage, and joy, but human beings have hundreds of different words for emotional states. Humans probably have so many different words for emotion because there are so many subtle differences in their emotional states. Being able to process so many subtly different ideas enables human emotion to be fine-tuned into many more subtly different grades of feeling.

Emotions are a vital help to people in navigating the long road to social acceptance. People who lack emotions do not fare well in human society. The distinctive complexity of human emotion is probably tied to some of the other tools we have seen that humans use to cultivate social acceptance. The human self, for example, is more elaborate and complex than what other animals have, and the complex self brings with it self-conscious emotions that inform and aid its activities. As an important example, the distinction between guilt and shame (doing a bad thing versus being a bad person) is probably beyond what most animals could understand; humans may be the only creatures who make use of that distinction.

Emotion is also linked to cognition (another tool used by humans on the road to social acceptance) in many and complex ways. We have already suggested that the human capacity for meaningful thought produces many more shades of emotional experience than would otherwise be possible, including many subtle distinctions between similar emotions (again, think of guilt versus shame). Humans are able to rely on anticipated emotion in their decision making, and even if their affective forecasting is sometimes off base, it can still inform and help human decision making in ways that would be impossible for almost any other creature.

The cognitive capabilities of human beings enable them to learn about their emotions too. Emotional intelligence is a concept that may be largely useless in discussing most other animals, but many people develop an emotional intelligence that can sometimes be more useful than other forms of intelligence. Emotional intelligence—using the ideas associated with emotions—enables people to function and succeed better amid the complexities of human society and culture. Although people high in narcissism, psychopathy, Machiavellianism, and sadism also tend to be high in emotional intelligence, they use it to manipulate others.

Emotional intelligence includes the power to regulate one's emotions (as in trying to control one's emotional state), and humans have cultivated that power much more than other animals.

People learn how to conceal their emotions, which may be an important manifestation of the general principle that nature says go (i.e., the same kinds of events produce the same emotions in all cultures) but culture says stop (i.e., people learn to hide or express their emotions differently depending on cultural norms and rules). Emotion regulation itself—such as in trying to stop feeling angry or to cheer up—shows how people deliberately exert control over their inner states. The very pursuit of happiness is also something that makes us human because it depends on several unique human abilities—such as the ability to think about a different emotional state from what one is currently feeling—to form a goal of moving from one state to another, to integrate inner states across time (remember, only humans can understand happiness in terms of broad satisfaction with one's life in general), and to save up information about how to move from one state into a happier one.

Ultimately, emotions make human life more meaningful and satisfying. A human life without emotion would be handicapped because a person without emotions would be without an important tool, but there is more to it than that: A life without emotion would be empty and dull. Human beings care about their emotional lives in ways that other animals almost certainly don't.

CHAPTER 6 SUMMARY

What Is Emotion?

- Emotions are mostly outside our conscious control, even though we may feel them consciously.
- An emotion is a conscious reaction to something; a mood is a feeling state that is not clearly linked to some event; affect is the automatic response that something is good or bad (liking versus disliking).
- Positive affect encompasses all good emotions, such as joy, bliss, love, and contentment; negative affect encompasses ; all bad emotions, such as anger, anxiety, fear, jealousy, and grief.

Emotional Arousal

- Emotions have both mental aspects (such as subjective feelings and interpretations) and physical ones (such as a racing heartbeat or tears).
- James and Lange proposed that the bodily processes of emotion come first, and then the mind's perception of these bodily reactions creates the subjective feeling of emotion. Proponents of the James–Lange theory of emotion failed to find specific arousal patterns for different emotions.
- According to the facial feedback hypothesis, feedback from the face muscles evokes or magnifies emotions.

- Schachter and Singer proposed that emotion has two components. One, the bodily state of arousal, is the same in all emotions. The other, the cognitive label, is different for each emotion.
- Sexual stimulation may affect the brain, the genitals, neither, or both.
- In excitation transfer, the arousal from one event transfers to a subsequent event.

Some Important Emotions

- Affect balance is the frequency of positive emotions minus the frequency of negative emotions.
- Couples who have children are less happy than couples who do not have children.
- People who are alone in the world are much less happy than people who have strong, rich social networks.
- The hedonic treadmill describes the tendency to revert to one's usual level of happiness soon after an emotional event.
- Happiness is rooted in one's outlook and approach to life, as well as in one's genes.
- Forgiving others, being grateful for blessings, practicing religious beliefs, sharing good feelings, and being optimistic can all increase happiness.

- Happiness is linked to a variety of good outcomes, including health and success in life.
- Anger is an emotional response to a real or imagined threat o provocation.
- The catharsis theory holds that expressing anger produces a healthy release of emotion and is therefore good for the psyche, but research demonstrates that catharsis increases anger and aggression and has negative health consequences.
- Shame is usually destructive, whereas guilt is usually constructive.
- Guilt motivates people to do good acts and make amends to repair damage to relationships.
- Disgust is a strong negative feeling of repugnance and revulsion. It motivates healthy behavior.

Why Do We Have Emotions?

- At least two basic arousal patterns—pleasant and unpleasant—underlie emotions.
- Emotions comprise an important and powerful feedback system, telling us whether something is good or bad.
- Positive emotions are linked to forming social bonds, whereas bad emotions are linked to various events that end, damage, or threaten relationships.
- Emotion rarely causes behavior directly.
- People who lack emotions have great difficulty adjusting to life and making decisions.
- Emotions help people learn from their mistakes. Without emotions, people don't learn.
- According to the affect-as-information hypothesis, people judge something as good or bad by asking themselves how they feel about it.
- Affective forecasting is the ability to predict one's emotional reactions to future events.
- According to the risk-as-feelings hypothesis, people react to risky situations based on how severe the situation is and how likely it is to occur.
- Strong conscious emotions can also influence people to engage in risky behavior and ignore future consequences. Emotions call attention to good and bad outcomes but seem to make people disregard probabilities and odds.
- The broaden-and-build theory of positive emotions suggests that positive emotions expand an individual's attention and mind-set, which, in turn, builds an individual's resources.

- Positive moods can increase flexibility, creativity, and problem-solving ability. People in a good mood perform better, are more persistent, try harder, and are more motivated than people in a neutral mood.
- Good moods can serve a protective function because individuals in a good mood tend to avoid taking risks.

Group Differences in Emotion

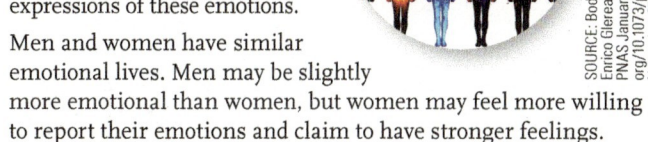

SOURCE: Bodily maps of emotions l Lauri Nummenmaa, Enrico Glerean, Riitta Hari, and Jari K. Hietanen PNAS January 14, 2014 111 (2) 646–651; https://doi.org/10.1073/pnas.1321664111 Contributed by Riitta Hari, November 27, 2013 (sent for review June 11, 2013).

- Six basic emotions have been observed in numerous cultures: anger, surprise, disgust, happiness, fear, and sadness. People of different cultures can reliably recognize posed facial expressions of these emotions.
- Men and women have similar emotional lives. Men may be slightly more emotional than women, but women may feel more willing to report their emotions and claim to have stronger feelings.
- Men fall in love faster than women, and women fall out of love faster than men.

Arousal, Attention, and Performance

- Arousal serves to narrow and focus attention. Some arousal is better than none, but too much arousal can hurt performance.

Emotional Intelligence (EI or EQ)

- Emotional intelligence is the ability to perceive emotions, to access and generate emotions so as to assist thought, to understand emotions and emotional knowledge, and to reflectively regulate emotions so as to promote emotional and intellectual growth.
- People high in narcissism, psychopathy, and Machiavellianism (called the "dark triad" of personality) tend to be high in emotional intelligence, but they use it to manipulate others.

Affect Regulation

- People attempt to regulate their emotions by doing things that feel good, distracting themselves from negative emotions, controlling their arousal, seeking social support, or dealing with the emotion-causing issue directly.

What Makes Us Human? Putting the Cultural Animal in Perspective

- In humans, emotion is tied to meaning.

key terms

affect 188
affect-as-information hypothesis 212
affect balance 196
affective forecasting 213
anger 201
arousal 190
automatic affect 189

broaden-and-build theory 215
catharsis theory 203
conscious emotion 189
dark tetrad of personality 221
disgust 206
emotion 188
emodiversity 200
emotional intelligence (EQ) 220

excitation transfer 192
facial feedback hypothesis 190
guilt 204
hedonic treadmill 197
James–Lange theory of emotion 190
life satisfaction 196
mood 188

risk-as-feelings hypothesis 214
Schachter–Singer theory of emotion 192
shame 204
survivor guilt 205
Yerkes–Dodson law 219

quiz yourself ANSWERS

1. What Is Emotion? p. 189
   answers: 1.b 2.a 3.a 4.b

2. Emotional Arousal p. 194
   answers: 1.b 2.c 3.d 4.b

3. Some Important Emotions p. 208
   answers: 1.c 2.b 3.a 4.d

4. Why Do We Have Emotions? p. 216
   answers: 1.b 2.a 3.c 4.b

5. Group Differences in Emotion p. 219
   answers: 1.c 2.d 3.c 4.c

6. Arousal, Attention, and Performance p. 220
   answers: 1.b 2.c 3.d 4.d

7. Emotional Intelligence (EI or EQ) p. 221
   answers: 1.b 2.c 3.a 4.d

8. Affect Regulation p. 225
   answers: 1.d 2.a 3.c 4.d

THE MISSION AND THE METHOD

MODULE E: APPLYING SOCIAL PSYCHOLOGY TO THE ENVIRONMENT

Richard L. Miller,
University of Nebraska at Kearney

CENGAGE TEAM

This book would not have been possible without the excellent in-house team at Cengage. Thanks to the following people for your belief in our vision for this book: Josh Parrott, Product Manager; Laura Ross, Product Director; Tangelique Williams-Grayer, Sr. Content Manager; Kat Wallace, Product Assistant; Bethany Bourgeois, Art Director; and Lori Hazzard, Senior Project Manager for MPS Limited.

We acknowledge our appreciation and debt to this full team, but we must single out one person who has had the most direct contact with us and who, at least from where we have sat for these several years, has made the most difference. Jeremy Judson was a patient, thoughtful, intelligent, and diplomatic editor who was remarkably effective at steering the manuscript through the nuts and bolts of the revision process. Often he would manage to sort through a dozen or more reviews, boiling the chaotic mass of suggestions down into the key targets for improvement and managing the process with reason and good humor.

- **Class activity/demonstration ideas.** Ideas and prompts for in-class activities.
- **Student projects/homework.** Short- and longer-term assignments, as well as substantial prompts for projects that students can do on their own as out-of-class assignments or short-term projects.
- **Video clip suggestions** our *Research in Action* video collection, YouTube, and other videoclip suggestions.
- **Handouts.** Each chapter includes helpful handouts correlated with suggested activities and homework.

Cognero Cengage Learning Testing Powered by Cognero is a flexible, online system that allows you to author, edit, and manage test bank content from multiple Cengage Learning solutions, create multiple test versions in an instant, and deliver tests from your Learning Management System (LMS), your classroom, or wherever you want.

PowerPoint The Online PowerPoint features lecture outlines and key images from the text.

Acknowledgments

We thank our colleagues for their diligent and thoughtful feedback on previous editions of this book. Their suggestions pointed the way to make this a better book.

CONTRIBUTORS OF APPLYING SOCIAL PSYCHOLOGY MODULES

Special thanks go to our colleagues who wrote the application modules. These are specialized topics outside our own expertise, and we could not have done these ourselves even half as well. These modules add to the breadth and flexibility of what can be taught with this textbook.

MODULE A: APPLYING SOCIAL PSYCHOLOGY TO CONSUMER BEHAVIOR

Curtis Haugtvedt,
The Ohio State University

MODULE B: APPLYING SOCIAL PSYCHOLOGY TO HEALTH

Regan A. R. Gurung,
Oregon State University

MODULE C: APPLYING SOCIAL PSYCHOLOGY TO THE WORKPLACE

Kathy Hanisch,
Iowa State University

MODULE D: APPLYING SOCIAL PSYCHOLOGY TO THE LAW

Margaret Bull Kovera,
John Jay College of Criminal Justice, City University of New York

For the fifth edition, like the third and fourth editions, we use the endnote reference style used in the top scientific journals (e.g., *Science, Nature, Proceedings of the National Academy of Science*). This is not a cosmetic change. This makes the text much more readable to students. It also changes the emphasis from *who* did the research to *what* the research found. The references in the endnotes are formatted according to the guidelines of the Publication Manual of the American Psychological Association (APA), so interested students can become familiar with APA formatting.

We hope you will enjoy the fifth edition of our textbook. If you have suggestions for improvement or discover errors in the text, please let us know by dropping us an email (r.baumeister@psy.uq.edu.au or bushman.20@osu.edu). Again, we are deeply grateful for the opportunity to share our love of social psychology with students and teachers around the world.

MindTap for Baumeister and Bushman's Social Psychology and Human Nature

MindTap is a personalized teaching experience with relevant assignments that guide students to analyze, apply, and improve thinking, allowing you to measure skills and outcomes with ease.

- **Personalized Teaching:** Becomes yours with a learning path that is built with key student objectives. Control what students see and when they see it. Use it as-is or match to your syllabus exactly—hide, rearrange, add, and create your own content.
- **Guide Students:** A unique learning path of relevant readings, multimedia, and activities that move students up the learning taxonomy from basic knowledge and comprehension to analysis and application.
- **Promote Better Outcomes:** Empower instructors and motivate students with analytics and reports that provide a snapshot of class progress, time in course, engagement and completion rates.

In addition to the benefits of the platform, MindTap for Baumeister and Bushman's *Social Psychology and Human Nature* features:

- **Videos, animations, and survey-type activities,** all based on key social psychology topics and concepts.
- **Chapter-opening activities that include** "choose-your-own-activity style exercises in which students progress through by answering questions and to indicate their next steps. At the end, their decision-based outcome is presented, along with related social psych research.
- **Quizzing for every** chapter, including multiple choice, true-false, and short response reflection questions to encourage application and critical thinking
- **Cerego Mastery Training** lessons to reinforce and help student learning of important topics

Supplements

Instructor's Resource Manual The Online Instructor's Research Manual includes the following tools for each chapter:

- **Chapter outline.** Detailed review of the chapter with key terms underlined and defined.
- **Lecture/discussion ideas.** Helpful ways to address topics in text, cover topics tangential to what is in text, or provide alternative examples to what are presented in the text.

MODULE A
Applying Social Psychology to Consumer Behavior

Dr. Haugtvedt included a new focus on general aspect of "social network analysis." He also included a discussion of *The Secret Life of Pronouns*, as well as a link to a website with text analysis exercises. A discussion of Luckin Coffee was added, which has quickly become a major competitor for Starbucks® in China and is considering U.S. locations as well. He added a link to a short TED talk by Adam Ostrow that focuses on Artificial Intelligence analysis of social media posts, which is related to the discussion of virtual memorials.

MODULE B
Applying Social Psychology to Health

A number of new major works of research have been published in the field of health psychology since the last edition. Most importantly, a major *Handbook of Health Psychology* (2019) highlights new directions in health psychology and key trends. Dr. Gurung's material added these new directions to the module. He also added new empirical studies. He removed some of the references to comfort food research because questions were raised about the validity of those results, and some studies were retracted. He has paid attention to the language used to discuss gender and pronoun use.

MODULE C
Applying Social Psychology to the Workplace

Module C now includes an added focus on organizational culture and its impact on employee recruitment, selection, the work environment, teams, leaders, performance management, and employee attitudes and behaviors. Dr. Hanisch also updated and expanded the section on optimal work environments and their design including modifying work areas to help with distress. Important factors to facilitate team effectiveness was added to the module, as well as new coverage of technology and culture adaptations by organizations.

MODULE D
Applying Social Psychology to the Law

Dr. Kovera updated the description of the effects of age on eyewitness memory to incorporate the results of a recent meta-analysis on the topic as well as a new identification procedure that is intended to help children make more accurate identifications. She updated the section on the relationship between witness confidence and accuracy to reflect the current understanding of their complex relationship. She expanded the section on the effects of fillers on eyewitness accuracy, including a discussion of the concept of propitious heterogeneity. She also expanded the section on double-blind lineup administration to incorporate more recent research that illuminates how administrator knowledge changes witnesses' identification choices, causing them to shift from filler picks to picking the suspect. She also included a new section on the effects of judicial instructions on the reliability of eyewitness identifications on juror decisions, noting that although the courts have adopted these instructions, they are generally ineffective. Finally, she deleted the section on how the lineup members are presented to witnesses (e.g., simultaneously vs. sequentially) because new science has questioned the conclusions of earlier research.

MODULE E
Applying Social Psychology to the Environment

Dr. Miller added a section on interventions based on Albert Bandura's social cognition theory that have been applied to promoting environmentalism. He added new content regarding attitudes toward climate change and noted gender differences regarding crowding and territoriality. He also addressed issues of sustainability and added new research on conservation.

extended. Findings on mimicry were extended to eating, indicating that people (especially young women) eat more when they see others eating more. Another study showed young male skateboarders taking more risks when observed by an attractive woman than a man. A recent study found that students learn more when their instructors are good-looking than when unattractive. Meanwhile, the rejection section was augmented with studies on the impact of having others remember vs. forget various things about you, such as your birthday.

CHAPTER 12
Close Relationships: Passion, Intimacy, and Sexuality

Chapter 12 incorporates some striking new findings that both push the theoretical understanding of relationships forward and offer information of practical use for students in their own lives and relationships. Although Chapter 11 showed that physical attractiveness makes it easier to form relationships, it also comes with a higher risk of divorce and breakup—perhaps even because the attractive person is often confident of being able to find someone new and better. In the sexuality section, new work has shown that each of act of sexual intercourse increases marital satisfaction for about two days thereafter (then it returns to its baseline). Marital satisfaction declines in step with a wife's diminishing sexual desire, which appears to be a normal pattern—so perhaps partners mistakenly blame each other when their appetites for sex diverge. (Husbands seem to stay at about the same level of desire for many years after marriage.)

To keep up with the changing times, we have upgraded our coverage of non-heterosexual sexuality. An exciting new theory about the continuing existence of homosexuality despite minimal help from either nature or culture has been added. The box on eating and sexual attraction was updated with new studies that included non-heterosexual participants. A brief section has been added to address non-binary gender theory, focusing on people who refuse to identify as either male or female. Research on this last is in its infancy, but we wanted to be among the first textbooks to add this coverage, and we anticipate expanding it in future editions. Our textbook is for everyone!

CHAPTER 13
Prejudice and Intergroup Relations

We expanded the section on anti-gay prejudice to be more inclusive of the LGBTQ+ community. Some students in our classes mentioned that our textbook treats gender as a binary construct, even though it is not. We also discuss some reasons why homosexuality can be adaptive from an evolutionary perspective. Given the rise of anti-Semitism around the world, we included a new section on Jews as a common target of prejudice. We also included another new target of common prejudice—"greedy" corporations. One way to reduce prejudice is through contact with outgroup members. We discuss new research showing that electronic contact or E-contact (e.g., texting) with outgroup members can reduce prejudice. We also deleted our extended discussion of the "Robber's Cave Study," because questions have been raised about the validity of those results.

CHAPTER 14
Groups

Chapter 14 was updated in several key places. New findings have shown that group performance benefits from diversity (specifically, Wikipedia entries were shown to have higher quality of the authors/editors had political diversity). The role of outgroups in making ingroups was attested in a new book reviewing all manner of societies, from bugs to apes to humankind. Some editions ago, we introduced the extended example of Robert Mugabe as a bad leader, and the story of Zimbabwe's decline under his leadership has been extended through subsequent editions. We were finally able to write a conclusion to that story in this edition, given the coup that removed him recently, though the saga has yet to have a truly happy ending in terms of the effects on the country.

indirectly through cognitive appraisals. Cognitive appraisals are evaluations, interpretations, and explanations of events in the environment, such as whether an event is a personal threat to your safety. We also discuss a new concept called **emodiversity**, which is the degree to which a person experiences a wide variety of emotions. We discuss how movements such as #BlackLivesMatter and #MeToo are fueled by anger, which motivates people to take action to solve injustices. Finally, we discuss two additional anger management techniques. Anger motivates people to approach things. Angry people often lean forward and are "in your face." Recent research has shown that doing the opposite (e.g., leaning backward in your chair) can reduce feelings of anger, especially for people who are prone to anger. Hungry people can also become angry (hungry + angry = hangry). Eating healthy food can reduce hunger-induced angry feelings by giving the brain the fuel it needs to regulate the anger.

CHAPTER 7
Attitudes, Beliefs, and Consistency

We open Chapter 7 with a new vignette about how people are often asked to express their attitudes on a wide range of topics on a fictional planet named Sargus 4 using vote badges, but also on the planet earth using computer and cell phones. In the digital media age, expressing attitudes seems more important than ever, even following purchases. We include a new section on how automatic attitudes are more difficult to measure than deliberate attitudes.

CHAPTER 8
Social Influence and Persuasion

We open Chapter 8 with a new vignette about fake news, which can even influence election results. The World Economic Form lists "the rapid spread of misinformation online" as one of the ten most pressing issues facing the world today. Unfortunately, misinformation spreads much faster than facts. Misinformation is also very difficult to correct once it has spread. In the field of medicine, inoculations (i.e., exposing to a small dose of virus) can make their immune systems stronger. Similarly, attitudes can be inoculated be exposing people to weak counterarguments so they can build up defenses against stronger counterarguments. We discuss new research showing that inoculation can provide cross-protection for related but untreated attitudes, kind of like a "blanket of protection."

CHAPTER 9
Prosocial Behavior: Doing What's Best for Others

Chapter 9 got a serious makeover in the previous version, so this one was merely updated with some recent findings. The idea of five moral foundations, with differential appeal based on political orientation, was nicely supported in a recent massive study of corporate lawsuits. A careful review of the previous edition's new material resulted in some streamlining to shorten the chapter, as well as clarifying some passages that readers found unclear or misleading.

CHAPTER 10
Aggression and Antisocial Behavior

We included a new section on **appetitive aggression**, which is a type of aggression characterized by the enjoyment of violence or bloodlust. We discuss the "dark tetrad" of personality that consists of four dark personality traits that are related to aggression: narcissism, psychopathy, Machiavellianism, and sadism. We also discuss eight reasons why people often deny violent media effects.

CHAPTER 11
Interpersonal Attraction and Rejection

This edition added several recent lines of work relevant to college student life. Coverage of social media use, including its relationship to belongingness and loneliness, was

CHAPTER 1
The Mission and the Method

We added a discussion of the **hindsight bias** or the **"knew it all along" phenomenon**, which can cause trouble for students who think social psychology is just common sense. We also discuss the "replication crisis" in science generally and in psychology specifically, and possible solutions to this crisis. We discuss the problem of HARKing (**H**ypothesizing **A**fter the **R**esults are **K**nown), and how pre-registering study hypotheses can eliminate HARKing. Finally, we talk about Open Science, which is a recent movement to make the results from scientific studies openly accessible to all people.

CHAPTER 2
Culture and Nature

Chapter 2 is the conceptual foundation of the book, so it does not change as rapidly as some of the other chapters. For this edition, we added some great new research on human brain evolution in response to different kinds of challenges. In a twist away from traditional evolutionary theory, it found competition among individuals to be a relatively minor factor, whereas cooperation to master the environment was a much more central factor. This fits our general theme that humans evolved to create culture. Further evidence has noted why humans live so much longer than chimpanzees, despite the extensive overlap in DNA: When someone is temporarily unable to hunt or forage because of injury or illness, humans will supply the person with food, thereby enabling the person to survive and recover — but chimps and other primates do not. This too fits the point that cooperation is a vital part of the evolution of humans as cultural animals.

CHAPTER 3
The Self

We added some new research findings, including some dramatic evidence on the importance of reputation concerns, new thinking on the differences between narcissism and high self-esteem, and what people do when their neighbors win the lottery.

CHAPTER 4
Choices and Actions: The Self in Action

This ever-popular chapter has been updated with new references and a couple exciting new findings. Some passages were streamlined for quicker, easier reading.

CHAPTER 5
Social Cognition

We added new research showing that the unconscious mind can process much more than we previously thought (e.g., effortful arithmetic computations, multiple-word expressions). Plus, we discuss perspective taking as another possible way to reduce the fundamental attribution error (i.e., the tendency for observers to attribute other people's behavior to personal causes and to downplay situational causes). When people try to put themselves in the shoes of others, they begin to understand how they feel, and they become more aware of the role of situational factors.

CHAPTER 6
Emotion and Affect

We open Chapter 6 with a new vignette on road rage, which is the leading cause of traffic fatalities (even ahead of texting and alcohol consumption). Indeed, traffic fatalities are the leading cause of death among 15 to 29 year olds worldwide.[3] We also discuss an additional emotion theory—cognitive mediation theory, which proposes that arousal influences emotions

Applying Social Psychology to the Law (Module D), and Applying Social Psychology to the Environment (Module E). These modules enable an instructor to tailor a course that can encompass some of the most important applied fields of study that have had long, close relationships with social psychology. Rather than writing these modules ourselves, we had content experts write these modules.

More With Less

When we embarked on this textbook, we made "doing more with less" one of our guiding mottos. As we saw it, social psychology was approaching a turning point. The early textbooks often went into great detail about many specific studies. That was possible because back then there wasn't a great deal of material to cover. Since then, the body of knowledge in the field has expanded year by year, with new findings being continuously documented in established journals along with new journals popping up all the time. It is no longer possible to cover all the influential studies in great detail.

Some textbooks have responded to information overload by packing more and more findings into the same amount of space. This clearly cannot go on forever. Either textbooks have to get longer and longer, or they have to become more and more selective. We chose the latter course. As things turned out, we were able to cover most of what has become standard in textbooks. But we do not claim or pretend to be exhaustive. Our model for this is introductory psychology. Once upon a time, perhaps, introductory textbooks could provide a comprehensive overview of psychology, but it has by now become standard practice for them merely to select a few topics for each chapter to illustrate rather than fully cover what that field has to offer. We think social psychology is reaching the same point as introductory psychology, and that the way forward is to accept the impossibility of covering it all.

To be sure, the review process did push us to be more thorough. One thing experts are very good at is saying, "Well, you could also cover topic X," and we heeded many such comments from our expert reviewers. But our goal all along has been to offer students an in-depth look at some information, with all its implications and connections highlighted, rather than to make sure to cite every relevant study. We hope instructors will add their personal favorite studies to the lectures, to augment what we have included. But to keep the textbook to a manageable length and still do justice to our goals, we had to leave out many important and worthy studies. Even some large topics ended up getting short shrift. Most notably, we devote fairly little space to the social neuroscience work that has become an important theme in the field. We don't dispute its importance. We simply think it is not what is best for introductory social psychology students. Our recommendation is that universities offer a subsequent course that can focus on brain processes and their link to social behavior. For an introductory social psychology course, we think students would prefer to learn about the more familiar and more readily understood questions about how people think, feel, and act in recognizable social situations.

What's New in the Fifth Edition?

We were delighted with the positive reception of the first four editions of our textbook. We are grateful for all the instructors and students who have used the textbook. Some of them have made suggestions for material to cover, noticed typos or other things to fix, or simply wanted to express their liking for the textbook. Thanks to all.

In that happy spirit, we set to work on the fifth edition. Our goals were to keep it current, to retain its core vision and best features, and to make substantial, targeted improvements in a few areas where we felt there were promising opportunities or recent developments in the field.

All chapters have come in for revision, especially updating their coverage with the addition of some recent research findings. We also made specific changes to each chapter, described briefly below.

Following are the *Money Matters* topics included in the textbook:

- Nature, Culture, and Money *(Chapter 2)*
- Doing It for Money, Not Love *(Chapter 3)*
- How Money Can Trick You into Making Bad Decisions *(Chapter 4)*
- Does Money Make a Difference? *(Chapter 5)*
- Emotions and Prices *(Chapter 6)*
- Would You Sell Your Soul For $1? *(Chapter 7)*
- Even a Penny Will Help *(Chapter 8)*
- Money, Prosocial Behavior, and Self-Sufficiency *(Chapter 9)*
- Money and Antisocial Behavior *(Chapter 10)*
- Is Manhood Measured in Dollars or Inches? *(Chapter 11)*
- Mating, Money, and Men *(Chapter 12)*
- Racial Discrimination in Sports: Paying More to Win *(Chapter 13)*
- Money, Power, and Laughter *(Chapter 14)*
- The Costs and Benefits of Environmental Protection *(Module E)*

Other themes run through the book without being formally reflected in specific boxes. The "duplex mind," divided into automatic versus deliberate processes, has become a powerful theme in the field's thinking about a great many issues, and we want students to appreciate it. It is a profound insight into how the human mind is organized. "The long road to social acceptance" reflects how much work humans have to do to gain and keep their places in society. "Nature says go, culture says stop" was not on our original list of themes but kept coming up as we wrote, and so we went back to revise our earlier chapters to recognize this common way that nature and culture interact to shape human behavior.

Pedagogical Features

Our textbook has also benefited from input and suggestions for what can help students master the material. We have kept what has worked well in other textbooks, such as including glossaries, tables, graphs, cartoons, and illustrations. Each chapter begins with a set of "Learning Objectives" and ends with a "Chapter Summary," where we present lists of bullet points summarizing key content in the chapter. A learning objective describes what students should know at the end of the chapter that they didn't know before they read it. Learning objectives should be useful for both instructors and students. They also set our textbook apart from other social psychology textbooks that do not include learning objectives.

Our textbook was one of the first to include self-quizzes. Each major header in each chapter ends with a series of four multiple-choice questions. These were very popular with students in the first four editions. We can understand why many textbooks don't include them—they were an immense amount of work to prepare, and we wrote them ourselves rather than hiring them out to someone less familiar with the content—but we think the effort was worth it. Every time students finish reading a section of a chapter, they can get a quick check on how well they understood it by answering those four questions and verifying whether their answers are correct. Research shows that taking quizzes is one of the best ways to learn new material,[1] far more effective than other techniques such as highlighting and underlining textbooks, rereading, and summarization.[2]

Another exciting feature of this textbook is the set of five application modules that can be assigned according to instructor preference. It is possible to get the textbook printed with or without these modules, or indeed with any combination of them. The five modules are: Applying Social Psychology to Consumer Behavior (Module A), Applying Social Psychology to Health (Module B), Applying Social Psychology to the Workplace (Module C),

There is no *The Social Side of Sex* box in Chapter 12 because half of that chapter is about sex.

A third box presents tradeoffs. In this box, we attempt to stimulate critical thinking. Many students come to social psychology wanting to find ways to change the world and solve its problems. We applaud that idealism, but we also think that many problems have their origin in the basic truth that solving one problem sometimes creates another problem. Many social psychology findings highlight tradeoffs in which each gain comes with a loss. We hope that the students will come away from these boxes with a heightened integrative capacity to see both sides of many problems and behaviors. Following are the *Tradeoffs* topics included in the textbook:

- **Research ethics** *(Chapter 1)*
- **Political Tradeoffs** *(Chapter 2)*
- **Self-Handicapping** *(Chapter 3)*
- **Now Versus Tomorrow: Delay of Gratification** *(Chapter 4)*
- **Conscious and Unconscious Thought** *(Chapter 5)*
- **Affect Intensity, or the Joys of Feeling Nothing** *(Chapter 6)*
- **What Is the Real Attitude?** *(Chapter 7)*
- **Should Speakers Talk Fast or Slow?** *(Chapter 8)*
- **The Prisoner's Dilemma** *(Chapter 9)*
- **Creativity and Cheating** *(Chapter 10)*
- **Testosterone—A Blessing and a Curse** *(Chapter 11)*
- **Sex In and Out of Marriage** *(Chapter 12)*
- **Competition Versus Cooperation** *(Chapter 13)*
- **Diversity in Groups** *(Chapter 14)*
- **Wrongful Convictions vs. Protecting Victims** *(Module D)*
- **The Tragedy of the Commons** *(Module E)*

We replaced the "Bad is Stronger Than Good" boxes in the first edition of our textbook with a series of boxes on money for subsequent editions. This set was stimulated in part by listening to Paul Rozin, a thoughtful contrarian who has criticized psychology for being out of step with the interests of most people. He would hold up a copy of *USA Today*, "the nation's newspaper," and note that its four sections (politics/crime, money, sports, and life/style) are presumably what American citizens are most interested in reading—yet these topics are scarcely even mentioned in the indexes of most psychology textbooks.

Money is highly relevant to our theme of humans as cultural animals. Other animals do not use money. Money is often spent on getting things that nature makes us want: food, shelter, warmth, comfort, and even health and sex. Social events, such as war, can greatly influence the value of money. Yet money is undeniably a cultural phenomenon. Thus, money shows how humankind has found cultural means of satisfying natural inclinations. Social psychologists (like intellectuals across the ages) have often been skeptical and critical of money, and especially of the desire for money. Money is a fact of life and an almost indispensable ingredient to the good life in modern society. We hope that this set of boxes will stimulate students to see money through the prism of social psychology's diverse interests.

dieting, drinking, and related concerns. We remember well our college days as "starving students." Eating is a microcosm of social processes. Following are the *Food for Thought* topics included in the textbook:

- **Does Chicken Soup Reduce Cold Symptoms?** *(Chapter 1)*
- **Virtuous Vegetarians** *(Chapter 2)*
- **Eating Binges and Escaping the Self** *(Chapter 3)*
- **Dieting as Self-Regulation** *(Chapter 4)*
- **It's the Thought That Counts (or Doesn't Count!) the Calories** *(Chapter 5)*
- **Mood and Food** *(Chapter 6)*
- **Would You Eat a Bug or a Worm?** *(Chapter 7)*
- **Convert Communicators and Health Messages** *(Chapter 8)*
- **Restaurants, Rules, and the Bad Taste of Nonconformity** *(Chapter 9)*
- **Is There a Link Between Diet and Violence?** *(Chapter 10)*
- **Social Rejection and the Jar of Cookies** *(Chapter 11)*
- **Eating in Front of a Cute Guy** *(Chapter 12)*
- **Prejudice Against the Obese** *(Chapter 13)*
- **Is Binge Eating Socially Contagious?** *(Chapter 14)*
- **Is Comfort Food Really Comforting?** *(Module B)*
- **Stress and Nutrition** *(Module C)*

The Social Side of *Sex*

The same can be said for sex as for food, and so each chapter has a box applying social psychology to sexuality. We suspect that few people leave college with their sexual selves unchanged since arrival, and so students' natural and personal interest in sexuality can be useful for illuminating many perspectives and patterns in social psychology. Our emphasis is, of course, not on the mechanics or techniques of sex but rather on the social context and influences, which the field of sexuality has often underappreciated. It is also helpful that human sexual behavior is a vivid, dramatic example of something that shows powerful influences of both nature and culture. One of us (Baumeister) has even written books on sexuality, including one with his wife (Dianne Tice). Following are *The Social Side of Sex* topics included in the textbook:

- **Sex and Culture** *(Chapter 2)*
- **Self-Esteem and Saying No to Sex** *(Chapter 3)*
- **Gender, Sex, and Decisions** *(Chapter 4)*
- **Counting Sex Partners** *(Chapter 5)*
- **Can People Be Wrong About Whether They Are Sexually Aroused?** *(Chapter 6)*
- **A–B Inconsistency and Erotic Plasticity** *(Chapter 7)*
- **Scared into Safe Sex?** *(Chapter 8)*
- **Helping, Sex, and Friends** *(Chapter 9)*
- **Sexual Aggression** *(Chapter 10)*
- **What Is Beauty?** *(Chapter 11)*
- **Roots of Anti-Gay Prejudice** *(Chapter 13)*
- **Is a Marriage a Group?** *(Chapter 14)*
- **Sex for Sale** *(Module A)*
- **Increasing Condom Use and Safe Sex Practices** *(Module B)*
- **Sexual Harassment** *(Module C)*

against obese people, Arabs and Muslims, Jews, atheists, and LGBTQ+ individuals. Special emphasis is given to the emerging and uplifting work on how people overcome prejudice.

CHAPTER 14
Groups

All over the world, human beings live in small groups. This chapter takes a fresh and exciting look at the social psychology of groups. The first part addresses one often-overlooked but basic question, namely why are some groups more and others less than the sum of their parts? Classic material on group processes is mixed with new research. Because many groups have leaders, this chapter also discusses leadership and power.

Concept Features

When we embarked on this book we listened long and hard to the complaints that fellow teachers of social psychology had regarding their textbooks and the way the field was taught. We also listened to the feedback from many students. Several features of our textbook are directly influenced by this feedback. We have sought to offer a new, positive alternative to existing textbooks.

The most common complaint, of course, was the lack of integration. Many instructors, and even those who liked their particular textbook, still felt that textbooks merely hopped from one finding and one phenomenon to another without any broad vision. Hence at the end of the term, as one colleague put it, the take-home message was "Social psychology is a large, interesting, and diverse field of study." Our overarching goal of putting the person back together was a direct response to this complaint and is, in our view, the defining feature of our textbook. The themes that run through the textbook help to flesh this out. These are developed in Chapter 2, "Culture and Nature," which we regard as the theoretical foundation of the book. We recommend that instructors assign this chapter early in the semester, which is why we put it early in our textbook. The subsequent chapters can be taught in almost any order. Thus, the textbook is not a linear sequence in which each chapter builds on the preceding one. We deliberately rejected that approach because we know many instructors like to adapt the sequence of topics to their own schedules, goals, and plans. Instead, the design of this textbook is like a wheel. Chapters 1 and 2 are the center, and all the other chapters are spokes.

Our chapters contain four box feature inserts. Although many textbooks have boxes, we are especially pleased with our set. In the first edition, they proved to be student favorites. We began with a fairly long list of possible boxes and gradually, based on input and feedback from students and instructors, trimmed these down to the list of four that run through the chapters. For the second edition, we kept three of the four boxes from the first edition. The fourth set, devoted to the broad theme that "Bad is stronger than good" in the first edition, was also well received, but was replaced by an even more exciting set called "Money Matters" in subsequent editions. Our readers liked this set of boxes very much, so we retained and updated them for the fifth edition. The Modules also contain some of these boxes.

One box in every chapter has to do with eating. One of us recalls a conversation years ago with Peter Herman, who observed that "Eating is the perfect social psychology variable, because it is connected to almost every social variable or process you can think of!" As we researched the various chapters and thought about the findings, we came to see he was right, and so each chapter has a box that covers some findings showing how the chapter's topic influences or is influenced by eating. We thought this would be especially appealing to today's students, for whom college often presents a novel set of challenges and opportunities for eating,

CHAPTER 8
Social Influence and Persuasion

Social influence and attempted persuasion are deeply woven into the fabric of human social life, and indeed it is the rare social interaction that has absolutely none. As information-using cultural animals, humans often find themselves wanting to influence others or being the targets of influence. This chapter covers how people exert that influence, why they do, and some strategies for resisting influence.

CHAPTER 9
Prosocial Behavior: Doing What's Best for Others

In this chapter, we look at what people do in order to make possible the success of their cultural and social groups. Many textbooks have a chapter on helping. We cover helping in this chapter, but the broad focus is on all prosocial behavior. The integrative focus helps resolve some long-running debates, such as whether helping is genuinely altruistic and prosocial or merely egoistic and selfish. We also break with the Milgram tradition of depicting obedience and conformity as bad, because culture and thus human social life would collapse without them. It also discusses morality.

CHAPTER 10
Aggression and Antisocial Behavior

Just as Chapter 9 replaced the traditional, narrow focus on helping with a broader focus on prosocial behavior, Chapter 10 replaces the traditional, narrow focus on aggression with a broader focus on antisocial behavior. Aggression is treated here as a holdover from the social animal stage—which is why cultures mainly struggle to reduce and prevent aggression, favoring nonviolent means of resolving conflicts. Other antisocial behaviors covered include cheating, lying, stealing, and littering.

CHAPTER 11
Interpersonal Attraction and Rejection

This chapter combines two very different but complementary sets of findings. The study of interpersonal attraction has a long history and, despite the occasional new finding, is a fairly well-established body of knowledge. The study of interpersonal rejection is far more recent but has become a thriving, fast-moving area. Together they constitute the two sides of the coin of people trying to connect with each other.

CHAPTER 12
Close Relationships: Passion, Intimacy, and Sexuality

In its first decades, social psychology mainly studied interactions among strangers—but most social life involves ongoing relationships. The study of close, intimate relationships blossomed in the 1980s from a small, underappreciated corner into a profound and exciting enterprise that changed the field. This chapter covers this work, much of it quite recent. It emphasizes romantic and sexual relationships, showcasing what social psychology has contributed to understanding of these grand, perennial human dramas. Human romance and sex are eternal problems that reveal our evolutionary background but also highlight the many striking ways in which humans are unique.

CHAPTER 13
Prejudice and Intergroup Relations

Prejudice occurs all over the world, often contributing to violence and oppression and other forms of misery. This chapter examines the many forms and faces of prejudice, ranging from the standard topics of racism and sexism to the less remarked prejudices

Content Overview

CHAPTER 1
The Mission and the Method
The opening chapter explains what social psychologists do and why students may want to learn about it. It explains social psychology's place among the different fields that study human behavior. It offers a brief introduction to the methods social psychologists use to tell the difference between right and wrong theories.

CHAPTER 2
Culture and Nature
Chapter 2 sets up the big picture. How do we explain people? Departing from the old and tired battle of nature against nurture, this textbook follows a newly emerging understanding: nature and culture worked together, such that nature designed the human being to be capable of culture. The stock notion of "the social animal" is shown to be correct but far too limited, whereas the "cultural animal" captures what is special about human beings.

This chapter then sets up many of the integrative themes that will run through the textbook to help make sense of the many facts and findings that will be covered.

CHAPTER 3
The Self
The human self is a complex and marvelous participant in the social world. This chapter provides a coherent understanding of the human self that is based on both classic and recent research in social psychology.

CHAPTER 4
Choices and Actions: The Self in Action
The self is not just an idea but also a doer. This chapter covers key social psychology topics of choice, decision-making, self-regulation, and the psychology of action. The remarkable recent progress in this work lends extra excitement to this material.

CHAPTER 5
Social Cognition
Social cognition revolutionized social psychology in the 1980s. Now it has settled into a core basis for understanding many spheres of social life. Cognition is vital to cultural animals, because cultures operate on the basis of information. This is a showcase for many of the great achievements of social psychology.

CHAPTER 6
Emotion and Affect
Our social psychology textbook is one of few on the market to include a chapter on emotion, despite the fact that emotions are an integral part of the human experience. It discusses both positive (e.g., happiness) and negative (e.g., anger) emotions. With each edition of our textbook, we are able to add more material on this important topic.

CHAPTER 7
Attitudes, Beliefs, and Consistency
The study of attitudes has a long and distinguished history in social psychology. This chapter brings together the influential early, classic studies with the latest advances.

Preface

the results of thousands of social psychology studies. So this time when publishers asked about writing a textbook, we thought it over. And then we decided to do it.

Some might think that explaining human nature isn't the job of social psychology and should be left to the personality psychologists. In our view, personality's claim to that question is not naturally any stronger than social psychology's. After all, personality psychologists mainly study differences between people, and so understanding the patterns common to all people isn't any more likely to arise from those data than from social psychology's data. *Au contraire*, learning about how people in general will respond to ordinary social dilemmas and events is at least as promising as studying individual differences in terms of being able to point toward general patterns of human nature.

Most general theories about human nature agonize over the competing explanations based on evolution and cultural influence. Our synthesis is based on the question: "What sort of picture of the human being emerges from the results of thousands of social psychology studies?" The answer is novel: Nature "made" human beings for culture. That is, we think human beings evolved specifically to belong to these complicated, information-using social systems that we call culture.

Our textbook has many themes that are mentioned occasionally in the various chapters to tie things together, and these are mostly derived from the central theme of human beings as cultural animals. The theme of putting people first is a subtle way of conveying what is biologically unique about humans: whereas most animals get what they need from their physical environment, people get what they need from each other. This message was implicit even in the classic Solomon Asch conformity experiments, in which people would disregard the direct evidence of their physical senses in order to go along with what other people (even a collection of strangers!) were saying.

Another central theme is that inner processes serve interpersonal functions. The conventional wisdom in psychology, going back to its Freudian roots, has been more or less that what happens to people is a result of what's inside them. We think the research in social psychology points toward the need to turn that on its head. What is inside people is a result of what happens between them. Even in terms of what evolution has built into the human psyche, what is there inside the person is there to help people thrive in their social and cultural groups. People are built to relate to other people. Even the "self," much discussed and invoked throughout social psychology, is designed to cultivate social acceptance and other forms of success that are valued in human cultures.

This is not a book about evolution, nor is it a book about cultural differences. It is a book about people. Toward that end, we occasionally use insights that emerge from cultural and evolutionary studies. But those remain mostly on the sidelines. We differ from the evolutionists in that we focus more on how humans are different from other animals rather than how they are similar to other animals. We differ from the cultural psychologists in that we focus more on what cultures have in common than on how they differ. These are fundamental and large differences of emphasis that set our book apart from other books.

The bottom line, for us, is a very positive view of human nature. Over the years, many of the major theories about people have emphasized the negative. They have depicted people as dominated by violent, destructive urges or by strivings for power, as souped-up rats in societal Skinner boxes, as spineless beings at the mercy of strong social forces or willy-nilly situational influences. We have been persuaded partly by the positive psychology movement that psychology loses much of its value when it focuses overly on the negative side. Besides, we like people! So the integrated picture we offer is a generally positive one, though we give the dark side of human nature its due.

Hence one important feature of this textbook is that every chapter ends with a brief section entitled "What Makes Us Human? Putting the Cultural Animal in Perspective" that provides a quick review of what answers have emerged in that chapter that makes human different from other animals. These were easy to write because we really do see that human social life is remarkably and importantly different from that of other animals. We do not shrink from discussing the flaws and biases in humanity, and we acknowledge humankind's vast capacity for petty malice and occasional capacity for great evil. But we think the final picture is mostly favorable. These end-of-chapter sections offer a brief reflection on what is special about human nature.

Preface

This textbook is simultaneously an expression of love and rebellion. The love is our feeling toward our field. We followed different paths into social psychology, but over the years we have developed an affectionate appreciation for it. We agreed to write this textbook partly because we thought we could contribute to the field by covering what we love about it. The process of writing strengthened those positive feelings, by helping us see the remarkably diverse and creative work that our fellow social psychologists have produced over the past several decades. We are also both very active social psychological researchers and teachers. We love doing social psychology research, and we love teaching social psychology classes.

The rebellion part begins with the title. Maybe social psychology has sold itself short by clinging to the message "it's all about the situation." We think it's partly about the situation, but to us social psychology is very much about people. We think students sign up for social psychology courses because they want to learn about people. And we think social psychologists actually have plenty to tell them about people. Hence the "human nature" part of our title.

In other words, we are rebelling against the old dogma that social psychology's truth requires treating people as blank slates who just respond to situations. Instead, we see people as highly complex, exquisitely designed, and variously inclined cultural animals who are influenced but not defined by situations. Our textbook will tell students plenty about the power of situations, but it also seeks to tell them about the people in those situations.

To us, the most exciting aspect of this project has been the attempt to "put the person back together," in the phrase that got us started on this textbook. We believe that social psychology can offer a remarkably new, coherent, and accurate vision of human nature.

In fact, this new vision of human nature was central to the story behind our textbook. Both of us had been approached many times by various publishers about possibly writing a social psychology textbook, and both of us had repeatedly brushed them off as quickly as possible. Back then we thought that writing a textbook sounded like a tedious, uncreative set of chores requiring reading and describing every part of the field, regardless of how interesting. Both of us loathe anything that is boring.

The turning point came when one of us (Baumeister) spent a year at an interdisciplinary institute and embraced the task of trying to package what social psychology has learned that could be useful to other fields. Scholars in those fields mostly want to know about people and why they act as they do. The response to this took the form of a book for general audiences called *The Cultural Animal* (Baumeister, 2005), but the realization slowly dawned that this new, more integrated understanding of the human being might provide a powerful basis for a social psychology textbook.

We have used many different textbooks in our own social psychology courses. Most of them are quite good. One dissatisfaction with them, however, and indeed one that we have heard echoed by many other instructors and students, is that they end up being just narrative lists of findings grouped by topic, rather like a handbook or encyclopedia. We wanted more. We wanted an integrated, coherent vision of human nature. And now we had a basis in the form of a new understanding of human nature that put together

Application Modules

A Applying Social Psychology to Consumer Behavior   A1
Curtis P. Haugtvedt, The Ohio State University

B Applying Social Psychology to Health   B1
Regan A. R. Gurung, Oregon State University

C Industrial and Organizational Psychology: Applying Social Psychology to the Workplace   C1
Kathy A. Hanisch, Iowa State University

D Applying Social Psychology to Law   D1
Margaret Bull Kovera, John Jay College of Criminal Justice, City University of New York

E Applying Social Psychology to the Environment   E1
Richard L. Miller, Texas A&M University–Kingsville

Glossary   G-1
Endnotes   EN-1
References   R-1
Name Index   N-1
Subject Index   S-1

13 Prejudice and Intergroup Relations 450

ABCs of Intergroup Relationships: Prejudice, Discrimination, and Stereotypes 453

Common Prejudices and Targets 457
Muslims 457
Jews 458
Atheists 460
People Who Are Overweight 461
Large "Greedy" Corporations and Profits 461
LGBTQ+ Individuals 462

Why Prejudice Exists 465
Us Versus Them: Groups in Competition 467
Ignorance? The Contact Hypothesis 469
Rationalizations for Oppression 470
Stereotypes as Heuristics 471
Prejudice and Self-Esteem 472

Content of Prejudice and Stereotypes 473
Are Stereotypes Always Wrong, Mostly Wrong, or Mostly Right? 473
Are Stereotypes Always Negative? 475

Inner Processes 475

Overcoming Stereotypes, Reducing Prejudice 478
Conscious Override 479
Contact 482
Common Goals 483

MONEY MATTERS 454
Racial Discrimination in Sports: Paying More to Win

FOOD FOR THOUGHT 461
Prejudice Against the Obese

THE SOCIAL SIDE OF SEX 464
Roots of Anti-Gay Prejudice

TRADEOFFS 468
Competition Versus Cooperation

WHAT MAKES US HUMAN? 490
Putting the Cultural Animal in Perspective

Impact of Prejudice on Targets 484
Self-Fulfilling Prophecies 484
Stigma and Self-Protection 485
Stereotype Threat 487

Are Social Psychologists Biased? 490

CHAPTER SUMMARY 491

14 Groups 494

What Groups Are and Do 498

Groups, Roles, and Selves 501

Group Action 503
Social Facilitation 504
Social Loafing 505
Punishing Cheaters and Free Riders 507
Deindividuation and Mob Violence 508
Shared Resources and the Commons Dilemma 508

How Groups Think 510
Brainstorming, and the Wisdom of Groups 510
Why Do People Love Teams? 512
Transactive Memory: Here, You Remember This 513
Groupthink 513
Foolish Committees 514
Group Polarization and the "Risky Shift" 515

Power and Leadership 517
Leadership 517
Toxic Leaders 518
What Is Power? 521
Effects of Power on Leaders 521
Preserving Power 525

THE SOCIAL SIDE OF SEX 499
Is a Marriage a Group?

TRADEOFFS 500
Diversity in Groups

FOOD FOR THOUGHT 506
Is Binge Eating Socially Contagious

MONEY MATTERS 526
Money, Power, and Laughter

WHAT MAKES US HUMAN? 527
Putting the Cultural Animal in Perspective

Effects of Power on Followers 525
Legitimate Leadership 526

CHAPTER SUMMARY 528

11 Interpersonal Attraction and Rejection 370

Need to Belong 373
ngingness as a Basic Need 373
Ingredients to ongingness 376
Belonging Is Bad for You 377
Friends, Lovers, and Groups 377

ction: Who Likes Whom? 378
larity, Complementarity, positeness 378
al Rewards: You Make Me Feel od 380
or Tat: Reciprocity and Liking 381
Seem Trustworthy: Moral its 382

You Again: Mere Exposure 383
Looking Good 384
Attraction in the 21st Century: Online Dating 387

Rejection 389
Effects of Rejection: Inner Reactions 390
Behavioral Effects of Rejection 393
Loneliness 394
What Leads to Social Rejection? 396
Romantic Rejection and Unrequited Love 397

CHAPTER SUMMARY 400

TRADEOFFS 374
Testosterone—A Blessing and a Curse

MONEY MATTERS 385
Is Manhood Measured in Dollars or Inches?

THE SOCIAL SIDE OF SEX 386
What Is Beauty?

FOOD FOR THOUGHT 392
Social Rejection and the Jar of Cookies

WHAT MAKES US HUMAN? 400
Putting the Cultural Animal in Perspective

12 Close Relationships 404

Is Love? 407
ionate and Companionate e 408
and Culture 408
Across Time 409
berg's Triangle 410
fits of Commitment 412

ent Types of Relationships 414
ange Versus Communal 414
hment 415
s of Attachment 415
Dimensions of Attachment? 416
g People Who Love mselves 417

Maintaining Relationships 419
I Love You More Each Day(?) 420
Investing in Relationships That Last 421
Are Married People Happier? 422
Thinking Styles of Couples 423
Being Yourself: Is Honesty the Best Policy? 425

Sexuality 427
Theories of Sexuality 428
Sex and Gender 431
Homosexuality 435
Challenging the Gender Binary 436
Extradyadic Sex 437

TRADEOFFS 411
Sex In and Out of Marriage

FOOD FOR THOUGHT 434
Eating in Front of a Cute Guy

MONEY MATTERS 442
Mating, Money, and Men

WHAT MAKES US HUMAN? 446
Putting the Cultural Animal in Perspective

Extradyadic Activity in Dating Relationships 439
Jealousy and Possessiveness 439
Culture, Female Sexuality, and the Double Standard 444

CHAPTER SUMMARY 447

Contents

9 Prosocial Behavior 290

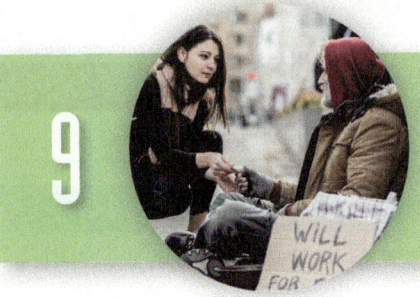

Is Helping Contagious? 292
What Is Prosocial Behavior? 293
  Born to Reciprocate 295
  Born to Be Fair 296
Morality 298
Cooperation, Forgiveness, Obedience, Conformity, and Trust 302
  Cooperation 302
  Forgiveness 305
  Obedience 307
  Conformity 310
  Trust 310
Why Do People Help Others? 313
  Evolutionary Benefits 313
  Two Motives for Helping: Altruism and Egoism 314
  Is Altruism Possible? 315
Who Helps Whom? 317
  Helpful Personality 317
  Similarity 318
  Gender 318
  Beautiful Victims 318
  Belief in a Just World 318
  Emotion and Mood 320
Bystander Helping in Emergencies 321
  Five Steps to Helping 321
  Too Busy to Help? 324
How Can We Increase Helping? 326
  Getting Help in a Public Setting 326

TRADEOFFS 304
The Prisoner's Dilemma

MONEY MATTERS 306
Money, Prosocial Behavior, and Self-Sufficiency

FOOD FOR THOUGHT 311
Restaurants, Rules, and the Bad Taste of Nonconformity

THE SOCIAL SIDE OF SEX 319
Helping, Sex, and Friends

WHAT MAKES US HUMAN? 327
Putting the Cultural Animal in Perspective

Provide Helpful Models 326
CHAPTER SUMMARY 328

10 Aggression & Antisocial Behavior 330

Defining Aggression, Violence, and Antisocial Behavior 334
  Is the World More or Less Violent Now Than in the Past? 335
Is Aggression Innate or Learned? 338
  Instinct Theories 338
  Learning Theories 339
  Nature and Nurture 340
Inner Causes of Aggression 342
  Frustration 342
  Being in a Bad Mood 342
  Appetitive Aggression 343
  Hostile Cognitive Biases 344
  Age and Aggression 346
  Gender Differences in Aggression and Violence 346
  Aggressive Personalities 348
Interpersonal Causes of Aggression 348
  Selfishness and Influence 348
  Domestic Violence: Hurting Those We Love 349
External Causes of Aggression 352
  Weapons Effect 352
  Violent Media 353
  Unpleasant Environments 355
  Chemical Influences 356
Self and Culture 358
  Norms and Values 358
  Self-Control 358
  Wounded Pride 359
  Culture of Honor 360

THE SOCIAL SIDE OF SEX 350
Sexual Aggression

FOOD FOR THOUGHT 357
Is There a Link Between Diet and Violence?

TRADEOFFS 363
Creativity and Cheating

MONEY MATTERS 364
Money and Antisocial Behavior

WHAT MAKES US HUMAN? 367
Putting the Cultural Animal in Perspective

Other Antisocial Behavior 362
Lying 362
Cheating 363
Stealing 364
Littering 366
CHAPTER SUMMARY 368

Contents

7 Attitudes, Beliefs, and Consistency 230

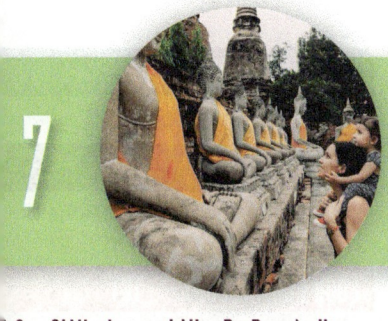

What Are Attitudes and Why Do People Have Them? 233
- Attitudes Versus Beliefs 233
- Dual Attitudes 233
- Why People Have Attitudes 235

How Attitudes Are Formed 236
- Formation of Attitudes 236
- Polarization 239

Consistency 240
- Cognitive Dissonance and Attitude Change 241
- Justifying Effort 241
- Justifying Choices 243
- Advances in Dissonance Theory 243
- Is the Drive for Consistency Rooted in Nature or Nurture? 245

Do Attitudes Really Predict Behaviors? 246
- Attacking Attitudes 246
- Defending Attitudes 246

Beliefs and Believing 249
- Believing Versus Doubting 249
- Belief Perseverance 249
- Belief and Coping 250
- Religious Belief 252
- Irrational Belief 253

TRADEOFFS 234
What Is the Real Attitude?

MONEY MATTERS 242
Would You Sell Your Soul for $1?

FOOD FOR THOUGHT 244
Would You Eat a Bug or a Worm?

THE SOCIAL SIDE OF SEX 247
A–B Inconsistency and Erotic Plasticity

WHAT MAKES US HUMAN? 254
Putting the Cultural Animal in Perspective

CHAPTER SUMMARY 255

8 Social Influence and Persuasion 258

Types of Social Influence 261
- Seeking Approval: Normative Influence 261
- Being Correct: Informational Influence 262

Techniques of Social Influence 264
- Techniques Based on Commitment and Consistency 264
- Techniques Based on Reciprocation 268
- Techniques Based on Scarcity 269
- Techniques Based on Capturing and Disrupting Attention 270

Persuasion 272
- Who: The Source 273
- Says What: The Message 276
- To Whom: The Audience 279
- Two Routes to Persuasion 280

Resisting Social Influence Techniques 283
- Attitude Inoculation 283
- Forewarned Is Forearmed 285
- Stockpile Resources 285

CHAPTER SUMMARY 286

MONEY MATTERS 267
Even a Penny Will Help

FOOD FOR THOUGHT 274
Convert Communicators and Health Messages

TRADEOFFS 275
Should Speakers Talk Fast or Slow?

THE SOCIAL SIDE OF SEX 277
Scared Into Safe Sex?

WHAT MAKES US HUMAN? 286
Putting the Cultural Animal in Perspective

5 Social Cognition 148

What Is Social Cognition? 151
Thinking About People: A Special Case? 151
Why People Think, and Why They Don't 152
Automatic and Deliberate Thinking 153
Thought Suppression and Ironic Processes 159

Attributions and Explanations: Why Did That Happen? 161
It's Not My Fault: Explaining Success and Failure 162
You Know I'm Right: The Actor/Observer Bias 163
Challenging Attribution Theory 165
Explaining Actions: A Different Approach 165

Heuristics: Mental Shortcuts 166
Representativeness Heuristic 166
Availability Heuristic 167
Simulation Heuristic 168
Anchoring and Adjustment Heuristic 168

Flawed or Clever Thinking? 170

(So-Called) Errors and Biases 171
Confirmation Bias 173
Illusory Correlations 173
Base Rate Fallacy 174
Gambler's Fallacy and the Hot Hand 175
False Consensus Effect 176
False Uniqueness Effect 176
Perseverance of Theories 177
Statistical Regression 177

MONEY MATTERS 158
Money in the Abstract

TRADEOFFS 160
Conscious and Unconscious Thought

FOOD FOR THOUGHT 161
It's the Thought That Counts (or Doesn't Count!) the Calories

THE SOCIAL SIDE OF SEX 172
Counting Sex Partners

WHAT MAKES US HUMAN? 181
Putting the Cultural Animal in Perspective

Illusion of Control 178
Counterfactual Thinking 178

Are Most People Really Stupid? 180
Reducing Cognitive Errors 180

CHAPTER SUMMARY 182

---

6 Emotion and Affect 186

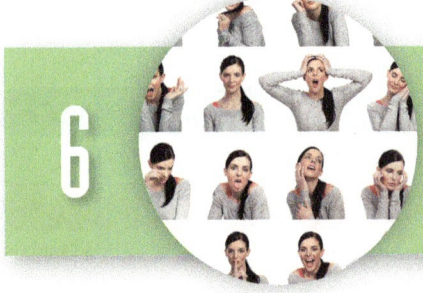

What Is Emotion? 188
Conscious Emotion Versus Automatic Affect 189

Emotional Arousal 190
James-Lange Theory of Emotion 190
Schachter–Singer Theory of Emotion 192
Misattribution of Arousal 192
Appraisal Theory of Emotion 194

Some Important Emotions 194
Happiness 195
Anger 201
Guilt and Shame 204
Disgust 206

Why Do We Have Emotions? 208
Emotions Promote Belongingness 209
Emotions Communicate Social Information 209
Emotions Cause Behavior—Sort Of 210
Emotions Guide Thinking and Learning 212
(Anticipated) Emotion Guides Decisions and Choices 213
Emotions Help and Hurt Decision Making 214
Positive Emotions Counteract Negative Emotions 215
Other Benefits of Positive Emotions 216

Group Differences in Emotion 217
Are Emotions Different Across Cultures? 217
Are Women More Emotional Than Men? 217

Arousal, Attention, and Performance 219

Emotional Intelligence (EI or EQ) 220

THE SOCIAL SIDE OF SEX 193
Can People Be Wrong About Whether They Are Sexually Aroused?

TRADEOFFS 200
Affect Intensity: Emotional Roller Coaster or Even Keel?

FOOD FOR THOUGHT 211
Mood and Food

MONEY MATTERS 215
Emotions and Prices

WHAT MAKES US HUMAN? 225
Putting the Cultural Animal in Perspective

Affect Regulation 222
How to Cheer Up 222
Affect Regulation Goals 223
Gender Differences in Emotion Con Strategies 224
Is Affect Regulation Safe? 224

CHAPTER SUMMARY 226

Contents

3 The Self 68

What Is the Self? 71
The Self's Main Jobs 71
Who Makes the Self: The Individual or Society? 72
Self-Awareness 75

Where Self-Knowledge Comes From 80
Looking Outside: The Looking-Glass Self 80
Looking Inside: Introspection 81
Looking at Others: Social Comparison 82
Self-Perception 83
The Fluctuating Image(s) of Self 84
Deliberately Seeking Self-Knowledge 86

Self and Information Processing 90
Anything That Touches the Self... 90
Can the Self-Concept Change? 91

Self-Esteem, Self-Deception, and Positive Illusions 94
Self-Esteem 94
Reality and Illusion 96
How People Fool Themselves 97
Benefits of Self-Esteem 98
Why Do We Care? 100
Is High Self-Esteem Always Good? 101
Pursuing Self-Esteem 103

Self-Presentation 104
Who's Looking? 105
Making an Impression 106
Self-Presentation and Risky Behavior 109

CHAPTER SUMMARY 111

FOOD FOR THOUGHT 79
Eating Binges and Escaping the Self

MONEY MATTERS 84
Doing It for Money, Not Love

TRADEOFFS 88
Self-Handicapping

THE SOCIAL SIDE OF SEX 99
Self-Esteem and Saying No to Sex

WHAT MAKES US HUMAN? 110
Putting the Cultural Animal in Perspective

---

4 Choices and Actions 114

What You Do, and What It Means 117
Making Choices 118
Why People Don't Choose 121
Freedom to Change 123

Freedom of Action 124
More or Less Free 125
Free Action Comes from Inside 125
Having an Out Versus No Escape 126

Goals, Plans, Intentions 127
Setting and Pursuing Goals 127
Hierarchy of Goals 129
Multiple Goals and Goal Shielding 130
Reaching Goals: What's the Plan? 131
Common Mistakes in Planning 132

Self-Regulation and Habits 133
Control and Willpower 133
Standards: Ideas That Guide Self-Regulation 134
Monitoring: Watching What You're Doing 135
Willpower for Change 136
Willpower and Decision Fatigue 138
Habits 139

Irrationality and Self-Destruction 140
Self-Defeating Acts: Being Your Own Worst Enemy 140
Suicide 143

CHAPTER SUMMARY 146

MONEY MATTERS 119
How Money Can Trick You Into Making Bad Decisions

THE SOCIAL SIDE OF SEX 121
Gender, Sex, and Decisions

FOOD FOR THOUGHT 137
Dieting as Self-Regulation

TRADEOFFS 142
Now Versus Tomorrow: Delay of Gratification

WHAT MAKES US HUMAN? 145
Putting the Cultural Animal in Perspective

Contents

1 The Mission and the Method 2

A Brief History of Social Psychology 5
What Do Social Psychologists Do? 8
Social Psychology's Place in the World 9
  Social Psychology's Place in the Social Sciences 10
  Social Psychology's Place Within Psychology 10
Why People Study Social Psychology 12
  Curiosity About People 12

Experimental Philosophy 13
Making the World Better 13
Social Psychology Is Fun! 14
How Do Social Psychologists Answer Their Own Questions? 15
  Accumulated Common Wisdom 15
  Overview of the Scientific Method 16
  Scientific Theories 16
  Research Design 18

FOOD FOR THOUGHT 17
Does Chicken Soup Reduce Cold Symptoms?

TRADEOFFS 20
Research Ethics

How Much of Social Psychology Is True? 27
  Self-Correcting Nature of Science 28
  HARKing (Hypothesizing After the Results are Known) 29
  Open Science 29
  Reliance on Student Samples 29
  Cultural Relativity 30

CHAPTER SUMMARY 31

2 Culture and Nature 34

Nature and Social Behavior 37
  Explaining the Psyche 37
  Nature Defined 38
  Evolution, and Doing What's Natural 38
  Social Animals 40
  The Social Brain 41
Culture and Human Social Life 43
  Social Animal or Cultural Animal? 43
  Culture Defined 43
  Nature and Culture Interacting 47
  What Makes Cultural Animals? 49

Are People the Same Everywhere? 50
Important Features of Human Social Life 52
  The Duplex Mind 52
  The Long Road to Social Acceptance 56
  Built to Relate 57
  Nature Says Go, Culture Says Stop 58
  Selfish Impulse Versus Social Conscience 59
  Tradeoffs: When You Can't Have It All 60

MONEY MATTERS 45
Nature, Culture, and Money

FOOD FOR THOUGHT 46
Virtuous Vegetarians

THE SOCIAL SIDE OF SEX 47
Sex and Culture

TRADEOFFS 62
Political Tradeoffs

WHAT MAKES US HUMAN? 65
Putting the Cultural Animal in Perspective

Putting People First 62

CHAPTER SUMMARY 65

Brief Contents

Preface xvii

CHAPTERS

1. The Mission and the Method 2
2. Culture and Nature 34
3. The Self 68
4. Choices and Actions: The Self in Control 114
5. Social Cognition 148
6. Emotion and Affect 186
7. Attitudes, Beliefs, and Consistency 230
8. Social Influence and Persuasion 258
9. Prosocial Behavior: Doing What's Best for Others 290
10. Aggression and Antisocial Behavior 330
11. Interpersonal Attraction and Rejection 370
12. Close Relationships: Passion, Intimacy, and Sexuality 404
13. Prejudice and Intergroup Relations 450
14. Groups 494

APPLICATION MODULES

A. Applying Social Psychology to Consumer Behavior A1
B. Applying Social Psychology to Health B1
C. Industrial and Organizational Psychology: Applying Social Psychology to the Workplace C1
D. Applying Social Psychology to Law D1
E. Applying Social Psychology to the Environment E1

Glossary G-1
Endnotes EN-1
References R-1
Name Index N-1
Subject Index S-1

in 2014). He lives in Columbus, Ohio, with his wife Tam Stafford and their youngest child. Their two oldest children share an apartment in Columbus. In his spare time, he likes to ride his bicycle, and listen to music, especially solo piano (e.g., Michiel Borstlap, Keith Jarrett), jazz (e.g., Miles Davis, John Coltrane, Sonny Rollins), and progressive rock (e.g., Patrick Moraz, Steve Hackett, Yes, Genesis, Deep Purple, Led Zeppelin, Pink Floyd).

About the Authors

ROY F. BAUMEISTER is currently a professor of psychology at the University of Queensland, Australia. He has taught introductory social psychology to thousands of undergraduate students. He received his Ph.D. from Princeton in 1978, and his teaching and research activities have included appointments at the University of California at Berkeley, Case Western Reserve University, Florida State University, the University of Texas at Austin, the University of Virginia, the Max Planck Institute in Munich (Germany), the VU University, Amsterdam (the Netherlands), King Abdulaziz University (Saudi Arabia), the University of Bamberg (Germany), the University of Melbourne (Australia), and the Center for Advanced Study in the Behavioral Sciences at Stanford. Baumeister is an active researcher whose work has been funded by the National Institutes of Health and by the Templeton Foundation. He has done research on the Self (including self-esteem and self-control), the need to belong, sexuality, aggression, and how people find meaning in life. In 2005, the Institute for Scientific Information concluded from a survey of published bibliographies that he was among the most influential psychologists in the world (the top 1%), and that status has been confirmed several times since then. According to Google Scholar, his works have been cited over 170,000 times in the scientific literature. In his (very rare) spare time, he likes to ski and play jazz. In 2013, he received the William James Award, the highest honor bestowed by the Association for Psychological Science in all of psychology, as recognition of his lifetime achievements and contributions to basic scientific research in psychology.

BRAD J. BUSHMAN is a professor of communication and psychology at The Ohio State University (since 2010), where he holds the Rinehart Chair of Mass Communication. Previously, he was a professor at Iowa State University (1990–2003) and at the University of Michigan (2003–2010). For over 30 years he has conducted research on aggression and violence. He was a member of President Obama's committee on gun violence, and he has testified before the United States Congress about youth violence. His research has challenged several myths (e.g., guns make people safer, venting anger reduces aggression, aggressive people suffer from low self-esteem, violence and sex sell products, media warning labels reduce audience size, exposure to violent media has a trivial effect on aggression). One of Bushman's colleagues even calls him the "myth buster." His research has been published in the top scientific journals (e.g., *Science, Nature, PNAS, JAMA*), and has been featured extensively in the mass media (e.g., *BBC, New York Times, NPR*). He has received honors for his teaching (e.g., G. Stanley Hall Lecture in 2018) and his research (e.g., Kurt Lewin Award from the Society for the Psychological Study of Social Issues for "outstanding contributions to the development and integration of psychological research and social action"; Distinguished Lifetime Contribution to Media Psychology and Technology from the American Psychological Association

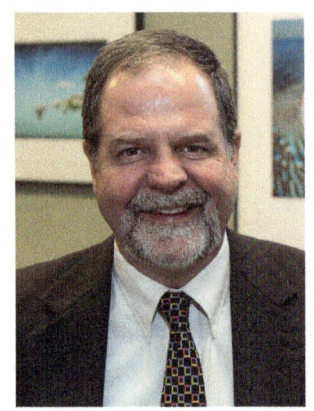

WE DEDICATE THIS TEXTBOOK TO OUR MENTORS AND TO THEIR MENTORS,
in appreciation of the teaching of psychology through these relationships.

APPLICATION MODULE C

Industrial and Organizational Psychology: Applying Social Psychology to the Workplace

Kathy A. Hanisch / Iowa State University

LEARNING OBJECTIVES

1 Summarize why work is an important part of life for many people and what benefits people get from work as well as the overarching role of the culture of an organization.

2 Identify the five components of the hiring process and describe the important features of each.

3 Evaluate the importance of work groups, leaders, and performance management on employee socialization and define the characteristics of a good leader in organizations.

4 Describe job satisfaction and organizational commitment and explain how they impact job performance.

5 Identify some common sources of employee stress and describe how employers can reduce the impact of these stressors to improve job performance.

6 Contrast organizational citizenship with organizational withdrawal and counterproductive behaviors.

THE SOCIAL SIDE OF SEX
Sexual Harassment
C10

TIPS FOR ORGANIZING YOUR DESK AND WORKSPACE
Designing your work area to foster productivity and health
C18

FOOD FOR THOUGHT
Stress and Nutrition
C28

WHAT MAKES US HUMAN?
Putting the Cultural Animal in Perspective
C32

You read a job post on LinkedIn, submitted your resume, and participated in a phone screen for the position. You took an online personality test and were then invited to the organization where you were interviewed by your potential supervisor and given a tour. The co-owners of the company have just offered you the position and proceed to tell you more about the job and benefits. They indicate that their organization is a great place to work; they tell you no one has quit their job in the last five years and employees are rarely absent. They also tell you that they have flexible policies including that you can work whatever hours you like, take vacation whenever you want, and if you decide to work for them you'll have access to spending cash as well as keys to the organization. At the end of the interview, the co-owners ask you what you are worth and indicate they will pay you whatever you wish. Does this sound too good to be true? Wouldn't this be ideal?

A very similar scenario was enacted by Arthur Friedman who was an Oakland appliance dealer in the 1970s. Friedman, the owner of the company, had some different ideas about how to run a business. Art, as reported in the *Washington Post*,[1] decided to change how he ran his business. At one of his staff meetings he announced that employees were able to work the hours they wanted, be paid what they thought they were worth, take vacation time when they wanted, and help themselves to petty cash if they were in need of spending money. New employees could set their own wages too. As you might imagine, the employees weren't sure how to take this news. It was reported that no one said anything during the meeting when Art first described his plan.[2] When he was asked why he was changing his business practices, Art replied, "I always said that if you give people what they want, you get what you want. You have to be willing to lose, to stick your neck out. I finally decided that the time had come to practice what I preached."[3]

It took about a month before any of the employees acted on what Art had said at the staff meeting. Then, many of the employees started asking for and receiving raises. Art told the payroll clerk to pay the employees what they wanted; he didn't approve the raises or even want to discuss them. Although many employees asked for $50 or $60 more per week, one employee, a truck driver, wanted $100 more per week; adjusted for inflation, $100 is equal to $666.40 in 2019.[4] Interestingly, this was a mediocre employee at best, but the raise made him a terrific employee. He felt he deserved more money; when his pay increased, so did his motivation and job performance. On the opposite side was a service man who was making less money than his coworkers; he said he didn't care because he didn't want to work that hard. He was happy being paid his wages and putting in the time and effort that he felt he owed the company. Both employees were able to make their jobs fit their working style.

In the final analysis, Friedman's experiment worked. He had changed the culture of the organization and the changes had positive results. The organization was profitable, union contracts were signed by him without reading them (the employees didn't need a union given the organizational culture), employees didn't quit, they didn't steal from the company, and they rarely were absent. The employees were happy, motivated, and worked to help the organization succeed. The employees realized that to make the organization work and remain in business they had to be reasonable in their requests and behavior.[5]

Imagine what you would do in a similar situation, for example, being asked to grade yourself in terms of the assignments and projects you do in a class. Would you grade yourself fairly, inflate your grade, or be more strict than your instructor? Research on self-evaluations of this type indicates that some students inflate their grades, but the likelihood of grade inflation decreases if students help determine how they will be graded, the instructor is involved in the assessment, and if the instructor has final control for determining the grades.[6] Student self-evaluations of performance and employees' determination of their own pay reflect accurate and honest assessments for most people; this would often be a function of the culture in the classroom or organization in terms of respect, integrity, and accountability. Employees who opt for less pay or students whose grades are low may accurately reflect the amount of time and effort they put toward work or their course, respectively.

A recent successful company as rated by *Fortune* in 2019 based on employee input is Hilton.[7] Since 1998, the Great Place to Work Institute has been producing *Fortune's* ranking based on survey questions where employees describe how their organization creates a Great Place to Work For All. Employees report about trust and reaching their full potential which makes up 85% of the evaluation; the remaining 15% consists of an assessment of the company's values, how effective the leaders are and the ability of employees to contribute new ideas.[8] To be eligible for consideration, companies must have at least 1000 employees in the United States and submit an application with over 200 datapoints documenting their human resources and practices; the evaluations are done for the previous year. The top company in 2019 was Hilton; 96% of employees say Hilton is a great place to work.[9]

Hilton's story is interesting because when Chris Nassetta, the CEO of Hilton, took over in 2007 he felt like corporate Hilton had lost touch with the front-line staff and the fact that their business is people serving people; he worked with his team to change that.[10] The attitudes of the executives at Hilton make their organization a place where employees are motivated to perform well because they are treated as the driving force behind the success of the business garnering similar reactions as Art Friedman's employees. The benefits at Hilton consist of the standard package of fringe benefits (e.g., competitive starting pay, retirement program benefits) plus generous parental leave, adoption assistance, travel perks, workspace upgrades, improved wardrobes, and more helpful continuing education and career development programs.[11,12] According to Nassetta, he is "...obsessed with taking care of his staff."[13]

1	Hilton (Hospitality)
2	Saleforce (Information Technology)
3	Wegmans Food Markets, Inc. (Retail)
4	Workday (Information Technology)
5	Kimpton Hotels & Restaurants (Hospitality)
6	Cisco (Information Technology)
7	Edward Jones (Financial Services & Insurance)
8	Ultimate Software (Information Technology)
9	Texas Health Resources (Health Care)
10	The Boston Consulting Group, Inc. (Professional Services)

2019 Best Fortune 100 Companies and Industries: Top 10

Great Place to Work Institute ranks organizations based on employee feedback and an assessment of company policies.

Source: https://www.hospitalitynet.org/news/4076889.html

Psychologists, known as industrial and organizational psychologists, are trained to help foster effective organizational cultures and to make improvements to the workplace through selection techniques that assist in matching employers and employees, performance management and evaluation systems that help foster the success of employees, the design of the job and work environment for performance, and changes in working conditions to influence positive employee attitudes and behaviors at work. The overall goal for I/O psychologists is to match the talents of the individual with the needs of the organization; if this happens, the organization will be successful from a profit and productivity standpoint, while the employee will be engaged and satisfied. Whether or not you decide to pursue a career in I/O psychology, you will, most likely, work at a job for pay at some time in your life so finding out how to get, keep, and enjoy a job are very important.

This module begins with an introduction to industrial and organizational psychology, a discussion of how important work is in our lives, and how psychologists seek to understand the interactions between the employee and the employer in the context of organizational culture. The next sections explore the life of employees beginning with developing appropriate and detailed job descriptions to facilitate recruitment and testing of job applicants in order to successfully select a good match between an employee and employer. Following that section, we'll examine how employees get used to and learn how the organization operates (employee socialization), a process that is centered around the culture of an organization that is often embodied in the employee's work team, work environment, leaders, and performance reviews. The module concludes with an examination of how employees' attitudes and stress affect their work behaviors as they impact the profit and loss numbers in organizations.

Industrial and Organizational Psychology

The Role of Social Psychology

In general terms, social psychology seeks a broad understanding of how normal adults think, feel, and behave when interacting with others (See Chapter 1). Industrial and organizational, or I/O, psychology seeks the same understanding about normal adults who work in organizations with a focus on the scientific study of individuals *at work*. Characteristics that define the field include (a) the focus on the individual, (b) normal behavior is of primary concern, (c) the use of the scientific research method with statistical analyses, and (d) theory-driven research is used to help solve applied (real-world) problems as well as problems are used to guide research. Some of the primary topics studied by I/O psychologists are organizational culture, employee selection, performance management and evaluation, training, job and workplace design, communication, work stress, motivation, leadership, groups and teams, organizational justice, human factors or system design, job attitudes, work-family conflict, and work behaviors.

I/O psychology is sometimes referred to as a part of applied social psychology. Both areas use psychological principles to evaluate normal individuals who interact with others, and the impact of their behaviors on individuals' perceptions, feelings, attitudes, and behaviors are studied. The fields overlap because similar topics such as motivation, leadership, and team or group performance are evaluated, but within different environments. Both are focused on understanding individuals' behaviors and the relations among individuals, but I/O psychology deals exclusively with employees in the workplace. The purpose of I/O psychology is "to enhance the dignity and performance of human beings, and the organizations they work in, by advancing the science and knowledge of human behavior."[14]

Work in Our Lives

You have learned about work since you were a small child. You may have asked where your mother was going when she took you to daycare or why your father left the house before 8 a.m. and did not return until after 5 p.m. You likely "played" at different jobs by dressing up to make you feel like an astronaut, firefighter, teacher, chef, or construction worker. As you got older, other sources of information about work may have come from your friends (who told you what their parents did), other family members, school, and the media. In high school, more education, a part-time job, and even social media may have given you additional details about the meaning of work. As you pursue a college degree, you will likely receive information about the work and jobs available in your chosen field through classes, career fairs, internships, practicums, or other job experiences.

Work is an important part of life for many people causing us to often ask people we meet what they *do*, which translates into, "what is your job and for whom do you work?" Many people identify with their work because they spend so much of their waking lives at work making it a central focus. Campbell (2017) provided statistics on how many years we spend doing different activities or events starting with an average life expectancy of almost 80 years.[15] Of that time, more than 13 years of one's life is spent at work; this comes in second only to sleeping which is about 26 years.[16]

Electrical workers!

Work is important because it provides many things people need and value. Work, for pay, provides us with the money necessary to satisfy our basic needs of food, shelter, and security (e.g., health care, retirement income), while the "leftover" money provides us with discretionary funds to use as we see fit. These funds may be used to buy a fancy coffee or a nice place to live, pay for a streaming service like Netflix or Spotify, support local or national charities, add to an existing book, movie, or music collection, attend fine art or athletic performances, or to save money for college. Money, typically from work, provides us with a standard of living that varies from person to person given our income and how we choose to spend it.

In addition, work provides much more. It provides a sense of accomplishment, satisfaction, the opportunities for social interactions (e.g., friendships), independence, a reason to get up in the morning, happiness, a sense of identity, recognition, and respect. For example, the most respected jobs of 2018 based on ratings (very high/high) of the honesty and ethical standards of occupations were nurses (84%), medical doctors (67%), pharmacists (66%), high school teachers (60%), and police officers (54%).[17] The professions receiving the lowest rankings on the very high/high ratings were members of Congress (8%), car salespeople (8%), telemarketers (9%), advertising practitioners (13%), stockbrokers (14%), and business executives (17%).[18] The ratings of respect for professions can sometimes be linked to heroism or scandals. For example, in 2001, firefighters received the highest respect ratings (90%) most likely because of their heroism after the 9/11 terror attacks; the ratings of respect for clergy dropped in 2002 and have, in general, been declining to 37% (2018) likely at least partially due to abuse scandals in the Catholic Church.[19]

Although most researchers and practitioners agree that money and recognition are nearly universal motivators,[20] others suggest that relatedness, autonomy, and competence are also common motivators.[21] However, many of the things valued or sought from work varies from person to person. For example, the respect of a job may not be important to you, but might be important to your best friend. Perhaps having your work provide you with a sense of accomplishment or a source of social interactions is what you desire, while those are valued much less by your sister or brother. It is important to understand what you want from your work and job as well as what your work and job can provide because the consequences of finding a good match and the alternative of not finding a good match have implications for your lifestyle, satisfactions, attitudes, stress, and behaviors that will be discussed in this module. From an employer's perspective it is useful to determine what employees want because satisfied employees compared to dissatisfied employees will be more likely to work to meet organizational goals and thereby help to ensure that the organization is profitable and viable. Part of a supervisor's job is to ascertain what employees value because those values may be used to motivate employees to perform well in their jobs. The process of determining the right match based on the talents and attitudes of a future employee starts early on in the hiring process for a position. This process will be described in the selecting employees section of this module.

Organizational Culture

An important component of your choice of organization will be the culture espoused and embodied by the organizational leaders and team members as well as the general climate or attitude adhered to by employees. **Organizational culture** definitions have been debated by researchers for a number of years. Denison defines culture as, "the deep structure of organizations, which is rooted in the values, beliefs, and assumptions held by organizational members."[22] Culture is thought to be stable and difficult to change. A related concept known as organizational climate, which is similar to culture because it is related to the organizational environment and influenced by the organization's value system, is more temporary and subject to direct influence by organizational members.[23] Managers do not make definitional distinctions when trying to influence, change, or deal with issues of climate, culture, or the work context and

organizational culture the cognitive component that includes the shared assumptions and beliefs of the organization often use these terms interchangeably in practice. For our purposes, we'll consider culture and climate together as they operate in concert to identify specific actions and behaviors that would represent the "normal behaviors" expected and desired from its employees by organizational leaders. For expanded discussions on culture and climate see Ostroff, Kinicki, and Tamkins.[24]

Organizational culture is important because it lets employees know what is expected of them and affects how they behave; this is critical in the recruitment, hiring, training, and socialization process for employees and will be discussed throughout this module. Culture is often determined by the founders of the organization and may be modified over time by the successes and failures of an organization. The work environment may impact the culture by determining appropriate behaviors allowed at work (e.g., socializing, collaboration; these issues and workspace design will be discussed later in this module).

There have been several case studies of organizations that have successfully changed their culture. Arthur Friedman allowed employees to set their own wages, decide the hours they worked, and required employees to belong to the union. The culture in Friedman's company changed resulting in better morale, increased productivity, and employee longevity. No one wanted to quit working in an organization with a culture where the employees were able to make their own decisions, which also impacted the organization's bottom line. Chris Nassetta, CEO of Hilton, is a leader that fosters the same type of culture as evidenced by the leap from 33rd to 1st in the Best Company to Work For in America ratings.[25] Changes at Hilton include free programs employees can use to better themselves such as earning their GEDs as well as workshops and training through Hilton University. In addition, there have been expansive upgrades to staff areas including better lighting, updated cafeteria (free for most employees), and nicer furnishings. After Nassetta donned a housekeeper's jacket and found out how heavy it was, he and his staff worked with Under Armour to design lighter and more comfortable work attire.[26] Hilton stock is up 274% from 2013 suggesting the organizational culture is supporting employees at being successful in their work.[27] Finding an organizational culture that fits your working style and organization expectations will have consequences for your morale, attitudes, performance, and tenure in an organization.

A positive organizational culture is critical to the success of an organization.

Types of Jobs

There are many types of work, in many types of jobs, in many different organizational settings. These settings include multi-international conglomerates, public and private companies, federal, state, and local government organizations, as well as home businesses. Individuals today have almost endless opportunities to pursue various avenues of employment.

People in the United States work a variety of schedules from extended workweeks (between 45 and 99 hours) to standard workweeks (between 35 and 44 hours) to part-time workweeks (fewer than 35 hours). Some people (e.g., police officers, nurses, factory workers), because of the nature of their jobs, work shifts other than the typical 8 a.m. to 5 p.m. shift. Others are offered flexible working schedules that often enable them to work the hours that best fit their lives as long as they accomplish the work. Telecommuting or working from home is becoming more popular with an increase in appropriate technology; some people work for virtual organizations that use communication technologies to outsource the majority of their functions.

In the United States, the **Occupational Information Network (O*NET)** consists of a comprehensive, detailed, and flexible set of job descriptors based on an extensive research program (find links to this resource on Psychology CourseMate at www.cengagebrain.com).[28] O*NET is a database that one can use to find details about occupations (e.g., tasks, knowledge, skills, work activities, wages, employment outlook;

Occupational Information Network or O*NET a comprehensive, detailed, and flexible set of job descriptors that can be used to learn about a position and find information to include in a job description; salary and occupational outlook are also provided see **FIGURE C.1** for an example) or select work activities or interests and locate corresponding occupations. It is a helpful starting point for individuals seeking details about the types of occupations that may interest them as well as the salary and occupational outlook for different occupations. It is also a useful starting point for employers who need to develop thorough job descriptions for the positions in their organizations. The O*NET is a major achievement in occupational information with over 970 occupations with database updates every year.[29]

Summary Report for:
19-3032.00-Industrial-Organizational Psychologists

Apply principles of psychology to human resources, administration, management, sales, and marketing problems. Activities may include policy planning; employee testing and selection, training and development; and organizational development and analysis. May work with management to organize the work setting to improve worker productivity.

Sample of reported Job Titles: Assessment Services Manager, Consultant, Consulting Psychologist, Industrial Psychologist, Industrial/Organizational Psychologist (I/O Psychologist), Management Consultant, Organizational Consultant, Organizational Development Consultant, Organizational Psychologist, Research Scientist

Tasks

- Formulate and implement training programs, applying principles of learning and individual differences.
- Conduct research studies of physical work environments, organizational structures, communication systems, group interactions, morale, or motivation to assess organizational functioning.
- Conduct presentations on research findings for clients or at research meetings.
- Provide expert testimony in employment lawsuits.
- Study consumers' reactions to new products and package designs, and to advertising efforts, using surveys and tests.
- Review research literature to remain current on psychological science issues.
- Develop interview techniques, rating scales, and psychological tests used to assess skills, abilities, and interests for the purpose of employee selection, placement, or promotion.
- Conduct individual assessments, including interpreting measures and providing feedback for selection, placement, or promotion.
- Write articles, white papers, or reports to share research findings and educate others.
- Develop new business by contacting potential clients, making sales presentations, and writing proposals.
- Develop and implement employee selection or placement programs.

Skills
Active Listening—Giving full attention to what other people are saying, taking time to understand the points being made, asking questions as appropriate, and not interrupting at inappropriate times.
Reading Comprehension—Understanding written sentences and paragraphs in work related documents.
Complex Problem Solving—Identifying complex problems and reviewing related information to develop and evaluate options and implement solutions.
Judgment and Decision Making—Considering the relative costs and benefits of potential actions to choose the most appropriate one.
Speaking—Talking to others to convey information effectively.
Critical Thinking—Using logic and reasoning to identify the strengths and weaknesses of alternative solutions, conclusions or approaches to problems.
Systems Analysis—Determining how a system should work and how changes in conditions, operations, and the environment will affect outcomes.
Systems Evaluation—Identifying measures or indicators of system performance and the actions needed to improve or correct performance, relative to the goals of the system.
Writing—Communicating effectively in writing as appropriate for the needs of the audience.
Monitoring—Monitoring/Assessing performance of yourself, other individuals, or organizations to make improvements or take corrective action.
Social Perceptiveness—Being aware of others' reactions and understanding why they react as they do.

Wages & Employment Trends

Median wages (2018)	$46.76 hourly, $97,260 annual
Employment (2016)	2,000 employees
Projected growth (2016-2026)	Average (5% to 9%)
Projected job openings (2016-2026)	100

FIGURE C.1
An abbreviated summary report from O*NET for an industrial and organizational psychologist.
Courtesy of o*net online.org/The American Job Center Network

Regardless of the type of job or your work schedule, you will spend most of your waking hours in some type of employment for many years. Because work is critical to who we are and what we do, studying the psychological principles and several topics examined by I/O psychologists will provide you with information that may be useful to you in your future careers.

QUIZ YOURSELF

Industrial and Organizational Psychology

1. Both I/O and social psychologists _____.
   - ⓐ apply psychological principles to the study of the interactions among people
   - ⓑ primarily study abnormal individuals
   - ⓒ conduct most of their research in the laboratory
   - ⓓ rely only on theory to solve their research questions

2. You could use O*NET to _____.
   - ⓐ find out what type of personality you have
   - ⓑ determine the employment outlook for a high school teacher
   - ⓒ find employers with job openings
   - ⓓ measure your networking skills

3. Spencer, Jenny, and Debbie are debating the merits of certain occupations. Spencer has always wanted to be a doctor, Debbie a business executive, and Jenny a police officer. Based on 2019 information, the rank order of the friends based on ratings of honesty for their occupations would be?
   - ⓐ Spencer, Debbie, and Jenny
   - ⓑ Debbie, Jenny, and Spencer
   - ⓒ Jenny, Spencer, and Debbie
   - ⓓ Spencer, Jenny, and Debbie

4. Nearly all individuals value _____ and _____ from their work.
   - ⓐ money; respect
   - ⓑ prestige; social interactions
   - ⓒ money; recognition
   - ⓓ satisfaction; prestige

answers: see pg C34

Selecting Employees

The Hiring Process

In the early 1900s when a man needed a job he would hang around the outside of a company and wait to see if management needed workers. Many times the people who worked for the company told their friends or relatives about possible job openings, prompting job seekers to show up for work. In those days, this often meant that individuals hired for the available jobs were similar to those working there (i.e., white males filled most positions at that time).

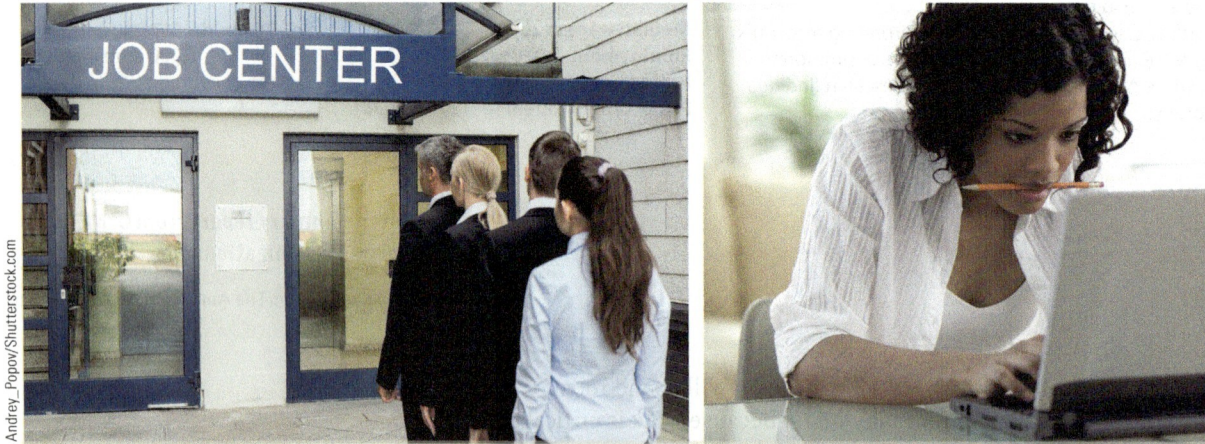

In the past century, applying for most jobs required a lot of legwork. For many modern jobs, job seekers let their fingers do the work keying in application information as well as sometimes taking online tests (e.g., personality) from home.

Industrial and organizational psychologists first became involved in the process of selecting employees when the U.S. government needed help selecting and placing officers and soldiers in World War I; they continued to help with similar selection decisions in World War II.[30] They used mental ability tests to determine who would become an officer (i.e., those with higher scores on the tests) and those who would be in the infantry (i.e., those whose tests scores were lower). There have been many advances since the two world wars so the process many employers use now to hire employees is very detailed, complicated, expensive, and time-consuming as well as legal, valid, accurate, and worthwhile. We will cover this area briefly and will divide the hiring process into five components: job analysis, legal issues, recruitment, testing, and the selection decision.

> "Acquiring the right talent is the most important key to growth. Hiring was – and still is – the most important thing we do."
> ~Marc Bennioff, founder, chairman, and co-CEO of Salesforce

Job Analysis

Job analysis is the identification of the critical elements of a job. I/O psychologists have been instrumental in devising effective strategies for evaluating the job itself to determine (1) what tasks and behaviors are necessary and how important each task or behavior is for the job, (2) the requirements (i.e., knowledge, skills, abilities, and other characteristics [KSAOs]) needed to perform the tasks of the job, and (3) the conditions (e.g., stress, safety, temperature) under which the job is performed. There are many ways to conduct a job analysis including interviewing current employees in the job, having job incumbents complete questionnaires, observing someone in the job, or asking subject matter experts (i.e., individuals knowledgeable about the job) to evaluate the job.[31] I/O psychologists continue to study effective job analysis techniques with current research suggesting that worker-oriented methods are best for employee selection given their focus on the worker as opposed to the job tasks.[32] One worker-oriented technique is the Critical Incident Technique (CIT) that uses critical incidents or behaviors that discriminate between excellent and poor behavior for someone performing the job.[33] For example, excellent behavior for a teacher might involve incorporating relevant and interesting material from the internet in a geography and landmark presentation such as using Google Earth to fly to the Pyramids of Giza in Egypt (excellent behavior) versus only going over information provided in the textbook (poor behavior).

job analysis the identification of the critical elements of a job; it documents the tasks, working conditions, and KSAOs needed to do the job

Title VII of the Civil Rights Act of 1964 federal legislation that prohibits discrimination based on sex, race, religion, color, and national origin (Big 5)

The data collected from a job analysis is used to provide useful information for many types of personnel functions including employee selection and placement, compensation, performance management and evaluation, training, promotions, and human resources or workforce planning. Specific to the hiring process, job analysis is used to write relevant job descriptions (including the job title) and recruitment materials (e.g., position ads), determine what tests should be used to help select employees with the appropriate KSAOs, and assist in meeting legal requirements for organizations.

Legal Issues

One of the most important pieces of federal legislation regarding employment and specifically the hiring of employees is **Title VII of the Civil Rights Act of 1964**. Title VII "prohibits discrimination based on sex, race, religion, color, and national origin"[34] or what will be referred to here as the "Big 5." Providing protection for people comprising the Big 5 helps to ensure that they have equal employment opportunities. There are exceptions to this act including national security, seniority systems, and bona fide occupational qualifications (BFOQs). BFOQs permit organizations to discriminate in hiring individuals in a protected class (e.g., any of the Big 5 as well as protected classes from other acts or laws) on the basis of a qualification that is deemed reasonably necessary to the operation of the business. For example, a woman can be discriminated against when hiring someone to model swimwear for men and vice versa. It is reasonably necessary to the marketing and selling of swimwear that organizations are permitted to require men to model male swimwear and women to model female swimwear; sex would be a BFOQ. It is not reasonably necessary, however, that a secretary in a church who does

Sex is a BFOQ in the case of women modeling maternity clothes.

quid pro quo a form of sexual harassment that means "in exchange for this, I'll give you that"

hostile work environment a form of sexual harassment when an employee experiences workplace harassment such as provocative pictures that make the environment an uncomfortable place to work

secretarial work and not religious (e.g., leading a Bible study) work be the same religion as the church that employs him; religion in this case would not be a BFOQ.

Abiding by laws that protect individuals against discrimination based on the Big 5 covered under the Civil Rights Act as well as age (i.e., Age Discrimination in Employment Act), disability (i.e., Americans with Disabilities Act), genetic information (i.e., Genetic Information Nondiscrimination Act), and others is important for employers as the costs of litigation can be very expensive both monetarily and in terms of an organization's reputation. Some organizations have stand-alone legal departments, others hire lawyers to assist them in making sure they abide by laws designed to protect employees and employers, and others rely on their human resource managers or I/O psychologists to ensure that they are following the law. Employment law in the United States is meant to protect and provide equal opportunities for individuals (see *The Social Side of Sex* for an example of such a protection).

The Social Side of *Sex*

Sexual Harassment

The Civil Rights Act of 1964 was originally designed to eliminate race discrimination, but sex was added at the last minute by a southern senator, Howard W. Smith. He said he added it to support women; however, his opponents said he was trying to kill the bill by adding sex.[35] Whatever the reason, this was the first protection afforded to working women who, as a result, have achieved more equality in the workplace.

In the early 1990s, Clarence Thomas was appointed to replace Thurgood Marshall as a lifetime member of the Supreme Court of the United States. His confirmation hearings were proceeding smoothly until Anita Hill, a law professor, reported to the FBI that she had been the subject of harassment by Clarence Thomas when she worked for him at the Equal Employment Opportunity Commission (EEOC). Her allegations were made public and for several days the nation watched televised hearings of Hill and Thomas answering questions. Hill alleged that because she had not accepted date invitations from Thomas, he subjected her to inappropriate discussions of sexual acts and pornographic material. Thomas vehemently denied her allegations and called the proceedings a "high-tech lynching of uppity Blacks."[36] Thomas was eventually confirmed as a member of the Supreme Court by a vote of 52 to 48.[37]

The Thomas hearings and Hill's testimony resulted in an increased awareness of sexual harassment across the United States. Men and women watched the hearings on television or saw reports on the evening news. Regardless of one's view on who was telling the truth, sexual harassment had assumed a new place in the consciousness of working Americans.

Sexual harassment exists in two forms: **Quid pro quo** and **hostile work environment**. An example of quid pro quo harassment is an offer by an employer of a promotion in exchange for sex. A single instance of this type of harassment is enough to constitute sexual harassment. Hostile work environment is exemplified by an employee who displays sexist photos in his locker that offend the women who work in the organization or an employee who tells jokes that are sexist; it typically alters the individual's employment because it is offensive. This type of harassment generally requires the harassment to be severe and pervasive; a single incident would not constitute a hostile work environment. Both types of harassment are inappropriate in the workplace and violate employees' civil rights.

It is in the best interest of employers to respond immediately and appropriately when they encounter a claim of sexual harassment in their organization. Employees who are sexually harassed are more likely to be absent from work, quit their jobs, and bring some type of legal action against their employers.[38] Claims of sexual harassment cost organizations in terms of money, reputation, and productivity; those costs can be very expensive.[39] The culture of the organization may be impacted greatly by sexual harassment and over time change the culture from one of trust to mistrust. Employee attitudes and behaviors may also be impacted and will be addressed in later sections of this module.[40,41]

The televised congressional hearings involving Clarence Thomas and Anita Hill made Americans aware of the realities of sexual harassment.

Recruitment

The development of job descriptions based on job analysis information and an understanding of legal issues prepares the organization for recruitment which is the next step in employee selection. **Recruitment** is the process organizations use to identify *qualified* individuals for a job. Depending on the job, an organization can recruit from inside the company (internal recruitment) or seek someone outside the organization (external recruitment). They may advertise on their company webpage or a site for specific types of jobs such as the official site for government jobs in the United States or careers in psychology (find links to these resources on Psychology CourseMate at www.cengagebrain.com). In addition, websites like monster.com, linkedin.com and careerbuilder.com help to foster a relationship between potential employees and employers in a variety of jobs and locations, while websites like siop.org are specific to positions available in the field of I/O psychology. Other recruitment sources include national and local newspapers, radio and television advertisements, trade magazines and professional publications (e.g., *The Industrial-Organizational Psychologist*), as well as employee referrals, and word of mouth.

Employee referral programs consist of current employees recommending friends or relatives for an open position in the organization. The referring employee typically receives some kind of reward (e.g., cash bonus) if the new employee works for the organization a set period of time (e.g., six months).[42] In an overall assessment of employee recruitment using multiple sources, employee referrals were found to be the best source in overall hiring volume, quality of hires, speed (application-to-hire time in days), and best employee retention after one and two years.[43] In addition, employee referrals have an impressive applicant-to-hire ratio at great organizations of 3:1, while average organizations have a 10:1 ratio; the average rate is 18:1 from all sources.[44] A meta-analysis (i.e., a statistical summary of studies), indicated that those employees recruited through inside sources (e.g., employee referrals, rehires) worked for the organization longer and had better job performance than those recruited through outside sources (e.g., advertisements, employment agencies, and recruiters).[45] Studies have supported the idea that those recruited using inside sources receive more accurate information (the good and bad) about the job, known as realistic job previews, than those recruited through external sources.[46,47] Research also shows that employees who stayed with the organization longer were referred by successful employees rather than unsuccessful employees.[48] Social psychology would suggest that our friends tend to be similar to us in some characteristics such as values, personality, attitudes, and interests, which may explain why successful employees make successful referrals and unsuccessful employees do not. Realistic job previews were also shown, in a meta-analysis, to enhance employees' perceptions of organizational honesty resulting in lower voluntary turnover of employees.[49]

Organizations are using social media (e.g., Facebook, LinkedIn) and emails to facilitate their employee referral programs.[50] These programs provide current employees with the tools to easily share information about jobs available in their workplace with their "friends" on social networking sites. For example, current employees may receive an email from the company informing them of jobs available at their workplace location. They will then be given the option of posting the information to their social networking site or forwarding the email to prospective job candidates. The system allows the employer to track the referrals and, if an applicant applies, contact the employee to provide an evaluation of his or her "referral." The entire process is monitored so that the referring employee is rewarded as is typically done with more traditional employee referral programs. Employers are hoping to reach those individuals best suited for their jobs and organization through their recruitment efforts.

After prospective employees have submitted either a resume or application with the company, someone from the organization (e.g., supervisor, selection committee, human resource manager) will determine which of the applicants should be considered further. In that process, he or she may make telephone inquiries of previous employers or other references, conduct background checks, or peruse professional and personal social

recruitment the process organizations use to identify qualified individuals for a job networking sites looking for both positive and negative information about the applicants on the internet using standard search engines.

Using the internet to seek information about applicants is inexpensive and these searches may be done based on the applicant's resume or application blank information and prior to contacting the applicant. The internet information may be used to provide useful information that results in further consideration of the applicant or it may eliminate the applicant from further consideration.[51] A 2018 national survey by The Harris Poll for CareerBuilder asked more than 1,000 hiring managers and human resource staff about their use of social media in the private sector.[52] The results indicated that 7 out of 10 employers conduct research on applicants through their social networking sites; the impact is seen in that 57% of them reported they found information that caused them not to hire the applicant.[53] Not surprising, those in information technology and manufacturing industries are more likely to check social media than those in retail. Interestingly, almost half of the employers surveyed also indicated they were unlikely to arrange an interview with an applicant if he/she does not have an online presence.[54] Specific things to avoid posting online, as noted by employers, are inappropriate photos and videos, drug and drinking use, discriminatory comments, criminal behavior, derogatory comments about previous or current employer/coworkers, and lying about qualifications.[55] Employers are also looking for information that provides them reasons to hire an applicant such as support for position qualifications, professionalism, and others' comments on the applicant.[56]

In sum, managers are using social networking sites to learn about how job candidates would fit with their organizational culture as well as their professionalism including communication skills and whether or not they denigrate a previous employer or organization.[57] Information, both positive and negative, that job applicants thought would only be viewed by their peers is making its way into the public arena at all levels, with, based on the research, many employers viewing the information without the knowledge of the job applicant.

Managers need to be cautious when perusing social networking sites so that their hiring decisions are not impacted by information that is illegal given federal and state laws that, for example, protect age, disability, and genetic information as well as protected classes under Title VII of the Civil Rights Act described previously. Some legal sources advocate that employers should seek information from social networking sites late in the hiring process so information that could discount what appears online would have been ascertained through various types of tests (more on this in the next section on testing).[58]

If you were considering these individuals for the jobs of airline pilot and teacher, respectively and they had posted these photos for public viewing on a social media sites, would you want to hire them? During the hiring process, organizations are searching social networking sites, such as Twitter and Facebook, to learn about their applicants from images as well as tweets that are posted to the sites.

It is likely that many organizations will prepare policies on the use of social networking sites for both recruiting new employees as well as the use of social networking sites by current employees; legal, privacy, and ethical issues will need to be dealt with by organizational managers as the number of people who use social networking sites continues to grow.[59]

Testing

You are familiar with tests and taking tests. **Tests** are defined here as the measurement of carefully chosen samples of behavior. Tests are vital to the success of organizations and are used to ascertain differences between applicants. These would include the paper-and-pencil or computer-based tests you are familiar with to determine your skill or ability in a class or general area (e.g., Scholastic Aptitude Test [SAT], Graduate Record Exam [GRE]). It would also include personality tests (e.g., openness to new experiences, conscientiousness), integrity or honesty tests, interviews, interest inventories, work samples (i.e., a performance test where the applicant does a replica of the work he will be asked to do on the job), and situational exercises (i.e., primarily for upper-level jobs where the test mirrors the job such as prioritizing tasks presented to an applicant as if she was the manager of an organization). The goal of these tests is to help employers choose those applicants best suited for the organization by tapping into their individual differences (see Chapter 3 regarding individual differences in self-esteem, self-presentation, and motivation).

Regardless of the type of test or how it is administered, the reliability and validity of a test are very important. **Reliability** is defined as consistency of measurement and can range from 0 to 1 with higher values representing more consistent measurement. It addresses the question: Does the test give you the same or very similar scores from one time to the next or consistent measurement of items within a test? Once you have determined that a test is reliable you can proceed to evaluate the validity of the test; reliability is a necessary but not sufficient condition for using a test. **Validity** is how accurate the test is with regard to what you are intending to measure and also has values ranging from 0 to 1 with higher values representing greater validity. For example, a test in your social psychology class that asked you about world religions or had you solve, using calculus, the greatest volume possible based on how a box was folded would not be a valid measure of what you learned in that class.

In addition to standard tests of abilities and skills, another form of testing for selection is the employee interview. Practically 100% of all organizations use some type of interview in their selection of employees even though they are often viewed as inherently subjective and flawed.[60] Interviews can be flawed if not conducted appropriately; almost 100 years of research has been completed on interviews providing evidence regarding when they are useful and when they are not.

Selection interviews can be broadly classified as unstructured and structured. **Unstructured interviews**, which are conducted by untrained interviewers, are characterized as informal and unplanned with random questions and no scoring key; **structured interviews** which are conducted by trained interviewers, have standardized questions based on a job analysis, a specific question order, and a predetermined scoring or answer key. Some typical and frequently asked questions during an informal interview are shown in **FIGURE C.2**. Examples of behavior or performance-based structured interview questions are shown in **FIGURE C.3**.

Structured interview questions may be scored based on benchmarks, which are expected answers based on the quality of the job candidate. These benchmarks may be an acceptable or unacceptable response or based on a five-point rating scale (more information on performance rating scales is provided later in this module). To illustrate the scoring used in a structured interview, assume a job applicant for a professional position. A structured question might ask him to, "Describe a time that you had to miss an important meeting due to an illness or family emergency. What did you do?" Possible benchmark responses might include: (a) I contacted the person in charge of the meeting and arranged for an appropriate

tests the measurement of carefully chosen samples of behavior

reliability consistency of measurement

validity the accuracy of a test in measuring what it is intended to measure

unstructured interview interview conducted by an untrained interviewer that is informal and unplanned with random questions and no scoring key

structured interview interview conducted by a trained interviewer that has standardized questions based on a job analysis, a specific question order, and a predetermined scoring or answer key

Selecting Employees | **C13**

> **Typical Unstructured Interview Questions**
> 1. What are your weaknesses?
> 2. Why should we hire you?
> 3. Why do you want to work here?
> 4. What are your goals?
> 5. Why did you leave (or why are you leaving) your job?
> 6. When were you most satisfied in your job?
> 7. What can you do for us that other candidates can't?
> 8. What are three positive things your last boss would say about you?
> 9. What salary are you seeking?
> 10. If you were an animal, which one would you want to be?

FIGURE C.2
Questions often asked by an untrained interviewer. Unstructured interview questions are often unrelated to the job, subjectively scored, and poor predictors of applicants' future job performance.

> **Structured Behavior-Based Interview Questions**
> 1. Tell me in specific detail about a time when you had to deal with a difficult customer.
> 2. Give me an example of a time when you had to make a decision without a supervisor present.
> 3. Give me a specific example of when you demonstrated your initiative in an employment setting.
> 4. Give me an example of a time when you had to work with a team.
> 5. Describe a time when you had to be creative at solving a problem.

FIGURE C.3
Situational or behavior-based interview questions with a carefully developed scoring system along with a trained interviewer make structured interviews useful in selecting employees.

"can-do" performance factors the maximum performance an employee can exhibit

"will-do" performance factors the normal or typical performance by an employee

person to attend the meeting for me (5 points), (b) I sent another employee to attend the meeting for me (3 points), and (c) I tried to find out what I missed at the meeting after I got back to work (1 point).[61] The standard scoring system for interviews results in a more objective evaluation of each job applicant than using no scoring system which is typical of unstructured interviews.

I/O psychologists have compared and evaluated the two types of interviews. Structured interviews, based on a job analysis, and often with behavior or performance-based questions have greater validity than unstructured interviews. Three separate meta-analysis investigations found validity coefficients corrected for unreliability and range restriction of .62,[62] .44,[63] and .57[64] for structured interviews predicting job performance. The corrected validity coefficient for the relationship between unstructured interviews and performance was .20.[65] I/O psychologists have helped to make interviews—the most popular type of test used by employers and expected by job applicants—more valid and reliable. When developed and conducted correctly, interviews can be useful selection tools.

Other commonly used tests, as measures of carefully chosen samples of behavior, and their corrected validity coefficients include measures of cognitive ability (.51),[66] motor work sample (.43),[67] integrity tests (.34),[68] grades (.32),[69] experience (.27),[70] overall personality (.17),[71] and education (.10).[72] Choosing the tests (evaluated for reliability and validity) for each position is done based on the job analysis to ensure that the tests chosen are appropriate and legal given the required tasks and activities; the goal is that they would assess the requisite knowledge, skills, abilities, and other characteristics needed for each specific job.

The Selection Decision

Employers when selecting employees are looking for a good match between the potential employee and the organization including the culture. They would like to match the requirements for excellent performance on the job with the person's knowledge, skills, abilities, personality, attitudes, and motivation for the job. They attempt to accomplish this by recruiting from a large pool of qualified applicants and then by using some of the different types of tests discussed earlier to predict which individuals will be outstanding, average, or poor performers. In addition, leaders and coworkers will also share information about the organizational culture to see if it fits applicants' wants and needs.

Researchers have posited two groups or factors that determine an employee's performance in the employment setting. They are the **"can-do" performance factors** (the maximum performance an employee can exhibit) and the **"will-do" performance factors** (the normal or typical performance by an employee).[73] The can-do factors are normally associated with one's general cognitive ability, reasoning, math and verbal abilities as well as the experience one brings to the job. These can-do factors suggest what an employee is capable of doing on the job if he is working to the best of his ability. Attitude, conscientiousness, and need for achievement as well as integrity are important will-do factors in performance. These factors in essence effect one's motivation or desire to perform well in the organization; the culture of the organization will also impact the will-do factors for employees. The truck driver described at the beginning of this module could do more, but until he was paid more he was unwilling to do so. A potential major influence on an employee's will-do factors are other individuals in the organization; these may be the owner/president of the company, immediate supervisor, coworkers, and subordinates. An individual's can-do and will-do factors may change as he or she moves from organization to organization and as she progresses through her career. Once job candidates are hired, the important process of their being accepted and socialized into the organizational culture at all levels including working in groups/teams and with their supervisors as well as learning about expectations for job performance begins.

QUIZ YOURSELF
Selecting Employees

1. Asking employees to describe their job is one way of conducting a _____.
   - (a) job evaluation
   - (b) job analysis
   - (c) performance appraisal
   - (d) job review

2. Alexander, a television reporter, wants access to the women's locker room right after the basketball game to conduct interviews with the team members. The women's team lets female reporters in to interview them but wants Alexander to wait until after they have showered and changed because they think he is too critical in his reporting style. Alexander argues he needs to be treated the same as the female reporters. What would be the likely outcome if this issue goes before a court?
   - (a) The team would win because sex is a BFOQ in this case.
   - (b) The team members would win because they can discriminate against Alexander's reporting style.
   - (c) Alexander would win because the team members can't discriminate against him because of his reporting style.
   - (d) Alexander would win because sex is not a BFOQ in this case.

3. Most organizations use interviews when hiring employees. Which of the following would you most likely find in a structured, performance-based interview?
   - (a) What is your biggest weakness?
   - (b) What are your long-term goals?
   - (c) Describe a situation in your last job where you had to confront a coworker because she was causing you problems.
   - (d) What types of extracurricular activities did you participate in during college?

4. Zachary is usually a conscientious and hard-working employee but the company hired a new boss who is really lazy and doesn't motivate his employees. It is likely that Zachary's ___ will be compromised in this situation.
   - (a) try-to factors
   - (b) will-do factors
   - (c) can-do factors
   - (d) must-do factors

answers: see pg C34

Socializing Employees Through Culture, Work Design, Groups, Leadership, and Performance Management

When you report for your first day of work in an organization, there will be many things you won't know and many things you'll need to learn to be successful in your job. The process of learning these things is called **organizational socialization**, which has been defined as "the process by which organizational members become a part of, or are absorbed into, the culture of the organization"[74] (culture was defined and discussed at the beginning of this module). In general terms, organizational socialization consists of new employees learning the ropes (i.e., how the organization operates) by relying on information provided by management, coworkers, observation, company handbooks, and websites. Both the culture of the organization and an employee's socialization can also be impacted by the workplace environment.

organizational socialization the process by which organizational members become a part of, or are absorbed into, the culture of the organization

Designing the Work Environment

Does the design of the work environment matter to employees? Do employers need to spend time and money designing the workspaces if they have provided employees with the equipment and resources needed to get the work done? Does the design of the office space impact performance, focus, engagement, innovation, and collaboration? Management at tech firms and data-driven companies believe that fostering innovation and creativity can be helped by providing employees with an appealing work environment. SAS, a leader in business analytics software and services, creates an energized environment with lots of windows, vibrant colors, a huge gymnasium, heated pool, and in some locations a college campus atmosphere.[75,76] Google's work environment in Manhattan boasts cafes, coffee bars, gourmet kitchens, sunny outdoor terraces, Broadway-themed conference rooms (with velvet drapes), vintage subway cars in which to have a conversation with a colleague, a secret room in the library, and a Lego play area.[77] The management at Google allows their software engineers to design their own work stations (sometimes they do so out of oversized Tinker Toys), choose a standing desk, or walk on a treadmill while they work.[78] Are these nice perks that are beneficial to employee performance and engagement? Or are these nice tokens from management, but not really necessary to drive employees to innovate, collaborate, and create in their jobs?

Four work modes have been described and include focus, collaboration, learning, and socializing; designing effective spaces for these different modes has been found to improve employees' performance, satisfaction and engagement.[79] For example, collaborating employees may want an open meeting space with in-office amenities (e.g., beverages, comfortable chairs) while an employee focusing on writing a final report may need a space with low noise level and good lighting plus functionality in a room with a pleasant design. For the socializing mode, a room that facilitates interactions among employees (e.g., game room, coffee lounge) where they can relax and share ideas with colleagues is necessary in organizations that rely on effective team performance. All of these modes are important in the workplace, although there is not one specific design for any one mode. Optimal work environments provide the capability for employees to choose the most appropriate environment for their current work mode. Employers who offer a wide-spectrum of space choices for employees to choose where they work have employees who perform better and are seen as innovative compared to those with little to no choice; employees are also more satisfied with their jobs and are more effective across all four modes of work.[80,81]

Designing a work environment with different types of workspace will help foster effective work modes.

While white-collar employees like those at SAS or Google may have their workspaces designed for effectiveness, what about the service industry? Returning once again to the management at Hilton, when they realized they had been neglecting their staff they decided to invest in their workspaces to make them more appealing to employees so they might be more committed to the organization, less likely to leave, and, as a result, increase profitability.[82] The upgrades were needed as the staff's area was described as "a dungeonous back of house" by Hilton's chief human resources officer.[83] As part of a major change to improve employee relations, Hilton has and is in the process of overhauling cafeterias and locker rooms as well as general maintenance like new paint and lighting that had been neglected for years.[84]

A lot of modern-day work has many employees either sitting (or standing; see health section later in this module) at their desks. Sometimes allowing something that seems simple in the work environment can lead to an increase in employee satisfaction and thus an increase in productive output particularly in certain types of work. A research study on computer information systems developers and their use of music while working found that positive affect and quality-of-work were lowest with no music and time-on-task was longest when music was removed.[85] The effects of music at work depend on many factors including the type of task (e.g., learning is negatively impacted by music), the type of music (e.g., classical vs. electronic, lyrics vs. no lyrics), and noise level to name a few.[86] Allowing workers to listen to music, particularly the type that doesn't infringe on other workers (i.e., music room, use of headphones), may become more popular in jobs where music does not interfere with the safety or performance of the job. Having happy, on-the-job workers who are able to control their work environments can contribute to an organization's success.

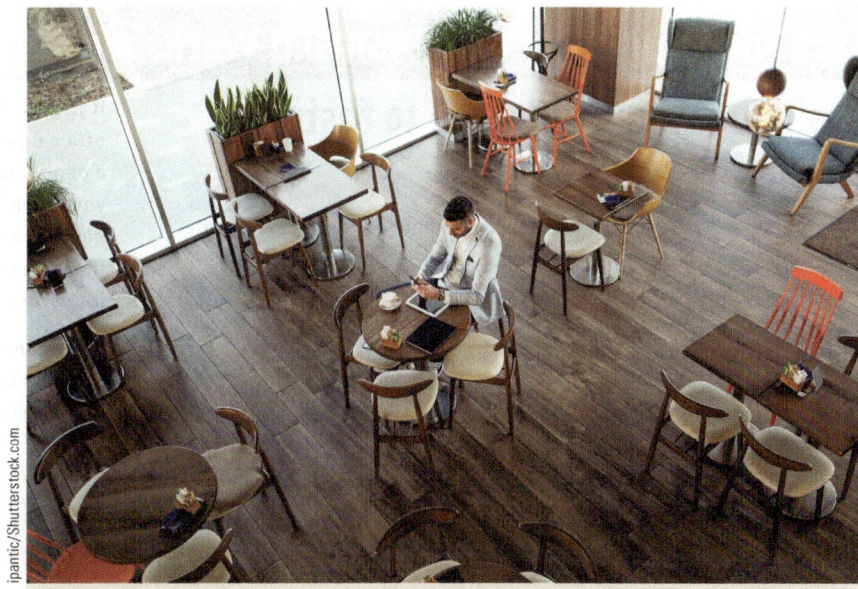

Redesigned cafeteria for employees at the Hilton Anatole in Dallas, Texas is similar to this employee eating area.

Interestingly, the use of music may impact workers' productivity, but the fairly recent Apple AirPods and their equivalents (i.e,, wireless headphones) may be having an unexpected effect on the role or function of the popular open-office work designs that have been assumed to foster collaboration. A survey conducted in 2017 estimated that 68% of the offices in America were designed to offer low or no separation between workers.[87] Although the open design saves money (no walls or cubicles, just desks or tables), employees seem to be trying to recapture some privacy and they may be doing so with wireless headphones. Without the tethering to a device, it is easier for employees to wear the headphones constantly and comfortably with some employees noting that they aren't even listening to anything, but are using them to appear that they are so they can avoid social interactions; some describe these interactions as a constant distraction.[88] Careful thought must be given to the design of the work environment and workspaces to ensure employees are able to function effectively. See tips for how you can get more done and have less stress by implementing some simple organization ideas for your desk and office.

Electronic technology has and will continue to change the way new employees are socialized.[94] The number of communication channels open to new employees include email, company websites, chat groups, and blogs. Many of these channels are also used by job applicants to learn about the organization before submitting their applications. These are also important given the changing nature of organizations where employees placed in different locations or in virtual organizations can learn information about their jobs, work environment, colleagues, and organizational culture information.

Supervisors and coworkers are important sources of socialization information, too. **Mentoring** is a form of training often used for a new employee. A current and often long-term employee (the mentor) is paired with a new employee. The mentor's role is to help the employee adapt to the job by assisting with information, resources, and advice about the job and organization. The veteran employee may provide information about how the organization works, how performance is managed and evaluated, and career advancement opportunities. Mentoring helps employees become successful on the job and learn the formal and informal rules of the organization as long as the mentor is a good trainer. Sometimes those who are excellent performers may not be able to teach someone else effectively; the choice of mentor and the employee-mentor match must be carefully determined.

mentoring training that occurs when a current and often long-term employee (the mentor) is paired with a new employee

Tips For Organizing Your Desk and Workspace

Designing your work area to foster productivity and health

Organization and productivity tips and tricks abound that may increase your effectiveness in your work or school which, if successful, would allow you to focus on tasks and lead to lower stress.[89,90] In terms of the health impact, disorganization signals to your brain that you are not in control of the work and you feel overwhelmed at what needs to get done.[91] Stress is triggered as a result of this so organizing your work area would result in a feeling of control.[92] A few do-it-yourself (DIY) ideas from Jeff Murphy, Director of Communications at SnackNation, provides suggestions for how you can revamp your work environment and organize your desk. A brief summary and description of five of his tips are provided below:

1. Hide the wires from all your devices. This will reduce visual clutter which will reduce that stress feeling.
2. Label everything including your cords. This should save time and frustration when you have to search for something for yourself or for others as well as knowing which cable belongs with each component.
3. Consider going paperless. This would eliminate notebooks and notes you leave lying around. Be sure to find a useful app or two that you can backup so you retain important information.
4. While number three above may not appeal to you, keep the paper but use a daily docket notepad so you can see what your day will be like at a glance. This type of notepad can distinguish and include information about tasks, meetings, errands, and notes.
5. If you still have walls (see the earlier discussion about open-office designs), use them to your advantage by implementing a pegboard design or shelving system to free up space on your desk. If you are in an open design situation without walls, perhaps a communal area to hang items that might be of use to the team or workgroup to which you belong could reduce clutter for several team members.[93]

There are many online and print resources about ways to declutter and organize your living and working spaces; the increase in efficiency and decrease in stress will be worth the time and effort spent.

Items can be stored on a pegboard in an open-office design to reduce clutter and so workgroup members can have easy access to them.

Research indicates that both mentors and those they mentor often benefit from the relationship. For example, researchers studied a sample of employees in a health care organization and found that those who were mentored reported higher salaries, greater promotion rates, and more positive career success than those who did not receive mentoring.[95] Employees who have been mentored compared to those with no mentoring have better compensation, advancement, career satisfaction, job satisfaction, job involvement, effective socialization, and organizational commitment.[96] In addition, informal or spontaneous mentoring relationships are more successful than formal, role-required mentoring.[97]

Given the advances in technology that make global organizations and workers able to interact across oceans easily, the importance of societal cultural norms within the organization's corporate culture may be an issue that must be dealt with from one country to another. From knowing the approach that should be used to facilitate a meeting to the appropriate gifts to exchange when visiting a subsidiary of the organization or a potential customer, cultural norms and the internal corporate culture may impact the success of the business relationship.

The giving of inexpensive gifts is considered proper etiquette when visiting possible client organizations and considered part of the corporate culture of many businesses here and abroad. The cultural norms when traveling outside the United States may make the gift choice, if not problematic, at least something that should be researched before visiting clients. For example, organizational managers visiting and/or working in China have learned that the color of gifts may be important in terms of the reactions and feelings that will be generated during a gift exchange. As a possible scenario, an organizational representative from the United States conducting work in China might take along green hats with the company logo on them that represent the organization's image to distribute to possible clients or new partners. This offer of a green hat may be considered offensive to a person in China because the wearing of a green hat indicates infidelity.[98] The interplay between corporate culture and being proud of an image or trademark may result in negative effects when operating in a global marketplace. Behaviors deemed acceptable within one's own country must be evaluated for any additional meaning and interpreted in the context of the global international environment.

The culture of an organization is generally stable, but may change with the passage of time as well as the current economy, economic outlook, and globalization of the organization. Work teams and the leadership of an organization have a large influence on the culture of an organization; their impact is described below.

Groups and Teams

Social psychologists have studied groups for more than 80 years (see Chapter 14).[99,100] Research has focused on group dynamic topics such as individual versus group problem solving,[101,102] and the effects of participation in decision making on group member satisfaction and performance.[103,104] Industrial and organizational psychologists have focused on studying groups or teams in organizations. The use of teams or groups in organizations has been increasing because work is more often than in the past being organized around team-based structures instead of individual jobs.[105]

Work groups can be defined as two or more employees who "(a) exist to perform organizationally relevant tasks, (b) share one or more common goals, (c) interact socially, (d) exhibit task interdependencies (i.e., work flow, goals, outcomes), (e) maintain and manage boundaries, and (f) are embedded in an organizational context that sets boundaries, constrains the team, and influences exchanges with other units in the broader entity."[106] Just as there can be a culture in an organization, work groups also exhibit cultures that may encourage or discourage certain types of work-related behaviors and these cultures form the basis for the socialization of new members of the group or team.

Several factors can impact group performance although the specific effects of each factor can vary from group to group based on the organizational culture and the individual group members. Two factors that have received research attention are group cohesiveness (i.e., how much group members like each other, feel pride in being part of the group, and are committed to their group's goals) and group homogeneity (i.e., how similar group members are to each other).[107] Research indicates that groups, in general, that are more cohesive have better decision quality,[108] greater productivity and efficiency,[109] and higher member satisfaction[110] than those that are less cohesive. Some organizations have uniforms as one way to facilitate employee cohesiveness.[111] Sometimes, however, group norms or the group's culture can result in cohesive groups conforming to a norm of lower productivity to satisfy the group norm even though the group could easily have higher performance.[112] Groups that are too cohesive may fall prey to groupthink, a generally ineffective process (see Chapter 14).

What factors contribute to group performance and how can we facilitate effective groups in organizations? While a lot of work has been done on groups, there is still more work to be done specifically in the area of dynamic team relationships in complex environments.[113] A few years ago researchers at Google decided to study what makes an effective team; they called it Project Aristotle, a nod to his quote, "the whole is greater than the sum of its parts."[114] They defined teams as being, "highly interdependent – they plan work, solve problems, make decisions, and review progress in service of a specific project."[115] In their research, they noted a difference between a team and a workgroup: team

work groups two or more employees who (a) exist to perform organizationally relevant tasks, (b) share one or more common goals, (c) interact socially, (d) exhibit task interdependencies, (e) maintain and manage boundaries, and (f) are embedded in an organizational context that sets boundaries, constrains the team, and influences exchanges with other units in the broader entity.

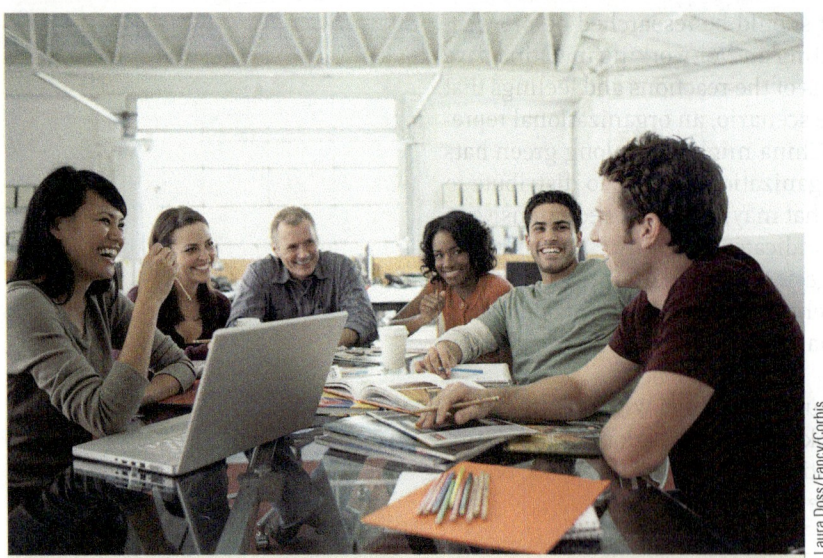

Team effectiveness has a lot to do with the interactions among the members with psychological safety and dependability being two important factors.

members need each other to get work done while work groups are less interdependent and may meet periodically.[116] Effectiveness was assessed by both quantitative (e.g., sales performance against quarterly quota) and qualitative (e.g., executive evaluation of the team) measures.[117] The sample size was 180 high- and low-performing teams in engineering and sales.[118] Using a number of measures including interviews and survey data, the results indicated that important factors in effective teams consisted of how the members worked together and not who was on the team. Specifically, five factors were identified as being important to team effectiveness in the following order: Psychological safety (i.e., safe to take risks around team members), dependability (i.e., team members honor their responsibilities and do so on time), structure and clarity (i.e., job expectations are understood and team members know how to fulfill those expectations), meaning (i.e., sense of purpose in the work or output), and impact (i.e., the work is making a difference).[119]

Do you like to work on group projects? Do you put in as much effort as you would if you were completing the assignment alone or are you a social loafer (i.e., do you put in less effort)? Many college courses require students to work in groups to complete some of the assignments, and students are graded as a group instead of as individuals. Some of the benefits of working in groups are that students gain insights into group dynamics, develop their interpersonal skills, and are exposed to other viewpoints.[120] Students with less experience with group assignments and grading, support group grading, whereas older students are less satisfied with a group experience than younger students, and students who work part-time versus those who work full-time view the group grading experience as more positive.[121] The odds are good that you will find yourself in groups in college classrooms that will prepare you for the almost inevitable work teams in your future.

Although organizations provide formal means of socializing new employees from the recruitment to selection process, the work group dynamics have immediate and direct effects on employees' socialization; the outcomes of organization socialization and work group socialization may be different.[122] For example, the management of the organization may set certain quotas for production, but because the work group thinks the quotas are unfair the members do not produce as much as they could. The members may favor the work group norms and because they all behave similarly, management cannot be certain whether the quotas are too high or whether the group is not capable of performing at the quota level. In technology organizations, the work group norms may be set higher than management norms because of the excitement and purpose the work group members have for what they are doing. Employees are socialized from many avenues so it is important for management to be aware of the different and perhaps varied information employees, particularly new employees, are receiving.

Work groups or teams may have leaders or may be self-managing. The latter are typically given whole work tasks and have autonomy and control over their work;[123] sometimes they have leaders but the role of the leader is to allow self-management. Outcomes of self-managing teams versus leader-led teams include better productivity, an increase in work quality, improved quality of life for employees, decreased absenteeism, and decreased turnover.[124] Sometimes these teams fail and often the failure is linked to the team leader who may be too autocratic, wielding too much power or influence; as a result the team does not realize the autonomy and control levels it needs to be successful.[125]

The functioning leaders of teams need to be involved in both "the development and shaping of the team processes, and the monitoring and management of ongoing team performance."[126] Developing a team may mean successfully integrating new employees into the team as well as helping with the transition of individuals in and out of the team depending on the team's function. Team leaders are critical to the success of group or team newcomers. Establishing and maintaining conditions wherein the team can perform well such as those found in the research on effective teams (discussed earlier) is also an important role for the team leader. Leaders are successful in this role by monitoring and taking action when appropriate.[127]

Leadership

Leadership has received a lot of attention in the organizational area of I/O psychology. Various definitions exist but in the context of understanding organizational socialization and culture, Katz and Kahn defined leadership as "the influential increment over and above mechanical compliance with the routine directives of the organization" (p. 528),[128] whereas Bryman summarizing the various leadership definitions in the literature stated that "... **leadership** involves a social influence process in which a person steers members of the group toward a goal" (p. 2).[129]

Although leadership has been studied for many years, it is still difficult to describe how to make or select the ideal or best leader because of the many factors that affect the success of the leader including the organizational culture, subordinate attributes (e.g., abilities, attitudes), and leader characteristics. Many theories exist and most have been useful in helping us to understand what makes a good leader and how to improve leadership style. Personality has been discussed as a defining characteristic of successful or unsuccessful leaders. Kirkpatrick and Locke's review suggests that drive, honesty and integrity, self-confidence, cognitive abilities, and knowledge are associated with successful leaders.[130] Poor cognitive abilities, poor social skills, indecisiveness, low self-confidence, low self-esteem, dishonesty, and lack of ambition are characteristics that lead to unsuccessful leadership.[131]

Several approaches and theories of leadership have been proposed and include the trait approach, skills approach, style approach, situational approach, contingency theory, path-goal theory, leader-member exchange theory, and transformational leadership.[132] Each theory has useful components and some recommend merging several of these theories/approaches to obtain the best understanding and identification of successful leadership.[133]

> "Leadership is the art of getting someone else to do something you want done because he wants to do it."
> — Dwight D. Eisenhower

leadership a social influence process in which a person steers members of the group toward a goal

Art Friedman's integrity likely made him a successful leader of the Friedman-Jacob's Co. He decided to give employees what he would want by providing them with the capabilities to make major decisions that could either make or break the organization. In his case, he created a self-managing group that had no need for external assistance from unions or other entities. As a result, Friedman demonstrated the transformational leadership approach.[134] Transformational leadership is characterized by high ethical standards, inspirational motivation, intellectual stimulation, and individual consideration—all clearly evident in Arthur Friedman's leadership style.

Chris Nassetta, the CEO of Hilton, can also be considered a transformational leader; he took over a struggling company in 2007 right before the global financial crisis and recession and some say he reinvented Hilton.[135] He had been involved before with helping troubled companies and identified Hilton's problem as "We had lost our way and we didn't have a purpose."[136] As the leader, Nassetta visited all the hotels and talked with employees in small and big groups;

Chris Nassetta became CEO of Hilton in 2007; in 2019 Hilton was rated the best place to work in the U.S.

they needed a vision and mission for turning around the company. From moving the corporate headquarters to cost cutting to layoffs, changes took six years; Hilton also became a public company in 2018.[137] A steady hand was kept at the wheel according to Nassetta; he kept his focus on the positives while being realistic and providing an effective strategy.[138] Given the number one ranking from Great Places to Work discussed at the beginning of this module, it does seem that Hilton's leader and team were able to turn things around for the hotel chain. Hilton, with the 2019 number one ranking, was the first hospitality organization to earn the honor. According to Nassetta, "...the focus is on creating an exceptional workplace culture for all."[139]

Leaders today and in the future must contend with information-based team environments requiring the capacities for sifting large amounts of information coming from computer networks.[140] Environmental turbulence (e.g., widely varying working environments as a result of economic issues) and global competition with potential culture issues as described earlier will require leaders to be learning agile.[141] These types of leaders know themselves well, like to experiment and learn, and can adeptly apply new knowledge leading to positive results in new and difficult situations.[142] The other important component in addition to quality that learning agile leaders have is that they surround themselves with others who have these same characteristics; the leader knows he or she won't make all the right decisions and will need to rely on others for help from time to time.[143] Leaders today need to be concerned with workforce planning and the appropriate management and evaluation of employee performance to ensure their organizations will be competitive and profitable.

Performance Management and Evaluation

Employees should continually be told about their job performance, both the good and the bad, from their employers as part of managing their day-to-day performance. Performance management has been defined as, "the broad collection of activities designed to maximize individual and, by extension, organizational performance. It includes setting expectations, measuring employee behaviors and results, providing coaching and feedback, and evaluating performance over time to use in decision-making."[144] Many organizations have focused on goal setting for the individual as a means to meet the goals of management as the leaders of the organization.

Formal employee performance evaluations are times for management to systematically evaluate employee performance and productivity on the job, set performance goals, and directly convey information about the culture of the organization.[145] Performance reviews are important for many reasons including: (1) determining areas of employees' work needing improvement, (2) accurately identifying levels of employees' performance so raises and promotions can be effectively managed, (3) dealing with unproductive employees in a fair and appropriate manner that may include termination, and (4) assisting in workforce planning that may be particularly important in difficult economic times, but should be done routinely to have the best employees in the organization.

Performance reviews vary in terms of their frequency with some organizations evaluating new employees 60 days after hire, whereas others evaluate new employees' performance six months after hire. Once an employee has been working for an organization for one year, most organizations formally evaluate performance annually or semi-annually.[146] A typical performance review consists of some type of form (i.e., for record-keeping and legal purposes) that is filled out by the supervisor of the employee; some organizations have both the employee and the employer fill out the same form to allow them to compare their views of the employee's performance. This is followed by a meeting between the employer and employee to discuss the employee's performance. This meeting should be held in a neutral, distraction-free location with an appropriate allotment of time devoted to the meeting.

performance reviews evaluations of employees' job performance usually conducted by their direct supervisor on an annual or semi-annual basis

Given that performance management and reviews will often clearly define the most important components of employees' jobs and help shape the culture of the organization, it would be important for job applicants to be given their performance review form during the hiring process. Providing the review form at that time will send a clear message to the applicants about the work that is valued by the organization and whether employees are being evaluated against a criterion set by management (this may suggest a more collaborative or cooperative culture) or will be appraised relative to their coworkers (this may suggest a more competitive culture). It is in the best interest of both the employer (for performance management) and the employee (as a road map to success) for the job performance requirements to be known at hire.

It is likely you have heard about the typical uses of performance reviews (e.g., raises, feedback), but one area where managers have less experience and expertise is using them in workforce planning particularly in times of economic crisis.[147] **Workforce planning** is a process used to assist managers in having a talented workforce to achieve their business goals.[148] In times of economic crisis or downturn, managers may be required to lay off employees or ask for or mandate a furlough from work, which would consist of employees taking time off without pay. These result in lower productivity for employees, but at a cost savings to the organization. Determining which employees should be laid off due to their low ability to perform their jobs effectively would be documented in their performance evaluations. Treating high performing employees the same as low performing employees in times of economic unrest (or really any time) will negatively impact the attitudes and behaviors of the high-performing employees. Having a workforce planning strategy in place will assist in making these important organizational decisions and likely enhance the culture of the organization. In the following section, information about work attitudes and behaviors is presented first with a subsequent evaluation of the relationship between attitudes and behaviors.

workforce planning the process used by managers to determine their needs with regard to human resources including retaining their talented employees, promoting employees, as well as removing poor performers

QUIZ YOURSELF

Socializing Employees Through Culture, Groups, Leadership, and Performance Appraisals

1. Mentoring of new employees, in general, has been found to have positive outcomes or consequences for _____.
   - (a) both the mentor and the employee
   - (b) the mentor
   - (c) the employee
   - (d) organizations with autocratic leaders

2. The norms for employees in the workplace are defined for them by all of the following except _____.
   - (a) the performance appraisal form
   - (b) the organizational culture
   - (c) their parents
   - (d) their work group

3. In the future, leaders will have to be concerned with which of the following?
   - (a) Environmental turbulence
   - (b) Global competition
   - (c) Information-based team environments
   - (d) All of the these

4. Carol is part of a successful self-managing team in an organization that produces handcrafted furniture. Compared to her coworkers who are in traditional leader-led teams, Carol and her work team should have _____.
   - (a) better productivity, lower work quality, and a decrease in absenteeism.
   - (b) an increase in work quality, decrease in work quantity, and better quality of life.
   - (c) an increase in absenteeism, lower work quality, and higher work quantity.
   - (d) better productivity, better work quality, and a better quality of life.

answers: see pg C34

Attitudes and Behaviors at Work

Given your skills and abilities matched the job for which you were hired (i.e., the selection process worked), one of the most important factors, in addition to organizational culture, influencing whether you will be motivated to do a good job hinges on your attitudes at work (see Chapter 7). Work attitudes have been extensively researched and have been shown to be related to a number of relevant work behaviors that influence how well employees do their jobs.[149] Some of the outcomes of positive work attitudes include volunteering for a project, helping out a coworker, showing up on time to work, and good performance. Quitting, absenteeism, tardiness, stealing from the organization, and early retirement are some of the outcomes that may be a result of poor work attitudes.

Attitudes, Organizational Justice, and Stress

Attitudes at work include satisfaction with the work itself, pay and benefits, supervision, coworkers, promotion opportunities, working conditions, and job security as well as organizational commitment. In general, you can be satisfied or dissatisfied with the work tasks and working conditions, with the people in your work environment, and the rewards you get from work. Employee satisfaction is important because it has been shown to be related to employee behaviors at work.[150] We'll examine two of the most commonly studied work attitudes: job satisfaction and organizational commitment. We'll follow this with a discussion of organizational justice and stress as important issues facing employees and employers given their impact on employees' behaviors.

Job Satisfaction

What makes you satisfied with a job or what types of things will you look for when you seek a job? For some individuals, interesting work is paramount; others place higher emphasis on having coworkers they like; and still others feel that the pay and benefits they receive is most important. Just as in selection, a match between what you want and what the organization can provide will result in a successful outcome for both parties. In an ideal economic environment, qualified candidates can be quite choosy; in a time when unemployment is high, qualified applicants can be selective while realizing certain sacrifices may need to be made to earn a living. These sacrifices will be more pronounced on the employee side relative to the employer side of the relationship. It is important for employers—even in times of high unemployment where workers are plentiful—to be concerned about the attitudes of their employees because they may make the difference in a successful versus unsuccessful employer-employee relationship and ultimately a profitable business.

I/O psychologists have conducted many studies on job satisfaction resulting in several suggestions for ways to improve the satisfaction of employees. Organizational leaders can influence the satisfaction levels of their employees by designing work environments that have some of the following attributes: Flexible working hours (discussed later with regard to work–family conflict), professional growth opportunities (e.g., training, college courses), interesting work (i.e., allowing employees to use a variety of skills and own their work),[151] autonomy in the job, job security, a good supervisor, good benefits, competitive pay, opportunities for promotion,[152] and an inspiring work environment (see earlier section on workplace design).[153] It is important to note that what makes one worker satisfied may not make another worker satisfied (see **FIGURE C.4**). Just as in selection, managers of organizations have to find the right match between what the employee wants and what the organization can offer with regard to satisfaction or attitudes in general.

As you may recall, Art Friedman allowed his employees to design their own work schedule, as well as to determine their own pay and work opportunities. Do you remember

attitudes at work satisfaction with the work itself, pay and benefits, supervision, coworkers, promotion opportunities, working conditions, and job security the truck driver who asked for a $100 raise which was equivalent to more than $650 today? Once he received the pay increase he thought he deserved, he became an excellent employee who put forth more time and effort in his job. In order for him to perform better he needed to be compensated better. This illustrates equity theory wherein an employee compares his inputs (e.g., knowledge, skills) to his outcomes (pay, work satisfaction).[154] If that comparison is equal, the employee is satisfied. If there is a discrepancy or inequity in the input to outcome comparison (i.e., one's inputs are viewed as greater than one's outcomes, I > O), the employee will be dissatisfied and likely reduce his inputs in one form (e.g., being absent from work) or another (e.g., being late to work; see discussion on withdrawal behaviors later in this module). Alternatively, do you recall the service man who did not ask for a raise and didn't want one? His response to being paid less than his coworkers was that he didn't want to work any harder than his current level; an example of that employee matching his inputs to his outcomes (I = O). Both men were satisfied with their specific situation and their performance reflected an equality in their inputs to their outcomes. As mentioned before, employees differ in their wants and needs; Art Friedman is a classic example of a leader letting employees decide what they want. In turn, his employees realized that for the organization to be successful, they needed to behave and perform in reasonable and appropriate ways.

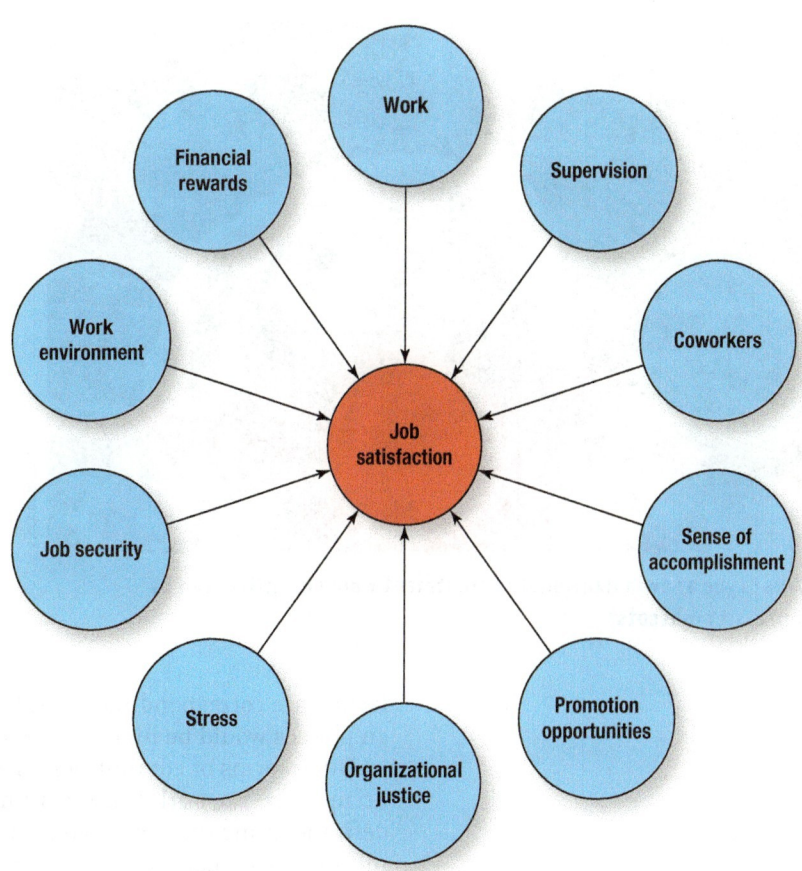

FIGURE C.4

An employee's job satisfaction may be impacted by many work-related factors. The importance of each factor will likely vary from employee to employee.

Organizational Commitment

The level of one's commitment or psychological attachment to an organization has been shown to be consistently related to employee retention within an organization. Researchers have defined and studied three types of organizational commitment: affective, normative, and continuance. Meyer and Allen define **affective commitment** as an employee's emotional attachment to the organization that makes the employee want to stay in the organization; **normative commitment** is a commitment based on feelings of obligation; and **continuance commitment** results when an employee remains with a company because of the high cost of losing organizational membership including monetary (e.g., retirement benefits) and social (e.g., friendships) costs.[155] Meyer and Herscovitch argue that employees have an organizational commitment profile at any given time in their job with varying levels on each of the three types of commitment.[156] In other words, an employee, for example, may have high levels of normative and continuance commitment, but have low levels of affective commitment. Depending on the profile, different behaviors may be engaged in by the employee such as quitting or volunteering to help a colleague with a work project.

Students may experience these different types of commitment to their university. Affective commitment would be when you, as a student, feel an emotional attachment or bond to your school because you really like your classes, the football team, and the town in which the university is located. You want to stay in that particular school because you are attached to it. Normative commitment might be exemplified by a student who feels he can't leave the university because his parents attended that university and he feels obligated to do the same thing regardless of whether it is

affective commitment an employee's emotional attachment to the organization that makes the employee want to stay in the organization

normative commitment a commitment to the organization based on feelings of obligation

continuance commitment commitment that results when an employee remains with a company because of the high cost of losing organizational membership including monetary and social costs the best school for him. Staying at a university because your friends are there and you have already paid for two years of college would typify someone acting under continuance commitment. You likely have some level of each type of commitment, and these could be represented as a commitment profile for you as a student. Students with low levels of commitment would be expected to leave the university before graduation.

One of the antecedents of organizational commitment is job satisfaction. People who are satisfied with their jobs are more committed to their organizations than those less satisfied.[157] Other causes of organizational commitment include trust in one's supervisor as well as human resources practices that are supportive of employees and a positive organizational culture.[158] Survivors of layoffs (i.e., those employees who remain on the job) have been found to report lower levels of organizational commitment after their coworkers have been laid off because of their own fear of job loss; their levels of job satisfaction are correspondingly low, too.[159] The organizational commitment of Friedman's employees would be high as evidenced by no turnover in five years.

Other forms of commitment have also been studied and include commitment to an occupation,[160] a work team,[161] a union, or a program (e.g., training program).[162] Many definitions and theories of commitment exist with ongoing research focusing on determining those that are most useful in the employment setting. In the next section on work behaviors, we'll examine research relevant to the consequences of organizational commitment.

What type of organizational commitment would be influenced by university mascots?

Organizational Justice

The perception of whether or not employees feel they have been treated fairly by their managers, coworkers, and other personnel (e.g., legal department) in a business is known as **organizational justice**; it is an antecedent of organizational commitment. The two widely accepted components of organizational justice are distributive justice and procedural justice. Distributive justice is the perception of fairness with regard to the outcomes one receives, whereas procedural justice is the perception of fairness with the process or means used to decide those outcomes.[163] One can perceive the outcome to be unfair but the process used to determine the outcome as fair. Research has found a relationship between fair treatment and job performance including task performance as well as citizenship and counterproductive behaviors.[164]

A meta-analytic research study evaluated perceived unfairness and employee health including stress.[165] Significant relations were found between perceptions of unfairness conceptualized in several ways and measures of stress and strain. The relations between organizational justice and work outcomes have also been studied across cultures. A study of Hong Kong Chinese and American employees from a large multinational organization matched in terms of sex, age, education, and tenure in the organization found that in both samples distributive and procedural justice were positively related to job satisfaction and performance and negatively related to absenteeism.[166] The work outcomes of justice perceptions were also evaluated across societal cultures and no differences were found between cultures. The relations between work outcomes and justice perceptions were found to be significantly higher for individuals with low power distance (an egalitarian

organizational justice employees' perceptions of fairness of treatment in the workplace approach to authority figures) than those with high power distance (authority figures are held in reverence). It was argued, based on the research results, that different cultures do not necessarily require different management styles with regard to organizational justice; practices and policies that promote fairness are required for all organizations to function effectively in the long term.[167] The immediate work environment, type of task and goals, as well as individuals' perceptions will likely have more impact on their perceptions of justice than a societal culture orientation. At least within the organizational justice area, broad generalizations against similar management practices across cultures may be inappropriate.

Stress

Just as organizations must manage and deal with employee satisfaction, commitment, and organizational justice, they also need to be aware of the work-related stress employees may be experiencing on the job. It is important to note that there are two kinds of stress: eustress and distress. Eustress is defined as good stress that helps us face challenges (e.g., job interview) and perform well in certain situations (e.g., making a presentation); this type of stress keeps us excited and motivated. Distress or bad stress results when individuals are not able to handle the demands of life, including work, well. The experience of eustress and distress varies from person to person as well as situation to situation; what one person finds stressful at work may not be stressful to her coworker.[168]

Stress experienced at work can be caused by being sexually harassed at work to not having enough time to get your work done to a chaotic and disorganized work environment.[169,170] As mentioned earlier, employees who perceive unfairness in their organization have been found to experience more stress and strain leading to potential health issues.[171] Stress has been shown to cause a decrease in productivity as well as health problems such as heart disease and diabetes.[172]

As college students you are familiar with stress. College students experience, typically, distress caused by academic challenges, financial problems, employment issues, relationships, socialization concerns, living away from home, and extracurricular activities. The American Institute of Stress notes that stress can influence emotions, moods, and behaviors and impact physical and mental functioning of students.[173] They provide eight broad categories of the impact of stress including physical symptoms, poor management skills, concentration difficulties, memory problems, constant worry, self-defeating thoughts, irritability and short temper, and social withdrawal.[174] Studies have found that stress impacts students' academic performance and has many health consequences.[175] Chronic stress may be related directly or indirectly to the following serious health problems that over time can significantly affect one's quality and enjoyment of life: heart disease, high blood pressure, heart attacks, strokes, depression, and anxiety.[176] Stress often leads to restless nights which impacts quality of sleep often setting up a cycle of sleepless nights (i.e., you are unable to sleep because you are under stress which leads to the lack of sleep causing you more stress).[177] (See *Food for Thought*).

Employee stress can be caused by role conflicts, role ambiguity, work overload, others in the work environment such as one's coworkers or supervisor, how well the person and the organization fit together in terms of values, attitudes, work requirements, abilities, and different types of change such as reorganization, downsizing, or layoffs.[178] Unemployment specifically can affect individuals with regard to potential stress in several different ways: the loss of one's job, the fear of losing one's job, the fear of never finding a job, and empathy for those around you who are in the throes of unemployment. All of these types of stressors have negative health outcomes similar to those experienced by students under stress.

FOOD FOR *Thought*

Stress and Nutrition

Do your eating behaviors change during finals week, before an important exam, or before taking a college entrance exam? Not surprisingly, stress may be a contributing factor to those changes. Researchers have studied work stress and its consequences for a number of years. One interesting area of study is how the work environment impacts snacking behavior, particularly between-meal snacking. O'Connor, Jones, Conner, and McMillan evaluated diaries completed by employees over a four-week period.[179]

The employees kept track of daily hassles, perceived daily variations in diet, and between-meal snacking.

The researchers found, in general, that daily hassles (e.g., lack of time to finish a project) were associated with a preference for high-fat and high-sugar between-meal snacks as well as a reduction in the consumption of vegetables and main meals.[180] Men and women were found to deal with their work environments differently with regard to their between-meal snacking. Specifically, women who work longer hours eat more high-fat and high-sugar snacks as well as exercise less, drink more caffeine, and smoke more (if they are smokers). Men who worked longer hours showed no negative effect on caffeine consumption, exercise, or smoking. Working longer hours was found to have one positive outcome for both men and women—their consumption of alcohol decreased.

Given the link between nutrition and health problems, the researchers concluded that hassles leading to stress have harmful effects on employees and workplace programs designed to reduce stress would help alleviate these concerns.[181] Suggestions about how to operate successful stress reduction programs are available to aid organizations in assisting employees in dealing with stress in the workplace.[182]

Another source of stress for many employees is the work–family balancing act oftentimes referred to as work–family conflict. As the number of dual-career couples has increased, work–family conflict has risen; this conflict has been negatively related to job performance, attendance, and health.[183] To help with work–family conflict, many organizations have become family friendly offering flexible hours, job sharing, telecommuting and family leave. In 2016 Hilton became an industry leader in parental leave policies for both salaried and hourly employees. Specifically, all new parents including adoptive parents are allowed up to two weeks of fully paid leave; new mothers who give birth are allowed an additional eight weeks of fully paid leave.[184]

Researchers have found that family-friendly businesses are more attractive to job applicants and result in higher employee retention rates. Breaugh and Frye evaluated family-friendly employment practices as well as family-supportive supervisors in relation to work-family conflict.[185] Their main findings were that both flexible hours and a supportive supervisor resulted in less work–family conflict. Where possible, employers should structure employees' work so they can have flexible schedules as well as provide training in supportive practices for managers; these together may be able to reduce the work–family conflict leading to better employee job performance, attendance, and attitudes as well as less stress.

Individuals need to develop their own stress management techniques to deal with stressful situations so they do not impinge on their health. Although there are differences in how individuals might manage their stress, some college students might participate in a physical activity such as tae kwon do, running, or lifting as exercise has been shown to be helpful in alleviating stress, whereas others might find that taking a short break from their work rejuvenates them, and still others may find alternative relaxation techniques such as yoga or meditation helpful.[186] In addition, social support

Engaging in physical exercise helps many students cope with stress in college.

can mitigate the effects of stress on both health-related ailments and attitudes.[187] Learning how to manage one's time, be organized, and prioritize activities are useful skills that can also help alleviate stress in college. Finally, having a strong support system of family and friends, eating and sleeping well, and laughter can be helpful in managing stress.[188] Learning how to deal with stress in college can make the inevitable work-related stress from employment easier to manage. All of these techniques for dealing with stress can be useful to employees as well. Employees' behaviors at work may be caused by both their attitudes and stress; these behaviors are discussed in the next section.

Behaviors at Work

Employers want their employees to engage in behaviors that will make them successful in the job because it assists in helping the organization meet its goals (e.g., profits, mission). Employees have control over two aspects of their work—their time and their effort.[189] Having employees at work instead of late or absent is important in performance and productivity; employees' attitudes will impact their will-do performance factors as described previously. Positive behaviors generally help an organization meet its goals, whereas negative behaviors detract from goal attainment.

Organizational Citizenship Behaviors

Organizational citizenship behaviors (OCBs) or prosocial behaviors have often been described as extra-role behaviors because they are behaviors not specifically required by the job and also not usually evaluated by employers during performance reviews. They have been described as behaviors that go beyond what is expected by the leaders of the organization.[190] Examples of these behaviors include staying late to finish a project, mentoring a new employee, volunteering for work, and helping a coworker. Some of the antecedents of OCBs are job satisfaction, jobs high in autonomy, a positive organizational culture, a good working environment, employees high in agreeableness (i.e., as a personality dimension),[191] and those high in conscientiousness.[192] Men who engage in OCBs are viewed positively, whereas women are viewed as just doing their jobs[193, 194]—this difference may result in an inappropriate gender disparity in the ratings of employee performance. OCBs have positive consequences for the organization and for employees in their day-to-day interactions with others in the organization.

You may engage in prosocial behaviors at your university by helping a student in a class by tutoring her or allowing her to study with you. You may also exhibit these types of behaviors in your personal life by donating blood or being a Big Brother or Big Sister to a boy or girl who needs a positive role model. Altruism and prosocial behaviors in your personal life are closely linked; they can carry over into the work environment.

Organizational Withdrawal and Counterproductive Behaviors

Unhappy employees cause problems for organizations because they sometimes choose to engage in behaviors that researchers refer to as organizational withdrawal[195] and counterproductive behaviors.[196] **Organizational withdrawal** has been defined as behaviors employees use to avoid their work or their job.[197,198,199] The two main components that comprise organizational withdrawal are **work withdrawal** and **job withdrawal**; the former are behaviors employees engage in to avoid their work and work tasks, whereas the latter includes behaviors employees use to remove themselves from the job itself.[200] Examples of work withdrawal include being absent from work, leaving work early, arriving to work late, missing meetings, and using work equipment for personal use without permission. Examples of job withdrawal behaviors include quitting one's job, transferring to another department within an organization, and retiring.

College students are familiar with withdrawal behaviors when it comes to certain college courses. Some classes may fail to keep your attention, and you may find yourself taking a nap in class or reading the newspaper. You may even look for legitimate reasons to not attend class such as offering to fill in for another employee at your workplace or deciding to attend an optional session for another class making it easier to miss class. Other students may just decide it's not worth attending class and stay home and sleep or study

organizational citizenship behaviors (OCBs) behaviors employees engage in that go beyond what is expected by the leaders of the organization

organizational withdrawal type of withdrawal comprised of work and job withdrawal

work withdrawal behaviors employees use to avoid their work

job withdrawal behaviors employees use to avoid their job for another class. These behaviors will likely be counterproductive to your performance (i.e., grade) in the course. Finally, some students drop (quit) a class or withdraw from the university; the latter is similar to quitting a job.

Counterproductive behaviors, although similar in some ways to withdrawal behaviors, are defined as "any intentional behavior on the part of an organizational member viewed by the organization as contrary to its legitimate interests."[201] An example of a counterproductive behavior would be an intentional violation of safety procedures; the behaviors may put the employee and members of the organization at risk in terms of health and financial consequences (e.g., liability). Categories of counterproductive behavior include theft, destruction of property, misuse of information, misuse of time and resources, unsafe behavior, poor attendance, poor quality work, alcohol use, drug use, and inappropriate physical actions (e.g., attacking a coworker). The next section integrates the attitudes and behaviors discussed previously and examines their relationships.

Attitude and Behavior Relations

Organizational citizenship behaviors are positively related to job satisfaction and organizational commitment; employees with good attitudes who feel more committed to their organization are more likely to help out a coworker or do other positive things to assist the organization.[202] As would be expected, a meta-analysis showed that those employees who demonstrated organizational citizenship behaviors were less likely to engage in counterproductive behaviors.[203]

Strong links have been found between job dissatisfaction and specific withdrawal or counterproductive behaviors such as absenteeism[204] and even stronger links with the aggregate behavior known as job withdrawal.[205] Counterproductive behaviors have also been linked as an outcome of distress with the counterproductive behaviors being described as a dysfunctional coping mechanism.[206] For example, an employee experiencing distress from having too much work responds by being absent from work to avoid it or sabotages his equipment so he cannot do his work. As a result of his withdrawal and counterproductive behaviors, he now has more work to complete and his stress level will be even higher. Stress also results from being a survivor of a layoff, which can lead to lower levels of commitment and satisfaction as well as lower productivity and intentions to quit.[207, 208] If you've accurately and appropriately evaluated your employees' performance, you can use that information to deal effectively with layoff decisions (i.e., ensuring positive perceptions of organizational justice); this will help to avoid the negative attitude and behavior changes among the survivors of a layoff that often occur.

Many years of research indicate a link between employees' attitudes and their behaviors at work. Sometimes the most revealing information about employees occurs when unforeseen circumstances arise, and employees have to choose how to behave without concern for what a supervisor, coworkers, or their work team might think. F. J. Smith took advantage of inclement weather to study the relationship between job attitudes and job behaviors.[209] He compared functional work groups in Chicago where a terrible snowstorm had occurred to work groups in New York where the weather was fine; all employees worked for the same organization. The comparison was done to determine which employees would choose (it was optional) to attend work the day after the storm in Chicago; employees had completed an organization-wide survey assessing work attitudes a few months earlier.

Examining both organizational sites provided a comparison not typically available and allowed the researcher to examine the relationship between work attitudes and attendance under difficult circumstances. Correlational results indicated a positive relationship between work attitudes and attendance for the employees headquartered in Chicago; those reporting higher satisfaction were more likely to attend work while those with lower satisfaction did not attend work (see **FIGURE C.5**). Interestingly, the relationship between the measures of work attitudes and attendance was not significant for the groups based in New York. It would have been up to the discretion of the individuals in the Chicago sample whether or not they attended work the day after the storm; the correlational results suggest

counterproductive behaviors any intentional behavior on the part of an organizational member viewed by the organization as contrary to its legitimate interests

FIGURE C.5

Correlations between job satisfaction levels and attendance levels on individual days for the Chicago and New York groups.[209]

Scale	Chicago (n= 27)[a]	New York (n=13)[b]
Supervision	.54**	.12
Amount of work	.36*	.01
Kind of work	.37*	.06
Financial rewards	.46**	.11
Career future	.60**	.14
Company identification	.42*	.02

*$p > .05$, one-tailed test **$p < .01$, one-tailed test [a]Group following storm [b]Group under normal working conditions

that those work groups with higher attitudes made an effort to attend work that day compared to those with lower attitudes even though they did not have to attend work.

Employers need to evaluate the organizational culture as well as the work environment and make modifications where necessary to ensure that they have employees who are satisfied, are committed, experience low distress, and have positive perceptions of organizational justice. Art Friedman and Chris Nassetta each made modifications in the work environment of their organization that led to employees who were satisfied and committed and who experienced low work stress. Hilton is now operating a very successful organization because they have turned their focus to their employees and the importance of them to a successful business. Employees need to learn how to seek out work that is satisfying as well as organizations they can commit to and to either manage the stress they are under or seek less stressful work. These in combination will help facilitate organizational citizenship behaviors and decrease withdrawal and counterproductive behaviors. Together the right employee attitudes and behaviors will help lead to successful organizational functioning.

QUIZ YOURSELF
Attitudes and Behaviors at Work

1. The two main components of organizational withdrawal are _____.
   - a) work withdrawal and quitting
   - b) job withdrawal and work withdrawal
   - c) quitting and job withdrawal
   - d) leaving and staying

2. Gordon is a survivor of a layoff, and his perception is that the layoffs were done fairly. What will likely happen to Gordon as a result of his organizational justice perceptions?
   - a) His job satisfaction will decrease.
   - b) He will be less likely to quit.
   - c) His organizational commitment will decrease.
   - d) He will be absent more often.

3. Jonathan's boss keeps adding more duties to his job each day and Jonathan is beginning to feel like he has way more to do than he can manage. He mentions to Doug, his friend, that he is under a great deal of stress and wants to know how he can manage it. Based on research, if you were Doug, what advice would you give Jonathan?
   - a) Quit your job; it's not going to get better.
   - b) Find a counterproductive behavior that will allow you to reduce your workload.
   - c) Find a relaxation technique that will help you deal with the stress better.
   - d) Drink more coffee to give you a boost to complete your job.

4. _____ would be an example of an organizational citizenship behavior, whereas _____ would be an example of a counterproductive behavior.
   - a) Mentoring a new employee, engaging in safe work practices
   - b) Being late, staying late to help a coworker
   - c) Missing a meeting, being late for work
   - d) Volunteering to serve on a committee, physically attacking your supervisor

answers: see pg C34

What Makes Us Human: Putting the Cultural Animal in Perspective

If we define work as the activity done not for the pleasure of doing it but rather to obtain the means of survival, then almost all animals do some work. Hunting food, building nests, digging caves, and other similar "work" is found throughout the animal kingdom. But human work is different in many important ways from the reasons we work (e.g., to experience satisfaction and achievement) to the central role and amount of time (second only to sleeping) in our lives.

The process of selecting employees is uniquely human. A pack of wolves does not use a structured interview to evaluate another wolf who wants to join the pack, nor does it give the new wolf standardized tests. Human organizations often perform complex assessments of both the person and the job in order to find the right match. The pack of wolves doesn't worry about complying with federal (or state and local) hiring laws, nor does it protect its members from sexual harassment. Animals do not go through the same performance management and review as humans; some animals may bully others resulting in the bullied animals leaving the herd, but this is not often easy to predict nor is it based on the performance of the animals or perceptions of justice.

Socialization processes show the cultural aspect of human work organizations.[210] Culture is all about information, and most new employees must often master a great deal of specialized information about what their job will consist of and how it fits into the big picture of what the organization does. (In contrast, a new wolf in the hunting pack can just follow the others and do what they do!) Mentoring is a special kind of relationship that occurs in human work groups because it helps new employees gain from the wisdom and experience of older ones—and, again, that is only necessary and even useful because of the informational complexity of human culture. There's not much mentoring in an anthill or flock of birds because it is not needed nor do they worry about their work environment as humans do.

The unique features of human groups do not end there. The effectiveness of team members is at least partially due to their interactions as well as stresses at work (e.g., financial pressures, deadlines, and conflict) that are unlike what any noncultural animal encounters. As a result of these stresses, they may choose to engage in withdrawal or counterproductive behaviors to manage, or in the short term, deal with the stressors. Many employees also exhibit positive, prosocial behaviors (such as the OCBs) at work and in their personal lives that exemplify some of the best features of human nature.

The complexity and organization of human work groups are remarkable. Human organizations are constantly changing in ways that no other non-cultural animal groups change. They add new roles (e.g., lawyers who ensure that hiring practices are consistent with new laws). They change the rules and procedures (as in the opening account about Arthur Friedman's changes). A group of leaders may make decisions to increase or decrease the organization's size, sometimes resulting in mass hirings or layoffs. These decisions give human work groups a flexibility to adapt to new opportunities or problems in ways that animal work groups do not.

Work is a central part of human life. As organizational cultures change, work will continue to change and evolve in new ways. For example, the technologies that enable people to do their work from home or at a distance from the work group's location are changing the experience of work for people in new and sometimes unpredictable ways. Such changes reflect the unique power of human culture. I/O psychology has and will continue to help employees and employers successfully navigate organizational culture and its many components.

MODULE C SUMMARY

Industrial and Organizational Psychology

- I/O psychology is the study of individuals' behavior using psychological principles in the workplace.
- I/O psychologists study organizational culture, employee selection, performance appraisal, training, job and workplace design, communication, work stress, motivation, leadership, groups and teams, organizational justice, human factors or system design, job attitudes, well-being, and work behaviors.
- Work is a central focus in many lives, and it provides us with things we need and value.
- In addition to satisfying our basic needs of food, shelter, and security, work also provides a sense of accomplishment, satisfaction, the opportunities for social interactions, independence, a reason to get up in the morning, happiness, a sense of identity, recognition, and respect.

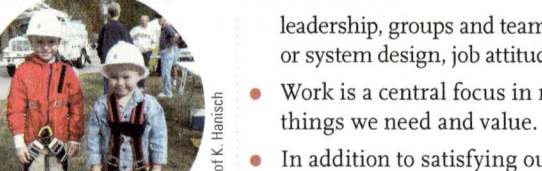
Courtesy of K. Hanisch

- Organizational culture is the climate or attitude in the organization. It provides information to employees about what is expected of them and impacts how they behave; it is critical to many processes discussed in this module.
- The O*NET is a comprehensive, detailed, and flexible set of job descriptors based on an extensive research program; it can be used to learn about different types of jobs and their economic and future outlook.
- There are many types of jobs available with different work schedules including shift work, flexible hours, and telecommuting.

Selecting Employees

- Industrial and organizational psychologists first became involved in selecting employees when the U.S. government needed help selecting and placing officers and soldiers in World War I.
- Job analysis is the identification of the critical elements of a job.
- Job analysis techniques include interviewing current employees in the job, having job incumbents complete questionnaires, observation of someone in the job, and having experts evaluate the job.
- Title VII of the Civil Rights Act of 1964 protects employees from discrimination in employment on the basis of sex, race, religion, color, and national origin.
- Sexual harassment has two forms: Quid pro quo and hostile work environment.
- Recruitment is the process of attracting qualified individuals to an organization.
- Employee recruitment can be either internal or external; employee referral programs are an effective form of internal recruitment.
- Tests are the measurement of carefully chosen samples of behavior; the reliability and validity of tests are important in assessing the quality of the test.
- Interviews are used routinely in organizations; interviews can typically be categorized as structured and unstructured.
- Structured interviews are much better in terms of the validity, or accuracy of assessment, than unstructured interviews.
- In personnel selection, employers are seeking to match the requirement for a job with the person's attributes that will result in successful performance on the job.

Socializing Employees Through Culture, Work Design, Groups, Leadership, and Performance Management and Evaluation

- Learning how an organization operates is one of the first things a new employee must do. Many avenues exist to accomplish this including supervisors, coworkers, mentors, memos, and company websites.
- Employees learn what is expected of them through the culture of an organization.
- Four work modes include focus, collaboration, learning, and socializing. Optimal work environments provide the capability for employees to choose the most appropriate environment for their current work mode.
- Providing standing desks and allowing employees to listen to music may increase employee satisfaction and commitment to the organization.
- Group performance, satisfaction, and turnover are impacted by the group's cohesiveness and homogeneity.
- Work groups or teams help socialize employees; sometimes the work group culture may be at odds with the organization's culture.
- Psychological safety, dependability, structure and clarity, sense of purpose, and impact are factors important to team effectiveness.
- Leaders of groups influence how well they function; different theories have been proposed that address what makes a good leader.
- Performance reviews can provide useful information about the type of culture present in the organization in addition to helping managers with workforce planning and other personnel decisions.

Attitudes and Behaviors at Work

- Attitudes at work include satisfaction with the work itself, pay and benefits, supervision, coworkers, promotion opportunities, working conditions, and job security.
- Organizational commitment profiles include employees' affective, normative, and continuance commitment; these in turn influence the behaviors employees engage in at work.
- Causes of employee stress include role conflicts, role ambiguity, work overload, different types of change such as reorganization, downsizing, or layoffs, others in the work environment such as one's coworkers or supervisor, how well the person and the organization fit together, and perceptions of organizational justice.
- Stress management activities may include physical exercise or relaxation techniques.
- Prosocial or organizational citizenship behaviors (OCBs) have often been described as extra-role behaviors because they are behaviors not specifically required by the job and also not usually evaluated by employers during performance reviews.
- Antecedents of OCBs include job satisfaction, jobs high in autonomy, a positive organizational culture, and employees high in agreeableness and conscientiousness.
- Organizational withdrawal includes work and job withdrawal; work withdrawal are behaviors employees use to avoid the work itself (e.g., being absent), whereas job withdrawal includes behaviors to remove themselves from their current job (e.g., retirement).
- Categories of counterproductive behavior include theft, destruction of property, misuse of information, misuse of time

- and resources, unsafe behavior, poor attendance, poor quality work, alcohol use, drug use, and inappropriate physical actions.
- OCBs are positively related to job satisfaction and organizational commitment; they are negatively related to counterproductive behaviors.
- Job dissatisfaction is linked to withdrawal behaviors such as absenteeism and quitting; it is strongly linked to work and job withdrawal as composite indicators of organizational withdrawal.
- Distress is one antecedent of counterproductive behaviors.
- Layoffs or mandatory furloughs may be implemented to help organizations remain viable in times of economic uncertainty or crisis for the organization; these can result in stress for the survivors of the layoff and impact their attitudes and behaviors.

What Makes Us Human? Putting the Cultural Animal in Perspective

- Human and animal work varies on many dimensions including the complexity of work groups and decision making.
- The assimilation and understanding of organizational culture makes humans unique and separates them from all other noncultural animals

key terms

affective commitment C25
attitudes at work C24
"can-do" performance factors C14
counterproductive behaviors C30
continuance commitment C25
hostile work environment C10
job analysis C9

job withdrawal C29
leadership C21
mentoring C17
normative commitment C25
occupational information network (O*NET) C6
organizational citizenship behaviors (OCBs) C29
organizational culture C5

organizational justice C26
organizational socialization C15
organizational withdrawal C29
performance reviews C22
quid pro quo C10
recruitment C11
reliability C13
structured interviews C13

tests C13
Title VII of the Civil Rights Act of 1964 C9
unstructured interviews C13
validity C13
"will-do" performance factors C14
workforce planning C23
work groups C19
work withdrawal C29

quiz yourself ANSWERS

1. Industrial and Organizational Psychology p. C8
   answers: 1.a 2.b 3.d 4.c
2. Selecting Employees p. C15
   answers: 1.b 2.d 3.c 4.b
3. Socializing Employees Through Culture, Groups, Leadership, and Performance Appraisals p. C23
   answers: 1.a 2.c 3.d 4.d
4. Attitudes and Behaviors at Work p. C31
   answers: 1.b 2b 3.c 4.d

APPLICATION MODULE D

Applying Social Psychology to Law

Margaret Bull Kovera / John Jay College of Criminal Justice, City University of New York

LEARNING OBJECTIVES

1. Distinguish estimator variables from system variables, and describe the estimator variables that were discussed.

2. Define system variables, and identify lineup conditions that produce better eyewitness evidence.

3. Summarize the research suggesting that eyewitness testimony is given undue influence in jury decisions.

4. Describe the process of jury selection, and analyze the psychological processes that influence it.

5. Evaluate the effect of social psychological processes on jury decision making.

6. Debate the use of repressed memories as evidence in a court of law.

Tradeoffs
Wrongful Convictions vs. Protecting Victims
D19

What Makes Us Human?
Putting the Cultural Animal in Perspective
D20

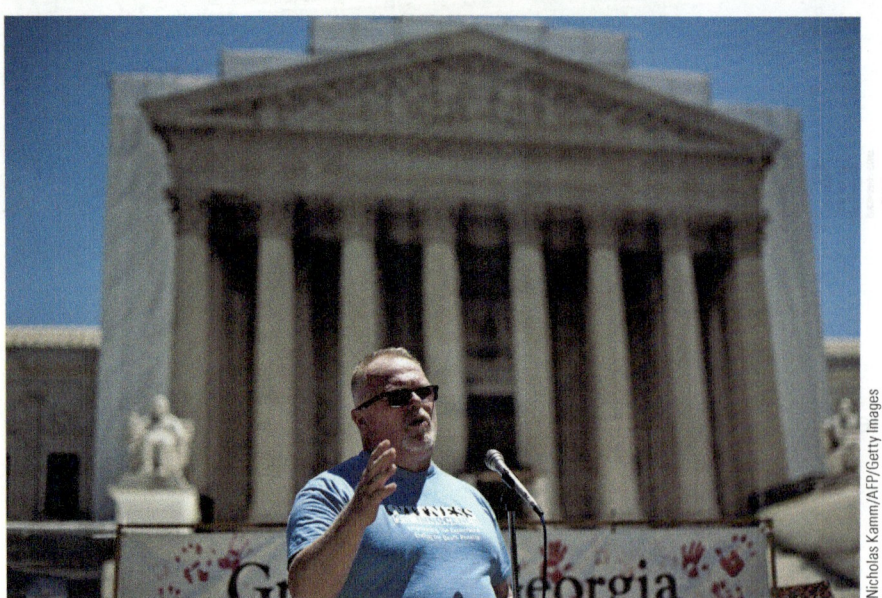

Kirk Bloodsworth was twice convicted for murdering 9-year-old Dawn Hamilton. After serving nine years in prison—two years on death row—for her murder he was exonerated by DNA sample testing.

There is no question that Dawn Hamilton suffered a horrible death. In the summer of 1984, 9-year-old Dawn was looking for one of her friends behind the apartment where she was spending the summer with her father. After stopping to watch two boys fish at the lake behind the apartment, Dawn was approached by a young man who told her that he would help her look for her friend. The two boys watched Dawn and this stranger enter the woods next to the lake. When Dawn had not returned home three hours later, her friends and relatives launched a search. Soon the police discovered her broken body in the woods where she had last been seen alive. She had been sodomized, vaginally penetrated with a stick, and a rock had crushed her skull. Several people who were near the lake that morning provided descriptions of the stranger seen with Dawn, and their descriptions generally agreed that the culprit was more than 6 feet tall, and thin, with curly blond hair. The boys who had last seen Dawn were taken to the police station, where they were questioned and helped produced a composite of the stranger who had taken Dawn into the woods. The composite was publicized, and eventually someone came forward and suggested that the composite looked like a local waterman, Kirk Noble Bloodsworth.

Bloodsworth was arrested, identified by five witnesses, tried for capital murder (meaning that he was eligible for the death penalty if convicted), and sentenced to death. It was eventually learned that the prosecution intentionally hid from the defense team information that suggested Bloodsworth's innocence, and a new trial was ordered. Bloodsworth was again convicted of Dawn Hamilton's murder, although the presiding judge in this case felt that there was not enough evidence to support a death sentence and sentenced him instead to two consecutive life terms in prison.

Although many people believed that this second conviction was the end of the story, there was a problem: Kirk Bloodsworth was not the man who killed Dawn Hamilton. After spending 9 years in a maximum-security prison, fearing for his life because of the constant threats he received from his fellow prisoners, Bloodsworth was released when the new science of DNA testing revealed that the semen left on Dawn's clothing could not have come from him.

How could this miscarriage of justice have happened? Not only did Bloodsworth, with his red hair, mutton-chop sideburns, and muscular build, not match the witnesses' descriptions of the culprit, but there also was no physical evidence tying him to the murder scene. How could two different juries find Kirk Bloodsworth guilty of the vicious murder of young Dawn Hamilton when he was not the person who committed the crime? Why did so many eyewitnesses mistakenly identify Bloodsworth as the man seen entering the woods with Dawn? Could their identifications have been influenced by the procedures the police used to collect this eyewitness evidence? Could the process used to select jurors for cases in which the death penalty is a sentencing option have affected jurors' decisions? Is it possible that the overwhelming media attention to the crime prejudiced the jury against Kirk Bloodsworth? These questions are at the heart of the application of social psychology to the legal system.

Long before reaching adulthood, most people understand that laws are developed to help regulate human behavior. Although self-interest may suggest that we steal from others who have what we want or aggress against people who prevent us from doing what we want to do, our culture has developed laws that prohibit these actions. Consistent with a central theme of this book, nature says go and culture says stop.

What people may not understand is the extent to which lawmakers, law enforcement personnel, judges, and jurors are social and cultural beings whose decisions about which behaviors need regulating and how to respond to people who break the law are influenced by their assumptions about human behavior. Lawmakers and the people who enforce those laws, much like the rest of us, are naïve social psychologists with theories about the factors that influence the accuracy of eyewitness memory and how jurors make decisions.

Thus, our criminal justice system is based on many psychological assumptions about behavior: Highly confident witnesses to a crime must have accurate memories. Jurors can follow instructions to disregard prejudicial information about a defendant that they learned from the news. But are highly confident witnesses necessarily accurate? Do people ever falsely confess to committing a crime that in fact was committed by someone else? Can jurors disregard information when judges instruct them to do so? Social psychologists are in a unique position to test whether these psychological assumptions are correct.

The best information can be obtained from a lineup in which there is one suspect and multiple people (fillers) who also match the culprit description but are known to be innocent. This is a bad lineup because the individuals differ dramatically on multiple dimensions (e.g., height, facial hair).

Eyewitness Memory

When the police arrest someone whom they suspect of committing a crime, they may have some evidence against that person, or they may just have a suspicion or a hunch that the person was involved in the criminal act. If there were witnesses to the crime, police may construct a photo array or a lineup to gather evidence from those witnesses about whether the suspect is in fact the culprit, the person who committed the crime. In a **lineup** procedure, a witness to the crime is shown the suspect (or a photo of the suspect) along with several other people (or photos of people) to see if the witness will identify the suspect as the culprit. It is important to remember that the suspect may or may not be the culprit. Police may suspect a person is the culprit, and the lineup procedure is a method of gaining evidence to support that suspicion. The other members of the lineup are known as **fillers**. In a properly constructed lineup, there should be only one suspect and the fillers should be people who are known to be innocent of the crime.[1]

When presented with a lineup, witnesses can make one of several identification decisions, depending on whether the suspect in the lineup is the culprit (known as a **culprit-present lineup**) or is innocent (known as a **culprit-absent lineup**). Witnesses make accurate identification decisions if they identify the suspect in a culprit-present lineup (a decision known as a **hit** or a **correct identification**) or if they state that the culprit is not present in a culprit-absent lineup (a decision known as a **correct rejection**). If the witness identifies a filler in either type of lineup, no charges will be brought against the filler because the fillers are known to be innocent. If, however, a witness fails to identify the suspect in a culprit-present lineup (a decision known as an **incorrect rejection**), then the police may not have the evidence they need to charge the person who committed the crime. Even more problematic is the situation in which a witness identifies the innocent suspect in a target-absent lineup (a decision known as a **false** or **mistaken identification**). In this case, not only will the witness's identification will likely result in charges being brought against an innocent person but also in the continued freedom of the guilty culprit.

lineup a police procedure in which a witness to the crime is shown a suspect (or a picture of the suspect) along with several other people (or photos of people) to see if the witness recognizes one of the lineup members as the person who committed the crime

fillers lineup members other than the suspect who are known to be innocent of the crime

culprit-present lineup a lineup in which the person who committed the crime is one of the lineup members

culprit-absent lineup a lineup in which the person who committed the crime is not present in the lineup

hit (correct identification) when a witness accurately identifies the person who committed a crime from a lineup

correct rejection when a witness correctly states that the person who committed the crime is not present in a lineup

incorrect rejection when a witness fails to identify the suspect in a target-present lineup

false (mistaken) identification when a witness incorrectly identifies an innocent suspect as the person who committed a crime

Estimator Variables

Two categories of variables that can increase or decrease eyewitness accuracy are known as system variables and estimator variables.[2] **System variables** are factors that are under the control of the criminal justice system, such as the instructions that the police officer gives to a witness during a lineup procedure or the fillers selected to appear with the suspect in the lineup. **Estimator variables** are not under the control of the justice system; they include characteristics of the culprit and the witness (e.g., whether the culprit and the witness are the same race, whether the culprit was wearing a disguise), the conditions present when the crime was witnessed (e.g., stress, lighting conditions), and characteristics of the witness's testimony (e.g., witness confidence) that may affect the accuracy of any subsequent eyewitness identification. The distinction between system and estimator variables has proved very important for the application of eyewitness research to criminal justice practice. Although research on estimator variables can help you evaluate how accurate the witness is likely to be, research on system variables provides the criminal justice system with information about changes that can be made to the system to reduce the chance that an innocent person will be mistakenly identified as a culprit.

Even though research on estimator variables cannot help improve the criminal justice system, it does provide information about the types of witness, event, and testimony characteristics that influence the reliability of eyewitness identifications. Thus, understanding the relationship of these variables to eyewitness accuracy will not reduce the number of people mistakenly identified, but it can help judges and juries estimate the accuracy of witnesses who testify before them.[3]

Witness Characteristics

When examining whether witness characteristics influence eyewitness accuracy, we are asking whether certain types of people make better witnesses than other types of people. For example, do women make more accurate identifications than men? A **meta-analysis** or statistical combination of a large number of studies, of the facial recognition literature suggests that women are more likely than men to make correct identifications when the culprit is present in the lineup; however, men are less likely than women to make a mistaken identification when the culprit is not in the lineup.[4] Basically, because women are more likely to choose someone from a lineup, they are more accurate than men in culprit-present lineups and less accurate than men in culprit-absent lineups. Overall, there is no evidence that either men or women have an advantage when it comes to the accuracy of eyewitness identifications. Tradeoffs are associated with each gender.

In contrast, younger adults are better witnesses than both children and older adults. In a meta-analysis of eyewitness identification studies that studied witnesses of varying ages, young adults were more likely to make a correct identification from a culprit-present lineup than were young children or older adults; they were also less likely to make a mistaken identification from a culprit-absent lineup.[5] Although one might expect that adults' superior identification accuracy may be due to their ability to provide more detailed descriptions of culprits, the length of a witness's description of the culprit appears unrelated to the accuracy of his or her identification, irrespective of whether the witness is an adult or a child.[6] Instead, the tendency of children to misidentify innocent suspects stems from their willingness to identify someone—anyone—from a lineup.[7] In attempts to identify a new identification procedure that will help children make more accurate identifications, researchers have tested a variety of procedures, like giving them a "Not Sure" response option, giving them instructions that motivate them to be accurate, or asking them to consider whether the photo whom they have judged looks most like the culprit is a picture of the culprit or someone else. All these procedures effectively reduce the number of identifications that children make, but they do not help children avoid making false identifications without also reducing the number of correct identifications that they make.[8,9]

As discussed in Chapter 13 on prejudice, 30 years of research show that people are better at identifying people of their own race or ethnicity than people of other races or ethnicities.[10] Even archival analyses of witnesses' decisions in actual criminal investigations,

---

system variables characteristics of a lineup administration that are under the control of the criminal justice system and that influence the accuracy of eyewitness identifications

estimator variables characteristics of the witness, the crime, and the witness's testimony that are not under the control of the justice system but that may provide information about the likely accuracy of an eyewitness identification

meta-analysis a quantitative method of reviewing a large research literature by statistical combination of the results across studies in which witnesses should be highly motivated to make correct identification decisions, show an **own-race bias**. Witnesses are more likely to identify a suspect (rather than a filler) when the suspect is the same race as the witness.[11]

Why are people better at recognizing criminals from their own ethnic or racial group? One explanation is that people are better at recognizing own-race culprits because they have greater interpersonal contact or experience with members of their ingroup (see Chapter 13 for more details relating to the contact hypothesis). Other studies suggest that people may devote more attention to own-race faces, encode them better, and consequently better recollect them than other race faces.[12] Indeed, decreasing the ability of participants to attend to faces eliminates the own-race bias in facial recognition, but does so by impairing the ability of people to recognize people from their own racial group.[13] Racial categorization of faces also plays a role in the own-race bias, with rapid categorization of a face as belonging to an outgroup interfering with the encoding of that face.[14] Rapid categorization of outgroup members interferes with memory for their faces even when group categories are relatively meaningless (e.g., participants were randomly assigned to Blue or Yellow groups), but the negative effects of outgroup categorization can be overcome by assigning people to roles (e.g., spy) that require paying attention to outgroup members faces.[15]

Event Characteristics

Crimes are often complex events, and characteristics of these events can influence the accuracy of an eyewitness identification. The ways in which some event characteristics influence the accuracy of memory are not surprising. People are more likely to recognize distinctive rather than nondistinctive faces,[16] faces that they have seen for longer lengths of time,[17] and faces seen more recently than those seen some time ago.[18] Disguises make accurate identifications more difficult. Even small alterations in appearance from the time of the witnessed event to the identification procedure, such as a culprit wearing a cap that covers the hairline during the crime but not during the lineup, can reduce the accuracy of eyewitnesses.[19] Witnesses also are less accurate identifying people who were wearing sunglasses during the witnessed event, unless the target also wears the sunglasses during the identification procedure.[20] Witnesses are less accurate identifying culprits wearing sunglasses than culprits wearing knit caps covering their hairline and least accurate when culprits wore both disguises.[21]

The amount of stress that people experience while witnessing a crime also varies based on features of the event. How does stress affect the accuracy of eyewitness memory? It appears to depend on how much stress the witness experiences. Current theories about the effects of stress on performance suggest that lower levels of stress may produce an orienting response, enabling people to narrowly focus on the most relevant aspects of a task. Higher levels of stress, however, include a somatic or physiological anxiety response that leads to a defensive orientation, which should decrease attention to surrounding stimuli and instead focus attention on identifying an escape route (see the Arousal, Attention, and Performance section in Chapter 6). When this somatic anxiety rises, performance decreases.[22] This theory explains the mixed pattern of results in the facial recognition literature. In studies containing a manipulation of stress that led participants to report increased arousal but did not produce a physiological change in participants (a manipulation that would produce an orienting response but not a defense orientation), witnesses' memory is more accurate for details that are central to the witnessed event but less accurate for peripheral details.[23] In contrast, a meta-analysis of the literature examining the relationship between high stress (arousal that is great enough to produce a defensive orientation) and eyewitness accuracy found that high levels of stress cause witnesses to make fewer correct identifications in target-present lineups but do not appear to affect the correct rejection rate in target-absent lineups.[24]

Increasingly researchers are taking advantage of circumstances that produce stress that cannot be ethically induced in the lab in their studies of the effects of stress on eyewitness accuracy. For example, military personnel subjected to high stress interrogations in mock prisoner of war camps are less accurate in identifying their interrogator than are those personnel subjected to less stressful interrogations.[25] Similarly, visitors to the Horror Labyrinth in the London Dungeon who were more anxious after their visit (as measured by a heart rate monitor)

own-race bias the finding that witnesses are more accurate in identifying members of their own race than members of another race gave descriptions of a person they saw in the labyrinth that were less accurate and were less likely to correctly identify him from a lineup than were visitors who were less anxious.[26]

The presence of a weapon during the witnessed crime, an event characteristic thought to produce stress, has received particular attention from researchers. Does the presence of a gun or other type of weapon attract witnesses' attention and distract them from attending to other relevant details of the crime such as the culprit's face? Research generally supports the existence of this **weapon focus** phenomenon.[27] In one study, researchers tracked participants' eye movements while they watched a slide show depicting an interaction between a customer and a cashier.[28] Half the participants saw the customer hand the cashier a check; the other half saw the customer point a gun at the cashier. The eye-tracking data showed that participants fixated more often and for a longer duration on the weapon than on the check, and this increased attention to the weapon was accompanied by decreases in identification accuracy. Even when weapons pose a threat, they are more memorable when they are unexpected in a given situation (e.g., a gun at a baseball game)[29] than expected (e.g., scissors at a hair salon),[30] which suggests that it is both the threat and the typicality of a weapon in a given situation that produce the weapon focus effect.[31] Adults are not the only ones who focus on a weapon; children also exhibit the weapon focus effect.[32]

Testimony Characteristics

Finally, characteristics of the witness's identification or testimony may serve as useful indicators of identification accuracy. For example, one might reasonably expect that confident witnesses are also more accurate witnesses. Indeed, the U.S. Supreme Court has ruled that witness confidence was one of five criteria that jurors should use to judge the accuracy of an eyewitness.[33] Yet the early research in this area suggested that witness confidence and accuracy were at best weakly related,[34] which led to some courts to adopt the position that there was little to no relationship between witness confidence and witness accuracy.[35,36]

The relationship between witness confidence and accuracy is more complicated than these court decisions suggest. One meta-analysis found little relationship between confidence and accuracy when witness accuracy was low because of poor witnessing conditions but a stronger relationship when witness accuracy was higher because of better witnessing conditions.[37] Another meta-analysis found that the accuracy–confidence relationship is stronger when you consider only those people who choose someone (either the suspect or a filler) during the identification task; the relationship diminishes if you include people who correctly or incorrectly reject the lineup.[38] This finding is significant because only those people who have positively identified someone (made a choice) who will be asked to testify at trial, so jurors will be evaluating these choosers based on their confidence. Moreover, it appears that you can increase the diagnosticity of choosers' confidence by having witnesses consider the conditions under which they witnessed the event and made the identification, or by asking them to generate hypotheses for why their identification decision may be inaccurate, before estimating their confidence.[39] Confidence is also more diagnostic of accuracy if the identification test and confidence rating are collected immediately after the witnesses have encoded the target face.[40]

What is the true relationship between witnesses' confidence and the accuracy of their identification? Increasingly, evidence suggests that confidence statements, made before there is a potential for contamination from outside sources, reliably predict witness accuracy.[41] There are even suggestions that estimator variables do not affect the accuracy of high-confidence witnesses.[42] However, many of the studies that find highly confident witnesses tend to be accurate have been conducted online, eliminating any suggestiveness that might come from lineup administrators interacting with witnesses, and with fair lineups that do not cause the suspect to stand out. Therefore, scholars have qualified their position on the witness confidence-accuracy relationship, arguing that witness confidence is related to their identification accuracy only when the identification and the confidence statement are taken under pristine conditions.[43] Pristine conditions include an identification procedure that includes only one suspect and a set of fillers that do not cause the suspect to stand out, instructions that warn the witness that the culprit may not be present in the lineup, double-blind administration of the identification procedure, and a confidence statement that is

weapon focus when a witness focuses on the weapon carried by a culprit, causing a decrease in accuracy for memory of the culprit's face taken immediately after the identification by an administrator who does not know which lineup member is the suspect.

Another testimony characteristic, the length of time it takes for a witness to make an identification decision, appears to be a promising indicator of accuracy.[44] Faster decision times for accurate witnesses may indicate that they are using a different cognitive process when engaging in the identification procedure. Perhaps witnesses who make quick identifications are using automatic processes that are not influenced by environmental concerns such as wanting to get criminals off the street. Perhaps increased time to make an identification indicates controlled processing and provides evidence that the witness is not relying on an internal memory of the culprit but is subject to situational pressures or other motivations that may taint the accuracy of the identification. Several studies have found that witnesses who report that the culprit "popped out" of the lineup or who report a subjectively easy process of identification tend to be more accurate than witnesses who report that they used a process of elimination to pick the lineup member who looked most like the culprit or that the identification task required a lot of cognitive effort.[45] Consistent with the duplex mind theme in this book, there appear to be two types of identifications: (a) fast, automatic identifications, and (b) slower, deliberate identifications. The automatic identifications appear to be more accurate.

Finally, a combination of confidence and time to identification may be a better predictor of eyewitness accuracy than either predictor on its own. A person walking by stopped to ask pedestrians for directions, and the pedestrians subsequently attempted to identify the direction seeker from a target-absent or target-present array. Witnesses who were fast to make an identification (6 seconds and under) and were highly confident (at least 90% confident) were very accurate. In contrast, witnesses who were slow and less confident were very inaccurate. These findings suggest that police officers may want to record both the time it takes a witness to make an identification and the witness's stated confidence before any other information is given to the witness so that this information can be used to make educated guesses about whether a witness is accurate.[46]

System Variables

The procedures that police investigators use when conducting a lineup can be thought of as being analogous to the procedures used by researchers conducting a social psychological experiment.[47] When gathering eyewitness evidence, investigators start with a hypothesis—namely, that the suspect is the culprit. Like researchers, investigators need to develop a procedure for testing this hypothesis. In this case, the procedure is the lineup. Just as in any social psychology experiment, the procedure will include instructions to the participant (the witness, in this case), the development of materials to present to the witness (selection of the fillers to include in the lineup or photo array), a protocol for presenting the materials, and a method of recording the participants' response (the identification decision). As you have already learned, many things can go awry when designing a social psychology experiment: Instructions can lead participants to behave in particular ways; **demand characteristics**—features of an experiment that communicate to the participant the experimenter's hypothesis—may be present in the study materials; and experimenters may leak hypotheses to participants. Not only may these flaws be present in psychology experiments, they also may be present in the procedures that police use to conduct lineups. The study of system variables in eyewitness identification studies is really an application of sound experimental methodology to police lineup procedures. Most of this research has focused on describing best practices for selecting lineup fillers, delivering lineup instructions, presenting the lineup to the witness, and eliminating behavioral influence of investigators on witnesses by limiting their knowledge of the suspect's identity.

Lineup Fillers

When the police conduct a lineup, they present the suspect along with some number of other people to the witness. Sometimes police present the witness with an all-suspect lineup, in which the police believe that every lineup member may possibly be the culprit.[48]

demand characteristics features of an experiment that communicate to the participant the experimenter's hypothesis

Any witness choice in an all-suspect lineup will result in charges against one of the suspects, and nothing can be learned about the accuracy of a witness's memory for the culprit. More can be learned when people who are known to be innocent serve as fillers.[49] Remember that in a real lineup, unlike in the laboratory, investigators can never be sure if the witness has an accurate memory of the culprit even when that witness chooses the suspect from the lineup. However, if a witness selects one of the fillers rather than the suspect, the police know that the witness's memory for the culprit is less than perfect.

There are two primary strategies for selecting fillers for lineups. The **match-to-suspect** strategy involves choosing fillers with features similar to those of the suspect. Matching fillers to the suspect may seem like a reasonable strategy, but let us take this strategy to the extreme. If we were to perfectly match fillers to the suspect, we could present the witness with a lineup of a suspect and clones of the suspect. Admittedly, a lineup of clones is not likely. However, a direct comparison of match-to-culprit (which can only be done in the lab where the culprit is known) and match-to-suspect strategies of filler selection for target-absent lineups showed that matching fillers to an innocent suspect rather than the culprit increases the likelihood of that innocent suspect's being mistakenly identified.[50]

Of course, a lineup constructed of people who look nothing like the suspect may cause the suspect to stand out as the only lineup member who matches the description of the culprit, increasing the rate of false identifications.[51] Thus, there must be some optimum level of filler similarity to suspect. The **match-to-culprit description** strategy, based on this concept, involves choosing fillers who share the features that the witness mentioned in his or her description of the culprit, but who vary on other features.[52] For example, if the witness's description mentioned that the culprit was in his mid-20s, around 6 feet tall, with a medium build, brown hair, and light eyes, then all the fillers should share these features. Let us say that the suspect has all these features, but also has curly hair. Using a match-to-culprit description strategy, the police officer would want to find fillers that share all the features of the description but vary on whether their hair is curly or straight and whether their eyes are blue or green (both light colors).

The choice of appropriate fillers for the lineup is very important because it can influence both the accuracy of witnesses' identifications and their confidence that the identification is accurate. Witnesses are more likely to identify the suspect from a lineup when the fillers that do not look very much like the suspect, irrespective of whether the suspect is guilty or innocent.[53] Thus, when the suspect is innocent, fillers that are dissimilar to the suspect increase mistaken identifications. In addition to increasing the possibility of a mistaken identification, witnesses who identify suspects from lineups containing dissimilar fillers are more confident in the accuracy of their identifications than are witnesses who identify suspects from more fairly constructed lineups, introducing error into witnesses' assessments of their confidence in the accuracy of the identification made.[54]

Recently, researchers have begun to explore whether it is possible for fillers to be too similar to the suspect. Although it is important that a suspect not stand out from the fillers, as would be the case if the suspect is the only lineup member who has a feature that a witness said the culprit had, it is also important that there be some ways in which the fillers differ from the suspect and each other. For an extreme example, imagine that the fillers are all clones of the suspect, who is also the culprit. In this scenario, the fillers would have all the same features as the guilty suspect, but there would be no way for a witness to find the culprit among the identical-looking fillers. Thus, some eyewitness identification experts have argued that a lineup should have **propitious heterogeneity**: variation in the physical features of the fillers that could help witnesses find the culprit among the fillers without biasing the lineup against an innocent suspect.[55] A lineup with fillers who are matched to the suspect has less propitious heterogeneity than a lineup with fillers who are matched to the witness's description of the culprit, making it more difficult to find the guilty culprit in a lineup.[56,57] The dangers associated with fillers who are highly similar to the suspect, resulting in a lineup that lacks propitious heterogeneity, maybe exacerbated by police departments that use facial recognition software to search large digital databases of photos to choose fillers. With larger databases (125,000 photos) as opposed to smaller (5,000 photos) databases, the fillers chosen by the software are more similar to the suspect, resulting in fewer correct identifications of guilty suspects.[58]

---

match-to-suspect choosing lineup fillers who have features that are similar to the features of the suspect the police have in custody

match-to-culprit description choosing lineup fillers who share features of the culprit mentioned in the witness's description of the culprit but who vary on other features

propitious heterogeneity variation in the physical features of the fillers that could help witnesses find the culprit among the fillers without biasing the lineup against an innocent suspect

Lineup Instructions

The lineup administrator's instructions to a witness have a powerful influence on the accuracy of the witness's decisions. Put yourself in the role of a witness who is called to the police station to view a lineup. Of course, you assume that the police have someone in custody whom they suspect of committing the crime that you witnessed. If there were no one in custody, why would you be asked to view a lineup? A meta-analysis of studies that manipulated whether lineup instructions were biased (e.g., implied that the witness's job was to pick the culprit from the lineup) or unbiased (e.g., reminded witnesses that the culprit may not be in the lineup) shows that unbiased instructions increase the likelihood that witnesses will correctly reject a lineup if the culprit is absent.[59] Even though more people fail to make a choice from a lineup when the instructions are unbiased, this meta-analysis demonstrated that instruction type does not affect the rate of correct identifications, which has resulted in the adoption of unbiased instructions as a recommended procedure by some police departments. However, a reconsideration of the studies included in the meta-analysis suggests that when instructions include a warning that the culprit may not be in the lineup, there is a small but significant drop in the number of correct identifications made by witnesses.[60] Given that any reduction in correct identifications is much smaller than the reduction in mistaken identifications, most scholars still recommend that instructions to witnesses include a warning that the culprit may not be in the lineup. The benefits of a warning that the culprit may not be in the lineup may be undone, however, by a pre-admonition suggestion that the witness should be able to identify the culprit from the lineup. Thus, it is important that the police remove any suggestion about the presence of the culprit from the identification procedure as it does not appear that a pre-identification warning can undo the harmful effects of a suggestion that the culprit will be present.[61]

Lineup Administrator Knowledge

A phenomenon related to eyewitness identification procedures that has only recently received attention from researchers is the effect of lineup administrator behavior on witness behavior. In many areas of science, **double-blind testing** is a model protocol.[62] A test is double-blind if neither the experimenter nor the research participant knows whether the participant is in the experimental or control condition. The purpose of double-blind testing is to ensure that the experimenter's behavior does not change systematically with the variable being tested. If it does, then any effects between conditions may be due to the experimenter's behavior and not the manipulated variable. The analogous situation in lineup procedures is that neither the lineup administrator nor the witness knows which lineup member is the suspect. This lack of knowledge eliminates the possibility that the administrator's behavior might communicate either knowingly or unwittingly to the witness the identity of the suspect.

Administrators who attempt to steer witnesses toward an identification of a suspect are more likely to obtain identifications of suspects from witnesses than are administrators who do not attempt to influence the witness.[63] Limiting contact between a witness and an administrator who knows the suspect's identity by having the administrator silently stand behind the witness during the procedure reduces mistaken identifications.[64] Single-blind lineup procedures result in more mistaken identifications than do double-blind procedures.[65] Moreover, if the lineup administrator knows the identity of the suspect and has reason to believe that the witness needs assistance in making an identification, the administrator's knowledge of the suspect's identity may influence that witness to mistakenly identify an innocent person.[66]

There are several conditions that magnify the effect of administrator influence in single-blind administrations. Single-blind administrators are more likely to influence the witness to identify the suspect when witnesses have weak memories, as is the case when the time between the witnessed event and the identification procedure is longer rather than shorter.[67] Similarly, administrators' influence is greater when the instructions to the witness are biased and the lineup members are presented at the same time rather than one at a time.[68] Biased instructions and **simultaneous lineup** presentation increase the chances that witnesses will make a guess when making an identification (rather than basing their identification on a clear memory of the culprit), increasing

double-blind testing a lineup administration in which neither the police officer nor the witness knows which lineup member is the suspect

simultaneous lineup a lineup in which all lineup members (or their photos) are presented to the witness at the same time the likelihood that witnesses will mistakenly identify a filler. Administrator influence tends not to change whether witnesses make an identification (as opposed to rejecting the lineup). Instead, witnesses who would have picked a filler under double-blind testing conditions are steered toward identifying the suspect in single-blind testing conditions.[69]

Besides influencing the accuracy of eyewitness identifications, lineup administrator knowledge of a suspect's identity may contribute to a weak relationship between confidence and accuracy, especially in actual cases, by influencing a witness's post-identification confidence.[70] Gary Wells and his colleagues have conducted a series of studies showing that it is extremely easy to manipulate witnesses' confidence in the accuracy of their identifications by providing post-identification information confirming their choice.[71,72] In these studies, witnesses were led to make mistaken identifications of an innocent suspect. What varied in these studies was the type of feedback given by the lineup administrator to the witness. In one condition, the administrator gave no feedback. In the other condition, the lineup administrator said, "Good, you identified the suspect." Not surprisingly, witnesses who received this confirming feedback were more confident in the accuracy of their identifications, which were all inaccurate, than were witnesses who received no feedback. This effect holds even when witnesses are specifically told that the culprit may not be present in the lineup.[73] Other types of confirming evidence, like a confession from the defendant or testimony from a jailhouse informant who testifies that the defendant confessed to him, also increase witnesses' confidence in the accuracy of their identifications.[74,75] Making witnesses suspicious about the motives of the administrator for giving the feedback appears to eliminate the post-identification feedback effect, and it does not seem to matter whether the suspicion is induced at the time the feedback is given or up to a week later.[76]

The post-identification feedback effect is very important because the law allows a judge to admit an eyewitness identification obtained using suggestive procedures if the judge rules that the eyewitness identification is nevertheless reliable. The judges are to gauge the reliability of an eyewitness by attending to five factors: the witness's opportunity to view the culprit, the witness's attention to the culprit, the quality of the witness's description of the culprit, the interval between the witnessed event and the identification procedure, and the certainty of the witness.[77] Confirmatory post-identification feedback alters not only witnesses' confidence in the accuracy of their identification but also their reports of their opportunity to view the culprit, the attention they paid to the culprit's face, and their estimations of the length of time they had to view the culprit.[78] Thus, three of the five factors that judges and jurors are asked to consider when evaluating the reliability of an eyewitness identification—opportunity to view, attention, and certainty—can be tainted by post-identification feedback.[79] In addition, post-identification feedback interferes with the ability of evaluators to tell the difference between accurate and inaccurate witnesses.[80] Thus, another crucial reason for requiring that administrators of lineups be blind to which member of a lineup is the suspect is that double-blind testing prevents post-identification feedback.

Controversy about Suggested System Reforms

Based on the evidence reviewed above, American Psychology–Law Society has endorsed a number of reforms to the criminal justice system intended to reduce mistaken identifications, including (among others) warning witnesses that the culprit may not be in a lineup, selecting fillers that do not cause the suspect to stand out from the other lineup member, conducting double-blind lineups, and collecting a confidence statement from the witness at the time of the identification and before confirming feedback can be provided.[81] Recently, some have begun to question the wisdom of these recommendations, noting that many suggested reforms (e.g., lineup warnings, higher filler similarity, double-blind administration) not only reduce mistaken identifications but also reduce the number of correct identifications that witness make. The one exception to this pattern is for the recommendation that police use lineups rather than showups (e.g., a single-person lineup) to collect eyewitness identification evidence. In this case, there is a reduction in mistaken identifications if lineups as opposed to show-ups are used without a corresponding drop in correct identifications.[82]

There is no doubt that many of these suggested reforms involve a tradeoff because the benefit of minimizing mistaken identifications using these reforms often comes with the cost of decreasing the number of correct identifications. But should we be concerned about these costs? Why are they occurring? As discussed earlier, a lineup is like an experiment designed to test the hypothesis that the suspect is the culprit. Like in all experiments, we should design a fair test of our hypothesis. In practice, however, lineups are not always fair tests of the hypothesis that the suspect is the person who committed a particular crime. Sometimes the fillers look nothing like the description given by the witness or the suspect, causing the suspect to stand out in the lineup. Sometimes the administrator may engage in behaviors, without meaning to do so, that draw attention to the suspect as is the case in single-blind lineup administration. These scenarios describe suggestive lineup procedures that encourage witnesses to pick someone, and at times a specific someone, from the lineup. Choosing fillers who match the description given by the witness and conducting double-blind lineups remove suggestiveness from the lineup procedure. Although these procedures reduce correct identifications in addition to reducing mistaken identifications, they do so through the removal of inappropriate suggestiveness.[83]

Persuasiveness of Eyewitness Memory

Jennifer Thompson studied the face of the man who raped her. During her assault, she told herself that if she got through this ordeal, she would remember every detail of her rapist's face. When Ronald Cotton was arrested for raping Thompson, she identified him from a photo array and later from a lineup as the person who brutally attacked her. Thompson said she was 100% confident that this was the man. The jury believed her and convicted Cotton, despite his continued protestations of innocence throughout the trial. Indeed, it is very powerful evidence when an eyewitness identifies a suspect from a lineup and then subsequently claims in court that she recognizes the person sitting at the defense table as the person who assaulted her for hours. How is a juror to argue with this witness? The juror was not present at the crime, and the witness was. The witness is confidently proclaiming that this is the person who raped her. The problem is that Cotton was not the man who raped her, as Thompson later learned when Bobby Poole, an inmate serving time with Cotton, bragged about raping her. Although Thompson was convinced she had never seen Poole before, DNA testing proved that he, and not Cotton, had raped her.[84]

Jennifer Thompson identified Ronald Cotton as the man who had raped her. DNA evidence proved that she was mistaken. The two are now friends and tour the country speaking about the problems with eyewitness identification evidence.

In another case, Troy Davis was convicted and sentenced to death for the murder of a police officer. Nine witnesses reported soon after the crime that they had seen Davis shoot the police officer. Jurors at Davis's trial heard testimony from these witnesses, convicted Davis of the murder, and sentenced him to death. Yet during the appeals process, doubts were raised about the accuracy of these witnesses' accounts, with seven of the witnesses recanting their earlier testimony.[85] One juror, Dorothy Ferrell, testified with certainty at the trial that Davis had pulled the trigger of the gun used to kill an off-duty police officer. Years later she claimed that she had identified Davis "to tell the police what they wanted to hear."[86] Despite this new information that eyewitnesses were claiming that their identifications of Davis were the result of coercive police actions, the judges reviewing Davis's appeals for a stay of execution were ultimately unmoved, and Davis was executed in September 2011.

Eyewitness identifications can be very powerful evidence, even when there are reasons to believe that the crime was witnessed or the identification was made under less than desirable circumstances. In an early study,[87] mock jurors read a summary of a trial in which the defendant was being tried for committing a grocery store robbery in which two people were killed. There were three different versions of the trial. Some mock jurors read that there was no eyewitness to the crime. Without an eyewitness, only 18% of the jurors voted to convict the defendant. Other jurors read that a store clerk had identified the defendant as the person who shot the two victims. With this eyewitness testimony, conviction rates rose to 72%. What is most remarkable is that conviction rates were almost identical (68%) for jurors who read that the defense attorney got the clerk to admit that he had 20/400 vision, was not wearing his glasses during the robbery, and therefore could not clearly see the shooter's face. Thus, even when an eyewitness could not have seen what he claimed to have seen, his identification of the defendant was very convincing evidence for jurors.

There are a number of approaches to investigating whether jurors can tell the difference between accurate and inaccurate eyewitness identifications. Survey research shows that laypeople misunderstand the effects of many variables on the accuracy of eyewitness identifications, including own-race bias, weapon focus, and the weak relationship between confidence and accuracy among other effects.[88] Other studies have asked laypeople to predict the outcomes of different eyewitness identification experiments after reading descriptions of their procedures and methods.[89,90] Participants in these studies underestimate the extent to which eyewitnesses make false identifications and lack an understanding of how some variables interact with one another to affect the accuracy of eyewitness memory.

A third method for testing juror sensitivity to factors that influence the reliability of eyewitness identifications is to conduct jury simulations. In these simulated trials, researchers manipulate characteristics of the witnessing conditions or the identification task that are known to affect eyewitness accuracy and then look to see whether these manipulations influence jurors' trial decisions. In one study, for example, jurors watched a trial in which the eyewitness identification was either an own-race or a cross-race identification; jurors' trial judgments, including verdict, were unaffected by the cross-race manipulation, suggesting that jurors are unaware of the own-race bias in identification accuracy.[91] Other studies have manipulated whether witnesses' confidence in their identification accuracy remains constant from identification to trial or increases during that time (perhaps due to post-identification confirming feedback); they have found that jurors' verdicts and evaluations of eyewitness accuracy are not affected by changes in witness confidence over time unless the change is challenged by the defense attorney.[92] Similarly, jurors judged mistaken witnesses who had received confirming feedback about their identification to be more accurate than those witnesses who did not, irrespective of whether evidence of the confirming feedback was presented in the testimony.[93] Confirming feedback also interferes with jurors' abilities to distinguish among witnesses who made accurate versus inaccurate identifications.[94]

Can any legal procedures be relied upon to increase jurors' ability to discriminate between accurate and inaccurate witnesses or to pay attention to factors that influence the reliability of eyewitness evidence? Some courts have recognized that eyewitness identifications can be unreliable and have held that judges should instruct jurors on the potential unreliability of eyewitness identification evidence obtained under certain circumstances.[95,96] Some courts have even developed science-based instructions designed to provide jurors with detailed information about fifteen factors that influence eyewitness identification accuracy.[97] Although the instructions are well-intentioned, tests of whether they help jurors evaluate eyewitness identifications suggest that they are ineffective in their original form.[98,99] Researchers have also tested a modified version of the instructions, which ask mock jurors to consider whether each factor discussed in the instructions applied to the case that they just heard. Although the standard instructions did not affect participants' verdicts, the modified instructions did help jurors render verdicts that reflected whether the witnessing conditions were good (no weapon, short exposure to culprit's face, and longer time between crime and the identification)

A jury convicted Troy Davis of shooting and killing an off-duty police officer based primarily on the testimony of nine eyewitnesses to the shooting. Although seven of the witnesses later recanted their identifications, claiming that they had been pressured by the police to identify Davis as the shooter, Davis was executed for this crime in September 2011.

or bad (weapon present, longer exposure time, and shorter retention interval). Specifically, the participants were more likely to convict when the witnessing conditions were good.[100]

Another possibility is that an expert might be called to testify about psychological research on the factors that influence the reliability of eyewitness testimony. There is some evidence that expert testimony on the psychology of eyewitness testimony can increase juror sensitivity to variations in witnessing conditions.[101] In most cases, jurors' verdicts and their estimates of the accuracy of the eyewitness were no different when the witnessing conditions were favorable or unfavorable to accuracy. However, when the eyewitness expert testified, jurors were less likely to convict and thought the eyewitness was less accurate when the witnessing conditions were poor than when they were good. The evidence that expert testimony may sensitize jurors to biased lineup procedures is mixed. One study found that expert testimony educated jurors about the effects of filler and instruction bias,[102] but another study found no effects of expert testimony, in part because jurors were sensitive to filler and instruction bias even in the no expert testimony conditions.[103] In light of these mixed results, some argue that the only purpose that expert testimony on eyewitness research serves is to make the jury more skeptical of all eyewitness identifications, even those made with favorable witnessing conditions and fair lineup procedures.[104]

QUIZ YOURSELF
Eyewitness Memory

1. _____ is an example of a system variable in eyewitness identifications, whereas _____ is an example of an estimator variable.
   - (a) Weapon focus; culprit's disguise
   - (b) Cross-racial identification; lineup instructions
   - (c) Investigator knowledge; filler selection
   - (d) Post-identification feedback; weapon focus

2. Which of the following statements best characterizes the relationship between witness confidence and accuracy?
   - (a) Witness confidence is influenced by external factors and is only slightly related to accuracy.
   - (b) Witness confidence is influenced by witnessing conditions and is a good index of a witness's accuracy.
   - (c) Witness confidence is solely a function of memory strength and is a good predictor of witness accuracy.
   - (d) Although witness confidence is not easily influenced by external factors, it is also unrelated to witness accuracy.

3. Which of the following instructions should police officers give to a witness if they want to increase the reliability of an identification?
   - (a) I need you to identify the suspect so that he will not be free to commit more crimes.
   - (b) We have evidence against a person in custody, and all you need to do is identify him.
   - (c) The suspect may or may not be in the lineup.
   - (d) Don't worry; they cannot see you from behind this mirror.

4. The weight that jurors give to eyewitness testimony when rendering verdicts is most influenced by _____.
   - (a) whether the witness had a good chance of viewing the culprit
   - (b) whether the witness had poor eyesight
   - (c) whether the lineup was conducted properly
   - (d) whether the witness was confident

answers: see pg D21

Jury Selection and Decision Making

When former professional football player O. J. Simpson was tried for the brutal deaths of his ex-wife, Nicole Brown, and her friend Ronald Goldman, both the prosecution and the defense hired trial consultants. The prosecution team, led by Marcia Clark, hired well-respected trial consultant Don Vinson to assist them in the jury selection process. Jo-Ellan Dimitrius, another high-profile consultant, assisted Robert Shapiro, Johnnie Cochran, and the rest of O. J. Simpson's "Dream Team." Although both teams initially hired consultants to assist in identifying jurors who would be favorable to one side, the two litigation teams differed in their use of the consultants they had hired. The prosecution team fired their consultant after a little more than a day of jury selection, whereas Dimitrius continued to assist the defense throughout the selection process.

Why did the prosecution fire Vinson? Reports suggest that Marcia Clark's intuition about the characteristics of an ideal pro-prosecution juror disagreed with the recommendations that Vinson was making based on research he had conducted before the trial. Vinson believed that the prosecution should try to remove African American women from the jury because his research showed that African American women were more likely to acquit than any other category of juror, including African American men. Unbeknownst to the prosecution team, the defense consultant's research supported similar conclusions.[105] In contrast, Marcia Clark believed that women would be more likely to have experienced intimate partner violence and therefore would judge Simpson more harshly because of the violence he had committed against Nicole in the past. The pretrial research conducted by these consultants also suggested that African Americans, men and women alike, would be more likely to accept the defense arguments of police misconduct than would jurors of other racial or ethnic backgrounds.[106]

At the end of jury selection, Marcia Clark had the jury she wanted: 10 women (8 African American and 2 European American) and 2 men (1 African American and 1 Hispanic). Yet this jury voted to acquit Simpson. Why? We may never know for sure, but the attitudes expressed by these jurors during the jury selection process reveal some clues. Five of the seated jurors reported during jury selection that they thought the use of physical force against a family member was sometimes acceptable. Nine members of the jury said that they believed Simpson was unlikely to have committed murder because he was an outstanding professional athlete. Although it is impossible to know whether Clark's failure to listen to her trial consultant contributed to her loss in the Simpson case, the different approaches used by Clark and Vinson to generate a profile of a pro-prosecution juror do illustrate some of the differences between traditional attorney-conducted jury

In the O. J. Simpson case, trial consultants for both the prosecution and the defense suggested that African American women would vote to acquit Simpson. The defense team, including Johnnie Cochran and Robert Shapiro, took the advice of their consultant, Jo-Ellan Dimitrius. In contrast, prosecutor Marcia Clark fired her consultant and ignored his advice.

selection and the jury selection practiced by social scientists. What kinds of theories do attorneys use to select jurors, and do these theories help them identify jurors who are favorable to their side? What methods do social scientists use to assist attorneys in jury selection, and what types of juror characteristics are predictive of verdict? Can the very process of selecting a juror change juror decision making? Let us find out.

Jury Selection

Before a trial begins, members of the community are called to the courthouse to form a jury pool, called a **venire** (pronounced veh-NEER). Once the venire has been assembled, a judge and attorneys for the two sides ask questions of a randomly drawn subset of these venirepersons to determine whether they hold any attitudes, preconceptions, or biases that would prevent them from fairly hearing the evidence in the case. This process of asking questions of venirepersons to uncover potential bias is called **voir dire** (pronounced vwar-deer), which comes from the French idiom "to speak the truth."

The goal of voir dire is to seat a jury of 6 or 12 people (depending on the type of trial) that can fairly hear the evidence against a defendant. The term *jury selection* is a bit of a misnomer, as jurors are not really selected for a jury; instead, potential jurors are eliminated from the venire in one of two ways. Attorneys may challenge a particular venireperson for cause if that potential juror has exhibited an easily identifiable bias during the course of voir dire. A judge must uphold a **challenge for cause**. The second method of excusing a potential juror is the **peremptory challenge** in which an attorney may excuse a venireperson for almost any reason, without specifying the reason. Attorneys use these challenges to eliminate any venireperson whom they judge to be unfavorable to their side but whose bias would not rise to the level required by a challenge for cause. Challenges for cause are limited only by an attorney's ability to convince the judge of a particular venireperson's bias; in contrast, each attorney is given a limited number of peremptory challenges.

What guides attorneys' decisions to exercise peremptory challenges? It appears as if attorneys hold **implicit personality theories**—a set of beliefs, developed through experience, about how demographic characteristics and attitudes are interrelated.[107] Some attorneys believe that wealthy people are more likely to convict criminal defendants unless the defendant is charged with a white-collar crime. Some defense attorneys believe that poor jurors are a good choice for civil juries because they are not used to large sums of money and will make smaller damage awards; others avoid poor jurors because they believe their poverty will lead them to deliver large awards, transferring money from rich defendants to poor plaintiffs like Robin Hood. Other defense attorneys believe that crime victims will be more punitive toward criminal defendants. The similarity leniency hypothesis argues that jurors who are similar to a defendant will be more lenient because they will have a greater ability to empathize with a similar individual.[108] The black sheep hypothesis suggests that defense attorneys should dismiss jurors who are similar to their clients because people may want to punish those with whom they share group membership because they reflect badly on the group.[109] Some of these hypotheses have received empirical support (e.g., victims of a crime are more punitive toward defendants being tried for the same crime),[110] but empirical support is limited at best for others, including the black sheep hypothesis[111] and the similarity leniency hypothesis.[112]

Even if attorneys' naïve theories about how venirepersons' attitudes influence their verdicts were correct, attorneys appear to be biased in the way that they ask questions and evaluate the information that they receive from potential jurors during voir dire in ways that can interfere with their ability to make good jury selection decisions. Specifically, attorneys ask venirepersons questions that will elicit answers that confirm the attorneys' preexisting hypotheses about the venirepersons' attitudes rather than more diagnostic questions that will elicit information about whether their hypotheses are true. Attorneys also overestimate the value of the answers that they receive from venirepersons when drawing conclusions about their likely attitudes.[113] As attorneys' hypotheses about venirepersons cause them to ask questions during voir dire that are likely to elicit confirming rather than accurate answers from venirepersons, attorneys could be making their

venire members of the community who are called to the courthouse to form a jury pool

voir dire the legal proceeding in which attorneys and judges attempt to uncover bias among those people who have been called for jury duty

challenge for cause a request made by an attorney that a potential juror be removed from the jury panel because he or she is clearly biased and will be unable to hear the case fairly

peremptory challenge a method of removing a potential juror from a jury panel in which the attorney need not specify the reason

implicit personality theories a set of beliefs, developed through experience, about how demographic characteristics and attitudes are interrelated challenge decisions based on unreliable information about the extent to which jurors are biased against a defendant.

Attorneys are not supposed to use peremptory challenges to eliminate jurors because of their race[114] or gender.[115] However, there is some evidence that race may play a role in attorneys' decisions to eliminate jurors from a venire.[116] To test whether venireperson race influences attorneys' use of peremptory challenges, researchers presented prosecuting attorneys with profiles of two potential jurors for a case in which a black defendant was charged with robbery and aggravated assault: a 43-year-old married man who wrote about police misconduct for his job as a journalist and a 40-year-old divorced man who worked as an advertising executive and stated that he distrusted statistics. Some attorneys read that the journalist was white and the advertising executive was black, whereas other attorneys read profiles that depicted the journalist as black and the advertising executive as white. Which potential jurors did the attorneys wish to exclude? Attorneys were more likely to exclude the black juror, irrespective of his other attributes. When asked why they chose to exclude the juror, however, the attorneys provided race-neutral explanations for their decision. If the black juror was the journalist, attorneys said they were excluding him because he had written about police misconduct; if the black juror was the advertising executive, attorneys said they were excluding him because he distrusted statistics. The gender of a prospective juror similarly influenced participants' jury selection decisions in a simulated case in which a battered woman killed her abusive partner, even when they were reminded that they were prohibited from using gender as a criterion for excluding them.[117]

In contrast to traditional attorney-conducted jury selection, attorneys may hire social scientists to assist them in identifying venirepersons who are likely to be biased against their side of the case. Whereas traditional voir dire is based on attorneys' naïve hypotheses about the relationships between juror characteristics and attitudes, scientific jury selection relies on the collection of survey data from the community in which the trial will be conducted to determine whether particular demographic characteristics or attitudes are related to venirepersons' beliefs about the likely guilt of the defendant. The question remains whether there are any reliable predictors of jury verdicts across different case types.

Attorneys find it attractive to use demographic characteristics when making decisions about which jurors to exclude because these characteristics are easily observable even in federal courts in which the rules limit the types of questions that attorneys can ask venirepersons. Unfortunately, most research demonstrates that demographic characteristics do not predict verdict across cases.[118] When demographics do predict verdict in cases, it is because the demographic serves as a proxy for a case-specific attitude. For example, women are consistently more likely to convict in cases involving rape[119] and child sexual abuse.[120] In contrast, women are less likely to convict when a woman is on trial for killing a spouse who has repeatedly battered her.[121] Differences in men's and women's attitudes may influence these outgroup bias effects on jurors' decisions.[122]

Using personality traits as predictors of verdicts across cases poses similar problems. Whether traits predict punitive or lenient verdict behavior often depends on case details. Thus, although individuals differ in whether they believe that the world is a just place and that bad things only happen to bad people (see Belief in a Just World section in Chapter 9), people who believe in a just world sometimes ascribe responsibility for harm to victims and sometimes are more punitive toward defendants.[123] Only the personality trait of authoritarianism seems to predict verdict across a wide variety of cases.[124] People with an **authoritarian personality** are more likely to hold conventional values, respect authority figures, and punish others who defy authority.[125] Authoritarian jurors are more likely to vote for conviction, especially when the trait is measured by scales specifically designed to tap legal authoritarianism, like the Revised Legal Attitudes Questionnaire.

The best predictor of verdict seems to be attitudes that are specific to a particular case.[126] As we learned in Chapter 7, if you want to predict a specific behavior, you should use a specific attitude. A number of scales have been developed to measure case-specific attitudes. People who support reforms to the civil justice system to prevent extremely large damage awards are more likely to side with the defense in a civil trial.[127] Attitudes toward the insanity defense predict verdict preferences in insanity defense cases.[128] Finally, attitudes toward drugs predict whether community members believe that a defendant is criminally responsible in a drug case.[129]

authoritarian personality a pattern of cross-situational attitudes and behaviors that reflects conventional values, respect for authority figures, and a desire to punish others who defy authority

Voir Dire in Capital Cases

Attitudes toward the death penalty are another example of a case-specific attitude that reliably predicts verdict.[130] When a defendant is subject to the death penalty, special jury selection procedures are taken to assess jurors' attitudes toward the death penalty to ensure that the seated jury can hear the case fairly knowing that if the defendant is convicted, he or she may be put to death. A capital case has two phases. As in all criminal trials, jurors are to consider whether the defendant is guilty of a crime. If the defendant is convicted of a capital crime, then there is a penalty phase during which jurors hear evidence that bears on whether the defendant's behavior warrants death. During the penalty phase in most states, jurors are asked to consider whether there is evidence of certain aggravating factors (e.g., a murder was committed in connection with another crime such as rape or a robbery, the victim was a police officer, there were multiple victims) that make the defendant's behavior worse and punishable by death. If there is evidence of aggravation, jurors must then consider whether there is mitigating evidence (e.g., the defendant has a history of being abused as a child, the crime was committed while the defendant was on drugs and lacked certain behavioral control) that would argue for sparing the defendant's life. Jurors who state that their attitudes toward the death penalty would render them incapable of following the law, either because they would never impose the death penalty or because they would be unable to fairly weigh the evidence of the defendant's guilt knowing that a conviction could result in death, are excused for cause. This special jury selection process is called **death qualification**.

death qualification the special jury selection process that occurs in capital cases with the purpose of excluding jurors who would not be able to weigh the evidence fairly because of their death penalty attitudes

The death qualification process results in a jury that differs demographically and attitudinally from juries seated in noncapital cases.[131] A random sample of more than 800 jury-eligible Californians showed that African Americans, women, Democrats, and the poor were significantly more likely to hold anti-death penalty attitudes that would exclude them from serving in a capital trial than were European Americans, men, Republicans, and the wealthy.[132] These findings have been repeated with other samples of community members[133] and with impaneled felony jurors.[134] Thus, the death qualification process removes specific groups of people from jury service, arguably interfering with a defendant's right to be tried by a jury of his or her peers.

Jurors who favor the death penalty are more likely to convict a defendant than are jurors who oppose the death penalty.[135] Three meta-analyses of the literature show that a juror favoring the death penalty is 25% to 44% more likely to vote guilty than is a juror who opposes the death penalty.[136,137,138] Moreover, juries consisting only of people who favor the death penalty are less critical of prosecution witnesses and remember less of the evidence than do juries containing people with a mix of attitudes toward the death penalty.[139]

Pretrial Publicity

In addition to using jury selection to exclude venirepersons who hold particular pretrial attitudes, attorneys also use jury selection to remove venirepersons whose exposure to pretrial publicity would prevent them from hearing the evidence impartially. Pretrial publicity can interfere with a defendant's right to a fair trial by exposing potential jurors to information that would be inadmissible as evidence during a trial, such as a prior criminal record or evidence produced by an illegal search. It is feared that exposure to this information could cause a juror to be biased against the defendant before ever hearing any of the evidence at trial. Our criminal justice system presumes the innocence of any defendant, and pretrial publicity represents a threat to a defendant's right to this presumption. A meta-analytic review showed that pretrial publicity has a small but reliable effect on juror judgments, resulting in higher conviction rates when jurors have been exposed to negative pretrial publicity.[140] When pretrial publicity contains information that is favorable to the defendant, conviction rates decrease.[141]

Pretrial publicity generally communicates negative information about a defendant to the potential jury pool.[142] We have seen throughout this book how difficult it is to overcome negative characterizations of people and their behavior. Moreover, it is natural to want to use all the information available to judge a defendant, but the laws of our culture attempt to restrict the use of certain information. The question is whether the

When pretrial publicity prejudices potential jurors against a defendant, judges should remove them for cause, but sometimes venirepersons hide their bias during voir dire. In the recent highly publicized trial of Joshua Komisarjevsky (the man convicted of a home invasion, arson, and murdering of three members of the Petit family in Cheshire, Connecticut), the judge refused to excuse a venireperson for cause, but she was later excused by the defense, using a peremptory challenge. As she exited the courtroom, she confronted the defendant, screaming, "Murderer!"

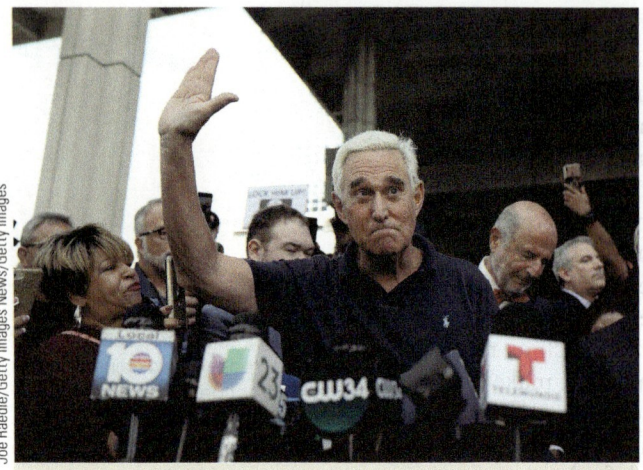

Pretrial publicity prejudices jurors against defendants. Might it have the same effects on judges?

laws provided to protect defendants against prejudicial pretrial publicity work. Given the relative advantage that negative information has over positive information, the answer is not particularly surprising.

Does jury selection provide an effective safeguard against the effects of pretrial publicity on juror decisions? There is an assumption that voir dire and jury selection can be used to educate jurors about the problem of using pretrial publicity when rendering verdicts and to identify and excuse jurors who have been inappropriately influenced by pretrial publicity. One study designed to test this assumption found that pretrial publicity equally affected mock jurors who had been through an extended voir dire and those who had not.[143] Another study found that judges might be able to reduce the effects of pretrial publicity by imploring venirepersons to suppress any thoughts of pretrial publicity they might have seen or heard and eliciting a commitment from them to do so.[144]

Other legal safeguards against the effects of pretrial publicity appear to be ineffective. Although one might expect that the presentation of trial evidence would provide additional information that would diminish the influence of pretrial information, jury simulation studies suggest that the negative effects of pretrial publicity linger even after jurors have heard the trial evidence.[145] Deliberations do not help jurors overcome their biases, as jurors ignore judges' instructions to ignore pretrial publicity and discuss information they learned from the media during their deliberations.[146,147] In addition, juries exposed to pretrial publicity that portrays the defendant in a negative light are more likely to discuss ambiguous trial evidence in a way that favors the prosecution.[148] Even delaying the trial, known as a **continuance** to allow time for the effects of pretrial publicity exposure to fade does not work as the courts intend; after a delay, pretrial publicity effects may be even stronger.[149] The most effective safeguard is a **change of venue** in which the trial is moved to a new location where the level of pretrial publicity was less than in the location where the crime was committed. Even in nationally high-profile cases, such as the case in which Timothy McVeigh detonated a truck bomb that blew up the federal building in Oklahoma City, regions of the country can be identified where there was less pretrial publicity,[150] and there does appear to be a relationship between amount of pretrial publicity and the size of its effect on jurors' verdicts.[151] The use of these safeguards to protect against wrongful conviction of the accused must be weighed against protecting victims. For more details on this fundamental tension, see *Tradeoffs*.

continuance delaying a trial until the level of media attention to the crime has decreased in order to reduce the prejudicial effects of pretrial publicity

change of venue moving a trial to a new location where there has been less pretrial publicity

QUIZ YOURSELF
Jury Selection and Decision Making

answers: see pg D21

1. The best predictor of trial verdicts is _____ .
   - ⓐ juror demographics
   - ⓑ personality traits
   - ⓒ attitudes toward crime
   - ⓓ case-specific attitudes

2. Which personality trait predicts verdict across a wide variety of cases?
   - ⓐ Belief in a just world
   - ⓑ Authoritarianism
   - ⓒ Extraversion
   - ⓓ Conscientiousness

3. Compared to jurors excused from serving in capital trials, death-qualified jurors _____ .
   - ⓐ are more likely to convict a defendant
   - ⓑ are more receptive to mitigating circumstances
   - ⓒ are more likely to be women
   - ⓓ are more likely to have concerns about the death penalty

4. Which of the following methods is the most effective at eliminating the effects of pretrial publicity on juror decisions?
   - ⓐ Voir dire
   - ⓑ Judicial instructions
   - ⓒ Continuance
   - ⓓ Change of venue

Wrongful Convictions Versus Protecting Victims

TRADE Offs

An early commentator on English common law once wrote that "it is better that ten guilty persons escape, than that one innocent suffer."[152] This quote illustrates the fundamental tension at the heart of the U.S. criminal justice system. Although our justice system is designed to control crime by deterring people from committing crimes and by identifying and punishing those who do, the founders of our country put into place legal protections that were designed to prevent the wrongful conviction of innocent people. Tension exists because if we create a system that ensures the punishment of all who are guilty, it is likely that some innocent people will be wrongly convicted. Alternatively, if we place a high value on acquitting those who are innocent, it is likely that some who have committed crimes will be let back on the streets, possibly to commit further crimes. Moreover, it is possible that the victims of those true culprits may experience additional harm at the thought of their attackers' walking free and possibly being able to harm them again.

This tradeoff between protecting the falsely accused from being wrongfully convicted and protecting victims by convicting the truly guilty is at the heart of debates regarding the reliability of recovered memories. This tension is illustrated by the story of Eileen and George Franklin.[153] One day, 29-year-old Eileen recalled a memory that had been buried in the recesses of her mind since childhood. She remembered watching her best friend, Susan Nason, sitting on a rock in the woods when a man brought a large rock down on her head, crushing her skull as Susan futilely attempted to block the blow with her hands. What was most disturbing to Eileen was the identity of the man: her father, George Franklin. Eventually, Eileen reported her memory of Susan's murder to the police, and on the sole basis of Eileen's recently recovered memory of 20 years earlier, George Franklin was charged with Susan Nason's murder. Despite evidence that the public knew every detail in Eileen's recovered memory through media reports at the time of the murder, George Franklin was convicted. The only evidence against him was the recovered memory of his daughter. Later the conviction was overturned on appeal.

If you disbelieve that something as traumatic as witnessing a friend's murder at the hands of one's own father can be forgotten for 20 years and then spontaneously recovered, then you are stripping support from someone who has possibly been traumatically victimized and needs help to heal the trauma suffered as a result of those experiences. On the other hand, if you judge the recovered memories to be reliable, you may protect the welfare of the victim, who honestly believes that she has been harmed, at the expense of prosecuting a man for a crime based on questionable evidence.

Not even a group of scholars convened in 1993 by the American Psychological Association to produce a consensus statement about the factors that contribute to the accuracy of recovered memories could resolve the tradeoff between protecting victims' rights and the rights of the accused. After 18 months of meetings, the disagreement among group members was so great that they insisted on releasing two reports: one authored by the clinicians in the group[154] and one authored by the memory researchers.[155] It is possible that one of the reasons that these two subgroups failed to reach consensus was their different orientations toward the relative importance of supporting victims by believing their accusations versus protecting the innocent from wrongful prosecution. The clinicians' report expressed concern that victims who report abuse after periods of memory loss will be routinely discredited or disbelieved. In contrast, the memory researchers focused on concerns over the role that therapists may play in the construction of recovered memories, arguing that misguided therapeutic techniques may result in the prosecution of innocent people.[156]

It is perhaps more surprising, given the different orientations of these groups, that the groups did find a few areas of agreement. They agreed that most people who were sexually abused as children retain memory for all or part of that abuse, but that abuse can be forgotten for a period and subsequently remembered. They also agreed that false memories—that is, memories for events that did not happen—might be constructed, and that this memory construction may be facilitated by poor therapeutic techniques. Most important, they agreed that much more research is needed to determine whether there are any characteristics that differentiate true from false memories of abuse. Until then, it will be difficult to evaluate the truth behind claims like those of Eileen Franklin and to know whether she was inadequately protected as a victim or her father was the victim of wrongful prosecution.

 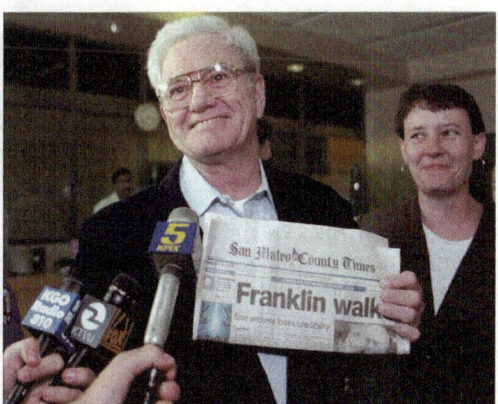

Eileen Franklin (left) accused her father, George Franklin (right), of murdering her friend Susan Nason. Although George was initially convicted of the crime, with his daughter's memory of the murder, recovered 20 years later, as the only evidence against him, his conviction was later overturned.

Jury Selection and Decision Making | D19

What Makes Us Human

Putting the Cultural Animal in Perspective

This module has emphasized how cultural prescriptions in the form of laws are based on psychological assumptions about human behavior. People's natural wants and needs may conflict with the cultural standards we have developed to regulate behavior. Not only might we have natural urges to behave in ways that are inconsistent with the law, but these tendencies could prevent us from faithfully following the law when judging the behaviors of those who might have broken the law.

At the heart of the U.S. legal system is the tradeoff between protecting citizens from those who fail to conform their behavior to legal prescriptions and protecting those same citizens from being wrongfully convicted and punished for the bad behavior of someone else. Mistaken identifications have proved to be the single largest threat to protecting citizens from wrongful conviction. Although biological factors such as stress can influence the accuracy of eyewitness identifications, police procedures that minimize the influence of these variables on the accuracy of eyewitness identifications can be adopted.

People have a natural tendency to attend to negative information and use that information when making decisions. Legal decisions about whether a person is responsible for committing a criminal act are no different; there is a tendency to be influenced by negative information, potentially resulting in an unfair trial. Pretrial media attention to unsavory characteristics of a defendant may be difficult for a juror to overlook when deciding whether that person is guilty of a crime. Jurors who are questioned about their death penalty attitudes and who see jurors opposed to the death penalty removed from jury service may find it difficult to overcome the effects of this questioning when determining whether the defendant before them is guilty of the crime of which he or she stands accused. Racial prejudices may automatically influence how jurors evaluate the evidence against defendants from certain minority groups, even when jurors make conscious attempts to overcome those prejudices.

The desire to protect citizens from wrongful convictions caused by juror biases, either naturally occurring or induced by pretrial publicity, is evident in legal protections. Jury selection procedures are designed to identify jurors who may be predisposed to view the defendant negatively, either because of automatic racial prejudices or because of pretrial publicity. Other potential remedies exist to deal with the negative influence of pretrial publicity on juror decisions, but few of these legal mechanisms seem to be particularly effective.

MODULE D SUMMARY

Eyewitness Memory

- Estimator variables are characteristics of the crime, the offender, the witness, or the person evaluating the quality of the eyewitness evidence that provide information about the likelihood that the witness has made an accurate identification.
- System variables are the many criminal justice procedures that can be manipulated to produce better eyewitness evidence. The rate of mistaken identifications is reduced when
  - Fillers are matched to a description of the culprit rather than to the suspect.
  - Lineup instructions note that the culprit may not be in the lineup.
  - Witnesses view lineup members sequentially rather than simultaneously.
  - The lineup administrator is not aware of the suspect's identity.

Jury Selection and Decision Making

- Despite evidence that eyewitness memory is not necessarily a faithful recording of events, jurors rely heavily on eyewitness identifications when making their decisions, especially when witnesses express confidence in the accuracy of their identifications.
- Traditional attorney-conducted jury selection is based on naïve stereotypes about human behavior. Scientific jury selection has identified few demographic characteristics that reliably predict verdicts. Better predictors include juror authoritarianism and case-specific attitudes.

- In death penalty cases, the jury selection process is used to identify jurors who, because of their opposition to the death penalty, would be unable to convict a defendant who is eligible for a death sentence even if the evidence proved his guilt. This death qualification process results in a jury that is more likely to convict the defendant.

- When the media present information about a case that is not admissible at trial, potential jurors may carry that information with them into the jury room. Research suggests that this pretrial publicity influences jurors' decisions, that jurors are unaware of this influence, and that most methods the courts use to counteract the effects of pretrial publicity are ineffective.

What Makes Us Human? Putting the Cultural Animal in Perspective

- Humans have wants and needs that may conflict with the cultural standards that regulate behavior. These urges may lead us to behave in ways that are inconsistent with the law and may also prevent us from faithfully following the law when judging the behaviors of those who may have broken the law.

key terms

authoritarian personality D16
challenge for cause D15
change of venue D18
continuance D18
correct rejection D3
culprit-absent lineup D3
culprit-present lineup D3
death qualification D17
demand characteristics D7
double-blind testing D9
estimator variables D4
false (mistaken) identification D3
fillers D3
hit (correct identification) D3
implicit personality
theories D15
incorrect rejection D3
lineup D3
match-to-culprit description D8
match-to-suspect D8
meta-analysis D4
own-race bias D5
peremptory challenge D15
propitious heterogeneity D8
simultaneous lineup D9
system variables D4
venire D15
voir dire D15
weapon focus D6

quiz yourself ANSWERS

1. Eyewitness Memory p. D13
   answers: 1.d 2.a 3.c 4.d

2. Jury Selection and Decision Making p. D18
   answers: 1.d 2.b 3.a 4.d

14

LEARNING OBJECTIVES

1. Explain how humans, as cultural animals, form groups that differ from the groups of other social animals, emphasizing how selves and roles alter the nature of human groups.

2. Discuss how roles and the inner processes of the self affect group behavior.

3. Describe group outcomes that result from being individually identified in the group versus feeling submerged in the group.

4. Describe how individuals within a group share information, including brainstorming and groupthink.

5. Describe the traits of successful leadership and the five crucial effects that power has on people.

Fuse/Corbis/Getty Images

THE SOCIAL SIDE OF SEX
Is a Marriage a Group?
499

TRADEOFFS
Diversity in Groups
500

FOOD FOR THOUGHT
Is Binge Eating Socially Contagious?
506

MONEY MATTERS
Money, Power, and Laughter
526

WHAT MAKES US HUMAN?
Putting the Cultural Animal in Perspective
527

In 1863 a well-to-do Michigan farming family gave birth to a son. As a boy, Henry never took to farming, instead showing an abiding interest in mechanical things. He became popular in his neighborhood for fixing people's watches. At age 16 he took a job as an apprentice machinist. Eventually he joined the Edison Engineering Company and at the age of 30 was their chief engineer.

Local travel at the time depended on horses, but clever inventors around the country were experimenting with ways to make self-propelled ("auto-mobile") vehicles. Henry began to tinker with internal combustion engines and began to work on a car (calling it the "Quadricycle," to link it with the popular bicycle). His neighbors had taken to calling him "Crazy Henry" because he spent his evenings and weekends shut up in his garage with his contraption. But they were impressed when late one night he got the car moving. According to legend, it smashed a hole in the side of the garage and drove around the neighborhood with Henry at the wheel.

The car market didn't seem very large. In the year 1900, barely 1 in 10,000 Americans owned an automobile. Nobody expected cars would someday swarm everywhere. Cars were in the news, though. A Vermont man, accompanied by a mechanic and a dog named Bud (all three wearing goggles) made the first coast-to-coast car trip in 65 days, after which they were hailed as national heroes.

Henry went to work for the fledgling Detroit Automobile Company. In two years, it didn't even manage to sell six cars. The company went bankrupt, and Henry was fired. Unemployed, he entered some automobile races and won them. This attention attracted some new financial backers. In 1903 Henry and some other men started the Ford Motor Company, with himself as vice president and chief engineer. A quiet banker named Gray was the first president, but Ford's racing fame dictated that they name the firm after him. The manufacturing system involved having two or three men work together to make a car. Obviously these men had to have enormous skill and knowledge, which made their work relatively expensive. The company was initially only able to make three cars per day, using parts made by other companies. Henry looked for ways to make the production more efficient. In 1907 Henry said that his goal was to create "a motor car for the great multitude."

The first coast-to-coast car trip included two men and a dog.

Up until this point, cars were rare and expensive machines, usually custom-made toys for the rich. More than 240 companies had been formed to build automobiles, so the prospects for great success by any one company were not good. It wasn't even clear that gasoline-powered engines would become the norm. In 1906, a steam-powered car (the Stanley Steamer) set the car speed record by going 127 miles per hour.

A big opportunity and challenge arose when the Ford company developed the Model T. This was the first practical car that ordinary people could afford. Henry threw out the tradition of custom-built cars and made them all exactly the same, even offering only one color. (Henry's remark, "The customer can have any color he wants so long as it's black," became famous.) The design of the Model T did not change from the first one built in 1908 until the final, 15-millionth one in 1927.

Four years after the first Model T was made, three out of every four cars in America were Model Ts. Even in 1918, half of all cars sold in the United States would be Model T Fords. But this escalating demand called for a much more efficient (and cheaper) system for making these cars.

Ford's solution to this problem is the reason we are featuring this story in the chapter on groups. Ford wrote, "Nothing is particularly hard if you divide it into small jobs."[1] Ford broke up the manufacture of

Henry Ford (1888) and his Quadricycle (1896).

In 1913 Henry Ford introduced the assembly line into his factory, which greatly improved productivity rates.

the car into 84 steps and assigned each one to a different worker. Thus, instead of two or three master craftsmen making each car, a great many men worked on each car. Each man, rather than knowing how to build an entire car, could specialize in just one small job. At first, Ford tried a system in which the cars being built were set up on a row of sawhorses. Each worker would do his part on the first vehicle and then move on to the next one. Runners brought parts for each job and left them next to each car. This cut production time down to about 17 hours per car, and Ford workers were soon producing 26,000 cars a month. But there were constant problems. The parts didn't all arrive at the same pace, so many workers had to stand around and wait before they could do their next task. In addition, a fair amount of time was lost as the workers moved around.

The biggest breakthrough came in 1913, with what became known as the assembly line. (Earlier versions had been tried, dating back to 1901.) Instead of having workers move from one car to another, with parts being delivered to constantly changing locations, Ford decided that each worker could stay in one place with a pile of ready parts. The cars would move along a conveyer belt. The initial experiment was done using ropes and pulleys to pull the cars along the belt, but the success of this plan quickly led to using a continuous chain pulled by a motor. Once this plan was adopted and a few bugs worked out, the time to make a new car dropped to 93 minutes. At the height of production, a new car rolled off the assembly line every 24 seconds. The car's price dropped as low as $99.

By dividing the task into many parts, Ford found that he could hire workers without expecting them to master a great deal of information about manufacturing cars. It takes a long time for a person to learn how to build an entire car; learning to do one small task might take only a few days. The assembly line was a tremendous success, and Ford became the largest car manufacturer in the world.

There was a problem, however: Many workers disliked the repetitious, boring, low-paid work. Many quit, and Ford was constantly hiring and training new workers. Henry came up with another stroke of genius to solve this problem. He would resist the temptation to pay the workers the minimum amount. He announced a new minimum wage of $5 per day, more than double the average at the time. This made him a hero to the working class, a role he accepted. "A business that makes nothing but money is a poor kind of business," he said in a later interview. Other capitalists called Ford "a traitor to his class," complaining that he was raising expectations and the cost of labor everywhere, but he ignored their complaints. Ordinary people flocked to work for him—and, with their higher wages, began buying Model T cars themselves. Business boomed. Ford reaped other benefits, including improved loyalty of his employees, and he saved money on training. Later he boasted that paying $5 a day was one of the smartest cost-cutting moves he had ever made.[2]

Can groups outperform individuals? Obviously, a group of 10 people can accomplish more than one person, but can a 10-person group outperform 10 people working alone? Culture enables human beings to form groups that can do things that no groups of other animals can, like build and operate a fishing boat, or publish a newspaper, or install artificial heat in everyone's home. To be sure, sometimes a group is less than the sum of its parts. But culture makes it possible (not guaranteed, but possible) for the group to become more than the sum of its parts, as illustrated in this story about Henry Ford.

What does this story exemplify about the social psychology of groups? A strong and persevering leader, experimenting with new ideas and methods, and good organization can breed success, of course. And by sharing rewards with his followers, Ford increased their loyalty, which also helped the group.

But most of all, the assembly line took division of labor to a new level. When ants or wolves hunt, they do so in a kind of swarm in which most individuals perform the same act. The individual acts are interchangeable. On the Ford moving assembly line, in contrast, each person performed a different job requiring some limited but specific knowledge or skill. Using this method, a group of people, each having minimal knowledge and skill, could produce something magnificent. The group was far more than the sum of its members. This is one important key to how human beings can use the power of culture to make groups that can achieve far more than collections of individuals operating alone. Interactive, complementary roles can make up a powerful system. ●

What Groups Are and Do

A **group** is a collection of people with something in common. Usually the group consists of people who have common interests and characteristics and periodically do something together. Still, some researchers use "group" to mean a category of people who do not all interact or even encounter each other, such as African Americans or athletes. Although most people think of a group as at least half a dozen members, many psychologists insist that, technically, two people (a "dyad") can be a group.

Indeed, the question of precisely what criteria need to be met in order for several people to qualify as a "group" is itself the target of research. That is because some groups seem more like groups than others, and so instead of a simple yes-or-no rule about what makes a group, it is more useful and accurate to think of group-ness as on a continuum. One could say that Canadians are a group, but that is a very large and diverse group, and most of the members don't know each other. Forty strangers on a bus don't make much of a group. Forty people waiting in line for football tickets may be a bit more like a group, given their common goal and perhaps their shared loyalty to their team. Forty people working together on an assembly line or football team make a much more coherent group. Yes, a dyad can be a group, but it is perhaps a special kind of group, and the processes and dynamics of a dyad (e.g., two people in a romantic relationship) are probably different from what goes on in a larger group. For one thing, two people can really relate as equals and make their decisions jointly so that each is satisfied, but a group of 100 probably cannot make decisions in that way; they will need either a leader who makes decisions or a democratic voting system that lets the preferences of the majority determine the decision.

What makes a group feel united? As we said, a football team is more like a group than 40 strangers on a bus, for several reasons.[3,4] They have a common identity, exemplified by the team name, whereas the strangers on the bus do not. The team members interact frequently with one another, unlike the strangers on the bus who often sit silently and don't talk to each other. The team members depend on one another, whereas the bus passengers do not. The team members work together toward common goals, again unlike the bus riders. The team members have common beliefs values, and practices, such as about the importance of football, and they are similar in other respects such as athleticism and gender, whereas the bus riders share only their faith that the bus will take them closer to their different destinations. The team members share emotionally powerful experiences, such as in winning or losing big games, whereas the bus riders do not.

In fact, if something emotionally powerful were to happen to the bus, such as being hijacked or having an accident, the riders might start to act and feel more like a group. One famous example was the United Airlines flight 93 that was hijacked by terrorists on that fateful September day in 2001. Several passengers and crew made telephone calls aboard the flight, learned about the terrorist attacks on the World Trade Center and the Pentagon, and made a joint effort to regain control of the plane. The plane crashed in a field near Shanksville, Pennsylvania, about 150 miles (240 km) northwest of Washington, D.C., killing all on board including 40 passengers and crew and 4 hijackers. An analysis of the flight recorders revealed that passengers and crew prevented the aircraft from reaching the hijackers' intended target, thought to be either the White House or U.S. Capitol.

group a collection of at least two people who are doing or being something together

Conflict between groups helps solidify feelings of belonging to a group.

The Social Side of Sex

Is a Marriage a Group?

The questions about what constitute a group have gone beyond technical debates among social science researchers. All known societies have some form of marriage, but they disagree about what kind of group can marry. In the modern world, most marriages are dyads: two people, a man and a woman. But other groups can be married too, such as same-sex dyads. Gay marriage has been legal in many countries for years, beginning with the Netherlands in 2001, and spreading across the world over the years we have published this textbook. In the past, most societies have included polygamy, a form of marriage in which one husband would have several wives. Today many Islamic countries, such as Saudi Arabia, permit a man to have up to four wives. Marriage systems in which one wife has multiple husbands are rare but not entirely unknown (especially in societies with shortages of women).

Should marriage be a dyad? Monogamy is often described as a benefit to women, and most women say they prefer it rather than polygamy, but it is not clear that this is rational. All else being equal, polygamy would seem to favor heterosexual women by offering more choices. It creates a surplus of single men, because a few men take up many wives, leaving far more single men than women. Even a woman who wants a monogamous marriage may be better off in a polygamous society, because polygamy creates a large selection of available men. Plus, of course, women have more options under polygamy: Some women would prefer to be the second or third wife of a rich, handsome man, rather than the sole wife of a homely, dull, poor one. In contrast, monogamy clearly favors the majority of men, especially the less powerful ones, because it enables every man to have a potential wife. Most likely, monogamy replaced polygamy in step with social reforms that favored greater equality among men.

Marriage fits many aspects of the definition of a group. It has a common identity (often symbolized by taking identical last names). Spouses interact frequently. They depend on each other. They work toward common goals, such as raising a family. They are often quite similar in many respects ranging from political and religious beliefs to intelligence and physical attractiveness. Yet they are also often different in many ways. Division of labor is common in marriage: Traditionally, the wife took care of the home, made and repaired the clothes, tended the sick, and stored and cooked the food, while the man did the heavy farm work (or, later, earned most of the money), provided protection, and built or repaired the dwelling. Today, spousal roles continue to change and adapt, but most married couples still divide up their tasks in some ways. Groups share emotional experiences, and marital love and sex would certainly count as such.

Indeed, it is possible to regard any couple engaging in sex as a dyad, at least a temporary one: Sex partners work together toward a common goal, share an intense experience, are typically similar to each other, often feel an emotional connection, and so forth. To be sure, sex sometimes occurs in larger groups, which raises the question of why most sex is dyadic.

Group sex, whether it is a matter of three people in bed together or a larger group having a wild orgy, often attracts attention but is fairly rare in practice.[5] It seems reasonable to estimate that over 99% of sex acts (not counting masturbation) in the world today involve just two people. Quite possibly this simply reflects the difficulty of getting multiple people to consent; it is often difficult for just two people to reach the point of agreeing that they want to have sex, and so getting seven or eight people to decide to jump in bed together might be much more difficult!

Thus, one factor is whether the members of a group feel similar to each other. For this reason, more diverse groups may find it harder to come together as a group, compared to groups that start off being similar. Then again, diversity brings other benefits; to appreciate these, see *Tradeoffs* on diversity.

Most likely another factor is the presence of an outgroup, especially a rival or enemy. Sports teams are often cohesive groups, not simply because they wear uniforms of the same color, but because they frequently have to work together for the common good against a common opponent. A team that merely practiced, without ever playing against an opponent, would probably not feel so unified. It is quite possible that the deeply rooted human impulse to form social groups was partly stimulated by competition among groups. Indeed, a recent major survey of all kinds of societies, from tiny bugs to humans to elephants, concluded that there is almost always an outgroup for every ingroup.[6] It is quite rare to have "us" without "them."

If a lone person wanted something—the fruit on a particular tree, for example—and a group also wanted it, the group would almost always win. Over evolutionary history, loners would therefore be losers, whereas the people who passed on their genes toward future generations would be the ones who formed groups.[7]

What, then, do groups accomplish? Answers to this can be found at both the social and cultural level. Social animals tend to live in groups, because groups provide several clear benefits. They promote safety, they find and share food, and they can do tasks that no one individual can do alone.

Diversity in Groups

TRADE Offs

The novelist Jerzy Kosinski filled his novels with vivid, moving stories from his personal life, which included many hardships. Kosinski himself eventually committed suicide. The title of his novel *The Painted Bird* refers to a story in which a character would capture a black bird and then, holding the blindfolded bird in one hand, dab it with different colors of paint until the bird was a collage of all colors of the rainbow. When no black feathers remained visible, he would remove the hood and release the frightened animal. The bird would quickly soar up into the sky, a beautiful spectacle of flying colors. Soon another black bird would come by and strike at it, however, and then another and another, until the painted bird disappeared in a mass of black birds that tore it to pieces.

The story captures a sad truth of nature: Often animals that look different from the others are targeted for rejection and outright violence. Animals do not seem to value diversity in their groups. They are not even content with excluding those who are different, but often actively destroy them.

American society has committed itself to promoting diversity, and there is much talk everywhere about how groups and institutions (work groups, universities, sports teams, and the like) will perform better if they are diverse. But is diversity always better? Is it safe for Americans to assume that they will always be able to outperform other, less diverse societies, such as the Chinese and Japanese? Diversity has both costs and benefits. Homogeneous (that is, not diverse) groups may have some advantages, too, along with their drawbacks. Many advocates of diversity oppose women's colleges or African American schools (because they exclude male or nonblack students), but such institutions have provided good educations for many students, and a cautious scientist would not insist that more diverse school populations always produce better results. (Of course, some people might oppose same-sex colleges on moral grounds even if they do provide a first-rate education.)

Research by social psychologists suggests that diversity involves tradeoffs.[8] On the plus side, diverse groups can be more flexible and creative than groups marked by greater similarity among the members. Greater diversity can bring together more perspectives and possibly more information. Groups can be smarter than the smartest individuals, but only if different people contribute different information to the mix.[9] Diverse groups, by definition, have a better chance of bringing together different information than similar groups.

One sign of benefits of diversity came in a study of Wikipedia entries. The ones edited by a politically diverse of editors scored higher in overall quality than ones where the editors agreed.[10] To be sure, this supports political diversity (e.g., getting input from both Democrats and Republicans), rather than ethnic diversity that is usually emphasized by the proponents of diversity. When editors all share the same political view, the product they produce has lower quality than when they are far apart and disagree about politics. The effect was strongest for articles on politics, but it was also found on articles about social issues and even to some extent on articles about science.

Recent research has confirmed that a group's collective wisdom can exceed the sum of its individual members, but only if the individual members have diverse and different views.[11] In fact, a group of diverse individuals can make better decisions than a group of similar individuals who are much smarter. The reason is that the errors of diverse people tend to cancel each other out, so when you average them you get the best answer. In contrast, similar individuals tend to make the same types of errors, so when you average them you really don't gain much.

On the minus side, diversity can make it harder for people to cooperate and work together. The different backgrounds can result in poor communication and misunderstandings. Often diverse groups perform less well than other groups. The difficulty in getting very different people to work together can result in frustration, resentment, low morale, and even feelings of alienation from (or reduced commitment to) the group.[12]

One way to resolve the conflict is to take into account different kinds of diversity. The benefits of diversity come from having people with different knowledge and skills, so they can complement each other. In contrast, groups benefit much less from other kinds of diversity, such as getting people with different ethnicities, nationalities, backgrounds, and the like.[13] The misunderstandings, distrust, and other communicative problems arise more readily given that sort of diversity.

This tradeoff helps explain one seeming paradox that will be seen throughout this chapter. Groups perform best if people are individually identified and perform their separate, distinct roles. Yet groups have all sorts of pressures that push everyone to be and become the same. Why are such widespread conformity pressures observed in so many groups, if diversity is superior? The tentative answer for now is that diversity can produce benefits, but it has costs as well. Indeed, the advantages of diversity in groups may be limited to cultural animals because they involve sharing information and role differentiation.

Human groups are not just social but also cultural, and culture greatly increases what groups can do.[14] Cultural groups preserve information in the group and pass it along to future generations, greatly increasing the benefit of being able to absorb and communicate information. Cultural groups also benefit from role differentiation. Everyone specializes at something, in effect becoming an expert at his or her role, and the result is that all of the jobs are performed by experts.

Ford's assembly line exemplifies these advantages of groups. Knowledge about how to make cars was accumulated and preserved by the group, so it gradually improved. The first assembly line had the workers, rather than the cars, move along the line. The second, improved version had the cars move down the line, pulled along by ropes. The third version had a motorized conveyor belt move the cars along. Furthermore, the company used information and reasoning to reorganize itself to make the assembly system better. And the essence of the assembly line is division of labor. Instead of having two or three men make the entire car, the new system used many workers, each of whom specialized in a few simple tasks. The result was impressive improvements in the ability to make more cars better, faster, and cheaper.

QUIZ YOURSELF
What Groups Are and Do

1. Which of the following is NOT a group?
   - (a) Three children; playing hide-and-go-seek
   - (b) Three neighbors; having a barbecue
   - (c) Three strangers; quietly waiting for a bus
   - (d) Three students; working together on a class project

2. In one high school class, the teacher lets students select their own groups to work on an important class project. As expected, similar students group themselves together. In another class, the teacher randomly divides students into groups, so dissimilar students are often grouped together. Which is likely to be the main advantage of the dissimilar groups over the homogeneous (similar) ones?
   - (a) The dissimilar (heterogeneous) groups will be more cooperative.
   - (b) The dissimilar groups will be more efficient.
   - (c) The dissimilar groups will generate a greater variety of information.
   - (d) The dissimilar groups will have higher morale.

3. Which of the following greatly increased the production of automobiles in Henry Ford's plants?
   - (a) The added health benefits workers received
   - (b) The assembly line
   - (c) The higher pay workers received
   - (d) The longer work week

4. Which of the following is an advantage of a group?
   - (a) Groups can provide safety in numbers.
   - (b) Groups can help each other find food.
   - (c) Groups can make difficult tasks easier to perform.
   - (d) All of the above

answers: see pg 529

Groups, Roles, and Selves

A vital feature of human groups is that many of them are made up of distinct, well-defined, individual roles. Each person has a different job to do, and each person can specialize and become an expert at that job. The different jobs complement each other, so the joint effort improves total performance. The assembly line thus reveals a crucial advantage that cultural groups have over merely social groups, such as wolves or bees. Complementary roles produce better results than simply having everyone chip in and do the same thing.

The advantages of specialized roles were recognized long before Henry Ford invented the assembly line. In medieval farming villages, for example, it was probably good to have a blacksmith. But if everyone tried to be a blacksmith, the village would starve. The same goes for musicians, artists, and priests. When human groups advanced to the point that they did not need every person to be producing as much food as possible all the time, they became able to support musicians, artists, and priests. But if everyone in a tribe or village wanted to be a musician, the group would be unable to survive. Today, the same goes for teachers, police officers, physicians, plumbers, fortune-tellers, prostitutes, computer repair technicians, comedians, airline flight attendants, and barbers. Human roles only work in the context of a large system when most other people do something else.

Identifying individual people with their unique roles within the group is an important key to the success of human groups. In this chapter, we will see repeatedly that groups do better when people are individually identified and perform their unique roles. In contrast, when people blend together into a group and lose their unique place, such as by submerging their identities into the group, the groups perform less well and sometimes produce downright ugly results.

Social psychologists coined the term **deindividuation** to refer to loss of self-awareness and of individual accountability in a group. The term, from the same root as "individual," implies a loss of individuality. Deindividuated participants in lab studies often behaved badly, such as stealing, aggressing, or doing other antisocial things.[15,16] We shall see repeatedly in this chapter that group processes can produce costly and destructive results when people submerge their individual identities in the group. As Stanislaus Lezczynski, King of Poland, observed: "No snowflake in an avalanche ever feels responsible."

Although this conclusion has emerged in a halting way from laboratory findings, it was also spectacularly confirmed by some of the major historical movements of the 20th century. For example, the essence of fascist movements was that the individual should be submerged in the group, and the individual's self-interest should be subordinated to the best interests of the group. The most successful fascists (at least for a while) were the German Nazis, who did achieve some impressive successes in rebuilding a shattered, starving nation and fighting a war against the combined great powers of the world, but whose inner dynamics degenerated into a level of shocking cruelty and evil that went beyond what had been seen in other places—and that ultimately resulted in the sweeping destruction of their own country. Germany's experiment with deindividuation was thus a disaster for all concerned.

Before closing this section, it is important to appreciate a few other important points about role differentiation. First, in a culture, the roles are defined by the system; they exist independently of the individual. The United States has one president, 100 senators,

deindividuation the loss of self-awareness and of individual accountability in a group

Movements such as National Socialism (Nazism) submerge individual identity into the group. The results have often been destructive, for themselves and others.

and nine Supreme Court justices. A select few individuals occupy those roles today, but after all those people are dead and gone, those roles will still exist and be occupied by other individuals. The system creates the role, and different human beings occupy it, each one coming and going. When you get a job, it will most likely be a position that someone else had before you and someone else will have after you.

The split between people and roles means that people must have selves that are flexible enough to adopt (and occasionally drop) roles. Ants, for example, benefit from a social system that has several different roles, but each ant is programmed by nature for only one role, and ants do not change jobs very often. In human society, new roles become available all the time. Individual humans often have careers that involve a series of different jobs and different roles.

Belonging to a human cultural group thus involves two separate demands. One is to find common values and other sources of similarity that can cement one's allegiance to the group. The other is to find some special or even unique role within the group.

Most individuals have multiple roles.

QUIZ YOURSELF

Groups, Roles, and Selves

1. When normally shy Devan is at a hockey game, he often gets swept away in the excitement. He is no longer self-conscious and, as a result, often does and says things that he later regrets. Hockey games seem to create in Devan a state of _____ .
   - (a) catharsis
   - (b) deindividuation
   - (c) excitation transfer
   - (d) pluralistic ignorance

2. Circumstances that increase _____ will decrease _____ .
   - (a) anonymity; empathy
   - (b) anonymity; diffusion of responsibility
   - (c) self-awareness; deindividuation
   - (d) self-awareness; empathy

3. What type of movement suggests that self-interest should be subordinated to the best interests of the group?
   - (a) Fascism
   - (b) Anarchy
   - (c) Capitalism
   - (d) Democracy

4. What is the most distinctive feature of human groups over nonhuman groups?
   - (a) Distinct well-defined, individual roles
   - (b) Collective roles that many individuals fill
   - (c) The existence of group leaders
   - (d) The existence of subordinates within the group

answers: see pg 529

Group Action

Many people do many things in groups. The effect of working in a group (as compared to working alone) is variable: Sometimes the group produces improvement; other times, disaster. Social psychologists have spent years mapping out these effects.

One theme we have already suggested is that the effects of groups are often negative when people are submerged in the group. In contrast, when people retain their individual identities and feel personally accountable for their actions, many of the bad effects of groups are prevented or reduced, and the positive effects of groups are more common. Identifying people and holding them accountable for their actions produces better outcomes. To be sure, accountability is not a cure-all for the broad range of lapses, mistakes, and mental biases people show in groups. But when people believe they may have to justify their actions and decisions to other people, they tend to be more careful and thorough in their thinking, including using all the information available to them and thinking about how they would respond to possible criticisms.[17] People cooperate more with others when they are individually identified, whereas the anonymity of groups produces more greed, fear, and other dangerous reactions.[18]

Social Facilitation

Many experts regard Norman Triplett's (1897–1898) work as the first social psychology experiments (see Chapter 1). While watching bicycle races, he noticed that cyclists who raced alone against the clock generally were slower than those who raced against competitors. In an early experiment, he instructed children to wind fishing reels as fast as they could. Those who did this task alone were slower than those who did it when someone else was competing against them. Triplett thought that the presence of others stimulated a competitive instinct, causing people to work harder.

But further work showed that competition was not necessary. Some people performed better merely because observers, as opposed to competitors, were present.[19,20] This finding led to the tentative conclusion that **evaluation apprehension** (concern about how others are evaluating you) is the driving factor. People increase effort when others are present because they want the others to evaluate them favorably.

A bigger problem for the theory is that the presence of others doesn't always make people perform better. Have you ever given a speech or performance in front of a large audience? Many people find that unnerving and make mistakes.[21,22,23,24,25] If an audience always made you do better, people would never "choke under pressure."

These diverse, seemingly conflicting sets of observations were integrated into an exciting theory proposed by social psychologist Robert Zajonc. His theory was rooted in observations of animal learning.[26] Zajonc proposed that being in the presence of other people (or, for animals, other members of the same species) is arousing: It makes one breathe faster, makes the heart beat faster, sends adrenaline through the system, and so forth. One well-known effect of arousal (note this is not sexual arousal, but any sort of physical excitement) is to increase the **dominant response**, which is defined as the most common response in that situation. Thus, whatever you normally tend to do, you will do it even more when in the presence of others. The essence of Zajonc's **social facilitation theory** (see **FIGURE 14.1**) is that the presence of others increases the dominant response tendency.[27] For example, if you usually (though not always) choose hamburgers over hot dogs, then choosing hamburgers is your dominant response in that situation. When others are present, you will be especially likely to choose a hamburger.

Social facilitation theory can explain both the good and the bad effects of the presence of others—both the faster cycling times in the presence of competition and the mistakes the amateur pianist makes when playing for an audience. For familiar, easy, and well-learned behaviors, the dominant response is to perform well, and so performance improves when others are watching. For difficult, unfamiliar tasks, the dominant response is to perform less well, so mistakes become more common when others are watching.

The social facilitation theory has been confirmed by many studies.[28] In fact, one investigation even found it among cockroaches

evaluation apprehension concern about how others are judging you and/or your performance

dominant response the most common reaction to a given situation

social facilitation theory proposition that the presence of others increases the dominant response tendency

FIGURE 14.1
Robert Zajonc's theory of social facilitation: The presence of others increases arousal. Arousal increases whatever response is dominant. If the dominant response is correct, performance increases. If the dominant response is incorrect, performance decreases.

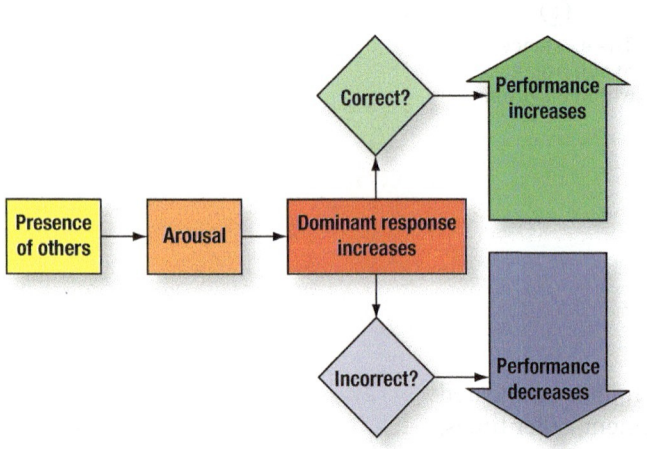

(see **FIGURE 14.2**).[29] Cockroaches probably do not suffer evaluation apprehension or other complex human motives, so this finding was best explained in the simple, basic terms of arousal increasing the dominant response.

Social facilitation theory has many applications to the real world. For example, many modern offices have more public shared space (such as large rooms where everyone is present) than private offices. Is this a good design decision? It depends. If the employees are working on simple or well-learned tasks, then this design works well because the presence of others should increase their performance. On the other hand, if the employees are working on complex or creative tasks, the design is bad because the presence of others is likely to decrease their performance. The Ford assembly line worked well in part because the tasks were simple, so the dominant response was to perform them correctly.

More recent work has concluded that social facilitation effects depend on three processes.[30] Bodily arousal confers more energy and increases the dominant response. Evaluation apprehension makes people strive to make a good impression (but also creates worries). And some degree of distraction occurs, insofar as people start paying attention to each other rather than the task. Evaluation apprehension and distraction both fit the "putting people first" orientation we have seen over and over in this textbook, because people care about what other people think of them.

The presence of others can also influence food consumption, as described in *Food for Thought*.

To be sure, evaluation apprehension does affect performance among humans, and it may intensify the effects of others' presence. A judgmental observer has a stronger effect than a blindfolded bystander.[31] The possibility of evaluation seems to inspire certain kinds of people to do their best. In particular, **narcissists** are individuals who regard themselves as better than others and are constantly trying to win the admiration of others. These glory hounds perform best when others are watching or when important rewards are riding on the outcome of their performance, whereas they tend to slack off when there is no opportunity to bring credit to themselves.[32] This pattern, however, can elicit resentment from other group members, who recognize that the narcissist is not a team player but rather is looking for individual honors.

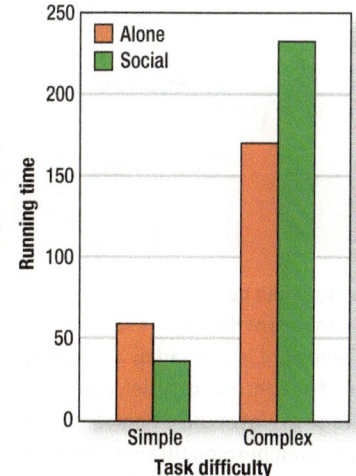

FIGURE 14.2

In a study, cockroaches completed simple mazes more quickly when they ran in the presence of four other cockroaches than when they ran alone. In contrast, cockroaches completed complex mazes more quickly when they ran alone than when they ran in the presence of four other cockroaches.[27]

Social Loafing

The preceding section showed that the presence of others can make people perform better, especially on easy and familiar tasks. But wait: Around the same time that Triplett was noticing that cyclists rode faster when other cyclists were present, a French engineer named Max Ringelmann was coming to a very different conclusion (see Chapter 1). Ringelmann observed farm workers and noticed that as new men were added, the total output didn't seem to increase as much as it should. He conducted experiments in which men pulled carts either alone or together. In theory, two men should pull twice as hard (200%) as one (and if social facilitation theory is at work here, two men should pull more than twice as hard!)—but in fact two men pulled only 186% as hard. When four men worked together, the drop in total effort was even bigger. In eight-man teams, each man was not even pulling half as hard as the lone men. Here was a clear example of a human group being less than the sum of its parts: Somehow the men didn't seem to work as hard in a team as they did when alone.[33] What went wrong?

Several factors reduce an individual's productivity when working in a group, such as difficulty coordinating efforts with others. But subsequent research confirmed a pattern that came to be known as **social loafing**. People reduce effort when working in a group, compared to when working alone.[34] In lab studies, for example, participants were assigned to make as much noise as possible by clapping and shouting. Recordings verified that they were louder (indicating greater effort) when working alone than in a group. Three people, each cheering alone, made about as much total noise as six people cheering together.

The pattern of social loafing has also been called the **free rider problem**.[35] This term is probably derived from trams, subways, and buses in Europe, which rely on the honor system for payment: People are supposed to buy a ticket and punch it or scan a debit card

narcissists individuals who regard themselves as better than others and are constantly trying to win the admiration of others

social loafing (free rider problem) the finding that people reduce effort when working in a group, compared to when working alone

Group Action | **505**

FOOD FOR *Thought*

Is Binge Eating Socially Contagious?

Binge eating has become a prominent problem in recent decades, especially among young women. It is defined by alternating periods of uncontrolled, lavish eating and of severe restraint marked sometimes by fasting or even purging through induced vomiting or taking laxatives. This pattern is notably unhealthy. Among other problems, frequent vomiting ruins one's teeth (because of stomach acid). It is associated with the clinical diagnosis of bulimia (based on Latin for "ox hunger"). These patterns were rarely noted or observed prior to the 1960s, but they have quickly become a serious problem. Recent estimates suggest that between 1 out of 20 and 1 out of 5 female college students engages in this behavior.

How could a pattern of problem behavior change so quickly from relatively unknown to widespread? Part of the answer lies in group processes. Research on college sororities found that binge-eating patterns seemed to be contagious, in the sense that they spread through the group.[36] Binge eating was most commonly noted when groups of young women, all about the same age, interacted regularly. Young women who joined sororities would adopt the behavior patterns of the group—sometimes including binge eating.

In fact, binge eating was associated with popularity in the sororities. There were two different patterns. In one, the more a young woman engaged in binge eating, the more popular she was. This suggests that women perceived binge eating as a pathway to social success. It also indicates that binge eating carried no social penalty. On the contrary, apparently the group rewarded binge eating, as the women who engaged in it most frequently were most highly regarded by the other group members.

The other pattern was only slightly less worrisome. One sorority apparently had norms for the optimal amount of binge eating. The most popular women were those who were closest to these norms. Thus, there was apparently at least some disapproval directed toward the most extreme binge eaters. Still, women who failed to engage in binge eating also paid a price in terms of lower popularity.

The second pattern, indicating social norms for binge eating, is consistent with the idea that women picked up the habit from their friends. Sure enough, the research on sororities found that a woman's tendency toward binge eating had typically become quite similar to that of her friends by the end of the academic year.[37] In other words, members of the group became more like their friends over time. Because the members of the sorority typically engaged in binge eating, new members adopted this pattern as they made friends.

Having a friend who binge eats increases the likelihood that you will binge eat.

---

when they climb on board. The money from these tickets pays for the transportation system. But some people simply get on and ride without paying. They thus take free rides, letting others provide the money that keeps the system going.

Free riders presumably know they are cheating the system and taking advantage of others. In lab studies, most social loafers say they are working as hard as they can, even though the experimental results prove that they aren't. Apparently, many people are not aware that they are socially loafing, or at least they are reluctant to admit it.[38]

Why does social loafing occur? One important factor is the feeling of being submerged in the group, and therefore not being individually accountable. When the contributions of individual group members are identified, so that everyone (or at least the leader) knows who did what, social loafing is greatly reduced.[39,40] People are less likely to steal free rides on the subway if they will be identified than if they think they can do it anonymously. Likewise, people work harder for their team or group if they believe that others will know if they slack off.[41] Ford's assembly line may have benefited from the fact that each person performed a different job, so it would be possible to identify a lazy employee who did poor work.

The importance of individual identification exemplifies the theme we have already noted: Groups produce more negative effects when individual identities are submerged in the group. During the 1980s and 1990s, "accountability" became a major buzzword in American businesses. Accountability meant that each person was held individually responsible for his or her decisions and job performance. The drive for accountability was fueled in part by the growing recognition that a lack of individual accountability contributes to social loafing.

The difference between feeling individually accountable and submerged in the group probably holds the key to the apparent contradiction between Ringelmann and Triplett. Remember, Triplett found that people performed better when others were present, but Ringelmann found the opposite. In Triplett's studies, performers were individually identified; in fact, they were often competing against one another. In Ringelmann's observations, the men were yoked together pulling carts, and no one could know how hard any individual man pulled. Competition and accountability lead to greater effort, but submersion in the group leads to social loafing.

A related cause of social loafing is the desire not to be a sucker.[42] Once members of a group begin to suspect that others are loafing, they loaf too, because they do not want to do all the work on behalf of others. If you and a friend had to paint the garage, and your friend spent most of the time texting and taking calls on her cell phone while you did most of the painting, you might well feel that you had been foolish to do more than your fair share of the work, especially if credit (and pay) was shared equally between the two of you. This pattern has also been called the **bad apple effect**,[43,44,45] based on the folk observation that one bad apple can spoil all the other apples. One loafer can thus cause other workers to loaf as well.

Again, individual identification helps overcome the tendency to loaf. People are less prone to copy a social loafer if they believe they will get credit or blame for their own work. When people believe their own contribution to the group is unique, especially if it is also important and meaningful, they are less likely to loaf.[46]

How is social loafing to be reconciled with social facilitation? The pattern of social facilitation is deeply rooted in nature and indeed is found in other species. Nature, apparently, has prepared people to become excited when others are around, and this can make for better performance. Social loafing and especially the bad apple effect appear to be much more distinctively human, insofar as people must often force themselves to do work that they dislike. Only humans worry about being a sucker, and perhaps only humans can reason through to the conclusion that they might as well enjoy the same benefit as others for half the effort, if they can get away with it.

Although it looks like these people are pulling the rope as hard as they can, research shows that they would pull harder if they were pulling alone.

Punishing Cheaters and Free Riders

Social psychologists have been using game-based methods to study people's motives for several decades, and recently economists have begun to adopt similar research methods. One influential finding is that when participants recognize that other players are showing signs of social loafing or free riding, they will punish them—even if it costs the participant money to punish the free rider.[47]

This finding was shocking to many economists. Certainly free riders can gradually undermine the system for everyone, but economists generally assume that rational human beings will maximize their own personal payoffs. Why would they give up some of their own money to punish a free rider, rather than just doing the best they can for themselves and leaving the free rider problem to others? Economists even came up with a name for this—**altruistic punishment**.[48] It is altruistic in the sense that the individual sacrifices his or her own gain for the betterment of all, by punishing people who cheat the system. This

bad apple effect the idea that one social loafer can cause other people to loaf as well

altruistic punishment the finding that people will sometimes sacrifice their own gain for the betterment of all, by punishing people who cheat the system

May I please see some ID?

might be compared to a bystander who risks injury in order to stop a crime, such as by attacking the criminal.

The irrationality of altruistic punishment suggests that it may involve something very deeply rooted in the psyche, which fits the theme of this book that natural selection has favored humans who are able to participate in a cultural society. One trait that would fit that description very well would be a deeply rooted impulse to punish people who cheat or beat the system. Culture depends on a system, and those who cheat the system can ruin it for everyone. Altruistic punishers may suffer in the short run, but in the long run they are likely to benefit. A group of people who are all willing to punish cheaters and free riders will have a safer, fairer system—and hence may survive and reproduce better—than a group of people who don't guard their culture against cheating and free riding.

Deindividuation and Mob Violence

Earlier in this chapter, we introduced another form of being submerged in the group: deindividuation. The term signifies a loss of individuality, and research now defines it as a loss of individual accountability and reduction of self-awareness, mainly due to the presence of others.[49,50,51] Social psychologists quickly reached the (preliminary) conclusion that deindividuation makes people more willing to act on their own impulses, which can increase antisocial behavior (see Chapter 10). We have seen that in many situations nature says go, whereas culture says stop. Apparently, one way that culture says "stop" is by holding people individually accountable for their actions, and when people become anonymous and not identifiable, they are less likely to heed the culture's pleas to stop. It is in a sense ironic that merging into the group can make people behave less in accordance with cultural values, because cultural values are group values. Thus, as people merge into the group, they sometimes feel freer to go against the group's values. Loss of individual accountability enables people to take advantage of the group for personal gain.

One review of all the published studies on deindividuation found that the effects of deindividuation are somewhat erratic, which calls into question any general conclusion such as "deindividuated people are more violent."[52] The review found that whether or not members of the group were anonymous to one another didn't seem to matter much, but being anonymous to outsiders did make people more willing to violate norms, such as by stealing and cheating. Likewise, what mattered in terms of self-awareness was whether people were attuned to how other people regarded them, not whether they were privately thinking about themselves. Thus, deindividuation makes people more willing to behave badly insofar as they cease worrying about what others think of them. Meanwhile, accountability emerged as the single biggest factor in predicting aggression. As we have said, people behave most in line with general social norms when they feel individually accountable for their acts. When not accountable, they will go along with what others are doing at the moment, even when these situational norms go against what is generally considered morally good. This is probably how looting happens during a riot: Most people believe stealing is wrong, but when one is submerged in the group and other members of the group are stealing, the individual goes along with the here-and-now group and steals, too.

Shared Resources and the Commons Dilemma

Land, food, money, tools, jewels, and other resources can be held in two ways. One is private property, in which a single person owns the resource. The other is to have resources shared by the group, so that people take what they need and leave the rest to others. The march of human history has seen a dramatic shift in ownership patterns. The earliest humans seem to have had relatively few possessions, and much of what they had was shared communally by the family, tribe, or other group. Modern Western civilizations, in contrast, have adopted private ownership of most goods, though communal ownership is still sometimes seen within families (e.g., any member of the family is permitted to take and eat food from the family refrigerator).

Private ownership has severe social costs. One is inequality. About 1% of the world population is estimated to hold 40% of world wealth.[53] Income disparity has been a regular cause for social protest movements, in the U.S. and elsewhere. Another possible inequality can occur when ambitious and greedy private owners take advantage of others to increase their share. Religious orders in many parts of the world have insisted that clergy and other people who devote their lives to spiritual striving renounce worldly possessions, sometimes taking a vow of poverty. In a very different manner, some social movements such as socialism and communism have advocated reducing or abolishing private property so that people will share ownership of valuable resources and not seek to exploit one another.

The Occupy movement was a protest against the wealthiest 1% (e.g., banks) by the other 99%.

Yet joint, communal ownership has costs too (thus indicating another tradeoff!). Resources that are not owned by anyone do not receive the preserving care that they get from individual owners. Communism became notorious for pollution and waste because individuals had no incentive to take care of the publicly owned resources. On a smaller scale, you might notice that your friends who live in dorm rooms or rental properties do not take care of these dwellings as carefully as they do their rooms at home or as carefully as people who own their own home.

Social psychologists became interested in the problems of communal resources under the name of the **commons dilemma**—the tendency for shared or jointly owned resources to be squandered and not used in an optimal or advantageous fashion. The term comes from the "tragedy of the commons," a pattern in which common grazing areas would get overused and become useless.[54] A more contemporary version is the worldwide dwindling of fish stocks. Because the fish in the sea belong to no one until they are caught, fishing boats just catch as many as they can, and eventually too few fish are left to reproduce and replenish the fish population.

Two kinds of conflict occur in the commons dilemma, both of which have been seen repeatedly in this book. The first is social conscience versus selfish impulse: People take things for themselves even when it hurts the group as a whole. The second involves time (again, the tradeoff of "now versus later"). To manage a resource for the long run, it is best to restrain oneself in the present. People could actually benefit their own selfish goals best if they would all simply go slowly, allowing the resource to replenish itself fully. But that is not what people do. They take most of the resource now, leaving little for later.

Communication helps. When people can communicate and urge each other to show restraint, they do not use up the resource as fast.[55] Unfortunately, they still tend to take too much, so the resource is still badly managed and ends up being depleted prematurely.

Another factor is the behavior of others. When people observe that others are greedily taking more for themselves rather than showing restraint in order to benefit everyone over the long term, they tend to copy this behavior. Earlier in this chapter we saw that the tendency to follow bad behavior is called the bad apple effect. When people observe others behaving well, they also tend to behave more favorably, but people copy bad behavior more quickly and readily than they copy good behavior.

commons dilemma the tendency for shared or jointly owned resources to be squandered and not used in an optimal or advantageous fashion

QUIZ YOURSELF
Group Action

1. The presence of others helps individual performance on _____ tasks and hurts individual performance on _____ tasks.
   - (a) boring; interesting
   - (b) interesting; boring
   - (c) easy; difficult
   - (d) difficult; easy

2. Professor Walleye Bass finds that having other faculty members observe his class improves his lectures. This improvement is the result of _____ .
   - (a) evaluation apprehension
   - (b) mere presence
   - (c) social loafing
   - (d) None of the above

3. Easy identification of the contributions of group members _____ .
   - (a) decreases group efficiency
   - (b) decreases evaluation apprehension
   - (c) decreases social facilitation
   - (d) decreases social loafing

4. Snap, Crackle, and Pop have a group project in their nutrition class. They write a paper on breakfast nutrition. Snap and Crackle do all the work, whereas Pop does little or no work. Because grades are assigned to groups of students, Snap, Crackle, and Pop all get "A"s. Pop's "A" grade illustrates _____ .
   - (a) a free ride
   - (b) downward social comparison
   - (c) the bad apple effect
   - (d) upward social comparison

answers: see pg 529

How Groups Think

Groups should seemingly be smarter than individuals. Folk wisdom says that two heads are better than one, so 10 heads ought to be better yet. The general principle is that groups are smarter than individuals. But are they? The following sections will reveal a mixture of answers.

Before we are too critical of groups, however, it is important to remember the theme that humans evolved to belong to cultural groups—groups that share and preserve information. It is normal and natural for people to share information and to look to others for information. Moreover, if information is to be shared through a group, members of human groups will have the natural tendency to think alike. Social psychologists have been good at finding absurd or destructive excesses of this tendency, such as when everyone in a group clings to a false belief. But these excesses are probably linked to basic tendencies that are neither absurd nor destructive. Groups do far more good than harm.

Brainstorming, and the Wisdom of Groups

Although fields such as advertising often borrow ideas from psychology, sometimes the advertising people get there first. Brainstorming is an idea that was developed by advertising executives in the 1950s to increase the creativity of their groups, and only after it had made its mark in ad groups did psychologists begin to conduct research on it. **Brainstorming** is a form of creative thinking in groups, using a procedure in which all group members are encouraged to generate as many ideas as possible without holding back or worrying about being wrong. They are also encouraged to build on each other's ideas. The core assumption is that creative people can feed off each other's thinking

brainstorming a form of creative thinking in groups, using a procedure in which all group members are encouraged to generate as many ideas as possible while interacting and stimulating each other processes and creative energy, thereby coming up with more and better ideas than could the same number of people working alone.

The benefits of brainstorming have been gradually confirmed by careful research. Compared against the same number of people working alone, people working together in a brainstorming group session enjoy the process of generating ideas more than people who toil alone. When they finish the work, they evaluate it more favorably, rating it as more creative and successful. People who work alone but hear about brainstorming groups also immediately recognize the advantages of brainstorming and express the belief that they would do better if they were in a brainstorming group.[56,57]

But that's all. If you read the preceding paragraph carefully, you probably noticed that it didn't say that the brainstorming groups actually performed better—only that they thought they were better, and they had more fun. When researchers actually check the quality and quantity of ideas, the performance of brainstorming groups is quite disappointing. A meta-analysis that combined the results of 18 separate studies concluded that the output of brainstorming groups is substantially lower than that of people working separately.[58] Eight people working individually produce more ideas than eight people brainstorming. Nor does brainstorming increase quality by sacrificing quantity; the quality of work coming out of the brainstorming groups is lower, too. In short, brainstorming doesn't improve creative output—it reduces it.

The brainstorming research was disappointing but not surprising. There is a long tradition of groups being regarded as having negative traits: immoral, dangerous, stupid, impulsive, violent, and even beastly.[59] The French writer Gustave le Bon[60] wrote in 1895 that when people come together in a group, they lose their ability to think as reasonable human beings and instead become dominated by the "group mind," which effectively moves them to a lower, more animalistic level of evolution.

Francis Galton (1822–1911), the pioneering scientist who stimulated much research in psychology, thought that most people were not very intelligent, and groups of people even less so. One day he attended a fair where there was a contest to guess the weight of a steer. The very large animal was there to be viewed, but the contest was made more difficult by the rule that the guess had to be how much the creature would weigh after being slaughtered and prepared for sale. People paid a small amount for a ticket, on which they would write their guesses, and the most accurate guess would win a prize. Some contestants were cattle farmers or butchers who might have had some knowledge of meat weights, but most others knew little about it and couldn't offer much more than a guess based on whim or a lucky number. After the contest, Galton obtained the 800 tickets and did some statistics on the guesses, hoping to provide more data on the foolishness and stupidity of the herd of common people.[61]

The correct answer was 1,198 pounds (543.4 kg). When Galton compiled the 800 guesses, thinking they would be way off, he found their average to be 1,197. He was stunned. How could all those unintelligent, uninformed people produce an almost perfect answer?

This anecdote was used by James Surowiecki to open his book *The Wisdom of Crowds*.[62] Surowiecki's work is an important counterweight to the long tradition of research indicating that groups produce stupid judgments. He has compiled an impressive list of patterns in which the collective wisdom turns out to be smarter than even the experts. For example, no expert on sports is consistently able to predict the outcome of sports events better than the final betting line, which is directly based on the bets of many individuals, even though those bets are distorted by wishful thinking, whims, guesses, and favorite colors. Likewise, almost no stockbroker can consistently pick winning stocks better than the market as a whole.

One of the most dramatic, if less scientific, illustrations of the power of collective wisdom comes from the television show *Who Wants to Be a Millionaire?* In this game show,

"O.K., we've set up the manufacturing facitlities, organized the distribution network, hired the marketing expertise, and allocated the advertising budget. Any ideas for a product?"

People enjoy brainstorming and think it works, but it does not.

In the television game show *Who Wants to Be a Millionaire?* people who are stumped get more questions correct when they poll the studio audience (91%) than when they ask an expert (65%). Surely they aren't smarter than a favorite expert!

contestants could win large sums of money by giving only correct answers to a series of multiple-choice question, each with four possible answers. When stumped, the contestant could either call an expert (selected in advance, usually the smartest or most knowledgeable person the contestant knows) or poll the studio audience. Surowiecki went through the statistics on how these "lifelines" worked out. Calling an expert was pretty good, producing the correct answer about two-thirds (65%) of the time. But polling the studio audience yielded the right answer 91% of the time! Thus, a crowd of random people sitting in a television studio was more likely to get the right answer than a carefully chosen expert.

It is remarkable to think that large groups of people are smarter than the smartest individuals, but under the right circumstances they are. "It's as if we've been programmed to be collectively smart," said Surowiecki[63]—a conclusion that resonates with our view of humans as cultural animals who learn about the world by sharing information. People assume that getting lots of independent opinions from average people simply multiplies mediocrity. But in fact it makes for collective wisdom. You'd need a super-expert, or possibly a very advanced technical problem (rocket scientists really do know a few crucial things!), before an expert would perform better than a crowd.

But the conditions that enable crowds to achieve this high level of intelligent functioning are often violated, as we will see below in connection with groupthink and other group processes. These conditions include diversity of opinion and independence. That is, each person must be able to think for himself or herself, and each person must be able to get some information from his or her own perspective. If everyone is forced or pressured to think the same thing, or if their main information is seeing what everyone else does, watch out—group wisdom may degenerate into group stupidity. On the other hand, the wisdom of crowds works well when individuals disagree, hold diverse opinions, and even have plenty of (various) biases.[64]

Recent findings have shown how fragile the "wisdom of crowds" effect is. If people are merely aware of what others are thinking, they start to conform, and the group as a whole becomes less accurate. Ironically, people become more confident as their answers converge with those of others, so the group as a whole feels surer of being accurate but is actually less accurate![65]

Many people working independently, all getting their own bits of information, often produce a surprisingly accurate average. If someone can pull together that information, the group can be wise. But when groups fall into the trap of following each other or conforming to dominant views, their power is lost. These conclusions fit this book's theme of regarding humans as cultural animals. In order to perform effectively, people must operate as separate, independent members of a group, pooling and sharing their diverse information. Only then do people become "collectively smart," in Surowiecki's words.

You may notice a seeming contradiction. Groups can be smarter than individuals, yet brainstorming groups don't perform as well as independent individuals. But brainstorming groups don't meet Surowiecki's criteria for success. Group members don't work independently and contribute their separate ideas—rather, they interact, which raises the likelihood that some will feel left out, will defer to the opinions of others, will be too shy to criticize the group, or in other ways will be held back from contributing what they can.

Why Do People Love Teams?

We have seen that groups often do not perform as well as a number of individuals working alone (though groups do usually outperform a single person). Why do people love the idea of working in groups? Why do American companies want everyone to be a "team player"? Why do they form teams?

The section on brainstorming suggested a partial answer. It noted that people believe teams will outperform the same number of people working individually (even though that belief often turns out to be wrong). Maybe people are just stuck in a mistaken view of reality and make their decisions based on that mistake.

A more complex and reasonable answer was furnished by research.[66] A large body of research finds a consistent pattern. Many people, including business managers, believe that teams are highly effective for improving performance, but in reality the majority of teams don't live up to their reputation (either in the lab or in real business organizations). If performance were the only measure, then most corporations and other organizations should forget about teamwork and cultivate individual excellence. But performance is not the only measure, and working in teams has many side benefits. People enjoy working with others rather than alone. Working in teams satisfies their need to belong. It enables them to feel confident, effective, and superior (if only because many members of teams think they are the star, or at least a crucial team member who deserves a large share of the credit for any success the team has). The enjoyment and other psychological benefits of teams may explain why people are so eager to form and join them, even if they really do not improve performance most of the time.

Transactive Memory: Here, You Remember This

As we have seen, groups are most likely to be "collectively smart" if members' minds work independently. The best strategy may be for members to specialize as to who remembers what. In a world of information overload, there is simply too much for any one person to remember. Hence, the solution: Different people should focus on different things. Remember Ford's assembly line: Instead of hiring mechanics who know how to build an entire car, he could hire people with little knowledge and just train them on a specific skill.

The idea that information is dispersed through the group runs directly contrary to the old "group mind" theories, according to which thinking in groups is mainly a matter of having everyone think the same thing. Noting this contradiction, some psychologists coined the term **transactive memory** to refer to a process by which members of a small group remember different kinds of information.[67,68] For example, when the electricity goes out and you need a candle, it helps if you can remember where the candles are. But it is almost as good if you know that your roommate remembers where they are. You don't have to remember everything yourself.

Groups are most effective when group members know about what they know and can shift responsibility for remembering to the best-suited individuals.[69] For example, a romantic couple moving in together might start off by having the woman do the cooking because that fits traditional roles and assumptions, but as they get to know each other, they might realize that the man is more interested in food and has a better memory for recipes, so they could reallocate the role to him. In lab studies, intimate couples who worked face to face performed the best on group memory tasks.[70] They did better than pairs of strangers and better than couples who were not face to face. The crucial difference was that by looking at each other, they could tell which of them knew the answer best.

Transactive memory begins at the learning stage, not just at the remembering stage. Groups perform better when they are trained together, in part because they can help slot people into particular roles for learning different things. That is, the group can speed its learning by figuring out who is good at what parts of the task. As a result, each person can concentrate on learning his or her specialty, rather than everyone trying to learn everything.[71,72]

Groupthink

The term **groupthink** was borrowed from novelist George Orwell, who used it in his novel about totalitarianism called *1984*. The term refers to the tendency of group members to think alike.[73,74] Social psychologists use it specifically to mean a style of thought in which

transactive memory a process by which members of a small group remember different kinds of information

groupthink the tendency of group members to think alike, which often leads to bad decisions the group clings to a shared but flawed or mistaken view of the world rather than being open to learning the truth. In decision making, groupthink means that the group sticks to its preferred course of action, refusing to consider alternatives fairly and refusing to recognize the dangers or flaws in its plan.

The roots of groupthink probably lie in the desire to get along. Members of a group do not want to spend all their time arguing, nor do they want the other members to dislike them. They most enjoy being together and working together when they all agree. In principle, a group will have the most information if people bring diverse viewpoints and air conflicting opinions (as noted in the preceding section), but such discussions can be difficult and unpleasant. Hence, people become reluctant to criticize the group, attack its basic beliefs, or question each other. This creates the illusion that everyone is in agreement.

Several aspects of a situation make groupthink more likely. First, the group tends to be fairly similar and cohesive to start with (and then becomes more so as a result of groupthink). That is, the members of the group share many views and ideas in common, and they tend to get along well with each other. Second, a strong, directive leader makes groupthink more likely. Third, the group may be isolated in some sense from others, so that it is not exposed to disturbing facts or contrary views. Fourth, the group may have high self-esteem, regarding itself as a superior, elite collection of people who do not need to worry about what outsiders think or want.

Social psychologists have identified several important signs that indicate when groupthink is occurring. First, there is pressure toward conformity. Groupthink originates in people's desire to get along and, toward that end, to hold the same views and opinions.

A second sign is an appearance of unanimous agreement. Because dissent is suppressed, people get the impression that everyone in the group agrees with the group's plans or views. In group meetings, members mainly express support and agreement. The illusion of consensus is sometimes furthered by **self-censorship** which means that individuals decide not to express their doubts or bring up information that goes against the group's plans and views. Thus, many individual members of the group may have doubts or know things that spell trouble for the group, but everyone thinks that no one else does, so each person decides not to rock the boat. This creates a vicious circle: Because no one is willing to express any doubts, the impression that no one (else) has any doubts becomes very strong.

An illusion of invulnerability is a third sign. When the experts all agree, it is easy to think that nothing can go wrong. Information about risks, costs, and dangers is suppressed, everyone expresses faith and optimism, and this creates the sense that the group can accomplish almost anything. Many of the worst disasters in history have arisen because this sort of illusion of invulnerability caused groups to make decisions without fully appreciating the flaws and dangers in their plan.

A sense of moral superiority is a fourth sign. Such groups regard themselves as good and virtuous. They hold high ideals and believe that they live up to them better than other people. This belief reinforces the patterns of self-censorship and pressure to conform that we have already noted.

A fifth sign is a tendency to underestimate opponents. Groupthink helps groups regard themselves as superior. The other side of the coin is that their opponents and enemies are regarded with disrespect, disdain, and contempt. Groups who are engaging in groupthink may refuse to negotiate with their enemies because they think they are evil. They do not fear their enemies because they regard them as weak. This can prove costly, because if you underestimate your enemies, your chances for success are much less than you think, and your plans will not go smoothly.

Foolish Committees

Most organizations rely on committees to study issues and make decisions. This approach is based on an eminently sensible principle: It may be hard for a single person to know all sides of an issue and all aspects of a problem. By bringing together a group of people with different knowledge and different viewpoints, the outcome can be improved. Ideally, each person contributes something different, the group members respect each

self-censorship choosing not to express doubts or other information that goes against a group's plans and views other's opinions, and the committee can achieve a broad level of wisdom and understanding that is above and beyond what anyone working alone could accomplish.

But ask anyone with extensive experience whether committees generally achieve high levels of wisdom and understanding. Most likely, the answer will be a laugh or a roll of the eyes. What goes wrong?

Careful laboratory studies of group decisions have begun to reveal the problems that cause committees to fail to live up to their promise. One important factor is that members of a committee want to get along with each other, so they focus more on what they have in common than on their different perspectives. These pressures toward group harmony end up stifling the free exchange of information.

In one set of studies, the experimenter told a group of participants to decide which of two job candidates should be hired. Each member of the group was given some information about the two candidates. There were seven reasons to hire Anderson and only four reasons to hire Baker, and the group had all of the reasons—so, logically, the committee should have chosen Anderson. Yet most groups ended up choosing Baker, who was objectively the poorer candidate.[75,76]

The roots of the wrong decision lay in how the information was distributed. The researchers gave each member of the group the same four reasons for choosing Baker, but they gave each person only one of the reasons for choosing Anderson. Each person got a different reason for choosing Anderson, so if the committee members managed to pool their knowledge, they would realize that there were more reasons to hire Anderson. After all, that is how committees are supposed to work, by bringing together all the different information that the various members have.

But they didn't manage to pool their information. Instead of talking about all seven different reasons for hiring Anderson, they mainly talked about the four reasons for hiring Baker. That is, their group discussion focused on what they all knew in common, rather than on the unique information each person had.

Thus, a committee can end up being less than the sum of its parts, even in purely informational terms. Instead of bringing together different views and information, committees often narrow their focus to what they have in common. Information is lost rather than gained.

Group Polarization and the "Risky Shift"

As we saw in the last section, committees are often formed on the principle that many people working together can be smarter and make better decisions than individuals working alone. Yet often the decisions of committees seem foolish. This has prompted research into how groups make decisions.

Early on, social psychologists stumbled onto a peculiar pattern in group decision making, which they dubbed the risky shift.[77,78] The **risky shift** was defined as a tendency for groups to take greater risks than the same individuals (on average) would have decided to take individually. Somehow the process of talking about the dilemma moved the group toward a more extreme, risky view. (If you read the earlier section on groupthink, this result will not surprise you!)

Rather soon after the risky shift was discovered, exceptions began to appear. Sometimes the group would shift toward more cautious decisions, which was the opposite of a risky shift. (Some social psychologists began to speak of a "stingy shift" or a "conservative shift.") For a time, the whole line of research was mired in arguments and confusion, but the correct principle began to emerge in later studies. The effect of groups is not invariably either a risky or a stingy shift. Rather, the primary effect is to drive the group toward a greater extreme in whatever direction it was already headed.[79] If the group leans initially toward risk, then group discussion will yield greater risk. If the group leans toward caution, discussion will make it all the more cautious.

The movement toward either extreme became known as the **group polarization effect**. (Polarization means moving away from the middle, toward either extreme. "Pole", as in North Pole, is another word for the extreme point.) It can be defined as a shift toward a more extreme position resulting from group discussion (illustrated in **FIGURE 14.3**).

risky shift a tendency for groups to take greater risks than the same individuals (on average) would have decided to take individually

group polarization effect a shift toward a more extreme position resulting from group discussion

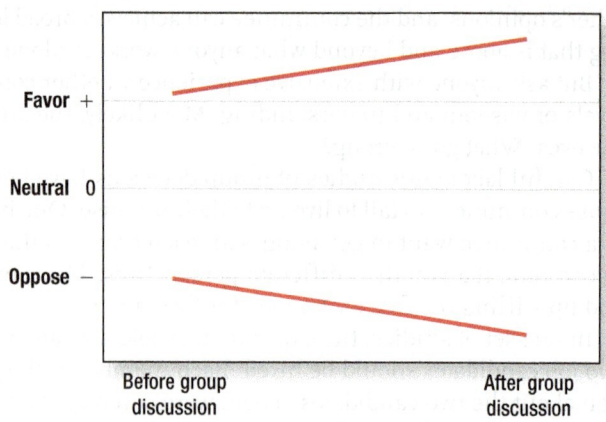

FIGURE 14.3

Group polarization occurs when group discussion leads people to become more extreme in the direction of their initial opinions.

Copyright © 2008 The McGraw-Hill Companies, Inc. Reprinted by permission.[125]

Group polarization depends on the fact that people in the group are fairly similar, so that they all initially lean in the same direction (e.g., they are all somewhat inclined to take a risk). This resembles what tends to happen in everyday life. Even when a large and diverse set of people are all thrown together, such as first-year students arriving at college, they soon sort themselves into groups of like-minded individuals. (As we saw in the chapter on attraction, similarity is a common and strong basis for forming friendships.) As a result, most people spend most of their time interacting with people who think and feel rather similarly. Hence, when they discuss issues, they accentuate each other's beliefs and feelings, thereby contributing to group polarization.

QUIZ YOURSELF
How Groups Think

1. Which of the following is not an effect of brainstorming in groups?
   - (a) People have more fun working in groups than alone.
   - (b) People think that the quality and quantity of answers are better when they work in groups than when they work alone.
   - (c) The quality and quantity of answers are better when people work in groups than when they work alone.
   - (d) All of the above are effects of brainstorming in groups.

2. Samantha is considering a new product line to compete with the leading manufacturer in her business. Although her staff wonders privately if the new product is a good idea, they support her decision rather than undermine her authority. This is an example of _____ .
   - (a) deindividuation
   - (b) group polarization
   - (c) groupthink
   - (d) risky shift

3. Which of the following is not a symptom of groupthink?
   - (a) Conformity pressure
   - (b) Overestimating opponents
   - (c) Illusion of unanimity
   - (d) Sense of moral superiority

4. The Department of Psychology is in the process of hiring a new faculty member. Although the individual members of the search committee tend to favor hiring Dr. Slight Favorite, most are still somewhat uncertain as to how they will finally vote. Friday afternoon they will discuss the candidate. What will be the most likely outcome of their deliberations?
   - (a) They will decide to hire Dr. Slight Favorite.
   - (b) They will decide not to hire Dr. Slight Favorite.
   - (c) They will be deadlocked.
   - (d) They will form another committee.

answers: see pg 529

Power and Leadership

Many groups strive for equality. In modern marriage, in particular, the ideal is that husband and wife own everything in common and make decisions equally, with respect and consideration for each other. In parallel, democracy is spreading through the world, with its similar emphasis on equality and joint decision making. In a democracy, each person's vote counts the same, and millions of votes may be counted in order to decide something important.

In practice, however, equality is not very efficient for making decisions, and it may have other drawbacks. Instead of full equality, most groups have leaders. Large groups don't just have leaders, they typically have a hierarchy of power, ranging from a leader at the top, down through several ranks of others who have some authority but must respect what the top leader says, down to the lowest levels of people who take orders and directives but cannot give them. Try to imagine, for example, an army that did away with all ranks and ascribed equal authority to every soldier, so that the army would never take action unless everyone (or at least a majority) voted in favor. No armies actually operate like this—and probably for very good reasons! Such an army would probably never manage to decide to fight a battle. And if it did, it would probably be hopeless at deciding what tactics to use amid the chaos, noise, trauma, and confusion of battle. Bad commanders have caused many battles to be lost, but an army without commanders would be even worse off, and it would probably lose every time.

> "Being powerful is like being a lady. If you have to tell people you are, you aren't."
> — Margaret Thatcher

Leadership

Leadership is vitally important but poorly understood. Bad leaders can ruin countries, organizations, or military units. One team of researchers sought to determine how big an impact the Chief Executive Officer (CEO, the highest ranking person in the organization) has on the performance of a company, as reflected in its profits. They concluded that the answer was about 14%, or one-seventh.[80] That is a huge impact for one person to have. Another study concluded that high-performing executives added an average of $25 million to the value of their company, as compared with average leaders.[81]

The importance of leadership emerged from an expansive study of corporate success called Good to Great.[82] The research group scanned the Fortune 1000 to identify companies that had 15 years of below-average performance followed by 15 years of above-average performance. They found 11 companies that had undergone this sort of sustained improvement, and then the research team tried to identify what these improving companies had in common. To the surprise of the researchers, the biggest common factor was leadership: All the companies had been transformed by a new CEO who took over the organization and improved its performance.

Moreover, two traits characterized the 11 CEOs who led their companies to lasting success. One was being modest and humble. This conclusion came as a shock at the time because the business world had been much enamored of celebrity CEOs with flamboyant, self-promoting styles and probably streaks of narcissism. The other important trait was extreme persistence, also known as "fierce resolve."[83] These leaders made decisions and stuck with them, even if the early results were disappointing. Recall the story about Henry Ford that opened this chapter: His first two car companies were failures, and his first attempt at a low-cost Ford, the Model N, was not very successful, but he stayed the course and achieved legendary success with the Model T.

Additional evidence suggests that most good leaders are perceived as having several basic traits.[84,85,86] Good leaders are decisive; they make a decision and stick with it. They are competent at the group's tasks. (Among hunter/gatherer tribes, which were the norm for most human beings in prehistoric times, the headman was usually one of the best hunters in the group.) Good leaders are seen as having integrity; they are honest and have good moral character (or at least they are perceived that way). Last, they have vision—some concept of what the group can become or achieve—and they use this vision to motivate other people to set aside self-interest in order to work toward the group's goals.

Recall, from the emotion chapter (Chapter 6), how guilt motivates concern for others and socially constructive behavior, whereas shame is generally antisocial? Being prone to guilt (and not shame) makes a better leader.[87] Guilt-prone people are seen as more desirable leaders, and they actually take charge more. Indeed, a study of performance in business organizations found that workers with higher guilt-proneness were rated as more effective leaders, as well as being more responsible for others, by their co-workers, supervisors, and subordinates. The guilt finding stands out in particular because much other research has found that people prefer leaders with plenty of positive emotions. But guilt's special link to responsible concern for others may be particularly helpful for leaders.

Another useful way of thinking about leadership divides the leader role into two components: task orientation and relationship orientation.[88] Task orientation means getting the job done well, and it is no accident that the best workers are often promoted into leader roles. Task-oriented leaders focus on planning, motivating, coordinating inputs from group members, setting goals, and providing feedback. Relationship orientation refers to maintaining good relationships among the group. Boosting morale, resolving conflicts, taking care of group members, and promoting group spirit are important parts of this component. Many leaders are good at one or the other of these two components of leadership, but a high-quality leader must be good at both.

Narcissists may not necessarily make great leaders, but that does not mean that narcissism and leadership are not linked. Narcissists may be more likely than others to become group leaders, for better or worse. In lab studies, groups of four strangers were assembled with no leader and assigned to discuss a problem and make a recommendation. The researchers tracked who emerged as a leader in each group. In every study, people scoring high on the trait of narcissism were most likely to emerge as leaders.[89] This appeared to be less a matter of seeking attention than of simply wanting to be in control and having the confidence to speak up frequently. Their confidence caused other group members to defer to them.

Speaking up and being assertive in other ways may help a person move into a leadership role, but it is not necessarily a recipe for successful leadership. Studies of MBA (master of business administration degree) students and actual business managers have found that as assertiveness increases, leadership quality first increases—and then decreases.[90] Assertiveness was defined as the tendency to speak up for, defend, and promote one's values and goals. Leaders who were low in assertiveness were seen as unable to motivate people and unable to get things done, so they were ineffective. At the other extreme, highly assertive leaders were viewed negatively in interpersonal terms (even if effective in some ways): unfriendly, bossy, manipulative, and generally not likable.

The mixed effects of assertiveness mesh well with the idea of the two components of leadership. Assertiveness may be helpful for the task dimension but harmful for the interpersonal dimension. The best leaders seem to strike the right balance of being somewhat but not too assertive.

Toxic Leaders

Bad leaders can be disastrous. History has many examples of leaders who have brought ruin, misery, and death to their followers (recall the example of Jim Jones in Chapter 8). One leader who went from an international hero to a despised pariah is Robert Mugabe, and his story is sobering.

Mugabe was a leader of the black uprising in Rhodesia, a relatively rich country in southern Africa. When his revolution succeeded, he became the first president of his country, newly renamed Zimbabwe. Representatives from 96 countries attended the independence ceremony in 1980, in which Mugabe promised peace and reconciliation, even assuring the 200,000 white citizens that he would be their friend and ally. The country had been impoverished by the war, but it had tremendous natural resources, including rich farmland and diamond mines, as well

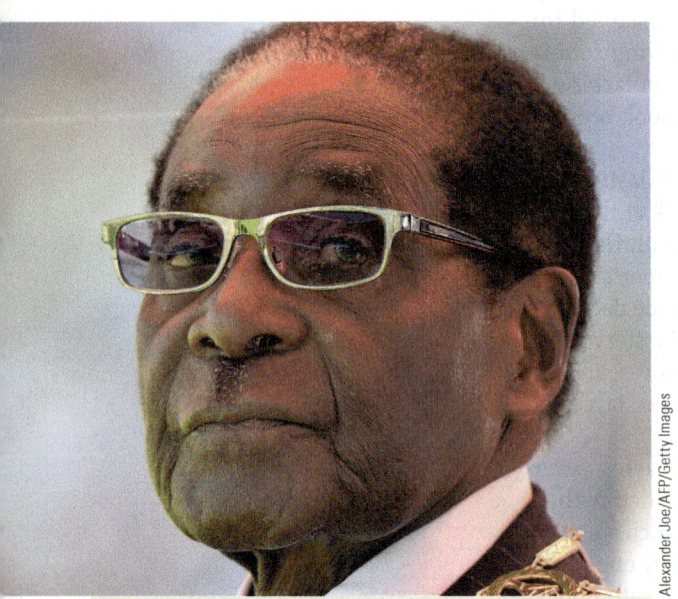
Robert Mugabe, former president of Zimbabwe.

as a strong industrial base. Zimbabwe was seen as the potential breadbasket of southern Africa, able to grow enough food to feed much of the rest of the continent.

Over time, Mugabe narrowed his goals and focused ever more on increasing and cementing his own power. In the process, he turned the once prosperous country from a breadbasket to a basket case. His talk of making the country rich through capitalism was abandoned in favor of Marxist politics, which brought poverty. Racial reconciliation was abandoned when the black majority grew impatient with Mugabe's policies, and in a transparent bid for popular support he announced that the government would confiscate farms owned by white people and give them to poor black peasants. This drove most of the white people out of the country, taking some knowledge and skills with them. Then, instead of giving the confiscated farms to poor and hungry black citizens, he gave the best to his cronies and loyalists, many of whom were already rich and few of whom knew anything about farming. Food production fell dramatically, and soon many Zimbabweans were starving. Instead of exporting food to other countries, as it had once done, Zimbabwe became dependent on donations of food from the outside world. Mugabe pressed ahead: "If I see anyone with cold feet," he said, "I'll put hot irons under them."

Zimbabwe could not even buy food because the economy was in a catastrophic state. Inflation reached such high levels that the money became virtually worthless. The majority of the workforce was unemployed. Meanwhile the corrupt government continued to pay lavish salaries to its leaders, along with other perks such as frequent brand-new Mercedes cars. Although the government was clearly going broke, Mugabe sent his army into a seemingly pointless civil war in the Congo, on the other side of Africa, at the cost of a million U.S. dollars a day. He sought to cheer up his impoverished citizens with publicity stunts, like conducting a lottery for a huge cash prize, selected from every citizen with a bank account. (By suspicious coincidence, the lottery officials found that Mugabe himself won the huge prize—a bit ironically, as he was one of the few Zimbabweans who did not need the money!) Another attempt to distract people from the economic failure was a campaign against homosexuals, whom Mugabe likened to unpleasant animals.

In 2002, Mugabe came up for reelection, and by now he faced a serious chance that the disillusioned masses would vote him out. He rigged the election shamelessly, including sponsoring systematic violence against members of the opposition party (and throwing the opposing presidential candidate into prison on trumped-up charges of treason). At the next election, in 2007, Mugabe came in second in the first round and looked certain to lose the runoff, whereupon his supporters became so violent against the opposition party that Mugabe's election opponent withdrew from the race.

The starving masses waited in line for food handouts from foreign donors, but Mugabe's men refused to give food to anyone who could not produce a membership card in their party. Many of the world's governments protested against how Mugabe had stolen the election, but he dismissed their accusations as nothing more than racism and continued to cement his hold on power while driving his country into ever greater ruin. When the Archbishop Desmond Tutu, a highly respected black leader who had won the Nobel Peace Prize, dared to call Mugabe a tyrant, Mugabe denounced him as an "angry, evil, and embittered little bishop." Most outsiders thought the archbishop was right. Finally, in 2017, the Zimbabwean military rose up and removed Mugabe from power. They offered to let him resign rather than be impeached, but he defied them, and so impeachment proceedings started, whereupon Mugabe finally did resign. He was allowed to continue living in luxury in the country. In 2019, he died at age 95.

Bosses can also make bad leaders. American business is home to plenty of bad bosses. Many surveys have found that between two-thirds and three-quarters of workers say the worst aspect of their job is their immediate boss.[91] Perhaps such surveys bring out a tendency to complain, but other, more objective methods of assessing managerial performance yield an average estimate that about half the bosses in the United States are inept.[92]

What makes some leaders so disastrous for their followers? Research has begun to fill in the picture of what makes a bad boss. After surveying many findings, one research study identified four patterns.[93] One was simply that the person was promoted above his or her abilities and never managed to adjust to the demands and responsibilities of the new job. A second pattern was failure to build a team, by making poor hiring choices. This may sound obvious, but it is often difficult to choose the right people for the team, especially because almost everyone knows that during a job interview you should try to project an image as a cooperative, reliable, talented, and motivated worker. Bad bosses may give top jobs to their friends and choose team members based on loyalty to the boss rather than competence (like Mugabe), or they may simply be unable to judge people effectively.

The third pattern of bad bosses involved poor interpersonal skills that created conflicts between the leader and subordinates. For example, some leaders may be arrogant and thus offend their group by demanding outward shows of respect and deference. ("Because I said so, that's why!") Others are simply insensitive—they don't know or don't care about the people who work for them. And the fourth pattern involved interpersonal actions that undermined the group's ability to work together, such as betraying someone's trust, failing to keep promises, taking advantage of subordinates, or frequently changing his or her mind.

One admirable attempt to distinguish dangerous leaders from others began by noting that politicians do not differ in mental health from the rest of the population, so a certain number of mentally ill people (even clinically insane) will come to power here and there. The successful ones may be able to think effectively, but the madness will be found in their emotional lives.[94]

In particular, the dangerous leaders suffer from "emotional disregard and disconnection from others."[95] This disconnection is not necessarily harmful in anyone, and even a leader with that characteristic will not necessarily turn to violence or evil, becoming instead a legalistic or technocratic ruler. However, when the emotional disconnection is combined with a proneness to violence, there is disaster in the making. Such a leader will be willing to undertake destructive projects, pursuing dreams of glory and grandeur (or even just vindictive grudges and hatreds) without worrying much about how his or her followers may be put at risk of intense suffering. Napoleon and Hitler are good examples. Although most histories focus on their conflicts with other nations and on the struggles and sufferings of their enemies and victims, it is instructive to recall what happened to their own followers. France suffered Napoleon's wars, and a generation had to cope with a lack of men who could serve as heirs, husbands, and fathers. Germany suffered even worse from Hitler's wars. Napoleon once responded to the news of the battlefield deaths of his own troops by saying that "soldiers are meant to be killed," a chilling comment that revealed how little emotional connection he felt with the agony and sacrifice of the young men who followed him.

Three characteristics seem typical of dangerous leaders.[96] First was the indifference toward the suffering of people, along with devaluation of other people in general. This allows the leader to manipulate, exploit, and even kill without regret. Second, the

Myself, Napolean, your glorious leader.

All in a day's work?

dangerous leader is intolerant of criticism, and they will often take steps to suppress dissent. Stifling the free press and imprisoning dissidents are often early signs of a dangerous leader. (Mugabe, for example, repeatedly arrested journalists who criticize his regime, and his opponent in the 2002 election was arrested for treason and could have been condemned to death.) Third, a dangerous leader has a grandiose sense of national entitlement. This corresponds to the egotism that we have already seen in Chapter 10 on aggression as characterizing violent and dangerous individuals.

What Is Power?

Power is an important aspect of leadership, insofar as leaders make decisions that affect the group. **Power** means one person's control over another person.

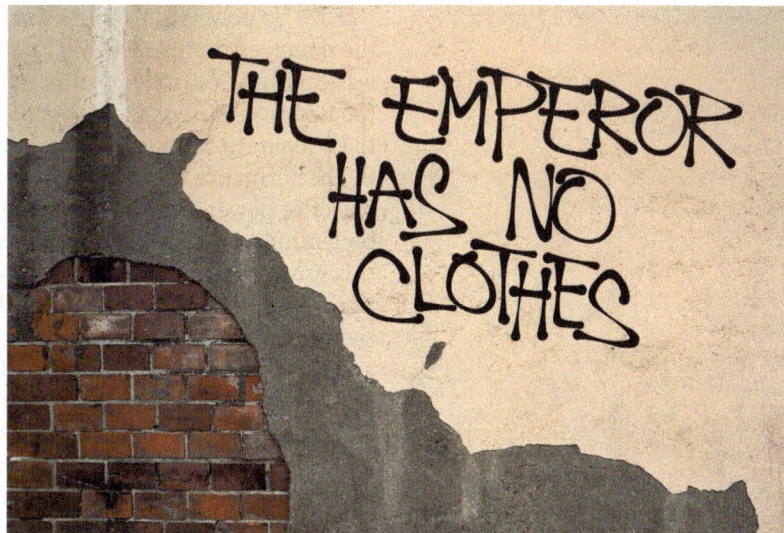

People are often afraid to question the leader.

Power can seem addictive. People who get a taste of power often show patterns of seeking more power. The careers of many powerful individuals, from Napoleon to John D. Rockefeller, suggest a steady rise in their grasping for ever greater power, even though the amount of power they already have seems enough to satisfy any normal person's needs and indeed far exceeds what normal folks can even dream of attaining. Napoleon, for example, was already emperor of France and held power over conquered territories all around Europe, including Germany, Austria, and Poland. Why did he need to attack Russia, too?

Although power is normally understood as an aspect of control, a famous essay by political scientist Hans Morgenthau proposed that it is linked to belongingness as well.[97] Morgenthau compared power to love, although at first blush the two may seem totally different. Yet both power and love effectively merge separate individuals. The difference is that love entails a more or less equal and mutual union, whereas power effects a one-sided union in which the will of the powerful person is imposed on the subordinate. Morgenthau went on to point out that this unequal merging (unlike love) ultimately fails to save the powerful person from loneliness because the self of the subordinate effectively disappears; even at the moment of peak domination, the powerful person finds himself or herself alone again after all. Morgenthau suggests that this dissatisfaction explains why powerful people seek even more power, thinking that this will help them escape from loneliness. It also explains why powerful people often insist on displays of love from their underlings ("our beloved leader"). Yet it continues to be lonely at the top.

Effects of Power on Leaders

The imbalance in power causes a variety of effects, many of which appear harmful. A British nobleman, Lord Acton, is credited with saying: "Power tends to corrupt, and absolute power corrupts absolutely." Is this a reason why it is good to keep changing one's leaders?

The corrupting effects of power have been studied by assigning participants to be managers over groups of workers. By random assignment, some of the managers had considerable power, such as the ability to give pay raises and bonuses, to deduct pay, to reassign workers, and even to fire them. The other, low-power managers had no such powers and simply had the title of manager. Both were supposed to get their workers to perform well.[98,99]

The managers without objective powers urged the workers to do better, praised them, proposed goals and targets, and gave advice. These tactics are quite reasonable ways to influence people, but the powerful managers spurned them. Instead they issued commands, made threats, and also made promises or offers of money (using the powers they held). The ones who were given power began to use it more and more over time. What they said was part of throwing their power around.

power one person's control over another person, including what happens to that person

How do powerful people perceive their underlings? These studies also measured how the managers in his research rated their workers. The actual performance of the workers was carefully controlled by the experimenter so that it was identical in the two conditions (powerful versus not-so-powerful managers). Yet the managers perceived these objectively identical workers in quite different ways. The managers with more power evaluated the performance of their workers much more poorly than did the managers who lacked objective power.[100] Powerful bosses gave their workers little credit for the work they did, preferring to see the workers as simply carrying out the commands of the manager. In this way, the powerful managers took credit for what was accomplished without forming a favorable view of the employees. In contrast, the managers with less power believed that the workers' own motivation and efforts were mainly responsible for what was achieved, and they rated the workers more favorably overall. Having power makes you look down on others and underestimate their worth.

Some of the detrimental effects of power on leaders are linked to how followers treat them. A study of American business CEOs (topmost leaders) found that their subordinates frequently flattered them and expressed agreement with their opinions even when the subordinates privately felt differently. This ingratiating flattery boosted the narcissistic egotism of the bosses. This in turn made the CEOs think they were doing great, to the extent that they downplayed problems in the company and failed to take action to solve them. In the long run, these egotistical mistakes increased the chance that the CEO be fired.[101] So if you find yourself in position of powerful leadership, don't listen too carefully to the flattery and agreement from your underlings!

Followers forgive and tolerate misbehavior by leaders much more readily than similar misbehavior by other group members. In several studies, for example, people read about a soccer player who broke the game's rules by yelling and cursing at the referee and the opposing team, also refusing to shake hands at the end of the game.[102] Participants rated that player more favorably if he was the leader than merely a member of the team. In another study, a team of participants played a lab game for money, and one of the players cheated to help the team. Again, that player was rated better if a leader than simply another member. It may be natural for group members to support their leader, but turning a blind eye to leader misdeeds is a potentially dangerous form of such support.

How do powerful people treat their followers? The prisoner's dilemma game (discussed in Chapter 9 on prosocial behavior) forces people to make a choice between two moves. One is cooperative; the other is exploitative, self-serving, and defensive. Researchers have used the game to see how powerful versus less powerful people treated each other. The highly powerful individuals favored self-serving responses rather than cooperative ones. Even when low-power people showed a consistent pattern of being willing to cooperate, high-power people would often continue to take advantage of them and pursue their individual goals.[103] Highly powerful people seem to disregard and even prey on the weak. These patterns certainly support Lord Acton's comment that power tends to corrupt.

Recent works suggest that the corrupting effect comes from the power, not the high status that often accompanies power. Status means that others respect and admire you. Experimental participants accorded high status were exceptionally fair and generous toward others. In contrast, power is control over others, and participants who were assigned high power were relatively unfair and unjust toward others.[104] The nastiest folks were the ones who got high power but low status. They treated others very badly. High status helped offset the negative effects of power.

Then again, not all power corrupts, and some people wield it in positive ways. Social psychologists have searched for a more balanced theory about power that can recognize its benefits as well as its costs. One general theory of power proposed that power has five crucial effects.[105]

Emotion

Power feels good. People with power are more likely to feel positive, pleasant emotions and to express these good feelings. For example, people who report feeling more dominant and powerful in life, such as those in leadership roles, generally report more positive and happy emotions.[106] People who lack power are more prone to feel and express negative emotions such as guilt and depression.

Rewards Versus Punishments

Power makes people attend more to rewards than to punishments, whereas lack of power has the opposite effect. Essentially, power focuses its possessors on the possibility of getting what they want. It makes them more likely to pursue whatever rewards appeal to them, including money, sex, attention, food, possessions, and success. Put another way, they look for opportunities.

They also ignore constraints. Lab studies show that people in power positions tend to overlook or forget information that might prevent them from reaching their goals.[107] Hence they may go ahead and pursue unrealistic or risky strategies, because they are not attuned to potential problems and obstacles. Power undermines caution.

Adaptability

Powerful people seem to think in terms of how they can use circumstances, benefit from them, or work with them. Powerful people change their behavior more across different situations than do powerless people.[108] You might think that low-power people bend to situations while high-power people remain true to their inner feelings, but the reverse seems to be true. Changing to fit the situation enables the powerful person to get the most out of it. For example, powerful people plan more leisure on weekends and more work during the week, compared to less powerful people. A low-power person might plan to spend a weekend reading a novel, for example, regardless of the season, but a powerful person will take more heed of the special opportunities of winter as opposed to summer (e.g., skiing, going to the beach).

Adapting one's plans and actions to get the most out of situational opportunities is not the same as being at the mercy of the situation. Even though powerful people may change how they act, they are not pushed around by the situation. As the title of a recent article states, "Power reduces the press [as in pressure] of the situation."[109] High- versus low-power participants in their studies responded in different ways to seemingly identical situations. High-power people perceived more choices, conformed less to the opinions expressed by others, and generated creative ideas that were further apart from what other people had already put forward, as compared to people low in power. In contrast, people who lack power shift their attention more to threats and dangers. Instead of thinking about how to get what they want, they focus more on how to avoid losing what they have, and they are more prone to see ambiguous situations as dangerous or threatening.

The phrase "thinking outside the box" has become something of a cliché in recent years; nonetheless, it is relevant here. If we think of the situation as the "box," then power enables people to think outside the box, but that includes finding ways to use the box to their own best advantage. People low in power remain inside the box in their thinking, and hence they may never fully appreciate what the box could do for them.

Deliberate Versus Automatic Thinking

As we have seen in this book's repeated references to the duplex mind, mental processes can be sorted into deliberate, controlled ones and relatively automatic ones. Power seems to make people rely more on automatic processing, whereas people who lack power engage in more deliberate thinking.[110] The reason is probably that the greater vulnerability of people low in power makes them feel the need to think carefully before acting. People who are held accountable for their actions—which is typical of people with low power—think in more complex ways, such as considering both sides of an issue rather than simply emphasizing the side they favor.[111,112] Powerful people are rarely told by others that they are wrong, so they become lazy in their thinking, and easy or lazy thinking is the specialty of the automatic system.

Approach Versus Inhibition

Last, power removes inhibitions against acting, whereas a lack of power makes people more inhibited. In a sense, this theme underlies all the others because it inclines powerful people to act assertively to pursue the rewards they want (including using others to help them get what they want), which brings the positive feeling of pursuing and getting these rewards.

The approach or action orientation makes powerful people more likely than others to engage in socially inappropriate behavior. Powerful people sometimes get into trouble when they act on their impulses without thinking about possible consequences. Many politicians (across the political spectrum!) have had their careers damaged because of minor sexual misdeeds. There is also some evidence that sexual harassment occurs because powerful men automatically think of sex in connection with power.[113] This automatic thinking, along with the tendency to act impulsively to pursue what one wants (and, perhaps crucially, the willingness to regard others as means toward one's own satisfaction), increases the likelihood of trying to pressure subordinates into granting sexual favors.

As we have seen, Henry Ford used his power to create a better system that enriched himself, his family, his workers, and his stockholders, and that also enriched society by providing a convenient and appealing mode of travel. Other leaders have brought disaster to their followers. Is power ultimately good or bad? Perhaps neither, according to some recent social psychology studies. These studies suggest that power increases the tendency to take action, and this can be for good or ill.

A series of studies suggested that power leads to action even if the power is logically irrelevant to the action.[114] That is, power seems to create a state of mind that favors action. Lacking power, in contrast, brings a wait-and-see mental state marked by inhibition and inaction. In one of these studies, participants played the card game blackjack after being assigned the role of either manager or worker (builder) on a separate task. Although being manager had nothing to do with the blackjack game, the managers were more likely to follow the active strategy of taking an additional card, whereas the low-power participants tended to stick with the cards they had been dealt and not ask for a new one. In another study, mental states were manipulated by having people remember and write about prior experiences in which they had either held power over someone or been subjected to another person's power. They performed this task while seated in a room in which an annoying fan was blowing directly on them. People in the high-power condition (those who were writing about having power over someone else) were more likely than those in the low-power condition to get up and move the fan or turn it off.

One of these studies is particularly relevant to the question of whether power is used for good or bad ends.[115] States of mind were manipulated again by having participants write about personal experiences of having power or being at the mercy of someone else's power. Half the participants played a commons dilemma game, in which people could passively allow the common resource to remain large (and grow) or could actively and selfishly take money for themselves. The other participants played a different kind of game in which the active response was to donate money for a public good, whereas the passive response was to keep one's own money and rely on others to be generous. In both games, the high-power participants took the active response, whereas the low-power participants tended to be more passive. Thus, power increased the tendency to take action both for selfish gain and for the benefit of others. Power doesn't always corrupt—sometimes it ennobles, too.

The idea that power can cut both ways was also supported in research that compared leaders who felt a communal bond with their followers and other leaders who were out for themselves without caring so much about

Feeling powerful makes you more likely to ask for another card. (But it doesn't make you more likely to win!)

others. The leaders who had a communal bond with their followers typically wanted to use their power to improve the lot of their underlings; in fact, many of them felt an obligation to do so. As a result, these leaders used their power to take care of their followers. In contrast, leaders who were out for themselves used their power for their own good, often to the harm or detriment of their followers.[116] Thus, again, power can be used to harm or to benefit those who are at the mercy of the powerful.

Preserving Power

Power can perhaps be addictive: People who get it gradually become increasingly concerned with preserving their power. The more they perceive a threat of losing power, the more they may concentrate on trying to conserve it. We saw in the example of Mugabe a case in which a ruler started out trying to do the best for all his citizens and over time became focused on advancing his cronies and consolidating his power, even to the detriment of the citizens. He may have been exceptionally bad, but he was far from unique in this. If you follow world news, you will read many stories about various leaders who seek to change their country's constitution to allow them to remain in power longer and longer, or who perform other damaging actions so as to preserve their position.

Lab studies have shed light on the power-clinging mentality. Leaders of experimental groups were faced with choices between doing what was best for the group and what was best for them, including maintaining their power position. Mostly, leaders did what was best for the group (though keep in mind that these were mainly student research participants who had just been assigned to be leaders, as opposed to people who had had years to become addicted to power). But when there was a threat to their power, many leaders changed their priorities to favor preserving their position.[117] For example, they might exclude a highly talented group member who could really help the group perform (but who might threaten the leader's authority). They blocked talented subordinates from having influence over the group's decisions. Also, following the ancient Chinese writer Sun-Tzu's advice to "keep your friends close, but your enemies closer," they took careful note of what other group members might threaten their situation (such as by performing really well) and tried to stay close to that person, presumably to keep a close eye on what that person did.[118]

There was one situation in which even the threatened leaders tended to do what is best, such as picking the best people even though these might outshine the leader. That was when they were competing against another group. Even leaders who put their own interests first will sometimes switch so as to take care of the group when it has to win a competition against an outgroup.

Effects of Power on Followers

Let us turn attention now from those with power to their subordinates. Being in a subordinate position, according to our definition of power, means that another person can decide what happens to you and that you may be forced to do things you do not want to do. Not surprisingly, subordinates pay extra attention to the powerful person and try to understand them. Careful laboratory studies have shown that when people are dependent on someone else, they spend extra time thinking about that person, analyzing that person's behavior, and trying to figure out that person's traits and personality.[119]

When there is conflict, the person with less power is at an obvious disadvantage. Hence, people with less power will be especially prone to foster peace and harmony. When subordinates ask for peace and cooperation, the powerful person may simply take this as a given and not be very responsive, whereas when the powerful person asks for peace and harmony, low-power people should be highly receptive. Some evidence for this was provided by laboratory studies with experimental games: Lab participants low in power responded very positively when the high-power person suggested cooperation and an end to conflict.[120]

Another fascinating study showed that people low in power adapt to the expectations of high-power people, even without realizing it.[121] Participants in this study were given randomly assigned, bogus information about the ostensible personality traits of their interaction partners. Power was manipulated in terms of which person was permitted to make decisions about the next phase of the study. The two participants then had a 10-minute conversation, which was recorded in such a way that each person was recorded on a separate channel. Judges who did not know the experimental manipulation then listened to what each person said and rated whether the person showed those traits that the partner had been anticipating. Low-power individuals ended up acting the way their high-power partners expected, more than the reverse. Many were unaware that they changed their behavior, and some of the changes were to the individual's own disadvantage. Thus, when power is unequal, the lower-ranking person may unwittingly make a variety of changes in behavior as influenced by the unstated expectations of the person high in power, even if the low-power person might not want to make those changes.

Sometimes power takes the form of controlling how much money people get. Lack of money is no laughing matter, yet people without money seem to laugh more (see *Money Matters*).

Legitimate Leadership

The maintenance of power often depends on legitimizing myths.[122] **Legitimizing myths** purport to explain and justify why people in power deserve to be in power. In an ostensible meritocracy, those in power have to contend that they have superior merit, such as by being smarter, more talented, or harder working than those who rank below them. After all, some degree of inequality is inevitable, and nearly all societies have power structures, so the crucial question is whether the inequality of power is fair and legitimate. The individuals or groups in power must typically find some reason that everyone will accept as establishing that their power is indeed fair and legitimate.

Indeed, the desire for legitimacy may be a common concern of powerful people, not least because it makes their job easier: Underlings will follow commands and cooperate better with leaders who are seen as legitimate than with others. When most nations were ruled by kings, many kings claimed "divine right," which is to say that they sought legitimacy by insisting that the supreme god had intended for them to rule. Indeed, the long and turbulent history of the relation between religion and politics has much to do

legitimizing myths explanations used to justify why people in power deserve to be in power

MONEY*Matters*

Money, Power, and Laughter

Who laughs more, rich and powerful people, or poor and dependent ones? Existing theories offer bases for predicting both answers. Rich and powerful people can do what they want, so perhaps they feel free to let go and laugh, whereas those low in power wait to see whether others laugh first. Alternatively, people low in power might laugh at the powerful person's jokes, as a way of ingratiating themselves.

To test these hypotheses, researchers assigned participants to high- or low-power roles and then measured how much they laughed at someone's jokes. Power was manipulated by control over money: Participants were told that a cash prize would be given to someone and either they or someone else would have the final decision. Then they interacted with someone who managed to tell several jokes, including both funny and unfunny ones. The researchers secretly recorded how much the participant laughed.

Low power led to more laughing. Apparently, having someone else control your money makes you more prone to laugh—regardless of whether the jokes are funny or not. Indeed, the researchers had difficulty coding the laughter according to whether the jokes were funny or not because low-power people seemed to laugh even at odd times when nothing funny had been said.[123]

Was this laughter a ploy to ingratiate themselves with the powerful person? Not necessarily. In one of the studies, participants merely watched a video of someone talking, so that nobody would seemingly know whether they laughed or not. They still laughed more. They also laughed more when they were interacting with a coworker who had no more money or power than they did.

Laughter may well be a strategy for making friends, because people like people who laugh.[124,125,126] Apparently, people who lack money and power are eager to make friends with anyone (not just those who are powerful). They become more prone to laugh at anybody's jokes—even if the jokes aren't funny!

with what the two systems offer each other: Religions offer legitimacy but lack power, while rulers have power but want legitimacy, so they make natural allies. In democratic systems, rulers claim legitimacy by virtue of being elected by a majority vote. But incompetent, immoral, or illegal actions can quickly rob an elected leader of this legitimacy.

In short, the quest to bolster legitimacy is typically an ongoing problem for those in power. Even as they hold and exercise power, they must remain on the lookout for ideas or values that can be used to justify their position of power and their influence over others.

QUIZ YOURSELF: Power and Leadership

1. What two traits are possessed by CEOs who lead their companies to lasting success? _____ .
   a. Good looks and intelligence
   b. Humility and persistence
   c. Persistence and intelligence
   d. Narcissism and persistence

2. Powerful is to powerlessness as _____ is to _____ .
   a. affect; cognition
   b. cognition; affect
   c. approach; inhibition
   d. inhibition; approach

3. Research has shown that in the prisoner's dilemma game, more powerful people choose to _____ and less powerful people choose to _____ .
   a. cooperate; cooperate
   b. cooperate; defect
   c. defect; cooperate
   d. defect; defect

4. Research shows that power leads to _____ .
   a. action
   b. competition
   c. cooperation
   d. inaction

answers: see pg 529

What Makes Us Human: Putting the Cultural Animal in Perspective

In this chapter we have glimpsed some of the best and the worst of human nature. Sometimes, as in violent lynch mobs and mass murder campaigns, groups bring out the worst in people and enable them to do things much more terrible than they would likely do alone. Other times, as on the assembly line, groups manage to achieve things that would be far beyond the powers of all the same group members acting individually.

One pattern we have seen is that submerging the individual in the group often leads to bad outcomes such as violence, groupthink, and the waste of resources in the commons dilemma, whereas keeping people individually identified and accountable helps to promote positive results. Humans are perhaps much better equipped than other animals to maintain separate, accountable identities, so humans can benefit from groups in ways that most other animals cannot.

Role differentiation and the division of labor help make human groups especially effective. People can take on and adapt to different roles, and they can design and function in a group that is a network of individually defined roles. Culture is especially powerful for creating such systems of interlocking, complementary roles. It is possible that human beings first created culture in order to enjoy some of these benefits of group systems. Groups of animals may have a couple of roles, such as leader and follower, but human groups such as corporations and universities can consist of hundreds of different roles with separate jobs and distinct functions.

The distinctively human traits make some effects stronger than those found in animals. We saw that social facilitation occurs in animals (even cockroaches!), but among humans the impact of others is intensified by evaluation apprehension. People are better than animals at anticipating how others will evaluate them and at adjusting their behavior accordingly.

Communication is important to the success of many groups. As language users, people can communicate much more effectively than other animals. To be sure, this does not always lead to good results because (as in groupthink) people can use their words to put pressure on others to conform to a faulty idea. By and large, though, good communication is central to the great success of human groups.

Power and leadership are found in the animal world, but they too take on new dimensions in human society. For one thing, the power of communication enables humans to preside over much larger groups. (Millions of U.S. citizens follow the laws made by their government, for example, even though they might never meet the president or any member of Congress face to face.)

More impressively, perhaps, humans have gradually developed means of transferring power without violence. Among most animals, power is held by the strongest male, who has his way with food and females until another male comes along and physically defeats him. Through most of human history, many rulers retained power until their death. A remarkable achievement of the modern era has been the democratic transfer of power, whereby the person or party that loses an election will peacefully turn over power to a new set of rulers. In some parts of the world, this has still never happened, but the tide of history seems to spread peaceful democratic transition to more and more places.

Restricting power has been one of the great achievements of human culture. As we saw, in groups of animals, the leader can do almost anything they want. Humans have gradually learned to hold their leaders accountable. The progress of culture has included imposing more and more restrictions on power, so that even the topmost leaders can be arrested, put on trial, and removed from office against their will. Even in the family, the husband or father no longer holds the extreme power over his wife and children that was common in many earlier societies, a power that at times has extended to life and death. Humans use laws—which are among the most powerful elements of culture—to restrict and restrain the uses of power. In this way, abuses of power can be reduced, and life can become better for the vast majority of people.

CHAPTER 14 SUMMARY

What Groups Are and Do

- Humans can use the power of culture to form groups that can achieve far more than collections of individuals operating alone.
- In human evolution, a tendency to form groups may have been beneficial because
  - Group members can find safety in numbers.
  - Group members can help each other find food.
  - Groups can accomplish tasks that would be too difficult for lone individuals.
- Cultural groups preserve information and pass it along to future generations.
- Cultural groups can use information, as well as reason from experience, to organize themselves.
- Cultural groups benefit from role differentiation and division of labor.

Groups, Roles, and Selves

- Complementary roles (as in the role differentiation of cultural groups) produce better results than simply having everyone do the same thing.
- Human roles work in the context of a large system in which most other people do something else.
- In fascist movements, the individual's self-interest is subordinated to the best interests of the group.
- Putting the best interests of the collective (that is, society as a whole) above those of the individual makes tyranny more likely.

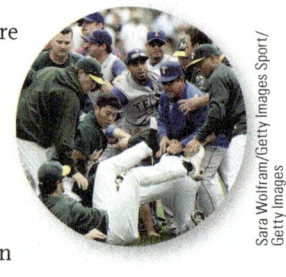

- Culture creates roles that are independent of the individuals who occupy those roles.
- Human selves are flexible enough to take on (and occasionally drop) roles.
- Identifying people in groups and holding them accountable for their actions produces better outcomes.

Group Action

- Zajonc's theory of social facilitation states that the presence of others increases arousal, which increases the dominant response tendency (the most common response in that situation).
- Social facilitation theory states that the presence of others can make people perform better, especially on easy and familiar tasks.
- The presence of others can change people's eating patterns.
- Narcissists are individuals who regard themselves as better than others and are constantly trying to win the admiration of others.
- Evaluation apprehension may intensify the effects of others' presence.
- Social loafing (also called the free rider problem) refers to the finding that people reduce effort when working in a group, compared to when working alone, especially if their work is not individually identifiable.
- The bad apple effect refers to the finding that one loafer can cause other workers to loaf as well.
- Deindividuation refers to a loss of self-awareness and of individual accountability in a group, which can lead to antisocial behavior.

- The commons dilemma is the tendency for shared or jointly owned resources to be squandered and not used in an optimal or advantageous fashion (the "tragedy of the commons").
- Communication, personality, mood, and the behavior of others all affect the tendency to overuse a common resource (the commons dilemma).

How Groups Think

- Brainstorming involves encouraging group members to share and generate as many ideas as possible without holding back or worrying about being wrong; it produces less creative output but is liked better than working separately.

- Large groups of people can make better predictions than the smartest members of the group if people operate as separate, independent members and then pool and share their diverse information.
- Transactive memory refers to a process by which the members of a small group remember different kinds of information.
- Groupthink refers to the tendency of group members to think alike. It is especially likely if the group
  - Is similar and cohesive.
  - Has a strong, directive leader.
  - Is isolated from other ideas.
  - Has high self-esteem.
- Groupthink is marked by these symptoms:
  - Pressure toward conformity.
  - An appearance of unanimous agreement.
  - An illusion of invulnerability.
  - A sense of moral superiority.
  - Underestimation of opponents.
- Groups tend to focus more on information held in common by all members than on unique information each person has.

- The risky shift is the tendency for groups to take greater risks than the same individuals (on average) would have decided to take individually.
- The group polarization effect is defined as a shift toward a more extreme position resulting from group discussion.

Power and Leadership

- Large groups typically have a hierarchy of power.
- Successful leaders are humble and extremely persistent.
- People who are perceived as good leaders have integrity, decisiveness, competence, and vision.
- Power refers to one person's control over another person's outcomes and behavior.
- Power has five crucial effects on the powerful: it feels good, it alters attention to rewards and punishments, it changes the relationships between people, it makes people rely more on automatic processing, and it removes inhibitions against taking action.
- People with less power are especially prone to fostering peace and harmony. They adapt to the expectations of high-power people, even without realizing it.
- Legitimizing myths purport to explain why those in power deserve to be in power.

What Makes Us Human? Putting the Cultural Animal in Perspective

- Submerging the individual in the group often leads to bad outcomes.
- Humans have gradually developed means of transferring power without violence.
- Restricting power has been one of the great achievements of human culture.

key terms

altruistic punishment 507
bad apple effect 507
brainstorming 510
commons dilemma 509
deindividuation 502

dominant response 504
evaluation apprehension 504
group 498
group polarization effect 515
groupthink 513

legitimizing myths 526
narcissists 505
power 521
risky shift 515
self-censorship 514

social facilitation theory 504
social loafing (free rider problem) 505
transactive memory 513

quiz yourself ANSWERS

1. What Groups Are and Do p.501
   answers: 1.c 2.c 3.b 4.d
2. Groups, Roles, and Selves p.503
   answers: 1.b 2.c 3.a 4.a
3. Group Action p.510
   answers: 1.c 2.a 3.d 4.a

4. How Groups Think p.516
   answers: 1.c 2.c 3.b 4.a
5. Power and Leadership p.527
   answers: 1.b 2.c 3.c 4.a

APPLICATION MODULE

Applying Social Psychology to Consumer Behavior

Curtis P. Haugtvedt, / The Ohio State University

LEARNING OBJECTIVES

1 Explain how individuals meet their needs (including basic, social, and self-actualizing needs) through the purchase of products and services.

2 Discuss how the internet and social media technology influence consumer behavior.

3 Describe how marketers use data from consumer activities on social media to influence purchase behavior.

4 Explain how paying with credit affects consumer behavior and how the simple presence of credit cards can influence decisions.

5 Analyze how store format influences how we shop and how much we spend, and identify ways in which the environment of the store influences consumer behavior.

6 Discuss how consumers make purchase decisions.

7 Discuss how terror management theory explains motivations underlying consumer behavior.

WHAT MAKES US HUMAN?
Putting the Cultural Animal in Perspective
A22

A1

Learning, Knowing, and Deciding What to Buy

Every minute of every day, most people around the world engage in activities that involve the purchase, use, or disposal of products or services. Companies engage in a wide range of marketing activities designed to influence your decisions as a consumer and as an individual and a member of a group, we do things that provide marketers with insights into the products and services to offer us. Almost all the students reading this book have multiple social media accounts (e.g., Facebook, Pinterest, Twitter, Instagram, Snapchat) and use various email services. Ever wonder how those social media tools can be provided to you for "free?" If you are like most people, you did not spend a great deal of time carefully reading the fine print of the user agreements for the services. Companies like Facebook and Google make money by doing extensive research in order to learn who you are, who your friends are, your favorite activities, the products you own or would like to own, where you are when you are posting something, and a long list of other things. That information is then used to send you certain promotional information, have specific advertisements show up on your screen, and after you buy a product, encourage feedback about your experiences so your experiences can influence other consumers.

As you are learning in this book, our behavior as humans is influenced by a wide variety of things. Physical surroundings, immediate social surroundings, how you are feeling at a given moment, and now the virtual influence of the likes and dislikes of others all influence human behavior.

Purchase decisions influence many things in our lives. They certainly have an influence on our financial well-being! The study of consumer behavior and consumer psychology covers many aspects of how the marketing process (exposure to ads and promotions) influence us, but consumer researchers also study broader concerns like the roles of ideal models on our self-image, the roles of buying material things versus buying experiences in our happiness and satisfaction in life. Consumer researchers and socially and environmentally conscious businesses also study ways in which changes in consumption behavior can have positive influences on our lives and health of the planet.

When did a quest for understanding consumer psychology and consumer behavior start? Persons working in marketplaces in ancient times certainly had knowledge about things related to successful selling and bartering. However, over most of history, needed products were relatively scarce. With the technological and manufacturing revolutions in the early 1900s, it became easier and cheaper to make products. Take cars, for example. Henry Ford's assembly-line processes greatly reduced the cost of cars (see Chapter 14). Yet, because of high demand his company easily sold every car they made. He did not see a need to offer a wide variety of products. People were simply happy to be able to purchase a car. He did not even have to paint the cars different colors. A famous saying attributed to Henry Ford is "customers can have any color car they want, as long as it is black."

Where does psychology come into the picture? After World War II, the United States had a lot of manufacturing capabilities, but companies learned that products were too similar to one another and consumers did not have reasons to pick one over the other. In order to be successful, companies needed to have a better understanding of what people wanted and needed. Because the wants and needs of individuals were sometimes quite different, marketers developed and used ways to find groups of consumers who were very similar to each other. Brands were then developed to match the preferences of these specific market segments. The automobile industry, for example, developed a range of brands from basic and economical to luxurious, expensive, and exclusive. Think basic Chevrolet to luxurious Cadillac, basic Ford to luxurious Lincoln, or basic Toyota to luxurious Lexus.

Not many years ago, marketing research about consumer behavior focused on surveys about the magazines people read, the TV shows they viewed, and the music they enjoyed, and used other data to understand lifestyles. Marketing research today includes a lot of information gleaned from social media, cell phone, and credit card use. Services like Pandora and Spotify even help you find music that you may enjoy by comparing your listening habits to people who are similar to you.

Just as people have different personalities, companies and research organizations work to develop personalities for different brands. The idea is that consumers will prefer brands that have "personalities" that reflect who they are or who they want to be. Companies like Apple gained market share by depicting their computer products as being different from the competition and showing how the users were also unique (see https://www.youtube.com/watch?v=VCL5UgxtoLs). As students reading this book know well, the demand for newly released Apple products is sometimes so high that crowd control is necessary!

While this book focuses on the general area of research and theory in social psychology, much of what we do as humans in the modern world involves our role as consumers. The things we buy are often a reflection of ourselves; in many of our interpersonal and social media conversations, we discuss our purchases with others and we often make inferences or judgments about the personality or lifestyle of people based on observing the products they own and their general consumption activities. Consistent with a fundamental principle of social psychology, other people influence us and we influence other people.

Marketers also have to be aware and, if possible, ahead of changing social trends. Teams of researchers are often used to interact with specific demographic groups. In this kind of **ethnographic** or qualitative approaches, researchers might become part of a group for an extended period. Harley-Davidson, for example, hires researchers to ride motorcycles and attend various events so they can learn more about the way enthusiasts talk about their products, to identify opinion leaders, and ultimately to have good ideas as to product modifications or new (and highly profitable) things like Harley-Davidson branded clothing and other accessories for motorcycles. Companies use **social network analysis** to help identify opinion leaders in social media by analyzing the nature and extent of their social network.

Companies routinely monitor online discussions about their products and services and use online marketing research techniques called **netnography** to better understand their current and future customers. They also use software that allows them to empirically analyze the online conversations to constantly monitor how consumers feel about their brands. This is called **sentiment analysis**. Social psychologist Jamie Pennebaker and his colleagues study individual personalities and interpersonal interaction through the analysis of words and things like Twitter posts. To understand how this research is conducted, complete some of the online exercises at https://www.secretlifeofpronouns.com by yourself and with your friends.

Companies seek to influence consumers, but consumers also seek to influence company policies. Consumers also use things like their social media posts to try to get to change policies with regard to where and how they get materials for the products as well as ways of disposing of the products (https://www.youtube.com/watch?v=uRGiGbX9lIo). Consumers and consumer groups are also quick to point out cases where they feel the advertisements for products are harmful to children or create or perpetuate stereotypes. Some groups even go so far as to call themselves "culture jammers" (see http://www.adbusters.org). They promote special events like "buy nothing day."

Consumer behavior and consumer psychology is a part of people's lives from beginning to end. Some expectant parents even go so far as to post ultrasound pictures of their babies. Reflecting the other end of life is a growing trend of **"online virtual memorials,"** which document a person's life and influence after they have died.

The field of consumer behavior encompasses much more than what is covered in this module. However, this module will focus on topics at the intersection of consumer behavior and social psychology. In the attitude and persuasion chapters (Chapters 7–8), the ways in which we may be persuaded to buy are thoroughly covered. In the next section, decision making will be briefly discussed. The remaining sections in this module focus more on the purchase and consumption situation and process. People who study consumer psychology and social psychology are interested in how personal and situational factors affect the purchase, use, and disposal of products.

ethnographic research method that attempts to provide a close understanding of people and cultures

social network analysis the process of studying the connections and activity levels between individuals, groups, or things. Social Network Analysis can be used in many areas but it is especially useful in tracking and and understanding social media connections. Social Analysis reports often include graphical representations of connections as well as visual depictions of activity levels

netnography ethnographic research applied to internet and social media communications to better understand the group and individual members

sentiment analysis use of software and analytical techniques, by companies, that allows them to empirically analyze online conversations to constantly monitor how consumers feel about their products and services

online virtual memorial online document of a person's life after they have died, or online version of cemeteries and other places to remember people

QUIZ YOURSELF

Learning, Knowing, and Deciding What to Buy

1. **Companies gather insights about consumer behavior from** _____.
   - (a) mail and telephone surveys
   - (b) social media activities
   - (c) ethnographic studies
   - (d) All of the above

2. **A brand** _____.
   - (a) can have a personality
   - (b) is usually cheaper than a generic product
   - (c) is mainly for wealthy consumers
   - (d) None of the above

3. **Sentiment analysis** _____.
   - (a) helps companies find out how consumers feel about their products
   - (b) measures profitability of a company
   - (c) reflects an old personal memory that has a lot of emotion
   - (d) helps companies reduce pollution

4. **Social Network Analysis** _____.
   - (a) is the study person-to-person connections potential
   - (b) sells expensive and exclusive brands
   - (c) monitors popular brands
   - (d) shows consumers how to reduce cell phone costs

answers: see pg A24

What Is for Sale?

In the modern world, companies are selling more than a product or service that meets a practical need. People tend to be emotionally involved in their purchases. Teenagers worldwide are targeted by advertising emphasizing American brands, so much so that the United States and its symbols are used in many global campaigns aimed at youth.[1] Clothes do more than protect us from the elements. The clothes you wear matter not only because others form impressions about the way you look (e.g., neat, pressed, well put together) but because we also form impressions based on the products a person chooses. Wearing different clothes can also affect how a person thinks about himself or herself. Different kinds or different aspects of advertisements influence some consumers more than others. In Chapter 11, you learned about the individual difference variable of self-monitoring. Research shows, for example, that high self-monitors tend to be more concerned with social aspects of products where whereas low self-monitors tend to be more concerned about product attributes or qualities of features.

Not only do advertisers target specific segments of consumers but the media organizations also sell access to consumers to companies. Most consumers rarely consider that they are being packaged and sold by networks, newspapers, radio stations, and their favorite social media sites. These media organizations work to place advertising in trade publications that product manufacturers and their marketing teams read. Tripod (a do-it-yourself website server) claims in one of their ads that they can deliver Generation X to the marketers. Radio station advertisements proclaim they have the ears (and thus the mind) of their audience. It is not enough for a network or radio station to say they have some consumers; they have to show they have the right consumers. The right consumers tend to be middle to upper class, 20 to 40 years old (preferably single and urban), with large disposable incomes. Male homosexual couples tend to have quite large disposable incomes and advertisers pay attention to them, though target marketing is done carefully so as not to upset the mainstream. TV programming that appeals to other, less wealthy demographic groups may be doomed to a short run if advertisers aren't interested in the viewers the show draws.

Social media is the new "word-of-mouth" advertising, combining the social verification of the product and the technology of the internet.[2] Increasingly companies are relying on their own social media pages to be "liked" and "shared" and hope they can find just one video commercial that will "go viral" on YouTube. More than 111 million people watched the Super Bowl and presumably saw the M&M's Super Bowl commercial,[3] but M&M's also received 15% of the social media attention including tweets, blogs, and posts that occurred during the Super Bowl.[4] The company posted the video on YouTube and received just over 2 million views, but when a popular YouTube channel also posted the video, they received over 17 million views. For social media to work for marketing, the company can only do so much and then must rely on others in the network to provide social validation. Watch the PBS Frontline Special "Generation Like" to see big changes in the way products are marketed to younger generations of consumers. (See http://www.pbs.org/wgbh/pages/frontline/generation-like/.)

While most market segments are based on generation, age, demographics, or even on shared values or interests, the green market segment is more challenging. Concern about the environment has been on the rise in the U.S. population. Historically, products that were marketed to "green consumers" focused on the products' components (e.g., 50% post-consumer recycled materials). The price of energy has led people to focus on how green products are saving money in addition to treading lightly on the environment. Focusing on the financial impact of buying a green product has increased this market segment to include a wide range of individuals. This makes the green market particularly diverse with dualistic motivations: Preserve the environment and reduce costs. The *Harvard Business Review* warns about targeting the green market too tightly.[5] Successful green marketing targets a larger population with products and services that anyone might be able to use while simultaneously saving money and reducing their impact on the environment. This strategy has worked with energy-efficient lightbulbs that fit standard light fixtures, save money, reduce energy use, and last much longer than traditional lightbulbs. People (with the exception of those who purchase carbon offsets) generally don't need to be green; they need products, and if those products happen to be environmentally friendly, then all the better.

Buying a "green" or healthy product is not always easy. Websites like Goodguide.com are beginning to provide detailed information to consumers who want to know more about the environmental, social, global, and health aspects of the products they buy.

While more common in Europe than in the United States, a growing trend is for consumers to share products. For example, instead of each person owing a car, three to four individuals can own a car and use their social media tools to make reservations to use or locate the car. Such practices make good economic and environmental sense.

Location, Location, Location

Besides advertising, many other factors influence marketplace behavior. Location of a store is a good predictor of whether or not you will shop there. The farther away a store is, the less likely a person is to shop at that store.[6] Since 1968 we have seen bustling downtown areas become ghost towns as people moved to suburbia and their trade dollars went with them to the shopping locations that sprouted up in neighborhoods. In addition, consumers have begun to expect certain types of stores to occur in clusters. For example, if you can find a Barnes and Noble, a Starbucks is likely nearby (or even inside the bookstore). This decreases the amount of effort that consumers have to exert to find the products they want for the price they want to pay. There may be a store that carries precisely the product you need, but if it is in a part of town you rarely frequent, you might do without or buy it online. In China, an upstart competitor to Starbucks is Luckin Coffee. Luckin Coffee rents small spaces in the corner of other retail stores. They typically focus on carryout and on delivery of hot coffee (on small electric motorcycles) in large cities in China. Chinese consumers use their cell phones to order and pay for the coffee. When they share their friend contact information with Luckin Coffee as part of the purchase process, their friends get a free cup of coffee! The network of consumers and fans of Luckin Coffee has grown very quickly.

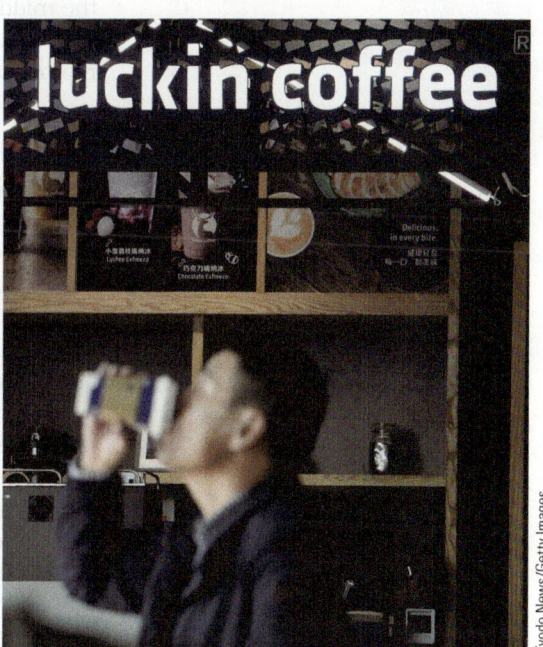

Luckin Coffee, a new competitor to Starbucks in China, uses creative marketing strategies involving social connections.

Another major factor that has helped to overcome the location problem is the internet, which allows us to shop anywhere in the world from our desk or laptop. Recent work has shown that regardless of location, loyalty to store format (layout, pricing, etc.) keeps people from switching between supermarkets.[7] This loyalty to store format is especially true for those who spend more money per trip and those who shop infrequently. That is not to say that the occasional sale doesn't cause a visit to a competing store, but a sale will not overwhelm the loyalty most people feel to their primary supermarket. It is likely that the same holds true for virtual store formats. A consumer who is accustomed to the format of Amazon.com may find the Waldenbooks or Hastings website less appealing or frustrating if the links they expect to have are difficult to find or not available.

While websites vary in how they display information, the physical store is often quite different from an online version of a store. Interesting virtual reality applications might make a future visit to an online version of a store more similar to a physical visit to a store. Thus, if a consumer has a preference for a certain physical store, he or she may be more loyal to the online version so store as well because of the ease of navigation. Going to the store virtually may be very similar to going to the store physically!

Store format influences how we shop and even how much we spend. That is, most people shop at the same locations again and again. Even if you live in a town with five grocery stores, chances are that you shop at one of them more often than you do the rest. You know this store's layout well and can easily locate the products you purchase most frequently, even when they are in disparate locations. One reason store layouts are grouped by product type is to cause consumers to search in the hope that during the search other products may catch their eye. However, most deli counters in grocery stores are now near the front of the store. This was a surprising finding worthy of magazine coverage in 1976, when a grocer found that moving the deli from the back of the store to the more high-traffic front area increased sales 300%.[8]

Other research has found that potential consumers at female apparel shops felt both discomfort and excitement when learning about a store design, layout, or concept that was incongruent with their expectations for clothing stores.[9] For example, in traditional female apparel stores, formal wear is often located near the lingerie section; professional, casual, and everyday wear is often toward the front of the store; and dressing rooms and sale racks are toward the back. However, newer stores may put the dressing rooms in the middle of the store or even in the middle of the space. The excitement may be good for business at first, but consumer discomfort would need to be eased quickly to ensure repeat business.

Environmental Influences: Sounds, Sights, and Smells

The environment of the store influences consumer behavior. Music, co-consumers, smells, and even associations between a brand and a specific commercial reminder can play a role. Research found that supermarket sales increased 38% when slower music was played.[10] Another study found that wine shoppers purchased more expensive wines when classical music was playing than when "Top 40" hits music was playing.[11] Not only does music pace our shopping, but it also provides a greater context of associative information about what sorts of products, schemas, and ultimately purchases are most appropriate. These associations probably influence consumers by influencing unconscious thought processes. For example, people probably do not consciously think that they should take their sweet time in a store if slow background music is playing. Rather, they probably unconsciously associate slow music with a more relaxed pace. Volkswagen (VW) dealerships often play progressive rock tunes from groups like Pink Floyd, Led Zeppelin, and Yes because people often associate VW cars with this genre of music. Indeed, in the past VW sponsored Pink Floyd concerts and gave away a free car at each concert. However, with personal music devices (e.g., iPods), brick-and-mortar stores are losing some of their ability to set the sound ambience for shoppers. Companies sometimes also employ creative techniques to capture the attention of consumers. In Amsterdam's Schiphol airport, for example, a motion-detecting device projects advertisements for products travelers are likely to need on the floor in front of a person as they walk in the airport!

Co-consumers also affect our shopping, eating, and consuming behavior. Donovan and Rossiter[12] used an environmental psychology approach to understanding our responses to busy shopping areas. Crowding tends to intensify whatever consumption experience we are already having. That is, if the atmosphere is pleasant and crowded, we may see it as even more pleasant and increase our time in that location, speak with others there, and ultimately consume more. However, if we find ourselves to be uncomfortable or irritated, the crowds are going to intensify that experience, causing us to leave as quickly as possible. Consider shopping during the winter holidays. This may be a fairly pleasant and happy experience, with our positive feelings enhanced by seeing others out also doing their gift shopping. However, anyone who waits until the 24th of December to purchase a major gift may have quite a different perspective on the crowds. The more pleasurable and arousing a store's environment, the more likely we are to spend more time (and more money) in the store. However, at heightened levels of arousal, people tend to enact their **dominant responses** (also see Chapter 14). If the dominant response is to leave the store, then that is what is most likely to occur when arousal becomes too high.[13] Our olfactory sense also plays a role in our perceptions of the consumption environment. Scented stores tend to be perceived as having better-quality products than unscented stores.[14] It is important, however, that the scent be congruent with the products available.[15] In the United Kingdom, McCain Foods has installed potato sculptures at 10 bus stops, with a built-in heating element that not only warms your hands but also emits the smell of freshly baked potatoes in an attempt to sell frozen potatoes.[16] However, smell may be more important when the product is being used than when the product is being selected.[17] Research shows that ambient scents that are present during encoding of brand/product information aid in recall and recognition brand-memory tests.[18] This means that product manufacturers and marketing professionals would do well to make sure that the smells that are present when you are learning about the brand are also present when you are choosing the brand.

When illumination is low, noise levels tend to drop, which increases the amount of time patrons will spend in a bar.[19] However, the time and money spent on store atmosphere is directly proportionate to how much of the purchase/consumption process is dependent on the environment. Taco Bell makes a profit by getting many consumers in and out of their establishment; whereas most bars and clubs make more money the longer the people stay. In some cases, the product is good enough to overwhelm a lack of ambience. Imagine great food vendors that provide only a busy and littered street corner, but have a booming business because they have a good food product that can be delivered and consumed quickly. However, some dining or club experiences have much more to do with the atmosphere than with the products being sold. Consider the cover charge just to enter some establishments, or the minimum purchase requirements, where consumers are buying the experience as much as they are buying the food or drink they plan to order. In the future, atmospherics may have to broaden in scope to include website design. The increasing use of the internet to make purchases in the comfort of one's own home may make "storefront" atmospherics a largely digital endeavor.[20]

Even the phonetic sounds making up the brand names of the products can influence perceptions of products and subsequently the purchase of these products. For example, researchers have found that the "ä" and "i" sounds are perceived differently.[21] The "ä" sound in Frosh is associated with perceptions that objects are bigger, heavier, slower, and duller, whereas the "i" in Frish is associated with perceptions that objects are smaller, lighter, livelier, and sharper. Participants in their study were presented with a press release announcing a new brand of ice cream and told that the brand name was either Frosh or Frish. In addition, they were told either that this was in fact the name of the product or that it was a name that was being used only for the test and not the name that would be used when the product was released to the public. The Frosh ice cream (when participants were told it was the actual brand name) was expected to be richer, smoother, and creamier than the Frish ice cream. Just the brand name phonetics can change people's perceptions of a product and ultimately their purchase decisions and behaviors.

dominant response a behavior that takes very little effort or thought and is frequently the default or habitual response to a specific situation

What Is for Sale?

It is clear that shopping environment impacts consumer behavior, but there is also evidence that the act of going shopping itself may be related to more positive health outcomes in later life. Recently, an analysis of data from Taiwan found that, among the oldest members of the population, those who shopped every day had 27% less risk of death compared to those who shopped less and that men benefited more from daily shopping.[22] There are likely a variety of explanations for this finding, but it is worth noting that shopping itself may fulfill needs beyond those fulfilled by the purchase.

Brand Allegiance

Brand loyalty also plays a role in understanding what products people will buy and what products are destined to expire on the shelf. Marketers are well aware of this and design any changes or modernization of logos, trademarks, and packaging with great care. For example, Betty Crocker has evolved over time and now has a more modern haircut, but the changes have occurred so gradually that the average consumer may not have noticed them. Today, Betty Crocker products rarely include the woman's image at all; in fact, the logo has evolved so that the red spoon is now the primary association with the brand. Imagine that Kit Kat bars were all of a sudden packaged in blue instead of orange wrappers. Chances are

brand loyalty the degree to which a customer holds a positive attitude toward a brand, has a commitment to it, and intends to continue purchasing it

Brands such as Betty Crocker must be careful that changes in the images associated with the brand change to reflect the current consumer, without appearing so suddenly different as to be unrecognizable to the brand loyal.

that people would assume something had changed about the product inside as well, and they might search for the "original" as denoted by packaging color.

Some marketing campaigns fail because a brand is so closely associated with some feature of the product that if it is changed, even the brand loyal consumer may stop buying. New Coke was one example. Coca-Cola came out with New Coke on April 23, 1985. The can changed slightly, and the new Coke formula was preferred in blind taste tests involving 200,000 people. However, people were loyal as much to the idea of Coke ("The Real Thing") as to the taste of the beverage itself, and by July 11, 1985, Coca-Cola Classic had returned as the "original" recipe Coke product. The New Coke formula can still be found in select markets as Coke II (not to be confused with the low-carbohydrate recipe in C2).

While some logos evolve to be something new, others make returns to past logo features in an effort to induce nostalgia for a time when the product experienced success. Pepsi-Cola has managed just such an evolution with a logo design change, appearing on cans in late 2008.[23] Consumer preferences and a desire for the way things used to be led to the marketing of products like Pepsi Throwback (a soda with real sugar instead of high-fructose corn sugar). Recognizing that sales of highly sugared sodas have been declining in recent years, companies like Pepsi have also begun to create product versions that have reduced amounts of sugar. One such product is Pepsi Next.

What leads up to the purchase may be a thoughtful considered process, or it may be an automatic one. The consumption process begins long before we choose a product and doesn't end until well after we have used it. As you can see in **FIGURE A.1**, the consumption process is much more elaborate than the typical consumer might imagine. The consumption process involves not only the persuasive attempts of advertisers and the specific purchase decisions of consumers but also consumer intentions for use and disposal.

Pepsi-Cola's latest logo design appeals to brand nostalgia.

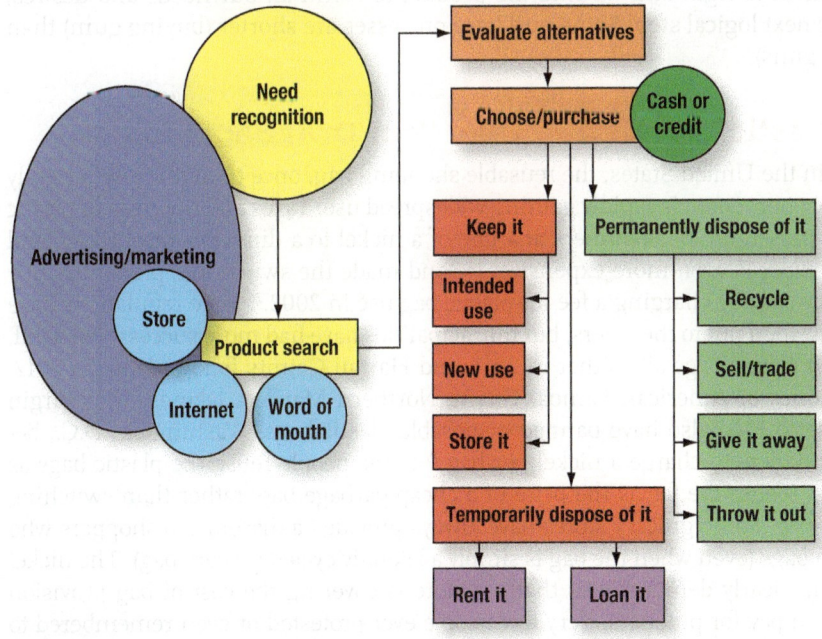

FIGURE A.1

The consumption process includes everything from advertising and need recognition to disposal of the product.

What Is for Sale? | **A9**

QUIZ YOURSELF
What Is for Sale?

1. **Margaret is designing an ad campaign for a new laundry detergent. If she wants to ensure repeat purchase, where should she place scratch-and-sniff stickers that smell like the laundry detergent?**
   - (a) On the boxes of detergent
   - (b) On the newspaper coupon ad inserts
   - (c) On the boxes and coupons
   - (d) In the laundry detergent aisle

2. **Dr. Hudson loves the holiday season and hopes to get all of her holiday shopping done before she leaves for her winter vacation. Based on what you've learned about atmospherics, Dr. Hudson is most likely to _____ .**
   - (a) shop primarily in familiar stores near her home
   - (b) be upset when she has to go to the crowded shopping mall to forage for gifts
   - (c) shop in a wide variety of stores regardless of how far they are from her home
   - (d) shop primarily in new stores where she is unfamiliar with the layout

3. **Kelly has been asked to design a website for a company that sells a wide variety of socks. Based on the research in this section, what would you suggest that Kelly do?**
   - (a) Provide as much information as possible about the socks.
   - (b) Give consumers a lot of details about the ways in which the socks are manufactured.
   - (c) Create a website that allows consumers to interact with the site and choose the information they see as most relevant.
   - (d) Use a very simple and basic design with photos of the socks and their prices.

4. **The "ä" sound in Frosh is associated with _____ .**
   - (a) bigger, heavier, slower, and duller
   - (b) newer, original, fresher, and innovative
   - (c) older, more mature, stale, and stable
   - (d) smaller, lighter, faster, and sharper

answers: see pg A24

Making the Purchase

If the environment is right and we find the product to fulfill all our needs and desires, purchase is the next logical step. Some purchase processes are shorter (buying gum) than others (buying guns).

Paper or Plastic? vs. BYOB (Bring Your Own Bag)

In some cities in the United States, the reusable shopping bag, once thought to be a trendy green market phenomenon, is rapidly gaining widespread use. Taxes and the costs of plastic bags are being passed on to consumers at a rate of a nickel to a dime per plastic bag, and in some states paper is even more expensive. Ireland made the switch to a predominantly BYOB consumer base by charging a fee for plastic bag use in 2002.[24] State regulations have not been passed when put to the voters, but municipalities have had more success. Portland, Oregon, banned plastic bags altogether in 2011, and Hawaii County followed suit in 2012. The U.S. territories of American Samoa, Guam, Northern Mariana Islands, U.S. Virgin Islands and Puerto Rico also have banned disposable plastic bags. Washington, D.C., began requiring retailers to charge a nickel per bag.[25] Some people reuse the plastic bags as trash can liners, seeing the fee as the price of a cheap garbage bag, rather than switching over to another bag. Some grocery stores have always provided a discount to shoppers who bring their own bags (even when the bag is simply a laterally cycled grocery bag). The nickel discount per bag clearly demonstrates that the store is covering the cost of bag provision through what you pay for products. Very few people ever protested or even remembered to bring in their own bags to save a nickel, but when the nickel is recapitulated as a fee, people take notice and in some cases even change their behavior.

Cash or Credit?

A situational factor that might influence how much (or if) a consumer spends is whether the purchase will be made with cash or on credit. "Cash or credit?" used to be the question that checkout employees asked right after "Paper or plastic?" Today the question is "Credit or debit?" The difference, of course, is that a debit is taking away from an existing supply of money that you have with a particular financial institution, whereas charging something to a credit card means you are essentially taking out a loan and (unless you pay the bill in full every month) will be charged interest. A 2009 study found that college students had an average credit card balance of $3,173.[26] According to a Gallup poll in 2008, the average American had around $3,848 in credit card debt.[27]

Shopping with a credit card often means spending more than you would if you had to hand over cash. In one study, Boston Celtic basketball tickets were auctioned online.[28] Half the bidders were informed they would have to pay cash; the other half were allowed to pay with a credit card. Participants who could pay with a credit card placed bids almost twice as high as the cash-only bidders did.

With the influx of credit availability and the organizations that have sprung up to help people manage their debt, we are encouraged to view debtors as we would someone who needs help to combat overeating or alcohol consumption—that there is something "wrong" with people who use credit. However, several studies indicate that credit card debt (at least among college students) is unrelated to impulsive buying or financial recklessness,[29] general self-destructiveness,[30] or the habitual feeling that one cannot control one's life.[31] Debt is related to time orientation (how long it will take to pay off the debt and a personal disposition to consider the distant future). That is, the less you think about the future or the more quickly you believe you can pay off the debt, the more likely you are to incur it. One series of studies demonstrated that participants felt that credit limits on credit cards were indicative of future earning potential, which supported the belief that more expensive purchases could be easily paid back in the future.[32] Optimistic credit card shoppers are likely to end up spending more than their pessimistic/realistic counterparts.

Of course, cash has quickly fallen by the wayside, as it is much quicker to slide one's debit card through the machine and key in a pin number than to wait for the cashier to make change or for you to count out your money. If you are buying online, you must have some electronic currency available. Indeed, the machines currently in use at some grocery stores have consumers enter their "club" number (to get the discounts of the day) and then present them with four options for payment—none of them cash. Of course, you *can* pay with cash—you simply have to ignore the screen and speak to the cashier directly.

Using credit seems quicker and less painful than using cash. However, credit purchases may extend the psychological experience of product satisfaction/dissatisfaction if you are still paying for the product months or even years after you made the decision to buy. The monthly payment serves as a reminder of your purchase decision and the product associations that go along with it. The way in which we pay for our purchases is, in effect, a tradeoff between convenience and being reminded of the purchase price for months.

Theories in basic social psychology can often be extended to help understand consumer behavior. Remember reading about the "weapons effect" research by Berkowitz and colleagues (see Chapter 10). In that research, it was shown that the mere presence of guns increased aggressive behavior. In a very interesting series of studies, one scholar used the research findings from the weapons effect to make predictions about the influence of credit cards on consumer decisions. He found that the presence of credit card stimuli was associated with making quicker decisions to spend and well as a willingness to pay higher prices for items![33]

Point-of-Purchase Perceptions

Once you are at the point of purchase, things quickly begin to change. As soon as you have chosen a product, you begin to like it more than you like its competitors. Even products that are low in desirability (e.g., soda can insulators) are suddenly imbued with a mere ownership effect and liked better once they belong to the person.³⁴ (See Chapters 3 and 7 for the related topics of endowment effect and cognitive dissonance, respectively.)

Choice is good, or so we believe. In the United States, there are a vast array of brands and products from which to choose. Rarely does one find only one product to fulfill a specific need. Most people probably believe that the more choices people have the better, and the more satisfied they should be. However, the impact of choice on consumer behavior may be more complex than we might at first imagine. Take a moment to consider how post-decision dissonance and cognitive dissonance might play out if you had to choose among many good alternatives. Participants in one study were asked to rate either 6 or 30 different Godiva chocolates.³⁵ They were then given the opportunity to buy chocolate. Those who had the choice of 30 chocolates reported they enjoyed their chocolate *less* than those who had only 6 choices. Perhaps participants felt they had a better chance of choosing the "best" available chocolate when there were only 6. Or it could be that they felt they "missed out" on less when there were 6 rather than 30 choices. One explanation that has received considerable attention is how much information people have about the choices before them. For example, it may be fairly straightforward to compare and choose among a few options, but a cost–benefit analysis with 30 choices would likely be cognitively taxing.

Making an informed decision seems like a great idea. Historically, a well-informed sales staff ensured that you could ask questions about a variety of products and the salesperson would be able to effectively address your concerns. However, with the advent of superstores, the salesperson is often reduced to answering questions about where something is rather than providing information about product features, qualities, or attributes. Online purchases provide us with better opportunities to make informed decisions by clicking on tabs providing product reviews by other consumers, specifications such as dimensions, colors, and features, and 360-degree views of the product. The vast amount of information about products that is available online is one way in which the internet makes up for the inability to "touch the product."

Virtual storefronts also offer a way to automate our purchases, so that we only have to be well-informed once and thereafter can simply make the identical purchase again and again. Automatically renewing movie rental subscriptions is one example. However, a more frequent use of this technology is online food orders. For example, the first time you visit an online pizza website, you can carefully specify your topping, sauce, and crust preferences and add any special notes about allergies or how to make it up your driveway. As you check out, you can specify that this is a favorite order. The next time you log in, you simply add your "favorite order" to the cart and click the checkout button. You can even save your payment information so that you do not have to debate about how to pay or locate your credit/debit card. Most websites also include the "order ahead" option, so you can place a detailed order for a future social event and have the pizza delivered several days later.

The internet provides an abundance of information and reports on a wide variety of products and consumer concerns. Researchers have investigated the amount of information provided by internet shopping sites.³⁶ Their findings indicate that if consumers are provided with a great deal of information about a product, they may experience overload and start to feel less confident in their decision, less satisfied, and more confused. The researchers suggest that allowing consumers to choose what specific attribute information to use when comparing products may reduce the potentially negative aspects of this effect. It has also been empirically demonstrated that websites that promote interactivity (activities, links to relevant information, opportunities for feedback/discussion, site maps) increase the potential consumer's comprehension of the material.³⁷ Although it may be important not to overwhelm consumers viewing websites, it may be beneficial to give them an opportunity to "interact" with the site to find the information they *do* consider important.

It is not only marketing executives who are aware of this process. The internet and websites such as eBay, craigslist, and Etsy have made it easier for individuals to buy from other individuals rather than from large companies or manufacturers. Bidders and buyers may quickly pass up a product if the photo is blurry or does not provide a view they find important. Other product-specific sites such as Half.com have a more hybrid approach to the amount of information that shoppers receive from individual sellers. Half.com provides some standard specifications about books and video games (e.g., edition, number of pages, ISBN, platform), and then individual sellers fill in information about the condition of the particular item they are selling (e.g., some highlighting, minor shelf wear, survived a flood).

When does an item become yours? The car is yours once you are off the lot (as anyone who has ever wrecked a brand-new car pulling out of the lot is well aware). Food items in the grocery store seem to become the property of the shopper as soon as the items are in the cart, but eating food not yet paid for in the grocery store seems strange to most people. In any case, we do have a sense of ownership of our purchases that when violated we clearly recognize. Suppose you take an empty cart from the front of the store, put a few items in it, and then briefly abandon it. If another person picks up an item out of your cart to examine it, you may feel the need to proclaim your ownership and demand that the item be put back in your cart. If an interloper attempts to make use of "your" cart, you will very likely say something. We often take ownership not only of the products we are buying but also of public property (such as shopping carts) during consumption processes.

The internet storefront at first lacked this sense of pre-purchase ownership that physical stores garner as people touch the products they would like to purchase and carry them to the counter. Many internet storefronts now use online "shopping carts" as a way of giving internet shoppers a feeling of ownership over the items in "their cart." By clicking on a link, you put the item in "your shopping cart"; another click allows you to "view the items in your cart." Using a virtual shopping cart may be a first step toward getting consumers committed to the purchase, giving them a sense of ownership over virtual images of products that can't be handled or touched.

Once the product is in your possession, product evaluation begins. While resources and our perceptions guide what and how much we purchase, the product must meet our expectations for the experience to be satisfying. If the product performs as expected, you probably will have neutral feelings regarding your purchase. If the product exceeds your expectations, this will result in feelings of satisfaction with the purchase. On the other hand, if the product does not meet your expectations, you will likely be dissatisfied. This is readily visible in children, who see a new toy in a commercial but play with it only a little bit and are disappointed when it doesn't work the way it did in the commercial (superhero dolls don't stay airborne as long when you throw them as they do in slow-motion commercial footage). The intensity of your post-purchase experiences is directly related to how "big" a purchase it was. If your breath strips taste bitter, you toss them out and think nothing more of it. However, if your new car interior smells "off," you will likely be heading back to the dealer.

These post-purchase experiences are not the sole predictor of repeat purchase. We are social creatures, and the reactions of our reference groups, friends, family, and even strangers will go a long way to determining whether we purchase the product or brand again. Subjective norms (what others believe you should do) are a strong predictor of whether consumers patronize fast-food restaurants.[38] If everyone you know has bought an iPad Pro, your purchase of an Android tablet will certainly make you unique, but the reactions of your iPad Pro–owning friends will factor into what you purchase the next time. If others seem to support your purchase decision, this increases the likelihood you will buy that product again; nothing guarantees that you will abandon the product line or be ostracized for owning it. Thus, the co-consumer is powerful not only as an aspect of the environment influencing repurchases but also as someone who sets norms for appropriate product consumption.

What does your purchase say about you? Making a purchase with the express purpose of making others aware of your ownership is called **conspicuous consumption**. The idea is that you are using the product to communicate something about yourself to others. For example, a Fossil watch can be set to tell the same time as a much less-expensive watch, but owning this particular brand communicates something to others about who you are (e.g., that you are cool). Cell phones are an excellent case in point, as they are often seen

conspicuous consumption the purchase and prominent display of luxury goods to provide evidence of a consumer's ability to afford them as status symbols. One study found that men tended to "display" their phones more as the number of men relative to women increased in a bar.[39] We may have preconceived impressions based on things that people eat, wear, or drive. For example, if you find out that a person drives a pickup truck with a gun rack, you might infer a great deal about that person from ownership of that vehicle and accessory.

Some products are strongly associated with stereotypes; other products are closely tied to ritual and have understood meaning. For example, a person wearing a ring on the third finger of the left hand is considered to be in a committed relationship (engaged or married); the absence of such a ring is taken to mean greater potential availability. With an increase in the age of first marriage, jewelers discovered a whole new market of women in their 30s with discretionary money and no "significant" jewelry. This led the Diamond Trading Company (a subsidiary of DeBeers) to launch an ad campaign urging women to "Raise your right hand" and buy a diamond ring for the right ring finger. "Your left hand says 'we,' your right hand says 'me'" and "Your left is your heart, your right is your voice" appeared in an advertisement to encourage single women to adorn themselves to show their independence.[40] Conspicuous consumption apparently is not just for the married and the single. There is also now a market for divorce jewelry. According to D Jewelry Company advertising, divorce rings are in the business of "Building self-esteem one person at a time" and that these rings are a "healing tool for broken hearts."[41] So what's a person to do with the wedding rings after the divorce? Several websites such as IDoNowIDont.com will purchase the rings, or you can buy a casket, a "Wedding Ring Coffin," if you can't bear to part with your marital jewels.

Terror management theory has been used to explain conspicuous consumption.[42] Terror management theory is essentially the idea that awareness of mortality (knowing we are going to die) leads humans to develop cultural worldviews and beliefs about reality that reduce the terror of existentialist thinking (see Chapter 3). Humans strive to remain in existence (even after death) via religious beliefs, reproduction, building lasting monuments, or "making a mark" on the world in some way. In the United States, one way to do this is by amassing wealth that can purchase these "marks," or at the very least be passed on in your name. Money can even stave off death, as it can be spent on quality medical care, life-sustaining medications, quality healthful foods, and gym memberships. One of the primary ways Americans, in particular, embrace their culture in the face of death is by spending money to possess material things. In the days following the terrorist attacks of 9/11, then President George W. Bush made a point of encouraging Americans to go shopping. In part, this was an attempt to keep the American economy going, but it is not quite the same as encouraging World War II–era citizens to buy war bonds.

Awareness of death makes us financially optimistic.[43] Participants were asked to think either about their own death or about listening to music; then they completed a questionnaire about their 15-year projections of their financial status. Those participants contemplating death believed they were more likely to have more money (especially to spend on luxury items). Also, most people believe that having a 20% increase in their income would make them happier.[44] Believing one is going to have more money in the future (and be happier) is likely to mean that it would be acceptable to spend more money in the present. Credit is based on just this idea: You can spend today and pay tomorrow (albeit with interest). The implication is not necessarily that Visa's next advertising campaign should include caskets. However, in a culture where conspicuous consumption runs rampant, your self-worth may be closely linked to your fiscal social comparisons.

There is some backlash against overconsumption, with magazines like *Real Simple* and websites such as The Simple Living Network encouraging people to value time and life experiences over money and extravagant purchases. The economic downturn, increase in foreclosures, and decrease in the availability of credit also impact attitudes toward buying, but perhaps also toward disposing of what we have and rate of replacement. Consider the television show *Hoarders*, which documents the experiences of individuals who have amassed so large a quantity of material goods or things that they often destroy their homes, and in some cases, their families. Often the narrative of the individual hoarder has origins in a time of financial uncertainty or remembering a time when such items were scarce. Other times people hoard items in an attempt to meet needs that may best be filled by interpersonal relationships, but after a lifetime of hearing that products can fulfill these needs, they choose instead to surround themselves with the material goods rather than people. The **usage situation** refers to the context in which a product is used. For some items, usage situations may vary. Laptops, cell phones, and iPads are some examples of products that were adapted specifically for a wide range of usage situations. Other items, such as laundry detergent or toothpaste, have more limited usage situations. Sometimes a usage situation is defined by the function of the product (requires electricity); in other cases, usage situations are limited by the "appropriate time" for the product to be used. Orange juice, for example, is still more popular for breakfast than with other meals or snacks, whereas bottled water has expanded its usage situation far beyond road trips and the gym.

In the case of gifts, a product must serve two usage situations. First, the product (together with appropriate wrappings) is to be used as a gift for the situation in which it is given and received (e.g., a party, in the mail). Second, the product is to be used by the recipient in other appropriate usage situations (e.g., wearing the gifted necklace to an appropriate function at a later date). Gift purchases are predicted by recipient reactions, not just buyer reactions. Certainly, what makes something a good product may not necessarily make it a good gift. In gift purchasing, the recipient's demographics and attitudes play as much of a role as the purchaser's. Research shows that both men and women feel more comfortable giving gifts to members of the same sex but have more intense feelings when giving gifts to members of the other sex.[45] Both givers and recipients experience "gifting anxiety," which sales staff can help to alleviate if they have a full understanding of the psychological processes underlying the gift-giving situation.[46]

Consumer behavior (and repeat purchasing) involves the entire relationship and interaction that a person has with the product and brand, from the moment the need is present until the product that is used to satisfy the need is out of the consumer's possession. Consumer needs have changed over time, and the consumption process and the ways consumers fulfill their needs have also evolved.

usage situation the context in which a product is used

QUIZ YOURSELF
Making the Purchase

1. **George is on a tight budget but has saved up just enough money to buy a new flash drive for his computer. If you want to ensure George isn't asking you for lunch money next week, what would you encourage him to do?**
   - (a) Put the flash drive on his credit card
   - (b) Use his debit card to buy the flash drive
   - (c) Withdraw cash at an ATM and then pay cash for the flash drive
   - (d) Do research on the internet to determine which flash drive has the best features

2. **Mindi and Mandi are identical twins, and their mother has bought them identical outfits for their birthday. Mindi insists that her mother write their names on the tags so they can tell them apart, even though they are identical. What effect explains this?**
   - (a) Mere exposure effect
   - (b) Cognitive dissonance
   - (c) Mere ownership effect
   - (d) Attributional theory

3. **College students are often inundated with credit card applications that promise free T-shirts for applying. What is it about college students that might draw creditors to seek applications from this population?**
   - (a) Optimism and future time orientation
   - (b) Past time orientation
   - (c) Cyclical time orientation
   - (d) Realism and linear time orientation

4. **What theory has been used to explain conspicuous consumption?**
   - (a) Cognitive dissonance theory
   - (b) Psychological reactance theory
   - (c) Self-awareness theory
   - (d) Terror management theory

answers: see pg A24

Consuming Today

Twenty-five years ago the internet was primarily an academic endeavor, and "unlimited" and "free" were not associated with telecommunications. The home was a comfortable retreat, a safe environment in which one could easily separate work from home life. Today, the home is a technological utopia with wireless networks, laptops, gaming systems, and cell phones connecting to a world that can come into any room of your home, your car, or your yard, removing the feasibility of separating work and home life by changing your location. Consumers can shop worldwide online and appear to have increasing needs to do more tasks in less and less time.

E-Commerce

It is now possible (especially in urban areas) to do all of one's shopping through an internet connection. Groceries can be ordered online and delivered to keyed freezers on your front porch. Pizza can be ordered online and delivered within 30 minutes. Clothes, shoes, music, books, condoms, shampoo, jewelry, and even cars can be ordered online and delivered to your home. Researchers in Hong Kong interviewed book buyers about their choice to purchase a book online or at a store.[47] The only factor they found that encouraged a visit to a physical bookstore was being able to "see" the item (in the tactile sense). The outcome for some brick-and-mortar storefronts is that they become a tactile kiosk for online purchasers. Although companies are always trying to give consumers the sense that they can "have it all," online consumption, like many other behaviors, has tradeoffs.

"There's an app for that!" ShopSavvy and RedLaser are smartphone apps that enable a shopper to scan the UPC or QR code of a product, engage in price comparison, and buy it from another store, while standing in the competitor's aisle. Perhaps it's not all bad news for stores who guarantee to beat a competitor's price; they may still get the sale at the reduced rate because they can instantly be presented with a price comparison from the competing store.

Even Black Friday sales, which used to provide brick-and-mortar businesses with a year-end boost, have found themselves competing with Cyber Monday, which is the day that online retailers roll out their biggest sales of the year. Of course, consumers who care more about sustainable economies will likely also do some shopping on Shop Local Saturday, which has cropped up in many smaller communities and occurs the Saturday before Cyber Monday.

Marketers make use of online and demographic information to engage in **geo-targeting**. Online advertising can be limited to appear on a widely available website only in certain regions (certain IP address ranges). This sort of direct marketing is relatively cheap and allows ad campaigns to be targeted to specific groups of consumers without much overhead.

Five internet consumer segments have been identified: confident/convenience-oriented/ comparison; store-preferred; highly involved; apathetic; and apprehensive.[48] These segments represent five basic attitudes that consumers have toward internet shopping. Interestingly, most of the respondents in this study were in the first segment (3 Cs); they were confident using the internet, considered it convenient, and thought it provided a good way to comparison shop. The smallest consumer segment was the store-preferred segment—individuals who preferred traditional brick-and-mortar shopping to online shopping. However, even this segment reported shopping online occasionally. When considering the impact of the internet on consumer behavior, it is important to consider the new "world brand" or global community implications of internet advertising and buying. Though not everyone has an outlet for a particular store in their vicinity, if they have internet access, they can still buy the product. Does this present special issues? Sure. Language doesn't always translate directly, such as when Chevrolet tried to sell its Nova automobile in the South American market only to realize later that in Spanish the word means "it doesn't run." Colors have different meanings in various cultures. Global mass marketing

---

geo-targeting the strategy of exposing only individuals within a specific geographic region to a particular ad campaign has moved beyond Coca-Cola, which sells essentially the same product worldwide. Ordering a Coke in Japan will get you the same formula you get in the United States. However, other corporations market globally in much the way that Nabisco markets Oreos. In Saudi Arabia, McDonald's closes five times a day for Muslim prayers. In India, McDonald's opened its first beefless outlet, also serving vegetable nuggets (instead of chicken).[49] It took more than 100 years for Coca-Cola to establish a global presence, but Starbucks went from 17 stores in the United States to 4,700 locations worldwide in a decade. The increase in the number of online consumers is likely to expand worldwide and make global brand presence almost instantaneous.

Do you like Oreo cookies? The company has worked hard to teach people about Oreo cookies, from demonstrating "how" to eat them, to developing unique flavors for different markets or traditions around the world. For example, there is a green tea–flavored Oreo that is very popular in China! Even U.S. high-sugar preferences must be significantly cut for the Japanese consumer, for whom Nabisco created Petit Oreo Non-Cream cookies.[50]

Buying Time: Cell Phones—Case in Point

One marketing strategy that has been increasingly used is to sell time. Discussion of the deadline technique in Chapter 8 showed how "limited time offers" can be used to encourage consumers to spend quickly. However, there is more to the interaction between situational time and consumer behavior than this advertising technique. Many consumers today are feeling time compression, or **time poverty** leading them to select products that will alleviate time pressure. As both adults and children continue to fill their days with more and more activities, they have less and less time to do things. As a result, speed, time, and products that allow for multitasking are in demand. Until the 1980s, it was common for someone to sit down, dial a phone with a rotary dial, and seek silence and solitude for making a phone call. However, the development of the cordless phone (and even more recently the phone headset) has made it possible for a person to have that telephone conversation while roaming the house doing a variety of chores.

The cell (or mobile) phone has furthered our ability to roam while talking on the phone so that we do not lose a moment of productivity while driving, shopping, or even "relaxing" at home. In 1997, there were fewer than 50 million cell phone users in the United States; as of 2011, the estimate is that there are more than 300 million cell phones in the United States, putting the United States third in line behind China (841 million) and India (729 million).[51] In the United States in June 2011, the Cellular Telecommunications Industry Association estimated that there were 2.12 trillion text messages sent per year and 2.25 trillion cell phone minutes used.[52] Text messaging filled a unique communication need for instant asynchronous and relatively private conversation that can occur in settings where a phone call would be inappropriate. For individuals with fewer social connections, the iPhone digital personal assistant, Siri, may be serving multiple purposes. Siri uses a conversational style that allows people to simply ask Siri to look up information, set up reminders, and carry out other digital tasks. For some consumers, this may provide social need fulfillment that keeps even the less socially inclined consumer engaged in the high-end smartphone market. The popularity of unlimited minutes and unlimited texting plans will likely lead to an increase in the amount of time spent on the phone, without necessarily decreasing the amount of time spent on other tasks. Our increasingly wireless lives have certainly made us busier and better equipped to multitask; in some respect, we are "buying time."

Some researchers are beginning to suggest that we spend too much time communicating via our electronic devices and not enough time talking to each other face-to-face. Watch Professor Sherry Turkle's TED talk, "Alone Together," and discuss reactions with your friends. http://www.ted.com/talks/sherry_turkle_alone_together.

Time is a precious, nonrefundable resource. Consumers are often most dissatisfied with services or products that have cost them time. Having a flight delayed several hours

time poverty a feeling of having less time available than is required to meet the demands of everyday living is usually much more dissatisfying than having a rough takeoff or landing. Products that manage to be complementary with other activities will have a larger market share than products that must be substituted for other products. For example, if a person uses Tide laundry detergent, he or she will not also use Era laundry detergent in the same load. Thus, Tide and Era are in direct competition for your laundry time. However, Febreze laundry additive is a product that is positioned to be complementary to laundry detergent and thus does not have to compete for your laundry time.

Orville Redenbacher popcorn has combined several of these ideas in their new Pop Up Bowl microwavable popcorn package. Not only does the microwave popcorn save you time as it always has, it now comes in a package that can be used as a bowl. This saves the consumer the time of waiting for the popcorn to cool or using up a bowl. It also provides an environmentally sound "dual use" package that green-minded consumers can feel good about. The bowl also meets a need for social interaction as their ultimate butter popcorn Pop Up Bowl product is touted with, "And now it's ultimate for sharing."[53]

As consumers have become increasingly mobile, food product manufacturers have noticed how much time is being spent in the car where food can be consumed only if it comes in the proper packaging. Campbell's Soup at Hand is designed to enable drivers to drink their soup from a disposable, single-serving, insulated, lidded container that fits nicely into any vehicle cup holder; when there is "No time for a meal," Yoplait encourages us to drink a Nouriche Yogurt Smoothie, which also fits into vehicle cup holders. If we can't find time to sit down to eat, we can certainly find time to drink a meal while driving. When cell phone companies found themselves competing for driving time, cell phone manufacturers came out with the hands-free Bluetooth headsets that allow cell phone use to be complementary with driving (or doing anything else you might need to do).

Companies aware of time poverty are essentially eliminating the need for consumers to make tradeoff choices. That is, you don't have to choose whether you want to spend your time driving or eating; you can now do both. The result, however, may be that you enjoy neither the drive nor the food as much as you might if you could find the time to do each separately. Tide now includes Downy or Febreze in their liquid detergent, so you don't even have to choose—you can have both at once. Eliminating the perception that you are trading one thing for another has been quite a successful marketing tactic, especially in the United States where "having it all" is paramount to achieving the "American Dream." Eliminating tradeoffs seems like an effective sales strategy.

Consider all the products we now rely on to save time: microwave ovens, garbage disposals, even fast wireless and in-home connections, all depend on consumers' valuing the irreplaceable, nonrefundable resource of time. Drive-through windows have appeared at banks, pharmacies, fast-food restaurants, and even some packaged liquor stores. ATMs and banking smartphone apps make sure your "workday" time does not have to be devoted to banking. Digital cameras mean that we have instant images and no longer need the one-hour photo processing that saved us the days we spent waiting for photos only a few years ago. Indeed, the only thing worse than a waste of money is a waste of time.

With the new Apple Watch on your wrist, you can save time by not having to take your cell phone out of your pocket to check your email or provide a basic response to a text.

Polychronic activity refers to being able to do more than one activity or task at a time. Many products are geared toward allowing us to do more than one thing at a time. Hair shampoo/conditioner formulas are meant to allow us to skip the second "conditioning" step by doing it all in one step; certain body washes allow us to wash our hair and our skin using a single product. Job ads often call for employees who can "multitask." The number of open windows on a computer desktop is often a good indicator of a person's multitasking skills. Computer manufacturers play to this by building faster and more capable machines that allow you to do "more at once." If we were all using only one or two programs at a time, we wouldn't need 16 GB of RAM to keep our computers running. It is becoming more common to have not just one monitor but also a second video card installed so that you can have dual monitors; certainly, this is not the configuration for one-program-at-a-time users.

polychronic activity engaging in more than one activity or behavior at a time

If we can't save time by doing more than one thing at once, we'd rather be in charge of our own time. Self-service has extended beyond gasoline pumps to checkout lanes where customers scan and bag their own items and then pay with a credit or debit card via an ATM-like interface. When first installed, these self-service lanes were intimidating (especially to market segments that are still suspicious of the computer), but those who use them often *feel* as though they have spent less time in line than those who have to stand idly by while someone else scans their purchases. Self-checkout has been present in many library systems for some time. In addition to the "time-saving" feature, self-checkout also increases the privacy of one's selections. Certainly, scanning your own condoms or that book on the joys of witchcraft will be less intimidating without the salesperson calling for a price check or asking if your rabbi knows what you are reading.

Technological advances have made us feel that our lives are full because they are busier and our time is more precious because there is more to do. Products and marketing campaigns that keep up with our perception that our lives are fast paced will likely prove most successful.

Consuming: The Dark Side

It is clear that cigarettes and other tobacco products are addictive. However, these are not the only "addictive" products being sold. To this point we have assumed that consumer behavior takes place on the up and up, in well-lit corporate-run stores or nicely designed websites. However, a great deal of consumption occurs on the street corner, in the local club, or even online across international borders. From prostitutes selling sexual gratification on the corner to the company selling growth hormones over the internet to 13-year-old boys who want to become stronger athletes, consumer behavior goes well beyond your local Walmart or shopping mall. These transactions, for ethical reasons, tend to go unstudied by psychologists and certainly aren't reliably tracked by government agencies.

Internet addiction, wherein one's virtual life (be it gaming, chatting, or just surfing) takes precedence over life in the real world, has also made headlines.[54] However, more recently it has been suggested that, rather than the internet itself being addictive, other addictions (e.g., pornographic or sexual addictions) are often played out online. If a person is losing sleep, work productivity, or relationships because of time spent online, this may be a sign that there is a problem, but the term *addiction* should be used carefully. Playing a game online with friends late into the night instead of going out to the local hangout for a beverage or two does not necessarily qualify as addiction.

Not all the "dark side" of consumer behavior involves addiction. **Product misuse** occurs when a product is not used for its intended purpose or in the intended way. Using a microwave to dry tennis shoes would be an example of product misuse. Although this might not be good for the shoes or the microwave, it's hardly on the same plane as huffing spray paint or using cold medicine to manufacture illegal narcotics. Another example of product misuse is overconsumption. This occurs when consumers purchase items to meet needs the product was not intended to fill. For example, eating an entire chocolate cake when one is depressed would be a misuse of the product, which has a much smaller suggested serving size. Overdosing on cough syrup for the intoxicating effects is yet another example of product misuse.

Another aspect of the "dark side" of consumer behavior is that consumers themselves are sometimes the product. This goes far beyond networks and magazines selling consumer audiences to advertisers; here we are discussing the actual marketing and selling of consumers physically. Frozen sperm (and artificial insemination supplies) can be purchased online for around $200 and delivered to your home within approximately three days. (Go to http://www.cengage.com/psychology/baumeister and select *Module Weblinks* to be directed to a current URL for this resource.) People can also sell their hair, sperm, and surrogate wombs. If you think you aren't for sale, you may be surprised that there are companies selling your personal information (e-mail address, phone number, credit history, and so on) to anyone who is willing to purchase this information—and the irony is, you aren't even profiting. (See Chapter 10 for a discussion of identity theft.)

product misuse using a product for an unintended purpose or without regard to instructions or usage suggestions

Shrinkage refers to a company's loss of money or inventory because of shoplifting and/or employee theft. This is particularly a problem for those in the retail business. Shoplifting at a local store "shrinks" the inventory of that store. If you are curious as to what items are most frequently pocketed without paying, look behind the counter of your local convenience store or in the keyed cases along the store walls. Items such as condoms, cigarettes, video games, and some cold medicines containing ingredients used to manufacture illicit drugs are often guarded by store personnel. These items are most at risk for being stolen. They aren't necessarily the most expensive items in the store, but they have the combined qualities of being small enough to conceal and somewhat taboo. The more embarrassed or ashamed you are to need or want the item, the more likely it is that you are going to have to ask the clerk to hand it to you.

QUIZ YOURSELF
Consuming Today

1. _____ has increasingly become an important nonrefundable resource.
   - (a) Money
   - (b) Education
   - (c) Technology
   - (d) Time

2. Margaret, who is part of the 3 C's market segment, is considering purchasing a new couch. If she is like the average American consumer, how will she include the Internet in this purchase?
   - (a) Complete the entire process online
   - (b) Search for information and comparison shop online, but then go to some stores to feel the product
   - (c) Complete the entire search and purchase process by going from store to store
   - (d) Not make use of the internet at all

3. Which of the following matches the consumer activity with the appropriate label?
   - (a) Francesca is engaging in shrinkage when she uses nail polish to stop a run in her hose.
   - (b) Fred is causing shrinkage for his employer by eating doughnuts he isn't paying for.
   - (c) Joe is engaging in product misuse by purchasing growth hormones on the internet.
   - (d) Kimberly is engaging in shrinkage by spending her downtime at work reorganizing shelves in the warehouse.

4. Polychronic activity refers to _____ .
   - (a) being able to do psychomotor tasks accurately
   - (b) being able to do psychomotor tasks quickly
   - (c) being able to do a sequence of consecutive tasks
   - (d) being able to do more than one activity or task at a time

answers: see pg A24

Post-Consumption Processes

What happens when a consumer is done with a product? There are several options: sell it, give it away, throw it away, or keep it with modifications.

Lateral cycling includes selling, giving, or trading an item to someone else to be used for its intended purpose. Purchasing a table at a garage sale that you intend to use as a table would be an example of lateral cycling. However, we wouldn't use this term if you took the table home and turned it into mulch. Flea markets are a great place to see lateral cycling at work. A suitcase purchased at an Australian flea market for $36 in July 2004 reportedly contained unreleased Beatles recordings and other Beatles memorabilia, so even lateral cycling shopping can be quite lucrative for the lucky. eBay is the perfect example of how the internet has changed our consumer disposal process. Recently, I was out with friends at a club where a marketing firm had sent surveyors with electronic notebooks and free Zippo

shrinkage the loss of money or inventory from shoplifting and/or employee theft

lateral cycling selling or giving a previously purchased product to someone else to use for its intended purpose cigarette lighters. Even though several people at the table did not smoke, they completed the survey and took the lighters, saying they would sell them on eBay. Thinking they were kidding, a few days later I looked up Zippos on eBay, and there they were being auctioned.

In the land of the automobile, how we recycle our cars is quite interesting. Different usage strategies often determine how our newest auto will make its way to the junkyard. Some people purchase a car with the intent of driving it only until they can trade it in for a newer model (at which point their car becomes someone else's problem). Others are inclined to drive their vehicle until it simply cannot make it one more inch down the road, and then sell it for scrap to whatever junkyard is willing to haul it away. Each year 10 million cars in the United States reach the end of their useful lives and must be recycled, parked, or abandoned.[55] At the same time, about 16.5 million new cars are put on the road each year in the United States.[56]

E-cycling, the recycling of electronic items, is becoming quite a newsworthy endeavor. The average U.S. household owns approximately 24 electronic items.[57] (Only 10% to 18% of these items are recycled; the rest are sent to landfills and termed e-waste.) The most environmentally sustainable choice is to reuse the item. Many women's shelters and charities are happy to receive used cell phones. These can provide a lifeline for individuals who may be in crisis but have no way to contact emergency services. Sprint has an e-cycling program that provides some financial incentive for newer cell phone models, which they redistribute to their employees for work purposes. Many schools are happy to receive slightly used computers for their technology courses or even for younger school children to make use of educational software. And, of course, buying a computer that can be easily upgraded not only is more economical in the long run but also can buy you some time until e-cycling processes can catch up with environmental safety standards. However, some electronics are simply too dated to be of much use to anyone.

Cell phones, computers, televisions, and other electronics are being recycled but because they contain many materials, the recycling process for these kinds of products not quite as clear as it is for single material products. Aluminum cans are melted down and remanufactured most frequently as aluminum cans. However, the multitude of materials used in a typical computer includes not only precious metals but also heavy metals (e.g., cadmium, lead, and mercury, which can release toxic fumes when extracted from the components). Recent coverage of the impact this toxicity has had in China has led some consumers to seek greener electronic alternatives.[58] Manufacturers are engaged in creating more environmentally neutral products. Intel and others are beginning to offer lead-free motherboards, and reduced heavy metals computers are coming from Dell and Hewlett-Packard.[59]

The few items that are not thrown out, laterally cycled, or recycled have traditionally been bought by others after we die: caskets, funeral sprays, tombstones. However, funeral homes have quickly stepped up to allow you to preselect your casket, tombstone, flowers, and service details while you are still among the living. The interesting thing about these purchases is that it would be hard to report dissatisfaction with them. It appears that the few items we buy that we take with us when we die are the ones we are least likely to complain about. Thus far, it is rare to hear of lateral cycling or recycling of most funeral items.

If you believe that lateral cycling is a reasonable thing to do with one's body, you will find that many research institutions, medical schools, and car manufacturers would be happy to make good use of your physical body. Donating your body to science can involve a range of activities.[60] Automobile manufacturers use cadavers to determine what safety standards can be improved; medical school gross anatomy courses always need more cadavers; surgeons learning new procedures often need some part of a body to practice on; and even emergency room interns can hone their medical procedure skills. There is no for-profit market for cadavers, and transporting cadavers requires many local and state licenses (not to mention if your body is posthumously transported across national borders), but this sort of donation would in effect be your last consumer behavior decision.

Having a better understanding of the consumer behavior process in its totality can be a great boon to one's own pocketbook as well as to a career in marketing, sales, business, or even as a professional shopper. Understanding how social psychology can be used to understand our consumer-focused social world is beneficial to our personal finances, economy, health, and environment.

QUIZ YOURSELF
Post-Consumption Processes

1. Environmentally conscious people often do much more than recycle. Their consumer behavior process might include _____.
   - (a) reusing and disposing
   - (b) recycling, reusing, and lateral cycling
   - (c) recycling and disposing
   - (d) lateral cycling and product misuse

2. Which of the following is an example of lateral cycling?
   - (a) Melting a box of old crayons to make candles
   - (b) Buying a coffee table at a flea market to use as a child's bench in your home
   - (c) Using old T-shirts as dust rags
   - (d) Giving your younger brother your old shoes to wear

3. Which of the following is the best estimate of the number of cars per year in the United States that can no longer be laterally cycled?
   - (a) 20 million
   - (b) 30 million
   - (c) 10.5 million
   - (d) 50,000

4. What type of cycling includes selling, giving, or trading an item to someone else to be used for its intended purpose?
   - (a) hierarchical cycling
   - (b) lateral cycling
   - (c) repetitive cycling
   - (d) vertical cycling

answers: see pg A24

What Makes Us Human

Putting the Cultural Animal in Perspective

Being a consumer is one of the things that makes human beings unique. This may sound odd because all animals need to consume certain things, such as food and water, in order to survive. But as this module has shown, consumer psychology focuses less on the consumption than on the purchasing of goods and services. A consumer participates in an economic system, a marketplace, and such systems are essentially unknown outside of humans. To human beings, however, the economy and marketplace are vitally important aspects of our culture, and they shape every day of our lives. In periods of economic downturn, when stock markets slump, even consumers with no shares may think more carefully about their purchases.

Consumer psychology incorporates many of this book's central themes. One theme is putting people first. Frequently, it is via the marketplace that we get what we need from other people and, more generally, from the cultural system, rather than directly from nature. As Chapter 2 pointed out, few modern individuals get their food directly from nature. Instead, they get it from the system: restaurants, grocery stores, room service. Consumers are hooked into the system in fundamental ways.

Another theme is that nature says go and culture says stop. People are naturally built to enjoy acquiring things, and so in a sense we are born to be consumers. It is evolutionary adaptive to acquire food and other accouterments that appeal to others. Being accepted socially improves our chance of survival. The main "stop" signal is financial: We are held back by the limits of our purchasing power. But modern cultures have begun to join with nature in saying "go" (in this case, "buy!") rather than stop. Credit cards allow people to continue purchasing when they are out of money. More broadly, the economy booms when people buy, so the culture has developed many features to encourage more buying and more consumption. Advertising, for example, is a huge, multibillion-dollar industry that encourages people to buy. When both nature and culture say "go!" it is no wonder that people have difficulty stopping, which is why many people end up deeply in debt or even bankrupt. The current economic situation in the United States demonstrates that this "go!" without a stop can lead not only people but entire corporations to be forced to stop. Certainly if there were a middle ground or cautionary light that would say "go slowly" or "proceed with caution," the layoffs and stock market crash might not be so devastating. The one item that hasn't been successfully sold to the U.S. consumer is the savings account. The amount of money that individuals save has fallen off dramatically in recent years and pointedly so among individuals in their 20s and 30s.[61] It doesn't seem to be a lack of desire, but rather increasing living costs paired with flattened wages that leads any extra money to go for bills, rather than into a rainy-day fund.

Tradeoffs, another theme of this book, are central to consumer decisions. Almost all purchasing decisions involve a tradeoff between keeping your money and acquiring something new. Choosing between products often invokes a tradeoff between price and quality, so that the consumer must balance the desire to avoid paying a high price against the desire to get something good.

Yet another theme is the long road to social acceptance, and in modern life at least, people travel big parts of this road as consumers. Homemade clothes may be inexpensive and practical but will not impress potential friends, lovers, or employers. If you do not watch the right shows or listen to popular music, you may not know what others are talking about. This module pointed out that advertisers often struggle to convince you that buying a product is a way to acquire and display your identity, but they are not entirely wrong. People do judge you by your possessions.

MODULE A SUMMARY

Learning, Knowing, and Deciding What to Buy

- The consumer behavior process begins at the point when a consumer recognizes a need and does not end until the product or service purchased to fulfill that need has expired.
- Advertisers and media corporations have symbiotic relationships whereby the media draw consumers in and deliver them to the advertiser and advertisements are delivered via the media to consumers.
- Products are often marketed and bought because they fulfill social, status, or esteem needs in addition to practical needs such as warmth.
- Consumers are also becoming increasingly aware of environmental concerns and may make product choices based on information about the company's environmental efforts and the green value of the product itself.
- Store layout, co-consumers, smells, sights, and sounds all make up the consumption environment and affect what people buy, how much they spend, and how much time and energy they devote to the process.
- The loyalty that consumers feel toward brands and products is robust and must be dealt with carefully by marketers to avoid alienating the consumer base associated with the product.

What Is for Sale?

- Consumers buy products for many reasons, some practical and some emotional.
- People tend to be emotionally involved in their purchases and advertisers know how draw on the emotions.
- In many cases, the products consumers own are part of their identity, for themselves and for others who interact with them.

Making the Purchase

- Once people have taken ownership of a product, they feel more positively toward it as part of the mere ownership effect and see alternative products as less valuable or appropriate.
- Paying with a credit card often means that consumers will spend more money. This is especially true if they are feeling optimistic about their future earning potential.

Consuming Today

- The internet is quickly changing the marketplace into a global endeavor and increasing the availability of products without geographical limitations.
- Today's consumer faces special issues with regard to time poverty and the increased need to engage in polychronic activities.
- The internet has also become a venue for shopping, gambling, and sexual addictions as it provides a ready access point with the added bonus of anonymity.

Post-Consumption Processes

- Increasingly, consumers are beginning to see that their purchases need to be disposed of in ways that conserve resources and are environmentally sustainable. In the future, more and more consumers will likely reuse, recycle, or laterally cycle before they dispose of their possessions.

What Makes Us Human? Putting the Cultural Animal in Perspective

- To human beings, the economy and marketplace are vitally important aspects of our culture, and they shape every day of our lives.

key terms

brand loyalty A8
conspicuous consumption A13
dominant response A7
ethnographic A3

geo-targeting A16
lateral cycling A20
netnography A3
online virtual memorials A3

polychronic activity A18
product misuse A19
sentiment analysis A3
shrinkage A20

social network analysis A3
time poverty A17
usage situation A15

quiz yourself ANSWERS

1. Learning, Knowing, and Deciding What to Buy p. A4
   answers: 1.c 2.a 3.c 4.a
2. What is for sale? p. A10
   answers: 1. 2. 3. 4.
3. Making the Purchase p. A15
   answers: 1.c 2.c 3.a 4.d
4. Consuming Today p. A20
   answers: 1.d 2.b 3.b 4.d
5. Post-Consumption Processes p. A22
   answers: 1.b 2.d 3.c 4.b

APPLICATION MODULE B

Applying Social Psychology to Health

Regan A. R. Gurung / Oregon State University

LEARNING OBJECTIVES

1. Identify the three broad segments of health psychology, and analyze the contributions of social psychology to each.

2. Compare the different definitions of stress, and contrast how the four major psychological theories of stress expand on our basic understanding of stress.

3. Differentiate approach and avoidant styles of coping, and explain how both problem-focused coping and emotion-focused coping help deal with stress.

4. Define social support, and summarize the three types of support others provide that help us to deal with stress.

5. Contrast the health belief model, the theory of planned behavior, the *transtheoretical* model, and the prototype/willingness model, and describe how each model explains behavior related to health.

6. Identify the social psychological processes that influence the recognition of symptoms and help to explain illness behavior.

7. Discuss how being a cultural animal has led humans to have special sorts of health problems as well as novel ways of dealing with health issues.

THE SOCIAL SIDE OF SEX
Increasing Condom Use and Safe Sex Practices
B12

FOOD FOR THOUGHT
Is Comfort Food Really Comforting?
B14

WHAT MAKES US HUMAN?
Putting the Cultural Animal in Perspective
B18

One of the biggest potential health threats today is e-cigarettes. They are billed as a way to help smokers quit. Is this true? Are there other negative effects?

Joe has some bad habits. Although a college student taking five classes, he spends large parts of his day watching television and often accompanies these sessions with generous helpings of potato chips, ice cream, and other fatty foods. When he is not watching television, he is surfing the internet, following Twitter feeds of his favorite athletes, updating his social media accounts, texting friends, or downloading music. As you can guess, he does not have much time for physical activity and is overweight. He is often stressed. To make matters worse, Joe likes to party a lot, and when out with his friends he is often pressured to binge drink, smoke, or do drugs. As a result of spending time with the wrong crowd all through high school and now in college, Joe smokes 10 to 15 cigarettes a day though he is considered switching to e-cigarettes. Based on this constellation of factors, Joe may not live to see the age of 40. (Enter "longevity game" into an internet search engine and calculate how long you can expect to live based on your lifestyle—don't be this average Joe!) Many of his bad habits are due to the situations Joe finds himself in and the people he associates with.

The situations we are in, and the people around us, can have implications for our health and well-being. Understanding the complex social psychological phenomena that influence our behaviors allows us to predict and modify our health behaviors. How important can this be? Consider this: If everyone in North America stopped smoking today, the death rates due to cancer would drop by close to 30%.[1] If more North Americans ate better, got more physical activity, and cut down on their alcohol consumption, death rates would drop even further.[2] This module will apply social psychology to health, with a focus on stress and coping and the role of situations and people in predicting our health behaviors.

Health is best defined as a state of complete physical, mental, and social well-being.[3] This broad definition is especially useful because it includes the mental component, which is particularly susceptible to psychological pressures from situations around us. One way to see health is as a continuum, with optimal health (broadly defined) at one end and poor health at the other. The number of healthy things we do in life determines our relative position on the continuum (closer to optimal health or closer to death) at a particular moment in time. The healthy things we do (eat and sleep well, exercise, take time to relax) move us toward the optimal health side. The unhealthy things we do (eat junk food, get stressed, smoke, drink excessively) make us slide toward the illness side. Of course, not everything can be compensated for. If you have smoked for 20 or 30 years, it is pretty hard to slide to the healthy other end. Furthermore, it is difficult to compare the extent to which different behaviors translate into longevity. Just because you do not smoke does not mean that you can drink excessively. Just because you exercise a lot does not mean you can afford to not eat a nutritious diet. Keeping your life moving toward optimal health is a daily challenge and a dynamic process, both strongly influenced by social psychological factors.

The challenge to achieve optimal health is made more difficult by the interaction of nature and culture, a theme you have encountered previously in this book. Many times nature pushes us in one direction, but our cultural background or the rules of the culture we are embedded in push us in another. Based on our evolutionary history, for example, we are all biologically wired to crave and enjoy fatty and salty foods. The tendency to eat as much fat and salt as we like, and consequently to grow heavier, runs into the cultural ideals of health and fitness we see in the media. Addicted smokers may want to light up a cigarette whenever they are out in public, but cultural smoking bans prevent them from doing so. Sometimes culture can work in the opposite direction as

health a state of complete physical, mental, and social well-being well. For example, in countries such as India and Japan, smoking is still normative as compared to North America. The same negative effects work for alcohol consumption. The state of Wisconsin has the highest number of deaths due to binge drinking and many adults do not think unhealthy levels of drinking is problematic. Although alcohol consumption is not a natural, innate urge, someone growing up in a culture where many people drink excessively may be more likely to drink excessively as well. Families are often such cultural settings, and young children are very likely to eat as well and be as physically active as their parents. Social psychology helps us navigate the connection between culture and health.

It was not until the early 20th century that psychology started to play a part in the examination of health. Psychologists, such as Freud, Alexander, and Dubar and organizations such as the Society for Behavioral Medicine, used the methods of psychology to examine health. Within mainstream psychology, researchers in social psychology, personality psychology, cognitive psychology, and clinical psychology realized that the basic theories that they derived to describe and predict behavior could be used in the study of health and well-being. As we will soon see, social psychological theories form one of the core foundations of health psychological research, and many social phenomena can explain why we do what we do. In fact, one of the individuals responsible for establishing the field of health psychology in psychology, Shelley Taylor, is trained as a social psychologist. Why are children likely to start smoking? What makes a person more or less likely to exercise or eat well? The answers to these and other questions come from theories derived from basic social psychological research.

Health psychology is an interdisciplinary subspecialty of psychology dedicated to promoting and maintaining health and preventing and treating illness.[4,5,6] Health psychologists play close attention to the way that thoughts, feelings, behaviors, and biological processes interact with each other to influence health and illness.[7] In many ways, health psychology is more than a subfield within the discipline of psychology, as it is built on theoretical ideas and research findings from many other areas of psychology. For example, many of the ways used to understand why we get stressed and how we cope come from social and personality psychology.[8]

The field of health psychology can be carved into three broad natural segments: (a) stress and coping, (b) health behaviors, and (c) issues in health care. The determinants of stress, and how these same factors can influence how we cope, are perhaps closest to the social psychological theories discussed earlier in this book. Social psychology also drove the derivation of the main theories relating to why we engage in various health-related behaviors. These include the good (such as physical activity), the bad (such as eating too much fast food), and the ugly (seen what smoking can do to a person's teeth and lungs?). This module will examine each of the three main areas of health psychology and discuss the contributions of social psychology to each.

What Is Stress?

Why do different people and cultures experience stress differently? What can we do to reduce stress? Stress can be defined in many different ways. It has been studied using different approaches, and everyone has a different notion of what is stressful. It is important that a definition of stress can be applied to many different people (and animals too). All negative events need not be stressful, and all positive events are not automatically free from stress. For example, losing your job may sound initially like a stressful event, but it may be a happy event if you hated your job. Similarly, although finding a romantic partner after a long period of being single sounds very positive, you may worry about how to make sure it lasts. As you can see, stress is subjective. What, then, is a convenient way to define stress? This is a good time to assess your own stress, using the questionnaire in **TABLE B.1**.

Most researchers contend that the best way to know when a person is stressed is to look at how the person's body responds to a situation. If the sympathetic nervous system activates in response to an event, then the person is under stress. This results in elevated heart rate, respiration, and circulation. Many early definitions of stress relied heavily on biological activity. Cannon[9] viewed stress as the biological mobilization of the body for

health psychology an interdisciplinary subspecialty of psychology dedicated to promoting and maintaining health and preventing and treating illness

TABLE B.1 The Student Stress Scale

Event	Life-Change Units	Event	Life-Change Units
Death of a close family member	100	Increased workload at school	37
Death of a close friend	73	Outstanding personal achievement	36
Divorce between parents	65	First quarter/semester in college	35
Jail term	63	Change in living conditions	31
Major personal injury or illness	63	Serious argument with instructor	30
Marriage	58	Lower grades than expected	29
Being fired from a job	50	Change in sleeping habits	29
Failing an important course	47	Change in social activities	29
Change in health of family member	45	Change in eating habits	28
Pregnancy	45	Chronic car trouble	26
Sex problems	44	Change in number of family get-togethers	26
Serious argument with close friend	40	Too many missed classes	25
Change in financial status	39	Change of college	24
Change of major	39	Dropping of more than one class	23
Trouble with parents	39	Minor traffic violations	20
New girl- or boyfriend	38		

action, involving sympathetic activation and endocrine activity. Selye[10] similarly viewed stress as the activation of a host of physiological systems. The later and more psychological theories defined stress as being caused when the perceived demands on the organism exceeded the resources to meet those demands.[1]

Although these different definitions have all been well supported, the simplest definition of **stress** is the upsetting of homeostasis.[11] Our bodies have an optimal level of functioning in regard to blood sugar level, body temperature, rate of circulation, and breathing. **Homeostasis** is the ideal level of bodily functions. Similar to the thermostat in homes, our body is designed to maintain its optimal level in all areas of functioning. We set our thermostats and if the temperature drops below the set level, the furnace starts. In this way a constant temperature is maintained. The hypothalamus in our brains similarly maintains set levels. Stress to our systems can thus be seen as something that upsets our ideal balance.

This simple but effective definition of stress harkens back to the origins of the word *stress*. Physicists long studied the effects of large forces on solid structures, and *stress* was originally used to describe the force exerted on a body that resulted in deformation or strain. Stress has similar effects on our body. This definition allows for subjectivity, as stressors can vary across individuals. If an event does not activate your stress response or disrupt your system, it is just another event. If an event disrupts you, it is a stressor. One person's event can be another person's stressor. For example, talking in public may not be stressful for you, but it could be very stressful for someone else. Four major psychological theories expand on this basic understanding of stress.

Fight-or-Flight Response

Walter Cannon applied the concept of homeostasis to the study of human interactions with the environment.[12] The basic idea is intuitive and can be remembered by a simple example. Imagine finding yourself face to face with a bear freshly escaped from the local zoo. You can

stress the upsetting of homeostasis
homeostasis the ideal level of bodily functions

probably guess what your body will do. Your heart pumps faster, your blood pressure rises, you breathe faster, your face is a little flushed, and your palms may be sweaty. All these reactions are caused by the sympathetic nervous system (SNS) that prepares your body for action. Activation of the SNS increases circulation, respiration, and metabolism, all factors that fuel your body to ready it to either fight the bear or flee, escaping as fast as you can. The higher respiration rate gets more oxygen into your lungs, the increased heart rate and blood pressure get the oxygenated blood to the muscles, and the increased metabolism breaks down energy for use by the fighting/fleeing muscles. The SNS also turns off certain systems in response to stress. Faced with a ravenous bear, you are probably not in a mood for food or sex. The SNS down regulates (turns off) the digestive system and the reproductive system in times of stress. The SNS activates the adrenal medulla, which secretes the major stress hormones adrenalin and noradrenalin (also called epinephrine and norepinephrine and collectively called the catecholamines) that stimulate the **fight-or-flight response**.

The reversal of this process (the activating of some systems and the deactivating of others), which helps your body recover from a stressor, is managed by the parasympathetic nervous system (PNS). The PNS decreases circulation and respiration and increases digestion and reproduction. Correspondingly, most stress management techniques work toward activating your PNS and slowing down breathing and heart rate. The PNS and SNS are both parts of the autonomic nervous system and are coordinated by higher brain structures such as the hypothalamus.

General Adaptation Syndrome

Hans Selye chanced on a new way of understanding stress after he unintentionally mishandled his lab rats. Selye was not an experienced animal handler, and he had much trouble weighing, injecting, and studying his rats. Through different forms of (unintended) mistreatment, he stressed both the experimental and control groups, and both groups developed ulcers. The rats also showed other physiological changes, including shrunken adrenal glands and deformed lymph nodes.[13] On realizing the cause of the ulcers, Selye exposed rats to a variety of stressors such as extreme heat and cold, sounds, and rain. He found that in every case the rats developed physiological problems similar to those of the mistreated rats. Selye concluded that organisms must have a general, nonspecific response to a variety of stressful events. Specifically, he hypothesized that no matter what the stressor, the body would react in the same way, and theorized that these responses were driven by the hypothalamic-pituitary-adrenal (HPA) axis. The hypothalamus activates the pituitary gland, which then activates the adrenal gland, which then secretes the chemical cortisol. See **FIGURE B.1** for a summary of the basic physiological reactions to stress.

fight-or-flight response Cannon's theory of stress explaining physiological responses in our body

FIGURE B.1

Physiological activity in Cannon's fight-or-flight response (left) and Selye's general adaptation system (right).

Selye argued that organisms have a general way of responding to all stressors, which he called a **general adaptation syndrome**. When faced with a stressor—whether a wild animal, a threatening mugger, or intense cold—the body first goes into a state of alarm. HPA activation takes place, and the body attempts to cope with the stressor during a period of resistance. If the stressor persists for too long, the body breaks down in a state of exhaustion. Many acute or short-term stressors can be successfully dealt with in the resistance stage. Chronic or long-term stressors drive us to exhaustion. Chronic stressors can exert true physiological and psychological damage on human brains and bodies, making real the phrase "stress can kill."[14,15]

Cognitive Appraisal Model

Richard Lazarus[16] devised the first psychological model of stress, known as the **cognitive appraisal model**. Lazarus saw stress as an imbalance between the demands placed on the individual and that individual's resources to cope. He argued that the experience of stress differs significantly across individuals, depending on how they interpret the event and the outcome of a specific sequence of thinking patterns called **appraisals**.

All of us are faced with demands. In college, you have papers to write and exams to take. At work, you may have projects and production deadlines to meet or a certain number of sales to make. Even in our personal lives, our family and friends rely on us and expect us to do various things. These different expectations, deadlines, and situations are all potential stressors. However, according to Lazarus, these expectations, deadlines, and situations are just events until we *deem* them to be stressful. The main cognitive process at work here is that of making appraisals.

Lazarus suggested that we make two major types of appraisals when we face any potentially stressful event. During *primary appraisals,* we ascertain whether the event is positive, negative, or neutral, and if negative, whether it is harmful, threatening, or challenging. A *harm* (or harm-loss) appraisal is made when we expect to lose something of great personal significance. For example, when we break up a close relationship, we lose a confidant. The event may involve the loss of psychological aspects, such as support from an ex-partner or the love of a parent who is dying; harm to one's self-esteem with the loss of a job; or even physical harm and loss, as in the diagnosis of a terminal illness. *Threat* appraisals are made when we believe the event will be extremely demanding and will put us at risk for damage. If you think that your bad performance on an upcoming project can severely ruin your reputation or that taking part in a certain race will hurt your body, you are seeing the project or race as a threat. *Challenge* appraisals occur when we believe that we can grow as a result of dealing with the event or when we look at positive ways in which we can benefit from it. For example, you can view an exam as harmful to your self-esteem and a threat if you expect to do badly, or you can view it as a challenge to your intelligence and how much you have studied. A primary appraisal can be heavily influenced by the stake we have in the outcome of the event.[17]

After we make a primary appraisal, we assess whether or not we have the necessary resources to cope with the event. During *secondary appraisal,* we determine whether we can deal with the event and how we can cope. We may think about the social support we have, who can help us, and what exactly can be done. We are asking ourselves the question, "Do I have what it takes to cope?" The answer is decisive. If our answer is no, we do not have the resources to cope, and we have appraised the event as harmful or threatening, then we appraise the event as a stressor. If our answer is yes, and we have appraised the event as a challenge, the event remains just that—an event. Throughout this process, we often engage in cognitive reappraisal, changing how we view the situation.

Many factors contribute to the appraisals of events. The *duration* of an event can play an important role in the process. Acute or short-term events may be appraised differently than chronic or long-term events. You may not worry too much if you know that the loud noise outside your window will stop in minutes. You may have an entirely different reaction if you live under the flight path of a nearby airport. Events can be either *negative* or *positive*. This dimension of stress is more straightforward. Some events are automatically

---

general adaptation syndrome Selye's stage theory of how we respond to all stressors in a similar way

cognitive appraisal model Lazarus's theory of how thinking plays a strong role in stress

appraisals how we think about a situation or event

threatening on the surface, such as having to speak in front of 500 people or being shot at by trigger-happy delinquents. Others may be positive on the surface, such as getting married, but may involve a great many demands on your mind and body, such as planning the wedding.

Control is another important factor in stress. When you believe that you have control over a situation, the situation is less likely to be stressful. Knowing that you are capable of changing the event is less stressful than not having any control over it. Nursing home residents who got extra control over their day-to-day activities, such as menus and recreational activities, were significantly better off.[18] *Predictability* is also related to control. You will fear going to class less if you know that your professor gives a quiz every Friday. If you have no idea when a quiz will be given, you will probably be more stressed.

Tend and Befriend

As we learned in Chapter 10, there are sex differences in stress responses: In addition to fighting or fleeing, women may **tend and befriend**.[19,20] Researchers noticed that diverse findings in the stress literature did not fit the fight-or-flight model. This model assumed that men and women faced the same challenges in our evolutionary history. However, this was not true. Females have always been primary caregivers of infants because of their greater investment in giving birth (nine months for women versus minutes for men) and ability to breast-feed. Men were able to fight or flee, but women often had to look after infants. If a woman fought and lost, she would leave her infant defenseless. If she ran, she would either have to leave her infant behind or the weight of the infant might slow her down and lead to capture. Instead, women developed additional stress responses aimed at protecting, calming, and quieting the child (tending) to remove it from harm's way and marshal resources to help. Essentially, women create social networks to provide resources and protection for themselves and their infants (befriending). The tend-and-befriend response is thus a more rational stress response for females than the basic fight-or-flight response. This theory builds on the brain's attachment/caregiving system, which counteracts the metabolic activity associated with the traditional fight-or-flight stress response—increased heart rate, blood pressure, and cortisol levels—and leads to nurturing and affiliative behavior.

In clear support of the theory, research shows that after a stressful day on the job, men wanted to be left alone and often fought with their spouses and children.[21] When stressed, women, on the other hand, actually tended to spend more time with their children and have more physical contact with them.

tend and befriend Taylor and colleagues' theory of how women react to stress differently than men

QUIZ YOURSELF
What Is Stress?

1. **Stress is best defined as _____ .**
   - (a) negative events that tax the body
   - (b) challenges to the body systems
   - (c) the perception of strain
   - (d) the upsetting of homeostasis

2. **During the fight-or-flight response, epinephrine _____ .**
   - (a) increases heart rate and blood pressure
   - (b) energizes the muscles
   - (c) converts fat into energy
   - (d) gets oxygen into the bloodstream

3. **According to Selye, the first brain structure to initiate the stress response is the _____ .**
   - (a) pituitary gland
   - (b) hippocampus
   - (c) amygdala
   - (d) hypothalamus

4. **During secondary appraisal in the cognitive appraisal model, individuals _____ .**
   - (a) evaluate their resources for dealing with stress
   - (b) unconsciously recall other similar stressful events
   - (c) engage in the use of defense mechanisms
   - (d) experience resistance and then exhaustion

answers: see pg B19

Coping

Coping is defined as the individual efforts made to manage distressing problems and emotions that affect the physical and psychological outcomes of stress.[22] Coping includes anything people do to manage problems or emotional responses, whether successful or not.[23] We have both broad general coping styles and more specific coping strategies. Coping styles are general predispositions to deal with stress. Similar to personality traits, coping styles tend to show a high level of stability across situations and time. The two most basic styles are approach coping and avoidant coping. An individual can approach the stressor and make active efforts to resolve it or try to avoid the stressor.[24]

Coping strategies are the specific behavioral and psychological efforts that people make to master, tolerate, reduce, or minimize stressful events.[25] Even though coping can refer to many different behaviors, it is easy to identify some main types of coping. Researchers have especially distinguished between problem-focused and emotion-focused strategies. Problem-focused coping involves directly facing the stressful situation and working hard to resolve it. For example, if you have a demanding, aggressive boss at work, you may experience a lot of stress at your job. If you have a direct conversation with your boss about the problem, you are taking concrete action to deal with the situation and follow a problem-focused approach. If you choose to stay away from work and call in sick, you are using emotion-focused coping, in which you use either mental or behavioral methods to deal with the feelings resulting from the stress. Although conceptually distinct, the two strategies are interdependent and work together, one supplementing the other in the overall coping process.[26]

How we cope with stress is often influenced by how much support we receive from others around us. **Social support**, generally defined as emotional, informational, or instrumental assistance from others,[27] has been tied to better health, more rapid recovery from illness, and a lower risk for mortality.[28,29,30,31]

Social support is assessed in two main ways. You can measure the social support that people report was provided to them, called *received support,* or the social support that people believe is available to them, called *perceived support.* These two forms of support vary in the functions they serve. When you are stressed, the type of support that you get and that will be helpful depends to a large extent on the type of stress you are under. If you are stressed because you have a big assignment due at school and do not even know how to begin, any information you can obtain about how to do it will be helpful. If you are stressed because your car broke down and you do not know how you will get to work, then someone giving you a ride will best help you cope. If someone close to you passes away or you have trouble in a close relationship, people showing you that you are esteemed, loved, and cared for by others will be the most supportive. These examples correspond to three main types of received support, and each has its counterpart form of perceived support. To summarize, received or perceived support can be

- Instrumental, also called tangible or material support (e.g., the loan of a car).
- Informational, or advice (e.g., how to do an assignment).
- Emotional (e.g., being told that people care for you).

Strong gender differences exist in the receipt and provision of social support.[32] This gender difference is so strong that following the early studies on affiliation in response to stress,[33] most subsequent research on affiliation under stress used only female participants. In a Dutch study of bullying, bullied girls were more likely to get depressed as they did not get social support after the event.[34]

Stress and coping are two major areas in which social psychology has been used to study health. Another major category, discussed in the next section, relates to behaviors that can keep us from getting sick.

coping individual efforts made to manage distressing problems and emotions that affect the physical and psychological outcomes of stress

social support emotional, informational, or instrumental assistance from others

QUIZ YOURSELF
Coping

1. Coping is best defined as _____.
   - (a) individual efforts made to manage the outcomes of stress
   - (b) processes designed to increase relaxation
   - (c) ways to prevent stressful events from occurring
   - (d) techniques to reduce the impact of stress

2. The two most basic styles of coping are _____.
   - (a) positive and negative
   - (b) acute and chronic
   - (c) approach and avoidant
   - (d) primary and secondary

3. The most basic coping strategies are _____.
   - (a) approach and avoidant
   - (b) active and passive
   - (c) indulgent and proactive
   - (d) problem-focused and emotion-focused

4. Social support is best defined as _____.
   - (a) the feeling of being cared for
   - (b) emotional, informational, or instrumental assistance from others
   - (c) having a number of people to turn to for help when needed
   - (d) an integrated caring network of friends, family, and resources when needed

answers: see pg B19

Increasing Healthy Behaviors

Healthy behaviors are defined as any specific actions that maintain and enhance health. These can range from the mundane (e.g., taking vitamins) to the critical (e.g., not smoking or not texting while driving). Many of our daily behaviors can influence our health and how long and how happily we live. Health psychologists use social psychological theories to explain why we perform healthy behaviors (and why we do not) and also to design and implement interventions to increase healthy behaviors.

An **intervention** can be defined as any program or message providing information or structure to change a behavior.[35] If psychologists design a billboard to get people to stop smoking, for example, the billboard is considered an intervention. The outcome (change in smoking) can be assessed to determine whether the intervention was successful. The design and success of interventions often rely on one of the key themes of this book, "putting people first." When people want to stop smoking, drink less, or exercise more, they often turn to others for help. Most interventions provide people with others to turn to for information or assistance.

Most common health problems are worsened, and in some cases even caused, by unhealthy behaviors. For example, eating a lot of fatty foods and not getting enough physical exercise increase the likelihood of getting Type II diabetes and coronary heart disease.[36] It is estimated that 50% of all deaths in the United States could have been postponed or avoided by changing unhealthy behaviors. Behavioral factors such as tobacco use, poor diet and activity patterns, and avoidable injuries are among the most prominent contributors to mortality.[37]

Health psychologists use a **biopsychosocial approach** to health, acknowledging that our health has biological, psychological, and social determinants. The *social* part of the term *biopsychosocial* is particularly important to social psychologists. For example, the media we are exposed to have a strong impact on the types of health behaviors we perform. The culture we live in and what we are surrounded by give us a lot of information about what is acceptable and what is not. As an example, consider movie watching.[38,39] You have probably noticed products placed in movies, but do you think you notice whether a character is smoking or not? Do you think it influences your likelihood to smoke?

healthy behaviors any specific behaviors that maintain and enhance health

intervention any program or message providing information or structure to change a behavior

biopsychosocial approach a model acknowledging that our health has biological, psychological, and social determinants

To find out, researchers in Argentina, focused on 33 secondary schools and studied 2502 boys and girls who had never smoked. There were two surveys 17 months apart. The researchers first examined the 100 films that made the most money each year between 2009 and 2013, assessing how much tobacco was used in each. The students then reported on whether they had seen the movies. At the second time point of the study, 34% of the students reported being susceptible to smoking, 24% reported having tried smoking, and 9% were currently smoking. The more smoking in movies the kids were exposed to, the more likely they were to becoming susceptible to smoking.[40] An interesting cultural difference? Compared to an average of 3.4 minutes of smoking in Argentine films, U.S.-produced films had 60 minutes of smoking on average.

Social psychology (see Chapter 3) also provides a mechanism for why movies are so important. Identifying with the movie characters is the problem. Men in one study watched movie clips with the male lead actor either smoking or not smoking.[41] The more the viewers identified with the actors, the greater the implicit associations between the self and smoking and the more the intention to smoke increased. The stronger associations uniquely predicted increases in smokers' intentions to smoke, over and above the effects of the viewer's explicit beliefs about smoking. This study establishes that exposure to smoking in movies is causally related to changes in smoking-related thoughts and that identifying with the actors is the key mechanism. Similar relationships between movie viewing and drinking have also been found.[42,43] Let's look at some of the theoretical approaches to changing health behaviors.

health belief model theory that posits that beliefs about the effectiveness, ease, and consequences of doing (or not doing) a certain behavior determine whether we do (or do not do) that behavior

The Health Belief Model

The **health belief model** represents one of the first theoretical approaches to studying the reasons people engage in healthy and unhealthy behaviors. According to the model, our beliefs concerning the effectiveness, ease, and consequences of doing (or not doing) a certain behavior will determine whether we do (or do not do) that behavior. It is one of the most widely used frameworks and has been used for both behavior change and maintenance. It all began when a group of social psychologists were brought together at the U.S. Public Health Service to try to explain why people did not participate in programs to prevent or detect disease.[44,45] The model was then extended to explain people's responses to illness symptoms[46] and then to explain what influences whether people follow their prescribed treatments.[47]

The formulation of the health belief model provides a nice illustration of how social, cognitive, and behaviorist views have influenced health psychology. For example, learning theorists such as Skinner[48] believed that we learned to do a certain behavior if it was followed by a positive outcome (a reinforcement). So if exercising made us feel healthy, we would be more likely to exercise. Cognitive theorists added a focus on the *value* of an outcome (e.g., health) and the *expectation* that a particular action (e.g., exercise) will achieve that outcome. The health belief model is a value-expectancy theory in which the values and expectations have been reformulated from abstract concepts into health-related behaviors and concepts. For example, in the 1950s, a large number of eligible adults did not get themselves screened for tuberculosis, although tuberculosis was a big health problem and the screenings were free. In one study involving more than 1,200 adults, researchers[49] found that 82% of the people who believed they were susceptible, and who believed early detection worked, had at least one voluntary chest X-ray. Only 21% of the people who had neither belief got an X-ray.

How does the model explain health behavior? The model suggests that individuals will perform healthy behaviors if they believe they are susceptible to the health issue, if they believe it will have severe consequences, if they believe that their behavior will be beneficial in reducing the severity or susceptibility, and if they believe that the anticipated benefits of the behavior

Teenagers and younger children often imitate behaviors they see in movies and other media.

outweigh its costs (or barriers). Another factor that has been added to the model is the concept of self-efficacy,[50] which you encountered earlier in this book (see Chapter 4). The key components of this model are summarized in **FIGURE B.2**.

Theory of Planned Behavior

Another way to try to predict whether someone is going to do something is to ascertain whether that person *intends* to do something. Behavioral intentions play a major role in many models of health behavior change, including the theory of reasoned action,[51] the theory of planned behavior[52] (see Chapter 7), the protection motivation theory,[53] and the concept of self-efficacy.[54]

So what is an intention? In these theories, intention is defined as a person's subjective probability that he or she will perform the behavior in question. It is essentially an estimate of the probability of your doing something. If you are asked if you want dessert at the start of a meal when you are hungry, the probability that you will say yes is higher than it will be after the meal when you are stuffed.

The **theory of planned behavior** assumes that people decide to behave a certain way on the basis of intentions that depend on their attitude toward the behavior and their perceptions of the social norms regarding the behavior. As in the health beliefs model, attitudes toward the behavior are based on what the person believes to be the consequences of the behavior and how important these consequences are (both costs and benefits). Will eating dessert make you put on weight? Perception of social norms is your assessment of what others think about the behavior. Do the people you know support eating sweet things? If you believe that everyone around you thinks that eating dessert is an acceptable thing, you are more likely to want to do it. Of course, you may not care what people around you think. Your motivation to comply with others' preference is also part of the perception of social norms. If you care about the people around you *and* they support dessert eating, you are more likely to eat dessert. The full model with its components is shown in **FIGURE B.3**. See *The Social Side of Sex* for how to increase the motivation to comply with safe sex practices.

Transtheoretical Model

You can only change if you are really ready to change. Using this basic idea, the **transtheoretical model**[55,56] of behavior change was developed to identify common themes across different intervention theories (hence *transtheoretical*). The model suggests that we progress through different stages as we think about, attempt to, and finally change any specific behavior.

This model sees change as a process occurring through a series of six stages. The main stages are summarized in **TABLE B.2**. If you know what stage a person is in, you can tailor your intervention to fit the state of mind that the stage describes. People who are unaware that they are practicing a behavior that is unhealthy or do not intend to take any action to change a behavior (at least not in the next six months) are said to be in the *precontemplation* stage. People may have tried to change before, failed, and become demoralized, or they may just be misinformed about the actual consequences of their behavior. Some teenage smokers are so confident about their own health that they do not believe smoking is a problem for them and have no intention of changing. People in this stage avoid reading, thinking, or talking about their unhealthy behaviors. Health promotion programs are often wasted on them because they either do not know they have a problem or do not really care.

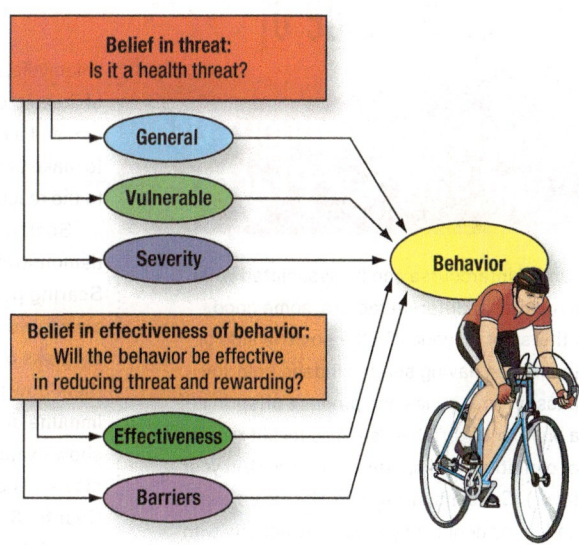

FIGURE B.2
Main components of the health beliefs model.

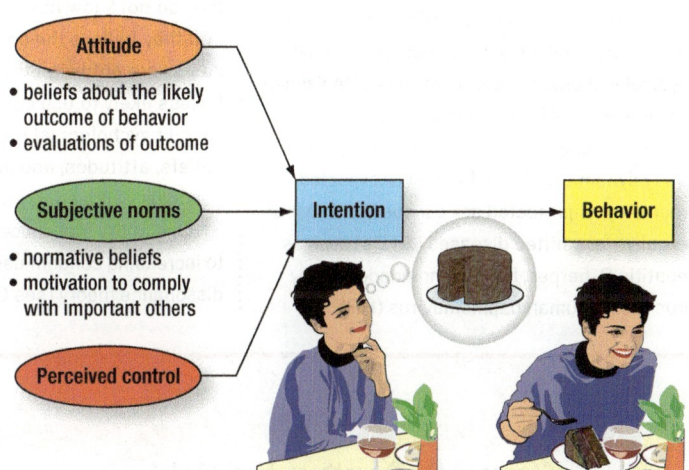

FIGURE B.3
Main components of the theory of planned behavior.

theory of planned behavior theory to explain how intentions predict behaviors

transtheoretical model the stages we progress through during behavior change

The Social Side of Sex

Increasing Condom Use and Safe Sex Practices

Sexual intercourse can be associated with a number of different factors, some good, others not so good. On the positive side of the ledger, having sex can indeed help you pass on your genes and produce offspring (if a number of variables such as fertility, timing of ovulation, and sperm motility work in your favor). Consensual sex can also be enjoyable, and many people engage in this activity with some frequency and with an interesting level of variety.[57] For example, an ABC news survey showed that 57% of Americans have had sex outdoors or in a public place, 50% talk about their sexual fantasies with their partners, and 43% call themselves sexually adventurous. Sex also has a dark side. Unwanted sexual activity such as rape and sexual harassment can lead to physical and psychological problems. Unplanned pregnancies can lead to negative attitudes toward the baby and have a negative impact on family dynamics.[58] Apart from an unexpected pregnancy, unprotected sex can lead to a host of sexually transmitted diseases (STDs) such as hepatitis B, herpes, human immunodeficiency virus (HIV), human papillomavirus (HPV), chlamydia, gonorrhea, and syphilis. The majority of these problems are due to risky, unprotected sex, and a key challenge for researchers has been to make sex safer. Social psychology can come to the rescue.

Social psychological research has demonstrated what does and does not work. Scaring people into using condoms has not always worked. Yes, you can tell people about the risks of unprotected sex, you can show them how many people die from acquired immune deficiency syndrome (AIDS), you can show examples of rashes from STDs, but they may still not use a condom when needed (see Chapter 8 for more information about fear appeals). Many of the theories discussed in this module have been adapted to increase condom use. For example, various elements of the health beliefs model have been shown to predict usage.[59,60] If people do not believe they are vulnerable to getting AIDS, or if they do not know how severe the disease is, or if they believe the costs of unprotected sex do not outweigh the benefits, they may be less likely to use condoms. Designing social psychological interventions to change beliefs, attitudes, and intentions toward using condoms can lead to increases in the behavior.

One of the first successful interventions to increasing condom use relied on cognitive dissonance theory (see Chapter 7). Researchers took the basic premise of cognitive dissonance theory—creating dissonance—and used it to get sexually active men and women to use condoms more often.[61] How did they create dissonance? They got participants to first give a lecture on the benefits of condom use and then, in effect, practice what they preached. The researchers recruited single, sexually active student volunteers to take part in a "campaign" supposedly designed to get other students who were just becoming sexually active to practice safe sex. The volunteers were asked to develop a persuasive speech about Acquired Immune Deficiency Syndrome (AIDS) and safer sex that was then videotaped. They also had to read through a list of reasons that might make it difficult to use a condom, which was designed to make them think of their own failures to do so in the past. The volunteers were essentially made to feel like hypocrites, speaking in favor of condom use while realizing they often failed to use condoms themselves. Sure enough, the dissonance caused by the hypocrisy was enough to get them to change their behavior. More volunteers in the experimental group than in a control group bought condoms, and the volunteers in the experimental group bought more condoms at the end of the study.

TABLE B.2 Stages of the Transtheoretical Model

Stage	Examples
1. **Precontemplation** Not aware of behavior, no intention to change	Thinking smoking is not harmful
2. **Contemplation** Aware that problem exists, thinking about change, weighing pros and cons	Seeing posters talking about dangers of smoking, wondering what can be done
3. **Preparation** Intend to change, modified but not committed	Starting to cut down on number smoked, comparing prices of the patch
4. **Action** Modified and commitment of time and energy	Using nicotine patch, not smoking
5. **Maintenance** Working to prevent relapse	Substituting safe behaviors when urge to smoke arises, staying away from smoky places
6. **Termination** No longer tempted by old behavior	No longer craving a cigarette

When people recognize they may be doing something unhealthy and intend to change (within the next month), they are said to be in the *contemplation* stage. Here they are more aware of the benefits of changing and are also very cognizant of the problems that changing may involve. For the dieter, it may be avoiding foods that she loves. For the smoker, it may mean not spending time with the buddies he always used to smoke with. The ambivalence of knowing the pros and cons of behavior change often keeps people in this stage for a long time and calls for unique interventions.

Preparation is the stage in which people are ready to take action to change their behavior. They generate plans and have specific ideas about how they are going to change. Someone who wants to lose weight may go out and buy new workout clothes and a gym membership. Someone who wants to drink less may give away all the alcohol in her house or have a talk with his doctor to get help. In essence, these people make a commitment to spend time and money on changing their behaviors. As you can guess, this is the stage in which people should be if an intervention is going to have any effect.[1]

Once people are actually changing their behavior, they are in the *action* stage. The change has to have taken place over the past six months, and should involve active efforts to change the behavior. For example, frequent trips to the gym characterize someone who is in the action stage of trying to lose weight. Does any attempt to change behavior, no matter how small, count as being in the action stage? No. People must reach a criterion that health professionals can agree is sufficient to reduce the risk for disease,[62] such as losing enough weight to no longer be classified as obese, or abstaining from smoking for a significant period of time.

Maintenance is the stage in which people try not to fall back into performing their unhealthy behaviors, or relapse. They may still be changing their behaviors and performing new behaviors, but they are not doing it as often as someone in the action stage. In this stage, the temptation to relapse is reduced, and there is often confidence that the new behavior changes can be continued for a period of time. For example, maintenance of abstinence from smoking can last from six months to five years.[63]

Finally, people may reach a stage in which they are no longer tempted by the unhealthy behavior they have changed. The ex-smoker who no longer craves a cigarette, the ex-fast-food addict who no longer feels like eating a burger and fries, and the once-couch-potato who now rides a bike to work every day are said to be in the *termination* stage. Can this state be achieved? One study found that fewer than 20% of former smokers and alcoholics reached this zero-temptation stage.[64] For the most part, this part of the model has been loosely interpreted as representing a lifetime of maintenance. See *Food for Thought* for ideas on how you might improve your eating behavior.

The Prototype-Willingness Model

The prototype-willingness model[65] is a model that is increasingly being adopted by health researchers around the world, as well as individuals who are conducting interventions and preventive interventions aimed at reducing and/or delaying the onset of health risk behavior in adolescents.[66] It is one of the most interesting and innovative theories of adolescent health behavior today, and bets are that it will continue to generate more attention and more value among health researchers internationally. It has been used in older populations as well and is one of the most widely cited health models. It makes a good final theory to know about.

The model is based on two primary assumptions about adolescent risk behavior that make intuitive sense. First, risky behavior is primarily a social activity. Second, risky behaviors are often reactions to situations that are conducive to risky behavior rather than deliberately planned. These two assumptions are reflected in the two focal constructs for the model: risk images (prototypes) and behavioral willingness. People, especially younger adolescents, have clear mental images of "typical" risk takers (smokers, drinkers). They also know that if they perform the risky behavior, they too will be associated with the image (or prototype). The more acceptable the image, the more likely the person is to perform the behavior that will make him or her like the image. Risk images have been shown to predict a variety of health risk behaviors, such as sexual risk taking, alcohol consumption, smoking, and reckless driving.[67] In addition to the role of the image, an adolescent is hypothesized to be more likely to attempt a risky behavior if he or she has a high level of behavioral willingness. Behavioral willingness is defined as an openness to risk opportunity, essentially what an adolescent might do under certain risky circumstances.[68] This is seen as an additional pathway to risk, on top of behavioral intention (as described in the theory of planned behavior above). This model has recently been used to predict behaviors such as contraceptive choice and marijuana use.[69,70]

FOOD FOR *Thought*

Is Comfort Food Really Comforting?

When you feel down, will some foods make you feel better than others? Do you find yourself indulging more in unhealthy foods to make you feel better? What are your "comfort foods"? What should you eat anyway?

First the big food answer. To help people figure out what is best to eat, the U.S. Department of Health and Human Services released an updated set of nutritional guidelines for Americans in 2011, complete with a new pictorial guide, a plate showing you what you should eat (**FIGURE B.4**). An important part of this guide is that it clearly shows amounts needed by age and sex, explicitly urging the consumption of more whole grains and a variety of fruits and vegetables, and including simple direct recommendations such as "make sure half your plate is fruits and vegetables." The MyPlate program is also explicit in that it is only one way to get health and focuses solely on eating.

OK, so you can use the plate, but what about when you feel down? Are there really comfort foods that can help you feel better? This is where social psychological experimentation comes in handy. In a recent study, researchers tested whether comfort foods were in fact comforting.[71]

In a series of smart studies, the researchers examined what makes us feel better and experimentally compared different types of food options. First participants completed an online survey and listed food stuffs they ate that made them feel good. The most commonly mentioned comfort foods were chocolate (26%), ice cream (18%), and cookies (11%). At least a week after they completed the surveys, participants came into the research lab and watched films that made them feel low. In a number of different studies, the participants then got their comfort food, no food, or some other food item. The researchers measured if their moods changed. There was good news and bad news.

Eating the comfort food did make participants feel better but so did eating the noncomfort food or no food. Mood essentially got better as time from watching the film increased whether food (comfort or not) was eaten or not. As you can tell from this research example, sometimes a lot of the effect of something is just in our heads. You may think that eating some foods, such as a pint of your favorite ice cream or a double serving of chicken wings, makes you feel better. This does not seem to be the case. Be smart and look back to the Coping section above for other ways to fight the blues.

FIGURE B.4
MyPlate provides recommendations of how much of what foods we should be eating.

QUIZ YOURSELF
Increasing Healthy Behaviors

1. **Healthy behaviors can be defined as behaviors that _____ .**
   - (a) reduce the risk of heart disease
   - (b) prevent illness
   - (c) maintain and enhance health
   - (d) increase physical and mental well-being

2. **A major part of a person's belief in the effectiveness of changing a behavior is _____ .**
   - (a) how rewarding the result is
   - (b) how punishing the result is
   - (c) the balance of rewards to punishment
   - (d) the balance of benefits to costs

3. **The theory of planned behavior focuses on a person's _____ .**
   - (a) attitudes toward health
   - (b) intention to change the behavior
   - (c) beliefs about the behavior
   - (d) plans to change the behavior

4. **Joaquin is a smoker. He knows this behavior is not very healthy, but he does not intend to change. He is in the _____ .**
   - (a) precontemplation stage
   - (b) contemplation stage
   - (c) preparation stage
   - (d) action stage

answers: see pg B19

Social Psychological Factors Surrounding Illness

Some basic social psychological theories also influence our behaviors when we are ill. Take recognizing symptoms: With physical problems, it is often clear when you need to see a doctor. A serious car or bike accident immediately brings medics to the spot. With other injuries, where the symptoms may not at first seem life threatening, people may first ignore the symptoms or delay going to a doctor. Why is this the case? Many social psychological factors help us understand some of the reasons.

The Confirmation Bias

Once we believe something is true, we often change the way we interpret new information and the way we look at the world. We tend to try to confirm our belief, which biases how we process information. As discussed in Chapter 5, we have a **confirmation bias**. Social psychologists have shown that if there is any ambiguity in a person's behavior, people are likely to interpret what they see in a way that is consistent with their bias.[72] If we believe that a change in our bodies is not a symptom of illness, we will probably look for information to support that belief. For example, if you are fair skinned and have spent too much time in the sun, there is a chance that you may develop some form of skin cancer. The first signs are often round discolorations of the skin. You could look at one of these developing spots and believe that it is a blemish or a pimple, or that it was always there. Now when you look at your skin, you may try to draw attention to parts that look great, ignoring the developing skin spots. You confirm your bias that you are fine and cancer free by thinking that you have often had those spots, off and on, and they never meant anything before. You may even think that you have been feeling especially great recently, so it could not be the beginning of a problem.

This confirmation bias can lead to misperceptions of the social world and an accentuation of symptoms that do get attention. If you believe that you do not need to go to a doctor to seek treatment for flulike symptoms or a cold, if you have managed to succeed on past occasions, or if you see others who do not seem to go in when they have symptoms, you may begin to overestimate how successful you can be by not going to a doctor. We not only find confirmation for what we expect to see, but we also tend to overestimate how often we are right.[73] This is the *illusory correlation* (see Chapter 5), in which you believe your

confirmation bias the tendency to look for information that supports our views expectation has been correct more times than it actually has been. Confirmation biases occur partly because we ignore disconfirmations of our biases and selectively remember information that supports our biases.[74]

Attributions and Misattributions

Another social psychological process that can influence the recognition of symptoms is related to how we determine the cause of events. The cognitive process of assigning meaning to a symptom or behavior, discussed in Chapter 5, is referred to as making **attributions**.[75] Many factors influence our attributions.[76] If your stomach hurts, you may attribute it to what you just ate. If you have not eaten anything different recently, you are more likely to worry about a stomach pain than if you have just tried something that is very different (spicier or oilier than you are used to). How you attribute a pain in your chest may depend on physical factors, such as your age, or psychological factors, such as beliefs that you hold about illness in general. A teenager may think of a chest pain as gas or a cramp; an older person may worry about a heart attack. The cause you attribute to your symptoms can influence whether or not you seek treatment.

Attributions vary across cultures.[77] Mexican American children may consider hearing voices to be evidence of a religious experience,[78] whereas European Americans are more likely to consider it a sign of mental illness. Hmong Americans consider epilepsy the mark of a shaman.[79] People's beliefs about the cause of a disease directly influence how they deal with it. If the spirits mean for you to have a certain pain, then it would be angering them and risking further pain if you tried to do something to alleviate it.

Sometimes we mistakenly label our physiological experiences based on external factors.[80] If you feel tired and a lot of people you work with have colds, you are likely to attribute your tiredness to your developing a cold, even though it could be due to your not getting enough sleep (see Chapter 6). This misattribution can increase your anxiety, and in combination with a confirmation bias (that you have a cold), you may soon find yourself accumulating more evidence to support your theory. Your belief that you are getting sick will, in essence, make you sick (a self-fulfilling prophecy; see Chapter 12).

Such self-fulfilling prophecies can contribute to the continued use of folk medicines and treatments (see Chapter 13). If you are biased against Western biomedicine, you will probably not try to get better after a visit to a doctor. If you are biased toward shamanism, you are probably going to feel a lot better after a shamanistic ritual is performed over you.

Personality

Perhaps the most common individual factor that influences the recognition of symptoms and the seeking of treatment is personality.[81] Personality is what defines each one of us. We have a unique and stable set of characteristics that relate to consistent patterns of behavior across situations. In general, different personality styles are related to a number of health outcomes,[82] but there are many personality characteristics that relate to seeking treatment.

Studies have shown that people who are relatively high in anxiety tend to report more symptoms of illness than others do.[83,84] Neuroticism is another key personality trait in this regard. People who are high in neuroticism experience higher levels of anxiety and tend to be high-strung. This often translates into an oversensitivity to symptoms and more complaining about ill health.[85] In fact, a thorough review of the personality and health literature suggests that people who experience long-term negative feelings (called *chronic negative affect*) show a disease-prone personality.[86]

Some people's personality types make them attend more to bodily sensations and report more symptoms than others.[87] People who monitor their symptoms to an extreme may be **hypochondriacs**, constantly worried about their health. Hypochondriacs believe that any minor change in their condition could be the sign of a major problem. They are constantly going to doctors to be checked. Even when they are told they are all right, they do not believe the diagnosis and may change doctors.[88]

attribution cognitive process of assigning meaning to a symptom or behavior

hypochondriacs people who are constantly worried about their health

Personality traits such as optimism and self-esteem normally buffer us against stress and illness, but may also delay seeking treatment. People with high self-esteem believe that they are very healthy and are optimistic in their outlook. They may also believe that their bodies can fight off infections or heal without specific medical treatment. People high in optimism may even downplay the negative symptoms they experience and expect things to turn around shortly. These people may wait and see if they get better, but sometimes they wait too long.

Understanding why we do or not do something is important because it provides us with a way to change and make a difference in our health. Armed with knowledge about the determinants of health behaviors and the methodological rigor of social psychology, researchers attempt to intervene to change behaviors. Psychologists have tried different techniques to get people to do what is healthy by designing interventions based on the theories discussed previously and using the scientific method to bring about change. Different interventions focus on different antecedents of behavior. Some health psychologists seek to change people's attitudes to change their behavior; others attempt to change their beliefs or intentions. The way an intervention is designed can depend on the specific behavior that needs to be changed, the funding available for the behavior change, and the number of people that the intervention has to reach.

As you can see, social psychological theories can be applied to understanding many different aspects of health, ranging from why we get stressed and how we cope with it to modifying our health behaviors and predicting how we recognize symptoms and report them. Applying a social psychological perspective to the study of health illustrates the benefits of considering people as active constructors of their own realities, with health behaviors depending on the interaction of the person and the situation. You may find these insights useful in optimizing your own health.

QUIZ YOURSELF
Social Psychological Factors Surrounding Illness

1. Many social psychological processes help explain illness behaviors (or their absence). If you do not think you are sick, you are likely to ignore symptoms and only look for evidence that you are healthy. This is called _____ .
   - (a) self-fulfilling prophecy
   - (b) selective attention
   - (c) confirmation bias
   - (d) impression management

2. The human tendency to want to assign a cause to an event or to symptoms is known as _____ .
   - (a) attribution
   - (b) misattribution
   - (c) self-fulfilling prophecy
   - (d) confirmation bias

3. Very often we do not realize or recognize the true causes of our symptoms. If you have been very stressed and as a result start putting on weight, you may instead blame a new diet. The underlying psychological process is known as _____ .
   - (a) confirmation bias
   - (b) attributional error
   - (c) misattribution
   - (d) illusory correlation

4. In some aboriginal tribes of Australia, a healthy man can get sick and die within days if he believes that he has been cursed. The underlying psychological phenomenon in this situation is _____ .
   - (a) misattribution
   - (b) confirmation bias
   - (c) illusory correlation
   - (d) self-fulfilling prophecy

answers: see pg B19

What Makes Us Human

Putting the Cultural Animal in Perspective

Health, stress, and illness are basic problems of life that humans share with a great many other creatures. Human beings, however, face special sorts of health problems and, more strikingly, have novel ways of dealing with them. Both of these reflect the importance of culture in human life.

The stresses that human beings suffer are quite different from those that other animals face, even if the effects of stress may be similar. Many animals never know where their next meal is coming from or whether predators will eat them that day. Culture has managed to erase those worries for a great many people. But in place of those concerns, we face a whole host of stresses that are the product of living in culture: pressures to meet deadlines or live up to the expectations of others, the danger of identity theft and terrorism, problems in the economy, lawsuits, warfare. The idea of living in a culture that puts an end to stress is still a remote fantasy.

One theme of this book has been that nature says go and culture says stop, but that doesn't always apply in the domain of health. At best, culture may send mixed messages that leave people torn between stop and go. For example, the temptations of junk food and sugary sweets, of tobacco and alcohol and dangerous drugs, and even of driving too fast are all provided by culture, even though the culture does warn people about those dangers.

Human culture, however, has come up with remarkable ways of fighting disease and promoting health. The accumulation of knowledge about health, injuries, and treatments has culminated in the nearly miraculous powers of modern medicine. Information about how to live a healthy life has also begun to spread rapidly. Medical testing can catch health problems early and enable people to avoid many of their worst effects, and medicines and surgery enable people to survive health problems that would have been fatal just a few generations ago.

One of the biggest signs of the power of human culture is that life expectancy has increased dramatically. Early humans often died quite young, and it was unusual for people to live to the age of 50. In modern Western cultures, at least, the average person born today can expect to live around 90 years, and only a small fraction die during childhood. No other species has been able to double or triple how long its members live by dint of its accumulated knowledge and socially promoted changes in behavior. In short, the progress of human culture has made it possible for you to live a much longer, healthier life than early humans could have dreamed.

MODULE B SUMMARY

What Is Stress?

- Stress is a disruption of our homeostatic balance. We are stressed anytime excessive demands are placed on our body and mind. Stressors are factors that disrupt our homeostasis.
- Stress activates the nervous system, especially the sympathetic nervous system, which in turn mobilizes the body for action. The parasympathetic system restores the body to rest after the stressor ends. The physiological stress response is characterized by the activation of different physiological pathways and the release of stress hormones.
- There are four major theories of stress:
  - Cannon described the fight-or-flight response, which involves sympathetic adrenal medulla activation and the release of catecholamines.

  - Selye described the general adaptation syndrome, involving hypothalamic pituitary adrenal activation and the release of cortisol.
  - Lazarus proposed a cognitive appraisal model, with primary and secondary appraisals of events determining stress.
  - Taylor and colleagues' tend-and-befriend model suggests that men and women have evolved different stress mechanisms.

Coping

- Coping is defined as the individual efforts made to manage distressing problems and emotions that affect the physical and psychological outcomes of stress. The two primary coping styles are problem-focused or approach coping and emotion-focused or avoidant coping.
- Social support is one of the most important factors influencing coping. Commonly defined as emotional, informational, or instrumental assistance from others, social support has been associated with a variety of positive health outcomes.

Increasing Healthy Behaviors

- Healthy behaviors are specific behaviors that maintain and enhance health. The most important are getting physical activity, limiting the consumption of alcohol, not smoking, and eating well.

- The health beliefs model suggests that our beliefs relating to the effectiveness, ease, and consequences of doing or not doing a behavior influence whether we do it or not. Our perception of susceptibility, the consequences of the illness, and the extent to which we believe behavior change is effective and worthwhile contributes to the likelihood of doing the behavior.

- The theory of planned behavior suggests that our intentions to perform a behavior are the most important predictors of whether we do it. These intentions are influenced by our attitudes toward the behavior and the perceptions of the social norms regarding the behavior.

- The transtheoretical model of behavior change suggests that there are key phases we pass through in regard to a behavior. We move from not thinking about changing (precontemplation) to contemplating change, to preparing to change, to changing (action stage), and then to maintaining the change.

Social Psychological Factors Surrounding Illness

- Many psychological factors such as conformation biases, personality styles, and attributional problems compounded by cultural differences interfere with accurate symptom recognition.

What Makes Us Human? Putting the Cultural Animal in Perspective

- Humans face special sorts of health problems and have novel ways of dealing with them, as evidenced by the dramatic increase in the life expectancy we enjoy today.

key terms

appraisals B6	coping B8	health psychology B3	social support B8
attribution B16	fight-or-flight response B5	healthy behaviors B9	stress B4
biopsychosocial approach B9	general adaptation syndrome B6	homeostasis B4	tend and befriend B7
cognitive appraisal model B6	health B2	hypochondriacs B16	theory of planned behavior B11
confirmation bias B15	health belief model B10	intervention B9	transtheoretical model B11

quiz yourself ANSWERS

1. What Is Stress? p. B7
   answers: 1.d 2.a 3.d 4.a

2. Coping p. B9
   answers: 1.a 2.c 3.d 4.b

3. Increasing Healthy Behaviors p. B15
   answers: 1.c 2.d 3.b 4.a

4. Social Psychological Factors Surrounding Illness p. B17
   answers: 1.c 2.a 3.c 4.d

7

LEARNING OBJECTIVES

1. Define attitudes, differentiating them from beliefs. Explain how people can hold dual attitudes and what the benefits and drawbacks of attitudes are.

2. Describe how attitudes are formed, distinguishing the different conditioning and cognitive processes that shape attitudes.

3. Identify the major consistency theories and describe how they relate to attitudes.

4. Explain how the duplex mind affects the drive toward consistency, and relate this to the idea discussed in Chapter 5 that human thinking and reasoning processes seem designed primarily for arguing.

5. Evaluate the evidence that attitudes predict behavior, summarizing the conditions that lead to the greatest attitude–behavior consistency.

6. Debate the role of attitudes in coping with trauma.

MONEY MATTERS
Would You Sell Your Soul for $1?
242

FOOD FOR THOUGHT
Would You Eat a Bug or a Worm?
244

THE SOCIAL SIDE OF SEX
A–B Inconsistency and Erotic Plasticity
247

WHAT MAKES US HUMAN?
Putting the Cultural Animal in Perspective
254

In the "Majority Rule" episode from science fiction comedy series *The Orville*, an exploratory space vessel from a 25th-century alliance of earth and many other planets visits a developing planet named Sargus 4 to find two missing anthropologists who visited the planet. Dressed like the planet's inhabitants, the landing team discovers that everyone on the planet wears a "Vote Badge" with a green upward arrow for positive votes and a red downward arrow for negative votes.

The Vote Badges are used to register public opinion on a variety of issues, including whether people approve or disapprove of your actions. The landing team quickly buys some Vote Badges from a vendor so they will fit in. Although the landing team is told to keep a low profile, one of the team members—John LaMarr—simulates a suggestive ("grindy") dance on a statue of a respected historical figure (Mella Giffendon) in the town square and is filmed doing it by several Saraguns. The films of LaMarr grinding with the statue are uploaded to Master Feed, and his Vote Badge quickly begins registering downvotes. The votes have serious consequences too. If you get 500,000 downvotes, you are denied service in restaurants; if you get over 1 million downvotes you have committed a "crime against the state" and must go on an apology tour where members of society judge your sincerity. If someone has over 10 million downvotes by the end of the apology tour, they are forcibly given "neurological readjustment" using a cap with shock electrodes, which makes them completely docile. The brain damage is irreversible too, as the ship's doctor discovers by examining one of the anthropologists who underwent the treatment. The other anthropologist tried to escape rather than receiving the treatment. LaMarr's Vote Badge quickly surpasses 1 million votes, so he must go on an apology tour, which doesn't go well because he knows nothing about the planet's hero Mella Giffendon. Fortunately, the USS *Orville* team is able to save LaMarr by breaking into the Master Feed and flooding it with doctored positive images and videos of LaMarr.

Although present-day earth is far cry from Sargun 4, people on earth do "register" their attitudes over a wide variety of topics. For example, one of your authors (Bushman) recently bought some mini cupcakes at *Kittie's Cakes* for his family, and immediately after paying for them received an email asking him to rate his experience.

In the digital age, people can express their attitudes and more easily and more often than ever before, and to much larger audiences, such as on social media. People use these ratings to determine what products they buy, what foods they eat, what movies and videos they watch, what books they read, what music they listen to, etc. Sometimes photos and videos even go viral (i.e., spread like a virus) and attract very large audiences. For example, the GANGNAM STYLE (강남스타일) M/V video by South Korean musician Psy has over 2 billion views. More recently, in 2018, 14-year-old girl named Evie Clair sang Christina Perri's song "Arms" on the program America's Got Talent for her dying father, and this has had over 150 million views. Even a 2018 Turkish Airlines advertisement video in which Dr. Oz talks about our 5 senses has about 100 million views. A video went

Vote Badge, worn by LaMarr, from "Majority Rule" episode of *The Orville*.

viral (over 1 million views) showing an airport baggage handler in South Africa straightening each suitcase after it fell onto the carousel belt, with handles out so passengers could easily grab their suitcase.[1]

Sometimes people use bad ratings to hurt businesses and might even face a lawsuit for doing so.[2] Sometimes people also engage in dangerous and even deadly behaviors chasing "likes" on social media. For example, two hikers at Hermit Falls in Angeles National Forest needed to be rescued after filming themselves jumping off a cliff into a pool of water below, one with a dislocated shoulder and one with two broken legs.[3] Indeed, between 2011 and 2017 over 250 people have died seeking the perfect selfie photo, a 2018 global study revealed.[4]

In this chapter, we discuss what attitudes are, how they are formed, what purpose they serve, and how they differ from beliefs. In the next chapter, we discuss attitude change, or persuasion. ●

What Are Attitudes and Why Do People Have Them?

Why are attitudes so important? And why specifically are they so important to social psychology? Some attitudes seem trivial, but others are clearly important. Attitudes can be important insofar as they predict behaviors. For example, does a person's attitude toward a political candidate predict whether he or she will vote for that person in an election? Does a person's attitude toward the environment predict whether he or she will recycle, take public transportation, ride a bike, car pool, use energy-efficient lightbulbs, and so on?

Attitudes Versus Beliefs

Attitudes differ from beliefs. **Beliefs** are pieces of information (facts or opinions) about something. **Attitudes** are global evaluations toward some object or issue (e.g., you like or dislike something, you are in favor of or opposed to some position).[6] If you think that a certain person is president or that it is cloudy outside, that's a belief. An attitude is whether you like this person as president, or the clouds. Logically, attitudes are for choosing, whereas beliefs are for explaining. Beliefs and attitudes both serve interpersonal functions. People need to influence how others choose, and people also need to explain things to others.

Dual Attitudes

"She says she likes jazz, but somehow she never seems to listen to it, and in fact when it comes on the radio, she usually changes the station!" **Dual attitudes** are defined as different evaluations of the same attitude object: an automatic attitude and a deliberate attitude.[7] This dual model of attitudes fits the duplex-mind theme of this book. **Automatic attitudes** (sometimes called **implicit attitudes** and/or **unconscious attitudes**) are very fast evaluative, "gut-level" responses that people don't think a great deal about. In contrast, **deliberate attitudes** (sometimes called **explicit attitudes** and/or **conscious attitudes**) are more reflective responses that people think more carefully about. Although this distinction between automatic and deliberate attitudes is very popular with current researchers, it has been around for a very long time.[8] Sometimes automatic and deliberate attitudes are inconsistent. In the United States, for example,

> "The concept of the attitude is probably the most distinctive and indispensable concept in contemporary American social psychology."
> — Gordon W. Allport[5]

beliefs pieces of information about something; facts or opinions

attitudes global evaluations toward some object or issue

dual attitudes different evaluations of the same attitude object held by the same person (perhaps one deliberate, the other automatic)

automatic attitudes (sometimes called **implicit attitudes** and/or **unconscious attitudes**) very fast evaluative, "gut-level" responses that people don't think a great deal about

deliberate attitudes (sometimes called **explicit attitudes** and/or **conscious attitudes**) reflective responses that people think more carefully about few people from any ethnic group admit to holding racial prejudices, and most sincerely espouse the ideals of racial equality, yet many people show negative automatic responses toward other races.[9]

Automatic attitudes are more difficult to measure than deliberate attitudes. Most measures of automatic attitudes involve measuring reaction times to stimuli. For example, automatic racial attitudes are often measured using reaction times to photos of black versus white people associated with negative (e.g., guns) versus neutral (e.g., cell phones) or positive (e.g., flowers) objects. Deliberate racial attitudes are often measured using self-report questionnaires such as the Symbolic Racism 2000 Scale,[10] which consists of 8 items [e.g., "It's really a matter of some people not trying hard enough; if blacks would only try harder they could be just as well off as whites" and "Generations of slavery and discrimination have created conditions that make it difficult for blacks to work their way out of the lower class" (reverse scored)] that are scored using a 4-point scale ranging from 1 = *strongly agree* to 4 = *strongly disagree*.

Racial attitudes seem very resistant to change. For example, exposure to high-status exemplars of black people such as former U.S. President Barack Obama has proven ineffective in shifting societal-level racial attitudes. However, the #BlackLivesMatter (#BLM) movement has led to both automatic and deliberate attitude changes.[11] In terms of automatic attitudes, white people became less pro-white, whereas black people showed little change. For deliberate attitudes, both white and black people moved toward a "no preference" position (i.e., white people became less pro-white and black people became less pro-black).

Some researchers have questioned the distinction between automatic and deliberate attitudes altogether.[12,13] They argue that it is inappropriate and unjustified to conclude that there are two different types of attitudes solely on the basis of automatic and deliberate measures leading to differing assessments of individuals' attitudes. They argue that the automatic/deliberate distinction applies to the level of measurement, not to the actual attitudes. For another question about dual attitudes, read the *Tradeoffs* box.

What Is the Real Attitude?

Dual attitudes present a dilemma for judging people. How do you judge someone whose dual attitudes conflict, which means that a person holds two different attitudes that are incompatible with one another? Should we judge a person based on the deliberate attitude—or based on the automatic one?

Suppose a person was brought up to endorse certain attitudes strongly, such as religious or political views. Then during adulthood the person thinks deeply about these issues and decides to change. The person's actions may reflect the new attitude, including voting and donating money—but the views learned from childhood are still strongly entrenched in the unconscious. Should we judge the person based on the automatic attitudes leftover from childhood, or the ones deliberately chosen by the adult?

Prejudice involves a particularly sensitive version of this dilemma. Hardly any Americans outwardly express racist attitudes any more, although they do seem to express more automatic racist attitudes. Do we judge a person based on explicit statements of being tolerant and egalitarian, or based on the reaction-time evidence suggesting an automatic racist bias?

Addiction presents another sensitive and complex case of dual attitudes. Many addicts desire their drugs (or whatever it is that they are addicted to) but also desire to recover from addiction and stop using. Do we judge them positively because of their earnest desire to be cured? Or do we judge them based on their automatic craving for destructive substances?

Further complicating the judgment question is the possibility of deception. People can lie about their true feelings, so in a sense explicit expressions of deliberate attitudes are less reliable than indicators of automatic attitudes (which are hard to fake). For example, a bigot might know that expressing prejudice is socially unacceptable and therefore might claim to be tolerant. Such possibilities make people more inclined to treat the automatic attitude as the "real" one. But in those cases, what was misleading was not the true, deliberate attitude, but only what the person expressed.

Why People Have Attitudes

Most animals don't need very many attitudes. They know what they like to eat (what tastes good), what fellow animals they like or dislike, and where they like to sleep. Their world is not very complex (compared to that of humans), and a few simple attitudes can serve them well.

In contrast, human life is now highly complex, and people need to have a broad assortment of attitudes. People are asked to vote on many issues and candidates in elections. When shopping, they are presented with literally thousands of different choices within one supermarket or department store. Even if they know they want a particular product, such as a pair of gloves, they face a vast array of potential choices, and having some attitudes can help (e.g., mittens are better than gloves because they are warmer, or gloves are better than mittens because the fingers are more usable; leather is fashionable, but harder to maintain, plus some animal had to die; brown gloves might clash with my blue coat). Attitudes are necessary and adaptive for humans. They help us adjust to new situations, seeking out those things in our environment that reward us and avoiding those things that punish us. Attitudes can even be a matter of life or death, influencing whether people take risks.

Attitudes are mainly used to sort things into "good" and "bad" categories. The world is full of information (see Chapter 5), but just figuring things out and understanding them isn't enough. You can only make your way through a complicated world if you can sort things into good and bad. Sure enough, good and bad are among the most basic categories of thought. Although these categories are abstract, children understand them very early in life, especially the category "bad." In one study of children 2 to 6 years old, bad pictures were more readily identified than good pictures at all ages beyond 2 years, 5 months.[14] This probably reflects one of the most basic psychological principles: Bad is stronger than good.[15,16]

As soon as you know what something is, you start to know whether you like or dislike it.[17] This initial evaluation is immediate and unconscious, occurring in the first microsecond of thought. This initial evaluation even occurs for things people have never encountered before, such as nonsense words. For example, the nonsense word *juvalamu* is very pleasing, the nonsense word *bargulum* is moderately pleasing, and the nonsense word *chakaka* is very displeasing.[18] Although people can easily override the initial, automatic evaluation with further thought, the initial evaluation stands if no further thought is given. According to John Bargh, who led this team of researchers (and no doubt inspired the word *bargulum!*), "We have yet to find something the mind regards with complete impartiality, without at least a mild judgment of liking or disliking."[19] Put another way, people have attitudes about everything.

Attitudes are tremendously helpful in making choices. Perhaps it doesn't matter what person you think ought to be eliminated next on TV shows such as *The Amazing Race, Top Chef, The Bachelor,* or *The Bachelorette.* When you have to choose what courses to take next semester, however, you will find that attitudes come in very handy. Without attitudes, you face a bewildering array of options, all respectable intellectual endeavors, all taught by presumably competent faculty, all offering useful knowledge or at least something interesting. How can you choose, unless you have attitudes that say this course will be more interesting, or that one will be more useful to your chosen career, or that one will lead to a higher paying job, and that other one is likely to be dreadfully boring?

Previous research has shown that possessing an attitude increases the ease, speed, and quality of decision making.[20] Thus, attitudes appear to have great functional value. Evidence for this came in a study in which first-year college students completed measures of negative life events and health at two points in time.[21] Students who entered college knowing their likes and dislikes on academically relevant issues experienced better physical and mental health in the new college setting than did other students. Thus, having plenty of attitudes is even good for your health!

QUIZ YOURSELF

What are Attitudes and Why do People Have Them?

1. **Which concept can be defined as pieces of information (facts or opinions) about something?**
   - (a) Attitudes
   - (b) Beliefs
   - (c) Intentions
   - (d) Values

2. **Which concept can be defined as a global evaluation?**
   - (a) Attitude
   - (b) Belief
   - (c) Intention
   - (d) Value

3. **Fast evaluation is to slow evaluation as _____ is to _____.**
   - (a) automatic attitude; deliberate attitude
   - (b) deliberate attitude; automatic attitude
   - (c) primacy effect; recency effect
   - (d) recency effect; primacy effect

4. **Dual attitudes refer to _____ and _____ attitudes.**
   - (a) automatic; deliberate
   - (b) new; old
   - (c) private; public
   - (d) rewarded; unrewarded

answers: see pg 257

How Attitudes Are Formed

Formation of Attitudes

Several explanations have been offered for how attitudes are formed. We shall look at relatively simple explanations (mere exposure, classical conditioning, body movements) and also at more complicated explanations (operant conditioning, social learning).

mere exposure effect the tendency for people to come to like things simply because they see or encounter them repeatedly

Mere Exposure Effect

Most people have heard the aphorism "familiarity breeds contempt." It is false. (Winston Churchill is said to have once rebutted the assertion that familiarity breeds contempt by pointing out that without a certain amount of familiarity, it is impossible to breed anything!) Hundreds of studies have shown that "familiarity breeds liking."[22] The **mere exposure effect** is the tendency for novel stimuli to be liked more after the individual has been repeatedly exposed to them. In 1968, social psychologist Robert Zajonc proposed that "mere repeated exposure of the individual to a stimulus is a sufficient condition for the enhancement of his attitude toward it."[23] In plainer terms, just seeing something over and over is enough to make you like it. To test his mere exposure hypothesis, Zajonc conducted a series of studies in which participants were exposed to novel stimuli (e.g., Turkish words, Chinese-like characters, and yearbook photos of strangers).[24] The more frequently participants saw each stimulus, the more they liked it (see **FIGURE 7.1**). Subsequent research has shown that mere exposure to more meaningful stimuli, such as faces of people from different races, can increase liking for similar faces that have never been seen.[25]

The mere exposure effect can also influence attitudes toward oneself. Female college students brought a close female friend with them to do an experiment.[26] The researchers took a photograph of each student and made two prints from it—a true print and a mirror (reversed) print. Participants liked the mirror print better than the true print, whereas their friends liked the true print better than the mirror print. A follow-up study found the same result when female participants brought their boyfriends. Why? Both groups liked what they had been exposed to most frequently. People most commonly see themselves

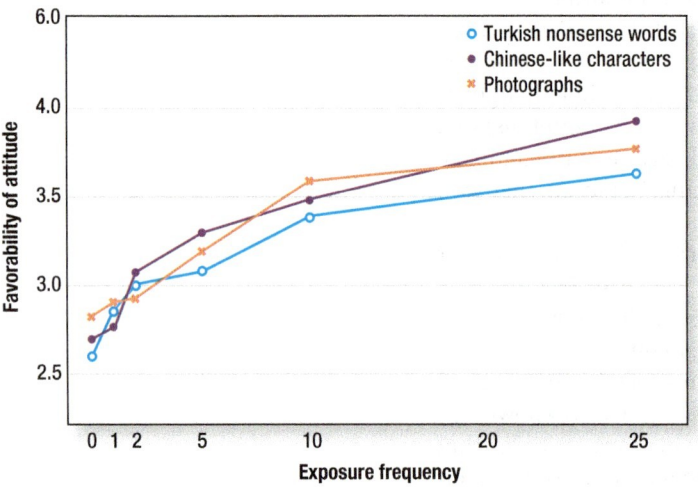

FIGURE 7.1

Relation between frequency of mere exposure to Turkish words, Chinese-like characters, and yearbook photos of strangers and attitudes toward these stimuli.

From R.S. Zajonc, "Attitudinal effects of mere exposure," *Journal of Personality and Social Psychology*, Monograph Supplement, 9, 1968, 1-27. Copyright © 1968 by the American Psychological Association. Reprinted by permission.

in a reversed image, as when they look in the mirror. In contrast, your friends mostly see your true image because they look directly at you rather than seeing you in a mirror. A recent real-world test of the mere exposure effect was conducted using the Eurovision Song Contest, in which TV viewers vote on what songs they like best from artists from different countries. The study found that songs played more frequently obtained more votes.[27]

The mere exposure effect appears to be quite robust. It even occurs for animals other than humans, such as crickets[28] and chickens.[29] Why does it occur? It seems that when people are exposed to novel stimuli over and over again, they feel more positively about them.[30]

This general rule has a couple of exceptions. If you initially dislike something, being exposed to it repeatedly will not make you like it more. In fact, it will make you like it less.[31,32] For example, if you hear a song on the radio that you hate, the more you hear it, the more you will hate it. The same is true for threatening stimuli (e.g., angry faces)—the more people are exposed to them, the less they like them.[33,34]

Embodied Attitudes

The famous biologist Charles Darwin thought attitudes were evident in bodily states, such as leaning toward or away from something. In an early classic demonstration,[35] college students were told that the researchers were conducting a marketing study for a headphone company "determined to create the ultimate headphones in terms of sound and comfort." After trying on six different headphones, participants listened to a simulated radio broadcast of an editorial commentator discussing tuition at their university. By the flip of a coin, half the participants heard the commentator argue that tuition should be increased, whereas the other half heard the commentator argue that tuition should be decreased. The experimenter said that it was important that headphones would function well despite movement, so participants were instructed to move their heads while listening. Some were told to move their heads up and down (like nodding agreement): These ended up agreeing with the message even if it meant their tuition would be increased. Others were told to move their heads from side to side (like shaking their head no). These ended up disagreeing with the message. Thus, the randomly assigned bodily movements shaped people's attitudes toward what they heard.

Even symbolically potent body movements can shape attitudes. Researchers had people write positive or negative thoughts about a new Mediterranean diet.[36] Some were then instructed to carry the paper on which their thoughts were written with them in their pocket, wallet, or purse. These people came to hold attitudes consistent with the positive or negative thoughts they had written. Others were told to rip up the paper and throw it in the trash. These people shifted in the opposite direction from what they had written. Thus, throwing their thoughts into the trash freed people from the influence of those thoughts.

Classical Conditioning

Research has shown that attitudes can be formed through **classical conditioning**.[37] Ivan Pavlov, a Nobel Prize–winning Russian scientist, developed the theory of classical conditioning and demonstrated it in his experiments with dogs. Meat powder (**unconditioned stimulus**) makes the dog's mouth water (**unconditioned response**). The first time a researcher rings a bell (**neutral stimulus**), the dog's mouth does not water. However, if the researcher rings the bell every time the dog gets meat powder, the dog begins to expect that every time it hears the bell it will be fed, and the bell becomes a **conditioned stimulus**. Eventually, the sound of the bell alone will make the dog's mouth water (**conditioned response**), even with no food around (see **FIGURE 7.2**). This principle is one of the foundations of the psychology of learning, and social psychologists have proposed that it could explain the formation of attitudes in humans. In a sense, Pavlov's dog developed a positive attitude toward the sound of the bell, where it had not had any attitude before, simply because the dog's positive attitude toward meat gradually became linked to the sound of the bell.

Classical conditioning may help explain the development of prejudice against social groups that are frequently associated with negative information in the media,[38] such as Muslims being associated with terrorism in the popular press.[39]

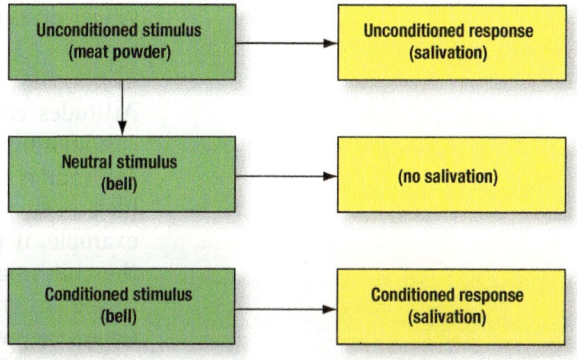

FIGURE 7.2

Ivan Pavlov proposed classical conditioning theory.

classical conditioning a type of learning in which, through repeated pairings, a neutral stimulus comes to evoke a conditioned response

unconditioned stimulus a stimulus (e.g., meat powder) that naturally evokes a particular response (e.g., salivation)

unconditioned response a naturally occurring response (e.g., salivation)

neutral stimulus a stimulus (e.g., Pavlov's bell) that initially evokes no response

conditioned stimulus a neutral stimulus that, through repeated pairings with an unconditioned stimulus, comes to evoke a conditioned response

conditioned response a response that, through repeated pairings, is evoked by a formerly neutral stimulus

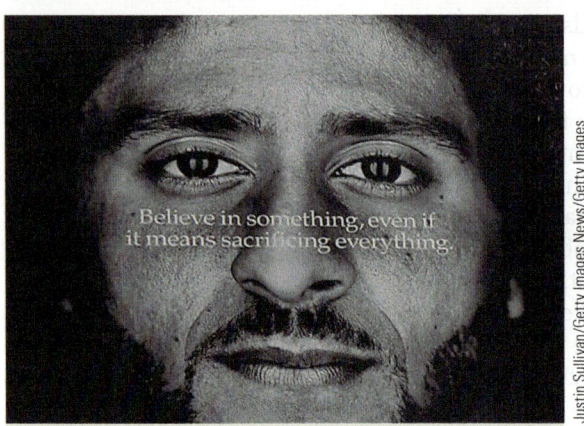

A Nike ad campaign featured Colin Kaepernick, the former NFL player who refused to stand for the national anthem to protest police brutality against black people. Nike sales surged as a result of the ad, although some people reacted negatively.

Advertisers use classical conditioning to their advantage by linking their products with famous or attractive people. For example, famous athletes such as Roger Federer, LeBron James, Christano Renaldo, Steph Curry, and Tiger Woods have endorsed Nike shoes, which should make attitudes toward Nike shoes more positive. That's also why advertisers may cancel their contracts with famous people who behave badly or illegally, so customers will not develop negative attitudes toward their products. For example, Nike (and other sponsors) dropped former bicyclist Lance Armstrong following his drug scandal,[40] and some National Football League (NFL) players after being convicted of domestic violence.[41,42] Likewise, Subway dropped spokesperson Jared Fogle after he pled guilty to paying minors for sex and receiving child pornography.[43] Sometimes an endorsement can endear some people and alienate others. For example, a Nike ad campaign featured Colin Kaepernick, the former NFL player who refused to stand for the national anthem to protest police brutality against black people. Although Nike sales surged as a result of the ad,[44] some people began cutting the Nike "swooshes" from their socks and some colleges dropped uniforms featuring the Nike logo to protest the Kaepernick ad.[45]

Other pairings seem questionable. For example, on the TV show *American Idol*, the "American Idol" logo is used to cover someone's mouth every time that person swears or makes an obscene gesture (e.g., sticking up their middle finger, mooning the camera). What might Dr. Pavlov have to say about associating the show's logo with vulgar, obscene swear words and actions?

Operant Conditioning

Attitudes can also be formed through **operant conditioning** (also called **instrumental conditioning**). In this type of conditioning, developed by behaviorists such as Edward Thorndike and B. F. Skinner, participants are more likely to repeat behaviors that have been rewarded and less likely to repeat behaviors that have been punished. For example, if parents or teachers praise a child for doing well on math problems, then the child may develop a more positive attitude toward math. Students in one study received either an "A" or a "D" (the grade was actually decided by the flip of a coin) on the essays each wrote.[46] Even though the grades were randomly determined, students who received an "A" reported more favorable attitudes toward the topic than did students who received a "D." (Don't worry; your social psychology instructor won't be assigning grades in your class randomly!) Parents, teachers, and other adults often use operant conditioning by praising children for expressing what they consider to be socially desirable attitudes.

Social Learning

By the early 1960s it became clear that conditioning by itself could not explain complex social behaviors. Psychologist Albert Bandura, who received the National Medal of Science from former President Barack Obama, theorized that the most powerful learning processes in understanding social behavior involved **social learning** (also called **observational learning**).[47,48,49] According to social learning theory, people learn how to behave by observing and imitating others. In several classic experiments, Bandura showed that young children imitated specific aggressive acts they observed in aggressive models, for example, hitting a "Bobo" doll (a large inflatable toy) that they had seen an actor hit. Furthermore, he developed the concept of vicarious learning of aggression by showing that children were especially likely to imitate other people who had been rewarded for behaving aggressively.[50,51] Bandura argued that this imitation was the key to social learning. The idea is that people do not just imitate the specific social behaviors they see, but they make cognitive inferences based on their observations, and these inferences lead to generalizations in behavior. What is important is how the child interprets social events, and how competent the child feels in responding in different ways.[52] These cognitions provide a basis for stability of behavior tendencies across a variety of situations. Watching Mommy hit Daddy (or vice versa) may not only increase a child's likelihood of hitting. It may also increase the child's belief that hitting is okay when someone provokes you. Once again, the capacity to learn from others is important for enabling humans to be cultural beings.

operant conditioning (instrumental conditioning) a type of learning in which people are more likely to repeat behaviors that have been rewarded and less likely to repeat behaviors that have been punished

social learning (observational learning) a type of learning in which people are more likely to imitate behaviors if they have seen others rewarded for performing them, and less likely to imitate behaviors if they have seen others punished for performing them.

Many viewers' attitudes about musical performances have been shaped by watching the judges on the TV program *American Idol*.

Of course, social learning theory can also explain how attitudes are developed. For example, many teens learn what attitudes are acceptable by watching whether other teens are rewarded or punished for endorsing certain music, clothing styles, hairstyles, and convictions.[53] Social media makes this process more efficient because one can learn about the attitudes of many other people. Indeed, the recording and tallying of "likes" has become a widely influential measure of popular attitudes, now reverberating through the business world too.

Polarization

Sometimes our attitudes about something can become stronger or weaker simply by thinking more about it. When we think about something, we may generate new ideas or insights that we did not consider when we formed our initial attitudes. Research suggests that as people reflect on their attitudes they become more extreme, an effect known as **attitude polarization**.[54,55,56,57] Even just thinking about an issue can move a person toward holding a more extreme attitude.

Furthermore, people who hold strong attitudes on certain issues are likely to evaluate relevant evidence in a biased manner. They tend to accept at face value evidence that confirms what they already believe, whereas they tend to be more critical of evidence that goes against what they believe. Thus, even if people see an equal amount of confirming and disconfirming evidence (so that logically their attitude should not change), they become even more convinced of their initial attitudes and adopt them more strongly. The attitude polarization effect is especially likely to occur in people who have strong initial attitudes.[58] Politics is one area in which attitude polarization is likely to occur, as illustrated by a study of populist attitudes in 11 countries.[59] Research on this important topic has a long history. In one early classic study,[60] proponents and opponents of the death penalty read studies about the death penalty. The results showed that both groups were biased in favor of studies that matched their initial opinion on the death penalty. As a result, their attitudes became more polarized—the proponents became more in favor of the death penalty, whereas the opponents became more opposed to it—even though all had read the same information! Attitude polarization also occurs sometimes because people are reluctant to admit they are wrong. As they think more about an issue, they tend to convince themselves that they were right all along.

Other studies show that people are more accepting of evidence presented by ingroup members (members of one's own group) than by outgroup members (members of a different group).[61] People are especially skeptical of evidence presented by outgroup

attitude polarization the finding that people's attitudes become more extreme as they reflect on them members who are different from themselves. All of this reflects another theme we have seen repeatedly in this book: putting people first. People rely on others for information, and they especially rely on people who are similar to themselves. If people are biased to accept information from ingroup members, then most groups will tend to hold fairly similar opinions on many issues. This may make it easier for the group to work together. Alternatively, it may foster poor decision making. These issues are discussed in more detail in the groups chapter (Chapter 14).

QUIZ YOURSELF
How Attitudes Are Formed

1. Alissa heard a new song on the radio that she likes. A company used the same song in its advertising jingle, and the song was played over and over, so she was repeatedly exposed to the song. Alissa's attitude toward the song is likely to _____.
   - ⓐ become ambivalent
   - ⓑ become more negative
   - ⓒ become more positive
   - ⓓ remain the same

2. If the word *pink* is followed by negative words and frowns from his mother, the toddler learns to respond negatively to the word *pink*. This is an example of _____.
   - ⓐ classical conditioning
   - ⓑ operant conditioning
   - ⓒ social learning
   - ⓓ verbal learning

3. Juan wasn't sure whether he was in favor of capital punishment or not. However, after receiving an "A" on a speech paper denouncing capital punishment, he decides that capital punishment is ineffective and inhumane. This is an example of _____.
   - ⓐ classical conditioning
   - ⓑ operant conditioning
   - ⓒ social learning
   - ⓓ verbal learning

4. After 3-year-old Davis sees his dad shaving, he covers his own face with shaving cream. This is an example of _____.
   - ⓐ classical conditioning
   - ⓑ operant conditioning
   - ⓒ social learning
   - ⓓ verbal learning

answers: see pg 257

Consistency

Inconsistency does not much trouble dogs or bugs, but people feel some inner pressure to resolve it. To reduce their feelings of inconsistency, people may have to seek out new information or reinterpret old information, realign or even abandon cherished beliefs, or change patterns of behavior. People don't like it when their beliefs, attitudes, and behaviors are inconsistent. (Nor do they approve of inconsistency in others!) This drive for consistency is a central component of several theories in social psychology.

Most consistency theories have three things in common. First, they specify the conditions that are required for consistency and inconsistency of cognitions. Second, they assume that inconsistency is unpleasant and therefore motivates people to restore consistency. Third, they specify the conditions that are needed to restore consistency. In general, people choose the path of least resistance to restore consistency. Because attitudes are easier to change than behaviors, people often change their attitudes. Next, we review the most influential consistency theory—cognitive dissonance theory. We then show how the duplex mind copes with inconsistency.

Cognitive Dissonance and Attitude Change

One of the most important applications of consistency to social phenomena is called **cognitive dissonance theory**. According to this theory, conflicting thoughts cause psychological discomfort (cognitive dissonance). It is a theory about how people rationalize their behavior so as to bring their attitudes into line with their actions.

The origins of cognitive dissonance theory lay in some confusing findings that emerged from persuasion research during its first flowering in the 1950s. At that time, psychology was dominated by operant conditioning theory (see "Formation of Attitudes" section earlier in this chapter), which was based on the simple idea that when people are rewarded, they will do more of whatever led to the reward. Applied to persuasion, operant conditioning theory held that the best way to get people to change their attitudes was to get them to act in the desired manner and then reward them for doing so. If you want people to like Brussels sprouts, get them to say they like Brussels sprouts, and then pay them big bucks for saying so. It sounded reasonable, but it never seemed to work very well. If anything, the people who said it for less money seemed to end up believing it more—opposite to what operant conditioning theory would predict.

Along came social psychologist Leon Festinger, who proposed that inconsistencies produce an unpleasant mental state called **cognitive dissonance**. He said that people want to maintain consistency, so when they catch themselves being inconsistent they feel bad. The reason that paying somebody big bucks to claim to like Brussels sprouts didn't produce any actual liking was that the money resolved the inconsistency: "I don't really like them, but if you pay me a lot to say I like them, I'll say so." The more interesting case, thought Festinger, was when the pay was minimal: "I didn't think I liked Brussels sprouts, but I said I like them, and I was willing to say so without getting much money. I'm not a liar. I must really like them after all." *Money Matters* describes how one classic experiment provided evidence for cognitive dissonance theory.

Justifying Effort

A second memorable study of cognitive dissonance, published the same year, introduced the idea of **effort justification**.[62] According to cognitive dissonance theory, people want to convince themselves that all their hard work and effort are worthwhile. This particular study was stimulated by controversies on college campuses surrounding "hazing" initiations at fraternities and sororities. People who wanted to join those organizations often had to go through embarrassing or painful initiation rituals, such as being spanked or performing demeaning tasks for the older members of the organization. College administrators often sought to clamp down on these practices, but fraternity and sorority members said that these experiences helped forge strong ties to the group. Dissonance researchers thought that perhaps the students were right.

The experiment was disguised as a group discussion on sex, which back in the 1950s was pretty racy stuff. The participants were all college women who had signed up to join one of these groups. When the participant arrived, the experimenter (a man) said that the group had met several times already, and one problem had surfaced, which was that some people were too embarrassed to talk about sex. Did the participant think she could talk freely? All the women said yes. In the control condition, the experimenter said okay, she could join the group. But in the other conditions, he said that she would have to pass an embarrassment test. Some participants were given a mild test, in which they merely had to say a few words such as *virgin* and *prostitute* out loud to the male experimenter. Others, however, were given a more severe initiation in which they had to recite obscene words and read sexually explicit passages from paperback novels out loud to the male experimenter, which was an embarrassing and unpleasant experience.

At the end of the test, the experimenter told each participant that she had passed and could join the interesting group—indeed could listen in on the discussion taking place right then. The supposedly interesting group turned out to consist of several biology graduate students droning on pointlessly about dull things like mating patterns among cockroaches. The measure was how well the participant liked what she heard and how

cognitive dissonance theory the theory that inconsistencies produce psychological discomfort, leading people to rationalize their behavior or change their attitudes

cognitive dissonance an unpleasant emotional state caused by conflicting or inconsistent thoughts

effort justification the finding that when people suffer or work hard or make sacrifices, they will try to convince themselves that it is worthwhile

MONEY Matters

Would You Sell Your Soul for $1?

In 1959, Leon Festinger and his colleague J. Merrill Carlsmith published a classic experiment to demonstrate how cognitive dissonance worked. It involved getting people to say they liked something they really didn't like by paying them to say it. The core question was how much pay would produce the most attitude change. Traditional reinforcement theory assumed that the more pay they received (the bigger the reward), the more people would come to believe what they said. Cognitive dissonance theory predicted the opposite: Small pay would produce the most attitude change.

Each participant came for a study called "Measures of Performance." The experimenter said it had to do with performing routine tasks, such as those found in factories. The experiment itself was excruciatingly boring. The participant spent the first half hour taking 12 little wooden spools off a tray one at a time, then putting them back on the tray, then off again, over and over and over. The second half hour was no better: The participant had to turn 48 square pegs a quarter turn clockwise, then again, and again, and again. Finally, when the participant was probably about bored to tears, the experimenter said that the study was over but then explained that there were some hidden wrinkles to the experiment—it was really about trying to motivate people to perform these routine, repetitious tasks. To do that, he employed a accomplice who pretended to be a previous participant in the study and who would tell real participants that the task was fun, exciting, interesting, fascinating, and great. The experimenter said the study's purpose was to see whether people who heard these glowing tributes performed better than others.

Then came the crucial part. The experimenter said that another participant was scheduled to arrive in a few minutes, and the accomplice who was supposed to be there had called to cancel. The experimenter asked the participant to "fill in" and perform the accomplice's job, which just entailed telling the next participant that the experiment was really interesting. Obviously this was false—the participant knew how deadly boring the task was—but the participant didn't want to refuse the request and so agreed to do what the experimenter asked. The experimenter paid the participant either $1 or $20 for performing this service. (Participants in the control group skipped this part of the experiment; they were not asked to lie and were paid nothing.) The next participant (who was actually an accomplice) came in, the participant told this person that the task was really interesting, the accomplice expressed some skepticism, the participant insisted, and the accomplice finally agreed.

Later, in a different room, another researcher asked the participant to rate how much he or she had enjoyed the experiment. The results are shown in **FIGURE 7.3**. Participants had essentially lied for either $1 or $20, and they had a chance to undo the lie by convincing themselves that they did find the experiment enjoyable. Those who had been paid $20 did not say the task was enjoyable; their ratings were no different from those of participants who had not been asked to lie. They had experienced no dissonance: They were willing to tell a lie for $20 (especially in the name of science; and $20 in 1959 would be equivalent to about $175 today). But those who had been paid only $1 still had some dissonance, and they changed their attitudes. They said the task really had been interesting. It was a way of rationalizing their behavior so as to resolve the inconsistency: They could reassure themselves that they had not actually lied.

Thus, people are willing to do questionable things for large sums of money. But when they perform the same actions for a small amount of money, people feel a need to rationalize and justify those actions, so they change their attitudes.

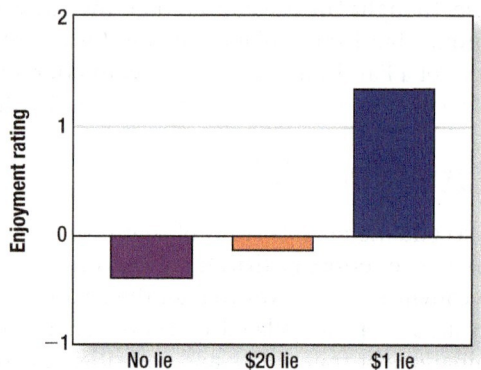

FIGURE 7.3

Participants who had been paid $1 to lie about how enjoyable the experiment was rated it as more enjoyable than did those in the other two groups, which were not significantly different from each other.

SOURCE: Festinger and Carlsmith (1959).

---

much she liked the group. The women who had had no test or only a mild test recognized how boring and useless it all was and said they didn't like the discussion or the group. But the women who had gone through the stressful, unpleasant initiation (the highly embarrassing test) rated the discussion and group much more favorably. As the fraternity members were saying, people who suffered more to get into a group ended up liking the group more. That was the only way to convince themselves that their suffering had been worthwhile. The mind's own drive for consistency is behind the process.

A rare and remarkable study confirmed the benefits of painful rituals for group identification. In connection with a religious festival in Mauritius, young adult men were randomly assigned to one of three roles. One group took part in ritual consisting of singing and praying. Another performed the Kavadi, a painful ritual requiring piercing the skin with needles, dragging a cart attached by hooks to the skin, and climbing a mountain barefoot. A third group observed the Kavadi. The men who performed or watched the painful Kavadi later donated more to the temple and identified more with Mauritius than the men who did the easy ritual.[63] Thus, taking part in the painful ritual made the men identify more with the large social group and act in a more prosocial manner.

Thus, dissonance makes people seek to justify and rationalize any suffering or effort they have made. Perhaps surprisingly, dissonance reduction processes can make people accept their suffering and even choose to continue it. *Food for Thought* describes how people will sometimes choose to suffer as a consequence of expecting to suffer, even if the choice is as unappealing as eating a worm!

Justifying Choices

The next big advance in cognitive dissonance theory was centered around having a choice, which is very important to people (see Chapter 4). (We also noted earlier in this chapter that attitudes are most helpful for choosing, so it would be useful and adaptive to review and revise attitudes when making choices.) If you perform an action but do not have any choice, you don't have to rationalize or justify it. In these studies,[64] students were encouraged to write an essay saying that various controversial speakers should be banned from college campuses, which was contrary to what most students believed (they supported free speech and their own freedom to listen). Some were told that this was their assigned task in the experiment. Others were told, "We would really appreciate it if you would do this, but it's entirely up to you to decide." Most people willingly agreed to the experimenter's request. However, only the people in the latter (high-choice) condition experienced dissonance and changed their attitudes toward greater agreement with their essays.

People also experience dissonance when they make difficult choices. For example, should you major in A or B? Should you attend college A or B? Should you accept the job offer from company A or B? Should you get married or remain single? Every decision involves tradeoffs (see Chapter 2), but people like to reduce their dissonance by justifying their choices. This type of dissonance is called **post-decision dissonance**. In particular, if the decision was a close call, you can reduce dissonance afterward by deciding that what you chose was far better than what you rejected.

"There are so many choices of socks to choose from. Which ones are best?"

Advances in Dissonance Theory

Another step forward came when researchers began to ask themselves what dissonance felt like. Was it an arousal state—that is, a bodily reaction in which the heart beats faster and in other respects the person seems more tense and nervous? In other words, does dissonance resemble an emotional reaction? A series of studies indicated that the answer is yes. When people performed actions contrary to their attitudes, they often felt acutely uncomfortable. If this feeling was blocked, they did not change their attitude. If they had this feeling but thought it was due to something else (specifically, a pill they had been given, along with instructions that the pill would make them feel tense and aroused), they did not change their attitudes.[65,66] Only people who felt discomfort *and* attributed it to their inconsistent behavior were driven to rationalize what they had done. They alone changed their attitudes to match their actions. Dissonance is marked not only by arousal, but also by an unpleasant arousal. It feels bad.

Another advance in dissonance theory linked the reaction to the interpersonal sphere. People may have some desire to be consistent in the privacy of their minds, but they have a much stronger desire to be seen by other people as consistent. We live in a social world in which people expect each other to be consistent, in a good way. (Of course, bad consistency is not valued, such as consistently being late, dishonest, or hostile.) People who say one thing one day and something else another day are criticized as liars, hypocrites, gullible

post-decision dissonance cognitive dissonance experienced after making a difficult choice, typically reduced by increasing the attractiveness of the chosen alternative and decreasing the attractiveness of rejected alternatives

FOOD FOR *Thought*

Would You Eat a Bug or a Worm?

Would you eat a worm? Television reality shows like *Survivor* typically include an episode in which people are asked to eat a variety of bugs, worms, and other foods that may be regarded as delicacies in some parts of the world but that strike most Americans as gross and unappealing, if not downright disgusting.

Yet social psychologists have found in multiple studies that if they set up the situational factors correctly, people—even modern American college students—will eat worms or bugs. This isn't because students think eating worms is about the same as eating dorm food! On the contrary, most start off with substantially negative attitudes toward eating such foods, but their attitudes can change.

One of the most thorough and revealing studies of worm eating looked at the underlying attitudes and beliefs that had to change.[67] On the first day of the study, participants filled out questionnaires. On the second day, each participant was ushered into a laboratory room and told the task would be performed there. In one condition, participants were told the task would involve weight discrimination—judging which of two items was heavier than the other. Other participants were told their assigned task would be to eat a worm. The lab was set up with a plate containing a (dead) worm, as well as a fork, a napkin, and a glass of water for the worm-eating task, and a scale, some weights, and some paper to record responses for the weights task. The participant was left alone for a while, to allow time to think about the impending task. Then came an attitude questionnaire, so the researchers could track people's attitudes about the task.

After a time, the experimenter returned and said he had made a mistake. Instead of being assigned the one task, the participant was supposed to be allowed to choose whether to do the worm-eating task or the weight discrimination task. Among the participants who had been told they were assigned to the weight discrimination task and then were given the chance to eat a worm instead, all (100%) said something to the effect of "no, thanks!" All these participants stuck with the emotionally neutral weight discrimination task.

Among those who had expected to eat the worm and then were given the chance to do the weight discrimination task, however, most (80%) stuck with the worm or at least said they did not have a preference. This may seem surprising, but the questionnaire data revealed that changed attitudes helped mediate the choice. Most of these people had changed their views by increasing their belief that (a) I am brave, (b) I deserve to suffer, or (c) eating a worm isn't so bad. The people who failed to change any of these beliefs made up the 20% who jumped at the chance to do the weight discrimination task instead.

Thus, this study shows that sometimes people will choose to suffer as a consequence of expecting to suffer—but only if they have coped by changing some of their relevant beliefs and attitudes.

Would you eat a worm?

weaklings, untrustworthy or unreliable chameleons, and worse. It is important to act consistently when in the presence of others. This interpersonal dimension invokes the importance of self-presentation, discussed in Chapter 3: What is inside is often driven by what happens between people. Consistency may be yet another case in which inner processes serve interpersonal relations. On the long road to social acceptance, people learn that others expect them to be consistent and may reject them if they are inconsistent.

Many studies have shown the importance of self-presentation (that is, the effort to make a good impression or keep a good reputation) in cognitive dissonance. For example, when people act in ways that are contrary to their attitudes, the effects depend on who is looking. Writing an essay that violates your beliefs has little effect if it is done privately and anonymously, whereas if you have to put your name on it, you are more likely to feel dissonance and to change your attitude to match what you wrote. Telling someone that a task was interesting doesn't seem to have an effect if that person doesn't listen or doesn't believe you, but if you actually convince someone, then you feel a much greater need to convince yourself, too.

Dissonance Theory and the Media

To avoid the dissonance that comes from hearing conflicting attitudes, people often purposely seek out media that confirm what they already believe—called **selective exposure**.[68]

selective exposure refers to the tendency of individuals to select information that supports their preexisting views and avoid information that contradicts their preexisting views

For example, conservative Americans might turn to media sources such as *The Washington Times*, *Fox News*, and *Breitbart*, whereas liberal Americans might turn to media sources such as *Huffington Post*, *Daily Kos*, and *Occupy Democrats*.[69] Indeed, some internet sites (e.g., Google) intentionally use algorithms to expose you to material that is consistent with your attitudes—called a **filter bubble**.[70] The use of filter bubbles could be considered forced selective exposure.

Is the Drive for Consistency Rooted in Nature or Nurture?

Social psychologists have debated for decades the question of whether consistency is rooted in nature or nurture. Cultural variation would be one indication that it is learned. Some evidence indicates that the same basic drive for consistency can be found in very different cultures,[71] but making choices does not seem to cause dissonance processes among East Asians the way it does for North Americans.[72,73,74] On the other hand, the influence of social pressures toward consistency probably strengthens the drive. Either way, the root probably lies in the fact that groups of people can get along better if the people understand each other, and understanding each other is easier if people are consistent. People expect and pressure each other to be consistent, and people respond to these pressures and expectations by seeking to be consistent. Quite possibly the drive for consistency is both rooted in our biological nature and strengthened by learning and socialization.

Indeed, the drive toward consistency may also embody a principle we saw in Chapter 5 (on social cognition): Human thinking and reasoning processes seem designed primarily for arguing. It is not that there is some peculiar feature of brain cells that renders them averse to contradiction. Rather, if you contradict yourself while arguing with someone, you are likely to lose the argument. Thus, evolution may have shaped the brain for arguing and thereby instilled a sensitivity toward inconsistency. Still, how people argue may be influenced by local, cultural conditions, so the consistency drive may vary somewhat from one culture to another.

Most likely the drive toward consistency involves both parts of the duplex mind. The automatic system can learn to detect inconsistencies and send out alarm signals (distress, arousal). The deliberate system then steps in and finds some resolution to the inconsistency by thinking about how to rationalize or rethink things. It is also possible that some modes of dissonance reduction are automatic.

filter bubbles are algorithms used on the internet to selectively guess what information a user would like to see based on information available about that use (e.g., previous web pages viewed, click behavior)

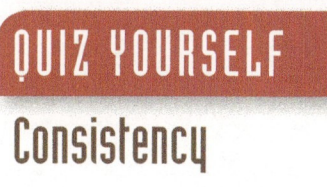

QUIZ YOURSELF
Consistency

1. Don says he values the environment. Someone reminds Don that he litters, wastes water, eats a lot of meat, drives a gas-guzzling car alone, and never uses public transportation. Don feels a certain amount of mental discomfort, which is most likely _____.
   - ⓐ attitude polarization
   - ⓑ cognitive dissonance
   - ⓒ effort justification
   - ⓓ negative attitude change

2. Cognitive dissonance theory predicts that when there is little external justification for having performed an act, dissonance will be _____ and attitude change will _____.
   - ⓐ high; occur
   - ⓑ high; not occur
   - ⓒ low; occur
   - ⓓ low; not occur

3. Which statement summarizes the basic idea underlying effort justification?
   - ⓐ Less leads to more.
   - ⓑ More leads to less.
   - ⓒ Suffering leads to liking.
   - ⓓ Liking leads to suffering.

4. The specific process of avoiding information that is different from what one already believes is called _____.
   - ⓐ cognitive dissonance
   - ⓑ predictive selection
   - ⓒ rationality
   - ⓓ selective exposure

answers: see pg 257

Do Attitudes Really Predict Behaviors?

Psychology calls itself a behavioral science, which means that it seeks to predict and explain behavior. Attitudes are supposedly worth studying because they guide behavior. People act on the basis of what they like and dislike. Or do they? This is an important question, because if attitudes can't predict behavior, there would be little point in studying them.

Researchers have been examining the link between attitudes and behaviors for decades. An early sign that this link might be weak came before World War II. In the 1930s, many Americans did not like the Chinese for a variety of reasons, including a common perception that Chinese immigrants were taking American jobs. In 1934, a social psychologist and a young Chinese couple drove 10,000 miles (16,000 km) across the United States.[75] They stopped at 184 restaurants and 66 hotels, auto camps, and tourist homes. They received service at all establishments, except for one dilapidated auto camp where the owner refused to lodge them and called them "Japs." Six months later, the social psychologist sent a questionnaire to the same establishments, asking whether they would accommodate Chinese guests. About 92% said they would *not* accommodate Chinese guests. This raised an early warning signal about attitudes: These business owners, at least, expressed attitudes that differed sharply from their actual behavior.

Attacking Attitudes

Up until the 1960s, most social psychologists had accepted Gordon Allport's assertion that the attitude is the most important concept in social psychology. Accordingly, they were surprised when Alan Wicker wrote an article in 1969 arguing that attitudes were a trivial, peripheral phenomenon.[76] After reviewing the results from 47 studies, Wicker concluded that attitudes did not cause behavior or even predict it very well. He even went so far as to suggest that social psychology should abandon the concept of attitude, and that researchers should study more important things instead! He wrote, "Taken as a whole, these studies suggest that it is considerably more likely that attitudes will be unrelated or only slightly related to overt behaviors than that attitudes will be closely related to actions."

Once you set aside the assumption that people are generally consistent, it is not hard to find evidence that attitudes can differ from behavior. For example, a prominent advocate of so-called "conversion therapy" (the scientifically discredited practice of trying to convert homosexuals into heterosexuals) says he now identifies as gay.[77] To read about some interesting studies on attitude–behavior (A–B) consistency in sexual behavior, see *The Social Side of Sex*.

Defending Attitudes

Wicker's 1969 critique provoked a crisis in the field. Many social psychologists had spent their careers studying attitudes, and they were very disturbed to hear that attitudes were just little ideas flitting around inside people's minds that had no connection to what the people actually did. Attitude researchers "circled the wagons" to defend themselves, seeking ways to show how attitudes actually might have a closer link to behavior.

General Attitudes and Specific Behaviors

A first response in defense of attitudes was that the gap between general attitudes and specific behaviors was too big.[78] Researchers might ask what someone's attitude was toward helping people and then measure whether the person was willing to donate blood. The problem is that someone might be in favor of helping people generally, but might be afraid of needles. In contrast, if researchers measured attitudes toward giving blood, these attitudes were much better predictors of whether the person would actually give blood. The solution, though it did help indicate that attitudes could predict behavior, sacrificed broad general attitudes and put a burden on researchers to measure a vast number of very specific attitudes rather than a few general ones.

The Social Side of Sex

A–B Inconsistency and Erotic Plasticity

As we have seen, attitude researchers have struggled with what they call the **A–B problem**, the inconsistency between attitudes (A) and behaviors (B). Sex provides ample room for contradictions between people's attitudes and their actual behaviors. One general prediction derives from the view that female sexuality is more open than male sexuality to influence from social, cultural, and situational factors, which is called **erotic plasticity**.[79] If that is correct, then women should show lower attitude–behavior consistency than men because women's sexual responses depend much more on the immediate situation and various other social influences. What a man wants may be the same regardless of context, but if the woman's sexual response depends on what it means, then her general attitude won't predict specific behaviors as accurately as his.

Same-gender sexual activity is one place where attitudes and behaviors diverge. A major survey asked people both about their attitudes toward homosexual activity ("Do you like the idea of having sex with someone of your own gender?") and about their actual behavior ("Have you had sex with someone of your own gender during the past year?") For men, the two questions overlapped heavily: A large majority (85%) of the men who favored homosexual activity had engaged in it during the past year. In contrast, attitudes and behaviors were much less consistent for women: Less than half the women who liked the idea had actually done it recently.[80]

The gender gap in consistency can be found in heterosexual behavior, too. Multiple studies have looked at whether people engage in sexual activity of which they do not approve, and all have found that women do this far more than men.[81,82,83]

Most people believe they should use condoms, especially when having sex with new or unfamiliar partners, but many people fail to do so. The gap between pro-condom attitudes and non-condom-using behaviors is larger among women than men (which is ironic, given that a condom detracts from male enjoyment more than female enjoyment).[84] Likewise, most people strongly favor being faithful to their partners if they have a committed relationship, but many people do occasionally indulge in kissing or sexual intercourse, or anything in between, with other partners. Again, women's behavior is more inconsistent than men's. In one study, men's attitudes regarding infidelity explained about 33% of their behavior, whereas women's attitudes explained only 11%.[85]

One solution to the A–B problem is for social psychologists to measure very specific attitudes. This doesn't resolve the gender problem, though. Several studies have measured whether people had sex on an occasion when they did not feel desire for sex. Both men and women do this (e.g., usually to please a partner who is feeling amorous), but more women than men do it.[86,87]

Apart from the special case of opportunity constraints, men's attitudes predict their sexual behavior much better than women's. The reason is not that women are generally inconsistent (indeed, no such general pattern exists outside of sexual activity). Rather, women's sexual responses are specific to the person, the situation, and what it all means, so their general attitudes are not highly relevant. In contrast, men tend to like and dislike the same things day in and day out, regardless of specific situations, so their general attitudes predict their behavior much better.

Behavior Aggregation

Another solution to the problem of attitude–behavior inconsistency comes from aggregating behavior, which means combining across many different behaviors on different occasions.[88] A person's attitude toward helping others might fare better if we didn't measure behavior by a single test, such as giving blood. Instead, we could add up whether the person gives blood, plus whether the person donates money to charity, plus whether the person volunteers to work with the homeless, plus whether the person stops to help a handicapped person cross the street, and so on. A person with a more positive attitude toward helping others will perform more of these behaviors, and this could add up to a substantial difference, even though the general attitude's link to any single behavior may be weak or unreliable.

Broad Attitude in Context

A third solution is that general attitudes can help cause behavior, but only if they are prominent in the person's conscious mind and influence how the person thinks about the choices he or she faces.[89] When asked to give blood, the person might say "no" despite having a favorable attitude toward helping others, because the person might not think of the question in terms of helping others. (The person might think of it in terms of being scared of needles, or of needing all his or her blood for a trip to the gym or hot date that night!) If you first caused the person to reflect on his or her attitude toward helping others, then when the request for a blood donation came along, the person would see it as an opportunity to help, and hence the person's willingness to give blood would be shaped by that broad attitude. The broad attitude can influence specific behavior, but only if it has a chance to shape how the person interprets and construes the specifics of the here-and-now situation.

A–B problem the problem of inconsistency between attitudes (A) and behaviors (B)

erotic plasticity degree to which social, cultural, and situational factors influence sexuality

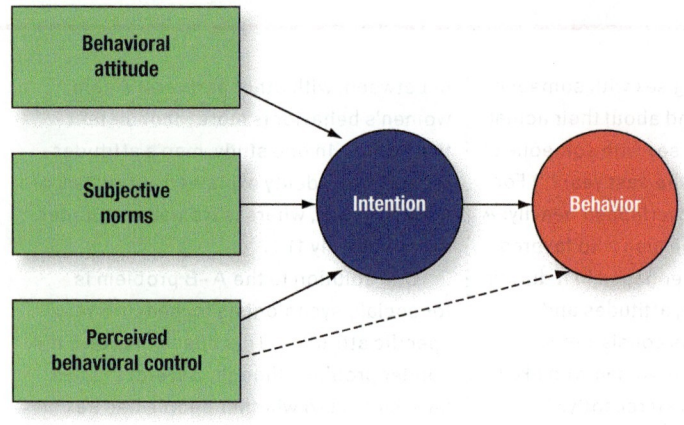

FIGURE 7.4

The theory of planned behavior. The dashed line indicates a direct effect of *Perceived behavioral control* on *Behavior*. The solid lines indicate indirect effects of *Behavioral attitude*, *Subjective norms*, and *Perceived behavioral control* through *Intention* on *Behavior*.

accessibility how easily something comes to mind

behavioral intentions an individual's plans to perform the behavior in question

subjective norms an individual's perceptions about whether significant others think he or she should (or should not) perform the behavior in question

perceived behavioral control an individual's beliefs about whether they can actually perform the behavior in question

Attitude Accessibility

Accessibility refers to how easily the attitude comes to mind. Highly accessible attitudes can be quite influential because they come to mind very easily.[90,91] Obviously, an attitude that does not easily come to mind will have little opportunity to exert influence on behavior. One meta-analysis of 88 studies found that attitudes that are certain, stable, consistent, accessible, and based on direct experience are especially effective in predicting behavior.[92]

Behavioral Intentions

Another approach was to consider the role of behavioral intentions on the link between attitudes and behaviors. Behavioral intentions are a key component of the theory of planned behavior, which is depicted in **FIGURE 7.4**.[93] As the title of this theory suggests, **behavioral intentions** refer to whether the person plans to perform the behavior in question. If a person intends to do a behavior, then it is likely that he or she will actually do it.

As can be seen in **FIGURE 7.4**, behavioral intentions are not only determined by the person's attitude but also by subjective norms and perceived behavioral control.

Subjective norms are the person's perceptions about whether significant others think he or she should perform the behavior in question or not. **Perceived behavioral control** refers to the person's beliefs about whether he or she can actually perform the behavior. A meta-analytic review of 185 studies found that the theory of planned behavior explained 27% of the variance in behavior—an impressive amount considering how difficult it is to predict human behavior.[94]

QUIZ YOURSELF
Do Attitudes Really Predict Behaviors?

1. In 1934, a social psychologist and a Chinese couple drove 10,000 miles across the country, stopping at numerous hotels and restaurants. The Chinese couple received service at all of the establishments except one. Six months later, LaPiere sent a questionnaire to the same establishments, asking whether they would accommodate Chinese guests. How many said they would accommodate Chinese guests?

   (a) More than 90%   (b) About 75% of them   (c) About 25% of them   (d) Less than 10%

2. After reviewing the results from 47 studies, what did Wicker conclude in his 1969 article about the relationship between attitudes and behaviors?

   (a) It is almost perfect.   (b) It is strong.   (c) It is moderate in size.   (d) It is so weak that the concept of attitudes should be abandoned.

3. According to Gordon Allport, what is the most important concept in psychology?

   (a) Aggression   (b) Attitudes   (c) Discrimination   (d) Social influence

4. The best way to predict whether people will go see the next Marvel movie is to assess their attitudes toward _____.

   (a) comics   (b) films   (c) previous Marvel movies   (d) Superheroes

answers: see pg 257

Beliefs and Believing

Consistency is an important issue for beliefs just as much as for attitudes. You want your beliefs about the world to be consistent with the world.

Believing Versus Doubting

"I understand what you're saying, but I don't believe it!" Clearly, the gap between understanding and believing appears to be big. Or is it? Research has suggested that doubting/disbelieving is separate from understanding—but believing immediately, *automatically* accompanies understanding. Consider the title of one article on this pattern: "You Can't Not Believe Everything You Read"![95] As soon as you understand it, you believe it; only then, and only maybe, do you take a second step of changing your mind. If someone tells you the moon is made of green cheese, you believe it for a brief moment, even though you probably quickly change your mind.

The difference is important. Believing and disbelieving are not on an equal par. If for some reason the mind is prevented from taking the second step of changing your mind, you might just go on believing that the earth is flat. It is very hard to take in information while withholding all judgment about whether it is correct. The first impulse is to believe what you hear (or read).

The duplex mind may be implicated here. The automatic system automatically believes the information it is given. The deliberate system can override this belief by deciding that it is false. If you only use automatic processing, you will believe lots of things that aren't true.[96,97]

Children, for example, are notoriously gullible. If believing and disbelieving were equal acts that occurred at the same step, then children would first learn to understand without either believing or disbelieving anything, and then gradually learn to judge information as true or false. But this is not what happens. Children first believe everything they are told, and only later learn to doubt and question.[98] Likewise, in lab studies, people who are supplied with information while they are distracted (such as when the experimenter tells them to remember a phone number for later) end up believing things they are told more than people who are not distracted. The distraction prevents them from taking the second step of thinking something like, "Wait a minute, this can't be right!"

Out in the world, religious and political cults are sometimes accused of "brainwashing" their members into believing strange things. To strengthen belief in their ideas, they often make sure their converts are tired or distracted (e.g., hungry from fasting) when the doctrines are presented. If you wanted people to understand your cult's ideas best, you would want them rested and alert when you presented your teachings, but if you want someone to believe everything, then you should present your ideas when the person is not at full mental power. Tired or distracted people do not make it to the second step (of doubt); they stop at the first step, which combines understanding and believing.[99,100]

In short, when you understand something, believing it is automatic, whereas to doubt and question it may require controlled, conscious thought. The automatic system is fairly uncritical and accepts as true whatever it is told. The deliberate mind can override this and change from belief to disbelief. But as we know, deliberate activity requires time and effort, which people do not always have.

Belief Perseverance

Once beliefs form, they are resistant to change. This is true even of false beliefs that have been discredited. This effect is called **belief perseverance**. In an influential study,[101] participants were given 25 real and fictitious suicide notes and were told to identify the real ones. By the flip of a coin, participants were told either that they had correctly identified 24 of the 25 (success feedback) or that they had correctly identified only 10 of the 25 (worse than random chance, the failure feedback). Both groups were told that the average

belief perseverance the finding that once beliefs form, they are resistant to change, even if the information on which they are based is discredited was 16 correct. At the end of the study, all participants were told that the feedback they had received was bogus. Nevertheless, participants who had received success feedback thought they were more accurate on the current test and that they would be more accurate on a future test than did participants who had received failure feedback. Participants thus continued to believe the feedback even though the researcher had discredited it.

A classic study about belief perseverance was mentioned in Chapter 5.[102] Half the participants read cases suggesting that risk-taking people make better firefighters than cautious people, whereas the other half read cases suggesting that cautious people make better firefighters than risk-taking people. Both groups of participants were told to come up with theories explaining the cases they had read. Then participants were told that the study was over and that the cases they had read were bogus. However, participants did not abandon their theories, even though the researcher had discredited the evidence on which they were based.

The good news is that there is a remedy for belief perseverance. Explaining the opposite theory (e.g., why a cautious person might make a better firefighter than a risk-taking person) reduces or eliminates belief perseverance.[103,104] If you want to understand things correctly, it is good to cultivate the habit of trying out the opposite theory to whatever theory you initially believe. Note that this trick makes use of the social cognition principle that reasoning is for arguing. To get a balanced, unbiased view in your mind, it helps to try to argue both sides. Put another way, try to play the "devil's advocate," is the popular phrase referring to deliberately arguing the opposite side. The term comes from group processes: The Catholic Church worried that someone with a checkered past might become pope, partly because none of the cardinals would dare criticize their possible future boss. Therefore, when choosing a new pope, they would appoint someone to be the "devil's advocate" whose sacred obligation was to argue that the candidate was unfit to be pope. That way all the objections would be heard.

Belief and Coping

Beliefs help people understand the world around them. This is especially apparent when people experience serious problems, such as misfortunes or disasters. The general term for how people attempt to deal with traumas and go back to functioning effectively in life is **coping**. The study of coping is an important opportunity for social psychologists to understand beliefs.

Something that puzzled psychologists for decades was that the psychological harm can be far more lasting, or even permanent, compared to the physical harm. People are sometimes quite upset over having their apartment robbed, even though they may not have lost much of value and most of the loss is repaid by an insurance company. Some rape victims may be traumatized for years even though they suffer no lasting or permanent physical harm. How can these processes be understood? Bodily injury and monetary loss may be two components of trauma, but clearly there is something else.

One important answer is that a crime affects a victim's beliefs about the world. These beliefs are called **assumptive worlds**, a term that expresses the view that people live in social worlds based on their assumptions about how things operate.[105] These include three main types of assumptions, all of which help people live healthy and happy lives, but any of which can be shattered when one is a victim of a crime:

1. **The world is benevolent.** Basically, people are nice, life is safe, and one can count on good things happening most of the time.
2. **The world is fair and just.** The world is fair, so people generally get what they deserve and deserve what they get. If you follow the rules and treat others with fairness and kindness, you can expect to be treated that way yourself.
3. **I am a good person.** I am someone of value and therefore deserve good things to happen to me.

If someone steals your wallet, or vandalizes your car, or assaults you during a stroll in the park, this creates a problem because it violates those beliefs. As you try to explain to yourself how such a thing can happen, you may feel that you cannot continue to maintain those three

coping how people attempt to deal with stressful traumas and go back to functioning effectively in life

assumptive worlds the view that people live in social worlds based on certain beliefs (assumptions) about reality beliefs as well as you did before. Ultimately, effective coping may involve figuring out how to explain the crime while still permitting yourself to continue believing that, by and large, the world is benevolent and fair and that you are a good person who deserves good things.

This view of coping helps explain a surprising finding that emerged from a study that showed blaming oneself is often a good way to cope.[106] That study interviewed individuals who had been paralyzed in serious accidents. All the victims had asked the question "why me?" and nearly all had come up with an answer. To the researchers' surprise, it did not seem to matter what explanation they came up with—fate, God's will, their own mistakes, the actions of others, or other factors. The big difference was whether they did or did not have an explanation. Those who had found an explanation coped better than those who had not, as rated by hospital staff and others. This finding was surprising because most psychologists at the time assumed that blaming oneself for misfortune or trauma would be bad for the person. Therapists who heard a patient blame themself would often rush in to insist that such an explanation was wrong, and the person should avoid self-blame. Yet self-blame seemed to work just fine in helping people cope. The researchers' explanation was that blaming oneself can actually help people achieve a sense of control. The paralyzed victims would say things like, "It was my fault; I was driving too fast" or "I wanted to impress my friends, so I jumped off the roof onto the trampoline, even though I knew it was risky." If people believe that their own foolish actions caused their misfortunes, it helps them feel that they can avoid future misfortunes by not repeating those mistakes. In contrast, people who cannot explain their misfortunes to themselves are more likely to think that something bad could happen to them again, regardless of what they do. They feel much more vulnerable and have a hard time getting over what happened.

Not all self-blame is good, of course. There is an important distinction between blaming oneself for bad actions and blaming oneself for being a bad person. Someone who reacts to being robbed or injured by thinking, "I am a worthless person and I deserve to have bad things happen to me" is not going to bounce back very effectively. This type of thinking is likely to lead to feelings of shame, which are destructive. It is much more helpful to think, "I am basically a good and competent person, and I foolishly took a risk that brought this harm to me—so if I act more wisely in the future, I can avoid further problems." This type of thinking is likely to lead to feelings of guilt and even confidence, which are constructive. (See Chapter 6 for a discussion on the difference between shame and guilt.)

The upshot is that mental processes play a central role in helping people cope with and recover from misfortunes. A broad theory of **cognitive coping** was put forward by Shelley Taylor, who outlined several kinds of beliefs that need to be bolstered or restored in the wake of trauma.[107] Her original work focused on women who had breast cancer, but the ideas have been applied in many other contexts since then.

One important type of cognitive coping is based on the belief that whatever happened could have been worse, so at least the person was somewhat lucky. The technical term for this is **downward comparison**.[108] People compare themselves and their situations to other people who are worse off, and this makes people feel better about themselves. For example, women whose breast cancer resulted in surgery to remove a lump from the breast compared themselves to others who had lost an entire breast, both breasts, or even died. The reverse comparison, called an **upward comparison**, was rare or absent: No woman who lost an entire breast compared herself with women who had only had the lumpectomy. In everyday life, many people seem to understand this principle because "it could have been a lot worse" is a standard phrase that people say to someone to whom something bad has just happened. (Upward and downward comparisons were also discussed in Chapter 3.)

Other beliefs in cognitive coping pertain to self-esteem and control. Victims of trauma and misfortune often need to find some way to restore their belief that they are good people and that they can exert control over what happens to them. Taylor observed that many women cultivated beliefs that they could control their cancer and prevent it from coming back, even though these beliefs often had little or no medical validity. The women thought that by eating certain foods or acting in a certain way (even by getting a divorce), they could keep themselves safe. These beliefs, although wrong according to medical knowledge (and many were later proven wrong because the cancer did eventually come back), were a great source of comfort that improved their well-being.

cognitive coping the idea that beliefs play a central role in helping people cope with and recover from misfortunes

downward comparison the act of comparing oneself to people who are worse off

upward comparison the act of comparing oneself to people who are better off

Still another type of helpful belief is that all things have some useful or higher purpose. The majority of women in Taylor's research sample reported positive changes in their lives that had come from having breast cancer. Many said they had learned to appreciate what was truly important in life, such as love and family, and had learned not to get upset over minor things. Religious beliefs are also helpful to people under these circumstances because people can accept on faith that God has some purpose for letting these misfortunes occur to them, or even that their suffering made them stronger or helped test and cement their faith. Others look to their own good deeds. A woman named Maureen Fischer suffered badly when her 3-year-old daughter died from a brain tumor, but she turned this tragedy into something good by raising money for and founding a hospitality lodge where families with very sick children could come for free vacations. In this way, her daughter's death helped her find a way to bring joy and comfort to many other suffering families.

When people encounter disasters or suffering, their beliefs must help them get by, and sometimes these beliefs must change. Even so, consistency is important in dictating whether beliefs will be helpful or not. Some traumas seem to contradict beliefs—such as assumptions about the world being a safe, benevolent, and fair place—that people need in order to go on living. Coping requires finding a way to make the trauma seem compatible or even consistent with those beliefs. Other beliefs help frame the problem in a way that makes it more tolerable, such as believing that the misfortune could have been much worse, or believing that the bad event led to some good purpose.

Religious Belief

Religion involves a very important category of beliefs. Science cannot generally say anything about whether religious beliefs are true or false. Regardless of objective truth, however, psychology can shed light on why some people accept religious beliefs whereas other people reject those same beliefs. It can also explore the benefits that people get from believing in religion, again regardless of whether those beliefs cannot be proven to be true.

The appeal of religion throughout history has been partly its ability to explain the world, especially those things that cannot be explained by science. Religion can explain both large and small things. It can explain grand issues, such as where the sun, earth, and moon came from, where the person (or soul) existed before birth, and what happens after death; but religion can also explain smaller things, such as why your child got sick. (Again, we are not saying the religious explanations are true or false—but remember, coping depends on having an explanation, regardless of whether it is true or false.)

Religious beliefs can help people cope with stress.[109,110] For example, people recover more quickly from being sexually assaulted if they use religion to cope with the traumatic event.[111] People who rely on religion to help them cope are also less likely to fall back on ineffective coping strategies, such as drinking alcohol.[112]

Research has shown that appealing to a superordinate (high, all-encompassing) principle or power is an effective way to reduce dissonance.[113] For example, doomsday prophet David Meade predicted that the world would end on April 23, 2018, but you are still here![114] Using verses from the Bible, Meade predicted the world would end on that day because he said the sun, the moon, and Jupiter would line up in the constellation Virgo. (Never mind that his astronomy was wrong.) Meade predicted that this celestial alignment would be the beginning of a cosmic catastrophe. Following the alignment, a rogue planet called Planet X or Nibiru (which does not exist) would pass by the earth in October 2018 causing things like volcanic eruptions, that would culminate in the return of Jesus Christ to the earth. Some people who believe such prophecies sell everything they own and try to warn others about the impending doom. When the dreaded day does not come, they reduce their cognitive dissonance by convincing themselves that their faith and prayers saved the world, and they try to convert others to their cause.[115]

Doomsday prophets come and go, and can cause cognitive dissonance when their prophecies fail.

Despite the benefits of religious beliefs, the road to religious belief sometimes contains stumbling blocks.[116,117] At a cognitive level, people may have trouble dealing with inconsistent doctrines or resolving existential questions. At a more emotional level, some religious doctrines and practices can elicit feelings of fear and guilt. People may also experience feelings of anger or resentment toward God when tragedies occur in their lives.[118] Religion offers great benefits to many believers, but maintaining faith is not always easy.

Irrational Belief

People believe lots of seemingly crazy things, even though they have no rational basis for these beliefs.[119] These include paranormal beliefs (about Bigfoot, UFOs, etc.), as well as beliefs that are logically and statistically flawed (e.g., the belief that you can influence the outcome of a sports event that you are watching on television, or the belief that random events even out in the short run). We explored some of these irrational beliefs in Chapter 5. When it comes to irrational beliefs, the minuses probably outweigh the pluses. People who hold irrational beliefs are more anxious,[120] cope less well with terminal illnesses,[121] are more likely to become depressed over time,[122] and have lower levels of self-esteem.[123] People who think they are lucky are more likely to gamble and may therefore squander their money trying to beat long odds or to recoup large amounts of money they have already lost.

How do gamblers sustain their optimism as their losses mount? After all, if you lose more than you win (as most gamblers do), you should logically conclude either that you aren't lucky or that gambling is a foolish thing to do with your money, so you should stop. An intriguing series of studies suggests that gamblers maintain their positive (irrational) beliefs by using a series of tricks. In particular, they convince themselves that many losses were "near wins," so they don't count those against themselves. Thus, if they bet on sports, they feel lucky and smart if they win the bet, and they feel unlucky or dumb if their team loses by a wide margin. But if they lose by a small margin, they tell themselves that they should have won. This permits them to remain confident that they will win in the future.[124]

QUIZ YOURSELF: Beliefs and Believing

1. Which is faster, believing or disbelieving?
   - (a) Believing
   - (b) Disbelieving
   - (c) They are equally fast.
   - (d) It depends on how old the person is.

2. Sometimes even social psychologists are reluctant to give up their pet theories, even when the data contradict those theories. This tendency is called _____.
   - (a) assumptive world beliefs
   - (b) belief perseverance
   - (c) mere exposure effect
   - (d) the A–B problem

3. Which of the following incidents would violate an assumptive world belief?
   - (a) Getting a flat tire
   - (b) Slipping and falling on the highway on the ice
   - (c) Getting beaten up by a bully at school
   - (d) All of the above

4. Trent was in a serious car crash. He totaled his car and broke his collarbone. Trent considered himself very unlucky. While in the hospital, he saw a story on the local news about another car accident in which the driver totaled his car and suffered serious brain damage. After hearing the news report, Trent now considers himself lucky rather than unlucky. What type of social comparison did Trent make?
   - (a) Downward
   - (b) Lateral
   - (c) Upward
   - (d) None of the above

answers: see pg 257

What Makes Us Human

Putting the Cultural Animal in Perspective

Humans are not unique in having attitudes. Animals have attitudes, at least in the sense that they like and dislike certain things. For example, one of your authors has a cat that likes poultry, but not beef, lamb, or pork. But humans have far more attitudes than other animals, and the mental processes associated with them are far more complex. The way attitudes and beliefs operate is much more complicated among humans. For one thing, consistency pressures seem much more central in human than in animal functioning. It is doubtful that animals can really understand inconsistency beyond very simple events (e.g., expecting something and suddenly not finding it). We have little reason to think that animals engage in rationalization, whereas humans are quick to rationalize, especially when they experience cognitive dissonance. Likewise, attempts to maintain consistency among multiple beliefs are much more prominent in human than in animal psychology.

One reason for the greater human concern with consistency is that we use language in dealing with each other. Humans explain their actions to each other and argue with each other. Inconsistency weakens arguments and explanations, and listeners are often quick to point out any inconsistencies. So people strive to be consistent as they prepare what to say.

The way people think creates other special processes involving attitudes and beliefs. People can hold dual attitudes, in which their deliberate attitude differs from their automatic response; animals that lack higher-level cognitions don't have that kind of inner conflict. We saw that simply thinking about an issue causes people's opinions to become polarized, but most animals would not be capable of that much thinking and hence wouldn't have to cope with its polarizing consequence. We also saw that doubting and questioning, and ultimately rejecting a belief as untrue, is often a second step in human thinking that may require conscious thought. Nonprimates probably lack the capacity to make true/false judgments. In practice, that probably means they believe everything that is presented to them and don't make judgments about whether something is true or false. Much of the great progress in human culture, from science to philosophy, involves carefully considering multiple views and rejecting those that are found to be false. Without the capacity to judge something as false, animals have been unable to develop science or philosophy.

Humans also use attitudes and beliefs much more extensively than other animals in how they relate to the world around them. We develop elaborate sets of beliefs to help us understand the world. (Again, only humans have developed science, religion, and philosophy.) Beliefs have another benefit, in that they can help people cope with misfortune. To an animal, a bad event (such as an injury) is just a practical matter, but for humans bad events affect their beliefs about the world, and people can use or modify those beliefs to help themselves bounce back.

CHAPTER 7 SUMMARY

What Are Attitudes and Why Do People Have Them?

- Beliefs are pieces of information, facts, or opinions; attitudes are broad evaluations (liking or disliking) toward some object or issue.
- Automatic attitudes are automatic, nonconscious, evaluative responses; deliberate attitudes are controlled, conscious, evaluative responses.
- Dual attitudes refer to having different, competing attitudes, one deliberate and the other automatic.
- People may not be aware of all their own attitudes.
- Attitudes help deal with the complex social world. People need far more attitudes than most animals.
- As soon as you know what something is, you start to know whether you like or dislike it (in the first microsecond of thought).
- To be impartial—as a judge or referee is supposed to—may require overcoming one's attitudes.
- Attitudes are tremendously helpful in making choices. Possessing an attitude increases the ease, speed, and quality of decision making.

How Attitudes Are Formed

- The mere exposure effect is the tendency for novel stimuli to be liked more after the individual has been repeatedly exposed to them. Familiarity breeds liking!
- Classical conditioning (also called Pavlovian conditioning) is the repeated pairing of an unconditioned stimulus with a conditioned stimulus, until the conditioned stimulus elicits a response similar to that elicited by the unconditioned stimulus.
- Classical conditioning may help explain the development of prejudiced attitudes against social groups that are frequently associated with negative information in the media.
- Advertisers use classical conditioning to direct attitudes by linking their products with famous or attractive people or with feeling good.
- Operant conditioning (also called instrumental conditioning) is a type of learning. People are more likely to repeat behaviors that have been rewarded and are less likely to repeat behaviors that have been punished.

- Social learning (also called observational learning, imitation, or vicarious learning) is the type of learning in which people are more likely to imitate behaviors if they have seen others rewarded for performing those behaviors, and are less likely to imitate behaviors if they have seen others punished for performing them.
- Attitudes can be formed or changed through operant conditioning, classical conditioning, or observational learning.
- Attitude polarization is the tendency for attitudes to become more extreme as people think about or reflect on their attitudes, especially if they held strong attitudes to begin with.
- If people see an equal amount of confirming and disconfirming evidence, they become even more convinced of their initial attitudes and adopt them more strongly.
- People are more accepting of evidence presented by ingroup members and more skeptical of evidence presented by outgroup members.

Consistency

- To reduce their feelings of inconsistency, people may have to seek out new or reinterpret old information, realign or abandon cherished beliefs, or change patterns of behavior. People will generally choose the easiest of these (the path of least resistance), which often means changing their attitudes.

  - Consistency theories have three parts:
  - They specify the conditions that are required for consistency and inconsistency of cognitions.
  - They assume that inconsistency is unpleasant and therefore motivates people to restore consistency.
  - They specify the conditions that are needed to restore consistency.
- According to cognitive dissonance theory, discrepancies between attitudes and behaviors produce psychological discomfort (cognitive dissonance), which causes people to rationalize their behavior so as to bring their attitudes into line with their actions.
- People who were paid a small amount to lie came to change their attitudes to believe their own lie; people who were paid a large amount to lie did not.
- Effort justification is the idea that people who expend a great deal of effort will want to convince themselves that their effort was worthwhile.

- People will sometimes choose to suffer as a consequence of expecting to suffer, if they have coped with their expectation by changing some of their relevant beliefs and attitudes.
- People who suffer more to get into a group end up liking the group more.
- Choice is necessary for dissonance and attitude change.
- Dissonance is marked by unpleasant arousal.
- People may have some desire to be consistent in the privacy of their minds, but they have a much stronger desire to be seen by other people as consistent.
- People selectively expose themselves to information that supports their preexisting views and avoid information that contradicts their preexisting views.
- Some internet sites use filter bubbles to expose users to information that they think the user will like.
- The drive for consistency may be rooted in our biological nature and strengthened by learning and socialization, and it may involve both parts of the duplex mind.

Do Attitudes Really Predict Behaviors?

- The A–B problem is the problem of inconsistency between attitudes (A) and behaviors (B). The link between attitudes and behaviors is often weak.
- Men's general attitudes predict their sexual behavior much better than women's.
- Attitudes predict behavior best if any or all of the following conditions are met:
  - Attitude measures are very specific.
  - Behaviors are aggregated across time and different situations.
  - Attitudes are consciously prominent and influence how the person thinks about the choices they face.
  - Attitudes are highly accessible (i.e., they come to mind easily).

Beliefs and Believing

- The automatic system just believes; the deliberate system can override this belief by deciding that it is false.
- Belief perseverance is the idea that once beliefs form, they are resistant to change.

- Explaining the opposite theory reduces or eliminates belief perseverance.
- *Coping* is the general term for how people attempt to deal with traumas and go back to functioning effectively in life.
- *Assumptive worlds* is a term for the view that people form a complex understanding of their world and live according to that. Their assumptions typically include the following, any of which can be violated by misfortune or trauma:
  - The world is benevolent.
  - The world is fair.
  - I am a good person.
- Blaming oneself can be a good way to cope, if one blames oneself for having made a mistake, as opposed to blaming oneself for being a bad person.
- Cognitive coping identifies several kinds of beliefs that need to be bolstered or restored in the wake of trauma, including the following:
  - Reevaluate the trauma using downward comparison, in which people compare themselves and their situations to other people who are worse off.
  - Restore self-esteem.
  - Restore belief in control.
  - Find positive changes resulting from the trauma.
- Irrational beliefs are often maintained despite contradictory evidence.

What Makes Us Human? Putting the Cultural Animal in Perspective

- Although animals have some attitudes (e.g., they have likes and dislikes), humans have many more attitudes.
- Humans also have far more complex attitudes than other animals do.
- Only humans rationalize their behaviors by changing their attitudes.
- Because humans have conscious thought, they can question, doubt, and reject a belief as untrue. Other animals lack this ability.
- Only humans develop elaborate sets of beliefs to help them understand the world.

key terms

A–B problem 247
accessibility 248
assumptive worlds 250
attitudes 233
attitude polarization 239
automatic attitudes 233
behavioral intentions 248
beliefs 233
belief perseverance 249
classical conditioning 237
cognitive coping 251
cognitive dissonance 241
cognitive dissonance theory 241
conditioned response 237
conditioned stimulus 237
coping 250
deliberate attitudes 233
downward comparison 251
dual attitudes 233
effort justification 241
filter bubbles 245
mere exposure effect 236
neutral stimulus 237
operant conditioning (instrumental conditioning) 238
perceived behavioral control 248
post-decision dissonance 243
selective exposure 244
social learning (observational learning, imitation, vicarious learning) 238
subjective norms 248
unconditioned response 237
unconditioned stimulus 237
upward comparison 251

quiz yourself ANSWERS

1. What Are Attitudes and Why Do People Have Them? p.236
   answers: 1.b 2.a 3.a 4.a
2. How Attitudes Are Formed p.240
   answers: 1.c 2.a 3.b 4.c
3. Consistency p.245
   answers: 1.b 2.a 3.c 4.d
4. Do Attitudes Really Predict Behaviors? p.248
   answers: 1.d 2.d 3.b 4.c
5. Beliefs and Believing p.254
   answers: 1.a 2.b 3.d 4.a

SOCIAL INFLUENCE AND PERSUASION

8

LEARNING OBJECTIVES

1. Distinguish normative and informational influence. Compare and contrast how being a cultural animal affects our susceptibility to each of these forms of influence.

2. Categorize the techniques of social influence in terms of the four basic principles and describe ways of resisting these techniques.

3. Explain how a persuasion attempt can be described by "who says what to whom," and identify which factors of each element are most likely to elicit successful persuasion.

4. Summarize the two routes to persuasion, applying the concept of the duplex mind to describe the two routes. Debate the efficacy of the two routes under different conditions such as strong versus weak messages or individual differences.

5. Describe some of the steps you can take to increase your resistance to persuasive attempts to change your attitudes.

6. Identify the terms sleeper effect, halo effect, inverted U-shaped relationship, and pluralistic ignorance and evaluate how they relate to social influence techniques.

MONEY MATTERS
Even a Penny Will Help
267

FOOD FOR THOUGHT
Convert Communicators and Health Messages
274

TRADEOFFS
Should Speakers Talk Fast or Slow?
275

THE SOCIAL SIDE OF SEX
Scared into Safe Sex?
277

WHAT MAKES US HUMAN?
Putting the Cultural Animal in Perspective
286

martin-dm/E+/Getty Images

Fake news is a form of news containing deliberate misinformation (or lies) that is spread through traditional channels. Although fake news has been around for a very long time, as the above illustration from 1894 shows, it seems more common today than ever before. For example, during a tropical storm that flooded the streets of the U.S. state of North Carolina, the Federal Emergency Management Agency (FEMA) had to dispel fake news that there were sharks swimming in the water-covered streets and highways.[1]

The World Economic Forum—a non-profit organization that is "committed to improving the world"—lists "the rapid spread of misinformation online" as one of the 10 most pressing issues facing the world.[2] The world today is described using terms such as "post-truth" and "post-fact." Indeed, the Oxford Dictionary chose the word "post-truth" as its word of the year in 2016.[3]

Research has shown that fake news actually spreads faster than real news. One study[4] examined tweets from 12 years of data from Twitter and found that 126,000 fake news stories were spread by about 3 million people. Fake news stories spread faster, farther, deeper, and broader than true news stories. Truthful news stories rarely reached more than 1000 Twitter users, whereas fake news stories routinely reach over 10,000 Twitter users.

Fake news stories are not always spread by people. Sometimes they are spread by "bots" (short for "robots"). For example, during the 2016 U.S. presidential election, Russians used armies of bots to spread fake news stories on social media in an attempt to influence election results.[5]

One tragic consequence of misinformation is that it causes people to stop believing in facts.[6,7] It also creates a sense of uncertainty about whether facts are knowable at all. In addition, misinformation can serve as a distraction from other, more important issues.[8]

Unfortunately, misinformation is very difficult to correct once it has spread.[9] In general, people seem to have difficulty ignoring information once it has been presented to them, even when that information is false.

As with other forms of media, people believe that fake news has a stronger effect on other people than on themselves,[10] called the "**third-person effect**."[11] At the end of the chapter, we discuss how people can inoculate themselves against social influence attempts, including fake news.

This chapter is about social influence. As social animals, people are exceptionally responsive to each other. As cultural animals, people rely on each other for information about the world and for guidance about how to act in uncertain situations. This dependency on others creates opportunities for social influence. ●

Fake news has been around for a very long time, as this 1894 illustration shows.

During a tropical storm that flooded the streets of the U.S. state of North Carolina, the Federal Emergency Management Agency (FEMA) had to dispel fake news that there were sharks swimming in the water-covered streets and highways.

Two Types of Social Influence

Social psychologists distinguish between two major categories of social influence: normative and informational.[12] Let us consider each of these in turn.

Seeking Approval: Normative Influence

Normative influence involves going along with the crowd in order to be liked and accepted. As Chapter 2 has emphasized, humans have a fundamental need to belong to social groups. Being accepted and included improves one's chances for survival (and improves life in many other ways). However, there is a long road to acceptance within the group. To live together, people usually need to agree on a set of common beliefs, values, attitudes, and behaviors that reduce ingroup threats and act for the common good. Therefore, people learn to conform to their group's rules. The more we see others behaving in a certain way or making particular decisions, the more we feel inclined to follow suit. This happens even when we are in a group of complete strangers: we will go along with the others to avoid looking like a fool.

The studies conducted by Solomon Asch illustrate the power of normative influence (also see Chapter 2).[13] Asch asked participants to judge which of three lines matched a comparison line. In some studies, the participant was asked last in a group of accomplices, all of whom had been instructed to give the same wrong answer. Asch found that many participants went along with the accomplices and gave the wrong answer, even though they could plainly see it was wrong, rather than deviating from the group. In some studies, Asch varied the discrepancy between the standard line and the comparison lines to discover the point at which the error made by the accomplices was so glaring that no participants would conform. These manipulations did not eliminate the effect: Participants went along with the group even when the group made flagrant errors. To be accepted by the group was more important to participants than to be correct, even though the other people were strangers.

Several factors influence whether people will conform to group norms. Asch varied the number of unanimous accomplices from 1 to 15.[14] He found that conformity increases as group size increases up to a point, then it levels off (see **FIGURE 8.1**).

third person effect occurs when people believe the media have a stronger impact on others than on themselves

normative influence going along with the crowd in order to be liked and accepted

In the studies conducted by Asch, participants chose line 1, 2, or 3 as matching the comparison line (line in the box to the left of lines 1, 2, and 3). During the experiment, six of the seven people were accomplices who gave the wrong answer (top right image). Many participants went along with the group even though the group gave an obviously wrong answer.

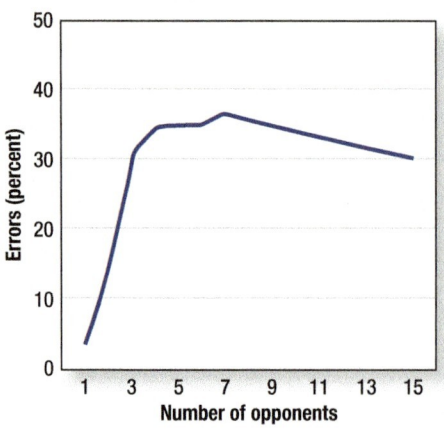

FIGURE 8.1

Effect of group size on conformity in the Asch experiment: As the number of accomplices increased from one to four, conformity increased dramatically; as more accomplices were added, conformity leveled off.

SOURCE: Asch (1955).

Size of the majority that opposed them had an effect on the participants. With a single opponent, the participant erred only 3.6% of the time; with two opponents, he erred 13.6%; three, 31.8%; four, 35.1%; six, 35.2%; seven, 37.1%; nine, 35.1%; fifteen, 31.2%.

autokinetic effect illusion, caused by very slight movements of the eye, that a stationary point of light in a dark room is moving

group norms the beliefs or behaviors that a group of people accepts as normal

FIGURE 8.2

Sherif used the autokinetic effect to study the development of group norms.

SOURCE: Sherif (1935).

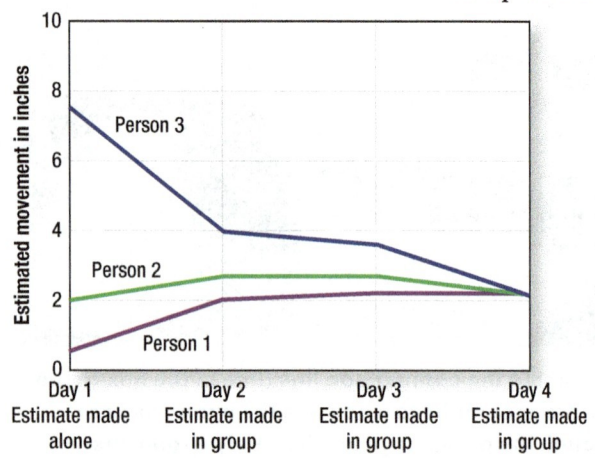

In another study, one of the accomplices was a "dissenter" who always gave the correct answer.[15] A single dissenter reduced conformity by about one-fourth. In addition, participants who gave the correct answer reported feelings of warmth and closeness toward the dissenter. Asch wondered whether the dissenter reduced conformity because he was accurate or because he deviated from the other accomplices. Thus, Asch conducted another study in which the dissenter disagreed with the other accomplices but chose another incorrect answer. Half the time the dissenter made a moderate error, choosing a line that was incorrect but not too far off; the other half of the time the dissenter made an extreme error. The results showed that when the dissenter made a moderate error, conformity decreased by about one-third; when the participants did make errors, most were moderate rather than extreme. When the dissenter made an extreme error, conformity decreased by almost three-fourths! Furthermore, when participants did make errors—and this occurred on only 9% of the trials—all of the errors were moderate, none extreme. Thus, the extreme dissenter had a remarkably freeing effect on participants. The implication is that people feel considerable pressure to conform to a group if everyone agrees, but if group members disagree about even the smallest point, then people become willing to stand up for what they believe.

When people deviate from group norms, they may pay a heavy price, including social rejection (see Chapter 11 for more on the psychology of rejection). Social rejection can be painful. Asch found that many people would agree with the group, even when they knew the group was wrong, rather than suffer social rejection. Other research has shown that people who deviate from the group do indeed run a heightened risk of being rejected. For example, in an early study,[16] groups of eight individuals discussed the case of a juvenile delinquent named Johnny Rocco. Each group consisted of five real participants and three accomplices. One accomplice, the "deviant," adopted the extreme position of punishing Rocco severely and did not deviate from this position during group discussion. A second accomplice, the "slider," first adopted the extreme position of punishing Rocco but then "slid" toward the position adopted by most group members. A third accomplice, the "mode," adopted the position of most group members. At the end of the group discussion, the experimenter told everyone that a smaller group was needed for the next group discussion, so that the group needed to vote one member out. Most groups voted out the deviant. A review of similar studies showed that groups are quick to reject deviants or nonconformists.[17] Rejection is more likely when there are only one or two nonconformists than when there are many nonconformists.[18]

Being Correct: Informational Influence

If you look at a pinpoint of light in a dark room, the light appears to move even though it does not actually move at all. This illusion of movement, caused by very slight movements of the eye, is called the **autokinetic effect**.

Muzafer Sherif used the autokinetic effect to study the formation of group norms.[19] **Group norms** are the beliefs or behaviors that a group of people accepts as normal. Sherif asked individual participants in a dark room to estimate how far the light moved. Their individual estimates ranged from about 1 inch to about 8 inches (2.54 to 20.32 centimeters). They repeated this process on subsequent days, but in the presence of two other participants. As participants heard the estimates provided by others, their individual answers converged and became more similar (see **FIGURE 8.2**). (Remember, the correct answer would have been zero, but the illusion is compelling.)

These social norms are not temporary, either; they can last at least one year.[20] These social norms can also be transmitted from one person to another. In another study that used the autokinetic effect,[21] researchers had a accomplice give an inflated estimate of how far the light moved in the presence of a real participant. The accomplice was then replaced by a real participant, who was in turn replaced by

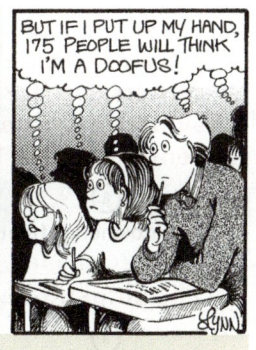

Pluralistic ignorance can paralyze students in the classroom and interfere with learning.

another real participant, and so on. The inflated estimate persisted over five generations of research participants. Thus, people ended up conforming to the (false) norms set by someone who was by this point long gone. If you have ever joined a club or organization and found that they have some strange practices that have been there for a long time, but no one can explain other than "We've always done it that way," this could be why!

The studies conducted by Sherif indicate a second type of social influence called informational influence. **Informational influence** involves going along with the crowd because you think the crowd knows more than you do (rather than because you want to be liked, as with normative social influence). It fits the "people first" theme we have seen throughout this book: People get valuable information from others, and sometimes they give more weight to what others think than to what their own eyes and ears tell them.

Two types of situations increase susceptibility to informational influence: (a) ambiguous situations, in which people do not know how to behave, and (b) crisis situations, in which people don't have time to think for themselves. In these situations, people conform to what others do because they assume that those other people must know what they are doing. Sometimes this assumption is wrong—others really do not know more than we do. In fact, others may assume that we know more than they do! In some cases, nobody knows anything, which is called a state of **pluralistic ignorance** (also see Chapter 9).

Pluralistic ignorance can be a big problem for college students. Have you ever sat through a class feeling completely lost and confused about the material being presented? You want to ask a question, but you're too embarrassed to ask it. No one else is saying anything, so you assume that everybody else understands the material. In fact, the other students are probably just as confused as you are. Pluralistic ignorance in the classroom can interfere with learning. Others often don't know as much as we give them credit for.

Pluralistic ignorance occurs when people attempt to match a group norm. Recent research suggests that college students consistently underestimate the amount of time their peers spend studying (the group norm), and the less time they think peers spend studying the less they prepare and the worse their own exam perform is.[22] The good news is that when the pluralistic ignorance is reduced by informing students how much time their peers actually study, students study more themselves and earn higher exam scores.

In short, there are two different kinds of social influence: normative and informational. A key difference is whether the conforming person comes to believe that others are right (informational) or believes they are wrong but conforms simply to avoid rejection, ridicule, hostility, or other kinds of punishment (normative). Informational social influence helps produce **private acceptance**—a genuine inner belief that others are right. Normative social influence may elicit mere **public compliance**—outwardly going along with the group but maintaining a private, inner belief that the group is wrong, or at least entertaining serious doubts about the group's decision. For example, some people become vegetarian because they believe it is a healthier lifestyle and better for the planet (private acceptance), whereas as others might become vegetarian because all their friends think it is trendy and cool, even though inwardly they still love to eat meat (public compliance).

informational influence going along with the crowd because you think the crowd knows more than you do

pluralistic ignorance looking to others for cues about how to behave, while they are looking to you; collective misinterpretation

private acceptance a genuine inner belief that others are right

public compliance outwardly going along with the group but maintaining a private, inner belief that the group is probably wrong

QUIZ YOURSELF
Two Types of Social Influence

1. Lucyna initially believes that when she becomes angry it is helpful to yell and scream to vent her anger. This emotional cleansing is called catharsis. After listening to her professor's lecture on the research evidence contradicting catharsis, Lucyna no longer believes that venting works. This change in belief illustrates _____.
   - (a) the autokinetic effect
   - (b) informational influence
   - (c) normative influence
   - (d) public compliance

2. The autokinetic effect is a(n) _____.
   - (a) false group consensus
   - (b) group norm
   - (c) illusion of perceived movement
   - (d) influential bias in social influence

3. The type of conformity based on a fear of social rejection is called _____.
   - (a) ingratiation
   - (b) modeling
   - (c) private acceptance
   - (d) public compliance

4. Tyrone plans to vote for candidate Duck in the local elections. Before he votes, his friends explain why they're going to vote for candidate Goose. In the voting booth, Tyrone votes for candidate Goose. This is an example of _____.
   - (a) private acceptance
   - (b) psychological reactance
   - (c) public compliance
   - (d) reciprocity

answers: see pg 288

Techniques of Social Influence

The previous section discussed influence as a matter of people feeling pressure to conform. In those cases, the influencer only offers information or dangles the possibility of social acceptance. In this section, we look at how influencers take a more active approach to altering another person's behavior, in ways that go far beyond conformity.

As Chapter 5 suggested, a primary purpose of human reasoning is to influence others, such as by arguing.[23] Most social influence techniques rely on four basic principles: (1) commitment and consistency, (2) reciprocation, (3) scarcity, and (4) capturing and disrupting attention. Not all the techniques in the following sections were discovered by social psychologists. As you will see, salespersons have been experimenting with ways of influencing people for a very long time.

Techniques Based on Commitment and Consistency

Several techniques of influence are based on the principle of commitment and consistency.[24] Once people make a commitment, they feel pressure (both internal pressure from inside themselves and external pressure from others) to behave consistently with that commitment. Inconsistent behavior causes a form of psychological discomfort called cognitive dissonance (see Chapter 7). The influence techniques in this section exploit that principle: Get the person to commit to what you want, then the person is more likely to do what you want. Seemingly trivial commitments can lead to substantial compliance on more important things.

Foot-in-the-Door Technique

Cult recruiters don't just ask a complete stranger on the street, "Hey, you! Do you want to give us all your belongings and join our cult today?" Instead, they start small. Consider, for example, the Jim Jones's Peoples Temple cult. Jones was able to persuade over 900 people to commit mass suicide.[25] Getting someone to join a cult and stay with it up through mass suicide takes powerful influence. How Jim Jones recruited followers is very revealing.[26] Members of the Peoples Temple would ask a passerby to help for just five minutes by stuffing and mailing a few envelopes. Jim Jones explained, "They came back for more. You know, once I get somebody, I can get them to do anything." When the person became a member of the Peoples Temple, monetary contributions were voluntary at first. Then, Jones asked for a 10% contribution, called a "tithe." After that, he required a 25% contribution. Finally, he required members to give him everything they had—a 100% contribution. Another example: Jones asked his followers to move from Indiana to California before he asked them to move to Jonestown in the jungles of Guyana, South America.

The technique Jim Jones used is called the **foot-in-the-door technique.** It is based on the principle of starting with a small request in order to get eventual compliance with a much larger request. The term refers to the efforts of old-fashioned door-to-door salespeople to get "one foot in the door" as a prerequisite to getting their whole body into the house. (The assumption was that the customer won't slam the door in your face as long as your foot is in the way.) Complying with small requests seems like no big deal, but it increases the likelihood of complying with larger requests later on. It is easier to comply the second time than the first time. If requests get bigger slowly and gradually, the person may be more willing to comply with each one than if the other had started with a large request.

In a classic study conducted in the 1960s,[27] researchers telephoned housewives in California and asked if they would answer a few questions about the household products they used. Three days later, the researcher called again. This time, the housewives were asked if a survey team of five or six men could come into their homes for two hours to catalog all their household products. The investigators found that the women who agreed to the small request were more than twice as likely to agree to the 2-hour request than a group of housewives who were asked only the larger request (53% versus 22%).

foot-in-the-door technique influence technique in which one starts with a small request in order to gain eventual compliance with a larger request

low-ball technique influence technique in which one first gets a person to comply with a seemingly low-cost request and only later reveals hidden additional costs

Low-Ball Technique

A second approach that shifts from a smaller request to a larger request is the **low-ball technique.** In this technique, the requester first gets a person to comply with a seemingly low-cost request and only later reveals hidden additional costs. Car salespeople sometimes try this technique on potential customers. You come into a car dealership and test drive a car you really want to buy. The salesperson quotes you an excellent price, and you agree to the deal. The salesperson goes to talk to the sales manager and then returns with some "bad news" (e.g., you will only get $400 on your trade-in, rather than the $2,000 you had been promised; the wireless audio system with 18 speakers costs extra, even though the salesperson had told you it came with the car; or perhaps the sales price you were offered was an error and must be raised $500). The original price is really a "low ball" that the salesperson threw at you to get you to buy the car.

In one test of the low-ball influence technique, college students were recruited to participate in a study on "thinking processes" that was to be conducted at 7:00 in the morning.[28] Half of the students were thrown a low ball: The researcher asked if they would be interested in participating in a study on thinking processes *before* telling them they would have to be at the lab at 7 a.m. After they agreed to participate, the researcher told them the bad news about the early starting time. Even though the researcher gave them a chance to change their minds, 56% agreed to participate. In contrast, among students who were told of the starting time before they made a commitment, only 24% agreed to participate. The low-balled participants were also more likely than the others to actually show up for the study. Thus, the low-ball technique increased both promises to comply and actual compliance.

Although the low-ball technique is considered unscrupulous, it often works. Why? As with the foot-in-the-door technique, it is based on the

"Would you like to super-size that?"

Car salespeople sometimes use the low-ball technique.

principle of commitment and consistency. Commitments have a tendency to "grow their own legs";[29] that is, people often add new reasons and justifications to support their initial commitment. One lesson we learned from cognitive dissonance theory is that people like to justify their decisions (see Chapter 7). Your initial decision to buy the car was based on a single "leg"—the great initial offer the salesperson quoted you. But then other legs start growing. You like the color. It's fast. It has that "new car smell" inside. The wireless sound system that connects to your new iPhone sounds great. And so on. The salesperson then throws a low ball that knocks over the leg that initially held up your decision to buy the car (the great initial offer), but the decision doesn't fall through because now all the new legs are holding it up. You fulfill your commitment and buy the car.

Bait-and-Switch Technique

Car salespeople also use a technique called **bait-and-switch**. The car dealership places an ad for a car at a great price, but when you get to the showroom that car is "sold out." The dealership placed the ad simply to get you into the showroom. Once you are there, they can try to sell you another car. You are baited with one car (usually a stripped-down model with no options, sold at an unbelievably low price), and then you are switched to another car (usually a fully loaded model that goes for a much higher price).

The bait-and-switch technique is used by businesses other than car sales. For example, you may go to a store because they advertised a product you want, but when you get to the store you discover that the product is sold out. Since you are already at the store, you decide to go shopping anyway. The ad served its purpose—it got you into the store.

The American Bar Association warns consumers that this technique is illegal and fraudulent. But that doesn't stop some businesses from using it.

The bait-and-switch technique, like the low-ball and foot-in-the-door techniques, is based on the principle of commitment and consistency.[30] It gets people to make a psychological commitment, and then relies on consistency pressures to keep them loyal to this commitment even when the influencer changes the terms.

Labeling Technique

The **labeling technique** is another way to induce compliance. It involves assigning a label to an individual and then requesting a favor that is consistent with the label. Former Egyptian President Anwar Sadat used the labeling technique to persuade those he negotiated with.[31] Before negotiations began, Sadat would tell his opponents that they and the citizens of their country were widely known for being cooperative and fair. In doing so, Sadat gave his opponents a label to live up to. According to former Secretary of State Henry Kissinger, Sadat was a successful negotiator because he understood how to get others to act on his behalf by giving them a reputation to uphold. People tend to live up to the positive labels others give them.

Research has shown that the labeling technique can persuade both children and adults. Elementary school children who are told by an adult "You look to me like the kind of girl (or boy) who understands how important it is to write correctly" were more likely to choose a penmanship task several days later than were children who were not labeled.[32] Similarly, adults who were previously told that they were "above average citizens" were more likely to vote several days later than were adults previously told that they were "average citizens."[33]

The labeling technique is also based on the commitment and consistency principle. Whether positive labels are assigned by oneself or by others, people like to live up to them. Labeling also uses the importance of self-concepts (see Chapter 3). How people think about themselves can influence their behavior. Thus, if you want to influence that person's behavior, an effective technique is to get the person to think of him- or herself in a manner that will produce the desired result. A person who thinks of herself as helpful will often be more helpful than a person who doesn't.

People also do not want to be labeled as cheap. Hence, they may find it hard to refuse a very small request. To see how this can lead to persuasion, please read the *Money Matters* box.

bait-and-switch influence technique in which one draws people in with an attractive offer that is unavailable and then switches them to a less attractive offer that is available

labeling technique influence technique in which one assigns a label to an individual and then requests a favor that is consistent with the label

MONEY Matters

Even a Penny Will Help

Asking for donations is hard work, and one gets used to refusals. Researchers developed a clever technique to make it harder for people to say no. In their study,[34] some accomplices simply asked for a donation to the American Cancer Society, while others added the phrase "Even a penny (cent) will help." Adding this phrase nearly doubled the rate at which people said yes and gave a donation.

Of course, getting donations of only a penny would not really be of much help to the American Cancer Society! But the researchers found that the average size of the donations did not change, even while more people donated. Thus, the even-a-penny method produced many more donations of the same approximate size, resulting in a big increase in total amount. This technique is called the **legitimization-of-paltry-favors technique**, and a meta-analytic review indicates that it is very effective.[35]

Why? Most reasons people give for refusing resemble, "I do not have enough money to donate," but such reasons do not work with the even-a-penny method. Everyone can afford to give a penny! To refuse a request when even a penny would be acceptable might make the refuser feel cheap and petty. Apparently, though, once people decide to go ahead and donate, they donate the amount they would normally give (rather than just giving a penny).

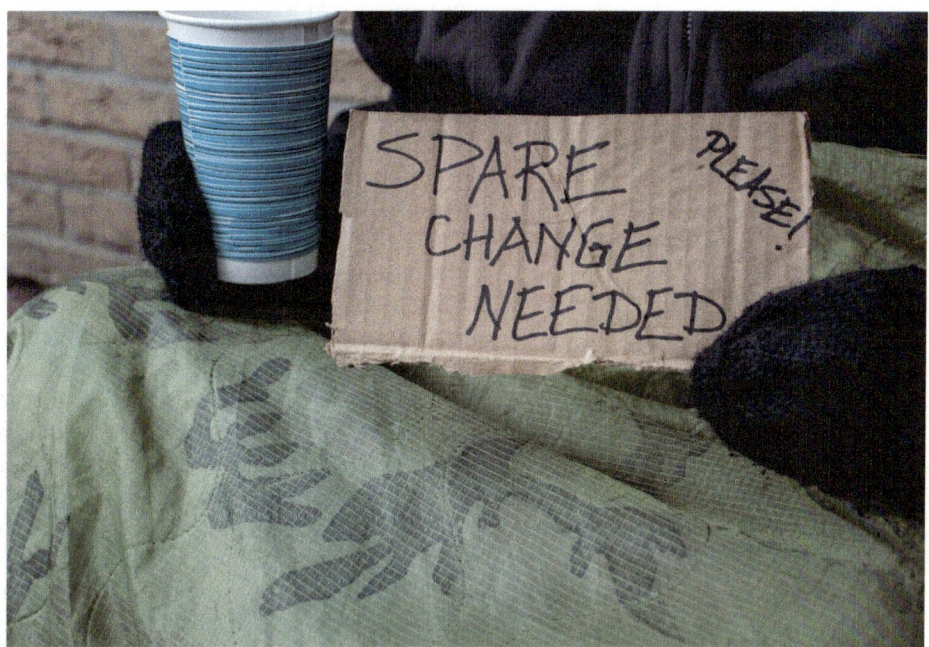

Defenses Against Techniques Based on Commitment and Consistency

Several influence techniques are based on the principle of commitment and consistency, including the foot-in-the-door technique, the low-ball technique, the bait-and-switch technique, the labeling technique, and the legitimization-of-paltry-favors technique (e.g., "even a penny will help"). The commitment and consistency principle is a great time saver. If people had to weigh the pros and cons of each decision, they would soon feel overwhelmed, and they would not be able to function. It is much easier to make a commitment once and then behave consistently with that commitment.

The power of the commitment and consistency principle comes from the sense of obligation it creates. When people freely make commitments, they feel obligated to behave consistently with those commitments. Behaving inconsistently has personal and interpersonal costs. Personally, inconsistency between one's attitudes and actions can result in cognitive dissonance, which is an unpleasant emotional response (see Chapter 7). Interpersonally, if your inconsistent behaviors affect others, you may suffer social rejection and ostracism, which don't feel good either (see Chapter 12). However, you should *not* feel obligated to behave consistently with a commitment that you were tricked into making. If it is not clear whether you were tricked into making a commitment, ask yourself this question: "Knowing what I know now, if I could go back in time, would I make the same commitment?"[36] If the answer is "yes," behave consistently with the commitment. If the answer is "no," don't do it!

Another way to resist influence is to make a public commitment to your position.[37] Commitments are much more binding when they are made in public than when they are made in private. Standing up for your convictions in public makes you less susceptible to what others have to say.

legitimization-of-paltry-favors technique influence technique that involves a phrase that suggests that even a very small amount of aid will help (e.g., "even a penny will help").

Techniques of Social Influence

Techniques Based on Reciprocation

Reciprocity—if you take care of me, I will take care of you—is one of the foundations of culture. All cultures understand reciprocity and expect people to obey its norms. The appreciation of reciprocity is deeply rooted in human nature; one sign of this is that people feel guilty if someone does them a favor and they cannot repay it in some way. This sentiment is the foundation for some of the best moral behavior and good treatment of others. Unfortunately, it is also something that sneaky people can exploit to influence others. Two influence techniques are based on reciprocation: door-in-the-face and that's-not-all.[38]

Door-in-the-Face Technique

An effective way to get people to comply with a request is to start by making an inflated request (that will most likely be rejected), and then retreat to a smaller request. The smaller request, the one that was desired all along, is likely to be accepted because it appears to be a concession. This is called the **door-in-the-face technique** because the first refusal is like slamming a door in the face of the person making the request. It is opposite of the foot-in-the door technique, which starts with a small request in order to get compliance to a larger request. In negotiations between labor and management, both sides often use this tactic. Both sides initially make extreme demands that they do not expect to get. Later they retreat to more reasonable demands. Although the expression "door in the face" vividly describes the procedure, the key to compliance is not the initial refusal but rather reciprocity. After the first offer is refused, the salesperson or negotiator makes a more reasonable offer, and people feel obliged to reciprocate this seemingly kind and generous offer by becoming more agreeable themselves.

To demonstrate the door-in-the-face method, researchers asked people if they would volunteer two hours per week for at least two years in a community mental health agency.[39] They all said "No." Next, they were asked if they would volunteer for two hours on a single occasion. About 76% of participants volunteered. In contrast, only 29% volunteered if they were just asked to work two hours on a single occasion (without the prior request for two years). Moreover, the door-in-the-face people were not simply agreeing without meaning to follow through. Among all those who volunteered, 85% of participants in the door-in-the-face group showed up, whereas only 50% of participants in the control group showed up, which coincides with the commitment and consistency principle described earlier.

The door-in-the-face technique does not work, however, if the first request is so extreme that it is seen as unreasonable.[40] The door-in-the-face technique also does not work if different people make the first and second requests.[41] This probably reflects the importance of reciprocation. The key to getting someone to agree is to pretend you are doing the person a favor by reducing your initial request to a much more reasonable request, so the person will feel an obligation to agree to it. If the second request comes from someone different, no sense of reciprocal obligation is created.

That's-Not-All Technique

The **that's-not-all technique**, like the door-in-the-face technique, begins with an inflated request. However, before the person can respond, the requester "sweetens" the deal by offering a discount or bonus. Perhaps you've seen this technique on television or in internet ads. First, the

door-in-the-face technique influence technique in which one starts with an inflated request and then retreats to a smaller request that appears to be a concession

that's-not-all technique influence technique in which one first makes an inflated request but, before the person can respond, sweetens the deal by offering a discount or bonus

The that's-not-all technique is effective, too.

"How much would you pay for all the secrets of the universe? Wait, don't answer yet. You also get this six-quart covered combination spaghetti pot and clam steamer. <u>Now</u> how much would you pay?"

"regular" price is reduced, and then several additional bonuses are added, such as getting two items for the price of one.

At cupcake booth on a college campus, researchers conducted a field experiment to test the that's-not-all technique.[42] Customers were randomly assigned to one of three groups. In the that's-not-all group, one researcher told the customer that the cupcakes cost $1.25. At this point, a second researcher tapped the first researcher on the shoulder. Before the customer could say anything, the first researcher raised his hand and said, "Wait a second." After a brief conversation with the second researcher, the first researcher told the customer that he would lower the price to $1.00 because they were planning to close the booth soon. In the bargain group, the participant was told, "These are only $1.00 now. We were selling them for $1.25 earlier." In the control group, customers were simply told that the cupcakes cost $1.00. The results showed that more customers in the "that's-not-all" group were more likely to buy cupcakes (55%) than in the bargain (25%) or control (20%) groups. Customers in the "that's-not-all" group most likely complied more because they felt as if the researcher were doing them a personal favor, whereas in the bargain group, the researcher did the same favor for everyone. People felt most obligated to reciprocate when they believed the seller was making an exception for them personally.

The that's-not-all technique, like the door-in-the-face technique, is based on reciprocal concessions and a sense of personal obligation. When a stranger or interaction partner does something kind for you, you feel an obligation to do something nice or kind in return. A discount or bonus can increase compliance by sweetening the deal. Reciprocity is one of the most basic traits of human beings because it goes to the essence of what a cultural animal is. It is in our genes to pay back what others do for us and to recognize when other people do—or do not—reciprocate. Thus, people can be readily exploited by unscrupulous salespeople who take advantage of their basic human tendency to reciprocate.

Defenses Against Techniques Based on Reciprocation

People feel obligated to repay favors and concessions. If people don't reciprocate, they feel guilty. Guilt often induces prosocial behavior (see Chapter 6). Generally, the principle of reciprocation is beneficial to society. It allows us to give, knowing that "what goes around comes around." The problem is that people who want to influence us expect something large for a small favor. For example, a charitable organization may give us inexpensive address labels and expect a large donation in return.

This chapter discussed two influence techniques based on reciprocal concessions: the door-in-the-face technique and the that's-not-all technique. How do we defend ourselves against people who use these techniques to manipulate us? Robert Cialdini, a social psychologist famous for his studies on influence, recommends that we accept initial favors or concessions in good faith, but be ready to define them as tricks if they prove to be tricks.[43] Once they are defined as tricks, we will no longer feel obligated to reciprocate them with a favor or concession. Nor should we feel guilty about not reciprocating. The reciprocation rule says that favors are to be repaid with favors. Tricks do not have to be repaid with favors!

Techniques Based on Scarcity

According to the scarcity principle, rare opportunities are more valuable than plentiful opportunities. Even everyday items can become valuable when they are scarce. For example, a rare collection of 6 stamps was listed for $6,000,000 on eBay!

Scarcity is sometimes used as a heuristic cue in decision making—what is rare is good. The scarcity heuristic is illustrated by the results of a consumer preferences study.[44] Participants were each given a cookie to taste and rate. Some participants received the cookie from a jar containing 10 cookies, whereas others received the cookie from a jar containing only 2 cookies. Even though the cookies were identical, the people who took the cookie from the jar containing only 2 cookies rated it higher than did the people who took the cookie from the jar containing 10 cookies.

> "What is rare is a greater good than what is plentiful."
> — Aristotle

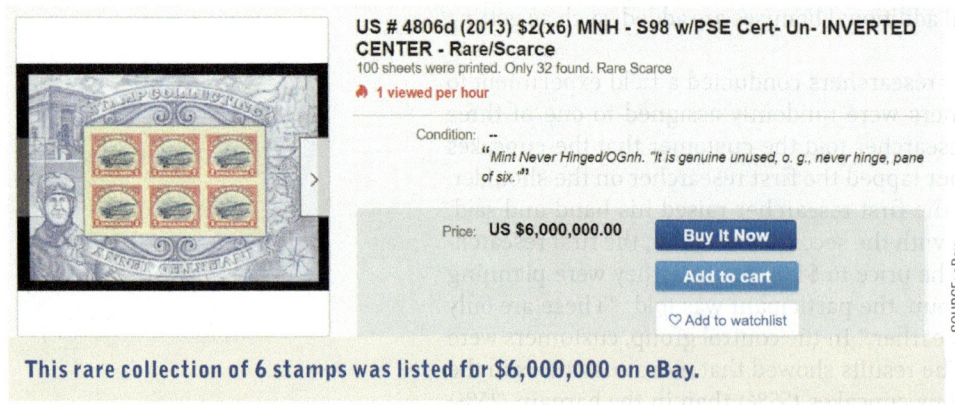

This rare collection of 6 stamps was listed for $6,000,000 on eBay.

One reason why the scarcity principle works is because it takes more effort to obtain rare items than plentiful items. Often, we have to compete with others for scarce opportunities. Perhaps that is why potential lovers and potential employees "play hard to get." They want others to think that they are a hot commodity with lots of options. If you don't agree to the person's request, you could lose a valuable partner or employee.

Another reason why the scarcity principle works is that people, especially those from individualistic cultures, value their freedom highly. As opportunities become scarce, we lose our freedom to obtain them. When our personal freedom is threatened, we experience an unpleasant emotional response called psychological reactance (see Chapter 4). This unpleasant emotion motivates us to obtain the scarce opportunity while we can.

Various influence techniques are based on scarcity. One is the **limited-number technique**, saying that only a limited number of these products will be available. Another is the **fast-approaching-deadline technique**, saying that an item or a price is only available for a limited time (e.g., last day of sale). The point of both is that your chances to buy the product are limited, either by how few there are or by the deadline.

Defenses Against Techniques Based on Scarcity

The principle of scarcity generally serves people well. Scarce items usually are more valuable than plentiful items. In the influence business, however, people often use the scarcity principle to convince us that their products are scarce and that we should get them now, while we can, even when plenty may be in stock.

We discussed two techniques based on scarcity: the limited-number technique and the fast-approaching-deadline technique. How do we defend ourselves against people who use these techniques to influence us? "Keep calm and carry on," as the British said during the bombings during World War II. It is easier said than done! Our natural response to scarcity is to panic. We want to seize the opportunity before it slips away. When our freedom is threatened, we experience psychological reactance (see Chapter 4). Unfortunately, this emotional response to scarcity interferes with our ability to think clearly. Robert Cialdini recommends a two-stage process of resistance.[45] First, we should use the tide of emotional arousal we feel in response to scarce items as a cue to stop short. We need to calm ourselves so we can think clearly and rationally. Second, we should ask why we want the item. Is it because it is scarce, or is it because of its own merits? "Because it is the last day of a sale" or "because it is the last one" is not a good reason for purchasing an item. We should buy something only if we really want it, not because it is scarce.

Techniques Based on Capturing and Disrupting Attention

Other influence techniques try to capture the attention of the target of influence or to distract the target of influence. When influencers have strong arguments, they want to attract the attention of targets because they want people to think about the convincing arguments. When influencers have weak arguments, they want to disrupt the attention of targets so they won't think too deeply about the unconvincing arguments (also see discussion of elaboration likelihood model in a later section of this chapter).

limited-number technique influence technique in which one tells people that an item is in short supply

fast-approaching-deadline technique influence technique in which one tells people an item or a price is only available for a limited time

Pique Technique

Often when panhandlers approach us, they ask, "Can you spare a quarter?" or "Can you spare any change?" People who live in large cities have heard these requests so many times that they often just ignore the panhandler and move on. Pedestrians have a refusal script in mind the instant they see a panhandler, such as "Sorry, I don't have any change." To be effective, the panhandler must disrupt this refusal script and capture the pedestrian's attention. The **pique technique** captures the pedestrian's attention by making the request novel. In a field study,[46] accomplices disguised as panhandlers asked pedestrians whether they had any change, or they asked them whether they had 17 cents. 37% of pedestrians complied with the 17 cents request, whereas only 23% complied with the spare change request. It helps to grab people's attention before they tune out.

The pique technique has also been used to influence drivers to slow down in residential areas. Aspen, Colorado, posted an unusual speed limit sign in its residential areas—14 miles per hour. "It gets people's attention," said Aspen's mayor. "I don't think many people even notice regular speed limit signs anymore."[47] Although the mayor is probably right, it did not pass because U.S. federal law requires speed limit signs to end in 0 or 5.

Disrupt-Then-Reframe

In the **disrupt-then-reframe technique**, a non sequitur or unexpected element is introduced to provide a momentary disruption. The disruption absorbs critical thinking functions and prevents individuals from processing the persuasive message. The requester then reframes the message in a positive light.

For example, researchers managed to disrupt attention by quoting the price of Christmas cards in pennies rather than dollars, followed by, "It's a bargain!"[48] When homeowners were told the cards cost 300 pennies (the disruption) and "which is a bargain" (the reframing), about 80% of the homeowners bought the cards. Compare that to about 40% of the homeowners who bought the cards when told that a package of eight cards cost $3.00. To work, this technique requires both the disruption and the reframing, in that order. Distraction prevents people from processing persuasive messages at a deep level.

As you may have noticed, many influence and persuasion techniques are based on the duplex mind. In many cases, persuaders want to influence someone to do something that one would not sensibly do if one thought long and hard about it. The deliberate mind is therefore the enemy, and the persuaders seek to neutralize and bypass it by working with the automatic mind. For example, your willingness to buy something ought to be the same regardless of whether its price is $3.00 or $.03. But it takes deliberate processing to recognize that those are the same and that one's willingness to buy should be the same. The automatic system is more susceptible to such tricks and biases, so persuaders prefer to work with it—and to keep the deliberate mind from getting involved.

Defenses Against Techniques Based on Capturing and Disrupting Attention

The pique technique is based on capturing attention. It catches people off guard, so they comply without thinking. Thus, the antidote is to stop and think before acting. Whether someone asks you for a quarter or for 17 cents should not determine whether you comply because the request is small in both cases.

The disrupt-then-reframe technique is based on disrupting attention. Distraction increases persuasion for weak messages and decreases persuasion for strong messages. The key, therefore, is to eliminate the distraction so you can process the message at a deep level.

pique technique influence technique in which one captures people's attention, as by making a novel request.

disrupt-then-reframe technique influence technique in which one disrupts critical thinking by introducing an unexpected element, then reframes the message in a positive light

QUIZ YOURSELF
Techniques of Social Influence

1. The technique in which an influencer prefaces the real request by first getting the person to agree to a smaller request is called the _____ technique.
   - (a) door-in-the-face
   - (b) foot-in-the-door
   - (c) low-ball
   - (d) pique

2. The class first asks their professor to cancel the next exam. The professor says, "No way!" The class then asks the professor to postpone the exam one week. The professor says, "Okay." This is an example of what technique?
   - (a) Disrupt-then-reframe
   - (b) Door-in-the-face
   - (c) Foot-in-the-door
   - (d) Low-ball

3. Mohamed accepts a job to shingle the roof of a house. He later learns that he also is expected to shingle the detached garage as part of the original agreement. This is an example of what technique?
   - (a) Door-in-the-face
   - (b) Legitimization of paltry favors
   - (c) Low-ball
   - (d) That's-not-all

4. Which of the following is an explanation of the fast-approaching-deadline technique?
   - (a) Capturing and disrupting attention
   - (b) Commitment and consistency
   - (c) Reciprocity
   - (d) Scarcity

answers: see pg 288

Persuasion

One important form of social influence is persuasion. A primary purpose of the human brain is to influence others and argue with them in an attempt to persuade them.[49] **Persuasion** is an attempt to change a person's attitude. (See Chapter 7 for a discussion on attitudes.) The scientific study of persuasion can be traced back to Carl Hovland, a social psychologist at Yale University. Hovland received a contract from the U.S. Army to study the morale of soldiers. President Franklin D. Roosevelt was worried that American soldiers would lose their will to fight Japan after defeating the German Nazis. White House adviser Lowell Mellett was told that the newly drafted soldiers "haven't the slightest enthusiasm for this war or this cause. They are not grouchy, they are not mutinous, they just don't give a tinker's dam."[50] The Army Morale Branch tried to improve soldier morale, but failed due to the "deadly effects of prepared lectures indifferently read to bored troops." The War Department hired Frank Capra, of Fox and Disney studios, to produce a series of films called *Why We Fight*. From 1942 to 1945 Hovland worked in Washington, D.C., to study the effects of these films on soldier morale.[51] Hovland conducted more than 50 experiments on persuasion and found that although the films were successful in helping soldiers understand the factual basis of the war, they were unsuccessful at motivating soldiers to fight the war. Soldiers were no more eager to die for America after watching films than before.

After the war, Hovland returned to Yale University. The Rockefeller Foundation gave him a grant to continue his studies on persuasion and communication. Hovland and his colleagues conducted a systematic program of research that analyzed the process and effectiveness of persuasion in terms of "who says what to whom."[52] The "who" component is the source of the message, such as a person who is making a speech. The "says what" component is the actual message, such as the content of the speech. The "to

persuasion an attempt to change a person's attitude

whom" component is the audience, the people who hear the speech. Whether persuasion succeeds or fails can be shaped by any and all of those factors.

Aristotle had proposed these same three components of persuasion more than 2,000 years before Hovland was born. In *Rhetoric*, Aristotle specified three components of the persuasive process: the speaker, the subject of the speech, and the hearer to whom the speech is addressed.[53] Aristotle also identified three elements necessary to persuade an audience: (a) emotional appeal (pathos), (b) intellectual appeal (logos), and (c) charisma (ethos). As we have seen, when social psychologists take up an idea, they often find they are not the first to have thought of it. But they can test and evaluate ideas using the experimental method and thereby make an important, original contribution to understanding. Aristotle was a brilliant philosopher, but he conducted no experiments. Many seemingly brilliant ideas turn out to be wrong, and only careful testing can determine which ones are correct.

Who: The Source

Perhaps the most important characteristics of the source of a message are credibility and likability. Let's look at both of these important characteristics.

Source Credibility

The **source** is the individual who delivers the message. A source can be credible or not credible. According to the Merriam-Webster dictionary, credibility is "the quality or power of inspiring belief." However, a source may inspire belief in some situations but not others. For example, an actor like Brad Pitt is a credible source for acting, but he is not a credible source on China or Tibet. Sometimes people are downright uncredible sources. For example, one California lawmaker who came to national prominence as an advocate for the #MeToo movement and was even featured on *Time* magazine's cover of its Persons of the Year: the "Silence Breakers" that spoke out against sexual misconduct, was later accused of sexual misconduct herself and resigned from her office.[54]

Speaker credibility was the topic of a famous early series of studies by Hovland and Weiss.[55] For example, participants read one speech advocating the development of atomic submarines. By random assignment, the speaker was said to be either a well-known physicist (Robert J. Oppenheimer, called the "father of the atomic bomb") or a writer for *Pravda* (the newspaper of the Communist Party in the former Soviet Union). Participants reported their opinions about the topics in the speeches before, immediately after, and a month after reading the speeches. The results showed that immediately after reading the speech, highly credible sources produced more opinion change than did less credible sources.

A month later, however, opinion for the less credible source increased and that for the highly credible source decreased. Therefore, in the long run, the overall amount of opinion change was about the same for the two sources. Hovland and Weiss called this the **sleeper effect**. Over time, people separated the message from the messenger. If they remembered the speech, they forgot who gave it. Subsequent research has shown that the sleeper effect is a very reliable effect.[56]

What makes a source credible? Hovland identified two characteristics: **expertise**, which is how much the source knows, and **trustworthiness**, which is whether the source will honestly tell you what he or she knows. Experts can influence us because we assume they know what they are talking about. But experts cannot be persuasive unless we trust them. A recent poll of American adults showed that the general public perceived lobbyists, car salespeople, members of Congress, and advertisers as the least trustworthy people.[57] Those considered most trustworthy were nurses, military officers, pharmacists, and grade school teachers. The main difference between the two groups of people is that the first group has something to sell, and therefore something to gain—your money! *Food for Thought* explains yet another way that communicators can be persuasive by being especially trustworthy.

> "You shouldn't speak until you know what you're talking about. Reporters ask me what I feel China should do about Tibet. Who cares what I think China should do? I'm an actor! They hand me a script. I act. I'm here for entertainment. Basically, when you whittle everything away, I'm a grown man who puts on makeup."
> — Brad Pitt, American actor

source is the individual who delivers the message

sleeper effect the finding that, over time, people separate the message from the messenger

expertise how much a source knows

trustworthiness whether a source will honestly tell you what he or she knows

Persuasion | 273

FOOD FOR *Thought*

Convert Communicators and Health Messages

Usually experts must be trustworthy to be credible. However, people can make up for their deficits in trustworthiness by arguing against their past transgressions. Such people are called **convert communicators**, and they can be quite persuasive.[60] This tactic is especially effective when used by low-status communicators that audiences might otherwise ignore. Because of the commitment and consistency principle, we take notice when people argue against their previously held attitudes and behaviors. Drug addicts, alcoholics, and chain smokers may lack status and prestige, but they can still be very credible sources when they tell us how they overcame their undesirable behaviors.

One example of a convert communicator is Geoffrey L. Turner, who passed away on February 13, 2019, from lung cancer at the age 66. Before he died, Turner wrote his own obituary, which read:

> I was an idiot who made the same stupid decision, day-after-day, multiple times per day. I was a smoker and even though I knew it may eventually kill me, I chose to deny the truth to myself. The pain and suffering I caused my family was not worth the perceived "satisfaction" that really did nothing more than waste money, separate me from my family, and eventually destroyed my body. I did many good things, helped lots of people, and even made a decent living. At 66 years old, I lived a decent life, but there are so many events and milestones I will not be able to share with my loved ones. The moral of this story—don't be an idiot. If you're a smoker – quit – now – your life depends on it and those that you love depend upon your life. …In lieu of flowers, donations are encouraged to the American Cancer Society or a children's charity of your choice.

Convert communicators are likable because they are similar to audience members. They also show a sense of mastery because they were able to overcome their undesirable behavior, which enhances their credibility. For example, research has shown that a reformed alcoholic is a much more persuasive source than a lifelong teetotaler on the subject of the importance of abstaining from alcohol.[61]

Powerful speakers are assumed to be credible sources.[58,59] Powerless speech, such as speech containing disclaimers (e.g., "I'm not an expert, but ..."), detracts from the speaker's credibility and therefore is less successful at exerting influence.

Although he didn't conduct any research on the topic, Aristotle recognized the importance of source credibility in persuasion. According to Aristotle, "Persuasion is accomplished by a character whenever the speech is held in such a way as to render the speaker worthy of credence." According to Aristotle, credible speakers display "(i) practical intelligence (*phronêsis*), (ii) a virtuous character, and (iii) good will."[62] Aristotle's list of characteristics resembles those proposed by Hovland's group. Practical intelligence is similar to expertise—expert sources are intelligent and know what they are talking about. "Virtuous character" and goodwill are similar to trustworthiness—trustworthy sources appear to be honest, virtuous, and goodwilled. Aristotle argued that if the speaker displayed practical intelligence without virtuosity and goodwill, the audience would doubt the speaker's aims, but that if the speaker displayed all three characteristics, "it cannot rationally be doubted that his suggestions are credible." It is not necessary that the speaker actually possess any of these characteristics—only that the audience believes that the speaker has these characteristics.

In addition to the perceived character of a speaker, other factors make a speaker more or less credible. One such factor is how fast the speaker talks. Does talking fast make a speaker more credible? To find out, see *Tradeoffs*.

Source Likability

We are also persuaded by sources we like. Two important factors that influence whether we like someone are similarity and physical attractiveness. In a study that examined source similarity, students at the University of California, Santa Barbara, read a speech advocating the use of standardized test scores in college admissions.[66] The arguments for using the scores were either strong or weak. Strong arguments were persuasive when the

---

convert communicators people perceived as credible sources because they are arguing against their own previously held attitudes and behaviors

Should Speakers Talk Fast or Slow?

TRADE Offs

People who are trying to persuade others, such as car salespeople and auctioneers, talk really fast. Is talking fast a good strategy or a bad one? Two early field experiments found that fast speakers were more persuasive than slow speakers.[63] In the first study, participants were adults in public locations such as parks and shopping malls. A researcher posing as a radio announcer stopped people and asked them to evaluate the radio program for that day, which was on "The danger of drinking coffee." The message argued that coffee was bad because it contains caffeine, a poisonous drug that causes heart damage, migraine headaches, stomach ulcers, and a host of other problems. The speaker who delivered the message was either a "locksmith" (low credibility source) or a biochemist (high credibility source). People either heard a slow speaker or one who spoke almost twice as many words per minute (102 vs. 195). Overall, the high-speed message was more persuasive than the low-speed message, and the high credible source was more persuasive than the low credible source.

In the second study, the researchers used an unfamiliar topic instead: "The Dangers of Hydroponically Grown Vegetables." Again, the faster the speech, the more persuasive the message was judged to be. Fast speakers were also judged to be more intelligent, knowledgeable, and objective. The authors concluded, "Beware of the fast talker" (p. 621).

According to these results, speaking fast makes people think you are more credible. This is good if thinking is shallow. But if thinking would have been deep, then fast talking distracts people from processing the arguments. This could reduce persuasion if the arguments supporting the message are strong, but it can increase persuasion if the arguments supporting the message are weak. The listener does not have time to figure out that the fast talker's arguments are flawed.

Fast talking can backfire.[64] Researchers approached undergraduate students and had them listen to a message about a recently passed law that raised the legal age for purchasing and consuming alcoholic beverages from 19 to 21 years. (Before conducting the study, the researchers found out that almost all students were opposed to the new law; they wanted to be able to drink legally at age 19 rather than 21.) By the flip of a coin, students heard a speech in favor of the new law (counter-attitudinal group) or a speech that opposed the new law (the pro-attitudinal group). The speech was delivered at a slow (144 words per minute), moderate (182 words per minute), or fast (214 words per minute) rate. As with earlier studies,[65] this study found that as speech rate increased, the perceived credibility of speakers also increased. The more important question is whether the speech influenced the students' attitudes. As can be seen in **FIGURE 8.3**, as speech rate increased, students showed more agreement with the counter-attitudinal message but less agreement with the pro-attitudinal message. Thus, persuaders should talk fast if their arguments are weak so listeners won't have time to think about the arguments. If their arguments are strong, persuaders should talk more slowly, so listeners can think about and appreciate the arguments. Perhaps this is why auctioneers talk really fast. They don't want the bidders to think too deeply about the money they are spending!

FIGURE 8.3

Speaking fast is good if the audience thinks your arguments are weak (because they won't have time to think about them), but it is bad if the audience thinks your arguments are strong.

SOURCE: Smith and Shaffer (1991).

From Smith, S.M. and Shaffer, D.R., "Celerity and cajolery: Rapid speech may promote or inhibit persuasion through its impact on message elaboration" Personality and Social Psychology Bulletin 17, 663, 669. Reprinted by permission of Sage Publications.

---

delegate who wrote the speech was a fellow student at the University of California, Santa Barbara, but not when the delegate was a student at the University of New Hampshire. (Weak arguments were not persuasive regardless of who wrote the speech.) Thus, overall, the similar source was more persuasive than the dissimilar source.

Physical attractiveness produces a positive reaction from others (see Chapter 11). We assume that attractive people also possess many other desirable traits—including traits that can influence how persuasive a person is, such as intelligence. This is called the **halo effect**. For example, attractive political candidates are more effective at persuading

halo effect the assumption that because people have one desirable trait (e.g., attractiveness), they also possess many other desirable traits (e.g., intelligence) people to vote for them than are unattractive candidates, even though many voters deny the impact of attractiveness on electability.[67,68]

Says What: The Message

Messages can vary on several dimensions. In this section, we examine some of the most important ones.

Reason Versus Emotion

There are two approaches in presenting a persuasive message. One can present the cold, hard facts, or one can appeal to emotions. Which approach works best? Well-educated and analytical people are more responsive to arguments based on logic and reason.[69]

Emotional responses can also be very effective. In *Rhetoric,* Aristotle wrote that the success of a persuasive message depends on the emotional state of the audience; "for we do not judge in the same way when we grieve and rejoice or when we are friendly and hostile."[70] Research has shown that people who are in a good mood are more receptive to persuasive messages than other people. One study found that persuasion was increased when college students were given snacks while reading the messages.[71]

Using humor is one way to put an audience in a good mood. About 40% of all ads employ humor.[72] Research shows that people pay more attention to humorous messages than to serious messages.[73] Humor can also make the source more likable.[74] On the downside, people may remember that a message was funny but forget what the message was about.[75]

Humor isn't the only emotional approach that speakers can use—fear is another option. Do scare tactics work to persuade people? If so, how much should you scare them? Should you just unnerve them a little, or scare the daylights out of them? Carl Hovland based his persuasion research on learning theory, which focuses on the link between the stimulus and the response. Hovland predicted that a frightening message (the stimulus) would increase arousal, attention, and comprehension of the message, which would result in attitude change (the response). Attitude change, in turn, should function as a reinforcement because it reduces the fear. Fear appeal and attitude change may have an **inverted (upside down) U-shaped relationship**, according to Irving Janis.[76] Attitude change is lowest for no fear and extremely high fear appeals, with the most attitude change occurring for moderate fear appeals. Subsequent research has shown that fear appeals are persuasive if they do not paralyze the audience with fear, if the audience is susceptible to the danger, and if the audience is told how to avoid the danger.[77] A meta-analysis of 105 studies involving about 18,000 participants found that fear appeals are especially effective if people feel vulnerable to the threat.[78] The research on fear appeals is affecting public policy. For example, the Canadian government now requires that half the surface on a cigarette pack be devoted to graphic images of the hazards of smoking. Research indicates that written warnings accompanied by pictures are 60 times more likely to inspire smokers to quit than are written warnings alone.[79] In this case, the target audience knows exactly how to avoid the danger—quit smoking. Even advertisers want to frighten us into buying their products. Who wants to get caught with bad breath, dandruff, and stinky armpits? Fear appeals can be persuasive, as long as people don't become too afraid. Other approaches might also be more effective than fear appeals, such as promoting efficacy (i.e., "I can do it!").[80] For an illustration of fear's effect on attitudes, see *Social Side of Sex*.

One-Sided Versus Two-Sided Messages

Another factor in persuasion is how a message is conveyed. That is, does the presenter offer only one side of the argument, or are both sides given? One interesting example of one-sided versus two-sided messages can be found in political campaigns. One-sided messages are more effective when audience members are less educated or have already made up their minds on the issue.

Should a political candidate talk only about his or her own strengths, or also about the opponent's weaknesses? In politics, negative campaigning is defined as trying to depict one's opponent as bad. Instead of focusing on what is good about one's own candidate, a negative advertisement talks mainly about the other side and tries to turn voters against

inverted (upside down) U-shaped relationship a relationship that looks like an upside down U when plotted

The Social Side of *Sex*

Scared Into Safe Sex?

The so-called sexual revolution of the 1960s produced a widespread increase in sexual activity in the 1970s. People began having sex at younger ages, more premarital and extramarital sex, and more sex partners. However, in the 1980s the AIDS epidemic burst into public consciousness. An incurable and fatal disease, AIDS made the free and easy sexual behavior of the 1970s seem dangerous and irresponsible.

Although some people did become more careful about their sex partners, it did not seem likely that entire nations would go back to the degree of sexual abstinence that had been the norm in the 1950s. (To be sure, attitudes about sex change more rapidly than realities, and many historians believe that both the sexual abstinence of the 1950s and the sexual freedom of the 1970s have been overstated.) Accordingly, there was a movement to influence people, perhaps especially young people, about the dangers of sexually transmitted infections. But what sort of influence would be most effective?

One approach used messages that would generate the maximum amount of fear, by emphasizing that one careless sex act can lead to a painful, grisly death. Many organizations thought this was the best way to go. However, they had not turned to social psychologists to learn whether inspiring fear is a good way to change attitudes and behaviors. Social psychologists had repeatedly found that strong fear-inspiring messages often backfire, failing to yield the desired changes in behavior.[81,82] People just "turn off" if you scare them too much.

In a series of studies on the specific effect of fear-inspiring anti-AIDS films, researchers reasoned that some people would find depictions of AIDS victims personally threatening and, as a result, would deny their fear and ignore the message.[83] Researchers showed emotionally powerful films about AIDS to sexually active college students. These films depicted young people discussing how they had gotten AIDS and how their lives had changed. The films were explicitly made to instill a sense of fear and vulnerability in young people so as to influence their sexual behavior toward more caution and restraint.

The films backfired. The sexually active young people who saw the films rejected the fear-inducing message. They rated their own risk of getting AIDS in the next five years as significantly lower than did a control sample of participants who had not seen any film. (Control participants in one study read pamphlets about AIDS prevention; in the other study they did not have any AIDS messages at all.) Thus, the film designed to make people worry more about their risk actually made them worry less.

Ironically, the films did succeed in increasing perceived risk among one group of people: Virgins (participants who had never had sex) who watched the same films rated their risk of AIDS as higher than virgins in the control conditions.

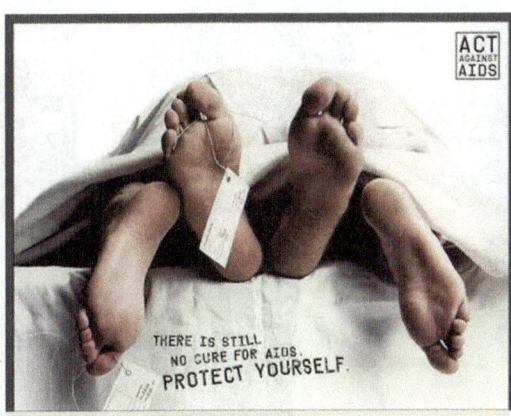

Strong fear appeals can often backfire.

At the end of the experimental session, the researchers offered all participants some informational pamphlets about AIDS to take home. These results confirmed the conclusion that some people were denying the reality of risk. Sexually active people who had watched the films took fewer pamphlets than control participants. Virgins who watched the film took more pamphlets than virgins in the control condition.

With sex, as with other behaviors, instilling fear is an unreliable mode of influence. People resist feeling bad, and they may resist the influence attempt that uses fear. Sexually active people do live with some risk of AIDS; in order to avoid facing that risk, they rejected the message and lowered their perception of danger. Only virgins, for whom AIDS is not a current danger, were able to attend to the fear-inducing message and respond with a plausibly increased awareness of risk.

him or her. Polls indicate that many voters disapprove of negative campaigning, and many candidates say they will refrain from criticizing their opponents. Nonetheless, one has only to watch television in the later stages of almost any major campaign to see negative advertisements.

Why are negative political ads so common? Do they really work? The results of social psychology research on negative campaigning have been mixed. In many cases, negative campaigning involves tradeoffs. One cost is that negative campaigning tends to produce lower evaluations of both candidates. In several laboratory studies, participants read campaign ads that were either positive or negative. When both sides used negative ads, the participants perceived both candidates more negatively.[84] Negative ads also made participants less likely to say they would vote, at least if voting was difficult (e.g., because of bad weather).[85] Negative

In the Clinton/Trump debates, both candidates focused on negative features of their opponent, as well as their own positive features.

campaigning may be most effective as a desperation measure by a candidate who is far behind in the polls and is willing to try anything to make the election closer. Even if a race is pretty close, candidates may turn negative in an attempt to get ahead.

Negative campaigning does not win very many votes, but perhaps that is not its goal—instead, the goal is to reduce the other side's votes. If voters for the other side stay home while one's own supporters are fanatical enough to vote despite an ugly, negative campaign, it might still work. Further research is needed before we can know whether the tradeoff yields more benefits than costs.

Overheard Messages

Other research has shown that if people think they are overhearing a message, they are more persuaded than if they see it as a sales pitch aimed directly at them.[86] People are more persuaded by messages that do not seem to be designed to influence them. Advertisers sometimes use this "overheard communicator trick" to persuade consumers.

Research has shown that advertisements with omitted conclusions are more persuasive than advertisements with conclusions.[87] Consumers appear to be more strongly influenced by the advertised message if they draw the conclusion on their own.

Because it is so easy to skip advertisements on television today, advertisers sometimes use product placement directly in television shows or movies. For example, the 2018 movie *Ocean's 8* contained several product placements (e.g., Cartier jewelry and watches, Budweiser beer, Beats headphones, Adidas shoes, Pines wheat grass tablets).[88] One reason product placements work so well is that people don't realize that advertisers are trying to influence them, so they let down their guard. Advertising executive David Ogilvy said, "A good advertisement is one which sells the product without drawing attention to itself."[89] Product placement occurs in most forms of media, including video games. For example, product placement is very prominent in racing video games. Players recall the products placed immediately after the game and also months later.[90] "Overheard" messages can be quite persuasive.

People from individualistic cultures are more influenced by person-focused ads. People from collectivistic cultures are more influenced by group-focused ads.

Repetition

Persuasive messages, such as advertisements, are often shown repeatedly. Does this help or hurt the message? Recall that the mere exposure effect is the tendency for novel stimuli to be liked more after the individual has been exposed to them repeatedly (see Chapter 7). Accumulated research confirms that repeated exposure to ads does influence memory for ads.[91] The initial attitude toward the product makes a difference.[92] If the person has a neutral or positive response to the message initially, then repeated exposure can make the message more persuasive; if the person hates the message right off the bat, hearing it again and again will only make things worse.

Even if audience members initially like the message, they don't want to hear it too many times, or advertisement wear-out might occur. **Advertisement wear-out** is defined as a "condition of inattention and possible irritation that occurs after an audience or target market has encountered a specific advertisement too many times."[93] A good example is Flo, the upbeat insurance expert (played by Stephanie Courtney) for the car insurance company Progressive, who debuted in 2008.[94] In 2009 the *Boston Herald* called her "the commercial break's new sweetheart" and said she was "attaining TV ad icon status."[95] Initially the ads were appealing, and people even dressed up as Flo for Halloween. After appearing in over 100 ads, however, Flo might

advertisement wear-out inattention and irritation that occurs after an audience has encountered the same advertisement too many times be losing her initial appeal. She now falls in the category of "love her or hate her."[96] Of course, it is possible that the advertising industry overstates the danger of wear-out, because the greater the perceived danger of wear-out, the faster companies buy new ad campaigns, and the more money advertisers make. Advertisers have to influence their clients as well as the people who watch their ads! One good way to prevent advertisement wear-out is to use **repetition with variation**—repeat the same information, but in a varied format.[97,98]

To Whom: The Audience

In studying persuasion, one cannot ignore the characteristics of audience members, such as how intelligent they are. Some people are easier to persuade than others, and certain persuasion techniques work better on some people than on others.

Intelligence

The studies conducted by Hovland and his colleagues showed that more intelligent soldiers learned more from the films, analyzed the ideas more thoroughly, and were more persuaded by two-sided arguments than by one-sided arguments.[99,100] Building on this research, Hovland's colleague William McGuire developed a model for persuasion that emphasized processes such as reception and yielding.[101] **Receptivity** refers to whether you "get" the message. (Did you pay attention to it? Do you understand it?) **Yielding** refers to whether you "accept" the message. (Did you believe it? Were you persuaded by it?) McGuire found that audience members with high self-esteem were receptive to persuasive messages because they had confidence in their initial positions. However, they did not yield to the message because they were satisfied with their existing attitudes. He also found that audience members with high intelligence were receptive to persuasive messages because they had longer attention spans and were better able to comprehend arguments. They too did not yield because they had confidence in their existing attitudes. Later work has largely confirmed McGuire's model.[102] Moderately intelligent people and people with moderate self-esteem levels are easiest to persuade. Thus, there is an inverted-U relationship between intelligence and persuasion and between self-esteem and persuasion.

Flo, the perky car insurance cashier, may be starting to lose her initial appeal after being featured in over 100 advertisements.

Need for Cognition

Most people are mentally lazy; they are cognitive misers (see Chapter 5). In contrast, people high in need for cognition like to think, analyze situations, and solve mental problems. **Need for cognition** is "the tendency for an individual to engage in and enjoy effortful thinking."[103] For example, people high in need for cognition may be more likely than others to watch the debates in a presidential election because they like to think about the issues and candidates.[104] Some sample items from the Need for Cognition scale are "I like to have the responsibility of handling a situation that requires a lot of thinking" and "I prefer my life to be filled with puzzles that I must solve." Research has shown that people high in need for cognition are more persuaded by strong arguments and are less persuaded by weak arguments than are people low in need for cognition.[105]

Concern about Public Image

Some people, such as those high on the traits of self-monitoring (see Chapter 11) and public self-consciousness (see Chapter 3), are very concerned about their public image (recall the discussion of self-presentation in Chapter 3). Persuasive messages that focus on name brands and stylish products appeal to such people. One study found that people high in public self-consciousness were even concerned about the brand

repetition with variation repeating the same information, but in a varied format

receptivity whether you "get" (pay attention to, understand) the message

yielding whether you "accept" (believe, and especially whether you change your attitude to agree with) the message

need for cognition a tendency to engage in and enjoy effortful thinking, analysis, and mental problem solving

TABLE 8.1 Major Findings of the Line of Persuasion Research Conducted by Hovland and His Colleagues

What Types of Sources Are Most Persuasive?	What Types of Messages Are Most Persuasive?	Who Is Receptive to Persuasive Messages?
Highly credible sources	Logical messages—mainly with educated, analytical people	People who are in a good mood
Likable sources	Moderately fear-inducing messages	People of average intelligence and self-esteem
Convert communicators	Two-sided messages	People concerned about their public image (high self-monitoring, high public self-consciousness)
Sources who argue against their own self-interest	Moderately discrepant messages	Very young or very old people
	Messages that are repeated (but may backfire). Overheard messages can be more effective because people "let their guard down."	

of peanut butter they ate.[106] Even though the jars contained the same peanut butter, individuals high in public self-consciousness gave the jar with the generic label very negative ratings and gave the jar with the name brand label very positive ratings. If publicly self-conscious people are concerned about the brand of peanut butter they buy, they are probably even more concerned about the clothes and shoes they wear and the cars they drive.

Cultural Differences

People from individualist cultures tend to place more emphasis on the individual, whereas people from collectivist cultures tend to place more emphasis on the group. One cross-cultural study tested what types of advertisements appealed to members of these two cultures.[107] One set of ads focused on the person (e.g., "Treat yourself to a breath-freshening experience"); the other set of advertisements focused on the group (e.g., "Share this breath-freshening experience"). Americans (from an individualistic culture) were more persuaded by the individualistic ads, whereas South Koreans (from a collectivistic culture) were more persuaded by the collectivist ads. Another study showed that Americans had more favorable attitudes toward products that offered "separateness," whereas Chinese had more favorable attitudes toward products that offered "togetherness."[108] The implication is that people are more persuaded by messages that match what their culture values. **TABLE 8.1.** summarizes the major results of persuasion studies conducted by Hovland, his colleagues, and other researchers.

Two Routes to Persuasion

One theme of this book has been the duplex mind: The mind has two systems, one deliberate and the other automatic. Influence attempts can operate using either system. That is, some forms of influence rely on appealing to conscious, rational, deliberate processing, whereas other forms rely on activating automatic responses. One appeals to enlightened self-interest; the other appeals to motivations or responses that may not be fully understood. Illicit or "tricky" forms of persuasion rely more on the latter. Both types of influence can be successful.

Social psychologists have avidly studied persuasion at least since the 1940s and have reported many findings, some of them seemingly contradictory or incompatible. For example, distraction sometimes increases and sometimes decreases persuasion. To resolve

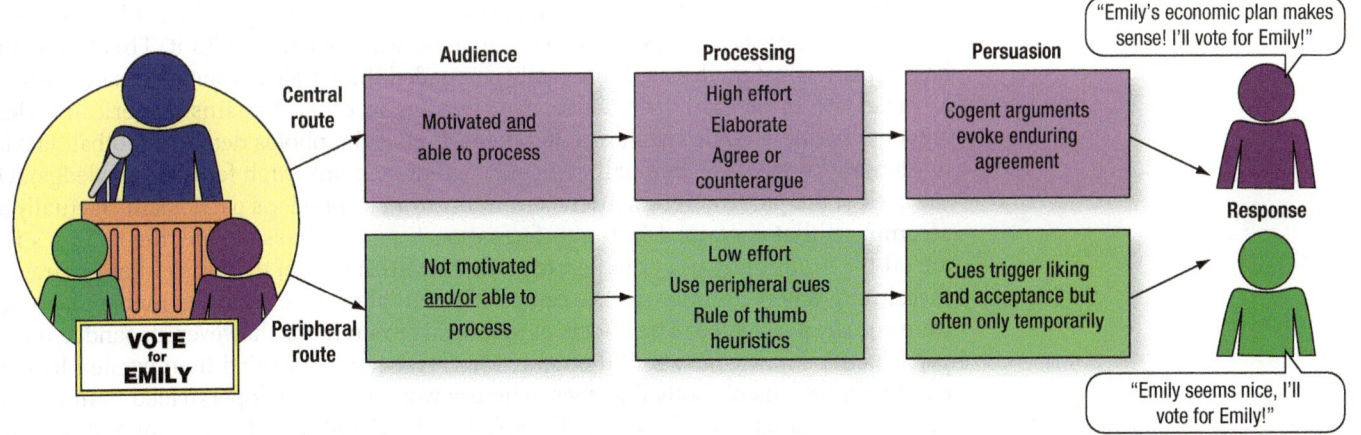

FIGURE 8.4
Elaboration likelihood model (ELM) of persuasion.

these problems, the **elaboration likelihood model**, or **ELM** for short[109] and the **heuristic/systematic model**[110] suggest two routes to persuasion. (The two theories are quite similar, and experts use either set of terms.) One route involves deliberate processing, whereas the other route involves automatic processing. These routes correspond with the duplex mind. We describe the ELM and refer to the heuristic/systematic model when the two models differ.

The route to persuasion that involves deliberate processing is called the **central route** (or **systematic processing** in the heuristic/systematic model); it is depicted on the top path in **FIGURE 8.4**. Persuasion that occurs along the central route involves careful and thoughtful consideration of the content of the persuasive message. The route that involves automatic processing is called the **peripheral route** (or **heuristic processing** in the heuristic/systematic model); it is depicted on the bottom path in Figure 8.4. Persuasion that occurs along the peripheral route involves the influence of some simple cue, such as how attractive the source is. We will start at the left side of the figure and work our way to the right side.

First, the person encounters a persuasive message (e.g., "Vote for Emily"). The first question is whether the person is motivated to process the message. This is influenced by two factors: personal relevance and need for cognition. **Personal relevance** refers to whether people expect the issue "to have significant consequences for their own lives."[111] The more personally relevant the issue, the more motivated people are to think about the persuasive message at a deep level. Some issues have personal relevance throughout our lives (e.g., the tax structure of the country we live in, the quality of water and air where we live); other issues have personal relevance for a certain period of time (e.g., raising college tuition and the price of textbooks when we are in college); still others have personal relevance only under very transient conditions (e.g., dishwasher ads are personally relevant only when a person is shopping for a dishwasher). The other factor that influences motivation to process the persuasive message is need for cognition. As mentioned previously, people high in need for cognition like to think and are therefore more likely than people low in need for cognition to think about the persuasive message at a deep level. Recent research shows that messages processed at a deep level are especially resistant to change.[112]

Just because people are motivated to process a message does not mean they will be able to process it. Two factors influence one's ability to process the message: distractions and knowledge. Distraction disrupts the ability to think about a persuasive message. Participants in one study were exposed to ads for a variety of consumer products.[113] Half the participants were distracted by having them count the number of random clicks on a tape recording. Weak arguments were more effective with distracted participants, probably because they were unable to think carefully about the message and discover its weaknesses. In contrast, strong arguments worked best on the central route—that is, when people were not distracted and could think consciously about the message.

elaboration likelihood model (ELM) theory that posits two routes to persuasion, via either conscious or automatic processing

heuristic/systematic model theory that posits two routes to persuasion, via either conscious or automatic processing

central route (systematic processing) the route to persuasion that involves careful and thoughtful consideration of the content of the message (conscious processing)

peripheral route (heuristic processing) the route to persuasion that involves some simple cue, such as attractiveness of the source (automatic processing)

personal relevance degree to which people expect an issue to have significant consequences for their own lives

Deliberate (central route) processing also depends on having sufficient knowledge to appreciate a message and possibly to understand what is wrong with it. This factor may help explain why females are more easily persuaded than males in some domains, whereas males are more easily persuaded than females in other domains. American college students in one study were shown 36 photos.[114] Half the photos depicted football tackles (high male knowledge), and half depicted current fashions (high female knowledge). On the back of the picture were written comments from a "previous participant" (actually an accomplice) that contained factual information (e.g., the dress is blue, the runner's feet are off the ground) or an evaluation (e.g., that's a great tackle) that was either accurate or inaccurate. When comments were completely factual or were accurate, men and women were equally persuaded. The effects of inaccurate evaluations, however, depended on the participant's knowledge about the topic. Men were less persuaded than women by inaccurate evaluations of football tackles, whereas women were less persuaded than men by inaccurate evaluations of fashion. Thus, both situational (i.e., distraction) and personal (i.e., knowledge) factors influence motivation.

If a person is motivated and able to process the message, the outcome of the processing that occurs depends on the quality of the arguments and the initial attitude. A persuasive message can be either strong or weak. When arguments are strong, thinking about them leads people to recognize their validity and to come up with further thoughts that support the message. In contrast, thinking about a message with weak arguments leads people to recognize its flaws and to come up with thoughts that argue against the message. Strong messages lead to strong positive attitude change, whereas weak messages can lead to strong negative attitude change.

Of course, the person's initial attitude sets some limits on how much the attitude can change. If the person has a very strong initial attitude, even a very strong opposing message may fail to change it. Additionally, people process information in a biased way: They are much more critical of messages that go against their views than of messages that agree with their views.[115] If people are not motivated or able to process a message, they may be persuaded by cues peripheral to the message. Some examples of peripheral cues are

- Experts know best.
- The more arguments, the better.
- Expensive products are good.
- Rare products are good.
- What is beautiful is good.

First-year college students read a message about senior comprehensive exams as part of an experiment.[116] Those in the high relevance group were told that the exams would be instituted at their university within two years. (*Yikes! I have to take the test to graduate!*) Students in the low relevance group were told that the exams would be instituted within 10 years. (*Who cares? I'll be gone by then!*) The source of the message was either an expert (a university dean) or a non-expert (a high school student). The source of the message had little or no impact on highly involved students. They had to take the exam regardless of the source of the message. Participants who were not highly involved, however, were more persuaded by the dean than by the high school student.

In summary, attitude change can take two routes. People who think about the message take the central route, whereas people who don't think about the message take the peripheral route. Attitude change that occurs via the peripheral route tends to be weak. It is temporary, is vulnerable to change, and does not predict future behavior very well. Persuasion by the central route produces much more durable and powerful attitude change, and it predicts behavior very well. But, of course, the central route is often the more difficult one to use because you actually have to have strong, effective arguments.

QUIZ YOURSELF

Persuasion

1. Pauline reads an article citing several reasons for having life insurance. When she notices that the article is really an insurance company advertisement, she decides that life insurance is a waste of money. When the topic of insurance comes up a few weeks later, Pauline thinks that life insurance is a good use of money. This change in attitude over time represents the _____ effect.
   - ⓐ primacy
   - ⓑ reactance
   - ⓒ recency
   - ⓓ sleeper

2. Maureen is very intelligent, Audrey is moderately intelligent, and Denise is not very intelligent. A two-sided persuasive message will probably be most effective on _____.
   - ⓐ Audrey
   - ⓑ Denise
   - ⓒ Maureen
   - ⓓ The three women should be equally affected.

3. While listening half-heartedly to a lecture, Jamaal hears his professor cite several reasons why playing violent video games increases aggression. Jamaal accepts these reasons solely because his professor has been correct before. In this example, Jamaal is using _____ processing.
   - ⓐ alpha
   - ⓑ central route
   - ⓒ omega
   - ⓓ peripheral route

4. Research shows that a person who is distracted from reading a weak message is more likely to be persuaded by that message. The elaboration likelihood model explains this by suggesting that _____.
   - ⓐ distractions take up most of the person's peripheral processing ability
   - ⓑ distractions serve as cues for rewards and punishments concerning being persuaded
   - ⓒ a distracting attitude makes the source more likable
   - ⓓ distractions prevent people from engaging in central route processing of information

answers: see pg 288

Resisting Social Influence Techniques

The Borg ("Cyborg") are among the evilest villains in space encountered by the *Star Trek* crew. They are a species that looks half human, half machine. When the Borg encounter a new species, they say, "This is the Borg Collective. Prepare to be assimilated. We will add your biological and technological distinctiveness to our own. You will adapt to service us. Resistance is futile." Sometimes the people who want to influence us seem like the Borg trying to assimilate us—resistance seems futile. In the case of persuasion, however, resistance need not be futile. You can take steps to increase your resistance to persuasive attempts to change your attitudes.

Attitude Inoculation

People brought up in a germ-free environment are highly vulnerable to diseases because their bodies have not built up antibodies to attack them. Medicine has helped to solve this problem by inoculating people: Exposing people to weakened doses of viruses (as in a flu shot) helps make their immune systems stronger. William McGuire and his colleagues transferred the concept of inoculation to the study of attitudes.[117,118,119,120] They

The Borg on *Star Trek* are a species that attempt to assimilate all other species (right). They live as a collective in a cube (left). When the Borg encounter a new species, they try to assimilate them. Sometimes the people who want to gain influence over us seem like The Borg. The good news is that you have defenses at your disposal to shield you against those who wield weapons of influence.

argued that cultural truisms (e.g., "Smoking is bad for your health") should be especially vulnerable to counterarguments because they exist in a kind of "germ-free" environment where their validity is never challenged. They argued that in order to immunize people against persuasion, it is good to expose them to some of the counterarguments against these cultural truisms and let them build up defenses against the counterarguments. Of course, being exposed to too many counterarguments, like too heavy a dose of the live virus, could have the opposite effect, reducing resistance rather than strengthening it.

Research has shown that inoculation works in the real world. For example, middle and high school students can be inoculated against peer pressure to smoke.[121,122,123] Researchers taught high school students to say "She is not really liberated if she is hooked on tobacco" in response to a cigarette ad that implied modern, liberated women smoke. The researchers also taught the students to role-play situations in which peers try to persuade them to smoke. After being called "chicken" for not taking a cigarette, they answer with statements like "I'd be a real chicken if I smoked just to impress you." In these studies, inoculated children are about half as likely as un-inoculated children to begin smoking.

Credit card debt is a growing problem worldwide, and college students aren't immune to it. Credit card companies often target college students because they are quick to use credit cards and slow to pay them back (because students don't have much money). A degree isn't the only thing students leave college with. Many also leave with a mountain of credit card debt. Fortunately, college students can be inoculated against persuasive attempts to acquire and use credit cards.[124] Students who were taught by researchers how to critically evaluate persuasive messages in credit card advertisements were able to resist these ads.[125] Inoculation also works against anti-vaccination attack messages.[125] Inoculation can even provide cross-protection for related but untreated attitudes, kind of like a "blanket of protection."[126] For example, practitioners using an inoculation message to target a specific pro-health attitude (e.g., benefits of regular exercise) could also help protect other related health attitudes (e.g., benefits of eating healthy food).

One theory of persuasion is based on the statement, "What doesn't kill me makes me stronger."[127] According to this theory, when people resist persuasion, they become more confident in their initial attitudes. When people think they have successfully resisted persuasion, they decide that their initial attitude is correct and therefore feel more certain about it. Such a pattern helps explain why inoculating people by exposing them to weak arguments can protect them against stronger arguments. Inoculation can help people counter-argue better.[128]

Forewarned Is Forearmed

Sneak attacks on attitudes can be devastating. If people know an attack is coming, however, they can prepare to defend themselves. High school students in a study were forewarned either 2 or 10 minutes in advance that they would hear a speech on "Why Teenagers Should Not Be Allowed to Drive" (not a very popular message, as you might guess).[129] The remaining students heard the same talk, but received no forewarning. The results showed that students who received no forewarning were persuaded the most, followed by those who received 2 minutes' warning, followed by those who received 10 minutes' warning. When people believe that someone is trying to persuade them (and take away their freedom of choice), they experience an unpleasant emotional response called psychological reactance, which motivates them to resist the persuasive attempt (see Chapter 4). Often people will do exactly the opposite of what they are being persuaded to do; this is called **negative attitude change** or a **boomerang effect**. The parents of Romeo and Juliet in Shakespeare's play found this out when their efforts to end the romance only drove the young lovebirds closer together.

College students are bombarded by ads from credit card companies. Fortunately, they can be inoculated against these ads.

Stockpile Resources

To deal with persuasion attempts, we should use all the resources at our disposal: physical, cognitive, and social. This includes getting plenty of sleep. Sleep deprivation is a very common tactic used on POWs (prisoners of war) during times of war. Although college students are not POWs, they are often sleep deprived.[130] We all function much better after a good night's sleep. People may be more susceptible to persuasion tactics when they are tired.[131] When we hear someone make a statement, we immediately accept the statement as being true, regardless of whether it is actually true. It is only with mental effort that we recognize the statement to be false and reject it. All of this happens in a fraction of a second. People usually have enough cognitive energy and motivation to mentally reject statements that sound false, but when people are tired, their mental energy levels drop, and they become more susceptible to false statements.

negative attitude change (boomerang effect) doing exactly the opposite of what one is being persuaded to do

QUIZ YOURSELF
Resisting Social Influence Techniques

1. When I am driving my car and someone tailgates me to make me go faster, I slow down. This is an example of _____.
   - ⓐ cognitive dissonance
   - ⓑ door-in-the-face
   - ⓒ low-balling
   - ⓓ psychological reactance

2. Knowing in advance that we are a target of a persuasive message is called _____.
   - ⓐ cognitive dissonance
   - ⓑ elaboration
   - ⓒ forewarning
   - ⓓ psychological reactance

3. The theory that exposure to weak versions of a persuasive message increases later resistance to that message is called _____.
   - ⓐ attitude inoculation
   - ⓑ negative attitude change
   - ⓒ psychological reactance
   - ⓓ the sleeper effect

4. Cialdini says that we should accept initial favors or concessions in good faith but be ready to define them as tricks if they prove to be tricks. This defense is most effective for techniques based on the _____ principle.
   - ⓐ capturing and disrupting attention
   - ⓑ commitment and consistency
   - ⓒ reciprocation
   - ⓓ scarcity

answers: see pg 288

What Makes Us Human

Putting the Cultural Animal in Perspective

All social animals rely on others for some of what they want and need, so they face the same basic problems of needing to influence others, at least sometimes. The need to exert social influence is not limited to human beings. But the need may be more extensive in humans than in other animals, given how much human activity depends on working together with others and participating in flexible social systems. Moreover, some methods of influence, and of resisting influence, are distinctly human.

The duplex mind is rather distinctively human, so only humans have two routes to persuasion. In particular, human beings have a special capacity for cognitive reasoning and thinking, so the central, or systematic, route to persuasion works better with humans than with any other animal. Likewise, logical reasoning and humor are only useful influence techniques with humans because only humans have logic and humor.

The extent to which people think about what others tell them, thereby elaborating on and embellishing a simple persuasive message, also reflects the extensive makeup of the human self. As we saw, getting people to label themselves as being a certain kind of person is an effective way to change their behavior. People have elaborate self-concepts that can be swayed in this way. With most other animals, the scope for influence by labeling the self-concept would be much smaller.

As cultural beings, humans are characterized by a social life filled with elaborate norms and implicit rules. Many persuasion techniques make use of these norms and rules. Humans everywhere recognize the norm of reciprocity, based on an abstract concept of fairness, and they accept obligations to reciprocate what is done for them. As we have seen, several influence techniques capitalize on norms of fairness and reciprocity. Although all human groups seem to have reciprocity norms, there may be important cultural differences in what needs to be reciprocated and what counts as reciprocation.

Another special dimension of the complexity of human social life is our ability to anticipate and care about how others perceive us, and to alter our behavior to make an impression. The distinction between private acceptance and public compliance is crucial to understanding human influence, but it is mostly irrelevant to understanding influence among other animals. Humans have a much more elaborate inner self and a more advanced understanding of the difference between inner sentiments and overt, expressive acts than other creatures. In plainer terms, only humans respond to social pressure by saying things they don't mean, or by going along with the crowd while keeping doubts to themselves.

The moral rules that are common to human cultures also capitalize on the human capacity for feeling guilty over violations of interpersonal norms, and persuaders can play on people's guilt to influence them. The door-in-the-face and foot-in-the-door techniques, for example, may well operate by making the person start to feel guilty.

Although we have focused on special opportunities to influence people, there is another side: People are uniquely able to resist influence and persuasion. Most of the means of resisting influence involve use of conscious control over responses (wait until your emotional reaction has subsided before making a decision), shifting among perspectives (consider an alternative view), and conscious reasoning (evaluate the message logically). These capacities are pretty much absent outside of our species. People, therefore, have special powers and weapons that enable them to avoid being swayed.

CHAPTER 8 SUMMARY

Two Types of Social Influence

- Normative influence involves going along with the crowd in order to be liked and accepted.
- People from collectivist countries are more likely to be influenced by group norms than are people from individualist countries.
- Conformity increases as group size increases (up to a point, then it levels off).
- People will conform to a group in which everyone agrees, but if group members disagree about even the smallest point, then people become willing to stand up for what they believe and go against the majority.
- People who deviate from a group are often rejected by the group.
- Group norms are the beliefs or behaviors a group of people accepts as normal.
- Informational influence involves going along with the crowd because you think the crowd knows more than you do, such as when
  - The situation is ambiguous, so people do not know how to behave.
  - There is a crisis, and people don't have time to think for themselves.

Techniques of Social Influence

- The foot-in-the-door technique gets someone to comply with a large request by first making a small request.
- The low-ball technique involves shifting from a smaller request to a larger request after the person has committed to the small request.

- The bait-and-switch technique involves making a great offer and then switching to a less desirable offer.
- The labeling technique involves assigning a label to an individual and then requesting a favor that is consistent with that label.
- The legitimization-of-paltry-favors technique involves asking for a very small contribution in order to get a larger contribution.
- The door-in-the-face technique involves making an inflated request (that will most likely be rejected) and then retreating to a smaller request. (It only works if the first request is not too extreme and if the same person makes both requests.)
- The that's-not-all technique begins with an inflated request that is quickly followed by a discount or bonus.
- According to the scarcity principle, rare opportunities are more valuable than plentiful opportunities.
- With the limited-number technique, the customer is told that items exist in a limited supply.
- With the fast-approaching-deadline technique, the customer is told that items can only be obtained for a limited time.
- When our personal freedom is threatened, we experience an unpleasant emotional response called psychological reactance, which motivates us to do what is forbidden.
- The pique technique captures the target's attention by making the request novel to increase the chances of compliance with the persuasive request.
- In the disrupt-then-reframe technique, a non sequitur or unexpected element is introduced to provide a momentary disruption that interrupts critical thinking and increases the chances of compliance with the persuasive request.

Persuasion

- Persuasion is an attempt to change a person's attitude.
- According to the sleeper effect, over time people separate the message from the messenger.
- Two characteristics can influence source credibility:
  - Expertise—how much the source knows.
  - Trustworthiness—how honest the source is.
- Fast talkers are assumed to be more credible and intelligent than slow talkers (as long as the speech is not too fast to be comprehended).
- Powerful speakers are believed to be credible.
- Powerless speech includes compound requests and disclaimers.
- Convert communicators make up for their deficits in trustworthiness by arguing against their past transgressions.
  - They can be very persuasive.
- They are likable because they are similar to audience members.
- They show a sense of mastery because they were able to overcome their undesirable behavior.
- Similarity and physical attractiveness increase liking and therefore increase persuasion.
- People who are in a good mood are more receptive to persuasive messages.
- Instilling fear is an unreliable mode of influence; moderate fear appeals are more persuasive than high or low fear appeals.
- One-sided persuasive messages work best when the audience is not able to process the message thoroughly; two-sided messages work best when the audience can process the message thoroughly.
- Message discrepancy is the difference between the initial attitude of the audience and the content of the speaker's message.
- Repetition polarizes initial responses to the persuasive message, although advertising wear-out can occur when an ad is repeated too many times.
- Overheard messages are more persuasive than direct attempts to change attitudes.
- If the message is weak, distraction makes the message more effective, but if the message is strong, then distraction makes the message less effective.
- Audience members with moderate levels of self-esteem and intelligence are most affected by persuasive messages.
- Need for cognition is the tendency for an individual to engage in and enjoy effortful thinking.
- People high in need for cognition are more persuaded by strong arguments and are less persuaded by weak arguments than are people low in need for cognition.
- The elaboration likelihood model (ELM) and the heuristic/systematic model are similar. They describe two routes to persuasion: one involving conscious processing and one involving automatic processing.
- The route that involves conscious processing is called the central route or systematic processing. The route that involves automatic processing is called the peripheral route or heuristic processing.
- Personal relevance is the degree to which people expect an issue to have significant consequences for their own lives.
- Two factors influence our ability to process a message: whether we are free from distractions and whether we have sufficient knowledge.
- Peripheral cues such as source expertise have no effect on people who are motivated to process a persuasive message, but they can have an effect on people who are not motivated to process the message.

Resisting Social Influence Techniques

- In order to immunize people against persuasion, it is good to expose them to some of the counterarguments and let them build up defenses against the counterarguments.
- When people resist persuasion, they become more confident in their initial attitudes.

- If people are forewarned that a persuasive message is coming, they are less persuaded by it.
- The boomerang effect (negative attitude change) results from psychological reactance to the persuasive attempt; the result is an attitude opposite to the persuasive message.

What Makes Us Human? Putting the Cultural Animal in Perspective

- The duplex mind is only found in humans, so only humans have two routes to persuasion.
- Inner traits and processes play a much bigger role in human influence than in influence in nonhuman animals.
- Many persuasion techniques rely on norms and implicit rules. Humans have far more elaborate norms and implicit rules than nonhuman animals.
- Probably only humans feel guilty if they break norms and rules.
- The distinction between private acceptance and public compliance plays a much bigger role in human influence than in influence in nonhuman animals.
- Humor can be a factor in persuasion, but nonhuman animals probably do not have a sense of humor.
- Only humans appear able to resist influence and persuasion.

key terms

advertisement wear-out 278
autokinetic effect 262
bait-and-switch 266
central route (systematic processing) 281
convert communicators 274
disrupt-then-reframe technique 271
door-in-the-face technique 268
elaboration likelihood model (ELM) 281
expertise 273
fast-approaching-deadline technique 270
foot-in-the-door technique 265
group norms 262
halo effect 275
heuristic/systematic model 281
informational influence 263
inverted U-shaped relationship 276
labeling technique 266
legitimization-of-paltry-favors technique 267
limited-number technique 270
low-ball technique 265
need for cognition 279
negative attitude change (boomerang effect) 285
normative influence 261
peripheral route (heuristic processing) 281
personal relevance 281
persuasion 272
pique technique 271
pluralistic ignorance 263
private acceptance 263
public compliance 263
receptivity 278
repetition with variation 278
sleeper effect 273
source 273
that's-not-all technique 268
trustworthiness 273
yielding 278

quiz yourself ANSWERS

1. Two Types of Social Influence p. 264
    answers: 1.b 2.c 3.d 4.a
2. Techniques of Social Influence p. 272
    answers: 1.b 2.b 3.c 4.d
3. Persuasion p. 283
    answers: 1.d 2.c 3.d 4.d
4. Resisting Social Influence Techniques p. 285
    answers: 1.d 2.c 3.a 4.c

PROSOCIAL BEHAVIOR
Doing What's Best for Others

9

LEARNING OBJECTIVES

1. Explain how reciprocity, social responsibility, equity, and equality create different motivations to help others.

2. Compare and contrast the different kinds of prosocial behaviors, such as cooperation, forgiveness, obedience, conformity and trust.

3. Analyze the different explanations and motives for helping.

4. Describe who is most likely to help and who is most likely to receive help.

5. Elucidate the five steps of bystander intervention.

6. Discuss the ways to increase helping.

TRADEOFFS
The Prisoner's Dilemma
304

MONEY MATTERS
Money, Prosocial Behavior, and Self-Sufficiency
306

FOOD FOR THOUGHT
Restaurants, Rules, and the Bad Taste of Nonconformity
311

THE SOCIAL SIDE OF SEX
Helping, Sex, and Friends
319

WHAT MAKES US HUMAN
Putting the Cultural Animal in Perspective
327

291

iStock.com/Halfpoint

In the 1999 novel by Catherine Ryan Hyde *Pay It Forward*, a 12-year-old boy does favors for three individuals and, when asked how they can repay him, tells them to "pay it forward" by doing favors for three others, who then are to be instructed to pay it forward to three more recipients. The book has been translated into at least 23 different languages, and was made into a movie in 2000. Many people have been inspired by the novel and movie.

For example, a 26-year-old named Dean Young from California decided to give a homeless man leftover homemade chocolate chip cookies from the restaurant he worked at, rather than throwing them away. Dean learned that when the man came back from serving overseas in the military, he discovered that his wife had sold everything he owned, emptied their joint bank account, and moved to Mexico with another man. He had no family either. After giving the man cookies for about a month, Dean took the man to a motel, gave him a small bag of toiletries (e.g., razor, toothbrush, scissors), and told him to get cleaned up and get a good sleep because they were going to look for jobs together the next day. When Dean dropped the man off at the motel he had "long scraggly beard and mane of mangy hair and so much dirt crusted on his skin that it made him look 80!" When he returned the next day, Dean was shocked to see how good the 25-year-old man looked. Dean bought the man a new suit and found him a good job working with computers, a skill the man possessed. The only problem was the job was in downtown Los Angeles. Dean said, "I'll pay your motel, meals, and get you passes for the Green Line to get to and from work until you can support yourself again." When he offered to pay the money back, Dean replied, "Tell you what, when you get to the point where you're back on your feet and financially secure enough to pay me back for what I've done for you, turn and go the opposite direction away from where I am. Keep going until you come across someone that can benefit from your kindness, your charity, your friendship and help them the way I helped you or anyway they need you to help them." A few years later, Dean saw the man at the restaurant where he worked. The man vigorously shook Dean's hand and told him how he "paid it forward." The former homeless man met an inner-city boy from a broken home. He became a big brother/father figure for the boy. The boy loved baseball. The man helped the boy and his friends form a baseball team, bought them uniforms and equipment, and even became their coach. He also took them to several Dodger games. Someday that inner-city boy might also "pay it forward" by helping someone else in need.

Social scientists call this "pay it forward" concept "upstream reciprocity," defined as passing benefits on to third parties instead of returning benefits to one's benefactors.[1] Many cities, states, provinces, and territories have issued *Pay it Forward* proclamations. The "pay it forward" concept has become a worldwide movement to send "ripples of kindness" around the world. In 2014, people from 70 countries participated in Pay It Forward Day. The response was so overwhelming that it has continued as an annual event since then, with now over 80 countries participating. ●

You do not know me but I saw that you needed some tires for your truck and I wanted to do something nice for a stranger because one day a stranger did the same for me. The receipt is in the envelope and all you have to do is go by Warehouse Tire on 3rd Street and ask for Steven Hodges and they will be put them on for free. All I ask is that one day you do something nice for a complete stranger.

The concept of "pay it forward"—doing a favor for someone and asking that person to do the same in the future—can promote prosocial behavior. For example, one person saw that tires on a truck were badly worn and bought new tires for the person, and left a note asking that the person do something nice for someone else.

Is Helping Contagious?

Sometimes social psychologists seem to focus on the negative things people do. The famous American historian Howard Zinn said:

> To be hopeful in bad times is not just foolishly romantic. It is based on the fact that human history is a history not only of cruelty, but also of compassion,

Fellow passengers saved a man by collectively lifting a train so he could get his leg out of the gap between the train and the platform.

sacrifice, courage, and kindness. What we choose to emphasize in this complex history will determine our lives. If we see only the worst, it destroys our capacity to do something. If we remember those times and places—and there are so many—where people have behaved magnificently, this gives us the energy to act, and at least the possibility of sending this spinning top of a world in a different direction. And if we do act, in however small a way, we don't have to wait for some grand utopian future. The future is an infinite succession of presents, and to live now as we think human beings should live, in defiance of all that is bad around us, is itself a marvelous victory.

As Zinn noted, people can and do behave magnificently. For example, a man was boarding a train in Perth, Australia, when he slipped and trapped his leg in the gap between the train and the platform. If the train left, the man might lose his leg or his life. Hundreds of fellow passengers pushed on the train and literally lifted it up so the man could get his leg out.[2]

The dying wish of Aaron Collins—a young man from Kentucky—was to leave an "awesome" tip of at least $500 to a waiter or waitress. Aaron's brother Seth and their mother Tina gave a $500 tip to a waitress at a pizza joint. They posted a video of it on a blog called "Aaron's Wish." Many strangers were moved by the video and began donating money to a foundation set up in Aaron's name (http://aaroncollins.org). So far, over 100 waiters or waitresses have received $500 tips in many states throughout the United States. Research has even shown that cooperative behavior can be contagious, passing from person to person to person.[3]

What Is Prosocial Behavior?

Prosocial behavior is defined as doing something that is good for other people or for society as a whole. Prosocial behavior includes behavior that respects others or allows society to operate. Culture is a whole that is more than the sum of its parts, but only if people

prosocial behavior doing something that is good for other people or for society as a whole cooperate and follow the rules will culture be able to yield its benefits. In a nutshell, prosocial behavior builds relationships. It is the opposite of antisocial behavior, which means doing something bad for others or for society. Antisocial behavior usually destroys relationships (see Chapter 10).

Social psychologists have had a peculiar relationship with prosocial behavior. Most social psychology textbooks feature helping as the main prosocial behavior while ignoring most other prosocial behaviors. When they discuss conformity, obedience, and other forms of following the rules, textbooks have often been sharply critical, suggesting that these are bad things. It is true that obedience and conformity can be bad—mindless obedience to a demented leader such as Hitler can produce all sorts of terrible consequences. For the most part, however, obedience and conformity are good things. Society would collapse if people didn't follow most of the rules most of the time. For example, consider what would happen if people decided to ignore traffic rules, such as "Stop," "Wrong Way," "Yield," and "Speed Limit" signs. Traffic accidents and fatalities would increase sharply! Likewise, imagine what would happen if most people just took things from stores without paying, or ignored the tax laws, or if restaurant employees did not wash their hands after using the bathroom, or if grocery stores disobeyed health regulations and sold rotten food.

Obeying the rules, conforming to socially accepted standards of proper behavior, and cooperating with others are important forms of prosocial behavior. Helping—which most social psychology textbooks treat as the quintessential form of prosocial behavior—is actually something of an "extra" or a luxury. We admire the spirit of "paying it forward," but society could function just fine if nobody did that. More broadly, society and culture can still bring immense benefits if people do not perform altruistic, self-sacrificing acts of helping. If no one obeys the rules, however, society will fall apart, and chaos will reign. Following rules is essential. Helping is less essential, though certainly helping makes the world a much nicer place, and some forms of helping (such as what parents do for their small children) are probably vital for the survival of the species.

We rely on other people to follow their own self-interest while obeying the rules. They sell us their food in exchange for our money, which is good for them and for us. No helping or self-sacrifice on their part is necessary, but it is vital that they obey the rules by not selling us spoiled meat or committing other fraudulent acts.

Imagine two societies, one in which people are happy and healthy, and another in which people are fearful, poor, and desperate. What might account for the difference? The happy society is likely full of people who cooperate with each other, respect each other, follow the rules, and contribute to the general welfare. The unhappy society is likely full of people who break the rules; its social life is marked by crime, corruption, distrust, betrayal, and wide-ranging general insecurity.

A society in which people respect and follow the rules is said to have an effective **rule of law**. If there are no laws, or if laws exist but are widely ignored and disobeyed, the rule of law is said to be lacking. The rule of law may occasionally annoy us, such as when you get a speeding ticket, but in reality, the rule of law is usually a huge boost to the quality of life. If you lived in a society where the rule of law had broken down, or had not yet appeared, you would find life hard and dangerous. Indeed, researchers have found a positive correlation between general happiness and rule of law, across many societies.[4]

Fairness and justice are also important factors in predicting prosocial behavior. If employees perceive the company they work for to be fair and just, they are more likely to be good "company citizens."[5] For example, they are more likely to voluntarily help others in the workplace and more likely to promote the excellence of their employer, without any promise of reward for these behaviors. The crucial point is that people behave better when they think the rules are fair.

The presence of others can stimulate prosocial behavior, such as when someone acts more properly because other people are watching. Dogs will stay off the furniture and out of the trash when their owners are present, but they blithely break those rules when alone. Humans may have more of a conscience, but they also still respond to the presence or absence of others. Public circumstances generally promote prosocial behavior, as shown by an interesting experiment. Participants[6] sat alone in a room and followed

rule of law when members of a society (including its most powerful leaders) respect and follow its rules

Others will see how much you contribute.

tape-recorded instructions. Half believed that they were being observed via a one-way mirror (public condition), whereas others believed that no one was watching (private condition). At the end of the experiment, the tape-recorded instructions invited the participant to make a donation by leaving some change in the jar on the table. The results showed that donations were seven times higher in the public condition than in the private condition. Apparently, one important reason for generous helping is to make (or sustain) a good impression on those who are watching.

One purpose of prosocial behavior, especially at cost to self, is to get oneself accepted into the group, so doing prosocial things without recognition is less beneficial. Self-interest dictates acting prosocially if it helps one belong to the group. That is probably why prosocial behavior increases when others are watching. Other studies have shown that favors increase compliance in both private and public settings, but compliance is greater in public settings.[7]

It may seem cynical to say that people's prosocial actions are motivated by wanting to make a good impression, but one can also see this pattern in a positive light. One theme of this book has been that people travel a long road to social acceptance. People do many things to get others to like them, and prosocial behavior is no exception.

Born to Reciprocate

Reciprocity is defined as the obligation to return in kind what another has done for us. Folk wisdom recognizes reciprocity with such sayings as "You scratch my back, and I'll scratch yours." Reciprocity norms are found in all cultures in the world.[8] If I do something for you, and you don't do anything back for me, I'm likely to be upset or offended, and next time around I may not do something for you. If you do something for me, and I don't reciprocate, I'm likely to feel guilty about it.

The reciprocity norm is so powerful that it even applies to situations in which you do not ask for the favor. Phil Kunz, a sociology professor at Brigham Young University in Provo, Utah, sent 578 Christmas cards to a sample of complete strangers living in Chicago, Illinois.[9] When somebody sends you a card, you feel obligated to send one back. Does this apply even to complete strangers? Apparently so, because Dr. Kunz received a total of 117 cards from people who had no idea who he was. He also received several

reciprocity the obligation to return in kind what another has done for us unexpected long-distance telephone calls from people who had received one of his Christmas cards. Although most of the cards just contained signatures, a significant number of them contained handwritten notes, long letters, and pictures of family and pets. Only 6 of the 117 people who sent Kunz cards said they couldn't remember him.

Most often people consider reciprocity to be direct—you help someone who may help you later. However, scientists have argued that some reciprocity may be indirect—help someone and receive help from someone else, even strangers who know you only through reputation.[10] Helping someone or refusing to help has an impact on one's reputation within the group. We all know people who are consistently helpful, and others who are not.

Does reciprocity apply to seeking help as well as giving help? Often you might need or want help, but you might not always accept help and certainly might not always seek it out. People's willingness to request or accept help often depends on whether they think they will be able to pay it back (i.e., reciprocity). If they don't think they can pay the helper back, they are less willing to let someone help them.[11] This is especially a problem among the elderly because their declining health and income are barriers to reciprocating.[12] As a result, elderly people may refuse to ask for help even when they need it, simply because they believe they will not be able to pay it back.

When someone helps you, you probably feel grateful for the assistance. **Gratitude** is defined as a positive emotion that results from the perception that one has benefited from the costly, intentional, voluntary action of another person.[13]

People often have an acute sense of fairness when they are on the receiving end of someone else's generosity or benevolence, and they prefer to accept help when they think they can pay the person back. We discuss this sense of fairness in the next section.

Born to Be Fair

The central theme of this book is that human beings are cultural animals, that the impulse to belong to culture is in our genes. Fairness is a cultural norm. **Norms** are standards established by society to tell its members what types of behavior are typical or expected. Norms that promote fairness can have an important influence on whether people contribute to the common good.[14] Two such norms are equity and equality. **Equity** means that each person receives benefits in proportion to what he or she has contributed (e.g., the person who does the most work gets the highest pay). **Equality** means that everyone gets the same amount. Both kinds of fairness are used and understood much more widely by humans than by any other animal.

According to some evolutionary theories, an individual's ability to reproduce depends largely on their position within the social group.[15] In order to maintain fitness-enhancing relationships, the individual must continually invest time, energy, and resources in building good relationships with others in the social group. To take without giving something back runs the risk that others might resent you and might ultimately reject or exclude you from the group. After all, few groups can afford to have lots of members (other than babies, perhaps) who take and take without contributing anything. It will be hard to pass on your genes to the next generation when the people you want to mate with shun you.

People are designed by nature (so to speak) to belong to a system based on fairness and social exchange. As one sign of the importance of fairness to human nature, the feeling that one has no value to others—that you are a taker rather than a giver—is a major cause of depression.[16] To be sure, there are plenty of obnoxious people who take more than they give, but most of them don't see themselves that way. People who do see themselves as taking more than they give may become depressed. To avoid depression, people may seek to contribute their fair share.

Some suicides may reflect the same concern with being fair and reciprocal. We saw in Chapter 4 that human beings differ from most other animals in that they commit suicide.

gratitude a positive emotion that results from the perception that one has benefited from the costly, intentional, voluntary action of another person

norms standards established by society to tell its members what types of behavior are typical or expected

equity the idea that each person receives benefits in proportion to what he or she contributes

equality the idea that everyone gets the same amount, regardless of what he or she contributes

One reason some people commit suicide is that they think they are a burden on other people—that others do things for them that they cannot reciprocate, so the others would be better off if they were dead.[17,18] Of course, people are not better off when someone commits suicide. Suicide has numerous negative effects on those left behind. Not only do the survivors miss the dead person, they may even blame themselves for the suicide.

The concern with fairness makes people feel bad when they don't contribute their fair share, but it can also affect people who think that their good performance makes others feel bad. When we outperform others, we may have mixed emotions. On the one hand, we may feel a sense of pride and pleasure because we have surpassed the competition. On the other hand, we may feel fear and anxiety because those we have outperformed might reject us or retaliate. Interpersonal concern about the consequences of outperforming others has been called **sensitivity about being the target of a threatening upward comparison**.[19] Outperformers often become distressed when they believe that others are envious that they did not perform as well. In reality, however, losers have more to worry about than winners. Research shows that participants are more aggressive against someone they beat (i.e., losers) than against someone who beat them (i.e., winners).[20]

Is reciprocity unique to humans? More simply, do animals understand the concept "fairness"? A study of monkeys provides a fascinating answer.[21] The researchers trained monkeys to fetch rocks. Each monkey was rewarded with a slice of cucumber for each rock it fetched. The monkeys could see each other getting these rewards, and they soon learned to keep fetching rocks to get cucumber slices. Then, however, the researchers randomly gave some monkeys a grape instead of a cucumber slice for their rocks. To a monkey, a grape is a much better treat than a slice of cucumber. The monkeys who got the grapes were very happy about this. The other monkeys were mad, however. They acted as if it were unfair that they only got the cucumber slice for the same act that earned other monkeys a grape. The ones who didn't get the grapes protested, such as by refusing to fetch more rocks ("going on strike") or by angrily flinging the cucumber slice away. This study attracted international media attention, with the implication being that monkeys understand fairness and object to unfairness.

But do they really? Perhaps the study was overinterpreted. Yes, a monkey is smart enough to protest when it is treated unfairly. If, however, unfairness per se is the problem, then the monkeys who received the grapes should have protested too. But they didn't. Researchers who study fairness distinguish between two kinds of unfairness, namely being **underbenefited** (getting less than you deserve) and being **overbenefited** (getting more than you deserve). Monkeys and several other animals seem to have an acute sense of when they are underbenefited. However, only humans seem to worry about being overbenefited. A full-blown sense of fairness, one that encompasses both aspects, is found only among humans. For people to be truly fair, they must object to being overbenefited as well as to being underbenefited (even if the latter is stronger).

People (unlike other animals) do feel guilty when they are overbenefited. In lab studies, people feel guilty if they receive a larger reward than others for performing the same amount or same quality of work.[22] Getting less than your fair share provokes anger and resentment, but getting more than your fair share produces guilt.[23] (See Chapter 6 for a discussion of anger and guilt.)

In fact, some researchers have questioned whether the monkeys genuinely thought they were unfairly underbenefited.[24] The monkeys' anger at not getting a grape might just be a frustration reaction, because they began to expect they would get a grape and then did not get one. Put another way, it wasn't the unfairness implicit in seeing another monkey getting something while they did not get the same—it was simply a matter of expecting something good and then being thwarted and frustrated.

People who harm others (perhaps without meaning to do so) prefer to do something nice for the person they harm, and they prefer the nice act to exactly match the harm they did, so that fairness and equity are restored.[25] They act as if the harm they did creates a debt to that person, and they desire to "pay it back" so as to get the relationship back on an even, fair footing.

Are human children born with an understanding of reciprocity and fairness? Babies cannot understand such things, but children seem to develop it rather early.

> "...it's better in fact to be guilty of manslaughter than of fraud about what is fair and just."
> — Plato, *The Republic and Other Works*

sensitivity about being the target of a threatening upward comparison interpersonal concern about the consequences of outperforming others

underbenefited getting less than you deserve

overbenefited getting more than you deserve

However, some important differences have emerged from research.[26] It appears that children between ages of 4 and 8 get the idea of paying back someone who has done something mean to them. Paying back positive things comes more slowly. Younger children notice when someone does something good for them, and it makes them more likely to do something nice themselves—but not necessarily for the same person who was nice to them. That is, researchers distinguished between direct reciprocity (paying back the same person) and generalized reciprocity (performing a similar act toward just anyone). With aggressive or antisocial acts, direct reciprocity appears early in child development: Being the target of unkind actions makes children do unkind things, but only toward the same person who was unkind to them. Being the target of prosocial actions makes them do prosocial things, but aimed at anyone. It is only later in child development that children understand the value of returning a favor specifically to the person who benefited them. This chapter began with the "pay it forward" story, and it seems children start off with something like a mindset to "pay it forward" when it comes to prosocial action. Quite possibly, receiving a good deed simply prompts them to do a good deed, regardless of who is involved. But as the next chapter will show, with antisocial and aggressive actions, "pay it back" is what comes first and naturally to small children.

QUIZ YOURSELF

What Is Prosocial Behavior?

1. Henrietta helped Maurille when her first child was born. When Henrietta has her first child, Maurille thinks she ought to help Henrietta. This type of helping illustrates the norm of _____.
   - (a) equity
   - (b) reciprocity
   - (c) social justice
   - (d) social responsibility

2. Albert thinks that because he has more job experience than others on his shift, he should make more money than they do. This illustrates the norm of _____.
   - (a) equality
   - (b) equity
   - (c) reciprocity
   - (d) social responsibility

3. At the local soup kitchen, volunteers give everyone one bowl of soup regardless of how much money they have or how hungry they are. This type of helping illustrates the norm of _____.
   - (a) equality
   - (b) equity
   - (c) reciprocity
   - (d) social responsibility

4. Feeling guilty about receiving more than one's fair share is found in _____.
   - (a) animals other than humans
   - (b) only humans
   - (c) both (a) and (b)
   - (d) neither (a) nor (b)

answers: see pg 329

Morality

This chapter is about prosocial behavior. One way to think of behavior is that it encompasses actions that are morally good. Thus, understanding morality is one key to understanding prosocial behavior. We have said that people seem to be born to reciprocate and to be fair. That suggests that they are born with a readiness to learn moral rules and act on them.

All known human societies have morals, which are a set of rules about what actions are right versus wrong. Moral rules tell people what they should do. In general, moral rules encourage people to do what is best for the social group, which often requires restraining selfish and other antisocial impulses. This sheds light on a key theme of this chapter, which is that in the long run everyone is better off when people cooperate—but people are often tempted to be selfish instead, and so it is necessary to encourage people to cooperate, such as by having and enforcing rules.

Moral issues arise frequently in everyday life. When researchers contacted people at randomly chosen moments during the day, one out of every three or four responses indicated that the person had experienced a moral or immoral action (by self or others, including just witnessing) within the past hour.[27] Having people do immoral things to you reduces your happiness significantly—and, conversely, happiness goes up when people do morally good things to you. Performing morally good actions is thus a way that people make each other feel better. It also increases one's sense of purpose.

One might assume that performing immoral actions would be a strong cause of unhappiness, not least because people would feel guilty and regretful. While it is true that performing immoral actions does tend to reduce levels of happiness, the effect is not strong or consistent. Inconsistency arises in part from the surprising fact that many people seem to get pleasure from doing immoral things—a "cheater's high," as described by one set of researchers.[28] They showed that people expect that dishonest and immoral behavior will make them feel bad, but contrary to their expectations, many of them feel a surge of positive emotion. This seems often to be based on a feeling of self-satisfaction, even perhaps a thrill, based on having cheated and gotten away with it.

Time of day seems to matter. Evidence for a "morning morality effect" shows that people seem to be at their virtuous best in the morning, and the likelihood of immoral actions increases later in the day.[29] One likely reason concerns self-control, which was covered in Chapter 4. It takes self-control to do what is morally right rather than acting on impulse or selfish motives. Self-control depends on an energy resource, which tends to be in good shape after a night's sleep but gets depleted during the day.

Morals often contribute to inner conflict—particularly when you are tempted to do something that will benefit yourself, but you know it would be morally wrong. For example, someone might be tempted to steal some money but holds back because stealing is immoral. An article with the simple title "Moral Actor, Selfish Agent" concluded that what many people do is try to appear to be moral (like an actor playing a role) while quietly being selfish.[30] The moral version of this self is thus an act that one puts on for others, because it is highly desirable to be perceived as a morally good person. People regard their moral actor self as idealistic, while they see their selfish agent self as realistic.

Many people associate morality with reasoning from principles. An early and influential line of research sought to classify people by the quality of their **moral reasoning**. This was done by presenting them with a dilemma and asking them to explain their judgment. A frequently used dilemma involved a man whose wife was deathly ill, and he could not afford the expensive medicine to save her life—but he had an opportunity to steal it. Should he steal? What mattered was not the specific answer of yes or no, but the quality of reasoning the person displayed while thinking about it.

But then psychologists began to notice that when people were confronted with moral dilemmas in their own lives, they often did not stop to engage in reasoning from principles. Instead, they seemed to be guided by a sense of what "feels right." Researchers began to study **moral intuitions** instead of moral reasoning.

Research began to show that people's moral intuitions have more influence than reasoning.[31] New dilemmas were devised, such as a case in which a brother and sister decided to have sex one time, used protection (and so had no consequences of pregnancy or disease), enjoyed it, never did it again, and ultimately felt their relationship had been strengthened by this one adventure. Most research participants condemned this as wrong. The reasons they gave were contradicted. For example, some pointed out that incest increases the odds of producing birth defects; but the example specified that the act did not cause pregnancy. Others said that incest might become habit-forming or damage the sibling relationship, but again the story ruled those out. Yet despite the failure of their reasons, most participants continued to condemn the incest as morally wrong. Some said things like, "I can't explain why, I just know it's wrong." Such sentiments capture the

moral reasoning using logical deductions to make moral judgments based on abstract principles of right and wrong

moral intuitions judgments (about whether an action is right or wrong) that occur automatically and rely on emotional feelings crucial point: The moral judgment was based on intuitive feelings, not reasoning from principles.

Are moral principles irrelevant? No. Often people must explain and justify their actions to others, and invoking shared moral principles is an effective way to do this.[32] People who perform immoral acts risk being excluded from important social groups: divorced, fired, even imprisoned.

Soon, researchers began to explore other irrational patterns of moral judgment. In one, people imagine a runaway trolley that is headed toward killing five people, and they are asked whether they would throw a switch to shift the trolley onto another track, where it will kill one person.[33] Many people say they would throw the switch, thereby killing an innocent person, in order to save the five.[34] However, if it were necessary to have physical contact with the victim (pushing him off a bridge in front of the trolley to stop it from killing the others ahead), they generally say they would not. The moral principle is the same: sacrificing one innocent person to save five other lives. But apparently moral intuitions respect a big difference between the two ways of killing someone (throwing a switch vs. pushing a human body off a bridge).

Another dilemma concerns the head of a large corporation who is told about a possible new venture that would increase profits and would either harm the environment or, in the other condition, would help the environment. He responds that he cares only about profits, not about the environment, and he approves the plan, which then does have the predicted effect on the environment.[35] If the outcome is harm, then research participants generally condemn him for having intentionally harmed the environment. But if the outcome is help, they do not give him credit for intentionally helping.[36] Again, the moral principle should seemingly predict no difference, because in both cases he explicitly said he did not care about the environment.

Political behavior is often guided by strong moral values. Research has proposed that moral differences may contribute to some of the disagreements between political liberals and conservatives. The broader idea is that moral judgments in general can be traced to five different foundations, which are like basic values. Liberals prize and use two of the five, whereas conservatives prize all five of them.[37]

One broad moral foundation is disapproval of people hurting each other. Another is the importance of fairness, which includes the assumption that people should generally reciprocate good treatment by others. These are the two that both liberals and conservatives uphold. The other three, which appeal mainly to conservatives, are respect for legitimate authority, loyalty to one's group (this includes patriotism), and purity/sanctity. Purity includes the value of cleanliness, in both the literal physical sense (e.g., wash hands before touching the flag or a holy book), and symbolic (e.g., ritual purification, sexual innocence). Subtle cues that evoke these values can affect people's political opinions. For example, when people encountered a dispenser of hand sanitizer, they expressed more conservative political views than when not thus reminded of purity.[38]

An impressive recent study of lawsuits against corporations has confirmed that different moral values contribute to different (im)moral actions. The researchers used a huge database (the National Archive of Criminal Justice Data), with over a million lawsuits during a 15-year period. They focused specifically on lawsuits and prosecutions of corporations. Crucially, the also checked the political contributions of each company's top management, to see whether the company leadership was predominantly Democrat or Republican.

Democrats place particular emphasis on moral issues such as civil rights, fairness to labor workers, and protecting the environment. Sure enough, firms with Democrat leadership were sued less often than Republican-led firms for civil rights issues, labor issues, and environmental violations. Meanwhile, Republicans place more emphasis property rights, market discipline, and self-reliance. Their firms were less likely than Democrat-led firms to be sued over securities fraud and intellectual property rights. These results fit the view that different people (with different political views) hold somewhat different ethical standards and act to uphold their own standards, while being less careful or scrupulous in relation to values they do not emphasize.Thus, morality is more than an abstract topic for debate by philosophers. It reaches into many corners of social life,

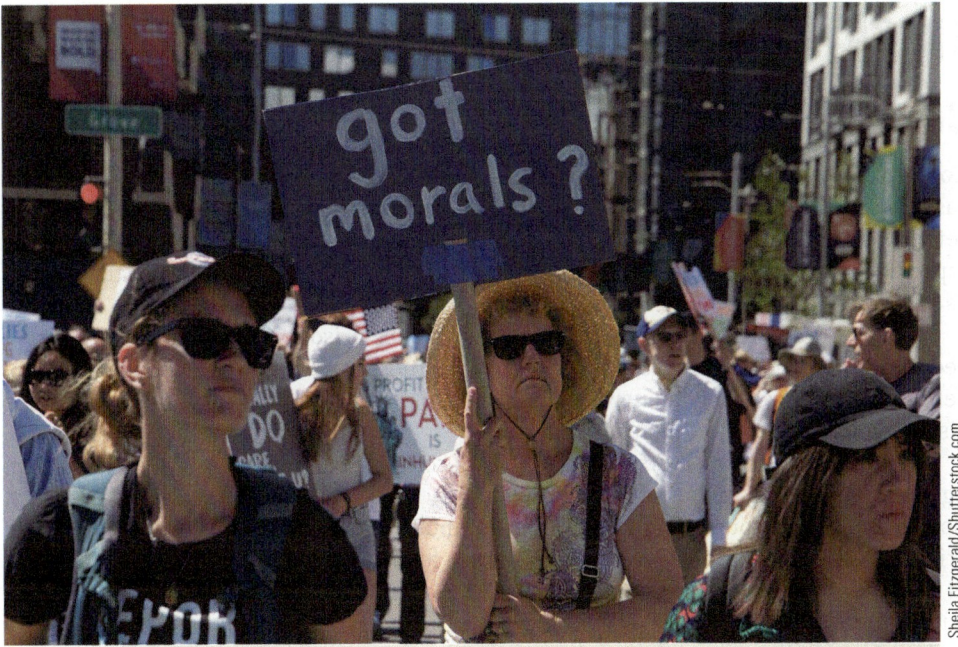

Sometimes the actions of politicians, large corporations, and other high-powered people prompt us to ask "Got morals?" Do you think they lack morals, or are their morals different than ours?

including emotion, judgment, impression formation, and politics. Morality is what enables people to agree that prosocial actions are indeed prosocial. More broadly, moral rules create the shared understandings of how to act—which are one of the foundations of human culture and society.

QUIZ YOURSELF
Morality

1. **What human societies have morals?**
   - (a) Developed countries
   - (b) Religious countries
   - (c) Third-world countries
   - (d) All of the above

2. **What time of day are people most moral?**
   - (a) Morning
   - (b) Afternoon
   - (c) Evening
   - (d) Morality does not depend on the time of day

3. **People expect to feel _____ when they engage in immoral behavior, and they actually feel _____ after engaging in immoral behavior.**
   - (a) bad; bad
   - (b) bad; good
   - (c) good; bad
   - (d) good; good

4. **Moral judgments in general can be traced to five different foundations: (1) disapproval of people hurting each other, (2) fairness, (3) respect for legitimate authority, (4) loyalty to one's group, and (5) purity/sanctity. Conservatives tend to value all five, whereas liberals tend to value which two?**
   - (a) disapproval of hurting others; fairness
   - (b) disapproval of hurting others; loyalty to one's group
   - (c) fairness; loyalty to one's group
   - (d) fairness; purity/sanctity

answers: see pg 329

Morality | **301**

Cooperation, Forgiveness, Obedience, Conformity, and Trust

Cooperation

Cooperation is a vital and relatively simple form of prosocial behavior. **Cooperation** is based on reciprocity: You do your part, and someone else does his or her part, and together you work toward common goals. Cooperating is vital for social groups to succeed, especially if they are to flourish in the sense of the whole being more than the sum of its parts.

Psychologists have studied cooperation by using the **prisoner's dilemma**, which forces people to choose between a cooperative act and another act that combines being competitive, exploitative, and defensive. The prisoner's dilemma, a widely studied tradeoff, is discussed in detail in the *Tradeoffs* box.

Political scientist Robert Axelrod once held a computer tournament designed to investigate the prisoner's dilemma situation using the payoff matrix shown in **TABLE 9.1**. Contestants in the tournament submitted computer programs that would compete in a prisoner's dilemma game for 200 rounds. These followed many different strategies, such as being antagonistic every round, cooperating every round, or deciding each move at random.

The strategy that gained the most points for the player was tit-for-tat:[39] Just do whatever the other player did last time. If the other player cooperated, then you should cooperate too. If the other player made the competitive move, then you should too. Obviously tit-for-tat is closely based on reciprocation, and it is no accident that reciprocation works so well: It promotes cooperation when the other person is cooperative, but it also protects you from being taken advantage of when the other person is exploitative.

Undoubtedly some people are more cooperative than others. One difference lies in how people interpret the situation. Cooperators see the prisoner's dilemma and related situations as an issue of good versus bad behavior (with cooperation being good). Competitors see it as weak versus strong, with cooperation being weak.[40,41] It is hardly surprising that people are more prone to cooperate if they think of cooperation as a sign of moral goodness than as a sign of weakness.

What happens when people with different approaches are matched in the prisoner's dilemma game? Sadly, the results show that exploitation trumps cooperation.[42,43,44] When both players favor cooperation, not surprisingly, they both tend to cooperate (and do pretty well). When both lean toward competition, then the game soon degenerates into everyone choosing the competitive response on every trial, and no one ends up doing well. When there is one of each, the game likewise degenerates into mutual exploitation and defensiveness. Thus, two virtuous people can do well by each other, but if either one plays selfishly, trust and cooperation are soon destroyed. This is an important and profound insight into how people relate to each other. If both people want to cooperate, they can succeed in doing so, for mutual benefit. If either one is not cooperative, then cooperation is typically doomed. Cooperation is a fragile tendency, easily destroyed. This probably reflects the facts of evolution: Across most species, competition is the norm and cooperation is rare. For example, research has shown that pigeons usually defect during

cooperation working together with someone for mutual or reciprocal benefit

prisoner's dilemma a game that forces people to choose between cooperation and competition

TABLE 9.1 Prisoner's Dilemma: Computer Tournament

	Player 1 (Antagonistic)	Player 2 (Cooperative)
Player 2 (Antagonistic)	Both get 1 point	Player 1 gets 0 points
		Player 2 gets 5 points
Player 2 (Cooperative)	Player 2 gets 0 points	Both get 3 points
	Player 1 gets 5 points	

a tit-for-tat condition of a prisoner's dilemma game even though it means earning only one-third of the food that they could have earned if they had cooperated.[45] Humans are much better at cooperating than most other animals, but this should be regarded as small progress in overcoming the naturally competitive tendencies that are still alive and well (and strong) in humans too.

Cooperation: The Big Picture

The prisoner's dilemma game offers a choice between cooperation and competition, as if those were on the same level. We noted that competition seems to be stronger, in the sense that if one person cooperates and the other competes, pretty soon both are competing. There may be important reasons for this.

In evolution, competition is much older and more deeply rooted than cooperation. Plenty of research with great apes (humankind's closest biological relatives) has shown that they compete very readily and cunningly, but the idea of cooperating with non-kin seems never even to occur to them.[46] Their few activities that sometimes look like cooperation (e.g., hunting in groups) are not truly cooperative, because each animal is really just out for itself.

Cooperation is a vital foundation of culture. The fact that animals do not cooperate probably contributes to the fact that they do not get very far at creating culture. The willingness to trust strangers and cooperate with them enabled humans to create civilization, with all its benefits. Indeed, although social psychologists have long emphasized research on helping, and stories about helpful people (including the "pay it forward" story with which this chapter opened) inspire admiration, helping is much less important than cooperation for the success of the human species.

The human tendency is not to trust and cooperate with everybody, indiscriminately. Rather, people tend to cooperate with members of their group. Often this is motivated by competition and threats from other groups. After all, if there were a battle between two groups, one of whom cooperated with each other and the other did not, the cooperators would likely win. Evidence shows that threats of violence make people more agreeable, trusting, and cooperative—but mainly with members of their own group.[47] In lab studies, threat made participants more willing to work with their own group and less willing to work with other groups. Even at the national level, countries that spent more money on their military forces showed more trust toward ingroup members and less toward outgroup members.

Cooperation requires each person to make sacrifices so that all can benefit. People who break these rules undermine the system and ruin it for everyone. For example, if lots of people started making and using counterfeit money, people would have to stop trusting the money they got, and society would lose the benefits of being able to use money. Social norms, moral principles, and laws help people know when it is appropriate to cooperate.

Unlike other animals, humans will punish someone who breaks rules, even if they were not personally victimized. A dog might try to bite another dog who takes its food, but no one has ever seen a third dog intervene to make the second dog respect the property of the first. Humans intervene in such ways, and even more. Some fascinating research using an economic game (similar to the prisoner's dilemma) has shown that many people will even accept costs, as in a reduction of their own pay, in order to punish someone else who breaks the rules.[48] This pattern is called "altruistic punishment," because the punisher is individually worse off as a result of punishing the rule-breaker, but the punisher helps the collective good by encouraging everyone to follow the rules. People engage in more altruistic punishment when they are thinking about how members of a group are similar to each other,[49] like a functioning social network.

Another way people help enforce rules is through gossip. Gossip has a bad reputation, but it is often used to communicate accurate information about others. People who break the rules develop bad reputations, and so others know not to trust them. When research participants saw another person betray someone's trust and refuse to cooperate, they passed this information along to others who might have to decide whether to trust and cooperate with that same person.[50] Indeed, it made people feel better to pass along this gossip. Moreover, when people know that gossip is likely to occur, they become more

The Prisoner's Dilemma

The prisoner's dilemma is a classic tradeoff that many psychologists have adapted for use in research. The dilemma arises in a story about two criminals, whom we will call Bart and Mack (see **TABLE 9.2**). They are arrested on suspicion of having committed armed robbery, and sure enough they are found to be carrying concealed weapons, but the police do not have enough evidence to link them to the robbery. Accordingly, the police question them separately. Both men are invited to confess to the crime and hence betray the other. What happens to either of them depends on how both of them react.

One possibility is that neither man confesses to the crime. This is the prosocial option (well, prosocial when crime isn't involved!): They cooperate with each other and reject the police's deals. If this happens, they can only be convicted of the minor charge of carrying concealed weapons. Both men will get a light jail sentence.

Another possibility is that one man will confess and the other will not. If Bart confesses and Mack holds out, then the police will let Bart turn state's evidence. In reward for his testimony against Mack, Bart can go free (the best possible outcome for Bart); the police will be able to get Mack convicted of the robbery, and he will get a long prison sentence (the worst possible outcome for Mack). Of course, the outcomes are reversed if Bart holds out and Mack confesses.

The last possibility is that both confess. The police then do not have to give anyone a free pass because both men have incriminated themselves. Both will go to prison for moderately long sentences, though perhaps not as long as the sentence that one gets if the other betrays him.

From the player's perspective, the dilemma is thus whether to confess and betray your partner or to hold out and cooperate with him. In a broader sense, your choice between a cooperative response and an antagonistic response. Confessing betrays your partner for your own benefit, and it also protects you in case your partner seeks to betray you. Cooperating (refusing to confess) involves taking a risk that could bring a good outcome for both people, but leaves you vulnerable to the longest sentence if your partner chooses to confess. Put another way, you will both be better off if both cooperate and refuse to confess because you both get light sentences. However, you can get the best outcome for yourself by confessing while your partner holds out, so many people will be tempted to try that route.

Yet another way of understanding the tradeoff is that it is between what is best for you versus what is best for everyone. What is best for you is to confess because you either get off totally free (if your partner holds out) or get a medium rather than a long sentence (if you both betray each other). But the best outcome for both partners is achieved if you both refuse to confess. This is the dilemma of human cultural life in a nutshell: whether to selfishly pursue your own impulses, regardless of the rules and other people's welfare, or instead to do what is best for all.

Researchers tested the prisoner's dilemma game with actual prisoners.[51] They compared female prisoners to female

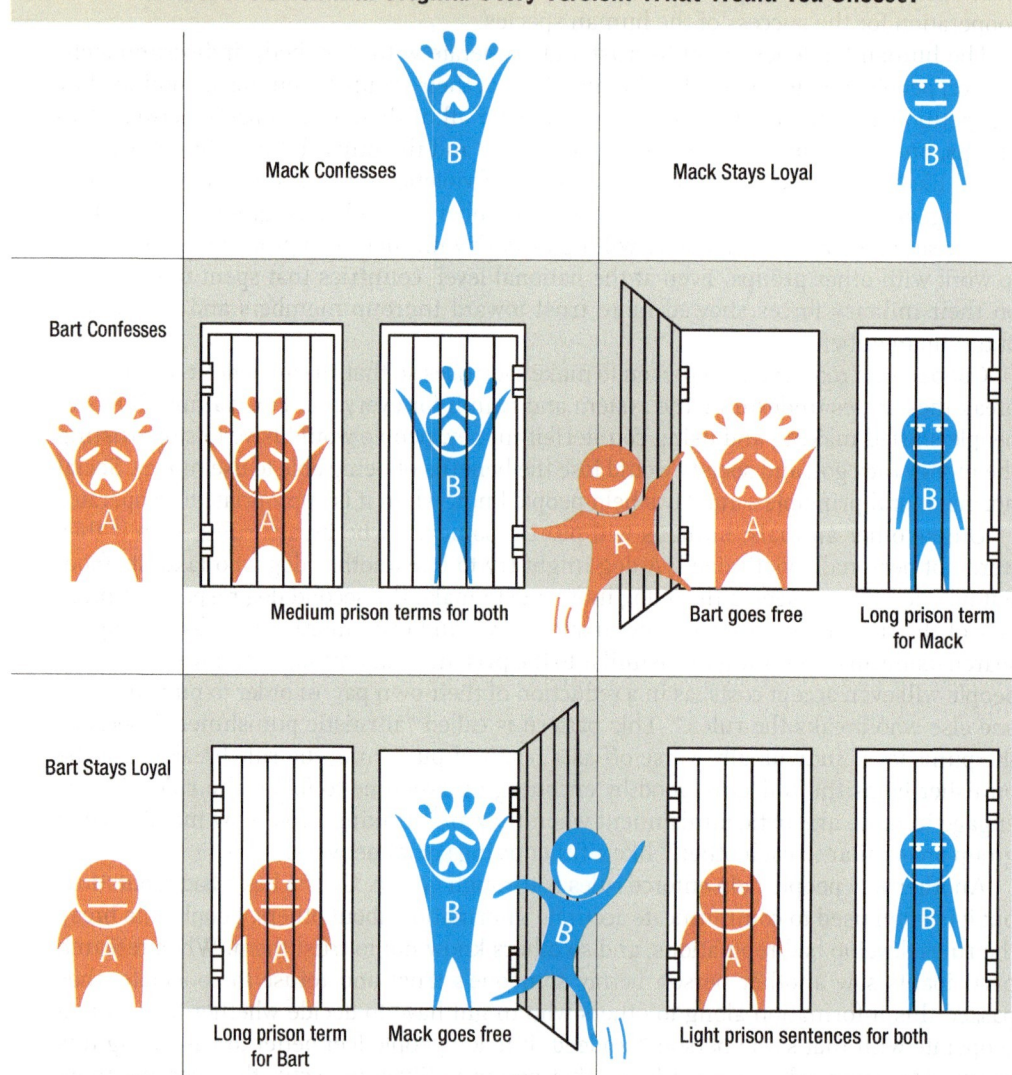

TABLE 9.2 Prisoner's Dilemma: Original Story Version: What Would You Choose?

college students in Germany. Surprisingly, they found that prisoners were far more cooperative than expected, even more cooperative than the college students.

The prisoner's dilemma is called a **non-zero-sum game**, a term from game theory with important implications for social life. **Zero-sum games** are those in which the winnings and losings add up to zero. Poker is zero-sum, because a certain amount of money changes hands, but there is no net change in the amount; what some people lose is precisely equal to what the others win. Likewise, tennis and chess are zero-sum, in the sense that one player wins (+1) and the other loses (–1), so the sum is zero (1 – 1=0). But in the prisoner's dilemma, both players can win, or both can lose. If more of human social life can be put on a non-zero-sum basis, so that everyone can win or gain something, life might be better overall.[52] Put more simply, when social interactions are zero-sum, my gain is your loss, so you and I are inevitably working against each other. Non-zero-sum interactions offer the possibility that we can both win, such as if we cooperate to help each other or solve each other's problems. Competing and fighting are often zero-sum because one side wins at the other's expense. Love, however, is often non-zero-sum because two people who love each other gain benefits from the relationship and are better off.

---

cooperative and less selfish. All these findings indicate how much human social behavior is attuned to the importance of cooperation and trust.

Although it is commonly believed that women are more cooperative than men, a meta-analysis of 50 years of research involving 31,642 participants in 18 different countries concluded that overall men are just as cooperative as women.[53] Nevertheless, there were some important differences in patterns. Male–male interactions are more cooperative than female–female interactions. In mixed-sex interactions, however, women were more cooperative than men. These findings make sense from an evolutionary perspective.[54] Ancestral men needed to cooperate to acquire resources, such as food and property. For example, if men did not cooperate during hunting and warfare, nobody would get any food, and wars would be lost. Ancestral women usually migrated between groups, and they would have been interacting mostly with women who tended not to be relatives. Such social interactions were likely rife with sexual competition, which could explain lower cooperation in female–female interactions.

According to the book *Warriors and Worriers: The Survival of the Sexes*,[55] men evolved to fight wars and battles together, whereas women evolved to bear and care for their children, which they cannot do alone. Men therefore form lasting bonds with other men, with whom they will work together and fight enemies together. Women seek someone to help provide for them and their children, and that usually means a man rather than another woman (who will have her own children who need support). Women therefore do not tend to form lasting, productive bonds with other women of their age. Rather, they seek to form attachments to men. This could account for the pattern of cooperation shown in prisoner's dilemma games (and much else). Still, there are many opinions and theories about gender differences, and not all of them would embrace this analysis.

Successful cooperation also seems to depend on communication. If communication is difficult, there is less cooperation.[56] Communication allows for the emergence of cooperation.[57] Cooperation drops sharply when partners avoid discussion during a prisoner's dilemma game.[58] Can money reduce cooperation and helping? To find out, see *Money Matters*.

Forgiveness

Forgiveness is an important category of prosocial behavior.[59] **Forgiveness** refers to ceasing to feel angry toward and ceasing to seek retribution against someone who has wronged you. According to theories of fairness, reciprocity, and equity, if someone does something bad to you, that person owes you a kind of debt—an obligation to do something positive for you to offset the bad deed. Forgiveness in that context involves releasing the person from this obligation, just as one might cancel a monetary debt. This does not mean that you condone what the person did. It just means that you won't hold it against him or her.

As we have seen, human beings have longer-lasting relationships than most other animals, and forgiveness is an important contributor to this. When people hurt,

non-zero-sum game an interaction in which both participants can win (or lose)

zero-sum game a situation in which one person's gain is another's loss

forgiveness ceasing to feel angry toward or seek retribution against someone who has wronged you

MONEY Matters

Money, Prosocial Behavior, and Self-Sufficiency

Human beings derive many benefits from cooperation, helping, forgiveness, and other prosocial acts. Money, however, can enable people to purchase many of the same benefits. Money may therefore make people less prone to engage in prosocial behavior. The idea that money promotes self-sufficiency was put forward and tested in a clever and well-designed set of experiments.[60] Researchers started with a common observation. When one doesn't have much money (such as when one is a student!) and has to move to a new apartment, one depends on the help of friends. Perhaps the person who is moving buys pizza and beer for the group, and everyone helps carry boxes and furniture to the new place. In contrast, when people have plenty of money, they hire professional movers instead of needing their friends to do the work.

The findings showed that the effects of money on self-sufficiency come from merely making people think about money. The manipulations included sitting participants in front of a computer that had a screen saver display with dollar bills (as compared to a blank screen or a display of fish), having participants unscramble groups of words to make sentences that referred to money (as opposed to neutral topics), and just simply displaying a stack of play money to participants. People who had been reminded of money were less likely than others to give help to someone who specifically asked for help. They were even less likely to help an accomplice who spilled a box of pencils and had to pick them up.

It wasn't just that money made people selfish or self-centered, however. In other studies in the same investigation, participants found themselves in difficulty, such as when they were assigned to work on puzzles that were quite difficult. They were told they could ask for help if they needed it. Participants who had been primed with the idea of money were less likely than others to ask for help and were slower to ask for help if they did ask.

Thus, money seemed to increase self-sufficiency: It made people less likely to give help or to ask for help. In a final study, participants were asked whether they wanted to work together with someone or alone. Those who had been primed with money were more likely than others to choose to work alone.

Money is a purely cultural phenomenon, but cultural attitudes toward money have always resulted in mixed feelings (e.g., regarding the love of money as the "root of all evil"[61]). The self-sufficiency findings suggest why that may be. Money provides benefits, but it also seems to pull people apart and reduce their prosocial inclinations.

---

disappoint, or betray each other, the bad feelings can damage the relationship and drive the people to leave it. Forgiveness can help heal the relationship and enable people to go on living or working together.[62] The more strongly someone is committed to a particular relationship, the more likely he or she is to forgive an offense by the other partner.[63]

Forgiveness is an important part of a successful romantic or marital relationship, as is increasingly recognized by both researchers and spouses themselves.[64,65] Couples that forgive each other have higher levels of relationship satisfaction.[66,67] But what causes what—the tendency to forgive or relationship satisfaction? Researchers have begun tracking couples over time, to see which comes first.[68] Partners who forgave each other for doing something wrong were happier than other couples six months later. In contrast, earlier satisfaction with the relationship did not predict later forgiveness. This pattern of findings indicates that forgiveness leads to better relationships, not vice versa.

The benefits of forgiveness have been well documented in research. It is fairly obvious that being forgiven is beneficial to the person who did something wrong because that person no longer needs to feel guilty or owes a debt to the one who has been hurt. Perhaps more surprisingly, forgiveness also has great benefits for the forgivers. They report better physical and mental health than victims who hold grudges.[69,70,71]

The downside of forgiveness may be that it invites people to offend again. So far, research has yielded mixed results. Some findings indicate that offenders are glad to be forgiven and often feel grateful, which may motivate them to perform more good deeds. For example, participants in one study[72] were led to believe they had accidentally broken some laboratory equipment. They received a message of forgiveness, or retribution, or both, or neither. Later, the experimenter asked for a favor. Those who had been forgiven were most willing to do the favor. Thus, instead of inviting repeat offenses, forgiveness

"FORGIVE YOU?... SURE I'LL FORGIVE YOU... THE MOMENT I SEE SOMETHING I REALLY WANT ON THE SHOPPING CHANNEL."

led to more prosocial behavior. On the other hand, a study of married couples found that spouses who were readily forgiven continued to engage in hurtful actions toward their partners.[73]

Mostly, though, forgiveness leads to more satisfying relationships. One pathway is that when someone refuses to forgive a loved one for doing something wrong, this tends to come up again in future conflicts, making them harder to resolve.[74] "It's just like when you forgot my birthday last year!" When each new conflict prompts the couple to bring up unforgiven old grudges, minor arguments quickly become major fights, and this sets the couple on the downward spiral that is typical of unhappy, problem-filled relationships (see Chapter 12). Forgiveness can help prevent this destructive pattern from starting.

Forgiveness is linked to seeing the other person's perspective and hence avoiding some cognitive biases that can drive people apart. When any two people have a conflict, especially if one does something to hurt the other, people tend to perceive and understand it in biased ways. The victim tends to emphasize all the bad consequences ("That really hurt my feelings"), whereas the perpetrator may focus on external factors that reduce his or her blame ("I couldn't help it"). Hence, they don't understand or sympathize with each other. People in highly satisfying dating relationships don't show those biases.[75] Instead, they see the other person's point of view better ("I know you couldn't help it"). Couples who think that way are more willing to forgive each other and hence better able to recover from a misdeed. Forgiveness helps couples get past even such relationship-threatening events as sexual infidelity, enabling the relationship to survive and recover.[76]

Why don't people forgive? Research has identified several major barriers that reduce willingness to forgive. One fairly obvious factor is the severity of the offense: The worse the person treated you, the harder it is to forgive.[77] Another is a low level of commitment to the relationship.[78] In a sense, forgiving is making a generous offer to renounce anger and claims for retribution as a way of helping to repair and strengthen the relationship, and people are more willing to do this for relationships that are more important to them. Apologies also help elicit forgiveness. When someone has wronged you but is sincerely remorseful and expresses an apology, you are much more willing to forgive than when no such apology or remorse is expressed.[79,80]

Inner processes also can lead toward or away from forgiveness. In particular, how the person thinks about the transgression can be decisive. If you think that you might easily have performed a similar offense, you become more willing to forgive.[81] In contrast, ruminating about what someone did to you can increase anger, which in turn makes forgiveness less likely.[82]

Some persons are also more forgiving than others. Religious people forgive more readily than nonreligious people,[83] in part because religions generally promote and encourage values that help people live together, and in fact some religions prominently extol forgiving as an important virtue. For example, the most famous and widely repeated prayer in the Christian religion couples a request for forgiveness with a promise to forgive others: "And forgive us our debts, as we forgive our debtors."[84]

Forgiving others requires inhibiting impulses to lash out aggressively at those who have harmed us. Cognitive executive functions are the mental abilities that help us attend to, organize, plan, and achieve goals. They also help us inhibit inappropriate behaviors. It is therefore not surprising that people with more advanced cognitive executive functions are more forgiving of others.[85] In a similar vein, people high in trait self-control are also more forgiving of others.[86]

In contrast, narcissistic individuals are less likely than others to forgive when they have been offended.[87,88] These conceited and self-centered individuals have a broad belief that they deserve special, preferential treatment, and they are outraged when someone offends them. They are easily offended and generally think they deserve some major compensation before they will consider forgiving.

Obedience

Obedience to orders can be prosocial, and in many respects it is highly desirable that people carry out the orders of their superiors. Groups such as military units, corporations,

obedience following orders from an authority figure

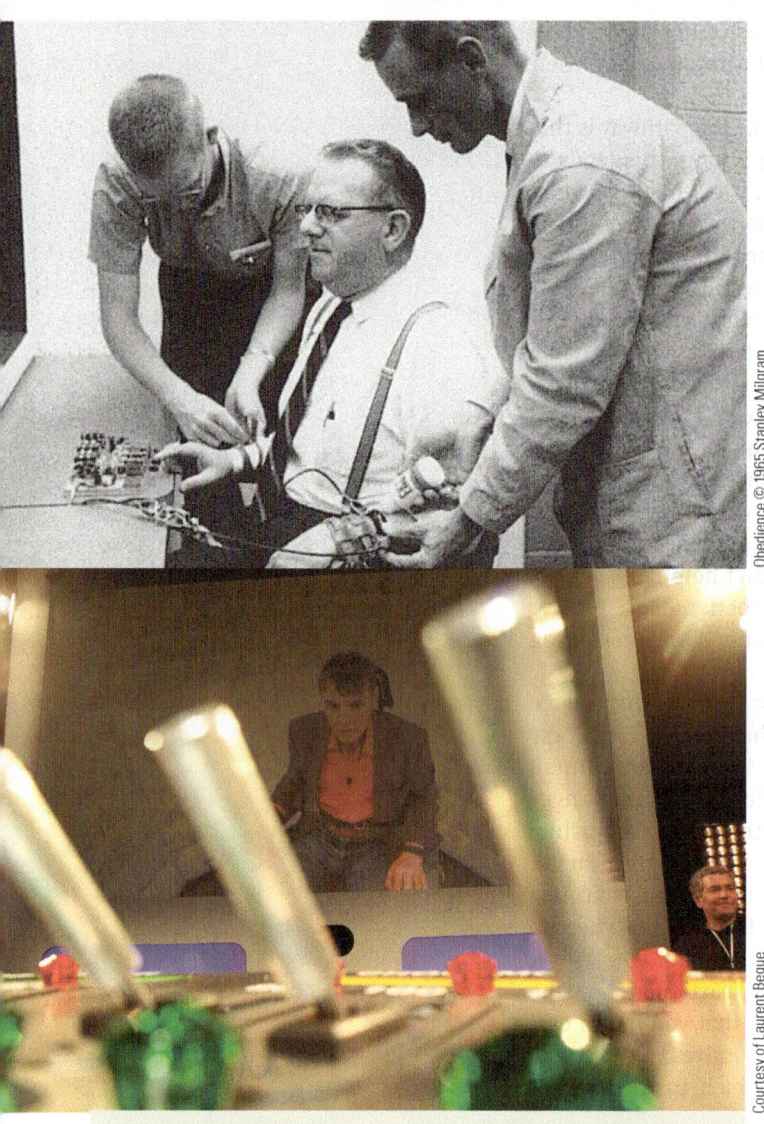

Conducting the Milgram study, the experimenter attaches shock electrodes to the wrists of the "learner" (actually an accomplice) while the "teacher" (the real participant) helps out.

surgical teams, and sports teams cannot function effectively without some degree of obedience. If people refuse to follow the leader's directions, the group degenerates into an ineffective collection of individuals.

Social psychologists have generally taken a dim view of obedience. This attitude can be traced to a classic series of studies conducted by Stanley Milgram in the 1960s.[89] His research interest, like that of many psychologists at the time, was shaped by the disturbing events of World War II, including large-scale massacres of civilians by Nazi German troops. After the war, the international outcry against these atrocities presented an ongoing challenge to social science to account for how seemingly ordinary, decent, well-intentioned individuals could do such things. Many of the killers defended themselves by saying "I was only following orders." The odds are that if someone asked you whether you might have helped kill Jews, homosexuals, Roma (gypsies), communists, and other defenseless civilians if you had lived in Nazi Germany, you would say "no way!" Yet these refusals stand in contrast to how so many German citizens actually behaved.

Milgram set up a study to see whether Americans would in fact follow orders that might injure or possibly kill someone. Participants were recruited for a study on learning, and when they arrived they were told that they would play the role of a teacher who would deliver electric shocks as punishment for mistakes made by a learner. They met the learner: a mild-mannered, middle-aged man who was actually an accomplice. The man mentioned that he had a heart condition.

The experimenter showed the participant an impressive-looking shock delivery apparatus, which had a row of switches with labels running from "Mild shock" up to "Danger: Severe shock" and then to "XXX." The experimenter said that each time the learner made a mistake, the participant should flick a switch, starting from the mildest shock (15 volts) and working upward toward the most severe shock (450 volts), in 15-volt increments. The experimenter said that although the shocks were painful, they would not be dangerous.

They started the exercise, and the learner kept making mistakes. The participant sat by the experimenter, who instructed him or her to deliver shocks. Although the learner was in another room, the participant could still hear him. (Subsequent studies showed that people were less willing to deliver severe shocks if the learner was in the same room with them, as opposed to being out of sight.) If the participant hesitated, the experimenter had a standard series of prods that commanded the participant to continue. To make it harder to continue, the learner followed a script that included groaning, screaming in pain, banging on the wall, and shouting that he had a heart condition, that his heart was starting to bother him, and that he did not want to continue the study. Eventually the learner stopped responding at all, so for all the participant knew, the learner had passed out or died. The experimenter, however, said to treat no response as a mistake and therefore to continue delivering higher shocks.

Before he conducted the study, Milgram surveyed a group of psychiatrists for predictions as to what would happen. How many participants would go all the way and deliver the most severe shock of 450 volts? The psychiatrists had faith that the participants would resist authority, and they predicted that only 1 in 1,000 (0.10%) would be willing to deliver the most severe shocks. In the actual study, the majority of participants (62.5%) went all the way up to the maximum shock (see **FIGURE 9.1**)! To be sure, this wasn't easy for them: Many showed acute signs of distress, such as sweating, making sounds, and

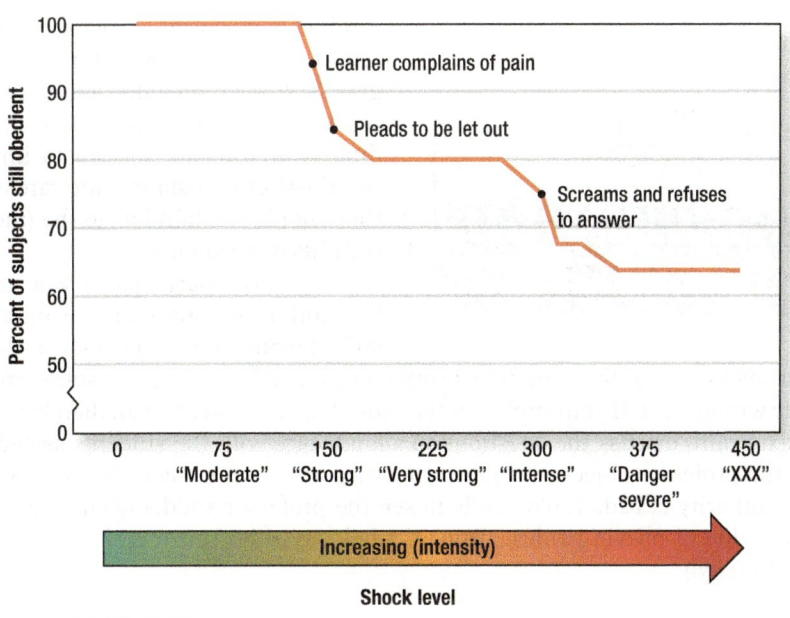

FIGURE 9.1

Results from the Milgram experiment, showing that most participants (62.5%) would deliver severe shocks to someone even if it harmed that person.

sometimes having fits of nervous laughter that seemed out of control, but they still did what they were told.

In 2009, social psychologist Jerry Burger replicated Milgram's findings and found nearly identical results, although he had to stop at 150 volts for ethical reasons.[90] Even after hearing cries of pain, 70% of participants kept shocking (Milgram found that 80% of participants kept shocking after 150 volts).

Much has been said and written about Milgram's studies (including some serious debates as to whether it is ethical for researchers to put their participants through such experiences). The intellectual community was deeply shocked (no pun intended) to learn how far American citizens would obey orders to hurt another person, despite the moral lessons of Nazi Germany. Many people use Milgram's studies to emphasize the point that human behavior is more strongly influenced by the situation than by the person. However, research suggests that there are important individual differences in obedience. For example, agreeable people are more obedient than others, whereas people who lean to the "left" (liberal) politically are less obedient than others.[91]

Milgram's research has given obedience a bad name. His study was published in the early 1960s, and the rest of that decade saw a broad countercultural movement in which many young and some older people became hostile to authority and asserted that disobedience was a positive good, a right, and even an obligation. Bumper stickers such as "Question Authority!" abounded.

Yet, again, obedience can usually be a good thing. As we have already noted, very few organizations can function properly without obedience. Even families would fall apart if children refused to obey their parents' rules. Milgram's study focused on a peculiar situation in which obedience has morally bad outcomes, but this is exceptional. In most situations, obedience produces good outcomes. For example, how could a football team win a game if the pass receivers refused to obey the quarterback's play calling, or indeed if they disobeyed the orders of the referees? What would happen if people refused to obey traffic signals?

The fact that people obeyed Milgram's instructions may reveal an important fact about human nature, and one that depicts it as less morally bankrupt than is often said. People are naturally inclined to belong to groups, to seek social acceptance, and to put other people first. When a seemingly legitimate authority figure gives them commands, they tend to obey. This tendency does contain some danger, such as when a misguided, power-hungry, or irresponsible leader gives immoral commands. But the willingness to obey authority figures is probably an important and positive aspect of human psychology that enables people to live effectively in large groups (and hence in culture). Obedience is

Homogeneous Originality by CIAgent

ultimately prosocial behavior because it supports group life and helps cultures to succeed. Milgram's studies provide cautionary evidence that obedience can be abused and can, under extraordinary circumstances, lead to immoral actions. But those circumstances are rare exceptions, and they should not blind us to the (mostly) prosocial benefits of obedience.

In a sense, participants who refused to obey the authority figure in a Milgram study were still obeying some rules—typically moral rules. Human cultural life sometimes contains conflicting rules, and sometimes people obey the wrong ones. If your professor tells you that obedience is bad, then try this: During the next exam, discuss the questions in a loud voice with the students seated near you, and if the professor objects, bring up the Milgram study's ostensible lesson that obedience to authority is bad. You're likely to see the professor suddenly change their tune about the value of obeying rules! (Don't actually try this. You might get expelled from your university!)

Conformity

Conformity is going along with the crowd (see Chapter 8). Like obedience, conformity has had a bad reputation among social psychologists, and this stems in part from influential early studies that depicted people doing foolish, irrational, or bad things in order to conform. The broader point, however, may be that conformity is prosocial, insofar as the studies show how people put other people first and exhibit a strong desire to get along with others. If people put themselves first, by being selfish, prosocial behavior decreases.[92]

People conform to the behavior of others more, and in general conform to social norms more, when others are watching than when unobserved.[93] For example, do people wash their hands after using the toilet in a public restroom? One study found that most women (77%) did—but only if they thought someone else was in the restroom too.[94] Among the women who thought they were alone, only a minority (39%) washed their hands. Presumably men would act about the same. (So if your date goes to the bathroom alone, you might think twice about holding hands!) The motivation behind socially desirable behavior (such as washing hands after using the toilet) can be to gain acceptance and approval from others.

Research shows that the presence of conformists dramatically increases the group size for which cooperation can be sustained.[95] In other words, a tendency toward conformity helps people to function well in large groups. Large groups are good for culture because there are more people (than in small groups) with which to share information, cooperate, exchange goods and services, and so forth.

Cultures vary in the degree to which they value conform. One study[96] compared conformity in several dozen countries and concluded that pressures to conform were strictest in places where the risk of disease was highest. Because many diseases are contagious, people can interact safely only if they trust that others are following safe practices to restrict disease (such as being clean). In places where there are few germs around, cultures tend to let people do whatever they want, but that sort of tolerant individualism risks allowing unsafe practices and spreading disease when there are many germs.

To learn more about conformity as it relates to restaurants, see *Food for Thought*. It includes information that might change the way you order your food for years to come.

Trust

Trust is a strong belief in the reliability and validity of someone or something. Trust is another vital part of prosocial behavior among humans. Trust enables strangers and other nonrelatives to cooperate. Economists say that every economic transaction involves

conformity going along with the crowd, that is, saying or doing whatever other people are doing

trust a confidence that others will provide benefits and/or not harm you, even if they may be tempted to do otherwise

FOOD FOR *Thought*

Restaurants, Rules, and the Bad Taste of Nonconformity

Earlier in this chapter we suggested that conforming to rules is an important form of prosocial behavior, without which society would disintegrate into chaos. For many years, the Outback Steakhouse restaurant advertised "No Rules" as its slogan. Do they really mean no rules apply? If you and six friends ate an ample meal there and then refused to pay, citing "no rules" as your justification, would the restaurant managers approve? Or how about if you grabbed food off the plates of other diners, or decided to run naked through their kitchen (violating Food and Drug Administration rules, which are in force regardless of the restaurant's advertising slogans or policies). If you were to try any or all of these behaviors at the nearest Outback Steakhouse, you'll quickly discover that they have plenty of rules after all.

Not all restaurant behavior involves conforming. In fact, psychologists have documented a curious pattern of deliberate nonconformity among restaurant diners. The surprising thing, though, is that it often leaves people less satisfied with their meal than they might otherwise have been.

"I'll have the chicken."

"Hey, I was going to order the chicken! But that's OK, I'll order something else."

Have you ever heard such an exchange? When people eat together in a restaurant, they often act as if there were only one of each item on the menu and feel some obligation not to order the same food that someone else in the party has already ordered. Of course, there is no need to order different things. The restaurant almost certainly has enough chicken for everyone who wants it. Nonetheless, people seem to feel they should order different things.

A careful research project confirmed that people do in fact order different foods.[97] In their first study, researchers tracked the orders of hundreds of diners at a restaurant, to see how often people ordered the same versus different entrees. They then used a computer simulation to form other groups at random, for comparison purposes. This comparison showed that people who eat together order different foods more often than they would by chance.

In a second experiment, they let people order from a menu of different beers. By random assignment, some of the groups had to order in secret, whereas the others ordered aloud in the usual manner. When diners didn't know what the others were having, they often ordered the same beer, but when they heard someone else order a particular beer, they switched to order something different.

This impulse to order something different makes people less satisfied with their food or drink. The researchers found that when diners ordered in secret (and therefore often ordered the same thing), they were pretty happy with what they had. When they ordered aloud, the person who ordered first (and therefore got what he or she wanted) was also pretty happy. But things weren't so good for the people who ordered later and often made a point of not ordering the same item that the first person had ordered. Those individuals were less satisfied with what they got.

It's not entirely clear why people feel the urge to order something different. Perhaps they just think that conformity is bad, so they try to avoid conforming to what someone else has done. But conformity is not really so bad. The people who order the same item, when it is their first choice, end up enjoying it more than the ones who switch to a second choice just to be different.

Apparently, the best practice is just to order your first choice, even if somebody else has already ordered it. Your second choice really won't taste as good, on average. Instead of trying to be different and nonconforming, just order what you would like best!

---

some degree of trust. (After all, when you buy something online, you are giving money to strangers you have not even seen, and you trust that they will send you the goods you paid for.) Yet economists also argue that rational people should not trust strangers, because they might get burned. However, research shows that people actually show an "excess" of trust to strangers.[98] That is, they trust strangers more than they probably should, including when they are not confident that the other stranger will do the right thing. The implication is that people (at least in many modern societies) respect a social norm that prohibits treating a stranger as untrustworthy, until and unless there is some reason to do so. People think they have an obligation to trust strangers, and they often feel guilty if they do not trust them. (To be sure, the trust is likely to be quickly withdrawn if the other person behaves badly. But to start off interacting with someone new, the norm in our culture is to show a willingness to trust.) Remember from Chapter 6 that guilt often motivates prosocial behavior. Trust links past, present, and future, and in that sense is particularly important for the kinds of cooperation that comprise human culture and social life.

Social psychologists have begun to study trust.[99] As the Dutch saying goes, "Trust comes by foot and leaves by horse!"—trust is slow to build up and then quick to unravel. The prisoner's dilemma game, for example, relies on trust: You make a cooperative play in the expectation that the other person will do likewise instead of betraying you for a bigger reward (see *Tradeoffs* box for a description of the prisoner's dilemma game). When people play the game over many rounds, trust is built up slowly as both continue to cooperate. A betrayal of trust early in the game usually spells the end of trust. If the same happens later in the game, after some trust has been established, it can recover.[100]

Research has found that people trust strangers with easier to pronounce names (e.g., "Andrian Babeshko" versus "Czeslaw Ratynska"), even when those strangers are from the same foreign country.[101] Comedian Stephen Colbert calls this effect "truthiness," defined as "truth that comes from the gut, not books." The effect might be due to the duplex mind. As lead researcher said, "information that's difficult to process signals danger," so weird names evoke an automatic distrust.

In general, people tend to be trusting, perhaps a bit more than is entirely safe. The "trust game," developed by behavioral economists, involves giving participants some money and telling them they can keep it or send any part of it off to someone else. Whatever they send will be tripled by the experimenter, and then the recipient can decide whether to keep it all or send part of it back. Obviously sending it off increases the money, and if the other person can be trusted to share the benefits, both people are better off. But there is no guarantee that you will get anything back, so trust is risky. In general, people send off a substantial amount of money, and others (strangers) generally reward their trust by splitting what they get.[102]

Although this work is in its early stages, some interesting facts have emerged. People trust others with good self-control, presumably because they can be expected to behave properly and resist selfish impulses.[103] People tend to distrust atheists, possibly because people think the fear of God is an important source of virtue (see Chapter 13).[104] Trust is an important factor in building commitment in close relationships.[105,106] Lonely people are much less trusting than other people.[107]

QUIZ YOURSELF
Cooperation, Forgiveness, Obedience, Conformity, and Trust

1. **Psychiatrists predicted that _____ participants would go all the way in Milgram's experiment, giving the maximum shock level (450 volts) to the accomplice.**
   - (a) 1 in 10
   - (b) 1 in 50
   - (c) 1 in 100
   - (d) 1 in 1,000

2. **A hockey coach orders a player to injure an opposing team's star player. Although the player is personally opposed to intentionally injuring other players, he follows the coach's order. This illustrates _____.**
   - (a) conformity
   - (b) compliance
   - (c) cooperation
   - (d) obedience

3. **The results from Milgram's experiments are generally taken to show that _____.**
   - (a) males are more physically aggressive than females
   - (b) people can be sadistic
   - (c) people often are resistant to situational pressures
   - (d) situational pressures can overwhelm individual differences

4. **The tendency for people to go along with the crowd is called _____.**
   - (a) compliance
   - (b) conformity
   - (c) cooperation
   - (d) obedience

answers: see pg 329

Why Do People Help Others?

People might have several different motives for helping. In this section we explore some of the possible reasons why people help others.

Evolutionary Benefits

It is clear that receiving help increases the likelihood of passing one's genes on to the next generation, but what about giving help? In the animal world, the costs of helping are easy to spot. A hungry animal that gives its food to another has less left for itself. Selfish animals (who don't share are) less likely to starve. Hence evolution should generally favor selfish, unhelpful creatures. Indeed, Richard Dawkins (1976) wrote a book titled *The Selfish Gene*.[108] According to Dawkins, genes are selfish in that they build "survival machines" (like human beings!) to increase the number of copies of themselves. In an interview, Dawkins said: "Genes try to maximize their chance of survival. The successful ones crawl down through the generations. The losers, and their hosts, die off. A gene for helping the group could not persist if it endangered the survival of the individual."[109]

One way that evolution might support some helping is between parents and children. Parents who helped their children more would be more successful at passing on their genes. Although evolution favors helping one's children, children have less at stake in the survival of their parents' genes. Thus, parents should be more devoted to their children, and more willing to make sacrifices to benefit them, than children should be to their parents. In general, we should help people who have our genes, a theory known as **kin selection**.[110,111] For example, you should be more likely to help a sibling (who shares one-half of your genes) than a nephew (who shares one-fourth of your genes) or a cousin (who shares one-eighth of your genes). Plenty of research evidence suggests that people do help their family members and close relatives more than they help other people. In both life-or-death and everyday situations, we are more likely to help others who share our genes.[112] However, life-or-death helping is affected more strongly by genetic relatedness than is everyday helping (see **FIGURE 9.2**).

Research has also shown that genetically identical twins (who share 100% of their genes) help each other significantly more than fraternal twins (who share 50% of their genes).[113] Likewise, survivors of a fire at a vacation complex said that when they realized the complex was on fire, they were much more likely to search for family members than for friends.[114]

Thus, the natural patterns of helping (that favor family and other kin) are still there in human nature. However, people do help strangers and non-kin much more than other animals do. People are not just like other animals, but they are not completely different either. Humans are cultural animals, selected by nature to participate with nonrelatives in a larger society. Our natural inclinations to help kin have been amplified via emotional responses to translate into more far-reaching actions, such as empathy.

Empathy is an emotional response that corresponds to the feelings of the other person. When people see a person in distress, they usually feel that person's distress; when they see a person who is sad, they feel that person's sadness. The sharing of feelings makes people want to help the sufferer to feel better. Empathy is an especially important emotion when it comes to understanding why people help. Dramatic evidence for this was provided in a study of 18-month-old toddlers.[115] When the adult researcher dropped something, the human toddlers immediately tried to help, such as by crawling over to where it was, picking it up, and giving it to him. (The babies also seemed to understand

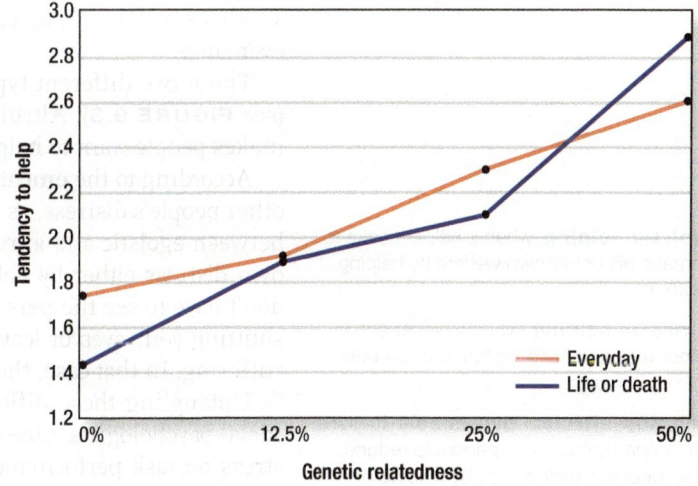

FIGURE 9.2

As genetic relatedness increases, helping also increases, in both everyday situations and life-or-death situations.[182]

kin selection the evolutionary tendency to help people who have our genes

empathy reacting to another person's emotional state by experiencing the same emotional state and empathize with the adult's mental state. If the researcher simply threw something on the floor, the babies didn't help retrieve it. They only helped if the adult seemed to want help.) The researchers then repeated this experiment with chimpanzees. The chimps were much less helpful, even though the human researcher was a familiar friend. This work suggests that humans are hardwired to cooperate and help each other from early in life, and that this is something that sets humans apart from even their closest animal relatives.

Unfortunately, some evidence suggests empathy levels are decreasing in college students.[116] Empathy scores have dropped 40% over the past 30 years or so. Compared with college students of the late 1970s, current students are less likely to agree with statements such as "I sometimes try to understand my friends better by imagining how things look from their perspective," and "I often have tender, concerned feelings for people less fortunate than me." The authors speculated, "College students today may be so busy worrying about themselves and their own issues that they don't have time to spend empathizing with others."[117] The media might also play a role in reducing empathy. For example, research shows that playing violent video games reduce feelings of empathy and makes people numb to the pain and suffering of others,[118] perhaps because violent games require players to adopt the role of the killer rather than the victim. Playing violent video games also decreases prosocial behavior such as cooperation and helping others.[119,120]

Two Motives for Helping: Altruism and Egoism

The 19th-century philosopher Auguste Comte (1875) described two forms of helping based on very different motives. One form he called **egoistic helping** in which the helper wants something in return for offering help. The helper's goal is to increase his or her own welfare (such as by making a friend, creating an obligation to reciprocate, or just making oneself feel good). The other form he called **altruistic helping** in which the helper expects nothing in return for offering help. The helper's goal in this case is to increase another's welfare. Psychologists, philosophers, and others have debated this distinction ever since.

These two different types of helping are produced by two different types of motives (see **FIGURE 9.3**). Altruistic helping is motivated by empathy. The sharing of feelings makes people want to help the sufferer to feel better.

According to the **empathy–altruism hypothesis**,[121] empathy motivates people to reduce other people's distress, as by helping or comforting them. How can we tell the difference between egoistic and altruistic motives? When empathy is low, people can reduce their own distress either by helping the person in need or by escaping the situation so they don't have to see the person suffer any longer. If empathy is high, however, then simply shutting your eyes or leaving the situation won't work because the other person is still suffering. In that case, the only solution is to help the victim feel better.

Untangling these different motives for helping has been an ongoing challenge for social psychologists. One study[122] was presented to participants as a test of the effects of stress on task performance. Through a rigged lottery, the "other participant" (actually an accomplice named Elaine) was assigned to perform 10 trials of a task while receiving

egoistic helping when a helper seeks to increase his or her own welfare by helping another

altruistic helping when a helper seeks to increase another's welfare and expects nothing in return

empathy–altruism hypothesis the idea that empathy motivates people to reduce other people's distress, as by helping or comforting

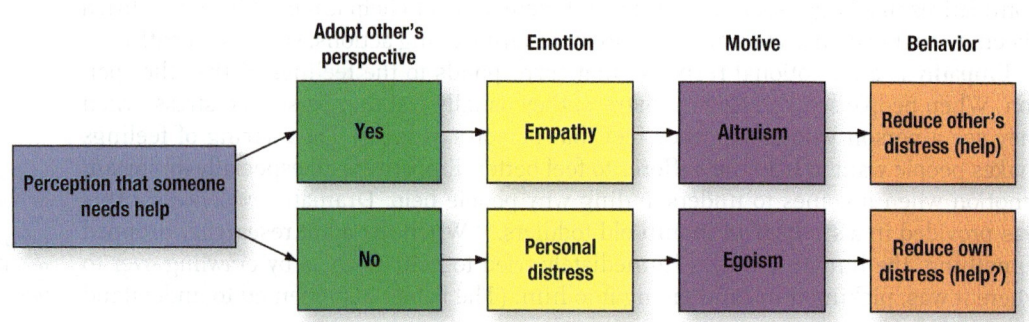

FIGURE 9.3
Two routes to helping: The top route is motivated by altruism, whereas the bottom route is motivated by egoism

random electric shocks (the stressor) on each trial. The real participant watched Elaine over a closed-circuit TV. Before the study began, the participant overheard a conversation in which Elaine told the experimenter that she was afraid of receiving the shocks because as a child she had been thrown from a horse into an electric fence. Ever since that experience, she had been terrified of electricity. The experimenter apologized but said Elaine would have to receive the shocks anyway because she had lost the coin toss.

To increase empathy, the researchers told half of the participants that Elaine's values and interests were very similar to their own (high-empathy condition). The other participants were told that Elaine's values and interests were quite different (low-empathy condition). People feel more empathy toward those they believe are similar to themselves than toward dissimilar people. To test for egoistic motives for helping, the researchers also manipulated how difficult it was to escape. In the easy-escape condition, participants were told that they could leave after watching Elaine get shocked on the first two trials. In the difficult-escape condition, participants were told that they would have to watch all 10 trials. Participants who were only concerned about their own feelings would not have to help Elaine in the easy-escape condition. Instead they could just walk away and forget about her suffering.

After watching Elaine suffer through two trials, the participant was asked whether she would be willing to trade places with Elaine as a way of helping her avoid further suffering. Consistent with empathy–altruism theory, almost all the participants in the high-empathy group traded places with Elaine, regardless of whether it was easy or difficult to escape (see **FIGURE 9.4**). In the low-empathy group, however participants did not offer to take Elaine's place if it was easy for them to escape the unpleasant task of watching Elaine suffer. If it was difficult to escape, more than half of them traded places with Elaine (rather than watch her suffer longer).

This study provided evidence for both kinds of helping. In the low-empathy condition, people helped only to make themselves feel good. If they could walk away and ignore the victim's suffering, many chose that path. In contrast, people who felt high empathy helped regardless of whether they were allowed to escape. High-empathy helping is centered on the victim's needs, not on one's own prospects for feeling good.

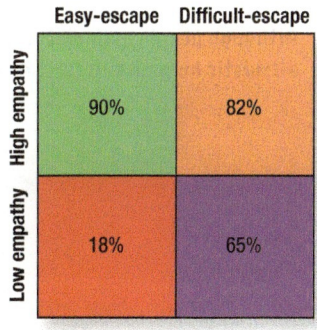

FIGURE 9.4

People in the high-empathy group helped regardless of whether escape was easy or difficulty. In the low-empathy group, people helped mainly when they could not escape.[183]

Is Altruism Possible?

As they conducted research on whether helping is driven by empathy and sympathy for victims or by the selfish desire to feel better, social psychologists gradually became involved in a centuries-old debate about whether people are basically good or evil—or, more to the point, basically unselfish or selfish. Many philosophers have asked whether people really perform morally good actions such as altruistic helping if they are motivated by a desire to feel good. In a nutshell, the argument is this: If you donate money to charity or help a needy victim because it makes you feel good to do so, aren't you really just being selfish and self-serving? Ultimately the question becomes: Is genuine altruism even possible? Skeptics would react to the "pay it forward" story at the start of this chapter by saying, for example, that Dean Young was just acting in a way that made himself feel good, even though it did genuinely help the other guy.

Social psychologists have split on this debate. Nobody disputes that some helping can be egoistical, in the sense that people sometimes help in order to gain benefits for themselves such as improved mood or a good reputation. They disagree as to whether egoism is the only motive. Some point out that people will help even when they could feel better by other, simpler means, such as by escaping the situation (as in the previous study with Elaine). They also think it is sad to dismiss so much genuine helping as mere selfishness—after all, helping someone for selfish reasons deserves to be recognized as something more positive and socially desirable than not helping or hurting someone for selfish reasons! Others have argued, however, that even empathic helping is a way to make oneself feel better. The debate goes on even today.

Our view is that the debate cannot be resolved because it asks the wrong question. It may well be true that people feel better when they help, and that these good feelings promote helping. But instead of supporting a negative conclusion about people—that

Although people assume that altruistic helping exists, it might not.

people are always basically selfish—this should foster a more positive, optimistic view. Isn't it great that natural selection influenced human beings to be able to get pleasure from helping others?

The idea that people are naturally designed to get pleasure from helping others has begun to gain support. An investigation compared people across 136 different countries, including lab studies in some quite different cultures (e.g., Canada, India, Uganda). Everywhere, people got pleasure from spending money on other people.[123] In one study, people were happier after being assigned to buy things for charity than after buying those same things for themselves. The researchers proposed that the joy of helping others may be a cross-cultural universal (that is, something true of people in all societies). This fits the view that it is built into human nature.

A study has suggested that the basic key to this sort of altruistic pleasure is seeing others receive help. Two-year-old children showed more physiological signs of pleasure when they helped an adult than when they were prevented from helping him. Crucially, they also showed pleasure when someone else came along and helped the adult.[124] That is only one study, but the implication is that people want others to be helped, more than they want to do the helping.

The conflict between selfish impulses and social conscience has been one theme of this book. Often people have to be socialized to resist selfish impulses so as to do what is best for society and culture.[125] Children must be taught to share, to take turns, and to respect the property of others, for example. The fact that nature has enabled people to feel empathy for the suffering of others and to feel good when they lend help is one (very welcome and constructive) way to avoid that conflict. The social conscience is there to make people do what is best for others (and best for society at large) even when doing so means overriding selfish impulses. The fact that people can get satisfaction from helping others makes it easier for the social conscience to accomplish this. If no one ever got any satisfaction from doing good deeds, there would probably be far fewer good deeds.

Selfishness may be part of human nature, but so is helpfulness. Human beings help their children and kin, their friends, and sometimes even total strangers. It is unfair to call them selfish just because this helping is often motivated by the fact that helping feels good. The innately prepared pleasure we get from helping is one important element in the basic goodness of human nature.[126,127]

Are some people more likely to help than others? If so, who are they? We discuss this topic in the next section.

QUIZ YOURSELF

Why Do People Help Others?

1. **Jean Luc's house is on fire. His grandparents, wife, children, and cousins are in the house. Based on kin selection theory, whom should he save first?**
   - (a) His children
   - (b) His cousins
   - (c) His grandparents
   - (d) His wife

2. **Eliza trips, falls, and begins to cry. When Mariah sees Eliza crying in pain, she starts to cry too. Mariah's response is called _____.**
   - (a) altruism
   - (b) egoism
   - (c) empathy
   - (d) reactance

3. **After seeing a victim of misfortune, empathy motivates us to _____.**
   - (a) gain the approval of bystanders
   - (b) gain the approval of the victim
   - (c) reduce our own discomfort
   - (d) reduce the discomfort of the victim

4. **After seeing a victim of misfortune, personal distress motivates us to _____.**
   - (a) gain the approval of bystanders
   - (b) gain the approval of the victim
   - (c) reduce our own discomfort
   - (d) reduce the discomfort of the victim

answers: see pg 329

Who Helps Whom?

Before we look at specific factors that differentiate who helps whom, let us consider the big picture. One thing that is special and remarkable about humans is their willingness to help others, even unrelated others. Imagine that you were offered a chance to get a nice reward for yourself, maybe money or good food. You could either get it just for yourself, or you could get a duplicate of your reward delivered to someone you had known for 15 years (and still get your own full reward). Which would you choose? Most people would eagerly choose to benefit a friend or acquaintance, especially if they could do so without cost to themselves.

Yet when this exact experiment was tried on chimps, the results were quite different. Chimps are biologically similar to human beings,[128] but they did not show any interest in helping their longtime (15-year) acquaintances. They took the reward for themselves, but they did not do the kind favor for others.[129] Thus, the basic motive to bring help and benefits to others who aren't blood relatives appears to be something that sets human beings apart from our closest animal relatives.

Helpful Personality

Eva Fogelman studied the family backgrounds of rescuers of Jews in Nazi-occupied Europe, where Jews were being rounded up and sent to death camps, and found some common denominators: "a nurturing, loving home: an altruistic parent or beloved caretaker who served as a role model for altruistic behavior; a tolerance for people who were different."[130] Other researchers studied 231 Gentiles who rescued Jews and 126 nonrescuers of the same age, gender, education, and geographic location during the war.[131] Rescuers had higher ethical values, had stronger beliefs in equity, had greater empathy, and were more likely to see all people as equal.

Some people are clearly more altruistic than others. In a typical questionnaire measure of altruistic personality,[132] respondents are asked to indicate the frequency with which they have engaged in specific prosocial behaviors within the past year, such as helping others (e.g., "I have donated blood") and giving to charity (e.g., "I have given money, goods, or clothes to a charity"). This scale, called the Self Report Altruism Scale, has been shown to correlate with peer ratings of altruism, completion of an organ donor card, and paper-and-pencil measures of prosocial orientation.[133] The altruistic personality also appears to have a genetic component.[134]

Similarity

Research has shown that people are more likely to help similar others than dissimilar others. (Even in the study reported above, with Elaine the accomplice, people who thought she was similar to them were more willing to help her than people who thought she was different.) The similarity bias especially works for outward symbols that are readily identifiable, such as similar apparel.[135] For example, research shows that international students are more likely to help other international students from similar countries than other international students from different countries.[136]

Gender

Research indicates that males are more helpful than females in the broader public sphere, toward strangers, and in emergency settings.[137] For example, since 1904 the Carnegie Hero Fund Commission has given awards to "heroes," defined as "a civilian who voluntarily risks his or her own life, knowingly, to an extraordinary degree while saving or attempting to save the life of another person."[138] More than 90% of the individuals who have received Carnegie medals have been men. Women are more helpful in the family sphere, in close relationships, and in situations that require repeated contact over a long period of time such as in volunteering.[139] Compared to males, females tend to feel more sympathy and empathy for people who need help.[140,141]

When it comes to receiving help, females are more likely to receive help than are males, regardless of whether the helper is male or female. If a car has a flat tire, for example, people are more likely to stop and help if the owner is female than if the owner is male.[142,143]

Males and females also differ in the types of help they offer their friends and relatives in sexual relationships. Read *The Social Side of Sex* to find out how.

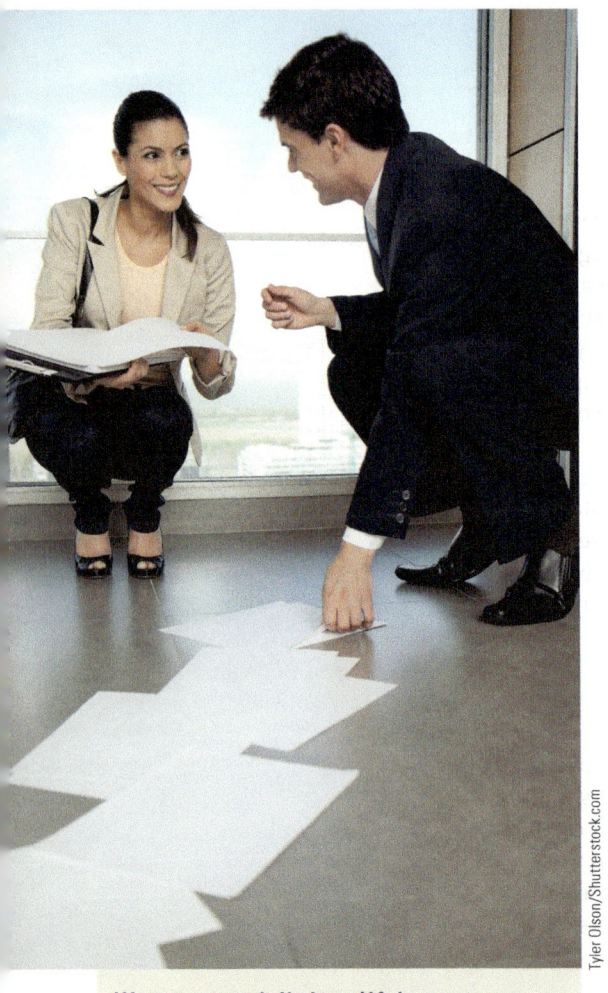

Women, especially beautiful women, are most likely to receive help.

Beautiful Victims

One of the most robust findings in the helping literature is that people are more likely to help attractive individuals than unattractive individuals. This holds true for male and female helpers and for males and females in need of help. This finding has been shown in both laboratory and field settings.[144] It has been shown in emergency situations and in nonemergency situations. In one study,[145] for example, people using phone booths at airports found a completed application form in the booth, a photograph of the applicant, and an addressed, stamped envelope. Half of the photos depicted an attractive applicant; the other half depicted an unattractive applicant. Callers were much more likely to mail applications for attractive applicants than for unattractive applicants.

In another study,[146] male college students walking by the student health center were approached by a woman who said she desperately needed money for a tetanus shot. Male students were more likely to give the woman money if she was attractive than if she was unattractive.

Belief in a Just World

When British soldiers marched a group of German civilians around the Belsen concentration camp at the end of World War II to show them what their soldiers had done, one civilian said, "What terrible criminals these prisoners must have

The Social Side of *Sex*

Helping, Sex, and Friends

A sexual relationship may seem like a private matter between two people, but in fact people depend on help from their friends and relatives in multiple ways. Just meeting sex partners is often a matter of relying on one's network. One landmark study of sexual practices found that less than half the people met their sex partners or marriage partners by introducing themselves, such as by approaching someone at a bar.[147] (Also, self-introductions were more likely to lead to short-term affairs rather than long-term relationships.) In contrast, many people were introduced to their lovers by friends, coworkers, or relatives. Family members were responsible for bringing together relatively few sex partners, but the likelihood of those relationships lasting was especially high, probably because your family knows you and will only introduce you to someone who is likely to be a good match. If your mother or brother introduces you to someone, it is probably not for the sake of casual sex but rather someone with whom you might have a stable and happy long-term relationship.

Online dating services, however, have reduced the need to rely on family members and friends to find partners. People even use online dating services to find sex partners.[148] A 2002 article from *Wired* magazine stated: "Twenty years from now, the idea that someone looking for love without looking for it online will be silly, akin to skipping the card catalog to instead wander the stacks because 'the right books are found only by accident.' Serendipity is the hallmark of inefficient markets, and the marketplace of love, like it or not, is becoming more efficient."[149] This prediction is accurate and seems to have come true before the 2022 target date.

Helping is also apparent in how people act on spring break, which for many college students is a brief, exciting time of intense partying and sexual opportunity. A team of researchers followed a sample of Canadian students who traveled to Florida for one spring break.[150] They found that most traveled in same-sex groups. On the way down, many of these groups made pacts or other agreements to help each other during the week. These agreements differed for men and women. The men generally promised to help each other find a partner to have sex with. They would agree that they all wanted to have sex and that they would support each other's efforts. If they were sharing a room, they would make plans as to how to keep it discreetly available in case one of them wanted to bring a woman there for sex. (For example, the others might agree to stay out late or even sleep on the beach if someone was there having sex.) The women, in contrast, made agreements to help each other avoid having sex. They usually agreed that their goal was to refrain from sex, unless one happened to find true love. They promised each other, for example, that if one of them got drunk and was being "hit on" (that is, targeted with romantic or sexual advances) by a particular man, the others would swoop in and bring her safely away. If they were sharing a room, they might promise not to leave one of them alone in it with a man. Thus, heterosexual men and women differ dramatically in how they help their friends in sexual situations.

Why? The most likely explanation is rooted in the social exchange theory of sex (see Chapter 12).[151] In that view, society treats heterosexual sex as something that men want from women, so men give women other resources (love, commitment, respect, attention, money) in exchange. Spring break sex is typically "free" sex that is not accompanied by commitment or other resources. From the exchange perspective, free sex signifies a good deal for men and a bad one for women. That is why men will try to support and help each other to engage in free sex, whereas women will try to support and help each other to avoid that sort of sex.

---

been to receive such treatment."[152] This statement was not made by a guard who was trying to justify his behavior to reduce cognitive dissonance; it was made by an innocent civilian. Why was this person blaming the victim? One possible explanation is that the person believed that the world is a just place where people get what they deserve and deserve what they get, a phenomenon referred to as **belief in a just world**.[153,154,155]

One unfortunate consequence of belief in a just world is that it leads people to blame the victim. They assume that those who suffer a bad fate had it coming to them. For example, people assume that rape victims must have behaved or dressed provocatively, that poor people are lazy, and that sick people are responsible for their illness. On the other hand, "blaming the victim" has become such a taboo and condemned response in the social sciences that many people today will refuse to blame a victim even when the victim does bear some of the blame. Research on violence and aggression has frequently shown, for example, that many violent acts stem from incidents in which both people provoked or attacked each other. Two patrons in a bar may start by exchanging insults, move along to shoving and hitting, and end up in a violent fight in which one is injured or killed. The killer is certainly to blame, but the so-called victim also deserves some blame under those circumstances. Victims generally deserve sympathy, and some are indeed entirely free from blame, but other victims do share responsibility for what happened to them.

belief in a just world the assumption that life is essentially fair, that people generally get what they deserve and deserve what they get

People who believe the world is just (fair) will help others, but only if they think those people deserve the help.[156] People who believe in a just world are not helpful toward victims who are perceived to be responsible for their own predicament.[157] People who believe most strongly in a just world express more negative attitudes toward helping the elderly because they believe that the elderly are responsible for meeting their own social, economic, and health needs.[158]

Belief in a just world can sometimes promote helping because the helper desires to deserve good outcomes. Again, the essence of believing in a just world is that people deserve what they get and get what they deserve. By extension, if you help others, you are a good and deserving person, so you can expect good things to happen to you. This can take on an almost superstitious aspect, as when people perform good or helpful acts in the expectation that they will be rewarded later.

Students sometimes show this sort of superstitious helping. Students at one college were asked to volunteer to do a good deed, such as serving as a reader for blind students or doing extra psychology experiments.[159] During the routine parts of the semester, helping was fairly low, and it made no difference whether the students had high or low belief in a just world. However, when the request came just before exam time, the students who believed in a just world were significantly more willing to help. Presumably they thought at some level that their good deeds would be rewarded by better luck and a better grade on the exam: If good things happen to good people, then it may help to do good deeds so as to become a good person.

Emotion and Mood

In general, positive feelings increase helping. Research has shown that helping is increased by all kinds of pleasant situations, such as sunny weather,[160] eating a cookie,[161] imagining a Hawaiian vacation,[162] and playing a relaxing video game.[163] One possible explanation for this phenomenon is that people want to maintain a good mood, and acting helpfully toward another person may allow them to sustain their good feelings (see Chapter 6).

On the other hand, bad emotions can sometimes increase helping. One way to resolve these findings is to suggest that some negative emotions may promote helping more than others. (Thus, perhaps guilt motivates helping, whereas shame or anger makes people unhelpful.) Another possibility is that the same emotion can have different effects. Focusing on yourself versus the victim can make a big difference, for example, even when the emotion is the same.

QUIZ YOURSELF
Who Helps Whom?

1. The trait that produces helping across a wide variety of settings is called the _____ personality.
   - (a) altruistic
   - (b) egoistic
   - (c) narcissistic
   - (d) overbenefited

2. When it comes to receiving help, males are more likely to help _____ and females are more likely to help _____.
   - (a) females; females
   - (b) females; males
   - (c) males; females
   - (d) males; males

3. People are especially inclined to help someone who is _____.
   - (a) altruistic
   - (b) authoritarian
   - (c) low in status
   - (d) physically attractive

4. People are especially likely to feel unsympathetic to a victim of misfortune if they _____.
   - (a) are in a good mood
   - (b) believe in a just world
   - (c) feel overbenefited
   - (d) feel underbenefited

answers: see pg 329

Bystander Helping in Emergencies

On March 13, 1964, a young woman named Kitty Genovese was attacked by a knife-wielding rapist outside her apartment in Queens, New York. News reports said her screams for help aroused 38 of her neighbors. Many watched from their windows while, for 35 minutes, she tried to escape. None called the police or sought to help in any other manner. In fact, her attacker left her twice and then returned each time; if someone had come to help her into the building during those intervals, she would have lived. Some of the witnesses didn't help because they thought it was a lover's quarrel. The *New York Times* article that described the event was titled "Thirty-Eight Who Saw Murder Didn't Call the Police."

The incident made the national news and ignited a storm of controversy. How could people just sit by and let a woman be murdered? Talking heads weighed in with their theories about urban decay, alienation, and other roots of the seemingly heartless indifference of the onlookers. Although some facts of this case have been disputed,[164] it led to a long line of social psychology studies on why bystanders might fail to help a victim in an emergency.

Most of the intellectuals who appeared on the news to discuss the Genovese murder assumed that the reasons for failing to help lay within the person. In a sense, they made what Chapter 5 described as the "fundamental attribution error": They underestimated the importance of situational factors and assumed behavior reflected the values and traits of the unresponsive bystanders. Even so, no news reporters could induce any of the bystanders to say, "I really didn't care whether that young woman lived or died." It fell to social psychologists to show that the special power of such emergency situations could explain what came to be known as the **bystander effect**. People are less likely to offer help when they are in the presence of others than when they are alone. Research shows the bystander effect even occurs in young children.[165]

On March 13, 1964, Kitty Genovese was attacked by a knife-wielding rapist outside her apartment in Queens, New York, while several of her neighbors watched from their windows.

Five Steps to Helping

Two social psychologists, John Darley and Bibb Latané, whose offices were a few minutes from the site of the Genovese murder, took the lead in studying the bystander effect. Gradually they came to recognize an absurd aspect of the controversy: the assumption that helping would be the normal, natural response. Instead, they proposed that there are at least five steps to helping in an emergency situation (see **FIGURE 9.5**). These amounted to five possible reasons that people would not help. A victim would only get help if the bystander resolved all five of these steps in the optimal way. Crucially, the presence of a crowd can interfere with helping at each of the five steps.

Step 1: Notice That Something Is Happening

The first step is to notice that something is happening. One obstacle to noticing the incident is being distracted: People who are busy or preoccupied are less likely to notice what is happening around them. Of course, people are more distracted when others are around than when alone. In a clever experiment,[166] male college students completed a questionnaire in a room, either alone or with two strangers. While they were working, smoke started coming into the room through a wall vent. Students who were alone noticed the smoke right away. In contrast, those in groups took about four times as long to notice the smoke. (Even though there were more people there to notice it!) The difference may be crucial in some emergency situations, such as a fire.

Step 2: Interpret Meaning of Event

Once you have noticed something is happening, the second step is to interpret the meaning of the event. Is it an emergency or not? Few people encounter emergencies on a

bystander effect the finding that people are less likely to offer help when they are in a group than when they are alone

FIGURE 9.5
Five steps to helping and the obstacles encountered at each step.[184]

regular basis, and emergencies do not usually come with obvious labels. How someone interprets these ambiguous situations can be decisive. For example, you notice a man stagger down the street and then slump onto the ground. Is he having a heart attack, so that your timely intervention might be needed to save his life? Or is he merely drunk, so that if you rush over to him your reward might be nothing more than having him puke on your shoes?

Sometimes it is hard to tell whether an event is an emergency. When it is easy to tell, people are more likely to intervene. To show the power of interpretations, researchers staged a physical fight between a man and a woman.[167] Bystanders offered help 65% of the time when she shouted, "Get away from me; I don't know you." Bystanders offered help only 19% of the time when she shouted, "Get away from me; I don't know why I ever married you." Perhaps they interpreted the event as a marital spat rather than as an emergency. Similarly, some of the bystanders who witnessed the Kitty Genovese murder thought it was only a lover's quarrel.

What are the obstacles to helping at this step? People often look to others for clues about how to behave. We think that others might know something that we don't know. If others do not react to an event, we conclude that it is not an emergency because otherwise they would be reacting. This phenomenon of collective misinterpretation is called **pluralistic ignorance** (also see Chapter 8). We forget that others, in turn, might be looking to us for clues about how to behave. They assume that we know more than they do. Nobody reacts, because everybody assumes that others know more than they do, when in reality nobody knows anything. Everybody is certain that nothing is wrong, when actually the event is an emergency! In simpler terms, "I'm not really sure what is going on, so I'll just mimic everyone else."

pluralistic ignorance looking to others for cues about how to behave, while they are looking to you; collective misinterpretation

Step 3: Take Responsibility for Providing Help

The third step is taking responsibility for providing help. You might notice that something is happening, and decide that it is an emergency, but that is not enough. You must be willing to take responsibility for helping. The obstacle to this step of helping is called **diffusion of responsibility**. With several potential helpers around, the personal responsibility of each bystander is reduced. If you are the only person present, 100% of the responsibility for providing help rests on your shoulders; if two people are present, each has 50% responsibility; if three people are present, each has about 33% responsibility; if four people are present, each has 25% responsibility; and so on. In crowds, people think, "Perhaps someone else will help; perhaps someone else has already called for help." With everyone thinking that someone else will help or has helped, nobody helps.

The importance of diffusion of responsibility was demonstrated in lab experiments conducted by researchers at New York University, not far from where Kitty Genovese was killed.[168] Participants believed they were taking part in a group discussion over an intercom system. During the session, another participant (actually a prerecorded voice) apparently started having a seizure and called for help. Participants who thought they were part of a six-person group generally did not help because they thought someone else would do so. In contrast, if the participant thought he or she was the only one who knew about the victim's seizure, the participant helped almost every time.

Step 4: Know How to Help

The fourth step is deciding how to help. Having assumed the responsibility to help, the person must now figure out what to do. An obstacle to offering direct help is the feeling of lack of competence—people don't feel qualified to help, or they think that somebody else is more qualified to help than they are. Researchers have shown that there is no bystander effect for those who feel competent to intervene directly. In one study,[169] female participants were either registered nurses or general education students. On their way to the lab, participants passed by a worker (actually an accomplice) who was standing on a ladder, fixing a light fixture. In the lab, participants worked on a task either alone or with an accomplice who was pretending to be another participant and whose instructions were to sit still and do nothing during the upcoming accident. In the hall, participants heard the ladder fall over, they heard a thud, and then they heard the worker groaning in pain. The vast majority of nurses helped, regardless of whether they were working alone or with a passive bystander. For them, lack of competence was no obstacle to helping. General education students were much more likely to help if they were working alone than if they were working with a passive bystander.

People who don't feel competent to offer direct help can still offer indirect help, which involves calling someone else to help. In the age of cell phones, offering indirect help is quite easy, and it may often be the wisest and safest course of action. Physical injuries are best handled by people with proper training, such as ambulance workers. Dangerous situations are best handled by people with proper training, such as police officers. Stalled motorist problems are best handled by people with proper training, such as the highway patrol. Calling others for help is still being helpful.

Step 5: Provide Help

The fifth and final step is to take action by offering help (see **TABLE 9.3**). There are obstacles to helping at this step also. One obstacle is called **audience inhibition**—people don't want to feel foolish in front of others if they offer help and the person does not want help. People also might not help if the costs outweigh the benefits.[170] For example, people might not want to get their hands or clothes dirty, or they might not have enough time. We discuss the issue of lack of time being an obstacle to helping in the next section.

diffusion of responsibility the reduction in feeling responsible that occurs when others are present

audience inhibition failure to help in front of others for fear of feeling like a fool if one's offer of help is rejected

Bystander Helping in Emergencies

Too Busy to Help?

One of the more moving and memorable stories from the New Testament in the Bible has come to be known as the parable of the Good Samaritan. It goes like this:

> A certain man went down from Jerusalem to Jericho, and fell among thieves, which stripped him of his raiment, and wounded him, and departed, leaving him half dead. And by chance there came down a certain priest that way: and when he saw him, he passed by on the other side. And likewise a Levite, when he was at the place, came and looked on him, and passed by on the other side. But a certain Samaritan, as he journeyed, came where he was: and when he saw him, he had compassion on him. And went to him, and bound up his wounds, pouring in oil and wine, and set him on his own beast, and brought him to an inn, and took care of him. And on the morrow when he departed, he took out two pence, and gave them to the host, and said unto him, Take care of him; and whatsoever thou spendest more, when I come again, I will repay thee. (Luke 10:30–35, King James Version)

TABLE 9.3 **Some Costs and Benefits of Helping**

	Helping	Not Helping
Costs	Lose time	Guilt
	Injury	Social disapproval
	Legal liability	Legal liability
	Worsen situation	
Benefits	Self praise	Avoid risk of injury
	Reward	Avoid risks of helping
	Social approval	

Would the parable of the Good Samaritan actually prompt bystanders to help in an emergency? To find out, researchers recruited students at the Princeton Theological Seminary who were studying to be ministers.[171] Half of them came to the psychology building expecting to give a talk about the Good Samaritan parable, so that the issue of helping needy victims should have been prominent in their minds. The remaining students were told to give a talk on job opportunities for seminary students.

Does being in a hurry make bystanders less likely to help in an emergency? To find out, students were also divided into low, moderate, and high "hurry" conditions. When they arrived at the lab for their appointment, they were told that their talk would be given in an auditorium in another building and were sent on their way. Those in the low-hurry condition were told that they were ahead of schedule and had plenty of time. Those in the moderate-hurry condition were told that they were right on schedule. Those in the high-hurry condition were told that they were late and that their audience was waiting for them. On the way to give their speech, all participants passed a man (actually an accomplice) who was slumped in a doorway, coughing and groaning. The measure of helping was whether students stopped to help the man.

The topic of the upcoming speech—and thus whether participants were thinking about career prospects or about the New Testament's most famous story of bystander helping—had no effect on helping. Several seminary students going to give a talk on the parable of the Good Samaritan literally stepped over the victim as they hurried on their way! Time pressures, however, had a significant effect on helping. Participants in the low-hurry condition were more than six times more likely to help than were participants in the high-hurry condition. The more time people had, the more likely they were to help.

QUIZ YOURSELF
Bystander Helping in Emergencies

1. **As the number of witnesses present at an emergency situation increases, the probability of any given individual helping _____.**
   - (a) decreases
   - (b) increases
   - (c) increases then levels off
   - (d) remains the same

2. **The fire alarm goes off. Nina doesn't move because she's uncertain about what's going on. She assumes that other people don't move because they know it's just a fire drill. Nina's thoughts illustrate _____.**
   - (a) diffusion of responsibility
   - (b) the discounting principle
   - (c) normative social influence
   - (d) pluralistic ignorance

3. **When Dick sees a neighbor's house on fire with a crowd of people standing around it, he doesn't call the fire department. He assumes that other neighbors who also saw the fire have already called the fire department. Dick's thoughts illustrate _____.**
   - (a) diffusion of responsibility
   - (b) the discounting principle
   - (c) normative social influence
   - (d) pluralistic ignorance

4. **In the Good Samaritan study,[172] participants varied in the amount of help that they offered to an (apparently) unconscious man as a function of their _____.**
   - (a) free time
   - (b) gender
   - (c) major
   - (d) religiosity

answers: see pg 329

How Can We Increase Helping?

Getting Help in a Public Setting

People aren't cold and uncaring when it comes to helping others; they are just uncertain about what to do. If you need help in an emergency setting, your best bet is to reduce the uncertainties of those around you concerning your condition and their responsibilities.[173] If you need emergency help when in a crowd of people, pick a face out of the crowd. Stare, speak, and point directly at that person. Say, "You, sir, in the red T-shirt, I need help. Call an ambulance now."

With that one statement you have reduced all the obstacles that might prevent or delay help.

- He notices you (reduces distraction).
- He understands that help is needed (reduces pluralistic ignorance).
- He understands that he, not someone else, is responsible for providing help (reduces diffusion of responsibility).
- He understands exactly how to provide help (reduces concerns about lack of competence).
- He should not be inhibited by an audience (reduces audience inhibition).

Decades of research have shown that if you follow this advice, you will maximize the likelihood of receiving help in a public setting.

Once people understand the situational factors that interfere with helping in emergency situations, they should be more likely to help. In one study,[174] students heard a lecture on why bystanders often don't help. Other students heard a different lecture or no lecture at all. As part of a different study in a different location, students found themselves walking with an unresponsive accomplice past someone sprawled beneath a bicycle. The group that heard the lecture was much more likely to help (67% vs. 27%). The researchers replicated the study by separating the lecture and the opportunity to help by two weeks. Two weeks later, when encountering a person slumped over, the group that had heard the lecture was still much more likely to help (43% vs. 25%). (See, taking a social psychology course can help you become a more helpful person!)

Provide Helpful Models

If unresponsive models interfere with helping, as often occurs in public when bystanders fail to offer help, can helpful models increase helping? The answer is a resounding yes. In one study,[175] fourth- and fifth-graders played a bowling game in which gift certificates could be earned. The gift certificates could be traded for candy and toys. Near the bowling game was a box labeled "Trenton Orphans Fund." The box also contained pictures of orphans in ragged clothing. Half the students were exposed to a helpful adult model, and half were not. Each time the adult model won gift certificates, he put half of them in the orphan box and said, "If you would like to give some of your gift certificates to them you can, but you do not have to." Students who were not exposed to the model were told the same thing. The students were then left alone to play the game. The results showed that 48% of students who were exposed to the adult model helped the orphans, whereas 0% of students who were not exposed to the adult model helped the orphans. If the researchers had included a child model condition, donations might have been even higher than for the adult model condition because people are more influenced by similar others.

The models don't need to be live either. Filmed models also work. Research has shown that prosocial television programs such as *Lassie, Mr. Rogers' Neighborhood, Barney,* and *Sesame Street* increase helpful behavior in children.[176] Prosocial video games[177] and music with prosocial lyrics[178] can also increase prosocial behavior. Another way to model helpful behavior is by **volunteering**. Over 1 in 4 Americans volunteer through or for an organization at least once a year.[179] The median amount of time spent on volunteering activities is

> "Example is not the main thing in influencing others. It is the only thing."
> — Albert Schweitzer, humanitarian, theologian, missionary, organist, and medical doctor

> "The more a soul is held captive by love, the more [that person] is identified with all humanity."
> — Mother Teresa

volunteering a planned, long-term, nonimpulsive decision to help others

50 hours; some possible activities included collecting, preparing, distributing, or serving food, fundraising, and tutoring or teaching others.

QUIZ YOURSELF

How Can We Increase Helping?

1. **At which stage do potential helpers weigh the costs of helping versus not helping before making their decisions?**
   - a. Assuming responsibility to help
   - b. Providing help
   - c. Interpreting the situation as an emergency
   - d. Noticing the emergency

2. **TV programs such as *Barney, Lassie,* and *Mr. Rogers' Neighborhood* have been shown to _____ helpful behavior in children.**
   - a. decrease
   - b. increase
   - c. have no effect on
   - d. Not enough research has been conducted to answer this question.

3. **Volunteerism is to other forms of helping as _____ is to _____.**
   - a. altruistic; egoistic
   - b. egoistic; altruistic
   - c. impulsive; nonimpulsive
   - d. nonimpulsive; impulsive

4. **Which of the following is NOT one of the five steps in the decision-tree model about whether bystanders lend help to victims in an emergency?**
   - a. Assuming responsibility
   - b. Feeling empathy for the victim.
   - c. Interpreting the event as an emergency
   - d. Notice that something is happening

answers: see pg 329

What Makes Us Human

Putting the Cultural Animal in Perspective

This chapter has given you a look at the brighter side of human nature. (But get ready for the darker side in the next chapter!) Prosocial behavior shows people doing things that bring benefits to others and help their culture and society to operate successfully. Traditionally, social psychologists have emphasized helping, but there are many other important forms of prosocial behavior. We may be inspired by the heroic acts, but society's successful functioning depends less on that sort of occasional, spectacular heroism than on everyday prosocial behavior like following rules, cooperating, reciprocating, forgiving, taking turns, and obeying legitimate authority. If most people do those things most of the time, the cultural system can succeed in making everyone better off. Recent centuries of human history have gradually seen power shift from individuals (such as kings who could command or decree whatever they wanted) to the rule of law, and in the process, life has gotten safer and happier for most people. Even today, happiness levels are higher in countries with a strong rule of law than in those that lack the rule of law.[180]

Perhaps the most sweeping and important difference in prosocial behavior between humans and other animals is that humans will do prosocial things for others who are not family members. As with most animals, human helping gives first priority to family members and loved ones, but human beings will also do nice things for total strangers. Sharing your food with your mother or your son does not indicate anything special about your humanity—many other animals would do the same. But donating money or blood to benefit people you will never meet is distinctively, and remarkably, human. In fact, we saw that 18-month-old human toddlers will even help non-kin voluntarily, and that they are more helpful than older chimps in similar situations. Nature seems to have prepared people to understand and care about each other and to offer help when possible.

Some animals can learn to follow rules, but usually these are very specific rules, made and enforced by another (typically bigger) animal whose presence is often essential for enforcing the rules. Rule following took a big leap with human evolution. People can follow laws, moral principles, and other rules even when they are alone, and they can apply them to novel situations, making following rules a vital form of prosocial behavior.

Obedience is related to following rules. Again, many animals can learn to obey specific commands. Only humans expect each other to tell the difference between legitimate and wrongful authority and to obey only the former. Even the military has come around (after atrocities such as the My Lai massacre during the Vietnam War and the Abu Ghraib prison abuses during the Iraq War) to advocating that soldiers have a duty to disobey orders that are improper. Studies such as Milgram's[181] have shown that it is hard for people to disobey direct orders from seemingly legitimate authority figures, but it can be done. The human being is (sometimes, at least) an autonomous, thinking, moral agent, even when receiving orders.

Conformity is simpler and cruder than following rules because all it requires is the ability to see what others are doing and the desire to do the same. Many animals exhibit a herd instinct sort of conformity, in which they unthinkingly copy the behavior of others. Unlike other animals, people exchange information with each other and rely on what others tell them to learn about the world.

Likewise, the beginnings of reciprocity can be seen among animals, but typically this involves sharing with kin. Humans can reciprocate with strangers. Cooperation, too, is more advanced in humans than in many other species. Some animals seem to cooperate, in that they do complementary things, but mostly these are fixed action patterns. Humans can decide to cooperate or not, and often they decide to cooperate.

Reciprocity and cooperation indicate some understanding of fairness. (If you don't pay it back, you're not being fair.) Some other animals have a crude understanding of fairness, but mostly they are upset when they are underbenefited. Humans often feel guilty or uncomfortable when they are overbenefited too.

Last, empathy may be more centrally important to human helping than to the prosocial behavior of other animals. People are much better than most other creatures at understanding what someone else is feeling, and this capacity to appreciate someone else's pain and suffering is an important factor in promoting helping behavior.

CHAPTER 9 SUMMARY

Is Helping Contagious?
- Helping and cooperative behavior can be contagious, passing from person to person to person.

What Is Prosocial Behavior?
- Prosocial behavior involves doing good for others or society; it builds relationships and allows society to function.
- Obeying rules, conforming to norms, cooperating, and helping are all forms of prosocial behavior.
- Public circumstances generally promote prosocial behavior. That is, people behave better when others are watching and know who they are.
- Reciprocity is the obligation to return in kind what another has done for us.
- Equity means that each person receives benefits in proportion to what he or she did. Equality means that everyone gets the same amount, regardless of performance.
- A full sense of fairness, recognizing both underbenefits and overbenefits, is important in humans but probably absent in other animals.

Cooperation, Forgiveness, Obedience, Conformity, and Trust
- Prisoner's dilemma is a game that consists of tradeoffs between cooperation and competition.
- Zero-sum games are those in which the winnings and losings add up to zero, so that one's gain is another's loss. Non-zero-sum games are those in which both participants can win (or lose).
- If one member of a pair is not cooperative, then cooperation is typically doomed.
- Communication improves the chances of cooperation.
- Forgiveness helps repair relationships and provides health benefits to both the forgiver and the forgiven person.
- Forgiveness is more likely when the offense or hurt was minor and when the offending person apologizes. People who are religious, are committed to the relationship, and are not self-centered or narcissistic are more willing to forgive than other people.
- A majority of participants in Milgram's experiments delivered extreme shocks to a screaming victim in obedience to an authority figure.
- Although mindless obedience can be bad, in most cases society is better off if people obey society's rules.
- Conformity means going along with the crowd. It can be good or bad.
- Conformity and obedience can be prosocial behaviors, in that they make it easier to get along with others and for society to function.

Why Do People Help Others?
- The evolutionary theory of kin selection suggests that we prefer to help others who are related to us.
- Altruistic helping is motivated by empathy, an emotional response that corresponds to the feelings of the other person because it motivates people to reduce others' distress.

Who Helps Whom?

- Many people get pleasure from helping others.
- People are more likely to help similar others than dissimilar others.
- Males are more helpful than females in the broader public sphere, toward strangers, and in emergencies, whereas females are more helpful in the family sphere, in close relationships, and in volunteering.
- Females are more likely to receive help than are males, regardless of whether the helper is male or female.
- People are more likely to help attractive individuals than unattractive individuals.
- Belief in a just world refers to the finding that people believe that the world is mostly fair and that people usually get what they deserve.
- People who believe the world is just will help others, but only if they think those people deserve the help.
- Positive moods generally increase helping, but some bad moods, such as guilt, can also promote helping.

Bystander Helping in Emergencies

- The bystander effect is the finding that people are less likely to offer help when they are in a group than when they are alone.
- The five steps to helping during an emergency are
  - Notice that something is happening.
  - Interpret the event as an emergency.
  - Take responsibility for providing help.
  - Know what to do.
  - Take action and provide help.
- Pluralistic ignorance involves thinking others know something that we don't know, even if others don't know it either.
- Diffusion of responsibility refers to the reduction in helping that occurs when multiple bystanders all assume that others will take the responsibility of helping.
- People who are in a hurry help less than those who aren't, even if those in a hurry are thinking about the Good Samaritan.

How Can We Increase Helping?

- Helping can be increased by
  - Reducing uncertainties
  - Educating others about bystander indifference
  - Providing helpful models
  - Teaching moral inclusion (making others a part of the ingroup)

What Makes Us Human? Putting the Cultural Animal in Perspective

- Humans, unlike other animals, frequently act in a prosocial manner toward others who are not family members.
- Rule following, obedience, and conformity are often depicted as negative acts, but for the most part are prosocial acts.

key terms

altruistic helping 314
audience inhibition 323
belief in a just world 319
bystander effect 321
conformity 310
cooperation 302
diffusion of responsibility 323
egoistic helping 314
empathy 313

empathy–altruism hypothesis 314
equality 296
equity 296
forgiveness 305
gratitude 296
kin selection 313
moral reasoning 299
moral inclusion 299

non-zero-sum game 305
norms 296
obedience 307
overbenefited 297
pluralistic ignorance 322
prisoner's dilemma 302
prosocial behavior 293
reciprocity 295
rule of law 294

sensitivity about being the target of a threatening upward comparison 297
trust 310
underbenefited 297
volunteering 326
zero-sum game 305

quiz yourself ANSWERS

1. What Is Prosocial Behavior? p.298
   answers: 1.b 2.b 3.a 4.b

2. Morality p.301
   answers: 1.d 2.a 3.b 4.a

3. Cooperation, Forgiveness, Obedience, Conformity, and Trust p.312
   answers: 1.d 2.d 3.d 4.b

4. Why Do People Help Others? p.317
   answers: 1.a 2.c 3.d 4.c

5. Who Helps Whom? p.320
   answers: 1.a 2.a 3.d 4.b

6. Bystander Helping in Emergencies p.325
   answers: 1.a 2.d 3.a 4.a

7. How Can We Increase Helping? p.327
   answers: 1.b 2.b 3.d 4.b

AGGRESSION & ANTISOCIAL BEHAVIOR

10

LEARNING OBJECTIVES

1. Define the different types of aggression.

2. Debate the role of nature versus nurture in human aggression, and analyze the effects of culture on aggressive impulses.

3. Identify the inner causes of aggression.

4. Describe the interpersonal causes of aggression.

5. Compare the external causes of aggression to the internal and interpersonal causes.

6. Discuss the role of culture and self-views in producing violence and aggression.

7. Identify other, nonaggressive forms of antisocial behavior.

THE SOCIAL SIDE OF SEX
Sexual Aggression
350

FOOD FOR THOUGHT
Is There a Link Between Diet and Violence?
357

TRADEOFFS
Creativity and Cheating
363

MONEY MATTERS
Money and Antisocial Behavior
364

WHAT MAKES US HUMAN?
Putting the Cultural Animal in Perspective
367

Rwanda, a country located in east-central Africa, was originally home to the Hutus.[1,2] About 600 years ago, the Tutsis, a tall warrior people that lived in Ethiopia, invaded and conquered the area and installed a king with extensive powers. Although the Hutus greatly outnumbered the Tutsis (about 85% to 15%), they agreed to raise crops for the Tutsis in exchange for protection from hostile intruders. In 1890, Rwanda became part of German East Africa. In 1916, during World War I, Belgium invaded the German territories, and after the war Rwanda came under Belgian rule.

Traditionally, the differences between Hutus and Tutsis were occupational rather than ethnic. The Hutus had the low-status farming jobs, whereas the Tutsis had the high-status cattle-herding jobs. In terms of appearance, the Hutus tended to be short and square, whereas the Tutsis were tall and thin. That may have been true 600 years ago, but today it is difficult (if not impossible) to tell them apart. The two groups not only look the same, they also speak the same language, inhabit the same parts of the country, follow the same traditions, intermarry, etc.

The Belgians considered the Tutsis as superior to the Hutus and even gave out identity cards classifying individuals as Hutu or Tutsi. Tutsis (not surprisingly) agreed with the Belgians and enjoyed better jobs, educational opportunities, and living conditions for decades. Resentment among the Hutus gradually built up, culminating in 1959 in a series of riots that overthrew the ruling Tutsi king. During these riots, more than 20,000 Tutsis were killed, and many more fled to nearby countries. When Belgium relinquished power and granted Rwanda independence in 1962, the Hutus took control of the country; many Tutsis left Rwanda and went to live in neighboring Burundi.

With the Hutus in power, the Tutsis were used as the scapegoats for every problem the country faced. Hate media fueled the fire. In 1993, Burundi President Melchior Ndadaye, a Hutu, was assassinated by hardline Tutsi soldiers. The media used the assassination to incite anger against Tutsis. The media falsely reported that the president had been tortured and castrated. (This harked back to cultural practices: In precolonial times, some Tutsi kings castrated defeated enemy rulers.)

On April 6, 1994, Rwandan President Juvenal Habyarimana, a Hutu, was killed when his plane was shot down above the airport. Nobody was sure who shot down the plane, but the Tutsis were blamed. Soon genocidal murders began, encouraged by media propaganda. Radio broadcasts called for a "final war" to "exterminate the (Tutsi) cockroaches." The United Nations (U.N.) commander in charge of peacekeeping operations at the time, General Romeo Dallaire, said: "Simply jamming [the] broadcasts and replacing them with messages of peace and reconciliation would have had a significant impact on the course of events."[3] As this chapter will discuss, the power of mass media to promote or restrain violence has been a lively topic of scientific research.

Not all broadcasters participated in the hate campaign. Thomas Kamilindi, a Hutu, resigned from a state-run radio station because he refused to broadcast hate messages. Kamilindi was called a "dog" and was almost killed for "sympathizing" with the Tutsis. A commander who happened to pass by just as a soldier pointed a gun at Kamilindi's head saved him. Kamilindi later discovered that his 5-year-old daughter had been murdered while she was visiting her Tutsi maternal grandparents, and his father had been murdered too. (One of your textbook authors—Bushman—was a mentor to Kamilindi for a year while he was a Knight-Wallace Journalism Fellow at the University of Michigan.)

In just 100 days, about 800,000 people, mostly of the Tutsi minority, were killed with guns, machetes, sticks, and stones. Hutus were given incentives for killing Tutsis, such as money, food, and even the dead Tutsis' houses and property. Imagine

Some of the victims of the 1994 massacre in Rwanda.

Today some Tutsis are forgiving the Hutus that murdered family members.

Unfortunately, violent and aggressive behavior often has unintended consequences. The 1994 genocide that occurred in Rwanda was the precipitating factor in starting the first Congo war, which resulted in 3.8 million deaths—the bloodiest war since World War II.[8] Beginning in April 1994, more than 2 million Rwandans fled to neighboring countries. Most went to Zaire (now called the Democratic Republic of Congo). Many of the refugees were Hutu militia forces (Interahamwe) who wanted to escape the Tutsi-led government that took control of Rwanda following the genocide. In October 1996, the Rwandan troops tried to forcibly oust President Mobutu Sese Seko, a dictator who had ruled Zaire for decades, which started the conflict.

The genocide in Rwanda illustrates several important points about aggression and violence. The mass media can promote aggression. Frustrated people can sometimes lash out at the source of their frustration in violent ways. Aggressors often dehumanize their victims, such as by calling them "cockroaches" or "dogs." Not just combatants but innocent people can be victims, in huge numbers. Women are also often the targets of sexual violence. Violent actions can have unintended consequences, such as stimulating further violent actions. On the other hand, it also illustrates that people can resist situational forces that increase aggression. For example, Thomas Kamilindi quit his job and refused to broadcast hate messages. During the genocide, hotel manager Paul Rusesabagina sheltered 1,268 Tutsis (and their sympathizers) while mobs outside his hotel shouted for their blood.[9] Among those saved were Kamilindi, his wife, and their surviving daughter. This true story formed the basis for the 2004 movie *Hotel Rwanda* and was held up as a positive ideal of manliness for ordinary men in the book *Is There Anything Good About Men?*, by one of your authors (Baumeister). Some Rwandans today are reconciling with those who participated in the genocide.[10] Forgiveness is possible, even for the most extreme actions.

the people in your hometown taking up their kitchen carving knives and carpentry tools to slaughter their neighbors.

Hate media were also used to incite rape and sexual assault against Tutsi women. For example, leaflets contained statements such as "You Tutsi women think that you are too good for us" and "Let us see what a Tutsi woman tastes like." A 1996 U.N. report stated that "rape was the rule and its absence the exception" and that "rape was systematic and was used as a 'weapon' by the perpetrators of the massacres." The report estimated that between 250,000 and 500,000 Tutsi women and girls had been raped, many by men who were HIV positive and knew it.[4]

The international community largely stood aside during the genocide. Initial reports were sporadic and difficult to believe, and international law generally discourages countries from interfering in the internal affairs of other countries. (Mass killings inside one country are thus more difficult to stop than an invasion of one country by another.) U.N. troops withdrew after the murder of 10 of their soldiers. The United States (U.S.) government was reluctant to involve itself in the "local conflict" in Rwanda and refused to label the killings as "genocide," a decision that former President Bill Clinton later came to regret. In a TV interview Clinton stated that he believes if he had sent 5,000 U.S. peacekeepers, more than 500,000 lives could have been saved.[5]

There was an ironic twist at the end, when the international community finally did send in troops to stop the bloodshed. A Tutsi army led by Paul Kagame (Rwanda's president today, since 2000) conquered the country. This stopped violence against Tutsis but sent the Hutus into a panic, for fear the Tutsis would extract brutal revenge. The U.N. troops had been told to stop all killings, and they found themselves in the peculiar position of having to protect mainly Hutus, including many who had taken part in the genocide.

Recently, journalists have reported that a second concurrent genocide was perpetrated by President Paul Kagame's troops that comprised the Rwandan Patriotic Front, against 500,000 or more Hutus.[6] Thus, according to these reports, a majority of the 800,000 or more Rwandans that were killed may have been Hutus. Former members of Kagame's staff, such as his former aide David Himbara, have made similar claims.[7] The ethnic composition of the victims of this tragedy and the role of Kagame's regime has become controversial.

333

Early psychological theories (such as Freud's) depicted aggression as the outburst of powerful inner forces. More recent theories have considered aggression as a kind of strategic behavior that people use to influence others, get what they want, and defend certain ideas that they see as under attack.[11,12]

Understanding aggression is important not only to social psychologists but also to society at large. One can adopt either a pessimistic or an optimistic view of aggression in human life. On the pessimistic side, there is a great deal of aggression, and it is sad to think how much avoidable suffering it causes all over the world. On the optimistic side, many situations could lead to aggression, but aggression arises in only a few of them, so somehow most people manage to inhibit their aggressive tendencies most of the time. And as we shall see, there is evidence that aggression and violence decrease as culture progresses.

Defining Aggression, Violence, and Antisocial Behavior

What is aggression? In everyday conversation, some people may describe a pushy salesperson who tries really hard to sell merchandise as "aggressive." The salesperson does not, however, want to harm potential customers. Most social psychologists define human **aggression** as any behavior intended to harm another person who does not want to be harmed.[13] This definition includes four important features. First, aggression is a behavior—you can see it. Aggression is not an emotion, such as anger (see Chapter 6 for a discussion of emotion). Aggression is not a thought, such as mentally rehearsing a murder (see Chapter 5 for a discussion of cognition). Second, aggression is intentional (not accidental), and the intent is to cause harm. For example, a dentist might intentionally give a patient a shot of anesthetic to numb the pain before filling a cavity (and the shot hurts!), but the goal is to help rather than hurt the patient. Note that behaviors that are intended to harm others are still acts of aggression even if they don't actually harm them. For example, if a person shoots a gun at you but misses, it is still an act of aggression. Third, the definition stipulates that the victim wants to avoid the harm. Thus, again, the dental patient is excluded because she or he is not seeking to avoid the harm (in fact, the patient probably booked the appointment weeks in advance and paid to have the dental work done). Suicide and sadomasochistic sex play are also not included because again the victim actively seeks to be harmed. Fourth, aggression involves at least two people—the perpetrator and the victim. Thus, suicide is once again excluded because it involves only one person.

It is useful to distinguish among various forms and functions of aggression. By "forms" we mean how the aggressive act is expressed, such as *physically* (e.g., hitting, kicking, stabbing, shooting) or *verbally* (e.g., yelling, screaming, swearing, name calling). In **displaced aggression**, the act is expressed against a substitute target.[14] For example, a man is berated by his boss at work but does not retaliate. When he gets home, he kicks his dog or yells at a family member instead. Recent research indicates that people may resort to displaced aggression when they lack other means to deal with frustrating situations.[15]

Different forms of aggression can be expressed directly or indirectly. In **direct aggression**, the victim is physically present; in **indirect aggression**, the victim is absent. For example, physical aggression can be direct (e.g., hitting a person in the face) or indirect (e.g., burning his house down while he is away). Likewise, verbal aggression can be direct (e.g., screaming in a person's face) or indirect (e.g., spreading rumors behind her back). Males are more likely than females to use direct aggression, whereas females are more likely than males to use indirect aggression.[16]

Aggressive acts may also differ in their function or motivation. Consider two examples. In the first, a husband finds his wife and her lover together in bed. He grabs his rifle from the closet and shoots and kills them both. In the second, a "hit man" uses a rifle to kill another person for money. The form of aggression is the same (shooting and killing victims with a rifle); however, the motives appear quite different. In the first example, the husband is probably motivated by anger. He is enraged when he finds his wife making love to another man, so he shoots them both. In the second example, the "hit man"

aggression any behavior intended to harm another person who is motivated to avoid the harm

displaced aggression any behavior that intentionally harms a substitute target rather than the provocateur

direct aggression any behavior that intentionally harms another person who is physically present

indirect aggression any behavior that intentionally harms another person who is physically absent is motivated by money. The "hit man" probably does not hate his victim, but he kills the person anyway for the money.

To capture different functions or motives for aggression, psychologists make a distinction between **reactive aggression** (also called hostile, affective, emotional, angry, impulsive, or retaliatory aggression) and **proactive aggression** (also called instrumental aggression or premeditated aggression).[17,18,19] Reactive aggression is "hot," impulsive, angry behavior that is motivated by a desire to harm someone. Proactive aggression is "cold," premeditated, calculated behavior that is motivated by some other goal (obtaining money, restoring one's image, restoring justice). Some scholars have argued that it is difficult (if not impossible) to distinguish between reactive and proactive aggression because they are highly correlated and because motives are often mixed.[20]

Bullying refers to persistent aggression by a perpetrator against a victim for the purpose of establishing a power relationship over the victim.[21] The key feature of bullying over other acts of aggression is its persistent nature—the bully repeatedly picks on the victim. People don't like to be bullied, and sometimes they retaliate. For example, one man from Tokyo, Japan sent more than 500 packages of rubbish (e.g., rotten tea leaves, dirt, women's underwear) in the mail to people who bullied him in primary school and in his boy scout troop.[22] **Cyberbullying** refers to the use of the internet (e.g., social media) to bully others. In cyberbullying the perpetrator can be anonymous, especially when using instant messaging. Although bullies at school tend to be bigger and stronger than their victims, cyberbullies can harm others regardless of how big and strong they are.

Researchers also use the term *violent* in a more precise way than the general public. A meteorologist might call a storm "violent" if it has intense winds, rain, thunder, lightning, or hail. Most social psychologists define **violence** as aggression that has as its goal extreme physical harm, such as injury or death. Thus, all violent acts are aggressive acts, but not all aggressive acts are violent—only the ones designed to cause extreme physical harm are violent. Likewise, not all crimes are violent, but most violent acts are crimes. For example, the U.S. Federal Bureau of Investigation (FBI) classifies four crimes as "violent"—homicide, aggravated assault, forcible rape, and robbery.

Acts of aggression and violence can be committed by individuals or by groups. As one scholar notes, "People fight and kill for personal reasons, but homicide is not war. War is social, with groups organized to kill people from other groups."[23]

Recent research indicates that violence is like a contagious disease that spreads from person to person.[24] As Dr. Martin Luther King Jr. noted, "violence begets violence."

Antisocial behavior is a term that social psychologists have used in casual and somewhat inconsistent ways (though clinical psychologists have a more precise definition). In general, it seems to refer to behavior that either damages interpersonal relationships or is culturally undesirable. Aggression is often equated with antisocial behavior.[25,26] Others have pointed out, however, that aggression is often a social as well as an antisocial strategy, in that it is a way that people seek to manage their social lives, such as by influencing the behavior of others to get what they want.[27] Littering, cheating, lying, and stealing, on the other hand, are behaviors that qualify as antisocial but may or may not be aggressive.

Is the World More or Less Violent Now Than in the Past?

Although the world seems more violent today than ever before, Daniel Webster was right—the world is actually less violent now than in the past. Quantitative studies of body counts, such as the proportion of prehistoric skeletons with axe and arrowhead wounds, suggest that prehistoric societies were far more violent than our own.[28] Although one can kill a lot more people with a bomb than with an axe, the death rates per battle were much higher in the past. Estimates show that if the wars of the 20th century had killed the same proportion of the population as ancient tribal wars, then the death toll would have been 20 times higher—2 billion rather than 100 million.[29]

More recent data also show that violence has declined over time. European murder rates have decreased dramatically since the Middle Ages.[30,31] For example, estimated murders

> "Let us thank God that we live in an age when something has influence besides the bayonet."
> —Daniel Webster

reactive aggression (also called hostile, affective, emotional, angry, impulsive, or retaliatory aggression) "hot," impulsive, angry behavior motivated by a desire to harm someone

proactive aggression (also called instrumental aggression) "cold," or premeditated, calculated harmful behavior that is a means to some practical or material end

bullying persistent aggression by a perpetrator against a victim for the purpose of establishing a power relationship over the victim

cyberbullying the use of the internet (e.g., email, social network sites, blogs) to bully others

violence aggression that has as its goal extreme physical harm, such as injury or death

antisocial behavior behavior that either damages interpersonal relationships or is culturally undesirable

Although modern weapons such as the bomb the Americans dropped on Hiroshima can kill a lot more people than ancient weapons, the world is actually a more peaceful place today than in the past.

in England dropped from 24 per 100,000 in the 14th century to 0.6 per 100,000 by the early 1960s. The major decline in violence seems to have occurred in the 17th century during the Age of Reason, beginning in The Netherlands and England and then spreading to other European countries.[32]

Global violence has been falling steadily since the middle of the 20th century (despite horrific episodes like the Rwanda massacres).[33] For example, the number of battle deaths in wars between countries has declined from more than 65,000 per year in the 1950s to fewer than 2,000 per year in the 2000s. Globally, the number of armed conflicts and combat deaths, the number of military coups, and the number of deadly violence campaigns waged against civilians have declined. As can be seen in **FIGURE 10.1**, violence levels have decreased worldwide in the 20th century.

A number of other observations are consistent with the idea that human society is becoming less violent over time. As Steven Pinker notes: "Cruelty as entertainment, human sacrifice to indulge superstition, slavery as a labor-saving device, conquest as the mission statement of government, genocide as a means of acquiring real estate, torture and mutilation as routine punishment, ... all were common features of life for most of human history. But, today, they are rare to nonexistent in the West, far less common elsewhere than they used to be, concealed when they do occur, and widely condemned when they are brought to light" (p. 18).[34]

In today's digital age, we certainly are more informed about wars and other acts of violence than in past ages. "If it bleeds, it leads" seems to be the rule used to determine what news stories to focus on. Citizen journalists around the world also make use of social media to "show and tell" the world about unjustified acts of violence. It is much more difficult for the perpetrators of violent acts to hide today than in the past. Because violent images are more available to us now than ever before, we might assume that violence levels are also higher. However, that perception might be due to the availability heuristic (see Chapter 5); when we can readily recall violent acts, we assume that violent acts are common. In reality, over time this planet is actually becoming a more peaceful place to live. (At least for humans; animals have not changed their behavior much, and species continue to go extinct at tragic rates, mostly due to loss of habitat caused by humans.)

FIGURE 10.1
Violence levels have decreased worldwide in the 20th century.

Country	Total deaths (high estimate)	Number of episodes
NAMIBIA	75,000	1
TURKEY	1,500,000	1
GERMANY	11,400,000	1
JAPAN	10,000,000	1
U.S.S.R.	20,000,000	1
INDIA	1,000,000	1
CHINA	30,000,000	3
SUDAN	2,850,000	3
ALGERIA	30,000	1
CHILE	10,000	1
RWANDA	1,020,000	2
ZAIRE	14,000	2
S. VIETNAM	500,000	1
INDONESIA	1,200,000	2
IRAQ	240,000	2
NIGERIA	2,000,000	1
EQ. GUINEA	50,000	1
PAKISTAN	3,010,000	2
UGANDA	900,000	2
PHILIPPINES	60,000	1
BURUNDI	210,000	3
CAMBODIA	1,700,000	1
ANGOLA	600,000	2
ARGENTINA	20,000	1
ETHIOPIA	10,000	1
BURMA	5,000	1
AFGHAN	1,800,000	1
GUATEMALA	200,000	1
EL SALVADOR	60,000	1
SYRIA	30,000	1
IRAN	20,000	1
SOMALIA	50,000	1
SRI LANKA	30,000	1
BOSNIA	225,000	1
YUGOSLAVIA	10,000	1

GERMANY During WWII, Nazis killed over 11 million.

U.S.S.R. Twenty million murdered, most under Stalin's reign.

CHINA Under Mao, 30 million killed, mainly in the Great Leap Forward.

SUDAN Mass murders continue today in the Darfur region.

IRAQ Under Saddam, perhaps 200,000 killed.

Century of Death

A grim account of the past century shows mass murder is a recurring tool used against political, ethnic, and religious groups.

○ Deaths per episode
— Duration of episode

Courtesy of Professor Barbara Harff

The fact that aggression and violence are decreasing over time is consistent with one of this book's key themes: Nature says yes and culture says no. One of the main goals of culture is to reduce aggression. When two social animals want the same thing, aggression is the main way of settling who gets it. Culture offers less aggressive ways of settling conflict: negotiation, property rights, money, courts of law, compromise, religious and moral rules, and the like. The main exception has been rivalries between cultures, which sometimes are settled with aggression. Even so, culture has sought to reduce these conflicts, such as with the Geneva Convention and other rules of war that constrain violence. World organizations such as the United Nations also try to reduce aggression between countries.

Defining Aggression, Violence, and Antisocial Behavior

QUIZ YOURSELF

Defining Aggression, Violence, and Antisocial Behavior

1. **Which of the following would be considered aggression?**
   - (a) A baseball batter's line drive accidentally hits the pitcher in the knee.
   - (b) A girl attempts to punch her little brother, but misses.
   - (c) A depressed man commits suicide.
   - (d) All of the above

2. **Which of the following would not be considered aggression?**
   - (a) A dentist giving a patient a shot of Novocain
   - (b) A depressed man committing suicide
   - (c) A sadomasochistic interaction
   - (d) All of the above

3. **Sander becomes so angry at his roommate for stealing the keg of beer he bought for a party that Sander starts kicking and hitting him repeatedly. Sander's actions are _____ .**
   - (a) aggressive
   - (b) violent
   - (c) aggressive and violent
   - (d) neither aggressive nor violent

4. **Over time, the level of violence in the world has _____ .**
   - (a) decreased
   - (b) remained the same
   - (c) increased linearly
   - (d) increased exponentially

answers: see pg 369

Is Aggression Innate or Learned?

> "The tendency of aggression ... constitutes the most powerful obstacle to culture."
> —Sigmund Freud (1856–1939)

The 19th and 20th centuries saw many attempts to improve society. The hope was to design a perfect society so that people could live together in peace, love, and harmony. Communism, democracy, and fascism were based on these ideals.

Aggression gradually emerged as the crux of the problem, however. If aggression only stems from frustration, exploitation, and injustice, then if one designed a perfect society, there would be no aggression. For example, if people were only aggressive because of injustice, then eliminating injustice would eliminate aggression. Even frustration might in theory be eliminated or at least significantly reduced, and much aggression along with it. (But don't count on it!)

On the other hand, if people are naturally, innately aggressive, then no amount of social engineering will be able to get rid of it. No matter how well a society is designed, people will still be aggressive. Perfect social harmony will prove elusive. If people are inherently aggressive, then aggression will always be with us, and society or culture needs to find ways of reducing it, such as by passing laws to punish wrongful aggression.

Instinct Theories

The instinct theory of aggression, first given scientific prominence by Charles Darwin,[35] views aggressive behavior as an evolutionary adaptation that had enabled creatures to survive better. This instinct presumably developed during the course of evolution because it promoted survival of individuals. Because fighting is closely linked to mating, the aggressive instinct helped ensure that only the strongest individuals would pass on their genes to future generations.

Sigmund Freud[36] argued that human motivational forces, such as sex and aggression, are based on instincts. An **instinct** is an innate (inborn, biologically programmed) tendency to seek a particular goal, such as food, water, or sex. In his early writings, Freud proposed the drive for sensory and sexual gratification as the primary human instinct, which he called **eros**. After witnessing the horrific carnage of World War I, however, Freud concluded that a single, positive life force could not be responsible for so much violence. He proposed, therefore, that humans also have a destructive, death instinct, which he called **thanatos**.

Freud's views undoubtedly influenced Konrad Lorenz,[37] whose instinct theory of aggression posited a buildup of aggressive urges (like hydraulic pressure inside a closed environment) that, if not released through some other activity, would inevitably lead to aggression. Although little empirical evidence has ever been found to support this "hydraulic" model of aggression, the theory that aggression results from the buildup of an internal drive or tension that must be released still has an influence on clinical psychology. It motivates popular venting and cathartic therapies even though numerous studies have found no evidence supporting the hydraulic model.[38,39,40]

Empirical evidence supporting the existence of innate, relatively automatic aggressive responses has been demonstrated for some species.[41] For example, in the male Stickleback fish, a red object triggers attack 100% of the time.[42] However, no such innate aggressive response has been demonstrated in humans.[43]

Learning Theories

According to social learning theory,[44,45,46] aggression is not an innate drive like hunger in search of gratification. People learn aggressive behaviors the same way they learn other social behaviors—by direct experience and by observing others. In social learning theory, the shift is from internal causes to external causes. According to this theory, people observe and copy or imitate the behavior of others—called **modeling**. Modeling can weaken or strengthen aggressive responding, depending on whether the model is rewarded or punished for behaving aggressively.

To demonstrate the social learning of aggression, Albert Bandura and his colleagues[47] allowed preschool children to watch an aggressive adult role model, a nonaggressive model, or no model. The aggressive model abused a large, inflated clown called a Bobo doll. The model laid the Bobo doll on its side, sat on it, punched it repeatedly in the nose, and said, "Sock him in the nose." The model then beat the doll on the head with a mallet and said, "Hit him down." The model tossed the doll up in the air and said, "Throw him in the air." The model kicked the doll about the room, saying, "Kick him" and "Pow." In contrast, the nonaggressive model played with nonviolent toys the entire time, so children in that condition saw no aggressive activity. After 10 minutes, the experimenter entered the room, informed the child that he or she would now go to another game room, and said good-bye to the model. The other room contained the Bobo doll as well as both aggressive (e.g., mallet, dart guns), and nonaggressive (e.g., tea set, crayons) toys. The children who had watched the aggressive model showed the highest levels of aggression (see **FIGURE 10.2**). Bandura and his colleagues replicated their findings using filmed models.[48]

To be sure, these studies do not meet our definition of human aggression because the aggressive act is targeted at an inanimate Bobo doll rather than a real person. However, many other studies have shown that aggressive models can influence people of all ages to behave more aggressively toward human targets. In one study,[49] children could help or hurt another child's chance of winning a prize by pressing either a green "HELP" button or a red "HURT" button. Participants were told that when they pressed the "HURT" button, a handle that the other child was turning would get really hot and burn them. (In reality, of course, there was no child

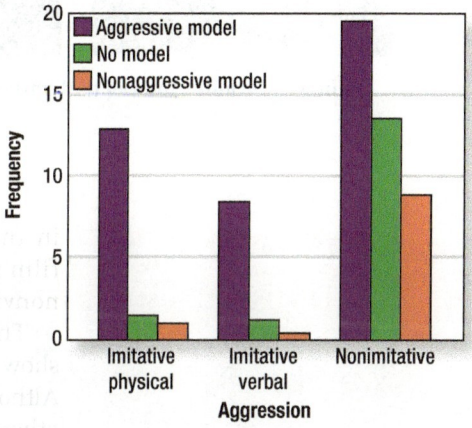

FIGURE 10.2

Results from a Bobo doll study conducted by Bandura and his colleagues. Children exposed to aggressive models behaved more aggressively than did children exposed to nonaggressive models or no models.[48]

instinct an innate (inborn, biologically programmed) tendency to seek a particular goal, such as food, water, or sex

eros in Freudian theory, the constructive, life-giving instinct

thanatos in Freudian theory, the destructive, death instinct

modeling observing and copying or imitating the behavior of others

Bandura's studies showed that children readily imitated filmed aggressive adult models.

in the other room, and no one got burned.) Children who had watched a violent film pressed the "HURT" button down longer than did children who had watched a nonviolent film.

These experiments don't exactly show that aggression is learned. They do, however, show that inhibitions against aggression can be overcome if a model acts aggressively. Although all creatures are innately disposed to learn some things better and faster than others, learning is still important. The impulse to lash out against someone who hurts or threatens or humiliates you may be natural and universal (nature says go), but the rules governing action or restraint depend heavily on culture (culture says stop). Some anthropologists and others believe that without cultural encouragement, there would be no aggression,[50] but the majority of social scientists disagree, partly because aggression has been found everywhere. The nonviolent human being, not the violent one, is the product of culture.

Nature *and* Nurture

Many experts on aggression (and your textbook authors) favor a middle ground in this nature-versus-nurture dispute. Both learning and instinct are relevant.

As already noted, learning clearly plays a role. People can learn how to behave aggressively. Even more important and more commonly, they learn how to restrain aggression. People learn and mostly obey complicated rules about aggression. Some remarkable evidence of this can be seen in American football games. Urged on by coaches and fans to "beat" and "destroy" their opponents, the defensive players charge at the quarterback as ferociously as they can, eager to slam into him and knock him to the ground. But they have to be able to stop this attempted aggression at a split-second's notice when the quarterback steps out of bounds, or he throws the ball, or the referee blows the whistle, to avoid being penalized for "roughing the passer."

As for nature, it is hard to dispute that aggression is found all over the world, and indeed some of its patterns are universal. For example, in all known societies, young adult men mainly perpetrate violence.[51] In no society do the majority of violent criminals turn out to be elderly women, for example.

Most likely, the Freudian theory of innate aggression needs a major overhaul. Freud and others thought aggression was like hunger: The need to aggress bubbles up from inside and has to be satisfied in some way. In that view, the aggressive drive is independent of circumstances. In contrast, perhaps natural selection has led to aggressive impulses as a way to respond to certain (social) events, such as someone else's getting something you want. To appreciate the difference, imagine what life would be like if you always got everything you wanted. According to the Freudian view, you would still have aggressive impulses, because the aggressive drive would still arise repeatedly and make you want to hit people or smash things. In contrast, if aggression is merely an innate response to not getting what you want, you might in principle never have an aggressive impulse if you always got what you wanted.

Humans don't have to learn to behave aggressively—rather, aggression seems to come quite naturally. Instead, they learn how to control their aggressive impulses. Thus, it may be natural to feel aggressive impulses in response to certain provocations. But cultural beings learn to bring those natural impulses under control so as to follow the rules. This fits the theme that nature says go, whereas culture says stop. All known human societies have rules against aggression, though they may consider some aggression acceptable. For human beings who live in culture, aggression is subject to rules and limits. And as we have seen, the gradual progress of human culture has led to a gradual but large reduction in rates of aggression and violence. Culture's "stop" message is slowly succeeding in making societies less aggressive over time.

Aggressive instincts can be modified so that even cats and rats can live together peacefully.

QUIZ YOURSELF

Is Aggression Innate or Learned?

1. **In Freud's theory, life-giving instinct is to death instinct as _____ is to _____.**
   - ⓐ eros; thanatos
   - ⓑ thanatos; eros
   - ⓒ id; superego
   - ⓓ superego; id

2. **Learning is to instinct as _____ is to _____.**
   - ⓐ external forces; internal forces
   - ⓑ internal forces; external forces
   - ⓒ Sigmund Freud; Konrad Lorenz
   - ⓓ Konrad Lorenz; Sigmund Freud

3. **Abdul believes that children are aggressive because they imitate what they see family members and media characters do. Abdul's beliefs are consistent with _____ theory.**
   - ⓐ Freudian
   - ⓑ frustration
   - ⓒ instinct
   - ⓓ social learning

4. **The wide variation in homicide rates across different countries illustrates the effect of _____ on violence and aggression.**
   - ⓐ aggressive cues
   - ⓑ frustration
   - ⓒ nature
   - ⓓ nurture

answers: see pg 369

Inner Causes of Aggression

Frustration

In 1939 a group of psychologists from Yale University published a book titled *Frustration and Aggression*.[52] In this book, they proposed the **frustration–aggression hypothesis**, which they summarized on the first page of their book with these two bold statements: (a) "the occurrence of aggressive behavior always presupposes the existence of frustration," and (b) "the existence of frustration always leads to some form of aggression." (Note the strong use of "always" in both sentences; social psychologists today hardly ever dare say "always" or "never"!) They defined **frustration** as blocking or interfering with a goal. The Yale group formulated the frustration-aggression hypothesis based on the early writings of Sigmund Freud.[53] Freud believed that people are primarily motivated to seek pleasure and avoid pain. People were presumed to be frustrated when their pleasure-seeking or pain-avoiding behavior was blocked. Freud regarded aggression as the "primordial reaction" to frustration. (As we saw earlier, Freud eventually revised his theory to include an aggressive instinct, but the Yale group favored his earlier theory.)

Neal Miller, one of the original authors of *Frustration and Aggression,* was quick to tone down the second statement of the frustration-aggression hypothesis.[54] He changed that statement to: "Frustration produces instigations to a number of different types of response, one of which is an instigation to some form of aggression" (p. 338). Miller continued to hold that the first statement of the hypothesis (aggression is *always* preceded by frustration) was true.

Most experts today think even Miller's revised theory goes to far. Aggression can exist without frustration. Still, there is no denying the basic truth that frustration often increases aggression.

The Rwanda genocide was triggered in part by frustration on the part of Hutus that the Tutsis were so much better off than they were, even though they were the minority group. The frustration of the majority Hutus dated back to having to submit to a Tutsi king. Of course, frustration does not justify the Hutus' slaughtering the Tutsis, but it may partly explain their actions.

Being in a Bad Mood

Angry, frustrated, distraught, upset people have long been regarded as being prone to aggressive behavior. As the previous section showed, psychologists have long believed that frustration causes aggression, and the data have confirmed that—but it is not the whole story because some aggression is not caused by frustration. More recently, Leonard Berkowitz (sometimes considered the grandfather of the social psychology of aggression, and also the academic grandfather of Bushman) proposed that all unpleasant events—not just frustration—deserve to be recognized as causes of aggression.[55] To be sure, not all varieties of negative affect have been tested for aggression-enhancing effects, but it is clear that some of them are quite capable of increasing aggression. When researchers want to elicit high levels of aggression in the laboratory, they typically start by inducing some aversive emotional state, such as anger or indignation. But perhaps it is too much to state that all negative emotions promote aggression. Indeed, guilt, which is a negative emotion, increases prosocial behavior[56] and decreases aggressive behavior.[57]

Why do unpleasant moods increase aggression? One possible explanation is that angry people aggress in the hope that doing so will enable them to feel better. Research has consistently shown that people who feel bad often try to remedy or repair their moods.[58] Because many people believe that venting is a healthy way to reduce anger and aggression

frustration–aggression hypothesis proposal that "the occurrence of aggressive behavior always presupposes the existence of frustration," and "the existence of frustration always leads to some form of aggression"

frustration blockage of or interference with a personal goal (see Chapter 6), they might vent by lashing out at others to improve their mood. Experimental research supports this hypothesis about trying to feel better.[59] These studies replicated the standard finding that anger increases aggression—but also found a revealing exception. When participants believed that their angry mood would not change for the next hour no matter what they did (ostensibly because of side effects of a pill they had taken, which temporarily "froze" their mood), anger did not lead to aggression. The implication is that anger does not *directly* or *inevitably* cause aggression. Rather, angry people attack others because they believe that lashing out will help get rid of their anger and enable them to feel better.

As we saw in Chapter 6, many emotions are characterized by a bodily state called arousal, which is a feeling of excitement or tenseness. (This does not refer to specifically sexual arousal, which is a special case.) Moreover, we saw that arousal caused by one event can sometimes be transferred to something else, thereby increasing one's reaction to it. Aggression can be increased by "excitation transfer." That is, arousal deriving from nonaggressive sources (such as physical exercise or an erotic nonviolent movie) can be mistaken for anger and can therefore increase aggression. Studies have randomly assigned participants to exercise by riding a stationary bike, or to skip the workout.[60] Afterward, participants were provoked or not provoked by an accomplice. Participants were then given an opportunity to punish the accomplice by shocking him. The highest levels of aggression were found among participants who had both ridden the bike and been provoked (see **FIGURE 10.3**). The provocation produced the anger, which was then fueled by excitation transfer from the workout.

The fact that aversive emotional states lead to aggression has been asserted for decades and supported by many research findings. However, it is important to point out that being in a bad mood is neither a necessary nor a sufficient condition (nor a justification) for aggression. There is negative affect without aggression, and vice versa.

FIGURE 10.3

Arousal from physical exercise can transfer to a provocation and therefore increase aggression. As shown in this figure, the most aggressive participants in this study were those who first exercised and were later provoked.[283]

Appetitive Aggression

Although feeling bad often leads to aggression, the reverse is not necessarily true. Some people feel good (rather than bad) after they behave in an aggressive or violent manner.[63] From an evolutionary perspective, succeeding at violent activities such as hunting, attacking rivals, and fighting over mates is functionally adaptive. Today, some people enjoy and even relish violent activities such as hunting, playing contact sports, and playing violent video games. This type of aggression is called **appetitive aggression**.[64] For example, a former U.S. Air Force member was sentenced to life in prison for killing a colleague by strangling her to death. In his journal, he wrote about how he had "a hunger, a thirst, a craving" to kill people, and "I just enjoy killing."[65] Persistent and childhood trauma are risk factors for appetitive aggression. Although males are more likely than females to engage in appetitive aggression, both genders are biologically attracted to it. For example, women have also been involved in bloody killings.[66]

People who have killed in combat often report that it is difficult in the beginning to overcome the moral barriers to killing. For example, people often experience nausea and anxiety for days afterward. Alcohol and drugs can help ease the pain. But it gets easier after each kill—a process called **desensitization**. Gradually, killing becomes appetitive, and can culminate in bloodlust. For example, 8% of the combatants in the Eastern Democratic Republic of the Congo reported having eaten the flesh of their enemies.[67] At the physiological level, the "thrill of the hunt" is accompanied by a surge of adrenalin, by the release of cortisol and especially endorphins, which block the pain and increase stamina.[68] Once the moral rules are adjusted through disinhibitory devices such as dehumanization (e.g., calling Tutsi's cockroaches)[69], killing becomes not only easier, but also pleasurable. Appetitive aggression makes massacres and genocides like the one in Rwanda possible.

It is interesting to note that some personality traits linked to aggression have the experience of positive emotions at their core, such as sensation-seeking and sadism.[70] Sensation seeking is the tendency to pursue pleasure excitement, such as by engaging in

> "If I hear the sounds of bullets I wish I could be fighting. This thirst to fight is in me. It is like the thirst of a person who likes Coca Cola. The thirst will not be satisfied until the person drinks a Coke."
>
> —Combatant of Eastern Democratic Republic of the Congo[61]

appetitive aggression aggression that is motivated, in part or whole, by an intrinsic enjoyment of the aggressive act

desensitization a psychological process that occurs when emotional reactions to a stimulus decrease following repeated exposure to it

> "Now, the passion to fight for your club and the adrenaline rush that comes with it was [sic] unbelievable. But I don't think that this addiction can be understood."
> —Football Hooligan Danny Brown in *Villains*[62]

> "Loving people live in a loving world. Hostile people live in a hostile world. Same world."
> — Wayne Dyer, American author and motivational speaker

thrilling or even risky activities (e.g., gambling, drugs, sex, reckless driving, sky diving, rock climbing). Most people experience distress after hurting an innocent person, but sadistic people instead experience pleasure, excitement, and perhaps even sexual arousal. It is interesting to note that about 18% of combatants agree that attacking humans can be sexually arousing for them.[71]

Hostile Cognitive Biases

As Wayne Dyer observed, loving people tend to view the world in a loving manner, whereas hostile people tend to view the world in hostile manner. Research has shown that aggressive individuals view the world in a more hostile manner than do nonaggressive individuals.[72] In other words, aggressive individuals have a hostile bias in the kinds of attributions they make. As we noted in Chapter 5, the attributions people make for another person's behavior can have a strong influence on their own behavior. Perceptions can be more important than reality when it comes to understanding human thought and behavior. People are more likely to behave aggressively when they perceive ambiguous behaviors from others as stemming from hostile intentions than when they perceive the same behaviors as coming from benign intentions. When an ambiguous event occurs, do we give others the benefit of the doubt, or do we assume they are out to get us? This is a question of attributions. Some people assume that others are out to attack them, even if they are not. That is, they automatically (and sometimes mistakenly) attribute hostile intent to other people.

The **hostile attribution bias** is the tendency to perceive ambiguous actions by others as indicating aggressive intent. For example, if someone bumps into you, a hostile attribution would be that the person did it on purpose to harm or annoy you. A meta-analysis of 41 studies involving more than 6,000 participants showed a strong relationship between hostile attribution of intent and aggressive behavior in children.[73] This relationship holds for adults, too.[74]

Two other related biases have been proposed: the hostile perception bias and the hostile expectation bias. The **hostile perception bias** is the tendency to perceive social

Some people have a hostile attribution bias—they interpret the ambiguous actions of others as hostile actions.

SOURCE: Tremblay (2000).

hostile attribution bias the tendency to perceive ambiguous actions by others as aggressive

hostile perception bias the tendency to perceive social interactions in general as being aggressive interactions in general as being aggressive. The hostile *attribution* bias pertains specifically to whether someone is attacking you, but the hostile *perception* bias pertains to whether other people are attacking each other, such as seeing two other people having a conversation and inferring that they are arguing or getting ready to fight. Research has shown that this bias is more prevalent in aggressive individuals than in nonaggressive individuals.[75] Even something as subtle as an advertisement for alcohol can increase hostile perceptions, perhaps because most people strongly associate alcohol with aggression.[76]

Aggressive people see the world as a hostile place. The **hostile expectation bias** is the tendency to expect others to react to potential conflicts with aggression. Individuals who are characteristically aggressive are more likely than nonaggressive individuals to expect others to behave in an aggressive manner.[77] For example, if you bump into another person, a hostile expectation would be that the person will assume that you did it on purpose and will attack you in return. Of course, people are more likely to behave aggressively themselves if they expect others to behave aggressively.

In summary, aggressive people have inner biases that make them (a) expect others to react aggressively, (b) view ambiguous acts as aggressive, and (c) assume that when someone does something to hurt or offend them, it was intentional rather than accidental. Such biases are an impediment to peace and harmony in our social world. If more people could give each other the benefit of the doubt more often, the world would be a less violent place.

Research suggests that hostile biases can be changed![78] Participants were teens in a youth program that were considered high risk for committing a crime. Indeed, 70% already had an official record of criminal convictions. Participants saw 15 faces on a continuum that ranged from clearly happy to clearly angry, with several ambiguous faces in between. First, teens indicated the point in the continuum when the faces changed from happy to angry. Next, teens were randomly assigned to treatment or control groups. The treatment consisted of telling the teens that two of the faces they

hostile expectation bias the tendency to assume that people will react to potential conflicts with aggression

Research shows that hostile biases can be changed so that they perceive faces to be less angry after training (bottom row) than before training (top row).[178]

Few dared to enter the territory of the dreaded "Cribs Gang."

thought were angry were in fact happy. They were told this each day for four days, just to make sure they got it. To measure the effect of the treatment, staff members recorded incidents of aggressive behavior the week prior to the experiment, and two weeks after the experiment. The results showed that teens in the treatment group were significantly less aggressive than those in the control group.

Although there are stable individual differences in the tendency to make hostile attributions, situational factors can also play a role. One obvious situational factor is exposure to violent media. Violence is a common in both real and fictional media. Theoretically, people who are immersed in violent media should come to view the world as a hostile place.[79,80] A recent meta-analysis of 37 studies involving over 10,000 participants found evidence consistent with this hypothesis.[81] The opposite is also true. Playing a prosocial video game can decrease the hostile expectation bias.[82]

Age and Aggression

Children do not commit many violent crimes, especially as compared to young adult men. Yet Richard Tremblay has provided evidence that very young children are in fact the most aggressive human beings on earth.[83] His research team observed toddlers in day-care settings and recorded that about 25% of interactions involve some kind of physical aggression (e.g., a child pushes another child out of the way and takes their toy). No adult group, not even violent youth gangs or hardened criminals, resorts to physical aggression 25% of the time. (Remember our definitions, though: Most toddler aggression isn't severe enough to qualify as violence, and it is sometimes difficult to determine intent in toddlers.) It is fortunate for all of us that toddlers are small, weak, and unlikely to be carrying guns!

The high level of aggression among toddlers again fits the theme that nature says go and culture says stop. Human children naturally rely on physical aggression to resolve their disputes, including influencing other toddlers to get what they want. Toddlers may resort to aggression 25% of the time, but as they grow up, they learn to inhibit aggression.

Although most people become less aggressive over time, a small subset of people become *more* aggressive over time. The most dangerous years for this small subset of individuals (and for society) are late adolescence and early adulthood. This is because aggressive acts become more extreme (e.g., weapons are used more frequently). Official records show that violent criminal offending is highest for individuals (especially men) between 15 and 30 years old, and declines significantly after that.[84]

Gender Differences in Aggression and Violence

Gender differences in aggression occur among most animals, including humans. For example, research shows that when male rats are under stress, they respond by either fighting or running away, called the **fight or flight syndrome**.[85] In contrast, female rats respond to stress by nurturing others and making friends, called the **tend and befriend syndrome**.[86]

In humans, gender differences in aggression are very noticeable by the preschool years, with boys showing higher levels of physical aggression than girls.[87] In later elementary grades and in adolescence, gender differences increase. Indirect aggression becomes much greater for girls than boys, physical aggression becomes much greater

Aggressiveness peaks at age 2. Fortunately, it is curtailed by nap times, curfews, limited strength, and general incompetence.
SOURCE: Tremblay (2000).

fight or flight syndrome a response to stress that involves aggressing against others or running away

tend and befriend syndrome a response to stress that involves nurturing others and making friends

Physical aggression is higher for boys than girls.

for boys than girls, and verbal aggression is about the same for girls and boys.[88,89] These gender differences culminate in dramatic differences in physically violent behavior in young adulthood, reflected in huge gender differences in murder rates. There is no known society in which women commit most of the violent crimes;[90] the gender difference in violence is universal.

Why? When something is universal, the common assumption is that it is at least partly innate. One answer would therefore be that males are innately more physically aggressive than females. A related answer is that during evolution, whether a male was able to reproduce depended on his status and rank among the males in his group—and those in turn depended on aggression. To get access to females and thereby have a chance to make babies, a male had to fight and dominate other males. Vestiges of this pattern have been shown in modern college students. After thinking about an intense sexual experience, college men (but not women) became more aggressive—and only toward other men, not toward women.[91] Thus, the thought of sex stimulates the male's concern with needing to dominate other males physically.

Nevertheless, it would be wrong to think that females are never physically aggressive. Females do display physical aggression in social interactions, particularly when other females provoke them.[92] Laboratory studies with college students often yield higher aggression by men, but provocation has a greater effect on aggression than does biological sex. Gender differences in lab aggression shrink under high provocation.[93] When it comes to heterosexual domestic partners, women are slightly *more* likely than men to use physical aggression against their partners![94,95] However, men are more likely than women to inflict serious injuries and death on their partners (i.e., violence), probably because men tend to be taller, heavier, and stronger than women on average.

Females are much more likely than males to engage in **relational aggression** (also called **social aggression**), defined as intentionally harming another person's social relationships, feelings of acceptance, or inclusion within a group.[96] Some examples of relational aggression include saying bad things about people behind their backs, withdrawing affection to get what you want, excluding others from your circle of friends, and giving someone the "silent treatment." Unfortunately, social aggression occurs in many cultures.[97] Twin studies have shown a genetic component of social aggression, as well as an environmental component.[98]

relational aggression (also called **social aggression**) behavior that involves intentionally harming another person's social relationships, feelings of acceptance, or inclusion within a group

Inner Causes of Aggression | **347**

Aggressive Personalities

Some people tend to be cranky, irritable, and aggressive almost all the time. Aggressiveness is a personality trait, and it is almost as stable over time as intelligence.[99] Aggressive children tend to grow up to be aggressive adults.

However, some scholars have argued that aggressiveness is not just one personality trait and have proposed instead that it consists of four dark personality traits: narcissism, psychopathy, Machiavellianism, and sadism.[100] Narcissism was discussed in Chapter 3. Narcissists have "thin skins" and are easily offended; they think they are special people who deserve special treatment. When they do not get the respect they believe they are entitled to, they often lash out at others in an aggressive manner. Psychopaths are callous and unemotional individuals who mainly focus on obtaining their own goals, regardless of whether they hurt other people in the process. They tend to be cold and calculating rather than impulsive. Thus, their aggressive responses tend to be proactive rather than reactive. The term "Machiavellianism" comes from the Italian philosopher and writer Niccolò Machiavelli, who advocated using any means necessary to gain raw political power, including aggression and violence. For Machiavellians, any means justify the ends. Sadism was discussed earlier in the chapter (see "Appetitive Aggression" section). Although the four dark traits are theoretically distinct, they share common features (e.g., lack of empathy, callous manipulation of others).

QUIZ YOURSELF
Inner Causes of Aggression

1. Interference with the attainment of a goal first results in _____.
   - ⓐ aggression
   - ⓑ catharsis
   - ⓒ violence
   - ⓓ frustration

2. Bernard is the class clown. Eberhard is the class genius. Adolf is the class bully. Otto is the class athlete ("jock"). The person most likely to assume that others are provoking him is _____.
   - ⓐ Adolf
   - ⓑ Bernard
   - ⓒ Eberhard
   - ⓓ Otto

3. Which group of people resorts to aggression most often?
   - ⓐ Toddlers
   - ⓑ Teenagers
   - ⓒ Young adults
   - ⓓ Adults

4. Females are more aggressive than males when it comes to _____.
   - ⓐ direct aggression
   - ⓑ indirect aggression
   - ⓒ physical aggression
   - ⓓ verbal aggression

answers: see pg 369

Interpersonal Causes of Aggression

Selfishness and Influence

One broad theory argues that aggression should be understood as a form of social influence.[101] Instead of a learned response, or a reaction to frustration, or an eruption of innate drives, aggression is mainly viewed as a means for people to get what they want. This theory highlights the social rather than the antisocial nature of aggression, because it depicts aggression as a way in which people relate to others.

Creatures that don't take care of themselves tend not to survive and reproduce, so evolution has made most animals (including humans) selfish.[102] Humans can rise above their selfishness, but the selfish core is still there. Social life inevitably breeds some degree of conflict between selfish beings, such as when two people want the same food or the same mate, when both want to occupy a nice spot, or even when both want to watch different programs on the same television set! Aggression is one means that social animals use to resolve some of these disputes.

When do people resort to aggression to get what they want? Several factors play a role.[103] The more they want the reward (think of saving the life of someone you love), the more willing people are to use violence to get it. People are more likely to resort to aggression when they believe it will bring success, such as if the other person seems unlikely to retaliate. (If the other person is bigger and stronger than you, then aggression does not seem a promising way to get what you want.) Some people regard physical violence as immoral and will not engage in it under almost any circumstances, whereas others are far less inhibited.

Blaming someone for unfair actions can lead to aggressive retaliation. The most commonly cited unfair things that people do include disloyalty, disregarding the feelings of others, hostility, breaking promises and other agreements, selfishness, rudeness, lateness, and vicious gossip.[104,105] People use many means to strike back or punish someone who has wronged them, ranging from directly hitting the person, to spreading nasty rumors, to committing property crimes such as burglary or vandalism. In fact, one study of arson (setting fires) in Houston concluded that three out of five arsons were done as a way of getting revenge for some perceived unjust mistreatment.[106] For example, people set fires to punish a bar or restaurant that had thrown them out, or to get back at an ex-lover.

In short, aggression is a strategy that many social animals (including humans) use to help them get what they want. To learn about one particular case—namely, sexual aggression—see *The Social Side of Sex*. Human culture may invoke laws and moral principles to try to get people to resolve their disputes using peaceful means, and most people probably agree that nonviolent means are better, but every day, all over the world, many people find themselves resorting to aggression or violence to get something or just to get even.

Domestic Violence: Hurting Those We Love

Domestic violence (also called **family violence** or **intimate-partner violence**) is violence that occurs within the home, between people who have a close relationship with each other. Examples of domestic violence include a husband beating his wife, a mother hurting her child, a parent sexually molesting a child, brothers and sisters hitting each other, a child witnessing parents fighting, a teenager hitting a parent, and an adult striking an elderly parent. If anything, aggression is highest between siblings.[107] The U.S. Surgeon General declared domestic violence to be the number one health risk in the United States. Women in non-committed relationships are especially at risk. The risk of being the victim of domestic violence for women who are separated, divorced, cohabiting with a partner, or never married is three times higher than the risk for married women.[108] It can occur in heterosexual, homosexual, or bisexual relationships. It is mainly women who report incidents of domestic violence to the police.[109]

Men are also victims of domestic violence, although it is often underreported. As was noted earlier, women actually attack their relationship partners slightly more often than men do, although women don't cause as much physical harm. The average husband is taller, stronger, and heavier than his wife, so if they get into a physical fight, she is much more likely to be injured or killed than he is. Domestic violence also occurs in relationships involving homosexual and bisexual men and women,[110] as well as transgender, genderqueer, and non-binary individuals.[111] Physically weaker family members, such as children or elderly parents, are especially at risk of becoming domestic violence victims because they cannot fight back. Domestic violence not only immediately harms victims, but it can also produce long-term harmful consequences (e.g., depression, anxiety, insomnia, loneliness, social dysfunction, somatic symptoms).[112,113]

The same factors that influence aggression against strangers also appear to influence aggression against loved ones. The "perfect storm" combination of causes for domestic violence appears to be a combination of strong instigating factors (e.g., provocation, rejection), strong impelling factors (e.g., trait aggressiveness, hostile attribution bias), and weak inhibitor factors (e.g., low self-control, alcohol intoxication).[114]

Research shows that husbands who want to control their wives are more likely to assault them.[115] Abusive spouses also tend to be abusive parents.[116] Parents who were abused

domestic violence (also called **family violence** or **intimate-partner violence**) physically harmful actions that occur within the home or family, between people who have a close relationship with each other

The Social Side of Sex

Sexual Aggression

We have seen that many people use aggression to get what they want from others, and one thing that people sometimes want—and use force to get—is sex. Most cultures recognize the problem that some men force women to have sex against their will. The #MeToo movement has raised awareness of this issue. The opposite problem, of women forcing men to have sex, has generally been ignored, though surveys suggest it also occurs.[117] Still, when women force men to have sex, the traumatic consequences appear to be much less than what female rape victims suffer.[118] Sometimes, too, men force other men to have sex, and women force other women. Male coercion of females is generally considered to be the most serious social problem, however. Of course, sexual coercion occurs within homosexual relationships as well as heterosexual relationships, and in relationships where the partners don't identify as male or female.

Defining rape or sexual coercion is a difficult issue that has compounded the problem of understanding, because sexual coercion consists of multiple phenomena that almost certainly have different causes. Some researchers have favored broad, loose definitions of sexual coercion, using one big category that includes everything from being attacked, beaten, and forced to have intercourse by a stranger to the case of a young man who kisses a woman against her will. Efforts to understand the causes of sexual coercion depend heavily on such definitions. Because there are far more cases resembling the stolen kiss than the forcible stranger rape, the stolen kiss data can crowd out the violent stranger rapes. The National Health and Social Life Survey[119] found that between 15% and 22% of women said they had been forced into some sexual activity against their will, but only 1% were forced by strangers. The majority of victims, in fact, said the person who forced them was someone they were in love with at the time.

Even if a woman is in love with the man who forced her, or has consented to kissing or petting with him, or even if she has previously (or subsequently) consented to sex with that man, that does not make any kind of forced sexual activity any less of a crime. Any person always has the right to refuse sexual advances from any person at any time, and it is both highly immoral and illegal to continue to demand sex when one's partner has indicated an unwillingness to go any further. It is upsetting and even traumatic to be subjected to unwanted sexual advances, whether one knows the attacker or not. However, researchers who use broad definitions of sexual coercion and then combine all acts when evaluating the harm done to victims may seriously underestimate the negative effects of some of the most atrocious acts of sexual violence.

How the victims fare depends on what definition of rape is used. Victims of violent rape, especially by strangers, often suffer lasting problems, including fear and anxiety, depression, and sexual problems.[120,121] Many victims blame themselves. Some withdraw from other people and become socially isolated. In contrast, when looser definitions of sexual coercion were used in other studies, the results suggested much less lasting trauma. Often the man apologized and the woman simply forgave him and went on to consider him a friend.[122] Three out of five rape victims said they had had consensual sex with the rapist on a previous occasion, and two out of five had some consensual activity (such as making out or oral sex) on the same day as the rape.[123] Two out of five rape victims said they would consent or had consented to having sex with the rapist on a later occasion.[124] Almost certainly these data are not based on violent stranger rapes—they refer instead to acquaintance and date rape patterns, which are different in some ways (though still immoral).

The old stereotype of the rapist was either a woman hater or a man who lacked social skills and could not get sex via romance and persuasion and therefore resorted to violence. Research, including studies on date rapists, has painted a very different picture.[125,126] Sexually coercive men generally have other sex partners and indeed may have more sex than noncoercive men. A sexually coercive man generally does not hate women, but he may devalue them, may have little empathy for their concerns or suffering, and is likely to feel that women have hurt or betrayed him in the past. His peer group places high emphasis on sexual conquests, and he wants to have some to boast about. He is therefore motivated to downplay his use of force or coercion and claim instead that he had consensual sex (because it bolsters his ego and reputation). In fact, he probably prefers not to use force, but he is willing to use any means he can, including trickery, false promises, untrue declarations of love, and force, to get sex. He has high sexual motivation and enjoys impersonal, uncommitted sex. If his crime was date rape, it was often preceded by some consensual activity such as oral sex; when the woman wanted to stop, he forced her to continue. He thinks very highly of himself and may well have narcissistic personality patterns, including the sense that he deserves special rewards such as sexual favors.[127] He may think the woman owes him sex and that he is only using a bit of force to claim what he deserves. Therefore, he may not even admit to himself that what he is doing is immoral and illegal.

---

as children are significantly more likely than others to abuse their own children.[128,129] However, one should not overstate this relationship, as is often done. By far, most victims of abuse do not become abusers themselves.

Domestic violence is not a recent phenomenon; it has a long history. One example is corporal or physical punishment of children. From an evolutionary perspective, agricultural and industrial societies used corporal punishment more frequently than hunter-gatherer societies, perhaps because hunter-gatherers had relatively few valuable physical possessions that children could damage.[130] Although corporal punishment was once

Qui aime bien châtie bien.

> An illustration from French caricaturist Jean Ignace Isidore Gérard's (pseudonym J. J. Grandville) *Les cent proverbs* captioned "Qui aime bien châtie bien" (*Who loves well, punishes well*), showing a man spanking a child in the foreground, and a husband beating his wife in the background.
>
> —J. J. Grandville "*Les cent proverbs*" 1845

quite common, culture is gradually intervening to prohibit and punish it. This indicates the slow process of culture entering more and more previously private spheres to say "stop" by exerting control over aggression. The American Puritan tradition regarded the nuclear family as sacrosanct and held that no one should intervene in how parents raise their children, but modern American culture is increasingly rejecting that view to insist that parents and teachers refrain from aggressive and violent treatment of children.[131]

QUIZ YOURSELF
Interpersonal Causes of Aggression

1. **What theory of aggression posits that people use aggression to restore justice?**
   - (a) Frustration–aggression theory
   - (b) Instinct theory
   - (c) Social influence theory
   - (d) Social learning theory

2. **Which group of people is especially at risk for domestic violence?**
   - (a) Men in committed relationships
   - (b) Men in noncommitted relationships
   - (c) Women in committed relationships
   - (d) Women in noncommitted relationships

3. **Which of the following statements is false?**
   - (a) Women attack their relationship partners more often than men do.
   - (b) In an attack, men cause more damage than women do.
   - (c) The average husband is taller, stronger, and heavier than his wife.
   - (d) All of the above are true.

4. **Domestic violence is especially likely to occur when instigating factors are _____, impelling factors are _____, and inhibiting factors are _____.**
   - (a) strong; strong; strong
   - (b) strong; strong; weak
   - (c) strong; weak; weak
   - (d) weak; weak; weak

answers: see pg 369

External Causes of Aggression

Weapons Effect

Obviously, using a weapon can increase aggression and violence, but can just seeing a weapon increase aggression? In 1967, Leonard Berkowitz and Anthony LePage conducted a study to find out.[132] Angry participants were seated at a table that had a shotgun and a revolver on it—or, in the control condition, badminton racquets and shuttlecocks. The items on the table were described as part of another experiment that the researcher had supposedly forgotten to put away. The participant was supposed to decide what level of electric shock to deliver to a accomplice, which were used to measure aggression. The experimenter told participants to ignore the items, but apparently, they could not. Participants who saw the guns were more aggressive than were participants who saw the sports items. Berkowitz and LePage dubbed this effect the **weapons effect**.

The weapons effect has been replicated many times, both inside and outside the lab. For example, the weapons effect can occur on the road. A representative survey of over 2,000 U.S. drivers found that those who had a gun in their car were significantly more likely to make obscene gestures at other drivers (23% vs. 16%), aggressively follow another car too closely (14% vs. 8%), or both (6.3% vs. 2.8%), even after controlling for several potential confounding factors (e.g., gender, age, urbanization, census region, driving frequency).[133] Of course, one cannot make the causal inferences from this survey (see Chapter 1). Guns could cause aggressive driving. But it could also be true that aggressive people are more likely to carry guns in their vehicles, or that some third factor is related to both aggressive driving and carrying guns in vehicles. But a recent driving simulation experiment found a causal link—people drove more aggressively when there was a gun on the passenger seat than when there was a tennis racket on the passenger seat.[134] These findings have practical implications. Driving a car is the most dangerous behavior most people engage in every day.[135] According to the World Health Organization (WHO), about 1.25 million people die each year as a result of road traffic crashes, and they are the leading cause of death among 15 to 29 year olds.[136] In the United States (U.S) alone, over 40,000 people are killed in motor vehicles each year. Although there are several causes of traffic accidents (e.g., texting, alcohol consumption, inclement weather), the leading cause is aggressive driving.[137] In the United States, aggressive driving accounts for more

> "Guns not only permit violence, they can stimulate it as well. The finger pulls the trigger, but the trigger may also be pulling the finger."
> —Leonard Berkowitz, Emeritus Professor of Psychology, University of Wisconsin

weapons effect the increase in aggression that occurs as a result of the mere presence of a weapon

Does the weapons effect extend to police officers who wear military gear?

than half of all traffic fatalities.[138] Thus, aggressive driving is an important applied health topic, especially for young drivers.

A recent meta-analysis of 151 effects from 78 studies involving 7,668 participants sheds light on why the weapons effect occurs.[139] Weapons prime aggressive thoughts in memory, including photos of weapons. It doesn't seem to matter whether a "good guy" (police officer, soldier) or a "bad guy" (criminal) is holding the gun. A recent field experiment found that the mere presence of a TASER (electroshock gun) more than doubled physical assaults against police officers in London, England,[140] even though logically people should avoid assaulting an officer with a TASER (or any other weapon). The authors recommended that officers conceal TASERs so they do not produce a weapons effect.

Indeed, you don't even need to be consciously aware of the fact that you have seen a weapon for it to affect you. In one study, participants who were exposed to words describing weapons (e.g., "gun") for only 17/100ths of a second were more aggressive afterward in comparison to participants exposed to nonaggressive words.[141] It is interesting to note that human beings are very good at quickly identifying potential threats, such as spiders and snakes. These responses are adaptive from an evolutionary perspective because some spiders and snakes are poisonous, and our ancient ancestors who could identify them quickly were more likely to avoid them and live to pass their genes on to the next generation. Recent research shows that people can identify guns as quickly as they can identify spiders and snakes.[142,143,144] These findings are very interesting because guns are modern threats and cannot be explained using evolutionary principles. Yet guns are a far bigger threat to more people today than spiders or snakes. Poisonous spiders (e.g., black widows, brown recluses) kill about 6–7 Americans each year.[145] Poisonous snakes (e.g., rattlesnakes, coral snakes) kill about 5 Americans each year.[146] In comparison, guns kill about 40,000 Americans each year.[147]

The weapons effect meta-analysis found that weapons can also increase hostile biases,[148] which can increase aggression (see Hostile Cognitive Biases section earlier in this chapter). For example, recent research shows that holding a gun makes people believe that others are also holding guns (as opposed to neutral objects such as a cell phone).[149]

Violent Media

As discussed in the previous section, the mere presence of a weapon can increase aggression—called the weapons effect. There are plenty of weapons in the mass media, and they are not merely present either. Media characters use weapons to kill and injure other characters. The use of weapons in the mass media is also increasing over time. For example, research shows that acts of gun violence in Hollywood movies rated PG-13 (for ages 13+) have nearly tripled since the rating was introduced in 1985.[150] Indeed, since 2012 PG-13 films contain more gun violence than movies rated R (for ages 17+).

Public debate on violent media effects can become especially contentious in the wake of a shooting rampage.[151] Following a rampage shooting, it is often revealed that the shooter spent an excessive amount of time consuming violent media (e.g., violent games). It is tempting for some to conclude that violent media caused the shooting rampage. However, it is impossible to make causal inferences about the link between exposure to violent media and violent criminal behavior because it is unethical to conduct experimental studies in which research participants can commit violent crimes in the lab (see Chapter 1). Violent behavior is complex and is caused by multiple factors, often acting together. The

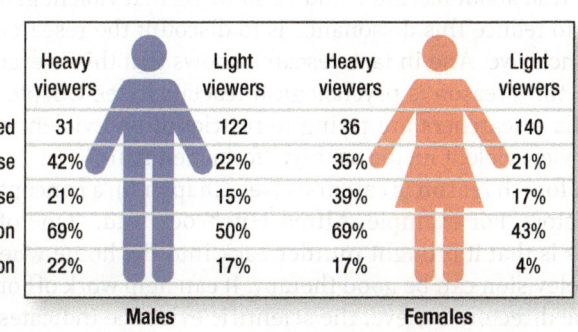

FIGURE 10.4

	Males		Females	
	Heavy viewers	Light viewers	Heavy viewers	Light viewers
Number interviewed	31	122	36	140
Pushed, grabbed, or shoved spouse	42%	22%	35%	21%
Threw something at spouse	21%	15%	39%	17%
Shoved another person	69%	50%	69%	43%
Bunched, beat, or choked another person	22%	17%	17%	4%

more extreme the violent behavior (e.g., from hitting, to shooting, to mass shooting), the more complex the causality may be. There is, however, a significant positive correlation between exposure to violent media and violent criminal behavior.[152] One can, however, draw causal inferences about the link between exposure to media violence and aggressive behavior in milder forms than violence. Hundreds of experiments have shown that exposure to media violence causes an increase in aggressive behavior.[153,154,155] Studies also have shown that parents who set limits on the amount and content of children's media use provide a powerful protective factor against aggression.[156] Longitudinal studies have shown that violent media effects persist over time (see Figure 10.4).[157,158]

One other type of media deserves special mention: violent media that contain sex, such as rape depictions. As we saw in the opening story, hate media may have contributed to the rape and sexual assault of women and girls during the 1994 genocide in Rwanda. Several social psychological experiments have found that violent sexual media increase aggression against women,[159,160] There are also long-term effects of viewing violent sexual media, such as desensitization to the pain and suffering experienced by women who have been the victims of sexual assault.[161,162]

Social scientists have extensively studied the effects of exposure to violent media on aggression. Some people think there is a "debate" about violent media effects. Although there is never complete consensus on any scientific topic, including violent media effects, the overwhelming majority of pediatricians (about 90%) and media researchers (about 67%) *strongly agree* or *agree* that violent screen media (i.e., television programs, movies, internet sites, video games) increase aggression in children.[163] The rest are about evenly divided between *disagree* or *strongly disagree* and *neither agree nor disagree*. In fact, numerous scientific and medical organizations have issued warning statements about the harmful effects of violent media, especially on children. These include the American Academy of Child and Adolescent Psychiatry, the American Academy of Family Physicians, the American Academy of Pediatrics, the American Medical Association, the American Psychiatric Association, the American Psychological Association, the Australian Psychological Society, the Canada Action Agenda, the International Society for Research on Aggression, the Society for the Psychological Study of Social Issues, the United Nations, and the U.S. Surgeon General.[164] For example, in 1972 the US Surgeon General issued the following statement: "It is clear to me that the causal relationship between televised violence and antisocial behavior is sufficient to warrant appropriate and immediate remedial action . . . There comes a time when the data are sufficient to justify action. That time has come."[165]

Given the fact that hundreds of studies have shown that violent media increase aggression, and numerous scientific and medical organizations have issued warnings about the harmful effects of violent media, one might wonder why people would deny these effects. There are at least reasons why,[166,167,168] several of which involve concepts we have already discussed in this textbook.

Some gamers claim, "I play violent video games, and I've never killed anyone." But this it is not surprising because very few people kill anyone (less than 5 people per 100,000 each year in the US, for example). People fail to consider the low base rates for rare events like murder (see base rate fallacy in Chapter 5). Research shows that playing violent games causes people to behave more aggressively, even if they don't kill anyone.

Cognitive dissonance is another reason why (see Chapter 7). If people frequently play violent video games and think the games are fun, they may feel uncomfortable when they read about research studies showing that violent games can be harmful. The easiest way to reduce this dissonance is to discount the research evidence as biased, flawed, or inconclusive. And in fact, research shows that this is exactly what gamers do.[169]

A third reason is psychological reactance (see Chapter 4). Gamers often think violent media researchers are trying to restrict or ban violent media. Younger children might also view violent media as tasty "forbidden fruit."

A fourth reason is catharsis (see Chapter 6), a concept embraced by many Hollywood directors. For example, Alfred Hitchcock said, "One of television's greatest contributions is that it brought murder back into the home where it belongs. Seeing a murder on television can be good therapy. It can help work off one's antagonism." Despite what these directors believe, the scientific evidence indicates that catharsis theory is false.

A fifth reason is called the **third-person effect**, which is the belief that the media have a much stronger effect on other people than on oneself.[170] People might also believe that violent media only affect some "susceptible" people (e.g., mentally ill people, aggressive people). Basically, people seem to think that they are somehow immune to media effects, including violent media effects.

A sixth reason is desensitzation, a concept discussed earlier in this chapter in the section on Appetitive Aggression. Through repeated exposure to violent media, people can become numb to it and think it is no big deal.

A seventh reason is that the media deny any link between exposure to violent media and aggression,[171,172] even though it is in their economic self-interest to make such claims. It is a paradox, though. On the one hand, the TV industry claims that a few minutes of advertising can sell just about anything. Indeed, a 30-second ad in the 2019 Super Bowl cost $5.25 million. On the other hand, the TV industry claims that the hours of programming surrounding the few minutes of advertising have no effect on viewers. But the tobacco industry said the same thing about cigarettes. Indeed, in 1994 all (even though the US Surgeon General began putting warning labels on cigarette packs in 1964) seven Tobacco CEOs testify before Congress that cigarettes are not addictive.[173]

An eighth reason is that journalists often report "both sides of the story," even if the scientific evidence is much stronger for one side than the other. And most lay people learn about studies from journalists than by reading the actual studies.

The ninth reason is that people do not understand psychological processes (e.g., priming, desensitization, social learning) as well as they understand biological processes. If one observes a player of violent video games assault another person, it is difficult to know the direct cause of the assault. Was it playing violent video games for hours on end, or was it something else? In contrast, if one sees a chain smoker die of lung cancer, it is much easier to believe that the direct cause of the lung cancer was smoking.

In summary, several psychological principles can explain why people often deny violent media effects. As we noted in Chapter 5, people tend to use "psycho-logic" rather than logic to make decisions. Of course, exposure to violent media is not the only risk factor for aggression, but it is not a trivial factor either.

Unpleasant Environments

One common belief shared by writers, philosophers, and laypersons alike is that hot temperatures increase aggression and violence. This belief has even crept into the English language, as indicated by common phrases such as "hot-headed," "hot-tempered," "hot under the collar," and "my blood is boiling." Research evidence is consistent with this belief. The evidence from laboratory experiments, field experiments, correlational studies, and archival studies of violent crimes indicates that hotter temperatures are associated with higher levels of aggression and violence.[174] Studies that compare the violence rates of regions that differ in climate have found that hotter regions have higher violent crime rates.[175] Time period studies generally have found higher violence rates in hot years, hot seasons, hot months, and hot days than cold ones.[176,177]

When people think of the consequences of global warming, they focus mainly on the impact of rising temperatures on droughts, agricultural crops, flooding, and extreme weather. However, there is also an impact of global warming on aggression and violence.[178] A comprehensive review of the 60 most rigorous studies conducted to date found strong causal evidence linking climate change to human conflict.[179]

Other unpleasant environmental events can also increase aggression[180], including traffic noise, foul odors, secondhand smoke, air pollution, pain, stress, unpleasant tastes, and crowding. It is important to distinguish between density and crowding. **Density** (the number of people in a given area) and **crowding** (the subjective and unpleasant feeling that there are too many people in a given area) are not the same thing. Crowding is a better predictor of aggression than density per se. In fact, high population density can produce positive emotions and behaviors in desirable environments, such as in football stadiums or concert halls. Crowding, on the other hand, can increase aggression in undesirable environments, such as in psychiatric wards[181] and prisons.[182]

third-person effect is the belief that media messages have a stronger impact on others than on oneself

density the number of people divided by the area of the space they share

crowding the subjective and unpleasant feeling that there are too many people in a given area

> "So, if anatomy is destiny then testosterone is doom."
> — Al Goldstein, pornographer

Chemical Influences

Hormones and Neurotransmitters

Like all behaviors, aggression is influenced by changes in chemical reactions and interactions within the brain. Two naturally occurring chemicals in the brain, testosterone and serotonin, have been closely linked with aggression. **Testosterone** is the male sex hormone. Although both males and females have testosterone, males have much more of it. Levels peak during puberty and begin to decline around age 23. Testosterone has repeatedly been linked to aggression. In his book *The Trouble with Testosterone*, Robert Sapolsky provides a concise description of the seemingly direct association between testosterone and aggression: "Remove the source of testosterone in species after species and levels of aggression typically plummet. Reinstate normal testosterone levels afterward with injections of synthetic testosterone, and aggression returns."[183]

One problem with establishing a link between testosterone and aggression is that behavioral outcomes closely related to aggression also affect circulating testosterone levels.[184] For example, laboratory studies of competitions have shown that males who win games usually experience an increase in testosterone, and some female winners do, too.[185,186,187] This research strongly suggests a reciprocal influence between testosterone and aggression in humans. Higher levels of plasma testosterone probably increase aggression slightly, but the outcome of winning and dominating affects testosterone levels just as much. To be sure, if high testosterone makes someone pick a fight that he or she lose, his or her testosterone may drop afterward.

In human brains, information is communicated between nerve cells (neurons) by the movement of chemicals across a small gap called the synapse. The chemical messengers are called neurotransmitters. **Serotonin** is one of these neurotransmitters; it has been called the "feel good" neurotransmitter. Not enough of it makes people feel bad and may therefore increase aggression. In correlational studies, levels of serotonin in the brain have been negatively related to aggression and violence in humans[188,189] and other animals.[190,191]

Alcohol and Other Drugs of Abuse

Alcohol is by far the chemical that has received the most attention from aggression researchers. Alcohol has long been associated with violent and aggressive behavior. In fact, it was standard practice for many centuries to issue soldiers some alcohol before they went into battle, both to reduce fear and to increase aggression.[192] There is ample evidence of a link between alcohol and aggression,[193] and experimental studies show the link is causal.[194,195,196]

There are several possible explanations for why alcohol increases aggressive tendencies. One explanation is that alcohol reduces inhibitions.[197] Normally people have strong inhibitions against behaving aggressively, and alcohol reduces these inhibitions. To use a car analogy, alcohol increases aggression by cutting the brake line rather than by stepping on the gas. Alcohol might increase aggression by decreasing glucose levels, which provide the brain with the fuel it needs to exercise self-control (see Chapter 4).[198] Alcohol might also increase aggression by decreasing serotonin levels.[199]

Another explanation is that alcohol has a "myopic" (nearsighted) or narrowing effect on attention.[200] This causes people to pay attention only on the most noticeable or salient features of a situation (e.g., provocation), and not pay attention to more subtle features. A third explanation is that alcohol increases aggression by decreasing self-awareness.[201] As was noted in Chapter 3, people become more aware of their internal standards when attention is focused on the self. Most people have internal standards against behaving aggressively, but alcohol reduces people's ability to focus on these internal standards. A fourth explanation is that alcohol disrupts executive functions such as self-control and emotion regulation.[202] A fifth explanation is that alcohol increases aggression because people expect it to. People who behave aggressively while intoxicated can therefore "blame the bottle" for their actions because they were "under the influence" of alcohol.

Does all of this mean that aggression is somehow contained in alcohol? No. Alcohol mainly seems to increase aggression in combination with other factors (e.g., provocation, frustration, aggressive cues).[203] For example, if someone insults or attacks you, your

testosterone the male sex hormone, high levels of which have been linked to aggression and violence in humans and other animals

serotonin the "feel good" neurotransmitter, low levels of which have been linked to aggression and violence in humans and other animals response will be more aggressive if you are drunk than sober. When there is no provocation, however, the effect of alcohol on aggression may be negligible. Plenty of people enjoy an occasional drink without turning aggressive.

If what you drink can affect aggression, what about what you eat? *Food for Thought* summarizes some intriguing findings about this link.

FOOD FOR *Thought*

Is There a Link Between Diet and Violence?

In his memoirs about his life as a violent youth gang member in Los Angeles, "Monster" Kody Scott reflected that whenever he started to spend a serious amount of time with his gang, he often began to feel grumpy and irritable after a few days.[204] He thought this might have something to do with what he ate at those times. Most gang members do not go home for dinner to eat a balanced meal with plenty of vegetables, fruit, vitamins, protein, fiber, and other nutritious foods. Instead, they eat erratically, often late at night, and almost exclusively from fast-food outlets that serve fatty, sweet, and fried foods. "Monster" thought that subsisting on junk food for weeks at a time might contribute to the readiness of gang members to react violently when provoked.

Is this plausible? Is there a link between diet and violence rates? During the early 1980s, a criminologist named Stephen Schoenthaler instituted dietary changes in a dozen juvenile correctional institutions. He simply removed two types of foods from their diets: fried foods (e.g., hamburgers, sausages, French fries) and sugary foods (e.g., cookies, milkshakes, soft drinks). His data, which involved 8,076 juvenile delinquents, showed that removing these unhealthy foods led to a 47% reduction in antisocial behavior, including assaults, insubordination, suicide attempts, and rule violations. Schoenthaler notes that "the more violent the bad behavior [before dietary interventions began], the more the improvement."[205]

Vitamin supplements also reduce antisocial behavior in juvenile delinquents. In a typical study, Schoenthaler gave a vitamin supplement to 71 inmates of a state juvenile detention facility. He compared antisocial behavior when prisoners were getting the supplement versus when they were getting a placebo. The result was a startling improvement in behavior with the supplement. Total violence fell by two-thirds. Escape attempts and going AWOL (absent without official leave) plummeted from 79 incidents to 13. Property crimes dropped by half.

The vitamin supplement results obtained for juvenile delinquents have also been obtained for adult prisoners. Researchers in the United Kingdom gave 231 young adult prisoners either a placebo or a vitamin supplement.[206] Prisoners receiving vitamin supplements for a minimum of two weeks were involved in 35% fewer violent and antisocial infractions than those who received a placebo. The lead author on the study, Dr. Bernard Gesch, a physiologist at Oxford University, said, "Since the 1950s there has been a ten-fold increase in offences. How else can we explain that but by diet? ... The main change over that period has been in nutrients." An over-the-counter vitamin supplement seems like an inexpensive way to reduce antisocial behavior.

So perhaps "Monster" was right: Junk food can help turn someone into a violent "monster." Much more research is needed, but at present the link between diet and violence appears to be real and significant.[207] Obviously, no one is suggesting that gang violence would disappear if only we could get a few young men to eat more fruits and vegetables. However, a recent review of the available evidence indicates that dietary interventions reduce aggressive behavior.[208]

QUIZ YOURSELF
External Causes of Aggression

1. Research suggests that the mere sight of a weapon can _____.
   - (a) elicit frustration
   - (b) increase aggression
   - (c) prevent violence
   - (d) produce catharsis

2. There is _____ relationship between alcohol and aggression.
   - (a) a negative
   - (b) no
   - (c) a positive
   - (d) None of the above

3. There is _____ relationship between hot temperatures and aggression.
   - (a) a negative
   - (b) no
   - (c) a positive
   - (d) None of the above

4. Low levels of _____ are associated with high levels of aggression.
   - (a) adrenaline
   - (b) alcohol
   - (c) serotonin
   - (d) testosterone

answers: see pg 369

Self and Culture

In this section we discuss the role of culture and self-views in aggression and violence.

Norms and Values

Amok is one of the few Malay words used in the English language. The term, which dates back to 1665, means "a murderous or violently uncontrollable frenzy that occurs chiefly among Malays."[209] **Running amok**, roughly translated, means going berserk. Historically, the typical pattern was that a young Malay man who had suffered some loss of face or other setback would run amok, heedlessly performing aggressive acts (and sometimes not-so-coincidentally damaging the property of the people who had done him wrong). The Malays believed that these responses were normal and that it was impossible for young men to restrain their wild, aggressive actions under those circumstances. However, when the British colonial administration disapproved of the practice and began to hold the young men responsible for their actions and to punish them for the harm they did, most Malays suddenly stopped running amok.[210]

The history of "running amok" thus reveals some important points about aggression. First, it shows the influence of culture: The aggression was accepted by one culture and prohibited by another; when the local culture changed, the practice died out. Second, it shows that cultures can promote aggression without placing a positive value on it. There is no sign that the Malays approved of running amok or thought it was a good thing to do, but positive value wasn't necessary. All that was needed was for the culture to believe that it was normal for people to lose control under some circumstances and act aggressively as a result. Third, it shows that when people believe their aggression is beyond control, they are often mistaken: The supposedly "uncontrollable" pattern of running amok died out when the British cracked down on it. The influence of culture was thus mediated through self-control.

Some cultures or subcultures place positive value on fighting and violence, at least in the sense of giving more respect to men who fight well. But researchers have not been successful at showing that people value fighting and violence. Even in youth gangs, most members say they don't like or approve of the violence. Violence is nowhere regarded as a positive good or end in itself. More often, violence may receive grudging acceptance as a necessary evil.

The link between culture and violence brings us back to the theme that nature says go and culture says stop. Some cultures condone losing control and engaging in violence under some circumstances, but they don't positively encourage it. For example, if a man catches his wife having sex with another man, many cultures forgive him for violence, up to and including killing one or both of them. Still, this is not the same as regarding killing them as a good thing. Nowhere are men given medals or prizes for killing their unfaithful wives and their lovers. When nature supplies the impulse to behave violently, culture sometimes tells people to stop; when culture falls silent, tolerating or condoning violence, then violence will rise. Cultures can become more violent without positively encouraging violence; all that is necessary is to stop saying no.

Self-Control

In 1990, two criminologists named Michael Gottfredson and Travis Hirschi published a book called *A General Theory of Crime*.[211] Such a brazen title was bound to stir controversy. After all, there are many crimes and many causes, so the idea of putting forward a single theory was pretty bold. What would their theory feature? Poverty? Frustration? Genetics? Violent media? Bad parenting? As it turned out, their main theory boiled down to poor self-control. Research has shown that poor self-control is one of the "strongest known correlates of crime" (p. 952).[212] And poor self-control is a better predictor of violent crimes than of nonviolent crimes.[213] Because self-control is covered in detail in Chapter 4, we discuss it only briefly here. The concept of self-control is related to other factors in

running amok according to Malaysian culture, refers to behavior of a young man who becomes "uncontrollably" aggressive after receiving a blow to his ego trol over their aggressive behavior than do sober people, perhaps because alcohol interferes with executive functions. Children 1 to 3 years old have difficulty controlling their behavior and are also quite aggressive.

The emphasis on poor self-control as a cause of crime is consistent with some themes of this book. We have seen that the conflict between selfish impulses and social conscience crops up over and over. Most crime is selfish because it seeks to benefit the individual at others' expense. Society mostly tries to socialize people to restrain aggressive and criminal impulses. (Indeed, by definition, culture and society try to get people to obey the norms and rules of good, law-abiding behavior. Even criminal parents do not usually teach or encourage their children to commit crimes, contrary to one stereotype.)

Gottfredson and Hirschi provided plenty of data to back up their theory. For one thing, criminals are not generally specialists; rather, people who break the law tend to break it in general. In the movies, criminals often specialize in one specific kind of crime, almost like any other job. But in reality, most criminals are arrested multiple times for different crimes. If self-control is a general capacity for bringing one's behavior into line with rules and standards, most criminals lack it.

Another sign is that the lives of criminals show low self-control even in behaviors that are not against the law. For example, they are more likely than law-abiding citizens to smoke cigarettes, to be involved in traffic accidents, to be involved in unplanned pregnancies, to fail to show up for work or school regularly, and the like.

Social psychology has found many risk factors for violence, such as being male, young, exposed to violence while growing up, poor, etc. Having many risk factors raises the odds of becoming violent, but it is hardly a guarantee.

This raises the question of why there isn't more violence than there is. After all, who hasn't been exposed to these risk factors? The answer lies in self-control. These factors may give rise to violent impulses, but mostly people restrain themselves. Violence starts when self-control stops.

Wounded Pride

For years, most social psychologists accepted the view that most aggression derived from low self-esteem. From murderers to playground bullies, violent individuals were assumed to have low opinions of themselves. Research, however, has contradicted that view.[214] If

Hitler probably did not have low self-esteem. In fact, the eminent psychoanalyst Erich Fromm said that Hitler had a narcissistic personality disorder. Most of the men seen here with Hitler also died before their time years because of his violent decisions. Tens of millions of others, too.

anything, violent individuals typically think they are better than others and have grandiose or inflated opinions of their own worth. Think of the most aggressive, violent person you know, from history or personal experience. That person probably did not have low self-esteem. For example, Adolf Hitler probably did not have low self-esteem.

Aggression often starts when someone comes along and questions or challenges those favorable self-views. Wounded pride seems to be the most apt descriptor of how self-views are linked to aggression.

This is not to say that high self-esteem causes aggression. Indeed, most people with high self-esteem are not aggressive. But violent individuals typically have the trait of narcissism, which is one of the "dark" personalities described above. For example, violent male prisoners who have murdered, raped, robbed, or assaulted someone have much higher narcissism scores than other men the same age.[215] Narcissists are especially likely to behave aggressively when they receive a blow to their egos.[216]

The wounded pride factor has found its way into so much aggression research that it is often scarcely noticed. Most laboratory studies on aggression include some kind of provocation in the form of an insult delivered to the participant by the person toward whom the participant will later be able to aggress. Without such an insult, most studies find hardly any aggression. Essentially, most studies of aggression simply show that other factors can increase or decrease the effect of wounded pride. Without an insult, alcohol and violent movies typically do not produce a significant increase in aggression. Even the contribution of narcissism depends on the insult. When narcissists receive praise, they are no more aggressive than anybody else.[217]

Both nature and culture may contribute to the importance of wounded pride in causing violence. In nature, many (mainly male) animals compete for status, and some fighting is required to reach and keep a high rank. Fighting is often a response to a challenge to one's favorable position. In humans, this translates into thinking you have to defend your good name or good opinion of yourself by lashing out at anyone who tries to attack it. As for culture, the concept of "honor" has often required violent action to maintain it, as explained in the next section.

Narcissists are especially likley to lash out aggressively against others when they are insulted, humiliated, criticized, or shamed.

Culture of Honor

Sam Houston needed his mother's permission to join the army in the War of 1812 because he was not yet 21 years old. His mother, Elizabeth Houston, agreed to let him join, and gave him two gifts before he left.[218] One was a gold ring with the word *honor* inscribed inside; Houston wore this ring until his death. The other gift was a musket (i.e., muzzle-loaded rifle used by infantry), which his mother gave him with the following admonition:

> My son, take this musket and never disgrace it; for remember, I had rather all my sons should fill one honorable grave, than that one of them should turn his back to save his life. Go, and remember, too, that while the door of my cottage is open to brave men, it is eternally shut against cowards.

Houston was from the southern United States. He was born in Virginia in 1793 and moved to Tennessee after his father died in 1807. In 1832 he moved to Texas and went on to become one of the heroes of that state. In fact, he was in command of the Texas soldiers who won their independence by defeating the Mexican army, shouting, "Remember the Alamo!" Texas later became the southern tip of the United States, and its largest city Houston was named after Sam Houston.

The southern United States has long been associated with higher levels of violent attitudes and behaviors than the northern United States. In comparison to northern states, southern states have more homicides per capita, have fewer restrictions on gun ownership, allow people to shoot assailants and burglars without retreating first, are more accepting of corporal punishment of children at home and in schools, and are more supportive of any wars involving U.S. troops.[219] People from southern states are also more tolerant of domestic violence.[220]

One theory proposes that these regional differences are caused by a **culture of honor**, which calls for a violent response to threats to one's honor.[221] This honor culture apparently dates back to the Europeans who first came to the United States. The northern U.S. was settled by English and Dutch farmers, whereas the southern U.S. was settled by Scottish and Irish herders. Sam Houston was of Scottish-Irish descent. A thief could become rich quickly by stealing another person's herd. The same was not true of agricultural crops in the North. For example, it is difficult to quickly steal 50 acres of corn! Men had to be ready to protect their herds with a violent response. A person who did not respond in this way would be branded as an "easy mark."

A similar culture of violence exists in the western United States, the so-called Wild West, where one could also lose one's wealth quickly by not protecting one's herd. (Cowboys herded cows, hence the name.) Even the names of places and businesses are more violent in the South and West than elsewhere.[222] One analysis concludes that 80% of the places with violent names were located in the South and West. Some examples are Gun Point, Florida; War, West Virginia; and Rifle, Colorado. Similarly, 68% of the businesses with violent names (e.g., "War Taxi" and "Rifle Realty," even "Shotgun Willy's Daycare Center") were located in the South and West. (Would you really want to leave your child with Shotgun Willy?)

Sam Houston at San Jacinto.

However, this violent culture isn't confined to the southern and western United States. Other examples of honor cultures include Latin American and Middle Eastern countries. Cultural anthropologists have observed that herding cultures throughout the world tend to be more violent than farming ones.[223,224,225]

The victims of cultures of honor are not always men. In some societies, women are killed if they bring "dishonor" to their family, such as by refusing to accept an arranged marriage, seeking a divorce (even from an abusive husband), committing adultery, or having sex before marriage (even if the man forced her). This practice, called **honor killing**, supposedly restores the family's honor from the disgrace caused by the woman. Thousands of women are killed each year in this way, mainly in Western Asia, North Africa, and parts of South Asia.[226]

Humiliation appears to be the primary cause of violence and aggression in honor cultures.[227] **Humiliation** is a state of disgrace or loss of self-respect (or of respect from others). It is related to the concept of shame that was discussed in Chapter 6, but humiliation and shame are not the same.[228] If someone insults you, and you judge the insult to be justified, then you feel shame (if you think you are a bad person, or you feel guilt if you do not think you are a bad person). If you judge the insult to be unjustified, then you feel humiliation. In honor cultures, there is nothing worse than being humiliated, and the culturally approved response to humiliation is violence.

In fact, the Holocaust, genocide, ethnic cleansing, terrorism, and suicide bombings may all have their roots in humiliation.[229] For example, World War II was triggered, at least in part, by the humiliation that the Versailles Treaty inflicted on Germany after World War I. Hitler attacked his neighbors in part to retaliate for past humiliations inflicted on Germany. Hitler may have perpetrated the Holocaust to avert future humiliation that he feared from "World Jewry." After World War II, the Marshall Plan was designed to bring dignity and respect rather than humiliation to Germany. Instead of starting World War III, Germany has become a cooperative and peaceful member of the European family.

culture of honor a society that places high value on individual respect, strength, and virtue, and accepts and justifies violent action in response to threats to one's honor

honor killing killing another individual who has brought "dishonor" to the family (e.g., a woman who has committed adultery)

humiliation a state of disgrace or loss of self-respect (or of respect from others)

QUIZ YOURSELF
Self and Culture

1. In their 1990 book *A General Theory of Crime*, criminologists Gottfredson and Hirschi identified _____ as the major cause of violence.
   - (a) frustration
   - (b) genetic factors
   - (c) poor self-control
   - (d) poverty

2. In what part of the United States is the culture of honor most prevalent?
   - (a) Midwest
   - (b) Northeast
   - (c) Northwest
   - (d) South

3. What personality trait is most strongly linked to violence and aggression?
   - (a) Narcissism
   - (b) Low self-esteem
   - (c) Both (a) and (b)
   - (d) Neither (a) nor (b)

4. Which of the following is the best predictor of violent crime in all cultures?
   - (a) Genetics
   - (b) Media violence
   - (c) Poor self-control
   - (d) Poverty

answers: see pg 369

Other Antisocial Behavior

Aggression and violence aren't the only forms of antisocial behaviors, although they are the forms social psychologists have studied the most. In this section we examine four other common forms of antisocial behavior: (1) lying, (2) cheating, (3) stealing, and (4) littering.

Lying

Lying is not telling the truth. Most people lie at least once per day.[230] However, about half of all lies are told by 5% of the population—so-called "habitual liars."[231]

Sometimes the stakes for lying are low, such as being embarrassed if one is caught. At other times the stakes are very high, such as lying to a spouse about infidelity or lying to a country about the reasons for going to war. When it comes to getting a job, people often lie about their qualifications and skills to increase the chance that they will be hired.[232] People also lie on social media to promote themselves.[233]

The cliché "all's fair in love and war" suggests that it is okay to lie to gain advantages in high-stakes situations. Social psychologists have done a lot more research on lying for love than on lying for war, and they have found that people are quick to tell lies if it will improve their love (or sex) lives. Both men and women are willing to lie to increase their chances of going out with an attractive partner.[234] The more attractive people are (as determined by independent judges), the more likely they are to lie about their height, weight, and age to online dating partners.[235] Lying is less common for very high-stakes issues in sexual relationships, such as whether the person has AIDS.[236] Lying in romantic relationships tends to be reciprocal—if one partner lies, the other also lies.[237] As expected, lying is associated with less commitment to the relationship.

Lying takes more cognitive resources than telling the truth.[238] Lying generally requires coordination between both parts of the duplex mind (Chapter 2): The automatic system knows what the truth is, and the deliberate system says something else while also concealing any telltale signs that what the person is saying is false.

Recent research shows that telling fewer lies is linked to better health and relationships. In this study, participants were randomly assigned to two groups. One group was told to stop telling lies during the duration of the study (10 weeks). The other (control) group

lying deliberately making a false statement, usually to mislead someone received no instructions about lying. The group that refrained from telling lies got sick less often over the course of 10 weeks, were less depressed, and said their social interactions with others were smoother.

Is it possible to reliably detect lying? "Liar, liar, pants on fire!" is a phrase that children like to use when they think another child is lying. It would be much easier to identify liars if their pants were on fire. Because pants don't spontaneously combust when people lie, more subtle cues must be used. Sometimes outside information is available, such as when facts or witnesses directly contradict the lie. When outside information is unavailable, people often rely on verbal and nonverbal cues. In one study, over 500 research participants were shown videotapes of college women who either lied or did not lie.[239] The participants included law enforcement personnel, including members of the U.S. Secret Service, Central Intelligence Agency (CIA), Federal Bureau of Investigation (FBI), National Security Agency, Drug Enforcement Agency, and California police and judges, as well as psychiatrists, college students, and working adults. Note that many of these deal with liars as part of their jobs. However, only the Secret Service personnel detected lying at better than chance levels. In general, people are not very good at detecting liars.[240] Even when children tell lies, adults have difficulty distinguishing them, and experts are no better than novices.[241] Textual analysis programs generally do better than people at detecting lying, even better than experts, correctly detecting liars at least 60% of the time (still far from perfect!).[242] Sometimes a mechanical device known as a polygraph (popularly called a lie detector) is used to "detect" lies, but in 1998 the U.S. Supreme Court concluded: "There is simply no consensus that polygraph evidence is reliable."

As was mentioned in Chapter 8, "fake news" is one common form of lying these days. Fortunately for the public, fact checkers often check what people say to determine whether it is accurate.

Cheating

Cheating is widely recognized as an antisocial, undesirable behavior, yet it is widespread. People even cheat on video games that are meant to be fun, as indicated by the popularity of cheat codes and websites.[243] Cheating occurs among some athletes, who take performance-enhancing drugs to increase their competitiveness.[244] It occurs among many students, who cheat out of a "desire to get ahead" in school.[245] Although most students acknowledge that cheating is wrong, more than 75% admit to having cheated in high

> "A thing worth having is a thing worth cheating for."
> — W. C. Fields (1880–1946), American comedian

Creativity and Cheating

TRADEOffs

Cheating involves breaking rules. As we have said, rules enable culture to function, so cheating is antisocial in a fundamental way, because it ruins the basis for civilization. Yet breaking rules can have positive benefits in some ways. Creativity often involves violating rules (though usually creativity does not harm innocent victims, like cheating does). Is there a link? Some fascinating experiments showed that people become more creative after cheating.[246] This is not just a matter of the type of person who breaks rules being both more creative and more willing to cheat. Ordinary people who were randomly assigned to engage in cheating (as opposed to being honest) went on to perform more creatively as a result. These results are no justification for the immoral act of cheating, but they do indicate a psychological link. Cheating makes people feel that rules do not matter, and this can boost their ability to think creatively.

Thus, cheating causes creativity. It works the other way, too: Creativity leads to cheating. The rule-breaking mind-set helps. Another factor is that a creative mentality finds it easier to come up with justifications for morally dubious behavior, as compared to an uncreative mind-set.[247] So creative people are able to rationalize their unethical actions.

Cheating does lead to more cheating, though. When people do dishonest things, their minds tend to shut down their knowledge of moral rules. Experimental participants who were induced to cheat after having read an honor code were less able than other participants to remember the honor code afterward—even when offered a chance to earn money for correctly remembering the moral rules.[248]

Cheating is sometimes done for money, as is stealing (which the next section will cover. To learn more about links between money and antisocial behavior, read the *Money Matters* box.

school or college.[249] Some students even cheat on free online courses that don't count toward anything.[250] Even some teachers cheat by raising test scores for students to create the illusion of educational gains.[251]

Although getting ahead is probably the primary reason why people cheat, there might also be other reasons. For example, recent research suggests that cheating can even trigger positive affect—called the "cheater's high."[252] For example, Frank Abagnale described the experience of cheating as "the most delightful sensation I'd ever experienced." Abagnale passed himself off as a pilot, a lawyer, and a physician, all before he turned 21. In 5 years, he had used 8 identities and passed bad checks worth over $2.5 million in 26 countries. To be sure, he benefited financially (at least until he was caught) by all that cheating—but he did also enjoy it. Experiments have shown that people can get pleasure by cheating even though they expected to feel guilty rather than self-satisfied, and even apart from the benefit of acquiring money.[253] Some of the enjoyment seems to come from getting away with something illicit and sneaky.

Stealing

Most companies lose about 5% of their annual revenue to employee theft.[254] The U.S. Chamber of Commerce[255] estimates that 75% of all employees steal at least once, and that 50% of those employees steal repeatedly. They may steal the company's product (e.g., waiters helping themselves to food) or just office supplies or money. Employees are especially likely to steal from employers when they feel they are being treated unfairly.[256] Employees can also steal time, such as by arriving to work late, leaving work early, taking longer lunches or breaks than company policy allows, and "surfing" the web or playing video games on company time. Research shows that employees who think such behavior is normal are more likely to engage in it.[257]

Not only do employees steal from employers, but customers steal too. Shoplifting (also known as a "five-finger discount") involves the theft of goods from a retail establishment. Retail theft is over $16 billion per year in the United States alone.[258] The average shoplifter who gets caught is found to have about $200 worth of stolen merchandise in his or her possession.[259] Stealing occurs online too.

> "But he that filches from me my good name
> Robs me of that which not enriches him
> And makes me poor indeed."
> — Shakespeare, Othello, Act iii. Sc. 3.

MONEY Matters

Money and Antisocial Behavior

No one will be surprised that people sometimes do dishonest things to get money. Indeed, many people have heard or read the Bible verse that "the love of money is the root of all kinds of evil."[260] But it seems that even the mere idea of money can be enough to elicit antisocial behavior. Merely thinking of the idea of money has been shown to increase cheating behavior.[261]

Then again, people do have moral scruples about money also. One study allowed students to solve problems and score their own answer sheets. Each correct solution earned them 50 cents. Some students were paid directly in cash. They cheated to some degree. Others were paid in tokens, which in a couple minutes they exchanged for cash. They cheated considerably more.[262] Thus, simply creating a mental separation between the cheating and the money (by using the tokens) increased cheating. Probably people have fewer scruples about taking extra tokens than extra money.

Some recent work has suggested that people have two sets of associations to the idea of money—with opposite moral effects. Chinese researchers tested this by having some people briefly handle old, dirty, crumpled money that had been buried in mud for several days. Other participants counted fresh, crisp, new banknotes. Compared to controls who handled only paper rather than money, those who handled the dirty money went on to behave in immoral, antisocial ways. But those who had handled clean, new money behaved in exceptionally moral, prosocial ways.[263] The explanation is that the use of money in society depends on fairness, trust, and honesty, and so money can evoke these positive values, even though ordinary, dirty money also evokes notions of selfish greed and unethical dirty tricks.

Desire for money has certainly been the root of much evil, but it also has motivated many positive things in society. The antisocial aspect of money seems to be the more prominent association for most people, but alongside it there is often a more positive view. As the lyrics in the Pink Floyd "Money" song state, "Money, so they say, is the root of all evil today. But if you ask for a raise, it's no surprise that they're giving none away."

As we saw with cheating, shoplifting is motivated by more than the desire to acquire material possessions. Many people do it for the excitement and thrill of getting away with something. The items they steal are often soon forgotten, left unused in a drawer or thrown away—which shows that the motivation to steal was not to acquire something important but rather for the temporary excitement of doing the deed.[264]

People can even steal your identity! **Identity theft** is defined as stealing someone else's personal information (e.g., Social Security number, bank account, credit card number) and using it without their permission, usually to obtain money or goods.[265] According to the Federal Trade Commission, "It is a serious crime that can wreak havoc with your finances, credit history, and reputation."[266]

One form of stealing is **plagiarism**, which means "to steal and pass off (the ideas or words of another) as one's own without crediting the source."[267] Some schools are cracking down on cheaters. At the University of California at Davis, for example, students receive No. 2 pencils with their exams that read, "Fill in your own bubble or be in trouble."[268] Other professors use plagiarism-checking websites to screen student papers.

Social psychologists have studied stealing and other antisocial behaviors and the factors that contribute to them. One such factor is the presence of others. The presence of others increases arousal (see Chapter 14 on groups). When people are in large groups, they become anonymous and lose their sense of individuality, a state called **deindividuation**. People in a deindividuated state are especially likely to engage in antisocial behaviors, such as theft. In a clever study,[269] children who were trick-or-treating on Halloween were greeted by an experimenter who said, "You may take one of the candies. I have to go back to my work in another room." Some children go trick-or-treating alone, and some go in groups. By the flip of a coin, half of the children were assigned to an identifiable group, and half were assigned to an anonymous group. The experimenter asked each child in the identifiable group what his or her name was and where he or she lived. The experimenter then carefully repeated each child's name and address to let the child know that he or she could be identified. The experimenter did not identify the children in the anonymous group. A hidden observer recorded whether each child took more than one piece of candy from a large bowl. Children were most likely to steal candy when they were in a group and when the experimenter could not identify them (see **FIGURE 10.5**). Research shows that theft can also be reduced when people believe that others are watching them, such as on closed-circuit television.[270]

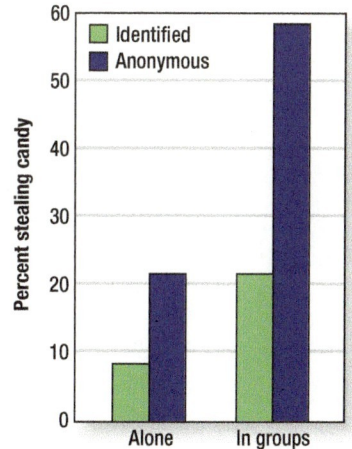

FIGURE 10.5
Children were most likely to steal candy when they were not identifiable and when they were in a group.[285]

identity theft consists of stealing someone's personal information (e.g., Social Security number, bank account, credit card number) and using it without their permission, usually to obtain money or goods.

plagiarize to claim the ideas or words of another person as one's own without crediting that person

deindividuation a sense of anonymity and loss of individuality, as in a large group, making people especially likely to engage in antisocial behaviors such as theft

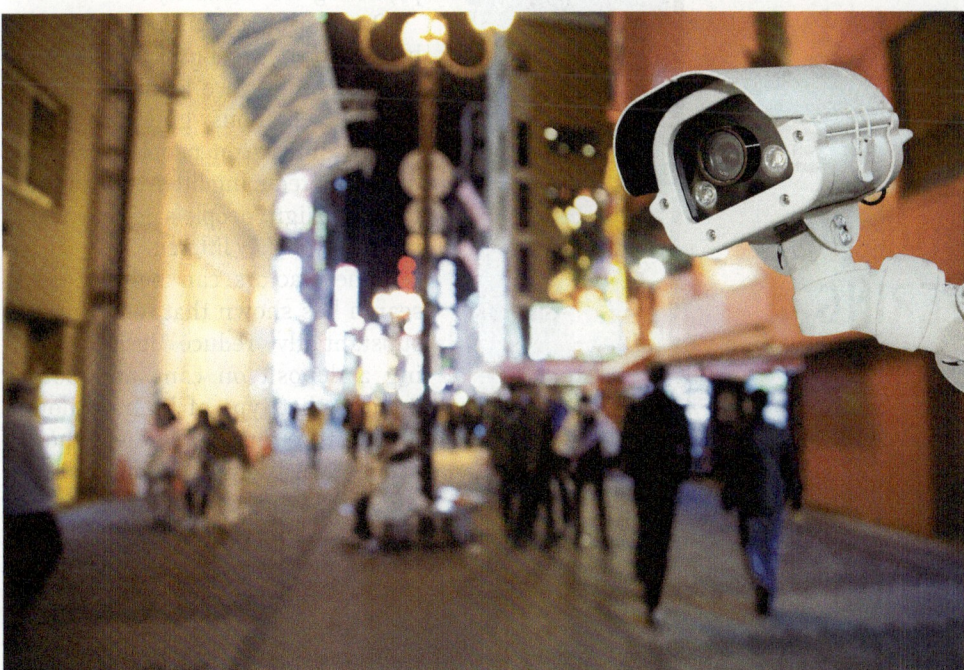

Be good. Someone is watching!

Littering

Litter is a big problem in many places. When everybody else seems to be littering, individuals are more likely to litter, too.[271,272] Cigarette butts are the most common form of litter in many states.[273] For example, each year 140 million cigarette butts are tossed onto Texas highways. Although convicts pick up some of the litter, hired crews (paid with taxpayer dollars) pick up 90% of it. To fight the problem, which was costing the state $20 million a year to clean up, the Texas Department of Transportation hired Mike Blair and Tim McClure, from an advertising company, to come up with a catchy anti-littering slogan.[274] The target audience was 18- to 24-year-old males who thought it was their "God-given right" to toss beer cans and other trash out the windows of their trucks. McClure came up with the slogan in an "aha" moment when he saw some garbage and remembered how his mother would always tell him his room was a mess and came up with the slogan "Don't Mess with Texas." The word litter is associated with animals like cats. "Mess seemed like it would resonate better," he said. This slogan plays on the pride of Texans in their home state—they love their state so much that they should not ruin it with litter. (The slogan was also designed to seem aggressive and macho, so as to appeal to the young men who were perceived as the source of much littering and who might not respond as well to a seemingly effeminate slogan such as "Please Be Clean." "Don't Mess with Texas" is well suited to a culture of honor state!)

Litter is not only unattractive, but it can also cause health problems to humans and animals. One recent study found that about 80% of smokers littered their cigarette butts, and that 74% of smokers did not extinguish their butts, sometimes before tossing them into a trashcan, which was a fire risk.[275] Litter such as broken bottles can also cause injuries and flat tires.[276] How can litter be reduced? One way is through anti-littering norms.[277,278,279] **Norms** are social standards that prescribe what people ought to do. Litter can be reduced by anti-littering norms, especially **injunctive norms** that specify what most others approve or disapprove of. In contrast, **descriptive norms**, which specify what most people do, seem ineffective at reducing littering. Messages that explicitly command people not to litter are less effective than messages that appeal to social norms.[280] This may be due to **psychological reactance**—the unpleasant emotional response people experience when someone is trying to restrict their freedom to engage in a behavior. Such threats frequently backfire (see Chapter 4 for a more detailed description of psychological reactance).

One reason norms might work is because people feel guilty if they don't follow them. As we learned in Chapter 6 on emotions, guilt can have a positive impact on people's behavior, including reducing litter. After a littering campaign, people said they would feel guilty if they littered.[281]

Other factors can help, too. Research has shown that recycling can substantially reduce litter.[282] Paying a deposit on cans and bottles reduces that type of litter, although it has little impact on other types of litter.[283] An adequate supply of trash cans also helps reduce litter.[284,285] In summary, making it convenient or rewarding for people to get rid of trash is effective.

norms social standards that prescribe what people ought to do

injunctive norms norms that specify what most others approve or disapprove of

descriptive norms norms that specify what most people do

psychological reactance the unpleasant emotional response people experience when someone is trying to restrict their freedom to engage in a desired behavior

The Texas Department of Transportation launched a campaign with the motto "Don't Mess with Texas" to combat the litter problem.

QUIZ YOURSELF: Other Antisocial Behavior

1. **What is the impact of the internet on school cheating?**
   - a) The internet has decreased school cheating.
   - b) The internet has not affected school cheating.
   - c) The internet has increased school cheating.
   - d) More research is needed to determine the impact of the internet on school cheating.

2. **Which of the following can increase self-awareness?**
   - a) Alcohol
   - b) Audience
   - c) Darkness
   - d) All of the above

3. **Tamika attends a football game, and her team wins. The fans rush the field and tear down a goal post. Tamika happily joins them and tears down a goal post with her fellow students. Tamika is probably experiencing _____.**
   - a) cognitive dissonance
   - b) deindividuation
   - c) psychological reactance
   - d) self-awareness

4. **What type of norm is most effective at reducing litter?**
   - a) Injunctive
   - b) Descriptive
   - c) Both (a) and (b)
   - d) Neither (a) nor (b)

answers: see pg 369

What Makes Us Human

Putting the Cultural Animal in Perspective

Aggression provides a curious perspective on what makes us human. In some ways, humans are far more aggressive than our biological relatives. Most fighting between animals of the same species stops far short of serious injury or death, whereas humans kill each other. Only humans have invented tools to increase aggression, and these (from spears and guns to nuclear weapons) have greatly escalated the harm people can do to each other. Only humans have been able to accumulate knowledge across generations (a hallmark of culture) so as to create weapons of mass destruction that are capable of destroying entire nations and possibly even wiping out the entire human population of the planet.

Only humans kill for ideas, such as religion or honor or political ideals. Only humans commit genocide, defined as the attempt to kill everyone in a particular racial or ethnic category. Only humans declare war on other groups, maintain military establishments to prepare for war in time of peace, and bestow honors on the individuals who kill their enemies most brilliantly or effectively. Only humans deliberately create chemical substances (such as alcohol) that make them more violent.

Still, human culture is unique in its devices for restraining aggression. Only humans commit crimes, in part because only humans can enact laws that define socially undesirable acts as crimes. The long history of culture is in part a story of placing ever more careful and thorough restraints on aggression, ranging from ancient moral laws ("Thou shalt not kill") to laws that forbid teachers from using corporal punishment on students or prohibit people from sending hostile email messages (i.e., cyberbullying). Only humans have police forces that deter and punish criminals—though, again, the police must often use violence to stop violence. This is the paradox of culture: Step by step, it has created the technology to do more harm while also creating laws and other devices to reduce and prevent harm, another example of a tradeoff (involving very high stakes). Yet the level of violence and aggression in the world has decreased over time, and continues to do so, mainly because of culture.

The elaborate mental apparatus that people have has transformed aggression, too. Factors such as the hostile attributional bias are probably unique to humans, because only humans make inferences about someone else's intentions. A hostile attributional bias is a way of interpreting the behavior of others—"I think you intended to hurt me!"—that increases the likelihood of an aggressive response. Animals know whether they were hurt or not, but they probably do not have much capacity to choose an aggressive or a nonaggressive reaction based on whether they think the hurt was inflicted intentionally or accidentally.

Aggression is not the only kind of antisocial behavior. The same paradox can be seen in other behaviors. Culture creates new opportunities for antisocial behavior, such as insurance fraud, insider trading, overcharging, and all sorts of scams. At the same time, culture seeks to promote and reward behavior that follows the rules. Insider trading was unknown in biblical times, but so were the laws against it.

The impulses to commit aggression and other antisocial acts are deeply rooted in the social nature of human beings. Social animals are generally selfish, and because they get what they want from other animals, they are often tempted to exploit or hurt others. The human capacity for self-control is probably much more extensive than what other animals have, and it is responsible for the fact that people mostly refrain from acting on their violent and antisocial impulses.

CHAPTER 10 SUMMARY

Defining Aggression, Violence, and Antisocial Behavior

- Aggression is any behavior that intentionally harms another person who is motivated to avoid the harm. Violence is aggression that has extreme harm as its goal.
- Antisocial behavior refers to behavior that either damages interpersonal relations or is culturally undesirable.
- Aggressive acts frequently fail to produce the intended, desired consequences and often bring about serious unintended consequences, mostly antisocial ones.
- Aggression is universal, but cultural rules restrict and govern aggression in different ways.
- Aggression evolved to help social animals deal with their social lives, but culture, as a better way of being social, offers new, nonviolent ways of resolving conflicts and problems.

Is Aggression Innate or Learned?

- Freud (and others) proposed that people have an innate instinct that causes them to behave aggressively.
- According to social learning theory, aggression is not an innate drive but rather a learned behavior.
- When people observe and copy the behavior of others, this is called modeling.
- Inhibitions against aggression can be overcome if a model acts out aggressively.
- Learning and cultural socialization can subdue or encourage innate aggressive impulses and aggressive action.
- Aggression is a product of both nature and learning.

Inner Causes of Aggression

- The original frustration-aggression hypothesis states that the occurrence of aggressive behavior always presupposes the existence of frustration and the existence of frustration always leads to some form of aggression.
- There can be aggression without frustration, and frustration without aggression, but aggression is increased by frustration.
- Unpleasant moods increase aggression, but being in a bad mood is neither a necessary nor a sufficient condition for aggression.
- Anger does not directly or inevitably cause aggression, but the belief that aggression will help get rid of anger does increase aggression.
- The hostile attribution bias is the tendency to perceive ambiguous actions by others as intentionally hostile.
- The hostile perception bias is the tendency to perceive social interactions in general as being aggressive.
- The hostile expectation bias is the tendency to expect others to react to potential conflicts with aggression.
- About 25% of toddler interactions in day-care settings involve some kind of physical aggression.
- In all known societies, young men just past the age of puberty commit most of the violent crimes and acts.

Interpersonal Causes of Aggression

JJ Grandville "Les cent proverbs" 1845

- Domestic violence (also called family violence or intimate-partner violence) is a violence that occurs within the home, between people who have a close relationship with each other (such as parents and children, spouses, and siblings).
- The sibling relationship is the most violent relationship in the world.
- In 1984, the U.S. Surgeon General declared domestic violence to be the number one health risk in the United States.
- Women attack their relationship partners slightly more often than men do, but women don't cause as much harm.

External Causes of Aggression

- People behave more aggressively in the mere presence of a weapon.
- Exposure to violent media increases aggression.
- Hotter temperatures are associated with higher levels of aggression and violence.
- Unpleasant environmental events, such as noise, crowding, foul odors, air pollution, and secondhand smoke, can increase aggression.
- Increases in testosterone, junk food, and alcohol lead to increased aggression. Decreases in serotonin and increases in vitamins reduce aggression.

Self and Culture

- Running amok, roughly translated, means going berserk. Cultural changes in running amok show that when people believe their aggression is beyond control, they are often mistaken.
- Poor self-control is an important cause of crime.
- Violent individuals, rather than having low self-esteem, typically think themselves better than other people and have grandiose or inflated opinions of their own worth.
- The term *narcissism* describes the condition of thinking oneself superior or special, feeling entitled to preferential treatment, being willing to exploit others, having low empathy with "lesser" human beings, and entertaining grandiose fantasies or other ideas about oneself as a great person.
- Much aggression involves wounded pride, so narcissists are especially likely to become aggressive.
- The southern United States has a culture of honor, which accepts and even calls for violent responses to threats to one's honor.
- Humiliation (a state of disgrace or loss of respect) appears to be a primary cause of violence and aggression in cultures of honor.

Other Antisocial Behavior

- Lying, swearing, cheating, stealing, and littering are forms of antisocial behavior.
- Deindividuated people are more likely to steal than people who can be readily identified.
- Norms are social standards that prescribe what people ought to do.
- Injunctive norms specify what most others approve or disapprove.

What Makes Us Human? Putting the Cultural Animal in Perspective

- Human cultures mostly attempt to restrain violence and aggression.

key terms

aggression 334
antisocial behavior 335
appetitive aggression 343
bullying 335
crowding 355
culture of honor 361
cyberbullying 335
deindividuation 365
density 355
descriptive norms 366
desensitization 343
direct aggression 334
displaced aggression 334
domestic violence (family violence, intimate-partner violence) 349
eros 339
fight or flight syndrome 346
frustration 342
frustration–aggression hypothesis 342
honor killing 361
hostile attribution bias 344
hostile expectation bias 345
hostile perception bias 344
humiliation 361
identity theft 365
indirect aggression 334
injunctive norms 366
instinct 339
lying 362
modeling 339
norms 366
plagiarize 365
proactive aggression (also called instrumental aggression) 335
psychological reactance 366
reactive aggression (also called hostile aggression) 335
relational aggression (also called social aggression) 347
running amok 358
serotonin 356
tend and befriend syndrome 346
testosterone 356
thanatos 339
third-person effect 355
violence 335
weapons effect 352

quiz yourself ANSWERS

1. Defining Aggression and Antisocial Behavior p.338
   answers: 1.b 2.d 3.c 4.a
2. Is Aggression Innate or Learned? p.341
   answers: 1.a 2.a 3.d 4.d
3. Inner Causes of Aggression p.348
   answers: 1.d 2.a 3.a 4.b
4. Interpersonal Causes of Aggression p.351
   answers: 1.c 2.d 3.d 4.b
5. External Causes of Aggression p.357
   answers: 1.b 2.c 3.c 4.c
6. Self and Culture p.362
   answers: 1.c 2.d 3.a 4.c
7. Other Antisocial Behavior p.367
   answers: 1.c 2.b 3.b 4.a

INTERPERSONAL ATTRACTION AND REJECTION

11

LEARNING OBJECTIVES

1 Differentiate the two ingredients for belongingness, and debate why the need to belong is a basic need for a cultural animal.

2 Contrast the variables that predict who will like whom.

3 Identify two strategies for getting someone to like you that confirm the importance of interpersonal rewards, and explain how reciprocity has a powerful effect on liking.

4 Compare the inner reactions to the behavioral effects of rejection.

5 Analyze what makes people feel lonely and describe the conditions that lead to social rejection.

Monkey Business Images/Shutterstock.com

TRADEOFFS
Testosterone—A Blessing and a Curse
374

MONEY MATTERS
Is Manhood Measured in Dollars or Inches?
385

THE SOCIAL SIDE OF SEX
What Is Beauty?
386

FOOD FOR THOUGHT
Social Rejection and the Jar of Cookies
392

WHAT MAKES US HUMAN?
Putting the Cultural Animal in Perspective
400

371

In 2003, an attractive young woman named Melana Scantlin signed up to be on one of those reality shows in which the female central character meets around 20 different guys, who compete for her affections. She was to eliminate them steadily and ideally end up marrying the winner.

She told the producers of the show that she wanted to meet and marry a man with good inner qualities. She said she cared little about physical attractiveness and was much more concerned with personality and other inner traits. Perhaps she sincerely thought that good looks and other superficial traits were not her concern, but when the show's bus opened and a series of very ordinary looking men came up to meet her, she struggled to hide her dismay, and hidden cameras later captured her complaining about the men's lack of physical charms. Some of the men were obese, others were bald, and few were genuinely handsome.

The men had been told that the woman was looking for personality rather than good looks, but they were soon disappointed. As one disgruntled suitor pointed out, by the second day of eliminations, she had sent home every man weighing over 200 pounds. Meanwhile, one man clearly regarded himself as better looking than everyone else, and this narcissistic fellow engaged in a variety of bullying maneuvers and putdowns that made most characters regard him as a jerk, but Melana went out of her way to convince herself that he was not a jerk. During the round in which she sent all the tubby and balding men home, she was seen lying on the floor with the narcissistic fellow with their arms around each other, kissing passionately.

Late in the game, after Melana had whittled the set of eligible men down to a handful of candidates, the producers surprised everyone by adding several new male suitors—this time all young and handsome, if rather shallow in some ways. This was the test to see how good looks would fare against the inner qualities she had presumably found among the average ones. After that point, whenever Melana had to choose someone for a date, she invariably chose one of the handsome young fellows. (She did say she already knew the original men and needed dates with the new guys to give them a fair chance.) More men were sent home, until she was down to the final two. One was the last of the original "average Joes"; the other was a handsome newcomer. On final dates, she discovered that Adam, the last of the average Joes, was not so average: He was in fact a millionaire who owned several luxury homes, had part-ownership in a bar, and had a successful career as an investor. He noticed that she suddenly warmed up to him, becoming more flirtatious and affectionate toward him when he revealed his assets. Perhaps it was too late, however. She chose the other finalist: Jason, a handsome but shallow waiter who at age 26 was still living with his parents. The relationship did not last, despite his looks.

Melana would not be the first person to choose physical attractiveness over other traits. What made her story so dramatic was that she had initially insisted that she was not interested in surface appearance and instead wanted inner qualities in a man.

Like most reality shows, *Average Joe* was about acceptance and rejection. The show revolved around a large group of people who were rejected one by one, or sometimes in groups, until at last the "winner" was the person who staved off rejection the longest (think *The Masked Singer, Dating Around, America's Got Talent, Survivor, The Bachelor, The Bachelorette,* and others). The woman in *Average Joe* could only accept one man, presumably as a husband or long-term relationship partner, and along the way she had to reject everyone else.

Like reality television (though perhaps the resemblance ends there!), this chapter is about attraction, social acceptance, and rejection. **Attraction** refers to anything that draws two or more people together, making them want to be together and possibly to form a lasting relationship. In social psychology, it is especially used to refer to what makes people like (or start to love) each other. **Social acceptance** means that other people

Melana and Jason.

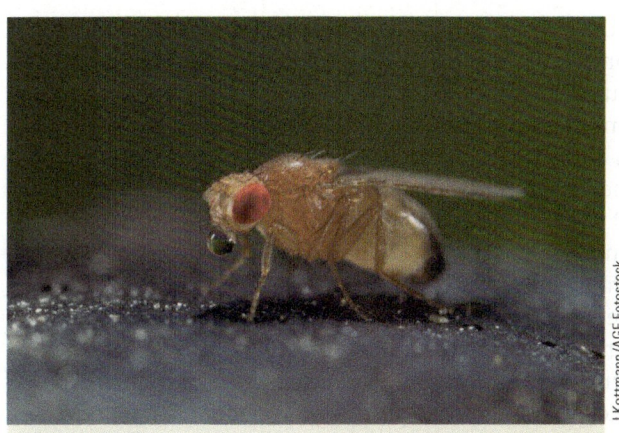

Rejected by females, male fruit flies turn to alcohol.

have come to like you, respect you, approve of you, and in general regard you in ways that will lead them to include you in their groups and relationships. **Rejection**, also known as **social exclusion**, is the opposite of acceptance: It means that others exclude you, so that you are not able to form or keep a social bond with them.

The quest for social acceptance is not limited to human beings. All social animals need to be accepted. Likewise, social rejection is a problem and a source of distress for many social animals as well as for human beings. Indeed, social rejection is even a problem for insects. Recent research found that male fruit flies that were spurned by female fruit flies drank more alcohol afterward![1] The basic patterns in this chapter—attraction based on similarity or good looks, rejection of those who are different—are more linked to the social than the cultural aspect of human nature.

It is not surprising that people have developed many ways to make themselves attractive to others. One cautionary note, which we suspect Melana Scantlin may someday recognize, is that the traits that make someone most attractive upon first meeting are not always the same traits that make for a successful relationship. Testosterone levels provide one example of this sort of tradeoff, as *Tradeoffs* explains. ●

The Need to Belong

Why is social attraction important? Forming bonds is a big part of human life. Social animals (including plenty of nonhuman ones) survive and reproduce mainly by way of their relationships with others. In order to survive, it is vital to form and maintain some relationships. Forming relationships involves securing acceptance, which often depends on getting others to feel and think positively about you. That (along with the flip side, rejection) is the focus of this chapter. Sustaining long-term close relationships will be the focus of the next chapter.

Belongingness as a Basic Need

People survive and reproduce better if they have relationships, but that doesn't mean they only want relationships for those reasons. Most likely, the "need to belong" is a powerful drive within the human psyche, and it affects people who are neither worried about survival nor urgently interested in reproduction. In our evolutionary past, the people who had a stronger need to belong probably fared better than other people, so that today's humans are mainly descended from ancestors who had a strong need to belong.[2,3,4] This book's theme of "putting people first" is probably linked to the need to belong. Human beings relate to their physical environment by relating to other people first. We get even our basic food and shelter from other people, rather than directly from nature. People who didn't care about being with other people probably didn't live as well or as long as those who formed strong social networks, and the need to belong helps make people want to form those networks. To enjoy the benefits of culture, people have to have an inner drive to connect with other people.

The universality of the need to belong was once aptly summarized by social psychologist Warren Jones in his research on loneliness: "In two decades of studying loneliness, I have met many people who say they have no friends. I have never met anyone who didn't want to have any friends."[5] Converging evidence from other sources casts doubt on the stereotype that some people are by nature loners or are indifferent to human social contact. True, some people may want many friends, whereas others are content with just a

attraction anything that draws two or more people together, making them want to be together and possibly to form a lasting relationship

social acceptance a situation in which other people have come to like you, respect you, approve of you, and include you in their groups and relationships

rejection (social exclusion) being prevented by others from forming or keeping a social bond with them; the opposite of acceptance few, but everybody needs somebody. Even religious hermits, who supposedly live alone in nature, typically rely heavily on one or two people who visit them regularly (e.g., in their cave) and supply much-needed human contact. Full deprivation of interpersonal contact is extremely stressful for everyone. That is why solitary confinement is considered an extreme form of punishment in prisons. It is said that prisoners at San Quentin who were sentenced to solitary confinement and had no communication with each other resorted to desperate measures just to achieve some connection with other humans: Many of the men learned to speak down into their toilets, so the sound could pass through the pipes into other cells. They generally did not know who they were talking with, probably could not communicate very effectively, and might not have much to talk about—and the prospect of talking with your head stuck inside your toilet would be off-putting to many—but it was worth it to them just to hear another voice and know that theirs was heard. If the only road to social acceptance requires putting your head into a toilet, many people will do it.

Talking into toilets may seem bizarre to you, or outside your realm of experience. More commonly, you probably know people who rely on the internet for much of their social life and social contact. The internet allows people to interact with strangers and feel as though they can form social connections without much risk or anxiety.[6,7,8] Some people manage to satisfy the need to belong by spending time in internet chat rooms, where they may have intimate conversations with other people. Some who suffer from

TRADE Offs

Testosterone—A Blessing and a Curse

Testosterone is a hormone associated with masculinity. Both men and women have it, though men have 9 or 10 times as much as women. (Women are somewhat more sensitive to it, though men are still more affected by testosterone overall, because they have so much more.) Most people, both men and women, tend to admire manly traits (especially in men), and they look upon testosterone as a good thing.

The researcher Jim Dabbs, one of psychology's leading experts on testosterone, reported that as he became known for this research, he received many inquiries from individuals about whether it was possible to increase their testosterone level. No one ever asked him about how to reduce it! Such one-sided interest suggests that people think very favorably of testosterone and will do almost anything for more of it. People don't seem to appreciate the tradeoffs, which come through much more clearly in Dabbs's book[9] on the hormone. In reality, testosterone is a very mixed blessing, both for the individual who has it and for others connected with that person. High-testosterone men are more exciting but less reliable. They are restless in many ways, shown by their frequent interest in exploring new places and meeting new people, but this also makes them less prone to stay at home and take care of their families (see **FIGURE 11.1**).

Nature seems to have recognized that testosterone is better suited for finding mates than for maintaining stable families, and it has made some remarkable adjustments.[10] First, testosterone reaches its peak in young men around the age of 20 and declines steadily after that, so that it is highest during the years of single male competition but lower over the more family-centered years that typically follow.

The right circumstances help turn it on: One study showed that males who simply came into contact with a female accomplice while waiting in line for an experiment had higher testosterone levels than men who came in contact with a male accomplice.[11] Second, when a young man becomes a father, his testosterone level typically drops. In fact, in one experiment, men who were

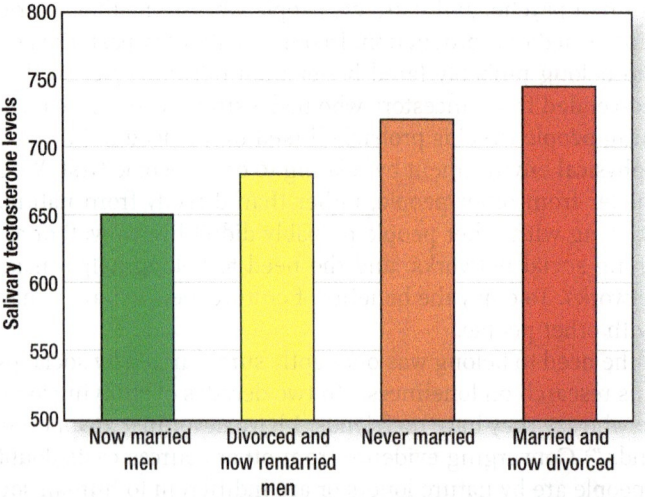

FIGURE 11.1 These data link low testosterone to a stable marriage; higher levels go with single status and divorce.

social anxiety or have feelings that society rejects and stigmatizes—so that opening up face to face with people they know is threatening, even dangerous—find they can communicate about their inner selves with complete strangers under the safe protection of anonymity that the internet offers. Nevertheless, on average across most populations, social media online interactions do not satisfy the need to belong, and if anything they seem to increase loneliness.[12] There may be a vicious circle in which lonely people spend more time on social media, with the result that they become even lonelier.[13] At best, some such interactions strengthen relationships with people one has met offline.[14]

Talking into toilets is just one extreme and vivid instance of how hard people will work to connect with others. The long road to social acceptance has been a repeated theme of this book, and this chapter will show the variety of ways in which people strive to gain acceptance—and the variety of ways they suffer when they fail to connect with others. Nobody wants to end up all alone in the world; in fact, most human beings could hardly survive by themselves. As this chapter will show, people work long and hard to secure acceptance by others and to avoid rejection.

Prisoners in San Quentin who were sentenced to solitary confinement and had no communication with each other resorted to desperate measures just to achieve some connection with other humans, such as speaking to other prisoners through toilet pipes.

soon to become fathers held a baby doll wrapped in a blanket that had previously been around a real baby (and therefore still had some baby smell), and after just a half hour these men experienced a significant decrease in their testosterone levels.[15]

Testosterone makes one more willing to take risks.[16] The tradeoffs there are obvious. High-testosterone men are more likely to perform heroic acts—and criminal ones, both of which involve risk taking. Competition also involves risk, and high-testosterone individuals are much more eager than others to compete in all sorts of spheres. If you don't compete, you can't win, but you can't lose either. The low-testosterone man may prefer to sit safely and comfortably on the sidelines, but the one with high testosterone wants to jump into the fray and test his mettle.

Testosterone seems to help promote high sex drive, in both men and women. Transsexuals who get testosterone shots (which help turn a woman into a man) report that they have more feelings of sexual desire and sexual interest.[17] Those who get testosterone blockers, which reduce the effect of testosterone, report a drop in sex drive. Among typical heterosexual individuals, higher levels of testosterone in both men and women are linked to higher sex drives in many studies, though some studies find no differences.[18] Whenever a relation is found, however, it links high testosterone to more desire.

Some of these go together. A notable experiment studied male skateboarders who tried out tricky jumps.[19] When these young men performed in front of an attractive female experimenter, they took greater risks and crashed more often, as compared to a male experimenter—and the risk taking was mediated by a rise in testosterone at the prospect of possibly showing off in front of a beautiful woman.

As we saw in Chapter 10, high-testosterone men are also more violent than others. The aggressive and sexual passions that come with high testosterone are accompanied by a corresponding lesser interest in simpler, gentler pleasures. Men with low testosterone are kinder, more trustworthy, and more affectionate.

High testosterone may lead to an exciting life, but a difficult one. The fascination with sex and violence can produce risky activities and problems. Probably such individuals have more active sex lives, but they also have shorter lives.[20] So all those people clamoring to raise their testosterone levels should be careful what they wish for!

"Give Mr. Fogarty his testosterone injection, Nurse, and then run like the dickens!"

People will do almost anything for more testosterone.

Bold adventures, passionate romances, but early graves.

A PLANET LIKE OURS

FOR THE LAST TIME, NO!

The need to belong is an important need!

Social animals probably developed a kind of "herd instinct" long ago, but the human need to belong goes beyond that. A herd is a large collection of animals that all do pretty much the same thing. In contrast, humans often play distinct roles and have all sorts of specific, individual relationships with other members of the group. We have some evidence that the animal species most closely related to human beings have more complex social lives than other kinds of animals, in part because they can understand relations among others. One monkey can recognize that two other monkeys have an alliance, or that they might form one, or that they are enemies who may be prone to fight against each other, and the monkey might adjust its own behavior toward these others accordingly. Humans do the same. In fact, one thought-provoking theory has proposed that the driving force behind the evolution of intelligence and the brain was social: Animals developed larger, smarter brains in order to keep track of more relationships and more complicated social networks.[21]

The **need to belong** is defined as the desire to form and maintain close, lasting relationships with some other individuals.[22,23,24,25,26,27] Without this motive, people might just live alone; they would certainly be willing to abandon a partner as soon as he or she became annoying. The need to belong drives people to affiliate, commit, and remain together, and it makes them reluctant to live alone. People usually form relationships easily and readily, such as with neighbors and work colleagues. They are reluctant to let relationships end, even if they do not see any clear purpose in continuing the relationship. For example, when workers at a corporation go through a training group exercise in which they meet regularly for a set period of time, the group typically resists its impending breakup, such as by promising to remain in touch with each other and even planning reunions.[28,29,30] The group's purpose will be over, and in fact most of these planned reunions never take place, but nobody wants to admit that the interpersonal connections are coming to an end. By the same token, when people break off a romantic relationship, they usually say they want to preserve some parts of their intimate connection despite terminating the romantic connection. "Let's just be friends" is the common breakup line, though in reality most ex-lovers do not sustain close friendships with each other.[31] Promising to remain friends is usually just a way to avoid the fact that a social bond is being broken.

Indeed, people are often reluctant to put an end even to bad relationships. People remain in relationships even with violent, abusive partners. This has been an enduring puzzle to psychologists and a source of vexation to therapists. A breathtaking variety of theories have been put forward to explain why women stay with men who humiliate or beat them, though it has been hard to prove any one of these theories correct, and many views (such as that some women have a masochistic desire to be beaten and abused) have been discredited. The broadest and simplest explanation is that breaking off relationships goes against the basic tendencies of human nature. We are designed to connect, not to separate, and even if the relationship is bad, we have a deeply rooted impulse not to terminate it. (Chapter 12 will cover more material about why people stay in bad relationships, especially in the section on the investment model.)

Two Ingredients to Belongingness

What exactly do people want? The need to belong has two parts.[32] First, people want some kind of regular social contacts. Of course, not all interactions are equally satisfying. Aversive social contacts, such as fighting and arguing, do not satisfy the need to belong. Positive social contacts are better, though neutral ones, such as watching television together or simply having breakfast together, are also satisfying. Second, people want the stable framework of some ongoing relationship in which the people share a mutual concern for each other.

Having either of these without the other produces partial satisfaction. For example, people who have many encounters with other people but without the relationship

need to belong the desire to form and maintain close, lasting relationships with other individuals framework are better off than people who are fully isolated, but they are not fully satisfied either. Imagine being a tollbooth collector who interacts with people all day long but never sees anyone for more than a minute or two and mostly just says the same few words over and over. The same goes for telemarketers, who may speak to many people on the phone but without any real connection. Prostitutes have rather intimate interactions with many individuals, but again without the context of an ongoing relationship that are not satisfying.[33,34,35]

Conversely, people who have the stable context without the frequent interactions also suffer from the lack of face-to-face contact, even though they may treasure the relationship. Long-distance relationships or so-called commuter marriages reveal this pattern: The partners place great value on the bond they have with their far-off lover, but they yearn to spend more time together.[36,37,38,39,40,41]

People may want to belong, but most do not seek to make new friends endlessly. Some people want more friends than others, but most people seem to think that having about four to six close relationships is enough.[42,43] That is, if you have about five people who care about you, whose company you enjoy, and with whom you can spend time on a regular basis, you probably feel fairly satisfied with your social life. (Most adults want at least one of those relationships to be a romantic pairing.) If you have fewer than that, you may be on the lookout for more. Few people seem eager to have more. In one survey, the majority of college students rated "having a few close friends" as extremely important, whereas "having lots of casual friends" was relatively unimportant.[44]

Another sign is how people act in people-rich settings such as universities. Because universities draw so many people, in principle, you could interact with someone new every day. As you may notice, that's not how people actually conduct their social lives. Most students form a social circle of about half a dozen other people and devote their time and energy to interacting with the members of this circle rather than to constantly seeking new friends.[45]

Not Belonging Is Bad for You

The need to belong is called a need, rather than merely a want, because when it is thwarted, people suffer more than just being unhappy. (A want is something that we can live without; a need is something that we have to have in order to be healthy.) Failure to satisfy the need to belong leads to significant health problems, including a higher risk of death. Death rates from all kinds of diseases are higher among people without social connections than among those with social connections.[46] People who are alone in the world have more physical and mental health problems than people who belong to a good social network.[47,48,49,50,51,52,53,54,55,56] Even apart from specific diseases, abundant evidence indicates that people who have more and better relationships live substantially longer than those who lack them.[57] Loneliness is hard on the body, impairing its natural powers including the immune system and its ability to recover from sickness or injury.[58]

There are plenty of other benefits to belonging (as if health and happiness were not enough!). Recent work has even linked belongingness to the meaning of life. Feeling connected to a strong network of relationships makes people see life as more meaningful.[59] Conversely, a lack of social connection can make life seem relatively meaningless.

Best Friends, Lovers, and Groups

Are close friends and romantic relationships the main or only way to satisfy the need to belong? In principle, cultural animals like human beings have another option: They can "belong" to a group or organization. Some people may find those social connections satisfying even if they do not form close friendships there.[60] As we shall see later in this chapter, some people can satisfy their wish for belongingness and keep loneliness at bay by feeling connected to a group or organization (even a university, or a professional sports team of which they are only fans). This seems to work better for men than for women.[61]

QUIZ YOURSELF
The Need to Belong

1. In the reality TV show *Average Joe,* Melana based her choice of partners on _____.
   - (a) personality
   - (b) physical attractiveness
   - (c) wealth
   - (d) All of the above

2. Which hormone has been linked with masculine traits such as aggressiveness and dominance?
   - (a) Cortisol
   - (b) Estrogen
   - (c) Progesterone
   - (d) Testosterone

3. The need to belong has two parts, _____ and _____.
   - (a) business contacts; pleasure contacts
   - (b) female contacts; male contacts
   - (c) regular social contacts; an ongoing relationship
   - (d) All of the above

4. Most people seem to think that having about _____ close relationships is enough.
   - (a) 1 to 3
   - (b) 4 to 6
   - (c) 7 to 9
   - (d) 10 to 12

answers: see pg 402

Attraction: Who Likes Whom?

Social psychologists have labored long and hard to study the start of possible friendships and other forms of liking. Two people who are just meeting may come to like each other, or they may not. Which way they go depends on a variety of factors. Social psychology's task has been to identify those factors.

Some social psychologists, such as the influential researcher Edward E. Jones,[62] approached the question of attraction by studying what people actively do to try to make someone like them. (The term **ingratiation** is used for this, although ingratiation also has the connotation of being something a bit sneaky or manipulative.) This is a useful complement to the simple studies of who likes whom. Imagine you met someone and wanted to get that person to like you, either as a friend or as a romantic partner. What would you do? Jones found that people seem to have an intuitive knowledge of what fosters attraction, and they use that knowledge to get other people to like them. We will see several examples in the coming sections.

Not much will prove surprising in these research findings. People like good-looking, friendly people who are similar to themselves in important ways, and they like people who are nice to them. Still, let us review the main conclusions.

Similarity, Complementarity, Oppositeness

Two old clichés make opposite predictions about who likes whom. "Birds of a feather flock together" suggests that people mainly like others who are similar to themselves, whereas "opposites attract" points to the contrary conclusion—that people are drawn to people dissimilar to themselves. Note that in such circumstances, whatever result social psychologists produce will look in retrospect like common sense. (This is why you shouldn't rely only on common sense when taking your social psychology exams! See Chapter 1 for a discussion on the weaknesses of common sense.)

In any case, decades of research by social psychologists have produced a clear and definitive winner in this battle of the clichés. Opposites do not attract very often. The birds of a feather are the ones who end up flocking together and staying together. In social psychology's terms, similarity is a common and potent cause of attraction.[63]

ingratiation what people actively do to try to make someone like them

matching hypothesis the proposition that people tend to pair up with others who are equally attractive

Most likely, you can see this yourself. Classify yourself on several major dimensions along which people differ. Choose ones that matter to you—perhaps age, race, level of education, liberal/conservative, religious or not, athletic or not, rich or poor. Then classify your several closest friends. The odds are that you and your close friends will fall in similar categories far more often than in different ones. People who want to influence us are well aware of this principle; sometimes they try to get us to like them by claiming that they are similar to us.

The appeal of similarity was illustrated in an amusing way by a news story. A man and a woman made contact via the internet and began to exchange emails. They discovered they had a great deal in common, and they became attracted to each other. They "dated" for about six months via email messages, though they did not reveal their names. The woman was also older than she had led the man to believe, so when he asked for her picture, she sent him a photo from a magazine. As their emotions grew stronger, the man pressured the woman to meet him for a romantic rendezvous. She finally relented and agreed to meet him on a dark beach. He went there, heart pounding, and saw a woman waiting for him as promised, wearing white shorts and a pink tank top. He spoke to her and she turned around, and they both got a shock: She was his mother! Obviously, nobody wants to date his own mother (especially because she was still married to his father, who became a laughingstock when the story hit the news and who took a very dim view of the whole episode).[64] But family members generally are quite similar to each other, so it is not surprising that when their identities were concealed they had many similarities that produced the attraction.

Similarity can promote liking in many spheres. Having friends who like to do the same things you like to do can be important. After all, if none of your friends likes to play tennis, how are you going to find someone to play with? Some people compartmentalize their social lives more than others. People who are high in **self-monitoring**[65,66,67,68] seek to maximize each social situation, whereas those low in that trait pay more attention to permanent connections and feelings rather than fluctuating ones. Hence, the high self-monitor tennis player would prefer to play tennis with the best (or most evenly matched) tennis player in his or her circle of friends, whereas the low self-monitor would prefer to play tennis with his or her best friend, regardless of tennis ability.

Some of the most striking effects of similarity are found in marriage, even though marriage, which usually binds together two people of opposite genders, is often assumed to be one of the spheres where opposite or at least complementary (thus different) traits promote attraction. In fact, most spouses are similar in many basic respects. For example, husband and wife tend to have similar levels of intelligence.[69] (When you get married, don't call your spouse an idiot, because your spouse's IQ probably is close to your own!) Married partners are also similar on other dimensions, including physical attractiveness, education, and socioeconomic status.[70] Similarity contributes not only to the initial attraction but to the development of close bonds. Couples who are more similar to each other in attractiveness are more likely to progress toward more loving and committed relationships[71] (see **FIGURE 11.2**).

The **matching hypothesis** states that people tend to pair up with others who are equally attractive.[72,73,74] This is especially true among lovers, but it also is true among friends. It occurs in same-sex and in opposite-sex relationships.

Why does similarity promote attraction? The pattern seems widespread and probably very deeply rooted in the psyche, so explanations should probably invoke simple, basic tendencies. If human beings were naturally selected "for" culture, and we evolved under conditions of competing cultures, people who attached themselves strongly to similar others would have an advantage. People who were drawn more to the different, the exotic, the foreign, might detach from their group and join another, but this would be risky. Newcomers aren't trusted as much as long-familiar mates.[75] Hence, people who preferred to form bonds with people very different from themselves might tend to leave behind fewer offspring than people who attached themselves to others like themselves. Another contributing factor is that most people start off life surrounded by family members, so we learn to love by loving people who are quite similar to us.

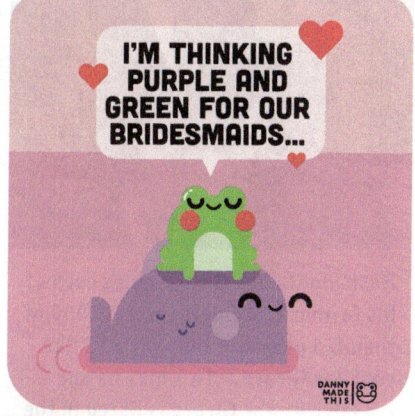

Daniel Vincenz

self-monitoring the ability to change one's behavior for different situations

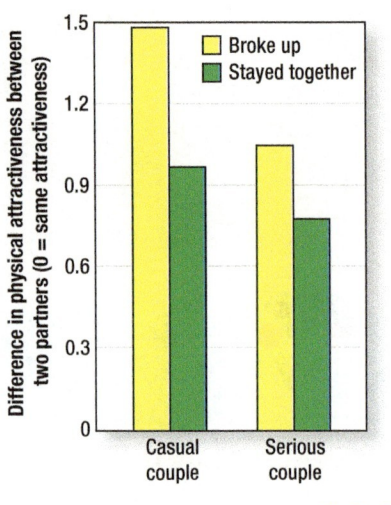

FIGURE 11.2

Dissimilarity in physical attractiveness increases the risk of breaking up.[71]

Some evidence indicates that matching is driven more by rejecting dissimilar others than by liking similar others.[76] In fact, as people get to know each other and find out about dissimilarities, liking diminishes. Most people believe that the more they know about someone, the more they like that person—but in reality, they tend to like someone less as they learn more. They start off assuming the other person will be similar. But once they find some dissimilarities, these seem to multiply, so that new evidence confirms dissimilarity and reduces liking. In an online dating study, researchers found, sure enough, that after the date was over people knew more about the dating partner but liked him or her less than previously.[77]

The attraction to similar others is probably social rather than cultural (see Chapter 2 for a discussion of the distinction between social and cultural animals). That is, the pattern that similarity promotes liking is not something that originates with human beings living in culture but rather something that originated among animals that formed into groups to help each other live better. Groups composed of similar animals would probably help each other live better. If anything, culture has raised the value of diversity and complementarity because cultural systems can take advantage of different roles and different talents.

Thus, as culture progresses and forms large, complex, interacting groups, there may be more need for complementarity. The movement toward diversity in organizations and the workplace may reflect an attempt to capitalize on the value of being different (see Chapter 14). But when people pick their friends and lovers, they still tend to look for those who are similar to themselves.

Social Rewards: You Make Me Feel Good

For several decades, psychological theory was dominated by **reinforcement theory**, which held that people and animals will perform behaviors that have been rewarded more than other behaviors. Applied to the issue of interpersonal attraction, this theory predicted that people would mainly like others who are rewarding to them—those who benefit them or make them feel good.

Two themes of ingratiation research confirm the importance of interpersonal rewards.[78] A first broad strategy for getting someone to like you is to do favors for that person. By definition, favors bring benefits to the recipient, and so favors make the person feel positively toward the person who did the favor. A man who wants a woman to like him will often do a broad variety of favors for her, such as sending her flowers, buying her dinner, and giving her gifts. Now and then people will recognize a favor as manipulative and resent it,[79] but in general favors are a good way to promote liking.

The second broad strategy involves praise. Most people feel good when they receive a compliment, so if you want someone to like you, you will probably be tempted to give that person plenty of compliments. Telling people what you like about them and what you see as their best traits is by and large a good way to go through life because it both reinforces the traits you approve of and makes people like you. The only limitation is that if people see the praise as manipulative or insincere, they may discount it. Otherwise, however, praising people is a reliable way to get them to like you.[80]

Consider Joe Girard, for example. Joe made a living by selling cars in Detroit, Michigan. He was so successful at his job that he was listed in the *Guinness Book of World Records* as the "Greatest Car Salesman." Every day he worked, Joe sold an average of five cars and trucks. Joe was once asked the secret of his success. His response was: "Finding the salesman you like, plus the price. Put them together, and you get a deal." In other words, getting people to like him was as important as money. He probably helped his business with repeat customers, too. Each month Joe would send a postcard to thousands of his former customers. The postcard contained only five words: "I like you! Joe Girard."[81] Praise can even help you sell cars.

Why do rewards promote liking? This is no big mystery. Rewards mean getting what you want. Any organism should learn to like people, places, animals, or things that provide it with what it wants and needs. This may be as simple as classical conditioning: You learn to associate feeling good with being with someone, so naturally you like that person more.

reinforcement theory the proposition that people and animals will perform behaviors that have been rewarded more than they will perform other behaviors

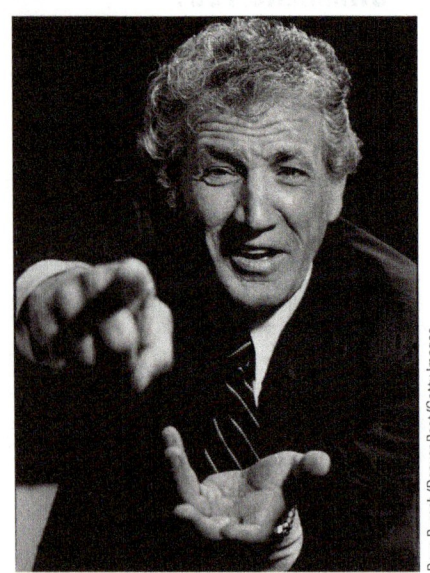

Each month Joe Girard sends each of his former customers (over 13,000 of them!) a postcard that says: "I like you! Joe Girard." This may be one reason why Joe Girard is listed in the *Guinness Book of World Records* as the "Greatest Car Salesman."

Tit for Tat: Reciprocity and Liking

Reciprocity is important for culture and therefore for human beings (see Chapters 8 and 9). Culture depends on reciprocity: If I do something for you, you should do something for me in return. Reciprocity is also important in liking. Having someone like you is powerful at a deep, gut level: It is hard to resist liking that person in return. The car salesman quoted above, Joe Girard, was on solid ground in thinking that telling people he liked them was a strong start.

If there is a single trait that stands out as most valued in social relationships, it is trustworthiness.[82] Why should trustworthiness be the single most important trait for social appeal? When you form a bond with someone, you expect to do positive things for that person. Trustworthiness means that you can expect the other person to reciprocate. That is an important and effective foundation for a good relationship.

Multiple studies have confirmed the simple principle that liking begets (reciprocal) liking, and it is so obvious and intuitively correct that few studies now bother to focus on it. Still, whenever participants receive feedback that someone else likes them, they almost invariably feel a surge of affection for that person. The power of reciprocal liking seems to be universal. Thus, even research that finds differences between cultures in how people think about friendships and how they attract new friends still finds the common principle: If someone likes you, it is hard to resist liking that person in return.[83]

Reciprocation can take other forms and in that respect can imply similarity. In nonverbal behavior, reciprocity can take the form of mimicking. In one well-known study,[84] participants interacted with an accomplice whom they wanted to like them. Sometimes the accomplice touched his or her face during the conversation, and other times the accomplice wiggled his or her foot. Without realizing what they were doing, participants mimicked these behaviors themselves. A follow-up study showed that mimicry is often successful as a means of increasing liking. Participants talked to an accomplice who had been trained to mimic the participant's nonverbal behavior (or not). When the accomplice performed the same nonverbal behaviors as the participant—for example, wiggling her foot in response to seeing the participant wiggle her foot—the participant ended up liking the accomplice more.[85] That may help explain why human babies quickly learn to mimic the people they see: Babies need people to like them!

Social mimicry shapes eating, too. Using experimental designs that measured how many M&M candies young women ate while working on problems together, researchers found that the women tended to match each other's eating habits.[86] This effect was especially strong among people with higher motivation to win the approval of others, and indeed making them feel socially accepted beforehand reduced the matching effect. Elsewhere, researchers taped parents having a meal with their adolescent daughters. The quantity of food was positively correlated: That is, the more the parent ate, the more the child ate. Moreover, when the parent took a bite of something, the daughter was likely to take a bite of the same food in the next few seconds.[87] These are not overwhelming effects, as if the daughter was copying the parent bite for bite. Plenty of bites were independent of each other. But if the mother took a bite of cheese, the chances went up slightly that the daughter would also take a bite of cheese pretty soon.

We started this chapter by describing the *Average Joe* television reality show that featured Melana Scantlin. The sequel, *Average Joe: Hawaii*, had another beautiful woman courted

I'm starting to like you more and more.

It's hard to say no to someone who really loves you.

by a bevy of ordinary-looking men. In this series, one of the nerdy-looking men adopted an unusual strategy, which was to declare himself wildly in love with the woman early in the game. It is a risky strategy, at least assuming that the declarations of love were truthful, because to fall in love with someone far more attractive than yourself (not to mention someone who was being courted by a couple of dozen other men!) makes you highly vulnerable to heartbreak. In this case, however, it had a powerful impact. The gorgeous young woman responded to the nerdy man's love for her, and she repeatedly selected him to continue in the game, even after the producers introduced a row of handsome young alternative suitors. The thoroughly smitten young man made it into the final round of two men, although she, like Melana Scantlin in the first game, ultimately chose the shallow but handsome fellow over the passionately devoted but average-looking guy. (Then the handsome guy dumped her.) Still, he had gone much further than he otherwise could have, simply by loving the woman unreservedly. It was hard for her to resist the fact that he loved her so much.

Reciprocation of liking may have a hugely powerful effect in everyday friendships. Its impact is more of a problem in romance, however. The difference may lie in the simple truth that you can have many friends but usually only one love relationship, in most cultures.

Research on one-sided, unrequited love has confirmed that people are positively attracted when they learn that someone else likes them—but if they do not want to reciprocate those feelings, they soon start to find the other person's attraction to them to be a burden or problem. If you were to find out that someone has a crush on you, your first reaction would almost certainly be positive because it is good to be loved. But if you did not really want that person as your partner, soon you would feel uncomfortable around them. Initially it is flattering to learn that someone likes you, but if you do not want to marry that person, your later reaction is a struggle with guilt and a search for ways to let the person down easily.[88]

Reciprocity brings us back to the broad theme of humans as cultural animals. If people liked those who liked them, this reciprocity would make people better suited to culture. Creatures who mainly liked those who disliked them would have a difficult time forming the network of relationships that makes culture possible. You are safer and better off among people who like you than among people who don't care about you one way or the other. Putting people first, to mention another theme of this book, seems to work best when it involves people who like us and are similar to us.

You Seem Trustworthy: Moral Traits

Many people can have fun with someone who is not particularly scrupulous about moral behavior, and they may even enjoy someone who breaks the rules now and then. But if you want to form a long-term relationship with someone, you will generally be happier if that person is a moral person.

Nobody disputes that people like people who are warm and friendly. But is that the main criterion? Recent evidence suggests that global impressions depend more on moral character than on warmth. Honest, trustworthiness, fairness, and courage have a big impact on the impressions people form—much more than warmth, sense of humor, sociability, and agreeableness.[89]

After all, liking is not the only thing that matters. Relationships need trust also, and trust depends on moral traits. People earn trust by having good self-control, which is a vital basis for moral behavior (see Chapter 4).[90] In fact, even people with low self-control choose partners with high self-control, contrary to the usual pattern of being attracted to similar others (which would predict that people with low self-control would be attracted to others who also have low self-control).[91] Again, this indicates judging people by moral traits, not friendliness.

Indeed, the importance of a person's moral character in interpersonal attraction is not just changing theories about attraction. It is also changing how psychologists think about morality. For decades, the focus has been on how people judge actions. Recent work has suggested, however, that morality may be more about judging people.[92] After all, an action is in the past, but the future may require a person to decide whether someone will make a good partner or not. Moral judgment, including blame and praise, may be a vital basis for making future choices about relationships.

You Again: Mere Exposure

What we have seen so far is hardly surprising. People like those who are similar to them, who like them back, and who make them feel good. But another pattern is less intuitively obvious. Apparently, people sometimes like others based on nothing more than familiarity. That is, they grow to like people whom they encounter on a regular basis. This **propinquity** (nearness) effect is robust and reliable. A classic study tracked friendship formation in a dormitory, and it found that people made friends (as well as enemies) most frequently among the people who lived close to them.[93]

Chapter 7 on attitudes described the mere exposure effect: People come to hold more positive attitudes toward familiar stimuli than toward novel, unfamiliar ones. Merely seeing or encountering something or someone on a regular basis increases liking (unless you dislike the person initially, then it leads to more disliking).

An extension of the mere exposure effect involves shared experiences. For example, many years from now in some far-off place you may meet a stranger and discover during the conversation that the two of you attended the same college or came from the same home town or had the same kind of pet. Logically, there is little reason that this should promote liking, but the odds are that you and this other person will begin to have friendly feelings toward each other based on this shared experience.

People seem to develop positive feelings toward someone even if the shared experiences were bad. Laboratory participants who are strangers and have no common bond except that they experience electric shock together end up liking each other more![94] A similar conclusion emerges from research on combat veterans. Going through combat is mostly a highly stressful, dangerous, sad, and terrifying experience, marked by loud noise, confusion, death and injury to friends, and uncertainty about one's own survival. Yet military groups who experience combat seem to bond to each other from the experience. One sign is that military reunions are better attended by groups who went through combat than by groups who did not.[95]

Why do familiarity and shared experiences promote liking? The effect of familiarity and shared experiences goes beyond simple explanations in terms of conditioning (positive associations). Most likely it is very deeply rooted in the psyche, which means its roots are far back in our evolutionary history. One should perhaps ask why even very simple animals would prefer familiar stimuli or familiar other animals. A tendency to grow fond of the familiar would help stamp in the preference for a stable environment (so animals might learn to like their homes). It would certainly promote stable social bonds. Imagine, for example, that nature programmed animals in the opposite way, so that familiarity led to contempt or some other form of disliking. How would families stay together? How would friendships, alliances, or other partnerships survive? If you always preferred a stranger to someone you knew, social life would be in constant turmoil and turnover. In contrast, if you automatically grew to like the people you saw regularly, you would soon prefer them over strangers, and groups would form and stabilize easily. Given the advantages of stable groups (e.g., people know each other, know how to work together, know how to make decisions together, know how to adjust to each other), it is not surprising that nature favored animals that grew to like (rather than dislike) each other on the basis of familiarity.

As with all these patterns, it is important not to overstate them. Of course, we do not grow to like everyone we see on a regular basis. Some people are a pain in the neck, and seeing them every day will not make them seem like adorable sweethearts. There is even an interesting pattern of research suggesting that a partner's annoying habits grow more annoying with repeated exposure (see **FIGURE 11.3**). This is called the **social allergy effect** based on the analogy to ordinary allergies, which grow worse over time. If you have

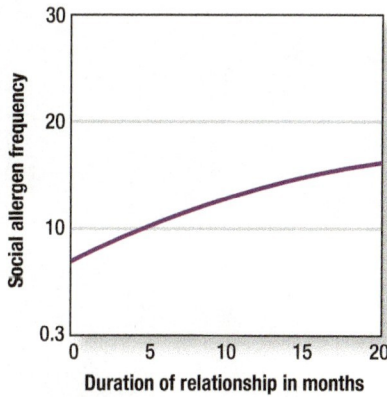

FIGURE 11.3
The longer the relationship continues, the more people are bothered by their partner's minor annoying habits, and the more negative emotion they have in response to them.

propinquity being near someone on a regular basis

social allergy effect the idea that a partner's annoying habits become more annoying over time

Attraction: Who Likes Whom? | 383

a slight allergy to cats and you move in with a romantic partner who has a cat, your cat allergy is likely to grow more severe as you are exposed to the cat more frequently. In the same way, early in a relationship you may be only slightly bothered by how your partner chews with her mouth open, or picks his toenails while watching television, or keeps repeating some stupid phrase such as "like, wow"—but this slight irritation will most likely grow more bothersome over time.[96,97,98,99] In short, familiarity and repeated exposure can sometimes make bad things worse. But the most common consequence is that people grow to like people (and places and things) that become familiar to them.

This increase in liking caused by familiarity, like nearly every social psychology effect, involves a shift in the odds rather than a black-and-white absolute difference. In this case, seeing someone regularly and becoming familiar with that person leads to a slight increase in the odds that you will end up liking that person. The mere exposure effect is probably an important part of the propinquity effect, noted earlier. We like those who live near us because we see them frequently.

Looking Good

In the Melana Scantlin story that started the chapter, a beautiful and desirable woman chose a physically attractive man over one with substance and success. Such a choice is not uncommon. When all else is equal, most people show a substantial preference for attractive over unattractive others. Even when all else is not equal, physical good looks count for a lot and can trump other good points.

Some of the advantages of good looks fall into the stereotype that has been called the **what is beautiful is good effect** (also called halo effect). That is, people assume that physically attractive people will be superior to others on many other traits. These traits include happiness, sexual warmth, popularity, and even intelligence and success.[100,101,102] To be sure, not all good traits are assumed to be linked to attractiveness. Attractive people are not assumed to be more honest than others, for example. Researchers have also found some evidence of cultural variation. South Koreans, for example, place more value than North Americans on honesty and compassionate concern for others, and South Koreans also are more likely to think that attractive people will rank higher than average on those traits.[103]

Good looks can outweigh other factors in attraction. (To see how one group of researchers tried to put a dollar value on physical attributes, read *Money Matters*.) Indeed, this fact produced one of the most famous disappointments in social psychology's research on attraction. A group of researchers set up a campus dating service to test their various theories about interpersonal liking.[104] They collected all sorts of information about the students in their pool; then they matched them at random and sent them out on dates. The researchers favored theories emphasizing similarity and reciprocity: They thought people who were most similar to each other on various attributes would enjoy their dates the most. This was not what happened. Instead, the main conclusion was that the dating partner's attractiveness was the strongest predictor of how much people enjoyed the date: The more attractive your partner was, the better you liked them. The fancy theories about matching and similarity and reciprocity couldn't shine through the overwhelming preference for the best-looking partners.

It is perhaps understandable that people want their dating partners and romantic partners to be physically attractive (see *The Social Side of Sex*). But good looks are valued in many other, nonromantic settings as well. Attractive children are more popular among other children than their less attractive peers, and teachers like them more, too.[105,106,107] Research even shows that 3-month-old babies prefer to look at more attractive faces.[108] Good-looking people do better in job interviews, including for jobs that are not based on looks.[109,110] We saw in the chapter on prosocial behavior that attractive people sometimes get more help in emergency situations (see Chapter 9).[111]

Students may even learn more when their teachers are attractive. In an experiment, students listened to a physics lecture on audiotape while viewing a photograph they were told was the lecturer. The photographs were actually randomly assigned and varied in

what is beautiful is good effect the assumption that physically attractive people will be superior to others on many other traits

MONEY Matters

Is Manhood Measured in Dollars or Inches?

What is the measure of a man? Women have long known that physical dimensions are a key component of their own attractiveness, and women's concern with losing weight and being thin is at least partly rooted in the competition to be desirable to men. One relevant measure is the ratio of waist size to hip size. Researchers have found that men are more attracted to women with a ratio of about 0.7, and they have clear preferences when they judge a woman only by her silhouette.[112] A low ratio like 0.7 is compatible with the so-called hourglass figure that men find desirable. If the ratio is higher, as it is for women with bigger bellies, attraction is less.

In an effort to see whether women would judge men by equally simple (some might say shallow!) criteria, researchers prepared silhouette drawings of men with varying waist-to-hip ratios and asked women to rate them for attractiveness.[113] Sure enough, women did have a slight preference for a certain body shape in men, with a waist-to-hip ratio of around 0.9 and normal overall weight. Of course, this doesn't necessarily mean very much because that was all the information the women had on which to judge the men, and the effect was small.

In a final study, therefore, researchers added a second variable: how much money the man earned. Waist-to-hip ratio still mattered, a little, but the amount of money the man made was much more important, especially when women were judging him as a partner for a long-term relationship or marriage. Women much preferred the men with high incomes over the low-paid ones. Dollars mattered more than inches, though for maximum appeal, both the right body and a high income were needed.

Of course, waistline is not the only part of a man that can be measured in inches. Being tall matters, and there is in fact some tradeoff between money and height, according to research done with an online dating service.[114] Women's choices depended on both men's height and their salaries. Taller was better, but money could compensate. Thus, a man who was 5 feet 8 inches (1.73 meters) tall could get as many dates as a man who was 6 feet (1.78 meters) tall, provided that the shorter man made more money—precisely, $146,000 per year more! For a 5-foot 2-inch (1.57 meters) man to do as well as a 6-footer, he would need to earn an extra $277,000 annually.

The news for short men is not all bad, however. Women may express some preference for dating tall men, but when they meet them, they do not find them any more attractive. Moreover, short men report having had just as many dates as tall men, so obviously they find ways of overcoming any prejudice against them.[115]

---

attractiveness. Students rated the attractive teacher more positively and performed better on a multiple-choice test when they had thought the teacher was attractive, as compared to the unattractive teacher.[116] The effect was true for both male and female students and both male and female teachers.

It may seem that everything is in favor of good-looking people. But as the next chapter will show, attractive people have higher rates of divorce and romantic breakup than others, and they do not work as hard as others (in some ways at least) to keep the relationship intact.[117] Most people want both a stable, lasting relationship and an attractive partner, but these goals may be in conflict.

For men, modern clothing is linked more to displaying wealth and status than showing off the body as a sex object. Women in one study were asked to rate how attractive they found men as potential husbands, dates, or lovers, based on seeing photographs of them.[118] The researchers had actually taken two photos of each man. In one photo, the man wore classy and expensive clothes, including a navy blue blazer, nice tie, and Rolex watch. For the other photo, each man put on a Burger King (fast food) server outfit, complete with hat. Women expressed very little desire to meet, date, sleep with, or marry the men they saw wearing Burger King outfits, probably because those outfits are associated with low status and not much money. The very same men attracted much more interest when dressed up in classy, expensive clothes.

Body shape is another component of attractiveness and sex appeal. A so-called hourglass figure composed of a narrow waist with wider hips and shoulders is most appealing in both men and women, though naturally the widest shoulders are seen as more attractive in a man than a woman. The ideal figure varies from culture to culture. For example, plump women are regarded as more attractive by some cultures than by others, though being very obese is not regarded as lovely by almost any culture. Even within a culture, standards of beauty change. For example, the weight of *Playboy* centerfolds and Miss America Pageant contestants and winners has decreased substantially since 1960.[119]

The Social Side of Sex

What Is Beauty?

Most people can agree fairly well on who is beautiful and who isn't, but it is much harder to say why someone is beautiful. Also, people agree more about women than about men, possibly because physical attractiveness counts more for women than for men.[120] In lab studies, both men and women automatically looked more at beautiful women (more than handsome men) in a group of faces.[121] Probably the reasons differed. The men see beautiful women as potential mates. The women see them as potential rivals and want to check out the competition. (Did it ever strike you as odd that not only are men's magazines filled with pictures of beautiful women—but so are women's magazines?)

Evolutionary psychologists generally think that female beauty is linked to signs of being a good mate and potential partner, which especially means being young and healthy. If cultural variation in beauty were random, you might expect that gray hair and wrinkled skin would be regarded as beautiful in some cultures, but no known culture treats old-looking women as more beautiful than younger-looking ones. A clear complexion is nearly always prized, possibly because it was a sign of health: Many infectious diseases such as pox left permanent marks on the skin, so clear skin would be one sign of a healthy mate. Today's men and women are descended from male ancestors who chose young and healthy-looking women.

Symmetry is a surprisingly powerful source of beauty. That is, people whose faces and bodies are exactly the same on both sides are regarded as more attractive than people whose right side is different from the left side. Symmetry is a sign of two important things: being healthy and having good genes. Faults or defects in someone's genes produce discrepancies between the left and right sides. The most symmetrical person presumably has the fewest genetic defects.

One of the most remarkable demonstrations of the power of symmetry began by measuring a series of body parts (such as earlobes and little fingers) of young adult men, to see how closely they matched. Then the researchers asked each man to sleep in a T-shirt some night when he did not use deodorant or cologne. Each man brought the T-shirt to the lab and left it there. A sample of young women then sniffed each T-shirt and rated how good it smelled (of course without knowing which men had worn them). They also informed the researchers of when they had had their last menstrual period. The most symmetrical men's T-shirts were rated as smelling the best, and this effect was mainly found among the women who were at the point in the menstrual cycle at which they would be most fertile. Thus, when women are most prone to get pregnant, they are most drawn to the bodily smell of men who were most symmetrical and hence would probably have the best genes.[122]

Researchers also demonstrated the importance of symmetry by doubling images. That is, researchers took facial photos of people, then cut each photo down the middle, threw out one side at random, and filled in the blank with the mirror image of the other side. For example, they might create a photo of you by taking the left side of your face, making a mirror image of it, and attaching the mirror image (as the right side) to the real left side. The result was faces that looked much like the original people but were more exactly symmetrical. Participants consistently rated these reworked images as more attractive than the original faces. Thus, increasing the symmetry of a face made it seem more attractive.

Another source of beauty is typicality. That is, people who look different from others are generally regarded as less attractive. This theory was proposed two centuries ago by the German philosopher Immanuel Kant,[123] who thought that the mind reviews all the faces it has ever seen, forms a sort of average or composite, and regards that as the most attractive. Recent advances in computer technology finally made it possible to test his theory by morphing faces together to make up an average. In a landmark study, researchers started with 16 different faces that varied in attractiveness. Then they combined pairs of faces using computer imaging software, so that they made 8 new faces, each of which was an "average" of two of the original faces. They then merged these again by pairs, and again, ultimately creating a single image that was the average of all 16. Participants consistently rated the original, actual faces as less attractive than the 2-face composites; the 4-face composites got even higher ratings; and the images that had been made by averaging all 16 faces were rated as the most beautiful.[124]

Further work has shown that the ultimate, most attractive faces are not really averages of everyone, but rather averages of the faces that are high on the other indices of beauty, such as youth and health. That is, a face that averages across the entire life span, including a baby, a little girl, an adolescent, a young adult, a middle-aged woman, and an old woman, is not as attractive as a face that is made by averaging a group of young adult women.

The preference for slender versus fuller figures seems to change fairly easily. In fact, men can change their preferences even within the same day! One study stopped Princeton students going to dinner or coming back from it to furnish ratings of attractiveness of women from photos. The hungry men (before dinner) preferred plumper women than the men who were full from dinner.[125]

Which photo is more attractive? The one on the left shows the actual face; the one on the right was made by duplicating the left side on the right, so that the face is perfectly symmetrical. Most people find the one on the right to be more attractive than the true picture.

The sources of cultural variation in ideal body weight are not fully known, although one factor may be whether food is scarce. That is, in a culture where there is often not enough to eat, a plump woman is probably rich and healthy, whereas a skinny woman is more in danger of starving or might have a disease. Men in such cultures might prefer slightly larger women because their bodies will be better able to support a baby. Of course, the men don't necessarily think about whether the woman can nurse a baby. It is just that the men who for whatever reason were attracted to the plumper women were more successful at passing on their genes, whereas the men who liked the skinniest women produced fewer surviving babies.

The ideal beauty standard for American women has become thinner over time.

Attraction in the 21st Century: Online Dating

Dogs, birds, and giraffes meet their mates today much the same way they always have, but human mating customs have changed repeatedly over the centuries. In the 1800s, much romance was conducted on the front porch, where the gentleman caller talked to the young lady with her mother present and sometimes with his romantic rivals also earnestly trying to dominate the conversation. The 20th century invented "dates" (the term originally referred to an encounter with a prostitute), especially as motorcars enabled young couples to seek livelier environments than Mom's front porch. Trips to the movies were a staple of mid-century dates. Dances have long been popular ways of getting to know romantic partners, though the settings and dances changed over the decades. Elsewhere in the world, the variety is even greater, including marriages arranged by parents so that the young couple first meet each other at their wedding, as well as people going to priests or professional matchmakers to get help finding a partner.

In the 21st century, many people seek romantic partners via online dating services (e.g., Zoosk, EliteSingles, eHarmony, SilverSingles, OurTime, Match). Not long ago, computers were owned by big corporations and operated mainly by professional nerds and their lackeys, but now young men and women use computers as instruments of romance. They can sign up to a service that lets them peruse information about large numbers of potential partners and contact ones they find appealing.

How has online dating changed romance? The Association for Psychological Science appointed a blue-ribbon panel of experts to review the latest research and draw some conclusions.[126]

To start with the obvious, the researchers documented several key differences between online dating and the more conventional (offline) sort. First, online dating greatly expands the range of potential partners and the ease of meeting them. College students can meet single people in classes and around campus, but once a person leaves college, the prospects for encountering eligible partners shrink markedly: One meets a few people at work, or is "set up" on a blind date by a third party, or chats up strangers in bars. In contrast, the online supply can seem almost limitless, at least in a large city.

Second, online dating enables people to communicate via computer before they meet in person, and in some cases these contacts can be extensive. You can send messages back and forth with a potential partner for days, weeks, even months before meeting face to face. This enables you to get to know much about the partner, make preliminary evaluations (perhaps finding out reasons not to meet, which are less awkwardly handled by email than in the middle of a romantic dinner), and build some degree of relationship before you are ever in the same room together.

Third, several online services offer to help you search out the best partners from your database. They use formulas and algorithms that select the people who will match up with you best.

Finding love has changed over time.

There are drawbacks, to be sure. People do not always tell the truth in their online profiles. One study checked online claims against actual measurements and found that 81% of the dating profiles contained lies about height, weight, or age.[127] Men tend to overstate their height, and women understate their weight.

On the harder question of whether online dating really improves outcomes, the panel's report had mixed answers. Yes, online dating vastly increases the number of potential partners, but one encounters them in the form of online profiles that can fail to include crucial information, and having thousands of potential partners may reduce the effort to work at getting to know any particular one. Communicating by computer can be helpful, but it is not a substitute for face-to-face interaction. As for the claims to find your soul mate by combing through the files with mathematical formulas—well, these are simply not plausible, as the panel concluded. Thus, online dating seems here to stay, and it does have its advantages, but it is not a magic recipe for finding love, and it may create its own set of problems and difficulties.

So far, we have focused on what makes people attractive and attracted to each other. In the next section, we turn to the other side of the coin: social rejection and exclusion.

QUIZ YOURSELF

Attraction: Who Likes Whom?

1. **Based on attraction research, which of these proverbs is most accurate?**
   - (a) "The early bird gets the worm."
   - (b) "Birds of a feather flock together."
   - (c) "Opposites attract."
   - (d) "Out of sight, out of mind."

2. **If you live next to someone, what outcome is most likely?**
   - (a) You will become friends with that person.
   - (b) You will become enemies with that person.
   - (c) Both (a) and (b)
   - (d) Neither (a) nor (b)

3. **If people are seated according to their last names using a seating chart, those with last names that start with the same letter often end up becoming good friends. This finding can be explained by _____.**
   - (a) ingratiation
   - (b) propinquity
   - (c) need for belonging
   - (d) similarity

4. **According to the what is beautiful is good effect, attractive people have a number of other desirable traits. Which of the following is not one of these traits, at least in Western cultures?**
   - (a) Happiness
   - (b) Honesty
   - (c) Intelligence
   - (d) Popularity

answers: see pg 402

Rejection

One day a young man named Kip Williams was walking through a park and unexpectedly saw a Frisbee spinning toward him. He caught it and looked about for its source. Two other guys waved to him, and he threw it back to them. Everyone smiled, and the three of them threw the Frisbee around for a few minutes. Then, oddly, the other two stopped throwing him the Frisbee and ignored him. He stood there for a few minutes, his smile gradually fading, until he realized that they weren't going to include him anymore. Feeling surprisingly sick and sad, he turned and slunk away.

In most cases that would have been the end of the story, but Williams went on to become a social psychologist. He remembered the experience and his emotional reaction. After all, why should he have expected the others to keep him in their game forever, and why should he even care? He hadn't gone to the park expecting to play Frisbee; he didn't know the guys, so they didn't owe him anything; and he didn't lose anything of importance or value. Yet somehow at a gut level he had been quite upset by the way the two fellows had excluded him. He turned his attention to the study of what happens when someone is rejected, excluded, or ignored. Kip Williams has even designed a virtual game called *Cyberball* that can be used to reproduce the situation of the excluded Frisbee player, for research purposes (see **FIGURE 11.4**).

Ostracism refers to being excluded, rejected, and ignored by others. The term comes from ancient Greece. One custom in Athens was that if a person behaved offensively or too aggressively, someone would write that person's name on a piece of broken pottery and put it in one of the large containers allocated in public places. These pieces of pottery, called *ostraka* (from which the word *ostracism* is derived) were collected and tallied, and if one person was named on 6,000 *ostraka*, the entire community agreed to give that person the silent treatment for 10 years: no one would speak to or interact with that person.

ostracism being excluded, rejected, and ignored by others

FIGURE 11.4

Psychologists have many ways to make participants feel socially excluded for short periods so they can evaluate the effects social exclusion has on everything from brain activity to sharing cookies. Many experiments use this *Cyberball* game, developed by Kip Williams of Purdue University. The participant, represented by the little hand in the foreground, is initially included in the game of catch with the other two players, who are really just part of a computer program. Midway through the game, the other players throw the ball between themselves, excluding the participant, whose little hand is left with nothing to do.

Lt. Henry Flipper was the first African American to graduate from West Point in 1877. He was ostracized the entire time he was a student at West Point.

Nowadays the term *ostracism* is used for smaller-scale practices of ignoring, as when a person refuses to speak to his or her spouse for a period of time. The close-knit Amish community will sometimes ostracize someone who is regarded as having violated the community's rules, such as by cheating someone, breaking religious rules, or misbehaving sexually. The silence is sometimes also used in military groups, such as if someone is believed to have cheated or broken the military code of honor. In such cases, no one speaks to the person or even acknowledges his existence. No one looks at you or responds to anything you say. Lt. Henry Flipper, the first black man to go to West Point, had to endure that treatment for his entire four years of college because the other cadets believed that it was inappropriate for an African American to study there to become an officer in the army.[128]

We opened this section with the brief story about Kip Williams being ostracized by strangers for a few minutes. Such experiences may be unpleasant, but when one is ostracized by significant others, or over a long period of time, the impact is almost certainly considerably worse.[129] The fact that some people (like Williams himself in the Frisbee story) feel bad after even a few minutes of ostracism attests to the power and importance that the human psyche attaches to being socially accepted. To be ostracized for months at a time by a spouse or parent can be devastating.

Much ostracism is informal, and some targets do not even know why they are being ostracized. One woman reported in an interview that her father had ostracized her off and on since she was 12, and she was now 40. Despairing of ever having a warm connection to her family again, she moved halfway around the world. Eventually her siblings contacted her and told her that her father was expected to die soon. This was one last chance to make up, so she made the long flight home, booked into a hotel, and finally went to the hospital. Even then she was torn between the desire to connect and the fear of being rejected again. She stood outside her father's hospital room struggling within herself as to what to say and whether to go in. Summoning all her courage, she finally walked in and looked at the now frail but still recognizable man lying on the bed. He was surprised to see her. "Oh Daddy, please don't leave me," she said. The old man's eyes filled with tears, but then he turned his face to the wall and never said a word to her. That was the last time she ever saw him. (As the researcher, Williams found these stories so hard to bear that he had to hire research assistants to take over the rest of the interviews.)

It is easy and appropriate to feel sorry for the victims of ostracism. Still, it is important to appreciate both perspectives. When someone is rude or offensive or behaves very badly, it may be appropriate to challenge their behavior in some way. However, simply refusing to interact with the offensive person may be easier than confronting him or her. Experiments have found that it depletes energy to confront someone who behaves badly, and some people may turn to ostracizing the bad person as a strategy that subtly expresses disapproval but also conserves energy.[130]

Recent work has extended rejection to forms less cruel and extreme than ostracism.[131] Many people experience being forgotten by someone else. This may be that someone you just met forgets your name or doesn't recognize you the next time they see you. It may also be that someone closer to you forgets something about you, like your birthday, or something you said or that the two of you did together. These experiences do not always bother people, but sometimes they do, and in more extreme cases, being completely forgotten by someone else causes one to feel a loss of meaningfulness in life.[132]

Effects of Rejection: Inner Reactions

Nobody thinks it's fun to be rejected, to be thrown out of a group, or to have your heart broken. The inner states that arise in response to rejection are almost uniformly negative. People who are repeatedly or continually ostracized by others over a long period report a broad variety of problems: pain, illness, depression, suicidal thoughts, eating disorders, helplessness, promiscuity.[133,134] Their self-esteem suffers, and they feel worthless. Some of them say life seems meaningless and pointless.[135,136] All of these findings underscore the central point that people are designed by nature to want to be accepted into social groups and relationships.

Being rejected repeatedly can cause people to develop expectations that other people will reject them too. This forms the basis of a personality trait called **rejection sensitivity**. Sometimes these expectations make people so hypersensitive to possible rejection that they become reluctant to open up or get close to others for fear of being hurt. This can set up a vicious circle in which rejection sensitivity causes people to push others away (so as to reduce the risk of getting hurt), which then damages relationships, causing more rejection and increasing the sensitivity.[137,138]

The common experience "you hurt my feelings" is usually tied to an implicit message that "you don't care about our relationship."[139] Anything a person does or says that suggests the person doesn't care about you as much as you care about him or her, or doesn't care about the relationship as much as you do, can hurt your feelings. Obviously, rejection almost always involves the sense that the rejecter doesn't care about the relationship—so hurt feelings are common. Perhaps surprisingly, it doesn't seem to matter much whether people actively try to reject you or do it more casually or thoughtlessly. Your feelings may be deeply hurt even if the other person never intended to hurt you and never thought about you at all, such as if your romantic partner forgot your birthday. Instead, the amount of hurt feelings depends on how much you care about the relationship and how clear a sign you received that the other person doesn't care as much.[140]

Not all rejection produces an immediate wave of emotional distress, however. In fact, the initial reaction to rejection is often closer to numbness, "feeling nothing," than anxiety or sadness.[141] This is possibly rooted in biology: The body reacts to the pain of social rejection with the same response it uses to physical pain, and severe pain often deadens the body to all feeling.[142,143,144,145,146,147] People who suffer terrible physical injuries, such as a broken bone or severe wound, may become numb, and sometimes athletes who are injured during a game don't fully feel the pain until the game is over. This could help explain why rejected people sometimes do antisocial things that might alienate other people further: They have become numb to the pain of social exclusion and hence don't realize that what they are doing might drive people away.

Indeed, social rejection affects the body in ways similar to physical injury. When people who have recently broken up with a romantic partner look at a photo or other reminder of that person, their brains respond with activity in the same places that respond to physical pain.[148] Social psychologist Nathan DeWall was struck by the parallels between social and physical pain, and he began to wonder whether taking a painkiller like aspirin or Tylenol (acetaminophen) would reduce suffering from social rejection just as it seems to reduce physical pain. He recruited samples of students to take a couple pills every day, by random assignment either Tylenol or a placebo. After a few days, those taking Tylenol reported fewer "hurt feelings" and other signs of being bothered by rejection. Their social self-esteem increased, even though other aspects of self-esteem (e.g., about their schoolwork) were unaffected. The placebo group showed no change. A lab study with brain scans showed the same benefit: Painkillers reduced responses to being rejected and ostracized.[149] Thus, distress over social events is really processed in the body in ways that resemble the response to physical injuries. Of course, one should not become addicted to painkillers just to numb social pain.

The numb or stunned feeling that comes from a strong (and especially an unexpected) rejection can interfere with normal psychological functioning. Rejection interferes with cognitive processing: In simple terms, rejection makes people temporarily stupid. They are less effective at processing complex information such as reasoning.[150] Rejection also undermines self-regulation: In the aftermath of rejection, people become more impulsive, more inclined to do something they will regret later (but that may seem appealing now).[151] Rejected people may, for example, blow their diets by eating a giant cake or a large serving of ice cream, or they may waste a large amount of money. See *Food for Thought* for some experimental findings on rejection and eating.

Other bodily effects of rejection have begun to be studied. At some unconscious level, people link temperature with social processes. Being surrounded by loving friends is

rejection sensitivity a tendency to expect rejection from others and to become hypersensitive to possible rejection

FOOD FOR *Thought*

Social Rejection and the Jar of Cookies

The love of your life, or at least the person you thought was the love of your life, storms out the door, saying, "I don't ever want to see you again!" and calling you a variety of names like loser, creep, and hopelessly inept lover. According to one stereotype, you might go home and eat an entire cheesecake, or a whole gallon of ice cream.

What does research say? The stereotype is actually fairly accurate. Social anxiety and fears of rejection are linked to eating binges and eating disorders.[152,153,154,155] In lab studies, rejected people are more prone to eat fattening or junk food.[156] This fits the more general pattern that rejection impairs self-regulation. People may want to eat cake, ice cream, or French fries much of the time, but usually they restrain these impulses because they know such foods are bad for them. After experiencing a rejection, however, the restraints are undermined. In one study, rejected people ate nearly twice as many cookies as people who had been accepted by a group (see **FIGURE 11.5**).[157] They also rated the cookies as tasting better, though the increased eating was statistically independent of the taste ratings, and some people ate more cookies even though they didn't find the taste particularly appealing. ("I didn't like the cookies, but I couldn't stop eating them!" said one participant who had been rejected by the group.)

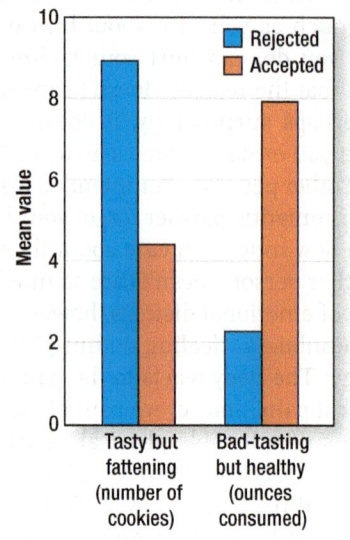

FIGURE 11.5

Rejection weakens self-control: Rejected persons ate more cookies but drank less of a healthy but bad-tasting beverage.[140]

The results seem to reflect a breakdown in control rather than an increase in hunger. If the food doesn't taste good but is good for you, rejection produces the opposite pattern (of reduced consumption). In one study, researchers exhorted participants (both verbally and with a cash incentive) to consume a healthy but very bad-tasting beverage consisting of unsweetened Kool-Aid mixed with both water and vinegar. The brew resembled some medicines and health drinks that taste bad but are worth consuming for their health benefits. (Vinegar is actually good for you.) Participants who had just experienced social acceptance or had received neutral feedback made themselves consume about 8 ounces of the gross-tasting drink, but rejected people averaged only about 2 ounces[158] (see **FIGURE 11.5**).

What these results have in common with the cookie-eating study is self-regulation. People need self-regulation to prevent themselves from eating junk foods, just as they need it to make themselves consume things they don't like but are good for them. On both counts, rejected people fared worse.

The bottom line is that rejected people do not self-regulate their eating as well as other people. They eat more junk food, and they consume less of what is good for them.

---

warm; being rejected is cold. Lonely people seem to feel physically cold, to the extent that they take more hot baths to warm up![159] Conversely, being physically cold can make people feel lonelier.

The conflict between social conscience and selfish impulse is an important theme of social psychology. Apparently, most people resolve this in favor of doing the sort of proper, generous, unselfish actions that society approves—but mainly if they enjoy and anticipate social acceptance. Rejection appears to change how people approach that conflict, making them more prone to favor the selfish impulse. Acting in a socially conscientious manner (such as waiting in line, paying taxes, or refraining from littering) often requires some degree of effort and sacrifice, and those sacrifices are compensated by the rewards of social acceptance. Accordingly, if people reject you, you may feel less inclined to make those efforts and sacrifices.

One more constructive response to rejection is to become more attuned to social cues and information about other people. Rejection makes people start to look about, cautiously, for new potential friends.[160] Participants in one experiment were rejected (or not) and then were permitted to read other people's diaries. The rejected people showed an increase in attention to the interpersonal events in the diaries, such as whether the diary writer had a date or played tennis with someone else.[161] When rejected people think they might have a chance to form a bond with someone or even to get back together with the person who rejected them, they focus their attention on this possibility and think at length about their possible relationship partners. Indeed, being able to think about people who do love you may shelter you from the pain of being rejected by someone else. Participants in another study who brought along a photograph of someone who loved them fared better and felt better after being rejected in the lab than did people who had no photos, and also better than someone who had brought photos of a favorite celebrity.[162]

What about outsiders who find their own way and thus create or discover things that people in the mainstream might miss? A provocative recent investigation showed that being rejected can actually increase creativity, though only for some people.[163] Participants who were rejected by a group scored higher on tests of creativity than others who were accepted. The increase in creativity was mainly found among people who desired to be different and unique, and those who thought of themselves as independent from others, so it is not safe to recommend rejecting people as a way of making everyone more creative! And measuring creativity is a tricky business, so the findings in these studies might not generalize to other measures. Still, it is encouraging to think that some people can respond to rejection in a positive manner, seeing the world in fresh, creative ways.

Behavioral Effects of Rejection

How should rejected people act? Conroy's novel *The Prince of Tides* tells the story of a young man from a rural area who went to a major state university in a big city. At the end of fraternity rush, he was stunned to learn that not a single fraternity offered him a bid. By chance he met a young woman who was in a similar predicament; the two formed a bond, eventually falling in love and marrying. They decided that if they were not to spend all their time at parties and other Greek life functions, they would devote themselves to their studies, and they achieved top grades (in fact the woman graduated first in her class). They also resolved to help others: The man became a teacher and the woman a physician. This story shows an ideal, exemplary response to rejection, marked by forming new social bonds, improving intellectual work, and engaging in prosocial behavior.

Social psychology studies have painted a very different picture of how people react to rejection, however. As we saw earlier in this chapter, rejected participants show decreases rather than increases in intelligent thought, and indeed IQ test performance often drops substantially among people who have just been rejected. Instead of seeking to form new social bonds, rejected people often treat new interaction partners with skepticism, aloofness, avoidance, or even outright hostility.[164] Instead of devoting themselves to others, rejected people are typically less generous, less cooperative, and less helpful than others, and they are more willing to cheat or break rules of good behavior.[165] They act in short-sighted, impulsive, even self-destructive ways.[166]

Repeated experiences of rejection or social exclusion (being left out of social groups) can create aggressive tendencies. One study surveyed high school students about various groups in their school, such as "jocks," "potheads," and popular kids. Students reported that they frequently imagined attacking, beating, shooting, and otherwise harming people in groups that had rejected or humiliated them.[167]

School violence grabbed America's attention in the 1990s, a sad trend that has continued ever since. The media publicized a series of incidents in which students took guns or other weapons to school and killed other students. Sometimes these were precisely targeted, such as when one killed his ex-girlfriend's new boyfriend. Other shootings seemed more random, such as when a student opened fire in a cafeteria where 400 students were dining, and the widely spraying bullets killed several students and wounded quite a few more.

What drove these students to lethal violence? One common theme was feeling socially excluded. It was never the most popular, well-loved students who brought guns to school and opened fire; rather, it was those who felt picked on, excluded, and rejected by others. A careful investigation of 15 of these incidents concluded that at least 13 of them involved young men who were going through long and painful experiences of being rejected by others.[168]

Aggression and rejection are linked in multiple ways. Aggression can lead to rejection. For example, young children in particular tend to exclude and avoid other children who start fights or engage in bullying (though as the students reach adolescence, this pattern

> School shooters are typically rejected teens who feel like social outcasts.

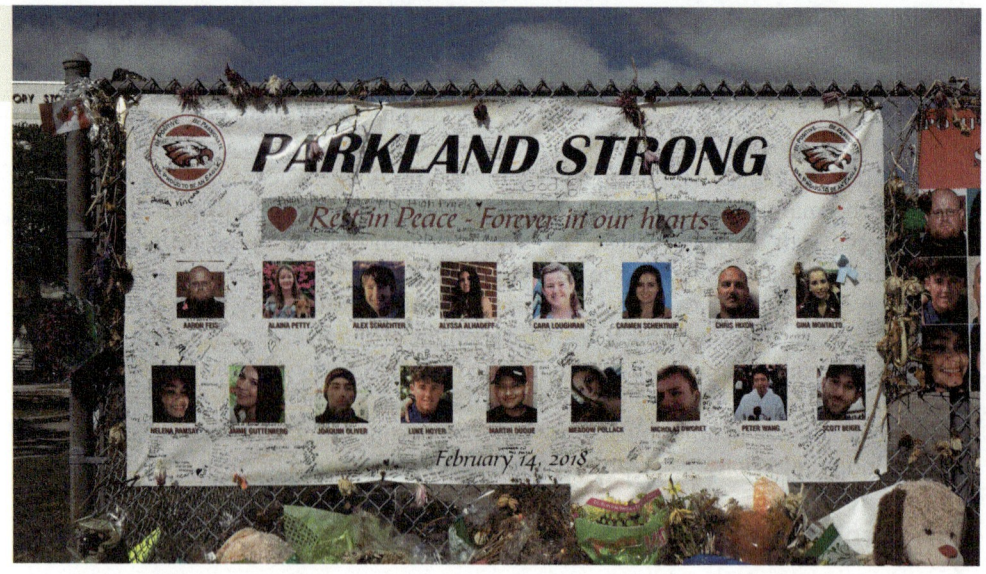

of rejection diminishes, and aggressive adolescents are sometimes accepted by others).[169] In lab studies, students who receive an experience of being rejected by others tend to show high levels of aggression toward someone who offends or provokes them—and, ominously, they are also more aggressive than average toward neutral people who haven't done anything bad to them.[170]

There are a few glimmers of hope. In particular, if the rejected person has some prospect of being accepted or included, either back into the group that excluded him or her or into a new group, then the rejected person's behavior is more positive and prosocial. If someone comes along and is kind to the rejected person, such as by praising the person or being nice in other ways, the rejected person may respond favorably, as by refraining from aggression, by cooperating, or by conforming.[171,172] Rejected people who have a chance to form a new friendship may engage in positive nonverbal behaviors, such as mimicking the nonverbal behavior of the new person;[173] as we have seen, nonverbal mimicry is a positive behavior that helps people come to like each other.

Loneliness

Loneliness is the painful feeling of wanting more human contact or connection than you have. The stereotype of the lonely person is a socially inept loser who doesn't know how to get along with others, who perhaps has little to offer other people, who has few or no friends, and who spends much of the time alone, perhaps envying other people who have friends and lovers. But recent research has begun to paint a very different picture. Lonely people are not that different from non-lonely people. They do not differ in intelligence or attractiveness. They spend about the same amount of time interacting with other people.[174] Thus, lonely does not mean alone: Loneliness is essentially independent of the quantity of relationships or social interaction.[175]

Not all lonely people are the same, either. Researchers have recognized variations in loneliness. It may be quite common for people to feel a temporary loneliness when they move to a new place and are separated from their friends and family. In many cases, those feelings go away as soon as the person starts making friends at the new home. Other people, however, suffer from chronic loneliness that may last for months or years. In general, when researchers speak of lonely people, they are referring to people who suffer chronic loneliness that has lasted for a substantial period of time and is not showing signs of letting up.

loneliness the painful feeling of wanting more human contact or connection than you have

> You can be lonely even when surrounded by people.

By and large, the lonely do not lack social skills, though they somehow fail to use them as much as others (they can get along well with others, but they don't).[176] The main deficiency that has been established is that lonely people are poorer at figuring out other people's emotional states.[177] This lack of emotional sensitivity could be either a cause of loneliness (because it makes it harder to attract and keep friends), or possibly a result, or perhaps both.

These findings indicate that loneliness is much more complex than simply a failure to find other people to be with. You can be lonely living in a densely populated city like New York. You can even be lonely when married, though married people are on average a bit less likely to be lonely than single people.[178,179] Being far from home is one strong predictor of loneliness,[180] which is probably one reason that in many cultures people live their entire lives close to their place of birth and are reluctant to relocate, even for a seemingly great career opportunity.

The long road to social acceptance is a theme to which we have returned repeatedly, and apparently some people find the road too long and difficult—but they pay a price for not making the full effort. Staying close to family is one strategy that seems to shorten the road, in the sense that if your family lives nearby, you have easier and readier access to some forms of social acceptance than if you live far away.

Loneliness originates in a gap between the amount or quality of social relationships that you have and the amount or quality that you want. In principle, this can be because you want a normal amount but have less than that—or because you have a normal amount but want a great deal more.[181]

In theory, loneliness can also be an issue of either the quality or the quantity of relationships. You might be lonely because you don't have enough contact with others, or because the time you spend with others does not satisfy your needs. In practice, the data suggest that most loneliness stems from a lack of close, satisfying relationships. Lonely people may spend plenty of time with other people, but just talking to many different people is not good enough, and people may suffer if they do not feel that enough people care about them and want to maintain a long-term, close relationship. Put another way, loneliness is typically rooted in the quality rather than the quantity of social interaction:[182] Lonely people spend plenty of time with others, but they do not come away from these interactions feeling satisfied. To be sure, most research on loneliness has focused on people who live in large cities or universities, and people who are lonely when there are many others around are probably suffering from a lack of quality rather than quantity. Living far from others, such as if you worked as a forest ranger in the Arctic, might produce loneliness for lack of quantity of interaction. Still, in the modern world, most loneliness is linked to quality rather than quantity of interaction.

Relationships to large groups or organizations are relevant for men, though apparently not for women. That is, a man who has few or no close friends but feels strongly connected to his corporation or university or sports team will probably not suffer from loneliness, but a woman in the same circumstance will typically still feel lonely because women tend to care less about large organizations than men do.[183]

Some people can even stave off loneliness by forming attachments to celebrities or people they see on television. Women who watch many situation comedies feel less lonely than other women who have the same number of friends and lovers but do not watch as many shows.[184] Apparently the televised characters come to feel like friends and family to them, especially if they watch the same shows regularly and develop feelings about the characters. Women tend to care more about close relationships with family and friends than men do.

Other people fight off loneliness by forming quasi-relationships with nonhuman entities. For example, they might bond with a dog or cat, or treat a potted plant like a person. Some people even name their cars and treat them like family members.[185] A vivid depiction of such a strategy was provided in the movie *Castaway*, in which Tom Hanks played a Federal Express worker who was stranded on a desert island for many months with no human contact at all. To keep himself sane and stave off loneliness, he painted a face on a volleyball that washed up on the island with him, named the ball "Wilson," and talked to it as if it were a close human friend. In fact, he risked his life to "rescue" Wilson when the ball floated away from his raft.

Loneliness takes its toll on the body. Lonely people sleep as much as non-lonely people, but the sleep is not as good or as refreshing, and they may end up feeling chronically tired. They spend the same amount of time in bed as others, but the lonely person is more prone to lie there awake or to wake up during the night.[186,187] Loneliness also seems to be bad for one's physical health. Lonely people take longer than others to recover from stress, illness, or injury.[188] The poor health stems from several factors, including sleep problems. As lonely people get older, they drink more alcohol and overeat more, and they fail to take care of themselves in many ways. They feel more stress and cope with it more poorly.[189]

What Leads to Social Rejection?

We have seen that being rejected or socially excluded is generally painful and harmful. Why do people inflict such rejection on each other? Several lines of research are starting to furnish answers.

Children are rejected by their peers for three main reasons.[190] First, aggressive children are rejected, possibly because children do not like violence and will avoid bullies and others whom they regard as dangerous. Second, some children withdraw from contact with others, and they in turn are rejected by others. The avoidance of withdrawn, isolated children escalates into adolescence, thereby creating a particular problem for people who move toward adulthood becoming more and more disconnected from social groups.

Third, and related to the other two, deviance leads to rejection. Children who are different in any obvious fashion are more likely to be rejected. Children reject others who look different, act differently, or otherwise seem different. Being handicapped, belonging to a racial minority, speaking differently, not knowing the locally favored style of music or clothing, not watching the same television shows or listening to the same music, having an unusual family arrangement (e.g., living with a grandmother rather than parents, or having two daddies or two mommies), or speaking with an accent—any of these can cause a child to be rejected by others. Even being clearly less intelligent or more intelligent than most of the other kids in the class can elicit rejection. This does not mean that the children make a deliberate or conscious decision that they do not approve of someone's personality or lifestyle. In terms of the duplex mind, the reaction against those who are different is probably automatic, and the reaction that leads children to reject others is probably rooted in automatic processes. Remember what you read in the section on attraction: People tend to like others who are similar to them and especially to dislike people who are different. The cruel, rejecting behavior of children may simply be an early form of this general pattern.

Among adults, the simplest and most general explanation for rejection is deviance.[191] Groups reject others who are different in important or meaningful ways from the rest of the group. Indeed, groups seem to find deviants threatening, and they are more bothered by a nonconformist or poor performer who is in the group than by one who is outside the group.[192] This is important evidence of the importance of group solidarity. Someone who is different from your group, but is not part of your group, doesn't threaten the unity of your group. In contrast, someone who is different to the same degree but still belongs to your group undermines group unity. Groups reject insiders more than outsiders for the same degree of deviance.[193]

Bad performance by a member of your own group is rated more negatively than an identically bad performance by someone who is not in the ingroup.[194,195] Conversely, good performance by an ingroup member of the ingroup is rated more positively than identically good performance by an outgroup member. Apparently, groups want their members to be successful, and they will reject members who are prone to failure.

Much deviance involves breaking the rules. Deviants don't do what they are

A relationship with your pet can stave off loneliness.

expected or supposed to do. As we saw in the chapter on prosocial behavior (Chapter 9), groups can only operate successfully if most people follow most of the rules most of the time, so each act of deviance presents some problem or threat to the success of the group. Deviants therefore undermine the quality of life for the rest of the group. If no one ever steals, for example, you don't need to worry about being robbed, so you don't need to lock your doors, buy security systems, pay for insurance, and take other precautions. The Qur'an (the holy book of Islam) prescribes that societies should cut off the hands of thieves, even someone who just steals a piece of fruit. This strikes many people in other cultures as unfair and excessive, but most likely the underlying sentiment is that the thief isn't just taking someone's piece of fruit—the thief is undermining the trust and security that everyone else would otherwise enjoy. A severe punishment might be justified if it would actually prevent people from doing things that spoil group life for everyone else. In other words, we miss the point if we view Islamic law as cruel or overly punitive for cutting off someone's hand as punishment for stealing a piece of fruit: The hand is cut off because stealing in general undermines trust and degrades the whole fabric of social relationships.

A further reason that groups may reject deviants lies in the so-called **bad apple effect**.[196] This effect is named after the cliché that one bad apple can spoil the whole barrel because the rot that infects one apple can spread to other apples. Applied to social behavior, the implication is that one person who breaks the rules can inspire other people to follow his or her example. As the example of stealing illustrated, the issue from the point of view of society as a whole is that if some people get away with stealing, then others may be tempted to steal also, and chaos can result. Sadly, bad apples seem to inspire more copycats than good apples: People are more easily swayed to follow the example of deviant misbehavior than of virtuous, exemplary, or heroic action.[197] Thus, if you break the group's rules, the group may believe it is best to reject or expel you, lest others follow your bad example.

The threat of being expelled or rejected does seem to be an important force in producing good behavior. When participants were expelled from a group after they had followed the example of a bad apple—and then were reinstated in the group, ostensibly due to an accident or technical problem—they subsequently behaved much better and more prosocially than others, generally following the example of the good rather than the bad apples.[198] Even the threat of being expelled is sometimes enough to discourage people from following bad apples.[199] This is probably an important explanation for why rejection is so powerful and important in life. Human groups need people to follow rules and conform to shared values, and the threat of rejection is a strong force encouraging them to do so.

The link between rejection and deviance has been confirmed in research on families. A large survey[200] asked people what were the worst things that family members do to each other, and how these behaviors related to being rejected by the family. The most commonly cited bad behaviors were seen as justifying expelling someone from the family. Most of these behaviors involved violating the basic rules or expectations that govern how family members are supposed to treat each other. These included rejection, abandonment, disloyalty, sexual abuse, and betrayal, in addition to watching your loved one become (or marry) a loser or criminal.

This research was not meant to pass moral judgment on whether such behaviors justify expulsion from the family. The point is simply that the threat of expulsion discourages people from doing those things to their loved ones. The net result is that family members treat each other better, and the family bonds remain stronger. The (very real) pain of rejection serves the function of holding families and other groups together.

Romantic Rejection and Unrequited Love

Most people experience romantic rejection at some point. They wanted someone for a romantic partner, but that person failed to match those feelings and declined any offers of a relationship. These failed romances can occasionally develop into serious problems, ranging from suicidal despair to violent stalking.

One impressive early paper on romantic rejection used attribution theory to understand the reasons women gave for refusing an offer of a date.[201] As we saw in Chapter 5,

bad apple effect the idea that one person who breaks the rules can inspire other people to break the rules also

Even adults are often threatened by people who look "different."

unrequited love a situation in which one person loves another but the other does not return that love

stalking persisting in romantic, courtship, or other behaviors that frighten and harass the rejecter in a relationship

many attributions can be sorted along two dimensions: internal/external and stable/unstable. The reasons the women privately held for refusing dates tended to be internal to the man and stable: There was something seriously wrong with him, as she saw it (internal). Also, his deficit was viewed as relatively permanent (stable). But the reasons women told the men for refusing the date were external and unstable. Thus, when a man she didn't fancy asked her for a date on Friday, she might say that she couldn't go out with him that night because her parents were coming to visit. This reason is external (it has nothing to do with him) and unstable (it pertains only to that particular night, or perhaps that weekend). People are often surprised when the romance-seekers they reject come around again and keep trying, but trying again would seem natural under those circumstances. She can't go out with him this Friday because her parents are coming to visit—so why not ask her out for next Friday? In contrast, if she said, "I can't go out with you because you're not very good-looking, you don't have enough money, you're not smart enough for me, and you smell bad," he would probably be much less likely to respond with "OK, then how about next Friday?" All those reasons for her refusing the offer for this Friday would also apply to next Friday.

Unrequited love is defined as a situation in which one person loves another but the other does not return that love. It is a common experience among adolescents and young adults, and most single people have at least one experience a year in which they have a crush on someone who does not have similar feelings toward them, or (conversely) in which they do not reciprocate someone else's feelings of romantic attraction toward them. The two roles are quite different and go with very different types of feelings. Most men and women have experience in both roles, though men have more experiences of being the rejected lovers, and women are more often in the rejecting role.[202,203]

The rejected lovers experience a kind of emotional roller coaster, in which they alternate between hopeful, exciting, passionate feelings, and insecure despair. They suffer intensely, but they are also drawn to the good parts, and they tend to look back on a failed love with some bittersweet affection. In contrast, the rejecters tend to think there was nothing good about the episode, and they are more likely to wish the whole thing had never happened.[204,205]

Rejection is felt as a blow to one's self-esteem. Broken-hearted lovers often wonder if something is wrong with them, or if they somehow have some inner flaw that prevented the other from becoming romantically attracted to them. They try to find some way to bolster their self-esteem, and nothing seems to work quite so well as finding a new lover.

Broken-hearted lovers may engage in stalking behaviors toward the rejecter. **Stalking** refers to persisting in romantic or courtship behavior (e.g., repeated phone calls) or other behaviors that frighten and harass the rejecter in the relationship.[206,207,208] Although unrequited love is something that both genders experience, women are disproportionately the victims of stalkers (possibly because they are more likely than men to be the rejecters). Data from the National Violence Against Women Survey showed that women report being stalked in the context of current or former romantic partners (marriage, cohabitation, or dating), whereas men rarely reported being stalked in the context of a current or former romantic relationship.[209] Male and female victims of stalking reported feeling that their safety was being threatened and some even carried weapons to protect themselves far more than nonvictims (45% vs. 29%) Thus, the sting of unrequited love may lead rejected people to stalk their rejecters, and this tendency is particularly strong among rejected men.

For the rejecters, the problem is not low self-esteem but guilt. As the concept of a need to belong implies, people are designed to form and maintain relationships, not to reject

Restraining orders for stalkers can sometimes be strict. Don't stalk!

them, and most people find that refusing someone's offer of love is difficult. They feel guilty for hurting the other person, and to minimize feelings of guilt they strive to convince themselves that they never led the other person on, so that the other person's love and resultant suffering were not their fault. Guilt is a central part of the difficulty of rejecting someone, and this difficulty is probably linked to a basic fact about human nature: Humans are programmed to form and maintain social bonds, and breaking bonds goes against the grain. Even if you don't want someone's love, it is difficult and sometimes painful to refuse it.

The message of rejection is difficult for both persons. The rejecter feels guilty and wants to avoid hurting the other person's feelings. The person who is about to be rejected is often eager to grasp at straws and seize on any sign of possible encouragement. It is therefore no wonder that the message often does not get communicated very well: The one doesn't want to say it, and the other doesn't want to hear it.

As we have seen, the road to social acceptance is often long. Rarely does it seem longer or harder than in unrequited love. Loving someone who does not return your feelings can be extremely discouraging and painful. And even rejecting someone's love is not usually easy.

QUIZ YOURSELF
Rejection

1. Being excluded, rejected, and ignored by others is what social psychologists call _____.
   - (a) propinquity
   - (b) loneliness
   - (c) ostracism
   - (d) bad apple effect

2. What personality trait is formed as a result of repeated rejection?
   - (a) Extraversion
   - (b) Introversion
   - (c) Rejection sensitivity
   - (d) Self-monitoring

3. What is the main difference between lonely and non-lonely people?
   - (a) Lonely people are less attractive.
   - (b) Lonely people are less emotionally sensitive.
   - (c) Lonely people are less intelligent.
   - (d) Lonely people are less socially skilled.

4. Loneliness is primarily determined by the _____ of relationships.
   - (a) quality
   - (b) quantity
   - (c) both (a) and (b)
   - (d) neither (a) nor (b)

answers: see pg 402

Rejection | 399

What Makes Us Human

Putting the Cultural Animal in Perspective

Much of what we have seen in this chapter is not unique to human beings. Many social animals seek social acceptance and try to avoid being rejected. Good-looking, rewarding, similar others are attractive. Deviants are vulnerable to rejection. Most social animals (and that category includes nearly all the close biological relatives of humankind) want to be allowed to belong to a group and want to avoid being rejected or excluded.

The human quest for belongingness has, however, some special features, or at least twists. The basic need to belong may be the same in humans as in other animals, but some of the processes are different. People use language to form and maintain relationships, and this enables them to disclose much more information about themselves. People can be similar or dissimilar on many dimensions that other animals cannot process: religion, favorite sports team, zodiac sign, political opinions, and many more. More broadly, humans traverse a long road to social acceptance, which means they have to spend a large and ongoing amount of time and energy to secure and maintain their place in the social group. A bird or frog can gain access to the group simply by being there and joining in, but humans who seek social acceptance need money, skills, the right clothes, an understanding of complex social norms, and much else.

Human social systems are more complex than those of other creatures, so there is more emphasis on being special or unique. We have seen that being similar is important for attraction, in humans as in other animals, but culture also places value on diversity. A culture is a system, and a system made up of all identical parts is not much of a system. Whether you are finding a niche in your career or persuading a loved one to choose you instead of a romantic rival, you may often feel some pressure to establish yourself as different or special. Put very simply, if you can do something useful that no one else in your small group can do (find a particular food, make fire, install plumbing, fix computers, prepare income tax returns, kick long field goals), you are safe: They cannot afford to exclude you. The strategy of promoting social acceptance via unique abilities is largely unknown outside of human beings, but it is very important in our human social life. Put more simply, most social animals seek acceptance via similarity, and humans do too, but only humans cultivate social acceptance by trying to be special or different.

Another striking difference is that human relationships are not just between the two people involved: They often require some validation or recognition by the culture. Animals have families, but these do not have legal status. If the father becomes separated from his offspring, he is not required—except among humans—to pay child support year after year. Both humans and animals experience romantic attraction and sexual mating, but only humans formalize the bond with a wedding license and a ceremony, so that every member of the large social group recognizes the bond and knows what it means. Animals can break up just by wandering off, whereas married humans require a divorce court. In the same vein, many animals neglect or even abuse their young, but only humans have formal systems to stop this, such as police or legal intervention. Animals may sometimes work together to build something, but only humans sign contracts or incorporate their partnerships or sue each other when the project fails.

Divorce courts, police interventions, and lawsuits may seem like an unpleasant aspect of human relationships. What have we done to ourselves? Yet these institutions represent something very positive: Human society has sought to protect people from betrayal and abuse by their relationship partners. Culture recognizes, validates, and encourages relationships, and ultimately it reduces some of the risk and suffering that go with the process of connecting with someone. If two animals work together to get some food and then the bigger one takes it all, the smaller one is simply out of luck. The more vulnerable human being, however, may go to court or try some other cultural recourse, and because the system is there, the stronger one is less likely to cheat or betray in the first place. In such ways, culture makes relationships stronger and better.

CHAPTER 11 SUMMARY

The Need to Belong

- Social acceptance means getting others to like you, respect you, approve of you, and in general want to have some kind of relationship with you.
- Rejection, also known as social exclusion, means that others exclude you, so that you are not able to form or keep a social bond with them.
- Testosterone, a hormone associated with masculinity, is a mixed blessing, both for the individual who has it and for others connected with that person; it is better suited to finding mates than to maintaining stable families.
- The need to belong, defined as the desire to form and maintain close, lasting relationships, is a powerful drive within the human psyche.

- According to social brain theory, the driving force behind the evolution of intelligence and the brain was the need to understand others so as to form and maintain social relationships.
- People usually form relationships easily and readily but are reluctant to let relationships end.
- The need to belong has two parts:
  - Regular social contact with others.
  - Close, stable, mutually intimate contact.
- Failure to satisfy the need to belong leads to significant health problems, up to and including a higher risk of death.

Attraction: Who Likes Whom?

- Ingratiation is actively to try to make someone like you.
- Similarity is a common and significant cause of attraction.
- People prepare for social interaction by shifting to become more similar to the people they expect to interact with.
- People with the trait of high self-monitoring seek to maximize each social situation, whereas those low in that trait pay more attention to permanent connections and feelings rather than fluctuating ones.
- The matching hypothesis states that people tend to pair up with others who are equally attractive.
- As culture progresses and forms large, complex, interacting groups, there may be more need for complementarity, but when people pick their friends and lovers, they still tend to look for those who are similar to themselves.
- In general, favors are a good way to promote liking.
- Praising people is a reliable way to get them to like you.
- Liking begets (reciprocal) liking.
- Mimicry is often successful as a means of increasing liking.
- Propinquity (being near someone on a regular basis) causes attraction, but it also can to lead to conflict and friction.
- Familiarity breeds liking.
- The social allergy effect refers to the finding that a partner's annoying habits grow more annoying with repeated exposure.
- When all else is equal, most people show a substantial preference for attractive over unattractive others.
- The what is beautiful is good effect suggests that people assume that physically attractive people will be superior to others on many other traits.
- Attractive children are more popular with other children than their less attractive peers, and teachers like them more, too.
- Evolutionary psychologists generally think that beauty is linked to signs of being a good mate and potential partner, which especially means being young and healthy.
- Symmetry is a powerful source of beauty.
- Average faces are more attractive than individual faces.
- Women are more attracted to men who look rich and successful.
- Many people find romantic partners online, which has both advantages (e.g., more potential partners to choose from) and disadvantages (e.g., easier for potential partners to mislead others or even lie to them).

Rejection

- Ostracism refers to being excluded, rejected, and ignored by others.
- Being rejected repeatedly can cause people to develop expectations that others will reject them, resulting in a personality trait called rejection sensitivity.

- "You hurt my feelings" is usually tied to an implicit message that "you don't care about our relationship."
- The initial reaction to rejection is often closer to numbness than to anxiety or sadness. It can interfere with normal psychological and cognitive functioning.
- Pain killers such as Tylenol can reduce social pain as well as physical pain.
- Rejection undermines self-regulation and often makes people behave selfishly rather than acting in a socially conscientious manner.
- Repeated experiences of rejection or social exclusion can create aggressive tendencies.
- Aggression can lead to rejection.
- Loneliness is the painful feeling of wanting more human contact or connection (either more quantity or quality of relationships) than you have.
- There are very few differences between lonely and non-lonely people, with the major exception that lonely people are poorer at figuring out other people's emotional states.
- Loneliness is bad for physical health.
- Children are rejected by their peers for three main reasons:
  - Because they are aggressive or violent.
  - Because they are withdrawn or socially isolated.
  - Because they are different from other children in some way.
- Among adults, the simplest and most general explanation for rejection is deviance.
- Groups reject insiders more than outsiders for the same degree of deviance.
- The bad apple effect suggests that one person who breaks the rules can inspire other people to follow his or her example.
- Humans are programmed to form and maintain social bonds; breaking them goes against the grain and makes the rejecter feel guilty.

What Makes Us Human? Putting the Cultural Animal in Perspective

- Human social systems are more complex than those of other creatures, so there is more emphasis on each individual being special or unique.
- Human relationships often require some validation or recognition by the culture.

key terms

attraction 373
bad apple effect 397
ingratiation 378
loneliness 394
matching hypothesis 379
need to belong 376
ostracism 389
propinquity 383
reinforcement theory 380
rejection (social exclusion) 373
rejection sensitivity 391
self-monitoring 379
social acceptance 373
social allergy effect 383
stalking 398
unrequited love 398
what is beautiful is good effect 384

quiz yourself ANSWERS

1. The Need to Belong p. 378
   answers: 1.b 2.d 3.c 4.b
2. Attraction: Who Likes Whom? p. 388
   answers: 1.b 2.c 3.b 4.b
3. Rejection p. 399
   answers: 1.c 2.c 3.b 4.a

CLOSE RELATIONSHIPS
Passion, Intimacy, and Sexuality

12

LEARNING OBJECTIVES

1. Describe the different types of love.
2. Differentiate exchange and communal relationships.
3. Describe the four styles of attachment.
4. Identify the factors that are important to maintaining relationships over time.
5. Use the theories of sexuality to explain sexual attitudes and behavior.
6. Summarize the work on sexual jealousy.

TRADEOFFS
Sex In and Out of Marriage
411

◆

FOOD FOR THOUGHT
Eating in Front of a Cute Guy
434

◆

MONEY MATTERS
Mating, Money, and Men
442

◆

WHAT MAKES US HUMAN?
Putting the Cultural Animal in Perspective
446

The Spencer family gave birth to their third daughter in July 1961. Her parents could hardly have suspected that their daughter would become a royal princess and the heartthrob of millions. Their own marriage crumbled, and years later Diana said she never forgot the sound of her mother's footsteps crunching on the gravel driveway as she left their home on the day of their divorce in 1969. In 1975 her father became the Earl of Spencer, which automatically elevated his family (including Diana) into the aristocracy. At school, Diana was a mediocre student but a good athlete. She did not go on to college. Instead, she worked at a series of dull jobs.

In 1977 Diana and her older sister Sarah were invited to a party, where they met Charles, the Prince of Wales. Sarah was originally regarded as the more promising girlfriend for him, and he dated her for a while, but soon Charles found himself attracted to the blossoming young beauty Diana. The attraction was mutual.

The match seemed improbable, which lent the entire episode the aura of a fairy tale. On their wedding day in 1981, he was 32 years old, whereas she was just 19. He was in line to become king of England, whereas she was working as a kindergarten assistant. The public continued to see him as a somewhat odd-looking and awkward fellow, whereas Diana was soon accepted as one of the world's great beauties, and her wardrobe became a source of fascination and imitation throughout the world. Their first public appearances were marked by an easygoing rapport between them and by a seemingly obvious pleasure in each other's company. When their engagement was announced, reporters asked them whether they were in love, and both said "Yes!" though Charles added "whatever love means" (a line that certainly won him no points as a dashing, romantic suitor!).

Their wedding, shortly before Diana's 20th birthday, was an international event. An estimated 600,000 people lined the streets to watch the wedding party go from Buckingham Palace to St. Paul's Cathedral. Millions of people around the world watched it on television. Diana later said that on that day she was "so in love with my husband that I couldn't take my eyes off him" and that she felt herself the luckiest woman in the world. And even if the prince did look a bit odd, the lavishly spectacular wedding seemed a perfect ending for a fairy tale in which an ordinary schoolgirl grew up, fell in love with a (sort of) handsome prince, married him in the so-called wedding of the century, thence to settle down and wait until they would someday become king and queen. In reality, the fairy tale was not over but would take a non-fairy-tale turn in the coming months.

Diana quickly became pregnant and produced a son who also would become heir to the throne, and two years later the couple had another son. The public took "Princess Di" into its heart, and she responded by trying to be perfect in her role. She supported charity causes, visited hospitals, and did other good deeds, all the while trying to raise their royal sons properly. Everything seemed perfect.

But things were not perfect, and indeed the marriage went downhill, first secretly, then more publicly. Her husband, Charles, did not come to love her as she wanted. Indeed, when they first got engaged, he privately told a friend he did not love her yet (though he expected that he would soon). More problematically, he retained strong ties to his mistress, Camilla Parker Bowles, even inviting her to the wedding, and continued his sexual affair with her after the wedding. Camilla Parker Bowles was also married at the time and had two children of her own. Diana later said in a BBC interview, "There were three of us in the marriage. It was a bit crowded." Her assessment won her widespread sympathy, though some subsequent reports have claimed that her comment was not entirely honest because at that time there was a fourth person in the marriage too—namely, Diana's lover.

Apparently, once the princess concluded that she was not getting the love she wanted from her husband, she sought it elsewhere. She had an affair with a handsome riding instructor on the palace staff. He fell hard for her. After five years, she broke it off. (The head of palace security took the riding instructor aside and told him how to deal with the breakup: "Well, look, you know, if it's over, consider yourself to have been in a very privileged position. Really, that's the end of it. Live with that memory.") She was hurt when he wrote a book about his affair with her.

Prince Charles and Diana, Princess of Wales, on their wedding day, July 29, 1981.

Prince Charles and his lover Camilla Parker Bowles who later became his second wife.

Another affair, this time with an art dealer, also ended badly when the man broke up with her and went back to his wife. The man started receiving nuisance hang-up calls, and after several hundred of these he went to the police, who traced the calls to the princess. (In some contexts, such behavior can be considered stalking, though no one is likely to prosecute a royal princess for it.) Another affair with a professional athlete also led to a highly publicized blowup.

These were hard times for Diana. She developed psychological symptoms, including eating disorders and self-mutilation (cutting herself). She worried that the royal family was plotting to ruin her image and even to kill her. She was intensely lonely and depressed. She heard her separation from Charles announced on the radio and thought "the fairy tale [has] come to an end." Four years later, in 1996, they were officially divorced.

In 1997, she thought she had finally found a new love to satisfy her. She told a friend, "I'm no longer lonely. I know what love is now." There were several men in her life, and there is some dispute as to which relationship she meant. We may never know, because on the last day of August she was killed in a car crash in the Pont de l'Alma road tunnel in Paris. Her death provoked an international outpouring of grief, including huge demonstrations of affection in London and elsewhere. The authorities were shocked by how many people came to express their grief and how many people's lives she had seemingly touched in some way. It is estimated that 6 million people crowded the streets of London for her funeral procession. A giant crowd listened via loudspeakers outside the funeral ceremony, and their applause was so loud that the people indoors were disturbed to hear it.

The public reaction to her death was so strong that the authorities planned a ceremony a year later to commemorate its anniversary. Turnout was much lower than expected. Apparently the public had gotten over its grief. The love of the public is short-lived, resembling passion more than intimacy or commitment. There was, however, a revival of affection for Diana in 2005, when Charles announced his intention to marry his longtime mistress Camilla. Diana's fans protested the marriage. Meanwhile, as of this writing Charles is still waiting for his chance to become king, even though he is already into his 70s.

Prince William, elder son of Prince Charles and Diana, Princess of Wales, with Miss Catherine Middleton on their wedding day.

What Is Love?

"I'm a 17-year-old girl and I think I'm in love, but my parents say I don't know what real love is. What is love and how can I tell if I'm really in love?"[1] Thus wrote a young woman to the Kinsey Institute, asking an earnest and personal question—and one that most people have struggled with at some point.

No simple answer can be given. Part of the problem is that there is more than one kind of love, so more than one phenomenon needs to be explained. The same person might feel different kinds of love toward several different people, even at the same point in his or her life. Most American adults say "I love you" into the telephone to their mothers on Mother's Day, for example, but what they mean by those three words is probably quite different from what they mean when saying "I love you" while kissing and hugging the person to whom they are engaged to be married.

Although the next section will distinguish two main types of love, recent research addressing the question of "What is love?" has produced one common feature that most people endorse. It is investment in the well-being of the other for his or her own sake. In other words, if James truly loves Angela, then he wants her to be happy, healthy, successful, and otherwise well off, regardless of any benefit to himself. In recent studies, participants rated this investment in the other's well-being as a common and essential feature of very different kinds of love relationship, including romantic love, parental love, nonsexual love between two adult female friends, and the caring love someone who takes care of a chronically ill man.[2] Caring for the other person regardless of one's personal gain may thus be a defining aspect of love in general.

Passionate and Companionate Love

An important distinction between two main kinds of love has emerged from many years of research.[3] The experts called the two kinds of love "passionate" and "companionate." By **passionate love** they mean having strong feelings of longing, desire, and excitement toward a special person. Passionate love (also called **romantic love**) makes people want to spend as much time as possible together, to touch each other and engage in other physical intimacies (often including sex), to think about each other and feel joy merely upon seeing each other, and to exhibit other patterns that suggest strong emotions.

In contrast, **companionate love** (sometimes called **affectionate love**) is less strongly emotional; it tends to be calmer and more serene. Companionate love means perceiving the other person as your soul mate or special partner. It signifies a high level of mutual understanding and caring and in many cases a commitment to make the relationship succeed. As the term implies, companionate love is what makes people want to remain each other's good companions. Someone high in companionate love is likely to say things like "My wife is my best friend." That kind of love is not the same as what usually motivates people to start a new sexual relationship, but it may be essential to a successful long-term marriage.

There is probably a physiological, even biochemical, difference between the two kinds of love. People who feel passionately in love have high levels of phenylethylamine (PEA), a neurotransmitter that enables information to travel from one brain cell to another.[4,5] This chemical produces strong emotional feelings, including those "tingling" sensations of excitement and euphoria that you get when the person you love walks into the room or holds your hand. It also helps produce high intensity and frequency of sexual desire. The emotional churning and the sense of being in an altered state (sometimes compared to being high on drugs) is very likely linked to some chemical in the body, and PEA is a leading candidate, although further research is needed, and passionate love may affect more than one chemical. In contrast, companionate love does not seem to be characterized by elevated levels of PEA.

Love and Culture

The PEA response suggests that passionate love involves something more basic than cultural learning, although undoubtedly culture can work with or against the biochemical responses to love objects. The question of whether romantic love is universal or is simply a product of Western culture has been fiercely debated. Some authorities[6] have argued that romantic love is a cultural construction, possibly introduced into Western culture by the Crusaders or troubadours, who brought it from the Middle East and elaborated it into its mythological status at the royal courts of Europe (where most marriages were arranged for political reasons, so passionate love flourished in extramarital affairs), and then embraced as one of the culture's main goals and values during the so-called Romantic Period (roughly 1775–1850). From the social constructionist view, cultural values and meanings have shaped personal feelings and changed the way people run their lives, and the cultural construction of love is an important case in point.

More recent cross-cultural work, however, suggests that passionate love is not merely a product of Western culture. In 1995, anthropologist William Jankowiak published a

Love changes over the years.

passionate love (romantic love) strong feelings of longing, desire, and excitement toward a special person

companionate love (affectionate love) mutual understanding and caring to make the relationship succeed painstaking, influential book titled *Romantic Passion: A Universal Experience?*[7] His answer was yes. Careful anthropological investigations led him to the conclusion that romantic love is indeed found nearly everywhere (that is, in the vast majority of cultures he surveyed around the world, though not in every single one). This is not to suggest that culture plays no role. The forms and expressions of romantic passion vary significantly, as does the culture's attitude toward passionate love. Modern Western culture (whose influence is certainly spreading through many parts of the world) has come to regard passionate love as an important part of life, so that if you never experience it, you will have missed out on a major form of fulfillment. Possibly, people in other cultures feel love as we do but do not place the same value on it and do not feel that a life without passionate love is by definition a lesser life.

Romantic love is not just an invention of Western culture.

In fact, passionate love may seem like a form of temporary insanity. Thus, although most cultures have recognized the existence of passionate love, different cultures and even different eras in Western culture have held very different attitudes toward it. One historian concluded that in bygone centuries in Europe, people regarded passionate love as a form of mental imbalance that made people feel and act in strange, even crazy ways. They did not think that passionate love was a good reason to marry someone; indeed, proposing marriage while in love would strike them as similar to making any major life decision while drunk or on drugs! And they certainly didn't think that passionate love made a good basis for marriage.[8] Companionate love seemed a much better bet.

Passionate love may therefore be found among humans everywhere, but how they experience it and how they regard it may depend on their culture. People are hooked into their cultural system, and the system can influence how they love.

Love Across Time

Companionate love may be harder to create than passionate love, which often arises spontaneously and without people trying to fall in love. Companionate love is what makes a good marriage or a stable, trustworthy, lasting relationship, but it takes sustained work and effort to build trust, intimacy, and other foundations of companionate love. Passionate love may be the most effective emotion for starting a relationship; companionate love may be the most effective emotion for making it succeed and survive in the long run.

One reason for skepticism about passionate love as the basis for marriage is that it tends to be temporary.[9] This is hard for most people to appreciate, especially young people who may not yet have spent many years in the same romantic relationship and who think that their passionate feelings are sure to be permanent. Popular songs, movies, and novels feed the impression that passionate love will last forever. But most people experience passionate love for a relatively brief period in a relationship—a year, perhaps, or two or three at most, if one is very lucky. A few lucky couples report still feeling passionate love even after many years together, but these are rare exceptions to the general pattern of declining passion.[10,11] If the relationship continues, it tends to rely more on companionate love. A successful long-term relationship thus depends on making an effective transition from one kind of love to the other.

A behavioral sign of the decrease in passion can be found in data about frequency of sexual intercourse. Many studies have found that as time goes by, the average married couple has sex less and less often.[12,13,14,15,16,17] Newlyweds generally live up to the stereotype of passionate young lovers who have relatively frequent sex. But this does not last.

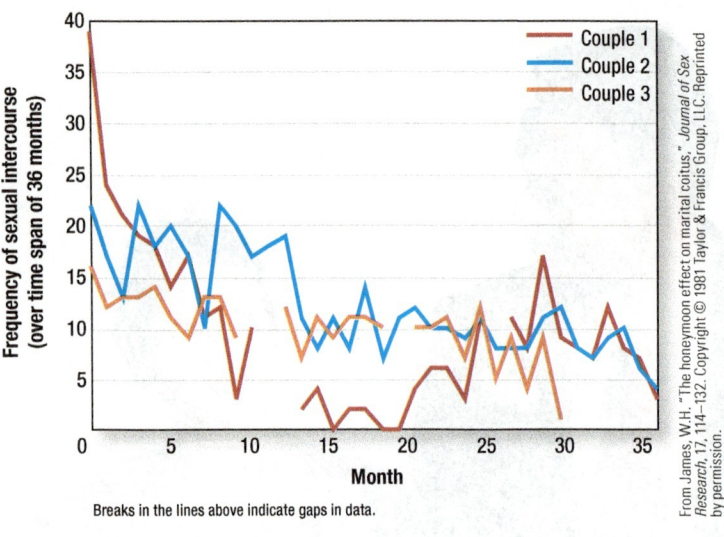

FIGURE 12.1
For most couples, sex is most frequent during the first month and first year after their wedding and declines after that.[237]

Research shows that the frequency of sexual intercourse declines by about half after the first year of marriage, from about 18 times per month during the first year to about 9 times per month in the second year.[18] It continues to decrease more slowly after that (see **FIGURE 12.1**). Likewise, studies that follow married couples over many years find that they start off having sex relatively often, but that this frequent rate decreases sharply at first and then continues to go down as the couple grows old together.[19] The decline in frequency of sex is not entirely due to aging. If a couple has a long marriage, their frequency of sex goes down, but if they then divorce and remarry, they typically show a big increase in sexual frequency with their new partners.[20] To learn more about the relationship between marriage and sex, see *Tradeoffs*.

The biochemical rush associated with high levels of PEA (if that is indeed the chemical component of love) is thus not destined to be permanent. It is probably a feature linked to new love and the forming of a new relationship bond. Unfortunately, many people probably mistake its normal and natural decline for a sign that they are no longer in love. They stop feeling swept away, and in particular their feelings of sexual desire for each other may dwindle to the individuals' normal, baseline levels, but the two people may mistake this process to mean that they have lost interest in each other or, even more ominously, that the other person has ceased to love them.

The story of Prince Charles and Diana, at the beginning of this chapter, illustrates the difference between passionate and companionate love. The start of their romance captured the world's imagination because it seemingly embodied the vital features of passionate love: a beautiful woman, a royal prince, blossoming attraction culminating in a spectacular wedding and then the birth of two handsome sons. Apparently, though, Charles and Diana failed to make the transition to companionate love, and their years together were not marked by intimacy, mutual devotion, and becoming each other's best friend. When passionate love fails to convert into companionate love (regardless of whether that is actually what transpired between Charles and Diana), the story line is likely to be one of a wonderful, romantic beginning followed by a downward spiral of stress, disappointment, estrangement, and ultimate failure. Fortunately, many people avoid that fate and do sustain a happy marriage for a long time or even a lifetime.

Sternberg's Triangle

A more elaborate theory of the nature of love was proposed by Robert Sternberg.[22] Instead of speaking of two different kinds of love, Sternberg proposed that love is composed of three different ingredients (see **FIGURE 12.2**). The first of these is **passion**, which he explained in terms of feelings of romantic attraction, physical attraction to the other person, and sexual interest. Passion is largely an emotional state and is characterized by high bodily arousal: When you feel passion, your heart beats more rapidly than usual, you become excited and alert, and you may also feel sexual arousal. Passion makes people want to be together and in many cases makes them want to kiss, hold hands, and perhaps have sex.

passion an emotional state characterized by high bodily arousal, such as increased heart rate and blood pressure

intimacy a feeling of closeness, mutual understanding, and mutual concern for each other's welfare and happiness

The second ingredient in Sternberg's scheme is **intimacy**. Intimacy, in his view, is the common core of all love relationships. It refers to feeling close to the other person. Empathy is important in intimacy; indeed, intimacy includes a sense of understanding the partner and being understood by him or her. Intimacy also entails a mutual concern for each other's welfare and happiness. When two people have a high degree of intimacy, they have a basic feeling of caring and concern about one another, they want each other to be happy and healthy, and they may often seek to

FIGURE 12.2
The triangle on the left represents a relationship that is high in intimacy and passion, but low in commitment. The triangle on the right represents a relationship that is high in intimacy and commitment but low in passion.

TRADE Offs

Sex In and Out of Marriage

It often seems as if married and single people envy each other. Single people think it must be wonderful to have a loving, devoted sex partner who sleeps with you every night, and they anticipate that getting married finally brings on a lifetime of great sex. Married people imagine that single life is full of sexual adventure and novelty, trying new acts and new partners anytime one wants instead of going to bed with the same old person according to the same old routine.

Of course, people have many reasons to marry (or not to marry), but we focus here on the links between marriage and sex, as indicated by the National Health and Social Life Survey.[21] The data suggest, first, that neither of the stereotypes invoked in the preceding paragraph is entirely correct. Frequent passionate sex, as seen in movies and novels, appears to be fairly unusual, and only a tiny fraction (8%) of married or single people have sex more than three times per week. Married people do have more sex than single people, or at least more than single people who are not cohabiting with a romantic partner. Living together without marriage is marked by the highest rates of sexual activity, though living together may not be the cause; unmarried cohabitation is mainly found among young people early in a relationship, and such individuals may have more sexual desire than older, long-married couples. Cohabitors also do not have many of the distractions of married life, such as small children, who can interfere with time and energy (and even privacy!) needed for sex. If you compare married people and single cohabitors of the same age, the frequency of sex is pretty similar, although the married people still have sex somewhat less often.

Thus, married people have more sex, in terms of quantity—but what about quality? Quality of sex is harder to measure, but one index might be how long people spend on a given sex act. By this measure, it looks as though single people have better sex. Married sex is more likely than unmarried sex to be finished in less than 15 minutes. Single persons are more likely than married ones to spend more than an hour on a single sexual event. Single people are also more likely than married ones to say that their most recent sex act included some activity beyond basic genital intercourse, which is another sign that they put effort and imagination into sex.

Not all signs of quality favor the single. When asked whether their most recent sex partner brought them physical or emotional satisfaction, married people are more likely than single ones to say yes. (Orgasm rates were nearly identical, however.) This may be partly because the marriage relationship contains love (and hence emotional satisfaction), and partly because a married spouse knows how to please you better than someone who is unfamiliar with your body. Single people are more likely than married ones to report consuming alcohol before sex, and alcohol does interfere with sexual responsiveness. Then again, at least the single people who drink before sex share the enjoyment of drinking; married people are prone to drink alone before sex, if at all.

One last and probably unsurprising difference is that single people have more sex partners than married ones. Though not all married people are faithful, most are, so marriage really does seem to entail settling down with one regular sex partner. Single people are more likely than married ones to have had several sex partners in the past year—then again, they are also more likely to have had none at all.

The relationship between marriage and sex thus appears to be a tradeoff. Married people have more frequent sex. Single people have more partners. Married people benefit from a partner who knows their responses and who loves them. Single people spend more time and energy on each sex act and try more things. For many single people, life alternates between periods of exciting sex with a new partner and periods of no sex with any partner. For many married people, sex conforms to a stable and regular pattern of familiar activities, once or twice a week.

---

do things that will benefit each other. Intimate partners try to take care of each other, and they emphasize communication about their lives, feelings, and problems.

The third ingredient is decision and **commitment**. Sternberg observed that when many people speak of love, they refer more to a conscious decision than to a feeling state. Emotions come and go, but commitments based on decisions remain constant unless they are deliberately revoked. For example, if you ask someone whether she loves her husband or her children, she may say, "Of course!" without having to think about it. If love referred only to passion, she would have to stop and examine her emotions at that moment to see whether she actually felt passionate attraction toward the other person. But if love means commitment, and she has made that commitment, then she can say, "Of course!" without requiring a survey of her current inner feelings.

Passion, intimacy, and commitment are not three different "kinds" of love. Instead, Sternberg proposed that any given love relationship can mix those three ingredients in any combination. Some love relationships might have high intimacy, high commitment, but low passion. Others might have plenty of passion and commitment but little intimacy. Can you think of examples of those types? The first (high intimacy and commitment but low passion) might describe a marriage that is still strong after many decades.

commitment a conscious decision that remains constant

This man is committed to his partner. Their relationship has high intimacy, high commitment, and high passion. Will the relationship last, or will he regret the tattoo later?

The second might describe a "whirlwind romance" in which two people fall madly in love and marry quickly, before they have gotten to know each other very well.

An ideal love might contain substantial measures of all three ingredients. If none of the three is present, Sternberg would say, there is no love. In his research, he concluded that intimacy is the most common ingredient; relatively few relationships utterly lack intimacy. Still, the feeling called "love at first sight" usually involves low intimacy; you hardly know the person yet, and passion is the main ingredient.

The three ingredients typically have different time courses. Passion can arise quickly—but as already noted, passion also tends to diminish after a while. Intimacy, in contrast, arises more slowly but can continue increasing for a long time, and it often remains high after it stops rising.[23,24] One theme of this book is the long road to social acceptance, and nowhere is the length of this road more obvious than in the slow, long-term development of an intimate relationship. The bond of intimacy continues to solidify for years. Last, decisions and commitments are typically made at particular points in time (such as agreeing to stop dating other people, or proposing marriage).

The shift from passionate to companionate love is explained by Sternberg's theory in terms of a change in the mixture of love's three ingredients (see **FIGURE 12.3**). Companionate love emphasizes intimacy and commitment, whereas passionate love consists mainly of passion (obviously). Commitment may help solidify the trust and mutual concern that contribute to companionate love. Thus, a typical long-term sexual relationship might start out consisting mainly of passion, but over time the intimacy grows stronger as passion grows weaker, and at some point a decision is made to solidify a long-range commitment. Commitment can help keep the couple together during periods of conflict or dissatisfaction, which many couples experience sooner or later. If the commitment is not made, or if intimacy does not grow, then the relationship is likely to break up after the early stage. The couple may still experience a great deal of passion, but once the passion dies down, there may be little to replace it, and they will run out of reasons to stay together.

Benefits of Commitment

Of the three components in Sternberg's theory of love, passion, and intimacy are familiar to everyone, but commitment may seem like a surprise as a third. Social psychologists have begun to explore relationship commitment more recently than the other two. What makes people make the leap and tie the knot?

An appealing relationship, with lots of passion and rising intimacy, is one factor that makes people ready to commit. But another may be fear of being single.[25] Many people have a deep fear of ending up alone in life. These fears motivate people to "settle for less": They lower their standards for relationship partners. They are more willing to pair up and stay with lower-quality partners, as compared to people with less fear of being single. If dissatisfied with a relationship, they are less likely to initiate a breakup, because they are afraid of being alone.

FIGURE 12.3

Passion and intimacy have different time courses over a relationship. Passion increases dramatically and then tends to decline steadily over time, whereas intimacy starts low and tends to increase over time.

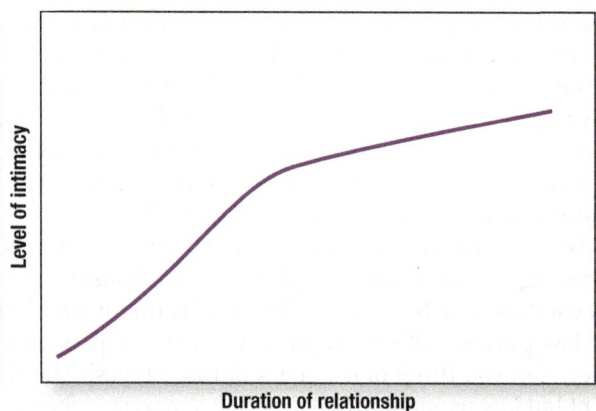

When a commitment is made, however, it changes the relationship, typically by making it stronger. Commitment may not matter much as long as both partners are deliriously happy together, but it helps when there are problems and conflicts. A commitment such as marriage may motivate a couple to work out their differences rather than splitting up. Even the problems may be contained better: Recent studies showed that romantic couples respond less aggressively to each other's provocations and misdeeds (such as criticizing the partner, flirting with someone else, or neglecting each other's needs and desires) to the extent that they were committed.[26] That is, commitment to the relationship reduced aggression within it.

That doesn't mean that commitment prevents problems. It can make them worse, in a way. After all, the more you care about the relationship, the more its problems will disturb you. The benefits of commitment are more visible over time than at once. A well-designed recent study found that higher levels of relationship commitment made people more sensitive and vulnerable to relationship problems in the short run—but also made them more resilient to these problems in the long run.[27] The two may go together. Being bothered by conflicts right away may motivate people to address them and solve them, which they can do better with a stronger commitment basis.

Weddings are themselves important devices for commitment, because the couple makes formal statements of commitment to each other. Weddings are of course something that only cultural animals do. Other animals may mate for long periods, even for life, but they do not cement the bond with a meaningful public ceremony. Some recent work has examined effects of wedding characteristics on commitment.[28] Perhaps surprisingly, spending a large amount of money on the ring or the wedding ceremony failed to reduce the likelihood of divorce and in fact may have increased it. That is, couples who spent more on the wedding and the ring had higher rates of divorce. What did reduce the likelihood of divorce was having a lot of people at the wedding. Thus, the beneficial effects of the wedding are more about the impact on one's social world than about spending a lot of money.

The role of physical attractiveness and sexual desire in marriage has been much disputed. Studies suggest that women whose male partners valued them for their bodies had higher satisfaction with the relationship than other women—provided that the man also valued her other traits and was committed.[29] Being valued for her body by a man whose commitment was low or who failed to appreciate other (non-body) qualities did lower the women's satisfaction. The implication for men who want happy wives and girlfriends is to show commitment and appreciate the woman's other qualities, but then also to express plenty of desire and appreciation for her physical charms too. Similar results are found for being valued for sex, as in being a good sex partner and engaging in frequent sex:[30] In a committed relationship, that increases the woman's satisfaction with the relationship, even though it decreases her satisfaction when commitment is weak.

QUIZ YOURSELF
What Is Love?

1. **Passionate love is an aspect of _____.**
   - (a) Eastern culture
   - (b) Western culture
   - (c) both Eastern and Western cultures
   - (d) neither Eastern nor Western cultures

2. **Passionate love is to companionate love as _____ love is to _____ love.**
   - (a) affectionate; romantic
   - (b) committed; intimate
   - (c) married; single
   - (d) romantic; affectionate

3. **People who feel passionately in love have high levels of _____.**
   - (a) acetylcholine
   - (b) dopamine
   - (c) epinephrine
   - (d) phenylethylamine

4. **In the triangle theory of love, what does companionate love stem from?**
   - (a) Commitment
   - (b) Intimacy
   - (c) Passion
   - (d) Both (a) and (b)

answers: see pg 449

Different Types of Relationships

Not all people are the same, nor are all relationships the same. Let us consider some of the basic differences in how people relate to each other.

Exchange Versus Communal

There are at least two different basic types of relationship. These can be called exchange and communal relationships.[31,32] **Exchange relationships** are based on reciprocity and fairness; each person does something for the other mainly in the expectation of getting some direct benefit in return. **Communal relationships**, in contrast, are based on mutual love and concern; in this type of relationship, people do things for each other without expecting to be repaid. The relationship between a family dentist and a regular customer would be one example of a long-term exchange relationship: The dentist and client may be friendly to each other and even enjoy seeing each other, but the basis of their interaction is still the exchange of dental care for money. In contrast, a long-term communal relationship might exist between two sisters, who help each other out during difficult times by giving emotional support and even money without expecting that the other will pay it back.

One difference between communal and exchange relationships is whether the people keep track. Thus, some couples that live together keep track of who pays which bills, who buys the groceries, and so forth, to make sure that everything is equal. Other couples live together in a more communal fashion, putting all their money into a joint bank account and letting either one spend it without having to check with the other. Even in terms of chores and doing favors for each other, some couples keep careful track, while others don't. In the lab, researchers have measured communal versus exchange orientation by having participants work on puzzles one after the other and noting whether they choose to use different colored pens (so each person's contribution is readily visible in a distinctive color) or the same colored pen (so that it becomes impossible to tell who did what). People who want or have communal relationships are more likely to use the same colored pen.[33,34] By doing that, they do not keep track of their respective contributions.

In general, social psychologists assume that communal relationships are more mature and desirable than exchange relationships. If you found out that a couple had been married for 10 years but still kept separate bank accounts and kept careful track of who paid for what, you would probably think something was wrong with the relationship, and you might question their commitment to each other. In fact, couples who pool their money in a communal fashion while living together are more likely to remain together and to get married than cohabiting couples who keep their relationship on an exchange basis by maintaining separate accounts.[35]

This bias in favor of communal relationships, however, is specific to close or intimate relationships. Across the broader society, exchange relationships seem much more powerful for driving progress and increasing wealth.[36] The communal societies in which possessions are shared freely by all tend to be simple, even relatively primitive cultures. The rich and flourishing cultures have all apparently become that way by taking advantage of social and economic exchange because the rewards for success encourage achievement, innovation, and risk taking. Thus, ultimately, there may be a tradeoff between the two types of relationship. Exchange relationships promote achievement, increase wealth, and ultimately drive progress, whereas communal relationships make people feel safe and secure and provide a haven where others care for you regardless of how much you achieve. This tradeoff may explain why most people in modern societies ultimately try to have some of both. They spend their working lives in a network of exchange relationships, where their salary and other rewards are directly proportional to what they accomplish, and where they do things for others specifically in order to get money or other rewards in return. Meanwhile, they try to set up their families on a communal basis, where people care for each other without keeping track of who contributed what and everyone shares with everyone else.

exchange relationships relationships based on reciprocity and fairness, in which people expect something in return

communal relationships relationships based on mutual love and concern, without expectation of repayment

In any case, communal interactions are healthier and more mature in close relationships. People in communal close relationships help each other more than do people in exchange close relationships.[37] They feel better about helping each other[38] and are more responsive to each other's emotional states.[39] They keep track of each other's needs rather than what the other does for them, and this attention to the other's needs reflects an ongoing concern to take care of each other.[40,41] Communal relationships also promote a greater sense of unity and shared identity, so the relationship feels more solid.

The underlying reality may be that communal and exchange relationships are based on different rules. Exchange relationships are based on reciprocity. In exchange relationships, you should only allow someone to do something for you if you are ready to repay that favor. Fairness and even exchange are uppermost concerns. In contrast, communal relationships are based on the norm of mutual concern. You can let the other person do things for you without any immediate idea of how to repay it, just as you would be willing to do a great deal for your partner without expecting anything in return. Instead of equality and repayment, the underlying rules involve caring for the other person and being available and ready to provide support, help, and other resources whenever the person needs you.

Attachment

During the dark days of World War II, London, England, endured daily bombings by the German air force. London was the nation's capital, and it was necessary for many people to remain at work there, but many parents decided to send their children to live out in the country, where the danger from bombs was much less. Although this practice promoted safety, it required many small children to be separated from their parents for significant periods of time. A British psychologist, John Bowlby, observed how the children dealt with these separations, and on this basis he began to formulate a theory about different styles of attachment.[42] This theory was revived by relationships researchers in the 1980s and has become an influential, powerful way of understanding all close relationships (including romantic ones).

Like many psychologists of his era, Bowlby was influenced by both Freudian and learning psychology, and these views treated adult behavior as shaped by early childhood experiences. Bowlby thought that how adults relate to others—romantic partners, work colleagues and bosses, even organizations—would essentially copy or repeat the style of interaction they had learned in childhood. He saw some children deal with separation from parents by clinging and crying and refusing to let go; others pretended they didn't like their parents and didn't care whether they were there or not; still others seemed to deal with the separation in a sad but accepting manner. He thought that these early experiences would shape how the children would later carry on their adult relationships. Bowlby's descriptions of the styles of interaction have influenced subsequent work, but today the weight of opinion does not favor the view that adult styles of interaction are strongly shaped by early childhood experiences. Many people change and develop new styles of relating long after early childhood. (Also, when research findings do indicate that a person has remained the same from childhood into adulthood, researchers today note that this could reflect some underlying genetic trait rather than the causal influence of childhood experiences.)

Types of Attachment

The original theory identified three types of attachment. John Bowlby's observations were extended by Phillip Shaver and his colleagues[43,44,45] to describe adult relationships, including love and romantic relationships. Shaver's group found that people could classify themselves reliably. It wasn't even necessary to use a long, fancy questionnaire; a single item (see **FIGURE 12.4**) was enough to sort people into categories. The categories range along a continuum from pulling close to pushing away. At one

FIGURE 12.4

Three attachment styles: avoidant (A), secure (B), and anxious/ambivalent (C)
SOURCE: Hazan and Shaver (1987).

Relationship questionnaire

_____ A. I am somewhat uncomfortable being close to others; I find it difficult to trust them completely, difficult to allow myself to depend on them. I am nervous when anyone gets too close, and often, others want me to be more intimate than I feel comfortable being.

_____ B. I find it relatively easy to get close to others and am comfortable depending on them and having them depend on me. I don't worry about being abandoned or about someone getting too close to me.

_____ C. I find that others are reluctant to get as close as I would like. I often worry that my partner doesn't really love me or won't want to stay with me. I want to get very close to my partner, and this sometimes scares people away.

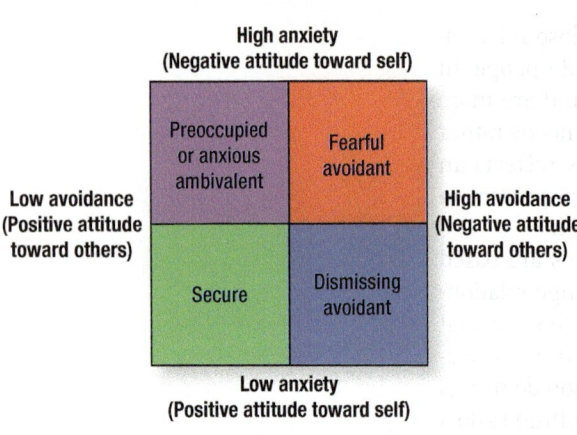

FIGURE 12.5
Two dimensions of attachment: anxiety and avoidance.

extreme lie the clinging types who want to be as close as possible, who ideally would like to experience a complete merger with someone else, and whose problems stem from the fact that others don't want to be as close as they do. This style of attachment is called anxious/ambivalent. At the other extreme one finds the *avoidant* individuals, who are uncomfortable when others want to get too close and who try to maintain some distance between themselves and relationship partners.

In the middle, between the anxious and avoidant styles, are the secure individuals. *Secure attachment* is characterized by a comfortable balance: The secure person is happy to become close and intimate with others and does not worry inordinately about being abandoned or hurt. Earlier, we noted that the difference between communal and exchange relationships is a kind of tradeoff, in that both have advantages in appropriate contexts. In that sense, neither communal nor exchange is inherently better than the other. All attachment styles are not equal, however. In almost all published studies, the secure attachment style produces the best outcomes.

The best that can be said for the other attachment styles is that they provide some limited kind of defense mechanisms or ways of coping with painful relationships. In fact, the avoidant attachment style is thought to start when parents (especially mothers) reject or neglect their babies, fail to express affection and other emotions, avoid physical contact, and fail to provide comfort when the babies are upset.[46] An upset baby whose mother fails to provide comfort may learn to turn off the desire to be close to the mother as a way of preventing itself from feeling worse.[47]

Two Dimensions of Attachment?

As the study of attachment styles evolved, researchers gradually moved from the single dimension (running from anxious/ambivalent to secure to avoidant) in favor of a two-dimensional **attachment theory**.[48,49,50,51,52] The two dimensions are now called *anxiety* and *avoidance*. A simple way to remember them is that one dimension (anxiety) refers to attitudes toward the self and the other dimension (avoidance) refers to attitudes toward the other person. Though both of these dimensions should be understood as a continuum, we can use a simple high-versus-low split on each dimension to create vivid images of four different attachment styles (see **FIGURE 12.5**). Thus, the new theory offers four styles, instead of the three in the earlier version, mainly by splitting the "avoidant" category into two.

The first of the four styles is, again, **secure attachment**. Securely attached people are low on anxiety and low on avoidance (or, to put it another way, they have favorable attitudes toward both self and others). They are good at close relationships. They trust their partners, share their feelings, provide support and comfort (and happily receive these as well), and enjoy their relationships. Their relationships tend to be stronger, more durable, more satisfying, and more intimate than those of people in the other categories.[53,54]

The second category is called **preoccupied attachment**, though some researchers still prefer the original term **anxious/ambivalent**. People in this category are low on avoidance, reflecting the fact that they want and enjoy closeness to the other person, but they tend to have high anxiety and a more negative attitude toward themselves. These individuals want to merge and cling but worry that their relationship partners will abandon them, possibly because they think their partners will discover their faults and flaws.[55,56,57,58,59] Preoccupied individuals tend to see partners as inconsistent, unreliable, and reluctant to commit. They seek more and more closeness, and their frequent efforts to force others to remain close to them can cause their partners to perceive them as overly controlling (or even "suffocating"). Preoccupied individuals may provide large amounts of comfort, support, and care to others, but sometimes they provide too much, partly because they provide care more to satisfy their own need to connect than out of any genuine sensitivity to their partner's needs.[60,61,62]

In the third type, **dismissing avoidant attachment**, people see themselves as worthy, adequate individuals (thus low anxiety) but seek to prevent relationships from becoming

---

attachment theory a theory that classifies people into four attachment styles (secure, preoccupied, dismissing avoidant, and fearful avoidant) based on two dimensions (anxiety and avoidance)

secure attachment style of attachment in which people are low on anxiety and low on avoidance; they trust their partners, share their feelings, provide and receive support and comfort, and enjoy their relationships

preoccupied (anxious/ambivalent) attachment style of attachment in which people are low on avoidance but high on anxiety; they want and enjoy closeness but worry that their relationship partners will abandon them

dismissing avoidant attachment style of attachment in which people are low on anxiety but high on avoidance; they tend to view partners as unreliable, unavailable, and uncaring too close.[63,64] They view partners as unreliable, unavailable, and uncaring. They seek to rely on themselves rather than on others. Their relationships are marked by more distance, lower commitment, and lower enjoyment than those of secure or preoccupied individuals. Their partners sometimes see them as withdrawn or aloof and as reluctant to open up (that is, they are slow to disclose personal feelings and experiences). They provide less care and support to their loved ones than do secure or preoccupied people.

Fourth, **fearful avoidant attachment** is characterized by both high anxiety and high avoidance. These people have low opinions of themselves and keep others from becoming close. They view potential relationship partners as untrustworthy, uncaring, and otherwise unavailable. They worry that they are unlovable. Given their issues with both self and others, this worry may not be entirely unfounded!

How firm are these styles? Although each person may have a habitual attachment style, anyone can occasionally have a relationship with a different style, partly because of the partner's influence.[65] You might normally be secure, for example, but you might find yourself preoccupied in a particular relationship, especially if the partner treats you in an erratic or anxiety-producing manner.

In many ways, the avoidant individuals (both dismissing and fearful) present the biggest theoretical puzzle.[66,67] We have said that the need to belong and the desire for close relationships are common to all human beings, yet at least on the surface avoidant people seem to push others away rather than keep them close. Do avoidant people thus lack the need to belong? Avoidant individuals do desire and seek out connections with others. But, they worry that if they give in to these wishes and become close to others, they will be hurt. Thus, the fear of closeness lies alongside the need to belong, and the two urges can come into conflict. Quite possibly their fear of closeness originates in previous experiences, whether very early in life such as having had a distant or rejecting mother, or as a result of early romantic experiences that ended in pain and suffering. Put another way, avoidant individuals have the same basic need to belong as other people, but they seem to learn to turn it off or disconnect it to avoid being hurt. Outwardly they may act as if they are indifferent to closeness with others, but secretly they often suffer a great deal during separations.[68,69]

Avoidance problems later in life may in part be due to being ignored as a child.

Avoidant individuals thus perform a delicate balancing act. They want contact and relationships with other people, but they seek to avoid becoming too close. In a sense, they want human connection and companionship but without allowing too much intimacy. Some deal with this by keeping multiple relationships going at the same time, so that if one partner starts to get too close, they can shift emphasis to another. Others manage the problem by frequently introducing conflict into a relationship, such as by getting into fights and arguments over seemingly minor things. That way they can stay connected to someone but prevent the relationship from becoming too close. Others simply set up their social lives so that they keep interactions relatively short, thus preventing intimacy from developing.[70]

Loving People Who Love Themselves

"First you must love yourself, and only then are you ready to love someone else"—this is a popular belief in our culture. It is variously attributed to the psychological thinkers Erik Erikson, Carl Rogers, and Abraham Maslow, but it is probably a misreading of their works. Erikson said that people must resolve their identity crisis and know who they are before they are ready to start working on intimacy.[71] He didn't say you had to love yourself—merely know yourself (and it is even questionable whether knowing yourself is a prerequisite for having a good relationship). Rogers focused on self-actualization (the global process of cultivating your talents and becoming a better person all around) rather than self-love. He also thought that people needed to receive unconditional love before they were ready to reach self-actualization.[72] This is in a sense the opposite of the idea that self-love comes first; instead, being loved comes first, self-esteem later. Maslow likewise proposed that belongingness and love needs were more basic than self-esteem needs;[73]

fearful avoidant attachment style of attachment in which people have both high anxiety and high avoidance; they have low opinions of themselves and keep others from getting close his views, too, run contrary to the theory that self-esteem comes first, love later.

Still, those theories are no more than theories. What do the facts and findings say about loving yourself and loving others? The evidence is at best weak and inconsistent in terms of showing that loving yourself contributes to loving others. In some cases, people who love themselves lavishly are less likely to love anyone else.

Let us begin with self-esteem. People with low self-esteem engage in a variety of behaviors that can undermine a relationship.[74,75] They are skeptical or distrustful when their partners express love or support, and sometimes they act as if they expect their partners to dump them. Still, these problematic behaviors do not seem to translate into breaking up faster. One possible reason is that people with high self-esteem do other, different things that are bad for relationships. When problems or conflicts occur in a relationship, people with high self-esteem are quicker to decide "I don't have to put up with this!" and to contemplate ending the relationship.[76,77] Probably the different levels of self-esteem contribute to those different reactions. People with low self-esteem doubt that they are lovable, so they expect others to leave them. People with high self-esteem think they are lovable, so they think they can find a new partner relatively easily. The net result may be that people who have either high or low self-esteem break up at about the same rate, but for different reasons. The other side of the coin is that people of all levels of self-esteem can have lasting, successful relationships.

Being in a relationship with a narcissist is no picnic. Because they are so full of themselves, they don't think about others.

The damage that self-love can do to relationship harmony is magnified if one looks at narcissism (see also Chapters 3 and 10), which is a personality type based on very high self-love. Narcissists have high self-esteem and a strong though somewhat unstable self-love, but these qualities do not make for good relationships; indeed, their selfishness and other qualities may harm relationships. They approach relationships in a game-playing spirit of having fun or as a pragmatic way of getting what they want (including sex).[78] They seek out successful, beautiful, admired people to date because they think they are similar to them, and they believe that the glamour or prestige of their partners makes them look good.[79]

Getting along with a narcissist is no picnic! Narcissists tend to hog the credit when things go well but blame their partners when things go badly,[80,81,82,83,84] which can certainly put a strain on a relationship. In an observational study in which couples discussed problems that threatened their self-esteem, narcissists had fewer positive interactions with their spouses than other people did.[85]

Ultimately, narcissists tend to be less committed to love relationships than other people are.[86] Narcissists tend to keep one eye on the relationship but another eye out to see whether a better partner might come along. Narcissists think they are superior beings and overestimate how attractive they are; as a result, they think they can and should have the most desirable romantic partners. A narcissist may love you for the time being, but he or she will dump you as soon as a better prospect comes along.

If self-love leads to loving others, narcissists should be the world's best lovers because they love themselves the most. The evidence suggests the opposite, however: In narcissists, at least, loving yourself detracts from loving others. Narcissists are interested in others mainly as a way of boosting their own inflated views of themselves. Hence, their relationships tend to be prone to breakup. This may help explain why marriages among celebrities often end in divorce: Being a celebrity tends to push people to become more narcissistic (partly because they are widely admired and highly paid), and this often leads to relationship problems, especially when new partners are constantly and readily available.

Although narcissism is one problematic extreme, some less extreme versions of self-love and self-esteem may be helpful for relationships. A more minimal form of self-love is **self-acceptance**, which means simply regarding yourself as being a reasonably good person as you are. The same study that found narcissism to be linked to fewer positive interactions with the spouse found that self-acceptance was linked to more positive interactions.[87] These findings suggest that having a very negative, critical attitude toward yourself can interfere with the capacity to love. The best summary of current knowledge on this issue is to say that either extreme of self-love or self-hate is likely to be detrimental to intimacy. Conversely, someone with a simple and secure appreciation of self, without being conceited or overblown, may be the best romantic partner.

QUIZ YOURSELF
Different Types of Relationships

1. Exchange relationship is to communal relationship as _____ is to _____ .
   - (a) concern; reciprocity
   - (b) passion; concern
   - (c) reciprocity; concern
   - (d) reciprocity; passion

2. What attachment style is associated with high levels of anxiety and high levels of avoidance?
   - (a) Dismissing avoidant
   - (b) Fearful avoidant
   - (c) Preoccupied
   - (d) Secure

3. Individuals who see themselves as worthy and adequate but seek to prevent relationships from becoming too close have what type of attachment style?
   - (a) Dismissing avoidant
   - (b) Fearful avoidant
   - (c) Preoccupied
   - (d) Secure

4. What personality trait is associated with a grandiose, inflated view of the self?
   - (a) Narcissism
   - (b) Self-acceptance
   - (c) Self-efficacy
   - (d) Self-esteem

answers: see pg 449

Maintaining Relationships

Information is available everywhere about how people form new relationships. Countless books, movies, and studies look at how people become attracted to each other and reach the point of making a commitment to carry on an intimate relationship. Most people have some idea about how to do this. In contrast, how people manage to keep a relationship going, sometimes for 40 years or more, seems a mystery. Social psychology is only gradually beginning to provide answers to the question of how people keep their relationships alive and well.

What goes on between partners in a long-term relationship? How do they keep it going? What causes some relationships to succeed while others fail? These processes have fascinated social psychologists in recent decades.

Whether relationships continue depends partly on how people deal with temptation, especially the temptation to seek other possible partners. One social psychologist had people in dating relationships look at photos of attractive members of the opposite sex and recorded how long they looked at them. He contacted the participants months later to see whether they were still together with the same relationship partner. The longer they had looked at the photos, the more likely they were to break up. Apparently, exposing yourself to temptation (even just by looking at photos of attractive members of the opposite sex) is one sign that the person may be drifting toward breaking up.[88]

self-acceptance regarding yourself as being a reasonably good person as you are

There is some evidence that men and women respond to relationship threats and temptations in different ways. In a series of studies, people who were in committed relationships were introduced to an attractive single person (or, in other studies, imagined this experience). Women reacted to meeting a desirable man by increasing their commitment to their current partner, such as by tolerating his faults more, thinking more positively about him, or increasing their commitment to him. Men, on the other hand, reacted to meeting an attractive single woman by reducing their commitment to their current partner and becoming more critical of her.[89] The implication is that meeting a tempting new partner makes men entertain the possibility of a new relationship instead of the one they have, whereas women try to defend their current relationship.

We saw in the previous chapter that physical good looks matter a great deal for initial attraction. Stereotypes suggest that beauty matters more to men than women, especially in the beginning, because other things take precedence in a long-term relationship. A classic rock song by Jimmy Soul that hit #1 on the Billboard and R&B charts in 1963 even advised men that "If you wanna be happy for the rest of your life, never make a pretty woman your wife!" and went on to advise men to "Get an ugly girl to marry you."

As usual, with the accumulation of data, the picture becomes more complicated. For marital satisfaction, the woman's physical attractiveness matters more than the man's.[90] That is, men with attractive wives were happier about the marriage and stayed higher in relationship satisfaction than men with less attractive wives. The man's looks had little impact on the woman's satisfaction. Further work suggests, however, that the part of indifference to male beauty can be chalked up to birth control pills. These pills alter women's hormones and change their patterns of sexual response. When women stop taking birth-control pills, their relationship satisfaction changes, depending on their partner's looks.[91] Women with good-looking husbands became more satisfied when they stopped taking the pill, but those with less handsome husbands experienced a decrease in satisfaction.

Other recent work has confirmed that physically attractive people are more likely than others to divorce or break up steady relationships.[92] For example, researchers rated how good-looking people were in their high school yearbook photos, and then found that the highly rated ones had shorter marriages and more divorces than the average ones. As we saw in the previous chapter, physical attractiveness makes one appealing to others, and so beautiful and handsome people have more options. Knowing they are attractive, they tend to be less satisfied than other people with the relationship they have and more interested in alternative options, such as exciting new partners. This adds another reason in support of Jimmy Soul's song about avoiding spouses who are too attractive—they will be prone to abandon you.

I Love You More Each Day(?)

Many people in happy marriages say that their relationships continue to grow and improve over the years. People striving to have good and lasting relationships want to know what secrets or actions enable this to happen. If you form a relationship when you are falling in love, everything seems wonderful and perfect. How can things continue to get even better than that?

The data suggest a very different picture. People may say and even believe their relationships are getting better, but usually they are mistaken. Evidence came from a study that had people report on their relationship quality year after year, and also report on changes. People in happy relationships consistently said their relationship was better each year. But if you compared how they rated it this year with how they rated it last year, there was no change. The ever-improving relationship is largely a myth. Good relationships essentially stay the same over long periods of time.[93]

Those were the happy relationships. Many longitudinal studies that track couples over years find essentially two outcomes: Some stay the same, and others get worse.[94,95,96] Relationships start off good, and either they stay good or they go downhill. The problem of how to have a good long-term relationship is therefore not finding a way to make it better and better—rather, the crucial thing is to avoid the downward spiral. Moreover, once relationships begin to deteriorate, it is apparently quite difficult and unusual to stop this process. The most important challenge is therefore to prevent the downward spiral from starting.

Which type will your relationship be? Intriguing findings suggest that it is possible to predict decline from early in the relationship. A longitudinal study tracked newlywed couples for four years. At the start of the study, they were all asked to rate their partners. They also did a complex task designed to assess unconscious, automatic attitudes. The simple, conscious ratings had no predictive power, but the relationships marked by positive unconscious attitudes toward each other held up better than the relationships with less positive automatic responses.[97] In a sense, then, the seeds of your divorce may be present at your wedding—but you won't be consciously aware of them. Put another way, most newlyweds have a conscious belief that they are happy together and the relationship is great, but these happy thoughts are there in roughly equal measure in the doomed relationships and in the ones that will thrive and last. The unconscious, however, already has begun to have the feelings that will predict which way the relationship will go.

In reality, most relationships do not improve steadily.

Many things can contribute to the downward spiral. These are especially likely when taking care of oneself and one's own needs is detrimental to the relationship. Making your partner feel guilty is one such process.[98,99] People who are insecure about the relationship are especially worried when the partner criticizes them or misbehaves in other ways. (Insecurity can be linked to anxious attachment styles; see above.) They respond to such conflicts and problems by expressing a high level of hurt feelings and other distress, which makes the partner feel guilty. Seeing the partner express remorse and guilt is reassuring to them, because it indicates that the partner is committed and cares about them. Unfortunately, exaggerating your distress to make your partner feel guilty has a negative effect in the long run, because it reduces the partner's satisfaction with the relationship.[100] Thus, before you make yourself feel better by inducing guilt in your partner, think twice about the damage that might do in the long run!

Investing in Relationships That Last

The question "Why do people stay with their long-term relationship partners?" was the focus of years of research by relationships expert Caryl Rusbult.[101] She began by noting the simpleminded answer: People stay with relationships when they are happy and satisfied. This is not wrong, but it is not a full explanation. People who were satisfied with their relationships were more likely than unsatisfied partners to stay together, but the statistical link was surprisingly weak—which meant that some other factors must be at work.

Eventually Rusbult and her colleagues developed a theory called the **investment model**, with three factors. The first factor, sure enough, is satisfaction. Do you like your partner? Are you glad you have this particular relationship? Do you enjoy spending time together? Does your partner please and satisfy you? If your answers are yes, the relationship is more likely to survive. This is hardly surprising.

The second factor is the quality of available alternatives. Maybe your relationship is not really satisfying, but you don't see anyone better available. In that case, you might remain in an unsatisfying relationship. Conversely, your relationship may be pretty good and satisfying, but if someone clearly better than your partner comes along and makes you an offer, you may be tempted to leave. Here, Rusbult's theory makes the important point that a decision on whether to stay or leave a particular relationship doesn't depend only on how you evaluate that relationship. The decision also depends on whether you could be happier with someone else.

investment model theory that uses three factors—satisfaction, alternatives, and investments—to explain why people stay with their long-term relationship partners

Commitment to one's relationship is weaker when many high-quality alternative partners are available.

The third factor is how much the individual has invested in the relationship. Rusbult notes that many investments are "sunk costs," which means that the person has put time, effort, emotion, and other resources into a relationship and cannot get them back out. If you have struggled for two years to get your partner to understand your feelings or respect your needs, and you then break up and start over with someone else, all that struggle is lost. You may have to repeat it all with your new partner. A couple that has spent 20 years together, amassing savings, coordinating careers, raising children, and the like, may be resistant to change simply because they have invested so much in the relationship and do not want to lose it. Even if another attractive partner comes along, they may cling to the relationship that they have worked hard to build. When an old married person dies, friends sometimes tell the widow or widower, "You don't get over it; you get used to it." The implication is that the lost partner is not replaceable. Even if you remarry, you cannot rebuild what you may have shared with someone for many decades of your adult life.

Each of these three factors alone has a weak (though significant) ability to predict whether couples stay together or break apart. Putting the three together provides a very (statistically) strong basis for prediction. If you are satisfied with the relationship, don't see appealing alternatives, and have invested a great deal in the relationship, you will almost certainly remain committed to it. Charles and Diana, whose relationship story opened this chapter, were clearly not satisfied and had plenty of alternatives, and these facts probably helped cause their relationship to break up even though they had invested a fair amount (public statements, time, money, love, plus the raising of children) in it.

The investment theory can even explain some of the phenomena that have puzzled psychologists for decades, including why people (especially women) remain in relationships with physically violent, abusive partners.[102] Logically, one would think that if your partner hits, hurts, or abuses you, you should immediately get out of that relationship and find someone else. Satisfaction is generally not very high in abusive relationships. But many abuse victims do not believe they have alternatives. Some believe they are not attractive enough to find someone else (a belief that the abusive spouse sometimes encourages). At the same time, many abuse victims invest a great deal in making the relationship work, often over long-term cycles in which brief episodes of violent abuse are followed by apologizing, making up, sharing feelings, and promising to do better in the future. The victim may be reluctant to toss aside all that has been achieved and take a chance on a new partner who may be no better.

Are Married People Happier?

Love and other close, intimate relationships make up a major part of life. Most people in North America today, and probably most people in most other modern cultures, believe that to miss out on love and intimacy would be to live a poorer, emptier life, compared to people who experience those things. In Chapter 11 we saw that having social bonds is linked to better mental and physical health on all sorts of measures. Many of those advantages have been specifically linked to marriage: People who marry live longer and healthier lives than people who never marry, and people who stay married live longer and better than those who divorce.[103,104,105]

Some qualifications are needed before you start thinking, "I'd better marry somebody, anybody, as soon as possible!" Unhappy marriages produce considerable stress and other bad effects that can nullify the advantages of marriage and in some cases leave people worse off married than alone.[106,107,108,109] Thus, not just marriage but happy marriage may be the most important thing. There may also be a gender difference, though more data are needed. To men, the big difference is being married versus not married, but for women, the quality of the relationship (happy versus unhappy) seems more powerful.[110]

Chapter 1 discussed how the conclusions from research depend on the methods. The data on the advantages of marriage have some built-in ambiguities because of the research methods. We saw in Chapter 1 that research cannot easily establish causality unless it uses random assignment to conditions, and of course no researchers can randomly assign people to be married versus single. It is possible that people who are healthier to start with are more likely to marry, so their better health might not be a result of the marriage. Research has shown that some inborn, genetic factors steer people toward marriage, whereas other genetic factors guide other people toward remaining single.[111] That is, married people are genetically different from lifelong single people, on average, and some of those differences could contribute to the differences in health and longevity. For example, a person born with a genetic problem that caused many health problems over the years might find it harder than a healthy person to marry (because people prefer to marry healthy, attractive partners) and also might be more likely to die at a young age (because of the health problems).

Still, some of the differences in outcomes are probably caused by the benefits of marriage. For example, Catholic priests do not live as long or as healthy lives as do Protestant ministers.[112] It does not seem likely that genetic traits steer men into Catholic versus Protestant faith—so the difference in how long they live is more likely due to the fact that only the Protestant clergy marry.

Thinking Styles of Couples

Certainly people do some things that help their relationships succeed. High on the list are ways in which the couple deals with problems and conflicts. If you live with someone for many years, there is a high likelihood that sooner or later the person will be unpleasant or difficult, at least occasionally. It is also likely that conflicts will arise when the two of you want different things, such as spending a vacation at the beach or visiting one person's parents, or when you disagree about money.

Some research has compared happy couples with unhappy couples. Seeing how those two types of couples differ, especially in how they deal with problems and conflicts, can shed light on what makes some couples happier than others.

Some of the crucial differences between happy and unhappy couples are based on the attributions they make. (As we saw in Chapter 5, attributions are inferences about the causes of events.) In strong, happy relationships, partners seem willing to give the partner the benefit of the doubt most of the time. For example, researchers asked people how they would respond when the partner did something unpleasant, as opposed to doing something pleasant.[113] The happy couples said they would probably attribute the partner's unpleasant behavior to some external factor, such as thinking that the person must be under stress at work. In contrast, when the partner does something pleasant, the member of a happy couple was likely to view this as further proof of what a good person the partner is. In short, good acts were attributed to the partner's inner qualities, whereas bad acts were dismissed as due to external factors. The researchers called this pattern (internal attributions for good behavior, external for bad) the **relationship-enhancing style of attribution** (see **FIGURE 12.6**). It strengthens the relationship by making the partners see each other in a positive light.

The unhappy couples interpreted events along the opposite lines. If the partner did something good, they tended to think it was due to external factors. For example, if the husband brought the wife flowers, she might think, "He must have just gotten those on sale" or even "He did something wrong and is trying to cover it up." If the partner did something bad, the person would think, "Well, that's just typical!" and see it as a reflection of the kind of person the partner was. Thus, bad acts were attributed to the partner's inner qualities, whereas good acts were dismissed as due to external factors. The researchers called this pattern the **distress-maintaining style of attribution** (see **FIGURE 12.6**).

These styles of thinking explain why it is often so difficult to save a relationship that is in trouble, even with the aid of professional marriage therapists. Getting people to change their actions and treat each other better is certainly an important first step, but

relationship-enhancing style of attribution tendency of happy couples to attribute their partner's good acts to internal factors and bad acts to external factors

distress-maintaining style of attribution tendency of unhappy couples to attribute their partner's good acts to external factors and bad acts to internal factors

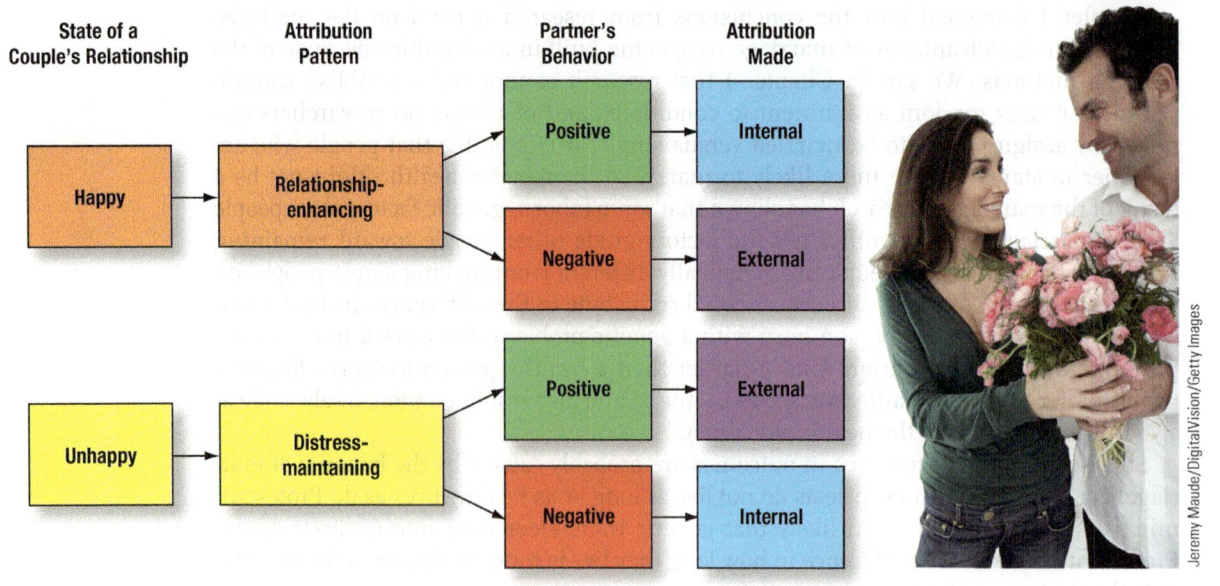

FIGURE 12.6
Happy and unhappy couples make different attributions for their partner's behavior.

once the distress-maintaining attributional pattern is in place, good actions tend to be discounted. You may decide to try to be nicer to your partner in order to try to strengthen the relationship, but your partner is likely to dismiss your positive acts. ("You're only being nice because the therapist told you to!") Meanwhile, even if you are trying to be good, you may occasionally slip up and say or do something unkind—in which case your distress-maintaining partner is likely to see this as the "real" you emerging again. You can't win, at least as long as your partner follows the distress-maintaining style of thinking.

Trust is an important factor that guides how people think about relationships and partners. People who trust their partners more can take more responsibility for conflicts (such as by accepting blame), because they are confident that the partner will act in their best interests in general. Lacking trust, one has to look out more for oneself. Several recent studies tracked couples over time and had them report on their conflicts and partner misdeeds both when they happened and then quite a bit later (from memory).[114] In high trust relationships, people's memories showed something much like the relationship-enhancing style of attribution: They remembered the partner's misdeeds less often and rated them as less severe than they had initially. In low-trust relationships, no such bias was apparent, and memories of partner misdeeds remain sharp and painful.

Other important thought processes include how people look at the relationship itself. Happy couples tend to exaggerate how wonderful the relationship is. When problems arise, they may see them as isolated incidents. In this way, they sustain a view that the relationship is great. People's ratings of their dating relationships tend to be more positive and optimistic than the ratings of those same relationships by the young lovers' parents and roommates.[115] (The roommates' predictions about whether the relationship would last were the most accurate!)

When couples start to move toward breaking up, the partners often reassess the relationship, wherein they go back and reinterpret past events as far less wonderful and positive than they seemed at the time.[116] For example, many happy couples maintain a highly romanticized story of how they first met, suggesting that they discovered that they were truly meant for each other and that they really turned each other on because they had a terrific rapport. When the same couple is preparing for breakup or divorce, they create a new version of the story of how they first met, suggesting that it was just an accident, that they happened to be lonely or sexually desperate and were willing to strike up a romance with anybody who happened to be there, or that the attraction was based on false impressions.

Another important process is devaluing alternatives. One study had people who were in relationships rate the attractiveness of several potential dating partners.[117] The people in the most committed relationships gave these potential partners low ratings, especially when the other person was attractive and would actually have been available as a possible dating partner. These circumstances were considered the most threatening, and so the devaluing of alternatives was probably a defensive response against the danger of becoming interested in someone else. Sure enough, in another study, those same researchers found that people who devalued alternatives were less likely to break up than people who refrained from devaluing. In other words, people in lasting relationships did not find other people appealing, whereas people in doomed relationships (the ones that later broke up) found other people appealing and even increased their attraction to them over time. Remember the study that let people look at attractive photos of opposite-sex individuals for as long as they wanted, the duration of looking predicted whether they broke up with their current partner: Those who looked longest were most likely to break up.[118]

In another study, young heterosexual participants who were in relationships rated photos of young opposite-sex persons as less attractive than did people who were not in relationships.[119] The two groups did not differ in how they rated young same-sex individuals or older opposite-sex individuals—neither of which constituted a potential threat to their current dating relationship. Thus, only the potential alternative partners were devalued. The implication is that closing your mind to other potential partners is one way to help keep your relationship safe.

Being Yourself: Is Honesty the Best Policy?

Listen to the discussions on television about what is best for long-term relationship success, and one common theme is honesty. The prevailing wisdom is that honesty is crucial, even essential, for relationship success. You have to be able to be yourself and show yourself as you really are, and your partner has to honestly accept this.

Then again, when you are shopping with your romantic partner and she or he asks, "Does this garment make me look fat?" should you honestly say, "Yes, but no more than most of your other clothes"? Honesty may be overrated. After all, people who are wildly, passionately in love often idealize and overestimate their partners—is that necessarily a bad thing? Why does love make us see each other as better than we are, if seeing each other accurately is best for relationship success?

There are in fact two very different views about honesty's role in successful relationships. One holds that honesty is the best policy: It is best if two people understand each other fully and correctly, communicate all their feelings, and accept each other for who they are. The other is that the people should idealize each other and see each other in a positively biased fashion.

During passionate love, two people generally take a very positive, even distorted view of each other. Friends will say, "What does he see in her?" or "I can't believe she thinks he's so brilliant." Moreover, the lovers tend to encourage and help each other to see each other in this idealized fashion. On dates, they wear their best clothes and are on their best behavior: thoughtful, charming, considerate, and proper. A woman might be careful that her new boyfriend only sees her when her hair is combed and she is wearing makeup. A man may clean up his language and monitor the opinions he expresses so as to make a good impression.

Because of these practices, people fall in love with an idealized version of each other. Such illusions may be difficult to sustain over the long run. Still, does that mean people should rush into honesty? Perhaps. You probably do want to be known and loved for who you really are. You might feel insecure if your partner has never seen the "real" you and instead has only known you on your best behavior. You may feel that if the other person ever found out what you are really like, he or she would reject and abandon you. The love between Charles and Diana may have started off with both people idealizing each other, but when the fairy tale ended and reality set in, the problems began.

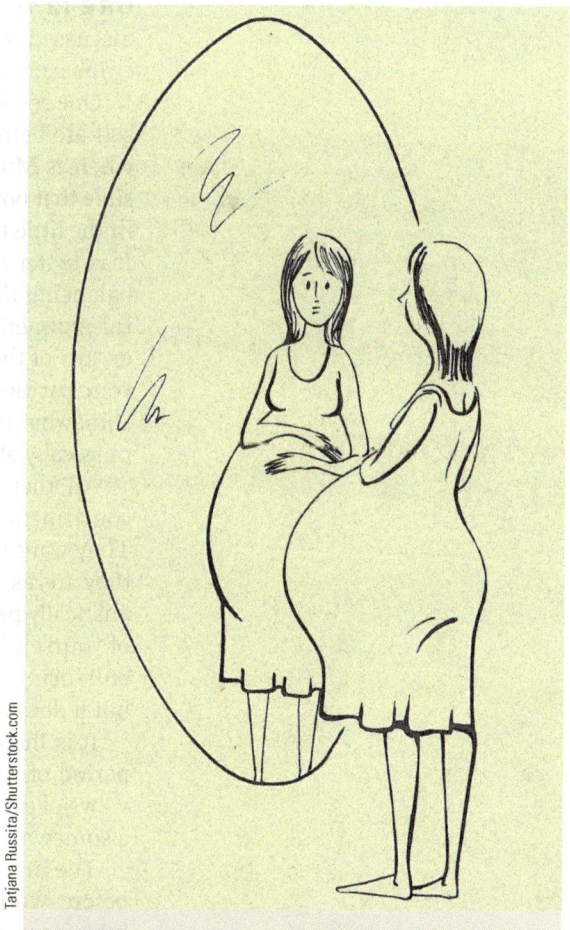

"Honey, do I look fat in these twins?" Honesty sometimes is not the best policy.

FIGURE 12.7
Idealize each other and you will stay together longer.

The question then becomes, should you try to preserve your partner's idealized version of you for as long as possible? Or should you reveal your true self, with all your flaws and failings, and seek to be accepted that way?

Research has provided conflicting answers. Work by William Swann and his colleagues[120,121] (see also Chapter 3) sought to show that people desire others to see them as they see themselves. (Admittedly, most people see themselves in a positively distorted fashion, so this is not the same as all-out honesty.) These researchers found that different rules apply in dating as opposed to marriage. When dating, people were most intimate with partners who viewed them most favorably. Within marriage, however, people were most intimate with partners who saw them as they saw themselves. In fact, people with low self-esteem were more intimate with partners who viewed them relatively less favorably than with partners who thought highly of them.[122]

In contrast, studies by Sandra Murray and John Holmes support the idealization view.[123,124,125,126] In their studies, couples were assessed on how much they idealized each other, as well as on relationship satisfaction. The researchers then followed up with the couples after many months to see whether they were still dating and, if so, how they were doing. They found that people who saw each other in the most positive fashion had the happiest relationships—and the most durable ones (that is, least likely to break up). Moreover, the idealization seemed to be the crucial cause. Having a very positive view of the other person at Time 1 led to a happier relationship (later) at Time 2, but a happy relationship at Time 1 did not predict a positive opinion of the partner at Time 2 (see **FIGURE 12.7**). This finding is consistent with the relationship-enhancing style of thought discussed in the previous section: People who downplay their partners' bad points and emphasize their partners' good points have the happiest relationships.

One resolution of these seemingly discrepant findings has to do with what aspects of self are being measured.[127] Swann's studies measured very specific features of the self, whereas Murray and Holmes measured global, overall appreciation. It is therefore plausible that both findings are correct. People may want their partner to see them accurately in the little things but to hold a broadly positive view of them in the vague, general sense. It is better for your partner to know accurately whether you are good at fixing the car, balancing the checkbook, being on time for a date, or acting in a charming and respectful manner in front of your partner's parents. If your partner vastly overestimates you on any of those, you may be headed for trouble! But at the same time, you probably want your partner to think that you are a wonderful person in general. If your partner has a somewhat inflated view of what a nice person you are, how intelligent you are, or how physically attractive you are, this may help the relationship to survive.

Another, perhaps deeper way to reconcile these findings is that people want selective confirmation of how they think of themselves—neither total honesty nor total illusion. They want their partners to see them at their best, which is a real and valid part of who they are, as opposed to seeing either the full nasty truth or a fictional version that is unrealistically perfect. The most attractive, brilliant, and charming, but still genuine, version of yourself is the one you'd like your partner to believe is the real you. The relationship-enhancing style of thought focuses on your partner's best traits and ignores the bad ones, but it does not fabricate nonexistent good traits.

It is therefore probably a good idea to stay on your best behavior for a relatively long period of time. Relationships do benefit when the people can sustain highly favorable views of each other. You want to allow your partner to see you at your best and to keep up a somewhat idealized view of the kind of person you are.

The marriages among the middle class during the Victorian period (late 19th century, before World War I) are often mocked these days as phony and pretentious. In those marriages, husband and wife would dress up for dinner together. They sometimes addressed each other in relatively formal terms. They did not necessarily pour out all their inner feelings to each other but kept some distance. They tried to keep up good, proper behavior even when alone together. In a sense, they remained on their best behavior, so that 5 or 25 years into a marriage they still acted almost as if they were still courting. To the modern sensibility, these practices seem like a silly way to go about having a close relationship with someone. The modern mind thinks that people should share everything about themselves.

But perhaps the Victorian practices deserve to be reconsidered. In fact, the middle-class Victorians had the longest lasting marriages in Western history, on average.[128,129,130] How can you make a relationship tolerable for 40 years? Perhaps the Victorians had a valid solution: Be on your best behavior. Research lends support to this view. Rather than requiring your partner to see you at your worst, such as sitting on the couch in dirty underwear and scratching yourself, or pouring forth all sorts of neurotically insecure thoughts and grumpy feelings, you want to help your partner continue to idealize you. On a first date, most people dress and act carefully so as to make the best impression they can. Perhaps if they continued to do this through many years of committed relationship and marriage, they would get better results.

QUIZ YOURSELF
Maintaining Relationships

1. Over the years, people in happy relationships say that their relationship _____; in fact, it _____ .
   - ⓐ is improving; does improve
   - ⓑ is improving; stays the same
   - ⓒ stays the same; does stay the same
   - ⓓ stays the same; improves

2. People want their partner to see them _____ in the little things and to see them _____ in general.
   - ⓐ accurately; accurately
   - ⓑ accurately; positively
   - ⓒ positively; accurately
   - ⓓ positively; positively

3. People who have a distress-maintaining attributional style make _____ attributions if their partner does something good, and _____ if their partner does something bad.
   - ⓐ external; external
   - ⓑ external; internal
   - ⓒ internal; external
   - ⓓ internal; internal

4. In order to have a happy long-term relationship with a significant other, it helps to have a _____ view of one's partner.
   - ⓐ negative
   - ⓑ neutral
   - ⓒ positive
   - ⓓ realistic

answers: see pg 449

Sexuality

Are love and sex the same thing? Undoubtedly, they overlap in many cases and are often intertwined. But a recent social theory proposes that they have two separate biological bases, which can sometimes result in confusion.

This theory was put forward by Lisa Diamond[131,132] based on her studies of female sexuality through time. Diamond's basic point is that humans form relationships based on two separate systems, which can reinforce each other or be in conflict. One of these is the attachment system (see the earlier section on attachment theory). This is an urge to connect and form close social bonds with a few individuals. The other system is the sex drive, based on the principles of mating. Diamond says that evolution probably shaped the sex drive to focus on the opposite gender (because only heterosexual sex can create children). The attachment drive, in contrast, is probably gender neutral. Most children form their first attachment to their mother, and later develop close friendships or attachments to other people, often primarily of their own gender.

If attachment and sexuality remained completely separate, there might be no problem, but most human beings mix intimacy with sex. The natural sex drive might dictate an initial preference for opposite-gender sex partners, but the attachment drive can promote intimacy between people of the same gender, and sometimes this can result in sexual attraction, too.

A curious pattern that Diamond observed in her data led her to conclude that attachment and sex were somewhat separate, independent systems that can produce these surprising effects. She found that many women identified themselves as heterosexual but then found themselves having a homosexual (lesbian) relationship. At that point, these women might identify themselves as lesbians. Crucially, however, the lesbian orientation often did not outlast the relationship: If the woman broke up with her girlfriend, she would not go looking for another woman, but instead would often find a man as her next romantic partner. Her affair with another woman was thus not a sign of a deep, fixed, unchangeably lesbian orientation. Instead, it was a result of her love and intimacy with a particular human being who happened to be a woman. She might have lesbian love with her, but when the relationship ended, she would revert to a heterosexual preference, and her next partner would be a man.

Diamond[133] concluded that if there is a "gay gene," love is not on it. Love comes from the attachment drive, and that drive is independent of gender. You can love both your mother and your father, both your son and your daughter, both your best male and best female friend. A gay gene (if it exists) would stipulate sexual orientation, so it might dictate which gender you would want to have sex with, but it would not limit your ability to experience love and intimacy with either gender. Attachment can lead to sexual desire, and sexual intimacy can promote attachment, so the two are not entirely independent—which is why sometimes people find themselves attracted to someone of the "wrong" gender, however they have defined it.

Nevertheless, love and sex are often deeply intertwined. Many people say that sex is best with a beloved partner. (The comedian Woody Allen joked that people should not disparage masturbation, because "it's sex with someone you love," namely yourself—the joke playing off the underlying recognition that love for others makes sex with them more enjoyable.) Not only does love improve sex. Sex also improves love. Careful research that tracked married couples over time found that their satisfaction with their relationship improves when they have sex, and this "afterglow" of loving each other more lasts for about two days.[134] Indeed, the stronger the afterglow, the happier the couple was with their relationship even six months later. Thus, couples who have sex at least every three days may be able to preserve their love better than others who do so less frequently. Indeed, many of the factors that gradually undermine marital love can be offset by having frequent sex.[135] Among other things, sex enables spouses to express their love for each other, and that can apparently keep love from fading.

Theories of Sexuality

Researchers have identified several basic theoretical approaches to sex. Especially popular and influential during the 1970s were **social constructionist theories**, which asserted that cultural forces and socialization shape how people assign meaning to their lives, with the result that sexual attitudes and behaviors vary widely based on culture.[136,137] It is no accident that this view was most influential during the peak years of the "sexual revolution" (1960s to 1970s). The sexual revolution had changed sexual attitudes and behaviors so rapidly in such a short time that it seemed as though almost any further changes would be possible. The rapid and extensive changes attested to the power of culture to shape the sex drive, contrary to views of sexual desire as innately programmed.

The social constructionist approach to sex acknowledges that there may be some biological foundations to sex, but most forms of sexual desire are seen as the result of cultural conditioning. Who wants to do what to whom (sexually) is seen as a result of social and political influences, including upbringing and media influence. Gender differences

social constructionist theories
theories asserting that attitudes and behaviors, including sexual desire and sexual behavior, are strongly shaped by culture and socialization

Constructionist theories emphasize that sexual attitudes and behaviors are shaped by cultural influences.

in sexuality are seen as highly changeable roles that are created by society to serve political or other goals. Feminist theory, which also reached a peak at this time, allied itself closely with the social constructionist approach to sex. In that view, women's sexuality was shaped by how men had long sought to control and oppress women; again, cultural influences (in this case, the influence of male-dominated culture on women) were seen as decisive.[138]

Evolutionary theory emerged in the 1970s and 1980s to provide a radically different view of sex. **Evolutionary theory** asserts that the sex drive has been shaped by natural selection and that its forms therefore tend to be innate.[139,140] Those patterns of sexual desire that led prehistoric men and women to have the most children would win in the evolutionary competition, with the result that people today are mainly descended from people who had those patterns of desire. For example, many prehistoric men might have been attracted to old women instead of young women, but old women usually do not have babies. The men who mated with old women would therefore not pass on their genes. As a result, today's men would all be descended from men who preferred younger women.[141]

The evolutionary approach sees gender differences as rooted in biology and hence as less flexible and less influenced by politics and culture than is suggested by the social constructionist view. One basis for gender differences lies in different reproductive strategies. People today are descended from those ancestors who raised the most children, but what succeeded best for one gender may not be the same as what worked best for the other. A woman can have only a few babies in her lifetime; each one occupies her body for about nine months and typically makes demands on her time and energy for years. Hence, a woman would by nature be cautious about sex and mating because each pregnancy is a huge investment for her. A man, on the other hand, can make a baby with only a few minutes of pleasure. Biologically, he could walk away and never expend any more time, effort, or other resources on that baby, yet still have passed along his genes. Hence, brief, casual, one-time sexual encounters will be more appealing to men than to women.[142]

Men can also be much less choosy than women about their partners, for the same reason. After all, the quality of your offspring depends on both your genes and those of your partner. If a woman gets pregnant by a low-quality man and then a better man comes along, she cannot make another baby for many months (by which time the better mate may be long gone). Hence, the most effective strategy for women would involve being cautious and choosy before consenting to sex. In contrast, if a man gets a low-quality woman

evolutionary theory theory of sexuality asserting that the sex drive has been shaped by natural selection and that its forms thus tend to be innate

A woman pays a higher biological price than a man for making a poor choice of sex partners, and so it behooves women to be more cautious than men about sex.

pregnant and then a better partner comes along, he can make a baby with the new woman almost immediately. Having sex with low-quality partners is thus more costly for women than for men.[143,144] As one sign of this, when researchers ask people what is the minimum IQ you would want to have in a sex partner, women give much higher numbers than men.[145] A recent and well-written blog by a prominent researcher reviewed large amounts of evidence to show that far more men than women wish to have sex with complete strangers.[146]

The same logic would predict differences in the desired number of sex partners. A woman can get pregnant only about once a year regardless of how many men she has sex with, whereas a man can make many different babies if he has sex with many different women. Moreover, for a woman, getting pregnant is not the only or main issue; she also wants a man to help provide for her and her children. (For example, if she has two small children and is pregnant with a third, she may find it hard to get food for her family by herself, especially if getting food requires chasing animals or climbing trees.) Hence, she may want to form a close relationship with a man whom she can trust to stick around and provide for her and her children. A woman with one intimate partner is more likely to receive male care over a long term than a woman who changes partners frequently. Nature may therefore have shaped women to desire sex mainly in the context of committed, lasting relationships. Men, in contrast, can be successful at passing on their genes by having sex with many different partners.

A third theoretical perspective on sexuality is based on **social exchange theory**, which seeks to understand social behavior by analyzing the costs and benefits of interacting with each other.[147,148,149,150] In this view, sex is a resource that women have and men want. Men therefore have to give women other resources in exchange for sex.[151,152] These resources may include money, attention, respect, love, and commitment. Male sexuality is not seen as having much value for social exchange, whereas most cultures place a high value on female sexuality. Most cultures do not place as much value on virginity or marital fidelity in men as in women. (Indeed, some commentators think that the marriage of Charles and Diana was partly shaped by pressure on Charles to marry a virgin, on the assumption that a future king should not marry someone who has already had other sex partners. It is doubtful that a female heir to the throne would be under similar pressure to marry a male virgin.) Likewise, in the extreme, women can sell sex for money—prostitution has been found all over the world in many different cultures—whereas that option is not widely available to men (except for a small number who, like women, cater to male customers).

Social exchange theory provides an economic perspective on sex. In essence, women's sexuality is the supply, and men's sexuality creates the demand. Moreover, people are hooked into the system, in the sense that their sexual decisions are affected by what other people in their peer group or community are doing. The "price" of sex, which is to say how much the man must invest before the woman consents to sex, may vary according to the standard laws of supply and demand. You may have noticed the difference if you have attended a school or college where one gender far outnumbers the other: The minority gender has much more influence. When men outnumber women (so that the supply of sex is lower than demand), the price is high: People have relatively little premarital or extramarital sex, and men must usually make a serious commitment before they can have sex. If a man doesn't want to make the commitment, he has

social exchange theory theory that seeks to understand social behavior by analyzing the costs and benefits of interacting with each other; it assumes that sex is a resource that women have and men want few alternatives available and will probably just not have much sex. In contrast, when women outnumber men (such as after a major war or in some low-income groups where many men have been lost to violence, prison, suicide, or outmigration), the price of sex drops, and women cannot usually demand much from the man in exchange for sex. If she refuses sex, he can just move on and get it from someone else. A recent major study of modern American campuses has shown that sexual norms have in fact shifted toward more readily available, low-commitment sex as the proportion of female students has increased.[153]

Sex and Gender

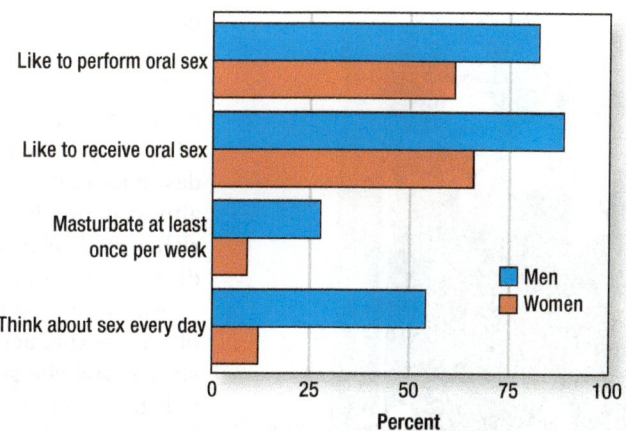

FIGURE 12.8
More men than women report high sexual desire on almost every measure, but some differences are bigger than others.

Stereotypes about gender and sexuality include the following: (a) Men want sex more than women. (b) Men separate love and sex more than women. (c) Women's sexuality is more natural, whereas men's sexuality reflects more cultural influence. (d) Women serve as "gatekeepers" who restrict the total amount of sex and decide whether and when sex will happen. Two of these are correct, and two are incorrect; can you pick which ones are which?

The first stereotype asserts that there is a gender difference in strength of sex drive. During the 1970s, sex was seen as an unmitigated good; to say that men had a stronger sex drive implied that they were somehow better than women. However, the notion that more sex is always better was soon discredited as AIDS, unwanted pregnancies, sexually transmitted diseases, and other problems surfaced. So it is perhaps possible now to take a fresh look at whether there is a gender difference in sex drive without worrying that some possible conclusions will be politically incorrect.

Nearly all the evidence supports the view that men have a stronger sex drive than women (see **FIGURE 12.8**). What behaviors do you think would reveal the strength of sex drive? Almost any form of overtly sexual behavior you might suggest is something men do more than women. Men think about sex more often, are aroused more often, desire sex more often, desire more sex partners, and desire more different kinds of sex acts than women. Men initiate sex more and refuse sex less than women. Men take more risks and expend more resources to get sex. Men want sex earlier in the relationship, want it more often during the relationship, and even want it more in old age. Men have more positive attitudes about their own genitals than do women, and they also have more positive attitudes about their partner's genitals than do women. Men find it harder to live without sex. (For example, some religious callings require people to give up sex, but all evidence suggests that men fail at this far more often than women.) And men rate their sex drives as stronger than women rate theirs. Essentially, every measure and every study point to greater sexual motivation among men.[154] Some experts still disagree,[155] though their work has come under fire for its methods.[156]

One of the largest and most consistent gender differences is in the desire for casual, uncommitted sex,[157] which is probably based in a simple desire to have sex with different partners. The term **Coolidge effect** was coined to refer to the sexually arousing power of a new partner. Specifically, a male animal would have sex and researchers would measure how long it took until he could become aroused again, as a function of having either the same partner or a new partner willing to copulate with him.[158] Males typically were more rapidly and more aroused by the new partner than by the familiar one.[159]

The term *Coolidge effect* is based on an amusing story about former U.S. President Calvin Coolidge, who was known for being a man of very few words. Once he and the First Lady toured a farm and were shown around separately. The First Lady noticed that the chicken area had many females but only one male. She inquired about this seeming imbalance, and the farmer assured her that the rooster was in fact able to perform sexually dozens of times every night. "Please point that out to Mr. Coolidge," she told the farmer. A short time later, when the president came to this area, the farmer dutifully said that the First Lady had specifically asked him to tell the president that the rooster was able to have sex over and over each night. "Same hen every time?" asked the president, and the

Coolidge effect the sexually arousing power of a new partner (greater than the appeal of a familiar partner)

Sexuality | 431

farmer answered that no, these prodigious sexual feats involved copulating with many different hens. "Point that out to Mrs. Coolidge," said the laconic president.

None of this should be taken to mean that women do not enjoy sex, or should not enjoy it. Enjoyment and desire are different. Also, at times (such as when newly falling in love) when women do desire sex almost as much as men, and certainly some women regularly desire more than some men. Many couples find that their sexual desires seem to match almost perfectly when they are falling in love, and they get married expecting a lifelong rich sexual relationship—but when the passionate phase wears off, they revert to their different baselines, and the husband usually wants sex more than the wife.

An Australian researcher persuaded a sample of married couples to keep daily reports of their sexual activities, for a book called *The Sex Diaries*.[160] She was hoping for steamy stories, and she got a few, but to her surprise the far more common report was that the wife had lost most of her interest in sex within a couple years after the wedding, while the husband continued to want to have sex. The researcher commented that many married women talk to each other about their clever little strategies for avoiding sex (e.g., starting an argument just before bedtime), without realizing how much anguish and disappointment their refusals caused the husbands. One husband had become so frustrated by his wife's rejection of his advances that he said he would wait until she initiated sex—with the result that they had had no sex for nine years! In such cases, one can feel sympathy for both persons. It is difficult for a wife to be subjected to frequent pressure to have intercourse when she does not want to. It is also difficult for a husband who never expected marriage to require him to give up most or all his sexual pleasure, especially if his wife both refuses most of his advances and disapproves of him finding other outlets such as masturbation or pornography.

Recent longitudinal studies of newlyweds confirmed that husbands and wives diverge over the early years of marriage[161]. Right after the wedding, husbands desired sex more than wives, but the difference was small. Over the five years, the husbands remained at the same level of desire, but on average the wives' desire diminished substantially. Moreover, both husbands and wives became less satisfied with the marriage, in direct correlation with the wife's declining interest in sex. (Husbands' desire for sex had no statistical relation to marital satisfaction.) One interpretation invokes attribution theory (Chapter 5): Husbands and wives attribute the wife's disinterest in sex to some problem in their marriage, perhaps often blaming each other. If they could realize that this is a normal pattern, they might be able to deal with it more constructively.

The second stereotype was that men can separate sex and love more than women. This stereotype probably arose from a valid observation, which was that men are much more interested than women in having sex without love. (The evolutionary theory, described earlier, offers a strong explanation for why this should be true.) Men do surpass women in seeking and enjoying sex without love.

On the other hand, love and sex can be separated in the opposite manner—enjoying love without sex—and it appears that women find this more acceptable. Thus, as to which gender can separate love from sex better, we have a seeming standoff: Men accept sex without love, whereas women accept love without sex. (Both genders, however, probably find love combined with sex to be the best.) To resolve this standoff, one national survey asked people whether they agreed with the statement "Love and sex are two different things."[162] More women than men agreed with this statement. In that sense, women separate sex and love more than men. Hence, the stereotype that men separate love from sex more easily than women is wrong.

The third stereotype has depicted women as closer to nature and men as closer to culture. This is relevant to the clash of theories we noted earlier: Is the sex drive mainly determined by culture, politics, and socialization, or by genes, hormones, and innate biological motivations? The answer does differ by gender—but in the way opposite to the stereotype.

To be sure, both nature and culture have an influence on every human being's sexuality. The balance between nature and culture can be expressed in terms of **erotic plasticity**, defined as the degree to which the sex drive can be shaped and altered by social, cultural, and situational forces. High plasticity indicates that culture can shape the person's sex

The Coolidge effect is named for an exchange between President Calvin Coolidge and First Lady Grace Coolidge about how a rooster can have sex with many hens (he can do it more times with different partners than with the same partner).

erotic plasticity the degree to which the sex drive can be shaped and altered by social, cultural, and situational forces

I'm ready when you're ready.

drive to a great extent, whereas a more "natural" and inflexible sex drive would have low plasticity.

Considerable evidence shows that women have higher erotic plasticity than men.[163,164] (It is not necessarily better or worse to have high plasticity.) Adult women often go through many changes in their sexual feelings and desires, whereas men remain much more constant through life.[165] Even switching back and forth between heterosexual and homosexual forms of sexuality is more common among women than men.[166,167] A man's sexual desires at age 20 are probably the same ones he will have at age 60, except for the natural diminishment due to aging. In contrast, a woman may have changed her desires and feelings several times along the way.[168,169] Another sign is that many social and cultural factors have a stronger influence on female than male sexuality. For example, highly educated women have quite different sex lives than uneducated women, and highly religious women have very different sex lives than nonreligious women—but for men, the corresponding differences are much smaller.[170,171] Thus, two powerful cultural forces (religion and education) affect female sexuality more strongly than male sexuality.

The difference in plasticity suggests a fairly basic difference in how the sex drive operates. We have seen that culture influences what things mean. Women's sexual responses typically depend on what sex means: who the partner is, what sex might signify about the relationship, what other couples are doing at similar stages, how she feels about the sexual partner, and what her sexual activity might signify about her as a person. Male sexuality seems much more to be a bodily, physical response. For example, a man who likes oral sex might well enjoy it whenever and wherever (and with whomever) the opportunity arises, but a woman who likes oral sex will only want it under certain circumstances and in contexts that carry the right meanings.

In short, the third stereotype is wrong, even specifically backward. Male sexuality is closer to nature and less affected by culture; women's sexuality is less biological and more closely tied to social and cultural meanings.

The fourth stereotype depicted women as the gatekeepers who restrict sex and decide whether and when it will happen. This is correct. Because men are not very choosy or cautious about sex, they are usually willing to have it under a wide variety of circumstances. Women are much more selective and hence become the ones who make the decision. Many findings confirm that women are the sexual gatekeepers. For example, a study of couples in various relationship stages[172] considered the category of "reluctant virgins"—people who had a dating partner and wanted to be having sex but were not having it because their partner did not consent. This category was filled almost entirely with men. The implication is that men were ready for sex fairly early, but whether sex happened depended on the woman's choice.

One revealing study surveyed dating couples at Pennsylvania State University. Researchers asked how many dates participants thought there should be before sex. They also asked each participant to estimate how many dates other people thought there should be before sex. The results were surprising: Nearly everyone thought that other people were leaping into bed faster than they themselves were. (For example, women thought that they would have sex after an average of 18 dates, but women typically estimated that other women would have sex after about 13 dates). Crucially, the researchers compared when the individual wanted to start having sex and when the couple actually did start having sex. The correlation between what men wanted and what happened was not significantly different from zero. In other words, the man's wishes were essentially irrelevant to whether or when the couple actually did have sex. In contrast, there was a very high correlation between the woman's preferences and the couple's activities.[173] Thus, a heterosexual couple starts having sex when the woman thinks it is appropriate; usually the man has been ready and waiting for some time.

Many dates involve eating together, and it is fair to assume that eating together usually precedes having sex together. To learn more about the effects of dieting on sex, read *Food for Thought*.

FOOD FOR *Thought*

Eating in Front of a Cute Guy

In the movie (and novel) *Gone With the Wind*, the heroine, Scarlett O'Hara, prepares for a dinner party by eating a meal at home. Asked about the seeming absurdity of eating just before dinner, she explains her behavior in self-presentational terms: A lady is expected to eat very little, so even though she is going to a dinner party, she will make the best impression if she hardly eats anything there. And because she is a hungry human being, the best way for her to refrain from eating the delicious food at the party is to be satiated before she goes!

Research has confirmed that people, perhaps especially women, eat sparingly in the presence of an attractive member of the opposite sex. In a laboratory study, college students ate a meal in the presence of an attractive male or female accomplice. Both men and women ate less in the presence of an opposite-gender than a same-gender accomplice.[174] Moreover, the reduced eating was correlated with the motive to gain social approval by doing what is socially desirable, for both men and women. For women, additionally, the restraint on eating was linked to the wish to seem feminine.

Thus, female eating in particular is tied to the pressures to please others and live up to cultural ideals of femininity. A more recent online study found that both heterosexual men and women said they would order less food (fewer total calories) when dining with opposite than same gender others—and the more attractive they found the other person, the less food they ordered.[175] (Non-heterosexual participants did not show significant differences in eating patterns depending on whom they imagined dining with.)

The importance of making a good impression on a potential dating partner was confirmed in other work where participants had the opportunity to eat snack foods (peanuts and M&M candies) while engaged in a get-acquainted conversation with a accomplice. The accomplice was either male or female. Half the time the accomplice was presented as a desirable and interesting person, but half the time the accomplice came across as something of a narrow-minded loser who had no hobbies or interests other than watching television, who had no career goals other than making money, and who claimed to already be in a romantic relationship. Female participants ate by far the least when in the presence of the attractive, desirable, and available man; they ate more in the presence of a woman or an unattractive man.[176] Thus, they seemed to restrain their eating for self-presentational reasons, mainly to make a good impression on a potential dating partner. The results were less clear-cut for male participants. They ate less in the presence of a woman than in the presence of a man, but the woman's availability and desirability did not seem to affect their eating. Men's restraint may be a matter of politeness and general norms that are activated by any woman, rather than a particular effort to make a good impression.

Thus, restraining one's food intake may be more important to women seeking to make a good impression on a potential dating partner than it is to men. This was confirmed in another study, in which female participants were given feedback suggesting that they had scored as either masculine or feminine in terms of their interests and personality. When women received private feedback that they were feminine, they ate less, consistent with the view that femininity operates as a cue to refrain from eating. But in another condition, the women were told that their male partners had seen their masculine/feminine scores. The women who thought their partner knew they had scored as "masculine" ate the lowest amount of any group in the experiment. Presumably they sought to reestablish their feminine image by eating lightly, thereby conforming to the cultural ideal of femininity.

Homosexuality

All these findings apply mainly to heterosexual relationships. In many respects, homosexual romance, sex, and love are quite similar to what happens between heterosexuals (for example, the desire for multiple partners is more common among male than female homosexuals),[177] but there are some unique aspects. For one, without clearly defined gender roles, homosexuals may feel freer to negotiate their roles in romance and sex without conforming to how society has trained people to act. Of course, this can also make things a bit more awkward, precisely because one does not have a culturally determined script. For example, if you are a heterosexual, you probably know how to act on a date with someone of the opposite sex, but if you were on a date with a member of your own sex, you would be constrained by fewer standard rules to say who should pay the bill, who should hold the door for whom, and so forth.

The basic fact that homosexuality exists all over the world and survives generation after generation poses a fundamental challenge to some of the major theories discussed so far. If sexuality is a product of cultural conditioning, how can homosexuality continue to exist? Most cultures have condemned homosexuality to varying degrees, and dominant cultures have often taken a fairly extreme position that homosexuality is sinful, illegal, and socially undesirable. If cultural socialization shapes sexuality, why is anyone a homosexual? On the other hand, if the sex drive is shaped by evolution based on natural selection and success at reproduction, then again homosexuality should have vanished long ago because homosexual sex does not produce children. How would a "gay gene" be passed along to future generations, if gay sex does not produce children?

At present we have no satisfactory answers. One intriguing theory, put forward by social psychologist Daryl Bem is known as EBE, for "exotic becomes erotic."[178,179] It is based on Schachter's theory of emotion,[180] discussed in Chapter 6, which holds that emotions arise when people have a bodily response of arousal and then put a label on it. Bem proposed that a specific gene for homosexuality does not exist but proposed that genes do contribute to temperament. Heterosexual development proceeds because boys and girls are temperamentally different and therefore play mainly with their own gender during childhood. To boys, therefore, other boys are familiar, whereas girls are different and "exotic." In adolescence, the boy may start to spend time around girls and will find himself nervous and otherwise aroused because they are different. He then learns to label this as sexual arousal. For heterosexual girls, the reverse applies: Boys seem different and exotic, so being around them is more arousing, and this arousal becomes labeled as romantic and sexual attraction.

Homosexuals, in Bem's theory, follow a similar process, except that during childhood they typically play with the other gender rather than their own. Some boys are temperamentally suited to prefer quiet play with girls rather than rough-and-tumble play with boys. When these boys reach adolescence, girls seem familiar, whereas other boys seem exotic. The nervousness arising from boys then gets labeled as sexual arousal. The reverse applies to girls, though as Bem noted, girls are more likely than boys to grow up having regular contact with and playmates of both genders.[181] (Bem suggested that women may be more bisexual than men precisely because they grow up around both boys and girls.)

At least one crucial step in Bem's theory—the labeling of nervousness as sexual arousal, leading to homosexual self-identification—has not yet been supported (or contradicted, for that matter) by data, probably because it is unethical to do properly controlled experiments that might transform someone from heterosexual to homosexual, or vice versa. Bem's theory fits well with the research findings available at the time he developed it (the 1990s), but at present it still rests partly on speculation. If Bem's theory does not turn out to be correct, then researchers must keep on looking for the mysterious combination of nature (genes, hormones) and social experiences that leads to homosexuality. Almost certainly there will be a combination of nature and nurture. For example, if one identical twin is gay, then the odds are about 50% that the other twin is gay.[182] This is far above chance, which indicates that genes have something to do with it. But it is far short of a full explanation: If identical twins share 100% of their genes, then they should share 100% of genetic traits (such as eye color), whereas homosexuality is only shared at 50%. Social influences and personal experiences must explain the 50% of cases in which one twin is gay and the other is not.

Another reason to be cautious about Bem's theory is that it says that attraction is based on being different. We saw in Chapter 11 that friendship and other forms of attraction are more commonly based on similarity than difference (that is, "opposites attract" is not usually correct, whereas "birds of a feather flock together" is usually correct). It is possible that sexual desire is different, and indeed sexual attraction to the opposite gender is more common than attraction to one's own gender. Sexual desire may therefore be a special case. Still, more research is needed before psychology can claim to have a solid understanding of these matters.

Another possible explanation for the continued existence of homosexuality has been put forward.[183] The notion of a single "gay gene" is now largely discredited, but there is evidence from very large samples that homosexual attraction and activity are linked to a cluster of different genes. Crucially, follow-up work[184] shows that people who have some of those genes have more sex partners than other people, which would account for why those genes continue to be passed on, and thus why homosexuality continues to exist despite the fact that it does not produce offspring. To put this in very simple terms, a super-non-feminine man who has none of these genes and the associated traits might have trouble relating to women, whereas a man who has some of them can relate better to women and will have plenty of children—while the man who has a great many of these genes may be sexually attracted to men. More work is needed on this, but it at least offers a plausible explanation.

Challenging the Gender Binary

In recent years, researchers and society itself have begun to recognize that some people do not identify themselves as either male or female. These are a small minority, and the vast majority of people go through life with a secure and stable sense of themselves as definitely male or female. But for some, the gender listed on their birth certificate does not fit how they feel about themselves. For people whose identity does not match the sex they were assigned at birth, dysphoria can be reduced by changing physical appearance. Some examples include clothing, cosmetics, chest binding, and medical options like hormone therapy and surgical procedures. Other people withdraw altogether from society's simple two-category system and refuse to think of themselves as either male or female.

Life may be more difficult for people who identify as neither male nor female. Even just using the restrooms in a public building can be complicated, given that most bathrooms are clearly marked for either males or females. Transgender people (that is, people who do not identify with the gender listed on their birth certificate) report relatively high levels of discrimination, harassment, rejection, social isolation, and other forms of victimization.[185] Trans women of color especially have very low life expectancies. They do not become transgender or non-binary in order to protest or make trouble. Indeed, they (like almost everyone else) experience very little or choice or control over their gender or sexual orientation. Their relationship to their own bodies is often complicated, and some seek to gain or lose weight in order to avoid looking like popular gender-typical bodies, reflecting a fundamental tendency to be dissatisfied with their own bodies. Some of this reflects the attitudes of society, in which many people object to those who fail to conform to standard patterns of male and female. Experiencing harassment, discrimination, or other forms of disapproval lead to unhappiness and low self-esteem, which then translate into feeling bad about one's body.[186]

There are undeniably stresses and problems associated with being a man, and others associated with being a woman. But people who do not fit neatly into male or female categories have even more stresses and problems. At present, far too little is known about this minority of people. With further research, however, they can expand our understanding not just of their own experiences but of key and fascinating aspects of humankind—starting by the challenge they pose to the common assumption that gender is always just a matter of one or the other.

Extradyadic Sex

In the course of long relationships, many couples have some conflicts about sex. One person may want to try some sex act that the other doesn't, or one may simply want sex more often than the other. In theory, the logical solution might be to find another partner. After all, if your husband doesn't want to play tennis with you, you just find another tennis partner and tell your husband about it later. Alas, that approach doesn't seem to work so well with sex.

In most long-term romantic relationships, the two partners expect each other to refrain from having sex with anyone else. When one person violates that expectation, the other is likely to be upset, and the relationship may be damaged or may even break up. This chapter began with the story of Charles and Diana, and though their marriage may have had multiple problems, it seems likely that the frequent infidelities by both of them contributed to their difficulties and eventual divorce. Even the term *infidelity* conveys a value judgment of disapproval (which is why many researchers prefer more neutral terms such as extramarital sex or even the broader term **extradyadic sex**, which is not limited to cases involving marriage).

Some couples have an "open" relationship, by which they mean that they are permitted to have sex with other people. During the sexual revolution of the 1970s, during which many people aspired to have such relationships and even to participate openly in sex with other people, extramarital sex was not regarded as being unfaithful.

Rare or Common?

Different surveys have reported different rates of extramarital sex. Some conclude that nearly half of married people eventually stray;[187] other studies conclude that extramarital sex is quite rare. There are several reasons for the different numbers, but two of them are important. First, the rate of extramarital sex has probably changed. It may have been more common and more tolerated in the 1970s than afterward, especially when the herpes and AIDS epidemics became widely known. Second, different studies use different sampling methods, and people who volunteer to answer a survey about sex are more likely to report extensive sexual experience than people who do not volunteer.[188,189,190]

The most reliable numbers suggest that there is far less extramarital sex (indeed far less sex altogether) than you might think from movies, novels, TV shows, and celebrity news. According to the National Health and Social Life Survey, more than 75% of husbands and 90% of wives claim to have been completely faithful over the entire period of their marriage.[191] Using another well-constructed national sample, researchers concluded that 23% of men and 12% of women have ever engaged in extramarital sex (including in a previous marriage).[192] Even if these numbers are precisely accurate, the actual rates of infidelity may end up being a little higher because some people who have not yet had an affair will eventually do so. Still, that is not likely to make a huge difference, so one must assume that monogamy and fidelity are the norm. Estimates that half of married men have affairs[193] are probably not accurate. The truth is closer to 1 out of 3 or 4 husbands, and 1 out of 9 or 10 wives, has sex with someone other than the spouse while married. Moreover, many of these are one-time occurrences in the course of a long marriage. In any given year, more than 90% of husbands and wives remain sexually faithful to their spouses.

To be sure, all these data are based on self-reports (what people are willing to tell an interviewer or report on a questionnaire), and it is hard to rule out the possibility that people claim to be more faithful than they are. In recent years, DNA tests have begun to confirm that many children (between 5% and 15%, according to most experts on paternity testing) are not biologically related to the man they believe is their father, presumably because the mother conceived the child through extramarital sex.[194] If that many women actually have children as a result of secret affairs, then the total amount of extramarital sex by women is probably much higher than we have assumed, and higher than many women are admitting.

Evolutionary psychologists[195] have pointed out that having such affairs and duping the husband into raising the children as if they were his own is a strategy that makes good

extradyadic sex having sex with someone other than one's regular relationship partner

Men are often surprised to learn they are not related to their children.

sense from the (admittedly amoral) standpoint of passing on one's genes. Highly successful and attractive men may have the best genes, and so a woman can make the best offspring by conceiving a child with such a man, even if he is not willing to marry her. To receive long-term financial support and care, she may need to marry a different man who might not have such good genes, but if he believes her children are his, he will take good care of them and provide for them. It does appear to be true that millions of men in North America and Western Europe have been fooled into raising children who are not their own.[196] Some experts have proposed that for a woman to dupe a man into raising children who were secretly conceived via extramarital sex is more immoral than rape.[197]

Extradyadic Sex and Breakups

Extramarital sex is a risk factor for breaking up. That is, people who remain faithful are more likely to stay together than people who have sex with other partners.[198] This is true even for couples who have an "open marriage" or other understanding that permits extramarital sex.[199] In a national survey, 38% of men who had had extramarital sex had also gotten a divorce, whereas only 15% of the fully faithful husbands had divorced. Among women, the corresponding numbers were 20% and 8%.[200] Thus, having extramarital sex was associated with more than double the divorce rate, as compared to fidelity.

One cannot leap to the conclusion, however, that extramarital sex causes divorce. After all, researchers cannot randomly assign people to have or not have extramarital sex, which is the sort of research design needed for firm conclusions about causality (see Chapter 1). Some people may be deeply unhappy about their marriage and have an affair as a result of their dissatisfaction. The affair could therefore be a symptom rather than a cause of the marital unhappiness, and perhaps those people would have gotten a divorce even if they had not had an affair.

People often view their own infidelities (if they have committed them) as a result rather than a cause of the problems in their relationships.[201] Their partner's infidelities, however, are seen as an important cause leading directly to the relationship problems and even to the breakup. This finding probably reflects a self-serving attributional bias (discussed in Chapter 5): People see their own misbehavior as being caused by external factors and not producing bad consequences but see their partner's actions in a less favorable light; in short, they would prefer to blame the divorce on their partner's actions rather than on their own. Still, these data do suggest that the causal arrow can point in either direction: Marital problems can lead to infidelity, or vice versa. In a famous television interview, Diana attributed her marital problems to Charles's infidelities, but she neglected to mention her own. If she was like most people, she was quick to say that her partner's sexual activities with others had damaged the marriage, whereas her own outside sexual activities were merely a result of the problems in the marriage—in effect, blaming him but not herself for similar actions.

We also should not overstate the link. Affairs do not lead inevitably to breaking up. In fact, only a small minority of extramarital affairs lead to divorce.[202] Infidelity is a risk factor, but the risk remains fairly small. Still, the affair is often a bigger risk than people anticipate. One researcher found that many people in her sample began their extramarital affairs with the firm belief that they could control the new sexual involvement and that their marriage would not be affected.[203] Often they were wrong. In particular, many people find themselves falling in love with their extramarital sex partners, especially when they have sex repeatedly or on a regular basis over a period of months. The strong emotional involvement often develops into a threat to the marriage, indeed more than the sex itself. Even if the marriage survives, it may be damaged or shaken by one person's love for someone else.

These patterns fit several themes. We saw earlier in this chapter that looking at tempting alternative partners can lead to breaking up one's current relationship, and now we see that having sex or romance with other partners likewise puts the relationship at risk. Avoiding those temptations is thus one constructive strategy to help preserve a relationship. One theme of this book is that nature says go and culture says stop. It is apparently natural to feel tempted from time to time to admire or even pursue alternative partners, but people can learn to resist and overcome these temptations (as culture prescribes). Another theme is the importance of self-regulation for overriding antisocial impulses. Being happily married or attached does not mean that the automatic system is indifferent to other possible partners. Self-regulation (here, in the form of stopping oneself from pursuing other partners) is a big part of the work that goes into making a relationship succeed.

Extradyadic Activity in Dating Relationships

Infidelity has also been studied in dating relationships. In dating relationships "extradyadic relations" is defined as erotic kissing, petting, or intercourse with someone other than your steady dating partner, and studies have found that 71% of men and 57% of women had experienced this (either by doing it or having their partner do it).[204] Despite the high frequency of experiences, most people expressed low tolerance and a negative attitude toward such activity. Many people disapproved of such activities but occasionally engaged in them anyway. The self-serving bias was apparent there too. In this research, people rated their own extradyadic relations as less bad than their partner's. When asked how much the extradyadic relations had caused pain and suffering, only 9% of men and 14% of women said their own infidelity had hurt their partner a great deal. In contrast, 45% of men and 30% of women said their partner's infidelity had hurt them a great deal. As usual, people seem more willing to make excuses for their own misbehavior than for their partner's!

Jealousy and Possessiveness

In medieval Europe, there were relatively few police and courts, and the system of law enforcement was not equal to the task of maintaining order. If people misbehaved or committed crimes, it often fell to the community itself to take action. One common form of punishment for less serious crimes and offenses was called the *charivari* (French word) or *shivaree* (English word). The whole village would gather together at some crucial place, such as outside the house of the offender. They would bring pots and other items and bang them together to make a loud noise. They would also shout or chant insulting remarks and might make embarrassing sounds. The point was to humiliate the offender.[205] The charivari was used to punish adultery. If a wife had sex with a man other than her husband, and enough people found out, the village would stage a charivari.

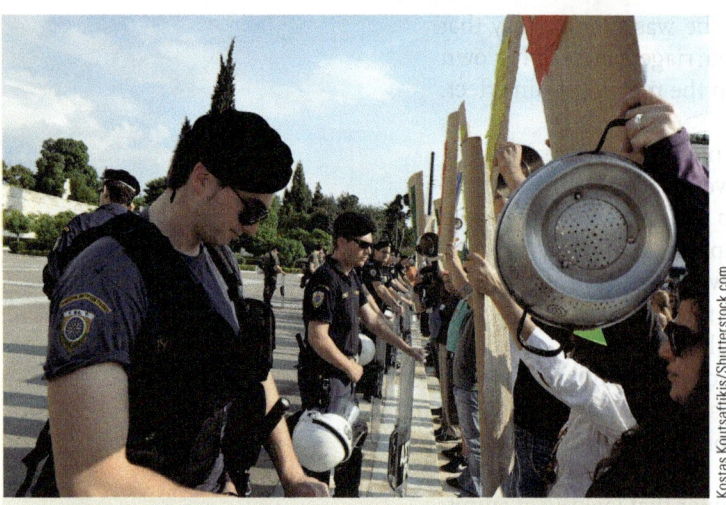

In medieval Europe, charivari involved banging pots and pans, as depicted here, to punish the husband of an adulterous woman, as well as less serious crimes. It is still practiced in some parts of the world today.

Ironically, though, the charivari was not generally used to punish the adulterous woman or her lover. Instead, the village would punish the husband. The implication was that he had not satisfied his wife sexually or exerted sufficient control over her behavior, so he needed to be punished. Apparently, if a man's wife had sex with another man, it was the husband's fault.[206]

The husband's humiliation, whether implicitly felt in the mere shame of his wife's infidelity, or explicitly recognized through the charivari, suggests an important link between jealousy and pride or self-esteem. When two people decide to have an extramarital affair, they often think mainly of themselves, and they may not intend any harm to their spouses. But if the affair comes to light, the spouses will have a variety of negative reactions, and these are often linked to a feeling of humiliation. Finding out that your spouse or romantic partner has been unfaithful is often a serious blow to your pride. Sure enough, people married to unfaithful partners have lower self-esteem than people married to faithful partners.[207]

Jealousy is a common response to partner infidelity, and many people feel jealous over even fairly minor signs that the partner might be interested in someone else, such as a flirtatious conversation at a party. Researchers distinguish jealousy from envy on the basis that jealousy is a fear of losing something that you have, whereas envy is a desire for something you do not have.[208]

Cultural Perspective

Some experts believe that jealousy is a product of social roles and expectations. In particular, some argue that Western societies have made men believe that women are their property, so men are jealous and sexually possessive of women. If only the culture taught people differently, the emotion of jealousy might disappear, according to this view.

Support for the cultural theory of jealousy came most famously from the anthropologist Margaret Mead's work *Coming of Age in Samoa,* though subsequent researchers have questioned her methods and conclusions and have even suggested that the handful of Samoans she interviewed were joking. Mead claimed that the Samoans did not have sexual jealousy or possessiveness. They allow their partners to share intimate interactions with others.[209] Similar observations have been made about Native American (Eskimo) cultures, in which male houseguests sometimes have sex with the hostess, with her husband's permission.

More recent work, however, has questioned those seemingly idyllic, nonpossessive attitudes. Sexual jealousy is found in all cultures and societies, although its forms, rules, and expressions may vary from one to another.[210,211] Eskimos do in fact have considerable sexual jealousy. The occasional sharing of a wife's sexual favors occurs only under certain circumstances, including consent by everyone involved and usually a desire to form a closer relationship between the two families. A cross-cultural study of 92 different societies and cultures found sexual jealousy in all of them, although again how they dealt with it varied.[212] In some, for example, a husband was permitted to beat or even kill his wife if he caught her having sex with another man, whereas other cultures prohibited such violent responses. Another survey found that different countries focused jealousy on different acts—for example, kissing someone other than your spouse elicits jealousy in some but is permitted in others—but again jealousy was found everywhere, and the various cultures were more similar than different.[213]

These findings suggest that society can modify and channel jealousy but cannot effectively eliminate it. Apparently, some degree of sexual possessiveness is deeply rooted in human nature. It is normal and natural to feel jealous if you find your partner has had sexual relations with someone else.

Evolutionary Perspective

The apparent universality of jealousy suggests that we should look to biological and evolutionary patterns to help explain it. Jealousy has a strong evolutionary basis, but the reasons differ somewhat for men as opposed to women.[214] These differences can be traced to the differences in male versus female reproductive systems. Both men and women supposedly want to pass on their genes, but the possibilities and dangers differ.

Men know that their wives can only have a few children, and normally just one at a time. Hence, a major threat to the man's reproductive goal is the possibility that another man might make his wife pregnant. Throughout most of history, it was difficult for men to know whether the children borne by their female partners were in fact the men's own offspring, so they faced a constant danger of raising the children of other men. The only solution was to keep strict control over the wife's sexual behavior. In various cultures, some men have kept their wives locked up and guarded, such as in a harem. Other men insisted that their wives wear iron chastity belts, which were originally designed as protection against rape but sometimes were adapted to help men retain confidence in their wives' fidelity. Such practices are largely absent in the modern Western world, though some men (and a few women) use threatened or actual physical violence to pressure their partners into remaining faithful. Because suspicions of jealousy can be unfounded, this violence sometimes hurts innocent victims. Even if the partner has been unfaithful (and, as noted above, DNA tests suggest that paternity fraud is still an important issue),[215] perpetrating or threatening physical violence against a romantic partner is immoral and illegal.

For women, the threat is different. If a woman's husband has sex with another woman, he has only expended a small quantity of sperm, and there is plenty more where that came from! The sperm itself is thus no great loss, and a single sex act does not therefore constitute much of a threat. On the other hand, the woman may depend on the man to provide her with food and other resources, as well as provide for her children. If he becomes involved with another woman, he may bestow some of his resources on her, which would leave the wife and her children in a poorer position. Men are well aware that women seek men who have resources, and this influences their behavior (see *Money Matters*). Hence, the greatest threat to the woman is the possibility that the man will become emotionally involved with someone else and therefore withhold these crucial resources.

This evolutionary theory about gender differences in sexual possessiveness was put to experimental tests in which students were asked a difficult question: Would it be worse for the person you love to have a one-time sexual encounter with another person without any emotional involvement, or for the person you love to have a lasting, emotionally intimate relationship with a member of your gender—but one that did not include sexual intercourse?

In the past men required women to use chastity belts to make sure they didn't have sex with other men.

MONEY Matters

Mating, Money, and Men

Women are attracted to men partly on the basis of thinking men will be generous providers. At some level, men seem to know this. Thoughts of women, sexuality, and mating change the way that men handle money.

One classic tradeoff involves now versus later. With money, people sometimes must choose between taking some money now versus getting a larger amount later. In research, as in life, the choice is often such that waiting for the larger amount will bring the best outcome in the long run, but when people feel money pressure in the heat of the moment, they will accept less in order to have it immediately. After men looked at sexy pictures or handled brassieres, they were more inclined to take the money now rather than waiting for more money later.[216]

The importance of sexual attraction was shown in a study where participants choose between receiving a modest amount of money (e.g., $15) right away and receiving a larger sum (e.g., $50) several weeks later. Most people in most conditions were willing to wait for the larger reward, but men who had looked at pictures of attractive women shifted toward taking the money right away.[217] No such shift was found if the men looked at pictures of unattractive women, or pictures of attractive or unattractive cars. Women looking at pictures of men likewise were unaffected. Thus, the urgency to have money now stems from male desire for attractive females.

The so-called ultimatum game (a popular research method) involves having one person decide how to divide payment between self and another person. The other person can then either accept the deal or refuse it, and if he or she refuses, neither person gets anything. The second person, "the responder," is thus sometimes faced with a choice between money and pride. For example, if both persons worked on the task, and the divider offers to split a $10 payment by keeping $8 and giving the responder only $2, the responder faces an unpleasant choice. The $2 is unfair and a bit humiliating, but then again it is arguably better to take $2 than nothing. In general, men tend to refuse such unfair offers in order to preserve their pride. But if the previous part of the experiment had involved having the men look at pictures of women in bikinis and lingerie, the men tend to swallow their pride and take the money.[218]

The underlying principle appears to be that when men are thinking about wooing women, they realize that money is important to have because women choose men on that basis. An early investigation showed that after men had looked at pictures of attractive women, they placed higher value on money and expressed greater ambition to become financially successful in life, as compared to men who looked at photos of older, relatively unattractive women.[219] Similar effects were found just by having men fill out the questionnaires in the presence of attractive women, as opposed to being in the presence of only other men. Thus, attraction to women makes men want money.

To be sure, neither men nor women were very happy with either possible scenario. But when forced to choose, they could do so—and their choices differed by gender. The majority of men (60%) objected more strongly to the sexual infidelity. In contrast, the women objected more to the emotional infidelity (only 17% objected more to the sexual infidelity).[220] These findings fit the evolutionary view: Male possessiveness focuses heavily on the sex act and is less concerned with intimate conversations, whereas female possessiveness emphasizes the emotional relationship and is less concerned with the sex act itself.

As is often the case, subsequent work has made the picture more complicated. In particular, men are often upset over both sexual and emotional relationships that link their wives or girlfriends with another man.[221,222,223] Also, some people assume that one form of infidelity will lead to the other, so the difference between sexual and emotional infidelity may not be as simple as the hypothetical dilemma posed by the experimenters makes it seem.[224] Nonetheless, researchers have reason to think that men and women do experience jealousy somewhat differently on average and may worry about different aspects of what their partners do with other lovers.

Causes of Jealousy

Jealousy thus seems to be a product of both the person and the situation. This impression is confirmed if we ask about the accuracy of people's jealous suspicions. To be sure, there are some cases of false jealousy; in particular, abusive individuals who have jealous rages and become physically violent toward their partners often are acting on suspicions that are completely unfounded.[225,226] Many jealous suspicions are, however, accurate.

In one large-scale investigation, researchers interviewed both husband and wife separately and then compared notes. Thus, they could ask the husband whether he believed his wife had ever been unfaithful and then check his response against his wife's actual (confidential) answer as to whether she had in fact strayed. They found that most suspicions of infidelity were justified. Only about 10% of wives' suspicions and 13% of husbands' suspicions were mistaken.[227] Thus, paranoid (false) jealousy is fairly unusual, although it certainly does exist. In marriage, at least, people who suspect their spouses of being unfaithful are usually correct. (The rates of unfounded suspicion were higher among couples who were living together without being married. For both men and women, slightly more than 20% of the people who suspected their cohabiting partners had been unfaithful were wrong.)

This is not to say that the partner always knows. In many cases, the partner falsely believed that the spouse had been faithful. Across various categories, these amounted to between 20% and 30% of unfaithful partners.[228] A study of college dating couples found that a large number were unaware of their partners' genuine infidelities.[229] Thus, a sizable minority of people manage to keep their affairs secret from their partners. But among spouses who suspected infidelity, most were correct. In any case, the evidence suggests that most but not all jealous suspicions have some valid basis.

Jealousy and Type of Interloper

The identity of the interloper (that is, the third person who has sex with one member of a romantic couple) also has an impact on how jealous people get. A common reaction to learning of a partner's infidelity is to disparage the interloper: "If you had to have an affair, did you have to choose such a loser?"[230] But such reactions tend to be irrational. After all, would you prefer your partner to have sex with someone who is not a suitable partner (and hence no competition to you)—or with somebody who is terrific? Remember, jealousy is essentially a response to a threat to your romantic attachment, so the less of a threat the interloper is, the less jealous you should feel. A loser won't steal your partner away, but a desirable, eligible person might.

This reasoning led some social psychologists to predict that people's jealousy would depend on how their own traits stacked up against those of the interloper. Their results fit very well with the view of jealousy as responding to threat. Even if the other person was reasonably talented, people were less jealous as long as those talents did not resemble their own. The worst jealousy occurred when the partner became involved with someone whose abilities exceeded their own, in the same area.[231,232] Thus, if you are a student in medical school, and your partner sleeps with an athlete, you may be unhappy about it, but your jealousy may remain at only a moderate level. Your jealousy would be much worse if your partner slept with someone who (like you) is also a medical student, and it will be worst of all if that other person has better grades than you or already has a medical degree. Similarly, if you are an athlete, then you'll be more jealous about your partner having sex with another athlete than with a medical student, and if the interloper's athletic skills surpass your own you will be extremely jealous.

Even the gender of the other person is important. Researchers found that men are less jealous and upset if their girlfriend has sex with a woman than with a man.[233] Probably this is because they believe that another man might steal the girlfriend away, whereas a woman would not be able to do so. Ironically, however, the same researchers found that women were less upset if their boyfriend had sex with another woman than with a man. In other words, both men and woman seem to object more strongly to a male interloper than to a female interloper. Women are regarded as less threatening. This fits the economic (exchange) theory of sexuality discussed earlier: In sex, women give something of value, whereas men take.

Social Reality

Thus far, however, we have not mentioned what may be the biggest factor of all in determining jealousy: the number of other people who know about the extradyadic sex.[234] If you learn that your partner has had a highly discreet, secret affair, you may well be upset, but your jealousy will not reach the highest levels. The worst situation is apparently to realize that you are the last person in your social network to learn about your partner's affair. By the time you find out, most of your friends already know about it, as do various other people. In simple terms, the more other people know about your partner's affair, the more upset and jealous you are likely to be.

Why does it matter so much what other people think? Probably this brings us back self-presentation and reputation. Your partner's affair makes you look bad. It makes you look like an incompetent lover who is unable to keep them satisfied. This is why other people's knowledge becomes so important. The more other people know about the affair, the more they know something that reflects badly on you. The textbook theme of "putting people first" entails that people care about what others think, and that applies very strongly to sex.

Researchers sometimes use the term **social reality** to refer to public awareness of some event.[235] If something happens but nobody knows about it, it does not have much social reality (although it has objective reality). It is therefore possible to go on with life afterward and more or less pretend that the whole episode never happened. In contrast, if other people know about it, it is harder to ignore it or put it behind you.

Social reality is thus an important determinant of jealousy. If many other people know about your partner's infidelity, you may find it difficult to continue with the relationship. You have to face them, after all, and you may wonder when you go out with your partner whether other people are looking at the two of you and thinking about your partner's infidelity.

Culture, Female Sexuality, and the Double Standard

All known cultures seek to regulate sex in some ways. The reason is not hard to guess. Unregulated sexual behavior produces all sorts of social turmoil and disruption: jealous partners committing acts of violence, collapsing marriages, unwanted babies, epidemics of sexually transmitted diseases. Some relevant evidence emerged from an anthropological study of one African society that was very permissive with regard to sex, so that both premarital and extramarital sex were common.[236] Although many individuals derived excitement and enjoyment from these activities, the social costs were huge. In particular, sexually transmitted diseases rendered around 40% of the woman unable to bear children—which was both a lasting source of heartbreak to these unfortunate individuals (and their husbands) and a significant disruption in how society would pass along resources from one generation to the next.

In sex, nature certainly says "go" whereas culture often pleads "stop!" These pleas have generally been directed more at women than at men, resulting in a widespread pattern called the cultural suppression of female sexuality. Why women? Different explanations have been put forward. One follows from what was said earlier about female erotic plasticity: Women's sexuality responds to cultural influences better than men's, so if a culture wants to control sexuality, it will be more successful focusing on women.

Another, more common explanation is that the cultural suppression of female sexuality is rooted in men's wish to control women. A related explanation has to do with **paternity uncertainty**—the fact that a man cannot be sure that the children born to his female partner are his. Aristotle once said, "Mothers are fonder than fathers of their children because they are more certain they are their own." To be sure, recent advances in DNA testing have finally made it possible for a man to be certain. Research with these techniques has consistently found that a great many women trick their husbands into supporting children fathered by an illicit lover, a fact that some feminists have regarded with pride,[237] though it has also spawned a men's rights movement that seeks to release divorced men from paying child support for children who are not genetically related to them. According to the paternity uncertainty view, men try to stifle female sexuality in order to make their wives less interested in having sex with other partners. This interpretation does not have much direct evidence, however.

Much discussion of the cultural suppression of female sexuality has focused on the so-called double standard of sexual morality. The **double standard** is defined as a pattern of moral judgment that says specific sexual behaviors (especially premarital sex) are acceptable for men but immoral for women. By the conventional view, this double standard is a mechanism by which men seek to control women's sexuality.

social reality beliefs held in common by several or many people; public awareness

paternity uncertainty the fact that a man cannot be sure that the children born to his female partner are his

double standard condemning women more than men for the same sexual behavior (e.g., premarital sex)

The view of the double standard as reflecting male control of women received a severe blow in one of the most comprehensive and influential reviews of published research on sexuality.[238] In every study that had found evidence of a double standard, women supported it more than men. Apparently, women are the ones who condemn other women while permitting men to do similar things. For example, a large national survey in 1965 (before the sexual revolution had gotten far) asked whether a woman who engaged in premarital sex was immoral.[239] "Yes" answers were received from 42% of men but from 91% of women (we will discuss this difference further in a few paragraphs). Thus, women condemned other women much more harshly than men condemned them. Subsequent work confirmed this in another way. Female college students were asked whether they themselves believed in the double standard (nearly all said no) and whether they thought others believed it (most said yes)—and if so, who these others were. Far more said the condemnation of women came from other women than from men.[240] (The rest said it came from both genders equally.)

In retrospect, evidence for the double standard has always been much weaker than is often assumed. A series of careful studies tried multiple ways of measuring it and found either no double standard or even a **reverse double standard**—that people condemned men more than women for the same sexual behavior.[241]

A methodological error in past work had created a false impression of widespread belief in a double standard. The error was rooted in the fact that women are generally less permissive than men about sexual morality in general. For example, national surveys from the 1930s to the 1950s asked people whether premarital sex was acceptable for everyone, acceptable for no one, or acceptable for men but not for women.[242] Only the last option indicates a true double standard, and only a tiny fraction of respondents endorsed it. But there was a gender difference: Women tended to say premarital sex was acceptable for no one, whereas men tended to say it was acceptable for everyone. Careless researchers were misled into thinking support for a double standard was widespread. They confused "being rated acceptable *by* men" as meaning "being rated acceptable *for* men." In reality, most men and most women made judgments that showed no double standard.

Thus, the double standard is weaker than assumed and, more surprisingly, is supported by women more than men. Moreover, the importance of women and the female community in restraining sex is not limited to these few moral judgments. In fact, the cultural control of female sexuality comes primarily from women, and the pressures on women to restrain their sexual activities come from other women. Thus, it is women who punish the sexually active woman or girl with gossip and a bad reputation, who promote religious or moral injunctions to refrain from sex, who tell girls about the dangers of sex and pregnancy, and who in some cultures support and carry out surgical procedures that impair the woman's physical capacity to enjoy sex.[243]

Why would women seek to restrain each other's sexuality? The answer is probably based neither on pathology nor on self-destructive motives, but rather may lie in a simple and rational response to women's situation. The social exchange theory of sex (described previously) offers a clear explanation. For most of history, women have lacked opportunities to acquire wealth, education, power, and other resources to provide themselves with a good life. A woman's sexuality has often been the main resource she had with which to bargain (by making a favorable marriage) for access to the good life. It was therefore important for each woman to maintain as high an exchange value as possible for her sexuality. As with any resource, the price depends on supply and demand; restricting the supply raises the price. To the extent that the community of women could restrain each other's sexuality, they all stood to benefit from the higher value.

When men can get sex without offering much in return, women derive relatively little benefit from their sexual favors. In contrast, when sex is not readily available, men may offer women a great deal in return for sex, including love and commitment, long-term financial support, and other resources. Such offerings have been crucial to women's well-being in cultures and historical periods in which women were unable to provide for themselves in other ways. Rather than being passive dupes or victims of culture, women appear to have responded in rational ways so as to make the best of their circumstances. Putting pressure on each other to restrain sexual behavior has sometimes been in women's best interests.

reverse double standard condemning men more than women for the same sexual behavior (e.g., premarital sex)

QUIZ YOURSELF: Sexuality

1. **Which theory proposes that sexual attitudes and behaviors are the result of cultural forces and socialization?**
   - (a) Attachment theory
   - (b) Evolutionary theory
   - (c) Social construction theory
   - (d) Social exchange theory

2. **When men outnumber women, the price of sex _____.**
   - (a) decreases
   - (b) increases
   - (c) increases then decreases
   - (d) stays the same

3. **Bjorn loves his wife, but he discovers that she has been unfaithful to him. To make matters worse, everyone knows she has been unfaithful to him. The common knowledge that Bjorn's wife has been unfaithful to him is called _____.**
   - (a) double standard
   - (b) reverse double standard
   - (c) social construction
   - (d) social reality

4. **Waldo believes that premarital sex is acceptable for men but unacceptable for women. This belief illustrates _____.**
   - (a) double standard
   - (b) erotic plasticity
   - (c) reverse double standard
   - (d) social construction

answers: see pg 449

What Makes Us Human: Putting the Cultural Animal in Perspective

Sexual attraction and mating are found throughout nature, but they take on new and added dimensions among human beings. For one thing, long-term monogamous mating is much more common among human beings than among other species, especially apes and other primates. The ability to stay sexually faithful to one partner for decades appears to be quite specific to humans.[244,245]

Culture helps. The view that humans are "naturally" monogamous is contradicted by data indicating that polygamy has been common in many societies and cultures. Only after some historical struggles did most modern cultures ban polygamy and insist that you can only marry one spouse at a time. Were people not thus influenced by culture, monogamy would be less common.

The effect of human culture on love and mating can perhaps be most plainly seen in divorce. If two animals have a sexual relationship that fails to satisfy them, especially if they frequently annoy and aggravate each other, they can dissolve their relationship just by walking away. Human beings require the culture's permission, which often entails hiring lawyers and negotiating for months over what will happen to their jointly owned property and their children.

The cultural control of close relationships extends far beyond divorce, of course. Many laws regulate what goes on in the family, affecting everything from hitting family members to bequeathing them money. Culture also shapes relationships via informal influence, such as how relationships and sex are depicted in the mass media, which in turn helps shape how people treat each other. No other species has ever changed or reinvented its gender roles to the extent that human beings have done. In general, these changes have been positive: Unlike some animals, for example, humans are culturally discouraged from eating or beating their offspring.

Sex itself has been profoundly affected by culture. Formal laws have prohibited various sex acts (for example, oral and anal sex have been illegal in many cultures) and various kinds of sex partners (same-gender partners, relatives, or underage children). The mixture of economic, moral, and religious factors that created the cultural control of female sexuality is almost impossible to imagine in any other species. Patterns of sexual activity changed in many ways during the 20th century, with its so-called sexual revolution(s), including vast increases in premarital sex and oral sex. Among the many factors contributing to these changes were the improvements in birth control technology. Only cultural (human) animals have been able to invent new ways of controlling pregnancy and to change their sexual norms on that basis.

Perhaps the biggest difference is in human intimacy. Having mastered language, people have been able to create complex, intricate selves. Forming a close relationship often begins with a great deal of talking, by which people reveal and disclose their inner selves to each other. Indeed, one theory of language has proposed that the reason humans evolved to use language was to promote close relationships[246] because talking enabled people to get to know each other and stay connected much more efficiently than the methods used by other primates. It is almost impossible to imagine a human marriage or other close relationship without language and conversation. The slow building of intimacy by talking to each other for years is an important aspect of the long road that people follow to form bonds with each other.

The seemingly endless human fascination with love and sex has also produced a steady stream of cultural activities to depict and celebrate them. The basic inclinations toward sex and mating may be rooted in biology and shared across many species, but in human art they are transformed into something grander and more meaningful. Most of the music you hear consists of songs about love. Most books and movies have some coverage of love, not even counting the pornography industry that finds a ready market for simple depictions of sex. In fact, if you took away love (including sex) and violence (including crime), it is hard to imagine the American film industry surviving at all! Poetry too has long favored themes of love and romance, whereas no baboons or turtles write love sonnets to their sweethearts.

Attractive nude young women (and men) have been favorite subjects for painters and sculptors. In short, much of human culture is about close relationships, love, and sexuality.

One of the most interesting and curious facts about human sex is that most people use a face-to-face position for intercourse. Most other mammals, including the great apes who are believed to be humans' closest biological relatives, rely on having the male enter the female from behind. Why are humans different? Possibly the more upright human posture for walking contributed by changing the direction of the internal organs. A more social explanation, however, points to something special and wonderful about human nature. The face-to-face position enables lovers to look into each other's eyes, kiss each other on the lips, and say sweet things to each other during sex. In that way, it is more compatible with promoting intimacy and sharing deep feelings of love. Quite possibly the earliest humans who began to make love in this position found that they were able to transform sex into a more meaningful act and one that would, by increasing love and intimacy, help build stronger families—and so perhaps their offspring fared better than people who still favored the older, animal positions for sex. If so, then the combination of love, intimacy, and sex is a crucial part of what makes us human.

CHAPTER 12 SUMMARY

What Is Love?

- Good relationships are good for you. Married people (especially happily married people) live longer, healthier lives than single or divorced people.
- Passionate love (also called romantic love) refers to having strong feelings of longing, desire, and excitement toward a special person.
- Companionate love (sometimes called affectionate love) refers to a high level of mutual understanding, caring, and commitment to make the relationship succeed.
- Passionate love is found all over the world, but the forms and expressions of romantic passion vary significantly from one culture to another.
- Companionate love is important for a long, happy marriage or a stable, trustworthy, lasting relationship.
- Married people have sex more often and more satisfyingly, but single people spend more time at each sexual episode and have more different partners.
- Sternberg proposed that love is composed of passion, intimacy, and commitment, and that these three ingredients can vary in strength in different relationships.

Different Types of Relationships

- Exchange relationships are based on reciprocity and fairness.
- Communal relationships are based on love and concern for each other, without expectation of direct, equal repayment.
- Communal relationships are more desirable in intimate relationships, but exchange relationships are more powerful for driving progress and increasing wealth in larger groups.
- The four kinds or styles of attachment are
  - Secure attachment, characterized by comfort with intimacy and no excessive fears of abandonment.
  - Dismissing avoidant attachment, characterized by avoidance of intimacy and discomfort with close relationships while viewing partners as unreliable, unavailable, and uncaring.
  - Fearful avoidant attachment, characterized by avoidance of intimacy and discomfort with close relationships while viewing the self as unlovable.
  - Preoccupied (or anxious/ambivalent) attachment, characterized by excessive desire for closeness to the point of desiring to merge with the partner, and worry about abandonment.

- Self-love and narcissism may not be beneficial to good relationships, but self-acceptance may help one get along with others.

Maintaining Relationships

- People in good relationships often think their relationships are getting better and better, but research suggests they actually stay at the same (good) level.
- The three factors of the investment model are
  - Satisfaction with the partner.
  - Quality of alternative partners.
- Investment (sunk costs) in the relationship.
- The relationship-enhancing style of attribution involves attributing good acts to the partner's inner qualities and attributing bad acts to external factors. The distress-maintaining style of attribution is just the opposite.
- People in love generally hold idealized versions of each other.
- Relationships can thrive when couples remain on their best behavior with each other.

Sexuality

- Diamond's work suggests that attachment/love and sex are two separate psychological systems in humans, so love and sex don't always match.
- Social constructionist theories of sex assert that sexual attitudes and behaviors vary widely based on culture and learning. These theories seek to understand how personal experiences and cultural influences shape sexual desire and behavior.
- Evolutionary theory emphasizes that the sex drive was shaped by natural selection. Evolutionary psychologists seek to understand innate patterns of sexual desire and behavior.
- The social exchange theory views sex as a resource that women have and that men want and are willing to exchange other resources for.
- On average, men have a stronger sex drive than women.
- The stereotype that men separate love from sex more easily than women is wrong.
- Women show more erotic plasticity than men, meaning that women's sex drive can be shaped and altered by social, cultural, and situational forces, whereas men are more driven by innate, biological needs.
- Women act as the gatekeepers who restrict sex and decide whether and when it will happen.
- Sexual jealousy is found in all cultures and societies, although its forms, rules, and expressions may vary from one to another, suggesting that some degree of sexual possessiveness is deeply rooted in human nature.
- Jealousy can focus on either a sexual or an emotional connection to an outsider. Men may focus more strongly on the sexual aspect than women.
- The more other people know about your partner's infidelity, the more upset and jealous you are likely to be.
- All known cultures seek to regulate sex in some ways.
- Paternity uncertainty refers to the fact that a man cannot be sure that the children born to his female partner are his (at least until recent advances in DNA testing).
- The sexual double standard is defined as a pattern of moral judgment that says specific sexual behaviors are acceptable for men but immoral for women. It is supported more by women than by men.
- Across different cultures, it has sometimes been in women's best interests to put pressure on each other to restrain sexual behavior.

What Makes Us Human? Putting the Cultural Animal in Perspective

- Long-term monogamous mating is much more common among human beings than among other species.

key terms

attachment theory 416
commitment 411
communal relationships 414
companionate love (affectionate love) 408
Coolidge effect 431
dismissing avoidant attachment 417
distress-maintaining style of attribution 423
double standard 444
erotic plasticity 432
evolutionary theory 429
exchange relationships 414
extradyadic sex 437
fearful avoidant attachment 417
intimacy 410
investment model 421
passion 410
passionate love (romantic love) 408
paternity uncertainty 444
preoccupied (anxious/ambivalent) attachment 416
relationship-enhancing style of attribution 423
reverse double standard 445
secure attachment 416
self-acceptance 419
social constructionist theories 428
social exchange theory 430
social reality 444

quiz yourself ANSWERS

1. What Is Love? p. 413
   answers: 1.c 2.d 3.d 4.d
2. Different Types of Relationships p. 419
   answers: 1.c 2.b 3.a 4.a
3. Maintaining Relationships p. 427
   answers: 1.b 2.b 3.b 4.c
4. Sexuality p. 446
   answers: 1.c 2.b 3.d 4.a

PREJUDICE AND INTERGROUP RELATIONS

13

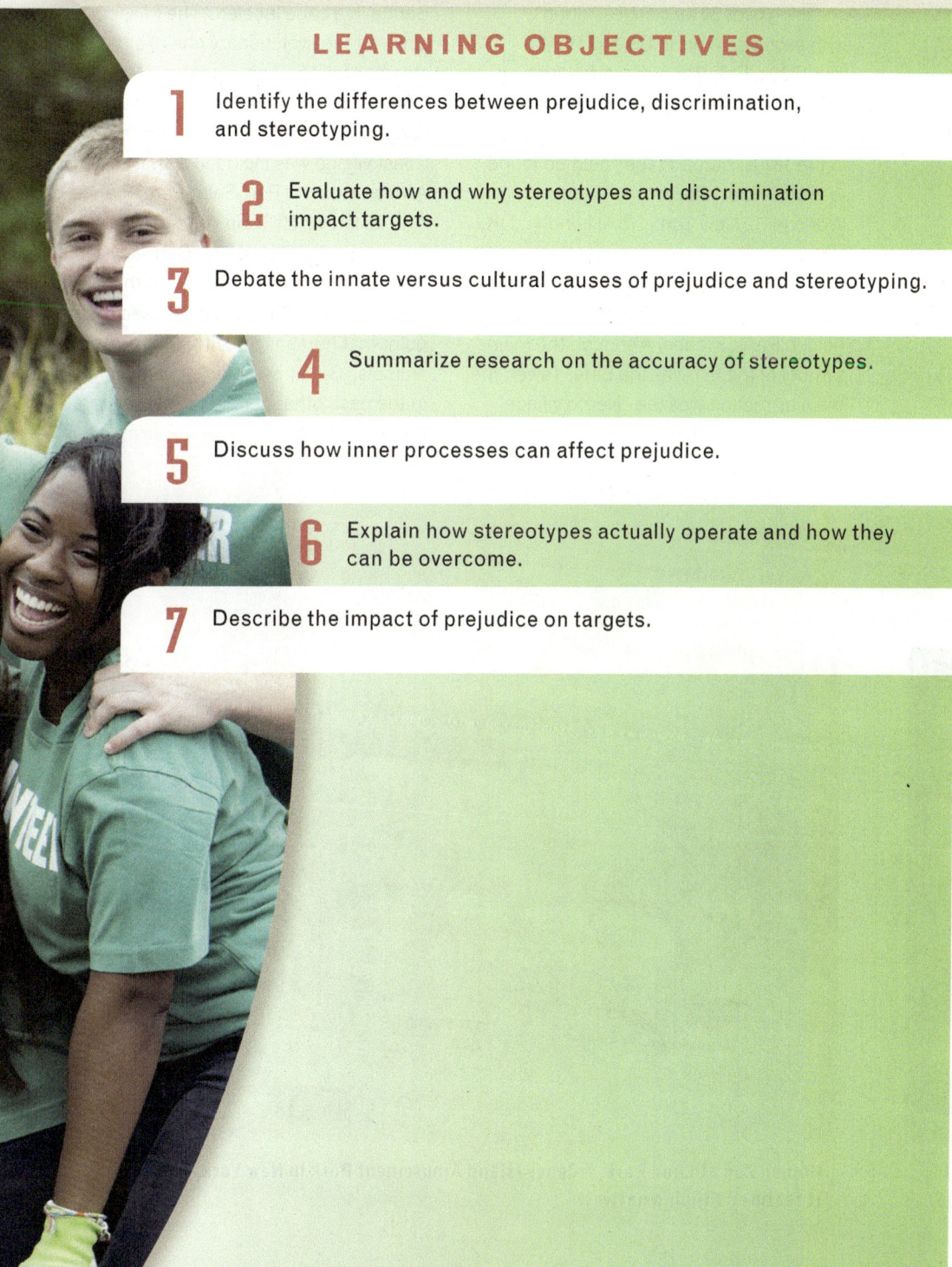

Ariel Skelley/Blend Images/Getty Images

LEARNING OBJECTIVES

1. Identify the differences between prejudice, discrimination, and stereotyping.
2. Evaluate how and why stereotypes and discrimination impact targets.
3. Debate the innate versus cultural causes of prejudice and stereotyping.
4. Summarize research on the accuracy of stereotypes.
5. Discuss how inner processes can affect prejudice.
6. Explain how stereotypes actually operate and how they can be overcome.
7. Describe the impact of prejudice on targets.

MONEY MATTERS
Racial Discrimination in Sports: Paying More to Win
454

FOOD FOR THOUGHT
Prejudice Against the Obese
461

THE SOCIAL SIDE OF SEX
Roots of Anti-Gay Prejudice
464

TRADEOFFS
Competition Versus Cooperation
468

WHAT MAKES US HUMAN?
Putting the Cultural Animal in Perspective
490

Most people are familiar with zoos in which animals are confined in pens and cages. People might be less familiar with the long history of human zoos in which Africans and conquered indigenous peoples were also kept in pens and cages as if they were animals.[1] The euphemistic term for these human zoos is "ethnological expositions." The crude term for them is "freak shows."

Regardless of what they were called, real people were "on display" for others to see. Human zoos have a very long history.

Christopher Columbus, the European who discovered the New World, in 1493 kidnapped indigenous Americans and brought them to the Spanish court. In the 16th century, the Aztec ruler Montezuma displayed humans such as dwarves, albinos, and hunchbacks, along with animals in his zoo in Tenochtitlán (now central Mexico City).[2] Also in the 16th century, the Italian Cardinal Hippolytus Medici had a collection of "Barbarians" speaking over 20 languages, along with exotic animals in his zoo.[3] In the mid-1800s, P. T. Barnum (co-founder of Barnum & Bailey Circus) had public displays of "human freaks" in his circus. In the 1870s, human zoos could be found in many major cities of the Western World (e.g., New York, USA; London, UK; Hamburg, Germany; Antwerp, Belgium; Barcelona, Spain; Milan, Italy; Warsaw, Poland).[4] In 1889, the World's Fair was held in Paris, France. Although the main symbol of the fair was the Eiffel Tower, the main attraction was the "Negro village" (village nègre) where 400 Africans were displayed for over 6.3 million visitors to see.[5] In 1896, the Cincinnati, Ohio Zoo invited 100 Native Americans from the Sioux tribe to establish a village at the zoo, where they lived for three months.[6] In 1904, the main exhibit of the World's Fair in St. Louis, Missouri was a display of "primitive" peoples from the Philippines, as well as the Apache Chief Geronimo.[7] In 1906, the Bronx Zoo in New York displayed the Congolese pygmy Ota Benga in a cage labeled "The Missing Link" (in the evolutionary chain) along with chimpanzees and an orangutan.[8] In 1958, the World's Fair in Brussels, Belgium, had a Congolese village.[9] In 1994, an Ivory Coast village was included as part of an African safari in Port-Saint-Père, France.[10] And as late as 2005, an African village was included in the Augsburg, Germany zoo, despite widespread protest that the village was racist.[11] This book has focused on the point that humans are different from other animals. But apparently, to many humans in the past, other people were less than fully human. ●

Ota Benga, a Congolese pygmy, at the Bronx Zoo in New York in 1906.

Human Zoo at Luna Park, a Coney Island Amusement Park in New York, 1905. It featured Filipino natives.

ABCs of Intergroup Relationships: Prejudice, Discrimination, and Stereotypes

Prejudice is derived from the Latin term for prejudging. It refers to evaluating a person or multiple persons based on membership in a group or category of people. Thus, prejudice involves attitudes toward categories of people, which can be used to judge individuals without being based on the individual's actions or personal traits.

Perhaps the best-known form of prejudice is **racism**, which is defined as having negative views toward people based on race (which is often, though not always, considered a biological category). Racism can take the form of overt, blanket statements of disliking and disparaging groups. In some settings, people are uncomfortable about their prejudices. This creates a pattern that some social psychologists have dubbed **aversive racism**.[12] Aversive racists simultaneously hold egalitarian values and negative (aversive or unpleasant) feelings toward people of other races. They believe in racial equality and equal opportunity, but they also feel uncomfortable around minorities and try to avoid them when possible. For example, when white Americans are talking to black Americans, they may sit farther away, maintain less eye contact, talk in a less friendly manner, and end discussions sooner than they do when talking to other white Americans.[13] Such a pattern may indicate that the white people were nervous and uncomfortable, but it could also mean that they felt inner conflict about having negative views toward black people.

Prejudiced feelings sometimes lead people to discriminate against others. **Discrimination** refers to unequal treatment of different people based on the groups or categories to which they belong. An example of discrimination against Native Americans would be the practice of keeping them on reservations instead of letting them live wherever they want. Prejudice can exist without discrimination, if people hold negative views but don't act unfairly. Sometimes discrimination can occur without prejudiced feelings. For example, suppose that a state police force sets a requirement that its officers must all be at least 6 feet (1.83 meters) tall, because it believes that "height equals might" and that criminals won't take short officers seriously. This height requirement would discriminate against women, Hispanics, and Asians because they are often shorter than 6 feet tall. To read about discrimination in paying athletes of different races, see the *Money Matters* box.

Stereotypes are beliefs that associate groups of people with certain traits. Stereotypes refer to what we believe or think about various groups. They can be good or bad. For example, one might stereotype older people as wise (good) or as slow (bad). Stereotypes are sometimes difficult to change. One reason is that people tend to throw exceptions to the stereotype's general rule into a separate category, called a **subtype**.[14] For example, if a man meets a woman who doesn't fit the stereotype of the warm and nurturing type, he can either discard or modify his stereotype of women, or he can put her into a subtype, such as "career woman" or an "athlete."[15]

Prejudice, discrimination, and stereotypes are the ABCs of intergroup relationships. The **A**ffective component is prejudice, the **B**ehavioral component is discrimination, and the **C**ognitive component is stereotyping.

The human mind seems naturally inclined to sort objects into groups rather than thinking about each object separately. This process of **categorization** makes it much easier to make sense of a complicated world. The process of sorting people into groups on the basis of characteristics they have in common (such as race, ethnicity, gender, age, religion, or sexual orientation) is called **social categorization**. As we saw in Chapter 5, people tend to be "cognitive misers," which means they generally think in easy, simple ways that minimize mental effort. Categorizing people is an easy and efficient way of simplifying the world and reducing mental effort. When people form an impression of a person, they typically use what personal information they have about the individual, but invoking stereotypes is a relatively easy way to fill in gaps in this knowledge.

prejudice a negative feeling toward an individual based solely on his or her membership in a particular group

racism prejudiced attitudes toward a particular race

aversive racism simultaneously holding egalitarian values and negative feelings toward people of other races

discrimination unequal treatment of different people based on the groups or categories to which they belong

stereotypes beliefs that associate groups of people with certain traits

subtypes categories that people use for individuals who do not fit a general stereotype

categorization the natural tendency of humans to sort objects into groups

social categorization the process of sorting people into groups on the basis of characteristics they have in common (e.g., race, gender, age, religion, sexual orientation)

MONEY Matters

Racial Discrimination in Sports: Paying More to Win

Many people argue that racial integration and diversity produce value for organizations. The evidence behind this claim has been mixed at best. But recent analyses of the economics of sport have begun to show that racial discrimination is in fact costly for some teams.

One of the best studies on the cost of discrimination in sports involved English football (soccer) teams.[16] These teams provided a useful test because teams were relatively free to hire athletes as they saw fit, which included the option of discriminating by race. There were also no salary caps, revenue sharing, and other financial regulations that distort the economic marketplace. In the 1970s, black players began to enter the major league, and some teams hired them eagerly, whereas others chose not to do so. Given the relatively free market for talent, the result was that black players got lower salaries than white players, regardless of ability. (This was the case because a player could get a higher salary when more teams wanted to bid for his services.) Another way of putting this is that black players cost less than white players, at any level of ability. It did not matter whether white or black players were better overall. All that mattered was that, whatever the player's talent level, his salary would be lower if he was black, so the team that hired him instead of a white player in effect got a bargain: a better player for the same money.

In general, teams with higher payrolls get better players and therefore win more games. But when the researcher analyzed teams for the number of black players they had, he found that using more black players allowed teams to win more games for the same amount of money. A team that had no black players would have to pay 5% more overall in player salaries to achieve the same win–loss record as a team that did have black players.

Thus, organizations do pay a price for racial discrimination. Hiring the best talent available regardless of race is the most effective strategy. To refuse to hire based on race means paying more or winning less, or both.

Modern objections to stereotyping and prejudice go far beyond the chance of an inaccurate prediction, of course. Today, people object to stereotyping and prejudice even if the stereotypes are reasonably accurate.

The view that prejudice and stereotyping are morally wrong is a product of modern Western culture. Several centuries ago, Western culture shifted to the view that each person had a right to be judged as an individual, regardless of their category. Prior to that, there was greater acceptance of judging people based on categories and groups. Even legal judgment followed such principles. For example, if a man rebelled against the local ruler, the ruler might have the man's entire extended family imprisoned or executed.[17] Nowadays, punishing the whole family for one individual's crime would seem unjust and unfair.

Women are stereotypically warm and nurturing. When a man sees a woman who does not meet this stereotype, such as these female Islamic State (IS) fighters, he can either discard or modify his stereotype of women, or he can put them into a subtype.

When viewing an ambiguous scene with a possibly dangerous man who may or may not be armed, participants are more likely to shoot at the man if he is black than if he is white.

Biased judgments based on stereotypes and prejudices are not only unfair and immoral; in some cases, they can have lethal consequences. For example, if a police officer possessed the stereotypic expectation that black men are more likely to be violent and aggressive than white men, it could influence split-second decisions whether to shoot black suspects, with tragic consequences. Indeed, research using computer simulations (similar to video games) has found that people, whether police officers or college students, are more likely to mistakenly shoot at unarmed black suspects than unarmed white suspects.[18,19,20,21,22,23] That is, when a research participant sees an ambiguous scene with a possibly dangerous man who may or may not be armed, the participant is more likely to shoot at the man if he is black than if he is white (even if he is not actually armed). Although it is tempting to treat this as an instance of anti-black prejudice among white people, the bias is not confined to white research participants: African Americans are also more likely to shoot at the possibly threatening man if he is black than if he is white.

One big difference between sorting people and sorting objects is the level of emotional involvement. For example, when sorting people into gender categories (e.g., male, female, non-binary), the sorter belongs to one of the categories and feels emotionally attached to it. In contrast, someone who sorts fruits into apples and oranges is probably not emotionally attached to these categories. **Outgroup members** ("them") are people who belong to a different group or category than we do. **Ingroup members** ("us") are people who belong to the same group or category as we do.

Most people assume that outgroup members are more similar to each other than ingroup members are to each other. This false assumption, known as the **outgroup homogeneity bias** is reflected in statements such as "They're all alike" and "If you've seen one, you've seen them all!"

In fact, "They all look alike." People see outgroup members as even looking similar to one another. Have you ever felt embarrassed because of confusing two people of a different racial group than your own? If so, you're not alone. Research has shown that eyewitnesses are more accurate at identifying people of their own racial group than at identifying people of a different racial group.[24,25] However, when outgroup members are angry, the opposite is true.[26] Angry outgroup members are easier to identify than are angry ingroup members. This finding reflects the importance of keeping track of

outgroup members people who belong to a different group or category than we do

ingroup members people who belong to the same group or category as we do

outgroup homogeneity bias the assumption that outgroup members are more similar to one another than ingroup members are to one another dangerous people. Angry members of another group may pose a major threat, so the human mind automatically pays close attention to them and makes a strong mental note of who those people are.

Outgroup homogeneity bias has a simple explanation: We don't have as much exposure to outgroup members as we do to ingroup members. Thus, we don't have much chance to learn about how outgroup members differ from one another. This lack of exposure can have several negative consequences such as prejudice.

QUIZ YOURSELF

ABCs of Intergroup Relationships: Prejudice, Discrimination, and Stereotypes

1. Prejudice is to discrimination as _____ is to _____ .
   - (a) affect; behavior
   - (b) affect; cognition
   - (c) cognition; affect
   - (d) cognition; behavior

2. Which of the following refers to the tendency that some people have to simultaneously (1) hold egalitarian values, and (2) experience negative feelings when interacting with minority groups?
   - (a) aversive racism
   - (b) contact hypothesis
   - (c) discontinuity effect
   - (d) social dominance orientation

3. One reason why people hold on to their stereotypes—even in the face of refuting evidence—is that they tend to view pieces of refuting evidence as "exceptions," which constitute their own (new) categories. That is, they tend to create _____ .
   - (a) biases
   - (b) prototypes
   - (c) subtypes
   - (d) typologies

4. Becca is a store clerk. While she is shopping at another store on her day off, she runs into a very rude store clerk and a very rude manager. Becca will probably conclude _____ .
   - (a) most store clerks and managers tend to be rude
   - (b) most store clerks but not necessarily managers tend to be rude
   - (c) most managers but not necessarily store clerks tend to be rude
   - (d) neither most store clerks nor most managers tend to be rude

answers: see pg 493

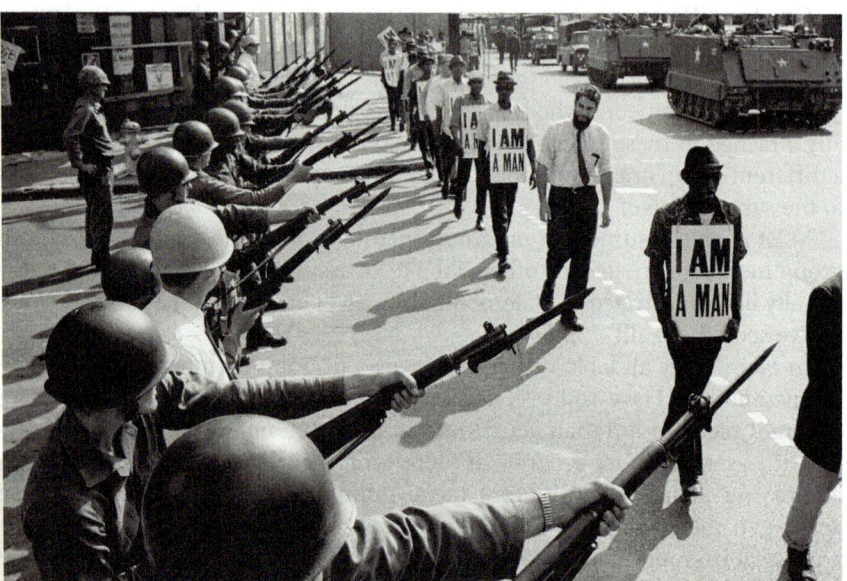

National Guard troops lined Beale Street in Memphis, Tennessee during a protest on March 29, 1968.

Common Prejudices and Targets

Prejudice is based on perceived differences among groups of people. Some prejudices build on external characteristics that are readily visible, such as race, gender, weight, or clothing (e.g., turbans worn by some Sikh and Muslim men; burqu and head scarves worn by some Muslim women; small hats called yarmulkes or kippas worn by some Jewish men). Probably the most widely discussed prejudice in modern North America is racial prejudice (racism), followed by gender prejudice (sexism). Racial prejudice has been an important social problem, particularly prejudices held by European Americans about African Americans.

Most people claim not to be prejudiced, but then again perhaps they just think that is the right thing to say. Sometimes behavior differs from expressed attitudes. One study of online dating found that 50% of the white women and 80% of the white men said that race didn't matter to them—hence they would be willing to date anyone from any race.[27] But if you look at how those people responded to dating ads, race did seem to matter. The white women who said race did not matter to them sent 97% of their responses to white men. Likewise, the white men who were supposedly open to any race sent 90% of their responses to white women. Thus, these people claimed not to care about race, but when actually contacting someone to date, they showed a strong preference for their own race.

Society has sought for decades to reduce or erase racial and gender prejudices. While people may at least strive to conceal if not overcome their racial and gender prejudices, other prejudices are often held with much less inner conflict or debate, such as against Muslims, Jews, atheists, obese individuals, large "greedy" corporations, and LGBTQ+ individuals.

> "If we were to wake up some morning and find that everyone was the same race, creed and color, we would find some other cause for prejudice by noon."
> — George Aiken, former Governor and U.S. Senator from Vermont

Muslims

In many parts of the Western world, Muslims are the targets of prejudice. For example, on March 15, 2019, a gunman killed 50 victims at the Al Noor mosque and the Linwood Islamic center in Christchurch, New Zealand. The prejudice against Muslims exists in many Western countries, where Muslims are often regarded as terrorists. Fill in the blank: Islamic ___. For many people living in the Western world, the words that come to mind are negative, violent ones such as "extremist," "fundamentalist," "insurgent," "militant," "jihadist," "mujahideen," or "terrorist." People rarely associate other religions with these negative, violent words. For example, when is the last time you heard about a Jehovah Witness terrorist? Adherents of the religion of Islam are called Muslims. The word Muslim means "one who submits to Allah (God)." There are about 1.8 billion Muslims, or 24% of the world's population, making Islam the second-largest religion after Christianity.[28] Islam began on the Arabian Peninsula in the 7th century. Although most Arabs are Muslims, a majority of the world's Muslims are not Arabs. Indonesia contains the largest percentage of the world Muslim population (about 13%).

Prejudice and discrimination against Arabs and Muslims living in the United States has increased dramatically since the terrorist attacks of September 11, 2001—"9/11."[29] For example, Muslims have been removed from airplanes without probable cause, out of fear they might be terrorists. Women in head scarves have been jeered and insulted. Mosques (Islamic places of worship) have been sprayed with graffiti and bullets. One study asked Americans to indicate whether they had "warm feelings" toward nine religious groups. The coldest feelings were for Muslims, followed closely by atheists (a group we discuss later in this chapter).[30]

Highly visible forms of discrimination (e.g., vandalism, assault) are relatively rare; pleas from the government, civil liberties groups, and others imply that such acts are socially and legally unacceptable. Less visible forms of discrimination, however, persist (e.g., workplace discrimination). One study focused on less visible forms of discrimination against Arabs.[31] The researchers used a modern variation

Since September 11, 2001, discrimination against Arabs has increased in the United States.

of Stanley Milgram's "lost letter" technique[32] to examine prejudice toward socially undesirable groups.[33] Milgram dropped self-addressed, stamped envelopes around a college campus and counted the number of lost letters that were mailed. People mailed more letters addressed to socially desirable groups (e.g., a medical research group) than to socially undesirable groups (e.g., a communist organization). In one study, white American college students received a "lost email" message addressed to a person with an Arab surname (e.g., Hameed) or a European American surname (e.g., Brice). The email stated that the intended recipient either had or had not won a prestigious four-year college scholarship. The email requested a reply within 48 hours. Thus, if the participant did not forward the email, the student would not be able to benefit from a scholarship worth tens of thousands of dollars. Participants had all completed a measure of prejudiced attitudes toward Arabs a few weeks before they received the email message. The scale had items such as "I can hardly imagine myself voting for an Arab-American who is running for an important political office." Prejudiced participants tended to pass along bad news but not pass along good news to the Arab target.

Other research has found similar results.[34] At a Swedish university, researchers dropped 100 unsealed envelopes around campus. Half the letters were addressed to a person with a common Swedish surname (A. Andersson), whereas the other half were addressed to a person with a common Muslim surname (A. Abdullah). Only initials were used for the first name to eliminate possible gender effects. The envelopes contained money (three SEK20 bills—about $9). The Swedish students returned 58% of the letters with a Swedish surname but only 36% of the letters with a Muslim surname.

The news media can play a key role in fueling prejudice against Muslims. By linking Islam with terror, the media can increase prejudice against all Muslims.[35]

Jews

Prejudice against Jewish people is called anti-Semitism, even though it is not directed against all Semitic people (e.g., Arabs, Ethiopians, Assyrians). The term was first used in 1860 by the Jewish scholar Moritz Steinschneider to refer to hatred or prejudice against Jews.[36] Steinschneider challenged French philosopher Ernest Renan's claim that the

In the Jewish cemetery in Quatzenheim, France, graves were desecrated with swastikas as part of a recent wave of anti-Semitism.

Aryan race (i.e., people of Indo-European heritage) is superior to all other races. Nazism is based on this view. In 1933, when the Nazis came to power in Germany, there were over 9 million Jews in Europe. By 1945, the Nazis had killed about two out of every three Jews—over 6 million Jews.[37] In *Mein Kampf*, Adolf Hitler conceptualized the German nation as a (*human*) body that had to be cured from a deadly disease caused by Jewish parasites.[38] The term *Holocaust* refers to the systematic state-sponsored extermination of Jews in Nazi Germany.

But Jews were hated long before 1860, and not just in Nazi Germany either. Jews have been persecuted and even massacred in many countries, including England in 1290, Spain in 1391 and 1492, Ukraine from 1648 to 1657, and Russia from 1821 to 1906. In the 1930s, Jews constituted a significant portion of the American Communist Party, and many Americans stereotyped Jews as Communists (a party viewed with disdain in the U.S.).[40] Historically, Jews have also been viewed as "outsiders" in U.S. colleges and universities.[41]

Today, a wave of anti-Semitism is sweeping the Western world.[42] For example, in France there has been a 74% increase in anti-Semitic incidents.[43] In one incident, vandals desecrated 90 graves in a Jewish cemetery in by painting swastikas on the headstones. In the United States, Neo-Nazis marched in Charlottesville, Virginia wearing swastikas and chanting "blood and soil." The "blood and soil" ("Blut und Boden") phrase invokes the Nazi philosophy that ethnic identity is based on blood descent and the territory where the individual lives.[44] Nazis believed (and still do believe) that the Aryan race is superior to all other races. At a party in California, high school teens were photographed laughing, toasting, and Sieg Heiling over a swastika formed by arranged red plastic cups.[45]

Of course, there is also a historical tension between the Jews and Arabs. Although they have a common father (called "Abraham" by the Jews and "Ibrahim" by the Muslims), the Jews come from his son Isaac, whereas the Arabs come from his son Ishmael, known as Isma'il. Today Israeli Jews and Palestinian Arabs both want the same land, and a compromise between the two groups has been difficult to achieve.

Social psychologists have been studying anti-Semitism since World War II. For example, in 1943 one social psychologist wrote: "Anti-Semitism gives rise to a stereotype of the Jew which exaggerates or distorts physiognomic characteristics and

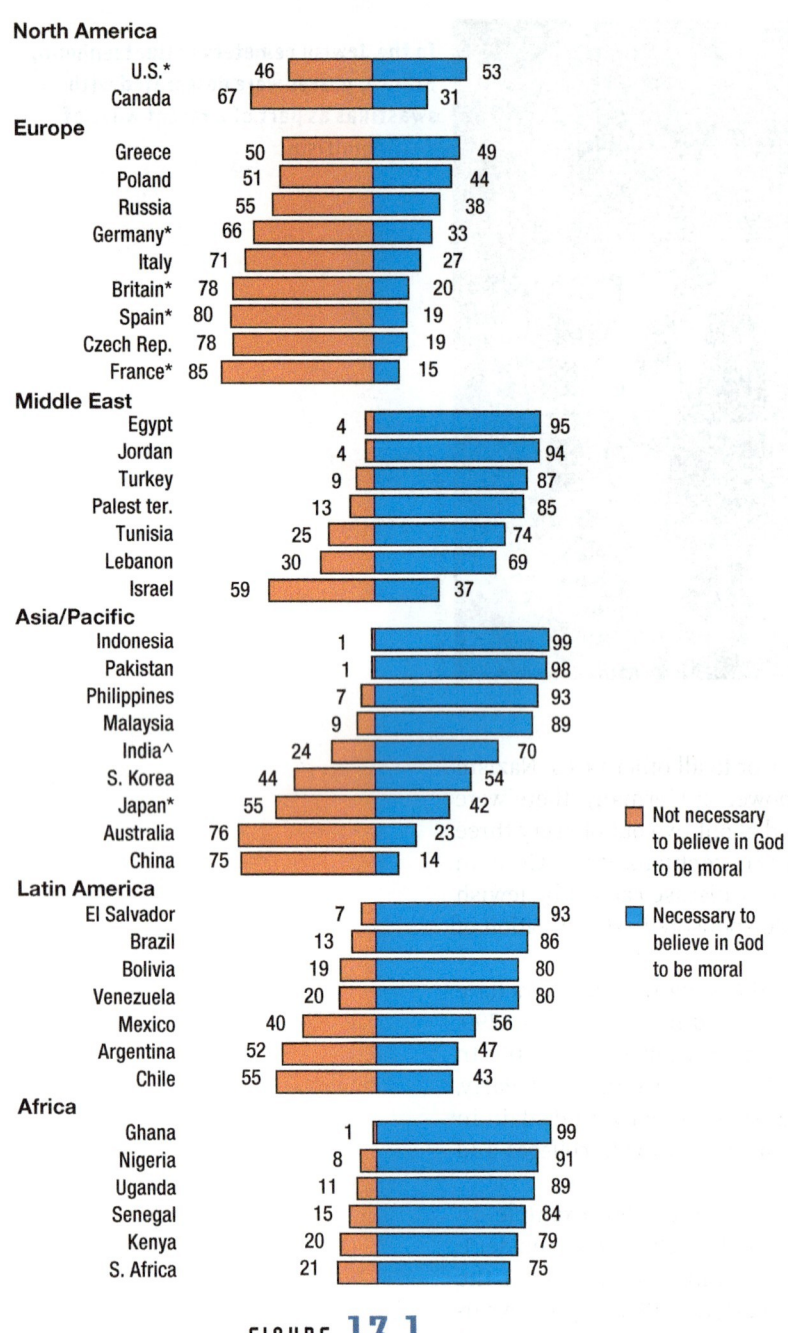

FIGURE 13.1
Is Belief in God Essential to Morality?

> "I don't know that atheists should be considered as citizens, nor should they be considered patriots. This is one nation under God."
> — George H.W. Bush, former U.S. President

culturally conditioned responses of some Jews, overgeneralizes these to pertain to all Jews, and completely omits other characteristics" (p. 352).[46] Some forms of anti-Semitism hold that Jewish people are conspiring to control society and even the world. In a study conducted in Poland, belief in Jewish conspiracy was related to fewer monetary donations to Jewish charities.[47]

Social psychological processes contributed to anti-Semitism as well. Jews often maintain their own cultural and religious traditions and are thus seen by some as constituting a unique cultural threat to many people's worldviews.[48] Throughout history, most ethnic groups cease to exist when their homeland is conquered, their government destroyed, and their people scattered abroad. The survivors blend into the local population. After the Romans extinguished the last of the Jewish rebellions, they scattered the population and disbanded the government. Remarkably, the Jews managed to preserve their identity despite that—in particular by resisting intermarriage. The result was that many places in Europe had Jewish ghettoes, so the majority Christians knew that Jews existed and were different. Moreover, medieval Christians did not bathe much, whereas Jews did, and this along with other hygienic practices meant that when plagues would come, the Jews would not suffer as badly. This prompted accusations that the Jews were somehow poisoning the Christians' water or in other ways helping the devil to kill Christians. Jews were also barred from many trades but did get into banking, with the result that they became rich, which fueled envy and antagonism.

Atheists

Atheists[49] are defined as people who do not believe in any god, and they are also disliked around the world in communities in which the majority of individuals are religious (see Figure 13.1).[50] As the title of one recent article suggests, people have more positive mental images of theists (believers) than atheists.[51] This might explain why many atheists refrain from outing themselves even in anonymous surveys, which leads to an underestimate of the number of atheists.[52]

Prejudice toward atheists seems to be rooted in distrust.[53] Religious people often consider belief in God a precondition for moral behavior. Scriptures such as this one from the Old Testament in the Bible reinforce such beliefs: "The fool hath said in his heart, *There is* no God. They are corrupt, they have done abominable works, *there is* none that doeth good."[54] One poll found that 22 of the 40 countries surveyed considered belief in God to be necessary for morality and good values.[55] Evolutionary theorists speculate that trusting kin comes more naturally than trusting people to whom one was not related, and religious communities may appeal to this by making people feel like they are related to each other. Many religions, for example, speak of their god as a father and address other members of the religion as "brother and sister." Atheists are seen as having no symbolic family and therefore cannot be trusted. Undoubtedly this dovetails with the suggestion that atheists have no fear of divine punishment, unlike believers. Moreover, some religious people believe that atheists will not change and are godless by nature.[56]

People Who Are Overweight

Another highly visible characteristic of individuals subject to prejudicial attitudes is obesity. Although some clothes may be "revealing" or "slimming," it is difficult to hide excessive weight. Unlike racist and sexist attitudes, many people will openly admit and even act upon their negative attitudes toward obese people (see *Food for Thought*).

Unfortunately, recent research confirms that there is indeed a bias against admitting overweight and obese students to college. In one study,[57] researchers obtained the height, weight, and recommendation letters for 97 people who had applied to a psychology graduate program. Researchers found that applicants (especially females) with a higher body weight had significantly fewer admission offers, even though body weight was unrelated to the overall quality of their recommendation letters. In another recent study,[58] male and female participants were asked to determine which female candidates they would be most and least likely to admit to a university on the basis of a variety of factors, including body size. Results showed only 6% of the overweight and obese women were selected for admission, compared to 60% of the underweight women.

Large "Greedy" Corporations and Profits

Many people hold negative stereotypes of large corporations and their profits. In Hollywood movies, in particular, businesspeople and corporations are often depicted as performing dangerous, exploitative, illegal acts to increase their profits.

> "Is fat really the worst thing a human being can be? Is fat worse than vindictive, jealous, shallow, boring, evil, or cruel? Not to me."
> — J. K. Rowling, British author of *Harry Potter* novels

stigma by association rejection of those who associate with stigmatized others

---

FOOD FOR *Thought*

Prejudice Against the Obese

In the United States, diet and activity level are the leading causes of death behind tobacco, and the gap is shrinking over time. Diet and activity are associated with almost every health risk known. However, obesity has other negative effects besides health risks, the biggest of which is the stigma associated with being fat. Anti-fat attitudes are strong, and they begin as early as preschool.[59] Five-year-old children say they would rather lose an arm than be fat.[60] Anti-fat attitudes are even stronger for adolescents than for children, especially among females.[61] The stigma is strong despite the fact that so many people are fat. In the United States, about two out of every three adults are considered either overweight or obese,[62] and the percent of obese people (about 40%) now exceeds the percent of overweight people.[63] (Overweight is defined as having a Body Mass Index or BMI greater than 25 but less than 30; obesity is defined as having a BMI greater than 30.)

Research has shown that compared to normal weight people, overweight people are considered to be less intelligent, less hardworking, less attractive, less popular, less successful, less strong-willed, and less trustworthy.[64,65,66,67,68] Obese people are also assumed to be less conscientious, less agreeable, less emotionally stable, and less extroverted than "normal weight" individuals, even though these stereotypes are false.[69] College students said they would rather marry a cocaine user, shoplifter, embezzler, or blind person than an obese person.[70]

The stigma associated with obesity is also contagious, as research has shown. Participants in one study[71] indicated whether they thought male job applicants should be hired. Half the participants saw a photo of the applicant sitting next to a normal-sized woman, whereas the other half saw the same applicant sitting next to an obese woman. The woman was actually the same person, but in the obese condition she wore an obese prosthesis (a "fat suit") to make her look fat. The results showed that the applicants were rated more negatively if they were shown sitting next to an obese woman. This effect is called **stigma by association**.

Being fat can even cost you money, especially if you are a woman.[72] Obese women earn about 6% less than other women, and obese men about 3% less than other men. The cumulative effect can be significant. An obese worker who is paid $1.25 less an hour over a 40-year career will end up earning $100,000 less.

In a nationally representative sample of Swedish adults, obese individuals were more likely to experience workplace and health care discrimination than normal weight individuals.[73] Even the nurses and doctors who treat them have strong negative attitudes and reactions toward obese patients.[74] Recent research found that medical students are also prejudiced against obese people.[75] "If doctors assume obese patients are lazy or lack willpower, they will be less likely to spend time counseling patients about lifestyle changes they could make," the lead author on the research said. "Doctors also may be less likely to recommend formal weight loss programs if they assume their patient is unlikely to follow through."[76]

Unlike many unfortunate fates that may befall a person, obesity is considered by many people to be self-inflicted.[77,78,79] Thus, people are likely to blame fat people for their plight.[80] Even nurses do this.[81] Obesity has many costs indeed!

Recent research found that the stereotyping extends to the profits themselves. People tend to assume that corporations that make greater profits are doing harm to society. People stereotype nonprofit organizations as morally good (although not especially competent), whereas for-profit firms are stereotyped as immoral (although fairly competent).[82] In particular, people readily believe that the pursuit of profit leads to unethical, exploitative, and dangerous practices.

The positive side of profits is apparently difficult for most people to appreciate. This is ironic, because in their daily lives people enjoy the immense benefits from using products produced by large corporations, such as mobile phones, computers, medicines, cars, and entertainment, not to mention a considerable portion of the food supply. People seem to lack the understanding that the primary way to make profits is to produce something that makes the world better, in the sense that it improves the daily life of ordinary people. They recognize the incentive to lie and cheat in order to make profits, but not the incentive to make something that people want to buy.[83]

LGBTQ+ Individuals

Although a person's sexual orientation or gender identity is not as readily visible as his or her race, gender, or weight, anti-LGBTQ+ prejudices are often quite strong. The intialism LGBTQ+ means Lesbian, Gay, Bisexual, Transgender, and Queer or Questionning. The + at the end incorporates several other groups (e.g., intersex, asexual, pansexual, agender, gender queer, bigender, gender variant, pangender). People are especially likely to feel prejudice toward gays and lesbians if they believe that homosexuality is a lifestyle choice rather than a biological predisposition.[84] However, the American Psychological Association pamphlet on the topic states, "most people experience little or no sense of choice about their sexual orientation."[85] The same applies for gender identity. After all, who would choose to be LGBTQ+ if it means being persecuted and rejected by society, peers, and possibly even family members? For example, 2 out of 3 gay people are afraid to hold hands in public, and many have been assaulted or even killed for doing so.[86]

> "Openness may not completely disarm prejudice, but it's a good place to start."
> — Jason Collins, first openly gay athlete in U.S. pro sports

Like other targets of prejudice, research has shown that LGBTQ+ individuals are not treated equally in the workplace, in the military, and even on the street. In one study of workplace discrimination against gay men,[87] pairs of fictitious résumés were sent in response to 1,769 job postings in seven states. One résumé in each pair was randomly assigned experience in either a gay campus organization or another liberal campus organization—Progressive and Socialist Alliance. Overall, gay applicants had a lower chance of being invited for an interview (7.2% versus 11.5%). The chance of a gay applicant being invited for an interview were much lower in the southern and midwestern states (Florida, Texas, Ohio) than in the western and northeastern states (California, Nevada, Pennsylvania, New York)—4.9% versus 9.0%, probably because the western and northeastern states are more supportive of gay rights. This finding is consistent with other research showing that gay bashing is higher when people think homosexuals' rights and benefits are illegitimate than when they think they are legitimate.[88]

Similarly, employers subject to antidiscrimination laws were more likely to invite a gay applicant for an interview than were employers not subject to antidiscrimination laws—6% versus 3%. Employers who mentioned masculine

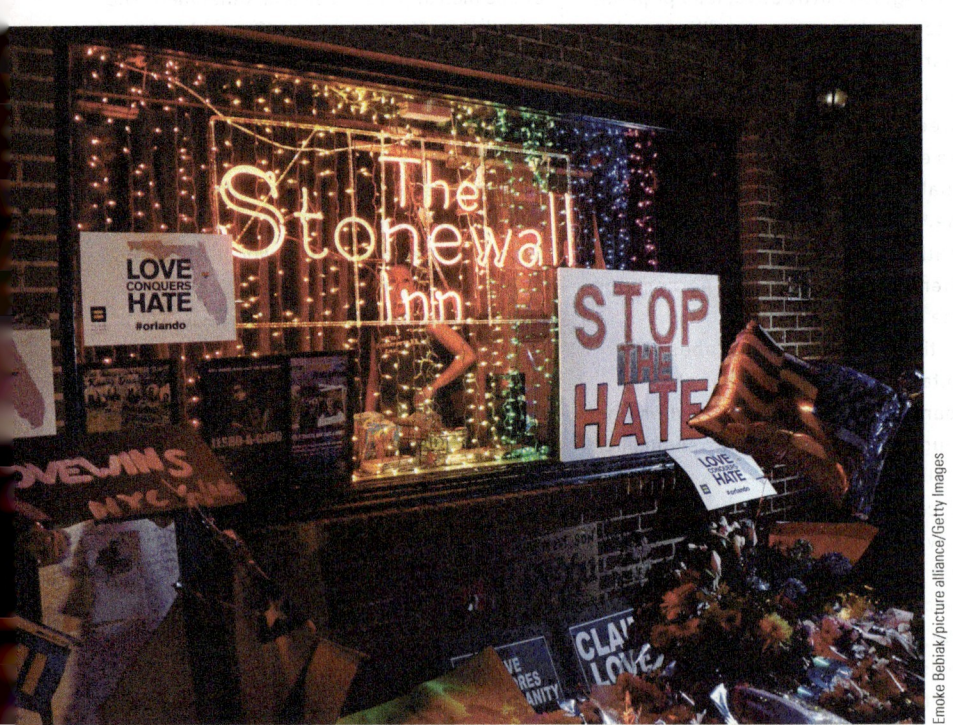

In 1969, gay people rioted in response to police raids at the Stonewall Inn, an LGBTQ bar in New York City. In 2016, in front of the Stonewall, thousands paid tribute to shooting victims at another gay nightclub, the Pulse, in Orlando, Florida.

J. C. Penney's decision to hire Ellen DeGeneres—a gay celebrity—as its spokesperson drew widespread support from some and threats of protest from others.

characteristics in the job ads (e.g., "makes decisions independently," "aggressive self-starter") were less likely to invite gay applicants for interviews than employers who did not mention masculine characteristics—4.8% versus 8.1%, perhaps because they thought gay men lacked these characteristics.

Some businesses even turn away gay customers, and in the United States, the U.S. Supreme Court ruled in favor of baker in Colorado who refused to bake a wedding cake for a same-sex couple for religious reasons, although the ruling did not fully resolve the issue.[89]

Of course, prejudice toward LGBTQ+ people isn't confined to businesses or formal organizations like the military. In one study,[90] male and female accomplices who wore either a black T-shirt without words or a black T-shirt with containing the words "Gay pride" in big, bright red letters asked pedestrians for change for a parking meter. Pedestrians were much less likely to help the accomplice if they wore a "Gay pride" T-shirt.

Many people who would never admit to holding a negative stereotype about another race will freely and openly say that they think homosexuals are bad.[91] Researchers have studied homophobia; phobias are excessive fears, so **homophobia** is an excessive fear of homosexuals or homosexual behavior. Research shows that participants with homophobic attitudes (e.g., "Gay people make me nervous" and "I would hit a homosexual for coming on to me") are more aggressive toward gay men.[92,93] Other research shows that homophobic participants were more likely to believe negative stereotypes about homosexuals (e.g., "Gays and lesbians are more promiscuous than straight people") and were less likely to believe positive stereotypes (e.g., "Gays and lesbians are more artistic than straight people").[94] (For information on the roots of anti-gay prejudice, see *The Social Side of Sex*.)

Opposition to gay rights is most pronounced among people with conservative political and religious beliefs,[95] and among people who are disgusted by homosexuality.[96] Indeed, if people are induced to feel disgusted, they are more prejudiced against homosexuals.[97] There are also cultural differences in tolerance toward homosexuality. For example, Dutch children living with lesbian parents are more open about growing up in a lesbian family, are less homophobic, and have fewer emotional and behavioral problems than American children in similar families.[98]

One sign of increasing tolerance concerns same-sex marriage. Support for same-sex marriage has increased dramatically over time, especially among younger Americans. Since 2011, the percent of Americans who favor same-sex marriage has been greater than the percent who oppose it.[99]

homophobia is an excessive fear of homosexuals or homosexual behavior

The Social Side of Sex

Roots of Anti-Gay Prejudice

Why are people prejudiced against homosexuals? The prejudice is strong, and many consider it normal and natural to abhor sexual deviance. Some people invoke religious or biblical statements condemning homosexuality, but most likely those statements are a result rather than an original cause of anti-gay bias. Other people think it is simple to say that homosexuality is unnatural, but in fact homosexual activity is quite natural and is found in hundreds of species besides humans, including mammals, birds, reptiles, amphibians, insects, molluscs, and nematodes.[100] There is no homophobia in the animal kingdom. Homosexuality is also found all over the world among humans. Nature, at least, does not regard homosexuality as unnatural. From an evolutionary perspective, homosexuality can be adaptive. For example, a third of all bonded Laytan albatrosses are female couples. Thus, colonies have far more female birds than male birds. But this helps the colony, because the females will share the parenting responsibilities while the males carry out opportunistic mating. As another example, homosexual penguins are much more likely to adopt and care for orphaned or abandoned young than are heterosexual penguins, which increases survival for the young who would almost certainly die if they were not adopted.[101] In humans, homosexual couples are also much more likely to adopt and become foster parents than are heterosexual couples.[102]

There are some curious facts about anti-gay prejudice. It is stronger among men than women,[103] even though men are more likely than women to take part in homosexual activity and to be homosexuals.[104] Then again, the apparently greater tolerance among women could be due to the fact that when people answer questions about homosexuality, they think mainly of male homosexuality. To correct for this methodological problem, researchers have asked participants separate questions about attitudes toward male versus female homosexuality, and found that both men and women were more intolerant of homosexuality in their own gender.[105,106]

Simple logic might dictate the opposite. After all, if you were the only heterosexual man in your town (because all the others were homosexual), you would be in a great position to choose the most desirable women for yourself. Put another way, every homosexual man reduces the competition for the number of available women for heterosexual men. Conversely, when people of the opposite sex turn out to be homosexual, a heterosexual's odds of finding

Some female Japanese macaques, like these two in Kyoto, prefer to be with females, even when males are present in their group.

an ideal mate are reduced. Heterosexuals ought logically to be delighted to learn that members of their own gender are homosexual and ought to be more opposed to homosexuality in the opposite gender. But that's not what the data say.

Some people object to homosexuality because their religion condemns it. To a social scientist, however, religious beliefs themselves require explanation: Why should a religion declare same-sex activity as a sin? A possible explanation is that religions adapt to help their groups compete against other groups, and in human history, the

---

QUIZ YOURSELF

Common Prejudices and Targets

1. The second leading cause of preventable death in the United States is _____.
   - (a) alcohol
   - (b) diet and activity level
   - (c) tobacco
   - (d) toxic agents

2. Research shows that atheists are considered to be _____ than religious people.
   - (a) less intelligent
   - (b) less trustworthy
   - (c) more noncommittal
   - (d) more cruel

3. Research shows that compared to non-obese people, obese people are less _____.
   - (a) agreeable
   - (b) conscientious
   - (c) emotionally stable
   - (d) None of the above

4. Which of the following is not thought to be a major motivator of anti-gay prejudice?
   - (a) Feelings of disgust
   - (b) Desire to have more possible relationship partners
   - (c) Fear of having to refuse homosexual advances
   - (d) Fear that one might enjoy homosexuality

answers: see pg 493

larger group often wins. Therefore, most successful religions advocate reproduction, and homosexual sex does not lead to reproduction. Yet that simple pragmatic explanation cannot easily account for the hostility and violence that have often characterized anti-gay attitudes.

One explanation is that people's attitudes are mainly rooted in fear that they themselves will be the target of romantic or sexual advances from homosexuals. Heterosexuals do not want to be in the awkward position of having to reject homosexual overtures.[107] That may be why they are more strongly opposed to homosexuality in their own gender.

A second explanation may be that they fear that they might have a positive response to homosexual advances. We saw in Chapter 6 that the men who expressed the strongest anti-gay views were also the most sexually aroused by watching gay pornography, though the men were reluctant to admit it, and their arousal was only verified by measuring their erectile responses.[108] The fear of one's own possible reactions might explain why people often treat homosexuals with such strong reactions of disgust and hatred, as if the homosexuals represented a dangerous threat.

A third (related) explanation may be fear of what others might think. Research shows that heterosexual men, but not heterosexual women, may exhibit prejudice against gays in order to distance themselves from gays and prove to others "I'm not gay ... I'm a real man!"[109] In fact, even people who do not express anti-gay prejudice may avoid spending time with openly gay people, such as by declining to work together on a class project.[110] This is because people fear that others will regard them gay if they are seen with gay friends. Heterosexual people do not want to be mistaken for homosexuals.

Then again, some of the prejudice may be unrelated to sex. Human men evolved to compete in groups against other men, including in battle, and so they seek out male friends with strong, manly qualities who can help them out in a fight. Heterosexual men have the stereotype that homosexual men may be weak or cowardly. Jason Collins, the first professional football player to come out as gay, described how he had spent years hearing other athletes insult each other with derogatory names for homosexuals, and so he worried about what his teammates would say to him when he returned after coming out. He said they treated him the same as ever, and moreover they simply switched to using non-homosexual insults for each other. More recently, lab studies have shown that heterosexual men will often choose a strong, manly gay man instead of a weak, effeminate heterosexual man to join their team,[111] especially for a physical competition.

Such findings suggest that prejudice against homosexuals is sometimes unrelated to their sexual activities. Many men want strong, manly friends rather than weak ones, and they stereotype homosexual men as lacking strength and courage. When assembling a team, they care less about the man's sexual tastes than about whether he's the sort you'd want beside you in a tough battle.

Many people believe homosexuality is unnatural, but in fact homosexual activity has been found all over the world in humans and in nonhuman species.

Of course there are other potential targets of prejudice besides the common targets we have discussed, such as people with stigmas. **Stigmas** include characteristics of individuals who are considered socially unacceptable. Besides homosexuality, other stigmas include being overweight (see above), mental illness, physical illness, physical blemishes, and poverty.

stigmas characteristics of individuals that are considered socially unacceptable (e.g., being overweight, mentally ill, sick, poor, or physically scarred)

Why Prejudice Exists

Why does prejudice exist? One view holds that prejudice is a product of a wicked culture. By this view, children start off innocent, trusting, and accepting of all others, but they are taught through socializing agents (e.g., parents, mass media) to dislike and reject certain groups.

There is certainly something correct in the view that stereotypes and prejudices are learned through socialization. Stereotypes often contain specific information about specific groups, and this information must be learned (as opposed to being innate knowledge). On the other hand, the tendency to hold stereotypes and prejudices may be innate. Children do not turn out on close inspection to be sweet, accepting, and tolerant. Even children as young as 6 months judge others based on race.[112] As we saw in Chapter 11, children everywhere seem instantly ready to reject anyone who is different in any way. There is even evidence that many primates naturally treat members of other groups as enemies.[113] Although the predisposition to categorize by stereotypes may be innate, the content of stereotypes is certainly learned through socialization.

At present, your authors have reluctantly come to the conclusion that prejudice is natural. As we shall see in the later section on overcoming prejudice, it seems that people automatically and normally know stereotypes and think of them, whereas they have to exert themselves to override them. More important perhaps, prejudices are found all over the world; we know of no culture in which gender stereotypes are unknown, or where members of rival groups view each other with only respect and admiration. That doesn't make prejudice right or acceptable, but as social scientists we should not be surprised to find it.

The conclusion is that the tendency to align with similar others and square off against different others, including forming negative stereotypes of them and discriminating against them, is deeply rooted in the human psyche. Some social psychologists noted early on that if two groups were involved in a laboratory study, and the experimenter allowed one person to decide how much to pay each participant, the person would usually give more money to members of his or her own group than to members of the other group, even if the groups were chosen completely at random.[114,115,116,117,118] Various theories were proposed to explain this finding. Was it because people felt similar to members of their own group? Was it because they had grown to like them? Was it because they had had conflict with the outgroup? Was it because they expected members of their own group to repay the good treatment later on?

A European research team led by Henri Tajfel decided to conduct a program of studies that would determine what caused these patterns of **ingroup favoritism** (preferential treatment of, or more favorable attitudes toward, people in one's own group, as compared to people in other groups). They formed an experimental plan: They would start out with groups that were so meaningless that people would not show any ingroup favoritism; then they would gradually add in other variables (such as the presumption that the group members were similar to each other, or had to depend on each other, or had common goals) and see at what point the ingroup favoritism started.

But the plan failed—for a very revealing reason. It failed because the research team could never get to the starting point. They were unable to make a group that seemed so arbitrary or trivial that no ingroup favoritism was found. If the experimenters did nothing more than flip a coin to assign participants to a "red team" and a "blue team," the red team members soon began to think that the blue team members were stupid or obnoxious or immoral, and they would favor other red team members if they could.[119] This automatic preference for members of one's own group even in the absence of pragmatic benefit or personal relationship is called the **minimal group effect**.

These findings suggest that people are normally and naturally ready to go along with dividing the world up into "us" and "them" and to adopt a negative stance toward "them." Prejudice and discrimination follow naturally from this tendency. As we said, the content of stereotypes may be learned, but the readiness to hold stereotypes is deeply rooted and not easily overcome.

Prejudice may be yet another sphere in which nature says go, whereas culture sometimes says "stop." Nature has prepared human beings to divide the world into "us" and "them" and to hold prejudices against "them." This mind-set may have been very helpful in early human evolution, during which people survived by belonging to groups that cooperated—and during which people in other groups were often dangerous.

Culture sometimes strives to teach people to overcome their prejudices. Modern diverse cultures in particular struggle to get people to set aside their prejudices and treat each other with fairness and tolerance. But no one seriously believes that prejudice has

ingroup favoritism preferential treatment of, or more favorable attitudes toward, people in one's own group

minimal group effect the finding that people show favoritism toward ingroup members even when group membership is randomly determined been fully eliminated from any society. Nevertheless, even some progress toward acceptance is welcome to stigmatized groups. As one example, in the middle of the 20th century homosexuality was regarded as a form of mental illness and was illegal in many American states. Although anti-homosexual attitudes remain (see *The Social Side of Sex* Box), homosexuality is no longer officially considered an illness, laws against have been repealed, same-sex marriage is now legal, and the majority of American citizens approve of tolerating it.

Of course, culture does not always say "stop." As we noted earlier, the content of stereotypes is almost always learned, and people learn from their culture what members of other groups are supposedly like. That goes for stereotypes that are fairly accurate and ones that are wildly distorted.

Us Versus Them: Groups in Competition

Several theories have been proposed to explain prejudice, including **realistic conflict theory**.[120] According to this theory, competition over scarce resources leads to intergroup hostility and conflict. A common example is a situation in which jobs are scarce and an established group blames immigrants for "taking the food out of our children's mouths." By **competition** we mean that some people attain their goals only if other people do not.[121] By **cooperation** we mean that people work together with others to help all of them achieve their goals.[122]

According to realistic conflict theory, groups should have the most negative attitudes toward their rivals, and these attitudes should be strongest, when resources are scarce and groups must compete for them. Everyone needs food, water, and air to live, but few groups fight over air because there is plenty for everyone. In contrast, fighting over food has a long history, and some predictions are that as the world's supply of freshwater begins to run short over the course of this century, conflicts over water will increase. Competition is not a part of every society. *Tradeoffs* describes 25 peaceful, cooperative, noncompetitive societies.

One could argue that realistic conflict theory is just frustration–aggression theory (see Chapter 10) applied to group conflict. Competition is a zero-sum game in which one side's gain is the other side's frustration. Hence people form negative attitudes toward competing outgroups because they frustrate your own group's efforts to get what you want.

Evolution may have had a hand in instilling the human readiness to form groups and hold prejudices against rival groups. Hunter-gatherer groups lived under conditions of fairly scarce resources, which is why they roamed over large areas. If two groups tried to spend the summer in the same area, there might not be enough food for both groups, so one group would have to leave. The groups would therefore be natural enemies. If one group contained people who readily formed prejudices against the others and acted quickly to drive the others out, whereas the other group failed to develop such attitudes, the more prejudiced group would very likely win the competition for scarce resources.

Most discussions of prejudice and stereotyping today focus on unfavorable treatment of the outgroup, but that is simply the other side of the coin of preferential or favorable treatment of the ingroup. For example, if a wealthy African American businessman gives a large sum of money to make scholarships available for African American students, is he discriminating against non-blacks (who are not eligible for his money) or helping members of his own group? Both are correct. When we understand prejudice as doing positive, favorable deeds for members of one's own group, it is easier to see how this could be favored in evolution and become part of human nature. Imagine human beings who didn't do anything special or nice for members of their own families or for the people with whom they lived and worked. Such people might well have lost out in natural selection, if pitted against groups in which most members helped and supported one another.

The idea of ingroup selection brings up the broader issue of whether prejudice is really based on love or hate. Hating the outgroup may be the flip side of the coin of loving

realistic conflict theory the idea that competition over scarce resources leads to intergroup hostility and conflict

competition situation in which people can attain their goals only if others do not

cooperation situation in which people must work together with others to help all achieve their goals

Competition Versus Cooperation

TRADE Offs

Many people in the United States and other Western societies perceive the world as a dog-eat-dog place in which people compete to survive and prosper. Not all societies adopt this view of competition. In an analysis of 25 cooperative, peaceful societies, researchers found that competition did not exist in 23 of the 25 societies.[123] In these 23 societies, even the games children play lack competition. For example, the !Kung children of Namibia and Botswana in southern Africa love to play a game called *zeni*. The children use a stick to throw into the air a weight attached by a thong to a feather. Then they use the stick to try to catch the object. Although the children exhibit widely different skill levels, they do not compete against each other. They just play the game for fun.[124]

The Piaroa of Venezuela are intensely opposed to competition and even put it in the same category of taboos such as cannibalism.[125] The Chewong of the Malay Peninsula are so opposed to competition that they don't even have a word for it in their language.[126] The Tristan Islanders had virtually no knowledge of competition until 1961, when they were forced to relocate to Great Britain for two years after a volcano erupted on their island. The Tristan Islanders did not fit in well with the highly competitive English society.[127] The Ifaluk, who live on a small Pacific atoll in the Federated States of Micronesia, value most highly a person who is *maluwelu* (calm, quiet, respectful, obedient, kind, gentle). The word *maluwelu* is also used to describe a lagoon when the wind is calm. They strongly devalue traits such as showing off, being disrespectful, and displaying personal possessions.[128] The Birhor, a tribal society of central India, do not compete for scarce resources and rarely accumulate possessions.[129]

Competition was found in 2 of the 25 peaceful societies, but it was limited to competition in business dealings. More than 100 years ago, the Fipa of western Tanzania transformed their society from one based on violence and war to one based on nonviolence and peace. The Fipa are very competitive in their business dealings, but the competition is constructive and peaceful.[130] The other competitive peaceful society is the Jains of India. The Jains believe in *ahimsa* (nonviolence), and they take vows to avoid any socially harmful acts, including stealing and lying. Yet they are quite competitive in the business world. An analysis of these studies does not prove that competition leads to violence, but it does show that cultures have the power to say "stop" even though our natural tendency is to compete for limited resources.

However, there might be a tradeoff to embracing cooperation and shunning competition. These 25 cooperative, peaceful societies are not very successful or powerful, in either economic or political terms. Competition may produce prejudice, hostility, and aggression, but it also produces progress and advancement. Communism sought to eliminate competition (at least based on greed) by eliminating private ownership and private property, but without incentives it was an economic failure. The effect can be summed up in one of the stock phrases that Soviet-bloc workers used to say before the collapse of European communism: "They pretend to pay us, and we pretend to work." Many small European countries competed for centuries for local power, at great cost in warfare and suffering, but as a result European military skills and technology so far surpassed those of the rest of the world that Europeans were able to conquer and colonize most other peoples they encountered. Indeed, according to some analyses, the competition among many small, neighboring countries was a central fact that enabled Europe to surpass and overpower other cultures that had once been clearly more powerful.[131] Competition has costs, but it also offers gains.

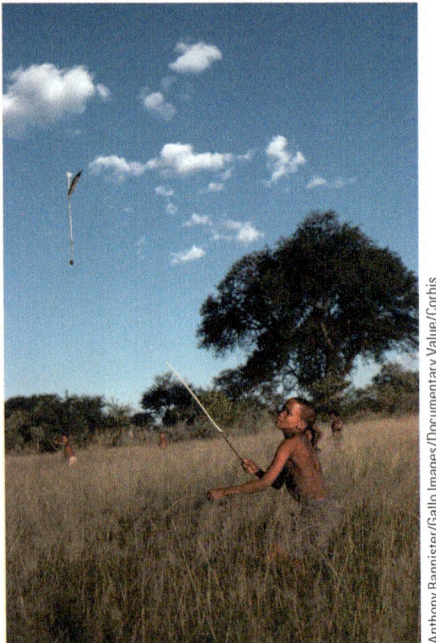

The !Kung children of Namibia and Botswana in southern Africa love to play a noncompetitive game called *zeni* where they use a stick to throw into the air a weight that is attached by a thong to a feather and then to try to catch the object.

Dancers from Ifaluk, one of the 25 peaceful, cooperative societies studied by Bruce Bonta found in the world (1997).

one's own group. Ironically, prejudice affects even judgments about whether people are motivated by love or hate. Participants in a series of studies rated their own group as motivated mainly by love, whereas they saw outgroups as motivated by hate.[132] Republicans and Democrats both saw each other as driven mainly by hate—and saw their own party members as motivated by love. Similar patterns emerged with Israelis and Palestinians, two groups with different religious and ethnic backgrounds that have clashed endlessly in the Middle East.

The challenges of living in a diverse society have sensitized modern individuals to the problems created by prejudices. People from different groups seem ready to distrust each other and develop negative views of each other. It is important to remember that humans evolved under conditions in which they interacted mainly with members of their own group, not other groups. (In other words, diverse societies are a fairly modern invention.) Groups whose members wanted to help and support one another probably flourished better than groups that didn't. But in modern life people have to live in harmony with people who belong to very different groups. This is not what we evolved for, but it is the reality of modern life.

Numerous studies have shown that groups are more prone to hostile competition than individuals are, called the **discontinuity effect**.[133] The discontinuity effect appears to be motivated by fear and greed.[134,135] People don't trust the members of other groups, so they grab as many resources as they can. If the outgroup is cooperative, they will take advantage of it. However, intergroup competitiveness is not inevitable. For example, we can reduce it by having people think about the long-term effects of their actions.[136] Making group members identifiable will also reduce intergroup competitiveness.[137] Recall from Chapter 10 that when people become deindividuated (identities are concealed), they are more likely to perform antisocial actions.

The crucial implication of the discontinuity effect is that groups won't usually get along as well as individuals. To illustrate, imagine two people from different races who have a dispute; they sit down, one-to-one, and try to reach an acceptable compromise. What are the odds that they can work it out? Now imagine that the dispute is between groups—six people of one race and six of the other. What are the odds that these groups can reach an acceptable compromise? The discontinuity effect holds that the two groups will be less likely to find a mutually agreeable compromise than the two individuals. One white person and one black person can perhaps find a mutually satisfactory compromise; six white people talking to six black people might not. This is not a reflection on the particular races but rather on universal human nature.

Ignorance? The Contact Hypothesis

Another view is that prejudice stems from ignorance. According to this view, people who have very little contact with other groups have no information about them, so they try to fill the gap by forming stereotypes. If people could resolve ignorance by having more interactions and getting more firsthand information about outgroups, prejudice would diminish or even disappear.

More than 50 years ago, Gordon Allport proposed the **contact hypothesis** which states that regular interaction between members of different groups reduces prejudice, providing that it occurs under favorable conditions.[138] According to this hypothesis, negative prejudices arise and survive because the two groups don't have much contact with each other. Bringing conflicting groups together supposedly reduces prejudicial feelings as members of different groups come to know and understand one another. For example, integrating children of different racial backgrounds should reduce prejudice as these students interact with one another and learn more about each other.

Research has shown some support for the contact hypothesis, provided that the contact is pleasant and positive and other conditions are met.[139,140] When the contact is not mutually satisfying, the result can be an increase in hostility and prejudice.[141] In line with the "bad is stronger than good" principle,[142] negative contact seems to outweigh positive contact.[143] When contact occurs under positive conditions, people feel good inside.

discontinuity effect the finding that groups are more extreme, and often more hostile, than individuals

contact hypothesis the idea that regular interaction between members of different groups reduces prejudice, providing that it occurs under favorable conditions

Over time, roommates of different races become less prejudiced.

This good feeling, in turn, leads to less prejudice.[144,145] These positive feelings, in turn, predicted less prejudiced behavior a year later. A longitudinal study of 1,655 secondary school students from Belgium, England, and Germany showed a reciprocal relationship between contact and prejudice.[146] Not only did contact reduce prejudice, but prejudiced people also avoid contact with minority group members. Contact can even work for common targets of prejudice, such as Muslims[147] and gays and lesbians.[148]

In fact, the positive contact need not be direct to work. Vicarious indirect contact through the media can work to reduce prejudice in direct contact situations.[149] Electronic contact, or e-contact, can also work.[150,151] Even imagining positive interactions with outgroup members can reduce prejudice toward them.[152] Some researchers have argued that it is time to rename the "contact hypothesis" as the "contact theory," because the scientific evidence has grown to a point that it is quite convincing.[153]

Rationalizations for Oppression

Some social psychologists have sought to explain prejudice and stereotyping on the basis of the political goals of the powerful group.[154] They propose, for example, that white Americans constructed stereotypes of African Americans as inferior beings to justify keeping them in an inferior position in society. Likewise, some feminists have suggested that men invented stereotypes of women simply to rationalize men's continued oppression of women. For example, the view that women were unsuited for higher education (even to the extent of bizarre medical theories proposing that if a woman studied too much, her uterus would come loose and wander aimlessly around inside her body) might have been invented so that men could justify refusing to admit women to universities. Traditional female stereotypes can be used to justify the oppression of women.[155] Today, in contrast, some groups promote negative stereotypes of men, which can be used to justify negative treatment of men, such as in legal and financial matters.

The fact that stereotypes can justify social inequality does not mean that stereotypes were deliberately invented as part of a conspiracy to oppress certain people. Rather, it suggests that people in positions of relative power and wealth find stereotypes to be an appealing way of explaining their superiority.

Stereotypes as Heuristics

The previous section presented stereotypes as a kind of conspiracy, claiming that people deliberately invented stereotypes for devious, manipulative ends. A simpler and less insidious view is that people often rely on stereotypes as mental shortcuts, just as they simplify the world in countless other ways. In Chapter 5, we saw that people use a variety of heuristics to help them understand the world in clear, simple ways. Stereotypes may be heuristics, too. Gordon Allport described stereotyping as "the law of least effort."[156] It is difficult and tiring to get to know each individual on his or her own merits, starting with a completely open mind, and to form a valid, carefully tested impression of each person. It is much easier to go through life prejudging people and assuming they will fit general stereotypes based on quickly recognizable categories. Such generalizations appeal to the lazy mind or cognitive miser.

Research has shown that stereotypes are energy-saving devices.[157] Participants performed two tasks at the same time. In one task, they were to form an impression of another person using a list of traits. Half of the participants saw only the name of the person they were to form an impression of (e.g., John), whereas the other half also saw a stereotypic label (e.g., John—skinhead). Underneath the name was a list of 10 traits, of which half were consistent with the stereotype (e.g., for skinheads: rebellious, aggressive, dishonest, untrustworthy, dangerous) and half were not (e.g., lucky, observant, modest, optimistic, curious). The other task involved listening to a prose passage (that had nothing to do with the stereotypes) and trying to remember what they heard. Participants' performance on both tasks was tested. Participants who saw a stereotype label recalled twice as many stereotypical traits as did participants who did not see the label. They also remembered more information about the prose passage. Thus, when people were encouraged to use stereotypes, they actually had better memory for other, unrelated information—because they were able to save mental energy by stereotyping the skinheads. Similar effects were obtained in a follow-up study even when the stereotype labels were presented subliminally. Using stereotypes enabled people to process more information, consistent with the view that stereotypes are useful tools that enable people to understand others more easily (and, in these cases, more accurately, too). In simple terms, people use stereotypes to simplify the process of thinking about other people.

People use stereotypes when their ability to judge is diminished. One clever study sorted participants into "morning people," who like to wake up early but get sleepy early in the evening, versus "night people," who have energy long after dark but find it hard to drag themselves out of bed in the morning.[158] Each group was tested for how much it used stereotype thinking in the morning versus at night. Morning people are more prone to use stereotypes at night (when they are tired) than in the morning (when they are alert). Night people do the opposite: They rely on stereotypes more in the morning than at night. These findings fit the broader point that people use stereotypes to conserve effort and energy.

People learn the content of stereotypes mainly from other people in their group. That is because people spend much more time with ingroup members than with outgroup members. This fits one of the themes of this book—"putting people first." People rely on other people for information about the world, rather than learn about the world through direct experience. If you have a stereotype about Russians, you probably learned it indirectly (e.g., from the media, from non-Russian friends) rather than directly from Russians.

Prejudice and Self-Esteem

We have seen that most stereotypes are negative and that most prejudices depict outgroups as inferior or as having bad traits. Several reasons for this have been suggested. One simple motivational explanation for the negative tone of most stereotypes is that people use them to boost self-esteem. The basic idea is that most people want to have high self-esteem, which is one of the most common assumptions underlying a great deal of research in social psychology. High self-esteem feels good. Applied to prejudice, the idea is that by regarding members of other groups as inferior, people enhance their self-esteem by virtue of belonging to their own group. Put another way, if all the other groups are inferior, then your own group must be superior—so you must be pretty good to belong to it. In this way, prejudice can be self-affirming. By using stereotypes to justify and act on prejudices, people can claim for themselves a feeling of mastery and self-worth.[159] For a summary of why prejudice exists, see **TABLE 13.1**.

TABLE 13.1 Explanations for Why Prejudice Exists

Explanation	Definition	Example
Competition	According to realistic conflict theory, competition over scarce resources leads to intergroup hostility and conflict.	Competition over good housing, schools, and jobs can lead to hostility toward outgroup members.
Ignorance	People who have very little contact with other groups have no information about them, and so they attempt to fill the gap by forming stereotypes.	People who have little contact with Muslims may assume that they all support the jihad against the West.
Rationalizations for oppression	To retain their status, powerful groups justify and rationalize prejudice against less powerful groups.	Some feminists have suggested that men invented stereotypes of women simply to rationalize continued oppression of women.
Stereotypes as heuristics	To simplify their world, people often rely on stereotypes as mental shortcuts or heuristics.	Rather than collect information about each African American individually, it requires less mental effort to stereotype them all as good at music and sports.
Prejudice boosts self-esteem	People can feel better about themselves if they consider their own group superior and all other groups inferior.	People might feel better about themselves if they think their own religion is the only true one and all others are false.

QUIZ YOURSELF
Why Prejudice Exists

1. **If some participants are randomly assigned to a "red group" and others are assigned to a "gray group," the "red group" members will think they are superior to the "gray group" members, whereas the "gray group" members will think they are superior to the "red group" members. What is this phenomenon called?**
   - ⓐ Discontinuity effect
   - ⓑ Minimal group effect
   - ⓒ Outgroup favoritism
   - ⓓ Outgroup homogeneity bias

2. **John hates immigrants because he believes they are taking American jobs. What idea can explain John's prejudice feelings toward immigrants?**
   - ⓐ contact hypothesis
   - ⓑ stereotypes as heuristics
   - ⓒ realistic conflict theory
   - ⓓ rationalization for oppression

3. **According to the discontinuity effect, _____.**
   - ⓐ both groups and individuals are influenced by competition
   - ⓑ groups are more influenced by competition than individuals are
   - ⓒ individuals are more influenced by competition than groups are
   - ⓓ neither groups nor individuals are influenced by competition

4. **What does the research indicate about the contact hypothesis?**
   - ⓐ Contact with outgroup members decreases prejudice, regardless of the context in which it occurs.
   - ⓑ Contact with outgroup members decreases prejudice in negative contexts.
   - ⓒ Contact with outgroup members decreases prejudice in positive contexts.
   - ⓓ Contact with outgroup members increases prejudice regardless of the context in which it occurs.

answers: see pg 493

Content of Prejudice and Stereotypes

In this section we examine the content of prejudice and stereotypes. One might say that people today have a stereotype about stereotypes, which is that stereotypes are typically both wrong and negative. Is that stereotype accurate?

Are Stereotypes Always Wrong, Mostly Wrong, or Mostly Right?

In the Stereotypes as Heuristics section, we covered the theory that stereotypes are heuristics. As we saw in Chapter 5, people use heuristics and other shortcuts in their thinking to conserve mental effort and time, and to help them make decisions when they lack full information. Heuristics can lead to errors, but heuristics survive because they often produce the right answer. This has led some researchers to wonder whether some stereotypes have some element of accuracy. For example, Italians are stereotypically viewed as fast and crazy drivers.[160] This stereotype might be accurate. For example, one Italian village installed speed cameras to catch fast drivers, and 58,000 infractions were recorded in just two weeks.[161] This number seems staggering, especially considering the population of the village is only 120 people!

Researchers have investigated the accuracy of stereotypes. In one analysis of gender stereotypes,[162] the findings suggested that people's stereotypes are accurate in both content and degree. Participants listed the traits men and women differed on, and indicated how large they thought the difference was. When these estimates were compared against published studies on actual gender differences, the results showed that the stereotypes were mostly quite accurate. That is, not only were participants correct about what traits were different between men and women—they were also pretty accurate at estimating the size of the differences.

A thorough review of stereotype accuracy and inaccuracy found remarkable accuracy, with some notable exceptions.[163] Most studies found that people's judgments about racial and ethnic differences averaged within 20% of the objective facts. Hence, severe inaccuracies were not common. Most studies found the same general level of accuracy for gender stereotypes. On the other hand, political stereotypes were consistently inaccurate: Democrats and Republicans do not perceive each other very accurately.[164] Stereotypes about personality traits based on countries were also not very accurate.[165] For example, if we were to ask you what sort of personality is typical among Germans, or Australians, or Brazilians, you might be able to come up with an answer, but it is not likely very accurate. Moreover, even the evidence of accuracy in general does not translate into everyone being correct. Although the average level of accuracy was high, in every study there were plenty of individuals who expressed wildly inaccurate stereotypes.

Research suggests that stereotypes of age differences in personality traits are accurate across 26 nations.[166] Adolescents were consistently seen as impulsive, rebellious, undisciplined, and open, whereas old people were consistently seen lower on these traits. These consensual age group stereotypes correlated strongly with actual personality test scores.

The high level of accuracy in modern stereotypes may also indicate that stereotyping has changed. Most participants in these studies were modern university students, who have been taught to be careful about using stereotypes and avoiding unfair prejudice. Decades ago, German Nazis stereotyped Jews as greedy, ruthless individuals conspiring to destroy their country as a step toward world domination—a mistaken notion that contributed to horrific mass murder called the Holocaust.

Even accurate stereotypes may be generalized unfairly and inaccurately. As we noted, a stereotype that women are shorter than men is accurate but may be wrong in many specific cases. A more dangerous version of that kind of mistake was found in connection with hurricanes. The National Hurricane Center alternates between assigning tropical cyclones in the Atlantic and Pacific oceans male names (e.g., Bret, Adrian) and female names (e.g., Arlene, Beatriz). Hurricanes with female names kill more people than hurricanes with male names.[167] This may seem surprising, as hurricanes are named in alternating fashion so that the gender is random. Plus, of course, hurricanes do not know their own names. The most likely explanation is that female hurricanes are no worse than male ones—but the names evoke the stereotypes that men are more violent and dangerous than women, so people take fewer precautions when the approaching hurricane has a female name than one that has a male name.

Another question regarding the accuracy of stereotypes is what happens when people judge a particular other person. Meta-analyses that combine the results of many different studies have generally concluded that there is a genuine effect of stereotypes on judgment of individual persons, but it is a pretty small one.[168] In contrast, people rely quite heavily on information specific to the person when making judgments about that person.[169] In other words, when people meet someone and form an impression of that person, they mostly rely on whatever they learn about that individual, and they may fill in the gaps with stereotypes to a small extent. This fits the view that stereotypes operate like heuristics; they are used to help make judgments when information is lacking or uncertain.

Prejudice has multiple roots. To the extent that prejudices are held as a heuristic way of understanding the social world, people may try to hold fairly accurate stereotypes. In contrast, to the extent that people hold prejudices in order to bolster their own self-esteem at the expense of others, or to rationalize the status quo and justify their oppression of disadvantaged minorities, stereotypes may be exaggerated or even entirely fabricated and hence have little or no factual basis.

Are Stereotypes Always Negative?

Are stereotypes always negative? No, of course not. Many people hold the stereotype that Asian Americans are good at math, or engineering, or schoolwork in general, or that African Americans have superior talents in a variety of culturally valued spheres such as music and sports. A once-popular stereotype that fat people were jolly contributed to how Santa Claus became depicted. If Santa were invented today, he would almost certainly be fashionably slim and debonair! Conversely, if a new character were introduced today as a fat old man with a long beard and a silly red pantsuit, he probably would be a bad guy or troublemaker.

Negative stereotypes generally present more of a cultural problem than positive ones, because they entail prejudging a person as having faults. But positive stereotypes can also be harmful, although the harm may not be as readily apparent.

> **QUIZ YOURSELF**
>
> **Content of Prejudice and Stereotypes**

1. Research has shown that stereotypes about women are _____ .
   - (a) accurate in content and degree
   - (b) accurate in content, but inaccurate in degree
   - (c) inaccurate in content, but accurate in degree
   - (d) inaccurate in content and degree

2. Joe is the kind of man who likes to hold doors open for women, buy them flowers and chocolates, pay for their meals, and in general put them on a pedestal. Joe is demonstrating _____ .
   - (a) benevolent sexism
   - (b) hostile sexism
   - (c) both benevolent and hostile sexism
   - (d) neither benevolent nor hostile sexism

3. What type of sexism leads to the greatest reductions on cognitive performance tests in women?
   - (a) Benevolent sexism leads to the greatest reductions in cognitive performance.
   - (b) Hostile sexism leads to the greatest reductions in cognitive performance.
   - (c) Reductions in cognitive performance are similar for benevolent and hostile sexism.
   - (d) Neither benevolent nor hostile sexism lead to reductions in cognitive performance.

4. Benevolent sexism is considered romantic in what part of the United States?
   - (a) Eastern
   - (b) Northern
   - (c) Southern
   - (d) Western

answers: see pg 493

Inner Processes

Inner processes (e.g., emotions) can also contribute to prejudice and stereotyping. Stereotypes can form simply on the basis of **salience**—a psychological term roughly meaning "obviousness."[170,171] We described one of these studies in Chapter 5 when we discussed illusory correlations.[172] That is, simply standing out can contribute to stereotyping. If you were, say, the first blond person to arrive on an island, people would pay extra attention to what you did, and if you did something memorable (say, you did something to disgrace a local church), people would remember that "blond people are against religion," and the next blonds to arrive would have to cope with that stereotype.

The research findings based on salience are interesting because they show how stereotypes can form from purely cognitive (mental) processes, without any influence of

salience being obvious or standing out

emotion or motivation. When motivation enters the picture, it can greatly increase the likelihood of prejudice. One classic formulation of motivated prejudice is scapegoat theory, first proposed by Gordon Allport in 1954.[173] In ancient times, on the Day of Atonement (Yom Kippur), Moses' older brother Aaron symbolically placed all the sins of the children of Israel on the head of a goat, who was then sent into the wilderness to perish.[174] The peoples' sins were supposed to perish along with the unfortunate scapegoat.

Scapegoat theory proposes that people blame their problems and misfortunes on outgroups, which contributes to negative attitudes toward these outgroups. This process is linked to attribution theory, discussed in Chapter 5, which looks at how people infer the causes of events. One theme introduced there was the **self-serving bias**. People like to take credit for success but refuse blame for problems and failures. When times are bad, people prefer to blame others (scapegoats) rather than their own bad judgment or incompetence.

Research suggests that scapegoating can derive from two different motivational roots.[174] One is a quest for moral affirmation and superiority. The person's responsibility for bad outcomes is transferred onto the scapegoat, so guilt and other feelings of moral inferiority are reduced. The other motivation is a desire for control. Many negative events have complex causes that are hard to fathom and even harder to control. In contrast, blaming a scapegoat is simple and straightforward, and it restores the person's sense of having control.

Scapegoating creates friction in any diverse society. Throughout Western history, the Jews have suffered repeatedly as a result of being blamed for the problems of Christian societies. Jews were blamed for the death of Jesus, even though he was a Jew and it was the Romans who actually performed the execution. Before long, however, Romans were European and Christian (and the pope himself lived in Rome), so the Christian community in Europe preferred to put the blame on the Jewish outgroup rather than on members of their own ingroup.

Even in the 20th century, Jews were scapegoats. Germans were shocked and baffled by their country's abrupt surrender in World War I (which, thanks in part to battlefield standstills and government propaganda, they had thought they were winning all along). When the Nazis accused the Jews of having stabbed the German war effort in the back, many Germans found this theory more believable and appealing than blaming their own leaders and politicians, and the wide acceptance of this theory helped fuel the hostility toward Jews that enabled the murderous Holocaust. Note that this likely served both motives for scapegoating: It enabled non-Jewish Germans to feel no responsibility for their nation's defeat and collapse, and it offered the false promise that Germans could regain control of their fate by treating the Jews as a dastardly enemy.

Social psychologists conducted a famous test of scapegoat theory using race relations in the United States. Researchers correlated the market price of cotton with the frequency of interracial lynching incidents in the southern United States over a period of 49 years, 1882 to 1930.[176] Lynching is execution by a vigilante mob. Typically, a group of people would hang or otherwise kill someone who has been accused of a crime but not legally convicted, and of course such killings are themselves both illegal and immoral. The researchers chose the price of cotton because many white families in the South made their living by growing cotton. Because the amount they could grow in a given year stayed about the same (given how much land they owned), a drop in cotton prices meant a big drop in income and hence financial problems for many. The researchers reasoned that when people were thus poorer than usual, they would want to blame their troubles on an outgroup, and they thought African Americans would make a convenient scapegoat. Hence, they reasoned, illegal violence against African Americans (as measured by lynching) would go up when cotton prices went down. That's what they found. Subsequent work with more elaborate statistical methods reconfirmed this hypothesis.[177]

To be sure, the correlation between cotton prices and interracial lynching is not necessarily a pattern of scapegoating. Recall that correlation does not mean causation. The relationship might be explained on other, related grounds, such as frustration (resulting from low cotton prices and less money) leading to aggression. Still, whatever the inner processes, it does suggest that harsh times cause people to behave more aggressively toward outgroups.

scapegoat theory the idea that blaming problems and misfortunes on outgroups contributes to negative attitudes toward these outgroups

self-serving bias the tendency for people to take credit for success but refuse blame for problems and failures

Research indicates that conflict and stress tend to bring out stereotypes. The subtitle of one set of studies is "She's fine if she praised me but incompetent if she criticized me."[177] In these studies, college students evaluated female university instructors as less competent than male instructors after receiving negative evaluations from them but not after receiving positive evaluations from them. Students who were praised by a woman or by students who watched someone else receive praise or criticism from a woman did not use the stereotype that women are less competent than men.

Similar findings have been reported for racial stereotypes. People are more likely to use racial stereotypes when there is a disagreement or conflict than when everyone agrees.[179] For example, white participants in one study read about a court case, gave their verdict, and then observed a videotape of a black or white fellow juror who either agreed or disagreed with the participant's verdict.[180] Later, on a computerized test, participants showed faster reaction times to black stereotypical words when black fellow jurors had disagreed with them. Thus, stereotypes may lie buried and forgotten much of the time, but when a black person disagrees with a white person, the stereotypes start leaping to mind.

Emotional stress can activate stereotypes and lead to distortions in how people see the world. A team of researchers collected facial photos of people of different races, including whites, Arabs, and blacks.[181] The photos were carefully chosen to have no particular expressions, and participants who were themselves in a calm or neutral state rated them all that way. However, in one experimental condition, participants first viewed scenes from a horror movie that induced fearful states. When these participants looked at the same faces, they saw the faces of people from other races as angry and threatening, though they did not show any change in how they perceived the faces of people from their own race. Moreover, these effects occurred mainly among people who held stereotypes of the other races as dangerous and threatening. For example, whites who regarded Arabs as dangerous tended to see the blank Arab faces as angry and threatening (when the white perceivers were already afraid). But whites who did not hold that stereotype of Arabs did not shift in how they perceived the Arab faces.

How does prejudice operate? One simple theory is that people simply prejudge others based on their assumptions. Some stereotypes may operate that way, but social psychology research has suggested that the actual process is often more subtle and complex. Some research shows that people use their stereotypes more as hypotheses to be tested than as rules that can be applied in all cases. In an influential experiment,[181] students were exposed to background information about a schoolgirl named Hannah. Some participants saw a videotape that depicted her as from a rich, privileged family, whereas others saw a videotape that depicted her as from a poor, working-class family. The participants were then asked to guess how well she was doing in school. The typical prejudice and stereotype would predict that the girl from the upper-class background would be doing better in school than the girl from the working-class background, but the researchers found no such difference. Participants were not willing to leap from knowing her background (and holding broad stereotypes) to making predictions or assumptions about her intellectual ability.

Meanwhile, other participants saw a second videotape. It depicted Hannah taking an oral test in school. There was only one version of this videotape, and it depicted Hannah's performance as inconsistent. Sometimes she seemed to perform quite well, but at other points she seemed bored by the test and not able to furnish the proper answers.

You might think that seeing someone take a test of intellectual ability would eliminate the effect of stereotypes, but in fact the Hannah experiment found exactly the opposite. The stereotypes based on family background emerged only among people who saw Hannah taking the test. The mechanism was probably one of **confirmation bias**, which we saw in Chapter 5 is a tendency to focus more on evidence that supports (confirms) one's expectations than on evidence that contradicts them. The participants who believed Hannah came from a rich family paid more attention to the parts of the test on which she was doing well, and so concluded that their expectations (that rich children do better in school) were confirmed. Meanwhile, the participants who believed she came from a poor family focused on the parts of the test on which she did poorly; they too concluded that their expectations (that poor children perform worse) were confirmed.

confirmation bias the tendency to focus more on evidence that supports one's expectations than on evidence that contradicts them

The participants did not truly prejudge Hannah. Their prejudices did not lead to firm assumptions about how smart she would be; instead, the prejudices functioned more like expectations, which they then sought to test against Hannah's behavior. Unfortunately, perhaps, they ended up viewing her behavior in a biased manner, so their ultimate impression of her was biased.

> **QUIZ YOURSELF**
>
> **Inner Processes**
>
> answers: see pg 493

1. The psychological term for obviousness is _____.
   - (a) heterogeneous
   - (b) homogeneous
   - (c) nonsalience
   - (d) salience

2. What theory proposes that people blame their problems and misfortunes on outgroups?
   - (a) Catharsis theory
   - (b) Realistic conflict theory
   - (c) Relative deprivation theory
   - (d) Scapegoat theory

3. In a famous 1940 study, researchers found that as cotton prices decreased, the number of lynchings _____.
   - (a) decreased
   - (b) increased
   - (c) increased and then decreased
   - (d) was not affected

4. Lea believes that all Muslims are terrorists. She searches for evidence on the internet and finds lots of "evidence" to support her belief. Lea is exhibiting _____.
   - (a) the confirmation bias
   - (b) the false consensus effect
   - (c) an illusory correlation
   - (d) the self-serving bias

Overcoming Stereotypes, Reducing Prejudice

> "The greatest and noblest pleasure which men can have in this world is to discover new truths; and the next is to shake off old prejudices."[183]
>
> — Frederick the Great, 18th-century King of Prussia

How prejudiced are Americans today? One view is that the United States is a deeply prejudiced, racist society. This view has been expressed by many, including U.S. Congressman John Lewis: "The scars and stains of racism are still deeply embedded in the American society." A contrary view is this:

> The sociological truths are that America, while still flawed in its race relations, is now the least racist white-majority society in the world; has a better record of legal protection of minorities than any other society, white or black; offers more opportunities to a greater number of black persons than any other society, including all those of Africa.[184]

This comment may sound as though it came from someone unfamiliar with American problems or unsympathetic to African Americans, but in fact the source was Orlando Patterson, a highly respected black scholar who was chair of the African American Studies program at Harvard University.

Which view is correct? Both could be. It depends on what the standard is. Compared to our American ideals of full tolerance and equality, there is still far too much prejudice, as the first characterization suggests. Compared to most other societies in the history of the world, however, the United States is remarkably tolerant, equal, and supportive, as Patterson's comment expresses.

It is undeniable that prejudice exists in the United States today. Indeed, to eliminate prejudice completely seems an impossible ideal. Still, modern Americans have come far in overcoming many prejudices and stereotypes. Most people now believe that prejudices based on race and gender are unfair and even immoral, and if people do know those stereotypes, they may try not to let them cloud their judgment of individuals. In most societies in world history, a person's race and gender would steer the person toward one sort of life, with one set of opportunities and not others, but modern American society has come remarkably far in removing those obstacles. Though the society was created by white men, and the government still is disproportionately composed of white men, the laws and court rulings issued by those men have changed society so that African Americans, women, and other categories of people can run for president (and win), serve on the Supreme Court, rise to the top of universities and corporations, represent their country in international diplomacy, and in other ways have access to the best positions and rewards the culture has to offer. Indeed, in some cases the white men made rules to give preferential treatment to women and people of color (e.g., affirmative action policies).

It is true that America elected its first non-white president, Barack Obama, in 2008. It is not true, however, that racism is no longer a problem in America.

None of this should be taken to imply that prejudice has been conquered or that cruel, immoral, and sometimes vicious acts of prejudice and discrimination have ceased. Prejudice is still a force in the United States; its influence ranges from hate crimes to demeaning ethnic jokes. The point is merely that American society has made considerable progress in fighting against some important kinds of prejudice, especially those based on race and gender. However, there is still a long way to go.

Conscious Override

If prejudice is natural, and culture sometimes wants to say "stop" to prejudice, those who hold prejudiced views must consciously override the response. The battle against prejudice is fought between the two halves of the duplex mind. The automatic system may often sustain prejudices, for many of the reasons we have already noted: Stereotypes simplify the world and help people make snap judgments; thus, they appeal to the automatic system (which is usually looking for ways to process information quickly). The conscious system can strive to overcome those prejudices and stereotypes so as to support equality and avoid prejudging individuals.

Numerous studies have shown that people harbor prejudiced attitudes toward particular social groups at the implicit or unconscious level, even though they honestly report having no prejudiced attitudes at the explicit or conscious level[185,186,187,188] (also see Chapter 7). Unconscious prejudiced attitude measures have been found to do a good job in predicting behavior, especially spontaneous behaviors.[189] Likewise, unconscious racist attitude measures have been shown to do a better job of predicting workplace discrimination in hiring practices than explicitly stated, conscious attitude measures.[190] Implicit attitude measures about alcohol did a better job of predicting drinking behavior than did explicit attitude measures.[191] Because people are reluctant to admit that they have racist attitudes or drinking problems, what they say in response to explicit questions is not always a good predictor of behavior.

Most implicit attitude measures compare prejudice toward blacks relative to whites. Thus, it is difficult to know whether racism is due to liking whites, disliking blacks, or both. Research shows that these measures indicate disliking blacks rather than liking whites.[192] Intriguing evidence about this inner struggle to overcome prejudice was provided in research examining the aftereffects of talking with someone of a different race.[193,194] As we saw in Chapter 4, self-regulation operates like a muscle that gets tired after use. Participants showed just such tiredness: They performed worse than other participants (who had spoken to someone of their own race) on a standard test of self-regulation (the Stroop task, which requires people to override their first impulse in order to give the correct response; see Chapter 5). The effect was strongest for participants who had the strongest prejudices. Thus, when people talk to someone from another race, they have to carefully regulate themselves in order to hide their prejudices and to make sure they do not say anything that could be interpreted as offensive or biased. This extra effort takes its toll, leaving people less able to self-regulate afterward. People do exert themselves consciously to overcome and hide their prejudices, even though the effort may be costly.

Of course, in many cases the conscious mind is quite comfortable hanging onto its prejudices and does not try to override the prejudicial reaction of the automatic system. The difference can perhaps be appreciated by comparing anti-black and anti-obese prejudices in the United States today. Most Americans regard racial prejudice as immoral and will consciously strive to avoid thinking or expressing negative stereotypes of African Americans. In contrast, many people are content to think and express negative stereotypes of obese people; they do not consciously try to override the automatic reaction (possibly unless they are talking to an obese person).

Mental Processes of Non-prejudiced People

The view that overcoming prejudice is based on conflict between conscious and automatic responses emerged from an important series of studies.[195] This research sought to find which mental processes underlay prejudice by seeking to ascertain what was different between prejudiced and non-prejudiced people. A questionnaire was used to classify people as either prejudiced or non-prejudiced, and people who were at both extremes took part. A series of tests were used to see where the difference lies.

The first hypothesis was that the difference lies in knowledge of stereotypes: Maybe non-prejudiced people are not familiar with the stereotypes. Upon testing both groups, however, the researcher found that they had equal knowledge of the content of stereotypes.

The second hypothesis was that the difference lies in whether the stereotype is activated (i.e., whether it springs to mind) when one encounters a member of the group. Non-prejudiced people might know the stereotype of African Americans, for example, but might not think of the stereotype when they encounter a real person. This too proved to be wrong: Both prejudiced and non-prejudiced people do think of the stereotype when they encounter someone from the stereotyped group. This suggested that the automatic system was at work, automatically retrieving the prejudicial information when it recognized a member of the category.

The third hypothesis, therefore, was that the automatic system operates in similar ways in both prejudiced and non-prejudiced people, but non-prejudiced people employ their conscious processing to override the stereotype and replace prejudiced thoughts with thoughts more in line with their values of tolerance, fairness, and equality. This hypothesis proved correct. Non-prejudiced people still know and think of stereotypes, but they override them. This fits our theme that nature says go and culture says "stop": It is normal and natural to have some degree of prejudice, but the conscious mind can learn to overcome these reactions and treat people in a fair and tolerant manner. Thus, the duplex mind was crucial. The automatic responses of prejudiced people are similar to those of non-prejudiced people. The difference lies in the conscious system and its override of automatic responses that conflict with conscious values.

Discrimination in Reverse

Research has shown that when people are accused of prejudice, they often exert themselves to prove the opposite. In an early laboratory study,[196] for example, white participants who thought of themselves as relatively unprejudiced were either accused or not accused by the experimenter of being racist. After leaving the study, participants encountered a black or white panhandler (actually an accomplice) who asked for money. The black panhandler received more money from participants who had been accused of racism than from other participants (not accused of racism). The white panhandler received an equal amount of money from the two groups of participants. Thus, white people gave more money to the black accomplice to prove they were not racists.

In another study,[197] black couples and white couples (actually accomplices) visited 40 different Canadian restaurants that had advertised dress code regulations, including jacket and tie for male diners. The male partner in each couple violated the dress code by wearing a turtleneck sweater instead of a dress shirt and tie; thus, according to restaurant policy, the restaurant could refuse service to them. When a black couple entered the restaurant first, they were served 75% of the time; when a white couple entered first, they were served only 30% of the time. The restaurant personnel may have had no conscious prejudices, but they subtly showed a reverse discrimination pattern. They treated the black couple more favorably in order to avoid the appearance of being biased.

There was a revealing twist in the restaurant study's data. About 45 minutes after the first couple arrived, the second couple from the other race arrived, and they too violated the dress code. In general, the second couple was treated the same as the first. However, the decision how to react depended on which couple arrived first, and this initial decision showed the reverse discrimination pattern. If the black couple arrived first, then they were seated despite breaking the rules; if later a white couple also broke the rules, they too were seated. If the white couple arrived first, they were usually turned away, and once the restaurant staff had refused service to the white couple, they felt justified in turning away the black couple on the same basis.

Thus, people overcome prejudice by making conscious efforts to be fair and equal in how they treat others. Many people try extra hard to avoid anything that could be interpreted as showing racism or sexism. People may not try as hard to overcome and override prejudices against LGBQ+ people, obese people, and others. But the progress in overcoming racism and sexism shows the way toward possibly reducing these other prejudices as well, so that Western society can live up to its ideals of judging each person as an individual rather than prejudging them as a member of a group or category.

Motives for Overcoming Prejudice

The previous sections have suggested two different reasons for wanting to overcome prejudice. One is a possibly heartfelt dedication to equality and a corresponding belief that prejudice is morally wrong. The other is an appreciation that expressing prejudice could elicit social disapproval. For example, most white Americans report that they do not want to respond with prejudice toward African Americans, but is this a sincere desire to promote equality or merely a strategic reluctance to say things that might make some people angry?

Both motives are real, but different people may emphasize one or the other (or neither).[198] A measure has been developed that can help classify people's responses according to these two motives. The measure assesses Internal Motivation to Respond Without Prejudice, which is understood as a motivation based on a strong inner belief that prejudice is wrong. It also assesses External Motivation to Respond Without Prejudice, which is essentially a sense that it is socially unwise to express opinions that others

Political correctness is the norm in the United States today.

FIGURE 13.2
Test yourself: What is your motivation to overcome prejudice?
Copyright © 1998 by the American Psychological Association. Reprinted by permission.[198]

Internal Motivation to Respond Without Prejudice
1. I attempt to act in nonprejudiced ways toward black people because it is personally important to me.
2. According to my personal values, using stereotypes about black people is OK (reverse scored.)
3. I am personally motivated by my beliefs to be nonprejudiced toward black people.
4. Because of my personal values, I believe that using stereotypes about black people is wrong.
5. Being nonprejudiced toward black people is important to my self-concept.

External Motivation to Respond Without Prejudice
1. Because of today's PC (politically correct) standards, I try to appear nonprejudiced toward black people.
2. I try to hide any negative thoughts about black people in order to avoid negative reactions from others.
3. If I acted prejudiced toward black people, I would be concerned that others would be angry with me.
4. I attempt to appear nonprejudiced toward black people in order to avoid disapproval from others.
5. I try to act nonprejudiced toward black people because of pressure from others.

Note: Answer each item on a scale running from 1= strongly disagree to 9 = strongly agree. For #2 on the Internal Motivation scale, subtract your answer from 10. Then add across items, and divide by the number of items. The average score for college students is about 8 for the Internal Motivation scale and about 5 for the External Motivation scale.[188]

will regard as socially undesirable or politically incorrect. **FIGURE 13.2** contains the items for both these scales. The scales can also be modified to assess motives to avoid prejudice against LGBTQ+ people, obese people, Muslims, Jews, or any other group. The internal and external motivations to avoid prejudice are not mutually exclusive. Some people have one, some have both, and others have neither.

People's source of motivation to respond without prejudice (i.e., the *reason* why they are motivated) has important implications for behavior. For example, people who are only externally motivated to respond without prejudice report low-prejudice attitudes and beliefs when they have to provide their responses publicly to an experimenter or another person. However, if they are allowed to write their answers privately on a questionnaire in an anonymous setting, they report attitudes that are more prejudiced. Thus, they shift their answers across settings depending on whether others will be privy to their responses. In contrast, people who are internally motivated to respond without prejudice report low-prejudice attitudes and beliefs regardless of how or to whom they provide their answers. Those neither internally nor externally motivated report moderately prejudiced attitudes regardless of the setting. (A much smaller number of present-day Americans consistently express strong racial prejudices.)

Although externally motivated people shift their responses to comply with social pressure to respond without prejudice, this public conformity comes at a price. White people who are primarily externally motivated to respond without prejudice become angry when they feel pressured to respond in a politically correct manner. When they are released from such pressure (i.e., when they are no longer under the watchful eye of a non-prejudiced audience), they respond with a backlash and actually express more prejudice than if they had not been pressured to respond without prejudice.[199]

White people who are primarily internally motivated to avoid prejudice have more deeply internalized, well-practiced non-prejudiced reactions than the other groups. This inner commitment to overcome prejudice allows them to override and replace any unwanted biased responses, including even very subtle biases that can occur automatically and with hardly any conscious recognition, resulting in more effective control of prejudice.[200,201]

Contact

As we learned earlier, prejudice can be reduced by positive contact with outgroup members.[202,203,204] Sometimes even vicarious contact can work, such as knowing that a good friend who is a member of your group has a close relationship with an outgroup member.[205] Although overt expressions of prejudice can be reduced by direct educational and attitude-change techniques (see Chapter 8), more covert expressions of prejudice, such as deliberate avoidance or mild harassment, can be reduced by intergroup contact.[206]

Common Goals

Cooperating to achieve common goals is one powerful antidote to intergroup conflict. In one study,[207] researchers found that when children play cooperative games, their aggressive behavior decreases, and their cooperative behavior increases. In contrast, when they play competitive games, their aggressive behavior increases and their cooperative behavior decreases.

One technique used to achieve a common goal is the jigsaw classroom. The **jigsaw classroom** is a cooperative learning technique developed to reduce feelings of prejudice.[208,209,210] Just as each piece of a jigsaw puzzle is necessary to complete the puzzle, some contribution from each student in a jigsaw classroom is necessary to complete an assignment. For example, if you want students to learn about Anne Frank, the jigsaw might contain six pieces: (1) her early childhood in Germany before moving to Amsterdam, the Netherlands, at age 4, (2) her life in Amsterdam before going into hiding, (3) her life in hiding from 1942 to 1944, (4) the family's arrest by the Gestapo in 1944, (5) her time in the Auschwitz and Bergen-Belsen concentration camps, and (6) how her father Otto (the only survivor) found and published her diary. After each person learns as much as possible about his or her assigned topic, students from different groups who were assigned the same topic meet together to become experts on their topic. Once each individual is up to speed, the jigsaw groups reconvene, and members share with each other what they have learned. Group members must work together as a team to accomplish a common goal. They cannot ignore outgroup members of their team or they will not be able to solve the puzzle as a team.

Several studies have shown positive outcomes for jigsaw classrooms. Research shows that participation in jigsaw classrooms decreases racial prejudice and increases academic performance.[211,212] The jigsaw classroom has been successfully applied in countries other than the United States.[213,214]

jigsaw classroom a cooperative learning technique for reducing feelings of prejudice by having students interact and cooperate to learn material

QUIZ YOURSELF
Overcoming Stereotypes, Reducing Prejudice

1. In the United States, people are most likely to consciously override prejudicial feelings for what group of individuals?
   - (a) African Americans
   - (b) Arab Americans
   - (c) LGBTQ+ people
   - (d) Obese individuals

2. A state police force has set a height requirement of 5 feet 10 inches (1.8 meters) for all officers. This requirement is not related to job effectiveness, but it generally excludes Hispanics, Asians, and women from the police force. The height requirement most clearly reflects _____.
   - (a) ingroup bias and outgroup homogeneity bias
   - (b) racism and sexism
   - (c) scapegoating and self-serving bias
   - (d) stereotyping and prejudice

3. Jett can think of many interesting ideas, but he isn't a very good writer. Kiowa is an excellent writer, but he is not very creative. In order to write a book, the two of them form a team. Writing a book in this example is a _____ goal.
   - (a) coordinate
   - (b) subordinate
   - (c) superordinate
   - (d) none of the above

4. What type of classroom has been shown to reduce prejudiced feelings?
   - (a) Active learning
   - (b) Integrated
   - (c) Jigsaw
   - (d) Segregated

answers: see pg 493

Impact of Prejudice on Targets

No culture seems immune to stereotypes, prejudice, and discrimination. Most cultures have stereotypes, at least of rival external groups. If two countries have recently fought against each other in a war, each will likely have some prejudices and stereotypes about the other, and most likely very negative ones. They can even within the same group, such as between Sunni and Shia Muslims.[215] In addition, diverse cultures typically have to contend with the fact that members of different groups or categories have stereotypes about the other groups. As one example, all societies have both men and women, and your textbook authors would be very surprised to find any society in which men and women do not hold some stereotypes about each other. Likewise, most democracies have different political parties, and the members of both parties hold prejudices and stereotypes about the opposing parties.

What effects do prejudices and stereotypes have on their targets? What is it like to grow up in a culture that regards you as unattractive, or incompetent, or dangerous? Or, for that matter, what is it like to live in a culture that expects you to be wise and kind? In his famous "I Have a Dream" speech, Martin Luther King Jr. said: "Being a Negro in America means trying to smile when you want to cry. It means the pain of watching your children grow up with clouds of inferiority in their mental skies. It means having your legs cut off, and then being condemned for being a cripple."

Probably the most common reaction is that people dislike being stereotyped; they want to be known and judged as individuals. Being stereotyped in a negative manner is especially unpleasant. In a series of studies, women who used feminist doctrines to express negative stereotypes of men elicited reactions that sometimes took the form of sexual harassment.[216] The experimenters instructed the men to select stimulus pictures to send to a woman via email. Some of the available pictures were of nature and animals and were thus neutral, but others were sexually explicit and even pornographic images, and in all conditions the women had indicated that they found such pictures offensive. To expose someone to sexual materials against that person's explicit wishes is a form of sexual harassment. Men were most likely to choose such pictures if the woman had stereotyped men in a degrading or insulting manner. Though this finding does not excuse or justify sexual harassment, it does indicate that reactions to being stereotyped can be quite negative and even hostile or aggressive. Some targets of prejudice and discrimination even attempt or commit suicide or are murdered. Consider, for example, the LGBTQ+ community. Suicide attempts are also about five times higher in LGBTQ+ youth than in other youth.[217] In the United States, homicides of LGBTQ+ people are at the highest levels since they began being recorded over 20-years ago.[218] Over half of female to male transgender people have attempted suicide.[219]

Self-Fulfilling Prophecies

Once we accept the expectations of others, we tend to behave in a manner that is consistent with those expectations, and as a result the expectations come true. This is called a **self-fulfilling prophecy**.[220] A self-fulfilling prophecy is an expectation about the future that tends to come true partly *because* it is expected.

A self-fulfilling prophecy involves three stages.[221] First, a person believes that a certain event will happen in the future. Second, this expectation, or prophecy, leads to a new behavior that the person would have not engaged in without the expectation. Third, the expected event takes place (partly as a result of the change in behavior), and the prophecy is fulfilled. A vivid example is the collapse of the Last National Bank, which was a stable and solvent financial institution in the early 1930s during the Great Depression in the United States. First, people began to believe (incorrectly) that the Last National Bank was on the verge of bankruptcy. Second, the people who had accounts at the bank panicked and withdrew all their money. Third, the bank collapsed. The initial

self-fulfilling prophecy a prediction that ensures, by the behavior it generates, that it will come true belief (that the bank was ready to collapse) was false, but once people withdrew all their money, the bank really did collapse.

Several studies have found results that are consistent with the self-fulfilling prophecy. In one famous research demonstration of this effect, participants were children from 18 classrooms.[222] The researchers gave all participants an IQ test and then randomly chose 20% of the children from each room and told the teachers they were "intellectual bloomers." Teachers were told that these bloomers would show remarkable gains in IQ during the coming year. By the end of the year, these randomly designated "intellectual bloomers" really did bloom. They improved their IQ scores by an average of 12 points, as compared with gains of 8 points among other students. Thus, teachers' expectations, which were initially false and baseless, became a reality, probably because the teachers focused more positive attention on the students whom they expected would bloom.

A comprehensive literature review found that although self-fulfilling prophecies do occur in the classroom, the effects are relatively small.[223] Teacher expectations do predict student performance, but that is because teacher's expectations are often accurate, not because the expectations become self-fulfilling prophecies.

The concept of the self-fulfilling prophecy offers one way to predict the effects of stereotypes on their targets. People often live up or down to what is expected of them, especially if others treat them in certain ways based on those expectations. Applied to stereotypes, a self-fulfilling prophecy would mean that people would come to act like the stereotypes others hold of them.[224]

Most social scientists have long assumed that self-fulfilling prophecy effects would be the main, most powerful way that stereotypes affect their targets. They assumed that people could not entirely resist internalizing the stereotypes that society held of them. However, people often can and do resist. One of the most surprising contradictions to the self-fulfilling prophecy effect formed the basis for a new line of theory and research, discussed in the next section.

Stigma and Self-Protection

Throughout much of American history, the culture has held stereotypes of African Americans as inferior to European Americans in various ways. Some of these probably originated during the period of slavery. Black people were stereotyped as lazy, intellectually backward, and childlike. These stereotypes most likely reflected the fundamental attribution error (see Chapter 5), which attributes people's behavior to their inner traits even when it was really caused by external circumstances. All over the world, slaves have generally been lazy as far as their masters are concerned,[225] and why shouldn't they be? People rise above laziness in response to incentives that reward hard work, such as money, power, and status, but these were all denied to slaves. Likewise, American slaves had almost no opportunity for schooling or education, without which intellectual attainments are difficult if not impossible. Many aspects of the slave's role resemble the child's role: few rights, utter dependency on others, inability to make decisions about one's own life, and the inability to express any striving for long-term future goals. Any sensible person would behave that way in that situation, and it is unfortunate but perhaps understandable that observers made the mistake of seeing those behaviors as reflecting slaves' innate traits rather than situational forces.

What survived into the 20th century, long after slavery had been abolished, was a general perception of African Americans as inferior to European Americans. What were the consequences for African Americans born in that new era? Most social scientists assumed that African Americans could not help internalizing those negative views to some degree, just as with any self-fulfilling prophecy. The broadest result of American prejudices would therefore be that African Americans would have low self-esteem. To live in a culture that regards you and treats you as a second-class citizen would, seemingly inevitably, cause you to see yourself that way. The low self-esteem could then perhaps explain many behavioral patterns that might be observed, from lower occupational attainment to crime and violence.

This line of thought was standard, but in the late 1980s it was turned upside down by a surprising finding. Researchers reviewed dozens of studies and established a startling conclusion: African Americans on average do not suffer from low self-esteem.[226] If anything, African Americans have higher self-esteem than white Americans. Subsequent work has verified this finding and shown that African Americans are actually somewhat different from other minority groups in this regard.[227] Most American minority groups do have somewhat lower self-esteem than mainstream European Americans, but African Americans continue to score consistently higher on self-esteem.[228]

How could this be? No one disputed the fact that American society had held prejudices that regarded black people as inferior. How did they manage not only to resist internalizing the message, but to end up with higher self-esteem than other groups? Researchers have offered three answers, each of which is rooted in cognitive strategies and processes similar to those covered in Chapter 5.[229]

The first involved social comparison—specifically, the choice of comparison targets. To an animal living in the forest, success and failure can probably be measured directly in terms of getting something to eat, but to cultural beings, success and failure are relative. Your salary, for example, might be a measure of how well you are doing, but by itself it doesn't mean much. Salary is an index of success only in comparison to what other people are earning. People compare themselves to those within their own group. The self-esteem of a minority group might therefore not suffer from the fact that its members earn less than members of other groups. The earnings of other groups are regarded as irrelevant. They mainly compare themselves against each other.

The second involves the criteria of self-worth. People judge themselves by many criteria. As we saw in Chapter 3 on the self, people often choose criteria on which they do well and avoid criteria that make them look bad. If you're good at basket weaving or meteorology, you may decide that those are important measures of self-worth, but if you are bad at them, you may decide that they are trivial and irrelevant. Groups, too, can reject or discount the standards that make them look bad, focusing instead on the things they do well.

The third process involves attribution theory. (Again!) We noted earlier in this chapter that the self-serving bias (making internal attributions for successes and external attributions for failures) can help explain the thinking and actions of people who hold stereotypes. It may also help explain reactions to prejudice. Some disadvantaged minority groups might protect their self-esteem by attributing their problems to other people's prejudices against them. Assume, for example, that most people's lives contain some successes and some failures, and that each individual's self-esteem will depend on how they add those up. If you can use the self-serving bias to dismiss your failures as irrelevant to your worth, your self-esteem can be higher than if you blame yourself for your failures. Despite all its costs and harm, prejudice does offer one advantage to the target—an external attribution for failure. Targets of prejudice can blame their failures and problems on prejudice. As a result, they can base their self-esteem mainly on their successes, and their self-esteem will rise.

A subsequent experiment confirmed that attributing failure to prejudice can protect self-esteem.[230] African American college students wrote an essay and received feedback that was critical and negative. This feedback came from a white American accomplice pretending to be another participant. Did the criticism cause a drop in self-esteem? It depended on attributions. Half the participants believed that the other participant knew who they were, including their race. These participants showed no drop in self-esteem, because they inferred that the bad evaluation reflected the prejudices of the evaluator. Criticism based on prejudice should not lower one's self-esteem, of course, so the participants who made this attribution (that the bad evaluation was caused by prejudice) shrugged it off. In contrast, the other participants were told that the evaluator knew nothing about them. They could not dismiss the evaluation as a result of racial prejudice because they thought the evaluator did not know their race. Their self-esteem did suffer (temporarily) as a result of the bad evaluation.

Thus, although both groups received exactly the same evaluation, only one group experienced a drop in self-esteem. Of course, those participants had no proof or evidence that the evaluation was motivated by racial prejudice, and in reality the evaluation (exactly the same for everyone) was decided by the experimental procedure. All that differed was that one group was able to conclude that prejudice might be one possible cause of it, and they apparently used this possibility as a basis for dismissing the criticism and maintaining their self-esteem.

If nothing else, these findings show that people are not just passive recipients of social influence. Cultures tell some groups that they are inferior, but many members of those groups successfully reject such messages.

Another form of self-protection against stigmas is to actively conceal them. Researchers have long recognized the important difference between visible and invisible stigmas. A woman who is black and a lesbian, for example, must deal with the fact that everyone can immediately see that she is black, whereas her homosexuality can be concealed. Recent work suggests that people who conceal their stigmatized identities "internalize the closet," which means that they become adept at keeping some parts of their self-concept secret.[231] In Chapter 3 we considered the important distinction between public self (the image one presents to the world) and private self (how one views oneself). Gay persons who keep their homosexuality secret learn to maintain a public (seemingly non-gay) identity, while also keeping a private concept of self that contains a sexual orientation that is not shared with the world. Similar patterns were found among people who concealed their strong religious beliefs from nonbelieving peers.

Competitive Victimhood

You might assume that nobody wants to be a victim. After all, being a victim is associated with being passive, with suffering mistreatment by others, and with general unhappiness. Yet in recent years various scholars have argued that in modern society, various people and groups compete to claim victim status.[232,233] Being a victim entitles a person to others' sympathy and emotional support, possibly extending to financial and legal entitlements. The victim's role enjoys a kind of moral privilege. It is considered taboo in many circles to reproach victims for any sort of misbehavior. No doubt this reflects the fact that many victims are innocent and both need and deserve help, and blaming them for their troubles could be seen as supporting the oppressors (who often blame their victims for sometimes completely made-up misdeeds).

Yet other people may claim victim status precisely because of the moral, legal, or financial advantages inherent in the role. Earlier work showed that claiming victim status reduces guilty feelings.[234] For example, Jews who were reminded of how many Jews were killed by Hitler's troops felt less guilty about Jews' harmful treatment of Palestinians. Likewise, Americans felt less guilty about their country's harmful actions in Iraq if the Americans had been reminded of terrorist attacks against America or even just reminded of the Pearl Harbor bombing by the Japanese in 1941. Claiming to be a victim—including based on events in the distant past—serves to reduce one's guilt, even for seemingly irrelevant acts.

Stereotype Threat

We have seen that people do not like being stereotyped and often strive extra hard to show that they do not fit negative stereotypes of their group. Sometimes stereotypes can even create **self-defeating prophecies**. This observation has been elaborated in a profound way by several social psychologists, who noted that when a stereotype might apply, people fear that their behavior will confirm it. This fear is called **stereotype threat**.[235] When people fear that they will be negatively stereotyped, their performance suffers.

Stereotype threat may operate most powerfully when it is difficult to contradict. Thus, if your group is stereotyped as liking greasy food, you can relatively easily show that it does not apply to you, simply by choosing healthier, nongreasy foods when others are watching. In contrast, if your group is stereotyped as being bad at singing, you would have to sing well in order to contradict it, and singing well in public (especially when you are nervous because of stereotype threat!) may be quite difficult.

self-defeating prophecy a prediction that ensures, by the behavior it generates, that it will not come true

stereotype threat the fear that one might confirm the stereotypes that others hold

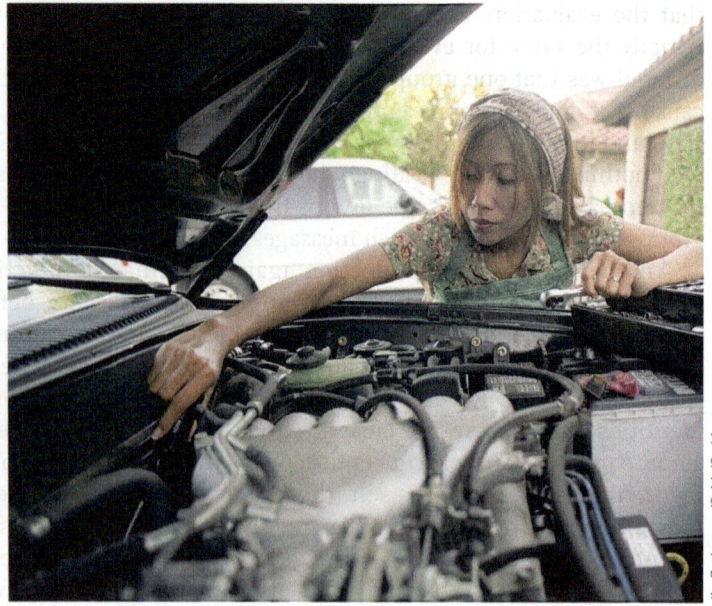

Can you identify the stereotype threats that these individuals face? In what way would failure be less bad if their genders were reversed?

Intellectual performance is of particular interest because of its importance in American culture and society. Girls score slightly lower than boys on math tests, even when they are gifted children.[236] The difference seems to be due to mathematical reasoning, because females can do simple arithmetical computations better than males. In a similar vein, African American students score lower on many tests than European American students.[237,238] Social psychologists wondered whether these gender and race differences might be partly due to stereotype threat, and they conducted a series of studies to test this hypothesis.

Several studies played on the stereotype that women perform worse than men on mathematical tests.[239] When the math test was described as producing no gender differences, women performed as well as men. However, when the math test was described as producing gender differences, women performed worse than men. Women feared that if they did poorly, it would reinforce people's beliefs about female inferiority at math, and the resulting worry contributed to lowering their performance. Even subtle cues can produce this effect, such as when the experimenter is male rather than female.[240] The effects are especially large if women are concerned that performing poorly will reflect badly on all women rather than on them personally.[241] The same thing happens to white men when the comparison group is Asian men (who are stereotyped to be good at math).[242]

Other studies have taken on the controversial issue of racial differences in intellectual performance. Although IQ tests have been accused of racial bias, defenders of the tests have argued that they are designed to predict performance in school, and the tests (which predict the performance of white students quite accurately) often predict higher grades for black students than the students actually end up achieving. Could that discrepancy be due to stereotype threat? In an important study,[243] researchers told some participants that the test had been shown to have no racial bias and no racial differences. In that condition, African American participants performed as well as their college admission standardized test scores would predict. Other participants received no such instruction, so the stereotype threat ("If I do badly, it will confirm people's stereotype of African Americans as intellectually inferior") remained an important force in the situation. In that situation, African Americans performed worse than others and worse than their college admission standardized test scores would predict. Other research has shown that under stereotype threat, African Americans experience an increase in blood pressure.[244] Eliminating the stereotype threat does not entirely eliminate the test-score gap between blacks and whites,[245,246,247] but it does eliminate the troubling pattern in which many students perform below what their college admission standardized test scores predict.

A meta-analytic review found that stereotype threat does impair test performance for women and minorities.[248] Why does the impairment occur? Anxiety appears to be the culprit. Confirming negative stereotypes makes people anxious, and the more anxious people are, the more their performance suffers.[249,250] When people become anxious, they try to calm down, but this takes a lot of effort and mental resources, which depletes people of the mental resources they need to perform well on the test.[251] Indeed, people who experience a stereotype threat show activity in the part of their brain involved in emotional processing rather than in the part of their brain involved in thinking and reasoning.[252]

Fortunately, there is a silver lining on this dark cloud of stereotype threat. Research shows that people can be inoculated against stereotype threat.[253] In one study, older people did better on a math test if they first interacted with their grandchildren than if they did not. Even imagining interacting with younger people improved performance. When older people interact with younger people, they feel less anxious about their test performance.

Nearly everyone is a member of some group that is sometimes the target of stereotyping. Stereotype threat can affect everyone. Minority groups sometimes hold the stereotype of European Americans as prejudiced, so in interracial interactions white people sometimes worry lest anything they say be interpreted as a sign of prejudice.

Indeed, this sort of stereotype threat makes interracial interactions more difficult for all concerned. Research on interactions between black and white people has found that both groups approached these interactions with heightened anxiety, for just these reasons.[254,255] Black people worried that their white interaction partners would be biased against them, so they feared behaving in ways that might justify these prejudices. Meanwhile, the white participants worried that they would be perceived as prejudiced by their black interaction partners, and they too feared that they might do something to confirm those stereotypes.

Stereotype threat should promote sympathy for minority groups, especially in difficult performance contexts. It is hard enough to perform well on your own, but it is that much more difficult to perform well while worrying that others will take failure as confirmation of negative stereotypes. No one likes to fail, and many people will avoid some risks in order to reduce the chances of failure. If failure reflects not only on you but also on an entire category of people to which you belong, the burden of failure is greatly increased, and it is not surprising that some people will withdraw in order to avoid such pressure.

QUIZ YOURSELF
Impact of Prejudice on Targets

1. Once we have adopted a certain expectation, we tend to behave in a manner that is consistent with that expectation, and the expectation comes true. This effect is called the _____.
   - (a) discontinuity effect
   - (b) false consensus effect
   - (c) minimal group effect
   - (d) self-fulfilling prophecy

2. Compared to European Americans, African Americans generally have _____ levels of self-esteem.
   - (a) higher
   - (b) more unstable
   - (c) lower
   - (d) similar

3. In a social interaction between blacks and whites, which group tends to become more anxious?
   - (a) Blacks
   - (b) Whites
   - (c) Both blacks and whites
   - (d) Neither blacks nor whites

4. Mr. Trig, a high school math teacher, communicates to his class that he thinks boys tend to do better in math than girls. As a result, some of the girls in his class become anxious about doing math problems. The girls are experiencing _____.
   - (a) stereotype threat
   - (b) discontinuity effect
   - (c) the scapegoating effect
   - (d) social identity threat

answers: see pg 493

Are Social Psychologists Biased?

Many social psychologists see their research as part of the battle against prejudice. This serves liberal ideals of fairness, justice, and equal opportunity, not to mention reducing hatred and violence. Simply put, most social psychologists would declare themselves opposed to prejudice.

That fact made the scientific community quite sensitive when some members began to suggest that the field of social psychology is biased—specifically, biased against political conservatives.[256] At the major national meeting of social psychology in 2001, one speaker asked for a show of hands indicating political affiliation. About 800 raised their hands to identify with liberalism, as compared with only 3 who admitted to being conservative. (In fact, only 20 claimed to be moderate or centrist, plus 12 libertarians.) More systematic surveys suggest that psychologists are about 10 to 15 times more likely to identify as liberals than conservatives—while in the general U.S. population, Gallup polls suggest that there are twice as many conservatives as liberals. Probably the 800-to-3 difference in the show of hands was so big because a few conservatives were afraid to express their views in public.

At present, the field of social psychology is debating whether its so-called "liberal bias" is a problem and what should be done about it. Almost certainly, a liberal bias shapes how research questions are asked and how data are interpreted. Editors may prefer to publish research findings that fit liberal rather than conservative views. In fact, liberals may even prevent research from being conducted if they do not approve of the political overtones. Disturbing evidence came from research on ethics boards, which all research-oriented universities have in order to decide whether a given study is safe and suitable to conduct with the student population. Researchers submitted identical research designs to 150 different universities' ethics boards, asking for permission to run the same study, which was concerned with prejudice and discrimination.[257,258] The applications were the same except for one detail: Half were described as attempting to study discrimination (i.e., against ethnic minorities), whereas the others were described as studying "reverse discrimination (i.e., against white males). There should have been no difference, because the procedures were exactly the same and thus equally safe, as well as equally valid in terms of scientific quality. But the boards rejected more applications that referred to "reverse discrimination," which goes against liberal bias, than when they referred simply to discrimination, which is congenial to liberal bias.

In writing this textbook, we have tried to be fair to both liberal and conservative political views. Still, we are covering the field as it is, and the body of scientific knowledge may itself be altered by liberal bias. This is a concern for anyone who prizes scientific truth above political ideals.

What Makes Us *Human*: Putting the Cultural Animal in Perspective

Conflict between groups is not unique to humans. As cultural animals, however, humans surround group conflict with meanings, values, and other ideas. Having a hostile feeling toward a rival group may be something that many animals experience, but creating a negative stereotype of the other group is something that requires the powerful mental apparatus of the human mind.

Moreover, the content of stereotypes and prejudices is generally learned, and as we saw, it is not so much learned by direct experience as from other people similar to oneself. Deliberately passing social ideas to the young is something that sets humans apart, and in general it is one of the wonders of human nature—but humans also teach stereotypes and prejudices to their children. This is not to say that children are naturally inclined toward love and tolerance of everyone. Human children seem all too ready to reject anyone who is different, so they quickly and readily acquire negative views of other groups.

Culture increases the scope and importance of prejudices. If a fish were prejudiced toward another group of fish, it might avoid interacting with them, but this would not affect the other fish very much. Humans, in contrast, rely on each other and their social network for their livelihoods. Prejudice can interfere with someone's chances to get a particular job, live in a desirable home, hold political office, and choose a desired mate. Victims of discrimination lose out on many cultural rewards, from prestige and self-esteem to money. People may use prejudices and stereotypes to strengthen the bonds within their group. This shows once again the theme that inner processes serve interpersonal relations: People form and maintain stereotypes because those mental structures help them deal with the social world.

But there is another, more positive side to human nature. Unlike other animals, humans can rise above their prejudices and feelings. People can reinvent and restructure the society in which they live—indeed, the processes of social change seem to go on relentlessly, at least in the modern world. People can also change themselves, by questioning their values and pushing themselves to think, feel, and act differently.

Thus, only humans have been able to rise above their natural antagonisms and create a society in which people from different, even formerly competing, groups can live together in peace, tolerance, and harmony. In the past century, the United States (like many other countries) has seen dramatic improvements in the social respect and opportunities offered to women, and it has moved far toward racial equality and tolerance, too. In many countries of the world, people from different groups that once hated, despised, and fought each other now live side by side and cooperate actively in a respectful, smoothly functioning system. The capacity for progress of this sort is one of the biggest advantages of human culture. The progress toward defeating prejudice and discrimination—though still incomplete and imperfect—is a very positive indication of what makes us human.

CHAPTER 13 SUMMARY

ABCs of Intergroup Relationships: Prejudice, Discrimination, and Stereotypes

- Prejudice is a negative feeling or attitude toward an individual based solely on his or her membership in a particular group.
- Discrimination refers to unequal treatment of different people based on the groups or categories to which they belong.
- Stereotypes are beliefs that associate groups of people with certain traits.
- The view that prejudice and stereotyping are morally wrong is a product of modern, Western culture. Many cultures tolerate stereotyping.
- Most stereotypes are negative, and most prejudices depict outgroups as inferior or as having bad traits.
- Outgroup members ("they") are people who belong to a different group or category than we do.
- Ingroup members ("we") are people who belong to the same group or category as we do.
- The outgroup homogeneity bias assumes that outgroup members are more similar to one another than ingroup members are to one another.
- Stigmas include characteristics of individuals that are considered socially unappealing, such as being overweight, mentally ill, sick, or poor, or having a physical blemish.
- Stigma by association shows that people are discriminated against for merely being associated with a stigmatized person.

Common Prejudices and Targets

- Both men and women are more intolerant of homosexuality in their own gender than in the opposite gender.

- Although stereotypes often contain culturally specific information, the tendency to form stereotypes and prejudices may be innate.
- People automatically and normally know stereotypes and think of them, whereas they have to exert themselves to override them.

Why Prejudice Exists

- Ingroup favoritism is preferential treatment of, or more favorable attitudes toward, people in one's own group, as compared to people in other groups.
- Realistic conflict theory suggests that competition over scarce resources leads to intergroup hostility and conflict; hostilities form when groups compete against each other.
- Some societies have little or no competition. These are typically peaceful, economically undeveloped groups.
- Competition has costs, but it also has benefits.
- Evolution may have had a hand in instilling the human readiness to form groups and hold prejudices against rival groups.
- The discontinuity effect suggests that groups are more prone to hostile competitiveness than individuals are.
- The contact hypothesis proposes that regular interaction between members of different groups reduces prejudice, providing that it occurs under favorable conditions.
- People often rely on stereotypes as heuristics (mental shortcuts).
- By using stereotypes to justify and act on prejudices, people can increase their feelings of self-worth.

Content of Prejudice and Stereotypes

- Some stereotypes are accurate, others are wrong, and others are partly true but overgeneralized.
- Stereotypes can form from purely cognitive processes, without any influence of emotion or motivation. Still, emotion or motivation can greatly increase the likelihood of prejudice.

Inner Processes

- Scapegoat theory proposes that people blame their problems and misfortunes on outgroups.
- Conflict and stress tend to bring out stereotypes and prejudice.
- People use their stereotypes more as hypotheses to be tested than as rules that can be applied in all cases.
- American society has made considerable progress in fighting against some important kinds of prejudice, especially those based on race and gender.
- The automatic system may often sustain prejudices, whereas the conscious system may strive to overcome those prejudices and stereotypes.
- When people are accused of prejudice, they often exert themselves to prove the opposite.

Overcoming Stereotypes, Reducing Prejudice

- People overcome prejudice by making conscious efforts to be fair and equal.
- The internal (belief that prejudice is morally wrong) and external (desire to avoid social disapproval) motivations for avoiding prejudice are not mutually exclusive.
- The jigsaw classroom, developed to reduce prejudice, is a cooperative learning technique in which group members must work together as a team and share unique information to accomplish a common goal.

Impact of Prejudice on Targets

- The self-fulfilling prophecy effect proposes that people will come to act in accordance with the stereotypes that others hold of them.
- Stereotypes can also create a self-defeating prophecy, which ensures, by the behavior it generates, that it will not come true.
- Cultures may tell some groups that they are inferior, but many members of those groups successfully reject such messages.
- Compared to European Americans, African Americans generally have higher levels of self-esteem.
- Stereotype threat is the fear that a stereotype might apply and that one's behavior might confirm it.
- Stereotype threat makes interracial interactions anxiety provoking for both races because both worry about confirming stereotypes about themselves.
- Unlike other animals, only humans have been able to rise above their natural antagonisms and create a society in which people from different, even formerly competing, groups can live together in peace, tolerance, and harmony.

What Makes Us Human?

- Although conflict between groups is not unique to humans, humans surround group conflict with meanings, values, and other ideas.
- Humans are the only animals that deliberately pass social ideas on to their young.
- People may use prejudices and stereotypes to strengthen the bonds within their group.
- Unlike other animals, humans can rise above their prejudices and feelings.

key terms

aversive racism 453
categorization 453
competition 467
confirmation bias 477
contact hypothesis 469
cooperation 467
discontinuity effect 469
discrimination 453

homophobia 463
ingroup favoritism 466
ingroup members 455
jigsaw classroom 483
minimal group effect 466
outgroup homogeneity bias 455
outgroup members 455
prejudice 453

racism 453
realistic conflict theory 467
salience 475
scapegoat theory 476
self-defeating prophecy 487
self-fulfilling prophecy 484
self-serving bias 476
social categorization 453

stereotype threat 487
stereotypes 453
stigma by association 461
stigmas 465
subtypes 453

quiz yourself ANSWERS

1. ABCs of Intergroup Relationships: Prejudice, Discrimination, and Stereotypes p.456
   answers: 1.a   2.a   3.c   4.c
2. Common Prejudices and Targets p.464
   answers: 1.b   2.b   3.b   4.d
3. Why Prejudice Exists p.473
   answers: 1.b   2.b   3.b   4.c
4. Content of Prejudice and Stereotypes p.475
   answers: 1.a   2.a   3.a   4.c
5. Inner Processes p.478
   answers: 1.d   2.d   3.b   4.a
6. Overcoming Stereotypes, Reducing Prejudice p.483
   answers: 1.a   2.b   3.c   4.c
7. Impact of Prejudice on Targets p.489
   answers: 1.d   2.a   3.c   4.a

GROUPS

APPLICATION MODULE E

Applying Social Psychology to the Environment

Richard L. Miller / Texas A&M University–Kingsville

LEARNING OBJECTIVES

1. Distinguish the four types of environmental problems, and identify barriers to solving these problems.

2. Explain the factors that lead to high density being interpreted as crowding, and identify some of the factors affecting our perception of crowding.

3. Evaluate how environmental quality factors such as weather, climate, noise, and pollution affect our psychological well-being.

4. Summarize the psychological principles that promote the conservation of scarce natural resources.

5. Describe the factors before, during, and after a disaster that impact the effects an environmental disaster has on people.

6. Analyze the ways in which social psychology can help promote environmentally sound behavior.

TRADEOFFS
The Tragedy of the Commons
E3

MONEY MATTERS
The Costs and Benefits of Environmental Protection
E21

WHAT MAKES US HUMAN?
Putting the Cultural Animal in Perspective
E22

Overview of Environmental Problems

Rick grew up on the Gulf Coast of Texas, and in the summer he would go out early in the morning and bring home fish for breakfast. When he was offered a job in Washington, D.C., he thought it would be great to live near the water again; looking at a map it appeared that a neighborhood bordering the Anacostia River might be just the thing. On his first trip to locate a place to live, he discovered there were no fish in the river. Rick asked how this could be and was told that the river was dead, that nothing could grow in it. He had never heard of a dead river before, but the real estate agent explained that industrial pollutants, sewage, and trash made the Anacostia one of the most polluted rivers in the nation. He looked at the river, and the water was black and ominous. He settled in a different part of town.

A few years ago, Bob Nixon, a former moviemaker, took on the task of cleaning up the river, with some success, but at a cost. The human environment surrounding the river is also very inhospitable to life, with a high crime rate, drug wars, and the full range of urban ills. Ten of the community development workers on Bob's team were murdered. The cycle of violence in the community is appalling. How have we allowed both the human environment and the natural environment to become so dangerous? Is this area an isolated case, or are there environmental problems that can affect all of us?

Our thoughts, emotions, and behavior are all influenced by our environment and it is important to understand that while we shape our environment, the environment in turn shapes us. We live in a world where environmental problems such as the effects of global warming on climate change, air pollution, water shortage, noise, and loss of biodiversity are the subject of constant debate.[1] Are we doing things that will make our world significantly less hospitable? Should we be concerned, or is much of what we read and hear about climate change, pollution, and toxic waste spills simply modern-day examples of Chicken Little saying, "The sky is falling"? Unfortunately, the problems are real, and the range of concerns is extensive and expanding.[2] Issues that few had heard of when the authors of your text were in college are now part of our common vocabulary. Some of these issues are global warming, which occurs because of the increasing concentration of greenhouse gases in the atmosphere; acid rain, which destroys marine and plant life; urban smog, which makes cities dangerous for those with respiratory weaknesses; toxic waste, which can be a lethal health hazard; and overpopulation, which depletes natural resources.[3] In this module, we will examine how social psychology can be used to understand and address environmental concerns related to overpopulation, environmental quality, the scarcity of natural resources, and environmental disasters. Addressing these issues involves tradeoffs such as the commons dilemma, discussed in *Tradeoffs*.

individual good–collective bad trap when a destructive behavior by one person is of little consequence but has disastrous results when repeated by many (e.g., overgrazing or overfishing)

one-person trap when the consequences of a destructive behavior affect only the individual (e.g., overeating)

missing hero trap when information of actual or potential disaster (e.g., toxic spill) is withheld from those affected by it

Four Types of Environmental Problems

Many environmental problems are a direct result of human behavior, and some of the problems are so severe that they seriously affect our way of life. For example, we live in a world of higher and higher population density. The rate of population increase is close to 80 million people annually. This population growth is significant for two reasons. First, the demand it places on the world's resources is unsustainable. In today's world, 25,000 people die of malnutrition and hunger-related diseases every day, most of who are children under the age of 5. Second, crowding has a direct effect on people as well as other animals. For example, research with rats forced to live in a highly crowded situation found that the normal

Anacostia River, Washington, D.C.

The Tragedy of the Commons

TRADE Offs

Why do factories pollute our air and water? Why are we rapidly depleting our supply of seafood? Why do people litter when we all know that someone will have to come and clean up our mess? These kinds of behaviors are characteristic of the commons dilemma (see Chapter 8), in which people's short-term selfish interests conflict with long-term societal needs.[4] A current example of this dilemma is the resistance of some Americans to be vaccinated against measles. As long as everyone else is vaccinated, then all can feel safe. However, if more and more people resist being vaccinated, the danger to all becomes more acute. If water is scarce, taking a shower may be good for you but harmful to the rest of the people needing water. In these situations, the gains to the individual appear to outweigh the costs, which create a form of social trap.[5] There are three types of social traps. The **individual good–collective bad trap** occurs when a destructive behavior by one person is of little consequence but when repeated by many, the result can be disastrous. Overgrazing, overfishing, and excessive water consumption are examples. The **one-person trap** occurs when the consequences of the action are only disastrous to the individual. For example, smoking or overeating seems momentarily pleasurable but has long-term negative consequences. The third type of trap is the **missing hero trap**. This trap occurs when information that people need is withheld. An example would be failure to notify nearby residents of a toxic waste spill or the harmful effects of pesticides.

How can the commons dilemma be avoided? One way is to change the consequences of the behavior to the individual involved by punishing what was previously reinforced and rewarding what was previously punished. Government regulations can limit the amount of a common good available to an individual; for example, permit systems for fishing and hunting. Similarly, many cities have created carpool lanes on highways, allowing faster movement for those who share their automobiles. A second technique is to change the structure of the commons by dividing previously shared resources into privately owned parcels. Fish farms are an example of this approach. However, many of our common resources such as air and water cannot be privatized.[6] A third technique is to provide feedback mechanisms so that individuals are aware when they are wasting precious resources.[7]

Promoting communication and a sense of identity based on membership in the group using the commons has been shown to increase conservation of the common resources. For example, in one study, farmers who were members of a cohesive rural community and strongly identified with one another were encouraged to discuss pro-ecological harvesting strategies. As a result, they made a number of harvesting choices that helped to conserve natural resources.[8] This approach may require breaking up a commons into smaller segments in order to promote cooperation in maintaining sustainability. Research on marine conservation has found that appeals to social equity can be effective, especially when the equity manipulation involves participation by the stakeholders in conservation planning[9] and financial considerations of the conservation intervention.[10]

Each of these techniques has its costs, benefits, and ease or difficulty of application. The least costly intervention is probably environmental education, but it may be one of the least effective as well. Reinforcement and punishment can have strong short-term effects, but many of these effects can dissipate over time when the reinforcement strategy is discontinued. Perhaps the most promising techniques have to do with increasing communication, promoting group identity, and encouraging individual commitment to solving the tragedy of the commons.

Many of the environmental problems we face today cross national boundaries. To solve global climate change, or water shortages around the world will take transnational efforts. For this to happen, key leaders need to view their country's fates as interconnected; understand the contribution their country makes to the problem; and take collective action to solve the problem. For this to happen requires a shift in the way governments, multinational corporations, and nongovernmental organizations think about the problem since according to Climate Action Tracker (see https://climateactiontracker.org/countries/) none of the top ten carbon-emitting countries is reaching their goal as set by the 2016 Paris agreement.

Five mechanisms have been identified that contribute to a shift in thinking. They are collective theorizing, issue linkage, active learning, legitimacy seeking, and catalytic amplification. The gradual acceptance of how human behavior impacts the environment is an outcome of collective theorizing. Issue linkage occurs as government policy begins to address environmental issues. Legitimacy seeking takes place as environmental protection groups abandon tactics that alienate others and begin to speak to the mainstream. Active learning occurs as various bodies begin to promote research in the causes, consequences and solutions to environmental problems. Finally, catalytic amplification is a result of cooperation among various stakeholders in promoting common solutions.[11]

In addition to the commons dilemma and social traps, a third social dilemma is the public goods problem. This problem arises when individuals consider the costs and benefits of helping with a project that will provide a benefit to the public good. This becomes a dilemma because one's contribution might not be needed or one's contribution is not enough for the project to succeed. This dilemma is fairly common, and when it is overcome, as in the recent case of Hurricane Harvey, where people from all walks of life pitched in to address the destruction, it is considered quite newsworthy.

New Orleans resident copes with the aftermath of Hurricane Katrina.

social order disintegrated and became what has been called a behavioral sink.[12] The animals exhibited heightened aggression, infant neglect and abuse, and sexual deviance, as well as hyperactivity among some and passivity among others. Similarly, humans who are crowded can become depressed,[13] anxious,[14] deviant,[15] withdrawn,[16] aggressive,[17] and both mentally and physically ill.[18] It is important to understand that crowding is a motivational state based on human perception and not simply a matter of density, which is a measure of physical space. For example, being in a mosh pit at a rock concert may be highly dense but not necessary feel crowded, unlike a supermarket with narrow aisles.

The quality of our environment is also affected by both natural and technological factors. Issues of weather and climate that have harmful effects on human behavior include the effects of longer, hotter summers. Heat has been shown to harm classroom performance;[19] to impair memory, attention, problem solving, and reaction time;[20] and to increase violent crime.[21]

Noise associated with our jobs and our homes has been shown to increase stress and impair people's health,[22] promote aggression,[23] and reduce helping behavior.[24] The most common occupational disease in the United States is noise-induced hearing loss and an estimated $242 million is spent each year to compensate workers for their hearing disabilities.[25]

Pollution also has harmful effects on both health and human judgment.[26] For example, the rate of childhood asthma has risen dramatically in the past 20 years.

Human beings obtain 91% of their energy from nonrenewable, nonsustainable resources such as oil, coal, and gas.[27] Energy sources are considered nonrenewable when they cannot be replenished in a short period of time and nonsustainable when their rate of depletion is greater than their rate of creation. The land area available for food production has shrunk dramatically due to urbanization, desertification, and overpopulation, and much of the remaining land has been damaged by inorganic fertilizers.[28] Clean water is becoming scarce, in part because of pollution and in part because of usage patterns that promote extensive irrigation and the decorative use of water for lawns, fountains, waterfalls, and artificial ponds and lakes.

A final area of concern involves environmental disasters, which have become more frequent and more intense lately due to climate change. Natural disasters such as hurricanes, typhoons, and earthquakes can have a profound effect on people, even on those not directly harmed by the disaster. The physical damage of a natural disaster is obvious, but the most profound effects are due to the social disruption caused by the disaster[29] that can continue to cause stress years after the disaster itself.[30] Technological disasters, including oil spills, mine accidents, nuclear power plant breakdowns, and exposure to toxins, can have obvious physical effects on the health and well-being of those involved. Long-term behavioral effects of technological disasters include anxiety, depression, anger, nightmares, and stress.[31] In addition, recent research has found that disasters can also cause deficits in cognitive performance.[32]

Barriers to Solving Environmental Problems

Some scientists argue that the impact of environmental problems has been overstated. Certainly, excessive claims have been made from time to time. Despite arguments about specific details related to environmental problems, the Union of Concerned Scientists has warned us about the consequences of leaving environmental problems unsolved.[33]

Given the urgency of environmental problems and their consequences, why have we not done everything in our power to eliminate these problems? There are several reasons. First, destruction of the environment is a global problem, difficult to overcome without cooperation among many nations. Second, the rate of environmental deterioration has increased rapidly in the past few decades. In fact, half of all the environmental changes that have occurred in the past 10,000 years have happened during our lifetime.[34] Third, fixing environmental problems can be costly, and inevitably there are vested interests that will suffer economically in the process. Fourth, it may take years of misuse and abuse before an environmental problem becomes apparent to everyone. Fifth, there are those who believe that environmental problems are so complicated that nothing can be done to prevent further degradation.[35] Finally, two recent meta-analyses have shown that ideology plays an important role in climate change denial and anti-environmentalism. Conservative ideology and party affiliation are associated with climate change denial regardless of demographic factors and knowledge about climate change.[36] Interestingly, it may not be that conservatives don't believe in climate change but that political polarization discourages them from endorsing what they see as a "liberal" issue.[37] Moreover, social dominance and authoritarianism are also associated with negative attitudes toward environmentalism and climate change.[38] Individuals who score high in social dominance orientation show a preference for a clearly defined social hierarchy and inequality. Individuals who score high on right-wing authoritarianism hold three interrelated attitudes: preference to submit to authority, conformity to traditional norms, and punishment of those who deviate from these norms (Altemeyer, 1998). In contrast, mindfulness, the process of focusing one's attention to experiences happening in the present moment, seems to promote pro-environmental attitudes and behavior[39] as does psychological ownership.[40]

Despite the many difficulties we will face in addressing environmental problems, the basic concern remains: "What kind of planet do we want? What kind of planet can we get?"[41]

The important question for students of psychology is how ordinary citizens, as well as those in business, government, and scientific laboratories can be encouraged to understand the nature of environmental problems, adopt practical solutions to those problems, and influence policy makers to address the problems in constructive ways.[42] Time is an important consideration in this process because many of the gains in technical efficiency that have come about from water-saving devices, improvements in home insulation, and energy-efficient appliances may be overtaken by increased consumption. To solve these problems will not only require that we change how we interact with the environment, but also how we come to understand and accept our role in environmental deterioration.[43]

The purpose of this module is to explore several areas in which psychology and the environment interact that may provide opportunities for positive change.

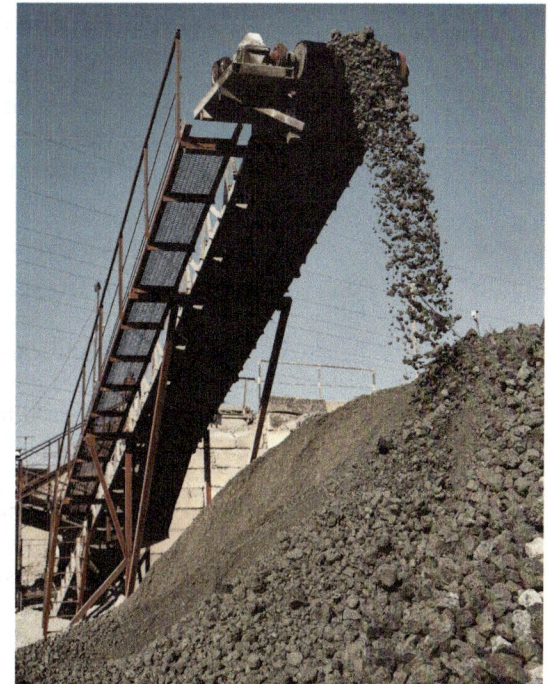

Will preserving the environment become institutionalized?

QUIZ YOURSELF
Overview of Environmental Problems

1. **Overpopulation is an environmental problem that can affect a person's _____ .**
   - (a) personality characteristics
   - (b) mental and physical health
   - (c) sleeping patterns
   - (d) cognitive problem solving ability

2. **Which of the following is the most sustainable source of energy?**
   - (a) Coal
   - (b) Oil
   - (c) Gas
   - (d) Sunlight

3. **Various explanations have been offered to account for why we are not more actively trying to solve our environmental problems. Which of the following is not one of those explanations?**
   - (a) The problems are often beyond the control of one nation.
   - (b) The cost of solving the problem is beyond easy reach.
   - (c) Most solutions have proven to be unworkable.
   - (d) The impact of the problems are not readily apparent.

4. **When rats were forced to live in a highly crowded situation, the result was a behavioral sink, which is characterized by _____ .**
   - (a) sexual deviance
   - (b) slower reaction time
   - (c) memory impairment
   - (d) altruistic behavior

answers: see pg E24

Problems Related to Overpopulation

The earth's population is growing at a logarithmic rate. Overpopulation can affect many aspects of the environment by contributing to pollution, depletion of natural resources including food and water, and environmental degradation, but the focus of this section is on the direct effects of overpopulation.

Crowding and Density

A few years ago, one of the bloodiest, most vicious prison riots in history took place in New Mexico. The overconcentration of inmates in a restricted environment contributed significantly to the carnage. How can crowding be so upsetting, and why is it that sometimes it is really enjoyable to lose yourself in a crowd? To understand this phenomenon, we need to make a distinction between **density**, which is the number of people who occupy a given space, and **crowding**, which is the subjective feeling that that there are too many people in the given space.[44]

One factor that turns density into crowding is the degree of control people feel they have over the presence of others. For example, when people were required to work in a crowded situation, their performance only suffered if they were unable to leave the situation.[45] Those who worked in the same crowded situation but were free to leave performed as well as those who worked in an uncrowded situation. A second factor is when the number of people interferes with a person's ability to achieve his or her objectives. When this happens, density turns into crowding.[46] A third factor that determines when density becomes crowding are the attributions (see Chapter 5) that people make regarding the arousal they experience when in the company of others. If people attribute their arousal to the presence of others, they will feel more crowded.[47] Finally, high density will become aversive if it leads to **sensory overload**,[48] which occurs when the amount of information to be processed exceeds the individual's capacity to sort out relevant information from information that is not. High-rise buildings, long narrow hallways and too few elevators can limit the amount of control residents have over the number and type of human interactions in which they engage. As a result, in crowded urban environments, people have been shown to ignore the needs of someone they pass on the street because they cope with the overload by only paying attention to the needs of those they have defined as important to them.

One of the most effective means for preventing the occurrence of crowding is to provide heightened cognitive control to people in high-density situations. **Cognitive control** is the sense people have about the predictability or controllability of their situation. For example, adding additional entrances to a mental health facility increased patient's sense of freedom and control along with a heightened sense of place among the therapists.[49]

density the number of people who occupy a given space

crowding the subjective feeling that there are too many people in a given space

sensory overload when the amount of information to be processed exceeds the individual's capacity to sort out what is relevant from what is not

cognitive control the sense people have about the predictability or controllability of their situation

People's expectations can change when it feels crowded.

Just learning that you are about to enter a crowded situation can be enough to reduce the aversion to that situation.[50] Moreover, a person's expectations about what is an appropriate level of crowding can make a difference. In the photos above, the picture on the left depicts a crowded environment that many people enjoy while the one on the right is aversive for most of us. Self-categorization theory suggests that social identification with a crowd should moderate the negative effects of crowding. Two studies, one at an outdoor music event and another at a demonstration march found support for the theory in that participants who identified with others in the crowd felt less crowded and displayed positive emotions, which increased over time.[51]

Personal Space

Another way we control the effects of crowding is by maintaining a certain distance, sometimes referred to as **personal space**, between ourselves and others. Personal space is an area with invisible boundaries that surrounds us. Its purposes are to avoid overstimulation, reduce stress, control unwanted arousal, achieve desired levels of privacy, and maintain our behavioral freedom.[52] Personal space can be understood as a form of nonverbal communication. It is the spatial component of interpersonal relationships and includes distance and angle (side-by-side, face-to-face, etc.) of human interactions.[53] The spacing between people communicates information about their relationship and the activities in which they are engaged. For example, think about telling someone about your sexual desires. Wouldn't it be odd to communicate this kind of intimate information at the typical 4- to 12-foot "social distance"? **TABLE E.1** summarizes how various relationships and activities relate to personal space among most North Americans. Other cultures may have different norms.

There are both individual and situational determinants of personal space. If people are attracted to one another, they are likely to interact at a closer physical distance, although it is women who are primarily responsible for reducing personal space.[54] People maintain a closer distance between themselves and others who are similar to them in age,[55] gender,[56] race,[57] religion,[58] sexual orientation,[59] and status.[60]

There are several individual differences in personal space preferences. In highly sensory "contact" cultures, such as Hispanic or Arabic cultures, individuals prefer to interact at closer distances than do northern Europeans or European Americans from "noncontact" cultures.[61] I recall a conversation I witnessed in a school playground between a teenager from Iran and his friend from Texas. As the Iranian moved closer to establish his preferred comfort zone, the Texan stepped back. Neither of them noticed what was happening, but by the time the 15-minute recess was over they had moved from one side of the playground to the other!

personal space an area with invisible boundaries that surrounds us

TABLE E.1 The Space Between Us[74]

Distance Zone	Intimate Relationships	Sensory Qualities
Intimate Distance (0 to 1½ feet)	Close personal contacts (e.g., dancing, making love, sports activities like wrestling)	Very aware of smell, heat from the other person; touch more important than talk
Personal Distance (1½ to 4 feet)	Contact with close friends; conversations closer with people we know well	Less aware of sensory input; vision and communication more important than touch
Social Distance (4 to 12 feet)	Contacts with strangers; impersonal and businesslike	Minimal sensory input; normal voice interaction; no touch possible
Public Distance (more than 12 feet)	Formal contacts between individuals and the public (e.g., actors, political debaters)	No sensory input; visual less detailed; nonverbal behaviors are exaggerated

Gender differences in personal space preferences are obvious. Two females will interact with one another at closer distances than will two males.[62] The personal space preferred by mixed-sex dyads depends on their relationship. Acquaintances maintain a distance somewhere between female–female and male–male pairs, whereas a man and a woman in a close relationship prefer distances closer than that used by either of the same-sex dyads.

Terror management theory (see Chapter 2) suggests that the fear of death creates existential anguish that underlies much of human motivation. Individuals who are confronted with reminders that they are going to die maintain closer personal space distances, especially if they have a strong need for affiliation.[63] Age also makes a difference in people's understanding of personal space. Awareness that there are personal space boundaries seldom occurs to us before our fourth birthday, and adult preferences are not usually evident until puberty.[64] As a result, most adults are fairly tolerant of spatial invasions by children. Our reaction when a child, even someone we don't know, attempts to get our attention by pulling the leg of our pants, is certainly different from what it would be if an adult stranger engaged in the same behavior.

Differences in personal space preferences are applied not only to our own behavior but also to the behavior of others. For example, students from North America have been shown to feel more comfortable the farther apart two brothers were sitting from one another, and the closer a brother and sister were sitting, whereas the Saudi students showed the opposite reaction. In conservative Muslim countries, greater distances between the sexes are preferred, even in intrafamily contact, but the aversion to public displays of male–male intimacy found in the United States and Europe is not universal.[65] What happens when someone invades our personal space? Among the many negative responses to the situation are a reduction in helping behavior,[66] negative evaluation of the invader,[67] performance deficits for complex tasks,[68] and compensatory reactions such as withdrawal or aggression.[69]

Territoriality

Territoriality is the tendency to stake out an area and a willingness to defend that area from intruders. Both humans and nonhuman animals practice territorial behavior. The purpose of territorial boundaries as a reaction to crowding is to make life more predictable, orderly, and stable.[70] For example, territorial cues have been shown to reduce crime.[71] Territories also provide people with feelings of distinctiveness, privacy, and a sense of personal identity.[72] Territorial boundaries can reduce the potential for conflict between people, but only if the boundaries are seen as legitimate and observed.[73]

How do we stake out the boundaries of our territory? Anyone who has ever owned a male dog is probably familiar with how they mark their territory using the bodily fluids available to them. Humans seldom use this technique, especially if they are sober. For humans, a backyard fence, cartoons on the wall outside their office door, a towel at the beach, their sweater draped over the back of a chair are all ways of signaling territorial ownership.

One of the most common ways we mark our territory is to personalize the area to be claimed. **Personalization**, in the form of improvements to our property or decorations that are unique reflections of our personal identity, can serve to facilitate neighborliness,[74] reduce problems with outsiders,[75] and proclaim our status within the community.[76] For example, among U.S. Army soldiers stationed in Germany, higher-ranking enlisted soldiers engaged in more personalization of their living quarters than lower-ranking soldiers.[77]

Interestingly, not all cultures promote a sense of personal identity based on territoriality. In the first place, some cultures do not claim territory. For instance, nomadic cultures can be hunter-gatherers who move from camp to camp following game and the availability of wild plants, pastoral nomads who move with their herds to gain better grazing

territoriality the tendency to stake out an area and a willingness to defend that area from intruders

personalization a way of marking our territory with improvements or decorations that are unique reflections of our personal identity land, or peripatetic nomads such as the Romani. Regarding personal identity, research shows that Turkish students are less likely than American students to think of their dorm rooms as an expression of who they are.[78] Cultures also differ in how they define territories. For example, German shop owners are legally responsible for keeping the street outside their shop clean and free of debris or snow, while in Spain the street is strictly public territory and cleaning it is the responsibility of government-funded organizations rather than the individual.[79]

To understand how territoriality works, it is useful to distinguish among three different types of territories. Your bedroom is a **primary territory**; as such, it is likely to be highly personalized and considered off limits to those not invited to enter. **Secondary territories** include the desk you usually sit at during class. You don't really own it, but you would be annoyed if someone came in early and sat in it. **Public territories** are open to anyone who is not specifically excluded. For example, a bar may be open to all except those who are not of legal age to drink.

Territoriality has implications for a variety of behaviors. Territoriality is central to understanding nationalism. When people seek self-government, they inevitably lay claim to a specified territory.[80] Thus, territoriality can encourage as well as prevent aggression. In a laboratory study, valued resources were distributed uniformly or clustered in patches throughout the environment. In the patchy condition, an ownership convention (i.e., the person who arrived first) determined who obtained the resource, but where resources were distributed uniformly, the ownership convention did not occur.[81]

A clearly marked, undisputed territory is likely to deter aggression,[82] whereas territories that are not well established can provoke aggressive behavior.[83] In his memoirs, Henry Kissinger recalls how he (as secretary of state) and General Alexander Haig fought for a room next to the president on a visit to the Soviet Union. Both men understood that other people's perception of their influence and prestige would be affected by their nearness to the seat of power. Another aspect of territoriality is that of "home turf," the feeling of relaxation, comfort, and control that occurs when you are interacting with visitors to your primary territory. And if those visitors are unwanted, you are more likely to assert yourself in interacting with them on your home turf than on either neutral ground or their territory.[84]

Some people are more territorial than others. One factor that affects territorial behavior is the extent to which a culture is either a low- or high-context culture. In a high-context culture, many things are left unsaid, letting the culture explain. Words and word choice become very important in a high-context communication because a few words can communicate a complex message very effectively to an ingroup (but less effectively outside that group). In a low-context culture, the communicator needs to be much more explicit and the value of a single word is less important.

People in low-context cultures tend to be more territorial. They are more likely to mark out the areas that are theirs and are more likely to engage in boundary wars with neighbors. For example, throughout history, Western society has shown considerable barbarity over ownership of land. Territoriality also extends to anything that is "mine," and ownership concerns extend to material things. Security thus becomes a subject of great concern for people who are highly territorial. People in high-context cultures tend to be less territorial. Individuals who are low in territoriality have less ownership of space and boundaries are less important to them. They will share territory and ownership. For example, Australian Aboriginal people will say that they belong to the land rather than the other way around. This may be a result of their success in living in harsh environmental conditions.[85]

There are also gender differences in human territoriality. Men are more likely to invade women's spaces than women are to invade men's spaces. Men seem to possess a stronger sense of territorial ownership and are more likely to challenge others' territorial boundaries[l]

primary territory area, such as a bedroom, that is highly personalized and considered off limits to those not invited to enter

secondary territory area, such as the desk you usually sit at, that you don't really own but nonetheless consider to be "yours"

public territory area that is open to anyone who is not specifically excluded

Problems Related to Overpopulation | **E9**

Some cultures are more territorial than others. The house on the left belongs to an American, whereas the one on the right belongs to an Australian Aborigine.

QUIZ YOURSELF
Problems Related to Overpopulation

1. Environmental psychologists consider _____ to be a physical state and _____ to be a psychological state.
   - ⓐ territoriality; personal space
   - ⓑ helplessness; sensory overload
   - ⓒ privacy; density
   - ⓓ density; crowding

2. The closest interaction distances are maintained by _____.
   - ⓐ male–male pairs
   - ⓑ female–female pairs
   - ⓒ male–female pairs who like one another
   - ⓓ male–female pairs who do not like each other

3. The three types of territory—primary, secondary, and public—differ on all of the following except _____.
   - ⓐ occupation by the owner
   - ⓑ degree of personalization
   - ⓒ how others perceive ownership
   - ⓓ concept of personal space

4. Just as Fatima is about to enter a store, she bumps into a friend leaving the store who tells her that the store is really crowded. Consequently, Fatima prepares herself for the crowd and is not too bothered by it. This example illustrates _____.
   - ⓐ cognitive control
   - ⓑ personalization
   - ⓒ primary territory
   - ⓓ sensory overload

answers: see pg E24

Environmental Quality

Imagine that you are sailing on a mountain lake on a crisp fall day in New England. The sun is glinting on the water, the leaves on the trees along the shoreline are turning gold and red, and a pleasant breeze is wafting you along. Now imagine that you are walking along the shore of the Anacostia River, picking up trash and stepping carefully to avoid the sludge and oil that mark the shore. You can hear the clanging of factories in the distance. These images can evoke very different emotional reactions that relate to the **ambient environment**, which includes temperature, odor, and sound. Although many aspects of the environment may go unnoticed, our mood, work performance, and physical

ambient environment sensory surroundings, including temperature, odor, and sound health can be affected by the sensory input we receive from the environment. In this section, we will examine the ways humans can be affected by weather, noise, and pollution.

Weather and Climate

The climate, elevation, and terrain where you live and work can affect your life profoundly. The skills you develop and the experiences that shape your life are strongly influenced by your environment. Climate may be the most important factor in shaping a culture's values and personality. For example, suicide rates have been associated with changes in barometric pressure. Atmospheric electricity seems to affect crime rates. Depression, nervousness, and even traffic accidents can occur because of wind conditions.[86] Human behavior is not only affected by individual weather events but also by sequences of weather events. For example, residents of Provence, France, will tell you that the cold, strong mistral wind blows for three days or multiples of three days. It is blamed for headaches, edginess, and bad behavior. Local legend has it that the painter Vincent van Gogh chopped off his ear after 17 days of the mistral.[87]

The most studied aspect of climate is heat, as suggested by the popular notion of "the long, hot summer." Heat is known to have a negative effect on performance in laboratory studies, the workplace, classrooms, and military settings. In addition, heat has been implicated in promoting civil war in sub-Saharan Africa, violence in East Africa, and civil conflict in the global tropics.[88] However, not all studies have shown negative effects. To explain the mixed findings, it has been suggested that heat may first lead to arousal and therefore improve performance, but continued exposure to high temperatures produces overarousal that leads to decreased performance. A second mitigating factor in the relationship between heat and performance is attention. As heat increases, arousal also increases, attention is narrowed, and people concentrate closely on the task at hand (see Chapter 6). Thus, performance on the primary task is not affected, but performance on secondary tasks deteriorates. As heat stress increases, individuals may feel less and less in control; as a result, performance deteriorates. As we saw in Chapter 9, hot temperatures are also linked to aggression and violence.

Noise

Noise is annoying, unwanted sound. How annoying depends on four factors: volume, predictability, perceived control and context. How loud is too loud? Noise above 90 decibels can be psychologically disturbing and, after hours of exposure, physically damaging. In general, noise that is irregular and unpredictable is more upsetting than constant, expected noise, especially if the noise is perceived as unnecessary or generated by those who seem unconcerned about the welfare of others.[89] Additional factors that moderate the effects of noise include the type of noise, the consistency of the noise, and the range of activities disrupted by the noise.[90]

The negative effects of lack of control have been well documented and include cognitive deficits, negative affect, and loss of motivation.[91] Control is important in coping with noise. In one study, participants were exposed to loud sound bursts at random intervals while they worked on a proofreading task. One group of participants had a button that they could use to stop the noise if they wanted to, although in this experiment, no one did. A second group did not have a stop button. A third group worked on the proofreading task without any noise. There were no differences in the performance of the groups during the noise, but the group that had worked without a stop button showed a substantial decrease in performance after the noise stopped. This result may be due to the **learned helplessness** that occurs when we believe that despite our efforts we are unable to control what happens to us (see Chapter 4 for more on learned helplessness). Several environmental stressors have been shown to contribute to learned helplessness, including noise, crowding, traffic congestion, and pollution.[92] For example, workers on the ground floor of a building near a noisy highway did not perform as well as workers on higher floors, and students going to school near the Los Angeles airport showed increases in blood pressure, distractibility, and long-term performance problems.[93]

noise annoying, unwanted sound

learned helplessness the belief that despite our efforts we are unable to control what happens to us

Environmental Quality | E11

Occupational noise and its impact on hearing loss has been the most frequently studied type of noise exposure. But in recent years, research has broadened to focus on social noise, such as noise heard in bars or through personal music players. Of course, what seems to be annoying noise to our neighbors may be music to our ears and therefore cause us less stress than those who don't appreciate our musical tastes. The study of social noise has increased our understanding of how different types of noise impact aspects of health other than hearing loss, including sleep, cardiovascular function, annoyance, and even a patient's ability to heal in a hospital environment.[94]

In addition to its effect on performance, noise can also influence social behavior. Are we really attracted to that person we see across the room in the noisy bar? Not likely, unless the person seems equally annoyed by the noise.[95] On the other hand, several studies have demonstrated that noise contributes to aggression (see Chapter 9). Noise can also reduce helping behavior. Noise that makes us irritable or uncomfortable may put us in a bad mood and therefore make us less likely to help others. Another explanation for the effects of noise on helping is that the noise overloads our senses and makes us less aware of what is happening around us, including signals that another person might need our help. In a field experiment, an individual who was wearing a cast on his arm dropped a box of books when getting out of a car. Noise was manipulated by having a lawn mower running nearby. The number of people who helped pick up the books dropped from 80% when the lawnmower had a muffler attached to 15% when the muffler was detached.[96]

Since noise has been shown to have a number of negative effects, should we take steps to try to reduce the amount of noise we live with? Is there value in implementing noise reduction programs? It has been found that reducing noise in the workplace increased job satisfaction.[97] In 2011, the World Health Organization in Europe put the cost of noise pollution for that continent at $30.8 billion a year. A recent study suggested that a 5-dB noise reduction scenario would reduce the prevalence of hypertension by 1.4% and coronary heart disease by 1.8%. The annual economic benefit was estimated at $3.9 billion.

Reducing noise in the community, especially noise associated with ground traffic and aircraft, has been shown to have positive effects, but people's response to noise reduction may depend on the extent to which they think the noise has implications for their health and well-being.[98]

Pollution

Perhaps the most serious health-related environmental concern is pollution. The main air pollutant warming the earth is carbon dioxide. Burning fossil fuels has pumped enough carbon dioxide into the atmosphere to raise levels of the pollutant higher than they have ever been. The effects of carbon dioxide depend on the extent of exposure as well as age, health, lifestyle, and other individual factors. Toxic effects include greater vulnerability to cardiac arrhythmias and seizures.[99] Of greater danger is the radiation and carcinogens found in our air and water, which are killing us at an ever-increasing rate (see **FIGURE E.1**). The World Health Organization estimates that approximately 800,000 people die prematurely each year because of air pollution. It is the thirteenth leading cause of mortality worldwide.[100] Current estimates are that one out of three Americans will get some form of cancer that is linked directly to environmental factors in 90% of the cases.[101] Air pollution affects the health of most people in the United States. Acute effects appear quickly; they range from headaches, rashes, and irritation to more serious effects such as convulsions and death. Chronic effects take longer to appear and are usually quite serious, especially for vulnerable populations such as children and the elderly.[102] Many of the components of polluted air can cause chronic effects.[103] Ozone contributes to skin cancer and aggravates respiratory problems by damaging the epithelial cells in the trachea. Arsenic and lead can disrupt children's development and cause problems with the central nervous system. Lead can cause liver disease. Cadmium retards fetal development. Carbon monoxide is implicated in visual and hearing impairment, heart disease, and neural disorders.

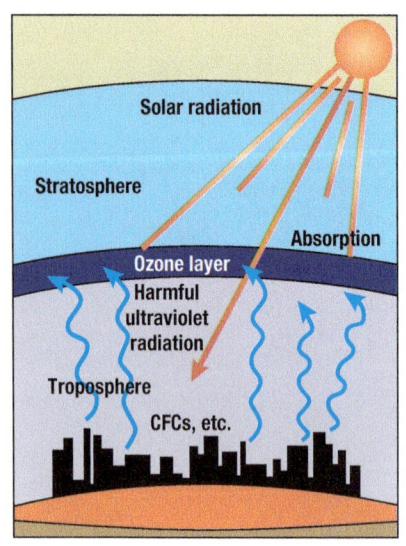

FIGURE E.1
Damage to the ozone layer.

Breathing polluted air can harm your performance. For example, participants who engaged in an information-processing task while breathing air that was drawn from a heavily used traffic site suffered decreased performance on three out of four of the tasks.[104]

Social behaviors can also be affected by air pollution, which has been shown to have an affect on depression,[105] anxiety and psychological stability,[106] and aggression (see Chapter 9).

QUIZ YOURSELF: Environmental Quality

1. Research indicates that heat may _____ attraction if the other person shares your discomfort and _____ attraction when it is not shared.
   - a) decrease; increase
   - b) increase; decrease
   - c) not affect; increase
   - d) not affect; decrease

2. The more predictable a noise is, _____ .
   - a) the more arousing the noise is
   - b) the more stressful the noise is
   - c) the easier the noise is to adapt to
   - d) the more likely it is to be disturbing

3. What percent of Americans will get some form of cancer that is directly linked to environmental factors?
   - a) 3%
   - b) 23%
   - c) 13%
   - d) 33%

4. Rodney lives in an apartment directly below the most commonly used flight path of airplanes on final approach to Chicago's O'Hare Airport. His schoolwork is likely to show _____ .
   - a) the effects of more supportive peer relationships
   - b) occasional performance deficits
   - c) long-term performance deficits
   - d) occasional flashes of creativity followed by stretches of mediocrity

answers: see pg E24

Scarcity of Natural Resources

The United States is the largest single consumer of the world's raw materials,[107] especially those materials involved in the production of energy, although the energy demands of Third World countries are rapidly increasing. The source of many of our society's resource and pollution problems is its insatiable appetite for energy. Although technological improvements can continue to provide better ways to conserve resources, changes in human behavior will also be required. One of the most important barriers to conservation is the lack of evidence available to policy makers,[108] which is further complicated by disagreements as to what constitutes valid evidence. Additional barriers to conservation include the cost of creating inexpensive alternative sources of energy, inefficient use of existing resources, the power of doing things the way they have always been done, and overreliance on inefficient means of transportation. In fact, one of the most wasteful uses of energy is transportation, especially the automobile. Despite programs that encourage people to use mass transit, North Americans are reluctant to give up the convenience and sense of control that a private automobile provides.

What can we do to promote conservation? Education and well-intentioned appeals to reduce water and energy consumption have had only limited success, in part because humans tend to be short-sighted about environmental issues and often perceive themselves as separate from the environment.[109] Furthermore, recent research on psychological reactance has found that in response to simple, yet prominently used factual messages about climate change, climate change skeptics become even more skeptical. This is especially true when the messages emphasize scientific conclusions.[110] However, the use of conservation **prompts**, cues that convey a message and remind people to do something, can influence conservation behaviors. Prompts are most effective when the message they convey is specific, well timed and placed, and when the requested behavior is easy.[111,112] For example, a specific prompt that reminds you to "turn off the lights when leaving the room" will be most effective if placed between the door you use when leaving the room and the light switch. Prompts are not always a matter of words. The presence of trashcans can act as a prompt to properly dispose of trash.[113]

Encouraging people to make a public commitment to conserving energy has been shown to be more effective than either education or prompts.[114] One way to do this is to provide opportunities for neighbors or co-workers to talk about conservation issues and to brainstorm specific actions that they could take to promote conservation. This can promote social comparison processes (see Chapter 3) in which uncertainty is replaced by a realization of what it will take to achieve the common good. Similarly, modeling and conformity pressures promote conservation.[115] Models are most effective when they are perceived positively and the model is similar to the individual who is targeted for influence. A video program on how to adapt to cooler temperatures at home used models who looked like ordinary people and who were rewarded for their conservation efforts. Those who watched the video reduced their consumption of energy used for heating by 26%. Another way to encourage conservation is to demonstrate the economic advantages of conservation activities. Incentives such as refunds on power bills for households that reduce their energy consumption can be effective.[116]

Social psychological techniques have also been shown to work. Researchers in one study examined various approaches to promoting conservation behaviors in a hotel.[117] Signs were placed in guests' bathrooms that encouraged the reuse of towels. Five different messages were used. The first provided an environmental focus that asked guests to "Help save the environment." The second message elicited cooperation and read: "Partner with us to help save the environment." The third message evoked the reciprocity norm and read: "We're doing our part for the environment, can we count on you?" The fourth message evoked a descriptive norm of guest behavior and read: "Join your fellow guests in helping save the environment, almost 75% of guests do so." The fifth message also evoked a descriptive norm, but this time the focus was on being a good citizen. It read: "Join your fellow citizens in helping save the environment, almost 75% do so." The most effective approaches were those evoking the reciprocity norm (46.7% of guests recycled their towels) and the descriptive norm of guest behavior (47.9% recycled their towels). Similarly, the use of a descriptive norm was compared to the use of an injunctive (you should) norm in prompting individuals to switch off lights after use. Men responded more to the injunctive norm while women responded to both types of normative messages.[118] While normative prompts can promote environmentalism, it is important that the

prompts cues that convey a message and remind people to do something

Direct conservation prompts.

The Home Energy Saver (HES) is one of several internet tools available to help homeowners and renters reduce their energy costs.

norm reference the target population's in-group.[119] In a recent study, an internet tool was used to encourage home owners to reduce their household energy use. The most effective technique provided the families with tailored information specific to their particular household, goal setting by the families involved, and tailored feedback on household energy use.[120]

QUIZ YOURSELF

Scarcity of Natural Resources

1. **Which of the following is not a barrier to conservation?**
   a. The cost of alternative forms of energy
   b. Inefficient means of transportation
   c. Habitual ways of doing things
   d. Extreme climate shifts

2. **Conservation models are most effective when they are perceived _____ and are _____ to the individual.**
   a. negatively; dissimilar
   b. negatively; similar
   c. positively; dissimilar
   d. positively; similar

3. **Which of the following is a prompt that can reduce litter?**
   a. Seeing a garbage can
   b. Seeing another person litter
   c. Seeing trash lying on the ground
   d. All of the above

4. **A new janitor is trying to get people to turn off the lights by putting a sign in the restroom. For the sign to be effective, where is the best place to put it?**
   a. In a private place, such as the toilet stall
   b. On the mirror
   c. Right next to the light switch
   d. All of the above should be equally effective

answers: see pg E24

Environmental Disasters

Despite our efforts to address the dangers of such natural disasters as earthquakes, tsunamis, hurricanes, tornados, and volcanic eruptions, the worldwide annual death toll is about a quarter of a million people killed by natural disasters.[121] Technological disasters that result from human actions include chemical spills, nuclear plant accidents, and lead contamination. Technological disasters are usually less dramatic and visible than natural disasters, but the death toll may be similar. People react somewhat differently to natural disasters and technological disasters. Individuals are more likely to experience long-term psychological distress when the disaster is human-made than when it occurs naturally. To understand the effects of environmental disasters, it is useful to look at factors that affect people before, during, and after the disaster occurs.

The Tohoku earthquake and tsunami that struck Japan in March 2011 and the subsequent nuclear disaster illustrate how disasters can be both natural and technological.

Before the Disaster

One of the important characteristics of a disaster situation is the extent to which people are warned ahead of time, even though not everyone takes these warnings seriously. In 2004, three hurricanes caused massive destruction in Florida. Evacuation orders were issued, and compliance was initially fairly good. However, people eventually became accustomed to the crisis, and fewer people were willing to leave their homes during the third hurricane. Similarly, many residents of New Orleans, especially those who had left the city the year before in anticipation of a hurricane that ultimately petered out, found the warning about Hurricane Katrina to be less than credible.

Why people will or won't evacuate is an important question. Many nonevacuators suggest that they are not convinced about the level of risk involved in staying behind. They may want to stay in order to protect their homes. Others who are separated from their families may be more concerned with finding family members than avoiding the impending disaster.[122] Another factor is the social comparison that occurs when respected neighbors decide to stay behind. Finally, local culture may influence how individuals react to a disaster. In New Orleans, it was common for long-term residents to ride out whatever hurricanes hit the Gulf coast. Community support networks were in place and individuals often felt that they needed to stay in order to fulfill their role within the support network. Furthermore, for many people, their sense of identity is tied closely to their living environment so to abandon one's home would cause them to lose a part of who they are.[123]

The extent to which you feel vulnerable in a disaster is influenced by how close you are to the source of danger. One form of closeness is physical proximity. For example, it has been found that individuals living 3 miles from a nuclear power plant indicated less fear than those living 64 miles away.[124] Cognitive dissonance theory suggests that when a hazard is difficult to control, individuals are likely to downplay or deny that a hazard is really dangerous (see Chapter 7). A second form of closeness has to do with how familiar the individual is with the hazard. For example, people who have experienced an earthquake are more likely to take an earthquake warning seriously. Conversely, individuals living in a community near a nuclear power plant were less concerned about the construction of a new plant than residents of other communities; those living close to the plant may have become used to it being there without incident. The third form of closeness involves place attachment. Long-term residents, especially those who are familiar with the risks of living where they do, are less likely to be concerned when warned of an impending disaster.[125] As a result, not one compulsory evacuation order in the past 40 years has ever been fully successful.[126] Individuals who don't comply with an evacuation order may believe they will be able to control the dangerous event. This illusion of control is strengthened when the individual is spared by fate while others nearby are not[127] or, in the case of Hurricane Katrina, there is a long history of being spared by what had initially appeared to be dangerous storms.

During the Disaster

Our immediate response to a disaster is usually to remain relatively calm and rational. Few people actually panic during a disaster. This is especially true of those with greater knowledge about the nature of the emergency.[128] Some typical behaviors when a disaster strikes are finding a protected place to wait out the disaster, helping others cope with the disaster, and not venturing far from where they were at the onset of the disaster.[129]

Of course, not all reactions to a disaster are going to be calm and rational. Some common negative reactions during and immediately after a disaster include irritability, lethargy, confusion, and withdrawal.[130] In addition, the case of Hurricane Katrina suggests that some people may take advantage of the confused circumstances to engage in looting, price gouging, and various forms of fraud.

Types of disaster victims: primary victims, secondary victims, and relief workers.

There are three types of disaster victims. Primary victims are directly affected by the event and must be able to cope with possible injury and loss. Secondary victims are those who are not in direct contact with the disaster but are connected through relationships with family or friends or have an economic stake in the disaster area. The lives of secondary victims are not at risk. A third category of disaster victims is the relief workers called in to assist the primary victims. These people usually work long hours under difficult conditions and are likely to be exposed to dead victims as well as those with serious injuries. Individuals who are repeatedly involved in disaster rescue efforts may show long-term stress symptoms including demoralization, helplessness, and depression.[131]

After the Disaster

What do people think and do when the worst of the disaster is over? They often think about who is responsible for the disaster, who will pay for disaster relief, and who will offer assistance in recovering from the disaster. In terms of who is to blame, survivors of a disaster usually want someone to pay for what has happened. People who are unaffected by the disaster may see the victims as those most responsible for what happened. This tendency to blame the victim can take the form of "Why were they living in that hazardous area? They should have known better."

Recovery from a disaster requires he reestablishment of patterns of everyday life. In general, most disaster relief efforts do not adequately address long-term recovery efforts, especially at the household level.[132] For example, in 2012 Hurricane Sandy devastated the Rockaway Peninsula with flood damage to thousands of homes and businesses. A year later, many grocery stores and other small businesses had still not reopened.[133]

A variety of post-disaster behavioral changes have been documented, including anxiety, depression, psychosomatic complaints, and sleep disorders, regardless of whether the disaster was a hurricane,[134] earthquake,[135] tornado,[136] volcanic eruption,[137] flood,[138] or technological disaster.[139] The effects of disasters can have long-term effects and have been observed to last as long as seven years.[140]

In general, women worry more than men in the aftermath of a disaster, which may also prompt them to cope more actively than men.[141] Czech children who lived in a heavily polluted area could not remember things as well as a matched group living outside of the polluted area.[142] Another behavioral change is **post-traumatic stress disorder**, which is characterized by sleep disorders, social withdrawal, uncontrollable thoughts about the event, and a desire to avoid thoughts of the event.[143] This disorder can last for many months following a disaster. Other stress-related reactions to a disaster include depression, phobias, amnesia, and even paralysis.[144] After the volcanic eruption of Mount St. Helens in 1980, residents who lived nearby showed increases in alcohol abuse, family stress, illness, and violence.[145]

One of the important coping mechanisms for individuals affected by a disaster involves social support. This is consistent with this textbook's theme of putting people first. People with more social and emotional support cope better and suffer fewer adjustment problems after a disaster. However, sometimes a disaster can reduce the availability of social support.

post-traumatic stress disorder post-disaster behavioral symptoms including sleep disorders, social withdrawal, uncontrollable thoughts about the event, and a desire to avoid thoughts of the event

If this happens, people will take steps to strengthen their support network. For example, after the 1976 Tangshan earthquake in China, two-thirds of those who were widowed remarried within a short time, despite cultural norms that discouraged remarriage.[146]

Age makes a difference in how we respond to disasters. Children generally respond in much the same way as their parents, although they may recover more rapidly.[147] For children, disasters often create specific fears and can result in regression to earlier forms of coping behavior. Older people who experience a disaster are more likely to be injured, less likely to evacuate, and more likely to lose possessions that have important sentimental value beyond their economic worth. In general, the financial burden of coping with the aftermath of a disaster tends to fall on the shoulders of the middle-aged, and research indicates that those most profoundly affected by a disaster are often middle-aged caregivers.[148]

QUIZ YOURSELF
Environmental Disasters

1. People may not evacuate after being warned because _____.
   - a) they do not think things will be as bad as is being suggested
   - b) they want to locate family members before leaving
   - c) they want to stay and protect their homes
   - d) all of the above

2. Research suggests that children who experience a disaster _____.
   - a) recover from the effects more quickly than adults
   - b) recover from the effects more slowly than adults
   - c) have a different set of reactions than do adults
   - d) are unlikely to experience post-traumatic stress disorder

3. People whose lives are directly threatened by a disaster are called _____.
   - a) primary victims
   - b) secondary victims
   - c) tertiary victims
   - d) disaster relief workers

4. Mary and her family lived in New Orleans. They lost everything when Hurricane Katrina devastated her neighborhood. As a result, her behavior shows many of the symptoms of post-traumatic stress disorder. Among the behavioral changes she exhibits are _____.
   - a) a desire to think about the event all the time
   - b) disordered sleep
   - c) memory loss
   - d) fears that another hurricane is likely to strike again

answers: see pg E24

Using Social Psychology to Save the Environment

Changing Attitudes and Behavior

All of us are faced with the need to make decisions about environmental issues every day. Do we leave the tap on while brushing our teeth, do we take a quick shower or a luxurious bath, do we replace the light bulbs in our kitchen with energy-saving ones, do we recycle? Considerable effort has been made to change environmental attitudes and behaviors through such means as public service announcements, despite the lack of evidence regarding their effectiveness. In fact, anti-littering spots on television that show people tossing trash out of a car window may suggest that such behavior is normal and act as a descriptive norm, thereby encouraging the behavior rather than eliminating it.[149] The most effective televised images are those that provide dramatic visualizations of the manifestations of environmental neglect and degradation. A second consideration in designing an effective attitude change program is to overcome the idea that there is nothing that one individual can do to change things. For example, to encourage conservation efforts, you could point out that buying a half-gallon container of milk instead of two quart containers is environmentally beneficial because that action, if practiced by all of us who buy milk, would reduce waste by 42 million pounds of paper and 6 million pounds of plastic per year.[150]

In trying to change environmental attitudes and behaviors, it is important to understand the somewhat tenuous relationship between attitudes and behaviors. Often, attitudes aren't very good predictors of behavior (see Chapter 7). Nevertheless, there are things we can do to increase attitude–behavior correspondence. The more specific the attitude, the more likely it is to lead to a corresponding behavior. Thus, a campaign that suggests you should be conscientious about recycling newspapers is more likely to increase recycling than a campaign that suggests you should be pro-environment.[151] Attitudes include affect as well as beliefs (see Chapter 7). To promote pro-environmental actions, it is important to address people's emotions as well as their beliefs. Public campaigns should provide affective appeals that associate positive emotional experiences with the pro-environmental behavior.[152] For attitudes to predict behavior, the attitude must be accessible when the behavior is elicited. Therefore, prompts that remind people of their attitudes at appropriate times can be effective. We also need to understand the costs of changing an attitude in a pro-environmental direction. If people are concerned about their health or comfort and a campaign suggests that they should sacrifice some of their health or comfort, it will not be successful. Attitudes vary in strength, and weak attitudes seldom predict behavior. The strongest attitudes are those acquired through direct experience. This suggests that getting people involved in an environmental action such as cleaning a river, or teaching students how to monitor their use of energy, can be effective in promoting environmentally responsible attitudes and behavior. (See Chapter 8 for more information about changing attitudes.)

The Role of Feedback

One promising approach to changing environmentally irresponsible behavior is to provide people with feedback about their actions. The most common form of environmental feedback is giving people information about their use of a particular resource, such as water or energy. This can be effective in promoting conservation because it tells people when they are doing a good job and when they could improve. The typical American could reduce the amount of energy consumed in the home by 50% to 75% by using conservation techniques that are relatively inexpensive. However, most Americans are not motivated to do so. Why not? People waste energy partly because they don't pay attention to their energy use, not because they set out to overuse energy.

Feedback helps people attend to their energy use. For example, to reduce transportation fuel use, signs were posted telling motorists the number of people that had exceeded the speed limit during the previous week and the best week on record. These signs were more effective in reducing traffic speed than other techniques, including increasing the number of tickets issued by police.[153] In a study conducted on a college campus, a sign was posted near a recycling bin that indicated the number of pounds collected each day. This feedback on how much was recycled increased the amount of recycling 76% initially, and even after the weekly update was discontinued, recycling continued well above what it had been prior to feedback. In general, the amount of energy conserved is directly related to the frequency with which people are provided feedback,[154] the perceived accuracy of the feedback,[155] and the extent to which energy conservation is a desired goal.[156]

Sometimes the most effective feedback is not just about our own behavior but also about how other people behave. For example, posting notices asking employees to conserve energy by closing windows during cold weather and turning off lights when leaving a room and providing weekly feedback about the amount of energy saved resulted in a modest improvement in energy conservation. However, when the weekly feedback included how other work groups were doing, the social comparison information resulted in dramatic improvements in energy conservation.[157] While the initial results of feedback approaches to conservation appear promising, a recent study in Australia found that the initial reduction in water consumption by participants in various feedback conditions returned to pre-intervention levels after one year. Feedback alone is not sufficient.

Moral Reasoning as a Determinant of Pro-Environmental Behavior

In addition to attitude change techniques and feedback mechanisms, a recent meta-analysis[158] identified a third predictor of pro-environmental behavior, personal moral norms. Individuals who feel a moral obligation to "save the planet" are much more likely to actually do something to address environmental problems. Feelings of guilt can provide the motivation to change one's behavior, although moral reasoning about the environment is enhanced when the individual feels empathy toward those being harmed by environmental inaction.[159] Moral reasoning about the environment is also enhanced when individuals feel more connected to the natural environment.[160] Research suggests that moral obligations can activate a personal norm related to the value of altruism that leads one to engage in specific behaviors.[161] For example research based on Value-Belief-Norm theory found that students who hold altruistic and biospheric values were more likely to engage in sustainability behaviors while those who held egoistic values were not.[162] Thus, an effective pro-environmental campaign could (1) discuss environmental issues in moral terms, (2) address the impact of inaction on those we care about, and (3) promote a general altruistic value orientation.

Overcoming the Tragedy of the Commons

How might we go about solving the tragedy of commons dilemma? Communication helps. In one study, participants were each given $6 and told that if they donated their share to a common pot, the amount would be doubled and distributed among the other participants. This would result in everyone doubling their money if all donated to the pot. However, few donated, so everyone lost out. In contrast, when participants were given 10 minutes to talk about the situation, the amount of giving doubled.[163] Communication can make a difference, especially with a small group of users, because it provides an opportunity to clarify the costs and benefits of collective action, reduces mistrust, and encourages public commitment to common goals.

With larger groups, making it easier for the individuals to monitor their own usage of the resource (thus, again, providing feedback) can be effective. A comparison of two communities experiencing a drought found that the community with water meters consumed less water than the community in which residents did not have water meters.[164]

Another approach to solving the commons dilemma is to make the individual's use of the endangered resource as public as possible in order to invoke normative conformity pressures and accountability. This is especially effective when a **hypocrisy induction** technique is employed. This technique involves confronting people with the inconsistency between their attitudes and their behavior. For example, during a water shortage, officials at the University of California posted signs in shower rooms asking students to take shorter showers. Less than 15% of the students complied. However, students who completed a questionnaire about water usage that made them mindful of water consumption and then signed their names to a public poster exhorting others to take shorter showers took significantly shorter showers.[165] Students felt that it was hypocritical to exhort others to conserve water and not conserve it themselves. Although this technique can be effective, individuals who are quick to perceive threats to their freedom of choice, may experience psychological reactance, and may react negatively to the implication that they are behaving hypocritically.[166]

hypocrisy induction a technique for effecting behavior change by confronting people with the inconsistency between their attitudes and their behavior

MONEY Matters

Interventions Based on Social Cognition Theory

During the past decade, interventions based on Albert Bandura's social cognitive theory (see Chapter 5) have addressed how to create a sustainable environmental future.[167] The means of achieving society-wide changes consists of three components. The first component is the theoretical model, which provides the mechanisms require for change. The second component addresses the means for implementing the theoretical model in the real world and the third component creates ways for the social diffusion of the changes in attitudes and behavior. The interventions require the creation of dramatic productions that capture public interest and provide positive role models of sympathetic characters. Interventions using this approach has been successfully implemented in Africa, Asia, and Latin America to stem a wide variety of environmental issues, including population growth, conservation such as sustainable farming and forestry, the protection of biodiversity and the preservation of natural resources.[168]

The Costs and Benefits of Environmental Protection

For many years, the debate on environmental issues focused on the out-of-pocket expenditures and other negative consequences associated with environmental protection. Recently, America and Europe have begun shifting to a "green culture" where citizens are embracing the fact that protecting our environment is everyone's responsibility. Part of this shift is an increasing awareness of environmental economics.

Central to environmental economics is the concept of market failure. An environmentally relevant market failure occurs when there is a wedge between what an individual does, given market prices and what society might want him or her to do to protect the environment.[169] Types of market failure include externality, nonrivalry, and nonexcludability.

Externality occurs when the cost to the individual does not take into account the cost to other people. For example, a company emitting pollution will typically not consider the health-related costs that its pollution imposes on others. Nonrivalry occurs when an environmental action paid for by some, also benefits others. For example, countries that have implemented carbon abatement programs are providing a benefit to those countries who have not. Nonexcludability occurs when it is too costly to prevent those who are not paying for a benefit from getting that benefit. Again, carbon abatement is a good example of nonexcludability.

Some of the solutions proposed to address environmentally relevant market failures are governmental treaties and regulations such as the Kyoto Protocol, pollution quotas including emissions trading, where polluting industries buy credits from less-polluting firms, taxes and tariffs on pollution, and better-defined property rights of individuals living in polluted areas, which could provide a right to be protected from polluted air or water.

Perhaps the most dramatic reason for the current movement to "go green" is that entrepreneurs are developing economic opportunities associated with environmental protection that provide new jobs and new industries that support environmental responsibility. The creation of renewable energy sources such as solar and wind power is one such opportunity and is being adopted more rapidly than many people realize. For example, in Denmark, more than 20% of power usage today comes from wind power alone. California provides a rebate on residents' electricity bills if they install a solar system as well as an income tax deduction for the interest paid on a loan to buy solar equipment. Another opportunity to promote renewable energy exists in the development of fuel-efficient and alternative fuel vehicles. Hybrid and battery electric vehicles are commercially available and are gaining wider industry and consumer acceptance. In 2008, there were 500,000 hybrid vehicles registered worldwide, and the number and variety of such vehicles is increasing.

According to one report, investment by Americans in renewable energy will create 1.4 million new jobs and an average household savings on energy bills of $1,275 per year by the year 2025.[170] Money matters and the public's awareness that there is a positive relationship between environmental responsibility and economic progress is making a difference in how environmentalism is viewed.

Environmental education can have an effect on the commons dilemma. In California, educational messages that emphasized either the long-term benefits of conservation, the short-term economic advantages, or the fact that the individual's water consumption was being monitored were delivered. The most effective message was the one that emphasized long-term benefits,[171] although a similar study in Michigan found that both economic and environmental rationales were effective in promoting conservation.[172] See *Money Matters* for more details on the costs and benefits of environmental protection.

Finally, given the urgent need to address serious environmental problems, the formation of small, self-organized institutions to regulate common pool resources on a local level should be encouraged. One approach to creating such institutions is "adaptive muddling," which promotes the use of small experiments that take into consideration personal and local knowledge of a situation in order to create a variety of potential solutions. This process reduces the costs of failure and provides tested techniques for widespread implementation.

QUIZ YOURSELF

Using Social Psychology to Save the Environment

1. The relationship between our attitudes and behavior can be strengthened if _____.
   - (a) the attitude is accessible when the behavior is elicited
   - (b) the attitude is not overly specific with regard to the behavior
   - (c) the cost of acting on the attitude is high
   - (d) the attitude is based on an emotional appeal

2. The strongest attitudes are those acquired from _____.
   - (a) family members
   - (b) close friends
   - (c) classroom instruction
   - (d) direct experience

3. The most effective form of feedback is _____.
   - (a) factual information about what we should do
   - (b) social comparison information about what others are doing
   - (c) visual representations of desired behaviors
   - (d) feedback that creates emotional arousal

4. Jane is involved in environmental causes and very conscientious about energy conservation. When her boyfriend points out to her that letting the water run while she brushes her teeth is not consistent with her beliefs, she changes her behavior. Her boyfriend has used a technique called _____.
   - (a) cognitive control
   - (b) sensory overload
   - (c) hypocrisy induction
   - (d) learned helplessness

answers: see pg E24

What Makes Us Human

Putting the Cultural Animal in Perspective

Humans are not the only creatures that have to deal with the environment—in fact, all living things depend on interacting effectively with the environment in order to survive. Environmental psychology is thus a cultural way of talking about a very basic and very natural set of problems.

Once again, though, human beings differ from other animals, and our participation in culture is central to what sets us apart. Our unique relationship to the environment begins with how we claim and mark territory. Thus, although many creatures claim and defend certain areas as their own, only humans do this with laws, deeds and leases, nameplates, and electronic security systems. Also, only humans personalize their territory in ways designed to express their individuality.

Humans use the environment in ways that no other animals can even imagine. We chop down trees to make fuel for fires, to make wood for building homes and constructing furniture, and to make paper on which we can write the thoughts and data of our cultural activities (including this textbook!). Humans can move mountains and rivers and create artificial lakes. Beavers make dams, but these would not pass the safety requirements or serve the long-term planning goals that human dams do.

Humans dig deep into the earth to mine for substances that can be used by our culture in many ways: gold and metals for making things, coal and oil to burn for energy.

In short, human technology has found ways to enrich human life by using all manner of the resources that our planet has to offer. Remember, however, that there are tradeoffs everywhere, as this book has shown over and over. The wonderful advantages that come with technology have also created problems. Most obviously, we are beginning to use up some of the planet's resources. In the United States in the 1960s, when the *Journal of Personality and Social Psychology* first began publishing, gasoline cost less than 30 cents per gallon, but the dwindling supply (and some other market factors) has pushed the price to 10 times as much, and even higher prices lie ahead—until eventually it may become difficult to find gasoline at any price.

Other side effects of human culture and technology include pollution of air and water, which ultimately may limit the ability of all creatures to survive. Global warming, now generally understood as partly caused by the heat generated by human activity, will change the planet in many ways and probably spell extinction for many other animals (though probably not for humans). It may also change where people can live—for example, if an increase in hurricanes renders tropical areas too dangerous.

The success of human culture has also created a huge indirect strain on the environment. Remember, one of the most basic purposes of culture is to help people survive and reproduce better, and human culture has been enormously successful. As the human population of earth approaches eight billion, it puts unprecedented strains on the environment to provide all the resources that these people need and want. It is safe to say that future humans will grapple increasingly with the problems of overpopulation—crowding, immigration, and all the problems that come with them, including traffic congestion, depletion of resources, demand for energy, and pollution.

The environment has many processes that enable it to recover from the harm people do, but these may be overwhelmed by the increasing numbers of people. For example, dirty water and air can slowly be cleaned by natural processes, and if only a few people pollute them, nature can recover. But when millions of people contribute to pollution, nature cannot keep up, and the environment will grow steadily worse.

Against these problems that human culture creates, culture also has begun to work toward solutions in uniquely human ways. Human beings make laws and exert social pressure on each other to reduce pollution, conserve limited resources, and recycle materials. No other animals have been known to cooperate to protect the environment in these ways. The international environmental movement reflects a high-minded concern to protect the planet (including, admittedly, from ourselves!) that is uniquely human. Human culture deals with the environment in ways that reflect both unique problems and novel solutions.

Even our response to natural disasters shows our uniquely human powers and institutions. After Hurricane Katrina devastated the Gulf Coast of the United States in 2005, offers of assistance in the form of money, housing opportunities, educational choices, and jobs came to the residents of the area from all over the country and the world. In other recent disasters, including the nuclear disaster in Japan and the earthquake in Pakistan, the unique network that binds humans, regardless of geographical location, has proved to be essential in staffing and funding the efforts to rescue the victims of those disasters.

Many environmental problems affect both humans and animals, but only humans think about what could happen and how we might overcome those problems. We create organizations that stockpile resources to help those caught in an environmental disaster. We rehearse scenarios of how to react if an environmental problem comes our way. We evaluate how well we have coped with a problem in order to better cope with the next problem. We sell and buy insurance. This ability to be proactive in our interaction with the environment certainly makes us human.

MODULE E SUMMARY

Overview of Environmental Problems

- Global warming, acid rain, urban smog, toxic waste, and overpopulation seriously threaten our quality of life.
- Social psychology can be applied to understanding and solving a wide range of environmental concerns, including overpopulation, environmental quality, the scarcity of natural resources, and environmental disasters.

Problems Related to Overpopulation

- High-population density can lead to the subjective feeling of crowding if the density leads to sensory overload or places constraints on human actions.
- People maintain a certain amount of personal space between themselves and others in order to avoid overstimulation, control unwanted arousal, reduce stress, and maintain behavioral freedom.
- The size and shape of an individual's personal space depends on age, gender, relationship, and cultural background.
- Human territoriality provides people with privacy and a sense of personal identity while making life more predictable and stable and less conflicted.
- The most common means to mark the boundaries of our territory is to personalize our area with improvements or decorations.

Environmental Quality

- The relationship between heat and aggression is curvilinear, meaning that, as temperature increases, aggression becomes more likely up to the point that it is so hot and uncomfortable that people are more interested in escaping the situation than in fighting.
- Irregular and unpredictable noise has been shown to have negative effects on learning and performance, interpersonal attraction, and helping behavior.
- Air pollution, including secondhand smoke, has a number of serious health consequences; it can also reduce helping behavior and heighten aggressive behavior.

Scarcity of Natural Resources

- The high demand for energy is one large barrier to conservation.
- Prompts have been used successfully to promote conservation-related behaviors by reminding us to do something that we intended to do.
- Public commitments can increase conservation.

Environmental Disasters

- People's response to a natural disaster is influenced by their proximity to the disaster, perceived control over its effects, and the reactions of others.
- Most people remain calm during a disaster, although they may exhibit negative reactions including confusion, lethargy, and withdrawal.
- Disaster victims can be classified as primary victims who bear the brunt of the disaster, secondary victims who are out of harm's way but are somehow connected to the disaster, and disaster relief workers whose job can produce long-term stress.
- The availability of social support is important in coping with a disaster.

Using Social Psychology to Save the Environment

- Programs designed to change attitudes and behavior work best if the targeted attitude is specific, if it is accessible when the behavior is elicited, and if information that can be clearly translated into a corresponding behavior is provided.
- Feedback mechanisms provide information about our actions and can be used to promote conservation-related behaviors. Feedback that includes information about the behavior of others can be particularly effective.
- The commons dilemma occurs when people act to maximize their individual outcomes at the expense of the common good. This is less likely to happen when individuals talk with one another about the common good, make commitments to promote the common good, and monitor the use of communal resources.
- Hypocrisy induction can be used to promote conservation by making people aware of the inconsistency between their beliefs and values and their behavior.

What Makes Us Human? Putting the Cultural Animal in Perspective

- Humans have a unique relationship with the environment that enables them to personalize their territory and mine resources from the environment to enrich life. The tradeoff is the huge indirect strain that human culture puts on the environment, but only humans are able to consider the potential impact of their actions and how we can overcome environmental problems.

key terms

ambient environment E10
cognitive control E6
crowding E6
density E6
hypocrisy induction E20
individual good–collective bad trap E2
learned helplessness E11
missing hero trap E2
noise E11
one-person trap E2
personal space E7
personalization E8
post-traumatic stress disorder E17
primary territory E9
prompts E14
public territory E9
secondary territory E9
sensory overload E6
territoriality E8

quiz yourself ANSWERS

1. Overview of Environmental Problems p. E5
   answers: 1.b 2.d 3.c 4.a
2. Problems Related to Overpopulation p. E10
   answers: 1.d 2.c 3.d 4.a
3. Environmental Quality p. E13
   answers: 1.b 2.c 3.d 4.c
4. Scarcity of Natural Resources p. E15
   answers: 1.d 2.d 3.a 4.c
5. Environmental Disasters p. E18
   answers: 1.d 2.a 3.a 4.b
6. Using Social Psychology to Save the Environment p. E22
   answers: 1.a 2.d 3.b 4.c

Glossary

A–B problem the problem of inconsistency between attitudes (A) and behaviors (B)

ABC triad Affect (how people feel inside), Behavior (what people do), Cognition (what people think about)

accessibility how easily something comes to mind

accomplice a research assistant pretending to be another participant in a study

actor/observer bias the tendency for actors to make external attributions and observers to make internal attributions

advertisement wear-out inattention and irritation that occurs after an audience has encountered the same advertisement too many times

affect the automatic response that something is good (positive affect) or bad (negative affect)

affect-as-information hypothesis the idea that people judge something as good or bad by asking themselves "How do I feel about it?"

affect balance the frequency of positive emotions minus the frequency of negative emotions

affective commitment an employee's emotional attachment to the organization that makes the employee want to stay in the organization

affective forecasting the ability to predict one's emotional reactions to future events

agent self (executive function) the part of the self involved in control, including both control over other people and self-control

aggression any behavior intended to harm another person who is motivated to avoid the harm

altruistic helping when a helper seeks to increase another's welfare and expects nothing in return

altruistic punishment the finding that people will sometimes sacrifice their own gain for the betterment of all, by punishing people who cheat the system

ambient environment sensory surroundings, including temperature, odor, and sound

anchoring and adjustment the tendency to judge the frequency or likelihood of an event by using a starting point (called an anchor) and then making adjustments up or down.

anger an emotional response to a real or imagined threat or provocation

anthropology the study of human culture—the shared values, beliefs, and practices of a group of people

antisocial behavior behavior that either damages interpersonal relationships or is culturally undesirable

appetitive aggression aggression that is motivated, in part or whole, by an intrinsic enjoyment of the aggressive act

applied research research that focuses on solving particular practical problems

appraisal motive the simple desire to learn the truth about oneself, whatever it is

appraisal theory of emotion the idea that emotion is determined by how an event in the environment is appraised (e.g., evaluated, interpreted, explained)

appraisals how we think about a situation or event

arousal a physiological reaction, including faster heartbeat and faster or heavier breathing, linked to most conscious emotions

assumptive worlds the view that people live in social worlds based on certain beliefs (assumptions) about reality

attachment theory a theory that classifies people into four attachment styles (secure, preoccupied, dismissing avoidant, and fearful avoidant) based on two dimensions (anxiety and avoidance)

attitude polarization the finding that people's attitudes become more extreme as they reflect on them

attitudes global evaluations toward some object or issue

attitudes at work satisfaction with the work itself, pay and benefits, supervision, co-workers, promotion opportunities, working conditions, and job security

attraction anything that draws two or more people together, making them want to be together and possibly to form a lasting relationship

attribution cognitive process of assigning meaning to a symptom or behavior

attributions the causal explanations people give for their own and others' behaviors, and for events in general

audience inhibition failure to help in front of others for fear of feeling like a fool if one's offer of help is rejected

authoritarian personality a pattern of cross-situational attitudes and behaviors that reflects conventional values, respect for authority figures, and a desire to punish others who defy authority

autokinetic effect illusion, caused by very slight movements of the eye, that a stationary point of light in a dark room is moving

automatic affect a quick response of liking or disliking toward something

automatic attitudes very fast evaluative, "gut-level" responses that people don't think a great deal about

automatic egotism response by the automatic system that "everything good is me, and everything bad is not me"

automatic system the part of the mind outside of consciousness that performs simple operations

availability heuristic the tendency to judge the frequency or likelihood of an event by the ease with which relevant instances come to mind

aversive racism simultaneously holding egalitarian values and negative feelings toward people of other races

bad apple effect the idea that one person who breaks the rules can inspire other people to break the rules also

bait-and-switch influence technique in which one draws people in with an attractive offer that is unavailable and then switches them to a less attractive offer that is available

base rate fallacy the tendency to ignore or underuse base rate information and instead to be influenced by the distinctive features of the case being judged

basic research research that focuses on a general understanding of basic principles that can be applied to many different problems

behavioral intentions an individual's plans to perform the behavior in question

behaviorism theoretical approach that seeks to explain behavior in terms of learning principles, without reference to inner states, thoughts, or feelings

belief in a just world the assumption that life is essentially fair, that people generally get what they deserve and deserve what they get

belief perseverance the finding that once beliefs form, they are resistant to change, even if the information on which they are based is discredited

beliefs pieces of information about something; facts or opinions

between-subjects design participants are exposed to only one level of the independent variable

biological psychology (physiological psychology, neuroscience) the study of what happens in the brain, nervous system, and other aspects of the body

biopsychosocial approach acknowledging that our health has biological, psychological, and social determinants

brainstorming a form of creative thinking in groups, using a procedure in which all group members are encouraged to generate as many ideas as possible while interacting and stimulating each other

brand loyalty the degree to which a customer holds a positive attitude toward a brand, has a commitment to it, and intends to continue purchasing it

broaden-and-build theory the proposition that positive emotions expand an individual's attention and mind-set and promote increasing one's resources

bullying persistent aggression by a perpetrator against a victim for the purpose of establishing a power relationship over the victim

bystander effect the finding that people are less likely to offer help when they are in a group than when they are alone

can-do factors the maximum performance an employee can exhibit

capacity for change the active phase of self-regulation; willpower

capacity to delay gratification the ability to make immediate sacrifices for later rewards

categorization the natural tendency of humans to sort objects into groups

catharsis theory the proposition that expressing negative emotions produces a healthy release of those emotions and is therefore good for the psyche

central route (systematic processing) the route to persuasion that involves careful and thoughtful consideration of the content of the message (conscious processing)

certainty effect in decision making, the greater weight given to definite outcomes than to probabilities

challenge for cause a request made by an attorney that a potential juror be removed from the jury panel because he or she is clearly biased and will be unable to hear the case fairly

change of venue moving a trial to a new location where there has been less pretrial publicity

classical conditioning a type of learning in which, through repeated pairings, a neutral stimulus comes to evoke a conditioned response

clinical psychology branch of psychology that focuses on behavior disorders and other forms of mental illness, and how to treat them

cognitive appraisal model Lazarus's theory of how thinking plays a strong role in stress

cognitive control the sense people have about the predictability or controllability of their situation

cognitive coping the idea that beliefs play a central role in helping people cope with and recover from misfortunes

cognitive dissonance the uncomfortable feeling people experience when they have two thoughts or cognitions conflict with one another

cognitive dissonance theory the theory that inconsistencies produce psychological discomfort, leading people to rationalize their behavior or change their attitudes

cognitive miser a term used to describe people's reluctance to do much extra thinking

cognitive psychology the study of thought processes, such as how memory works and what people notice

commitment a conscious decision that remains constant

commons dilemma the tendency for shared or jointly owned resources to be squandered and not used in an optimal or advantageous fashion

communal relationships relationships based on mutual love and concern, without expectation of repayment

companionate love (affectionate love) mutual understanding and caring to make the relationship succeed

competition situation in which people can attain their goals only if others do not

conditioned response a response that, through repeated pairings, is evoked by a formerly neutral stimulus

conditioned stimulus a neutral stimulus that, through repeated pairings with an unconditioned stimulus, comes to evoke a conditioned response

confirmation bias the tendency to notice and search for information that confirms one's beliefs and to ignore information that disconfirms one's beliefs

conformity going along with the crowd, that is, saying or doing whatever other people are doing

confounding occurs when two the effects of variables cannot be separated

conscious emotion a powerful and clearly unified feeling state, such as anger or joy

consent form a document that participants receive before a study begins; the form contains enough information about the study procedures, including any potential harm they (or others) might experience, so participants can decide if they want to participate

consistency motive a desire to get feedback that confirms what the person already believes about themself

conspicuous consumption the purchase and prominent display of luxury goods to provide evidence of a consumer's ability to afford them

construct validity of the cause extent to which the independent variable is a valid representation of the theoretical stimulus

construct validity of the effect extent to which the dependent variable is a valid representation of the theoretical response

contact hypothesis the idea that regular interaction between members of different groups reduces prejudice, providing that it occurs under favorable conditions

continuance commitment commitment that results when an employee remains with a company because of the high cost of losing organizational membership including monetary and social costs

continuance delaying a trial until the level of media attention to the crime has decreased in order to reduce the prejudicial effects of pretrial publicity

convert communicators people perceived as credible sources because they are arguing against their own previously held attitudes and behaviors

Coolidge effect the sexually arousing power of a new partner (greater than the appeal of a familiar partner)

cooperation working together with someone for mutual or reciprocal benefit

coping individual efforts made to manage distressing problems and emotions that affect the physical and psychological outcomes of stress

correct rejection when a witness correctly states that the person who committed the crime is not present in a lineup

correlation the relationship or association between two variables

correlation coefficient (r) the statistical relationship or association between two variables

correlational approach a nonexperimental method in which the researcher merely observes whether variables are associated or related

counterfactual thinking imagining alternatives to past or present events or circumstances

counterproductive behaviors any intentional behavior on the part of an organizational member viewed by the organization as contrary to its legitimate interests

counterregulation the "what the heck" effect that occurs when people indulge in a behavior they are trying to regulate after an initial regulation failure

crowding the subjective and unpleasant feeling that there are too many people in a given area

culprit-absent lineup a lineup in which the person who committed the crime is not present in the lineup

culprit-present lineup a lineup in which the person who committed the crime is one of the lineup members

culture an information-based system that includes shared ideas and common ways of doing things

culture of honor a society that places high value on individual respect, strength, and virtue, and accepts and justifies violent action in response to threats to one's honor

cyberbullying the use of the internet (e.g., email, social network sites, blogs) to bully others

dark triad of personality consists of narcissism, psychopathy, and Machiavellianism

death qualification the special jury selection process that occurs in capital cases with the purpose of excluding jurors who would not be able to weigh the evidence fairly because of their death penalty attitudes

debiasing reducing errors and biases by getting people to use deliberate processing rather than automatic processing

debriefing an oral or written statement participants receive at the end of a psychological study; it serves two main purposes: (1) to fully inform participants about the study and answer any questions they have, and (2) to reduce or eliminate any stress or harm the participant experienced by being in the study

deception studies research studies that withhold information from participants or intentionally mislead them about the purpose of the study

decision fatigue a state of depleted willpower caused by making decisions, which can affect subsequent decisions by causing people to fail to think and choose carefully

deindividuation a sense of anonymity and loss of individuality, as in a large group, making people especially likely to engage in antisocial behaviors such as theft

deliberate attitudes reflective responses that people think more carefully about

deliberate system the part of the mind that performs complex operations

demand characteristics features of an experiment that communicate to the participant the experimenter's hypothesis

density the number of people divided by the area of the space they share

dependent variable the variable in a study that represents the result of the events and processes

desensitization a psychological process that occurs when emotional reactions to a stimulus decrease following repeated exposure to it

descriptive norms norms that specify what most people do

developmental psychology the study of how people change across their lives, from conception and birth to old age and death

diffusion of responsibility the reduction in feeling responsible that occurs when others are present

direct aggression any behavior that intentionally harms another person who is physically present

discontinuity effect the finding that groups are more extreme, and often more hostile, than individuals

discrimination unequal treatment of different people based on the groups or categories to which they belong

disgust a strong negative feeling of repugnance and revulsion

dismissing avoidant attachment style of attachment in which people are low on anxiety but high on avoidance; they tend to view partners as unreliable, unavailable, and uncaring

displaced aggression any behavior that intentionally harms a substitute target rather than the provocateur

disrupt-then-reframe technique influence technique in which one disrupts critical thinking by introducing an unexpected element, then reframes the message in a positive light

distress-maintaining style of attribution tendency of unhappy couples to attribute their partner's good acts to external factors and bad acts to internal factors

domestic violence (also called **family violence** or **intimate-partner violence**) physically harmful actions that occur within the home or family, between people who have a close relationship with each other

dominant response a behavior that takes very little effort or thought and is frequently the default or habitual response to a specific situation

door-in-the-face technique influence technique in which one starts with an inflated request and then retreats to a smaller request that appears to be a concession

double standard condemning women more than men for the same sexual behavior (e.g., premarital sex)

double-blind testing a lineup administration in which neither the police officer nor the witness knows which lineup member is the suspect

downward comparison the act of comparing oneself to people who are worse off

downward counterfactuals imagining alternatives that are worse than actuality

downward social comparison comparing yourself to people worse off than you

dual attitudes different evaluations of the same attitude object held by the same person (perhaps one deliberate, the other automatic)

duplex mind the idea that the mind has two different processing systems (deliberate and automatic)

economics the study of the production, distribution, and consumption of goods and services, and the study of money

effort justification the finding that when people suffer or work hard or make sacrifices, they will try to convince themselves that it is worthwhile

egoistic helping when a helper seeks to increase his or her own welfare by helping another

elaboration likelihood model (ELM) theory that posits two routes to persuasion, via either conscious or automatic processing

emotion a conscious evaluative reaction that is clearly linked to some event

emotional intelligence the ability to perceive, access and generate, understand, and reflectively regulate emotions

empathy reacting to another person's emotional state by experiencing the same emotional state

empathy–altruism hypothesis the idea that empathy motivates people to reduce other people's distress, as by helping or comforting

endowment effect the finding that items gain in value to the person who owns them

entity theorists those who believe that traits are fixed, stable things (entities) that are not subject to change

equality the idea that everyone gets the same amount, regardless of what he or she contributes

equity the idea that each person receives benefits in proportion to what he or she contributes

eros in Freudian theory, the constructive, life-giving instinct

erotic plasticity the degree to which the sex drive can be shaped and altered by social, cultural, and situational forces

error management theory the idea that both men and women seek to minimize the costliest type of error, but that men's and women's goals, and hence worst errors, differ

estimator variables characteristics of the witness, the crime, and the witness's testimony that are not under the control of the justice system but that may provide information about the likely accuracy of an eyewitness identification

ethnographic a research method that attempts to provide a close understanding of people and cultures

evaluation apprehension concern about how others are judging you and/or your performance

evolutionary theory theory of sexuality asserting that the sex drive has been shaped by natural selection and that its forms thus tend to be innate

exchange relationships relationships based on reciprocity and fairness, in which people expect something in return

excitation transfer the idea that arousal from one event can transfer to a later event

experiment a study in which the researcher manipulates an independent variable and randomly assigns people to groups (levels of the independent variable)

experimental realism the extent to which study participants get so caught up in the procedures that they forget they are in an experiment

expertise how much a source knows

external validity the extent to which the findings from a study can be generalized to other people, other settings, and other time periods

extradyadic sex having sex with someone other than one's regular relationship partner

extrinsic motivation performing an activity because of something that results from it

facial feedback hypothesis the idea that feedback from the face muscles evokes or magnifies emotions

false (mistaken) identification when a witness incorrectly identifies an innocent suspect as the person who committed a crime

false consensus effect the tendency to overestimate the number of other people who share one's opinions, attitudes, values, and beliefs

false uniqueness effect the tendency to underestimate the number of other people who share one's most prized characteristics and abilities

fast-approaching-deadline technique influence technique in which one tells people an item or a price is only available for a limited time

fearful avoidant attachment style of attachment in which people have both high anxiety and high avoidance; they have low opinions of themselves and keep others from getting close

field experiment an experiment conducted in a real-world setting

fight-or-flight syndrome a response to stress that involves aggressing against others or running away

fight-or-flight response Cannon's theory of stress explaining physiological responses in our body

fillers lineup members other than the suspect who are known to be innocent of the crime

filter bubbles are algorithms used on the internet to selectively guess what information a user would like to see based on information available about that use (e.g., previous web pages viewed, click behavior)

first instinct fallacy the false belief that it is better not to change one's first answer on a test even if one starts to think that a different answer is correct

foot-in-the-door technique influence technique in which one starts with a small request in order to gain eventual compliance with a larger request

forgiveness ceasing to feel angry toward or seek retribution against someone who has wronged you

framing how information is presented to others

Freudian psychoanalysis theoretical approach that seeks to explain behavior by looking at the deep unconscious forces inside the person

frustration blockage of or interference with a personal goal

frustration–aggression hypothesis proposal that "the occurrence of aggressive behavior always presupposes the existence of frustration," and "the existence of frustration always leads to some form of aggression"

fundamental attribution error (correspondence bias) the tendency for observers to attribute other people's behavior to internal or dispositional causes and to downplay situational causes

gain-framed appeal focuses on how doing something will add to your health

gambler's fallacy the tendency to believe that a particular chance event is affected by previous events and that chance events will "even out" in the short run

general adaptation syndrome Selye's stage theory of how we respond to all stressors in a similar way

generalized other a combination of other people's views that tells you who and what you are

geo-targeting the strategy of exposing only individuals within a specific geographic region to a particular ad campaign

goal an idea of some desired future state

goal shielding occurs when the activation of a focal goal the person is working on inhibits the accessibility of alternative goals

gratitude a positive emotion that results from the perception that one has benefited from the costly, intentional, voluntary action of another person

group a collection of at least two people who are doing or being something together

group norms the beliefs or behaviors that a group of people accepts as normal

group polarization effect a shift toward a more extreme position resulting from group discussion

groupthink the tendency of group members to think alike, which often leads to bad decisions

guilt an unpleasant moral emotion associated with a specific instance in which one has acted badly or wrongly

habit an acquired behavior that, if followed regularly, will become almost automatic

halo effect the assumption that because people have one desirable trait (e.g., attractiveness), they also possess many other desirable traits (e.g., intelligence)

HARKing (Hypothesizing After the Results are Known) when a hypothesis is formulated after the data are collected and analyzed, but presented as if it was formulated before the data were collected

health a state of complete physical, mental, and social well-being

health belief model theory that posits that beliefs about the effectiveness, ease, and consequences of doing (or not doing) a certain behavior determine whether we do (or do not do) that behavior

health psychology an interdisciplinary subspecialty of psychology dedicated to promoting and maintaining health and preventing and treating illness

healthy behaviors any specific behaviors that maintain and enhance health

hedonic treadmill a theory proposing that people stay at about the same level of happiness regardless of what happens to them

heuristic/systematic model theory that posits two routes to persuasion, via either conscious or automatic processing

heuristics mental shortcuts that provide quick estimates about the likelihood of uncertain events

hindsight bias or the "knew it all along" phenomenon is the tendency, *after* an event has occurred, to overestimate one's ability to have foreseen the outcome

history the study of past events

hit (correct identification) when a witness accurately identifies the person who committed a crime from a lineup

homeostasis the ideal level of bodily functions

homophobia an excessive fear of homosexuals or homosexual behavior

honor killing killing another individual who has brought "dishonor" to the family (e.g., a woman who has committed adultery)

hostile attribution bias the tendency to perceive ambiguous actions by others as aggressive

hostile expectation bias the tendency to assume that people will react to potential conflicts with aggression

hostile perception bias the tendency to perceive social interactions in general as being aggressive

hostile work environment a form of sexual harassment when an employee experiences workplace harassment such as provocative pictures that make the environment an uncomfortable place to work

hot hand the tendency for gamblers who get lucky to think they have a "hot" hand and their luck will continue

humiliation a state of disgrace or loss of self-respect (or of respect from others)

hypochondriacs people who are constantly worried about their health

hypocrisy induction a technique for effecting behavior change by confronting people with the inconsistency between their attitudes and their behavior

hypothesis an idea about the possible nature of reality; a prediction tested in an experiment

identity theft consists of stealing someone's personal information (e.g., Social Security number, bank account, credit card number) and using it without their permission, usually to obtain money or goods

illusion of control the false belief that one can influence certain events, especially random or chance ones

illusory correlation the tendency to overestimate the link between variables that are related only slightly or not at all

implicit personality theories a set of beliefs, developed through experience, about how demographic characteristics and attitudes are interrelated

incorrect rejection when a witness fails to identify the suspect in a target-present lineup

incremental theorists those who believe that traits are subject to change and improvement

independent self-construal a self-concept that emphasizes what makes the self different and sets it apart from others

independent variable the variable manipulated by the researcher that is assumed to lead to changes in the dependent variable

indirect aggression any behavior that intentionally harms another person who is physically absent

individual good–collective bad trap when a destructive behavior by one person is of little consequence but has disastrous results when repeated by many (e.g., overgrazing)

informational influence going along with the crowd because you think the crowd knows more than you do

ingratiation what people actively do to try to make someone like them

ingroup favoritism preferential treatment of, or more favorable attitudes toward, people in one's own group

ingroup members people who belong to the same group or category as we do

injunctive norms norms that specify what most others approve or disapprove of

instinct an innate (inborn, biologically programmed) tendency to seek a particular goal, such as food, water, or sex

Institutional Review Board (IRB) is a committee that makes sure that a research study conducted in university settings is ethical. The board must contain at least one scientist, one nonscientist, and one person not affiliated with the university

interdependent self-construal a self-concept that emphasizes what connects the self to other people and groups

internal validity the extent to which changes in the independent variable caused changes in the dependent variable

interpersonal self (public self) the image of the self that is conveyed to others

intervention any program or message providing information or structure to change a behavior

intimacy a feeling of closeness, mutual understanding, and mutual concern for each other's welfare and happiness

intrinsic motivation wanting to perform an activity for its own sake

introspection the process by which a person examines the contents of his or her mind and mental states

inverted (upside-down) U-shaped relationship a relationship that looks like an upside-down U when plotted

investment model theory that uses three factors—satisfaction, alternatives, and investments—to explain why people stay with their long-term relationship partners

James–Lange theory of emotion the proposition that the bodily processes of emotion come first and the mind's perception of these bodily reactions then creates the subjective feeling of emotion

jigsaw classroom a cooperative learning technique for reducing feelings of prejudice by having students interact and cooperate to learn material

job analysis the identification of the critical elements of a job; it documents the tasks, working conditions, and human attributes needed to do the job

job withdrawal behaviors employees use to avoid their job

kin selection the evolutionary tendency to help people who have our genes

knowledge structures organized packets of information that are stored in memory

labeling technique influence technique in which one assigns a label to an individual and then requests a favor that is consistent with the label

lateral cycling selling or giving a previously purchased product to someone else to use for its intended purpose

leadership a social influence process in which a person steers members of the group toward a goal

learned helplessness belief that one's actions will not bring about desired outcomes, leading one to give up and quit trying

legitimization-of-paltry-favors technique influence technique that involves a phrase that suggests that even a very small amount of aid will help (e.g., "even a penny will help")

legitimizing myths explanations used to justify why people in power deserve to be in power

life satisfaction an evaluation of how one's life is generally and how it compares to some standard

limited-number technique influence technique in which one tells people that an item is in short supply

lineup a police procedure in which a witness to the crime is shown a suspect (or a picture of the suspect) along with several other people (or photos of people) to see if the witness recognizes one of the lineup members as the person who committed the crime

loneliness the painful feeling of wanting more human contact or connection than you have

looking-glass self the idea that people learn about themselves by imagining how they appear to others

loss-framed appeal focuses on how not doing something will subtract from your health

low-ball technique influence technique in which one first gets a person to comply with a seemingly low-cost request and only later reveals hidden additional costs

lying deliberately making a false statement, usually to mislead someone.

margin of error a statistic measure of the amount of random sampling error in a survey's results—for example, a 3% margin of error means that the survey's result could be 3% lower or 3% higher than the average response—the larger the sample is, the smaller the margin of error is

match-to-culprit description choosing lineup fillers who share features of the culprit mentioned in the witness's description of the culprit but who vary on other features

match-to-suspect choosing lineup fillers who have features that are similar to the features of the suspect the police have in custody

matching hypothesis the proposition that people tend to pair up with others who are equally attractive

mentoring training that occurs when a current and often long-term employee (the mentor) is paired with a new employee

mere exposure effect the tendency for people to come to like things simply because they see or encounter them repeatedly

meta-analysis a quantitative literature review that combines the statistical results (e.g., correlation coefficients) from all studies conducted on a topic

meta-cognition reflecting on one's own thought processes

minimal group effect the finding that people show favoritism toward ingroup members even when group membership is randomly determined

missing hero trap when information of actual or potential disaster (e.g., toxic spill) is withheld from those affected by it

modeling observing and copying or imitating the behavior of others

monitoring keeping track of behaviors or responses to be regulated

mood a feeling state that is not clearly linked to some event

moral inclusion involves treating all people as ingroup members

moral intuitions judgments (about whether an action is right or wrong) that occur automatically and rely on emotional feelings

moral reasoning using logical deductions to make moral judgments based on abstract principles of right and wrong

mundane realism refers to whether the setting of an experiment physically resembles the real world

mutation a new gene or combination of genes

narcissism excessive self-love and a selfish orientation

natural selection the process whereby those members of a species that survive and reproduce most effectively are the ones that pass along their genes to future generations

nature the physical world around us, including its laws and processes

need for cognition a tendency to engage in and enjoy effortful thinking, analysis, and mental problem solving

need to belong the desire to form and maintain close, lasting relationships with other individuals

negative attitude change (boomerang effect) doing exactly the opposite of what one is being persuaded to do

netnography ethnographic research applied to internet and social media communications to better understand the group and individual members

neuroscience the study of what happens in the brain, nervous system, and other aspects of the body

neutral stimulus a stimulus (e.g., Pavlov's bell) that initially evokes no response

noise annoying, unwanted sound

non-zero-sum game an interaction in which both participants can win (or lose)

normative commitment a commitment to the organization based on feelings of obligation

normative influence going along with the crowd in order to be liked and accepted

norms standards established by society to tell its members what types of behavior are typical or expected

obedience following orders from an authority figure

Occupational Information Network, or O*NET a comprehensive, detailed, and flexible set of job descriptors that can be used to find information to include in a job description; salary and occupational outlook are also provided

omission bias the tendency to take whatever course of action does not require you to do anything (also called the default option)

one-person trap when the consequences of a destructive behavior affect only the individual (e.g., overeating)

one-shot illusory correlation an illusory correlation that occurs after exposure to only one unusual behavior performed by only one member of an unfamiliar group

online virtual memorial online document of a person's life after they have died, or online version of cemeteries and other places to remember people

open science is a movement to make the results from scientific studies openly accessible to all people.

operant conditioning (instrumental conditioning) a type of learning in which people are more likely to repeat behaviors that have been rewarded and less likely to repeat behaviors that have been punished

operational definitions observable operations, procedures, and measurements that are based on the independent and dependent variables

organizational citizenship behaviors (OCBs) behaviors employees engage in that go beyond what is expected by the leaders of the organization.

organizational culture the cognitive component that includes the shared assumptions and beliefs of the organization

organizational justice employees' perceptions of fairness of treatment in the workplace

organizational socialization the process by which organizational members become a part of, or are absorbed into, the culture of the organization

organizational withdrawal type of withdrawal comprised of work and job withdrawal

ostracism being excluded, rejected, and ignored by others

outgroup homogeneity bias the assumption that outgroup members are more similar to one another than ingroup members are to one another

outgroup members people who belong to a different group or category than we do

overbenefited getting more than you deserve

overjustification effect the tendency for intrinsic motivation to diminish for activities that have become associated with rewards

own-race bias the finding that witnesses are more accurate in identifying members of their own race than members of another race

panic button effect a reduction in stress or suffering due to a belief that one has the option of escaping or controlling the situation, even if one doesn't exercise it

passion an emotional state characterized by high bodily arousal, such as increased heart rate and blood pressure

passionate love (romantic love) strong feelings of longing, desire, and excitement toward a special person

paternity uncertainty the fact that a man cannot be sure that the children born to his female partner are his

perceived behavioral control an individual's beliefs about whether they can actually perform the behavior in question

peremptory challenge a method of removing a potential juror from a jury panel for which the attorney need not specify the reason

performance reviews evaluations of employees' job performance usually conducted by their direct supervisor on an annual or semi-annual basis

peripheral route (heuristic processing) the route to persuasion that involves some simple cue, such as attractiveness of the source (automatic processing)

personal relevance degree to which people expect an issue to have significant consequences for their own lives

personal space an area with invisible boundaries that surrounds us

personality psychology the branch of psychology that focuses on important differences between individuals

personalization a way of marking our territory with improvements or decorations that are unique reflections of our personal identity

persuasion an attempt to change a person's attitude

phenomenal self (working self-concept) the image of self that is currently active in the person's thoughts

philosophy "love of wisdom"; the pursuit of knowledge about fundamental matters such as life, death, meaning, reality, and truth

physiological psychology the study of what happens in the brain, nervous system, and other aspects of the body

pique technique influence technique in which one captures people's attention, as by making a novel request.

plagiarize to claim the ideas or words of another person as one's own without crediting that person

planning fallacy the tendency for plans to be overly optimistic because the planner fails to allow for unexpected problems

pluralistic ignorance looking to others for cues about how to behave, while they are looking to you; collective misinterpretation

political science the study of political organizations and institutions, especially governments

polychronic activity engaging in more than one activity or behavior at a time

population the total number of people under consideration

post-decision dissonance cognitive dissonance experienced after making a difficult choice, typically reduced by increasing the attractiveness of the chosen alternative and decreasing the attractiveness of rejected alternatives

post-traumatic stress disorder post-disaster behavioral symptoms including sleep disorders, social withdrawal, uncontrollable thoughts about the event, and a desire to avoid thoughts of the event

power one person's control over another person, including what happens to that person

praxis practical ways of doing things

prejudice a negative feeling toward an individual based solely on his or her membership in a particular group

preoccupied (anxious/ambivalent) attachment style of attachment in which people are low on avoidance but high on anxiety; they want and enjoy closeness but worry that their relationship partners will abandon them

primary territory area, such as a bedroom, that is highly personalized and considered off limits to those not invited to enter

priming activating an idea in someone's mind so that related ideas are more accessible

prisoner's dilemma a game that forces people to choose between cooperation and competition

private acceptance a genuine inner belief that others are right

private self-awareness looking inward on the private aspects of the self, including emotions, thoughts, desires, and traits

proactive aggression (also called instrumental aggression) "cold," or premeditated, calculated harmful behavior that is a means to some practical or material end

product misuse using a product for an unintended purpose or without regard to instructions or usage suggestions

prompts cues that convey a message and remind people to do something

propinquity being near someone on a regular basis

propitious heterogeneity variation in the physical features of the fillers that could help witnesses find the culprit among the fillers without biasing the lineup against an innocent suspect

prosocial behavior doing something that is good for other people or for society as a whole

psyche a broader term for mind, encompassing emotions, desires, perceptions, and all other psychological processes

psychological reactance the unpleasant emotional response people experience when someone is trying to restrict their freedom to engage in a desired behavior

psychology the study of human behavior

public compliance outwardly going along with the group but maintaining a private, inner belief that the group is probably wrong

public self-awareness looking outward on the public aspects of the self that others can see and evaluate

public self-consciousness about how others perceive you

public territory area that is open to anyone who is not specifically excluded

quasi-experiment a type of study in which the researcher can manipulate an independent variable but cannot random assign participants to conditions

quid pro quo a form of sexual harassment that means "in exchange for this, I'll give you that"

racism prejudiced attitudes toward a particular race

random assignment procedure whereby each study participant has an equal chance of being in each treatment group

random sample a sample wherein each person in the population has an equal chance of being selected

reactance an unpleasant emotional response that people often experience when someone is trying to restrict their freedom

reactance theory the idea that people are distressed by loss of freedom or options and seek to reclaim or reassert them

reactive aggression (also called hostile, affective, emotional, angry, impulsive, or retaliatory aggression) "hot," impulsive, angry behavior motivated by a desire to harm someone

realistic conflict theory the idea that competition over scarce resources leads to intergroup hostility and conflict

receptivity whether you "get" (pay attention to, understand) the message

reciprocity the obligation to return in kind what another has done for us

recruitment the process organizations use to identify qualified individuals for a job

regret involves feeling sorry for one's misfortunes, limitations, losses, transgressions, shortcomings, or mistakes

reinforcement theory the proposition that people and animals will perform behaviors that have been rewarded more than they will perform other behaviors

rejection (social exclusion) being prevented by others from forming or keeping a social bond with them; the opposite of acceptance

rejection sensitivity a tendency to expect rejection from others and to become hypersensitive to possible rejection

relational aggression (also called **social aggression**) behavior that involves intentionally harming another person's social relationships, feelings of acceptance, or inclusion within a group

relationship-enhancing style of attribution tendency of happy couples to attribute their partner's good acts to internal factors and bad acts to external factors

reliability consistency of measurement

repetition with variation repeating the same information, but in a varied format

replication repeating a study to see if the effect is reliable

representativeness heuristic the tendency to judge the frequency or likelihood of an event by the extent to which it resembles the typical case

reproduction producing babies that survive long enough to also reproduce

reverse double standard condemning men more than women for the same sexual behavior (e.g., premarital sex)

risk-as-feelings hypothesis the idea that people rely on emotional processes to evaluate risk, with the result that their judgments may be biased by emotional factors

risk aversion in decision making, the greater weight given to possible losses than possible gains

risky shift a tendency for groups to take greater risks than the same individuals (on average) would have decided to take individually

rule of law when members of a society (including its most powerful leaders) respect and follow its rules

running amok according to Malaysian culture, refers to behavior of a young man who becomes "uncontrollably" violent after receiving a blow to his ego

salience being obvious or standing out

scapegoat theory the idea that blaming problems and misfortunes on outgroups contributes to negative attitudes toward these outgroups

Schachter–Singer theory of emotion the idea that emotion has two components: a bodily state of arousal and a cognitive label that specifies the emotion

schemas knowledge structures that represent substantial information about a concept, its attributes, and its relationships to other concepts

scripts knowledge structures that define situations and guide behavior

secondary territory area, such as the desk you usually sit at, that you don't really own but nonetheless consider to be "yours"

secure attachment style of attachment in which people are low on anxiety and low on avoidance; they trust their partners, share their feelings, provide and receive support and comfort, and enjoy their relationships

selective exposure refers to the tendency of individuals to select information that supports their preexisting views and avoid information that contradicts their preexisting views

self-acceptance regarding yourself as being a reasonably good person as you are

self-awareness attention directed at the self

self-censorship choosing not to express doubts or other information that goes against a group's plans and views

self-deception strategies mental tricks people use to help them believe things that are false

self-defeating behavior any action by which people bring failure, suffering, or misfortune on themselves

self-defeating prophecy a prediction that ensures, by the behavior it generates, that it will not come true

self-determination theory the theory that people need to feel at least some degree of autonomy and internal motivation

self-enhancement motive the desire to learn favorable or flattering things about the self

self-esteem how favorably someone evaluates himself or herself

self-fulfilling prophecy a prediction that ensures, by the behavior it generates, that it will come true

self-handicapping putting obstacles in the way of one's own performance so that anticipated or possible failure can be blamed on the obstacle instead of on lack of ability

self-knowledge (self-concept) a set of beliefs about oneself

self-monitoring the ability to change one's behavior for different situations

self-perception theory the theory that people observe their own behavior to infer what they are thinking and how they are feeling

self-presentation any behavior that seeks to convey some image of self or some information about the self to other people

self-protection trying to avoid loss of esteem

self-reference effect the finding that information bearing on the self is processed more thoroughly and more deeply, and hence remembered better, than other information

self-regulation the process people use to control and change their thoughts, feelings, and behaviors

self-serving bias the tendency to take credit for success but deny blame for failure; or internal attributions for success, external attributions for failure

sensitivity about being the target of a threatening upward comparison interpersonal concern about the consequences of outperforming others

sensory overload when the amount of information to be processed exceeds the individual's capacity to sort out what is relevant from what is not

sentiment analysis often using computers and analytical techniques on words in postings, this type of analysis provides companies with information about how people feel about their products or services

serotonin the "feel good" neurotransmitter, low levels of which have been linked to aggression and violence in both humans and animals

sex guilt feeling guilty about sexual thoughts, acts, or fantasies

shame a moral emotion that, like guilt, involves feeling bad but, unlike guilt, spreads to the whole person

shrinkage the loss of money or Inventory from shoplifting and/or employee theft

simulation heuristic the tendency to judge the frequency or likelihood of an event by the ease with which you can imagine (or mentally simulate) it

simultaneous lineup a lineup in which all lineup members (or their photos) are presented to the witness at the same time

sleeper effect the finding that, over time, people separate the message from the messenger

social acceptance a situation in which other people have come to like you, respect you, approve of you, and include you in their groups and relationships

social allergy effect the idea that a partner's annoying habits become more annoying over time

social animals animals that seek connections to others and prefer to live, work, and play with other members of their species

social categorization the process of sorting people into groups on the basis of characteristics they have in common (e.g., race, gender, age, religion, sexual orientation)

social cognition a movement in social psychology that began in the 1970s that focused on thoughts about people and about social relationships

social comparison examining the difference between oneself and another person

social constructionist theories theories asserting that attitudes and behaviors, including sexual desire and sexual behavior, are strongly shaped by culture and socialization

social exchange theory theory that seeks to understand social behavior by analyzing the costs and benefits of interacting with each other; it assumes that sex is a resource that women have and men want

social facilitation theory proposition that the presence of others increases the dominant response tendency

social learning (observational learning) a type of learning in which people are more likely to imitate behaviors if they have seen others rewarded for performing them, and less likely to imitate behaviors if they have seen others punished for performing them

social loafing (free rider problem) the finding that people reduce effort when working in a group, compared to when working alone

Social Network Analysis the process of studying the connections and activity levels between individuals, groups, or things. Social Network Analysis can be used in many areas but it is especially useful in tracking and understanding social media connections. Social Analysis reports often include graphical representations of connections as well as visual depictions of activity levels

social psychology the scientific study of how people affect and are affected by others

social reality beliefs held in common by several or many people; public awareness

social roles the different roles a person plays, as in a play or a movie

social support emotional, informational, or instrumental assistance from others

sociology the study of human societies and the groups that form those societies

sociometer a measure of how desirable one would be to other people

source the individual who delivers the message

stalking persisting in romantic, courtship, or other behaviors that frighten and harass the rejecter in a relationship

standards ideas (concepts) of how things might possibly be

statistical regression (regression to the mean) the statistical tendency for extreme scores or extreme behavior to be followed by others that are less extreme and closer to average

status quo bias the preference to keep things the way they are rather than change

stereotype threat the fear that one might confirm the stereotypes that others hold

stereotypes beliefs that associate groups of people with certain traits

stigma by association rejection of those who associate with stigmatized others

stigmas characteristics of individuals that are considered socially unacceptable (e.g., being overweight, mentally ill, sick, poor, or physically scarred)

stimulus sampling using more than one exemplar of a stimulus (e.g., more than one violent video game)

stress the upsetting of homeostasis

Stroop effect in the Stroop test, the finding that people have difficulty overriding the automatic tendency to read the word rather than name the ink color

Stroop test a standard measure of effortful control over responses, requiring participants to identify the color of a word (which may name a different color)

structured interview interview conducted by a trained interviewer that has standardized questions based on a job analysis, a specific question order, and a predetermined scoring or answer key

subjective norms an individual's perceptions about whether significant others think he or she should (or should not) perform the behavior in question

subtypes categories that people use for individuals who do not fit a general stereotype

survival living longer

survivor guilt an unpleasant emotion associated with living through an experience during which other people died

system variables characteristics of a lineup administration that are under the control of the criminal justice system and that influence the accuracy of eyewitness identifications

target-absent lineup a lineup in which the person who committed the crime is not present in the lineup

target-present lineup a lineup in which the person who committed the crime is one of the lineup members

temporal discounting in decision making, the greater weight given to the present over the future

tend and befriend syndrome a response to stress that involves nurturing others and making friends

tend and befriend Taylor and colleagues' theory of how women react to stress differently than men

territoriality the tendency to stake out an area and a willingness to defend that area from intruders

testosterone the male sex hormone, high levels of which have been linked to aggression and violence in both humans and animals

tests the measurement of carefully chosen samples of behavior

thanatos in Freudian theory, the destructive, death instinct

that's-not-all technique influence technique in which one first makes an inflated request but, before the person can respond, sweetens the deal by offering a discount or bonus

theories unobservable constructs that are linked together in some logical way

theory of evolution a theory proposed by Charles Darwin to explain how change occurs in nature

theory of planned behavior theory to explain how intentions predict behaviors

theory perseverance proposes that once the mind draws a conclusion, it tends to stick with that conclusion unless there is overwhelming evidence to change it

third-person effect the belief that media messages have a stronger impact on others than on oneself

time poverty a feeling of having less time available than is required to meet the demands of everyday living

Title VII of the Civil Rights Act of 1964 federal legislation that prohibits discrimination based on race, color, religion, sex, and national origin (Big 5)

TOTE the self-regulation feedback loop of Test, Operate, Test, Exit

tradeoff a choice in which taking or maximizing one benefit requires either accepting a cost or sacrificing another benefit

transactive memory a process by which members of a small group remember different kinds of information

transtheoretical model the stages we progress through during behavior change

trust a confidence that others will provide benefits and/or not harm you, even if they may be tempted to do otherwise

trustworthiness whether a source will honestly tell you what he or she knows

unconditioned response a naturally occurring response (e.g., salivation)

unconditioned stimulus a stimulus (e.g., meat powder) that naturally evokes a particular response (salivation)

underbenefited getting less than you deserve

unrequited love a situation in which one person loves another but the other does not return that love

unstructured interview interview conducted by an untrained interviewer that is informal and unplanned, with random questions and no scoring key

upward comparison the act of comparing oneself to people who are better off

upward counterfactuals imagining alternatives that are better than actuality

upward social comparison comparing yourself to people better than you

usage situation the context in which a product is used.

validity the accuracy of a test in measuring what it is intended to measure

venire members of the community who are called to the courthouse to form a jury pool

violence aggression that has as its goal extreme physical harm, such as injury or death

voir dire the legal proceeding in which attorneys and judges attempt to uncover bias among those people who have been called for jury duty

volunteering a planned, long-term, nonimpulsive decision to help others

weapon focus when a witness focuses on the weapon carried by a culprit, causing a decrease in accuracy for memory of the culprit's face

weapons effect the increase in aggression that occurs as a result of the mere presence of a weapon

what is beautiful is good effect the assumption that physically attractive people will be superior to others on many other traits

will-do factors the normal or typical performance by an employee

within-subjects design participants are exposed to all levels of the independent variable

work groups two or more employees who (a) exist to perform organizationally relevant tasks, (b) share one or more common goals, (c) interact socially, (d) exhibit task interdependencies, (e) maintain and manage boundaries, and (f) are embedded in an organizational context that sets boundaries, constrains the team, and influences exchanges with other units in the broader entity

work withdrawal behaviors employees use to avoid their work

workforce planning the process used by managers to determine their needs with regard to human resources including retaining their talented employees, promoting employees, as well as removing poor performers.

Yerkes-Dodson law the proposition that some arousal is better than none, but too much can hurt performance

yielding whether you "accept" (believe, and especially whether you change your attitude to agree with) the message

Zeigarnik effect a tendency to experience automatic, intrusive thoughts about a goal whose pursuit has been interrupted

zero-sum game a situation in which one person's gain is another's loss

Endnotes

CHAPTER 1
Social Psychology and Human Nature

1. Carpenter, C. S., & Stehr, M. F. (2010). Intended and unintended effects of youth bicycle helmet laws. The National Bureau of Econonomic Research. Retrieved from https://www.nber.org/papers/w15658
2. The Economist (2015, October 22). Death on the roads.
3. Halderman, P. (2018, July 4). The secret price of pets. *New York Times*. Retrieved from https://www.nytimes.com/2018/07/04/style/how-to-pamper-your-pet.html
4. Ailes, E. (2016, April 4). 13 of the world's most stupid criminals. BBC News. Retrieved from http://www.bbc.com/news/uk-35785834
5. Triplett, N. (1897). The dynamogenic factors in peacemaking and competition. *American Journal of Psychology, 9*, 507–533.
6. Ringelmann, M. (1913). Recherches sur les moteurs animés: Travail de l'homme. *Annales de l'Institut National Argonomique*, 2e srie, tom 12, 1–40.
7. McDougall, William (1960. Original work published 1908), *An Introduction to Social Psychology* (23rd ed.), University Paperbacks. Imprint of Methuen & Co (London) and Barnes & Noble (New York), pp. xxi–xxii (Note: Preface to 23rd edition commences p. xxi, with date of this preface [October 1936] on p. xxii.)
8. Ross, Edward A. (1974. Original work published 1908). *Social Psychology*. New York: Arno Press.
9. Allport, F. H. (1924). *Social psychology*. Boston: Houghton Mifflin Company.
10. Allport, G. W. (1954). The historical background of modern social psychology. In G. Lindzey (Ed.), *Handbook of social psychology* (Vol. 1, pp. 3–56). Cambridge, MA: Addison-Wesley.
11. Lewin, K. (1936). *Principles of topological psychology*. New York: McGraw-Hill.
12. Milgram, S. (1974). *Obedience to authority; An experimental view*. New York: Harper and Row.
13. Milgram, S. (1973, December). The perils of obedience. *Harper's*, 62–66.
14. Bargh, J. A., Chen, M., & Burrows, L. (1996). Automaticity of social behavior: Direct effects of trait construct and stereotype activation on action. *Journal of Personality and Social Psychology, 71*(2), 230–244.
15. O'Brien, E. H., Anastasio, P. A., & Bushman, B. J. (2011). Time crawls when you're not having fun: Feeling entitled makes dull tasks drag on. *Personality and Social Psychology Bulletin, 37*(10), 1287–1296.
16. George Santayana (1905) *Reason in Common Sense*, p. 284, volume 1 of The Life of Reason. Unabridged Dover Press.
17. Stephan, C. W. & Stephan, W. G. (1985). *Two social psychologies: An integrative approach*. Homewood, IL: Dorsey.
18. Funder, D. C. (2001). Personality. *Annual Review of Psychology, 52*, 197–221.
19. Lewin, K. (1951). *Field theory in social science: Selected theoretical papers* (D. Cartwright, Ed.). New York: Harper Torchbooks. Quote on p. 169.
20. Rogow, A. A, Carey, G. L., & Farrell, C. (1957). The significance of aphorisms in American culture. *Sociology and Social Research, 41*, 417–420.
21. Teigen, H. (1986). Old truths or fresh insights? A study of student's evaluations of proverbs. *British Journal of Social Psychology, 25*, 43–50.
22. Garrett, R. K., & Weeks, B. E. (2017). Epistemic beliefs' role in promoting misperceptions and conspiracist ideation. *PLOS ONE*. doi:10.1371/journal.pone.0184733
23. McLeod, J. M., & Pan, Z. (2005). Concept explication and theory construction. In S. Dunwoody, L. B. Becker, D. M. McLeod, & G. M. Kosicki (Eds.), *The evolution of key mass communication concepts* (pp. 13–76). Creskill, NJ: Hampton Press.
24. Buss, A. H. (1961). *The psychology of aggression*. New York: John Wiley.
25. Dollard, J., Doob, L., Miller, N., Mowrer, O., & Sears, R. (1939). *Frustration and aggression*. New Haven, CT: Yale University Press.
26. Bushman, B. J., & Anderson. C. A. (1998). Methodology in the study of human aggression: Integrating experimental and nonexperimental findings. In R. G. Geen & E. I. Donnerstein (Eds.), *Human aggression: Theories, research, and implications for policy* (pp. 23–48). New York: Academic Press.
27. Harris, M. B. (1974). Mediators between frustration and aggression in a field experiment. *Journal of Experimental Social Psychology, 10*(6), 561–571.
28. Harris, M. B. (1976). Instigators and inhibitors of aggression in a field experiment. *Journal of Social Psychology, 98*(1), 27–38.
29. Cook, T. D., & Campbell, D. T. (1979). *Quasi-experimentation* (pp. 37–94). Boston: Houghton Mifflin.
30. Orne, M. T. (1962). On the social psychology of the psychological experiment: With particular reference to demand characteristics and their implications. *American Psychologist, 17*(11), 776–783.
31. Epley, N., & Huff, C. (1998). Suspicion, affective response, and educational benefit as a result of deception in psychology research. *Personality and Social Psychology Bulletin, 24*, 759–768.
32. Cook, T. D., & Campbell, D. T. (1979). *Quasi-experimentation* (pp. 37–94). Boston: Houghton Mifflin.
33. Wells, G. L., & Windschitl, P. D. (1999). Stimulus sampling and social psychological experimentation. *Personality and Social Psychology Bulletin, 25*, 1115–1125.
34. Brehm, J. W. (1966). *A theory of psychological reactance*. New York: Academic Press.
35. Ruback, R. B. & Juieng, D. (1997). Territorial defense in parking lots: Retaliation against waiting drivers. *Journal of Applied Social Psychology, 27*, 821–834.
36. Harris, M. B. (1974). Mediators between frustration and aggression in a field experiment. *Journal of Experimental Social Psychology, 10*(6), 561–571.
37. Aronson, E., & Carlsmith, J. M. (1968). Experimentation in social psychology. In G. Lindzey & E. Aronson (Eds.), *Handbook of Social Psychology* (2nd ed., Vol. 2, pp. 1–79). Reading, MA: Addison-Wesley.
38. Berkowitz, L., & Donnerstein, E. (1982). External validity is more than skin deep. *American Psychologist, 37*, 245–257.
39. Wynder, E. L., & Graham, E. A. (1950). Tobacco smoking as a possible etiological factor in bronchiogenic carcinoma. *Journal of the American Medical Association, 143*, 329–336.
40. Anderson, C. A., & Dill, K. E. (2000). Video games and aggressive thoughts, feelings, and behavior in laboratory and real life. *Journal of Personality and Social Psychology, 78*(4), 772–790.
41. Cohen, J. (1988). *Statistical power analysis for the behavioral sciences* (2nd ed.). New York: Academic Press.
42. The Onion (2014, June 24). Report: Only Predictor Of Happy Marriage Is If Husband Ever Won Wife Big Stuffed Animal At Amusement Park. Retrieved from: http://www.theonion.com/articles/report-only-predictor-of-happy-marriage-is-if-husb,36353/
43. Election polls—Accuracy record in presidential elections. Retrieved from http://www.gallup.com/poll/9442/election-polls-accuracy-record-presidential-elections.aspx
44. Geiger, A. (2018, January 5). About six-in-ten Americans support marijuana legalization. *Pew Research Center*. Retrieved from http://www.pewresearch.org/fact-tank/2018/01/05/americans-support-marijuana-legalization/
45. Schuman, H., & Scott, J. (1987). Problems in the use of survey questions to measure public opinion. *Science, 236*(4804), 957–959.
46. Schwarz, N. (1999). Self-reports: How the questions shape the answers. *American Psychologist, 54*(2), 93–105. doi: 10.1037/0003-066X.54.2.93
47. Kim, J., Glaser, P., & Smith, T. W. (2011). The polls—trends: Trends in surveys on surveys. *Public Opinion Quarterly, 75*(1), 165–191.
48. Henrich, J., Heine, S. J., & Norenzayan, A. (2010). The weirdest people in the world? *Behavioral and Brain Sciences, 33*, 61–83. doi:10.1017/S0140525X0999152X
49. Koole, S. L., & Lakens, D. (2012). Rewarding replications: A sure and simple way to improve psychological science. *Perspectives in Psychological Science, 7*(6), 608–614. doi: 10.1177/1745691612462586
50. Baker, M. (2016, 26 May). 1,500 scientists lift the lid on reproducibility *Nature, 533*, 452–454. http://dx.doi.org/10.1038/533452a
51. Open Science Collaboration (2015). Estimating the reproducibility of psychological science. *Science, 349*(6251), 1–8. http://dx.doi.org/10.1126/science.aac4716
52. Hawkins, R. X. D., Smith, E. N., Au, C., Arias, J. M., Catapano, R., Hermann, E., ...Frank, M. C. (2018). Improving the replicability of psychological science through pedagogy. *Advances in Methods and Practices in Psychological Science, 1*, 7-18.10.1177/2515245917740427
53. Lilienfeld, S. O. (2017). Psychology's replication crisis and the grant culture: Righting the ship. *Perspectives on Psychological Science, 12*, 660–664. http://dx.doi.org/10.1177/1745691616687745
54. Simmons, J. P., Nelson, L. D., & Simonsohn, U. (2011). False-positive psychology: Undisclosed flexibility in data collection and analysis allows presenting anything as significant. *Psychological Science, 22*, 1359–1366. doi:10.1177/0956797611417632
55. Anderson, S. F., & Maxwell, S. E. (2017). Addressing the 'replication crisis': Using original studies to design replication studies with appropriate statistical power. *Multivariate Behavioral Research, 52*, 305–324. doi:10.1080/00273171.2017.1289361
56. Archer, J., & Bushman, B. J. (invited review). The uses of meta-analysis in psychology. *Current Directions in Psychological Science*.
57. Shadish, W. R., Cook, T. D., & Campbell, D. T. (2002). *Experimental and quasi-experimental designs for generalized causal inference*. New York: Houghton Mifflin Company.
58. Kerr, N. L. (1998). HARKing: Hypothesizing after the results are known. *Personality And Social Psychology Review, 2*(3), 196–217. doi:10.1207/s15327957pspr0203_4
59. Nosek, B. A., Ebersole, C. R., DeHaven, A. C., & Mellor, D. T. (2018). The preregistration revolution. *PNAS Proceedings of the National Academy of Sciences of the United States of America, 115*(11), 2600–2606. doi:10.1073/pnas.1708274114
60. OSF Home. https://osf.io
61. Adolph, K. E., Gilmore, R. O., Freeman, C., Sanderson, P., & Millman, D. (2012). Toward open behavioral science. *Psychological Inquiry, 23*(3), 244–247. doi:10.1080/1047840X.2012.705133
62. Hesse, B. W. (2018). Can psychology walk the walk of open science? *American Psychologist, 73*(2), 126–137. doi:10.1037/amp0000197

63. McAbee, S. T., Grubbs, J. B., & Zickar, M. J. (2018). Open science is robust science. *Industrial And Organizational Psychology: Perspectives On Science And Practice, 11*(1), 54–61. doi:10.1017/iop.2017.85
64. Grahe, J. E. (2014). Announcing open science badges and reaching for the sky. *The Journal of Social Psychology, 154*(1), 1–3. doi:10.1080/00224545.2014.853582
65. Oakes, W. (1972). External validity and the use of real people as subjects. *American Psychologist, 27,* 959–962.
66. Sears, D. O. (1986). College sophomores in the laboratory: Influences of a narrow data base on social psychology's view of human nature. *Journal of Personality and Social Psychology, 51,* 515–530.
67. Anderson, C. A., Suzuki, K., Swing, E. L., Groves, C. L., Gentile, D. A., Prot, S., Lam, C. P., Sakamoto, A., . . . Petrescu, P. (2017). Media violence and other aggression risk factors in seven nations. *Personality and Social Psychology Bulletin, 43,* 986–998. doi: 10.1177/0146167217703064
68. Anderson, C. A., Shibuya, A., Ihori, N., Swing, E. L., Bushman, B. J., Sakamoto, A., Rothstein, H. R., Saleem, M., & Barlett, C. P. (2010). Violent video game effects on aggression, empathy, and prosocial behavior in Eastern and Western countries: A meta-analytic review. *Psychological Bulletin, 136*(2), 151–173.
69. Bond, R., & Smith, P. B (1996). Culture and conformity: A meta-analysis of studies using Asch's (1952b 1956) line judgment task. *Psychological Bulletin, 119* (1), 111–137.

CHAPTER 2
Culture and Nature

1. Colapinto, J. (2000). *As nature made him: The boy who was raised as a girl.* New York: HarperCollins.
2. Colapinto, J. (2000). *As nature made him: The boy who was raised as a girl.* New York: HarperCollins.
3. Joiner, T. (2005). *Why people die by suicide.* Cambridge, MA: Harvard University Press.
4. de Waal, F. B. M. (2002). Evolutionary psychology: The wheat and the chaff. *Current Directions in Psychological Science, 11,* 187–191.
5. Buss, D. M. (1994). *The evolution of desire: Strategies of human mating.* New York: Basic Books.
6. Symons, D. (1979). *The evolution of human sexuality.* New York: Oxford University Press.
7. Trivers, R. (1972). Parental investment and sexual selection. In B. Campbell (Ed.), *Sexual selection and the descent of man: 1871–1971* (pp. 136–179). Chicago: Aldine.
8. Schmitt, D. P. (2003). Universal sex differences in the desire for sexual variety: Tests from 52 nations, 6 continents, and 13 islands. *Journal of Personality and Social Psychology, 85,* 85–104.
9. Dunbar, R. I. M. (1993). Coevolution of neocortical size, group size, and language in humans. *Behavioral and Brain Sciences, 16,* 681–694.
10. Dunbar, R. I. M. (1996). *Grooming, gossip, and the evolution of language.* Cambridge, MA: Harvard University Press.
11. Powell, J., Lewis, P.A., Roberts, N., Garcia-Finana, M., & Dunbar, R.I.M. (2012). Orbital prefrontal cortex volume predicts social network size: An imaging study of individual differences in humans. *Proceedings of the Royal Society B, 279,* 2157–2162.
12. Gonzalez-Forero, M., & Gardner, A. (2018). Inference of ecological and social drivers of human brain-size evolution. *Nature, 557,* 554–557.
13. Sugiyama, L.S. (2004). Illness, injury, and disability among Shiwiar forager-horticulturalists: Implications of health-risk buffering for the evolution of human life history. *American Journal of Physical Anthropology, 123,* 371–389.
14. Aronson, E. (2007). *The social animal.* New York: Worth.
15. de Waal, F. B. M. (2002). Evolutionary psychology: The wheat and the chaff. *Current Directions in Psychological Science, 11,* 187–191.
16. Boyd, R., & Richerson, P. J. (1985). *Culture and the evolutionary process.* Chicago: University of Chicago Press.
17. Shteynberg, G., Hirsh, J. B., Apfelbaum, E. P., Larsen, J. T., Galinsky, A. D., & Roese, N. J. (2014, August 25). Feeling more together: Group attention intensifies emotion. *Emotion.* Advance online publication. http://dx.doi.org/10.1037/a0037697
18. Shteynberg, G., & Apfelbaum, A. P. (2013). The power of shared experience: Simultaneous observation with similar others facilitates social learning. *Social Psychological and Personality Science, 4,* 738–744.
19. Thomas, K. A., DeScioli, P., Haque, O. S., & Pinker, S. (2014). The psychology of coordination and common knowledge. *Journal of Personality and Social Psychology,* Advance online publication. http://dx.doi.org/10.1037/a0037037
20. Davies, G. (2002). *A history of money from ancient times to the present day.* Cardiff: University of Wales Press.
21. Lea, S. E. G., & Webley, P. (2006). Money as tool, money as drug: The biological psychology of a strong incentive. *Behavioral and Brain Sciences, 29,* 161–209.
22. Lea, S. E. G., & Webley, P. (2006). Money as tool, money as drug: The biological psychology of a strong incentive. *Behavioral and Brain Sciences, 29,* 161–209.
23. Levitt, S. J., & Dubner, S. D. (2005). *Freakonomics: A rogue economist explores the hidden side of everything.* New York: Morrow.
24. Van Boven, L., & Gilovich, T. (2003). To do or to have? That is the question. *Journal of Personality and Social Psychology, 85,* 1193–1202.
25. Caprariello, P. A. & Reis, H. T. (2013). To do, to have, or to share? Valuing experiences over material possessions depends on the involvement of others. *Journal of Personality and Social Psychology, 104,* 199–215.
26. Blackwell, B., & Hutchins, I. (1994). *Delights of the garden.* New York: Doubleday.
27. Frey, R. G. (1983). *Rights, killing, and suffering: Moral vegetarianism and applied ethics.* Oxford: Blackwell.
28. Ritson, J. (1802). *An essay on abstinence from animal food, as a moral duty.* London: Richard Phillips.
29. Tansey, G., & D'Silva, J. (1999). *The meat business: Devouring a hungry planet.* New York: St. Martin's Press.
30. Walters, K. S., & Portmess, L. (Eds.). (1999). *Ethical vegetarianism: From Pythagoras to Peter Singer.* Albany: State University of New York Press.
31. Grondin, S., Deshaies, P., & Nault, L. P. (1984). Trimestres de naissance et participation au hockey et au volleyball. *La Revue Quebecoise de l'Activité Physique, 2,* 97–103.
32. Musch, J., & Grondin, S. (2001). Unequal competition as an impediment to personal development: A review of the relative age effect in sport. *Developmental Review, 21,* 147–167.
33. Pedersen, W. C., Miller, L. C., Putcha-Bhagavatula, A. D., & Yang, Y. (2002). Evolved sex differences in the number of partners desired? The long and short of it. *Psychological Science, 13,* 157–161.
34. Tannahill, R. (1980). *Sex in history.* London: Scarborough House.
35. Frayser, S. G. (1985). *Varieties of sexual experience: An anthropological perspective on human sexuality.* New Haven, CT: HRAF Press.
36. Herdt, G. (1984). Ritualized homosexual behavior in the male cults of Melanesia, 1862–1983: An introduction. In G. Herdt (Ed.), *Ritualized homosexuality in Melanesia* (pp. 1–82). Berkeley: University of California Press.
37. Musch, J., & Grondin, S. (2001). Unequal competition as an impediment to personal development: A review of the relative age effect in sport. *Developmental Review, 21,* 147–167.
38. Dickinson, D. J., & Larsen, J. D. (1963). The effects of chronological age in months on school achievement. *Journal of Educational Research, 56,* 492–493.
39. Hauck, A., & Finch, A. (1993). The effect of relative age on achievement in middle school. *Psychology in the Schools, 30,* 74–79.
40. Maddux, C. D., Stacy, D., & Scott, M. (1981). School entry age in a group of gifted children. *Gifted Child Quarterly, 25,* 180–184.
41. DeMeis, J., & Stearns, E. (1992). Relationship of school entrance age to academic and social performance. *Journal of Educational Research, 86,* 21–27.
42. Vandello, J. A., Bosson, J. K., Cohen, D., Burnaford, R. M., & Weaver, J. R. (2008). Precarious manhood. *Journal of Personality and Social Psychology, 95,* 1325–1339.
43. Vandello, J. A., Bosson, J. K., Cohen, D., Burnaford, R. M., & Weaver, J. R. (2008). Precarious manhood. *Journal of Personality and Social Psychology, 95,* 1325–1339.
44. Harris, M. (1974). *Cows, pigs, wars, and witches: The riddles of culture.* New York: Random House.
45. Harris, M. (1977). *Cannibals and kings: The origins of culture.* New York: Random House.
46. Murray, D. R., Trudeau, R., & Schaller, M. (2011). On the origins of cultural differences in conformity: Four tests of the pathogen prevalence hypothesis. *Personality and Social Psychology Bulletin, 37,* 318–329.
47. Fincher, C. L., Thornhill, R., Murray, D. R., & Schaller, M. (2008). Pathogen prevalence predicts human cross-cultural variability in individualism /collectivism. *Proceedings of the Royal Society B, 275,* 1279–1285.
48. Park, J. H., & Schaller, M. (2009). Parasites, minds and cultures. *The Psychologist, 22,* 942–945.
49. Schaller, M., & Murray, D. R. (2008). Pathogens, personality, and culture: Disease prevalence predicts worldwide variability in sociosexuality, extraversion, and openness to experience. *Journal of Personality and Social Psychology, 95,* 212–221.
50. Schaller, M., & Murray, D. R. (2008). Pathogens, personality, and culture: Disease prevalence predicts worldwide variability in sociosexuality, extraversion, and openness to experience. *Journal of Personality and Social Psychology, 95,* 212–221.
51. Boyd, R., & Richerson, P. J. (1985). *Culture and the evolutionary process.* Chicago: University of Chicago Press.
52. Boyd, R., & Richerson, P. J. (2005). *The origin and evolution of cultures.* New York: Oxford University Press
53. Baumeister, R. F. (2005). *The cultural animal: Human nature, meaning, and social life.* New York: Oxford University Press.
54. Baumeister, R. F. (2005). *The cultural animal: Human nature, meaning, and social life.* New York: Oxford University Press.
55. Boyd, R., & Richerson, P. J. (1985). *Culture and the evolutionary process.* Chicago: University of Chicago Press.
56. Litt, C. J. (1981). Children's attachment to transitional objects: A study of two pediatric populations. *American Journal of Orthopsychiatry, 51,* 131–139.
57. Barry, H., III, & Paxson, L. M. (1971). Infancy and early childhood: Cross-cultural codes II. *Ethnology, 10,* 466–508.
58. Leung, K., & Bond, M. H. (2004). Social axioms: A model for social beliefs in multicultural perspective. In M. Zanna (Ed.), *Advances in experimental social psychology* (Vol. 36, pp. 119–197). New York: Academic Press.
59. Koider, S., Andrillon, T., Barbosa, L. S., Goupil L., & Bekinschtein, T. A. (2014). Inducing task-relevant responses to speech in the sleeping brain. *Current Biology, 24,* 1–7.
60. Oswald, I., Taylor, A. M., & Treisman, M. (1960). Discriminative responses to stimulation during human sleep. *Brain, 83,* 440–453.
61. Strack, F., & Deutsch, R. (2004). Reflective and impulsive determinants of social behavior. *Personality and Social Psychology Review, 8*(3), 220–247.
62. Gazzaniga, M. S. (1998). *The mind's past.* Berkeley: University of California Press.

63. Gazzaniga, M. S. (2003, January). *The when, where, what, and why of conscious experience.* Paper presented at the 25th Annual National Institute on the Teaching of Psychology Convention, St. Petersburg Beach, FL.
64. Wegner, D. M. (2002). *The illusion of conscious will.* Cambridge, MA: MIT Press.
65. Bargh, J. A. (1982). Attention and automaticity in the processing of self-relevant information. *Journal of Personality and Social Psychology, 43,* 425–436.
66. Bargh, J. A. (1994). The four horsemen of automaticity: Awareness, intention, efficiency, and control in social cognition. In R. S. Wyer, Jr., & T. K. Srull (Eds.), *Handbook of social cognition* (pp. 1–40). Hillsdale, NJ: Erlbaum.
67. Bargh, J. A., Chen, M., & Burrows, L. (1996). Automaticity of social behavior: Direct effects of trait construct and stereotype activation on action. *Journal of Personality and Social Psychology, 71,* 230–244.
68. Bargh, J. A., Gollwitzer, P. M., Lee-Chai, A., Barndollar, K., & Trötschel, R. (2001). The automated will: Nonconscious activation and pursuit of behavioral goals. *Journal of Personality and Social Psychology, 81,* 1014–1027.
69. Lieberman, M. D., Gaunt, R., Gilbert, D. T., & Trope, Y. (2002). Reflection and reflexion: A social cognitive neuroscience approach to attributional inference. *Advances in Experimental Social Psychology, 34,* 199–249.
70. Bargh, J. A. (1994). The four horsemen of automaticity: Awareness, intention, efficiency, and control in social cognition. In R. S. Wyer, Jr., & T. K. Srull (Eds.), *Handbook of social cognition* (pp. 1–40). Hillsdale, NJ: Erlbaum.
71. Lieberman, M. D., Gaunt, R., Gilbert, D. T., & Trope, Y. (2002). Reflection and reflexion: A social cognitive neuroscience approach to attributional inference. *Advances in Experimental Social Psychology, 34,* 199–249.
72. Van der Wal, R.C., & van Dillen, L.F. (2013). Leaving a flat taste in your mouth: Task load reduces taste perception. *Psychological Science, 24,* 1277–1284.
73. DeWall, C. N., Baumeister, R. F., & Masicampo, E. J. (2008). Evidence that logical reasoning depends on conscious processing. *Consciousness and Cognition. 17,* 628–645.
74. Kahneman, D., & Frederick, S. (2002). Representativeness revisited: Attribute substitution in intuitive judgment. In T. Gilovich, D. Griffin, & D. Kahneman (Eds.), *Heuristics and biases* (pp. 49–81). New York: Cambridge University Press.
75. Kahneman, D. (2011). *Thinking, fast and slow.* New York: Farrar, Straus, and Giroux.
76. Strack, F., & Deutsch, R. (2004). Reflective and impulsive determinants of social behavior. *Personality and Social Psychology Review, 8*(3), 220–247.
77. Baumeister, R. F., Masicampo, E. J., & Vohs, K. D. (2011). Do conscious thoughts cause behavior? *Annual Review of Psychology, 62,* 331–361.
78. Peters, K., & Kashima, Y. (2007). From social talk to social action: Shaping the social triad with emotion sharing. *Journal of Personality and Social Psychology, 93,* 780–797.
79. Walton, G. M., Cohen, G. L., Cwir, D., & Spencer, S. J. (2012). Mere belonging: The power of social connections. *Journal of Personality and Social Psychology, 102,* 513–532.
80. Cesario, J., Plaks, J. E., & Higgins, E. T. (2006). Automatic social behavior as motivated preparation to interact. *Journal of Personality and Social Psychology, 90,* 893–910.
81. Loersch, C., & Arbuckle, N.L. (2013). Unraveling the mystery of music: Music as an evolved group process. *Journal of Personality and Social Psychology, 105,* 777–798.
82. Freud, S. (1961). *Civilization and its discontents* (standard ed.). London: Norton. (Original work published 1930).
83. Baumeister, R. F., Heatherton, T. F., & Tice, D. M. (1994). *Losing control: How and why people fail at self-regulation.* San Diego: Academic Press.
84. Ridley, M. (1993). *The red queen: Sex and evolution in human nature.* New York: Penguin.
85. Ridley, M. (2004). *Evolution* (3rd ed.). Oxford: Blackwell Science.
86. Baumeister, R. F., Reis, H. T., & Delespaul, P. A. E. G. (1995). Subjective and experiential correlates of guilt in everyday life. *Personality and Social Psychology Bulletin, 21,* 1256–1268.
87. Tangney, J. P., & Dearing, R. L. (2002). *Shame and guilt.* New York: Guilford Press.
88. Rozin, P., Markwith, M., & McCauley, C. (1994). Sensitivity to indirect contacts with other persons: AIDS aversion as a composite of aversion to strangers, infection, moral taint, and misfortune. *Journal of Abnormal Psychology, 103,* 495–505.
89. Pryor, J. B., Reeder, G. D., Yeadon, C., & Hesson-McInnis, M. (2004). A dual-process model of reactions to perceived stigma. *Journal of Personality and Social Psychology, 87,* 436–452.
90. Mischel, W. (1974). Processes in delay of gratification. In L. Berkowitz (Ed.), *Advances in experimental social psychology* (Vol. 7, pp. 249–292). San Diego: Academic Press.
91. Mischel, W. (1996). From good intentions to willpower. In P. Gollwitzer & J. Bargh (Eds.), *The psychology of action* (pp. 197–218). New York: Guilford Press.
92. Dion, J., & Mellor, B. (2004, August). Is sport really good for you? *EnRoute,* pp. 33–34.
93. Roberts, W. A. (2002). Are animals stuck in time? *Psychological Bulletin, 128,* 473–489.
94. Luce, M. F. (1998). Choosing to avoid: Coping with negatively emotion-laden consumer decisions. *Journal of Consumer Research, 24,* 409–433.
95. Luce, M. F., Bettman, J. R., & Payne, J. W. (1997). Choice processing in emotionally difficult decisions. *Journal of Experimental Psychology: Learning, Memory, and Cognition, 23,* 384–405.
96. Luce, M. F., Bettman, J. R., & Payne, J. W. (2001). *Emotional decisions: Tradeoff difficulty and coping in consumer choice.* Chicago: University of Chicago Press.
97. Tetlock, P. E. (1981). Pre- to post-election shifts in presidential rhetoric: Impression management or cognitive adjustment? *Journal of Personality and Social Psychology, 41,* 207–212.
98. Tetlock, P. E. (2000). Coping with trade-offs: Psychological constraints and political implications. In S. Lupia, M. McCubbins, & S. Popkin (Eds.), *Political reasoning and choice.* Berkeley: University of California Press.
99. Van Beest, I., & Williams, K. D. (2006). When inclusion costs and ostracism pays, ostracism still hurts. *Journal of Personality and Social Psychology, 91,* 918–928.
100. Asch, S. E. (1955, November). Opinions and social pressure. *Scientific American,* 31–35.
101. Asch, S. E. (1956). Studies of independence and conformity: I. A minority of one against a unanimous majority. *Psychological Monographs, 70* (No. 416).
102. Bond, R. A., & Smith, P. B. (1996). Culture and conformity: A meta-analysis of studies using Asch's (1952, 1956) line judgment task. *Psychological Bulletin, 119,* 111–137.
103. Hilmert, C. J., Kulik, J. A., & Christenfeld, N. J. (2006). Positive and negative opinion modeling: The influence of another's similarity and dissimilarity. *Journal of Personality and Social Psychology, 90,* 440–452.

CHAPTER 3
The Self

1. Turnbull, S. (2003). *The Ottoman Empire 1326–1699.* New York: Routledge.
2. James, W. (1948). *Psychology.* Cleveland, OH: World Publishing. (Original work published 1892).
3. Sennett, R. (1974). *The fall of public man.* New York: Random House.
4. Stone, L. (1977). *The family, sex and marriage in England: 1500–1800.* London: Perennial.
5. Weintraub, K. J. (1978). *The value of the individual: Self and circumstance in autobiography.* Chicago: University of Chicago Press.
6. Baumeister, R. F. (1987). How the self became a problem: A psychological review of historical research. *Journal of Personality and Social Psychology, 52,* 163–176.
7. Turner, R. H. (1976). The real self: From institution to impulse. *American Journal of Sociology, 81,* 989–1016.
8. Goffman, E. (1959). *The presentation of self in everyday life.* New York: Doubleday Anchor.
9. Markus, H. R., & Kitayama, S. (1991). Culture and the self: Implications for cognition, emotion, and motivation. *Psychological Review, 98,* 224–253. See also Triandis, H. C. (1989). The self and social behavior in differing cultural contexts. *Psychological Review, 96,* 506–520.
10. Clark, D. (1986). *The missing link.* New York: Humansphere.
11. Biddle, B. J., & Thomas, E. J. (1966). *Role theory: Concepts and research.* New York: Wiley.
12. Mead, G. H. (1934). *Mind, self and society.* Chicago: University of Chicago Press.
13. Goffman, E. (1959). *The presentation of self in everyday life.* New York: Doubleday Anchor.
14. Duval, S., & Wicklund, R. (1972). *A theory of objective self-awareness.* New York: Academic Press.
15. Fenigstein, A., Scheier, M. F., & Buss, A. H. (1975). Public and private self-consciousness: Assessment and theory. *Journal of Consulting and Clinical Psychology, 43,* 522–527.
16. Carver, C. S., & Scheier, M. F. (1981). *Attention and self-regulation: A control theory approach to human behavior.* New York: Springer Press.
17. Kagan, J. (1981). *The second year: The emergence of self-awareness.* Cambridge, MA: Harvard University Press.
18. Becker, A. E., Burwell, R. A., Herzog, D. B., Hamburg, P., & Gilman, S. E. (2002). Eating behaviours and attitudes following prolonged exposure to television among ethnic Fijian adolescent girls. *British Journal of Psychiatry, 180,* 509–514.
19. Botta, R. A. (2000). The mirror of television: A comparison of black and white adolescents' body image. *Journal of Communication, 50,* 144–159.
20. Harrison, K. (2000). The body electric: Thin-ideal media and eating disorders in adolescents. *Journal of Communication, 50,* 119–143.
21. Harrison, K. (2001). Ourselves, our bodies: Thin-ideal media, self-discrepancies, and eating disorder symptomatology in adolescents. *Journal of Social and Clinical Psychology, 20,* 289–323.
22. Harrison, K. (2003). Television viewers' ideal body proportions: The case of the curvaceously thin woman. *Sex Roles, 48,* 255–264.
23. Lavine, H., Sweeney, D., & Wagner, S. H. (1999). Depicting women as sex objects in television advertising: Effects on body dissatisfaction. *Personality and Social Psychology Bulletin, 25,* 1049–1058.
24. Tiggemann, M., & Pickering, A. S. (1996). Role of television in adolescent women's body dissatisfaction and drive for thinness. *International Journal of Eating Disorders, 20,* 199–220.
25. Silvia, P. J., & Duval, T. S. (2001). Objective self-awareness theory: Recent progress and enduring problems. *Personality and Social Psychology Review, 5,* 230–241.
26. Diener, E., & Wallbom, M. (1976). Effects of self-awareness on antinormative behavior. *Journal of Research in Personality, 10,* 107–111.
27. Sentyrz, S. M., & Bushman, B. J. (1998). Mirror, mirror on the wall, who's the thinnest one of all? Effects of self-awareness on consumption of fatty, reduced-fat, and fat-free products. *Journal of Applied Psychology, 83,* 944–949.
28. Heatherton, T. F., Polivy, J., Herman, C. P., & Baumeister, R. F. (1993). Self-awareness, task failure and disinhibition: How attentional focus affects eating. *Journal of Personality, 61,* 49–61.

29. Scheier, M. F., Fenigstein, A., & Buss, A. H. (1974). Self-awareness and physical aggression. *Journal of Experimental Social Psychology, 10,* 264–273.
30. Smith, G. E., Gerrard, M., & Gibbons, F. X. (1997). Self-esteem and the relation between risk behavior and perceptions of vulnerability to unplanned pregnancy in college women. *Health Psychology, 16,* 137–146.
31. Pryor, J. B., Gibbons, F. X., Wicklund, R. A., Fazio, R. H., & Hood, R. (1977). Self-focused attention and self-report validity. *Journal of Personality, 45,* 513–527.
32. Greenberg, J., & Musham, C. (1981). Avoiding and seeking self-focused attention. *Journal of Research in Personality, 15,* 191–200.
33. Hull, J. G. (1981). A self-awareness model of the causes and effects of alcohol consumption. *Journal of Abnormal Psychology, 90,* 586–600.
34. Hull, J. G., Levenson, R. W., Young, R. D., & Scher, K. J. (1983). Self-awareness-reducing effects of alcohol consumption. *Journal of Personality and Social Psychology, 44,* 461–473.
35. Baumeister, R. F. (1990). Suicide as escape from self. *Psychological Review, 97,* 90–113.
36. Chatard, A., & Selimbegovic, L. (2011). When self-destructive thoughts flash through the mind: Failure to meet standards affects the accessibility of suicide-related thoughts. *Journal of Personality and Social Psychology, 100,* 587–605.
37. Carver, C. S., & Scheier, M. F. (1981). *Attention and self-regulation: A control therapy approach to human behavior.* New York: Springer Press.
38. Carver, C. S., & Scheier, M. F. (1990). Origins and functions of positive and negative affect: A control-process view. *Psychological Review, 97,* 19–35.
39. Heatherton, T. F., & Baumeister, R. F. (1991). Binge eating as escape from self-awareness. *Psychological Bulletin, 110,* 86–108.
40. Blanchard, F. A., & Frost, R. O. (1983). Two factors of restraint: Concern for dieting and fluctuations. *Behavior Research and Therapy, 21,* 259–267.
41. Heatherton, T. F., Polivy, J., & Herman, C. P. (1989). Restraint and internal responsiveness: Effects of placebo manipulations of hunger state on eating. *Journal of Abnormal Psychology, 98,* 89–92.
42. Cooley, C. H. (1902). *Human nature and the social order.* New York: Charles Scribner's Sons.
43. Mead, G. H. (1934). *Mind, self and society.* Chicago: University of Chicago Press.
44. Shrauger, J. S., & Shoeneman, T. J. (1979). Symbolic interactionist view of self-concept: Through the looking glass darkly. *Psychological Bulletin, 86,* 549–573.
45. Tesser, A., & Rosen, S. (1975). The reluctance to transmit bad news. In L. Berkowitz (Ed.), *Advances in experimental social psychology* (Vol. 8, pp. 193–232). New York: Academic Press.
46. Rosenberg, M. (1979). *Conceiving the self.* New York: Basic Books.
47. Nisbett, R. E., & Wilson, T. D. (1977). Telling more than we can know: Verbal reports on mental processes. *Psychological Review, 84,* 231–259.
48. Nisbett, R. E., & Wilson, T. D. (1977). Telling more than we can know: Verbal reports on mental processes. *Psychological Review, 84,* 231–259.
49. Smith, G. H., & Engel, R. (1968). Influence of a female model on perceived characteristics of an automobile. *Proceedings of the Annual Convention of the American Psychological Association, 3,* 681–682.
50. Nisbett, R. E., & Wilson, T. D. (1977). Telling more than we can know: Verbal reports on mental processes. *Psychological Review, 84,* 231–259.
51. Vazire, S. (2010). Who knows what about a person? The Self-Other Knowledge Asymmetry (SOKA) model. *Journal of Personality and Social Psychology, 98,* 281–300.
52. Festinger, L. (1954). A theory of social comparison processes. *Human Relations, 7,* 117–140.
53. Tesser, A. (1988). Toward a self-evaluation maintenance model of social behavior. In L. Berkowitz (Ed.), *Advances in experimental social psychology* (Vol. 21, pp. 181–227). San Diego: Academic Press.
54. Agarwal, S., Mikhed, V., & Scholnick, B. (2016) Does inequality cause financial distress? Evidence from lottery winners and neighboring bankruptcies. Working paper, Federal Reserve Bank of Philadelphia.
55. Bem, D. J. (1965). An experimental analysis of self-persuasion. *Journal of Experimental Social Psychology, 1,* 199–218. Jones, E. E., & Gerard, H. B. (1967). *Foundations of social psychology.* New York: Wiley.
56. Jones, E. E., & Gerard, H. B. (1967). *Foundations of social psychology.* New York: Wiley.
57. Markus, H. R., & Kunda, Z. (1986). Stability and malleability in the self-concept in the perception of others. *Journal of Personality and Social Psychology, 51,* 858–866.
58. Deci, E. L. (1971). The effects of externally mediated rewards on intrinsic motivation. *Journal of Personality and Social Psychology, 18,* 105–115.
59. Deci, E. L., Koestner, R., & Ryan, R. M. (1999). A meta-analytic review of experiments examining the effects of extrinsic rewards on intrinsic motivation. *Psychological Bulletin, 125,* 627–668.
60. Cameron, J., Banko, K. M., & Pierce, W. D. (2001). Pervasive negative effects of rewards on intrinsic motivation: The myth continues. *The Behavior Analyst, 24,* 1–44.
61. Deci, E. L. (1971). The effects of externally mediated rewards on intrinsic motivation. *Journal of Personality and Social Psychology, 18,* 105–115.
62. Lepper, M. P., Greene, D., & Nisbett, R. E. (1973). Undermining children's intrinsic interest with extrinsic reward: A test of the "overjustification" hypothesis. *Journal of Personality and Social Psychology, 28,* 129–137.
63. Deci, E. L., Koestner, R., & Ryan, R. M. (1999). A meta-analytic review of experiments examining the effects of extrinsic rewards on intrinsic motivation. *Psychological Bulletin, 125,* 627–668.
64. Cameron, J., Banko, K. M., & Pierce, W. D. (2001). Pervasive negative effects of rewards on intrinsic motivation: The myth continues. *The Behavior Analyst, 24,* 1–44.
65. Rosenfeld, D. L., Folger, R., & Adelman, H. F. (1980). When rewards reflect competence: A qualification of the overjustification effect. *Journal of Personality and Social Psychology, 39,* 368–376.
66. Cameron, J., Banko, K. M., & Pierce, W. D. (2001). Pervasive negative effects of rewards on intrinsic motivation: The myth continues. *The Behavior Analyst, 24,* 1–44.
67. Deci, E. L., Koestner, R., & Ryan, R. M. (1999). A meta-analytic review of experiments examining the effects of extrinsic rewards on intrinsic motivation. *Psychological Bulletin, 125,* 627–668.
68. Wrzesniewski, A., Schwartz, B., Cong, X., Kane, M., Omar, A., & Kolditz, T. (2014). Multiple types of motives don't multiply the motivation of West Point cadets. *PNAS, 111,* 10990–10995.
69. McGuire, W. J., McGuire, C. V., Child, P., & Fujioka, T. (1978). Salience of ethnicity in the spontaneous self-concept as a function of one's ethnic distinctiveness in the social environment. *Journal of Personality and Social Psychology, 36,* 511–520.
70. McGuire, W. J., McGuire, C. V., Child, P., & Winton, W. (1979). Effects of household gender composition on the salience of one's gender in the spontaneous self-concept. *Journal of Experimental Social Psychology, 15,* 77–90.
71. Lord, C. G., & Saenz, D. S. (1985). Memory deficits and memory surfeits: Differential cognitive consequences of tokenism for tokens and observers. *Journal of Personality and Social Psychology, 49,* 918–926.
72. Wakslak, C. J., Nussbaum, S., Liberman, N., & Trope, Y. (2008). Representations of the self in the near and distant future. *Journal of Personality and Social Psychology, 95,* 751–773.
73. Kirkpatrick, L. A., & Ellis, B. J. (2001). An evolutionary-psychological perspective on self-esteem: Multiple domains and multiple functions. In G. J. O. Fletcher & M. S. Clark (Eds.), *Blackwell handbook of social psychology: Vol. 2. Interpersonal processes* (pp. 411–436). Oxford: Blackwell.
74. Trope, Y. (1983). Self-assessment in achievement behavior. In J. Suls & A. Greenwald (Eds.), *Psychological perspectives on the self* (Vol. 2, pp. 93–121). Hillsdale, NJ: Erlbaum.
75. Trope, Y. (1986). Self-enhancement and self-assessment in achievement behavior. In R. Sorrentino & E. T. Higgins (Eds.), *Handbook of motivation and cognition* (Vol. 2, pp. 350–378). New York: Guilford Press.
76. Sedikides, C. S., & Gregg, A. P. (2008). Self-enhancement: Food for thought. *Perspectives on Psychological Science, 3,* 102–116.
77. Swann, W. B., Jr. (1985). The self as architect of social reality. In B. Schlenker (Ed.), *The self and social life* (pp. 100–125). New York: McGraw-Hill.
78. Swann, W. B., Jr. (1987). Identity negotiation: Where two roads meet. *Journal of Personality and Social Psychology, 53,* 1038–1051.
79. Sedikides, C. (1993). Assessment, enhancement, and verification determinants of the self-evaluation process. *Journal of Personality and Social Psychology, 65,* 317–338.
80. Kim, Y.-H., Chiu, C., & Zou, Z. (2010). Know thyself: Misperceptions of actual performance undermine achievement motivation, future performance, and subjective well-being. *Journal of Personality and Social Psychology, 99,* 395–409.
81. Kim, Y.-H., Chiu, C., & Zou, Z. (2010). Know thyself: Misperceptions of actual performance undermine achievement motivation, future performance, and subjective well-being. *Journal of Personality and Social Psychology, 99,* 395–409.
82. Kwan, V. S., John, O., Robin, R., & Kuang, L. (2008). Conceptualizing and assessing self-enhancement bias: A componential approach. *Journal of Personality and Social Psychology, 94,* 1062–1077.
83. Jussim, L., HsiuJu, Y., & Aiello, J. R. (1995). Self-consistency, self-enhancement, and accuracy in reactions to feedback. *Journal of Experimental Social Psychology, 31,* 322–356.
84. McFarlin, D. B., & Blascovich, J. (1981). Effects of self-esteem and performance on future affective preferences and cognitive expectations. *Journal of Personality and Social Psychology, 40,* 521–531.
85. Shrauger, J. S. (1975). Responses to evaluation as a function of initial self-perceptions. *Psychological Bulletin, 82,* 581–596.
86. Swann, W. B., Jr., Griffin, J. J., Predmore, S., & Gaines, B. (1987). The cognitive-affective crossfire: When self-consistency confronts self-enhancement. *Journal of Personality and Social Psychology, 52,* 881–889.
87. Hirt, E. R., Deppe, R. K., & Gordon, L. J. (1991). Self-reported versus behavioral self-handicapping: Empirical evidence for a theoretical distinction. *Journal of Personality and Social Psychology, 61,* 981–991.
88. Jones, E. E., & Berglas, S. (1978). Control of attributions about the self through self-handicapping strategies: The appeal of alcohol and the role of underachievement. *Personality and Social Psychology Bulletin, 4,* 200–206.
89. Smith T. W., Snyder C. R., & Perkins S. C. (1983). The self-serving function of hypochondriacal complaints: Physical symptoms as self-handicapping strategies. *Journal of Personality and Social Psychology, 44,* 787–797.
90. Snyder, C. R., & Higgins, R. L. (1990). *Self-handicapping: The paradox that isn't.* Norwell, MA: Kluwer.
91. Kolditz, T., & Arkin, R. M. (1982). An impression management interpretation of the self-handicapping phenomenon. *Journal of Personality and Social Psychology, 43,* 492–502.
92. Paulhus, D. L., & Levitt, K. (1987). Desirable responding triggered by affect: Automatic egotism? *Journal of Personality and Social Psychology, 52,* 245–259.

93. Swann, W. B., Jr., Hixon, J. G., Stein-Seroussi, A., & Gilbert, D. T. (1990). The fleeting gleam of praise: Cognitive processes underlying behavioral reactions to self-relevant feedback. *Journal of Personality and Social Psychology, 59*, 17–26.

94. Swann, W. B., Jr., Stein-Seroussi, A., & Giesler, R. B. (1992). Why people self-verify. *Journal of Personality and Social Psychology, 62*, 392–401.

95. Tice, D. M. (1991). Esteem protection or enhancement? Self-handicapping motives and attributions differ by trait self-esteem. *Journal of Personality and Social Psychology, 60*, 711–725.

96. Berglas, S., & Jones, E. E. (1978). Drug choice as a self-handicapping strategy in response to non-contingent success. *Journal of Personality and Social Psychology, 36*, 405–417.

97. Berglas, S. C., & Baumeister, R. F. (1993). *Your own worst enemy: Understanding the paradox of self-defeating behavior*. New York: Basic Books.

98. Rogers, T. B., Kuiper, N. A., & Kirker, W. S. (1977). Self-reference and the encoding of personal information. *Journal of Personality and Social Psychology, 35*, 677–688.

99. Rogers, T. B., Kuiper, N. A., & Kirker, W. S. (1977). Self-reference and the encoding of personal information. *Journal of Personality and Social Psychology, 35*, 677–688.

100. Greenwald, A. G., & Banaji, M. R. (1989). The self as a memory system: Powerful, but ordinary. *Journal of Personality and Social Psychology, 57*, 41–54.

101. Higgins, E. T., & Bargh, J. A. (1987). Social cognition and social perception. *Annual Review of Psychology, 38*, 369–425.

102. Klein, S. B., & Kihlstrom, J. F. (1986). Elaboration, organization, and the self-reference effect in memory. *Journal of Experimental Psychology: General, 115*, 26–39.

103. Symons, C. S., & Johnson, B. T. (1997). The self-reference effect in memory: A meta-analysis. *Psychological Bulletin, 121*, 371–394.

104. Kahneman, D., Knetsch, J. L., & Thaler, R. H. (1990). Experimental tests of the endowment effect and the Coase theorem. *Journal of Political Economy, 98*(6), 1325–1348.

105. Beggan, J. K. (1992). On the social nature of nonsocial perception: The mere ownership effect. *Journal of Personality and Social Psychology, 62*, 229–237.

106. Langer, E. J. (1975). The illusion of control. *Journal of Personality and Social Psychology, 32*, 311–328.

107. Jones, E. E., Rhodewalt, F., Berglas, S., & Skelton, J. A. (1981). Effects of strategic self-presentation on subsequent self-esteem. *Journal of Personality and Social Psychology, 41*, 407–421.

108. Rhodewalt, F., & Agustdottir, S. (1986). Effects of self-presentation on the phenomenal self. *Journal of Personality and Social Psychology, 50*, 47–55.

109. Jones, E. E., & Nisbett, R. E. (1971). *The actor and the observer: Divergent perceptions of the causes of behavior*. New York: General Learning Press.

110. Backteman, G., & Magnusson, D. (1981). Longitudinal stability of personality characteristics. *Journal of Personality, 49*, 148–160.

111. Caspi, A., & Roberts, B. W. (2001). Personality development across the life course: The argument for change and continuity. *Psychological Inquiry, 12*, 49–66.

112. Epstein, S. (1979). The stability of behavior: I. On predicting most of the people much of the time. *Journal of Personality and Social Psychology, 37*, 1097–1126.

113. Eron, L. D., & Huesmann, L. R. (1990). The stability of aggressive behavior—even into the third generation. In M. Lewis & S. M. Miller (Eds.), *Handbook of developmental psychopathology* (pp. 147–156). New York: Plenum Press.

114. Harter, S. (1993). Causes and consequences of low self-esteem in children and adolescents. In R. F. Baumeister (Ed.), *Self-esteem: The puzzle of low self-regard* (pp. 87–116). New York: Plenum Press.

115. Group for the Advancement of Psychiatry. (1957). *Methods of forceful indoctrination: Observations and interviews*. New York: Author.

116. Heatherton, T. F., & Nichols, P. A. (1994). Personal accounts of successful versus failed attempts at life change. *Personality and Social Psychology Bulletin, 20*, 664–675.

117. Fazio, R. H., Effrein, E. A., & Falender, V. J. (1981). Self-perceptions following social interaction. *Journal of Personality and Social Psychology, 41*, 232–242.

118. Tice, D. M. (1992). Self-presentation and self-concept change: The looking-glass self is also a magnifying glass. *Journal of Personality and Social Psychology, 63*, 435–451.

119. Schlenker, B. R., Dlugolecki, D. W., & Doherty, K. J. (1994). The impact of self-presentations on self-appraisals and behaviors: The power of public commitment. *Personality and Social Psychology Bulletin, 20*, 20–33.

120. Ross, M. (1989). The relation of implicit theories to the construction of personal histories. *Psychological Review, 96*, 341–357.

121. Conway, M., & Ross, M. (1984). Getting what you want by revising what you had. *Journal of Personality and Social Psychology, 47*, 738–748.

122. Ross, M. (1989). The relation of implicit theories to the construction of personal histories. *Psychological Review, 96*, 341–357.

123. McFarlin, D. B., & Blascovich, J. (1981). Effects of self-esteem and performance on future affective preferences and cognitive expectations. *Journal of Personality and Social Psychology, 40*, 521–531.

124. Campbell, J. D. (1990). Self-esteem and clarity of the self-concept. *Journal of Personality and Social Psychology, 59*, 538–549.

125. Baumeister, R. F., Hutton, D. G., & Tice, D. M. (1989). Cognitive processes during deliberate self-presentation: How self-presenters alter and misinterpret the behavior of their interaction partners. *Journal of Experimental Social Psychology, 25*, 59–78.

126. Campbell, J. D., Chew, B., & Scratchley, L. S. (1991). Cognitive and emotional reactions to daily events: The effects of self-esteem and self complexity. *Journal of Personality, 59*, 473–505.

127. Branden, N. (1994). *The six pillars of self-esteem*. New York: Bantam Books.

128. Bushman, B. J., Moeller, S. J., & Crocker, J. (2011). Sweets, sex, or self-esteem? Comparing the value of self-esteem boosts with other pleasant rewards. *Journal of Personality, 79*(5), 993–1012.

129. Bushman, B. J., Moeller, S. J., Konrath, S., & Crocker, J. (2012). Investigating the link between liking versus wanting self-esteem and depression in a nationally representative sample of American adults. *Journal of Personality, 80*(5), 1455–1471. DOI: 10.1111/j.1467-6494.2012.00781.x.

130. Twenge, J. M. (2006). *Generation me*. New York: Free Press.

131. Twenge, J. M., & Campbell, W. K. (2001). Age and birth cohort differences in self-esteem: A cross-temporal meta-analysis. *Personality and Social Psychology Review, 5*, 321–344.

132. Svenson, O. (1981). Are we less risky and more skillful than our fellow drivers? *Acta Psychologica, 47*, 143–51.

133. College Board. (1976–1977). *Student descriptive questionnaire*. Princeton, NJ: Educational Testing Service.

134. Gilovich, T. (1991). *How we know what isn't so*. New York: Free Press.

135. Kling, K. C., Hyde, J. S., Showers, C. J., & Buswell, B. N. (1999). Gender differences in self-esteem: A meta-analysis. *Psychological Bulletin, 125*, 470–500.

136. Crocker, J., & Major, B. (1989). Social stigma and self-esteem: The self-protective properties of stigma. *Psychological Review, 96*, 608–630.

137. Gray-Little, B., & Hafdahl, A. R., (2000). Factors influencing racial comparisons of self-esteem: A quantitative synthesis. *Psychological Bulletin, 126*, 26–54.

138. Twenge, J., & Crocker, J. (2002). Race, ethnicity, and self-esteem: Meta-analyses comparing whites, blacks, Hispanics, Asians, and Native Americans, including a commentary on Gray-Little and Hafdahl (2000). *Psychological Bulletin, 128*, 371–408.

139. Twenge, J., & Crocker, J. (2002). Race, ethnicity, and self-esteem: Meta-analyses comparing whites, blacks, Hispanics, Asians, and Native Americans, including a commentary on Gray-Little and Hafdahl (2000). *Psychological Bulletin, 128*, 371–408.

140. Sedikides, C., Meek, R., Alicke, M. D., & Taylor, S. (2013). Behind bars but above the bar: Prisoners consider themselves more prosocial than non-prisoners. *British Journal of Social Psychology, 53*, 396–403.

141. Beck, A. T. (1976). *Cognitive therapy and the emotional disorders*. New York: Meridian.

142. Beck, A. T. (1988). *Cognitive therapy of depression: A personal reflection*. The Malcolm Millar Lecture in Psychotherapy. Aberdeen: Scottish Cultural Press.

143. Beck, A. T., & Burns, D. (1978). Cognitive therapy of depressed suicidal outpatients. In J. O. Cole, A. F. Schatzberg, & S. H. Frazier (Eds.), *Depression: Biology, psychodynamics, and treatment* (pp. 199–211). New York: Plenum Press.

144. Clark, D. A., Beck, A. T., & Brown, G. (1989). Cognitive mediation in general psychiatric outpatients: A test of the content specificity hypothesis. *Journal of Personality and Social Psychology, 56*, 958–964.

145. Ottaviani, R., & Beck, A. T. (1987). Cognitive aspects of panic disorders. *Journal of Anxiety Disorders, 1*, 15–28.

146. Shaw, B. F., & Beck, A. T. (1977). The treatment of depression with cognitive therapy. In A. Ellis & R. Grieger (Eds.), *Handbook of rational emotive therapy* (pp. 309–326). New York: Springer.

147. Moore, M. T., & Fresco, D. M. (2012). Depressive realism: A meta-analytic review. *Clinical Psychology Review, 32*, 496–509.

148. Alloy, L. B., & Abramson, L. Y. (1979). Judgment of contingency in depressed and nondepressed students: Sadder but wiser? *Journal of Experimental Psychology: General, 108*(4), 441–485.

149. Lewinsohn, P. M., Mischel, W., Chaplin, W., & Barton, R. (1980). Social competence and depression: The role of illusory self-perceptions. *Journal of Abnormal Psychology, 89*, 203–212.

150. Taylor, S. E., & Brown, J. D. (1988). Illusion and well-being: A social psychological perspective on mental health. *Psychological Bulletin, 103*, 193–210.

151. Gollwitzer, P. M., & Kinney, R. F. (1989). Effects of deliberative and implemental mind-sets on the illusion of control. *Journal of Personality and Social Psychology, 56*, 531–542.

152. Taylor, S. E., & Gollwitzer, P. M. (1995). Effects of mindset on positive illusions. *Journal of Personality and Social Psychology, 69*, 213–226.

153. Gonzales, M., Pederson, J., Manning, D., & Wetter, D. (1990). Pardon my gaffe: Effects of sex, status, and consequence severity on accounts. *Journal of Personality and Social Psychology, 58*, 610–621.

154. Weary, G. (1980). Examination of affect and egotism as mediators of bias in causal attributions. *Journal of Personality and Social Psychology, 38*, 348–357.

155. Zuckerman, M. (1979). Attribution of success and failure revisited, or: The motivational bias is alive and well in attribution theory. *Journal of Personality, 47*, 245–287.

156. Kunda, Z. (1990). The case for motivated reasoning. *Psychological Bulletin, 108*, 480–498.

157. Pyszczynski, T., Greenberg, J., & Holt, K. (1985). Maintaining consistency between self-serving beliefs and available data: A bias in information processing. *Personality and Social Psychology Bulletin, 11*, 179–190.

158. Wyer, R. S., & Frey, D. (1983). The effects of feedback about self and others on the cognitive processing of feedback-relevant information. *Journal of Experimental Social Psychology, 19*, 540–559.

159. Baumeister, R. F., & Cairns, K. J. (1992). Repression and self-presentation: When audiences interfere with self-deceptive strategies. *Journal of Personality and Social Psychology, 62*, 851–862.
160. Crary, W. G. (1966). Reactions to incongruent self-experiences. *Journal of Consulting Psychology, 30*, 246–252.
161. Kuiper, N. A., & Derry, P. A. (1982). Depressed and nondepressed content self-reference in mild depression. *Journal of Personality, 50*, 67–79.
162. Mischel, W., Ebbesen, E. B., & Zeiss, A. R. (1976). Determinants of selective memory about the self. *Journal of Consulting and Clinical Psychology, 44*, 92–103.
163. Crocker, J., & Major, B. (1989). Social stigma and self-esteem: The self-protective properties of stigma. *Psychological Review, 96*, 608–630.
164. Taylor, S. E. (1983). Adjustment to threatening events: A theory of cognitive adaptation. *American Psychologist, 38*, 1161–1173.
165. Wills, T. A. (1981). Downward comparison principles in social psychology. *Psychological Bulletin, 90*, 245–271.
166. Campbell, J. D. (1986). Similarity and uniqueness: The effects of attribute type, relevance, and individual differences in self-esteem and depression. *Journal of Personality and Social Psychology, 50*, 281–294.
167. Marks, G. (1984). Thinking one's abilities are unique and one's opinions are common. *Personality and Social Psychology Bulletin, 10*, 203–208.
168. Suls, J., & Wan, C. K. (1987). In search of the false uniqueness phenomenon: Fear and estimates of social consensus. *Journal of Personality and Social Psychology, 52*, 211–217.
169. Dunning, D., & McElwee, R. O. (1995). Idiosyncratic trait definitions: Implications for self-description and social judgment. *Journal of Personality and Social Psychology, 68*, 936–946.
170. Dunning, D., Meyerowitz, J. A., & Holzberg, A. D. (1989). Ambiguity and self-evaluation: The role of idiosyncratic trait definitions in self-serving assessments of ability. *Journal of Personality and Social Psychology, 57*, 1082–1090.
171. Dunning, D., Perie, M., & Story, A. L. (1991). Self-serving prototypes of social categories. *Journal of Personality and Social Psychology, 61*, 957–968.
172. Dunning, D., & Perretta, S. (2002). Automaticity and eyewitness accuracy: A 10-to-12 second rule for distinguishing accurate from inaccurate positive identifications. *Journal of Applied Psychology, 87*, 951–962.
173. Gabriel, M. T., Critelli, J. W., & Ee, J. S. (1994). Narcissistic illusions in self-evaluations of intelligence and attractiveness. *Journal of Personality, 62*, 143–155.
174. Bowles, T. (1999). Focusing on time orientation to explain adolescent self concept and academic achievement: Part II. Testing a model. *Journal of Applied Health Behaviour, 1*, 1–8.
175. Diener, E., Wolsic, B., & Fujita, F. (1995). Physical attractiveness and subjective well-being. *Journal of Personality and Social Psychology, 69*, 120–129.
176. Gabriel, M. T., Critelli, J. W., & Ee, J. S. (1994). Narcissistic illusions in self-evaluations of intelligence and attractiveness. *Journal of Personality, 62*, 143–155.
177. Miller, C. T., & Downey, K. T. (1999). A meta-analysis of heavyweight and self-esteem. *Personality and Social Psychology Review, 3*, 68–84.
178. Bachman, J. G., & O'Malley, P. M. (1977). Self-esteem in young men: A longitudinal analysis of the impact of educational and occupational attainment. *Journal of Personality and Social Psychology, 35*, 365–380.
179. Bachman, J. G., & O'Malley, P. M. (1986). Self-concepts, self-esteem, and educational experiences: The frog pond revisited (again). *Journal of Personality and Social Psychology, 50*, 35–46.
180. Baumeister, R. F., Campbell, J. D., Krueger, J. I., & Vohs, K. D. (2003). Does high self-esteem cause better performance, interpersonal success, happiness, or healthier lifestyles? *Psychological Science in the Public Interest, 4*, 1–44.
181. Forsyth, D. R., & Kerr, N. A. (1999, August). *Are adaptive illusions adaptive?* Poster presented at the annual meeting of the American Psychological Association, Boston, MA.
182. Maruyama, G., Rubin, R. A., & Kingsbury, G. G. (1981). Self-esteem and educational achievement: Independent constructs with a common cause? *Journal of Personality and Social Psychology, 40*, 962–975.
183. Pottebaum, S. M., Keith, T. Z., & Ehly, S. W. (1986). Is there a causal relation between self-concept and academic achievement? *Journal of Educational Research, 79*, 140–144.
184. Rosenberg, M., Schooler, C., & Schoenbach, C. (1989). Self-esteem and adolescent problems: Modeling reciprocal effects. *American Sociological Review, 54*, 1004–1018.
185. Scheirer, M. A., & Kraut, R. E. (1979). Increased educational achievement via self-concept change. *Review of Educational Research, 49*, 131–150.
186. Skaalvik, E. M., & Hagtvet, K. A. (1990). Academic achievement and self-concept: An analysis of causal predominance in a developmental perspective. *Journal of Personality and Social Psychology, 58*, 292–307.
187. Wylie, R. C. (1979). *The self-concept: Vol. 2. Theory and research on selected topics.* Lincoln: University of Nebraska Press.
188. Adams, G. R., Ryan, B. A., Ketsetzis, M., & Keating, L. (2000). Rule compliance and peer sociability: A study of family process, parent-child school-focused interactions and children's classroom behavior. *Journal of Family Psychology, 14*, 237–250.
189. Battistich, V., Solomon, D., & Delucchi, K. (1993). Interaction processes and student outcomes in cooperative learning groups. *The Elementary School Journal, 94*, 19–32.
190. Baumeister, R. F., Campbell, J. D., Krueger, J. I., & Vohs, K. D. (2003). Does high self-esteem cause better performance, interpersonal success, happiness, or healthier lifestyles? *Psychological Science in the Public Interest, 4*, 1–44.
191. Bishop, J. A., & Inderbitzen, H. M. (1995). Peer acceptance and friendship: An investigation of their relation to self-esteem. *Journal of Early Adolescence, 15*, 476–489.
192. Brockner, J., & Lloyd, K. (1986). Self-esteem and likability: Separating fact from fantasy. *Journal of Research in Personality, 20*, 496–508.
193. Buhrmester, D., Furman, W., Wittenberg, M. T., & Reis, H. T. (1988). Five domains of interpersonal competence in peer relationships. *Journal of Personality and Social Psychology, 55*, 991–1008.
194. Campbell, J. D., & Fehr, B. A. (1990). Self-esteem and perceptions of conveyed impressions: Is negative affectivity associated with greater realism? *Journal of Personality and Social Psychology, 58*, 122–133.
195. Glendenning, A., & Inglis, D. (1999). Smoking behaviour in youth: The problem of low self-esteem? *Journal of Adolescence, 22*, 673–682.
196. Keefe, K., & Berndt, T. J. (1996). Relations of friendship quality to self-esteem in early adolescence. *Journal of Early Adolescence, 16*, 110–129.
197. Heatherton, T. F., & Vohs, K. D. (2000). Interpersonal evaluations following threats to self: Role of self-esteem. *Journal of Personality and Social Psychology, 78*, 725–736.
198. Colvin, C. R., Block, J., & Funder, D. C. (1995). Overly positive evaluations and personality: Negative implications for mental health. *Journal of Personality and Social Psychology, 68*, 1152–1162.
199. Baumeister, R. F., Campbell, J. D., Krueger, J. I., & Vohs, K. D. (2003). Does high self-esteem cause better performance, interpersonal success, happiness, or healthier lifestyles? *Psychological Science in the Public Interest, 4*, 1–44.
200. Brockner, J. (1983). Low self-esteem and behavioral plasticity: Some implications. In L. Wheeler & P. Shaver (Eds.), *Review of personality and social psychology, Vol. 4* (pp. 237–271). Beverly Hills, CA: Sage.
201. Janis, I. L. (1954). Personality correlates of susceptibility to persuasion. *Journal of Personality, 22*, 504–518.
202. Janis, I. L., & Field, P. (1959). Sex differences and personality factors related to persuasibility. In C. Hovland & I. Janis (Eds.), *Personality and persuasibility* (pp. 55–68, 300–302). New Haven, CT: Yale University Press.
203. Paul, C., Fitzjohn, J., Herbison, P., & Dickson, N. (2000). The determinants of sexual intercourse before age 16. *Journal of Adolescent Health, 27*, 136–147.
204. Langer, L. M., & Tubman, J. G. (1997). Risky sexual behavior among substance-abusing adolescents: Psychosocial and contextual factors. *American Journal of Orthopsychiatry, 67*, 315–322.
205. McGee, R., & Williams, S. (2000). Does low self-esteem predict health compromising behaviours among adolescents? *Journal of Adolescence, 23*, 569–582.
206. Sprecher, S., & Regan, P. C. (1996). College virgins: How men and women perceive their sexual status. *Journal of Sex Research, 33*, 3–15.
207. Walsh, A. (1991). Self-esteem and sexual behavior: Exploring gender differences. *Sex Roles, 25*, 441–450.
208. Smith, G. E., Gerrard, M., & Gibbons, F. X. (1997). Self-esteem and the relation between risk behavior and perceptions of vulnerability to unplanned pregnancy in college women. *Health Psychology, 16*, 137–146.
209. Diener, E., & Diener, M. (1995). Cross-cultural correlates of life satisfaction and self-esteem. *Journal of Personality and Social Psychology, 68*, 653–663.
210. Orth, U., Robins, R. W., & Widaman, K. F. (2012). Life-span development of self-esteem and its effects on important life outcomes. *Journal of Personality and Social Psychology, 102*, 1271–1288.
211. Leary, M. R., Tambor, E. S., Terdal, S. K., & Downs, D. L. (1995). Self-esteem as an interpersonal monitor: The sociometer hypothesis. *Journal of Personality Psychology, 68*, 518–530.
212. Leary, M. R., & Baumeister, R. F. (2000). The nature and function of self-esteem: Sociometer theory. In M. Zanna (Ed.), *Advances in experimental social psychology* (Vol. 32, pp. 1–62). San Diego: Academic Press.
213. Greenberg, J., Solomon, S., & Pyszczynski, T. (1997). Terror management theory of self-esteem and cultural worldviews: Empirical assessments and conceptual refinements. In M. P. Zanna (Ed.), *Advances in experimental social psychology* (Vol. 29, pp. 61–139). San Diego: Academic Press.
214. Koch, E. J., & Shepperd, J. A. (2008). Testing competence and acceptance explanations of self-esteem. *Self and Identity, 7*, 54–74.
215. Twenge, J. M., Konrath, S., Foster, J. D., Campbell, W. K., & Bushman, B. J. (2008). Egos inflating over time: A cross-temporal meta-analysis of the Narcissistic Personality Inventory. *Journal of Personality, 76*, 875–901.
216. Trzesniewski, K. H., Donnellan, M. B., & Robins, R. W. (2008). Is "Generation Me" really more narcissistic than previous generations? *Journal of Personality, 76*, 903–917.
217. Twenge, J. M. (2006). *Generation Me.* New York: Free Press.
218. DeWall, C. N., Pond, R. S., Campbell, W. K., & Twenge, J. M. (2011). Tuning in to psychological change: Linguistic markers of psychological traits and emotions over time in popular U.S. song lyrics. *Psychology of Aesthetics, Creativity, and the Arts, 5*, 200–207.
219. Morf, C. C., & Rhodewalt, F. (2001). Unraveling the paradoxes of narcissism: A dynamic self-regulatory processing model. *Psychological Inquiry, 12*, 177–196.

220. Brummelman, E., Thomaes, S., & Sedikides, C. (2016). Separating narcissism from self-esteem. *Current Directions in Psychological Science, 25,* 8–13.
221. Bushman, B. J., & Baumeister, R. F. (1998). Threatened egotism, narcissism, self-esteem, and direct and displaced aggression: Does self-love or self-hate lead to violence? *Journal of Personality and Social Psychology, 75,* 219–229.
222. Bushman, B. J., & Baumeister, R. F. (2002). Does self-love or self-hate lead to violence. *Journal of Research in Personality, 36,* 543–545.
223. Bushman, B. J., Bonacci, A. M., Van Dijk, M., & Baumeister, R. F. (2003). Narcissism, sexual refusal, and sexual aggression: Testing a narcissistic reactance model of sexual coercion. *Journal of Personality and Social Psychology, 84,* 1027–1040.
224. Aberson, C. L., Healy, M., & Romero, V. (2000). Ingroup bias and self-esteem: A meta-analysis. *Personality and Social Psychology Review, 4,* 157–173.
225. Crocker, J., & Schwartz, I. (1985). Prejudice and ingroup favoritism in a minimal intergroup situation: Effects of self-esteem. *Personality and Social Psychology Bulletin, 11,* 379–386.
226. Buss, D. M., & Shackelford, T. K. (1997). From vigilance to violence: Mate retention tactics in married couples. *Journal of Personality and Social Psychology, 72,* 346–361.
227. Campbell, W. K. (1999). Narcissism and romantic attraction. *Journal of Personality and Social Psychology, 77,* 1254–1270.
228. Campbell, W. K. (2005). *When you love a man who loves himself.* Naperville, IL: Sourcebooks.
229. Campbell, W. K., & Foster, C. A. (2002). Narcissism and commitment in romantic relationships: An Investment Model analysis. *Personality and Social Psychology Bulletin, 28,* 484–495.
230. Campbell, W. K., Foster, C. A., & Finkel, E. J. (2002). Does self-love lead to love for others? A story of narcissistic game playing. *Journal of Personality and Social Psychology, 83,* 340–354.
231. Campbell, W. K. (2005). *When you love a man who loves himself.* Naperville, IL: Sourcebooks.
232. Olweus, D. (1994). Bullying at school: Long-term outcomes for the victims and an effective school-based intervention program. In R. Huesmann (Ed.), *Aggressive behavior: Current perspectives* (pp. 97–130). New York: Plenum Press.
233. Salmivalli, C., Kaukiainen, A., Kaistaniemi, L., & Lagerspetz, K. M. J. (1999). Self-evaluated self-esteem, peer-evaluated self-esteem, and defensive egotism as predictors of adolescents' participation in bullying situations. *Personality and Social Psychology Bulletin, 25,* 1268–1278.
234. Perez, R. C. (1973). The effect of experimentally induced failure, self-esteem and sex on cognitive differentiation. *Journal of Abnormal Psychology, 81,* 74–79.
235. Shrauger, J. S., & Sorman, P. B. (1977). Self-evaluations, initial success and failure, and improvement as determinants of persistence. *Journal of Consulting and Clinical Psychology, 45,* 784–795.
236. Janoff-Bulman, R., & Brickman, P. (1982). Expectations and what people learn from failure. In N. T. Feather (Ed.), *Expectations and actions: Expectancy-value models in psychology* (pp. 207–237). Hillsdale, NJ: Erlbaum.
237. McFarlin, D. B. (1985). Persistence in the face of failure: The impact of self-esteem and contingency information. *Personality and Social Psychology Bulletin, 11,* 153–163.
238. McFarlin, D. B., Baumeister, R. F., & Blascovich, J. (1984). On knowing when to quit: Task failure, self-esteem, advice, and nonproductive persistence. *Journal of Personality, 52,* 138–155.
239. Sandelands, L. E., Brockner, J., & Glynn, M. A. (1988). If at first you don't succeed, try, try again: Effects of persistence-performance contingencies, ego involvement, and self-esteem on task persistence. *Journal of Applied Psychology, 73,* 208–216.
240. Di Paula, A., & Campbell, J. D. (2002). Self-esteem and persistence in the face of failure. *Journal of Personality and Social Psychology, 83,* 711–724.
241. McFarlin, D. B. (1985). Persistence in the face of failure: The impact of self-esteem and contingency information. *Personality and Social Psychology Bulletin, 11,* 153–163.
242. Crocker, J., & Park, L. E. (2004). The costly pursuit of self-esteem. *Psychological Bulletin, 130,* 392–414.
243. Crocker, J., & Park, L. E. (2004). The costly pursuit of self-esteem. *Psychological Bulletin, 130,* 392–414.
244. Tesser, A. (1988). Toward a self-evaluation maintenance model of social behavior. In L. Berkowitz (Ed.), *Advances in experimental social psychology* (Vol. 21, pp. 181–227). San Diego: Academic Press.
245. Crocker, J., Sommers, S. R., & Luhtanen, R. K. (2002). Hopes dashed and dreams fulfilled: Contingencies of self-worth and admissions to graduate school. *Personality and Social Psychology Bulletin, 28,* 1275–1286.
246. Von Hippel, W., & Trivers, R. (2011). The evolution and psychology of self-deception. *Behavioral and Brain Sciences, 34,* 1–56.
247. Baumeister, R. F. (1982). A self-presentational view of social phenomena. *Psychological Bulletin, 91,* 3–26.
248. Goffman, E. (1959). *The presentation of self in everyday life.* New York: Doubleday Anchor.
249. Schlenker, B. R. (1980). *Impression management: The self-concept, social identity, and interpersonal relations.* Monterey, CA: Brooks/Cole.
250. Vonasch, A. J., Reynolds, T., Winegard, B. M., & Baumeister, R. F. (2018). Death before dishonour: Incurring costs to protect moral reputation. *Social Psychology and Personality Science, 9,* 604–613.
251. Tufekci, Z. (2008). Grooming, gossip, Facebook, and Myspace: What can we learn about these sites from those who won't assimilate? *Information, Communication & Society, 11,* 544–564.
252. Tamir, D. I., & Mitchell, J. P. (2012). Disclosing information about the self is intrinsically rewarding. *PNAS, 109,* 8038–3043.
253. Baumeister, R. F., & Tice, D. M. (1984). Role of self-presentation and choice in cognitive dissonance under forced compliance: Necessary or sufficient causes? *Journal of Personality and Social Psychology, 46,* 5–13.
254. Tedeschi, J. T., Schlenker, B. R., & Bonoma, T. V. (1971). Cognitive dissonance: Private ratiocination or public spectacle? *American Psychologist, 26,* 685–695.
255. Baumeister, R. F., & Cairns, K. J. (1992). Repression and self-presentation: When audiences interfere with self-deceptive strategies. *Journal of Personality and Social Psychology, 62,* 851–862.
256. Baumeister, R. F., & Jones, E. E. (1978). When self-presentation is constrained by the target's knowledge: Consistency and compensation. *Journal of Personality and Social Psychology, 36,* 608–618.
257. Greenberg, J., & Pyszczynski, J. (1985). Compensatory self-inflation: A response to the threat to self-regard of public failure. *Journal of Personality and Social Psychology, 49,* 273–280.
258. Munger, K., & Harris, S. J. (1989). Effects of an observer on handwashing in a public restroom. *Perceptual and Motor Skills, 69,* 733–734.
259. Heatherton, T. F., personal communication, 1993.
260. Braginski, B. M., Braginski, D. D., & Ring, K. (1969). *Methods of madness: The mental hospital as a last resort.* New York: Holt, Rinehart & Winston.
261. Goffman, E. (1959). *The presentation of self in everyday life.* New York: Doubleday Anchor.
262. Schlenker, B. R. (1980). *Impression management: The self-concept, social identity, and interpersonal relations.* Monterey, CA: Brooks/Cole.
263. Schlenker, B. R. (1980). *Impression management: The self-concept, social identity, and interpersonal relations.* Monterey, CA: Brooks/Cole.
264. Faith, heroics and bedtime snacks hailed at Columbine funerals. (1999, April 26). *CNN.* Retrieved August 25, 2019 from http://www.cnn.com/US/9904/26/school.shooting.funeral/
265. Wicklund, R. A., & Gollwitzer, P. M. (1982). *Symbolic self-completion.* Hillsdale, NJ: Erlbaum.
266. Wicklund, R. A., & Gollwitzer, P. M. (1982). *Symbolic self-completion.* Hillsdale, NJ: Erlbaum.
267. Bryan, C. J., Walton, G. M., Rogers, T., & Dweck, C. S. (2011). Motivating voter turnout by invoking the self. *PNAS, 108*(31), 12653–12656.
268. Griskevicius, V., Tybur, J. M., & Van den Bergh, B. (2010). Going green to be seen: Status, reputation, and conspicuous conservation. *Journal of Personality and Social Psychology, 98,* 392–404.
269. Schlenker, B. R. (1975). Self-presentation: Managing the impression of consistency when reality interferes with self-enhancement. *Journal of Personality and Social Psychology, 32,* 1030–1037.
270. Schlenker, B. R. (1975). Self-presentation: Managing the impression of consistency when reality interferes with self-enhancement. *Journal of Personality and Social Psychology, 32,* 1030–1037.
271. Schlenker, B. R. (1980). *Impression management: The self-concept, social identity, and interpersonal relations.* Monterey, CA: Brooks/Cole.
272. Paulhus, D. L., & Levitt, K. (1987). Desirable responding triggered by affect: Automatic egotism? *Journal of Personality and Social Psychology, 52,* 245–259.
273. Tice, D. M., Butler, J. L., Muraven, M. B., & Stillwell, A. M. (1995). When modesty prevails: Differential favorability of self-presentation to friends and strangers. *Journal of Personality and Social Psychology, 69,* 1120–1138.
274. Van Damme, C., Deschrijver, E., Van Geert, E., & Hoorens, V. (2017). When praising yourself insults others: Self-superiority claims provoke aggression. *Personality and Social Psychology Bulletin, 43,* 1008–1019.
275. Heine, S. J., Lehman, D. R., Markus, H. R., & Kitayama, S. (1999). Is there a universal need for positive self-regard? *Psychological Review, 106,* 766–794.
276. Sedikides, C., Gaertner, L., & Toguchi, Y. (2003). Pancultural self-enhancement. *Journal of Personality and Social Psychology, 84,* 60–70.
277. Leary, M. R., Tchividjian, L. R., & Kraxberger, B. E. (1994). Self-presentation can be hazardous to your health: Impression management and health risk. *Health Psychology, 13,* 461–470.

CHAPTER 4
Choices and Actions: The Self in Control

1. Hee, K. H. (1993). *The tears of my soul.* New York: Morrow.
2. James, W. (1890). *Principles of psychology.* New York: Holt.
3. Fiske, S. T. (1992). Thinking is for doing: Portraits of social cognition from daguerreotype to laser-photo. *Journal of Personality and Social Psychology, 63,* 877–889.
4. Baumeister, R. F., & Masicampo, E. J. (2010). Conscious thought is for facilitating social and cultural interactions: How mental simulations serve the animal-culture interface. *Psychological Review, 117,* 945–971.
5. Anderson, C. A. (1983). Imagination and expectation: The effect of imagining behavioral scripts on personal intentions. *Journal of Personality and Social Psychology, 45,* 293–305.
6. Anderson, C. A., & Sechler, E. S. (1986). Effects of explanation and counter and explanation on the development and use of social theories. *Journal of Personality and Social Psychology, 20,* 24–34.
7. Carroll, J. S. (1978). The effect of imagining an event on expectations for the event: An interpretation in terms of the availability heuristic. *Journal of Experimental Social Psychology, 14,* 88–96.
8. Gregory, L. W., Cialdini, R. B., & Carpenter, K. M. (1982). Self-relevant scenarios as mediator of likelihood estimates and compliance: Does

imagining make it so? *Journal of Personality and Social Psychology, 43,* 89–99.

9. Hirt, E. R., & Sherman, S. J. (1985). The role of prior knowledge in explaining hypothetical events. *Journal of Experimental Social Psychology, 21,* 519–543.

10. Sherman, S. T., Zehner, K. S., Johnson, J., & Hirt, E. R. (1983). Social explanation: The role of timing, set, and recall on subjective likelihood estimates. *Journal of Personality and Social Psychology, 44,* 1127–1143.

11. Taylor, S. E., & Pham, L. B. (1996). Mental simulation, motivation, and action. In P. M. Gollwitzer & J. A. Bargh (Eds.), *The psychology of action: Linking cognition and motivation to behavior* (pp. 219–235). New York: Guilford Press.

12. Waldman, S. (1992, January 27). The tyranny of choice: Why the consumer revolution is ruining your life. *New Republic,* 22–25.

13. Kahneman, D., & Tversky, A. (1979). Prospect theory: An analysis of decision under risk. *Econometrica, 47,* 263–291.

14. Kahneman, D., & Tversky, A. (1984). Choices, values, and frames. *American Psychologist, 39,* 341–350.

15. Tversky, A., & Kahneman, D. (1983). Extensional vs. intuitive reasoning: The conjunction fallacy in probability judgment. *Psychological Review, 91,* 293–315.

16. Hsee, C. K., & Zhang, J. (2004). Distinction bias: Misprediction and mischoice due to joint evaluation. *Journal of Personality and Social Psychology, 86*(5), 680–695.

17. Bazerman, M. H., Loewenstein, G. F., & White, S. B. (1992). Reversals of preference in allocation decisions: Judging an alternative versus choosing among alternatives. *Administrative Science Quarterly, 37*(2), 220–240.

18. Hsee, C. K. (1996). The evaluability hypothesis: An explanation for preference reversals between joint and separate evaluations of alternatives. *Organizational Behavior and Human Decision Processes, 67*(3), 247–257.

19. Atthowe, J. M. (1960). Types of conflict and their resolution: A reinterpretation. *Journal of Experimental Psychology, 59,* 1–9.

20. Kahneman, D., & Tversky, A. (1979). Prospect theory: An analysis of decision under risk. *Econometrica, 47,* 263–291.

21. Haselton, M. G., & Buss, D. M. (2000). Error management theory: A new perspective on biases in cross-sex mind reading. *Journal of Personality and Social Psychology, 78,* 81–91.

22. Wilson, M., & Daly M. (2003). Do pretty women inspire men to discount the future? *Biology Letters (Proc. R. Soc. Lond. B; Suppl.* doi: 10.1098/rsbl.2003.0134, online 12/12/2003)

23. Shin, J., & Ariely, D. (2004). Keeping doors open: The effect of unavailability on incentives to keep options open. *Management Science, 50,* 575–586.

24. Anderson, C. J. (2003). The psychology of doing nothing: Forms of decision avoidance result from reason and emotion. *Psychological Bulletin, 129,* 139–167.

25. Anderson, C. J. (2003). The psychology of doing nothing: Forms of decision avoidance result from reason and emotion. *Psychological Bulletin, 129,* 139–167.

26. Iyengar, S. S., & Lepper, M. R. (2000). When choice is demotivating: Can one desire too much of a good thing? *Journal of Personality and Social Psychology, 79,* 995–1006.

27. Schwartz, B. (2004, April). The tyranny of choice. *Scientific American,* 72–75.

28. Scheibehenne, B., Greifeneder, R., & Todd, P. M. (2008, November). *Can there ever be too many options? Re-assessing the effect of choice overload.* Paper presented at the annual meeting of the Society for Judgment and Decision Making, Chicago.

29. Mochon, D. (2008, November). *Single option aversion: When the illusion of choices reduces deferral.* Paper presented at the annual meeting of the Society for Judgment and Decision Making, Chicago.

30. White, C. M., Reisen, N., & Hoffrage, U. (2008, November). *Choice deferral can arise from absolute evaluation or relative comparison.* Paper presented at the annual meeting of the Society for Judgment and Decision Making, Chicago.

31. Brehm, J. W. (1966). *A theory of psychological reactance.* New York: Academic Press.

32. Brehm, J. W. (1972). *Responses to loss of freedom: A theory of psychological reactance.* Morristown, NJ: General Learning Press.

33. Brehm, S. S., & Brehm, J. W. (1981). *Psychological reactance.* New York: Wiley.

34. Wicklund, R. A. (1974). *Freedom and reactance.* Potomac, MD: Erlbaum.

35. Wortman, C. B., & Brehm, J. W. (1975). Responses to uncontrollable outcomes: An integration of reactance theory and the learned helplessness model. In L. Berkowitz (Ed.), *Advances in experimental social psychology* (Vol. 8, pp. 277–336). New York: Academic Press.

36. Brehm, J. W. (1966). *A theory of psychological reactance.* New York: Academic Press.

37. Brehm, S. S., & Brehm, J. W. (1981). *Psychological reactance.* New York: Wiley.

38. Bushman, B. J., & Cantor, J. (2003). Media ratings for violence and sex: Implications for policy makers and parents. *American Psychologist, 58,* 130–141.

39. Baumeister, R. F., Catanese, K. R., & Wallace, H. M. (2002). Conquest by force: A narcissistic reactance theory of rape and sexual coercion. *Review of General Psychology, 6,* 92–135.

40. Bushman, B. J., Bonacci, A. M., Van Dijk, M., & Baumeister, R. F. (2003). Narcissism, sexual refusal, and sexual aggression: Testing a narcissistic reactance model of sexual coercion. *Journal of Personality and Social Psychology, 84,* 1027–1040.

41. Heine, S. J., Lehman, D. R., Markus, H. R., & Kitayama, S. (1999). Is there a universal need for positive self-regard? *Psychological Review, 106,* 766–794.

42. Dweck, C. S. (1996). Implicit theories as organizers of goals and behavior. In P. Gollwitzer & J. Bargh (Eds.), *The psychology of action: Linking cognition and motivation to behavior* (pp. 69–91). New York: Guilford Press.

43. Dweck, C. S., & Leggett, E. L. (1988). A social-cognitive approach to motivation and personality. *Psychological Review, 95,* 256–273.

44. Henderson, V., & Dweck, C. S. (1990). Achievement and motivation in adolescence: A new model and data. In S. Feldman & G. Elliott (Eds.), *At the threshold: The developing adolescent* (pp. 308–329). Cambridge, MA: Harvard University Press.

45. Zhao, W., & Dweck, C. S. (1994). *Implicit theories and vulnerability to depression-like responses.* Unpublished manuscript, Columbia University, New York. Cited in Dweck, C. S. (1996). Implicit theories as organizers of goals and behavior. In P. Gollwitzer & J. Bargh (Eds.), *The psychology of action: Linking cognition and motivation to behavior* (pp. 69–91). New York: Guilford Press.

46. Dweck, C. S. (1996). Implicit theories as organizers of goals and behavior. In P. Gollwitzer & J. Bargh (Eds.), *The psychology of action: Linking cognition and motivation to behavior* (pp. 69–91). New York: Guilford Press.

47. Kant, I. (1967). *Kritik der praktischen Vernunft* [Critique of practical reason]. Hamburg: Felix Meiner Verlag. (Original work published 1797).

48. Vohs, K. D., & Schooler, J. (2008). The value of believing in free will: Encouraging a belief in determinism increases cheating. *Psychological Science, 19,* 49–54.

49. Baumeister, R. F., Masicampo, E. J., & DeWall, C. N. (2009). Prosocial benefits of feeling free: Disbelief in free will increases aggression and reduces helpfulness. *Personality and Social Psychology Bulletin, 35,* 260–268.

50. Monroe, A. E. & Malle, B. F. (2010). From uncaused will to conscious choice: The need to study, not speculate about people's folk concept of free will. *Review of Philosophy and Psychology, 9,* 211–224.

51. Deci, E. L., & Ryan, R. M. (1985). *Intrinsic motivation and self-determination in human behavior.* New York: Plenum Press.

52. Deci, E. L., & Ryan, R. M. (2000). The "what" and "why" of goal pursuits: Human needs and the self-determination of behavior. *Psychological Inquiry, 11,* 227–268.

53. Ryan, R. M., & Deci, E. L. (2000). Self-determination theory and the facilitation of intrinsic motivation, social development, and well-being. *American Psychologist, 55,* 68–78.

54. deCharms, R. (1968). *Personal causation.* New York: Academic Press.

55. Deci, E. L. (1975). *Intrinsic motivation.* New York: Plenum Press.

56. Deci, E. L., Koestner, R., & Ryan, R. M. (1999). A meta-analytic review of experiments examining the effects of extrinsic rewards on intrinsic motivation. *Psychological Bulletin, 125,* 627–668.

57. Fisher, C. D. (1978). The effects of personal control, competence, and extrinsic reward systems on intrinsic motivation. *Organizational Behavior and Human Performance, 21,* 273–288.

58. Ryan, R. M. (1982). Control and information in the intrapersonal sphere: An extension of cognitive evaluation theory. *Journal of Personality and Social Psychology, 43,* 450–461.

59. Ryan, R. M., & Deci, E. L. (2000). Self-determination theory and the facilitation of intrinsic motivation, social development, and well-being. *American Psychologist, 55,* 68–78.

60. Amabile, T. M. (1996). *Creativity in context.* Boulder, CO: Westview Press.

61. Deci, E. L., Nezlek, J., & Sheinman, L. (1981). Characteristics of the rewarder and the intrinsic motivation of the rewardee. *Journal of Personality and Social Psychology, 40,* 1–10.

62. Deci, E. L., Koestner, R., & Ryan, R. M. (1999). A meta-analytic review of experiments examining the effects of extrinsic rewards on intrinsic motivation. *Psychological Bulletin, 125,* 627–668.

63. Flink, C., Boggiano, A. K., & Barrett, M. (1990). Controlling teaching strategies: Undermining children's self-determination and performance. *Journal of Personality and Social Psychology, 59*(5), 916–924.

64. Grolnick, W. S., & Ryan, R. M. (1987). Autonomy in children's learning: An experimental and individual differences investigation. *Journal of Personality and Social Psychology, 52,* 890–898.

65. Ryan, R. M., & Deci, E. L. (2000). Self-determination theory and the facilitation of intrinsic motivation, social development, and well-being. *American Psychologist, 55,* 68–78.

66. Ryan, R. M., & Grolnick, W. S. (1986). Origin and pawns in the classroom: Self-report and projective assessments of individual differences in children's perceptions. *Journal of Personality and Social Psychology, 50,* 550–558.

67. Utman, C. H. (1997). Performance effects of motivational state: A meta-analysis. *Personality and Social Psychology Review, 1,* 170–182.

68. Kasser, T., & Ryan, R. M. (2001). Be careful what you wish for: Optimal functioning and the relative attainment of intrinsic and extrinsic goals. In P. Schmuck & K. Sheldon (Eds.), *Life goals and well-being* (pp. 116–131). Göttingen: Hogrefe.

69. Sheldon, K. M., & Kasser, T. (1998). Pursuing personal goals: Skills enable progress but not all progress is beneficial. *Personality and Social Psychology Bulletin, 24,* 1319–1331.

70. Glass, D. C., Singer, J. E., & Friedman, L. N. (1969). Psychic cost of adaptation to an environmental stressor. *Journal of Personality and Social Psychology, 12,* 200–210. Retrieved from http://www.quotationspage.com/quote/34212.html

71. Oettingen, G., & Gollwitzer, P. M. (2001). Goal setting and goal striving. In A. Tesser & N. Schwarz (Eds.), *Blackwell handbook of social psychology: Intraindividual processes* (pp. 329–348). Oxford: Blackwell.

72. Locke, E. A., & Kristof, A. L. (1996). Volitional choices in the goal achievement process. In P. M. Gollwitzer & J. A. Bargh (Eds.), *The psychology of*

action: Linking cognition and motivation to behavior (pp. 363–384). New York: Guilford Press.

73. Locke E. A., & Latham, G. P. (1990). *A theory of goal setting and task performance.* Englewood Cliffs, NJ: Prentice Hall.

74. Little, B. R. (1989). Personal projects analysis: Trivial pursuits, magnificent obsessions, and the search for coherence. In D. Buss & N. Cantor (Eds.), *Personality psychology: Recent trends and emerging directions* (pp. 15–31). New York: Springer Verlag.

75. Emmons, R. A. (1989). The personal striving approach to personality. In L. Pervin (Ed.), *Goal concepts and personality and social cognition* (pp. 87–126). Hillsdale, NJ: Erlbaum.

76. Little, B. R. (1989). Personal projects analysis: Trivial pursuits, magnificent obsessions, and the search for coherence. In D. Buss & N. Cantor (Eds.), *Personality psychology: Recent trends and emerging directions* (pp. 15–31). New York: Springer Verlag.

77. Tomasello, M., & Call, J. (1997). *Primate cognition.* New York: Oxford University Press.

78. Roberts, W. A. (2002). Are animals stuck in time? *Psychological Bulletin, 128,* 473–489.

79. Bonezzi, A., Brendl, C.M., & De Angelis, M. (2011). Stuck in the middle: The psychophysics of goal pursuit. *Psychological Science, 22,* 607–612.

80. Farrell, W. (1993). *The myth of male power.* New York: Berkley Books.

81. Kasser, T., & Ryan, R. M. (1993). A dark side of the American Dream: Correlates of financial success as a central life aspiration. *Journal of Personality and Social Psychology, 65,* 410–422.

82. Gollwitzer, P. M. (1996). The volitional benefits of planning. In P. M. Gollwitzer & J. A. Bargh (Eds.), *The psychology of action: Linking cognition and motivation to behavior* (pp. 287–312). New York: Guilford Press.

83. Locke, E. A., & Kristof, A. L. (1996). Volitional choices in the goal achievement process. In P. M. Gollwitzer & J. A. Bargh (Eds.), *The psychology of action: Linking cognition and motivation to behavior* (pp. 363–384). New York: Guilford Press.

84. Locke E. A., & Latham, G. P. (1990). *A theory of goal setting and task performance.* Englewood Cliffs, NJ: Prentice Hall.

85. Gollwitzer, P. M., & Kinney, R. F. (1989). Effects of deliberative and implemental mind-sets on the illusion of control. *Journal of Personality and Social Psychology, 56,* 531–542.

86. Taylor, S. E., & Gollwitzer, P. M. (1995). Effects of mindset on positive illusions. *Journal of Personality and Social Psychology, 69,* 213–226.

87. Gollwitzer, P. M. (1996). The volitional benefits of planning. In P. M. Gollwitzer & J. A. Bargh (Eds.), *The psychology of action: Linking cognition and motivation to behavior* (pp. 287–312). New York: Guilford Press.

88. Masicampo, E. J., & Baumeister, R. F. (2011). Consider it done! Plan making can eliminate the cognitive effects of unfulfilled goals. *Journal of Personality and Social Psychology.* Online publication doi: 10.1037/a0024192

89. Locke, E. A., & Kristof, A. L. (1996). Volitional choices in the goal achievement process. In P. M. Gollwitzer & J. A. Bargh (Eds.), *The psychology of action: Linking cognition and motivation to behavior* (pp. 363–384). New York: Guilford Press.

90. Locke E. A., & Latham, G. P. (1990). *A theory of goal setting and task performance.* Englewood Cliffs, NJ: Prentice Hall.

91. Bandura, A., & Schunk, D. H. (1981). Cultivating competence, self-efficacy, and intrinsic interest through proximal self-motivation. *Journal of Personality and Social Psychology, 41,* 586–598.

92. Bandura, A., & Schunk, D. H. (1981). Cultivating competence, self-efficacy, and intrinsic interest through proximal self-motivation. *Journal of Personality and Social Psychology, 41,* 586–598.

93. Shah, J. Y., Friedman, R., & Kruglanski, A. W. (2002). Forgetting all else: On the antecedents and consequences of goal shielding. *Journal of Personality and Social Psychology, 83,* 1261–1280.

94. Fitzsimons, G. M., & Bargh, J. A. (2003). Thinking of you: Nonconscious pursuit of interpersonal goals associated with relationship partners. *Journal of Personality and Social Psychology, 84,* 148–164.

95. Shah, J. Y. (2003). Automatic for the people: How representations of significant others implicitly affect goal pursuit. *Journal of Personality and Social Psychology, 84,* 661–681.

96. Shah, J. Y. (2003). Automatic for the people: How representations of significant others implicitly affect goal pursuit. *Journal of Personality and Social Psychology, 84,* 661–681.

97. Fitzsimons, G. M., & Shah, J. Y. (2008). How goal instrumentality shapes relationship evaluations. *Journal of Personality and Social Psychology, 95,* 319–337.

98. Gollwitzer, P. M. (1996). The volitional benefits of planning. In P. M. Gollwitzer & J. A. Bargh (Eds.), *The psychology of action: Linking cognition and motivation to behavior* (pp. 287–312). New York: Guilford Press.

99. Gollwitzer, P. M. (1996). The volitional benefits of planning. In P. M. Gollwitzer & J. A. Bargh (Eds.), *The psychology of action: Linking cognition and motivation to behavior* (pp. 287–312). New York: Guilford Press.

100. Kirschenbaum, D., Humphrey, L., & Malett, S. (1981). Specificity of planning in adult self-control: An applied investigation. *Journal of Personality and Social Psychology, 40,* 941–950.

101. Kirschenbaum, D., Malett, S., Humphrey, L., & Tomarken, A. (1982). Specificity of planning and maintenance of self-control: 1 year follow-up of a study improvement program. *Behavior Therapy, 13,* 232–240.

102. Kirschenbaum, D., Malett, S., Humphrey, L., & Tomarken, A. (1982). Specificity of planning and maintenance of self-control: 1 year follow-up of a study improvement program. *Behavior Therapy, 13,* 232–240.

103. Buehler, R., Griffin, D., & Ross, M. (1994). Exploring the "planning fallacy": Why people underestimate their task completion times. *Journal of Personality and Social Psychology, 67,* 366–381.

104. Buehler, R., Griffin, D., & Ross, M. (1994). Exploring the "planning fallacy": Why people underestimate their task completion times. *Journal of Personality and Social Psychology, 67,* 366–381.

105. Kahneman, D., & Tversky, A. (1979). Prospect theory: An analysis of decision under risk. *Econometrica, 47,* 263–291.

106. Buehler, R., Griffin, D., & Ross, M. (1994). Exploring the "planning fallacy": Why people underestimate their task completion times. *Journal of Personality and Social Psychology, 67,* 366–381.

107. Liberman, N., & Trope, Y. (1998). The role of feasibility and desirability considerations in near and distant future decisions: A test of temporal construal theory. *Journal of Personality and Social Psychology, 75,* 5–18.

108. Liberman, N., Sagristano, M. C., & Trope, Y. (2002). The effect of temporal perspective on level of construal. *Journal of Experimental Social Psychology, 38,* 524–534.

109. Baumeister, R. F., Stillwell, A. M., & Heatherton, T. F. (1994). Guilt: An interpersonal approach. *Psychological Bulletin, 115,* 243–267.

110. Mischel, W., Shoda, Y., & Peake, P. K. (1988). The nature of adolescent competencies predicted by preschool delay of gratification. *Journal of Personality and Social Psychology, 54,* 687–696.

111. Shoda, Y., Mischel, W., & Peake, P. K. (1990). Predicting adolescent cognitive and self-regulatory competencies from preschool delay of gratification: Identifying diagnostic conditions. *Developmental Psychology, 26,* 978–986.

112. Tangney, J. P., Baumeister, R. F., & Boone, A. L. (2004). High self-control predicts good adjustment, less pathology, better grades, and interpersonal success. *Journal of Personality, 72,* 271–322.

113. Olivola, C. Y., & de Neve, J. E. (2012). Going with your gut feelings lands you in the gutter: Decision making style in adolescence predicts financial well-being in adulthood. Manuscript submitted for publication. University of Warwick, United Kingdom.

114. Carver, C. S., & Scheier, M. F. (1982). Control theory: A useful conceptual framework for personality-social, clinical and health psychology. *Psychological Bulletin, 92,* 111–135.

115. Carver, C. S., & Scheier, M. F. (1981). *Attention and self-regulation: A control therapy approach to human behavior.* New York: Springer.

116. Carver, C. S., & Scheier, M. F. (1982). Control theory: A useful conceptual framework for personality-social, clinical and health psychology. *Psychological Bulletin, 92,* 111–135.

117. Powers, W. T. (1973). *Behavior: The control of perception.* Chicago: Aldine.

118. Leon, G., & Chamberlain, K. (1973). Emotional arousal, eating patterns, and body image as differential factors associated with varying success in maintaining a weight loss. *Journal of Consulting and Clinical Psychology, 40,* 474.

119. Logue, A. W. (1991). *The psychology of eating and drinking: An introduction* (2nd ed.). New York: W. H. Freeman.

120. Polivy, J. (1976). Perception of calories and regulation of intake in restrained and unrestrained subjects. *Addictive Behaviors, 1,* 237–243.

121. Hull, J. G. (1981). A self-awareness model of the causes and effects of alcohol consumption. *Journal of Abnormal Psychology, 90,* 586–600.

122. Abraham, S. F., & Beumont, P. J. V. (1982). How patients describe bulimia or binge eating. *Psychological Medicine, 12,* 625–635.

123. Ashton, H., & Stepney, R. (1982). *Smoking: Psychology and pharmacology.* London: Tavistock.

124. Baumeister, R. F., Stillwell, A. M., & Heatherton, T. F. (1994). Guilt: An interpersonal approach. *Psychological Bulletin, 115,* 243–267.

125. Bushman, B. J., & Cooper, H. M. (1990). Effects of alcohol on human aggression: An integrative research review. *Psychological Bulletin, 107,* 341–354.

126. Steele, C. M., & Southwick, L. (1985). Alcohol and social behavior: I. The psychology of drunken excess. *Journal of Personality and Social Psychology, 48,* 18–34.

127. Baumeister, R. F., Bratslavsky, E., Muraven, M., & Tice, D. M. (1998). Ego depletion: Is the active self a limited resource? *Journal of Personality and Social Psychology, 74,* 1252–1265.

128. Baumeister, R. F., Bratslavsky, E., Muraven, M., & Tice, D. M. (1998). Ego depletion: Is the active self a limited resource? *Journal of Personality and Social Psychology, 74,* 1252–1265.

129. Baumeister, R. F., & Tierney, J. (2011). *Willpower: Rediscovering the greatest human strength.* New York: Penguin Press.

130. Grandey, A.A., Frone, M.R., Melloy, R.C., & Sayre, G.M. (2019). When are fakers also drinkers? A self-control view of emotional labor and alcohol consumption among U.S. service workers. *Journal of Occupational Health Psychology,* advance online publication, http://dx.doi.org/10.1037/ocp0000147

131. Baumeister, R. F. (2002). Ego depletion and self-control failure: An energy model of the self's executive function. *Self and Identity, 1,* 129–136.

132. Vohs, K. D., Baumeister, R. F., Schmeichel, B. J., Twenge, J. M., Nelson, N. M., & Tice, D. M. (2008). Making choices impairs subsequent self-control: A limited-resource account of decision making, self-regulation, and active initiative. *Journal of Personality and Social Psychology, 94,* 883–898. doi: 10.1037/0022-3514.94.5.883

133. Pocheptsova, A., Amir, O., Dhar, R., & Baumeister, R. F. (2009). Deciding without resources: Resource depletion and choice in context. *Journal of Marketing Research, 46,* 344–355. doi: 10.1509/jmkr.46.3.344

134. Levav, J., Heitmann, H., Herrmann, A., & Iyengar, S. S. (2010). Order in product customization

134. decisions: Evidence from field experiments. *Journal of Political Economy, 118,* 274–299.
135. Danziger, S., Levav, J., & Avnaim-Pesso, L. (2011). Extraneous factors in judicial decisions. *PNAS, 108,* 6889–6892.
136. Wing, R. R., Tate, D. F., Gorin, A. A., Raynor, H. A., Fava, J. L., & Machan, J. (2007). "STOP regain": Are there negative effects of daily weighing? *Journal of Consulting and Clinical Psychology, 75,* 652–656.
137. Vohs, K. D. & Heatherton, T. F. (2000). Self-regulatory failure: A resource depletion approach. *Psychological Science, 11,* 249–254.
138. Wood, W. & Neal, D. (2007). A new look at habits and the habit-goal interface. *Psychological Review, 114,* 843–863.
139. Wood, W. & Neal, D. (2007). A new look at habits and the habit-goal interface. *Psychological Review, 114,* 843–863.
140. Wood, W., & Neal, D. T. (2009). The habitual consumer. *Journal of Consumer Psychology, 19,* 579–592.
141. Wood, W., & Rünger, D. (2016). Psychology of habit. *Annual Review of Psychology, 67,* 289–314.
142. Ouellette, J. A., & Wood, W. (1998). Habit and intention in everyday life: The multiple processes by which past behavior predicts future behavior. *Psychological Bulletin, 124,* 54–74.
143. Neal, D.T., Wood, W., & Drolet, A. (2013). How do people adhere to goals when willpower is low? The profits (and pitfalls) of strong habits. *Journal of Personality and Social Psychology, 104,* 959–975.
144. Neal, D. T., & Wood, W. (2007). Automaticity *in situ:* Direct context cuing of habits in daily life. In J. Bargh, P. Gollwitzer, & E. Morsella (Eds.), *Psychology of action (Vol. 2): Mechanisms of human action.* London: Oxford University Press.
145. Freud, S. (1964). *Beyond the pleasure principle* (J. Strachey, Trans.). New York: Norton. (Original work published 1920).
146. Horner, M. (1972). Toward an understanding of achievement related conflicts in women. *Journal of Social Issues, 28,* 157–176.
147. Hyland, M. E. (1989). There is no motive to avoid success: The compromise explanation for success-avoiding behavior. *Journal of Personality, 57,* 665–693.
148. Jones, E. E., & Berglas, S. (1978). Control of attributions about the self through self-handicapping strategies: The appeal of alcohol and the role of underachievement. *Personality and Social Psychology Bulletin, 4,* 200–206.
149. Mischel, W. (1996). From good intentions to willpower. In P. M. Gollwitzer & J. Bargh (Eds.), *The psychology of action: Linking cognition and motivation to behavior* (pp. 197–218). New York: Guilford Press.
150. Mischel, W., & Mendoza-Denton, R. (2002). Harnessing willpower and socio-emotional intelligence to enhance human agency and potential. In L. G. Aspinwall & U. M. Staudinger (Eds.), *A psychology of human strengths: Fundamental questions and future directions for a positive psychology* (pp. 245–256). Washington, DC: American Psychological Association.
151. Mischel, W., Shoda, Y., & Peake, P. K. (1988). The nature of adolescent competencies predicted by preschool delay of gratification. *Journal of Personality and Social Psychology, 54,* 687–696.
152. Shoda, Y., Mischel, W., & Peake, P. K. (1990). Predicting adolescent cognitive and self-regulatory competencies from preschool delay of gratification: Identifying diagnostic conditions. *Developmental Psychology, 26,* 978–986.
153. Gottfredson, M. R., & Hirschi, T. (1990). *A general theory of crime.* Stanford, CA: Stanford University Press.
154. Kidd, C., Palmeri, H., & Aslin, R.N. (2013). Rational snacking: Young children's decision-making on the marshmallow task is moderated by beliefs about environmental reliability. *Cognition, 126,* 109–114.
155. Ferrari, J. R., Johnson, J. L., & McCown, W. G. (1995). *Procrastination and task avoidance: Theory, research, and treatment.* New York: Plenum Press.
156. Tice, D. M., & Baumeister, R. F. (1997). Longitudinal study of procrastination, performance, stress, and health: The costs and benefits of dawdling. *Psychological Science, 8,* 454–458.
157. Ferrari, J. R. (2001). Procrastination as self-regulation failure of performance: Effects of cognitive load, self-awareness, and time limits on "working under pressure." *European Journal of Personality, 15,* 391–406.
158. Joiner, T. (2005). *Why people die by suicide.* Cambridge, MA: Harvard University Press.
159. Davis, P. A. (1983). *Suicidal adolescents.* Springfield, IL: C. C. Thomas.
160. Farberow, N. L. (1975). Cultural history of suicide. In N. L. Farberow (Ed.), *Suicide in different cultures* (pp. 1–16). Baltimore: University Park Press.
161. Hendin, H. (1982). *Suicide in America.* New York: Norton.
162. Maris, R. (1969). *Social forces in urban suicide.* Homewood, IL: Dorsey.
163. Maris, R. (1981). *Pathways to suicide: A survey of self-destructive behaviors.* Baltimore: Johns Hopkins University Press.
164. Rothberg, J. M., & Jones, F. D. (1987). Suicide in the U.S. Army: Epidemiological and periodic aspects. *Suicide and Life-Threatening Behavior, 17,* 119–132.
165. Baumeister, R. F. (1990). Suicide as escape from self. *Psychological Review, 97,* 90–113.
166. Gottschalk, L. A., & Gleser, G. C. (1960). An analysis of the verbal content of suicide notes. *British Journal of Medical Psychology, 33,* 195–204.
167. Hendin, H. (1982). *Suicide in America.* New York: Norton.
168. Henken, V. J. (1976). Banality reinvestigated: A computer-based content analysis of suicidal and forced-death documents. *Suicide and Life-Threatening Behavior, 6,* 36–43.
169. Shneidman, E. S. (1981). Suicide thoughts and reflections, 1960–1980. *Suicide and Life-Threatening Behavior, 11,* 197–360.
170. Joiner, T. (2005). *Why people die by suicide.* Cambridge, MA: Harvard University Press.

CHAPTER 5
Social Cognition

1. Iannelli, V. (2014, September 7). International measles outbreaks. About Health. Retrieved from http://pediatrics.about.com/od/measles/a/measles-outbreak.htm
2. Texas Department of State Health Services (2018, January 23). *Measles outbreak in Ellis County.* Retrieved from https://www.dshs.texas.gov/news/releases/2018/HealthAdvisory-01232018.aspx
3. Iannelli, V. (2014, September 7). International measles outbreaks. About Health. Retrieved from http://pediatrics.about.com/od/measles/a/measles-outbreak.htm
4. Belluz, J. (2018, October 16). This autism dad has a warning for anti-vaxers. *Vox.* Retrieved from https://www.vox.com/science-and-health/2018/10/16/17964992/vaccine-autism-book-peter-hotez
5. Molina, B. (2019, January 17). People choosing not to vaccinate is now a global health threat, says WHO. *USA Today.* Retrieved from https://amp.usatoday.com/amp/260114000 2?fbclid=IwAR3TFBddtV6AYzlNS4ldYllfE-2NO1R2LIpnegPVeZMnz8XjceRUr2UhUXE
6. Centers for Disease Control and Prevention (2014). Q&As about vaccination options for preventing measles, mumps, rubella, and varicella. Retrieved from http://www.cdc.gov/vaccines/vpd-vac/combo-vaccines/mmrv/vacopt-faqs-hcp.htm
7. Wakefield, A., Murch, S., Anthony, A. *et al.* (1998). Ileal-lymphoid-nodular hyperplasia, non-specific colitis, and pervasive developmental disorder in children. *Lancet, 351* (9103): 637–641. doi:10.1016/ S0140-6736(97)11096-0
8. Rubin, D. B. (2008). Fanning the vaccine–autism link. *Neurology Today, 8* (15), 3. doi:10.1097/01. NT.0000335577.64245.34
9. Mansell, W. (2018, December 12). Republican congressman-elect suggests autism linked to vaccines, without evidence, wants to get 'real data' from CDC. *Newsweek.* Retrieved from https://www .newsweek.com/vaccines-autism-link-children-cdc -report-mark-green-congressman-tennessee-1256259
10. Demicheli, V., Rivetti, A., Debalini, M. G., & Di Pietrantonj, C. (2012). Vaccines for measles, mumps and rubella in children. *Cochrane Database Systematic Reviews,* 2. Art. No.: CD004407. doi:10.1002/14651858.CD004407.pub3
11. Hviid A, Hansen JV, Frisch M, & Melbye M. (2019). Measles, mumps, rubella vaccination and autism: A nationwide cohort study. *Annals of Internal Medicine* [Epub ahead of print] doi: 10.7326/M18-2101
12. Taylor, L. E., Swerdfeger, A. L., & Eslick, G. D. (2014). Vaccines are not associated with autism: An evidence-based meta-analysis of case-control and cohort studies. *Vaccine, 32*(29), 3623–3629. doi: 10.1016/j.vaccine.2014.04.085
13. Doja, A., & Roberts, W. (2006). Immunizations and autism: A review of the literature. *Canadian Journal of Neurological Sciences, 33* (4), 341–346. PMID 17168158
14. Murch, S. H., Anthony, A., Casson, D. H. et al. (2004). Retraction of an interpretation. *Lancet,* 363 (9411), 750. doi:10.1016/S0140-6736(04)15715-2
15. Boseley, S. (2010, January 28). Andrew Wakefield found 'irresponsible' by GMC over MMR vaccine scare. *The Guardian* (London). Retrieved from https://www.theguardian.com/society/2010/jan /28/andrew-wakefield-mmr-vaccine
16. The Editors of *The Lancet* (2010, February). Retraction—Ileal-lymphoid-nodular hyperplasia, non-specific colitis, and pervasive developmental disorder in children. *The Lancet* 375 (9713), 445. doi:10.1016/S0140-6736(10)60175-4
17. Stein, R. (2011, January 11). Wakefield tried to capitalize on autism-vaccine link, report says. *The Washington Post.* Retrieved from http://voices .washingtonpost.com/checkup/2011/01/wakefield _tried_to_capitalize.html.
18. Flaherty, D. K. (2011). The vaccine-autism connection: a public health crisis caused by unethical medical practices and fraudulent science. *Annals of Pharmacotherapy* 45 (10): 1302–1304. doi:10.1345/aph.1Q318
19. Parikh, R. (2011, January 20). Make anti-vaccine parents pay higher premiums. CNN. Retrieved from http://edition.cnn.com/2011/OPINION/01 /20/parikh.childhood.immunizations/index.html ?_s=PM:OPINION
20. Belluz, J. (2018, October 16). This autism dad has a warning for anti-vaxers. *Vox.* Retrieved from https://www.vox.com/science-and -health/2018/10/16/17964992/vaccine-autism -book-peter-hotez
21. Belluz, J. (2018, October 16). This autism dad has a warning for anti-vaxers. *Vox.* Retrieved from https://www.vox.com/science-and -health/2018/10/16/17964992/vaccine-autism -book-peter-hotez
22. Lewandowsky, S., Ecker, U. K. H., Seifert, C., Schwarz, N., & Cook, J. (2012). Misinformation and its correction: Continued influence and successful debiasing. *Psychological Science in the Public Interest, 13,* 106–131. doi: 10.1177/1529100612451018
23. Fiske, S. T., & Taylor, S. E. (1991). *Social cognition* (2nd ed.). New York: Random House.
24. Fiske, S. T., & Taylor, S. E. (1991). *Social cognition* (2nd ed.). New York: Random House.
25. Mercier, H., & Sperber, D. (2011). Why do humans reason? Arguments for an argumentative theory. *Behavioral and Brain Sciences, 34*(2), 57–74.
26. Baumeister, R. F., & Masicampo, E. J. (2010). Conscious thought is for facilitating social and cultural interactions: How mental simulations serve the animal-culture interface. *Psychological Review, 117,* 945–971.

27. Deacon, T. (1997). What makes the human brain different? *Annual Review of Anthropology, 26,* 337–357.
28. Heinz, S., Baron, G., & Frahm, H. (1988). Comparative size of brains and brain components. In H. D. Steklis & J. Erwin (Eds.), *Comparative Primate Biology: Vol. 4. Neurosciences.* New York: Wiley.
29. Macphail, E. (1982). *Brain and intelligence in vertebrates.* Oxford: Clarendon Press.
30. Wilson, T. D., Reinhard, D. A., Westgate, E. C., Gilbert, D. T., Ellerbeck, N., Hahn, C., Brown, C. L., & Shaked, A. (2014). Just think: The challenges of the disengaged mind. *Science, 345,* 75–77.
31. Fiske, S. T., & Taylor, S. E. (1984). *Social cognition.* New York: Random House.
32. Gilbert, D. T., Pelham, B. W., & Krull, D. S. (1988). On cognitive business: When person perceivers meet persons perceived. *Journal of Personality and Social Psychology, 54,* 733–740.
33. Stroop, J. R. (1935). Studies of interference in serial verbal reactions. *Journal of Experimental Psychology, 28,* 643–662.
34. Smith, J. D., Boomer, J., Zakrzewski, A. C., Roeder, J. L., Church, B. A., & Ashby, F. G. (2014). Deferred feedback sharply dissociates implicit and explicit category learning. *Psychological Science, 25*(2), 447–457. doi: 10.1177/0956797613509112
35. Mata, A., Ferreira, M. B., & Sherman, S.J. (2013). The metacognitive advantage of deliberative thinkers: A dual-process perspective on overconfidence. *Journal of Personality and Social Psychology, 105,* 353–373.
36. Meyer, D. E., & Schvaneveldt, R. W. (1971). Facilitation in recognizing pairs of words: Evidence of a dependence between retrieval operations. *Journal of Experimental Psychology, 90,* 227–234.
37. Neely, J. H. (1991). Semantic priming effects in visual word recognition: A selective review of current findings and theories. In D. Besner & G. Humphreys (Eds.), *Basic processes in reading: Visual word recognition* (pp. 264–336). Hillsdale, NJ: Erlbaum.
38. Gibson, B., & Zielaskowski, K. (2013). Subliminal priming of winning images prompts increased betting in slot machine play. *Journal of Applied Social Psychology, 43*(1), 106–115. doi:10.1111/j.1559-1816.2012.00985.x
39. Higgins, E. T., Rholes, W. S., & Jones, C. R. (1977). Category accessibility and impression formation. *Journal of Experimental Social Psychology, 13,* 141–154.
40. Bargh, J. A., Chen, M., & Burrows, L. (1996). Automaticity of social behavior: Direct effects of trait construct and stereotype activation on action. *Journal of Personality and Social Psychology, 71,* 230–244.
41. Hansen, J., Kutzner, F., & Wänke, M. (2013). Money and thinking: Reminders of money trigger abstract construal and shape consumer judgments. *Journal of Consumer Research, 39,* 1154–1166.
42. Epley, N., & Gneezy, A. (2007). The framing of financial windfalls and implications for public policy. *Journal of Socio-Economics, 36,* 36–47.
43. Epley, N., Mak, D., & Idson, L. C. (2006). Bonus or rebate? The impact of income framing on spending and saving. *Journal of Behavioral Decision Making, 19*(3), 213–227. Mata, A., Ferreira, M. B., & Sherman, S. J. (2013). The metacognitive advantage of deliberative thinkers: A dual-process perspective on overconfidence. *Journal of Personality and Social Psychology, 105,* 353–373.
44. Rothman, A. J., Bartels, R. D., Wlaschin, J., & Salovey, P. (2006). The strategic use of gain- and loss-framed messages to promote healthy behavior: How theory can inform practice. *Journal of Communication, 56*(Suppl. 1), S202–S220.
45. Werle, C.O.C., Wansink, B., & Payne, C.R. (2014). Is it fun or exercise? The framing of physical activity biases subsequent snacking. *Marketing Letters,* DOI 10.1007/s11002-014-9301-6.
46. Wegner, D. M. (1994). Ironic processes of mental control. *Psychological Review, 101,* 34–52.
47. Biryukov, P. (1911). *Leo Tolstoy: His life and work.* New York: Charles Scribner's Sons.
48. Wegner, D. M. (1989). *White bears and other unwanted thoughts: Suppression, obsession, and the psychology of mental control.* New York: Viking/Penguin.
49. Wegner, D. M., Schneider, D. J., Carter, S. R., & White, T. L. (1987). Paradoxical effects of thought suppression. *Journal of Personality and Social Psychology, 53*(1), 5–13.
50. Wenzlaff, R. M., & Wegner D. M. (2000). Thought suppression. *Annual Review of Psychology, 51,* 59–91.
51. Toll, B. A., Sobell, M. B., Wagner, E. F., & Sobell, L. C. (2001). The relationship between thought suppression and smoking cessation. *Addictive Behaviors, 26,* 509–515.
52. Riley, B. (2014). Experiential avoidance mediates the association between thought suppression and mindfulness with problem gambling. *Journal of Gambling Studies, 30*(1), 163–171. doi:10.1007/s10899-012-9342-9
53. Garland, E. L., Brown, S. M., & Howard, M. O. (2016). Thought suppression as a mediator of the association between depressed mood and prescription opioid craving among chronic pain patients. *Journal of Behavioral Medicine, 39*(1), 128–138. doi:10.1007/s10865-015-9675-9
54. Najmi, S., & Wegner, D. M. (2008). Thought suppression and psychopathology. In A. J. Elliot (Ed.), *Handbook of approach and avoidance motivation* (pp. 447–459). New York: Psychology Press.
55. Schmidt, R. E., & Gendolla, G. H. E. (2008). Dreaming of white bears: The return of the suppressed at sleep onset. *Consciousness and Cognition, 17*(3), 714–724.
56. Wegner, D. M., Wenzlaff, R. M., & Kozak, M. (2004). Dream rebound: The return of suppressed thoughts in dreams. *Psychological Science, 15,* 232–236.
57. Malinowski, J. (2017). High thought suppressors dream more of their negative waking-life experiences than low thought suppressors. *Dreaming, 27*(4), 269–277. doi:10.1037/drm0000061
58. Abramowitz, J. S., Tolin, D. F., & Street, G. P. (2001). Paradoxical effects of thought suppression: A meta-analysis of controlled studies. *Clinical Psychology Review, 21,* 683–705.
59. Lin, Y. J., & Wicker, F. W. (2007). A comparison of the effects of thought suppression, distraction and concentration. *Behaviour Research and Therapy, 45*(12):2924–2937.
60. Dijksterhuis, A., & Nordgren, L. F. (2006). A theory of unconscious thought. *Perspectives on Psychological Science, 1,* 95–109.
61. Dijksterhuis, A., & Nordgren, L. F. (2006). A theory of unconscious thought. *Perspectives on Psychological Science, 1,* 95–109.
62. Gonzalez-Vallejo, C., Lassiter, G. D., Bellezza, F. S., & Lindberg, M. J. (2008). "Save angels perhaps": A critical examination of Unconscious Thought Theory and the Deliberation-Without-Attention effect. *Review of General Psychology, 12,* 282–296.
63. DeWall, C. N., Baumeister, R. F., & Masicampo, E. J. (2008). Evidence that logical reasoning depends on conscious processing. *Consciousness and Cognition, 17,* 628–645.
64. Sklar, A. Y., Levy, N., Goldstein, A., Mandel, R., Maril, A., & Hassin, R. R. (2012). Reading and doing arithmetic nonconsciously. *PNAS Proceedings of the National Academy of Sciences of the United States of America, 109*(48), 19614–19619. doi:10.1073/pnas.1211645109
65. Sklar, A. Y., Levy, N., Goldstein, A., Mandel, R., Maril, A., & Hassin, R. R. (2012). Reading and doing arithmetic nonconsciously. *PNAS Proceedings of the National Academy of Sciences of the United States of America, 109*(48), 19614–19619. doi:10.1073/pnas.1211645109
66. Hassin, R. R., & Sklar, A. Y. (2015). The human unconscious: A functional perspective. In J. W. Sherman, B. Gawronski, & Y. Trope (Eds.), *Dual-process theories of the social mind.* New York: Guilford Press
67. Herman, C. P., & Mack, D. (1975). Restrained and unrestrained eating. *Journal of Personality, 43,* 647–660.
68. Herman, C. P., & Mack, D. (1975). Restrained and unrestrained eating. *Journal of Personality, 43,* 647–660.
69. Knight, L. J., & Boland, F. J. (1989). Restrained eating: An experimental disentanglement of disinhibiting variables of perceived calories and food type. *Journal of Abnormal Psychology, 98,* 412–420.
70. Soetens, B., Braet, C., Dejonckheere, P., & Roets, A. (2006). When suppression backfires: The ironic effects of suppressing eating-related thoughts. *Journal of Health Psychology, 11*(5), 655–668.
71. Soetens, B., Braet, C., & Moens, E. (2008). Thought suppression in obese and non-obese restrained eaters: Piece of cake or forbidden fruit? *European Eating Disorders Review, 16*(1), 67–76.
72. Heider, F. (1958). *The psychology of interpersonal relations.* New York: John Wiley.
73. Burger, J. M., Cooper, H. M., & Good, T. L. (1982). Teacher attributions of student performance: Effects of outcome. *Personality and Social Psychology Bulletin, 8,* 685–690.
74. Weiner, B. (1972). *Theories of motivation: From mechanism to cognition.* Chicago: Rand McNally.
75. Obach, M. S. (2003). A longitudinal-sequential study of perceived academic competence and motivational beliefs for learning among children in middle school. *Educational Psychology, 23,* 323–338.
76. Platt, C. W. (1988). Effects of causal attributions for success on first-term college performance: A covariance structure model. *Journal of Educational Psychology, 80,* 569–578.
77. Armbrister, R. C. (2002). A cross-cultural comparison of student social attributions. *Psychology in the Schools, 39,* 39–49.
78. Holloway, S. D., Kashiwagi, K., Hess, R. D., & Azuuma, H. (1986). Causal attributions by Japanese and American mothers and children about performance in mathematics. *International Journal of Psychology, 21,* 269–286.
79. Campbell, W. K., & Sedikides, C. (1999). Self-threat magnifies the self-serving bias: A meta-analytic integration. *Review of General Psychology, 3,* 23–43.
80. Zuckerman, M. (1979). Attribution of success and failure revisited, or: The motivational bias is alive and well in attribution theory. *Journal of Personality, 47,* 245–287.
81. Bradley, G. W. (1978). Self-serving biases in the attribution process: A reexamination of the fact or fiction question. *Journal of Personality and Social Psychology, 36,* 56–71.
82. Tetlock, P. E. (1980). Explaining teacher explanations for pupil performance: A test of the self-presentation position. *Social Psychology Quarterly, 43,* 283–290.
83. Ross, M., & Sicoiy, F. (1979). Egocentric biases in availability and attribution. *Journal of Personality and Social Psychology, 37,* 322–336.
84. Savitsky, K., Van Boven, L., Epley, N., & Wight, W. (2005). The unpacking effect in responsibility allocations for group tasks. *Journal of Experimental Social Psychology, 41,* 447–457.
85. Van Boven, L., & Epley, N. (2003). The unpacking effect in evaluative judgments: When the whole is less than the sum of its parts. *Journal of Experimental Social Psychology, 39,* 263–269.
86. Jones, E. E., & Nisbett, R. E. (1971). *The actor and the observer: Divergent perceptions of the causes of behavior.* New York: General Learning Press.
87. Jones, E. E., & Harris, V. A. (1967). The attribution of attitudes. *Journal of Experimental Social Psychology, 3,* 1–24.
88. Choi, I., & Nisbett, R. E. (1998). Situational salience and cultural differences in the correspondence bias and actor-observer bias. *Personality and Social Psychology Bulletin, 24*(9), 949–960.
89. Miyamoto, Y., & Kitayama, S. (2002). Cultural variation in correspondence bias: The critical role

of attitude diagnosticity of socially constrained behavior. *Journal of Personality and Social Psychology, 83*(5), 1239–1248.

90. Masuda, T., & Kitayama, S. (2004). Perceiver-induced constraint and attitude attribution in Japan and the US: A case for the cultural dependence of the correspondence bias. *Journal of Experimental Social Psychology, 40*(3), 409–416.

91. Van Boven, L., Kamada, A., & Gilovich, T. (1999). The perceiver as perceived: Everyday intuitions about the correspondence bias. *Journal of Personality and Social Psychology, 77*(6), 1188–1199.

92. Zhou, X., He, L., Yang, Q., Lao, J., & Baumeister, R. F. (2012). Control deprivation and styles of thinking. *Journal of Personality and Social Psychology, 102*, 460–478. doi: 10.1037/a0026316

93. Hooper, N., Erdogan, A., Keen, G., Lawton, K., & McHugh, L. (2015). Perspective taking reduces the fundamental attribution error. *Journal of Contextual Behavioral Science, 4*(2), 69–72. doi:10.1016/j.jcbs.2015.02.002

94. Malle, B. F. (2006). The actor-observer asymmetry in causal attribution: A (surprising) meta-analysis. *Psychological Bulletin, 132*, 895–919.

95. Malle, B. F., Knobe, J. M., & Nelson, S. E. (2007). Actor-observer asymmetries in explanations of behavior: New answers to an old question. *Journal of Personality and Social Psychology, 93*, 491–514.

96. Kruger, J., & Gilovich, T. (2004). Actions, intentions, and self-assessment: The road to self-enhancement is paved with good intentions. *Personality and Social Psychology Bulletin, 30*(3), 328–339.

97. Pronin, E., Berger, J., & Molouki, S. (2007). Alone in a crowd of sheep: Asymmetric perceptions of conformity and their roots in an introspection illusion. *Journal of Personality and Social Psychology, 92*, 585–595.

98. Pronin, E., Berger, J., & Molouki, S. (2007). Alone in a crowd of sheep: Asymmetric perceptions of conformity and their roots in an introspection illusion. *Journal of Personality and Social Psychology, 92*, 585–595.

99. Pronin, E., Berger, J., & Molouki, S. (2007). Alone in a crowd of sheep: Asymmetric perceptions of conformity and their roots in an introspection illusion. *Journal of Personality and Social Psychology, 92*, 585–595.

100. Malle, B. F. (2011). Time to give up the dogmas of attribution: An alternative theory of behavior explanation. *Advances of Experimental Social Psychology, 44*, 297–352.

101. Fiske, S. T. (2004). *Social beings: A core motives approach to social psychology.* New York: Wiley.

102. Geurten, M., Willems, S., Germain, S., & Meulemans, T. (2015). Less is more: The availability heuristic in early childhood. *British Journal of Developmental Psychology, 33*(4), 405-410. doi:10.1111/bjdp.12114

103. Fischhoff, B., Lichtenstein, S., Slovic, P., Derby, S. L., & Keeney, R. L. (1981). *Acceptable risk.* New York: Cambridge University Press.

104. World Health Organization. (2019, May 29). Tobacco. Retrieved from http://www.who.int/en/news-room/fact-sheets/detail/tobacco

105. Doyle, A. C. (1974). *The memoirs of Sherlock Holmes.* London: J. Murray; Cape. (Original work published 1894)

106. Kahneman, D., & Tversky, A. (1982). The psychology of preferences. *Scientific American, 246*, 160–173.

107. Medvec, V. H., Madey, S. F., & Gilovich, T. (1995). When less is more: Counterfactual thinking and satisfaction among Olympic medalists. *Journal of Personality and Social Psychology, 69*, 603–610.

108. Slovic, P., & Lichtenstein, S. (1971). Comparison of Bayesian and regression approaches to the study of information processing in judgment. *Organizational Behavior and Human Performance, 6*, 649–744.

109. Tversky, A., & Kahneman, D. (1974) Judgment under uncertainty: Heuristics and biases. *Science, 185*, 1124–1131.

110. Jansen, Bart (2018, April 19). Miracle on the Hudson pilot Sully Sullenberger: Southwest crew worked seamlessly to land jet. USA Today. Retrieved from https://www.usatoday.com/story/news/2018/04/19/sully-sullenberger-southwest-airlines-emergency-landing/533821002/

111. Fiske, S. T., & Taylor, S. E. (1991). *Social cognition* (2nd ed.). New York: Random House.

112. Laumann, E. O., Gagnon, J. H., Michael, R. T., & Michaels, S. (1994). *The social organization of sexuality: Sexual practices in the United States.* Chicago: University of Chicago Press.

113. Morokoff, P. J. (1986). Volunteer bias in the psychophysiological study of female sexuality. *Journal of Sex Research, 22*, 35–51.

114. Centers for Disease Control and Prevention. Key Statistics from the National Survey of Family Growth—N Listing. Retrieved from https://www.cdc.gov/nchs/nsfg/key_statistics/n.htm

115. Janus, S. S., & Janus, C. L. (1993). *The Janus report on sexual behavior.* New York: Wiley.

116. Laumann, E. O., Gagnon, J. H., Michael, R. T., & Michaels, S. (1994). *The social organization of sexuality: Sexual practices in the United States.* Chicago: University of Chicago Press.

117. Baumeister, R. F., & Vohs, K. D. (2004). Sexual economics: Sex as female resource for social exchange in heterosexual interactions. *Personality and Social Psychology Review, 8*(4), 339–363.

118. Buss, D. M., & Schmitt, D. P. (1993). Sexual strategies theory: An evolutionary perspective on human mating. *Psychological Review, 100*, 204–232.

119. Miller, L. C., & Fishkin, S. A. (1997). On the dynamics of human bonding and reproductive success: Seeking windows on the adapted-for-human environmental interface. In J. Simpson & D. Kenrick (Eds.), *Evolutionary social psychology* (pp. 197–235). Mahwah, NJ: Erlbaum.

120. Galperin, A., Haselton, M.G., Frederick, D.A., Poore, J., von Hippel, W., Buss, D.M., & Gonzaga, G.C. (2013). Sexual regret: evidence for evolved sex differences. *Archives of Sexual Behavior, 42*, 1145–1161.

121. Alexander, M. G., & Fisher, T. D. (2003). Truth and consequences: Using the bogus pipeline to examine sex differences in self-reported sexuality. *The Journal of Sex Research, 40*, 27–35.

122. Einon, D. (1994). Are men more promiscuous than women? *Ethology and Sociobiology, 15*(3), 131–143.

123. Phillis, D. E., & Gromko, M. H. (1985). Sex differences in sexual activity: Reality or illusion? *Journal of Sex Research, 21*, 437–443.

124. Phillis, D. E., & Gromko, M. H. (1985). Sex differences in sexual activity: Reality or illusion? *Journal of Sex Research, 21*, 437–443.

125. Brown, N. R., & Sinclair, R. C. (1999). Estimating number of lifetime sexual partners: Men and women do it differently. *Journal of Sex Research, 36*, 292–297.

126. Sinclair, R. C., & Brown, N. R. (1999, April–May). *Discrepant partner reports: Do women encode sexual experiences more deeply than men do?* Paper presented at the annual convention of the Midwestern Psychological Association, Chicago.

127. Wiederman, M. W. (1997). The truth must be in here somewhere: Examining the gender discrepancy in self-reported lifetime number of sex partners. *Journal of Sex Research, 34*, 375–386.

128. Sanders, S. A., & Reinisch, J. M. (1999). Would you say you "had sex" if ...? *Journal of the American Medical Association, 281*, 275–277.

129. Dunning, D. (1999). A newer look: Motivated social cognition and the schematic representation of social concepts. *Psychological Inquiry, 10*, 1–11.

130. Smith, D. (2004, June 20). Sign writer. *Observer.* Retrieved from http://observer.guardian.co.uk/comment/story/0,6903,1243121,00.html

131. Baggini, J. (2004). Bad moves: Confirmation bias. Retrieved from http://www.butterfliesandwheels.com/badmovesprint.php?num=42

132. Rudski, J. M. (2002). Hindsight and confirmation biases in an exercise in telepathy. *Psychological Reports, 91*, 899–906.

133. Nickerson, R. S. (1998). Confirmation bias: A ubiquitous phenomenon in many guises. *Review of General Psychology, 2*, 175–220.

134. Mercier, H., & Sperber, D. (2011). Why do humans reason? Arguments for an argumentative theory. *Behavioral and Brain Sciences, 34*(2), 57–74.

135. Golding, S. L., & Rorer, L. G. (1972). Illusory correlation and subjective judgment. *Journal of Abnormal Psychology, 80*, 249–260.

136. Hamilton, D. L., & Gifford, R. K. (1976). Illusory correlation in interpersonal perception: A cognitive basis of stereotypic judgments. *Journal of Experimental Social Psychology, 12*, 392–407.

137. Risen, J. L., Gilovich, T., & Dunning, D. (2007). One-shot illusory correlations and stereotype formation. *Personality and Social Psychology Bulletin, 33*(11), 1492–1502.

138. Appelbaum, P., & Swanson, J. (2010). Gun laws and mental illness: How sensible are the current restrictions. *Psychiatric Services, 61*, 652–654. doi: 10.1176/appi.ps.61.7.652

139. Kahneman, D., Slovic, P., & Tversky, A. (Eds.). (1982). *Judgment under uncertainty: Heuristics and biases.* New York: Cambridge University Press.

140. Sundali, J., & Croson, R. (2006). Biases in casino betting: The hot hand and the gambler's fallacy. *Judgment and Decision Making, 1*(1), 1–12.

141. Krueger, J., & Clement, R. W. (1994). The truly false consensus effect: An ineradicable and egocentric bias in social perception. *Journal of Personality and Social Psychology, 67*, 596–610.

142. Marks, G., & Miller, N. (1987). Ten years of research on the false consensus effect: An empirical and theoretical review. *Psychological Bulletin, 102*, 72–90.

143. Ross, L., Greene, D. & House, P. (1977). The false consensus effect: An egocentric bias in social perception and attributional processes. *Journal of Experimental Social Psychology, 13*, 279–301.

144. Goel, S., Mason, W., & Watts, D. J. (2010). Real and perceived attitude agreement in social networks. *Journal of Social and Personality Psychology, 99*(4), 611–621.

145. Coleman, M. D. (2016). Emotion and the false consensus effect. *Current Psychology: A Journal for Diverse Perspectives on Diverse Psychological Issues,* doi:10.1007/s12144-016-9489-0

146. Goethals, G. R., Messick, D. M., & Allison, S. T. (1991). The uniqueness bias: Studies of constructive social comparison. In J. Suls & T. A. Wills (Eds.), *Social conparison: Contemporary theory and research.* Hillsdale, NJ: Erlbaum.

147. Kulig, J. W. (2013). What's in a name? Our false uniqueness! *British Journal of Social Psychology, 52*(1), 173–179. doi:10.1111/bjso.12001

148. Suls, J., Wan, C. K., & Sanders, G. S. (1988). False consensus and false uniqueness in estimating the prevalence of health-protective behaviors. *Journal of Applied Social Psychology, 18*, 66–79.

149. Anderson, C. A., Lepper, M. R., & Ross, L. (1980). The perseverance of social theories: The role of explanation in the persistence of discredited information. *Journal of Personality and Social Psychology, 39*, 1037–1049.

150. Lewandowsky, S., Ecker, U. K. H., Seifert, C., Schwarz, N., & Cook, J. (2012). Misinformation and its correction: Continued influence and successful debiasing. *Psychological Science in the Public Interest, 13*, 106–131. doi: 10.1177/1529100612451018

151. Ruscio, J. (2002). *Clear thinking with psychology: Separating sense from nonsense.* Pacific Grove, CA: Wadsworth.

152. Gilovich, T. (1991). *How we know what isn't so.* New York: Free Press.

153. Langer, E. J. (1975). The illusion of control. *Journal of Personality and Social Psychology, 32*, 311–328.

154. Langer, E. J., & Roth, J. (1975). Heads I win, tails it's chance: The illusion of control as a function of the sequence of outcomes in a purely chance task. *Journal of Personality and Social Psychology, 32*, 951–955.

155. Fenton-O'Creevy, M., Nicholson, N., Soane, E., & Willman, P. (2003). Trading on illusions: Unrealistic perceptions of control and trading

156. Cowley, E., Briley, D. A., & Farrell, C. (2015). How do gamblers maintain an illusion of control? *Journal of Business Research, 68*(10), 2181–2188. doi:10.1016/j.jbusres.2015.03.018
157. Kahneman, D., & Tversky, A. (1982). The psychology of preferences. *Scientific American, 246,* 160–173.
158. Hofstadter, D. R. (1979). *Gödel, Escher, Bach: An eternal golden braid.* New York: Basic Books.
159. Kray, L. J., George, L., Liljenquist, K., Galinsky, A., Tetlock, P., & Roese, N. (2010). From what *might* have been to what *must* have been: Counterfactual thinking creates meaning. *Journal of Personality and Social Psychology, 98,* 106–118.
160. Krueger, J., Wirtz, D., & Miller, D. T. (2005). Counterfactual thinking and the first instinct fallacy. *Journal of Personality and Social Psychology, 88,* 725–735.
161. Brownstein, S. C., Wolf, I. K., & Green, S. W. (2000). *Barron's how to prepare for the GRE: Graduate Record Examination.* Hauppauge, NY: Barron's Education Series, p. 6.
162. Krueger, J., Wirtz, D., & Miller, D. T. (2005). Counterfactual thinking and the first instinct fallacy. *Journal of Personality and Social Psychology, 88,* 725–735.
163. Markman, K., Gavanski, I., Sherman, S., & McMullen, M. (1993). The mental simulation of better and worse possible worlds. *Journal of Experimental Social Psychology, 29,* 87–109.
164. McMullen, M. N., Markman, K. D., & Gavanski, I. (1995). Living in neither the best nor the worst of all possible worlds: Antecedents and consequences of upward and downward counterfactual thinking. In N. J. Roese & J. M. Olson (Eds.), *What might have been: The social psychology of counterfactual thinking* (pp. 133–167). Mahwah, NJ: Erlbaum.
165. Roese, N. J., & Olson, J. M. (1997). Counterfactual thinking: The intersection of affect and function. In M. P. Zanna (Ed.), *Advances in experimental social psychology* (Vol. 29, pp. 1–59). New York: Academic Press.
166. Taylor, S. E. (1983). Adjustment to threatening events: A theory of cognitive adaptation. *American Psychologist, 38,* 1161–1173.
167. Gilovich, T., & Medvec, V. H. (1995). The experience of regret: What, when, and why. *Psychological Review, 102,* 379–395.
168. Landman, J. (1993). *Regret: The persistence of the possible.* New York: Oxford University Press.
169. Cosmides, L. (1989). The logic of social exchange: Has natural selection shaped how humans reason? Studies with the Wason selection task. *Cognition, 31,* 187–276.
170. Cosmides, L., & Tooby, J. (1992). Cognitive adaptations for social exchange. In J. Barkow, L. Cosmides, & J. Tooby (Eds.), *The adapted mind: Evolutionary psychology and the generation of culture* (pp. 163–228). Oxford: Oxford University Press.
171. Fiddick, L., Cosmides, L., & Tooby, J. (2000). No interpretation without representation: The role of domain-specific representations and inferences in the Wason selection task. *Cognition, 77,* 1–79.
172. Case, D. A., Fantino, E., & Goodie, A. S. (1999). Base-rate training without case cues reduces base-rate neglect. *Psychonomic Bulletin and Review, 6*(2), 319–327.
173. Lopes, L. L. (1987). Procedural debiasing. *Acta Psychologica, 64,* 167–185.
174. Williams, A. D. (1992). Bias and debiasing techniques in forensic psychology. *American Journal of Forensic Psychology, 10,* 19–26.
175. Hirt, E. R., Kardes, F. R., & Markman, K. D. (2004). Activating a mental simulation mind-set through generation of alternatives: Implications for debiasing in related and unrelated domains. *Journal of Experimental Social Psychology, 40,* 374–383.
176. Hirt, E. R., & Markman, K. D. (1995). Multiple explanation: A consider-an-alternative strategy for debiasing judgments. *Journal of Personality and Social Psychology, 69,* 1069–1086.
177. Sanna, L. J., & Schwarz, N. (2003). Using the hindsight bias: The role of accessibility experiences and (mis)attributions. *Journal of Experimental Social Psychology, 39,* 287–295.
178. Arkes, H. R. (1991). Costs and benefits of judgment errors: Implications for debiasing. *Psychological Bulletin, 110,* 486–498.
179. Williams, A. D. (1992). Bias and debiasing techniques in forensic psychology. *American Journal of Forensic Psychology, 10,* 19–26.
180. Arkes, H. R. (1991). Costs and benefits of judgment errors: Implications for debiasing. *Psychological Bulletin, 110,* 486–498.
181. Williams, A. D. (1992). Bias and debiasing techniques in forensic psychology. *American Journal of Forensic Psychology, 10,* 19–26.
182. Kray, L. J., & Galinsky, A. D. (2003). The debiasing effect of counterfactual mind-sets: Increasing the search for disconfirmatory information in group decisions. *Organizational Behavior and Human Decision Processes, 91,* 69–81.
183. Croskerry, P. (2003). The importance of cognitive errors in diagnosis and strategies to minimize them. *Academic Medicine, 78,* 775–780.
184. Lench, H. C., Bench, S. W., & Davis, E. L. (2016). Distraction from emotional information reduces biased judgements. *Cognition and Emotion, 30*(4), 638–653. doi:10.1080/02699931.2015.1020767

CHAPTER 6
Emotion and Affect

1. Pegues, J. (2018, August 31). Violent road rage incident involving a car jack caught on camera. *CBS News.* Retrieved from https://www.cbsnews.com/news/violent-road-rage-incident-car-jack-caught-on-camera-washington-dc/
2. American Automobile Association (AAA). Are you an aggressive driver? Retrieved from https://www.aaafoundation.org/are-you-aggressive-driver
3. Fehr, B., & Russell, J. A. (1984). Concept of emotion viewed from a prototype perspective. *Journal of Experimental Psychology: General, 113,* 464–486. Quote on p. 484
4. Cacioppo, J. T., & Gardner, W. L. (1999). Emotion. *Annual Review of Psychology, 50,* 191–214.
5. Watson, D., & Clark, L. A. (1991). Self-versus peer ratings of specific emotional traits: Evidence of convergent and discriminant validity. *Journal of Personality and Social Psychology, 60,* 927–940.
6. Watson, D., & Clark, L. A. (1992). Affects separable and inseparable: On the hierarchical arrangement of the negative affects. *Journal of Personality and Social Psychology, 62,* 489–505.
7. Watson, D., & Tellegen, A. (1985). Toward a consensual structure of mood. *Psychological Bulletin, 98,* 219–235.
8. Gallagher, J. (2011). Babies can "hear" emotion as early as three months old. *BBC News Health.* June 30. Retrieved from http://www.bbc.co.uk/news/health-13962068
9. Baumeister, R. F., Bratslavsky, E., Finkenauer, C., & Vohs, K. D. (2001). Bad is stronger than good. *Review of General Psychology, 5,* 323–370.
10. Goleman, D. (1995, August 8). Brain may tag all perceptions with a value. *New York Times,* 1–10.
11. Bargh, J. A., Chaiken, S., Raymond, P., & Hymes, C. (1996). The automatic evaluation effect: Unconditional automatic attitude activation with a pronunciation task. *Journal of Experimental Social Psychology, 32,* 104–128.
12. James, W. (1884). What is an emotion? *Mind, 9,* 188–205.
13. James, W. (1890). *Principles of psychology* (p. 190). New York: Holt.
14. Izard, C. E. (1971). *The face of emotion.* New York: Appleton-Century-Crofts.
15. Izard, C. E. (1990). The substrates and functions of emotion feelings: William James and current emotion theory. *Personality and Social Psychology Bulletin, 16,* 626–635.
16. Tomkins, S. S. (1962). *Affect, imagery, consciousness: Vol. 1. The positive affects.* New York: Springer.
17. Strack, F., Martin, L., & Stepper, S. (1988). Inhibiting and facilitating conditions of the human smile: A nonobtrusive test of the facial feedback hypothesis. *Journal of Personality and Social Psychology, 54,* 768–777.
18. Marsh, A. A., Rhoads, S. A., & Ryan, R. M. (2018). A multi-semester classroom demonstration yields evidence in support of the facial feedback effect. *Emotion.* https://doi-org.proxy.lib.umich.edu/10.1037/emo0000532.supp (Supplemental)
19. Neal, D., & Chartrand, T. L. (2011). Embodied emotion perception: Amplifying and dampening facial feedback modulates emotion perception accuracy. *Social Psychological and Personality Science, 2,* 673–678.
20. Schachter, S. (1964). The interaction of cognitive and physiological determinants of emotional state. In L. Berkowitz (Ed.), *Advances in experimental social psychology* (pp. 49–79). New York: Academic Press.
21. Schachter, S., & Singer, J. E. (1962). Cognitive, social, and physiological determinants of emotional state. *Psychological Review, 69,* 379–399.
22. Zillmann, D. (1979). *Hostility and aggression.* Hillsdale, NJ: Erlbaum.
23. Schachter, S., & Singer, J. E., (1962). Cognitive, social, and physiological determinants of emotional state. *Psychological Review, 69,* 379–399.
24. Chivers, M. L., Seto, M. C., Laan, E., Lalumière, M. L., & Grimbos, T. (2010). Agreement of genital and subjective measures of sexual arousal: A meta-analysis. *Archives of Sexual Behavior, 39*(1), 5–56.
25. Cohen, J. (1988). *Statistical power analysis for the behavioral sciences* (2nd ed.). New York: Academic Press.
26. Adams, H. E., Wright, L. W., Jr., & Lohr, B. A. (1996). Is homophobia associated with homosexual arousal? *Journal of Abnormal Psychology, 105,* 440–446.
27. Morokoff, P. J. (1985). Effects of sex guilt, repression, sexual "arousability," and sexual experience on female sexual arousal during erotica and fantasy. *Journal of Personality and Social Psychology, 49,* 177–187.
28. Marshall, G. D., & Zimbardo, P. G. (1979). Affective consequences of inadequately explained arousal. *Journal of Personality and Social Psychology, 37,* 970–988.
29. Maslach, C. (1979). Negative and emotional biasing of unexplained arousal. *Journal of Personality and Social Psychology, 37,* 953–969.
30. Zanna, M., Higgins, E., & Taves, P. (1976). Is dissonance phenomenologically aversive? *Journal of Experimental Social Psychology, 12,* 530–538.
31. Arnold, M. B. (1960). *Emotion and personality.* New York, NY: Columbia University Press.
32. Lazarus, R.S. (1991). *Emotion and adaptation.* New York, NY: Oxford University Press
33. Moors, A., Ellsworth, P. C., Scherer, K. R., & Frijda, N. H. (2013). Appraisal theories of emotion: State of the art and future development. *Emotion Review, 5*(2), 119–124. doi:10.1177/1754073912468165
34. Wamsley, L. (2017, October 25). Einstein's note on happiness, given to bellboy in 1922, fetches $1.6 million. *NPR.* Retrieved from https://www.npr.org/sections/thetwo-way/2017/10/25/560004689/einsteins-note-on-happiness-given-to-bellboy-in-1922-fetches-1-6-million
35. Twenge, J. M., Campbell, W. K., & Foster, C. A. (2003). Parenthood and marital satisfaction: A meta-analytic review. *Journal of Marriage and Family, 65,* 574–583.
36. Baumeister, R. F. (1991). *Meanings of life.* New York: Guilford Press.
37. Baumeister, R. F. (1991). *Meanings of life.* New York: Guilford Press.
38. Prior, E., Lew, R., Hammarberg, K., & Johnson, L. (in press). Fertility facts, figures and future plans: An online survey of university students. *Human Fertility.* DOI: 10.1080/14647273.2018.1482569
39. Campbell, A. (1981). *The sense of well-being in America.* New York: McGraw-Hill.
40. Hicken, M. (2013, August 14). Average cost to raise a kid: $241,080. *CNN Money.* Retrieved from http://money.cnn.com/2013/08/14/pf/cost-children/

41. Brickman, P., & Campbell, D. T. (1971). Hedonic relativism and planning the good society. In M. H. Apley (Ed.), *Adaptation-level theory: A symposium* (pp. 287–302). New York: Academic Press.
42. Brickman, P., Coates, D., & Janoff-Bulman, R. (1978). Lottery winners and accident victims: Is happiness relative? *Journal of Personality and Social Psychology, 36*, 917–927.
43. Diener, E., Lucas, R. E., & Scollon, C. N. (2006). Beyond the hedonic treadmill: Revisions to the adaptation theory of well-being. *American Psychologist, 61*, 305–314.
44. Kahneman, D. (1999). Objective happiness. In D. Kahneman, E. Diener, & N. Schwartz (Eds.), *Well-being: The foundations of hedonic psychology* (pp. 3–25). New York: Russell Sage Foundation.
45. Kahneman, D., Knetsch, J. L., & Thaler, R. H. (1990). Experimental tests of the endowment effect and the Coase theorem. *Journal of Political Economy, 98*(6), 1325–1348.
46. Kahneman, D., Wakker, P. P., & Sarin, R. (1997). Back to Bentham? Explorations of experienced utility. *Quarterly Journal of Economics, 62*, 375–406.
47. Diener, E., Lucas, R. E., & Scollon, C. N. (2006). Beyond the hedonic treadmill: Revisions to the adaptation theory of well-being. *American Psychologist, 61*, 305–314.
48. Brickman, P., Coates, D., & Janoff-Bulman, R. (1978). Lottery winners and accident victims: Is happiness relative? *Journal of Personality and Social Psychology, 36*, 917–927.
49. Lucas, R. E. (2007). Long-term disability is associated with lasting changes in subjective well-being: Evidence from two nationally representative longitudinal studies. *Journal of Personality and Social Psychology, 92*(4), 717–730.
50. Costa, P. T., & McCrae, R. R. (1980). Influence of extraversion and neuroticism on subjective well-being: Happy and unhappy people. *Journal of Personality and Social Psychology, 38*, 668–678.
51. Costa, P. T., & McCrae, R. R. (1984). Personality as a lifelong determinant of wellbeing. In C. Z. Malatesta & C. E. Izard (Eds.), *Emotion in adult development* (pp. 141–157). Beverly Hills, CA: Sage.
52. Costa, P. T., McCrae, R. R., & Zonderman, A. B. (1987). Environmental and dispositional influences on well-being: Longitudinal follow-up of an American national sample. *British Journal of Psychology, 78*, 299–306.
53. Costa, P. T., McCrae, R. R., & Zonderman, A. B. (1987). Environmental and dispositional influences on well-being: Longitudinal follow-up of an American national sample. *British Journal of Psychology, 78*, 299–306.
54. Brown, K. W., & Ryan, R. M. (2003). The benefits of being present: Mindfulness and its role in psychological well-being. *Journal of Personality and Social Psychology, 84*, 822–848.
55. McCullough, M. E. (2008). *Beyond revenge: The evolution of the forgiveness instinct*. San Francisco: Jossey-Bass.
56. McCullough, M. E., Emmons, R. A., & Tsang, J. (2002). The grateful disposition: A conceptual and empirical topography. *Journal of Personality and Social Psychology, 82*, 112–127.
57. McCullough, M. E., Rachal, K. C., Sandage, S. J., Worthington, E. L., Brown, S. W., & Hight, T. L. (1998). Interpersonal forgiving in close relationships: II. Theoretical elaboration and measurement. *Journal of Personality and Social Psychology, 75*, 1586–1603.
58. Ryff, C. D. (1995). Psychological well-being in adult life. *Current Directions in Psychological Science, 4*, 99–104.
59. Sheldon, K. M., & Lyubomirsky, S. (2004). Achieving sustainable new happiness: Prospects, practices, and prescriptions. In P. A. Linley & S. Joseph (Eds.), *Positive psychology in practice* (pp. 127–145). Hoboken, NJ: Wiley.
60. Thrash, T. M., & Elliot, A. J. (2003). Inspiration as a psychological construct. *Journal of Personality and Social Psychology, 84*, 871–889.
61. Lyubomirsky, S. (2001). Why are some people happier than others? The role of cognitive and motivational processes in well-being. *American Psychologist, 56*, 239–249.
62. Danner, D., Snowdon, D., & Friesen, W. (2001). Positive emotions in early life and longevity: Findings from the Nun Study. *Journal of Personality and Social Psychology, 80*, 804–813.
63. Abel, E. L., & Kruger, M. L. (2010). Smile intensity in photographs predicts longevity. *Psychological Science, 21*(4), 542–544.
64. Alcock, I., White, M. P., Wheeler, B. W., Fleming, L. E., & Depledge, M. H. (2014). Longitudinal effects on mental health of moving to greener and less green urban areas. *Environmental Science & Technology, 48*(2), 1247–1255. doi: 10.1021/es403688w
65. Ryan, R. M., Weinstein, N., Bernstein, J., Brown, K. W., Mistretta, L., & Gagné, M. (2010). Vitalizing effects of being outdoors and in nature. *Journal of Environmental Psychology, 30* (2), 159–168. doi: 10.1016/j.jenvp.2009.10.009
66. For review, see Gruber, J., Mauss, I. B., & Tamir, M. (2011). A dark side of happiness? How, when, and why happiness is not always good. *Perspectives on Psychological Science, 6*, 222–233.
67. Lyubomirsky, S., King, L. A., & Diener, E. (2005). The benefits of frequent positive affect: Does happiness lead to success? *Psychological Bulletin, 131*, 803–855.
68. Forgas, J. P. (2013). Don't worry, be sad! On the cognitive, motivational, and interpersonal benefits of negative mood. *Current Directions in Psychological Science, 22*, 225–232.
69. Schooler, J. W., Ariely, D., & Loewenstein, G. (2003). The pursuit and assessment of happiness may be self-defeating. In J. Carrillo & I. Brocas (Eds.), *The psychology of economic decisions* (pp. 41–70). Oxford: Oxford University Press.
70. Tamir, M., Schwartz, S. H., Oishi, S., & Kim, M. Y. (2017). The secret to happiness: Feeling good or feeling right? *Journal of Experimental Psychology: General, 146*(10), 1448–1459. doi:10.1037/xge0000303
71. Silver, K. (2017, August 14). Anger and hatred can make us feel happy, says study. *BBC*. Retrieved from https://www.bbc.com/news/health-40900811
72. Quoidbach, J., Gruber, J., Mikolajczak, M., Kogan, A., Kotsou, I., & Norton, M. I. (2014) Emodiversity and the emotional ecosystem. *Journal of Experimental Psychology: General, 143*(6), 2057–2066. doi:10.1037/a0038025
73. Larsen, R. J., & Diener, E. (1987). Affect intensity as an individual difference characteristic: A review. *Journal of Research in Personality, 21*, 1–39.
74. Sheldon, K. M. (1994). Emotionality differences between artists and scientists. *Journal of Research in Personality, 28*, 481–491.
75. Aries, P. (1962). *Centuries of childhood: A social history of family life* (Trans. R. Baldick). New York: Random House.
76. Stone, L. (1977). *The family, sex and marriage in England: 1500–1800*. London: Perennial.
77. Berkowitz, L. (1993). *Aggression: Its causes, consequences, and control*. New York: McGraw-Hill.
78. Krizan, Z., & Hisler, G. (2018). Sleepy anger: Restricted sleep amplifies angry feelings. *Journal of Experimental Psychology: General*. https://doi-org.proxy.lib.umich.edu/10.1037/xge0000522
79. Peterson, C. K., & Harmon-Jones, E. (in press). Anger and testosterone: Evidence that situationally-induced anger relates to situationally-induced testosterone. *Emotion*.
80. Carver, C. S., & Harmon-Jones, E. (2009). Anger is an approach-related affect: Evidence and implications. *Psychological Bulletin, 135*, 183–204.
81. Averill, J. R. (1982). *Anger and aggression: An essay on emotion*. New York: Springer-Verlag.
82. Tice, D. M., & Baumeister, R. F. (1993). Controlling anger: Self-induced emotion change. In D. M. Wegner & J. W. Pennebaker (Eds.), *Handbook of mental control* (pp. 393–409). Englewood Cliffs, NJ: Prentice-Hall.
83. Berkowitz, L. (1993). *Aggression: Its causes, consequences, and control*. New York: McGraw-Hill.
84. Van Dijk, E., Van Kleef, G. A., Steinel, W., & Van Beest, I. (2008). A social functional approach to emotions in bargaining: When communicating anger pays and when it backfires. *Journal of Personality and Social Psychology, 94*(4), 600–614.
85. Van Kleef, G. A., De Dreu, C. K. W., & Manstead, A. S. R. (2004a). The interpersonal effects of anger and happiness in negotiations. *Journal of Personality and Social Psychology, 86*(1), 57–76.
86. Van Kleef, G. A., De Dreu, C. K. W., & Manstead, A. S. R. (2004b). The interpersonal effects of emotions in negotiations: A motivated information processing approach. *Journal of Personality and Social Psychology, 87*(4), 510–528.
87. Tamir, M., Mitchell, C., & Gross, J. J. (2008). Hedonic and instrumental motives in anger regulation. *Psychological Science, 19*(4), 324–328.
88. Ellis, A. (1977). *How to live with—and without— anger*. New York: Reader's Digest Press.
89. Geen, R. G., & Quanty, M. B. (1977). The catharsis of aggression: An evaluation of a hypothesis. In L. Berkowitz (Ed.), *Advances in experimental social psychology* (Vol. 10, pp. 1–37). New York: Academic Press.
90. Lewis, W. A., & Bucher, A. M. (1992). Anger, catharsis, the reformulated frustration-aggression hypothesis, and health consequences. *Psychotherapy, 29*, 385–392.
91. Rosenman, R. H., & Chesney, M. A. (1982). Stress, Type A behavior and coronary heart disease. In L. Goldberger & S. Breznitz (Eds.), *Handbook of stress: Theoretical and clinical aspects* (pp. 547–565). New York: Free Press.
92. Miller, T. Q., Smith, T. W., Turner, C. W., Guijarro, M. L., & Hallet, A. J. (1996). A meta-analytic review of research on hostility and physical health. *Psychological Bulletin, 119*, 322–348.
93. Bushman, B. J., Baumeister, R. F., & Stack, A. D. (1999). Catharsis, aggression, and persuasive influence: Self-fulfilling or self-defeating prophecies? *Journal of Personality and Social Psychology, 76*, 367–376.
94. Bushman, B. J. (2002). Does venting anger feed or extinguish the flame? Catharsis, rumination, distraction, anger, and aggressive responding. *Personality and Social Psychology Bulletin, 28*, 724–731.
95. Zillmann, D. (1979). *Hostility and aggression*. Hillsdale, NJ: Erlbaum.
96. Mischkowski, D., Kross, E., & Bushman, B. J. (2012). Flies on the wall are less aggressive: Self-distanced reflection reduces angry feelings, aggressive thoughts, and aggressive behaviors. *Journal of Experimental Social Psychology, 48*(5), 1187–1191. DOI: 10.1016/j.jesp.2012.03.012
97. Baron, R. A. (1976). The reduction of human aggression: A field study of the influence of incompatible reactions. *Journal of Applied Social Psychology, 6*, 260–274.
98. Veenstra, L., Schneider, I. K., Bushman, B. J., & Koole, S. L. (2017). Drawn to danger: Trait anger predicts automatic approach behavior to angry faces. *Cognition and Emotion, 31*(4), 765–771. DOI: 10.1080/02699931.2016.1150256
99. Veenstra, L., Bushman, B. J., & Koole, S. L. (2018). The facts on the furious: A brief review of the psychology of trait anger. *Current Opinion in Psychology, 19*, 98–103. DOI: 10.1016/j.copsyc.2017.03.014
100. DeWall, C. N., Deckman, T., Gailliot, M. T., & Bushman, B. J. (2011). Sweetened blood cools hot tempers: Physiological self-control and aggression. *Aggressive Behavior, 37*(1), 73–80. DOI: 10.1002/ab.20366
101. Bushman, B. J., DeWall, C. N., Pond, R. S. Jr., & Hanus, M. D. (2014). Low glucose relates to greater aggression in married couples. *Proceedings of the National Academy of Sciences (PNAS), 111*(17), 6254–6257. DOI: 10.1073/pnas.1400619111

102. Michaud, S. G., & Aynesworth, H. (2000). *Ted Bundy: Conversations with a killer*. Irving, TX: Authorlink. Quote on p. 320
103. Michaud, S. G., & Aynesworth, H. (2000). *Ted Bundy: Conversations with a killer*. Irving, TX: Authorlink. Quote on p. 263
104. Hare, R. D. (1998). *Without conscience: The disturbing world of the psychopaths among us*. New York: Guilford Press.
105. Cryder, C. E, Springer, S., & Morewedge, C. M. (2012), Guilty feelings, targeted actions. *Personality and Social Psychology Bulletin, 38*(5), 607–618. doi: 10.1177/0146167211435796
106. Tangney, J. P., & Dearing, R. L. (2002). *Shame and guilt*. New York: Guilford Press.
107. Sznycer et al. (2018). Cross-culture invariances in the architecture of shame. *PNAS, 115*(39), 9702–9707. doi: 10.1073/pnas.1805016115
108. Baumeister, R. F., Stillwell, A. M., & Heatherton, T. F. (1994). Guilt: An interpersonal approach. *Psychological Bulletin, 115*, 243–267.
109. Tangney, J. P., & Dearing, R. L. (2002). *Shame and guilt*. New York: Guilford Press.
110. Tangney, J. P., & Fischer, K. W. (1995). *Self-conscious emotions: The psychology of shame, guilt, embarrassment, and pride*. New York: Guilford Press.
111. McMillen, D. L., & Austin, J. B. (1971). Effect of positive feedback on compliance following transgression. *Psychonomic Science, 24*, 59–61.
112. Cialdini, R. B., Darby, B. L., & Vincent, J. E. (1973). Transgression and altruism: A case for hedonism. *Journal of Experimental Social Psychology, 9*, 502–516.
113. Harris, M. B., Benson, S. M., & Hall, C. L. (1975). The effects of confession on altruism. *Journal of Social Psychology, 96*, 187–192.
114. Katzev, R., Edelsack, L., Reynolds, R., Steinmetz, G., Walker, T., & Wright, R. (1978). The effect of reprimanding transgressions on subsequent helping behavior: Two field experiments. *Personality and Social Psychology Bulletin, 4*, 326–329.
115. Goldsmith, K., Cho, E.K., & Dhar, R. (2012). When guilt begets pleasure: The positive effect of a negative emotion. *Journal of Marketing Research, 49*, 872–881.
116. BBC (2016, June 14). Orlando survivor: 'The guilt of being alive is heavy.' *BBC*. Retrieved from https://www.bbc.com/news/av/world-us-canada-36532267/orlando-survivor-the-guilt-of-being-alive-is-heavy
117. Arnold, A. (2019, March 23). A Parkland Survivor took her own life. *The Cut*. Retrieved from https://www.thecut.com/2019/03/parkland-survivor-sydney-aiello-has-taken-her-own-life.html?utm_medium=s1&utm_source=fb&utm_campaign=nym&fbclid=IwAR2q5zNbWQscLt3zCS8hYu6u3B5N1CJtCBdXyB7OeYH-CGy15_nU9BxuG4s
118. Brockner, J., Greenberg, J., Brockner, A., Bortz, J., Davy, J., & Carter, C. (1986). Layoffs, equity theory, and work performance: Further evidence of the impact of survivor guilt. *Academy of Management Journal, 29*, 373–384.
119. Baumeister, R. F., Reis, H. T., & Delespaul, P. A. E. G. (1995). Subjective and experiential correlates of guilt in everyday life. *Personality and Social Psychology Bulletin, 21*, 1256–1268.
120. Nelissen, R.M.A. (2014). Relational utility as a moderator of guilt in social interactions. *Journal of Personality and Social Psychology, 106*, 257–271.
121. Baumeister, R. F., Stillwell, A. M., & Heatherton, T. F. (1994). Guilt: An interpersonal approach. *Psychological Bulletin, 115*, 243–267.
122. Matthew 27:24.
123. Zhong, C. B., & Liljenquist, K. A. (2006). Washing away your sins: Threatened morality and physical cleansing. *Science, 313*, 1451–1452.
124. Xu, H., Bègue, L., & Bushman, B. J. (2014). Washing the guilt away: Effects of personal versus vicarious cleansing on guilty feelings and prosocial behavior. *Frontiers in Human neuroscience, 8*, 97. doi: 10.3389/fnhum.2014.00097
125. Haidt, J., & Joseph, C. (2008). The moral mind: How five sets of innate intuitions guide the development of many culture-specific virtues, and perhaps even modules. In P. Carruthers, S. Laurence, & S. Stich (Eds.), *The innate mind* (Vol. 3, pp. 367–392). New York: Oxford University Press.
126. Lee, S. W. S., & Schwarz, N. (2011). Wiping the slate clean: Psychological consequences of physical cleansing. *Current Directions in Psychological Science, 20*(5), 307–311.
127. Hutcherson, C. A., & Gross, J. J. (2011). The moral emotions: A social-functionalist account of anger, disgust, and contempt. *Journal of Personality and Social Psychology, 100*(4), 719–737.
128. Curtis, V. (2011). Why disgust matters. *Philosophical Transactions of the Royal Society B, 366*, 3478–3490. Quote on p. 3486
129. Curtis, V. (2011). Why disgust matters. *Philosophical Transactions of the Royal Society B, 366*, 3478–3490.
130. Skolnick, A., Bascom, K. L., & Wilson, D. T. (2013). Gender role expectations of disgust: Men are low and women are high. *Sex Roles, 69*(1–2), 72–88. doi: 10.1007/s11199-013-0279-y
131. Schaller, M. (2011). The behavioural immune system and the psychology of human sexuality. *Philosophical Transactions of the Royal Society B, 366*, 3418–3426.
132. Schaller, M. (2011). The behavioural immune system and the psychology of human sexuality. *Philosophical Transactions of the Royal Society B, 366*, 3418–3426.
133. Vartanian, L. R., Thomas, M. A, & Vanman, E. J. (2013). Disgust, contempt, and anger and the stereotypes of obese people. *Eating and Weight Disorders, 18*(4), 377–382. doi: 10.1007/s40519-013-0067-2
134. Taylor, K. (2007). Disgust is a factor in extreme prejudice. *British Journal of Social Psychology, 46*(3), 597–617.
135. Morrison, T. G., Kiss, M. J., Bishop, C., & Morrison, M. A. (2018). "We're disgusted with queers, not fearful of them": The interrelationships among disgust, gay men's sexual behavior, and homonegativity. *Journal of Homosexuality*, doi:10.1080/00918369.2018.1490576
136. O'Handley, B. M., Blair, K. L., & Hoskin, R. A. (2017). What do two men kissing and a bucket of maggots have in common? Heterosexual men's indistinguishable salivary α-amylase responses to photos of two men kissing and disgusting images. *Psychology & Sexuality, 8*(3), 173–188. doi:10.1080/19419899.2017.1328459
137. Choma, B. L., Hodson, G., & Costello, K. (2012). Intergroup disgust sensitivity as a predictor of islamophobia: The modulating effect of fear. *Journal of Experimental Social Psychology, 48*(2), 499–506.
138. Ritter, R. S., & Preston, J. L. (2011). Gross gods and icky atheism: Disgust responses to rejected religious beliefs. *Journal of Experimental Social Psychology, 47*(6), 1225–1230.
139. Buckles, E. E., & Trapnell, P. D. (2013). Disgust facilitates outgroup dehumanization. *Group Processes & Intergroup Relations, 16*(6), 771–780. 10.1177/1368430212471738
140. Chapman, H. A., & Anderson, A. K. (2013). Things Rank and Gross in Nature: A Review and Synthesis of Moral Disgust. *Psychological Bulletin, 139*(2), 300–327. doi: 10.1037/a0030964
141. Horberg, E. J., Oveis, C., Keltner, D., & Cohen, A. B. (2009). Disgust and the moralization of purity. *Journal of Personality and Social Psychology, 97*(6), 963–976.
142. Schnall, S., Haidt, J., Clore, G. L., & Jordan, A. H. (2008). Disgust as embodied moral judgment. *Personality and Social Psychology Bulletin, 34*(8), 1096–1109.
143. Damasio, A. R. (1994). *Descartes' error*. London: Picador.
144. Anderson, S. A., Russell, C. S., & Schumm, W. R. (1983). Perceived marital quality and family life-cycle categories: A further analysis. *Journal of Marriage and the Family, 45*, 127–139.
145. Baumeister, R. F., & Leary, M. R. (1995). The need to belong: Desire for interpersonal attachments as a fundamental human motivation. *Psychological Bulletin, 117*, 497–529.
146. Belsky, J. (1985). Exploring individual differences in marital change across the transition to parenthood: The role of violated expectations. *Journal of Marriage and the Family, 47*, 1037–1044.
147. Belsky, J., Lang, M. E., & Rovine, M. (1985). Stability and change in marriage across the transition to parenthood: A second study. *Journal of Marriage and the Family, 47*, 855–865.
148. Belsky, J., Spanier, G. B., & Rovine, M. (1983). Stability and change in marriage across the transition to parenthood. *Journal of Marriage and the Family, 45*, 567–577.
149. Bernard, J. (1982). *The future of marriage*. New Haven, CT: Yale University Press.
150. Campbell, A., Converse, P. E., & Rogers, W. L. (1976). *The quality of American life: Perceptions, evaluations, and satisfactions*. New York: Russell Sage.
151. Glenn, N. D., & McLanahan, S. (1982). Children and marital happiness: A further specification of the relationship. *Journal of Marriage and the Family, 44*, 63–72.
152. Glenn, N. D., & Weaver, C. N. (1978). A multi-variate multisurvey study of marital happiness. *Journal of Marriage and the Family, 40*, 269–282.
153. Ruble, D. N., Fleming, A. S., Hackel, L. S., & Stangor, C. (1988). Changes in the marital relationship during the transition to first time motherhood: Effects of violated expectations concerning division of household labor. *Journal of Personality and Social Psychology, 55*, 78–87.
154. Spanier, G. B., & Lewis, R. A. (1980). Marital quality: A review of the seventies. *Journal of Marriage and the Family, 42*, 825–839.
155. Twenge, J. M., Campbell, W. K., & Foster, C. A. (2003). Parenthood and marital satisfaction: A meta-analytic review. *Journal of Marriage and Family, 65*, 574–583.
156. Gable, S. L., & Reis, H. T. (2001). Appetitive and aversive social interaction. In J. Harvey (Ed.), *Close romantic relationships: Maintenance and enhancement* (pp. 169–194). Mahwah, NJ: Erlbaum.
157. Leary, M. R., & Springer, C. A. (2000). Hurt feelings: The neglected emotion. In R. Kowalski (Ed.), *Aversive behaviors and interpersonal transgression*. Washington, DC: American Psychological Association.
158. Coan, J. A., Schaefer, H. S., & Davidson, R. J. (2006). Lending a hand: Social regulation of the neural response to threat. *Psychological Science, 17*(12), 1032–1039.
159. Koole, S. L., Tjew A Sin, M., & Schneider, I. K.. (2014). Embodied terror management: (Simulated) Interpersonal touch alleviates existential concerns among individuals with low self-esteem. *Psychological Science, 25*(1), 30–37. doi: 10.1177/0956797613483478
160. Hatfield, E., Cacioppo, J.T., & Rapson, R.L. (1993). Emotional contagion. *Current Directions in Psychological Science, 2*, 96–100.
161. Kramer, A.D.I., Guillory, J.E., & Hancock, J.T. (2014). Experimental evidence of massive-scale emotional contagion through social networks. *Proceedings of the National Academy of Science, 111*, 24–26.
162. Coviello, L., Sohn, Y., Kramer, A. D. I., Marlow, C., Franceschetti, M., Christakis, N. A., & Fowler, J. H. (2014). Detecting emotional contagion in massive social networks. *PLOS ONE, 9*(3), doi: 10.1371/journal.pone.0090315
163. Frijda, N. H. (1986). *The emotions*. New York: Cambridge University Press.
164. Frijda, N. H., Kuipers, P., & ter Schure, E. (1989). Relations among emotion, appraisal, and emotional action readiness. *Journal of Personality and Social Psychology, 57*, 212–228.
165. Frijda, N. H. (1986). *The emotions*. New York: Cambridge University Press.

166. Berkowitz, L. (1993). *Aggression: Its causes, consequences, and control.* New York: McGraw-Hill.
167. Cialdini, R. B., & Kenrick, D. T. (1976). Altruism as hedonism: A social development perspective on the relationship of negative mood state and helping. *Journal of Personality and Social Psychology, 34,* 907–914.
168. Hornstein, H. A. (1982). Promotive tension: Theory and research. In V. Derlega & J. Grzelak (Eds.), *Cooperation and helping behavior: Theories and research* (pp. 229–248). New York: Academic Press.
169. Lerner, M. J. (1982). The justice motive in human relations and economic model of man: A radical analysis of facts and fictions. In V. Derlega & J. Grzelak (Eds.), *Cooperation and helping behavior: Theories and research* (pp. 249–278). New York: Academic Press.
170. Reykowski, J. (1982). Motivation and prosocial behavior. In V. Derlega & J. Grzelak (Eds.), *Cooperation and helping behavior: Theories and research* (pp. 352–375). New York: Academic Press.
171. Gardner, M. P., Wansink, B., & Kim, J. (2014). Better moods for better eating?: How mood influences food choice. *Journal of Consumer Psychology, 24*(3), 320-335. doi: 10.1037/t01397-000
172. Agras, W. S., & Telch, C. F. (1998). The effects of caloric deprivation and negative affect on binge eating in obese binge-eating disordered women. *Behavior Therapy, 29,* 491–503.
173. Agras, W. S., & Telch, C. F. (1998). The effects of caloric deprivation and negative affect on binge eating in obese binge-eating disordered women. *Behavior Therapy, 29,* 491–503.
174. Telch, C. F., & Agras, W. S. (1996). Do emotional states influence binge eating in the obese? *International Journal of Eating Disorders, 20,* 271–279.
175. Johnson, W. G., Schlundt, D. G., Barclay, D. R., Carr-Nangle, R. E., & Engler, L. B. (1995). A naturalistic functional analysis of binge eating. *Behavior Therapy, 26,* 101–118.
176. Turner, S. A., Luszczynska, A., Warner, L., & Schwarzer, R. (2010). Emotional and uncontrolled eating styles and chocolate chip cookie consumption. A controlled trial of the effects of positive mood enhancement. *Appetite, 54*(1), 143–149.
177. Tice, D. M., Bratslavsky, E., & Baumeister, R. F. (2001). Emotional distress regulation takes precedence over impulse control: If you feel bad, do it! *Journal of Personality and Social Psychology, 80,* 53–67.
178. Handley, I. M., Lassiter, G. D., Nickell, E. F., & Herchenroeder, L. M. (2004). Affect and automatic mood maintenance. *Journal of Experimental Social Psychology, 40,* 106–112.
179. Manucia, G. K., Baumann, D. J., & Cialdini, R. B. (1984). Mood influences on helping: Direct effects or side effects? *Journal of Personality and Social Psychology, 46,* 357–364.
180. Van Dijk, W. W., & Zeelenberg, M. (2002). Investigating the appraisal patterns of regret and disappointment. *Motivation and Emotion, 26,* 321–331.
181. Damasio, A. R. (1994). *Descartes' error.* London: Picador.
182. Bechara, A., Damasio, H., Tranel, D., & Damasio, A. R. (1997). Deciding advantageously before knowing the advantageous strategy. *Science, 275,* 1293–1295.
183. Sakaki, M., Fryker, K., & Mather, M. (2014). Emotion strengthens high-priority memory traces but weakens low-priority memory traces. *Psychological Science, 25,* 387–395.
184. Roese, N. J., & Olson, J. M. (1997). Counterfactual thinking: The intersection of affect and function. In M. P. Zanna (Ed.), *Advances in experimental social psychology* (Vol. 29, pp. 1–59). New York: Academic Press.
185. Clore, G. L., Gasper, K., & Garvin, E. (2001). Affect as information. In J. P. Forgas (Ed.), *Handbook of affect and social cognition* (pp. 122–144). Mahwah, NJ: Erlbaum.
186. Schwarz, N., & Clore, G. L. (1983). Mood, misattribution, and judgments of well-being: Informative and directive functions of affective states. *Journal of Personality and Social Psychology, 45,* 513–523.
187. Niedenthal, P. M., Halberstadt, J. B., & Innes-Ker, A. H. (1999). Emotional response categorization. *Psychological Review, 106,* 337–361.
188. DeWall, C. N., Baumeister, R. F., Chester, D. S., & Bushman, B. J. (in press). How often does currently felt emotion predict social behavior and judgment? A meta-analytic test of two theories. *Emotion Review.*
189. Gilbert, D. T., Pinel, E. C., Wilson, T. D., Blumberg, S. J., & Wheatley, T. P. (1998). Immune neglect: A source of durability bias in affective forecasting. *Journal of Personality and Social Psychology, 75,* 617–638.
190. Buehler, R., & McFarland, C. (2001). Intensity bias in affective forecasting: The role of temporal focus. *Personality and Social Psychology Bulletin, 27,* 1480–1493.
191. Wilson, T. D., Wheatley, T., Meyers, J. M., Gilbert, D. T., & Axsom, D. (2000). Focalism: A source of durability bias in affective forecasting. *Journal of Personality and Social Psychology, 78,* 821–836.
192. Fiske, S. (2002, November/December). Forecasting the future. *Psychology Today.* Retrieved from http://www.psychologytoday.com/articles/pto-20021125-000001.html
193. Carlsmith, K. M., Wilson, T. D., & Gilbert, D. T. (2008). The paradoxical consequences of revenge. *Journal of Personality and Social Psychology, 95*(6), 1316–1324.
194. Nisbet, E. K., & Zelenski, J. M. (2011). Underestimating nearby nature: Affective forecasting errors obscure the happy path to sustainability. *Psychological Science, 22*(9), 1101–1106.
195. Mellers, B. A., Schwartz, A., Ho, K., & Ritov, I. (1997). Elation and disappointment: Emotional responses to risky options. *Psychological Science, 8,* 423–429.
196. Connolly, T. (2002). Regret in decision making. *Current Directions in Psychological Science, 11,* 212–216.
197. Barlow, D. H. (1988). *Anxiety and its disorders: The nature and treatment of anxiety and panic.* New York: Guilford Press.
198. Loewenstein, G. F., Weber, E. U., Hsee, C. K., & Welch, N. (2001). Risk as feelings. *Psychological Bulletin, 127,* 267–286.
199. Blanton, H., & Gerrard, M. (1997). Effect of sexual motivation on men's risk perception for sexually transmitted disease: There must be 50 ways to justify a lover. *Health Psychology, 16,* 374–379.
200. Lerner, J. S., Small, D. A., & Loewenstein, G. (2004). Heart strings and purse strings: Carryover effects of emotions on economic decisions. *Psychological Science, 15*(5), 337–341.
201. Rozin, P., Haidt, J., & McCauley, C. R. (1993). Disgust. In M. Lewis & J. M. Haviland (Eds.), *Handbook of emotions* (pp. 575–594). New York: Guilford Press.
202. Rozin, P., Haidt, J., & McCauley, C. R. (2009). Disgust: The body and soul emotion in the 21st century. In B. O. Olatunji & D. McKay (Eds.), *Disgust and its disorders: Theory, assessment, and treatment implications* (pp. 9–29). Washington, DC: American Psychological Association.
203. Gerrard, M., Gibbons, F. X., & McCoy, S. B. (1993). Emotional inhibition of effective contraception. *Anxiety, Stress & Coping: An International Journal, 6,* 73–88.
204. Okwumabua, J. O., & Duryea, E. J. (2003). Depressive symptoms and decision making among African American youth. *Journal of Adolescent Research, 18,* 436–453.
205. Fredrickson, B. L. (2003). The value of positive emotions. *American Scientist, 91,* 330–335.
206. Fredrickson, B. L. (1998). What good are positive emotions? *Review of General Psychology, 2,* 300–319.
207. Fredrickson, B. L. (2001). The role of positive emotions in positive psychology: The broaden-and-build theory of positive emotions. *American Psychologist, 56,* 218–226.
208. Fredrickson, B. L. (2003). The value of positive emotions. *American Scientist, 91,* 330–335.
209. Ellsworth, P. C., & Smith, C. A. (1988). Shades of joy: Patterns of appraisal differentiating pleasant emotions. *Cognition and Emotion, 2,* 301–331.
210. Frijda, N. H. (1986). *The emotions.* New York: Cambridge University Press.
211. Gable, S. L., Reis, H. T., & Elliot, A. J. (2000). Behavioral activation and inhibition in everyday life. *Journal of Personality and Social Psychology, 78,* 1135–1149.
212. David, J. P., Green, P. J., Martin, R., & Suls, J. (1997). Differential roles of neuroticism, extraversion, and event desirability for mood in daily life: An integrative model of top-down and bottom-up influences. *Journal of Personality and Social Psychology, 73,* 149–159.
213. Major, B., Zubek, J. M., Cooper, M. L., Cozzarelli, C., & Richards, C. (1997). Mixed messages: Implications of social conflict and social support within close relationships for adjustment to a stressful life event. *Journal of Personality and Social Psychology, 72,* 1349–1363.
214. Estrada, C. A., Isen, A. M., & Young, M. J. (1997). Positive affect facilitates integration of information and decreases anchoring in reasoning among physicians. *Organizational Behavior and Human Decision Processes, 72,* 117–135.
215. Isen, A. M. (2000). Positive affect and decision making. In M. Lewis & J. M. Haviland-Jones (Eds.), *Handbook of emotions* (2nd ed., pp. 417–435). New York: Guilford Press.
216. Erez, A., & Isen, A. M. (2002). The influence of positive affect on the components of expectancy motivation. *Journal of Applied Psychology, 87,* 1055–1067.
217. Nadler, R. T., Rabi, R., & Minda, J. P. (2010). Better mood and better performance: Learning rule-described categories is enhanced by positive mood. *Psychological Science, 21*(12), 1770–1776.
218. Isen, A. M., & Patrick, R. (1983). The effect of positive feelings and risk taking: When the chips are down. *Organizational Behavior and Human Performance, 31,* 194–202.
219. de Vries, M., Holland, R. W., Corneille, O., Rondeel, E., & Witteman, C. L. M. (2012). Mood effects on dominated choices: Positive mood induces departures from logical rules. *Journal of Behavioral Decision Making, 25*(1), 74–81.
220. Martin, E. A., & Kerns, J. G. (2011). The influence of positive mood on different aspects of cognitive control. *Cognition and Emotion, 25*(2), 265–279.
221. Biss, R. K., Hasher, L., & Thomas, R. C. (2010). Positive mood is associated with the implicit use of distraction. *Motivation and Emotion, 34*(1), 73–77.
222. Ekman, P., Friesen, W. V., O'Sullivan, M., Chan, A., Diacoyanni-Tarlatzis, I., Heider, K., et al. (1987). Universals and cultural differences in the judgments of facial expressions of emotion. *Journal of Personality and Social Psychology, 53,* 712–717.
223. Elfenbein, H. A., & Ambady, N. (2002). On the universality and cultural specificity of emotion recognition: A meta-analysis. *Psychological Bulletin, 128,* 203–235.
224. Nummenmaa, L., Glerean, E., Hari, R., & Hietanen, J. K. (2014). Bodily maps of emotions., PNAS, *111*(2), 646–651, doi: 10.1073/pnas.1321664111
225. Benitez-Quiroz, C. F., Wilbur, R. B., & Martinez, A. M. (2016). The not face: A grammaticalization of facial expressions of emotion. *Cognition, 15077-84.* doi:10.1016/j.cognition.2016.02.004
226. Dimeo-Ediger, W. (2016, March 30). It's A Small World When It Comes to :-/ NPR. Retrieved from https://www.npr.org/sections/goatsandsoda/2016/03/30/472452258/its-a-small-world-when-it-comes-to

227. Larson, R. W., & Pleck, J. (1999). Hidden feelings: Emotionality in boys and men. In D. Bernstein (Ed.), *Nebraska Symposium on Motivation: Vol. 45. Gender and motivation* (pp. 25–74). Lincoln: University of Nebraska Press.
228. Larson, R. W., & Pleck, J. (1999). Hidden feelings: Emotionality in boys and men. In D. Bernstein (Ed.), *Nebraska Symposium on Motivation: Vol. 45. Gender and motivation* (pp. 25–74). Lincoln: University of Nebraska Press.
229. Larson, R. W., & Pleck, J. (1999). Hidden feelings: Emotionality in boys and men. In D. Bernstein (Ed.), *Nebraska Symposium on Motivation: Vol. 45. Gender and motivation* (pp. 25–74). Lincoln: University of Nebraska Press.
230. LaFrance, M., & Banaji, M. (1992). Toward a reconsideration of the gender-emotion relationship. In M. S. Clark (Ed.), *Emotion and social behavior: Review of personality and social psychology* (Vol. 14, pp. 178–201). Newbury Park, CA: Sage.
231. LaFrance, M., & Banaji, M. (1992). Toward a reconsideration of the gender-emotion relationship. In M. S. Clark (Ed.), *Emotion and social behavior: Review of personality and social psychology* (Vol. 14, pp. 178–201). Newbury Park, CA: Sage.
232. Goodenough, F. L. (1931). *Anger in young children.* Minneapolis: University of Minnesota Press.
233. Brody, L. R. (1996). Gender, emotional expression, and parent-child boundaries. In R. D. Kavanaugh, B. Zimmerberg, & S. Fein (Eds.), *Emotion: Interdisciplinary perspectives* (pp. 139–170). Mahwah, NJ: Eribaum.
234. Buss, A. H. (1989). Temperaments as personality traits. In C. A. Kohnstamm, J. E. Bates, & M. Rothbart (Eds.), *Temperament in childhood* (pp. 49–58). Chichester, West Sussex, UK: Wiley.
235. Rothbart, M. K. (1989). Temperament and development. In G. A. Kohnstamm, J. E. Bates, & M. K. Rothbart (Eds.), *Temperament in childhood* (pp. 187–247). New York: Wiley.
236. Gottman, J. M. (1994). *What predicts divorce?* Hillsdale, NJ: Erlbaum.
237. Gottman, J. M. (1994). *What predicts divorce?* Hillsdale, NJ: Erlbaum.
238. Eisenberg, N., & Lennon, R. (1983). Sex differences in empathy and related capacities. *Psychological Bulletin, 94,* 100–131.
239. Ackerman, J. M., Griskevicius, V., & Li, N. P. (2011). Let's get serious: Communicating commitment in romantic relationships. *Journal of Personality and Social Psychology, 100*(6), 1079–1094.
240. Hill, C. T., Rubin, Z., & Peplau, L. A. (1976). Breakups before marriage: The end of 103 affairs. *Journal of Social Issues, 32,* 147–168.
241. Huston, T. L., Surra, C., Fitzgerald, N. M., & Cate, R. (1981). From courtship to marriage: Mate selection as an interpersonal process. In S. Duck & R. Gilmour (Eds.), *Personal relationships. 2: Developing personal relationships.* New York: Academic Press.
242. Kanin, E. J., Davidson, K. D., & Scheck, S. R. (1970). A research note on male-female differentials in the experience of heterosexual love. *Journal of Sex Research, 6,* 64–72.
243. Baumeister, R. F., Wotman, S. R., & Stillwell, A. M. (1993). Unrequited love: On heartbreak, anger, guilt, scriptlessness, and humiliation. *Journal of Personality and Social Psychology, 64,* 377–394.
244. Hill, C. T., Rubin, Z., & Peplau, L. A. (1976). Breakups before marriage: The end of 103 affairs. *Journal of Social Issues, 32,* 147–168.
245. Yerkes, R. M., & Dodson, J. D. (1908). The relation of strength of stimulus to rapidity of habit formation. *Journal of Comparative Neurology and Psychology, 18,* 459–482.
246. Easterbrook, J. A. (1959). The effect of emotion on the utilization and the organization of behavior. *Psychological Review, 66,* 183–201.
247. Chajut, E., & Algom, D. (2003). Selective attention improves under stress: Implications for theories of social cognition. *Journal of Personality and Social Psychology, 85,* 231–248.
248. Keinan, G. (1987). Decision making under stress: Scanning of alternatives under controllable and uncontrollable threats. *Journal of Personality and Social Psychology, 52,* 639–644.
249. Keinan, G., Friedland, N., & Ben-Porath, Y. (1987). Decision making under stress: Scanning of alternatives under physical threat. *Acta Psychologica, 64,* 219–228.
250. Paul, A. M. (1999, June 28). Promotional intelligence. *Ivory Tower.* Retrieved August 11, 2004, from http://www.salon.com/books/it/1999/06/28/emotional/index1.html
251. Salovey, P., & Mayer, J. D. (1990). Emotional intelligence. *Imagination, Cognition, and Personality, 9,* 185–211.
252. Mayer, J. D., & Salovey, P. (1997). What is emotional intelligence? In P. Salovey & D. Sluyter (Eds.), *Emotional development and emotional intelligence: Implications for educators* (pp. 3–31). New York: Basic Books.
253. Dunn, E. W., Brackett, M. A., Ashton-James, C., Schneiderman, E., & Salovey, P. (2007). On emotionally intelligent time travel: Individual differences in affective forecasting ability. *Personality and Social Psychology Bulletin, 33*(1), 85–93.
254. Hoerger, M., Chapman, B. P., Epstein, R. M., & Duberstein, P. R. (2012). Emotional intelligence: A theoretical framework for individual differences in affective forecasting. *Emotion, 12*(4), 716–725. doi:10.1037/a0026724
255. Lopes, P. N., Brackett, M. A., Nezlek, J. B., Schütz, A., Sellin, I., & Salovey, P. (2004). Emotional intelligence and social interaction. *Personality and Social Psychology Bulletin, 30,* 1018–1034.
256. O'Boyle, E. H., Jr., Humphrey, R. H., Pollack, J. M., Hawver, T. H., & Story, P. A. (2011). The relation between emotional intelligence and job performance: A meta-analysis. *Journal of Organizational Behavior, 32*(5), 788–818.
257. Zhang, H.-H., & Wang, H. (2011). A meta-analysis of the relationship between individual emotional intelligence and workplace performance. *Acta Psychologica Sinica, 43*(2), 188–202.
258. Harms, P. D., & Credé, M. (2010). Emotional intelligence and transformational and transactional leadership: A meta-analysis. *Journal of Leadership & Organizational Studies, 17*(1), 5–17.
259. Martins, A.; Ramalho, N.; Morin, E. (2010). A comprehensive meta-analysis of the relationship between emotional intelligence and health. *Personality and Individual Differences, 49,* 554–564.
260. Peterson, K., Malouff, J., & Thorsteinsson, E. B. (2011). A meta-analytic investigation of emotional intelligence and alcohol involvement. *Substance Use & Misuse, 46*(14), 1726–1733.
261. Malouff, J. M., & Schutte, N. S. (2014). Trait emotional intelligence and romantic relationship satisfaction: A meta-analysis. *American Journal of Family Therapy, 42*(1), 53–66. doi: 10.1080/01926187.2012.748549
262. Perera, H. N., & DiGiacomo, M. (2013). The relationship of trait emotional intelligence with academic performance: A meta-analytic review. *Learning and Individual Differences, 28*(12), 20–33. doi: 10.1016/j.lindif.2013.08.002
263. Schlaerth, A., Ensari, N., & Christian, J. (2013). A meta-analytical review of the relationship between emotional intelligence and leaders' constructive conflict management. *Group Processes & Intergroup Relations, 16*(1), 126–136. doi: 10.1177/1368430212439907
264. Paulhus, D. L. (2014). Toward a taxonomy of dark personalities. *Current Directions in Psychological Science, 23,* 421–426.
265. Nagler, U. K. J., Reiter, K. J., Furtner, M. R., & Rauthmann, J. F. (2014). Is there a "dark intelligence"? Emotional intelligence is used by dark personalities to emotionally manipulate others. *Personality and Individual Differences, 65*(7), 47–52. doi: 10.1016/j.paid.2014.01.025
266. Konrath, S., Corneille, O., Bushman, B. J., & Luminet, O. (2014). The relationship between narcissistic exploitativeness, dispositional empathy, and emotion recognition abilities. *Journal of Nonverbal Behavior, 38*(1), 129–143. doi: 10.1007/s10919-013-0164-y
267. Plouffe, R. A., Saklofske, D. H., & Smith, M. M. (2017). The Assessment of Sadistic Personality: Preliminary psychometric evidence for a new measure. *Personality and Individual Differences, 104,* 166–171. doi:10.1016/j.paid.2016.07.043
268. Bradley, S. J. (1990). Affect regulation and psychopathology: Bridging the mind-body gap. *Canadian Journal of Psychiatry, 35,* 540–547.
269. Greenspan, S. I., & Porges, S. W. (1984). Psychopathology in infancy and early childhood: Clinical perspectives on the organization of sensory and affective-thematic experience. *Child Development, 55,* 49–70.
270. Van Praag, H. M. (1990). Two-tier diagnosing in psychiatry. *Psychiatry Research, 34,* 1–11.
271. Thayer, R. E., Newman, R., & McClain, T. M. (1994). Self-regulation of mood: Strategies for changing a bad mood, raising energy, and reducing tension. *Journal of Personality and Social Psychology, 67,* 910–925.
272. Cohen, J., & Andrade, E. B. (2004). Affect, intuition, and task-contingent affect regulation. *Journal of Consumer Research, 31,* 358–367.
273. Mick, D. G., & DeMoss, M. (1990). Self-gifts: Phenomenological insights from four contexts. *Journal of Consumer Research, 17,* 322–332.
274. Thayer, R. E., Newman, R., & McClain, T. M. (1994). Self-regulation of mood: Strategies for changing a bad mood, raising energy, and reducing tension. *Journal of Personality and Social Psychology, 67,* 910–925.
275. Rippere, V. (1977). "What's the thing to do when you're feeling depressed?" A pilot study. *Behaviour Research and Therapy, 15,* 185–191.
276. Bremner, R. H., Koole, S. L., & Bushman, B. J. (2011). "Pray for those who mistreat you:" Effects of prayer on anger and aggression. *Personality and Social Psychology Bulletin, 37*(6), 830–837.
277. Mischkowski, D., Kross, E., & Bushman, B. J. (2012). Flies on the wall are less aggressive: Self-distanced reflection reduces angry feelings, aggressive thoughts, and aggressive behaviors. *Journal of Experimental Social Psychology, 48*(5), 1187–1191. doi: 10.1016/j.jesp.2012.03.012
278. Thayer, R. E., Newman, R., & McClain, T. M. (1994). Self-regulation of mood: Strategies for changing a bad mood, raising energy, and reducing tension. *Journal of Personality and Social Psychology, 67,* 910–925.
279. Bushman, B. J. (2002). Does venting anger feed or extinguish the flame? Catharsis, rumination, distraction, anger, and aggressive responding. *Personality and Social Psychology Bulletin, 28,* 724–731.
280. Tice, D. M., & Bratslavsky, E. (2000). Giving in to feel good: The place of emotion regulation in the context of general self-control. *Psychological Science, 11,* 149–159.
281. Erber, R., Wegner, D. M., & Therriault, N. (1996). On being cool and collected: Mood regulation in anticipation of social interaction. *Journal of Personality and Social Psychology, 70,* 757–766.
282. Erber, R., & Erber, M. W. (2000). The self-regulation of moods: Second thoughts on the importance of happiness in everyday life. *Psychological Science, 11,* 142–148.
283. Tamir, M., Mitchell, C., & Gross, J. J. (2008). Hedonic and instrumental motives in anger regulation. *Psychological Science, 19*(4), 324–328.
284. Larsen, R. J. (2000). Toward a science of mood regulation. *Psychological Inquiry, 11*(3), 129–141.
285. Thayer, R. E., Newman, R., & McClain, T. M. (1994). Self-regulation of mood: Strategies for changing a bad mood, raising energy, and reducing tension. *Journal of Personality and Social Psychology, 67,* 910–925.

286. Hyde, J. S. (2005). The gender similarities hypothesis. *American Psychologist, 60,* 581–592.
287. Nolen-Hoeksema, S. (1991). Responses to depression and their effects on the duration of depressive episodes. *Journal of Abnormal Psychology, 100,* 569–582.
288. Forster, J. L. & Jeffery, R. W. (1986). Gender differences related to weight history, eating patterns, efficacy expectations, self-esteem, and weight loss among participants in a weight reduction program. *Addictive Behaviors, 11,* 141–147.
289. Grunberg, N. E., & Straub, R. O. (1992). The role of gender and taste class in the effects of stress on eating. *Health Psychology, 11,* 97–100.
290. Berkowitz, A. D., & Perkins, H. W. (1987). Recent research on gender differences in collegiate alcohol use. *Journal of American College Health, 36,* 123–129.
291. Dube, K. C., Kumar, A., Kumar, N., & Gupta, S. P. (1978). Prevalence and pattern of drug use amongst college students. *Acta Psychiatrica Scandinavica, 57,* 336–356.
292. Engs, R. C., & Hanson, D. J. (1990). Gender differences in drinking patterns and problems among college students: A review of the literature. *Journal of Alcohol and Drug Education, 35,* 36–47.
293. Richman, J. A., & Flaherty, J. A. (1986). Sex differences in drinking among medical students: Patterns and psychosocial correlates. *Journal of Studies on Alcohol, 47,* 283–289.
294. Thayer, R. E., Newman, R., & McClain, T. M. (1994). Self-regulation of mood: Strategies for changing a bad mood, raising energy, and reducing tension. *Journal of Personality and Social Psychology, 67,* 910–925.
295. Larsen, R. J. (2000). Toward a science of mood regulation. *Psychological Inquiry, 11*(3), 129–141. Quote on p. 129
296. Schachter, S., & Singer, J. E., (1962). Cognitive, social, and physiological determinants of emotional state. *Psychological Review, 69,* 379–399.
297. Moors, A., Ellsworth, P. C., Scherer, K. R., & Frijda, N. H. (2013). Appraisal theories of emotion: State of the art and future development. *Emotion Review, 5*(2), 119–124. doi:10.1177/1754073912468165

CHAPTER 7
Attitudes, Beliefs, and Consistency

1. Airport baggage handler goes viral (19 September 2018). *CNN.* Retrieved from https://www.cnn.com/videos/travel/2018/09/19/south-africa-baggage-handler-viral-video-vpx.hln
2. Deabler, A. (2018, December 19). Restaurant sues customer over bad Facebook review: "This is slander'" *Fox News.* Retrieved from https://www.foxnews.com/food-drink/restaurant-sues-customer-over-bad-facebook-review
3. Cosgrove, J. (2018, September 23). Chasing 'likes' on Instagram, hikers break limbs—and need rescuing. *Los Angeles Times.* Retrieved from https://www.latimes.com/local/lanow/la-me-rescue-mission-increase-20180924-story.html
4. Bansal, A., Garg, C., Pakhare, A., & Gupta, S. (2018). Selfies: A boon or bane? *Journal of Family Medicine and Primary Care, 7*(4), 828-831. doi: 10.4103/jfmpc.jfmpc_109_18
5. Allport, G. (1935). Attitudes. In C. Murchinson (Ed.). *A Handbook of Social Psychology* (pp. 789–844). Worchester, MA: Clark University Press.
6. Eagly, A. H., & Chaiken, S. (1998). Attitude structure and function. In D. T. Gilbert, S. T. Fiske, & G. Lindzey (Eds.), *Handbook of social psychology* (4th ed., Vol. 1, pp. 269–322). New York: McGraw-Hill.
7. Wilson, T. D., Lindsey, S., & Schooler, T. Y. (2000). A model of dual attitudes. *Psychological Review, 107,* 101–126.
8. Hovland, C. I., Janis, I. L., & Kelley, H. H. (1953). *Communications and persuasion: Psychological studies in opinion change,* New Haven: Yale University Press.
9. Fazio, R. H., Jackson, J. R., Dunton, B. C., & Williams, C. J. (1995). Variability in automatic activation as an unobtrusive measure of racial attitudes: A bona fide pipeline? *Journal of Personality and Social Psychology, 69,* 1013–1027.
10. Henry, P. J., & Sears, D. O. (2002). The symbolic racism 2000 scale. *Political Psychology, 23,* 253–283. https://doi.org/10.1111/0162-895X.00281
11. Sawyer, J., & Gampa, A. (2018). Implicit and explicit racial attitudes changed during Black Lives Matter. *Personality and Social Psychology Bulletin, 44*(7), 1039–1059. https://doi-org.proxy.lib.umich.edu/10.1177/0146167218757454
12. Fazio, R. H., & Olson, M. A. (2003). Implicit measures in social cognition research: Their meaning and use. *Annual Review of Psychology, 54,* 297–327.
13. Olson, M. A., & Fazio, R. H. (2009). Implicit and explicit measures of attitudes: The Perspective of the MODE model. In R. E. Petty, R. H. Fazio, & P. Briñol (Eds.), *Insights from the new implicit measures* (pp. 19–63). New York: Psychology Press.
14. Rhine, R. J., Hill, S. J., & Wandruff, S. E. (1967). Evaluative responses of preschool children. *Child Development, 38,* 1035–1042.
15. Baumeister, R. F., Bratslavsky, E., Finkenauer, C., & Vohs, K. D. (2001). Bad is stronger than good. *Review of General Psychology, 5,* 323–370.
16. Rozin, P., & Royzman, E. B. (2001). Negativity bias, negativity dominance, and contagion. *Personality and Social Psychology Review, 5,* 296–320.
17. Goleman, D. (1995, August 8). Brain may tag all perceptions with a value. *New York Times,* 1–10.
18. Bargh, J. A., Chaiken, S., Raymond, P., & Hymes, C. (1996). The automatic evaluation effect: Unconditional automatic attitude activation with a pronunciation task. *Journal of Experimental Social Psychology, 32,* 104–128.
19. Cited in Goleman, D. (1995, August 8). Brain may tag all perceptions with a value. *New York Times,* 1–10.
20. Fazio, R. H., Blascovich, J., & Driscoll, D. M. (1992). On the functional value of attitudes: The influence of accessible attitudes on the ease and quality of decision making. *Personality and Social Psychology Bulletin, 18,* 388–401.
21. Fazio, R. H., & Powell, M. C. (1997). On the value of knowing one's likes and dislikes: Attitude accessibility, stress, and health in college. *Psychological Science, 8,* 430–436.
22. Bornstein, R. F. (1989). Exposure and affect: Overview and meta-analysis of research, 1968–1987. *Psychological Bulletin, 106,* 265–289.
23. Zajonc, R. B. (1968). Attitudinal effects of mere exposure. *Journal of Personality and Social Psychology, 9*(2, Pt. 2), 1–27.
24. Zajonc, R. B. (1968). Attitudinal effects of mere exposure. *Journal of Personality and Social Psychology, Monograph Supplement, 9,* 1–27.
25. Zebrowitz, L. A., White, B., & Wieneke, K. (2008). Mere exposure and racial prejudice: Exposure to other-race faces increases liking for strangers of that race. *Social Cognition, 26*(3), 259–275.
26. Mita, T. H., Dermer, M., & Knight, J. (1977). Reversed facial images and the mere-exposure hypothesis. *Journal of Personality and Social Psychology, 35,* 597–601.
27. Abakoumkin, G. (2018). Mere exposure effects in the real world: Utilizing natural experiment features from the Eurovision Song Contest. *Basic and Applied Social Psychology, 40*(4), 236–247. https://doi-org.proxy.lib.umich.edu/10.1080/01973533.2018.1474742
28. Harrison, A. A., & Fiscaro, S. A. (1974). Stimulus familiarity and alley illumination as determinants of approach response latencies of house crickets. *Perceptual and Motor Skills, 39,* 147–152.
29. Zajonc, R. B., Reimer, D. J., & Hausser, D. (1973). Imprinting and the development of object preference in chicks by mere repeated exposure. *Journal of Comparative Physiological Psychology, 83,* 434–440.
30. Harmon-Jones, E., & Allen, J. J. B. (2001). The role of affect in the mere exposure effect: Evidence from psychophysiological and individual differences approaches. *Personality and Social Psychology Bulletin, 27*(7), 889–898.
31. Cacioppo, J. T., & Petty, R. E. (1989). Effects of message repetition on argument processing, recall and persuasion. *Basic and Applied Social Psychology, 10,* 3–12.
32. Klinger, M. R., & Greenwald, A. G. (1994). Preferences need no inferences? The cognitive basis for unconscious emotional effects. In P. M. Niedenthal & S. Kitayama (Eds.), *The heart's eye: Emotional influences in perception and attention* (pp. 67–85). Orlando, FL: Academic Press.
33. Young, S. G., & Claypool, H. M. (2010). Mere exposure has differential effects on attention allocation to threatening and neutral stimuli. *Journal of Experimental Social Psychology, 46*(2), 424–427.
34. Crisp, R. J., Hutter, R. R. C., & Young, B. (2009). When mere exposure leads to less liking: The incremental threat effect in intergroup contexts. *British Journal of Psychology, 100*(1), 133–149.
35. Wells, G. L., & Petty, R. E. (1980). The effects of overt head movements on persuasion: Compatibility and incompatibility of responses. *Basic and Applied Social Psychology, 1,* 219–230.
36. Briñol, P., Gascó, M., Petty, R. E., & Horcajo, J. (2013). Treating thoughts as material objects can increase or decrease their impact on evaluation. *Psychological Science, 24*(1), 41–47. https://doi-org.proxy.lib.umich.edu/10.1177/0956797612449176
37. Olson, M. A., & Fazio, R. H. (2001). Implicit attitude formation through classical conditioning. *Psychological Science, 12,* 413–417.
38. Jonas, K., Eagly, A. H., & Stroebe, W. (1995). Attitudes and persuasion. In M. Argyle & A. M. Colman (Eds.), *Social psychology.* Harlow, UK: Longman.
39. Das, E., Bushman, B. J., Bezemer, M. D., Kerkhof, P., & Vermeulen, I. E. (2009). How terrorism news reports increase prejudice against outgroups: A Terror Management account. *Journal of Experimental Social Psychology, 45,* 453–459.
40. Albergotti, R., O'Connell, V., & Vranica, S. (2012, October 18). Lance Armstrong gets dumped: Nike, RadioShack, others distance themselves from cyclist amid drug scandal. *The Wall Street Journal.* Retrieved from http://online.wsj.com/news/articles/SB10000872396390444868204578062313532317222
41. Pendleton, M. (2014, September 9). Nike drops endorsement deal with Ray Rice. *FSS.* Retrieved from http://fullscalesports.com/2014/09/09/nike-drops-endorsement-deal-with-ray-rice/
42. Manfred, T. (2014, September 17). Nike drops Adrian Peterson. *Business Insider.* Retrieved from http://www.businessinsider.com/nike-drops-adrian-peterson-2014-9
43. Littlefield, C. (2015, July 7). Subway suspends spokesman Jared Fogle, who's been crucial to the brand. *Los Angeles Times.* Retrieved from https://www.latimes.com/nation/nationnow/la-na-nn-subway-on-jared-fogle-reports-we-are-shocked-20150707-story.html
44. Whitten, S. (2018, September 7). Nike's online sales surge in days after Kaepernick ad debut. *CNBC.* Retrieved from https://www.cnbc.com/2018/09/07/nikes-online-sales-surge-in-days-after-kaepernick-ad-debut.html
45. O'Kane, C. (2018, September 7). College drops uniforms featuring Nike logo to protest Kaepernick ad. *CBS News.* Retrieved from https://www.cbsnews.com/news/college-of-the-ozarks-drops-uniforms-featuring-nike-logo-to-protest-nikes-kaepernick-ad/
46. Bostrom, R. N., Vlandis, J. W., & Rosenbaum, M. E. (1961). Grades as reinforcing contingencies and attitude change. *Journal of Educational Psychology, 52*(2), 112–115.
47. Bandura, A. (1977). *Social learning theory.* Englewood Cliffs, NJ: Prentice Hall.
48. Bandura, A., Ross, D., & Ross, S. A. (1961). Transmission of aggression through imitation of aggressive models. *Journal of Abnormal and Social Psychology, 63,* 575–582.

49. Bandura, A., Ross, D., & Ross, S. A. (1963). Vicarious reinforcement and imitative learning. *Journal of Abnormal and Social Psychology, 67*, 601–607.

50. Bandura, A. (1965). Influence of models' reinforcement contingencies on the acquisition of imitative responses. *Journal of Abnormal and Social Psychology, 66*, 575–582.

51. Bandura, A., Ross, D., & Ross, S. A. (1963). Vicarious reinforcement and imitative learning. *Journal of Abnormal and Social Psychology, 67*, 601–607.

52. Bandura, A. (1986). *Social foundations of thought and action: A social-cognitive theory*. Englewood Cliffs, NJ: Prentice-Hall.

53. Fiske, S. T. (2004). *Social beings: A core motives approach to social psychology*. New York: Wiley.

54. Miller, A. G., McHoskey, J. W., Bane, C. M., & Dowd, T. G. (1993). The attitude polarization phenomenon: Role of response measure, attitude extremity, and behavioral consequences of reported attitude change. *Journal of Personality and Social Psychology, 64*, 561–574.

55. Tesser, A. (1976). Attitude polarization as a function of thought and reality constraints. *Journal of Research in Personality, 10*, 183–194.

56. Wilson, T. D., Dunn, D. S., Kraft, D., & Lisle, D. J. (1989). Introspection, attitude change, and attitude-behavior consistency: The disruptive effects of explaining why we feel the way we do. In M. P. Zanna (Ed.), *Advances in experimental social psychology* (Vol. 22, pp. 287–343). San Diego: Academic Press.

57. Wilson, T. D., Hodges, S. D., & LaFleur, S. J. (1995). Effects of introspecting about reasons: Inferring attitudes from accessible thoughts. *Journal of Personality and Social Psychology, 69*, 16–28.

58. Miller, A. G., McHoskey, J. W., Bane, C. M., & Dowd, T. G. (1993). The attitude polarization phenomenon: Role of response measure, attitude extremity, and behavioral consequences of reported attitude change. *Journal of Personality and Social Psychology, 64*, 561–574.

59. Schulz, A. (2018). Where populist citizens get the news: An investigation of news audience polarization along populist attitudes in 11 countries. *Communication Monographs*. https://doi-org.proxy.lib.umich.edu/10.1080/03637751.2018.1508876

60. Lord, C. G., Ross, L., & Lepper, M. R. (1979). Biased assimilation and attitude polarization: The effects of prior theories on subsequently considered evidence. *Journal of Personality and Social Psychology, 37*, 2098–2109.

61. Mackie, D., & Cooper, J. (1984). Attitude polarization: Effects of group membership. *Journal of Personality and Social Psychology, 46*, 575–585.

62. Aronson, E., & Mills, J. (1959). The effect of severity of initiation on liking for a group. *Journal of Abnormal and Social Psychology, 59*, 177–181.

63. Xygalatas, D., Mitkidis, P., Fischer, R., Reddish, P., Skewes, J., Geertz, A.W., Roepstorff, A., & Builbulia, J. (2013). Extreme rituals promote prosociality. *Psychological Science, 24*, 1602–1605.

64. Linder, D. E., Cooper, J., & Jones, E. E. (1967). Decision freedom as a determinant of the role of incentive magnitude in attitude change. *Journal of Personality and Social Psychology, 6*, 245–254.

65. Zanna, M. P., & Cooper, J. (1974). Dissonance and the pill: An attribution approach to studying the arousal properties of dissonance. *Journal of Personality and Social Psychology, 29*, 703–709.

66. Zanna, M., Higgins, E. & Taves, P. (1976). Is dissonance phenomenologically aversive? *Journal of Experimental Social Psychology, 12*, 530–538.

67. Comer, R., & Laird, J. D. (1975). Choosing to suffer as a consequence of expecting to suffer: Why do people do it? *Journal of Personality and Social Psychology, 32*, 92–101.

68. Knobloch-Westerwick, S. (2014). *Choice and preference in media use: Advances in selective exposure theory and research*. New York: Routledge.

69. Otero, V. (2019). Media Bias Chart: Version 4. Retrieved August 16, 2019 from https://www.adfontesmedia.com

70. Pariser, E. (2011). *The filter bubble: What the Internet is hiding from you*. New York: Penguin Press.

71. Kitayama, S., & Markus, H. R. (1999). Yin and Yang of the Japanese self: The cultural psychology of personality coherence. In D. Cervone (Ed.), *The coherence of personality: Social-cognitive bases of consistency, variability, and organization* (pp. 242–302). New York: Guilford Press.

72. Heine, S. J., & Lehman, D. R. (1997). Culture, dissonance, and self-affirmation. *Personality and Social Psychology Bulletin, 23*, 389–400.

73. Hoshino-Browne, E., Zanna, A. S., Spencer, S. J., Zanna, M. P., Kitayama, S., & Lackenbauer, S. (2005). On the cultural guises of cognitive dissonance: The case of Easterners and Westerners. *Journal of Personality and Social Psychology, 89*, 294–310.

74. Kitayama, S., Snibbe, A. C., Markus, H. R., & Suzuki, T. (2004). Is there any "free" choice? Cognitive dissonance in two cultures. *Psychological Science, 15*, 527–533.

75. LaPiere, R. T. (1934). Attitudes vs. actions. *Social Forces, 13*, 230–237.

76. Wicker, A. W. (1969). Attitudes versus actions: The relationship of verbal and overt behavioral responses to attitude object. *Journal of Social Issues, 25*, 41–78.

77. Forrest, A. (2019, January 24). Prominent 'gay conversion therapist' comes out as gay and offers apology. *Independent*. Retrieved from https://www.independent.co.uk/news/world/americas/gay-conversion-therapy-therapist-comes-out-utah-mormon-david-matthews-lgbtq-a8744361.html?fbclid=IwAR3nTByKLsoFInD7SXP4RTu5HROalUHU7Vd5novMKlmsoLZCh4Gpjfz9Rpg

78. Ajzen, I., & Fishbein, M. (1977). Attitude-behavior relations: A theoretical analysis and review of empirical research. *Psychological Bulletin, 84*, 888–918.

79. Baumeister, R. F. (2000). Gender differences in erotic plasticity: The female sex drive as socially flexible and responsive. *Psychological Bulletin, 126*, 347–374.

80. Laumann, E. O., Gagnon, J. H., Michael, R. T., & Michaels, S. (1994). *The social organization of sexuality: Sexual practices in the United States*. Chicago: University of Chicago Press.

81. Antonovsky, H. F., Shoham, I., Kavenocki, S., Modan, B., & Lancet, M. (1978). Sexual attitude-behavior discrepancy among Israeli adolescent girls. *Journal of Sex Research, 14*, 260–272.

82. Christensen, H. T., & Carpenter, G. R. (1962). Value-behavior discrepancies regarding premarital coitus in three Western cultures. *American Sociological Review, 27*, 66–74.

83. Croake, J. W., & James, B. (1973). A four year comparison of premarital sexual attitudes. *Journal of Sex Research, 9*, 91–96.

84. Herold, E. S., & Mewhinney, D.-M. K. (1993). Gender differences in casual sex and AIDS prevention: A survey of dating bars. *Journal of Sex Research, 30*, 36–42.

85. Hansen, G. L. (1987). Extradyadic relations during courtship. *Journal of Sex Research, 23*, 382–390.

86. Beck, J. G., Bozman, A. W., & Qualtrough, T. (1991). The experience of sexual desire: Psychological correlates in a college sample. *Journal of Sex Research, 28*, 443–456.

87. O'Sullivan, L. F., & Allgeier, E. R. (1998). Feigning sexual desire: Consenting to unwanted sexual activity in heterosexual dating relationships. *Journal of Sex Research, 35*, 234–243.

88. Rushton, J. P., Brainerd, C. J., & Pressley, M. (1983). Behavioral development and construct validity: The principle of aggregation. *Psychological Bulletin, 94*, 18–38.

89. Fazio, R. H., & Towles-Schwen, T. (1999). The MODE model of attitude-behavior processes. In S. Chaiken (Ed.), *Dual-process theories in social psychology* (pp. 97–116). New York: Guilford Press.

90. Ajzen, I. (2001). Nature and operation of attitudes. In T. Fiske, D. L. Schacter, & C. Zahn-Waxler (Eds.), *Annual review of psychology* (Vol. 52, pp. 27–58). Palo Alto, CA: Annual Reviews.

91. Fazio, R. H. (1990). Multiple processes by which attitudes guide behavior: The MODE model as an integrative frame work. In P. Zanna (Ed.), *Advances in experimental social psychology* (Vol. 23, pp. 75–109). San Diego: Academic Press.

92. Kraus, S. J. (1995). Attitudes and the prediction of behavior: A meta-analysis of the empirical literature. *Personality and Social Psychology Bulletin, 21*, 58–75.

93. Ajzen, I. (2012). The theory of planned behavior. In P. A. M. Lange, A. W. Kruglanski, & E. T. Higgins (Eds.), *Handbook of theories of social psychology* (Vol. 1, pp. 438–459). London, U.K.: Sage.

94. Armitage, C. J., & Conner, M. (2001). Efficacy of the theory of planned behaviour: A meta-analytic review. *British Journal of Social Psychology, 40*, 471–499.

95. Gilbert, D. T., Tafarodi, R. W., & Malone, P. S. (1993). You can't not believe everything you read. *Journal of Personality and Social Psychology, 65*, 221–233.

96. Gilbert, D. T. (1991). How mental systems believe. *American Psychologist, 46*, 107–119.

97. Gilbert, D. T. (1993). The assent of man: Mental representation and the control of belief. In D. Wegner & J. Pennebaker (Eds.), *Handbook of mental control* (pp. 57–87). Englewood Cliffs, NJ: Prentice-Hall.

98. Gilbert, D. T. (1991). How mental systems believe. *American Psychologist, 46*, 107–119.

99. Gilbert, D. T. (1991). How mental systems believe. *American Psychologist, 46*, 107–119.

100. Gilbert, D. T. (1993). The assent of man: Mental representation and the control of belief. In D. Wegner & J. Pennebaker (Eds.), *Handbook of mental control* (pp. 57–87). Englewood Cliffs, NJ: Prentice-Hall.

101. Ross, L., Lepper, M. R., & Hubbard, M. (1975). Perseverance in self-perception and social perception: Biased attributional processes in the debriefing paradigm. *Journal of Personality and Social Psychology, 32*, 880–892.

102. Anderson, C. A., Lepper, M. R., & Ross, L. (1980). The perseverance of social theories: The role of explanation in the persistence of discredited information. *Journal of Personality and Social Psychology, 39*, 1037–1049.

103. Anderson, C. A., & Sechler, E. S. (1986). Effects of explanation and counterexplanation on the development and use of social theories. *Journal of Personality and Social Psychology, 20*, 24–34.

104. Lord, C. G., Lepper, M. R., & Preston, E. (1984). Considering the opposite: A corrective strategy for social judgment. *Journal of Personality and Social Psychology, 47*, 1231–1243.

105. Janoff-Bulman, R. (1992). *Shattered assumptions: Towards a new psychology of trauma*. New York: Free Press.

106. Bulman, R. J., & Wortman, C. B. (1977). Attributions of blame and coping in the "real world": Severe accident victims react to their lot. *Journal of Personality and Social Psychology, 35*, 351–363.

107. Taylor, S. E. (1983). Adjustment to threatening events: A theory of cognitive adaptation. *American Psychologist, 38*, 1161–1173.

108. Wills, T. A. (1981). Downward comparison principles in social psychology. *Psychological Bulletin, 90*, 245–271.

109. Pargament, K. I. (1997). *The psychology of religion and coping. Theory, research, practice*. New York: Guilford Press.

110. Smith, T. B., McCullough, M. E., & Poll, J. (2003). Religiousness and depression: Evidence for a main effect and the moderating influence of stressful life events. *Psychological Bulletin, 129*, 614–636.

111. Frazier, P., Tashiro, T., Berman, M., Steger, M., & Long, J. (2004), Correlates of levels and patterns

111. of positive life changes following sexual assault. *Journal of Consulting and Clinical Psychology, 72,* 19–30.
112. Bazargan, S., Sherkat, D. E., & Bazargan, M. (2004). Religion and alcohol use among African-American and Hispanic inner-city emergency care patients. *Journal for the Scientific Study of Religion, 43,* 419–428.
113. Burris, C. T., Harmon-Jones, E., & Tarpley, W. R. (1997). "By faith alone": Religious agitation and cognitive dissonance. *Basic and Applied Social Psychology, 19,* 17–31.
114. Bryner, J. (2018, April 23). The "end of the world" is today. Here's why we're still here. Live Science. Retrieved from https://www.livescience.com/62378-doomsday-april-23.html
115. Festinger, L., Riecken, H. W., & Schachter, S. (1956). *When prophecy fails: A social and psychological study of a modern group that predicted the destruction of the world.* New York: Harper-Torchbooks.
116. Exline, J. J. (2002). Stumbling blocks on the religious road: Fractured relationships, nagging vices, and the inner struggle to believe. *Psychological Inquiry, 13,* 182–189.
117. Exline, J. J., & Rose, E. (2005). Religious and spiritual struggles. In R. F. Paloutzian & C. L. Park (Eds.), *Handbook of the psychology of religion* (pp. 315–330). New York: Guilford Press.
118. Exline, J. J., Park, C. L., Smyth, J. M., & Carey, M. P. (2011). Anger toward God: Social-cognitive predictors, prevalence, and links with adjustment to bereavement and cancer. *Journal of Personality and Social Psychology, 100*(1), 129–148.
119. Tobacyk, J., & Milford, G. (1983). Belief in paranormal phenomena: Assessment instrument development and implications for personality functioning. *Journal of Personality and Social Psychology, 44,* 1029–1037.
120. Tobacyk, J. J., & Downs, A. (1986). Personal construct threat and irrational beliefs as cognitive predictors of increases in musical performance anxiety. *Journal of Personality and Social Psychology, 51*(4), 779–782.
121. Thompson, M. P., Norris, F. H., & Hanacek, B. (1993). Age differences in the psychological consequences of Hurricane Hugo. *Psychology and Aging, 8,* 606–616.
122. Persons, J. B., & Rao, P. A. (1985). Longitudinal study of cognitions, life events, and depression in psychiatric inpatients. *Journal of Abnormal Psychology, 94,* 51–63.
123. Daly, M. J., & Burton, R. L. (1983). Self-esteem and irrational beliefs: An exploratory investigation with implications for counseling. *Journal of Counseling Psychology, 30,* 361–366.
124. Gilovich, T. (1983). Biased evaluation and persistence in gambling. *Journal of Social and Personal Psychology, 44,* 1110–1126.

CHAPTER 8
Social Influence and Persuasion

1. Naylor, B. (2018, September 14). Sharks in the water? FEMA tries to fight "fake news" as Florence hits. *NPR.* Retrieved from https://www.npr.org/2018/09/14/647935099/sharks-in-the-water-fema-tries-to-fight-fake-news-as-florence-hits
2. World Economic Forum (2013). Top 10 trends of 2014. Retrieved from http://reports.weforum.org/outlook-14/top-ten-trends-category-page/top-10-trends-of-2014-introduction/
3. Flood, A. (2016). "Post-truth" named word of the year by Oxford Dictionaries. *The Guardian.* Retrieved from https://www.theguardian.com/books/2016/nov/15/post-truth-named-word-of-the-year-by-oxford-dictionaries
4. Vosoughi, S., Roy, D. & Aral, S. (2018). The spread of true and false news online. *Science, 359*(6380), 1146–1151. DOI: 10.1126/science.aap9559
5. O'Connor, G. (2017, April 3). How Russian Twitter bots pumped out fake news during the 2016 election. *NPR.* Retrieved from https://www.npr.org/sections/alltechconsidered/2017/04/03/522503844/how-russian-twitter-bots-pumped-out-fake-news-during-the-2016-election
6. van der Linden, S., Leiserowitz, A., Rosenthal, S., & Maibach, E. (2017). Inoculating the public against misinformation about climate change. *Global Challenges, 1,* 1600008. http://dx.doi.org/10.1002/gch2.201600008
7. McCright, A. M., Charters, M., Dentzman, K., & Dietz, T. (2016). Examining the effectiveness of climate change frames in the face of a climate change denial counter-frame. *Topics in Cognitive Science, 8,* 76–97. http://dx.doi.org/10.1111/tops.12171
8. Lewandowsky, S., Ecker, U. H., & Cook, J. (2017). Beyond misinformation: Understanding and coping with the 'post-truth' era. *Journal of Applied Research in Memory and Cognition, 6*(4), 353–369. doi:10.1016/j.jarmac.2017.07.00
9. Lewandowsky, S., Ecker, U. H., & Cook, J. (2017). Beyond misinformation: Understanding and coping with the 'post-truth' era. *Journal of Applied Research in Memory and Cognition, 6*(4), 353–369. doi:10.1016/j.jarmac.2017.07.00
10. Jang, S. M., & Kim, J. K. (2018). Third person effects of fake news: Fake news regulation and media literacy interventions. *Computers in Human Behavior,* 80295-302. doi:10.1016/j.chb.2017.11.034
11. Davison, W. P. (1983). The third-person effect in communication. *Public Opinion Quarterly, 47,* 1–15.
12. Deutsch, M., & Gerard, H. B. (1955). A study of normative and informational social influences upon individual judgment. *Journal of Abnormal and Social Psychology, 51,* 629–636.
13. Asch, S. E. (1955, November). Opinions and social pressure. *Scientific American,* 31–35.
14. Asch, S. E. (1955, November). Opinions and social pressure. *Scientific American,* 31–35.
15. Asch, S. E. (1955, November). Opinions and social pressure. *Scientific American,* 31–35.
16. Schachter, S. (1951). Deviation, rejection, and communication. *Journal of Abnormal and Social Psychology, 46*(2), 190–207.
17. Tata, J., Anthony, T., Lin, H., Newman, B., Tang, S., Millson, M., & Suvakumar, K. (1996). Proportionate group size and rejection of the deviate: A meta-analytic integration. *Journal of Social Behavior and Personality, 11,* 739–752.
18. Tata, J., Anthony, T., Lin, H., Newman, B., Tang, S., Millson, M., & Suvakumar, K. (1996). Proportionate group size and rejection of the deviate: A meta-analytic integration. *Journal of Social Behavior and Personality, 11,* 739–752.
19. Sherif, M. (1935). A study of some social factors in perception. *Archives of Psychology* (Columbia University), *187,* 60.
20. Rohrer, J. H., Baron, S. H., Hoffman, E. L., & Swander, D. V. (1954). The stability of autokinetic judgments. *Journal of Abnormal and Social Psychology, 49*(4, Pt. 1), 595–597.
21. Jacobs, R. C., & Campbell, D. T. (1961). The perpetuation of an arbitrary tradition through several generations of a laboratory microculture. *Journal of Abnormal and Social Psychology, 62,* 649–658.
22. Buzinski, S. G., Clark, J., Cohen, M., Buck, B., & Roberts, S. P. (2018). Insidious assumptions: How pluralistic ignorance of studying behavior relates to exam performance. *Teaching of Psychology, 45*(4), 333–339. https://doi-org.proxy.lib.umich.edu/10.1177/0098628318796919
23. Mercier, H., & Sperber, D. (2011). Why do humans reason? Arguments for an argumentative theory. *Behavioral and Brain Sciences, 34*(2), 57–74.
24. Cialdini, R. B. (2001). *Influence: Science and practice* (4th ed.). Boston: Allyn and Bacon.
25. Hall, J. R. (1987). *Gone from the promised land: Jonestown in American cultural history.* New Brunswick: Transaction Books.
26. Ornstein, R. (1991). *The evolution of consciousness: Of Darwin, Freud, and cranial fire: The origins of the way we think.* New York: Prentice Hall.
27. Freedman, J. L. & Fraser, S. C. (1966). Compliance without pressure: The foot-in-the-door technique. *Journal of Personality and Social Psychology, 4*(2), 195–202. DOI: 10.1037/h0023552
28. Cialdini, R. B., Cacioppo, J. T., Bassett, R., & Miller, J. A. (1978). Low-ball procedure for producing compliance: Commitment then cost. *Journal of Personality and Social Psychology, 36,* 463–476.
29. Cialdini, R. B. (2001). *Influence: Science and practice* (4th ed.). Boston: Allyn and Bacon.
30. Cialdini, R. B. (2001). *Influence: Science and practice* (4th ed.). Boston: Allyn and Bacon.
31. Cialdini, R. B. (2001). *Influence: Science and practice* (4th ed.). Boston: Allyn and Bacon.
32. Cialdini, R. B., Eisenberg, N., Green, B. L., Rhoads, K., & Bator, R. (1998). Undermining the undermining effect of reward on sustained interest: When unnecessary conditions are sufficient. *Journal of Applied Social Psychology, 28,* 249–263.
33. Tybout, A. M., & Yalch, R. F. (1980). The effect of experience: A matter of salience? *Journal of Consumer Research, 6,* 406–413.
34. Cialdini, R. B., & Schroeder, D. A. (1976). Increasing compliance by legitimizing paltry contributions: When even a penny helps. *Journal of Personality and Social Psychology, 34*(4), 599–604.
35. Lee, S., Moon, S.-I., & Feeley, T. H. (2016). A meta-analytic review of the legitimization of paltry favors compliance strategy. *Psychological Reports, 118*(3), 748–771. https://doi-org.proxy.lib.umich.edu/10.1177/0033294116647690
36. Cialdini, R. B. (2001). *Influence: Science and practice* (4th ed.). Boston: Allyn and Bacon.
37. Myers, D. G. (2006). *Social psychology* (8th ed.). New York: McGraw Hill.
38. Cialdini, R. B. (2001). *Influence: Science and practice* (4th ed.). Boston: Allyn and Bacon.
39. Miller, R. L., Seligman, C., Clark, N. T., & Bush, M. (1976). Perceptual contrast versus reciprocal concession as mediators of induced compliance. *Journal of Behavioral Science, 7,* 401–409.
40. Schwarzwald, J., Raz, M., & Zvibel, M. (1979). The applicability of the door-in-the-face technique when established behavioral customs exist. *Journal of Applied Social Psychology, 9,* 576–586.
41. Cialdini, R. B., Vincent, J., Lewis, S., Catalan, J., Wheeler, D., & Darby, B. L. (1975). Reciprocal concessions procedure for inducing compliance: The door-in-the-face technique. *Journal of Personality and Social Psychology, 31,* 206–215.
42. Burger, J. M. (1986). Increasing compliance by improving the deal: The that's-not-all technique. *Journal of Personality and Social Psychology, 51,* 277–283.
43. Cialdini, R. B. (2001). *Influence: Science and practice* (4th ed.). Boston: Allyn and Bacon.
44. Worchel, S., Lee, J., & Adewole, A. (1975). Effects of supply and demand on ratings of object value. *Journal of Personality and Social Psychology, 32,* 906–914.
45. Cialdini, R. B. (2001). *Influence: Science and practice* (4th ed.). Boston: Allyn and Bacon.
46. Santos, M. D., Leve, C., & Pratkanis, A. R. (1994). Hey buddy, can you spare seventeen cents? Mindful persuasion and the pique technique. *Journal of Applied Social Psychology, 24,* 755–764.
47. Glionna, J. M. (2013, January 30). New Aspen speed limit—14 miles an hour? *Los Angeles Times.* Retrieved from http://articles.latimes.com/2013/jan/30/nation/la-na-nn-new-aspen-speed-limit-14-miles-an-hour-20130130
48. Davis, B. P., & Knowles, E. S. (1999). A disrupt-then-reframe technique of social influence. *Journal of Personality and Social Psychology, 76,* 192–199.
49. Mercier, H., & Sperber, D. (2011). Why do humans reason? Arguments for an argumentative theory. *Behavioral and Brain Sciences, 34*(2), 57–74.
50. *Why We Fight.* Retrieved from http://history.acusd.edu/gen/filmnotes/whywefight.html
51. Hovland, C., Lumsdaine, A., & Sheffield, F. (1949). *Experiments on mass communication: Studies in social psychology in World War II* (Vol. 3). Princeton, NJ: Princeton University Press.

52. Hovland, C. I., Janis, I. L., & Kelley, H. H. (1953). *Communication and persuasion.* New Haven: Yale University Press.
53. *Rhet.* I.3, 1358a37ff.
54. McCausland, P. (2018, February 9). #MeToo advocate and California lawmaker accused of sexual misconduct. *NBC News.* Retrieved from https://www.nbcnews.com/storyline/sexual-misconduct/metoo-advocate-california-lawmaker-accused-sexual-misconduct-n846421
55. Hovland, C. I., & Weiss, W. (1951). The influence of source credibility on communication effectiveness. *Public Opinion Quarterly, 15,* 635–650.
56. Pratkanis, A. R., Greenwald, A. G., Leippe, M. R., & Baumgardner, M. H. (1988). In search of reliable persuasion effects: III. The sleeper effect is dead: Long live the sleeper effect. *Journal of Personality and Social Psychology, 54,* 203–218.
57. Brenan, M. (2017, December 26). Nurses keep healthy lead as most honest, ethical profession. *Gallup Economy.* https://news.gallup.com/poll/224639/nurses-keep-healthy-lead-honest-ethical-profession.aspx?g_source=Economy&g_medium=newsfeed&g_campaign=tiles
58. Erickson, B., Lind, E. A., Johnson, B. C., & O'Barr, W. M. (1978). Speech style and impression formation in a court setting: The effects of "powerful" and "powerless'" speech. *Journal of Experimental Social Psychology, 14,* 266–279.
59. Newcombe, D., & Arnkoff, D. B. (1979). Effects of speech style and sex of speaker on person perception. *Journal of Personality and Social Psychology, 37,* 1293–1303.
60. Levine, J. M., & Valle, R. S. (1975) The convert as a credible communicator. *Social Behavior and Personality, 3,* 81–90.
61. Levine, J. M., & Valle, R. S. (1975). The convert as a credible communicator. *Social Behavior and Personality, 3,* 81–90.
62. *Rhet.* II.1, 1378a6ff.
63. Miller, N., Maruyama, G., Beaber, R. J., & Valone, K. (1976). Speed of speech and persuasion. *Journal of Personality and Social Psychology, 34,* 615–624.
64. Smith, S. M., & Shaffer, D. R. (1991). Celerity and cajolery: Rapid speech may promote or inhibit persuasion through its impact on message elaboration. *Personality and Social Psychology Bulletin, 17,* 663–669.
65. Miller, N., Maruyama, G., Beaber, R. J., & Valone, K. (1976). Speed of speech and persuasion. *Journal of Personality and Social Psychology, 34,* 615–624.
66. Mackie, D. M., Worth L. T., & Asuncion, A. G. (1990). Processing of persuasive in-group messages. *Journal of Personality and Social Psychology, 58,* 812–822.
67. Budesheim, T. L., & DePaola, S. J. (1994). Beauty or the beast? The effects of appearance, personality and issue information on evaluations of political candidates. *Personality and Social Psychology Bulletin, 20,* 339–348.
68. Efran, M. G., & Patterson, E. W. J. (1974). Voters vote beautiful: The effects of physical appearance on a national election. *Canadian Journal of Behavioral Science, 6,* 352–356.
69. Hovland, C., Lumsdaine, A., & Sheffield, F. (1949). *Experiments on mass communication: Studies in social psychology in World War II* (Vol. 3). Princeton, NJ: Princeton University Press.
70. cp. *Rhet.* II.1, 1378a1ff.
71. Janis, I. L., Kaye, D., & Kirschner, P. (1965). Facilitating effects of "eating-while-reading" on responsiveness to persuasive communications. *Journal of Personality and Social Psychology, 1*(2), 181–186.
72. Unger, L. S. (1996). The potential for using humor in global advertising. *Humor, 9,* 143–168.
73. Duncan, C. P., & Nelson, J. E. (1985). Effects of humor in a radio advertising experiment. *Journal of Advertising, 14,* 33–40, 64.
74. Gruner, C. R. (1985). Advice to the beginning speaker on using humor: What the research tells us. *Communication Education, 34,* 142–147.
75. Cantor, J. R., & Venus, P. (1980). The effect of humor on recall of a radio advertisement. *Journal of Broadcasting, 24,* 13–22.
76. Janis, I. L. (1967). Effects of fear arousal on attitude change: Recent developments in theory and experimental research. *Advances in Experimental Social Psychology, 4,* 166–224.
77. Rogers, E. M. (1983). *Diffusion of innovations.* New York: Free Press.
78. De Hoog, N., Stroebe, W., & De Wit, J. B. F. (2007). The impact of vulnerability to and severity of a health risk on processing and acceptance of fear-arousing communications: A meta-analysis. *Review of General Psychology, 11*(3), 258–285.
79. Newman, A. (2001, February 4). Anti-smoking campaign: Rotten teeth and dead babies. *New York Times Magazine,* p. 16. Available at www.nytimes.com/
80. Ort, A., & Fahr, A. (2018). Using efficacy cues in persuasive health communication is more effective than employing threats—An experimental study of a vaccination intervention against Ebola. *British Journal of Health Psychology, 23*(3), 665–684. https://doi-org.proxy.lib.umich.edu/10.1111/bjhp.12310
81. Hovland, C. I., Janis, I. L., & Kelley, H. H. (1953). *Communication and persuasion.* New Haven: Yale University Press.
82. Janis, I. L., & Feshbach, S. (1953). Effects of fear-arousing communications. *Journal of Abnormal and Social Psychology, 48,* 78–92.
83. Morris, K. A., & Swann, W. B., Jr. (1996). Denial and the AIDS crisis: Wishing away the threat of aids. In S. Oskamp & S. Thompson (Eds.), *Safer sex in the '90s* (pp. 57–79). New York: Sage.
84. Budesheim, T. L., Houston, D. A., & DePaola, S. J. (1996). The persuasiveness of in-group and out-group political messages: The case of negative political campaigning. *Journal of Personality and Social Psychology, 70,* 523–534.
85. Houston, D. A., Doan, K. A., & Roskos-Ewoldsen, D. (1999). Negative political advertising and choice conflict. *Journal of Experimental Psychology: Applied, 5,* 3–16.
86. Walster, E., & Festinger, L. (1962). The effectiveness of "overheard" persuasive communication. *Journal of Abnormal and Social Psychology, 65,* 395–402.
87. Kardes, F. R. (1988). Spontaneous inference processes in advertising: The effects of conclusion omission and involvement on persuasion. *Journal of Consumer Research, 15,* 225–233.
88. Ocean's 8 (2018) product placement scenes. *Product Placement Blog.* Retrieved from https://productplacementblog.com/tag/oceans-8-2018/page/4/
89. Thinkexist.com Retrieved from http://thinkexist.com/quotation/a_good_advertisement_is_one_which_sells_the/202773.html[COMP: Please pass query on to pages. AU: Please provide full source information.]
90. Nelson, M. R. (2002). Recall of brand placements in computer/video games. *Journal of Advertising Research, 42,* 80–92.
91. Janiszewski, C., Noel, H., & Sawyer, A. G. (2003). A meta-analysis of the spacing effect in verbal learning: Implications for research on advertising repetition and consumer memory. *Journal of Consumer Research, 30,* 138–149.
92. Cacioppo, J. T., & Petty, R. E. (1989). Effects of message repetition on argument processing, recall and persuasion. *Basic and Applied Social Psychology, 10,* 3–12.
93. *Dictionary of Marketing Terms* (2004).
94. Parsley, A. (2009). 5 Things to Know About TV's Progressive Insurance Lady. *People.* Retrieved from http://www.people.com/people/article/0,,20301774,00.html
95. Falcone, L. B.(2009, October 7). Insurance pitchgirl a surprise TV hit: Going with the flo. *Boston Herald.* Retrieved from http://bostonherald.com/news_opinion/columnists/2009/10/insurance_pitchgirl_surprise_tv_hit
96. Northrup, L. (2012, October 24). I hate Progressive Insurance for waking me up over and over. *Consumerist.* Retrieved from https://consumerist.com/2012/10/24/i-hate-progressive-insurance-for-waking-me-up-over-and-over/
97. Pratkanis, A. R., & Aronson, E. (1992). *Age of propaganda: The everyday use and abuse of persuasion.* New York: Henry Holt.
98. Smith, G. F., & Dorfman, D. D. (1975). The effect of stimulus uncertainty on the relationship between frequency of exposure and liking. *Journal of Personality and Social Psychology, 31,* 150–155.
99. Hovland, C., Lumsdaine, A., & Sheffield, F. (1949). *Experiments on mass communication: Studies in social psychology in World War II* (Vol. 3). Princeton, NJ: Princeton University Press.
100. Hovland, C. I., & Weiss, W. (1951). The influence of source credibility on communication effectiveness. *Public Opinion Quarterly, 15,* 635–650.
101. McGuire, W. J. (1968). Personality and susceptibility to social influence. In E. F. Borgotta & W. W. Lambert (Eds.), *Handbook of personality theory and research* (pp. 1130–1187). Chicago: Rand McNally.
102. Rhodes, N., & Wood, W. (1992). Self-esteem and intelligence affect influenceability: The mediating role of message reception. *Psychological Bulletin, 111,* 156–171.
103. Cacioppo, J. T., & Petty, R. E. (1982). The need for cognition. *Journal of Personality and Social Psychology, 42,* 116–131. Quote from p. 116.
104. Ahlering, R. F. (1987). Need for cognition, attitudes, and the 1984 Presidential election. *Journal of Research in Personality, 21,* 100–102.
105. Cacioppo, J. T., & Petty, R. E. (1982). The need for cognition. *Journal of Personality and Social Psychology, 42,* 116–131. Quote from p. 116.
106. Bushman, B. J. (1993). What's in a name? The moderating role of public self-consciousness on the relation between brand label and brand preference. *Journal of Applied Psychology, 78,* 857–861.
107. Hang-Pil, S., & Shavitt, S. (1994). Persuasion and culture: Advertising appeals in individualistic and collectivistic societies. *Journal of Experimental Social Psychology, 30,* 326–350.
108. Wang, C. L., Bristol, T., Mowen J. C., & Chakraborty, G. (2000). Alternative modes of self-construal: Dimensions of connectedness-separateness and advertising appeals to the cultural and gender-specific self. *Journal of Consumer Psychology, 9,* 107–115.
109. Petty, R. E., & Cacioppo, J. T. (1986). *Communication and persuasion: Central and peripheral routes to attitude change.* New York: Springer-Verlag.
110. Eagly, A. H., & Chaiken, S. (1998). Attitude structure and function. In D. T. Gilbert, S. T. Fiske, & G. Lindzey (Eds.), *Handbook of social psychology* (4th ed., Vol. 1, pp. 269–322). New York: McGraw-Hill.
111. Apsler, R., & Sears, D. O. (1968). Warning, personal involvement, and attitude change. *Journal of Personality and Social Psychology, 9,* 162–168.
112. Blankenship, K. L., & Wegener, D. T. (2008). Opening the mind to close it: Considering a message in light of important values increases message processing and later resistance to change. *Journal of Personality and Social Psychology, 94*(2), 196–213.
113. Tsal, Y. (1984). *The role of attention in processing information from advertisements.* Unpublished manuscript, Cornell University, Ithaca, NY.
114. Cacioppo, J. T., & Petty, R. E. (1980). Sex differences in influenceability: Toward specifying the underlying processes. *Personality and Social Psychology Bulletin, 6*(4), 651–656.
115. Lord, C. G., Ross, L., & Lepper, M. R. (1979). Biased assimilation and attitude polarization: The effects of prior theories on subsequently considered evidence. *Journal of Personality and Social Psychology, 37,* 2098–2109.
116. Petty, R. E., & Cacioppo, J. T. (1979). Issue involvement can increase or decrease persuasion by

116. enhancing message-relevant cognitive responses. *Journal of Personality and Social Psychology, 37*, 1915–1926.
117. McGuire, W. J. (1961). The effectiveness of supportive refutational defenses in immunizing and restoring beliefs against persuasion. *Sociometry, 24*, 184–197.
118. McGuire, W. J. (1964). Inducing resistance to persuasion: Some contemporary approaches. *Advances in Experimental Social Psychology, 1*, 191–229.
119. McGuire, W. J., & Papageorgis, D. (1961). The relative efficacy of various types of prior belief-defense in producing immunity against persuasion. *Journal of Abnormal Social Psychology, 62*, 327–337.
120. Papageorgis, D., & McGuire, W. J. (1961). The generality of immunity to persuasion produced by pre-exposure to weakened counterarguments. *Journal of Abnormal and Social Psychology, 62*, 475–481.
121. Perry, C. L., Killen, J., Slinkard, L. A., & McAlister, A. L. (1980). Peer teaching and smoking prevention among junior high students. *Adolescence, 15*, 277–281.
122. Chassin, L., Presson, C. C., Sherman, S. J., & Edwards, D. A. (1990). The natural history of cigarette smoking: Predicting young-adult smoking outcomes from adolescent smoking patterns. *Health Psychology, 9*, 701–716.
123. Falck, R., & Craig, R. (1988). Classroom-oriented primary prevention programming for drug abuse. *Journal of Psychoactive Drugs, 20*, 403–408.
124. Compton, J. A., & Pfau, M. (2004). Use of inoculation to foster resistance to credit card marketing targeting college students. *Journal of Applied Communication Research, 32*(4), 343–364.
125. Wong, N. C. H. (2016). "Vaccinations are safe and effective": Inoculating positive HPV vaccine attitudes against antivaccination attack messages. *Communication Reports, 29*(3), 127–138. https://doi-org.proxy.lib.umich.edu/10.1080/08934215.2015.10
126. Parker, K. A., Rains, S. A., & Ivanov, B. (2016). Examining the "blanket of protection" conferred by inoculation: The effects of inoculation messages on the cross-protection of related attitudes. *Communication Monographs, 83*(1), 49–68. https://doi-org.proxy.lib.umich.edu/10.1080/036377 51.2015.1030681
127. Tormala, Z. L., & Petty, R. E. (2002). What doesn't kill me makes me stronger: The effects of resisting persuasion on attitude certainty. *Journal of Personality and Social Psychology, 83*, 1298–1313.
128. Parker, K. A., Rains, S. A., & Ivanov, B. (2016). Examining the "blanket of protection" conferred by inoculation: The effects of inoculation messages on the cross-protection of related attitudes. *Communication Monographs, 83*(1), 49–68. https://doi-org.proxy.lib.umich.edu/10.1080/036377 51.2015.1030681
129. Freedman, J. L., & Sears, D. O. (1965). Warning, distraction, and resistance to influence. *Journal of Personality and Social Psychology, 1*(3), 262–266.
130. For college students, yes, sleep matters. *WebMD*. Retrieved from https://www.webmd.com/sleep -disorders/features/for-college-students-sleep -matters
131. Gilbert, D. T. (1991). How mental systems believe. *American Psychologist, 46*, 107–119.

CHAPTER 9
Prosocial Behavior: Doing What's Best for Others

1. Nowak, M., & Roch, S. (2006). Upstream reciprocity and the evolution of gratitude. *Proceedings of the Royal Society of London, Series B: Biological Sciences, 274*, 605–609.
2. Tran, C. (2014, August 6). All heave! Commuters work together to free with their bare hands man whose leg had become stuck between platform and train. *DailyMail*. Retrieved August 26, 2019 from http:// www.dailymail.co.uk/news/article-2717511/Train -commuters-managed-free-man-leg-stuck-to.html
3. Fowler, J. H., & Christakis, N. A. (2010). Cooperative behavior cascades in human social networks. *PNAS, 107*(12), 5334–5338. doi: 10.1073/pnas.0913149107
4. Veenhoven, R. (2004). *World database of happiness: Continuous register of scientific research on subjective appreciation of life*. Retrieved August 26, 2019 from http://www.eur.nl/fsw/research/happiness
5. Lee, C. (1995). Prosocial organizational behaviors: The roles of workplace justice, achievement striving, and pay satisfaction. *Journal of Business and Psychology, 10*, 197–206.
6. Satow, K. L. (1975). Social approval and helping. *Journal of Experimental Social Psychology, 11*, 501–509.
7. Whatley, M. A., Webster, J. M., Smith, R. H., & Rhodes, A. (1999). The effect of a favor on public and private compliance: How internalized is the norm of reciprocity? *Basic and Applied Social Psychology, 21*, 251–259.
8. Triandis, H. C. (1978). Some universals of social behavior. *Personality and Social Psychology Bulletin, 4*, 1–16.
9. Kunz, P. R., & Woolcott, M. (1976). Season's greetings: From my status to yours. *Social Science Research, 5*, 269–278.
10. Ferriere, R. (1998, June 11). Help and you shall be helped. *Nature, 393*, 517–519.
11. Fisher, J. D., & Nadler, A. (1976). Effects of donor resources on recipient self-esteem and self-help. *Journal of Experimental Social Psychology, 12*(2), 139–150.
12. Dowd, J. J. (1975). Aging as exchange: A preface to theory. *Journal of Gerontology, 30*(5), 584–594.
13. McCullough, M. E., Kimeldorf, M. B., & Cohen, A. D. (2008). An adaptation for altruism? The social causes, social effects, and social evolution of gratitude. *Current Directions in Psychological Science, 17*(4), 281–285.
14. Biel, A., Eek, D., & Gaerling, T. (1999). The importance of fairness for cooperation public-goods dilemmas. In P. Juslin (Ed.), *Judgment and decision making: Neo-Brunswikian and process-tracing approaches* (pp. 245–259). Mahwah, NJ: Erlbaum.
15. Buss, D. M. (1999). *Evolutionary psychology: The new science of the mind*. New York: Allen & Bacon.
16. Allen, N. B., & Badcock, P. B. T. (2003). The social risk hypothesis of depressed mood: Evolutionary, psychosocial, and neurobiological perspectives. *Psychological Bulletin, 129*, 887–913.
17. Filiberti, A., Ripamonti, C., Totis, A., Ventafridda, V., De Conno, F., Contiero, P., & Tamburini, M. (2001). Characteristics of terminal cancer patients who committed suicide during a home palliative care program. *Journal of Pain and Symptom Management, 22*, 544–553.
18. Join Joiner, T., Pettit, J. W., Walker, R. L., Voelz, Z. R., Cruz, J., Rudd, M. D., & Lester, D. (2002). Perceived burdensomeness and suicidality: Two studies on the suicide notes of those attempting and those completing suicide. *Journal of Social & Clinical Psychology, 21*, 531–545.
19. Exline, J. J., & Lobel, M. (1999). The perils of outperformance: Sensitivity about being the target of a threatening upward comparison. *Psychological Bulletin, 125*, 307–337.
20. Muller, D., Bushman, B. J., Subra, B., & Ceaux, E. (2012). Are people more aggressive when they are worse off or better off than others? *Social Psychological and Personality Science, 3*(6), 754-759. DOI: 10.1177/1948550612436984
21. de Waal, F. B. M., & Davis, J. M. (2003). Capuchin cognitive ecology: Cooperation based on projected returns. *Neuropsychologia, 41*, 221–228.
22. Austin, W., McGinn, N. C., & Susmilch, C. (1980). Internal standards revisited: Effects of social comparisons and expectancies on judgments of fairness and satisfaction. *Journal of Experimental Social Psychology, 16*, 426–441.
23. Hassebrauck, M. (1986). Ratings of distress as a function of degree and kind of inequity. *Journal of Social Psychology, 126*, 269–270.
24. Tomasello, M. (2016) *A natural history of morality*. Cambridge, MA: Harvard.
25. Berscheid, E., & Walster, E. (1967). When does a harm-doer compensate a victim? *Journal of Personality and Social Psychology, 6*, 433–441.
26. Chemyak, N., Leimgruber, K.L., Dunham, Y.C., Hu, J., & Blake, P.R. (in press). Paying back those who harmd us but not those who helped us: Direct negative reciprocity precedes direct positive reciprocity in early development. *Psychological Science*.
27. Hofmann, W., Wisneski, D.C., Brandt, M.J., & Skitka, L.J. (2014). Morality in everyday life. *Science, 345*, 1340–1343.
28. Ruedy, N.E., Moore, C., Gino, F., & Schweitzer, M.E. (2013). The cheater's high: The unexpected affective benefits of unethical behavior. *Journal of Personality and Social Psychology, 105*, 531–548.
29. Kouchaki, M., & Smith, I.H. (2014). The Morning Morality Effect: The influence of time of day on unethical behavior. *Psychological Science, 25*, 95–102.
30. Frimer, J. A., Schaefer, N. K., & Oakes, H. (2014). Moral actor, selfish agent. *Journal of Personality and Social Psychology, 106*, 790–802.
31. Haidt, J. (2001). The emotional dog and its rational tail: A social intuitionist approach to moral judgment. *Psychological Review, 108*, 814–834.
32. Haidt, J. (2007). The new synthesis in moral psychology. *Science, 316*, 998–1002.
33. Foot, P. (1967). The problem of abortion and the doctrine of double effect. *Oxford Review, 5*, 5–15.
34. Greene, J. D., Sommerville, R. B., Nystrom, L. E., Darley, J. M., Cohen, J. D. (2001). An fMRI investigation of emotional engagement in moral judgment. *Science, 293*, 2105–2108.
35. Knobe, J. (2003). Intentional action and side effects in ordinary language. *Analysis, 63*, 190–194.
36. Knobe, J. (2010). Person as scientist, person as moralist. *Behavioral and Brain Sciences, 33*, 315–329.
37. Graham, J., Haidt, J., & Nosek, B. A. (2009). Liberals and conservatives rely on different sets of moral foundations. *Journal of Personality and Social Psychology, 96*, 1029–1046.
38. Helzer, E. G., & Pizarro, D. A. (2011). Dirty liberals! Reminders of physical cleanliness influence moral and political attitudes. *Psychological Science, 22*, 517–522.
39. Axelrod. R. (1980). More effective choice in the prisoner's dilemma. *Journal of Conflict Resolution, 24*, 3–25.
40. Beggan, J. K., Messick, D. M., & Allison, S. T. (l988). Social values and egocentric bias: Two tests of the might over morality hypothesis. *Journal of Personality and Social Psychology, 55*, 606–611.
41. Liebrand, W. B. G., Wilke, H. A. M., & Wolters, F. J. M. (1986). Value orientation and conformity. A study using three types of social dilemma games. *Journal of Conflict Resolution, 30*, 77–97.
42. Kelley, H. H., & Stahelski, A. J. (1970). Social interaction basis of cooperators' and competitors' beliefs about others. *Journal of Personality and Social Psychology, 16*, 66–91.
43. Miller, D. T., & Holmes, J. G. (1975). The role of situational restrictiveness on self-fulfilling prophecies: A theoretical and empirical extension of Kelley and Stahelski's triangle hypothesis. *Journal of Personality & Social Psychology, 31*, 661–673.
44. Misra, S, & Kalro, A. (1979). Triangle effect and the connotative meaning of trust in prisoner's dilemma: A cross cultural study. International *Journal of Psychology, 14*, 255–263.
45. Green, L., Price, P. C., & Hamburger, M. E. (1995). Prisoner's dilemma and the pigeon: Control by immediate consequences. *Journal of the Experimental Analysis of Behavior, 64*, 1–17.

46. For excellent summary, see Tomasello, M. (2013) *A natural history of human thinking*. Cambridge, MA: Harvard University Press.
47. White, A. E., Kenrick, D. T., Li, Y. J., Mortensen, C. R., Neuberg, S. L., & Cohen, A. B. (2012). When nasty breeds nice: Threats of violence amplify agreeableness at national, individual, and situational levels. *Journal of Personality and Social Psychology, 103*, 622–634.
48. Fehr, E., & Gächter, S. (2002). Altruistic punishment in humans. *Nature, 415*, 137–140.
49. Mussweiler, T., & Ockenfels, A. (2013). Similarity increases altruistic punishment in humans. *PNAS*, early edition, http://www.pnas.org/cgi/doi/10.1073/pnas.1215443110.
50. Feinberg, M., Willer, R., Stellar, J., & Keltner, D. (2012). The virtues of gossip: Reputational information sharing as prosocial behavior. *Journal of Personality and Social Psychology, 102*, 1015–1030.
51. Khadjavi, M., & Lange, A. (2013). Prisoners and their dilemma. *Journal of Economic Behavior & Organization, 92*(8), 163–175. doi: 10.1016/j.jebo.2013.05.015
52. Wright R. (2000). *Non zero: The logic of human destiny*. New York: Pantheon.
53. Balliet, D., Li, N. P., Macfarlan, S. J., Van Vugt, M. (2011). Sex differences in cooperation: a meta-analytic review of social dilemmas. *Psychological Bulletin, 137*(6), 881–909.
54. http://www.apa.org/news/press/releases/2011/09/cooperate-equally.aspx
55. Benenson, J. F. (2014). *Warriors and worriers: The survival of the sexes*. Oxford, UK: Oxford University Press.
56. Steinfatt, T. M. (1973). The Prisoner's Dilemma and a creative alternative game: The effects of communications under conditions of real reward. *Simulation and Games, 4*, 389–409.
57. Miller, J., Butts, C. T., & Rodes, D. (2002). Communication and cooperation. *Journal of Economic Behavior and Organization, 47*, 179–195.
58. Kiesler, S., Sproull, L., & Waters, K. (1996). A prisoner's dilemma experiment on cooperation with people and human-like computers. *Journal of Personality and Social Psychology, 70*, 47–65.
59. Exline, J. J., Worthington, E. L., Hill, P., & McCullough, M. E. (2003). Forgiveness and justice: A research agenda for social and personality psychology. *Personality and Social Psychology Review, 7*, 337–348.
60. Vohs, K. D., Mead, N. L., & Goode, M. R. (2006, November). The psychological consequences of money. *Science, 314*(5802), 1154–1156.
61. 1 Timothy 6:10 (Bible).
62. McCullough, M. E., Pargament, K. I., & Thoresen, C. E. (Eds.) (2000). *Forgiveness: Theory, research, and practice*. New York: Guilford.
63. Finkel, E. J., Rusbult, C. E., Kumashiro, M., & Hannon, P. (2002). Dealing with betrayal in close relationships: Does commitment promote forgiveness? *Journal of Personality and Social Psychology, 82*, 956–974.
64. Fenell, D. (1993). Characteristics of long-term first marriages. *Journal of Mental Health Counseling, 15*, 446–460.
65. Fincham, F. D., Hall, J. H., & Beach, S. R. H. (2005). 'Til lack of forgiveness doth us part: Forgiveness in marriage. In E. L. Worthington (Ed.), *Handbook of forgiveness* (pp. 207–226). New York: Wiley.
66. Kachadourian, L. K., Fincham, F. D., & Davila, J. (2004). The tendency to forgive in dating and married couples: Association with attachment and relationship satisfaction. *Personal Relationships, 11*, 373–393.
67. Kachadourian, L. K., Fincham, F. D., & Davila, J. (2005). Attitudinal ambivalence, rumination and forgiveness of partner transgressions in marriage. *Personality and Social Psychology Bulletin, 31*, 334–342.
68. Paleari, G., Regalia, C., & Fincham, F. D. (2005). Marital quality, forgiveness, empathy, and rumination: A longitudinal analysis. *Personality and Social Psychology Bulletin, 31*, 368–378.
69. Coyle, C. T., & Enright, R. D. (1997). Forgiveness intervention with post-abortion men. *Journal of Consulting and Clinical Psychology, 65*, 1042–1046.
70. Freedman, S. R., & Enright, R. D. (1996). Forgiveness as an intervention goal with incest survivors. *Journal of Consulting and Clinical Psychology, 64*, 983–992.
71. Witvliet, C. V. O., Ludwig, T. E., & Van der Laan, K. L. (2001). Granting forgiveness or harboring grudges: Implications for emotion, physiology, and health. *Psychological Science, 121*, 117–123.
72. Kelln, B. R. C., & Ellard, J. H. (1999). An equity theory analysis of the impact of forgiveness and retribution on transgressor compliance. *Personality and Social Psychology Bulletin, 25*, 864–872; see also Wallace, H. M., Exline, J. J., & Baumeister, R. F. (2008). Interpersonal consequences of forgiveness: Does forgiveness deter or encourage repeat offenses? *Journal of Experimental Social Psychology, 44*, 453–460.
73. McNulty, J. K. (2011). The dark side of forgiveness: The tendency to forgive predicts continued psychological and physical aggression in marriage. *Personality and Social Psychology Bulletin, 37*(6), 770–783.
74. Fincham, F. D., Beach, S. R., & Davila, J. (2004). Forgiveness and conflict resolution in marriage. *Journal of Family Psychology, 18*, 72–81.
75. Kearns, J. N., & Fincham, F. D. (2005). Victim and perpetrator accounts of interpersonal transgressions: Self-serving or relationship-serving biases? *Personality and Social Psychology Bulletin, 31*, 321–333.
76. Hall, J. H., & Fincham, F. D. (2006). Relationship dissolution following infidelity: The roles of attributions and forgiveness. *Journal of Social and Clinical Psychology, 25*, 508–522.
77. Exline, J. J., Worthington, E. L., Hill, P., & McCullough, M. E. (2003). Forgiveness and justice: A research agenda for social and personality psychology. *Personality and Social Psychology Review, 7*, 337–348.
78. Exline, J. J., Worthington, E. L., Hill, P., & McCullough, M. E. (2003). Forgiveness and justice: A research agenda for social and personality psychology. *Personality and Social Psychology Review, 7*, 337–348.
79. Darby, B. W., & Schlenker, B. R. (1982). Children's reactions to apologies. *Journal of Personality and Social Psychology, 43*, 742–753.
80. Gonzales, M. H., Haugen, J. A., & Manning, D. J. (1994). Victims as "narrative critics": Factors influencing rejoinders and evaluative responses to offenders' accounts. *Personality and Social Psychology Bulletin, 20*, 691–704.
81. Exline, J. J., Baumeister, R. F., Zell, A. L., Kraft, A. J., & Witvliet, C. V. O. (2008). Not so innocent: Does seeing one's own capability for wrongdoing predict forgiveness? *Journal of Personality and Social Psychology, 94*, 495–515.
82. McCullough, M. E., Bono, G., & Root, L. M. (2007). Rumination, emotion, and forgiveness: Three longitudinal studies. *Journal of Personality and Social Psychology, 92*, 490–505.
83. Tsang, J.-A., McCullough, M. E., & Hoyt, W. T. (2005). Psychometric and rationalization accounts for the religion-forgiveness discrepancy. *Journal of Social Issues. 61*, 785–805.
84. Matthew 6:12 (Bible).
85. Pronk, T. M., Karremans, J. C., Overbeek, G., Vermulst, A. A., & Wigboldus, D. H. J. (2010). What it takes to forgive: When and why executive functioning facilitates forgiveness. *Journal of Personality and Social Psychology, 98*(1), 119–131.
86. Balliet, D., Li, N. P., & Joireman, J. (2011). Relating trait self-control and forgiveness within prosocials and proselfs: Compensatory versus synergistic models. *Journal of Personality and Social Psychology, 101*(5), 1090–1105.
87. Exline, J. J., Baumeister, R. F., Bushman, B. J., Campbell, W. K., & Finkel, E. J. (2004). Too proud to let go: Narcissistic entitlement as a barrier to forgiveness. *Journal of Personality and Social Psychology, 87*, 894–912.
88. Exline, J. J., & Zell, A. L. (2009). Empathy, self-affirmation, and forgiveness: The moderating roles of gender and entitlement. *Journal of Social and Clinical Psychology, 28*(9), 1071–1099.
89. Milgram, S. (1963). Behavioral study of obedience. *Journal of Abnormal and Social Psychology, 67*, 371–378.
90. Burger, J. M. (2009). Replicating Milgram: Would people still obey today? *American Psychologist, 64*(1), 1–11.
91. Bègue, L., Beauvois J.-L., Courbet, D., Oberlé, D., Lepage, J., & Duke, A. A. (2015). Personality predicts obedience in a Milgram paradigm. *Journal of Personality, 83*(3), 299–306. doi: 10.1111/jopy.12104
92. Silfver, M., Helkama, K., Lönnqvist, J.-E., & Verkasalo, M. (2008). The relation between value priorities and proneness to guilt, shame, and empathy. *Motivation and Emotion, 32*(2), 69–80.
93. Insko, C. A., Smith, R. H., Alicke, M. D., Wade, J., & Taylor, S. (1985). Conformity and group size: The concern with being right and the concern with being liked. *Personality and Social Psychology Bulletin, 11*, 41–50.
94. Munger, K., & Harris, S. J. (1989). Effects of an observer on handwashing in a public restroom. *Perceptual and Motor Skills, 69*, 733–734.
95. Guzmán, R. A., Rodríguez-Sickert, C., & Rowthorn, R. (2007). When in Rome, do as the Romans do: The coevolution of altruistic punishment, conformist learning, and cooperation. *Evolution and Human Behavior, 28*(2), 112–117.
96. Murray, D. R., Trudeau, R., & Schaller, M. (2011). On the origins of cultural differences in conformity: Four tests of the pathogen prevalence hypothesis. *Personality and Social Psychology Bulletin, 37*(3), 318–329.
97. Ariely, D., & Levav, J. (2000). Sequential choice in group settings: Taking the road less traveled and less enjoyed. *Journal of Consumer Research, 27*, 279–290.
98. Dunning, D., Anderson, J. E., Schlösser, T., Ehlebracht, D., & Fetchenhauer, D. (2014). Trust at zero acquaintance: More a matter of respect than expectation of reward. *Journal of Personality and Social Psychology, 107*(1), 122–141. doi: 10.1037/a0036673
99. Simpson, J. A. (2007). Foundations of interpersonal trust. In A. W. Kruglanski & E. T. Higgins (Eds.), *Social psychology: Handbook of basic principles* (2nd ed., pp. 587–607) New York: Guilford Press.
100. Miller, J. E., & Rempel, J. K. (2004) Trust and partner-enhancing attributions in close relationships. *Personality and Social Psychology Bulletin, 30*, 695–705.
101. Newman, E. J., Sanson, M., Miller, E. K., Quigley-McBride, A., Foster, J. L., Bernstein, D. M., & Garry, M. (2014). People with easier to pronounce names promote truthiness of claims. *PLOS ONE, 9*(2): e88671. doi: 10.1371/journal.pone.0088671. Retrieved August 26, 2019 from http://www.plosone.org/article/info%3Adoi%2F10.1371%2Fjournal.pone.0088671
102. Fetchenhauer, D., & Dunning, D. (2009). Do people trust too much or too little? *Journal of Economic Psychology, 30*, 263–276.
103. Righetti, F., & Finkenauer, C. (2011). If you are able to control yourself, I will trust you: The role of perceived self-control in interpersonal trust. *Journal of Personality and Social Psychology, 100*, 874–886.
104. Gervais, W. M., Shariff, A. F., & Norenzayan, A. (2011). Do you believe in atheists? Distrust is central to anti-atheist prejudice. *Journal of Personality and Social Psychology, 101*, 1189–1206.
105. Murray, S. L., Holmes, J. G., & Collins, N. L. (2006). Optimizing assurance: The risk regulation system in relationships. *Psychological Bulletin, 132*, 641–666.

106. Wieselquist, J., Rusbult, C. E., Foster, C. A., & Agnew, C. R. (1999). Commitment, pro-relationship behavior, and trust in close relationships. *Journal of Personality and Social Psychology, 77*, 942–966.
107. Rotenberg, K. J., Addis, N., Betts, L. R., Corrigan, A., Fox, C., Hobson, Z., Rennison, S., Trueman, M., & Boulton, M. J. (2010). The relation between trust beliefs and loneliness during early childhood, middle childhood, and adulthood. *Personality and Social Psychology Bulletin, 36*, 1086–1100.
108. Dawkins, R. (1976/1989). *The selfish gene.* New York: Oxford University Press.
109. Richard Dawkins, an original thinker who bashes orthodoxy. (2011, 19 September). *New York Times.* Retrieved August 26, 2019 from http://www.nytimes.com/2011/09/20/science/20dawkins.html?pagewanted5all
110. Darwin, C. (1859). *The origin of species by means of natural selection, or the preservation of favoured races in the struggle for life.* Reprinted from the 6th edition in New York, A. L. Burt Company, not dated.
111. Hamilton, W. D. (1964). The genetical evolution of social behaviour I and II. *Journal of Theoretical Biology, 7*, 1–16 and 17–52.
112. Burnstein, E., Crandall, C., & Kitayama, S. (1994). Some neo-Darwinian decision rules for altruism: Weighing cues for inclusive fitness as a function of the biological importance of the decision. *Journal of Personality and Social Psychology, 67*, 773–789.
113. Segal, N. L. (1984). Cooperation, competition and altruism within twin sets: A reappraisal. *Ethology and Sociobiology, 5*, 163–177.
114. Sime, J. D. (1983). Affiliative behavior during escape to building exits. *Journal of Environmental Psychology, 3*, 21–41.
115. Warneken, F., & Tomasello, M. (2006). Altruistic helping in human infants and young chimpanzees. *Science, 311*, 1301–1303.
116. Konrath, S., O'Brien, E., & Hsing, C. (2011). Changes in dispositional empathy in American college students over time: A meta-analysis. *Personality and Social Psychology Review, 15*, 180–198.
117. Bryner, J. (2010, May 28). Today's college students lack empathy. *LiveScience.* Retrieved August 26, 2019 from http://www.livescience.com/9918-today-college-students-lack-empathy.html
118. Anderson, C. A., Shibuya, A., Ihori, N., Swing, E. L., Bushman, B. J., Sakamoto, A., Rothstein, H. R., Saleem, M., & Barlett, C. P. (2010). Violent video game effects on aggression, empathy, and prosocial behavior in Eastern and Western countries: A meta-analytic review. *Psychological Bulletin, 136*(2), 151–173. doi: 10.1037/a0018251
119. Anderson, C. A., Shibuya, A., Ihori, N., Swing, E. L., Bushman, B. J., Sakamoto, A., Rothstein, H. R., Saleem, M., & Barlett, C. P. (2010). Violent video game effects on aggression, empathy, and prosocial behavior in Eastern and Western countries: A meta-analytic review. *Psychological Bulletin, 136*(2), 151–173. doi: 10.1037/a0018251
120. Greitemeyer, T., & Mügge, D. O. (2014). Video games do affect social outcomes: A meta-analytic review of the effects of violent and prosocial video game play. *Personality and Social Psychology Bulletin, 40*(5), 578–589. doi: 10.1177/0146167213520459
121. Batson, C. D., Batson, J. G., Slingsby, J. K., Harrell, K. L., Peekna, H. M., & Todd, R. M. (1991). Empathic joy and the empathy-altruism hypothesis. *Journal of Personality and Social Psychology, 61*, 413–426.
122. Batson, C. D., Duncan, B. D., Ackerman, P., Buckley, T., & Birch, K. (1981). Is empathic emotion a source of altruism motivation? *Journal of Personality and Social Psychology, 40*, 290–302.
123. Aknin, L. B., Barrington-Leigh, C. P., Dunn, E. W., Helliwell, J. F., Burns, J., Biswas-Diener, R., Kemerza, I., Nyende, P., Ashton-James, C. E., & Norton, M. I. (2013). Prosocial spending and well-being: Cross-cultural evidence for a psychological universal. *Journal of Personality and Social Psychology, 104*, 635–652.
124. Hepach, R., Vaish, A., & Tomasello, M. (2012). Young children are intrinsically motivated to see others helped. *Psychological Science, 23*, 967–972.
125. Baumeister, R. F. (2005). *The cultural animal: Human nature, meaning, and social life.* New York: Oxford University Press.
126. Peterson, C., & Seligman, M. E. P. (2004). *Character strengths and virtues.* New York: Oxford University Press.
127. Snyder, C. R., & Lopez, S. (Eds.) (2002). *Handbook of positive psychology.* New York: Oxford University Press.
128. "Junk DNA" defines differences between humans and chimps. (2011, October 25). *ScienceDaily.* Retrieved August 26, 2019 from http://www.sciencedaily.com/releases/2011/10/111025122615.htm
129. Silk, J. B., Brosnan, S. F., Vonk, J., Henrich, J., Povinelli, D. J., Richardson, A. S., Lambeth, S. P., Mascaro, J., & Schapiro, S. J. (2005, October 27). Chimpanzees are indifferent to the welfare of unrelated group members. *Nature, 437*, 1357–1359.
130. Cited in Robinson, P. (1995). *Schindler's List teaching guide.* Available August 26, 2019 at http://www.southerninstitute.info/holocaust_education/schind.html
131. Oliner, S. P., & Oliner, P. M. (1988). *The altruistic personality: Rescuers of Jews in Nazi Europe.* New York: The Free Press. Also see Midlarsky, E., Jones, S. F., & Corley, R. P. (2005). Personality correlates of heroic rescue during the holocaust. *Journal of Personality, 73*, 907–934.
132. Rushton, J. P., Fulker, D. W., Neale, M. C., Nias, D. K. B., & Eysenck, H. J. (1986). Altruism and aggression: The heritability of individual differences. *Journal of Personality and Social Psychology, 50*, 1192–1198.
133. Rushton, J. P., Chrisjohn, R. D., & Fekken, G. C. (1981). The altruistic personality and the Self-Report Altruism Scale. *Personality and Individual Differences, 2*, 293–302.
134. Rushton, J. P., Fulker, D. W., Neale, M. C., Nias, D. K. B., & Eysenck, H. J. (1986). Altruism and aggression: The heritability of individual differences. *Journal of Personality and Social Psychology, 50*, 1192–1198.
135. Emswiller, T., Deaux, K., & Willits, J. E. (1971). Similarity, sex, and requests for small favors. *Journal of Applied Social Psychology, 1*, 284–291.
136. Siem, B., & Stürmer, S. (2012). Cross-cultural volunteerism: Examining the effects of intercultural (dis)similarities on volunteers' motivations to support international students. *Basic and Applied Social Psychology, 34*(6), 544–557. doi: 10.1080/01973533.2012.727316
137. Eagly, A. H. & Crowley, M. (1986). Gender and helping behavior: A meta-analytic view of the social psychological literature. *Psychological Bulletin, 100*, 283–308.
138. Carnegie Hero Fund Commission. (2002). Requirements for a Carnegie Medal. Available August 26, 2019 at http://www.carnegiehero.org/nominate.php
139. Aries, E. J., & Johnson, F. L. (1983). Close friendship in adulthood: Conversational content between same-sex friends. *Sex Roles, 9*, 1183–1196.
140. Eisenberg, N., & Lennon, R. (1983). Sex differences in empathy and related capacities. *Psychological Bulletin, 94*, 100–131.
141. Hoffman, M. L. (1977). Sex differences in empathy and related behaviors. *Psychological Bulletin, 84*, 712–722.
142. Penner, L. A., Dertke, M. C., & Achenbach, C. J. (1973). The "flash" system: A field study of altruism. *Journal of Applied Social Psychology, 3*, 362–370.
143. Pomazal, R. J. & Clore, G. L. (1973). Helping on the highway: The effects of dependency and sex. *Journal of Applied Social Psychology, 3*, 150–164.
144. Harrell, W. A. (1978). Physical attractiveness, self-disclosure, and helping behavior. *Journal of Social Psychology, 104*, 15–17.
145. Benson, P. L., Karabenick, S. A., & Lerner, R. M. (1976). Pretty pleases: The effects of physical attractiveness, race, and sex on receiving help. *Journal of Experimental Social Psychology, 12*, 409–415.
146. West, S. G., & Brown, T. J. (1975). Physical attractiveness, the severity of the emergency and helping: A field experiment and interpersonal simulation. *Journal of Experimental Social Psychology, 11*, 531–538.
147. Laumann, E. O., Gagnon, J. H., Michael, R. T., & Michaels, S. (1994). *The social organization of sexuality: Sexual practices in the United States.* Chicago: University of Chicago Press.
148. Couch, D., & Liamputtong, P. (2008). Online dating and mating: The use of the internet to meet sexual partners. *Qualitative Health Research, 18*(2), 268–279.
149. Griscom, R. (2002, November). Why are online personals so hot? *Wired.* Retrieved August 26, 2019 from http://www.wired.com/wired/archive/10.11/view.html?pg52
150. Maticka-Tyndale, E., Herold, E. S., & Mewhinney, D. (1998). Casual sex on spring break: Intentions and behaviors of Canadian students. *The Journal of Sex Research, 35*, 254–264.
151. Also see Baumeister, R. F., & Vohs, K. D. (2004). Sexual economics: Sex as female resource for social exchange in heterosexual interactions. *Personality and Social Psychology Review, 8*(4), 339–363.
152. Hewstone, M. (1990). The "Ultimate Attribution Error"? A review of the literature on intergroup causal attribution. *European Journal of Social Psychology, 20*, 311–335.
153. Furnham, A. (2003). Belief in a just world: Research progress over the past decade. *Personality and Individual Differences, 34*, 795–817.
154. Lerner, M. J., & Miller, D. T. (1978). Just world research and the attribution process: Looking back and ahead. *Psychological Bulletin, 85*, 1030–1051.
155. Lerner, M. J., & Simmons, C. H. (1966). Observer's reaction to the "innocent victim": Compassion or rejection? *Journal of Personality and Social Psychology, 4*, 203–210.
156. Zuckerman, M. (1975). Belief in a just world and altruistic behavior. *Journal of Personality and Social Psychology, 31*, 972–997.
157. DePalma, M. T., Madey, S. F., Tillman, T. C., & Wheeler, J. (1999). Perceived patient responsibility and belief in a just world affect helping. *Basic and Applied Social Psychology, 21*, 131–137.
158. MacLean, M. J. & Chown, S. M. (1988). Just world beliefs and attitudes toward helping elderly people: A comparison of British and Canadian university students. *International Journal of Aging and Human Development, 26*, 249–260.
159. Zuckerman, M. (1975). Belief in a just world and altruistic behavior. *Journal of Personality and Social Psychology, 31*, 972–997.
160. Cunningham, M. R. (1979). Mood, and helping behavior: Quasi experiments with the Sunshine Samaritan. *Journal of Personality and Social Psychology 37*, 1947–1956.
161. Isen, A. M., & Levin, P. F. (1972). Effect of feeling good on helping: Cookies and kindness. *Journal of Personality and Social Psychology, 21*, 384–388.
162. Rosenhan, D. L., & White, G. M. (1967). Observation and rehearsal as determinants of prosocial behavior. *Journal of Personality and Social Psychology, 5*, 424–431.
163. Whitaker, J. L., & Bushman, B. J. (2012). "Remain calm. Be kind": Effects of relaxing video games on aggressive and prosocial behavior. *Social Psychological and Personality Science, 3*(1), 88–92. doi: 10.1177/1948550611409760
164. Manning, R., Levine, M., & Collins, A. (2007). The Kitty Genovese murder and the social psychology of helping: The parable of the 38 witnesses. *American Psychologist, 62*, 555–562.
165. Plötner, M., Over, H., Carpenter, M., and Tomasello, M. (2015, April). Young children show the bystander effect in helping situations. *Psychological Science, 26*, 499–506.

166. Latané, B., & Darley, J. (1968). Group inhibition of bystander intervention in emergencies. *Journal of Personality and Social Psychology, 10,* 215–221.
167. Shotland, R. L., & Straw, M. K. (1976). Bystander response to an assault: When a man attacks a woman. *Journal of Personality and Social Psychology, 34,* 990–999.
168. Darley, J. M., & Latané, B. (1968). Bystander intervention in emergencies: *Journal of Personality & Social Psychology, 8,* 377–383.
169. Cramer, R. E., McMaster, M. R., Bartell, P. A., & Dragna, M. (1988). Subject competence and minimization of the bystander effect. *Journal of Applied Social Psychology, 18,* 1133–1148.
170. Piliavin, I. M., Piliavin, J. A. & Rodin, J. (1975). Costs, diffusion, and the stigmatized victim. *Journal of Personality and Social Psychology, 32,* 429–438.
171. Darley, J. M. & Batson, C. D. (1973). From Jerusalem to Jericho: A study of situational and dispositional variables in helping behavior. *Journal of Personality and Social Psychology, 27,* 100–108.
172. Darley, J. M. & Batson, C. D. (1973). From Jerusalem to Jericho: A study of situational and dispositional variables in helping behavior. *Journal of Personality and Social Psychology, 27,* 100–108.
173. Cialdini, R. B. (1993) *Influence: Science and practice* (3rd ed.) (p. 113). New York: Harper-Collins.
174. Beaman, A. L., Barnes, P. J., & Klentz, B. (1978). Increasing helping rates through information dissemination: Teaching pays. *Personality and Social Psychology Bulletin, 4,* 406–411.
175. Rosenhan, D. L., & White, G. M. (1967). Observation and rehearsal as determinants of prosocial behavior. *Journal of Personality and Social Psychology, 5,* 424–431.
176. Hearold, S. (1986). A synthesis of 1043 effects of television on social behavior. In G. Comstock (Ed.), *Public communication and behavior* (pp. 65–133). New York: Academic Press.
177. Gentile, D. A., Anderson, C. A., Yukawa, S., Ihori, N., Saleem, M., Ming, L. K., Liau, A. K., Khoo, A., Bushman, B. J., Huesmann, L. R., & Sakamoto, A. (2009). The effects of prosocial video games on prosocial behaviors: International evidence from correlational, longitudinal, and experimental studies. *Personality and Social Psychology Bulletin, 35*(6), 752–763.
178. Greitemeyer, T. (2009). Effects of songs with prosocial lyrics on prosocial thoughts, affect, and behavior. *Journal of Experimental Social Psychology, 45*(1), 186–190.
179. Bureau of Labor Statistics (2014; February 25). Volunteering in the United States, 2013. Retrieved August 26, 2019 from http://www.bls.gov/news.release/volun.nr0.htm
180. Veenhoven, R. (2004). Challenges for Quality of Life in the Contemporary World. *World database of happiness: Continuous register of scientific research on subjective appreciation of life* (pp. 75–89). Retrieved August 25, 2019 from https://link.springer.com/chapter/10.1007/978-1-4020-2903-5_6
181. Milgram, S. (1963). Behavioral study of obedience. *Journal of Abnormal and Social Psychology, 67,* 371–378.

CHAPTER 10
Aggression & Antisocial Behavior

1. Rwanda: How the genocide happened. (2004, December 18). *BBC News.* Retrieved August 25, 2019 from http://news.bbc.co.uk/2/hi/africa/1288230.stm
2. Timeline: Rwanda. (2008, August 8). *BBC News.* Retrieved August 25, 2019 from http://news.bbc.co.uk/2/hi/africa/1070329.stm
3. Smith, R. (2003, December 3). The impact of hate media in Rwanda. *BBC News.* Retrieved August 25, 2019 from http://news.bbc.co.uk/2/hi/africa/3257748.stm
4. De Brouwer, A.-M. (2005). *Supranational criminal prosecution of sexual violence: The ICC and the practice of the ICTY and the ICTR.* Mortsel, Belgium: Intersentia.
5. The triumph of evil. (1995). *PBS Frontline.* Retrieved from http://www.pbs.org/wgbh/pages/frontline/shows/evil
6. Rever, J. (2018). *In praise of blood: The crimes of the Rwandan Patriotic Front.* Toronto, Canada. Random House Canada.
7. Himbara, D. (2017). *Kagame's killing fields.* North Charleston, South Carolina. CreateSpace Independent Publishing Platform.
8. http://www.globalsecurity.org/military/world/war/congo.htm
9. Paul Rusesabagina. (2006, September 29). *BBC nNews.* Retrieved October 20, 2019 from http://news.bbc.co.uk/2/hi/programmes/hardtalk/5393104.htm
10. Coward, J. (2011, November 7). My Take: If Rawandans can forgive killings, we can forgive the waitress. *CNN.* Retrieved October 20, 2019 from http://religion.blogs.cnn.com/2011/11/07/my-take-if-rwandans-can-forgive-killings-we-can-forgive-the-waitress/
11. Baumeister, R. F. (1997). *Evil: Inside human cruelty and violence.* New York: W. H. Freeman.
12. Tedeschi, J. T., & Felson, R. B. (1994). *Violence, aggression, and coercive actions.* Washington, DC: American Psychological Association.
13. Baron, R. A., & Richardson, D. R. (1994). *Human aggression* (2nd ed.). New York: Plenum Press.
14. Marcus-Newhall, A., Pedersen, W. C., Carlson, M., & Miller, N. (2000). Displaced aggression is alive and well: A meta-analytic review. *Journal of Personality and Social Psychology, 78,* 670–689.
15. Leander, N. P., & Chartrand, T. L. (2017). On thwarted goals and displaced aggression: A compensatory competence model. *Journal of Experimental Social Psychology, 72,* 88–100. DOI: 10.1016/j.jesp.2017.04.010
16. Lagerspetz, K. M., Bjorkqvist, K., & Peltonen, T. (1988). Is indirect aggression typical of females? Gender differences in aggressiveness in 11- to 12-year-old children. *Aggressive Behavior, 14,* 403–414.
17. Buss, A. H. (1961). *The psychology of aggression.* New York: Wiley.
18. Dodge, K. A., & Coie, J. D. (1987). Social-information-processing factors in reactive and proactive aggression in children's peer groups. *Journal of Personality and Social Psychology, 53,* 1146–1158.
19. Feshbach, S. (1964). The function of aggression and the regulation of aggressive drive. *Psychological Review, 71,* 257–272.
20. Bushman, B. J., & Anderson, C. A. (2001). Is it time to pull the plug on the hostile versus instrumental aggression dichotomy? *Psychological Review, 108,* 273–279.
21. Olweus, D. (1978). *Aggression in the schools: Bullies and whipping boys.* Washington, DC: Hemisphere (Wiley).
22. Japanese man sends rubbish to revenge school 'bullies'. (2016, December 2). *BBC.* Retrieved August 25, 2019 from https://www.bbc.com/news/world-asia-38188618
23. Ferguson, R. B. (2018, September 1). War is not part of human nature. *Scientific American.* Retrieved August 25, 2019 from https://www.scientificamerican.com/article/war-is-not-part-of-human-nature/
24. Bond, R. M., & Bushman, B. J. (2017). The contagious spread of violence through social networks in U.S. adolescents. *American Journal of Public Health, 107*(2), 288-294. doi:10.2105/AJPH.2016.303550
25. American Psychiatric Association. (1994). *Diagnostic and statistical manual of mental disorders* (4th ed.). Washington, DC: Author.
26. Paik, H., & Comstock, G. (1994). The effects of television violence on antisocial behavior: A meta-analysis. *Communication Research, 21,* 516–546.
27. Tedeschi, J. T., & Felson, R. B. (1994). *Violence, aggression, and coercive actions.* Washington, DC: American Psychological Association.
28. Pinker, S. (2007, March 19). A history of violence. *New Republic, 236*(12), 18.
29. Pinker, S. (2007, March 19). A history of violence. *New Republic, 236*(12), 18.
30. Eisner, M. (2001). Modernization, self-control and lethal violence: The long-term dynamics of European homicide rates in theoretical perspective. *British Journal of Criminology, 41,* 618–638.
31. Gurr, T. R. (1981). Historical trends in violent crime: A critical review of the evidence. *Crime and Justice, 3,* 295.
32. Pinker, S. (2007, March 19). A history of violence. *New Republic, 236*(12), 18.
33. http://www.humansecuritybrief.info/
34. Pinker, S. (2007, March 19). A history of violence. *New Republic, 236*(12), 18.
35. Darwin, C. (1948). *Origin of species.* New York: Modern Library. (Original work published 1871).
36. Freud, S. (1933/1950). Why war? In *Collected works of Sigmund Freud* (Vol. 16). London: Imagio.
37. Lorenz, K. (1966). *On aggression* (M. K. Wilson, Trans.) New York: Harcourt, Brace.
38. Berkowitz, L. (1993). *Aggression: Its causes, consequences, and control.* New York: McGraw-Hill.
39. Geen, R. G., & Quanty, M. B. (1977). The catharsis of aggression: An evaluation of a hypothesis. In L. Berkowitz (Ed.), *Advances in experimental social psychology* (Vol. 10, pp. 1–37). New York: Academic Press.
40. Scott, J. P. (1958). *Aggression.* Chicago: University of Chicago Press.
41. Lorenz, K. (1966). *On aggression* (M. K. Wilson, Trans.) New York: Harcourt, Brace.
42. Timbergen, N. (1952). The curious behavior of the Stickleback. *Scientific American, 187,* 22–26.
43. Hinde, R. A. (1970). *Animal behavior.* New York: McGraw-Hill.
44. Bandura, A. (1973). *Aggression: A social learning theory analysis.* Englewood Cliffs, NJ: Prentice-Hall.
45. Mischel, W. (1973). Toward a cognitive social learning reconceptualization of personality. *Psychological Review, 80,* 252–283.
46. Mischel, W., & Shoda, Y. (1995). A cognitive-affective system theory of personality: Reconceptualizing situations, dispositions, dynamics, and invariance in personality structure. *Psychological Review, 102,* 246–268.
47. Bandura, A., Ross, D., & Ross, S. A. (1961). Transmission of aggression through imitation of aggressive models. *Journal of Abnormal and Social Psychology, 63,* 575–582.
48. Bandura, A., Ross, D., & Ross, S. A. (1963). Vicarious reinforcement and initiative learning. *Journal of Abnormal and Social Psychology, 67,* 601–607.
49. Liebert, R., & Baron, R. (1972). Some immediate effects of televised violence on children's behavior. *Developmental Psychology, 6,* 469–475.
50. Alland, A., Jr. (1972). *The human imperative.* New York: Columbia University Press.
51. U.S. Federal Bureau of Investigation. (2012). *Uniform crime reports.* Washington, DC: U.S. Government Printing Office.
52. Dollard, J., Doob, L., Miller, N., Mowrer, O., & Sears, R. (1939). *Frustration and aggression.* New Haven, CT: Yale University Press.
53. Freud, S. (1961). *Mourning and melancholia* (standard ed.). London: Norton. (Original work published 1917).
54. Miller, N. E. (1941). The frustration-aggression hypothesis. *Psychological Review, 48,* 337–342.
55. Berkowitz, L. (1989). Frustration-aggression hypothesis: Examination and reformulation. *Psychological Bulletin, 106,* 59–73.
56. Xu, H., Bègue, L., & Bushman, B. J. (2014). Washing the guilt away: Effects of personal versus vicarious cleansing on guilty feelings and prosocial behavior. *Frontiers in Human Neuroscience, 8.* doi: 10.3389/fnhum.2014.00097
57. Tangney, J. P., Wagner, P., Fletcher, C., & Gramzow, R. (1992). Shamed into anger? The relation of shame and guilt to anger and self-reported aggression. *Journal of Personality and Social Psychology, 62*(4), 669–675. doi: 10.1037/0022-3514.62.4.669

58. Morris, W. N., & Reilly, N. P. (1987). Toward the self-regulation of mood: Theory and research. *Motivation and Emotion, 11*, 215–249.
59. Bushman, B. J., Baumeister, R. F., & Phillips, C. M. (2001). Do people aggress to improve their mood? Catharsis beliefs, affect regulation opportunity, and aggressive responding. *Journal of Personality and Social Psychology, 81*, 17–32.
60. Zillmann, D., Katcher, A. H., & Milavsky, B. (1972). Excitation transfer from physical exercise to subsequent aggressive behavior. *Journal of Experimental Social Psychology, 8*, 247–259.
61. Elbert T, Moran J, & Schauer M. (2017). Appetitive aggression. In B. J. Bushman (Ed) *Aggression and violence*. (pp. 119–136). New York: Taylor & Francis/Routledge.
62. Elbert T, Moran J, & Schauer M. (2017). Appetitive aggression. In B. J. Bushman (Ed) *Aggression and violence*. (pp. 119–136). New York: Taylor & Francis/Routledge.
63. Chester, D. S. (2017). The role of positive affect in aggression. *Current Directions in Psychological Science, 26*(4), 366–370. DOI: 10.1177/0963721417700457
64. Elbert, T., Schauer, M., & Moran, J. K. (2018). Two pedals drive the bi-cycle of violence: Reactive and appetitive aggression. *Current Opinion in Psychology, 19*, 135–138. DOI: 0.1016/j.copsyc.2017.03.016
65. Pelisek, C. (2018, April 13). 'I just enjoy killing': Airman gets life in prison for strangling another Air Force member. *People*. Retrieved August 25, 2019 from https://people.com/crime/air-force-member-strangled-female-airman-journal-described-murder/
66. Elbert T, Moran J, & Schauer M. (2017). Appetitive aggression. In B. J. Bushman (Ed) *Aggression and violence*. (pp. 119–136). New York: Taylor & Francis/Routledge.
67. Elbert, T., Schauer, M., Hinkel, H., Riedke, H., Maedl, A., Winkler, N., . . . & Hecker, T. (2013). *Sexual and gender-based violence in the Kivu Provinces of the DRC*. Washington, DC: The International Bank for Reconstruction and Development/The World Bank.
68. Elbert, T., Schauer, M., & Moran, J. K. (2018). Two pedals drive the bi-cycle of violence: Reactive and appetitive aggression. *Current Opinion in Psychology, 19*, 135–138. DOI: 0.1016/j.copsyc.2017.03.016
69. Bandura, A. (1999). Moral disengagement in the perpetration of inhumanities. *Personality and Social Psychology Review, 3*, 193–209. DOI: 10.1207/s15327957pspr0303_3
70. Chester, D. S. (2017). The role of positive affect in aggression. *Current Directions in Psychological Science, 26*(4), 366–370. DOI: 10.1177/0963721417700457
71. Weierstall, R., Haer, R., Banholzer, L., & Elbert, T. (2013). Becoming cruel: Appetitive aggression released by detrimental socialisation in former Congolese soldiers. *International Journal of Behavioral Development, 37*(6), 505–513. DOI: 10.1177/0165025413499126
72. Dill, K. E., Anderson, C. A., Anderson, K. B., & Deuser, W. E. (1997). Effects of aggressive personality on social expectations and social perceptions. *Journal of Research in Personality, 31*, 272–292.
73. Orobio de Castro, B., Veerman, J. W., Koops, W., Bosch, J. D., & Monshouwer, H. J. (2002). Hostile attribution of intent and aggressive behavior: A meta‐analysis. *Child Development, 73*, 916–934.
74. Epps, J., & Kendall, P. C. (1995). Hostile attribution bias in adults. *Cognitive Therapy and Research, 19*, 159–178.
75. Dill, K. E., Anderson, C. A., Anderson, K. B., & Deuser, W. E. (1997). Effects of aggressive personality on social expectations and social perceptions. *Journal of Research in Personality, 31*, 272–292.
76. Bartholow, B. D., & Heinz, A. (2006). Alcohol and aggression without consumption: Alcohol cues, aggressive thoughts, and hostile perception bias. *Psychological Science, 17*, 30–37.
77. Dill, K. E., Anderson, C. A., Anderson, K. B., & Deuser, W. E. (1997). Effects of aggressive personality on social expectations and social perceptions. *Journal of Research in Personality, 31*, 272–292.
78. Penton-Voak I. S., Thomas, J., Gage, S. H., McMurran, M., McDonald, S., & Munafò M. R. (2013). Increasing recognition of happiness in ambiguous facial expressions reduces anger and aggressive behavior. *Psychological Science, 24*(5), 688–697. doi: 10.1177/0956797612459657
79. Gerbner, G. (1998). Cultivation analysis: An overview. *Mass Communication & Society, 1*(3-4), 175-194. DOI:10.1080/15205436.1998.9677855
80. Gerbner, G., & Gross, L. (1976). Living with television: The violence profile. *Journal of Communication, 26*(2), 172–199. DOI:10.1111/j.1460-2466.1976.tb01397.x
81. Bushman, B. J. (2016). Violent media exposure and hostile appraisals: A meta-analytic review. *Aggressive Behavior, 42*(6), 605-613. DOI: 10.1002/ab.21655
82. Greitemeyer, T., & Osswald, S. (2009). Prosocial video games reduce aggressive cognitions. *Journal of Experimental Social Psychology, 45*(4), 896–900.
83. Tremblay, R. E. (2000). The development of aggressive behavior during childhood: What have we learned in the past century? *International Journal of Behavioral Development, 24*(2), 129–141.
84. U.S. Federal Bureau of Investigation. (2018). *Uniform crime reports*. Washington, DC: U.S. Government Printing Office.
85. Taylor, S. E., Klein, L. C., Lewis, B. P., Gruenewald, T. L., Gurung, R. A R, & Updegraff, J. A. (2000). Biobehavioral responses to stress in females: Tend-and-befriend, not fight-or-flight. *Psychological Review, 107*, 441–429.
86. Taylor, S. E., Klein, L. C., Lewis, B. P., Gruenewald, T. L., Gurung, R. A R, & Updegraff, J. A. (2000). Biobehavioral responses to stress in females: Tend-and-befriend, not fight-or-flight. *Psychological Review, 107*, 441–429.
87. Loeber, R., & Hay, D. (1997). Key issues in the development of aggression from childhood to early adulthood. *Annual Review of Psychology, 48*, 371–410.
88. Crick, N. R., & Grotpeter, J. K. (1995). Relational aggression, gender, and social-psychological adjustment. *Child Development, 66*, 710–722.
89. Vaillancourt, R. (2005). Indirect aggression among humans: Social construct or evolutionary adaption? In R. E. Tremblay, W. W. Hartup, & J. Archer (Eds.), *Developmental origins of aggression* (pp. 158–177). New York: Guilford Press.
90. Steffensmeier, D., & Allan, E. (1996). Gender and crime: Toward a gendered theory of female offending. *Annual Review of Sociology, 22*, 459–487.
91. Ainsworth, S. E., & Maner, J. K. (2012). Sex begets violence: Mating motives, social dominance, and physical aggression in men. *Journal of Personality and Social Psychology, 103*, 819–829.
92. Collins, R. L., Quigley, B., & Leonard, K. (2007). Women's physical aggression in bars: An event-based examination of precipitants and predictors of severity. *Aggressive Behavior, 33*(4), 304–313.
93. Bettencourt, B. A., & Miller, N. (1996). Gender differences in aggression as a function of provocation: A meta-analysis. *Psychological Bulletin, 119*, 422–447.
94. Archer, J. (2000). Sex differences in aggression between heterosexual partners: A meta-analytic review. *Psychological Bulletin, 126*, 651–680.
95. Straus, M. A. (1997). Physical assaults by women partners: A major social problem. In M. R. Walsh (Ed.), *Women, men and gender: Ongoing debates* (pp. 210–221). New Haven, CT: Yale University Press.
96. Crick, N. R., & Grotpeter, J. K. (1995). Relational aggression, gender, and social-psychological adjustment. *Child Development, 66*, 710–722.
97. Bass, E. C., Saldarriaga, L., Cunha, J., Chen, B.-B., Santo, J. B., & Bukowski, W. M. (2018). A cross-cultural analysis of the relations of physical and relational aggression with peer victimization. *International Journal of Behavioral Development, 42*(1), 132–142. https://doi-org.proxy.lib.umich.edu/10.1177/0165025416677846
98. Slawinski, B. L., Klump, K. L., & Burt, S. A. (2018). The etiology of social aggression: A nuclear twin family study. *Psychological Medicine*. DOI: 10.1017/S0033291718000697
99. Olweus, D. (1979). The stability of aggressive reaction patterns in males: A review. *Psychological Bulletin, 86*, 852–875.
100. Paulhus, D. L., Curtis, S. R., & Jones, D. N. (2018). Aggression as a trait: the Dark Tetrad alternative. *Current Opinion in Psychology, 19*, 88–92. doi:10.1016/j.copsyc.2017.04.007
101. Tedeschi, J. T., & Felson, R. B. (1994). *Violence, aggression, and coercive actions*. Washington, DC: American Psychological Association.
102. Dawkins, R. (1989). *The selfish gene*. New York: Oxford University Press. (Original work published 1976).
103. Tedeschi, J. T., & Felson, R. B. (1994). *Violence, aggression, and coercive actions*. Washington, DC: American Psychological Association.
104. Messick, D. M., Bloom, S., Boldizar, J. P., & Samuelson, C. D. (1985). Why we are fairer than others. *Journal of Experimental Social Psychology, 21*, 480–500.
105. Mikula, G., Petri, B., & Tanzer, N. (1989). What people regard as unjust: Types, structures and everyday experiences of injustice. *European Journal of Social Psychology, 20*, 133–149.
106. Pettiway, L. E. (1987). Arson for revenge: The role of environmental situation, age, sex, and race. *Journal of Quantitative Criminology, 3*(2), 169–184.
107. Wiehe, V. R. (1991). *Perilous rivalry: When siblings become abusive*. Lexington, MA: Heath/Lexington Books.
108. Zalar, R. W., Harris, R. B., Kyriacou, D. N., Anglin, D., & Minow, M. (2000). Domestic violence. *New England Journal of Medicine, 342*, 1450–1453.
109. Stanko, E. A. (2000). The day to count: Reflections on a methodology to raise awareness about the impact of domestic violence in the UK. *Caribbean Journal of Criminology & Social Psychology, 5*(1–2), 103–118.
110. Anderson, P. B., & Struckman-Johnson, C. (Eds.). (1998). *Sexually aggressive women: Current perspectives and controversies*. New York: Guilford Press.
111. Anderson, P. B., & Struckman-Johnson, C. (Eds.). (1998). *Sexually aggressive women: Current perspectives and controversies*. New York: Guilford Press.
112. Matud, M. P. (2005). The psychological impact of domestic violence on Spanish women. *Journal of Applied Social Psychology, 35*(11), 2310–2322.
113. Kunst, M., Bogaerts, S., & Winkel, F. W. (2010). Domestic violence and mental health in a Dutch community sample: The adverse role of loneliness. *Journal of Community & Applied Social Psychology, 20*(5), 419–425.
114. Finkel, E. J., DeWall, C. N., Slotter, E. B., McNulty, J. K., Pond, R. S., Jr., & Atkins, D. C. (2012). Using I³ theory to clarify when dispositional aggressiveness predicts intimate partner violence perpetration. *Journal of Personality and Social Psychology, 102*(3), 533–549.
115. Felson, R. B., & Messner, S. F. (2000). The control motive in intimate partner violence. *Social Psychology Quarterly, 63*(1), 86–94.
116. Ross, S. M. (1996). Risk of physical abuse to children of spouse abusing parents. *Child Abuse and Neglect, 20*, 589–598.
117. Caesar, P. L. (1988). Exposure to violence in the families-of-origin among wife-abusers and maritally nonviolent men. *Violence and Victims, 3*, 49–63.

118. Cappell, C., & Heiner, R. B. (1990). The intergenerational transmission of family aggression. *Journal of Family Violence, 5,* 135–152.
119. Laumann, E. O., Gagnon, J. H., Michael, R. T., & Michaels, S. (1994). *The social organization of sexuality: Sexual practices in the United States.* Chicago: University of Chicago Press.
220. Meyer, C. B., & Taylor, S. E. (1986). Adjustment to rape. *Journal of Personality and Social Psychology, 50,* 1226–1234.
221. Rynd, N. (1988). Incidence of psychometric symptoms in rape victims. *Journal of Sex Research, 24,* 155–161.
222. Murnen, S. K., Perot, A., & Byrne, D. (1989). Coping with unwanted sexual activity: Normative responses, situational determinants, and individual differences. *Journal of Sex Research, 26,* 85–106.
123. O'Sullivan, L. F., Byers, E. S., & Finkelman, L. (1998). A comparison of male and female college students' experiences of sexual coercion. *Psychology of Women Quarterly, 22*(2), 177–195.
124. Koss, M. P. (1988). Hidden rape: Sexual aggression and victimization in the national sample of students in higher education. In M. A. Pirog-Good & J. E. Stets (Eds.), *Violence in dating relationships: Emerging social issues* (pp. 145–168). New York: Praeger.
125. Baumeister, R. F., Catanese, K. R., & Wallace, H. M. (2002). Conquest by force: A narcissistic reactance theory of rape and sexual coercion. *Review of General Psychology, 6,* 92–135.
126. Felson, R. B. (2002). *Violence and gender reexamined.* Washington, DC: American Psychological Association.
127. Bushman, B. J., Bonacci, A. M., Van Dijk, M., & Baumeister, R. F. (2003). Narcissism, sexual refusal, and sexual aggression: Testing a narcissistic reactance model of sexual coercion. *Journal of Personality and Social Psychology, 84,* 1027–1040.
128. Pitt, E. L. (2000). Domestic violence in gay and lesbian relationships. *Journal of the Gay and Lesbian Medical Association, 4,* 195–196.
129. Yerke, A. F., & DeFeo, J. (2016). Redefining intimate partner violence beyond the binary to include transgender people. *Journal of Family Violence, 31*(8), 975–979. https://doi-org.proxy.lib.umich.edu/10.1007/s10896-016-9887-y
130. Diamond, J. (2013). *The world until yesterday.* Viking.
131. http://www.endcorporalpunishment.org
132. Berkowitz, L., & LePage, A. (1967). Weapons as aggression-eliciting stimuli. *Journal of Personality and Social Psychology, 7,* 202–207.
133. Hemenway, D., Vriniotis, M., & Miller, M. (2006). Is an armed society a polite society? Guns and road rage. *Accident Analysis and Prevention, 38*(4), 687–695.
134. Bushman, B. J., Kerwin, T., Whitlock, T., & Weisenberger, J. M.(2017). The weapons effect on wheels: Motorists drive more aggressively when there is a gun in the vehicle. *Journal of Experimental Social Psychology, 73,* 82-85. DOI: 10.1016/j.jesp.2017.06.007
135. Groeger, J. A. (2000). *Understanding driving – Applying cognitive psychology to a complex everyday task*: Psychology Press, Taylor and Francis, Hove, UK.
136. World Health Organization (2016). Road traffic injuries. Retrieved August 25, 2019 from www.who.int/mediacentre/factsheets/fs358/en/
137. American Automobile Association (AAA, n.d.). *Aggressive driving.* Retrieved from https://www.aaafoundation.org/aggressive-driving]
138. American Automobile Association (AAA, n.d.). *Aggressive driving.* Retrieved from https://www.aaafoundation.org/aggressive-driving
139. Benjamin, A. J., Jr., Kepes, S., & Bushman, B. J. (2018). Effects of weapons on aggressive thoughts, angry feelings, hostile appraisals, and aggressive behavior: A meta-analytic review of the weapons effect literature. *Personality and Social Psychology Review, 22*(4), 347-377. DOI: 10.1177/1088868317725419
140. Ariel, B., Lawes, D., Weinborn, C., Henry, R. Chen, K., & Sabthe, H. B. (2019). The "less-than-lethal weapons effect": Introducing tasers to routine police operations in England and Wales. *Criminal Justice and Behavior, 46*(2), 280–300. DOI: 10.1177/0093854818812918
141. Subra, B., Muller, D., Bègue, L., Bushman, B. J., & Delmas, F. (2010). Automatic effects of alcohol and weapon cues on aggressive thoughts and behaviors. *Personality and Social Psychology Bulletin, 36*(8), 1052–1057. doi: 10.1177/0146167210374725
142. Blanchette, I. (2006). Snakes, spiders, guns, and syringes: How specific are evolutionary constraints on the detection of threatening stimuli? *The Quarterly Journal of Experimental Psychology, 59*(8), 1484–1504.
143. Carlson, J. M., Fee, A. L., & Reinke, K. S. (2009). Backward masked snakes and guns modulate spatial attention. *Evolutionary Psychology, 7*(4), 534–544.
144. Fox, E., Griggs, L., & Mouchlianitis, E. (2007). The detection of fear-relevant stimuli: Are guns noticed as quickly as snakes? *Emotion, 7*(4), 691–696.
145. Langley, R.L. (2005). Animal-Related Fatalities in the United States - An Update Wilderness and Environmental Medicine, 16, 67–74.
146. Centers for Disease Control and Prevention. (n.d.). Venomous Snakes. Retreived from https://www.cdc.gov/niosh/topics/snakes/
147. Everytown (2019, April 4). Gun violence in America. Retrieved August 25, 2019 from https://everytownresearch.org/gun-violence-america/
148. Benjamin, A. J., Jr., Kepes, S., & Bushman, B. J. (2018). Effects of weapons on aggressive thoughts, angry feelings, hostile appraisals, and aggressive behavior: A meta-analytic review of the weapons effect literature. *Personality and Social Psychology Review, 22*(4), 347-377. DOI: 10.1177/1088868317725419
149. Biggs, A. T., Brockmole, J. R., & Witt, J. K. (2013). Armed and attentive: Holding a weapon can bias attentional priorities during scene viewing. *Attention, Perception, & Psychophysics, 75*(8), 1715–1724.
150. Bushman, B. J., Jamieson, P. E., Weitz, I., & Romer, D. (2013). Gun violence trends in movies. *Pediatrics, 132*(6), 1014–1018. doi: 10.1542/peds.2013-1600
151. Bushman, B. J., Newman, K., Calvert, S. L., Downey, G., Dredze, M., Gottfredson, M., Jablonski, N. G., Masten, A., Morrill, C., Neill, D. B., Romer, D., & Webster, D. (2016). Youth violence: What we know and what we need to know. *American Psychologist, 71*(1), 17–39. DOI: 10.1037/a0039687
152. Bushman, B. J., & Anderson, C. A. (2015). Understanding causality in the effects of media violence. *American Behavioral Scientist, 59*(14), 1807–1821. DOI: 10.1177/0002764215596554
153. Anderson, C. A., Shibuya, A., Ihori, N., Swing, E. L., Bushman, B. J., Sakamoto, A., Rothstein, H. R., Saleem, M., & Barlett, C. P. (2010). Violent video game effects on aggression, empathy, and prosocial behavior in Eastern and Western countries: A meta-analytic review. *Psychological Bulletin, 136*(2), 151–173. doi: 10.1037/a0018251
154. Greitemeyer, T., & Mügge, D. O. (2014). Video games do affect social outcomes: A meta-analytic review of the effects of violent and prosocial video game play. *Personality and Social Psychology Bulletin, 40,* 578–589. doi: 10.1177/0146167213520459
155. Bushman, B. J., & Huesmann, L. R. (2006). Short-term and long-term effects of violent media on aggression in children and adults. *Archives of Pediatrics & Adolescent Medicine, 160*(4), 348–352. doi: 10.1001/archpedi.160.4.348
156. Gentile, D. G., & Bushman, B. J. (2012). Reassessing media violence effects using a risk and resilience approach to understanding aggression. *Psychology of Popular Media Culture, 1*(3), 138–151. doi:10.1037/a0028481
157. Huesmann, L. R., Moise, J., Podolski, C. P., & Eron, L. D. (2003). Longitudinal relations between childhood exposure to media violence and adult aggression and violence: 1977–1992. *Developmental Psychology, 39,* 201–221.
158. Prescott, A. T., Sargent, J. D., & Hull, J. G. (2018). Metaanalysis of the relationship between violent video game play and physical aggression over time. *PNAS Proceedings of the National Academy of Sciences of the United States of America, 115*(40), 9882–9888. https://doi-org.proxy.lib.umich.edu/10.1073/pnas.1611617114
159. Donnerstein, E., & Berkowitz, L. (1981). Victim reactions in aggressive erotic films as a factor in violence against women. *Journal of Personality and Social Psychology, 41,* 710–724.
160. Burnay, J., Bushman, B. J., & Larøi, F. (2019). Effects of sexualized video games on online sexual harassment. *Aggressive Behavior, 45*(2), 214–223. DOI: 10.1002/ab.21811
161. Malamuth, N. M., & Check, J. V. P. (1981). The effects of mass media exposure on acceptance of violence against women: A field experiment. *Journal of Research in Personality, 15,* 436–446.
162. Mullin, C. R., & Linz, D. (1995). Desensitization and resensitization to violence against women: Effects of exposure to sexually violent films on judgments of domestic violence victims. *Journal of Personality and Social Psychology, 69,* 449–459.
163. Bushman, B. J., Gollwitzer, M., & Cruz, C. (2015). There is broad consensus: Media researchers agree that violent media increase aggression in children, and pediatricians and parents concur. *Psychology of Popular Media Culture, 4*(3), 200–214. DOI: 10.1037/ppm0000046
164. Bushman, B. J., (2019). Media violence statements. Retrieved August 25, 2019 from http://u.osu.edu/bushman.20/statements-on-media-violence-effects-by-major-scientific-groups/
165. Steinfeld, J. (1972). *Statement in hearings before Subcommittee on Communications of Committee on Commerce* (United States Senate, Serial #92–52, pp. 25–27). Washington, DC: United States Government.
166. Huesmann, L. R., & Taylor, L. D. (2003). The case against the case against media violence. In D. Gentile (Ed.), *Media violence and children* (pp. 107–130). Westport, CT: Greenwood Press.
167. Strasburger, V. C., Donnerstein, E. I., & Bushman, B. J. (2014). Why is it so hard to believe that media affect children and adolescents? *Pediatrics, 133,* 571–573. doi:10.1542/peds.2013-2334
168. Bushman, B. J. (2018). Teaching students about violent media effects. *Teaching of Psychology, 45*(2), 200–206. DOI: 10.1177/0098628318762936
169. Nauroth, P., Gollwitzer, M., Bender, J., & Rothmund, T. (2014). Gamers against science: The case of the violent video games debate. *European Journal of Social Psychology, 44,* 104-116. doi:10.1002/ejsp.1998
170. Davison, W. P. (1983). The third-person effect in communication. *Public Opinion Quarterly, 47,* 1–15. doi:10.1086/268763
171. Bushman, B. J., & Anderson, C. A. (2001). Media violence and the American public: Scientific facts versus media misinformation. *American Psychologist, 56,* 477–489. doi:10.1037/0003-066X.56.6-7.477
172. Martins, N., Weaver, A. J., Yeshua-Katz, D., Lewis, N. H., Tyree, N. E., & Jensen, J. D. (2013). A content analysis of print news coverage of media violence and aggression research. *Journal of Communication, 63,* 1070–1087. doi:10.1111/jcom.12052
173. Julepea. (2010, January 4). Big Tobacco executive "Nicotine Is Not Addictive." https://www.youtube.com/watch?v=A6B1q22R438
174. Anderson, C. A., Anderson, K. B., Dorr, N., DeNeve, K. M., & Flanagan, M. (2000). Temperature and aggression. In M. Zanna (Ed.), *Advances in experimental social psychology* (Vol. 32, pp. 63–133). New York: Academic Press.
175. Anderson, C. A., & Anderson, K. B. (1996). Violent crime rate studies in philosophical context: A

destructive testing approach to heat and southern culture of violence effects. *Journal of Personality and Social Psychology, 70,* 740–756.

176. Anderson, C. A., Bushman, B. J., & Groom, R. W. (1997). Hot years and serious and deadly assault: Empirical tests of the heat hypothesis. *Journal of Personality and Social Psychology, 73,* 1213–1223.

177. Leffingwell, A. (1892). *Illegitimacy and the influence of the seasons upon conduct.* New York: Scribner's.

178. Anderson, C. A., Bushman, B. J., & Groom, R. W. (1997). Hot years and serious and deadly assault: Empirical tests of the heat hypothesis. *Journal of Personality and Social Psychology, 73*(6), 1213–1223. doi: 10.1037//0022-3514.73.6.1213

179. Hsiang, S. M., Burke, M., & Miguel, E. (2013). Quantifying the influence of climate on human conflict. *Science, 341*(6151):1235367. doi: 10.1126/science.1235367

180. Groves, C. L., & Anderson, C. A. (2018). Aversive events and aggression. *Current Opinion in Psychology, 19,* 144-148. doi: 10.1016/j.copsyc.2017.03.027

181. Nijman, H. L. I., & Rector, G. (1999). Crowding and aggression on inpatient psychiatric wards. *Psychiatric Services, 50*(6), 830–831.

182. Lawrence, C., & Andrews, K. (2004). The influence of perceived prison crowding on male inmates' perception of aggressive events. *Aggressive Behavior, 30*(4), 273–283.

183. Sapolsky, R. M. (1998). *The trouble with testosterone: And other essays on the biology of the human predicament* (p. 150). New York: Scribner.

184. Archer, J. (1988). *The behavioral biology of aggression.* Cambridge: Cambridge University Press.

185. Gladue, B. A., Boechler, M., & McCaul, K. D. (1989). Hormonal responses to competition in human males. *Aggressive Behavior, 17,* 313–326.

186. Mazur, A., Susman, E. J., & Edelbrock, S. (1997). Sex differences in testosterone response to a video game contest. *Evolution and Human Behavior, 18,* 317–326.

187. McCaul, K. D., Gladue, B. A., & Joppa, M. (1992). Winning, losing, mood, and testosterone. *Hormones and Behavior, 26,* 486–504.

188. Moffitt, T., Brammer, G., Caspi, A., Fawcett, J., Raleigh, M., Yuwiler, A., & Silva, P. (1998). Whole blood serotonin relates to violence in an epidemiological study. *Biological Psychiatry, 43,* 446–457.

189. Goveas, J. S., Csernansky, J. G., & Coccaro, E. F. (2004). Platelet serotonin content correlates inversely with life history of aggression in personality-disordered subjects. *Psychiatry Research, 126,* 23–32.

190. Higley, J. D., Mehlman, P. T., Taub, D. M., Higley, S. B., Suomi, S. J., Vickers, J. H., & Linnoila, M. (1992). Cerebrospinal fluid mono-amine and adrenal correlates of aggression in free-ranging Rhesus monkeys. *Archives of General Psychiatry, 49,* 436–441.

191. Westergaard, G. C., Mehlman, P. T., Suomi, S. J., & Higley, J. D. (1999). CSF 5-HIAA and aggression in female macaque monkeys: Species and interindividual differences. *Psychopharmacology, 146,* 440–446.

192. Keegan, J. (1993). *A history of warfare.* New York: Knopf.

193. Lipsey, M. W., Wilson, D. B., Cohen M. A., & Derzon, J. H. (1997). Is there a causal relationship between alcohol use and violence? A synthesis of the evidence. In M. Galanter (Ed.), *Recent developments in alcoholism: Vol. 13. Alcohol and violence: Epidemiology, neurobiology, psychology, and family issues* (pp. 245–282). New York: Plenum Press.

194. Lipsey, M. W., Wilson, D. B., Cohen M. A., & Derzon, J. H. (1997). Is there a causal relationship between alcohol use and violence? A synthesis of the evidence. In M. Galanter (Ed.), *Recent developments in alcoholism: Vol. 13. Alcohol and violence: Epidemiology, neurobiology, psychology, and family issues* (pp. 245–282). New York: Plenum Press.

195. Bushman, B. J., & Cooper, H. M. (1990). Effects of alcohol on human aggression: An integrative research review. *Psychological Bulletin, 107,* 341–354.

196. Ito, T. A., Miller, N., & Pollock, V. E. (1996). Alcohol and aggression: A meta-analysis on the moderating effects of inhibitory cues, triggering events, and self-focused attention. *Psychological Bulletin, 120,* 60–82.

197. Graham, K. (1980). Theories of intoxicated aggression. *Canadian Journal of Behavioral Science, 12,* 141–158.

198. Gailliot, M. T., & Baumeister, R. F. (2007). The physiology of willpower: Linking blood glucose to self-control. *Personality and Social Psychology Review, 11*(4), 303–327.

199. Badawy, A. A.-B. (2003). Alcohol and violence and the possible role of serotonin. *Criminal Behaviour and Mental Health, 13*(1), 31–44. doi: 10.1002/cbm

200. Steele, C. M., & Josephs, R. A. (1990). Alcohol myopia: Its prized and dangerous effects. *American Psychologist, 45,* 921–933.

201. Hull, J. G. (1981). A self-awareness model of the causes and effects of alcohol consumption. *Journal of Abnormal Psychology, 90,* 586–600.

202. Giancola, P. R. (2000). Executive functioning: A conceptual framework for alcohol-related aggression. *Experimental Clinical Psychopharmacology, 8,* 576–597.

203. Bushman, B. J. (1997). Effects of alcohol on human aggression: Validity of proposed explanations. In D. Fuller, R. Dietrich, & E. Gottheil (Eds.), *Recent developments in alcoholism: Alcohol and violence* (Vol. 13, pp. 227–243). New York: Plenum Press.

204. Shakur, S. (1993). *Monster: The autobiography of an L.A. gang member.* New York: Atlantic Monthly Press.

205. New studies show strong link between diet and behavior. (1998). *Crime Times, 4*(1). Retrieved August 25, 2019 from http://www.autismwebsite.com/crimetimes/98a/w98ap2.htm

206. Gesch, B. C., Hammond, S. M., Hampson, S. E., Eves, A., & Crowder, M. J. (2002). Influence of supplementary vitamins, minerals and essential fatty acids on the antisocial behaviour of young adult prisoners: Randomised, placebo-controlled trial. *British Journal of Psychiatry, 181,* 22–28.

207. Benton, D. (2007). The impact of diet on anti-social, violent and criminal behaviour. *Neuroscience & Biobehavioral Reviews, 31*(5), 752–774.

208. Zaalberg, A. (in press). The effects of nutrients and neurotoxicants on aggressive behavior. *Journal of Criminal Justice.* DOI: 10.1016/j.jcrimjus.2018.10.001

209. Amok. (n.d.) in *Merriam-Webster Dictionary.* Retrieved August 25, 2019 from https://www.merriam-webster.com/dictionary/amok

210. Carr, J. E., & Tann, E. K. (1976). In search of the true Amok: Amok as viewed within Malay culture. *American Journal of Psychiatry, 133*(11), 1295–1299.

211. Gottfredson, M. R., & Hirschi, T. (1990). *A general theory of crime.* Stanford, CA: Stanford University Press. Also see DeWall, C. N., Finkel, E. J., & Denson, T. F. (2011). Self-control inhibits aggression. *Social and Personality Psychology Compass, 5*(7), 458–472.

212. Pratt, T. C., & Cullen, F. T. (2000). The empirical status of Gottfredson and Hirschi's general theory of crime: A meta-analysis. *Criminology, 38,* 931–964.

213. Henry, B., Caspi, A., Moffitt, T. E., & Silva, P. A. (1996). Temperamental and familial predictors of violent and nonviolent criminal convictions: Age 3 to age 18. *Developmental Psychology, 32,* 614–623.

214. Baumeister, R. F., Smart, L., & Boden, J. M. (1996). Relation of threatened egotism to violence and aggression: The dark side of high self-esteem. *Psychological Review, 103,* 5–33.

215. Bushman, B. J., & Baumeister, R. F. (2002). Does self-love or self-hate lead to violence? *Journal of Research in Personality, 36,* 543–545.

216. Bushman, B. J., & Baumeister, R. F. (1998). Threatened egotism, narcissism, self-esteem, and direct and displaced aggression: Does self-love or self-hate lead to violence? *Journal of Personality and Social Psychology, 75,* 219–229.

217. Bushman, B. J., & Baumeister, R. F. (1998). Threatened egotism, narcissism, self-esteem, and direct and displaced aggression: Does self-love or self-hate lead to violence? *Journal of Personality and Social Psychology, 75,* 219–229.

218. Day, D., & Ullom, H. H. (Eds.). (1947). *The autobiography of Sam Houston.* Norman: University of Oklahoma Press.

219. Cohen, D., & Nisbett, R. E. (1997). Field experiments examining the culture of honor: The role of institutions in perpetuating norms about violence. *Personality and Social Psychology Bulletin, 23,* 1188–1199.

220. Vandello, J. A., & Cohen, D. (2003). Male honor and female fidelity: Implicit cultural scripts that perpetuate domestic violence. *Journal of Personality and Social Psychology, 84*(5), 997–1010.

221. Cohen, D., & Nisbett, R. E. (1997). Field experiments examining the culture of honor: The role of institutions in perpetuating norms about violence. *Personality and Social Psychology Bulletin, 23,* 1188–1199.

222. Kelly, M. H. (1999). Regional naming patterns and the culture of honor. *Names, 47,* 3–20.

223. Campbell, J. K. (1965). Honour and the devil. In J. G. Peristiany (Ed.), *Honour and shame: The values of Mediterranean society* (pp. 112–175). London: Weidenfeld & Nicolson.

224. Edgerton, R. (1971). *The individual in cultural adaptation.* Berkeley: University of California Press.

225. Peristiany, J. G. (Ed.). (1965). *Honour and shame: The values of Mediterranean society.* London: Weidenfeld & Nicolson.

226. United Nations Population Fund. (2007/2008). A human rights and health priority. Retrieved October 17, 2008, from http://www.unfpa.org/swp/2000/english/ch03.html

227. William, I. M. (1993). *Humiliation: And other essays on honor, social discomfort, and violence.* Ithaca, NY: Cornell University Press.

228. http://www.emotionalcompetency.com/humiliation.htm

229. Lindner, E. G. (2002). Healing the cycles of humiliation: How to attend to the emotional aspects of "unsolvable" conflicts and the use of "humiliation entrepreneurship." *Peace and Conflict: Journal of Peace Psychology, 8,* 125–138.

230. Serota, K. B., Levine, T. R., & Boster, F. J. (2010). The prevalence of lying in America: Three studies of self-reported lies. *Human Communication Research, 36*(1), 2–25.

231. Weiss, B., & Feldman, R. S. (2006). Looking good and lying to do it: Deception as an impression management strategy in job interviews. *Journal of Applied Social Psychology, 36*(4), 1070–1086.

232. Underwood, J. D. M., Kerlin, L., & Farrington-Flint, L. (2011). The lies we tell and what they say about us: Using behavioural characteristics to explain Facebook activity. *Computers in Human Behavior, 27*(5), 1621–1626.

233. Rowatt, W. C., Cunningham, M. R., & Druen, P. B. (1999). Lying to get a date: The effect of facial physical attractiveness on the willingness to deceive prospective dating partners. *Journal of Social and Personal Relationships, 16*(2), 209–223.

234. Toma, C. L., & Hancock, J. T. (2010). Looks and lies: The role of physical attractiveness in online dating self-presentation and deception. *Communication Research, 37*(3), 335–351.

235. Williams, S. S. (2001). Sexual lying among college students in close and casual relationships. *Journal of Applied Social Psychology, 31*(11), 2322–2338.

236. Cole, R. (2001). Lying to the one you love: The use of deception in romantic relationships. *Journal of Social and Personal Relationships, 18*(1), 107–129.
237. van 't Veer, A. E., Stel, M., & van Beest, I. (2014). Limited capacity to lie: Cognitive load interferes with being dishonest. *Judgment and Decision Making, 9*(3), 199–206. doi: 10.2139/ssrn.2351377
238. Ekman, P., & O'Sullivan, M. (1991). Who can catch a liar? *American Psychologist, 46*(9), 913–920.
239. Bond, C. F., Jr., & DePaulo, B. M. (2008). Individual differences in judging deception: Accuracy and bias. *Psychological Bulletin, 134*(4), 477–492.
240. Nysse-Carris, K. L., Bottoms, B. L., & Salerno, J. M. (2011). Experts' and novices' abilities to detect children's high-stakes lies of omission. *Psychology, Public Policy, and Law, 17*(1), 76–98.
241. Newman, M. L., Pennebaker, J. W., Berry, D. S., & Richards, J. M. (2003). Lying words: Predicting deception from linguistic styles. *Personality and Social Psychology Bulletin, 29*(5), 665–675.
242. Fields, D. A., & Kafai, Y. B. (2010). "Stealing from grandma" or generating cultural knowledge? Contestations and effects of cheating in a tween virtual world. *Games and Culture: A Journal of Interactive Media, 5*(1), 64–87.
243. Honour, J. W. (2004, July 8). The fight for fair play: Can athletes be held responsible for every substance they take? *Nature, 430,* 143–144.
244. Simkin, M. G., & McLeod, A. (2010). Why do college students cheat? *Journal of Business Ethics, 94*(3), 441–453.
245. Davis, S. F., Grover, C. A., Becker, A. H., & McGregor, L. N. (1992). Academic dishonesty: Prevalence, determinants, techniques, and punishments. *Teaching of Psychology, 19,* 16–20.
246. Bosch, T. (2012, August 20). Why would someone cheat on a free online class that doesn't count toward anything? *Slate.* Retrieved from http://www.slate.com/blogs/future_tense/2012/08/20/coursera_plagiarism_why_would_students_cheat_in_a_free_online_class_that_doesn_t_over_academic_credit_.html
247. Chait, J. (2013, April 2). Teachers cheating on tests: Not a big deal. *New York Magazine.* Retrieved from http://nymag.com/daily/intelligencer/2013/04/teachers-cheating-on-tests-not-a-big-deal.html
248. Park, C. (2003). In other (people's) words: Plagiarism by university students—literature and lessons. *Assessment and Evaluation in Higher Education, 28,* 471–488.
249. Ruedy, N. E., Moore, C., Gino, F., & Schweitzer, M. E. (2013). The cheater's high: The unexpected affective benefits of unethical behavior. *Journal of Personality and Social Psychology, 105*(4), 531–548. doi: 10.1037/a0034231
250. Vohs, K. D., & Schooler, J. W. (2008). The value of believing in free will: Encouraging a belief in determinism increases cheating. *Psychological Science, 19,* 49–54.
251. Gino, F., & Ariely, D. (2012). The dark side of creativity: Original thinkers can be more dishonest. *Journal of Personality and Social Psychology, 102,* 445–459.
252. Shu, L. L., & Gino, F. (2012). Sweeping dishonesty under the rug: How unethical actions lead to forgetting of moral rules. *Journal of Personality and Social Psychology, 102,* 1164–1177.
253. Henle, C. A., Reeve, C. L., & Pitts, V. E. (2010). Stealing time at work: Attitudes, social pressure, and perceived control as predictors of time theft. *Journal of Business Ethics, 94*(1), 53–67.
254. Shteir, R. (2011). *The steal: a cultural history of shoplifting.* New York: Penguin Press.
255. Hagan, F. E. (2010). *Crime types and criminals.* Thousand Oaks, CA: Sage Publications.
256. 1 Timothy 6:10 (Bible).
257. Gino, F., & Mogilner, C. (2014). Time, money, and morality. *Psychological Science, 25,* 414–421.
258. Mazar, N., Amir, O., & Ariely, D. (2008). The dishonesty of honest people: A theory of self-concept maintenance. *Journal of Marketing Research, 45,* 633–644.
259. Yang, Q., Wu, X., Zhou, X., Mead, N. L., Vohs, K. D., & Baumeister, R. F. (2013). Diverging effects of clean versus dirty money on attitudes, values, and interpersonal behavior. *Journal of Personality and Social Psychology, 104,* 473–489.
260. Russakoff, R., & Goodman, M. (2011, July 14). Employee theft: Are you blind to it? *CBS Money Watch.* Retrieved from http://www.cbsnews.com/news/employee-theft-are-you-blind-to-it/
261. Umphress, E. E., Ren, L. R., Bingham, J. B., & Gogus, C. I. (2009). The influence of distributive justice on lying for and stealing from a supervisor. *Journal of Business Ethics, 86,* 507–518.
262. Umphress, E. E., Ren, L. R., Bingham, J. B., & Gogus, C. I. (2009). The influence of distributive justice on lying for and stealing from a supervisor. *Journal of Business Ethics, 86*(4), 507–518.
263. Katz, J. (1988). *Seductions of crime: Moral and sensual attractions in doing evil.* New York: Basic Books.
264. Federal Trade Commission (2019). *Consumer information.* Retrieved August 25, 2019 from https://www.consumer.ftc.gov
265. Federal Trade Commission: Consumer information. Retrieved from http://www.consumer.ftc.gov/features/feature-0014-identity-theft
266. U.S. Department of Justice. (2019). *Identity theft.* Retrieved August 25, 2019 from http://www.justice.gov/criminal/fraud/websites/idtheft.html
267. Altschuler, G. C. (2001, January 7). Battling the cheats. *New York Times.* Retrieved from https://www.nytimes.com/2001/01/07/education/college-prep-battling-the-cheats.html
268. Roberts, J. (2013, November 2). Three pages of Rand Paul's book were plagiarized from think tanks. *Reuters.* Retrieved August 25, 2019 from http://www.buzzfeed.com/andrewkaczynski/entire-section-of-rand-pauls-book-copied-verbatim-from-case#1m04yi5
269. Hayes, R., & Downs, D. M. (2011). Controlling retail theft with CCTV domes, CCTV public view monitors, and protective containers: A randomized controlled trial. *Security Journal, 24*(3), 237–250.
270. Yap, A., Wazlawek, A. S., Lucas, B. J., Cuddy, A. J. C., & Carney, D. R. (2013). The ergonomics of dishonesty: The effect of incidental posture on stealing, cheating, and traffic violations. *Psychological Science, 24*(11), 2281-2289. doi: 10.1177/0956797613492425
271. Krauss, R. M., Freedman, J. L., & Whitcup, M. (1978). Field and laboratory studies of littering. *Journal of Experimental Social Psychology, 14,* 109–122.
272. Reiter, S. M., & Samuel, W. (1980). Littering as a function of prior litter and the presence or absence of prohibitive signs. *Journal of Applied Social Psychology, 10,* 45–55.
273. Bator, R. J., Bryan, A. D., & Schultz, P. W. (2011). Who gives a hoot? Intercept surveys of litterers and disposers. *Environment and Behavior, 43*(3), 295–315.
274. Texas Municipal League Intergovernmental Risk Pool. (2018, April 20). Don't Mess with Texas - The story behind the slogan. https://blog.tmlirp.org/dont-mess-with-texas-the-story-behind-the-slogan
275. Patel, V., Thomson, G. W., & Wilson, N. (2013). Cigarette butt littering in city streets: A new methodology for studying and results. *Tobacco Control: An International Journal, 22*(1), 59–62. doi: 10.1136/tobaccocontrol-2012-050529
276. Forsyth, A. J. M., & Davidson, N. (2010). The nature and extent of illegal drug and alcohol-related litter in Scottish social housing community: A photographic investigation. *Addiction Research & Theory, 18*(1), 71–83.
277. Cialdini, R. B., Reno, R. R., & Kallgren, C. A. (1990). A focus theory of normative conduct: Recycling the concept of norms to reduce littering in public places. *Journal of Personality and Social Psychology, 58,* 1015–1026.
278. Kallgren, C. A., Reno, R. R., & Cialdini, R. B. (2000). Littering can be reduced by anti-littering norms: A focus theory of normative conduct: When norms do and do not affect behavior. *Personality and Social Psychology Bulletin, 26,* 1002–1012.
279. Reno, R. R., Cialdini, R. B., & Kallgren, C. A. (1993). The trans-situational influence of social norms. *Journal of Personality and Social Psychology, 64,* 104–112.
280. Reich, J. W., & Robertson, J. L. (1979). Reactance and norm appeal in anti-littering messages. *Journal of Applied Social Psychology, 9,* 91–101.
281. Grasmick, H. G., Bursik, R. J., & Kinsey, K. A. (1991). Shame and embarrassment as deterrents to noncompliance with the law: The case of an antilittering campaign. *Environment and Behavior, 23,* 233–251.
282. Reams, M. A., Geaghan, J. P., & Gendron, R. C. (1996). The link between recycling and litter: A field study. *Environment and Behavior, 28,* 92–110.
283. Trinkaus, J. (1984). A bottle law: An informal look. *Perceptual and Motor Skills, 59,* 806.
284. Finnie, W. C. (1973). Field experiments and litter control. *Environment and Behavior, 5,* 123–143.
285. de Kort, Y. A. W., McCalley, L. T., & Midden, C. J. H. (2008). Persuasive trash cans: Activation of littering norms by design. *Environment and Behavior, 40*(6), 870–891.

CHAPTER 11
Interpersonal Attraction and Rejection

1. Shohat-Ophir, G., Kaun, K. R., Azanchi, R., & Heberlein, U. (2012). Sexual deprivation increases ethanol intake in Drosophila. *Science, 335,* 1351–1355.
2. Bowlby, J. (1969). *Attachment and loss: Vol. 1. Attachment.* New York: Basic Books.
3. Bowlby, J. (1973). *Attachment and loss: Vol. 2. Separation anxiety and anger.* New York: Basic Books.
4. Baumeister, R. F., & Leary, M. R. (1995). The need to belong: Desire for interpersonal attachments as a fundamental human motivation. *Psychological Bulletin, 117,* 497–529.
5. Jones, W. (1989, August). Address given at the annual convention of the American Psychological Association, New Orleans.
6. McKenna, K. Y. A., & Bargh, J. A. (1998). Coming out in the age of the Internet: Identity "demarginalization" through virtual group participation. *Journal of Personality and Social Psychology, 75,* 681–694.
7. McKenna, K. Y. A., & Bargh, J. A. (1999). Causes and consequences of social interaction on the Internet: A conceptual framework. *Media Psychology, 1,* 249–269.
8. McKenna, K. Y. A., & Bargh, J. A. (2000). Plan 9 from Cyberspace: The implications of the Internet for personality and social psychology. *Personality and Social Psychology Review, 4,* 57–75.
9. Dabbs, J. M. (2000). *Heroes, rogues, and lovers: Testosterone and behavior.* New York: McGraw-Hill.
10. Dabbs, J. M. (2000). *Heroes, rogues, and lovers: Testosterone and behavior.* New York: McGraw-Hill.
11. Roney, J. R., Mahler, S. V., & Maestripieri, D. (2003). Behavioral and hormonal responses of men to brief interactions with women. *Evolution and Human Behavior, 24,* 365–375.
12. Liu, D., & Baumeister, R. F. (2017). Social networking and personality if self-worth: A meta-anaylsis. *Journal of Research in Personality, 64,* 79-89.
13. Kross, E., Verduyn, P., Demiralp, E., Park, J., Lee, D. S., Lin, N., et al. (2013). Facebook use predicts declines in subjective well-being in young adults. *PLoS ONE, 8,* e69841.
14. Liu, D., Ainsworth, S. E., & Baumeister, R. F. (2016). A meta-analysis of social networking online and social capital. *Review of General Psychology, 20,* 369-391.
15. Storey, A. E., Walsh, C. L., Quinton, R. L., & Wynne-Edward, K. E. (2000). Hormonal correlates of paternal responsiveness in new and expectant fathers. *Evolution and Human Behavior, 21,* 79–95.
16. Dabbs, J. M. (2000). *Heroes, rogues, and lovers: Testosterone and behavior.* New York: McGraw-Hill.

17. Van Goozen, S. H. M., Cohen-Kettenis, P. T., Gooren, L. J. G. M., Frijda, N. H., & Can de Poll, N. E. (1995). Gender differences in behaviour: Activating effects of cross-sex hormones. *Psychoneuroendocrinology, 20,* 343–363.
18. For a review, see Baumeister, R. F., Catanese, K. R., & Vohs, K. D. (2001). Is there a gender difference in strength of sex drive? Theoretical views, conceptual distinctions, and a review of relevant evidence. *Personality and Social Psychology Review, 5,* 242–273.
19. Ronay, R., & von Hippel, W. (2010). The presence of an attractive woman elevates testosterone and physical risk taking in young men. *Social Psychological and Personality Science, 1,* 57–64.
20. Worthman, C. M. (1999). Faster, farther, higher: Biology and the discourses on human sexuality. In D. Suggs & A. Miracle (Eds.), *Culture, biology, and sexuality* (pp. 64–75). Athens: University of Georgia Press.
21. Dunbar, R. I. M. (1998). The social brain hypothesis. *Evolutionary Anthropology, 6,* 178–190.
22. Ainsworth, M. D. (1989). Attachments beyond infancy. *American Psychologist, 44,* 709–716.
23. Axelrod, R., & Hamilton, W. D. (1981). The evolution of cooperation. *Science, 211,* 1390–1396.
24. Baumeister, R. F., & Leary, M. R. (1995). The need to belong: Desire for interpersonal attachments as a fundamental human motivation. *Psychological Bulletin, 117,* 497–529.
25. Bowlby, J. (1969). *Attachment and loss: Vol. 1. Attachment.* New York: Basic Books.
26. Buss, D. M. (1990). The evolution of anxiety and social exclusion. *Journal of Social and Clinical Psychology, 9,* 196–210.
27. Buss, D. M. (1991). Evolutionary personality psychology. *Annual Review of Psychology, 42,* 459–491.
28. Egan, G. (1970). *Encounter: Group processes for interpersonal growth.* Monterey, CA: Brooks/Cole.
29. Lacoursiere, R. B. (1980). *The life cycles of groups: Group developmental stage theory.* New York: Human Sciences Press.
30. Lieberman, M. A., Yalom, I. D., & Miles, M. B. (1973). *Encounter groups: First facts.* New York: Basic Books.
31. Baumeister, R. F., & Wotman, S. R. (1992). *Breaking hearts: The two sides of unrequited love.* New York: Guilford Press.
32. Baumeister, R. F., & Leary, M. R. (1995). The need to belong: Desire for interpersonal attachments as a fundamental human motivation. *Psychological Bulletin, 117,* 497–529.
33. Adler, P. (1980). On becoming a prostitute. In E. Muga (Ed.), *Studies in prostitution* (pp. 22–26). Nairobi: Kenya Literature Bureau.
34. McLeod, E. (1982). *Women working: Prostitution today.* London: Croom Helm.
35. Symanski, R. (1980). Prostitution in Nevada. In E. Muga (Ed.), *Studies in prostitution* (pp. 246–279). Nairobi: Kenya Literature Bureau.
36. Bunker, B. B., Zubek, J. M., Vanderslice, V. J., & Rice, R. W. (1992). Quality of life in dual-career families: Commuting versus single-residence couples. *Journal of Marriage and the Family, 54,* 399–407.
37. Gerstel, N., & Gross, H. (1982). Commuter marriages: A review. *Marriage and Family Review, 5,* 71–93.
38. Gerstel, N., & Gross, H. (1984). *Commuter marriage: A study of work and family.* New York: Guilford Press.
39. Govaerts, K., & Dixon, D. N. (1988). ... Until careers do us part: Vocational and marital satisfaction in the dual-career commuter marriage. *International Journal for the Advancement of Counseling, 11,* 265–281.
40. Harrison, A. A., & Connors, M. M. (1984). Groups in exotic environments. In L. Berkowitz (Ed.), *Advances in Experimental Social Psychology* (Vol. 18, pp. 49–87). New York: Academic Press.
41. Winfield, F. E. (1985). *Commuter marriage.* New York: Columbia University Press.
42. Caldwell, M. A., & Peplau, L. A. (1982). Sex differences in same-sex friendships. *Sex Roles, 8,* 721–732.
43. Wheeler, L., & Nezlek, J. (1977). Sex differences in social participation. *Journal of Personality and Social Psychology, 35,* 742–754.
44. Reis, H. T. (1990). The role of intimacy in interpersonal relations. *Journal of Social and Clinical Psychology, 9,* 15–30.
45. Wheeler, L., & Nezlek, J. (1977). Sex differences in social participation. *Journal of Personality and Social Psychology, 35,* 742–754.
46. Lynch, J. J. (1979). *The broken heart: The medical consequences of loneliness.* New York: Basic Books.
47. Bhatti, B., Derezotes, D., Kim, S., & Specht, H. (1989). The association between child maltreatment and self-esteem. In A. M. Mecca, N. J. Smelser, & J. Vasconcellos (Eds.), *The social importance of self-esteem* (pp. 24–71). Berkeley: University of California Press.
48. Cacioppo, J. T., Hawkley, L. C., Berntson, G. G., Ernst, J. M., Gibbs, A. C., Stickgold, R., et al. (2002). Lonely days invade the nights: Social modulation of sleep efficiency. *Psychological Science, 13,* 385–388.
49. Cacioppo, J. T., Hawkley, L. C., Crawford, L. E., Ernst, J. M., Burleson, M. H., Kowalewski, R. B., et al. (2002). Loneliness and health: Potential mechanisms. *Psychosomatic Medicine, 64,* 407–417.
50. DeLongis, A., Folkman, S., & Lazarus, S. (1988). The impact of daily stress on health and mood: Psychosocial and social resources as mediators. *Journal of Personality and Social Psychology, 54,* 486–495.
51. Goodwin, J. S., Hunt, W. C., Key, C. R., & Samet, J. M. (1987). The effect of marital status on stage, treatment, and survival of cancer patients. *Journal of the American Medical Association, 258,* 3125–3130.
52. Hawkley, L. C., Burleson, M. H., Berntson, G. G., & Cacioppo, J. T. (2003). Loneliness in everyday life: Cardiovascular activity, psychosocial context, and health behaviors. *Journal of Personality and Social Psychology, 85,* 105–120.
53. Herlitz, J., Wiklund, I., Caidahl, K., Hartford, M., Haglid, M., Karlsson, B. W., et al. (1998). The feeling of loneliness prior to coronary artery bypass grafting might be a predictor of short- and long-term postoperative mortality. *European Journal of Vascular and Endovascular Surgery, 16,* 120–125.
54. Kiecolt-Glaser, J. K., Fisher, L. D., Ogrocki, P., Stout, J. C., Speicher, C. E., & Glaser, R. (1987). Marital quality, marital disruption, and immune function. *Psychosomatic Medicine, 49,* 13–34.
55. Kiecolt-Glaser, J. K., Garner, W., Speicher, C., Penn, G. M., Holliday, J., & Glaser, R. (1984). Psychosocial modifiers of immunocompetence in medical students. *Psychosomatic Medicine, 46,* 7–14.
56. For review, see Uchino, B. N., Cacioppo, J. T., & Kiecolt-Glaser, J. K. (1996). The relationship between social support and physiological processes: A review with emphasis on underlying mechanisms and implications for health. *Psychological Bulletin, 119,* 488–531.
57. Holt-Lunstad, J., Smith, T. B., & Layton, J. B. (2010). Social relationships and mortality risk: A meta-analytic review. *PLOS Medicine, 7,* e1000316.
58. Cacioppo, J. T., & Hawkley, L. C. (2005). People thinking about people: The vicious cycle of being a social outcast in one's own mind. In K. D. Williams, J. P. Forgas, & W. von Hippel (Eds.), *The social outcast: Ostracism, social exclusion, rejection, and bullying* (pp. 91–108). New York: Psychology Press.
59. Lambert, N. M., Stillman, T. F., Hicks, J. A., Baumeister, R. F., Kamble, S., & Fincham, F. D. (2013). To belong is to matter: Sense of belonging enhances meaning in life. *Personality and Social Psychology Bulletin, 39,* 1418–1427.
60. Gardner, W. L., Pickett, C. L., & Knowles, M. (2005). Social snacking and shielding: Using social symbols, selves, and surrogates in the service of belonging needs. In K. D. Williams, J. P. Forgas, & W. von Hippel (Eds.), *The social outcast: Ostracism, social exclusion, rejection, and bullying* (pp. 227–242). New York: Psychology Press.
61. Gardner, W., Seeley, E., Gabriel, S., Pennington, G., Solomon, J., Ernst, J., et al. (2002). The role of "his" and "her" forms of interdependence in everyday life: Gender, belonging, and social experience. Unpublished manuscript, Northwestern University.
62. Jones, E. E. (1964). *Ingratiation.* New York: Irvington.
63. Byrne, D. (1971). *The attraction paradigm.* New York: Academic Press.
64. Green, G. (2005, December 9). Man dates gal on Internet for six months—and it turns out she's his mother! Retrieved September 2, 2019 from http://entertainment.tv.yahoo.com/news/wwn
65. Gangestad, S. W., & Snyder, M. (2000). Self-monitoring: Appraisal and reappraisal. *Psychological Bulletin, 126,* 530–555.
66. Lennox, R. D., & Wolfe, R. N. (1984). Revision of the self-monitoring scale. *Journal of Personality and Social Psychology, 46,* 1349–1364.
67. Snyder, M. (1974). Self monitoring of expressive behavior. *Journal of Personality and Social Psychology, 30,* 526–537.
68. Snyder, M., & Gangestad, S. (1986). On the nature of self-monitoring: Matters of assessment, matters of validity. *Journal of Personality and Social Psychology, 51,* 125–139.
69. Jensen, A. (1977). Genetic and behavioral effects of nonrandom mating. In C. Noble, R. Osborne, & N. Weyl (Eds.), *Human variation: Biogenetics of age, race, and sex.* New York: Academic Press.
70. Murstein, B. I., & Christy, P. (1976). Physical attractiveness and marriage adjustment in middle-aged couples. *Journal of Personality and Social Psychology, 34,* 537–542.
71. White, G. L. (1980). Physical attractiveness and courtship progress. *Journal of Personality and Social Psychology, 39,* 660–668.
72. Feingold, A. (1988). Matching for attractiveness in romantic partners and same-sex friends: A meta-analysis and theoretical critique. *Psychological Bulletin, 104,* 226–235.
73. McKillip, J., & Reidel, S. L. (1983). External validity of matching on physical attractiveness for same and opposite sex couples. *Journal of Applied Social Psychology, 13,* 328–337.
74. Walster, E., Aronson, V., Abrahams, D., & Rottmann, L. (1966). Importance of physical attractiveness in dating behavior. *Journal of Personality and Social Psychology, 4,* 508–516.
75. Fukuyama, F. (1999). *Trust.* New York: Free Press.
76. Rosenbaum, M. E. (1986). The repulsion hypothesis: On the nondevelopment of relationships. *Journal of Personality and Social Psychology, 51,* 1156–1166.
77. Norton, M. I., Frost, J. H., & Ariely, D. (2007). Less is more: The lure of ambiguity, or why familiarity breeds contempt. *Journal of Personality and Social Psychology, 92,* 97–105.
78. Jones, E. E., & Wortman, E. (1973). *Ingratiation: An attributional approach.* Morristown, NJ: General Learning Press.
79. Brehm, J. W., & Cole, A. H. (1966). Effect of a favor which reduces freedom. *Journal of Personality and Social Psychology, 3,* 420–426.
80. Jones, E. E., & Wortman, E. (1973). *Ingratiation: An attributional approach.* Morristown, NJ: General Learning Press.
81. Cialdini, R. B. (2001). *Influence: Science and practice* (4th ed.). Boston: Allyn and Bacon.
82. Cottrell, C. A., Neuberg, S. L., & Li, N. P. (2007). What do people desire in others? A sociofunctional perspective on the importance of different valued characteristics. *Journal of Personality and Social Psychology, 92,* 208–231.
83. Fiske, S. T., & Yamamoto, M. (2005). Coping with rejection: Core social motives, across cultures and individuals. In K. D. Williams, J. P. Forgas, & W. von Hippel (Eds.), *The social outcast: Ostracism, social exclusion, rejection, and bullying* (pp. 185–199). New York: Psychology Press.

84. Chartrand, T. L., & Bargh, J. A. (1999). The chameleon effect: The perception-behavior link and social interaction. *Journal of Personality and Social Psychology, 76*, 893–910.
85. Lakin, J. L., & Chartrand, T. L. (2005). Exclusion and nonconscious behavioral mimicry. In K. D. Williams, J. P. Forgas, & W. von Hippel (Eds.), *The social outcast: Ostracism, social exclusion, rejection, and bullying* (pp. 279–296). New York: Psychology Press.
86. Robinson, E., Tobias, T., Shaw, L., Freeman, E., Higgs, S. (2011). Social matching of food intake and the need for social acceptance. *Appetite, 56*, 747–752.
87. Sharps, M., Higgs, S., Blissett, J., Nouwen, A., Chechlacz, M., Allen, H. A., & Robinson, E. (2015). Examining evidence for behavioural mimicry of parental eating by adolescent females. An observational study. *Appetite, 89*, 56–61.
88. Baumeister, R. F., Wotman, S. R., & Stillwell, A. M. (1993). Unrequited love: On heartbreak, anger, guilt, scriptlessness, and humiliation. *Journal of Personality and Social Psychology, 64*, 377–394.
89. Goodwin, G. P., Piazza, J., & Rozin, P. (2013). Moral character predominates in person perception and evaluation. *Journal of Personality and Social Psychology, 106*, 148–168.
90. Righetti, F., & Finkenauer, C. (2011). If you are able to control yourself, I will trust you: The role of perceived self-control in interpersonal trust. *Journal of Personality and Social Psychology, 100*, 874–886.
91. Shea, C. T., Davisson, E. K., & Fitzsimons, G. (2013). Riding other people's coattails: Individuals with low self-control value self-control in other people. *Psychological Science, 24*, 1031–1036.
92. Uhlmann, E. L., Pizarro, D. A., & Diermeier, D. (2015). A person-centered approach to moral judgment. *Perspectives on Psychological Science, 10*, 72–81.
93. Festinger, L., Schachter, S., & Back, K. W. (1950) *Social pressures in informal groups: A study of human factors in housing*. New York: Harper.
94. Latane, B., Eckman, J., & Joy, V. (1966). Shared stress and interpersonal attraction. *Journal of Experimental Social Psychology Supplement, 1*, 80–94.
95. Elder, G. H., Jr., & Clipp, E. C. (1988). Combat experience, comradeship, and psychological health. In J. P. Wilson, Z. Harel, & B. Kahana (Eds.), *Human adaptation to extreme stress: From the Holocaust to Vietnam* (pp. 131–156). New York: Plenum Press.
96. Barbee, A. P., Lawrence, T., & Cunningham, M. R. (1998). When a friend is in need: Feelings about seeking, giving, and receiving social support. In P. Anderson & L. Guerro (Eds.), *Handbook of communication and emotion* (pp. 282–298). New York: Academic Press.
97. Cunningham, M. R. (2009). Social allergies. In H. Reis & S. Sprecher (Eds.), *Handbook of human relationships*. Thousand Oaks, CA: Sage.
98. Cunningham, M. R., Barbee, A. P., & Druen, P. B. (1997). Social antigens and allergies: The development of hypersensitivity in close relationships. In R. Kowalski (Ed.), *Aversive interpersonal behaviors* (pp. 190–215). New York: Plenum Press.
99. Cunningham, M. R., Barbee, A. P., & Mandal, E. (2009). Hurtful behaviors in the workplace. In R. Kowalski (Ed.), *Feeling hurt in close relationships* (pp. 417–456). Cambridge: Cambridge University Press.
100. Eagly, A. H., Ashmore, R. D., Makhijani, M. G., & Longo, L. C. (1991). What is beautiful is good, but...: A meta-analytic review of the physical attractiveness stereotype. *Psychological Bulletin, 110*, 109–128.
101. Feingold, A. (1992). Gender differences in mate selection preferences: A test of the parental investment model. *Psychological Bulletin, 112*, 125–139.
102. Jackson, L. A., Hunter, J. E., & Hodge, C. N. (1995). Physical attractiveness and intellectual competence: A meta-analytic review. *Social Psychology Quarterly, 58*, 108–122.
103. Wheeler, L., & Kim, Y. (1997). What is beautiful is culturally good: The physical attractiveness stereotype has different content in collectivistic cultures. *Personality and Social Psychology Bulletin, 23*, 795–802.
104. Walster, E., Aronson, V., Abrahams, D., & Rottmann, L. (1966). Importance of physical attractiveness in dating behavior. *Journal of Personality and Social Psychology, 4*, 508–516.
105. Clifford, M., & Walster, E. (1973). The effect of physical attractiveness on teacher expectations. *Sociology of Education, 46*, 248–258.
106. Dion, K. (1973). Young children's stereotyping of facial attractiveness. *Developmental Psychology, 9*, 183–188.
107. Dion, K. K., Berscheid, E., & Walster, F. H. (1972). What is beautiful is good. *Journal of Personality and Social Psychology, 24*, 285–290.
108. Langlois, J. H., Roggman, L. A., Casey, R. J., & Ritter, J. M. (1987). Infant preferences for attractive faces: Rudiments of a stereotype? *Developmental Psychology, 23*, 363–369.
109. Cash, T. F., & Janda, L. H. (1984). The eye of the beholder. *Psychology Today, 18*, 46–52.
110. Mack, D., & Rainey, D. (1990). Female applicants' grooming and personnel selection. *Journal of Social Behavior and Personality, 5*, 399–407.
111. West, S. G., & Brown, T. J. (1975). Physical attractiveness, the severity of the emergency and helping: A field experiment and interpersonal simulation. *Journal of Experimental Social Psychology, 11*, 531–538.
112. Singh, D. (1993). Adaptive significance of female physical attractiveness: Role of waist-to-hip ratio. *Journal of Personality and Social Psychology, 65*(2), 293–307.
113. Singh, D. (1995). Female judgment of male attractiveness and desirability for relationships: Role of waist-to-hip ratio and financial status. *Journal of Personality and Social Psychology, 69*(6), 1089–1101.
114. Hitsch, G. J., Hortaçsu, A., & Ariely, D. (2006). What makes you click? Mate preferences and matching outcomes in online dating. MIT Sloan Research Paper No. 4603–06. Available at http://home.uchicago.edu/hortacsu/onlinedating.pdf
115. Shepperd, J. A., & Strathman, A. J. (1989). Attractiveness and height: The role of stature in dating preference, frequency of dating, and perceptions of attractiveness. *Personality and Social Psychology Bulletin, 15*(4), 617–627.
116. Westfall, R., Millar, M., & Walsh, M. (2016) Effects of instructor attractiveness on learning. *Journal of General Psychology, 143*, 161–171.
117. Ma-Kellams, C., Wang, M. C., & Cardiel, H. (2017). Attractiveness and relationship longevity: Beauty is not what it is cracked up to be. *Personal Relationships, 24*, 146–161.
118. Grammer, K., Fink, B., Moller A. P., & Thornhill, R. (2003). Darwinian aesthetics: Sexual selection and the biology of beauty. *Biological Reviews, 78*, 385–407.
119. Garner, D. M., Garfinkel, P. E., Schwartz, D., & Thompson, M. (1980). Cultural expectations of thinness in women. *Psychological Reports, 47*, 483–491.
120. Buss, D. M. (1994). *The evolution of desire: Strategies of human mating*. New York: Basic Books.
121. Maner, J. K., Gailliot, M. T., & DeWall, C. N. (2007). Adaptive attentional attunement: Evidence for mating-related perceptual bias. *Evolution and Human Behavior, 28*(1), 28–36.
122. Thornhill, R., & Gangestad, S. W. (1999). The scent of symmetry: A human sex pheromone that signals fitness? *Evolution and Human Behavior, 20*, 175–201.
123. Kant, I. (1924). *Critique of judgment*. Hamburg: Felix Meiner Verlag. (Original work published 1790).
124. Langlois, J. H., Roggman, L. A., Casey, R. J., & Ritter, J. M. (1987). Infant preferences for attractive faces: Rudiments of a stereotype? *Developmental Psychology, 23*, 363–369.
125. Nelson, L. D., & Morrison, E. L. (2005). The symptoms of resource scarcity: Judgments of food and finances impact preferences for potential partners. *Psychological Science, 16*(2), 167–173.
126. Finkel, E. J., Eastwick, P. W., Karney, B. R., Reis, H. T., & Sprecher, S. (2012). Online dating: A critical analysis from the perspective of psychological science. *Psychological Science in the Public Interest, 13*, 3–66.
127. Toma, C. L., Hancock, J. T., & Ellison, N. B. (2008). Separating fact from fiction: An examination of deceptive self-presentation on online dating profiles. *Personality and Social Psychology Bulletin, 34*, 1023–1036.
128. Williams, K. D. (2001). *Ostracism: The power of silence*. New York: Guilford Press.
129. Williams, K. D. (2001). *Ostracism: The power of silence*. New York: Guilford Press.
130. Sommer, K. L., & Yoon, J. (2013). When silence is golden: Ostracism as resource conservation during aversive interactions. *Journal of Social and Personal Relationships, 30*, 901–918.
131. Ray, D. G., Gomillion, S., Pintea, A. I., & Hamlin, I. (2018). On being forgotten: Memory and forgetting serve as signals of interpersonal importance. *Journal of Personality and Social Psychology, 116*, 259–276.
132. King, L. A., & Geise, A. C. (2011). Being forgotten: Implications for the experience of meaning in life. *Journal of Social Psychology, 151*, 696–709.
133. Williams, K. D. (2001). *Ostracism: The power of silence*. New York: Guilford Press.
134. Williams, K. D., & Zadro, L. (2005). Ostracism: The indiscriminate early detection system. In K. D. Williams, J. P. Forgas, & W. von Hippel (Eds.), *The social outcast: Ostracism, social exclusion, rejection, and bullying* (pp. 19–34). New York: Psychology Press.
135. Williams, K. D. (2001). *Ostracism: The power of silence*. New York: Guilford Press.
136. Williams, K. D., & Zadro, L. (2005). Ostracism: The indiscriminate early detection system. In K. D. Williams, J. P. Forgas, & W. von Hippel (Eds.), *The social outcast: Ostracism, social exclusion, rejection, and bullying* (pp. 19–34). New York: Psychology Press.
137. Romero-Canyas, R., & Downey, G. (2005). Rejection sensitivity as a predictor of affective and behavioral responses to interpersonal stress: A defensive motivational system. In K. D. Williams, J. P. Forgas, & W. von Hippel (Eds.), *The social outcast: Ostracism, social exclusion, rejection, and bullying* (pp. 131–154). New York: Psychology Press.
138. Sommer, K. L., & Rubin, Y. (2005). Maintaining self-esteem in the face of rejection. In K. D. Williams, J. P. Forgas, & W. von Hippel (Eds.), *The social outcast: Ostracism, social exclusion, rejection, and bullying* (pp. 171–184). New York: Psychology Press.
139. Leary, M. R., Springer, C., Negel, L., Ansell, E., & Evans, K. (1998). The causes, phenomenology, and consequences of hurt feelings. *Journal of Personality and Social Psychology, 74*, 1225–1237.
140. Leary, M. R. (2005). Varieties of interpersonal rejection. In K. D. Williams, J. P. Forgas, & W. von Hippel (Eds.), *The social outcast: Ostracism, social exclusion, rejection, and bullying* (pp. 35–54). New York: Psychology Press.
141. Twenge, J. M., Catanese, K. R., & Baumeister, R. F. (2002). Social exclusion causes self-defeating behavior. *Journal of Personality and Social Psychology, 83*, 606–615.
142. MacDonald, G., & Leary M. R. (2005). Why does social exclusion hurt? The relationship between social and physical pain. *Psychological Bulletin, 131*, 202–223.
143. Panksepp, J. (1998). *Affective neuroscience: The foundations of human and animal emotions*. London: Oxford University Press.
144. Panksepp, J., Herman, B. H., Conner, R., Bishop, P., & Scott, J. P. (1978). The biology of social

attachments: Opiates alleviate separation distress. *Biological Psychiatry, 13,* 607–618.

145. Panksepp, J., Najam, N., & Soares, F. (1980). Morphine reduces social cohesion in rats. *Pharmacology, Biochemistry, and Behavior, 11,* 131–134.

146. Panksepp, J., Vilberg, T., Bean, N. J., Coy, D. H., & Kastin, A. J. (1978). Reduction of distress vocalization in chicks by opiate-like peptides. *Brain Research Bulletin, 3,* 663–667.

147. DeWall, C. N., & Baumeister, R. F. (2006). Alone but feeling no pain: Effects of social exclusion on physical pain tolerance and pain threshold, affective forecasting, and interpersonal empathy. *Journal of Personality and Social Psychology, 91,* 1–15.

148. Kross, E., Berman, M. G., Mischel, W., Smith, E. E., and Wager, T. D. (2011). Social rejection shares somatosensory representations with physical pain. *Proceedings of the National Academy of Sciences, 108,* 6270–6275.

149. DeWall, C. N., MacDonald, G., Webster, G. D., Masten, C., Baumeister, R. F., Powell, C., Combs, D., Schurtz, D. R., Stillman, T. F., Tice, D. M., & Eisenberger, N. I. (2010). Tylenol reduces social pain: Behavioral and neural evidence. *Psychological Science, 21,* 931–937.

150. Baumeister, R. F., Twenge, J. M., & Nuss, C. K. (2002). Effects of social exclusion on cognitive processes: Anticipated aloneness reduces intelligent thought. *Journal of Personality and Social Psychology, 83,* 817–827.

151. Baumeister, R. F., DeWall, C. N., Ciarocco, N. J., & Twenge, J. M. (2005). Social exclusion impairs self-regulation. *Journal of Personality and Social Psychology, 88,* 589–684.

152. Blanchard, F. A., & Frost, R. O. (1983). Two factors of restraint: Concern for dieting and fluctuations. *Behavior Research and Therapy, 21,* 259–267.

153. Chiodo, J. (1987). Bulimia: An individual behavioral analysis. *Journal of Behavior Therapy and Experimental Psychiatry, 18,* 41–49.

154. Gross, J., & Rosen, J. C. (1988). Bulimia in adolescents: Prevalence and psychosocial correlates. *International Journal of Eating Disorders, 7,* 51–61.

155. Strober, M., & Humphrey, L. L. (1987). Familial contributions to the etiology and course of anorexia nervosa and bulimia. *Journal of Consulting and Clinical Psychology, 55,* 654–659.

156. Twenge, J. M., Catanese, K. R., & Baumeister, R. F. (2003). Social exclusion and the deconstructed state: Time perception, meaninglessness, lethargy, lack of emotion, and self-awareness. *Journal of Personality and Social Psychology, 85,* 409–423.

157. Baumeister, R. F., DeWall, C. N., Ciarocco, N. J., & Twenge, J. M. (2005). Social exclusion impairs self-regulation. *Journal of Personality and Social Psychology, 88,* 589–684.

158. Baumeister, R. F., DeWall, C. N., Ciarocco, N. J., & Twenge, J. M. (2005). Social exclusion impairs self-regulation. *Journal of Personality and Social Psychology, 88,* 589–684.

159. Bargh, J. A., & Shaley, I. (2012). The substitutability of physical and social warmth in daily life. *Emotion, 12,* 154–162.

160. Maner, J. K., DeWall, C. N., Baumeister, R. F., & Schaller, M. (2007). Does social exclusion motivate interpersonal reconnection? Resolving the "porcupine problem." *Journal of Personality and Social Psychology, 92*(1), 42–55.

161. Gardner, W. L., Pickett, C. L., & Brewer, M. B. (2000). Social exclusion and selective memory: How the need to belong influences memory for social events. *Personality and Social Psychology Bulletin, 26,* 486–496.

162. Gardner, W. L., Pickett, C. L., & Knowles, M. (2005). Social snacking and shielding: Using social symbols, selves, and surrogates in the service of belonging needs. In K. D. Williams, J. P. Forgas, & W. von Hippel (Eds.), *The social outcast: Ostracism, social exclusion, rejection, and bullying* (pp. 227–242). New York: Psychology Press.

163. Kim, S. H., Vincent, L. C., & Goncalo, J. A. (2012). Outside advantage: Can social rejection fuel creative thought? *Journal of Experimental Psychology: General, 142,* 605–611.

164. Twenge, J. M., Baumeister, R. F., Tice, D. M., & Stucke, T. S. (2001). If you can't join them, beat them: Effects of social exclusion on aggressive behavior. *Journal of Personality and Social Psychology, 81,* 1058–1069.

165. Twenge, J. M., Ciarocco, N. J., Cuervo, D., Bartels, J. M., & Baumeister, R. F. (2004). Social exclusion reduces prosocial behavior. *Journal of Personality and Social Psychology, 92,* 56–66.

166. Twenge, J. M., Catanese, K. R., & Baumeister, R. F. (2002). Social exclusion causes self-defeating behavior. *Journal of Personality and Social Psychology, 83,* 606–615.

167. Gaertner, L., & Iuzzini, J. (2005). Rejection and entitativity: A synergistic model of mass violence. In K. D. Williams, J. P. Forgas, & W. von Hippel (Eds.), *The social outcast: Ostracism, social exclusion, rejection, and bullying* (pp. 307–320). New York: Psychology Press.

168. Leary, M. R., Kowalski, R. M., Smith, L., & Phillips, S. (2003). Teasing, rejection, and violence: Case studies of the school shootings. *Aggressive Behavior, 29,* 202–214.

169. Juvonen, J., & Gross, E. F. (2005). The rejected and the bullied: Lessons about social misfits from developmental psychology. In K. D. Williams, J. P. Forgas, & W. von Hippel (Eds.), *The social outcast: Ostracism, social exclusion, rejection, and bullying* (pp. 155–170). New York: Psychology Press.

170. Twenge, J. M., Baumeister, R. F., Tice, D. M., & Stucke, T. S. (2001). If you can't join them, beat them: Effects of social exclusion on aggressive behavior. *Journal of Personality and Social Psychology, 81,* 1058–1069.

171. Ouwerkerk, J. W., Kerr, N. L., Gallucci, M., & Van Lange, P. A. M. (2005). Avoiding the social death penalty: Ostracism and cooperation in social dilemmas. In K. D. Williams, J. P. Forgas, & W. von Hippel (Eds.), *The social outcast: Ostracism, social exclusion, rejection, and bullying* (pp. 321–332). New York: Psychology Press.

172. Williams, K. D., & Zadro, L. (2005). Ostracism: The indiscriminate early detection system. In K. D. Williams, J. P. Forgas, & W. von Hippel (Eds.), *The social outcast: Ostracism, social exclusion, rejection, and bullying* (pp. 19–34). New York: Psychology Press.

173. Lakin, J. L., & Chartrand, T. L. (2005). Exclusion and nonconscious behavioral mimicry. In K. D. Williams, J. P. Forgas, & W. von Hippel (Eds.), *The social outcast: Ostracism, social exclusion, rejection, and bullying* (pp. 279–296). New York: Psychology Press.

174. Cialdini, J. T., & Patrick, W. (2008). *Loneliness.* New York: Norton.

175. Wheeler, L., Reis, H., & Nezlek, J. B. (1983). Loneliness, social interaction, and sex roles. *Journal of Personality and Social Psychology, 45*(4), 943–953.

176. Cacioppo, J. T., & Hawkley, L. C. (2005). People thinking about people: The vicious cycle of being a social outcast in one's own mind. In K. D. Williams, J. P. Forgas, & W. von Hippel (Eds.), *The social outcast: Ostracism, social exclusion, rejection, and bullying* (pp. 91–108). New York: Psychology Press.

177. Pickett, C. L., & Gardner, W. L. (2005). The social monitoring system: Enhanced sensitivity to social cues and information as an adaptive response to social exclusion and belonging need. In K. D. Williams, J. P. Forgas, & W. von Hippel (Eds.), *The social outcast: Ostracism, social exclusion, rejection, and bullying* (pp. 213–226). New York: Psychology Press.

178. Peplau, L. A., & Perlman, D. (Eds.). (1982). *Loneliness: A sourcebook of current theory, research, and therapy.* New York: Wiley.

179. Russell, D., Peplau, L. A., & Cutrona, C. E. (1980). The revised UCLA Loneliness Scale: Concurrent and discriminant validity evidence. *Journal of Personality and Social Psychology, 39,* 472–480.

180. Cacioppo, J. T., Ernst, J. M., Burleson, M. H., McClintock, M. K., Malarkey, W. B., Hawkley, L. C., et al. (2000). Lonely traits and concomitant physiological processes: The MacArthur Social Neuroscience Studies. *International Journal of Psychophysiology, 35,* 143–154.

181. Gardner, W. L., Pickett, C. L., & Knowles, M. (2005). Social snacking and shielding: Using social symbols, selves, and surrogates in the service of belonging needs. In K. D. Williams, J. P. Forgas, & W. von Hippel (Eds.), *The social outcast: Ostracism, social exclusion, rejection, and bullying* (pp. 227–242). New York: Psychology Press.

182. Cacioppo, J. T., & Hawkley, L. C. (2005). People thinking about people: The vicious cycle of being a social outcast in one's own mind. In K. D. Williams, J. P. Forgas, & W. von Hippel (Eds.), *The social outcast: Ostracism, social exclusion, rejection, and bullying* (pp. 91–108). New York: Psychology Press.

183. Gardner, W., Seeley, E., Gabriel, S., Pennington, G., Solomon, J., Ernst, J., et al. (2002). The role of "his" and "her" forms of interdependence in everyday life: Gender, belonging, and social experience. Unpublished manuscript, Northwestern University.

184. Kanazawa, S. (2002). Bowling with our imaginary friends. *Evolution and Human Behavior, 23,* 167–171.

185. Gardner, W. L., Pickett, C. L., & Knowles, M. (2005). Social snacking and shielding: Using social symbols, selves, and surrogates in the service of belonging needs. In K. D. Williams, J. P. Forgas, & W. von Hippel (Eds.), *The social outcast: Ostracism, social exclusion, rejection, and bullying* (pp. 227–242). New York: Psychology Press.

186. Cacioppo, J. T., Hawkley, L. C., Berntson, G. G., Ernst, J. M., Gibbs, A. C., Stickgold, R., et al. (2002). Lonely days invade the nights: Social modulation of sleep efficiency. *Psychological Science, 13,* 385–388.

187. Cacioppo, J. T., Hawkley, L. C., Crawford, L. E., Ernst, J. M., Burleson, M. H., Kowalewski, R. B., et al. (2002). Loneliness and health: Potential mechanisms. *Psychosomatic Medicine, 64,* 407–417.

188. Cacioppo, J. T., & Hawkley, L. C. (2005). People thinking about people: The vicious cycle of being a social outcast in one's own mind. In K. D. Williams, J. P. Forgas, & W. von Hippel (Eds.), *The social outcast: Ostracism, social exclusion, rejection, and bullying* (pp. 91–108). New York: Psychology Press.

189. Cialdini, J. T., & Patrick, W. (2008). *Loneliness.* New York: Norton.

190. Juvonen, J., & Gross, E. F. (2005). The rejected and the bullied: Lessons about social misfits from developmental psychology. In K. D. Williams, J. P. Forgas, & W. von Hippel (Eds.), *The social outcast: Ostracism, social exclusion, rejection, and bullying* (pp. 155–170). New York: Psychology Press.

191. Wright, J. C., Giammarino, M., & Parad, H. W. (1986). Social status in small groups: Individual-group similarity and the social "misfit." *Journal of Personality and Social Psychology, 50,* 523–536.

192. Hogg, M. A. (2005). All animals are equal but some animals are more equal than others: Social identity and marginal membership. In K. D. Williams, J. P. Forgas, & W. von Hippel (Eds.), *The social outcast: Ostracism, social exclusion, rejection, and bullying* (pp. 243–262). New York: Psychology Press.

193. Marques, J. M., & Yzerbyt, V. Y. (1988). The black sheep effect: Judgmental extremity in inter- and intra-group situations. *European Journal of Social Psychology, 18,* 287–292.

194. Marques, J. M., Abrams, D., Páez, D., & Hogg, M. A. (2001). Social categorization, social identification, and rejection of deviant group members. In M. A. Hogg & R. S. Tindale (Eds.), *Blackwell handbook of social psychology: Group processes* (pp. 400–424). Oxford: Blackwell.

195. Marques, J. M., & Páez, D. (1994). The "black sheep effect": Social categorization, rejection of ingroup deviates and perception of group variability. *European Review of Social Psychology, 5*, 37–68.
196. Colman, A. M. (1982). *Game theory and experimental games: The study of strategic interaction*. Oxford: Pergamon Press.
197. Ouwerkerk, J. W., Kerr, N. L., Gallucci, M., & Van Lange, P. A. M. (2005). Avoiding the social death penalty: Ostracism and cooperation in social dilemmas. In K. D. Williams, J. P. Forgas, & W. von Hippel (Eds.), *The social outcast: Ostracism, social exclusion, rejection, and bullying* (pp. 321–332). New York: Psychology Press.
198. Ouwerkerk, J. W., Kerr, N. L., Gallucci, M., & Van Lange, P. A. M. (2005). Avoiding the social death penalty: Ostracism and cooperation in social dilemmas. In K. D. Williams, J. P. Forgas, & W. von Hippel (Eds.), *The social outcast: Ostracism, social exclusion, rejection, and bullying* (pp. 321–332). New York: Psychology Press.
199. Kerr, N. L., Rumble, A. C., Park, E. S., Ouwerkerk, J. W., Parks, C. D., Gallucci, M., & Van Lange, P. A. M. (2009). "How many bad apples does it take to spoil the whole barrel": Social exclusion and tolerance for bad apples. *Journal of Experimental Social Psychology, 45*(4), 603–613.
200. Fitness, J. (2005). Bye, bye, black sheep: The causes and consequences of rejection in family relationships. In K. D. Williams, J. P. Forgas, & W. von Hippel (Eds.), *The social outcast: Ostracism, social exclusion, rejection, and bullying* (pp. 263–277). New York: Psychology Press.
201. Folkes, V. S. (1982). Communicating the reasons for social rejection. *Journal of Personality and Social Psychology, 18*, 235–252.
202. Baumeister, R. F., & Wotman, S. R. (1992). *Breaking hearts: The two sides of unrequited love*. New York: Guilford Press.
203. Hill, C. A., Blakemore, J. E. O., & Drumm, P. (1997). Mutual and unrequited love in adolescence and adulthood. *Personal Relationships, 4*(1), 15–23.
204. Baumeister, R. F., & Wotman, S. R. (1992). *Breaking hearts: The two sides of unrequited love*. New York: Guilford Press.
205. Baumeister, R. F., Wotman, S. R., & Stillwell, A. M. (1993). Unrequited love: On heartbreak, anger, guilt, scriptlessness, and humiliation. *Journal of Personality and Social Psychology, 64*, 377–394.
206. Bjerregaard, B. (2000). An empirical study of stalking victimization. *Violence and Victims, 15*, 389–406.
207. Cupach, W. R., & Spitzberg, B. H. (2000). Obsessive relational intrusion: Incidence, perceived severity, and coping. *Violence and Victims, 15*, 357–372.
208. Davis, K. E., & Frieze, I. H. (2000). Research on stalking: What do we know and where do we go? *Violence and Victims, 15*, 473–487.
209. Tjaden, P., & Thoennes, N. (1998). *Stalking in America: Findings from the National Violence Against Women Survey* (NCJ Report no. 169592). Washington, DC: National Institute of Justice and Centers for Disease Control and Prevention.

CHAPTER 12

Close Relationships Passion, Intimacy, and Sexuality

1. Reinisch, J. (1990). *The Kinsey Institute new report on sex: What you must know to be sexually literate*. Stuttgart: St. Martin's Press. (Quotation on p. 89).
2. Hegi, K. E., & Bergner, R. M. (2010). What is love? An empirically-based essentialist account. *Journal of Social and Personal Relationships, 27*, 620–636.
3. See Hatfield, E., & Rapson, R. L. (1987). Passionate love: New directions in research. In W. H. Jones & D. Perlman (Eds.), *Advances in personal relationships* (Vol. 1, pp. 109–139). Greenwich, CT: JAI Press.
4. Liebowitz, M. R. (1983). *The chemistry of love*. Boston: Little & Brown.
5. Walsh, A. (1991). The biological relationship between sex and love. *Free Inquiry, 11*, 20–24.
6. For example, de Rougemont, D. (1956). *Love in the Western world*. New York: Schoeken.
7. Jankowiak, W. (Ed.). (1995). *Romantic passion: A universal experience?* New York: Columbia University Press.
8. Stone, L. (1977). *The family, sex, and marriage in England 1500–1800*. London: Perennial.
9. For example, Acker, M., & Davis, M. H. (1992). Intimacy, passion and commitment in adult romantic relationships: A test of the triangular theory of love. *Journal of Social and Personality Relationships, 9*, 21–50.
10. Aron, A., Fisher, H., & Strong, G. (2006). Romantic love. In A. Vangelisti & D. Perlman (Eds.), *Cambridge handbook of personal relationships* (pp. 595–614). New York: Cambridge University Press.
11. Karney, B. R., & Bradbury, T. N. (1997). Neuroticism, marital interaction, and the trajectory of marital satisfaction. *Journal of Personality and Social Psychology, 72*, 1075–1092.
12. Blumstein, P., & Schwartz, P. (1983). *American couples: Money, work, and sex*. New York: Morrow.
13. Greenblat, C. (1983). The salience of sexuality in the early years of marriage. *Journal of Marriage and the Family, 45*, 277–288.
14. Griffitt, W. (1981). Sexual intimacy in aging marital partners. In J. Marsh & S. Kiesler (Eds.), *Aging: Stability and change in the family* (pp. 301–315). New York: Academic Press.
15. James, W. H. (1981). The honeymoon effect on marital coitus. *Journal of Sex Research, 17*, 114–123.
16. Laumann, E. O., Gagnon, J. H., Michael, R. T., & Michaels, S. (1994). *The social organization of sexuality: Sexual practices in the United States*. Chicago: University of Chicago Press.
17. Udry, J. R. (1980). Changes in the frequency of marital intercourse from panel data. *Archives of Sexual Behavior, 9*, 319–325.
18. James, W. H. (1981). The honeymoon effect on marital coitus. *Journal of Sex Research, 17*, 114–123.
19. Ard, B. N. (1977). Sex in lasting marriages: A longitudinal study. *Journal of Sex Research, 13*, 274–285.
20. Call, V., Sprecher, S., & Schwartz, P. (1995). The incidence and frequency of marital sex in a national sample. *Journal of Marriage and the Family, 57*, 639–650.
21. Laumann, E. O., Gagnon, J. H., Michael, R. T., & Michaels, S. (1994). *The social organization of sexuality: Sexual practices in the United States*. Chicago: University of Chicago Press.
22. Sternberg, R. J. (1986). A triangular theory of love. *Psychological Review, 93*, 119–135.
23. Acker, M., & Davis, M. H. (1992). Intimacy, passion and commitment in adult romantic relationships: A test of the triangular theory of love. *Journal of Social and Personality Relationships, 9*, 21–50.
24. Baumeister, R. F., & Bratslavsky, E. (1999). Passion, intimacy, and time: Passionate love as a function of change in intimacy. *Personality and Social Psychology Review, 3*, 49–67.
25. Spielmann, S. S., MacDonald, G., Maxwell, J. A., Joel, S., Peragine, D., Muise, A., & Impett, E. A. (2013). Settling for less out of fear of being single. *Journal of Personality and Social Psychology, 105*, 1049–1073.
26. Slotter, E. B., Finkel, E. J., DeWall, C. N., Pond, R. S., Lambert, N. M., Bodenhausen, G. V., & Fincham, F. D. (2011). Putting the brakes on aggression toward a romantic partner: The inhibitory influence of relationship commitment. *Journal of Personality and Social Psychology, 102*, 291–305.
27. Li, T., & Fung, H. H. (2012). How negative interactions affect relationship satisfaction: The paradoxical short-term and long-term effects of commitment. *Social Psychological and Personality Science, 4*, 274–281.
28. Francis, A. M., & Mialon, H. M. (2014). "A diamond is forever" and other fairy tales: The relationship between wedding expenses and marriage duration. Unpublished paper, Emory University, Atlanta, GA (Andrew.francis@emory.edu).
29. Meltzer, A. L., & McNulty, J. K. (2013). "Tell me I'm sexy... and otherwise valuable": Body evaluation and relationship satisfaction. *Personal Relationships, 21*, 68–87.
30. Meltzer, A.L., McNulty, J.K., & Maner, J.K. (2017). Women like being valued for sex by their partner and engaging in frequent sex, as long as their partner is committed to a long-term relationship. *Archives of Sexual Behavior, 46*(2), 475-488. doi: 10.1007/s10508-015-0622-1
31. Clark, M. S. (1984). Record keeping in two types of relationships. *Journal of Personality and Social Psychology, 47*, 549–557.
32. Clark, M. S., & Mills, J. (1979). Interpersonal attraction in exchange and communal relationships. *Journal of Personality and Social Psychology, 37*, 12–24.
33. Clark, M. S. (1984). Record keeping in two types of relationships. *Journal of Personality and Social Psychology, 47*, 549–557.
34. Clark, M. S., & Mills, J. (1979). Interpersonal attraction in exchange and communal relationships. *Journal of Personality and Social Psychology, 37*, 12–24.
35. Blumstein, P., & Schwartz, P. (1983). *American couples: Money, work, and sex*. New York: Morrow.
36. For example, Seabright, P. (2004). *The company of strangers: A natural history of economic life*. Princeton, NJ: Princeton University Press.
37. Clark, M. S., Ouellette, R., Powell, M., & Milberg, S. (1987). Recipients' mood, relationship type, and helping. *Journal of Personality and Social Psychology, 53*, 94–103.
38. Williamson, G. M., & Clark, M. S. (1989). Providing help and desired relationship type as determinants of changes in moods and self-evaluations. *Journal of Personality and Social Psychology, 56*(5), 722–734.
39. Clark, M. S., Ouellette, R., Powell, M., & Milberg, S. (1987). Recipients' mood, relationship type, and helping. *Journal of Personality and Social Psychology, 53*, 94–103.
40. Clark, M. S., Ouellette, R., Powell, M., & Milberg, S. (1987). Recipients' mood, relationship type, and helping. *Journal of Personality and Social Psychology, 53*, 94–103.
41. Clark, M. S., Mills, J., & Corcoran, D. (1989). Keeping track of needs and inputs of friends and strangers. *Personality and Social Psychology Bulletin, 15*, 533–542.
42. Bowlby, J. (1969). *Attachment and loss: Vol 1. Attachment*. New York: Basic Books.
43. Bartholomew, K., & Shaver, P. R. (1998). Measures of attachment: Do they converge? In J. A. Simpson & W. S. Rholes (Eds.), *Attachment theory and close relationships* (pp. 25–45). New York: Guilford Press.
44. Cooper, M. L., Shaver, P. R., & Collins, N. L. (1998). Attachment styles, emotion regulation, and adjustment in adolescence. *Journal of Personality and Social Psychology, 74*, 1380–1397.
45. Hazan, C., & Shaver, P. R. (1987). Romantic love conceptualized as an attachment process. *Journal of Personality and Social Psychology, 52*, 511–524.
46. Ainsworth, M. D. S., Blehar, M. C., Waters, E., & Wall, S. (1978). *Patterns of attachment: A psychological study of the strange situation*. Hillsdale, NJ: Erlbaum.
47. Edelstein, R. S., & Shaver, P. R. (2004). Avoidant attachment: Exploration of an oxymoron. In D. Mashek & A. Aron (Eds.), *Handbook of closeness and intimacy* (pp. 397–412). Mahwah, NJ: Erlbaum.
48. Bartholomew, K., & Horowitz, L. M. (1991). Attachment styles among young adults: A test of a four-category model. *Journal of Personality and Social Psychology, 61*, 226–244.
49. Brennan, K. A., Clark, C. L., & Shaver, P. R. (1998). Self-report measures of adult attachment. In J. A. Simpson & W. S. Rholes (Eds.), *Attachment theory and close relationships* (pp. 46–76). New York: Guilford Press.
50. Brennan, K. A., & Shaver, P. R. (1995). Dimensions of adult attachment, affect regulation, and romantic

relationship functioning. *Personality and Social Psychology Bulletin, 21,* 267–283.

51. Collins, N. L., & Feeney, B. C. (2000). A safe haven: An attachment theory perspective on support-seeking and caregiving in adult romantic relationships. *Journal of Personality and Social Psychology, 58,* 644–663.
52. Edelstein, R. S., & Shaver, P. R. (2004). Avoidant attachment: Exploration of an oxymoron. In D. Mashek & A. Aron (Eds.), *Handbook of closeness and intimacy* (pp. 397–412). Mahwah, NJ: Erlbaum.
53. Collins, N. L., & Feeney, B. C. (2000). A safe haven: An attachment theory perspective on support-seeking and caregiving in adult romantic relationships. *Journal of Personality and Social Psychology, 58,* 644–663.
54. Collins, N. L., & Feeney, B. C. (2004). An attachment theory perspective on closeness and intimacy. In D. Mashek & A. Aron (Eds.), *Handbook of closeness and intimacy* (pp. 163–187). Mahwah, NJ: Erlbaum.
55. Bartholomew, K., & Horowitz, L. M. (1991). Attachment styles among young adults: A test of a four-category model. *Journal of Personality and Social Psychology, 61,* 226–244.
56. Collins, N. L., & Feeney, B. C. (2004). An attachment theory perspective on closeness and intimacy. In D. Mashek & A. Aron (Eds.), *Handbook of closeness and intimacy* (pp. 163–187). Mahwah, NJ: Erlbaum.
57. Collins, N. L., & Read, S. J. (1990). Adult attachment, working models and relationship quality in dating couples. *Journal of Personality and Social Psychology, 58,* 644–663.
58. Hazan, C., & Shaver, P. R. (1987). Romantic love conceptualized as an attachment process. *Journal of Personality and Social Psychology, 52,* 511–524.
59. Simpson, J. A. (1990). Influence of attachment styles on romantic relationships. *Journal of Personality and Social Psychology, 59,* 971–980.
60. Feeney, B. C., & Collins, N. L. (2001). Predictors of caregiving in adult intimate relationships. *Journal of Personality and Social Psychology, 80,* 972–994.
61. Feeney, J. A. (1996). Attachment, caregiving, and marital satisfaction. *Personal Relationships, 3,* 401–416.
62. Kunce, L. J., & Shaver, P. R. (1994). An attachment-theoretical approach to caregiving in romantic relationships. In K. Bartholomew & D. Perlman (Eds.), *Advances in personal relationships* (Vol. 5, pp. 205–237). London: Kingsley.
63. Bartholomew, K. (1990). Avoidance of intimacy: An attachment perspective. *Journal of Social and Personal Relationships, 7,* 147–178.
64. Collins, N. L., & Feeney, B. C. (2004). An attachment theory perspective on closeness and intimacy. In D. Mashek & A. Aron (Eds.), *Handbook of closeness and intimacy* (pp. 163–187). Mahwah, NJ: Erlbaum.
65. Baldwin, M. W. (1992). Relational schemas and the processing of social information. *Psychological Bulletin, 112,* 461–474.
66. Collins, N. L., & Feeney, B. C. (2004). An attachment theory perspective on closeness and intimacy. In D. Mashek & A. Aron (Eds.), *Handbook of closeness and intimacy* (pp. 163–187). Mahwah, NJ: Erlbaum.
67. Edelstein, R. S., & Shaver, P. R. (2004). Avoidant attachment: Exploration of an oxymoron. In D. Mashek & A. Aron (Eds.), *Handbook of closeness and intimacy* (pp. 397–412). Mahwah, NJ: Erlbaum.
68. Spangler, G., & Grossman, K. E. (1993). Biobehavioral organization in securely and insecurely attached infants. *Child Development, 64,* 1439–1450.
69. Sroufe, L. A., & Waters, E. (1977). Heart rate as a convergent measure in clinical and developmental research. *Merrill-Palmer Quarterly, 23,* 3–27.
70. Tidwell, M., Reis, H. T., & Shaver, P. R. (1996). Attachment styles, attractiveness, and emotions in social interactions: A diary study. *Journal of Personality and Social Psychology, 71,* 729–745.
71. Erikson, E. H. (1950). *Childhood and society*. New York: Norton.
72. Rogers, C. R. (1961). *On becoming a person*. Boston: Houghton Mifflin.
73. Maslow, A. H. (1968). *Toward a psychology of being*. New York: Van Nostrand.
74. Murray, S., Bellavia, G., Rose, P., & Griffin, D. (2003). Once hurt, twice hurtful: How perceived regard regulates daily marital interactions. *Journal of Personality and Social Psychology, 84,* 126–147.
75. Murray, S., Rose, P., Bellavia, G., Holmes, J., & Kusche, A. (2002). When rejection stings: How self-esteem constrains relationship enhancement processes. *Journal of Personality and Social Psychology, 83,* 556–573.
76. Rusbult, C. E., Morrow, G. D., & Johnson, D. J. (1987). Self-esteem and problem solving behavior in close relationships. *British Journal of Social Psychology, 26,* 293–303.
77. Sommer, K. L., Williams, K. D., Ciarocco, N. J., & Baumeister, R. F. (2001). When silence speaks louder than words: Explorations into the intra-psychic and interpersonal consequences of social ostracism. *Basic and Applied Social Psychology, 23,* 225–243.
78. Campbell, W. K., & Foster, C. A. (2002). Narcissism and commitment in romantic relationships: An investment model analysis. *Personality and Social Psychology Bulletin, 28,* 484–495.
79. Campbell, W. K. (1999). Narcissism and romantic attraction. *Journal of Personality and Social Psychology, 77,* 1254–1270.
80. Campbell, W. K., Reeder, G. D., Sedikides, C., & Elliot, A. J. (2000). Narcissism and comparative self-enhancement strategies. *Journal of Research in Personality, 34,* 329–347.
81. Farwell, L., & Wohlwend-Lloyd, R. (1998). Narcissistic processes: Optimistic expectations, favorable self-evaluations, and self-enhancing attributions. *Journal of Personality, 66,* 65–83.
82. Morf, C. C., & Rhodewalt, F. (2001). Unraveling the paradoxes of narcissism: A dynamic self-regulatory processing model. *Psychological Inquiry, 12,* 177–196.
83. Schütz, A. (2000). *Selbstwertgefühl: Zwischen Selbstakzeptanz und Arroganz*. Stuttgart: Kohlhammer.
84. Schütz, A. (2001). Self-esteem and interpersonal strategies. In J. P. Forgas, K. D. Williams, & L. Wheeler (Eds.), *The social mind: Cognitive and motivational aspects of interpersonal behavior* (pp. 157–176). New York: Cambridge University Press.
85. Schütz, A. (1999). It was your fault! Self-serving biases in autobiographical accounts of esteem threatening conflicts in married couples. *Journal of Social and Personal Relationships, 16,* 193–209.
86. Campbell, W. K., & Foster, C. A. (2002). Narcissism and commitment in romantic relationships: An investment model analysis. *Personality and Social Psychology Bulletin, 28,* 484–495.
87. Schütz, A. (1999). It was your fault! Self-serving biases in autobiographical accounts of esteem threatening conflicts in married couples. *Journal of Social and Personal Relationships, 16,* 193–209.
88. Miller, R. S. (1997). Inattentive and contented: Relationship commitment and attention to alternatives. *Journal of Personality and Social Psychology, 73,* 758–766.
89. Lydon, J. E., Menzies-Toman, D., Burton, K., & Bell, C. (2008). If-then contingencies and the differential effects of the availability of an attractive alternative on relationship maintenance for men and women. *Journal of Personality and Social Psychology, 95,* 50–65.
90. Meltzer, A. L., McNulty, J. K., Jackson, G. L., & Karney, B. R. (2014). Sex differences in the implications of partner physical attractiveness in the trajectory of marital satisfaction. *Journal of Personality and Social Psychology, 106,* 418–428.
91. Russell, V. M., McNulty, J. K., Baker, L. R., & Meltzer, A. L. (2014). The association between discontinuing hormonal contraceptives and wives' marital satisfaction depends on husbands' facial attractiveness. *PNAS, 111,* 17081–17086.
92. Ma-Kellams, C., Wang, M. C., & Cardiel, H. (2017). Attractiveness and relationship longevity: Beauty is not what it is cracked up to be. *Personal Relationships, 24,* 146–161.
93. Sprecher, S. (1999). "I love you more today than yesterday": Romantic partners' perceptions of changes in love and related affect over time. *Journal of Personality and Social Psychology, 76,* 46–53.
94. Levenson, R. W., & Gottman, J. M. (1983). Marital interaction: Physiological linkage and affective exchange. *Journal of Personality and Social Psychology, 45,* 587–597.
95. Levenson, R. W., & Gottman, J. M. (1985). Physiological and affective predictors of change in marital satisfaction. *Journal of Personality and Social Psychology, 49,* 85–94.
96. Sprecher, S. (1999). "I love you more today than yesterday": Romantic partners' perceptions of changes in love and related affect over time. *Journal of Personality and Social Psychology, 76,* 46–53.
97. McNulty, J. K., Olson, M. A., Meltzer, A. L., & Shaffer, M. J. (2014). Though they may be unaware, newlyweds implicitly know whether their marriage will be satisfying. *Science, 342,* 1149–1120.
98. Baumeister, R. F., Stillwell, A. M., & Heatherton, T. F. (1995). Personal narratives about guilt: Role in action control and interpersonal relationships. *Basic and Applied Social Psychology, 17,* 173–198. doi: 10.1207/s15324834basp1701&2_10
99. Baumeister, R. F., Stillwell, A. M., & Heatherton, T. F. (1994). Guilt: An interpersonal approach. *Psychological Bulletin, 115,* 243–267. doi:10.1037/0033-2909.115.2.243
100. Overall, N. C., Girme, Y. U., Lemay, E. P., & Hammond, M. D. (2014). Attachment anxiety and reactions to relationship threat: The benefits and costs of inducing guilt in romantic partners. *Journal of Personality and Social Psychology, 106,* 235–256.
101. Rusbult, C. E. (1983). A longitudinal test of the investment model: The development (and deterioration) of satisfaction and commitment in heterosexual involvements. *Journal of Personality and Social Psychology, 45,* 101–117.
102. For example, Rusbult, C. E., & Martz, J. M. (1995). My relationship is better than—and not as bad as—yours is: The perception of superiority in close relationships. *Personality and Social Psychology Bulletin, 21,* 558–571.
103. Horowitz, A. V., White, H. R., & Howell-White, S. (1997). Becoming married and mental health: A longitudinal study of a cohort of young adults. *Journal of Marriage and the Family, 58,* 895–907.
104. Hu, Y., & Goldman, M. (1990). Mortality differentials by marital status: An international comparison. *Demography, 27,* 233–250.
105. See also Johnson, W., McGue, M., Krueger, R. F., & Bouchard, T. J. (2004). Marriage and personality: A genetic analysis. *Journal of Personality and Social Psychology, 86,* 285–294.
106. Coyne, J. C., & DeLongis, A. (1986). Going beyond social support: The role of social relationships in adaptation. *Journal of Consulting and Clinical Psychology, 54,* 454–460.
107. DeLongis, A., Folkman, S., & Lazarus, S. (1988). The impact of daily stress on health and mood: Psychological and social resources as mediators. *Journal of Personality and Social Psychology, 54,* 486–495.
108. Kiecolt-Glaser, J. K., Fisher, L. D., Ogrocki, P., Stout, J. C., Speicher, C. E., & Glaser, R. (1987). Marital quality, marital disruption, and immune function. *Psychosomatic Medicine, 49,* 13–34.
109. Myers, D. G. (1992). The secrets of happiness. *Psychology Today, 25,* 38–46.
110. Kiecolt-Glaser, J. K., & Newton, T. L. (2001). Marriage and health: His and hers. *Psychological Bulletin, 127,* 472–503.
111. Johnson, W., McGue, M., Krueger, R. F., & Bouchard, T. J. (2004). Marriage and personality: A genetic analysis. *Journal of Personality and Social Psychology, 86,* 285–294.
112. Bernard, J. (1982). *The future of marriage*. New Haven, CT: Yale University Press.

113. Holtzworth-Munroe, A., & Jacobson, N. S. (1985). Causal attributions of married couples: When do they search for causes? What do they conclude when they do? *Journal of Personality and Social Psychology, 48,* 1398–1412.
114. Luchies, L. B., Wieselquist, J., Rusbult, C. E., Kumasiro, M., Eastwick, P. W., Coolsen, M. K., & Finkel, E. J. (2013). Trust and biased memory of transgressions in romantic relationships. *Journal of Personality and Social Psychology, 104,* 673–694.
115. MacDonald, T. K., & Ross, M. (1999). Assessing the accuracy of predictions about dating relationships: How and why do lovers' predictions differ from those made by observers? *Personality and Social Psychology Bulletin, 25,* 1417–1429.
116. Vaughan, D. (1986). *Uncoupling: Turning points in intimate relationships.* New York: Oxford University Press.
117. Johnson, D. J., & Rusbult, C. E. (1989). Resisting temptation: Devaluation of alternative partners as a means of maintaining commitment in close relationships. *Journal of Personality and Social Psychology, 57,* 967–980.
118. Miller, R. S. (1997). Inattentive and contented: Relationship commitment and attention to alternatives. *Journal of Personality and Social Psychology, 73,* 758–766.
119. Simpson, J. A., Gangestad, S., & Lerma, M. (1990). Perception of physical attractiveness: Mechanisms involved in the maintenance of romantic relationships. *Journal of Personality and Social Psychology, 59,* 1192–1201.
120. For example, Swann, W. B., Jr. (1985). The self as architect of social reality. In B. Schlenker (Ed.), *The self and social life* (pp. 100–125). New York: McGraw-Hill.
121. Swann, W. B., Jr. (1987). Identity negotiation: Where two roads meet. *Journal of Personality and Social Psychology, 53,* 1038–1051.
122. Swann, W. B., De La Ronde, C., & Hixon, J. G. (1994). Authenticity and positivity strivings in marriage and courtship. *Journal of Personality and Social Psychology, 66,* 857–869.
123. Murray, S., Holmes, J. G., & Griffin, D. W. (1996). The benefits of positive illusions: Idealization and the construction of satisfaction in close relationships. *Journal of Personality and Social Psychology, 70,* 79–98.
124. Murray, S., & Holmes, J. G. (1993). See virtues in faults: Negativity and the transformation of interpersonal narratives in close relationships. *Journal of Personality and Social Psychology, 65,* 707–722.
125. Murray, S., & Holmes, J. G. (1994). Story-telling in close relationships: The construction of confidence. *Personality and Social Psychology Bulletin, 20,* 663–676.
126. Holmes, J. G. (2004, October). The power of positive thinking in close relationships. Paper presented at the Third International Positive Psychology Summit, Washington, DC.
127. Swann, W. B., Jr. (1998). The self and interpersonal relationships. Paper presented at the meeting of the Society of Experimental Social Psychologists, Lexington, KY.
128. Macfarlane, A. (1986). *Marriage and love in England: Modes of reproduction, 1300–1840.* New York: Basil Blackwell.
129. Shorter, E. (1975). *The making of the modern family.* New York: Basic Books.
130. Stone, L. (1977). *The family, sex, and marriage in England 1500–1800.* London: Perennial.
131. Diamond, L. M. (2003). What does sexual orientation orient? A biobehavioral model distinguishing romantic love and sexual desire. *Psychological Review, 110,* 173–192.
132. Diamond, L. M. (2004). Emerging perspectives on distinctions between romantic love and sexual desire. *Current Directions in Psychological Science, 13,* 116–119.
133. Diamond, L. M. (2003). An attachment perspective on female sexual fluidity. Paper presented at the Women's Sexualities Conference: Historical, Interdisciplinary, and International Perspectives, sponsored by the Kinsey Institute for Research in Sex, Gender, and Reproduction, Bloomington, IN.
134. Melter, A. L., Makhanova, A., Hicks, L. L., French, J. E., McNulty, J. K., & Bradbury, T. N. (2017). Quantifying the sexual afterglow: The lingering benefits of sex and their implications for pair-bonded relationships. *Psychological Science, 28,* 587–598.
135. Maxwel, J. A., & McNulty, J. K. (2019). No longer in a 'dry spell': The developing understanding of how sex influences romantic relationships. *Current Directions in Psychological Science, 28,* 102–107.
136. DeLamater, J., & Hyde, J. S. (1998). Essentialism vs. social constructionism in the study of human sexuality. *Journal of Sex Research, 35,* 10–18.
137. Staples, R. (1973). *Black women in America: Sex, marriage, and family.* Chicago: Nelson-Hall.
138. For example, Kitzinger, C. (1987). *The social construction of lesbianism.* London: Sage.
139. Symons, D. (1979). *The evolution of human sexuality.* New York: Oxford University Press.
140. Symons, D. (1995). Beauty is in the adaptations of the beholder: The evolutionary psychology of human female sexual attractiveness. In P. R. Abramson & S. D. Pinkerton (Eds.), *Sexual nature/sexual culture* (pp. 80–118). Chicago: University of Chicago Press.
141. Buss, D. M. (1994). *The evolution of desire: Strategies of human mating.* New York: Basic Books.
142. Trivers, R. (1972). Parental investment and sexual selection. In B. Campbell (Ed.), *Sexual selection and the descent of man: 1871–1971* (pp. 136–179). Chicago: Aldine.
143. Symons, D. (1979). *The evolution of human sexuality.* New York: Oxford University Press.
144. Buss, D. M., & Schmitt, D. P. (1993). Sexual strategies theory: An evolutionary perspective on human mating. *Psychological Review, 100,* 204–232.
145. Buss, D. M., & Schmitt, D. P. (1993). Sexual strategies theory: An evolutionary perspective on human mating. *Psychological Review, 100,* 204–232.
146. Schmitt, D. P. (2017). What type of person would agree to have sex with a stranger? Psychology Today blogs. https://www.psychologytoday.com/intl/blog/sexual-personalities/201706/what-type-person-would-agree-have-sex-stranger
147. Blau, P. N. (1964). *Exchange and power in social life.* New York: Wiley.
148. Homans, G. C. (1950). *The human group.* New York: Harcourt, Brace, & World.
149. Homans, G. C. (1961). *Social behavior: Its elementary forms.* New York: Harcourt, Brace, & World.
150. Sprecher, S. (1998). Social exchange theories and sexuality. *Journal of Sex Research, 35,* 32–43.
151. Baumeister, R. F., & Vohs, K. D. (2004). Sexual economics: Sex as female resource for social exchange in heterosexual interactions. *Personality and Social Psychology Review, 8*(4), 339–363.
152. Symons, D. (1979). *The evolution of human sexuality.* New York: Oxford University Press.
153. Regnerus, M. (2011). *Premarital sex in America: How young Americans meet, mate, and think about marrying.* New York: Oxford University Press.
154. Baumeister, R. F., Catanese, K. R., & Vohs, K. D. (2001). Is there a gender difference in strength of sex drive? Theoretical views, conceptual distinctions, and a review of relevant evidence. *Personality and Social Psychology Review, 5,* 242–273.
155. Conley, T. D., Moors, A. C., Matsick, J. L., Ziegler, A., & Valentine, B. A. (2011). Women, men, and the bedroom: Methodological and conceptual insights that narrow, reframe, and eliminate gender differences in sexuality. *Current Directions in Psychological Science, 20,* 296–300.
156. Schmitt, D. P., Jonason, P. K., Byerley, G. J., Flores, S. D., Illbeck, B. E., O'Leary, K. N., & Qudrat, A. (2012). A reexamination of sex differences in sexuality: New studies reveal old truths. *Current Directions in Psychological Science, 21,* 135–139.
157. Oliver, M. B., & Hyde, J. S. (1993). Gender differences in sexuality: A meta-analysis. *Psychological Bulletin, 114,* 29–51.
158. For example, Wilson, J., Kuehn, R., & Beach, F. (1963). Modifications in the sexual behavior of male rats produced by changing the stimulus female. *Journal of Comparative and Physiological Psychology, 56,* 636–644.
159. Francoeur, R. T., Perper, T., Scherzer, N. A., Sellmer, G. P., & Cornog, M. (1991). *A descriptive dictionary and atlas of sexology,* p. 130. New York: Greenwood Press.
160. Arndt, B. (2009). *The Sex Diaries.* Melbourne: Melbourne University Press.
161. McNulty, J., Maxwell, J., Meltzer, A., & Baumeister, R. F. (in press). The honeymoon is over: Sex-differentiated changes in sexual desire predict marital dissatisfaction. *Archives of Sexual Behaviour.*
162. Janus, S. S., & Janus, C. L. (1993). *The Janus report on sexual behavior.* New York: Wiley.
163. Baumeister, R. F. (2000). Gender differences in erotic plasticity: The female sex drive as socially flexible and responsive. *Psychological Bulletin, 126,* 347–374.
164. Diamond, L. M. (2008). *Sexual fluidity: Understanding women's love and desire.* Cambridge, MA: Harvard University Press.
165. For example, Kinsey, A. C., Pomeroy, W. B., Martin, C. E., & Gebhard, P. H. (1953). *Sexual behavior in the human female.* Philadelphia: Saunders.
166. For example, Savin-Williams, R. C. (1990). *Gay and lesbian youth: Expressions of identity.* New York: Hemisphere.
167. Whisman, V. (1996). *Queer by choice.* New York: Routledge.
168. Adams, C. G., & Turner, B. F. (1985). Reported change in sexuality from young adulthood to old age. *Journal of Sex Research, 21,* 126–141.
169. Ard, B. N. (1977). Sex in lasting marriages: A longitudinal study. *Journal of Sex Research, 13,* 274–285.
170. Adams, C. G., & Turner, B. F. (1985). Reported change in sexuality from young adulthood to old age. *Journal of Sex Research, 21,* 126–141.
171. Laumann, E. O., Gagnon, J. H., Michael, R. T., & Michaels, S. (1994). *The social organization of sexuality: Sexual practices in the United States.* Chicago: University of Chicago Press.
172. McCabe, P. (1987). Desired and experienced levels of premarital affection and sexual intercourse during dating. *Journal of Sex Research, 23,* 23–33.
173. Cohen, L. L., & Shotland, R. L. (1996). Timing of first sexual intercourse in a relationship: Expectations, experiences, and perceptions of others. *Journal of Sex Research, 33,* 291–299.
174. Pliner, P., & Chaiken, S. (1990). Eating, social motives, and self-presentation in women and men. *Journal of Experimental Social Psychology, 26,* 240–254.
175. Baker, M., Strickland, A., & Fox, N. D. (2019). Choosing a meal to increase your appeal: How relationship status, sexual orientation, dining partner sex, and attractiveness impact nutritional choices in social dining scenarios. *Appetite, 133,* 262–269.
176. Mori, D., Chaiken, S., & Pliner, P. (1987). "Eating lightly" and the self-presentation of femininity. *Journal of Personality and Social Psychology, 53,* 693–702.
177. Bell, A. P., & Weinberg, M. S. (1978). *Homosexualities: A study of diversity among men and women.* New York: Simon & Schuster.
178. Bem, D. J. (1996). Exotic becomes erotic: A developmental theory of sexual orientation. *Psychological Review, 103,* 320–335.
179. Bem, D. J. (1998). Is EBE theory supported by evidence? Is it androcentric? A reply to Peplau et al. (1998). *Psychological Review, 105,* 395–398.
180. Schachter, S. (1964). The interaction of cognitive and physiological determinants of emotional state.

In L. Berkowitz (Ed.), *Advances in Experimental Social Psychology* (pp. 49–79). New York: Academic Press.
181. Bem, D. J. (1998). Is EBE theory supported by evidence? Is it androcentric? A reply to Peplau et al. (1998). *Psychological Review, 105,* 395–398.
182. Bailey, J. M., & Pillard, R. C. (1995). Genetics of human sexual orientation. *Annual Review of Sex Research, 6,* 126–150.
183. Ganna, A., Verweij, K. J. H., ... & Zietsch, B. (in press). Large-scale GWAS reveals insights into the genetic architecture of same-sex sexual behaviour. *Science.*
184. As this book went to press, the follow-up work by the same team as in the previous footnote (Ganna et al.) was not yet available. The authors learned of it from presentations by Zietsch (last author).
185. This is widely reported; see long list of sources noted by Tabaac, A., Perrin, P. B., & Benotsch, E. G. (2018). Discrimination, mental health, and body image among transgender and gender-non-binary indivdiuals: Constructing a multiple mediational path model. *Journal of Gay & Lesbian Social Services, 30,* 1–16.
186. Tabaac, A., Perrin, P. B., & Benotsch, E. G. (2018). Discrimination, mental health, and body image among transgender and gender-non-binary indivdiuals: Constructing a multiple mediational path model. *Journal of Gay & Lesbian Social Services, 30,* 1–16.
187. For example, Thompson, A. P. (1983). Extramarital sex: A review of the research literature. *Journal of Sex Research, 19,* 1–22.
188. Morokoff, P. J. (1986). Volunteer bias in the psychophysiological study of female sexuality. *Journal of Sex Research, 22,* 35–51.
189. Wiederman, M. W. (1993). Demographic and sexual characteristics of nonresponders to sexual experience items in a national survey. *Journal of Sex Research, 30,* 27–35.
190. Wiederman, M. W. (2004). Self-control and sexual behavior. In R. Baumeister & K. Vohs (Eds.), *Handbook of self-regulation* (pp. 537–552). New York: Guilford Press.
191. Laumann, E. O., Gagnon, J. H., Michael, R. T., & Michaels, S. (1994). *The social organization of sexuality: Sexual practices in the United States.* Chicago: University of Chicago Press.
192. Wiederman, M. W. (1997). The truth must be in here somewhere: Examining the gender discrepancy in self-reported lifetime number of sex partners. *Journal of Sex Research, 34,* 375–386.
193. For example, Thompson, A. P. (1983). Extramarital sex: A review of the research literature. *Journal of Sex Research, 19,* 1–22.
194. Abraham, C. (2002, December 14). Mommy's little secret. *The Globe and Mail* (Toronto), pp. F1, F6.
195. For example, Buss, D. M. (1994). *The evolution of desire: Strategies of human mating.* New York: Basic Books.
196. Abraham, C. (2002, December 14). Mommy's little secret. *The Globe and Mail* (Toronto), pp. F1, F6.
197. Abraham, C. (2002, December 14). Mommy's little secret. *The Globe and Mail* (Toronto), pp. F1, F6.
198. Laumann, E. O., Gagnon, J. H., Michael, R. T., & Michaels, S. (1994). *The social organization of sexuality: Sexual practices in the United States.* Chicago: University of Chicago Press.
199. Blumstein, P., & Schwartz, P. (1983). *American couples: Money, work, and sex.* New York: Morrow.
200. Wiederman, M. W. (1997). The truth must be in here somewhere: Examining the gender discrepancy in self-reported lifetime number of sex partners. *Journal of Sex Research, 34,* 375–386.
201. Spanier, G. P., & Margolis, R. L. (1983). Marital separation and extramarital sexual behavior. *Journal of Sex Research, 19,* 23–48.
202. Lawson, A. (1988). *Adultery: An analysis of love and betrayal.* New York: Basic Books.
203. Lawson, A. (1988). *Adultery: An analysis of love and betrayal.* New York: Basic Books.
204. Hansen, G. L. (1987). Extradyadic relations during courtship. *Journal of Sex Research, 23,* 382–390.
205. Shorter, E. (1975). *The making of the modern family.* New York: Basic Books.
206. Shorter, E. (1975). *The making of the modern family.* New York: Basic Books.
207. Shackelford, T. K. (2001). Self-esteem in marriage: An evolutionary psychological analysis. *Personality and Individual Differences, 30,* 371–390.
208. Pines, A., & Aronson, E. (1983). Antecedents, correlates, and consequences of sexual jealousy. *Journal of Personality, 51,* 108–136.
209. Mead, M. (1928). *Coming of age in Samoa: A psychological study of primitive youth for Western civilization.* New York: Morrow.
210. Reiss, I. L. (1986). *Journey into sexuality.* New York: Prentice Hall.
211. Reiss, I. L. (1986). A sociological journey into sexuality. *Journal of Marriage and the Family, 48,* 233–242.
212. Hupka, R. B. (1981). Cultural determinants of jealousy. *Alternative Lifestyles, 4,* 310–356.
213. Buunk, B. P. & Hupka, R. B. (1987). Cross-cultural differences in the elicitation of sexual jealousy. *Journal of Sex Research, 23,* 12–22.
214. Buss, D. M. (1994). *The evolution of desire: Strategies of human mating.* New York: Basic Books.
215. Abraham, C. (2002, December 14). Mommy's little secret. *The Globe and Mail* (Toronto), pp. F1, F6.
216. Van den Bergh, B., Dewitte, S., & Warlop, L. (2008). Bikinis instigate generalized impatience in intertemporal choice. *Journal of Consumer Research, 35*(1), 85–97.
217. Wilson, M., & Daly M. (2003). Do pretty women inspire men to discount the future? Biology Letters. *Proceedings of the Royal Society, London. B (Suppl.).* doi: 10.1098/rsbl.2003.0134
218. Van den Bergh, B., Dewitte, S., & Warlop, L. (2008). Bikinis instigate generalized impatience in intertemporal choice. *Journal of Consumer Research, 35*(1), 85–97.
219. Roney, J. R. (2003). Effects of visual exposure to the opposite sex: Cognitive aspects of mate attraction in human males. *Personality and Social Psychology Bulletin, 29*(3), 393–404.
220. Buss, D. M., Larsen, R. J., Westen, D., & Semmelroth, J. (1992). Sex differences in jealousy: Evolution, physiology, and psychology. *Psychological Science, 3,* 251–255.
221. Buunk, B. P., Angleitner, A., Oubaid, V., & Buss, D. M. (1996). Sex differences in jealousy in evolutionary and cultural perspective: Tests from the Netherlands, Germany, and the United States. *Psychological Science, 7,* 1103–1116.
222. DeSteno, D. A., Bartlett, M. Y., Braverman, J., & Salovey, P. (2002). Sex differences in jealousy: Evolutionary mechanisms or artifact of measurement. *Journal of Personality and Social Psychology, 83,* 1103–1116.
223. Harris, C. R. (2000). Psychophysiological responses to imagined infidelity: The specific innate modular view of jealousy reconsidered. *Journal of Personality and Social Psychology, 75,* 1082–1091.
224. DeSteno, D. A., Bartlett, M. Y., Braverman, J., & Salovey, P. (2002). Sex differences in jealousy: Evolutionary mechanisms or artifact of measurement. *Journal of Personality and Social Psychology, 83,* 1103–1116.
225. For example, Gondolf, E. W. (1985). *Men who batter: An integrated approach for stopping wife abuse.* Holmes Beach, CA: Learning Publications.
226. Renzetti, C. M. (1992). *Violent betrayal: Partner abuse in lesbian relationships.* Newbury Park, CA: Sage.
227. Blumstein, P., & Schwartz, P. (1983). *American couples: Money, work, and sex.* New York: Morrow.
228. Blumstein, P., & Schwartz, P. (1983). *American couples: Money, work, and sex.* New York: Morrow.
229. Seal, D. W. (1997). Interpartner concordance of self-reported sexual behavior among college dating couples. *Journal of Sex Research, 34,* 39–55.
230. Lawson, A. (1988). *Adultery: An analysis of love and betrayal.* New York: Basic Books.
231. DeSteno, D. A., & Salovey, P. (1996). Evolutionary origins of sex differences in jealousy? Questioning the "fitness" of the model. *Psychological Science, 7,* 367–372.
232. Salovey, P., & Rodin, J. (1991). Provoking jealousy and envy: Domain relevance and self-esteem threat. *Journal of Social and Clinical Psychology, 10,* 395–413.
233. Wiederman, M. W., & LaMar, L. (1998). "Not with him you don't!": Gender and emotional reactions to sexual infidelity during courtship. *Journal of Sex Research, 34,* 375–386.
234. Pines, A., & Aronson, E. (1983). Antecedents, correlates, and consequences of sexual jealousy. *Journal of Personality, 51,* 108–136.
235. Wicklund, R. A., & Gollwitzer, P. M. (1982). *Symbolic self-completion.* Hillsdale, NJ: Erlbaum.
236. Bailey, R. C., & Aunger, R. V. (1995). Sexuality, infertility and sexually transmitted disease among farmers and foragers in central Africa. In P. Abramson & S. Pinkerton (Eds.), *Sexual nature/sexual culture* (pp. 195–222). Chicago: University of Chicago Press.
237. For example, Ehrenreich, B. (1999, March 8). The real truth about the female. *Time, 153*(9), 57–91.
238. Oliver, M. B., & Hyde, J. S. (1993). Gender differences in sexuality: A meta-analysis. *Psychological Bulletin, 114,* 29–51.
239. King, K., Balswick, J. O., & Robinson, I. E. (1977). The continuing premarital sexual revolution among college females. *Journal of Marriage and the Family, 39,* 455–459.
240. Millhausen, R. R., & Herold, E. S. (1999). Does the sexual double standard still exist? Perceptions of university women. *Journal of Sex Research, 36,* 361–368.
241. Sprecher, S. (1989). Premarital sexual standards for different categories of individuals. *Journal of Sex Research, 19,* 23–48.
242. Smith, T. (1994). Attitudes toward sexual permissiveness: Trends, correlates, and behavioral connections. In A. S. Rossi (Ed.), *Sexuality across the life course* (pp. 63–97). Chicago: University of Chicago Press.
243. For a review, see Baumeister, R. F., & Twenge, J. M. (2002). Cultural suppression of female sexuality. *Review of General Psychology, 6,* 166–203.
244. Barash, D. P., & Lipton, J. E. (2002). *Myth of monogamy: Fidelity and infidelity in animals and people.* New York: W. H. Freeman.
245. Smuts, B. (1996). Male aggression against women: An evolutionary perspective. In D. Buss & N. Malamuth (Eds.), *Sex, power, conflict* (pp. 231–268). New York: Oxford University Press.
246. Dunbar, R. I. M. (1996). *Grooming, gossip, and the evolution of language.* Cambridge, MA: Harvard University Press.

CHAPTER 13
Prejudice and Intergroup Relations

1. David, M. B. (2013, February 13). Deep racism: The forgotten history of human zoos. *Popular Resistance.* Retrieved from http://www.popularresistance.org/deep-racism-the-forgotten-history-of-human-zoos/
2. Mullan, B., & Marvin, G. (1998). *Zoo culture: The book about watching people watch animals* (2nd ed.). Urbana, IL: University of Illinois Press.
3. Harskamp, J., & Dijstelberge, P. (2012, April 12). The human zoo. Retrieved from http://abeautifulbook.wordpress.com/2012/04/21/the-human-zoo/
4. Mullan, B., & Marvin, G. (1998). *Zoo culture: The book about watching people watch animals* (2nd ed.). Urbana, IL: University of Illinois Press.
5. Harskamp, J., & Dijstelberge, P. (2012, April 12). The human zoo. Retrieved from http://abeautifulbook.wordpress.com/2012/04/21/the-human-zoo/
6. Cincinnati zoo and botanical garden. Retrieved from http://www.ohiohistorycentral.org/w/Cincinnati_Zoo_and_Botanical_Garden?rec5685

7. Missouri Historical Society. The *1904 World's Fair: Looking back at looking forward.* Retrieved from http://mohistory.org/Fair/WF/HTML/Overview/page3.html
8. Keller, M. (2006, August 6). The scandal at the zoo. *New York Times.* Retrieved from http://www.nytimes.com/2006/08/06/nyregion/thecity/06zoo.html?ex=51155009600&en=5c2cc9b84edc068cd&ei=5087%0A
9. Political Blind Spot (2014, February 13). Through the 1950s, Africans and Native Americans were kept in zoos as exhibits. Retrieved from http://politicalblindspot.com/through-the-1950s-africans-and-native-americans-were-kept-in-zoos-as-exhibits/
10. Political Blind Spot (2014, February 13). Through the 1950s, Africans and Native Americans were kept in zoos as exhibits. Retrieved from http://politicalblindspot.com/through-the-1950s-africans-and-native-americans-were-kept-in-zoos-as-exhibits/
11. Hawley, C. (2005, June 9). German zoo scandal: "African Village" accused of putting humans on display. *Der Spiegel.* Retrieved from http://www.spiegel.de/international/german-zoo-scandal-african-village-accused-of-putting-humans-on-display-a-359799.html
12. Gaertner, S. L., & Dovidio, J. F. (1986). The aversive form of racism. In J. F. Dovidio & S. L. Gaertner (Eds.), *Prejudice, discrimination, and racism* (pp. 61–89). San Diego: Academic Press.
13. Word, C. O., Zanna, M. P., & Cooper, J. (1974). The nonverbal mediation of self-fulfilling prophecies in interracial interaction. *Journal of Experimental Social Psychology, 10,* 109–120.
14. Richards, Z., & Hewstone, M. (2001). Subtyping and subgrouping: Processes for the prevention and promotion of stereotype change. *Personality and Social Psychology Review, 5,* 52–73.
15. Altermatt, T. W., & DeWall, C. N. (2003). Agency and virtue: Dimensions underlying subgroups of women. *Sex Roles, 49,* 631–641.
16. Szymanski, S. (2000). A market test for discrimination in the English professional soccer leagues. *Journal of Political Economy, 108*(3), 590–603.
17. Stone, L. (1977). *The family, sex and marriage in England: 1500–1800.* London: Perennial.
18. Correll, J., Park, B., Judd, C. M., & Wittenbrink, B. (2002). The police officer's dilemma: Using ethnicity to disambiguate potentially threatening individuals. *Journal of Personality and Social Psychology, 86,* 1314–1329.
19. Greenwald, A. G., Oakes, M. A., & Hoffman, H. G. (2003). Targets of discrimination: Effects of race on responses to weapons holders. *Journal of Experimental Social Psychology, 39,* 399–340.
20. Payne, B. K. (2001). Prejudice and perception: The role of automatic and controlled processes in misperceiving a weapon. *Journal of Personality and Social Psychology, 81,* 181–192.
21. Plant, E. A., & Peruche, B. M. (2005). The consequences of race for police officers' responses to criminal suspects. *Psychological Science, 16,* 180–183.
22. Butz, D. A., Plant, E. A., & Doerr, C. (2007). Liberty and justice for all? The implications of exposure to the United States flag for intergroup relations. *Personality and Social Psychology Bulletin, 33,* 396–408.
23. Mekawi, Y., & Bresin, K. (2015). Is the evidence from racial bias shooting task studies a smoking gun? Results from a meta-analysis. *Journal of Experimental Social Psychology, 61,* 120–130. DOI: 10.1016/j.jesp.2015.08.002
24. Devine, P. G., & Malpass, R. S. (1985). Orienting strategies in differential face recognition. *Personality and Social Psychology Bulletin, 11*(1), 33–40.
25. Meissner, C. A., & Brigham, J. C. (2001). Thirty years of investigating the own-race bias in memory for faces: A meta-analytic review. *Psychology, Public Policy, and Law, 7,* 3–35.
26. Ackerman, J. M., Shapiro, J. R., Neuberg, S. L., Kenrick, D. T., Schaller, M., Becker, D. V., et al. (2006). They all look the same to me (unless they're angry): From out-group homogeneity to out-group heterogeneity. *Psychological Science, 17*(10), 836–840.
27. Levitt, S. D., & Dubner, S. J. (2005). *Freakonomics.* New York: Morrow HarperCollins.
28. Hackett, C., & McClendon, D. (2017, April 5). Christians remain world's largest religious group, but they are declining in Europe. *Pew Research Center.* Retrieved from http://www.pewresearch.org/fact-tank/2017/04/05/christians-remain-worlds-largest-religious-group-but-they-are-declining-in-europe/
29. Hendricks, N. J., Ortiz, C. W., Sugie, N., & Miller, J. (2007). Beyond the numbers: Hate crimes and cultural trauma within Arab American immigrant communities. *International Review of Victimology, 14*(1), 95–113.
30. Pew Research Center (2017, February 15). Americans express increasingly warm feelings toward religious groups. Retrieved from http://www.pewforum.org/2017/02/15/americans-express-increasingly-warm-feelings-toward-religious-groups/
31. Bushman, B. J., & Bonacci, A. M. (2004). You've got mail: Using e-mail to examine the effect of prejudiced attitudes on discrimination against Arabs. *Journal of Experimental Social Psychology, 40,* 753–759.
32. Milgram, S. (1977). *The individual in a social world.* New York: McGraw-Hill.
33. Stern, S. E., & Faber, J. E. (1997). The lost e-mail method: Milgram's lost-letter technique in the age of the Internet. *Behavior Research Methods, Instruments, and Computers, 29,* 260–263.
34. Ahmed, A. M. (2010). Muslim discrimination: Evidence from two lost-letter experiments. *Journal of Applied Social Psychology, 40*(4), 888–898.
35. Das, E., Bushman, B. J., Bezemer, M. D., Kerkhof, P., & Vermeulen, I. E. (2009). How terrorism news reports increase prejudice against outgroups: A terror management account. *Journal of Experimental Social Psychology, 45,* 453–459.
36. Bein, A. (1990). The Jewish question: Biography of a world problem. Fairleigh Dickinson University Press.
37. Introduction to the Holocaust. *U.S. Holocaust Memorial Museum.* Retrieved from https://encyclopedia.ushmm.org/content/en/article/introduction-to-the-holocaust
38. Musolff, A. (2007). What role do metaphors play in racial prejudice? The function of antisemitic imagery in Hitler's Mein Kampf. *Patterns of Prejudice, 41*(1), 21–43. DOI: 10.1080/00313220601118744
39. Glick, P. (2002). Sacrificial lambs dressed in wolves' clothing: Envious prejudice, ideology, and the scapegoating of Jews. In L. S. Newman & R. Erber (Eds.), *Understanding genocide: The social psychology of the Holocaust.* (pp. 113–142). New York, NY: Oxford University Press.
40. Beim, A., & Fine, G. A. (2007). The cultural frameworks of prejudice: Reputational images and the postwar disjuncture of Jews and Communism. *The Sociological Quarterly, 48*(3), 373–397. DOI: 10.1111/j.1533-8525.2007.00082.x
41. Horowitz, H. L. (1987). *Campus life: Undergraduate cultures from the end of the eighteenth century to the present.* Chicago, IL: University of Chicago Press.
42. Bergmann, W., & Bowman, P. (2008). Anti-Semitic attitudes in Europe: A comparative perspective. *Journal of Social Issues, 64*(2), 343–362. DOI: 10.1111/j.1540-4560.2008.00565.x
43. Giordano, C. (2019, February 19). Vandals desecrate 90 Jewish graves in Paris as antisemitism marches about to take place. *Independent.* Retrieved from https://www.independent.co.uk/news/world/europe/france-antisemitism-vandals-jewish-graves-paris-gilets-jaunes-swastikas-marches-a8786226.html
44. Wagner, M. (2017). 'Blood and soil': Protesters chant Nazi slogan in Charlottesville. CNN. Retrieved from https://www.cnn.com/2017/08/12/us/charlottesville-unite-the-right-rally/index.html
45. Nazi-saluting teens provoke outrage in California after photos flood internet. *NPR.* Retrieved from https://www.npr.org/2019/03/04/700168758/nazi-saluting-teens-provoke-outrage-in-california-after-photos-flood-internet
46. Brown, J. F. (1943). Social and psychological factors in the anti-Semitic attitude. *Journal of Educational Sociology, 16,* 351–354. https://doi-org.proxy.lib.umich.edu/10.2307/2261771
47. Bilewicz, M., Winiewski, M., Kofta, M., & Wójcik, A. (2013). Harmful ideas, the structure and consequences of anti-Semitic beliefs in Poland. *Political Psychology, 34*(6), 821–839. DOI: 10.1111/pops.12024
48. Cohen, F., Jussim, L., Harber, K. D., & Bhasin, G. (2009). Modern anti-Semitism and anti-Israeli attitudes. *Journal of Personality and Social Psychology, 97*(2), 290–306. DOI: 10.1037/a0015338
49. Schiavone, S. R., & Gervais, W. M. (2017). Atheists. *Social and Personality Psychology Compass, 11*(12), 1–13. DOI: 10.1111/spc3.12365
50. Gervais, W. M. & Norenzayan, A. (2013). Religion and the origins of anti-atheist prejudice. Chapter to appear in S. Clarke, R. Powell, & J. Savulescu (Eds.), *Intolerance and conflict: A scientific and conceptual investigation.* Oxford: Oxford University Press.
51. Brown-Iannuzzi, J. L., McKee, S., & Gervais, W. M. (2018). Atheist horns and religious halos: Mental representations of atheists and theists. *Journal of Experimental Psychology: General, 147*(2), 292–297. DOI: 10.1037/xge0000376.supp (Supplemental)
52. Gervais, W. M., & Najle, M. B. (2018). How many atheists are there? *Social Psychological and Personality Science, 9*(1), 3–10. DOI: 10.1177/1948550617707015
53. Gervais, W. M., Shariff, A. F., & Norenzayan, A. (2011). Do you believe in atheists? Distrust is central to anti-atheist prejudice. *Journal of Personality and Social Psychology, 101,* 1189–1206. doi: 10.1037/a0025882
54. Psalms 14: 1 (Bible; King James version).
55. Pew Research Global Attitudes Project. (2014, March 13). Worldwide, many see belief in God as essential to morality. Retrieved from http://www.pewglobal.org/2014/03/13/worldwide-many-see-belief-in-god-as-essential-to-morality/
56. Simpson, A., Rios, K., & Cowgill, C. M. (2017). Godless in essence? Psychological essentialism, theistic meta-beliefs, and anti-atheist prejudice. *Personality and Individual Differences, 119,* 35–45. DOI: 10.1016/j.paid.2017.06.029
57. Burmeister, J. M., Kiefner, A. E., Carels, R. A., & Musher-Eizenman, D. R. (2013). Weight bias in graduate school admissions. *Obesity, 21*(5), 918–920. doi: 10.1002/oby.20171
58. Swami, V., & Monk, R. (2013). Weight bias against women in a university acceptance scenario. *Journal of General Psychology, 140*(1), 45–56. doi: 10.1080/00221309.2012.726288
59. Cramer, P., & Steinwert, T. (1998). Thin is good, fat is bad: How early does it begin? *Journal of Applied Developmental Psychology, 19,* 429–451.
60. Kolata, G. (1992, November 22). The burdens of being overweight: Mistreatment and misconceptions. *New York Times,* A1.
61. Klaczynski, P., Daniel, D. B., & Keller, P. S. (2009). Appearance idealization, body esteem, causal attributions, and ethnic variations in the development of obesity stereotypes. *Journal of Applied Developmental Psychology, 30*(4), 537–551.
62. Centers for Disease Control. (2012). Overweight and obesity. Retrieved from http://www.cdc.gov/obesity/data/trends.HTML
63. Adult obesity facts. *CDC.* Retrieved from https://www.cdc.gov/obesity/data/adult.html
64. Harris, M. B., Harris, R. J., & Bochner, S. (1982). Fat, four-eyed and female: Stereotypes of obesity glasses and gender. *Journal of Applied Social Psychology, 12,* 503–516.
65. Hebl, M. R., & Heatherton, T. F. (1997). The stigma of obesity: The differences are black and white. *Personality and Social Psychology Bulletin, 24,* 417–426.

66. Larwood, L., & Gattiker, U. E. (1995). Rational bias and interorganizational power in the employment of management consultants. *Group and Organization Studies, 10*, 3–17.
67. Lerner, R. (1969). Some female stereotypes of male body build–behavior relations. *Perceptual and Motor Skills, 28*, 363–366.
68. Staffieri, J. (1967). A study of social stereotype of body image in children. *Journal of Personality and Social Psychology, 7*, 101–104.
69. Roehling, M. V., Roehling, P. V., & Odland, L. M. (2008). Investigating the validity of stereotypes about overweight employees: The relationship between body weight and normal personality traits. *Group and Organization Management, 33*(4), 392–424.
70. Tiggemann, M., & Rothblum, E. D. (1988). Gender differences in social consequences of perceived overweight in the United States and Australia. *Sex Roles, 18*, 75–86.
71. Hebl, M. R., & Mannix, L. M. (2003). The weight of obesity in evaluating others: A mere proximity effect. *Personality and Social Psychology Bulletin, 29*, 28–38.
72. Vermeulen, F. (2011, March 22). The price of obesity: How your salary depends on your weight. *Forbes*. Retrieved from https://www.forbes.com/sites/freekvermeulen/2011/03/22/the-price-of-obesity-how-your-salary-depends-on-your-weight/#36861f4a3d9a
73. Hansson, L. M., Näslund, E., & Rasmussen, F. (2010). Perceived discrimination among men and women with normal weight and obesity. A population-based study from Sweden. *Scandinavian Journal of Public Health, 38*(6), 587–596.
74. Bejciy-Spring, S. M. (2008). R-E-S-P-E-C-T: A model for the sensitive treatment of the bariatric patient. *Bariatric Nursing and Surgical Patient Care, 3*(1), 47–56.
75. Miller, D. P., Spangler, J. G., Vitolins, M. Z., Davis, S. W., Ip, E. H., Marion, G. S., & Crandall, S. J. (2013). Are medical students aware of their anti-obesity bias? *Academic Medicine, 88*(7), 978–982. doi: 10.1097/ACM.0b013e318294f817
76. Palca, J. (2013, May 23). The weight of a med student's subconscious bias. *NPR*. Retrieved from http://www.npr.org/blogs/health/2013/05/23/186294402/the-weight-of-a-med-students-subconscious-bias
77. Clayson, D. E., & Klassen, M. L. (1989). Perception of attractiveness by obesity and hair color. *Perceptual and Motor Skills, 68*, 199–202.
78. DeJong, W. (1980). The stigma of obesity: The consequences of naive assumptions concerning the causes of physical deviance. *Journal of Health and Social Behavior, 21*(1), 75–87.
79. DeJong, W. (1993). Obesity as a characterological stigma: The issue of responsibility and judgments of task performance. *Psychological Reports, 73*, 963–970.
80. Crandall, C. S. (1994). Prejudice against fat people: Ideology and self-interest. *Journal of Personality and Social Psychology, 66*, 882–894.
81. Tanneberger, A., & Ciuputu-Plath, C. (2018). Nurses' weight bias in caring for obese patients: Do weight controllability beliefs influence the provision of care to obese patients? *Clinical Nursing Research, 27*(4), 414–432. DOI: 10.1177/1054773816687443
82. Aaker, J., Vohs, K. D., & Mogilner, C. (2010). Nonprofits are seen as warm and for-profits as competent: Firm stereotypes matter. *Journal of Consumer Research, 37*, 224–237.
83. Bhattacharjee, A., Dana, J., & Baron, J. (2017). Anti-profit beliefs: How people neglect the societal benefits of profit. *Journal of Personality and Social Psychology, 113*, 671–696.
84. Wood, P. B., & Bartkowski, J. P. (2004). Attribution style and public policy attitudes toward gay rights. *Social Science Quarterly, 85*(1), 58–74.
85. American Psychological Association. (2008). Answers to your questions: For a better understanding of sexual orientation and homosexuality. Washington, DC: Author. Retrieved from http://www.apa.org/topics/sorientation.pdf
86. Stopera, M. (2019, March 19). 15 things all straight people do that 2/3 of gay people are still afraid to. *BuzzFeed*. Retrieved from https://www.buzzfeed.com/mjs538/straight-people-do-this-but-23-of-gay-people-are
87. Tilcsik, A. (2011). Pride and prejudice: Employment discrimination against openly gay men in the United States. *American Journal of Sociology, 117*(2), 586–626.
88. Bahns, A. J., & Branscombe, N. R. (2011). Effects of legitimizing discrimination against homosexuals on gay bashing. *European Journal of Social Psychology, 41*(3), 388–396.
89. Wolf, R. (2018, June 4). Supreme Court rules on narrow grounds for baker who refused to create same-sex couple's wedding cake. *USA Today*. Retrieved from https://www.usatoday.com/story/news/politics/2018/06/04/supreme-court-rules-against-gay-wedding-exemptions/1052989001/
90. Hendren, A., & Blank, H. (2009). Prejudiced behavior toward lesbians and gay men: A field experiment on everyday helping. *Social Psychology, 40*(4), 234–238.
91. Herek, G. M. (2000). The psychology of sexual prejudice. *Current Directions in Psychological Science, 9*, 19–22.
92. Bernat, J. A., Calhoun, K. S., Adams, H. E., & Zeichner, A. (2001). Homophobia and physical aggression toward homosexual and heterosexual individuals. *Journal of Abnormal Psychology, 110*, 179–187.
93. Parrott, D. J. (2009). Aggression toward gay men as gender role enforcement: Effects of male role norms, sexual prejudice, and masculine gender role stress. *Journal of Personality, 77*(5), 1137–1166.
94. Brown, M. J., & Groscup, J. L. (2009). Homophobia and acceptance of stereotypes about gays and lesbians. *Individual Differences Research, 7*(3), 159–167.
95. Wood, P. B., & Bartkowski, J. P. (2004). Attribution style and public policy attitudes toward gay rights. *Social Science Quarterly, 85*(1), 58–74.
96. Olatunji, B. O. (2008). Disgust, scrupulosity and conservative attitudes about sex: Evidence for a mediational model of homophobia. *Journal of Research in Personality, 42*(5), 1364–1369.
97. Terrizzi, J. A., Jr., Shook, N. J., & Ventis, W. L. (2010). Disgust: A predictor of social conservatism and prejudicial attitudes toward homosexuals. *Personality and Individual Differences, 49*(6), 587–592.
98. Bos, H. M. W., Gartrell, N. K., Van Balen, F., Peyser, H., & Sandfort, T. G. M. (2008). Children in planned lesbian families: A cross-cultural comparison between the United States and the Netherlands. *American Journal of Orthopsychiatry, 78*(2), 211–219.
99. Pew Research Center (2014, February 23). *Gay marriage*. Retrieved from http://www.pewresearch.org/data-trend/domestic-issues/attitudes-on-gay-marriage/
100. Bailey, N. W., & Zuk, M. (2009). Same-
101. BBC. Gay penguins in Kent zoo are 'the best parents.' *BBC News*. Retrieved from https://www.bbc.com/news/uk-england-kent-27405652
102. Avery, D. (2018, August 11). Gay couples are four times more likely to adopt, so of course congress wants to stop them. *Hornet*. Retrieved from https://hornet.com/stories/gay-parents-adoption/
103. Herek, G. M., & Capitanio, J. P. (1996). "Some of my best friends": Intergroup contact, concealable stigma, and heterosexuals' attitudes toward gay men and lesbians. *Personality and Social Psychology Bulletin, 22*(4), 412–424.
104. Laumann, E. O., Gagnon, J. H., Michael, R. T., & Michaels, S. (1994). *The social organization of sexuality: Sexual practices in the United States*. Chicago: University of Chicago Press.
105. Whitley, B. E. (1988). Sex differences in heterosexuals' attitudes toward homosexuals: It depends upon what you ask. *Journal of Sex Research, 24*, 287–291.
106. Herek, G. M., & Capitanio, J. P. (1999). AIDS stigma and sexual prejudice. *American Behavioral Scientist, 42*, 1126–1143.
107. Whitley, B. E. (1988). Sex differences in heterosexuals' attitudes toward homosexuals: It depends upon what you ask. *Journal of Sex Research, 24*, 287–291.
108. Adams, H. E., Wright, L. W., Jr., & Lohr, B. A. (1996). Is homophobia associated with homosexual arousal? *Journal of Abnormal Psychology, 105*, 440–446.
109. Falomir-Pichastor, J. M., & Mugny, G. (2009). "I'm not gay ... I'm a real man!": Heterosexual men's gender self-esteem and sexual prejudice. *Personality and Social Psychology Bulletin, 35*(9), 1233–1243.
110. Buck, D. M., Plant, E. A., Ratcliff, J., Zielaskowski, K., & Boerner, P. (2013). Concern over the misidentification of sexual orientation: Social contagion and the avoidance of sexual minorities. *Journal of Personality and Social Psychology, 105*, 941–960.
111. Winegard, B., Reynolds, T., Baumeister, R. F., & Plant, E. A. (2016). The coalitional value theory of anti-gay bias. *Evolutionary Behavioral Sciences, 10*, 245–265.
112. Bronson, P., & Merryman, A. (2009, September 4). Even babies discriminate: A nurtureshock excerpt. *Newsweek*. Retrieved from http://www.newsweek.com/even-babies-discriminate-nurtureshock-excerpt-79233
113. Pinker, S. (2011). *The better angels of our nature: Why violence has declined*. New York: Viking Adult.
114. Billig, M., & Tajfel, H. (1973). Social categorization and similarity in intergroup behaviour. *European Journal of Social Psychology, 3*(1), 27–52.
115. Brewer, M. B. (1979). In-group bias in the minimal intergroup situation: A cognitive-motivational analysis. *Psychological Bulletin, 86*(2), 307–324.
116. Brewer, M. B., & Silver, M. (1978). Ingroup bias as a function of task characteristics. *European Journal of Social Psychology, 8*(3), 393–400.
117. Tajfel, H., & Billig, M. (1974). Familiarity and categorization in intergroup behavior. *Journal of Experimental Social Psychology, 10*(2), 159–170.
118. Tajfel, H., Billig, M. G., Bundy, R. P., & Flament, C. (1971). Social categorization and intergroup behaviour. *European Journal of Social Psychology, 1*(2), 149–178.
119. Locksley, A., Ortiz, V., & Hepburn, C. (1980). Social categorization and discriminatory behavior: Extinguishing the minimal intergroup discrimination effect. *Journal of Personality and Social Psychology, 39*(5), 773–783.
120. Sherif, M. (1966) *In common predicament: Social psychology of intergroup conflict and cooperation*. Boston: Houghton-Mifflin.
121. Johnson, D. W., & Johnson, R. T. (1983). The socialization and achievement crises: Are cooperative learning experiences the solution? *Applied Social Psychology Annual, 4*, 119–164.
122. Johnson, D. W., & Johnson, R. T. (1983). The socialization and achievement crises: Are cooperative learning experiences the solution? *Applied Social Psychology Annual, 4*, 119–164.
123. Bonta, B. D. (1997). Cooperation and competition in peaceful societies. *Psychological Bulletin, 121*, 299–320.
124. Draper, P. (1976). Social and economic constraints on child life among the !Kung. In R. B. Lee & I. DeVore (Eds.), *Kalahari hunter-gatherers: Studies of the !Kung San and their neighbors* (pp. 199–217). Cambridge, MA: Harvard University Press.
125. Overing, J. (1986). Images of cannibalism, death and domination in a "non-violent" society. In D. Riches (Ed.), *The anthropology of violence* (pp. 86–101). Oxford: Blackwell.
126. Howell, S. (1989). "To be angry is not to be human, but to be fearful is": Chewong concepts of human nature. In S. Howell & R. Willis (Eds.), *Societies at peace: Anthropological perspectives* (pp. 45–59). London: Routledge.
127. Keir, G. (1966). The psychological assessment of the children from the island of Tristan da Cunha. In C. Banks & P. L. Broadhurst (Eds.), *Stephanos: Studies in psychology presented to Cyril Burt* (pp. 129–172). New York: Barnes & Noble.
128. Bonta, B. D. (1997). Cooperation and competition in peaceful societies. *Psychological Bulletin, 121*, 299–320.
129. Adhikary, A. K. (1984). *Society and world view of the Birhor: A nomadic hunting and gathering community of Orissa*. Calcutta: Anthropological Survey of India.
130. Willis, R. (1989). The "peace puzzle" in Ufipa. In S. Howell & R. Willis (Eds.), *Societies at peace: Anthropological perspectives* (pp. 133–145). London: Routledge.

131. McNeill, W. H. (1982). *The pursuit of power: Technology, armed force, and society since A.D. 1000.* Chicago: University of Chicago Press.

132. Waytz, A., Young, L.L., & Ginges, J. (2014). Motive attribution asymmetry for love vs. hate drives intractable conflict. *PNAS*, early edition.

133. Schopler, J., & Insko, C. A. (1992). The discontinuity effect in interpersonal and intergroup relations: Generality and mediation. *European Review of Social Psychology, 3*, 121–151.

134. Insko, C. A., Schopler, J., Hoyle, R. H., & Dardis, G. J. (1990). Individual-group discontinuity as a function of fear and greed. *Journal of Personality and Social Psychology, 58*, 68–79.

135. Schopler, J., Insko, C. A., Drigotas, S., & Graetz, K. A. (1993). Individual-group discontinuity: Further evidence for mediation by fear and greed. *Personality and Social Psychology Bulletin, 19*, 419–431.

136. Insko, C. A., Schopler, J., Pemberton, M. B., Wieselquist, J., McIlraith, S. A., Currey, D. P., et al. (1998). Long-term outcome maximization and the reduction of interindividual-intergroup discontinuity. *Journal of Personality and Social Psychology, 75*, 695–711.

137. Schopler, J., Insko, C. A., Drigotas, S. M., & Wieselquist, J. (1995). The role of identifiability in the reduction of interindividual-intergroup discontinuity. *Journal of Experimental Social Psychology, 31*, 553–574.

138. Allport, G. W. (1954) *The nature of prejudice.* Reading, MA: Addison-Wesley.

139. Pettigrew, T. F., & Tropp, L. R. (2005). Allport's intergroup contact hypothesis: Its history and influence. In J. F. Dovidio, P. Glick, & L. A. Rudman (Eds.), *On the nature of prejudice: Fifty years after Allport* (pp. 262–277). Malden, MA: Blackwell.

140. Pettigrew, T. F., & Tropp, L. R. (2006). A meta-analytic test of intergroup contact theory. *Journal of Personality and Social Psychology, 90*, 751–783.

141. Paolini, S., Harwood, J., & Rubin, M. (2010). Negative intergroup contact makes group memberships salient: Explaining why intergroup conflict endures. *Personality and Social Psychology Bulletin, 36*(12) 1723–1738. doi: 10.1177/0146167210388667

142. Baumeister, R. F., Bratslavsky, E., Finkenauer, C., & Vohs, K. D. (2001). Bad is stronger than good. *Review of General Psychology, 5*(4), 323–370. doi: 10.1037//1089-2680.5.4.323

143. Barlow, F. K., Paolini, S., Pedersen, A., Hornsey, M. J., Radke, H. R. M., Harwood, J., Rubin, M., & Sibley, C. G. (2012). The contact caveat: Negative contact predicts increased prejudice more than positive contact predicts reduced prejudice. *Personality and Social Psychology Bulletin, 38*(12), 1629–1643. doi: 10.1177/0146167212457953

144. Pettigrew, T. F., & Tropp, L. R. (2008). How does intergroup contact reduce prejudice? Meta-analytic tests of three mediators. *European Journal of Social Psychology, 38*, 922–934.

145. Swart, H., Hewstone, M., Christ, O., & Voci, A. (2011). Affective mediators of intergroup contact: A three-wave longitudinal study in South Africa. *Journal of Personality and Social Psychology, 101*(6), 1221–1238.

146. Binder, J., Zagefka, H., Brown, R., Funke, F., Kessler, T., Mummendey, A., et al. (2009). Does contact reduce prejudice or does prejudice reduce contact? A longitudinal test of the contact hypothesis among majority and minority groups in three European countries. *Journal of Personality and Social Psychology, 96*(4), 843–856.

147. Hutchison, P., & Rosenthal, H. E. S. (2011). Prejudice against Muslims: Anxiety as a mediator between intergroup contact and attitudes, perceived group variability and behavioural intentions. *Ethnic and Racial Studies, 34*(1), 40–61.

148. Baunach, D. M., Burgess, E. O., & Muse, C. S. (2010). Southern (dis)comfort: Sexual prejudice and contact with gay men and lesbians in the south. *Sociological Spectrum, 30*(1), 30–64.

149. Mazziotta, A., Mummendey, A., & Wright, S. C. (2011). Vicarious intergroup contact effects: Applying social-cognitive theory to intergroup contact research. *Group Processes & Intergroup Relations, 14*(2), 255–274.

150. White, F. A., Verrelli, S., Maunder, R. D., & Kervinen, A. (2018). Using electronic contact to reduce homonegative attitudes, emotions, and behavioral intentions among heterosexual women and men: A contemporary extension of the contact hypothesis. *Journal of Sex Research*. DOI: 10.1080/00224499.2018.1491943

151. Cao, B., & Lin, W.-Y. (2017). Revisiting the contact hypothesis: Effects of different modes of computer-mediated communication on intergroup relationships. *International Journal of Intercultural Relations, 58*, 23–30. DOI: 10.1016/j.ijintrel.2017.03.003

152. Crisp, R. J., Birtel, M. D., & Meleady, R. (2011). Mental simulations of social thought and action: Trivial tasks or tools for transforming social policy? *Current Directions in Psychological Science, 20*(4), 261–264.

153. Hewstone, M., & Swart, H. (2011). Fifty-odd years of inter-group contact: From hypothesis to integrated theory. *British Journal of Social Psychology, 50*(3), 374–386.

154. Sidanius, J., & Pratto, F. (1999). *Social dominance: An intergroup theory of social hierarchy and oppression.* New York: Cambridge University Press.

155. Jost, J. T., & Kay, A. C. (2005). Exposure to benevolent sexism and complementary gender stereotypes: Consequences for specific and diffuse forms of system justification. *Journal of Personality and Social Psychology, 88*, 498–509.

156. Allport, G. W. (1954) *The nature of prejudice.* Reading, MA: Addison-Wesley.

157. Macrae, C. N., Milne, A. B., & Bodenhausen, G. V. (1994). Stereotypes as energy-saving devices: A peek inside the cognitive toolbox. *Journal of Personality and Social Psychology, 66*, 37–47.

158. Bodenhausen, G. V. (1990). Stereotypes as judgmental heuristics: Evidence of circadian variations in discrimination. *Psychological Science, 1*, 319–322.

159. Fein, S., & Spencer, S. J. (1997). Prejudice as self-image maintenance: Affirming the self through derogating others. *Journal of Personality and Social Psychology, 73*, 31–44.

160. Giuffrida, A. (2015, March 26). Why are Italians such crazy drivers? The Local it. Retrieved from https://www.thelocal.it/20150326/why-are-italians-such-crazy-drivers

161. Kennedy, M. (2018, November 19). Italian Village Installs Speed Cameras, Records 58,000 Infractions In 2 Weeks. NPR. Retrieved from https://www.npr.org/2018/11/19/669224810/italian-village-installs-speed-cameras-records-58-000-infractions-in-2-weeks

162. Swim, J. K. (1994). Perceived versus meta-analytic effect sizes: An assessment of the accuracy of gender stereotypes. *Journal of Personality and Social Psychology, 66*, 21–36.

163. Jussim, L., Cain, T. R., Crawford, J. T., Harber, K., & Cohen, F. (2009). The unbearable accuracy of stereotypes. In T. Nelson (Ed.), *Handbook of prejudice, stereotyping, and discrimination* (pp. 199–228). Mahwah, NJ: Erlbaum.

164. Judd, C., & Park, B. (1993). The assessment of accuracy of social stereotypes. *Psychological Review, 100*, 109–128.

165. Terracianno, A., et al. (2005). National character does not reflect mean personality trait levels in 49 cultures. *Science, 310*, 96–100.

166. Chan, W., McCrae, R. R., De Fruyt, F., Jussim, L., Löckenhoff, C. E., De Bolle, M., ... et al. (2012). Stereotypes of age differences in personality traits: Universal and accurate? *Journal of Personality and Social Psychology. 103*, 1050–1066. doi: 10.1037/a0029712

167. Jung, K., Shavitt, S., Viswanathan, M., & Hilbe, J. M. (2014). Female hurricanes are deadlier than male hurricanes. *PNAS, 111*, 8782–8787.

168. Jussim, L., Cain, T. R., Crawford, J. T., Harber, K., & Cohen, F. (2009). The unbearable accuracy of stereotypes. In T. Nelson (Ed.), *Handbook of prejudice, stereotyping, and discrimination* (pp. 199–228). Mahwah, NJ: Erlbaum.

169. Kunda, Z., & Thagard, P. (1996). Forming impressions from stereotypes, traits, and behaviors: A parallel-constraint-satisfaction theory. *Psychological Review, 103*, 284–308.

170. Hamilton, D. L., Dugan, P. M., & Trolier, T. K. (1985). The formation of stereotypic beliefs: Further evidence for distinctiveness-based illusory correlations. *Journal of Personality and Social Psychology, 48*, 5–17.

171. Hamilton, D. L., & Gifford, R. K. (1976). Illusory correlation in interpersonal perception: A cognitive basis of stereotypic judgments. *Journal of Experimental Social Psychology, 12*, 392–407.

172. Hamilton, D. L., & Gifford, R. K. (1976). Illusory correlation in interpersonal perception: A cognitive basis of stereotypic judgments. *Journal of Experimental Social Psychology, 12*, 392–407.

173. Allport, G. W. (1954) The nature of prejudice. Reading, MA: Addison-Wesley.

174. Leviticus 16: 7–10 (Bible).

175. Rothschild, Z. K., Landau, M. J., Sullivan, D., & Keefer, L. A. (2012). A dual-motive model of scapegoating: Displacing blame to reduce guilt or increase control. *Journal of Personality and Social Psychology, 102*, 1148–1163.

176. Hovland, C. I., & Sears, R. (1940). Minor studies of aggression: Correlation of lynchings with economic conditions. *Journal of Psychology, 9*, 301–310.

177. Hepworth, J. T., & West, S. G. (1988). Lynchings and the economy: A time-series reanalysis of Hovland and Sears (1940). *Journal of Personality and Social Psychology, 55*, 239–247.

178. Sinclair, L., & Kunda, Z. (2000). Motivated stereotyping of women: She's fine if she praised me but incompetent if she criticized me. *Personality and Social Psychology Bulletin, 26*, 1329–1342.

179. Sinclair, L., & Kunda, Z. (1999). Reactions to a black professional: Motivated inhibition and activation of conflicting stereotypes. *Journal of Personality and Social Psychology, 77*, 885–904.

180. Kunda, Z., Davies, P. G., Adams, B. D., & Spencer, S. J. (2002). The dynamic time course of stereotype activation: Activation, dissipation, and resurrection. *Journal of Personality and Social Psychology, 82*, 283–299.

181. Maner, J. K., Kenrick, D. T., Neuberg, S. L., Becker, D. V., Robertson, T., Hofer, B., et al. (2005). Functional projection: How fundamental social motives can bias interpersonal perception. *Journal of Personality and Social Psychology, 88*, 63–78.

182. Darley, J. M., & Gross, P. H. (1983). A hypothesis-confirming bias in labeling effects. *Journal of Personality and Social Psychology, 44*(1), 20–33.

183. http://thinkexist.com/quotes/frederick_the_great/

184. Quoted by Krauthammer, C. (1997, June 29). Apology is not ours to give. *Cleveland Plain Dealer*, p. 2–E.

185. Fazio, R. H., Jackson, J. R., Dunton, B. C., & Williams, C. J. (1995). Variability in automatic activation as an unobstrusive measure of racial attitudes: A bona fide pipeline? *Journal of Personality and Social Psychology, 69*, 1013–1027.

186. Fazio, R. H., & Olson, M. A. (2003). Implicit measures in social cognition research: Their meaning and uses. *Annual Review of Psychology, 54*, 297–327.

187. Greenwald, A. G., McGhee, D. E., & Schwartz, J. K. L. (1998). Measuring individual differences in implicit cognition: The implicit association test. *Journal of Personality and Social Psychology, 74*, 1464–1480.

188. Payne, B. K. (2001). Prejudice and perception: The role of automatic and controlled processes in misperceiving a weapon. *Journal of Personality and Social Psychology, 81*, 181–192.

189. Rydell, R. J., & McConnell, A. R. (2006). Understanding implicit and explicit attitude change: A systems of reasoning analysis. *Journal of Personality and Social Psychology, 91*, 995–1008.

190. Ziegert, J. C., & Hanges, P. J. (2005). Employment discrimination: The role of implicit attitudes, motivation, and a climate for racial bias. *Journal of Applied Psychology, 90*, 553–562.

191. Payne, B. K., Govorun, O., & Arbuckle, N. L. (2008). Automatic attitudes and alcohol: Does implicit liking predict drinking? *Cognition and Emotion, 22*, 238–271.

192. Scherer, L. D., & Lambert, A. J. (2012). Implicit race bias revisited: On the utility of task context in assessing implicit attitude strength. *Journal of Experimental Social Psychology, 48*, 366–370.

193. Richeson, J. A., & Shelton, J. N. (2003). When prejudice doesn't pay: Effects of interracial contact on executive function. *Psychological Science, 14,* 287–290.
194. Richeson, J. A., Trawalter, S., & Shelton, J. N. (2005). African Americans' implicit racial attitudes and the depletion of executive function after interracial interactions. *Social Cognition, 23,* 336–352.
195. Devine, P. G. (1989). Stereotypes and prejudice: Their automatic and controlled components. *Journal of Personality and Social Psychology, 56,* 5–18.
196. Dutton, D. G., & Lake, R. A. (1973). Threat of own prejudice and reverse discrimination in interracial situations. *Journal of Personality and Social Psychology, 28,* 94–100.
197. Dutton, D. G. (1971). Reactions of restaurateurs to blacks and whites violating restaurant dress requirements. *Canadian Journal of Behavioural Science, 3,* 298–302.
198. Plant, E. A., & Devine, P. G. (1998). Internal and external motivation to respond without prejudice. *Journal of Personality and Social Psychology, 75,* 811–832.
199. Plant, E. A., & Devine, P. G. (2001). Responses to other-imposed pro-black pressure: Acceptance or backlash? *Journal of Experimental Social Psychology, 37,* 486–501.
200. Amodio, D. M., Harmon-Jones, E., & Devine, P. G. (2003). Individual differences in the activation and control of affective race bias as assessed by startle eyeblink response and self-report. *Journal of Personality and Social Psychology, 84,* 738–753.
201. Devine, P. G., Plant, E. A., Amodio, A. M., Harmon-Jones, E., & Vance, S. L. (2002). Exploring the relationship between implicit and explicit prejudice: The role of motivations to respond without prejudice. *Journal of Personality and Social Psychology, 82,* 835–848.
202. Binder, J., Zagefka, H., Brown, R., Funke, F., Kessler, T., Mummendey, A., et al. (2009). Does contact reduce prejudice or does prejudice reduce contact? A longitudinal test of the contact hypothesis among majority and minority groups in three European countries. *Journal of Personality and Social Psychology, 96,* 843–856.
203. Pettigrew, T. F., & Tropp, L. R. (2006). A meta-analytic test of intergroup contact theory. *Journal of Personality and Social Psychology, 90,* 751–783.
204. Shook, N. J., & Fazio, R. H. (2008). Interracial roommate relationships: An experimental field test of the contact hypothesis. *Psychological Science, 19,* 717–723.
205. Wright, S. C., Aron, A., McLaughlin-Volpe, T., & Ropp, S. A. (1997). The extended contact effect: Knowledge of cross-group friendships and prejudice. *Journal of Personality and Social Psychology, 73,* 73–90.
206. Dovidio, J. F., & Gaertner, S. L. (1999). Reducing prejudice: Combating intergroup biases. *Current Directions in Psychological Science, 8,* 101–105.
207. Bay-Hinitz, A. K., Peterson, R. F., & Quilitch, H. R. (1994). Cooperative games: A way to modify aggressive and cooperative behaviors in young children. *Journal of Applied Behavior Analysis, 27,* 435–446.
208. Aronson, E. (2000). *Nobody left to hate: Teaching compassion after Columbine.* New York: W. H. Freeman.
209. Aronson, E., Blaney, N., Stephin, C., Sikes, J., & Snapp, M. (1978). *The jigsaw classroom.* Beverly Hills, CA: Sage.
210. Aronson, E., & Patnoe, S. (1997). *The jigsaw classroom: Building cooperation in the classroom* (2nd ed.). New York: Addison Wesley Longman.
211. Aronson, E., & Osherow, N. (1980). Cooperation, prosocial behavior, and academic performance: Experiments in the desegregated classroom. *Applied Social Psychology Annual, 1,* 163–196.
212. Walker, I., & Crogan, M. (1998). Academic performance, prejudice, and the jigsaw classroom: New pieces to the puzzle. *Journal of Community and Applied Social Psychology, 8,* 381–393.
213. Walker, I., & Crogan, M. (1998). Academic performance, prejudice, and the jigsaw classroom: New pieces to the puzzle. *Journal of Community and Applied Social Psychology, 8,* 381–393.
214. Alebiosu, K. A. (2001). Cooperative learning and students' affective learning outcome in Nigerian chemistry classrooms. *IFE Psychologia, 9,* 135–142.
215. BBC. (2016, January 4). *BBC News.* Sunnis and Shia: Islam's ancient schism. Retrieved from https://www.bbc.com/news/world-middle-east-16047709.
216. Maass, A., Cadinu, M., Guarnieri, G., & Grasselli, A. (2003). Sexual harassment under social identity threat: The computer harassment paradigm. *Journal of Personality and Social Psychology, 85,* 853–870.
217. Centers for Disease Control. (2016). *Sexual identity, sex of sexual contacts, and health-risk behaviors among students in grades 9-12: youth risk behavior surveillance.* Atlanta, GA: U.S. Department of Health and Human Services.
218. Anti-Violence Project. A crisis of hate: A report on lesbian, gay, bisexual, transgender and queer hate violence homicides in 2017. Retrieved from https://avp.org/a-crisis-of-hate-january/
219. Toomey, R. B., Syvertsen, A. K., & Shramko, M. (2018). Transgender adolescent suicide behavior. *Pediatrics, 142*(4), 1–8.
220. Merton, R. K. (1948). The self-fulfilling prophecy. *Antioch Review,* pp. 193–210.
221. Merton, R. K. (1948). The self-fulfilling prophecy. *Antioch Review,* pp. 193–210.
222. Rosenthal, R., & Jacobson, L. (1968). *Pygmalion in the classroom: Teacher expectation and pupils' intellectual development.* New York: Rinehart and Winston.
223. Jussim, L., & Harber, K. D. (2005). Teacher expectations and self-fulfilling prophecies: Knowns and unknowns, resolved and unresolved controversies. *Personality and Social Psychology Review, 9*(2), 131–155.
224. Jussim, L., & Harber, K. D. (2005). Teacher expectations and self-fulfilling prophecies: Knowns and unknowns, resolved and unresolved controversies. *Personality and Social Psychology Review, 9*(2), 131–155.
225. Patterson, O. (1982). *Slavery and social death.* Cambridge, MA: Harvard University Press.
226. Crocker, J., & Major, B. (1989). Social stigma and self-esteem: The self-protective properties of stigma. *Psychological Review, 96,* 608–630.
227. Judd, C., & Park, B. (1993). The assessment of accuracy of social stereotypes. *Psychological Review, 100,* 109–128.
228. Twenge, J. M., & Crocker, J. (2002). Race and self-esteem: Meta-analyses comparing Whites, Blacks, Hispanics, Asians, and American Indians. *Psychological Bulletin, 128,* 371–408.
229. Crocker, J., & Major, B. (1989). Social stigma and self-esteem: The self-protective properties of stigma. *Psychological Review, 96,* 608–630.
230. Crocker, J., Voelkl, K., Testa, M., & Major, B. (1991). Social stigma: The affective consequences of attributional ambiguity. *Journal of Personality and Social Psychology, 60,* 218–228.
231. Sedlovskaya, A., Purdie-Vaughn, V., Eibach, R.P., LaFrance, M., Romero-Canyas, R., & Camp, N.P. (2013). Internalizing the closet: Concealment heightens the cognitive distinction between public and private selves. *Journal of Personality and Social Psychology, 104,* 695–715.
232. Bawer, B. (2012). *The victims' revolution: The rise of identity studies and the closing of the liberal mind.* New York: Broadside Books.
233. Cole, A.M. (2007). *The cult of true victimhood.* Palo Alto, CA: Stanford University Press.
234. Wohl, M. J. A., & Branscombe, N. R. (2008). Remembering historical victimization: Collective guilt for current ingroup transgressions. *Journal of Personality and Social Psychology, 94,* 988–1006.
235. Steele, C. M., & Aronson, J. A. (1995). Stereotype threat and the intellectual test performance of African Americans. *Journal of Personality and Social Psychology, 69,* 797–811.
236. Benbow, C. P., Lubinski, D., Shea, D. L., & Eftekhari-Sanjani, H. (2000). Sex differences in mathematical reasoning ability: Their status 20 years later. *Psychological Science, 11,* 474–480.
237. Gottfredson, L. (Ed.). (1997). Intelligence and social policy. *Intelligence, 24,* 1–320.
238. Jencks, C., & Phillips, M. (Eds.). (1998). *The Black–White test score gap.* Washington, DC: Brookings Institution.
239. Spencer, S. J., Steele, C. M., & Quinn, D. M. (1999). Stereotype threat and women's math performance. *Journal of Experimental Social Psychology, 35,* 4–28.
240. Stone, J., & McWhinnie, C. (2008). Evidence that blatant versus subtle stereotype threat cues impact performance through dual processes. *Journal of Experimental Social Psychology, 44*(2), 445–452.
241. Wout, D., Danso, H., Jackson, J., & Spencer, S. (2008). The many faces of stereotype threat: Group- and self-threat. *Journal of Experimental Social Psychology, 44*(3), 792–799.
242. Aronson, J., Lustina, M. J., Good, C., Keough, K., Steele, C. M., & Brown, J. (1999). When white men can't do math: Necessary and sufficient factors in stereotype threat. *Journal of Experimental Social Psychology, 35,* 29–46.
243. Steele, C. M., & Aronson, J. A. (1995). Stereotype threat and the intellectual test performance of African Americans. *Journal of Personality and Social Psychology, 69,* 797–811.
244. Blascovich, J., Spencer, S. J., Quinn, D., & Steele, C. (2001). African Americans and high blood pressure: The role of stereotype threat. *Psychological Science, 12,* 225–229.
245. Sackett, P. R., Hardison, C. M., & Cullen, M. J. (2004). On interpreting stereotype threat as accounting for African American–White differences on cognitive tests. *American Psychologist, 59,* 7–13.
246. Sackett, P. R., Hardison, C. M., & Cullen, M. J. (2004b). On the value of correcting mischaracterizations of stereotype threat research. *American Psychologist, 59,* 48–49.
247. Steele, C. M., & Aronson, J. A. (2004). Stereotype threat does not live by Steele and Aronson (1995) alone. *American Psychologist, 59,* 47–55.
248. Nguyen, H.-H. D., & Ryan, A. M. (2008). Does stereotype threat affect test performance of minorities and women? A meta-analysis of experimental evidence. *Journal of Applied Psychology, 93*(6), 1314–1334.
249. Abrams, D., Crisp, R. J., Marques, S., Fagg, E., Bedford, L., & Provias, D. (2008). Threat inoculation: Experienced and imagined intergenerational contact prevents stereotype threat effects on older people's math performance. *Psychology and Aging, 23*(4), 934–939.
250. Brodish, A. B., & Devine, P. G. (2009). The role of performance-avoidance goals and worry in mediating the relationship between stereotype threat and performance. *Journal of Experimental Social Psychology, 45*(1), 180–185.
251. Johns, M., Inzlicht, M., & Schmader, T. (2008). Stereotype threat and executive resource depletion: Examining the influence of emotion regulation. *Journal of Experimental Psychology: General, 137*(4), 691–705.
252. Krendl, A. C., Richeson, J. A., Kelley, W. M., & Heatherton, T. F. (2008). The negative consequences of threat: A functional magnetic resonance imaging investigation of the neural mechanisms underlying women's underperformance in math. *Psychological Science, 19*(2), 168–175.
253. Abrams, D., Crisp, R. J., Marques, S., Fagg, E., Bedford, L., & Provias, D. (2008). Threat inoculation: Experienced and imagined intergenerational contact prevents stereotype threat effects on older people's math performance. *Psychology and Aging, 23*(4), 934–939.

254. Plant, E. A. (2004). Responses to interracial interactions over time. *Personality and Social Psychology Bulletin, 30,* 1458–1471.
255. Shelton, J. N. (2003). Interpersonal concerns in social encounters between majority and minority group members. *Group Processes and Intergroup Relations, 6,* 171–185.
256. All material in this section is taken from: Duarte, J. L., Crawford, J. T., Stern, C., Haidt, J., Jussim, L., & Tetlock, P. E. (in press/2015). Political diversity will improve social psychological science. *Behavioral and Brain Sciences.*
257. Ceci, S. J., Peters, D., & Plotkin, J. (1985). Human subjects review, personal values, and the regulation of social sciences research. *American Psychologist, 51,* 768–784.
258. From Plant, E. A., & Devine, P. G. (1998). Internal and external motivation to respond without prejudice. *Journal of Personality and Social Psychology, 75,* 811–832.

CHAPTER 14
Groups

1. Quotes – Henry Ford. Retrieved from http://quotes4all.net/henry%20ford:3.html
2. Gross, D. (1996). *Forbes greatest business stories of all time.* New York: Wiley.
3. Campbell, D. T. (1958). Common fate, similarity, and other indices of the status of aggregates of persons as social entities. *Behavioral Science, 3,* 14–25.
4. Lickel, B., Hamilton, D. L., Wieczorkowska, G., Lewis, A., Sherman, S. J., & Uhles, A. N. (2000). Varieties of groups and the perception of group entitativity. *Journal of Personality and Social Psychology, 78,* 223–246.
5. Laumann, E. O., Gagnon, J. H., Michael, R. T., & Michaels, S. (1994). *The social organization of sexuality: Sexual practices in the United States.* Chicago, IL: University of Chicago Press.
6. Moffett, M.W. (2019). *The human swarm: How our socities arise, thrive, and fall.* New York: Basic Books.
7. Hoyle, R. H., Pinkley, R. L., & Insko, C. A. (1989). Perceptions of social behavior: Evidence of differing expectations for interpersonal and intergroup interaction. *Personality and Social Psychology Bulletin, 15,* 365–376.
8. For a review, see Levine, J. M., & Moreland, R. L. (1998). Small groups. In D. Gilbert, S. Fiske, & G. Lindzey (Eds.), *Handbook of social psychology* (4th ed., Vol. 2, pp. 415–469). Boston: McGraw-Hill.
9. Surowiecki, J. (2004). *The wisdom of crowds: Why the many are smarter than the few and how collective wisdom shapes business, economics, societies, and nations.* New York: Doubleday.
10. Shi, F., Teplitskiy, M., Duede, E., & Evans, J. A. (2019). The wisdom of polarized crowd. Nature Human Behaviour, advance online publication, doi.org/10.1038/s41562-019-0541-6.
11. Page, S. E. (2008). *The difference: How the power of diversity creates better groups, firms, schools, and societies.* Princeton, NJ: Princeton University Press.
12. Levine, J. M., & Moreland, R. L. (1998). Small groups. In D. Gilbert, S. Fiske, & G. Lindzey (Eds.), *Handbook of social psychology* (4th. ed., Vol. 2, pp. 415–469). Boston: McGraw-Hill.
13. Mannix, E., & Neale, M.A. (2005). What differences make a difference? The promise and reality of diverse teams in organizations. *Psychological Science in the Public Interest, 6,* 31–55.
14. Baumeister, R. F. (2005). *The cultural animal: Human nature, meaning, and social life.* New York: Oxford University Press.
15. Diener, E., Fraser, S. C., Beaman, A. L., & Kelem, R. T. (1976). Effects of deindividuation variables on stealing among Halloween trick-or-treaters. *Journal of Personality and Social Psychology, 33,* 178–183.
16. Zimbardo, P. G. (1970). The human choice: Individuation, reason, and order versus deindividuation, impulse, and chaos. In W. J. Arnold & D. Levine (Eds.), *Nebraska Symposium on Motivation* (pp. 237–307). Lincoln: University of Nebraska Press.
17. Lerner, J. S., & Tetlock, P. E. (1999). Accounting for the effects of accountability. *Psychological Bulletin, 125,* 255–275.
18. Schopler, J., Insko, C. A., Drigotas, S. M., Wieselquist, J., Pemberton, M. B., & Cox, C. (1995). The role of identifiability in the reduction of interindividual-intergroup discontinuity. *Journal of Experimental Social Psychology, 31,* 553–574.
19. Cottrell, N. B., Wack, D. L., Sekerak, G. J, & Rittle, R. H. (1968). Social facilitation of dominant responses by the presence of an audience and the mere presence of others. *Journal of Personality and Social Psychology, 9,* 245–250.
20. Seta, C. E., & Seta, J. J. (1995). When audience presence is enjoyable: The influences of audience awareness of prior success on performance and task interest. *Basic and Applied Social Psychology, 16*(1–2), 95–108.
21. Beilock, S. L., & Carr, T. H. (2001). On the fragility of skilled performance: What governs choking under pressure? *Journal of Experimental Psychology: General, 130,* 701–725.
22. Butler, J. L., & Baumeister, R. F. (1998). The trouble with friendly faces: Skilled performance with a supportive audience. *Journal of Personality and Social Psychology, 75,* 1213–1230.
23. Wallace, H. M., & Baumeister, R. F. (2002). The performance of narcissists rises and falls with perceived opportunity for glory. *Journal of Personality and Social Psychology, 82,* 819–834.
24. Wright, E. F., & Jackson, W. (1991). The home-course disadvantage in golf championships: Further evidence for the undermining effect of supportive audiences on performance under pressure. *Journal of Sport Behavior, 14,* 51–60.
25. Wright, E. F., & Voyer, D. (1995). Supporting audiences and performance under pressure: The home-ice disadvantage in hockey championships. *Journal of Sport Behavior, 18,* 21–28.
26. For example, Spence, K. W. (1956). *Behavior theory and conditioning.* New Haven, CT: Yale University Press.
27. Zajonc, R. B. (1965). Social facilitation. *Science, 149,* 269–274.
28. Bond, C. F., & Titus, L. J. (1983). Social facilitation: A meta-analysis of 241 studies. *Psychological Bulletin, 94,* 265–292.
29. Zajonc, R. B., Heingartner, A., & Herman, E. M. (1969). Social enhancement and impairment of performance in the cockroach. *Journal of Personality and Social Psychology, 13,* 83–92.
30. Aiello, J. R., & Douthitt, E. A. (2001). Social facilitation: From Triplett to electronic performance monitoring. *Group Dynamics: Theory, Research, and Practice, 5,* 163–180.
31. Cottrell, N. B., Wack, D. L., Sekerak, G. J., & Rittle, R. H. (1968). Social facilitation of dominant responses by the presence of an audience and the mere presence of others. *Journal of Personality and Social Psychology, 9,* 245–250.
32. Wallace, H. M., & Baumeister, R. F. (2002). The performance of narcissists rises and falls with perceived opportunity for glory. *Journal of Personality and Social Psychology, 82,* 819–834.
33. Ringelmann, M. (1913). Recherches sur les moteurs animés: Travail de l'homme. *Annales de l'Institut National Argonomique,* 2e srie, tom 12, 1–40. Published in French, cited in Kravitz, D. A., & Martin, B. (1986). Ringelmann rediscovered: The original article. *Journal of Personality and Social Psychology, 50,* 936–941.
34. Latane, B., Williams, K., & Harkins, S. (1979). Many hands make light the work: The causes and consequences of social loafing. *Journal of Personality and Social Psychology, 37,* 822–832.
35. For example, Kerr, N. L., & Bruun, S. E. (1983). Dispensability of member effort and group motivation losses: Free-rider effects. *Journal of Personality and Social Psychology, 44,* 78–94.
36. Crandall, C. S. (1988). Social contagion of binge eating. *Journal of Personality and Social Psychology, 55,* 588–598.
37. Crandall, C. S. (1988). Social contagion of binge eating. *Journal of Personality and Social Psychology, 55,* 588–598.
38. Karau, S. J., & Williams, K. D. (1993). Social loafing: A meta-analytic review and theoretical integration. *Journal of Personality and Social Psychology, 65,* 681–706.
39. Kerr, N. L., & Bruun, S. E. (1981). Ringelmann revisited: Alternative explanations for the social loafing effect. *Personality and Social Psychology Bulletin, 7*(2), 224–231.
40. Williams, K., Harkins, S. G., & Latané, B. (1981). Identifiability as a deterrant to social loafing: Two cheering experiments. *Journal of Personality and Social Psychology, 40*(2), 303–311.
41. Karau, S. J., & Williams, K. D. (1993). Social loafing: A meta-analytic review and theoretical integration. *Journal of Personality and Social Psychology, 65,* 681–706.
42. Kerr, N. L. (1983). Motivation losses in small groups: A social dilemma analysis. *Journal of Personality and Social Psychology, 45,* 819–828.
43. Kerr, N. L., Rumble, A. C., Park, E. S., Ouwerkerk, J. W., Parks, C. D., Gallucci, M., & Van Lange, P. A. M. (2009). "How many bad apples does it take to spoil the whole barrel?" Social exclusion and tolerance for bad apples. *Journal of Experimental Social Psychology. 45*(4), 603–613. Retrieved from http://www.sciencedirect.com/science/article/pii/S0022103109000390
44. Kurzban, R., & Leary, M. R. (2001). Evolutionary origins of stigmatization: The functions of social exclusion. *Psychological Bulletin, 127,* 187–208.
45. Ouwerkerk, J. W., Van Lange, P. A., Gallucci, M., & Kerr, N. L. (2005). Avoiding the social death penalty: Ostracism and cooperation in social dilemmas. In K. D. Williams, J. P. Forgas, & W. von Hippel (Eds.), *The social outcast: Ostracism, social exclusion, rejection, and bullying* (pp. 321–332). New York: Psychology Press.
46. Kerr, N. L., & Bruun, S. E. (1983). Dispensability of member effort and group motivation losses: Free-rider effects. *Journal of Personality and Social Psychology, 44,* 78–94.
47. Fehr, E., & Gächter, S. (2002). Altruistic punishment in humans. *Nature, 415*(6868), 137–140.
48. Fehr, E., & Gächter, S. (2002). Altruistic punishment in humans. *Nature, 415*(6868), 137–140.
49. Diener, E., Fraser, S. C., Beaman, A. L., & Kelem, R. T. (1976). Effects of deindividuation variables on stealing among Halloween trick-or-treaters. *Journal of Personality and Social Psychology, 33*(2), 178–183.
50. Festinger, L., Pepitone, A., & Newcomb T. (1952). Some consequences of deindividuation in a group. *Journal of Abnormal and Social Psychology, 47,* 382–389.
51. Zimbardo, P. G. (1970). The human choice: Individuation, reason, and order versus deindividuation, impulse, and chaos. In W. J. Arnold & D. Levine (Eds.), *Nebraska Symposium on Motivation, 1969*(237–307). Lincoln: University of Nebraska Press.
52. Postmes, T., & Spears, R. (1998). Deindividuation and antinormative behavior: A meta-analysis. *Psychological Bulletin, 123,* 238–259.
53. Davies, J. B., Sandström, S., Shorrocks, A., & Wolff, E. N. (2008). The World Distribution of Household Wealth. UNU-WIDER. Retrieved from http://www.wider.unu.edu/publications/working-papers/discussion-papers/2008/en_GB/dp2008-03/
54. Hardin, G. (1968). The tragedy of the commons. *Science, 162,* 1243–1248.
55. For example, Brechner, K. C. (1977). An experimental analysis of social traps. *Journal of Experimental Social Psychology, 13,* 552–564.
56. Paulus, P. B., Dzindolet, M. T., Poletes, G., & Camacho, L. M. (1993). Perception of performance

Endnotes | EN-41

56. in group brainstorming: The illusion of group productivity. *Personality and Social Psychology Bulletin, 19*, 78–89.
57. Stroebe, W., Diehl, M., & Abakoumkin, G. (1992). The illusion of group effectivity. *Personality and Social Psychology Bulletin, 18*, 643–650.
58. Mullen, B., Johnson, C., & Salas, E. (1991). Productivity loss in brainstorming groups: A meta-analysis. *Basic and Applied Social Psychology, 12*, 3–23.
59. Mackay, C. (1932). *Extraordinary popular delusions and the madness of crowds*. New York: Farrar, Straus and Cudahy. (Original work published 1841).
60. Le Bon, G. (1908). *The crowd: A study of the popular mind*. London: T Fisher Unwin.
61. Surowiecki, J. (2004). *The wisdom of crowds: Why the many are smarter than the few and how collective wisdom shapes business, economics, societies, and nations*. New York: Doubleday.
62. Surowiecki, J. (2004). *The wisdom of crowds: Why the many are smarter than the few and how collective wisdom shapes business, economics, societies, and nations*. New York: Doubleday.
63. Surowiecki, J. (2004). *The wisdom of crowds: Why the many are smarter than the few and how collective wisdom shapes business, economics, societies, and nations*. New York: Doubleday. (Quotation on p. 11).
64. Davis-Stober, C.P., Budescu, D.V., Dana, J., & Broomell, S.B. (2014). When is a crowd wise? *Decision, 1*, 79–101.
65. Lorenz, J., Rauhut, H., Schweitzer, F., & Helbing, D. (2011). How social influence can undermine the wisdom of crowd effect. *PNAS (Proceedings of the National Academy of Sciences), 108*, 9020–9025.
66. Allen, N. J., & Hecht, T. D. (2004). The "romance of teams": Toward an understanding of its psychological underpinnings and implications. *Journal of Occupational and Organizational Psychology, 77*, 439–461.
67. Wegner, D. M. (1986). Transactive memory: A contemporary analysis of the group mind. In B. Mullen & G. R. Goethals (Eds.), *Theories of group behavior* (pp. 185–208). New York: Springer-Verlag.
68. Wegner, D. M., Giuliano, T., & Hertel, P. (1985). Cognitive interdependence in close relationships. In W. Ickes (Ed.), *Compatible and incompatible relationships* (pp. 253–276). New York: Springer-Verlag.
69. Hollingshead, A. B., & Brandon, D. P. (2003). Potential benefits of communication in transactive memory systems. *Human Communication Research, 29*, 607–615.
70. Hollingshead, A. B. (1998). Retrieval processes in transactive memory systems. *Journal of Personality and Social Psychology, 74*, 659–671.
71. Liang, D. W., Moreland, R. L., & Argote, L. (1995). Group versus individual training and group performance: The mediating role of transactive memory. *Personality and Social Psychology Bulletin, 21*, 384–393.
72. Moreland, R. L., Argote, L., & Krishnan, R. (1998). Training people to work in groups. In R. Tindale, L. Heath, J. Edwards, E. Posavac, F. Bryant, Y. Suarez-Balcazar, et al. (Eds.), *Theory and research on small groups* (pp. 37–60). New York: Plenum Press.
73. Janis, I. (1982). *Groupthink* (2nd ed.). Boston: Houghton Mifflin.
74. Janis, I. (1982). *Groupthink* (2nd ed.). Boston: Houghton Mifflin.
75. Stasser, G., & Titus, W. (1985). Pooling of unshared information in group decision making: Biased information sampling during discussion. *Journal of Personality and Social Psychology, 48*, 1467–1478.
76. Stasser, G., & Titus, W. (1987). Effects of information load and percentage of shared information on the dissemination of unshared information during group discussion. *Journal of Personality and Social Psychology, 53*, 81–93.
77. Stoner, J. A. F. (1961). *A comparison of individual and group decisions involving risk*. Unpublished master's thesis, Massachusetts Institute of Technology.
78. Wallach, M. A., Kogan, N., & Bem, D. J. (1962). Group influence on individual risk-taking. *Journal of Abnormal and Social Psychology, 65*, 75–86.
79. Moscovici, S., & Zavalloni, M. (1969). The group as a polarizer of attitudes. *Journal of Personality and Social Psychology, 12*, 125–135.
80. Joyce, W. F., Nohria, N., & Roberson, B. (2003). *What really works: The 4+2 formula for sustained business success*. New York: HarperBusiness.
81. Barrick, M. R., Day, D. V., Lord, R. G., & Alexander, R. A. (1991). Assessing the utility of executive leadership. *Leadership Quarterly, 2*, 9–22.
82. Collins, J. (2001). *Good to great*. New York: HarperCollins.
83. Collins, J. (2001). *Good to great*. New York: HarperCollins.
84. Hogan, R., & Kaiser, R. B. (2005). What we know about leadership. *Review of General Psychology, 9*(2), 169–180.
85. Kouzes, J. M., & Posner, B. Z. (2002). *The leadership challenge* (3rd ed.). San Francisco: Jossey-Bass.
86. Lord, R. G., Foti, R. J., & DeVader, C. L. (1984). A test of leadership categorization theory: Internal structure, information processing, and leadership perceptions. *Organizational Behavior and Human Performance, 34*, 343–378.
87. Schaumberg, R.L., & Flynn, F.J. (2012). Uneasy lies the head that wears the crown: The link between guilt proneness and leadership. *Journal of Personality and Social Psychology, 103*, 327–342.
88. Yukl, G. (2006). *Leadership in organizations*. Upper Saddle River, NJ: Prentice-Hall.
89. Brunell, A. B., Gentry, W. A., Campbell, W. K., Hoffman, B. J., Kuhnert, K. W., & DeMarree, K. G. (2008). Leadership emergence: The case of the narcissistic leader. *Personality and Social Psychology Bulletin, 34*, 1663–1676.
90. Ames, D. R., & Flynn, F. J. (2007). What breaks a leader: The curvilinear relation between assertiveness and leadership. *Journal of Personality and Social Psychology, 92*, 307–324.
91. Hogan, R., & Kaiser, R. B. (2005). What we know about leadership. *Review of General Psychology, 9*(2), 169–180.
92. DeVries, D., & Kaiser, R. B. (2003, November). Going sour in the suite. Paper presented at the Maximizing Executive Effectiveness workshop, Miami, FL.
93. Leslie, J. B., & Van Velsor, E. (1996). *A look at derailment today*. Greensboro, NC: Centre for Creative Leadership.
94. Mayer, J. D. (1993). The emotional madness of the dangerous leader. *Journal of Psychohistory, 20*, 331–348.
95. Mayer, J. D. (1993). The emotional madness of the dangerous leader. *Journal of Psychohistory, 20*, 331–348. (Quotation on p. 337).
96. Mayer, J. D. (1993). The emotional madness of the dangerous leader. *Journal of Psychohistory, 20*, 331–348.
97. Morgenthau, H. (1962). Love and power. *Commentary, 33*, 247–251.
98. Kipnis, D. (1972). Does power corrupt? *Journal of Personality and Social Psychology, 24*, 33–41.
99. Kipnis, D. (1976). *The powerholders*. Chicago: University of Chicago Press.
100. Kipnis, D. (1972). Does power corrupt? *Journal of Personality and Social Psychology, 24*, 33–41.
101. Park, S. H., Westphal, J. D., & Stern, I. (2011). Set up for a fall: The insidious effects of flattery and opinion conformity toward corporate leaders. *Administrative Science Quarterly, 56*, 2257–2302.
102. Abrams, D., de Moura, G., & Travaglino, G. (2013) A double standard when group members behave badly: Transgression credit to ingroup leaders. *Journal of Personality and Social Psychology, 105*, 799–815.
103. Lindskold, S., & Aronoff, J. R. (1980). Conciliatory strategies and relative power. *Journal of Experimental Social Psychology, 16*, 187–198.
104. Blader, S. L., & Chen, Y. (2012). Differentiating the effects of status and power: A justice perspective. *Journal of Personality and Social Psychology, 102*, 994–1014.
105. Keltner, D., Gruenfeld, D. H., & Anderson, C. (2003). Power, approach, and inhibition. *Psychological Review, 110*, 265–284.
106. Watson, D., & Clark, L. A. (1997). Extraversion and its positive emotional core. In R. Hogan, J. Johnson, & S. Briggs (Eds.), *Handbook of personality psychology* (pp. 767–793). New York: Academic Press.
107. Whitson, J. A., Liljenquist, K. A., Galinsky, A. D., Magee, J. C., Gruenfeld, D. H., & Cadena, B. (2013). The blind leading: Power reduces awareness of constraints. *Journal of Experimental Social Psychology, 49*, 579–582.
108. Guinote, A. (2008). Power and affordances: When the situation has more power over powerful than powerless individuals. *Journal of Personality and Social Psychology, 95*, 237–252.
109. Galinsky, A. D., Magee, J. C., Gruenfeld, D. H., Whitson, J. A., & Liljenquist, K. A. (2008). Power reduces the press of the situation: Implications for creativity, conformity, and dissonance. *Journal of Personality and Social Psychology, 95*, 1450–1466.
110. Keltner, D., Gruenfeld, D. H., & Anderson, C. (2003). Power, approach, and inhibition. *Psychological Review, 110*, 265–284.
111. Lerner, J. S., & Tetlock, P. E. (1999). Accounting for the effects of accountability. *Psychological Bulletin, 125*, 255–275.
112. Tetlock, P. E. (1992). The impact of accountability on judgment and choice: Toward a social contingency model. In M. P. Zanna (Ed.), *Advances in experimental social psychology* (Vol. 25, pp. 331–376). San Diego: Academic Press.
113. Bargh, J. A., Raymond, P., Pryor, J. B., & Strack, F. (1995). The attractiveness of the underling: An automatic power-sex association and its consequences for sexual harassment. *Journal of Personality and Social Psychology, 68*, 768–781.
114. Galinsky, A. D., Gruenfeld, D. H., & Magee, J. C. (2003). From power to action. *Journal of Personality and Social Psychology, 85*, 453–466.
115. Galinsky, A. D., Gruenfeld, D. H., & Magee, J. C. (2003). From power to action. *Journal of Personality and Social Psychology, 85*, 453–466.
116. Lee-Chai, A. Y., Chen, S., & Chartrand, T. L. (2001). From Moses to Marcos: Individual differences in the use and abuse of power. In A. Y. Lee-Chai & J. A. Bargh (Eds.), *The use and abuse of power: Multiple perspectives on the causes of corruption* (pp. 57–74). New York: Psychology Press.
117. Maner, J. K., & Mead, N. L. (2010). The essential tension between leadership and power: When leaders sacrifice group goals for the sake of self-interest. *Journal of Personality and Social Psychology, 99*, 482–497.
118. Mead, N. L., & Maner, J. K. (2012) On keeping your enemies close: Powerful leaders seek proximity to ingroup power threats. *Journal of Personality and Social Psychology, 102*, 576–591.
119. Erber, R., & Fiske, S. T. (1984). Outcome dependency and attention to inconsistent information. *Journal of Personality and Social Psychology, 47*, 709–726.
120. Lindskold, S., & Aronoff, J. R. (1980). Conciliatory strategies and relative power. *Journal of Experimental Social Psychology, 16*, 187–198.
121. Copeland, J. T. (1994). Prophecies of power: Motivational implications of social power for behavioral confirmation. *Journal of Personality and Social Psychology, 67*, 264–277.
122. Chen, E. S., & Tyler, T. R. (2001). Cloaking power: Legitimizing myths and the psychology of the advantaged. In A. Y. Lee-Chai & J. Bargh (Eds.), *The use and abuse of power: Multiple perspectives on the causes of corruption* (pp. 241–261). Philadelphia: Psychology Press.
123. Stillman, T. F., Baumeister, R. F., & DeWall, C. N. (2007). What's so funny about not having money? The effects of power on laughter. *Personality and Social Psychology Bulletin, 33*, 1547–1558.

124. Fraley, B., & Aron, A. (2004). The effect of a shared humorous experience on closeness in initial encounters. *Personal Relationships, 11,* 61–78.

125. Sprecher, S., & Regan, P. (2002). Liking some things (in some people) more than others: Partner preferences in romantic relationships and friendships. *Journal of Social and Personal Relationships, 19,* 463–481.

126. Zajonc, R. B., Heingartner, A., & Herman, E. M. (1969). Social enhancement and impairment of performance in the cockroach. *Journal of Personality and Social Psychology, 13*(2), 83–92. doi:10.1037/h0028063

MODULE A
Applying Social Psychology to Consumer Behavior

1. Frith, K. T., & Mueller, B. (2003). *Advertising and society: Global issues.* New York: Peter Lang.

2. Burgess, J. (2008) "All your chocolate rain are belong to us?" Viral video, YouTube and the dynamics of participatory culture. In UNSPECIFIED (Ed.), *Video vortex reader: Responses to YouTube.* Institute of Network Cultures, Amsterdam, pp. 101–109. Retrieved from http://eprints.qut.edu.au/18431/1/18431.pdf

3. Elliott, S. (2012). M&M's to Unveil New Speaking Role at Super Bowl. *New York Times.* Retrieved from http://www.nytimes.com/2012/01/17/business/media/mms-to-unveil-a-new-speaking-role-at-super-bowl.html?_r51

4. Roberts, J. (2012, February 28). *How to begin analyzing social media.* Retrieved August 20, 2012, from http://www.collectiveintellect.com/blog/brand-tracker-super-bowl-2012.

5. Bishop, S. (2008, January 23). Don't bother with the "green" consumer. *Harvard Business Report.* Retrieved from http://www.hbrgreen.org/2008/01/dont_bother_with_the_green_con.html

6. Bruner, J. A., & Mason, J. L. (1968). The influence of driving time upon shopping center preference. *Journal of Marketing, 32*(2), 57–61.

7. Rhee, H., & Bell, D. R. (2002). The inter-store mobility of supermarket shoppers. *Journal of Retailing, 78,* 225–237.

8. Store of the month. (1976, October). *Progressive Grocer,* 104.

9. Babin, B. J., & Babin, L. (2001). Seeking something different? A model of schema typicality, consumer affect, purchase intentions and perceived shopping value. *Journal of Business Research, 54,* 89–96.

10. Milliman, R. E. (1982). Using background music to affect the behavior of supermarket shoppers. *Journal of Marketing, 46,* 86–91.

11. Areni, C. S., & Kim, D. (1993). The influence of background music on shopping behavior: Classical versus Top-Forty. In L. McAlister & M. L. Rothschild (Eds.), *Advances in consumer research* (pp. 336–340). Provo, UT: Association for Consumer Research.

12. Donovan, R., & Rossiter, J. (1982). Store atmosphere: An environmental psychology approach. *Journal of Retailing, 58,* 34–57.

13. Spangenberg, E. R., Crowley, A. E., & Henderson, P. W. (1996). Improving the store environment: Do olfactory cues affect evaluations and behaviors? *Journal of Marketing, 60,* 67–80.

14. Mitchell, D. J., Kahn, B. E., & Knasko, S. C. (1995). There's something in the air: Effects of congruent or incongruent ambient odor on consumer decision making. *Journal of Consumer Research, 22,* 229–238.

15. Steinmetz, K. (2012). Follow your nose: Food company launches 'smell-vertising' for potato ads. *Time NewsFeed.* Retrieved from http://newsfeed.time.com/2012/02/10/follow-your-nose-food-company-launches-smell-vertising-for-potato-ads/

16. Schifferstein, H. N. J., & Michaut, A. M. K. (2002). Effects of appropriate and inappropriate odors on product evaluation. *Perceptual and Motor Skills, 95,* 1199–1214.

17. Morrin, M., & Ratnewshwar, S. (2003). Does it make sense to use scents to enhance brand memory? *Journal of Marketing Research, 40,* 10–25.

18. Sommer, R. (1969). *Personal space: The behavioral basis of design.* Englewood Cliffs, NJ: Prentice-Hall.

19. Koernig, S. K. (2003). E-scapes: The electronic physical environment and service tangibility. *Psychology and Marketing, 20,* 151–167.

20. Koernig, S. K. (2003). E-scapes: The electronic physical environment and service tangibility. *Psychology and Marketing, 20,* 151–167.

21. Yorkston, E., & Menon, G. (2004). A sound idea: Phonetic effects of brand names on consumer judgments. *Journal of Consumer Research, 31,* 43–51.

22. Chang, Y., Chen, R. C., Wahlqvist, M. L., & Lee, M. (2011). Frequent shopping by men and women increases survival in the older Taiwanese population. *Journal of Epidemial Community Health.* Retrieved from http://jech.bmj.com/content/early/2011/03/17/jech.2010.126698.abstract

23. New image. Retrieved from http://logos.wikia.com/wiki/Pepsi

24. Rosenthal, E. (2008, February 2). Motivated by a tax, Irish spurn plastic bags. *New York Times.* Retrieved from http://www.nytimes.com/2008/02/02/world/europe/02bags.html?_r51&pagewanted51

25. See http://www.campaignforrecycling.org/our_issues/plastic/plastic_bags/current_laws for a complete listing.

26. Sallie Mae. (2009). *How undergraduate students use credit cards: Sallie Mae's National Study of Usage Rates and Trends 2009.* Retrieved August 20, 2012, from http://static.mgnetwork.com/rtd/pdfs/20090830_iris.pdf

27. Jacobe, D. (2008, June 11). Nearly one-third of credit-card owners hold high balances. Retrieved from http://www.gallup.com/poll/107833/nearly-onethird-americans-hold-high-credit-balances.aspx

28. Prelec, D., & Simester, D. (2001). Always leave home without it. *Marketing Letters, 12,* 5–12.

29. Boddington, L., & Kemp, S. (1999). Student debt, attitudes towards debt, impulsive buying, and financial management. *New Zealand Journal of Psychology, 28,* 89–93.

30. Politano, J., & Lester, D. (1997). Self-destructiveness and credit card debt. *Psychological Reports, 81,* 634.

31. Lea, S. E. G., & Webley, P. (2006). Money as tool, money as drug: The biological psychology of a strong incentive. *Behavioral and Brain Sciences, 29,* 161–209.

32. Soman, D., & Cheema, A. (2002). The effect of credit on spending decisions: The role of the credit limit and credibility. *Marketing Science, 21,* 32–53.

33. Feinberg, R. (1986). Credit cards as spending facilitating stimuli: A conditioning interpretation. *Journal of Consumer Research, 3,* 348–356.

34. Beggan, J. K. (1992). On the social nature of nonsocial perception: The mere ownership effect. *Journal of Personality and Social Psychology, 62,* 229–237.

35. Iyengar, S. S., & Lepper, M. R. (2000). When choice is demotivating: Can one desire too much of a good thing? *Journal of Personality and Social Psychology, 79,* 995–1006.

36. Lee, B. K., & Lee, W. N. (2004). The effect of information overload on consumer choice quality in an on-line environment. *Psychology and Marketing, 21,* 159–183.

37. Macias, W. (2003). A beginning look at the effects of interactivity, product involvement, and web experience on comprehension: Brand web sites as interactive advertising. *Journal of Current Issues and Research in Advertising, 25,* 31–44.

38. Bagozzi, R. P., Wong, N., Abe, S., & Bergami, M. (2000). Cultural and situational contingencies and the theory of reasoned action: Application to fast food restaurant consumption. *Journal of Consumer Psychology, 9,* 97–106.

39. Cell phone or pheromone? New props for mating game. (2000, November 7). *New York Times.*

40. Right hand diamonds marketed to women as power sign. (2003, December 2). *Sacramento Bee.* Retrieved from http://www.sacbee.com/content/business/story/7887166p-8825882c.html

41. Newman, A. (May 26, 2010). With this ring, I thee what? *New York Times.* Retrieved February 18, 2012, from http://www.nytimes.com/2010/05/27/fashion/27rings.html?adxnnl51&adxnnlx51329596054-/Hwober8MpThtkMeSSX7pA

42. Solomon, S., Greenberg, J., & Pyszczynski, T. A. (2004). Lethal consumption: Death-denying materialism. In T. Kasser & A. D. Kanner (Eds.), *Psychology and consumer culture: The struggle for a good life in a materialistic world* (pp. 127–146). Washington, DC: American Psychological Association.

43. Kasser, T., & Sheldon, K. M. (2000). Of wealth and death: Materialism, mortality salience, and consumption behavior. *Psychological Science, 11,* 348–351.

44. Myers, D. G. (1993, July/August). Pursuing happiness. *Psychology Today,* pp. 32–35, 66–67.

45. Gould, S. J., & Weil, C. E. (1991). Gift-giving and gender self-concepts. *Gender Role, 24,* 617–637.

46. Wooten, D. B. (2000). Qualitative steps toward an expanded model of anxiety in gift-giving. *Journal of Consumer Research, 27,* 84–95.

47. Tse, A. C. B., & Yim, F. (2001). Factors affecting the choice of channels: Online vs. conventional. *Journal of International Consumer Marketing, 14,* 137–152.

48. McKinney, L. N. (2004). Internet shopping orientation segments: An exploration of differences in consumer behavior. *Family and Consumer Sciences Research Journal, 32,* 408–433.

49. Frith, K. T., & Mueller, B. (2003). *Advertising and society: Global issues.* New York: Peter Lang.

50. Some kids won't eat the middle of an Oreo. (1991, November 20). *Wall Street Journal,* p. B1.

51. Kwan, M. (2010). How many cell phones are in the US? Retrieved from http://cellphones.lovetoknow.com/how-many-cell-phones-are-us

52. CTIA.org. (2012). Background on CTIA's semiannual wireless industry survey. Retrieved from http://www.ctia.org/media/industry_info/index.cfm/AID/10323

53. Orville Redenbacher Company Website. Retrieved August 20, 2012, from http://www.orville.com/homemade-popcorn

54. DeAngelis, T. (2000). Is Internet addiction real? *Monitor on Psychology, 31.* Retrieved from http://www.apa.org/monitor/apr00/addiction.html

55. Lakin, A. (2009). Recyclable cars. *DriverSide.com.* Retrieved from http://www.driverside.com/auto-library/recyclable_cars-257

56. U.S. Census Bureau. (2009). New motor vehicle sales and car production. *The 2009 statistical abstract: National data book.* Retrieved from http://www.census.gov/compendia/statab/tables/09s1021.pdf

57. Consumer Electronics Association. (2008, April). *Market research report: Trends in CE reuse, recycle and removal.*

58. China's hi-tech toxics. (2002). *BBC News.* Retrieved from http://news.bbc.co.uk/hi/english/static/in_depth/world/2002/disposable_planet/waste/chinese_workshop

59. Sarrel, M. D. (2006, November 29). Recycling e-waste. *PCMag.com.* Retrieved from http://www.pcmag.com/article2/0,2817,2064151,00.asp

60. Roach, M. (2004). *Stiff: The curious lives of human cadavers.* New York: W. W. Norton.

61. Fetterman, M., & Hausen, B. (2006, November 19). Young people struggle to deal with kiss of debt. *USA Today.* Retrieved from http://www.usatoday.com/money/perfi/credit/2006-11-19-young-and-in-debt-cover_x.htm

MODULE B
Applying Social Psychology to Health

1. Gurung, R. A. R. (2019). *Health psychology: Well-being in a diverse world* (4th ed.). Thousand Oaks, CA: SAGE.
2. Centers for Disease Control. (2018). Alcohol and public health. Retrieved from https://www.cdc.gov/alcohol/onlinetools.htm
3. World Health Organization (2003). WHO definition of health. Preamble to the Constitution of the World Health Organization as adopted by the International Health Conference, New York, 19–22 June, 1946; signed on 22 July 1946 by the representatives of 61 States (Official Records of the World Health Organization, no. 2, p. 100) and entered into force on 7 April 1948. Retrieved from http://www.who.int/about/definition/en/print.html
4. Friedman, H., & Silver, R. (Eds.). (2007). *Foundations of health psychology*. New York: Oxford University Press.
5. Matarazzo, J. D. (1982). "Behavioral health" challenge to academic, scientific and professional psychology. *American Psychologist, 37*(1), 1–14.
6. Revenson, T. A., & Gurung, R. A. R. (Eds.). (2019). *Handbook of health psychology*. New York: Routledge.
7. Gurung, R. A. R. (2012). Health psychology. In D. S. Dunn (Ed.), *Oxford Bibliographies in Psychology*. New York: Oxford University Press.
8. Contrada, R., & Baum, A. (Eds.). (2011). *The handbook of stress science: Biology, psychology, and health*. New York: Springer.
9. Cannon, W. B. (1929). *Bodily changes in pain, hunger, fear and rage*. Oxford: Appleton.
10. Seyle, H. (1956). *The stress of life*. New York: McGraw-Hill.
11. Gruenewald, T., & Wang, D. (2019). Stress and health. In T. A. Revenson & R. A. R. Gurung (Eds.), *Handbook of health psychology* (pp. 213–224). New York: Routledge.
12. Cannon, W. B. (1914). The interrelations of emotions as suggested by recent physiological researches. *American Journal of Physiology, 25,* 256–282.
13. Sapolsky, R. (2004). *Why zebras don't get ulcers: The acclaimed guide to stress, stress-related disease, and coping*. New York: Holt.
14. Eiland, L., & McEwen, B. S. (2012). Early life stress followed by subsequent adult chronic stress potentiates anxiety and blunts hippocampal structural remodeling. *Hippocampus, 22*(1), 82–91. doi: 10.1002/hipo.20862
15. Mocayar Marón, F. J., Ferder, L., Saraví, F. D., & Manucha, W. (2018). Hypertension linked to allostatic load: From psychosocial stress to inflammation and mitochondrial dysfunction. *Stress: The International Journal on the Biology of Stress,* doi:http://dx.doi.org/10.1080/10253890.2018.1542683
16. Lazarus, R. S. (1966). *Psychological stress and the coping process*. New York: McGraw-Hill.
17. Lazarus, R. S. (1991). Progress on a cognitive-motivational-relational theory of emotion. *American Psychologist, 46*(8), 819–834.
18. Langer, E. J., & Rodin, J. (1976). The effects of choice and enhanced personal responsibility for the aged: A field experiment in an institutional setting. *Journal of Personality and Social Psychology, 34*(2), 191–198.
19. Taylor, S. E., Klein, L. C., Lewis, B. P., Gruenewald, T. L., Gurung, R. A. R., & Updegraff, J. A. (2000). Biobehavioral responses to stress in females: Tend-and-befriend, not fight-or-flight. *Psychological Review, 107*(3), 411–429.
20. Taylor, S. E., & Master, S. L. (2011). Social responses to stress: The tend-and-befriend model. In R. J. Contrada, A. Baum, R. J. Contrada, A. Baum (Eds.), *The handbook of stress science: Biology, psychology, and health* (pp. 101–109). New York: Springer.
21. Repetti, R. L., & Saxbe, D. E. (2019). The influence of chronic family stressors on adult health. In B. H. Fiese, M. Celano, K. Deater-Deckard, E. N. Jouriles & M. A. Whisman (Eds.), *APA handbook of contemporary family psychology: Applications and broad impact of family psychology (vol. 2); APA handbook of contemporary family psychology: Applications and broad impact of family psychology (vol. 2)* (pp. 121–136). Washington, DC.: American Psychological Association, doi:http://dx.doi.org/10.1037/0000100-008
22. Aldwin, C. M., Lee, H., Choun, S, & Kang, S. (2019). Coping. In T. A. Revenson & R. A. R. Gurung (Eds.), *Handbook of health psychology* (pp. 225–238). New York: Routledge.
23. Carver, C. S., & Scheier, M. F. (1994). Situational coping and coping dispositions in a stressful transaction. *Journal of Social and Personality Psychology, 56,* 267–283.
24. Moos, R. H., & Schaefer, J. A. (1993). Coping resources and processes: Current concepts and measures. In L. Goldberger & S. Breznitz (Eds.), *Handbook of stress: Theoretical and clinical aspects* (2nd ed., pp. 234–257). New York: Free Press.
25. Lazarus, R. S., & Launier, R. (1978). Stress-related transactions between person and environment. In L. A. Pervin & M. Lewis (Eds.), *Perspectives in interactional psychology* (pp. 287–322). New York: Plenum.
26. Tennen, H., Affleck, G., Armeli, S., & Carney, M. A. (2000). A daily process approach to coping: Linking theory, research, and practice. *American Psychologist, 55*(6), 626–636.
27. Knoll, N., Scholz, & Ditzen, B. (2019). Social support, family processes, and health. In T. A. Revenson & R. A. R. Gurung (Eds.), *Handbook of health psychology* (pp. 279–289). New York: Routledge.
28. House, J. S., Umberson, D., & Landis, K. R. (1988). Structures and processes of social support. *Annual Review of Sociology, 14,* 293–318.
29. Lett, H. S., Blumenthal, J. A., Babyak, M. A., Catellier, D. J., Carney, R. M., Berkman, L. F., & ... Schneiderman, N. (2008). Perceived social support predicts outcomes following myocardial infarction: A call for screening?: Response. *Health Psychology, 27*(1), 1–3. doi: 10.1037/0278-6133.27.1.1b
30. Sarason, B. R., Sarason, I. G., & Gurung, R. A. R. (2001). Close personal relationships and health outcomes: A key to the role of social support. In B. R. Sarason & S. Duck (Eds.), *Personal relationships. Implications for clinical and community psychology* (pp. 15–41). Chichester: Wiley.
31. Uchino, B. N., Cacioppo, J. T., & Kiecolt-Glaser, J. K. (1996). The relationship between social support and physiological processes: A review with emphasis on underlying mechanisms and implications for health. *Psychological Bulletin, 119*(3), 488–531.
32. Rosenthal, L., & Gronich, B. (2019). Gender and health. In T. A. Revenson & R. A. R. Gurung (Eds.), *Handbook of health psychology* (pp. 303–314). New York: Routledge.
33. Schachter, S. (1959). *The psychology of affiliation: Experimental studies of the sources of gregariousness*. Oxford: Stanford University Press.
34. Pouwelse, M., Bolman, C., Lodewijkx, H., & Spaa, M. (2011). Gender differences and social support: Mediators or moderators between peer victimization and depressive feelings. *Psychology in the Schools, 48*(8), 800–814. doi: 10.1002/pits.20589
35. Michie, S., Marques, M. M., Norris, E., & Johnson, M. (2019). Theories and interventions in health behavior change. In T. A. Revenson & R. A. R. Gurung (Eds.), *Handbook of health psychology* (pp. 69–88). New York, NY: Routledge.
36. Halliday, D. M., Epperson, A. E., & Song, A. V. (2019). Weight loss, obesity, and health. In T. A. Revenson & R. A. R. Gurung (Eds.), *Handbook of health psychology* (pp. 91–104). New York: Routledge.
37. Murphy, S. L., Xu, J. Q., Kochanek, K. D., Arias, E. (2018). *Mortality in the United States, 2017*. NCHS Data Brief, no 328. Hyattsville, MD: National Center for Health Statistics.
38. Wills, T., Sargent, J., Stoolmiller, M., Gibbons, F., & Gerrard, M. (2008). Movie smoking exposure and smoking onset: A longitudinal study of mediation processes in a representative sample of U.S. adolescents. *Psychology of Addictive Behaviors, 22*(2), 269–277.
39. Sargent, J. D., Dalton, M. A., Heatherton, T. & Beach, M. (2003). Modifying exposure to smoking depicted in movies: A novel approach to preventing adolescent smoking. *Archives of Pediatrics and Adolescent Medicine, 157*(7), 643–648.
40. Mejia, R., Pérez, A., Peña, L., Kollath-Cattano, C., Morello, P., Braun, S., et al. (2017). Smoking in movies and adolescent smoking initiation: A longitudinal study among argentinean adolescents. The Journal of Pediatrics, 180, 222–228. doi:http://dx.doi.org/10.1016/j.jpeds.2016.10.001
41. Dal Cin, S., Gibson, B., Zanna, M., Shumate, R., & Fong, G. (2007). Smoking in movies, implicit associations of smoking with the self, and intentions to smoke. *Psychological Science, 18*(7), 559–563.
42. Dal Cin, S., Worth, K., Dalton, M., & Sargent, J. (2008). Youth exposure to alcohol use and brand appearances in popular contemporary movies. *Addiction, 103*(12), 1925–1932.
43. Jackson, K. M., Janssen, T., Barnett, N. P., Rogers, M. L., Hayes, K. L., & Sargent, J. (2018). Exposure to alcohol content in movies and initiation of early drinking milestones. *Alcoholism: Clinical and Experimental Research, 42*(1), 184–194. doi: http://dx.doi.org/10.1111/acer.13536
44. Hochbaum, G. M. (1958). *Public participation in medical screening programs: A sociopsychological study*. PHS publication no. 572. Washington, DC: Government Printing Office. Holder-Perkins & Wise.
45. Rosenstock, I. M. (1960). What research in motivation suggests for public health. *American Journal of Public Health, 50,* 295–301.
46. Kirscht, J. P. (1971). Social and psychological problems of surveys on health and illness. *Social Science and Medicine, 5*(6), 519–526.
47. Becker, M. H. (Ed.). (1974). The health belief model and personal health behavior. *Health Education Monographs, 2,* entire issue.
48. Skinner, B. F. (1938). *The behavior of organisms*. Englewood Cliffs, NJ: Appleton-Century-Crofts.
49. Kirscht, J. P., Haefner, D. P., & Kegeles, S. S. (1966). A national study of health beliefs. *Journal of Health & Human Behavior, 7*(4), 248–254. doi:http://dx.doi.org/10.2307/2948771
50. Rosenstock, I. M., Strecher, & Becker, M. H. (1988). The health belief model and HIV risk behavior change. In J. Peterson & R. DiClemente (Eds.), *Preventing AIDS: Theory and practice of behavior interventions* (pp. 5–24). New York: Plenum Press.
51. Fishbein, M., & Ajzen, I. (1975). *Belief, attitude, intention and behavior: An introduction to theory and research*. Boston: Addison-Wesley.
52. Ajzen, I. (1988). *Attitudes, personality, and behavior*. Homewood, IL: Dorsey Press.
53. Rogers, E. M. (1983). *Diffusion of innovations*. New York: Free Press.
54. Bandura, A. (1977). *Social learning theory*. Englewood Cliffs, NJ: Prentice Hall.
55. Prochaska, J. O., Wright, J. A., & Velicer, W. F. (2008). Evaluating theories of health behavior change: A hierarchy of criteria applied to the transtheoretical model. *Applied Psychology: An International Review, 57*(4), 561–588. doi: 10.1111/j.1464-0597.2008.00345.x
56. Prochaska, J. O., & Prochaska, J. M. (2010). Self-directed change: A transtheoretical model. In *Social psychological foundations of clinical psychology* (pp. 431–440). New York: Guilford Press.
57. Langer, G., Arndet, C., & Sussman, D. (2004). A peek beneath the sheets. Retrieved from http://www.abcnews.go.com/Primetime/News
58. Gurung, R. A. R., Dunkel-Schetter, C., Collins, N., Rini, C., & Hobel. (2005). Psychosocial predictors of perceived prenatal stress. *Journal of Social and Clinical Psychology, 24,* 497–519.
59. Li, X., Lei, Y., Wang, H., He, G., & Williams, A. B. (2016). The health belief model: A qualitative

study to understand high-risk sexual behavior in chinese men who have sex with men. *JANAC: Journal of the Association of Nurses in AIDS Care, 27*(1), 66-76. doi:http://dx.doi.org/10.1016/j.jana.2015.10.005

60. Fauk, N. K., Kustanti, C. Y., Liana, D. S., Indriyawati, N., Crutzen, R., & Mwanri, L. (2018). Perceptions of determinants of condom use behaviors among male clients of female sex workers in indonesia: A qualitative inquiry. *American Journal of Men's Health, 12*(4), 666-675. doi:http://dx.doi.org/10.1177/1557988318756132

61. Stone, J., Aronson, E., Crain, A. L., Winslow, M. P., & Fried, C. B. (1994). Inducing hypocrisy as a means of encouraging young adults to use condoms. *Personality and Social Psychology Bulletin, 20*, 116–128.

62. Prochaska, J. O., Redding, C. A., & Evers, K. E. (2002). The transtheoretical model and stages of change. In K. Glanz, B. K. Rimer, & F. M. Lewis (Eds.), *Health behavior and health education: Theory, research, and practice* (pp. 99–120). San Francisco: Jossey-Bass.

63. Centers for Disease Control and Prevention. (2014). Best practices for comprehensive tobacco control programs-2014. Retrieved from https://www.cdc.gov/tobacco/stateandcommunity/best_practices/pdfs/2014/comprehensive.pdf

64. Snow, M. G., Prochaska, J. O., & Rossi, J. S. (1992). Stages of change for smoking cessation among former problem drinkers: A cross-sectional analysis. *Journal of Substance Abuse, 4*(2), 107–116.

65. Gibbons, F. X., & Gerrard, M. (1997). Health images and their effects on health behavior. In B. P. Buunk & F. X. Gibbons (Eds.), *Health, coping, and well-being: Perspectives from social comparison theory* (pp. 63–94). Mahwah, NJ: Erlbaum.

66. Dohnke, B., Steinhilber, A., & Fuchs, T. (2015). Adolescents' eating behaviour in general and in the peer context: Testing the prototype-willingness model. *Psychology & Health, 30*(4), 381–399. doi: 10.1080/08870446.2014.974604

67. Litt, D. M., & Lewis, M. A. (2013). The prototype willingness model: A review. In J. Assailly (Ed.), *Psychology of risk-taking; psychology of risk-taking* (pp. 83–98). Hauppauge, NY: Nova Science Publishers.

68. Gerrard, M., Gibbons, F., Houlihan, A., Stock, M., & Pomery, E. (2008). A dual-process approach to health risk decision making: The prototype willingness model. *Developmental Review, 28*(1), 29–61.

69. Peterson, L. M., Campbell, M. A. T., & Laky, Z. E. (2019). The next frontier for men's contraceptive choice: College men's willingness to pursue male hormonal contraception. *Psychology of Men & Masculinities, 20*(2), 226–237. doi:http://dx.doi.org/10.1037/men0000174

70. Lewis, M. A., Litt, D. M., King, K. M., Garcia, T. A., Waldron, K. A., & Lee, C. M. (2018). Consideration of future consequences as a moderator of the willingness-behavior relationship for young adult marijuana use and consequences. *Addictive Behaviors, 87*, 8–16. doi:http://dx.doi.org/10.1016/j.addbeh.2018.06.010

71. Wagner, H. S., Ahlstrom, B., Redden, J. P., Vickers, Z., & Mann, T. (2014). The myth of comfort food. *Health Psychology, 33*(12), 1552–1557. doi: 10.1037/hea0000068

72. Olson, J. M., Roese, N. J., & Zanna, M. P. (1996). Expectancies. In E. T. Higgins, & A. W. Kruglanski (Eds.), *Social psychology: Handbook of basic principles* (pp. 211–239). New York: Guilford Press.

73. Shavitt, S., Sanbonmatsu, D. M., Smittipatana, S., & Posavac, S. S. (1999). Broadening the conditions for illusory correlation formation: Implications for judging minority groups. *Basic and Applied Social Psychology, 21*(4), 263–279.

74. Fiske, S. T. (2004). *Social beings: A core motives approach to social psychology*. New York: Wiley.

75. Jones, E. E., Kannouse, D. E., Kelley, H. H., Nisbett, R. E., Valins, S., & Weiner, B. (Eds.). (1972). *Attribution: Perceiving the causes of behavior*. Morristown, NJ: General Learning Press.

76. Miller, S. M., & Diefenbach, M. A. (1998). The Cognitive-Social Health Information-Processing (C-SHIP) model: A theoretical framework for research in behavioral oncology. In D. S. Krantz, & A. Baum (Eds.), *Technology and methods in behavioral medicine* (pp. 219–244). Mahwah, NJ: Lawrence Erlbaum.

77. Gurung, R. A. R. (Ed.). (2014). *Multicultural approaches to health and wellness in America: Major issues and cultural groups*. Westport, CT: Praeger Publishers.

78. Abraido-Lanza, Mendoza, S., & Armbrister, A. N. (2019). *Latino health.* In T. A. Revenson, & R. A. R. Gurung (Eds.), *Handbook of health psychology* (pp. 342–354). New York: Routledge.

79. Fadiman, A. (1997). *The spirit catches you and you fall down: A Hmong child, her American doctors, and the collusion of two cultures*. New York: Farrar, Straus and Giroux.

80. Schachter, S., & Singer, J. E., (1962). Cognitive, social, and physiological determinants of emotional state. *Psychological Review, 69*, 379–399.

81. Smith, T. W., & Parkhurst, K. A. (2019). Personality and health. In T. A. Revenson & R. A. R. Gurung (Eds.), *Handbook of health psychology* (pp. 195–213). New York: Routledge.

82. Contrada, R. J., & Guyll, M. (2001). On who gets sick and why: The role of personality, stress, and disease. In A. Baum, T. A. Revenson, & J. E. Singer (Eds.), *Handbook of health psychology* (pp. 59–81). Hillsdale, NJ: Erlbaum.

83. Feldman, P. J., Cohen S., Gwaltney, J. M., Jr., Doyle, W. J., & Skoner, D. P. (1999). The impact of personality on the reporting of unfounded symptoms and illness. *Journal of Personality and Social Psychology, 77*, 370–378.

84. Broadbent, E. (2019). Illness cognitions and beliefs. In T. A. Revenson & R. A. R. Gurung (Eds.), *Handbook of health psychology* (pp. 252–262). New York: Routledge.

85. Brown, K. W., & Moskowitz, D. S. (1997). Does unhappiness make you sick? The role of affect and neuroticism in the experience of common physical symptoms. *Journal of Personality and Social Psychology, 72*(4), 907–917.

86. Friedman, H. S., & Booth-Kewley, S. (1987). The "disease-prone personality": A meta-analytic view of the construct. *American Psychologist, 42*, 539–555.

87. Barsky, A. J. (1988). *Worried sick: Our troubled quest for wellness.* New York: Little Brown and Co.

88. Holder-Perkins, V., & Wise, T. N. (2001). Somatization disorder. In K. A. Phillips (Eds.), *Somatoform and factitious disorders* (pp. 1–26). Washington, DC: American Psychiatric Association.

MODULE C

Industrial and Organizational Psychology: Applying Social Psychology to the Workplace

1. Koughan, M. (1975, February 23). Arthur Friedman's outrage: Employees decide their pay. *Washington Post.*

2. Koughan, M. (1975, February 23). Arthur Friedman's outrage: Employees decide their pay. *Washington Post.*

3. Koughan, M. (1975, February 23). Arthur Friedman's outrage: Employees decide their pay. *Washington Post.*

4. DollarTimes. (2019). Calculate the value of $100 in 1970. Retrieved from https://www.dollartimes.com/inflation/inflation.php?amount=100&year=1970.

5. Koughan, M. (1975, February 23). Arthur Friedman's outrage: Employees decide their pay. *Washington Post.*

6. Ross, J. A. (2006, November). The reliability, validity, and utility of self-assessment. *Practical assessment, Research & Evaluation, 11*(10). Retrieved from http://pareonline.net/pdf/v11n10.pdf

7. Great Place to Work. (2019). 100 best companies to work for. Retrieved from https://www.greatplacetowork.com/certified-company/1000367.

8. Fortune 100 Best. (2019). Identifying best places to work: US and globally. *Fortune.* Retrieved from http://fortune.com/best-companies/.

9. Great Place to Work. (2019). 100 best companies to work for. Retrieved from https://www.greatplacetowork.com/certified-company/1000367.

10. Fortune 100 Best. (2019). Hilton. *Fortune.* Retrieved from http://fortune.com/best-companies/hilton-worldwide-holdings/

11. Glassdoor. (2019). Hilton. Retrieved from https://www.glassdoor.com/Benefits/Hilton-US-Benefits-EI_IE330.0,6_IL.7,9_IN1.htm

12. Hilton. (2019). Hilton named the #1 company to work for in the U.S. Retrieved from https://newsroom.hilton.com/corporate/news/employees-rank-hilton-the-best-place-to-work-in-the-us

13. Fortune 100 Best. (2019). Hilton. *Fortune.* http://fortune.com/best-companies/hilton-worldwide-holdings/

14. Rucci, A. J. (2008). I-O psychology's "core purpose": Where science and practice meet. *The Industrial and Organizational Psychologist, 46*(1), 17–34.

15. Campbell, L. (2017). We've broken down your entire life into years spent doing tasks. *Huffington Post.* Retrieved from https://www.huffingtonpost.com.au/2017/10/18/weve-broken-down-your-entire-life-into-years-spent-doing-tasks_a_23248153/

16. Campbell, L. (2017). We've broken down your entire life into years spent doing tasks. *Huffington Post.* Retrieved from https://www.huffingtonpost.com.au/2017/10/18/weve-broken-down-your-entire-life-into-years-spent-doing-tasks_a_23248153/

17. Brenan, M. (2018, December 20). Nurses again outpace other professions for honesty, ethics. *Gallup.* https://news.gallup.com/poll/245597/nurses-again-outpace-professions-honesty-ethics.aspx

18. Brenan, M. (2018, December 20). Nurses again outpace other professions for honesty, ethics. *Gallup.* https://news.gallup.com/poll/245597/nurses-again-outpace-professions-honesty-ethics.aspx

19. Brenan, M. (2018, December 20). Nurses again outpace other professions for honesty, ethics. *Gallup.* https://news.gallup.com/poll/245597/nurses-again-outpace-professions-honesty-ethics.aspx

20. Clark, R. E. (2003). Fostering the work motivation of individuals and teams. *Performance Improvement, 42*(3), 21–29.

21. Baard, P.P., Deci, E.L., & Ryan, R.M. (2004). Intrinsic need satisfaction: A motivational basis of performance and well-being in two work settings. *Journal of Applied Social Psychology, 34*(10), 2045-2068.

22. Denison, D. R. (1996). What is the difference between organizational culture and organizational climate? A native's point of view on a decade of paradigm wars. *The Academy of Management Review, 21*(3), 619–654.

23. Denison, D. R. (1996). What is the difference between organizational culture and organizational climate? A native's point of view on a decade of paradigm wars. *The Academy of Management Review, 21*(3), 619–654.

24. Ostroff, C., Kinicki, A. J., & Tamkins, M. M. (2003). Organizational culture and climate. In W. C. Borman, D. R. Ilgen, & R. J. Klimoski (Eds.), *Handbook of psychology: Industrial and organizational psychology, 12*, 565–593. New York: Wiley.

25. Fortune 100 Best. (2019). Hilton. *Fortune.* Retrieved from http://fortune.com/best-companies/hilton-worldwide-holdings/

26. Fortune 100 Best. (2019). Hilton. *Fortune.* Retrieved from http://fortune.com/best-companies/hilton-worldwide-holdings/

27. Fortune 100 Best. (2019). Hilton. *Fortune.* Retrieved from http://fortune.com/best-companies/hilton-worldwide-holdings/

28. Peterson, N. G., Mumford, M. D., Borman, W. C., Jeanneret, P. R., & Fleishmann, E. A. (1999). *An occupational information system for the 21st century: The development of O*NET*. Washington, D.C.: American Psychological Association.

29. O*NET Resource Center. (2014). Production Database – O*NET 19.0. Retrieved from http://www.onetcenter.org/database.html

30. Aamodt, M. G. (2016). *Industrial/Organizational Psychology: An Applied Approach.* Belmont, CA: Wadsworth, Cengage Learning.

31. Gael, S. A. (1988). *The job analysis handbook for business, industry, and government* (Vols. 1 and 2). New York: Wiley.

32. Aamodt, M. G. (2016). *Industrial/Organizational Psychology: An Applied Approach.* Belmont, CA: Wadsworth, Cengage Learning.

33. Flanagan, J. C. (1954). The critical incident technique. *Psychological Bulletin, 51,* 327–358.

34. U.S. Equal Employment Opportunity Commission. (2012). Laws & guidance. Retrieved from http://www.eeoc.gov/laws/index.cfm

35. National Archives. (2012). Teaching with documents: The Civil Rights Act of 1964 and the Equal Employment Opportunity Commission. Retrieved from http://www.archives.gov/education/lessons/civil-rights-act/

36. Roy Rosenzweig Center for History and New Media. (2006, December). *An outline of the Anita Hill and Clarence Thomas controversy.* Retrieved from http://chnm.gmu.edu/courses/122/hill/hillframe.htm

37. Roy Rosenzweig Center for History and New Media. (2006, December). *An outline of the Anita Hill and Clarence Thomas controversy.* Retrieved from http://chnm.gmu.edu/courses/122/hill/hillframe.htm

38. Hanisch, K.A. (1996). An integrated framework for studying the outcomes of sexual harassment: Consequences for individuals and organizations. In M.S. Stockdale (Ed.), *Women and Work: A Research and Policy Series, Volume 5: Sexual harassment in the workplace: Perspectives, frontiers, and response strategies* (pp. 174–199). Thousand Oaks, CA: Sage.

39. Knapp, D.E., & Kustis, G.A. (1996). The real "disclosure": Sexual harassment and the bottom line. In M.S. Stockdale (Ed.), *Women and Work: A Research and Policy Series, Volume 5: Sexual harassment in the workplace: Perspectives, frontiers, and response strategies* (pp. 199–215). Thousand Oaks, CA: Sage.

40. Jablin, F. M. (1982). Organizational communication: An assimilation approach. In M. E. Rolff & C. R. Berger (Eds.), *Social cognition and communication* (pp. 255–286). Beverly Hills, CA: Sage.

41. Hanisch, K. A. (1995). Behavioral families and multiple causes: Matching the complexity of responses to the complexity of antecedents. *Current Directions in Psychological Science, 4*(5), 156–162.

42. Pogorzelski, S., & Harriott, J. (2007). *Finding keepers: The Monster guide to hiring and holding the world's best employees.* New York: McGraw Hill.

43. Sullivan, J. (2012). 10 compelling numbers that reveal the power of employee referrals. Retrieved from http://www.ere.net/2012/05/07/10-compelling-numbers-that-reveal-the-power-of-employee-referrals/

44. Sullivan, J. (2012). 10 compelling numbers that reveal the power of employee referrals. Retrieved from http://www.ere.net/2012/05/07/10-compelling-numbers-that-reveal-the-power-of-employee-referrals/

45. Zottoli, M. A., & Wanous, J. P. (2000). Recruitment source research: Current status and future directions. *Human Resource Management Review, 10,* 435–451.

46. McManus, M. A., & Baratta, J. E. (1992). *The relationship of recruiting source to performance and survival.* Paper presented at the annual meeting of the Society for Industrial and Organizational Psychology, Montreal, Canada.

47. Rupert, G. (1989). Employee referrals as a source of recruitment and job performance. *Proceedings of the 10th Annual Graduate Conference in Industrial/Organizational Psychology and Organizational Behavior.*

48. Aamodt, M.G., & Carr, K. (1988). Relationship between recruitment source and employee behavior. *Proceedings of the 12th Annual Meeting of the International Personnel Management Association Assessment Council,* 143–146.

49. Earnest, D. R., Allen, D. G., & Landis, R. S. (2011). Mechanisms linking realistic job previews with turnover: A meta-analytic path analysis. *Personnel Psychology, 64*(4), 865–897.

50. Raphael, T. (2010, June 22). Employee referral programs using more social media. Retrieved from www.ere.net/2010/06/22/employee-referral-programs-using-more-social-media/

51. Hargis, M. (2008). Social networking sites dos and don'ts. *CNN* Retrieved from http://edition.cnn.com/2008/LIVING/worklife/11/05/cb.social.networking/index.html

52. PRNewswire. (2018). More than half of employers have found content on social media that caused them NOT to hire a candidate, according to recent CareerBuilder survey. Retrieved from https://www.prnewswire.com/news-releases/more-than-half-of-employers-have-found-content-on-social-media-that-caused-them-not-to-hire-a-candidate-according-to-recent-careerbuilder-survey-300694437.html

53. PRNewswire. (2018). More than half of employers have found content on social media that caused them NOT to hire a candidate, according to recent CareerBuilder survey. Retrieved from https://www.prnewswire.com/news-releases/more-than-half-of-employers-have-found-content-on-social-media-that-caused-them-not-to-hire-a-candidate-according-to-recent-careerbuilder-survey-300694437.html

54. PRNewswire. (2018). More than half of employers have found content on social media that caused them NOT to hire a candidate, according to recent CareerBuilder survey. Retrieved from https://www.prnewswire.com/news-releases/more-than-half-of-employers-have-found-content-on-social-media-that-caused-them-not-to-hire-a-candidate-according-to-recent-careerbuilder-survey-300694437.html

55. PRNewswire. (2018). More than half of employers have found content on social media that caused them NOT to hire a candidate, according to recent CareerBuilder survey. Retrieved from https://www.prnewswire.com/news-releases/more-than-half-of-employers-have-found-content-on-social-media-that-caused-them-not-to-hire-a-candidate-according-to-recent-careerbuilder-survey-300694437.html

56. PRNewswire. (2018). More than half of employers have found content on social media that caused them NOT to hire a candidate, according to recent CareerBuilder survey. Retrieved from https://www.prnewswire.com/news-releases/more-than-half-of-employers-have-found-content-on-social-media-that-caused-them-not-to-hire-a-candidate-according-to-recent-careerbuilder-survey-300694437.html

57. Hargis, M. (2008). Social networking sites dos and don'ts. *CNN.* Retrieved from http://edition.cnn.com/2008/LIVING/worklife/11/05/cb.social.networking/index.html

58. The Believeau Law Group. (2012). Can companies use social media to screen job applicants? Retrieved from www.beliveaulaw.net/2012/02/can-companies-use-social-media-to-screen-job-applicants/

59. Waring, R. L., & Buchanan, F. R. (2010). Social networking web sites: The legal and ethical aspects of pre-employment screening and employee surveillance. *Journal of Human Resources Education, 4*(2), 14–23.

60. Salgado, J. F., Viswesvaran, C., & Ones, D. (2001). Predictors used for personnel selection: An overview of constructs, methods and techniques. In N. Anderson, D. S. Ones, H. K. Sinangil, & C. Viswesvaran, *Handbook of industrial, work and organizational psychology* (vol. 1, pp. 166–199). Thousand Oaks, CA: Sage.

61. West Virginia Division of Personnel. (2004, September). Selection interviewing: Developing and administering structured behavioral interviews. Retrieved from http://webcache.googleusercontent.com/search?q=cache:khtpGpmt7vwJ:www.state.wv.us/admin/personnel/emprel/toolbox/quiz/interviewing.pdf+&cd=1&hl=en&ct=clnk&gl=us

62. Arvey, R. D., & Campion, J. E. (1982). The employment interview: A summary and review of recent research. *Personnel Psychology, 35,* 281–322.

63. McDaniel, M. A., Whetzel, D. L., Schmidt, F. L., & Maurer, S. D. (1994). The validity of employment interviews: A comprehensive review and meta-analysis. *Journal of Applied Psychology, 79,* 599–616.

64. Huffcutt, A. I., & Arthur, W., Jr. (1994). Hunter and Hunter (1984) revisited: Interview validity for entry-level jobs. *Journal of Applied Psychology, 79,* 184–190.

65. Huffcutt, A. I., & Arthur, W., Jr. (1994). Hunter and Hunter (1984) revisited: Interview validity for entry-level jobs. *Journal of Applied Psychology, 79,* 184–190.

66. Schmidt, F. L., & Hunter, J. E. (1998). The validity and utility of selection methods in personnel psychology: Practical and theoretical implications of 85 years of research findings. *Psychological Bulletin, 124*(2), 262–274.

67. Hardison, C. M., Kim, D., & Sackett, P. R. (2005, April). *Meta-analysis of work sample criterion related validity: Revisiting anomalous findings.* Paper presented at the 20th annual conference of the Society for Industrial-Organizational Psychology, Los Angeles.

68. Ones, D. S., Viswesvaran, C., & Schmidt, F. L. (1993). Comprehensive meta-analysis of integrity test validities: Findings for personnel selection and theories of job performance. *Journal of Applied Psychology, 78*(4), 679–703.

69. Roth, P. L, BeVier, C. A., Switzer, F. S., & Schippmann, J. S. (1996). Meta-analyzing the relationship between grades and job performance. *Journal of Applied Psychology, 81*(5), 548–556.

70. Quinones, M. A., Ford, J. K., & Teachout, M. S. (1995). The relationship between work experience and job performance: A conceptual and meta-analytic review. *Personnel Psychology, 48*(4), 887–910.

71. Tett, R. P., Jackson, D. N., Rothstein, M., & Reddon, J. R. (1994). Meta-analysis of personality-job performance relations: A reply to Ones, Mount, Barrick, & Hunter (1994). *Personnel Psychology, 47*(1), 157–172.

72. Hunter, J. E., & Hunter, R. E. (1984). Validity and utility of alternative predictors of job performance. *Psychological Bulletin, 96*(1), 72–98.

73. Schmitt, N., Cortina, J. M., Ingerick, M. J., & Wiechmann, D. (2003). Personnel selection and employee performance. In W. C. Borman, D. R. Ilgen, & R. J. Klimoski (Eds.), *Handbook of psychology: Industrial and organizational psychology* (vol. 12, pp. 77–105). New York: Wiley.

74. Jablin, F. M. (1982). Organizational communication: An assimilation approach. In M. E. Rolff & C. R. Berger (Eds.), *Social cognition and communication* (pp. 255–286). Beverly Hills, CA: Sage.

75. Crowley, M.C. (2015). How SAS became the world's best place to work. Fast Company. Retrieved from http://www.sas.com/en_us/careers/life-at-sas.html

76. SAS. (2015). Life at SAS. *Fast Company.* Retrieved from http://www.fastcompany.com/3004953/how-sas-became-worlds-best-place-work

77. Stewart, J.B. (2013, March 15). Looking for a lesson in Google's perks. *New York Times.* Retrieved from http://www.nytimes.com/2013/03/16/business/at-google-a-place-to-work-and-play.html?pagewanted=all&_r=0

78. Stewart, J.B. (2013, March 15). Looking for a lesson in Google's perks. *New York Times.* Retrieved from http://www.nytimes.com/2013/03/16/business/at-google-a-place-to-work-and-play.html?pagewanted=all&_r=0

79. Sullivan, M. (2013, June 28). More proof office space design impacts productivity, focus and collaboration. Retrieved from http://www.officingtoday.com/2013/06/more-proof-office-space-design-impacts-productivity-focus-and-collaboration/
80. Van Horne, T. (2013, December 5). Workplace design impacts performance, employee engagement and innovation. Retrieved from http://www.canadaone.com/ezine/2013/workplace_design_impacts_performance.html
81. Sullivan, M. (2013, June 28). More proof office space design impacts productivity, focus and collaboration. Retrieved from http://www.officingtoday.com/2013/06/more-proof-office-space-design-impacts-productivity-focus-and-collaboration/
82. Staley, O. (2018). Hilton Hotels' newest upgrades are strictly for staff. Retrieved from https://qz.com/work/1233750/hilton-hotels-has-new-upgrades-strictly-for-service-workers
83. Staley, O. (2018). Hilton Hotels' newest upgrades are strictly for staff. Retrieved from https://qz.com/work/1233750/hilton-hotels-has-new-upgrades-strictly-for-service-workers
84. Staley, O. (2018). Hilton Hotels' newest upgrades are strictly for staff. Retrieved from https://qz.com/work/1233750/hilton-hotels-has-new-upgrades-strictly-for-service-workers
85. Lesiuk, T. (2005). The effect of music listening on work performance. *Psychology of Music, 33*(2), 173–191.
86. Ciotti, G. (2015). How music affects your productivity. Sparring Mind. Retrieved from http://www.sparringmind.com/music-productivity/
87. Sanders, A. (2017, September 29). Space and project management benchmarks. IFMA Research Report #34. Retrieved from https://slidex.tips/download/space-and-project-management-benchmarks-ifma-research-report-34
88. Mull, A. (2019). Workers love AirPods because employers stole their wall. *The Atlantic*. Retrieved from https://www.theatlantic.com/health/archive/2019/04/airpods-open-plan-offices/588112/?utm_source=pocket-newtab
89. McMains, S. & Kastner, S. (2011). Interactions of top-down and bottom-up mechanisms in human visual cortex. *Journal of Neuroscience, 31*(2), 587–597.
90. Murphy, J. (2019). Get more done & stress less with these simple office organization ideas. Retrieved https://www.snacknation.com/blog/office-organization-ideas.
91. Murphy, J. (2019). Get more done & stress less with these simple office organization ideas. Retrieved https://www.snacknation.com/blog/office-organization-ideas.
92. Murphy, J. (2019). Get more done & stress less with these simple office organization ideas. Retrieved https://www.snacknation.com/blog/office-organization-ideas.
93. Eion, K. (2019). 20 awesome DIY office organization ideas that boost efficiency. Retrieved https://www.lifehack.org/articles/productivity/20-awesome-diy-office-organization-ideas-that-boost-efficiency.html.
94. Flanagin, A, J., & Waldeck, J. H. (2004). Technology use and organizational newcomer socialization. *Journal of Business Communication, 41*(2), 137–165.
95. Allen, T. D., Lentz, E., & Day, R. (2006). Career success outcomes associated with mentoring others: A comparison of mentors and nonmentors. *Journal of Career Development, 32*(3), 272–285.
96. Greenhaus, J. H. (2003). Career dynamics. In W. C. Borman, D. R. Ilgen, & R. J. Klimoski (Eds.), *Handbook of psychology: Industrial and organizational psychology* (vol. 12, pp. 519–540). New York: Wiley.
97. Ragins, B. R., & Cotton, J. L. (1999). Mentor functions and outcomes: A comparison of men and women in formal and informal mentoring relationships. *Journal of Applied Psychology, 84*(4), 529–550.
98. Illuminant. (2011, January 17). Avoiding insult and injury when using color in China. Retrieved from http://www.illuminantpartners.com/2011/01/17/color/
99. Hare, A. P. (1962). *Handbook of small group research.* New York: The Free Press of Glencoe.
100. McGrath, J. E. (1966). *Small group research.* New York: Holt, Rinehart, & Winston.
101. Hill, G. W. (1982). Group versus individual performance: Are N + 1 heads better than one? *Psychological Bulletin, 91*(3), 517–539.
102. Paulus, P. B. (2000). Groups, teams, and creativity: The creative potential of idea-generating groups. *Applied Psychology: An International Review, 49*(2), 237–262.
103. Likert, R. (1967). *The human organization: Its management and value.* New York: McGraw-Hill.
104. Sagie, A. (1997). Leader direction and employee participation in decision making: Contradictory or compatible practices? *Applied Psychology: An International Review, 46*(4), 387–452.
105. Lawler, E. E., Mohrman, S. A., & Ledford, G. E. (1995). *Creating high performance organizations: Practices and results of employee involvement and total quality management in Fortune 1000 companies.* San Francisco: Jossey-Bass.
106. Kozlowski, S. W., & Bell, B. S. (2003). Work groups and teams in organizations. In W. C. Borman, D. R. Ilgen, & R. J. Klimoski (Eds.), *Handbook of Psychology: Industrial and Organizational Psychology* (vol. 12, pp. 333–375). New York: Wiley.
107. Aamodt, M. G. (2016). *Industrial/Organizational Psychology:* An Applied Approach. Belmont, CA: Wadsworth, Cengage Learning.
108. Mullen, B., Anthony, T., Salas, E., & Driskell, J. E. (1994). Group cohesiveness and quality of decision making: An integration of the groupthink hypothesis. *Small Group Research, 25*(2), 189–204.
109. Beal, D. J., Cohen, R. R., Burke, M. J., & McLendon, C. L. (2003). Cohesion and performance in groups: A meta-analytic clarification of construct relations. *Journal of Applied Psychology, 88*(6), 989–1004.
110. Brawley, L. R., Carron, A. V., & Widmeyer, W. N. (1993). The influence of the group and its cohesiveness on perceptions of group goal-related variables. *Journal of Sport and Exercise Psychology, 15*(3), 245–260.
111. Aamodt, M. G. (2016). *Industrial/organizational psychology: An applied approach.* Belmont, CA: Wadsworth, Cengage Learning.
112. Forsyth, D. R. (2010). *Group dynamics* (5th ed.). Belmont, CA: Wadsworth.
113. Mathieu, J. E., Hollenbeck, J. R., van Knippenberg, D., & Ilgen, D. R. (2017). A century of work teams in the *Journal of Applied Psychology, 102*(3), 452–467.
114. Duhigg, C. (2016, February 25). What Google learned from its quest to build the perfect team. *The New York Times Magazine,* Retrieved from https://www.nytimes.com/2016/02/28/magazine/what-google-learned-from-its-quest-to-build-the-perfect-team.html?smid=pl-share
115. Duhigg, C. (2016, February 25). What Google learned from its quest to build the perfect team. *The New York Times Magazine.* Retrieved from https://www.nytimes.com/2016/02/28/magazine/what-google-learned-from-its-quest-to-build-the-perfect-team.html?smid=pl-share
116. Re: Work (2019). Guide: Understand team effectiveness. Retrieved from https://rework.withgoogle.com/guides/understanding-team-effectiveness/steps/introduction.
117. Re: Work (2019). Guide: Understand team effectiveness. Retrieved from https://rework.withgoogle.com/guides/understanding-team-effectiveness/steps/introduction.
118. Re: Work (2019). Guide: Understand team effectiveness. Retrieved from https://rework.withgoogle.com/guides/understanding-team-effectiveness/steps/introduction.
119. Re: Work (2019). Guide: Understand team effectiveness. Retrieved from https://rework.withgoogle.com/guides/understanding-team-effectiveness/steps/introduction.
120. Mello, J. A. (1993). Improving individual member accountability in small group settings. *Journal of Management Education, 17*(2), 253–259.
121. Barfield, R. L. (2003). Students' perceptions of and satisfaction with group grades and the group experience in the college classroom. *Assessment and Evaluation in Higher Education, 28*(4), 355–369.
122. Anderson, N., & Thomas, H. D. C. (1996). Work group socialization. In M. A. West (Ed.), *Handbook of work group psychology* (pp. 423–450). Chichester, UK: Wiley.
123. Manz, C. C. (1992). Self-leading work teams: Moving beyond self-management myths. *Human Relations, 45*, 1119–1140.
124. Cohen, S. G., & Ledford, G. E., Jr. (1994). The effectiveness of self-managing teams: A quasi-experiment. *Human Relations, 47*, 13–43.
125. Stewart, G. L., & Manz, C. C. (1995). Leadership for self-managing work teams: A typology and integrative model. *Human Relations, 48*, 347–370.
126. Kozlowski, S. W., & Bell, B. S. (2003). Work groups and teams in organizations. In W. C. Borman, D. R. Ilgen, & R. J. Klimoski (Eds.), *Handbook of Psychology: Industrial and Organizational Psychology* (vol. 12, pp. 333–375). New York: Wiley.
127. Kozlowski, S. W., Gully, S. M., McHugh, P. P., Salas, E., & Cannon-Bowers, J. A. (1996). A dynamic theory of leadership and team effectiveness: Developmental and task contingent leader roles. In G. R. Ferris (Ed.), *Research in personnel and human resource management* (vol. 14, pp. 253–305). Greenwich, CT: JAI Press.
128. Katz, D., & Kahn, R. L. (1978). *The social psychology of organizations* (2nd ed.). New York: Wiley.
129. Bryman, A. S. (1996). The importance of context: Qualitative research and the study of leadership. *Leadership Quarterly, 7*, 353–370.
130. Kirkpatrick, S. A., & Locke, E. A. (1991). Leadership: Do traits matter? *Academy of Management Executive, 5*, 48–60.
131. Kaplan, R. E., Drath, W. H., & Kofodimos, J. R. (1991). *Beyond ambition: How driven managers can lead better and live better.* San Francisco: Jossey-Bass.
132. Northouse, P. G. (2004). *Leadership: Theory and practice.* Thousand Oaks, CA: Sage Publications.
133. Aamodt, M. G. (2016). *Industrial/organizational psychology: An applied approach.* Belmont, CA: Wadsworth, Cengage Learning.
134. Bass, B. M. (1990). From transactional to transformational leadership: Learning to share the vision. *Organizational Dynamics, 18*(3), 19–31.
135. Bass, B. M. (1990). From transactional to transformational leadership: Learning to share the vision. *Organizational Dynamics, 18*(3), 19–31.
136. Gharib, S. (2019, January 31). Hilton CEO says the key leadership lesson in the hotel's turnaround: "We kept a steady hand on the wheel." *Fortune.* Retrieved from http://fortune.com/2019/01/31/hilton-ceo-on-leading-leadership.
137. Gharib, S. (2019, January). Hilton CEO says the key leadership lesson in the hotel's turnaround: "We kept a steady hand on the wheel." *Fortune* Retrieved from http://fortune.com/2019/01/31/hilton-ceo-on-leading-leadership.
138. Gharib, S. (2019, January 31). Hilton CEO says the key leadership lesson in the hotel's turnaround: "We kept a steady hand on the wheel." *Fortune.* Retrieved from http://fortune.com/2019/01/31/hilton-ceo-on-leading-leadership.
139. Hospitalitynet. (2019, February 15). Employees rank Hilton the best place to work in the U.S. February 15. Retrieved from https://www.hospitalitynet.org/news/4091997.html.
140. Avolio, B. J., Kahai, S. S., & Dodge, G. (2000). E-leading in organizations and it implications for theory, research and practice. *Leadership Quarterly, 11*, 615–670.
141. Lombardo, M. M., & Eichinger, R. W. (2000). High potentials as high learners. *Human Resource Management, 39*(4), 321–329.
142. Lombardo, M. M., & Eichinger, R. W. (2000). High potentials as high learners. *Human Resource Management, 39*(4), 321–329.

143. Ryan, J. R. (2009, February 27). Learning agility equals leadership success, *Bloomberg Businessweek*. Retrieved from http://www.businessweek.com/managing/content/feb2009/ca20090227_893956.htm
144. Dorsey, D. & Mueller-Hanson, R. (2017). Performance management that makes a difference: An evidence-based approach. Society for Human Resource Management. Retrieved from: Learning agility equals leadership success, *Bloomberg Businessweek*. Retrieved from https://www.shrm.org/hr-today/trends-and-forecasting/special-reports-and-expert-views/Documents/Performance%20Management.pdf.
145. Fletcher, C., & Perry, E. L. (2001). Performance appraisal and feedback: A consideration of national culture and a review of contemporary research and future trends. In N. Anderson, D. S. Ones, H. K. Sinangil, & C. Viswesvaran, *Handbook of industrial, work and organizational psychology* (vol. 1, pp. 127–144). Thousand Oaks, CA: Sage.
146. Aamodt, M. G. (2016). *Industrial/organizational psychology: An applied approach*. Belmont, CA: Wadsworth, Cengage Learning.
147. Sullivan, J. (2009, February 9). Employee furloughs can be a bad alternative to layoffs. Ere.net. Retrieved from http://www.ere.net/tags/furloughs
148. Tarquinio, M. (2009, January 27). Workforce planning research: How to strengthen your job in today's economy. Ere.net. Retrieved from http://www.ere.net/2009/01/27/workforce-planning-research-how-to-strengthen-your-job-in-today%e2%80%99s-economy
149. Hanisch, K. A. (1995). Behavioral families and multiple causes: Matching the complexity of responses to the complexity of antecedents. *Current Directions in Psychological Science*, 4(5), 156–162.
150. Hanisch, K. A. (1995). Behavioral families and multiple causes: Matching the complexity of responses to the complexity of antecedents. *Current Directions in Psychological Science*, 4(5), 156–162.
151. Hackman, J. R., & Oldham, G. R. (1976). Motivation through the design of work: A test of a theory. *Organizational Behavior and Human Performance*, 16(2), 250–279.
152. Cranny, C. J., Smith, P. C., & Stone, E. F. (1992). *Job satisfaction: How people feel about their jobs and how it affects their performance*. New York: Lexington Books.
153. Sullivan, M. (2013, June 28). More proof office space design impacts productivity, focus and collaboration. Retrieved from http://www.officingtoday.com/2013/06/more-proof-office-space-design-impacts-productivity-focus-and-collaboration.
154. Adams, J. S. (1965). Inequity in social change. In L. Berkowitz (Ed.), *Advances in experimental social psychology* (Vol. 2, pp. 267–299). New York: Academic Press.
155. Meyer, J. P., & Allen, N. J. (1991). A three-component conceptualization of organizational commitment. *Human Resource Management Review*, 1, 61–89.
156. Meyer, J. P. & Herscovitch, L. (2001). Commitment in the workplace: Toward a general model. *Human Resource Management Review*, 11, 299–326.
157. Mueller, C. W., Boyer, E. M., Price, J. L. & Iverson, R. D. (1994). Employee attachment and non-coercive conditions of work: The case of dental hygienists. *Work and Occupations*, 21, 179–212.
158. Arthur, J. B. (1994). Effects of human resource systems on manufacturing performance and turnover. *Academy of Management Journal*, 37, 670–687.
159. Roskies, E., & Louis-Guerin, C. (1990). Job insecurity in managers: Antecedents and consequences. *Journal of Organizational Behavior*, 11, 345–359.
160. Meyer, J. P., Allen, N. J., & Smith, C. A. (1993). Commitments to organizations and occupations: Extension and test of a three component conceptualization. *Journal of Applied Psychology*, 78, 538–551.
161. Ellemers, N., de Gilder, D., & van den Heuvel, H. (1998). Career-oriented vs. team-oriented commitment and behavior at work. *Journal of Applied Psychology*, 83, 717–730.
162. Cooper-Hakim, A., & Viswesvaran, C. (2005). The construct of work commitment: Testing an integrative framework. *Journal of Applied Psychology*, 131, 241–259.
163. Greenberg J. (1990). Organizational justice: Yesterday, today and tomorrow. *Journal of Management* 16, 399–432.
164. Rupp, D. E., & Cropanzano, R. (2002). The mediating effects of social exchange relationships in predicting workplace outcomes from multifoci organizational justice. *Organizational Behavior and Human Decision Processes*, 89, 925–946.
165. Robbins, J. M., Ford, M.T., & Tetrick, L.E. (2012). Perceived unfairness and employee health: A meta-analytic integration. *Journal of Applied Psychology*, 97(2), 235–272.
166. Lam, S. S. K., Schaubroeck, J., & Aryee, S. (2002). Relationship between organizational justice and employee work outcomes: A cross-national study. *Journal of Organizational Behavior*, 23, 1–18.
167. Lam, S. S. K., Schaubroeck, J., & Aryee, S. (2002). Relationship between organizational justice and employee work outcomes: A cross-national study. *Journal of Organizational Behavior*, 23, 1–18.
168. Mills, H., Reiss, N., & Dombeck, M. (2008, Jun 30). Types of stressors (eustress vs. distress). Retrieved from http://www.mentalhelp.net/poc/view_doc.php?type=doc&id=15644
169. Sonnentag, S., & Frese, M. (2003). Stress in organizations. In W. C. Borman, D. R. Ilgen, & R. J. Klimoski (Eds.), Handbook of psychology (vol. 12, pp. 453–491). Hoboken, NJ: John Wiley & Sons.
170. Murphy, J. (2019). Get more done & stress less with these simple office organization ideas. Retrieved https://www.snacknation.com/blog/office-organization-ideas.
171. Robbins, J. M., Ford, M. T., & Tetrick, L. E. (2012). Perceived unfairness and employee health: A meta-analytic integration. *Journal of Applied Psychology*, 97(2), 235–272.
172. Chandola, T., Brunner, E., & Marmot, M. (2006). Chronic stress at work and the metabolic syndrome: Prospective study. *British Medical Journal*. Retrieved from http://www.bmj.com/content/early/2005/12/31/bmj.38693.435301.80
173. The American Institute of Stress. (2019). 50 common signs and symptoms of stress. Retrieved from https://www.stress.org/stress-effects.
174. The American Institute of Stress. (2019). 50 common signs and symptoms of |stress. Retrieved from https://www.stress.org/stress-effects.
175. The American College Health Association. (2008). American College Health Association – National college health assessment spring 2007 reference group data report (abridged). *Journal of American College Health*, 56(5), 469–479. Retrieved from http://www.acha-ncha.org/docs/JACH%20March%202008%20SP%2007%20Ref%20Grp.pdf
176. WebMD (2015). Stress symptoms. Retrieved from http://www.webmd.com/balance/stress-management/stress-symptoms-effects_of-stress-on-the-body?page=2
177. Holmes, L. (2014, September 17). 5 ways stress wrecks your sleep (and what to do about it). *Huffington Post*. Retrieved from http://www.huffingtonpost.com/2014/09/17/stress-and-sleep_n_5824506.html
178. Aamodt, M. G. (2016). *Industrial/organizational psychology: An applied approach*. Belmont, CA: Wadsworth, Cengage Learning.
179. O'Connor, D. B., Jones, F., Conner, M., McMillan, B., & Ferguson, E. (2008). Effects of daily hassles and eating style on eating behavior. *Health Psychology*, 27(1), S20–S31.
180. O'Connor, D. B., Jones, F., Conner, M., McMillan, B., & Ferguson, E. (2008). Effects of daily hassles and eating style on eating behavior. *Health Psychology*, 27(1), S20–S31.
181. O'Connor, D. B., Jones, F., Conner, M., McMillan, B., & Ferguson, E. (2008). Effects of daily hassles and eating style on eating behavior. *Health Psychology*, 27(1), S20–S31.
182. American Psychological Association. (2018). Coping with stress at work. October. Retrieved from https://www.apa.org/helpcenter/work-stress.
183. Eby, L. T., Casper, W. J., Lockwood, A., Bordeaux, C., & Brinley, A. (2005). Work and family research in IO/OB: Content analysis and review of the literature (1980–2002). *Journal of Vocational Behavior*, 66, 124–197.
184. Hilton. (2016). Hilton launches new industry-leading parental leave policies. January. Retrieved from https://newsroom.hilton.com/corporate/news/hilton-launches-new-industryleading-parental-leave-policies
185. Breaugh, J. A., & Frye, N. K. (2008). Work-family conflict: The importance of family-friendly employment practices and family-supportive supervisors. *Journal of Business Psychology*, 22, 345–353.
186. American Psychological Association (2015). Five tips to help manage stress. Retrieved from http://www.apa.org/helpcenter/manage-stress.aspx
187. Atkinson, T., Liem, R., & Liem, J. H. (1986). The social costs of unemployment: Implications for social support. *Journal of Health and Social Behavior*, 27, 317–331.
188. American Psychological Association (2015). Five tips to help manage stress. Retrieved from http://www.apa.org/helpcenter/manage-stress.aspx
189. Naylor, J. C., Pritchard, R. D., & Ilgen, D. R. (1980). *A theory of behavior in organizations*. New York: Academic Press.
190. Smith, C. A., Organ, D. W., & Near, J. P. (1983). Organizational citizenship behavior: Its nature and antecedents. *Journal of Applied Psychology*, 68, 653–663.
191. Witt, L. A., Kacmar, M., Carlson, D. S., & Zivnuska, S. (2002). Interactive effects of personality and organizational politics on contextual performance. *Journal of Organizational Behavior*, 23, 911–926.
192. Borman, W. C., Penner, L. A., Allen, T.D., & Motowidlo, S. J. (2001). Personality predictors of citizenship performance. *International Journal of Selection and Assessment*, 9, 52–69.
193. Heilman, M. E., & Chen, J. J. (2005). Same behavior, different consequences: Reactions to men's and women's altruistic citizenship behaviors. *Journal of Applied Psychology*, 90, 431–441.
194. Kidder, D. L., & Parks, J. M. (2001). The good soldier: Who is s(he)? *Journal of Organizational Behavior*, 22, 939–959.
195. Hanisch, K. A., Hulin, C. L., & Roznowski, M. A. (1998). The importance of individuals' repertoires of behaviors: The scientific appropriateness of studying multiple behaviors and general attitudes. *Journal of Organizational Behavior*, 19, 463–480.
196. Sackett, P. R., & DeVore, C. J. (2001). Counterproductive behaviors at work. In N. Anderson, D. S. Ones, H. K. Sinangil, & C. Viswesvaran, *Handbook of Industrial, Work and Organizational Psychology*, 1, 145–165.
197. Hanisch, K. A., & Hulin, C. L. (1990). Job attitudes and organizational withdrawal: An examination of retirement and other voluntary withdrawal behaviors. *Journal of Vocational Behavior*, 37(1), 60–78.
198. Hanisch, K. A., & Hulin, C. L. (1991). General attitudes and organizational withdrawal: An evaluation of a causal model. *Journal of Vocational Behavior*, 39, 110–128.

199. Hanisch, K. A. (1995). Behavioral families and multiple causes: Matching the complexity of responses to the complexity of antecedents. *Current Directions in Psychological Science, 4*(5), 156–162.
200. Hanisch, K. A., & Hulin, C. L. (1990). Job attitudes and organizational withdrawal: An examination of retirement and other voluntary withdrawal behaviors. *Journal of Vocational Behavior, 37*(1), 60–78.
201. Sackett, P. R., & DeVore, C. J. (2001). Counterproductive behaviors at work. In N. Anderson, D. S. Ones, H. K. Sinangil, & C. Viswesvaran, *Handbook of Industrial, Work and Organizational Psychology, 1*, 145–165. Thousand Oaks, CA: Sage.
202. LePine, J. A., Erez, A., & Johnston, D. E. (2002). The nature and dimensionality of organizational citizenship behavior: A critical review and a meta-analysis. *Journal of Applied Psychology, 87*(1), 52–65.
203. Dalal, R. S. (2006). A meta-analysis of the relationship between organizational citizenship behavior and counterproductive work behavior. *Journal of Applied Psychology, 90*(6), 1241–1255.
204. Hackett, R. D. (1989). Work attitudes and employee absenteeism: A synthesis of the literature. *Journal of Occupational Psychology, 62*(3), 235–248.
205. Hanisch, K. A., & Hulin, C. L. (1990). Job attitudes and organizational withdrawal: An examination of retirement and other voluntary withdrawal behaviors. *Journal of Vocational Behavior, 37*(1), 60–78.
206. Lennings, C. J. (1997). Police and occupationally related violence: A review. *Policing: An International Journal of Police Strategies and Management, 20*(3), 555–566.
207. Hanisch, K. A. (1999). Job loss and unemployment research from 1994–1998: A review and recommendations for research and intervention. *Journal of Vocational Behavior, 55*(2), 188–220.
208. Wanberg, C. R., Kammeyer-Mueller, J. D., & Shi, K. (2001). Job loss and the experience of unemployment: International research and perspectives. In N. Anderson, D. S. Ones, H. K. Sinangil, & C. Viswesvaran (Eds.), *Handbook of Industrial, Work and Organizational Psychology* (vol. 2, pp. 253–269). Thousand Oaks, CA: Sage.
209. Smith, F. J. (1977). Work attitudes as a predictor of attendance on a specific day. *Journal of Applied Psychology, 62*(1), 16–19.
210. Schein, E. H. (1990). Organizational culture. *American Psychologist, 45*(2), 109–119.

MODULE D

Applying Social Psychology to Law

1. Cutler, B. L., & Kovera, M. B. (2010). *Evaluating eyewitness identification*. New York: Oxford University Press.
2. Wells, G. L. (1984). The psychology of lineup identifications. *Journal of Applied Social Psychology, 14*, 89–103.
3. Wells, G. L., & Olson, E. A. (2003). Eyewitness testimony. *Annual Review of Psychology, 54*, 277–295.
4. Shapiro, P. N., & Penrod, S. D. (1986). Meta-analysis of facial identification studies. *Psychological Bulletin, 100*, 139–156.
5. Fitzgerald, R. J., & Price, H. L. (2015). Eyewitness identification across the life span: A meta-analysis of age differences. *Psychological Bulletin, 141*, 1228–1265.
6. Pozzulo, J. D., & Warren, K. L. (2003). Descriptions and identifications of strangers by youth and adult eyewitnesses. *Journal of Applied Psychology, 88*, 315–323.
7. Keast, A., Brewer, N., & Wells, G. L. (2007). Children's metacognitive judgments in an eyewitness identification task. *Journal of Experimental Child Psychology, 9*, 286–314.
8. Brewer, N., Keast, A., & Sauer, J. D. (2010). Children's eyewitness identification performance: Effects of a Not Sure response option and accuracy motivation. *Legal and Criminological Psychology, 15*, 261–277.
9. Price, H. L., & Fitzgerald, R. J. (2016). Face-off: A new identification procedure for child eyewitnesses. *Journal of Experimental Psychology: Applied, 22*, 366–380.
10. Meissner, C. A., & Brigham, J. C. (2001). Thirty years of investigating the own-race bias in memory for faces: A meta-analytic review. *Psychology, Public Policy, and Law, 7*, 3–35.
11. Behrman, B. W., & Davey, S. L. (2001). Eyewitness identification in actual criminal cases: An archival analysis. *Law and Human Behavior, 25*, 475–491.
12. Marcon, J. L., Susa, K. J., & Meissner, C. A. (2009). Assessing the influence of recollection and familiarity in memory for own- versus other-race faces. *Psychonomic Bulletin & Review, 16*, 99–103.
13. Zhou, G., Pu, X., Young, S. G., & Tse, C.-S. (2015). Effects of divided attention and social categorization on the own-race bias in face recognition. *Visual Cognition, 22*, 1296–1310.
14. Susa, K. J., Meissner, C. A., & deHeer, H. (2010). Modeling the role of social-cognitive processes in the recognition of own- and other-race faces. *Social Cognition, 28*, 523–537.
15. Van Bavel, J. J., & Cunningham, W. A. (2012). A social identity approach to person memory: Group membership, collective identification, and social role shape attention and memory. *Personality and Social Psychology Bulletin, 38*, 1566–1578.
16. Light, L. L., Kayra-Stuart, F., & Hollander, S. (1979). Recognition memory for typical and unusual faces. *Journal of Experimental Psychology: Human Learning and Memory, 5*, 212–228.
17. Bornstein, B. H., Deffenbacher, K. A., Penrod, S. D., & McGorty, E. (2012). Effects of exposure time and cognitive operations on facial identification accuracy: A meta-analysis of two variables associated with initial memory strength. *Psychology, Crime, & Law, 18*, 473–490.
18. Deffenbacher, K. A., Bornstein, B. H., McGorty, E. K., & Penrod, S. D. (2008). Forgetting the once-seen face: Estimating the strength of an eyewitness's memory representation. *Journal of Experimental Psychology: Applied, 14*, 139–150.
19. Cutler, B. L., Penrod, S. D., & Martens, T. K. (1987). The reliability of eyewitness identification: The role of system and estimator variables. *Law and Human Behavior, 11*, 233–258.
20. Hockley, W. E., Hemsworth, D. H., & Consoli, A. (1999). Shades of the mirror effect: Recognition of faces with and without sunglasses. *Memory and Cognition, 27*, 128–138.
21. Mansour, J. K., Beaudry, J. L., Bertrand, M. I., Kalmet, N., Melsom, E. I., & Lindsay, R. C. L. (2012). Impact of disguise on identification decisions and confidence with simultaneous and sequential lineups. *Law and Human Behavior, 36*, 513–526.
22. Deffenbacher, K. A. (1994). Effects of arousal on everyday memory. *Human Performance, 7*, 141–161.
23. Safer, M. A., Christianson, S.-A., Autry, M. W., & Osterlund, K. (1998). Tunnel memory for traumatic events. *Applied Cognitive Psychology, 12*, 99–117.
24. Deffenbacher, K. A., Bornstein, B. H., Penrod, S. D., & McGorty, E. K. (2004). A meta-analytic review of the effects of high stress on eyewitness memory. *Law and Human Behavior, 28*, 687–706.
25. Morgan, C. A., III, Hazlett, G., Doran, A., Garrett, S., Hoyt, G., Thomas, P., Baranoski, M., & Southwick, S. M. (2004). Accuracy of eyewitness memory for persons encountered during exposure to highly intense stress. *International Journal of Law and Psychiatry, 27*, 265–279.
26. Valentine, T., & Mesout, J. (2009). Eyewitness identification under stress in the London Dungeon. *Applied Cognitive Psychology, 23*, 151–161.
27. Fawcett, J. M., Peace, K. A., Greve, A. (2016). Looking down the barrel of a gun: What do we know about the weapon focus effect? *Journal of Applied Research in Memory and Cognition, 5*, 257–263.
28. Loftus, E. F., Loftus, G. R., & Messo, J. (1987). Some facts about "weapon focus." *Law and Human Behavior, 11*, 55–62.
29. Pickel, K. L. (1999). The influence of context on the "weapon focus" effect. *Law and Human Behavior, 23*, 299–311.
30. Pickel, K. L. (1998). Unusualness and threat as possible causes of "weapon focus." *Memory, 6*, 277–295.
31. Hope, L., & Wright, D. (2007). Beyond unusual? Examining the role of attention in the weapon focus effect. *Applied Cognitive Psychology, 21*, 951–961.
32. Davies, G. M., Smith, S., & Blincoe, C. (2008). A "weapon focus" effect in children. *Psychology, Crime, & Law, 14*, 19–28.
33. Neil v. Biggers, 409 U. S. 188 (1972).
34. Cutler, B. L., Penrod, S. D., & Martens, T. K. (1987). The reliability of eyewitness identification: The role of system and estimator variables. *Law and Human Behavior, 11*, 233–258.
35. State v. Guilbert. Supreme Court of Connecticut, 306 Conn. 218 (2012).
36. *State v. Henderson*, 208 N.J. 208 (2011)
37. Bothwell, R. K., Deffenbacher, K. A., & Brigham, J. C. (1987). Correlations of eyewitness accuracy and confidence: Optimality hypothesis revisited. *Journal of Applied Psychology, 72*, 691–695.
38. Sporer, S. L., Penrod, S. D., Read, J. D., & Cutler, B. L. (1995). Choosing, confidence, and accuracy: A meta-analysis of the confidence-accuracy relation in eyewitness identification studies. *Psychological Bulletin, 118*, 315–327.
39. Brewer, N., Keast, A., & Rishworth, A. (2002). The confidence-accuracy relationship in eyewitness identification: The effects of reflection and disconfirmation on correlation and calibration. *Journal of Experimental Psychology: Applied, 8*, 44–56.
40. Sauer, J., Brewer, N., Zweck, T., & Weber, N. (2010). The effect of retention interval on the confidence-accuracy relationship for eyewitness identification. *Law and Human Behavior, 34*, 337–347. doi: 10.1007/s10979-009-9192-x
41. Wixted, J. T., Mickes, L., Clark, S. E., Gronlund, S. D., & Roediger, H. L. III (2015). Initial eyewitness confidence reliably predicts eyewitness identification accuracy. *American Psychologist, 70*, 515–526.
42. Semmler, C., Dunn, J., Mickes, L., & Wixted, J. T. (2018). The role of estimator variables in eyewitness identification. *Journal of Experimental Psychology: Applied, 24*, 700–415.
43. Wixted, J. T., & Wells, G. L. (2017). The relationship between eyewitness confidence and identification accuracy: A new synthesis. *Psychological Science in the Public Interest, 18*, 10–65.
44. Weber, N., Brewer, N., Wells, G. L., Semmler, C., & Keast, A. (2004). Eyewitness identification accuracy and response latency: The unruly 10–12-second rule. *Journal of Experimental Psychology: Applied, 10*, 139–147.
45. Dunning, D., & Stern, L. B. (1994). Distinguishing accurate from inaccurate identifications via inquiries about decision processes. *Journal of Personality and Social Psychology, 67*, 818–835.
46. Sauerland, M., & Sporer, S. L. (2009). Fast and confident: Postdicting eyewitness identification accuracy in a field study. *Journal of Experimental Psychology: Applied, 15*, 46–62.
47. Wells, G. L., & Luus, C. A. E. (1990). Police lineups as experiments: Social methodology as a framework for properly conducted lineups. *Personality and Social Psychology Bulletin, 16*, 106–117.
48. Wells, G. L., & Turtle, J. W. (1986). Eyewitness identification: The importance of lineup models. *Psychological Bulletin, 99*, 320–329.
49. Luus, C. A. E., & Wells, G. L. (1991). Eyewitness identification and the selection of distractors for lineups. *Law and Human Behavior, 15*, 43–57.
50. Clark, S. E., & Tunnicliff, J. L. (2001). Selecting lineup foils in eyewitness identification: Experimental control and real-world simulation. *Law and Human Behavior, 25*, 199–216.
51. Lindsay, R. C. L., & Wells, G. L. (1980). What price justice? Exploring the relationship between lineup fairness and identification accuracy. *Law and Human Behavior, 4*, 303–314.

52. Luus, C. A. E., & Wells, G. L. (1991). Eyewitness identification and the selection of distractors for lineups. *Law and Human Behavior, 15,* 43–57.
53. Fitzgerald, R. J., Price, H. L., Oriet, C., & Charman, S. D. (2013). The effect of suspect-filler similarity on eyewitness identification decisions: A meta-analysis. *Psychology, Public Policy, and Law, 19,* 151–164.
54. Charman, S. D., Wells, G. L., & Joy, S. W. (2011). The dud effect: Adding highly dissimilar fillers increases confidence in lineup identifications. *Law and Human Behavior, 35,* 479–500.
55. Wells, G. L. (1993). What do we know about eyewitness identification? *American Psychologist, 48,* 553–571.
56. Carlson, C. A., Jones, A. R., Whittington, J. E., Locamyeir, R. F., Carlson, M. A., & Wooten, A. R. (2019). Lineup fairness: Propitious heterogeneity and the diagnostic feature-detection hypothesis. *Cognitive Research: Principles and Implications,* 4:2.
57. Fitzgerald, R. J., Oriet, C., & Price, H. L. (2015). Suspect filler similarity in eyewitness lineups: A literature review and a novel methodology. *Law and Human Behavior, 39,* 62–74.
58. Bergold, A. N., & Heaton, P. (2018). Does filler database size influence identification accuracy? *Law and Human Behavior, 42,* 227–243.
59. Steblay, N. M. (1997). Social influence in eyewitness recall: A meta-analytic review of lineup instruction effects. *Law and Human Behavior, 21,* 283–297.
60. Clark, S. E. (2005). A re-examination of the effects of biased lineup instructions in eyewitness identification. *Law and Human Behavior, 29,* 395–424.
61. Quinlivan, D. S., Neuschatz, J. S., Cutler, B. L., Wells, G. L., McClung, J., & Harker, D. L. (2012). Do pre-admonition suggestions moderate the effect of unbiased lineup instructions? *Legal and Criminological Psychology, 17,* 165–176.
62. Rosenthal, R. (2002). Covert communication in classrooms, clinics, courtrooms, and cubicles. *American Psychologist, 57,* 839–849.
63. Clark, S. E., Brower, G. L., Rosenthal, R., Hicks, J. M., & Moreland, M. B. (2013). Lineup administrator influences on eyewitness identification and eyewitness confidence. *Journal of Applied Research in Memory and Cognition, 2,* 158–165.
64. Haw, R. M., & Fisher, R. P. (2004). Effects of administrator-witness contact on eyewitness identification accuracy. *Journal of Applied Psychology, 89,* 1106–1112.
65. Charman, S. D., & Quiroz, V. (2016). Blind sequential lineup administration reduces both false identifications and confidence in those false identifications. *Law and Human Behavior, 40,* 477–487.
66. Douglass, A. B., Smith, C., & Fraser-Thill, R. (2005). A problem with double-blind photospread procedures: Photospread administrators use one eyewitness's confidence to influence the identification of another eyewitness. *Law and Human Behavior, 29,* 543–562.
67. Zimmerman, D. M., Chorn, J. A., Rhead, L. M., Evelo, A. J., & Kovera, M. B. (2017). Memory strength and lineup presentation moderate effects of administrator influence on mistaken identifications. *Journal of Experimental Psychology: Applied, 23,* 460–473.
68. Greathouse, S. M., & Kovera, M. B. (2009). Instruction bias and lineup presentation moderate the effects of administrator knowledge on eyewitness identification. *Law and Human Behavior, 33,* 70–82.
69. Kovera, M. B., & Evelo, A. J. (2017). The case for double-blind administration. *Psychology, Public Policy, and Law,* 421–437.
70. Garrioch, L., & Brimacombe, C. A. E. (2001). Lineup administrators' expectations: Their impact on eyewitness confidence. *Law and Human Behavior, 25,* 299–315.
71. Wells, G. L., & Bradfield, A. L. (1998). "Good, you identified the suspect": Feedback to eyewitnesses distorts their reports of the witnessing experience. *Journal of Applied Psychology, 83,* 360–376.
72. Wells, G. L., Olson, E. A., & Charman, S. D. (2003). Distorted retrospective eyewitness reports as functions of feedback and delay. *Journal of Experimental Psychology: Applied, 9,* 42–52.
73. Semmler, C., Brewer, N., & Wells, G. L. (2004). Effects of postidentification feedback on eyewitness identification and nonidentification confidence. *Journal of Applied Psychology, 89,* 334–346.
74. Erickson, W. B., Lampinen, J. M., Wooten, A., Wetmore, S., & Neuschatz, J. (2016). When snitches corroborate: Effects of post-identification feedback from a potentially compromised source. *Psychiatry, Psychology and Law, 23,* 148–160.
75. Mote, P. M., Neuschatz, J. S., Bornstein, B. H., Wetmore, S. A., & Key, K. N. (2018). Secondary confessions as post-identification feedback: How jailhouse informant testimony can alter eyewitnesses' identification decisions. *Journal of Police and Criminal Psychology.* Online publication in advance of print.
76. Neuschatz, J. S., Lawson, D. S., Fairless, A. H., Powers, R. A., Neuschatz, J. S., Goodsell, C. A., & Toglia, M. P. (2007). The mitigating effects of suspicion on post-identification feedback and on retrospective eyewitness memory. *Law and Human Behavior, 31,* 231–247.
77. Manson v. Braithwaite, 1977, 432 U.S. 98.
78. Steblay, N. K., Wells, G. L., & Douglass, A. B. (2014). The eyewitness post identification effect 15 years later: Theoretical and policy implications. *Psychology, Public Policy, and Law, 20,* 1–18.
79. Wells, G. L., & Quinlivan, D. S. (2009). Suggestive eyewitness identification procedures and the Supreme Court's reliability test in light of eyewitness science: 30 years later. *Law and Human Behavior, 33,* 1–24.
80. Smalarz, L., & Wells, G. L. (2014). Post-identification feedback to eyewitnesses impairs evaluators' abilities to discriminate between accurate and mistaken testimony. *Law and Human Behavior, 38,* 194–202.
81. Wells, G. L., Kovera, M. B., Douglass, A. B., Brewer, N., Meissner, C. A., & Wixted, J. (2020). Policy and procedure recommendations for the collection and preservation of eyewitness identification evidence. *Law and Human Behavior.*
82. Clark, S. E. (2012). Costs and benefits of eyewitness identification reform: Psychological science and public policy. *Perspectives on Psychological Science, 7,* 238–259.
83. Wells, G. L., Steblay N. K., & Dysart, J. E. (2012). Eyewitness identification reforms: Are suggestiveness-induced hits and guesses true hits? *Perspectives on Psychological Science, 7,* 264–271.
84. Thompson-Cannino, J., Cotton, R., & Torneo, E. (2009). *Picking Cotton: Our memoir of injustice and redemption.* New York: St. Martin's Press.
85. Associated Press. Troy Davis execution fuels eyewitness ID debate. (2011, September 27). *USA Today.* Retrieved from http://www.usatoday.com/news/nation/story/2011-09-27/troy-davis-eyewitness-testimony/50563754/1
86. Loftus, E. (1974). Reconstructing memory: The incredible eyewitness. *Psychology Today, 8*(7), 116–119.
87. Desmarais, S. L., & Read, J. D. (2011). After 30 years, what do we know about what jurors know? A meta-analytic review of lay knowledge regarding eyewitness factors. *Law and Human Behavior, 35,* 200–210.
88. Brigham, J. C., & Bothwell, R. K. (1983). The ability of prospective jurors to estimate the accuracy of eyewitness identification. *Law and Human Behavior, 7,* 19–30.
89. McAuliff, B. D., & Kovera, M. B. (2007). Estimating the effects of misleading information on witness accuracy: Can experts tell jurors something they don't already know? *Applied Cognitive Psychology, 21,* 849–870.
90. Abshire, J., & Bornstein, B. J. (2003). Juror sensitivity to the cross-race effect. *Law and Human Behavior, 27,* 471–480.
91. Bradfield, A., & McQuiston, D. E. (2004). When does evidence of eyewitness confidence inflation affect judgments in a criminal trial? *Law and Human Behavior, 28,* 369–387.
92. Douglass, A. B., Neuschatz, J. S., Imrich, J., & Wilkinson, M. (2010). Does post-identification feedback affect evaluations of eyewitness testimony and identification procedures? *Law and Human Behavior, 34,* 282–294.
93. Smalarz, L., & Wells, G. L. (2014). Post-identification feedback to eyewitnesses impairs evaluators' abilities to discriminate between accurate and mistaken testimony. *Law and Human Behavior, 38,* 194–202.
94. Cutler, B. L., Penrod, S. D., & Dexter, H. R. (1989). The eyewitness, the expert psychologist, and the jury. *Law and Human Behavior, 13,* 311–332.
95. Commonwealth v. Gomes, 470 Mass. 352 (2015).
96. State v. Henderson, 27 A. 3d 872 (N. J. 2011).
97. State v. Henderson, 27 A. 3d 872 (N. J. 2011).
98. Dillon, M. K., Jones, A. M., Bergold, A. N., Hui, C. Y. T., & Penrod, S. D. (2017). *Henderson* instructions: Do they enhance evidence evaluation? *Journal of Forensic Psychology Research and Practice, 17,* 1–24.
99. Jones, A. M., Bergold, A. N., Dillon, M. K., & Penrod, S. D. (2017). Comparing the effectiveness of *Henderson* instructions and expert testimony: Which safeguard improves jurors' evaluations of eyewitness evidence? *Journal of Experimental Criminology, 13,* 29–52.
100. Jones, A. M., & Penrod, S. (2018). Improving the effectiveness of the *Henderson* instruction safeguard against unreliable eyewitness identification. *Psychology, Crime & Law, 24,* 177–193.
101. Devenport, J. L., Stinson, V., Cutler, B. L., & Kravitz, D. A. (2002). How effective are the cross-examination and expert testimony safeguards? Jurors' perceptions of the suggestiveness and fairness of biased lineup procedures. *Journal of Applied Psychology, 87,* 1042–1054.
102. Devenport, J. L., & Cutler, B. L. (2004). Impact of defense-only and opposing eyewitness experts on juror judgments. *Law and Human Behavior, 28,* 569–576.
103. Leippe, M. R., Eisenstadt, D., Rauch, S. M., & Seib, H. M. (2004). Timing of eyewitness expert testimony, jurors' need for cognition, and case strength as determinants of trial verdicts. *Journal of Applied Psychology, 89,* 524–541.
104. Kressel, N. J., & Kressel, D. R. (2002). *Stack and sway.* Boulder, CO: Westview Press.
105. Davis, D., & Loftus, E. F. (2006). Psychologists in the forensic world. In S. I. Donaldson, D. E. Berger, & K. Pezdek (Eds.), *Applied psychology: New frontiers and rewarding careers* (pp. 171–200). Mahwah, NJ: Lawrence Erlbaum Associates.
106. Fulero, S. M., & Penrod, S. D. (1990a). Attorney jury selection folklore: What do they think and how can psychologists help? *Forensic Reports, 3,* 233–259.
107. Blue, L. A. (1991). Jury selection in a civil case. *Trial Lawyers Quarterly, 21,* 11–25.
108. Marques, J. M., Abrams, D., Páez, D., & Martinez-Taboada, C. (1998). The role of categorization and in-group norms in judgments of groups and their members. *Journal of Personality and Social Psychology, 75,* 976–988.
109. Culhane, S. E., Hosch, H. M., & Weaver, W. G. (2004). Crime victims serving as jurors: Is there bias present? *Law and Human Behavior, 28,* 649–659.
110. Culhane, S. E., Hosch, H. M., & Weaver, W. G. (2004). Crime victims serving as jurors: Is there bias present? *Law and Human Behavior, 28,* 649–659.
111. Taylor, T. S., & Hosch, H. M. (2004). An examination of jury verdicts for evidence of a similarity-leniency effect, an out-group punitiveness effect, or a black sheep effect. *Law and Human Behavior, 28,* 587–598.
112. Kerr, N. L., Hymes, R. W., Anderson, A. B., & Weathers, J. E. (1995). Defendant-juror similarity and mock juror judgments. *Law and Human Behavior, 19,* 545–567.

113. Otis, C. C., Greathouse, S. M., Kennard, J. B., & Kovera, M. B. (2014). Hypothesis testing in attorney-conducted voir dire. *Law and Human Behavior, 38,* 392–404.
114. Batson v. Kentucky, 106 S.Ct. 1712 (1986).
115. J.E.B. v. Alabama *ex rel.* T.B., 114 S.Ct. 1419 (1994).
116. Sommers, S. R., & Norton, M. I. (2007). Race-based judgments, race-neutral justifications: Experimental examination of peremptory use and the Batson challenge procedure. *Law and Human Behavior, 31,* 261–273.
117. Norton, M. I., Sommers, S. R., & Brauner, S. (2007). Bias in jury selection: Justifying prohibited peremptory challenges. *Journal of Behavioral Decision Making, 20,* 467–479. doi: 10.1002/bdm.571
118. Kovera, M. B., & Cutler, B. L. (2013). *Jury selection.* New York: Oxford University Press.
119. Wenger, A. A., & Bornstein, B. H. (2006). The effects of victim's substance use and relationship closeness on mock jurors' judgments in an acquaintance rape case. *Sex Roles, 54,* 547–555.
120. Quas, J. A., Bottoms, B. L., Haegerich, T. M., & Nysse-Carris, K. L. (2002). Effects of victim, defendant, and juror gender on decisions in child sexual assault cases. *Journal of Applied Social Psychology, 32,* 1993–2021.
121. Schuller, R. A., & Hastings, P. A. (1996). Trials of battered women who kill: The impact of alternative forms of expert evidence. *Law and Human Behavior, 20,* 167–187.
122. Bottoms, B. L., Kalder, A. K., Stevenson, M. C., Oudekerk, B. A., Wiley, T. R., & Perona, A. (2011). Gender differences in jurors' perceptions of infanticide involving disabled and non-disabled infant victims. *Child Abuse & Neglect, 35,* 127–141.
123. Bègue, L., & Bastounis, M. (2003). Two spheres of belief in justice: Extensive support for the bidimensional model of belief in a just world. *Journal of Personality, 71,* 435–463.
124. Narby, D. J., Cutler, B. L., & Moran, G. (1993). A meta-analysis of the association between authoritarianism and jurors' perceptions of defendant culpability. *Journal of Applied Psychology, 78,* 3442.
125. Kravitz, D. A., Cutler, B. L., & Brock, P. (1993). Reliability and validity of the original and revised Legal Attitudes Questionnaire. *Law and Human Behavior, 17,* 661–667.
126. Kovera, M. B., & Cutler, B. L. (2013). *Jury selection.* New York: Oxford University Press.
127. Moran, G., Cutler, B. L., & De Lisa, A. (1994). Attitudes toward tort reform, scientific jury selection, and juror bias: Verdict inclination in criminal and civil trials. *Law and Psychology Review, 18,* 309–328.
128. Crocker, C. B., & Kovera, M. B. (2010). The effects of rehabilitative voir dire on juror bias and decision making. *Law and Human Behavior, 34,* 212–226.
129. Moran, G., Cutler, B. L., & Loftus, E. F. (1990). Jury selection in major controlled substance trials: The need for extended voir dire. *Forensic Reports, 3,* 331–348.
130. O'Neil, K. M., Patry, M. W., & Penrod, S. D. (2004). Exploring the effects of attitudes toward the death penalty on capital sentencing verdicts. *Psychology, Public Policy, and Law, 10,* 443–470.
131. Moran, G., & Comfort, J. C. (1986). Neither "tentative nor fragmentary": Verdict preference of impaneled felony jurors as a function of attitude toward capital punishment. *Journal of Applied Psychology, 71,* 146–155.
132. Fitzgerald, R., & Ellsworth, P. C. (1984). Due process vs. crime control: Death qualification and jury attitudes. *Law and Human Behavior, 8,* 31–51.
133. Haney, C., Hurtado, A., & Vega, L. (1994). Modern death qualification: New data on its biasing effects. *Law and Human Behavior, 18,* 619–633.
134. Moran, G., & Comfort, J. C. (1986). Neither "tentative nor fragmentary": Verdict preference of impaneled felony jurors as a function of attitude toward capital punishment. *Journal of Applied Psychology, 71,* 146–155.
135. Cowan, C. L., Thompson, W. C., & Ellsworth, P. C. (1984). The effects of death qualification on jurors: Predisposition to convict and on the quality of deliberation. *Law and Human Behavior, 8,* 53–79.
136. Allen, M., Mabry, E., & McKelton, D. (1998). Impact of juror attitudes about the death penalty on juror evaluations of guilt and punishment: A meta-analysis. *Law and Human Behavior, 22,* 715–731.
137. Filkins, J. W., Smith, C. M., & Tindale, R. S. (1998). An evaluation of the biasing effects of death qualification: A meta-analytic/computer simulation approach. In R. S. Tindale et al. (Eds.), *Theory and research on small groups.* New York: Plenum Press.
138. Nietzel, M. T., McCarthy, D. M., & Kern, M. J. (1999). Juries: The current state of the empirical literature. In R. Roesch, S. D. Hart, & J. R. P. Ogloff (Eds.), *Psychology and law: The state of the discipline* (pp. 23–52). Dordrecht, Netherlands: Kluwer Academic Publishers.
139. Cowan, C. L., Thompson, W. C., & Ellsworth, P. C. (1984). The effects of death qualification on jurors: Predisposition to convict and on the quality of deliberation. *Law and Human Behavior, 8,* 53–79.
140. Steblay, N. M., Besirevic, J., Fulero, S. M., & Jimenez-Lorente, B. (1999). The effects of pretrial publicity on juror verdicts: A meta-analytic review. *Law and Human Behavior, 23,* 219–235.
141. Daftary-Kapur, T., Penros, S. D., O'Connor, M., & Wallace, B. (2014). Examining pretrial publicity in a shadow jury paradigm: Issues of slant, quantity, persistence and generalizability. *Law and Human Behavior, 38,* 462–477.
142. Bakhshay, S., & Haney, C. (2018). The media's impact on the right to a fair trial: A content analysis of pretrial publicity in capital cases. *Psychology, Public Policy, and Law, 24,* 326–340.
143. Dexter, H. R., Cutler, B. L., & Moran, G. (1992). A test of voir dire as a remedy for the prejudicial effects of pretrial publicity. *Journal of Applied Social Psychology, 22,* 819–832.
144. Crocker, C. B. (2010). *An investigation of the psychological processes involved in juror rehabilitation.* (Unpublished doctoral dissertation.) The City University of New York.
145. Ruva, C. L., McEvoy, C., & Bryant, J. B. (2007). Effects of pre-trial publicity and jury deliberation on juror bias and source memory errors. *Applied Cognitive Psychology, 21,* 45–67.
146. Ruva, C. L., & Guenther, C. C. (2015). From the shadows into the light: How pretrial publicity and deliberation affect mock jurors' decisions, impressions, and memory. *Law and Human Behavior, 39,* 294–310.
147. Ruva, C. L., & LeVasseur, M. A. (2012). Behind closed doors: The effect of pretrial publicity on jury deliberations. *Psychology, Crime & Law, 18,* 431–452.
148. Ruva, C. L., & Guenther, C. C. (2015). From the shadows into the light: How pretrial publicity and deliberation affect mock jurors' decisions, impressions, and memory. *Law and Human Behavior, 39,* 294–310.
149. Steblay, N. M., Besirevic, J., Fulero, S. M., & Jimenez-Lorente, B. (1999). The effects of pretrial publicity on juror verdicts: A meta-analytic review. *Law and Human Behavior, 23,* 219–235.
150. Studebaker, C. A., Robbennolt, J. K., Pathak-Sharma, M. K., & Penrod, S. D. (2000). Assessing pretrial publicity effects: Integrating content analytic results. *Law and Human Behavior, 24,* 317–336.
151. Steblay, N. M., Besirevic, J., Fulero, S. M., & Jimenez-Lorente, B. (1999). The effects of pretrial publicity on juror verdicts: A meta-analytic review. *Law and Human Behavior, 23,* 219–235.
152. Blackstone, W. (1783). *Commentaries on the Laws of England* (9th ed., Vol. 4, p. 358). London: Strahan, Cadell & Prince.
153. Loftus, E. F., & Ketcham, K. (1994). *The myth of repressed memory.* New York: St. Martin's Press.
154. Alpert, J. L., Brown, L. S., & Courtois, C. A. (1998). Symptomatic clients and memories of childhood abuse: What the trauma and child sexual abuse literature tells us. *Psychology, Public Policy, and Law, 4,* 941–995.
155. Ornstein, P. A., Ceci, S. J., & Loftus, E. F. (1998). Adult recollections of childhood abuse: Cognitive and developmental perspectives. *Psychology, Public Policy, and Law, 7,* 1025–1051.
156. Ornstein, P. A., Ceci, S. J., & Loftus, E. F. (1998). Adult recollections of childhood abuse: Cognitive and developmental perspectives. *Psychology, Public Policy, and Law, 7,* 1025–1051.

MODULE E
Applying Social Psychology to the Environment

1. Viek, C., & Steg, L. (2007). Human behavior and environmental sustainability: problems, driving forces and research topics. *Journal of Social Issues, 63,* 1–19.
2. Kates, R. W., Clark, W. C., Corell, R., Hall, J. M., Jaeger, C. C., Lowe, I., McCarthy, J. J., Schellnhuber, H. J., Bolin, B., Dickson, N. M., Faucheux, S., Gallopin, G. C., Grubler, A., Huntley, B., Jager, J., Jodha, N. S., Kasperson, R. E., Mabogunje, A., Matson, P., Mooney, H., Moore, B., III, O'Riordan, T., & Svedin, U. (2001). Sustainability science. *Science, 292,* 641–642.
3. Nickerson, R. S. (2003). *Psychology and environmental change.* Mahway, NJ: Erlbaum.
4. Hardin, G. (1968). The tragedy of the commons. *Science, 162,* 1243–1248.
5. Platt, J. (1973). Social traps. *American Psychologist, 28,* 641–651.
6. Martichuski, D. K., & Bell, P. A. (1991). Reward, punishment, privatization, and moral suasion in a commons dilemma. *Journal of Applied Social Psychology, 21,* 1356–1369.
7. Jorgenson, D. O., & Papciak, A. S. (1981). The effects of communication, resource feedback, and identifiability on behavior in a simulated commons. *Journal of Experimental Social Psychology, 17,* 373–385.
8. Kramer, R. M., & Brewer, M. B. (1984). Effects of group identity on resource use in a simulated commons dilemma. *Journal of Personality and Social Psychology, 46,* 1044–1057.
9. Twohey, R. J. (2018). Strategically integrating human dimensions into marine conservation decision making. UC Santa Barbara. ProQuest ID: Twohey_ucsb_0035D_14094. Merritt ID: ark:/13030/m58q0zgz. Retrieved from https://escholarship.org/uc/item/6m64p2wg
10. Klein, C., McKinnon, M. C., Twohey-Wright, N. Possingham, H. P., & Halpern, B. S. (2015). Social equity and the probability of success of biodiversity conservation. *Global Environmental Change, 35,* 299–306.
11. Ansari, S., Wijen, F., & Gray, B. (2013). Constructing a climate change logic: An institutional perspective on the "tragedy of the commons." *Organization Science, 24,* 1014–1040.
12. Calhoun, J. B. (1962). Population density and social pathology. *Scientific American, 206,* 139–148.
13. Schwab, J., Nadeau, S. E., & Warheit, G. J. (1979). Crowding and mental health. *Pavlovian Journal of Biological Science, 14,* 226–233.
14. Saegert, S., MacIntosh, E., & West, S. (1975). Two studies of crowding in urban public spaces. *Environment and Behavior, 1,* 159–184.
15. Schmidt, C. (1969). Urban crime areas: Part I. *American Sociological Review, 25,* 527–542.
16. Evans, G. W., & Lepore, S. J. (1993). Household crowding and social support: A quasi-experimental analysis. *Journal of Personality and Social Psychology, 65,* 308–316.
17. Sundstrom, E. (1978). Crowding as a sequential process: Review of research on the effects of population density on humans. In A. Baum & Y. M.

Epstein (Eds.), *Human response to crowding* (pp. 31–116). Hillsdale, NJ: Erlbaum.

18. Baum, A., & Paulus, P. B. (1987). Crowding. In D. Stokols & I. Altman (Eds.), *Handbook of environmental psychology* (Vol. 1, pp. 533–570). New York: Wiley-Interscience.

19. Benson, G. P., & Zieman, G. L. (1981). *The relationship of weather to children's behavior problems.* Unpublished manuscript, Colorado State University, Fort Collins, CO.

20. Bell, P. A., & Greene, T. C. (1982). Thermal stress: Physiological comfort, performance, and social effects of hot and cold environments. In G. W. Evans (Ed.), *Environmental stress* (pp. 75–105). London: Cambridge University Press.

21. Anderson, C. A., Bushman, B. J., & Groom, R. W. (1997). Hot years and serious and deadly assault: Empirical tests of the heat hypothesis. *Journal of Personality and Social Psychology, 73,* 1213–1223.

22. Fay, T. H. (Ed.). (1991). *Noise and health.* New York: New York Academy of Medicine.

23. Cohen, S., & Spacapan, S. (1984). The social psychology of noise. In D. M. Jones & A. J. Chapman (Eds.), *Noise and society* (pp. 221–245). New York: Wiley.

24. Matthews, K. E., & Canon, L. K. (1975). Environmental noise level as a determinant of helping behavior. *Journal of Personality and Social Psychology, 32,* 571–577.

25. Basner, M., Babisch, W., Davis, A., Brink, M., Clark, C., Janssen, S., & Stansfeld, S. (2014). Auditory and non-auditory effects of noise on health. *Lancet, 383,* 1325–1332.

26. Evans, G. W., Jacobs, S. V., Dooley, D., & Catalano, R. (1987). The interaction of stressful life events and chronic strains on community mental health. *American Journal of Community Psychology, 15,* 23–34.

27. Miller, P. V. (2002). The authority and limitation of polls. In J. Manza, F. L. Cook, & B. I. Page (Eds.), *Navigating public opinion* (pp. 221–231). New York: Oxford University Press.

28. Engelman, R., Halweil, B., & Nierenberg, D. (2002). Rethinking population, improving lives. In C. Flavin, H. French, & G. Gardner (Eds.), *State of the world 2002: A Worldwatch Institute report on progress toward a sustainable society* (p. 127). New York: Norton.

29. Quarantelli, E. L. (1998). *What is a disaster?* New York: Routledge.

30. Bland, S. H., O'Leary, E. S., Farinaro, E., Fabrizio, J., & Trevisan, M. (1996). Long-term psychological effects of natural disasters. *Psychosomatic Medicine, 58,* 18–24.

31. Tichener, J. L., & Kapp, F. T. (1976). Family and character change at Buffalo Creek. *American Journal of Psychiatry, 33*(3), 295–299.

32. Helton, W. S., Head, J., & Kemp, S. (2011). Natural disaster induced cognitive disruption: Impacts on action slips. *Consciousness and Cognition, 20,* 1732–1737.

33. Union of Concerned Scientists. (1993). *World scientists warning to humanity.* Cambridge, MA: Union of Concerned Scientists.

34. Kates, R. W. (1994). Sustaining life on the earth. *Scientific American, 271*(4), 114–122.

35. Ehrenfeld, D. (1981). *The arrogance of humanism.* New York: Oxford University Press.

36. Hornsey, M. J., Harris, E. A., Bain, P. G. & Fielding, K. S. (2016). Meta-analyses of the determinants and outcomes of belief in climate change. *Nature Climate Change, 6,* 622–626.

37. van Boven, L., Ehret, P. J., & Sherman, D. K. (2018). Psychological barriers to bipartisan public support for climate policy. *Perspectives on Psychological Science, 13,* 492–507.

38. Stanley, S. K., & Wilson, M. S. (2019). Meta-analysing the association between social dominance orientation, authoritarianism, and attitudes on the environment and climate change. *Journal of Environmental Psychology, 61,* 46–56.

39. Panno, A., Giacomantonio, M., Carrus, G., Maricchiolo, F., Pirchio, S., Mannetti, L. (2017). Mindfulness, pro-environmental behavior, and belief in climate change: The mediating role of social dominance. *Environment and Behavior, 50,* 864–888.

40. Sussenbach, S., & Kameleitner, B. (2016). Psychological ownership as a facilitator of sustainable behaviors. In J. Peck and S. Shu (Eds.), *Psychological Ownership.* New York: Springer.

41. Clark, W. C. (1989). Managing planet earth. *Scientific American, 261*(3), 47–54.

42. Kraft, M. (2006). *Environmental policies and politics.* Englewood Cliffs, NJ: Prentice Hall.

43. Midden, C., Kaiser, F., & McCalley, T. (2007). Technology's four roles in understanding individuals' conservation of natural resources. *Journal of Social Issues, 63,*155–174.

44. Stokols, D. (1972) On the distinction between density and crowding: Some implications for future research. *Psychological Review, 79,* 275–277.

45. Sherrod, D. R. (1974). Crowding, perceived control, and behavioral aftereffects. *Journal of Applied Social Psychology, 4,* 171–186.

46. Schopler, J., & Stockdale, J. (1977). An interference analysis of crowding. *Environmental Psychology and Nonverbal Behavior, 1,* 81–88.

47. Paulus, P. B., & Matthews, R. (1980). Crowding, attribution, and task performance. *Basic and Applied Social Psychology, 1,* 3–13.

48. Saegert, S. (1978). High density environments: Their personal and social consequences. In A. Baum & Y. M. Epstein (Eds.), *Human response to crowding* (pp. 259–276). Hillsdale, NJ: Erlbaum.

49. Gutkowski, S., Ginath, Y. & Guttmann, F. (1992). Improving psychiatric environments through minimal architectural change. *Hospital and Community Psychiatry, 43,* 920–923.

50. Langer, E. J., & Saegert, S. (1977). Crowding and cognitive control. *Journal of Personality and Social Psychology, 35,* 175–182.

51. Novelli, D., Drury, J., Reicher, S., & Stott, C. (2013). Crowdedness mediates the effect of social identification on positive emotion in a crowd: A survey of two crowd events. *PLoS ONE, 8*(11), 1–7.

52. Hayduk, L. A. (1994). Personal space: Understanding the simplex model. *Journal of Nonverbal Behavior, 18,* 245–260.

53. Gifford, R. (2017). *Applying social psychology to the environment.* Thousand Oaks, CA: Sage.

54. Edwards, D. J. A. (1972). Approaching the unfamiliar: A study of human interaction distances. *Journal of Behavioral Sciences, 1,* 249–250.

55. Latta, R. M. (1978). Relation of status incongruous to personal space. *Personality and Social Psychology Bulletin, 4,* 143–146.

56. Kaya, N., & Erkip, F. E. (1999). Invasion of personal space under the condition of short-term crowding: A case study on an automatic teller machine. *Journal of Environmental Psychology, 19,* 183–189.

57. Aiello, J. R. (1987). Human spatial behavior. In D. Stokols & I. Altman (Eds.), *Handbook of environmental psychology* (Vol. 1, pp. 505–531). New York: Wiley.

58. Balogun, S. K. (1991). Personal space as affected by religions of the approaching and the approached people. *Indian Journal of Behaviour, 15,* 45–50.

59. Barrios, B. A., Corbitt, L. C., Estes, J. P., & Topping, J. S. (1976). Effect of social stigma on interpersonal distance. *The Psychological Record, 26,* 342–348.

60. Dean, L. M., Willis, F. N., & Hewitt, J. (1975). Initial interaction distance among individuals equal and unequal in military rank. *Journal of Personality and Social Psychology, 32,* 294–299.

61. Remland, M. S., Jones, T. S., & Brinkman, H. (1995). Interpersonal distance, body orientation, and touch: Effects of culture, gender, and age. *Journal of Social Psychology, 135,* 281–297.

62. Barnard, W. A., & Bell, P. A. (1982). An unobtrusive apparatus for measuring interpersonal distance. *Journal of General Psychology, 107,* 85–90.

63. Mulligan, R., Burmood, C., O'Hara, S., & Warren, C. (2004). Personal space preferences: The role of mortality salience and affiliation motivation. *Journal of Psychological Inquiry, 9*(1), 14–20.

64. Duke, M. P., & Wilson, J. (1973). The measurement of interpersonal distance in pre-school children. *Journal of Genetic Psychology, 123,* 361–362.

65. Hewitt, J., & Alqahtani, M. A. (2003). Differences between Saudi and U.S. students in reaction to same- and mixed-sex intimacy by others. *Journal of Social Psychology, 143,* 233–242.

66. Smith, R. J., & Knowles, E. S. (1979). Affective and cognitive mediators of reactions to spatial invasions. *Journal of Experimental Social Psychology, 15,* 437–452.

67. Murphy-Berman, V., & Berman, J. (1978). Importance of choice and sex invasions of personal space. *Personality and Social Psychology Bulletin, 4,* 424–428.

68. Evans, G. W., & Howard, H. R. B. (1972). A methodological investigation of personal space. In W. J. Mitchell (Ed.), *Environmental design: Research and practice,* Proceedings of EDRA3/ AR8 Conference. University of California, Los Angeles, CA.

69. Konecni, V. J., Libuser, L., Morton, H., & Ebbesen, E. G. (1975). Effects of a violation of personal space on escape and helping response. *Journal of Experimental Social Psychology, 11,* 288–299.

70. Brown, B. (1987). Territoriality. In D. Stokols & I. Altman (Eds.), *Handbook of environmental psychology* (Vol. 1, pp. 505–531). New York: Wiley-Interscience.

71. Wortley, R., & McFarlane, M. (2011). The role of territoriality in crime prevention: A field experiment. *Security Journal, 24,* 149–156.

72. Harris, P. B., & Brown, B. B. (1996). The home and identity display: Interpreting resident territoriality from home exteriors. *Journal of Environmental Psychology, 16,* 187–203.

73. Childress, H. (2004). Teenagers, territories and the appropriation of space. *Childhood, 11,* 195–205.

74. Brown, B. B., & Werner, C. M. (1985). Social cohesiveness, territoriality, and holiday decorations: The influence of cul-de-sacs. *Environment and Behavior, 17,* 539–565.

75. Taylor, R. B., Gottfredson, S. D., & Brower, S. (1981). Territorial cognitions and social climate in urban neighborhoods. *Basic and Applied Social Psychology, 2,* 289–303.

76. Reinsch, J., & Spotanski, C. (2005). Human territoriality: The effects of status on personalization and demarcation. *Journal of Psychological Inquiry 10*(1), 16–21.

77. Miller, R. L. (1979). Middle class residents in ghetto housing: Attitudes & behavior. *Proceedings of the International Conference on Environmental Psychology,* Guildford, England, 75.

78. Kaya, N., & Weber, M. J. (2003). Cross-cultural differences in the perception of crowding and privacy regulation: American and Turkish students. *Journal of Environmental Psychology, 23,* 301–309.

79. Miller, R. L. (2013). Territoriality. In K. Keith (Ed.), *Encyclopedia of cross-cultural psychology* (pp. 1276–1278). New York, NY: Wiley-Blackwell.

80. Etherington, J. (2010). Nationalism, territoriality, and national territorial belonging. *Papers. Revista de Sociología, 95,* 321–339.

81. DeScioli, P., & Wilson, B. J. (2011). The territorial foundations of human property. *Evolution and Human Behavior, 32,* 297–304.

82. Altman, I., Nelson, P. A., & Lett, E. E. (1972, Spring). The ecology of home environments. *Catalog of Selected Documents in Psychology* (No. 150).

83. Ley, D., & Cybriwsky, R. (1974). The spatial ecology of stripped cars. *Environment and Behavior, 6,* 53–68.

84. Martindale, D. A. (1971). Territorial dominance behavior in dyadic verbal interactions. *Proceedings of the Annual Convention of the American Psychological Association, 6,* 305–306.

85. Hall, E. T. (1976). *Beyond culture.* New York, NY: Anchor Books.

86. Sommers, P., & Moos, R. (1976). The weather and human behavior. In R. H. Moos (Ed.), *The human context: Environmental determinants of behavior* (pp. 73–107). New York: Wiley.
87. Sommers, P., & Moos, R. (1976). The weather and human behavior. In R. H. Moos (Ed.), *The human context: Environmental determinants of behavior* (pp. 73–107). New York: Wiley.
88. Hsiang, S. M., Burke, M., & Miquel, E. (2013). Quantifying the influence of climate on human conflict. *Science, 341*, 1212–1226.
89. Green, D. M., & Fidell, S. (1991). Variability in the criterion for reporting annoyance in community noise surveys. *Journal of the Acoustical Society of America, 89*, 234–243.
90. Szalma, J. L., & Hancock, P. A. (2011). Noise effects on human performance: A meta-analytic synthesis. *Psychological Bulletin, 137*, 682–707.
91. Basner, M., Babisch, W., Davis, A., Brink, M., Clark, C., Janssen, S., & Stansfeld, S. (2014). Auditory and non-auditory effects of noise on health. *Lancet, 383*, 1325–1332.
92. Glass, D. C., & Singer, J. E. (1972). *Urban stress: Experiments on noise and social stressors*. New York: Academic Press.
93. Evans, G. W., & Stecker, R. (2004). The motivational consequences of environmental stress. *Journal of Environmental Psychology, 24*, 143–165.
94. Basner, M., Babisch, W., Davis, A., Brink, M., Clark, C., Janssen, S., & Stansfeld, S. (2014). Auditory and non-auditory effects of noise on health. *Lancet, 383*, 1325–1332.
95. Cohen, S. (1978). Environmental load and the allocation of attention. In A. Baum, J. S. Singer, & S. Valins (Eds.), *Advances in environmental psychology* (Vol. 1, pp. 1–29). Hillsdale, NJ: Erlbaum.
96. Kenrick, D. T., & Johnson, G. A. (1979). Interpersonal attraction in aversive environments. A problem for the classical conditioning paradigm. *Journal of Personality and Social Psychology, 87*, 572–579.
97. Sundstrom, E., Town, J. P., Rice, R. W., Osborn, D. P., & Brill, M. (1994). Office noise, satisfaction, and performance. *Environment and Behavior, 26*, 195–222.
98. Staples, S. L. (1997). Public policy and environmental noise: Modeling exposure or understanding. *American Journal of Public Health, 87*, 2063–2067.
99. Basner, M., Babisch, W., Davis, A., Brink, M., Clark, C., Janssen, S., & Stansfeld, S. (2014). Auditory and non-auditory effects of noise on health. *Lancet, 383*, 1325–1332.
100. Anderson, J. O., Thundiyll, J. G., & Stobach, A. (2012). Clearing the air: A review of the effects of particulate matter air pollution on human health. *Journal of Medical Toxicology, 8*, 166–175.
101. Miller, G. T. (1990). *Living in the environment* (6th ed.). Belmont, CA: Wadsworth.
102. Guxens, M., & Sunyer, J. (2012). A review of epidemiological studies on neuropsychological effects of air pollution. *Swiss Medical Weekly, 141*, 1–7.
103. Holgate, S. T., Samet, J. M., Maynard, R. L., & Koren, H. S. (Eds.) (1999). *Air pollution and health*. San Diego: Academic Press.
104. Lewis, J., Baddeley, A. D., Bonham, K. G., & Lovett, D. (1970). Traffic pollution and mental efficiency. *Nature, 225*, 95–97.
105. Jacobs, S. V., Evans, G. W., Catalano, R., & Dooley, D. (1984). Air pollution and depressive symptomatology: Exploratory analyses of intervening psychosocial factors. *Population & Environment, 7*, 260–272.
106. Lundberg, A. (1996). Psychiatric aspects of air pollution. *Otolaryngology-Head and Neck Surgery, 114*(2), 227–231.
107. Brown, L. R. (1994). *State of the world 1994*. New York: Norton.
108. Rose, D. C., Sutherland, W. J., Amano, T., GonzálezaVaro, J. P., Robertson, R. J., Simmons, B. I., …Mukherjee, N. (2018). The major barriers to evidence-informed conservation policy and possible solutions. *Conservation Letters, 11*, e12564.
109. Schultz, P. W. (2011). Conservation means behavior. *Conservation Biology, 25*, 1080–1083.
110. Ma, Y., Dixon, G., & Hmielowski, J. D. (2019). Psychological reactance from reading basic facts on climate change: The role of prior view and political identification. *Environmental Communication, 13*, 71–86.
111. Barker, M. R., Bailey, J. S., & Lee, N. (2004). The impact of verbal prompts on child safety-belt use in shopping carts. *Journal of Applied Behavior Analysis, 37*, 527–530.
112. Geller, E. S., Winett, R. A., & Everett, P. B. (1982). *Preserving the environment: Strategies for behavior change*. New York: Pergamon.
113. Finnie, W. C. (1973). Field experiments and litter control. *Environment and Behavior, 5*, 123–143.
114. Leonard-Barton, D. (1980, September). *The role of interpersonal communication networks in the diffusion of energy conserving practices and technologies*. Paper presented at the International Conference of Consumer Behavior and Energy Policy, Banff, Alberta, Canada.
115. Florin, P., & Wandersman, A. (1983). A psychosocial perspective on neighborhood conservation. In N. R. Feimer & E. S. Geller (Eds.), *Environmental psychology: Directions and perspectives*. New York: Praeger.
116. Kohlenberg, R. J., Phillips, T., & Proctor, W. (1976). A behavioral analysis of peaking in residential electricity energy consumption. *Journal of Applied Behavior Analysis, 9*, 13–18.
117. Goldstein, N. J., Cialdini, R. B., & Griskevicius, V. (2004). *A room with a viewpoint: Using norm-based appeals to motivate conservation behaviors in a hotel setting*. Paper presented at the annual meeting of the Society for Personality and Social Psychology, Austin, TX.
118. Krzysztof, J., & Leoniak, W. (2019) The role of normative prompts and norm support cues in promoting light-switching behavior: A field study. *Journal of Environmental Psychology, 64*, 1–11.
119. Lede, E., Meleady, R., & Seger, C. R. (2019). Optimizing the influence of social norms interventions: Applying social identity insights to motivate residential water conservation. *Journal of Environmental Psychology, 62*, 105–114.
120. Abrahamse, W., Steg, L., Vlek, C., & Rothengatter, T. (2007). The effect of tailored information, goal setting, and tailored feedback on household energy use, energy-related behaviors, and behavioral antecedents. *Journal of Environmental Psychology, 27*, 265–276.
121. Baum, A., & Fleming, I. (1993). Implications of psychological research on stress and technological accidents. *American Psychologist, 48*, 665–672.
122. Drabek, T. E., & Stephenson, J. S. (1971). When disaster strikes. *Journal of Applied Social Psychology, 1*, 187–203.
123. Kotani, H., & Yokomatsu, M. (2013). Inheritance of local culture and disaster: Identity-formation-model approach. *Journal of Integrated Disaster Risk Management, 3*, 107–125.
124. Spielberg, W. E. (1986). Living with Indian Point: A study in investigating the relationship between stress, time distortion, ideology, coping style and expressed vulnerability of high school students in close residence to a nuclear power plant. *Dissertation Abstracts International, 47*(9–B), 3971–3972.
125. Stout-Wiegand, N., & Trent, R. B. (1984–1985). Comparison of students' and non-student residents' attitudes toward local energy developments: Environmentalism versus economic interest. *Journal of Environmental Education, 16*, 29–35.
126. Davis, I. (1978). *Shelter after disaster*. Oxford, UK: Oxford Polytechnic Press.
127. Parker, S. D., Brewer, M. B., & Spencer, J. R. (1980). Natural disaster, perceived control and attributions to fate. *Personality & Social Psychology Bulletin, 6*, 454–459.
128. Hansson, R. O., Noulles, D., & Bellovich, S. J. (1982). Knowledge warning and stress: A study of comparative roles in an urban floodplain. *Environment and Behavior, 14*, 171–185.
129. Archea, J. (1990). Two earthquakes: Three human conditions. In Y. Yoshitake, R. B. Bechtel, T. Takahashi, & M. Asai (Eds.), *Current issues in environment-behavior research*. Tokyo: University of Tokyo.
130. Weinrich, S., Hardin, S. B., & Johnson, M. (1990). Nurses respond to hurricane Hugo victims: Disaster stress. *Archives of Psychiatric Nursing, 4*, 195–205.
131. Fullerton, C. S., McCarroll, J. E., Ursano, R. S., & Wright, K. M. (1992). Psychological responses of rescue workers: Fire fighters and trauma. *American Journal of Orthopsychiatry, 62*, 371–378.
132. Chandrasekhar, D. (2010). Setting the stage: How policy institutions create the scope for participation in planning. *Journal of Disaster Research, 5*, 130–137.
133. American Planning Association-New York Metro Chapter. (2013). Getting back to business: Addressing the needs of Rockaway businesses impacted by Superstorm Sandy. Retrieved from http://www.nyplanning.org/docs/APANYM%20Business%20Recovery%20Report%20to%20RDRC.pdf.
134. Wang, P. S., Gruber, M. J., Powers, R. E., Schoenbaum, M., Speier, A. H., Wells, K. B., et al. (2007). Mental health service use among Hurricane Katrina survivors in the eight months after the disaster. *Psychiatric Services, 58*, 1403–1411.
135. Giannopoulou, I., Dikaiakou, A., Yule, W. (2006). Cognitive-behavioural group intervention for PTSD symptoms in children following the Athens 1999 earthquake: A pilot study. *Clinical Child Psychology and Psychiatry, 2011*, 543–553.
136. Lochman, J. E., Vernberg, E., Boxmeyer, C., & Powell, N. (2012, May). Tornado effects on children's behavioral, emotional and psychophysiological functioning and parents' depression. Paper to be presented in a symposium (R. Guadagno, Chair) at the Association of Psychological Science Annual Convention, Chicago, IL.
137. Doocy, S., Daniels, A., Dooling, S., & Gorokhovich, Y. (2013). The human impact of volcanoes: A historical review of events 1900–2009 and systematic literature review. *PLoS Currents, 16*, 5.
138. Doocy, S., Daniels, A., Murray, S., & Kirsch, T. D. (2013). The human impact of floods: A historical review of events 1980–2009 and systematic literature review. *PLoS Currents Disasters, 16*, doi: 10.1371/currents.dis.f4deb457904936b07c09daa98ee8171a
139. Bowler, R., Meqler, D., Huel, G., & Cone, J. (1994). Psychological, psychosocial, and psychophysiological sequelae in a community affected by a railroad chemical disaster. *Journal of Traumatic Stress, 7*, 601–624.
140. Bland, S. H., O'Leary, E. S., Farinaro, E., Jossa, F., & Trevisan, M. (1996). Long-term psychological effects of natural disasters. *Psychosomatic Medicine, 58*, 18–25.
141. Mardberg, B., Carlstedt, L., Stalberg-Carlstedt, B., & Shalit, B. (1987). Sex differences in perception of threat from the Chernobyl accident. *Perceptual & Motor Skills, 65*, 228.
142. Arochova, O., Kontrova, J., Lipkova, V., & Liska, J. (1988). Effect of toxic atmosphere emissions on cognitive performance by children. *Studia Psychologica, 30*, 101–114.
143. Solomon, S. D., & Canino, G. J. (1990). Appropriateness of the DSM-III-R criteria for Posttraumatic Stress Disorder. *Comprehensive Psychiatry, 31*, 227–237.
144. Escobar, J. I., Canino, G., Rubio-Stipec, M., & Bravo, M. (1992). Somatic symptoms after a natural disaster: A prospective study. *American Journal of Psychiatry, 149*, 965–967.

145. Adams, P. R., & Adams, G. R. (1984). Mount St. Helens ashfall: Evidence for a disaster stress reaction, *American Psychologist, 39,* 252–260.
146. Chen, X., Dai, K., & Parnell, A. (1992). Disaster tradition and change: Remarriage and family reconstruction in a post-earthquake community in the People's Republic of China. *Journal of Comparative Family Studies, 23,* 115–132.
147. Green, B. L., Grace, M. C., Vary, M. G., Krammer, T. L., Gleser, G. C., & Leonard, A. C. (1994). Children of disaster in the second decade: A 17-year follow-up of Buffalo Creek survivors. *Journal of the American Academy of Child and Adolescent Psychiatry, 33,* 71–79.
148. Thompson, M. P., Norris, F. H., & Hanacek, B. (1993). Age differences in the psychological consequences of Hurricane Hugo. *Psychology and Aging, 8,* 606–616.
149. Cialdini, R. B. (1989). Littering: When every litter bit hurts. In R. E. Rice & C. K. Atkin (Eds.), *Public communication campaigns* (2nd ed., pp. 221–223). London: Sage.
150. Purcell, A. H. (1981, February). The world's trashiest people: Will they clean up their act or throw away their future? *The Futurist, 2,* 51–59.
151. Tarrant, M. A., & Cordell, H. K. (1997). The effect of respondent characteristics on general environmental attitude-behavior correspondence. *Environment and Behavior, 29,* 618–637.
152. Carrus, G., Passafaro, P., & Bonnes, M. (2008). Emotions, habits and rational choices in ecological behaviours: The case of recycling and use of public transportation. *Journal of Environmental Psychology, 28,* 51–62.
153. Van Houten, R., & Nau, P. A. (1981). A comparison of the effects of posted feedback and increased police surveillance on highway speeding. *Journal of Applied Behavior Analysis, 14,* 261–271.
154. Seligman, C., & Darley, J. M. (1977). Feedback as a means of decreasing residential energy consumption. *Journal of Applied Psychology, 62,* 363–368.
155. Stern, P. C., & Oskamp, S. (1987). Managing scarce environmental resources. In D. Stokols & I. Altman (Eds.), *Handbook of environmental psychology* (Vol. 2, pp. 1043–1088). New York: Wiley.
156. Becker, L. J. (1978). The joint effect of feedback and goal setting on performance: A field study of residential energy conservation. *Journal of Applied Psychology, 63,* 228–233.
157. Siero, F. W., Bakker, A. B., Dekker, G. B., & Van Den Burg, M. T. C. (1996). Changing organizational energy consumption behavior through comparative feedback. *Journal of Environmental Psychology, 16,* 235–246.
158. Bamberg, S., & Moser, G. (2007). Twenty years after Hines, Hungerford, and Tomera: A new meta-analysis of psycho-social determinants of pro-environmental behaviour. *Journal of Environmental Psychology, 27,* 14–25.
159. Berenguer, J. (2010). The effect of empathy in environmental moral reasoning. *Environment and Behavior, 42,* 110–134.
160. Nisbet, E. K., Zelenski, J. M., & Murphy, S. A. (2009). The nature relatedness scale: Linking individuals' connection with nature, environmental concern, and behavior. *Environment and Behavior, 41,* 715–740.
161. Schwartz, S. H. (1977). Normative influences on altruism. *Advances in Experimental Social Psychology, 10,* 221–279.
162. Whitley, C. T., Takahashi, B., Zwickle, A., Besley, J. C., & Lertpratchya, A. P. (2018). Sustainability behaviors among college students: An application of the VBN theory. *Environmental Education Research, 24,* 245–262.
163. Orbell, J. M., van de Kragt, A. J. C., & Dawes, R. M. (1988). Explaining discussion-induced comparison. *Journal of Personality and Social Psychology, 54,* 811–819.
164. Van Vugt, M., & Samuelson, C. (1999). The impact of personal metering in the management of a natural resource crisis: A social dilemma analysis. *Personality and Social Psychology Bulletin, 25,* 731–745.
165. Dickerson, C., Thibodeau, R., Aronson, E., & Miller, D. (1992). Using cognitive dissonance to encourage water conservation. *Journal of Applied Social Psychology, 22,* 841–854.
166. Clancy, B., & Milam, H. (2012). How psychological reactance modifies the effects of hypocrisy induction. *Journal of Psychological Inquiry, 17,* 36–39.
167. Bandura, A. (2009). Social cognitive theory goes global. *The Psychologist, 22,* 504–506.
168. Bandura, A. (2019). Applying theory for human betterment. *Perspectives on Psychological Science, 14,* 12–15.
169. Hanley, N., Shogren, J., & White, B. (2007). *Environmental economics in theory and practice.* London, UK: Palgrave.
170. Hoerner, J. A., & Barrett, J. (2004, September). *Smarter, cleaner, stronger: Secure jobs, a clean environment, and less foreign oil.* Retrieved from http://www.rprogress.org/publications/2004/SmartCleanStrong_National.pdf
171. Thompson, S. C. G., & Stoutemyer, K. (1991). Water use as a commons dilemma: The effects of education that focuses on long-term consequences and individual action. *Environment and Behavior, 23,* 314–333.
172. De Young, R., Duncan, A., Frank, J., Gill, N., Rothman, S., Shenot, J., Shotkin, A., & Zweizig, M. (1993). Promoting source reduction behavior: The role of motivational behavior. *Environment and Behavior, 25,* 70–85. ªStokols, D. (1972) On the distinction between density and crowding: Some implications for future research. *Psychological Review, 79,* 275-–277.

References

1 Timothy 6:10.

Aaker, J., Vohs, K. D., & Mogilner, C. (2010). Nonprofits are seen as warm and for-profits as competent: Firm stereotypes matter. *Journal of Consumer Research, 37,* 224–237.

Aamodt, M. G. (2016). *Industrial/organizational psychology: An applied approach.* Belmont, CA: Wadsworth, Cengage Learning.

Aamodt, M.G., & Carr, K. (1988). Relationship between recruitment source and employee behavior. *Proceedings of the 12th Annual Meeting of the International Personnel Management Association Assessment Council,* 143–146.

Abakoumkin, G. (2018). Mere exposure effects in the real world: Utilizing natural experiment features from the Eurovision Song Contest. *Basic and Applied Social Psychology, 40*(4), 236–247. https://doi-org.proxy.lib.umich.edu/10.1080/01973533.2018.1474742

Abel, E. L., & Kruger, M. L. (2010). Smile intensity in photographs predicts longevity. *Psychological Science, 21*(4), 542–544.

Aberson, C. L., Healy, M., & Romero, V. (2000). Ingroup bias and self-esteem: A meta-analysis. *Personality and Social Psychology Review, 4,* 157–173.

Abraham, C. (2002, December 14). Mommy's little secret. *The Globe and Mail* (Toronto), pp. F1, F6.

Abraham, S. F., & Beumont, P. J. V. (1982). How patients describe bulimia or binge eating. *Psychological Medicine, 12,* 625–635.

Abrahamse, W., Steg, L., Vlek, C., & Rothengatter, T. (2007). The effect of tailored information, goal setting, and tailored feedback on household energy use, energy-related behaviors, and behavioral antecedents. *Journal of Environmental Psychology, 27,* 265–276.

Abraido-Lanza, Mendoza, S., & Armbrister, A. N. (2019). Latino health. In T. A. Revenson, & R. A. R. Gurung (Eds.), *Handbook of health psychology* (pp. 342–354). New York: Routledge.

Abramowitz, J. S., Tolin, D. F., & Street, G. P. (2001). Paradoxical effects of thought suppression: A meta-analysis of controlled studies. *Clinical Psychology Review, 21,* 683–705.

Abrams, D., Crisp, R. J., Marques, S., Fagg, E., Bedford, L., & Provias, D. (2008). Threat inoculation: Experienced and imagined intergenerational contact prevents stereotype threat effects on older people's math performance. *Psychology and Aging, 23*(4), 934–939.

Abrams, D., de Moura, G., & Travaglino, G. (2013) A double standard when group members behave badly: Transgression credit to ingroup leaders. *Journal of Personality and Social Psychology, 105,* 799–815.

Abshire, J., & Bornstein, B. J. (2003). Juror sensitivity to the cross-race effect. *Law and Human Behavior, 27,* 471–480.

Acker, M., & Davis, M. H. (1992). Intimacy, passion and commitment in adult romantic relationships: A test of the triangular theory of love. *Journal of Social and Personality Relationships, 9,* 21–50.

Ackerman, J. M., Griskevicius, V., & Li, N. P. (2011). Let's get serious: Communicating commitment in romantic relationships. *Journal of Personality and Social Psychology, 100*(6), 1079–1094.

Ackerman, J. M., Shapiro, J. R., Neuberg, S. L., Kenrick, D. T., Schaller, M., Becker, D. V., et al. (2006). They all look the same to me (unless they're angry): From out-group homogeneity to out-group heterogeneity. *Psychological Science, 17*(10), 836–840.

Adams, C. G., & Turner, B. F. (1985). Reported change in sexuality from young adulthood to old age. *Journal of Sex Research, 21,* 126–141.

Adams, G. R., Ryan, B. A., Ketsetzis, M., & Keating, L. (2000). Rule compliance and peer sociability: A study of family process, parent-child school-focused interactions and children's classroom behavior. *Journal of Family Psychology, 14,* 237–250.

Adams, H. E., Wright, L. W., Jr., & Lohr, B. A. (1996). Is homophobia associated with homosexual arousal? *Journal of Abnormal Psychology, 105,* 440–446.

Adams, J. S. (1965). Inequity in social change. In L. Berkowitz (Ed.), *Advances in experimental social psychology* (Vol. 2, pp. 267–299). New York: Academic Press.

Adams, P. R., & Adams, G. R. (1984). Mount St. Helens ashfall: Evidence for a disaster stress reaction, *American Psychologist, 39,* 252–260.

Adhikary, A. K. (1984). *Society and world view of the Birhor: A nomadic hunting and gathering community of Orissa.* Calcutta: Anthropological Survey of India.

Adler, P. (1980). On becoming a prostitute. In E. Muga (Ed.), *Studies in prostitution* (pp. 22–26). Nairobi: Kenya Literature Bureau.

Adolph, K. E., Gilmore, R. O., Freeman, C., Sanderson, P., & Millman, D. (2012). Toward open behavioral science. *Psychological Inquiry, 23*(3), 244–247. doi: 10.1080/1047840X.2012.705133

Adult obesity facts. *CDC.* Retrieved from https://www.cdc.gov/obesity/data/adult.html

Agarwal, S., Mikhed, V., & Scholnick, B. (2016). Does inequality cause financial distress? Evidence from lottery winners and neighboring bankruptcies. Working paper, Federal Reserve Bank of Philadelphia.

Agras, W. S., & Telch, C. F. (1998). The effects of caloric deprivation and negative affect on binge eating in obese binge-eating disordered women. *Behavior Therapy, 29,* 491–503.

Ahlering, R. F. (1987). Need for cognition, attitudes, and the 1984 Presidential election. *Journal of Research in Personality, 21,* 100–102.

Ahmed, A. M. (2010). Muslim discrimination: Evidence from two lost-letter experiments. *Journal of Applied Social Psychology, 40*(4), 888–898.

Aiello, J. R. (1987). Human spatial behavior. In D. Stokols & I. Altman (Eds.), *Handbook of environmental psychology* (Vol. 1, pp. 505–531). New York: Wiley.

Aiello, J. R., & Douthitt, E. A. (2001). Social facilitation: From Triplett to electronic performance monitoring. *Group Dynamics: Theory, Research, and Practice, 5,* 163–180.

Ailes, E. (2016, April 4). 13 of the world's most stupid criminals. BBC News. Retrieved from http://www.bbc.com/news/uk-35785834

Ainsworth, M. D. (1989). Attachments beyond infancy. *American Psychologist, 44,* 709–716.

Ainsworth, M. D. S., Blehar, M. C., Waters, E., & Wall, S. (1978). *Patterns of attachment: A psychological study of the strange situation.* Hillsdale, NJ: Erlbaum.

Ainsworth, S. E., & Maner, J. K. (2012). Sex begets violence: Mating motives, social dominance, and physical aggression in men. *Journal of Personality and Social Psychology, 103,* 819–829.

Airport baggage handler goes viral (19 September 2018). *CNN.* Retrieved from https://www.cnn.com/videos/travel/2018/09/19/south-africa-baggage-handler-viral-video-vpx.hln

Ajzen, I. (1988). *Attitudes, personality, and behavior.* Homewood, IL: Dorsey Press.

Ajzen, I. (2001). Nature and operation of attitudes. In T. Fiske, D. L. Schacter, & C. Zahn-Waxler (Eds.), *Annual review of psychology* (Vol. 52, pp. 27–58). Palo Alto, CA: Annual Reviews.

Ajzen, I. (2012). The theory of planned behavior. In P. A. M. Lange, A. W. Kruglanski, & E. T. Higgins (Eds.), *Handbook of theories of social psychology* (Vol. 1, pp. 438–459). London, U.K.: Sage.

Ajzen, I., & Fishbein, M. (1977). Attitude-behavior relations: A theoretical analysis and review of empirical research. *Psychological Bulletin, 84,* 888–918.

Aknin, L. B., Barrington-Leigh, C. P., Dunn, E. W., Helliwell, J. F., Burns, J., Biswas-Diener, R., Kemerza, I., Nyende, P., Ashton-James, C. E., & Norton, M. I. (2013). Prosocial spending and well-being: Cross-cultural evidence for a psychological universal. *Journal of Personality and Social Psychology, 104,* 635–652.

Albergotti, R., O'Connell, V., & Vranica, S. (2012, October 18). Lance Armstrong gets dumped: Nike, RadioShack, others distance themselves from cyclist amid drug scandal. The Wall Street Journal. Retrieved from http://online.wsj.com/news/articles/SB10000872396390444868204578062313532317222

Alcock, I., White, M. P., Wheeler, B. W., Fleming, L. E., & Depledge, M. H. (2014). Longitudinal effects on mental health of moving to greener and less green urban areas. *Environmental Science & Technology, 48*(2), 1247–1255. doi: 10.1021/es403688w

Aldwin, C. M., Lee, H., Choun, S, & Kang, S. (2019). Coping. In T. A. Revenson & R. A. R. Gurung (Eds.), *Handbook of health psychology* (pp. 225–238). New York: Routledge.

Alebiosu, K. A. (2001). Cooperative learning and students' affective learning outcome in Nigerian chemistry classrooms. *IFE Psychologia, 9,* 135–142.

Alexander, M. G., & Fisher, T. D. (2003). Truth and consequences: Using the bogus pipeline to examine sex differences in self-reported sexuality. *The Journal of Sex Research, 40,* 27–35.

Alland, A., Jr. (1972). *The human imperative.* New York: Columbia University Press.

Allen, M., Mabry, E., & McKelton, D. (1998). Impact of juror attitudes about the death penalty on juror evaluations of guilt and punishment: A meta-analysis. *Law and Human Behavior, 22,* 715–731.

Allen, N. B., & Badcock, P. B. T. (2003). The social risk hypothesis of depressed mood: Evolutionary, psychosocial, and neurobiological perspectives. *Psychological Bulletin, 129,* 887–913.

Allen, N. J., & Hecht, T. D. (2004). The "romance of teams": Toward an understanding of its psychological underpinnings and implications. *Journal of Occupational and Organizational Psychology, 77,* 439–461.

Allen, T. D., Lentz, E., & Day, R. (2006). Career success outcomes associated with mentoring others: A comparison of mentors and nonmentors. *Journal of Career Development, 32*(3), 272–285.

Alloy, L. B., & Abramson, L. Y. (1979). Judgment of contingency in depressed and nondepressed students: Sadder but wiser? *Journal of Experimental Psychology: General, 108*(4), 441–485.

Allport, F. H. (1924). *Social psychology.* Boston: Houghton Mifflin Company.

Allport, G. (1935). Attitudes. In C. Murchinson (Ed.). *A Handbook of Social Psychology* (pp. 789–844). Worchester, MA: Clark University Press.

Allport, G. W. (1954). *The nature of prejudice.* Reading, MA: Addison-Wesley.

Allport, G. W. (1954). The historical background of modern social psychology. In G. Lindzey (Ed.), *Handbook of social psychology* (Vol. 1, pp. 3–56). Cambridge, MA: Addison-Wesley.

Alpert, J. L., Brown, L. S., & Courtois, C. A. (1998). Symptomatic clients and memories of childhood abuse: What the trauma and child sexual abuse literature tells us. *Psychology, Public Policy, and Law, 4,* 941–995.

Altermatt, T. W., & DeWall, C. N. (2003). Agency and virtue: Dimensions underlying subgroups of women. *Sex Roles, 49,* 631–641.

Altman, I., Nelson, P. A., & Lett, E. E. (1972, Spring). The ecology of home environments. *Catalog of Selected Documents in Psychology* (No. 150).

Altschuler, G. C. (2001, January 7). Battling the cheats. *New York Times*. Retrieved from https://www.nytimes.com/2001/01/07/education/college-prep-battling-the-cheats.html

Amabile, T. M. (1996). *Creativity in context*. Boulder, CO: Westview Press.

American Automobile Association (AAA). Are you an aggressive driver? Retrieved from https://www.aaafoundation.org/are-you-aggressive-driver

American Automobile Association (AAA, n.d.). *Aggressive driving*. Retrieved from https://www.aaafoundation.org/aggressive-driving

American College Health Association. (2008). American College Health Association – National college health assessment spring 2007 reference group data report (abridged). *Journal of American College Health, 56*(5), 469–479. Retrieved from http://www.acha-ncha.org/docs/JACH%20March%202008%20SP%2007%20Ref%20Grp.pdf

American Institute of Stress. (2019). 50 common signs and symptoms of stress. Retrieved from https://www.stress.org/stress-effects.

stress. Retrieved from https://www.stress.org/stress-effects.

American Planning Association-New York Metro Chapter. (2013). Getting back to business: Addressing the needs of Rockaway businesses impacted by Superstorm Sandy. Retrieved from http://www.nyplanning.org/docs/APANYM%20Business%20Recovery%20Report%20Report%20to%20RDRC.pdf.

American Psychiatric Association. (1994). *Diagnostic and statistical manual of mental disorders* (4th ed.). Washington, DC: Author.

American Psychological Association (2015). Five tips to help manage stress. Retrieved from http://www.apa.org/helpcenter/manage-stress.aspx

American Psychological Association. (2008). Answers to your questions: For a better understanding of sexual orientation and homosexuality. Washington, DC: Author. Retrieved from http://www.apa.org/topics/sorientation.pdf

American Psychological Association. (2018). Coping with stress at work. October. Retrieved from https://www.apa.org/helpcenter/work-stress.

Ames, D. R., & Flynn, F. J. (2007). What breaks a leader: The curvilinear relation between assertiveness and leadership. *Journal of Personality and Social Psychology, 92*, 307–324.

Amodio, D. M., Harmon-Jones, E., & Devine, P. G. (2003). Individual differences in the activation and control of affective race bias as assessed by startle eyeblink response and self-report. *Journal of Personality and Social Psychology, 84*, 738–753.

Amok. (n.d.) in *Merriam-Webster Dictionary*. Retrieved August 25, 2019 from https://www.merriam-webster.com/dictionary/amok

Anderson, C. A. (1983). Imagination and expectation: The effect of imagining behavioral scripts on personal intentions. *Journal of Personality and Social Psychology, 45*, 293–305.

Anderson, C. A., & Anderson, K. B. (1996). Violent crime rate studies in philosophical context: A destructive testing approach to heat and southern culture of violence effects. *Journal of Personality and Social Psychology, 70*, 740–756.

Anderson, C. A., & Dill, K. E. (2000). Video games and aggressive thoughts, feelings, and behavior in laboratory and real life. *Journal of Personality and Social Psychology, 78*(4), 772–790.

Anderson, C. A., & Sechler, E. S. (1986). Effects of explanation and counter and explanation on the development and use of social theories. *Journal of Personality and Social Psychology, 20*, 24–34.

Anderson, C. A., Anderson, K. B., Dorr, N., DeNeve, K. M., & Flanagan, M. (2000). Temperature and aggression. In M. Zanna (Ed.), *Advances in experimental social psychology* (Vol. 32, pp. 63–133). New York: Academic Press.

Anderson, C. A., Bushman, B. J., & Groom, R. W. (1997). Hot years and serious and deadly assault: Empirical tests of the heat hypothesis. *Journal of Personality and Social Psychology, 73*(6), 1213–1223. doi: 10.1037//0022-3514.73.6.1213

Anderson, C. A., Lepper, M. R., & Ross, L. (1980). The perseverance of social theories: The role of explanation in the persistence of discredited information. *Journal of Personality and Social Psychology, 39*, 1037–1049.

Anderson, C. A., Shibuya, A., Ihori, N., Swing, E. L., Bushman, B. J., Sakamoto, A., Rothstein, H. R., Saleem, M., & Barlett, C. P. (2010). Violent video game effects on aggression, empathy, and prosocial behavior in Eastern and Western countries: A meta-analytic review. *Psychological Bulletin, 136*(2), 151–173. doi: 10.1037/a0018251

Anderson, C. A., Suzuki, K., Swing, E. L., Groves, C. L., Gentile, D. A., Prot, S., Lam, C. P., Sakamoto, A., et al.. (2017). Media violence and other aggression risk factors in seven nations. *Personality and Social Psychology Bulletin, 43*, 986–998. doi: 10.1177/0146167217703064

Anderson, C. J. (2003). The psychology of doing nothing: Forms of decision avoidance result from reason and emotion. *Psychological Bulletin, 129*, 139–167.

Anderson, J. O., Thundiyll, J. G., & Stobach, A. (2012). Clearing the air: A review of the effects of particulate matter air pollution on human health. *Journal of Medical Toxicology, 8*, 166–175.

Anderson, N., & Thomas, H. D. C. (1996). Work group socialization. In M. A. West (Ed.), *Handbook of work group psychology* (pp. 423–450). Chichester, UK: Wiley.

Anderson, P. B., & Struckman-Johnson, C. (Eds.). (1998). *Sexually aggressive women: Current perspectives and controversies*. New York: Guilford Press.

Anderson, S. A., Russell, C. S., & Schumm, W. R. (1983). Perceived marital quality and family life-cycle categories: A further analysis. *Journal of Marriage and the Family, 45*, 127–139.

Anderson, S. F., & Maxwell, S. E. (2017). Addressing the 'replication crisis': Using original studies to design replication studies with appropriate statistical power. *Multivariate Behavioral Research, 52*, 305–324. doi:10.1080/00273171.2017.1289361

Ansari, S., Wijen, F., & Gray, B. (2013). Constructing a climate change logic: An institutional perspective on the "tragedy of the commons." *Organization Science, 24*, 1014–1040.

Anti-Violence Project. A crisis of hate: A report on lesbian, gay, bisexual, transgender and queer hate violence homicides in 2017. Retrieved from https://avp.org/a-crisis-of-hate-january/

Antonovsky, H. F., Shoham, I., Kavenocki, S., Modan, B., & Lancet, M. (1978). Sexual attitude-behavior discrepancy among Israeli adolescent girls. *Journal of Sex Research, 14*, 260–272.

Appelbaum, P., & Swanson, J. (2010). Gun laws and mental illness: How sensible are the current restrictions. *Psychiatric Services, 61*, 652–654. doi: 10.1176/appi.ps.61.7.652

Apsler, R., & Sears, D. O. (1968). Warning, personal involvement, and attitude change. *Journal of Personality and Social Psychology, 9*, 162–168.

Archea, J. (1990). Two earthquakes: Three human conditions. In Y. Yoshitake, R. B. Bechtel, T. Takahashi, & M. Asai (Eds.), *Current issues in environment-behavior research*. Tokyo: University of Tokyo.

Archer, J. (1988). *The behavioral biology of aggression*. Cambridge: Cambridge University Press.

Archer, J. (2000). Sex differences in aggression between heterosexual partners: A meta-analytic review. *Psychological Bulletin, 126*, 651–680.

Archer, J., & Bushman, B. J. (invited review). The uses of meta-analysis in psychology. *Current Directions in Psychological Science*.

Ard, B. N. (1977). Sex in lasting marriages: A longitudinal study. *Journal of Sex Research, 13*, 274–285.

Areni, C. S., & Kim, D. (1993). The influence of background music on shopping behavior: Classical versus Top-Forty. In L. McAlister & M. L. Rothschild (Eds.), *Advances in consumer research* (pp. 336–340). Provo, UT: Association for Consumer Research.

Ariel, B., Lawes, D., Weinborn, C., Henry, R. Chen, K., & Sabthe, H. B. (2019). The "less-than-lethal weapons effect": Introducing tasers to routine police operations in England and Wales. *Criminal Justice and Behavior, 46*(2), 280–300. DOI: 10.1177/0093854818812918

Ariely, D., & Levav, J. (2000). Sequential choice in group settings: Taking the road less traveled and less enjoyed. *Journal of Consumer Research, 27*, 279–290.

Aries, E. J., & Johnson, F. L. (1983). Close friendship in adulthood: Conversational content between same-sex friends. *Sex Roles, 9*, 1183–1196.

Aries, P. (1962). *Centuries of childhood: A social history of family life* (Trans. R. Baldick). New York: Random House.

Arkes, H. R. (1991). Costs and benefits of judgment errors: Implications for debiasing. *Psychological Bulletin, 110*, 486–498.

Armbrister, R. C. (2002). A cross-cultural comparison of student social attributions. *Psychology in the Schools, 39*, 39–49.

Armitage, C. J., & Conner, M. (2001). Efficacy of the theory of planned behaviour: A meta-analytic review. *British Journal of Social Psychology, 40*, 471–499.

Arndt, B. (2009). *The Sex Diaries*. Melbourne: Melbourne University Press.

Arnold, A. (2019, March 23). A Parkland Survivor took her own life. *The Cut*. Retrieved from https://www.thecut.com/2019/03/parkland-survivor-sydney-aiello-has-taken-her-own-life.html?utm_medium=s1&utm_source=fb&utm_campaign=nym&fbclid=IwAR2q5zNbWQscLt3zCS8hYu6u3B5N1CJtCBdXyB7OeYH-CGy15_nU9BxuG4s

Arnold, M. B. (1960). *Emotion and personality*. New York, NY: Columbia University Press.

Arochova, O., Kontrova, J., Lipkova, V., & Liska, J. (1988). Effect of toxic atmosphere emissions on cognitive performance by children. *Studia Psychologica, 30*, 101–114.

Aron, A., Fisher, H., & Strong, G. (2006). Romantic love. In A. Vangelisti & D. Perlman (Eds.), *Cambridge handbook of personal relationships* (pp. 595–614). New York: Cambridge University Press.

Aronson, E. (2000). *Nobody left to hate: Teaching compassion after Columbine*. New York: W. H. Freeman.

Aronson, E. (2007). *The social animal*. New York: Worth.

Aronson, E., & Carlsmith, J. M. (1968). Experimentation in social psychology. In G. Lindzey & E. Aronson (Eds.), *Handbook of Social Psychology* (2nd ed., Vol. 2, pp. 1–79). Reading, MA: Addison-Wesley.

Aronson, E., & Mills, J. (1959). The effect of severity of initiation on liking for a group. *Journal of Abnormal and Social Psychology, 59*, 177–181.

Aronson, E., & Osherow, N. (1980). Cooperation, prosocial behavior, and academic performance: Experiments in the desegregated classroom. *Applied Social Psychology Annual, 1*, 163–196.

Aronson, E., & Patnoe, S. (1997). *The jigsaw classroom: Building cooperation in the classroom* (2nd ed.). New York: Addison Wesley Longman.

Aronson, E., Blaney, N., Stephin, C., Sikes, J., & Snapp, M. (1978). *The jigsaw classroom*. Beverly Hills, CA: Sage.

Aronson, J., Lustina, M. J., Good, C., Keough, K., Steele, C. M., & Brown, J. (1999). When white men can't do math: Necessary and sufficient factors in stereotype threat. *Journal of Experimental Social Psychology, 35*, 29–46.

Arthur, J. B. (1994). Effects of human resource systems on manufacturing performance and turnover. *Academy of Management Journal, 37*, 670–687.

Arvey, R. D., & Campion, J. E. (1982). The employment interview: A summary and review of recent research. *Personnel Psychology, 35*, 281–322.

Asch, S. E. (1955, November). Opinions and social pressure. *Scientific American*, 31–35.

Asch, S. E. (1956). Studies of independence and conformity: I. A minority of one against a unanimous majority. *Psychological Monographs, 70* (No. 416).

Ashton, H., & Stepney, R. (1982). *Smoking: Psychology and pharmacology*. London: Tavistock.

Associated Press. Troy Davis execution fuels eyewitness ID debate. (2011, September 27). *USA Today*. Retrieved from http://www.usatoday.com/news/nation/story/2011-09-27/troy-davis-eyewitness-testimony/50563754/1

Atkinson, T., Liem, R., & Liem, J. H. (1986). The social costs of unemployment: Implications for social support. *Journal of Health and Social Behavior, 27*, 317–331.

Atthowe, J. M. (1960). Types of conflict and their resolution: A reinterpretation. *Journal of Experimental Psychology, 59*, 1–9.

Austin, W., McGinn, N. C., & Susmilch, C. (1980). Internal standards revisited: Effects of social comparisons and expectancies on judgments of fairness and satisfaction. *Journal of Experimental Social Psychology, 16*, 426–441.

Averill, J. R. (1982). *Anger and aggression: An essay on emotion*. New York: Springer-Verlag.

Avery, D. (2018, August 11). Gay couples are four times more likely to adopt, so of course congress wants to stop them. *Hornet*. Retrieved from https://hornet.com/stories/gay-parents-adoption/

Avolio, B. J., Kahai, S. S., & Dodge, G. (2000). E-leading in organizations and it implications for theory, research and practice. *Leadership Quarterly, 11*, 615–670.

Axelrod, R., & Hamilton, W. D. (1981). The evolution of cooperation. *Science, 211*, 1390–1396.

Axelrod. R. (1980). More effective choice in the prisoner's dilemma. *Journal of Conflict Resolution, 24*, 3–25.

Baard, P.P., Deci, E.L., & Ryan, R.M. (2004). Intrinsic need satisfaction: A motivational basis of performance and well-being in two work settings. *Journal of Applied Social Psychology, 34*(10), 2045–2068.

Babin, B. J., & Babin, L. (2001). Seeking something different? A model of schema typicality, consumer affect, purchase intentions and perceived shopping value. *Journal of Business Research, 54*, 89–96.

Bachman, J. G., & O'Malley, P. M. (1977). Self-esteem in young men: A longitudinal analysis of the impact of educational and occupational attainment. *Journal of Personality and Social Psychology, 35*, 365–380.

Bachman, J. G., & O'Malley, P. M. (1986). Self-concepts, self-esteem, and educational experiences: The frog pond revisited (again). *Journal of Personality and Social Psychology, 50*, 35–46.

Backteman, G., & Magnusson, D. (1981). Longitudinal stability of personality characteristics. *Journal of Personality, 49*, 148–160.

Badawy, A. A.-B. (2003). Alcohol and violence and the possible role of serotonin. *Criminal Behaviour and Mental Health, 13*(1), 31–44. doi: 10.1002/cbm

Baggini, J. (2004). Bad moves: Confirmation bias. Retrieved from http://www.butterfliesandwheels.com/badmovesprint.php?num=42

Bagozzi, R. P., Wong, N., Abe, S., & Bergami, M. (2000). Cultural and situational contingencies and the theory of reasoned action: Application to fast food restaurant consumption. *Journal of Consumer Psychology, 9*, 97–106.

Bahns, A. J., & Branscombe, N. R. (2011). Effects of legitimizing discrimination against homosexuals on gay bashing. *European Journal of Social Psychology, 41*(3), 388–396.

Bailey, J. M., & Pillard, R. C. (1995). Genetics of human sexual orientation. *Annual Review of Sex Research, 6*, 126–150.

Bailey, N. W., & Zuk, M. (2009). Same- sex sexual behavior and evolution. *Trends in Ecology & Evolution, 24*(8), 439–446. DOI: 10.1016/j.tree.2009.03.014

Bailey, R. C., & Aunger, R. V. (1995). Sexuality, infertility and sexually transmitted disease among farmers and foragers in central Africa. In P. Abramson & S. Pinkerton (Eds.), *Sexual nature/sexual culture* (pp. 195–222). Chicago: University of Chicago Press.

Baker, M. (2016, 26 May). 1,500 scientists lift the lid on reproducibility *Nature, 533*, 452–454. http://dx.doi.org/10.1038/533452a

Baker, M., Strickland, A., & Fox, N. D. (2019). Choosing a meal to increase your appeal: How relationship status, sexual orientation, dining partner sex, and attractiveness impact nutritional choices in social dining scenarios. *Appetite, 133*, 262–269.

Bakhshay, S., & Haney, C. (2018). The media's impact on the right to a fair trial: A content analysis of pretrial publicity in capital cases. *Psychology, Public Policy, and Law, 24*, 326–340.

Baldwin, M. W. (1992). Relational schemas and the processing of social information. *Psychological Bulletin, 112*, 461–474.

Balliet, D., Li, N. P., & Joireman, J. (2011). Relating trait self-control and forgiveness within prosocials and proselfs: Compensatory versus synergistic models. *Journal of Personality and Social Psychology, 101*(5), 1090–1105.

Balliet, D., Li, N. P., Macfarlan, S. J., Van Vugt, M. (2011). Sex differences in cooperation: a meta-analytic review of social dilemmas. *Psychological Bulletin, 137*(6), 881–909.

Balogun, S. K. (1991). Personal space as affected by religions of the approaching and the approached people. *Indian Journal of Behaviour, 15*, 45–50.

Bamberg, S., & Moser, G. (2007). Twenty years after Hines, Hungerford, and Tomera: A new meta-analysis of psycho-social determinants of pro-environmental behaviour. *Journal of Environmental Psychology, 27*, 14–25.

Bandura, A. (1965). Influence of models' reinforcement contingencies on the acquisition of imitative responses. *Journal of Abnormal and Social Psychology, 66*, 575–582.

Bandura, A. (1973). *Aggression: A social learning theory analysis*. Englewood Cliffs, NJ: Prentice-Hall.

Bandura, A. (1977). *Social learning theory*. Englewood Cliffs, NJ: Prentice Hall.

Bandura, A. (1986). *Social foundations of thought and action: A social-cognitive theory*. Englewood Cliffs, NJ: Prentice-Hall.

Bandura, A. (1999). Moral disengagement in the perpetration of inhumanities. *Personality and Social Psychology Review, 3*, 193–209. DOI: 10.1207/s15327957pspr0303_3

Bandura, A. (2009). Social cognitive theory goes global. *The Psychologist, 22*, 504–506.

Bandura, A. (2019). Applying theory for human betterment. *Perspectives on Psychological Science, 14*, 12–15.

Bandura, A., & Schunk, D. H. (1981). Cultivating competence, self-efficacy, and intrinsic interest through proximal self-motivation. *Journal of Personality and Social Psychology, 41*, 586–598.

Bandura, A., Ross, D., & Ross, S. A. (1961). Transmission of aggression through imitation of aggressive models. *Journal of Abnormal and Social Psychology, 63*, 575–582.

Bandura, A., Ross, D., & Ross, S. A. (1963). Vicarious reinforcement and imitative learning. *Journal of Abnormal and Social Psychology, 67*, 601–607.

Bansal, A., Garg, C., Pakhare, A., & Gupta, S. (2018). Selfies: A boon or bane? *Journal of Family Medicine and Primary Care, 7*(4), 828–831. doi: 10.4103/jfmpc.jfmpc_109_18

Barash, D. P., & Lipton, J. E. (2002). *Myth of monogamy: Fidelity and infidelity in animals and people*. New York: W. H. Freeman.

Barbee, A. P., Lawrence, T., & Cunningham, M. R. (1998). When a friend is in need: Feelings about seeking, giving, and receiving social support. In P. Anderson & L. Guerro (Eds.), *Handbook of communication and emotion* (pp. 282–298). New York: Academic Press.

Barfield, R. L. (2003). Students' perceptions of and satisfaction with group grades and the group experience in the college classroom. *Assessment and Evaluation in Higher Education, 28*(4), 355–369.

Bargh, J. A. (1982). Attention and automaticity in the processing of self-relevant information. *Journal of Personality and Social Psychology, 43*, 425–436.

Bargh, J. A. (1994). The four horsemen of automaticity: Awareness, intention, efficiency, and control in social cognition. In R. S. Wyer, Jr., & T. K. Srull (Eds.), *Handbook of social cognition* (pp. 1–40). Hillsdale, NJ: Erlbaum.

Bargh, J. A., & Shaley, I. (2012). The substitutability of physical and social warmth in daily life. *Emotion, 12*, 154–162.

Bargh, J. A., Chaiken, S., Raymond, P., & Hymes, C. (1996). The automatic evaluation effect: Unconditional automatic attitude activation with a pronunciation task. *Journal of Experimental Social Psychology, 32*, 104–128.

Bargh, J. A., Chen, M., & Burrows, L. (1996). Automaticity of social behavior: Direct effects of trait construct and stereotype activation on action. *Journal of Personality and Social Psychology, 71*(2), 230–244.

Bargh, J. A., Gollwitzer, P. M., Lee-Chai, A., Barndollar, K., & Trötschel, R. (2001). The automated will: Nonconscious activation and pursuit of behavioral goals. *Journal of Personality and Social Psychology, 81*, 1014–1027.

Bargh, J. A., Raymond, P., Pryor, J. B., & Strack, F. (1995). The attractiveness of the underling: An automatic power-sex association and its consequences for sexual harassment. *Journal of Personality and Social Psychology, 68*, 768–781.

Barker, M. R., Bailey, J. S., & Lee, N. (2004). The impact of verbal prompts on child safety-belt use in shopping carts. *Journal of Applied Behavior Analysis, 37*, 527–530.

Barlow, D. H. (1988). *Anxiety and its disorders: The nature and treatment of anxiety and panic*. New York: Guilford Press.

Barlow, F. K., Paolini, S., Pedersen, A., Hornsey, M. J., Radke, H. R. M., Harwood, J., Rubin, M., & Sibley, C. G. (2012). The contact caveat: Negative contact predicts increased prejudice more than positive contact predicts reduced prejudice. *Personality and Social Psychology Bulletin, 38*(12), 1629–1643. doi: 10.1177/0146167212457953

Barnard, W. A., & Bell, P. A. (1982). An unobtrusive apparatus for measuring interpersonal distance. *Journal of General Psychology, 107*, 85–90.

Baron, R. A. (1976). The reduction of human aggression: A field study of the influence of incompatible reactions. *Journal of Applied Social Psychology, 6*, 260–274.

Baron, R. A., & Richardson, D. R. (1994). *Human aggression* (2nd ed.). New York: Plenum Press.

Barrick, M. R., Day, D. V., Lord, R. G., & Alexander, R. A. (1991). Assessing the utility of executive leadership. *Leadership Quarterly, 2*, 9–22.

Barrios, B. A., Corbitt, L. C., Estes, J. P., & Topping, J. S. (1976). Effect of social stigma on interpersonal distance. *The Psychological Record, 26*, 342–348.

Barry, H., III, & Paxson, L. M. (1971). Infancy and early childhood: Cross-cultural codes II. *Ethnology, 10*, 466–508.

Barsky, A. J. (1988). *Worried sick: Our troubled quest for wellness*. New York: Little Brown and Co.

Bartholomew, K. (1990). Avoidance of intimacy: An attachment perspective. *Journal of Social and Personal Relationships, 7*, 147–178.

Bartholomew, K., & Horowitz, L. M. (1991). Attachment styles among young adults: A test of a four-category model. *Journal of Personality and Social Psychology, 61*, 226–244.

Bartholomew, K., & Shaver, P. R. (1998). Measures of attachment: Do they converge? In J. A. Simpson & W. S. Rholes (Eds.), *Attachment theory and close relationships* (pp. 25–45). New York: Guilford Press.

Bartholow, B. D., & Heinz, A. (2006). Alcohol and aggression without consumption: Alcohol cues, aggressive thoughts, and hostile perception bias. *Psychological Science, 17*, 30–37.

Basner, M., Babisch, W., Davis, A., Brink, M., Clark, C., Janssen, S., & Stansfeld, S. (2014). Auditory and non-auditory effects of noise on health. *Lancet, 383*, 1325–1332.

Bass, B. M. (1990). From transactional to transformational leadership: Learning to share the vision. *Organizational Dynamics, 18*(3), 19–31.

B., Santo, J. B., & Bukowski, W. M. (2018). A cross-cultural analysis of the relations of physical and relational aggression with peer victimization.

Batora, R. J., Bryan, A. D., & Schultz, P. W. (2011). Who gives a hoot? Intercept surveys of litterers and disposers. *Environment and Behavior, 43*(3), 295–315.

Batson v. Kentucky, 106 S.Ct. 1712 (1986).

Batson, C. D., Batson, J. G., Slingsby, J. K., Harrell, K. L., Peekna, H. M., & Todd, R. M. (1991). Empathic joy and the empathy-altruism hypothesis. *Journal of Personality and Social Psychology, 61,* 413–426.

Batson, C. D., Duncan, B. D., Ackerman, P., Buckley, T., & Birch, K. (1981). Is empathic emotion a source of altruism motivation? *Journal of Personality and Social Psychology, 40,* 290–302.

Battistich, V., Solomon, D., & Delucchi, K. (1993). Interaction processes and student outcomes in cooperative learning groups. *The Elementary School Journal, 94,* 19–32.

Baum, A., & Fleming, I. (1993). Implications of psychological research on stress and technological accidents. *American Psychologist, 48,* 665–672.

Baum, A., & Paulus, P. B. (1987). Crowding. In D. Stokols & I. Altman (Eds.), *Handbook of environmental psychology* (Vol. 1, pp. 533–570). New York: Wiley-Interscience.

Baumeister, R. F. (1982). A self-presentational view of social phenomena. *Psychological Bulletin, 91,* 3–26.

Baumeister, R. F. (1987). How the self became a problem: A psychological review of historical research. *Journal of Personality and Social Psychology, 52,* 163–176.

Baumeister, R. F. (1990). Suicide as escape from self. *Psychological Review, 97,* 90–113.

Baumeister, R. F. (1991). *Meanings of life.* New York: Guilford Press.

Baumeister, R. F. (1997). *Evil: Inside human cruelty and violence.* New York: W. H. Freeman.

Baumeister, R. F. (2000). Gender differences in erotic plasticity: The female sex drive as socially flexible and responsive. *Psychological Bulletin, 126,* 347–374.

Baumeister, R. F. (2002). Ego depletion and self-control failure: An energy model of the self's executive function. *Self and Identity, 1,* 129–136.

Baumeister, R. F. (2005). *The cultural animal: Human nature, meaning, and social life.* New York: Oxford University Press.

Baumeister, R. F., & Bratslavsky, E. (1999). Passion, intimacy, and time: Passionate love as a function of change in intimacy. *Personality and Social Psychology Review, 3,* 49–67.

Baumeister, R. F., & Cairns, K. J. (1992). Repression and self-presentation: When audiences interfere with self-deceptive strategies. *Journal of Personality and Social Psychology, 62,* 851–862.

Baumeister, R. F., & Jones, E. E. (1978). When self-presentation is constrained by the target's knowledge: Consistency and compensation. *Journal of Personality and Social Psychology, 36,* 608–618.

Baumeister, R. F., & Leary, M. R. (1995). The need to belong: Desire for interpersonal attachments as a fundamental human motivation. *Psychological Bulletin, 117,* 497–529.

Baumeister, R. F., & Masicampo, E. J. (2010). Conscious thought is for facilitating social and cultural interactions: How mental simulations serve the animal-culture interface. *Psychological Review, 117,* 945–971.

Baumeister, R. F., & Tice, D. M. (1984). Role of self-presentation and choice in cognitive dissonance under forced compliance: Necessary or sufficient causes? *Journal of Personality and Social Psychology, 46,* 5–13.

Baumeister, R. F., & Tierney, J. (2011). *Willpower: Rediscovering the greatest human strength.* New York: Penguin Press.

Baumeister, R. F., & Twenge, J. M. (2002). Cultural suppression of female sexuality. *Review of General Psychology, 6,* 166–203.

Baumeister, R. F., & Vohs, K. D. (2004). Sexual economics: Sex as female resource for social exchange in heterosexual interactions. *Personality and Social Psychology Review, 8*(4), 339–363.

Baumeister, R. F., & Wotman, S. R. (1992). *Breaking hearts: The two sides of unrequited love.* New York: Guilford Press.

Baumeister, R. F., Bratslavsky, E., Finkenauer, C., & Vohs, K. D. (2001). Bad is stronger than good. *Review of General Psychology, 5*(4), 323–370. doi: 10.1037//1089-2680.5.4.323

Baumeister, R. F., Bratslavsky, E., Muraven, M., & Tice, D. M. (1998). Ego depletion: Is the active self a limited resource? *Journal of Personality and Social Psychology, 74,* 1252–1265.

Baumeister, R. F., Campbell, J. D., Krueger, J. I., & Vohs, K. D. (2003). Does high self-esteem cause better performance, interpersonal success, happiness, or healthier lifestyles? *Psychological Science in the Public Interest, 4,* 1–44.

Baumeister, R. F., Catanese, K. R., & Vohs, K. D. (2001). Is there a gender difference in strength of sex drive? Theoretical views, conceptual distinctions, and a review of relevant evidence. *Personality and Social Psychology Review, 5,* 242–273.

Baumeister, R. F., Catanese, K. R., & Wallace, H. M. (2002). Conquest by force: A narcissistic reactance theory of rape and sexual coercion. *Review of General Psychology, 6,* 92–135.

Baumeister, R. F., DeWall, C. N., Ciarocco, N. J., & Twenge, J. M. (2005). Social exclusion impairs self-regulation. *Journal of Personality and Social Psychology, 88,* 589–684.

Baumeister, R. F., Heatherton, T. F., & Tice, D. M. (1994). *Losing control: How and why people fail at self-regulation.* San Diego: Academic Press.

Baumeister, R. F., Hutton, D. G., & Tice, D. M. (1989). Cognitive processes during deliberate self-presentation: How self-presenters alter and misinterpret the behavior of their interaction partners. *Journal of Experimental Social Psychology, 25,* 59–78.

Baumeister, R. F., Masicampo, E. J., & DeWall, C. N. (2009). Prosocial benefits of feeling free: Disbelief in free will increases aggression and reduces helpfulness. *Personality and Social Psychology Bulletin, 35,* 260–268.

Baumeister, R. F., Masicampo, E. J., & Vohs, K. D. (2011). Do conscious thoughts cause behavior? *Annual Review of Psychology, 62,* 331–361.

Baumeister, R. F., Reis, H. T., & Delespaul, P. A. E. G. (1995). Subjective and experiential correlates of guilt in everyday life. *Personality and Social Psychology Bulletin, 21,* 1256–1268.

Baumeister, R. F., Smart, L., & Boden, J. M. (1996). Relation of threatened egotism to violence and aggression: The dark side of high self-esteem. *Psychological Review, 103,* 5–33.

Baumeister, R. F., Stillwell, A. M., & Heatherton, T. F. (1994). Guilt: An interpersonal approach. *Psychological Bulletin, 115,* 243–267. doi:10.1037/0033-2909.115.2.243

Baumeister, R. F., Stillwell, A. M., & Heatherton, T. F. (1995). Personal narratives about guilt: Role in action control and interpersonal relationships. *Basic and Applied Social Psychology, 17,* 173–198. doi: 10.1207/s15324834basp1701&2_10

Baumeister, R. F., Twenge, J. M., & Nuss, C. K. (2002). Effects of social exclusion on cognitive processes: Anticipated aloneness reduces intelligent thought. *Journal of Personality and Social Psychology, 83,* 817–827.

Baumeister, R. F., Wotman, S. R., & Stillwell, A. M. (1993). Unrequited love: On heartbreak, anger, guilt, scriptlessness, and humiliation. *Journal of Personality and Social Psychology, 64,* 377–394.

Baunach, D. M., Burgess, E. O., & Muse, C. S. (2010). Southern (dis)comfort: Sexual prejudice and contact with gay men and lesbians in the south. *Sociological Spectrum, 30*(1), 30–64.

Bawer, B. (2012). *The victims' revolution: The rise of identity studies and the closing of the liberal mind.* New York: Broadside Books.

Bay-Hinitz, A. K., Peterson, R. F., & Quilitch, H. R. (1994). Cooperative games: A way to modify aggressive and cooperative behaviors in young children. *Journal of Applied Behavior Analysis, 27,* 435–446.

Bazargan, S., Sherkat, D. E., & Bazargan, M. (2004). Religion and alcohol use among African-American and Hispanic inner-city emergency care patients. *Journal for the Scientific Study of Religion, 43,* 419–428.

Bazerman, M. H., Loewenstein, G. F., & White, S. B. (1992). Reversals of preference in allocation decisions: Judging an alternative versus choosing among alternatives. *Administrative Science Quarterly, 37*(2), 220–240.

BBC (2016, June 14). Orlando survivor: 'The guilt of being alive is heavy.' *BBC.* Retrieved from https://www.bbc.com/news/av/world-us-canada-36532267/orlando-survivor-the-guilt-of-being-alive-is-heavy

BBC. (2014, May 14). Gay penguins in Kent zoo are 'the best parents.' *BBC News.* Retrieved from https://www.bbc.com/news/uk-england-kent-27405652

BBC. (2016, January 4). *BBC News.* Sunnis and Shia: Islam's ancient schism. Retrieved from https://www.bbc.com/news/world-middle-east-16047709.

Beal, D. J., Cohen, R. R., Burke, M. J., & McLendon, C. L. (2003). Cohesion and performance in groups: A meta-analytic clarification of construct relations. *Journal of Applied Psychology, 88*(6), 989–1004.

Beaman, A. L., Barnes, P. J., & Klentz, B. (1978). Increasing helping rates through information dissemination: Teaching pays. *Personality and Social Psychology Bulletin, 4,* 406–411.

Bechara, A., Damasio, H., Tranel, D., & Damasio, A. R. (1997). Deciding advantageously before knowing the advantageous strategy. *Science, 275,* 1293–1295.

Beck, A. T. (1976). *Cognitive therapy and the emotional disorders.* New York: Meridian.

Beck, A. T. (1988). *Cognitive therapy of depression: A personal reflection.* The Malcolm Millar Lecture in Psychotherapy. Aberdeen: Scottish Cultural Press.

Beck, A. T., & Burns, D. (1978). Cognitive therapy of depressed suicidal outpatients. In J. O. Cole, A. F. Schatzberg, & S. H. Frazier (Eds.), *Depression: Biology, psychodynamics, and treatment* (pp. 199–211). New York: Plenum Press.

Beck, J. G., Bozman, A. W., & Qualtrough, T. (1991). The experience of sexual desire: Psychological correlates in a college sample. *Journal of Sex Research, 28,* 443–456.

Becker, A. E., Burwell, R. A., Herzog, D. B., Hamburg, P., & Gilman, S. E. (2002). Eating behaviours and attitudes following prolonged exposure to television among ethnic Fijian adolescent girls. *British Journal of Psychiatry, 180,* 509–514.

Becker, L. J. (1978). The joint effect of feedback and goal setting on performance: A field study of residential energy conservation. *Journal of Applied Psychology, 63,* 228–233.

Becker, M. H. (Ed.). (1974). The health belief model and personal health behavior. *Health Education Monographs, 2,* entire issue.

Beggan, J. K. (1992). On the social nature of nonsocial perception: The mere ownership effect. *Journal of Personality and Social Psychology, 62,* 229–237.

Beggan, J. K., Messick, D. M., & Allison, S. T. (1988). Social values and egocentric bias: Two tests of the might over morality hypothesis. *Journal of Personality and Social Psychology, 55,* 606–611.

Bègue, L., & Bastounis, M. (2003). Two spheres of belief in justice: Extensive support for the bidimensional model of belief in a just world. *Journal of Personality, 71,* 435–463.

Bègue, L., Beauvois J.-L., Courbet, D., Oberlé, D., Lepage, J., & Duke, A. A. (2015). Personality predicts obedience in a Milgram paradigm. *Journal of Personality, 83*(3), 299–306. doi: 10.1111/jopy.12104

Behrman, B. W., & Davey, S. L. (2001). Eyewitness identification in actual criminal cases: An archival analysis. *Law and Human Behavior, 25,* 475–491.

Beilock, S. L., & Carr, T. H. (2001). On the fragility of skilled performance: What governs choking under pressure? *Journal of Experimental Psychology: General, 130,* 701–725.

Beim, A., & Fine, G. A. (2007). The cultural frameworks of prejudice: Reputational images and the postwar disjuncture of Jews and Communism. *The Sociological Quarterly, 48*(3), 373–397. DOI: 10.1111/j.1533-8525.2007.00082.x

Bein, A. (1990). *The Jewish question: Biography of a world problem.* Fairleigh Dickinson University Press.

Bejciy-Spring, S. M. (2008). R-E-S-P-E-C-T: A model for the sensitive treatment of the bariatric patient. *Bariatric Nursing and Surgical Patient Care, 3*(1), 47–56.

Bell, A. P., & Weinberg, M. S. (1978). *Homosexualities: A study of diversity among men and women.* New York: Simon & Schuster.

Bell, P. A., & Greene, T. C. (1982). Thermal stress: Physiological comfort, performance, and social effects of hot and cold environments. In G. W. Evans (Ed.), *Environmental stress* (pp. 75–105). London: Cambridge University Press.

Belluz, J. (2018, October 16). This autism dad has a warning for anti-vaxers. *Vox.* Retrieved from https://www.vox.com/science-and-health/2018/10/16/17964992/vaccine-autism-book-peter-hotez

Belsky, J. (1985). Exploring individual differences in marital change across the transition to parenthood: The role of violated expectations. *Journal of Marriage and the Family, 47,* 1037–1044.

Belsky, J., Lang, M. E., & Rovine, M. (1985). Stability and change in marriage across the transition to parenthood: A second study. *Journal of Marriage and the Family, 47,* 855–865.

Belsky, J., Spanier, G. B., & Rovine, M. (1983). Stability and change in marriage across the transition to parenthood. *Journal of Marriage and the Family, 45,* 567–577.

Bem, D. J. (1965). An experimental analysis of self-persuasion. *Journal of Experimental Social Psychology, 1,* 199–218. Jones, E. E., & Gerard, H. B. (1967). *Foundations of social psychology.* New York: Wiley.

Bem, D. J. (1996). Exotic becomes erotic: A developmental theory of sexual orientation. *Psychological Review, 103,* 320–335.

Bem, D. J. (1998). Is EBE theory supported by evidence? Is it androcentric? A reply to Peplau et al. (1998). *Psychological Review, 105,* 395–398.

Benbow, C. P., Lubinski, D., Shea, D. L., & Eftekhari-Sanjani, H. (2000). Sex differences in mathematical reasoning ability: Their status 20 years later. *Psychological Science, 11,* 474–480.

Benenson, J. F. (2014). *Warriors and worriers: The survival of the sexes.* Oxford, UK: Oxford University Press.

Benitez-Quiroz, C. F., Wilbur, R. B., & Martinez, A. M. (2016). The not face: A grammaticalization of facial expressions of emotion. *Cognition, 15077-*84. doi:10.1016/j.cognition.2016.02.004

Benjamin, A. J., Jr., Kepes, S., & Bushman, B. J. (2018). Effects of weapons on aggressive thoughts, angry feelings, hostile appraisals, and aggressive behavior: A meta-analytic review of the weapons effect literature. *Personality and Social Psychology Review, 22*(4), 347–377. DOI: 10.1177/1088868317725419

Benson, G. P., & Zieman, G. L. (1981). *The relationship of weather to children's behavior problems.* Unpublished manuscript, Colorado State University, Fort Collins, CO.

Benson, P. L., Karabenick, S. A., & Lerner, R. M. (1976). Pretty pleases: The effects of physical attractiveness, race, and sex on receiving help. *Journal of Experimental Social Psychology, 12,* 409–415.

Benton, D. (2007). The impact of diet on anti-social, violent and criminal behaviour. *Neuroscience & Biobehavioral Reviews, 31*(5), 752–774.

Berenguer, J. (2010). The effect of empathy in environmental moral reasoning. *Environment and Behavior, 42,* 110–134.

Berglas, S. C., & Baumeister, R. F. (1993). *Your own worst enemy: Understanding the paradox of self-defeating behavior.* New York: Basic Books.

Berglas, S., & Jones, E. E. (1978). Drug choice as a self-handicapping strategy in response to non-contingent success. *Journal of Personality and Social Psychology, 36,* 405–417.

Bergmann, W., & Bowman, P. (2008). Anti-Semitic attitudes in Europe: A comparative perspective. *Journal of Social Issues, 64*(2), 343–362. DOI: 10.1111/j.1540-4560.2008.00565.x

Bergold, A. N., & Heaton, P. (2018). Does filler database size influence identification accuracy? *Law and Human Behavior, 42,* 227–243.

Berkowitz, A. D., & Perkins, H. W. (1987). Recent research on gender differences in collegiate alcohol use. *Journal of American College Health, 36,* 123–129.

Berkowitz, L. (1989). Frustration-aggression hypothesis: Examination and reformulation. *Psychological Bulletin, 106,* 59–73.

Berkowitz, L. (1993). *Aggression: Its causes, consequences, and control.* New York: McGraw-Hill.

Berkowitz, L., & Donnerstein, E. (1982). External validity is more than skin deep. *American Psychologist, 37,* 245–257.

Berkowitz, L., & LePage, A. (1967). Weapons as aggression-eliciting stimuli. *Journal of Personality and Social Psychology, 7,* 202–207.

Bernard, J. (1982). *The future of marriage.* New Haven, CT: Yale University Press.

Bernat, J. A., Calhoun, K. S., Adams, H. E., & Zeichner, A. (2001). Homophobia and physical aggression toward homosexual and heterosexual individuals. *Journal of Abnormal Psychology, 110,* 179–187.

Berscheid, E., & Walster, E. (1967). When does a harm-doer compensate a victim? *Journal of Personality and Social Psychology, 6,* 433–441.

Bettencourt, B. A., & Miller, N. (1996). Gender differences in aggression as a function of provocation: A meta-analysis. *Psychological Bulletin, 119,* 422–447.

Bhattacharjee, A., Dana, J., & Baron, J. (2017). Anti-profit beliefs: How people neglect the societal benefits of profit. *Journal of Personality and Social Psychology, 113,* 671–696.

Bhatti, B., Derezotes, D., Kim, S., & Specht, H. (1989). The association between child maltreatment and self-esteem. In A. M. Mecca, N. J. Smelser, & J. Vasconcellos (Eds.), *The social importance of self-esteem* (pp. 24–71). Berkeley: University of California Press.

Biddle, B. J., & Thomas, E. J. (1966). *Role theory: Concepts and research.* New York: Wiley.

Biel, A., Eek, D., & Gaerling, T. (1999). The importance of fairness for cooperation public-goods dilemmas. In P. Juslin (Ed.), *Judgment and decision making: Neo-Brunswikian and process-tracing approaches* (pp. 245–259). Mahwah, NJ: Erlbaum.

Biggs, A. T., Brockmole, J. R., & Witt, J. K. (2013). Armed and attentive: Holding a weapon can bias attentional priorities during scene viewing. *Attention, Perception, & Psychophysics, 75*(8), 1715–1724.

Bilewicz, M., Winiewski, M., Kofta, M., & Wójcik, A. (2013). Harmful ideas, the structure and consequences of anti-Semitic beliefs in Poland. *Political Psychology, 34*(6), 821–839. DOI: 10.1111/pops.12024

Billig, M., & Tajfel, H. (1973). Social categorization and similarity in intergroup behaviour. *European Journal of Social Psychology, 3*(1), 27–52.

Binder, J., Zagefka, H., Brown, R., Funke, F., Kessler, T., Mummendey, A., et al. (2009). Does contact reduce prejudice or does prejudice reduce contact? A longitudinal test of the contact hypothesis among majority and minority groups in three European countries. *Journal of Personality and Social Psychology, 96*(4), 843–856.

Biryukov, P. (1911). *Leo Tolstoy: His life and work.* New York: Charles Scribner's Sons.

Bishop, J. A., & Inderbitzen, H. M. (1995). Peer acceptance and friendship: An investigation of their relation to self-esteem. *Journal of Early Adolescence, 15,* 476–489.

Bishop, S. (2008, January 23). Don't bother with the "green" consumer. *Harvard Business Report.* Retrieved from http://www.hbrgreen.org/2008/01/dont_bother_with_the_green_con.html

Biss, R. K., Hasher, L., & Thomas, R. C. (2010). Positive mood is associated with the implicit use of distraction. *Motivation and Emotion, 34*(1), 73–77.

Bjerregaard, B. (2000). An empirical study of stalking victimization. *Violence and Victims, 15,* 389–406.

Blackstone, W. (1783). *Commentaries on the Laws of England* (9th ed., Vol. 4, p. 358). London: Strahan, Cadell & Prince.

Blackwell, B., & Hutchins, I. (1994). *Delights of the garden.* New York: Doubleday.

Blader, S. L., & Chen, Y. (2012). Differentiating the effects of status and power: A justice perspective. *Journal of Personality and Social Psychology, 102,* 994–1014.

Blanchard, F. A., & Frost, R. O. (1983). Two factors of restraint: Concern for dieting and fluctuations. *Behavior Research and Therapy, 21,* 259–267.

Blanchette, I. (2006). Snakes, spiders, guns, and syringes: How specific are evolutionary constraints on the detection of threatening stimuli? *The Quarterly Journal of Experimental Psychology, 59*(8), 1484–1504.

Bland, S. H., O'Leary, E. S., Farinaro, E., Jossa, F., & Trevisan, M. (1996). Long-term psychological effects of natural disasters. *Psychosomatic Medicine, 58,* 18–25.

Blankenship, K. L., & Wegener, D. T. (2008). Opening the mind to close it: Considering a message in light of important values increases message processing and later resistance to change. *Journal of Personality and Social Psychology, 94*(2), 196–213.

Blanton, H., & Gerrard, M. (1997). Effect of sexual motivation on men's risk perception for sexually transmitted disease: There must be 50 ways to justify a lover. *Health Psychology, 16,* 374–379.

Blascovich, J., Spencer, S. J., Quinn, D., & Steele, C. (2001). African Americans and high blood pressure: The role of stereotype threat. *Psychological Science, 12,* 225–229.

Blau, P. N. (1964). *Exchange and power in social life.* New York: Wiley.

Blue, L. A. (1991). Jury selection in a civil case. *Trial Lawyers Quarterly, 21,* 11–25.

Blumstein, P., & Schwartz, P. (1983). *American couples: Money, work, and sex.* New York: Morrow.

Boddington, L., & Kemp, S. (1999). Student debt, attitudes towards debt, impulsive buying, and financial management. *New Zealand Journal of Psychology, 28,* 89–93.

Bodenhausen, G. V. (1990). Stereotypes as judgmental heuristics: Evidence of circadian variations in discrimination. *Psychological Science, 1,* 319–322.

Bond, C. F., & Titus, L. J. (1983). Social facilitation: A meta-analysis of 241 studies. *Psychological Bulletin, 94,* 265–292.

Bond, C. F., Jr., & DePaulo, B. M. (2008). Individual differences in judging deception: Accuracy and bias. *Psychological Bulletin, 134*(4), 477–492.

Bond, R. A., & Smith, P. B. (1996). Culture and conformity: A meta-analysis of studies using Asch's (1952, 1956) line judgment task. *Psychological Bulletin, 119,* 111–137.

Bond, R. M., & Bushman, B. J. (2017). The contagious spread of violence through social networks in U.S. adolescents. *American Journal of Public Health, 107*(2), 288–294. doi:10.2105/AJPH.2016.303550

Bond, R., & Smith, P. B (1996). *Culture and conformity: A meta-analysis of studies using Asch's (1952b 1956) line judgment task.* Psychological Bulletin, 119 (1), 111–137.

Bonezzi, A., Brendl, C.M., & De Angelis, M. (2011). Stuck in the middle: The psychophysics of goal pursuit. *Psychological Science, 22,* 607–612.

Bonta, B. D. (1997). Cooperation and competition in peaceful societies. *Psychological Bulletin, 121,* 299–320.

Borman, W. C., Penner, L. A., Allen, T.D., & Motowidlo, S. J. (2001). Personality predictors of citizenship performance. *International Journal of Selection and Assessment, 9,* 52–69.

Bornstein, B. H., Deffenbacher, K. A., Penrod, S. D., & McGorty, E. C. (2012). Effects of exposure time and cognitive operations on facial identification accuracy: A meta-analysis of two variables associated with initial memory strength. *Psychology, Crime, & Law, 18,* 473–490.

Bornstein, R. F. (1989). Exposure and affect: Overview and meta-analysis of research, 1968–1987. *Psychological Bulletin, 106,* 265–289.

Bos, H. M. W., Gartrell, N. K., Van Balen, F., Peyser, H., & Sandfort, T. G. M. (2008). Children in planned lesbian families: A cross-cultural comparison between the United States and the Netherlands. *American Journal of Orthopsychiatry, 78*(2), 211–219.

Bosch, T. (2012, August 20). Why would someone cheat on a free online class that doesn't count toward anything? *Slate.* Retrieved from http://www.slate.com/blogs/future_tense/2012/08/20/coursera_plagiarism_why_would_students_cheat_in_a_free_online_class_that_doesn_t_over_academic_credit_.html

Boseley, S. (2010, January 28). Andrew Wakefield found 'irresponsible' by GMC over MMR vaccine scare. *The Guardian* (London). Retrieved from https://www.theguardian.com/society/2010/jan/28/andrew-wakefield-mmr-vaccine

Bostrom, R. N., Vlandis, J. W., & Rosenbaum, M. E. (1961). Grades as reinforcing contingencies and attitude change. *Journal of Educational Psychology, 52*(2), 112–115.

Bothwell, R. K., Deffenbacher, K. A., & Brigham, J. C. (1987). Correlations of eyewitness accuracy and confidence: Optimality hypothesis revisited. *Journal of Applied Psychology, 72,* 691–695.

Botta, R. A. (2000). The mirror of television: A comparison of black and white adolescents' body image. *Journal of Communication, 50,* 144–159.

Bottoms, B. L., Kalder, A. K., Stevenson, M. C., Oudekerk, B. A., Wiley, T. R., & Perona, A. (2011). Gender differences in jurors' perceptions of infanticide involving disabled and non-disabled infant victims. *Child Abuse & Neglect, 35,* 127–141.

Bowlby, J. (1969). *Attachment and loss: Vol. 1. Attachment.* New York: Basic Books.

Bowlby, J. (1973). *Attachment and loss: Vol. 2. Separation anxiety and anger.* New York: Basic Books.

Bowler. R, Meqler, D., Huel. G., & Cone, J. (1994). Psychological, psychosocial, and psychophysiological sequelae in a community affected by a railroad chemical disaster. *Journal of Traumatic Stress, 7,* 601–624.

Bowles, T. (1999). Focusing on time orientation to explain adolescent self concept and academic achievement: Part II. Testing a model. *Journal of Applied Health Behaviour, 1,* 1–8.

Boyd, R., & Richerson, P. J. (2005). *The origin and evolution of cultures.* New York: Oxford University Press.

Bradfield, A., & McQuiston, D. E. (2004). When does evidence of eyewitness confidence inflation affect judgments in a criminal trial? *Law and Human Behavior, 28,* 369–387.

Bradley, G. W. (1978). Self-serving biases in the attribution process: A reexamination of the fact or fiction question. *Journal of Personality and Social Psychology, 36,* 56–71.

Bradley, S. J. (1990). Affect regulation and psychopathology: Bridging the mind-body gap. *Canadian Journal of Psychiatry, 35,* 540–547.

Braginski, B. M., Braginski, D. D., & Ring, K. (1969). *Methods of madness: The mental hospital as a last resort.* New York: Holt, Rinehart & Winston.

Branden, N. (1994). *The six pillars of self-esteem.* New York: Bantam Books.

Brawley, L. R., Carron, A. V., & Widmeyer, W. N. (1993). The influence of the group and its cohesiveness on perceptions of group goal-related variables. *Journal of Sport and Exercise Psychology, 15*(3), 245–260.

Breaugh, J. A., & Frye, N. K. (2008). Work-family conflict: The importance of family-friendly employment practices and family-supportive supervisors. *Journal of Business Psychology, 22,* 345–353.

Brechner, K. C. (1977). An experimental analysis of social traps. *Journal of Experimental Social Psychology, 13,* 552–564.

Brehm, J. W. (1966). *A theory of psychological reactance.* New York: Academic Press.

Brehm, J. W. (1972). *Responses to loss of freedom: A theory of psychological reactance.* Morristown, NJ: General Learning Press.

Brehm, J. W., & Cole, A. H. (1966). Effect of a favor which reduces freedom. *Journal of Personality and Social Psychology, 3,* 420–426.

Brehm, S. S., & Brehm, J. W. (1981). *Psychological reactance.* New York: Wiley.

Bremner, R. H., Koole, S. L., & Bushman, B. J. (2011). "Pray for those who mistreat you:" Effects of prayer on anger and aggression. *Personality and Social Psychology Bulletin, 37*(6), 830–837.

Brenan, M. (2017, December 26). Nurses keep healthy lead as most honest, ethical profession. *Gallup Economy.* https://news.gallup.com/poll/224639/nurses-keep-healthy-lead-honest-ethical-profession.aspx?g_source=Economy&g_medium=newsfeed&g_campaign=tiles

Brenan, M. (2018, December 20). Nurses again outpace other professions for honesty, ethics. *Gallup.* https://news.gallup.com/poll/245597/nurses-again-outpace-professions-honesty-ethics.aspx

Brennan, K. A., & Shaver, P. R. (1995). Dimensions of adult attachment, affect regulation, and romantic relationship functioning. *Personality and Social Psychology Bulletin, 21,* 267–283.

Brennan, K. A., Clark, C. L., & Shaver, P. R. (1998). Self-report measures of adult attachment. In J. A. Simpson & W. S. Rholes (Eds.), *Attachment theory and close relationships* (pp. 46–76). New York: Guilford Press.

Brewer, M. B. (1979). In-group bias in the minimal intergroup situation: A cognitive-motivational analysis. *Psychological Bulletin, 86*(2), 307–324.

Brewer, M. B., & Silver, M. (1978). Ingroup bias as a function of task characteristics. *European Journal of Social Psychology, 8*(3), 393–400.

Brewer, N., Keast, A., & Rishworth, A. (2002). The confidence-accuracy relationship in eyewitness identification: The effects of reflection and disconfirmation on correlation and calibration. *Journal of Experimental Psychology: Applied, 8,* 44–56.

Brewer, N., Keast, A., & Sauer, J. D. (2010). Children's eyewitness identification performance: Effects of a Not Sure response option and accuracy motivation. *Legal and Criminological Psychology, 15,* 261–277.

Brickman, P., & Campbell, D. T. (1971). Hedonic relativism and planning the good society. In M. H. Apley (Ed.), *Adaptation-level theory: A symposium* (pp. 287–302). New York: Academic Press.

Brickman, P., Coates, D., & Janoff-Bulman, R. (1978). Lottery winners and accident victims: Is happiness relative? *Journal of Personality and Social Psychology, 36,* 917–927.

Brigham, J. C., & Bothwell, R. K. (1983). The ability of prospective jurors to estimate the accuracy of eyewitness identification. *Law and Human Behavior, 7,* 19–30.

Briñol, P., Gascó, M., Petty, R. E., & Horcajo, J. (2013). Treating thoughts as material objects can increase or decrease their impact on evaluation. *Psychological Science, 24*(1), 41–47. https://doi-org.proxy.lib.umich.edu/10.1177/0956797612449176

Broadbent, E. (2019). Illness cognitions and beliefs. In T. A. Revenson & R. A. R. Gurung (Eds.), *Handbook of health psychology* (pp. 252–262). New York: Routledge.

Brockner, J. (1983). Low self-esteem and behavioral plasticity: Some implications. In L. Wheeler & P. Shaver (Eds.), *Review of personality and social psychology, Vol. 4* (pp. 237–271). Beverly Hills, CA: Sage.

Brockner, J., & Lloyd, K. (1986). Self-esteem and likability: Separating fact from fantasy. *Journal of Research in Personality, 20,* 496–508.

Brockner, J., Greenberg, J., Brockner, A., Bortz, J., Davy, J., & Carter, C. (1986). Layoffs, equity theory, and work performance: Further evidence of the impact of survivor guilt. *Academy of Management Journal, 29,* 373–384.

Brodish, A. B., & Devine, P. G. (2009). The role of performance-avoidance goals and worry in mediating the relationship between stereotype threat and performance. *Journal of Experimental Social Psychology, 45*(1), 180–185.

Brody, L. R. (1996). Gender, emotional expression, and parent-child boundaries. In R. D. Kavanaugh, B. Zimmerberg, & S. Fein (Eds.), *Emotion: Interdisciplinary perspectives* (pp. 139–170). Mahwah, NJ: Eribaum.

Bronson, P., & Merryman, A. (2009, September 4). Even babies discriminate: A nurtureshock excerpt. *Newsweek.* Retrieved from http://www.newsweek.com/even-babies-discriminate-nurtureshock-excerpt-79233

Brown, B. (1987). Territoriality. In D. Stokols & I. Altman (Eds.), *Handbook of environmental psychology* (Vol. 1, pp. 505–531). New York: Wiley-Interscience.

Brown, B. B., & Werner, C. M. (1985). Social cohesiveness, territoriality, and holiday decorations: The influence of cul-de-sacs. *Environment and Behavior, 17,* 539–565.

Brown, J. F. (1943). Social and psychological factors in the anti-Semitic attitude. *Journal of Educational Sociology, 16,* 351–354. https://doi-org.proxy.lib.umich.edu/10.2307/2261771

Brown, K. W., & Moskowitz, D. S. (1997). Does unhappiness make you sick? The role of affect and neuroticism in the experience of common physical symptoms. *Journal of Personality and Social Psychology, 72*(4), 907–917.

Brown, K. W., & Ryan, R. M. (2003). The benefits of being present: Mindfulness and its role in psychological well-being. *Journal of Personality and Social Psychology, 84,* 822–848.

Brown, L. R. (1994). *State of the world 1994.* New York: Norton.

Brown, M. J., & Groscup, J. L. (2009). Homophobia and acceptance of stereotypes about gays and lesbians. *Individual Differences Research, 7*(3), 159–167.

Brown, N. R., & Sinclair, R. C. (1999). Estimating number of lifetime sexual partners: Men and women do it differently. *Journal of Sex Research, 36,* 292–297.

Brown-Iannuzzi, J. L., McKee, S., & Gervais, W. M. (2018). Atheist horns and religious halos: Mental representations of atheists and theists. *Journal of Experimental Psychology: General, 147*(2), 292–297. DOI: 10.1037/xge0000376.supp (Supplemental)

Brownstein, S. C., Wolf, I. K., & Green, S. W. (2000). *Barron's how to prepare for the GRE: Graduate Record Examination.* Hauppauge, NY: Barron's Education Series, p. 6.

Brummelman, E., Thomaes, S., & Sedikides, C. (2016). Separating narcissism from self-esteem. *Current Directions in Psychological Science, 25,* 8–13.

Brunell, A. B., Gentry, W. A., Campbell, W. K., Hoffman, B. J., Kuhnert, K. W., & DeMarree, K. G. (2008). Leadership emergence: The case of the narcissistic leader. *Personality and Social Psychology Bulletin, 34,* 1663–1676.

Bruner, J. A., & Mason, J. L. (1968). The influence of driving time upon shopping center preference. *Journal of Marketing, 32*(2), 57–61.

Bryan, C. J., Walton, G. M., Rogers, T., & Dweck, C. S. (2011). Motivating voter turnout by invoking the self. *PNAS, 108*(31), 12653–12656.

Bryman, A. S. (1996). The importance of context: Qualitative research and the study of leadership. *Leadership Quarterly, 7,* 353–370.

Bryner, J. (2010, May 28). Today's college students lack empathy. *LiveScience.* Retrieved August 26, 2019 from http://www.livescience.com/9918-today-college-students-lack-empathy.html

Bryner, J. (2018, April 23). The "end of the world" is today. Here's why we're still here. Live Science. Retrieved from https://www.livescience.com/62378-doomsday-april-23.html

Buck, D. M., Plant, E. A., Ratcliff, J., Zielaskowski, K., & Boerner, P. (2013). Concern over the misidentification of sexual orientation: Social contagion and the avoidance of sexual minorities. *Journal of Personality and Social Psychology, 105,* 941–960.

Buckles, E. E., & Trapnell, P. D. (2013). Disgust facilitates outgroup dehumanization. *Group Processes & Intergroup Relations, 16*(6), 771–780. 10.1177/1368430212471738

Budesheim, T. L., & DePaola, S. J. (1994). Beauty or the beast? The effects of appearance, personality and issue information on evaluations of political candidates. *Personality and Social Psychology Bulletin, 20,* 339–348.

Budesheim, T. L., Houston, D. A., & DePaola, S. J. (1996). The persuasiveness of in-group and out-group political messages: The case of negative political campaigning. *Journal of Personality and Social Psychology, 70,* 523–534.

Buehler, R., & McFarland, C. (2001). Intensity bias in affective forecasting: The role of temporal focus. *Personality and Social Psychology Bulletin, 27,* 1480–1493.

Buehler, R., Griffin, D., & Ross, M. (1994). Exploring the "planning fallacy": Why people underestimate their task completion times. *Journal of Personality and Social Psychology, 67,* 366–381.

Buhrmester, D., Furman, W., Wittenberg, M. T., & Reis, H. T. (1988). Five domains of interpersonal competence in peer relationships. *Journal of Personality and Social Psychology, 55,* 991–1008.

Bulman, R. J., & Wortman, C. B. (1977). Attributions of blame and coping in the "real world": Severe accident victims react to their lot. *Journal of Personality and Social Psychology, 35,* 351–363.

Bunker, B. B., Zubek, J. M., Vanderslice, V. J., & Rice, R. W. (1992). Quality of life in dual-career families: Commuting versus single-residence couples. *Journal of Marriage and the Family, 54,* 399–407.

Bureau of Labor Statistics (2014; February 25). Volunteering in the United States, 2013. Retrieved August 26, 2019 from http://www.bls.gov/news.release/volun.nr0.htm

Burger, J. M. (1986). Increasing compliance by improving the deal: The that's-not-all technique. *Journal of Personality and Social Psychology, 51,* 277–283.

Burger, J. M. (2009). Replicating Milgram: Would people still obey today? *American Psychologist, 64*(1), 1–11.

Burger, J. M., Cooper, H. M., & Good, T. L. (1982). Teacher attributions of student performance: Effects of outcome. *Personality and Social Psychology Bulletin, 8,* 685–690.

Burgess, J. (2008) *"All your chocolate rain are belong to us?" Viral video, YouTube and the dynamics of participatory culture.* In UNSPECIFIED (Ed.), *Video vortex reader: Responses to YouTube.* Institute of Network Cultures, Amsterdam, pp. 101–109. Retrieved from http://eprints.qut.edu.au/18431/1/18431.pdf

Burmeister, J. M., Kiefner, A. E., Carels, R. A., & Musher-Eizenman, D. R. (2013). Weight bias in graduate school admissions. *Obesity, 21*(5), 918–920. doi: 10.1002/oby.20171

Burnay, J., Bushman, B. J., & Larøi, F. (2019). Effects of sexualized video games on online sexual harassment. *Aggressive Behavior, 45*(2), 214–223. DOI: 10.1002/ab.21811

Burnstein, E., Crandall, C., & Kitayama, S. (1994). Some neo-Darwinian decision rules for altruism: Weighing cues for inclusive fitness as a function of the biological importance of the decision. *Journal of Personality and Social Psychology, 67,* 773–789.

Burris, C. T., Harmon-Jones, E., & Tarpley, W. R. (1997). "By faith alone": Religious agitation and cognitive dissonance. *Basic and Applied Social Psychology, 19,* 17–31.

Bushman, B. J. (1993). What's in a name? The moderating role of public self-consciousness on the relation between brand label and brand preference. *Journal of Applied Psychology, 78,* 857–861.

Bushman, B. J. (1997). Effects of alcohol on human aggression: Validity of proposed explanations. In D. Fuller, R. Dietrich, & E. Gottheil (Eds.), *Recent developments in alcoholism: Alcohol and violence* (Vol. 13, pp. 227–243). New York: Plenum Press.

Bushman, B. J. (2002). Does venting anger feed or extinguish the flame? Catharsis, rumination, distraction, anger, and aggressive responding. *Personality and Social Psychology Bulletin, 28,* 724–731.

Bushman, B. J. (2016). Violent media exposure and hostile appraisals: A meta-analytic review. *Aggressive Behavior, 42*(6), 605–613. DOI: 10.1002/ab.21655

Bushman, B. J. (2018). Teaching students about violent media effects. *Teaching of Psychology, 45*(2), 200–206. DOI: 10.1177/0098628318762936

Bushman, B. J. (2019). Media violence statements. Retrieved August 25, 2019 from http://u.osu.edu/bushman.20/statements-on-media-violence-effects-by-major-scientific-groups/

Bushman, B. J., & Anderson, C. A. (2001). Is it time to pull the plug on the hostile versus instrumental aggression dichotomy? *Psychological Review, 108,* 273–279.

Bushman, B. J., & Anderson, C. A. (2001). Media violence and the American public: Scientific facts versus media misinformation. *American Psychologist, 56,* 477–489. doi:10.1037/0003-066X.56.6–7.477

Bushman, B. J., & Anderson, C. A. (2015). Understanding causality in the effects of media violence. *American Behavioral Scientist, 59*(14), 1807–1821. DOI: 10.1177/0002764215596554

Bushman, B. J., & Anderson, C. A. (1998). Methodology in the study of human aggression: Integrating experimental and nonexperimental findings. In R. G. Geen & E. I. Donnerstein (Eds.), *Human aggression: Theories, research, and implications for policy* (pp. 23–48). New York: Academic Press.

Bushman, B. J., & Baumeister, R. F. (1998). Threatened egotism, narcissism, self-esteem, and direct and displaced aggression: Does self-love or self-hate lead to violence? *Journal of Personality and Social Psychology, 75,* 219–229.

Bushman, B. J., & Baumeister, R. F. (2002). Does self-love or self-hate lead to violence. *Journal of Research in Personality, 36,* 543–545.

Bushman, B. J., & Bonacci, A. M. (2004). You've got mail: Using e-mail to examine the effect of prejudiced attitudes on discrimination against Arabs. *Journal of Experimental Social Psychology, 40,* 753–759.

Bushman, B. J., & Cantor, J. (2003). Media ratings for violence and sex: Implications for policy makers and parents. *American Psychologist, 58,* 130–141.

Bushman, B. J., & Cooper, H. M. (1990). Effects of alcohol on human aggression: An integrative research review. *Psychological Bulletin, 107,* 341–354.

Bushman, B. J., & Huesmann, L. R. (2006). Short-term and long-term effects of violent media on aggression in children and adults. *Archives of Pediatrics & Adolescent Medicine, 160*(4), 348–352. doi: 10.1001/archpedi.160.4.348

Bushman, B. J., Baumeister, R. F., & Phillips, C. M. (2001). Do people aggress to improve their mood? Catharsis beliefs, affect regulation opportunity, and aggressive responding. *Journal of Personality and Social Psychology, 81,* 17–32.

Bushman, B. J., Baumeister, R. F., & Stack, A. D. (1999). Catharsis, aggression, and persuasive influence: Self-fulfilling or self-defeating prophecies? *Journal of Personality and Social Psychology, 76,* 367–376.

Bushman, B. J., Bonacci, A. M., Van Dijk, M., & Baumeister, R. F. (2003). Narcissism, sexual refusal, and sexual aggression: Testing a narcissistic reactance model of sexual coercion. *Journal of Personality and Social Psychology, 84,* 1027–1040.

Bushman, B. J., DeWall, C. N., Pond, R. S. Jr., & Hanus, M. D. (2014). Low glucose relates to greater aggression in married couples. *Proceedings of the National Academy of Sciences (PNAS), 111*(17), 6254–6257. DOI: 10.1073/pnas.1400619111

Bushman, B. J., Gollwitzer, M., & Cruz, C. (2015). There is broad consensus: Media researchers agree that violent media increase aggression in children, and pediatricians and parents concur. *Psychology of Popular Media Culture, 4*(3), 200–214. DOI: 10.1037/ppm0000046

Bushman, B. J., Jamieson, P. E., Weitz, I., & Romer, D. (2013). Gun violence trends in movies. *Pediatrics, 132*(6), 1014–1018. doi: 10.1542/peds.2013–1600

Bushman, B. J., Moeller, S. J., & Crocker, J. (2011). Sweets, sex, or self-esteem? Comparing the value of self-esteem boosts with other pleasant rewards. *Journal of Personality, 79*(5), 993–1012.

Bushman, B. J., Moeller, S. J., Konrath, S., & Crocker, J. (2012). Investigating the link between liking versus wanting self-esteem and depression in a nationally representative sample of American adults. *Journal of Personality, 80*(5), 1455–1471. DOI: 10.1111/j.1467-6494.2012.00781.x.

Bushman, B. J., Newman, K., Calvert, S. L., Downey, G., Dredze, M., Gottfredson, M., Jablonski, N. G., Masten, A., Morrill, C., Neill, D. B., Romer, D., & Webster, D. (2016). Youth violence: What we know and what we need to know. *American Psychologist, 71*(1), 17–39. DOI: 10.1037/a0039687

Bushman, B. J., Kerwin, T., Whitlock, T., & Weisenberger, J. M.(2017). The weapons effect on wheels: Motorists drive more aggressively when there is a gun in the vehicle. *Journal of Experimental Social Psychology, 73,* 82–85. DOI: 10.1016/j.jesp.2017.06.007

Buss, A. H. (1961). *The psychology of aggression.* New York: John Wiley.

Buss, A. H. (1989). Temperaments as personality traits. In G. A. Kohnstamm, J. E. Bates, & M. Rothbart (Eds.), *Temperament in childhood* (pp. 49–58). Chichester, West Sussex, UK: Wiley.

Buss, D. M. (1990). The evolution of anxiety and social exclusion. *Journal of Social and Clinical Psychology, 9,* 196–210.

Buss, D. M. (1991). Evolutionary personality psychology. *Annual Review of Psychology, 42,* 459–491.

Buss, D. M. (1994). *The evolution of desire: Strategies of human mating.* New York: Basic Books.

Buss, D. M. (1999). *Evolutionary psychology: The new science of the mind.* New York: Allen & Bacon.

Buss, D. M., & Schmitt, D. P. (1993). Sexual strategies theory: An evolutionary perspective on human mating. *Psychological Review, 100,* 204–232.

Buss, D. M., & Shackelford, T. K. (1997). From vigilance to violence: Mate retention tactics in married couples. *Journal of Personality and Social Psychology, 72,* 346–361.

Buss, D. M., Larsen, R. J., Westen, D., & Semmelroth, J. (1992). Sex differences in jealousy: Evolution, physiology, and psychology. *Psychological Science, 3,* 251–255.

Butler, J. L., & Baumeister, R. F. (1998). The trouble with friendly faces: Skilled performance with a supportive audience. *Journal of Personality and Social Psychology, 75,* 1213–1230.

Butz, D. A., Plant, E. A., & Doerr, C. (2007). Liberty and justice for all? The implications of exposure to the United States flag for intergroup relations. *Personality and Social Psychology Bulletin, 33,* 396–408.

Buunk, B. P. & Hupka, R. B. (1987). Cross-cultural differences in the elicitation of sexual jealousy. *Journal of Sex Research, 23,* 12–22.

Buunk, B. P., Angleitner, A., Oubaid, V., & Buss, D. M. (1996). Sex differences in jealousy in evolutionary and cultural perspective: Tests from the Netherlands, Germany, and the United States. *Psychological Science, 7,* 1103–1116.

Buzinski, S. G., Clark, J., Cohen, M., Buck, B., & Roberts, S. P. (2018). Insidious assumptions: How pluralistic ignorance of studying behavior relates to exam performance. *Teaching of Psychology, 45*(4), 333–339. https://doi-org.proxy.lib.umich.edu/10.1177/0098628318796919

Byrne, D. (1971). *The attraction paradigm.* New York: Academic Press.

Cacioppo, J. T., & Gardner, W. L. (1999). Emotion. *Annual Review of Psychology, 50,* 191–214.

Cacioppo, J. T., & Hawkley, L. C. (2005). People thinking about people: The vicious cycle of being a social outcast in one's own mind. In K. D. Williams, J. P. Forgas, & W. von Hippel (Eds.), *The social outcast: Ostracism, social exclusion, rejection, and bullying* (pp. 91–108). New York: Psychology Press.

Cacioppo, J. T., & Petty, R. E. (1980). Sex differences in influenceability: Toward specifying the underlying processes. *Personality and Social Psychology Bulletin,* 6(4), 651–656.

Cacioppo, J. T., & Petty, R. E. (1982). The need for cognition. *Journal of Personality and Social Psychology, 42,* 116–131.

Cacioppo, J. T., & Petty, R. E. (1989). Effects of message repetition on argument processing, recall and persuasion. *Basic and Applied Social Psychology, 10,* 3–12.

Cacioppo, J. T., Ernst, J. M., Burleson, M. H., McClintock, M. K., Malarkey, W. B., Hawkley, L. C., et al. (2000). Lonely traits and concomitant physiological processes: The MacArthur Social Neuroscience Studies. *International Journal of Psychophysiology, 35,* 143–154.

Cacioppo, J. T., Hawkley, L. C., Berntson, G. G., Ernst, J. M., Gibbs, A. C., Stickgold, R., et al. (2002). Lonely days invade the nights: Social modulation of sleep efficiency. *Psychological Science, 13,* 385–388.

Cacioppo, J. T., Hawkley, L. C., Crawford, L. E., Ernst, J. M., Burleson, M. H., Kowalewski, R. B., et al. (2002). Loneliness and health: Potential mechanisms. *Psychosomatic Medicine, 64,* 407–417.

Caesar, P. L. (1988). Exposure to violence in the families-of-origin among wife-abusers and maritally nonviolent men. *Violence and Victims, 3,* 49–63.

Caldwell, M. A., & Peplau, L. A. (1982). Sex differences in same-sex friendships. *Sex Roles, 8,* 721–732.

Calhoun, J. B. (1962). Population density and social pathology, *Scientific American, 206,* 139–148.

Call, V., Sprecher, S., & Schwartz, P. (1995). The incidence and frequency of marital sex in a national sample. *Journal of Marriage and the Family, 57,* 639–650.

Cameron, J., Banko, K. M., & Pierce, W. D. (2001). Pervasive negative effects of rewards on intrinsic motivation: The myth continues. *The Behavior Analyst, 24,* 1–44.

Campbell, A. (1981). *The sense of well-being in America.* New York: McGraw-Hill.

Campbell, A., Converse, P. E., & Rogers, W. L. (1976). *The quality of American life: Perceptions, evaluations, and satisfactions.* New York: Russell Sage.

Campbell, D. T. (1958). Common fate, similarity, and other indices of the status of aggregates of persons as social entities. *Behavioral Science, 3,* 14–25.

Campbell, J. D. (1986). Similarity and uniqueness: The effects of attribute type, relevance, and individual differences in self-esteem and depression. *Journal of Personality and Social Psychology, 50,* 281–294.

Campbell, J. D. (1990). Self-esteem and clarity of the self-concept. *Journal of Personality and Social Psychology, 59,* 538–549.

Campbell, J. D., & Fehr, B. A. (1990). Self-esteem and perceptions of conveyed impressions: Is negative affectivity associated with greater realism? *Journal of Personality and Social Psychology, 58,* 122–133.

Campbell, J. D., Chew, B., & Scratchley, L. S. (1991). Cognitive and emotional reactions to daily events: The effects of self-esteem and self complexity. *Journal of Personality, 59,* 473–505.

Campbell, J. K. (1965). Honour and the devil. In J. G. Peristiany (Ed.), *Honour and shame: The values of Mediterranean society* (pp. 112–175). London: Weidenfeld & Nicolson.

Campbell, L. (2017). We've broken down your entire life into years spent doing tasks. *Huffington Post.* Retrieved from https://www.huffingtonpost.com.au/2017/10/18/weve-broken-down-your-entire-life-into-years-spent-doing-tasks_a_23248153/

Campbell, W. K. (1999). Narcissism and romantic attraction. *Journal of Personality and Social Psychology, 77,* 1254–1270.

Campbell, W. K. (2005). *When you love a man who loves himself.* Naperville, IL: Sourcebooks.

Campbell, W. K., & Foster, C. A. (2002). Narcissism and commitment in romantic relationships: An Investment Model analysis. *Personality and Social Psychology Bulletin, 28,* 484–495.

Campbell, W. K., & Sedikides, C. (1999). Self-threat magnifies the self-serving bias: A meta-analytic integration. *Review of General Psychology, 3,* 23–43.

Campbell, W. K., Foster, C. A., & Finkel, E. J. (2002). Does self-love lead to love for others? A story of narcissistic game playing. *Journal of Personality and Social Psychology, 83,* 340–354.

Campbell, W. K., Reeder, G. D., Sedikides, C., & Elliot, A. J. (2000). Narcissism and comparative self-enhancement strategies. *Journal of Research in Personality, 34,* 329–347.

Cannon, W. B. (1914). The interrelations of emotions as suggested by recent physiological researches. *American Journal of Physiology, 25,* 256–282.

Cannon, W. B. (1929). *Bodily changes in pain, hunger, fear and rage.* Oxford: Appleton.

Cantor, J. R., & Venus, P. (1980). The effect of humor on recall of a radio advertisement. *Journal of Broadcasting, 24,* 13–22.

Cao, B., & Lin, W.-Y. (2017). Revisiting the contact hypothesis: Effects of different modes of computer-mediated communication on intergroup relationships. *International Journal of Intercultural Relations, 58,* 23–30. DOI: 10.1016/j.ijintrel.2017.03.003

Cappell, C., & Heiner, R. B. (1990). The intergenerational transmission of family aggression. *Journal of Family Violence, 5,* 135–152.

Caprariello, P. A. & Reis, H. T. (2013). To do, to have, or to share? Valuing experiences over material possessions depends on the involvement of others. *Journal of Personality and Social Psychology, 104,* 199–215.

Carlsmith, K. M., Wilson, T. D., & Gilbert, D. T. (2008). The paradoxical consequences of revenge. *Journal of Personality and Social Psychology, 95*(6), 1316–1324.

Carlson, C. A., Jones, A. R., Whittington, J. E., Locameir, R. F., Carlson, M. A., & Wooten, A. R. (2019). Lineup fairness: Propitious heterogeneity and the diagnostic feature-detection hypothesis. *Cognitive Research: Principles and Implications, 4:*2.

Carlson, J. M., Fee, A. L., & Reinke, K. S. (2009). Backward masked snakes and guns modulate spatial attention. *Evolutionary Psychology, 7*(4), 534–544.

Carnegie Hero Fund Commission. (2002). Requirements for a Carnegie Medal. Available August 26, 2019 at http://www.carnegiehero.org/nominate.php

Carpenter, C. S., & Stehr, M. F. (2010). Intended and unintended effects of youth bicycle helmet laws. The National Bureau of Economonic Research. Retrieved from https://www.nber.org/papers/w15658

Carr, J. E., & Tann, E. K. (1976). In search of the true Amok: Amok as viewed within Malay culture. *American Journal of Psychiatry, 133*(11), 1295–1299.

Carroll, J. S. (1978). The effect of imagining an event on expectations for the event: An interpretation in terms of the availability heuristic. *Journal of Experimental Social Psychology, 14,* 88–96.

Carrus, G., Passafaro, P., & Bonnes, M. (2008). Emotions, habits and rational choices in ecological behaviours: The case of recycling and use of public transportation. *Journal of Environmental Psychology, 28,* 51–62.

Carver, C. S., & Harmon-Jones, E. (2009). Anger is an approach-related affect: Evidence and implications. *Psychological Bulletin, 135,* 183–204.

Carver, C. S., & Scheier, M. F. (1981). *Attention and self-regulation: A control therapy approach to human behavior.* New York: Springer Press.

Carver, C. S., & Scheier, M. F. (1982). Control theory: A useful conceptual framework for personality-social, clinical and health psychology. *Psychological Bulletin, 92,* 111–135.

Carver, C. S., & Scheier, M. F. (1990). Origins and functions of positive and negative affect: A control-process view. *Psychological Review, 97,* 19–35.

Carver, C. S., & Scheier, M. F. (1994). Situational coping and coping dispositions in a stressful transaction. *Journal of Social and Personality Psychology, 56,* 267–283.

Case, D. A., Fantino, E., & Goodie, A. S. (1999). Base-rate training without case cues reduces base-rate neglect. *Psychonomic Bulletin and Review, 6*(2), 319–327.

Cash, T. F., & Janda, L. H. (1984). The eye of the beholder. *Psychology Today, 18,* 46–52.

Caspi, A., & Roberts, B. W. (2001). Personality development across the life course: The argument for change and continuity. *Psychological Inquiry, 12,* 49–66.

Ceci, S. J., Peters, D., & Plotkin, J. (1985). Human subjects review, personal values, and the regulation of social sciences research. *American Psychologist, 51,* 768–784.

Cell phone or pheromone? New props for mating game. (2000, November 7). *New York Times.*

Centers for Disease Control and Prevention (2014). Q&As about vaccination options for preventing measles, mumps, rubella, and varicella. Retrieved from http://www.cdc.gov/vaccines/vpd-vac/combo-vaccines/mmrv/vacopt-faqs-hcp.htm

Centers for Disease Control and Prevention. (2014). Best practices for comprehensive tobacco control programs-2014. Retrieved from https://www.cdc.gov/tobacco/stateandcommunity/best_practices/pdfs/2014/comprehensive.pdf

Centers for Disease Control and Prevention. (n.d.). Venomous Snakes. Retrieved from https://www.cdc.gov/niosh/topics/snakes/

Centers for Disease Control and Prevention. Key Statistics from the National Survey of Family Growth—N Listing. Retrieved from https://www.cdc.gov/nchs/nsfg/key_statistics/n.htm

Centers for Disease Control. (2012). Overweight and obesity. Retrieved from http://www.cdc.gov/obesity/data/trends.HTML

Centers for Disease Control. (2016). *Sexual identity, sex of sexual contacts, and health-risk behaviors among students in grades 9–12: youth risk behavior surveillance.* Atlanta, GA: U.S. Department of Health and Human Services.

Centers for Disease Control. (2018). Alcohol and public health. Retrieved from https://www.cdc.gov/alcohol/onlinetools.htm

Cesario, J., Plaks, J. E., & Higgins, E. T. (2006). Automatic social behavior as motivated preparation to interact. *Journal of Personality and Social Psychology, 90,* 893–910.

Chait, J. (2013, April 2). Teachers cheating on tests: Not a big deal. *New York Magazine.* Retrieved from http://nymag.com/daily/intelligencer/2013/04/teachers-cheating-on-tests-not-a-big-deal.html

Chajut, E., & Algom, D. (2003). Selective attention improves under stress: Implications for theories of social cognition. *Journal of Personality and Social Psychology, 85,* 231–248.

Chan, W., McCrae, R. R., De Fruyt, F., Jussim, L., Löckenhoff, C. E., De Bolle, M., et al. (2012). Stereotypes of age differences in personality traits: Universal and accurate? *Journal of Personality and Social Psychology. 103,* 1050–1066. doi: 10.1037/a0029712

Chandola, T., Brunner, E., & Marmot, M. (2006). Chronic stress at work and the metabolic syndrome: Prospective study. *British Medical Journal.* Retrieved from http://www.bmj.com/content/early/2005/12/31/bmj.38693.435301.80

Chandrasekhar, D. (2010). Setting the stage: How policy institutions create the scope for participation in planning. *Journal of Disaster Research, 5,* 130–137.

Chang, Y., Chen, R. C., Wahlqvist, M. L., & Lee, M. (2011). Frequent shopping by men and women increases survival in the older Taiwanese population. *Journal of Epidemial Community Health.* Retrieved from http://jech.bmj.com/content/early/2011/03/17/jech.2010.126698.abstract

Chapman, H. A., & Anderson, A. K. (2013). Things Rank and Gross in Nature: A Review and Synthesis of Moral Disgust. *Psychological Bulletin, 139*(2), 300–327. doi: 10.1037/a0030964

Charman, S. D., & Quiroz, V. (2016). Blind sequential lineup administration reduces both false identifications and confidence in those false identifications. *Law and Human Behavior, 40,* 477–487.

Charman, S. D., Wells, G. L., & Joy, S. W. (2011). The dud effect: Adding highly dissimilar fillers increases confidence in lineup identifications. *Law and Human Behavior, 35,* 479–500.

Chartrand, T. L., & Bargh, J. A. (1999). The chameleon effect: The perception-behavior link and social interaction. *Journal of Personality and Social Psychology, 76*, 893–910.

Chassin, L., Presson, C. C., Sherman, S. J., & Edwards, D. A. (1990). The natural history of cigarette smoking: Predicting young-adult smoking outcomes from adolescent smoking patterns. *Health Psychology, 9*, 701–716.

Chatard, A., & Selimbegovic, L. (2011). When self-destructive thoughts flash through the mind: Failure to meet standards affects the accessibility of suicide-related thoughts. *Journal of Personality and Social Psychology, 100*, 587–605.

Chemyak, N., Leimgruber, K.L., Dunham, Y.C., Hu, J., & Blake, P.R. (in press). Paying back those who harmed us but not those who helped us: Direct negative reciprocity precedes direct positive reciprocity in early development. *Psychological Science.*

Chen, E. S., & Tyler, T. R. (2001). Cloaking power: Legitimizing myths and the psychology of the advantaged. In A. Y. Lee-Chai & J. Bargh (Eds.), *The use and abuse of power: Multiple perspectives on the causes of corruption* (pp. 241–261). Philadelphia: Psychology Press.

Chen, X., Dai, K., & Parnell, A. (1992). Disaster tradition and change: Remarriage and family reconstruction in a post-earthquake community in the People's Republic of China. *Journal of Comparative Family Studies, 23*, 115–132.

Chester, D. S. (2017). The role of positive affect in aggression. *Current Directions in Psychological Science, 26*(4), 366–370. DOI: 10.1177/0963721417700457

Childress, H. (2004). Teenagers, territories and the appropriation of space. *Childhood, 11*, 195–205.

China's hi-tech toxics. (2002). *BBC News*. Retrieved from http://news.bbc.co.uk/hi/english/static/in_depth/world/2002/disposable_planet/waste/chinese_workshop

Chiodo, J. (1987). Bulimia: An individual behavioral analysis. *Journal of Behavior Therapy and Experimental Psychiatry, 18*, 41–49.

Chivers, M. L., Seto, M. C., Laan, E., Lalumière, M. L., & Grimbos, T. (2010). Agreement of genital and subjective measures of sexual arousal: A meta-analysis. *Archives of Sexual Behavior, 39*(1), 5–56.

Choi, I., & Nisbett, R. E. (1998). Situational salience and cultural differences in the correspondence bias and actor-observer bias. *Personality and Social Psychology Bulletin, 24*(9), 949–960.

Choma, B. L., Hodson, G., & Costello, K. (2012). Intergroup disgust sensitivity as a predictor of islamophobia: The modulating effect of fear. *Journal of Experimental Social Psychology, 48*(2), 499–506.

Christensen, H. T., & Carpenter, G. R. (1962). Value-behavior discrepancies regarding premarital coitus in three Western cultures. *American Sociological Review, 27*, 66–74.

Cialdini, J. T., & Patrick, W. (2008). *Loneliness.* New York: Norton.

Cialdini, R. B. (1989). Littering: When every litter bit hurts. In R. E. Rice & C. K. Atkin (Eds.), *Public communication campaigns* (2nd ed., pp. 221–223). London: Sage.

Cialdini, R. B. (1993) *Influence: Science and practice* (3rd ed.) (p. 113). New York: Harper-Collins.

Cialdini, R. B. (2001). *Influence: Science and practice* (4th ed.). Boston: Allyn and Bacon.

Cialdini, R. B., & Kenrick, D. T. (1976). Altruism as hedonism: A social development perspective on the relationship of negative mood state and helping. *Journal of Personality and Social Psychology, 34*, 907–914.

Cialdini, R. B., & Schroeder, D. A. (1976). Increasing compliance by legitimizing paltry contributions: When even a penny helps. *Journal of Personality and Social Psychology, 34*(4), 599–604.

Cialdini, R. B., Cacioppo, J. T., Bassett, R., & Miller, J. A. (1978). Low-ball procedure for producing compliance: Commitment then cost. *Journal of Personality and Social Psychology, 36*, 463–476.

Cialdini, R. B., Darby, B. L., & Vincent, J. E. (1973). Transgression and altruism: A case for hedonism. *Journal of Experimental Social Psychology, 9*, 502–516.

Cialdini, R. B., Eisenberg, N., Green, B. L., Rhoads, K., & Bator, R. (1998). Undermining the undermining effect of reward on sustained interest: When unnecessary conditions are sufficient. *Journal of Applied Social Psychology, 28*, 249–263.

Cialdini, R. B., Reno, R. R., & Kallgren, C. A. (1990). A focus theory of normative conduct: Recycling the concept of norms to reduce littering in public places. *Journal of Personality and Social Psychology, 58*, 1015–1026.

Cialdini, R. B., Vincent, J., Lewis, S., Catalan, J., Wheeler, D., & Darby, B. L. (1975). Reciprocal concessions procedure for inducing compliance: The door-in-the-face technique. *Journal of Personality and Social Psychology, 31*, 206–215.

Cincinnati zoo and botanical garden. Retrieved from http://www.ohiohistorycentral.org/w/Cincinnati_Zoo_and_Botanical_Garden?rec5685

Ciotti, G. (2015). How music affects your productivity. Sparring Mind. Retrieved from http://www.sparringmind.com/music-productivity.

Clancy, B., & Milam, H. (2012). How psychological reactance modifies the effects of hypocrisy induction. *Journal of Psychological Inquiry, 17*, 36–39.

Clark, D. (1986). *The missing link.* New York: Humansphere.

Clark, D. A., Beck, A. T., & Brown, G. (1989). Cognitive mediation in general psychiatric outpatients: A test of the content specificity hypothesis. *Journal of Personality and Social Psychology, 56*, 958–964.

Clark, M. S. (1984). Record keeping in two types of relationships. *Journal of Personality and Social Psychology, 47*, 549–557.

Clark, M. S., & Mills, J. (1979). Interpersonal attraction in exchange and communal relationships. *Journal of Personality and Social Psychology, 37*, 12–24.

Clark, M. S., Mills, J., & Corcoran, D. (1989). Keeping track of needs and inputs of friends and strangers. *Personality and Social Psychology Bulletin, 15*, 533–542.

Clark, M. S., Ouellette, R., Powell, M., & Milberg, S. (1987). Recipients' mood, relationship type, and helping. *Journal of Personality and Social Psychology, 53*, 94–103.

Clark, R. E. (2003). Fostering the work motivation of individuals and teams. *Performance Improvement, 42*(3), 21–29.

Clark, S. E. (2005). A re-examination of the effects of biased lineup instructions in eyewitness identification. *Law and Human Behavior, 29*, 395–424.

Clark, S. E. (2012). Costs and benefits of eyewitness identification reform: Psychological science and public policy. *Perspectives on Psychological Science, 7*, 238–259.

Clark, S. E., & Tunnicliff, J. L. (2001). Selecting lineup foils in eyewitness identification: Experimental control and real-world simulation. *Law and Human Behavior, 25*, 199–216.

Clark, S. E., Brower, G. L., Rosenthal, R., Hicks, J. M., & Moreland, M. B. (2013). Lineup administrator influences on eyewitness identification and eyewitness confidence. *Journal of Applied Research in Memory and Cognition, 2*, 158–165.

Clark, W. C. (1989). Managing planet earth. *Scientific American, 261*(3), 47–54.

Clayson, D. E., & Klassen, M. L. (1989). Perception of attractiveness by obesity and hair color. *Perceptual and Motor Skills, 68*, 199–202.

Clifford, M., & Walster, E. (1973). The effect of physical attractiveness on teacher expectations. *Sociology of Education, 46*, 248–258.

Clore, G. L., Gasper, K., & Garvin, E. (2001). Affect as information. In J. P. Forgas (Ed.), *Handbook of affect and social cognition* (pp. 122–144). Mahwah, NJ: Erlbaum.

Coan, J. A., Schaefer, H. S., & Davidson, R. J. (2006). Lending a hand: Social regulation of the neural response to threat. *Psychological Science, 17*(12), 1032–1039.

Cohen, D., & Nisbett, R. E. (1997). Field experiments examining the culture of honor: The role of institutions in perpetuating norms about violence. *Personality and Social Psychology Bulletin, 23*, 1188–1199.

Cohen, F., Jussim, L., Harber, K. D., & Bhasin, G. (2009). Modern anti-Semitism and anti-Israeli attitudes. *Journal of Personality and Social Psychology, 97*(2), 290–306. DOI: 10.1037/a0015338

Cohen, J. (1988). *Statistical power analysis for the behavioral sciences* (2nd ed.). New York: Academic Press.

Cohen, J., & Andrade, E. B. (2004). Affect, intuition, and task-contingent affect regulation. *Journal of Consumer Research, 31*, 358–367.

Cohen, L. L., & Shotland, R. L. (1996). Timing of first sexual intercourse in a relationship: Expectations, experiences, and perceptions of others. *Journal of Sex Research, 33*, 291–299.

Cohen, S. (1978). Environmental load and the allocation of attention. In A. Baum, J. S. Singer, & S. Valins (Eds.), *Advances in environmental psychology* (Vol. 1, pp. 1–29). Hillsdale, NJ: Erlbaum.

Cohen, S. G., & Ledford, G. E., Jr. (1994). The effectiveness of self-managing teams: A quasi-experiment. *Human Relations, 47*, 13–43.

Cohen, S., & Spacapan, S. (1984). The social psychology of noise. In D. M. Jones & A. J. Chapman (Eds.), *Noise and society* (pp. 221–245). New York: Wiley.

Colapinto, J. (2000). *As nature made him: The boy who was raised as a girl.* New York: HarperCollins.

Cole, A.M. (2007). *The cult of true victimhood.* Palo Alto, CA: Stanford University Press.

Cole, R. (2001). Lying to the one you love: The use of deception in romantic relationships. *Journal of Social and Personal Relationships, 18*(1), 107–129.

Coleman, M. D. (2016). Emotion and the false consensus effect. *Current Psychology: A Journal for Diverse Perspectives on Diverse Psychological Issues*, doi:10.1007/s12144-016-9489-0

College Board. (1976–1977). *Student descriptive questionnaire.* Princeton, NJ: Educational Testing Service.

Collins, J. (2001). *Good to great.* New York: HarperCollins.

Collins, N. L., & Feeney, B. C. (2000). A safe haven: An attachment theory perspective on support-seeking and caregiving in adult romantic relationships. *Journal of Personality and Social Psychology, 58*, 644–663.

Collins, N. L., & Feeney, B. C. (2004). An attachment theory perspective on closeness and intimacy. In D. Mashek & A. Aron (Eds.), *Handbook of closeness and intimacy* (pp. 163–187). Mahwah, NJ: Erlbaum.

Collins, N. L., & Read, S. J. (1990). Adult attachment, working models and relationship quality in dating couples. *Journal of Personality and Social Psychology, 58*, 644–663.

Collins, R. L., Quigley, B., & Leonard, K. (2007). Women's physical aggression in bars: An event-based examination of precipitants and predictors of severity. *Aggressive Behavior, 33*(4), 304–313.

Colman, A. M. (1982). *Game theory and experimental games: The study of strategic interaction.* Oxford: Pergamon Press.

Colvin, C. R., Block, J., & Funder, D. C. (1995). Overly positive evaluations and personality: Negative implications for mental health. *Journal of Personality and Social Psychology, 68*, 1152–1162.

Comer, R., & Laird, J. D. (1975). Choosing to suffer as a consequence of expecting to suffer: Why do people do it? *Journal of Personality and Social Psychology, 32*, 92–101.

Commonwealth v. Gomes, 470 Mass. 352 (2015).

Compton, J. A., & Pfau, M. (2004). Use of inoculation to foster resistance to credit card marketing targeting college students. *Journal of Applied Communication Research, 32*(4), 343–364.

Conley, T. D., Moors, A. C., Matsick, J. L., Ziegler, A., & Valentine, B. A. (2011). Women, men, and the bedroom: Methodological and conceptual insights that narrow, reframe, and eliminate gender differences in sexuality. *Current Directions in Psychological Science, 20*, 296–300.

Connolly, T. (2002). Regret in decision making. *Current Directions in Psychological Science, 11,* 212–216.

Consumer Electronics Association. (2008, April). *Market research report: Trends in CE reuse, recycle and removal.*

Contrada, R. J., & Guyll, M. (2001). On who gets sick and why: The role of personality, stress, and disease. In A. Baum, T. A. Revenson, & J. E. Singer (Eds.), *Handbook of health psychology* (pp. 59–81). Hillsdale, NJ: Erlbaum.

Contrada, R., & Baum, A. (Eds.). (2011). *The handbook of stress science: Biology, psychology, and health.* New York: Springer.

Conway, M., & Ross, M. (1984). Getting what you want by revising what you had. *Journal of Personality and Social Psychology, 47,* 738–748.

Cook, T. D., & Campbell, D. T. (1979). *Quasi-experimentation* (pp. 37–94). Boston: Houghton Mifflin.

Cooley, C. H. (1902). *Human nature and the social order.* New York: Charles Scribner's Sons.

Cooper, M. L., Shaver, P. R., & Collins, N. L. (1998). Attachment styles, emotion regulation, and adjustment in adolescence. *Journal of Personality and Social Psychology, 74,* 1380–1397.

Cooper-Hakim, A., & Viswesvaran, C. (2005). The construct of work commitment: Testing an integrative framework. *Journal of Applied Psychology, 131,* 241–259.

Copeland, J. T. (1994). Prophecies of power: Motivational implications of social power for behavioral confirmation. *Journal of Personality and Social Psychology, 67,* 264–277.

Correll, J., Park, B., Judd, C. M., & Wittenbrink, B. (2002). The police officer's dilemma: Using ethnicity to disambiguate potentially threatening individuals. *Journal of Personality and Social Psychology, 86,* 1314–1329.

Cosgrove, J. (2018, September 23). Chasing 'likes' on Instagram, hikers break limbs—and need rescuing. *Los Angeles Times.* Retrieved from https://www.latimes.com/local/lanow/la-me-rescue-mission-increase-20180924-story.html

Cosmides, L. (1989). The logic of social exchange: Has natural selection shaped how humans reason? Studies with the Wason selection task. *Cognition, 31,* 187–276.

Cosmides, L., & Tooby, J. (1992). Cognitive adaptations for social exchange. In J. Barkow, L. Cosmides, & J. Tooby (Eds.), *The adapted mind: Evolutionary psychology and the generation of culture* (pp. 163–228). Oxford: Oxford University Press.

Costa, P. T., & McCrae, R. R. (1980). Influence of extraversion and neuroticism on subjective well-being: Happy and unhappy people. *Journal of Personality and Social Psychology, 38,* 668–678.

Costa, P. T., & McCrae, R. R. (1984). Personality as a lifelong determinant of wellbeing. In C. Z. Malatesta & C. E. Izard (Eds.), *Emotion in adult development* (pp. 141–157). Beverly Hills, CA: Sage.

Costa, P. T., McCrae, R. R., & Zonderman, A. B. (1987). Environmental and dispositional influences on well-being: Longitudinal follow-up of an American national sample. *British Journal of Psychology, 78,* 299–306.

Cottrell, C. A., Neuberg, S. L., & Li, N. P. (2007). What do people desire in others? A sociofunctional perspective on the importance of different valued characteristics. *Journal of Personality and Social Psychology, 92,* 208–231.

Cottrell, N. B., Wack, D. L., Sekerak, G. J, & Rittle, R. H. (1968). Social facilitation of dominant responses by the presence of an audience and the mere presence of others. *Journal of Personality and Social Psychology, 9,* 245–250.

Couch, D., & Liamputtong, P. (2008). Online dating and mating: The use of the Internet to meet sexual partners. *Qualitative Health Research, 18*(2), 268–279.

Coviello, L., Sohn, Y., Kramer, A. D. I., Marlow, C., Franceschetti, M., Christakis, N. A., & Fowler, J. H. (2014). Detecting emotional contagion in massive social networks. *PLoS ONE, 9*(3), doi: 10.1371/journal.pone.0090315

Cowan, C. L., Thompson, W. C., & Ellsworth, P. C. (1984). The effects of death qualification on jurors: Predisposition to convict and on the quality of deliberation. *Law and Human Behavior, 8,* 53–79.

Cowley, E., Briley, D. A., & Farrell, C. (2015). How do gamblers maintain an illusion of control? *Journal of Business Research, 68*(10), 2181–2188. doi:10.1016/j.jbusres.2015.03.018

Coyle, C. T., & Enright, R. D. (1997). Forgiveness intervention with post-abortion men. *Journal of Consulting and Clinical Psychology, 65,* 1042–1046.

Coyne, J. C., & DeLongis, A. (1986). Going beyond social support: The role of social relationships in adaptation. *Journal of Consulting and Clinical Psychology, 54,* 454–460.

Cramer, P., & Steinwert, T. (1998). Thin is good, fat is bad: How early does it begin? *Journal of Applied Developmental Psychology, 19,* 429–451.

Cramer, R. E., McMaster, M. R., Bartell, P. A., & Dragna, M. (1988). Subject competence and minimization of the bystander effect. *Journal of Applied Social Psychology, 18,* 1133–1148.

Crandall, C. S. (1988). Social contagion of binge eating. *Journal of Personality and Social Psychology, 55,* 588–598.

Crandall, C. S. (1994). Prejudice against fat people: Ideology and self-interest. *Journal of Personality and Social Psychology, 66,* 882–894.

Cranny, C. J., Smith, P. C., & Stone, E. F. (1992). *Job satisfaction: How people feel about their jobs and how it affects their performance.* New York: Lexington Books.

Crary, W. G. (1966). Reactions to incongruent self-experiences. *Journal of Consulting Psychology, 30,* 246–252.

Crick, N. R., & Grotpeter, J. K. (1995). Relational aggression, gender, and social-psychological adjustment. *Child Development, 66,* 710–722.

Crisp, R. J., Birtel, M. D., & Meleady, R. (2011). Mental simulations of social thought and action: Trivial tasks or tools for transforming social policy? *Current Directions in Psychological Science, 20*(4), 261–264.

Crisp, R. J., Hutter, R. R. C., & Young, B. (2009). When mere exposure leads to less liking: The incremental threat effect in intergroup contexts. *British Journal of Psychology, 100*(1), 133–149.

Croake, J. W., & James, B. (1973). A four year comparison of premarital sexual attitudes. *Journal of Sex Research, 9,* 91–96.

Crocker, C. B. (2010). *An investigation of the psychological processes involved in juror rehabilitation.* (Unpublished doctoral dissertation.) The City University of New York.

Crocker, C. B., & Kovera, M. B. (2010). The effects of rehabilitative voir dire on juror bias and decision making. *Law and Human Behavior, 34,* 212–226.

Crocker, J., & Major, B. (1989). Social stigma and self-esteem: The self-protective properties of stigma. *Psychological Review, 96,* 608–630.

Crocker, J., & Park, L. E. (2004). The costly pursuit of self-esteem. *Psychological Bulletin, 130,* 392–414.

Crocker, J., & Schwartz, I. (1985). Prejudice and ingroup favoritism in a minimal intergroup situation: Effects of self-esteem. *Personality and Social Psychology Bulletin, 11,* 379–386.

Crocker, J., Sommers, S. R., & Luhtanen, R. K. (2002). Hopes dashed and dreams fulfilled: Contingencies of self-worth and admissions to graduate school. *Personality and Social Psychology Bulletin, 28,* 1275–1286.

Crocker, J., Voelkl, K., Testa, M., & Major, B. (1991). Social stigma: The affective consequences of attributional ambiguity. *Journal of Personality and Social Psychology, 60,* 218–228.

Croskerry, P. (2003). The importance of cognitive errors in diagnosis and strategies to minimize them. *Academic Medicine, 78,* 775–780.

Crowley, M.C. (2015). How SAS became the world's best place to work. *Fast Company.* Retrieved from http://www.sas.com/en_us/careers/life-at-sas.html

Cryder, C. E, Springer, S., & Morewedge, C. M. (2012), Guilty feelings, targeted actions. *Personality and Social Psychology Bulletin, 38*(5), 607–618. doi: 10.1177/0146167211435796

CTIA.org. (2012). Background on CTIA's semiannual wireless industry survey. Retrieved from http://www.ctia.org/media/industry_info/index.cfm/AID/10323

Culhane, S. E., Hosch, H. M., & Weaver, W. G. (2004). Crime victims serving as jurors: Is there bias present? *Law and Human Behavior, 28,* 649–659.

Cunningham, M. R. (1979). Mood, and helping behavior: Quasi experiments with the Sunshine Samaritan. *Journal of Personality and Social Psychology 37,* 1947–1956.

Cunningham, M. R. (2009). Social allergies. In H. Reis & S. Sprecher (Eds.), *Handbook of human relationships.* Thousand Oaks, CA: Sage.

Cunningham, M. R., Barbee, A. P., & Druen, P. B. (1997). Social antigens and allergies: The development of hypersensitivity in close relationships. In R. Kowalski (Ed.), *Aversive interpersonal behaviors* (pp. 190–215). New York: Plenum Press.

Cunningham, M. R., Barbee, A. P., & Mandal, E. (2009). Hurtful behaviors in the workplace. In R. Kowalski (Ed.), *Feeling hurt in close relationships* (pp. 417–456). Cambridge: Cambridge University Press.

Cupach, W. R., & Spitzberg, B. H. (2000). Obsessive relational intrusion: Incidence, perceived severity, and coping. *Violence and Victims, 15,* 357–372.

Curtis, V. (2011). Why disgust matters. *Philosophical Transactions of the Royal Society B, 366,* 3478–3490. Quote on p. 3486

Cutler, B. L., & Kovera, M. B. (2010). *Evaluating eyewitness identification.* New York: Oxford University Press.

Cutler, B. L., Penrod, S. D., & Dexter, H. R. (1989). The eyewitness, the expert psychologist, and the jury. *Law and Human Behavior, 13,* 311–332.

Cutler, B. L., Penrod, S. D., & Martens, T. K. (1987). The reliability of eyewitness identification: The role of system and estimator variables. *Law and Human Behavior, 11,* 233–258.

Dabbs, J. M. (2000). *Heroes, rogues, and lovers: Testosterone and behavior.* New York: McGraw-Hill.

Daftary-Kapur, T., Penros, S. D., O'Connor, M., & Wallace, B. (2014). Examining pretrial publicity in a shadow jury paradigm: Issues of slant, quantity, persistence and generalizability. *Law and Human Behavior, 38,* 462–477.

Dal Cin, S., Gibson, B., Zanna, M., Shumate, R., & Fong, G. (2007). Smoking in movies, implicit associations of smoking with the self, and intentions to smoke. *Psychological Science, 18*(7), 559–563.

Dal Cin, S., Worth, K., Dalton, M., & Sargent, J. (2008). Youth exposure to alcohol use and brand appearances in popular contemporary movies. *Addiction, 103*(12), 1925–1932.

Dalal, R. S. (2006). A meta-analysis of the relationship between organizational citizenship behavior and counterproductive work behavior. *Journal of Applied Psychology, 90*(6), 1241–1255.

Daly, M. J., & Burton, R. L. (1983). Self-esteem and irrational beliefs: An exploratory investigation with implications for counseling. *Journal of Counseling Psychology, 30,* 361–366.

Damasio, A. R. (1994). *Descartes' error.* London: Picador.

Danner, D., Snowdon, D., & Friesen, W. (2001). Positive emotions in early life and longevity: Findings from the Nun Study. *Journal of Personality and Social Psychology, 80,* 804–813.

Danziger, S., Levav, J., & Avnaim-Pesso, L. (2011). Extraneous factors in judicial decisions. *PNAS, 108,* 6889–6892.

Darby, B. W., & Schlenker, B. R. (1982). Children's reactions to apologies. *Journal of Personality and Social Psychology, 43,* 742–753.

Darley, J. M. & Batson, C. D. (1973). From Jerusalem to Jericho: A study of situational and dispositional variables in helping behavior. *Journal of Personality and Social Psychology, 27,* 100–108.

Darley, J. M., & Gross, P. H. (1983). A hypothesis-confirming bias in labeling effects. *Journal of Personality and Social Psychology, 44*(1), 20–33.

Darley, J. M., & Latané, B. (1968). Bystander intervention in emergencies: *Journal of Personality & Social Psychology, 8,* 377–383.

Darwin, C. (1859). *The origin of species by means of natural selection, or the preservation of favoured races in the struggle for life.* Reprinted from the 6th edition in New York, A. L. Burt Company, not dated.

Darwin, C. (1948). *Origin of species.* New York: Modern Library. (Original work published 1871).

Das, E., Bushman, B. J., Bezemer, M. D., Kerkhof, P., & Vermeulen, I. E. (2009). How terrorism news reports increase prejudice against outgroups: A terror management account. *Journal of Experimental Social Psychology, 45,* 453–459.

David, J. P., Green, P. J., Martin, R., & Suls, J. (1997). Differential roles of neuroticism, extraversion, and event desirability for mood in daily life: An integrative model of top-down and bottom-up influences. *Journal of Personality and Social Psychology, 73,* 149–159.

David, M. B. (2013, February 13). Deep racism: The forgotten history of human zoos. *Popular Resistance.* Retrieved from http://www.popularresistance.org/deep-racism-the-forgotten-history-of-human-zoos/

Davies, G. (2002). *A history of money from ancient times to the present day.* Cardiff: University of Wales Press.

Davies, G. M., Smith, S., & Blincoe, C. (2008). A "weapon focus" effect in children. *Psychology, Crime, & Law, 14,* 19–28.

Davies, J. B., Sandström, S., Shorrocks, A., & Wolff, E. N. (2008). The World Distribution of Household Wealth. UNU-WIDER. Retrieved from http://www.wider.unu.edu/publications/working-papers/discussion-papers/2008/en_GB/dp2008-03/

Davis, B. P., & Knowles, E. S. (1999). A disrupt-then-reframe technique of social influence. *Journal of Personality and Social Psychology, 76,* 192–199.

Davis, D., & Loftus, E. F. (2006). Psychologists in the forensic world. In S. I. Donaldson, D. E. Berger, & K. Pezdek (Eds.), *Applied psychology: New frontiers and rewarding careers* (pp. 171–200). Mahwah, NJ: Lawrence Erlbaum Associates.

Davis, I. (1978). *Shelter after disaster.* Oxford, UK: Oxford Polytechnic Press.

Davis, K. E., & Frieze, I. H. (2000). Research on stalking: What do we know and where do we go? *Violence and Victims, 15,* 473–487.

Davis, P. A. (1983). *Suicidal adolescents.* Springfield, IL: C. C. Thomas.

Davis, S. F., Grover, C. A., Becker, A. H., & McGregor, L. N. (1992). Academic dishonesty: Prevalence, determinants, techniques, and punishments. *Teaching of Psychology, 19,* 16–20.

Davison, W. P. (1983). The third-person effect in communication. *Public Opinion Quarterly, 47,* 1–15. doi:10.1086/268763

Davis-Stober, C.P., Budescu, D.V., Dana, J., & Broomell, S.B. (2014). When is a crowd wise? *Decision, 1,* 79–101.

Dawkins, R. (1976/1989). *The selfish gene.* New York: Oxford University Press.

Dawkins, R. (1989). *The selfish gene.* New York: Oxford University Press. (Original work published 1976).

Day, D., & Ullom, H. H. (Eds.). (1947). *The autobiography of Sam Houston.* Norman: University of Oklahoma Press.

De Brouwer, A.-M. (2005). *Supranational criminal prosecution of sexual violence: The ICC and the practice of the ICTY and the ICTR.* Mortsel, Belgium: Intersentia.

De Hoog, N., Stroebe, W., & De Wit, J. B. F. (2007). The impact of vulnerability to and severity of a health risk on processing and acceptance of fear-arousing communications: A meta-analysis. *Review of General Psychology, 11*(3), 258–285.

de Kort, Y. A. W., McCalley, L. T., & Midden, C. J. H. (2008). Persuasive trash cans: Activation of littering norms by design. *Environment and Behavior, 40*(6), 870–891.

de Rougemont, D. (1956). *Love in the Western world.* New York: Schoeken.

de Vries, M., Holland, R. W., Corneille, O., Rondeel, E., & Witteman, C. L. M. (2012). Mood effects on dominated choices: Positive mood induces departures from logical rules. *Journal of Behavioral Decision Making, 25*(1), 74–81.

de Waal, F. B. M. (2002). Evolutionary psychology: The wheat and the chaff. *Current Directions in Psychological Science, 11,* 187–191.

de Waal, F. B. M., & Davis, J. M. (2003). Capuchin cognitive ecology: Cooperation based on projected returns. *Neuropsychologia, 41,* 221–228.

De Young, R., Duncan, A., Frank, J., Gill, N., Rothman, S., Shenot, J., Shotkin, A., & Zweizig, M. (1993). Promoting source reduction behavior: The role of motivational behavior. *Environment and Behavior, 25,* 70–85.

Deabler, A. (2018, December 19). Restaurant sues customer over bad Facebook review: "This is slander'" *Fox News.* Retrieved from https://www.foxnews.com/food-drink/restaurant-sues-customer-over-bad-facebook-review

Deacon, T. (1997). What makes the human brain different? *Annual Review of Anthropology, 26,* 337–357.

Dean, L. M., Willis, F. N., & Hewitt, J. (1975). Initial interaction distance among individuals equal and unequal in military rank. *Journal of Personality and Social Psychology, 32,* 294–299.

DeAngelis, T. (2000). Is Internet addiction real? *Monitor on Psychology, 31.* Retrieved from http://www.apa.org/monitor/apr00/addiction.html

deCharms, R. (1968). *Personal causation.* New York: Academic Press.

Deci, E. L. (1971). The effects of externally mediated rewards on intrinsic motivation. *Journal of Personality and Social Psychology, 18,* 105–115.

Deci, E. L. (1975). *Intrinsic motivation.* New York: Plenum Press.

Deci, E. L., & Ryan, R. M. (1985). *Intrinsic motivation and self-determination in human behavior.* New York: Plenum Press.

Deci, E. L., & Ryan, R. M. (2000). The "what" and "why" of goal pursuits: Human needs and the self-determination of behavior. *Psychological Inquiry, 11,* 227–268.

Deci, E. L., Koestner, R., & Ryan, R. M. (1999). A meta-analytic review of experiments examining the effects of extrinsic rewards on intrinsic motivation. *Psychological Bulletin, 125,* 627–668.

Deci, E. L., Nezlek, J., & Sheinman, L. (1981). Characteristics of the rewarder and the intrinsic motivation of the rewardee. *Journal of Personality and Social Psychology, 40,* 1–10.

Deffenbacher, K. A. (1994). Effects of arousal on everyday memory. *Human Performance, 7,* 141–161.

Deffenbacher, K. A., Bornstein, B. H., McGorty, E. K., & Penrod, S. D. (2008). Forgetting the once-seen face: Estimating the strength of an eyewitness's memory representation. *Journal of Experimental Psychology: Applied, 14,* 139–150.

Deffenbacher, K. A., Bornstein, B. H., Penrod, S. D., & McGorty, E. K. (2004). A meta-analytic review of the effects of high stress on eyewitness memory. *Law and Human Behavior, 28,* 687–706.

DeJong, W. (1980). The stigma of obesity: The consequences of naive assumptions concerning the causes of physical deviance. *Journal of Health and Social Behavior, 21*(1), 75–87.

DeJong, W. (1993). Obesity as a characterological stigma: The issue of responsibility and judgments of task performance. *Psychological Reports, 73,* 963–970.

DeLamater, J., & Hyde, J. S. (1998). Essentialism vs. social constructionism in the study of human sexuality. *Journal of Sex Research, 35,* 10–18.

DeLongis, A., Folkman, S., & Lazarus, S. (1988). The impact of daily stress on health and mood: Psychosocial and social resources as mediators. *Journal of Personality and Social Psychology, 54,* 486–495.

DeMeis, J., & Stearns, E. (1992). Relationship of school entrance age to academic and social performance. *Journal of Educational Research, 86,* 21–27.

Demicheli, V., Rivetti, A., Debalini, M. G., & Di Pietrantonj, C. (2012). Vaccines for measles, mumps and rubella in children. Cochrane Database Systematic Reviews, 2. Art. No.: CD004407. doi:10.1002/14651858.CD004407.pub3

Denison, D. R. (1996). What is the difference between organizational culture and organizational climate? A native's point of view on a decade of paradigm wars. *The Academy of Management Review, 21*(3), 619–654.

Denison, D. R. (1996). What is the difference between organizational culture and organizational climate? A native's point of view on a decade of paradigm wars. *The Academy of Management Review, 21*(3), 619–654.

DePalma, M. T., Madey, S. F., Tillman, T. C., & Wheeler, J. (1999). Perceived patient responsibility and belief in a just world affect helping. *Basic and Applied Social Psychology, 21,* 131–137.

DeScioli, P., & Wilson, B. J. (2011). The territorial foundations of human property. *Evolution and Human Behavior, 32,* 297–304.

Desmarais, S. L., & Read, J. D. (2011). After 30 years, what do we know about what jurors know? A meta-analytic review of lay knowledge regarding eyewitness factors. *Law and Human Behavior, 35,* 200–210.

DeSteno, D. A., & Salovey, P. (1996). Evolutionary origins of sex differences in jealousy? Questioning the "fitness" of the model. *Psychological Science, 7,* 367–372.

DeSteno, D. A., Bartlett, M. Y., Braverman, J., & Salovey, P. (2002). Sex differences in jealousy: Evolutionary mechanisms or artifact of measurement. *Journal of Personality and Social Psychology, 83,* 1103–1116.

Deutsch, M., & Gerard, H. B. (1955). A study of normative and informational social influences upon individual judgment. *Journal of Abnormal and Social Psychology, 51,* 629–636.

Devenport, J. L., & Cutler, B. L. (2004). Impact of defense-only and opposing eyewitness experts on juror judgments. *Law and Human Behavior, 28,* 569–576.

Devenport, J. L., Stinson, V., Cutler, B. L., & Kravitz, D. A. (2002). How effective are the cross-examination and expert testimony safeguards? Jurors' perceptions of the suggestiveness and fairness of biased lineup procedures. *Journal of Applied Psychology, 87,* 1042–1054.

Devine, P. G. (1989). Stereotypes and prejudice: Their automatic and controlled components. *Journal of Personality and Social Psychology, 56,* 5–18.

Devine, P. G., & Malpass, R. S. (1985). Orienting strategies in differential face recognition. *Personality and Social Psychology Bulletin, 11*(1), 33–40.

Devine, P. G., Plant, E. A., Amodio, A. M., Harmon-Jones, E., & Vance, S. L. (2002). Exploring the relationship between implicit and explicit prejudice: The role of motivations to respond without prejudice. *Journal of Personality and Social Psychology, 82,* 835–848.

DeVries, D., & Kaiser, R. B. (2003, November). Going sour in the suite. Paper presented at the Maximizing Executive Effectiveness workshop, Miami, FL.

DeWall, C. N., & Baumeister, R. F. (2006). Alone but feeling no pain: Effects of social exclusion on physical pain tolerance and pain threshold, affective forecasting, and interpersonal empathy. *Journal of Personality and Social Psychology, 91,* 1–15.

DeWall, C. N., Baumeister, R. F., & Masicampo, E. J. (2008). Evidence that logical reasoning depends on conscious processing. *Consciousness and Cognition, 17,* 628–645.

DeWall, C. N., Baumeister, R. F., Chester, D. S., & Bushman, B. J. (in press). How often does currently felt emotion predict social behavior and judgment? A meta-analytic test of two theories. *Emotion Review.*

DeWall, C. N., Deckman, T., Gailliot, M. T., & Bushman, B. J. (2011). Sweetened blood cools hot tempers: Physiological self-control and aggression. *Aggressive Behavior, 37*(1), 73–80. DOI: 10.1002/ab.20366

DeWall, C. N., Finkel, E. J., & Denson, T. F. (2011). Self-control inhibits aggression. *Social and Personality Psychology Compass, 5*(7), 458–472.

DeWall, C. N., MacDonald, G., Webster, G. D., Masten, C., Baumeister, R. F., Powell, C., Combs, D., Schurtz, D. R., Stillman, T. F., Tice, D. M., & Eisenberger, N. I. (2010). Tylenol reduces social pain: Behavioral and neural evidence. *Psychological Science, 21,* 931–937.

DeWall, C. N., Pond, R. S., Campbell, W. K., & Twenge, J. M. (2011). Tuning in to psychological change: Linguistic markers of psychological traits and emotions over time in popular U.S. song lyrics. *Psychology of Aesthetics, Creativity, and the Arts, 5,* 200–207.

Dexter, H. R., Cutler, B. L., & Moran, G. (1992). A test of voir dire as a remedy for the prejudicial effects of pretrial publicity. *Journal of Applied Social Psychology, 22,* 819–832.

Di Paula, A., & Campbell, J. D. (2002). Self-esteem and persistence in the face of failure. *Journal of Personality and Social Psychology, 83,* 711–724.

Diamond, J. (2013). *The world until yesterday.* New York: Viking.

Diamond, L. M. (2003). An attachment perspective on female sexual fluidity. Paper presented at the Women's Sexualities Conference: Historical, Interdisciplinary, and International Perspectives, sponsored by the Kinsey Institute for Research in Sex, Gender, and Reproduction, Bloomington, IN.

Diamond, L. M. (2003). What does sexual orientation orient? A biobehavioral model distinguishing romantic love and sexual desire. *Psychological Review, 110,* 173–192.

Diamond, L. M. (2004). Emerging perspectives on distinctions between romantic love and sexual desire. *Current Directions in Psychological Science, 13,* 116–119.

Diamond, L. M. (2008). *Sexual fluidity: Understanding women's love and desire.* Cambridge, MA: Harvard University Press.

Dickerson, C., Thibodeau, R., Aronson, E., & Miller, D. (1992). Using cognitive dissonance to encourage water conservation. *Journal of Applied Social Psychology, 22,* 841–854.

Dickinson, D. J., & Larsen, J. D. (1963). The effects of chronological age in months on school achievement. *Journal of Educational Research, 56,* 492–493.

Dictionary of Marketing Terms (2004).

Diener, E., & Diener, M. (1995). Cross-cultural correlates of life satisfaction and self-esteem. *Journal of Personality and Social Psychology, 68,* 653–663.

Diener, E., & Wallbom, M. (1976). Effects of self-awareness on antinormative behavior. *Journal of Research in Personality, 10,* 107–111.

Diener, E., Fraser, S. C., Beaman, A. L., & Kelem, R. T. (1976). Effects of deindividuation variables on stealing among Halloween trick-or-treaters. *Journal of Personality and Social Psychology, 33,* 178–183.

Diener, E., Lucas, R. E., & Scollon, C. N. (2006). Beyond the hedonic treadmill: Revisions to the adaptation theory of well-being. *American Psychologist, 61,* 305–314.

Diener, E., Wolsic, B., & Fujita, F. (1995). Physical attractiveness and subjective well-being. *Journal of Personality and Social Psychology, 69,* 120–129.

Dijksterhuis, A., & Nordgren, L. F. (2006). A theory of unconscious thought. *Perspectives on Psychological Science, 1,* 95–109.

Dill, K. E., Anderson, C. A., Anderson, K. B., & Deuser, W. E. (1997). Effects of aggressive personality on social expectations and social perceptions. *Journal of Research in Personality, 31,* 272–292.

Dillon, M. K., Jones, A. M., Bergold, A. N., Hui, C. Y. T., & Penrod, S. D. (2017). Henderson instructions: Do they enhance evidence evaluation? *Journal of Forensic Psychology Research and Practice, 17,* 1–24.

Dimeo-Ediger, W. (2016, March 30). It's A Small World When It Comes to :-/ NPR. Retrieved from https://www.npr.org/sections/goatsandsoda/2016/03/30/472452258/its-a-small-world-when-it-comes-to

Dion, J., & Mellor, B. (2004, August). Is sport really good for you? *EnRoute,* pp. 33–34.

Dion, K. (1973). Young children's stereotyping of facial attractiveness. *Developmental Psychology, 9,* 183–188.

Dion, K. K., Berscheid, E., & Walster, F. H. (1972). What is beautiful is good. *Journal of Personality and Social Psychology, 24,* 285–290.

Dodge, K. A., & Coie, J. D. (1987). Social-information-processing factors in reactive and proactive aggression in children's peer groups. *Journal of Personality and Social Psychology, 53,* 1146–1158.

Dohnke, B., Steinhilber, A., & Fuchs, T. (2015). Adolescents' eating behaviour in general and in the peer context: Testing the prototype-willingness model. *Psychology & Health, 30*(4), 381–399. doi: 10.1080/08870446.2014.974604

Doja, A., & Roberts, W. (2006). Immunizations and autism: A review of the literature. *Canadian Journal of Neurological Sciences, 33*(4), 341–346. PMID 17168158

Dollard, J., Doob, L., Miller, N., Mowrer, O., & Sears, R. (1939). *Frustration and aggression.* New Haven, CT: Yale University Press.

DollarTimes. (2019). Calculate the value of $100 in 1970. Retrieved from https://www.dollartimes.com/inflation/inflation.php?amount=100&year=1970.

Donnerstein, E., & Berkowitz, L. (1981). Victim reactions in aggressive erotic films as a factor in violence against women. *Journal of Personality and Social Psychology, 41,* 710–724.

Donovan, R., & Rossiter, J. (1982). Store atmosphere: An environmental psychology approach. *Journal of Retailing, 58,* 34–57.

Doocy, S., Daniels, A., Dooling, S., & Gorokhovich, Y. (2013). The human impact of volcanoes: A historical review of events 1900–2009 and systematic literature review. *PLoS Currents, 16,* 5.

Doocy, S., Daniels, A., Murray, S., & Kirsch, T. D. (2013). The human impact of floods: A historical review of events 1980–2009 and systematic literature review. *PLoS Currents Disasters, 16,* doi: 10.1371/currents.dis.f4deb457904936b07c09daa98ee8171a

Dorsey, D. & Mueller-Hanson, R. (2017). Performance management that makes a difference: An evidence-based approach. Society for Human Resource Management. Retrieved from: Learning agility equals leadership success, *Bloomberg Businessweek.* Retrieved from https://www.shrm.org/hr-today/trends-and-forecasting/special-reports-and-expert-views/Documents/Performance%20Management.pdf.

Douglass, A. B., Neuschatz, J. S., Imrich, J., & Wilkinson, M. (2010). Does post-identification feedback affect evaluations of eyewitness testimony and identification procedures? *Law and Human Behavior, 34,* 282–294.

Douglass, A. B., Smith, C., & Fraser-Thill, R. (2005). A problem with double-blind photospread procedures: Photospread administrators use one eyewitness's confidence to influence the identification of another eyewitness. *Law and Human Behavior, 29,* 543–562.

Dovidio, J. F., & Gaertner, S. L. (1999). Reducing prejudice: Combating intergroup biases. *Current Directions in Psychological Science, 8,* 101–105.

Dowd, J. J. (1975). Aging as exchange: A preface to theory. *Journal of Gerontology, 30*(5), 584–594.

Doyle, A. C. (1974). *The memoirs of Sherlock Holmes.* London: J. Murray; Cape. (Original work published 1894)

Drabek, T. E., & Stephenson, J. S. (1971). When disaster strikes. *Journal of Applied Social Psychology, 1,* 187–203.

Draper, P. (1976). Social and economic constraints on child life among the !Kung. In R. B. Lee & I. DeVore (Eds.), *Kalahari hunter-gatherers: Studies of the !Kung San and their neighbors* (pp. 199–217). Cambridge, MA: Harvard University Press.

Duarte, J. L., Crawford, J. T., Stern, C., Haidt, J., Jussim, L., & Tetlock, P. E. (in press/2015). Political diversity will improve social psychological science. *Behavioral and Brain Sciences.*

Dube, K. C., Kumar, A., Kumar, N., & Gupta, S. P. (1978). Prevalence and pattern of drug use amongst college students. *Acta Psychiatrica Scandinavica, 57,* 336–356.

Duhigg, C. (2016, February 25). What Google learned from its quest to build the perfect team. *The New York Times Magazine.* Retrieved from https://www.nytimes.com/2016/02/28/magazine/what-google-learned-from-its-quest-to-build-the-perfect-team.html?smid=pl-share

Duke, M. P., & Wilson, J. (1973). The measurement of interpersonal distance in pre-school children. *Journal of Genetic Psychology, 123,* 361–362.

Dunbar, R. I. M. (1993). Coevolution of neocortical size, group size, and language in humans. *Behavioral and Brain Sciences, 16,* 681–694.

Dunbar, R. I. M. (1996). *Grooming, gossip, and the evolution of language.* Cambridge, MA: Harvard University Press.

Dunbar, R. I. M. (1998). The social brain hypothesis. *Evolutionary Anthropology, 6,* 178–190.

Duncan, C. P., & Nelson, J. E. (1985). Effects of humor in a radio advertising experiment. *Journal of Advertising, 14,* 33–40, 64.

Dunn, E. W., Brackett, M. A., Ashton-James, C., Schneiderman, E., & Salovey, P. (2007). On emotionally intelligent time travel: Individual differences in affective forecasting ability. *Personality and Social Psychology Bulletin, 33*(1), 85–93.

Dunning, D. (1999). A newer look: Motivated social cognition and the schematic representation of social concepts. *Psychological Inquiry, 10,* 1–11.

Dunning, D., & McElwee, R. O. (1995). Idiosyncratic trait definitions: Implications for self-description and social judgment. *Journal of Personality and Social Psychology, 68,* 936–946.

Dunning, D., & Perretta, S. (2002). Automaticity and eyewitness accuracy: A 10-to-12 second rule for distinguishing accurate from inaccurate positive identifications. *Journal of Applied Psychology, 87,* 951–962.

Dunning, D., & Stern, L. B. (1994). Distinguishing accurate from inaccurate identifications via inquiries about decision processes. *Journal of Personality and Social Psychology, 67,* 818–835.

Dunning, D., Anderson, J. E., Schlösser, T., Ehlebracht, D., & Fetchenhauer, D. (2014). Trust at zero acquaintance: More a matter of respect than expectation of reward. *Journal of Personality and Social Psychology, 107*(1), 122–141. doi: 10.1037/a0036673

Dunning, D., Meyerowitz, J. A., & Holzberg, A. D. (1989). Ambiguity and self-evaluation: The role of idiosyncratic trait definitions in self-serving assessments of ability. *Journal of Personality and Social Psychology, 57,* 1082–1090.

Dunning, D., Perie, M., & Story, A. L. (1991). Self-serving prototypes of social categories. *Journal of Personality and Social Psychology, 61,* 957–968.

Dutton, D. G. (1971). Reactions of restaurateurs to blacks and whites violating restaurant dress requirements. *Canadian Journal of Behavioural Science, 3,* 298–302.

Dutton, D. G., & Lake, R. A. (1973). Threat of own prejudice and reverse discrimination in interracial situations. *Journal of Personality and Social Psychology, 28,* 94–100.

Duval, S., & Wicklund, R. (1972). *A theory of objective self-awareness.* New York: Academic Press.

Dweck, C. S. (1996). Implicit theories as organizers of goals and behavior. In P. Gollwitzer & J. Bargh (Eds.), *The psychology of action: Linking cognition and motivation to behavior* (pp. 69–91). New York: Guilford Press.

Dweck, C. S., & Leggett, E. L. (1988). A social-cognitive approach to motivation and personality. *Psychological Review, 95,* 256–273.

Eagly, A. H. & Crowley, M. (1986). Gender and helping behavior: A meta-analytic view of the social psychological literature. *Psychological Bulletin, 100,* 283–308.

Eagly, A. H., & Chaiken, S. (1998). Attitude structure and function. In D. T. Gilbert, S. T. Fiske, & G. Lindzey (Eds.), *Handbook of social psychology* (4th ed., Vol. 1, pp. 269–322). New York: McGraw-Hill.

Eagly, A. H., & Chaiken, S. (1998). Attitude structure and function. In D. T. Gilbert, S. T. Fiske, & G.

Lindzey (Eds.), *Handbook of social psychology* (4th ed., Vol. 1, pp. 269–322). New York: McGraw-Hill.

Eagly, A. H., Ashmore, R. D., Makhijani, M. G., & Longo, L. C. (1991). What is beautiful is good, but...: A meta-analytic review of the physical attractiveness stereotype. *Psychological Bulletin, 110,* 109–128.

Earnest, D. R., Allen, D. G., & Landis, R. S. (2011). Mechanisms linking realistic job previews with turnover: A meta-analytic path analysis. *Personnel Psychology, 64*(4), 865–897.

Easterbrook, J. A. (1959). The effect of emotion on the utilization and the organization of behavior. *Psychological Review, 66,* 183–201.

Eby, L. T., Casper, W. J., Lockwood, A., Bordeaux, C., & Brinley, A. (2005). Work and family research in IO/OB: Content analysis and review of the literature (1980–2002). *Journal of Vocational Behavior, 66,* 124–197.

Edelstein, R. S., & Shaver, P. R. (2004). Avoidant attachment: Exploration of an oxymoron. In D. Mashek & A. Aron (Eds.), *Handbook of closeness and intimacy* (pp. 397–412). Mahwah, NJ: Erlbaum.

Edgerton, R. (1971). *The individual in cultural adaptation.* Berkeley: University of California Press.

Edwards, D. J. A. (1972). Approaching the unfamiliar: A study of human interaction distances. *Journal of Behavioral Sciences, 1,* 249–250.

Efran, M. G., & Patterson, E. W. J. (1974). Voters vote beautiful: The effects of physical appearance on a national election. *Canadian Journal of Behavioral Science, 6,* 352–356.

Egan, G. (1970). *Encounter: Group processes for interpersonal growth.* Monterey, CA: Brooks/Cole.

Ehrenfeld, D. (1981). *The arrogance of humanism.* New York: Oxford University Press.

Ehrenreich, B. (1999, March 8). The real truth about the female. *Time, 153*(9), 57–91.

Eiland, L., & McEwen, B. S. (2012). Early life stress followed by subsequent adult chronic stress potentiates anxiety and blunts hippocampal structural remodeling. *Hippocampus, 22*(1), 82–91. doi: 10.1002/hipo.20862

Einon, D. (1994). Are men more promiscuous than women? *Ethology and Sociobiology, 15*(3), 131–143.

Eion, K. (2019). 20 awesome DIY office organization ideas that boost efficiency. Retrieved https://www.lifehack.org/articles/productivity/20-awesome-diy-office-organization-ideas-that-boost-efficiency.html

Eisenberg, N., & Lennon, R. (1983). Sex differences in empathy and related capacities. *Psychological Bulletin, 94,* 100–131.

Eisner, M. (2001). Modernization, self-control and lethal violence: The long-term dynamics of European homicide rates in theoretical perspective. *British Journal of Criminology, 41,* 618–638.

Ekman, P., & O'Sullivan, M. (1991). Who can catch a liar? *American Psychologist, 46*(9), 913–920.

Ekman, P., Friesen, W. V., O'Sullivan, M., Chan, A., Diacoyanni-Tarlatzis, I., Heider, K., et al. (1987). Universals and cultural differences in the judgments of facial expressions of emotion. *Journal of Personality and Social Psychology, 53,* 712–717.

Elbert T, Moran J, & Schauer M. (2017). Appetitive aggression. In B. J. Bushman (Ed). *Aggression and violence.* (pp. 119–136). New York: Taylor & Francis/Routledge.

Elbert, T., Schauer, M., & Moran, J. K. (2018). Two pedals drive the bi-cycle of violence: Reactive and appetitive aggression. *Current Opinion in Psychology, 19,* 135–138. DOI: 10.1016/j.copsyc.2017.03.016

Elbert, T., Schauer, M., Hinkel, H., Riedke, H., Maedl, A., Winkler, N., et al. (2013). *Sexual and gender-based violence in the Kivu Provinces of the DRC.* Washington, DC: The International Bank for Reconstruction and Development/The World Bank.

Elder, G. H., Jr., & Clipp, E. C. (1988). Combat experience, comradeship, and psychological health. In J. P. Wilson, Z. Harel, & B. Kahana (Eds.), *Human adaptation to extreme stress: From the Holocaust to Vietnam* (pp. 131–156). New York: Plenum Press.

Election polls—Accuracy record in presidential elections. Retrieved from http://www.gallup.com/poll/9442/election-polls-accuracy-record-presidential-elections.aspx

Elfenbein, H. A., & Ambady, N. (2002). On the universality and cultural specificity of emotion recognition: A meta-analysis. *Psychological Bulletin, 128,* 203–235.

Ellemers, N., de Gilder, D., & van den Heuvel, H. (1998). Career-oriented vs. team-oriented commitment and behavior at work. *Journal of Applied Psychology, 83,* 717–730.

Elliott, S. (2012). M&M's to Unveil New Speaking Role at Super Bowl. *New York Times.* Retrieved from http://www.nytimes.com/2012/01/17/business/media/mms-to-unveil-a-new-speaking-role-at-super-bowl.html?_r51

Ellis, A. (1977). *How to live with—and without—anger.* New York: Reader's Digest Press.

Ellsworth, P. C., & Smith, C. A. (1988). Shades of joy: Patterns of appraisal differentiating pleasant emotions. *Cognition and Emotion, 2,* 301–331.

Emmons, R. A. (1989). The personal striving approach to personality. In L. Pervin (Ed.), *Goal concepts and personality and social cognition* (pp. 87–126). Hillsdale, NJ: Erlbaum.

Emswiller, T., Deaux, K., & Willits, J. E. (1971). Similarity, sex, and requests for small favors. *Journal of Applied Social Psychology, 1,* 284–291.

Engelman, R., Halweil, B., & Nierenberg, D. (2002). Rethinking population, improving lives. In C. Flavin, H. French, & G. Gardner (Eds.), *State of the world 2002: A Worldwatch Institute report on progress toward a sustainable society* (p. 127). New York: Norton.

Engs, R. C., & Hanson, D. J. (1990). Gender differences in drinking patterns and problems among college students: A review of the literature. *Journal of Alcohol and Drug Education, 35,* 36–47.

Epley, N., & Gneezy, A. (2007). The framing of financial windfalls and implications for public policy. *Journal of Socio-Economics, 36,* 36–47.

Epley, N., & Huff, C. (1998). Suspicion, affective response, and educational benefit as a result of deception in psychology research. *Personality and Social Psychology Bulletin, 24,* 759–768.

Epley, N., Mak, D., & Idson, L. C. (2006). Bonus or rebate? The impact of income framing on spending and saving. *Journal of Behavioral Decision Making, 19*(3), 213–227. Mata, A., Ferreira, M. B., & Sherman, S. J. (2013). The metacognitive advantage of deliberative thinkers: A dual-process perspective on overconfidence. *Journal of Personality and Social Psychology, 105,* 353–373.

Epps, J., & Kendall, P. C. (1995). Hostile attribution bias in adults. *Cognitive Therapy and Research, 19,* 159–178.

Epstein, S. (1979). The stability of behavior: I. On predicting most of the people much of the time. *Journal of Personality and Social Psychology, 37,* 1097–1126.

Erber, R., & Erber, M. W. (2000). The self-regulation of moods: Second thoughts on the importance of happiness in everyday life. *Psychological Science, 11,* 142–148.

Erber, R., & Fiske, S. T. (1984). Outcome dependency and attention to inconsistent information. *Journal of Personality and Social Psychology, 47,* 709–726.

Erber, R., Wegner, D. M., & Therriault, N. (1996). On being cool and collected: Mood regulation in anticipation of social interaction. *Journal of Personality and Social Psychology, 70,* 757–766.

Erez, A., & Isen, A. M. (2002). The influence of positive affect on the components of expectancy motivation. *Journal of Applied Psychology, 87,* 1055–1067.

Erickson, B., Lind, E. A., Johnson, B. C., & O'Barr, W. M. (1978). Speech style and impression formation in a court setting: The effects of "powerful" and "powerless'" speech. *Journal of Experimental Social Psychology, 14,* 266–279.

Erickson, W. B., Lampinen, J. M., Wooten, A., Wetmore, S., & Neuschatz, J. (2016). When snitches corroborate: Effects of post-identification feedback from a potentially compromised source. *Psychiatry, Psychology and Law, 23,* 148–160.

Erikson, E. H. (1950). *Childhood and society.* New York: Norton.

Eron, L. D., & Huesmann, L. R. (1990). The stability of aggressive behavior—even into the third generation. In M. Lewis & S. M. Miller (Eds.), *Handbook of developmental psychopathology* (pp. 147–156). New York: Plenum Press.

Escobar, J. I., Canino, G., Rubio-Stipec, M., & Bravo, M. (1992). Somatic symptoms after a natural disaster: A prospective study. *American Journal of Psychiatry, 149,* 965–967.

Estrada, C. A., Isen, A. M., & Young, M. J. (1997). Positive affect facilitates integration of information and decreases anchoring in reasoning among physicians. *Organizational Behavior and Human Decision Processes, 72,* 117–135.

Etherington, J. (2010). Nationalism, territoriality, and national territorial belonging. *Papers. Revista de Sociología, 95,* 321–339.

Evans, G. W., & Howard, H. R. B. (1972). A methodological investigation of personal space. In W. J. Mitchell (Ed.), *Environmental design: Research and practice,* Proceedings of EDRA3/ AR8 Conference. University of California, Los Angeles, CA.

Evans, G. W., & Lepore, S. J. (1993). Household crowding and social support: A quasi-experimental analysis. *Journal of Personality and Social Psychology, 65,* 308–316.

Evans, G. W., & Stecker, R. (2004). The motivational consequences of environmental stress. *Journal of Environmental Psychology, 24,* 143–165.

Evans, G. W., Jacobs, S. V., Dooley, D., & Catalano, R. (1987). The interaction of stressful life events and chronic strains on community mental health. *American Journal of Community Psychology, 15,* 23–34.

Everytown (2019, April 4). Gun violence in America. Retrieved August 25, 2019 from https://everytownresearch.org/gun-violence-america/

Exline, J. J. (2002). Stumbling blocks on the religious road: Fractured relationships, nagging vices, and the inner struggle to believe. *Psychological Inquiry, 13,* 182–189.

Exline, J. J., & Lobel, M. (1999). The perils of outperformance: Sensitivity about being the target of a threatening upward comparison. *Psychological Bulletin, 125,* 307–337.

Exline, J. J., & Rose, E. (2005). Religious and spiritual struggles. In R. F. Paloutzian & C. L. Park (Eds.), *Handbook of the psychology of religion* (pp. 315–330). New York: Guilford Press.

Exline, J. J., & Zell, A. L. (2009). Empathy, self-affirmation, and forgiveness: The moderating roles of gender and entitlement. *Journal of Social and Clinical Psychology, 28*(9), 1071–1099.

Exline, J. J., Baumeister, R. F., Bushman, B. J., Campbell, W. K., & Finkel, E. J. (2004). Too proud to let go: Narcissistic entitlement as a barrier to forgiveness. *Journal of Personality and Social Psychology, 87,* 894–912.

Exline, J. J., Baumeister, R. F., Zell, A. L., Kraft, A. J., & Witvliet, C. V. O. (2008). Not so innocent: Does seeing one's own capability for wrongdoing predict forgiveness? *Journal of Personality and Social Psychology, 94,* 495–515.

Exline, J. J., Park, C. L., Smyth, J. M., & Carey, M. P. (2011). Anger toward God: Social-cognitive predictors, prevalence, and links with adjustment to bereavement and cancer. *Journal of Personality and Social Psychology, 100*(1), 129–148.

Exline, J. J., Worthington, E. L., Hill, P., & McCullough, M. E. (2003). Forgiveness and justice: A research agenda for social and personality psychology. *Personality and Social Psychology Review, 7,* 337–348.

Fadiman, A. (1997). *The spirit catches you and you fall down: A Hmong child, her American doctors, and the collusion of two cultures.* New York: Farrar, Straus and Giroux.

Faith, heroics and bedtime snacks hailed at Columbine funerals. (1999, April 26). *CNN.* Retrieved August 23, 2019 from http://www.cnn.com/US/9904/26/school.shooting.funeral/

Falck, R., & Craig, R. (1988). Classroom-oriented primary prevention programming for drug abuse. *Journal of Psychoactive Drugs, 20,* 403–408.

Falcone, L. B.(2009, October 7). Insurance pitchgirl a surprise TV hit: Going with the flo. *Boston Herald.* Retrieved from http://bostonherald.com/news_opinion/columnists/2009/10/insurance_pitchgirl_surprise_tv_hit

Falomir-Pichastor, J. M., & Mugny, G. (2009). "I'm not gay ... I'm a real man!": Heterosexual men's gender self-esteem and sexual prejudice. *Personality and Social Psychology Bulletin, 35*(9), 1233–1243.

Farberow, N. L. (1975). Cultural history of suicide. In N. L. Farberow (Ed.), *Suicide in different cultures* (pp. 1–16). Baltimore: University Park Press.

Farrell, W. (1993). *The myth of male power.* New York: Berkley Books.

Farwell, L., & Wohlwend-Lloyd, R. (1998). Narcissistic processes: Optimistic expectations, favorable self-evaluations, and self-enhancing attributions. *Journal of Personality, 66,* 65–83.

Fauk, N. K., Kustanti, C. Y., Liana, D. S., Indriyawati, N., Crutzen, R., & Mwanri, L. (2018). Perceptions of determinants of condom use behaviors among male clients of female sex workers in indonesia: A qualitative inquiry. *American Journal of Men's Health, 12*(4), 666–675. doi:http://dx.doi.org/10.1177/1557988318756132

Fawcett, J. M., Peace, K. A., Greve, A. (2016). Looking down the barrel of a gun: What do we know about the weapon focus effect? *Journal of Applied Research in Memory and Cognition, 5,* 257–263.

Fay, T. H. (Ed.). (1991). *Noise and health.* New York: New York Academy of Medicine.

Fazio, R. H. (1990). Multiple processes by which attitudes guide behavior: The MODE model as an integrative frame work. In P. Zanna (Ed.), *Advances in experimental social psychology* (Vol. 23, pp. 75–109). San Diego: Academic Press.

Fazio, R. H., & Olson, M. A. (2003). Implicit measures in social cognition research: Their meaning and uses. *Annual Review of Psychology, 54,* 297–327.

Fazio, R. H., & Powell, M. C. (1997). On the value of knowing one's likes and dislikes: Attitude accessibility, stress, and health in college. *Psychological Science, 8,* 430–436.

Fazio, R. H., & Towles-Schwen, T. (1999). The MODE model of attitude-behavior processes. In S. Chaiken (Ed.), *Dual-process theories in social psychology* (pp. 97–116). New York: Guilford Press.

Fazio, R. H., Blascovich, J., & Driscoll, D. M. (1992). On the functional value of attitudes: The influence of accessible attitudes on the ease and quality of decision making. *Personality and Social Psychology Bulletin, 18,* 388–401.

Fazio, R. H., Effrein, E. A., & Falender, V. J. (1981). Self-perceptions following social interaction. *Journal of Personality and Social Psychology, 41,* 232–242.

Fazio, R. H., Jackson, J. R., Dunton, B. C., & Williams, C. J. (1995). Variability in automatic activation as an unobtrusive measure of racial attitudes: A bona fide pipeline? *Journal of Personality and Social Psychology, 69,* 1013–1027.

Federal Trade Commission (2019). *Consumer information.* Retrieved August 25, 2019 from https://www.consumer.ftc.gov

Federal Trade Commission: Consumer information. Retrieved from http://www.consumer.ftc.gov/features/feature-0014-identity-theft

Feeney, B. C., & Collins, N. L. (2001). Predictors of caregiving in adult intimate relationships. *Journal of Personality and Social Psychology, 80,* 972–994.

Feeney, J. A. (1996). Attachment, caregiving, and marital satisfaction. *Personal Relationships, 3,* 401–416.

Fehr, B., & Russell, J. A. (1984). Concept of emotion viewed from a prototype perspective. *Journal of Experimental Psychology: General, 113,* 464–486. Quote on p. 484

Fehr, E., & Gáchter, S. (2002). Altruistic punishment in humans. *Nature, 415*(6868), 137–140.

Fein, S., & Spencer, S. J. (1997). Prejudice as self-image maintenance: Affirming the self through derogating others. *Journal of Personality and Social Psychology, 73,* 31–44.

Feinberg, M., Willer, R., Stellar, J., & Keltner, D. (2012). The virtues of gossip: Reputational information sharing as prosocial behavior. *Journal of Personality and Social Psychology, 102,* 1015–1030.

Feinberg, R. (1986). Credit cards as spending facilitating stimuli: A conditioning interpretation. *Journal of Consumer Research, 3,* 348–356.

Feingold, A. (1988). Matching for attractiveness in romantic partners and same-sex friends: A meta-analysis and theoretical critique. *Psychological Bulletin, 104,* 226–235.

Feingold, A. (1992). Gender differences in mate selection preferences: A test of the parental investment model. *Psychological Bulletin, 112,* 125–139.

Feldman, P. J., Cohen S., Gwaltney, J. M., Jr., Doyle, W. J., & Skoner, D. P. (1999). The impact of personality on the reporting of unfounded symptoms and illness. *Journal of Personality and Social Psychology, 77,* 370–378.

Felson, R. B. (2002). *Violence and gender reexamined.* Washington, DC: American Psychological Association.

Felson, R. B., & Messner, S. F. (2000). The control motive in intimate partner violence. *Social Psychology Quarterly, 63*(1), 86–94.

Fenell, D. (1993). Characteristics of long-term first marriages. *Journal of Mental Health Counseling, 15,* 446–460.

Fenigstein, A., Scheier, M. F., & Buss, A. H. (1975). Public and private self-consciousness: Assessment and theory. *Journal of Consulting and Clinical Psychology, 43,* 522–527.

Fenton-O'Creevy, M., Nicholson, N., Soane, E., & Willman, P. (2003). Trading on illusions: Unrealistic perceptions of control and trading performance. *Journal of Occupational and Organizational Psychology, 76,* 53–68.

Ferguson, R. B. (2018, September 1). War is not part of human nature. *Scientific American.* Retrieved August 25, 2019 from https://www.scientificamerican.com/article/war-is-not-part-of-human-nature/

Ferrari, J. R. (2001). Procrastination as self-regulation failure of performance: Effects of cognitive load, self-awareness, and time limits on "working under pressure." *European Journal of Personality, 15,* 391–406.

Ferrari, J. R., Johnson, J. L., & McCown, W. G. (1995). *Procrastination and task avoidance: Theory, research, and treatment.* New York: Plenum Press.

Ferriere, R. (1998, June 11). Help and you shall be helped. *Nature, 393,* 517–519.

Feshbach, S. (1964). The function of aggression and the regulation of aggressive drive. *Psychological Review, 71,* 257–272.

Festinger, L. (1954). A theory of social comparison processes. *Human Relations, 7,* 117–140.

Festinger, L., & Maccoby, N. (1964). On resistance to persuasive communications. *Journal of Abnormal and Social Psychology, 68,* 359–366.

Festinger, L., Pepitone, A., & Newcomb T. (1952). Some consequences of deindividuation in a group. *Journal of Abnormal and Social Psychology, 47,* 382–389.

Festinger, L., Schachter, S., & Back, K. W. (1950) *Social pressures in informal groups: A study of human factors in housing.* New York: Harper.

Festinger, L., Riecken, H. W., & Schachter, S. (1956). *When prophecy fails: A social and psychological study of a modern group that predicted the destruction of the world.* New York: Harper-Torchbooks.

Fetchenhauer, D., & Dunning, D. (2009). Do people trust too much or too little? *Journal of Economic Psychology, 30,* 263–276.

Fetterman, M., & Hausen, B. (2006, November 19). Young people struggle to deal with kiss of debt. *USA Today.* Retrieved from http://www.usatoday.com/money/perfi/credit/2006-11-19-young-and-in-debt-cover_x.htm

Fiddick, L., Cosmides, L., & Tooby, J. (2000). No interpretation without representation: The role of domain-specific representations and inferences in the Wason selection task. *Cognition, 77,* 1–79.

Fields, D. A., & Kafai, Y. B. (2010). "Stealing from grandma" or generating cultural knowledge? Contestations and effects of cheating in a tween virtual world. *Games and Culture: A Journal of Interactive Media, 5*(1), 64–87.

Filiberti, A., Ripamonti, C., Totis, A., Ventafridda, V., De Conno, F., Contiero, P., & Tamburini, M. (2001). Characteristics of terminal cancer patients who committed suicide during a home palliative care program. *Journal of Pain and Symptom Management, 22,* 544–553.

Filkins, J. W., Smith, C. M., & Tindale, R. S. (1998). An evaluation of the biasing effects of death qualification: A meta-analytic/computer simulation approach. In Tindale, R. S., Heath, L., Edwards, J., Posavac, E. J., Bryant, F. B., Suarez-Balcazar, Y., et al. (Eds.), *Theory and research on small groups.* New York: Plenum Press.

Fincham, F. D., Beach, S. R., & Davila, J. (2004). Forgiveness and conflict resolution in marriage. *Journal of Family Psychology, 18,* 72–81.

Fincham, F. D., Hall, J. H. & Beach, S. R. H. (2005). 'Til lack of forgiveness doth us part: Forgiveness in marriage. In E. L. Worthington (Ed.), *Handbook of forgiveness* (pp. 207–226). New York: Wiley.

Fincher, C. L., Thornhill, R., Murray, D. R., & Schaller, M. (2008). Pathogen prevalence predicts human cross-cultural variability in individualism/collectivism. *Proceedings of the Royal Society B, 275,* 1279–1285.

Finkel, E. J., DeWall, C. N., Slotter, E. B., McNulty, J. K., Pond, R. S., Jr., & Atkins, D. C. (2012). Using I theory to clarify when dispositional aggressiveness predicts intimate partner violence perpetration. *Journal of Personality and Social Psychology, 102*(3), 533–549.

Finkel, E. J., Eastwick, P. W., Karney, B. R., Reis, H. T., & Sprecher, S. (2012). Online dating: A critical analysis from the perspective of psychological science. *Psychological Science in the Public Interest, 13,* 3–66.

Finkel, E. J., Rusbult, C. E., Kumashiro, M., & Hannon, P. (2002). Dealing with betrayal in close relationships: Does commitment promote forgiveness? *Journal of Personality and Social Psychology, 82,* 956–974.

Finnie, W. C. (1973). Field experiments and litter control. *Environment and Behavior, 5,* 123–143.

Fischhoff, B., Lichtenstein, S., Slovic, P., Derby, S. L., & Keeney, R. L. (1981). *Acceptable risk.* New York: Cambridge University Press.

Fishbein, M., & Ajzen, I. (1975). *Belief, attitude, intention and behavior: An introduction to theory and research.* Boston: Addison-Wesley.

Fisher, C. D. (1978). The effects of personal control, competence, and extrinsic reward systems on intrinsic motivation. *Organizational Behavior and Human Performance, 21,* 273–288.

Fisher, J. D., & Nadler, A. (1976). Effects of donor resources on recipient self-esteem and self-help. *Journal of Experimental Social Psychology, 12*(2), 139–150.

Fiske, S. (2002, November/December). Forecasting the future. *Psychology Today.* Retrieved from http://www.psychologytoday.com/articles/pto-20021125-000001.html

Fiske, S. T. (1992). Thinking is for doing: Portraits of social cognition from daguerreotype to laser-photo. *Journal of Personality and Social Psychology, 63,* 877–889.

Fiske, S. T. (2004). *Social beings: A core motives approach to social psychology.* New York: Wiley.

Fiske, S. T., & Taylor, S. E. (1984). *Social cognition.* New York: Random House.

Fiske, S. T., & Taylor, S. E. (1991). *Social cognition* (2nd ed.). New York: Random House.

Fiske, S. T., & Yamamoto, M. (2005). Coping with rejection: Core social motives, across cultures and individuals. In K. D. Williams, J. P. Forgas, & W. von Hippel (Eds.), *The social outcast: Ostracism, social exclusion, rejection, and bullying* (pp. 185–199). New York: Psychology Press.

Fitness, J. (2005). Bye, bye, black sheep: The causes and consequences of rejection in family relationships. In K. D. Williams, J. P. Forgas, & W. von Hippel (Eds.), *The social outcast: Ostracism, social exclusion, rejection, and bullying* (pp. 263–277). New York: Psychology Press.

Fitzgerald, R. J., & Price, H. L. (2015). Eyewitness identification across the life span: A meta-analysis of age differences. *Psychological Bulletin, 141,* 1228–1265.

Fitzgerald, R. J., Oriet, C., & Price, H. L. (2015). Suspect filler similarity in eyewitness lineups: A literature review and a novel methodology. *Law and Human Behavior, 39,* 62–74.

Fitzgerald, R. J., Price, H. L., Oriet, C., & Charman, S. D. (2013). The effect of suspect-filler similarity on eyewitness identification decisions: A meta-analysis. *Psychology, Public Policy, and Law, 19,* 151–164.

Fitzgerald, R., & Ellsworth, P. C. (1984). Due process vs. crime control: Death qualification and jury attitudes. *Law and Human Behavior, 8,* 31–51.

Fitzsimons, G. M., & Bargh, J. A. (2003). Thinking of you: Nonconscious pursuit of interpersonal goals associated with relationship partners. *Journal of Personality and Social Psychology, 84,* 148–164.

Fitzsimons, G. M., & Shah, J. Y. (2008). How goal instrumentality shapes relationship evaluations. *Journal of Personality and Social Psychology, 95,* 319–337.

Flaherty, D. K. (2011). The vaccine-autism connection: a public health crisis caused by unethical medical practices and fraudulent science. Annals of Pharmacotherapy 45 (10): 1302–1304. doi:10.1345/aph.1Q318

Flanagan, J. C. (1954). The critical incident technique. *Psychological Bulletin, 51,* 327–358.

Flanagin, A., J., & Waldeck, J. H. (2004). Technology use and organizational newcomer socialization. *Journal of Business Communication, 41*(2), 137–165.

Fletcher, C., & Perry, E. L. (2001). Performance appraisal and feedback: A consideration of national culture and a review of contemporary research and future trends. In N. Anderson, D. S. Ones, H. K. Sinangil, & C. Viswesvaran, *Handbook of industrial, work and organizational psychology* (vol. 1, pp. 127–144). Thousand Oaks, CA: Sage.

Flink, C., Boggiano, A. K., & Barrett, M. (1990). Controlling teaching strategies: Undermining children's self-determination and performance. *Journal of Personality and Social Psychology, 59*(5), 916–924.

Flood, A. (2016). "Post-truth" named word of the year by Oxford Dictionaries. *The Guardian.* Retrieved from https://www.theguardian.com/books/2016/nov/15/post-truth-named-word-of-the-year-by-oxford-dictionaries

Florin, P., & Wandersman, A. (1983). A psychosocial perspective on neighborhood conservation. In N. R. Feimer & E. S. Geller (Eds.), *Environmental psychology: Directions and perspectives.* New York: Praeger.

Folkes, V. S. (1982). Communicating the reasons for social rejection. *Journal of Personality and Social Psychology, 18,* 235–252.

Foot, P. (1967). The problem of abortion and the doctrine of double effect. *Oxford Review, 5,* 5–15.

For college students, yes, sleep matters. *WebMD.* Retrieved from https://www.webmd.com/sleep-disorders/features/for-college-students-sleep-matters

Forgas, J. P. (2013). Don't worry, be sad! On the cognitive, motivational, and interpersonal benefits of negative mood. *Current Directions in Psychological Science, 22,* 225–232.

Forrest, A. (2019, January 24). Prominent 'gay conversion therapist' comes out as gay and offers apology. *Independent.* Retrieved from https://www.independent.co.uk/news/world/americas/gay-conversion-therapy-therapist-comes-out-utah-mormon-david-matthews-lgbtq-a8744361.html?fbclid=IwAR3nTByKLsoFIn D7SXP4RTu5HROalUHU7Vd5novMKlmsoLZCh4 Gpjfz9Rpg

Forster, J. L. & Jeffery, R. W. (1986). Gender differences related to weight history, eating patterns, efficacy expectations, self-esteem, and weight loss among participants in a weight reduction program. *Addictive Behaviors, 11,* 141–147.

Forsyth, A. J. M., & Davidson, N. (2010). The nature and extent of illegal drug and alcohol-related litter in Scottish social housing community: A photographic investigation. *Addiction Research & Theory, 18*(1), 71–83.

Forsyth, D. R. (2010). *Group dynamics* (5th ed.). Belmont, CA: Wadsworth.

Forsyth, D. R., & Kerr, N. A. (1999, August). *Are adaptive illusions adaptive?* Poster presented at the annual meeting of the American Psychological Association, Boston, MA.

Fortune 100 Best. (2019). Hilton. *Fortune.* Retrieved from http://fortune.com/best-companies/hilton-worldwide-holdings/

Fortune 100 Best. (2019). Identifying best places to work: US and globally. *Fortune.* Retrieved from http://fortune.com/best-companies/.

Fowler, J. H., & Christakis, N. A. (2010). Cooperative behavior cascades in human social networks. *PNAS, 107*(12), 5334–5338. doi: 10.1073/pnas.0913149107

Fox, E., Griggs, L., & Mouchlianitis, E. (2007). The detection of fear-relevant stimuli: Are guns noticed as quickly as snakes? *Emotion, 7*(4), 691–696.

Fraley, B., & Aron, A. (2004). The effect of a shared humorous experience on closeness in initial encounters. *Personal Relationships, 11,* 61–78.

Francis, A. M., & Mialon, H. M. (2014). "A diamond is forever" and other fairy tales: The relationship between wedding expenses and marriage duration. Unpublished paper, Emory University, Atlanta, GA (Andrew.francis@emory.edu).

Francoeur, R. T., Perper, T., Scherzer, N. A., Sellmer, G. P., & Cornog, M. (1991). *A descriptive dictionary and atlas of sexology,* p. 130. New York: Greenwood Press.

Frayser, S. G. (1985). *Varieties of sexual experience: An anthropological perspective on human sexuality.* New Haven, CT: HRAF Press.

Frazier, P., Tashiro, T., Berman, M., Steger, M., & Long, J. (2004), Correlates of levels and patterns of positive life changes following sexual assault. *Journal of Consulting and Clinical Psychology, 72,* 19–30.

Fredrickson, B. L. (1998). What good are positive emotions? *Review of General Psychology, 2,* 300–319.

Fredrickson, B. L. (2001). The role of positive emotions in positive psychology: The broaden-and-build theory of positive emotions. *American Psychologist, 56,* 218–226.

Fredrickson, B. L. (2003). The value of positive emotions. *American Scientist, 91,* 330–335.

Freedman, J. L. & Fraser, S. C. (1966). Compliance without pressure: The foot-in-the-door technique. *Journal of Personality and Social Psychology, 4*(2), 195–202. DOI: 10.1037/h0023552

Freedman, J. L., & Sears, D. O. (1965). Warning, distraction, and resistance to influence. *Journal of Personality and Social Psychology, 1*(3), 262–266.

Freedman, S. R., & Enright, R. D. (1996). Forgiveness as an intervention goal with incest survivors. *Journal of Consulting and Clinical Psychology, 64,* 983–992.

Freud, S. (1933/1950). Why war? In *Collected works of Sigmund Freud* (Vol. 16). London: Imagio.

Freud, S. (1961). *Civilization and its discontents* (standard ed.). London: Norton. (Original work published 1930).

Freud, S. (1961). *Mourning and melancholia* (standard ed.). London: Norton. (Original work published 1917).

Freud, S. (1964). *Beyond the pleasure principle* (J. Strachey, Trans.). New York: Norton. (Original work published 1920).

Frey, R. G. (1983). *Rights, killing, and suffering: Moral vegetarianism and applied ethics.* Oxford: Blackwell.

Friedman, H. S., & Booth-Kewley, S. (1987). The "disease-prone personality": A meta-analytic view of the construct. *American Psychologist, 42,* 539–555.

Friedman, H., & Silver, R. (Eds.). (2007). *Foundations of health psychology.* New York: Oxford University Press.

Frijda, N. H. (1986). *The emotions.* New York: Cambridge University Press.

Frijda, N. H., Kuipers, P., & ter Schure, E. (1989). Relations among emotion, appraisal, and emotional action readiness. *Journal of Personality and Social Psychology, 57,* 212–228.

Frimer, J. A., Schaefer, N. K., & Oakes, H. (2014). Moral actor, selfish agent. *Journal of Personality and Social Psychology, 106,* 790–802.

Frith, K. T., & Mueller, B. (2003). *Advertising and society: Global issues.* New York: Peter Lang.

Fukuyama, F. (1999). *Trust.* New York: Free Press.

Fulero, S. M., & Penrod, S. D. (1990a). Attorney jury selection folklore: What do they think and how can psychologists help? *Forensic Reports, 3,* 233–259.

Fullerton, C. S., McCarroll, J. E., Ursano, R. S., & Wright, K. M. (1992). Psychological responses of rescue workers: Fire fighters and trauma. *American Journal of Orthopsychiatry, 62,* 371–378.

Funder, D. C. (2001). Personality. *Annual Review of Psychology, 52,* 197–221.

Furnham, A. (2003). Belief in a just world: Research progress over the past decade. *Personality and Individual Differences, 34,* 795–817.

Gable, S. L., & Reis, H. T. (2001). Appetitive and aversive social interaction. In J. Harvey (Ed.), *Close romantic relationships: Maintenance and enhancement* (pp. 169–194). Mahwah, NJ: Erlbaum.

Gable, S. L., Reis, H. T., & Elliot, A. J. (2000). Behavioral activation and inhibition in everyday life. *Journal of Personality and Social Psychology, 78,* 1135–1149.

Gabriel, M. T., Critelli, J. W., & Ee, J. S. (1994). Narcissistic illusions in self-evaluations of intelligence and attractiveness. *Journal of Personality, 62,* 143–155.

Gael, S. A. (1988). *The job analysis handbook for business, industry, and government* (Vols. 1 and 2). New York: Wiley.

Gaertner, L., & Iuzzini, J. (2005). Rejection and entitativity: A synergistic model of mass violence. In K. D. Williams, J. P. Forgas, & W. von Hippel (Eds.), *The social outcast: Ostracism, social exclusion, rejection, and bullying* (pp. 307–320). New York: Psychology Press.

Gaertner, S. L., & Dovidio, J. F. (1986). The aversive form of racism. In J. F. Dovidio & S. L. Gaertner (Eds.), *Prejudice, discrimination, and racism* (pp. 61–89). San Diego: Academic Press.

Gailliot, M. T., & Baumeister, R. F. (2007). The physiology of willpower: Linking blood glucose to self-control. *Personality and Social Psychology Review, 11*(4), 303–327.

Galinsky, A. D., Gruenfeld, D. H., & Magee, J. C. (2003). From power to action. *Journal of Personality and Social Psychology, 85,* 453–466.

Galinsky, A. D., Magee, J. C., Gruenfeld, D. H., Whitson, J. A., & Liljenquist, K. A. (2008). Power reduces the press of the situation: Implications for creativity, conformity, and dissonance. *Journal of Personality and Social Psychology, 95,* 1450–1466.

Gallagher, J. (2011). Babies can "hear" emotion as early as three months old. BBC News Health. June 30. Retrieved from http://www.bbc.co.uk/news/health-13962068

Galperin, A., Haselton, M.G., Frederick, D.A., Poore, J., von Hippel, W., Buss, D.M., & Gonzaga, G.C. (2013). Sexual regret: evidence for evolved sex differences. *Archives of Sexual Behavior, 42,* 1145–1161.

Gangestad, S. W., & Snyder, M. (2000). Self-monitoring: Appraisal and reappraisal. *Psychological Bulletin, 126,* 530–555.

Ganna, A., Verweij, K. J. H., & Zietsch, B. (2019). Large-scale GWAS reveals insights into the genetic architecture of same-sex sexual behaviour. *Science.* Vol. 365, Issue 6456, DOI: 10.1126/science.aat7693. https://science.sciencemag.org/content/365/6456/eaat7693

Gardner, M. P., Wansink, B., & Kim, J. (2014). Better moods for better eating?: How mood influences food choice. *Journal of Consumer Psychology, 24*(3), 320–335. doi: 10.1037/t01397-000

Gardner, W. L., Pickett, C. L., & Brewer, M. B. (2000). Social exclusion and selective memory: How the need to belong influences memory for social events. *Personality and Social Psychology Bulletin, 26,* 486–496.

Gardner, W. L., Pickett, C. L., & Knowles, M. (2005). Social snacking and shielding: Using social symbols, selves, and surrogates in the service of belonging needs. In K. D. Williams, J. P. Forgas, & W. von Hippel (Eds.), *The social outcast: Ostracism, social exclusion, rejection, and bullying* (pp. 227–242). New York: Psychology Press.

Gardner, W., Seeley, E., Gabriel, S., Pennington, G., Solomon, J., Ernst, J., et al. (2002). The role of "his" and "her" forms of interdependence in everyday life: Gender, belonging, and social experience. Unpublished manuscript, Northwestern University.

Garland, E. L., Brown, S. M., & Howard, M. O. (2016). Thought suppression as a mediator of the association between depressed mood and prescription opioid craving among chronic pain patients. *Journal of Behavioral Medicine, 39*(1), 128–138. doi:10.1007/s10865-015-9675-9

Garner, D. M., Garfinkel, P. E., Schwartz, D., & Thompson, M. (1980). Cultural expectations of thinness in women. *Psychological Reports, 47,* 483–491.

Garrett, R. K., & Weeks, B. E. (2017). Epistemic beliefs' role in promoting misperceptions and conspiracist ideation. *PLoS ONE.* doi:10.1371/journal.pone.0184733

Garrioch, L., & Brimacombe, C. A. E. (2001). Lineup administrators' expectations: Their impact on eyewitness confidence. *Law and Human Behavior, 25,* 299–315.

Gazzaniga, M. S. (1998). *The mind's past.* Berkeley: University of California Press.

Gazzaniga, M. S. (2003, January). *The when, where, what, and why of conscious experience.* Paper presented at the 25th Annual National Institute on the Teaching of Psychology Convention, St. Petersburg Beach, FL.

Geen, R. G., & Quanty, M. B. (1977). The catharsis of aggression: An evaluation of a hypothesis. In L. Berkowitz (Ed.), *Advances in experimental social psychology* (Vol. 10, pp. 1–37). New York: Academic Press.

Geen, R. G., & Quanty, M. B. (1977). The catharsis of aggression: An evaluation of a hypothesis. In L. Berkowitz (Ed.), *Advances in experimental social psychology* (Vol. 10, pp. 1–37). New York: Academic Press.

Geiger, A. (2018, January 5). About six-in-ten Americans support marijuana legalization. *Pew Research Center.* Retrieved from http://www.pewresearch.org/fact-tank/2018/01/05/americans-support-marijuana-legalization/

Geller, E. S., Winett, R. A., & Everett, P. B. (1982). *Preserving the environment: Strategies for behavior change.* New York: Pergamon.

Gentile, D. A., Anderson, C. A., Yukawa, S., Ihori, N., Saleem, M., Ming, L. K., Liau, A. K., Khoo, A., Bushman, B. J., Huesmann, L. R., & Sakamoto, A. (2009). The effects of prosocial video games on prosocial behaviors: International evidence from correlational, longitudinal, and experimental studies. *Personality and Social Psychology Bulletin, 35*(6), 752–763.

Gentile, D. G., & Bushman, B. J. (2012). Reassessing media violence effects using a risk and resilience approach to understanding aggression. *Psychology of Popular Media Culture, 1*(3), 138–151. doi:10.1037/a0028481

George Santayana (1905) Reason in Common Sense, p. 284, volume 1 of The Life of Reason. New York: Unabridged Dover Press.

Georgia Institute of Technology. "Junk DNA" defines differences between humans and chimps. (2011, October 25). *ScienceDaily.* Retrieved from http://www.sciencedaily.com/releases/2011/10/111025122615.htm

Gerbner, G. (1998). Cultivation analysis: An overview. *Mass Communication & Society, 1*(3–4), 175–194. DOI: 10.1080/15205436.1998.9677855

Gerbner, G., & Gross, L. (1976). Living with television: The violence profile. *Journal of Communication, 26*(2), 172–199. DOI:10.1111/j.1460-2466.1976.tb01397.x

Gerrard, M., Gibbons, F. X., & McCoy, S. B. (1993). Emotional inhibition of effective contraception. *Anxiety, Stress & Coping: An International Journal, 6,* 73–88.

Gerrard, M., Gibbons, F., Houlihan, A., Stock, M., & Pomery, E. (2008). A dual-process approach to health risk decision making: The prototype willingness model. *Developmental Review, 28*(1), 29–61.

Gerstel, N., & Gross, H. (1982). Commuter marriages: A review. *Marriage and Family Review, 5,* 71–93.

Gerstel, N., & Gross, H. (1984). *Commuter marriage: A study of work and family.* New York: Guilford Press.

Gervais, W. M. & Norenzayan, A. (2013). Religion and the origins of anti-atheist prejudice. Chapter to appear in S. Clarke, R. Powell, & J. Savulescu (Eds.), *Intolerance and conflict: A scientific and conceptual investigation.* Oxford: Oxford University Press.

Gervais, W. M., & Najle, M. B. (2018). How many atheists are there? *Social Psychological and Personality Science, 9*(1), 3–10. DOI: 10.1177/1948550617707015

Gervais, W. M., Shariff, A. F., & Norenzayan, A. (2011). Do you believe in atheists? Distrust is central to anti-atheist prejudice. *Journal of Personality and Social Psychology, 101,* 1189–1206. doi: 10.1037/a0025882

Gesch, B. C., Hammond, S. M., Hampson, S. E., Eves, A., & Crowder, M. J. (2002). Influence of supplementary vitamins, minerals and essential fatty acids on the antisocial behaviour of young adult prisoners: Randomised, placebo-controlled trial. *British Journal of Psychiatry, 181,* 22–28.

Geurten, M., Willems, S., Germain, S., & Meulemans, T. (2015). Less is more: The availability heuristic in early childhood. *British Journal of Developmental Psychology, 33*(4), 405–410. doi:10.1111/bjdp.12114

Gharib, S. (2019, January 31). Hilton CEO says the key leadership lesson in the hotel's turnaround: "We kept a steady hand on the wheel." *Fortune.* Retrieved from http://fortune.com/2019/01/31/hilton-ceo-on-leading-leadership.

Giancola, P. R. (2000). Executive functioning: A conceptual framework for alcohol-related aggression. *Experimental Clinical Psychopharmacology, 8,* 576–597.

Giannopoulou, I., Dikaiakou, A., Yule, W. (2006). Cognitive-behavioural group intervention for PTSD symptoms in children following the Athens 1999 earthquake: A pilot study. *Clinical Child Psychology and Psychiatry, 2011,* 543–553.

Gibbons, F. X., & Gerrard, M. (1997). Health images and their effects on health behavior. In B. P. Buunk & F. X. Gibbons (Eds.), *Health, coping, and well-being: Perspectives from social comparison theory* (pp. 63–94). Mahwah, NJ: Erlbaum.

Gibson, B., & Zielaskowski, K. (2013). Subliminal priming of winning images prompts increased betting in slot machine play. *Journal of Applied Social Psychology, 43*(1), 106–115. doi:10.1111/j.1559-1816.2012.00985.x

Gifford, R. (2017). *Applying social psychology to the environment.* Thousand Oaks, CA: Sage.

Gilbert, D. T. (1991). How mental systems believe. *American Psychologist, 46,* 107–119.

Gilbert, D. T. (1993). The assent of man: Mental representation and the control of belief. In D. Wegner & J. Pennebaker (Eds.), *Handbook of mental control* (pp. 57–87). Englewood Cliffs, NJ: Prentice-Hall.

Gilbert, D. T., Pelham, B. W., & Krull, D. S. (1988). On cognitive business: When person perceivers meet persons perceived. *Journal of Personality and Social Psychology, 54,* 733–740.

Gilbert, D. T., Pinel, E. C., Wilson, T. D., Blumberg, S. J., & Wheatley, T. P. (1998). Immune neglect: A source of durability bias in affective forecasting. *Journal of Personality and Social Psychology, 75,* 617–638.

Gilbert, D. T., Tafarodi, R. W., & Malone, P. S. (1993). You can't not believe everything you read. *Journal of Personality and Social Psychology, 65,* 221–233.

Gilovich, T. (1983). Biased evaluation and persistence in gambling. *Journal of Personal and Social Psychology, 44,* 1110–1126.

Gilovich, T. (1991). *How we know what isn't so.* New York: Free Press.

Gilovich, T., & Medvec, V. H. (1995). The experience of regret: What, when, and why. *Psychological Review, 102,* 379–395.

Gino, F., & Ariely, D. (2012). The dark side of creativity: Original thinkers can be more dishonest. *Journal of Personality and Social Psychology, 102,* 445–459.

Gino, F., & Mogilner, C. (2014). Time, money, and morality. *Psychological Science, 25,* 414–421.

Giordano, C. (2019, February 19). Vandals desecrate 90 Jewish graves in Paris as antisemitism marches about to take place. *Independent.* Retrieved from https://www.independent.co.uk/news/world/europe/france-antisemitism-vandals-jewish-graves-paris-gilets-jaunes-swastikas-marches-a8786226.html

Giuffrida, A. (2015, March 26). Why are Italians such crazy drivers? The Local it. Retrieved from https://www.thelocal.it/20150326/why-are-italians-such-crazy-drivers

Gladue, B. A., Boechler, M., & McCaul, K. D. (1989). Hormonal responses to competition in human males. *Aggressive Behavior, 17,* 313–326.

Glass, D. C., & Singer, J. E. (1972). *Urban stress: Experiments on noise and social stressors.* New York: Academic Press.

Glass, D. C., Singer, J. E., & Friedman, L. N. (1969). Psychic cost of adaptation to an environmental stressor. *Journal of Personality and Social Psychology, 12,* 200–210. Retrieved from http://www.quotationspage.com/quote/34212.html

Glassdoor. (2019). Hilton. Retrieved from https://www.glassdoor.com/Benefits/Hilton-US-Benefits-EI_IE330.0,6_IL.7,9_IN1.htm

Glendenning, A., & Inglis, D. (1999). Smoking behaviour in youth: The problem of low self-esteem? *Journal of Adolescence, 22,* 673–682.

Glenn, N. D., & McLanahan, S. (1982). Children and marital happiness: A further specification of the relationship. *Journal of Marriage and the Family, 44,* 63–72.

Glenn, N. D., & Weaver, C. N. (1978). A multi-variate multisurvey study of marital happiness. *Journal of Marriage and the Family, 40,* 269–282.

Glick, P. (2002). Sacrificial lambs dressed in wolves' clothing: Envious prejudice, ideology, and the scapegoating of Jews. In L. S. Newman & R. Erber (Eds.), *Understanding genocide: The social psychology of the Holocaust.* (pp. 113–142). New York, NY: Oxford University Press.

Glionna, J. M. (2013, January 30). New Aspen speed limit—14 miles an hour? *Los Angeles Times.* Retrieved from http://articles.latimes.com/2013/jan/30/nation/la-na-nn-new-aspen-speed-limit-14-miles-an-hour-20130130

Goel, S., Mason, W., & Watts, D. J. (2010). Real and perceived attitude agreement in social networks. *Journal of Social and Personality Psychology, 99*(4), 611–621.

Goethals, G. R., Messick, D. M., & Allison, S. T. (1991). The uniqueness bias: Studies of constructive social comparison. In J. Suls & T. A. Wills (Eds.), *Social conparison: Contemporary theory and research.* Hillsdale, NJ: Erlbaum.

Goffman, E. (1959). *The presentation of self in everyday life.* New York: Doubleday Anchor.

Golding, S. L., & Rorer, L. G. (1972). Illusory correlation and subjective judgment. *Journal of Abnormal Psychology, 80,* 249–260.

Goldsmith, K., Cho, E.K., & Dhar, R. (2012). When guilt begets pleasure: The positive effect of a negative emotion. *Journal of Marketing Research, 49,* 872–881.

Goldstein, N. J., Cialdini, R. B., & Griskevicius, V. (2004). *A room with a viewpoint: Using norm-based appeals to motivate conservation behaviors in a hotel setting.* Paper presented at the annual meeting of the Society for Personality and Social Psychology, Austin, TX.

Goleman, D. (1995, August 8). Brain may tag all perceptions with a value. *New York Times,* 1–10.

Gollwitzer, P. M. (1996). The volitional benefits of planning. In P. M. Gollwitzer & J. A. Bargh (Eds.), *The psychology of action: Linking cognition and motivation to behavior* (pp. 287–312). New York: Guilford Press.

Gollwitzer, P. M., & Kinney, R. F. (1989). Effects of deliberative and implemental mind-sets on the illusion of control. *Journal of Personality and Social Psychology, 56,* 531–542.

Gondolf, E. W. (1985). *Men who batter: An integrated approach for stopping wife abuse*. Holmes Beach, CA: Learning Publications.

Gonzales, M. H., Haugen, J. A., & Manning, D. J. (1994). Victims as "narrative critics": Factors influencing rejoinders and evaluative responses to offenders' accounts. *Personality and Social Psychology Bulletin, 20*, 691–704.

Gonzales, M., Pederson, J., Manning, D., & Wetter, D. (1990). Pardon my gaffe: Effects of sex, status, and consequence severity on accounts. *Journal of Personality and Social Psychology, 58*, 610–621.

Gonzalez-Forero, M., & Gardner, A. (2018). Inference of ecological and social drivers of human brain-size evolution. *Nature, 557*, 554–557.

Gonzalez-Vallejo, C., Lassiter, G. D., Bellezza, F. S., & Lindberg, M. J. (2008). "Save angels perhaps": A critical examination of Unconscious Thought Theory and the Deliberation-Without-Attention effect. *Review of General Psychology, 12*, 282–296.

Goodenough, F. L. (1931). *Anger in young children*. Minneapolis: University of Minnesota Press.

Goodwin, G. P., Piazza, J., & Rozin, P. (2013). Moral character predominates in person perception and evaluation. *Journal of Personality and Social Psychology, 106*, 148–168.

Goodwin, J. S., Hunt, W. C., Key, C. R., & Samet, J. M. (1987). The effect of marital status on stage, treatment, and survival of cancer patients. *Journal of the American Medical Association, 258*, 3125–3130.

Gottfredson, L. (Ed.). (1997). Intelligence and social policy, *Intelligence, 24*, 1–320.

Gottfredson, M. R., & Hirschi, T. (1990). *A general theory of crime*. Stanford, CA: Stanford University Press

Gottman, J. M. (1994). *What predicts divorce?* Hillsdale, NJ: Erlbaum.

Gottschalk, L. A., & Gleser, G. C. (1960). An analysis of the verbal content of suicide notes. *British Journal of Medical Psychology, 33*, 195–204.

Gould, S. J., & Weil, C. E. (1991). Gift-giving and gender self-concepts. *Gender Role, 24*, 617–637.

Govaerts, K., & Dixon, D. N. (1988). ... Until careers do us part: Vocational and marital satisfaction in the dual-career commuter marriage. *International Journal for the Advancement of Counseling, 11*, 265–281.

Goveas, J. S., Csernansky, J. G., & Coccaro, E. F. (2004). Platelet serotonin content correlates inversely with life history of aggression in personality-disordered subjects. *Psychiatry Research, 126*, 23–32.

Graham, J., Haidt, J., & Nosek, B. A. (2009). Liberals and conservatives rely on different sets of moral foundations. *Journal of Personality and Social Psychology, 96*, 1029–1046.

Graham, K. (1980). Theories of intoxicated aggression. *Canadian Journal of Behavioral Science, 12*, 141–158.

Grahe, J. E. (2014). Announcing open science badges and reaching for the sky. *The Journal of Social Psychology, 154*(1), 1–3. doi:10.1080/00224545.2014.853582

Grammer, K., Fink, B., Moller A. P., & Thornhill, R. (2003). Darwinian aesthetics: Sexual selection and the biology of beauty. *Biological Reviews, 78*, 385–407.

Grandey, A.A., Frone, M.R., Melloy, R.C., & Sayre, G.M. (2019). When are fakers also drinkers? A self-control view of emotional labor and alcohol consumption among U.S. service workers. *Journal of Occupational Health Psychology*, advance online publication, http://dx.doi.org/10.1037/ocp0000147

Grasmick, H. G., Bursik, R. J., & Kinsey, K. A. (1991). Shame and embarrassment as deterrents to noncompliance with the law: The case of an antilittering campaign. *Environment and Behavior, 23*, 233–251.

Gray-Little, B., & Hafdahl, A. R., (2000). Factors influencing racial comparisons of self-esteem: A quantitative synthesis. *Psychological Bulletin, 126*, 26–54.

Great Place to Work. (2019). 100 best companies to work for. Retrieved from https://www.greatplacetowork.com/certified-company/1000367

Great Place to Work. (2019). 100 best companies to work for. Retrieved from https://www.greatplacetowork.com/certified-company/1000367

Greathouse, S. M., & Kovera, M. B. (2009). Instruction bias and lineup presentation moderate the effects of administrator knowledge on eyewitness identification. *Law and Human Behavior, 33*, 70–82.

Green, B. L., Grace, M. C., Vary, M. G., Krammer, T. L., Gleser, G. C., & Leonard, A. C. (1994). Children of disaster in the second decade: A 17-year follow-up of Buffalo Creek survivors. *Journal of the American Academy of Child and Adolescent Psychiatry, 33*, 71–79.

Green, D. M., & Fidell, S. (1991). Variability in the criterion for reporting annoyance in community noise surveys. *Journal of the Acoustical Society of America, 89*, 234–243.

Green, G. (2005, December 9). Man dates gal on Internet for six months—and it turns out she's his mother! Retrieved September 2, 2019 from http://entertainment.tv.yahoo.com/news/wwn

Green, L., Price, P. C., & Hamburger, M. E. (1995). Prisoner's dilemma and the pigeon: Control by immediate consequences. *Journal of the Experimental Analysis of Behavior, 64*, 1–17.

Greenberg J. (1990). Organizational justice: Yesterday, today and tomorrow. *Journal of Management 16*, 399–432.

Greenberg, J., & Musham, C. (1981). Avoiding and seeking self-focused attention. *Journal of Research in Personality, 15*, 191–200.

Greenberg, J., & Pyszczynski, J. (1985). Compensatory self-inflation: A response to the threat to self-regard of public failure. *Journal of Personality and Social Psychology, 49*, 273–280.

Greenberg, J., Solomon, S., & Pyszczynski, T. (1997). Terror management theory of self-esteem and cultural worldviews: Empirical assessments and conceptual refinements. In M. P. Zanna (Ed.), *Advances in experimental social psychology* (Vol. 29, pp. 61–139). San Diego: Academic Press.

Greenblat, C. (1983). The salience of sexuality in the early years of marriage. *Journal of Marriage and the Family, 45*, 277–288.

Greene, J. D., Sommerville, R. B., Nystrom, L. E., Darley, J. M., Cohen, J. D. (2001). An fMRI investigation of emotional engagement in moral judgment. *Science, 293*, 2105–2108.

Greenhaus, J. H. (2003). Career dynamics. In W. C. Borman, D. R. Ilgen, & R. J. Klimoski (Eds.), *Handbook of psychology: Industrial and organizational psychology* (vol. 12, pp. 519–540). New York: Wiley.

Greenspan, S. I., & Porges, S. W. (1984). Psychopathology in infancy and early childhood: Clinical perspectives on the organization of sensory and affective-thematic experience. *Child Development, 55*, 49–70.

Greenwald, A. G., & Banaji, M. R. (1989). The self as a memory system: Powerful, but ordinary. *Journal of Personality and Social Psychology, 57*, 41–54.

Greenwald, A. G., McGhee, D. E., & Schwartz, J. K. L. (1998). Measuring individual differences in implicit cognition: The implicit association test. *Journal of Personality and Social Psychology, 74*, 1464–1480.

Greenwald, A. G., Oakes, M. A., & Hoffman, H. G. (2003). Targets of discrimination: Effects of race on responses to weapons holders. *Journal of Experimental Social Psychology, 39*, 399–340.

Gregory, J. W., Cialdini, R. B., & Carpenter, K. M. (1982). Self-relevant scenarios as mediator of likelihood estimates and compliance: Does imagining make it so? *Journal of Personality and Social Psychology, 43*, 89–99.

Greitemeyer, T. (2009). Effects of songs with prosocial lyrics on prosocial thoughts, affect, and behavior. *Journal of Experimental Social Psychology, 45*(1), 186–190.

Greitemeyer, T., & Mügge, D. O. (2014). Video games do affect social outcomes: A meta-analytic review of the effects of violent and prosocial video game play. *Personality and Social Psychology Bulletin, 40*(5), 578–589. doi: 10.1177/0146167213520459

Greitemeyer, T., & Osswald, S. (2009). Prosocial video games reduce aggressive cognitions. *Journal of Experimental Social Psychology, 45*(4), 896–900.

Griffitt, W. (1981). Sexual intimacy in aging marital partners. In J. Marsh & S. Kiesler (Eds.), *Aging: Stability and change in the family* (pp. 301–315). New York: Academic Press.

Griscom, R. (2002, November). Why are online personals so hot? *Wired*. Retrieved August 26, 2019 from http://www.wired.com/wired/archive/10.11/view.html?pg52

Griskevicius, V., Tybur, J. M., & Van den Bergh, B. (2010). Going green to be seen: Status, reputation, and conspicuous conservation. *Journal of Personality and Social Psychology, 98*, 392–404.

Groeger, J. A. (2000). *Understanding driving – Applying cognitive psychology to a complex everyday task*: Psychology Press, Taylor and Francis, Hove, UK.

Grolnick, W. S., & Ryan, R. M. (1987). Autonomy in children's learning: An experimental and individual differences investigation. *Journal of Personality and Social Psychology, 52*, 890–898.

Grondin, S., Deshaies, P., & Nault, L. P. (1984). Trimestres de naissance et participation au hockey et au volleyball. *La Revue Quebecoise de l'Activité Physique, 2*, 97–103.

Gross, D. (1996). *Forbes greatest business stories of all time*. New York: Wiley.

Gross, J., & Rosen, J. C. (1988). Bulimia in adolescents: Prevalence and psychosocial correlates. *International Journal of Eating Disorders, 7*, 51–61.

Group for the Advancement of Psychiatry. (1957). *Methods of forceful indoctrination: Observations and interviews*. New York: Author.

Groves, C. L., & Anderson, C. A. (2018). Aversive events and aggression. *Current Opinion in Psychology, 19*, 144–148. doi: 10.1016/j.copsyc.2017.03.027

Gruber, J., Mauss, I. B., & Tamir, M. (2011). A dark side of happiness? How, when, and why happiness is not always good. *Perspectives on Psychological Science, 6*, 222–233.

Gruenewald, T., & Wang, D. (2019). Stress and health. In T. A. Revenson & R. A. R. Gurung (Eds.), *Handbook of health psychology* (pp. 213–224). New York: Routledge.

Grunberg, N. E., & Straub, R. O. (1992). The role of gender and taste class in the effects of stress on eating. *Health Psychology, 11*, 97–100.

Gruner, C. R. (1985). Advice to the beginning speaker on using humor: What the research tells us. *Communication Education, 34*, 142–147.

Guinote, A. (2008). Power and affordances: When the situation has more power over powerful than powerless individuals. *Journal of Personality and Social Psychology, 95*, 237–252.

Gurr, T. R. (1981). Historical trends in violent crime: A critical review of the evidence. *Crime and Justice, 3*, 295.

Gurung, R. A. R. (2012). Health psychology. In D. S. Dunn (Ed.), *Oxford Bibliographies in Psychology*. New York: Oxford University Press.

Gurung, R. A. R. (2019). *Health psychology: Well-being in a diverse world* (4th ed.). Thousand Oaks, CA: SAGE.

Gurung, R. A. R. (Ed.). (2014). *Multicultural approaches to health and wellness in America: Major issues and cultural groups*. Westport, CT: Praeger Publishers.

Gurung, R. A. R., Dunkel-Schetter, C., Collins, N., Rini, C., & Hobel. (2005). Psychosocial predictors of perceived prenatal stress. *Journal of Social and Clinical Psychology, 24*, 497–519.

Gutkowski, S., Ginath, Y. & Guttmann, F. (1992). Improving psychiatric environments through minimal architectural change. *Hospital and Community Psychiatry, 43*, 920–923.

Guxens, M., & Sunyer, J. (2012). A review of epidemiological studies on neuropsychological effects of air pollution. *Swiss Medical Weekly, 141*, 1–7.

Guzmán, R. A., Rodríguez-Sickert, C., & Rowthorn, R. (2007). When in Rome, do as the Romans do: The coevolution of altruistic punishment, conformist learning, and cooperation. *Evolution and Human Behavior, 28*(2), 112–117.

Hackett, C., & McClendon, D. (2017, April 5). Christians remain world's largest religious group, but they are declining in Europe. *Pew Research Center*. Retrieved from http://www.pewresearch.org/fact-tank/2017/04/05/christians-remain-worlds-largest-religious-group-but-they-are-declining-in-europe/

Hackett, R. D. (1989). Work attitudes and employee absenteeism: A synthesis of the literature. *Journal of Occupational Psychology, 62*(3), 235–248.

Hackman, J. R., & Oldham, G. R. (1976). Motivation through the design of work: A test of a theory. *Organizational Behavior and Human Performance, 16*(2), 250–279.

Hagan, F. E. (2010). *Crime types and criminals*. Thousand Oaks, CA: Sage Publications.

Haidt, J. (2001). The emotional dog and its rational tail: A social intuitionist approach to moral judgment. *Psychological Review, 108*, 814–834.

Haidt, J. (2007). The new synthesis in moral psychology. *Science, 316*, 998–1002.

Haidt, J., & Joseph, C. (2008). The moral mind: How five sets of innate intuitions guide the development of many culture-specific virtues, and perhaps even modules. In P. Carruthers, S. Laurence, & S. Stich (Eds.), *The innate mind* (Vol. 3, pp. 367–392). New York: Oxford University Press.

Halderman, P. (2018, July 4). The secret price of pets. *New York Times*. Retrieved from https://www.nytimes.com/2018/07/04/style/how-to-pamper-your-pet.html

Hall, E. T. (1976). *Beyond culture*. New York, NY: Anchor Books.

Hall, J. H., & Fincham, F.D. (2006). Relationship dissolution following infidelity: The roles of attributions and forgiveness. *Journal of Social and Clinical Psychology, 25*, 508–522.

Hall, J. R. (1987). *Gone from the promised land: Jonestown in American cultural history*. New Brunswick: Transaction Books.

Halliday, D. M., Epperson, A. E., & Song, A. V. (2019). Weight loss, obesity, and health. In T. A. Revenson & R. A. R. Gurung (Eds.), *Handbook of health psychology* (pp. 91–104). New York: Routledge.

Hamilton, D. L., & Gifford, R. K. (1976). Illusory correlation in interpersonal perception: A cognitive basis of stereotypic judgments. *Journal of Experimental Social Psychology, 12*, 392–407.

Hamilton, D. L., Dugan, P. M., & Trolier, T. K. (1985). The formation of stereotypic beliefs: Further evidence for distinctiveness-based illusory correlations. *Journal of Personality and Social Psychology, 48*, 5–17.

Hamilton, W. D. (1964). The genetical evolution of social behaviour I and II. *Journal of Theoretical Biology, 7*, 1–16 and 17–52.

Handley, I. M., Lassiter, G. D., Nickell, E. F., & Herchenroeder, L. M. (2004). Affect and automatic mood maintenance. *Journal of Experimental Social Psychology, 40*, 106–112.

Haney, C., Hurtado, A., & Vega, L. (1994). Modern death qualification: New data on its biasing effects. *Law and Human Behavior, 18*, 619–633.

Hang-Pil, S., & Shavitt, S. (1994). Persuasion and culture: Advertising appeals in individualistic and collectivistic societies. *Journal of Experimental Social Psychology, 30*, 326–350.

Hanisch, K. A. (1995). Behavioral families and multiple causes: Matching the complexity of responses to the complexity of antecedents. *Current Directions in Psychological Science, 4*(5), 156–162.

Hanisch, K. A. (1999). Job loss and unemployment research from 1994–1998: A review and recommendations for research and intervention. *Journal of Vocational Behavior, 55*(2), 188–220.

Hanisch, K. A., & Hulin, C. L. (1990). Job attitudes and organizational withdrawal: An examination of retirement and other voluntary withdrawal behaviors. *Journal of Vocational Behavior, 37*(1), 60–78.

Hanisch, K. A., & Hulin, C. L. (1991). General attitudes and organizational withdrawal: An evaluation of a causal model. *Journal of Vocational Behavior, 39*, 110–128.

Hanisch, K. A., Hulin, C. L., & Roznowski, M. A. (1998). The importance of individuals' repertoires of behaviors: The scientific appropriateness of studying multiple behaviors and general attitudes. *Journal of Organizational Behavior, 19*, 463–480.

Hanisch, K.A. (1996). An integrated framework for studying the outcomes of sexual harassment: Consequences for individuals and organizations. In M.S. Stockdale (Ed.), *Women and Work: A Research and Policy Series, Volume 5: Sexual harassment in the workplace: Perspectives, frontiers, and response strategies* (pp. 174–199). Thousand Oaks, CA: Sage.

Hanley, N., Shogren, J., & White, B. (2007). *Environmental economics in theory and practice*. London, UK: Palgrave.

Hansen, G. L. (1987). Extradyadic relations during courtship. *Journal of Sex Research, 23*, 382–390.

Hansen, J., Kutzner, F., & Wänke, M. (2013). Money and thinking: Reminders of money trigger abstract construal and shape consumer judgments. *Journal of Consumer Research, 39*, 1154–1166.

Hansson, L. M., Náslund, E., & Rasmussen, F. (2010). Perceived discrimination among men and women with normal weight and obesity. A population-based study from Sweden. *Scandinavian Journal of Public Health, 38*(6), 587–596.

Hansson, R. O., Noulles, D., & Bellovich, S. J. (1982). Knowledge warning and stress: A study of comparative roles in an urban floodplain. *Environment and Behavior, 14*, 171–185.

Hardin, G. (1968). The tragedy of the commons. *Science, 162*, 1243–1248.

Hardison, C. M., Kim, D., & Sackett, P. R. (2005, April). *Meta-analysis of work sample criterion related validity: Revisiting anomalous findings*. Paper presented at the 20th annual conference of the Society for Industrial-Organizational Psychology, Los Angeles.

Hare, A. P. (1962). *Handbook of small group research*. New York: The Free Press of Glencoe.

Hare, R. D. (1998). *Without conscience: The disturbing world of the psychopaths among us*. New York: Guilford Press.

Hargis, M. (2008). Social networking sites dos and don'ts. *CNN*. Retrieved from http://edition.cnn.com/2008/LIVING/worklife/11/05/cb.social.networking/index.html

Harmon-Jones, E., & Allen, J. J. B. (2001). The role of affect in the mere exposure effect: Evidence from psychophysiological and individual differences approaches. *Personality and Social Psychology Bulletin, 27*(7), 889–898.

Harms, P. D., & Credé, M. (2010). Emotional intelligence and transformational and transactional leadership: A meta-analysis. *Journal of Leadership & Organizational Studies, 17*(1), 5–17.

Harrell, W. A. (1978). Physical attractiveness, self-disclosure, and helping behavior. *Journal of Social Psychology, 104*, 15–17.

Harris, C. R. (2000). Psychophysiological responses to imagined infidelity: The specific innate modular view of jealousy reconsidered. *Journal of Personality and Social Psychology, 75*, 1082–1091.

Harris, M. (1974). *Cows, pigs, wars, and witches: The riddles of culture*. New York: Random House.

Harris, M. (1977). *Cannibals and kings: The origins of culture*. New York: Random House.

Harris, M. B. (1974). Mediators between frustration and aggression in a field experiment. *Journal of Experimental Social Psychology, 10*(6), 561–571.

Harris, M. B. (1976). Instigators and inhibitors of aggression in a field experiment. *Journal of Social Psychology, 98*(1), 27–38.

Harris, M. B., Benson, S. M., & Hall, C. L. (1975). The effects of confession on altruism. *Journal of Social Psychology, 96*, 187–192.

Harris, M. B., Harris, R. J., & Bochner, S. (1982). Fat, four-eyed and female: Stereotypes of obesity glasses and gender. *Journal of Applied Social Psychology, 12*, 503–516.

Harris, P. B., & Brown, B. B. (1996). The home and identity display: Interpreting resident territoriality from home exteriors. *Journal of Environmental Psychology, 16*, 187–203.

Harrison, A. A., & Connors, M. M. (1984). Groups in exotic environments. In L. Berkowitz (Ed.), *Advances in Experimental Social Psychology* (Vol. 18, pp. 49–87). New York: Academic Press.

Harrison, A. A., & Fiscaro, S. A. (1974). Stimulus familiarity and alley illumination as determinants of approach response latencies of house crickets. *Perceptual and Motor Skills, 39*, 147–152.

Harrison, K. (2000). The body electric: Thin-ideal media and eating disorders in adolescents. *Journal of Communication, 50*, 119–143.

Harrison, K. (2001). Ourselves, our bodies: Thin-ideal media, self-discrepancies, and eating disorder symptomatology in adolescents. *Journal of Social and Clinical Psychology, 20*, 289–323.

Harrison, K. (2003). Television viewers' ideal body proportions: The case of the curvaceously thin woman. *Sex Roles, 48*, 255–264.

Harskamp, J., & Dijstelberge, P. (2012, April 12). The human zoo. Retrieved from http://abeautifulbook.wordpress.com/2012/04/21/the-human-zoo/

Harter, S. (1993). Causes and consequences of low self-esteem in children and adolescents. In R. F. Baumeister (Ed.), *Self-esteem: The puzzle of low self-regard* (pp. 87–116). New York: Plenum Press.

Haselton, M. G., & Buss, D. M. (2000). Error management theory: A new perspective on biases in cross-sex mind reading. *Journal of Personality and Social Psychology, 78*, 81–91.

Hassebrauck, M. (1986). Ratings of distress as a function of degree and kind of inequity. *Journal of Social Psychology, 126*, 269–270.

Hassin, R. R., & Sklar, A. Y. (2015). The human unconscious: A functional perspective. In J. W. Sherman, B. Gawronski, & Y. Trope (Eds.), *Dual-process theories of the social mind*. New York: Guilford Press

Hatfield, E., & Rapson, R. L. (1987). Passionate love: New directions in research. In W. H. Jones & D. Perlman (Eds.), *Advances in personal relationships* (Vol. 1, pp. 109–139). Greenwich, CT: JAI Press.

Hatfield, E., Cacioppo, J.T., & Rapson, R.L. (1993). Emotional contagion. *Current Directions in Psychological Science, 2*, 96–100.

Hauck, A., & Finch, A. (1993). The effect of relative age on achievement in middle school. *Psychology in the Schools, 30*, 74–79.

Haw, R. M., & Fisher, R. P. (2004). Effects of administrator-witness contact on eyewitness identification accuracy. *Journal of Applied Psychology, 89*, 1106–1112.

Hawkins, R. X. D., Smith, E. N., Au, C., Arias, J. M., Catapano, R., Hermann, E., et al. (2018). Improving the replicability of psychological science through pedagogy. *Advances in Methods and Practices in Psychological Science, 1*, 7–18.10.1177/2515245917740427

Hawkley, L. C., Burleson, M. H., Berntson, G. G., & Cacioppo, J. T. (2003). Loneliness in everyday life: Cardiovascular activity, psychosocial context, and health behaviors. *Journal of Personality and Social Psychology, 85*, 105–120.

Hawley, C. (2005, June 9). German zoo scandal: "African Village" accused of putting humans on display. *Der Spiegel*. Retrieved from http://www.spiegel.de/international/german-zoo-scandal-african-village-accused-of-putting-humans-on-display-a-359799.html

Hayduk, L. A. (1994). Personal space: Understanding the simplex model. *Journal of Nonverbal Behavior, 18*, 245–246.

Hayes, R., & Downs, D. M. (2011). Controlling retail theft with CCTV domes, CCTV public view monitors, and protective containers: A randomized controlled trial. *Security Journal, 24*(3), 237–250.

Hazan, C., & Shaver, P. R. (1987). Romantic love conceptualized as an attachment process. *Journal of Personality and Social Psychology, 52*, 511–524.

Hearold, S. (1986). A synthesis of 1043 effects of television on social behavior. In G. Comstock (Ed.), *Public communication and behavior* (pp. 65–133). New York: Academic Press.

Heatherton, T. F., & Baumeister, R. F. (1991). Binge eating as escape from self-awareness. *Psychological Bulletin, 110,* 86–108.

Heatherton, T. F., & Nichols, P. A. (1994). Personal accounts of successful versus failed attempts at life change. *Personality and Social Psychology Bulletin, 20,* 664–675.

Heatherton, T. F., & Vohs, K. D. (2000). Interpersonal evaluations following threats to self: Role of self-esteem. *Journal of Personality and Social Psychology, 78,* 725–736.

Heatherton, T. F., personal communication, 1993.

Heatherton, T. F., Polivy, J., & Herman, C. P. (1989). Restraint and internal responsiveness: Effects of placebo manipulations of hunger state on eating. *Journal of Abnormal Psychology, 98,* 89–92.

Heatherton, T. F., Polivy, J., Herman, C. P., & Baumeister, R. F. (1993). Self-awareness, task failure and disinhibition: How attentional focus affects eating. *Journal of Personality, 61,* 49–61.

Hebl, M. R., & Heatherton, T. F. (1997). The stigma of obesity: The differences are black and white. *Personality and Social Psychology Bulletin, 24,* 417–426.

Hebl, M. R., & Mannix, L. M. (2003). The weight of obesity in evaluating others: A mere proximity effect. *Personality and Social Psychology Bulletin, 29,* 28–38.

Hee, K. H. (1993). *The tears of my soul.* New York: Morrow.

Hegi, K. E., & Bergner, R. M. (2010). What is love? An empirically-based essentialist account. *Journal of Social and Personal Relationships, 27,* 620–636.

Heider, F. (1958). *The psychology of interpersonal relations.* New York: John Wiley.

Heilman, M. E., & Chen, J. J. (2005). Same behavior, different consequences: Reactions to men's and women's altruistic citizenship behaviors. *Journal of Applied Psychology, 90,* 431–441.

Heine, S. J., & Lehman, D. R. (1997). Culture, dissonance, and self-affirmation. *Personality and Social Psychology Bulletin, 23,* 389–400.

Heine, S. J., Lehman, D. R., Markus, H. R., & Kitayama, S. (1999). Is there a universal need for positive self-regard? *Psychological Review, 106,* 766–794.

Heinz, S., Baron, G., & Frahm, H. (1988). Comparative size of brains and brain components. In H. D. Steklis & J. Erwin (Eds.), *Comparative Primate Biology: Vol. 4. Neurosciences.* New York: Wiley.

Helton, W. S., Head, J., & Kemp, S. (2011). Natural disaster induced cognitive disruption: Impacts on action slips. *Consciousness and Cognition, 20,* 1732–1737.

Helzer, E. G., & Pizarro, D. A. (2011). Dirty liberals! Reminders of physical cleanliness influence moral and political attitudes. *Psychological Science, 22,* 517–522.

Hemenway, D., Vriniotis, M., & Miller, M. (2006). Is an armed society a polite society? Guns and road rage. *Accident Analysis and Prevention, 38*(4), 687–695.

Henderson, V., & Dweck, C. S. (1990). Achievement and motivation in adolescence: A new model and data. In S. Feldman & G. Elliott (Eds.), *At the threshold: The developing adolescent* (pp. 308–329). Cambridge, MA: Harvard University Press.

Hendin, H. (1982). *Suicide in America.* New York: Norton.

Hendren, A., & Blank, H. (2009). Prejudiced behavior toward lesbians and gay men: A field experiment on everyday helping. *Social Psychology, 40*(4), 234–238.

Hendricks, N. J., Ortiz, C. W., Sugie, N., & Miller, J. (2007). Beyond the numbers: Hate crimes and cultural trauma within Arab American immigrant communities. *International Review of Victimology, 14*(1), 95–113.

Henken, V. J. (1976). Banality reinvestigated: A computer-based content analysis of suicidal and forced-death documents. *Suicide and Life-Threatening Behavior, 6,* 36–43.

Henle, C. A., Reeve, C. L., & Pitts, V. E. (2010). Stealing time at work: Attitudes, social pressure, and perceived control as predictors of time theft. *Journal of Business Ethics, 94*(1), 53–67.

Henrich, J., Heine, S. J., & Norenzayan, A. (2010). The weirdest people in the world? *Behavioral and Brain Sciences, 33,* 61–83. doi:10.1017/S0140525X0999152X

Henry Ford. Retrieved from http://quotes4all.net/henry%20ford:3.html

Henry, B., Caspi, A., Moffitt, T. E., & Silva, P. A. (1996). Temperamental and familial predictors of violent and nonviolent criminal convictions: Age 3 to age 18. *Developmental Psychology, 32,* 614–623.

Henry, P. J., & Sears, D. O. (2002). The symbolic racism 2000 scale. *Political Psychology, 23,* 253–283. https://doi.org/10.1111/0162-895X.00281

Hepach, R., Vaish, A., & Tomasello, M. (2012). Young children are intrinsically motivated to see others helped. *Psychological Science, 23,* 967–972.

Hepworth, J. T., & West, S. G. (1988). Lynchings and the economy: A time-series reanalysis of Hovland and Sears (1940). *Journal of Personality and Social Psychology, 55,* 239–247.

Herdt, G. (1984). Ritualized homosexual behavior in the male cults of Melanesia, 1862–1983: An introduction. In G. Herdt (Ed.), *Ritualized homosexuality in Melanesia* (pp. 1–82). Berkeley: University of California Press.

Herek, G. M. (2000). The psychology of sexual prejudice. *Current Directions in Psychological Science, 9,* 19–22.

Herek, G. M., & Capitanio, J. P. (1996). "Some of my best friends": Intergroup contact, concealable stigma, and heterosexuals' attitudes toward gay men and lesbians. *Personality and Social Psychology Bulletin, 22*(4), 412–424.

Herek, G. M., & Capitanio, J. P. (1999). AIDS stigma and sexual prejudice. *American Behavioral Scientist, 42,* 1126–1143.

Herlitz, J., Wiklund, I., Caidahl, K., Hartford, M., Haglid, M., Karlsson, B. W., et al. (1998). The feeling of loneliness prior to coronary artery bypass grafting might be a predictor of short- and long-term postoperative mortality. *European Journal of Vascular and Endovascular Surgery, 16,* 120–125.

Herman, C. P., & Mack, D. (1975). Restrained and unrestrained eating. *Journal of Personality, 43,* 647–660.

Herold, E. S., & Mewhinney, D.-M. K. (1993). Gender differences in casual sex and AIDS prevention: A survey of dating bars. *Journal of Sex Research, 30,* 36–42.

Hesse, B. W. (2018). Can psychology walk the walk of open science? *American Psychologist, 73*(2), 126–137. doi:10.1037/amp0000197

Hewitt, J., & Alqahtani, M. A. (2003). Differences between Saudi and U.S. students in reaction to same- and mixed-sex intimacy by others. *Journal of Social Psychology, 143,* 233–242.

Hewstone, M. (1990). The "Ultimate Attribution Error"? A review of the literature on intergroup causal attribution. *European Journal of Social Psychology, 20,* 311–335.

Hewstone, M., & Swart, H. (2011). Fifty-odd years of inter-group contact: From hypothesis to integrated theory. *British Journal of Social Psychology, 50*(3), 374–386.

Hicken, M. (2013, August 14). Average cost to raise a kid: $241,080. *CNN Money.* Retrieved from http://money.cnn.com/2013/08/14/pf/cost-children/

Higgins, E. T., & Bargh, J. A. (1987). Social cognition and social perception. *Annual Review of Psychology, 38,* 369–425.

Higgins, E. T., Rholes, W. S., & Jones, C. R. (1977). Category accessibility and impression formation. *Journal of Experimental Social Psychology, 13,* 141–154.

Higley, J. D., Mehlman, P. T., Taub, D. M., Higley, S. B., Suomi, S. J., Vickers, J. H., & Linnoila, M. (1992). Cerebrospinal fluid mono-amine and adrenal correlates of aggression in free-ranging Rhesus monkeys. *Archives of General Psychiatry, 49,* 436–441.

Hill, C. A., Blakemore, J. E. O., & Drumm, P. (1997). Mutual and unrequited love in adolescence and adulthood. *Personal Relationships, 4*(1), 15–23.

Hill, C. T., Rubin, Z., & Peplau, L. A. (1976). Breakups before marriage: The end of 103 affairs. *Journal of Social Issues, 32,* 147–168.

Hill, G. W. (1982). Group versus individual performance: Are N + 1 heads better than one? *Psychological Bulletin, 91*(3), 517–539.

Hilmert, C. J., Kulik, J. A., & Christenfeld, N. J. (2006). Positive and negative opinion modeling: The influence of another's similarity and dissimilarity. *Journal of Personality and Social Psychology, 90,* 440–452.

Hilton. (2016). Hilton launches new industry-leading parental leave policies. January. Retrieved from https://newsroom.hilton.com/corporate/news/hilton-launches-new-industryleading-parental-leave-policies

Hilton. (2019). Hilton named the #1 company to work for in the U.S. Retrieved from https://newsroom.hilton.com/corporate/news/employees-rank-hilton-the-best-place-to-work-in-the-us

Himbara, D. (2017). *Kagame's killing fields.* North Charleston, South Carolina. CreateSpace Independent Publishing Platform.

Hinde, R. A. (1970). *Animal behavior.* New York: McGraw-Hill.

Hirt, E. R., & Markman, K. D. (1995). Multiple explanation: A consider-an-alternative strategy for debiasing judgments. *Journal of Personality and Social Psychology, 69,* 1069–1086.

Hirt, E. R., & Sherman, S. J. (1985). The role of prior knowledge in explaining hypothetical events. *Journal of Experimental Social Psychology, 21,* 519–543.

Hirt, E. R., Deppe, R. K., & Gordon, L. J. (1991). Self-reported versus behavioral self-handicapping: Empirical evidence for a theoretical distinction. *Journal of Personality and Social Psychology, 61,* 981–991.

Hirt, E. R., Kardes, F. R., & Markman, K. D. (2004). Activating a mental simulation mind-set through generation of alternatives: Implications for debiasing in related and unrelated domains. *Journal of Experimental Social Psychology, 40,* 374–383.

Hitsch, G. J., Hortaçsu, A., & Ariely, D. (2006). What makes you click? Mate preferences and matching outcomes in online dating. MIT Sloan Research Paper No. 4603–06. Available at http://home.uchicago.edu/,hortacsu/onlinedating.pdf

Hochbaum, G. M. (1958). *Public participation in medical screening programs: A sociopsychological study.* PHS publication no. 572. Washington, DC: Government Printing Office. Holder-Perkins & Wise.

Hockley, W. E., Hemsworth, D. H., & Consoli, A. (1999). Shades of the mirror effect: Recognition of faces with and without sunglasses. *Memory and Cognition, 27,* 128–138.

Hoerger, M., Chapman, B. P., Epstein, R. M., & Duberstein, P. R. (2012). Emotional intelligence: A theoretical framework for individual differences in affective forecasting. *Emotion, 12*(4), 716–725. doi:10.1037/a0026724

Hoerner, J. A., & Barrett, J. (2004, September). *Smarter, cleaner, stronger: Secure jobs, a clean environment, and less foreign oil.* Retrieved from http://www.rprogress.org/publications/2004/SmartCleanStrong_National.pdf

Hoffman, M. L. (1977). Sex differences in empathy and related behaviors. *Psychological Bulletin, 84,* 712–722.

Hofmann, W., Wisneski, D.C., Brandt, M.J., & Skitka, L.J. (2014). Morality in everyday life. *Science, 345,* 1340–1343.

Hofstadter, D. R. (1979), *Gödel, Escher, Bach: An eternal golden braid.* New York: Basic Books.

Hogan, R., & Kaiser, R. B. (2005). What we know about leadership. *Review of General Psychology, 9*(2), 169–180.

Hogg, M. A. (2005). All animals are equal but some animals are more equal than others: Social identity and marginal membership. In K. D. Williams, J. P. Forgas, & W. von Hippel (Eds.), *The social outcast: Ostracism, social exclusion, rejection, and bullying* (pp. 243–262). New York: Psychology Press.

Holder-Perkins, V., & Wise, T. N. (2001). Somatization disorder. In K. A. Phillips (Ed.), *Somatoform and factitious disorders* (pp. 1–26). Washington, DC: American Psychiatric Association.

Holgate, S. T., Samet, J. M., Maynard, R. L., & Koren, H. S. (Eds.) (1999). *Air pollution and health.* San Diego: Academic Press.

Hollingshead, A. B. (1998). Retrieval processes in transactive memory systems. *Journal of Personality and Social Psychology, 74,* 659–671.

Hollingshead, A. B., & Brandon, D. P. (2003). Potential benefits of communication in transactive memory systems. *Human Communication Research, 29,* 607–615.

Holloway, S. D., Kashiwagi, K., Hess, R. D., & Azuuma, H. (1986). Causal attributions by Japanese and American mothers and children about performance in mathematics. *International Journal of Psychology, 21,* 269–286.

Holmes, J. G. (2004, October). The power of positive thinking in close relationships. Paper presented at the Third International Positive Psychology Summit, Washington, DC.

Holmes, L. (2014, September 17). 5 ways stress wrecks your sleep (and what to do about it). *Huffington Post.* Retrieved from http://www.huffingtonpost.com/2014/09/17/stress-and-sleep_n_5824506.html

Holt-Lunstad, J., Smith, T. B., & Layton, J. B. (2010). Social relationships and mortality risk: A meta-analytic review. *PLoS Medicine, 7,* e1000316.

Holtzworth-Munroe, A., & Jacobson, N. S. (1985). Causal attributions of married couples: When do they search for causes? What do they conclude when they do? *Journal of Personality and Social Psychology, 48,* 1398–1412.

Homans, G. C. (1950). *The human group.* New York: Harcourt, Brace, & World.

Homans, G. C. (1961). *Social behavior: Its elementary forms.* New York: Harcourt, Brace, & World.

Honour, J. W. (2004, July 8). The fight for fair play: Can athletes be held responsible for every substance they take? *Nature, 430,* 143–144.

Hooper, N., Erdogan, A., Keen, G., Lawton, K., & McHugh, L. (2015). Perspective taking reduces the fundamental attribution error. *Journal of Contextual Behavioral Science, 4*(2), 69–72. doi:10.1016/j.jcbs.2015.02.002

Hope, L., & Wright, D. (2007). Beyond unusual? Examining the role of attention in the weapon focus effect. *Applied Cognitive Psychology, 21,* 951–961.

Horberg, E. J., Oveis, C., Keltner, D., & Cohen, A. B. (2009). Disgust and the moralization of purity. *Journal of Personality and Social Psychology, 97*(6), 963–976.

Horner, M. (1972). Toward an understanding of achievement related conflicts in women. *Journal of Social Issues, 28,* 157–176.

Hornsey, M. J., Harris, E. A., Bain, P. G. & Fielding, K. S. (2016). Meta-analyses of the determinants and outcomes of belief in climate change. *Nature Climate Change, 6,* 622–626.

Hornstein, H. A. (1982). Promotive tension: Theory and research. In V. Derlega & J. Grzelak (Eds.), *Cooperation and helping behavior: Theories and research* (pp. 229–248). New York: Academic Press.

Horowitz, A. V., White, H. R., & Howell-White, S. (1997). Becoming married and mental health: A longitudinal study of a cohort of young adults. *Journal of Marriage and the Family, 58,* 895–907.

Horowitz, H. L. (1987). *Campus life: Undergraduate cultures from the end of the eighteenth century to the present.* Chicago, IL: University of Chicago Press.

Hoshino-Browne, E., Zanna, A. S., Spencer, S. J., Zanna, M. P., Kitayama, S., & Lackenbauer, S. (2005). On the cultural guises of cognitive dissonance: The case of Easterners and Westerners. *Journal of Personality and Social Psychology, 89,* 294–310.

Hospitalitynet. (2019, February 15). Employees rank Hilton the best place to work in the U.S. February 15. Retrieved from https://www.hospitalitynet.org/news/4091997.html.

House, J. S., Umberson, D., & Landis, K. R. (1988). Structures and processes of social support. *Annual Review of Sociology, 14,* 293–318.

Houston, D. A., Doan, K. A., & Roskos-Ewoldsen, D. (1999). Negative political advertising and choice conflict. *Journal of Experimental Psychology: Applied, 5,* 3–16.

Hovland, C. I., & Sears, R. (1940). Minor studies of aggression: Correlation of lynchings with economic conditions. *Journal of Psychology, 9,* 301–310.

Hovland, C. I., & Weiss, W. (1951). The influence of source credibility on communication effectiveness. *Public Opinion Quarterly, 15,* 635–650.

Hovland, C. I., Janis, I. L., & Kelley, H. H. (1953). *Communication and persuasion.* New Haven: Yale University Press.

Hovland, C. I., Lumsdaine, A., & Sheffield, F. (1949). *Experiments on mass communication: Studies in social psychology in World War II* (Vol. 3). Princeton, NJ: Princeton University Press.

Howell, S. (1989). "To be angry is not to be human, but to be fearful is": Chewong concepts of human nature. In S. Howell & R. Willis (Eds.), *Societies at peace: Anthropological perspectives* (pp. 45–59). London: Routledge.

Hoyle, R. H., Pinkley, R. L., & Insko, C. A. (1989). Perceptions of social behavior: Evidence of differing expectations for interpersonal and intergroup interaction. *Personality and Social Psychology Bulletin, 15,* 365–376.

Hsee, C. K. (1996). The evaluability hypothesis: An explanation for preference reversals between joint and separate evaluations of alternatives. *Organizational Behavior and Human Decision Processes, 67*(3), 247–257.

Hsee, C. K., & Zhang, J. (2004). Distinction bias: Misprediction and mischoice due to joint evaluation. *Journal of Personality and Social Psychology, 86*(5), 680–695.

Hsiang, S. M., Burke, M., & Miguel, E. (2013). Quantifying the influence of climate on human conflict. *Science, 341*(6151): 1212–1226. doi: 10.1126/science.1235367

http://thinkexist.com/quotes/frederick_the_great/

http://www.apa.org/news/press/releases/2011/09/cooperate-equally.aspx

http://www.emotionalcompetency.com/humiliation.htm

http://www.endcorporalpunishment.org

http://www.globalsecurity.org/military/world/war/congo.htm

http://www.humansecuritybrief.info/

Hu, Y., & Goldman, M. (1990). Mortality differentials by marital status: An international comparison. *Demography, 27,* 233–253.

Huesmann, L. R., & Taylor, L. D. (2003). The case against the case against media violence. In D. Gentile (Ed.), *Media violence and children* (pp. 107–130). Westport, CT: Greenwood Press.

Huesmann, L. R., Moise, J., Podolski, C. P., & Eron, L. D. (2003). Longitudinal relations between childhood exposure to media violence and adult aggression and violence: 1977–1992. *Developmental Psychology, 39,* 201–221.

Huffcutt, A. I., & Arthur, W., Jr. (1994). Hunter and Hunter (1984) revisited: Interview validity for entry-level jobs. *Journal of Applied Psychology, 79,* 184–190.

Hull, J. G. (1981). A self-awareness model of the causes and effects of alcohol consumption. *Journal of Abnormal Psychology, 90,* 586–600.

Hull, J. G., Levenson, R. W., Young, R. D., & Scher, K. J. (1983). Self-awareness-reducing effects of alcohol consumption. *Journal of Personality and Social Psychology, 44,* 461–473.

Hunter, J. E., & Hunter, R. E. (1984). Validity and utility of alternative predictors of job performance. *Psychological Bulletin, 96*(1), 72–98.

Hupka, R. B. (1981). Cultural determinants of jealousy. *Alternative Lifestyles, 4,* 310–356.

Huston, T. L., Surra, C., Fitzgerald, N. M., & Cate, R. (1981). From courtship to marriage: Mate selection as an interpersonal process. In S. Duck & R. Gilmour (Eds.), *Personal relationships. 2: Developing personal relationships.* New York: Academic Press.

Hutcherson, C. A., & Gross, J. J. (2011). The moral emotions: A social-functionalist account of anger, disgust, and contempt. *Journal of Personality and Social Psychology, 100*(4), 719–737.

Hutchison, P., & Rosenthal, H. E. S. (2011). Prejudice against Muslims: Anxiety as a mediator between intergroup contact and attitudes, perceived group variability and behavioural intentions. *Ethnic and Racial Studies, 34*(1), 40–61.

Hviid A, Hansen JV, Frisch M, & Melbye M. (2019). Measles, mumps, rubella vaccination and autism: A nationwide cohort study. *Annals of Internal Medicine* [Epub ahead of print] doi: 10.7326/M18-2101

Hyde, J. S. (2005). The gender similarities hypothesis. *American Psychologist, 60,* 581–592.

Hyland, M. E. (1989). There is no motive to avoid success: The compromise explanation for success-avoiding behavior. *Journal of Personality, 57,* 665–693.

Iannelli, V. (2014, September 7). International measles outbreaks. About Health. Retrieved from http://pediatrics.about.com/od/measles/a/measles-outbreak.htm

Illuminant. (2011, January 17). Avoiding insult and injury when using color in China. Retrieved from http://www.illuminantpartners.com/2011/01/17/color/

Insko, C. A., Schopler, J., Hoyle, R. H., & Dardis, G. J. (1990). Individual-group discontinuity as a function of fear and greed. *Journal of Personality and Social Psychology, 58,* 68–79.

Insko, C. A., Schopler, J., Pemberton, M. B., Wieselquist, J., McIlraith, S. A., Currey, D. P., et al. (1998). Long-term outcome maximization and the reduction of interindividual-intergroup discontinuity. *Journal of Personality and Social Psychology, 75,* 695–711.

Insko, C. A., Smith, R. H., Alicke, M. D., Wade, J., & Taylor, S. (1985). Conformity and group size: The concern with being right and the concern with being liked. *Personality and Social Psychology Bulletin, 11,* 41–50.

Introduction to the Holocaust. *U.S. Holocaust Memorial Museum.* Retrieved from https://encyclopedia.ushmm.org/content/en/article/introduction-to-the-holocaust

Isen, A. M. (2000). Positive affect and decision making. In M. Lewis & J. M. Haviland-Jones (Eds.), *Handbook of emotions* (2nd ed., pp. 417–435). New York: Guilford Press.

Isen, A. M., & Levin, P. F. (1972). Effect of feeling good on helping: Cookies and kindness. *Journal of Personality and Social Psychology, 21,* 384–388.

Isen, A. M., & Patrick, R. (1983). The effect of positive feelings and risk taking: When the chips are down. *Organizational Behavior and Human Performance, 31,* 194–202.

Ito, T. A., Miller, N., & Pollock, V. E. (1996). Alcohol and aggression: A meta-analysis on the moderating effects of inhibitory cues, triggering events, and self-focused attention. *Psychological Bulletin, 120,* 60–82.

Iyengar, S. S., & Lepper, M. R. (2000). When choice is demotivating: Can one desire too much of a good thing? *Journal of Personality and Social Psychology, 79,* 995–1006.

Izard, C. E. (1971). *The face of emotion.* New York: Appleton-Century-Crofts.

Izard, C. E. (1990). The substrates and functions of emotion feelings: William James and current emotion theory. *Personality and Social Psychology Bulletin, 16,* 626–635.

J.E.B. v. Alabama *ex rel.* T.B., 114 S.Ct. 1419 (1994).

Jablin, F. M. (1982). Organizational communication: An assimilation approach. In M. E. Rolff & C. R. Berger (Eds.), *Social cognition and communication* (pp. 255–286). Beverly Hills, CA: Sage.

Jackson, K. M., Janssen, T., Barnett, N. P., Rogers, M. L., Hayes, K. L., & Sargent, J. (2018). Exposure to alcohol content in movies and initiation of early drinking milestones. *Alcoholism: Clinical and Experimental Research, 42*(1), 184–194. doi:http://dx.doi.org/10.1111/acer.13536

Jackson, L. A., Hunter, J. E., & Hodge, C. N. (1995). Physical attractiveness and intellectual competence:

A meta-analytic review. *Social Psychology Quarterly, 58,* 108–122.

Jacobe, D. (2008, June 11). Nearly one-third of credit-card owners hold high balances. Retrieved from http://www.gallup.com/poll/107833/nearly-onethird-americans-hold-high-credit-balances.aspx

Jacobs, R. C., & Campbell, D. T. (1961). The perpetuation of an arbitrary tradition through several generations of a laboratory microculture. *Journal of Abnormal and Social Psychology, 62,* 649–658.

Jacobs, S. V., Evans, G. W., Catalano, R., & Dooley, D. (1984). Air pollution and depressive symptomatology: Exploratory analyses of intervening psychosocial factors. *Population & Environment, 7,* 260–272.

James, W. (1884). What is an emotion? *Mind, 9,* 188–205.

James, W. (1890). *Principles of psychology.* New York: Holt.

James, W. (1948). *Psychology.* Cleveland, OH: World Publishing. (Original work published 1892).

James, W. H. (1981). The honeymoon effect on marital coitus. *Journal of Sex Research, 17,* 114–123.

Jang, S. M., & Kim, J. K. (2018). Third person effects of fake news: Fake news regulation and media literacy interventions. *Computers in Human Behavior,* 80295-302. doi:10.1016/j.chb.2017.11.034

Janis, I. (1982). *Groupthink* (2nd ed.). Boston: Houghton Mifflin.

Janis, I. L. (1954). Personality correlates of susceptibility to persuasion. *Journal of Personality, 22,* 504–518.

Janis, I. L. (1967). Effects of fear arousal on attitude change: Recent developments in theory and experimental research. *Advances in Experimental Social Psychology, 4,* 166–224.

Janis, I. L., & Feshbach, S. (1953). Effects of fear-arousing communications. *Journal of Abnormal and Social Psychology, 48,* 78–92.

Janis, I. L., & Field, P. (1959). Sex differences and personality factors related to persuasibility. In C. Hovland & I. Janis (Eds.), *Personality and persuasibility* (pp. 55–68, 300–302). New Haven, CT: Yale University Press.

Janis, I. L., Kaye, D., & Kirschner, P. (1965). Facilitating effects of "eating-while-reading" on responsiveness to persuasive communications. *Journal of Personality and Social Psychology, 1*(2), 181–186.

Janiszewski, C., Noel, H., & Sawyer, A. G. (2003). A meta-analysis of the spacing effect in verbal learning: Implications for research on advertising repetition and consumer memory. *Journal of Consumer Research, 30,* 138–149.

Jankowiak, W. (Ed.). (1995). *Romantic passion: A universal experience?* New York: Columbia University Press.

Janoff-Bulman, R. (1992). *Shattered assumptions: Towards a new psychology of trauma.* New York: Free Press.

Janoff-Bulman, R., & Brickman, P. (1982). Expectations and what people learn from failure. In N. T. Feather (Ed.), *Expectations and actions: Expectancy-value models in psychology* (pp. 207–237). Hillsdale, NJ: Erlbaum.

Jansen, Bart (2018, April 19). Miracle on the Hudson pilot Sully Sullenberger: Southwest crew worked seamlessly to land jet. USA Today. Retrieved from https://www.usatoday.com/story/news/2018/04/19/sully-sullenberger-southwest-airlines-emergency-landing/533821002/

Janus, S. S., & Janus, C. L. (1993). *The Janus report on sexual behavior.* New York: Wiley.

Japanese man sends rubbish to revenge school 'bullies'. (2016, December 2). *BBC.* Retrieved August 25, 2019 from https://www.bbc.com/news/world-asia-38188618

Jencks, C., & Phillips, M. (Eds.). (1998). *The Black–White test score gap.* Washington, DC: Brookings Institution.

Jensen, A. (1977). Genetic and behavioral effects of nonrandom mating. In C. Noble, R. Osborne, & N. Weyl (Eds.), *Human variation: Biogenetics of age, race, and sex.* New York: Academic Press.

Johns, M., Inzlicht, M., & Schmader, T. (2008). Stereotype threat and executive resource depletion: Examining the influence of emotion regulation. *Journal of Experimental Psychology: General, 137*(4), 691–705.

Johnson, D. J., & Rusbult, C. E. (1989). Resisting temptation: Devaluation of alternative partners as a means of maintaining commitment in close relationships. *Journal of Personality and Social Psychology, 57,* 967–980.

Johnson, D. W., & Johnson, R. T. (1983). The socialization and achievement crises: Are cooperative learning experiences the solution? *Applied Social Psychology Annual, 4,* 119–164.

Johnson, W. G., Schlundt, D. G., Barclay, D. R., Carr-Nangle, R. E., & Engler, L. B. (1995). A naturalistic functional analysis of binge eating. *Behavior Therapy, 26,* 101–118.

Johnson, W., McGue, M., Krueger, R. F., & Bouchard, T. J. (2004). Marriage and personality: A genetic analysis. *Journal of Personality and Social Psychology, 86,* 285–294.

Joiner, T., Pettit, J. W., Walker, R. L., Voelz, Z. R., Cruz, J., Rudd, M. D., & Lester, D. (2002). Perceived burdensomeness and suicidality: Two studies on the suicide notes of those attempting and those completing suicide. *Journal of Social & Clinical Psychology, 21,* 531–545.

Joiner, T. (2005). *Why people die by suicide.* Cambridge, MA: Harvard University Press.

Jonas, K., Eagly, A. H., & Stroebe, W. (1995). *Attitudes and persuasion.* In M. Argyle & A. M. Colman (Eds.), *Social psychology.* Harlow, UK: Longman.

Jones, A. M., & Penrod, S. (2018). Improving the effectiveness of the *Henderson* instruction safeguard against unreliable eyewitness identification. *Psychology, Crime & Law, 24,* 177–193.

Jones, A. M., Bergold, A. N., Dillon, M. K., & Penrod, S. D. (2017). Comparing the effectiveness of *Henderson* instructions and expert testimony: Which safeguard improves jurors' evaluations of eyewitness evidence? *Journal of Experimental Criminology, 13,* 29–52.

Jones, E. E. (1964). *Ingratiation.* New York: Irvington.

Jones, E. E., & Berglas, S. (1978). Control of attributions about the self through self-handicapping strategies: The appeal of alcohol and the role of underachievement. *Personality and Social Psychology Bulletin, 4,* 200–206.

Jones, E. E., & Gerard, H. B. (1967). *Foundations of social psychology.* New York: Wiley.

Jones, E. E., & Harris, V. A. (1967). The attribution of attitudes. *Journal of Experimental Social Psychology, 3,* 1–24.

Jones, E. E., & Nisbett, R. E. (1971). *The actor and the observer: Divergent perceptions of the causes of behavior.* New York: General Learning Press.

Jones, E. E., & Wortman, E. (1973). *Ingratiation: An attributional approach.* Morristown, NJ: General Learning Press.

Jones, E. E., Kannouse, D. E., Kelley, H. H., Nisbett, R. E., Valins, S., & Weiner, B. (Eds.). (1972). *Attribution: Perceiving the causes of behavior.* Morristown, NJ: General Learning Press.

Jones, E. E., Rhodewalt, F., Berglas, S., & Skelton, J. A. (1981). Effects of strategic self-presentation on subsequent self-esteem. *Journal of Personality and Social Psychology, 41,* 407–421.

Jones, W. (1989, August). Address given at the annual convention of the American Psychological Association, New Orleans.

Jorgenson, D. O., & Papciak, A. S. (1981). The effects of communication, resource feedback, and identifiability on behavior in a simulated commons. *Journal of Experimental Social Psychology, 17,* 373–385.

Jost, J. T., & Kay, A. C. (2005). Exposure to benevolent sexism and complementary gender stereotypes: Consequences for specific and diffuse forms of system justification. *Journal of Personality and Social Psychology, 88,* 498–509.

Joyce, W. F., Nohria, N., & Roberson, B. (2003). *What really works: The 4+2 formula for sustained business success.* New York: HarperBusiness.

Judd, C., & Park, B. (1993). The assessment of accuracy of social stereotypes. *Psychological Review, 100,* 109–128.

Julepea. (2010, January 4). Big Tobacco executive "Nicotine Is Not Addictive." https://www.youtube.com/watch?v=A6B1q22R438

Jung, K., Shavitt, S., Viswanathan, M., & Hilbe, J. M. (2014). Female hurricanes are deadlier than male hurricanes. *PNAS, 111,* 8782–8787.

Jussim, L., & Harber, K. D. (2005). Teacher expectations and self-fulfilling prophecies: Knowns and unknowns, resolved and unresolved controversies. *Personality and Social Psychology Review, 9*(2), 131–155.

Jussim, L., Cain, T. R., Crawford, J. T., Harber, K., & Cohen, F. (2009). The unbearable accuracy of stereotypes. In T. Nelson (Ed.), *Handbook of prejudice, stereotyping, and discrimination* (pp. 199–228). Mahwah, NJ: Erlbaum.

Jussim, L., HsiuJu, Y., & Aiello, J. R. (1995). Self-consistency, self-enhancement, and accuracy in reactions to feedback. *Journal of Experimental Social Psychology, 31,* 322–356.

Juvonen, J., & Gross, E. F. (2005). The rejected and the bullied: Lessons about social misfits from developmental psychology. In K. D. Williams, J. P. Forgas, & W. von Hippel (Eds.), *The social outcast: Ostracism, social exclusion, rejection, and bullying* (pp. 155–170). New York: Psychology Press.

Kachadourian, L. K., Fincham, F. D., & Davila, J. (2004). The tendency to forgive in dating and married couples: Association with attachment and relationship satisfaction. *Personal Relationships, 11,* 373–393.

Kachadourian, L. K., Fincham, F. D., & Davila, J. (2005). Attitudinal ambivalence, rumination and forgiveness of partner transgressions in marriage. *Personality and Social Psychology Bulletin, 31,* 334–342.

Kagan, J. (1981). *The second year: The emergence of self-awareness.* Cambridge, MA: Harvard University Press.

Kahneman, D. (1999). Objective happiness. In D. Kahneman, E. Diener, & N. Schwartz (Eds.), *Well-being: The foundations of hedonic psychology* (pp. 3–25). New York: Russell Sage Foundation.

Kahneman, D. (2011). *Thinking, fast and slow.* New York: Farrar, Straus, and Giroux.

Kahneman, D., & Frederick, S. (2002). Representativeness revisited: Attribute substitution in intuitive judgment. In T. Gilovich, D. Griffin, & D. Kahneman (Eds.), *Heuristics and biases* (pp. 49–81). New York: Cambridge University Press.

Kahneman, D., & Tversky, A. (1979). Prospect theory: An analysis of decision under risk. *Econometrica, 47,* 263–291.

Kahneman, D., & Tversky, A. (1982). The psychology of preferences. *Scientific American, 246,* 160–173.

Kahneman, D., & Tversky, A. (1984). Choices, values, and frames. *American Psychologist, 39,* 341–350.

Kahneman, D., Knetsch, J. L., & Thaler, R. H. (1990). Experimental tests of the endowment effect and the Coase theorem. *Journal of Political Economy, 98*(6), 1325–1348.

Kahneman, D., Slovic, P., & Tversky, A. (Eds.). (1982). *Judgment under uncertainty: Heuristics and biases.* New York: Cambridge University Press.

Kahneman, D., Wakker, P. P., & Sarin, R. (1997). Back to Bentham? Explorations of experienced utility. *Quarterly Journal of Economics, 62,* 375–406.

Kallgren, C. A., Reno, R. R., & Cialdini, R. B. (2000). Littering can be reduced by anti-littering norms: A focus theory of normative conduct: When norms do and do not affect behavior. *Personality and Social Psychology Bulletin, 26,* 1002–1012.

Kanazawa, S. (2002). Bowling with our imaginary friends. *Evolution and Human Behavior, 23,* 167–171.

Kanin, E. J., Davidson, K. D., & Scheck, S. R. (1970). A research note on male-female differentials in the experience of heterosexual love. *Journal of Sex Research, 6,* 64–72.

Kant, I. (1924). *Critique of judgment.* Hamburg: Felix Meiner Verlag. (Original work published 1790).

Kant, I. (1967). *Kritik der praktischen Vernunft* [Critique of practical reason]. Hamburg: Felix Meiner Verlag. (Original work published 1797).

Kaplan, R. E., Drath, W. H., & Kofodimos, J. R. (1991). *Beyond ambition: How driven managers can lead better and live better*. San Francisco: Jossey-Bass.

Karau, S. J., & Williams, K. D. (1993). Social loafing: A meta-analytic review and theoretical integration. *Journal of Personality and Social Psychology, 65*, 681–706.

Kardes, F. R. (1988). Spontaneous inference processes in advertising: The effects of conclusion omission and involvement on persuasion. *Journal of Consumer Research, 15*, 225–233.

Karney, B. R., & Bradbury, T. N. (1997). Neuroticism, marital interaction, and the trajectory of marital satisfaction. *Journal of Personality and Social Psychology, 72*, 1075–1092.

Kasser, T., & Ryan, R. M. (1993). A dark side of the American Dream: Correlates of financial success as a central life aspiration. *Journal of Personality and Social Psychology, 65*, 410–422.

Kasser, T., & Ryan, R. M. (2001). Be careful what you wish for: Optimal functioning and the relative attainment of intrinsic and extrinsic goals. In P. Schmuck & K. Sheldon (Eds.), *Life goals and well-being* (pp. 116–131). Göttingen: Hogrefe.

Kasser, T., & Sheldon, K. M. (2000). Of wealth and death: Materialism, mortality salience, and consumption behavior. *Psychological Science, 11*, 348–351.

Kates, R. W. (1994). Sustaining life on the earth. *Scientific American, 271*(4), 114–122.

Kates, R. W., Clark, W. C., Corell, R., Hall, J. M., Jaeger, C. C., Lowe, I., McCarthy, J. J., Schellnhuber, H. J., Bolin, B., Dickson, N. M., Faucheux, S., Gallopin, G. C., Grubler, A., Huntley, B., Jager, J., Jodha, N. S., Kasperson, R. E., Mabogunje, A., Matson, P., Mooney, H., Moore, B., III, O'Riordan, T., & Svedin, U. (2001). Sustainability science. *Science, 292*, 641–642.

Katz, D., & Kahn, R. L. (1978). *The social psychology of organizations* (2nd ed.). New York: Wiley.

Katz, J. (1988). *Seductions of crime: Moral and sensual attractions in doing evil*. New York: Basic Books.

Katzev, R., Edelsack, L., Reynolds, R., Steinmetz, G., Walker, T., & Wright, R. (1978). The effect of reprimanding transgressions on subsequent helping behavior: Two field experiments. *Personality and Social Psychology Bulletin, 4*, 326–329.

Kaya, N., & Erkip, F. E. (1999). Invasion of personal space under the condition of short-term crowding: A case study on an automatic teller machine. *Journal of Environmental Psychology, 19*, 183–189.

Kaya, N., & Weber, M. J. (2003). Cross-cultural differences in the perception of crowding and privacy regulation: American and Turkish students. *Journal of Environmental Psychology, 23*, 301–309.

Kearns, J. N., & Fincham, F. D. (2005). Victim and perpetrator accounts of interpersonal transgressions: Self-serving or relationship-serving biases? *Personality and Social Psychology Bulletin, 31*, 321–333.

Keast, A., Brewer, N., & Wells, G. L. (2007). Children's metacognitive judgments in an eyewitness identification task. *Journal of Experimental Child Psychology, 9*, 286–314.

Keefe, K., & Berndt, T. J. (1996). Relations of friendship quality to self-esteem in early adolescence. *Journal of Early Adolescence, 16*, 110–129.

Keegan, J. (1993). *A history of warfare*. New York: Knopf.

Keinan, G. (1987). Decision making under stress: Scanning of alternatives under controllable and uncontrollable threats. *Journal of Personality and Social Psychology, 52*, 639–644.

Keinan, G., Friedland, N., & Ben-Porath, Y. (1987). Decision making under stress: Scanning of alternatives under physical threat. *Acta Psychologica, 64*, 219–228.

Keir, G. (1966). The psychological assessment of the children from the island of Tristan da Cunha. In C. Banks & P. L. Broadhurst (Eds.), *Stephanos: Studies in psychology presented to Cyril Burt* (pp. 129–172). New York: Barnes & Noble.

Keller, M. (2006, August 6). The scandal at the zoo. *New York Times*. Retrieved from http://www.nytimes.com/2006/08/06/nyregion/thecity/06zoo.html?ex51155009600&en5c2cc9b84edc068cd&ei55087%0A

Kelley, H. H., & Stahelski, A. J. (1970). Social interaction basis of cooperators' and competitors' beliefs about others. *Journal of Personality and Social Psychology, 16*, 66–91.

Kelln, B. R. C., & Ellard, J. H. (1999). An equity theory analysis of the impact of forgiveness and retribution on transgressor compliance. *Personality and Social Psychology Bulletin, 25*, 864–872; see also Wallace, H. M., Exline, J. J., & Baumeister, R. F. (2008). Interpersonal consequences of forgiveness: Does forgiveness deter or encourage repeat offenses? *Journal of Experimental Social Psychology, 44*, 453–460.

Kelly, M. H. (1999). Regional naming patterns and the culture of honor. *Names, 47*, 3–20.

Keltner, D., Gruenfeld, D. H., & Anderson, C. (2003). Power, approach, and inhibition. *Psychological Review, 110*, 265–284.

Kennedy, M. (2018, November 19). Italian Village Installs Speed Cameras, Records 58,000 Infractions In 2 Weeks. NPR. Retrieved from https://www.npr.org/2018/11/19/669234810/italian-village-installs-speed-cameras-records-58-000-infractions-in-2-weeks

Kenrick, D. T., & Johnson, G. A. (1979). Interpersonal attraction in aversive environments. A problem for the classical conditioning paradigm. *Journal of Personality and Social Psychology, 87*, 572–579.

Kerr, N. L. (1983). Motivation losses in small groups: A social dilemma analysis. *Journal of Personality and Social Psychology, 45*, 819–828.

Kerr, N. L. (1998). HARKing: Hypothesizing after the results are known. *Personality And Social Psychology Review, 2*(3), 196–217. doi:10.1207/s15327957p-spr0203_4

Kerr, N. L., & Bruun, S. E. (1981). Ringelmann revisited: Alternative explanations for the social loafing effect. *Personality and Social Psychology Bulletin, 7*(2), 224–231.

Kerr, N. L., & Bruun, S. E. (1983). Dispensability of member effort and group motivation losses: Free-rider effects. *Journal of Personality and Social Psychology, 44*, 78–94.

Kerr, N. L., Hymes, R. W., Anderson, A. B., & Weathers, J. E. (1995). Defendant-juror similarity and mock juror judgments. *Law and Human Behavior, 19*, 545–567.

Kerr, N. L., Rumble, A. C., Park, E. S, Ouwerkerk, J. W., Parks, C. D., Gallucci, M., & Van Lange, P. A. M. (2009). "How many bad apples does it take to spoil the whole barrel": Social exclusion and tolerance for bad apples. *Journal of Experimental Social Psychology, 45*(4), 603–613.

Kerr, N. L., Rumble, A. C., Park, E. S., Ouwerkerk, J. W., Parks, C. D., Gallucci, M., & Van Lange, P. A. M. (2009). "How many bad apples does it take to spoil the whole barrel?" Social exclusion and tolerance for bad apples. *Journal of Experimental Social Psychology. 45*(4), 603–613. Retrieved from http://www.sciencedirect.com/science/article/pii/S0022103109000390

Khadjavi, M., & Lange, A. (2013). Prisoners and their dilemma. *Journal of Economic Behavior & Organization, 92*(8), 163–175. doi: 10.1016/j.jebo.2013.05.015

Kidd, C., Palmeri, H., & Aslin, R.N. (2013). Rational snacking: Young children's decision-making on the marshmallow task is moderated by beliefs about environmental reliability. *Cognition, 126*, 109–114.

Kidder, D. L., & Parks, J. M. (2001). The good soldier: Who is s(he)? *Journal of Organizational Behavior, 22*, 939–959.

Kiecolt-Glaser, J. K., & Newton, T. L. (2001). Marriage and health: His and hers. *Psychological Bulletin, 127*, 472–503.

Kiecolt-Glaser, J. K., Fisher, L. D., Ogrocki, P., Stout, J. C., Speicher, C. E., & Glaser, R. (1987). Marital quality, marital disruption, and immune function. *Psychosomatic Medicine, 49*, 13–34.

Kiecolt-Glaser, J. K., Garner, W., Speicher, C., Penn, G. M., Holliday, J., & Glaser, R. (1984). Psychosocial modifiers of immunocompetence in medical students. *Psychosomatic Medicine, 46*, 7–14.

Kiesler, S., Sproull, L., & Waters, K. (1996). A prisoner's dilemma experiment on cooperation with people and human-like computers. *Journal of Personality and Social Psychology, 70*, 47–65.

Kim, J., Glaser, P., & Smith, T. W. (2011). The polls—trends: Trends in surveys on surveys. *Public Opinion Quarterly, 75*(1), 165–191.

Kim, S. H., Vincent, L. C., & Goncalo, J. A. (2012). Outside advantage: Can social rejection fuel creative thought? *Journal of Experimental Psychology: General, 142*, 605–611.

Kim, Y.-H., Chiu, C., & Zou, Z. (2010). Know thyself: Misperceptions of actual performance undermine achievement motivation, future performance, and subjective well-being. *Journal of Personality and Social Psychology, 99*, 395–409.

Kim, Y.-H., Chiu, C., & Zou, Z. (2010). Know thyself: Misperceptions of actual performance undermine achievement motivation, future performance, and subjective well-being. *Journal of Personality and Social Psychology, 99*, 395–409.

King, K., Balswick, J. O., & Robinson, I. E. (1977). The continuing premarital sexual revolution among college females. *Journal of Marriage and the Family, 39*, 455–459.

King, L. A., & Geise, A. C. (2011). Being forgotten: Implications for the experience of meaning in life. *Journal of Social Psychology, 151*, 696–709.

Kinsey, A. C., Pomeroy, W. B., Martin, C. E., & Gebhard, P. H. (1953). *Sexual behavior in the human female*. Philadelphia: Saunders.

Kipnis, D. (1972). Does power corrupt? *Journal of Personality and Social Psychology, 24*, 33–41.

Kipnis, D. (1976). *The powerholders*. Chicago: University of Chicago Press.

Kirkpatrick, L. A., & Ellis, B. J. (2001). An evolutionary-psychological perspective on self-esteem: Multiple domains and multiple functions. In G. J. O. Fletcher & M. S. Clark (Eds.), *Blackwell handbook of social psychology: Vol. 2. Interpersonal processes* (pp. 411–436). Oxford: Blackwell.

Kirkpatrick, S. A., & Locke, E. A. (1991). Leadership: Do traits matter? *Academy of Management Executive, 5*, 48–60.

Kirschenbaum, D., Humphrey, L., & Malett, S. (1981). Specificity of planning in adult self-control: An applied investigation. *Journal of Personality and Social Psychology, 40*, 941–950.

Kirschenbaum, D., Malett, S., Humphrey, L., & Tomarken, A. (1982). Specificity of planning and maintenance of self-control: 1 year follow-up of a study improvement program. *Behavior Therapy, 13*, 232–240.

Kirscht, J. P. (1971). Social and psychological problems of surveys on health and illness. *Social Science and Medicine, 5*(6), 519–526.

Kirscht, J. P., Haefner, D. P., & Kegeles, S. S. (1966). A national study of health beliefs. *Journal of Health & Human Behavior, 7*(4), 248–254. doi:http://dx.doi.org/10.2307/2948771

Kitayama, S., & Markus, H. R. (1999). Yin and Yang of the Japanese self: The cultural psychology of personality coherence. In D. Cervone (Ed.), *The coherence of personality: Social-cognitive bases of consistency, variability, and organization* (pp. 242302). New York: Guilford Press.

Kitayama, S., Snibbe, A. C., Markus, H. R., & Suzuki, T. (2004). Is there any "free" choice? Cognitive dissonance in two cultures. *Psychological Science, 15*, 527–533.

Kitzinger, C. (1987). *The social construction of lesbianism*. London: Sage.

Klaczynski, P., Daniel, D. B., & Keller, P. S. (2009). Appearance idealization, body esteem, causal attributions, and ethnic variations in the development of obesity stereotypes. *Journal of Applied Developmental Psychology, 30*(4), 537–551.

Klein, C., McKinnon, M. C., Twohey-Wright, N. Possingham, H. P., & Halpern, B. S. (2015). Social equity and the probability of success of biodiversity conservation. *Global Environmental Change, 35*, 299–306.

Klein, S. B., & Kihlstrom, J. F. (1986). Elaboration, organization, and the self-reference effect in memory. *Journal of Experimental Psychology: General, 115*, 26–39.

Kling, K. C., Hyde, J. S., Showers, C. J., & Buswell, B. N. (1999). Gender differences in self-esteem: A meta-analysis. *Psychological Bulletin, 125*, 470–500.

Klinger, M. R., & Greenwald, A. G. (1994). Preferences need no inferences? The cognitive basis for unconscious emotional effects. In P. M. Niedenthal & S. Kitayama (Eds.), *The heart's eye: Emotional influences in perception and attention* (pp. 67–85). Orlando, FL: Academic Press.

Knapp, D. E., & Kustis, G. A. (1996). The real "disclosure": Sexual harassment and the bottom line. In M.S. Stockdale (Ed.), *Women and Work: A Research and Policy Series, Volume 5: Sexual harassment in the workplace: Perspectives, frontiers, and response strategies* (pp. 199–215). Thousand Oaks, CA: Sage.

Knight, L. J., & Boland, F. J. (1989). Restrained eating: An experimental disentanglement of disinhibiting variables of perceived calories and food type. *Journal of Abnormal Psychology, 98*, 412–420.

Knobe, J. (2003). Intentional action and side effects in ordinary language. *Analysis, 63*, 190–194.

Knobe, J. (2010). Person as scientist, person as moralist. *Behavioral and Brain Sciences, 33*, 315–329.

Knobloch-Westerwick, S. (2014). Choice and preference in media use: Advances in selective exposure theory and research. New York: Routledge.

Knoll, N., Scholz, U., & Ditzen, B. (2019). Social support, family processes, and health. In T. A. Revenson & R. A. R. Gurung (Eds.), *Handbook of health psychology* (pp. 279–289). New York: Routledge.

Koch, E. J., & Shepperd, J. A. (2008). Testing competence and acceptance explanations of self-esteem. *Self and Identity, 7*, 54–74.

Koernig, S. K. (2003). E-scapes: The electronic physical environment and service tangibility. *Psychology and Marketing, 20*, 151–167.

Kohlenberg, R. J., Phillips, T., & Proctor, W. (1976). A behavioral analysis of peaking in residential electricity energy consumption. *Journal of Applied Behavior Analysis, 9*, 13–18.

Koider, S., Andrillon, T., Barbosa, L. S., Goupil L., & Bekinschtein, T. A. (2014). Inducing task-relevant responses to speech in the sleeping brain. *Current Biology, 24*, 1–7.

Kolata, G. (1992, November 22). The burdens of being overweight: Mistreatment and misconceptions. *New York Times*, A1.

Kolditz, T., & Arkin, R. M. (1982). An impression management interpretation of the self-handicapping phenomenon. *Journal of Personality and Social Psychology, 43*, 492–502.

Konecni, V. J., Libuser, L., Morton, H., & Ebbesen, E. G. (1975). Effects of a violation of personal space on escape and helping response. *Journal of Experimental Social Psychology, 11*, 288–299.

Konrath, S., Corneille, O., Bushman, B. J., & Luminet, O. (2014). The relationship between narcissistic exploitativeness, dispositional empathy, and emotion recognition abilities. *Journal of Nonverbal Behavior, 38*(1), 129–143. doi: 10.1007/s10919-013-0164-y

Konrath, S., O'Brien, E., & Hsing, C. (2011). Changes in dispositional empathy in American college students over time: A meta-analysis. *Personality and Social Psychology Review, 15*, 180–198.

Koole, S. L., & Lakens, D. (2012). Rewarding replications: A sure and simple way to improve psychological science. *Perspectives in Psychological Science, 7*(6), 608–614. doi: 10.1177/1745691612462186

Koole, S. L., Tjew A Sin, M., & Schneider, I. K. (2014). Embodied terror management: (Simulated) Interpersonal touch alleviates existential concerns among individuals with low self-esteem. *Psychological Science, 25*(1), 30–37. doi: 10.1177/0956797613483478

Koss, M. P. (1988). Hidden rape: Sexual aggression and victimization in the national sample of students in higher education. In M. A. Pirog-Good & J. E. Stets (Eds.), *Violence in dating relationships: Emerging social issues* (pp. 145–168). New York: Praeger.

Kotani, H., & Yokomatsu, M. (2013). Inheritance of local culture and disaster: Identity-formation-model approach. *Journal of Integrated Disaster Risk Management, 3*, 107–125.

Kouchaki, M., & Smith, I.H. (2014). The Morning Morality Effect: The influence of time of day on unethical behavior. *Psychological Science, 25*, 95–102.

Koughan, M. (1975, February 23). Arthur Friedman's outrage: Employees decide their pay. *Washington Post*.

Kouzes, J. M., & Posner, B. Z. (2002). *The leadership challenge* (3rd ed.). San Francisco: Jossey-Bass.

Kovera, M. B., & Cutler, B. L. (2013). *Jury selection*. New York: Oxford University Press.

Kovera, M. B., & Evelo, A. J. (2017). The case for double-blind administration. *Psychology, Public Policy, and Law*, 421–437.

Kozlowski, S. W., & Bell, B. S. (2003). Work groups and teams in organizations. In W. C. Borman, D. R. Ilgen, & R. J. Klimoski (Eds.), *Handbook of Psychology: Industrial and Organizational Psychology* (vol. 12, pp. 333–375). New York: Wiley.

Kozlowski, S. W., & Bell, B. S. (2003). Work groups and teams in organizations. In W. C. Borman, D. R. Ilgen, & R. J. Klimoski (Eds.), *Handbook of Psychology: Industrial and Organizational Psychology* (vol. 12, pp. 333–375). New York: Wiley.

Kozlowski, S. W., Gully, S. M., McHugh, P. P., Salas, E., & Cannon-Bowers, J. A. (1996). A dynamic theory of leadership and team effectiveness: Developmental and task contingent leader roles. In G. R. Ferris (Ed.), *Research in personnel and human resource management* (vol. 14, pp. 253–305). Greenwich, CT: JAI Press.

Kraft, M. (2006). *Environmental policies and politics*. Englewood Cliffs, NJ: Prentice Hall.

Kramer, A.D.I., Guillory, J.E., & Hancock, J.T. (2014). Experimental evidence of massive-scale emotional contagion through social networks. *Proceedings of the National Academy of Science, 111*, 24–26.

Kramer, R. M., & Brewer, M. B. (1984). Effects of group identity on resource use in a simulated commons dilemma. *Journal of Personality and Social Psychology, 46*, 1044–1057.

Kraus, S. J. (1995). Attitudes and the prediction of behavior: A meta-analysis of the empirical literature. *Personality and Social Psychology Bulletin, 21*, 58–75.

Krauss, R. M., Freedman, J. L., & Whitcup, M. (1978). Field and laboratory studies of littering. *Journal of Experimental Social Psychology, 14*, 109–122.

Kravitz, D. A., Cutler, B. L., & Brock, P. (1993). Reliability and validity of the original and revised Legal Attitudes Questionnaire. *Law and Human Behavior, 17*, 661–667.

Kray, L. J., & Galinsky, A. D. (2003). The debiasing effect of counterfactual mind-sets: Increasing the search for disconfirmatory information in group decisions. *Organizational Behavior and Human Decision Processes, 91*, 69–81.

Kray, L. J., George, L., Liljenquist, K., Galinsky, A., Tetlock, P., & Roese, N. (2010). From what *might* have been to what *must* have been: Counterfactual thinking creates meaning. *Journal of Personality and Social Psychology, 98*, 106–118.

Krendl, A. C., Richeson, J. A., Kelley, W. M., & Heatherton, T. F. (2008). The negative consequences of threat: A functional magnetic resonance imaging investigation of the neural mechanisms underlying women's underperformance in math. *Psychological Science, 19*(2), 168–175.

Kressel, N. J., & Kressel, D. R. (2002). *Stack and sway*. Boulder, CO: Westview Press.

Krizan, Z., & Hisler, G. (2018). Sleepy anger: Restricted sleep amplifies angry feelings. *Journal of Experimental Psychology: General*. https://doi-org.proxy.lib.umich.edu/10.1037/xge0000522

Kross, E., Berman, M. G., Mischel, W., Smith, E. E., and Wager, T. D. (2011). Social rejection shares somatosensory representations with physical pain. *Proceedings of the National Academy of Sciences, 108*, 6270–6275.

Kross, E., Verduyn, P., Demiralp, E., Park, J., Lee, D. S., Lin, N., et al. (2013). Facebook use predicts declines in subjective well-being in young adults. *PLoS ONE, 8*, e69841.

Krueger, J., & Clement, R. W. (1994). The truly false consensus effect: An ineradicable and egocentric bias in social perception. *Journal of Personality and Social Psychology, 67*, 596–610.

Krueger, J., Wirtz, D., & Miller, D. T. (2005). Counterfactual thinking and the first instinct fallacy. *Journal of Personality and Social Psychology, 88*, 725–735.

Kruger, J., & Gilovich, T. (2004). Actions, intentions, and self-assessment: The road to self-enhancement is paved with good intentions. *Personality and Social Psychology Bulletin, 30*(3), 328–339.

Krzysztof, J., & Leoniak, W. (2019) The role of normative prompts and norm support cues in promoting light-switching behavior: A field study. *Journal of Environmental Psychology, 64*, 1–11.

Kuiper, N. A., & Derry, P. A. (1982). Depressed and non-depressed content self-reference in mild depression. *Journal of Personality, 50*, 67–79.

Kulig, J. W. (2013). What's in a name? Our false uniqueness! *British Journal of Social Psychology, 52*(1), 173–179. doi:10.1111/bjso.12001

Kunce, L. J., & Shaver, P. R. (1994). An attachment-theoretical approach to caregiving in romantic relationships. In K. Bartholomew & D. Perlman (Eds.), *Advances in personal relationships* (Vol. 5, pp. 205–237). London: Kingsley.

Kunda, Z. (1990). The case for motivated reasoning. *Psychological Bulletin, 108*, 480–498.

Kunda, Z., & Thagard. P. (1996). Forming impressions from stereotypes, traits, and behaviors: A parallel-constraint-satisfaction theory. *Psychological Review, 103*, 284–308.

Kunda, Z., Davies, P. G., Adams, B. D., & Spencer, S. J. (2002). The dynamic time course of stereotype activation: Activation, dissipation, and resurrection. *Journal of Personality and Social Psychology, 82*, 283–299.

Kunst, M., Bogaerts, S., & Winkel, F. W. (2010). Domestic violence and mental health in a Dutch community sample: The adverse role of loneliness. *Journal of Community & Applied Social Psychology, 20*(5), 419–425.

Kunz, P. R., & Woolcott, M. (1976). Season's greetings: From my status to yours. *Social Science Research, 5*, 269–278.

Kurzban, R., & Leary, M. R. (2001). Evolutionary origins of stigmatization: The functions of social exclusion. *Psychological Bulletin, 127*, 187–208.

Kwan, M. (2010). How many cell phones are in the US? Retrieved from http://cellphones.lovetoknow.com/how-many-cell-phones-are-us

Kwan, V. S., John, O., Robin, R., & Kuang, L. (2008). Conceptualizing and assessing self-enhancement bias: A componential approach. *Journal of Personality and Social Psychology, 94*, 1062–1077.

Lacoursiere, R. B. (1980). *The life cycles of groups: Group developmental stage theory*. New York: Human Sciences Press.

LaFrance, M., & Banaji, M. (1992). Toward a reconsideration of the gender-emotion relationship. In M. S. Clark (Ed.), *Emotion and social behavior: Review of personality and social psychology* (Vol. 14, pp. 178–201). Newbury Park, CA: Sage.

Lagerspetz, K. M., Bjorkqvist, K., & Peltonen, T. (1988). Is indirect aggression typical of females? Gender differences in aggressiveness in 11- to 12-year-old children. *Aggressive Behavior, 14*, 403–414.

Lakin, A. (2009). Recyclable cars. *DriverSide.com*. Retrieved from http://www.driverside.com/auto-library/recyclable_cars-257

Lakin, J. L., & Chartrand, T. L. (2005). Exclusion and nonconscious behavioral mimicry. In K. D. Williams, J. P. Forgas, & W. von Hippel (Eds.), *The social outcast: Ostracism, social exclusion, rejection, and bullying* (pp. 279–296). New York: Psychology Press.

Lam, S. S. K., Schaubroeck, J., & Aryee, S. (2002). Relationship between organizational justice and employee work outcomes: A cross-national study. *Journal of Organizational Behavior, 23*, 1–18.

Lambert, N. M., Stillman, T. F., Hicks, J. A., Baumeister, R. F., Kamble, S., & Fincham, F. D. (2013). To belong is to matter: Sense of belonging enhances meaning in life. *Personality and Social Psychology Bulletin, 39*, 1418–1427.

Landman, J. (1993). *Regret: The persistence of the possible.* New York: Oxford University Press.

Langer, E. J. (1975). The illusion of control. *Journal of Personality and Social Psychology, 32*, 311–328.

Langer, E. J., & Rodin, J. (1976). The effects of choice and enhanced personal responsibility for the aged: A field experiment in an institutional setting. *Journal of Personality and Social Psychology, 34*(2), 191–198.

Langer, E. J., & Roth, J. (1975). Heads I win, tails it's chance: The illusion of control as a function of the sequence of outcomes in a purely chance task. *Journal of Personality and Social Psychology, 32*, 951–955.

Langer, E. J., & Saegert, S. (1977). Crowding and cognitive control. *Journal of Personality and Social Psychology, 35*, 175–182.

Langer, G., Arnedt, C., & Sussman, D. (2004). A peek beneath the sheets. Retrieved from http://www.abcnews.go.com/Primetime/News

Langer, L. M., & Tubman, J. G. (1997). Risky sexual behavior among substance-abusing adolescents: Psychosocial and contextual factors. *American Journal of Orthopsychiatry, 67*, 315–322.

Langley, R.L. (2005). *Animal-Related Fatalities in the United States—An Update* Wilderness and Environmental Medicine, *16*, 67–74.

Langlois, J. H., Roggman, L. A., Casey, R. J., & Ritter, J. M. (1987). Infant preferences for attractive faces: Rudiments of a stereotype? *Developmental Psychology, 23*, 363–369.

LaPiere, R. T. (1934). Attitudes vs. actions. *Social Forces, 13*, 230–237.

Larsen, R. J. (2000). Toward a science of mood regulation. *Psychological Inquiry, 11*(3), 129–141.

Larsen, R. J., & Diener, E. (1987). Affect intensity as an individual difference characteristic: A review. *Journal of Research in Personality, 21*, 1–39.

Larson, R. W., & Pleck, J. (1999). Hidden feelings: Emotionality in boys and men. In D. Bernstein (Ed.), *Nebraska Symposium on Motivation: Vol. 45. Gender and motivation* (pp. 25–74). Lincoln: University of Nebraska Press.

Larwood, L., & Gattiker, U. E. (1995). Rational bias and interorganizational power in the employment of management consultants. *Group and Organization Studies, 10*, 3–17.

Latané, B., & Darley, J. (1968). Group inhibition of bystander intervention in emergencies. *Journal of Personality and Social Psychology, 10*, 215–221.

Latane, B., Eckman, J., & Joy, V. (1966). Shared stress and interpersonal attraction. *Journal of Experimental Social Psychology Supplement, 1*, 80–94.

Latane, B., Williams, K., & Harkins, S. (1979). Many hands make light the work: The causes and consequences of social loafing. *Journal of Personality and Social Psychology, 37*, 822–832.

Latta, R. M. (1978). Relation of status incongruous to personal space. *Personality and Social Psychology Bulletin, 4*, 143–146.

Laumann, E. O., Gagnon, J. H., Michael, R. T., & Michaels, S. (1994). *The social organization of sexuality: Sexual practices in the United States.* Chicago, IL: University of Chicago Press.

Lavine, H., Sweeney, D., & Wagner, S. H. (1999). Depicting women as sex objects in television advertising: Effects on body dissatisfaction. *Personality and Social Psychology Bulletin, 25*, 1049–1058.

Lawler, E. E., Mohrman, S. A., & Ledford, G. E. (1995). *Creating high performance organizations: Practices and results of employee involvement and total quality management in Fortune 1000 companies.* San Francisco: Jossey-Bass.

Lawrence, C., & Andrews, K. (2004). The influence of perceived prison crowding on male inmates' perception of aggressive events. *Aggressive Behavior, 30*(4), 273–283.

Lawson, A. (1988). *Adultery: An analysis of love and betrayal.* New York: Basic Books.

Lazarus, R. S. (1966). *Psychological stress and the coping process.* New York: McGraw-Hill.

Lazarus, R. S. (1991). Progress on a cognitive-motivational-relational theory of emotion. *American Psychologist, 46*(8), 819–834.

Lazarus, R. S., & Launier, R. (1978). Stress-related transactions between person and environment. In L. A. Pervin & M. Lewis (Eds.), *Perspectives in interactional psychology* (pp. 287–322). New York: Plenum.

Lazarus, R.S. (1991). *Emotion and adaptation.* New York, NY: Oxford University Press

Le Bon, G. (1908). *The crowd: A study of the popular mind.* London: T Fisher Unwin.

Lea, S. E. G., & Webley, P. (2006). Money as tool, money as drug: The biological psychology of a strong incentive. *Behavioral and Brain Sciences, 29*, 161–209.

Leander, N. P., & Chartrand, T. L. (2017). On thwarted goals and displaced aggression: A compensatory competence model. *Journal of Experimental Social Psychology, 72*, 88–100. DOI: 10.1016/j.jesp.2017.04.010

Leary, M. R. (2005). Varieties of interpersonal rejection. In K. D. Williams, J. P. Forgas, & W. von Hippel (Eds.), *The social outcast: Ostracism, social exclusion, rejection, and bullying* (pp. 35–54). New York: Psychology Press.

Leary, M. R., & Baumeister, R. F. (2000). The nature and function of self-esteem: Sociometer theory. In M. Zanna (Ed.), *Advances in experimental social psychology* (Vol. 32, pp. 1–62). San Diego: Academic Press.

Leary, M. R., & Springer, C. A. (2000). Hurt feelings: The neglected emotion. In R. Kowalski (Ed.), *Aversive behaviors and interpersonal transgression.* Washington, DC: American Psychological Association.

Leary, M. R., Kowalski, R. M., Smith, L., & Phillips, S. (2003). Teasing, rejection, and violence: Case studies of the school shootings. *Aggressive Behavior, 29*, 202–214.

Leary, M. R., Springer, C., Negel, L., Ansell, E., & Evans, K. (1998). The causes, phenomenology, and consequences of hurt feelings. *Journal of Personality and Social Psychology, 74*, 1225–1237.

Leary, M. R., Tambor, E. S., Terdal, S. K., & Downs, D. L. (1995). Self-esteem as an interpersonal monitor: The sociometer hypothesis. *Journal of Personality Psychology, 68*, 518–530.

Leary, M. R., Tchividjian, L. R., & Kraxberger, B. E. (1994). Self-presentation can be hazardous to your health: Impression management and health risk. *Health Psychology, 13*, 461–470.

Lede, E., Meleady, R., & Seger, C. R. (2019). Optimizing the influence of social norms interventions: Applying social identity insights to motivate residential water conservation. *Journal of Environmental Psychology, 62*, 105–114.

Lee, B. K., & Lee, W. N. (2004). The effect of information overload on consumer choice quality in an on-line environment. *Psychology and Marketing, 21*, 159–183.

Lee, C. (1995). Prosocial organizational behaviors: The roles of workplace justice, achievement striving, and pay satisfaction. *Journal of Business and Psychology, 10*, 197–206.

Lee, S. W. S., & Schwarz, N. (2011). Wiping the slate clean: Psychological consequences of physical cleansing. *Current Directions in Psychological Science, 20*(5), 307–311.

Lee, S., Moon, S.-I., & Feeley, T. H. (2016). A meta-analytic review of the legitimization of paltry favors compliance strategy. *Psychological Reports, 118*(3), 748–771. https://doi-org.proxy.lib.umich.edu/10.1177/0033294116647690

Lee-Chai, A. Y., Chen, S., & Chartrand, T. L. (2001). From Moses to Marcos: Individual differences in the use and abuse of power. In A. Y. Lee-Chai & J. A. Bargh (Eds.), *The use and abuse of power: Multiple perspectives on the causes of corruption* (pp. 57–74). New York: Psychology Press.

Leffingwell, A. (1892). *Illegitimacy and the influence of the seasons upon conduct.* New York: Scribner's.

Leippe, M. R., Eisenstadt, D., Rauch, S. M., & Seib, H. M. (2004). Timing of eyewitness expert testimony, jurors' need for cognition, and case strength as determinants of trial verdicts. *Journal of Applied Psychology, 89*, 524–541.

Lench, H. C., Bench, S. W., & Davis, E. L. (2016). Distraction from emotional information reduces biased judgements. *Cognition and Emotion, 30*(4), 638–653. doi:10.1080/02699931.2015.1020767

Lennings, C. J. (1997). Police and occupationally related violence: A review. *Policing: An International Journal of Police Strategies and Management, 20*(3), 555–566.

Lennox, R. D., & Wolfe, R. N. (1984). Revision of the self-monitoring scale. *Journal of Personality and Social Psychology, 46*, 1349–1364.

Leon, G., & Chamberlain, K. (1973). Emotional arousal, eating patterns, and body image as differential factors associated with varying success in maintaining a weight loss. *Journal of Consulting and Clinical Psychology, 40*, 474.

Leonard-Barton, D. (1980, September). *The role of interpersonal communication networks in the diffusion of energy conserving practices and technologies.* Paper presented at the International Conference of Consumer Behavior and Energy Policy, Banff, Alberta, Canada.

LePine, J. A., Erez, A., & Johnston, D. E. (2002). The nature and dimensionality of organizational citizenship behavior: A critical review and a meta-analysis. *Journal of Applied Psychology, 87*(1), 52–65.

Lepper, M. P., Greene, D., & Nisbett, R. E. (1973). Undermining children's intrinsic interest with extrinsic reward: A test of the "overjustification" hypothesis. *Journal of Personality and Social Psychology, 28*, 129–137.

Lerner, J. S., & Tetlock, P. E. (1999). Accounting for the effects of accountability. *Psychological Bulletin, 125*, 255–275.

Lerner, J. S., Small, D. A., & Loewenstein, G. (2004). Heart strings and purse strings: Carryover effects of emotions on economic decisions. *Psychological Science, 15*(5), 337–341.

Lerner, M. J. (1982). The justice motive in human relations and economic model of man: A radical analysis of facts and fictions. In V. Derlega & J. Grzelak (Eds.), *Cooperation and helping behavior: Theories and research* (pp. 249–278). New York: Academic Press.

Lerner, M. J., & Miller, D. T. (1978). Just world research and the attribution process: Looking back and ahead. *Psychological Bulletin, 85*, 1030–1051.

Lerner, M. J., & Simmons, C. H. (1966). Observer's reaction to the "innocent victim": Compassion or rejection? *Journal of Personality and Social Psychology, 4*, 203–210.

Lerner, R. (1969). Some female stereotypes of male body build–behavior relations. *Perceptual and Motor Skills, 28*, 363–366.

Lesiuk, T. (2005). The effect of music listening on work performance. *Psychology of Music, 33*(2), 173–191.

Leslie, J. B., & Van Velsor, E. (1996). *A look at derailment today.* Greensboro, NC: Centre for Creative Leadership.

Lett, H. S., Blumenthal, J. A., Babyak, M. A., Catellier, D. J., Carney, R. M., Berkman, L. F., et al. (2008). Perceived social support predicts outcomes following myocardial infarction: A call for screening?: Response. *Health Psychology, 27*(1), 1–3. doi: 10.1037/0278-6133.27.1.1b

R-24 | References

Leung, K., & Bond, M. H. (2004). Social axioms: A model for social beliefs in multicultural perspective. In M. Zanna (Ed.), *Advances in experimental social psychology* (Vol. 36, pp. 119–197). New York: Academic Press.

Levav, J., Heitmann, H., Herrmann, A., & Iyengar, S. S. (2010). Order in product customization decisions: Evidence from field experiments. *Journal of Political Economy, 118,* 274–299.

Levenson, R. W., & Gottman, J. M. (1983). Marital interaction: Physiological linkage and affective exchange. *Journal of Personality and Social Psychology, 45,* 587–597.

Levenson, R. W., & Gottman, J. M. (1985). Physiological and affective predictors of change in marital satisfaction. *Journal of Personality and Social Psychology, 49,* 85–94.

Levine, J. M., & Moreland, R. L. (1998). Small groups. In D. Gilbert, S. Fiske, & G. Lindzey (Eds.), *Handbook of social psychology* (4th ed., Vol. 2, pp. 415–469). Boston: McGraw-Hill.

Levine, J. M., & Valle, R. S. (1975). The convert as a credible communicator. *Social Behavior and Personality, 3,* 81–90.

Leviticus 16: 7–10 (Bible).

Levitt, S. J., & Dubner, S. D. (2005). *Freakonomics: A rogue economist explores the hidden side of everything.* New York: Morrow.

Lewandowsky, S., Ecker, U. K. H., Seifert, C., Schwarz, N., & Cook, J. (2012). Misinformation and its correction: Continued influence and successful debiasing. *Psychological Science in the Public Interest, 13,* 106–131. doi: 10.1177/1529100612451018

Lewandowsky, S., Ecker, U. H., & Cook, J. (2017). Beyond misinformation: Understanding and coping with the 'post-truth' era. *Journal of Applied Research in Memory and Cognition, 6*(4), 353–369. doi:10.1016/j.jarmac.2017.07.00

Lewin, K. (1936). *Principles of topological psychology.* New York: McGraw-Hill.

Lewin, K. (1951). *Field theory in social science: Selected theoretical papers* (D. Cartwright, Ed.). New York: Harper Torchbooks. Quote on p. 169.

Lewinsohn, P. M., Mischel, W., Chaplin, W., & Barton, R. (1980). Social competence and depression: The role of illusory self-perceptions. *Journal of Abnormal Psychology, 89,* 203–212.

Lewis, J., Baddeley, A. D., Bonham, K. G., & Lovett, D. (1970). Traffic pollution and mental efficiency. *Nature, 225,* 95–97.

Lewis, M. A., Litt, D. M., King, K. M., Garcia, T. A., Waldron, K. A., & Lee, C. M. (2018). Consideration of future consequences as a moderator of the willingness-behavior relationship for young adult marijuana use and consequences. *Addictive Behaviors, 87,* 8–16. doi:http://dx.doi.org/10.1016/j.addbeh.2018.06.010

Lewis, W. A., & Bucher, A. M. (1992). Anger, catharsis, the reformulated frustration-aggression hypothesis, and health consequences. *Psychotherapy, 29,* 385–392.

Ley, D., & Cybriwsky, R. (1974). The spatial ecology of stripped cars. *Environment and Behavior, 6,* 53–68.

Li, T., & Fung, H. H. (2012). How negative interactions affect relationship satisfaction: The paradoxical short-term and long-term effects of commitment. *Social Psychological and Personality Science, 4,* 274–281.

Li, X., Lei, Y., Wang, H., He, G., & Williams, A. B. (2016). The health belief model: A qualitative study to understand high-risk sexual behavior in chinese men who have sex with men. *JANAC: Journal of the Association of Nurses in AIDS Care, 27*(1), 66–76. doi:http://dx.doi.org/10.1016/j.jana.2015.10.005

Liang, D. W., Moreland, R. L., & Argote, L. (1995). Group versus individual training and group performance: The mediating role of transactive memory. *Personality and Social Psychology Bulletin, 21,* 384–393.

Liberman, N., & Trope, Y. (1998). The role of feasibility and desirability considerations in near and distant future decisions: A test of temporal construal theory. *Journal of Personality and Social Psychology, 75,* 5–18.

Liberman, N., Sagristano, M. C., & Trope, Y. (2002). The effect of temporal perspective on level of construal. *Journal of Experimental Social Psychology, 38,* 524–534.

Lickel, B., Hamilton, D. L., Wieczorkowska, G., Lewis, A., Sherman, S. J., & Uhles, A. N. (2000). Varieties of groups and the perception of group entitativity. *Journal of Personality and Social Psychology, 78,* 223–246.

Lieberman, M. A., Yalom, I. D., & Miles, M. B. (1973). *Encounter groups: First facts.* New York: Basic Books.

Lieberman, M. D., Gaunt, R., Gilbert, D. T., & Trope, Y. (2002). Reflection and reflexion: A social cognitive neuroscience approach to attributional inference. *Advances in Experimental Social Psychology, 34,* 199–249.

Liebert, R., & Baron, R. (1972). Some immediate effects of televised violence on children's behavior. *Developmental Psychology, 6,* 469–475.

Liebowitz, M. R. (1983). *The chemistry of love.* Boston: Little & Brown.

Liebrand, W. B. G., Wilke, H. A. M., & Wolters, F. J. M. (1986). Value orientation and conformity. A study using three types of social dilemma games. *Journal of Conflict Resolution, 30,* 77–97.

Light, L. L., Kayra-Stuart, F., & Hollander, S. (1979). Recognition memory for typical and unusual faces. *Journal of Experimental Psychology: Human Learning and Memory, 5,* 212–228.

Likert, R. (1967). *The human organization: Its management and value.* New York: McGraw-Hill.

Lilienfeld, S. O. (2017). Psychology's replication crisis and the grant culture: Righting the ship. *Perspectives on Psychological Science, 12,* 660–664. http://dx.doi.org/10.1177/1745691616687745

Lin, Y. J., & Wicker, F. W. (2007). A comparison of the effects of thought suppression, distraction and concentration. *Behaviour Research and Therapy, 45*(12):2924–2937.

Linder, D. E., Cooper, J., & Jones, E. E. (1967). Decision freedom as a determinant of the role of incentive magnitude in attitude change. *Journal of Personality and Social Psychology, 6,* 245–254.

Lindner, E. G. (2002). Healing the cycles of humiliation: How to attend to the emotional aspects of "unsolvable" conflicts and the use of "humiliation entrepreneurship." *Peace and Conflict: Journal of Peace Psychology, 8,* 125–138.

Lindsay, R. C. L., & Wells, G. L. (1980). What price justice? Exploring the relationship between lineup fairness and identification accuracy. *Law and Human Behavior, 4,* 303–314.

Lindskold, S., & Aronoff, J. R. (1980). Conciliatory strategies and relative power. *Journal of Experimental Social Psychology, 16,* 187–198.

Lipsey, M. W., Wilson, D. B., Cohen M. A., & Derzon, J. H. (1997). Is there a causal relationship between alcohol use and violence? A synthesis of the evidence. In M. Galanter (Ed.), *Recent developments in alcoholism: Vol. 13. Alcohol and violence: Epidemiology, neurobiology, psychology, and family issues* (pp. 245–282). New York: Plenum Press.

Lipsey, M. W., Wilson, D. B., Cohen M. A., & Derzon, J. H. (1997). Is there a causal relationship between alcohol use and violence? A synthesis of the evidence. In M. Galanter (Ed.), *Recent developments in alcoholism: Vol. 13. Alcohol and violence: Epidemiology, neurobiology, psychology, and family issues* (pp. 245–282). New York: Plenum Press.

Litt, C. J. (1981). Children's attachment to transitional objects: A study of two pediatric populations. *American Journal of Orthopsychiatry, 51,* 131–139.

Litt, D. M., & Lewis, M. A. (2013). The prototype willingness model: A review. In J. Assailly (Ed.), *Psychology of risk-taking; psychology of risk-taking* (pp. 83–98). Hauppauge, NY: Nova Science Publishers.

Little, B. R. (1989). Personal projects analysis: Trivial pursuits, magnificent obsessions, and the search for coherence. In D. Buss & N. Cantor (Eds.), *Personality psychology: Recent trends and emerging directions* (pp. 15–31). New York: Springer Verlag.

Littlefield, C. (2015, July 7). Subway suspends spokesman Jared Fogle, who's been crucial to the brand. *Los Angeles Times.* Retrieved from https://www.latimes.com/nation/nationnow/la-na-nn-subway-on-jared-fogle-reports-we-are-shocked-20150707-story.html

Liu, D., & Baumeister, R. F. (2017). Social networking and personality if self-worth: A meta-anaylsis. *Journal of Research in Personality, 64,* 79–89.

Liu, D., Ainsworth, S. E., & Baumeister, R. F. (2016). A meta-analysis of social networking online and social capital. *Review of General Psychology, 20,* 369–391.

Lochman, J. E., Vernberg, E., Boxmeyer, C., & Powell, N. (2012, May). Tornado effects on children's behavioral, emotional and psychophysiological functioning and parents' depression. Paper to be presented in a symposium (R. Guadagno, Chair) at the Association of Psychological Science Annual Convention, Chicago, IL.

Locke E. A., & Latham, G. P. (1990). *A theory of goal setting and task performance.* Englewood Cliffs, NJ: Prentice Hall.

Locke, E. A., & Kristof, A. L. (1996). Volitional choices in the goal achievement process. In P. M. Gollwitzer & J. A. Bargh (Eds.), *The psychology of action: Linking cognition and motivation to behavior* (pp. 363–384). New York: Guilford Press.

Locksley, A., Ortiz, V., & Hepburn, C. (1980). Social categorization and discriminatory behavior: Extinguishing the minimal intergroup discrimination effect. *Journal of Personality and Social Psychology, 39*(5), 773–783.

Loeber, R., & Hay, D. (1997). Key issues in the development of aggression from childhood to early adulthood. *Annual Review of Psychology, 48,* 371–410.

Loersch, C., & Arbuckle, N.L. (2013). Unraveling the mystery of music: Music as an evolved group process. *Journal of Personality and Social Psychology, 105,* 777–798.

Loewenstein, G. F., Weber, E. U., Hsee, C. K., & Welch, N. (2001). Risk as feelings. *Psychological Bulletin, 127,* 267–286.

Loftus, E. (1974). Reconstructing memory: The incredible eyewitness. *Psychology Today, 8*(7), 116–119.

Loftus, E. F., & Ketcham, K. (1994). *The myth of repressed memory.* New York: St. Martin's Press.

Loftus, E. F., Loftus, G. R., & Messo, J. (1987). Some facts about "weapon focus." *Law and Human Behavior, 11,* 55–62.

Logue, A. W. (1991). *The psychology of eating and drinking: An introduction* (2nd ed.). New York: W. H. Freeman.

Lombardo, M. M., & Eichinger, R. W. (2000). High potentials as high learners. *Human Resource Management, 39*(4), 321–329.

Lopes, L. L. (1987). Procedural debiasing. *Acta Psychologica, 64,* 167–185.

Lopes, P. N., Brackett, M. A., Nezlek, J. B., Schütz, A., Sellin, I., & Salovey, P. (2004). Emotional intelligence and social interaction. *Personality and Social Psychology Bulletin, 30,* 1018–1034.

Lord, C. G., & Saenz, D. S. (1985). Memory deficits and memory surfeits: Differential cognitive consequences of tokenism for tokens and observers. *Journal of Personality and Social Psychology, 49,* 918–926.

Lord, C. G., Lepper, M. R., & Preston, E. (1984). Considering the opposite: A corrective strategy for social judgment. *Journal of Personality and Social Psychology, 47,* 1231–1243.

Lord, C. G., Ross, L., & Lepper, M. R. (1979). Biased assimilation and attitude polarization: The effects of prior theories on subsequently considered evidence. *Journal of Personality and Social Psychology, 37,* 2098–2109.

Lord, R. G., Foti, R. J., & DeVader, C. L. (1984). A test of leadership categorization theory: Internal structure, information processing, and leadership perceptions. *Organizational Behavior and Human Performance, 34,* 343–378.

Lorenz, J., Rauhut, H., Schweitzer, F., & Helbing, D. (2011). How social influence can undermine the wisdom of crowd effect. *PNAS (Proceedings of the National Academy of Sciences), 108*, 9020–9025.

Lorenz, K. (1966). *On aggression* (M. K. Wilson, Trans.) New York: Harcourt, Brace.

Lucas, R. E. (2007). Long-term disability is associated with lasting changes in subjective well-being: Evidence from two nationally representative longitudinal studies. *Journal of Personality and Social Psychology, 92*(4), 717–730.

Luce, M. F. (1998). Choosing to avoid: Coping with negatively emotion-laden consumer decisions. *Journal of Consumer Research, 24*, 409–433.

Luce, M. F., Bettman, J. R., & Payne, J. W. (1997). Choice processing in emotionally difficult decisions. *Journal of Experimental Psychology: Learning, Memory, and Cognition, 23*, 384–405.

Luce, M. F., Bettman, J. R., & Payne, J. W. (2001). *Emotional decisions: Tradeoff difficulty and coping in consumer choice*. Chicago: University of Chicago Press.

Luchies, L. B., Wieselquist, J., Rusbult, C. E., Kumasiro, M., Eastwick, P. W., Coolsen, M. K., & Finkel, E. J. (2013). Trust and biased memory of transgressions in romantic relationships. *Journal of Personality and Social Psychology, 104*, 673–694.

Lundberg, A. (1996). Psychiatric aspects of air pollution. *Otolaryngology-Head and Neck Surgery, 114*(2), 227–231.

Luus, C. A. E., & Wells, G. L. (1991). Eyewitness identification and the selection of distractors for lineups. *Law and Human Behavior, 15*, 43–57.

Lydon, J. E., Menzies-Toman, D., Burton, K., & Bell, C. (2008). If-then contingencies and the differential effects of the availability of an attractive alternative on relationship maintenance for men and women. *Journal of Personality and Social Psychology, 95*, 50–65.

Lynch, J. J. (1979). *The broken heart: The medical consequences of loneliness*. New York: Basic Books.

Lyubomirsky, S. (2001). Why are some people happier than others? The role of cognitive and motivational processes in well-being. *American Psychologist, 56*, 239–249.

Lyubomirsky, S., King, L. A., & Diener, E. (2005). The benefits of frequent positive affect: Does happiness lead to success? *Psychological Bulletin, 131*, 803–855.

Ma, Y., Dixon, G., & Hmielowkski, J. D. (2019). Psychological reactance from reading basic facts on climate change: The role of prior view and political identification. *Environmental Communication, 13*, 71–86.

Maass, A., Cadinu, M., Guarnieri, G., & Grasselli, A. (2003). Sexual harassment under social identity threat: The computer harassment paradigm. *Journal of Personality and Social Psychology, 85*, 853–870.

MacDonald, G., & Leary M. R. (2005). Why does social exclusion hurt? The relationship between social and physical pain. *Psychological Bulletin, 131*, 202–223.

MacDonald, T. K., & Ross, M. (1999). Assessing the accuracy of predictions about dating relationships: How and why do lovers' predictions differ from those made by observers? *Personality and Social Psychology Bulletin, 25*, 1417–1429.

Macfarlane, A. (1986). *Marriage and love in England: Modes of reproduction, 1300–1840*. New York: Basil Blackwell.

Macias, W. (2003). A beginning look at the effects of interactivity, product involvement, and web experience on comprehension: Brand web sites as interactive advertising. *Journal of Current Issues and Research in Advertising, 25*, 31–44.

Mack, D., & Rainey, D. (1990). Female applicants' grooming and personnel selection. *Journal of Social Behavior and Personality, 5*, 399–407.

Mackay, C. (1932). *Extraordinary popular delusions and the madness of crowds*. New York: Farrar, Straus and Cudahy. (Original work published 1841).

Mackie, D. M., Worth L. T., & Asuncion, A. G. (1990). Processing of persuasive in-group messages. *Journal of Personality and Social Psychology, 58*, 812–822.

Mackie, D., & Cooper, J. (1984). Attitude polarization: Effects of group membership. *Journal of Personality and Social Psychology, 46*, 575–585.

MacLean, M. J. & Chown, S. M. (1988). Just world beliefs and attitudes toward helping elderly people: A comparison of British and Canadian university students. *International Journal of Aging and Human Development, 26*, 249–260.

Macphail, E. (1982). *Brain and intelligence in vertebrates*. Oxford: Clarendon Press.

Macrae, C. N., Milne, A. B., & Bodenhausen, G. V. (1994). Stereotypes as energy-saving devices: A peek inside the cognitive toolbox. *Journal of Personality and Social Psychology, 66*, 37–47.

Maddux, C. D., Stacy, D., & Scott, M. (1981). School entry age in a group of gifted children. *Gifted Child Quarterly, 25*, 180–184.

Major, B., Zubek, J. M., Cooper, M. L., Cozzarelli, C., & Richards, C. (1997). Mixed messages: Implications of social conflict and social support within close relationships for adjustment to a stressful life event. *Journal of Personality and Social Psychology, 72*, 1349–1363.

Ma-Kellams, C., Wang, M. C., & Cardiel, H. (2017). Attractiveness and relationship longevity: Beauty is not what it is cracked up to be. *Personal Relationships, 24*, 146–161.

Malamuth, N. M., & Check, J. V. P. (1981). The effects of mass media exposure on acceptance of violence against women: A field experiment. *Journal of Research in Personality, 15*, 436–446.

Malinowski, J. (2017). High thought suppressors dream more of their negative waking-life experiences than low thought suppressors. *Dreaming, 27*(4), 269–277. doi:10.1037/drm0000061

Malle, B. F. (2006). The actor-observer asymmetry in causal attribution: A (surprising) meta-analysis. *Psychological Bulletin, 132*, 895–919.

Malle, B. F. (2011). Time to give up the dogmas of attribution: An alternative theory of behavior explanation. *Advances of Experimental Social Psychology, 44*, 297–352.

Malle, B. F., Knobe, J. M., & Nelson, S. E. (2007). Actor-observer asymmetries in explanations of behavior: New answers to an old question. *Journal of Personality and Social Psychology, 93*, 491–514.

Malouff, J. M., & Schutte, N. S. (2014). Trait emotional intelligence and romantic relationship satisfaction: A meta-analysis. *American Journal of Family Therapy, 42*(1), 53–66. doi: 10.1080/01926187.2012.748549

Maner, J. K., & Mead, N. L. (2010). The essential tension between leadership and power: When leaders sacrifice group goals for the sake of self-interest. *Journal of Personality and Social Psychology, 99*, 482–497.

Maner, J. K., DeWall, C. N., Baumeister, R. F., & Schaller, M. (2007). Does social exclusion motivate interpersonal reconnection? Resolving the "porcupine problem." *Journal of Personality and Social Psychology, 92*(1), 42–55.

Maner, J. K., Gailliot, M. T., & DeWall, C. N. (2007). Adaptive attentional attunement: Evidence for mating-related perceptual bias. *Evolution and Human Behavior, 28*(1), 28–36.

Maner, J. K., Kenrick, D. T., Neuberg, S. L., Becker, D. V., Robertson, T., Hofer, B., et al. (2005). Functional projection: How fundamental social motives can bias interpersonal perception. *Journal of Personality and Social Psychology, 88*, 63–78.

Manfred, T. (2014, September 17). Nike drops Adrian Peterson. *Business Insider*. Retrieved from http://www.businessinsider.com/nike-drops-adrian-peterson-2014-9

Manning, R., Levine, M., & Collins, A. (2007). The Kitty Genovese murder and the social psychology of helping: The parable of the 38 witnesses. *American Psychologist, 62*, 555–562.

Mannix, E., & Neale, M.A. (2005). What differences make a difference? The promise and reality of diverse teams in organizations. *Psychological Science in the Public Interest, 6*, 31–55.

Mansel, W. (2018, December 12). Republican congressman-elect suggests autism linked to vaccines, without evidence, wants to get 'real data' from CDC. *Newsweek*. Retrieved from https://www.newsweek.com/vaccines-autism-link-children-cdc-report-mark-green-congressman-tennessee-1256259

Manson v. Braithwaite, 1977, 432 U.S. 98.

Mansour, J. K., Beaudry, J. L., Bertrand, M. I., Kalmet, N., Melsom, E. I., & Lindsay, R. C. L. (2012). Impact of disguise on identification decisions and confidence with simultaneous and sequential lineups. *Law and Human Behavior, 36*, 513–526.

Manucia, G. K., Baumann, D. J., & Cialdini, R. B. (1984). Mood influences on helping: Direct effects or side effects? *Journal of Personality and Social Psychology, 46*, 357–364.

Manz, C. C. (1992). Self-leading work teams: Moving beyond self-management myths. *Human Relations, 45*, 1119–1140.

Marcon, J. L., Susa, K. J., & Meissner, C. A. (2009). Assessing the influence of recollection and familiarity in memory for own- versus other-race faces. *Psychonomic Bulletin & Review, 16*, 99–103.

Marcus-Newhall, A., Pedersen, W. C., Carlson, M., & Miller, N. (2000). Displaced aggression is alive and well: A meta-analytic review. *Journal of Personality and Social Psychology, 78*, 670–689.

Mardberg, B., Carlstedt, L., Stalberg-Carlstedt, B., & Shalit, B. (1987). Sex differences in perception of threat from the Chernobyl accident. *Perceptual & Motor Skills, 65*, 228.

Maris, R. (1969). *Social forces in urban suicide*. Homewood, IL: Dorsey.

Maris, R. (1981). *Pathways to suicide: A survey of self-destructive behaviors*. Baltimore: Johns Hopkins University Press.

Markman, K., Gavanski, I., Sherman, S., & McMullen, M. (1993). The mental simulation of better and worse possible worlds. *Journal of Experimental Social Psychology, 29*, 87–109.

Marks, G. (1984). Thinking one's abilities are unique and one's opinions are common. *Personality and Social Psychology Bulletin, 10*, 203–208.

Marks, G., & Miller, N. (1987). Ten years of research on the false consensus effect: An empirical and theoretical review. *Psychological Bulletin, 102*, 72–90.

Markus, H. R., & Kitayama, S. (1991). Culture and the self: Implications for cognition, emotion, and motivation. *Psychological Review, 98*, 224–253. See also Triandis, H. C. (1989). The self and social behavior in differing cultural contexts. *Psychological Review, 96*, 506–520.

Markus, H. R., & Kunda, Z. (1986). Stability and malleability in the self-concept in the perception of others. *Journal of Personality and Social Psychology, 51*, 858–866.

Marques, J. M., & Páez, D. (1994). The "black sheep effect": Social categorization, rejection of ingroup deviates and perception of group variability. *European Review of Social Psychology, 5*, 37–68.

Marques, J. M., & Yzerbyt, V. Y. (1988). The black sheep effect: Judgmental extremity in inter- and intra-group situations. *European Journal of Social Psychology, 18*, 287–292.

Marques, J. M., Abrams, D., Páez, D., & Hogg, M. A. (2001). Social categorization, social identification, and rejection of deviant group members. In M. A. Hogg & R. S. Tindale (Eds.), *Blackwell handbook of social psychology: Group processes* (pp. 400–424). Oxford: Blackwell.

Marques, J. M., Abrams, D., Páez, D., & Martinez-Taboada, C. (1998). The role of categorization and in-group norms in judgments of groups and their members. *Journal of Personality and Social Psychology, 75*, 976–988.

Marsh, A. A., Rhoads, S. A., & Ryan, R. M. (2018). A multi-semester classroom demonstration yields evidence in support of the facial feedback effect. *Emotion*. https://doi-org.proxy.lib.umich.edu/10.1037/emo0000532.supp (Supplemental)

Marshall, G. D., & Zimbardo, P. G. (1979). Affective consequences of inadequately explained arousal. *Journal of Personality and Social Psychology, 37*, 970–988.

Martichuski, D. K., & Bell, P. A. (1991). Reward, punishment, privatization, and moral suasion in a commons dilemma. *Journal of Applied Social Psychology, 21*, 1356–1369.

Martin, E. A., & Kerns, J. G. (2011). The influence of positive mood on different aspects of cognitive control. *Cognition and Emotion, 25*(2), 265–279.

Martindale, D. A. (1971). Territorial dominance behavior in dyadic verbal interactions. *Proceedings of the Annual Convention of the American Psychological Association, 6*, 305–306.

Martins, A.; Ramalho, N.; Morin, E. (2010). A comprehensive meta-analysis of the relationship between emotional intelligence and health. *Personality and Individual Differences, 49*, 554–564.

Martins, N., Weaver, A. J., Yeshua-Katz, D., Lewis, N. H., Tyree, N. E., & Jensen, J. D. (2013). A content analysis of print news coverage of media violence and aggression research. *Journal of Communication, 63*, 1070–1087. doi:10.1111/jcom.12052

Maruyama, G., Rubin, R. A., & Kingsbury, G. G. (1981). Self-esteem and educational achievement: Independent constructs with a common cause? *Journal of Personality and Social Psychology, 40*, 962–975.

Masicampo, E. J., & Baumeister, R. F. (2011). Consider it done! Plan making can eliminate the cognitive effects of unfulfilled goals. *Journal of Personality and Social Psychology.* Online publication doi: 10.1037/a0024192

Maslach, C. (1979). Negative and emotional biasing of unexplained arousal. *Journal of Personality and Social Psychology, 37*, 953–969.

Maslow, A. H. (1968). *Toward a psychology of being*. New York: Van Nostrand.

Masuda, T., & Kitayama, S. (2004). Perceiver-induced constraint and attitude attribution in Japan and the US: A case for the cultural dependence of the correspondence bias. *Journal of Experimental Social Psychology, 10*(3), 409–416.

Mata, A., Ferreira, M. B., & Sherman, S.J. (2013). The metacognitive advantage of deliberative thinkers: A dual-process perspective on overconfidence. *Journal of Personality and Social Psychology, 105*, 353–373.

Matarazzo, J. D. (1982). "Behavioral health" challenge to academic, scientific and professional psychology. *American Psychologist, 37*(1), 1–14.

Mathieu, J. E., Hollenbeck, J. R., van Knippenberg, D., & Ilgen, D. R. (2017). A century of work teams in the *Journal of Applied Psychology, 102*(3), 452–467.

Maticka-Tyndale, E., Herold, E. S., & Mewhinney, D. (1998). Casual sex on spring break: Intentions and behaviors of Canadian students. *The Journal of Sex Research, 35*, 254–264.

Matthew 27:24.

Matthew 6:12.

Matthews, K. E., & Canon, L. K. (1975). Environmental noise level as a determinant of helping behavior. *Journal of Personality and Social Psychology, 32*, 571–577.

Matud, M. P. (2005). The psychological impact of domestic violence on Spanish women. *Journal of Applied Social Psychology, 35*(11), 2310–2322.

Maxwel, J. A., & McNulty, J. K. (2019). No longer in a 'dry spell': The developing understanding of how sex influences romantic relationships. *Current Directions in Psychological Science, 28*, 102–107.

Mayer, J. D. (1993). The emotional madness of the dangerous leader. *Journal of Psychohistory, 20*, 331–348.

Mayer, J. D., & Salovey, P. (1997). What is emotional intelligence? In P. Salovey & D. Sluyter (Eds.), *Emotional development and emotional intelligence: Implications for educators* (pp. 3–31). New York: Basic Books.

Mazar, N., Amir, O., & Ariely, D. (2008). The dishonesty of honest people: A theory of self-concept maintenance. *Journal of Marketing Research, 45*, 633–644.

Mazur, A., Susman, E. J., & Edelbrock, S. (1997). Sex differences in testosterone response to a video game contest. *Evolution and Human Behavior, 18*, 317–326.

Mazziotta, A., Mummendey, A., & Wright, S. C. (2011). Vicarious intergroup contact effects: Applying social-cognitive theory to intergroup contact research. *Group Processes & Intergroup Relations, 14*(2), 255–274.

McAbee, S. T., Grubbs, J. B., & Zickar, M. J. (2018). Open science is robust science. *Industrial and Organizational Psychology: Perspectives on Science and Practice, 11*(1), 54–61. doi:10.1017/iop.2017.85

McAuliff, B. D., & Kovera, M. B. (2007). Estimating the effects of misleading information on witness accuracy: Can experts tell jurors something they don't already know? *Applied Cognitive Psychology, 21*, 849–870.

McCabe, P. (1987). Desired and experienced levels of premarital affection and sexual intercourse during dating. *Journal of Sex Research, 23*, 23–33.

McCaul, K. D., Gladue, B. A., & Joppa, M. (1992). Winning, losing, mood, and testosterone. *Hormones and Behavior, 26*, 486–504.

McCausland, P. (2018, February 9). #MeToo advocate and California lawmaker accused of sexual misconduct. *NBC News.* Retrieved from https://www.nbcnews.com/storyline/sexual-misconduct/metoo-advocate-california-lawmaker-accused-sexual-misconduct-n846421

McCright, A. M., Charters, M., Dentzman, K., & Dietz, T. (2016). Examining the effectiveness of climate change frames in the face of a climate change denial counter-frame. *Topics in Cognitive Science, 8*, 76–97. http://dx.doi.org/10.1111/tops.12171

McCullough, M. E. (2008). *Beyond revenge: The evolution of the forgiveness instinct*. San Francisco: Jossey-Bass.

McCullough, M. E., Bono, G., & Root, L. M. (2007). Rumination, emotion, and forgiveness: Three longitudinal studies. *Journal of Personality and Social Psychology, 92*, 490–505.

McCullough, M. E., Emmons, R. A., & Tsang, J. (2002). The grateful disposition: A conceptual and empirical topography. *Journal of Personality and Social Psychology, 82*, 112–127.

McCullough, M. E., Kimeldorf, M. B., & Cohen, A. D. (2008). An adaptation for altruism? The social causes, social effects, and social evolution of gratitude. *Current Directions in Psychological Science, 17*(4), 281–285.

McCullough, M. E., Pargament, K. I., & Thoresen, C. E. (Eds.) (2000). *Forgiveness: Theory, research, and practice*. New York: Guilford.

McCullough, M. E., Rachal, K. C., Sandage, S. J., Worthington, E. L., Brown, S. W., & Hight, T. L. (1998). Interpersonal forgiving in close relationships: II. Theoretical elaboration and measurement. *Journal of Personality and Social Psychology, 75*, 1586–1603.

McDaniel, M. A., Whetzel, D. L., Schmidt, F. L., & Maurer, S. D. (1994). The validity of employment interviews: A comprehensive review and meta-analysis. *Journal of Applied Psychology, 79*, 599–616.

McDougall, William (1960. Original work published 1908), *An Introduction to Social Psychology* (23rd ed.), University Paperbacks. Imprint of Methuen & Co (London) and Barnes & Noble (New York), pp. xxi–xxii (Note: Preface to 23rd edition commences p. xxi, with date of this preface [October 1936] on p. xxii.)

McFarlin, D. B. (1985). Persistence in the face of failure: The impact of self-esteem and contingency information. *Personality and Social Psychology Bulletin, 11*, 153–163.

McFarlin, D. B., & Blascovich, J. (1981). Effects of self-esteem and performance on future affective preferences and cognitive expectations. *Journal of Personality and Social Psychology, 40*, 521–531.

McFarlin, D. B., Baumeister, R. F., & Blascovich, J. (1984). On knowing when to quit: Task failure, self-esteem, advice, and nonproductive persistence. *Journal of Personality, 52*, 138–155.

McGee, R., & Williams, S. (2000). Does low self-esteem predict health compromising behaviours among adolescents? *Journal of Adolescence, 23*, 569–582.

McGrath, J. E. (1966). *Small group research*. New York: Holt, Rinehart, & Winston.

McGuire, W. J. (1961). The effectiveness of supportive refutational defenses in immunizing and restoring beliefs against persuasion. *Sociometry, 24*, 184–197.

McGuire, W. J. (1964). Inducing resistance to persuasion: Some contemporary approaches. *Advances in Experimental Social Psychology, 1*, 191–229.

McGuire, W. J. (1968). Personality and susceptibility to social influence. In E. F. Borgotta & W. W. Lambert (Eds.), *Handbook of personality theory and research* (pp. 1130–1187). Chicago: Rand McNally.

McGuire, W. J., & Papageorgis, D. (1961). The relative efficacy of various types of prior belief-defense in producing immunity against persuasion. *Journal of Abnormal Social Psychology, 62*, 327–337.

McGuire, W. J., McGuire, C. V., Child, P., & Fujioka, T. (1978). Salience of ethnicity in the spontaneous self-concept as a function of one's ethnic distinctiveness in the social environment. *Journal of Personality and Social Psychology, 36*, 511–520.

McGuire, W. J., McGuire, C. V., Child, P., & Winton, W. (1979). Effects of household gender composition on the salience of one's gender in the spontaneous self-concept. *Journal of Experimental Social Psychology, 15*, 77–90.

McKenna, K. Y. A., & Bargh, J. A. (1998). Coming out in the age of the Internet: Identity "demarginalization" through virtual group participation. *Journal of Personality and Social Psychology, 75*, 681–694.

McKenna, K. Y. A., & Bargh, J. A. (1999). Causes and consequences of social interaction on the Internet: A conceptual framework. *Media Psychology, 1*, 249–269.

McKenna, K. Y. A., & Bargh, J. A. (2000). Plan 9 from Cyberspace: The implications of the Internet for personality and social psychology. *Personality and Social Psychology Review, 4*, 57–75.

McKillip, J., & Reidel, S. L. (1983). External validity of matching on physical attractiveness for same and opposite sex couples. *Journal of Applied Social Psychology, 13*, 328–337.

McKinney, L. N. (2004). Internet shopping orientation segments: An exploration of differences in consumer behavior. *Family and Consumer Sciences Research Journal, 32*, 408–433.

McLeod, E. (1982). *Women working: Prostitution today*. London: Croom Helm.

McLeod, J. M., & Pan, Z. (2005). Concept explication and theory construction. In S. Dunwoody, L. B. Becker, D. M. McLeod, & G. M. Kosicki (Eds.), *The evolution of key mass communication concepts* (pp. 13–76). Creskill, NJ: Hampton Press.

McMains, S. & Kastner, S. (2011). Interactions of top-down and bottom-up mechanisms in human visual cortex. *Journal of Neuroscience, 31*(2), 587–597.

McManus, M. A., & Baratta, J. E. (1992). *The relationship of recruiting source to performance and survival*. Paper presented at the annual meeting of the Society for Industrial and Organizational Psychology, Montreal, Canada.

McMillen, D. L., & Austin, J. B. (1971). Effect of positive feedback on compliance following transgression. *Psychonomic Science, 24*, 59–61.

McMullen, M. N., Markman, K. D., & Gavanski, I. (1995). Living in neither the best nor the worst of all possible worlds: Antecedents and consequences of upward and downward counterfactual thinking. In N. J. Roese & J. M. Olson (Eds.), *What might have been: The social psychology of counterfactual thinking* (pp. 133–167). Mahwah, NJ: Erlbaum.

McNeill, W. H. (1982). *The pursuit of power: Technology, armed force, and society since A.D. 1000*. Chicago: University of Chicago Press.

McNulty, J. K. (2011). The dark side of forgiveness: The tendency to forgive predicts continued psychological and physical aggression in marriage. *Personality and Social Psychology Bulletin, 37*(6), 770–783.

McNulty, J. K., Olson, M. A., Meltzer, A. L., & Shaffer, M. J. (2014). Though they may be unaware, newlyweds implicitly know whether their marriage will be satisfying. *Science, 342*, 1149–1120.

McNulty, J., Maxwell, J., Meltzer, A., & Baumeister, R. F. (in press). The honeymoon is over: Sex-differentiated changes in sexual desire predict marital dissatisfaction. *Archives of Sexual Behaviour*.

Mead, G. H. (1934). *Mind, self and society*. Chicago: University of Chicago Press.

Mead, M. (1928). *Coming of age in Samoa: A psychological study of primitive youth for Western civilization*. New York: Morrow.

Mead, N. L., & Maner, J. K. (2012) On keeping your enemies close: Powerful leaders seek proximity to in-group power threats. *Journal of Personality and Social Psychology, 102*, 576–591.

Medvec, V. H., Madey, S. F., & Gilovich, T. (1995). When less is more: Counterfactual thinking and satisfaction among Olympic medalists. *Journal of Personality and Social Psychology, 69*, 603–610.

Meissner, C. A., & Brigham, J. C. (2001). Thirty years of investigating the own-race bias in memory for faces: A meta-analytic review. *Psychology, Public Policy, and Law, 7*, 3–35.

Mejia, R., Pérez, A., Peña, L., Kollath-Cattano, C., Morello, P., Braun, S., et al. (2017). Smoking in movies and adolescent smoking initiation: A longitudinal study among argentinean adolescents. *The Journal of Pediatrics, 180*, 222–228. doi:http://dx.doi.org/10.1016/j.jpeds.2016.10.001.

Mekawi, Y., & Bresin, K. (2015). Is the evidence from racial bias shooting task studies a smoking gun? Results from a meta-analysis. *Journal of Experimental Social Psychology, 61*, 120–130. DOI: 10.1016/j.jesp.2015.08.002

Mellers, B. A., Schwartz, A., Ho, K., & Ritov, I. (1997). Elation and disappointment: Emotional responses to risky options. *Psychological Science, 8*, 423–429.

Mello, J. A. (1993). Improving individual member accountability in small group settings. *Journal of Management Education, 17*(2), 253–259.

Melter, A. L., Makhanova, A., Hicks, L. L., French, J. E., McNulty, J. K., & Bradbury, T. N. (2017). Quantifying the sexual afterglow: The lingering benefits of sex and their implications for pair-bonded relationships. *Psychological Science, 28*, 587–598.

Meltzer, A. L., & McNulty, J. K. (2013). "Tell me I'm sexy . . . and otherwise valuable": Body evaluation and relationship satisfaction. *Personal Relationships, 21*, 68–87.

Meltzer, A. L., McNulty, J. K., Jackson, G. L., & Karney, B. R. (2014). Sex differences in the implications of partner physical attractiveness in the trajectory of marital satisfaction. *Journal of Personality and Social Psychology, 106*, 418–428.

Meltzer, A.L., McNulty, J.K., & Maner, J.K. (2017). Women like being valued for sex by their partner and engaging in frequent sex, as long as their partner is committed to a long-term relationship. *Archives of Sexual Behavior, 46*(2), 475–488. doi: 10.1007/s10508-015-0622-1

Mercier, H., & Sperber, D. (2011). Why do humans reason? Arguments for an argumentative theory. *Behavioral and Brain Sciences, 34*(2), 57–74.

Merton, R. K. (1948). The self-fulfilling prophecy. *Antioch Review*, pp. 193–210.

Messick, D. M., Bloom, S., Boldizar, J. P., & Samuelson, C. D. (1985). Why we are fairer than others. *Journal of Experimental Social Psychology, 21*, 480–500.

Meyer, C. B., & Taylor, S. E. (1986). Adjustment to rape. *Journal of Personality and Social Psychology, 50*, 1226–1234.

Meyer, D. E., & Schvaneveldt, R. W. (1971). Facilitation in recognizing pairs of words: Evidence of a dependence between retrieval operations. *Journal of Experimental Psychology, 90*, 227–234.

Meyer, J. P. & Herscovitch, L. (2001). Commitment in the workplace: Toward a general model. *Human Resource Management Review, 11*, 299–326.

Meyer, J. P., & Allen, N. J. (1991). A three-component conceptualization of organizational commitment. *Human Resource Management Review, 1*, 61–89.

Meyer, J. P., Allen, N. J., & Smith, C. A. (1993). Commitments to organizations and occupations: Extension and test of a three component conceptualization. *Journal of Applied Psychology, 78*, 538–551.

Michaud, S. G., & Aynesworth, H. (2000). *Ted Bundy: Conversations with a killer*. Irving, TX: Authorlink.

Michie, S., Marques, M. M., Norris, E., & Johnson, M. (2019). Theories and interventions in health behavior change. In T. A. Revenson & R. A. R. Gurung (Eds.), *Handbook of health psychology* (pp. 69–88). New York, NY: Routledge.

Mick, D. G., & DeMoss, M. (1990). Self-gifts: Phenomenological insights from four contexts. *Journal of Consumer Research, 17*, 322–332.

Midden, C., Kaiser, F., & McCalley, T. (2007). Technology's four roles in understanding individuals' conservation of natural resources. *Journal of Social Issues, 63*, 155–174.

Mikula, G., Petri, B., & Tanzer, N. (1989). What people regard as unjust: Types, structures and everyday experiences of injustice. *European Journal of Social Psychology, 20*, 133–149.

Milgram, S. (1963). Behavioral study of obedience. *Journal of Abnormal and Social Psychology, 67*, 371–378.

Milgram, S. (1973, December). The perils of obedience. *Harper's*, 62–66.

Milgram, S. (1974). *Obedience to authority; An experimental view*. New York: Harper and Row.

Milgram, S. (1977). *The individual in a social world*. New York: McGraw-Hill.

Miller, A. G., McHoskey, J. W., Bane, C. M., & Dowd, T. G. (1993). The attitude polarization phenomenon: Role of response measure, attitude extremity, and behavioral consequences of reported attitude change. *Journal of Personality and Social Psychology, 64*, 561–574.

Miller, C. T., & Downey, K. T. (1999). A meta-analysis of heavyweight and self-esteem. *Personality and Social Psychology Review, 3*, 68–84.

Miller, D. P., Spangler, J. G., Vitolins, M. Z., Davis, S. W., Ip, E. H., Marion, G. S., & Crandall, S. J. (2013). Are medical students aware of their anti-obesity bias? *Academic Medicine, 88*(7), 978–982. doi: 10.1097/ACM.0b013e318294f817

Miller, D. T., & Holmes, J. G. (1975). The role of situational restrictiveness on self-fulfilling prophecies: A theoretical and empirical extension of Kelley and Stahelski's triangle hypothesis. *Journal of Personality & Social Psychology, 31*, 661–673.

Miller, G. T. (1990). *Living in the environment* (6th ed.). Belmont, CA: Wadsworth.

Miller, J. E., & Rempel, J. K. (2004) Trust and partner-enhancing attributions in close relationships. *Personality and Social Psychology Bulletin, 30*, 695–705.

Miller, J., Butts, C. T., & Rodes, D. (2002). Communication and cooperation. *Journal of Economic Behavior and Organization, 47*, 179–195.

Miller, L. C., & Fishkin, S. A. (1997). On the dynamics of human bonding and reproductive success: Seeking windows on the adapted-for-human environmental interface. In J. Simpson & D. Kenrick (Eds.), *Evolutionary social psychology* (pp. 197–235). Mahwah, NJ: Erlbaum.

Miller, N. E. (1941). The frustration-aggression hypothesis. *Psychological Review, 48*, 337–342.

Miller, N., Maruyama, G., Beaber, R. J., & Valone, K. (1976). Speed of speech and persuasion. *Journal of Personality and Social Psychology, 34*, 615–624.

Miller, P. V. (2002). The authority and limitation of polls. In J. Manza, F. L. Cook, & B. I. Page (Eds.), *Navigating public opinion* (pp. 221–231). New York: Oxford University Press.

Miller, R. L. (1979). Middle class residents in ghetto housing: Attitudes & behavior. *Proceedings of the International Conference on Environmental Psychology, Guildford, England*, 75.

Miller, R. L. (2013). Territoriality. In K. Keith (Ed.), *Encyclopedia of cross-cultural psychology* (pp. 1276–1278). New York, NY: Wiley-Blackwell.

Miller, R. L., Seligman, C., Clark, N. T., & Bush, M. (1976). Perceptual contrast versus reciprocal concession as mediators of induced compliance. *Journal of Behavioral Science, 7*, 401–409.

Miller, R. S. (1997). Inattentive and contented: Relationship commitment and attention to alternatives. *Journal of Personality and Social Psychology, 73*, 758–766.

Miller, S. M., & Diefenbach, M. A. (1998). The Cognitive-Social Health Information-Processing (C-SHIP) model: A theoretical framework for research in behavioral oncology. In D. S. Krantz, & A. Baum (Eds.), *Technology and methods in behavioral medicine* (pp. 219–244). Mahwah, NJ: Lawrence Erlbaum.

Miller, T. Q., Smith, T. W., Turner, C. W., Guijarro, M. L., & Hallet, A. J. (1996). A meta-analytic review of research on hostility and physical health. *Psychological Bulletin, 119*, 322–348.

Millhausen, R. R., & Herold, E. S. (1999). Does the sexual double standard still exist? Perceptions of university women. *Journal of Sex Research, 36*, 361–368.

Milliman, R. E. (1982). Using background music to affect the behavior of supermarket shoppers. *Journal of Marketing, 46*, 86–91.

Mills, H., Reiss, N., & Dombeck, M. (2008, Jun 30). Types of stressors (eustress vs. distress). Retrieved from http://www.mentalhelp.net/poc/view_doc.php?type=doc&id=15644

Mischel, W. (1973). Toward a cognitive social learning reconceptualization of personality. *Psychological Review, 80*, 252–283.

Mischel, W. (1974). Processes in delay of gratification. In L. Berkowitz (Ed.), *Advances in experimental social psychology* (Vol. 7, pp. 249–292). San Diego: Academic Press.

Mischel, W. (1996). From good intentions to willpower. In P. Gollwitzer & J. Bargh (Eds.), *The psychology of action* (pp. 197–218). New York: Guilford Press.

Mischel, W., & Mendoza-Denton, R. (2002). Harnessing willpower and socio-emotional intelligence to enhance human agency and potential. In L. G. Aspinwall & U. M. Staudinger (Eds.), *A psychology of human strengths: Fundamental questions and future directions for a positive psychology* (pp. 245–256). Washington, DC: American Psychological Association.

Mischel, W., & Shoda, Y. (1995). A cognitive-affective system theory of personality: Reconceptualizing situations, dispositions, dynamics, and invariance in personality structure. *Psychological Review, 102*, 246–268.

Mischel, W., Ebbesen, E. B., & Zeiss, A. R. (1976). Determinants of selective memory about the self. *Journal of Consulting and Clinical Psychology, 44*, 92–103.

Mischel, W., Shoda, Y., & Peake, P. K. (1988). The nature of adolescent competencies predicted by preschool delay of gratification. *Journal of Personality and Social Psychology, 54*, 687–696.

Mischkowski, D., Kross, E., & Bushman, B. J. (2012). Flies on the wall are less aggressive: Self-distanced reflection reduces angry feelings, aggressive thoughts, and aggressive behaviors. *Journal of Experimental Social Psychology, 48*(5), 1187–1191. doi: 10.1016/j.jesp.2012.03.012

Misra, S, & Kalro, A. (1979). Triangle effect and the connotative meaning of trust in prisoner's dilemma: A cross cultural study. International *Journal of Psychology, 14*, 255–263.

Missouri Historical Society. The *1904 World's Fair: Looking back at looking forward*. Retrieved from http://mohistory.org/Fair/WF/HTML/Overview/page3.html

Mita, T. H., Dermer, M., & Knight, J. (1977). Reversed facial images and the mere-exposure hypothesis. *Journal of Personality and Social Psychology, 35*, 597–601.

Mitchell, D. J., Kahn, B. E., & Knasko, S. C. (1995). There's something in the air: Effects of congruent or incongruent ambient odor on consumer decision making. *Journal of Consumer Research, 22*, 229–238.

Miyamoto, Y., & Kitayama, S. (2002). Cultural variation in correspondence bias: The critical role of attitude diagnosticity of socially constrained behavior. *Journal of Personality and Social Psychology, 83*(5), 1239–1248.

Mocayar Marón, F. J., Ferder, L., Saraví, F. D., & Manucha, W. (2018). Hypertension linked to allostatic load: From psychosocial stress to inflammation and mitochondrial dysfunction. *Stress: The International Journal on the Biology of Stress*, doi:http://dx.doi.org/10.1080/10253890.2018.1542683

Mochon, D. (2008, November). *Single option aversion: When the illusion of choices reduces deferral*. Paper presented at the annual meeting of the Society for Judgment and Decision Making, Chicago.

Moffett, M.W. (2019). *The human swarm: How our societies arise, thrive, and fall.* New York: Basic Books.

Moffitt, T., Brammer, G., Caspi, A., Fawcett, J., Raleigh, M., Yuwiler, A., & Silva, P. (1998). Whole blood serotonin relates to violence in an epidemiological study. *Biological Psychiatry, 43,* 446–457.

Molina, B. (2019, January 17). People choosing not to vaccinate is now a global health threat, says WHO. *USA Today.* Retrieved from https://amp.usatoday.com/amp/2601140002?fbclid=IwAR3TFBddtV6AYzlNS4ldYllfE-2NO1R2LIpnegPVeZMnz8XjceRUr2UhUXE

Monroe, A. E. & Malle, B. F. (2010). From uncaused will to conscious choice: The need to study, not speculate about people's folk concept of free will. *Review of Philosophy and Psychology, 9,* 211–224.

Moore, M. T., & Fresco, D. M. (2012). Depressive realism: A meta-analytic review. *Clinical Psychology Review, 32,* 496–509.

Moors, A., Ellsworth, P. C., Scherer, K. R., & Frijda, N. H. (2013). Appraisal theories of emotion: State of the art and future development. *Emotion Review, 5*(2), 119–124. doi:10.1177/1754073912468165

Moos, R. H., & Schaefer, J. A. (1993). Coping resources and processes: Current concepts and measures. In L. Goldberger & S. Breznitz (Eds.), *Handbook of stress: Theoretical and clinical aspects* (2nd ed., pp. 234–257). New York: Free Press.

Moran, G., & Comfort, J. C. (1986). Neither "tentative nor fragmentary": Verdict preference of impaneled felony jurors as a function of attitude toward capital punishment. *Journal of Applied Psychology, 71,* 146–155.

Moran, G., Cutler, B. L., & De Lisa, A. (1994). Attitudes toward tort reform, scientific jury selection, and juror bias: Verdict inclination in criminal and civil trials. *Law and Psychology Review, 18,* 309–328.

Moran, G., Cutler, B. L., & Loftus, E. F. (1990). Jury selection in major controlled substance trials: The need for extended voir dire. *Forensic Reports, 3,* 331–348.

Moreland, R. L., Argote, L., & Krishnan, R. (1998). Training people to work in groups. In R. Tindale, L. Heath, J. Edwards, E. Posavac, F. Bryant, Y. Suarez-Balcazar, et al. (Eds.), *Theory and research on small groups* (pp. 37–60). New York: Plenum Press.

Morf, C. C., & Rhodewalt, F. (2001). Unraveling the paradoxes of narcissism: A dynamic self-regulatory processing model. *Psychological Inquiry, 12,* 177–196.

Morgan, C. A., III, Hazlett, G., Doran, A., Garrett, S., Hoyt, G., Thomas, P., Baranoski, M., & Southwick, S. M. (2004). Accuracy of eyewitness memory for persons encountered during exposure to highly intense stress. *International Journal of Law and Psychiatry, 27,* 265–279.

Morgenthau, H. (1962). Love and power. *Commentary, 33,* 247–251.

Mori, D., Chaiken, S., & Pliner, P. (1987). "Eating lightly" and the self-presentation of femininity. *Journal of Personality and Social Psychology, 53,* 693–702.

Morokoff, P. J. (1985). Effects of sex guilt, repression, sexual "arousability," and sexual experience on female sexual arousal during erotica and fantasy. *Journal of Personality and Social Psychology, 49,* 177–187.

Morokoff, P. J. (1986). Volunteer bias in the psychophysiological study of female sexuality. *Journal of Sex Research, 22,* 35–51.

Morrin, M., & Ratnewshwar, S. (2003). Does it make sense to use scents to enhance brand memory? *Journal of Marketing Research, 40,* 10–25.

Morris, K. A., & Swann, W. B., Jr. (1996). Denial and the AIDS crisis: Wishing away the threat of aids. In S. Oskamp & S. Thompson (Eds.), *Safer sex in the '90s* (pp. 57–79). New York: Sage.

Morris, W. N., & Reilly, N. P. (1987). Toward the self-regulation of mood: Theory and research. *Motivation and Emotion, 11,* 215–249.

Morrison, T. G., Kiss, M. J., Bishop, C., & Morrison, M. A. (2018). "We're disgusted with queers, not fearful of them": The interrelationships among disgust, gay men's sexual behavior, and homonegativity. *Journal of Homosexuality,* doi:10.1080/00918369.2018.1490576

Moscovici, S., & Zavalloni, M. (1969). The group as a polarizer of attitudes. *Journal of Personality and Social Psychology, 12,* 125–135.

Mote, P. M., Neuschatz, J. S., Bornstein, B. H., Wetmore, S. A., & Key, K. N. (2018). Secondary confessions as post-identification feedback: How jailhouse informant testimony can alter eyewitnesses' identification decisions. *Journal of Police and Criminal Psychology.* Online publication in advance of print.

Mueller, C. W., Boyer, E. M., Price, J. L. & Iverson, R. D. (1994). Employee attachment and non-coercive conditions of work: The case of dental hygienists. *Work and Occupations, 21,* 179–212.

Mull, A. (2019). Workers love AirPods because employers stole their wall. *The Atlantic.* Retrieved from https://www.theatlantic.com/health/archive/2019/04/airpods-open-plan-offices/588112/?utm_source=pocket-newtab

Mullan, B., & Marvin, G. (1998). *Zoo culture: The book about watching people watch animals* (2nd ed.). Urbana, IL: University of Illinois Press.

Mullen, B., Anthony, T., Salas, E., & Driskell, J. E. (1994). Group cohesiveness and quality of decision making: An integration of the groupthink hypothesis. *Small Group Research, 25*(2), 189–204.

Mullen, B., Johnson, C., & Salas, E. (1991). Productivity loss in brainstorming groups: A meta-analysis. *Basic and Applied Social Psychology, 12,* 3–23.

Muller, D., Bushman, B. J., Subra, B., & Ceaux, E. (2012). Are people more aggressive when they are worse off or better off than others? *Social Psychological and Personality Science, 3*(6), 754–759. DOI: 10.1177/1948550612436984

Mulligan, R., Burmood, C., O'Hara, S., & Warren, C. (2004). Personal space preferences: The role of mortality salience and affiliation motivation. *Journal of Psychological Inquiry, 9*(1), 14–20.

Mullin, C. R., & Linz, D. (1995). Desensitization and resensitization to violence against women: Effects of exposure to sexually violent films on judgments of domestic violence victims. *Journal of Personality and Social Psychology, 69,* 449–459.

Munger, K., & Harris, S. J. (1989). Effects of an observer on handwashing in a public restroom. *Perceptual and Motor Skills, 69,* 733–734.

Murch, S. H., Anthony, A., Casson, D. H., Malik, M., Berelowitz, M., Dhillon, A. P., et al. (2004). Retraction of an interpretation. *Lancet, 363* (9411), 750. doi:10.1016/S0140-6736(04)15715-2

Murnen, S. K., Perot, A., & Byrne, D. (1989). Coping with unwanted sexual activity: Normative responses, situational determinants, and individual differences. *Journal of Sex Research, 26,* 85–106.

Murphy, J. (2019). Get more done & stress less with these simple office organization ideas. Retrieved https://www.snacknation.com/blog/office-organization-ideas.

Murphy, S. L., Xu, J. Q., Kochanek, K. D., Arias, E. (2018). *Mortality in the United States, 2017.* NCHS Data Brief, no 328. Hyattsville, MD: National Center for Health Statistics.

Murphy-Berman, V., & Berman, J. (1978). Importance of choice and sex invasions of personal space. *Personality and Social Psychology Bulletin, 4,* 424–428.

Murray, D. R., Trudeau, R., & Schaller, M. (2011). On the origins of cultural differences in conformity: Four tests of the pathogen prevalence hypothesis. *Personality and Social Psychology Bulletin, 37,* 318–329.

Murray, S. L., Holmes, J. G., & Collins, N. L. (2006). Optimizing assurance: The risk regulation system in relationships. *Psychological Bulletin, 132,* 641–666.

Murray, S., & Holmes, J. G. (1993). See virtues in faults: Negativity and the transformation of interpersonal narratives in close relationships. *Journal of Personality and Social Psychology, 65,* 707–722.

Murray, S., & Holmes, J. G. (1994). Story-telling in close relationships: The construction of confidence. *Personality and Social Psychology Bulletin, 20,* 663–676.

Murray, S., Bellavia, G., Rose, P., & Griffin, D. (2003). Once hurt, twice hurtful: How perceived regard regulates daily marital interactions. *Journal of Personality and Social Psychology, 84,* 126–147.

Murray, S., Holmes, J. G., & Griffin, D. W. (1996). The benefits of positive illusions: Idealization and the construction of satisfaction in close relationships. *Journal of Personality and Social Psychology, 70,* 79–98.

Murray, S., Rose, P., Bellavia, G., Holmes, J., & Kusche, A. (2002). When rejection stings: How self-esteem constrains relationship enhancement processes. *Journal of Personality and Social Psychology, 83,* 556–573.

Murstein, B. I., & Christy, P. (1976). Physical attractiveness and marriage adjustment in middle-aged couples. *Journal of Personality and Social Psychology, 34,* 537–542.

Musch, J., & Grondin, S. (2001). Unequal competition as an impediment to personal development: A review of the relative age effect in sport. *Developmental Review, 21,* 147–167.

Musolff, A. (2007). What role do metaphors play in racial prejudice? The function of antisemitic imagery in Hitler's Mein Kampf. *Patterns of Prejudice, 41*(1), 21–43. DOI: 10.1080/00313220601118744

Mussweiler, T., & Ockenfels, A. (2013). Similarity increases altruistic punishment in humans. *PNAS,* early edition, http://www.pnas.org/cgi/doi/10.1073/pnas.1215443110.

Myers, D. G. (1992). The secrets of happiness. *Psychology Today, 25,* 38–46.

Myers, D. G. (1993, July/August). Pursuing happiness. *Psychology Today,* pp. 32–35, 66–67.

Myers, D. G. (2006). *Social psychology* (8th ed.). New York: McGraw Hill.

Nadler, R. T., Rabi, R., & Minda, J. P. (2010). Better mood and better performance: Learning rule-described categories is enhanced by positive mood. *Psychological Science, 21*(12), 1770–1776.

Nagler, U. K. J., Reiter, K. J., Furtner, M. R., & Rauthmann, J. F. (2014). Is there a "dark intelligence"? Emotional intelligence is used by dark personalities to emotionally manipulate others. *Personality and Individual Differences, 65*(7), 47–52. doi: 10.1016/j.paid.2014.01.025

Najmi, S., & Wegner, D. M. (2008). Thought suppression and psychopathology. In A. J. Elliot (Ed.), *Handbook of approach and avoidance motivation* (pp. 447–459). New York: Psychology Press.

Narby, D. J., Cutler, B. L., & Moran, G. (1993). A meta-analysis of the association between authoritarianism and jurors' perceptions of defendant culpability. *Journal of Applied Psychology, 78,* 3442.

National Archives. (2012). Teaching with documents: The Civil Rights Act of 1964 and the Equal Employment Opportunity Commission. Retrieved from http://www.archives.gov/education/lessons/civil-rights-act/

Nauroth, P., Gollwitzer, M., Bender, J., & Rothmund, T. (2014). Gamers against science: The case of the violent video games debate. *European Journal of Social Psychology, 44,* 104–116. doi:10.1002/ejsp.1998

Naylor, B. (2018, September 14). Sharks in the water? FEMA tries to fight "fake news" as Florence hits. *NPR.* Retrieved from https://www.npr.org/2018/09/14/647935099/sharks-in-the-water-fema-tries-to-fight-fake-news-as-florence-hits

Naylor, J. C., Pritchard, R. D., & Ilgen, D. R. (1980). *A theory of behavior in organizations.* New York: Academic Press.

Nazi-saluting teens provoke outrage in California after photos flood internet. (2019, March 4). *NPR.* Retrieved from https://www.npr.org/2019/03/04/700168758/nazi-saluting-teens-provoke-outrage-in-california-after-photos-flood-internet

Neal, D., & Chartrand, T. L. (2011). Embodied emotion perception: Amplifying and dampening facial feedback modulates emotion perception accuracy. *Social Psychological and Personality Science, 2,* 673–678.

Neal, D. T., & Wood, W. (2007). Automaticity in situ: Direct context cuing of habits in daily life. In J. Bargh, P. Gollwitzer, & E. Morsella (Eds.), *Psychology of action (Vol. 2): Mechanisms of human action.* London: Oxford University Press.

Neal, D. T., Wood, W., & Drolet, A. (2013). How do people adhere to goals when willpower is low? The profits (and pitfalls) of strong habits. *Journal of Personality and Social Psychology, 104,* 959–975.

Neely, J. H. (1991). Semantic priming effects in visual word recognition: A selective review of current findings and theories. In D. Besner & G. Humphreys (Eds.), *Basic processes in reading: Visual word recognition* (pp. 264–336). Hillsdale, NJ: Erlbaum.

Neil v. Biggers, 409 U. S. 188 (1972).

Nelissen, R.M.A. (2014). Relational utility as a moderator of guilt in social interactions. *Journal of Personality and Social Psychology, 106,* 257–271.

Nelson, L. D., & Morrison, E. L. (2005). The symptoms of resource scarcity: Judgments of food and finances impact preferences for potential partners. *Psychological Science, 16*(2), 167–173.

Nelson, M. R. (2002). Recall of brand placements in computer/video games. *Journal of Advertising Research, 42,* 80–92.

Neuschatz, J. S., Lawson, D. S., Fairless, A. H., Powers, R. A., Neuschatz, J. S., Goodsell, C. A., & Toglia, M. P. (2007). The mitigating effects of suspicion on post-identification feedback and on retrospective eyewitness memory. *Law and Human Behavior, 31,* 231–247.

New studies show strong link between diet and behavior. (1998). *Crime Times, 4*(1). Retrieved August 25, 2019 from http://www.autismwebsite.com/crimetimes/98a/w98ap2.htm

Newcombe, D., & Arnkoff, D. B. (1979). Effects of speech style and sex of speaker on person perception. *Journal of Personality and Social Psychology, 37,* 1293–1303.

Newman, A. (2001, February 4). Anti-smoking campaign: Rotten teeth and dead babies. *New York Times Magazine,* p. 16. Available at www.nytimes.com/

Newman, A. (2010, May 26). With this ring, I thee what? *New York Times.* Retrieved February 18, 2012, from http://www.nytimes.com/2010/05/27/fashion/27rings.html?adxnnl51&adxnnlx51329596054-/Hwober8MpThtkMeSSX7pA

Newman, E. J., Sanson, M., Miller, E. K., Quigley-McBride, A., Foster, J. L., Bernstein, D. M., & Garry, M. (2014). People with easier to pronounce names promote truthiness of claims. *PLoS ONE, 9*(2): e88671. doi: 10.1371/journal.pone.0088671. Retrieved August 26, 2019 from http://www.plosone.org/article/info%3Adoi%2F10.1371%2Fjournal.pone.0088671

Newman, M. L., Pennebaker, J. W., Berry, D. S., & Richards, J. M. (2003). Lying words: Predicting deception from linguistic styles. *Personality and Social Psychology Bulletin, 29*(5), 665–675.

Nguyen, H.-H. D., & Ryan, A. M. (2008). Does stereotype threat affect test performance of minorities and women? A meta-analysis of experimental evidence. *Journal of Applied Psychology, 93*(6), 1314–1334.

Nickerson, R. S. (1998). Confirmation bias: A ubiquitous phenomenon in many guises. *Review of General Psychology, 2,* 175–220.

Nickerson, R. S. (2003). *Psychology and environmental change.* Mahway, NJ: Erlbaum.

Niedenthal, P. M., Halberstadt, J. B., & Innes-Ker, A. H. (1999). Emotional response categorization. *Psychological Review, 106,* 337–361.

Nietzel, M. T., McCarthy, D. M., & Kern, M. J. (1999). Juries: The current state of the empirical literature. In R. Roesch, S. D. Hart, & J. R. P. Ogloff (Eds.), *Psychology and law: The state of the discipline* (pp. 23–52). Dordrecht, Netherlands: Kluwer Academic Publishers.

Nijman, H. L. I., & Rector, G. (1999). Crowding and aggression on inpatient psychiatric wards. *Psychiatric Services, 50*(6), 830–831.

Nisbet, E. K., & Zelenski, J. M. (2011). Underestimating nearby nature: Affective forecasting errors obscure the happy path to sustainability. *Psychological Science, 22*(9), 1101–1106.

Nisbet, E. K., Zelenski, J. M., & Murphy, S. A. (2009). The nature relatedness scale: Linking individuals' connection with nature, environmental concern, and behavior. *Environment and Behavior, 41,* 715–740.

Nisbett, R. E., & Wilson, T. D. (1977). Telling more than we can know: Verbal reports on mental processes. *Psychological Review, 84,* 231–259.

Nolen-Hoeksema, S. (1991). Responses to depression and their effects on the duration of depressive episodes. *Journal of Abnormal Psychology, 100,* 569–582.

Northouse, P. G. (2004). *Leadership: Theory and practice.* Thousand Oaks, CA: Sage Publications.

Northrup, L. (2012, October 24). I hate Progressive Insurance for waking me up over and over. *Consumerist.* Retrieved from https://consumerist.com/2012/10/24/i-hate-progressive-insurance-for-waking-me-up-over-and-over/

Norton, M. I., Frost, J. H., & Ariely, D. (2007). Less is more: The lure of ambiguity, or why familiarity breeds contempt. *Journal of Personality and Social Psychology, 92,* 97–105.

Norton, M. I., Sommers, S. R., & Brauner, S. (2007). Bias in jury selection: Justifying prohibited peremptory challenges. *Journal of Behavioral Decision Making, 20,* 467–479. doi: 10.1002/bdm.571

Nosek, B. A., Ebersole, C. R., DeHaven, A. C., & Mellor, D. T. (2018). The preregistration revolution. *PNAS Proceedings of the National Academy of Sciences of the United States of America, 115*(11), 2600-2606. doi:10.1073/pnas.1708274114

Novelli, D., Drury, J., Reicher, S., & Stott, C. (2013). Crowdedness mediates the effect of social identification on positive emotion in a crowd: A survey of two crowd events. *PLoS ONE, 8*(11), 1–7.

Nowak, M., & Roch, S. (2006). Upstream reciprocity and the evolution of gratitude. *Proceedings of the Royal Society of London, Series B: Biological Sciences, 274,* 605–609.

Nummenmaa, L., Glerean, E., Hari, R., & Hietanen, J. K. (2014). Bodily maps of emotions., *PNAS, 111*(2), 646–651, doi: 10.1073/pnas.1321664111

Nysse-Carris, K. L., Bottoms, B. L., & Salerno, J. M. (2011). Experts' and novices' abilities to detect children's high-stakes lies of omission. *Psychology, Public Policy, and Law, 17*(1), 76–98.

O*NET Resource Center. (2014). Production Database – O*NET 19.0. Retrieved from http://www.onetcenter.org/database.html

O'Boyle, E. H., Jr., Humphrey, R. H., Pollack, J. M., Hawver, T. H., & Story, P. A. (2011). The relation between emotional intelligence and job performance: A meta-analysis. *Journal of Organizational Behavior, 32*(5), 788–818.

O'Brien, E. H., Anastasio, P. A., & Bushman, B. J. (2011). Time crawls when you're not having fun: Feeling entitled makes dull tasks drag on. *Personality and Social Psychology Bulletin, 37*(10), 1287–1296.

O'Connor, D. B., Jones, F., Conner, M., McMillan, B., & Ferguson, E. (2008). Effects of daily hassles and eating style on eating behavior. *Health Psychology, 27*(1), S20–S31.

O'Connor, G. (2017, April 3). How Russian Twitter bots pumped out fake news during the 2016 election. *NPR.* Retrieved from https://www.npr.org/sections/alltechconsidered/2017/04/03/522503844/how-russian-twitter-bots-pumped-out-fake-news-during-the-2016-election

O'Kane, C. (2018, September 7). College drops uniforms featuring Nike logo to protest Kaepernick ad. *CBS News.* Retrieved from https://www.cbsnews.com/news/college-of-the-ozarks-drops-uniforms-featuring-nike-logo-to-protest-nikes-kaepernick-ad/

O'Neil, K. M., Patry, M. W., & Penrod, S. D. (2004). Exploring the effects of attitudes toward the death penalty on capital sentencing verdicts. *Psychology, Public Policy, and Law, 10,* 443–470.

O'Sullivan, L. F., & Allgeier, E. R. (1998). Feigning sexual desire: Consenting to unwanted sexual activity in heterosexual dating relationships. *Journal of Sex Research, 35,* 234–243.

O'Sullivan, L. F., Byers, E. S., & Finkelman, L. (1998). A comparison of male and female college students' experiences of sexual coercion. *Psychology of Women Quarterly, 22*(2), 177–195.

Oakes, W. (1972). External validity and the use of real people as subjects. *American Psychologist, 27,* 959–962.

Obach, M. S. (2003). A longitudinal-sequential study of perceived academic competence and motivational beliefs for learning among children in middle school. *Educational Psychology, 23,* 323–338.

Ocean's 8 (2018) product placement scenes. *Product Placement Blog.* Retrieved from https://productplacementblog.com/tag/oceans-8-2018/page/4/

Oettingen, G., & Gollwitzer, P. M. (2001). Goal setting and goal striving. In A. Tesser & N. Schwarz (Eds.), *Blackwell handbook of social psychology: Intraindividual processes* (pp. 329–348). Oxford: Blackwell.

O'Handley, B. M., Blair, K. L., & Hoskin, R. A. (2017). What do two men kissing and a bucket of maggots have in common? Heterosexual men's indistinguishable salivary α-amylase responses to photos of two men kissing and disgusting images. *Psychology & Sexuality, 8*(3), 173–188. doi:10.1080/19419899.2017.1328459

Okwumabua, J. O., & Duryea, E. J. (2003). Depressive symptoms and decision making among African American youth. *Journal of Adolescent Research, 18,* 436–453.

Olatunji, B. O. (2008). Disgust, scrupulosity and conservative attitudes about sex: Evidence for a mediational model of homophobia. *Journal of Research in Personality, 42*(5), 1364–1369.

Oliner, S. P., & Oliner, P. M. (1988). *The altruistic personality: Rescuers of Jews in Nazi Europe.* New York: The Free Press. Also see Midlarsky, E., Jones, S. F., & Corley, R. P. (2005). Personality correlates of heroic rescue during the holocaust. *Journal of Personality, 73,* 907–934.

Oliver, M. B., & Hyde, J. S. (1993). Gender differences in sexuality: A meta-analysis. *Psychological Bulletin, 114,* 29–51.

Olivola, C. Y., & de Neve, J. E. (2012). Going with your gut feelings lands you in the gutter: Decision making style in adolescence predicts financial well-being in adulthood. Manuscript submitted for publication. University of Warwick, United Kingdom.

Olson, J. M., Roese, N. J., & Zanna, M. P. (1996). Expectancies. In E. T. Higgins, & A. W. Kruglanski (Eds.), *Social psychology: Handbook of basic principles* (pp. 211–239). New York: Guilford Press.

Olson, M. A., & Fazio, R. H. (2001). Implicit attitude formation through classical conditioning. *Psychological Science, 12,* 413–417.

Olson, M. A., & Fazio, R. H. (2009). Implicit and explicit measures of attitudes: The Perspective of the MODE model. In R. E. Petty, R. H. Fazio, & P. Briñol (Eds.), *Insights from the new implicit measures* (pp. 19–63). New York: Psychology Press.

Olweus, D. (1978). *Aggression in the schools: Bullies and whipping boys.* Washington, DC: Hemisphere (Wiley).

Olweus, D. (1979). The stability of aggressive reaction patterns in males: A review. *Psychological Bulletin, 86,* 852–875.

Olweus, D. (1994). Bullying at school: Long-term outcomes for the victims and an effective school-based intervention program. In R. Huesmann (Ed.), *Aggressive behavior: Current perspectives* (pp. 97–130). New York: Plenum Press.

Ones, D. S., Viswesvaran, C., & Schmidt, F. L. (1993). Comprehensive meta-analysis of integrity test validities: Findings for personnel selection and theories of job performance. *Journal of Applied Psychology, 78*(4), 679–703.

Open Science Collaboration (2015). Estimating the reproducibility of psychological science. *Science, 349*(6251), 1–8. http://dx.doi.org/10.1126/science.aac4716

Orbell, J. M., van de Kragt, A. J. C., & Dawes, R. M. (1988). Explaining discussion-induced comparison. *Journal of Personality and Social Psychology, 54,* 811–819.

Orne, M. T. (1962). On the social psychology of the psychological experiment: With particular reference to demand characteristics and their implications. *American Psychologist, 17*(11), 776–783.

Ornstein, P. A., Ceci, S. J., & Loftus, E. F. (1998). Adult recollections of childhood abuse: Cognitive and developmental perspectives. *Psychology, Public Policy, and Law, 7*, 1025–1051.

Ornstein, R. (1991). *The evolution of consciousness: Of Darwin, Freud, and cranial fire: The origins of the way we think*. New York: Prentice Hall.

Orobio de Castro, B., Veerman, J. W., Koops, W., Bosch, J. D., & Monshouwer, H. J. (2002). Hostile attribution of intent and aggressive behavior: A meta-analysis. *Child Development, 73*, 916–934.

Ort, A., & Fahr, A. (2018). Using efficacy cues in persuasive health communication is more effective than employing threats—An experimental study of a vaccination intervention against Ebola. *British Journal of Health Psychology, 23*(3), 665–684. https://doi-org.proxy.lib.umich.edu/10.1111/bjhp.12310

Orth, U., Robins, R. W., & Widaman, K. F. (2012). Lifespan development of self-esteem and its effects on important life outcomes. *Journal of Personality and Social Psychology, 102*, 1271–1288.

Orville Redenbacher Company Website. Retrieved August 20, 2012, from http://www.orville.com/homemade-popcorn

Ostroff, C., Kinicki, A. J., & Tamkins, M. M. (2003). Organizational culture and climate. In W. C. Borman, D. R. Ilgen, & R. J. Klimoski (Eds.), *Handbook of psychology: Industrial and organizational psychology, 12*, 565–594. New York: Wiley.

Oswald, I., Taylor, A. M., & Treisman, M. (1960). Discriminative responses to stimulation during human sleep. *Brain, 83*, 440–453.

OSF Home. https://osf.io

Otero, V. (2019). Media Bias Chart: Version 4. Retrieved August 16, 2019 from https://www.adfontesmedia.com

Otis, C. C., Greathouse, S. M., Kennard, J. B., & Kovera, M. B. (2014). Hypothesis testing in attorney-conducted voir dire. *Law and Human Behavior, 38*, 392–404.

Ottaviani, R., & Beck, A. T. (1987). Cognitive aspects of panic disorders. *Journal of Anxiety Disorders, 1*, 15–28.

Ouellette, J. A., & Wood, W. (1998). Habit and intention in everyday life: The multiple processes by which past behavior predicts future behavior. *Psychological Bulletin, 124*, 54–74.

Ouwerkerk, J. W., Kerr, N. L., Gallucci, M., & Van Lange, P. A. M. (2005). Avoiding the social death penalty: Ostracism and cooperation in social dilemmas. In K. D. Williams, J. P. Forgas, & W. von Hippel (Eds.), *The social outcast: Ostracism, social exclusion, rejection, and bullying* (pp. 321–332). New York: Psychology Press.

Ouwerkerk, J. W., Van Lange, P. A., Gallucci, M., & Kerr, N. L. (2005). Avoiding the social death penalty: Ostracism and cooperation in social dilemmas. In K. D. Williams, J. P. Forgas, & W. von Hippel (Eds.), *The social outcast: Ostracism, social exclusion, rejection, and bullying* (pp. 321–332). New York: Psychology Press.

Overall, N. C., Girme, Y. U., Lemay, E. P., & Hammond, M. D. (2014). Attachment anxiety and reactions to relationship threat: The benefits and costs of inducing guilt in romantic partners. *Journal of Personality and Social Psychology, 106*, 235–256.

Overing, J. (1986). Images of cannibalism, death and domination in a "non-violent" society. In D. Riches (Ed.), *The anthropology of violence* (pp. 86–101). Oxford: Blackwell.

Page, S. E. (2008). *The difference: How the power of diversity creates better groups, firms, schools, and societies.* Princeton, NJ: Princeton University Press.

Paik, H., & Comstock, G. (1994). The effects of television violence on antisocial behavior: A meta-analysis. *Communication Research, 21*, 516–546.

Palca, J. (2013, May 23). The weight of a med student's subconscious bias. *NPR*. Retrieved from http://www.npr.org/blogs/health/2013/05/23/186294402/the-weight-of-a-med-students-subconscious-bias

Paleari, G., Regalia, C., & Fincham, F. D. (2005). Marital quality, forgiveness, empathy, and rumination: A longitudinal analysis. *Personality and Social Psychology Bulletin, 31*, 368–378.

Panksepp, J. (1998). *Affective neuroscience: The foundations of human and animal emotions*. London: Oxford University Press.

Panksepp, J., Herman, B. H., Conner, R., Bishop, P., & Scott, J. P. (1978). The biology of social attachments: Opiates alleviate separation distress. *Biological Psychiatry, 13*, 607–618.

Panksepp, J., Najam, N., & Soares, F. (1980). Morphine reduces social cohesion in rats. *Pharmacology, Biochemistry, and Behavior, 11*, 131–134.

Panksepp, J., Vilberg, T., Bean, N. J., Coy, D. H., & Kastin, A. J. (1978). Reduction of distress vocalization in chicks by opiate-like peptides. *Brain Research Bulletin, 3*, 663–667.

Panno, A., Giacomantonio, M., Carrus, G., Maricchiolo, F., Pirchio, S., Mannetti, L. (2017). Mindfulness, pro-environmental behavior, and belief in climate change: The mediating role of social dominance. *Environment and Behavior, 50*, 864–888.

Paolini, S., Harwood, J., & Rubin, M. (2010). Negative intergroup contact makes group memberships salient: Explaining why intergroup conflict endures. *Personality and Social Psychology Bulletin, 36*(12) 1723–1738. doi: 10.1177/0146167210388667

Papageorgis, D., & McGuire, W. J. (1961). The generality of immunity to persuasion produced by pre-exposure to weakened counterarguments. *Journal of Abnormal and Social Psychology, 62*, 475–481.

Pargament, K. I. (1997). *The psychology of religion and coping. Theory, research, practice.* New York: Guilford Press.

Parikh, R. (2011, January 20). Make anti-vaccine parents pay higher premiums. CNN. Retrieved from http://edition.cnn.com/2011/OPINION/01/20/parikh.childhood.immunizations/index.html?_s=PM:OPINION

Pariser, E. (2011). *The filter bubble: What the Internet is hiding from you*. New York: Penguin Press.

Park, C. (2003). In other (people's) words: Plagiarism by university students—literature and lessons. *Assessment and Evaluation in Higher Education, 28*, 471–488.

Park, J. H., & Schaller, M. (2009). Parasites, minds and cultures. *The Psychologist, 22*, 942–945.

Park, S. H., Westphal, J. D., & Stern, I. (2011). Set up for a fall: The insidious effects of flattery and opinion conformity toward corporate leaders. *Administrative Science Quarterly, 56*, 2257–2302.

Parker, K. A., Rains, S. A., & Ivanov, B. (2016). Examining the "blanket of protection" conferred by inoculation: The effects of inoculation messages on the cross-protection of related attitudes. *Communication Monographs, 83*(1), 49–68. https://doi-org.proxy.lib.umich.edu/10.1080/03637751.2015.1030681

Parker, S. D., Brewer, M. B., & Spencer, J. R. (1980). Natural disaster, perceived control and attributions to fate. *Personality & Social Psychology Bulletin, 6*, 454–459.

Parrott, D. J. (2009). Aggression toward gay men as gender role enforcement: Effects of male role norms, sexual prejudice, and masculine gender role stress. *Journal of Personality, 77*(4), 1137–1166.

Parsley, A. (2009). 5 Things to Know About TV's Progressive Insurance Lady. *People*. Retrieved from http://www.people.com/people/article/0,,20301774,00.html

Patel, V., Thomson, G. W., & Wilson, N. (2013). Cigarette butt littering in city streets: A new methodology for studying and results. *Tobacco Control: An International Journal, 22*(1), 59–62. doi: 10.1136/tobaccocontrol-2012-050529

Patterson, O. (1982). *Slavery and social death*. Cambridge, MA: Harvard University Press.

Paul, A. M. (1999, June 28). Promotional intelligence. *Ivory Tower*. Retrieved August 11, 2004, from http://www.salon.com/books/it/1999/06/28/emotional/index1.html

Paul, C., Fitzjohn, J., Herbison, P., & Dickson, N. (2000). The determinants of sexual intercourse before age 16. *Journal of Adolescent Health, 27*, 136–147.

Paulhus, D. L. (2014). Toward a taxonomy of dark personalities. *Current Directions in Psychological Science, 23*, 421–426.

Paulhus, D. L., & Levitt, K. (1987). Desirable responding triggered by affect: Automatic egotism? *Journal of Personality and Social Psychology, 52*, 245–259.

Paulhus, D. L., Curtis, S. R., & Jones, D. N. (2018). Aggression as a trait: the Dark Tetrad alternative. *Current Opinion in Psychology, 19*, 88–92. doi:10.1016/j.copsyc.2017.04.007

Paulus, P. B. (2000). Groups, teams, and creativity: The creative potential of idea-generating groups. *Applied Psychology: An International Review, 49*(2), 237–262.

Paulus, P. B., & Matthews, R. (1980). Crowding, attribution, and task performance. *Basic and Applied Social Psychology, 1*, 3–13.

Paulus, P. B., Dzindolet, M. T., Poletes, G., & Camacho, L. M. (1993). Perception of performance in group brainstorming: The illusion of group productivity. *Personality and Social Psychology Bulletin, 19*, 78–89.

Payne, B. K. (2001). Prejudice and perception: The role of automatic and controlled processes in misperceiving a weapon. *Journal of Personality and Social Psychology, 81*, 181–192.

Payne, B. K., Govorun, O., & Arbuckle, N. L. (2008). Automatic attitudes and alcohol: Does implicit liking predict drinking? *Cognition and Emotion, 22*, 238–271.

Pedersen, W. C., Miller, L. C., Putcha-Bhagavatula, A. D., & Yang, Y. (2002). Evolved sex differences in the number of partners desired? The long and short of it. *Psychological Science, 13*, 157–161.

Pegues, J. (2018, August 31). Violent road rage incident involving a car jack caught on camera. *CBS News*. Retrieved from https://www.cbsnews.com/news/violent-road-rage-incident-car-jack-caught-on-camera-washington-dc/

Pelisek, C. (2018, April 13). 'I just enjoy killing': Airman gets life in prison for strangling another Air Force member. *People*. Retrieved August 25, 2019 from https://people.com/crime/air-force-member-strangled-female-airman-journal-described-murder/

Pendleton, M. (2014, September 9). Nike drops endorsement deal with Ray Rice. *FSS*. Retrieved from http://fullscalesports.com/2014/09/09/nike-drops-endorsement-deal-with-ray-rice/

Penner, L. A., Dertke, M. C., & Achenbach, C. J. (1973). The "flash" system: A field study of altruism. *Journal of Applied Social Psychology, 3*, 362–370.

Penton-Voak I. S., Thomas, J., Gage, S. H., McMurran, M., McDonald, S., & Munafò M. R. (2013). Increasing recognition of happiness in ambiguous facial expressions reduces anger and aggressive behavior. *Psychological Science, 24*(5), 688–697. doi: 10.1177/0956797612459657

Peplau, L. A., & Perlman, D. (Eds.). (1982). *Loneliness: A sourcebook of current theory, research, and therapy*. New York: Wiley.

Perera, H. N., & DiGiacomo, M. (2013). The relationship of trait emotional intelligence with academic performance: A meta-analytic review. *Learning and Individual Differences, 28*(12), 20–33. doi: 10.1016/j.lindif.2013.08.002

Perez, R. C. (1973). The effect of experimentally induced failure, self-esteem and sex on cognitive differentiation. *Journal of Abnormal Psychology, 81*, 74–79.

Peristiany, J. G. (Ed.). (1965). *Honour and shame: The values of Mediterranean society*. London: Weidenfeld & Nicolson.

Perry, C. L., Killen, J., Slinkard, L. A., & McAlister, A. L. (1980). Peer teaching and smoking prevention among junior high students. *Adolescence, 15*, 277–281.

Persons, J. B., & Rao, P. A. (1985). Longitudinal study of cognitions, life events, and depression in psychiatric inpatients. *Journal of Abnormal Psychology, 94*, 51–63.

Peters, K., & Kashima, Y. (2007). From social talk to social action: Shaping the social triad with emotion sharing. *Journal of Personality and Social Psychology, 93*, 780–797.

Peterson, C. K., & Harmon-Jones, E. (in press). Anger and testosterone: Evidence that situationally-induced anger relates to situationally-induced testosterone. *Emotion*.

Peterson, C., & Seligman, M. E. P. (2004). *Character strengths and virtues.* New York: Oxford University Press.

Peterson, K., Malouff, J., & Thorsteinsson, E. B. (2011). A meta-analytic investigation of emotional intelligence and alcohol involvement. *Substance Use & Misuse, 46*(14), 1726–1733.

Peterson, L. M., Campbell, M. A. T., & Laky, Z. E. (2019). The next frontier for men's contraceptive choice: College men's willingness to pursue male hormonal contraception. *Psychology of Men & Masculinities, 20*(2), 226–237. doi:http://dx.doi.org/10.1037/men0000174

Peterson, N. G., Mumford, M. D., Borman, W. C., Jeanneret, P. R., & Fleishmann, E. A. (1999). *An occupational information system for the 21st century: The development of O*NET.* Washington, D.C.: American Psychological Association.

Pettigrew, T. F., & Tropp, L. R. (2005). Allport's intergroup contact hypothesis: Its history and influence. In J. F. Dovidio, P. Glick, & L. A. Rudman (Eds.), *On the nature of prejudice: Fifty years after Allport* (pp. 262–277). Malden, MA: Blackwell.

Pettigrew, T. F., & Tropp, L. R. (2006). A meta-analytic test of intergroup contact theory. *Journal of Personality and Social Psychology, 90,* 751–783.

Pettigrew, T. F., & Tropp, L. R. (2008). How does intergroup contact reduce prejudice? Meta-analytic tests of three mediators. *European Journal of Social Psychology, 38,* 922–934.

Pettiway, L. E. (1987). Arson for revenge: The role of environmental situation, age, sex, and race. *Journal of Quantitative Criminology, 3*(2), 169–184.

Petty, R. E., & Cacioppo, J. T. (1979). Issue involvement can increase or decrease persuasion by enhancing message-relevant cognitive responses. *Journal of Personality and Social Psychology, 37,* 1915–1926.

Petty, R. E., & Cacioppo, J. T. (1986). *Communication and persuasion: Central and peripheral routes to attitude change.* New York: Springer-Verlag.

Pew Research Center (2014, February 23). *Gay marriage.* Retrieved from http://www.pewresearch.org/data-trend/domestic-issues/attitudes-on-gay-marriage/

Pew Research Center (2017, February 15). Americans express increasingly warm feelings toward religious groups. Retrieved from http://www.pewforum.org/2017/02/15/americans-express-increasingly-warm-feelings-toward-religious-groups/

Pew Research Global Attitudes Project. (2014, March 13). Worldwide, many see belief in God as essential to morality. Retrieved from http://www.pewglobal.org/2014/03/13/worldwide-many-see-belief-in-god-as-essential-to-morality/

Phillis, D. E., & Gromko, M. H. (1985). Sex differences in sexual activity: Reality or illusion? *Journal of Sex Research, 21,* 437–443.

Pickel, K. L. (1998). Unusualness and threat as possible causes of "weapon focus." *Memory, 6,* 277–295.

Pickel, K. L. (1999). The influence of context on the "weapon focus" effect. *Law and Human Behavior, 23,* 299–311.

Pickett, C. L., & Gardner, W. L. (2005). The social monitoring system: Enhanced sensitivity to social cues and information as an adaptive response to social exclusion and belonging need. In K. D. Williams, J. P. Forgas, & W. von Hippel (Eds.), *The social outcast: Ostracism, social exclusion, rejection, and bullying* (pp. 213–226). New York: Psychology Press.

Piliavin, I. M., Piliavin, J. A. & Rodin, J. (1975). Costs, diffusion, and the stigmatized victim. *Journal of Personality and Social Psychology, 32,* 429–438.

Pines, A., & Aronson, E. (1983). Antecedents, correlates, and consequences of sexual jealousy. *Journal of Personality, 51,* 108–136.

Pinker, S. (2007, March 19). A history of violence. *New Republic, 236*(12), 18.

Pinker, S. (2011). *The better angels of our nature: Why violence has declined.* New York: Viking Adult.

Pitt, E. L. (2000). Domestic violence in gay and lesbian relationships. *Journal of the Gay and Lesbian Medical Association, 4,* 195–196.

Plant, E. A. (2004). Responses to interracial interactions over time. *Personality and Social Psychology Bulletin, 30,* 1458–1471.

Plant, E. A., & Devine, P. G. (1998). Internal and external motivation to respond without prejudice. *Journal of Personality and Social Psychology, 75,* 811–832.

Plant, E. A., & Devine, P. G. (2001). Responses to other-imposed pro-black pressure: Acceptance or backlash? *Journal of Experimental Social Psychology, 37,* 486–501.

Plant, E. A., & Peruche, B. M. (2005). The consequences of race for police officers' responses to criminal suspects. *Psychological Science, 16,* 180–183.

Platt, C. W. (1988). Effects of causal attributions for success on first-term college performance: A covariance structure model. *Journal of Educational Psychology, 80,* 569–578.

Platt, J. (1973). Social traps. *American Psychologist, 28,* 641–651.

Pliner, P., & Chaiken, S. (1990). Eating, social motives, and self-presentation in women and men. *Journal of Experimental Social Psychology, 26,* 240–254.

Plötner, M., Over, H., Carpenter, M., and Tomasello, M. (2015, April). Young children show the bystander effect in helping situations. *Psychological Science, 26,* 499–506.

Plouffe, R. A., Saklofske, D. H., & Smith, M. M. (2017). The Assessment of Sadistic Personality: Preliminary psychometric evidence for a new measure. *Personality and Individual Differences, 104,* 166–171. doi:10.1016/j.paid.2016.07.043

Pocheptsova, A., Amir, O., Dhar, R., & Baumeister, R. F. (2009). Deciding without resources: Resource depletion and choice in context. *Journal of Marketing Research, 46,* 344–355. doi: 10.1509/jmkr.46.3.344

Pogorzelski, S., & Harriott, J. (2007). *Finding keepers: The Monster guide to hiring and holding the world's best employees.* New York: McGraw Hill.

Politano, J., & Lester, D. (1997). Self-destructiveness and credit card debt. *Psychological Reports, 81,* 634.

Political Blind Spot (2014, February 13). Through the 1950s, Africans and Native Americans were kept in zoos as exhibits. Retrieved from http://political-blindspot.com/through-the-1950s-africans-and-native-americans-were-kept-in-zoos-as-exhibits/

Polivy, J. (1976). Perception of calories and regulation of intake in restrained and unrestrained subjects. *Addictive Behaviors, 1,* 237–243.

Pomazal, R. J. & Clore, G. L. (1973). Helping on the highway: The effects of dependency and sex. *Journal of Applied Social Psychology, 3,* 150–164.

Postmes, T., & Spears, R. (1998). Deindividuation and antinormative behavior: A meta-analysis. *Psychological Bulletin, 123,* 238–259.

Pottebaum, S. M., Keith, T. Z., & Ehly, S. W. (1986). Is there a causal relation between self-concept and academic achievement? *Journal of Educational Research, 79,* 140–144.

Pouwelse, M., Bolman, C., Lodewijkx, H., & Spaa, M. (2011). Gender differences and social support: Mediators or moderators between peer victimization and depressive feelings. *Psychology in the Schools, 48*(8), 800–814. doi: 10.1002/pits.20589

Powell, J., Lewis, P.A., Roberts, N., Garcia-Finana, M., & Dunbar, R.I.M. (2012). Orbital prefrontal cortex volume predicts social network size: An imaging study of individual differences in humans. *Proceedings of the Royal Society B, 279,* 2157–2162.

Powers, W. T. (1973). *Behavior: The control of perception.* Chicago: Aldine.

Pozzulo, J. D., & Warren, K. L. (2003). Descriptions and identifications of strangers by youth and adult eyewitness. *Journal of Applied Psychology, 88,* 315–323.

Pratkanis, A. R., & Aronson, E. (1992). *Age of propaganda: The everyday use and abuse of persuasion.* New York: Henry Holt.

Pratkanis, A. R., Greenwald, A. G., Leippe, M. R., & Baumgardner, M. H. (1988). In search of reliable persuasion effects: III. The sleeper effect is dead: Long live the sleeper effect. *Journal of Personality and Social Psychology, 54,* 203–218.

Pratt, T. C., & Cullen, F. T. (2000). The empirical status of Gottfredson and Hirschi's general theory of crime: A meta-analysis. *Criminology, 38,* 931–964.

Prelec, D., & Simester, D. (2001). Always leave home without it. *Marketing Letters, 12,* 5–12.

Prescott, A. T., Sargent, J. D., & Hull, J. G. (2018). Meta-analysis of the relationship between violent video game play and physical aggression over time. *PNAS Proceedings of the National Academy of Sciences of the United States of America, 115*(40), 9882–9888. https://doi-org.proxy.lib.umich.edu/10.1073/pnas.1611617114

Price, H. L., & Fitzgerald, R. J. (2016). Face-off: A new identification procedure for child eyewitnesses. *Journal of Experimental Psychology: Applied, 22,* 366–380.

Prior, E., Lew, R., Hammarberg, K., & Johnson, L. (in press). Fertility facts, figures and future plans: An online survey of university students. *Human Fertility.* DOI: 10.1080/14647273.2018.1482569

PRNewswire. (2018). More than half of employers have found content on social media that caused them NOT to hire a candidate, according to recent CareerBuilder survey. Retrieved from https://www.prnewswire.com/news-releases/more-than-half-of-employers-have-found-content-on-social-media-that-caused-them-not-to-hire-a-candidate-according-to-recent-careerbuilder-survey-300694437.html

Prochaska, J. O., & Prochaska, J. M. (2010). Self-directed change: A transtheoretical model. In *Social psychological foundations of clinical psychology* (pp. 431–440). New York: Guilford Press.

Prochaska, J. O., Redding, C. A., & Evers, K. E. (2002). The transtheoretical model and stages of change. In K. Glanz, B. K. Rimer, & F. M. Lewis (Eds.), *Health behavior and health education: Theory, research, and practice* (pp. 99–120). San Francisco: Jossey-Bass.

Prochaska, J. O., Wright, J. A., & Velicer, W. F. (2008). Evaluating theories of health behavior change: A hierarchy of criteria applied to the transtheoretical model. *Applied Psychology: An International Review, 57*(4), 561–588. doi: 10.1111/j.1464-0597.2008.00345.x

Pronin, E., Berger, J., & Molouki, S. (2007). Alone in a crowd of sheep: Asymmetric perceptions of conformity and their roots in an introspection illusion. *Journal of Personality and Social Psychology, 92,* 585–595.

Pronk, T. M., Karremans, J. C., Overbeek, G., Vermulst, A. A., & Wigboldus, D. H. J. (2010). What it takes to forgive: When and why executive functioning facilitates forgiveness. *Journal of Personality and Social Psychology, 98*(1), 119–131.

Pryor, J. B., Gibbons, F. X., Wicklund, R. A., Fazio, R. H., & Hood, R. (1977). Self-focused attention and self-report validity. *Journal of Personality, 45,* 513–527.

Pryor, J. B., Reeder, G. D., Yeadon, C., & Hesson-McInnis, M. (2004). A dual-process model of reactions to perceived stigma. *Journal of Personality and Social Psychology, 87,* 436–452.

Psalms 14:1.

Purcell, A. H. (1981, February). The world's trashiest people: Will they clean up their act or throw away their future? *The Futurist, 2,* 51–59.

Pyszczynski, T., Greenberg, J., & Holt, K. (1985). Maintaining consistency between self-serving beliefs and available data: A bias in information processing. *Personality and Social Psychology Bulletin, 11,* 179–190.

Quarantelli, E. L. (1998). *What is a disaster?* New York: Routledge.

Quas, J. A., Bottoms, B. L., Haegerich, T. M., & Nysse-Carris, K. L. (2002). Effects of victim, defendant, and juror gender on decisions in child sexual assault cases. *Journal of Applied Social Psychology, 32,* 1993–2021.

Quinlivan, D. S., Neuschatz, J. S., Cutler, B. L., Wells, G. L., McClung, J., & Harker, D. L. (2012). Do pre-admonition suggestions moderate the effect of unbiased lineup instructions? *Legal and Criminological Psychology, 17,* 165–176.

Quinones, M. A., Ford, J. K., & Teachout, M. S. (1995). The relationship between work experience and job performance: A conceptual and meta-analytic review. *Personnel Psychology, 48*(4), 887–910.

Quoidbach, J., Gruber, J., Mikolajczak, M., Kogan, A., Kotsou, I., & Norton, M. I. (2014). Emodiversity and the emotional ecosystem. *Journal of Experimental Psychology: General, 143*(6), 2057–2066. doi:10.1037/a0038025

Quoted by Krauthammer, C. (1997, June 29). Apology is not ours to give. *Cleveland Plain Dealer*, p. 2-E.

Ragins, B. R., & Cotton, J. L. (1999). Mentor functions and outcomes: A comparison of men and women in formal and informal mentoring relationships. *Journal of Applied Psychology, 84*(4), 529–550.

Raphael, T. (2010, June 22). Employee referral programs using more social media. Retrieved from www.ere.net/2010/06/22/employee-referral-programs-using-more-social-media/

Ray, D. G., Gomillion, S., Pintea, A. I., & Hamlin, I. (2018). On being forgotten: Memory and forgetting serve as signals of interpersonal importance. *Journal of Personality and Social Psychology, 116*, 259–276.

Re: Work (2019). Guide: Understand team effectiveness. Retrieved from https://rework.withgoogle.com/guides/understanding-team-effectiveness/steps/introduction.

Reams, M. A., Geaghan, J. P., & Gendron, R. C. (1996). The link between recycling and litter: A field study. *Environment and Behavior, 28*, 92–110.

Regnerus, M. (2011). *Premarital sex in America: How young Americans meet, mate, and think about marrying.* New York: Oxford University Press.

Reich, J. W., & Robertson, J. L. (1979). Reactance and norm appeal in anti-littering messages. *Journal of Applied Social Psychology, 9*, 91–101.

Reinisch, J. (1990). *The Kinsey Institute new report on sex: What you must know to be sexually literate.* Stuttgart: St. Martin's Press. (Quotation on p. 89).

Reinsch, J., & Spotanski, C. (2005). Human territoriality: The effects of status on personalization and demarcation. *Journal of Psychological Inquiry 10*(1), 16–21.

Reis, H. T. (1990). The role of intimacy in interpersonal relations. *Journal of Social and Clinical Psychology, 9*, 15–30.

Reiss, I. L. (1986). A sociological journey into sexuality. *Journal of Marriage and the Family, 48*, 233–242.

Reiss, I. L. (1986). *Journey into sexuality.* New York: Prentice Hall.

Reiter, S. M., & Samuel, W. (1980). Littering as a function of prior litter and the presence or absence of prohibitive signs. *Journal of Applied Social Psychology, 10*, 45–55.

Remland, M. S., Jones, T. S., & Brinkman, H. (1995). Interpersonal distance, body orientation, and touch: Effects of culture, gender, and age. *Journal of Social Psychology, 135*, 281–297.

Reno, R. R., Cialdini, R. B., & Kallgren, C. A. (1993). The trans-situational influence of social norms. *Journal of Personality and Social Psychology, 64*, 104–112.

Renzetti, C. M. (1992). *Violent betrayal: Partner abuse in lesbian relationships.* Newbury Park, CA: Sage.

Repetti, R. L., & Saxbe, D. E. (2019). The influence of chronic family stressors on adult health. In B. H. Fiese, M. Celano, K. Deater-Deckard, E. N. Jouriles & M. A. Whisman (Eds.), *APA handbook of contemporary family psychology: Applications and broad impact of family psychology (vol. 2); APA handbook of contemporary family psychology: Applications and broad impact of family psychology (vol. 2)* (pp. 121–136). Washington, DC.: American Psychological Association. doi:http://dx.doi.org/10.1037/0000100-008

Revenson, T. A., & Gurung, R. A. R. (Eds.). (2019). *Handbook of health psychology.* New York: Routledge.

Rever, J. (2018). *In praise of blood: The crimes of the Rwandan Patriotic Front.* Toronto, Canada. Random House Canada.

Reykowski, J. (1982). Motivation and prosocial behavior. In V. Derlega & J. Grzelak (Eds.), *Cooperation and helping behavior: Theories and research* (pp. 352–375). New York: Academic Press.

Rhee, H., & Bell, D. R. (2002). The inter-store mobility of supermarket shoppers. *Journal of Retailing, 78*, 225–237.

Rhet. I.3, 1358a37ff.

Rhet. II.1, 1378a6ff.

Rhine, R. J., Hill, S. J., & Wandruff, S. E. (1967). Evaluative responses of preschool children. *Child Development, 38*, 1035–1042.

Rhodes, N., & Wood, W. (1992). Self-esteem and intelligence affect influenceability: The mediating role of message reception. *Psychological Bulletin, 111*, 156–171.

Rhodewalt, F., & Agustdottir, S. (1986). Effects of self-presentation on the phenomenal self. *Journal of Personality and Social Psychology, 50*, 47–55.

Richard Dawkins, an original thinker who bashes orthodoxy. (2011, 19 September). *New York Times.* Retrieved August 26, 2019 from http://www.nytimes.com/2011/09/20/science/20dawkins.html?pagewanted5all

Richards, Z., & Hewstone, M. (2001). Subtyping and subgrouping: Processes for the prevention and promotion of stereotype change. *Personality and Social Psychology Review, 5*, 52–73.

Richeson, J. A., & Shelton, J. N. (2003). When prejudice doesn't pay: Effects of interracial contact on executive function. *Psychological Science, 14*, 287–290.

Richeson, J. A., Trawalter, S., & Shelton, J. N. (2005). African Americans' implicit racial attitudes and the depletion of executive function after interracial interactions. *Social Cognition, 23*, 336–352.

Richman, J. A., & Flaherty, J. A. (1986). Sex differences in drinking among medical students: Patterns and psychosocial correlates. *Journal of Studies on Alcohol, 47*, 283–289.

Ridley, M. (1993). *The red queen: Sex and evolution in human nature.* New York: Penguin.

Ridley, M. (2004). *Evolution* (3rd ed.). Oxford: Blackwell Science.

Righetti, F., & Finkenauer, C. (2011). If you are able to control yourself, I will trust you: The role of perceived self-control in interpersonal trust. *Journal of Personality and Social Psychology, 100*, 874–886.

Righetti, F., & Finkenauer, C. (2011). If you are able to control yourself, I will trust you: The role of perceived self-control in interpersonal trust. *Journal of Personality and Social Psychology, 100*, 874–886.

Right hand diamonds marketed to women as power sign. (2003, December 2). *Sacramento Bee.* Retrieved from http://www.sacbee.com/content/business/story/7887166p-8825882c.html

Riley, B. (2014). Experiential avoidance mediates the association between thought suppression and mindfulness with problem gambling. *Journal of Gambling Studies, 30*(1), 163–171. doi:10.1007/s10899-012-9342-9

Ringelmann, M. (1913). Recherches sur les moteurs animés: Travail de l'homme. *Annales de l'Institut National Argonomique*, 2e srie, tom 12, 1–40. Published in French, cited in Kravitz, D. A., & Martin, B. (1986). Ringelmann rediscovered: The original article. *Journal of Personality and Social Psychology, 50*, 936–941.

Rippere, V. (1977). "What's the thing to do when you're feeling depressed?" A pilot study. *Behaviour Research and Therapy, 15*, 185–191.

Risen, J. L., Gilovich, T., & Dunning, D. (2007). One-shot illusory correlations and stereotype formation. *Personality and Social Psychology Bulletin, 33*(11), 1492–1502.

Ritson, J. (1802). *An essay on abstinence from animal food, as a moral duty.* London: Richard Phillips.

Ritter, R. S., & Preston, J. L. (2011). Gross gods and icky atheism: Disgust responses to rejected religious beliefs. *Journal of Experimental Social Psychology, 47*(6), 1225–1230.

Roach, M. (2004). *Stiff: The curious lives of human cadavers.* New York: W. W. Norton.

Robbins, J. M., Ford, M. T., & Tetrick, L. E. (2012). Perceived unfairness and employee health: A meta-analytic integration. *Journal of Applied Psychology, 97*(2), 235–272.

Roberts, J. (2012, February 28). *How to begin analyzing social media.* Retrieved August 20, 2012, from http://www.collectiveintellect.com/blog/brand-tracker-super-bowl-2012.

Roberts, J. (2013, November 2). Three pages of Rand Paul's book were plagiarized from think tanks. *Reuters.* Retrieved August 25, 2019 from http://www.buzzfeed.com/andrewkaczynski/entire-section-of-rand-pauls-book-copied-verbatim-from-case#1m04yi5

Roberts, W. A. (2002). Are animals stuck in time? *Psychological Bulletin, 128*, 473–489.

Robinson, E., Tobias, T., Shaw, L., Freeman, E., Higgs, S. (2011). Social matching of food intake and the need for social acceptance. *Appetite, 56*, 747–752.

Robinson, P. (1995). *Schindler's List teaching guide.* Available August 26, 2019 at http://www.southerninstitute.info/holocaust_education/schind.html

Roehling, M. V., Roehling, P. V., & Odland, L. M. (2008). Investigating the validity of stereotypes about overweight employees: The relationship between body weight and normal personality traits. *Group and Organization Management, 33*(4), 392–424.

Roese, N. J., & Olson, J. M. (1997). Counterfactual thinking: The intersection of affect and function. In M. P. Zanna (Ed.), *Advances in experimental social psychology* (Vol. 29, pp. 1–59). New York: Academic Press.

Roese, N. J., & Olson, J. M. (1997). Counterfactual thinking: The intersection of affect and function. In M. P. Zanna (Ed.), *Advances in experimental social psychology* (Vol. 29, pp. 1–59). New York: Academic Press.

Rogers, C. R. (1961). *On becoming a person.* Boston: Houghton Mifflin.

Rogers, E. M. (1983). *Diffusion of innovations.* New York: Free Press.

Rogers, T. B., Kuiper, N. A., & Kirker, W. S. (1977). Self-reference and the encoding of personal information. *Journal of Personality and Social Psychology, 35*, 677–688.

Rogow, A. A, Carey, G. L., & Farrell, C. (1957). The significance of aphorisms in American culture. *Sociology and Social Research, 41*, 417–420.

Rohrer, J. H., Baron, S. H., Hoffman, E. L., & Swander, D. V. (1954). The stability of autokinetic judgments. *Journal of Abnormal and Social Psychology, 49*(4, Pt. 1), 595–597.

Romero-Canyas, R., & Downey, G. (2005). Rejection sensitivity as a predictor of affective and behavioral responses to interpersonal stress: A defensive motivational system. In K. D. Williams, J. P. Forgas, & W. von Hippel (Eds.), *The social outcast: Ostracism, social exclusion, rejection, and bullying* (pp. 131–154). New York: Psychology Press.

Ronay, R., & von Hippel, W. (2010). The presence of an attractive woman elevates testosterone and physical risk taking in young men. *Social Psychological and Personality Science, 1*, 57–64.

Roney, J. R. (2003). Effects of visual exposure to the opposite sex: Cognitive aspects of mate attraction in human males. *Personality and Social Psychology Bulletin, 29*(3), 393–404.

Roney, J. R., Mahler, S. V., & Maestripieri, D. (2003). Behavioral and hormonal responses of men to brief interactions with women. *Evolution and Human Behavior, 24*, 365–375.

Rose, D. C., Sutherland, W. J., Amano, T., González-Varo, J. P., Robertson, R. J., Simmons, B. I., et al. (2018). The major barriers to evidence-informed conservation policy and possible solutions. *Conservation Letters, 11*, e12564.

Rosenbaum, M. E. (1986). The repulsion hypothesis: On the nondevelopment of relationships. *Journal of Personality and Social Psychology, 51*, 1156–1166.

Rosenberg, M. (1979). *Conceiving the self.* New York: Basic Books.

Rosenberg, M., Schooler, C., & Schoenbach, C. (1989). Self-esteem and adolescent problems: Modeling reciprocal effects. *American Sociological Review, 54*, 1004–1018.

Rosenfeld, D. L., Folger, R., & Adelman, H. F. (1980). When rewards reflect competence: A qualification of the overjustification effect. *Journal of Personality and Social Psychology, 39*, 368–376.

Rosenhan, D. L., & White, G. M. (1967). Observation and rehearsal as determinants of prosocial behavior. *Journal of Personality and Social Psychology, 5,* 424–431.

Rosenman, R. H., & Chesney, M. A. (1982). Stress, Type A behavior and coronary heart disease. In L. Goldberger & S. Breznitz (Eds.), *Handbook of stress: Theoretical and clinical aspects* (pp. 547–565). New York: Free Press.

Rosenstock, I. M. (1960). What research in motivation suggests for public health. *American Journal of Public Health, 50,* 295–301.

Rosenstock, I. M., Strecher, & Becker, M. H. (1988). The health belief model and HIV risk behavior change. In J. Peterson & R. DiClemente (Eds.), *Preventing AIDS: Theory and practice of behavior interventions* (pp. 5–24). New York: Plenum Press.

Rosenthal, E. (2008, February 2). Motivated by a tax, Irish spurn plastic bags. *New York Times.* Retrieved from http://www.nytimes.com/2008/02/02/world/europe/02bags.html?_r51&pagewanted51

Rosenthal, L., & Gronich, B. (2019). Gender and health. In T. A. Revenson & R. A. R. Gurung (Eds.), *Handbook of health psychology* (pp. 303–314). New York: Routledge.

Rosenthal, R. (2002). Covert communication in classrooms, clinics, courtrooms, and cubicles. *American Psychologist, 57,* 839–849.

Rosenthal, R., & Jacobson, L. (1968). *Pygmalion in the classroom: Teacher expectation and pupils' intellectual development.* New York: Rinehart and Winston.

Roskies, E., & Louis-Guerin, C. (1990). Job insecurity in managers: Antecedents and consequences. *Journal of Organizational Behavior, 11,* 345–359.

Ross, Edward A. (1974. Original work published 1908). *Social Psychology.* New York: Arno Press.

Ross, J. A. (2006, November). The reliability, validity, and utility of self-assessment. *Practical assessment, Research & Evaluation, 11*(10). Retrieved from http://pareonline.net/pdf/v11n10.pdf

Ross, L., Greene, D., & House, P. (1977). The false consensus effect: An egocentric bias in social perception and attributional processes. *Journal of Experimental Social Psychology, 13,* 279–301.

Ross, L., Lepper, M. R., & Hubbard, M. (1975). Perseverance in self-perception and social perception: Biased attributional processes in the debriefing paradigm. *Journal of Personality and Social Psychology, 32,* 880–892.

Ross, M. (1989). The relation of implicit theories to the construction of personal histories. *Psychological Review, 96,* 341–357.

Ross, M., & Sicoiy, F. (1979). Egocentric biases in availability and attribution. *Journal of Personality and Social Psychology, 37,* 322–336.

Ross, S. M. (1996). Risk of physical abuse to children of spouse abusing parents. *Child Abuse and Neglect, 20,* 589–598.

Rotenberg, K. J., Addis, N., Betts, L. R., Corrigan, A., Fox, C., Hobson, Z., Rennison, S., Trueman, M., & Boulton, M. J. (2010). The relation between trust beliefs and loneliness during early childhood, middle childhood, and adulthood. *Personality and Social Psychology Bulletin, 36,* 1086–1100.

Roth, P. L, BeVier, C. A., Switzer, F. S., & Schippmann, J. S. (1996). Meta-analyzing the relationship between grades and job performance. *Journal of Applied Psychology, 81*(5), 548–556.

Rothbart, M. K. (1989). Temperament and development. In G. A. Kohnstamm, J. E. Bates, & M. K. Rothbart (Eds.), *Temperament in childhood* (pp. 187–247). New York: Wiley.

Rothberg, J. M., & Jones, F. D. (1987). Suicide in the U.S. Army: Epidemiological and periodic aspects. *Suicide and Life-Threatening Behavior, 17,* 119–132.

Rothman, A. J., Bartels, R. D., Wlaschin, J., & Salovey, P. (2006). The strategic use of gain- and loss-framed messages to promote healthy behavior: How theory can inform practice. *Journal of Communication, 56*(Suppl. 1), S202–S220.

Rothschild, Z. K., Landau, M. J., Sullivan, D., & Keefer, L. A. (2012). A dual-motive model of scapegoating: Displacing blame to reduce guilt or increase control. *Journal of Personality and Social Psychology, 102,* 1148–1163.

Rowatt, W. C., Cunningham, M. R., & Druen, P. B. (1999). Lying to get a date: The effect of facial physical attractiveness on the willingness to deceive prospective dating partners. *Journal of Social and Personal Relationships, 16*(2), 209–223.

Roy Rosenzweig Center for History and New Media. (2006, December). *An outline of the Anita Hill and Clarence Thomas controversy.* Retrieved from http://chnm.gmu.edu/courses/122/hill/hillframe.htm

Rozin, P., & Royzman, E. B. (2001). Negativity bias, negativity dominance, and contagion. *Personality and Social Psychology Review, 5,* 296–320.

Rozin, P., Haidt, J., & McCauley, C. R. (1993). Disgust. In M. Lewis & J. M. Haviland (Eds.), *Handbook of emotions* (pp. 575–594). New York: Guilford Press.

Rozin, P., Haidt, J., & McCauley, C. R. (2009). Disgust: The body and soul emotion in the 21st century. In B. O. Olatunji & D. McKay (Eds.), *Disgust and its disorders: Theory, assessment, and treatment implications* (pp. 9–29). Washington, DC: American Psychological Association.

Rozin, P., Markwith, M., & McCauley, C. (1994). Sensitivity to indirect contacts with other persons: AIDS aversion as a composite of aversion to strangers, infection, moral taint, and misfortune. *Journal of Abnormal Psychology, 103,* 495–505.

Ruback, R. B. & Juieng, D. (1997). Territorial defense in parking lots: Retaliation against waiting drivers. *Journal of Applied Social Psychology, 27,* 821–834.

Rubin, D. B. (2008). Fanning the vaccine–autism link. *Neurology Today, 8* (15), 3. doi:10.1097/01.NT.0000335577.64245.34

Ruble, D. N., Fleming, A. S., Hackel, L. S., & Stangor, C. (1988). Changes in the marital relationship during the transition to first time motherhood: Effects of violated expectations concerning division of household labor. *Journal of Personality and Social Psychology, 55,* 78–87.

Rucci, A. J. (2008). I-O psychology's "core purpose": Where science and practice meet. *The Industrial and Organizational Psychologist, 46*(1), 17–34.

Rudski, J. M. (2002). Hindsight and confirmation biases in an exercise in telepathy. *Psychological Reports, 91,* 899–906.

Ruedy, N. E., Moore, C., Gino, F., & Schweitzer, M. E. (2013). The cheater's high: The unexpected affective benefits of unethical behavior. *Journal of Personality and Social Psychology, 105*(4), 531–548. doi: 10.1037/a0034231

Ruedy, N.E., Moore, C., Gino, F., & Schweitzer, M.E. (2013). The cheater's high: The unexpected affective benefits of unethical behavior. *Journal of Personality and Social Psychology, 105,* 531–548.

Rupert, G. (1989). Employee referrals as a source of recruitment and job performance. *Proceedings of the 10th Annual Graduate Conference in Industrial/Organizational Psychology and Organizational Behavior.*

Rupp, D. E., & Cropanzano, R. (2002). The mediating effects of social exchange relationships in predicting workplace outcomes from multifoci organizational justice. *Organizational Behavior and Human Decision Processes, 89,* 925–946.

Rusbult, C. E. (1983). A longitudinal test of the investment model: The development (and deterioration) of satisfaction and commitment in heterosexual involvements. *Journal of Personality and Social Psychology, 45,* 101–117.

Rusbult, C. E., & Martz, J. M. (1995). My relationship is better than—and not as bad as—yours is: The perception of superiority in close relationships. *Personality and Social Psychology Bulletin, 21,* 558–571.

Rusbult, C. E., Morrow, G. D., & Johnson, D. J. (1987). Self-esteem and problem solving behavior in close relationships. *British Journal of Social Psychology, 26,* 293–303.

Ruscio, J. (2002). *Clear thinking with psychology: Separating sense from nonsense.* Pacific Grove, CA: Wadsworth.

Rushton, J. P., Brainerd, C. J., & Pressley, M. (1983). Behavioral development and construct validity: The principle of aggregation. *Psychological Bulletin, 94,* 18–38.

Rushton, J. P., Chrisjohn, R. D., & Fekken, G. C. (1981). The altruistic personality and the Self-Report Altruism Scale. *Personality and Individual Differences, 2,* 293–302.

Rushton, J. P., Fulker, D. W., Neale, M. C., Nias, D. K. B., & Eysenck, H. J. (1986). Altruism and aggression: The heritability of individual differences. *Journal of Personality and Social Psychology, 50,* 1192–1198.

Russakoff, R., & Goodman, M. (2011, July 14). Employee theft: Are you blind to it?. *CBS Money Watch.* Retrieved from http://www.cbsnews.com/news/employee-theft-are-you-blind-to-it/

Russell, D., Peplau, L. A., & Cutrona, C. E. (1980). The revised UCLA Loneliness Scale: Concurrent and discriminant validity evidence. *Journal of Personality and Social Psychology, 39,* 472–480.

Russell, V. M., McNulty, J. K., Baker, L. R., & Meltzer, A. L. (2014). The association between discontinuing hormonal contraceptives and wives' marital satisfaction depends on husbands' facial attractiveness. *PNAS, 111,* 17081–17086.

Ruva, C. L., & Guenther, C. C. (2015). From the shadows into the light: How pretrial publicity and deliberation affect mock jurors' decisions, impressions, and memory. *Law and Human Behavior, 39,* 294–310.

Ruva, C. L., & LeVasseur, M. A. (2012). Behind closed doors: The effect of pretrial publicity on jury deliberations. *Psychology, Crime & Law, 18,* 431–452.

Ruva, C. L., McEvoy, C., & Bryant, J. B. (2007). Effects of pre-trial publicity and jury deliberation on juror bias and source memory errors. *Applied Cognitive Psychology, 21,* 45–67.

Rwanda: How the genocide happened. (2004, December 18). *BBC News.* Retrieved August 25, 2019 from http://news.bbc.co.uk/2/hi/africa/1288230.stm

Ryan, J. R. (2009, February 27). Learning agility equals leadership success, *Bloomberg Businessweek.* Retrieved from http://www.businessweek.com/managing/content/feb2009/ca20090227_893956.htm

Ryan, R. M. (1982). Control and information in the intrapersonal sphere: An extension of cognitive evaluation theory. *Journal of Personality and Social Psychology, 43,* 450–461.

Ryan, R. M., & Deci, E. L. (2000). Self-determination theory and the facilitation of intrinsic motivation, social development, and well-being. *American Psychologist, 55,* 68–78.

Ryan, R. M., & Grolnick, W. S. (1986). Origin and pawns in the classroom: Self-report and projective assessments of individual differences in children's perceptions. *Journal of Personality and Social Psychology, 50,* 550–558.

Ryan, R. M., Weinstein, N., Bernstein, J., Brown, K. W., Mistretta, L., & Gagné, M. (2010). Vitalizing effects of being outdoors and in nature. *Journal of Environmental Psychology, 30* (2), 159–168. doi: 10.1016/j.jenvp.2009.10.009

Rydell, R. J., & McConnell, A. R. (2006). Understanding implicit and explicit attitude change: A systems of reasoning analysis. *Journal of Personality and Social Psychology, 91,* 995–1008.

Ryff, C. D. (1995). Psychological well-being in adult life. *Current Directions in Psychological Science, 4,* 99–104.

Rynd, N. (1988). Incidence of psychometric symptoms in rape victims. *Journal of Sex Research, 24,* 155–161.

Sackett, P. R., & DeVore, C. J. (2001). Counterproductive behaviors at work. In N. Anderson, D. S. Ones, H. K. Sinangil, & C. Viswesvaran, *Handbook of Industrial, Work and Organizational Psychology, 1,* 145–165. Thousand Oaks, CA: Sage.

Sackett, P. R., Hardison, C. M., & Cullen, M. J. (2004). On interpreting stereotype threat as accounting for African American–White differences on cognitive tests. *American Psychologist, 59,* 7–13.

Sackett, P. R., Hardison, C. M., & Cullen, M. J. (2004b). On the value of correcting mischaracterizations of stereotype threat research. *American Psychologist, 59,* 48–49.

Saegert, S. (1978). High density environments: Their personal and social consequences. In A. Baum & Y. M. Epstein (Eds.), *Human response to crowding* (pp. 259–276). Hillsdale, NJ: Erlbaum.

Saegert, S., MacIntosh, E., & West, S. (1975). Two studies of crowding in urban public spaces. *Environment and Behavior, 1,* 159–184.

Safer, M. A., Christianson, S.-A., Autry, M. W., & Osterlund, K. (1998). Tunnel memory for traumatic events. *Applied Cognitive Psychology, 12,* 99–117.

Sagie, A. (1997). Leader direction and employee participation in decision making: Contradictory or compatible practices? *Applied Psychology: An International Review, 46*(4), 387–452.

Sakaki, M., Fryker, K., & Mather, M. (2014). Emotion strengthens high-priority memory traces but weakens low-priority memory traces. *Psychological Science, 25,* 387–395.

Salgado, J. F., Viswesvaran, C., & Ones, D. (2001). Predictors used for personnel selection: An overview of constructs, methods and techniques. In N. Anderson, D. S. Ones, H. K. Sinangil, & C. Viswesvaran, *Handbook of industrial, work and organizational psychology* (vol. 1, pp. 166–199). Thousand Oaks, CA: Sage.

Sallie Mae. (2009). *How undergraduate students use credit cards: Sallie Mae's National Study of Usage Rates and Trends 2009.* Retrieved August 20, 2012, from http://static.mgnetwork.com/rtd/pdfs/20090830_iris.pdf

Salmivalli, C., Kaukiainen, A., Kaistaniemi, L., & Lagerspetz, K. M. J. (1999). Self evaluated self-esteem, peer-evaluated self-esteem, and defensive egotism as predictors of adolescents' participation in bullying situations. *Personality and Social Psychology Bulletin, 25,* 1268–1278.

Salovey, P., & Mayer, J. D. (1990). Emotional intelligence. *Imagination, Cognition, and Personality, 9,* 185–211.

Salovey, P., & Rodin, J. (1991). Provoking jealousy and envy: Domain relevance and self-esteem threat. *Journal of Social and Clinical Psychology, 10,* 395–413.

Sandelands, L. E., Brockner, J., & Glynn, M. A. (1988). If at first you don't succeed, try, try again: Effects of persistence-performance contingencies, ego involvement, and self-esteem on task persistence. *Journal of Applied Psychology, 73,* 208–216.

Sanders, A. (2017, September 29). Space and project management benchmarks. IFMA Research Report #34. Retrieved from https://slidex.tips/download/space-and-project-management-benchmarks-ifma-research-report-34.

Sanders, S. A., & Reinisch, J. M. (1999). Would you say you "had sex" if ...? *Journal of the American Medical Association, 281,* 275–277.

Sanna, L. J., & Schwarz, N. (2003). Using the hindsight bias: The role of accessibility experiences and (mis)attributions. *Journal of Experimental Social Psychology, 39,* 287–295.

Santos, M. D., Leve, C., & Pratkanis, A. R. (1994). Hey buddy, can you spare seventeen cents? Mindful persuasion and the pique technique. *Journal of Applied Social Psychology, 24,* 755–764.

Sapolsky, R. (2004). *Why zebras don't get ulcers: The acclaimed guide to stress, stress-related disease, and coping.* New York: Holt.

Sapolsky, R. M. (1998). *The trouble with testosterone: And other essays on the biology of the human predicament* (p. 150). New York: Scribner.

Sarason, B. R., Sarason, I. G., & Gurung, R. A. R. (2001). Close personal relationships and health outcomes: A key to the role of social support. In B. R. Sarason & S. Duck (Eds.), *Personal relationships. Implications for clinical and community psychology* (pp. 15–41). Chichester: Wiley.

Sargent, J. D., Dalton, M. A., Heatherton, T. & Beach, M. (2003). Modifying exposure to smoking depicted in movies: A novel approach to preventing adolescent smoking. *Archives of Pediatrics and Adolescent Medicine, 157*(7), 643–648.

Sarrel, M. D. (2006, November 29). Recycling e-waste. *PCMag.com.* Retrieved from http://www.pcmag.com/article2/0,2817,2064151,00.asp

SAS. (2015). Life at SAS. *Fast Company.* Retrieved from http://www.fastcompany.com/3004953/how-sas-became-worlds-best-place-work

Satow, K. L. (1975). Social approval and helping. *Journal of Experimental Social Psychology, 11,* 501–509.

Sauer, J., Brewer, N., Zweck, T., & Weber, N. (2010). The effect of retention interval on the confidence-accuracy relationship for eyewitness identification. *Law and Human Behavior, 34,* 337–347. doi: 10.1007/s10979-009-9192-x

Sauerland, M., & Sporer, S. L. (2009). Fast and confident: Postdicting eyewitness identification accuracy in a field study. *Journal of Experimental Psychology: Applied, 15,* 46–62.

Savin-Williams, R. C. (1990). *Gay and lesbian youth: Expressions of identity.* New York: Hemisphere.

Savitsky, K., Van Boven, L., Epley, N., & Wight, W. (2005). The unpacking effect in responsibility allocations for group tasks. *Journal of Experimental Social Psychology, 41,* 447–457.

Sawyer, J., & Gampa, A. (2018). Implicit and explicit racial attitudes changed during Black Lives Matter. *Personality and Social Psychology Bulletin, 44*(7), 1039–1059. https://doi-org.proxy.lib.umich.edu/10.1177/0146167218757454

Schachter, S. (1951). Deviation, rejection, and communication. *Journal of Abnormal and Social Psychology, 46*(2), 190–207.

Schachter, S. (1959). *The psychology of affiliation: Experimental studies of the sources of gregariousness.* Oxford: Stanford University Press.

Schachter, S. (1964). The interaction of cognitive and physiological determinants of emotional state. In L. Berkowitz (Ed.), *Advances in experimental social psychology* (pp. 49–79). New York: Academic Press.

Schachter, S., & Singer, J. E., (1962). Cognitive, social, and physiological determinants of emotional state. *Psychological Review, 69,* 379–399.

Schaller, M. (2011). The behavioural immune system and the psychology of human sexuality. *Philosophical Transactions of the Royal Society B, 366,* 3418–3426.

Schaller, M., & Murray, D. R. (2008). Pathogens, personality, and culture: Disease prevalence predicts worldwide variability in sociosexuality, extraversion, and openness to experience. *Journal of Personality and Social Psychology, 95,* 212–221.

Schaumberg, R.L., & Flynn, F.J. (2012). Uneasy lies the head that wears the crown: The link between guilt proneness and leadership. *Journal of Personality and Social Psychology, 103,* 327–342.

Scheibehenne, B., Greifeneder, R., & Todd, P. M. (2008, November). *Can there ever be too many options? Reassessing the effect of choice overload.* Paper presented at the annual meeting of the Society for Judgment and Decision Making, Chicago.

Scheier, M. F., Fenigstein, A., & Buss, A. H. (1974). Self-awareness and physical aggression. *Journal of Experimental Social Psychology, 10,* 264–273.

Schein, E. H. (1990). Organizational culture. *American Psychologist, 45*(2), 109–119.

Scheirer, M. A., & Kraut, R. E. (1979). Increased educational achievement via self-concept change. *Review of Educational Research, 49,* 131–150.

Scherer, L. D., & Lambert, A. J. (2012). Implicit race bias revisited: On the utility of task context in assessing implicit attitude strength. *Journal of Experimental Social Psychology, 48,* 366–370.

Schiavone, S. R., & Gervais, W. M. (2017). Atheists. *Social and Personality Psychology Compass, 11*(12), 1–13. DOI: 10.1111/spc3.12365

Schifferstein, H. N. J., & Michaut, A. M. K. (2002). Effects of appropriate and inappropriate odors on product evaluation. *Perceptual and Motor Skills, 95,* 1199–1214.

Schlaerth, A., Ensari, N., & Christian, J. (2013). A meta-analytical review of the relationship between emotional intelligence and leaders' constructive conflict management. *Group Processes & Intergroup Relations, 16*(1), 126–136. doi: 10.1177/1368430212439907

Schlenker, B. R. (1975). Self-presentation: Managing the impression of consistency when reality interferes with self-enhancement. *Journal of Personality and Social Psychology, 32,* 1030–1037.

Schlenker, B. R. (1980). *Impression management: The self-concept, social identity, and interpersonal relations.* Monterey, CA: Brooks/Cole.

Schlenker, B. R., Dlugolecki, D. W., & Doherty, K. J. (1994). The impact of self-presentations on self-appraisals and behaviors: The power of public commitment. *Personality and Social Psychology Bulletin, 20,* 20–33.

Schmidt, C. (1969). Urban crime areas: Part I. *American Sociological Review, 25,* 527–542.

Schmidt, F. L., & Hunter, J. E. (1998). The validity and utility of selection methods in personnel psychology: Practical and theoretical implications of 85 years of research findings. *Psychological Bulletin, 124*(2), 262–274.

Schmidt, R. E., & Gendolla, G. H. E. (2008). Dreaming of white bears: The return of the suppressed at sleep onset. *Consciousness and Cognition, 17*(3), 714–724.

Schmitt, D. P. (2003). Universal sex differences in the desire for sexual variety: Tests from 52 nations, 6 continents, and 13 islands. *Journal of Personality and Social Psychology, 85,* 85–104.

Schmitt, D. P. (2017). What type of person would agree to have sex with a stranger? Psychology Today blogs. https://www.psychologytoday.com/intl/blog/sexual-personalities/201706/what-type-person-would-agree-have-sex-stranger

Schmitt, D. P., Jonason, P. K., Byerley, G. J., Flores, S. D., Illbeck, B. E., O'Leary, K. N., & Qudrat, A. (2012). A reexamination of sex differences in sexuality: New studies reveal old truths. *Current Directions in Psychological Science, 21,* 135–139.

Schmitt, N., Cortina, J. M., Ingerick, M. J., & Wiechmann, D. (2003). Personnel selection and employee performance. In W. C. Borman, D. R. Ilgen, & R. J. Klimoski (Eds.), *Handbook of psychology: Industrial and organizational psychology* (vol. 12, pp. 77–105). New York: Wiley.

Schnall, S., Haidt, J., Clore, G. L., & Jordan, A. H. (2008). Disgust as embodied moral judgment. *Personality and Social Psychology Bulletin, 34*(8), 1096–1109.

Schooler, J. W., Ariely, D., & Loewenstein, G. (2003). The pursuit and assessment of happiness may be self-defeating. In J. Carrillo & I. Brocas (Eds.), *The psychology of economic decisions* (pp. 41–70). Oxford: Oxford University Press.

Schopler, J., & Insko, C. A. (1992). The discontinuity effect in interpersonal and intergroup relations: Generality and mediation. *European Review of Social Psychology, 3,* 121–151.

Schopler, J., & Stockdale, J. (1977). An interference analysis of crowding. *Environmental Psychology and Nonverbal Behavior, 1,* 81–88.

Schopler, J., Insko, C. A., Drigotas, S. M., Wieselquist, J., Pemberton, M. B., & Cox, C. (1995). The role of identifiability in the reduction of interindividual-intergroup discontinuity. *Journal of Experimental Social Psychology, 31,* 553–574.

Schopler, J., Insko, C. A., Drigotas, S., & Graetz, K. A. (1993). Individual-group discontinuity: Further evidence for mediation by fear and greed. *Personality and Social Psychology Bulletin, 19,* 419–431.

Schuller, R. A., & Hastings, P. A. (1996). Trials of battered women who kill: The impact of alternative forms of expert evidence. *Law and Human Behavior, 20,* 167–187.

Schultz, P. W. (2011). Conservation means behavior. *Conservation Biology, 25,* 1080–1083.

Schulz, A. (2018). Where populist citizens get the news: An investigation of news audience polarization along populist attitudes in 11 countries. *Communication Monographs.* https://doi-org.proxy.lib.umich.edu/10.1080/03637751.2018.1508876

Schuman, H., & Scott, J. (1987). Problems in the use of survey questions to measure public opinion. *Science, 236*(4804), 957–959.

Schütz, A. (1999). It was your fault! Self-serving biases in autobiographical accounts of esteem threatening conflicts in married couples. *Journal of Social and Personal Relationships, 16,* 193–209.

Schütz, A. (2000). *Selbstwertgefühl: Zwischen Selbstakzeptanz und Arroganz.* Stuttgart: Kohlhammer.

Schütz, A. (2001). Self-esteem and interpersonal strategies. In J. P. Forgas, K. D. Williams, & L. Wheeler (Eds.), *The social mind: Cognitive and motivational aspects of interpersonal behavior* (pp. 157–176). New York: Cambridge University Press.

Schwab, J., Nadeau, S. E., & Warheit, G. J. (1979). Crowding and mental health. *Pavlovian Journal of Biological Science, 14,* 226–233.

Schwartz, B. (2004, April). The tyranny of choice. *Scientific American,* 72–75.

Schwartz, S. H. (1977). Normative influences on altruism. *Advances in Experimental Social Psychology, 10,* 221–279.

Schwarz, N. (1999). Self-reports: How the questions shape the answers. *American Psychologist, 54*(2), 93–105. doi: 10.1037/0003-066X.54.2.93

Schwarz, N., & Clore, G. L. (1983). Mood, misattribution, and judgments of well-being: Informative and directive functions of affective states. *Journal of Personality and Social Psychology, 45,* 513–523.

Schwarzwald, J., Raz, M., & Zvibel, M. (1979). The applicability of the door-in-the-face technique when established behavioral customs exist. *Journal of Applied Social Psychology, 9,* 576–586.

Scott, J. P. (1958). *Aggression.* Chicago: University of Chicago Press.

Seabright, P. (2004). *The company of strangers: A natural history of economic life.* Princeton, NJ: Princeton University Press.

Seal, D. W. (1997). Interpartner concordance of self-reported sexual behavior among college dating couples. *Journal of Sex Research, 34,* 39–55.

Sears, D. O. (1986). College sophomores in the laboratory: Influences of a narrow data base on social psychology's view of human nature. *Journal of Personality and Social Psychology, 51,* 515–530.

Sedikides, C. (1993). Assessment, enhancement, and verification determinants of the self-evaluation process. *Journal of Personality and Social Psychology, 65,* 317–338.

Sedikides, C. S., & Gregg, A. P. (2008). Self-enhancement: Food for thought. *Perspectives on Psychological Science, 3,* 102–116.

Sedikides, C., Gaertner, L., & Toguchi, Y. (2003). Pan-cultural self-enhancement. *Journal of Personality and Social Psychology, 84,* 60–70.

Sedikides, C., Meek, R., Alicke, M. D., & Taylor, S. (2013). Behind bars but above the bar: Prisoners consider themselves more prosocial than non-prisoners. *British Journal of Social Psychology, 53,* 396–403.

Sedlovskaya, A., Purdie-Vaughn, V., Eibach, R.P., LaFrance, M., Romero-Canyas, R., & Camp, N.P. (2013). Internalizing the closet: Concealment heightens the cognitive distinction between public and private selves. *Journal of Personality and Social Psychology, 104,* 695–715.

Segal, N. L. (1984). Cooperation, competition and altruism within twin sets: A reappraisal. *Ethology and Sociobiology, 5,* 163–177.

Seligman, C., & Darley, J. M. (1977). Feedback as a means of decreasing residential energy consumption. *Journal of Applied Psychology, 62,* 363–368.

Semmler, C., Brewer, N., & Wells, G. L. (2004). Effects of postidentification feedback on eyewitness identification and nonidentification confidence. *Journal of Applied Psychology, 89,* 334–346.

Semmler, C., Dunn, J., Mickes, L., & Wixted, J. T. (2018). The role of estimator variables in eyewitness identification. *Journal of Experimental Psychology: Applied, 24,* 700–415.

Sennett, R. (1974). *The fall of public man.* New York: Random House.

Sentyrz, S. M., & Bushman, B. J. (1998). Mirror, mirror on the wall, who's the thinnest one of all? Effects of self-awareness on consumption of fatty, reduced-fat, and fat-free products. *Journal of Applied Psychology, 83,* 944–949.

Serota, K. B., Levine, T. R., & Boster, F. J. (2010). The prevalence of lying in America: Three studies of self-reported lies. *Human Communication Research, 36*(1), 2–25.

Seta, C. E., & Seta, J. J. (1995). When audience presence is enjoyable: The influences of audience awareness of prior success on performance and task interest. *Basic and Applied Social Psychology, 16*(1–2), 95–108.

Seyle, H. (1956). *The stress of life.* New York: McGraw-Hill.

Shackelford, T. K. (2001). Self-esteem in marriage: An evolutionary psychological analysis. *Personality and Individual Differences, 30,* 371–390.

Shadish, W. R., Cook, T. D., & Campbell, D. T. (2002). *Experimental and quasi-experimental designs for generalized causal inference.* New York: Houghton Mifflin Company.

Shah, J. Y. (2003). Automatic for the people: How representations of significant others implicitly affect goal pursuit. *Journal of Personality and Social Psychology, 84,* 661–681.

Shah, J. Y., Friedman, R., & Kruglanski, A. W. (2002). Forgetting all else: On the antecedents and consequences of goal shielding. *Journal of Personality and Social Psychology, 83,* 1261–1280.

Shakur, S. (1993). *Monster: The autobiography of an L.A. gang member.* New York: Atlantic Monthly Press.

Shapiro, P. N., & Penrod, S. D. (1986). Meta-analysis of facial identification studies. *Psychological Bulletin, 100,* 139–156.

Sharps, M., Higgs, S., Blissett, J., Nouwen, A., Chechlacz, M., Allen, H. A., & Robinson, E. (2015). Examining evidence for behavioural mimicry of parental eating by adolescent females. An observational study. *Appetite, 89,* 56–61.

Shavitt, S., Sanbonmatsu, D. M., Smittipatana, S., & Posavac, S. S. (1999). Broadening the conditions for illusory correlation formation: Implications for judging minority groups. *Basic and Applied Social Psychology, 21*(4), 263–279.

Shaw, B. F., & Beck, A. T. (1977). The treatment of depression with cognitive therapy. In A. Ellis & R. Grieger (Eds.), *Handbook of rational emotive therapy* (pp. 309–326). New York: Springer.

Shea, C. T., Davisson, E. K., & Fitzsimons, G. (2013). Riding other people's coattails: Individuals with low self-control value self-control in other people. *Psychological Science, 24,* 1031–1036.

Sheldon, K. M. (1994). Emotionality differences between artists and scientists. *Journal of Research in Personality, 28,* 481–491.

Sheldon, K. M., & Kasser, T. (1998). Pursuing personal goals: Skills enable progress but not all progress is beneficial. *Personality and Social Psychology Bulletin, 24,* 1319–1331.

Sheldon, K. M., & Lyubomirsky, S. (2004). Achieving sustainable new happiness: Prospects, practices, and prescriptions. In P. A. Linley & S. Joseph (Eds.), *Positive psychology in practice* (pp. 127–145). Hoboken, NJ: Wiley.

Shelton, J. N. (2003). Interpersonal concerns in social encounters between majority and minority group members. *Group Processes and Intergroup Relations, 6,* 171–185.

Shepperd, J. A., & Strathman, A. J. (1989). Attractiveness and height: The role of stature in dating preference, frequency of dating, and perceptions of attractiveness. *Personality and Social Psychology Bulletin, 15*(4), 617–627.

Sherif, M. (1935). A study of some social factors in perception. *Archives of Psychology* (Columbia University), *187,* 60.

Sherif, M. (1966) *In common predicament: Social psychology of intergroup conflict and cooperation.* Boston: Houghton-Mifflin.

Sherman, S. T., Zehner, K. S., Johnson, J., & Hirt, E. R. (1983). Social explanation: The role of timing, set, and recall on subjective likelihood estimates. *Journal of Personality and Social Psychology, 44,* 1127–1143.

Sherrod, D. R. (1974). Crowding, perceived control, and behavioral aftereffects. *Journal of Applied Social Psychology, 4,* 171–186.

Shi, F., Teplitskiy, M., Duede, E., & Evans, J. A. (2019). The wisdom of polarized crowd. *Nature Human Behaviour,* advance online publication, doi.org/10.1038/s41562-019-0541-6.

Shin, J., & Ariely, D. (2004). Keeping doors open: The effect of unavailability on incentives to keep options open. *Management Science, 50,* 575–586.

Shneidman, E. S. (1981). Suicide thoughts and reflections, 1960–1980. *Suicide and Life-Threatening Behavior, 11,* 197–360.

Shoda, Y., Mischel, W., & Peake, P. K. (1990). Predicting adolescent cognitive and self-regulatory competencies from preschool delay of gratification: Identifying diagnostic conditions. *Developmental Psychology, 26,* 978–986.

Shohat-Ophir, G., Kaun, K. R., Azanchi, R., & Heberlein, U. (2012). Sexual deprivation increases ethanol intake in *Drosophila. Science, 335,* 1351–1355.

Shook, N. J., & Fazio, R. H. (2008). Interracial roommate relationships: An experimental field test of the contact hypothesis. *Psychological Science, 19,* 717–723.

Shorter, E. (1975). *The making of the modern family.* New York: Basic Books.

Shotland, R. L., & Straw, M. K. (1976). Bystander response to an assault: When a man attacks a woman. *Journal of Personality and Social Psychology, 34,* 990–999.

Shrauger, J. S. (1975). Responses to evaluation as a function of initial self-perceptions. *Psychological Bulletin, 82,* 581–596.

Shrauger, J. S., & Shoeneman, T. J. (1979). Symbolic interactionist view of self-concept: Through the looking glass darkly. *Psychological Bulletin, 86,* 549–573.

Shrauger, J. S., & Sorman, P. B. (1977). Self-evaluations, initial success and failure, and improvement as determinants of persistence. *Journal of Consulting and Clinical Psychology, 45,* 784–795.

Shteir, R. (2011). *The steal: a cultural history of shoplifting.* New York: Penguin Press.

Shteynberg, G., & Apfelbaum, A. P. (2013). The power of shared experience: Simultaneous observation with similar others facilitates social learning. *Social Psychological and Personality Science, 4,* 738–744.

Shteynberg, G., Hirsh, J. B., Apfelbaum, E. P., Larsen, J. T., Galinsky, A. D., & Roese, N. J. (2014, August 25). Feeling more together: Group attention intensifies emotion. *Emotion.* Advance online publication. http://dx.doi.org/10.1037/a0037697

Shu, L. L., & Gino, F. (2012). Sweeping dishonesty under the rug: How unethical actions lead to forgetting of moral rules. *Journal of Personality and Social Psychology, 102,* 1164–1177.

Sidanius, J., & Pratto, F. (1999). *Social dominance: An intergroup theory of social hierarchy and oppression.* New York: Cambridge University Press.

Siem, B., & Stürmer, S. (2012). Cross-cultural volunteerism: Examining the effects of intercultural (dis)similarities on volunteers' motivations to support international students. *Basic and Applied Social Psychology, 34*(6), 544–557. doi: 10.1080/01973533.2012.727316

Siero, F. W., Bakker, A. B., Dekker, G. B., & Van Den Burg, M. T. C. (1996). Changing organizational energy consumption behavior through comparative feedback. *Journal of Environmental Psychology, 16,* 235–246.

Silfver, M., Helkama, K., Lönnqvist, J-E., & Verkasalo, M. (2008). The relation between value priorities and proneness to guilt, shame, and empathy. *Motivation and Emotion, 32*(2), 69–80.

Silk, J. B., Brosnan, S. F., Vonk, J., Henrich, J., Povinelli, D. J., Richardson, A. S., Lambeth, S. P., Mascaro, J., & Schapiro, S. J. (2005, October 27). Chimpanzees are indifferent to the welfare of unrelated group members. *Nature, 437,* 1357–1359.

Silver, K. (2017, August 14). Anger and hatred can make us feel happy, says study. *BBC.* Retrieved from https://www.bbc.com/news/health-40900811

Silvia, P. J., & Duval, T. S. (2001). Objective self-awareness theory: Recent progress and enduring problems. *Personality and Social Psychology Review, 5,* 230–241.

Sime, J. D. (1983). Affiliative behavior during escape to building exits. *Journal of Environmental Psychology, 3,* 21–41.

Simkin, M. G., & McLeod, A. (2010). Why do college students cheat? *Journal of Business Ethics, 94*(3), 441–453.

Simmons, J. P., Nelson, L. D., & Simonsohn, U. (2011). False-positive psychology: Undisclosed flexibility in data collection and analysis allows presenting anything as significant. *Psychological Science, 22,* 1359–1366. doi:10.1177/0956797611417632

Simpson, A., Rios, K., & Cowgill, C. M. (2017). Godless in essence? Psychological essentialism, theistic meta-beliefs, and anti-atheist prejudice. *Personality and Individual Differences, 119,* 35–45. DOI: 10.1016/j.paid.2017.06.029

Simpson, J. A. (1990). Influence of attachment styles on romantic relationships. *Journal of Personality and Social Psychology, 59,* 971–980.

Simpson, J. A. (2007). Foundations of interpersonal trust. In A. W. Kruglanski & E. T. Higgins (Eds.), *Social psychology: Handbook of basic principles* (2nd ed., pp. 587–607) New York: Guilford Press.

Simpson, J. A., Gangestad, S., & Lerma, M. (1990). Perception of physical attractiveness: Mechanisms involved in the maintenance of romantic relationships. *Journal of Personality and Social Psychology, 59,* 1192–1201.

Sinclair, L., & Kunda, Z. (1999). Reactions to a black professional: Motivated inhibition and activation of conflicting stereotypes. *Journal of Personality and Social Psychology, 77,* 885–904.

Sinclair, L., & Kunda, Z. (2000). Motivated stereotyping of women: She's fine if she praised me but incompetent if she criticized me. *Personality and Social Psychology Bulletin, 26,* 1329–1342.

Sinclair, R. C., & Brown, N. R. (1999, April–May). *Discrepant partner reports: Do women encode sexual experiences more deeply than men do?* Paper presented at the annual convention of the Midwestern Psychological Association, Chicago.

Singh, D. (1993). Adaptive significance of female physical attractiveness: Role of waist-to-hip ratio. *Journal of Personality and Social Psychology, 65*(2), 293–307.

Singh, D. (1995). Female judgment of male attractiveness and desirability for relationships: Role of waist-to-hip ratio and financial status. *Journal of Personality and Social Psychology, 69*(6), 1089–1101.

Skaalvik, E. M., & Hagtvet, K. A. (1990). Academic achievement and self-concept: An analysis of causal predominance in a developmental perspective. *Journal of Personality and Social Psychology, 58,* 292–307.

Skinner, B. F. (1938). *The behavior of organisms.* Englewood Cliffs, NJ: Appleton-Century-Crofts.

Sklar, A. Y., Levy, N., Goldstein, A., Mandel, R., Maril, A., & Hassin, R. R. (2012). Reading and doing arithmetic nonconsciously. *PNAS Proceedings of the National Academy of Sciences of the United States of America, 109*(48), 19614–19619. doi:10.1073/pnas.1211645109

Skolnick, A., Bascom, K. L., & Wilson, D. T. (2013). Gender role expectations of disgust: Men are low and women are high. *Sex Roles, 69*(1–2), 72–88. doi: 10.1007/s11199-013-0279-y

Slawinski, B. L., Klump, K. L., & Burt, S. A. (2018). The etiology of social aggression: A nuclear twin family study. *Psychological Medicine.* DOI: 10.1017/S0033291718000697

Slotter, E. B., Finkel, E. J., DeWall, C. N., Pond, R. S., Lambert, N. M., Bodenhausen, G. V., & Fincham, F. D. (2011). Putting the brakes on aggression toward a romantic partner: The inhibitory influence of relationship commitment. *Journal of Personality and Social Psychology, 102,* 291–305.

Slovic, P., & Lichtenstein, S. (1971). Comparison of Bayesian and regression approaches to the study of information processing in judgment. *Organizational Behavior and Human Performance, 6,* 649–744.

Smalarz, L., & Wells, G. L. (2014). Post-identification feedback to eyewitnesses impairs evaluators' abilities to discriminate between accurate and mistaken testimony. *Law and Human Behavior, 38,* 194–202.

Smith T. W., Snyder C. R., & Perkins S. C. (1983). The self-serving function of hypochondriacal complaints: Physical symptoms as self-handicapping strategies. *Journal of Personality and Social Psychology, 44,* 787–797.

Smith, C. A., Organ, D. W., & Near, J. P. (1983). Organizational citizenship behavior: Its nature and antecedents. *Journal of Applied Psychology, 68,* 653–663.

Smith, D. (2004, June 20). Sign writer. *Observer.* Retrieved from http://observer.guardian.co.uk/comment/story/0,6903,1243121,00.html

Smith, F. J. (1977). Work attitudes as a predictor of attendance on a specific day. *Journal of Applied Psychology, 62*(1), 16–19.

Smith, G. E., Gerrard, M., & Gibbons, F. X. (1997). Self-esteem and the relation between risk behavior and perceptions of vulnerability to unplanned pregnancy in college women. *Health Psychology, 16,* 137–146.

Smith, G. F., & Dorfman, D. D. (1975). The effect of stimulus uncertainty on the relationship between frequency of exposure and liking. *Journal of Personality and Social Psychology, 31,* 150–155.

Smith, G. H., & Engel, R. (1968). Influence of a female model on perceived characteristics of an automobile. *Proceedings of the Annual Convention of the American Psychological Association, 3,* 681–682.

Smith, J. D., Boomer, J., Zakrzewski, A. C., Roeder, J. L., Church, B. A., & Ashby, F. G. (2014). Deferred feedback sharply dissociates implicit and explicit category learning. *Psychological Science, 25*(2), 447–457. doi: 10.1177/0956797613509112

Smith, R. (2003, December 3). The impact of hate media in Rwanda. *BBC News.* Retrieved August 25, 2019 from http://news.bbc.co.uk/2/hi/africa/3257748.stm

Smith, R. J., & Knowles, E. S. (1979). Affective and cognitive mediators of reactions to spatial invasions. *Journal of Experimental Social Psychology, 15,* 437–452.

Smith, S. M., & Shaffer, D. R. (1991). Celerity and cajolery: Rapid speech may promote or inhibit persuasion through its impact on message elaboration. *Personality and Social Psychology Bulletin, 17,* 663–669.

Smith, T. (1994). Attitudes toward sexual permissiveness: Trends, correlates, and behavioral connections. In A. S. Rossi (Ed.), *Sexuality across the life course* (pp. 63–97). Chicago: University of Chicago Press.

Smith, T. B., McCullough, M. E., & Poll, J. (2003). Religiousness and depression: Evidence for a main effect and the moderating influence of stressful life events. *Psychological Bulletin, 129,* 614–636.

Smith, T. W., & Parkhurst, K. A. (2019). Personality and health. In T. A. Revenson & R. A. R. Gurung (Eds.), *Handbook of health psychology* (pp. 195–213). New York: Routledge.

Smuts, B. (1996). Male aggression against women: An evolutionary perspective. In D. Buss & N. Malamuth (Eds.), *Sex, power, conflict* (pp. 231–268). New York: Oxford University Press.

Snow, M. G., Prochaska, J. O., & Rossi, J. S. (1992). Stages of change for smoking cessation among former problem drinkers: A cross-sectional analysis. *Journal of Substance Abuse, 4*(2), 107–116.

Snyder, C. R., & Higgins, R. L. (1990). *Self-handicapping: The paradox that isn't.* Norwell, MA: Kluwer.

Snyder, C. R., & Lopez, S. (Eds.) (2002). *Handbook of positive psychology.* New York: Oxford University Press.

Snyder, M. (1974). Self monitoring of expressive behavior. *Journal of Personality and Social Psychology, 30,* 526–537.

Snyder, M., & Gangestad, S. (1986). On the nature of self-monitoring: Matters of assessment, matters of validity. *Journal of Personality and Social Psychology, 51,* 125–139.

Soetens, B., Braet, C., & Moens, E. (2008). Thought suppression in obese and non-obese restrained eaters: Piece of cake or forbidden fruit? *European Eating Disorders Review, 16*(1), 67–76.

Soetens, B., Braet, C., Dejonckheere, P., & Roets, A. (2006). When suppression backfires: The ironic effects of suppressing eating-related thoughts. *Journal of Health Psychology, 11*(5), 655–668.

Solomon, S. D., & Canino, G. J. (1990). Appropriateness of the DSM-III-R criteria for Posttraumatic Stress Disorder. *Comprehensive Psychiatry, 31,* 227–237.

Solomon, S., Greenberg, J., & Pyszczynski, T. A. (2004). Lethal consumption: Death-denying materialism. In T. Kasser & A. D. Kanner (Eds.), *Psychology and consumer culture: The struggle for a good life in a materialistic world* (pp. 127–146). Washington, DC: American Psychological Association.

Soman, D., & Cheema, A. (2002). The effect of credit on spending decisions: The role of the credit limit and credibility. *Marketing Science, 21,* 32–53.

Some kids won't eat the middle of an Oreo. (1991, November 20). *Wall Street Journal,* p. B1.

Sommer, K. L., & Rubin, Y. (2005). Maintaining self-esteem in the face of rejection. In K. D. Williams, J. P. Forgas, & W. von Hippel (Eds.), *The social outcast: Ostracism, social exclusion, rejection, and bullying* (pp. 171–184). New York: Psychology Press.

Sommer, K. L., & Yoon, J. (2013). When silence is golden: Ostracism as resource conservation during aversive interactions. *Journal of Social and Personal Relationships, 30,* 901–918.

Sommer, K. L., Williams, K. D., Ciarocco, N. J., & Baumeister, R. F. (2001). When silence speaks louder than words: Explorations into the intra-psychic and interpersonal consequences of social ostracism. *Basic and Applied Social Psychology, 23,* 225–243.

Sommer, R. (1969). *Personal space: The behavioral basis of design.* Englewood Cliffs, NJ: Prentice-Hall.

Sommers, P., & Moos, R. (1976). The weather and human behavior. In R. H. Moos (Ed.), *The human context: Environmental determinants of behavior* (pp. 73–107). New York: Wiley.

Sommers, S. R., & Norton, M. I. (2007). Race-based judgments, race-neutral justifications: Experimental examination of peremptory use and the Batson challenge procedure. *Law and Human Behavior, 31,* 261–273.

Sonnentag, S., & Frese, M. (2003). Stress in organizations. In W. C. Borman, D. R. Ilgen, & R. J. Klimoski (Eds.), *Handbook of psychology* (vol. 12, pp. 453–491). Hoboken, NJ: John Wiley & Sons.

Spangenberg, E. R., Crowley, A. E., & Henderson, P. W. (1996). Improving the store environment: Do olfactory cues affect evaluations and behaviors? *Journal of Marketing, 60,* 67–80.

Spangler, G., & Grossman, K. E. (1993). Biobehavioral organization in securely and insecurely attached infants. *Child Development, 64,* 1439–1450.

Spanier, G. B., & Lewis, R. A. (1980). Marital quality: A review of the seventies. *Journal of Marriage and the Family, 42,* 825–839.

Spanier, G. P., & Margolis, R. L. (1983). Marital separation and extramarital sexual behavior. *Journal of Sex Research, 19,* 23–48.

Spence, K. W. (1956). *Behavior theory and conditioning.* New Haven, CT: Yale University Press.

Spencer, S. J., Steele, C. M., & Quinn, D. M. (1999). Stereotype threat and women's math performance. *Journal of Experimental Social Psychology, 35,* 4–28.

Spielberg, W. E. (1986). Living with Indian Point: A study in investigating the relationship between stress, time distortion, ideology, coping style and expressed vulnerability of high school students in close residence to a nuclear power plant. *Dissertation Abstracts International, 47*(9–B), 3971–3972.

Spielmann, S. S., MacDonald, G., Maxwell, J. A., Joel, S., Peragine, D., Muise, A., & Impett, E. A. (2013). Settling for less out of fear of being single. *Journal of Personality and Social Psychology, 105,* 1049–1073.

Sporer, S. L., Penrod, S. D., Read, J. D., & Cutler, B. L. (1995). Choosing, confidence, and accuracy: A meta-analysis of the confidence-accuracy relation in eyewitness identification studies. *Psychological Bulletin, 118,* 315–327.

Sprecher, S. (1989). Premarital sexual standards for different categories of individuals. *Journal of Sex Research, 19*, 23–48.

Sprecher, S. (1998). Social exchange theories and sexuality. *Journal of Sex Research, 35*, 32–43.

Sprecher, S. (1999). "I love you more today than yesterday": Romantic partners' perceptions of changes in love and related affect over time. *Journal of Personality and Social Psychology, 76*, 46–53.

Sprecher, S., & Regan, P. (2002). Liking some things (in some people) more than others: Partner preferences in romantic relationships and friendships. *Journal of Social and Personal Relationships, 19*, 463–481.

Sprecher, S., & Regan, P. C. (1996). College virgins: How men and women perceive their sexual status. *Journal of Sex Research, 33*, 3–15.

Sroufe, L. A., & Waters, E. (1977). Heart rate as a convergent measure in clinical and developmental research. *Merrill-Palmer Quarterly, 23*, 3–27.

Staffieri, J. (1967). A study of social stereotype of body image in children. *Journal of Personality and Social Psychology, 7*, 101–104.

Staley, O. (2018). Hilton Hotels' newest upgrades are strictly for staff. Retrieved from https://qz.com/work/1233750/hilton-hotels-has-new-upgrades-strictly-for-service-workers

Stanko, E. A. (2000). The day to count: Reflections on a methodology to raise awareness about the impact of domestic violence in the UK. *Caribbean Journal of Criminology & Social Psychology, 5*(1–2), 103–118.

Stanley, S. K., & Wilson, M. S. (2019). Meta-analysing the association between social dominance orientation, authoritarianism, and attitudes on the environment and climate change. *Journal of Environmental Psychology, 61*, 46–56.

Staples, R. (1973). *Black women in America: Sex, marriage, and family.* Chicago: Nelson-Hall.

Staples, S. L. (1997). Public policy and environmental noise: Modeling exposure or understanding. *American Journal of Public Health, 87*, 2063–2067.

Stasser, G., & Titus, W. (1985). Pooling of unshared information in group decision making: Biased information sampling during discussion. *Journal of Personality and Social Psychology, 48*, 1467–1478.

Stasser, G., & Titus, W. (1987). Effects of information load and percentage of shared information on the dissemination of unshared information during group discussion. *Journal of Personality and Social Psychology, 53*, 81–93.

State v. Guilbert. Supreme Court of Connecticut, 306 Conn. 218 (2012).

State v. Henderson, 208 N.J. 208 (2011)

State v. Henderson, 27 A. 3d 872 (N. J. 2011).

Steblay, N. K., Wells, G. L., & Douglass, A. B. (2014). The eyewitness post identification effect 15 years later: Theoretical and policy implications. *Psychology, Public Policy, and Law, 20*, 1–18.

Steblay, N. M. (1997). Social influence in eyewitness recall: A meta-analytic review of lineup instruction effects. *Law and Human Behavior, 21*, 283–297.

Steblay, N. M., Besirevic, J., Fulero, S. M., & Jimenez-Lorente, B. (1999). The effects of pretrial publicity on juror verdicts: A meta-analytic review. *Law and Human Behavior, 23*, 219–235.

Steele, C. M., & Aronson, J. A. (1995). Stereotype threat and the intellectual test performance of African Americans. *Journal of Personality and Social Psychology, 69*, 797–811.

Steele, C. M., & Aronson, J. A. (2004). Stereotype threat does not live by Steele and Aronson (1995) alone. *American Psychologist, 59*, 47–55.

Steele, C. M., & Josephs, R. A. (1990). Alcohol myopia: Its prized and dangerous effects. *American Psychologist, 45*, 921–933.

Steele, C. M., & Southwick, L. (1985). Alcohol and social behavior: I. The psychology of drunken excess. *Journal of Personality and Social Psychology, 48*, 18–34.

Steffensmeier, D., & Allan, E. (1996). Gender and crime: Toward a gendered theory of female offending. *Annual Review of Sociology, 22*, 459–487.

Stein, R. (2011, January 11). Wakefield tried to capitalize on autism-vaccine link, report says. The Washington Post. Retrieved from http://voices.washingtonpost.com/checkup/2011/01/wakefield_tried_to_capitalize.html.

Steinfatt, T. M. (1973). The Prisoner's Dilemma and a creative alternative game: The effects of communications under conditions of real reward. *Simulation and Games, 4*, 389–409.

Steinfeld, J. (1972). *Statement in hearings before Subcommittee on Communications of Committee on Commerce* (United States Senate, Serial #92–52, pp. 25–27). Washington, DC: United States Government.

Steinmetz, K. (2012). Follow your nose: Food company launches 'smell-vertising' for potato ads. *Time NewsFeed.* Retrieved from http://newsfeed.time.com/2012/02/10/follow-your-nose-food-company-launches-smell-vertising-for-potato-ads/

Stephan, C. W. & Stephan, W. G. (1985). *Two social psychologies: An integrative approach.* Homewood, IL: Dorsey.

Stern, P. C., & Oskamp, S. (1987). Managing scarce environmental resources. In D. Stokols & I. Altman (Eds.), *Handbook of environmental psychology* (Vol. 2, pp. 1043–1088). New York: Wiley.

Stern, S. E., & Faber, J. E. (1997). The lost e-mail method: Milgram's lost-letter technique in the age of the Internet. *Behavior Research Methods, Instruments, and Computers, 29*, 260–263.

Sternberg, R. J. (1986). A triangular theory of love. *Psychological Review, 93*, 119–135.

Stewart, G. L., & Manz, C. C. (1995). Leadership for self-managing work teams: A typology and integrative model. *Human Relations, 48*, 347–370.

Stewart, J. B. (2013, March 15). Looking for a lesson in Google's perks. *New York Times.* Retrieved from http://www.nytimes.com/2013/03/16/business/at-google-a-place-to-work-and-play.html?pagewanted=all&_r=0

Stillman, T. F., Baumeister, R. F., & DeWall, C. N. (2007). What's so funny about not having money? The effects of power on laughter. *Personality and Social Psychology Bulletin, 33*, 1547–1558.

Stokols, D. (1972) On the distinction between density and crowding: Some implications for future research. *Psychological Review, 79*, 275–-277.

Stone, J., & McWhinnie, C. (2008). Evidence that blatant versus subtle stereotype threat cues impact performance through dual processes. *Journal of Experimental Social Psychology, 44*(2), 445–452.

Stone, J., Aronson, E., Crain, A. L., Winslow, M. P., & Fried, C. B. (1994). Inducing hypocrisy as a means of encouraging young adults to use condoms. *Personality and Social Psychology Bulletin, 20*, 116–128.

Stone, L. (1977). *The family, sex and marriage in England: 1500–1800.* London: Perennial.

Stoner, J. A. F. (1961). *A comparison of individual and group decisions involving risk.* Unpublished master's thesis, Massachusetts Institute of Technology.

Stopera, M. (2019, March 19). 15 things all straight people do that 2/3 of gay people are still afraid to. *BuzzFeed.* Retrieved from https://www.buzzfeed.com/mjs538/straight-people-do-this-but-23-of-gay-people-are

Store of the month. (1976, October). *Progressive Grocer,* 104.

Storey, A. E., Walsh, C. L., Quinton, R. L., & Wynne-Edward, K. E. (2000). Hormonal correlates of paternal responsiveness in new and expectant fathers. *Evolution and Human Behavior, 21*, 79–95.

Stout-Wiegand, N., & Trent, R. B. (1984–1985). Comparison of students' and non-student residents' attitudes toward local energy developments: Environmentalism versus economic interest. *Journal of Environmental Education, 16*, 29–35.

Strack, F., & Deutsch, R. (2004). Reflective and impulsive determinants of social behavior. *Personality and Social Psychology Review, 8*(3), 220–247.

Strack, F., Martin, L., & Stepper, S. (1988). Inhibiting and facilitating conditions of the human smile: A nonobtrusive test of the facial feedback hypothesis. *Journal of Personality and Social Psychology, 54*, 768–777.

Strasburger, V. C., Donnerstein, E. I., & Bushman, B. J. (2014). Why is it so hard to believe that media affect children and adolescents? *Pediatrics, 133*, 571–573. doi:10.1542/peds.2013-2334

Straus, M. A. (1997). Physical assaults by women partners: A major social problem. In M. R. Walsh (Ed.), *Women, men and gender: Ongoing debates* (pp. 210–221). New Haven, CT: Yale University Press.

Strober, M., & Humphrey, L. L. (1987). Familial contributions to the etiology and course of anorexia nervosa and bulimia. *Journal of Consulting and Clinical Psychology, 55*, 654–659.

Stroebe, W., Diehl, M., & Abakoumkin, G. (1992). The illusion of group effectivity. *Personality and Social Psychology Bulletin, 18*, 643–650.

Stroop, J. R. (1935). Studies of interference in serial verbal reactions. *Journal of Experimental Psychology, 28*, 643–662.

Studebaker, C. A., Robbennolt, J. K., Pathak-Sharma, M. K., & Penrod, S. D. (2000). Assessing pretrial publicity effects: Integrating content analytic results. *Law and Human Behavior, 24*, 317–336.

Subra, B., Muller, D., Bègue, L., Bushman, B. J., & Delmas, F. (2010). Automatic effects of alcohol and weapon cues on aggressive thoughts and behaviors. *Personality and Social Psychology Bulletin, 36*(8), 1052–1057. doi: 10.1177/0146167210374725

Sugiyama, L. S. (2004). Illness, injury, and disability among Shiwiar forager-horticulturalists: Implications of health-risk buffering for the evolution of human life history. *American Journal of Physical Anthropology, 123*, 371–389.

Sullivan, J. (2009, February 9). Employee furloughs can be a bad alternative to layoffs. Ere.net. Retrieved from http://www.ere.net/tags/furloughs

Sullivan, J. (2012). 10 compelling numbers that reveal the power of employee referrals. Retrieved from http://www.ere.net/2012/05/07/10-compelling-numbers-that-reveal-the-power-of-employee-referrals/

Sullivan, M. (2013, June 28). More proof office space design impacts productivity, focus and collaboration. Retrieved from http://www.officingtoday.com/2013/06/more-proof-office-space-design-impacts-productivity-focus-and-collaboration/

Suls, J., & Wan, C. K. (1987). In search of the false uniqueness phenomenon: Fear and estimates of social consensus. *Journal of Personality and Social Psychology, 52*, 211–217.

Suls, J., Wan, C. K., & Sanders, G. S. (1988). False consensus and false uniqueness in estimating the prevalence of health-protective behaviors. *Journal of Applied Social Psychology, 18*, 66–79.

Sundali, J., & Croson, R. (2006). Biases in casino betting: The hot hand and the gambler's fallacy. *Judgment and Decision Making, 1*(1), 1–12.

Sundstrom, E. (1978). Crowding as a sequential process: Review of research on the effects of population density on humans. In A. Baum & Y. M. Epstein (Eds.), *Human response to crowding* (pp. 31–116). Hillsdale, NJ: Erlbaum.

Sundstrom, E., Town, J. P., Rice, R. W., Osborn, D. P., & Brill, M. (1994). Office noise, satisfaction, and performance. *Environment and Behavior, 26*, 195–222.

Surowiecki, J. (2004). *The wisdom of crowds: Why the many are smarter than the few and how collective wisdom shapes business, economics, societies, and nations.* New York: Doubleday.

Susa, K. J., Meissner, C. A., & deHeer, H. (2010). Modeling the role of social-cognitive processes in the recognition of own- and other-race faces. *Social Cognition, 28*, 523–537.

Sussenbach, S., & Kameleitner, B. (2016). Psychological ownership as a facilitator of sustainable behaviors. In J. Peck and S. Shu (Eds.), *Psychological Ownership.* New York: Springer.

Svenson, O. (1981). Are we less risky and more skillful than our fellow drivers? *Acta Psychologica, 47*, 143–51.

Swami, V., & Monk, R. (2013). Weight bias against women in a university acceptance scenario. *Journal of General Psychology, 140*(1), 45–56. doi: 10.1080/00221309.2012.726288

Swann, W. B., De La Ronde, C., & Hixon, J. G. (1994). Authenticity and positivity strivings in marriage and courtship. *Journal of Personality and Social Psychology, 66*, 857–869.

Swann, W. B., Jr. (1985). The self as architect of social reality. In B. Schlenker (Ed.), *The self and social life* (pp. 100–125). New York: McGraw-Hill.

Swann, W. B., Jr. (1998). The self and interpersonal relationships. Paper presented at the meeting of the Society of Experimental Social Psychologists, Lexington, KY.

Swann, W. B., Jr., Griffin, J. J., Predmore, S., & Gaines, B. (1987). The cognitive-affective crossfire: When self-consistency confronts self-enhancement. *Journal of Personality and Social Psychology, 52*, 881–889.

Swann, W. B., Jr., Hixon, J. G., Stein-Seroussi, A., & Gilbert, D. T. (1990). The fleeting gleam of praise: Cognitive processes underlying behavioral reactions to self-relevant feedback. *Journal of Personality and Social Psychology, 59*, 17–26.

Swann, W. B., Jr., Stein-Seroussi, A., & Giesler, R. B. (1992). Why people self-verify. *Journal of Personality and Social Psychology, 62*, 392–401.

Swart, H., Hewstone, M., Christ, O., & Voci, A. (2011). Affective mediators of intergroup contact: A three-wave longitudinal study in South Africa. *Journal of Personality and Social Psychology, 101*(6), 1221–1238.

Swim, J. K. (1994). Perceived versus meta-analytic effect sizes: An assessment of the accuracy of gender stereotypes. *Journal of Personality and Social Psychology, 66*, 21–36.

Symanski, R. (1980). Prostitution in Nevada. In E. Muga (Ed.), *Studies in prostitution* (pp. 246–279). Nairobi: Kenya Literature Bureau.

Symons, C. S., & Johnson, B. T. (1997). The self-reference effect in memory: A meta-analysis. *Psychological Bulletin, 121*, 371–394.

Symons, D. (1979). *The evolution of human sexuality*. New York: Oxford University Press.

Symons, D. (1995). Beauty is in the adaptations of the beholder: The evolutionary psychology of human female sexual attractiveness. In P. R. Abramson & S. D. Pinkerton (Eds.), *Sexual nature/sexual culture* (pp. 80–118). Chicago: University of Chicago Press.

Szalma, J. L., & Hancock, P. A. (2011). Noise effects on human performance: A meta-analytic synthesis. *Psychological Bulletin, 137*, 682–707.

Sznycer, D., Xygalatas, D., Agey, E., Alami, S., An, X-F, Ananyeva, K. I., et al. (2018). Cross-cultural invariances in the architecture of shame. *PNAS, 115*(39), 9702–9707. doi: 10.1073/pnas.1805016115

Szymanski, S. (2000). A market test for discrimination in the English professional soccer leagues. *Journal of Political Economy, 108*(3), 590–603.

Tabaac, A., Perrin, P. B., & Benotsch, E. G. (2018). Discrimination, mental health, and body image among transgender and gender-non-binary indivdiuals: Constructing a multiple mediational path model. *Journal of Gay & Lesbian Social Services, 30*, 1–16.

Tajfel, H., & Billig, M. (1974). Familiarity and categorization in intergroup behavior. *Journal of Experimental Social Psychology, 10*(2), 159–170.

Tajfel, H., Billig, M. G., Bundy, R. P., & Flament, C. (1971). Social categorization and intergroup behaviour. *European Journal of Social Psychology, 1*(2), 149–178.

Tamir, D. I., & Mitchell, J. P. (2012). Disclosing information about the self is intrinsically rewarding. *PNAS, 109*, 8038–3043.

Tamir, M., Mitchell, C., & Gross, J. J. (2008). Hedonic and instrumental motives in anger regulation. *Psychological Science, 19*(4), 324–328.

Tamir, M., Schwartz, S. H., Oishi, S., & Kim, M. Y. (2017). The secret to happiness: Feeling good or feeling right? *Journal of Experimental Psychology: General, 146*(10), 1448–1459. doi:10.1037/xge0000303

Tangney, J. P., & Dearing, R. L. (2002). *Shame and guilt*. New York: Guilford Press.

Tangney, J. P., & Fischer, K. W. (1995). *Self-conscious emotions: The psychology of shame, guilt, embarrassment, and pride*. New York: Guilford Press.

Tangney, J. P., Baumeister, R. F., & Boone, A. L. (2004). High self-control predicts good adjustment, less pathology, better grades, and interpersonal success. *Journal of Personality, 72*, 271–322.

Tangney, J. P., Wagner, P., Fletcher, C., & Gramzow, R. (1992). Shamed into anger? The relation of shame and guilt to anger and self-reported aggression. *Journal of Personality and Social Psychology, 62*(4), 669–675. doi: 10.1037/0022-3514.62.4.669

Tannahill, R. (1980). *Sex in history*. London: Scarborough House.

Tanneberger, A., & Ciupitu-Plath, C. (2018). Nurses' weight bias in caring for obese patients: Do weight controllability beliefs influence the provision of care to obese patients? *Clinical Nursing Research, 27*(4), 414–432. DOI: 10.1177/1054773816687443

Tansey, G., & D'Silva, J. (1999). *The meat business: Devouring a hungry planet*. New York: St. Martin's Press.

Tarquinio, M. (2009, January 27). Workforce planning research: How to strengthen your job in today's economy. Ere.net. Retrieved from http://www.ere.net/2009/01/27/workforce-planning-research-how-to-strengthen-your-job-in-today%e2%80%99s-economy

Tarrant, M. A., & Cordell, H. K. (1997). The effect of respondent characteristics on general environmental attitude-behavior correspondence. *Environment and Behavior, 29*, 618–637.

Tata, J., Anthony, T., Lin, H., Newman, B., Tang, S., Millson, M., & Suvakumar, K. (1996). Proportionate group size and rejection of the deviate: A meta-analytic integration. *Journal of Social Behavior and Personality, 11*, 739–752.

Taylor, K. (2007). Disgust is a factor in extreme prejudice. *British Journal of Social Psychology, 46*(3), 597–617.

Taylor, L. E., Swerdfeger, A. L., & Eslick, G. D. (2014). Vaccines are not associated with autism: An evidence-based meta-analysis of case-control and cohort studies. Vaccine, 32(29), 3623–3629. doi: 10.1016/j.vaccine.2014.04.085

Taylor, R. B., Gottfredson, S. D., & Brower, S. (1981). Territorial cognitions and social climate in urban neighborhoods. *Basic and Applied Social Psychology, 2*, 289–303.

Taylor, S. E. (1983). Adjustment to threatening events: A theory of cognitive adaptation. *American Psychologist, 38*, 1161–1173.

Taylor, S. E., & Brown, J. D. (1988). Illusion and well-being: A social psychological perspective on mental health. *Psychological Bulletin, 103*, 193–210.

Taylor, S. E., & Gollwitzer, P. M. (1995). Effects of mindset on positive illusions. *Journal of Personality and Social Psychology, 69*, 213–226.

Taylor, S. E., & Master, S. L. (2011). Social responses to stress: The tend-and-befriend model. In R. J. Contrada, A. Baum, R. J. Contrada, A. Baum (Eds.), *The handbook of stress science: Biology, psychology, and health* (pp. 101–109). New York: Springer.

Taylor, S. E., & Pham, L. B. (1996). Mental simulation, motivation, and action. In P. M. Gollwitzer & J. A. Bargh (Eds.), *The psychology of action: Linking cognition and motivation to behavior* (pp. 219–235). New York: Guilford Press.

Taylor, S. E., Klein, L. C., Lewis, B. P., Gruenewald, T. L., Gurung, R. A. R, & Updegraff, J. A. (2000). Biobehavioral responses to stress in females: Tend-and-befriend, not fight-or-flight. *Psychological Review, 107*, 441–429.

Taylor, T. S., & Hosch, H. M. (2004). An examination of jury verdicts for evidence of a similarity-leniency effect, an out-group punitiveness effect, or a black sheep effect. *Law and Human Behavior, 28*, 587–598.

Tedeschi, J. T., & Felson, R. B. (1994). *Violence, aggression, and coercive actions*. Washington, DC: American Psychological Association.

Tedeschi, J. T., Schlenker, B. R., & Bonoma, T. V. (1971). Cognitive dissonance: Private ratiocination or public spectacle? *American Psychologist, 26*, 685–695.

Teigen, H. (1986). Old truths or fresh insights? A study of student's evaluations of proverbs. *British Journal of Social Psychology, 25*, 43–50.

Telch, C. F., & Agras, W. S. (1996). Do emotional states influence binge eating in the obese? *International Journal of Eating Disorders, 20*, 271–279.

Tennen, H., Affleck, G., Armeli, S., & Carney, M. A. (2000). A daily process approach to coping: Linking theory, research, and practice. *American Psychologist, 55*(6), 626–636.

Terracciano, A., Abdel-Khalek, A. M., Adam, N., Adamovova, L., Ahn, C.-K., Ahn, H.-N., et al. (2005). National character does not reflect mean personality trait levels in 49 cultures. *Science, 310*, 96–100.

Terrizzi, J. A., Jr., Shook, N. J., & Ventis, W. L. (2010). Disgust: A predictor of social conservatism and prejudicial attitudes toward homosexuals. *Personality and Individual Differences, 49*(6), 587–592.

Tesser, A. (1976). Attitude polarization as a function of thought and reality constraints. *Journal of Research in Personality, 10*, 183–194.

Tesser, A. (1988). Toward a self-evaluation maintenance model of social behavior. In L. Berkowitz (Ed.), *Advances in experimental social psychology* (Vol. 21, pp. 181–227). San Diego: Academic Press.

Tesser, A., & Rosen, S. (1975). The reluctance to transmit bad news. In L. Berkowitz (Ed.), *Advances in experimental social psychology* (Vol. 8, pp. 193–232). New York: Academic Press.

Tetlock, P. E. (1980). Explaining teacher explanations for pupil performance: A test of the self-presentation position. *Social Psychology Quarterly, 43*, 283–290.

Tetlock, P. E. (1981). Pre- to post-election shifts in presidential rhetoric: Impression management or cognitive adjustment? *Journal of Personality and Social Psychology, 41*, 207–212.

Tetlock, P. E. (1992). The impact of accountability on judgment and choice: Toward a social contingency model. In M. P. Zanna (Ed.), *Advances in experimental social psychology* (Vol. 25, pp. 331–376). San Diego: Academic Press.

Tetlock, P. E. (2000). Coping with trade-offs: Psychological constraints and political implications. In S. Lupia, M. McCubbins, & S. Popkin (Eds.), *Political reasoning and choice*. Berkeley: University of California Press.

Tett, R. P., Jackson, D. N., Rothstein, M., & Reddon, J. R. (1994). Meta-analysis of personality-job performance relations: A reply to Ones, Mount, Barrick, & Hunter (1994). *Personnel Psychology, 47*(1), 157–172.

Texas Department of State Health Services (2018, January 23). Measles outbreak in Ellis County. Retrieved from https://www.dshs.texas.gov/news/releases/2018/HealthAdvisory-01232018.aspx

Texas Municipal League Intergovernmental Risk Pool. (2018, April 20). Don't Mess with Texas - The story behind the slogan. https://blog.tmlirp.org/dont-mess-with-texas-the-story-behind-the-slogan

Thayer, R. E., Newman, R., & McClain, T. M. (1994). Self-regulation of mood: Strategies for changing a bad mood, raising energy, and reducing tension. *Journal of Personality and Social Psychology, 67*, 910–925.

The Believeau Law Group. (2012). Can companies use social media to screen job applicants? Retrieved from www.beliveaulaw.net/2012/02/can-companies-use-social-media-to-screen-job-applicants/

The Economist (2015, October 22). Death on the roads.

The Editors of The Lancet. (2010, February). Retraction—Ileal-lymphoid-nodular hyperplasia, non-specific colitis, and pervasive developmental disorder in children. The Lancet 375 (9713), 445. doi:10.1016/S0140-6736(10)60175-4

The Onion. (2014, June 24). Report: Only Predictor Of Happy Marriage Is If Husband Ever Won Wife Big Stuffed Animal At Amusement Park. Retrieved from: http://www.theonion.com/articles/report-only-predictor-of-happy-marriage-is-if-husb,36353/

The triumph of evil. (1995). *PBS Frontline*. Retrieved from http://www.pbs.org/wgbh/pages/frontline/shows/evil

Thinkexist.com Retrieved from http://thinkexist.com/quotation/a_good_advertisement_is_one_which_sells_the/202773.html

Thomas, K. A., DeScioli, P., Haque, O. S., & Pinker, S. (2014). The psychology of coordination and common knowledge. *Journal of Personality and Social Psychology*, Advance online publication. http://dx.doi.org/10.1037/a0037037

Thompson, A. P. (1983). Extramarital sex: A review of the research literature. *Journal of Sex Research, 19*, 1–22.

Thompson, M. P., Norris, F. H., & Hanacek, B. (1993). Age differences in the psychological consequences of Hurricane Hugo. *Psychology and Aging, 8*, 606–616.

Thompson, S. C. G., & Stoutemyer, K. (1991). Water use as a commons dilemma: The effects of education that focuses on long-term consequences and individual action. *Environment and Behavior, 23*, 314–333.

Thompson-Cannino, J., Cotton, R., & Torneo, E. (2009): *Picking Cotton: Our memoir of injustice and redemption*. New York: St. Martin's Press.

Thornhill, R., & Gangestad, S. W. (1999). The scent of symmetry: A human sex pheromone that signals fitness? *Evolution and Human Behavior, 20*, 175–201.

Thrash, T. M., & Elliot, A. J. (2003). Inspiration as a psychological construct. *Journal of Personality and Social Psychology, 84*, 871–889.

Tice, D. M. (1991). Esteem protection or enhancement? Self-handicapping motives and attributions differ by trait self-esteem. *Journal of Personality and Social Psychology, 60*, 711–725.

Tice, D. M. (1992). Self-presentation and self-concept change: The looking-glass self is also a magnifying glass. *Journal of Personality and Social Psychology, 63*, 435–451.

Tice, D. M., & Baumeister, R. F. (1993). Controlling anger: Self-induced emotion change. In D. M. Wegner & J. W. Pennebaker (Eds.), *Handbook of mental control* (pp. 393–409). Englewood Cliffs, NJ: Prentice-Hall.

Tice, D. M., & Baumeister, R. F. (1997). Longitudinal study of procrastination, performance, stress, and health: The costs and benefits of dawdling. *Psychological Science, 8*, 454–458.

Tice, D. M., & Bratslavsky, E. (2000). Giving in to feel good: The place of emotion regulation in the context of general self-control. *Psychological Science, 11*, 149–159.

Tice, D. M., Bratslavsky, E., & Baumeister, R. F. (2001). Emotional distress regulation takes precedence over impulse control: If you feel bad, do it! *Journal of Personality and Social Psychology, 80*, 53–67.

Tice, D. M., Butler, J. L., Muraven, M. B., & Stillwell, A. M. (1995). When modesty prevails: Differential favorability of self-presentation to friends and strangers. *Journal of Personality and Social Psychology, 69*, 1120–1138.

Tichener, J. L., & Kapp, F. T. (1976). Family and character change at Buffalo Creek. *American Journal of Psychiatry, 33*(3), 295–299.

Tidwell, M., Reis, H. T., & Shaver, P. R. (1996). Attachment styles, attractiveness, and emotions in social interactions: A diary study. *Journal of Personality and Social Psychology, 71*, 729–745.

Tiggemann, M., & Pickering, A. S. (1996). Role of television in adolescent women's body dissatisfaction and drive for thinness. *International Journal of Eating Disorders, 20*, 199–220.

Tiggemann, M., & Rothblum, E. D. (1988). Gender differences in social consequences of perceived overweight in the United States and Australia. *Sex Roles, 18*, 75–86.

Tilcsik, A. (2011). Pride and prejudice: Employment discrimination against openly gay men in the United States. *American Journal of Sociology, 117*(2), 586–626.

Timbergen, N. (1952). The curious behavior of the Stickleback. *Scientific American, 187*, 22–26.

Timeline: Rwanda. (2008, August 8). *BBC News*. Retrieved August 25, 2019 from http://news.bbc.co.uk/2/hi/africa/1070329.stm

Tjaden, P., & Thoennes, N. (1998). *Stalking in America: Findings from the National Violence Against Women Survey* (NCJ Report no. 169592). Washington, DC: National Institute of Justice and Centers for Disease Control and Prevention.

Tobacyk, J. J., & Downs, A. (1986). Personal construct threat and irrational beliefs as cognitive predictors of increases in musical performance anxiety. *Journal of Personality and Social Psychology, 51*(4), 779–782.

Tobacyk, J., & Milford, G. (1983). Belief in paranormal phenomena: Assessment instrument development and implications for personality functioning. *Journal of Personality and Social Psychology, 44*, 1029–1037.

Toll, B. A., Sobell, M. B., Wagner, E. F., & Sobell, L. C. (2001). The relationship between thought suppression and smoking cessation. *Addictive Behaviors, 26*, 509–515.

Toma, C. L., & Hancock, J. T. (2010). Looks and lies: The role of physical attractiveness in online dating self-presentation and deception. *Communication Research, 37*(3), 335–351.

Toma, C. L., Hancock, J. T., & Ellison, N. B. (2008). Separating fact from fiction: An examination of deceptive self-presentation on online dating profiles. *Personality and Social Psychology Bulletin, 34*, 1023–1036.

Tomasello, M. (2013) *A natural history of human thinking*. Cambridge, MA: Harvard University Press.

Tomasello, M. (2016) *A natural history of morality*. Cambridge, MA: Harvard.

Tomasello, M., & Call, J. (1997). *Primate cognition*. New York: Oxford University Press.

Tomkins, S. S. (1962). *Affect, imagery, consciousness: Vol. 1. The positive affects*. New York: Springer.

Toomey, R. B., Syvertsen, A. K., & Shramko, M. (2018). Transgender adolescent suicide behavior. *Pediatrics, 142*(4), 1–8.

Tormala, Z. L., & Petty, R. E. (2002). What doesn't kill me makes me stronger: The effects of resisting persuasion on attitude certainty. *Journal of Personality and Social Psychology, 83*, 1298–1313.

Tran, C. (2014, August 6). All heave! Commuters work together to free with their bare hands man whose leg had become stuck between platform and train. *DailyMail*. Retrieved August 26, 2019 from http://www.dailymail.co.uk/news/article-2717511/Train-commuters-managed-free-man-leg-stuck-to.html

Tremblay, R. E. (2000). The development of aggressive behavior during childhood: What have we learned in the past century? *International Journal of Behavioral Development, 24*(2), 129–141.

Triandis, H. C. (1978). Some universals of social behavior. *Personality and Social Psychology Bulletin, 4*, 1–16.

Trinkaus, J. (1984). A bottle law: An informal look. *Perceptual and Motor Skills, 59*, 806.

Triplett, N. (1897). The dynamogenic factors in peacemaking and competition. *American Journal of Psychology, 9*, 507–533.

Trivers, R. (1972). Parental investment and sexual selection. In B. Campbell (Ed.), *Sexual selection and the descent of man: 1871–1971* (pp. 136–179). Chicago: Aldine.

Trope, Y. (1983). Self-assessment in achievement behavior. In J. Suls & A. Greenwald (Eds.), *Psychological perspectives on the self* (Vol. 2, pp. 93–121). Hillsdale, NJ: Erlbaum.

Trope, Y. (1986). Self-enhancement and self-assessment in achievement behavior. In R. Sorrentino & E. T. Higgins (Eds.), *Handbook of motivation and cognition* (Vol. 2, pp. 350–378). New York: Guilford Press.

Trzesniewski, K. H., Donnellan, M. B., & Robins, R. W. (2008). Is "Generation Me" really more narcissistic than previous generations? *Journal of Personality, 76*, 903–917.

Tsal, Y. (1984). *The role of attention in processing information from advertisements*. Unpublished manuscript, Cornell University, Ithaca, NY.

Tsang, J.-A., McCullough, M. E., & Hoyt, W. T. (2005). Psychometric and rationalization accounts for the religion-forgiveness discrepancy. *Journal of Social Issues. 61*, 785–805.

Tse, A. C. B., & Yim, F. (2001). Factors affecting the choice of channels: Online vs. conventional. *Journal of International Consumer Marketing, 14*, 137–152.

Tufekci, Z. (2008). Grooming, gossip, Facebook, and Myspace: What can we learn about these sites from those who won't assimilate? *Information, Communication & Society, 11*, 544–564.

Turnbull, S. (2003). *The Ottoman Empire 1326–1699*. New York: Routledge.

Turner, R. H. (1976). The real self: From institution to impulse. *American Journal of Sociology, 81*, 989–1016.

Turner, S. A., Luszczynska, A., Warner, L., & Schwarzer, R. (2010). Emotional and uncontrolled eating styles and chocolate chip cookie consumption. A controlled trial of the effects of positive mood enhancement. *Appetite, 54*(1), 143–149.

Tversky, A., & Kahneman, D. (1974) Judgment under uncertainty: Heuristics and biases. *Science, 185*, 1124–1131.

Tversky, A., & Kahneman, D. (1983). Extensional vs. intuitive reasoning: The conjunction fallacy in probability judgment. *Psychological Review, 91*, 293–315.

Twenge, J. M. (2006). *Generation me*. New York: Free Press.

Twenge, J. M., & Campbell, W. K. (2001). Age and birth cohort differences in self-esteem: A cross-temporal meta-analysis. *Personality and Social Psychology Review, 5*, 321–344.

Twenge, J. M., & Crocker, J. (2002). Race and self-esteem: Meta-analyses comparing Whites, Blacks, Hispanics, Asians, and American Indians. *Psychological Bulletin, 128*, 371–408.

Twenge, J. M., Baumeister, R. F., Tice, D. M., & Stucke, T. S. (2001). If you can't join them, beat them: Effects of social exclusion on aggressive behavior. *Journal of Personality and Social Psychology, 81*, 1058–1069.

Twenge, J. M., Campbell, W. K., & Foster, C. A. (2003). Parenthood and marital satisfaction: A meta-analytic review. *Journal of Marriage and Family, 65*, 574–583.

Twenge, J. M., Catanese, K. R., & Baumeister, R. F. (2002). Social exclusion causes self-defeating behavior. *Journal of Personality and Social Psychology, 83*, 606–615.

Twenge, J. M., Catanese, K. R., & Baumeister, R. F. (2003). Social exclusion and the deconstructed state: Time perception, meaninglessness, lethargy, lack of emotion, and self-awareness. *Journal of Personality and Social Psychology, 85*, 409–423.

Twenge, J. M., Ciarocco, N. J., Cuervo, D., Bartels, J. M., & Baumeister, R. F. (2004). Social exclusion reduces prosocial behavior. *Journal of Personality and Social Psychology, 92*, 56–66.

Twenge, J. M., Konrath, S., Foster, J. D., Campbell, W. K., & Bushman, B. J. (2008). Egos inflating over time: A cross-temporal meta-analysis of the Narcissistic Personality Inventory. *Journal of Personality, 76*, 875–901.

Twenge, J., & Crocker, J. (2002). Race, ethnicity, and self-esteem: Meta-analyses comparing whites, blacks, Hispanics, Asians, and Native Americans, including a commentary on Gray-Little and Hafdahl (2000). *Psychological Bulletin, 128*, 371–408.

Twohey, R. J. (2018). Strategically integrating human dimensions into marine conservation decision making. UC Santa Barbara. ProQuest ID: Twohey_ucsb_0035D_14094. Merritt ID: ark:/13030/m58q0zgz. Retrieved from https://escholarship.org/uc/item/6m64p2wg

Tybout, A. M., & Yalch, R. F. (1980). The effect of experience: A matter of salience? *Journal of Consumer Research, 6*, 406–413.

U.S. Census Bureau. (2009). New motor vehicle sales and car production. *The 2009 statistical abstract: National data book*. Retrieved from http://www.census.gov/compendia/statab/tables/09s1021.pdf

U.S. Department of Justice. (2019). *Identity theft*. Retrieved August 25, 2019 from http://www.justice.gov/criminal/fraud/websites/idtheft.html

U.S. Equal Employment Opportunity Commission. (2012). *Laws & guidance*. Retrieved from http://www.eeoc.gov/laws/index.cfm

U.S. Federal Bureau of Investigation. (2012). *Uniform crime reports.* Washington, DC: U.S. Government Printing Office.

U.S. Federal Bureau of Investigation. (2018). *Uniform crime reports.* Washington, DC: U.S. Government Printing Office.

Uchino, B. N., Cacioppo, J. T., & Kiecolt-Glaser, J. K. (1996). The relationship between social support and physiological processes: A review with emphasis on underlying mechanisms and implications for health. *Psychological Bulletin, 119,* 488–531.

Udry, J. R. (1980). Changes in the frequency of marital intercourse from panel data. *Archives of Sexual Behavior, 9,* 319–325.

Uhlmann, E. L., Pizarro, D. A., & Diermeier, D. (2015). A person-centered approach to moral judgment. *Perspectives on Psychological Science, 10,* 72–81.

Umphress, E. E., Ren, L. R., Bingham, J. B., & Gogus, C. I. (2009). The influence of distributive justice on lying for and stealing from a supervisor. *Journal of Business Ethics, 86,* 507–518.

Underwood, J. D. M., Kerlin, L., & Farrington-Flint, L. (2011). The lies we tell and what they say about us: Using behavioural characteristics to explain Facebook activity. *Computers in Human Behavior, 27*(5), 1621–1626.

Unger, L. S. (1996). The potential for using humor in global advertising. *Humor, 9,* 143–168.

Union of Concerned Scientists. (1993). *World scientists warning to humanity.* Cambridge, MA: Union of Concerned Scientists.

United Nations Population Fund. (2007/2008). A human rights and health priority. Retrieved October 17, 2008, from http://www.unfpa.org/swp/2000/english/ch8.html

Utman, C. H. (1997). Performance effects of motivational state: A meta-analysis. *Personality and Social Psychology Review, 1,* 170–182.

Vaillancourt, R. (2005). Indirect aggression among humans: Social construct or evolutionary adaption? In R. E. Tremblay, W. W. Hartup, & J. Archer (Eds.), *Developmental origins of aggression* (pp. 158–177). New York: Guilford Press.

Valentine, T., & Mesout, J. (2009). Eyewitness identification under stress in the London Dungeon. *Applied Cognitive Psychology, 23,* 151–161.

van 't Veer, A. E., Stel, M., & van Beest, I. (2014). Limited capacity to lie: Cognitive load interferes with being dishonest. *Judgment and Decision Making, 9*(3), 199–206. doi: 10.2139/ssrn.2351377

Van Bavel, J. J., & Cunningham, W. A. (2012). A social identity approach to person memory: Group membership, collective identification, and social role shape attention and memory. *Personality and Social Psychology Bulletin, 38,* 1566–1578.

Van Beest, I., & Williams, K. D. (2006). When inclusion costs and ostracism pays, ostracism still hurts. *Journal of Personality and Social Psychology, 91,* 918–928.

Van Boven, L., & Epley, N. (2003). The unpacking effect in evaluative judgments: When the whole is less than the sum of its parts. *Journal of Experimental Social Psychology, 39,* 263–269.

Van Boven, L., & Gilovich, T. (2003). To do or to have? That is the question. *Journal of Personality and Social Psychology, 85,* 1193–1202.

Van Boven, L., Ehret, P. J., & Sherman, D. K. (2018). Psychological barriers to bipartisan public support for climate policy. *Perspectives on Psychological Science, 13,* 492–507.

Van Boven, L., Kamada, A., & Gilovich, T. (1999). The perceiver as perceived: Everyday intuitions about the correspondence bias. *Journal of Personality and Social Psychology, 77*(6), 1188–1199.

Van Damme, C., Deschrijver, E., Van Geert, E., & Hoorens, V. (2017). When praising yourself insults others: Self-superiority claims provoke aggression. *Personality and Social Psychology Bulletin, 43,* 1008-1019.

Van den Bergh, B., Dewitte, S., & Warlop, L. (2008). Bikinis instigate generalized impatience in intertemporal choice. *Journal of Consumer Research, 35*(1), 85–97.

van der Linden, S., Leiserowitz, A., Rosenthal, S., & Maibach, E. (2017). Inoculating the public against misinformation about climate change. *Global Challenges, 1,* 1600008. http://dx.doi.org/10.1002/gch2.201600008

Van der Wal, R.C., & van Dillen, L.F. (2013). Leaving a flat taste in your mouth: Task load reduces taste perception. *Psychological Science, 24,* 1277–1284.

Van Dijk, E., Van Kleef, G. A., Steinel, W., & Van Beest, I. (2008). A social functional approach to emotions in bargaining: When communicating anger pays and when it backfires. *Journal of Personality and Social Psychology, 94*(4), 600–614.

Van Dijk, W. W., & Zeelenberg, M. (2002). Investigating the appraisal patterns of regret and disappointment. *Motivation and Emotion, 26,* 321–331.

Van Goozen, S. H. M., Cohen-Kettenis, P. T., Gooren, L. J. G. M., Frijda, N. H., & Can de Poll, N. E. (1995). Gender differences in behaviour: Activating effects of cross-sex hormones. *Psychoneuroendocrinology, 20,* 343–363.

Van Horne, T. (2013, December 5). Workplace design impacts performance, employee engagement and innovation. Retrieved from http://www.canadaone.com/ezine/2013/workplace_design_impacts_performance.html

Van Houten, R., & Nau, P. A. (1981). A comparison of the effects of posted feedback and increased police surveillance on highway speeding. *Journal of Applied Behavior Analysis, 14,* 261–271.

Van Kleef, G. A., De Dreu, C. K. W., & Manstead, A. S. R. (2004a). The interpersonal effects of anger and happiness in negotiations. *Journal of Personality and Social Psychology, 86*(1), 57–76.

Van Kleef, G. A., De Dreu, C. K. W., & Manstead, A. S. R. (2004b). The interpersonal effects of emotions in negotiations: A motivated information processing approach. *Journal of Personality and Social Psychology, 87*(4), 510–528.

Van Praag, H. M. (1990). Two-tier diagnosing in psychiatry. *Psychiatry Research, 34,* 1–11.

Van Vugt, M., & Samuelson, C. (1999). The impact of personal metering in the management of a natural resource crisis: A social dilemma analysis. *Personality and Social Psychology Bulletin, 25,* 731–745.

Vandello, J. A., & Cohen, D. (2003). Male honor and female fidelity: Implicit cultural scripts that perpetuate domestic violence. *Journal of Personality and Social Psychology, 84*(5), 997–1010.

Vandello, J. A., Bosson, J. K., Cohen, D., Burnaford, R. M., & Weaver, J. R. (2008). Precarious manhood. *Journal of Personality and Social Psychology, 95,* 1325–1339.

Vartanian, L. R., Thomas, M. A, & Vanman, E. J. (2013). Disgust, contempt, and anger and the stereotypes of obese people. *Eating and Weight Disorders, 18*(4), 377–382. doi: 10.1007/s40519-013-0067-2

Vaughan, D. (1986). *Uncoupling: Turning points in intimate relationships.* New York: Oxford University Press.

Vazire, S. (2010). Who knows what about a person? The Self-Other Knowledge Asymmetry (SOKA) model. *Journal of Personality and Social Psychology, 98,* 281–300.

Veenhoven, R. (2004). Challenges for Quality of Life in the Contemporary World. *World database of happiness: Continuous register of scientific research on subjective appreciation of life* (pp. 75–89). Retrieved August 25, 2019 from https://link.springer.com/chapter/10.1007/978-1-4020-2903-5_6

Veenstra, L., Bushman, B. J., & Koole, S. L. (2018). The facts on the furious: A brief review of the psychology of trait anger. *Current Opinion in Psychology, 19,* 98–103. DOI: 10.1016/j.copsyc.2017.03.014

Veenstra, L., Schneider, I. K., Bushman, B. J., & Koole, S. L. (2017). Drawn to danger: Trait anger predicts automatic approach behavior to angry faces. *Cognition and Emotion, 31*(4), 765–771. DOI: 10.1080/02699931.2016.1150256

Vermeulen, F. (2011, March 22). The price of obesity: How your salary depends on your weight. *Forbes.* Retrieved from https://www.forbes.com/sites/freekvermeulen/2011/03/22/the-price-of-obesity-how-your-salary-depends-on-your-weight/#36861f4a3d9a

Viek, C., & Steg, L. (2007). Human behavior and environmental sustainability: problems, driving forces and research topics. *Journal of Social Issues, 63,* 1–19.

Vohs, K. D. & Heatherton, T. F. (2000). Self-regulatory failure: A resource depletion approach. *Psychological Science, 11,* 249–254.

Vohs, K. D., & Schooler, J. (2008). The value of believing in free will: Encouraging a belief in determinism increases cheating. *Psychological Science, 19,* 49–54.

Vohs, K. D., Baumeister, R. F., Schmeichel, B. J., Twenge, J. M., Nelson, N. M., & Tice, D. M. (2008). Making choices impairs subsequent self-control: A limited-resource account of decision making, self-regulation, and active initiative. *Journal of Personality and Social Psychology, 94,* 883–898. doi: 10.1037/0022-3514.94.5.883

Vohs, K. D., Mead, N. L., & Goode, M. R. (2006, November). The psychological consequences of money. *Science, 314*(5802), 1154–1156.

Von Hippel, W., & Trivers, R. (2011). The evolution and psychology of self-deception. *Behavioral and Brain Sciences, 34,* 1–56.

Vonasch, A.J., Reynolds, T., Winegard, B.M., & Baumeister, R.F. (2018). Death before dishonour: Incurring costs to protect moral reputation. *Social Psychology and Personality Science, 9,* 604–613.

Vosoughi, S., Roy, D. & Aral, S. (2018). The spread of true and false news online. *Science, 359*(6380), 1146–1151. DOI: 10.1126/science.aap9559

Wagner, H. S., Ahlstrom, B., Redden, J. P., Vickers, Z., & Mann, T. (2014). The myth of comfort food. *Health Psychology, 33*(12), 1552–1557. doi: 10.1037/hea0000068

Wagner, M. (2017). 'Blood and soil': Protesters chant Nazi slogan in Charlottesville. CNN. Retrieved from https://www.cnn.com/2017/08/12/us/charlottesville-unite-the-right-rally/index.html

Wakefield, A., Murch, S., Anthony, A., Linnell, J., Casson, D. M., Malik, M., et al. (1998). Ileal-lymphoid-nodular hyperplasia, non-specific colitis, and pervasive developmental disorder in children. Lancet, 351 (9103): 637–641. doi:10.1016/S0140-6736(97)11096-0

Wakslak, C. J., Nussbaum, S., Liberman, N., & Trope, Y. (2008). Representations of the self in the near and distant future. *Journal of Personality and Social Psychology, 95,* 751–773.

Waldman, S. (1992, January 27). The tyranny of choice: Why the consumer revolution is ruining your life. *New Republic,* 22–25.

Walker, I., & Crogan, M. (1998). Academic performance, prejudice, and the jigsaw classroom: New pieces to the puzzle. *Journal of Community and Applied Social Psychology, 8,* 381–393.

Wallace, H. M., & Baumeister, R. F. (2002). The performance of narcissists rises and falls with perceived opportunity for glory. *Journal of Personality and Social Psychology, 82,* 819–834.

Wallach, M. A., Kogan, N., & Bem, D. J. (1962). Group influence on individual risk-taking. *Journal of Abnormal and Social Psychology, 65,* 75–86.

Walsh, A. (1991). Self-esteem and sexual behavior: Exploring gender differences. *Sex Roles, 25,* 441–450.

Walsh, A. (1991). The biological relationship between sex and love. *Free Inquiry, 11,* 20–24.

Walster, E., & Festinger, L. (1962). The effectiveness of "overheard" persuasive communication. *Journal of Abnormal and Social Psychology, 65,* 395–402.

Walster, E., Aronson, V., Abrahams, D., & Rottmann, L. (1966). Importance of physical attractiveness in dating behavior. *Journal of Personality and Social Psychology, 4,* 508–516.

Walters, K. S., & Portmess, L. (Eds.). (1999). *Ethical vegetarianism: From Pythagoras to Peter Singer.* Albany: State University of New York Press.

Walton, G. M., Cohen, G. L., Cwir, D., & Spencer, S. J. (2012). Mere belonging: The power of social connections. *Journal of Personality and Social Psychology, 102,* 513–532.

Wamsley, L. (2017, October 25). Einstein's note on happiness, given to bellboy in 1922, fetches $1.6 million. *NPR*. Retrieved from https://www.npr.org/sections/thetwo-way/2017/10/25/560004689/einsteins-note-on-happiness-given-to-bellboy-in-1922-fetches-1-6-million

Wanberg, C. R., Kammeyer-Mueller, J. D., & Shi, K. (2001). Job loss and the experience of unemployment: International research and perspectives. In N. Anderson, D. S. Ones, H. K. Sinangil, & C. Viswesvaran (Eds.), *Handbook of Industrial, Work and Organizational Psychology* (vol. 2, pp. 253–269). Thousand Oaks, CA: Sage.

Wang, C. L., Bristol, T., Mowen J. C., & Chakraborty, G. (2000). Alternative modes of self-construal: Dimensions of connectedness-separateness and advertising appeals to the cultural and gender-specific self. *Journal of Consumer Psychology, 9*, 107–115.

Wang, P. S., Gruber, M. J., Powers, R. E., Schoenbaum, M., Speier, A. H., Wells, K. B., et al. (2007). Mental health service use among Hurricane Katrina survivors in the eight months after the disaster. *Psychiatric Services, 58*, 1403–1411.

Waring, R. L., & Buchanan, F. R. (2010). Social networking web sites: The legal and ethical aspects of pre-employment screening and employee surveillance. *Journal of Human Resources Education, 4*(2), 14–23.

Warneken, F., & Tomasello, M. (2006). Altruistic helping in human infants and young chimpanzees. *Science, 311*, 1301–1303.

Watson, D., & Clark, L. A. (1991). Self-versus peer ratings of specific emotional traits: Evidence of convergent and discriminant validity. *Journal of Personality and Social Psychology, 60*, 927–940.

Watson, D., & Clark, L. A. (1992). Affects separable and inseparable: On the hierarchical arrangement of the negative affects. *Journal of Personality and Social Psychology, 62*, 489–505.

Watson, D., & Clark, L. A. (1997). Extraversion and its positive emotional core. In R. Hogan, J. Johnson, & S. Briggs (Eds.), *Handbook of personality psychology* (pp. 767–793). New York: Academic Press.

Watson, D., & Tellegen, A. (1985). Toward a consensual structure of mood. *Psychological Bulletin, 98*, 219–235.

Waytz, A., Young, L.L., & Ginges, J. (2014). Motive attribution asymmetry for love vs. hate drives intractable conflict. *PNAS*, early edition.

Weary, G. (1980). Examination of affect and egotism as mediators of bias in causal attributions. *Journal of Personality and Social Psychology, 38*, 348–357.

Weber, N., Brewer, N., Wells, G. L., Semmler, C., & Keast, A. (2004). Eyewitness identification accuracy and response latency: The unruly 10–12-second rule. *Journal of Experimental Psychology: Applied, 10*, 139–147.

WebMD (2015). Stress symptoms. Retrieved from http://www.webmd.com/balance/stress-management/stress-symptoms-effects_of-stress-on-the-body?page=2

Wegner, D. M. (1986). Transactive memory: A contemporary analysis of the group mind. In B. Mullen & G. R. Goethals (Eds.), *Theories of group behavior* (pp. 185–208). New York: Springer-Verlag.

Wegner, D. M. (1989). *White bears and other unwanted thoughts: Suppression, obsession, and the psychology of mental control*. New York: Viking/Penguin.

Wegner, D. M. (1994). Ironic processes of mental control. *Psychological Review, 101*, 34–52.

Wegner, D. M. (2002). *The illusion of conscious will*. Cambridge, MA: MIT Press.

Wegner, D. M., Giuliano, T., & Hertel, P. (1985). Cognitive interdependence in close relationships. In W. Ickes (Ed.), *Compatible and incompatible relationships* (pp. 253–276). New York: Springer-Verlag.

Wegner, D. M., Schneider, D. J., Carter, S. R., & White, T. L. (1987). Paradoxical effects of thought suppression. *Journal of Personality and Social Psychology, 53*(1), 5–13.

Wegner, D. M., Wenzlaff, R. M., & Kozak, M. (2004). Dream rebound: The return of suppressed thoughts in dreams. *Psychological Science, 15*, 232–236.

Weierstall, R., Haer, R., Banholzer, L., & Elbert, T. (2013). Becoming cruel: Appetitive aggression released by detrimental socialisation in former Congolese soldiers. *International Journal of Behavioral Development, 37*(6), 505–513. DOI: 10.1177/0165025413499126

Weiner, B. (1972). *Theories of motivation: From mechanism to cognition*. Chicago: Rand McNally.

Weinrich, S., Hardin, S. B., & Johnson, M. (1990). Nurses respond to hurricane Hugo victims: Disaster stress. *Archives of Psychiatric Nursing, 4*, 195–205.

Weintraub, K. J. (1978). *The value of the individual: Self and circumstance in autobiography*. Chicago: University of Chicago Press.

Weiss, B., & Feldman, R. S. (2006). Looking good and lying to do it: Deception as an impression management strategy in job interviews. *Journal of Applied Social Psychology, 36*(4), 1070–1086.

Wells, G. L. (1984). The psychology of lineup identifications. *Journal of Applied Social Psychology, 14*, 89–103.

Wells, G. L. (1993). What do we know about eyewitness identification? *American Psychologist, 48*, 553–571.

Wells, G. L., & Bradfield, A. L. (1998). "Good, you identified the suspect": Feedback to eyewitnesses distorts their reports of the witnessing experience. *Journal of Applied Psychology, 83*, 360–376.

Wells, G. L., & Luus, C. A. E. (1990). Police lineups as experiments: Social methodology as a framework for properly conducted lineups. *Personality and Social Psychology Bulletin, 16*, 106–117.

Wells, G. L., & Olson, E. A. (2003). Eyewitness testimony. *Annual Review of Psychology, 54*, 277–295.

Wells, G. L., & Petty, R. E. (1980). The effects of overt head movements on persuasion: Compatibility and incompatibility of responses. *Basic and Applied Social Psychology, 1*, 219–230.

Wells, G. L., & Quinlivan, D. S. (2009). Suggestive eyewitness identification procedures and the Supreme Court's reliability test in light of eyewitness science: 30 years later. *Law and Human Behavior, 33*, 1–24.

Wells, G. L., & Turtle, J. W. (1986). Eyewitness identification: The importance of lineup models. *Psychological Bulletin, 99*, 320–329.

Wells, G. L., & Windschitl, P. D. (1999). Stimulus sampling and social psychological experimentation. *Personality and Social Psychology Bulletin, 25*, 1115–1125.

Wells, G. L., Kovera, M. B., Douglass, A. B., Brewer, N., Meissner, C. A., & Wixted, J. (2020). Policy and procedure recommendations for the collection and preservation of eyewitness identification evidence. *Law and Human Behavior*.

Wells, G. L., Olson, E. A., & Charman, S. D. (2003). Distorted retrospective eyewitness reports as functions of feedback and delay. *Journal of Experimental Psychology: Applied, 9*, 42–52.

Wells, G. L., Steblay N. K., & Dysart, J. E. (2012). Eyewitness identification reforms: Are suggestiveness-induced hits and guesses true hits? *Perspectives on Psychological Science, 7*, 264–271.

Wenger, A. A., & Bornstein, B. H. (2006). The effects of victim's substance use and relationship closeness on mock jurors' judgments in an acquaintance rape case. *Sex Roles, 54*, 547–555.

Wenzlaff, R. M., & Wegner D. M. (2000). Thought suppression. *Annual Review of Psychology, 51*, 59–91.

Werle, C.O.C., Wansink, B., & Payne, C.R. (2014). Is it fun or exercise? The framing of physical activity biases subsequent snacking. *Marketing Letters*, DOI 10.1007/s11002-014-9301-6.

West Virginia Division of Personnel. (2004, September). Selection interviewing: Developing and administering structured behavioral interviews. Retrieved from http://webcache.googleusercontent.com/search?q=cache:khtpGpmt7vwJ:www.state.wv.us/admin/personnel/emprel/toolbox/quiz/interviewing.pdf+&cd=1&hl=en&ct=clnk&gl=us

West, S. G., & Brown, T. J. (1975). Physical attractiveness, the severity of the emergency and helping: A field experiment and interpersonal simulation. *Journal of Experimental Social Psychology, 11*, 531–538.

Westergaard, G. C., Mehlman, P. T., Suomi, S. J., & Higley, J. D. (1999). CSF 5-HIAA and aggression in female macaque monkeys: Species and interindividual differences. *Psychopharmacology, 146*, 440–446.

Westfall, R., Millar, M., & Walsh, M. (2016) Effects of instructor attractiveness on learning. *Journal of General Psychology, 143*, 161–171.

Whatley, M. A., Webster, J. M., Smith, R. H., & Rhodes, A. (1999). The effect of a favor on public and private compliance: How internalized is the norm of reciprocity? *Basic and Applied Social Psychology, 21*, 251–259.

Wheeler, L., & Kim, Y. (1997). What is beautiful is culturally good: The physical attractiveness stereotype has different content in collectivistic cultures. *Personality and Social Psychology Bulletin, 23*, 795–802.

Wheeler, L., & Nezlek, J. (1977). Sex differences in social participation. *Journal of Personality and Social Psychology, 35*, 742–754.

Wheeler, L., Reis, H., & Nezlek, J. B. (1983). Loneliness, social interaction, and sex roles. *Journal of Personality and Social Psychology, 45*(4), 943–953.

Whisman, V. (1996). *Queer by choice*. New York: Routledge.

Whitaker, J. L., & Bushman, B. J. (2012). "Remain calm. Be kind": Effects of relaxing video games on aggressive and prosocial behavior. *Social Psychological and Personality Science, 3*(1), 88–92. doi: 10.1177/1948550611409760

White, A. E., Kenrick, D. T., Li, Y. J., Mortensen, C. R., Neuberg, S.L., & Cohen, A. B. (2012). When nasty breeds nice: Threats of violence amplify agreeableness at national, individual, and situational levels. *Journal of Personality and Social Psychology, 103*, 622–634.

White, C. M., Reisen, N., & Hoffrage, U. (2008, November). *Choice deferral can arise from absolute evaluation or relative comparison*. Paper presented at the annual meeting of the Society for Judgment and Decision Making, Chicago.

White, F. A., Verrelli, S., Maunder, R. D., & Kervinen, A. (2018). Using electronic contact to reduce homonegative attitudes, emotions, and behavioral intentions among heterosexual women and men: A contemporary extension of the contact hypothesis. *Journal of Sex Research*. DOI: 10.1080/00224499.2018.1491943

White, G. L. (1980). Physical attractiveness and courtship progress. *Journal of Personality and Social Psychology, 39*, 660–668.

Whitley, B. E. (1988). Sex differences in heterosexuals' attitudes toward homosexuals: It depends upon what you ask. *Journal of Sex Research, 24*, 287–291.

Whitley, C. T., Takahashi, B., Zwickle, A., Besley, J. C., & Lertpratchya, A. P. (2018). Sustainability behaviors among college students: An application of the VBN theory. *Environmental Education Research, 24*, 245–262.

Whitson, J. A., Liljenquist, K. A., Galinsky, A. D., Magee, J. C., Gruenfeld, D. H., & Cadena, B. (2013). The blind leading: Power reduces awareness of constraints. *Journal of Experimental Social Psychology, 49*, 579–582.

Whitten, S. (2018, September 7). Nike's online sales surge in days after Kaepernick ad debut. *CNBC*. Retrieved from https://www.cnbc.com/2018/09/07/nikes-online-sales-surge-in-days-after-kaepernick-ad-debut.html

Why We Fight. Retrieved from http://history.acusd.edu/gen/filmnotes/whywefight.html

Wicker, A. W. (1969). Attitudes versus actions: The relationship of verbal and overt behavioral responses to attitude object. *Journal of Social Issues, 25*, 41–78.

Wicklund, R. A. (1974). *Freedom and reactance*. Potomac, MD: Erlbaum.

Wicklund, R. A., & Gollwitzer, P. M. (1982). *Symbolic self-completion*. Hillsdale, NJ: Erlbaum.

Wiederman, M. W. (1993). Demographic and sexual characteristics of nonresponders to sexual experience items in a national survey. *Journal of Sex Research, 30*, 27–35.

Wiederman, M. W. (1997). The truth must be in here somewhere: Examining the gender discrepancy in self-reported lifetime number of sex partners. *Journal of Sex Research, 34,* 375–386.

Wiederman, M. W. (2004). Self-control and sexual behavior. In R. Baumeister & K. Vohs (Eds.), *Handbook of self-regulation* (pp. 537–552). New York: Guilford Press.

Wiederman, M. W., & LaMar, L. (1998). "Not with him you don't!": Gender and emotional reactions to sexual infidelity during courtship. *Journal of Sex Research, 34,* 375–386.

Wiehe, V. R. (1991). *Perilous rivalry: When siblings become abusive.* Lexington, MA: Heath/Lexington Books.

Wieselquist, J., Rusbult, C. E., Foster, C. A., & Agnew, C. R. (1999). Commitment, pro-relationship behavior, and trust in close relationships. *Journal of Personality and Social Psychology, 77,* 942–966.

William, I. M. (1993). *Humiliation: And other essays on honor, social discomfort, and violence.* Ithaca, NY: Cornell University Press.

Williams, A. D. (1992). Bias and debiasing techniques in forensic psychology. *American Journal of Forensic Psychology, 10,* 19–26.

Williams, K. D. (2001). *Ostracism: The power of silence.* New York: Guilford Press.

Williams, K. D., & Zadro, L. (2005). Ostracism: The indiscriminate early detection system. In K. D. Williams, J. P. Forgas, & W. von Hippel (Eds.), *The social outcast: Ostracism, social exclusion, rejection, and bullying* (pp. 19–34). New York: Psychology Press.

Williams, K., Harkins, S. G., & Latané, B. (1981). Identifiability as a deterrant to social loafing: Two cheering experiments. *Journal of Personality and Social Psychology, 40*(2), 303–311.

Williams, S. S. (2001). Sexual lying among college students in close and casual relationships. *Journal of Applied Social Psychology, 31*(11), 2322–2338.

Williamson, G. M., & Clark, M. S. (1989). Providing help and desired relationship type as determinants of changes in moods and self-evaluations. *Journal of Personality and Social Psychology, 56*(5), 722–734.

Willis, R. (1989). The "peace puzzle" in Ufipa. In S. Howell & R. Willis (Eds.), *Societies at peace: Anthropological perspectives* (pp. 133–145). London: Routledge.

Wills, T. A. (1981). Downward comparison principles in social psychology. *Psychological Bulletin, 90,* 245–271.

Wills, T., Sargent, J., Stoolmiller, M., Gibbons, F., & Gerrard, M. (2008). Movie smoking exposure and smoking onset: A longitudinal study of mediation processes in a representative sample of U.S. adolescents. *Psychology of Addictive Behaviors, 22*(2), 269–277.

Wilson, J., Kuehn, R., & Beach, F. (1963). Modifications in the sexual behavior of male rats produced by changing the stimulus female. *Journal of Comparative and Physiological Psychology, 56,* 636–644.

Wilson, M., & Daly M. (2003). Do pretty women inspire men to discount the future? Biology Letters. *Proceedings of the Royal Society, London. B (Suppl.).* doi: 10.1098/rsbl.2003.0134

Wilson, T. D., Dunn, D. S., Kraft, D., & Lisle, D. J. (1989). Introspection, attitude change, and attitude-behavior consistency: The disruptive effects of explaining why we feel the way we do. In M. P. Zanna (Ed.), *Advances in experimental social psychology* (Vol. 22, pp. 287–343). San Diego: Academic Press.

Wilson, T. D., Hodges, S. D., & LaFleur, S. J. (1995). Effects of introspecting about reasons: Inferring attitudes from accessible thoughts. *Journal of Personality and Social Psychology, 69,* 16–28.

Wilson, T. D., Lindsey, S., & Schooler, T. Y. (2000). A model of dual attitudes. *Psychological Review, 107,* 101–126.

Wilson, T. D., Reinhard, D. A., Westgate, E. C., Gilbert, D. T., Ellerbeck, N., Hahn, C., Brown, C. L., & Shaked, A. (2014). Just think: The challenges of the disengaged mind. *Science, 345,* 75–77.

Wilson, T. D., Wheatley, T., Meyers, J. M., Gilbert, D. T., & Axsom, D. (2000). Focalism: A source of durability bias in affective forecasting. *Journal of Personality and Social Psychology, 78,* 821–836.

Winegard, B., Reynolds, T., Baumeister, R. F., & Plant, E.A. (2016). The coalitional value theory of anti-gay bias. *Evolutionary Behavioral Sciences, 10,* 245–269.

Winfield, F. E. (1985). *Commuter marriage.* New York: Columbia University Press.

Wing, R. R., Tate, D. F., Gorin, A. A., Raynor, H. A., Fava, J. L., & Machan, J. (2007). "STOP regain": Are there negative effects of daily weighing? *Journal of Consulting and Clinical Psychology, 75,* 652–656.

Witt, L. A., Kacmar, M., Carlson, D. S., & Zivnuska, S. (2002). Interactive effects of personality and organizational politics on contextual performance. *Journal of Organizational Behavior, 23,* 911–926.

Witvliet, C. V. O., Ludwig, T. E., & Van der Laan, K. L. (2001). Granting forgiveness or harboring grudges: Implications for emotion, physiology, and health. *Psychological Science, 121,* 117–123.

Wixted, J. T., & Wells, G. L. (2017). The relationship between eyewitness confidence and identification accuracy: A new synthesis. *Psychological Science in the Public Interest, 18,* 10–65.

Wixted, J. T., Mickes, L., Clark, S. E., Gronlund, S. D., & Roediger, H. L. III (2015). Initial eyewitness confidence reliably predicts eyewitness identification accuracy. *American Psychologist, 70,* 515–526.

Wohl, M. J. A., & Branscombe, N. R. (2008). Remembering historical victimization: Collective guilt for current ingroup transgressions. *Journal of Personality and Social Psychology, 94,* 988–1006.

Wolf, R. (2018, June 4). Supreme Court rules on narrow grounds for baker who refused to create same-sex couple's wedding cake. *USA Today.* Retrieved from https://www.usatoday.com/story/news/politics/2018/06/04/supreme-court-rules-against-gay-wedding-exemptions/1052989001/

Wong, N. C. H. (2016). "Vaccinations are safe and effective": Inoculating positive HPV vaccine attitudes against antivaccination attack messages. *Communication Reports, 29*(3), 127–138. https://doi-org.proxy.lib.umich.edu/10.1080/08934215.2015.10

Wood, P. B., & Bartkowski, J. P. (2004). Attribution style and public policy attitudes toward gay rights. *Social Science Quarterly, 85*(1), 58–74.

Wood, W. & Neal, D. (2007). A new look at habits and the habit-goal interface. *Psychological Review, 114,* 843–863.

Wood, W., & Neal, D. T. (2009). The habitual consumer. *Journal of Consumer Psychology, 19,* 579–592.

Wood, W., & Rünger, D. (2016). Psychology of habit. *Annual Review of Psychology, 67,* 289–314.

Wooten, D. B. (2000). Qualitative steps toward an expanded model of anxiety in gift-giving. *Journal of Consumer Research, 27,* 84–95.

Worchel, S., Lee, J., & Adewole, A. (1975). Effects of supply and demand on ratings of object value. *Journal of Personality and Social Psychology, 32,* 906–914.

Word, C. O., Zanna, M. P., & Cooper, J. (1974). The nonverbal mediation of self-fulfilling prophecies in interracial interaction. *Journal of Experimental Social Psychology, 10,* 109–120.

World Economic Forum (2013). Top 10 trends of 2014. Retrieved from http://reports.weforum.org/outlook-14/top-ten-trends-category-page/top-10-trends-of-2014-introduction/

World Health Organization (2003). WHO definition of health. Preamble to the Constitution of the World Health Organization as adopted by the International Health Conference, New York, 19–22 June, 1946; signed on 22 July 1946 by the representatives of 61 States (Official Records of the World Health Organization, no. 2, p. 100) and entered into force on 7 April 1948. Retrieved from http://www.who.int/about/definition/en/print.html

World Health Organization (2016). Road traffic injuries. Retrieved from www.who.int/mediacentre/factsheets/fs358/en/

World Health Organization. (2019, May 29). Tobacco. Retrieved August 25, 2019 from http://www.who.int/en/news-room/fact-sheets/detail/tobacco

Worthman, C. M. (1999). Faster, farther, higher: Biology and the discourses on human sexuality. In D. Suggs & A. Miracle (Eds.), *Culture, biology, and sexuality* (pp. 64–75). Athens: University of Georgia Press.

Wortley, R., & McFarlane, M. (2011). The role of territoriality in crime prevention: A field experiment. *Security Journal, 24,* 149–156.

Wortman, C. B., & Brehm, J. W. (1975). Responses to uncontrollable outcomes: An integration of reactance theory and the learned helplessness model. In L. Berkowitz (Ed.), *Advances in experimental social psychology* (Vol. 8, pp. 277–336). New York: Academic Press.

Wout, D., Danso, H., Jackson, J., & Spencer, S. (2008). The many faces of stereotype threat: Group- and self-threat. *Journal of Experimental Social Psychology, 44*(3), 792–799.

Wright R. (2000). *Non zero: The logic of human destiny.* New York: Pantheon.

Wright, E. F., & Jackson, W. (1991). The home-course disadvantage in golf championships: Further evidence for the undermining effect of supportive audiences on performance under pressure. *Journal of Sport Behavior, 14,* 51–60.

Wright, E. F., & Voyer, D. (1995). Supporting audiences and performance under pressure: The home-ice disadvantage in hockey championships. *Journal of Sport Behavior, 18,* 21–28.

Wright, J. C., Giammarino, M., & Parad, H. W. (1986). Social status in small groups: Individual-group similarity and the social "misfit." *Journal of Personality and Social Psychology, 50,* 523–536.

Wright, S. C., Aron, A., McLaughlin-Volpe, T., & Ropp, S. A. (1997). The extended contact effect: Knowledge of cross-group friendships and prejudice. *Journal of Personality and Social Psychology, 73,* 73–90.

Wrzesniewski, A., Schwartz, B., Cong, X., Kane, M., Omar, A., & Kolditz, T. (2014). Multiple types of motives don't multiply the motivation of West Point cadets. *PNAS, 111,* 10990–10995.

Wyer, R. S., & Frey, D. (1983). The effects of feedback about self and others on the cognitive processing of feedback-relevant information. *Journal of Experimental Social Psychology, 19,* 540–559.

Wylie, R. C. (1979). *The self-concept: Vol. 2. Theory and research on selected topics.* Lincoln: University of Nebraska Press.

Wynder, E. L., & Graham, E. A. (1950). Tobacco smoking as a possible etiological factor in bronchiogenic carcinoma. *Journal of the American Medical Association, 143,* 329–336.

Xu, H., Bègue, L., & Bushman, B. J. (2014). Washing the guilt away: Effects of personal versus vicarious cleansing on guilty feelings and prosocial behavior. *Frontiers in Human Neuroscience, 8.* doi: 10.3389/fnhum.2014.00097

Xygalatas, D., Mitkidis, P., Fischer, R., Reddish, P., Skewes, J., Geertz, A.W., Roepstorff, A., & Builbulia, J. (2013). Extreme rituals promote prosociality. *Psychological Science, 24,* 1602–1605.

Yang, Q., Wu, X., Zhou, X., Mead, N. L., Vohs, K. D., & Baumeister, R. F. (2013). Diverging effects of clean versus dirty money on attitudes, values, and interpersonal behavior. *Journal of Personality and Social Psychology, 104,* 473–489.

Yap, A., Wazlawek, A. S., Lucas, B. J., Cuddy, A. J. C., & Carney, D. R. (2013). The ergonomics of dishonesty: The effect of incidental posture on stealing, cheating, and traffic violations. *Psychological Science, 24*(11), 2281–2289. doi: 10.1177/0956797613492425

Yerke, A. F., & DeFeo, J. (2016). Redefining intimate partner violence beyond the binary to include transgender people. *Journal of Family Violence, 31*(8), 975–979. https://doi-org.proxy.lib.umich.edu/10.1007/s10896-016-9887-y

Yerkes, R. M., & Dodson, J. D. (1908). The relation of strength of stimulus to rapidity of habit formation. *Journal of Comparative Neurology and Psychology, 18,* 459–482.

Yorkston, E., & Menon, G. (2004). A sound idea: Phonetic effects of brand names on consumer judgments. *Journal of Consumer Research, 31,* 43–51.

Young, S. G., & Claypool, H. M. (2010). Mere exposure has differential effects on attention allocation to threatening and neutral stimuli. *Journal of Experimental Social Psychology, 46*(2), 424–427.

Yukl, G. (2006). *Leadership in organizations*. Upper Saddle River, NJ: Prentice-Hall.

Zaalberg, A. (in press). The effects of nutrients and neurotoxicants on aggressive behavior. *Journal of Criminal Justice*. DOI: 10.1016/j.jcrimjus.2018.10.001

Zajonc, R. B. (1965). Social facilitation. *Science, 149*, 269–274.

Zajonc, R. B. (1968). Attitudinal effects of mere exposure. *Journal of Personality and Social Psychology, 9*(2, Pt. 2), 1–27.

Zajonc, R. B., Heingartner, A., & Herman, E. M. (1969). Social enhancement and impairment of performance in the cockroach. *Journal of Personality and Social Psychology, 13*(2), 83–92. doi:10.1037/h0028063

Zajonc, R. B., Reimer, D. J., & Hausser, D. (1973). Imprinting and the development of object preference in chicks by mere repeated exposure. *Journal of Comparative Physiological Psychology, 83*, 434–440.

Zalar, R. W., Harris, R. B., Kyriacou, D. N., Anglin, D., & Minow, M. (2000). Domestic violence. *New England Journal of Medicine, 342*, 1450–1453.

Zanna, M. P., & Cooper, J. (1974). Dissonance and the pill: An attribution approach to studying the arousal properties of dissonance. *Journal of Personality and Social Psychology, 29*, 703–709.

Zanna, M., Higgins, E. & Taves, P. (1976). Is dissonance phenomenologically aversive? *Journal of Experimental Social Psychology, 12*, 530–538.

Zebrowitz, L. A., White, B., & Wieneke, K. (2008). Mere exposure and racial prejudice: Exposure to other-race faces increases liking for strangers of that race. *Social Cognition, 26*(3), 259–275.

Zhang, H.-H., & Wang, H. (2011). A meta-analysis of the relationship between individual emotional intelligence and workplace performance. *Acta Psychologica Sinica, 43*(2), 188–202.

Zhao, W., & Dweck, C. S. (1994). *Implicit theories and vulnerability to depression-like responses*. Unpublished manuscript, Columbia University, New York. Cited in Dweck, C. S. (1996). Implicit theories as organizers of goals and behavior. In P. Gollwitzer & J. Bargh (Eds.), *The psychology of action: Linking cognition and motivation to behavior* (pp. 69–91). New York: Guilford Press.

Zhong, C. B., & Liljenquist, K. A. (2006). Washing away your sins: Threatened morality and physical cleansing. *Science, 313*, 1451–1452.

Zhou, G., Pu, X., Young, S. G., & Tse, C.-S. (2015). Effects of divided attention and social categorization on the own-race bias in face recognition. *Visual Cognition, 22*, 1296–1310.

Zhou, X., He, L., Yang, Q., Lao, J., & Baumeister, R. F. (2012). Control deprivation and styles of thinking. *Journal of Personality and Social Psychology, 102*, 460–478. doi: 10.1037/a0026316

Ziegert, J. C., & Hanges, P. J. (2005). Employment discrimination: The role of implicit attitudes, motivation, and a climate for racial bias. *Journal of Applied Psychology, 90*, 553–562.

Zillmann, D. (1979). *Hostility and aggression*. Hillsdale, NJ: Erlbaum.

Zillmann, D., Katcher, A. H., & Milavsky, B. (1972). Excitation transfer from physical exercise to subsequent aggressive behavior. *Journal of Experimental Social Psychology, 8*, 247–259.

Zimbardo, P. G. (1970). The human choice: Individuation, reason, and order versus deindividuation, impulse, and chaos. In W. J. Arnold & D. Levine (Eds.), *Nebraska Symposium on Motivation* (1969; pp. 237–307). Lincoln: University of Nebraska Press.

Zimmerman, D. M., Chorn, J. A., Rhead, L. M., Evelo, A. J., & Kovera, M. B. (2017). Memory strength and lineup presentation moderate effects of administrator influence on mistaken identifications. *Journal of Experimental Psychology: Applied, 23*, 460–473.

Zottoli, M. A., & Wanous, J. P. (2000). Recruitment source research: Current status and future directions. *Human Resource Management Review, 10*, 435–451.

Zuckerman, M. (1975). Belief in a just world and altruistic behavior. *Journal of Personality and Social Psychology, 31*, 972–997.

Zuckerman, M. (1979). Attribution of success and failure revisited, or: The motivational bias is alive and well in attribution theory. *Journal of Personality, 47*, 245–287.

Name Index

A

Aaker, J., 462n82
Aamodt, M. G., C9n30, C9n32, C11n48, C19n107, C21n133, C22n146, C27n178, C19111
Abakoumkin, G., 237n27, 511n57
Abe, S., A13n38
Abel, E. L, 198n63
Aberson, C. L., 102n224
Abraham, C., 437n194, 438n196, 438n197, 441n215
Abraham, S. F., 136n122
Abrahams, D., 379n74, 384n104
Abrahamse, W., E15n120
Abraido-Lanza, A., B16n78
Abramowitz, J. S., 159n58
Abrams, D., 396n194, 489n247, 489n251, 522n102, D15n108
Abramson, L. Y., 96n148
Abshire, J., D12n90
Achenbach, C. J., 318n142
Acker, M., 409n9, 412n23
Ackerman, J. M., 218n239, 455n26
Ackerman, P., 314n122
Adams, B. D., 477n178
Adams, C. G., 433n168, 433n170
Adams, G. R., 98n188, E17n145
Adams, H. E., 193n26, 463n92, 464n108
Adams, J. S., C25n154
Adams, P. R., E17n145
Addis, N., 312n107
Adelman, H. F., 85n65
Adewole, A., 269n44
Adhikary, A. K., 468n129
Adler, P., 377n33
Adolph, K. E., 29n61
Affleck, G., B8n26
Agarwal, S., 83n54
Agnew, C. R., 312n106
Agras, W. S., 211n172, 211n173, 211n174
Agustdottir, S., 91n108
Ahlering, R. F., 279n104
Ahlstrom, B., B14n71
Ahmed, A. M., 458n34
Aiello, J. R., 88n83, 505n30, E7n57
Ailes, E., 4n4
Ainsworth, M. D., 376n22
Ainsworth, M. D. S., 416n46
Ainsworth, S. E., 347n89, 375n14
Ajzen, I., 246n78, 248n90, 248n93, B11n51, B11n52
Aknin, L. B., 316n123
Albergotti, R., 238n40
Alcock, I., 199n64
Aldwin, C. M., B8n22
Alebiosu, K. A., 483n212
Alexander, M. G., 172n121
Alexander, R. A., 517n81
Algom, D., 220n247

Alicke, M. D., 95n140, 310n93
Allan, E., 347n88
Alland, A., Jr., 339n48
Allen, D. G., C11n49
Allen, H. A., 381n87
Allen, J. J. B., 237n30
Allen, M., D17n136
Allen, N. B., 296n16
Allen, N. J., 513n66, C25n155, C26n160
Allen, T. D., C18n95, C29n192
Allgeier, E. R., 247n87
Allison, S. T., 176n146, 302n40
Alloy, L. B., 96n148
Allport, F. H., 6n9
Allport, G., 233n5
Allport, G. W., 6n10, 469n138, 471n156
Alpert, J. L., D19n154
Alqahtani, M. A., E8n65
Altermatt, T. W., 453n15
Altman, I., E9n82
Altschuler, G. C., 365n265
Amabile, T. M., 126n60
Amano, T., E13n108
Ambady, N., 217n223
Ames, D. R., 518n90
Amir, O., 138n133, 364n256
Amodio, A. M., 482n199
Amodio, D. M., 482n198
Anastasio, P. A., 9n15
Anderson, A. B., D15n112
Anderson, A. K., 208n140
Anderson, C., 522n105, 523n110
Anderson, C. A., 18n26, 23n40, 30n67, 30n68, 117n5, 117n6, 177n149, 250n102, 250n103, 314n118, 314n119, 326n177, 335n18, 344n73, 345n75, 353n150, 353n151, 354n169, 355n172, 355n173, 355n174, 355n176, 355n178, E4n21
Anderson, C. E., 343n70
Anderson, C. J., 121n24, 122n25
Anderson, J. E., 311n98
Anderson, J. O., E12n100
Anderson, K. B., 343n70, 344n73, 345n75, 355n172, 355n173
Anderson, N., C20n122
Anderson, P. B., 349n108, 349n109
Anderson, S. A., 209n144
Anderson, S. F., 28n55
Andrade, E. B., 222n272
Andrews, K., 355n180
Andrillon, T., 53n59
Angleitner, A., 442n221
Anglin, D., 349n106
Ansari, S., E3n11
Ansell, E., 391n139
Anthony, A., 150n7, 150n14
Anthony, T., 262n17, 262n18, C19n108

Antonovsky, H. F., 247n81
Apfelbaum, E. P., 44n17, 44n18
Appelbaum, P., 174n138
Apsler, R., 281n111
Aral, S., 260n4
Arbuckle, N. L., 58n81, 479n189
Archea, J., E16n129
Archer, J., 28n56, 347n92, 355n182
Ard, B. N., 410n19, 433n169
Areni, C. S., A6n11
Argote, L., 513n71, 513n72
Arias, E., B9n37
Arias, J. M., 28n52
Ariel, B., 353n138
Ariely, D., 121n23, 200n69, 311n97, 364n249, 364n256, 380n77, 385n114
Aries, E. J., 318n139
Aries, P., 200n75
Arkes, H. R., 181n178, 181n180
Arkin, R. M., 89n91
Armbrister, A. N., B16n78
Armbrister, R. C., 162n77
Armeli, S., B8n26
Armitage, C. J., 248n94
Arndt, B., 432n160
Arnett, C., B12n57
Arnkoff, D. B., 274n59
Arnold, A., 205n117
Arnold, M. B., 194n31
Aron, A., 409n10, 482n203, 526n124
Aronoff, J. R., 252n120, 522n103
Aronson, E., 23n37, 43n14, 241n62, 279n97, 440n208, 443n234, 483n206, 483n207, 483n208, 483n209, B12n61, E20n165
Aronson, J., 488n240
Aronson, J. A., 487n233, 488n241, 488n245
Aronson, V., 379n74, 384n104
Arthur, J. B., C26n158
Arthur, W., Jr., C14n64, C14n65
Arvey, R. D., C14n62
Aryee, S., C26n166, C27n167
Asch, S. E., 64n100, 64n101, 261n13, 262n15
Ashby, F. G., 154n34
Ashmore, R. D., 384n100
Ashton-James, C., 221n253
Ashton-James, C. E., 316n123
Ashton, H., 136n123
Aslin, R. N., 142n154
Asuncion, A. G., 274n66
Atkins, D. C., 349n112
Atkinson, T., C29n187
Atthowe, J. M., 120n19
Au, C., 28n52
Aunger, R. V., 444n236
Austin, J. B., 205n111
Austin, W., 297n22
Autry, M. W., D5n23

Antonovsky, H. F., 247n81
Averill, J. R., 201n81
Avery, D., 464n102
Avnaim-Pesso, L., 138n135
Avolio, B. J., C22n140
Axelrod, R., 302n39, 376n23
Axsom, D., 213n191
Aynesworth, H., 204n102, 204n103
Azanchi, R., 373n1
Azuuma, H., 162n78

B

Baard, P. P., C5n21
Babin, B. J., A6n9
Babin, L., A6n9
Babisch, W., E4n25, E11n91, E12n94, E12n99
Babyak, M. A., B8n29
Bachman, J. G., 98n178, 98n179
Back, K. W., 383n93
Backteman, G., 91n110
Badawy, A. A.-B., 356n197
Badcock, P. B. T., 296n16
Baddeley, A. D., E13n104
Baggini, J., 173n131
Bagozzi, R. P., A13n38
Bahns, A. J., 462n88
Bailey, J. M., 435n182
Bailey, J. S., E14n111
Bailey, R. C., 444n236
Bain, P. G., E5n36
Bakhshay, S., D17n142
Bakker, A. B., E20n157
Baldwin, M. W., 417n65
Balliet, D., 305n53, 307n86
Balogun, S. K., E7n58
Balswick, J. O., 445n239
Bamberg, S., E20n158
Banaji, M., 218n230, 218n231
Banaji, M. R., 90n100
Bandura, A., 129n91, 129n92, 238n47, 238n48, 238n49, 238n50, 238n51, 238n52, 339n42, 339n45, 339n46, 343n67, B11n54, E21n167, E21n168
Bane, C. M., 239n54, 239n58
Banholzer, L., 343n69
Banko, K. M., 84n60, 85n64, 85n66
Bansal, A., 233n4
Baranoski, M., D5n25
Barash, D. P., 446n244
Baratta, J. E., C11n46
Barbee, A. P., 384n96, 384n98, 384n99
Barbosa, L. S., 53n59
Barclay, D. R., 211n175
Barfield, R. L., C20n121
Bargh, J. A., 9n14, 54n65, 54n66, 54n67, 54n68, 54n70, 90n101, 130n94, 157n40, 189n11, 235n18, 374n6, 374n7, 374n8, 381n84, 392n159, 524n113

Barker, M. R., E14n111
Barlett, C. P., 30n68, 314n118, 314n119, 353n151
Barlow, D. H., 214n197
Barlow, F. K., 469n143
Barnard, W. A., E8n62
Barndollar, K., 54n68
Barnes, P. J., 326n174
Barnett, N. P., B10n43
Baron, G., 152n28
Baron, J., 462n83
Baron, R., 339n47
Baron, R. A., 203n97, 334n11
Baron, S. H., 262n20
Barrett, J., E21n170
Barrett, M., 126n63
Barrick, M. R., 517n81
Barrington-Leigh, C. P., 316n123
Barrios, B. A., E7n59
Barry, H., III, 51n57
Barsky, A. J., B16n87
Bartell, P. A., 323n169
Bartels, J. M., 393n165
Bartels, R. D., 158n44
Bartholomew, K., 415n43, 416n48, 416n55, 417n63
Bartholow, B. D., 344n74
Bartkowski, J. P., 463n95
Bartlett, M. Y., 442n222, 442n224
Barton, R., 96n149
Bartowski, J. P., 462n84
Bascom, K. L., 207n130
Basner, M., E4n25, E11n91, E12n94, E12n99
Bass, B. M., C21n134, C21n135
Bass, E. C., 347n95
Bassett, R., 265n28
Bastounis, M., D16n123
Bator, R., 266n32
Bator, R. J., 366n271
Batson, C. D., 314n121, 314n122, 325n171, 325n172
Batson, J. G., 314n121
Battistich, V., 98n189
Baum, A., B3n8, E4n18, E15n121
Baumann, D. J., 211n179
Baumeister, R. F., 49n53, 49n54, 55n73, 55n77, 59n83, 59n86, 72n6, 77n28, 78n35, 79n39, 89n97, 95n125, 97n159, 98n180, 98n190, 98n199, 100n212, 102n221, 102n222, 102n223, 102n238, 104n247, 104n250, 105n253, 105n255, 105n256, 117n4, 123n39, 123n40, 125n49, 128n88, 133n109, 134n112, 136n124, 136n127, 136n128, 136n129, 138n131, 138n132, 138n133, 143n156, 143n165, 152n26, 160n63, 164n92, 172n117, 189n9, 196n36, 196n37, 201n82, 203n93, 204n108, 206n119, 206n121, 209n145, 211n177, 213n188, 218n243, 235n15, 247n79, 306n72, 307n81, 307n87, 316n125, 319n151, 333n9, 342n57, 350n123, 350n125, 356n196, 358n212, 358n213, 359n214, 360n215, 364n257, 373n4, 375n12,
375n14, 375n18, 376n24, 376n31, 376n32, 377n59, 382n88, 391n141, 391n147, 391n149, 391n150, 391n151, 392n156, 392n157, 392n158, 392n160, 393n164, 393n165, 393n166, 394n170, 398n202, 398n204, 398n205, 412n24, 418n77, 421n98, 421n99, 430n151, 431n154, 431n161, 433n163, 445n243, 465n111, 469n142, 500n14, 504n22, 504n23, 505n32, 526n123
Baumgardner, M. H., 273n56
Baunach, D. M., 470n148
Bawer, B., 487n230
Bay-Hinitz, A. K., 483n205
Bazargan, M., 252n112
Bazargan, S., 252n112
Bazerman, M. H., 119n17
Beaber, R. J., 275n63, 275n65
Beach, F., 431n158
Beach, M., B9n39
Beach, S. R., 307n74
Beach, S. R. H., 306n65
Beal, D. J., C19n109
Beaman, A. L., 326n174, 502n15, 508n49
Bean, N. J., 391n146
Beaudry, J. L., D5n21
Beauvois, J-L., 309n91
Bechara, A., 212n182
Beck, A. T., 96n141, 96n142, 96n143, 96n144, 96n145, 96n146
Beck, J. G., 247n86
Becker, A. E., 76n18
Becker, A. H., 363n243
Becker, D. V., 455n26, 477n179
Becker, L. J., E19n156
Becker, M. H., B10n47, B11n50
Bedford, L., 489n247, 489n251
Beggan, J. K., 91n105, 302n40, A12n34
Bègue, L., 206n124, 309n91, 342n54, 353n139, D16n123
Behrman, B. W., D5n11
Beilock, S. L., 504n21
Beim, A., 459n40
Bein, A., 458n36
Bejciy-Spring, S. M., 461n74
Bekinschtein, T. A., 53n59
Bell, A. P., 435n177
Bell, B. S., C19n106, C20n126
Bell, C., 420n89
Bell, D. R., A6n7
Bell, P. A., E3n6, E4n20, E8n62
Bellavia, G., 418n74, 418n75
Bellezza, F. S., 160n62
Bellovich, S. J., E16n128
Belluz, J., 150n4, 151n20, 151n21
Belsky, J., 209n146, 209n147, 209n148
Bem, D. J., 83n55, 435n178, 435n179, 435n181, 515n78
Ben-Porath, Y., 220n249
Benbow, C. P., 487n234
Bench, S. W., 181n184
Bender, J., 354n167
Benenson, J. F., 305n55
Benitez-Quiroz, C. F., 217n225
Benjamin, A. J., Jr., 352n137, 353n146
Benotsch, E. G., 436n185, 436n186
Benson, G. P., E4n19
Benson, P. L., 318n145
Benson, S. M., 205n113
Benton, D., 357n205
Berenguer, J., E20n159
Bergami, M., A13n38
Berger, J., 165n97, 165n98, 165n99
Berglas, S., 88n88, 89n96, 91n107, 141n148
Berglas, S. C., 89n97
Bergmann, W., 459n42
Bergner, R. M., 408n2
Bergold, A. N., D8n58, D12n98, D12n99
Berke, M., E11n88
Berkman, L. F., B8n29
Berkowitz, A. D., 224n290
Berkowitz, L., 23n38, 201n77, 202n83, 210n166, 339n36, 342n53, 350n130, 354n157
Berman, J., E8n67
Berman, M., 252n111
Berman, M. G., 391n148
Bernard, J., 209n149, 423n112
Bernat, J. A., 463n92
Berndt, T. J., 98n196
Bernstein, D. M., 312n101
Bernstein, I., 199n65
Berntson, G. G., 377n48, 377n52, 396n186
Berry, D. S., 363n239
Berscheid, E., 297n25, 384n107
Bertrand, M. I., D5n21
Besirevic, J., D17n140, D18n149, D18n151
Besley, J. C., E20n162
Bettencourt, B. A., 347n91
Bettman, J. R., 61n95, 61n96
Betts, L. R., 312n107
Beumont, P. J. V., 136n122
BeVier, C. A., C14n69
Bezemer, M. D., 237n39, 458n35
Bhasin, G., 460n48
Bhattacharjee, A., 462n83
Bhatti, B., 377n47
Biddle, B. J., 75n11
Biel, A., 296n14
Biggs, A. T., 353n147
Bilewicz, M., 460n47
Billig, M., 466n114, 466n117
Billig, M. G., 466n118
Binder, J., 470n146, 482n200
Bingham, J. B., 364n259, 364n260
Birch, K., 314n122
Birtel, M. D., 470n152
Biryukov, P., 159n47
Bishop, C., 207n135
Bishop, J. A., 98n191
Bishop, P., 391n144
Bishop, S., A5n5
Biss, R. K., 216n221
Biswas, Diener, R., 316n123
Bjerregaard, B., 398n206
Bjorkqvist, K., 334n14
Blackstone, W., D19n152
Blackwell, B., 46n26
Blader, S. L., 522n104
Blair, K. L., 207n136
Blake, P. R., 298n26
Blakemore, J. E. O., 398n203
Blanchard, F. A., 79n40, 392n152
Blanchette, I., 353n140
Bland, S. H., E4n30, E17n140
Blaney, N., 483n207
Blank, H., 463n90
Blankenship, K. L., 281n112
Blanton, H., 214n199
Blascovich, J., 88n84, 94n123, 102n238, 235n20, 488n242
Blau, P. N., 430n147
Blehar, M. C., 416n46
Blincoe, C., D6n32
Blissett, J., 381n87
Block, J., 98n198
Bloom, S., 348n102
Blue, L. A., D15n107
Blumberg, S. J., 213n189
Blumenthal, J. A., B8n29
Blumstein, P., 409n12, 414n35, 438n199, 443n227, 443n228
Bochner, S., 461n64
Boddington, L., A11n29
Boden, J. M., 358n212
Bodenhausen, G. V., 413n26, 471n157, 472n158
Boechler, M., 356n183
Boerner, P., 464n110
Bogaerts, S., 349n111
Boggiano, A. K., 126n63
Boland, F. J., 161n69
Boldizar, J. P., 348n102
Bolin, B., E2n2
Bolman, C., B8n34
Bonacci, A. M., 102n223, 123n40, 350n125, 457n31
Bond, C. F., 504n28
Bond, C. F., Jr., 362n237
Bond, M. H., 51n58
Bond, R., 30n69
Bond, R. A., 64n102
Bond, R. M., 335n22
Bonezzi, A., 127n79
Bonham, K. G., E13n104
Bonnes, M., E19n152
Bono, G., 307n82
Bonoma, T. V., 105n254
Bonta, B. D., 468n123, 468n128
Boomer, J., 154n34
Boone, A. L., 134n112
Booth-Kewley, S., B16n86
Bordeaux, C., C28n183
Borman, W. C., C6n28, C29n192
Bornstein, B. H., D5n17, D5n18, D5n24, D10n75, D16n119
Bornstein, B. J., D12n90
Bornstein, R. F., 236n22
Bortz, J., 205n118
Bos, H. M. W., 463n98
Bosch, J. D., 344n71
Bosch, T., 363n244
Boseley, S., 150n15
Bosson, J. K., 48n42, 48n43
Boster, F. J., 361n228
Bostrom, R. N., 238n46
Bothwell, R. K., D6n37, D12n88

Botta, R. A., 76n19
Bottoms, B. L., 362n238, D16n120, D16n122
Bouchard, T. J., 422n105, 423n111
Boulton, M. J., 312n107
Bowlby, J., 373n2, 373n3, 376n25, 415n42
Bowler, R., E17n139
Bowles, T., 98n174
Bowman, P., 459n42
Boxmeyer, C., E17n136
Boyd, R., 43n16, 49n51, 49n52, 49n55
Boyer, E. M., C26n157
Bozman, A. W., 247n86
Brackett, M. A., 221n253, 221n255
Bradbury, T. N., 409n11, 428n134
Bradfield, A., D12n91
Bradfield, A. L., D10n71
Bradley, G. W., 163n81
Bradley, S. J., 222n268
Braet, C., 161n70, 161n71
Braginski, B. M., 105n260
Braginski, D. D., 105n260
Brainerd, C. J., 247n88
Brammer, G., 356n186
Branden, N., 95n127
Brandon, D. P., 513n69
Brandt, M. J., 299n27
Branscombe, N. R., 462n88, 487n232
Bratslavsky, E., 136n127, 136n128, 189n9, 211n177, 223n280, 235n15, 412n24, 469n142
Braun, S., B10n40
Brauner, S., D16n117
Braverman, J., 442n222, 442n224
Bravo, M., E17n144
Brawley, L. R., C19n110
Breaugh, J. A., C28n185
Brechner, K. C., 509n55
Brehm, J. W., 22n34, 122n31, 122n32, 122n33, 122n35, 123n36, 123n37, 380n79
Brehm, S. S., 122n33, 123n37
Bremner, R. H., 222n276
Brenan, M., 273n57, C5n17, C5n18, C5n19
Brendl, C. M., 127n79
Brennan, K. A., 416n49, 416n50
Bresin, K., 455n23
Brewer, M. B., 392n161, 466n115, 466n116, E3n8, E16n127
Brewer, N., D4n7, D4n8, D6n39, D6n40, D7n44, D10n73, D10n81
Brickman, P., 102n236, 197n41, 197n42, 197n48
Brigham, J. C., 455n25, D4n10, D6n37, D12n88
Briley, D. A., 178n156
Brill, M., E12n97
Brimacombe, C. A. E., D10n70
Brink, M., E4n25, E11n91, E12n94, E12n99
Brinkman, H., E7n61
Brinley, A., C28n183
Briñol, P., 237n36
Bristol, T., 280n108
Broadbent, E., B16n84
Brock, P., D16n125
Brockmole, J. R., 353n147

Brockner, A., 205n118
Brockner, J., 98n192, 99n200, 102n239, 205n118
Brodish, A. B., 489n248
Brody, L. R., 218n233
Bronson, P., 466n112
Broomell, S. B., 512n64
Brosnan, S. F., 317n129
Brower, G. L., D9n63
Brower, S., E8n75
Brown-Iannuzzi, J. L., 460n51
Brown, B., E8n70
Brown, B. B., E8n72, E8n74
Brown, C. L., 153n30
Brown, G., 96n144
Brown, J., 488n240
Brown, J. D., 96n150
Brown, J. F., 460n46
Brown, K. W., 198n54, 199n65, B16n85
Brown, L. R., E13n107
Brown, L. S., D19n154
Brown, M. J., 463n94
Brown, N. R., 172n125, 172n126
Brown, R., 470n146, 482n200
Brown, S. M., 159n53
Brown, S. W., 198n57
Brown, T. J., 318n146, 384n111
Brownstein, S. C., 178n161
Brummelman, E., 102n220
Brunell, A. B., 518n89
Bruner, J. A., A5n6
Brunner, E., C27n172
Bruun, S. E., 505n35, 506n39, 507n46
Bryan, A. D., 366n271
Bryan, C. J., 108n267
Bryant, J. B., D18n145
Bryman, A. S., C21n129
Bryner, J., 252n114, 314n117
Buchanan, F. R., C13n59
Bucher, A. M., 203n90
Buck, B., 263n22
Buck, D. M., 464n110
Buckles, E. E., 207n139
Buckley, T., 314n122
Budescu, D. V., 512n64
Budesheim, T. L., 276n67, 277n84
Buehler, R., 131n103, 132n104, 132n106, 213n190
Buhrmester, D., 98n193
Builbulia, J., 243n63
Bukowki, W. M., 347n95
Bulman, R. J., 251n106
Bundy, R. P., 466n118
Bunker, B. B., 377n36
Burger, J. M., 162n73, 269n42, 309n90
Burgess, E. O., 470n148
Burgess, J., A4n2
Burke, M., 355n177
Burke, M. J., C19n109
Burleson, M. H., 377n49, 377n52, 395n180, 396n187
Burmeister, J. M., 461n57
Burmood, C., E8n63
Burnaford, R. M., 48n42, 48n43
Burnay, J., 354n158
Burns, D., 96n143

Burns, J., 316n123
Burnstein, E., 313n112
Burris, C. T., 252n113
Burrows, L., 9n14, 54n67, 157n40
Bursik, R. J., 366n279
Burt, S. A., 347n96
Burton, K., 420n89
Burton, R. L., 253n123
Burwell, R. A., 76n18
Bush, M., 268n39
Bushman, B. J., 9n15, 18n26, 28n56, 30n68, 77n27, 95n128, 95n129, 101n215, 102n221, 102n222, 102n223, 123n38, 123n40, 136n125, 203n93, 203n94, 203n96, 203n98, 203n99, 203n100, 203n101, 206n124, 213n188, 221n266, 222n276, 222n277, 223n279, 237n39, 280n106, 297n20, 307n87, 314n118, 314n119, 320n163, 326n177, 335n18, 335n22, 342n54, 342n57, 346n79, 350n125, 352n132, 352n137, 353n139, 353n146, 353n148, 353n149, 353n150, 353n151, 354n153, 354n154, 354n158, 354n161, 354n162, 354n165, 354n166, 354n169, 355n174, 355n176, 356n193, 356n201, 358n213, 359n214, 360n215, 457n31, 458n35, E4n21
Buss, A. H., 17n24, 76n15, 77n29, 218n234, 334n15
Buss, D. M., 40n5, 102n226, 121n21, 172n118, 172n120, 296n15, 376n26, 376n27, 386n120, 429n141, 430n144, 430n145, 437n195, 441n214, 442n220, 442n221
Buswell, B. N., 95n135
Butler, J. L., 108n273, 504n22
Butts, C. T., 305n57
Butz, D. A., 455n22
Buunk, B. P., 440n213, 442n221
Buzinski, S. G., 263n22
Byerley, G. J., 431n156
Byers, E. S., 350n121
Byrne, D., 350n120, 378n63

C

Cacioppo, J. T., 189n4, 210n160, 237n31, 265n28, 278n92, 279n103, 279n105, 281n109, 282n114, 282n116, 377n48, 377n49, 377n52, 377n56, 377n58, 395n176, 395n180, 395n182, 396n186, 396n187, 396n188, B8n31
Cadena, B., 523n107
Cadinu, M., 484n214
Caesar, P. L., 349n115
Caidahl, K., 377n53
Cain, T. R., 474n163, 474n168
Cairns, K. J., 97n159, 105n255
Caldwell, M. A., 377n42
Calhoun, J. B., E4n12
Calhoun, K. S., 463n92

Call, J., 127n77
Call, V., 410n20
Calvert, S. L., 353n149
Camacho, L. M., 511n56
Cameron, J., 84n60, 85n64, 85n66
Camp, N. P., 486n229
Campbell, A., 197n39, 209n150
Campbell, D. T., 18n29, 21n32, 28n57, 197n41, 262n21, 498n3
Campbell, J. D., 95n124, 95n126, 98n166, 98n180, 98n190, 98n194, 98n199, 103n240
Campbell, J. K., 361n221
Campbell, L., C4n15, C4n16
Campbell, M. A. T., B14n69
Campbell, W. K., 95n131, 101n215, 101n218, 102n227, 102n228, 102n229, 102n230, 102n231, 163n79, 196n35, 209n155, 307n87, 418n78, 418n79, 418n80, 418n86, 518n89
Campion, J. E., C14n62
Can de Poll, N. E., 375n17
Canino, G., E17n144
Canino, G. J., E17n143
Cannon-Bowers, J. A., C21n127
Cannon, W. B., B3n9, B4n12
Canon, L. K., E4n24
Cantor, J., 123n38
Cantor, J. R., 276n75
Cao, B., 470n151
Capitanio, J. P., 464n106
Capitanio, M. P., 464n103
Cappell, C., 349n116
Caprariello, P. A., 46n25
Cardiel, H., 385n117, 420n92
Carels, R. A., 461n57
Carey, G. L., 15n20
Carey, M. P., 253n118
Carlsmith, J. M., 23n37
Carlsmith, K. M., 213n193
Carlson, C. A., D8n56
Carlson, D. S., C29n191
Carlson, J. M., 353n141
Carlson, M., 334n12
Carlson, M. A., D8n56
Carlstedt, L., E17n141
Carney, D. R., 365n268
Carney, M. A., B8n26
Carney, R. M., B8n29
Carpenter, C. S., 4n1
Carpenter, G. R., 247n82
Carpenter, K. M., 117n8
Carpenter, M., 321n165
Carr-Nangle, R. E., 211n175
Carr, J. E., 357n208
Carr, K., C11n48
Carr, T. H., 504n21
Carroll, J. S., 117n7
Carron, A. V., C19n110
Carrus, G., E5n39, E19n152
Carter, C., 205n118
Carter, S. R., 159n49
Carver, C. S., 76n16, 78n37, 78n38, 135n114, 135n115, 135n116, 201n80, B8n23
Case, D. A., 181n172
Casey, R. J., 384n108, 386n124

Name Index | N-3

Cash, T. F., 384n109
Casper, W. J., C28n183
Caspi, A., 91n111, 356n186, 358n211
Casson, D. H., 150n14
Catalan, J., 268n41
Catalano, R., E4n26, E13n105
Catanese, K. R., 123n39, 350n123, 375n18, 391n141, 392n156, 393n166, 431n154
Catapano, R., 28n52
Cate, R., 218n241
Catellier, D. J., B8n29
Ceaux, E., 297n20
Ceci, S. J., 490n255, D19n155, D19n156
Cesario, J., 57n80
Chaiken, S., 189n11, 233n6, 235n18, 281n110, 434n174, 434n176
Chait, J., 363n245
Chajut, E., 220n247
Chakraborty, G., 280n108
Chamberlain, K., 135n118
Chan, A., 217n222
Chan, W., 474n166
Chandola, T., C27n172
Chandrasekhar, D., E17n132
Chang, Y., A8n22
Chaplin, W, 96n149
Chapman, B. P., 221n254
Chapman, H. A., 208n140
Charman, S. D., D8n53, D8n54, D9n65, D10n72
Charters, M., 260n7
Chartrand, T. L., 191n19, 334n13, 381n84, 381n85, 394n173, 525n116
Chassin, L., 284n122
Chatard, A., 78n36
Chechlacz, M., 381n87
Check, J. V. P., 354n159
Cheema, A., A11n32
Chemyak, N., 298n26
Chen, B.-B., 347n95
Chen, E. S., 526n122
Chen, J. J., C29n193
Chen, K., 353n138
Chen, M., 9n14, 54n67, 157n40
Chen, R. C., A8n22
Chen, S., 525n116
Chen, X., E18n146
Chen, Y., 522n104
Chesney, M. A., 203n91
Chester, D. S., 213n188, 343n61, 343n68
Chew, B., 95n126
Child, P., 85n69, 85n70
Childress, H., E8n73
Chiodo, J., 392n153
Chiu, C., 87n80, 87n81
Chivers, M. L., 193n24
Cho, E. K., 205n115
Choi, I., 164n88
Choma, B. L., 207n137
Chorn, J. A., D9n67
Choun, S., B8n22
Chown, S. M., 320n158
Chrisjohn, R. D., 318n133
Christ, O., 470n145
Christakis, N. A., 210n162, 293n3

Christenfeld, N. J., 64n103
Christensen, H. T., 247n82
Christian, J., 221n263
Christianson, S.-A., D5n23
Christy, P., 379n70
Church, B. A., 154n34
Cialdini, J. T., 394n174, 396n189
Cialdini, R. B., 117n8, 205n112, 210n167, 211n179, 264n24, 265n28, 266n29, 266n30, 266n31, 266n32, 267n34, 267n36, 268n38, 268n41, 269n43, 270n45, 326n173, 366n275, 366n276, 366n277, 380n81, E14n117, E18n149
Ciarocco, N. J., 391n151, 392n157, 392n158, 393n165, 418n77
Ciotti, G., C17n86
Ciupitu-Plath, C., 461n81
Clancy, B., E20n166
Clark, C., E4n25, E11n91, E12n94, E12n99
Clark, C. L., 416n49
Clark, D., 74n10
Clark, D. A., 96n144
Clark, J., 263n22
Clark, L. A., 189n5, 189n6, 523n106
Clark, M. S., 414n31, 414n32, 414n33, 414n34, 415n37, 415n38, 415n39, 415n40, 415n41
Clark, N. T., 268n39
Clark, R. E., C5n20
Clark, S. E., D6n41, D8n50, D9n60, D9n63, D11n82
Clark, W. C., E2n2, E5n41
Claypool, H. M., 237n33
Clayson, D. E., 461n77
Clement, R. W., 176n141
Clifford, M., 384n105
Clipp, E. C., 383n95
Clore, G. L., 208n142, 212n185, 318n143
Coan, J. A., 209n158
Coates, D., 197n42, 197n48
Coccaro, E. F., 356n187
Cohen-Kettenis, P. T., 375n17
Cohen, A. B., 208n141, 303n47
Cohen, A. D., 296n13
Cohen, D., 48n42, 48n43, 360n217, 360n218, 361n219
Cohen, F., 460n48, 474n163, 474n168
Cohen, G. L., 57n79
Cohen, J., 24n41, 193n25, 222n272
Cohen, J. D., 300n34
Cohen, L. L., 434n173
Cohen, M., 263n22
Cohen, M. A., 356n191, 356n192
Cohen, R. R., C19n109
Cohen, S., B16n83, E4n23, E12n95
Cohen, S. G., C20n124
Coie, J. D., 334n16
Colapinto, J., 36n1, 36n2
Cole, A. H., 380n79
Cole, A. M., 487n231
Cole, R., 362n234
Coleman, M. D., 176n145
Collins, A., 321n164
Collins, J., 517n82, 517n83
Collins, N., B12n58

Collins, N. L., 312n105, 415n44, 416n51, 416n53, 416n54, 416n56, 416n57, 416n60, 417n64, 417n66
Collins, R. L., 347n90
Colman, A. M., 397n196
Colvin, C. R., 98n198
Combs, D., 391n149
Comer, R., 244n67
Comfort, J. C., D17n131, D17n134
Compton, J. A., 284n124
Comstock, G., 335n24
Cone, J., E17n139
Cong, X., 85n68
Conley, T. D., 431n155
Conner, M., 248n94, C28n179, C28n180, C28n181
Conner, R., 391n144
Connolly, T., 214n196
Connors, M. M., 377n40
Consoli, A., D5n20
Contiero, P., 297n17
Contrada, R., B3n8
Contrada, R. J., B16n82
Converse, P. E., 209n150
Conway, M., 93n121
Cook, J., 151n22, 177n150, 260n8, 260n9
Cook, T. D., 18n29, 21n32, 28n57
Cooley, C. H., 80n42
Coolsen, M. K., 424n114
Cooper-Hakim, A., C26n162
Cooper, H. M., 136n125, 162n73, 356n193
Cooper, J., 239n61, 243n64, 243n65, 453n13
Cooper, M. L., 215n213, 415n44
Copeland, J. T., 525n121
Corbitt, L. C., E7n59
Corcoran, D., 415n41
Cordell, H. K., E19n151
Corell, R., E2n2
Corneille, O., 216n219, 221n266
Cornog, M., 431n159
Correll, J., 455n18
Corrigan, A., 312n107
Cortina, J. M., C14n73
Cosgrove, J., 233n3
Cosmides, L., 180n169, 180n170, 180n171
Costa, P. T., 198n50, 198n51, 198n52, 198n53
Costello, K., 207n137
Cotton, J. L., C18n97
Cotton, R., D11n84
Cottrell, C. A., 381n82
Cottrell, N. B., 504n19, 505n31
Couch, D., 319n148
Courbet, D., 309n91
Courtois, C. A., D19n154
Coviello, L., 210n162
Cowan, C. L., D17n135, D17n139
Cowgill, C. M., 460n56
Cowley, E., 178n156
Cox, C., 504n18
Coy, D. H., 391n146
Coyle, C. T., 306n69
Coyne, J. C., 422n106
Cozzarelli, C., 215n213
Craig, R., 284n123

Crain, A. L., B12n61
Cramer, P., 461n59
Cramer, R. E., 323n169
Crandall, C., 313n112
Crandall, C. S., 461n80, 506n36, 506n37
Crandall, S. J., 461n75
Cranny, C. J., C24n152
Crary, W. G., 97n160
Crawford, J. T., 474n163, 474n168
Crawford, L. E., 377n49, 396n187
Credé, M., 221n258
Crick, N. R., 346n86, 347n94
Crisp, R. J., 237n34, 470n152, 489n247, 489n251
Critelli, J. W., 98n173, 98n176
Croake, J. W., 247n83
Crocker, C. B., D16n128, D18n144
Crocker, J., 95n128, 95n129, 95n136, 95n138, 95n139, 97n163, 102n225, 103n242, 103n243, 103n245, 485n224, 486n226, 486n227, 486n228
Crogan, M., 483n210, 483n211
Cropanzano, R., C26n164
Croskerry, P., 181n183
Croson, R., 175n140
Crowder, M. J., 357n204
Crowley, A. E., A7n13
Crowley, M., 318n137
Crowley, M. C., C16n75
Crutzen, R., B12n60
Cruz, C., 354n161
Cruz, J., 297n18
Cryder, C. E., 204n105
Csernansky, J. G., 356n187
Cuddy, A. J. C., 365n268
Cuervo, D., 393n165
Culhane, S. E., D15n109, D15n110
Cullen, F. T., 358n210
Cullen, M. J., 488n243, 488n244
Cunha, J., 347n95
Cunningham, M. R., 320n160, 362n231, 384n96, 384n97, 384n98, 384n99
Cunningham, W. A., D5n15
Cupach, W. R., 398n207
Currey, D. P., 469n136
Curtis, S. R., 347n98
Curtis, V., 206n128, 207n129
Cutler, B. L., D3n1, D5n19, D6n34, D6n38, D9n61, D12n94, D13n101, D13n102, D16n118, D16n124, D16n125, D16n126, D16n127, D16n129, D18n143
Cutrona, C. E., 395n179
Cwir, D., 57n79
Cybriwsky, R., E9n83

D
D'Silva, J., 46n29
Dabbs, J. M., 374n9, 374n10, 375n16
Daftary-Kapur, T., D17n141
Dai, K., E18n146
Dal Cin, S., B10n41, B10n42
Dalal, R. S., C30n203
Dalton, M., B10n42
Dalton, M. A., B9n39

Daly, M., 121n22, 442n217
Daly, M. J., 253n123
Damasio, A. R., 209n143, 212n181, 212n182
Damasio, H., 212n182
Dana, J., 462n83, 512n64
Daniel, D. B., 461n61
Daniels, A., E17n137, E17n138
Danner, D., 198n62
Danso, H., 488n239
Danziger, S., 138n135
Darby, B. L., 205n112, 268n41
Darby, B. W., 307n79
Dardis, G. J., 469n134
Darley, J., 321n166
Darley, J. M., 300n34, 323n168, 325n171, 325n172, 477n180, E19n154
Darwin, C., 313n110, 336n33
Das, E., 237n39, 458n35
Davey, S. L., D5n11
David, J. P., 215n212
David, M. B., 452n1
Davidson, K. D., 218n242
Davidson, N., 366n274
Davidson, R. J., 209n158
Davies, G., 45n20
Davies, G.M., D6n32
Davies, J. B., 509n53
Davila, J., 306n66, 306n67, 307n74
Davis-Stober, C. P., 512n64
Davis, A., E4n25, E11n91, E12n94, E12n99
Davis, B. P., 271n48
Davis, D., D14n105
Davis, E. L., 181n184
Davis, I., E16n126
Davis, J. M., 297n21
Davis, K. E., 398n208
Davis, M. H., 409n9, 412n23
Davis, P. A., 143n159
Davis, P. G., 477n178
Davis, S. F., 363n243
Davis, S. W., 461n75
Davison, W. P., 260n11, 354n168
Davisson, E. K., 382n91
Davy, J., 205n118
Dawes, R. M., E20n163
Dawkins, R., 313n108, 348n100
Day, D., 360n216
Day, D. V., 517n81
Day, R., C18n95
De Angelis, M., 127n79
De Bolle, M., 474n166
De Brouwer, A.-M., 333n4
De Conno, F., 297n17
De Dreu, C. K. W., 202n85, 202n86
De Fruyt, F., 474n166
De Gilder, D., C26n161
De Hoog, N., 276n78
De Kort, Y. A. W., 366n283
De La Ronde, C., 426n122
De Lisa, A., D16n127
De Moura, G., 522n102
De Never, J. E., 134n113
De Rougemont, D., 408n6
De Vries, M., 216n219
De Waal, F. B. M., 38n4, 43n15, 297n21

De Wit, J. B. F., 276n78
De Young, R., E21n172
Deabler, A., 233n2
Deacon, T., 152n27
Dean, L. M., E7n60
DeAngelis, T., A19n54
Dearing, R. L., 59n87, 204n106, 204n109
Deaux, K., 318n135
Debalini, M. G., 150n10
DeCharms, R., 126n54
Deci, E. L., 84n58, 84n59, 85n61, 85n63, 85n67, 125n51, 125n52, 125n53, 126n55, 126n56, 126n59, 126n61, 126n62, 126n65, C5n21
Deckman, T., 203n100
DeFeo, J., 350n127
Deffenbacher, K. A., D5n17, D5n18, D5n22, D5n24, D6n37
DeHaven, A. C., 29n59
DeHeer, H., D5n14
Dejonckheere, P., 161n70
DeJong, W., 461n78, 461n79
Dekker, G. B., E20n157
DeLamater, J., 428n136
Delespaul, P. A. E. G., 59n86, 206n119
Delmas, F., 353n139
DeLongis, A., 377n50, 422n106, 422n107
Delucchi, K., 98n189
DeMarree, K. G., 518n89
DeMeis, J., 48n41
Demicheli, V., 150n10
Demiralp, E., 375n13
DeMoss, M., 222n273
DeNeve, K. M., 355n172
Denison, D. R., C5n22, C5n23
Dentzman, K., 260n7
DePalma, M. T., 320n157
DePaola, S. J., 276n67, 277n84
DePaulo, B. M., 362n237
Depledge, M. H., 199n64
Deppe, R. K., 88n87
Derby, S. L., 167n103
Derezotes, D., 377n47
Dermer, M., 236n26
Derry, P. A., 97n161
Dertke, M. C., 318n142
Derzon, J. H., 356n191, 356n192
Deschrijver, E., 108n274
DeScioli, P., 44n19, E9n81
Deshaies, P., 47n31
Desmarais, S. L., D11n87
DeSteno, D. A., 442n222, 442n224, 443n231
Deuser, W. E., 343n70, 344n73, 345n75
Deutsch, M., 261n12
Deutsch, R., 53n61, 55n76
DeVader, C. L., 517n86
Devenport, J. L., D13n101, D13n102
Devine, P. G., 455n24, 479n193, 480n196, 481n197, 482n198, 482n199, 489n248, 490n256
DeVore, C. J., C29n196, C30n201
DeVries, D., 519n92
DeWall, C. N., 55n73, 101n218, 125n49, 160n63, 203n100, 203n101, 213n188, 349n112,
386n121, 391n147, 391n149, 391n151, 392n157, 392n158, 392n160, 413n26, 453n15, 526n123
Dewitte, S., 442n216, 442n218
Dexter, H. R., D12n94, D18n143
Dhar, R., 205n115
Di Paula, A., 103n240
Di Pietrantonj, C., 150n10
Diacoyanni-Tarlatzis, I., 217n222
Diamond, J., 350n128
Diamond, L. M., 427n131, 427n132, 428n133, 433n164
Dickerson, C., E20n165
Dickinson, D. J., 48n38
Dickson, N., 99n203
Dickson, N. M., E2n2
Diefenbach, M. A., B16n76
Diehl, M., 511n57
Diener, E., 77n26, 98n175, 99n209, 197n43, 197n47, 199n67, 200n73, 502n15, 508n49
Diener, M., 99n209
Diermeier, D., 383n92
Dietz, T., 260n7
DiGiacomo, M., 221n262
Dijksterhuis, A., 160n60, 160n61
Dijstelberge, P., 452n3, 452n5
Dikaiakou, A., E17n135
Dill, K. E., 23n40, 343n70, 344n73, 345n75
Dillon, M. K., D12n98, D12n99
Dimeo-Ediger, W., 217n226
Dion, J., 61n92
Dion, K., 384n106
Dion, K. K., 384n107
Ditzen, B., B8n27
Dixon, D. N., 377n39
Dixon, G., E14n110
Dlugolecki, D. W., 93n119
Doan, K. A., 277n85
Dodge, G., C22n140
Dodge, K. A., 334n16
Dodson, J. D., 219n245
Doerr, C., 455n22
Doherty, K. J., 93n119
Dohnke, B., B13n66
Doja, A., 150n13
Dollard, J., 17n25, 340n50
Dombeck, M., C27n168
Donnellan, M. B., 101n216
Donnerstein, E., 23n38, 354n157
Donnerstein, E. I., 354n165
Donovan, R., A7n12
Doob, L., 17n25, 340n50
Doocy, S., E17n137, E17n138
Dooley, D., E4n26, E13n105
Dooling, S., E17n137
Doran, A., D5n25
Dorfman, D. D., 279n98
Dorr, N., 355n172
Dorsey, D., C22n144
Douglass, A. B., D9n66, D10n78, D10n81, D12n92
Douthitt, E. A., 505n30
Dovidio, J. F., 453n12, 483n204
Dowd, J. J., 296n12
Dowd, T. G., 239n54, 239n58
Downey, G., 353n149, 391n137

Downey, K. T., 98n177
Downs, A., 253n120
Downs, D. L., 100n211
Downs, D. M., 365n267
Doyle, A. C., 167n105
Doyle, W. J., B16n83
Drabek, T. E., E16n122
Dragna, M., 323n169
Draper, P., 468n124
Drath, W. H., C21n131
Dredze, M., 353n149
Drigotas, S., 469n135
Drigotas, S. M., 469n137, 504n18
Driscoll, D. M., 235n20
Driskell, J. E., C19n108
Drolet, A., 139n143
Druen, P. B., 362n231, 384n98
Drumm, P., 398n203
Drury, J., E7n51
Dube, K. C., 224n291
Duberstein, P. R., 221n254
Dubner, S. D., 45n23
Dubner, S. J., 457n27
Duede, E., 500n10
Dugan, P. M., 475n170
Duhigg, C., C19n114, C19n115
Duke, A. A., 309n91
Duke, M. P., E8n64
Dunbar, R. I. M., 41n9, 41n10, 41n11, 376n21, 447n246
Duncan, A., E21n172
Duncan, B. D., 314n122
Duncan, C. P., 276n73
Dunham, Y. C., 298n26
Dunkel-Schetter, C., B12n58
Dunn, D. S., 239n56
Dunn, E. W., 221n253, 316n123
Dunn, J., D6n42
Dunning, D., 98n169, 98n170, 98n171, 98n172, 172n129, 174n137, 311n98, 312n102, D7n45
Dunton, B. C., 234n9, 478n183
Duryea, E. J., 215n204
Dutton, D. G., 480n194, 480n195
Duval, S., 75n14
Duval, T. S., 76n25
Dweck, C. S., 108n267, 123n42, 123n43, 124n44, 124n45, 124n46
Dysart, J. E., D11n83
Dzindolet, M. T., 511n56

E

Eagly, A. H., 233n6, 237n38, 281n110, 318n137, 384n100
Earnest, D. R., C11n49
Easterbrook, J. A., 219n246
Eastwick, P. W., 387n126, 424n114
Ebbesen, E. B., 97n162
Ebbesen, E. G., E8n69
Ebersole, C. R., 29n59
Eby, L. T., C28n183
Ecker, U. H., 260n8, 260n9
Ecker, U. K. H., 151n22, 177n150
Eckman, J., 383n94
Edelbrock, S., 356n184
Edelsack, L., 205n114

Edelstein, R. S., 416n47, 416n52, 417n67
Edgerton, R., 361n222
Edwards, D. A., 284n122
Edwards, D. J. A., E7n54
Ee, J. S., 98n173, 98n176
Eek, D., 296n14
Effrein, E. A., 92n117
Efran, M. G., 276n68
Eftekhari-Sanjani, H., 487n234
Egan, G., 376n28
Ehlebracht, D., 311n98
Ehly, S. W., 98n183
Ehrenfeld, D., E5n35
Ehrenreich, B., 444n237
Ehret, P. J., E5n37
Eibach, R. P., 486n229
Eichinger, R. W., C22n141, C22n142
Eiland, L., B6n14
Einon, D., 172n122
Eion, K., C18n93
Eisenberg, N., 218n238, 266n32, 318n140
Eisenberger, N. I., 391n149
Eisenstadt, D., D13n103
Eisner, M., 335n28
Ekman, P., 217n222, 362n236
Elbert, T., 343n59, 343n60, 343n64, 343n65, 343n66, 343n69, 344n62
Elder, G. H., Jr., 383n95
Elfenbein, H. A., 217n223
Ellard, J. H., 306n72
Ellemers, N., C26n161
Ellerbeck, N., 153n30
Elliot, A. J., 198n60, 215n211, 418n80
Elliott, S., A5n3
Ellis, A., 202n88
Ellis, B. J., 86n73
Ellison, N. B., 388n127
Ellsworth, P. C., 194n33, 215n209, 225n297, D17n132, D17n135, D17n139
Emmons, R. A., 127n75, 198n56
Emswiller, T., 318n135
Engel, R., 82n49
Engelman, R., E4n28
Engler, L. B., 211n175
Engs, R. C., 224n292
Enright, R. D., 306n69, 306n70
Ensari, N., 221n263
Epley, N., 21n31, 158n42, 158n43, 163n84, 163n85
Epperson, A. E., B9n36
Epps, J., 344n72
Epstein, R. M., 221n254
Epstein, S., 91n112
Erber, M. W., 223n282
Erber, R., 223n281, 223n282, 525n119
Erdogan, A., 165n93
Erez, A., 216n216, C30n202
Erickson, B., 274n58
Erickson, W. B., D10n74
Erikson, E. H., 417n71
Erkip, F. E., E7n56
Ernst, J., 377n61, 395n183
Ernst, J. M., 377n48, 377n49, 395n180, 396n186, 396n187
Eron, L. D., 91n113, 354n155

Escobar, J. I., E17n144
Eslick, G. D., 150n12
Estes, J. P., E7n59
Estrada, C. A., 216n214
Etherington, J., E9n80
Evans, G. W., E4n16, E4n26, E8n68, E11n93, E13n105
Evans, J. A., 500n10
Evans, K., 391n139
Evelo, A. J., D9n67, D10n69
Everett, P. B., E14n112
Evers, K. E., B13n62
Eves, A., 357n204
Exline, J. J., 253n116, 253n117, 253n118, 297n19, 305n59, 306n72, 307n77, 307n78, 307n81, 307n87, 307n88
Eysenck, H. J., 317n132, 318n134

F

Faber, J. E., 458n33
Fabrizio, J., E4n30
Fadiman, A., B16n79
Fagg, E., 489n247, 489n251
Fahr, A., 276n80
Fairless, A. H., D10n76
Falck, R., 284n123
Falcone, L. B., 278n95
Falender, V. J., 92n117
Falomir-Pichastor, J. M., 464n109
Fantino, E., 181n172
Farberow, N. L., 143n160
Farinaro, E., E4n30, E17n140
Farrell, C., 15n20, 178n156
Farrell, W., 127n80
Farrington-Flint, L., 362n230
Farwell, L., 418n81
Faucheux, S., E2n2
Fauk, N. K., B12n60
Fava, J. L., 138n136
Favio, R. H., 482n202
Fawcett, J., 356n186
Fawcett, J. M., D6n27
Fay, T. H., E4n22
Fazio, R. H., 77n31, 92n117, 234n9, 234n12, 234n13, 235n20, 235n21, 237n37, 247n89, 248n91, 478n183, 479n184
Fee, A. L., 353n141
Feeley, T. H., 267n35
Feeney, B. C., 416n51, 416n53, 416n54, 416n56, 416n60, 416n61, 417n64, 417n66
Fehr, B., 188n3
Fehr, B. A., 98n194
Fehr, E., 303n48, 507n47, 507n48
Fein, S., 472n159
Feinberg, M., 303n50
Feinberg, R., A11n33
Feingold, A., 379n72, 384n101
Feinke, K. S., 353n141
Fekken, G. C., 318n133
Feldman, P. J., B16n83
Feldman, R. S., 361n229
Felson, R. B., 333n10, 335n25, 348n99, 348n101, 349n113, 350n124
Fenell, D., 306n64
Fenigstein, A., 76n15, 77n29

Fenton-O'Creevy, M., 178n155
Ferder, L., B6n15
Ferguson, E., C28n179, C28n180, C28n181
Ferguson, R. B., 335n21
Ferrari, J. R., 142n155, 143n157
Ferreira, M. B., 154n35
Ferriere, R., 296n10
Feshbach, S., 277n82, 335n17
Festinger, L., 82n52, 252n115, 278n86, 383n93, 508n50
Fetchenhauer, D., 311n98, 312n102
Fetterman, M., A22n61
Fiddick, L., 180n171
Fidell, S., E11n89
Field, P., 99n202
Fielding, K. S., E5n36
Fields, D. A., 363n240
Filiberti, A., 297n17
Filkins, J. W., D17n137
Finch, A., 48n39
Fincham, F. D., 306n65, 306n66, 306n67, 306n68, 307n74, 307n75, 307n76, 377n59, 413n26
Fincher, C. L., 49n47
Fine, G. A., 459n40
Fink, B., 385n118
Finkel, E. J., 102n230, 306n63, 307n87, 349n112, 387n126, 413n26, 424n114
Finkelman, L., 350n121
Finkenauer, C., 189n9, 235n15, 312n103, 382n90, 469n142
Finnie, W. C., 366n282, E14n113
Fiscaro, S. A., 237n28
Fischer, K. W., 204n110
Fischer, R., 243n63
Fischhoff, B., 167n103
Fishbein, M., 246n78, B11n51
Fisher, C. D., 126n57
Fisher, H., 409n10
Fisher, J. D., 296n11
Fisher, L. D., 377n54, 422n108
Fisher, R. P., D9n64
Fisher, T. D., 172n121
Fishkin, S. A., 172n119
Fiske, S., 213n192
Fiske, S. T., 117n3, 151n23, 152n24, 153n31, 166n101, 171n111, 239n53, 381n83, 525n119, B16n74
Fitness, J., 397n200
Fitzgerald, N. M., 218n241
Fitzgerald, R., D17n132
Fitzgerald, R. J., D4n5, D4n9, D8n53, D8n57
Fitzjohn, J., 99n203
Fitzsimons, G., 382n91
Fitzsimons, G. M., 130n94, 130n97
Flaherty, D. K., 150n18
Flaherty, J. A., 224n293
Flament, C., 466n118
Flanagan, J. C., C9n33
Flanagan, M., 355n172
Flanagin, A. J., C17n94
Fleishmann, E. A., C6n28
Fleming, A. S., 209n153
Fleming, I., E15n121
Fleming, L. E., 199n64
Fletcher, C., 342n55, C22n145

Flink, C., 126n63
Flood, A., 260n3
Flores, S. D., 431n156
Florin, P., E14n115
Flynn, F. J., 518n87, 518n90
Folger, R., 85n65
Folkes, V. S., 397n201
Folkman, S., 377n50, 422n107
Fong, G., B10n41
Foot, P., 300n33
Ford, J. K., C14n70
Ford, M. T., C26n165, C27n171
Forgas, J. P., 199n68
Forrest, A., 246n77
Forster, J. L., 224n288
Forsyth, A. J. M., 366n274
Forsyth, D. R., 98n181, C19n112
Foster, C. A., 102n229, 102n230, 196n35, 209n155, 312n106, 418n78, 418n86
Foster, J. D., 101n215
Foster, J. L., 312n101
Foti, R. J., 517n86
Fowler, J. H., 210n162, 293n3
Fox, C., 312n107
Fox, E., 353n142
Fox, N. D., 434n175
Frahm, H., 152n28
Fraley, B., 526n124
Franceschetti, M., 210n162
Francis, A. M., 413n28
Francoeur, R. T., 431n159
Frank, J., E21n172
Frank, M. C., 28n52
Fraser-Thill, R., D9n66
Fraser, S. C., 265n27, 502n15, 508n49
Frayser, S. G., 47n35
Frazier, P., 252n111
Frederick, D. A., 172n120
Frederick, S., 55n74
Fredrickson, B. L., 215n205, 215n206, 215n207, 215n208
Freedman, J. L., 265n27, 285n129, 365n269
Freedman, S. R., 306n70
Freeman, C., 29n61
Freeman, E., 381n86
French, J. E., 428n134
Fresco, D. M., 96n147
Frese, M., C27n169
Freud, S., 59n82, 140n145, 336n34, 341n51
Frey, D., 97n158
Frey, R. G., 46n27
Fried, C. B., B12n61
Friedland, N., 220n249
Friedman, H., B3n4
Friedman, H. S., B16n86
Friedman, L. N., 126n70
Friedman, R., 130n93
Friesen, W., 198n62
Friesen, W. V., 217n222
Frieze, I. H., 398n208
Frijda, N. H., 194n33, 210n163, 210n164, 210n165, 215n210, 225n297, 375n17
Frimer, J. A., 299n30
Frisch, M., 150n11

N-6 | Name Index

Frith, K. T., A4n1, A17n49
Frone, M. R., 137n130
Frost, J. H., 380n77
Frost, R. O., 79n40, 392n152
Frye, N. K., C28n185
Fryker, K., 212n183
Fuchs, T., B13n66
Fujioka, T., 85n69
Fujita, F., 98n175
Fukuyama, F., 379n75
Fulero, S. M., D14n106, D17n140, D18n149, D18n151
Fulker, D. W., 317n132, 318n134
Fullerton, C. S., E17n131
Funder, D. C., 11n18, 98n198
Fung, H. H., 413n27
Funke, F., 470n146, 482n200
Furman, W., 98n193
Furnham, A., 319n153
Furtner, M. R., 221n265

G

Gable, S. L., 209n156, 215n211
Gabriel, M. T., 98n173, 98n176
Gabriel, S., 377n61
Gächter, S., 303n48, 507n47, 507n48
Gael, S. A., C9n31
Gaerling, T., 296n14
Gaertner, L., 108n276, 393n167
Gaertner, S. L., 453n12, 483n204
Gage, S. H., 345n76
Gagnon, J. H., 172n112, 172n116, 247n80, 319n147, 350n117, 409n16, 411n21, 433n171, 437n191, 438n198, 464n104, 499n5
Gailliot, M. T., 203n100, 356n196, 386n121
Gaines, B., 88n86
Galinsky, A., 178n159
Galinsky, A. D., 44n17, 181n182, 523n107, 523n109, 524n114, 524n115
Gallagher, J., 189n7, 189n8
Gallopin, G. C., E2n2
Gallucci, M., 394n171, 397n197, 397n198, 397n199, 507n43, 507n45
Galperin, A., 172n120
Gampa, A., 234n11
Gangé, M., 199n65
Gangestad, S., 379n68, 425n119
Gangestad, S. W., 379n65, 386n122
Ganna, A., 436n183
Garbriel, S., 395n183
Garcia-Finana, M., 41n11
Garcia, T. A., B14n70
Gardner, A., 42n12
Gardner, M. P., 211n171
Gardner, W., 377n61, 395n183
Gardner, W. L., 189n4, 377n60, 392n161, 393n162, 395n177, 395n181, 395n185
Garfinkel, P. E., 385n119
Garg, C., 233n4
Garland, E. L., 159n53
Garner, D. M., 385n119
Garner, W., 377n55
Garrett, R. K., 15n22
Garrett, S., D5n25

Garrioch, L., D10n70
Garry, M., 312n101
Gartrell, N. K., 463n98
Garvin, E., 212n185
Gascó, M., 237n36
Gasper, K., 212n185
Gattiker, U. E., 461n66
Gaunt, R., 54n69, 54n71
Gavanski, I., 178n163, 178n164
Gazzaniga, M. S., 54n62, 54n63
Geaghan, J. P., 366n280
Gebhard, P. H., 433n165
Geen, R. G., 203n89, 339n37
Geertz, A. W., 243n63
Geiger, A., 26n44
Geise, A. C., 390n132
Geller, E. S., E14n112
Gendolla, G. H. E., 159n55
Gendron, R. C., 366n280
Gentile, D. A., 30n67, 326n177
Gentile, D. G., 354n154
Gentry, W. A., 518n89
George, L., 178n159
Gerard, H. B., 84n56, 261n12
Gerbner, G., 345n77, 345n78
Gerrard, M., 77n30, 99n208, 214n199, 215n203, B9n38, B13n65, B14n68
Gerstel, N., 377n37, 377n38
Gervais, W. M., 312n104, 460n49, 460n50, 460n51, 460n52, 460n53
Gesch, B. C., 357n204
Geurten, M., 167n102
Gharib, S., C21n136, C22n137, C22n138
Giacomantonio, M., E5n39
Giammarino, M., 396n191
Giancola, P. R., 356n200
Giannopoulou, I., E17n135
Gibbons, F., B9n38, B14n68
Gibbons, F. X., 77n30, 77n31, 99n208, 215n203, B13n65
Gibbs, A. C., 377n48, 396n186
Gibson, B., 157n38, B10n41
Giesler, R. B., 89n94
Gifford, R., E7n53
Gifford, R. K., 173n136, 475n171, 475n172
Gilbert, D. T., 54n69, 54n71, 89n93, 153n30, 153n32, 213n189, 213n191, 213n193, 249n95, 249n96, 249n97, 249n98, 249n99, 249n100, 285n131
Gill, N., E21n172
Gilman, S. E., 76n18
Gilmore, R. O., 29n61
Gilovich, T., 46n24, 95n134, 164n91, 165n96, 168n107, 174n137, 177n152, 179n167, 253n124
Ginath, Y., E6n49
Ginges, J., 469n132
Gino, F., 299n28, 363n247, 364n249, 364n250, 364n255
Giordano, C., 459n43
Giuffrida, A., 473n160
Giuliano, T., 513n68
Gladue, B. A., 356n183, 356n185
Glaser, P., 26n47

Glaser, R., 377n54, 377n55, 422n108
Glass, D. C., 126n70, E11n92
Glendenning, A., 98n195
Glenn, N. D., 209n151, 209n152
Glerean, E., 217n224
Gleser, G. C., 144n166, E18n147
Glick, P., 476n39
Glionna, J. M., 271n47
Glore, G. L., 212n186
Glynn, M. A., 102n239
Gneezy, A., 158n42
Goel, S., 176n144
Goethals, G. R., 176n146
Goffman, E., 73n8, 75n13, 104n248, 106n261
Gogus, C. I., 364n259, 364n260
Golding, S. L., 173n135
Goldman, M., 422n104
Goldsmith, K., 205n115
Goldstein, A., 160n64, 160n65
Goldstein, N. J., E14n117
Goleman, D., 189n10, 235n17, 235n19
Gollwitzer, M., 354n161, 354n167
Gollwitzer, P. M., 54n68, 96n151, 96n152, 107n265, 107n266, 127n71, 128n82, 128n85, 128n86, 128n87, 131n98, 131n99, 444n235
Gomillion, S., 390n131
Goncalo, J. A., 393n163
Gondolf, E. W., 442n225
Gonzaga, G. C., 172n120
Gonzales, M., 97n153
Gonzales, M. H., 307n80
Gonzalez-Forero, M., 42n12
Gonzalez-Vallejo, C., 160n62
GonzálezáVaro, J. P., E13n108
Good, C., 488n240
Good, T. L., 162n73
Goode, M. R., 306n60
Goodenough, F. L., 218n232
Goodie, A. S., 181n172
Goodman, M., 364n258
Goodsell, C. A., D10n76
Goodwin, G. P., 382n89
Goodwin, J. S., 377n51
Gooren, L. J. G. M., 375n17
Gordon, L. J., 88n87
Gorin, A. A., 138n136
Gorokhovich, Y., E17n137
Gottfredson, L., 488n235
Gottfredson, M., 353n149
Gottfredson, M. R., 142n153, 358n209
Gottfredson, S. D., E8n75
Gottman, J. M., 218n236, 218n237, 420n94, 420n95
Gottschalk, L. A., 144n166
Gould, S. J., A15n45
Goupil, L., 53n59
Govaerts, K., 377n39
Goveas, J. S., 356n187
Govorun, O., 479n189
Grace, M. C., E18n147
Graetz, K. A., 469n135
Graham, E. A., 23n39
Graham, J., 300n37
Graham, K., 356n195
Grahe, J. E., 29n64
Grammer, K., 385n118

Gramzow, R., 342n55
Grandey, A. A., 137n130
Grasmick, H. G., 366n279
Grasselli, A., 484n214
Gray-Little, B., 95n137
Gray, B., E3n11
Greathouse, S. M., D9n68, D15n113
Green, B. L., 266n32, E18n147
Green, D. M., E11n89
Green, G., 379n64
Green, L., 303n45
Green, P. J., 215n212
Green, S. W., 178n161
Greenberg, J., 77n32, 97n157, 100n213, 105n257, 205n118, A14n42, C26n163
Greenblat, C., 409n13
Greene, D., 85n62, 176n143
Greene, J. D., 300n34
Greene, T. C., E4n20
Greenhaus, J. H., C18n96
Greenspan, S. I., 222n269
Greenwald, A. G., 90n100, 237n32, 273n56, 455n19, 479n185
Gregg, A. P., 87n76
Gregory, L. W., 117n8
Greifeneder, R., 122n28
Greitemeyer, T., 314n120, 326n178, 346n80, 354n152
Greve, A., D6n27
Griffin, D., 131n103, 132n104, 132n106, 418n74
Griffin, D. W., 426n123
Griffin, J. J., 88n86
Griffitt, W., 409n14
Griggs, L., 353n142
Grimbos, T., 193n24
Grime, Y. U., 421n100
Griskevicius, V., 108n268, 218n239, E14n117
Grisom, R., 319n149
Groeger, J. A., 352n133
Grolnick, W. S., 126n64, 126n66
Gromko, M. H., 172n123, 172n124
Grondin, S., 47n31, 47n32, 48n37
Gronich, B., B8n32
Gronlund, S. D., D6n41
Groom, R. W., 355n174, 355n176, E4n21
Groscup, J. L., 463n94
Gross, D., 497n2
Gross, E. F., 394n169, 396n190
Gross, H., 377n37, 377n38
Gross, J., 392n154
Gross, J. J., 202n87, 206n127, 223n283
Gross, L., 345n78
Gross, P. H., 477n180
Grossman, K. E., 417n68
Grotpeter, J. K., 346n86, 347n94
Grover, C. A., 363n243
Groves, C. L., 30n67, 355n178
Grubbs, J. B., 29n63
Gruber, J., 199n66, 200n72
Gruber, M. J., E17n134
Grubler, A., E2n2
Gruenewald, T., B4n11
Gruenewald, T. L., 346n83, 346n84, B7n19

Gruenfeld, D. H., 522n105, 523n107, 523n109, 523n110, 524n114, 524n115
Grunberg, N. E., 224n289
Gruner, C. R., 276n74
Guarnieri, G., 484n214
Guenther, C. C., D18n146, D18n148
Guijarro, M. L., 203n92
Guillory, J. E., 210n161
Guinote, A., 523n108
Gully, S. M., C21n127
Gupta, S., 233n4
Gupta, S. P., 224n291
Gurr, T. R., 335n29
Gurung, R. A. R., 346n83, 346n84, B2n1, B3n6, B3n7, B7n19, B8n30, B12n58, B16n77
Gutkowski, S., E6n49
Guttmann, F., E6n49
Guxens, M., E12n102
Guyll, M., B16n82
Guzmán, R. A., 310n95
Gwaltney, J. M., Jr., B16n83

H

Hackel, L. S., 209n153
Hackett, C., 457n28
Hackett, R. D., C30n204
Hackman, J. R., C24n151
Haefner, D. P., B10n49
Haegerich, T. M., D16n120
Haer, R., 343n69
Hafdahl, A. R., 95n137
Hagan, F. E., 364n253
Haglid, M., 377n53
Hagtvet, K. A., 98n186
Hahn, C., 153n30
Haidt, J., 206n125, 208n142, 215n201, 215n202, 299n31, 300n32, 300n37
Halberstadt, J. B., 213n187
Halderman, P., 4n3
Hall, C. L., 205n113
Hall, E. T., E9n85
Hall, J. H., 306n65, 307n76
Hall, J. M., E2n2
Hall, J. R., 265n25
Hallet, A. J., 203n92
Halliday, D. M., B9n36
Halpern, B. S., E3n10
Halweil, B., E4n28
Hamburg, P., 76n18
Hamburger, M. E., 303n45
Hamilton, D. L., 173n136, 475n170, 475n171, 475n172, 498n4
Hamilton, W. D., 313n111, 376n23
Hamlin, I., 390n131
Hammarberg, K., 197n38
Hammond, M. D., 421n100
Hammond, S. M., 357n204
Hampson, S. E., 357n204
Hanacek, B., 253n121, E18n148
Hancock, J. T., 210n161, 362n232, 388n127
Hancock, P. A., E11n90
Handley, I. M., 211n178
Haney, C., D17n133, D17n142
Hang-Pil, S., 280n107
Hanges, P. J., 479n188

Hanisch, K. A., C10n38, C10n41, C24n149, C24n150, C29n195, C29n197, C29n198, C29n199, C29n200, C30n205, C30n207
Hanley, N., E21n169
Hannon, P., 306n63
Hansen, G. L., 247n85, 439n204
Hansen, J., 158n41
Hansen, J. V., 150n11
Hanson, D. J., 224n292
Hansson, L. M., 461n73
Hansson, R. O., E16n128
Haque, O. S., 44n19
Harber, K., 474n163, 474n168
Harber, K. D., 460n48, 485n221, 485n222
Hardin, G., 509n54, E3n4
Hardin, S. B., E16n130
Hardison, C. M., 488n243, 488n244, C14n67
Hare, A. P., C19n99
Hare, R. D., 204n104
Hargis, M., C12n51, C12n57
Hari, R., 217n224
Harker, D. L., D9n61
Harkins, S., 505n34
Harkins, S. G., 506n40
Harmon-Jones, E., 201n79, 201n80, 237n30, 252n113, 482n198, 482n199
Harms, P. D., 221n258
Harrell, K. L., 314n121
Harrell, W. A., 318n144
Harriott, J., C11n42
Harris, C. R., 442n223
Harris, E. A., E5n36
Harris, M., 48n44, 48n45
Harris, M. B., 18n27, 18n28, 23n36, 205n113, 461n64
Harris, P. B., E8n72
Harris, R. B., 349n106
Harris, R. J., 461n64
Harris, S. J., 105n258, 310n94
Harris, V. A., 164n87
Harrison, A. A., 237n28, 377n40
Harrison, K., 76n20, 76n21, 76n22
Harskamp, J., 452n3, 452n5
Harter, S., 92n114
Hartford, M., 377n53
Harwood, J., 469n141, 469n143
Haselton, M. G., 121n21, 172n120
Hasher, L., 216n221
Hassebrauck, M., 297n23
Hassin, R. R., 160n64, 160n65, 160n66
Hastings, P. A., D16n121
Hatfield, E., 210n160, 408n3
Hauck, A., 48n39
Haugen, J. A., 307n80
Hausen, B., A22n61
Hausser, D., 237n29
Haw, R. M., D9n64
Hawkins, R. X. D., 28n52
Hawkley, L. C., 377n48, 377n49, 377n52, 377n58, 395n176, 395n180, 395n182, 396n186, 396n187, 396n188
Hawley, C., 452n11
Hawver, T. H., 221n256

Hay, D., 346n85
Hayduk, L. A., E7n52
Hayes, K. L., B10n43
Hayes, R., 365n267
Hazan, C., 415n45, 416n58
Hazlett, G., D5n25
He, G., B12n59
He, L., 164n92
Head, J., E4n32
Healy, M., 102n224
Hearold, S., 326n176
Heatherton, F., B9n39
Heatherton, T. F., 59n83, 77n28, 79n39, 79n41, 92n116, 98n197, 105n259, 133n109, 136n124, 137n137, 204n108, 206n121, 421n98, 421n99, 461n65, 489n250
Heaton, P., D8n58
Heberlein, U., 373n1
Hebl, M. R., 461n65, 461n71
Hecker, T., 343n65
Hee, K. H., 116n1
Hegi, K. E., 408n2
Heider, F., 162n72
Heider, K., 217n222
Heilman, M. E., C29n193
Heine, S. J., 28n48, 108n275, 123n41, 245n72
Heiner, R. B., 349n116
Heingartner, A., 505n29, 526n126
Heinz, A., 344n74
Heinz, S., 152n28
Heitmann, H., 138n134
Helbing, D., 512n65
Helkama, K., 310n92
Helliwell, J. F., 316n123
Helton, W. S., E4n32
Helzer, E. G., 300n38
Hemenway, D., 351n131
Hemsworth, D. H., D5n20
Henderson, P. W., A7n13
Henderson, V., 124n44
Hendin, H., 143n161, 144n167
Hendren, A., 463n90
Hendricks, N. J., 457n29
Henken, V. J., 144n168
Henle, C. A., 364n251
Henrich, J., 28n48, 317n129
Henry, B., 358n211
Henry, P. J., 234n10
Henry, R., 353n138
Hepach, R., 316n124
Hepburn, C., 466n119
Hepworth, J. T., 476n175
Herbison, P., 99n203
Herchenroeder, L. M., 211n178
Herdt, G., 47n36
Herek, G. M., 463n91, 464n103, 464n106
Herlitz, J., 377n53
Herman, B. H., 391n144
Herman, C. P., 77n28, 79n41, 161n67, 161n68
Herman, E. M., 505n29, 526n126
Hermann, E., 28n52
Herold, E. S., 247n84, 319n150, 445n240
Herrmann, A., 138n134
Herscovitch, L., C25n156

Hertel, P., 513n68
Herzog, D. B., 76n18
Hess, R. D., 162n78
Hesse, B. W., 29n62
Hesson-McInnis, M., 60n89
Hewitt, J., E7n60, E8n65
Hewstone, M., 319n152, 453n14, 470n145, 470n153
Hicken, M., 197n40
Hicks, J. A., 377n59
Hicks, J. M., D9n63
Hicks, L. L., 428n134
Hietanen, J. K., 217n224
Higgins, E., 193n30, 243n66
Higgins, E. T., 57n80, 90n101, 157n39
Higgins, R. L., 88n90
Higgs, S., 381n86, 381n87
Hight, T. L., 198n57
Higley, J. D., 356n188, 356n189
Higley, S. B., 356n188
Hilbe, J. M., 474n167
Hill, C. A., 398n203
Hill, C. T., 218n240, 218n244
Hill, G. W., C19n101
Hill, P., 305n59, 307n77, 307n78
Hill, S. J., 235n14
Hilmert, C. J., 64n103
Himbara, D., 333n7
Hinde, R. A., 339n41
Hinkel, H., 343n65
Hirschi, T., 142n153, 358n209
Hirsh, J. B., 44n17
Hirt, E., 117n10
Hirt, E. R., 88n87, 117n9, 181n175, 181n176
Hisler, G., 201n78
Hitsch, G. J., 385n114
Hixon, J. G., 89n93, 426n122
Hmielowski, J. D., E14n110
Ho, K., 214n195
Hobel, C. J., B12n58
Hobson, Z., 312n107
Hochbaum, G. M., B10n44
Hockley, W. E., D5n20
Hodge, C. N., 384n102
Hodges, S. D., 239n57
Hodson, G., 207n137
Hoerger, M., 221n254
Hoerner, J. A., E21n170
Hofer, B., 477n179
Hoffman, B. J., 518n89
Hoffman, E. L., 262n20
Hoffman, H. G., 455n19
Hoffman, M. L., 318n141
Hoffrage, U., 122n30
Hofmann, W., 299n27
Hofstadter, D. R., 178n158
Hogan, R., 517n84, 519n91
Hogg, M. A., 396n192, 396n194
Holder-Perkins, V., B16n88
Holgate, S. T., E12n103
Holland, R. W., 216n219
Hollander, S., D5n16
Hollenbeck, J. R., C19n113
Holliday, J., 377n55
Hollingshead, A. B., 513n69, 513n70
Holloway, S. D., 162n78
Holmes, J., 418n75

Holmes, J. G., 302n43, 312n105, 426n123, 426n124, 426n125, 426n126
Holmes, L., C27n177
Holt-Lundstad, J., 377n57
Holt, K., 97n157
Holtzworth-Munroe, A., 423n113
Holzberg, A. D., 98n170
Homans, G. C., 430n148, 430n149
Honour, J. W., 363n241
Hood, R., 77n31
Hooper, N., 165n93
Hoorens, V., 108n274
Hope, L., D6n31
Horbert, E. J., 208n141
Horcajo, J., 237n36
Horner, M., 141n146
Hornsey, M. J., 469n143, E5n36
Hornstein, H. A., 210n168
Horowitz, A. V., 422n103
Horowitz, H. L., 459n41
Horowitz, L. M., 416n48, 416n55
Hortaçsu, A., 385n114
Hosch, H. M., D15n109, D15n110, D15n111
Hoshino-Browne, E., 245n73
Hoskin, R. A., 207n136
Houlihan, A., B14n68
House, J. S., B8n28
House, P., 176n143
Houston, D. A., 277n84, 277n85
Hovland, C., 272n51, 276n69, 279n99
Hovland, C. I., 233n8, 272n52, 273n55, 277n81, 279n100, 476n174
Howard, H. R. B., E8n68
Howard, M. O., 159n53
Howell-White, S., 422n103
Howell, S., 468n126
Hoyle, R. H., 469n134, 499n7
Hoyt, G., D5n25
Hoyt, W. T., 307n83
Hsee, C. K., 119n16, 119n18, 214n198
Hsiang, S. M., 355n177, E11n88
Hsing, C., 314n116
HsiuJu, Y., 88n83
Hu, J., 298n26
Hu, Y., 422n104
Hubbard, M., 249n101
Huel, G., E17n139
Huesmann, L. R., 91n113, 326n177, 354n153, 354n155, 354n164
Huff, C., 21n31
Huffcutt, A. I., C14n64, C14n65
Hui, C. Y. T., D12n98
Hulin, C. L., C29n195, C30n205, C296n197, C296n198, C296n200
Hull, J. G., 78n33, 78n34, 135n121, 354n156, 356n199
Humphrey, L., 131n100, 131n101, 131n102
Humphrey, L. L., 392n155
Humphrey, R. H., 221n256
Hunt, W. C., 377n51
Hunter, J. E., 384n102, C14n66, C14n72
Hunter, R. E., C14n72
Huntley, B., E2n2
Hupka, R. B., 440n212
Hurtado, A., D17n133

Huston, T. L., 218n241
Hutcherson, C. A., 206n127
Hutchins, I., 46n26
Hutchison, P., 470n147
Hutter, R. R. C., 237n34
Hutton, D. G., 95n125
Hviid, A., 150n11
Hyde, J. S., 95n135, 224n286, 428n136, 431n157, 445n238
Hyland, M. E., 141n147
Hymes, C., 189n11, 235n18
Hymes, R. W., D15n112

I

Iannelli, V., 150n1, 150n3
Idson, L. C., 158n43
Ihori, N., 30n68, 314n118, 314n119, 326n177, 353n151
Ilgen, D. R., C19n113, C29n189
Illbeck, B. E., 431n156
Impett, E. A., 412n25
Imrich, J., D12n92
Inderbitzen, H. M., 98n191
Indriyawati, N., B12n60
Ingerick, M. J., C14n73
Inglis, D., 98n195
Innes-Ker, A. H., 213n187
Insko, C. A., 310n93, 469n133, 469n134, 469n135, 469n136, 469n137, 499n7, 504n18
Inzlicht, M., 489n249
Ip, E. H., 461n75
Isen, A. M., 216n214, 216n215, 216n216, 216n218, 320n161
Ito, T. A., 356n194
Iuzzini, J., 393n167
Ivanov, B., 284n126, 285n128
Iverson, R. D., C26n157
Iyengar, S. S., 122n26, 138n134, A12n35
Izard, C. E., 190n14, 190n15

J

Jablin, F. M., C10n40, C15n74
Jablonski, N. G., 353n149
Jackson, D. N., C14n71
Jackson, G. O., 420n90
Jackson, J., 488n239
Jackson, J. R., 234n9, 478n183
Jackson, K. M., B10n43
Jackson, L. A., 384n102
Jackson, W., 504n24
Jacobe, D., A11n27
Jacobs, R. C., 262n21
Jacobs, S. V., E4n26, E13n105
Jacobson, L., 484n220
Jaeger, C. C., E2n2
Jager, J., E2n2
James, B., 247n83
James, W., 72n2, 117n2, 190n12, 190n13
James, W. H., 409n15, 410n18
Jamieson, P. E., 353n148
Janda, L. H., 384n109
Jang, S. M., 260n10
Janis, I., 513n73, 513n74
Janis, I. L., 99n201, 99n202, 233n8, 272n52, 276n71, 276n76, 277n81, 277n82

Janiszewski, C., 278n91
Jankowiak, W., 409n7
Janoff-Bulman, R., 102n236, 197n42, 197n48, 250n105
Jansen, B., 170n110
Janssen, S., E4n25, E11n91, E12n94, E12n99
Janssen, T., B10n43
Janus, C. L., 172n115, 432n162
Janus, M. D., 203n101
Janus, S. S., 172n115, 432n162
Jeanneret, P. R., C6n28
Jeffery, R. W., 224n288
Jencks, C., 488n236
Jensen, A., 379n69
Jensen, J. D., 355n170
Jimenez-Lorente, B., D17n140, D18n149, D18n151
Jodha, N. S., E2n2
Joel, S., 412n25
John, O., 87n82
Johns, M., 489n249
Johnson, B. C., 274n58
Johnson, B. T., 90n103
Johnson, C., 511n58
Johnson, D. J., 418n76, 424n117
Johnson, D. W., 467n121, 467n122
Johnson, F. L., 318n139
Johnson, G. A., E12n96
Johnson, J., 117n10
Johnson, J. L., 142n155
Johnson, L., 197n38
Johnson, M., B9n35, E16n130
Johnson, N. S., 423n113
Johnson, R. T., 467n121, 467n122
Johnson, W., 422n105, 423n111
Johnson, W. G., 211n175
Johnston, D. E., C30n202
Join Joiner, T., 297n18
Joiner, T., 36n3, 143n158, 144n170
Joireman, J., 307n86
Jonas, K., 237n38
Jonason, P. K., 431n156
Jones, A. M., D12n98, D12n99, D13n100
Jones, A. R., D8n56
Jones, C. R., 157n39
Jones, D. N., 347n98
Jones, E. E., 84n56, 88n88, 89n96, 91n107, 91n109, 105n256, 141n148, 163n86, 164n87, 243n64, 378n62, 380n78, 380n80, B16n75
Jones, F., C28n179, C28n180, C28n181
Jones, F. D., 143n164
Jones, T. S., E7n61
Jones, W., 373n5
Joppa, M., 356n185
Jordan, A. H., 208n142
Jorgenson, D. O., E3n7
Joseph, C., 206n125
Josephs, R. A., 356n198
Jossa, F., E17n140
Jost, J. T., 470n155
Joy, S. W., D8n54
Joy, V., 383n94
Joyce, W. F., 517n80
Judd, C., 474n164, 486n225
Judd, C. M., 455n18

Juieng, D., 22n35
Jung, K., 474n167
Jussim, L., 88n83, 460n48, 474n163, 474n166, 474n168, 485n221, 485n222
Juvonen, J., 394n169, 396n190

K

Kachadourian, L. K., 306n66, 306n67
Kacmar, M., C29n191
Kafai, Y. B., 363n240
Kagan, J., 76n17
Kahleman, D., 132n105
Kahn, B. E., A7n14
Kahn, R. L., C21n128
Kahneman, D., 55n74, 55n75, 90n104, 118n13, 118n14, 118n15, 120n20, 168n106, 168n109, 174n139, 178n157, 197n44, 197n45, 197n46
Kaiser, F., E5n43
Kaiser, R. B., 517n84, 519n91, 519n92
Kaistaniemi, L., 102n233
Kalder, A. K., D16n122
Kallgren, C. A., 366n275, 366n276, 366n277
Kalmet, N., D5n21
Kalro, A., 302n44
Kamada, A., 164n91
Kamble, S., 377n59
Kameleitner, B., E5n40
Kammeyer-Mueller, J. D., C30n208
Kanazawa, S., 395n184
Kane, M., 85n68
Kang, S., B8n22
Kanin, E. J., 218n242
Kannouse, D. E., B16n75
Kant, I., 124n47, 386n123
Kaplan, R. E., C21n131
Kapp, F. T., E4n31
Karabenick, S. A., 318n145
Karau, S. J., 506n38, 506n41
Kardes, F. R., 181n175, 278n87
Karlsson, B. W., 377n53
Karney, B. R., 387n126, 409n11, 420n90
Karremans, J. C., 307n85
Karlsson, Y., 57n78
Kashiwagi, K., 162n78
Kasperson, R. E., E2n2
Kasser, T., 126n68, 126n69, 128n81, A14n43
Kastin, A. J., 391n146
Kastner, S., C18n89
Katcher, A. H., 342n58
Kates, R. W., E2n2, E4n34
Katz, D., C21n128
Katz, J., 364n261
Katzev, R., 205n114
Kaukiainen, A., 102n233
Kaun, K. R., 373n1
Kavenocki, S., 247n81
Kay, A. C., 470n155
Kaya, N., E7n56, E9n78
Kaye, D., 276n71
Kayra-Stuart, F., D5n16
Kearns, J. N., 307n75

Keast, A., D4n7, D4n8, D6n39, D7n44
Keating, L., 98n188
Keefe, K., 98n196
Keefer, L. A., 476n173
Keegan, J., 356n190
Keen, G., 165n93
Keeney, R. L., 167n103
Kegeles, S. S., B10n49
Keinan, G., 220n248, 220n249
Keir, A., 468n127
Keith, T. Z., 98n183
Kelem, R. T., 502n15, 508n49
Keller, M., 452n8
Keller, P. S., 461n61
Kelley, H. H., 233n8, 272n52, 277n81, 302n42, B16n75
Kelley, W. M., 489n250
Kelln, B. R. C., 306n72
Kelly, M. H., 361n220
Keltner, D., 208n141, 303n50, 522n105, 523n110
Kemerza, I., 316n123
Kemp, S., A11n29, E4n32
Kendall, P. C., 344n72
Kennard, J. B., D15n113
Kennedy, M., 473n161
Kenrick, D. T., 210n167, 303n47, 455n26, 477n179, E12n96
Keough, K., 488n240
Kepes, S., 352n137, 353n146
Kerkhof, P., 237n39, 458n35
Kerlin, L., 362n230
Kern, M. J., D17n138
Kerns, J. G., 216n220
Kerr, N. A., 98n181
Kerr, N. L., 29n58, 394n171, 397n197, 397n198, 397n199, 505n35, 506n39, 507n42, 507n43, 507n45, 507n46, D15n112
Kervinen, A., 470n150
Kerwin, T., 352n132
Kessler, T., 470n146, 482n200
Ketcham, K., D19n153
Ketsetzis, M., 98n188
Key, C. R., 377n51
Key, K. N., D10n75
Khadjavi, M., 304n51
Khoo, A., 326n177
Kidd, C., 142n154
Kidder, D. L., C29n194
Kiecolt-Glaser, J. K., 377n54, 377n55, 377n56, 422n108, 422n110, B8n31
Kiefner, A. E., 461n57
Kiesler, S., 305n58
Kihlstrom, J. F., 90n102
Killen, J., 284n121
Kim, D., A6n11, C14n67
Kim, J., 26n47, 211n171
Kim, J. K., 260n10
Kim, M. Y., 200n70
Kim, S., 377n47
Kim, S. H., 393n163
Kim, Y., 384n103
Kim, Y.-H., 87n80, 87n81
Kimeldorf, M. B., 296n13
King, K., 445n239
King, K. M., B14n70
King, L. A., 199n67, 390n132

Kingsbury, G. G., 98n182
Kinicki, A. J., C6n24
Kinney, R. F., 96n151, 128n85
Kinsey, A. C., 433n165
Kinsey, K. A., 366n279
Kipnis, D., 521n98, 521n99, 522n100
Kirker, W. S., 90n98, 90n99
Kirkpatrick, L. A., 86n73
Kirkpatrick, S. A., C21n130
Kirsch, T. D., E17n138
Kirschenbaum, D., 131n100, 131n101, 131n102
Kirschner, P., 276n71
Kirscht, J. P., B10n46, B10n49
Kiss, M. J., 207n135
Kitayama, S., 74n9, 108n275, 123n41, 164n89, 164n90, 245n71, 245n73, 245n74, 313n112
Kitzinger, C., 429n138
Klaczynski, P., 461n61
Klassen, M. L., 461n77
Klein, C., E3n10
Klein, L. C., 346n83, 346n84, B7n19
Klein, S. B., 90n102
Klentz, B., 326n174
Kling, K. C., 95n135
Klinger, M. R., 237n32
Klump, K. L., 347n96
Knapp, D. E., C10n39
Knasko, S. C., A7n14
Knetsch, J. L., 90n104, 197n45
Knight, J., 236n26
Knight, L. J., 161n69
Knobe, J., 300n35, 300n36
Knobe, J. M., 165n95
Knobloch-Westerwick, S., 244n68
Knoll, N., B8n27
Knowles, E. S., 271n48, E8n66
Knowles, M., 377n60, 393n162, 395n181, 395n185
Koch, E. J., 100n214
Kochanek, K. D., B9n37
Koernig, S. K., A7n19, A7n20
Koestner, R., 84n59, 85n63, 85n67, 126n56, 126n62
Kofodimos, J. R., C21n131
Kofta, M., 460n47
Kogan, A., 200n72
Kogan, N., 515n78
Kohlenberg, R. J., E14n116
Koider, S., 53n59
Kolata, G., 461n60
Kolditz, T., 85n68, 88n91
Kollath-Cattano, C., B10n40
Konecni, V. J., E8n69
Konrath, S., 95n129, 101n215, 221n266, 314n116
Kontrova, J., E17n142
Koole, S., 222n276
Koole, S. L., 28n49, 203n98, 203n99, 209n159
Koops, W., 344n71
Koren, H. S., E12n103
Koss, M. P., 350n122
Kotani, H., E16n123
Kotsou, I., 200n72
Kouchaki, M., 299n29
Koughan, M., C2n1, C2n2, C2n3, C2n5

Kouzes, J. M., 517n85
Kovera, M. B., D3n1, D9n67, D9n68, D10n69, D10n81, D12n89, D15n113, D16n118, D16n126, D16n128
Kovett, D., E13n104
Kowalewski, R. B., 377n49, 396n187
Kowalski, R., 393n168
Kozak, M., 159n56
Kozlowski, S. W., C19n106, C20n126, C21n127
Kraft, A. J., 307n81
Kraft, D., 239n56
Kraft, M., E5n42
Kramer, A. D. I., 210n161, 210n162
Kramer, R. M., E3n8
Krammer, T. L., E18n147
Kraus, S. J., 248n92
Krauss, R. M., 365n269
Kraut, R. E., 98n185
Krauthammer, C., 478n182
Kravitz, D. A., D13n101, D16n125
Kraxberger, B. E., 109n277
Kray, L. J., 178n159, 181n182
Krendl, A. C., 489n250
Kressel, D. R., D13n104
Kressel, N. J., D13n104
Krishnan, R., 513n72
Kristof, A. L., 127n72, 128n83, 129n89
Krizan, Z., 201n78
Kross, E., 203n96, 222n277, 375n13, 391n148
Krueger, J., 176n141, 178n160, 178n162
Krueger, J. I., 98n180, 98n190, 98n199
Krueger, R. F., 422n105, 423n111
Kruger, J., 165n96
Kruger, M. L., 198n63
Kruglanski, A. W., 130n93
Krull, D. S., 153n32
Krzysztof, J., E14n118
Kuang, L., 87n82
Kuehn, R., 431n158
Kuhnert, K. W., 518n89
Kuiper, N. A., 90n98, 90n99, 97n161
Kuipers, P., 210n164
Kulig, J. W., 176n147
Kulik, J. A., 64n103
Kumar, A., 224n291
Kumar, N., 224n291
Kumashiro, M., 306n63
Kumasiro, M., 424n114
Kunce, L. J., 416n62
Kunda, Z., 84n57, 97n156, 474n169, 476n176, 477n177, 477n178
Kunst, M., 349n111
Kunz, P. R., 295n9
Kurzban, R., 507n44
Kusche, A., 418n75
Kustanti, C. Y., B12n60
Kustis, G. A., C10n39
Kutzner, F., 158n41
Kwan, M., A17n51
Kwan, V. S., 87n82
Kyriacou, D. N., 349n106

L

Laan, E., 193n24
Lackenbauer, S., 245n73
Lacoursiere, R. B., 376n29
LaFleur, S. J., 239n57
LaFrance, M., 218n230, 218n231, 486n229
Lagerspetz, K. M., 334n14
Lagerspetz, K. M. J., 102n233
Laird, J. D., 244n67
Lake, R. A., 4809n194
Lakens, D., 28n49
Lakin, A., A21n55
Lakin, J. L., 381n85, 394n173
Laky, Z. E., B14n69
Lalumière, M. L., 193n24
Lam, C. P., 30n67
Lam, S. S. K., C26n166, C27n167
LaMar, L., 443n233
Lambert, A. J., 479n190
Lambert, N. M., 377n59, 413n26
Lambeth, S. P., 317n129
Lampinen, J. M., D10n74
Lancet, M., 247n81
Landau, M. J., 476n173
Landis, K. R., B8n28
Landis, R. S., C11n49
Landman, J., 179n168
Lang, M. E., 209n147
Lange, A., 304n51
Langer, E. J., 91n106, 178n153, 178n154, B7n18, E7n50
Langer, G., B12n57
Langer, L. M., 99n204
Langley, R. L., 353n143
Langlois, J. H., 384n108, 386n124
Lao, J., 164n92
LaPiere, R. T., 246n75
Larøi, F., 354n158
Larsen, J. D., 48n38
Larsen, J. T., 44n17
Larsen, R. J., 200n73, 224n284, 224n295, 442n220
Larson, R. W., 217n227, 218n228, 218n229
Larwood, L., 461n66
Lassiter, G. D., 160n62, 211n178
Latane, B., 383n94, 505n34
Latané, B., 321n166, 321n168, 506n40
Latham, G. P., 127n73, 128n84, 129n90
Latta, R. M., E7n55
Laumann, E. O., 172n112, 172n116, 247n80, 319n147, 350n117, 409n16, 411n21, 433n171, 437n191, 438n198, 464n104, 499n5
Launier, R., B8n25
Lavine, H., 76n23
Lawes, D., 353n138
Lawler, E. E., C19n105
Lawrence, C., 355n180
Lawrence, T., 384n96
Lawson, A., 439n202, 439n203, 443n230
Lawson, D. S., D10n76
Lawton, K., 165n93
Layton, J. B., 377n57

Lazarus, R. S., 194n32, B6n16, B6n17, B8n25
Lazarus, S., 377n50, 422n107
Le Bon, G., 511n60
Lea, S. E. G., 45n21, 45n22, A11n31
Leander, N. P., 334n13
Leary, M. R., 100n211, 100n212, 109n277, 209n145, 209n157, 373n4, 376n24, 376n32, 391n139, 391n140, 391n142, 393n168, 507n44
Lede, E., E15n119
Ledford, G. E., C19n105
Ledford, G. E., Jr., C20n124
Lee-Chai, A., 54n68
Lee-Chai, A. Y., 525n116
Lee, B. K., A12n36
Lee, C., 294n5
Lee, C. M., B14n70
Lee, D. S., 375n13
Lee, H., B8n22
Lee, J., 269n44
Lee, M., A8n22
Lee, N., E14n111
Lee, S., 267n35
Lee, S. W. S., 206n126
Lee, W. N., A12n36
Leffingwell, A., 355n175
Leggett, E. L., 123n43
Lehman, D. R., 108n275, 123n41, 245n72
Lei, Y., B12n59
Leimgruber, K. L., 298n26
Leippe, M. R., 273n56, D13n103
Leiserowitz, A., 260n6
Lemay, E. P., 421n100
Lench, H. C., 181n184
Lennings, C. J., C30n206
Lennon, R., 218n238, 318n140
Lennox, R. D., 379n66
Lentz, E., C18n95
Leon, G., 135n118
Leonard-Barton, D., E14n114
Leonard, A. C., E18n147
Leonard, K., 347n90
Leoniak, W., E14n118
LePage, A., 350n130
Lepage, J., 309n91
LePine, J. A., C30n202
Lepore, S. J., E4n16
Lepper, M. P., 85n62
Lepper, M. R., 122n26, 177n149, 239n60, 249n101, 250n102, 250n104, 282n115, A12n35
Lerma, M., 425n119
Lerner, J. S., 215n200, 504n17, 523n111
Lerner, M. J., 210n169, 319n154, 319n155
Lerner, R., 461n67
Lerner, R. M., 318n145
Lertpratchya, A. P., E20n162
Lesiuk, T., C17n85
Leslie, J. B., 519n93
Lester, D., 297n18, A11n30
Lett, E. E., E9n82
Lett, H. S., B8n29
Leung, K., 51n58
LeVasseur, M. A., D18n147

Levav, J., 138n134, 138n135, 311n97
Leve, C., 271n46
Levenson, R. W., 78n34, 420n94, 420n95
Levin, P. F., 320n161
Levine, J. M., 274n60, 274n61, 500n8, 500n12
Levine, M., 321n164
Levine, T. R., 361n228
Levitt, K., 89n92, 108n272
Levitt, S. D., 457n27
Levitt, S. J., 45n23
Levy, N., 160n64, 160n65
Lewandowsky, S., 151n22, 177n150, 260n8, 260n9
Lewin, K., 6n11, 14n19
Lewinsohn, P. M., 96n149
Lewis, A., 498n4
Lewis, B. P., 346n83, 346n84, B7n19
Lewis, J., E13n104
Lewis, M. A., B14n67, B14n70
Lewis, N. H., 355n170
Lewis, P. A., 41n11
Lewis, R. A., 209n154
Lewis, S., 268n41
Lewis, W. A., 203n90
Ley, D., E9n83
Li, N. P., 218n239, 305n53, 307n86, 381n82
Li, T., 413n27
Li, X., B12n59
Li, Y. J., 303n47
Liamputtong, P., 319n148
Liana, D. S., B12n60
Liang, D. W., 513n71
Liau, A. K., 326n177
Liberman, N., 86n72, 132n107, 133n108
Libuser, L., E8n69
Lichtenstein, S., 167n103, 168n108
Lickel, B., 498n4
Lieberman, M. A., 376n30
Lieberman, M. D., 54n69, 54n71
Liebert, R., 339n47
Liebowitz, M. R., 408n4
Liebrand, W. B. G., 302n41
Liem, J. H., C29n187
Liem, R., C29n187
Light, L. L., D5n16
Likert, R., C19n103
Lilienfeld, S. O., 28n53
Liljenquist, K., 178n159
Liljenquist, K. A., 206n123, 523n107, 523n109
Lin, H., 262n17, 262n18
Lin, N., 375n13
Lin, W.-Y., 470n151
Lin, Y. J., 159n59
Lind, E. A., 274n58
Lindberg, M. J., 160n62
Linder, D. E., 243n64
Lindner, E. G., 361n227
Lindsay, R. C. L., D5n21, D8n51
Lindskold, S., 522n103, 525n120
Linnoila, M., 356n188
Linsey, S., 233n7
Linz, D., 354n160
Lipkova, V., E17n142
Lipsey, M. W., 356n191, 356n192

Lipton, J. E., 446n244
Liska, J., E17n142
Lisle, D. J., 239n56
Litt, C. J., 51n56
Litt, D. M., B14n67, B14n70
Little, B. R., 127n74, 127n76
Littlefield, C., 238n43
Liu, D., 375n12, 375n14
Lloyd, K., 98n192
Lobel, M., 297n19
Locamyeir, R. F., D8n56
Lochman, J. E., E17n136
Locke, E. A., 127n72, 127n73, 128n83, 128n84, 129n89, 129n90, C21n130
Löckenhoff, C. E., 474n166
Locksley, A., 466n119
Lockwood, A., C28n183
Lodewijkx, H., B8n34
Loeber, R., 346n85
Loersch, C., 58n81
Loewenstein, G., 200n69, 215n200
Loewenstein, G. F., 119n17, 214n198
Loftus, E., D11n86
Loftus, E. F., D6n28, D14n105, D16n129, D19n153, D19n155, D19n156
Loftus, G. R., D6n28
Logue, A. W., 135n119
Lohr, B. A., 193n26, 464n108
Lombardo, M. M., C22n141, C22n142
Long, J., 252n111
Longo, L. C., 384n100
Lönnqvist, J-E., 310n92
Lopes, L. L., 181n173
Lopes, P. N., 221n255
Lopez, S., 316n127
Lord, C. G., 86n71, 239n60, 250n104, 282n115
Lord, R. G., 517n81, 517n86
Lorenz, J., 512n65
Lorenz, K., 338n35, 339n39
Louis-Guerin, C., C26n159
Lowe, I., E2n2
Lubinski, D., 487n234
Lucas, B. J., 365n268
Lucas, R. E., 197n43, 197n47, 198n49
Luce, M. F., 61n94, 61n95, 61n96
Luchies, L. B., 424n114
Ludwig, T. E., 306n71
Luhtanen, R. K., 103n245
Luminet, O., 221n266
Lumsdaine, A., 272n51, 276n69, 279n99
Lundberg, A., E13n106
Lustina, M. J., 488n240
Luszczynska, A., 211n176
Luus, C. A. E., D7n47, D8n49, D8n52
Lydon, J. E., 420n89
Lynch, J. J., 377n46
Lyubomirsky, S., 198n59, 198n61, 199n67

M

Ma-Kellams, C., 385n117, 420n92
Ma, Y., E14n110
Maass, A., 484n214
Mabogunje, A., E2n2
Mabry, E., D17n136

MacDonald, G., 391n142, 391n149, 412n25
MacDonald, T. K., 424n115
Macfarlan, S. J., 305n53
Macfarlane, A., 427n128
Machan, J., 138n136
Macias, W., A12n37
MacIntosh, E., E4n14
Mack, D., 161n67, 161n68, 384n110
Mackay, T., 511n59
Mackie, D., 239n61
Mackie, D. M., 274n66
MacLean, M. J., 320n158
Macphail, E., 152n29
Macrae, C. N., 471n157
Maddux, C. D., 48n40
Madey, S. F., 168n107, 320n157
Maedl, A., 343n65
Maestripieri, D., 374n11
Magee, J. C., 523n107, 523n109, 524n114, 524n115
Magnusson, D., 91n110
Mahler, S. V., 374n11
Maibach, E., 260n6
Major, B., 95n136, 97n163, 215n213, 485n224, 486n227, 486n228
Mak, D., 158n43
Makhanova, A., 428n134
Makhijani, M. G., 384n100
Malamuth, N. M., 354n159
Malarkey, W. B., 395n180
Malett, S., 131n100, 131n101, 131n102
Malinowski, J., 159n57
Malle, B. F., 125n50, 165n94, 165n95, 165n100
Malone, P. S., 249n95
Malouff, J., 221n260
Malouff, J. M., 221n261
Malpass, R. S., 455n24
Mandal, E., 384n99
Mandel, R., 160n64, 160n65
Maner, J. K., 347n89, 386n121, 392n160, 413n30, 477n179, 525n117, 525n118
Manfred, T., 238n42
Mann, T., B14n71
Mannetti, L., E5n39
Manning, D., 97n153
Manning, D. J., 307n80
Manning, R., 321n164
Mannix, E., 500n13
Mannix, L. M., 461n71
Mansell, W., 150n9
Mansour, J. K., D5n21
Manstead, A. S. R., 202n85, 202n86
Manucha, W., B6n15
Manucia, G. K., 211n179
Manz, C. C., C20n123, C20n125
Marcon, J. L., D5n12
Marcus-Newhall, A., 334n12
Mardberg, B., E17n141
Maricchiolo, F., E5n39
Maril, A., 160n64, 160n65
Marion, G. S., 461n75
Maris, R., 143n162, 143n163
Markkus, H. R., 108n275
Markman, K., 178n163
Markman, K. D., 178n164, 181n175, 181n176

Marks, G., 98n167, 176n142
Markus, H. R., 74n9, 84n57, 123n41, 245n71, 245n74
Markwith, M., 60n88
Marlow, C., 210n162
Marmot, M., C27n172
Marques, J. M., 396n193, 396n194, 396n195, D15n108
Marques, M. M., B9n35
Marques, S., 489n247, 489n251
Marsh, A. A., 190n18
Marshall, G. D., 193n28
Martens, T. K., D5n19, D6n34
Martichuski, D. K., E3n6
Martin, C. E., 433n165
Martin, E. A., 216n220
Martin, L., 190n17
Martin, R., 215n212
Martindale, D. A., E9n84
Martinez-Taboada, C., D15n108
Martinez, A. M., 217n225
Martins, A., 221n259
Martins, N., 355n170
Martz, J. M., 422n102
Maruyama, G., 98n182, 275n63, 275n65
Marvin, G., 452n2, 452n4
Mascaro, J., 317n129
Masicampo, E. J., 55n73, 55n77, 117n4, 125n49, 128n88, 152n26, 160n63
Maslach, C., 193n29
Maslow, A. H., 417n73
Mason, J. L., A5n6
Mason, W., 176n144
Masten, A., 353n149
Masten, C., 391n149
Master, S. L., B7n20
Masuda, T., 164n90
Mata, A., 154n35
Matarazzo, J. D., B3n5
Mather, M., 212n183
Mathieu, J. E., C19n113
Maticka-Tyndale, E., 319n150
Matsick, J. L., 431n155
Matson, P., E2n2
Matthews, K. E., E4n24
Matthews, R., E6n47
Matud, M. P., 349n110
Maunder, R. D., 470n150
Maurer, S. D., C14n63
Mauss, I. B., 199n66
Maxwel, J. A., 428n135
Maxwell, J., 431n161
Maxwell, J. A., 412n25
Maxwell, S. E., 28n55
Mayer, J. D., 220n251, 221n252, 520n94, 520n95, 520n96
Maynard, R. L., E12n103
Mazar, N., 364n256
Mazur, A., 356n184
Mazziotta, A., 470n149
McAbee, S. T., 29n63
McAlister, A. L., 284n121
McAuliff, B. D., D12n89
McCabe, P., 433n172
McCalley, L. T., 366n283
McCalley, T., E5n43
McCarroll, J. E., E17n131

McCarthy, D. M., D17n138
McCarthy, J. J., E2n2
McCaul, K. D., 356n183, 356n185
McCauley, C., 60n88
McCauley, C. R., 215n201, 215n202
McCausland, P., 273n54
McClain, T. M., 222n271, 222n274, 223n278, 224n285, 224n294
McClendon, D., 457n28
McClintock, M. K., 395n180
McClung, J., D9n61
McConnell, A. R., 479n187
McCown, W. G., 142n155
McCoy, S. B., 215n203
McCrae, R. R., 198n50, 198n51, 198n52, 474n166
McCright, A. M., 260n7
McCullough, M. E., 198n55, 198n56, 198n57, 252n110, 296n13, 305n59, 306n62, 307n77, 307n78, 307n82, 307n83
McDaniel, M. A., C14n63
McDonald, S., 345n76
McDougall, W., 6n7
McElwee, R. O., 98n169
McEvoy, C., D18n145
McEwan, B. S., B6n14
McFarland, C., 213n190
McFarlane, M., E8n71
McFarlin, D. B., 88n84, 94n123, 102n237, 102n238, 103n241
McGee, R., 99n205
McGhee, D. E., 479n185
McGinn, N. C., 297n22
McGorty, E., D5n17, D5n18
McGorty, E. K., D5n24
McGrath, J. E., C19n100
McGregor, L. N., 363n243
McGue, J., 423n111
McGue, M., 422n105
McGuire, C. V., 85n69, 85n70
McGuire, W. J., 85n69, 85n70, 279n101, 283n117, 283n118, 283n119, 283n120
McHoskey, J. W., 239n54, 239n58
McHugh, L., 165n93
McHugh, P. P., C21n127
McIlraith, S. A., 469n136
McKee, S., 460n51
McKelton, D., D17n136
McKenna, K. Y. A., 374n6, 374n7, 374n8
McKillip, J., 379n73
McKinney, L. N., A16n48
McKinnon, M. C., E3n10
McLanahan, S., 209n151
McLaughlin-Volpe, T., 482n203
McLendon, C. L., C19n109
McLeod, A., 363n242
McLeod, E., 377n34
McLeod, J. M., 16n23
McMains, S., C18n89
McManus, M. A., C11n46
McMaster, M. R., 323n169
McMillan, B., C28n179, C28n180, C28n181
McMillen, D. L., 205n111
McMullen, M., 178n163
McMullen, M. N., 178n164

McMurran, M., 345n76
McNeill, W. H., 468n131
McNulty, J., 431n161
McNulty, J. K., 307n73, 349n112, 413n29, 413n30, 420n90, 420n91, 421n97, 428n134, 428n135
McQuiston, D. E., D12n91
McWhinnie, C., 488n238
Mead, G. H., 75n12, 80n43
Mead, M., 440n209
Mead, N. L., 306n60, 364n257, 525n117, 525n118
Medvec, V. H., 168n107, 179n167
Meek, R., 95n140
Mehlman, P. T., 356n188, 356n189
Meissner, C. A., 455n25, D4n10, D5n12, D5n14, D10n81
Mejia, R., B10n40
Mekawi, Y., 455n23
Melbye, M., 150n11
Meleady, R., 470n152, E15n119
Mellers, B. A., 214n195
Mello, J. A., C20n120
Mellor, B., 61n92
Mellor, D. T., 29n59
Melloy, R. C., 137n130
Melsom, E. I., D5n21
Melter, A. L., 428n134
Meltzer, A., 431n161
Meltzer, A. L., 413n29, 413n30, 420n90, 420n91, 421n97
Mendoza-Denton, R., 142n150
Mendoza, S., B16n78
Menon, G., A7n21
Menzies, Toman, D., 420n89
Meqler, D., E17n139
Mercier, H., 152n25, 173n134, 264n23, 272n49
Merryman, A., 466n112
Merton, R. K., 484n218, 484n219
Mesout, J., D6n26
Messick, D. M., 176n146, 302n40, 348n102
Messner, S. F., 349n113
Messo, J., D6n28
Meulemans, T., 167n102
Mewhinney, D., 319n150
Mewhinney, D.-M. K., 247n84
Meyer, C. B., 350n118
Meyer, D. E., 157n36
Meyer, J. P., C25n155, C25n156, C26n160
Meyerowitz, J. A., 98n170
Meyers, J. M., 213n191
Mialon, H. M., 413n28
Michael, R. T., 172n112, 172n116, 247n80, 319n147, 350n117, 409n16, 411n21, 433n171, 437n191, 438n198, 464n104, 499n5
Michaels, S., 172n112, 172n116, 247n80, 319n147, 350n117, 409n16, 411n21, 433n171, 437n191, 438n198, 464n104, 499n5
Michaud, S. G., 204n102, 204n103
Michaut, A. M. K., A7n16
Michie, S., B9n35
Mick, D. G., 222n273
Mickes, L., D6n41, D6n42
Midden, C., E5n43

Midden, C. J. H., 366n283
Miguel, E., 355n177
Mikhed, V., 83n54
Mikolajczak, M., 200n72
Mikula, G., 349n103
Milam, H., E20n166
Milavsky, B., 342n58
Milberg, S., 415n37, 415n39, 415n40
Miles, M. B., 376n30
Milford, G., 253n119
Milgram, S., 7n12, 7n13, 308n89, 328n181, 458n32
Millar, M., 385n116
Miller, A. G., 239n54, 239n58
Miller, C. T., 98n177
Miller, D., E20n165
Miller, D. P., 461n75
Miller, D. T., 178n160, 178n162, 302n43, 319n154
Miller, E. K., 312n101
Miller, G. T., E12n101
Miller, J., 305n57, 457n29
Miller, J. A., 265n28
Miller, J. E., 312n100
Miller, L. C., 47n33, 172n119
Miller, M., 351n131
Miller, N., 17n25, 176n142, 275n63, 275n65, 334n12, 340n50, 347n91, 356n194
Miller, N. E., 342n52
Miller, P. V., E4n27
Miller, R. L., 268n39, E8n77, E9n79
Miller, R. S., 419n88, 425n118
Miller, S. M., B16n76
Miller, T. Q., 203n92
Millhausen, R. R., 445n240
Milliman, R. E., A6n10
Millman, D., 29n61
Mills, H., C27n168
Mills, J., 241n62, 414n32, 414n34, 415n41
Millson, M., 262n17, 262n18
Milne, A. B., 471n157
Minda, J. P., 216n217
Ming, L. K., 326n177
Minow, M., 349n106
Miquel, E., E11n88
Mischel, W., 60n90, 60n91, 96n149, 97n162, 134n110, 134n111, 141n149, 142n150, 142n151, 142n152, 339n43, 339n44, 391n148
Mischkowski, D., 203n96, 222n277
Misra, S., 302n44
Mistretta, L., 199n65
Mita, T. H., 236n26
Mitchell, C., 202n87, 223n283
Mitchell, D. J., A7n14
Mitchell, J. P., 105n252
Mitkidis, P., 243n63
Miyamoto, Y., 164n89
Mocayar Marón, F. J., B6n15
Mochon, D., 122n29
Modan, B., 247n81
Moeller, S. J., 95n128, 95n129
Moens, E., 161n71
Moffett, M. W., 499n6
Moffitt, T., 356n186
Moffitt, T. E., 358n211

Mogilner, C., 364n255, 462n82
Mohrman, S. A., C19n105
Moise, J., 354n155
Molina, B., 150n5
Moller, A. P., 385n118
Molouki, S., 165n97, 165n98, 165n99
Monk, R., 461n58
Monroe, A. E., 125n50
Monshouwer, H. J., 344n71
Moon, S.-I., 267n35
Mooney, H., E2n2
Moore, B., III, E2n2
Moore, C., 299n28, 363n247
Moore, M. T., 96n147
Moors, A., 194n33, 225n297
Moors, A. C., 431n155
Moos, R., E11n86, E11n87
Moos, R. H., B8n24
Moran, G., D16n124, D16n127, D16n129, D17n131, D17n134, D18n143
Moran, J., 343n59, 343n60, 343n64
Moran, J. K., 343n66, 344n62
More, P. M., D10n75
Moreland, M. B., D9n63
Moreland, R. L., 500n8, 500n12, 513n71, 513n72
Morello, P., B10n40
Morewedge, C. M., 204n105
Morf, C. C., 101n219, 418n82
Morgan, C. A., III, D5n25
Morgenthau, H., 521n97
Mori, D., 434n176
Morin, E., 221n259
Morokoff, P. J., 172n113, 193n27, 437n188
Morrill, C., 353n149
Morrin, M., A7n17
Morris, K. A., 277n83
Morris, W. N., 342n56
Morrison, E. L., 386n125
Morrison, M. A., 207n135
Morrison, T. G., 207n135
Morrow, G. D., 418n76
Mortensen, C. R., 303n47
Morton, H., E8n69
Moscovici, S., 515n79
Moser, G., E20n158
Moskowitz, D., B16n85
Motowidlo, S., C29n192
Mouchlianitis, E., 353n142
Mowen, J. C., 280n108
Mowrer, O., 17n25, 340n50
Mueller-Hanson, R., C22n144
Mueller, B., A4n1, A17n49
Mueller, C. W., C26n157
Mügge, D. O., 314n120, 354n152
Mugny, G., 464n109
Muise, A., 412n25
Mukherjee, N., D13n108
Mull, A., C17n88
Mullan, B., 452n2, 452n4
Mullen, B., 511n58, C19n108
Muller, D., 297n20, 353n139
Mulligan, R., E8n63
Mullin, C. R., 354n160
Mumford, M. D., C6n28
Mummendey, A., 470n146, 470n149, 482n200

Munafò, M. R., 345n76
Munger, K., 105n258, 310n94
Muraven, M., 136n127, 136n128
Muraven, M. B., 108n273
Murch, S., 150n7
Murch, S. H., 150n14
Murnen, S. K., 350n120
Murphy-Berman, V., E8n67
Murphy, J., C18n90, C18n91, C18n92, C27n170
Murphy, S. A., E20n160
Murphy, S. L., B9n37
Murray, D. R., 49n46, 49n47, 49n49, 49n50, 310n96
Murray, S., 418n74, 418n75, 426n123, 426n124, 426n125, E17n138
Murray, S. L., 312n105
Murstein, B. I., 379n70
Musch, J., 47n32, 48n37
Muse, S. E., 470n148
Musham, C., 77n32
Musher-Eizenman, D. R., 461n57
Musolff, A., 459n38
Mussweiler, T., 303n49
Mwanri, L., B12n60
Myers, D. G., 267n37, 422n109, A14n44

N

Nadeau, S. E., E4n13
Nadler, A., 296n11
Nadler, R. T., 216n217
Nagler, U. K. J., 221n265
Najam, N., 391n145
Najile, M. B., 460n52
Najmi, S., 159n54
Narby, D. J., D16n124
Näslund, E., 461n73
Nau, P. A., E19n153
Nault, L. P., 47n31
Nauroth, P., 354n167
Naylor, B., 260n1
Naylor, J. C., C29n189
Neal, D., 137n138, 139n139, 139n140, 191n19
Neal, D. T., 139n143, 139n144
Neale, M. A., 500n13
Neale, M. C., 317n132, 318n134
Near, J. P., C29n190
Necht, T. D., 513n66
Neely, J. H., 157n37
Negel, L., 391n139
Neill, D. B., 353n149
Nelissen, R. M. A., 206n120
Nelson, J. E., 276n73
Nelson, L. D., 28n54, 386n125
Nelson, M. R., 278n90
Nelson, N. M., 138n132
Nelson, P. A., E9n82
Nelson, S. E., 165n95
Neuberg, S. L., 303n47, 381n82, 455n26, 477n179
Neuschatz, J., D10n74
Neuschatz, J. S., D9n61, D10n75, D10n76, D12n92
Newcomb, T., 508n50
Newcombe, D., 274n59
Newman, A., 276n79, A14n41
Newman, B., 262n17, 262n18

Newman, E. J., 312n101
Newman, K., 353n149
Newman, M. L., 363n239
Newman, R., 222n271, 222n274, 223n278, 224n285, 224n294
Newton, T. L., 422n110
Nezlek, J., 126n61, 377n43, 377n45
Nezlek, J. B., 221n255, 394n175
Nguyen, H.-H. D., 488n246
Nias, D. K. B., 317n132, 318n134
Nichols, P. A., 92n116
Nicholson, N., 178n155
Nickell, E. F., 211n178
Nickerson, R. S., 173n133, E2n3
Niedenthal, P. M., 213n187
Nierenberg, D., E4n28
Nietzel, M. T., D17n138
Nijman, H. L. I., 355n179
Nisbet, E. K., 214n194, E20n160
Nisbett, R. E., 81n47, 82n48, 82n50, 85n62, 91n109, 163n86, 164n88, 360n217, 361n219, B16n75
Noel, H., 278n91
Nohria, N., 517n80
Nolen-Hoeksema, S., 224n287
Nordgren, L. F., 160n60, 160n61
Norenzayan, A., 28n48, 312n104, 460n50, 460n53
Norris, E., B9n35
Norris, F. H., 253n121, E18n148
Northouse, P. G., C21n132
Northrup, L., 279n96
Norton, M. I., 200n72, 316n123, 380n77, D16n116, D16n117
Nosek, B. A., 29n59, 300n37
Noulles, D., E16n128
Nouwen, A., 381n87
Novelli, D., E7n51
Nowak, M., 292n1
Nummenmaa, L., 217n224
Nuss, C. K., 391n150
Nussbaum, S., 86n72
Nyende, P., 316n123
Nysse-Carris, K. L., 362n238, D16n120
Nystrom, L. E., 300n34

O

O'Barr, W. M., 274n58
O'Boyle, E. H., Jr., 221n256
O'Brien, E., 314n116
O'Brien, E. H., 9n15
O'Connell, V., 238n40
O'Connor, D. B., C28n179, C28n180, C28n181
O'Connor, G., 260n5
O'Connor, M., D17n141
O'Handley, B. M., 207n136
O'Hara, S., E8n63
O'Kane, C., 238n45
O'Leary, E. S., E4n30, E17n140
O'Leary, K. N., 431n156
O'Malley, P. M., 98n178, 98n179
O'Neil, K. M., D17n130
O'Riordan, T., E2n2
O'Sullivan, L. F., 247n87, 350n121
O'Sullivan, M., 217n222, 362n236
Oakes, H., 299n30
Oakes, M. A., 455n19

Oakes, W., 30n65
Obach, M. S., 162n75
Oberlé, D., 309n91
Ockenfels, A., 303n49
Odland, L. M., 461n69
Oettingen, G., 127n71
Ogrocki, P., 377n54, 422n108
Oishi, S., 200n70
Okwumabua, J. O., 215n204
Olatunji, B. O., 463n96
Oldham, G. R., C24n151
Oliner, P. M., 317n131
Oliner, S. P., 317n131
Oliver, M. B., 431n157, 445n238
Olivola, C. Y., 134n113
Olson, E. A., D4n3, D10n72
Olson, J. M., 178n165, 212n184, B15n72
Olson, M. A., 234n12, 234n13, 237n37, 421n97, 479n184
Olweus, D., 102n232, 335n19, 347n97
Omar, A., 85n68
Ones, D., C13n60
Ones, D. S., C14n68
Orbell, J. M., E20n163
Organ, D. W., C29n190
Oriet, C., D8n53, D8n57
Orne, M. T., 19n30
Ornstein, P. A., D19n155, D19n156
Ornstein, R., 265n26
Orobio de Castro, B., 344n71
Ort, A., 276n80
Ortiz, C. W., 457n29
Ortiz, V., 466n119
Osborn, D. P., E12n97
Osherow, N., 483n209
Oskamp, S., E19n155
Osswald, S., 346n80
Osterlund, K., D5n23
Ostroff, C., C6n24
Oswald, I., 53n60
Otero, V., 245n69
Otis, C. C., D15n113
Ottaviani, R., 96n145
Oubaid, V., 442n221
Oudekerk, B. A., D16n122
Ouellette, J. A., 139n142
Ouellette, R., 415n37, 415n39, 415n40
Ouwerkerk, J. W., 394n171, 397n197, 397n198, 397n199, 507n43, 507n45
Oveis, C., 208n141
Over, H., 321n165
Overall, N. C., 421n100
Overbeek, G., 307n85
Overing, J., 468n125

P

Páez, D., 396n194, 396n195, D15n108
Page S. E., 500n11
Paik, H., 335n24
Pakhare, A., 233n4
Palca, J., 461n76
Paleari, G., 306n68
Palmeri, H., 142n154
Pan, Z., 16n23
Panksepp, J., 391n143, 391n144, 391n145, 391n146

Panno, A., E5n39
Paolini, S., 469n141, 469n143
Papageorgis, D., 283n119, 283n120
Papciak, A. S., E3n7
Parad, H. W., 396n191
Pargament, K. I., 252n109, 306n62
Parikh, R., 151n19
Pariser, E., 245n70
Park, B., 455n18, 474n164, 486n225
Park, C., 363n246
Park, C. L., 253n118
Park, E. S., 397n199, 507n43
Park, J., 375n13
Park, J. H., 49n48
Park, S. H., 522n101
Park. L. E., 103n242, 103n243
Parker, K. A., 284n126, 285n128
Parker, S. D., E16n127
Parkhurst, K. A., B16n81
Parks, C. D., 397n199, 507n43
Parks, J. M., C29n194
Parnell, A., E18n146
Parrott, D. J., 463n93
Parsley, A., 278n94
Passafaro, P., E19n152
Patel, V., 366n273
Pathak-Sharma, M. K., D18n150
Patnoe, S., 483n208
Patrick, R., 216n218
Patrick, W., 394n174, 396n189
Patry, M. W., D17n130
Patterson, E. W. J., 276n68
Patterson, O., 485n223
Paul, A. M., 220n250
Paul, C., 99n203
Paulhus, D. L., 89n92, 108n272, 221n264, 347n98
Paulus, P. B., 511n56, C19n102, E4n18, E6n47
Paxson, L. M., 51n57
Payne, B. K., 455n20, 479n186, 479n189
Payne, C. R., 158n45
Payne, J. W., 61n95, 61n96
Peace, K. A., D6n27
Peake, P. K., 134n110, 134n111, 142n151, 142n152
Pedersen, A., 469n143
Pedersen, W. C., 47n33, 334n12
Pederson, J., 97n153
Peekna, H. M., 314n121
Pegues, J., 188n1
Pelham, B. W., 153n32
Pelisek, C., 343n63
Peltonen, T., 334n14
Pemberton, M. B., 469n136, 504n18
Peña, L., B10n40
Pendleton, M., 238n41
Penn, G. M., 377n55
Pennebaker, J. W., 363n239
Penner, L. A., 318n142, C29n192
Pennington, G., 377n61, 395n183
Penrod, S., D13n100
Penrod, S. D., D4n4, D5n17, D5n18, D5n19, D5n24, D6n34, D6n38, D12n94, D12n98, D12n99, D14n106, D17n130, D18n150
Penros, S. D., D17n141
Penton-Voak, I. S., 345n76

Pepitone, A., 508n50
Peplau, L. A., 218n240, 218n244, 377n42, 395n178, 395n179
Peragine, D., 412n25
Perera, H. N., 221n262
Pérez, A., B10n40
Perez, R. C., 102n234
Perie, M., 98n171
Peristiany, J. G., 361n223
Perkins, H. W., 224n290
Perkins, S. C., 88n89
Perlman, D., 395n178
Perona, A., D16n122
Perot, A., 350n120
Perper, T., 431n159
Perretta, S., 98n172
Perrin, P. B., 436n185, 436n186
Perry, C. L., 284n121
Perry, E. L., C22n145
Persons, J. B., 253n122
Peruche, B. M., 455n21
Peters, D., 490n255
Peters, K., 57n78
Peterson, C., 316n126
Peterson, C. K., 201n79
Peterson, K., 221n260
Peterson, L. M., B14n69
Peterson, N. G., C6n28
Peterson, R. F., 483n205
Petrescu, P., 30n67
Petri, B., 349n103
Pettigrew, T. F., 469n139, 469n140, 470n144, 482n201
Pettit, J. W., 297n18
Pettiway, L. E., 349n104
Petty, R. E., 237n31, 237n35, 237n36, 278n92, 279n103, 279n105, 281n109, 282n114, 282n116, 284n127
Peyser, H., 463n98
Pfau, M., 284n124
Pham, L. B., 118n11
Phillips, C. M., 342n57
Phillips, M., 488n236
Phillips, S., 393n168
Phillips, T., E14n116
Phillis, D. E., 172n123, 172n124
Piazza, J., 382n89
Pickel, K. L., D6n29, D6n30
Pickering, A. S., 76n24
Pickett, C. L., 377n60, 392n161, 393n162, 395n177, 395n181, 395n185
Pierce, W. D., 84n60, 85n64, 85n66
Piliavin, I. M., 323n170
Piliavin, J. A., 323n170
Pillard, R. C., 435n182
Pinel, E. C., 213n189
Pines, A., 440n208, 443n234
Pinker, S., 44n19, 335n26, 335n27, 335n30, 336n32, 466n113
Pinkley, R. L., 499n7
Pintea, A. I., 390n131
Pirchio, S., E5n39
Pitt, E. L., 350n126
Pitts, V. E., 364n251
Pizarro, D. A., 300n38, 383n92
Plaks, J. E., 57n80

Plant, E. A., 455n21, 455n22, 464n110, 465n111, 480n196, 481n197, 482n199, 489n252, 490n256
Platt, C. W., 162n76
Platt, J., E3n5
Pleck, J., 217n227, 218n228, 218n229
Pliner, P., 434n174, 434n176
Plotkin, J., 490n255
Plötner, M., 321n165
Plouffe, R. A., 221n267
Pocheptsova, A., 138n133
Podolski, C. P., 354n155
Pogorzelski, S., C11n42
Poletes, G., 511n56
Politano, J., A11n30
Polivy, J., 77n28, 79n41, 135n120
Poll, J., 252n110
Pollack, J. M., 221n256
Pollock, V. E., 356n194
Pomazal, R. J., 318n143
Pomeroy, W. B., 433n165
Pomery, E., B14n68
Pond, R. S., 101n218, 413n26
Pond, R. S., Jr., 203n101, 349n112
Poore, J., 172n120
Porges, S. W., 222n269
Portmess, L., 46n30
Posavac, S. S., B15n73
Posner, B. Z., 517n85
Possingham, H. P., E3n10
Postmes, T., 508n52
Pottebaum, S. M., 98n183
Pouwelse, M., B8n34
Povinelli, D. J., 317n129
Powell, C., 391n149
Powell, J., 41n11
Powell, M., 415n37, 415n39, 415n40
Powell, M. C., 235n21
Powell, N., E17n136
Powers, R. A., D10n76
Powers, R. E., E17n134
Powers, W. T., 135n117
Pozzulo, J. D., D4n6
Pratkanis, A. R., 271n46, 273n56, 279n97
Pratt, T. C., 358n210
Pratto, F., 470n154
Predmore, S., 88n86
Prelec, D., A11n28
Prescott, A. T., 354n156
Pressley, M., 247n88
Presson, C. C., 284n122
Preston, K., 250n104
Preston, J. L., 207n138
Price, H. L., D4n5, D4n9, D8n53, D8n57
Price, J. L., C26n157
Price, P. C., 303n45
Prior, E., 197n38
Pritchard, R. D., C29n189
Prochaska, J. M., B11n56
Prochaska, J. O., B11n55, B11n56, B13n62, B13n64
Proctor, W., E14n116
Pronin, E., 165n97, 165n98, 165n99
Pronk, T. M., 307n85
Prot, S., 30n67
Provias, D., 489n247, 489n251

Pryor, J. B., 60n89, 77n31, 524n113
Pu, X., D5n13
Purcell, A. H., E19n150
Purdie-Vaughn, V., 486n229
Putcha-Bhagavatula, A. D., 47n33
Pyszczynski, J., 105n257
Pyszczynski, T., 97n157, 100n213
Pyszczynski, T. A., A14n42

Q

Qualtrough, T., 247n86
Quanty, M. B., 203n89, 339n37
Quarantelli, E. L., E4n29
Quas, J. A., D16n120
Qudrat, A., 431n156
Quigley-McBride, A., 312n101
Quigley, B., 347n90
Quilitch, H. R., 483n205
Quinlivan, D. S., D9n61, D10n79
Quinn, D., 488n242
Quinn, D. M., 488n237
Quinones, M. A., C14n70
Quinton, R. L., 375n15
Quiroz, V., D9n65
Quoidbach, J., 200n72

R

Rabi, R., 216n217
Rachal, K. C., 198n57
Radke, H. R. M., 469n143
Ragins, B. R., C18n97
Rainey, D., 384n110
Rains, S. A., 284n126, 285n128
Raleigh, M., 356n186
Ramalho, N., 221n259
Rao, P. A., 253n122
Raphael, T., C11n50
Rapson, R. L., 210n160, 408n3
Rasmussen, F., 461n73
Ratcliff, J., 464n110
Ratnewshwar, S., A7n17
Rauch, S. M., D13n103
Rauhut, H., 512n65
Rauthmann, J. F., 221n265
Ray, D. G., 390n131
Raymond, P., 189n11, 235n18, 524n113
Raynor, H. A., 138n136
Raz, M., 268n40
Read, J. D., D6n38, D11n87
Read, S. J., 416n57
Reams, M. A., 366n280
Rector, G., 355n179
Redden, J. P., B14n71
Redding, C. A., B13n62
Reddish, P., 243n63
Reddon, J. R., C14n71
Reeder, G. D., 60n89, 418n80
Reeve, C. L., 364n251
Regalia, C., 306n68
Regan, P., 526n125
Regan, P. C., 99n206
Regnerus, M., 431n153
Reich, J. W., 366n278
Reicher, S., E7n51
Reicken, H. W., 252n115
Reidel, S. L., 379n73
Reidke, H., 343n65
Reilly, N. P., 342n56

Reimer, D. J., 237n29
Reinhard, D. A., 153n30
Reinisch, J., 407n1
Reinisch, J. M., 172n128
Reinsch, J., E8n76
Reis, H., 394n175
Reis, H. T., 46n25, 59n86, 98n193, 206n119, 209n156, 215n211, 377n44, 387n126, 417n70
Reisen, N., 122n30
Reiss, I. L., 440n210, 440n211
Reiss, N., C27n168
Reiter, K. J., 221n265
Reiter, S. M., 365n270
Remland, M. S., E7n61
Rempel, J. K., 312n100
Ren, L. R., 364n259, 364n260
Rennison, S., 312n107
Reno, R. R., 366n275, 366n276, 366n277
Renzetti, C. M., 442n226
Repetti, R. L., B7n21
Revenson, T. A., B3n6
Rever, J., 333n6
Reykowski, J., 210n170
Reynolds, R., 205n114
Reynolds, T., 104n250, 465n111
Rhead, L. M., D9n67
Rhee, H., A6n7
Rhine, R. J., 235n14
Rhoads, K., 266n32
Rhoads, S. A., 190n18
Rhodes, A., 295n7
Rhodes, N., 279n102
Rhodewalt, F., 91n107, 91n108, 101n219, 418n82
Rholes, W. S., 157n39
Rice, R. W., 377n36, E12n97
Richards, C., 215n213
Richards, J. M., 363n239
Richards, Z., 453n14
Richardson, A. S., 317n129
Richardson, D. R., 334n11
Richerson, P. J., 43n16, 49n51, 49n52, 49n55
Richeson, J. A., 479n191, 479n192, 489n250
Richman, J. A., 224n293
Ridley, M., 59n84, 59n85
Righetti, F., 312n103, 382n90
Riley, B., 159n52
Ring, K., 105n260
Ringelmann, M., 5n6, 505n33
Rini, C., B12n58
Rios, K., 460n56
Ripamonti, C., 297n17
Rippere, V., 222n275
Risen, J. L., 174n137
Rishworth, A., D6n39
Ritov, I., 214n195
Ritson, J., 46n28
Ritter, J. M., 384n108, 386n124
Ritter, R. S., 207n138
Rittle, R. H., 504n19, 505n31
Rivetti, A., 150n10
Roach, M., A21n60
Robbennolt, J. K., D18n150
Robbins, J. M., C26n165, C27n171
Roberson, B., 517n80

Roberts, B. W., 91n111
Roberts, J., 365n266, A5n4
Roberts, N., 41n11
Roberts, S. P., 263n22
Roberts, W., 150n13
Roberts, W. A., 61n93, 127n78
Robertson, J. L., 366n278
Robertson, R. J., E13n108
Robertson, T., 477n179
Robin, R., 87n82
Robins, R. W., 100n210, 101n216
Robinson, E., 381n86, 381n87
Robinson, I. E., 445n239
Robinson, P., 317n130
Roch, S., 292n1
Rodes, D., 305n57
Rodin, J., 323n170, 443n232, B7n18
Rodriguez-Sickert, C., 310n95
Roeder, J. L., 154n34
Roediger, H. L., III, D6n41
Roehling, M. V., 461n69
Roehling, P. V., 461n69
Roepstorff, A., 243n63
Roese, N., 178n159
Roese, N. J., 44n17, 178n165, 212n184, B15n72
Roets, A., 161n70
Rogers, C. R., 417n72
Rogers, E. M., 276n77, B11n53
Rogers, M. L., B10n43
Rogers, T., 108n267
Rogers, T. B., 90n98, 90n99
Rogers, W. L., 209n150
Roggman, L. A., 384n108, 386n124
Rogow, A. A., 15n20
Rohrer, J. H., 262n20
Romer, D., 353n148, 353n149
Romero-Canyas, R., 391n137, 486n229
Romero, V., 102n224
Ronay, R., 375n19
Rondeel, E., 216n219
Roney, J. R., 374n11, 442n219
Root, L. M., 307n82
Ropp, S. A., 482n203
Rorer, L. G., 173n135
Rose, D. C., E13n108
Rose, E., 253n117
Rose, P., 418n74, 418n75
Rosen, J. C., 392n154
Rosen, S., 81n45
Rosenbaum, M. E., 238n46, 380n76
Rosenberg, M., 81n46, 98n184
Rosenfeld, D. L., 85n65
Rosenhan, D. L., 320n162, 326n175
Rosenman, R. H., 203n91
Rosenstock, I. M., B10n45, B11n50
Rosenthal, E., A10n24
Rosenthal, H. E. S., 470n147
Rosenthal, L., B8n32
Rosenthal, R., 484n220, D9n62, D9n63
Rosenthal, S., 260n6
Roskies, E., C26n159
Roskos-Ewoldsen, D., 277n85
Ross, D., 238n48, 238n49, 238n51, 339n45, 339n46
Ross, E. A., 6n8

Ross, J. A., C2n6
Ross, L., 176n143, 177n149, 239n60, 249n101, 250n102, 282n115
Ross, M., 93n120, 93n121, 93n122, 131n103, 132n104, 132n106, 163n83, 424n115
Ross, S. A., 238n48, 238n49, 238n51, 339n45, 339n46
Ross, S. M., 349n114
Rossi, J. S., B13n64
Rossiter, J., A7n12
Rotenberg, K. J., 312n107
Roth, J., 178n154
Roth, P. L., C14n69
Rothbart, M. K., 218n235
Rothberg, J. M., 143n164
Rothblum, E. D., 461n70
Rothengatter, T., E15n120
Rothman, A. J., 158n44
Rothman, S., E21n172
Rothmund, T., 354n167
Rothschild, Z. K., 476n173
Rothstein, H. R., 30n68, 314n118, 314n119, 353n151
Rothstein, M., C14n71
Rottmann, L., 379n74, 384n104
Rovine, M., 209n147, 209n148
Rowatt, W. C., 362n231
Rowthorn, R., 310n95
Roy, D., 260n4
Royzman, E. B., 235n16
Rozin, P., 60n88, 215n201, 215n202, 235n16, 382n89
Roznowski, M. A., C26n195
Ruback, R. B., 22n35
Rubin, D. B., 150n8
Rubin, M., 469n141, 469n143
Rubin, R. A., 98n182
Rubin, Y., 391n138
Rubin, Z., 218n240, 218n244
Rubio-Stipec, M., E17n144
Ruble, D. N., 209n153
Rucci, A. J., C4n14
Rudd, M. D., 297n18
Rudski, J. M., 173n132
Ruedy, N. E., 299n28, 363n247
Rumble, A. C., 397n199, 507n43
Rünger, D., 139n141
Rupert, G., C11n47
Rupp, D. E., C26n164
Rusbult, C. E., 306n63, 312n106, 418n76, 421n101, 422n102, 424n114, 424n117
Ruscio, J., 177n151
Rushton, J. P., 247n88, 317n132, 318n133, 318n134
Russakoff, R., 364n258
Russell, C. S., 209n144
Russell, D., 395n179
Russell, J. A., 188n3
Russell, V. M., 420n91
Ruva, C. L., D18n145, D18n146, D18n147, D18n148
Ryan, A. M., 488n246
Ryan, B. A., 98n188
Ryan, J. R., C22n143
Ryan, R. M., 84n59, 85n63, 85n67, 125n51, 125n52, 125n53, 126n56, 126n58, 126n59, 126n62, 126n64, 126n65, 126n66, 126n68, 128n81, 190n18, 198n54, 199n65, C5n21
Rydell, R. J., 479n187
Ryff, C. D., 198n58
Rynd, N., 350n119

S

Sabthe, H. B., 353n138
Sackett, P. R., 488n243, 488n244, C14n67, C29n196, C30n201
Saegert, S., E4n14, E6n48, E7n50
Saenz, D. S., 86n71
Safer, M. A., D5n23
Sagie, A., C19n104
Sagristano, M. C., 133n108
Sakaki, M., 212n183
Sakamoto, A., 30n67, 30n68, 314n118, 314n119, 326n177, 353n151
Saklofske, D. H., 221n267
Salas, E., 511n58, C19n108, C21n127
Saldarriaga, L., 347n95
Saleem, M., 30n68, 314n118, 314n119, 326n177, 353n151
Salerno, J. M., 362n238
Salgado, J. F., C13n60
Salmivalli, C., 102n233
Salovey, P., 158n44, 220n251, 221n252, 221n253, 221n255, 442n222, 442n224, 443n231, 443n232
Samet, J. M., 377n51, E12n103
Samuel, W., 365n270
Samuelson, C., E20n164
Samuelson, C. D., 348n102
Sanbonmatsu, D. M., B15n73
Sandage, S. J., 198n57
Sandelands, L. E., 102n239
Sanders, A., C17n87
Sanders, G. S., 176n148
Sanders, S. A., 172n128
Sanderson, P., 29n61
Sandfort, T. G. M., 463n98
Sandström, S., 509n53
Sanna, L. J., 181n177
Sanson, M., 312n101
Santayana, G., 10n16
Santo, J. B., 347n95
Santos, M. D., 271n46
Sapolsky, R., B5n13
Sapolsky, R. M., 355n181
Sarason, B. R., B8n30
Sarason, I. G., B8n30
Saraví, F. D., B6n15
Sargent, J., B9n38, B10n42, B10n43
Sargent, J. D., 354n156, B9n39
Sarin, R., 197n46
Sarrel, M. D., A21n59
Satow, K. L., 294n6
Sauer, J., D6n40
Sauer, J. D., D4n8
Sauerland, M., D7n46
Savin-Williams, R. C., 433n166
Savitsky, K., 163n84
Sawyer, A. G., 278n91
Sawyer, J., 234n11
Saxbe, D. E., B7n21
Sayre, G. M., 137n130

Schachter, S., 192n20, 192n21, 192n23, 225n296, 252n115, 262n16, 383n93, 435n180, B8n33, B16n78, B16n80
Schaefer, H. S., 209n158
Schaefer, J. A., B8n24
Schaefer, N. K., 299n30
Schaller, M., 49n46, 49n47, 49n48, 49n49, 49n50, 207n131, 207n132, 310n96, 392n160, 455n26
Schapiro, S. J., 317n129
Schaubroeck, J., C26n166, C27n167
Schauer, M., 343n59, 343n60, 343n64, 343n65, 343n66, 344n62
Schaumberg, R. L., 518n87
Scheck, S. R., 218n242
Scheibehenne, B., 122n28
Scheier, M. F., 76n15, 76n16, 77n29, 78n37, 78n38, 135n114, 135n115, 135n116, B8n23
Schein, E. H., C32n210
Scheirer, M. A., 98n185
Schellnhuber, H. J., E2n2
Schemeichel, B. J., 138n132
Schenider, D. J., 159n49
Scher, K. J., 78n34
Scherer, K. R., 194n33, 225n297
Scherer, L. D., 479n190
Scherzer, N. A., 431n159
Schiavone, S. R., 460n49
Schifferstein, H. N. J., A7n16
Schippmann, J. S., C14n69
Schlaerth, A., 221n263
Schlenker, B. R., 93n119, 104n249, 105n254, 106n262, 106n263, 108n269, 108n270, 108n271, 307n79
Schlösser, T., 311n98
Schlundt, D. G., 211n175
Schmader, T., 489n249
Schmidt, C., E4n15
Schmidt, F. L., C14n63, C14n66, C14n68
Schmidt, R. E., 159n55
Schmitt, D., 172n118
Schmitt, D. P., 40n8, 430n144, 430n145, 430n146, 431n156
Schmitt, N., C14n73
Schnall, S., 208n142
Schneider, I. K., 203n98, 209n159
Schneiderman, E., 221n253
Schneiderman, N., B8n29
Schoenbach, C., 98n184
Schoenbaum, M., E17n134
Scholnick, B., 83n54
Scholz, U., B8n27
Schooler, C., 98n184
Schooler, J., 125n48
Schooler, J. W., 200n69, 363n248
Schooler, T. Y., 233n7
Schopler, J., 469n133, 469n134, 469n135, 469n136, 469n137, 504n18, E6n46
Schroeder, D. A., 267n34
Schuller, R. A., D16n121
Schultz, P. W., 366n271, E13n109
Schulz, A., 239n59
Schuman, H., 26n45
Schumm, W. R., 209n144

Schunk, D. H., 129n91, 129n92
Schurtz, D. R., 391n149
Schutte, N. S., 221n261
Schütz, A., 221n255, 418n83, 418n84, 418n85, 419n87
Schvaneveldt, R. W., 157n36
Schwab, J., E4n13
Schwartz, A., 214n195
Schwartz, B., 85n68, 122n27
Schwartz, D., 385n119
Schwartz, I., 102n225
Schwartz, J. K. L., 479n185
Schwartz, P., 409n12, 410n20, 414n35, 438n199, 443n227, 443n228
Schwartz, S. H., 200n70, E20n161
Schwarz, N., 26n46, 151n22, 177n150, 181n177, 206n126, 212n186
Schwarzer, R., 211n176
Schwarzwald, J., 268n40
Schweitzer, F., 512n65
Schweitzer, M. E., 299n28, 363n247
Scollon, C. N., 197n43, 197n47
Scott, J., 26n45
Scott, J. P., 339n38, 391n144
Scott, M., 48n40
Scratchley, L. S., 95n126
Seabright, P., 414n36
Seal, D. W., 443n229
Sears, D. O., 30n66, 234n10, 281n111, 285n129
Sears, R., 17n25, 340n50, 476n174
Sechler, E. S., 117n6, 250n103
Sedikides, C., 87n79, 95n140, 102n220, 108n276, 163n79, 418n80
Sedikides, C. S., 87n76
Sedlovskaya, A., 486n229
Seeley, E., 377n61, 395n183
Segal, N. L., 313n113
Seger, C. R., E15n119
Seib, H. M., D13n103
Seifert, C., 151n22, 177n150
Sekerak, G. J., 504n19, 505n31
Seligman, C., 268n39, E19n154
Seligman, M. E. P., 316n126
Selimbegovic, L., 78n36
Sellin, I., 221n255
Sellmer, G. P., 431n159
Semmelroth, J., 442n220
Semmler, C., D6n42, D7n44, D10n73
Sennett, R., 72n3
Sentyrz, S. M., 77n27
Serota, K. B., 361n228
Seta, C. E., 504n20
Seta, J. J., 504n20
Seto, M. C., 193n24
Seyle, H., B4n10
Shackelford, T. K., 102n226, 440n207
Shadish, W. R., 28n57
Shaffer, D. R., 275n64
Shaffer, M. J., 421n97
Shah, J. Y., 130n93, 130n95, 130n96, 130n97
Shaked, A., 153n30
Shakur, S., 356n202
Shaley, I., 392n159
Shalit, B., E17n141

Shapiro, J. R., 455n26
Shapiro, P. N., D4n4
Shariff, A. F., 312n104, 460n53
Sharps, M., 381n87
Shaver, P. R., 415n43, 415n44, 415n45, 416n47, 416n49, 416n50, 416n52, 416n58, 416n62, 417n67, 417n70
Shavitt, S., 280n107, 474n167, B15n73
Shaw, B. F., 96n146
Shaw, L., 381n86
Shea, C. T., 382n91
Shea, D. L., 487n234
Sheffield, F., 272n51, 276n69, 279n99
Sheinman, L., 126n61
Sheldon, K. M., 126n69, 198n59, 200n74, A14n43
Shelton, J. N., 479n191, 479n192, 489n253
Shenot, J., E21n172
Shepperd, J. A., 100n214, 385n115
Sherif, M., 262n19, 467n120
Sherkat, D. E., 252n112
Sherman, D. K., E5n37
Sherman, S., 178n163
Sherman, S. J., 117n9, 154n35, 284n122, 498n4
Sherman, S. T., 117n10
Sherrod, D. R., E6n45
Shi, F., 500n10
Shi, K., C30n208
Shibuya, A., 30n68, 314n118, 314n119, 353n151
Shin, J., 121n23
Shneidman, E. S., 144n169
Shoda, Y., 134n110, 134n111, 142n151, 142n152, 339n44
Shoeneman, T. J., 80n44
Shogren, J., E21n169
Shoham, I., 247n81
Shohat-Ophir, G., 373n1
Shook, N. J., 463n97, 482n202
Shorrocks, A., 509n53
Shorter, E., 427n129, 439n205, 440n206
Shotkin, A., E21n172
Shotland, R. L., 322n167, 434n173
Showers, C. J., 95n135
Shramko, M., 484n217
Shrauger, J. S., 80n44, 88n85, 102n235
Shteir, R., 364n252
Shteynberg, G., 44n17, 44n18
Shu, L. L., 364n250
Shumate, R., B10n41
Sibley, C. G., 469n143
Sicoiy, F., 163n83
Sidanius, J., 470n154
Siem, B., 318n136
Siero, F. W., E20n157
Sikes, J., 483n207
Silfver, M., 310n92
Silk, J. B., 317n129
Silva, P., 356n186
Silva, P. A., 358n211
Silver, K., 200n71
Silver, M., 466n116
Silver, R., B3n4
Silvia, P. J., 76n25
Sime, J. D., 313n114

Simester, D., A11n28
Simkin, M. G., 363n242
Simmons, B. I., E13n108
Simmons, C. H., 319n155
Simmons, J. P., 28n54
Simonsohn, U., 28n54
Simpson, A., 460n56
Simpson, J. A., 311n99, 416n59, 425n119
Sinclair, L., 476n176, 477n177
Sinclair, R. C., 172n125, 172n126
Singer, J. E., 126n70, 192n21, 192n23, 225n296, B16n80, E11n92
Singh, D., 385n112, 385n113
Skaalvik, E. M., 98n186
Skelton, J. A., 91n107
Skewes, J., 243n63
Skinner, B. F., B10n48
Skitkan, L. J., 299n27
Sklar, A. Y., 160n64, 160n65, 160n66
Skolnick, A., 207n130
Skoner, D. P., B16n83
Slawinski, B. L., 347n96
Slingsby, J. K., 314n121
Slinkard, L. A., 284n121
Slotter, E. B., 349n112, 413n26
Slovic, P., 167n103, 168n108, 174n139
Smalarz, L., D10n80, D12n93
Small, D. A., 215n200
Smart, L., 358n212
Smith, C., D9n66
Smith, C. A., 215n209, C26n160, C29n190
Smith, C. M., D17n137
Smith, D., 173n130
Smith, E. E., 391n148
Smith, E. N., 28n52
Smith, F. J., C30n209
Smith, G. E., 77n30, 99n208
Smith, G. F., 279n98
Smith, G. H., 82n49
Smith, I. H., 299n29
Smith, J. D., 154n34
Smith, L., 393n168
Smith, M. M., 221n267
Smith, P. B., 30n69, 64n102
Smith, P. C., C24n152
Smith, R., 332n3
Smith, R. H., 295n7, 310n93
Smith, R. J., E8n66
Smith, S., D6n32
Smith, S. M., 275n64
Smith, T., 445n242
Smith, T. B., 252n110, 377n57
Smith, T. W., 26n47, 88n89, 203n92, B16n81
Smittipatana, S., B15n73
Smuts, B., 446n245
Smyth, J. M., 253n118
Snapp, M., 483n207
Snibbe, A. C., 245n74
Snow, M. G., B13n64
Snowdon, D., 198n62
Snyder, C. R., 88n89, 88n90, 316n127
Snyder, M., 379n65, 379n67, 379n68
Soane, E., 178n155
Soares, F., 391n145
Sobell, L. C., 159n51
Sobell, M. B., 159n51

Soetens, B., 161n70, 161n71
Sohn, Y., 210n162
Solomon, D., 98n189
Solomon, J., 377n61, 395n183
Solomon, S., 100n213, A14n42
Solomon, S. D., E17n143
Soman, D., A11n32
Sommer, K. L., 390n130, 391n138, 418n77
Sommer, R., A7n18
Sommers, P., E11n86
Sommers, S. R., 103n245, D16n116, D16n117
Sommerville, R. B., 300n34
Song, A. V., B9n36
Sonnentag, S., C27n169
Sorman, P. B., 102n235
Southwick, L., 136n126
Southwick, S. M., D5n25
Spaa, M., B8n34
Spacapan, S., E4n23
Spangenberg, E. R., A7n13
Spangler, G., 417n68
Spangler, J. G., 461n75
Spanier, G. B., 209n148, 209n154
Spanier, G. P., 438n201
Spears, R., 508n52
Specht, H., 377n47
Speicher, C. E., 377n54, 377n55, 422n108
Speier, A. H., E17n134
Speilmann, S. S., 412n25
Spence, K. W., 504n26
Spencer, J. R., E16n127
Spencer, S., 488n239
Spencer, S. J., 57n79, 245n73, 472n159, 477n178, 488n237, 488n242
Sperber, D., 152n25, 173n134, 264n23, 272n49
Spielberg, W. E., E16n124
Spitzberg, B. H., 398n207
Sporer, S. L., D6n38, D7n46
Spotanski, C., E8n76
Sprecher, S., 99n206, 387n126, 410n20, 420n93, 420n96, 430n150, 445n241, 526n125
Springer, C., 391n139
Springer, C. A., 209n157
Springer, S., 204n105
Sproull, L., 305n58
Sroufe, L. A., 417n69
Stack, A. D., 203n93
Stacy, D., 48n40
Staffieri, J., 461n68
Stahelski, A. J., 302n42
Staley, O., C16n82, C16n83, C16n84
Stalberg-Carlstedt, B., E17n141
Stangor, C., 209n153
Stanko, E. A., 349n107
Stanley, S. K., E5n38
Stansfeld, S., E11n91, E12n94, E12n99
Stansfelt, S., E4n25
Staples, R., 428n137
Staples, S. L., E12n98
Stasser, G., 515n75, 515n76
Stearns, E., 48n41
Steblay, N. K., D10n78, D11n83

Steblay, N. M., D9n59, D17n140, D18n149, D18n151
Stecker, R., E11n93
Steele, C., 488n242
Steele, C. M., 136n126, 356n198, 487n233, 488n237, 488n240, 488n241, 488n245
Steffensmeier, D., 347n88
Steg, L., E2n1, E15n120
Steger, M., 252n111
Stehr, M. F., 4n1
Stein-Seroussi, A., 89n93, 89n94
Stein, R., 150n17
Steinel, W., 202n84
Steinfatt, T. M., 305n56
Steinfeld, J., 354n163
Steinhilber, A., B13n66
Steinmetz, G., 205n114
Steinmetz, K., A7n15
Steinwert, T., 461n59
Stel, M., 362n235
Stellar, J., 303n50
Stephan, C. W., 10n17
Stephan, W. G., 10n17
Stephenson, J. S., E16n122
Stephin, C., 483n207
Stepney, R., 136n123
Stepper, S., 190n17
Stern, I., 522n101
Stern, L. B., D7n45
Stern, P. C., E19n155
Stern, S. E., 458n33
Sternberg, R. J., 411n22
Stevenson, M. C., D16n122
Stewart, G. L., C20n125
Stewart, J. B., C16n77, C16n78
Stickgold, R., 377n48, 396n186
Stillman, T. F., 377n59, 391n149, 526n123
Stillwell, A. M., 108n273, 133n109, 136n124, 204n108, 206n121, 218n243, 382n88, 398n205, 421n98, 421n99
Stinson, V., D13n101
Stobach, A., E12n100
Stock, M., B14n68
Stockdale, J., E6n46
Stokols, D., E6n44
Stone, E. F., C24n152
Stone, J., 488n238, B12n61
Stone, J. A. F., 515n77
Stone, L., 72n4, 200n76, 409n8, 427n130, 454n17
Stoolmiller, M., B9n38
Stopera, M., 462n86
Storey, A. E., 375n15
Story, A. L., 98n171
Story, P. A., 221n256
Stott, C., E7n51
Stout-Wiegand, N., E16n125
Stout, J. C., 377n54, 422n108
Stoutemyer, K., E21n171
Strack, F., 53n61, 55n76, 190n17, 524n113
Strasburger, V. C., 354n165
Strathman, A. J., 385n115
Straub, R. O., 224n289
Straus, M. A., 347n93
Straw, M. K., 322n167

Strecher, V. J., B11n50
Street, G. P., 159n58
Strickland, A., 434n175
Strober, M., 392n155
Stroebe, W., 237n38, 276n78, 511n57
Strong, G., 409n10
Stroop, J. R., 154n33
Struckman-Johnson, C., 349n108, 349n109
Stucke, T. S., 393n164, 394n170
Studebaker, C. A., D18n150
Stürmer, S., 318n136
Subra, B., 297n20, 353n139
Sugie, N., 457n29
Sugiyama, L. S., 42n13
Sullivan, D., 476n173
Sullivan, J., C11n43, C11n44, C23n147
Sullivan, M., C16n79, C16n81, C24n153
Suls, J., 98n168, 176n148, 215n212
Sundali, J., 175n140
Sundstrom, E., E4n17, E12n97
Sunyer, J., E12n102
Suomi, S. J., 356n188, 356n189
Surowiecki, J., 500n9, 511n61, 511n62, 512n63
Surra, C., 218n241
Susa, K. J., D5n12, D5n14
Susman, E. J., 356n184
Susmilch, C., 297n22
Sussenbach, S., E5n40
Sussman, D., B12n57
Sutherland, W. J., E13n108
Suvakumar, K., 262n17, 262n18
Suzuki, K., 30n67
Suzuki, T., 245n74
Svedin, U., E2n2
Svenson, O., 95n132
Swami, V., 461n58
Swander, D. V., 262n20
Swann, W. B., 426n122
Swann, W. B., Jr., 87n77, 87n78, 88n86, 89n93, 89n94, 277n83, 426n120, 426n121, 426n127
Swanson, J., 174n138
Swart, H., 470n145, 470n153
Sweeney, D., 76n23
Swerdfeger, A. L., 150n12
Swim, J. K., 473n162
Swing, E. L., 30n67, 30n68, 314n118, 314n119, 353n151
Switzer, F. S., C14n69
Symanski, R., 377n35
Symons, C. S., 90n103
Symons, D., 40n6, 429n139, 429n140, 430n143, 430n152
Syvertsen, A. K., 484n217
Szalma, J. L., E11n90
Sznycer, D., 204n107
Szymanski, S., 454n16

T

Tabaac, A., 436n185, 436n186
Tafarodi, R. W., 249n95
Tajfel, H., 466n114, 466n117, 466n118
Takahashi, B., E20n162
Tambor, E. S., 100n211
Tamburini, M., 297n17

Tamir, D. I., 105n252
Tamir, M., 199n66, 200n70, 202n87, 223n283
Tamkins, M. M., C6n24
Tang, S., 262n17, 262n18
Tangney, J. P., 59n87, 134n112, 204n106, 204n109, 204n110, 342n55
Tann, E. K., 357n208
Tannahill, R., 47n34
Tanneberger, A., 461n81
Tansey, G., 46n29
Tanzer, N., 349n103
Taplitskiy, M., 500n10
Tarpley, W. R., 252n113
Tarquinio, M., C23n148
Tarrant, M. A., E19n151
Tashiro, T., 252n111
Tata, J., 262n17, 262n18
Tate, D. F., 138n136
Taub, D. M., 356n188
Taves, P., 193n30, 243n66
Taylor, A. M., 53n60
Taylor, K., 207n134
Taylor, L. E., 150n12
Taylor, R. B., E8n75
Taylor, S., 95n140, 310n93
Taylor, S. E., 96n150, 96n152, 97n164, 118n11, 128n86, 151n23, 152n24, 153n31, 171n111, 179n166, 251n107, 346n83, 346n84, 350n118, B7n19, B7n20
Taylor, T. S., D15n111
Tchividjian, L. R., 109n277
Teachout, M. S., C14n70
Tedeschi, J. T., 105n254, 333n10, 335n25, 348n99, 348n101
Teigen, H., 15n21
Telch, C. F., 211n172, 211n173, 211n174
Tellegen, A., 189n7
Tennen, H., B8n26
Ter Schure, E., 210n164
Terdal, S. K., 100n211
Terraccianno, A., 474n165
Terrizzi, J. A., 463n97
Tesser, A., 81n45, 83n53, 103n244, 239n55
Testa, M., 486n228
Tetlock, P., 178n159
Tetlock, P. E., 62n97, 62n98, 504n17, 523n111, 523n112
Tetrick, L. E., C26n165, C27n171
Tetrock, P. E., 163n82
Tett, R. P., C14n71
Thagard, P., 474n169
Thaler, R. H., 90n104, 197n45
Thayer, R. E., 222n271, 222n274, 223n278, 224n285, 224n294
Therriault, N., 223n281
Thibodeau, R., E20n165
Thoennes, N., 398n209
Thomaes, S., 102n220
Thomas, E. J., 75n11
Thomas, H. D. C., C20n122
Thomas, J., 345n76
Thomas, K. A., 44n19
Thomas, M. A., 207n133
Thomas, P., D5n25

Thomas, R. C., 216n221
Thompson-Cannino, J., D11n84
Thompson, A. P., 437n187, 437n193
Thompson, M., 385n119
Thompson, M. P., 253n121, E18n148
Thompson, S. C. G., E21n171
Thompson, W. C., D17n135, D17n139
Thomson, G. W., 366n273
Thoresen, C. E., 306n62
Thornhill, R., 49n47, 385n118, 386n122
Thorsteinsson, E. B., 221n260
Thrash, T. M., 198n60
Thundiyll, J. G., E12n100
Tice, D. M., 59n83, 89n95, 93n118, 95n125, 105n253, 108n273, 136n127, 136n128, 138n132, 143n156, 201n82, 211n177, 223n280, 391n149, 393n164, 394n170
Tichener, J. L., E4n31
Tidwell, M., 417n70
Tierney, J., 136n129
Tiggemann, M., 76n24, 461n70
Tikcsik, A., 462n87
Tillman, T. C., 320n157
Timbergen, N., 339n40
Tindale, R. S., D17n137
Titus, L. J., 504n28
Titus, W., 515n75, 515n76
Tjaden, P., 398n209
Tjew, A. Sin M., 209n159
Tobacyk, J., 253n119
Tobacyk, J. J., 253n120
Tobias, T., 381n86
Todd, P. M., 122n28
Todd, R. M., 314n121
Toglia, M. P., D10n76
Toguchi, Y., 108n276
Tolin, D. F., 159n58
Toll, B. A., 159n51
Toma, C. L., 362n232, 388n127
Tomarken, A., 131n101, 131n102
Tomasello, M., 127n77, 297n24, 303n46, 313n115, 316n124, 321n165
Tomkins, S. S., 190n16
Tooby, J., 180n170, 180n171
Toomey, R. B., 484n217
Topping, J. S., E7n59
Tormala, Z. L., 284n127
Torneo, E., D11n84
Totis, A., 297n17
Towles, Schwen, T., 247n89
Town, J. P., E12n97
Tran, C., 293n2
Tranel, D., 212n182
Trapnell, P. D., 207n139
Travaglino, G., 522n102
Trawalter, S., 479n192
Traylor, L. D., 354n164
Treisman, M., 53n60
Tremblay, R. E., 346n81
Trent, R. B., E16n125
Trevisan, M., E4n30, E17n140
Triandis, H. C., 295n8
Trinkaus, J., 366n281
Triplett, N., 5n5
Trivers, R., 40n7, 104n246, 429n142

Trolier, T. K., 475n170
Trope, Y., 54n69, 54n71, 86n72, 87n74, 87n75, 132n107, 133n108
Tropp, L. R., 469n139, 469n140, 470n144, 482n201
Trötschel, R., 54n68
Trudeau, R., 49n46, 310n96
Trueman, M., 312n107
Trzesniewski, K. H., 101n216
Tsal, Y., 281n113
Tsang, J., 198n56
Tsang, J.-A., 307n83
Tse, A. C. B., A16n47
Tse, C.-S., D5n13
Tubman, J. G., 99n204
Tufekci, Z., 105n251
Tunnicliff, J. L., D8n50
Turnbull, S., 70n1
Turner, B. F., 433n168, 433n170
Turner, C. W., 203n92
Turner, R. H., 73n7
Turner, S. A., 211n176
Turtle, J. W., D7n48
Tversky, A., 118n13, 118n14, 118n15, 120n20, 132n105, 168n106, 168n109, 174n139, 178n157
Twenge, J., 95n138, 95n139
Twenge, J. M., 95n130, 95n131, 101n215, 101n217, 101n218, 138n132, 196n35, 209n155, 391n141, 391n150, 391n151, 392n156, 392n157, 392n158, 393n164, 393n165, 393n166, 394n170, 445n243, 486n226
Twohey-Wright, N., E3n10
Twohey, R. J., E3n9
Tybout, A. M., 266n33
Tybur, J. M., 108n268
Tyler, T. R., 526n122
Tyree, N. E., 355n170

U

Uchino, B. N., 377n56, B8n31
Udry, J. R., 409n17
Uhles, A. N., 498n4
Uhlmann, E. L., 383n92
Ullon, H. H., 360n216
Umberson, D., B8n28
Umphress, E. E., 364n259, 364n260
Underwood, J. D. M., 362n230
Unger, L. S., 276n72
Updegraff, J. A., 346n83, 346n84, B7n19
Ursano, R. S., E17n131
Utman, C. H., 126n67

V

Vaillancourt, R., 346n87
Vaish, A., 316n124
Valentine, B. A., 431n155
Valentine, T., D6n26
Valins, S., B16n75
Valle, R. S., 274n60, 274n61
Valone, K., 275n63, 275n65
Van 't Veer, A. E., 362n235
Van Balen, F., 463n98
Van Bavel, J. J., D5n15

Van Beest, I., 63n99, 202n84, 362n235
Van Boven, L., 46n24, 163n84, 163n85, 164n91, E5n37
Van Damme, C., 108n274
Van de Kragt, A. J. C., E20n163
Van den Bergh, B., 108n268, 442n216, 442n218
Van Den Burg, M. T. C., E20n157
Van den Heuvel, H., C26n161
Van der Laan, K. L., 306n71
Van der Linden, S., 260n6
Van der Wal, R. C., 54n72
Van Dijk, E., 202n84
Van Dijk, M., 102n223, 123n40, 350n125
Van Dijk, W. W., 211n180
Van Dillen, L. F., 54n72
Van Geert, E., 108n274
Van Goozen, S. H. M., 375n17
Van Horne, T., C16n80
Van Houten, R., E19n153
Van Kleef, G. A., 202n84, 202n85, 202n86
Van Knippenberg, D., C19n113
Van Lange, P. A., 507n45
Van Lange, P. A. M., 394n171, 397n197, 397n198, 397n199, 507n43
Van Praag, H. M., 222n270
Van Velsor, E., 519n93
Van Vugt, M., 305n53, E20n164
Vance, S. L., 482n199
Vandello, J. A., 48n42, 48n43, 360n218
Vanderslice, V. J., 377n36
Vanman, E. J., 207n133
Vartanian, L. R., 207n133
Vary, M. G., E18n147
Vaughan, D., 424n116
Vazire, S., 82n51
Veenhoven, R., 294n4, 327n180
Veenstra, L., 203n98, 203n99
Veerman, J. W., 344n71
Vega, L., D17n133
Velicer, W. F., B11n55
Ventafridda, V., 297n17
Ventis, W. L., 463n97
Venus, P., 276n75
Verduyn, P., 375n13
Verkasalo, M., 310n92
Vermeulen, F., 461n72
Vermeulen, I. E., 237n39, 458n35
Vermulst, A. A., 307n85
Vernberg, E., E17n136
Verrelli, S., 470n150
Verweij, K. J. H., 436n183
Vickers, J. H., 356n188
Vickers, Z., B14n71
Viek, C., E2n1
Vilberg, T., 391n146
Vincent, J., 268n41
Vincent, J. E., 205n112
Vincent, L. C., 393n163
Viswanathan, M., 474n167
Viswesvaran, C., C13n60, C14n68, C26n162
Vitolins, M. Z., 461n75
Vlandis, J. W., 238n46

Vlek, C., E15n120
Voci, A., 470n145
Voelkl, K., 486n228
Voelz, Z. R., 297n18
Vohs, K. D., 55n77, 98n180, 98n190, 98n197, 98n199, 125n48, 137n137, 138n132, 172n117, 189n9, 235n15, 306n60, 319n151, 363n248, 364n257, 375n18, 430n151, 431n154, 462n82, 469n142
Von Hippel, W., 104n246, 172n120, 375n19
Vonasch, A. J., 104n250
Vonk, J., 317n129
Vosoughi, S., 260n4
Voyer, D., 504n25
Vranica, S., 238n40
Vriniotis, M., 351n131

W

Wack, D. L., 504n19, 505n31
Wade, J., 310n93
Wager, T. D., 391n148
Wagner, E. F., 159n51
Wagner, H. S., B14n71
Wagner, M., 459n44
Wagner, P., 342n55
Wagner, S. H., 76n23
Wahlqvist, M. L., A8n22
Wakefield, A., 150n7
Wakker, P. P., 197n46
Wakslak, C. J., 86n72
Waldeck, J. H., C17n94
Waldman, S., 118n12
Waldron, K. A., B14n70
Walker, I., 483n210, 483n211
Walker, R. L., 297n18
Walker, T., 205n114
Wall, S., 416n46
Wallace, B., D17n141
Wallace, H. M., 123n39, 306n72, 350n123, 504n23, 505n32
Wallach, M. A., 515n78
Wallbom, M., 77n26
Walsh, A., 99n207, 408n5
Walsh, C. L., 375n15
Walsh, M., 385n116
Walster, E., 278n86, 297n25, 379n74, 384n104, 384n105
Walster, F. H., 384n107
Walters, K. S., 46n30
Walton, G. M., 57n79, 108n267
Wamsley, L., 195n34
Wan, C. K., 98n168, 176n148
Wanberg, C. R., C30n208
Wandersman, A., E14n115
Wandruff, S. E., 235n14
Wang, C. L., 280n108
Wang, D., B4n11
Wang, H., 221n257, B12n59
Wang, M. C., 385n117, 420n92
Wang, P. S., E17n134
Wänke, M., 158n41
Wanous, J. P., C11n45
Wansink, B., 158n45, 211n171
Warheit, G. J., E4n13
Waring, R. L., C13n59
Warlop, L., 442n216, 442n218
Warneken, F., 313n115

Warner, L., 211n176
Warren, C., E8n63
Warren, K. L., D4n6
Waters, E., 416n46, 417n69
Waters, K., 305n58
Watson, D., 189n5, 189n6, 189n7, 523n106
Watts, D. J., 176n144
Waytz, A., 469n132
Wazlawek, A. S., 365n268
Weary, G., 97n154
Weathers, J. E., D15n112
Weaver, A. J., 355n170
Weaver, C. N., 209n152
Weaver, J. R., 48n42, 48n43
Weaver, W. G., D15n109, D15n110
Weber, E. U., 214n198
Weber, M. J., E9n78
Weber, N., D6n40, D7n44
Webley, P., 45n21, 45n22, A11n31
Webster, D., 353n149
Webster, G. D., 391n149
Webster, J. M., 295n7
Weeks, B. E., 15n22
Wegener, D. T., 281n112
Wegner, D. M., 54n64, 159n46, 159n48, 159n49, 159n50, 159n54, 159n56, 223n281, 513n67, 513n68
Wcicratall, R., 343n69
Weil, C. E., A15n45
Weinberg, M. S., 435n177
Weinborn, C., 353n138
Weiner, B., 162n74, B16n75
Weinrich, S., E16n130
Weinstein, N., 199n65
Weintraub, K. J., 72n5
Weisenberger, J. M., 352n132
Weiss, B., 361n229
Weiss, W., 273n55, 279n100
Weitz, I., 353n148
Welch, N., 214n198
Wells, G. L., 21n33, 237n35, D4n2, D4n3, D4n7, D6n43, D7n44, D7n47, D7n48, D8n49, D8n51, D8n52, D8n54, D8n55, D9n61, D10n71, D10n72, D10n73, D10n78, D10n79, D10n80, D10n81, D11n83, D12n93
Wells, K. B., E17n134
Wenger, A. A., D16n119
Wenzlaff, R. M., 159n50, 159n56
Werle, C. O. C., 158n45
Werner, C. M., E8n74
West, S., E4n14
West, S. G., 318n146, 384n111, 476n175
Westen, D., 442n220
Westergaard, G. C., 356n189
Westfall, R., 385n116
Westgate, E. C., 153n30
Westphal, J. D., 522n101
Wetmore, S., D10n74
Wetmore, S. A., D10n75
Wetter, D., 97n153
Whatley, M. A., 295n7
Wheatley, T., 213n191
Wheatley, T. P., 213n189
Wheeler, B. W., 199n64
Wheeler, D., 268n41

Wheeler, J., 320n157
Wheeler, L., 377n43, 377n45, 384n103, 394n175
Whetzel, D. L., C14n63
Whisman, V., 433n167
Whitaker, J. L., 320n163
Whitcup, M., 365n269
White, A. E., 303n47
White, B., 236n25, E21n169
White, C. M., 122n30
White, F. A., 470n150
White, G. L., 379n71
White, G. M., 320n162, 326n175
White, H. R., 422n103
White, M. P., 199n64
White, S. B., 119n17
White, T. L., 159n49
Whitley, B. E., 464n105, 464n107
Whitley, C. T., E20n162
Whitlock, T., 352n132
Whitson, J. A., 523n107, 523n109
Whitten, S., 238n44
Whittington, J. E., D8n56
Wicker, A. W., 246n76
Wicker, F. W., 159n59
Wicklund, R., 75n14
Wicklund, R. A., 77n31, 107n265, 107n266, 122n34, 444n235
Widaman, K. F., 100n210
Widmeyer, W. N., C19n110
Wiechmann, D., C14n73
Wieczorkowska, G., 498n4
Wiederman, M. W., 172n127, 437n189, 437n190, 437n192, 438n200, 443n233
Wiehe, V. R., 349n105
Wieneke, K., 236n25
Wieselquist, J., 312n106, 424n114, 469n136, 469n137, 504n18
Wigboldus, D. H. J., 307n85
Wight, W., 163n84
Wijen, F., E3n11
Wiklund, I., 377n53
Wilbur, R. B., 217n225
Wiley, T. R., D16n122
Wilke, H. A. M., 302n41
Wilkinson, M., D12n92
Willems, S., 167n102
Willer, R., 303n50
William, I. M., 361n225
Williams, A. B., B12n59
Williams, A. D., 181n174, 181n179, 181n181
Williams, C. J., 234n9, 478n183
Williams, K., 505n34, 506n40
Williams, K. D., 63n99, 390n128, 390n129, 390n133, 390n134, 391n135, 391n136, 394n172, 418n77, 506n38, 506n41
Williams, S., 99n205
Williams, S. S., 362n233
Williamson, G. M., 415n38
Willis, F. N., E7n60
Willis, R., 468n130
Willis, T. A., 97n165
Willits, J. E., 318n135
Willman, P., 178n155
Wills, T., B9n38
Wills, T. A., 251n108

Wilson, B. J., E9n81
Wilson, D. B., 356n191, 356n192
Wilson, D. T., 207n130
Wilson, J., 431n158, E8n64
Wilson, M., 121n22, 442n217
Wilson, M. S., E5n38
Wilson, N., 366n273
Wilson, T. D., 81n47, 82n48, 82n50, 153n30, 213n189, 213n191, 213n193, 233n7, 239n56, 239n57
Windschitl, P. D., 21n33
Winegard, B., 465n111
Winegard, B. M., 104n250
Winett, R. A., E14n112
Winfield, F. E., 377n41
Wing, R. R., 138n136
Winiewski, M., 460n47
Winkel, F. W., 349n111
Winkler, N., 343n65
Winslow, M. P., B12n61
Winton, W., 85n70
Wirtz, D., 178n160, 178n162
Wise, T. N., B16n88
Wisneski, D. C., 299n27
Witeman, C. L. M., 216n219
Witt, J. K., 353n147
Witt, L. A., C29n191
Wittenberg, M. T., 98n193
Wittenbrink, B., 455n18
Witvliet, C. V. O., 306n71, 307n81
Wixted, J., D10n81
Wixted, J. T., D6n41, D6n42, D6n43
Wlaschin, J., 158n44
Wohl, M. J. A., 487n232
Wohlwend-Lloyd, R., 418n81
Wójcik, A., 460n47
Wolf, I. K., 178n161
Wolf, R., 463n89
Wolfe, R. N., 379n66
Wolff, E. N., 509n53
Wolsic, B., 98n175
Wolters, F. J. M., 302n41
Wong, N., A13n38
Wong, N. C. H., 284n125
Wood, P. B., 462n84, 463n95
Wood, W., 137n138, 139n139, 139n140, 139n141, 139n142, 139n143, 139n144, 279n102
Woolcott, M., 295n9
Wooten, A., D10n74
Wooten, A. R., D8n56
Wooten, D. B., A15n46
Word, C. O., 453n13
Worschel, S., 269n44
Worth, K., B10n42
Worth, L. T., 274n66
Worthington, E. L., 198n57, 305n59, 307n77, 307n78
Worthman, C. M., 375n20
Wortley, R., E8n71
Wortman, C. B., 122n35, 251n106
Wortman, E., 380n78, 380n80
Wotman, S. R., 218n243, 376n31, 382n88, 398n202, 398n204, 398n205
Wout, D., 488n239
Wright, D., D6n31
Wright, E. F., 504n24, 504n25

Wright, J. A., B11n55
Wright, J. C., 396n191
Wright, K. M., E17n131
Wright, L. W., Jr., 193n26, 464n108
Wright, R., 205n114, 305n52
Wright, S. C., 470n149, 482n203
Wrzesniewski, A., 85n68
Wu, X., 364n257
Wyer, R. S., 97n158
Wylie, R. C., 98n187
Wynder, E. L., 23n39
Wynne-Edward, K. E., 375n15

X
Xu, H., 206n124, 342n54
Xu, J. Q., B9n37
Xygalatas, D., 243n63

Y
Yalch, R. F., 266n33
Yalom, I. D., 376n30
Yamamoto, M., 381n83
Yang, Q., 164n92, 364n257
Yang, Y., 47n33
Yap, A., 365n268
Yeadon, C., 60n89
Yerke, A. F., 350n127
Yerkes, R. M., 219n245
Yeshua-Katz, D., 355n170
Yim, F., A16n47
Yokomatsu, M., E16n123
Yoon, J., 390n130
Yorkston, E., A7n21
Young, B., 237n34
Young, L. L., 469n132
Young, M. J., 216n214
Young, R. D., 78n34
Young, S. G., 237n33, D5n13
Yukawa, S., 326n177
Yukl, G., 518n88
Yule, W., E17n135
Yuwiler, A., 356n186
Yzerbyt, V. Y., 396n193

Z
Zaalberg, A., 357n206
Zadro, L., 390n134, 391n136, 394n172
Zagefka, H., 470n146, 482n200
Zajonc, R. B., 236n23, 236n24, 237n29, 504n27, 505n29, 526n126
Zakrzewski, A. C., 154n34
Zalar, R. W., 349n106
Zanna, A. S., 245n73
Zanna, M., 193n30, 243n66, B10n41
Zanna, M. P., 243n65, 245n73, 453n13, B15n72
Zavalloni, M., 515n79
Zebrowitz, L. A., 236n25
Zeelenberg, M., 211n180
Zehner, K. S., 117n10
Zeichner, A., 463n92
Zeiss, A. R., 97n162
Zelenski, J. M., 214n194, E20n160

Name Index | N-19

Zell, A. L., 307n81, 307n88
Zhang, H.-H., 221n257
Zhang, J., 119n16
Zhao, W., 124n45
Zhong, C. B., 206n123
Zhou, G., D5n13
Zhou, X., 164n92, 364n257
Zickar, M. J., 29n63
Ziegert, J. C., 479n188
Ziegler, A., 431n155
Zielaskowski, K., 157n38, 464n110
Zieman, G. L., E4n19
Zietsch, B., 436n183
Zillmann, D., 192n22, 203n95, 342n58
Zimbardo, P. G., 193n28, 502n16, 508n51
Zimmerman, D. M., D9n67
Zivnuska, S., C29n191
Zonderman, A. B., 198n52, 198n53
Zottoli, M. A., C11n45
Zou, Z., 87n80, 87n81
Zubek, J. M., 215n213, 377n36
Zuckerman, M., 97n155, 163n80, 320n156, 320n159
Zvibel, M., 268n40
Zweck, T., D6n40
Zweizig, M., E21n172
Zwickle, A., E20n162

Subject Index

A

Abagnale, Frank, 364
ABC triad, 8, 453–456
Ability, 162–163
Abnormal behavior, 11
A–B problem, 247
Absenteeism, C30
Academic performance
   age effect, 48
   cheating, 363–364
   self-esteem effects on, 98
   self-fulfilling prophecies, 485
   stereotype threat and, 488–489
   stereotyping and, 477
   test taking, 178
Acceptance. *See* Social acceptance
Accessibility, 248
Accomplices, 18, 64
Accountability
   in business, 506–507
   deindividualism and, 502, 508
   in groups, 504
Accumulated common wisdom, 15
Action orientation to power, 524
Actions. *See* Choices and actions
Action stage of transtheoretical model, B12, B13
Actor/observer bias, 163–165
Adaptability, power and, 523
Addiction, A19
Adolescents, 346, 393, 398
   risky behavior, B13–B14
   smoking, B9–B10
Advertisement wear-out, 278–279
Advertising. *See also* Persuasion
   classical conditioning, 238
   cultural differences in preferences, 280
   global focus, A16–A17
   introspection failure, 82
   political ads, 277–278
   social media, A4–A5
Affairs, 437–439, 442–444
Affect. *See also* Emotions and affect
   defined, 8, 188–189
   intensity, 200
   in intergroup relations, 453
   regulation of, 222–225
Affect-as-information hypothesis, 212–213
Affect balance, 196
Affect Intensity Measure (AIM), 200
Affectionate love, 408. *See also* Companionate love
Affective commitment, C25
Affective forecasting, 213–214, 221
Affect regulation, 222–224
African Americans
   on juries, D14
   lynching of, 476
   self-esteem of, 95, 485–486
   stereotypes of, 470, 485
   stereotype threat and, 488–489
   and West Point, first at, 390

Age differences
   aggression for, 346
   disaster response, E18
   eyewitness memory, D4
   personal space, E8
Age effect, 48
Agent self (executive function), 71, 72, 307
Age of Reason, 336
Aggression, 16–17, 334, 338–341. *See also* Violence
   accountability and, 508
   age differences for, 346
   anger and, 201, 202
   appetitive, 343–344
   automatic processes and, 57
   chemical influences on, 356–357
   conscious override and, 56
   crowding and, E4
   cultural differences, 58, 358–362
   defined, 334–335
   external causes, 352–357
   frustration-aggression theory, 18, 23, 342, 467
   frustration and, 342
   gender differences, 346–347
   instinct theories of, 338–339
   interpersonal causes of, 348–351
   learning theories of, 339–340
   mass media's promotion of, 332, 333, 353–355
   mood and, 342–343
   narcissism and, 102, 348, 360
   outperformance and, 297
   personality trait of, 348
   rejection and, 393–394
   sexual aggression, 349, 350
   social learning theory, 238–239
   territoriality and, E9
   and video games, 16, 19–22
Aggressive driving, 352–353
Aiello, Sydney, 205
AIM (Affect Intensity Measure), 200
Air pollution, E12–E13
Alcohol use or abuse
   aggression and, 356–357
   as emotion control strategy, 224
   implicit attitudes about, 479
   loneliness and, 396
   self-awareness reduction from, 77–78, 136
   self-handicapping explanation, 88–89
Allport, Gordon, 6, 246, 469, 471, 476
Altruism, 315–316
Altruistic helping, 314
Altruistic personality, 317–318
Altruistic punishment, 303, 507–508
Ambient environment, E10–E11
Ambiguous situations, 263
American Idol, 238
American political beliefs, 44
Amish community, 390
Anchoring and adjustment heuristic, 168–169
Anger, 201–203, 342–343
   management of, 202–203, 223–224
   and outgroup members, 455–456

Animals
   attitudes of, 254
   cultural animals, 43, 49–50
   goals of, 127
   herd instinct, 376
   homosexuality in, 464
   loneliness and pets, 395
   reciprocity of, 297
   selfishness, 313, 317
   sensory systems, 62–63
   social animals, 40–41
Anorexia. *See* Eating disorders
Anthropology, 10
Anticipated emotion, 213–214
Anti-gay prejudice, 462–465
Anti-Semitism, 458–460
Antisocial behavior, 330–369
   aggression (*See* Aggression)
   cheating, 363–364
   defined, 335
   littering, 366
   lying, 362–363
   money and, 364
   prosocial behavior *vs.*, 294
   stealing, 364–365
Anxiety, 214, 489
Anxious/ambivalent attachment, 416
Apologies, 204, 307
Appetitive aggression, 343–344
Applied research, 14
Appraisal motive, 87, 88
Appraisals, B6–B7
Appraisal theory of emotion, 194
Approach orientation to power, 524
Approach tendency, 201
Arabs, prejudice against, 457–458
Aristotle, 272, 274
Arousal, emotional, 190–194
   affect regulation strategy, 222
   aggression and, 343
   attention and, 219–220
   cognitive dissonance, 243
   defined, 190
   learning and, 212
   performance and, 219–220
   pleasant *vs.* unpleasant states, 193
   sexual arousal, 193, 214, 435
   shopping, A7
   social facilitation theory, 504
Arsenic, E12
Arson, 349
Asch, Solomon, 64, 261–262
Asian Americans and selfhood, 74
As Nature Made Him: The Boy Who Was Raised as a Girl (Colapinto), 36
Assembly lines, 497, 500–501
Assertiveness, 518
Association for Psychological Science, 387
Assumptive worlds, 250
Atheists, 312, 460
Attachment, 415–417, 427–428
Attachment theory, 416–417

Attention, 270–271
    alcohol use impact, 356
    emotional arousal and, 219–220
    self-esteem and, 97
Attitude polarization, 239–240
Attitudes, 233–240, 246–248
    accessibility of, 248
    Allport's work, 6
    as behavior predictor, 246–248
    beliefs vs., 233
    change through persuasion, 282
    defined, 233
    dual attitudes, 233–234
    environmental issues, E18–E19
    formation of, 236–240
    inoculation of, 283–285
    polarization of, 239–240
    reasons for, 235
    social media and expression of, 232–233
Attitudes at work, C24–C29, C30–C31
Attraction, 378–388
    defined, 372, 373
    importance of, 373
    long-term relationships and, 420
    online dating, 387–388
Attractiveness
    helpfulness and, 318
    persuasive speaker and, 275–276
    what is beautiful is good effect, 384
Attributions and attribution theory, 97, 161–166
    actions, explaining, 165
    actor/observer bias, 163–165, 438
    aggression and, 344–345
    history of, 7, 170
    illness symptoms, B16
    model of, 162
    racism, 486
    romantic rejection, 397–398
    self-serving bias, 486
    success and failure, explanations of, 162–163
Audience, 279–280
Audience inhibition, 323
Australian Aborigines, E9
Authoritarian personality, D16
Authority, obedience to, 7, 307–310
Autism and vaccination link, 150–151
Autokinetic effect, 262
Automatic affect, 189, 194, 210
Automatic attitudes, 233–234
Automatic egotism, 89, 108
Automatic system of the mind, 153–155, 171. See also Heuristics
    conscious override of, 56, 60, 89, 479–480
    defined, 53
    vs. deliberate system, 53–56
    and goals, 129–130
    habits, 140
    and persuasion, 281
    power, 523
    prejudice, 479–480
Automobile industry, A2
Autonomy, 125–126
Availability heuristic, 167, 169, 176, 336
Available alternatives and lasting relationships, 421
Average Joe, 372, 381–382
Aversive racism, 453
Avoidance tendency, 201
Avoidant attachment, 416, 417

Awareness, 155. *See also* Self-awareness
Axelrod, Robert, 302

B

Babies, 189, 381. *See also* Children
Bacon, Francis, 173
Bad apple effect, 397, 507, 509
Bait-and-switch technique, 266
Bandura, Albert, 238, 339
Bargh, John, 235
Baseball players, 198–199
Base rate fallacy, 174–175, 179
Basic research, 14
Beauty, 386. *See also* Attractiveness
Behavior. *See also* Choices and actions
    antisocial behavior (*See* Antisocial behavior)
    attitudes as predictor of, 246–248
    consumer behavior (*See* Consumer behavior)
    defined, 8
    emotional causes, 210–211
    environmental issues, E18–E19
    and intergroup relations, 453
    Lewin's work, 6
    natural, 58–59
    prosocial behavior (*See* Prosocial behavior)
    rejection and, 392–394
    risky behavior (*See* Risky behavior)
    self-awareness and, 77
    self-defeating behavior, 140–143
    self-presentation, 104–110
    sexual behavior (*See* Sexuality and sexual behavior)
    at work, C30–C31
Behavioral intentions, 248
Behaviorism, 7, 117, 151, 238
Belief in a just world, 318–320
Belief perseverance, 249–250
Beliefs, 249–254
    attitudes vs., 233
    coping and, 250–252
    defined, 233
    doubting vs., 249
    health belief model, B10–B11
    irrational beliefs, 253
    in just world, 318–320
    perseverance of, 249–250
    religious beliefs, 252–253
Belongingness, 209, 373–378, 521
Bem, Daryl, 435
Benefits, employee, C3, C28
Berkowitz, Leonard, 342, 352, A11
Bernall, Cassie, 106, 107, 108
Betty Crocker, A8
Between-subjects design, 17
BFOQs (bona fide occupational qualifications), C9–C10
Biases and errors, 171–180
    actor/observer bias, 163–165, 438
    attitude polarization, 239–240
    base rate fallacy, 174–175
    cognitive errors, common, 179
    confirmation bias, 173, 477–478, B15–B16
    correspondence bias, 164
    counterfactual thinking, 178–179
    false consensus effect, 176
    false uniqueness effect, 176–177
    friends' opinions, 171–172
    fundamental attribution error, 164–165, 321
    gambler's fallacy, 175

hostile cognitive biases, 344–345
    illusion of control, 178
    illusory correlations, 173–174
    liberal bias, 490
    omission bias, 122
    optimism bias, 132
    outgroup homogeneity bias, 455–456
    own-race bias, D4–D5
    self-serving bias, 97, 163, 476, 486
    statistical regression, 177–178
    status quo bias, 121–122
    theory perseverance, 177
Binary gender, challenges to assumption of, 436
Binge eating, 79, 135–136, 211, 506
    rejection and, 392
Biological psychology, 10–11
Biology, influence of, 7
Biopsychosocial approach to health, B9
Birhor people, 468
Birth control, 420
Bisexuality, 435
Black people. *See* African Americans
Black sheep hypothesis, D15
Blame, 251
    scapegoat theory, 476
    of victims, 319, 350
Bloodsworth, Kirk, C2
Bobo doll study, 339–340
Bodily topography of emotions, 217
Body odor, 386
Body shape, 385
Body weight, 386
Bona fide occupational qualifications (BFOQs), C9–C10
Boomerang effect, 285
Bosses, 519–520, 521–522
Botox injections, 191
Bowlby, John, 415
Brain, 41–42, 152. *See also* Duplex mind
Brainstorming, 510–512
Brainwashing, 92, 249
Brand loyalty, A8–A9
Break-ups of close relationships, 424–425
Breast cancer, 251–252
Brehm, Jack, 122
Broaden-and-build theory, 215
Brown, Jonathon, 96
Bullies and bullying, 102, 335, 393
Bundy, Ted, 204
Burdensomeness, 144
Burger, Jerry, 309
Busyness, 325
Bystander effect, 321–325

C

Cadmium, E12
Cainer, Jonathan, 173
Cancer, 251–252, B2
Can-do performance factors, C14
Capacity for change, 136–138
Capacity to delay gratification, 142
Capital cases, voir dire in, D17
Capra, Frank, 272
Carbon monoxide, E12
Carlsmith, J. Merrill, 242
Carnegie Hero Fund Commission, 318
Cash purchases, A11
Castaway, 395
Castro, Fidel, 164

Casual sex, 431
Categorization, 453
Catharsis theory, 203, 354
Catholic nuns and happiness, 198
Catholic priests and health, 423
Cause-effect conclusions, 17
Celebrities, 418
Cell phones, A17–A19, A21
Central route to persuasion, 281, 282
Certainty effect, 120
Challenge appraisals, B6
Challenge for cause, D15
Change, 92–93, 143
    capacity for, 136–138
    environmental attitudes and behaviors, E18–E19
    freedom to, 123–124
    in self-knowledge, 91–93
Change of venue, D18
Charivari, 439–440
Charles, Prince of Wales, 406–407
Chastity belts, 441
Cheater's high, 299, 364
Cheating, 77, 363–364, 506, 507–508
Chewong people, 468
Chicken soup and colds, 17
Chief executive officers (CEOs), 517, 522
Childlessness, 196–197
Children, 266
    abuse of, 349 350
    aggression, 339–340, 346–247, 396
    attitudes, 235
    beliefs, 249
    birthdays and achievement, 48
    capacity to delay gratification, 142
    disaster response, E18
    empathy, 313–314
    English, in World War II, 415
    happiness and, 196–197, 200
    punishment of, 350–351
    rejection of, 393–394, 396
    self-knowledge, 81
    smoking inoculation, 284
Chimpanzee studies, 61, 314
Chinese in America, 246
Choices and actions, 114–147, 165
    choosing process, 118–121
    consumer behavior (*See* Consumer behavior)
    decision avoidance, 121–122
    decisiveness, 517
    emotions and, 213–215
    equality and, 517
    irrational behavior, 140–145
    justification of, 243
    meaning of, 117–124
    money's influence, 119
    self-destructive behavior, 140–145
    self-regulation (*See* Self-regulation)
    terrorism example, 116–117
    tradeoffs, 60–61
Chronic negative affect, B16
Churchill, Winston, 236
Cialdini, Robert, 269, 270
CIT (Critical Incident Technique), C9
Civil Rights Act of 1964, C9, C10, C12
Classical conditioning, 237–238
Climate, E11
Clinical psychology, 11
Clinton, Bill, 333
Closeness to danger, E16

Close relationships, 404–449
    break-ups, 376, 424–425, 438–439
    dating (*See* Dating)
    growth of, 420–421
    honesty in, 425–427
    investment model, 421–422
    jealousy in, 439–444
    love (*See* Love)
    maintenance of, 419–427
    marriage (*See* Marriage)
    sexual behavior (*See* Sexuality and sexual behavior)
    thinking styles of couples, 423–425
    types of, 414–419
Clothing, 385
Coca-Cola, A9
Co-evolution, 49
Cognition, 279, 281
    defined, 8
    and intergroup relations, 453
    rejection and, 391
Cognitive appraisal model, B6–B7
Cognitive biases and errors. *See* Biases and errors
Cognitive control, E6–E7
Cognitive coping, 251
Cognitive dissonance, 241
Cognitive dissonance theory, 241, 243–245
    choice justification, 243
    and condom use, B12
    consumer behavior, A12
    effort justification, 241–243
    media and, 244–245
    money and, 242
    natural disasters, E16
    religious views and, 252–253
    violence, 354
Cognitive errors, reducing, 180–181
Cognitive miser, 152–153, 164, 279, 453
Cognitive psychology, 11
Cohesiveness of groups, C19
Colbert, Stephen, 312
Colds, chicken soup and, 17
Collective wisdom, 511–512
Collectivism, 49, 108, 164
College students
    aggression, 347
    cheating, 363–364
    choice justification, 244
    delay of gratification, 61, 142
    effort justification, 241–242
    embodied attitudes, 237
    empathy, 314
    mere exposure effect, 236
    narcissism of, 101
    persuasion, 282
    pluralistic ignorance of, 263
    reliance on for research, 27–28, 29–30
    self-esteem, 95
    sexual norms, 430–431
    social circles, 377
    stress, C27, C28–C29
    withdrawal behaviors of, C29–C30
Collins, Jason, 465
Comfort foods, 211, B14
Coming of Age in Samoa (Mead), 440
Commitment, 411, 412–413, 420
    organizational commitment, C25–C26, C30
    social influence techniques based on, 264–267
    in Sternberg's triangle of love, 411

Committees, 514–515
Commons dilemma, 508–509, 524, E3, E20–E21
Common wisdom, 15
Communal relationships, 414–415
Communication
    commons dilemma and, 509
    of criticism, 81
    environmental issues, E20
    nonverbal communication, E6
    by social animals, 50
Communism, 7, 468, 509
Commuter marriages, 377
Companionate love, 408
    across time, 409–410
    vs. passionate love, 408
    Sternberg's triangle of love theory, 412
Company citizens, 294
Comparison, social, 82–83, 97, 486
Competence, 102
Competence and helping, 323
Competition, 467, 504
    vs. cooperation, 468
    prejudice and, 467–469, 472
Competition machine, 5
Competitive victimhood, 487
Compliance, public, 263
Compliments, 95, 380
Comte, Auguste, 314
Conditioned response, 237
Conditioned stimulus, 237
Condoms, 247, B12
Confirmation bias, 173, 179, 477–478, B15–B16
Conflicts, 48, 59–60, 525–526
Conformity, 310
    Asch's research on, 64, 261–262
    assumptions about, 165
    and cultural development, 49
    as groupthink indication, 514
    as prosocial behavior, 294
    restaurant diners, 311
Confounding, 21, 22
Conscious attitudes, 233
Conscious emotion, 189, 194
Consciousness, 53–54, 55
Conscious override, 56, 60, 89, 479–482
Conscious system, 53. *See also* Deliberate system of the mind
Conscious thought, 52, 160
Consent forms, 20, 21
Conservation, E13–E15
Conservatism, 463
Conservatives, moral foundation of, 300
Consistency, 240–245, 264–267
Consistency motive, 87–88
Conspicuous consumption, A13–A14
Constructs, 16–17
Construct validity of the cause, 18
Construct validity of the effect, 18
Consumer behavior, A1–A24
    cell phones, A17–A19
    consumption process, A9
    dark side of, A19–A20
    decision making, A2–A4
    e-commerce, A12–A13, A16–A17
    post-consumption process, A20–A21
    purchase making, A10–A15
Consumer Reports, 171
Consumer segments, e-commerce, A16
Consumption process, A9

Contact hypothesis, 469–470, 482–483
Contemplation stage of transtheoretical model, B12, B13
Contingent success, 89
Continuance commitment, C25
Continuance (trials), D18
Control, 126, 155
    in cognitive appraisal model, B7
    illusion of, 175–176
    of noise, E11
    over female sexuality, 444–445
    rejection and, 392
Controls, experimental, 23
Conversion therapy, 246
Convert communicators, 274
Convictions, wrongful, D2–D3
Cooley, Charles Horton, 80
Coolidge, Calvin, 431–432
Coolidge effect, 431–432
Cooperation, 302, 467
    vs. competition, 468
    as prosocial behavior, 294, 302–305
Coping, 416
    beliefs and, 250–252
    defined, 250, B8
    with natural disasters, E17–E18
Corporal punishment, 350–351
Corporations. *See also* Work and workplace
    prejudice against, 461–462
Correct identification, D3
Correct rejection, D3
Correlation, 23, 193
Correlational approach, 23–25
Correlation coefficient *(r)*, 23–24
Correlations, illusory, 173–174, B15–B16
Correspondence bias, 164
Corruption, 521–522
Cotton, Ronald, D11
Counterfactual thinking, 178–179, 212
Counterproductive behaviors, C30
Counter-regulation effect, 161
Creativity and cheating, 363
Credibility, source, 273–274
Credit cards, 284, A11
Crimes
    eyewitness memory, D3–D13
    hot temperatures and, 355
    rape, 333, 350, 354
    self-control and, 358–359
    stealing, 364–365, A20
    violent crimes, 335
Crisis situations, 263
Critical Incident Technique (CIT), C9
Criticism, 81, 105, 520–521
Crowding, 355, E2–E3, E5–E6
Crystal, Billy, 104
Cues, 57–58, 392, E14
Culprit-absent lineups, D3, D4
Culprit-present lineups, D3, D4
Cults, 264–265
Cultural animals, 43, 49–50. *See also* Humans as cultural animals
Cultural groups, 500
Cultural relativity, 30
Culture and cultural differences, 51–52
    advantages of, 65
    aggression, 58, 358–362
    altruism in, 316
    anger, 201

    attributions in illness, B16
    vs. being social, 49–50
    body weight, ideal, 385–386
    competition *vs.* cooperation, 303, 468
    conformity, 310
    conscious override, importance of, 56
    consistency, 245
    defined, 43–46
    eating habits, 46
    emotions, 217
    gender roles, 47
    groups, 500
    healthy choices, B2–B3
    homosexuality and, 435–436
    information, meaningful, 46
    intergroup relationships, 490–491
    jealousy, 440
    love, 408–409
    meaning learned through, 117
    money, 45
    nature and, 47–49
    organizational culture, C5–C6
    personal space, E6, E8
    persuasion, 280
    physical attractiveness, 384
    as praxis, 45
    prejudice, 466–467, 484
    putting people first, 63–65
    self, 73–74
    self-control from, 58–59
    selfishness *vs.* social conscience, 59–60
    sexual behavior, 47, 58, 428–429, 430, 432–433, 444–446
    shared ideas of, 43–44
    sleep, 50–51
    social acceptance, 56–57
    social behavior and, 37–38
    as social system, 44–45
    standards of, 134, 135
    territoriality, E8–E9
    tradeoffs, 61
    violence and, 337, 358–362
Culture of honor, 360–361
Curiosity, 12–13, 87
Cyberball, 389
Cyberbullying, 335

D

Dabbs, Jim, 374
Dark tetrad of personality, 221
Darley, John, 321
Darwin, Charles, 38, 237, 338
Date rape, 350
Dating
    attractiveness of partner and, 384
    eating, 434
    idealization of partner, 426
    infidelity, 439
    interracial dating, 457
    number of dates before sex, 434
    online dating, 387–388
Davis, Troy, D11, D12
Dawkins, Richard, 313
Death and dying, 39, 377
    behavioral risks, B9
    from cancer, B2
    donating body to science, A21
    by guns, 353
    personal space and, E8

    and purchasing decisions, A14
    suicide (*See* Suicide)
"Death drive," 141
Death penalty, 239, D17
Death qualification, D17
Debiasing, 181
Debriefing, 21
Debt, consumer, A11
Deception studies, 21
Deci, Ed, 125
Decision avoidance, 121–122
Decision fatigue, 138–139
Decision-making. *See* Choices and actions
Defense mechanism, 416
DeGeneres, Ellen, 463
Deindividuation, 365, 502, 508
Delay of gratification, 60, 142
Deliberate attitudes, 233–234
Deliberate system of the mind, 153–155, 523
    vs. automatic system, 53–56
    conscious override by, 56, 60, 89
    defined, 53
    and goals, 129–130
    and persuasion, 281, 282
Demand characteristics, 20, 21, D7
Democratic business leaders, 300
Demographics in juries, D16
Density of population, 355, E5–E6
Dependent variables, 18, 19
Depression
    gender differences, 224
    helpfulness and, 210–211
    powerlessness and, 523
    self-esteem and, 96
Deschappelles, 89
Descriptive norms, 366
Desensitization, 343, 355
Devaluation of others, 520
    potential partners, 424–425
Developmental psychology, 11
Deviance, 396–397
de Waal, Frans, 38
DeWall, Nathan, 391
Diamond, Lisa, 427–428
Diets and dieting, 135–136, 137, 161. *See also* Eating
    self-awareness and, 79
    self-presentation influence, 105
Diffusion of responsibility, 323
Direct aggression, 334
Direct reciprocity, 298
Disasters, natural, E4, E15–E18
Disconnection from others, 520
Discontinuity effect, 469
Discounting, temporal, 120, 121
Discrimination, 453
    against Arab Americans, 457–458
    employment, C9–C10
    against LGBTQ+ individuals, 462–465
    reverse discrimination, 481
    in sports, 454
Disease. *See* Illness
Disgust, 58, 206–208, 215, 463
Dismissing avoidant attachment, 416–417
Displaced aggression, 334
Disrupt-then-reframe technique, 271
Dissimilarities, 380
Dissonance. *See* Cognitive dissonance theory
Distal goals, 129–130

Distraction, 281, 321, 505
Distress, C27
Distress-maintaining style of attribution, 423–424
Diversity, 380, 499, 500
Division of labor, 49
Divorce, 438, 446, A14
DNA testing, D2, D11
    paternity testing, 437, 444
Dodson, John, 219
Domestic violence, 349–351
    victiim staying with abuser, 376, 422
Dominant responses, 504, A7
Donations, 267, 295
Doomsday prophets, 252, 253
Door-in-the-face technique, 268
Double-blind testing, D9
Double standard, 444–445
Doubting, 249
Downward counterfactuals, 178–179
Downward social comparison, 83, 251
Doyle, Arthur Conan, 167
Driving, aggressive, 352–353
Driving ability, 95
Drug use, 60–61
Dual attitudes, 233–234
Dunbar, Robin, 41
Duplex mind, 52–56, 153
    automatic system (*See* Automatic system of the mind)
    beliefs, 249
    biases and errors of, 171
    consciousness, 53
    consistency, 245
    defined, 52
    deliberate system (*See* Deliberate system of the mind)
    goal hierarchies, 129
    power, 523
    prejudice, 479, 480
    self-knowledge and, 89
    social influence techniques and, 271, 280
Dweck, Carol, 123
Dyads, 498
Dyer, Wayne, 344
Dysphoria, 436

E

Easterbrook, J.A., 219–220
Eating. *See also* Diets and dieting
    comfort foods, B14
    counter-regulation, 161
    cultural influences, 46, 58, 117
    on dates, 434
    disgusting foods, 244
    emotional eating, 224
    habits, 139–140
    mimicking and, 381
    mood and, 211
    rejection and, 391, 392
    self-awareness and, 76, 79
    stress and, C28
    vegetarianism, 46
    violence and, 357
Eating disorders, 76, 392
    binge eating, 79, 135–136, 211, 506
EBE (exotic becomes erotic), 435
E-cigarettes, B2
E-commerce, A12–A13, A16–A17

Economics, 10, E21. *See also* Money
The Economist, 4
E-cycling, A21
Education. *See also* Academic performance; College students
    environmental education, E21
    jigsaw classroom, 483
    sexual behavior and, 433
    of spouses, 379
Efficiency, in thinking, 155
Effort, 155
Effort justification, 241–243
Egoistic helping, 314, 315
Egotism, 89, 104. *See also* Self-esteem
Eichmann, Adolf, 6
Einstein, Albert, 153, 166, 195
Ekman, Paul, 217
Elaboration likelihood model (ELM), 281–282
Elderly, A8, E18
Electronics, e-cycling of, A21
ELM (Elaboration likelihood model), 281–282
Embodied attitudes, 237
Emergencies, E4, E15–E18
    helping in, 321–325
Emodiversity, 200
Emotional infidelity, 441–442
Emotional intelligence (EI or EQ), 220–221, 222
Emotion and persuasive messages, 276
Emotions and affect, 186–228, 435
    anger (*See* Anger)
    appraisal theory of, 194
    arousal (*See* Arousal, emotional)
    and behavior, 210–211
    belongingness, 209
    chronic negative affect, B16
    control of, 222–224
    and culture, 44, 217
    decisions and, 213–215
    defined, 188–189
    depression, 96, 210–211, 224, 523
    disgust, 58, 206–208, 215
    fear, 276, 277, 469
    guilt (*See* Guilt)
    happiness (*See* Happiness)
    helping behavior and, 320
    mood (*See* Mood)
    negative, 215–216
    positive, 215–216
    power and, 522–523
    purpose of, 208–216
    regulation of, 222–224
    rejection and, 390–391
    sadness, 210–211, 215
    self-esteem and, 95, 100
    shame, 204
    social functions, 57
    social information and, 209–210
    of suicidal people, 143
    thinking and learning, 212–213
    uniqueness to human beings, 225–226
Empathy, 210, 218, 313–314, 410
Empathy-altruism hypothesis, 314–315
Employees and employment. *See* Work and workplace
Endowment effect, 90–91
Energy conservation, E13–E15, E19–E20
Energy sources, E4

England
    children in World War II, 415
    murder rates, 335–336
Entity theorists, 123–124
Environment. *See also* Environmental problems; Nature
    aggression, effect on, 355
    consumer behavior influences, A6–A8
    tradeoffs, 62
    of workplace, C16–C19
Environmentally-conscious products, 108, A2, A5
Environmental problems, E1–E24
    attitude and behavioral changes, E18–E19
    barriers to solving, E4–E5
    costs and benefits of protection, E21
    natural disasters, E15–E18
    overpopulation, E6–E9
    overview of, E2–E4
    quality of environment, E10–E13
    scarcity of natural resources, E13–E15
Environmental protection, E21
Environmental psychology, A7
EQ (emotional intelligence), 220–221, 222
Equality, 296, 517
Equity, 296
Erikson, Erik, 417
Eros, 339
Erotic plasticity, 247, 432–433, 444
Error, margin of, 26
Error management theory, 121
Errors in thinking. *See* Biases and errors
Escape options, 126
Eskimos, 440
ESP (extrasensory perception), 167
Estimator variables, D4–D7
Ethical issues, research, 20–21
Ethnicity. *See* Race and ethnicity
Ethnographic approach, A3
Eustress, C27
Evacuations, E16
Evaluation apprehension, 504, 505
Evolution, 38–40
    altruistic punishment, 508
    of brain size, 42
    cooperation and competition, 303, 305
    decision making, 180
    and emotions, 210, 211
    fairness, 296
    helping behavior, 313–314
    homosexuality, 435–436
    jealousy, 441–442
    prejudice and, 467
    selfishness and, 59
    self-knowledge, 86
    sexuality, 427–428, 429, 437–438
    and suicide, 143
Evolutionary theory, 429–430
Exchange relationships, 414–415
Excitation transfer, 192–193, 343
Exclusion. *See* Rejection
Executive function, 71, 72, 307
Exercise, 222, 223
    and aggression, 343
    for anger management, 203
Exotic becomes erotic (EBE), 435
Experiment, defined, 19
Experimental philosophy, 13
Experimental realism, 23

Experimental studies, 19–22
    design flaws, 28
    early, 5
    ethical issues, 20–21
    field experiments, 22–23
    laboratory experiments, 22–23
Expertise, 273
Expert testimony, D13
Explicit attitudes, 233
Externality, E21
External Motivation to Respond Without Prejudice, 481–482
External validity, 23, 28
Extradyadic sex, 437–439, 442–444
Extramarital sex, 437–439, 442–444
Extrasensory perception (ESP), 167
Extraversion, 11
Extrinsic motivation, 84–85, 125–126
Eyewitness memory, D3–D13
    confidence of, D6–D7
    estimator variables, D4–D7
    events, characteristics of, D5–D6
    eyewitnesses, characteristics of, D4–D5
    persuasiveness of, D11–D13
    system variables, D7–D10
    testimony, characteristics of, D6–D7

F

Facebook, 176, 210
Facial expression-emotion link, 217
Facial expressions, 217
Facial feedback hypothesis, 190–191
Facilitating thought, 221
Failure, 102–103, 162–163
Fairness, 294, 296–298
    evolution of, 296
    in relationships, 414
    stress and, C26
Fake news, 260, 363
False consensus effect, 176, 179
False (mistaken) identification, D3
False uniqueness effect, 176–177, 179
Familiarity, 383–384
Families. *See also* Marriage; Parents and parenting
    loneliness caused by separation from, 394
    rejection in, 390, 397
    similarity in, 378
Family-friendly employment practice, C28
Family violence, 349. *See also* Domestic violence
Fascism, 502. *See also* Nazi Germany
Fast-approaching-deadline technique, 270
Fast talking and persuasiveness, 275
Favorability *vs.* plausibility tradeoff, 108
Favors, 380
FBI (U.S. Federal Bureau of Investigation), 335
Fear, 469
    as persuasion tactic, 276, 277
Fearful avoidant attachment, 417
Fear of success theory, 141
Feedback
    belief perseverance and, 249–250
    energy conservation role, E19–E20
    facial feedback hypothesis, 191–192
    and self-esteem, 97
    self-knowledge from, 80–81
Feedback loop, 135
Feelings. *See* Emotions and affect
Feminism, 428, 470

Festinger, Leon, 241, 242
Field experiments, 22–23
Fierce resolve, 517
Fight or flight syndrome, 346, B4–B5
Fillers, D3
Filter bubble, 245
Fipa people, 468
First instinct fallacy, 178
Fischer, Maureen, 252
Flexible work schedule, C6, C28
Flipper, Henry, 390
Flukes, 16, 22
Fogelman, Eva, 317
Food, 63. *See also* Eating
Food pyramid, B14
Foot-in-the-door technique, 264–265
Ford, Henry, 496–497, 501, 517, 524, A2
Ford Motor Company, 496–497, 500–501
Forecasting, affective, 213–214
Forewarning about persuasion tactics, 285
Forgiveness, 305–307
Framing, 158
Freedom of action, 124–126
Free rider problem, 505–506, 507–508
Free will, 124–126
French culture, 43
Freud, Sigmund, 141, 334, 339, 341, 342
Freudian psychoanalysis, 7, 8
Friedman, Arthur, C2, C6, C21, C24–C25
Friendship. *See also* Relationships
    formation of, 383
    ideal number of friends, 377
    reciprocation of liking, 381
    self-presentation, 108
Fromm, Erich, 359
Frustration, 17, 342
Frustration-aggression theory, 18, 23, 342, 467
Frustration and Aggression (Dollard, et al.), 342
Fujimoto, Shun, 74, 75
Fundamental attribution error, 164–165, 321
Future self-concept, 86

G

Gain-framed appeals, 158
Gallup poll, 25–26
Galton, Francis, 177, 511
Gambler's fallacy, 175, 179
Gambling, 216, 253
"Gay gene," 428, 435, 436. *See also* Homosexuality
Gender and gender differences
    academic performance, 488
    aggression, 343, 346–347
    anti-gay prejudice, 464
    attraction, 385–386
    belongingness, 377
    binary, challenges to, 436
    brain size, 42
    cooperation, 305
    cultural differences, 47
    depression, 224
    domestic violence, 349–350
    eating, 434
    emotional expression, 217–218
    emotion control strategies, 224
    evolutionary theory on, 40, 429–430
    extramarital sex, 437, 443
    eyewitness memory, D4
    in goal setting, 127–128
    helpfulness, 318

    homosexual experiences, 433
    jealousy, 442
    loneliness, 395
    love, 218
    marriage and, 422
    organizational citizenship behaviors and, C29
    personal space, E8
    self-esteem, 95
    sexual aggression, 350
    sexual behavior, 121, 172, 247, 431–434, 444–445
    socialization and, 36–37
    in social support, B8
    stalking, 398
    stereotypes based on, 473–474, 484
    stress response, B7
    violence, 346–347
General adaptation syndrome, B5–B6
Generalized other, 80
Generalized reciprocity, 298
A General Theory of Crime (Gottfredson & Hirschi), 358
Genetic factors, 429, 435–436. *See also* Nature
    for marriage, 423
Genocide, in Rwanda, 332–334, 342
Genovese, Kitty, 321
Geo-targeting, A16
Gesch, Bernard, 357
Gifts and gift giving, A15, C18–C19
Gilbert, Dan, 213
Girard, Joe, 380, 381
Glamour magazine poll, 26
Globalization, A17, C19
Global warming, 355
Goals, 127–131, 197
    vs. habits, 139–140
    hierarchy of, 129–130
    multiple, 130–131
    self-awareness and, 78
    setting, 127–129
Goal shielding, 130–131
Gone With the Wind, 434
Good Samaritan parable, 324–325
Google, C16, C19–C20
Gossip, 303–305
Gottfredson, Michael, 358–359
Gratification, delay of, 60, 142
Gratitude, 296
Greed, 469
Green market segment, A5
Green products, 108
Group norms, 262–263
Group polarization effect, 515–516
Groups, 494–529
    actions of, 503–509
    attitude polarization, 239–240
    conformity, 310
    defined, 498–501
    diversity in, 500
    expulsion from, 397
    intergroup relations (*See* Intergroup relations)
    leadership, 517–521, 526–527, C21–C22
    marriages as, 499
    membership in and loneliness, 395
    need to belong and, 377
    power, 521–526
    prosocial behavior of, 295, 309–310
    rejection in, 396

roles, 501–503
  thinking of, 510–516
  unity of, 498
  in workplace, 376, C19–C21
Group selection, 59
Group sex, 499
Groupthink, 512, 513–514
Guilt, 59, 188, 204–206
  anticipated, 213
  from being overbenefited, 297
  defined, 204
  effects of, 204–205
  and leadership, 518
  littering and, 366
  and rejection, 399
  and relationships, 205–206, 421
  self-blame and, 251
  and sexual arousal, 193
  vs. shame, 204
  washing away, 205
Guns, 352–353

H

Habits, 139–140
Halo effect, 275–276, 384
Hamilton, Dawn, C2
Hand washing, 105, 206, 310
Hangry, 203
Hanks, Tom, 395
Happiness, 195–200
  in close relationships, 423–425
  constant, 199
  defined, 195–196
  hedonic treadmill, 197–198
  increasing, 198–199
  marriage and, 422–423
  pursuit of, 200
  roots of, 196–197, 198
  rule of law and, 294
HARKing (Hypothesizing After the Results are Known), 29
Harm appraisals, B6
Harvard Business Review, A5
Hate media, 332, 333, 354
Head scarves, 457
Health, 274, B1–B19
  crowding and, E3
  defined, B2
  disgust reaction and, 207
  domestic violence risks, 349
  framing of messages about, 158
  happiness impact, 198–199
  improvement approaches, B9–B14
  loneliness and, 377, 396
  marriage and, 423
  self-esteem impact, 103
  self-presentation and, 109
  stress (*See* Stress)
Health belief model, B10–B11
Health psychology, B3
Healthy behaviors, B9–B14
Hearing, 62–63
Heart disease, 203
Heat, 355, E3, E11
Hedonic treadmill, 197–198
Hee, Kim Hyun, 116–117
Heider, Fritz, 162, 165
Height and discrimination, 453
Helpful personality, 317–318

Helping, 294. *See also* Prosocial behavior
  bystander effect, 321–325
  contagious quality of, 292–293
  increasing, 326
  likeliness of, 317–320
  reasons for, 313–317
Herd instinct, 376
Heroic acts, 318
Heuristic processing, 281
Heuristics, 153, 166–169, 170
  anchoring and adjustment, 168–169
  availability heuristic, 167
  defined, 166
  representativeness heuristic, 166–167, 169, 175
  scarcity heuristic, 269–270
  simulation heuristic, 168
  stereotypes as, 471–472, 473
Heuristic/systematic model, 281
Hierarchy of goals, 129–130
High-context cultures, E9
High-empathy people, 315
Higher purpose, belief in, 252
Hill, Anita, C10
Hilton, C3, C16, C28
Hindsight bias, 15, 29
Hiring process, C8–C14. *See also* Work and workplace
Hirschi, Travis, 358–359
History, 10
  of social psychology, 5–7
Hit (correct identification), D3
Hitler, Adolf, 6, 359, 360, 459, 520
HIV/AIDS, 277, 362, B12
Hoarding, A14–A15
Hofstadter, Douglas, 178
Holmes, John, 426
Holmes, Sherlock, 167
Holocaust, 7, 317, 361, 459
Homeostasis, B4
Homogeneity of groups, C19
Homophobia, 463
  and homosexual feelings, 193
Homosexuality, 435–436
  attachment and sexuality, 428
  attitudes toward, 193, 247
  gender differences, 433
  prejudice, 462–465, 467
Honesty, 425–427
Honor, culture of, 360–361
Honor killings, 361
Hormones, 356–357, 374–375
Horner, Matina, 141
Hostile aggression, 335
Hostile attribution bias, 344–345
Hostile expectation bias, 345
Hostile perception bias, 344–345
Hostile work environment, C10
Hotez, Peter, 151
Hot hand, 175, 179
Hot temperatures, E3, E11
Hourglass figures, 385
Houston, Sam, 360
Hovland, Carl, 272–273, 276, 279
Humans as cultural animals, 65
  antisocial behavior, 367
  attitudes, 254–455
  attraction, 400
  choice and actions, 145
  close relationships, 446–447

  consumer behavior, A22–A23
  emotions, 225–226
  environmental problems, E22–E23
  groups, 527–528
  health, B18
  intergroup relations, 490–491
  laws, D20
  prosocial behavior, 327–328
  rejection, 400
  self, 110–111
  social cognition, 181–182
  social influence, 286
  work and workplace, C32
Human zoos, 452
Humiliation, 361, 439–440
Humility, 108, 517
Humor, 222, 224, 276
Hurricanes, 474, E16
Hurt feelings, 391
Hydraulic model of aggression, 339
Hypochondriacs, B16
Hypocrisy, 106
Hypocrisy induction, E20
Hypothesis, 16, 17, 28
Hypothesizing After the Results are Known (HARKing), 29

I

Idealization, 425–427
Ideas and culture, 43–44, 58
Identity, 107–108, 502
Identity theft, 365
Ifaluk people, 468
Ignorance, 469–470, 472
Illness. *See also* Mental illness
  attributions and, B16
  behavior and attitudes in cultures with more disease, 49
  cancer, 251–252, B2
  confirmation bias, B15–B16
  disgust reaction and, 207
  heart disease, 203
  loneliness and, 377
  personality and, B16–B17
  vaccinations and, 150–151, E3
Illusion of control, 178, 179
Illusions, 96–97, 128
Illusory correlations, 173–174, 179, B15–B16
Imagination, 117–118
Imitation and learning, 238
Immoral actions, 299. *See also* Morality
Implicit attitudes, 233, 479
Implicit personality theories, D15
Impressions, 106–107
Impulses, 59–60
Impulsive system of the mind, 53. *See also* Automatic system of the mind
Incorrect rejection, D3
Incremental theorists, 123–124
Independent self-construal, 73–74
Independent variables, 17, 19
Indirect aggression, 334
Individual good-collective bad trap, E2, E3
Individualism, 49, 108, 164
Industrial and organizational (I/O) psychology, C3–C7
Inequality, 509, 526
Infants, 218, 381. *See also* Children
Infidelity, 437–444

Subject Index | S-7

Influence. *See* Social influence
Information, 46, 63–64
Informational influence, 262–263
Information processing, self and, 90–93
Ingratiation, 378, 380
Ingroup favoritism, 466
Ingroup members, 455
Inhibition orientation to power, 523–525
Initiative, 98, 102
Injunctive norms, 366
Inner processes serving interpersonal relations theory, 57–58
    choices and actions, 117, 125
    emotions, 194–195, 209
    forgiveness, 307
    prejudice and stereotyping, 475–478
    self-awareness, 77
    self-esteem, 100
Inoculation of attitudes, 283–285
Instinct, 338–339
    defined, 339
    first instinct fallacy, 178
    herd instinct, 376
Institutional Review Board (IRB), 20, 21
Instrumental aggression, 335
Instrumental conditioning, 238
Intelligence
    of audience, 279
    emotional intelligence, 220–221, 222
    of groups, 510–512
    rejection and, 391
    self-fulfilling prophecies, 485
    sex partner choice and, 430
    of spouses, 379
    stereotype threat and, 488
    stereotyping and, 477–478
Intentions, behavioral, 155, 248
Interdependent self-construal, 73–74
Intergroup relations, 450–493. *See also* Discrimination; Prejudice; Stereotypes
Internalization, 93
Internal Motivation to Respond Without Prejudice, 481–482
Internal validity, 19
Internet
    addiction to, A19
    e-commerce, A12–A13, A16–A17
    energy saving and, E15
    job candidates, searching on, C12
    sex for sale on, A19
    social connections, 374
    social media (*See* Social media)
Interpersonal attraction. *See* Attraction
Interpersonal self, 71, 72
Interpretation and helping, 321–322
Interracial dating, 457
Interventions, B9
Interviews, C13–C14
Intimacy, 410–411, 412
    attachment and, 416–417
    sexuality and, 428 (*See also* Sexuality and sexual behavior)
    in Sternberg's triangle of love, 410
Intimate-partner violence, 349–350
Intrinsic motivation, 84–85, 103, 125–126
Introspection, 81–82
Introversion, 11
Intuition, 15, 55
Inverted U-shaped relationship, 276, 279

Investment model, 421–422
Invulnerability, 514
I/O (industrial and organizational) psychology, C3–C7
iPhone, A17
IRB (Institutional Review Board), 20, 21
Ironic processes, 159
Irrational behavior, 140–145
Irrational beliefs, 253
Irrational bets, 118–120
Islam. *See* Muslims

J

Jackson, Reggie, 84
Jains, 468
James, William, 117, 156, 190
James-Lange Theory of Emotion, 190–191
Jankowiak, William, 408–409
Japan, 51, 74, 108, 123
Jealousy, 439–444
    causes of, 442–443
    cultural perspective of, 440
    evolutionary perspective of, 441–442
Jefferson, Thomas, 203
Jews and Judaism, 474, 476, 487. *See also* Holocaust
    prejudice against, 458–460
Jigsaw classroom, 483
Job analysis, C9
Job interviews, C13–C14
Jobs. *See also* Work and workplace
    most respected, C5
    types of, C6–C7
Job satisfaction, C24–C25, C26, C30–C31
Job withdrawal, C29
Jones, Edward E., 12, 378
Jones, Jim, 265
Jones, Warren, 373
Junk food, 357
Juries, D11–D18
Just world, belief in, 318–320

H

Kagame, Paul, 333
Kahneman, Daniel, 55
Kamilindi, Thomas, 332, 333
Kant, Immanuel, 386
Kierkegaard, Søren, 15
King, Martin Luther, Jr., 335, 484
Kin selection, 313
"Knew it all along" phenomenon, 15
Knowledge, 49–50
    persuasion and, 281
    of self (*See* Self-knowledge)
Knowledge structures, 155
Koch, Ed, 86
Kosinski, Jerzy, 500
!Kung people, 468
Kunz, Phil, 295–296

L

Labeling technique, 266
Laboratory experiments, 22–23
Landon, Alf, 25, 26
Lange, Carl, 190
Language, 46, 49
Last National Bank, 484–485
Latané, Bibb, 321
Lateral cycling, A20–A21
Laughter, 526

Law, D1–D21
    and employment, C9–C10
    eyewitness memory, D3–D13
    jury selection, D14–D16
    pretrial publicity, D17–D18
    rule of law, 294
    system reforms, suggestions for, D10–D13
    tradeoffs, 62
    wrongful convictions, D19
Law of least effort, 471
Lazarus, Richard, B6
Lazarus' Cognitive-Mediational Theory, 191
Lead, E12
Leadership, 517–521, 526–527, C21–C22
Learned helplessness, 124, E11
Learning, 238–239, 339–340
    aggression, theories of, 339–340
    emotions and, 212–213
Leary, Mark, 100
Le Bon, Gustave, 511
Legal system. *See* Law
Legitimization-of-paltry-favors technique, 267
Legitimizing myths, 526
LePage, Anthony, 352
Lewin, Kurt, 6, 12, 14
Lewis, John, 478
LGBTQ+ individuals, 462–465, 484
Liberal bias, 490
Liberals, moral foundation of, 300
Life, prolonging, 39
Life satisfaction, 196
Likability, of sources, 274–276
Liking, 381–382. *See also* Attraction
Limited-number technique, 270
Lineups, D3, D7–D10
    administrator knowledge of, D9–D10
    fillers for, D7–D8
    instructions, D9
Literary Digest poll, 25
Littering, 366
Loneliness, 373–374, 394–396
    health impact, 377, 396
    of powerful people, 521
    trust and, 312
Long-distance relationships, 377
Long-term goals, 129–130
Long-term relationships, 419–427
Looking-glass self, 80–81, 92
Lorenz, Konrad, 339
Loss-framed appeals, 158
Lost letter study, 457–458
Lotteries and happiness, 197
Love, 407–415
    companionate love, 408
    culture and, 408–409
    gender differences, 218
    lying for, 362
    passionate love, 408
    of self, 417–419
    sex separated from, 432
    and sexual intimacy, 428
    Sternberg's triangle, 410–412
    unrequited love, 382, 397–399
Low-ball technique, 265–266
Low-context cultures, E9
Low-empathy people, 315
Luckin Coffee, A5
Lying, 362–363
Lynching, 476

M

Machiavellianism, 221, 348
Maintenance stage of transtheoretical model, B12, B13
Malay culture, 358
Malle, Bertram, 165
Managing emotions, 221
Manhood, 385
    cultural concepts of, 48
Margin of error, 26
Market failure, E21
Marriage
    commuter marriages, 377
    forgiveness in, 306–307
    genetic factors for, 423
    as a group, 499
    happiness and, 422–423
    idealization of spouse, 426
    infidelity, 437–444
    loneliness in, 395
    long-distance, 377
    love as basis for, 409–410
    of Prince Charles and Princess Diana, 406–407, 410, 422, 425, 437, 438–439
    self and, 73
    sexual behavior in, 409–410, 411, 432
    similarity of couple's characteristics, 379
    in Victorian period, 426–427
Maslow, Abraham, 417
Mass media. *See also* Social media; Television
    aggression and, 332, 333, 346, 353–355
    dissonance theory and, 244–245
    framing of stories, 158
    illusory correlations by, 174
    prejudice against Muslims, 458
Matching hypothesis, 378, 379
Match-to-culprit description, D8
Match-to-suspect strategy, D8
Mathematics, 488
Mayer, John, 220–221
McGuire, William, 279, 283–284
Mead, George Herbert, 80
Mead, Margaret, 440
Meade, David, 252
Meaning, 117–124, 125, 127
    choices, making, 118–121
    choices, not making, 121–123
    freedom to change, 123–124
Measles, mumps, and rubella (MMR) vaccine, 150–151
Media. *See* Mass media; Social media
Mein Kampf (Hitler), 459
Mellett, Lowell, 272
Memory, 93, 513
    of eyewitnesses, D3–D13
    priming, 156–157
    recovered memory, D19
    self-esteem and, 97
Men. *See also* Gender and gender differences
    brain size, 42
    disgust reaction, 207
    domestic violence and, 349–350
    emotional control strategies, 224
    emotional expression, 217–218
    goal setting, 127–128
    self-esteem, 95
    sexual arousal, 193, 214
    testosterone and aggression, 356
    urination delay study, 20–21

Menstrual periods, 93
Mental illness, 105–106, 222
    depression, 96, 210–211, 224, 523
    leaders with, 520
    in the mass media, 174
    passionate love as, 409
Mental shortcuts. *See* Heuristics
Mentoring, C17–C18
Mere exposure effect, 236–237, 383–384
Messages
    one-sided *vs.* two-sided messages, 276–278
    overheard messages, 278
    reason *vs.* emotion, 276
    repetition, 278–279
Meta-analysis, 24, 28, D4
Meta-cognition, 181
Methodology, 15–27
    accumulated common wisdom, 15
    common wisdom, 15
    research design, 18–27
    scientific method, 9, 13, 16
    scientific theories, 16–18
    theories, 16–18
Mexico, sleep patterns in, 51
Milgram, Stanley, 6–7, 308–309, 458
Milgram experiments, 308–309
Military
    bonding in, 383
    eyewitness memory, D5
    morale of soldiers, 272
Miller, Neal, 342
Mimicking, 381
Mind-sets and goals, 128
Minimal group effect, 466
Minorities. *See* Race and ethnicity
Mirrors, and self-awareness, 76, 77
Misattribution of arousal, 192–194
Misattributions, B16
Mischel, Walter, 142
Missing hero trap, E2
Mistaken identification, D3
MMR (measles, mumps, and rubella) vaccine, 150–151
Mob violence, 508
Modeling, 326–327, 339
Modesty, 89, 108, 517
Money
    antisocial behavior and, 364
    cognitive dissonance and, 242
    cultural significance of, 45
    decision-making impact, 119
    emotional decisions, 215
    environmental problems, E21
    happiness and, 197
    laughter and, 526
    manhood and, 385
    motivation for making, 84
    priming with, 158
    prosocial behavior and, 306
    questionable behavior for, 242
    self-sufficiency and, 306
    sexual attraction based on, 442
    social acceptance and, 63
    in sports teams, 454
Monitoring, 135–136, 279, 379
Monogamy, 446
Mood, 188, 222–224
    aggression and, 342–343
    bad mood effects, 199
    eating and, 211

    good mood benefits, 216
    helping behavior and, 320
    persuasion receptivity and, 276
Moral intuitions, 299
Morality, 59, 298–301
    environmental issues, E20
    self-presentation and, 108
    sexuality, 444–445
Moral judgment, 299–300
Moral reasoning, 299, E20
Moral superiority, 514
Moral traits, 382–383
Morgenthau, Hans, 521
Morning morality effect, 299
Motivation, 125–126
    for aggression, 334–335
    and goals, 127
    guilt as, 204–205
    for helping, 314–315
    for overcoming prejudice, 481–482
    self-perception and, 84–85
Mugabe, Robert, 518–519, 521, 525
Mundane realism, 23
Murder rates, 337
    in England, 335–336
Murray, Sandra, 426
Music, 326
    consumer behavior effects, A6
    group connection and, 57–58
    at work, C17
Muslims, 397
    prejudice against, 457–458
Mutations, 40

N

Napoleon Bonaparte, 520, 521
Narcissism
    aggression and, 102, 348, 360
    close relationships and, 418–419
    forgiveness, 307
    high self-esteem and, 101–102
    inflated self-knowledge and, 87
    leadership and, 518
Narcissists, 123, 221, 418–419, 505
Nassetta, Chris, C3, C6, C21–C22
National Health and Social Life Survey, 350, 437
National Violence Against Women Survey, 398
Natural disasters, E4, E15–E18
Natural resources, scarcity of, E13–E15
Natural selection, 39–40, 61
Nature
    aggression, 341
    behavior from, 58–59
    culture and, 47–49
    defined, 38
    eating habits, 46
    and evolution, 38–40
    homosexuality and, 435–436
    prejudice and, 466
    sexuality and, 432–433
    social behavior and, 37–42
Nature-nurture debate
    aggression, 340–341
    children raised as different gender, 36–37
    consistency, drive for, 245
    criticisms of, 38
Nazi Germany, 6. *See also* Holocaust
    deindividuation in, 502
    and Jews, 459, 474, 476

Need for cognition, 279, 281
Need to belong, 373–376, 417, 513
Negative attitude change, 285
Negative emotions or affect, 188–189, 215–216, 342–343. See also Anger; Fear
Negotiations, 199, 202
Nervous system, B5
Netnography, A3
Networks, 44
Neuroscience, 7, 10
Neuroticism, B16
Neurotransmitters, 356–357, 408
Neutral stimulus, 237
Night and Fog, 216
1984 (Orwell), 513
Nisbett, Richard, 81–82
Noise, A7, E4, E11–E12
Noncontingent success, 89
Nonexperimental studies, 23–25
Non-prejudiced people, 480
Nonverbal communication, E6
Non-zero-sum game, 305
Normative commitment, C25–C26
Normative influence, 261–262, 263
Norms, 296, 366
    aggression and, 358
    of fairness, 296–298
    group norms, 262–263
    of reciprocity, 295–296
    subjective norms, 248
Numbness, 391

O

Obama, Barack, 234, 479
Obedience, 294, 307–310
    as justification for inflicting pain, 6–7
Obesity, 461
Objective predictors of happiness, 196–197, 198
Observable variables, 17
Observational learning, 238
OCBs (organizational citizenship behaviors), C29, C30
Occupational Information Network (O*NET), C6–C7
Occupy movements, 509
Oil drilling, 13
Oklahoma City bombing, D18
Omission bias, 122
One Day in the Life of Ivan Denisovich (Solzhenitzyn), 195
One-person trap, E2, E3
One-shot illusory correlation, 174
One-sided messages, 276–278
O*NET (Occupational Information Network), C6–C7
Online dating, 319, 387–388
Online shopping, A5, A12–A13, A16–A17
Online virtual memorials, A3
Open relationships, 437, 438
Open science, 29
Operant conditioning, 238, 241
Operational definitions, 18
Opposites attract, 378
Oppression, rationalizations for, 470, 472
Optimism
    and illness, B17
    over-optimism, 96, 132–133
Options, keeping open, 120–121

Organizational citizenship behaviors (OCBs), C29, C30
Organizational climate, C5
Organizational commitment, C25–C26, C30
Organizational culture, C5–C6
Organizational justice, C26–C27
Organizational socialization, C15
Organizational withdrawal, C29–C30
The Orville, 232
Orwell, George, 513
Ostracism, 389–390
Outback Steakhouse, 311
Outgroup homogeneity bias, 455–456
Outgroup members, 455
Outperformers, 297
Overbenefited, 297
Overconsumption, A14–A15
Overheard messages, 278
Overjustification effect, 84–85
Overpopulation, E4, E6–E9
Overweight people, 461, 480
Ownership, A13
Own-race bias, D4–D5
Ozone, E12

P

Pain of rejection, 391
The Painted Bird (Kosinski), 500
Panic button effect, 126
Parasympathetic nervous system (PNS), B5
Parents and parenting
    attachment, 416, 417
    emotional bonds, 200
    happiness of, 196–197
    punishment, 350–351
    sleeping with children, 51
Parikh, Rahul, 150–151
Parking lot field experiment, 22–23
Passion, 410, 411–412
Passionate love, 408, 409–410. See also Close relationships
    vs. companionate love, 408
    cultural differences, 408–409
    Sternberg's triangle of love theory, 411
    view of lover, 425–426
Paternity tests, 437, 444
Paternity uncertainty, 444
Pathogens and culture, 48–49
Patterson, Orlando, 478
Pavlov, Ivan, 237
Pay It Forward, 292
PEA (phenylethylamine), 408
Peer pressure, 99
Peoples Temple cult, 265
Pepsi-Cola, A9
Perceived behavioral control, 248
Perceived support, B8
Perceiving emotions, 221
Peremptory challenges, D15
Performance, 219–220
    CEO's impact on, 517
    of teams, 512–513
Performance reviews, C22–C23
Peripheral cues, 282
Peripheral route, 281, 282
Persistence, 102–103, 517
Personality
    for aggression, 348
    happiness and, 198

    helpful, 317–318
    illness and symptoms, B16–B17
    jury selection, D16
Personality psychology, 11–12
Personalization, E8
Personal relevance, 281
Personal space, E6–E7
Persuasion, 272–283
    audience, 279–280
    defined, 272–273
    eyewitness memory, D11–D13
    messages, 276–278
    models of, 280–282
    resistance to, 283–285
    sources, 273–276
Pets, 395. See also Animals
Phelps, Michael, 83
Phenomenal self, 84–85
Phenylethylamine (PEA), 408
Philosophy, 13
Phobias, 463
Physical aggression, 334. See also Aggression
Physical attractiveness. See Attractiveness
Physiological psychology, 10
Piaroa people, 468
Pinker, Steven, 336
Pique technique, 271
Pitt, Brad, 273
Plagiarism, 365
Planned behavior theory, 248, B11
Planning, 131–133
Planning fallacy, 132
Plastic bags, A10
Plausibility *vs.* favorability tradeoff, 108
Pluralistic ignorance, 263, 322
PNS (parasympathetic nervous system), B5
Point of purchase perceptions, A11–A15
Polarization
    of attitudes, 239–240
    of group, 515–516
Political correctness, 481–482
Political issues and attitudes, 276–278
    American beliefs and practices, 44
    on environmental problems, E5
    and morality, 300
    polling, 25–26
    self-presentation, 107–108
    of social psychologists, 13–14
    stereotypes, 474
    tradeoffs, 62
Political science, 10
Polls, election, 25–26
Pollution, E4, E12–E13
Polychronic activity, A18
Polygamy, 499
Polygraph, 363
Poor people, laughter and, 526
Population, 26, E2–E3, E6–E9
Positive affect or emotions, 188–189, 215–216. See also Happiness
Positive illusions, 96–97, 128
Positive psychology movement, 198
Possessiveness, 439–444
Post-consumption process, A20–A21
Post-decision dissonance, 243
Post-traumatic stress disorder (PTSD), E17
Power, 521–526
    preserving, 525
Praise, 380

Praxis, 45
Prayer, 222
Precarious manhood, 48
Precontemplation stage of transtheoretical model, B11, B12
Predictability, in cognitive appraisal model, B7
Pregnancy, 429–430, 441
   of prison inmates, 62
Prejudice, 457–464
   as affective component of intergroup relations, 453
   in America, 478–479, 480
   against atheists, 460
   competition and, 467–469
   contact hypothesis, 469–470, 482–483
   content of, 473–475
   defined, 453
   disgust reaction and, 207
   explanations for, 465–473
   impact of, 484–489
   inner processes behind, 475–478
   against Jews, 458–460
   against LGBTQ+ individuals, 462–465
   against Muslims, 457–458
   against obese people, 461, 480
   overcoming, 481–482
   racial prejudice, 234, 453, 454, 457, 479–482
   rationalizations for, 471
   reduction of, 478–483
   self-esteem and, 102, 472
   socialization and, 465–466
   societal objections to, 454
Premarital sex, 444–445
Preoccupied attachment, 416
Preparation stage of transtheoretical model, B12, B13
Pretrial publicity, D17–D18
Pride and aggression, 359–360
Primary appraisals, B6
Primary territories, E9
Prime the pump, 156
Priming, 156–157, 158
The Prince of Tides (Conroy), 393
Prisoner's dilemma, 302, 303, 304–305
   and power, 522
   trust in, 311–312
Prisons and prisoners, 62, 95–96, 357, 374
Private acceptance, 263
Private condition, 295
Private ownerships, 509
Private self-awareness, 76
Private self-consciousness, 78, 79
Privileged access, 81, 83
Proactive aggression, 335
Procrastination, 143
Product, human beings as, A19
Product misuse, A19
Product placement, 278
Profits and corporations, 461–462
Prompts, E14
Propinquity, 383–384
Propitious heterogeneity, D8
Prosocial behavior, 290–329
   altruism, 315–316
   bystander effect, 321–325
   conformity, 310
   cooperation, 302–305
   defined, 293–298
   depression and, 210–211
   fairness, 294, 296–298
   forgiveness, 305–307
   increasing, 326
   likeliness of, 317–320
   morality, 298–301
   obedience, 307–310
   organizational citizenship behaviors, C29, C30
   reasons for, 313–317
   reciprocity, 295–296
   trust, 310–312
Prototype-willingness model, B13–B14
Proximal goals, 129–130
Psyche, 37–38, 63
Psychoanalysis, 7, 8
Psychological reactance theory, 22, 270, 285, 354, 366
Psychology, 10–11
Psychopathy, 221, 348
PTSD (post-traumatic stress disorder), E17
Public compliance, 263
Public condition, 295
Public image, concern for, 279–280
Public self, 72
Public self-awareness, 76
Public self-consciousness, 78, 79
Public settings, and prosocial behavior, 326
Public territories, E9
Punishment, 523
   of children, 350–351
   of social loafers, 507–508
Purity and disgust, 208
Putting people first, 62–64, 82
   and attitude polarization, 78
   self-awareness and, 78
   self-knowledge, 80, 88

Q

Quadricycle, 496
Quasi-experiments, 19
Quatro, Charles John, 173
Quid pro quo, C10

R

Race and ethnicity
   peremptory challenges based on, D16
   phenomenal self, 85–86
   research issues, 20–21
   scapegoat theory, 476
   self-esteem, 95
Racism, 457
   attitudes about, 234
   conscious override, 479–482
   defined, 453
   in sports, 454
Radio, A4
Random assignment, 19, 22, 23
Random sample, 26
Rape, 333, 350, 354
Rational bets, 118–120
Reactance, 22, 270, 285, 366
Reactance theory, 122–123
Reactive aggression, 335
Realism in experiments, 23
Realistic conflict theory, 467
Reality, 96
Reality shows, 372, 381–382
Real self, 72–73
Reason and persuasive messages, 276
Received support, B8
Receptivity, 279
Reciprocity, 268–269, 295–296
   of animals, 297
   cooperation, 302
   defined, 295
   energy conservation promotion, E14
   in exchange relationships, 414, 415
   liking and, 381–382
Recovered memory, D19
Recruitment of employees, C11–C13
Recycling, 366, A21
Referrals, employee, C11
Reflective system of the mind, 53. *See also* Deliberate system of the mind
Regression to the mean, 177
Regret, 179
   anticipated, 122, 214
Reinforcement histories, 8–9
Reinforcement theory, 380
Rejection, 389–399
   defined, 373
   effects of, 390–393
   ostracism, 389–390
   reasons for, 396–397
   and social influence, 262
Rejection sensitivity, 391
Relational aggression, 347
Relationship-enhancing style of attribution, 423–424
Relationship orientation, 518
Relationships
   attraction (*See* Attraction)
   belongingness, 209, 373–376
   close relationships (*See* Close relationships)
   communal relationships, 414–415
   emotions in, 209
   exchange relationships, 414–415
   forgiveness, 306–307
   friendship, 108, 377, 381, 383
   guilt and, 204–205, 421
   happiness and, 197
   loneliness and, 394–396
   maintaining, 419–427
   narcissists, 101–102
   self-esteem and, 102
   self-presentation, 108
   social allergy effect, 383–384
Relative age effect, 47–48
Relevance, and persuasion impact, 281
Reliability, 26–27, C13
Relief workers, E17
Religion, 108, 222
   beliefs, 250–252
   brainwashing, 249
   forgiveness, 307
   sexual behavior and, 433
Renewable energy, E21
Rennard, Stephen, 17
Repetition, 278–279
Repetition with variation, 279
Replication, 28
Replication crisis, 28
Representativeness heuristic, 166–167, 169, 175
Reproduction and evolution, 39, 40, 41, 296, 429–430
Republican business leaders, 300

Research, 19–22, 25–27
    ethical issues, 20–21
    laboratory and field experiments, 22–23
    nonexperimental studies, 23–25
Resistance to social influence, 283–285
Responsibility, diffusion of, 323
Restaurants and conformity, 311
Retail stores, A5–A6
Retaliation, 349
Revenge, 213–214
Reverse discrimination, 481, 490
Reverse double standard, 445
Reverse psychology, 122
Rewards, 349
    attraction and, 380
    overjustification effect, 84–85
    power and, 523
Rhetoric (Aristotle), 273, 276
Ringelmann, Max, 5, 505, 507
Risk-as-feelings hypothesis, 214
Risk aversion, 118–120
Risk images, B13–B14
Risky behavior
    of adolescents, B13–B14
    good mood impact, 216
    self-presentation impact, 109–110
    sexual arousal and, 214–215
    testosterone and, 375
Risky shift, 515–516
Road Rage, 188
Rogers, Carl, 417
Roles, 74–75, 501–503
Romantic love, 408. *See also* Passionate love
Romantic Passion: A Universal Experience? (Jankowiak), 408–409
Romantic Period, 408
Romantic relationships. *See* Close relationships
Roosevelt, Franklin D., 25, 26, 272
Rozin, Paul, 207
Rule breaking, 396–397
Rule of law, 294
Rules, in relationships, 415
Running amok, 358
Rusbult, Caryl, 421–422
Russell, Bill, 84
Russian roulette, 120
Rwanda genocide, 332–334, 342
Ryan, Richard, 125

S

Sadat, Anwar, 266
Sadism, 221, 343–344, 348
Sadness, 210–211, 215. *See also* Depression
Safe sex practices, 277, B12
Salience, 475
Salovey, Peter, 220–221
Same-sex marriage, 463, 467
Samoans, 440
Sanderson, Cael, 131
Sapolsky, Robert, 356
Satisfaction with relationship, 421
Scantlin, Melana, 372, 384
Scapegoat theory, 476
Scarcity, 269–270
    of natural resources, E13–E15
Scare tactics, for persuasion, 276
Schachter, Stanley, 192
Schachter-Singer theory of emotion, 191, 192, 435
Schemas, 155–156

Schoenthaler, Stephen, 357
Schools. *See* Education
Scientific method, 9, 13, 16
Scott, "Monster" Kody, 357
Scripts, 156
Secondary appraisals, B6
Secondary territories, E9
Secure attachment, 416
Selective confirmation, 426
Selective exposure, 244–245
Self, 68–113
    awareness of (*See* Self-awareness)
    censorship of, 514
    control of (*See* Self-control)
    creation of, 72–75
    defined, 71
    esteem of (*See* Self-esteem)
    fluctuating images of, 84–86
    handicapping of, 88–89, 141
    information processing and, 90–94
    knowledge of (*See* Self-knowledge)
    presentation of (*See* Self-presentation)
    purpose of, 71–72
    study of, 7
    uniqueness to human beings, 110–111
Self-acceptance, 419
Self-actualization, 417
Self-awareness, 71–72, 75–78, 110–111
    alcohol use, effect on, 356
    deindividuation and, 502
Self-awareness theory, 77
Self-blame, 251
Self-censorship, 514
Self-concept. *See* Self-knowledge
Self-concept confusion, 94
Self-consciousness, 279–280
Self-construal, 74
Self-control, 58–59. *See also* Self-regulation
    aggression and, 358–359
    forgiveness and, 307
    trust and, 312
Self-deception strategies, 96–97, 104
Self-defeating behavior, 140–143
Self-defeating prophecies, 487
Self-destructive behavior, 140–145
    suicide, 143–144
Self-determination theory, 125–126
Self-efficacy, B11
Self-enhancement motive, 87–88, 108
Self-esteem, 94–96
    aggression and, 359–360
    benefits of, 98–100
    changes in, 92
    close relationships and, 418–419
    depression and, 96
    high, 98–100, 101–103
    illness and, B17
    and persuasion, 279
    prejudice and, 102, 472, 486–487
    pursuit of, 103
    reality *vs.* illusions, 96–97
    sexual behavior and, 98, 99
Self-fulfilling prophecies, 484–485, B16
Self-handicapping, 88–89, 141
Self-interest, 59, 60
Selfishness, 313–314
    aggression and, 348–249
    rejection and, 392
    vs. social conscience, 59–60

The Selfish Gene (Dawkins), 313
Self-knowledge, 71–72, 80–90
    beginnings of, 86–87
    changes in, 91–93
    fluctuating images of self, 84–86
    introspection, 81–82
    looking-glass self, 80–81, 92
    reasons for seeking, 87
    seeking, 86–89
    self-perception, 83–84
    social comparison, 82–83
Self-love, 417–419
Self-monitoring, 279, 379
Self-perception theory, 83–84
Self-presentation, 104–110
    cognitive dissonance and, 244
    Count Zrínyi example, 70
    defined, 104
    impression-making, 106–108
    risky behavior, 109–110
    social media, 104–105
Self-protection, 95, 485–487
Self-reference effect, 90, 91
Self-regulation, 133–139, 145, 222
    for breaking bad habits, 140
    defined, 78, 133
    dieting, 137
    monitoring, 135–136
    prejudice and, 479–480
    rejection and, 391, 392
    standards of, 134
    willpower, 133–134, 136–139
Self Report Altruism Scale, 318
Self-service, in stores, A19
Self-serving bias, 97, 163, 476, 486
Self-sufficiency, 306
Self-verification motive, 87
Self-worth, 486
Selye, Hans, B5–B6
Sensation-seeking, 343–344
Sensitivity about being the target of a threatening upward comparison, 297
Sensory overload, E6
Sensory system, 63
Sentiment analysis, A3
September 11, 2001, 144, 457, 498
Serotonin, 356
The Sex Diaries, 432
Sexism, 457
Sexual aggression, 349, 350. *See also* Rape
Sexual arousal, 193, 214–215, 435
Sexual harassment, 484, 524, C10
Sexual intercourse, 409–410
Sexuality and sexual behavior, 427–446
    A–B problem, 247
    aggression, 349, 350 (*See also* Rape)
    arousal, 193, 214–215, 435
    attachment and, 427–428
    biological basis for, 427–428
    cultural differences, 47, 58, 428–429, 430, 432–433, 444–445
    disgust reaction, 207
    evolutionary theory of, 427–428, 429, 437–438
    frequency of sexual intercourse, 409–410
    gender differences, 121, 172, 247, 431–434, 444–445
    in groups, 499
    harassment, 484, 524, C10
    helpfulness of friends and family, 319

jealousy, 439–444
  marriage and, 409–410, 411, 413
  money, attraction based on, 442
  number of sex partners, 172
  power and, 524
  safe sex practices, 277, B12
  self-esteem and, 98, 99
  of single people, 411
  testosterone and, 375
  theories of, 428–431
Sexual orientation, prejudice based on, 462–465
Sexual revolution, 428
Shame, 204
Shared experiences, 383
Shared ideas of cultures, 43–44
Shared resources, 508–509
Shaver, Phillip, 415–416
Sherif, Muzafer, 262–263
Shivaree, 439
Shoplifting, 364, A20
Shopping, 119. See also Consumer behavior
Shopping bags, A10
Short-term goals, 129–130
Shrinkage, A20
Sidney Opera House, 132
Sight, A6–A8
Similarity
  attraction and, 378–379
  helpfulness and, 318
  persuasive speaker and, 274–275
  prejudice and, 466
Similarity leniency hypothesis, D15
Simpson, O. J., trial of, D14
Simulation heuristic, 168, 169
Simultaneous lineups, D8–D9
Singer, Jerome, 192
Situational factors, 8, 9, 17
Skateboarders, 375
Skinner, B.F., 117, 238
Skinnerian behaviorism, 117
Slavery, 485
Sleep, 50–51, 396
  deprivation, 285
Sleeper effect, 273
Slow talking and persuasiveness, 275
Smell, sense of, A7
Smiling and life expectancy, 198–199
Smoking, B2, B9–B10
  cigarette butts, 366
  inoculation against, 284
  labeling of cigarette packages, 207, 276
  as self-defeating behavior, 141
SNS (sympathetic nervous system), B5
Social acceptance, 372–373
  loneliness and, 395
  money pitted against, 63
  self-awareness and, 78
  self-knowledge and, 86
  self-presentation and, 106
  struggle for, 56–57
Social aggression, 347
Social allergy effect, 383–384
Social animals, 40–41
  defined, 43
  humans vs. other animals, 65
  vs.cultural animals, 43
Social behavior, 37–42
  of animals, 40–41
  and the brain, 41–42

evolution, 38–40
  nature, defined, 38
  the psyche, 37–38
Social brain theory, 41–42, 57
Social categorization, 453
Social cognition, 11, 148–185
  attributions (See Attributions and attribution theory)
  biases and errors (See Biases and errors)
  defined, 151
  described, 151–159
  environmental problems, E21
  heuristics (See Heuristics)
Social comparison, 82–83, 97, 486
Social conscience, 59–60
Social constructionist theories of sexuality, 428–429
Social exchange theory of sexuality, 319, 430–431, 445
Social exclusion, 373. See also Rejection
Social facilitation theory, 5, 504–505, 507
Social influence, 258–288
  aggression as a form of, 348–249
  defenses against techniques of, 267, 269, 270, 271
  informational influence, 262–263
  leadership, C21–C22
  normative influence, 261–262, 263
  persuasion (See Persuasion)
  resistance to, 283–285
  self-esteem and, 99
  techniques of, 264–272
Social information, 209–210
Social interaction, 52–64
  affect regulation prior to, 223–224
  vs. cultural, 49–50
  rejection and, 394, 395
  selfhood and, 74–75
Socialization, 316
  of employees, C15
  gender, 36–37
  organizational, C15
  prejudice, 465–466
Social learning, 238–239
  and aggression, 339–340
Social loafing, 5, 505–508
Social media
  advertising, A4–A5
  attitudes expressed on, 232–233, 239
  employee recruitment, C11
  Facebook, 176, 210
  self-presentation on, 104–105
  violent acts, coverage of, 336
Social network analysis, A3
Social neuroscience, 7
Social psychologists, 8–9
  liberal bias of, 490
Social psychology, 5–7
  criticisms of, 27–28
  defined, 4
  importance of, 4
  methodologies, 15–27
  vs. other social sciences, 10
  psychology and, 10–12
  reasons for study, 12–14
  validity of, 27–30
Social Psychology (McDougall), 6
Social Psychology (Ross), 6
Social reality, 443–444

Social rejection. See Rejection
Social rewards, 380
Social roles, 74–75
Social sciences, 10
Social support, 222, B8, E17–E18. See also Relationships
Sociology, 10
Sociometer theory, 100
Soldiers, 272, 383
Solitary confinement, 374
Solzhenitsyn, Alexander, 195
Sorting into groups, 453, 455
Sound, A6–A8, E11–E12
Sources, 273–276
Speaker, persuasive, 272–276
Speaking, speed of, 275
Speech and culture, 49
Spencer, Diana, 406–407
Spencer, Herbert, 39
Spin, 158
Split brain studies, 53–54
Sports
  age effect, 47–48
  drug use tradeoff, 60–61
  racial discrimination, 454
Sports Illustrated jinx, 177
Spring break sex, 319
Stalking, 398
Standards, 76–77, 134, 135
Starbucks, 4
Star Trek, 283, 284
Statistical regression, 177–178, 179
Status quo bias, 121–122, 214
Stealing, 364–365
Steinschneider, Moritz, 458–459
Stereotypes, 453–455
  of African Americans, 470, 485–486
  as cognitive component of intergroup relations, 453
  content of, 473–475
  of gender and sexuality, 431–434, 473–474
  as heuristics, 471–472, 473
  of homosexuals, 463, 465
  inner processes behind, 475–478
  of Jews, 474
  overcoming, 478–483
  of overweight people, 461
  positive, 475
  rationalizations for, 470
  socialization and, 465–466
  societal objections to, 454
  of women, 470
Stereotype threat, 86, 487–489
Sternberg, Robert, 410–412
Sternberg's triangle, 410–412
Stigmas, 465
  by association, 461
  avoidance of, 59–60
  self-protection and, 485–487
Stimulus sampling, 21–22
Stocking buying and self-knowledge, 81–82
Stockpiling resources, 285
Stress, B3–B4
  cognitive appraisal model, B6–B7
  eating habits and, C28
  eyewitness memory and, D5–D6
  fight-or-flight response, B4–B5
  general adaptation syndrome, B5–B6
  management of, 209

Stress, B3–B4 (*continued*)
   questionnaire for, B4
   stereotyping and, 477
   tend and befriend syndrome, B7
   thinking and, 220
   unfairness and, C26
   at work, C27–C29
Strong arguments, 282
Stroop, James Ridley, 154
Stroop effect, 154
Stroop test, 153–154
Structured interviews, C13–C14
Study skills, 93
Stupidity, 180–181
Subjective norms, 248
Subjective predictors of happiness, 198
Subordinates, effects of power on, 525–526
Subtypes, 453, 454
Success, 162–163
Suicide, 78, 143–144
   by Peoples Temple cult, 265
   reasons for committing, 144, 296–297
   survivor guilt and, 205
Suicide bombers, 144
Supermarkets, A6
Suppression of thought, 159
Surowiecki, James, 511
Survey research, 25–27
Survival, 39–40
Survivor guilt, 205
Swann, William, 426
Symbolic Racism 2000 Scale, 234
Symmetry, 386
Sympathetic nervous system (SNS), B5
Systematic processing, 281
System variables, D4, D7–D10

T

Tajfel, Henri, 466
Talking, fast-slow tradeoff, 275
Task orientation, 518
Taylor, Shelley, 96, 251
Teams, 512–513, C19–C21
The Tears of My Soul (Hee), 116
Teenagers. *See* Adolescents
Television, 326. *See also* specific shows
   reality shows, 372, 381–382
   standards depicted on, 76
   violence on, 354
Temperature, E3, E11
Temporal discounting, 120, 121
Ten Commandments, 58, 59, 134
Tend and befriend syndrome, 346, B7
Termination stage of transtheoretical model, B12, B13
Territoriality, 22–23, E8–E9
Terrorism
   Korean Airlines, 116–117
   September 11, 2001, 457, 498
   suicide bombers, 144
Terror management theory, 100, A14, E8
Testosterone, 201, 356, 374–375
Tests, employment, C13–C14
Test taking, 178
Tetlock, Phillip, 62
Thanatos, 339
That's-not-all technique, 268–269
Theft, 364–365, A20

Theories, scientific, 16–18. *See also* specific theories
Theory of evolution, 38–40
Theory of planned behavior, B11
Theory perseverance, 177, 179
Thinking. *See also* Social cognition
   about money, 158
   about people, 151–152
   biases and errors in (*See* Biases and errors)
   in close relationships, styles of, 423–425
   conscious-unconscious tradeoff, 160
   duplex mind (*See* Duplex mind)
   emotions undermining, 212–213
   flawed or clever, 170
   in groups, 510–516
   meaning obtained through, 117
   reasons for, 152–153
   stress effect on, 220
   suppression of, 159
Thinking outside the box, 523
Third-person effect, 260, 355
Thomas, Clarence, C10
Thompson, Jennifer, D11
Thorndike, Edward, 238
Threat appraisals, B6
Time
   selling of, A17–A19
   tradeoffs on, 60
Time poverty, A17–A18
Tit-for-tat strategy, 302, 381–382
Title VII of the Civil Rights Act of 1964, C9, C12
Tolstoy, Leo, 159
TOTE (Test, Operate, Test, and Exit), 135
Toxic leaders, 518–521
Tradeoffs, 60–62
   affect intensity, 200
   competition *vs.* cooperation, 468
   conscious-unconscious thought, 160
   creativity and cheating, 363
   defined, 60
   delay of gratification, 142
   diversity, 500
   fast or slow speaking, 275
   favorability *vs.* plausibility, 108
   political, 62
   prisoner's dilemma, 304–305
   real attitude, 234
   research ethics, 20–21
   self-defeating behavior, 141–143
   self-handicapping, 88–89
   sex and marriage, 411
   testosterone, 374–375
   tragedy of commons, E3
   wrongful convictions *vs.* protecting victims, D19
Tragedy of the commons, 509, E3, E20–E21
Transactive memory, 513
Transformational leadership, C21
Transgender people, 436
Transtheoretical model, B11–B13
Trauma, coping with, 250–251
Tremblay, Richard, 346
Trial consultants, D14
Trials
   capital cases, D17
   eyewitness memory, D11–D12
   jury selection, D14–D16
   pretrial publicity, D17–D18
Triplett, Norman, 5, 504, 507

Tristan Islanders, 468
The Trouble with Testosterone (Sapolsky), 356
True self, 72–73
Trump, Donald, 93
Trust, 310–312, 424
Trust game, 312
Trustworthiness, 273, 381, 382–383
Truth, 15–16
Truthiness, 312
Turner, Geoffrey L., 274
Turner, Ralph, 73
Tuskegee syphilis study, 21
Tutu, Desmond, 519
Twain, Mark, 84
Twin studies, 435–436
Two-sided messages, 276–278
Two Social Psychologies: An Integrative Approach (Stephan and Stephan), 10

U

Ultimatum game, 442
Unanimous agreement, 514
Unconditioned response, 237
Unconditioned stimulus, 237
Unconscious attitudes, 233
Unconscious thought, 8, 160. *See also* Automatic system of the mind
Underbenefited, 297
Understanding emotions, 221
United States
   political beliefs, 44
   sleeping habits of, 50–51
Unobservable constructs, 17
Unrequited love, 382, 397–399
Unstructured interviews, C13–C14
Upstream reciprocity, 292
Upward counterfactuals, 178
Upward social comparison, 83, 251
Urination delay study, 20–21
U.S. Census Bureau, 61
U.S. Federal Bureau of Investigation (FBI), 335
Usage situation, A15

V

Vaccination, 150–151, E3
Validity, 26–27, C13, C14
Values, 358
Variables
   dependent variables, 18, 19
   estimator variables, D4–D7
   independent variables, 17, 19
   system variables, D4, D7–D10
Vegetarianism, 46
Venire, D15–D16
Venting, 342–343
Verbal aggression, 334
Vicarious learning, 238
Victims
   blaming of, 319
   competitive, 487
   of disasters, E17
   helping (*See* Helping)
   protection of, D19
Victorian period, 426–427
Video games, 326
   empathy, lack of, 314
   violence in, 16, 19–22, 30, 354, 355
Violence
   alcohol use and, 356–357

culture and, 358–362
defined, 335
domestic violence, 349–351
eating habits and, 357
gender differences, 346–347
historical levels of, 335–337
hot temperatures and, 355
jealousy and, 441
media depictions, 353–355
mob violence, 508
prejudice and stereotypes, 455
U.S. regional differences, 360–361
in video games, 16, 19–22, 30, 354, 355
Viral marketing, A5
Virginity, 99, 430
Vitamin supplements, 357
Voir dire, D15, D18
Volunteering, 326–327

W

Wakefield, Andrew, 150
Wants, as different from needs, 377
War
    deaths in, 336
    killing desensitization, 343
    military, 272, 383
    persuasion of troops in, 272
    World War II, 4, 361 (See also Holocaust)
Washing away guilt, 206
Water, E4
Weak arguments, 282
Wealth. See also Money
    laughter and, 526
    private ownership, 509
    and relationships, 414
Weapon focus, D6
Weapons effect, 352–353
Weather, E11
Webster, Daniel, 335
Weddings, 413
Weiner, Bernard, 162
What is beautiful is good effect, 384

Who Wants to Be a Millionaire?, 507–511
WHO (World Health Organization), 150, 352
Wicker, Alan, 246
Will-do performance factors, C14
Williams, Kip, 389
Willpower, 133–134, 136–139
Wilson, Timothy, 81–82
Wind conditions, E11
Wisdom, 13, 15
    of groups, 510–512
The Wisdom of Crowds (Surowiecki), 511
Within-subjects design, 17
Witnesses. *See* Eyewitness memory
Women. *See also* Gender and gender differences
    beauty, 386
    body, ideal, 385–387
    brain size, 42
    disgust reaction, 207
    domestic violence and, 349–350
    emotional expression, 217–218
    emotion control strategies, 224
    goal setting, 127–128
    marriage and, 413
    menstrual periods, 93
    self-esteem, 95
    sexual arousal, 193
    stereotypes of, 470
Word-of-mouth marketing, A4–A5
Words, use of, 9
Work and workplace, C1–C34
    attitudes at, C24–C29
    bad bosses, 519–520
    behaviors, C30–C31
    committees, 514–515
    discrimination, 462–463, C9–C10
    emotional intelligence, 221
    employee benefits, C3, C28
    employee selection, C8–C14
    environment of, C16–C19
    groups, 376, C19–C21
    hours, C6

industrial and organizational psychology, C3–C7
leadership, 517–518, C21–C22
mentoring, C17–C18
organizational citizenship behaviors, C29
organizational culture, C5–C6
organizational justice, C26–C27
performance reviews, C22–C23
schedules, C6, C28
significance of work, C4–C5
teams, 512–513
theft by employees, 364
Work-family balance, C28
Work-family conflict, C28
Workforce planning, C23
Work groups, 376, C19–C21
Working self-concept, 84
Work withdrawal, C29
World Economic Forum, 260
World Health Organization (WHO), 150, 352
World War II, 4, 6, 361, 415. *See also* Holocaust
Worm eating, 244
Wounded pride, 359–360
Wrongful convictions, D2–D3, D19

Y

Yerkes, Robert, 219
Yerkes-Dodson law, 219
Yielding, 279
Youth, targeting advertising to, A4. *See also* Adolescents
YouTube, A5

Z

Zajonc, Robert, 236, 504
Zappa, Frank, 180
Zeigarnik effect, 129
Zero-sum game, 305
Zimbabwe, toxic leadership in, 518–519
Zinn, Howard, 292–293
Zrínyi, Miklós, 70, 76, 104